Twelfth Five Year Plan (2012–2017)

Faster, More Inclusive and Sustainable Growth

Volume I

Copyright © Planning Commission (Government of India) 2013

All rights reserved. No part of this book may be reproduced or utilised in any form or by any means, electronic or mechanical, including photocopying, recording or by any information storage or retrieval system, without permission in writing from the Planning Commission, Government of India.

First published in 2013 by

SAGE Publications India Pvt Ltd
B1/I-1 Mohan Cooperative Industrial Area
Mathura Road, New Delhi 110 044, India
www.sagepub.in

SAGE Publications Inc
2455 Teller Road
Thousand Oaks, California 91320, USA

SAGE Publications Ltd
1 Oliver's Yard, 55 City Road
London EC1Y 1SP, United Kingdom

SAGE Publications Asia-Pacific Pte Ltd
33 Pekin Street
#02-01 Far East Square
Singapore 048763

Published by Vivek Mehra for SAGE Publications India Pvt Ltd, Phototypeset in 11/13pt Minion Pro by RECTO Graphics, Delhi and printed at Saurabh Printers, New Delhi.

Second Printing 2014

Library of Congress Cataloging-in-Publication Data
India. Planning Commission
  Twelfth five year plan (2012/2017)/Planning Commission, Government of India.
    Volumes cm
  1. India—Economic Policy—1991–92. Finance, Public—India. I. Title.
HC435.3.I39   338.954009'0512—dc23   2013   2013009870

ISBN: 978-81-321-1368-3 (PB)

The SAGE Team: Rudra Narayan, Archita Mandal, Rajib Chatterjee and Dally Verghese

Twelfth Five Year Plan (2012–2017)

Faster, More Inclusive and Sustainable Growth

Volume I

Planning Commission
Government of India

Thank you for choosing a SAGE product! If you have any comment, observation or feedback, I would like to personally hear from you. Please write to me at contactceo@sagepub.in

—Vivek Mehra, Managing Director and CEO,
SAGE Publications India Pvt Ltd, New Delhi

Bulk Sales

SAGE India offers special discounts for purchase of books in bulk. We also make available special imprints and excerpts from our books on demand.

For orders and enquiries, write to us at

Marketing Department
SAGE Publications India Pvt Ltd
B1/I-1, Mohan Cooperative Industrial Area
Mathura Road, Post Bag 7
New Delhi 110044, India
E-mail us at marketing@sagepub.in

Get to know more about SAGE, be invited to SAGE events, get on our mailing list. Write today to marketing@sagepub.in

This book is also available as an e-book.

प्रधान मंत्री
Prime Minister

Foreword

The Twelfth Plan period presents both challenges and opportunities. The Plan commenced at a time when the global economy was going through a second financial crisis, precipitated by the sovereign debt problems of the Eurozone which erupted in the last year of the Eleventh Plan. The crisis affected all countries including India. Our growth slowed down to 6.2 percent in 2011-12 and the deceleration continued into the first year of the Twelfth Plan, when the economy is estimated to have grown by only 5 percent.

This poses an immediate challenge of bringing the economy back to a higher growth path. Short term downturns occur in all economies. They do not necessarily indicate an erosion of longer term potential, but they do call for urgent corrective action. The Twelfth Plan therefore emphasizes that our first priority must be to bring the economy back to rapid growth while ensuring that the growth is both inclusive and sustainable.

The potential of the economy to grow much more rapidly is evident from the Eleventh Plan experience, which produced an average growth rate of 8 percent for the period 2007-08 to 2011-12. This was lower than the Eleventh Plan target of 9 percent, but higher than the Tenth Plan achievement of 7.6 percent and also the highest growth rate ever recorded by the Indian economy in any Plan period. The slow down witnessed in the first year of the Plan is partly due to the global environment, which has affected all countries, but it is also due to a number of domestic constraints which have arisen. While we cannot do much about the global slowdown, we can address domestic constraints and this must have top priority.

The economy faces macro economic imbalances, because the fiscal deficit expanded sharply after 2008. There has also been a parallel widening of the current account deficit of our balance of payments which is expected to reach about 5 percent of GDP in 2012-13. This must be contained as quickly as possible. A number of infrastructure projects have run into implementation problems and this, combined with the depressed mood of investors in industrialized countries, has affected animal spirits of investors.

The Twelfth Plan has therefore proposed a two pronged strategy focusing initially on the need to bring the macro economic imbalances under control and to reverse the slow down, while also pushing for structural reforms in many areas that are critical for maintaining medium term growth.

The Government has commenced the process of macro-economic rebalancing. It is firmly committed to bringing the fiscal deficit under control and a medium term road map for fiscal correction has been announced. This aims at reducing the Central government deficit to no more than 3 percent by the end of the plan period in line with the macro-economic projections in the Plan.

The high current account deficit is another macro-economic aspect of imbalance. Our foreign exchange reserves position is strong, but the reserves cannot be a source for financing prolonged deficits. It is therefore essential to bring the current account deficit down to more manageable levels. The expansion in the current account deficit was partly on account of the expansion in the fiscal deficit and the targeted reduction in the fiscal deficit is an important instrument for bringing the current account deficit under control. It is expected to decline in 2013-14, but it will still be high. However, it will be on a perceptibly downward path, reaching comfortable levels in the next two years.

This poses the challenge of having to ensure financing of a somewhat elevated deficit for two more years. This must be done through long term capital flows, including especially FDI. Strong signals have been given to assure foreign investors that the government is keen to attract both FDI and FII flows in order to finance the current account deficit even as we work to reduce the size of the deficit over time. Caps on the permitted level of FDI in a number of sectors have been relaxed, and a broader review of policies is being undertaken with a view to facilitate an easier flow of foreign investment.

The Government has also acted on the supply side to tackle implementation problems holding up large infrastructure projects. A Cabinet Committee on Investment has been established to deal with situations where clearances are unduly delayed and this has succeeded in removing many bottlenecks. This will accelerate clearance of projects and help revive the pace of investment which should bring about a reversal of the slowdown.

The Twelfth Plan has set a target of 8 percent growth over the five year period 2012-13 to 2016-17. With a growth of only 5 percent in the first year and perhaps 6.5 percent in the second, it will require a very sharp acceleration in the later years to achieve an average of 8 percent over the entire Plan period. Growth will have to be pushed to over 9 percent in the last two years. The economy did grow at over 9 percent for five years before 2008, but that was at a time when the global economy was booming. To achieve this level over the next two years, given the uncertain prospects of the global economy in the years ahead, poses challenges. The Plan therefore emphasizes that returning to 9 percent growth by the end of the Plan period will not be easy.

The Plan document makes it amply clear that a return to high growth will not come from following a business as usual approach. It will require policy action on many fronts, by both the central and the state governments. The Plan provides a detailed outline of the key steps needed in each area. Some of the policy changes called for are difficult, but they are necessary if we want inclusive and sustainable growth. We need to accelerate growth in agriculture to continue the trend initiated in the Eleventh Plan. We need much faster growth in manufacturing to provide employment to our young and increasingly educated population which has high expectations and aspirations. We need to address the challenge of managing the infrastructure sectors to ensure that these sectors expand sufficiently to support growth. We also need to face up to the enormous challenges posed by urbanization.

In all this, we must keep in mind that growth must not only be rapid, it must be inclusive and sustainable. The benefits of growth must reach the SCs, STs, OBC, Minorities and other disadvantaged groups in our society. All these groups must get a fair share of the benefits of growth and must have a stake in the process. The issue of environmental sustainability cannot be ignored. We need a growth process that is consistent with protecting our environment.

One of the problems with our plans in the past has been that they have focused on outlining an attractive future, with not enough focus on what is needed to achieve it and the consequences of failing in this regard. Recognizing that outcomes will be the result of actions, the Twelfth Plan, for the first time, has resorted to scenarios to indicate the implications of different types of behaviour. Our objective should be to achieve the scenario of "strong inclusive growth" which can yield an average growth rate of around 8 percent of GDP and significant improvements in various inclusiveness indicators. Significantly, the Plan warns that if we fail to do what is necessary, we may slip into a scenario of "Policy logjam" which will lead to growth of 5 to 5.4 percent, with a much worse outcome for inclusiveness.

The objectives of the Twelfth Plan are ambitious and achieving them will be difficult. This is a challenge for our democratic system. We have to prove that vigorously competitive politics in a democracy can achieve a sufficient consensus to be able to implement the difficult but necessary policy choices we face. This is a national challenge that the entire political and intellectual leadership of our country must come to grips with. It is a challenge for the central government and also for state governments.

One of the important achievements of the past decade is that India has broken out of a long period of relatively slow growth to show that it can grow more rapidly. The Eleventh Plan experience has also shown that this growth can be much more inclusive than in the past.

If we can continue this performance for the next twenty years, we will have ensured the re-emergence of India as major economic player in the world, and also one committed to its democratic, secular and pluralistic traditions. We will have demonstrated that this ancient land of India can re-emerge as a modem nation, uplifting millions out of poverty, empowering each and every citizen, unleashing individual talent and liberating enterprise, within the framework of a democratic Constitution and under the Rule of Law. We have a long way to go, but I believe we have shown that the creative energies of the Indian people can propel the economy forward at much faster rates than was thought possible thus far, and with greater inclusiveness than in the past. I am confident that the rise of a new India will have beneficial consequences for the whole world. It will inspire millions around the world, especially in Asia, Africa and Latin America, to seek their own destiny within the framework of a plural, secular and liberal democracy.

(Manmohan Singh)

New Delhi
10 May, 2013

Planning Commission

(As on 27th July, 2013)

Dr. Manmohan Singh, Prime Minister	Chairman
Shri Montek Singh Ahluwalia	Deputy Chairman
Shri P. Chidambaram, Minister of Finance	Member
Shri Sharad Pawar, Minister of Agriculture and Food Processing Industries	Member
Shri Sushil Kumar Shinde, Minister of Home Affairs	Member
Shri Mallikarjun Kharge, Minister of Railways	Member
Shri Gulam Nabi Azad, Minister of Health & Family Welfare	Member
Shri Kamal Nath, Minister of Urban Development & Parliamentary Affairs	Member
Shri Kapil Sibal, Minister of Communications & IT & Minister of Law & Justice	Member
Shri M.M. Pallam Raju, Minister of Human Resource Development	Member
Shri Jairam Ramesh, Minister of Rural Development	Member
Shri Rajeev Shukla, Minister of State for Parliamentary Affairs and Planning	Member
Shri B.K. Chaturvedi	Member
Dr. Saumitra Chaudhuri	Member
Dr. (Ms.) Syeda Hameed	Member
Dr. Narendra Jadhav	Member
Prof. Abhijit Sen	Member
Dr. Mihir Shah	Member
Dr. K. Kasturirangan	Member
Sh. Arun Maira	Member

सत्यमेव जयते

Preface

National planning is a process of setting national targets, and preparing programmes and policies that will help achieve those targets. The policies and programmes must be consistent with each other, ensure optimal use of national resources both financial and real, and be based on an understanding of the response of the economy to these interventions. This exercise has become more complex over time for several reasons. First, the setting of targets is not just a technocratic process. It must reflect the aspirations of an increasingly aware public and a vocal civil society to command the broadest possible social and political support. Second, the strategies outlined by the plan must reflect the growing complexity and maturity of the economy, including its growing integration with the rest of the world, and the changing role of the public and private sectors. Finally, plan strategies are only as good as our ability to implement them and therefore implementation capability is very important.

The Twelfth Five Year Plan has been formulated keeping all these factors in mind. Some reflections on each of these three aspects are offered in this preface.

The Multi-Dimensional Nature of Plan Targets

Traditionally, public discussion of plan targets has tended to focus narrowly on targets for GDP growth, leading to the criticism that planners are obsessed with economic growth as an end in itself. This has never been true of Indian plans, and it is certainly not true of the Twelfth Plan. Our plans have consistently emphasised that higher rates of growth of GDP are a necessary, but not a sufficient condition for raising the living standards of the population as a whole.

The Twelfth Plan is firmly anchored in this tradition. Rapid growth is viewed as a necessary condition because it ensures an expansion in the productive capacity of the economy without which a broad based improvement in living standards is not possible. However, it recognises that faster growth is not a sufficient condition simply because one can easily imagine a growth process which may not be sufficiently inclusive to ensure a spread of benefits to the mass of the population. For example, any growth process which ignores agriculture will miss out on opportunities to improve incomes for a large part of the population. Hence the Twelfth Plan target of accelerating GDP growth is accompanied by a specific target to accelerate growth of agricultural GDP. The Twelfth Plan aims at catalyzing a growth process which has the structural characteristics that will promote inclusiveness. The Eleventh Plan started the process of accelerating agricultural growth by achieving 3.6 percent growth component with 2.4 percent in the Tenth. The Twelfth Plan aims at accelerating agricultural growth further to 4 percent.

The proportion of the population depending mainly on agriculture has been falling, but it is still too large, given the shrinking contribution of agriculture as a percentage of GDP. We must therefore plan for a substantial percentage of those currently engaged in agriculture to shift to higher productivity non-agricultural occupations. This can only happen if the non-agricultural sector can provide gainful employment not only to the growing number of people who will be entering the labour force, but those moving out of agriculture. To be truly inclusive the growth process must therefore be job creating. A growth based on growth from highly capital intensive sectors areas such as petrochemicals, steel, mining, etc., or one that is dependent on high end skills, e.g., software development, information technology etc. cannot provide a sufficient expansion in employment to the large numbers of the labour force with mid level skills who need better employment opportunities. This calls for robust growth in the manufacturing sector, including especially in small and medium enterprises. The Twelfth Plan therefore seeks to achieve a faster growth in manufacturing, with particular emphasis on the medium, small and micro enterprises, which provide the best scope for absorbing labour currently employed in low productivity occupations.

An employment generating growth process will generate a broad based growth of incomes, but this by itself does not assure the achievement of other important targets in terms of access to education, health, sanitation and clean drinking water. These are not only essential elements of welfare, but also for ensuring a healthy and productive labour force, which raises medium term growth capacity. The Twelfth Plan places special emphasis on expanding access to these services and views it as a critical role of government in the development process.

The private sector now has a demonstrable capability to invest in and stimulate growth in many areas of the economy and public sector initiatives in these areas are therefore no longer necessary. However, the provision of education, health and essential services for the bulk of the population has to be the responsibility of the State. Thus, while the state should withdraw from areas where the private sector is able to deliver well, this does amount to advocating a reduction in the role of the State: what is needed is a restructuring in the role of the State, reducing its role in some areas but increasing it in others.

The objective of inclusiveness also calls for pro-active intervention to bridge the many "divides" which segment our society. The Plan must retain its traditional focus on reducing poverty – an area where the results in the Eleventh Plan have been heartening. It must also focus on promoting productive employment to meet the aspirations of youth. It must ensure upliftment of specific groups such as the SCs/STs/OBCs, minorities and other marginalised groups that suffer from historical exclusion. It must systematically close the gender gap which is a blot on our social structure. It must also ensure balanced development of all the regions. Finally it must ensure that the growth strategy is consistent with sustainability concerns which are now gaining importance.

These multi-dimensional objectives are reflected in the adoption of 25 monitorable targets in the Twelfth Plan of which growth of GDP is only one. The other targets cover the many features of development which measure inclusiveness and sustainability. Individual states have also been encouraged to set state specific targets in the same areas.

Participation in Planning

The process of fixing Plan targets and also defining Plan strategies can no longer be viewed as purely technical functions. There is a widespread desire on the part of many stakeholders to participate in the process. The Planning Commission has therefore consulted widely not only with the Central Ministries and State Governments, but also with sector experts, economists, sociologists, political scientists and civil society organisations. About 146 Working Groups were established under the chairmanship of Secretary of the Ministry concerned, and included sector experts from within and outside the Government. Their reports were reviewed by a steering Group chaired by the respective Member of the Planning Commission. Each steering group included representatives of different Ministries, non government experts and other stakeholders. The reports of the steering groups were used as inputs into the Plan formulation, and the reports are also available on the website of the Planning Commission.

Regional meetings were held with Chief Ministers of groups of states to get the views of State Governments. These regional meetings were also used for interacting with the civil society groups. As many as 900 civil society organisations have been consulted in various ways.

A radical departure from the past was the use of social media on various aspects of the Plan, and also as a form of outreach. The Planning Commission organized several events to increase awareness of the planning process amongst the youth. During a Google Hangout, which was widely telecast on television, senior officials from the Commission answered a variety of questions taken live from social media users, on topics such as governance, industrialization, agriculture, infrastructure, and even the relevance of the Planning Commission itself.

Subsequently, over a thousand young students and professionals came together in ten locations across the country to 'Hack' the Twelfth Plan, and develop creative ways of communicating its message to the public. These initiatives reflect Planning Commission's sincere desire to engage more directly with the stakeholders. More broadly, they are part of an evolution of the Planning Commission itself, as it strives to become an 'exercise in persuasion'.

The Role of Programmes

Traditionally, our Plans have been viewed as synonymous with the collection of government programmes designed to promote one or other plan objective. There is much interest in this context in the total size of the Plan, and the allocation of financial resources to different sectors and programmes. There is not enough focus on the role of policies in achieving plan objectives by influencing the decisions taken by the households and firms and this issue is discussed in the next section.

The Twelfth Plan relies on an extensive range of government programmes, which cover a wide variety of sectors, to help achieve the inclusive and sustainable growth. There are programmes in health, education, drinking water and sanitation, provision of critical infrastructure in rural and urban areas, programmes of livelihood support for the weaker sections and special programmes for the historically disadvantaged sections of our population, particularly the Scheduled Castes, Scheduled Tribes, OBCs, Minorities, and other marginalised groups. Plan programmes can be classified into three groups. There are central sector programmes, administered directly by agencies of the central government. There are state sector programmes, administered by state agencies, which form part of the State Plan. There are also Centrally Sponsored Schemes (CSS), operating in areas that are, constitutionally the domain of the States, but the Central Government provides resources to the states to support these programmes while the programmes themselves are implemented by the State Government and its agencies.

This public sector component of our development effort, taking the Centre and the States together, amounts to about 12 percent of GDP. About half of this takes the form of capital expenditure or investment, with the rest is accounted for salaries for the delivery of services, or pure transfers, as in the case of provision of resources for mid day meals for school children or nutrition for pre school children; scholarships for disadvantaged groups, pensions for the poor, etc. Economists have traditionally focused on investment, as a key driver of growth, but once it is recognized that access to essential services such as, health, education, and nutritional support for children are critical contributors to growth in the medium term, it is obvious that non investment expenditures in the sectors are critical to achieve access.

While these programmes are important, it is important to recognise that merely expanding expenditure in these programmes will not necessarily achieve the objectives of the Plan. We also need to look beyond expenditures, at the outcomes achieved. This calls for rigorous and independent evaluations of the effectiveness of our programmes in achieving the desired outcomes and an analysis of why they fall short. A common explanation of why results have fallen short of expectations is that the programmes are underfunded. This is often true but there are also problems because of design flaws, and shortcomings in implementation capacity at the ground level which needs to be remedied to improve outcomes. Both the Centre and the States should undertake such evaluations systematically, and especially, at the end of each Plan period.

The Role of Policy Restructuring

Along with programmes, the policy content of the Plan deserves much greater attention than it typically gets. In an economy in which the private sector has grown in scale, decisions taken by individuals and firms determine many critical economic outcomes, and the policies which influence these decisions are therefore important. This is especially so since private investment by farmers, unorganised enterprises and the corporate sector, accounts for 75 percent of total investment in the economy.

One aspect of policy emphasised in the Prime Minister's Foreword, is the achievement of a sound macro-economic framework. This essentially boils down to having a reasonable fiscal deficit, a financeable current account deficit, a moderate rate of inflation and high rates of domestic savings. The Twelfth Plan has commenced at a time when there are weaknesses in these areas but it outlines a macro economic strategy for correction. Success in these efforts will be critical to creating an environment in which the high levels of investment and capital inflows needed for high growth can materialise.

In addition to policies for macro-economic stability, policy restructuring is needed in many sectors if we are to make progress towards achieving Plan objectives. The Plan document outlines an ambitious agenda for policy change. This includes policies aimed at supporting the diversification of agriculture, and greater involvement of the private sector in marketing agricultural produce. It also includes policies related to energy pricing, and greater involvement of the private sector in exploration and development of primary energy sources. Industrial growth can be greatly helped by policies aimed at improving the ease of doing business, and also, policies that would encourage a flow of both risk capital and debt into small and medium industries. Rationalisation of tax policies, including especially, the introduction of GST, is another very important area, as is the rationalisation of subsidy policy to progressively reduce dysfunctional subsidies, and make essential subsidies better targeted through the use of Aadhar. The Plan emphasises the need to design policies regarding the efficient use of water through a combination of regulation and appropriate pricing. These policies will have to be supported by well designed public investment to encourage effective conservation of water. Policies for effective management of urbanisation are increasingly important and this is a new challenge facing the economy.

Since the total resources available to the Government is limited, and there are heavy demands on such resources from sectors such as health and education, there is an obvious need to leverage private resources to achieve public ends. This is particularly important in the area of infrastructure development where it leads to some important policy departures. One such departure is the adoption in the Eleventh Plan of Public Private Partnership as a strategy for developing infrastructure.

Traditionally, infrastructure used to be created by the public sector but increasingly, all over the world, countries have experimented with different forms of public private partnership, particularly in situations where users are willing to pay a user charge which generates a potential revenue stream. Emphasising PPPs where possible, does not imply a blind pursuit of PPPs as the only means of implementing infrastructure projects. Private investors are unlikely to be interested in investing in the remoter or more backward parts of the country and the development of infrastructure in these parts will have to rely dominantly on public investment. However it is possible to follow the PPP option for many projects in roads, airports, ports, power generation and distribution, etc. The Central Government has evolved procedures and bidding documents which seek to achieve the objectives of transparency and robust competitive bidding for PPP projects and has encouraged state Governments to proceed on the same basis.

Both the Central Government and many State Governments have embarked on ambitious programmes of developing infrastructure through PPPs. As a result, India now has the largest number of PPP projects of all emerging market countries. However, as the number of PPP projects expands, there will be unexpected problems in the course of implementation. Both the Centre and the States must evolve mechanisms to monitor PPP projects closely to ensure that they come up to the expected standards of service delivery and also to identify problems in project implementation so that these can be resolved as speedily as possible in a fair and transparent manner.

Many of the policies on the policy agenda outlined in the Plan lie in the domain of the Central Government but many also lie in the domain of the States. Some, such as the implementation of the GST, which is an extremely important initiative, depend upon joint action, since it involves a constitutional amendment. States are likely to differ in the speed at which they implement policy changes recommended in different areas since action in some areas may be easier for a particular State than in others. However a substantial effort in the broad directions indicated in the Plan, will have a significant effect on outcomes and experience of success in some States will encourage others to follow suit.

Implementation is the Key

The success of any Plan depends heavily on the quality of implementation, and it is here that our planning process is perhaps the weakest. It is often said that our plans are very good, but implementation is poor. This is actually a contradiction. Planning can only be called good if it is based on a realistic assessment of what can be implemented, with concrete proposals to increase implementation capacity as part of the strategy.

As far as Plan programmes are concerned, it is often said that the programmes are inadequately funded, and such funds as are available are often not well spent. Some element of under funding is unavoidable because resources are calculated on the basis of likely growth of revenue, which depends on the overall growth of the economy. When growth falls short of the targets, resources are also likely to be lower than projected. The solution lies in clearer prioritisation, so that shortfalls in resources do not lead to proportional under funding of all programmes but rather that the least productive programmes are scaled back. An important precondition for implementing this approach is a candid assessment of what are the most effective programmes based on periodic independent evaluation and constant concurrent evaluation. The role of evaluation needs to be greatly strengthened in our planning process. The Planning Commission has created a new mechanism with an Independent Evaluation Office headed by a Director General at the level of Member of the Planning Commission.

One reason why implementation is poor is that the capacity to implement is lacking at the operational level. Development programmes, in areas that have constitutionally been devolved to the Panchayati Raj Institutions, or Urban Local Bodies, should be implemented with these institutions playing a major role, both in the design of the programme, and its actual implementation on the ground. Unfortunately, although States have generally devolved "functions" to the PRI institutions, they have done much less to devolve "funds". In many cases, even the devolution of "functionaries" to the level needed for effectiveness has not really taken place. The PRIs also lack the capacity to design, implement, and monitor programmes. This is true not only for the Panchayats in rural areas, but also for urban local bodies, as revealed by the experience of the JNNURM. The Twelfth Plan, therefore, provides for a portion of the funds in many programmes to be used to build implementation capacity. A new Centrally Sponsored Scheme for strengthening the capacity of the Panchayats, the Rajiv Gandhi Panchayat Shashaktikaran Abhiyan has also been introduced.

A major new initiative taken in the Twelfth Plan, to improve implementation of the Centrally Sponsored Schemes is to rationalise the number of the CSS, reducing them from 142 to 66, and also permitting greater flexibility in the guidelines. Recognising the fact that "one size fits all" national guidelines do not take into account the characteristics of different States, which justifies a differentiated approach, a new system has been introduced with two major changes. First, each state will be able to propose modifications in the national guidelines to suit the particular circumstances of the state. Second, each state will be allowed full flexibility for ten percent of its allocation under each scheme, which can be used for projects, which depart even from the modified state specific guidelines. The only requirement will be that the project must be within the broad objectives of the scheme. This is designed to encourage innovation at the state level.

Problems of implementation also arise in implementing the policy agenda of the Plan. Progress in this are often suffers from a lack of understanding of the need for policy change and the pressure of vested interests. And yet, effective implementation of these policy changes is critical to achieve the productivity increases which are essential for achieving high growth. The mid term review of the Twelfth Plan should focus specifically on the success achieved in this dimension. An assessment should be made of success achieved by the Centre, in implementing the policy restructuring envisaged with a parallel exercise for each State.

Scenario Analysis

An important innovation in the Twelfth Plan is the recourse to scenario analysis. Instead of adopting a set of notional targets, and outlining what is necessary to achieve them, the Plan outlines three scenarios. The first is the scenario in which we are able to achieve highly substantial implementation of the programmes and policies outlined in the Plan. This is a scenario of "strong inclusive growth", which would yield an average growth rate of around 8 percent in the Plan period, and would also be sufficiently inclusive to show significant progress in each of the 25 monitorable indicators, which reflect the multi-dimensionality of targets that have been fixed for the Twelfth Plan. This is clearly the outcome we should aim at.

However, the Plan also notes, that although technically feasible, Scenario 1 is by no means an assured outcome. Success will depend on our ability to fund Plan programmes on the scale envisaged, while maintaining macro economic stability, and also implementing the broad ranging policy changes, which are needed to achieve higher levels of productivity and the investment needed. If this agenda is only partially implemented the economy will progress as in Scenario 2, with growth around 6.0 percent and much low levels of inclusiveness. The Plan also indicates the consequences of failing to make any significant progress by outlining a Scenario 3 called Policy Logjam. In this case, the growth rate could fall to around 5 percent with very little progress on the inclusiveness agenda.

The requirements for achieving the Twelfth Plan's Scenario-1 are extremely demanding, especially at a time when the external environment is highly uncertain. However, these difficulties affecting the first two years of the Plan should be viewed as a short term impediment. With determined effort to correct macro-economic imbalances, and to achieve effective implementation of both the programmes and sectoral policies outlined in the Plan, there is a good chance of bringing the economy back to an 8 percent growth path, which is warranted by the underlying fundamentals. As the Plan points out, it is difficult, but not impossible. With a strong national effort, we should be able to put the economy on a path which achieves the transition we all want.

New Delhi
10th May 2013

(Montek Singh Ahluwalia)
Deputy Chairman

Contents

List of Figures — xxi
List of Tables — xxii
List of Boxes — xxiv
List of Acronyms — xxv
List of Annexures — xxxiv

1. Twelfth Plan: An Overview — 1
2. Macroeconomic Framework — 37
3. Financing the Plan — 70
4. Sustainable Development — 112
5. Water — 144
6. Land Issues — 191
7. Environment, Forestry and Wildlife — 202
8. Science and Technology — 235
9. Innovation — 278
10. Governance — 286
11. Regional Equality — 302

Figures

2.1	Systems Analysis for Twelfth Plan Scenarios	40
2.2	Investment Rate—Ratio to GDP at Current Prices—Over the Years	43
2.3.	Domestic Savings Rate—Ratio to GDP—Over the Years	48
2.4	Annualised Reduction in Poverty Ratio between 1993–94, 2004–05 and 2009–10 for Alternate Measures of PL in Percentage Points	68
2.5	Annualised Rate of Decline as Proportion of the Initial Ratio in that Expenditure Class	68
3.1	Central Subsidies as Per Cent to GDP	76
3.2	Private Sector Investment in Infrastructure (Per Cent Share)	86
3.3	Investment in Infrastructure as a Per Cent of GDP	87
4.1	Policy Alternatives for Sustainable Growth	113
4.2	Iron and Steel Industry	123
4.3	Cement Industry: Historical Trends of Total Energy (in PJ) and Specific Energy Consumption (GJ/tonne)	124
4.4	Modal share of freight transport in India	131
4.5	Passenger Transport Activity and Emissions in 2007	132
4.6	Sector-wise Electricity Consumption in India	135
5.1	Incomplete MMI Projects across Plan Periods	147
5.2	Increasing Gap between Irrigation Potential Created and Utilised	149
5.3	Groundwater Abstraction Trends in Selected Countries (in km3/year)	155
5.4	Water Saving Potential in Industry	168
7.1	Sanctioned Outlay vs Actual Expenditure in the Eleventh Plan (₹ Crore)	207
7.2	Sector-wise Allocations/Expenditure during the Eleventh Plan (₹ Crore)	208
7.3	Strategies for the Twelfth Plan	212
7.4	Rationalisation of Schemes from the Eleventh to the Twelfth Five Year Plan	216
7.5	Global Temperature Rise—Effect of Increase in GHG Concentration	222
11.1	Convergence of GDP Growth Rates during Successive Plans	304
11.2	Trends in Inter-State Inequality	306
11.3	Inter-State Income Inequalities (Bases on States' GSDP Per Capita on Current Price)	307
11.4	Growth during 2001–10 and Income in 2001	308

Tables

2.1	Annual Growth Rate of GDP by Industry of Origin at Constant (2004–05) Prices	42
2.2	Investment and Consumption Expenditure as Proportion of GDP at Constant 2004–05 Prices	44
2.3	Domestic Savings and Components Thereof in Per Cent of GDP at Current Prices	49
2.4	External Payments—Current and Capital Account	52
2.5	Fiscal Position of Centre and States and Subsidy Quanta	54
2.6	General Government Balance and Government Debt as Per Cent of GDP	55
2.7	Trends in Global GDP Growth	59
2.8	Decile-wise annual growth in $MPCE_{URP}$ at constant prices (2004–05)	69
3.1	Projected vis-à-vis Realised Financing Pattern of the Plan Outlay of the Centre	71
3.2	NPRE and Its Components	72
3.3	Gross Fiscal Deficit	72
3.4	Eleventh Plan Resources of States and UTs	73
3.5	Projection of the Twelfth Plan Resources of the Centre	76
3.6	Resources of the Centre in Eleventh and Twelfth Plan	77
3.7	Twelfth Plan Resources of States and UTs	77
3.8	Eleventh Plan Realisation and Twelfth Plan Projection of Resources of States and UTs	78
3.9	Overall Financing Pattern: Eleventh and Twelfth Plans	79
3.10	Plan Resources as Per Cent of GDP	79
3.11	Public Sector Allocation for Twelfth Plan	81
3.12	GBS Allocation in Eleventh and Twelfth Plans	81
3.13	Allocation of Centre's GBS by Major Sectors—Eleventh Plan Realisation and Twelfth Plan Projection	82
3.14	Projected CA to States/UTs' Plan for Twelfth Plan	83
3.15	Sector-Wise Investments: Tenth Plan and Eleventh Plan	85
3.16	Investment during the Eleventh Plan as Percentage of GDP	87
3.17	Projected Investment in Infrastructure—Twelfth Plan	89
3.18	Source-Wise Projected Investment	90
3.19	Likely Sources of Debt	91
4.1	Sector-wise Annual Energy Consumption of Designated Consumers	125
4.2	Initial Estimate of Energy Consumption and Energy Reduction Targets	126
4.3	Cap-and-Trade vs Carbon Tax	128
4.4	Coverage of Green Building Rating System up to October 2012	137
5.1	Top 10 Groundwater-Abstracting Countries as of 2010	155

5.2	Physical and Financial Progress in Watershed Projects of DOLR	159
5.3	Nagpur's Water Highway: Losing as It Travels	162
5.4	Sanitation Facilities in Urban India	163
5.5	Waste Treatment Capacity in Indian Cities	163
5.6	Sector-wise allocation of JNNURM Funds (as on 21.9.2011) 100th CSMC	165
5.7	Potential Water Saving from Various Measures in Industry	169
7.1	Thematic Schemes under Implementation at the End of the Eleventh Plan	206
7.2	Categories along with indicators selected for Planning Commission's EPI	219
7.3	Different Levels of Global Mean Temperature Increase above Pre-industrial Levels	222
7.4	Policy Interventions Optimal for Various Technologies	232
8.1	Plan Outlays and Expenditure of Central Scientific Ministries/Departments/Agencies During Eleventh Five Year Plan and Indicative Outlay for Twelfth Five Year Plan	273
10.1	Year-Wise Damage Caused Due to Floods, Cyclonic Storms, Landslides and so on during Last 10 Years in India	300
10.2	Gross Budgetary Support for the Twelfth Five Year Plan	301
11.1	Comparative Growth Rates in GSDP for Selected Low-Income States	304
11.2	Growth Rates in SDP in Different States	305
11.3	Convergence of GDP Growth Rates in Successive Plans	306
11.4	Disparity in PCI (Per Capita NSDP) at 2004–05 Prices	307
11.5	Disparities in Human Development Indicators	309
11.6	Human Development Index (1999–2000 and 2007–08)	310
11.7	Weighted Coefficient of Variation in District-level Domestic Product	311
11.8	Ratio of Per Capita GDDP in Richest District to Poorest District	311
11.9	Index of Infrastructure	314
11.10	Rank Correlation between Infrastructure Index, Poverty Ratio and Per Capita Income of States	315
11.11	State-wise and Sector-wise Growth Rates for the Twelfth Five Year Plan (2012–2017)	316
11.12	Financial Transfers under Normal Central Assistance (Plan) and Thirteenth Finance Commission	317
11.13	Criteria and Weights for Tax Devolution	318
11.14	Criteria and Weights under Gadgil-Mukherjee Formula	318
11.15	Statewise Central Releases under Important Flagship Schemes as Per Cent of Total	319
11.16	Eleventh Plan Expenditure	321
11.17	Total Plan Expenditure by the Centre and States of NE, Including NEC	331
11.18	Growth Rate in SDP in the NE States	332

Boxes

1.1	Prime Minister Dr Manmohan Singh at the 57th NDC	6
1.2	Eleventh Plan Achievements on Inclusive Growth	9
3.1	Infrastrcuture Debt Fund	92
3.2	Model Concession Agreements for PPP	92
3.3	Model Bidding Documents for PPP Projects	93
3.4	Guidelines and Manuals	93
3.5	Global Ranking in PPP	94
3.6	Hyderabad Metro Rail Project	95
3.7	India Front-Runner in the PPP Race: ADB	98
4.1	Twelve Focus Areas for the Twelfth Plan	118
4.2	Importance of Clean Coal Technology: Ultra-super Critical Power Plants	119
5.1	IIM Lucknow Evaluates AIBP for Planning Commission	148
5.2	Participatory Groundwater Management in India	156
5.3	Bengaluru: The Best?	164
5.4	A 'Wave' of Change in Tiruchirapally	164
5.5	Water Use Efficiency in UK Industry	169
7.1	Vision	202
7.2	Waste Disposal in PPP Mode	204
7.3	Monitorable Targets for the Twelfth Plan	209
7.4	Goals	210
7.5	Tribal Families Jointly Manage '*Yepuru*' Forests, Nellore District, Andhra Pradesh for One and Half Decade, for Sustainable Livelihood	220
7.6	Bundelkhand Model for Farmland Productivity Enhancement in Rain-fed Areas of the Country through Water Harvesting	221
7.7	Suggested Re-organisation of the National Action Plan for Climate Change	229
7.8	Framework for Understanding Finance Strategies	231
8.1	Discovery of Higgs Boson—Indian Contribution	242
8.2	Significant Achievements/Development of DST during Eleventh Plan Period	244
8.3	Leveraging International Collaboration for Strengthening National Programmes Journey From Stanford–India Biodesign Programme—A Novel Collaborative Technology Innovation to Launching National Biodesign Alliance	249
8.4	Significant Achievements/Development of DBT during the Eleventh Plan Period	250
8.5	Significant Achievements/Development of MoES/ESSO during the Eleventh Plan Period	254
8.6	Significant Achievements of DSIR/CSIR during the Eleventh Plan Period	259
8.7	Significant Achievements/Development of DOS during the Eleventh Plan Period	264
8.8	Significant Achievements/Development of DAE during the Eleventh Plan Period	269
11.1	From the Report of the Twelfth Plan Working Group on Special Area Programmes	328

Acronyms

AAGR	Average Annual Growth Rate	ASEAN	Association of Southeast Asian Nations
AAI	Airport Authority of India		
AAS	Agromet Advisory Services	ATTF	AHWR Thermal Hydraulics Test Facility
ACA	Additional Central Assistance		
AcSIR	Academy of Scientific and Innovative Research	AWSs	Automatic Weather Stations
		AYUSH	Ayurveda, Yoga & Naturopathy, Unani, Siddha and Homoeopath
ACTREC-TMC	Advanced Centre for Treatment, Research and Education in Cancer at Tata Memorial Centre	BADP	Border Area Development Programme
ACWADAM	Advanced Centre for Water Resources Development and Management	BARC	Bhabha Atomic Research Centre
		BC Ratio	Benefit-Cost Ratio
		BCM	Billion Cubic Metre
ADB	Asian Development Bank	BCR	Balance from Current Revenues
AHWR	Advanced Heavy Water Reactor	BCRLIP	Biodiversity Conservation & Rural Livelihood Improvement Project
AIBP	Accelerated Irrigation Benefit Programme		
		BE	Budget Estimates/Budgeted Expenditure
AIIMS	All India Institute for Medical Sciences		
		BEE	Bureau of Energy Efficiency
ALICE	A Large Ion Collider Experiment	BEL	Bharat Electronics Limited
ALTM	Airborne Laser Terrain Mapper	BIMARU	Bihar, Madhya Pradesh, Rajasthan and Uttar Pradesh
AMA	Aquifer Management Association		
AMIs	Airport Meteorological Instruments	BIPP	Biotechnology Industry Partnership Programme
ANUSAT	Anna University Satellite	BIRAC	Biotechnology Industry Research Assistance Council
APFAMGS	Andhra Pradesh Farmers Managed Groundwater System		
		BIRD	Building Industrial R&D and Common Research Facilities
APM	Administered Pricing Mechanism		
APPRC	Action Plan for Preparation of Regulations, CBRs (Conduct of Business Regulations) and Criteria	BLY	Bachat Lamp Yojana
		BMCs	Biodiversity Management Committees
		BOD	Bio-chemical Oxygen Demand/ Biological Oxygen Demand
ARC	Administrative Reforms Commission		
ARGs	Automatic Rain Gauges	BOT	Build-Operate-Transfer
ASCI	Administrative Staff College of India	BRAI	Biotechnology Regulatory Authority of India

BRGF	Backward Regions Grant Fund	CETPs	Continuous Effluent Treatment Plants
BRLF	Bharat Rural Livelihoods Foundation	CFLs	Compact Fluorescent Lamps
BRNS	Board of Research in Nuclear Sciences	CFT	Cluster Facilitation Teams
		CGP	Cluster of Gram Panchayats
BSI	Botanical Survey of India	CHTR	Compact High Temperature Reactor
BTIA	Broad-based Trade and Investment Agreement	CICC	Cable-In-Conduit-Conductor
CA	Cascade Associations/Central Assistance	CICs	Cluster Innovation Centres
		CITES	Convention on International Trade Endangered Species of Fauna and Flora
CAAQMS	Continuous Ambient Air Quality Monitoring Stations		
CAGR	Compound Annual Growth Rate	CKMNT	Centre for Knowledge Management of Nano Science and Technology
CAMPA	Compensatory Afforestation Fund Management and Planning Authority		
		CMIE	Centre for Monitoring of Indian Economy
CAT	Centre for Atmospheric Technology	CMS	Compact Muon Solenoid
CBD	Convention on Biological Diversity	CO_2	Carbon Dioxide
		CO_2 eq	Carbon Dioxide equivalent
CBDR	Common But Differentiated Responsibility	CoE	Centres of Excellence
		CPCB	Central Pollution Control Board
CBF	Central Board of Forestry	CPSE	Central Public Sector Enterprises
CBIPM	Capacity Building for Industrial Pollution Management project	CPSMS	Central Plan Schemes Monitoring System
CBS	Core Banking Solutions	CRZ	Coastal Regulation Zone
CCAS	Climate Change Assessment Studies	CS	Central Sector
		CSIR	Council of Scientific and Industrial Research
CCCR	Centre for Climate Change Research	CSIR-CSMCRI	Central Salt and Marine Chemicals Research Institute
CCI	Cabinet Committee on Infrastructure		
		CSOs	Civil Society Organisations
CCL	Climate Change Levy	CSR	Corporate Social Responsibility
CDM	Clean Development Mechanism	CSS	Centrally Sponsored Scheme
CDMA	Code Division Multiple Access	CSTRI	Council for Science and Technology for Rural India
CECA	Comprehensive Economic Cooperation Agreement		
		CURIE	Consolidation of University Research, Innovation and Excellence
CEL	Central Electronics Ltd		
CEMS	Continuous Emission Monitoring System		
		CVD	Chemical Vapour Deposition
CEPA	Comprehensive Economic Partnership Agreement	CWG	Common Wealth Games
		DAE	Department of Atomic Energy
CER	Certified Emission Reduction	DAE-SRC	Department of Atomic Energy–Science Research Council
CERC	Central Electricity Regulatory Commission		
		DBFOT	Design, Build, Finance, Operate and Transfer
CERN	European Organization for Nuclear Research		
		DBT	Department of Biotechnology

DCs	Designated Consumers	ERI	Ecosystem Research Institute
DFCCIL	Dedicated Freight Corridor Corporation of India Limited	ESSO	Earth System Science Organisation
DFIs	Development Finance Institutions	EWS	Economically Weaker Section
DIET	District Institute of Education and Training	FAIR	Facility for Anti-proton and Ion Research
DIPP	Department of Industrial Policy and Promotion	FBR	Fast Breeder Reactor
		FC	Finance Commission
DMS	Disaster Management Support	FDI	Foreign Direct Investment
DO	Dissolved Oxygen	FEEED	Framework for Energy Efficient Economic Development
DOCS	Distributed Organic Chemical Synthesis	FIIs	Foreign Institutional Investors
DOM	Dissolved Organic Matter	FIST	Fund for Improvement of S&T Infrastructure
DOS	Department of Space		
DRDO	Defence Research and Development Organisation	FMS	Focus Market Scheme
		FMTF	Fuelling Machine Test Facility
DSSCs	Dye Sensitised Solar Cells	FRA	Forest Rights Act
DST	Department of Science & Technology	FRBMA	Fiscal Responsibility and Budget Management Act
DTAA	Double Taxation Avoidance Agreement	FSI	Forest Survey of India
		FTC	Forest and Tree Cover
DWRs	Doppler Weather Radars	FTE	Full-Time Equivalent
EAPs	External Aided Projects	FTP	Foreign Trade Policy
EBR	Extra-Budgetary Resources	FYP	Five Year Plan
ECB	European Central Bank/External Commercial Borrowings	GA	Geographic Area
		GAP-1	Ganga Action Plan-1
ECBC	Energy Conservation Building Codes	GBPIHED	G.B. Pant Institute for Himalayan Environment and Development
ECVs	Essential Climate Variables	GBS	Gross Budgetary Support
EEFP	Energy Efficiency Financing Platform	GCNEP	Global Centre for Nuclear Energy Partnership
EER	Energy Efficiency Ratio	GDCF	Gross Domestic Capital Formation
EEZ	Exclusive Economic Zone		
EI	Empowered Institution	GDDP	Gross District Domestic Product
EIA	Environment Impact Assessment	GDP	Gross Domestic Product
EIP	Eco-Industrial Park	GFCF	Gross Fixed Capital Formation
EMP	Environmental Management Plan	GHG	Greenhouse Gas
EMPOWER	Encouraging and Motivating Pursuit of World Class Exploratory Research	GHG-IMS	GHG Inventory Management System
		GHGs	Green House Gases
ENVIS	Environmental Information System	GIM	National Mission for a Green India
Eos	Earth Observations	GIS	Geographic Information System
EPC	Engineering, Procurement and Construction	GISAT	Geo Imaging Satellite
		GLP	Good Laboratory Practice
EPI	Environmental Performance Index	GM	Genetic Modification/Genetically Modified
EPO	European Patent Office	GMP	Genetically Modified Products

GNSS	Global Navigation Satellite System	ICTS	International Centre for Theoretical Sciences
GOI	Government of India		
GPS	Global Positioning System	ICZM	Integrated Coastal Zone Management
GRIHA	Green Rating for Integrated Habitat Assessment	IDFs	Infrastructure Development Funds
GSDP	Gross State Domestic Product		
GSLV	Geosynchronous Satellite Launch Vehicle	IDWH	Integrated Development of Wildlife Habitats
GSO	Geostationary Earth Orbit	IEA	International Energy Agency
GST	Goods and Services Tax	IEBR	Internal & Extra Budgetary Resources
HADP	Hill Areas Development Programme		
		IEO	Independent Evaluation Office
HAGAR	High Altitude Gamma Ray	IEP	Integrated Energy Policy
HBNI	Homi Bhabha National Institute	IERMON	Indian Environmental Radiation Monitoring Network
HCR	Head Count Ratio		
HDI	Human Development Index	IFMS	Intensification of Forest Management Scheme
HDN	Hemolytic Disease of the New born		
		IGBC	Indian Green Building Council
HDRs	Human Development Reports	IGCAR	Indira Gandhi Centre for Atomic Research
HFRR	High Flux Research Reactor		
HLEC	High Level Expert Committee	IGVdb	Indian Genome Variation database
HLEG	High Level Expert Group		
HLNRA	High-Level Natural Background Radiation Areas	IICs	Inter-Institutional Centres
		IID	Integrated Infrastructure Development
HRD	Human Resource Development		
HUD	Head Up Display	IIFCL	India Infrastructure Finance Company Limited
HVAC	Heating, Ventilation and Air Conditioning		
		IIIF	India Inclusive Innovation Funds
IAP	Integrated Action Plan	IIPDF	India Infrastructure Project Development Fund
IARCI	International Advanced Research Centre for Powder Metallurgy and New Materials		
		IIST	Indian Institute of Space Science and Technology
IBIN	Indian Bio-resource Information System		
		IIT	Indian Institute of Technology
		IMD	India Meteorological Department
IBIS	Indian Biodiversity Information System	IMF	International Monetary Fund
		IMR	Infant Mortality Rate
IBP	India Biodiversity Portal	INCCA	Indian Network for Climate Change Assessment
ICAR	Indian Council of Agricultural Research		
		India-WRIS	India-Water Resource Information System
ICDS	Integrated Child Development Services		
		INGO	Indian Geographical Organisation
ICFRE	Indian Council of Forestry Research and Education	INO	India-based Neutrino Observatory
		INSAT	Indian National Satellite System
ICMR	Indian Council of Medical Research	IOCoML	Indian Ocean Census of Marine Life
ICT	Information and Communication Technology	IP	Intellectual property
		IPR	Intellectual Property Rights

IR	Internal Resources	MIS	Micro Irrigation Systems
IRNSS	Indian Regional Navigational Satellite System	MLD	Million litres per day
		MLFPS	Market-Linked Focus Product Scheme
IRS	Indian Remote Sensing		
ISRO	Indian Space Research Organisation	MMR	Maternal Mortality Rate
		MNCs	Multinational Companies
IT	Income Tax	MoEF	Ministry of Environment and Forests
ITER	International Thermonuclear Experimental Reactor		
		MoES	Ministry of Earth Sciences
ITES	IT enabled services	MoP	Ministry of Power
ITIs	Industrial Training Institutes	MoRD	Ministry of Rural Development
IUCs	Inter-University Centres	MoU	Memorandum of Understanding
JFM	Joint Forest Management	MoUD	Ministry of Urban Development
JNCASR	Jawaharlal Nehru Centre for Advanced Scientific Research	MOX	Mixed oxide
		MPLADs	Member of Parliament's Local Area Development Programme
JNNSM	Jawaharlal Nehru National Solar Mission		
		MSME	Micro, Small and Medium Enterprises
JNNURM	Jawaharlal Nehru National Urban Renewal Mission		
		Mt	Million Tonnes
JNPT	Jawaharlal Nehru Port Trust	MTEE	Market Transformation for Energy Efficiency
KNN	Kanpur Nagar Nigam		
KYC	Know Your Customer	Mtoe/MTOE	Million Tonnes of Oil Equivalent
LAC	Latin America and the Caribbean	MTPA	Million Tonnes Per Annum
LCA	Light Combat Aircraft	MTs	Metric Tonnes
LDCs	Less Developed Countries	MW	Mega Watt
LED	Light Emitting Diode	NAAQS	National Ambient Air Quality Standards
LEHIPA	Linear Proton Accelerator		
LHC	Large Hadron Collider	NABL	National Accreditation Board for Testing Laboratories
LIGO	Laser Interferometer Gravitational Wave Observatory		
		NAEB	National Afforestation and Eco Development Board
LNG	Liquefied Natural Gas		
LPG	Liquefied Petroleum Gas	NAP	National Action Plan/National Afforestation Programme
LTROs	Longer-Term Refinancing Operations		
		NAP	National Agricultural Policy
LTTD	Low Temperature Thermal Desalination	NAPCC	National Action Plan on Climate Change
LWE	Left Wing Extremism	NASSCOM	National Association of Software and Services Companies
LWR	Light Water Reactor		
MCAs	Model Concession Agreements	NATCOMS	National Communications
MCR	Miscellaneous Capital Receipts	NATMO	National Atlas and Thematic Organisation
MDMs	Mid Day Meals		
MFA	Multifibre Agreement	NBC	National Building Code
MFP/NTFP	Minor Forest Produce/Non Timber Forest Produce	NCA	Normal Central Assistance
		NCAD	National Civil Aircraft Development
MGNREGA	Mahatma Gandhi National Rural Employment Guarantee Act		
		NCDMA	National CDM Authority
MHRD	Ministry of Human Resource Development	NCEF	National Clean Energy Fund
		NCS	National Centre for Seismology

NCSM	National Council of Science Museums	NMEEE	National Mission on Enhanced Energy Efficiency
NDC	National Development Council	NMITLI	New Millennium Indian Technology Leadership Initiative
NDEM	National Database for Emergency Management	NMNH	National Museum of Natural History
NE	North East		
NEAMA	National Environment Assessment and Monitoring Authority	NNRMS	National Natural Resources Management System
		NOx	Nitrogen Oxides
NEC	North Eastern Council	NPA	Non-Performing Assets
NECA	National Elephant Conservation Authority	NPCA	National Plan for Conservation of Aquatic Ecosystems
NEERI	National Environmental Engineering Research Institute	NPRE	Non Plan Revenue Expenditure
		NRAA	National Rainfed Area Authority
NEFC	National Environment and Forestry Council	NRCD	National River Conservation Directorate
NeGAP	National e-Governance Assistance Programme	NRCP	National River Conservation Plan
		NRDMS	Natural Resources Data Management System
NELP	New Exploration Licensing Policy		
NEMP	National Environmental Monitoring Programme	NREGA	National Rural Employment Guarantee Act
NEP	National Electricity Policy	NRHM	National Rural Health Mission
NEPA	National Environment Protection Authority	NRLM	National Rural Livelihoods Mission
NERF	National Environment Restoration Fund	NSAP	National Social Assistance Programme
NFHS	National Family Health Survey	NSDI	National Spatial Data Infrastructure
NGIS	National Geographic Information Systems		
		NSDP	Net State Domestic Product
NGOs	Non-Governmental Organisations	NSERB	National Science and Engineering Research Board
NGRBA	National Ganga River Basin Authority		
		NSS	National Service Scheme
NGT	National Green Tribunal	NSSO	National Sample Survey Office
NHDP	National Highway Development Projects	NUIS	National Urban Information System
NHM	National Health Mission	NWC	National Water Commission
NIF	National Innovation Foundation	NWCP	National Wetland Conservation Programme
NIMS	National Inventory Management System		
		NWFL	National Water Framework Law
NISER	National Institute of Science Education Research	NWM	National Water Mission
		NWP	National Water Policy/Numerical Weather Prediction
NITs	National Institutes of Technology		
NKN	National Knowledge Network	NWR-IC	National Water Resources – Information Centre
NLCP	National Lake Conservation Plan		
NLDCs	Non-Least Developed Countries	O&M	Operation & Maintenance
NLSRC	National Life Sciences Resource Centre	OBCs	Other Backward Classes
		OCM	Ocean Colour Monitor

Acronym	Expansion
ODS	Oxide Dispersion Strengthened
OfWat	Office of Water, Regulator
OMCs	Oil Marketing Companies
OOS	Ocean Observation System
OSDD	Open Source Drug Discovery
PACE	Patent Acquisition and Collaborative Research and Technology Development
PAs	Protected Areas
PAT	Perform, Achieve and Trade/Perform-Achieve-Trade
PCI	Per Capita Income
PCTs	Patent Cooperation Treaties
PDS	Public Distribution System
PEO	Programme Evaluation Organisation
PESA	Panchayats (Extension to the Scheduled Areas) Act 1996
PET	Potential Evapo-Transpiration
PFBR	Prototype Fast Breeder Reactor
PFZs	Potential Fishing Zones
PHWR	Pressurised Heavy Water Reactor
PIM	Participatory Irrigation Management
PMGSY	Pradhan Mantri Grameen Sadak Yojana
PMN	Polymetallic Manganese Nodule
PPC	Portland Pozzolana Cement
PPP	Public–Private Partnership
PPPAC	Public–Private Partnership Appraisal Committee
PPPPs	People–Public–Private Partnerships
PRIs	Panchayati Raj Institutions
PRISM	Promoting Innovations in Individuals, Start-ups and MSMEs
PSEs	Public Sector Enterprises
PSLV	Polar Satellite Launch Vehicle
PSUs	Public Sector Undertakings
PTAs	Preferential Trade Agreements
PUFAs	Pooly Unsaturated Fatty Acids
PURSE	Promotion of University Research and Scientific Excellence
R&D	Research and Development
R&R	Resettlement & Rehabilitation
RBI	Reserve Bank of India
RDF	Refuse Derived Fuel
RE	Revised Estimates
REC	Renewable Energy Certificate
REDD+	Reduced Emissions from Deforestation and Forest Degradation
RF	Radio Frequency
RFD	Results Framework Document
RFP	Model Request for Proposal
RFQ	Request for Qualification
RISK	Research Initiative to Scale New Knowledgebase
RKVY	Rashtriya Krishi Vikas Yojana
RLV	Reusable launch vehicle
RO	Reverse Osmosis
ROV	Remotely Operated Vehicle
RRCAT	Raja Ramanna Centre for Advanced Technology
RRI	Raman Research Institute
RRR	Repair, Renovation and Restoration
RS	Restricted Service
RSBY	Rashtriya Swasthya Bima Yojana
RSDP	Remote Sensing Data Policy
RSPM	Respirable Suspended Particulate Matter
RSVY	Rashtriya Sam Vikas Yojana
RTE	Right to Education
S&T	Science and Technology
SAARC	South Asian Association for Regional Corporation
SACEP	South Asia Co-operative Environment Programme
SACU	Southern African Customs Union
SAFTA	South Asia Free Trade Area
SAPCC	State Action Plans on Climatic Change
SBIRI	Small Business Innovative Research Initiative
SC	State Water Regulatory and Development Council/Super Critical
SCA	Special Central Assistance
SCI	Science Citation Index
SCs	Scheduled Castes
SDP	State Domestic Product
SDRs	Special Drawing Rights
SEC	Specific Energy Consumption

SEEP	Super-Efficient Equipment Programme	TECHVILS	Technology Enabled Villages
SEFC	State Environment and Forest Council	TEM	Transmission Electron Microscope
SEWA	Self Employed Women's Association	TePP	Technopreneur Promotion Programme
SEZs	Special Economic Zones	TFP	Total Factor Productivity
SGDP	State Gross Domestic Product	THSTI	Translational Health Science and Technology Institute
SGSY	Swaranjayanti Gram Swarojgar Yojana	TIFAC	Technology Information, Forecasting and Assessment Council
SHGs	Self Help Groups		
SIROs	Scientific & Industrial Research Organisations	TIFR	Tata Institute of Fundamental Research
SIS-DP	Space-based Information Support for Decentralised Planning	TK	Traditional Knowledge
		TKDL	Traditional Knowledge Digital Library
SIWEA	State Independent Water Expert Authority	TLP	Tariff Liberalization Programme
SKA	Square Kilometre Array	TMT	Thirty Metre Telescope
SMC	Soil Moisture Conservation	TQM	Total Quality Management
SMEs	Small and Medium Scale Enterprises	TRGs	Tele-metred Automatic Rain Gauges
SMS	Short Message Service	TRIPS	Trade-Related Aspects of Intellectual Property Rights
SNP	Satellite Navigation Programme		
SoI	Survey of India	TTC	Telemetry, Tracking and Command
SOTEF	Solar Test Facility		
SOx	Sulphur Oxides	U-Excel	Unit for Excellence
SPA	Special Plan Assistance	UGC-DAE	University Grants Commission-Department of Atomic Energy
SPCAs	Society for Prevention of Cruelty to Animals		
		UHC	Universal Health Care
SPM	Suspended Particulate Matter	UID	Unique Identification
SPS	Standard Positioning Service	UIDSSMT	Urban Infrastructure Development Scheme for Small and Medium Towns
SPV	Solar Photovoltaic		
SSA	Sarva Shiksha Abhiyan/Sub-Saharan Africa		
		UK	United Kingdom
SSI	Small Scale Industries	ULBs	Urban Local Bodies
ST	Solar Thermal	UMPPs	Ultra Mega Power Projects
STI	Technology and Innovation	UN	United Nations
STPs	Sewage Treatment Plants	UNCED	United Nations Conference on Environment and Development
STs	Scheduled Tribes		
TBM	Test blanket module	UNDP	United Nations Development Programme
TCC	Trichy City Corporation		
TCIS	TIFR Centre for Interdisciplinary Sciences	UNEP	United Nations Environment Programme
TDB	Technology Development Board	UNFCCC	United Nations Framework Convention on Climate Change
TDDP	Technology Development and Demonstration Programme		
		USC	Ultra Super Critical
TDEM	Time Domain Electromagnetic	USOF	Universal Services Obligation Fund

USPTO	United States Patent and Trademark Office	WAVE	Women's Action for Village Empowerment
UTs	Union Territories	WBCSD	World Business Council for Sustainable Development
UVIT	Ultraviolet Imaging Telescope		
VAT	Value Added Tax	WGDP	Western Ghat Development Programme
VGF	Viability Gap Funding		
VOL	Vinati Organics Limited	WHO	World Health Organisation
VP	Vigyan Prasar	WMC	Waste Minimization Circles
VSAT	Very Small Aperture Terminal	WRIS	Water Resources Information System
VSF	Viability Support Funding		
VSS	Van Samrakshana Samithi	WTO	World Trade Organisation
WALMIs	Water and Land Management Institutes	WUAs	Water Users Associations
		WUGs	Water Users Groups
WASSAN	Watershed Support Services and Activities Network	ZBB	Zero based budgeting
		ZSI	Zoological Survey of India

Annexures

2.1	Poverty—Measures and Changes Therein	67
3.1	Sectoral Allocation for Public Sector's Resources—Eleventh Plan (2007–12) Realisation and Twelfth Plan (2012–17) Projections	99
3.2	Budget Support, IEBR and Outlay for Central Ministry/Department—Eleventh Plan (2007–12) Realisation and Twelfth Plan (2012–17) Projections	100
3.3	Proposed Sectoral Allocations for States and Union Territories in the Twelfth Plan	103
4.1	Estimated Energy Savings due to Electrical Appliances Programme in the Twelfth Plan	140
4.2	Co-Benefits Framework for Low Carbon Strategies	141
5.1	Plan-wise Expenditure on Irrigation and Flood Control	181
5.2	Plan-wise Proliferation of Schemes in MMI Sector	181
5.3	Spillover of Major, Medium and ERM Projects into the Twelfth Plan	182
5.4	CLA/Grant and Irrigation Potential Created through AIBP, 1996–2012	182
5.5	Plan-Wise Irrigation Potential Created and Utilised	183
5.6	Physical and Financial Achievements of CAD Programme	184
5.7	Water Use Efficiency of Completed Major/Medium Irrigation Projects Based on Field Measurements of Losses	185
5.8	Water Data Base Development and Management in the Twelfth Plan	186
8.1	National Targets for S&T Sector for the Twelfth Plan	274

1

Twelfth Plan: An Overview

INTRODUCTION

1.1. India's 1.25 billion citizens have higher expectations about their future today, than they have ever had before. They have seen the economy grow much faster in the past 10 years than it did earlier, and deliver visible benefits to a large number of people. This has understandably raised the expectations of all sections, especially those who have benefited less. Our people are now much more aware of what is possible, and they will settle for no less. The Twelfth Five Year Plan must rise to the challenge of meeting these high expectations.

The Initial Conditions

1.2. Though expectations have mounted, the circumstances in which the Twelfth Plan has commenced are less favourable than at the start of the Eleventh Plan in 2007–08. At that time, the economy was growing robustly, the macroeconomic balance was improving and global economic developments were supportive. The situation today is much more difficult. The global economy is going through what looks like a prolonged slowdown. The domestic economy has also run up against several internal constraints. Macro-economic imbalances have surfaced following the fiscal expansion undertaken after 2008 to give a fiscal stimulus to the economy. Inflationary pressures have built up. Major investment projects in energy and transport have slowed down because of a variety of implementation problems. Some changes in tax treatment in the 2012–13 have caused uncertainty among investors.

1.3. These developments have produced a reduction in the rate of investment, and a slowing down of economic growth to 6.2 per cent in 2011–12, which was the last year of the Eleventh Plan. The growth rate in the first half of 2012–13, which is the first year of the Twelfth Plan, is even lower. The downturn clearly requires urgent corrective action but it should not lead to unwarranted pessimism about the medium term. India's economic fundamentals have been improving in many dimensions, and this is reflected in the fact that despite the slowdown in 2011–12, the growth rate of the economy averaged 8 per cent in the Eleventh Plan period. This was lower than the Plan target of 9 per cent, but it was better than the achievement of 7.8 per cent in the Tenth Plan. The fact that this growth occurred in a period which saw two global crises, one in 2008 and another in 2011, is indicative of the resilience which the economy has developed.

The Policy Challenge

1.4. The policy challenge in the Twelfth Plan is, therefore, two-fold. The immediate challenge is to reverse the observed deceleration in growth by reviving investment as quickly as possible. This calls for urgent action to tackle implementation constraints in infrastructure which are holding up large projects, combined with action to deal with tax related issues which have created uncertainty in the investment climate. From a longer term perspective, the Plan must put in place policies that can leverage the many strengths of the economy to bring it back to its real growth potential. This will take time but the aim should be to get back to 9 per cent growth by the end of the Twelfth Plan period.

1.5. The preparation of a Five Year Plan for the country is an opportunity to step back, take stock of the 'big picture', identify the strengths that can be leveraged to enable the country to move forward, and the constraints that could hold it back, and on this basis develop a strategic agenda. In developing such an agenda, the Planning Commission has relied on four key elements.

- First, the strategy must be firmly grounded in an understanding of the complexities of the development challenges that India faces, recognising the transformation that is taking place in the economy and in the world. This understanding of the ground reality must be used to identify the critical leverage points where government action could have the maximum impact. The focus must be on identifying the strategic leverage points where successful action could trigger many supportive reactions rather than fixing everything everywhere.
- Second, progress will be achieved through a combination of government action in both policies and public programmes, and the efforts of many private actors that are important in the economy. Much of the inclusive growth we hope to achieve depends on investment in the private sector which accounts for over 70 per cent of total investment. This includes not only the organised corporate sector, but also Micro, Small and Medium Enterprises (MSMEs), individual farmers and myriads of small businessmen who add to Gross Domestic Product (GDP) and create jobs. The dynamism of this segment, and its ability to seize economic opportunities, is critical for inclusive growth and the Plan must address the constraints faced by all these private actors in achieving better results.
- Third, the outlay on government programmes has to increase in many areas but this must be accompanied by improved implementation. For this, it is necessary to focus on capacity building and governance reforms, including system change that will increase accountability in the public sector. The Twelfth Plan must back this focus by making specific allocations to improve the ability of government to work better.
- Finally, the planning process must serve as a way of getting different stakeholders to work together to achieve broad consensus on key issues. These stakeholders include (*i*) different levels of the government sector: Centre, States and Panchayati Raj Institutions (PRIs)/Urban Local Bodies (ULBs); (*ii*) the private sector, both big companies and small businesses, whose investments will drive our growth and (*iii*) citizens' groups and the voluntary sector, who bring the key element of people's participation and can greatly help improve the quality of government action.

1.6. The Planning Commission has consulted widely over the past two years with other Ministries, with State Governments, with experts and also with Civil Society Organisations (CSOs). As many as 900 CSOs have been consulted through workshops and other fora. Several expert groups were set up to advice on various aspects of the economy and their reports are important inputs. These include the High Level Expert Group (HLEG) on Health, the HLEG on Transport, the Expert Group on Infrastructure Financing, the Expert Group on the Low Carbon Economy, the Expert Group on Venture Capital and Angel Investors, and the Expert Group on Management of Public Enterprises.

1.7. This Chapter is not an executive summary. Rather it provides an overview of the basic rationale of the Plan and the key areas of intervention. The Chapter is organised as follows:

- Section 1.2 presents the basic vision and aspirations which drive the Plan and which are captured in the sub-title 'Faster, sustainable and More Inclusive Growth'.
- Section 1.3 focuses on the development of capabilities—both human and institutional—to achieve the vision.
- Section 1.4 focuses on the challenge of managing our national resources rationally; a critical area for planning if we want growth to be sustainable.
- Section 1.5 deals with India's engagement with the world in the Twelfth Plan and beyond.

- Section 1.6 presents a summary of some of the major policy initiatives that taken together would contribute a strategy for achieving faster, more inclusive and sustainable growth.

VISION AND ASPIRATIONS

1.8. The broad vision and aspirations which the Twelfth Plan seeks to fulfil are reflected in the subtitle: 'Faster, Sustainable, and More Inclusive Growth'. The simultaneous achievement of each of these elements is critical for the success of the Plan.

The Need for Faster Growth

1.9. Planners are sometimes criticised for focusing too much on GDP growth, when the real objective should be to achieve an improved quality of life of the people across both economic and non-economic dimensions. The Twelfth Plan fully recognises that the objective of development is broad-based improvement in the economic and social conditions of our people. However, rapid growth of GDP is an essential requirement for achieving this objective.

1.10. There are two reasons why GDP growth is important for the inclusiveness objective. First, rapid growth of GDP produces a larger expansion in total income and production which, if the growth process is sufficiently inclusive, will directly raise living standards of a large section of our people by providing them with employment and other income enhancing activities. Our focus should not be just on GDP growth itself, but on achieving a growth process that is as inclusive as possible. For example, rapid growth which involves faster growth in agriculture, and especially in rain-fed areas where most of the poor live, will be much more inclusive than a GDP growth that is driven entirely by mining or extraction of minerals for exports. Similarly, rapid growth which is based on faster growth for the manufacturing sector as a whole, including MSME, will generate a much broader spread of employment and income earning opportunities and is therefore more inclusive than a growth which is largely driven by extractive industries.

1.11. The second reason why rapid growth is important for inclusiveness is that it generates higher revenues, which help to finance critical programmes of inclusiveness. There are many such programmes which either deliver benefits directly to the poor and the excluded groups, or increase their ability to access employment and income opportunities generated by the growth process. Examples of such programmes are the Mahatma Gandhi National Rural Employment Guarantee Act (MGNREGA), Sarva Siksha Abhiyan (SSA), Mid Day Meals (MDMs), Pradhan Mantri Gram Sadak Yojana (PMGSY), Integrated Child Development Services (ICDS), National Rural Health Mission (NRHM), and so on. This is also relevant for the sustainability objective since programmes aimed at making development more sustainable also involve additional costs.

Growth Prospects

1.12. The Approach Paper to the Twelfth Plan, approved by the National Development Council (NDC) in 2011, had set a target of 9 per cent average growth of GDP over the Plan period. That was before the Eurozone crisis in that year triggered a sharp downturn in global economic prospects, and also before the extent of the slowdown in the domestic economy was known. A realistic assessment of the growth prospects of the economy in the Twelfth Plan period is given in Chapter 2. It concludes that the current slowdown in GDP growth can be reversed through strong corrective action, including especially an expansion in investment with a corresponding increase in savings to keep inflationary pressures under control. However, while our full growth potential remains around 9 per cent, acceleration to this level can only occur in a phased manner, especially since the global economy is expected to remain weak for the first half of the Plan period. Taking account of all these factors, the Twelfth Plan should work towards bringing GDP growth back to an inclusive 9 per cent in the last two years of the Plan, which will yield an average growth rate of about 8 per cent over the entire Plan period. The outcome is conditional on many policy actions as is described in scenario one.

1.13. Within the aggregate GDP growth target, two sub-targets are especially important for inclusiveness. These are a growth rate of 4 per cent for the agricultural sector over the Twelfth Plan period and around 10 per cent in the last two years of the Plan for the manufacturing sector. The policies needed to achieve these sectoral targets are summarised in Section 1.6.

1.14. The Twelfth Plan's strategy for growth depends crucially on productivity gains as one of the key drivers of growth. Productivity is the additional contribution to growth after taking account of the effect of capital accumulation and growth in labour. These traditional sources of growth are not likely to be enough for India in the coming years and we must therefore focus much more on productivity improvements among all constituents: big businesses, MSMEs, farmers and even government. This can be done by improving the business regulatory environment, strengthening the governance capacity of States, investing more in infrastructure rather than subsidies, and by using Science and Technology (S&T) to drive innovation.

Alternative Scenarios

1.15. The projection of 8 per cent growth in the Twelfth Plan period should not be viewed as a 'business as usual' outcome that can be realised with relatively little effort. It is in fact a projection of what is possible if we take early steps to reverse the current slowdown and also take other policy actions needed to address other key constraints that will otherwise prevent the economy from returning to a higher growth path. Failure to act firmly on these policies will lead to lower growth and also poorer outcomes on inclusiveness.

1.16. To illustrate the consequences of inaction on key growth promoting policies, the Planning Commission has undertaken a systematic process of 'scenario planning' based on diverse views and disciplines to understand the interplay of the principal forces, internal and external, shaping India's progress. This analysis suggests three alternative scenarios of how India's economy might develop titled, 'Strong Inclusive Growth', 'Insufficient Action' and 'Policy Logjam'.

1.17. The first scenario 'Strong Inclusive Growth', describes the conditions that will emerge if a well-designed strategy is implemented, intervening at the key leverage points in the system. This in effect is the scenario underpinning the Twelfth Plan growth projections of 8 per cent, starting from below 6 per cent in the first year to reach 9 per cent in the last two years. The second scenario 'Insufficient Action' describes the consequences of half hearted action in which the direction of policy is endorsed, but sufficient action is not taken. The growth in this scenario declines to around 6 per cent to 6.5 per cent. The third scenario 'Policy Logjam', projects the consequences of Policy Inaction persisting too long. The growth rate in this scenario can drift down to 5 per cent to 5.5 per cent.

1.18. The scenarios are discussed in greater detail in Chapter 2 and presented in another document complementing the Plan. Public discussion of these scenarios could help to generate a discourse going beyond the parameters of the Twelfth Five Year Plan and assist in building a national consensus about the policies that are necessary if India's future is to unfold as we want. It is important to emphasise that the scenarios are not presented an alternative option form which we can choose. In fact, the only scenario that will meet the aspiration of the people is scenario one. The other scenarios are only presented to illustrate the consequences of inaction.

1.19. Ours is a diverse society and also an argumentative one. We are suspicious when decisions that affect us are not taken transparently and we resent too much centralisation of decision-making. But we all believe in democracy, we respect the views of others and, although we may disagree, we admire and learn from those who work together to offer any vision of a better India. We need to do more to build a greater consensus around a common national goal.

1.20. The Twelfth Plan should aim at a growth process that preserves emphasis on inclusion and sustainability while minimising downside effects on growth. Plans are traditionally viewed as being about what governments should do, but that is a narrow view since most investment today is private, and much of that is corporate. The Twelfth Plan must provide a competitive environment in which the private sector, including the corporate sector but also all Indians, both as individuals and in the collective, are enable to reach their full potential. The objective must be to stimulate new entrepreneurship while enabling existing MSMEs, including in agriculture, to invest more and grow faster. For this, we need to meet their needs for infrastructure and for easier, cheaper and faster access to capital.

1.21. India is fortunate that it is richly endowed in entrepreneurial talent. At a rough estimate, the number of non-agricultural establishments in the country increases by about 8 million every 10 years. While many of these enterprises are very small, and reflect basic survival strategies, many are not. The past decade has shown the dynamism that is possible in this sector under the right circumstances. Many of the leading corporates today belonged to the MSME category at the turn of the century. In this context, the Twelfth Plan's overarching priority on developing human capital can, with the proper prioritisation of infrastructure and with innovative use of technology and finance, unleash a truly inclusive growth story.

1.22. This inclusive strategy involves a much greater role of the States, and closer coordination between the Centre and the States, than would be needed for a purely corporate-led growth strategy. This is because most of the policy measures and institutional support required for small and medium entrepreneur-led growth lie in the domain of State Governments and local bodies. The Centre's contributions would lie mainly in creating the appropriate macroeconomic framework, financial sector policies and national level infrastructure.

The Meaning of Inclusiveness

1.23. Inclusiveness means many different things and each aspect of inclusiveness poses its own challenges for policy.

Inclusiveness as Poverty Reduction

1.24. Distributional concerns have traditionally been viewed as ensuring an adequate flow of benefits to the poor and the most marginalised. This must remain an important policy focus in the Twelfth Plan. It is worth noting that the record in this dimension of inclusiveness is encouraging. The percentage of the population below the official poverty line has been falling but even as that happens, the numbers below the poverty line remain large. According to the latest official estimates of poverty based on the Tendulkar Committee poverty line, as many as 29.8 per cent of the population, that is, 350 million people were below the poverty line in 2009–10. Questions have been raised about the appropriateness of the Tendulkar poverty line which corresponds to a family consumption level of ₹3,900 per month in rural areas and ₹4,800 per month in urban areas (in both cases for a family of five). There is no doubt that the Tendulkar Committee poverty line represents a very low level of consumption and the scale of poverty even on this basis is substantial. An Expert committee under Dr. C. Rangarajan has been set up to review all issues related to the poverty line keeping in view international practices.

1.25. Chapter 2 reports on the progress made in reducing poverty over time. It is well established that the percentage of the population in poverty has been falling consistently but the rate of decline was too slow. The rate of decline in poverty in the period 2004–05 to 2009–10 was 1.5 percentage points per year, which is twice the rate of decline of 0.74 percentage points per year observed between 1993–94 and 2004–05. Normally, large sample surveys used for official estimates of poverty are conducted every five years, but because 2009–10 was a drought year, the National Sample Survey Office (NSSO) felt that it would tend to overstate poverty and it was therefore decided to advance the next large sample survey to 2011–12. The results of this survey will yield an official estimate of the extent of poverty in 2011–12, that is, the position at the end of the Eleventh Plan period, but this will be available only in mid-2013. However, preliminary results from the survey have been published and they suggest that the percentage of the population in poverty will decline significantly compared to 2009–10. According to some non-official estimates, the rate of decline in poverty between 2004–05 and 2011–12 will be close to 2 per cent per year, which was the Eleventh Plan target. If this turns out to be the case, it can be claimed that the Eleventh Plan has indeed delivered on inclusiveness.

Inclusiveness as Group Equality

1.26. Inclusiveness is not just about bringing those below an official fixed poverty line to a level above it. It is also about a growth process which is seen to be 'fair' by different socio-economic groups that constitute our society. The poor are certainly one target group, but inclusiveness must also embrace the concern of other groups such as the Scheduled Castes (SCs), Scheduled Tribes (STs), Other Backward Classes (OBCs), Minorities, the differently abled and other marginalised groups. Women can also be viewed as a disadvantaged group for this purpose. These distinct 'identity groups' are sometimes correlated with income slabs—the SCs and STs, for example, are in the lower income category—and all poverty alleviation strategies help them directly. Women on the other hand span the entire income spectrum, but there are gender-based issues of inclusiveness that are relevant all along the spectrum.

1.27. Inclusiveness from a group perspective obviously goes beyond a poverty reduction perspective and includes consideration of the status of the group as a whole relative to the general population. For example, narrowing the gap between the SCs or STs and the general population must be part of any reasonable definition of inclusiveness, and this is quite distinct from the concern with poverty, or inequality. For example, it is perfectly possible for anti-poverty strategies to be reducing income poverty among SCs and STs without reducing the income gap between these groups and the general population.

1.28. Ending of gender based inequities, discrimination and all forms of violence against girls and women is being accorded overriding priority in the Twelfth Plan. This is fundamental to enabling women participate fully in the development process, and in fulfilling their social, economic, civil and political rights.

Inclusiveness as Regional Balance

1.29. Another aspect of inclusiveness relates to whether all States, and indeed all regions, are seen to benefit from the growth process. The regional dimension has grown in importance in recent years. On the positive side, as documented in Chapter 11, many of the erstwhile backward States have begun to show significant improvement in growth performance and the variation in growth rates across States has narrowed. However, both the better performing and other States are increasingly concerned about their backward regions, or districts, which may not share the general improvement in living standards experienced elsewhere. Many of these districts have unique characteristics including high concentration of tribal population in forested areas, or Minorities in urban areas. Some districts are also affected by left wing extremism, making the task of development much more difficult.

1.30. In the Twelfth Plan, we must pay special attention to the scope for accelerating growth in the States that are lagging behind. This will require strengthening of States' own capacities to plan, to implement and to bring greater synergies within their own administration and with the Central Government. As a first step, the Planning Commission is working with it's counterpart Planning Boards and Planning Departments in all State Governments to improve their capabilities. An important constraint on the growth of backward regions in the country is the poor state of infrastructure, especially road connectivity, schools and health facilities and the availability of electricity, all of which combine to hold back

---

Box 1.1
Prime Minister Dr Manmohan Singh at the 57th NDC

Gender inequality is an aspect which deserves special attention. Women and girls represent half the population and our society has not been fair to this half. Their socio-economic status is improving, but gaps persist.... There can be no meaningful development without the active participation of half the population and this participation simply cannot take place if their security and safety are not assured. I urge all Chief Ministers to pay special attention to this critical area in their states.

development. Improvement in infrastructure must therefore be an important component of any regionally inclusive development strategy.

Inclusiveness and Inequality

1.31. Inclusiveness also means greater attention to income inequality. The extent of inequality is measured by indices such as the Gini coefficient, which provide a measure of the inequality in the distribution on a whole, or by measures that focus on particular segments such as the ratio of consumption of the top 10 per cent or 20 per cent of the population to that of the bottom 10 per cent or 20 per cent of the population, or in terms of rural–urban, such as the ratio of mean consumption in urban *versus* rural areas. An aspect of inequality that has come sharply into focus in industrialised countries, in the wake of the financial crisis, is the problem of extreme concentration of income at the very top, that is, the top 1 per cent and this concern is also reflected in the public debate in India.

1.32. Perfect equality is not found anywhere and there are many reasons why it may not even be a feasible objective. However, there can be no two opinions on the fact that inequality must be kept within tolerable limits. Some increase in inequality in a developing country during a period of rapid growth and transformation may be unavoidable and it may even be tolerated if it is accompanied by sufficiently rapid improvement in the living standards of the poor. However, an increase in inequality with little or no improvement in the living standards of the poor is a recipe for social tensions. Static measures of inequality do not capture the phenomenon of equality of opportunity which needs special attention. Any given level of inequality of outcomes is much more socially acceptable if it results from a system which provides greater equality of opportunity. As a society, we therefore need to move as rapidly as possible to the ideal of giving every child in India a fair opportunity in life, which means assuring every child access to good health and quality education. While this may not be possible to achieve in one Plan period, the Twelfth Plan should aim at making substantial progress in this dimension.

Inclusiveness as Empowerment

1.33. Finally, inclusiveness is not just about ensuring a broad-based flow of benefits or economic opportunities, it is also about empowerment and participation. It is a measure of the success we have achieved in building a participatory democracy that people are no longer prepared to be passive recipients of benefits doled out by the Government. They are slowly beginning to demand these benefits and opportunities as rights and they also want a say in how they are administered. This brings to the fore issues of governance, accountability and peoples participation to much greater extent than before. This also covers areas like access to information about government schemes, knowledge of the relevant laws and how to access justice. The growing concern with governance has also focused attention on corruption. How to tackle corruption is now at the centre stage of policy debates.

Inclusiveness through Employment Programmes

1.34. One of the most important interventions for fostering inclusion during Eleventh Plan was the MGNREGA. While its achievements in ameliorating poverty and preventing acute distress during times of drought have been recorded and appreciated, there are also some complaints against MGNREGA, primarily on the grounds that it is a dole, involving huge expenditures that could have been spent more productively. There are also complaints that it is leading to increase in wages of agricultural labour and construction workers.

1.35. The view that rising wages by themselves represent a problem is not credible since this is the only mechanism through which landless agricultural labour can benefit from economic growth. If rising wages squeeze farm profitability, the solution lies in raising farm productivity to accommodate higher wages. Several initiatives in this regard are discussed in Chapter 12. In any case, rural labour relations in large parts of the country continue to be feudal, and use of migrant labour for both agriculture and construction continues to be exploitative. These inequities would not get corrected by themselves. We should not be looking to perpetuate a situation where low-cost labour provides the necessary profit margins for farmers, removing incentives to invest in efficiency improvement.

1.36. The main point to note is that employment schemes are not new in India, and they have a well-established poverty reducing impact. With National Sample Survey showing an eightfold increase in employment in public works after MGNREGA, there is no doubt that its impact on rural wage earnings and poverty has been much larger than all previous rural employment schemes. What is less appreciated is that this has been achieved with a rather modest increase in the share spent on rural employment schemes out of total Central Plan expenditures. It has increased from an average of 11.8 per cent in the three years before MGNREGA (2002–03 to 2004–05) to 13.3 per cent in the last three (2009–10 to 2011–12). This means that although MGNREGA is not free of leakages, these have declined considerably. Thus, far from opening a bottomless pit as some critics still claim, the provision of employment as a legal right, has greatly improved the share of intended beneficiaries in what government spends for development of rural areas.

1.37. There is also evidence that wherever land productivity has improved and greater water security been delivered, small and marginal farmers working in MGNREGA sites have reverted back to farming and allied livelihoods. There is also evidence that MGNREGA is enabling crop diversification, particularly into horticulture, wherever it has adequately converged with schemes of Agricultural Departments. An important lesson from this experience is that it is the quality of assets created, which will determine whether MGNREGA can go beyond the safety net to become a springboard for entrepreneurship, even at the lowest income levels.

1.38. Each of the dimensions of inclusiveness discussed above is relevant, and public attention often focuses on one or the other at different times. We should aim at achieving steady progress in each of these dimensions. Accelerated growth in recent years has yielded distinct benefits to many and the prosperity which this has generated is visible to all, raising the expectations of all sections of the population, and creating a demand for a fair share of the benefits of growth. Policymaking has to be watchful of developments in each dimension of fairness and be quick to take corrective steps as soon as the need arises. Box 1.2 provides an assessment of trends in some key variables which point to the greater inclusiveness of growth in recent years.

Environmental Sustainability

1.39. While striving for faster and more inclusive growth, the Twelfth Plan must also pay attention to the problem of sustainability. No development process can afford to neglect the environmental consequences of economic activity, or allow unsustainable depletion and deterioration of natural resources. Unfortunately, the experience of development in many countries, and our own past experience in some respects, suggests that this can easily happen unless appropriate corrective steps are taken at early stages. The Twelfth Plan must devise a strategy of development which effectively reconciles the objective of development with the objective of protecting the environment.

1.40. Development cannot take place without additional energy and the energy requirement of development will have to be reconciled with the objective of protection of environment. The economy depends heavily on coal and hydro power to meet its energy needs and the development of each of these energy sources involves potential trade-offs with conservation of forests and the objective of avoiding displacement of people. We need to manage these conflicting objectives more efficiently, with adequate compensation for those dispossessed and appropriate remedial steps to correct for loss of forest cover where this is unavoidable. Nuclear energy is another important energy source for the country, and has the greatest potential over the next 20 years, of providing a substitute for coal-based electricity. However, here too environmental and safety issues have arisen, especially after the Fukushima accident. These concerns are being addressed.

1.41. The achievement of environmental sustainability will impact the life of communities in several dimensions. It will require the need development of new energy efficient practices in urban housing and transport to contain the growth in the demand for energy. It would mean use of far more energy

Box 1.2
Eleventh Plan Achievements on Inclusive Growth

The following are some important indicators showing the extent to which the Eleventh Plan succeeded in fulfilling the objective of inclusive growth. (In some cases, where the data relate to the NSSO surveys, the time period for comparison is before and after 2004–05.)

- GDP growth in the Eleventh Plan 2007–08 to 2011–12 was 8 per cent compared with 7.6 per cent in the Tenth Plan (2002–03 to 2006–07) and only 5.7 per cent in the Ninth Plan (1997–98 to 2001–02). The growth rate of 7.9 per cent in the Eleventh Plan period is one of the highest of any country in that period which saw two global crises.
- Agricultural GDP growth accelerated in the Eleventh Plan, to an average rate of 3.7 per cent, compared with 2.4 per cent in the Tenth Plan, and 2.5 per cent in the Ninth Plan.
- The percentage of the population below the poverty line declined at the rate of 1.5 percentage points (ppt) per year in the period 2004–05 to 2009–10, twice the rate at which it declined in the previous period 1993–94 to 2004–05. (When the data for the latest NSSO survey for 2011–12 become available, it is likely that the rate of decline may be close to 2 ppt per year.)
- The rate of growth of real consumption per capita in rural areas in the period 2004–05 to 2011–12 was 3.4 per cent per year which was four times the rate in the previous period 1993–94 to 2004–05.
- The rate of unemployment declined from 8.2 per cent in 2004–05 to 6.6 per cent in 2009–10 reversing the trend observed in the earlier period when it had actually increased from 6.1 per cent in 1993–94 to 8.2 per cent in 2004–05.
- Rural real wages increased 6.8 per cent per year in the Eleventh Plan (2007–08 to 2011–12) compared to an average 1.1 per cent per year in the previous decade, led largely by the government's rural policies and initiatives.
- Complete immunization rate increased by 2.1 ppt per year between 2002–04 and 2007–08, compared to a 1.7 ppt fall per year between 1998–99 and 2002–04. Similarly, institutional deliveries increased by 1.6 ppt per year between 2002–04 and 2007–08 higher than the 1.3 ppt increase per year between 1998–99 and 2002–04.
- Net enrolment rate at the primary level rose to a near universal 98.3 per cent in 2009–10. Dropout rate (classes I–VIII) also showed improvements, falling 1.7 ppt per year between 2003–04 and 2009–10, which was twice the 0.8 ppt fall between 1998–99 and 2003–04.

efficient technologies in coal-based electricity generation such as the introduction of super critical and ultra super critical boilers. It would require active promotion of energy efficiency in industries, farms and offices, and the promotion of more energy efficient appliances through policies of branding and mandatory standards. Transport policies and related technologies for more energy efficient vehicles will need to be developed and adopted.

1.42. The issue of sustainability also has a global dimension because of the threat of climate change caused by the accumulation of carbon dioxide and other Greenhouse Gases (GHG) in the atmosphere due to human activity. Since GHG emission in any country accelerates the process of global warming, this is obviously an area where a global cooperative solution is needed. No country will have sufficient incentive to contain its own emissions unless it is part of a global compact. Such a compact in turn is possible only if there is a fair distribution of the burden. Developing countries have consistently argued that since it is the industrialised countries that have historically contributed the bulk of the accumulated stock of GHG, and are also the most able to pay, they must bear burden of global mitigation and adjustment. India is participating in the ongoing international negotiations under the UN Framework Convention on Climate Change, but progress thus far has been minimal.

1.43. We cannot, however, abstain from taking action to deal with climate change until an international solution is found. It is known that India will be one of the countries most severely affected if global warming proceeds unchecked and as such appropriate domestic action is necessary. A National Action Plan for climate change has been evolved with eight component Missions. Implementation of these missions must be an integral part of the Twelfth Plan. Policies should be closely monitored to ensure that we achieve the stated objective of reducing the emissions intensity of our GDP by 20 per cent to 25 per cent between 2005 and 2020.

1.44. Resolving the conflict between energy and the environment is not without cost. It involves additional upfront costs both of mitigating the adverse impact on the environment and of switching to more expensive renewable energy sources. These costs must be built into the cost and the pricing of the energy produced. The reluctance to bear these costs arises largely because the cost of environmental damage is not properly measured. It is only when this is done that the cost of avoiding such damage can be compared with the environmental benefits to reach a rational decision on whether the costs are worth it. Part of the problem is that the conventional ways of measuring GDP in terms of production do not take account of environmental damage caused by production of certain goods which should properly be reflected as a subtraction from GDP. Only if GDP is adjusted in this way for environmental costs that growth of adjusted GDP can be called a measure of the increase in total production in the economy. Recognising this problem, the Planning Commission has commissioned an Expert Group under Professor Partha Dasgupta to prepare a template for estimating green national accounts which would measure national production while allowing for negative effects on national resources.

1.45. To summarise, the Twelfth Plan must be guided by a vision of India moving forward in a way that would ensure a broad-based improvement in living standards of all sections of the people through a growth process which is faster than in the past, more inclusive and also more environmentally sustainable. What is needed to achieve this objective is outlined in subsequent sections of this chapter.

DEVELOPING CAPABILITIES

1.46. In this section, we focus on the capabilities we need to develop to achieve the objective of faster, more inclusive and sustainable growth. We first consider the development of human capabilities, which are in many ways the most important. Then we focus on institutional capabilities and the development of infrastructure which is a general capability enhancer for all agents. Both the Central and State Governments have a large role to play in developing these capabilities and the Twelfth Plan at the Central and State level should accord high importance to this effort.

Development of Human Capabilities

1.47. The development of human capabilities must be the first priority, for three reasons. First, these capabilities are actually ends in themselves. Second, they are also important instrumentalities which interact positively with others to raise the productive capacity of our economy and therefore its ability to satisfy the material needs of our population. Third, proper development of human capabilities will also ensure that our growth is more inclusive in the sense that the marginalised and disadvantaged sections of our society will be more able to access the opportunities thrown up by the growth process.

Life and Longevity

1.48. The most fundamental of all human capabilities is life itself and the steady rise in life expectation in the country suggests that significant progress has been made in this dimension. Life expectancy which was only 32 years at the time of Independence is now 67 years. In other words, every Indian can expect to live twice as long as was the case at Independence! Nevertheless, the level of life expectancy in India remains lower than in many emerging market economies and it is appropriate to plan for significant further improvements in this important dimension.

1.49. The infant mortality rate (IMR) is another dimension of human capability where we are making progress. IMR fell from 80 in 1991 to 66 in 2001 and at a faster rate thereafter to 47 in 2010. The rate of decline was 14 in the first period and 19 in the second period. Nevertheless, the level of IMR remains high and we need to do much better for our children. We must strive to bring the IMR down to 28 by the end of the Twelfth Plan. Maternal mortality rates (MMRs) are another indication of weakness in our performance. MMR has been falling over time, thanks to the initiatives for promoting institutional deliveries under the NRHM. The percentage of women giving birth in institutions with the benefit of skilled birth attendants has increased from 53 per cent in 2005 to 73 per cent in 2009. We need to do even better, and the Twelfth Plan must bring MMR down to 1 per 1,000 by the end of the Plan period.

1.50. While there has been progress in the dimensions discussed above, the decline in the child sex ratio rings an urgent alarm. This is an area of grave concern since it implies that society is denying life to female children, and increasingly resorting to female foeticide. The spread of diagnostic and medical facilities has paradoxically actually worsened the situation, as the falling child sex rate is being seen in the more developed areas and cities.

Education

1.51. India has a young population, and consequently, the labour force, which is expected to decline in most developed countries and even in China, is expected to increase over the next 20 years. This 'demographic dividend' can add to our growth potential through its impact on the supply of labour and also, via the falling dependency ratio, on the rate of domestic savings. Besides, a young population brings with it the aspirations and the impatience of youth, which in turn can become strong drivers for bringing about change and innovation. To reap this demographic dividend we must ensure that our younger citizens come into the labour force with higher levels of education and the skills needed to support rapid growth. The SSA has brought us close to the target of universalisation of primary education and the Right to Education Act (RTE) 2009 makes eight years of elementary education a fundamental right for all the children. The MDM Scheme has ensured that retention in schools has improved greatly. However, the learning outcomes for a majority of children continue to be disappointing. Addressing the quality issue in our schools is critical for the effective development of human capabilities and for achieving the objective of equality of opportunities. The quality of teachers and, even more important, their motivation and accountability will need to be improved. Many of the children who are presently in school are first-generation learners, and these children need supplementary instruction. This is not easy due to shortage of qualified teachers in many schools across the country. New and innovative approaches such as multigrade learning, which has been successfully tried in Tamil Nadu, could be adopted in such cases.

1.52. The success of the SSA has put pressure on expanding the capacity of secondary schools and the Rashtriya Madhyamik Shiksha Abhiyan (RMSA) addresses this issue. Although there is considerable focus on providing secondary school access, the dropout rates between elementary and secondary schools continue to be high, and between the secondary and post-secondary stage they are even higher. This is a particularly serious problem for girls, who have to travel longer distances to attend secondary schools. Curricular and examination reforms in secondary schooling would receive special attention aimed at fostering critical thinking and analytical skills, and preparing students for further education. All this requires innovative approaches, some of which are already in evidence in certain States.

1.53. The last decade has also seen a huge increase in the demand for higher education and this is expected to increase further as more children complete school and more and more jobs are seen to require higher-level qualifications. However, our higher education institutions also suffer from problems of quality. Too many of our universities are producing graduates in subjects that are not required by the changing job market, and the quality is also not what it should be. Higher education policy has to be driven by three 'E's: expansion, equity and excellence. Of these, the third E, 'excellence', is the most difficult to achieve. India cannot hope to be competitive in an increasingly knowledge driven world if our higher education institutions do not come up to the high standards of excellence needed to be able to be globally competitive. Not even one Indian university figures in the latest list of the top 200 universities in the world. We should work towards ensuring that there are at least five by the end of the Twelfth Plan. For this, universities at the top of the quality hierarchy should be identified and generously supported so that they can reach the top league. Centres of excellence within existing universities should be created. A special initiative should be launched to attract high calibre faculty from around the world on non-permanent teaching assignments. All these initiatives should be pooled into an India Excellence Initiative in the Twelfth Plan.

Skill Development

1.54. The Skill Development Mission is being launched to skill at least 50 million individuals by the end of the Twelfth Plan. Skill development programmes in the past have been run mainly by the government, with insufficient connection with market demand. To ensure that skills match demand, special efforts are needed to ensure that employers and enterprises play an integral role in the conception and implementation of vocational training programmes, including managing Industrial Training Institutes (ITIs) and in the development of faculty. An enabling framework is needed that would attract private investment in Vocational Training through Public–Private Partnership (PPP). We should try to optimise on the respective strengths of the public and private sector entities engaged in skill development. Mobilising the required investments, setting up first rate ITIs, ensuring efficiency in operations and management and enabling post-training employment will be the primary responsibilities of private sector entities while the government will provide the enabling framework and the requisite financial support especially in respect of SC, ST, Minorities and differently abled persons and other deprived sections of society.

Nutrition

1.55. Poor learning outcomes in our schools are partly because of poor quality of teaching but they are also partly due to high incidence of child malnutrition, which reduces learning ability. India has had the largest and the longest running child development programme in the world in the form of ICDS, but the problem of malnutrition remains large. Unfortunately, the latest data on child malnutrition are from the National Family Health Survey (NFHS-3) conducted in the period 2005–07 which pre-dates the Eleventh Plan. The full impact of the Eleventh Plan programmes on this aspect of human capability is therefore not yet known. Surveys undertaken by the State Governments seem to suggest that malnutrition has fallen in many States. The next Annual Health Survey for 2012–13 will include data on malnutrition and these data will provide a reliable basis for assessing what has happened since NFHS-3. Meanwhile, the ICDS programme will be expanded and comprehensively restructured in the Twelfth Plan to make it more effective.

1.56. Malnutrition is also a problem among adults, especially women. The incidence of anaemia and low body mass among women is very high in the country. The causes of this persistent malnutrition are not well understood. The availability of food, especially better quality food products such as fruits, vegetables and dairy products, is significantly better today than it was in the past. Nevertheless, the incidence of malnutrition remains high. There is a need to bring this dimension of human capability to the fore front of policy attention. The Food Security Bill under consideration will address some of these issues, but the problem of nutrition is actually much more complex and a multidimensional approach is necessary.

Health

1.57. Health is another critical dimension of human capability, which needs much greater attention in the Twelfth Plan. At present, less than 30 per cent of outpatient and less than half of inpatient health care capacity of the country is in the public sector, and the majority of the population relies on private health care provision which often imposes a heavy financial burden. It is, therefore, essential to expand public sector capacity in health care especially in the rural areas. The NRHM, launched during the Tenth Plan, made an important start in expanding health care facilities in rural areas. While additional infrastructure has been created, there are large shortages of personnel, especially specialists in rural health facilities, reflecting the fact that trained human resources in health are in short supply and it takes many years to set up new medical colleges to train the required number of doctors.

1.58. Ideally, the public health care system must be expanded to address the health needs of the vast majority of citizens, recognising that upper-income groups may opt for private health care. The Twelfth Plan will therefore see the transformation of the NRHM into a National Health Mission, covering both rural and urban areas. Unlike rural residents, those in urban areas have access to private health care providers, but private health care is costly and large numbers of urban residents especially slum dwellers cannot afford it. An important component of the National Health Mission will be the Urban Health Initiative for the Poor, providing public sector primary care facilities in selected low-income urban areas. This will require additional resources in the public sector from the budgets of both the Centre and the States, and cities.

1.59. There is a massive shortage of healthcare professionals in the country and their supply must therefore be expanded rapidly if we want to fulfil our commitments in this sector. We must therefore plan for an expansion of teaching and training programmes for healthcare professionals, particularly in the public sector institutions.

1.60. Finally, attainment of good health outcomes is not just a matter of providing curative care. We need to give much greater attention to public health which has traditionally suffered from neglect. We also need to focus much more on a provision of clean drinking water and sanitation, which can make a major contribution to improved health. This was the experience in industrialised countries over a hundred years ago, and this is also true for us today.

1.61. The longer-term objective of Health Policy must be the provision of Universal Health Care (UHC), whereby any one who wants it is assured of access to a well defined set of health care entitlements. Putting a UHC system in place will take time, but we need to start building an appropriate architecture.

Drinking Water and Sanitation

1.62. The problem of providing safe drinking water is particularly acute in the rural areas. Successive plans have emphasised programmes for expanding the coverage of rural drinking water but they have not had as much success, as desired. The incidence of 'slipped back' habitations appears to be accelerating and serious problems of water quality have emerged in many areas. Part of the problem is that rural drinking water schemes are not fully integrated with national system of aquifer management. Excessive drawal of groundwater for irrigation is leading to lowering of water tables causing drinking water hand pumps to run dry and lowering of the water table is also causing salinity and chemical pollution, making the water non-potable. A sustainable solution to the rural drinking water problem has to be found as part of a holistic approach for aquifer management.

1.63. Sanitation and clean drinking water are critical determinants of health and are complementary to each other. Without proper sanitation, the incidence of diarrhoeal diseases due to contaminated drinking water will not come down, and without adequate water supply, improved sanitation is generally not possible. It is, therefore, necessary to adopt a habitation approach to sanitation and to institutionalise the integration of water supply with sanitation in each habitation. The problem of sanitation in urban areas is also very serious since almost all our cities, including even the State capitals and major metros, have a large percentage of the population (45 per cent in Delhi) not connected to the sewer system. Urban development must give top priority to planning for water, toilets and sewerage as an integrated whole taking into account the likely expansion of the urban population.

Enhancing Human Capabilities through Information Technology

1.64. The ability to access information is an important institutional capability we need to develop. Lack of ready access information is often a major impediment in efforts to improve the well-being of the people. With improvement in literacy and education, and developments in information technology, we are in a position to provide our people with access to information, including obtaining birth records, land records, payment records for utilities and so on.

1.65. The rapid spread of mobile telephony, including in rural areas has facilitated innumerable innovations which directly benefit the ordinary citizen. Farmers in some parts of the country are able to subscribe to commercial services which deliver relevant information for a particular crop to the farmer through Short Message Service (SMS). The parents of babies born in municipal hospitals in Bengaluru get an SMS alert, when the next vaccination is due. Such innovations need to be encouraged. Yet another human capability that is important is the ease and effectiveness of establishing identity. The

Aadhar project, which provides a unique identification (UID) number, backed by biometric data capture, to establish identity unambiguously, is a major step forward. Identity can be difficult to establish, especially for the poor, when they move from their place of origin, whether by choice or by compulsion. The UID project has already enrolled 200 million persons. Experiments with using Aadhar to make payments under MGNREGS electronically into no frill bank accounts which can be accessed through mobile phones have begun in 51 districts. It will soon be possible for large-scale use of the Aadhar platform to make various types of government payments due to individuals in a seamless manner electronically, avoiding problems of misuse and leakage.

1.66. The Aadhar platform will also facilitate a shift from the physical delivery of subsidised commodities through the Public Distribution System (PDS) to a system of cash payment, if desired. Some States have indicated that they would be interested in such a shift. Adoption of a target to move the major subsidies and beneficiary payments to a cash basis linked to Aadhar by the end of the Twelfth Plan period would be a major step towards improving efficiency.

Development of Institutional Capabilities

1.67. The Twelfth Plan also needs to focus on developing the capabilities of our institutions to perform the increasingly complex and demanding tasks expected of them. We have three pillars of governance (Legislature, Executive and Judiciary) and three tiers of government (Centre, State and Panchayats/ULBs). The capabilities of these institutions to deliver on their mandate need to be greatly improved. The gaps are most evident at the lowest level of PRIs and ULBs, where trained personnel are lacking and the training systems are also inadequate. It is also true at higher levels, where trained personnel may be available, but the capability of the systems is poor because they are not performance oriented and motivation is low.

Implementation Capability

1.68. The consultations undertaken by the Planning Commission in the course of preparing the Twelfth Plan have revealed a near universal perception that the capacity to implement is low at all levels of government. The government simply does not function with the efficiency that is required in the twenty-first century. This is partly because of the lack of motivation at various levels, but it is primarily because governmental systems and procedures are largely process-driven. They are not outcome-oriented. Accountability is often viewed as adhering to procedures with no incentive to depart from procedures to secure better results. Unless this weakness is overcome, mere provision of more funds for programmes implemented in the same old way will not help.

1.69. Where implementation rests within one Ministry, there are problems of (*i*) insufficient attention to evidence-based analysis in the design of policies and programmes, (*ii*) insufficient concurrent evaluation that would give feedback on outcomes achieved and (*iii*) lack of willingness or ability to bring about systemic changes needed to improve outcomes. Even when it is known that a change in procedures will help, it takes very long to bring about that change. The problem is greatly multiplied when the effectiveness of a programme depends, as it often does, on actions that have to be taken by several different Ministries. Inter-ministerial consultations take far too long, and more importantly, are typically not oriented to resolving problems. This is because each Ministry works in a silo, applying its own rules and procedures. The effort is to seek a consensus if possible, with little ability to over rule positions taken by individual Ministries in the interest of a holistic problem solving approach. Resolving conflicting stands by consensus is of course desirable if possible, but beyond a point, it may not be possible, and some systems for conflict resolution are needed.

1.70. To deal effectively with these problems it may be necessary to redesign governmental decision-making systems. There has been a great deal of system redesign in the private sector in response to the new environment created by economic reforms. A similar redesign of government is needed. For example, one way of accelerating the processing of large infrastructure projects is to set up a National Investment Approval Board chaired by the Prime Minister and including all key Ministers and to amend the Transaction of Business Rules so that statutory clearances under various Acts for all infrastructure projects above a given size are given by the Board, taking into account the views of all Ministries. The allocation of business rules could provide that such clearances would be issued by the Cabinet Secretariat based on the decision of the Board. This would be a systemic change which would ensure a holistic consideration of complex issues and greatly accelerate decision-making. Several other changes are discussed in Chapter 6 including in particular the need for greater reliance on industry specialists with domain knowledge.

Delivery of Public Services

1.71. Delivery of public services in many States is hampered by weak institutional capacity. Thus, although public hospitals may have trained doctors and nurses, and public schools may have trained teachers, neither of these institutions will have administrators who are trained in the operation of health care or educational institutions. Too much of the knowledge needed to manage public service delivery is learnt on the job, which detracts from the institution's effective functioning.

1.72. The first step in reforming public service delivery is to devise mechanisms for measuring the extent of public satisfaction with public services and publicising the results. The Public Affairs Centre at Bengaluru has done excellent work in conducting systematic surveys of public perception or satisfaction with various types of public services ranging from water and sanitation, health and education, public transport, police and so on. Such surveys periodically conducted produce valuable information for the political leadership on where performance is felt to be poor and where it is improving.

1.73. Greater involvement of citizens' organisations can help focus government attention on these problem areas. The Delhi Government's experiment with Bhagidhari is example of citizen involvement and consultation operating through Resident Welfare Associations.

Regulatory Institutions

1.74. An area where the lack of institutional capability is beginning to manifest itself is in our expanding system of regulatory bodies. As areas that were earlier dominated by the public sector have been opened up for private operators, often competing among themselves or with existing public sector operators, independent regulatory institutions have been established to oversee the functioning of the players in the system. The effectiveness of regulatory organisations depends critically upon the quality of the personnel running the institutions and the degree of independence established. Too many of the regulatory agencies are staffed by former bureaucrats and there is not enough induction of specialists with domain knowledge. A thorough review of the regulatory system established in different sectors is needed to determine the weaknesses of the system currently in place and recommend ways of correcting them. This is especially true as the next two five year Plans are likely to see faster change in the global economy and in the structure of the Indian economy too.

Development of Infrastructure

1.75. Infrastructure provides the basic support system for other sectors of the economy expanding capabilities everywhere. A distinguishing characteristic of infrastructure is that where imports can meet the gap between demand and supply, deficiencies in infrastructure cannot be made good through imports. Infrastructure requirements can only be met through development of the relevant infrastructure capacity in the domestic economy. Furthermore, Good quality infrastructure is important not only for faster growth but also to ensure that growth is inclusive. Small businesses spread throughout the country need access to good quality and reliable infrastructure services to compete effectively. Large enterprises can often develop their own infrastructure as they often do with captive power, and being large can even locate themselves *ab initio* where other infrastructure is better, that is, nearer ports and near transport hubs. Small enterprises on the other hand

Power

1.76. Electric power is a critical input into all economic activity and rapid and inclusive growth is only possible if reliable electricity is made available everywhere. It is essential not only for agriculture, industry and commercial business but also for basic household lighting. The percentage of households with electricity has increased from 56 in 2001 to 67 in 2011, but even so almost 45 per cent of rural households have no electricity connection. Furthermore, those that do typically do not have assured power, even in urban areas.

1.77. The Eleventh Plan added 55,000 MW of generation capacity which, though short of the target, was more than twice the capacity added in the Tenth Plan. The Twelfth Plan aims to add another 88,000 MW. This level of additional capacity is not infeasible but delivery of power depends critically on solving serious fuel availability problems that have arisen relating to coal and natural gas. Uncertainties about fuel availability would seriously dampen investment activity, especially since about half the generation capacity is expected to come from the private sector, and they will not be able to achieve financing if fuel supply issues are not resolved. The problem is not that fuel cannot be made available since domestic shortfalls can be met by imports but since imports are at much higher prices, power producers are reluctant to accept. The problem can be resolved by resorting to some form of price pooling and this must be explored. Equally important is the need to address the financial weakness of the distribution segment of the power sector. Almost all the distribution companies (discoms) are running large financial losses, reflecting high transmission and distribution losses and also an unwillingness to raise tariffs in line with rising cost. Some discoms have recently raised tariffs after many years, which is a welcome development but most have yet to do so. Some of the critical policy correctives to deal with these problems are outlined in Section 1.6.

1.78. Renewable energy, especially wind energy and solar energy are potentially promising alternatives to conventional fossil fuel-based electric power. They are more expensive at present, but given likely trends in fossil fuel prices globally, and technological developments in these sectors there is a need to expand the contribution from these sectors. The scope for doing so is discussed in detail in Chapter 10.

Telecommunications

1.79. Telecommunications has seen impressive expansion and large investments in the past several years with a tele-density increasing from 26.2 per cent in 2008 to 78.7 per cent in 2012. The expansion has been led by private sector service providers whose market share (in terms of number of connections) increased in this period from 73.5 per cent to 86.3 per cent. Unfortunately, issues related to alleged improprieties in the allocation of spectrum in 2008 have dominated public discussions. Several 2G licenses and associated spectrum allotted in 2008 were cancelled by the Supreme Court in 2011 and the court ordered the government to auction the spectrum. This process of auctioning is currently underway and is expected to be completed by January 2013.

1.80. There is tremendous scope for further expansion in telecommunications, especially with the introduction of 3G services. Telecommunications, and the associated increase in Internet connectivity is clearly a productivity enhancing development, and India is well placed to benefit from this. Already, a large number of services benefiting ordinary people have come into being. For a small fee, farmers can sign up for a service which provides customer specific information through SMS on market prices in nearby markets, conditions and possible disease outbreaks in specific crops in which the farmer is currently interested. Mobile banking, through business correspondents acting as agents, is giving ordinary people in villages, far from a brick and mortar bank branch, virtually direct access to simple banking service.

1.81. There is scope for using the Universal Services Obligation Fund (USOF) creatively to enhance access to mobile telephone including especially as a platform for delivery of a range of services to the underserved in rural areas.

Road Transport

1.82. In the area of transport, there has been some progress in the roads sector, both in the development of national highways and in rural roads, but much more needs to be done. The National Highway Development Programme needs to be stepped up with an aggressive pursuit of PPP to construct toll roads on a Build-Operate-Transfer (BOT) basis. The States too need to expand their road programmes to provide good quality connectivity in all areas. Many States have resorted successfully to PPP as a mode of road development.

1.83. A special effort is needed to speed up road connectivity in Jammu & Kashmir, the North East and other Special Category States. A good start has been made in the SARDP-NE in the Eleventh Plan and this needs to be pursued with greater vigour in the Twelfth Plan. Enhanced connectivity of the North East should be a high priority. This is also true for districts affected by Left-Wing Extremism.

Railways

1.84. Development of capability in the Railways is another urgent priority for the Twelfth Plan. Capacity in the Railways has lagged far behind what is needed and feasible, especially given the need to shift from road transport to rail in the interest of improving energy efficiency, and reducing the carbon footprint of our development. Expansion of the system must be accompanied by technological modernisation, greater attention to safety and steps to ensure financial viability. Several important new initiatives are underway which will materialise in the course of the Twelfth Plan. These include flagship projects such as the Western and Eastern Freight Corridor, the Mumbai Elevated Rail Corridor and the High Speed Corridor. Given the scarcity of resources, there is need and also considerable scope, for pursing PPP initiatives in this sector along the lines outlined in Chapter 9.

Airports

1.85. Airport development is a basic infrastructure requirement for connectivity, especially since the demand for air travel is projected to grow rapidly. This area has seen a sea change in the Eleventh Plan with the development of four new airports through private participation in the PPP mode (Bengaluru, Hyderabad, Delhi and Mumbai), the upgradation of two metro airports by Airport Authority of India (AAI) (Chennai and Kolkata) and the development of 35 non-metro airports by AAI. There is need for further expansion in the Twelfth Plan with the creative use of PPP wherever possible. Several projects are likely to be taken up in the Twelfth Plan. These include the Navi Mumbai Airport, the Goa Airport and the Kannur Airport. A policy to make some of our airports into international hubs is also being considered.

Ports

1.86. Ports are another critical capability for international trade connectivity. Progress in this area in the Eleventh Plan was disappointing as for as major ports were concerned because several institutional issues had to be resolved for the proposed PPP expansion plans to materialise. These have now been resolved and it is expected that the Twelfth Plan will see a much greater expansion. In contrast minor ports (which come under State Governments) have done very well in the Eleventh Plan. An aggressive expansion of port capacity in the major ports based on PPP is essential in the Twelfth Plan. In addition, two entirely new PPP ports are proposed by the Central Government; one in West Bengal and the other in Andhra Pradesh.

Financing Infrastructure

1.87. Traditionally, infrastructure development used to occur through the public sector. However, given the scarcity of public resources, and the need to shift scarce public resources into health and education, efforts have been made to induct private participation in the development of infrastructure. These efforts have met with a fair degree of success. As of 31 March 2012, 390 PPP projects have been approved involving an investment of ₹3,05010 crore. According to a report published by the World Bank, India has been the top recipient of PPP investment since 2006 and has accounted for almost half of the investment in new PPP projects implemented in the first half of 2011 in developing countries. An Asian Development Bank report states that India stands in the same league as developed economies like South Korea and Japan on implementation of PPP projects and the Model Concession Agreements prepared in India and used in our PPP projects have also been commended.

1.88. The total investment in infrastructure sectors in the Twelfth Plan is estimated to be ₹55.7 lakh crore, which is roughly one trillion dollars at prevailing exchange rates. The share of private investment in the total investment in infrastructure rose from 22 per cent in the Tenth Plan to 36.61 per cent in the Eleventh Plan. It will have to increase to about 48 per cent during the Twelfth Plan if the infrastructure investment target is to be met. These projections have also been validated by the high level committee on infrastructure set up under the chairmanship of Shri Deepak Parekh. The committee has however qualified its projections as dependent on several policy initiatives that the government would need to take for ensuring this level of investment.

1.89. The Twelfth Plan lays special emphasis on the development of social sectors in view of their impact on human development and quality of life. Unlike the case with other infrastructure, experiments with PPP in the social sector have been more limited. Many States have experimented with PPPs in health and education. The Central Government has approved setting up of 2,500 Model Schools in PPP mode and a proposal for setting up 3,000 ITIs through PPP is under consideration. These initiatives will be strengthened during the Twelfth Plan.

1.90. Resort to PPPs in the social sector often raises concerns about the commercialisation of services that are normally expected to be provided free or highly subsidised. These are important concerns but they can be addressed by well-drafted concession agreements and strict monitoring to ensure that PPP concessionaires abide by their commitments. This must be reinforced with penalties for non compliance. While extending the concept of PPP to social and urban sector projects, the need for 'people's' participation in the design and monitoring of PPP schemes becomes crucial. Local citizens are direct stakeholders in such projects and therefore their support becomes crucial. Therefore, some cities and States have begun to shape PPPs in the social and urban sectors as People–Public–Private Partnerships (PPPPs). This is a valuable innovation which should be applauded.

The Reach of Banking and Insurance

1.91. Like infrastructure, development of an efficient financial services system is a key enabler of capabilities which affects how well individuals can manage life cycle needs and also affect the functioning of enterprises and their prospects of growth. More broadly, it affects the extent of entrepreneurship and of competition. India is underserved by financial services on every parameter. More than 40 per cent of households avail no banking service at all. The ratio of total bank credit outstanding to GDP is only about 57 per cent as against over 140 per cent in East Asia and Pacific. Insurance premia account for less than 1 per cent of GDP, which is only about a third of the international average. The organised financial sector does not reach out to large segments of the population which are serviced if at all by all manner of informal financial entities at terms and costs that retard their growth prospects.

1.92. Lack of insurance products is an example of under-supply of financial services. It can be nobody's case that the Indian economy has lower inherent risks than others, or that life cover is any less important. It is rather that costs of providing cover and assessing claims are currently so high relative to the cover itself that either premium-to-cover ratios become exorbitant or appropriate insurance products are simply not created. High transactions costs relative to size of accounts are also the main reason for low banking coverage and this is compounded by high risk perception of banks, in part because of lack of insurance. Agriculture and other forms of MSMEs are particularly ill-served and the situation has in fact deteriorated in some ways over the last two decades because of problems afflicting the cooperative banking sector.

1.93. In recent years, financial inclusion has come back into focus, partly because technology (such as the IT-infrastructure, set-up of a core banking network, mobile phones, satellite imagery and automatic weather stations) now permits solutions such as banking correspondents and weather insurance which cut down on overhead costs; and partly because the power of cooperation, whether through SHG–bank linkage, Joint Liability Groups or simply the old fashioned Primary Agricultural Co-operative Society is again being revitalised. Cooperatives still have the widest credit reach and their local knowledge and risk sharing potential is an asset for the financial sector as a whole which has not been fully exploited. They should be given increased prominence during Twelfth Plan because potential benefits and cost of inaction are both very high. An area that government should take a lead is in creation of suitable databases of registry information both for easier collateral and finer actuarial calculations. The UID project can help with this, but there are also more basic requirements such as proper land records and property titling which should not meet the same fate as the so far disappointing record on registering births and deaths.

1.94. In the industrial sector smaller firms are credit constrained. The size distribution of firms in India shows that there are a number of large firms, as in other countries, but there are not enough firms in the middle range with employees ranging from 100 to 500. Instead an overwhelming number of firms are concentrated at the small end with less than 50 employees. This suggests that our small firms do not operate in an environment in which they can graduate to the middle category. One of the constraints is finance. Banks and other financial institutions have to be more creative to respond to the needs of potentially dynamic entrepreneurs capable of rapid growth. Indian banks typically do not exercise judgement in expanding credit limits in a manner which favours companies that are more likely to grow.

1.95. The capital market has been an important source of funding for larger companies and the opening of the economy to portfolio flows from Foreign Institutional Investors (FIIs) in recent years has produced a buoyant capital market where companies have raised significant funds through new issues. However, this mechanism has been used mainly by the larger companies to raise funds. We do not have effective institutions that can channel equity funding to smaller companies and start-ups. In a knowledge economy, we need to do much more to encourage the growth of venture capital funds and angel investors. The Planning Commission had appointed a Committee on Angel Investment and Early Stage Venture Capital which has since submitted its report. The Committee has made a number of recommendations which are discussed in Chapter 2 and which need to be given serious consideration.

Science and Technology

1.96. S&T is a vital aspect of national capability. Science Departments/Agencies have played a significant role in solving the socio-economic issues. The Department of Space through satellite-based system has provided nationwide land use/land cover mapping for natural resources management, thematic mapping for national urban information system, the process of measuring forest and wasteland, locating potential drinking water zones and potential fishing zone and crop production forecasting. The Twelfth Five Year Plan must build on the scientific base created by earlier Plans and give a renewed thrust to emphasise creative and relevant research and innovation. The central focus must be to ensure that S&T becomes a major driver in the process of the national development.

1.97. The Twelfth Plan programmes of the Indian Science should aim at three outcomes:

1. Realisation of the Indian vision to emerge as global leader in advanced science;
2. Encourage and facilitate Indian Science to address the major developmental needs of the country like food security, energy and environmental needs, addressing the water challenges and providing technological solutions to affordable health care requirements and
3. Gain global competitiveness through a well-designed innovation ecosystem, encouraging global research centres of multinational corporations (MNCs) to be set up in India.

1.98. To realise these objectives, it will be necessary to build technology partnerships with States and socio-economic ministries through new models of technological solutions, design, development and delivery. India's aspiration to emerge as a stronger scientific power at the end of the Twelfth Plan period will require additional funding and also an effort to interconnect available resources and competitiveness. Indian researchers must also be able to gain access to the large global Research and Development (R&D) infrastructure and work in collaboration with others to develop necessary indigenous capabilities. There is need for much greater flexibility in the way scientific establishments work. We need to encourage collaboration with universities, with private and public sector corporations and also with global research centres. The Twelfth Plan must also experiment with new models of funding scientific research. Instead of all government research funds being allocated to the budget of different scientific departments, there is a case for creating a new National Research Fund which can receive competing research proposals from different research institutions, or combinations of institutions, and select from these proposals to fund the most promising on a project basis. Research funding for particular projects should be continued only on the basis of periodic peer reviews which indicate whether progress is satisfactory and also point to corrective steps which might help.

1.99. S&T endeavours over the last decade have placed increasing emphasis on contributing to the societal development and improving the quality of life of citizens. Such new initiatives in turn have also created in some cases societal reactions stemming from issues like health and environmental safety. In the recent past, introduction of genetically modified (GM) foods and Nuclear Energy are two such examples. The Twelfth Plan envisages a more effective institutional framework in linking S&T with society through a variety of outreach strategies. This is proposed to be carried out both through the scientific establishments as well as through educational programmes including initiatives from non-governmental organisations (NGOs).

MANAGING NATURAL RESOURCES AND THE ENVIRONMENT

1.100. Achievement of rapid and sustainable growth is critically dependent on our ability to manage our natural resources effectively. India is not liberally endowed with natural resources. In fact, we are among the lowest in the world on almost all measures of resource availability on a per capita basis. In recent years, the deficiencies in the way in which we manage natural resources have come under increasingly critical scrutiny. Agitations around land acquisition, deforestation, water use, air and water pollution, and also our response to natural disasters, have become more common. These are no longer peripheral issues: They are issues which demand mainstream attention and pose challenges which this Plan must address squarely.

Soil Health and Productivity

1.101. Soil is one of the basic natural resources that support life on earth and this resource is under threat in India from soil erosion due to natural factors compounded by deforestation which increases run off and also from excessive use of chemical fertilisers. The soil ecosystem is a living self-balancing system and excessive use of synthetic chemical fertilisers disturbs this balance often causing long-term damage to the soil.

1.102. Chemical fertilisers, especially urea, are highly subsidised and the fertiliser subsidy has grown exponentially during the last three decades. These heavy subsidies on some fertilisers prompt overuse of the subsidised chemical fertilisers which has resulted in severe depletion of micronutrients and degradation of soil in many parts of the country. Chemical fertilisers should be used with great care and in conjunction with other means of using organic sources to replenish the soil. The way forward is to rejuvenate the soil and restore soil health through addition of organic matter in large quantities. Use of organic manures will gradually bring down the dependence on chemical fertilisers. However, the use of organic manures is discouraged because they receive no subsidy while urea is heavily subsidised. This price distortion is an important factor discouraging the shift.

1.103. More generally, support for ecological/organic fertilisation is scattered under various schemes and hence it is not getting its due. The best practices of soil fertility management need to be adopted, which include generation of biomass for bulk addition of organic matter in the soil to maintain proper soil health, *in situ* degeneration of biomass through sole cropping/inter-cropping/bund cropping of green manure crops, recycling of farm and household waste through use of intensive nutrient recycling methods such as composting, production of bio-fertilisers at regional and local levels, adoption of bio-dynamic farming methods and crop rotations to enrich the soil.

Rational Use of Land

1.104. Land is a fixed resource and its availability in India on a per capita basis is relatively low compared with most countries. Furthermore, the country's population is likely to continue to grow till at least 2040 whereas the land mass may actually shrink with increased coastal erosion and flooding due to climate change. In these circumstances, the rational and planned use of land must be an issue that needs the highest priority, and should be made a central focus of our resource planning. Land is a state subject, but the issues are so critical that there is need for better coordination at the national level.

1.105. There are three main areas of conflict that need to be addressed. The first relates to the allocation of available land between agriculture, industry and urban use. The second potential conflict arises from the fact that allocation across different uses cannot occur simply through market processes and some land acquisition is therefore necessary, but the terms on which this had been done in the past are no longer acceptable. The third potential conflict arises because most of our mineral resources are in areas, which are forested and the effective exploitation of these resources calls for acquisition, which may disrupt some tribal communities.

1.106. As far as the allocation to alternative sectors is concerned, it is important to recognise that diversion of land from agricultural to non-agricultural uses is inevitable in any development process since industry must expand and cities must also expand and in both cases land needed for this expansion can only come from agriculture. Concern is often raised in this context about the impact on food security. This problem is greatly exaggerated because the productivity of land in agriculture at present is very low and the shift of some land from agriculture to non-agricultural use can easily be offset by productivity increases, which are feasible and have been seen in many other developing countries. We need a clearer articulation of a strategy for dealing with such shifts while ensuring the continuing increase in the supply of agricultural products of the appropriate mix of grains, horticulture products and cash crops. The scope for achieving productivity increases in agriculture is discussed in detail in Chapter 12.

1.107. If the shift of land from agriculture to non-agricultural use could take place without any compulsory acquisition it would not pose a major problem since all such shifts would be voluntary. Unfortunately, this is not always possible. Land required for constructing a road or a railway line or even a dam has to be location specific and this effectively gives the landowner a veto right over the project. Given the large number of landowners involved, problems can arise even if the vast majority of the landowners are adequately compensated which is why compulsory acquisition provisions are unavoidable and exist in every country. Compulsory acquisition is unavoidable where there is a genuine public purpose such as acquiring land for infrastructure development. There may be a case for using acquisition for certain lands of privately owned facilities which serve a public purpose but this needs to be carefully defined. To remedy the deficiencies in the existing legislation for land acquisition which dates back to colonial times, the government has introduced the Land Acquisition Relief and Rehabilitation Bill in Parliament which is expected to create a much more balanced framework protecting the rights of those whose land is being acquired, as well as those whose livelihood will be disrupted.

1.108. The third potential conflict between accessing our mineral resources and minimising disturbance to forests also poses difficult problems. The services that are rendered by forests are unique and cannot be easily replaced. They include sustaining the life styles of the adivasis, but go well beyond that to include critical ecological services such as acting as a carbon sink and as a natural harvester of water through enhanced groundwater recharging. Mining encroaches on forest land and involves displacement of tribals, but the conflict can be reconciled if mining is combined with scientific replanting or regeneration, plus compensatory forestation on a larger scale, which may enable effective exploitation of our mineral resources with an actual increase in total forest cover. There may be some areas of forests that we view as sacrosanct, such as special reserves and biodiversity hotspots, where no intrusion is allowed, but other than these it should be possible to reconcile the two conflicting objectives, extracting valuable minerals and protecting the forests, through scientific methods of exploitation combined with steps which can protect and even enhance forest cover.

1.109. Resolution of this conflict is particularly necessary in view of the energy challenge facing the country. Most of our coal resources and hydro potential are in ecologically sensitive areas and a successful resolution of these problems is critical if we are to be able to exploit our potential energy resources. The alternative is to either accept a much lower rate of growth, or rely even more than we already do on imported energy, which has implications for both the balance of payments and energy security.

1.110. Alternative energy sources, including a variety of renewable energy sources, provide another route for energy security especially in the longer run. However, its quantitative potential over the next 10 years is small at present though it is expected to expand to 50,000 MW by the end of the Twelfth Plan. The costs of these sources are also are much higher though they are falling. This is a potentially profitable area for further research, which is of special interest for us.

1.111. Expansion of nuclear energy as an important potential alternative to coal-based electricity poses a new set of concerns following the Fukushima accident in Japan which has heightened fears of possible accidents with leakages in radiation. This has promoted agitations against nuclear power in some parts of the country but it is an option that cannot be closed if we are to meet the essential energy needs of the country. However, much greater attention will have to be paid towards improving the confidence of the people and especially in providing world-class systems to counter the risks associated with this form of energy.

Water as a Scarce Natural Resource

1.112. Water is another key natural resource in fixed supply and its availability is now at a level which is just about equal to demand on average. Availability in some areas is greater than demand but there are other areas which are seriously water-stressed. While intensive use of groundwater made a great contribution to the Green Revolution, today in large parts of west, central and south India there is a man-made crisis of falling water tables. Economic growth at between 8 per cent and 9 per cent a year will only be possible if the water requirements of the expanding population, with a growing degree of urbanisation and the water requirement of expanding GDP can be met. Detailed studies suggest that on a business as usual basis, the total demand for water by 2031 is likely to be 50 per cent higher than today. This gap has to be bridged if the projected GDP growth is not to be choked. It is estimated that about 20 per cent of the gap at most can be bridged by taking steps to augment available supply through additional storage and groundwater retention. The rest of the deficit has to be bridged through greater water use efficiency.

1.113. Fortunately, there is large scope for improving water use efficiency in our economy. Agriculture consumes around 80 per cent of our available water resources at present and its water use efficiency is among the lowest in the world. Absence of rational pricing for canal water, combined with free or very cheap power for agriculture, has encouraged agricultural practices which are extremely wasteful. Cheap power has encouraged excess drawal of groundwater leading to falling water tables in large parts of the country. However, the man-made crisis of falling water tables is forcing some change as farmers are beginning to recognise the need to adopt technologies that economise on water.

1.114. The Twelfth Plan must break new ground in bringing sustainable management of our aquifers to the forefront of policymaking. Although efforts are being made for recharging of groundwater sources, these are yet to show sustained results across most parts of the country. An aquifer mapping programme that would enable more informed participatory management and better alignment of cropping patterns to water availability across the country will need to be the starting point of our efforts. This must be combined with a massive groundwater recharge programme based on integrating a reformulated MGNREGS with programmes on watershed development and restoration of water bodies.

1.115. It is also necessary to consider whether a new legislative framework is necessary to help manage our water resources better. Water, except for inter-state rivers, is a state subject and as such, it is largely up to the States to consider what initiatives are feasible to avoid a steady intensification of the problem. A framework law, that is, an umbrella statement of general principles governing the exercise of legislative and/or executive (or devolved) powers by the Centre, the States and the local governance institutions needs to be developed. Such a framework law is not intended to either centralise water management or change Centre–State relations or alter the Constitutional position on water in any way. It is intended to be justiciable, in the sense that the laws are passed, and the executive actions are taken by the Central and State Governments, and the devolved functions exercised by PRIs conform to the general principles and priorities laid down in the framework law, and that deviations can be challenged in a court of law. These are, indeed, sensitive issues, and action on them must be receded by the largest possible consensus across States. However, the urgency of moving forward on these critical matters can no longer be disputed.

1.116. New model legislation is needed for protection, conservation, management and regulation of groundwater. The present model bill amounts to little more than grandfathering existing uses. What is remarkable is that some of the most important legal principles governing groundwater even today were laid down in British common law as early as the middle of the nineteenth century and have not been updated since then. The new model bill would need to recognise that over the last two decades, not only has the groundwater situation in India acquired crisis proportions, new developments in jurisprudence have created the basis as well as the necessity to redefine the legal framework for use of groundwater. These include the Public Trust Doctrine enunciated by the Supreme Court, principles of environmental law and the 73rd and 74th amendments to the Constitution. These issues are discussed in detail in Chapter 4.

1.117. Parallel efforts are needed to contain pollution of surface water and contamination of groundwater, which is reaching serious proportions. Industry must be pushed to adopt the best international practices to improve water use efficiency. Consumption of fresh water can be substantively reduced through use of water-efficient technologies or changed processes in various manufacturing activities and also by reusing and recycling the waste water from water using industrial processes and making the reclaimed water available for use in the secondary activities within or outside the industry. Enforcing pollution control measures in a context where the vast majority of producers are small and widely dispersed is not easy. However, this is a challenge in policy design, which cannot be ignored. States have to ensure that it is fully integrated into local planning.

1.118. Increased urbanisation will also pose additional problems for water management since urban populations need to be serviced with piped water systems available on a 24 × 7 basis and these systems should be accompanied by sewerage systems, which ensure that only cleaned water is returned to rivers or other disposal sites. At present, no Indian city is in a position to boast of a complete sewerage system. We have installed capacity to treat only about 30 per cent of the human waste we generate. Just two cities, Delhi and Mumbai, which generate around 17 per cent of the country's urban sewage, have nearly 40 per cent of the country's installed capacity. The Twelfth Plan must ensure that no water scheme in urban India will be sanctioned without an integrated sewage treatment component, which ensures that city waste does not pollute our fresh water sources.

ENGAGEMENT WITH THE WORLD

1.119. Economic reforms over the past two decades have made India a much more open economy. The share of exports of goods and services in total GDP has increased from 6.9 per cent in 1991 to 24.6 per cent in 2012. Imports of goods and services as a percentage of GDP have also increased from 8.3 per cent to 29.8 per cent in the same period. These changes are the result of conscious efforts to open up the economy. Import duties have been reduced over time and a number of preferential trading arrangements have been introduced as part of Comprehensive Economic Partnership Arrangements with individual countries and groups of countries, especially Association of Southeast Asian Nations (ASEAN), Japan, Korea, Singapore and Sri Lanka. More such agreements are being negotiated with the European Union and with Australia. Investment into India, and also from India to other countries has increased.

For all these reasons, India's growth prospects in the years ahead cannot be viewed in isolation from what is happening in the world economy.

Global Economic Prospects

1.120. The global economy is currently going through a very difficult phase. The financial crisis of 2008–09 interrupted what had been a long period of global growth. Initially, the global economy appeared to respond well to the stimulus policies introduced by many countries in 2009, but the horizon was again clouded by the Eurozone crisis which is currently seen as a major fault line in the world economy. Many European countries are facing severe social and economic pain in their effort to introduce fiscal discipline aimed at regaining market confidence. The International Monetary Fund (IMF) projects zero growth in the Eurozone in 2012 with only a gradual improvement thereafter, on the assumption that a disruptive outcome is avoided.

1.121. The major industrialised and developing countries, meeting at Summit level in the G20, have repeatedly emphasised the importance of avoiding disruptive outcomes and the need for all countries to act in concert and cooperation to bring the global economy back on a path of sustainable growth. It is to be hoped that global economic cooperation will prove strong enough to avoid a hard landing. Although uncertainty remains high, and downside risks are significant, the most reasonable assumption on which to plan is that the global economy will recover gradually. However, the structural change that has been underway for some time, with industrialised countries growing more slowly while the emerging market countries, especially in Asia, grow more rapidly, will continue in the foreseeable future. We must, therefore, plan for a world in which the share of global GDP will therefore shift steadily away from the current industrialised countries and towards the faster growing emerging economies, especially in Asia.

Implications for the Balance on Current Account

1.122. Slower growth in industrialised countries will mean that our exports to these countries may be adversely affected. Our exports to Europe fell 9 per cent in April–December 2012, undoubtedly affected by economic conditions there. Fortunately, India's export basket is relatively diversified and since emerging market countries are expected to grow more rapidly in the years ahead, we may be able to benefit from this. There is also scope for increasing our share in industrialised country markets by competing more aggressively with countries like China, which will experience loss of competitiveness because of rising labour costs at home. This is especially true of services, where India's increasing sophistication will allow it to win more business from cost-conscious developed countries However, there is no room for complacency, because other developing countries, such as the Philippines, are improving their capabilities and there are moves within developed countries to 'on shore' services hitherto outsourced. It is difficult to quantify the net effect of all these factors, but it is reasonable to plan for merchandise exports growing at an average annual rate of about 15 per cent in the Twelfth Plan than compared with 20.7 per cent in the Eleventh Plan. Growth of earnings from tourism and also remittances are likely to be subdued.

1.123. On the import side, the targeted GDP growth of average 8 per cent per annum will require a rapid growth of imports, particularly because of our incremental energy needs. The impact on the balance of payments will of course depend on what happens to oil and gas prices, but these are not expected to moderate significantly in the short to medium term, and indeed may even go up as the world economy recovers gradually from the global crisis, or due to any sudden shocks in the Middle East. High import payments combined with modest export growth means that the current account deficit will be an important source of stress in the coming years.

1.124. Another contingency that we have to keep in mind is the likely trend in global food prices. For a variety of reasons, most notably rising demand from emerging markets as their incomes expand, combined with lagging agricultural productivity in many emerging market countries and possible diversion of land to production of renewable energy in industrialised countries, global food prices are likely to be high in the years ahead. Fortunately, our domestic food grain production has been expanding but food security considerations may require import in certain conditions. Domestic import and export policies and our buffer stock policy have to be calibrated to meet domestic demand while responding to developments in global markets.

1.125. India's current account deficit was a surplus 2.3 per cent of GDP in 2003–04. Since then it has gone into deficit, reaching 2.7 per cent of GDP in 2010–11 and 4.2 per cent in 2011–12. As pointed out in Chapter 2, a large part of the increase in 2011–12 was due to imports of gold, which are not expected to be repeated. Even so, the current account deficit in the first year of the Twelfth Plan will be around 5 per cent, which exceeds what has traditionally been regarded as a sustainable level. The macroeconomic analysis in Chapter 2 prescribes that policies must be calibrated to ensure that the current account deficit in the Twelfth Plan period averages around 2.9 per cent. On current prospects, it is likely to be somewhat higher. The ability to finance this deficit through stable capital flows is therefore critical.

Capital Flows

1.126. India has followed a calibrated policy of opening up the capital account, differentiating according to the nature of capital flows. Foreign Direct Investment (FDI) is regarded as the most stable capital flow which also provides technology and marketing links, and has therefore been most freely allowed. Portfolio flows are not as stable as FDI, but they are also not as volatile as short-term debt and have been allowed freely from qualified FIIs. Short-term debt from abroad is the least stable form of capital flow and is, therefore, highly controlled except for trade credit. Longer-term external borrowing is allowed more liberally, but subject to caps. This policy produced good results in the Eleventh Plan, yielding an annual average net capital inflow of 4.1 per cent of GDP during the Eleventh Plan. Since the average current account deficit was 2.7 per cent of GDP, the net capital inflows exceeded what was required to finance the current account deficit and contributed to a build up of forex reserves.

1.127. Looking ahead, if we assume that worst case outcomes will be avoided, then even though Europe may grow very slowly in the coming years, world financial markets can be expected to stabilise. On this assumption, it is reasonable to assume that India can finance a current account deficit of around 2.5 per cent of GDP relying mainly on FDI and FII flows, with some recourse to long-term borrowing. Since the projected current account deficit for 8 per cent growth is somewhat higher, financing the deficit will be a stress point in the years ahead. Capital flows from Europe may well be subdued, but there is scope for diversifying to tap other markets, notably Japan and also the sovereign wealth funds in the Middle East. The key element that will make this possible is that India must be seen to be set on a high growth path, with macroeconomic balances coming under control over the medium term, and policies towards foreign investment being viewed as supportive. The specific policy requirements for achieving this outcome are discussed in Section 1.6.

Other Aspects of External Engagement

1.128. There are several other aspects of engagement with the world economy, which are relevant for achieving our overall growth objectives. First and the most important relates to energy supply and energy security. India's dependence on imported energy is high and is generally expected to increase. Apart from our traditional dependence upon oil imports, the import of natural gas and coal will also need to increase significantly. The price of imported energy will obviously have an impact on our growth capacity in the sense that high energy prices impose a cost on the economy and make it more difficult to generate domestic surpluses for investment. Dependence on energy imports also raises concern about energy security. We need to have sufficient flexibility to be able to alter our fuel composition to respond to movements in energy prices. We also need to develop stable long-term steady sources of supply for different fuels relying on long-term supply agreements with countries in different geographies, and through asset acquisition abroad.

1.129. Second, non-financial aspects of India's engagement with the world need to be strengthened. S&T is an important area to project India's engagement with the world. India has the potential to emerge as a major scientific power, provided the right policies and frameworks are implemented. The need for more global collaboration and partnerships in research on the part of our universities, research institutes and the corporate sector has been mentioned earlier. Such activity needs to be strongly encouraged.

1.130. Finally, India needs to engage more proactively with the global community at bilateral, regional and multilateral levels. In the last 10 years India has worked on several bilateral agreements—these take time to show impact, and positive effects of these will start showing up soon. Special attention needs to be paid to our immediate neighbours. The South Asian Association for Regional Cooperation (SAARC) mechanism is yet to achieve the necessary degree of salience. The bilateral efforts have certainly been more fruitful but much greater emphasis needs to be placed on the regional cooperation agenda as the benefits can go well beyond what is possible through the bilateral route. While this is largely a political issue, it may be desirable to begin the process of instituting dialogue between the apex planning agencies of neighbouring countries.

1.131. Looking beyond our immediate neighbourhood, India needs to be proactive in traditional multilateral forums such as the United Nations (UN), and also participate proactively in new emerging forums of importance such as the G20, IBSA, BASIC and so on. This will sometimes require us to go beyond our comfort zone and be prepared for out-of-the-box modes of engagement. India will also need to play an active role in breaking deadlocks and ensuring progress on two economically important multilateral forums, the World Trade Organization (WTO) and United Nations Framework Convention on Climate Change (UNFCCC).

KEY POLICY INITIATIVES NEEDED

1.132. In this section, we discuss some of the major policy initiatives needed to achieve rapid, more inclusive and sustainable growth. Policies and programmes to improve human capabilities, institutional capabilities and to develop infrastructure, have been discussed in Section 1.3. They are all necessary for achieving the Twelfth Plan objectives and should have high priority.

Immediate Priorities: Reviving Investor Sentiments

1.133. An immediate policy objective in the very first year of the Plan must be to revive animal spirits, which have suffered for a variety of reasons. Some of the reasons for a downturn in investor sentiment can be easily corrected. For example, the perception among investors, that some of the tax changes introduced in the Budget are anti-investor need to be allayed as quickly as possible. The Finance Ministry has appointed two expert committees to look into these issues and it is hoped that the recommendations of these committees will provide a reasonable basis for reviving investor confidence on these issues. A firm decision on the recommendations of the Committee should be announced as early as possible.

1.134. The next important short-term action must be to remove the impediments to implementation of projects in infrastructure, especially in the area of energy. The following steps are especially urgent.

Fuel Supply to Power Stations

1.135. The fuel supply problem affecting electric power generation stations that have been commissioned but do not have adequate assurance of supply of coal or gas, and the problems of power stations currently under implementation which have yet to tie up fuel supply agreements, need to be addressed urgently. Coal India is the dominant domestic producer of coal because of nationalisation. It must take on the responsibility of making coal available to all power plants which are governed by regulated tariffs or have entered into PPAs based on competitive bidding for tariffs. Coal India must take steps to enhance its domestic production capability as much as possible, including by exploring possible PPP arrangements with mine development operators working on a contract basis. In the short run, however, the shortage can only be made up by imports. Additional imports are possible but the fact that imported coal is available only at much higher prices discourages potential consumers. One way of resolving this problem is through a system of pricing pooling. This should be explored and it should be implemented urgently.

Financial Problems of Discoms

1.136. Many discoms have accumulated high volumes of debt to finance their large current losses. Commercial banks are increasingly unwilling to finance the losses any further. This in turn has created unwillingness on the part of banks to finance power generation projects that are being set up because of doubts that they will be paid by the discoms. A debt restructuring plan, in which State Governments take over a large part of the burden of paying back the debt has been approved by the Cabinet and must be implemented by all the affected Sates. The commercial banks will have to bear part of the burden by restructuring the loans, and the Reserve Bank of India (RBI) may have to allow some regulatory forbearance relieving the banks of treating the restructured loans as non-performing assets (NPA) and making suitable provisions for them. As envisaged in the package, these steps must be combined with credible steps on the part of the State Governments and the discoms to ensure restoration of the operational viability of the discoms in future. An early implementation of open access would help create an environment that would promote efficiency and competitiveness.

Clarity in Terms of NELP Contracts

1.137. Several problems have arisen in interpreting existing New Exploration Licensing Policy (NELP) contracts especially related to the process for approving expenditure on the development plan and the approval for gas prices. This uncertainty is not conducive to attracting private investment in this very important part of the energy sector. A committee under Dr. C. Rangarajan has been set up to make recommendations on future NELP contracts, which would avoid uncertainty and establish clear rules regarding the pricing of oil and gas from future NELP fields. An early decision on this issue should be taken within calendar year 2012.

The Size of the Public Sector Plan

1.138. Although planning should cover both the activities of the government and those of the private sector, a great deal of the public debate on planning in India takes place around the size of the public sector plan. The Twelfth Plan lays out an ambitious set of government programmes, which will help to achieve the objective of rapid and inclusive growth. These programmes add up to a total plan size for the Centre of ₹43,33,739 crores including both budget resources and the resources of the public sector enterprises which comes to about 6.35 per cent of GDP. This compares with ₹20,25,130 crores in the Eleventh Plan, which was 5.96 per cent of GDP. The total plan size of the States is ₹37,16,385 crore or 5.45 per cent of GDP, as compared to ₹17,25,848 crore in the Eleventh Plan, which was 5 per cent of GDP.

1.139. Although the proposed Plan size is large, the demand from various sectors is also very high. However, resource constraints are a reality and even the plan size projected is conditional on high growth rate of revenue and a significant degree of control over subsidies. If for any reason these assumptions prove too optimistic, the size of the Plan may have to be trimmed at the time of the Mid Term Review.

1.140. In view of the scarcity of resources, it is essential to take bold steps to improve the efficiency of public expenditure through plan programmes. To this end the Planning Commission had established a Committee under Member, B. K. Chaturvedi to make recommendations for rationalisation and to increase efficiency of Centrally Sponsored Schemes (CSSs) and for improving their efficiency. There has been a proliferation of CSS over the years, many of which are quite small. The Chaturvedi Committee had recommended that the number of CSSs should be drastically reduced and the guidelines under which the schemes are implemented should be made much more flexible. The recommendations have been discussed with the Ministries and the States and have generally been welcomed. It is proposed to implement these recommendations with effect from 2013–14.

Longer-Term Increase in Investment and Saving Rates

1.141. Bringing the economy back to 9 per cent growth by the end of the Twelfth Plan requires fixed investment rate to rise to 35 per cent of GDP by the end of the Plan period. This will require action to revive private investment, including private corporate investment, and also action to stimulate public investment, especially in key areas of infrastructure especially, energy, transport, water supply and water resource management.

1.142. The strategy of expanding investment will help to counter the weakening of external demand on account of the global downturn. It is important that the expansion in domestic demand should not be in the form of consumption, but in the form of higher levels of investment. This not only provides demand in the short run to support higher levels production but also strengthens the longer-term growth potential of the economy. We should also ensure that a large part of the increase in investment goes into infrastructure as this would have a positive effect on reviving private investment in other sectors and would ease supply constraints, which limit future growth. The Eleventh Plan succeeded in raising investment in infrastructure from 5.04 per cent of GDP in the Tenth Plan to 7.2 per cent of GDP in the Eleventh Plan. The Twelfth Plan aims to raise it further to 9 per cent of GDP by 2016–17.

1.143. Higher levels of investment have to be supported by a sufficient expansion in domestic savings to keep the investment savings gap, which is also the current account deficit, at a level which can be financed through external capital. India's domestic savings capacity has been an important strength of the economy, although recent years saw a distinct weakening in this area because of deterioration in both government and corporate savings. Household savings, however, have remained strong and are likely to increase in the future, both because of our age composition and as result of increased financial inclusion. Nonetheless, reversal of the combined deterioration in government and corporate savings has to be a key element in our strategy.

The Need for Fiscal Correction

1.144. The decline in public savings in the past few years is largely a reflection of the stimulus policies that were followed, which are reflected in the expansion in the fiscal deficit. The Central Government fiscal deficit was 5.9 per cent of GDP in 2011–12. Allowing for a fiscal deficit of just under 3 per cent for the States, the combined deficit of the Centre and the State Governments, which had fallen to 4.7 per cent in 2007–08, expanded to just under 9 per cent in 2011–12. This has to be reversed through a credible correction over the medium term. The Finance Ministry has set up an Independent Expert Committee to advise on a credible medium-term road map for fiscal correction. The Committee has recommended a new road map for fiscal deficit reduction to bring the Central Government deficit down to 3 per cent by the end of the Twelfth Plan. It will be necessary to take action on two fronts:

1. The Centre must persevere with reforms of the tax structure, notably the introduction of Good and Services Tax (GST), which will represent a major modernisation of the indirect tax system. GST will greatly simplify the system and improve revenue mobilisation, primarily by plugging loopholes. Since introduction of GST requires a Constitutional amendment, it needs a broad political support which has taken time to build. However, if it can be introduced soon, it will give a boost to efficiency and to revenue mobilisation without raising rates.
2. It will require a reversal of the trend witnessed in recent years for Central Government subsidies to grow as a percentage of GDP. It must be emphasised that the objective is not to eliminate subsidies. Subsidies can even increase in absolute terms as the GDP grows, but they must be reduced as a percentage of the GDP. There is a role for targeted subsidies that advance the cause of inclusiveness, but such subsidies can be contained within a predetermined level of affordability. It should be possible to do this without hurting the poor. Some subsidies such as under the proposed Food Security Act will be predetermined. Others such as on fertiliser can be redesigned to serve their purpose at less cost. Subsidies, on petroleum products are untargeted and do not benefit the poor and the most needy. They will have to be reduced.

1.145. The State Governments also need to take steps to reduce the growing burden of subsidies, most especially the large and growing losses in the power sector.

Managing the Current Account Deficit

1.146. The initiatives described above to increase government savings and corporate savings will create conditions conducive to keeping the current account deficit at 2.5 per cent of GDP. This level of deficit can be financed through long-term capital flows as long as India's macroeconomic parameters are seen to be improving and GDP growth recovers above 7 per cent. India is still under weight in most global portfolios given its economic size and growth potential and positive signals about the revival of growth, combined with a credible commitment to improve macroeconomic balances and a welcoming stance towards foreign investment will ensure the financing needed to maintain a current account deficit of 2.5 per cent.

1.147. The steps taken to liberalise FDI, especially in areas where there is evident investor interest such as for example, FDI in retail, would help by sending the right signals. We must build on the success of previous liberalisation in FDI in other sectors, such as insurance, and before that telecom.

Economic Reforms and Efficiency of Resource Use

1.148. While higher investment is necessary for faster growth, it is equally important to ensure efficiency in resource use, both in the public and private sectors. The implementation of the reform relating to CSSs mentioned above will help achieve greater efficiency to implement in the public sector.

1.149. In the private sector—which accounts for over 70 per cent of total investment—the main instrument available for improved efficiency of resource use is to continue economic reforms, which increase competitive pressure in the system and give producers the flexibility and freedom they need to upgrade technology and expand capacity. In this context, it is worth noting that the global experience with the financial crisis, and the policy rethinking it has triggered, a backlash against market based reform in the financial sector. We need to consider what implications this has for our own policies of economic reforms.

1.150. There is no doubt that the financial excesses in the United States, the United Kingdom and Europe have revealed deep institutional weaknesses in the financial system in these countries and this has produced a backlash against 'Wall Street', 'greedy capitalism' and also against 'markets' generally. What this implies for the pursuit of efficiency promoting economic reforms in emerging market countries needs careful consideration. The principal lesson from the global financial crisis is that financial systems are prone to vulnerability if internal controls are weak; the structure of incentives does not incentivise risk-averse behaviour and if the structure of regulation and the quality of supervision is poor. Since financial integration has made financial systems highly interconnected, vulnerability in one part of the system can extend rapidly to others. These weaknesses explain the severity of the crisis in the industrialised countries. However, our financial system was not exposed to these problems, partly because the degree of integration with global financial markets was low (that is, capital controls were in place which limited cross border banking activity) and partly also because the banking system was much more tightly regulated. On both issues, the cautious approach of the Government of India (GOI) and the RBI towards capital account liberalisation and the maintenance of fairly tight regulatory control on the banks stand vindicated.

1.151. The principal lesson we should learn is that we should continue with our strategy of gradual liberalisation in the financial sector. There is no case for reversing this process of gradual liberalisation, or even stopping it. Countries that had gone too far towards adopting 'light touch regulation' are quite correctly tightening their regulatory standards though it should be noted that concern is beginning to be expressed in these countries that this process may be going too far. India was never at that end of the spectrum. In fact, we were if anything at the other end where control over banks and financial institutions is much stronger than in most other jurisdictions and is sometimes excessive.

1.152. However, there is one aspect that does require attention. The global financial crisis highlights the moral hazard problems of following universal banking principles and has brought back into prominence the issue of segregating the commercial and investment banking functions. Our efforts to liberalise the financial sector in the past have meant that Indian banks are today required to undertake investments lending less by design than by default. With the demise of development finance institutions (DFIs), the function of term lending has devolved on the commercial banking sector, which may not be entirely prepared to carry out this function. First, it is not clear whether the Indian banking sector has acquired the requisite risk assessment and project appraisal skills for term loans, without which financing long-duration projects can be hazardous. Second, the entire sector is now more vulnerable to asset–liability imbalance, requiring more frequent recapitalisation particularly as global regulatory norms tighten following the crisis. Third, since there has been no change in the sources from which banks can raise their resources, all increases in term lending are at the cost of funds available for working capital purposes. This leads to smaller and weaker clients being crowded out from the credit space whenever norms stiffen or investment increases. This makes our banking system less inclusive than it would otherwise have been. It is an opportune time, therefore, to blend further gradual liberalisation with a broader consideration of the design of our banking sector and ensure that the laws are consistent with the intentions.

1.153. Looking beyond the financial sector, to the real sector, there is no reason to backtrack on the use of market mechanisms to achieve efficiency or from an open economy, including a freer flow of foreign direct investment. No such reversal is taking place anywhere in the world and we should act no differently. Protectionist noises have certainly increased in industrialised countries, which is disturbing, but actions have been relatively contained thus far. The G20, of which India is a part, have regularly called in their summits for an avoidance of new protectionist measures. It is to be hoped that this high level consensus will be translated into action. None of this justifies a retreat from international openness on our part. Those arguing for protectionism in industrialised countries are fighting to protect their economies from the loss of competitiveness vis-à-vis emerging markets. It is not in India's interest to support such voices by willingly redirecting our own policies in that direction. On the contrary, it is in our interest, as we gain in competitiveness, to ensure that global markets remain open.

Transparency in Allocating Scarce Natural Resources

1.154. The economic reforms successfully eliminated discretionary decision-making in areas such as industrial licenses and import licenses. The process of extending transparent policies and mechanisms to allocation of scarce natural resouces to private companies for commercial purposes has also been initiated. This is an extremely important gain. It will be further carried forward during the Twelfth Plan.

Agricultural Growth

1.155. It is well recognised that faster growth of agriculture makes the overall growth process more inclusive. A positive feature of the experience is that agricultural growth increased from 2.4 per cent in the Tenth Plan to 3.7 per cent in the Eleventh Plan. Further acceleration to 4 per cent is essential to ensure inclusiveness.

1.156. Action is needed on several fronts including provision of basic support services such as technology and irrigation infrastructure, access to credit, good and reliable seeds and improved post-harvest technology. The latter is particularly important since the bulk of the acceleration in growth will come from diversification towards horticulture, animal husbandry and fisheries. The greatest potential for improving productivity is in the rain-fed areas, which account for 55 per cent of net sown area and where most of the poor live. Land productivity is low in these areas, but a combination of effective water management combined with better seeds, promotion of soil health and critical on farm investments combined with public sector efforts to improve infrastructure can make a big difference. Rain-fed farming requires a natural resource management perspective with a farming systems approach focusing on producing diverse products that mutually reinforce each other and stabilise the system. These areas are ecologically fragile and highly vulnerable to the vagaries of climate, so the resilience of the system has to be increased. They require knowledge and institutional investments to improve soil moisture management, enhance soil productivity, revitalise common pool resources, provide appropriate seed and low external input systems as also farm mechanisation, along with diverse livelihood options such as livestock and fisheries. Some of the government's key inclusiveness promoting programmes, such as MGNREGA, can make a major contribution to improving land productivity, if the projects under it are structured to increase on farm productivity. Properly designed and converged, MGNREGA can contribute to creating positive synergy with agricultural growth.

1.157. In addition, the Twelfth Plan must address some basic imbalances. First, to increase rice productivity in Eastern India and at same time relieve North-West India from the stress on groundwater caused by this water-intensive crop. Second, to focus on growing imbalances in nutrient use that can affect productivity seriously. Third, to ensure that there is enough parity between procurement operations for crops such as oilseeds and pulses as for rice and wheat, so that we can avoid situations like at present when huge stocks of the latter coexist with huge imports of the former. Fourth, to put at the centre of our agricultural policies. These matters are discussed in Chapter 12.

Manufacturing

1.158. The manufacturing sector provides the best opportunity for creating quality jobs, which require skills which are relatively easily imparted to someone who has finished secondary school. However, this is also an area where business as usual will not produce rapid growth and a paradigm shift is needed. The reasons why manufacturing in India has not grown sufficiently rapidly and also not created as much employment in the formal sector as might have been expected, have been analysed in Chapter 9. The following are some of the initiatives needed to correct this performance:

- First, India ranks towards the bottom of international comparisons of ease of doing business. The business regulatory environment in the country is intimidating for manufacturers, especially small-scale enterprises. It saps their productivity and deters further investments. The Plan proposes some initiatives to tune up India's business regulatory environment. Much of the action needed lies with State Governments.
- Second is the state of the physical infrastructure—power and transport, in particular—on which manufacturing enterprises depend much more than IT-based service enterprises, strategies for improving infrastructure are a core of the Plan and they will make a difference to performance of manufacturing as a whole.
- Third, India needs to increase the technological depth of its manufacturing sector to improve its competitiveness and also the country's trade balance. India is increasingly importing high-tech and capital goods and exporting raw materials in return. Strategies are required to induce more depth and value-addition in India's manufacturing sector that are not 'protectionist' and that leverage FDI and are compatible with an open global trade regime.
- Fourth is a rethinking of the role of human resources in manufacturing. Successful manufacturing requires learning and absorption of technologies and the ability to improve them and this takes place principally through the human side of the enterprise. Sustainable competitiveness will also require a new way of dealing with labour Refurbishing of India's outdated labour laws is necessary, but improvement of industrial relations and the collaboration that is necessary between employees and management will not be obtained merely by changing the laws. It will require a new social contract founded on a developmental orientation and on partnerships in India's Manufacturing and Industrial sectors and in the enterprises within them.
- Fifth, the growth of the MSME sector must be a central focus of India's manufacturing strategy. This sector is the foundation for a strong manufacturing sector providing more employment with less capital. It has a complementary relationship with large industries because it supplies components and inputs to them. It is the entry point for workers and entrepreneurs who move through it to larger-scale enterprises. Whereas much government attention is given to consult with and address the issues of larger enterprises, the development of the MSME sector must become more central to the deliberations about the challenges of Indian industry and the Indian economy. The sector must be viewed not as a static and weak sector, requiring constant support and protection, but as an integral part of the industrial system with upward mobility for individual units within it.
- Lastly, many of the changes in policy and implementation that are required to improve the environment for manufacturing—in the business regulatory environment, in implementing infrastructure projects, in industrial relations, and the requirements of SMEs—are within the domains of the States. This includes the quality of power supply, much of road connectivity, implementation of sales tax administration, implementation of laws relating to safety, pollution control and labour, industrial parks and so on. The Centre also has a critical role to play in areas such as rail

transportation, income tax, Cenvat, export regulation and the functioning of the financial system.

1.159. These issues are also relevant for India's entire business sector, which apart from manufacturing, covers services and off-farm rural enterprises. All of them will benefit from better business regulation and better infrastructure.

Energy Policies for Long-Term Growth

1.160. A growth rate of 8 per cent in GDP requires a growth rate of about 6 per cent in total energy use from all sources. Unfortunately, our capacity to expand domestic energy supplies to meet this demand is severely limited. We are not well-endowed with energy resources except for coal and the existence of policy distortions make management of demand and supply more difficult. Some of these problems have already been discussed earlier in this Chapter in connection with the immediate need to revive investor sentiment. There are also longer-term constraints that need to be addressed.

Coal Production

1.161. Coal is the most abundant primary energy source available in the country, but most of the country's coal resources are in forest areas, traditionally inhabited by our tribal population. Coal production for supply to third parties is nationalised but projects in some sectors are allowed to have captive coal mines. Coal India was not able to meet its coal production targets in the Eleventh Plan and, as pointed out earlier, domestic coal supplies are not assured for coal-based power projects coming on stream in the Twelfth Plan. It is absolutely essential to ensure that domestic production of coal increases from 540 million tonnes in 2011–12 to the target of 795 million tonnes at the end of the Plan. This increase of 255 million tonnes assumes an increase of 64 million tonnes of captive capacity with the rest being met by Coal India Limited. However, even with this increase, we will need to import 185 million tonnes of coal in 2016–17. Environmental and forest clearances of coal projects have presented problems. A special mechanism for inter-Ministerial coordination needs to be set up to accelerate processing of these projects in a time bound manner. Unless this is done, India's energy needs will be in jeopardy and investor sentiment will weaken irreversibly, at least for the duration of the Twelfth Plan. Taking a longer-term view, the policy of nationalisation of coal itself needs to be reviewed as was pointed out in the Eleventh Plan. If private sector producers are allowed in petroleum, which is a more valuable resource, there is no reason why they should not be allowed in coal. They are allowed to a small extent in the State of Meghalaya, which has private ownership of coal, because the tribal land there is not government land.

Petroleum Price Distortions

1.162. The petroleum sector suffers from a serious distortion in product prices which lead to huge under-recoveries and discourage private investment. Domestic prices for diesel charged by Oil Marketing Companies (OMCs) was 35.3 per cent lower than trade parity prices before the recent price adjustment. Prices for kerosene and LPG are 72.6 per cent and 53.6 per cent lower than they should be.

1.163. Continuation of these systems indefinitely, without provision of a budgetary subsidy, would seriously damage the petroleum industry, limiting its ability to invest in the discovery and development of new oil sources and discouraging all new private investment. If on the other hand, the gap is covered by a budgetary subsidy, it will impose an impossible burden on the budget, necessitating either a sharp cut in other government expenditures or a highly destabilising increase in the fiscal deficit. It is in this context that the diesel prices had to be raised to reduce the gap or a cap was placed on the number of subsidised cylinders. The Twelfth Plan must ensure a move to more rational petroleum product pricing, It may not be possible to remove all distortions immediately, but a phased price adjustment is needed that would reduce subsidy to manageable levels. As a general rule small increases in prices effected over time can help reduce the gap by manageable levels.

Natural Gas Pricing

1.164. Natural gas also faces problems of price misalignment. At present, the price of gas paid to domestic producers is $4.25 per MMBtu, whereas the spot imported liquefied natural gas (LNG) price is around $11–14 per MMBtu. Producers argue that unless they are assured of prices linked to world prices, no investment will take place in this sector. The government has appointed an expert committee under Dr. C. Rangarajan to advise on the form of NELP contracts. The Committee is expected to submit its report very shortly and it is hoped that it will recommend steps to introduce clarity about the policy regarding pricing of gas without which new investment may be inhibited.

Urbanisation

1.165. More effective management of the process of urbanisation in the country will be critical for more inclusive, more sustainable and faster economic growth. Urbanisation is a natural part of the development process because cities provide substantial economics of scale and of agglomeration. In India the cities are also effective drivers of inclusiveness because barriers of caste, creed, and language are bridged in interconnected efforts by residents to earn better livelihoods. At present, about 31 per cent of the population, that is, about 380 million, live in urban areas and this will increase to about 600 million by 2030. Providing reasonable quality services to the growing urban population presents a major challenge. Urban services are very poor, particularly sanitation, solid waste removal, water, roads and public transportation. Affordable, decent housing is woefully inadequate in all Indian cities, leading to the formation of slums, health and living conditions in which are aggravated by poor water and sanitation services.

1.166. The Jawaharlal Nehru National Urban Renewal Mission-II (JNNURM-II) was a landmark initiative because it put India's urban agenda centre stage. It set about providing resources to the States linked to incentives for reforms which would trigger to focus on improvements to cities and towns. The seven years' experience with JNNURM has been a substantial learning experience which has also revealed weaknesses in the governance systems and the capabilities of cities, States and even the Centre to manage the process of urbanisation. Urban governance is very weak, with poor coordination amongst the many agencies that must work together to create and maintain good functioning habitats. Personnel and institutional capabilities for urban management have to be developed on a massive scale across the country. Capabilities for planning locally are woefully inadequate, which is leading to projects not aligned with local priorities and poor coordination amongst separate initiatives.

1.167. Since overall government resources are limited and must be applied to other priority sectors such as health and education, it is necessary that cities, especially the larger ones, and progressively even the smaller ones, are encouraged and enabled to draw resources from the market and the private sector. For this, they must improve their governance and ability to implement projects. They will also have to manage their land resources more strategically, both to ensure better land use and to secure what will be a principal resource for their future financial needs. They must become able to recover adequate service charges, and equitably, from their inhabitants, which will require them to demonstrate an ability to deliver better and more reliable services. The concept of PPPPs, which systematically put local citizens into the partnership framework must be applied.

1.168. The strategies for improving the management of urbanisation are explained in Chapter 14. A new JNNURM-II incorporating the learning from JNNURM-I will be a major feature of the Twelfth Plan. It must give priority to the strengthening of human and institutional capabilities, local planning and improvements in governance, which are the foundations for a more financially and environmentally sustainable and a more inclusive process of governance.

MONITORABLE TARGETS FOR THE PLAN

1.169. The aspirations and challenges that guide the Twelfth Plan have been discussed in the body of this chapter and strategies for meeting these aspirations are spelt out in detail in the individual Chapters of the Plan. To focus the energies of the government and other stakeholders in development, it is desirable to identify monitorable indicators, which can be used to track the progress of our efforts. Given the complexity of the country and the development process, there are a very large number of targets that can and should be used. Most of these are discussed in the sectoral chapters. However, there is a core set of indicators which could form the objectives towards which all development partners can work, which includes not only the Central and State Governments, but also local governments, CSOs and international agencies.

1.170. Twenty-five core indicators that are listed below reflect the vision of rapid, sustainable and more inclusive growth:

Economic Growth
1. Real GDP Growth Rate of 8.0 per cent.
2. Agriculture Growth Rate of 4.0 per cent.
3. Manufacturing Growth Rate of 10.0 per cent.
4. Every State must have an average growth rate in the Twelfth Plan preferably higher than that achieved in the Eleventh Plan.

Poverty and Employment
5. Head-count ratio of consumption poverty to be reduced by 10 percentage points over the preceding estimates by the end of Twelfth Five Year Plan.
6. Generate 50 million new work opportunities in the non-farm sector and provide skill certification to equivalent numbers during the Twelfth Five Year Plan.

Education
7. Mean Years of Schooling to increase to seven years by the end of Twelfth Five Year Plan.
8. Enhance access to higher education by creating two million additional seats for each age cohort aligned to the skill needs of the economy.
9. Eliminate gender and social gap in school enrolment (that is, between girls and boys, and between SCs, STs, Muslims and the rest of the population) by the end of Twelfth Five Year Plan.

Health
10. Reduce IMR to 25 and MMR to 1 per 1,000 live births, and improve Child Sex Ratio (0–6 years) to 950 by the end of the Twelfth Five Year Plan.
11. Reduce Total Fertility Rate to 2.1 by the end of Twelfth Five Year Plan.
12. Reduce under-nutrition among children aged 0–3 years to half of the NFHS-3 levels by the end of Twelfth Five Year Plan.

Infrastructure, Including Rural Infrastructure
13. Increase investment in infrastructure as a percentage of GDP to 9 per cent by the end of Twelfth Five Year Plan.
14. Increase the Gross Irrigated Area from 90 million hectare to 103 million hectare by the end of Twelfth Five Year Plan.
15. Provide electricity to all villages and reduce AT&C losses to 20 per cent by the end of Twelfth Five Year Plan.
16. Connect all villages with all-weather roads by the end of Twelfth Five Year Plan.
17. Upgrade national and state highways to the minimum two-lane standard by the end of Twelfth Five Year Plan.
18. Complete Eastern and Western Dedicated Freight Corridors by the end of Twelfth Five Year Plan.
19. Increase rural tele-density to 70 per cent by the end of Twelfth Five Year Plan.
20. Ensure 50 per cent of rural population has access to 40 lpcd piped drinking water supply, and 50 per cent *gram panchayat*s achieve Nirmal Gram Status by the end of Twelfth Five Year Plan.

Environment and Sustainability
21. Increase green cover (as measured by satellite imagery) by 1 million hectare every year during the Twelfth Five Year Plan.
22. Add 30,000 MW of renewable energy capacity in the Twelfth Plan.

23. Reduce emission intensity of GDP in line with the target of 20 per cent to 25 per cent reduction over 2005 levels by 2020.

Service Delivery
24. Provide access to banking services to 90 per cent Indian households by the end of Twelfth Five Year Plan.
25. Major subsidies and welfare related beneficiary payments to be shifted to a direct cash transfer by the end of the Twelfth Plan, using the Aadhar platform with linked bank accounts.

1.171. States are encouraged to set state-specific targets corresponding to the above, taking account of what is the reasonable degree of progress given the initial position. Sector-wise growth targets for each State are given in Chapter 11.

2

Macroeconomic Framework

INTRODUCTION

2.1. The Eleventh Plan (2007–12) had targeted an average annual growth of 9 per cent, significantly higher than the realised rate of 7.6 per cent in the Tenth Plan (2002–07), but broadly in line with the acceleration of economic activity and growth experienced after 2004–05. The Plan began well, with 9.3 per cent growth in 2007–08, but the global financial crisis of 2008 reduced growth to 6.7 per cent in 2008–09. The economy rebounded well initially, to record 8.6 per cent growth in 2009–10, and then 9.3 per cent in 2010–11. However, the downturn in the global economy in 2011 due to the sovereign debt crisis in Europe combined with the emergence of domestic constraints on investment in infrastructure reduced gross domestic product (GDP) growth to 6.2 per cent in 2011–12. As a result, the average growth over the five years of the Eleventh Plan was 8.0 per cent.

2.2. Achieving 8.0 per cent growth in a period which saw two global crises, one in 2008 and another in 2011 is commendable. However, the deceleration is also a matter of concern, especially since growth in 2011–12 showed a continuous deceleration quarter by quarter during the year, with the last quarter of 2011–12 registering a year on year growth rate of only 5.3 per cent. The preliminary estimates for the first half of 2012–13 show a growth of 5.4 per cent, which is only marginally higher, suggesting that the first year of the Twelfth Plan will see relatively low growth momentum. However, weak short-term performance should not lead to pessimism about the medium term. There is good reason to believe that the fundamentals of the Indian economy remain strong, and the economy can return to 8–9 per cent growth path depending on the state of the global economy and the domestic policy response to overcome growth constraints.

THE DETERMINANTS OF GROWTH

2.3. The growth potential of the economy over a five year period depends upon a number of factors. These include the capacity of the economy to maintain high rates of investment, while also ensuring productive use of capital. This in turn depends upon investor expectations and the ability to mobilise financing for investment. The existence of a dynamic entrepreneurial and managerial class capable of taking risks and dealing with competitive pressure is an important positive feature of our economy. It also depends upon the quality of public sector managers responsible for investment and productivity in the public sector, which remains important in many areas of the economy. We have good reason to be optimistic on all these counts as evidenced by the fact that we grew rapidly between 2003–04 and 2008–09, and the Indian enterprise has also begun to expand its global presence.

2.4. Growth also depends on the availability of labour in adequate quantities, and with the right kind of skills to support rapid growth. We have the benefit of a demographic dividend because the age structure of the population ensures that the labour force will be growing in India even as it is falling in most industrialised countries, and even in China. However, the level of skills of the labour force needs to be enhanced. Skill shortages did emerge during our period of high growth and this is an area to which the government is according high priority.

2.5. The external environment also affects the growth potential since it determines the scope for exports to grow and thus contribute to the expansion of domestic economic activity. It also determines the extent to which the economy can finance a current account deficit through non-debt flows, especially Foreign Direct Investment (FDI), which often serves as an instrument for technological up-gradation and modernisation.

2.6. The acceleration of economic growth has been examined in detail in many studies. The accumulation of capital and labour stocks, as well as the manner in which these stocks are used, that is productivity, has been the subject of intensive study. Global experience suggests that different countries have drawn their growth acceleration in somewhat different proportions from factor accumulation and from Total Factor Productivity (TFP). The latter is the residual that is not explained by factor accumulation and represents an array of elements from technology (both that embodied in capital and that which is disembodied), to education and skills, to institutions and public policy.

2.7. It is well known that emerging market countries have the potential to accelerate growth substantially by accelerating growth in TFP because they are generally not at the productivity frontier, though their ability to do so is not independent of the rate of investment. The higher the TFP, the better is the use of labour and capital stock. Economic reforms have also increased efficiency of resource use in many sectors and studies show that there has been an increase in TFP in the Indian economy over time, and that this improvement was greater in the past two decades, especially in the past decade as compared to the previous periods. There is also considerable scope for further efficiency gains especially from use of IT-based technology, such as geographic information system (GIS) based systems, to increase the efficiency with which we create and operating public investments. These are important reasons for being optimistic about future growth in India.

Growth Prospects in the Twelfth Plan

2.8. Ideally, we should be able to explore the interaction of different determinants of growth through the use of quantitative economic models, which could illustrate the effect of different policy alternatives. However, it is well recognised that no single model will capture all possible interactions. The Planning Commission, therefore, relies upon a number of different models constructed by different research institutions which emphasise different aspects of the interaction between growth variables. The synthesis view that emerges from this exercise, and, from internal discussions within the Commission, is that it is possible for the economy to work its way out of the current slowdown and restore high growth, but this will take time and a number of hard policy decisions. The macroeconomic conclusions which emerge from this exercise are summarised in this Chapter.

2.9. Since the growth in the first year of the Plan is likely to range around 6 per cent, and the international economy is also expected to remain weak for the next two years, we need to plan for a gradual build up to high growth in the succeeding two years, accelerating thereafter to take the economy back to 9 per cent growth in the last years of the Plan. This backloaded trajectory of acceleration implies that growth in the Twelfth Plan period as a whole will at best average around 8.0 per cent. Any target that may be set now is bound to be subject to some uncertainty and downside risks, but it can be said that given the past record of growth, a target of 8.0 per cent is certainly feasible provided the worse case assumptions about the global economy do not materialise, and positive assumptions about our own ability to take hard decisions necessary to achieve a rapid and inclusive growth does.

2.10. The need to take hard decisions to return to high growth follows from the fact that we cannot assume the earlier rapid growth will readily re-emerge in the future. This is because several critical constraints, which emerged as the economy accelerated, and which visibly constrain our growth potential, have to be effectively tackled. Among these constraints are macroeconomic constraints that limit our ability to increase investment and savings, and to finance the current account deficit, which is the difference between the two. These are discussed in greater detail in this Chapter. There are also sectoral constraints relating to the availability of energy, transport, water, land and employable skills, and constraints relating to the business environment. These are discussed in other chapters of the Plan document.

2.11. Before discussing the macroeconomic constraints or achieving 8.0 per cent growth, it is useful to point out that growth is also affected by social and political forces, which are not easy to quantify. These forces determine the acceptability of economic policies and consequently the pace at which they can be implemented, all of which affect the determinants of growth such as investment rates and the pace of productivity improvement. Indeed, the decline in investment and growth in recent years is attributed to the country's internal social and political environment, which is preventing India from realising what pure economics would suggest is its full growth potential. These influences are not easy to build into quantitative models. However, the Planning Commission has attempted, for the first time, to reflect the impact of these forces by using the technique of 'scenario planning'.

Defining Alternative Scenarios

2.12. Scenario planning is designed to make a qualitative assessment of the forces that affect the economy, but cannot be easily quantified, such as social and political forces and conditions of institutions. Scenario planning cannot predict exact numerical outcomes of different scenarios, but it can project the trends of the economy, depending on how the principal sociopolitical forces take shape.

2.13. Figure 2.1 is a graphic presentation of some of the interconnections that were analysed to explain the principal forces shaping India's economy in different scenarios. The arrows indicate the primary direction of influence, though in many cases, the influence is circular over time generating 'feedback loops' within a system. Consider the interactions between 'Lack of Trust in Institutions', 'Impatience and Protest' and 'Political LogJam'. Lack of trust in institutions can cause increasing impatience in the country, especially amongst younger people, and leads to protests, sometimes turning violent. (The increasing impatience and protest is fuelled by the ubiquity of media and the explosion of information.) The lack of trust can create a political logjam, which makes reforms that the system needs that much more difficult. This reduces performance which in turn increases impatience and further reduces the credibility of the country's institutions, and trust in them.

2.14. This type of systems' analysis helps locate the 'leverage points' at which decision-makers can act to break the system out of its negatively reinforcing loops. For example, merely asking citizens to be more patient and trust their leaders will not increase trust and patience. However, credible improvement in the conduct of government (and business) institutions can increase citizens' trust, dampen protest, ease the political logjam and enable policy reforms that are required to improve the condition of government's finances and induce economic growth. Thus, analysis locates the leverage points as also the forces on which action can be taken to influence the condition of others. These are seen in the middle of Figure 2.1.

2.15. Figure 2.1 shows that in the present situation one of the key leverage points lie in the design and conduct of institutions of governance and business, including the policy framework with which business works and the signals to which it responds. Change at these leverage points can affect other conditions of the system positively, generating positive feedback loops. Economists, such as Nobel Laureates Douglass North and Elinor Ostrom have explained that 'institutions' are both the guiding ideas and norms of societies as also the 'organisations' with significant roles in governance. In our analysis, we have described these combinations as 'Governance Models' and 'Business Models'. The analysis of scenarios for India has revealed three critical features of governance and business models that are impacting the pace of inclusion, equitable use of our natural resources, environmental sustainability and economic growth. These are:

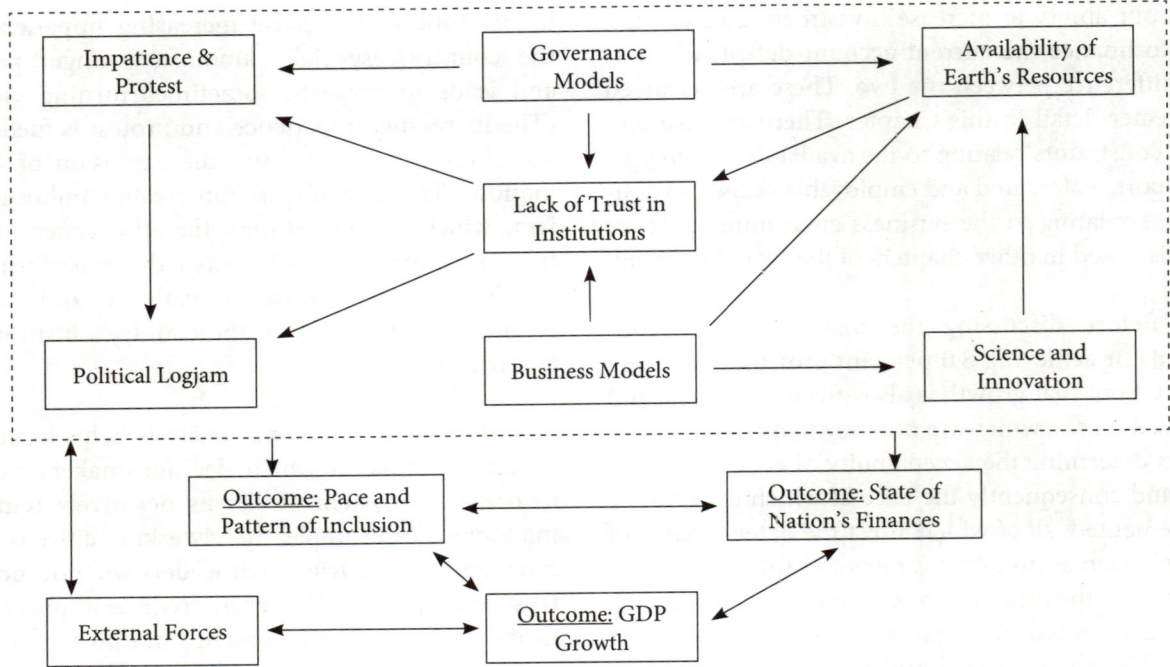

FIGURE 2.1: Systems Analysis for Twelfth Plan Scenarios

1. The approach we take to 'Inclusion': More subsidies or more widespread generation of opportunities for better livelihoods?
2. The approach we take to 'Governance': Will we strengthen local, community-based and collaborative governance rapidly?
3. The strategies we adopt towards energy and environment (as well as structure of programmes and enterprises): Big projects and centralised programmes, or more community-based solutions and enterprises?

2.16. Scenarios are not predictions. They are projections of plausible outcomes of alternative courses of action. They point to strategies that have more likelihood of producing the desired results. Therefore, depending on the strategies we choose and implement, we can envisage different outcomes for the country's progress. Three alternative scenarios are described in the following paragraphs.

Scenario 1

2.17. **Strong Inclusive Growth**: This is the future of India if we can implement a well-designed strategy addressing the key constraints holding back the economy. With appropriate steps taken to deal with implementation and governance problems, the wheels of government at all levels begin to move more smoothly. Local governance institutions and small enterprises are nurtured and have an opportunity to grow effectively, along with larger enterprises. Livelihood opportunities, along with community-based solutions and enterprises for addressing environmental issues, are seen to be sprouting. Many virtuous circles begin to operate in this scenario, raising confidence and trust. In this scenario, growth could average 8.0 per cent and inclusiveness would be assured.

Scenario 2

2.18. **Insufficient Action**: This scenario reflects the outcome of insufficient policy action. While broad direction of policy may be endorsed at different levels, action is incomplete or implementation is poor, with the result that outcomes are weaker than anticipated. Centralised government systems do not provide sufficient flexibility to cope with demands for decentralisation. Small enterprises and new entrepreneurs need to be encouraged, but unless the business environment necessary for them to flourish is effectively transformed, the outcome will fall short of expectations. The policy conflict between subsidies and financial stability of the economy remains unresolved. In this scenario, growth of 8.2 per cent is not feasible. Growth could decline to between 6 per cent and 6.5 per cent, and inclusiveness would suffer.

Scenario 3

2.19. *Policy Logjam*: This scenario reflects a situation where very little can be done for whatever reason on many of the policy fronts identified in the Twelfth Plan. It will be difficult to build growth momentum if critical supply constraints relating to energy and transport are not overcome. Investor confidence is likely to be severely eroded, and the lack of inclusiveness that results will lead to increased impatience and political logjam, putting the economy under severe stress. Vicious cycles begin to operate and the growth rate can drift down to 5–5.5 per cent with serious loss on the inclusiveness front. In some ways, there is a danger of insufficient action scenario degenerating into a policy logjam scenario, if it persists too long.

2.20. Clearly, Scenario 1: Strong inclusive growth is the only way for the country to go and the policy agenda laid out in the Plan is designed to achieve this objective. The outcomes of the three scenarios, in terms of the pace of inclusion, the confidence of people in country's institutions, as also the government's finances and the GDP, are not easily quantified, but their broad direction can be clearly seen. More information is available in the document, 'Scenarios: Shaping India's Future', that accompanies this Plan document, and is posted on the Planning Commission's website.

2.21. It is difficult to predict what the precise impact of different scenarios on poverty will be. However, past trends indicate what 'strong inclusive growth' can achieve on this front. Consumption Poverty in India is measured on the basis of Household Consumption Survey, conducted quinquennially (after a gap of every five years). Evidence suggests decline in poverty headcount ratio between 2004–05 and 2009–10 was twice as fast as that between 1993–94 and 2004–05. For details see the analytic note on 'Poverty—Measures and Changes Therein' in Annexure 2.1.

Sectoral Pattern of Growth

2.22. The sectoral pattern of growth associated with the 8.0 per cent growth scenario is summarised in Table 2.1. The Agriculture Forestry and Fishing Sector is projected to grow at 4 per cent, an improvement over the 3.7 per cent rate achieved in the Eleventh Plan. A detailed analysis of the constraints on growth and policy imperatives in the sector is given in Chapter 12 which concludes that 4 per cent growth is feasible.

2.23. The Mining and Quarrying Sector grew by only 3.2 per cent in the Eleventh Plan, the growth rate being pushed down by negative growth of 0.6 per cent in 2011–12 reflecting problems in the iron ore sector, gas production and also coal. The Twelfth Plan assumes a substantial improvement with the growth rate averaging 5.7 per cent. This will require serious attention to the many constraints that have bedevilled growth in this sector.

2.24. The manufacturing sector decelerated in the course of the Eleventh Plan with a growth rate of only 2.7 per cent in 2011–12. A robust reversal of this trend is essential for a return to rapid growth and especially the growth with inclusiveness since the growth of manufacturing job opportunities depends critically on this revival. The Plan projects a steady acceleration with the growth rate close to 10 per cent in the last two years. The average growth rate in the Twelfth Plan period is projected at over 7 per cent which is a significant improvement over the situation in 2011–12 and 2012–13. An average growth rate of 7 per cent in manufacturing is relatively low, but it reflects the fact that the Twelfth Plan begins with a base year growth of only 2.7 per cent in 2011–12 and perhaps lower in 2012–13. Over the longer run, the aim should be to achieve a sustained double digit growth in manufacturing sector.

2.25. Electricity, gas and water supply are projected to grow at 7.3 per cent on an average compared with 6.1

TABLE 2.1
Annual Growth Rate of GDP by Industry of Origin at Constant (2004–05) Prices

(Unit: Per Cent)

		Eleventh Plan period						Twelfth Plan period					
		2007–08	2008–09	2009–10	2010–11	2011–12	Average	2012–13	2013–14	2014–15	2015–16	2016–17	Average
1	Agriculture, forestry and fishing	5.8	0.1	0.8	7.9	3.6	3.7	2.0	4.5	4.5	4.5	4.5	4.0
2	Mining and quarrying	3.7	2.1	5.9	4.9	−0.6	3.2	1.0	5.0	7.0	7.0	8.5	5.7
3	Manufacturing	10.3	4.3	11.3	9.7	2.7	7.7	2.2	6.0	8.5	9.5	9.5	7.1
4	Electricity, gas and water supply	8.3	4.6	6.2	5.2	6.5	6.1	5.2	7.5	8.0	8.0	8.0	7.3
5	Construction	10.8	5.3	6.7	10.2	5.6	7.7	8.0	8.0	8.5	10.0	11.0	9.1
6	Trade, hotels and restaurant	10.1	5.7	7.9	11.5	6.2	8.3	5.5	6.0	8.0	8.7	8.7	7.4
7	Transport, storage and communication	12.5	10.8	14.8	13.8	8.4	12.0	7.3	11.1	13.0	13.6	14.1	11.8
8	Financing, insurance, real estate and business services	12.0	12.0	9.7	10.1	11.7	11.1	9.8	9.5	10.0	10.0	10.0	9.9
9	Community, social and personal services	6.9	12.5	11.7	4.3	6.0	8.3	7.3	7.2	7.2	7.2	7.2	7.2
	Total GDP	9.3	6.7	8.6	9.3	6.2	8.0	5.8	7.3	8.5	9.0	9.2	8.0
	Industry (2–5)	9.7	4.4	9.2	9.2	3.5	7.2	4.0	6.6	8.4	9.4	9.8	7.6
	Services (6–9)	10.3	10.0	10.5	9.8	8.2	9.7	7.6	8.3	9.4	9.7	9.9	9.0

per cent achieved in the Eleventh Plan. Construction, which grew at 7.7 per cent in the Eleventh Plan, is projected to grow at an average rate of 9.1 per cent. The other service sectors are projected to grow fairly robustly with Trade Hotels and Restaurants at 7.4 per cent; Transport, Storage and Communication at 11.8 per cent; Insurance and Business Service at 9.9 per cent, and, finally, Community and Personal Services at 7.2 per cent.

INVESTMENT

2.26. The ability to raise the rate of investment (ratio of gross fixed capital formation [GFCF] to GDP) is widely regarded as critical for the achievement of high growth. As shown in Figure 2.2, the period when the economy grew rapidly after 2003–04 and up to 2007–08 was a period when the investment rate increased. The fixed investment rate (at current prices) rose steadily after 2003–04 and was close to 34 per cent in 2007–08. Total capital formation—which includes inventories and investment in valuables—was higher at 39 per cent in that year, but for growth what matters is the fixed investment.

2.27. The fixed investment rate fell after 2007–08, initially on account of global factors, and later also owing to difficulties in the domestic arena which affected the pace of implementation of projects. The estimate for the GFCF rate in 2011–12 at constant prices is 33.7 per cent. The rate of gross domestic capital formation (GDCF), which includes stocks and valuables, but not other errors and omissions, is 37.9 per cent, of which valuables is 2.4 per cent of GDP.

2.28. For annual output growth to average 8.0 per cent in the Twelfth Plan period, and to cross 9 per cent in the closing year, it is estimated that the fixed investment rate will have to increase by about 1.5 percentage points of GDP over the level in 2011–12. The resulting trajectory of fixed investment over the Plan period is shown in Table 2.2. The fixed investment rate should increase to 35 per cent of GDP (at constant prices) by the end of the Twelfth Plan, yielding an average fixed investment rate of over 34 per cent of GDP for the Twelfth Plan period as a whole. These levels are marginally higher than what was achieved in the Eleventh Plan but they are broadly consistent with achieving an average

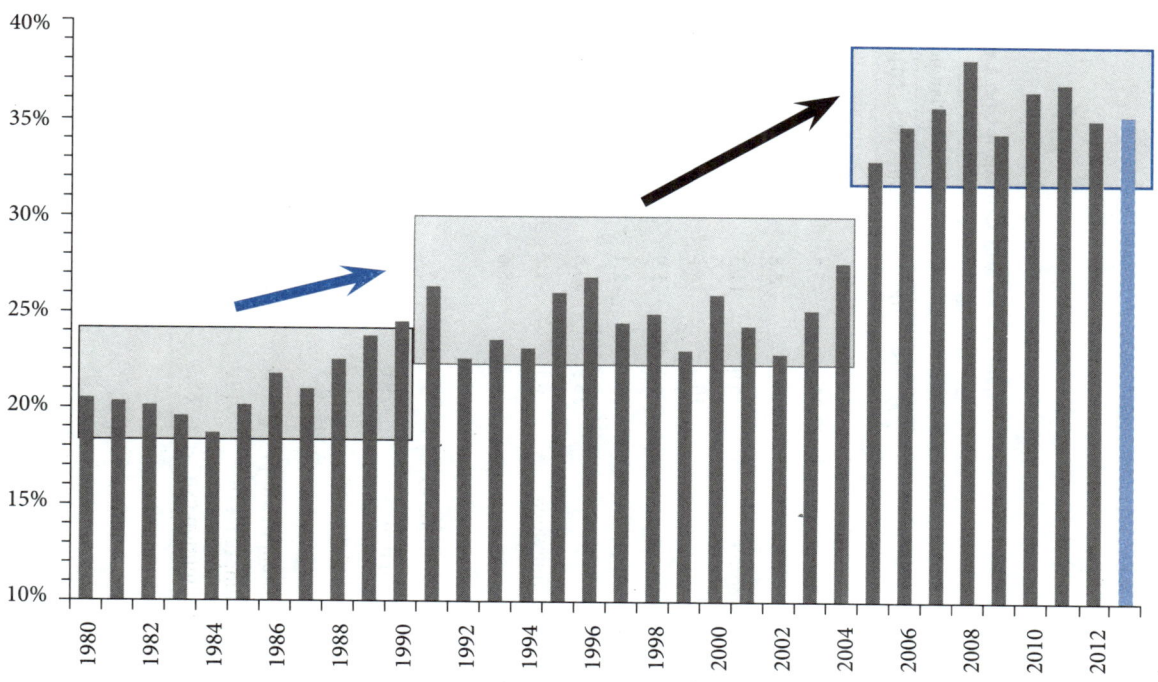

FIGURE 2.2: Investment Rate—Ratio to GDP at Current Prices—Over the Years

TABLE 2.2
Investment and Consumption Expenditure as Proportion of GDP at Constant 2004–05 Prices

	Eleventh Plan period						Twelfth Plan period					
	2007–08	2008–09	2009–10	2010–11	2011–12	Average	2012–13	2013–14	2014–15	2015–16	2016–17	Average
Ratio to GDP in Per Cent												
Fixed investment rate	33.7	33.5	33.3	34.3	33.7	33.7	33.0	33.9	34.4	34.5	35.0	34.2
Public	8.2	8.8	8.6	8.1	7.8	8.3	8.0	8.4	8.4	8.5	8.5	8.4
Private corporate	15.0	11.3	11.3	12.8	11.6	12.4	11.3	12.5	14.0	14.5	15.0	13.5
Household	10.5	13.5	13.4	13.4	14.3	13.0	13.5	13.0	12.0	11.5	11.5	12.3
Stocks	4.1	1.9	3.0	3.5	2.3	3.0	2.3	2.9	3.1	3.1	3.1	2.9
Valuables	1.1	1.4	2.0	2.4	2.4	1.8	2.2	1.9	1.6	1.6	1.6	1.8
GDCF	38.9	36.8	38.3	40.2	38.4	38.5	37.5	38.7	39.1	39.2	39.7	38.8
Errors and omissions	0.1	−1.3	0.2	−0.2	−0.5	−0.3						
Investment rate	39.0	35.6	38.4	40.0	37.9	38.2	37.5	38.7	39.1	39.2	39.7	38.8
Annual Real Growth Rate Per Cent												
Private consumption exp.	9.4	7.2	7.4	8.6	8.0	8.1	6.5	7.5	7.5	8.0	8.0	7.5
Govt consumption exp.	9.6	10.4	13.9	5.9	8.6	9.7	5.1	5.5	5.5	5.5	5.5	5.4
Total consumption exp.	9.7	7.7	8.4	8.1	8.1	8.3	6.3	6.8	7.3	7.8	7.8	7.2
Ratio to GDP in Per Cent												
Private consumption exp.	58.1	60.0	59.4	58.3	59.2	59.0	59.5	59.1	58.8	58.3	57.8	58.7
Govt consumption exp.	10.3	11.0	11.5	11.0	11.3	11.0	11.2	10.9	10.6	10.3	10.0	10.6
Total consumption exp.	68.5	71.0	70.9	69.4	70.5	70.0	70.6	70.0	69.4	68.6	67.8	69.3

real growth rate of little above 8 per cent, allowing for acceleration in growth in the course of the Plan period, and implying a significant relaxation in the physical constraints that limit the economy in infrastructure and other key sectors.

2.29. Over the past decade and a half, price inflation in capital goods has lagged that in the overall economy. As a consequence, the rates of capital formation at constant prices have tended to exceed that when measured at current prices. In the base year of the Twelfth Plan, the investment rate at constant prices is about 1.2 percentage points higher than in current prices. The savings investment balancing must of course be achieved at current prices.

Composition of Investment

2.30. The composition of fixed investment by source is also shown in Table 2.2. The public fixed investment rate (mostly investment by public enterprises) averaged 8.3 per cent in the Eleventh Plan, with a range of 7.8–8.8 per cent. It is projected to remain roughly in this range in the Twelfth Plan period averaging 8.4 per cent. Household fixed investment (which includes unincorporated business) averaged 13.0 per cent in the Eleventh Plan, with a range of 10.5–14.3 per cent. For the Twelfth Plan, household fixed investment is projected to average 12.3 per cent for the Plan period as a whole, it begins higher at 13.5 per cent in the first two years, slowly reducing to 11.5 per cent in the final two years of the Plan as the corporate sector expands its share.

2.31. Private corporate investment has been the major driver of investment in recent years. In 2003–04 private corporate fixed investment (at constant 1999–2000 prices) was only 6.2 per cent of GDP, while the overall fixed investment rate was 27.1 per cent. It rose to 9.1 per cent (at constant 2004–05 prices) in 2004–05 and 11.9 per cent in 2005–06. The overall fixed investment rate increased to 28.7 per cent in 2004–05 and to 30.5 per cent in 2005–06. Private corporate investment averaged 12.4 per cent in the Eleventh Plan but it was at a peak of 15.0 per cent in 2007–08, that is, the first year of the Eleventh Plan and declined in subsequent years to 11.6 per cent in 2011–12. If the overall fixed investment rate has to pick up in the Twelfth Plan, there has to be a recovery in private corporate fixed investment. Table 2.2 shows a gradual build-up in private corporate investment from 11.3 per cent in 2012–13 rising steadily to touch 15.0 per cent—the peak value achieved in 2007–08—in the last year of the Twelfth Plan. This would produce an average of 13.5 per cent for the Twelfth Plan as a whole; higher than the average of 12.4 per cent in the Eleventh Plan.

2.32. It must be noted that a large part of private corporate investment is now in the field of infrastructure—power generation, roads, ports, airports and telecommunications—and a lot of it is in the Public–Private Partnership (PPP) mode. The robust growth in private corporate investment is in part a reflection of the strategy of increasing the share of investment devoted to infrastructure and the recognition that private investment has to play a large part in this. Higher investment in infrastructure is critical for the revival of the investment climate as it would lead to enhanced investment in manufacturing.

Gross Capital Formation

2.33. To move from GFCF to gross capital formation we need to add increase in inventory and investment in valuables. Increase in inventory averaged 3.0 per cent of GDP in the Eleventh Plan, at constant (2004–05) prices. If the crisis year of 2008–09 is excluded (there is very large drawing down of inventories in crisis periods, as indeed had occurred in 2008–09), the average for the Eleventh Plan period is 3.2 per cent of GDP. For the Twelfth Plan period the increase in inventories is projected to account for close to 3.0 per cent.

2.34. Investment by households in valuables refers mainly to gold and silver. Import of gold and silver aggregated about $60 billion in 2011–12, most of which was 'investment' made by households. Until 2007–08, this represented around 1.0–1.3 per cent of GDP and even in the crisis year of 2008–09 the ratio was 1.4 per cent. Thereafter, it has increased very sharply perhaps reflecting the assessment that inflation had increased and the rupee was likely to come under pressure, combined with a fall in the penetration of other financial savings products, thereby making gold an attractive asset. It is estimated at constant prices to be 2.4 per cent of GDP in 2011–12. With the exchange rate depreciation that has occurred, and the initiatives to improve the availability of financial savings products and expected moderation in inflation, the proportion of investments in valuables is expected to steadily decline to 1.6 per cent of GDP in 2016–17. The average for the Twelfth Plan period is projected to be around 1.8 per cent, about the same as in the Eleventh Plan period.

2.35. As shown in Table 2.2, the aggregate GDCF in the Eleventh Plan at constant 2004–05 prices amounted to 38.2 per cent of GDP (including errors and omissions item of (–)0.3 per cent). The projections as outlined above for the Twelfth Plan would result in a higher average of 38.8 per cent of GDP. However, in the first year of the Plan, the ratio is likely to be lower than the Eleventh Plan average, but it is then expected to move up close to 40 per cent by the end of the Twelfth Plan. At current prices, the increase in GDCF would be somewhat less, moving up from 36.1 per cent of GDP in the Eleventh Plan to 36.9 per cent in the Twelfth Plan period. It is this ratio that is relevant for financing.

The Role of Infrastructure Investment in Accelerating Growth

2.36. A key component of the overall strategy for raising the rate of fixed investment is an increase in public and private investment in infrastructure. This is because enhanced investment in infrastructure will ease some of the key supply constraints on growth and it is also the area where progress is most likely to increase investor confidence. Several things need to be accomplished in order to facilitate this.

2.37. The most important sector in infrastructure is the power sector. There is about 90 GW of capacity under various stages of construction and attending to the outstanding issues facing these projects must be given a high priority. However, given the time lag involved in implementing power projects, it is necessary to ensure that projects which will be commissioned only in the Thirteenth Plan can also move ahead satisfactorily. Almost half the capacity in the Twelfth Plan is projected to come from the private sector and the position is likely to be the same in the Thirteenth Plan. Private sector investors in power generation have faced many problems in recent times. They include (*i*) inadequate supply of domestic coal and unanticipated increase in prices of imported coal; (*ii*) difficulties with clearances for captive mines, as well as for generating stations; (*iii*) land availability; (*iv*) poor financial health of some state electricity distribution companies which are the main customers, and which suffer from insufficient tariff adjustment plus inefficiencies in collection; (*v*) inadequate availability of domestic natural gas; (*vi*) inadequate fuel supply agreements for coal and (*vii*) more recently, difficulties in obtaining finance from both external and domestic sources. Several steps have been taken to resolve the problems that are negatively impacting fresh private investment in the power sector. A strict timeline needs to be maintained to achieve all of these measures. These issues are discussed in detail in Chapter 14.

2.38. Investment in road development has seen successes in both the Central and State Sectors. There was a return to buoyancy in 2011–12, with contracts awarded for nearly 8,000 km as against the target of 7,300 km. We need to be able to accelerate the pace of progress in the coming years. The Railways also require considerable investment to achieve the expansion in capacity needed and also to modernise and improve safety. The Delhi Mumbai Freight Corridor has external funding, but other investments are constrained by inadequacies of internal resources of the Railways, largely the consequence of frozen and uneconomic tariffs on passenger routes. On the freight side, Railways make a surplus, but transport services need to adapt more to customer requirements. There is a lot of potential and need for constructive change.

2.39. Many ocean port projects are pending due to clearances and other decisions that are in the domain of government. It is vital that we smoothen out the path ahead for the port sector. The New Mumbai International Airport is yet to be bid out. There are several problems involved, but we need to get the process off the ground. There are many other airports, small and big, that need to be developed in the Twelfth Plan. The Airport Authority has completed several terminal buildings and modernised these airports. The rest need to be taken up, if possible with private partners. In addition, there are many small airports and landing strips which hold potential for the purpose of extending connectivity and spreading of business opportunities. However, we have to work out a framework for executing of these projects and also develop a sub-model for air transport linkages to these dispersed and smaller airports.

2.40. Inland water transport has been neglected and needs to be accelerated. There are large gains to be had in terms of efficiency, if we can get some of the river-ways to become meaningfully functional. Coastal shipping also has considerable potential.

2.41. Connectivity is especially crucial to our northeastern region, both between themselves and to Myanmar and Bangladesh. We are working on a multi-modal connection through Ashuganj in Bangladesh to Tripura and the Sithwe–Kaladan River Project to Lunglei in Mizoram. We need to energise the reconditioning and reconnections of the other road networks through Moreh (Manipur) and Ledo (Assam) to Myanmar. This can then link up further to Thailand and to the road network system in South East Asia. Our development partners including Association of Southeast Asian Nations (ASEAN) and Asian Development Bank (ADB) are likely to be supportive of this.

2.42. Infrastructure capacity creation has suffered from implementation problems. It is vitally important that government makes strenuous efforts to ensure that buoyancy of private investment in infrastructure is returned. If that is achieved, it will catalyse balancing investments in a host of manufacturing activities and enable the economy's fixed investment rate to slowly return to its pre-2008 trajectory (as also the overall growth rate of the Indian economy). Investment in infrastructure is sometimes seen as running into environmental problems. The reconciliation of these objectives may require higher levels of investment than otherwise but this additional cost of compliance is perhaps a necessary cost that will have to be borne and can be partly offset by greater efficiency elsewhere.

SAVINGS

2.43. The high levels of investment projected for the Twelfth Plan have to be financed through a combination of domestic savings and net foreign inflow. The prospects of each of these components playing their expected role in the Twelfth Plan period and facilitating the level of investment projected are discussed in the following sections.

Trends in Domestic Savings

2.44. A strong domestic savings performance has been one of the strengths of the Indian economy for several years. As evident from Figure 2.2, the savings rate has undergone deep transformation rising from less than 20 per cent of GDP in 1980 to around 25 per cent in the 1990s and to over 30 per cent in the second half of the last decade. It reached a peak value of 36.8 per cent in 2007–08, after which it dropped to 33.7 per cent in 2009–10, but picked up a bit to 34.0 per cent in 2010–11. It has come down to 30.8 per cent in 2011–12. Thus the aggregate savings rate declined by 6.0 percentage points between 2007–08 and 2011–12.

2.45. Two factors were principally responsible for raising the domestic savings rate in the period up to 2007–08. One was the big improvement in government finances and the other was the improvement in the level of retained earnings of the private corporate sector. Between 2001–02 and 2007–08, the savings of government administration improved from *minus* 6.0 per cent of GDP to *plus* 0.5 per cent of GDP—an improvement of 6.5 percentage points. This was equal to almost half of the 13.4 percentage point improvement in the overall savings rate. The retained earnings of the private corporate sector improved from 3.4 to 9.4 per cent of GDP—an increase of about 6.0 percentage points. There were also small increases in the savings by households and that by public sector enterprises. Household savings comprise financial savings as well as physical savings that are directly made by households and unincorporated enterprises such as house building,

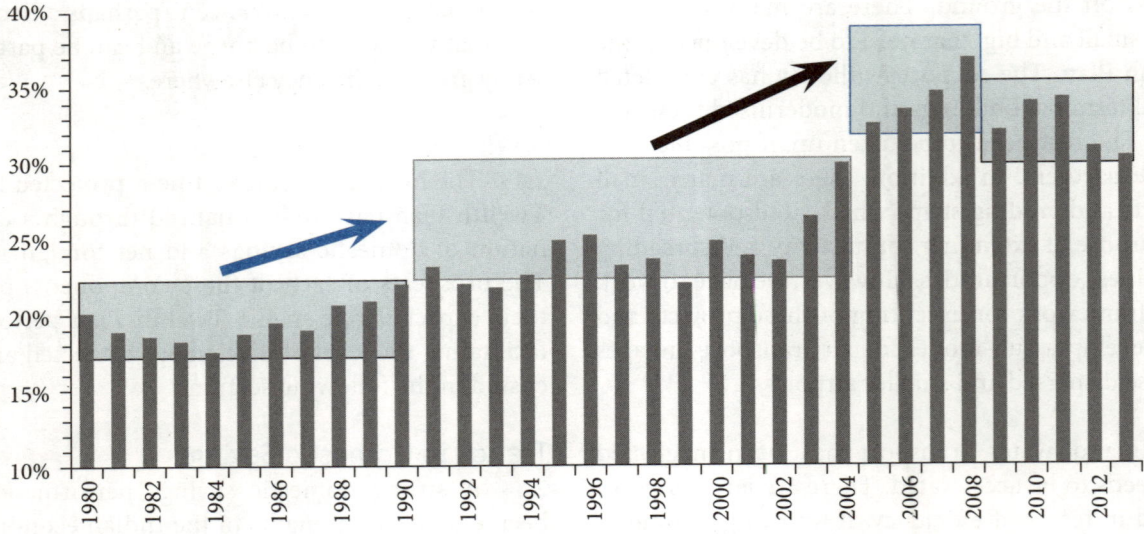

FIGURE 2.3.: Domestic Savings Rate—Ratio to GDP—Over the Years

farm improvement and asset creation by unincorporated businesses. Gross financial savings by households improved by 2.3 percentage points, but then so did the sector's liabilities (mortgage, automobile and other kinds of borrowing), so that net financial savings of the household sector increased by just 0.7 percentage points. However, the savings made by the household sector directly in physical assets declined by about 0.5 percentage points. The total savings of this sector therefore, remained more or less unchanged during this period as a percentage of GDP.

2.46. The decline in domestic savings rates after the crisis of 2008 reflects deterioration in precisely the two elements, which had accounted for the increase earlier. Between 2007–08 and 2011–12 the deterioration in the savings of government—flowing from the fiscal stimulus given in the wake of the crisis—amounted to 2.5 percentage points. Combined with lower retained earnings by departmental and non-departmental enterprises, this reduced the savings of the public sector by as much as 3.7 percentage points of GDP accounting for nearly two-thirds of the fall of 6.0 percentage points in the domestic savings rate. Savings by the private corporate sector declined by 2.2 percentage points while households savings remaied largely unchanged.

A Savings Strategy for the Twelfth Plan

2.47. The savings strategy in the Twelfth Plan must be to reverse the decline in savings that occurred after 2007–08 in order to finance the increase in the rate of investment projected for the Twelfth Plan period. The Working Group on Savings for the Twelfth Plan had made several projections based on alternative values for economic growth and inflation. It had projected the gross domestic savings rate to range between 36–37 per cent of GDP for the Twelfth Plan period, depending on whether GDP growth is 8 per cent or 9 per cent. On reviewing these estimates, it was felt that it would suffice if the savings rate reaches 36.0 per cent in the last year of the Plan as shown in Table 2.3. The projected average level of the domestic savings rate for the Twelfth Plan is 33.6 per cent, slightly higher than the 33.5 per cent recorded in the Eleventh Plan.

2.48. Factoring in capital inflows from abroad to cover the projected current account deficit of 3.4 per cent of GDP, the average investment rate for the Twelfth Plan period that can be sustained

TABLE 2.3
Domestic Savings and Components Thereof in Per Cent of GDP at Current Prices

	Eleventh Plan period							Twelfth Plan period					
	2007–08	2008–09	2009–10	2010–11	2011–12	Average		2012–13	2013–14	2014–15	2015–16	2016–17	Average
Gross Savings in Financial Assets	15.4	13.0	15.1	13.9	11.1	13.7		12.4	13.8	15.0	16.1	16.4	14.7
Increase in Financial Liabilities	3.8	2.9	3.1	3.6	3.1	3.3		3.4	3.8	4.2	4.5	4.5	4.1
Net Household Financial Savings	11.6	10.1	12.0	10.4	8.0	10.4		9.0	10.0	10.8	11.6	11.9	10.7
Household saving in physical assets	10.5	13.5	13.2	13.4	14.3	13.0		13.2	12.7	12.2	11.7	11.7	12.3
Household savings total	22.4	23.6	25.2	23.5	22.3	23.4		22.8	22.7	23.0	23.3	23.6	23.0
Savings by the private corporate sector	9.4	7.4	8.4	7.9	7.2	8.1		7.3	7.7	8.0	8.5	8.5	8.2
Savings by the public sector	5.0	1.0	0.2	2.6	1.3	2.0		1.5	2.0	2.5	3.1	3.9	2.7
Savings of government administration	0.5	-2.8	-3.1	-0.6	-2.0	-1.6		-1.8	-1.5	-1.2	-0.9	-0.3	-1.2
Savings of departmental enterprises	0.6	0.4	0.4	0.3	0.4	0.4		0.3	0.4	0.4	0.5	0.5	0.4
Savings of non-departmental enterprises	3.9	3.3	2.8	2.9	3.0	3.2		3.0	3.1	3.3	3.5	3.7	3.3
Gross Domestic Savings	36.8	32.0	33.7	34.0	30.8	33.5		31.0	32.4	33.5	34.9	36.0	33.6
Net Savings from Abroad	1.3	2.3	2.8	2.8	4.2	2.7		4.8	3.8	3.0	2.8	2.5	3.4
Finance for Investment	38.1	34.3	36.5	36.8	35.0	36.1		35.8	36.2	36.5	37.7	38.5	36.9

comes to about 36.9 per cent of GDP. This is roughly equal to the rate of GDCF in current prices, of 36.8 per cent.

Household Savings

2.49. The gross financial savings of the household sector is expected to average 14.7 per cent in the Twelfth Plan going up from 13.9 per cent in 2010–11 (and 11.1 per cent in 2011–12), to 16.4 per cent at the end of the Twelfth Plan (2016–17). The borrowings of the household sector from the financial system are expected to increase from 3.6 per cent in 2010–11, and 3.1 per cent in 2011–12 to 4.5 per cent in 2016–17. Thus, the net financial savings of the household sector is expected to go up from 10.4 per cent in 2010–11, and 8.0 per cent in 2011–12 to 11.9 per cent in 2016–17, while the average for the Plan period is likely to be 10.7 per cent. Investment by households in physical assets is expected to average 12.3 per cent of GDP in the Twelfth Plan. Thus, the total household savings including both net financial and physical assets are projected to average 23.0 per cent for the Twelfth Plan period, about the same as in the Eleventh Plan period.

Private Corporate Savings

2.50. Savings of the private corporate sector reached a peak of 9.4 per cent of GDP in 2007–08, from which it came down as profits came under pressure from the crisis, growth slowed down and input costs rose. The average for the Eleventh Plan period was 8.1 per cent. It is expected that a gradual recovery in the savings of the private corporate sector from 7.9 per cent in 2010–11 to 8.0–8.5 per cent in the final three years of the Plan would give an average of 8.2 per cent for the full Plan period. This is about the same as that in the Eleventh Plan.

Public Sector Savings

2.51. The savings of the public sector comprise of the savings of government administration, surpluses of departmental undertakings and retained earnings of public sector enterprises. The first two are a function of the extent of operating deficit in government finance, and the third has been adversely impacted by losses arising from selling prices not increasing in line with rising costs. More specifically, this has been the case with government-owned petroleum companies and state owned electricity distribution companies. The Working Group on Savings had projected that savings of the public sector would be around 2 per cent in 2012–13, and would average 3.5 per cent over the Twelfth Plan period. However, it now appears that savings in the public sector would be significantly lower at about 1.5 per cent in 2012–13, which would improve gradually to over 4 per cent in 2016–17, yielding a Plan average of 2.7 per cent. A better performance would yield large positive potential results since the government borrowing needs could be curtailed freeing resources for productive uses in the economy. This is only possible if we can curb the subsidy bill, particularly that associated with refined petroleum products, which has become so large that it is undermining the financial capacity of the government to spend on more socially worthwhile activities.

2.52. The overall domestic savings rate is projected to increase from an estimated 30.8 per cent in 2011–12 to 36.0 per cent in 2016–17, and average 33.6 per cent for the Twelfth Plan period. This would be slightly higher than the 33.5 per cent recorded in the Eleventh Plan period. Since the projected average investment rate (GDCF, including errors and omissions) in the Twelfth Plan (at current prices) is 36.9 per cent and the projected gross domestic savings is 33.6 per cent, the net external financing needed for macroeconomic balance should average 3.4 per cent. This would be a significant reduction over the course of the Plan period from 4.2 per cent reported in 2011–12, the last year of the Eleventh Plan and the anticipated higher level in 2012–13.

Projected Current Account Deficit

2.53. In this section, we review trends in the external sector to see whether the financing gap viewed from the balance of payments side is broadly consistent with the investment savings gap described above. The opening up of the Indian economy has greatly increased the role of trade in the economy. The ratio of merchandise exports to GDP in 1999–2000 was 8.3 per cent and that of import was 12.3 per cent, while the net service export was 0.9 per cent. The sum of these three items in that year (which has sometimes been used as a measure of openness) was 21.5 per cent. The extent of trade integration with the rest of the world has expanded very significantly since 1999–2000. For the Tenth Plan (2002–07) period as a whole, merchandise exports and imports rose to 11.7 and 15.7 per cent of GDP respectively, and net service exports to 2.1 per cent, taking the aggregate of external trade activities to 29.5 per cent of GDP. In the Eleventh Plan the share of merchandise exports and imports rose further to 14.4 and 22.7 per cent respectively. Adding in net service export, the proportion of external trade to GDP rose to 40.3 per cent of GDP for the Eleventh Plan period as a whole. In the final year of the Eleventh Plan, that is 2011–12, this figure touched 45.8 per cent of GDP.

2.54. India is greatly dependant on import of crude petroleum and more recently of Liquefied Natural Gas and hence our external payments are seen to be particularly vulnerable on this count. Though crude oil prices have more than quadrupled over the past decade (from $25 per barrel to $115 per barrel at present), our merchandise exports and other imports have tended to keep pace. On the import side, the value of total oil imports as a ratio of aggregate merchandise imports have risen from less than 27 per cent in 2003–04 and 2004–05 to 31.7 per cent in 2007–08, before easing up a bit, before once again hitting 31.7 per cent in 2011–12 and perhaps exceed 34 per cent in 2012–13. India exports a large volume of refined petroleum products and it is the net oil import bill (after reducing the value of exported refined petroleum products from the oil import bill) that should be germane. The net oil import bill was less than 21 per cent of total merchandise imports in 2004–05 and increased only slightly to 22 per cent in 2008–09 and is expected to be around 23 per cent in 2012-13.

2.55. However, the key issue from the point of view of sustainability is the proportion that these oil imports bear in relation to merchandise exports. The value of net oil imports to that of merchandise exports excluding refined petroleum products was 28 to 30 per cent in 2003–04 and 2004–05 and steadily rose thereafter to peak at 40 per cent in 2007–08 and 2008–09. It dipped slightly, but was back up close to this level in 2011–12. In the current year (2012–13) the ratio has risen to 48.7 per cent in the first ten months. Clearly the adverse situation in our balance of trade is significantly on account of the stress arising from the rising proportion of net oil imports relative to our capacity to export other products.

2.56. As trade integration has increased, the merchandise trade deficit has widened from 4.7 per cent of GDP in 2004–05 to 6.5 per cent in 2006–07, and further to 7.1 per cent and 9.5 per cent in the two succeeding years. It declined a little in subsequent years, but hit 9.9 per cent in 2011–12. This high trade deficit was offset by a growing net balance on service trade, and a high level of remittances. In the Eleventh Plan period, the average merchandise trade deficit was 8.3 per cent of GDP, the net services export was 3.2 per cent, and private remittances 3.5 per cent of GDP. The sum of the net services export and private remittances thus averaged 6.7 per cent of GDP, which funded 80 per cent of the merchandise trade deficit. However, it must be kept in mind that as the stock of foreign investment builds up in India, the net investment income is increasingly becoming a larger negative number, going from (–)0.6 per cent of GDP in 2004–05 to (–)0.9 per cent in 2011–12. It should, however, be noted that this negative item does not necessarily result in an actual outflow. In Balance of Payments accounting, if the income accrues, but is not remitted abroad and is retained in the enterprise, it will show up as positive FDI inflow.

2.57. The net effect of all these developments has been an expansion of the current account deficit from 1.2 per cent of GDP in 2005–06 and 1.3 per cent in 2007–08, before going to over 2.5 per cent in each of the years after 2008–09. In 2011–12 the current account deficit was at a record high of 4.2 per cent of GDP though this reflects abnormally high gold imports. For the Eleventh Plan as a whole the average current account deficit was 2.7 per cent of GDP.

2.58. Projections of trade and other balances for the Twelfth Plan period are presented in Table 2.4. Merchandise exports as a proportion of GDP are expected to remain around 16.0 per cent GDP during the course of the Twelfth Plan. In 2016–17, exports would be over $570 billion. The average of the Twelfth Plan would be 16 per cent. Merchandise imports are expected to stabilise a proportion of

TABLE 2.4
External Payments—Current and Capital Account

(All Figures as Per Cent of GDP at Current Prices)

	Eleventh Plan period						Twelfth Plan period					
	2007–08	2008–09	2009–10	2010–11	2011–12	Average	2012–13	2013–14	2014–15	2015–16	2016–17	Average
Merchandise Exports	13.2	14.9	13.1	14.7	16.3	14.4	15.7	16.0	16.1	16.0	15.9	16.0
Merchandise Imports	20.3	24.4	21.1	21.6	26.1	22.7	26.5	25.8	25.1	24.5	24.0	25.2
Merchandise Trade Deficit	−7.1	−9.5	−8.0	−6.9	−9.9	−8.3	−10.8	−9.7	−9.0	−8.5	−8.1	−9.2
Net Service export	3.1	4.4	2.6	2.6	3.4	3.2	3.5	3.5	3.5	3.4	3.4	3.5
Merchandise. Exports (X) + Imports (M)	33.4	39.3	34.1	36.3	42.4	37.1	42.2	41.8	41.2	40.5	39.9	41.1
Total of X, M and Net Services Export	36.6	43.8	36.7	38.8	45.8	40.3	45.7	45.3	44.7	43.9	43.3	44.6
Private remittances	3.4	3.6	3.8	3.1	3.4	3.5	3.6	3.6	3.5	3.4	3.4	3.4
Net Investment Income	−0.4	−0.5	−0.4	−0.9	−0.9	−0.6	−1.2	−1.1	−1.1	−1.1	−1.0	−1.1
Current Account Balance	−1.3	−2.3	−2.8	−2.8	−4.2	−2.7	−4.8	−3.8	−3.0	−2.8	−2.5	−3.4
FDI Net	1.3	2.1	1.4	0.4	1.2	1.3	1.4	1.4	1.3	1.1	1.0	1.3
FDI Inward	2.8	4.2	2.4	1.4	1.8	2.5	2.0	1.9	1.8	1.7	1.6	1.8
FDI Outward	1.5	2.1	1.0	0.9	0.6	1.2	0.5	0.5	0.5	0.5	0.6	0.5
Portfolio equity	2.4	−1.7	2.4	1.8	0.9	1.2	1.3	1.2	0.9	0.6	0.5	0.9
Loans	3.4	0.5	1.0	1.6	1.0	1.5	1.3	1.3	1.1	0.9	0.8	1.1
Banking	0.9	−0.4	0.1	0.3	0.9	0.4	1.3	1.1	0.9	0.7	0.5	0.9
Other	0.7	0.5	−1.0	−0.6	−0.4	−0.1	−0.3	−0.2	−0.2	−0.1	−0.1	−0.2
Capital Account Balance	8.7	1.0	3.9	3.6	3.7	4.2	4.9	4.8	3.9	3.2	2.7	3.9

GDP at about 25 per cent of GDP during the Plan period. The merchandise trade deficit would therefore average a little over 9 per cent of GDP.

2.59. The net positive balance on trade in services is expected to increase only slightly to 3.5 per cent of GDP from 3.2 per cent in the Eleventh Plan. Private remittances averaged 3.1 per cent of GDP in the Tenth Plan, which increased to 3.5 per cent in the Eleventh Plan. Net investment income was (–)0.4 per cent in the Tenth Plan and (–)0.6 per cent in the Eleventh Plan, but as pointed out previously, has gone up to nearly (–)0.9 per cent in 2010–11 and 2011–12. In the Twelfth Plan, private remittances are expected to average an almost unchanged level of 3.4 per cent of GDP, while net investment income is expected to grow to a slightly larger negative number of (–)1.1 per cent.

2.60. The resultant current account deficit emerging from these projections average 3.4 per cent of GDP for the Twelfth Plan period as a whole. It is projected to be higher in the first two years and moderate slightly thereafter towards the end of the period. The projected current account deficit is higher than the normal comfort level, according to which it should be restricted to less than 2.5 per cent of GDP. This would reduce the risk of non-availability of external financing conditions for both domestic and overseas investors. Having a higher than comfort level of current account deficit, for at least the first two years, has implications for the way the capital account is managed to facilitate capital inflows.

Prospects for Mobilising External Finance

2.61. The capital inflow required to finance a projected average current account deficit of 3.4 per cent of GDP can take several forms including FDI, Foreign Institutional Investor (FII) flows, and various types of debt including short-term trade credit and official external assistance. Our objective should be to finance the deficit as much as possible through stable foreign inflows. This means emphasising FDI and minimising short-term debt in particular. The pattern of capital flows in the Eleventh Plan period and projection for the Twelfth Plan are summarised in Table 2.3.

2.62. In the Eleventh Plan, inflows by way of FDI ranged between 1.4 and 4.2 per cent of GDP, averaging 2.5 per cent of GDP. In the same period, there were also outflows as Indian companies acquired overseas assets and this ranged between 0.6 and 2.1 per cent in various years, being much higher in 2007–08 and 2008–09, averaging 1.2 per cent for the Eleventh Plan period as a whole. In 2011–12, outbound FDI flows were much lower at 0.6 per cent of GDP.

2.63. Portfolio equity inflows fluctuated to a greater extent, from (–)1.7–2.4 per cent of GDP in the Eleventh Plan period, and averaged 1.2 per cent of GDP for the Plan period as a whole. It is worth noting that they were lowest at (–)1.7 per cent in 2008–09, the year of the financial crisis but otherwise they were positive and sizeable in every year. This suggests that while FII flows are more volatile, than FDI, they are not the same as 'hot money'.

2.64. Loan capital inflows occur mostly through external commercial borrowings (ECBs) of Indian private and public sector companies and non-resident bank deposits. Short-term trade loans as well as FII investment in Indian government and corporate debt securities are also significant. Net inbound official assistance now forms a relatively small component of capital inflows. These sources taken together accounted for 1.5 per cent of GDP in the course of the Eleventh Plan. Net inflow through the banking channels was just 0.4 per cent of GDP during the course of the Eleventh Plan.

2.65. Total capital inflows from all sources thus averaged 4.2 per cent of GDP in the Eleventh Plan period. This volume of capital inflows was significantly higher than the financing required for the 2.7 per cent current account deficit, and the excess was accumulated in the foreign currency assets (including special drawing rights [SDRs] and gold) of the Reserve Bank of India (RBI).

2.66. The baseline projections made for the Twelfth Plan, as presented in Table 2.4, are based on conservative assumptions, keeping in mind the current uncertain conditions in the global economic environment. This uncertainty is bound to lead to risk aversion, and also conservative assessment of the relative attractiveness of India as a destination for global capital in present circumstances. On this basis, the inbound FDI flows are projected to be slightly less than that in the Eleventh Plan, to average 1.8 per cent of GDP. It is likely that outbound FDI will also be lower than in the Eleventh Plan level, and is projected to be 0.5 per cent of GDP, and as a result the net inflow of FDI will remain almost unchanged at 1.3 per cent of GDP.

2.67. Portfolio equity inflows are volatile and given the global conditions that have been prevalent for some time, our projections assume that the total of such inflows would be only around 0.9 per cent of GDP, lower than the 1.2 per cent recorded in the Eleventh Plan. This assumption is almost certainly unduly cautious. Early resolution of some of the uncertainties that have arisen in the mind of foreign investors in India, combined with a visible resumption of growth momentum in 2013–14, could easily lead to stronger inflows in the remaining years. An average of over 1 per cent of GDP over the Plan period is not at all infeasible.

2.68. Loan and banking capital inflows (including NRI deposits), net of repayments, taken together are expected to be 1.1 per cent of GDP, lower than that the 1.3 per cent recorded in the Eleventh Plan. Taking all the flows together, the total of capital inflows in the Twelfth Plan is expected to be 3.9 per cent of GDP, lower than the 4.2 per cent experienced in the Eleventh Plan, but about adequate to finance the current account deficit of 3.4 per cent. This only reinforces the lack of slack on the external payments side.

2.69. To summarise, the capital inflow, projection on which the Twelfth Plan is based is deliberately conservative. It is not at all unreasonable to conclude that if growth proceeds as planned in Scenario 1, and policies towards foreign investment are seen to be positive, is encouraged, we could expect additional flows of at least 0.5 per cent of GDP. This would allow us some build up foreign exchange reserves in line with rising levels of trade and external liabilities. However, to achieve this outcome, it is imperative to improve investment conditions at home and to encourage more capital inflows, while at the same time work on ways to contain the current account deficit.

The Importance of Fiscal Consolidation

2.70. Since the Twelfth Plan strategy involves mobilising external finance to meet a current account deficit, which is likely to significantly exceed the comfort level of 2.5 per cent of GDP, it is important to emphasise that international analysts focus on the fiscal situation as a key indicator of macroeconomic balance. India's domestic macroeconomic balances must be seen to inspire confidence in the international market. The key indicator in this context is the fiscal deficit. Table 2.5 presents the fiscal position of both the Centre and the States.

2.71. The deficit of the Centre has risen from 2.5 per cent of GDP in the first year of the Eleventh Plan to 5.7 per cent in the last year, with the Plan average at 5.3 per cent. Taking the fiscal deficit of the Centre and the States together, it has increased from just under 4 per cent of GDP in 2007–08 to a little over 8 per cent, a deterioration of 4 percentage points.

2.72. The initial increase in the fiscal deficit in 2007–08 seemed justified on the grounds that all countries were embarking on a fiscal expansion as a countercyclical move. However, India's fiscal deficit expansion continued even after the crisis, and although a reversal was attempted in 2011–12, the projected fiscal deficit target of 5.1 per cent of GDP in 2011–12 was considerably overshot. The increase in the Centre's

TABLE 2.5
Fiscal Position of Centre and States and Subsidy Quanta

	Gross Fiscal Deficit % GDP		
	Centre	States	Total
2007–08	2.54	1.49	3.97
2008–09	5.99	2.26	8.17
2009–10	6.48	3.02	9.46
2010–11	4.87	2.15	6.99
2011–12 (LE)[a]	5.68	2.32	8.00
Total Eleventh Plan	5.29	2.25	7.54

Note: [a]LE: The figures for 2011–12 are provisional actual for Centre and RE for States.

fiscal deficit after 2008–09 has been shaped by a combination of two factors. The first is the slowing down of growth that has adversely impacted tax collections along with fiscal concessions in the form of lower excise duty and service tax rates given by the government at the time of the global crisis. The second factor has been the build-up in subsidies. The subsidy burden is a matter of particular concern because a substantial part of the subsidy on petroleum products is not reflected in the budget of the Centre as indeed the real losses of the power sector are not reflected in the budgets of the State Governments.

2.73. Table 2.6 presents a comparison between India's fiscal deficit and debt to GDP ratio with that of other major industrialised and developing countries. India's fiscal deficit, though not as high as some industrialised countries, is much higher than the other emerging markets. India's debt to GDP ratio is also lower than that of many industrialised countries but is higher than that of emerging market countries.

TABLE 2.6
General Government Balance and Government Debt as Per Cent of GDP

	General Government Balance % of GDP	General Government Debt % of GDP
	2011	2011
All Advanced	−7.2	110.3
Euro Area	−4.1	88.1
Spain	−8.5	68.5
Germany	−1.0	81.5
UK	−8.7	82.5
France	−5.3	86.3
US	−9.6	102.9
Ireland	−9.9	105.0
Portugal	−4.0	106.8
Italy	−3.9	120.1
Japan	−10.1	229.8
All Emerging	−2.2	37.0
Brazil	−2.6	66.2
Russia	1.6	9.6
India	−8.7	68.1
China	−1.2	25.8

Source: Fiscal Monitor (IMF, April 2012).

To some extent, the extent of fiscal stress in India is less than it seems because India's likely growth rate is much higher than expected by other countries except China. However, considering that the fiscal position had improved in the years before 2008, and there is need to release resources for investment in infrastructure, there can be no doubt that the Twelfth Plan must aim at a credible fiscal consolidation path that would bring the central government's fiscal deficit back to tolerable levels.

2.74. The compression in the deficit does not have to be brought about immediately. The Finance Ministry's original fiscal consolidation path envisaged reducing the fiscal deficit from the targeted 5.1 per cent of GDP in 2011–12 to 3 per cent of GDP by 2014–15, that is, an adjustment of a little over 0.6 percentage points per year. The end point envisaged may no longer be feasible in present circumstances, but it should be possible to get to 3 per cent of GDP by the end of the Plan period. As pointed out in Chapter 3, this will require a substantial increase in tax revenues, and also a reduction in subsidies as a percentage of GDP.

2.75. The ratio of Central Government revenues to GDP declined by over 2 percentage points of GDP over the Eleventh Plan period. The increase in tax revenues needed to accelerate growth, therefore, requires the tax revenue to GDP ratio to rise by the same percentage points, taking it a little above the level that prevailed in 2007–08. This should not be onerous and can be achieved primarily through efforts to improve tax administration. The implementation of Good and Services Tax (GST) is the most promising prospect in this regard. It will not only modernise the indirect tax system, greatly increasing efficiency and the ease of doing business, but also that will increase the revenues of both the Centre and the States.

2.76. As far as subsidies are concerned, it requires a reduction in subsidies from about 2.4 per cent of GDP in 2011–12 to around 1.5 per cent of GDP in the terminal year of the Twelfth Plan. It is important to emphasise that subsidies are not being abolished, but only reduced as a percentage of GDP in order to accommodate Plan expenditure which is now largely directed at inclusiveness promoting schemes, and can be better targeted than most of the existing subsidies.

2.77. The consequences of not achieving fiscal consolidation need to be carefully considered. It is important to avoid complacency that the concern with fiscal consolidation is a purely technical concern, which can be ignored if the corrective steps needed are politically difficult. It needs to be kept in mind that global perceptions about our macroeconomic stability are critical for maintaining access to capital flows and, as pointed out above, the fiscal deficit is a performance parameter of critical importance. Failure to take credible action towards fiscal consolidation risks an erosion of confidence leading to lower capital inflows and greater exchange rate depreciation, which will either force large adjustments in petroleum prices, or would lead to a further worsening of the fiscal deficit.

EFFICIENT FINANCIAL INTERMEDIATION

2.78. While availability of savings in the aggregate is an important part of macroeconomic balance, it is also important to have an efficient financial system that can channel savings to the most productive uses, and also ensure inclusiveness. The past two decades have seen far-reaching change in the character and structure of the country's banking system and the capital markets. These changes have addressed the management of credit risk, provisioning against delinquent loans and a greater focus on fee-based income. The interest rate regime that used to be highly regulated was systematically replaced by a commercially determined framework that helped price-in credit quality, duration and diversification of risk. The kind of loan products available and the servicing of these for the commercial sector have also become more efficient. Retail banking, that is, personal loans for buying homes and other durable assets, and payment and settlement facilities, have become an important and rapidly growing component of banking. Lending to small borrowers typified by the self-help group (SHG) and microfinance has come some distance towards making financial inclusion meaningful.

2.79. These changes have also changed the behaviour of corporate borrowers. In many ways, financial risk was not meaningful in the years before 1991. It changed subsequently, and with it the incentives to maintain a clean credit record and a lower leverage. Dismantling of the production licensing system, lower import tariffs and the end of quantitative restrictions on imports made competition a reality in India, that is, both domestic competition and competition vis-à-vis the global producers. Finally, the decline in the ownership functions of government and quasi-governmental agencies, and the enhanced role of capital markets in raising finance has given new importance to the interests of shareholders, especially minority shareholders. Associated with this is the challenge of corporate control, which now has to face up to proactive mergers, acquisition and sale.

2.80. The combination of all of these developments was in full play between 1997 and 2003. The large-scale expansion by Indian corporates in the immediate follow-up of the economic liberalisation was subject to some weaknesses. As these assets came into production, commodity prices worldwide came under pressure, first on account of low-priced supply from the former USSR, and later on account of the Asian Currency Crisis. For the first time, starting 1997 there were large-scale corporate defaults in India. This led to a round of restructuring, with assets being sold and corporate ownership changing hands. Once the process was complete, the corporate manufacturing sector came out well-equipped to deal with business and financial risk, challenges to corporate control, and became more competitive globally. The Information Technology Sector evolved post-liberalisation and has focused on export business, with funding secured mostly from equity. It has, therefore, developed in an entirely different environment than did the manufacturing sector, and was therefore always globally competitive, receptive to new ideas, with very little leverage on its balance sheet.

2.81. A large number of today's manufacturing units (and some service sector ones too) originally began as small scale industries (SSI), and have grown into much larger establishments, including many in engineering, chemicals, pharmaceuticals and textiles. In many ways, the emergence of a modern corporate establishment in India gained from the horizontal expansion of SSI units in years past. Small and medium scale enterprises (SMEs)—which do exceed even the current definitions of SSI by a wide margin—will nevertheless be a continuing source of entrepreneurial talent and a source of great strength for the Indian economy in the years to come.

Banking and Finance

2.82. Although the financial sector in India has grown fairly rapidly in recent years, in terms of the conventional metrics of financial deepening—such as a ratio of total financial claims or bank loans to GDP—India appears to be considerably behind other emerging markets. It is not entirely certain whether the data can be interpreted thus, and whether we should necessarily follow the contours of bigger the better. Capital, unlike labour, is perpetually recycled, and the shorter the cycle, the more efficient is the use of such capital. The loan to GDP ratio, which is used as a measure of the role of banking, reflects end balance sheet totals, and does not tell us anything about the extent of turnover during the year.

2.83. However, this is not to say that there are no challenges facing the development of the Indian financial sector. Possibly, the most troubling in the present context is the manner in which gold has resurfaced as a vehicle of choice for households to invest their savings in. Gold and land were the only vehicles of investment in the past. Since Independence, we have striven to encourage not just thrift, but the confidence of the Indian citizen in financial products so that their savings become available for productive use by the rest of the economy. That over six decades later, gold would resurface to such an important extent as a preferred mode of holding savings, speaks of the serious deficiencies in the distribution and perhaps regulatory structure of our financial framework that channels household savings.

2.84. This is closely related to the larger issue of instruments of long-term savings—life insurance, pensions, provident funds and so on. As both personal disposable incomes and life expectancy increases, the need for perceived safe instruments that offer a reasonable real return has, and will continue to play an increasingly important role in the financial life of the nation and its citizens. The development of this industry has to be seen in an appropriately longer time frame, inherent financial sustainability and the quality of assurance that it gives investors with regard to their concerns. The government has been considering steps to increase the scale of FDI permitted in the insurance sector but a lack of political consensus has held back change.

2.85. The need for long-term savings products is the mirror image of the other important need—that of long-term finance for long gestation products, namely physical infrastructure. Without the first, the latter becomes hard. Commercial banks mostly hold short-term liabilities and their assets ought to reflect this duration too. However, in the absence of adequate sources of long-term finance, much of infrastructure lending has been coming from banks. A secondary market for bank loans through conversion to securities offers an exit to banks without excessively stretching their asset–liability mismatch. That is an important objective of the policy to promote infrastructure debt funds, which is now close to being in place.

2.86. The secondary market for corporate bonds has yet to take off in a significant manner, especially in the medium to long term. This has been a matter long identified as a priority and several regulatory issues have since been resolved. Possibly the non-development of ancillary markets or the continued excess of supply of gilts is preventing this market from taking off. The market for infrastructure debt generically belongs to the corporate bond market and without movement on the latter, movement in the former is not likely. In the financial sector, deep markets reduce the market (duration, illiquidity and so on) risk, and thus in the final analysis, total risks, which eventually lower the cost of capital to the borrower. For several independent and interrelated reasons, in the Twelfth Plan, special efforts must be made to ensure that the corporate bond market takes off.

2.87. There is also an issue of access. Small businesses find it hard to raise finance, and poorer households find it hard to access the organised savings and credit industry. These are not problems of India alone or for that matter of developing countries only. Even in developed economies these challenges are in evidence. In some contrast to most of the world, Indian banks actually have much greater exposure to small credits and experience in dealing with such exposure. This has arisen from the mandates with regard to lending to the farm sector and to SSI.

2.88. The banking system, with its larger overheads, is perhaps not best suited to deal with small credits. This is where SHGs and similar collective guarantee credit schemes have a big role to play. Microfinance institutions are another vehicle. There have been some unfortunate developments in the case of microfinance, but we must be alive to the danger of throwing the baby out with the bathwater. The Microfinance Regulation Act which has been introduced in Parliament will establish a regulatory framework which would allay suspicions and allow the industry to develop unhindered with due regulatory oversight. We do need other kinds of mezzanine financial agencies—SHG, microfinance, cooperative—which permit the banks an easier way to fund the capital needs of small creditors.

2.89. The well-intentioned Know Your Customer (KYC) requirements have made it even harder for the poor to enter our banks. This is not acceptable. The Aadhar number must become a passport for ordinary people to be able to use the savings and payments facilities of our banking system, or for that matter, all other regulated savings products—mutual funds, insurance and so on.

2.90. The financing of small businesses is an intrinsic challenge because of heightened perception of credit risks. The system of refinancing through government agencies like SIDBI, in conjunction with the use of credit information databases, offers some solutions. Raising the cost to wilful defaulters is intrinsic to combat moral hazard that may creep in from well-intentioned official compassion. Otherwise the cost to the competent small businesspersons from the indiscipline of their competitors is debilitating.

2.91. However, a large part of the problem lies with the inadequacy of equity in the sector. To increase access to equity—especially for small businesses—venture capital, private equity finance and similar agencies have been encouraged. However, notwithstanding the sharp increase in the extent of this kind of activity, only the surface has been scratched. Regulatory encouragement to the providers of equity to small business is therefore essential.

Venture Capital

2.92. One of the most important gaps in our existing financial structure is the lack of a sufficiently large venture capital and angel investor community, who play a very important role in financing start-ups, especially in areas where technology is the key to success and risk capital is needed. To explore ways of filling this gap, Planning Commission had constituted a Committee on Angel Investment and Early Stage Venture Capital under the Chairmanship of Shri Sunil Mitra, former Finance Secretary. The committee included members from traditional financing bodies, venture/PE capital, consulting firms and National Association of Software and Services Companies (NASSCOM). The report of the committee is available at the Planning Commission website under the link 'reports'. The committee has made a number of recommendations that would help to create a strong ecosystem for innovation and early stage entrepreneurship to flourish. The recommendations include tax-related incentives and various relaxations on the regulatory side that would enable banks and insurance companies to be a little more active in this area. It also makes recommendations for setting up, technology parks and incubators of various types through PPP.

THE EXTERNAL ENVIRONMENT

2.93. Macroeconomic balance in an open economy is powerfully affected by the external environment. This is particularly relevant at the start of the Twelfth Plan because the Indian economy is now much more globally integrated and the global economy is experiencing serious short term difficulties in the midst of some fundamental longer term changes.

2.94. As shown in Table 2.6 the rate at which the world economy expanded did not change much in the decade of the 1990s vis-à-vis the 1980s. However, in the period after 2000 and just before the global crisis broke out, the average annual rate of increase in world output increased by 1.2 percentage points: This increase in global growth, in the period 2000–07 reflected an interesting asymmetry. The advanced economies slowed marginally from 2.7 per cent in the 1990s to an average growth of 2.6 per cent per year in 2000–07. However, the developing world growth accelerated sharply from 3.6 per cent in the 1990s to 6.5 per cent per year. Although the bulk of the growth occurred in Asia alone, the rest of the developing world in Africa and Latin America also benefited. This period represents the extension of economic opportunity to the world as a whole, and almost every country raised itself up to seize these opportunities. This favourable period come to an end in 2008.

2.95. Between 2008 and 2011, the US and the Eurozone economies have virtually stagnated. While the US economy is picking up, the recovery is weaker than what was expected, and is certainly disproportionate to the size of the fiscal and monetary stimulus that was used. The problems inherent in the European Monetary Union, and fiscally overweight governments, were prised open by the crisis. Though economic conditions seem to have stabilised for the moment, it is clear that it will take several years for the Eurozone economy to return to health. The trends in global growth are shown in Table 2.7.

TABLE 2.7
Trends in Global GDP Growth

GDP Growth (Constant Prices)	1980s	1990s	2000–2007	2008–2011
World	3.2	3.0	4.2	2.8
Advanced economies	3.1	2.7	2.6	0.3
Emerging and developing economies	3.5	3.6	6.5	5.6
Developing Asia	6.7	7.2	8.4	8.1
India	5.4	5.6	7.1	7.7
Brazil	3.0	1.7	3.5	3.8
China	9.8	10.0	10.5	9.6
Russia	–	–	7.2	1.5

Source: WEO database (IMF, October 2012).

2.96. A positive feature of the global scene is that many developing economies, and a handful of strong developed economies, have developed an autonomous momentum of their own. However, they are obviously not immune to what happens in the United States and Eurozone—on account of trade effects, the likely turbulence in the world's financial markets and the effect of all this on business confidence. It is therefore prudent to look at the general global economic outlook in terms of different time segments—the short term (up to two years), then the medium to longer term (3–15 years).

The Short-Term Prospects

2.97. The IMF World Economic Outlook of October 2012, continues to emphasise the downside risks that can emerge, primarily from the Eurozone. It is our view that while there continues to be serious problems in the developed world and that these will persist, the downside risks have reduced significantly compared to 2011. The manner in which matters have been handled in Europe in 2012 reflects the learning from the difficulties of dealing in an atmosphere of excessive public scrutiny and unduly high expectations. Issues have crystallised to a much greater extent, and notwithstanding the change in political leadership in France, the direction of Franco-German cooperative leadership does not appear to have shifted significantly. The European Central Bank (ECB) has provided large amount of finance to the banking system through the Longer-Term Refinancing Operations (LTROs) and together with the IMF appears to have constructed a 'firewall' in excess of $1 trillion. The explicit determination to intervene on such a large scale is indeed important. This offsets the potential risks that emanate from de-leveraging of an estimated $2.6 trillion mostly by European banks. Many adaptive changes that limit the damage can reasonably be expected to transpire. The Fiscal Deficits and Public Debt, in general, remain high in the developed countries, as would be evident from Table 2.6.

2.98. The Eurozone member countries seem to recognise the need for a coordinated move towards a fiscal union though it is unclear whether, in the final analysis, this fiscal union will indeed materialise. However, they are most likely to tread this path for the next few years, in which period the two other large Eurozone economies—Italy and Spain—are expected to stabilise. It is possible that Greece will have to leave the monetary union, but it will not imperil the Eurozone as long as they can stabilise Italy and Spain.

2.99. In the United States, the recovery has been weaker than projected. However, there are clear signs that the economy is on the mend, and the IMF has raised its growth estimate for 2012 to 2.3 per cent. Going forward, conditions are likely to stabilise in 2013. However, the United States will continue to have the problem of adopting an internally consistent and non-disruptive path for fiscal consolidation, and for rolling back the enormously extended monetary stance.

2.100. It is possible that the unprecedented loose monetary stance in the United States and in the European Union may continue for some years, and this, may create problems for others, as indeed has been the case with commodity prices. However, the main concern is shocks—not persistent weaknesses in these economies. The shocks, are not likely to happen because: (i) In the Eurozone, the direction that member countries, under the leadership of Germany and France, have taken, are expressly designed to keep things on hold for the next few years; (ii) the large amount of liquidity that has been created by the US Federal Reserve, and more recently by the ECB, will prevent any recurrence of the financial crisis. However, conditions in the European Union will continue to negatively impact the European bank financing, which has been significant for the Indian private sector infrastructure projects in the past.

2.101. It is difficult to assess how this environment will affect us. The slower growth in the United States and in the European Union will undoubtedly have an adverse impact on expansion of our markets for exports—of both goods and services—to these countries. In the short run, therefore, we are likely to face continuing pressure on the balance of payments in the form of high trade deficits and higher than comfortable current account deficit estimated at about 3.4 per cent of GDP on average.

The Medium and Longer Term

2.102. The medium- and longer-term perspective is better. It is reasonable to assume that the economies of the United States and Eurozone will recover over a period of time and disastrous outcomes, that is, shocks, are unlikely to happen, because the major players have too much to lose and a lot of preparation has gone into creating the ground to expressly avoid such an event. However, there will be periodical upheavals in the financial markets because certain things will go wrong, and some unexpected developments will happen. While these will be managed and contained, it is reasonable to expect sporadic volatility continuing in financial markets and investment sentiments, on account of bad news that will come out from time to time from the advanced economies.

2.103. China, India and other emerging markets in Asia and also in Africa are posed to grow more rapidly. The twenty-first Century has been referred to as the 'Asian Century' and it could well be, but it is imperative to underscore that this is not pre-ordained. It will depend on whether the emerging market economies of Asia are able to make the effort to overcome obstacles, to where they have got to, by dint of their own efforts. The opportunities exist, but it is always possible to fail to make the best of opportunity. It is vitally important that we show the resolve not to miss the opportunity by taking the outcome for granted.

2.104. It is relevant in this context, to recall what happened at the end of the Multifibre Agreement (MFA) in 2004. Before the end of MFA there was a belief in informed policy circles that India and China would reap the whole of the benefit and that the least developed economies may gain little. In fact, China was the principal beneficiary: Share of exports of apparel was 18.3 per cent in 2000 and this doubled to 36.9 per cent in 2010. The less-developed economies such as Bangladesh, Vietnam and Cambodia gained significantly[1] in line with what was desired by policy. However, India's share increased from 3.0 per cent in 2000 to only 3.2 per cent in 2010. In other words, opportunities do a rise, but countries can fail to seize them.

Changing Global Economic Structure

2.105. India, China and other Asian economies, are poised to reverse the huge declines in their relative share in world economic output. Between 1500 and 1700, India and China had each accounted for about one quarter of world economic output, while the share of Asia as a whole was over 60 per cent.[2] At the end of the colonial era in 1950, the shares in world output of India, China and the rest of Asia (excluding Japan) were 5.1 per cent, 4.8 per cent and 3.6 per cent respectively.[3] Between 1950 and 1980, there was not much that changed in output shares—except of course for the post-war boom in Japan, and later rapid export led growth in Korea, Hong Kong, Taiwan and Singapore. In the two decades between 1980 and 2000, while East and South East Asian economies expanded at a rapid pace and successfully improved their respective shares of world economic activity, the developed world as a whole, also gained ground, with the share of world output originating in the advanced economies increased from 73 per cent to 80 per cent. This was largely at the expense of the former Soviet bloc. There was, however, a sharp pick up in the rate of growth in the advanced economies of the West flowing for the most part from the deep changes in economic policies adopted by these economies in the 1980s which reinvigorated them. There were also small declines in the relative shares of Latin America, Middle East and sub-Saharan Africa in addition to the substantial decline in the former Soviet bloc.

2.106. Post-2000, it has been an altogether different story. The share of the advanced economies fell from 80 per cent in 2000 to 64 per cent in 2011, while that of the developing world increased from 20 to 36 per cent. Not only is this a development of enormous moment in the economic polarity of the world, but there is every reason to believe that it will progress further. Some projections envisage an equally balanced split between the advanced and developing economies around 2025–30.

2.107. The underlying trend of shifting economic polarity will continue. As mentioned previously, the share of developed economies in world GDP is likely to fall further towards 50 per cent by 2025–30. China which has been the biggest gainer in terms of altered share of world GDP is likely to see her share of world output rise to about 15 per cent by 2020 and to around 18 per cent by around 2025. This would bring her close to the projected GDP of the USA.

2.108. India's share of world GDP was 1.5 per cent in 2000, which increased to 2.4 per cent in 2011. By 2017, we may be at 3.5 per cent ($3.3 trillion), 4.2–4.5 per cent ($4.5–5.0 trillion) by 2020 and 5.5–6.0 per cent ($8 trillion) by 2025. This is based on somewhat modest assumptions. It is self-evident that projections made over this kind of time horizon are likely to come up short. However, in the absence of any cataclysmic event, the broad contour of future economic geography is most likely to approximate this.

2.109. It is important to emphasise that even if developing countries are able to harvest their economic potential, they will still not become rich economies in the next 10 or even 20 years. China, for instance, has made the greatest advance in terms of income and output experiencing 34 years of rapid economic growth (average annual rate of 10 per cent) that has propelled her from being the sixth-largest in 2000 to being the second largest economy in the world. Nevertheless, China in 2012 had a per capita income of $6,000, much ahead of India at $1,600 but still far behind middle-income economies in Eastern Europe and Latin America. Even if she is able to sustain a rapid pace of expansion, by 2025 China will still at best be able to secure a position in the highest 60–65 economies, but yet be lower in per capita income compared to many economies in East Europe, Latin America and Asia. India will at best be a middle-income country, but with the important difference that problems of poverty as currently defined will be well behind us.

Change in the Character of Capital Flows

2.110. The structure of the international capital market has changed considerably and this has implications for India's strategy in the years ahead. The developed world, particularly the USA, has run persistent current account deficits, which have been matched by persistent current account surpluses in the oil exporting nations, Japan, China and several other East and South East Asian economies.

2.111. The aggregate of the absolute values of current account deficits and surpluses amounted to 2.2 per cent of world GDP in 1990, which then went on to a peak value of 5.8 per cent in 2006; from where it declined to 4.1 per cent in 2010. In absolute terms the sum of the global aggregate of current account deficits and surpluses has increased from $1.2 trillion in 2000 to $2.8 trillion in 2006 and 2007 and now stands at $2.9 trillion in 2011.[4] This represents the sum of the net flows between surplus and deficit national economies. However, the volume of gross flows is much greater than represented by these net flows. Further, cross-border capital flows over the years have accumulated and the stock of cross-border capital has been estimated to be as large as $100 trillion today.[5]

2.112. One of the interesting developments in international capital markets is the emergence of a much wider array of instruments, both debt and non-debt. Bond issuance and risk capital in the form of equity, as also some kinds of hybrid instruments have come to form a very significant component of capital flows. Further, the nature and direction of these capital flows no longer follow the traditional North–South contours and are also not unidirectional. Capital flows from the advanced to the developing economies and also from developing to advanced economy and indeed amongst the developing economies themselves.

2.113. In 1990, as much as 95 per cent of the FDI outflows originated in advanced economies. In 2011 this share had fallen to 73 per cent, even as the total value of flows rose from $242 billion to $1.7 trillion. The volume of FDI outflows peaked at $2.2 trillion or almost 4 per cent of world GDP in 2007, the year before the global crisis. On the destination side, the share of developing economies saw a rapid increase from 17 per cent in 1990 to 45 per cent in 2011, of which the inflow into Asia increased over the two decades from 11 to 28 per cent. The large increase in the proportion of total FDI originating in the developing world from 4.5 per cent in 1990 to 23 per cent in 2011, translates in absolute terms to an increase from $11 billion to $384 billion, of which $280 billion was from developing Asia.[6] It must be noted that while there was understandably a sizeable decline in the FDI flow from advanced economies, after 2008 that from developing Asia continued to rise without interruption.

2.114. The regional difference in current account balances is a manifestation of major differences in the national savings rates in the respective countries. It is quite possible that there will be some mitigation in the magnitude of these differentials. However, it is rather likely that in the foreseeable future, the magnitude of incremental savings arising in Asia and other developing economies will be proportionately larger than that which may reasonably be expected to arise in the advanced economies. To a great extent Asia has come to be a major locus of capital flows with several centres acquiring considerable significance as the focus of financial intermediation.

2.115. The shift in the polarity and geography of both capital flows and of their intermediation will be as powerful and notable as the shift in the geography of production and international trade. The dominance of conventional centres in New York, London and Frankfurt will yield to a growing role for centres in the developing world—most particularly in Asia. Hong Kong and Singapore have already acquired increasingly important roles as centres of financial mobilisation. Asia is simultaneously a major source of savings as also of demand for investment financing. Skills have gradually become internalised, and regulation and market structures seem to be supportive of these two island centres to expand very much more. It is not certain to what extent mainland centres like Shanghai, or for that matter Mumbai, will be able to keep pace. In any event a financial network within Asia is already there and will take on a much greater role. Increasingly larger increments of the stock of savings of the developed economies are entering into this network, and this process too will continue and deepen.

2.116. The changing structure of global capital markets and India's need for financing capital flows raises the issue of what should be India's policy towards capital flows. India has followed a policy of calibrated opening to capital inflows, which has served the country well. FDI is regarded as the most stable form of capital inflow and one that brings with it technology, productivity enhancement and international market linkage. Portfolio flows are more volatile than FDI but past experience shows that they are much less so than commonly feared. The real area of vulnerability is debt denominated in foreign exchange, especially short-term debt. India's policy has reflected this hierarchical preference with the greatest openness to FDI and the strongest control over short-term debt. This basic policy of calibrated opening up of the capital account should continue.

2.117. Looking ahead, it needs to be kept in mind that as Indian industry globalises, and acquires assets abroad; Indian firms will need much more flexibility in capital transactions including especially access to risk management instruments. Unwillingness to allow such instruments to be developed in domestic market only pushes this activity abroad, and in the longer run this weakens India's ability to serve as a potential centre for financial transaction. There is a case for comprehensively reviewing the present policy and laying out a clearer road map of calibrated liberalisation over the Twelfth Plan period and beyond.

Changes in Trade Patterns

2.118. The large ongoing changes in the pattern of economic activity described above have expectedly been mirrored in the changes in the pattern of trade in merchandise and services. In the decades following the end of colonial rule, the share of developing economies in world merchandise exports fell from 34 per cent in 1948 to 24 per cent in 1973, as exports of manufactures from the developed world increased rapidly. Thereafter, as many developing countries turned into increasingly important exporters of manufactured goods, their shares in aggregate merchandise exports recovered to 33 per cent in 2003 and further to 44 per cent by 2010.[7]

2.119. Most dramatic has been the increase in the share of global merchandise imports accounted for by Asia (excluding Japan) which has risen from 17 to 25 per cent between 1993 and 2010. If we take Asia (excluding Japan), Latin America, Africa and the Middle East together, we will find that their share of global merchandise imports increased from 28 to 38 per cent between 1993 and 2010. The share of the developed western economies and Japan dropped from 71 to 59 per cent in the same period. This process will only deepen further in the coming decades. The market for services—which includes transportation, travel, financial and telecommunication, besides IT-related businesses—is actually more evenly spread out than that for merchandise, with developing economies accounting for almost half of the import market. However, even here there will be proportionately more rapid expansion in the IT-related business in the developing economies.

2.120. The other notable development in international trade is the increasing regional concentration of merchandise trade. In 2010, the second-largest regional trade was located in Asia (excluding Middle East) amounting in value to $2.9 trillion or 63 per cent of the regional trade concentration of Europe, which amounted to $4.7 trillion. Expectedly, the proportion of Asian origin exports to other Asian markets has increased from 47 per cent in 1999 to 53 per cent in 2011. Not only is the developing world as a whole and Asia in particular, becoming proportionately more important in international trade, but the trade within the region, and potentially with Africa and Latin America holds the promise of further expansion in future.

2.121. This has implications for our longer-term trade strategy. Although our markets in the industrialised world may not grow rapidly, other markets will expand to a greater extent and we need to be present in these markets to take the advantage.

Four Lessons

2.122. Four lessons emerge from this brief review which are relevant for developing economies as a whole:

- First, a window of opportunity exists and domestic conditions have supportive so far, and, therefore, may reasonably be expected to continue to support a rapid pace of expansion.
- Second, the initial conditions are so disparate that many decades of sustained high economic growth can bridge, but only a part of the gap.
- Third, with almost all developing economies expanding at a fast pace, even with a rapid and sustained pace, an individual country may fail to do as well as many of her comparators.
- Fourth, some kind of end state may emerge within a few decades and there is a strong probability that

this will in some sense become the new economic hierarchy. Thereafter, flexibility and opportunity may become diminished. We need to hasten to make as much use of these opportunities, while they are still open.

Strategy for Trade and Commerce

2.123. The long-term vision of the government is to make India a major player in world trade by 2020, and assume a role of leadership in the international trade organisations commensurate with India's growing economic and demographic profile. In consonance with its vision of ensuring sustained accelerated growth of exports and making India a major player of world trade, the government announces a Foreign Trade Policy (FTP) every five years. FTP is annually reviewed to incorporate changes necessary to take care of emerging economic scenarios both domestically and globally.

2.124. The underlying philosophy of India's FTP is based on seven broad principles:

1. Give a focused thrust to exports of employment-intensive industries.
2. Encourage domestic manufacturing for inputs to export industry and reduce the dependence on imports.
3. Promote technological up-gradation of exports to retain a competitive edge in global markets.
4. Persist with a strong market diversification strategy to hedge the risks against global uncertainty.
5. Encourage exports from the North-Eastern Region given its special place in India's economy.
6. Provide incentives for manufacturing of green goods recognising the imperative of building capacities for environmental sustainability.
7. Endeavour to reduce transaction cost through procedural simplification and reduction of human interface.

2.125. To boost exports, supportive measures are necessary as is adequate infrastructure. Simultaneously, concerted efforts need to be directed at creating domestic capacity in production of goods where India's import dependency is high and increasing. Given this background, the objectives on exports for the Twelfth Plan are:

- Substantial increase in exports to balance the Trade Deficit
- Enhancing the proportion of Manufacturing in the export basket (61.5 per cent at present) to realise higher value addition

These objectives entail drawing up of country and commodity specific strategies, with a medium- and long-term perspective. The products strategies are discussed in Chapter 9.

Territorial Strategy for Exports

2.126. Trade flows within the South has increased substantially. However, the share of India, though increasing rapidly, is still much lower as compared to countries like China and those in South East Asia in particular. Thus, there is substantial potential for increasing India's trade with the South and with Latin America, Africa and CIS.

2.127. During the Eleventh Plan, America and Europe continued to be important destinations of Indian exports although their combined share declined from 39.8 to 35.4 per cent. India is negotiating a Broad-based Trade and Investment Agreement (BTIA) with European Union and on its completion it would result in increase bilateral trade and flows of investment between the two trading partners. The share of Asia and ASEAN after showing steady increase have shown some decline during the last two years of Eleventh Plan and the region still accounted for more than half of India's exports during the Plan period. Exports to Africa also registered a steady increase after showing some decline in initial years of the plan.

2.128. India has been pursuing a policy of market diversification directing her export promotion efforts at Asia and ASEAN, Latin America and Africa through Focus Market initiatives and bilateral trade agreements.

Commercial Relations and Trade Agreements

2.129. While the multilateral trade negotiations progressed slowly, India pursued regional and bilateral trade negotiations with vigour. In pursuance of its 'Look East Policy', a continuous dialogue is maintained with the ASEAN and the countries of South East Asia at summit-level engagements. Having signed the India–ASEAN Trade in Goods Agreement, negotiations on Agreements on Trade in Services and Investment continued with a view to be concluded by end 2012.

2.130. Some of the Major bilateral agreements which have been concluded in the recent past include: Comprehensive Economic Partnership Agreement (CEPA) with Republic of Korea, Comprehensive Economic Cooperation Agreement (CECA) with Malaysia, India–Thailand Free Trade Agreement, conclusion of CEPA with Japan, continuing relations with the United States, USA remains one of India's major trade partner and India–EU BTIA Negotiations and so on; so far as, the focus areas are concerned, these are:

South Asian Association of Regional Cooperation (SAARC)

2.131. In a major initiative the Government of India (GOI) completely eliminated negative list for less developed countries (LDCs) in South Asia Free Trade Area (SAFTA) leaving only tobacco and alcohol on the list. This is expected to give a big boost to exports from SAARC LDC countries to India. India further reduced 30 per cent (264 tariff lines) of the SAFTA Sensitive list maintained by it for non-least developed countries (NLDCs) allowing the peak tariff rates to reduce to 5 per cent within three years, as per SAFTA process of tariff liberalisation. This shall reduce India's Sensitive list for Pakistan from 878 to 614 tariff lines. Agreement on SAFTA, inter alia, prescribes a phased Tariff Liberalization Programme (TLP) according to which peak tariff rate maintained by India for all items other than those included in the sensitive list is 8 per cent which will reduce to 5 per cent with effect from 1 January 2013.

2.132. *India–Bangladesh Trade Relations*: India–Bangladesh relations intensified during the year. A Memorandum of Understanding (MoU) on establishment of border haats at Baliamari-Kalaichar (Pillar No. 1,072) and Lauwaghar-Balat (Pillar No. 1,213) at Meghalaya, India–Bangladesh border was signed on 2010. The first border haat at Kalaichar was inaugurated on 2011 and both the border haats are now operational.

2.133. *India–Nepal Trade Relations*: India and Nepal have special relations and regular consultations take place between the governments. Double Taxation Avoidance Agreement (DTAA) with Nepal was signed, which will help exporters and investors of both the countries in further improving mutual business engagements.

Focus Latin American Countries Programme

2.134. An integrated programme 'Focus: LAC' which was launched in November 1997 has been extended up to March 2014 in order to consolidate the gains of the previous years and significantly enhance India's trade with the Latin America and the Caribbean (LAC) region. Latin America has been given special 'focus' status to diversify our trade basket and offset the inherent disadvantages for our exporters such as credit risk, higher freight cost and so on. The new FTP (2009–2014), pays special attention to LAC and 16 new markets of LAC region have been incorporated under Focus Market Scheme (FMS) bringing the total 231. Under the Market-Linked Focus Product Scheme (MLFPS), 13 markets have been identified, includes Brazil. The Preferential Trade Agreements (PTAs) with Mercosur and Chile are being expanded.

'Focus Africa' Programme

2.135. The 'Focus Africa' Programme was initially launched with focus on seven countries of Sub-Saharan African (SSA) Region, namely South Africa, Nigeria, Mauritius, Tanzania, Kenya, Ghana and Ethiopia. With a view to further widen and deepen India's trade with Africa, the scope of this Programme was further extended to include Angola, Botswana, Ivory Coast, Madagascar, Mozambique, Senegal, Seychelles, Uganda, Zambia, Namibia and Zimbabwe, along with the six countries of North Africa, namely Egypt, Libya, Tunisia, Sudan, Morocco and Algeria. *India and Southern African Customs Union* (SACU) are also negotiating a *PTA*. SACU consists of a group of five countries, namely Botswana, Lesotho, Namibia, Swaziland and South Africa.

2.136. Till now, three *'India Show' events* have been held in Africa. The first India Show was in South Africa in 2010, Next one was held in Addis Ababa, Ethiopia in 2011 and in the current year, 'India Show' was organised at Accra, Ghana.

2.137. India hosted the first ever *India–Africa Forum Summit* in 2008 at New Delhi. The second Africa–India Forum Summit was held at Addis Ababa from 24–25 May 2011. These Summits have been built upon the foundations of the historical relationship that exists between India and Africa, and designed a new architecture for a structured engagement, interaction and co-operation between India and Africa in the twenty-first century.

2.138. The first India–Africa Trade Ministers Meet was convened at Addis Ababa in May 2011, just ahead of the second India–Africa Forum Summit. The second meeting of the Trade Ministers from India and Africa was held on March 2012 at New Delhi, which was attended by 12 ministers from African countries. During this meeting, the Ministers launched the *India–Africa Business Council (IABC)*. The Council will suggest the way forward on enhancing economic and commercial relations between India and Africa and also identify and address issues which hinder growth of economic partnership between India and Africa.

WTO Negotiations

2.139. The Doha Round of negotiations at the World Trade Organization (WTO), which began in 2001, is still under way. The scope of the negotiations includes agriculture, market access for non-agricultural products, services trade, trade-related aspects of intellectual property rights (TRIPS), rules (covering anti-dumping and subsidies), trade facilitation and so on. The conduct, conclusion and entry into force of the outcome of the negotiations are parts of a single undertaking, that is, 'nothing is agreed until everything is agreed'.

2.140. Progress has been very slow due to wide gaps in the expectations of the members. There have been several attempts to bring the talks back on track and to build on the results already achieved in the negotiations. There have been constant attempts in the WTO and in other forums like the G20 to resolve the impasse. During the Ministerial Conference of the WTO held in December 2011, members once again reaffirmed their belief in rules based multilateral trade and their commitment to resolve the issues in a transparent way through consensus.

2.141. In keeping with its commitment towards the legitimate interests of developing economies, LDCs and vulnerable economies, India has been working closely with various coalition groups in the WTO towards an early development-oriented conclusion of the Doha Round.

2.142. However, developed countries no longer appear interested in concluding the Round as a single undertaking. They are using the prolonged financial and economic crisis and the relatively better performance of a few developing countries to justify their demands for a change in mandate of the Doha talks and for new issues such as food security and climate change to be brought into the negotiations. Over the last several months, they have been making efforts to selectively conclude areas of the Doha negotiations in which they have a particular interest, for example trade facilitation and services.

2.143. The prolonged hiatus in the Doha Round talks in a matter of concern. It is not for want of willingness on the part of developing countries to engage, but is the result of an apparent perception among some developed countries that they will not gain much from the Round. The neglect of the Doha Round is unfortunate and jeopardises an opportunity to strengthen multilateral trade rules. Trade liberalisation will take place in any case driven by global market dynamics. Many countries, including India, have autonomously lowered tariffs and simplified border procedures. However, the multilateral trading regime treats trade as a tool of economic growth and development and not merely as a tool to serve commercial interests. The Doha Round offers a chance to strengthen this regime.

ANNEXURE 2.1

Poverty—Measures and Changes Therein

Household consumption expenditure surveys of the National Sample Survey Office (NSSO) have formed the basis of our analysis and conclusions about family consumption baskets and from that of consumption poverty. Till recently, the official estimates of poverty was based on the recommendations of the expert committee chaired by the late Professor D.T. Lakdawala which had submitted its recommendations in 1993. Over the years the findings on poverty made in line with the methodology of the Lakdawala Committee began to be criticised as being 'too low' and not in line with the general advancement of the economy.

In 2005, the Planning Commission appointed a new expert committee chaired by the late Professor Suresh Tendulkar which submitted its recommendations in late 2009. The Tendulkar Committee made several deep-rooted changes in the methodology for adjusting poverty lines to price changes and substantially revised upward the rural poverty line vis-à-vis the Lakdawala Committee, both for 1993–94 as well as for 2004–05, which was the latest large survey of the NSSO on household consumption expenditures then available.

What constitutes a 'fair' poverty line has always been a contentious issue. This primarily flows from the fact that poverty and in a broader sense deprivation is a cultural construct specific to a point in time. It is inconceivable that the sense of what constitutes poverty would remain unchanged as society becomes wealthier, incomes rise and modern amenities become widely available. Progress by its very nature inherently does and should recalibrate the very notion of what constitutes poverty and deprivation.

The recommendations of the Expert Committee chaired by the late Professor Suresh Tendulkar were adopted by the Planning Commission. Applying this methodology to the NSSO large survey of 2009–10 showed that the poverty ratio had declined by 7 percentage points for the country as a whole between 2004–05 and 2009–10. The annual rate of decline in this period was double that for previous periods.

This finding was criticised by some for using a poverty line that was variously described as being too 'low'. Some points need to be made in this regard. First, what we have is the NSSO data which is collected on the basis of household surveys that seek to assess family expenditure budgets. Since households are of different sizes, the NSSO normalises the data by expressing their finding in per capita terms. These neither relate to single member households nor to family income.

Second, the finding that poverty has declined much faster in the period 2004–05 to 2009–10 is valid irrespective of where we choose to draw the poverty line. If we use the Tendulkar poverty line (PL), the decline in the period is found to be 7.3 percentage points. If we use a poverty line 30 per cent higher, the decline would be 7.8 percentage points. Likewise at 50 per cent higher the decline is 6.5 percentage points.

In fact, the decline in the poverty ratio for different levels higher and lower than the Tendulkar PL shows that the decline not only occurs at every level higher or lower than the Tendulkar PL, but that the decline is noticeably faster at lower levels of PL, particularly in rural areas, namely within the range of ±30 per cent of the Tendulkar PL, that is amongst the lower end of the consumption distribution (Figure 2.4).

At the left hand tail of the distribution it appears that the pace of reduction is lower both for rural and urban areas. However, this is because the reduction is being measured as the annualised rate of decline in percentage points of poverty. If the initial poverty ratio is low, then the decline in terms of percentage points cannot be other than small. To see what the pace of decline at the lowest income groups, the rate of decline has been normalised by expressing it in terms of a ratio of the initial percentage of persons falling under that PL or expenditure class. This is depicted at Figure 2.5.

From the charts in Figure 2.5, it is clear that the rate of decline has if anything been faster amongst the lowest income groups in rural areas and this phenomenon is even more marked in the urban areas. The positive distributive implications of the reduction of poverty at the overall level, and even more so the greater impact on the relatively poor at the lower end of the income distribution, is a matter of satisfaction.

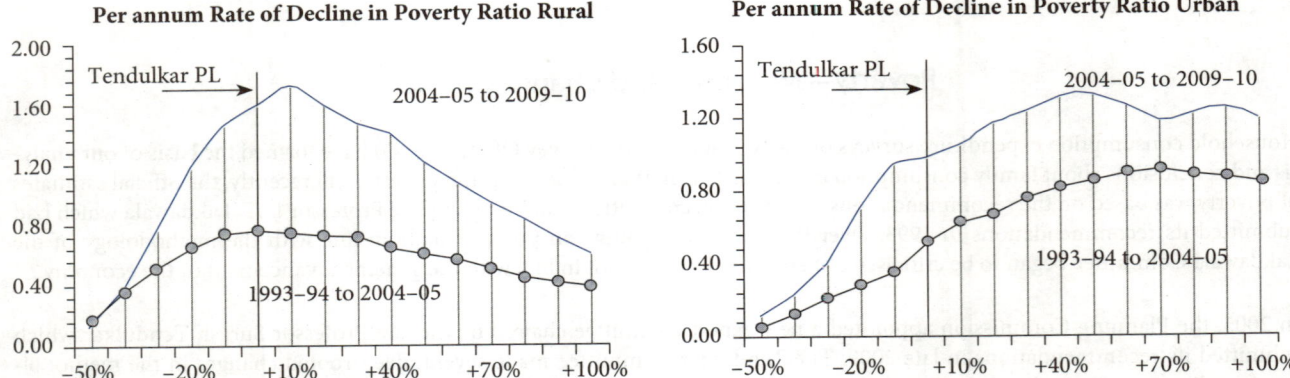

FIGURE 2.4: Annualised Reduction in Poverty Ratio between 1993–94, 2004–05 and 2009–10 for Alternate Measures of PL in Percentage Points

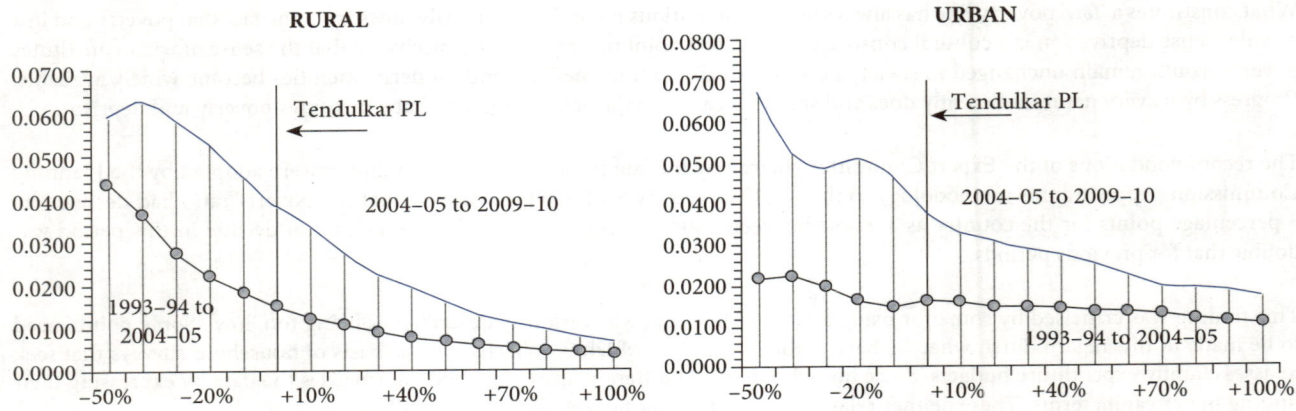

FIGURE 2.5: Annualised Rate of Decline as Proportion of the Initial Ratio in that Expenditure Class

Third, is that the difference in the NSSO consumption expenditure total and that of the private final consumption expenditure estimate of National Accounts Statistics (NAS) has been large and widening, from being over 90 per cent of the latter in the 1970s to less than 50 per cent now. Some of this is explicable, some not. In any case, the data available is the NSSO data as reported has been used without making any adjustment. Finally, these are actual data and about actual families who live below these consumption expenditure levels.

In view of the debate on the issue of measuring poverty, it has been decided to (*i*) de-link the benefits that are intended for the poor from the PLs computed from the NSSO household consumption surveys using the Tendulkar methodology; and (*ii*) set up a fresh Committee to go into every aspect of the issue.

The 68th Round of the NSSO Household Consumption Expenditure for 2011–12 has been just completed. Detailed household unit wise data will only become available after some time. The NSSO has however released some preliminary summary estimates on Uniform Recall Period (URP) both at current and at constant prices. The methodology now in use follows the Tendulkar Committee which is based on Mixed Recall Period (MRP). However, the URP distribution by decile categories is available. From the NSSO summary data release it appears that Monthly Per Capital Consumption Expenditure (MPCE) at constant (2004–05) prices increased in the two year period between 2009–10 and 2011–12 by 18.1 per cent and 13.3 per cent in rural and urban areas. This corresponds to an annualised rate of increase of 8.7 and 6.5 in rural and urban areas respectively, which is much higher than the 1.4 per cent and 2.7 per cent respective annual increases in rural and urban households between 2004–05 and 2009–10.

The 30th percentile (that is the third decile from the bottom of the distribution) of MPCE (URP) in the 68th Round show that at constant prices the increase between 2009–10 and 2011–12 was 14.5 per cent and 15.3 per cent for rural and urban households respectively, which translate to annualised rates of increase of 7.0 per cent and 7.4 per cent for urban and rural households. These are much higher than the corresponding values for the period 2004–05 to 2009–10 which was 1.7 per cent and 1.9 per cent respectively.

A large part of the reason for the much higher growth in real MPCE in the most recent period may well have been that conditions in 2009–10 was unusually depressed on account of the combination of the global crisis that had occurred a year earlier and the very poor monsoon of 2009. The initial findings of the 68th Round fully justifies the decision that was taken to go in for a large sample survey in 2011–12 (before the results for the 2009–10 survey was available) instead of the normal five-year interval.

From this, the inference is that the rate of decline in poverty in the period 2009–10 to 2011–12 would be much higher than that which emerged from the NSSO surveys for the periods 2004–05 to 2009–10. Or to put it another way the rate of decline in poverty in the period 2004–05 to 2011–12 would be much higher than that for the period 1993–94 to 2004–05.

Decile-wise annual growth in real MPCE for the periods 1993–94 to 2004–05 and 2004–05 to 2011–12 as given in Table 2.8 shows that growth in consumption across deciles was much more inclusive in the period 2004–05 to 2011–12 as compared to the period 1993–94 to 2004–05.

TABLE 2.8
Decile-wise annual growth in $MPCE_{URP}$ at constant prices (2004–05)

(%)

Deciles (% of population)	Rural		Urban	
	1993–94 to 2004–05	2004–05 to 2011–12	1993–94 to 2004–05	2004–05 to 2011–12
First (0–10)	0.70	2.91	0.66	2.96
Second (10–20)	0.49	3.00	0.54	3.28
Third (20–30)	0.56	3.15	0.66	3.39
Fourth (30–40)	0.55	3.17	0.91	3.42
Fifth (40–50)	0.54	3.17	1.00	3.41
Sixth (50–60)	0.55	3.30	1.24	3.35
Seventh (60–70)	0.52	3.40	1.36	3.30
Eighth (70–80)	0.61	3.45	1.35	3.40
Ninth (80–90)	0.71	3.48	1.47	3.45
Tenth (90–100)	1.61	3.71	2.30	4.52
Average	0.85	3.40	1.49	3.72

NOTES

1. The shares of Bangladesh, Vietnam and Cambodia rose from 2.6 per cent, 0.9 per cent and 0.5 per cent in 2000 to 4.5 per cent, 3.1 per cent and 0.9 per cent respectively (*International Trade Statistics 2011*, WTO).
2. Angus Maddison, *Contours of the World Economy 1-2030 AD* (Oxford University Press, 2007). The regional identifier 'Asia' does not include Middle East/West Asia in conformity with conventional practice.
3. For purposes of comparison, India in 1950 is the sum of India, Pakistan and Bangladesh (then East Pakistan) and that of China the sum of mainland China, Hong Kong and Taiwan.
4. Computed from balance of payment data in the *World Economic Outlook* database of the IMF.
5. Stephen G. Cecchetti, *Global Imbalances: Current Accounts and Financial Flows* (Myron Scholes Global Markets Forum, University of Chicago, September 2011).
6. *World Investment Report* (UNCTAD, 2012).
7. Data on trade flows in this sections are from International Trade Statistics (WTO, 2011).

3
Financing the Plan

INTRODUCTION

3.1. This Chapter presents projections of the public sector resources for the Twelfth Plan period given the target Gross Domestic Product (GDP) growth rate of 8 per cent. The estimates show resource availability for the Twelfth Plan of ₹80,50,123 crore at current prices for the Centre and States taken together.

3.2. These projections imply that public sector resources for the Plan will be at 11.80 per cent of GDP in the Twelfth Plan as against 10.96 per cent realised in the Eleventh Plan. However, the outcome will depend critically on achievement of buoyancy in tax revenue, effective control over subsidies and an improvement in the resource mobilising capacity of Public Sector Enterprises (PSEs) both at the Central and State levels.

PUBLIC SECTOR RESOURCES IN THE ELEVENTH PLAN

3.3. This section presents an overview of the resources of the Centre and States in the Eleventh Plan period.

Centre's Plan Resources

3.4. The Gross Budgetary Support (GBS) in Eleventh Plan was projected at ₹14,21,711 crore at 2006–07 prices. This included ₹3,24,851 crore of Central Assistance (CA) to the States and Union Territories (UTs). With the Eleventh Plan resources of Central Public Sector Enterprises (CPSEs) projected at ₹10,59,711 crore, total resources available for the Central Plan was fixed at ₹21,56,571 crore.

3.5. As shown in Table 3.1, the realised GBS for the Plan was 89.23 per cent of the projected amount. Realised CA to States and UTs at ₹3,38,913 crore was 104.33 per cent of the projected level. As a percentage of GBS, this increased from 22.85 per cent to 26.72 per cent. This increase in the share of CA to States and UTs is a reflection of the stimulus packages offered by the Government as counter-cyclical measures, resulting in increased resource transfers to States through CSS in health, education and rural development, which expanded well beyond what was originally projected. Central Public Sector Enterprises (CPSEs) achieved 64.57 per cent of resources projected in the Plan. A large part of the shortfall is accounted for by under-recoveries of the public sector enterprises (PSEs) due to market price controls imposed by the Government.

3.6. The total resources available for the Central Plan, consisting of GBS for the Central Plan plus PSEs' resources, worked out to be 74.84 per cent of the projected level, that is, ₹16,13,882 crore at 2006–07 prices.

3.7. The composition of the GBS in the Eleventh Plan as actually realised reflects a significant deterioration of non-debt contribution compared to the Plan projections. The share of Balance from Current Revenues (BCRs) in GBS was projected to be 46 per cent, but deteriorated sharply to (−)14.01 per cent. Therefore, to bridge the gap, the realised share of borrowings had to increase to 108.92 per cent as against the projected share of 54.00 per cent.

TABLE 3.1
Projected vis-à-vis Realised Financing Pattern of the Plan Outlay of the Centre

(₹ Crore at 2006–07 Prices)

Sources of Funding Projection		Eleventh Plan (2007–12)		
		Projection	Realisation	% Realisation
1	BCR	6,53,989	–1,77,679	–27.17
		(46.00)	(–14.01)	
2	Borrowings including net MCR*	7,67,722	13,81,639	179.97
		(54.00)	(108.92)	
3	Net flow from abroad	0	64,563	
4	Gross Budgetary Support for the Plan (1 + 2 + 3)	14,21,711	12,68,523	89.23
5	CA to States and UTs' Plan	3,24,851	3,38,913	104.33
		(22.85)	(26.72)	
6	GBS for Central Plan (4 – 5)	10,96,860	9,29,610	84.75
		(77.15)	(73.28)	
7	Resources of PSEs	10,59,711	6,84,272	64.57
8	Resources for Central Plan (6 + 7)	21,56,571	16,13,882	74.84

Note: Figures in parentheses are percentages of GBS to Plan (S. No. 4). * MCR: Miscellaneous Capital Receipts.

3.8. The overall negative BCR during the Eleventh Plan as against the projection of substantial positive BCR was partly due to global financial crisis slowing down economic growth and partly due to counter cyclical fiscal measures and Sixth Pay Commission awards. The BCR, which turned out to be positive in the last year of the Tenth Plan, had improved further in the first year of the Eleventh Plan. However, BCR turned negative in next two years, as well as in the last year of the Eleventh Plan.

Revenue Receipts

3.9. Gross Tax Revenue of the Centre which grew at an Average Annual Growth Rate (AAGR) of 20.5 per cent in the Tenth Plan, declined to 14.23 per cent in the Eleventh Plan. Net of the share of the States, the tax revenues of the Centre grew at 13.31 per cent. Non-tax revenue has grown at an AAGR of 16.55 per cent in the Eleventh Plan as against 4.31 per cent in the Tenth Plan. However, much of the increase was due to one off nature of proceeds of 3G/BWA Telecom Spectrum auction in 2010–11. The average annual growth of revenue receipts of the Central Government during the Eleventh Plan was 13.08 per cent.

3.10. An important factor underlying the poor resource mobilisation performance in the Eleventh Plan was the fact that revenue receipts of the Centre decreased by 2.20 percentage points of GDP from 10.87 per cent in 2007–08 to 8.66 per cent in 2011–12. Between 2007–08 and 2011–12, gross tax revenue as a proportion of GDP decreased by about 1.71 percentage points, of which 0.16 percentage points was the decrease in the share of the States. The gross tax GDP ratio continuously declined from 11.89 per cent in 2007–08 to 10.33 per cent in 2010–11 and further to 10.18 per cent in 2011–12. Tax revenues (net of States' shares) decreased by about 1.56 percentage points from 8.81 per cent in 2007–08 to 7.25 per cent in 2011–12. Non-tax revenue fell by about 0.64 percentage points from 2.05 per cent of GDP in 2007–08 to 1.41 per cent of GDP in 2011–12. The decline in non-tax revenue has been largely due to a steep decline in interest receipts by about two percentage points owing to debt consolidation and resetting of interest rates, and disintermediation in borrowings arising from the award of the 12th Finance Commission (FC).

Non-Plan Revenue Expenditure

3.11. The Non-Plan Revenue Expenditure (NPRE) increased by 0.77 percentage points from 8.44 per cent of GDP in 2007–08 to 9.21 per cent of GDP in 2011–12 (refer to Table 3.2). This was mainly because

TABLE 3.2
NPRE and Its Components

Items		2007–08	2011–12
		Actual	RE
1	Interest	1,71,030	2,75,618
		(3.43)	(3.11)
2	Pension	24,261	56,190
		(0.49)	(0.63)
3	Salary	44,361	99,716
		(0.89)	(1.13)
4	Subsidies	70,926	2,16,297
		(1.42)	(2.44)
5	Other NPRE	1,10,283	1,67,919
		(2.21)	(1.90)
6	(Total) NPRE	4,20,861	8,15,740
		(8.44)	(9.21)

Source: Planning Commission.
Note: Figures in parentheses are percentages of GDP.

of an increase in salary payments due to Sixth Pay Commission award and sharp increase in subsidies by 1.02 per cent of GDP. Subsidies increased sharply from 1.42 per cent of GDP in 2007–08 to 2.44 per cent of GDP in 2011–12.

3.12. During the Eleventh Plan, expenditure on subsidies increased by 205 per cent from ₹70,926 crore in 2007–08 to ₹2,16,297 crore in 2011–12. The food subsidy and petroleum subsidy increased by about 139 per cent and 1,445 per cent respectively over this period. The sharp increase in petroleum subsidies was due to rise in international crude oil prices, rupee depreciation and inadequate passing of the increase in retail prices. The abolition of the practice of providing subsidies in securities and bringing subsidies transparently into budget accounting by cash subsidies, particularly for petroleum and fertilisers is another important factor for increase in subsidy expenditure. Subsidy rationalisation, including direct transfer of cash subsidy to the poor, is a priority policy objective of the Government and some initiatives are under consideration.

3.13. The borrowings of the Central Government have been much higher than the projected borrowing by the Centre due to economic slowdown caused by global financial crisis. The percentage of interest payments to revenue receipts increased from 31.56 per cent in 2007–08 to 37.2 per cent in 2009–10 and only marginally declined to 35.94 per cent in 2011–12. However, the debt burden of the Centre has declined by almost 2 percentage points from 46.2 per cent in 2007–08 to 44.2 per cent of GDP as per 2011–12 (BE).

Fiscal Deficit

3.14. The gross fiscal deficit of the Centre, as a per cent of GDP, increased from 2.54 per cent in 2007–08 to 5.89 per cent in 2011–12 (RE). The Fiscal position at the State level, on the other hand, was stable primarily because borrowing of the States are controlled by the Centre. The gross fiscal deficit of the States, as a per cent of GDP, has been within the projected level, except in 2009–10. Nevertheless, the combined fiscal deficit of the Centre and States increased from 3.97 per cent in 2007–08 to 8.09 per cent in 2011–12 (RE). The average combined fiscal deficit for the Eleventh Plan, as a percentage of GDP, was 7.34 per cent with 5.15 per cent for the Centre, and 2.23 per cent for the States. The year-wise figures of fiscal deficit are provided in Table 3.3.

3.15. The net flow from abroad for externally aided projects is another source of plan financing. The share of the net inflow from abroad, through this route was 2.2 per cent of GBS in the Tenth Plan. This was expected to decline due to early repayment of costlier debt. No specific target was fixed for the

TABLE 3.3
Gross Fiscal Deficit

Year	Centre	States	Combined
2007–08	2.54	1.49	3.97
2008–09	5.99	2.26	8.17
2009–10	6.48	3.02	9.46
2010–11	4.87	2.15	6.99
2011–12 (RE)	5.89	2.21	8.09
Eleventh Plan Average (2007–12)	5.15	2.23	7.34

Source: Indian Public Finance Statistics 2010–11 (Ministry of Finance) and *Annual Financial Statement 2012–13.*
Note: RE stands for Revised Estimates.

Eleventh Plan. But net inflow from abroad contributed about 5.09 per cent of the GBS in the Eleventh Plan, which was 0.24 per cent of the GDP.

Central Public Sector Enterprises

3.16. The Internal and Extra Budgetary Resources (IEBR) of the CPSEs was projected to provide ₹10,59,711 crore, but the actual realisation was only ₹6,84,272 crore which was 64.57 per cent of the projected amount. As a result, the realised share of IEBR in the Central Plan resources was only 42.4 per cent, much lower than the projected share of 49.14 per cent.

3.17. The investment by CPSEs is financed through budgetary support provided by the Central Government, which is a part of GBS and IEBR raised by CPSEs on their own. IEBR comprises of Internal Resources (IR) and Extra-Budgetary Resources (EBR). IR comprise retained profits—net of dividend paid to Government, depreciation provision, carried forward reserves and surpluses. EBR consist of receipts from the issue of bonds, debentures, External Commercial Borrowings (ECB), suppliers' credit, deposit receipts and term loans from financial institutions.

3.18. IEBR contributed 64.3 per cent of the Plan outlay of CPSEs during the Eleventh Plan, the rest being budgetary support. Of this, IR contributed 55.28 per cent and EBR 44.72 per cent. In the original projections, IR were to contribute 45.53 per cent and EBR were to contribute only about 54.47 per cent. The Eleventh Plan realisation of IR has been relatively better than the EBR. Consequently, EBR have been well within the Eleventh Plan target of 54.47 per cent.

States Resources in the Eleventh Plan

3.19. The Eleventh Plan resources of the States and UTs were projected at ₹14,88,147 crore at 2006–07 prices. The realisation at 2006–07 prices is placed at ₹13,47,842 crore which is 90.57 per cent of the projected level. The realised pattern of funding shows a considerable shortfall over the projected levels (as shown in Table 3.4). BCR was realised only at about 71.26 per cent over the projected level. With resources of the PSEs being slightly higher by about 4.2 per cent and borrowings restricted to 92.44 per cent of the projected level, the share of States' own resources in the aggregate plan resources has shown

TABLE 3.4
Eleventh Plan Resources of States and UTs

(₹ Crore at 2006–07 Prices)

	Sources of Funding	Projection	Realisation	% Realisation
1	Balance from current revenues	3,85,050	2,74,400	71.26
		(25.87)	(20.36)	
2	Resources of PSEs	1,28,824	1,34,234	104.20
		(8.66)	(9.96)	
3	Borrowings including net MCR	6,49,422	6,00,295	92.44
		(43.64)	(44.54)	
4	State's own resources (1 + 2 + 3)	11,63,296	10,08,929	86.73
		(78.17)	(74.86)	
5	CA to States' and UTs' Plan	3,24,851	3,38,913	104.33
		(21.83)	(25.14)	
6	Aggregate plan resources (4 + 5)	14,88,147	13,47,842	90.57
7	GBS to Plan (6 − 2)	13,59,323	12,13,608	89.28
8	GBS as percentage of GDP	**5.06**	**4.51**	

Source: Planning Commission.
Note: Figures in parentheses are percentages of Aggregate Plan Resources.

marginal decline to 74.86 per cent against the projection of 78.17 per cent.

3.20. Performance of the States can be analysed, broadly, in terms of three components, namely the BCR reflecting non-debt resources, States' borrowings reflecting debt-based funding, and CA, which is now all grant.

3.21. The BCR of the States was expected to be ₹3,85,050 crore and the actual realisation was only 71.26 per cent of the amount. The States' own tax revenues have increased due to improvements made possible through the introduction of value-added tax (VAT). The share of Central taxes devolved to the States has also improved owing to increased share recommended by 13th FC. However, compression of Non-Plan expenditure has not been as expected. This was largely due to salary increase of State/UT Government employees following the Sixth Pay Commission award.

3.22. As a consequence, reliance on borrowing increased marginally. Against a projected contribution of 43.64 per cent of the Plan resources, borrowing in the Eleventh Plan was marginally higher at 44.54 per cent. CA to States and UTs in the Eleventh Plan was 104.33 per cent of the projected level, and its contribution to Plan resources has been 25.14 per cent as against the projection of about 21.83 per cent. This has been the consequence of the increased expenditure on social sector through stimulus package offered by the Central Government.

PUBLIC SECTOR RESOURCES IN THE TWELFTH PLAN

Centre's Resources

3.23. There have been several important developments during the Eleventh Plan that have implications for financing of the Twelfth Plan. The Indian Economy resiliently faced the global financial crisis of 2008. However, slower growth adversely impacts growth in Centre's resources, particularly taxes. The Sixth Central Pay Commission award has been implemented. The 13th FC award for 2011–15 is under implementation with some changes in the fiscal responsibility and budget management framework targets. Service tax has emerged as a very promising source of revenue. Efforts are being made to introduce unified Goods and Service Tax (GST) in consultation with States. This will be a major reform of the indirect tax system.

Effect of Fiscal Responsibility and Budget Management Act (FRBMA)

3.24. FRBMA, 2003 and the associated rules which came into force with effect from 5 July 2004, enjoined the Central Government to lay down before the Parliament, the Medium Term Fiscal Policy Statement. During 2011–12, the fiscal deficit target of the Centre could not be met due to decline in economic growth impacting tax collection and high international crude prices leading to increase in subsidy-related expenditure. With proposal for additional mobilisation of indirect tax resource, fiscal deficit is estimated to decline during the Twelfth Plan. The gradual scaling down of the fiscal deficit will inevitably restrict the Government from making larger public investments through borrowing, but it will certainly pay in the long run. Borrowings which increase resource availability also increase the outstanding debt, and thereby increase the interest burden. High fiscal deficits also lead to other undesirable consequences such as uncertainty about macro-fundamentals which can affect investor confidence and make the climate unsuitable for private investment with adverse effects upon economic growth.

3.25. The projection of fiscal deficits based on Medium Term Fiscal Policy Statement 2012–13 indicates that debt resources for funding of GBS for the Twelfth Plan will be higher initially but is projected to decline gradually. The Centre's net borrowing which was 5.9 per cent of GDP in 2011–12 (RE) is estimated to decline to 5.1 per cent of GDP in 2012–13 (BE). The fiscal deficit as percent of GDP is further projected to decline to 4.5 per cent in 2013–14, 3.9 per cent in 2014–15, 3.2 per cent in 2015–16 and 3.0 per cent of GDP in the last year of the Twelfth Plan.

Effect of the 14th FC

3.26. The recommendations of the 13th FC had important implications for Plan financing. The 13th FC Award increased the devolution to the States from 30.5 per cent to 32 per cent of divisible pool. This has increased the State Share to Gross Tax Revenue of the Centre (exclusive of cesses, surcharge and cost of collection which does not constitute shareable pool) from about 26 per cent to more than 28 per cent, thereby increasing their capacity to finance the Plan. This increased capacity is kept in mind when determining the Plan resources of the States/UTs.

3.27. The 13th FC recommendations cover the period up to 2014–15, which includes the first three years of the Twelfth Plan. The projections of resources for the Twelfth Plan have been made assuming 28.45 per cent of tax devolutions of the Gross Tax revenue. This has been assumed by factoring in the surcharges being phased out and keeping the same ratio beyond 13th FC period till the terminal year of the Twelfth Plan. This might change later after the recommendations of 14th FC are available.

Effect of Service Tax and GST

3.28. The introduction of service tax has provided a promising source of revenue, but there are some caveats which have to be kept in mind before making projections for the Twelfth Plan. First, the scope for expanding the service tax net to more and more services gets narrower as the net is widened. The contribution of the expanding net will, therefore, reduce over time. Second, the preponderance of small service providers below the taxable limit of turnover constrains the scope of revenue mobilisation beyond a certain level. The introduction of GST will usher in major reforms of indirect taxes in the Centre and States. The Central Government is working with Empowered Committee of States to work out a consensus in this regard. The Twelfth Plan assumptions on tax resources of the Centre and States envisage revenue neutrality of GST although there might be positive spin-off effects of GST mainly through better tax compliance.

3.29. Keeping in mind the implication of the Mid-Term Fiscal Policy Statement and also the prospects for higher collection of taxes including service tax, an assessment has been made of the likely GBS of the Centre. The resource projection based on the estimates made by the Working Group on the Centre's resources with some changes given the changed economic scenario, yields a projection of GBS of the Centre, which indicates that it will grow from 5.13 per cent of GDP in 2012–13 to 5.22 per cent of GDP in 2016–17. The average GBS for the Central Plan in the Twelfth Plan period stands at 5.23 per cent of GDP as against 4.69 per cent of GDP realised in the Eleventh Plan.

3.30. The Gross Tax Revenue as a percentage of GDP is estimated to increase from 10.62 per cent in 2012–13 (BE) to at least the levels achieved in 2007–08. The tax revenue (net of States' share) increases from 7.60 per cent of GDP in 2012–13 to 8.79 per cent of GDP in 2016–17, averaging 8.27 per cent during the Twelfth Plan. Collection of direct tax has remained higher than the indirect tax collection since 2008–09 and projected to have similar trend during Twelfth Plan. Corporate tax collection averages 69.37 per cent of direct tax collection during the Twelfth Plan. It increases from 4.25 per cent of GDP in 2012–13 to 4.83 per cent of GDP in 2016–17 averaging 4.57 per cent of GDP, that is, 0.76 percentage points increase over the average Eleventh Plan realisation.

3.31. Subsidies in the first year of the Twelfth Plan have been taken as per 2012–13 (BE), which is likely to be somewhat higher when the final figures become available. With the reforms being undertaken, the total subsidies, as a proportion of GDP, are projected to decline to 1.5 per cent by 2016–17. Inability to pass on increases in global oil prices to the consumers would have a substantial impact on resources for the Plan, if this situation is not rectified urgently. The realised subsidies in the Eleventh Plan and projection for the Twelfth Plan are shown graphically in Figure 3.1.

3.32. Twelfth Plan resources for the Centre and its funding are summarised in Table 3.5. The GBS available for the Plan is estimated at ₹35,68,626 crore at current prices. CA to the States' and UTs' Plan works out to be ₹8,57,786 crore. IEBR of Central public sector enterprises (CPSEs) is estimated at ₹16,22,899 crore. The total resources available for the Central Plan outlay are, therefore, projected at ₹43,33,739 crore. This is only an indicative outlay. The actual realisation can change depending on how

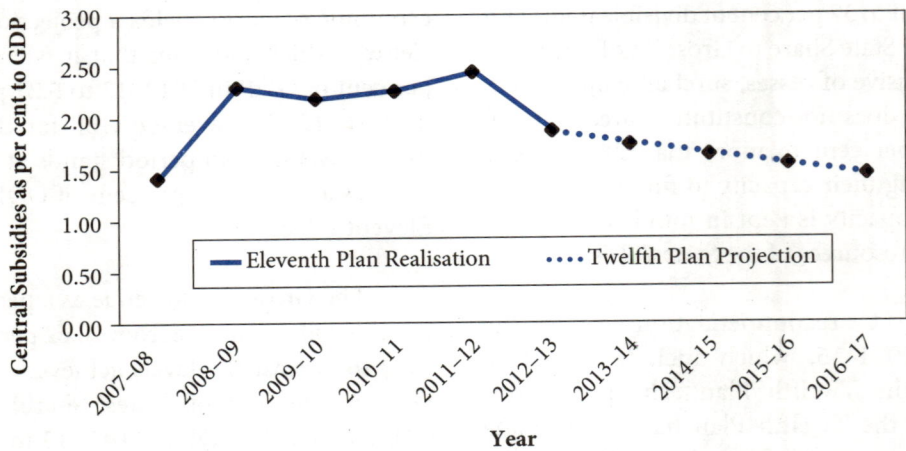

FIGURE 3.1: Central Subsidies as Per Cent to GDP

TABLE 3.5
Projection of the Twelfth Plan Resources of the Centre

(₹ Crore at Current Prices)

	Sources of Funding	Projection
1	Balance from current revenues	13,87,371 (38.88)
2	Borrowings including net MCR	21,81,255 (61.12)
3	Gross Budgetary Support to Plan (1 + 2)	35,68,626 (100)
4	CA to States and UTs' Plan	8,57,786 (24.04)
5	Total GBS for Central Plan (3 − 4)	27,10,840 (75.96)
6	Resources of PSEs including Borrowed Resource	16,22,899 (45.48)
7	**Total Resources for Central Plan** (5 + 6)	43,33,739

Source: Planning Commission.
Note: Figures in parentheses are percentages of GBS to Plan (S. No. 3).

the resource position evolves from year to year. The financial position will be reviewed at the time of Mid-term Appraisal.

3.33. Table 3.6 compares the funding pattern in the Twelfth Plan with the Eleventh Plan realisation as percentages of GDP. The BCR as percent of GDP was projected at 2.31 per cent for the Eleventh Plan which turned negative by (−)0.61 per cent. However, with good buoyancy in tax revenue and a decline in non-plan expenditure, BCR is estimated to be 1.88 per cent of the GDP for the Twelfth Plan. The imposition of the fiscal deficit ceiling ensures that borrowings, including net miscellaneous capital receipts, decline from 5.06 per cent of GDP in Eleventh Plan to 3.35 per cent in the Twelfth Plan.

States' Resources

3.34. The fiscal deficit of the States as a whole remained below 3 per cent of GDP during the Eleventh Plan period. While prescribing different fiscal paths for individual States, the 13th FC has also set the fiscal deficits target of 3 per cent of GDP to be achieved by 2014–15 by all the States. Accordingly, the fiscal deficit limit of all States which has been a little over 3 per cent of the GDP in 2012–13 is projected to remain around 2.22 per cent during the Twelfth Plan period. This inevitably limits the scope for mobilising debt resources of the States, therefore, have to look at improving revenue realisation and controlling non-Plan expenditure.

3.35. The Aggregate Plan resources of the States and UTs including PSE resources have been projected to be ₹37,16,385 crore at current prices (see Table 3.7). This comprises of ₹28,58,599 crore of own resources (including borrowings) and ₹8,57,786 crore of CA.

TABLE 3.6
Resources of the Centre in Eleventh and Twelfth Plan

(as % of GDP)

	Sources of Funding	Eleventh Plan Realisation	Twelfth Plan Projections	% Increases (+)/ Decreases (−)
1	Balance from Current Revenues	−0.61	1.88	2.49
2	Borrowings including net MCR	5.06	3.35	−1.71
3	Net Flow from Abroad	0.24	0.00	−0.24
4	**Gross Budgetary Support to Plan (1 to 3)**	**4.69**	**5.23**	**0.54**
5	CA to States and UTs' Plan	1.26	1.26	0.00
6	**GBS for Central Plan (4 − 5)**	**3.43**	**3.97**	**0.54**
7	Resources of PSEs	2.53	2.38	−0.15
8	**Resources for Central Plan (6 + 7)**	**5.96**	**6.35**	**0.39**

Source: Planning Commission.

TABLE 3.7
Twelfth Plan Resources of States and UTs

(₹ Crore at Current Prices)

	Sources of Funding	Projection		
		State	UTs	Total
1	Balance from Current Revenues	8,85,939	74,040	9,59,979
		(24.80)	(51.39)	(25.83)
2	Resources of PSEs	3,76,043	4,276	3,80,319
		(10.53)	(2.97)	(10.23)
3	Borrowings	14,94,258	24,043	15,18,301
		(41.83)	(16.69)	(40.85)
4	**State's Own Resources (1 to 3)**	**27,56,240**	**1,02,359**	**28,58,599**
		(77.16)	(71.05)	(76.92)
5	CA to States' and UTs' Plan	8,16,083	41,703	8,57,786
		(22.84)	(28.95)	(23.08)
6	**Aggregate Plan Resources (4 + 5)**	**35,72,323**	**1,44,062**	**37,16,385**
		(100.00)	(100.00)	(100.00)

Source: Planning Commission.
Note: Percentage of Total is in the parentheses.

UTs account for 3.88 per cent of the combined aggregate Plan resources of the States and UTs.

3.36. As a proportion of GDP, aggregate Plan resources of the States and UTs are projected at 5.45 per cent of GDP, registering an increase of 0.44 percentage points over the Eleventh Plan realisation (refer to Table 3.8). The BCR, which was ₹2,74,400 crore at 2006–07 prices in the Eleventh Plan, is projected to increase to ₹9,59,979 crore at current prices. This represents an increase of 0.39 percentage points of GDP over the Eleventh Plan. However, projections of resources of PSEs show a growth of 0.06 percentage points as compared with the Eleventh Plan. CA to the States remains almost at the same level as percentage of GDP.

TABLE 3.8
Eleventh Plan Realisation and Twelfth Plan Projection of Resources of States and UTs

(% of GDP)

	Sources of Funding	Eleventh Plan Realisation	Twelfth Plan Projections	% Increases (+)/ Decreases (−)
1	Balance from Current Revenues	1.02	1.41	**0.39**
2	Resources of PSEs	0.50	0.56	0.06
3	Borrowings	2.23	2.22	0.01
4	**States' Own Resources (1 to 3)**	**3.75**	**4.19**	**0.44**
5	CA to States' and UTs' Plan	1.26	1.26	0.00
6	**Aggregate Plan Resources (4 + 5)**	**5.01**	**5.45**	**0.44**

Source: Planning Commission.

3.37. Mobilisation of resources of such a magnitude for the Twelfth Plan is contingent upon significant improvement in the States' own resources, mainly through improved BCR. The States will have to step up efforts to increase their own tax and non-tax revenue collections through better tax administration, plugging the scope for leakages and levying of cost-based user charges. It is assumed that there would not be any additional burden on account of Pay-Commission related salary increase for majority of the States during the Plan period. Further, the devolution of taxes have been assumed at the 13th FC level for the last two years of the Plan.

3.38. As shown in Table 3.8, the CA being transferred to the States in the Twelfth Plan amounts to 1.26 per cent of GDP which is same as the Eleventh Plan. However, CA is not the only means of Plan transfer. Substantial plan transfers take place through the Centrally Sponsored Schemes (CSS) which have been greatly expanded in the Twelfth Plan. Accordingly, the States will receive larger transfer of total plan resources from the Centre.

3.39. Table 3.9 compares the structure of financing projected in the Twelfth Plan for the Centre and States, combined with that actually realised in the Eleventh Plan. The most notable feature is that the Twelfth Plan projections show relatively modest dependence on borrowings amounting to 45.96 per cent of the total Plan resources compared with 66.77 per cent in the Eleventh Plan realisation. The higher dependence on borrowings during the Eleventh Plan was the outcome of expansionary fiscal measures of the Centre to counter economic slowdown affected by global financial crisis and inevitable increase in expenditure. With sharp fall in revenue collection, the Centre had to mobilise more resources through borrowings. As against this, tighter fiscal discipline is envisaged both for Centre and States during the Twelfth Plan period. Assuming that the economy will return to a higher growth trajectory and with good revenue buoyancies, the revenue collection is projected to grow annually by about 17 per cent on average. This is reflected in the large improvement in BCR which is projected to increase from 3.71 per cent of the total public sector plan resources in the Eleventh Plan to 29.16 per cent of the total public sector plan resources for Centre and States taken together in the Twelfth Plan.

3.40. The financing plan outlined above will pose major challenges. As shown in Table 3.10, the total resources for the Central and State Plans taken together have to increase from an average of 10.96 per cent of GDP in the Eleventh Plan to an average of 11.80 per cent of GDP in the Twelfth Plan. The increase of 0.84 per cent of GDP in total resources for the Plan has to be achieved keeping borrowing within the stipulated limit and reducing the fiscal deficit of the Centre and States to 3 per cent on each account in the last year of the Twelfth Plan. Taking account of the resources mobilised by the public sector, the combined BCR of the Centre and the States has to increase by more than the projected increase in Plan resources.

TABLE 3.9
Overall Financing Pattern: Eleventh and Twelfth Plans

(₹ Crore at Current Prices)

	Sources of Funding	Eleventh Plan Realisation			Twelfth Plan Projection		
		Centre	States and UTs	Total	Centre	States and UTs	Total
1	Balance from Current Revenues	−2,42,390	3,81,536	1,39,146	13,87,371	9,59,979	23,47,350
		(−11.97)	(22.11)	(3.71)	(32.01)	(25.83)	(29.16)
2	Borrowings including net MCR	17,51,691	7,52,815	25,04,506	21,81,255	15,18,301	36,99,556
		(86.50)	(43.62)	(66.77)	(50.33)	(40.85)	(45.96)
3	Net Inflow from Abroad	80,043	0.00	80,043	–	–	–
		(3.95)		(2.13)			
4	Centre's GBS (1 + 2 + 3)	15,89,344	–	15,89,344	35,68,626	–	35,68,626
		(78.48)	–	(42.37)	(82.35)	–	(44.33)
5	Resources of PSEs/Local Bodies	8,57,244	1,70,039	10,27,283	16,22,899	3,80,319	20,03,218
		(42.33)	(9.85)	(27.39)	(37.45)	(10.23)	(24.88)
6	State's Own Resources (1 + 2 + 5)	–	13,04,390	13,04,390	–	28,58,599	28,58,599
		–	(75.58)	(34.77)	–	(76.92)	(35.51)
7	CA to States and UTs' Plan	−4,21,458	4,21,458	–	−8,57,786	8,57,786	–
		(−20.81)	(24.42)	–	(−19.79)	(23.08)	–
8	Resources of the Public Sector Plan (1 + 2 + 3 + 5 + 7)	20,25,130	17,25,848	37,50,978	43,33,739	37,16,385	80,50,123

Source: Planning Commission.
Note: Figures in parentheses are percentages of Resources of the Public Sector Plan.

TABLE 3.10
Plan Resources as Per Cent of GDP

S. No.	Item	Eleventh Plan	Twelfth Plan	Increase over Eleventh Plan
I	**Aggregate Plan Resources**			
	Centre	5.96	6.35	0.39
	States	5.00	5.45	0.45
	Centre and States	10.96	11.80	0.84
II	**Balance from Current Revenues**			
	Centre	−0.61	1.88	2.49
	States	1.02	1.41	0.39
	Centre and States	0.41	3.29	2.88

Source: Planning Commission.

3.41. The Centre's BCR, realised in the Eleventh Plan, averaged (−)0.61 per cent of GDP. It is projected to average 1.88 per cent of GDP in the Twelfth Plan, that is, an improvement of 2.49 percentage points of GDP. Similarly, the BCR of the States is also expected to improve from 1.02 per cent of GDP as realised in the Eleventh Plan to 1.41 per cent of GDP in the Twelfth Plan. As can be seen from Table 3.10, the projected improvement required in the combined BCR of the Centre and States taken together is, therefore, 2.88 percentage points of GDP. It must be emphasised that achievement of these BCR targets is a key element in the financing of the Plan.

3.42. Underlying the projected BCR is a projection that tax revenues (net to Centre) would grow from 7.60 per cent of GDP in 2012–13 to 8.79 per cent of GDP in 2016–17. NPRE is expected to decline from 8.53 per cent of GDP in 2012–13 to 7.09 per cent in 2016–17. Thus the projected improvement of 2.49 per cent of GDP in BCR of the Centre is expected to come slightly more from contraction in NPRE than growth in taxes.

3.43. The assumption of growth in tax revenues of the Centre and the States built into the projections is not unreasonable. Tax revenues recorded in the recent past has shown a lot of swings due to economic slowdown affected by the global financial crisis. The annual growth of gross tax revenue collection which dipped to 2–3 per cent in 2008–09 and 2009–10, returned to a healthy growth of 27 per cent in 2010–11 followed by 13.69 per cent in 2011–12 (RE). With the recovery of the economy and proposal to mobilise additional tax revenues, gross tax revenue is estimated to grow by about 19.5 per cent in 2012–13 (BE) over the previous year. Efforts will continue in the Twelfth Plan period towards achieving the targeted tax-to-GDP ratios. However, the BCR projections are equally dependent upon the ability to moderate the growth in NPRE and this aspect of the projections deserves focused attention.

3.44. There are several factors which could make it difficult to contain expenditures to the projected level. There is inevitable upward pressure of increasing expenditure on subsidies, particularly on fertiliser and petroleum due to increasing international crude oil prices, and also on food owing to proposed food security legislation. The subsidy regime needs to be urgently reformed to keep the total subsidy within the ceiling of 1.5 per cent of GDP in 2016–17 that the resources projections have built in.

Allocation of Public Sector Resources

3.45. The projection of the overall resources for the Twelfth Plan has been presented in the preceding section. This section focuses on the allocation of Public Sector Resources for the Twelfth Plan between the Centre and the States/UTs and the proposed sectoral distribution of the resources in keeping with the objective of achieving faster and more inclusive growth.

3.46. The projected assessment of resources of the public sector for the Twelfth Plan at ₹80,50,123 crore at current prices comprises of the Centre's share at ₹43,33,739 crore and the States/UTs share at ₹37,16,385 crore. The resources for the Central Plan includes the GBS component of ₹27,10,840 crore and the IEBR component of ₹16,22,899 crore at current prices. Resource allocation in the Central sector according to different Heads of Development is indicated in Annexure 3.1 and the Ministry/Department-wise details of budgetary support and IEBR are indicated in Annexure 3.2. Table 3.11 indicates the sources of funding public sector outlays for Centre and States for the Twelfth Plan.

3.47. The Twelfth Plan resources of the States and UTs are projected at ₹37,16,385 crore at current prices, out of which States' own resources are ₹28,58,599 crore and the CA to States and UTs is ₹8,57,786 crore at current prices. Head of Development-wise allocation for the States/UTs with States/UTs-wise core plan details are furnished in Annexure 3.3. These allocations would be finalised in consultation with the States.

3.48. A comparison of the distribution of the total GBS in the Eleventh and the Twelfth Plan has been shown in Table 3.12. In comparison to the Eleventh Plan realisation, there is an increase of 132.12 per cent in the projected GBS for the Centre for the Twelfth Plan. CA to State/UT Plans for State sector programmes is about 103.53 per cent higher than the grant component realised during the Eleventh Plan. The share of the projected grant component of the CA to States/UTs plan in the total GBS for Twelfth Plan has slightly decreased from the level realised in the Eleventh Plan (from 26.52 per cent to 24.04 per cent).

3.49. The projection of GBS allocation to different sectors, Ministries/Departments and the support to

TABLE 3.11
Public Sector Allocation for Twelfth Plan

(₹ Crore at Current Prices)

	Sources of Funding	Allocation
	Centre	
1	Budgetary Support	27,10,840
2	IEBR	16,22,899
3	Total Centre (1 + 2)	43,33,739
	States and UTs	
	Sources of Funding	Allocation
4	States' Own Resources	28,58,599
5	CA to State/UT Plan	8,57,786
6	Total States and UTs (4 + 5)	37,16,385
	Total Public Sector Outlay	
7	Grand Total (3 + 6)	80,50,123

Source: Planning Commission.

TABLE 3.12
GBS Allocation in Eleventh and Twelfth Plans

(₹ Crore at Current Prices)

Items	Eleventh Plan Realisation		Twelfth Plan Projections		
	Amount	% Share in Total GBS	Amount	% Share in Total GBS	% Increase over Eleventh Plan
Central Plan (Central Sector and Centrally Sponsored Schemes)	11,67,886	73.48	27,10,840	75.96	132.12
CA to State Plan	4,21,458	26.52	8,57,786	24.04	103.53
Total	**15,89,344**	**100.00**	**35,68,626**	**100.00**	**124.53**

Source: Planning Commission.

the State/UT Plan has been made in tune with the approach adopted for the Twelfth Plan for *'faster, sustainable and inclusive growth'*. The Twelfth Plan aims at putting the economy on a sustainable growth trajectory with a growth rate of 9.1 per cent by the end of the Plan period by targeting robust growth in agriculture at 4 per cent per year and by creating productive employment at a faster pace than before. The Twelfth Plan focuses on poverty reduction, ensuring access to basic physical infrastructure, health and education facilities to all while giving importance to bridging the regional/social/gender disparities and attending to the marginalised and the weaker social groups. Accordingly, a major structural shift across sectors has been proposed by allocating more resources to the priority areas identified for ensuring inclusiveness. A broad picture of the structural change in terms of sectoral allocation of Centre's budgetary resources (GBS including CA to State Plans for major sectoral programmes) in Twelfth Plan as compared to Eleventh Plan has been shown in the Table 3.13.

3.50. It may be noted that the biggest increase in allocation of Centre's GBS is for Health and Child Development, Urban Development and Education. The share of Health and Child Development in Centre's GBS goes up to 11.45 per cent as compared to 7.09 per cent in the Eleventh Plan. The share of Urban Development increases from

TABLE 3.13
Allocation of Centre's GBS by Major Sectors—Eleventh Plan Realisation and Twelfth Plan Projection

(₹ Crore in Current Prices)

S. No.	Major Sectors	Eleventh Plan Realisation	% Share	Twelfth Plan Projection	% Share	% Increase over Eleventh Plan
1	Agriculture and Water Resources	1,16,554	7.33	2,84,030	7.96	143.69
2	Rural Development and Panchayati Raj	3,97,524	25.01	6,73,034	18.86	69.31
3	Scientific Departments	58,690	3.69	1,42,167	3.98	142.23
4	Transport and Energy	2,04,076	12.84	4,48,736	12.57	119.89
5	Education	1,77,538	11.17	4,53,728	12.71	155.57
6	Health and Child Development	1,12,646	7.09	4,08,521	11.45	262.66
7	Urban Development	63,465	3.99	1,64,078	4.60	158.53
8	Others	4,58,849	28.87	9,94,333	27.86	116.70
	Total Plan Allocation	15,89,342	100.00	35,68,626	100.00	124.53

Source: Planning Commission.

3.99 per cent in the Eleventh Plan to 4.60 per cent in the Twelfth Plan. The share of Education goes up to 12.71 per cent in Twelfth Plan. The percentage increase in GBS for Scientific Departments, Agriculture and Water Resources is also substantial. The increase in budgetary support for Infrastructure in Transport and Energy Sectors is impressive considering that a large proportion of investments in these sectors would be made from the resources of CPSEs (IEBR) and through Public–Private Partnerships (PPPs). The resources for Rural Development Programmes in the areas of Housing, Employment and livelihood had been substantially increased during the Eleventh Plan as compared to the initial allocations. Even a moderate increase in resources for these programmes proposed in the Twelfth Plan over this high base means a substantial budgetary support for these programmes.

3.51. The Twelfth Plan proposes to provide ₹8,57,786 crore at current prices as CA to State/UT Plans. Table 3.14 indicates the details of sector-wise CA component of the resources of the States/UTs. Out of the total CA to States/UTs of ₹8,57,786 crore at current prices, 20.84 per cent (that is, ₹1,78,739 crore) has been earmarked for the Gadgil-Mukherjee Formula driven NCA. Special Plan Assistance (SPA) for Special Category States and Special Central Assistance (SCA) for the Border Areas Development Programme (BADP)/Hill Area Development Programme (HADP)/North East Council (NEC) accounts for 14.31 of the total CA. The remaining 64.85 per cent of CA to the States is assigned to Additional Central Assistance (ACA) for various flagship programmes and other schemes in accordance with the priority set for the Twelfth Plan, such as the AIBP, National Social Assistance Programme (NSAP), BRGF, RKVY and JNNURM including MP's Local Area Development Programme.

3.52. The overall plan outlay of all the States and UTs is projected to increase from ₹17,25,848 crore in the Eleventh Plan to ₹37,16,385 crore in the Twelfth Plan (both at current prices), an increase of 115.34 per cent on a comparable basis. The aggregate picture indicates that the States would be allocating more than proportionate increase to social services (41.68 per cent), transport (11.53 per cent) and agriculture and allied activities (6.85 per cent). The aggregate picture, it must be noted, conceals wide inter-State variations in terms of Plan sizes relative to GSDP, per capita plan expenditure and percentage sectoral outlays.

ISSUES IN PLAN FINANCING

3.53. Several conceptual issues that have a bearing on the structure of the Plan financing and public expenditure management were discussed in the Eleventh Plan document. These issues included

TABLE 3.14
Projected CA to States/UTs' Plan for Twelfth Plan

(₹ Crore at Current Prices)

Sectors	Programme	Allocation
State Development Plan	Normal CA	1,78,739
Special Category States	Special Plan Assistance	36,436
	Special CA (Untied to any project)	63,858
	Central Pool for North East and Sikkim	6,218
Agriculture	Rashtriya Krishi Vikas Yojana	63,246
SCA	Border Area Development Programme/Hill Area Development	10,122
	Programme/North Eastern Council	6,108
Irrigation	Accelerated Irrigation Benefit Programme	91,435
Urban/Local Area Development	Jawaharlal Nehru Urban Renewal Mission	1,01,917
	MPs' Local Area Development Programme	19,775
Balanced Regional Development	Backward Region Grant Fund	76,677
	Bodoland Territory Council	340
Elderly and Weaker Section	National Social Assistance Programme	48,642
Infrastructure	Roads and Bridges	12,410
Externally Aided Projects	Various EAPs	81,912
E-Governance	National e-Governance Action Plan	3,537
Tribal Development	Tribal Sub-Plan	7,787
	Grants-in-aid under Article 275 (1)	6,924
UT Plans		41,073
Total		**8,57,786**

the classification of expenditure into Plan and Non-Plan, Revenue and Capital, fund transfers of Centrally Sponsored Schemes (CSS) as Central Plan rather than as CA to State Plans, mode of fund transfer to States (consolidated fund versus societies route), monitoring of plan expenditure, scope of the Public Sector Plan and the problems posed by the FRBM framework to constrain grants for capital assets.

3.54. A High Level Expert Committee (HLEC) on Efficient Management of Public Expenditure was constituted by the Planning Commission under the Chairmanship of Dr. C. Rangarajan to look into various issues mentioned above and suggest measures for efficient management of public expenditure. The HLEC has made 25 recommendations across the 5 terms of reference.

3.55. The HLEC has recommended abolition of Plan and Non-Plan distinction in the Budget and a shift in the approach of public expenditure management to a more holistic view, from one year horizon to a multi-year horizon, and from input-based budgeting to the budgeting linked to outputs and outcomes. The HLEC has also outlined broad redefinition of roles of Ministry of Finance, Planning Commission, Administrative Ministries of the Central Government and State Governments. It has proposed a change in the annual budgeting process.

3.56. The HLEC has supported the proposal to introduce a new multidimensional budget and accounting classification for Union and State Governments in respect of functions, programmes and schemes. It has recommended extension of Central Plan Scheme Monitoring System (CPSMS) through interfaces with

State treasuries and Core Banking Solution (CBS) to enable real-time tracking of all Schemes for which resources are transferred to States and their agencies. These measures will enable a comprehensive view of the resources transferred to States and their agencies as well as utilisation across different Schemes.

3.57. The HLEC has recommended phase out of direct mode of transfer to autonomous societies/agencies so as to fully ensure treasury mode of transfer of Central Plan funds for better accountability. In the transition period, till the complete switch over to treasury mode, several measures have been recommended in respect of accounting, auditing and submission of utilisation reports by the societies/agencies.

3.58. The HLEC is in favour of continuing the Revenue-Capital categorisation. It recommends that all transfers should be treated as revenue expenditure in accounts, but there was a merit in excluding the grants for capital assets for the purpose of FRBM compliance. The Committee recommends that aggregate control for FRBM compliance may shift from the conventional Revenue Deficit to 'Adjusted Revenue Deficit' (revenue deficit adjusted to the extent of grants for capital assets). This should, however, be subject to rigid compliance to the definitional requirements of capital assets as well as maintenance of asset records/registers available in public domain.

3.59. As regards the scope of the Public Sector Plan, the HLEC has recommended inclusion of investment outlays funded by IEBR of PSEs. The scope of Public Sector Plan, according to the Committee, should also include the resources of local bodies. As regards the PPP projects, the Committee recommends that only the annuity commitments or Viability Gap Funding (VGF) should be a part of the Plan, but there should be a separate supplement to the Central/State budgets providing comprehensive information on PPPs.

3.60. Some recommendations of the HLEC have been accepted. The ongoing CPSMS would be expanded to facilitate better tracking and utilisation of funds. The amendments have been made in the FRBM Act of the Centre to give statutory recognition to the concept of 'Effective Revenue Deficit' and to introduce medium-term expenditure framework statement along with the other three statements envisaged under the FRBMA. This would help Ministries/Departments to reallocate resources on priority schemes and weed out those which have outlived their utility. The Committee constituted to review the list of the Heads of Accounts of Union and States has submitted its Report. The recommendation on transfer of Plan resources to States only through the Consolidated Fund (Treasury) route will be implemented along with other recommendations to improve accountability of resources. The recommendation of the HLEC relating to abolition of Plan and Non-Plan classification is under consideration to determine its feasibility, especially in so far as it relates to interaction with the States.

FINANCING INFRASTRUCTURE: THE SHIFT TO PPP

3.61. It is widely recognised that adequate investment in the development of infrastructure is a prerequisite for higher growth. In this context, steps have been taken by the government to create an enabling environment to promote investment in infrastructure.

ACHIEVEMENTS OF THE ELEVENTH PLAN

3.62. To meet the infrastructure deficit at the beginning of the Eleventh Plan, an increase in investment in physical infrastructure was envisaged from about 5 per cent of GDP witnessed during the Tenth Plan to about 9 per cent of GDP by 2011–12 (terminal year of the Eleventh Plan). This was estimated to require an investment of ₹20,56,150 crore during the Eleventh Plan as compared to an estimated investment of ₹9,16,176 crore during the Tenth Plan. Further, the contribution of the private sector in infrastructure investment was expected to rise from about 22 per cent in the Tenth Plan to about 30 per cent in the Eleventh Plan.

Sector-Wise Investments

3.63. On the basis of the figures of actual investment for the first four years of the Eleventh Plan and provisional figures for the fifth year, it is expected that the total investment in infrastructure during the Eleventh Plan would be ₹19,35,058 crore (as against projected investment of ₹20,56,150 crore) at 2006–07 prices. The contribution of the private sector would be about 36 per cent compared to 30 per cent originally projected for the Eleventh Plan which is much higher than 22.04 per cent realised in the Tenth Plan. The details of investment over the Tenth Plan and Eleventh Plan periods are shown in Table 3.15. The investment realised during the Eleventh Plan period has been about 94 per cent of the original projections, with the public sector under-performing at 86 per cent of the target and the private sector over-performing to reach 113 per cent. The achievement was not uniform across all sectors. While Telecommunication, Oil and Gas Pipelines, Roads and Bridges sectors exceeded their investment targets, investment in Ports, Railways, Water Supply and Sanitation and Storage was much below expectations. The share of private investment in different sectors over the Eleventh Plan period is given in Figure 3.2.

TABLE 3.15
Sector-Wise Investments: Tenth Plan and Eleventh Plan

(₹ Crore at 2006–07 Prices)

Sectors	Tenth Plan	Total Eleventh Plan			
	Actual	Original Projections	Anticipated	% Increase of Eleventh Plan Anticipated over Tenth Plan Actuals	Anticipated % of Original Projections
Electricity (incl. RE)	2,74,661	6,66,525	6,45,835	135.14	96.90
Centre	1,03,431	2,55,316	1,93,619	87.20	75.84
States	1,02,054	2,25,697	1,48,819	45.94	65.94
Private	69,176	1,85,512	3,03,396	338.59	163.55
Roads and Bridges	1,52,616	3,14,152	3,61,822	137.08	115.17
Centre	71,536	1,07,359	1,55,367	117.19	144.72
States	68,143	1,00,000	1,34,246	97.01	134.25
Private	12,937	1,06,792	72,209	458.14	67.62
Telecommunications	1,44,669	2,58,439	3,09,271	113.78	119.97
Centre	50,626	80,753	68,628	35.56	84.99
Private	94,042	1,77,686	2,40,643	155.89	135.43
Railways (incl. MRTS)	1,03,493	2,61,808	1,95,340	88.75	74.61
Centre	1,00,077	2,01,453	1,72,113	71.98	85.44
States	2,743	10,000	11,727	327.44	117.27
Private	672	50,354	11,501	1,610.14	22.84
Irrigation (incl. WS)	1,21,475	2,53,301	1,95,688	61.09	77.26
Centre	9,661	24,759	11,629	20.37	46.97
States	1,11,814	2,28,543	1,84,059	64.61	80.54
Water Supply and SN	60,577	1,43,730	97,351	60.71	67.73
Centre	21,508	42,003	37,243	73.16	88.67
States	37,958	96,306	59,989	58.04	62.29
Private	1,111	5,421	119	−89.33	2.20
Ports (incl. ILW)	22,351	87,995	35,536	58.99	40.38
Centre	2,630	29,889	4,398	67.24	14.71
States	916	3,627	2,216	141.95	61.10
Private	18,805	54,479	28,922	53.80	53.09

(Contd)

(Table 3.15 Contd)

Sectors	Tenth Plan	Total Eleventh Plan			
	Actual	Original Projections	Anticipated	% Increase of Eleventh Plan Anticipated over Tenth Plan Actuals	Anticipated % of Original Projections
Airports	7,354	30,968	29,282	298.20	94.56
Centre	3,855	9,288	9,708	151.85	104.52
States	717	50	929	29.64	1,858.00
Private	2,782	21,630	18,644	570.20	86.20
Storage	5,591	22,378	14,203	154.03	63.47
Centre	3,065	4,476	4,709	53.64	105.21
States	124	6,713	1,669	1,250.17	24.86
Private	2,402	11,189	7,825	225.72	69.93
Oil and Gas pipelines	23,389	16,855	50,730	116.90	300.98
Centre	21,088	10,327	27,818	31.91	269.37
States	2,279	–	3,335	46.35	–
Private	23	6,528	19,578	85,737.54	299.91
Grand Total	**9,16,176**	**20,56,150**	**19,35,058**	**111.21**	**94.11**
Centre	3,87,477	7,65,622	6,85,234	76.84	89.50
States	3,26,748	6,70,937	5,46,989	67.40	81.53
Private	2,01,951	6,19,591	7,02,836	248.02	113.43
Grand Total	**9,16,176**	**20,56,150**	**19,35,058**	**111.21**	**94.11**
Public	7,14,225	14,36,559	12,32,222	72.53	85.78
Private	2,01,951	6,19,591	7,02,836	248.02	113.43
GDPmp	1,82,46,267	2,70,44,506	2,69,34,373	–	–
Investment as % of GDP con. mp	**5.02**	**7.60**	**7.18**	–	–

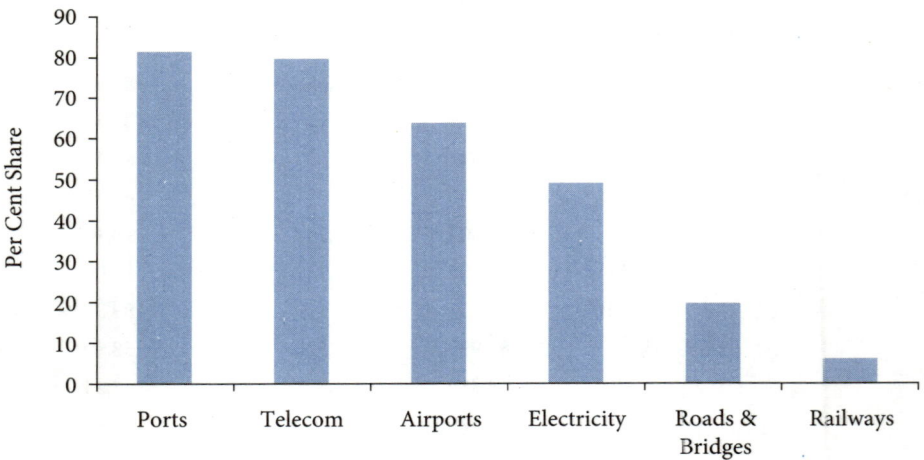

FIGURE 3.2: Private Sector Investment in Infrastructure (Per Cent Share)

Infrastructure Investment and GDP

3.64. Table 3.16 depicts the share of infrastructure as a percentage of GDP. This has increased from 5.04 per cent in the Tenth Plan to about 7.21 per cent of GDP in the Eleventh Plan. It can also be seen that the share of private sector as percentage of GDP has gone up from 1.12 per cent to 2.64 per cent during the same period.

3.65. Starting from a base of 5.61 per cent of GDP in 2006–07, infrastructure investment reached an all-time high of 8.41 per cent of GDP in 2010–11, part of which was contributed by telecom operators investing in the auction of 3G spectrum. The percentage dipped to 6.90 per cent of GDP in the terminal year of the Eleventh Plan period primarily due to slowdown in the Telecommunication sector. The Eleventh Plan as a whole is likely to see an increase of about 2.17 per cent of GDP in infrastructure investment as compared to the Tenth Plan. About 70 per cent of this increase is because of higher private participation. The relative share of public and private investment as percentage of GDP is given in Figure 3.3.

STRATEGY FOR THE TWELFTH PLAN

3.66. The strategy for the Twelfth Plan encourages private sector participation directly as well as through various forms of PPPs, wherever desirable

TABLE 3.16
Investment during the Eleventh Plan as Percentage of GDP

(₹ Crore at Current Prices)

Years	Tenth Plan (Actual)	Base Year of Eleventh Plan (2006–07) (Actual)	2007–08 (Actual)	2008–09 (Actual)	2009–10 (Actual)	2010–11 (Actual)	2011–12 (RE)	Total Eleventh Plan
GDPmp	1,65,98,847	42,94,706	49,87,090	56,30,063	64,57,352	76,74,148	88,55,797	3,36,04,450
Public Investment	6,51,136	1,79,415	2,16,178	2,73,796	2,96,924	3,59,185	3,90,689	15,36,773
Private Investment	1,86,023	61,621	96,177	1,40,568	1,44,665	2,85,990	2,20,104	8,87,504
Total Investment	8,37,159	2,41,116	3,12,355	4,14,364	4,41,590	6,45,175	6,10,793	24,24,277
Investment as Per Cent of GDP								
Public Investment	3.92	4.18	4.33	4.86	4.60	4.68	4.41	4.57
Private Investment	1.12	1.43	1.93	2.50	2.24	3.73	2.49	2.64
Total Investment	5.04	5.61	6.26	7.36	6.84	8.41	6.90	7.21

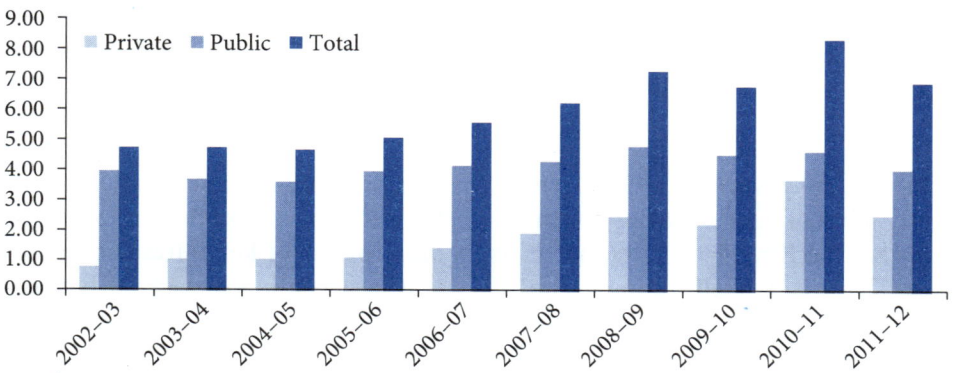

FIGURE 3.3: Investment in Infrastructure as a Per Cent of GDP

and feasible. The share of private sector in infrastructure investment will have to rise substantially from about 36.61 per cent anticipated in the Eleventh Plan to about 48 per cent in the Twelfth Plan. It is expected that competition and private investment will not only expand capacity, but also improve the quality of service, besides minimising cost and time overruns in implementation of infrastructure projects. The year and Sector-wise projections for the Twelfth Plan are given in Table 3.17.

3.67. The Central share in the overall infrastructure investment is likely to decline from 35.34 per cent in the Eleventh Plan to 28.72 per cent in the Twelfth Plan, and the States' share is likely to decline to 23.13 per cent compared to 28.05 per cent in the Eleventh Plan. The share of the private sector is expected to increase from 36.61 per cent in the Eleventh Plan to 48.14 per cent in the Twelfth Plan.

Financing Infrastructure Investment in the Twelfth Plan

3.68. The total public sector investment in infrastructure envisaged in the Twelfth Plan is ₹16,01,061 crore by the Centre and ₹12,89,762 crore by the States. Investment by the private sector, which includes PPP projects, makes up the balance of ₹26,83,840 crore, which is 48.14 per cent of the required investment during the Twelfth Plan, a much higher share than the anticipated 36.61 per cent during the Eleventh Plan. Of the projected investment of ₹16,01,061 crore by the Central Government, ₹9,47,083 crore is likely to be funded out of IEBR. In the case of States, ₹7,30,569 crore is expected from budgetary resources, while about ₹5,59,194 crore is expected from their IEBR, as per details in Table 3.18. This would require a much higher scale of effort by the public sector undertakings, especially for raising debt on commercial terms.

3.69. The total requirement of debt by the public and private sectors is likely to be ₹27,75,641 crore. However, the availability of debt financing for infrastructure during the Twelfth Plan is estimated at ₹22,65,171 crore. There is a likely funding gap of about ₹5,00,000 crore for the debt component, the details of which are given in Table 3.19. Measures would have to be taken for addressing this gap.

3.70. The projected investment in infrastructure over the Twelfth Plan would be possible only if there is a substantial expansion in internal generation and extra-budgetary resources of the public sector, in addition to a significant rise in private investment. The scale of private investment would require a significant reinforcement of the enabling policy and regulatory environment.

Institutional Framework for PPP

Cabinet Committee on Infrastructure

3.71. The approach to PPPs must remain firmly grounded in principles which ensure that PPPs are formulated and executed in public interest with a view to achieving additional capacity and delivery of quality public services at reasonable costs. These partnerships must ensure investment for supplementing scarce public resources while improving efficiencies. The government's current initiatives in the area of PPPs are designed to achieve these objectives.

3.72. The following steps have been taken to promote private investment in infrastructure sector:

1. Setting up robust institutional structure for appraising and approving PPP projects
2. Developing standardised documents such as model concession agreements across infrastructure sectors
3. Increasing availability of finance by creating dedicated institutions and providing viability gap funding

3.73. The Committee on Infrastructure (CoI) was constituted in August 2004 under the Chairmanship of the Prime Minister, with the objectives of initiating policies that would ensure time-bound creation of world class infrastructure, delivering services matching international standards, developing structures that maximise the role of PPPs and monitoring the progress of key infrastructure projects to ensure that targets are achieved. In July 2009, the CoI was replaced by a Cabinet Committee on Infrastructure (CCI) under the Chairmanship of the Prime Minister. CCI reviews and approves policies and projects across

TABLE 3.17
Projected Investment in Infrastructure—Twelfth Plan

(₹ Crore at Current Prices)

Sectors	Total Eleventh Plan	Twelfth Plan Projections					
		2012–13	2013–14	2014–15	2015–16	2016–17	Total Twelfth Plan
Electricity	7,28,494	2,28,405	2,59,273	2,94,274	3,33,470	3,86,244	15,01,666
Centre	2,33,501	69,059	77,650	87,228	97,616	1,09,242	4,40,796[1]
States	1,84,696	56,338	62,337	68,909	75,888	83,572	3,47,043
Private	3,10,297	1,03,008	1,19,286	1,38,137	1,59,966	1,93,429	7,13,827
Renewable Energy	89,220	31,199	42,590	58,125	79,075	1,07,637	3,18,626
Centre	9,630	3,631	4,739	6,179	8,027	10,427	33,003
States	1,018	744	886	1,056	1,253	1,487	5,425
Private	78,572	26,825	36,965	50,890	69,795	95,724	2,80,198
Roads and Bridges	4,53,121	1,50,466	1,64,490	1,80,415	1,98,166	2,21,000	9,14,536
Centre[2]	1,94,678	61,920	64,567	67,272	69,833	72,502	3,36,094
States	1,65,903	47,844	51,222	54,786	58,377	62,204	2,74,433
Private	92,540	40,702	48,702	58,357	69,955	86,294	3,04,010
Telecommunications[3]	3,84,962	1,05,949	1,36,090	1,76,489	2,30,557	2,94,814	9,43,899
Centre	86,375	15,203	14,827	14,446	14,023	13,611	72,110
Private	2,98,586	90,746	1,21,263	1,62,042	2,16,535	2,81,203	8,71,789
Railways	2,01,237	64,713	78,570	96,884	1,21,699	1,57,355	5,19,221
Centre	1,92,147	59,988	70,202	82,078	95,601	1,11,351	4,19,221
Private	9,090	4,725	8,368	14,806	26,098	46,003	1,00,000
MRTS	41,669	13,555	17,148	22,298	29,836	41,322	1,24,158
Centre	21,469	5,889	6,784	7,808	8,953	10,266	39,700
States	14,786	4,732	5,451	6,274	7,194	8,249	31,901
Private	5,414	2,934	4,912	8,215	13,688	22,806	52,557
Irrigation (incl. Watershed)	2,43,497	77,113	87,386	99,178	1,12,506	1,28,186	5,04,371
Centre	14,426	4,679	5,952	7,713	10,161	13,666	42,171
States	2,29,071	72,434	81,434	91,466	1,02,346	1,14,520	4,62,200
Water Supply and Sanitation	1,20,774	36,569	42,605	49,728	58,084	68,333	2,55,319
Centre[4]	46,003	13,999	16,423	19,248	22,473	26,240	98,382
States[5]	74,607	22,335	25,732	29,617	33,959	38,939	1,50,582
Private	164	235	451	864	1,651	3,154	6,355
Ports (+ILW)	44,536	18,661	25,537	35,260	49,066	69,256	1,97,781
Centre	5,480	2,888	3,415	4,034	4,747	5,586	20,670
States	2,759	794	930	1,089	1,269	1,480	5,563
Private	36,298	14,979	21,192	30,138	43,050	62,189	1,71,548
Airports	36,311	7,691	10,716	15,233	21,959	32,116	87,714
Centre	11,873	2,456	2,710	2,988	3,282	3,605	15,041
States	1,030	268	351	458	596	776	2,449
Private	23,408	4,967	7,655	11,787	18,081	27,735	70,224

(Contd)

(Table 3.17 Contd)

Sectors	Total Eleventh Plan	Twelfth Plan Projections					Total Twelfth Plan
		2012–13	2013–14	2014–15	2015–16	2016–17	
Oil and Gas pipelines	62,534	12,211	16,604	23,833	36,440	59,845	1,48,933
Centre	35,179	9,335	11,367	13,827	16,757	20,308	71,594
States	4,070	832	985	1,164	1,372	1,616	5,969
Private	23,284	2,044	4,253	8,842	18,311	37,921	71,370
Storage	17,921	4,480	6,444	9,599	14,716	23,202	58,441
Centre	5,956	1,711	2,026	2,396	2,823	3,326	12,280
States	2,116	623	717	826	947	1,085	4,198
Private	9,850	2,146	3,701	6,377	10,947	18,791	41,963
Grand Total	24,24,277	7,51,012	8,87,454	10,61,316	12,85,573	15,89,308	55,74,663
Centre	8,56,717	2,50,758	2,80,662	3,15,217	3,54,296	4,00,129	16,01,061
States	6,80,056	2,06,944	2,30,045	2,55,645	2,83,201	3,13,928	12,89,762
Private	8,87,504	2,93,310	3,76,747	4,90,455	6,48,077	8,75,251	26,83,840
Grand Total	24,24,277	7,51,012	8,87,454	10,61,316	12,85,573	15,89,308	55,74,663
Public	15,36,773	4,57,702	5,10,707	5,70,862	6,37,497	7,14,057	28,90,823
Private	8,87,504	2,93,310	3,76,747	4,90,455	6,48,077	8,75,251	26,83,840
GDPmp	3,36,04,450	1,01,50,618	1,16,45,987	1,33,58,028	1,53,47,089	1,76,61,485	6,81,63,208
Investment as % of GDPmp	7.21	7.40	7.62	7.95	8.38	9.00	8.18

1. Excludes projections for DAE (Power) and NLC (Power) but these are included in the Eleventh Plan.
2. Includes PMGSY.
3. Includes spectrum auction charges.
4. Includes projections for Integrated Low Cost Sanitation (ILCS) Scheme.
5. Includes JnNURM.

TABLE 3.18
Source-Wise Projected Investment

(₹ Crore at Current Prices)

	2012–13	2013–14	2014–15	2015–16	2016–17	Total Twelfth Plan
Centre	2,50,758	2,80,662	3,15,217	3,54,296	4,00,129	16,01,061
Central budget	1,07,664	1,17,805	1,29,245	1,42,220	1,57,044	6,53,978
Internal generation	68,200	75,519	83,919	93,145	1,03,931	4,24,713
Borrowings	74,894	87,338	1,02,052	1,18,931	1,39,154	5,22,370
States	2,06,944	2,30,045	2,55,645	2,83,201	3,13,928	12,89,762
States budget	1,27,290	1,36,027	1,45,413	1,55,499	1,66,340	7,30,569
Internal generation	23,429	27,652	32,422	37,560	43,409	1,64,472
Borrowings	56,225	66,365	77,810	90,142	1,04,179	3,94,722
Private	2,93,310	3,76,747	4,90,455	6,48,077	8,75,251	26,83,840
Internal accruals/Equity	87,992	1,13,024	1,52,042	2,00,904	2,71,328	8,25,291
Borrowings	2,05,318	2,63,723	3,38,413	4,47,172	6,03,923	18,58,549
Total projected investment	7,51,012	8,87,454	10,61,316	12,85,573	15,89,308	55,74,663
Non-debt	4,14,575	4,70,027	5,43,041	6,29,328	7,42,052	27,99,022
Debt	3,36,437	4,17,426	5,18,275	6,56,246	8,47,256	27,75,641

TABLE 3.19
Likely Sources of Debt

(₹ Crore at Current Prices)

	2012–13	2013–14	2014–15	2015–16	2016–17	Total Twelfth Plan
Domestic Bank Credit	1,19,066	1,62,663	2,16,015	2,85,513	3,81,389	11,64,646
NBFCs	56,973	81,027	1,12,014	1;54,124	2,14,325	6,18,462
Pension/Insurance funds	21,681	25,694	29,602	33,941	39,331	1,50,248
ECBs	46,799	56,020	65,182	75,484	88,349	3,31,834
Likely Total Debt Resources	2,44,519	3,25,231	4,22,590	5,49,007	7,23,823	22,65,171
Estimated Requirement of Debt	3,36,437	4,17,426	5,18,275	6,56,246	8,47,256	27,75,641
Gap between Estimates and Likely Requirement	91,918	92,195	95,685	1,07,239	1,23,433	5,10,470

infrastructure sectors. It considers and decides on financial, institutional and legal measures required to enhance investment in infrastructure sectors.

PPP Appraisal Committee and Empowered Institution

3.74. A Public–Private Partnership Appraisal Committee (PPPAC) consisting of the Secretary, Department of Economic Affairs, as Chairman, and Secretaries of the Planning Commission, Department of Expenditure, Department of Legal Affairs and the Administrative Department concerned, as Members was constituted for speedy approval of PPP projects. The project proposals are appraised by the Planning Commission and approved by the PPPAC. The Empowered Institution (EI) approves projects for providing Viability Gap Funding to the infrastructure projects at the State level.

Regulatory Framework

3.75. In recent years, independent regulatory authorities have been established in the power, telecom, and civil aviation sectors. Tariffs in the port sector are also fixed by an independent authority. These authorities discharge numerous responsibilities, which were earlier in the domain of the government. For initiating further improvements in the regulatory structures and practices, Regulatory Reforms Bill is under consideration of the Government.

Advisory Services

3.76. PPP projects are based on long-term contracts and may involve delegation of governmental authority such as for toll collection, besides enabling private control over monopolistic services. Implementation of PPP projects, therefore, requires appropriate advisory services in terms of preparation of project agreements, structuring of projects and so on. Planning Commission has operationalised a scheme for technical assistance to project authorities by providing consultants for projects. The Ministry of Finance has also created an India Infrastructure Project Development Fund (IIPDF) to provide loans for meeting development expenses, including the cost of engaging consultants for PPP projects.

Viability Gap Funding

3.77. The VGF Scheme was notified in 2006 to enhance the financial viability of competitively bid infrastructure projects, which are justified by economic returns, but do not pass the standard thresholds of financial returns. Under the scheme, grant assistance of up to 20 per cent of capital costs is provided by the Central Government to PPP projects undertaken by any Central Ministry, State Government, statutory entity or local body, thus leveraging budgetary resources to access a larger pool of private capital. An additional grant of up to 20 per cent of project costs can be provided by the sponsoring Ministry, State Government or project authority.

India Infrastructure Finance Company Limited (IIFCL)

3.78. IIFCL was incorporated by the Ministry of Finance in consultation with the Planning

> **Box 3.1**
> **Infrastructure Debt Fund**
>
> Infrastructure projects are capital intensive and have long payback periods, and, therefore, require long-term funds at comparatively low costs. Infrastructure projects in India are financed mainly by commercial banks, as insurance and pension funds do not normally lend for new projects. The present bond market lacks depth to address the needs for a long-term debt. With a view to overcoming these shortcomings, Infrastructure Development Funds (IDFs) are being set up for channelising long-term debt from domestic and foreign pension and insurance funds, as well as from other sources. These IDFs will also carry adequate credit enhancement in terms of implicit government guarantees for repayment of debt. The Reserve Bank of India, and the Securities and Exchange Board of India have already laid down regulatory framework for the IDFs.
>
> Besides augmenting debt resources for financing infrastructure, the IDFs would refinance PPP projects after their construction is completed and operations have stabilised. By refinancing bank loans of existing projects, the IDFs are expected to take over a significant volume of the existing bank debt, and this will release an equivalent volume of fresh lending for infrastructure projects.

Commission in 2006 for providing long-term loans for financing infrastructure projects that typically involve long gestation periods. IIFCL provides financial assistance up to 20 per cent of the project cost both through direct lending to project companies, and by refinancing banks and financial institutions. IIFCL raises funds from both domestic and overseas markets on the strength of government guarantees. IIFCL has sanctioned loans aggregating ₹40,373 crore for 229 projects involving a total investment of ₹3,52,047 crore and disbursed ₹20,377 crore till 31 March 2012.

3.79. IIFCL is expected to graduate in the Twelfth Plan from the existing role of a normal lender to that of a catalyst mobilising additional resources for financing of infrastructure. This could be achieved by IIFCL providing guarantees for bonds issued by private infrastructure companies rather than expanding its direct lending operations. This would enable mobilisation of insurance and pension funds, external debt and household savings. IIFCL would also make subordinated debt available as an additional source of finance. Further, IIFCL may also substitute its take-out financing scheme with an Infrastructure Debt Fund. Please refer to Box 3.1.

High Level Committee on Financing Infrastructure

3.80. In order to review the existing framework for financing of infrastructure and to make recommendations in this regard, a High Level Committee on Financing Infrastructure has been constituted. The Committee is expected to give its report by 31 March 2013.

Standardised Documents and Processes

3.81. The government has decided to formulate standard documents for bidding and award of PPP concessions. Adoption of a standardised framework ensures transparency in the allocation of risks, costs and obligations while minimising the potential for disputes and malfeasance.

3.82. The Model Concession Agreements (MCAs) published by the Secretariat for PPP and Infrastructure at the Planning Commission for various sectors are listed in Box 3.2. MCAs for PPPs in electricity distribution, power generation, modern storage facilities, hospitals, school education, drip

> **Box 3.2**
> **Model Concession Agreements for PPP**
>
> - National Highways
> - State Highways
> - Operation and Maintenance of Highways
> - National Highways (six laning)
> - Operation of Container Trains
> - Re-development of Railway Stations
> - Procurement-cum-Maintenance Agreement for Locomotives
> - Non-metro Airports
> - Greenfield Airports
> - Port Terminals
> - Transmission of Electricity
> - Urban Metro Rail

irrigation and Industrial Training Institutes are under preparation.

3.83. Standardised guidelines and model documents that incorporate key principles relating to the bid process for PPP projects have also been developed. These are indicated in Box 3.3.

> **Box 3.3**
> **Model Bidding Documents for PPP Projects**
>
> - Model Request for Qualification (RFQ) Document for PPP projects
> - Model Request for Proposal (RFP) Document for PPP projects
> - Model RFP Document for Selection of Technical Consultants
> - Model RFP Document for Selection of Legal Advisers
> - Model RFP Document for Selection of Financial Consultants and Transaction Advisers
> - Model RFP Document for Selection of Transmission Consultants

3.84. The government has identified several areas for reform of policies and processes. A number of Guidelines and Manuals have been issued in pursuance of the initiatives described above. These are listed in Box 3.4.

3.85. The government has recently issued Guidelines for Monitoring of PPP Projects. These Guidelines seek to establish a two-tier institutional mechanism for monitoring of PPP projects that would ensure compliance of the contractual framework contained in the concession agreements with a view to safeguarding the interests of the public exchequer and the users. The Central Ministries are expected to submit quarterly reports relating to defaults on the part of the concessionaires and the project authorities which would be placed before the Cabinet Committee on Infrastructure for review.

Engineering, Procurement, Construction (EPC) Contract

3.86. The conventional item-rate contracts are generally prone to time and cost overruns, particularly in the national highway sector, resulting in enhanced cost to the exchequer, as also considerable delays in the completion of projects. Developed countries have moved to Engineering, Procurement and Construction (EPC) contracts where the contractor is responsible for design and construction on a turnkey basis and for a fixed price. The Planning Commission has published a model EPC contract for Highways. It is expected that about 20,000 km of two-lane National Highways would be developed under this model. A similar document is also being prepared for Dedicated Freight Corridor of the Indian Railways.

PPPs in Infrastructure

3.87. Private investment in infrastructure is being encouraged in an environment which ensures competition and transparency. Protection of public interest is being ensured by institutionalising the necessary frameworks and processes for due diligence, checks and balances. However, it is recognised that unless governance issues, such as those related to competition in service provision, collection of user charges, institutional capacity, regulation, and dispute resolution continue to be adequately addressed, mobilisation of sufficient resources for the requisite infrastructure investment may not be possible.

> **Box 3.4**
> **Guidelines and Manuals**
>
> - Guidelines for Financial Support to PPPs in Infrastructure (VGF Scheme)
> - Guidelines on Formulation, Appraisal and Approval of PPP Projects (PPPAC)
> - Guidelines for Establishing Joint Ventures in Infrastructure
> - Guidelines for Monitoring of PPP Projects
> - Scheme for Financing Infrastructure Projects through the IIFCL
> - Manual of Specifications and Standards for Two-laning of Highways
> - Manual of Specifications and Standards for Four-laning of Highways

3.88. Till 31 March 2012, the PPPAC had approved 285 PPP projects involving an investment of ₹2,47,300 crore. The Empowered Institution has approved 105 projects involving an investment of ₹57,710 crore (for global ranking in PPP, refer to Box 3.5).

> **Box 3.5**
> **Global Ranking in PPP**
>
> According to a World Bank Report on Private Participation in Infrastructure, private participation in the first semester of 2011 was highly concentrated in just one country, India. The Report further states that India has been the top recipient of PPI activity since 2006 and has implemented 43 new projects which attracted total investment of US$20.7 billion in 2011. India alone accounted for almost half of the investment in new PPI projects in developing countries implemented in the first semester of 2011. The Report maintained that India remained the largest market for PPI in the developing world. In the South Asian region, India attracted 98 per cent of regional investment and implemented 43 of the 44 new projects in the region.

PPP in Highways

3.89. The National Highway network of the country spans about 70,548 km. The National Highway Development Project (NHDP), covering a length of about 54,000 km of highways, is India's largest road development programme in its history. The government has encouraged increased private sector participation in upgrading the arterial road network of the country to world class standards. More than 60 per cent of the estimated investment requirement is expected to be financed through PPP. With several key projects on the anvil spanning a length of about 45,000 km (including six-laning of four-laned roads, expressways and port connectivity projects) and a large number of projects in States, there are increasing opportunities for the domestic and foreign players in the sector. The government has decided to widen 20,000 km of less than two-lane National Highways to two-lane standard in the EPC mode.

PPP in Civil Aviation

3.90. During the Eleventh Plan, the private sector played a major role in the development of metro airports through PPP. The development of greenfield international airports at Hyderabad and Bengaluru along with the redevelopment of the Delhi International airport was successfully completed during this period. The redevelopment of Mumbai International airport, which was also taken up through PPP, is at an advanced stage of completion. Investment by the private sector on the four metro airports during the Eleventh Plan period was ₹23,187 crore. Further, it was observed that introduction of PPP has led to a significant rise in the collection of revenues, especially non-aviation revenues.

3.91. Airports Authority of India has identified 15 operational Airports for taking up operation and maintenance of both terminal and air side through PPP. This would be taken up in two phases. In the first phase, nine airports, namely Guwahati, Jaipur, Ahmedabad, Bhubhaneshwar, Lucknow, Gaya, Udaipur, Khajuraho and Amritsar would be taken up; and in the second phase, six airports would be taken up for operation and maintenance through PPP. Kolkata and Chennai airports have been constructed by AAI with an investment of about ₹4,200 crore. PPP in management and operation of airports is not only preferable for reasons of efficiency and superior services but also important for keeping passenger charges low, because of the ability of private entities to raise non-aviation revenues that cross-subsidise airport charges. This proposition is borne out by the international experience and the experience of PPP metro airports in India. It is, therefore, recommended that these large airports should be awarded under the PPP mode for their management and operation.

3.92. Five green field airports including Navi Mumbai, Goa, Kannur, Chandigarh and Kota have been identified for development through PPP. For building and operating a Greenfield airport on PPP basis, a precise policy and regulatory framework has now been spelt out in the Model Concession Agreement for Greenfield Airports.

PPP in Urban Infrastructure

3.93. Private sector participation needs to be encouraged in urban infrastructure sectors like water supply and sewerage and solid waste management. In urban transport, private sector can provide more efficient transport services, construct and maintain modern bus terminals with commercial complexes, over bridges, city roads and so on. PPP initiatives are also being undertaken to develop metro rail systems in Indian cities (refer to Box 3.6 for details on Hyderabad Metro Rail Project).

Box 3.6
Hyderabad Metro Rail Project

Hyderabad Metro Rail Project is presently under construction on PPP mode with a total project cost of ₹12,132 crore. The project is spread over three high density traffic corridors of Hyderabad with total length of 71 km and is being developed on Design, Build, Finance, Operate and Transfer (DBFOT) mode. The project was awarded to the successful bidder for a VGF of ₹1,458 crore which will be provided by the Central Government while the remaining investment will be made by the concessionaire. This will be the single largest private investment in a PPP project in India. It is also one of the largest metro rail projects built and operated by a private entity anywhere in the world. The project demonstrates how large volumes of private capital can be deployed in public projects in a transparent, efficient and competitive manner. The concession has been awarded on the basis of the Model Concession Agreement for Urban Transit developed by the Planning Commission.

PPP in Ports

3.94. The government has encouraged private sector participation in port development and operations. Foreign direct investment up to 100 per cent is permitted under the automatic route for port development projects. Private investment has been envisaged on PPP basis in ports of Kolkata, Haldia, Paradip, Vizag, Ennore, Chennai, Tuticorin, Cochin, New Mangalore, Mormugao, Mumbai, JNPT and Kandla.

PPP in Power

3.95. To attract private sector participation, government has permitted the private sector to set up coal, gas or liquid-based thermal, hydel, wind or solar projects with foreign equity participation up to 100 per cent under the automatic route. The government has also launched Ultra Mega Power Projects (UMPPs) with an initial capacity of 4,000 MW to attract ₹160–200 billion of private investment. Out of the total nine UMPPs, four UMPPs at Mundra (Gujarat), Sasan (Madhya Pradesh), Krishnapatnam (Andhra Pradesh) and Tilaiya Dam (Jharkhand) have already been awarded. The remaining five UMPPs, namely in Sundergarh District (Orissa), Cheyyur (Tamil Nadu), Girye (Maharashtra), Tadri (Karnataka) and Akaltara (Chattisgarh) are yet to be awarded. To create Transmission Super Highways, the government has allowed private sector participation in the transmission sector. A PPP project at Jhajjar in Haryana for transmission of electricity was awarded under the PPP mode. Further, to enable private participation in distribution of electricity, especially by way of PPP, a model framework is being developed by the Planning Commission.

PPP in Railways

3.96. Dedicated Freight Corridor Corporation of India Limited (DFCCIL) has been set up for implementing the Dedicated Freight project and the Ministry of Railways would explore the possibilities of attracting private investment in some segments of this project. Indian Railways has decided to redevelop 50 railway stations in the metropolitan cities and major tourist centers like Delhi, Jaipur, Chandigarh, Patna, Bypanahalli, Bhubneshwar, Mumbai CST, Howrah and so on as world-class stations through PPP. The proposal to set up of production units for manufacturing of electric and diesel locomotives at Madhepura and Marhowra respectively and passenger coaches at Kanchrapara through PPP has already been approved. Further, movement of container trains has already been opened to the private sector, and this has acquired more than 25 per cent share of the market. Construction of an elevated metro rail project in Mumbai is being undertaken through PPP.

PPP in Sports Infrastructure

3.97. The Planning Commission, in consultation with the Ministry of Sports and Youth Affairs, is developing a model for operation and management of sports infrastructure through PPP. Large public funds were invested to create world class facilities in the stadia for CWG Delhi in 2010. It is proposed to take up management and operation of existing stadia as well as development of new stadia through PPP. The objective is to utilise these facilities optimally throughout the year and also generate revenues for their operation and maintenance.

PPP in Micro Irrigation

3.98. A scheme for setting up Micro Irrigation Systems (MIS) through PPP will be launched in pursuance of the government's objective to enhance irrigation efficiency, productivity and farm incomes by employing more efficient means of irrigation in integrated clusters. The absence of organised operations in the farm sector would be overcome by farmers coming together for the purpose of implementing this scheme through a single entity in every village. The existing subsidies which are provided by the Central and State Governments for on-farm MIS equipment and solar systems would be availed of under this scheme. Similarly, budgetary support would continue to be provided for the development of infrastructure. PPP in MIS would help in doubling the irrigation efficiency as compared to flow irrigation.

PPP in Storage of Foodgrains

3.99. A scheme for setting up modern storage facilities through PPP under the VGF has been formulated in pursuance of the Government decision to create 2MMT of modern storage facilities in the form of silos. This would enhance food security, reduce wastage and improve the quality of stored foodgrains.

3.100. Silos will be constructed and operated under the PPP mode across several states. Land for construction and operation of silos would be provided on licence to the private entity and up to 20 per cent of the total project cost will be provided as VGF. For storage of foodgrains at the Silos, the Concessionaire will be entitled to receive a recurring storage charge which shall be payable on adherence to performance and maintenance standards. It is expected that in the first phase, a capacity of 2 million MT of silo capacity would be created under the PPP mode.

PPPs in Social Sectors

3.101. The Twelfth Plan lays special emphasis on the development of social sectors in view of their impact on human development and quality of life, especially of the underpreviliged sections. The physical targets set in the Plan cannot be met out of public resources alone. It is, therefore, imperative that resources have to be attracted from the private sector to ensure that targets, in physical and financial terms, are met by the end of the Twelfth Plan period.

3.102. In the social sectors, it may not be possible to adopt the user-charge-based concessions, although they may not be completely ruled out. However, concessions which would provide reimbursement of service costs could attract considerable private investment. The main advantages of adopting the PPP approach in the social sectors would be enhanced investment, reduction in time and cost over-runs, improvement in efficiencies and better quality of performance.

PPP in Education

3.103. A scheme for setting up 2,500 schools under PPP mode is being rolled out in the Twelfth Plan. The purpose of the scheme is to meet the government's objective of establishing world-class schools for providing quality education to underprivileged children who cannot afford to pay the tuition fee that good private schools charge. It is expected that the scheme will help in creating capacity for providing quality education to 40 lakh children, out of which 25 lakh will be from the underprivileged category.

3.104. The respective rights and obligations of the private entity and the government will be codified in an agreement with the former undertaking to deliver the agreed service on the payment of a unitary charge by the government. Recurring tuition support would be provided for up to 1,000 students from under privileged categories at par with the amount that the Central Government spends on a student in Kendriya Vidyalaya. There would be no capital support and land would have to be procured by the private entity. Infrastructure support shall be made available by the government for the underprivileged students at the rate of 25 per cent of the recurring tuition support. The concession would be for a period of 10 years. There will be no financial bidding. Predetermined criteria relating to capacity and track record of the respective applicants will be taken into account in selection of the private entities.

3.105. The scheme for 2,500 PPP schools should be viewed as an opportunity to evolve innovative ways to empower and enable non-government players to engage in providing world-class education, especially to children from low-income families. The objective should be to combine the respective strengths of the public and private sectors to complement each other in pursuit of the shared goal of good education for all. In particular, adoption of the PPP mode would lead to rapid expansion of access to world-class education by low-income families.

PPP in Health Care Services

3.106. Several State Governments are experimenting with delivery of health services through different models. Planning Commission is also in the process of preparing a scheme for setting up secondary and tertiary care hospitals through PPPs at various District Headquarters. The principle objective of the scheme is to create a health care delivery mechanism comprising multi-specialty hospital to meet the growing health care needs of the poor, and for supplementing human resources in the sector by setting up nursing schools and medical colleges.

3.107. It is expected that in the Twelfth Plan, the proposed scheme will be rolled out by the Government, and a 200-bed district-level hospital would serve a catchment area of about 8–10 lakh of population (20 lakh for a 300-bed tertiary care hospital). This will help families from the economically disadvantaged groups get access to quality health care through hospitals set up under this scheme, especially those who are covered under the Rashtriya Swasthya Bima Yojna (RSBY).

PPP in Skill Development

3.108. As part of the government's initiative to augment the programmes for skill development, the Prime Minister had announced setting up of 1,500 ITIs through PPP in unserved blocks. The objective is to create centres of excellence in vocational education especially for the youth from low-income families in order to improve their prospects of gainful employment. The programme will be expanded to cover a total of 3,000 blocks during the Twelfth Plan.

3.109. A major proportion of the costs incurred by an ITI are of a recurring nature, and it is therefore, proposed to provide support for the recurring expenditure incurred by an ITI towards training students from underprivileged families. Further, it is proposed to provide capital grant to meet a part of the cost of creating the infrastructure for setting up the ITIs. It is expected that 30 lakh youth, including 15 lakh youth from socially and economically disadvantaged groups would be initiated into vocational training and will acquire skills through the ITIs set up under this scheme.

Financial Support to PPPs in Social Sectors

3.110. A scheme for financial support to PPPs in the social sectors is being formulated as part of the Twelfth Plan initiative to enhance investments and coverage in social sectors, and also to expand the role of private participation.

3.111. The scheme envisages that capital investment and recurring costs to be incurred by a non-government entity on the delivery of services to EWS families, based on a concession agreement between government (or a statutory authority) and a non-government entity, will be provided by the respective State Governments, who in turn will be eligible for Viability Support Funding (VSF) from the Central Government.

Capacity Building in the States

3.112. The State Governments generally do not have dedicated staff resources for handling PPP projects or for building the requisite capacity. Such capacity is critical for conceptualising project proposals, engaging consultants, interacting with and supervising consultants, analysing and processing their advice for government approvals, interacting with prospective investors, executing the project documents and monitoring implementation. Therefore, the Planning Commission may need to provide financial assistance (ACA) to the State Governments for the setting up a nodal Secretariat for PPP in each State.

3.113. The aforesaid PPP Secretariat in each State would be responsible for identifying areas in the respective States amenable to PPP, conceptualise the projects, initiate and approve feasibility studies, appraise and approve bid documentation, guide the process and so on. This would enable capacity building in the States. The total expenditure on this scheme over the next five years would be limited to about ₹100 crore.

> **Box 3.7**
> **India Front-Runner in the PPP Race: ADB**
>
> According to a study by the Economic Intelligence Unit of the Economist commissioned by Asian Development Bank (ADB), while UK and Australia have been categorised as mature economies, India is positioned in the league of developed economies like Republic of Korea and Japan on implementation of PPP projects for infrastructure development. India has outscored China and Japan to rank second on PPP projects performance among the Asian nations and fourth in the Asia-Pacific nations. As per the Report, PPP development in India has been driven by strong political will and advances in public capacity and processes.
>
> The Report states that PPP projects have a huge level of overall acceptance and use in India. It states that government agencies have a relatively high level of proficiency in PPP projects and that as a result of introduction of Model Concession Agreements, the risk allocation has been improving. In terms of finance, matters have improved, with a variety of initiatives (such as the creation of the Viability Gap Funding and the India Infrastructure Finance Company Limited) enabling greater participation of private finance in infrastructure.

3.114. *To conclude*, the gains of private participation in meeting the policy objectives of the Government have been significant during the Eleventh Plan. These initiatives will be expanded and reinforced during the Twelfth Plan, especially in social sectors such as health, education, skill development and so on with a view to meeting the investment targets, while also ensuring inclusiveness. It is envisaged that by the end of the Twelfth Plan, not only will there be ₹55,74,663 crore worth of investment in infrastructure sectors, but also that PPPs would have successfully forayed into the social sectors to promote universal access, while ensuring quality in the delivery of services.

ANNEXURE 3.1
Sectoral Allocation for Public Sector's Resources—Eleventh Plan (2007–12) Realisation and Twelfth Plan (2012–17) Projections

(in ₹ Crore)

S. No.	Heads of Development	Centre								States and UTs						Centre, States and UTs		
		Budgetary Support			IEBR			Total Outlay			Budgetary Resources			Total Outlay		Total Outlay		
		Eleventh Plan	Twelfth Plan	% Increase	Eleventh Plan	Twelfth Plan	% Increase	Eleventh Plan	Twelfth Plan	% Increase	Eleventh Plan*	Twelfth Plan$	% Increase	Eleventh Plan	Twelfth Plan	% Increase	Eleventh Plan	Twelfth Plan	% Increase
1	Agriculture and Allied Activities	60,339	1,33,965	122.02	344	671	95.04	60,683	1,34,636	121.87	1,02,422	2,28,637	123.23	1,63,105	3,63,273	122.72			
2	Rural Development	1,79,925	2,67,047	48.42	0	0	0	1,79,925	2,67,047	48.42	1,08,284	1,90,417	75.85	2,88,209	4,57,464	58.73			
3	Special Area Programmes	0	0	0	0	0	0	0	0	0	42,817	80,370	87.71	42,817	80,370	87.71			
4	Irrigation and Flood Control	2,325	17,212	640.30	1	0	0	2,326	17,212	639.98	2,27,008	4,04,800	78.32	2,29,334	4,22,012	84.02			
5	Energy	43,374	98,541	127.19	4,60,709	9,87,456	114.33	5,04,083	10,85,997	115.44	1,80,188	3,52,468	95.61	6,84,271	14,38,466	110.22			
6	Industry and Minerals	50,452	1,20,372	138.59	97,058	1,71,718	76.92	1,47,510	2,92,090	98.01	38,143	85,212	123.40	1,85,653	3,77,302	103.23			
7	Transport	2,27,637	4,91,713	116.01	1,82,232	3,27,769	79.86	4,09,869	8,19,482	99.94	2,03,316	3,84,690	89.21	6,13,185	12,04,172	96.38			
8	Communications	5,308	29,699	459.51	53,208	51,285	−3.61	58,516	80,984	38.40	0	0	0	58,516	80,984	38.40			
9	Science, Technology and Environment	50,615	1,30,054	156.95	0	0	0	50,615	1,30,054	156.95	18,682	37,296	99.64	69,297	1,67,350	141.50			
10	Economic Services	45,706	1,81,321	296.71	18	155	761.11	45,724	1,81,476	296.89	43,652	1,24,136	184.38	89,376	3,05,612	241.94			
11	Social Services	4,92,408	11,90,416	141.75	63,672	83,845	31.68	5,56,080	12,74,261	129.15	6,41,496	13,90,582	116.77	11,97,576	26,64,843	122.52			
12	General Services	9,795	50,500	415.57	2	0	0	9,797	50,500	415.46	45,800	57,459	25.46	55,597	1,07,959	94.18			
	Total	**11,67,884**	**27,10,840**	**132.12**	**8,57,244**	**16,22,899**	**89.32**	**20,25,128**	**43,33,739**	**114.00**	**16,51,808**	**33,36,068**	**101.96**	**36,76,936**	**76,69,807**	**108.59**			

Note: * Sectoral outlays for states/UTs are based on data given by states. The total of all states arrived from sectoral outlays differs from the total given in Table 3.9 due to several reasons including accounting differences for some scheme of Central Assistance and differences in data provided by states on resources side and outlay side.
$ Excludes IEBR of SPSEs and Local Bodies.

ANNEXURE 3.2

Budget Support, IEBR and Outlay for Central Ministry/Department—Eleventh Plan (2007–12) Realisation and Twelfth Plan (2012–17) Projections

(₹ Crore in Current Prices)

S. No.	Ministry/Department	Budgetary Support			IEBR			Total Outlay		
		Eleventh Plan	Twelfth Plan	% Increase	Eleventh Plan	Twelfth Plan	% Increase	Eleventh Plan	Twelfth Plan	% Increase
1	Department of Agriculture and Cooperation	38,003	71,500	88.14	0	0		38,003	71,500	88.14
2	Department of Agriculture Research and Education	9,989	25,553	155.81	0	0		9,989	25,553	155.81
3	Department of Animal Husbandry, Dairying and Fisheries	4,970	14,179	185.29	0	0		4,970	14,179	185.29
4	Department of Health and Family Welfare	84,339	2,68,551	218.42	0	0		84,339	2,68,551	218.42
5	Department of Ayurveda, Yoga and Naturopathy, Unani, Siddha and Homoeopathy (AYUSH)	3,032	10,044	231.27	0	0		3,032	10,044	231.27
6	Department of Health Research	1,894	10,029	429.51	0	0		1,894	10,029	429.51
7	Department of Aids Control	1,500	11,394	659.60	0	0		1,500	11,394	659.60
8	Department of School Education and Literacy	1,37,734	3,43,028	149.05	0	0		1,37,734	3,43,028	149.05
9	Department of Higher Education	39,804	1,10,700	178.12	0	0		39,804	1,10,700	178.12
10	Ministry of Power	31,102	54,279	74.52	1,75,090	3,86,517	120.75	2,06,192	4,40,796	113.78
11	Ministry of Road Transport and Highways	77,498	1,44,769	86.80	17,891	64,834	262.38	95,389	2,09,603	119.73
12	Department of Rural Development[a]	2,81,438	4,12,965	46.73	17,707	0		2,99,146	4,12,965	38.04
13	Department of Land Resources	10,244	30,296	195.75	0	0		10,244	30,296	195.75
14	Ministry of Drinking Water and Sanitation	45,711	98,015	114.42	0	0		45,711	98,015	114.42
15	Department of Science and Technology	8,636	21,596	150.07	0	0		8,636	21,596	150.07
16	Department of Scientific and Industrial Research	6,941	17,896	157.85	0	0		6,941	17,896	157.85
17	Department of Biotechnology	4,840	11,804	143.89	0	0		4,840	11,804	143.89
18	Department of Space	15,836	39,750	151.01	0	0		15,836	39,750	151.01
19	Ministry of Women and Child Development	47,396	1,17,707	148.35	0	0		47,396	1,17,707	148.35

20	Railways	75,976	1,94,221	155.64	1,13,863	2,25,000	97.61	1,89,838	4,19,221	120.83
21	Ministry of Urban Development	25,133	54,311	116.09	11,002	11,489	4.43	36,135	65,800	82.10
22	Department of Posts	1,714	5,527	222.55	0	0	–	1,714	5,527	222.55
23	Department of Telecommunications	3,416	20,825	509.54	53,208	51,285	-3.61	56,625	72,110	27.35
24	Department of Information Technology	9,634	36,078	274.49	1,810	3,944	117.90	11,444	40,022	249.72
25	Ministry of Home Affairs	10,323	52,839	411.83	0	0		10,323	52,839	411.83
26	Ministry of Housing and Urban Poverty Alleviation	3,537	7,850	121.92	41,465	71,355	72.09	45,002	79,205	76.00
27	Ministry of Micro, Small and Medium Enterprises	9,175	24,124	162.93	1,072	1,890	76.34	10,247	26,014	153.87
28	Ministry of Tribal Affairs	4,558	7,746	69.93	0	0		4,558	7,746	69.93
29	Ministry of Social Justice and Empowerment	16,271	32,684	100.87	0	0		16,271	32,684	100.87
30	Ministry of Minority Affairs	7,283	17,323	137.85	0	0		7,283	17,323	137.85
31	Ministry of Labour & Employment	4,321	13,223	205.98	0	0		4,321	13,223	205.98
32	Ministry of Information & Broadcasting	2,873	7,583	163.95	0	1,000		2,873	8,583	198.75
33	Department of Atomic Energy	19,211	41,615	116.62	12,601	65,572	420.36	31,812	1,07,187	236.94
34	Department of Chemicals and Petrochemicals	2,629	2,890	9.93	12	3	-74.61	2,641	2,893	9.53
35	Department of Pharmaceuticals	249	2,968	1,090.72	0	127		249	3,095	1,141.48
36	Department of Fertilisers	728	1,484	103.78	6,027	15,437	156.14	6,755	16,921	150.50
37	Ministry of Civil Aviation	4,353	16,983	290.15	28,525	16,215	-43.15	32,877	33,198	0.97
38	Ministry of Coal	1,454	4,617	217.59	25,169	1,08,244	330.07	26,623	1,12,861	323.92
39	Department of Commerce	7,743	15,133	95.43	0	0		7,743	15,133	95.43
40	Department of Industrial Policy and Promotion	4,457	12,601	182.74	0	0		4,457	12,601	182.74
41	Department of Consumer Affairs	761	1,260	65.63	0	0		761	1,260	65.63
42	Department of Food and Public Distribution	323	1,523	370.88	345	671	94.53	668	2,194	228.27
43	Ministry of Corporate Affairs	211	233	10.57	0	0		211	233	10.57
44	Ministry of Culture	3,098	7,275	134.85	0	0		3,098	7,275	134.85
45	Ministry of Development of North Eastern Region	459	955	108.02	0	0		459	955	108.02

(Contd)

(Annexure 3.2 Contd)

S. No.	Ministry/Department	Budgetary Support			IEBR			Total Outlay		
		Eleventh Plan	Twelfth Plan	% Increase	Eleventh Plan	Twelfth Plan	% Increase	Eleventh Plan	Twelfth Plan	% Increase
46	Ministry of Earth Sciences	3,226	9,506	194.67	0	0		3,226	9,506	194.67
47	Ministry of Environment and Forests	8,545	17,874	109.17	0	0		8,545	17,874	109.17
48	Ministry of External Affairs	3,347	18,467	451.80	0	0		3,347	18,467	451.80
49	Department of Economic Affairs	7,675	21,379	178.54	0	0		7,675	21,379	178.54
50	Department of Financial Services	23,530	1,03,261	338.85	0	0		23,530	1,03,261	338.85
51	Department of Expenditure	24	23	−4.33	0	0		24	23	−4.33
52	Ministry of Food Processing Industries	1,615	5,990	270.79	0	0		1,615	5,990	270.79
53	Department of Heavy Industry	1,153	4,680	305.78	7,636	17,543	129.74	8,790	22,223	152.84
54	Department of Public Enterprises	45	50	11.41	0	0		45	50	11.41
55	Ministry of Law & Justice	1,555	5,802	273.22	0	0		1,555	5,802	273.22
56	Ministry of Mines	1,070	2,332	117.95	5,535	18,221	229.22	6,605	20,553	211.19
57	Ministry of New and Renewable Energy	3,605	19,113	430.17	6,025	13,890	130.55	9,630	33,003	242.72
58	Ministry of Panchayati Raj	636	6,437	912.41	0	0		636	6,437	912.41
59	Ministry of Personnel, Public Grievances and Pensions	788	1,385	75.65	0	0		788	1,385	75.65
60	Ministry of Petroleum and Natural Gas	126	5,147	3,984.92	2,58,953	4,36,541	68.58	2,59,079	4,41,688	70.48
61	Ministry of Planning	1,808	14,717	714.21	0	0		1,808	14,717	714.21
62	Ministry of Shipping	2,146	6,960	224.33	15,718	21,990	39.90	17,864	28,950	62.05
63	Ministry of Statistics and Programme Implementation	792	3,709	368.20	0	0		792	3,709	368.20
64	Ministry of Steel	134	200	49.04	57,572	90,975	58.02	57,706	91,175	58.00
65	Ministry of Textiles	19,922	25,931	30.16	0	0		19,922	25,931	30.16
66	Ministry of Tourism	4,913	15,190	209.14	18	155	761.11	4,932	15,345	211.13
67	Ministry of Water Resources	2,603	18,118	595.98	0	0		2,603	18,118	595.98
68	Ministry of Youth Affairs and Sports	7,830	6,648	−15.10	0	0		7,830	6,648	−15.10
	Grand Total	**11,67,885**	**27,10,840**	**132.12**	**8,57,244**	**16,22,899**	**89.32**	**20,25,129**	**43,33,739**	**114.00**

Note: ^aIncludes ₹28,000 crore as central share of Rural Development Flexi Fund (DoRD + DoLR + DoDWS).

ANNEXURE 3.3
Proposed Sectoral Allocations for States and Union Territories in the Twelfth Plan

Proposed Sectoral Allocations for States and Union Territories in the Twelfth Plan
(Current Prices) (₹ in Crore)

S. No.	Head of Development	Andhra Pradesh	%age of Total Budgetary Plan	Arunachal Pradesh	%age of Total Budgetary Plan	Assam	%age of Total Budgetary Plan	Bihar	%age of Total Budgetary Plan
1	2	3		4		5		6	
I	Agriculture and Allied Activities	17,137.88	5.00	1,113.93	5.27	3,272.60	5.90	15,612.62	6.83
II	Rural Development	33,706.50	9.83	203.57	0.96	3,674.63	6.62	12,774.42	5.59
III	Special Area Programmes	91.98	0.03	855.25	4.05	10,755.61	19.39	7,515.45	3.29
IV	Irrigation and Flood Control	75,000.00	21.88	544.40	2.58	8,050.63	14.51	21,784.52	9.54
V	Energy	40,000.00	11.67	1,332.00	6.31	4,408.27	7.95	17,381.47	7.61
VI	Industry and Minerals	10,000.00	2.92	104.50	0.49	1,169.89	2.11	4,077.45	1.78
VII	Transport	22,351.89	6.52	1,511.70	7.16	5,285.66	9.53	41,437.54	18.14
VIII	Communication	0.00		0.00		0.00		0.00	
IX	Science, Technology and Environment	64.39	0.02	106.80	0.51	1,126.07	2.03	2,418.15	1.06
X	General Economic Services	8,736.86	2.55	12,996.92	61.52	2,259.49	4.07	19,729.70	8.64
XI	Social Services	1,33,247.35	38.87	2,165.43	10.25	13,369.39	24.10	79,595.51	34.84
1	Education	24,084.32	7.02	539.10	2.55	4,125.29	7.44	29,957.34	13.11
2	Medical and Public Health	11,795.20	3.44	275.00	1.30	1,332.45	2.40	5,125.57	2.24
3	Water Supply and Sanitation	6,505.30	1.90	500.00	2.37	865.45	1.56	4,334.34	1.90
4	Housing	11,755.24	3.43	268.43	1.27	91.50	0.17	10,116.31	4.43
5	Urban Development	40,000.00	11.67	401.85	1.90	3,951.50	7.12	7,749.48	3.39
6	Others Social Services	39,107.29	11.41	181.05	0.86	3,003.20	5.41	22,312.47	9.77
XII	General Services	2,505.15	0.73	191.50	0.91	2,108.11	3.80	6,125.16	2.68
XIII	**Total Bugedtary Plan (I to XII)**	**3,42,842.00**	**100.00**	**21,126.00**	**100.00**	**55,480.35**	**100.00**	**2,28,452.00**	**100.00**
XIV	Local Bodies Resources	0.00	—	0.00	—	0.00	—	0.00	—
XV	PSEs Resources	0.00	—	0.00	—	0.00	—	0.00	—
XVI	**Total Plan Outlay (XIII + XIV + XV)**	**3,42,842.00**		**21,126.00**		**55,480.35**		**2,28,452.00**	

Note: Sectoral allocations in respect of some States/UTs are provisional and may undergo changes in consultation with concerned States/UTs.

Proposed Sectoral Allocations for States and UTs in the Twelfth Plan (Current Prices) (₹ in Crore)

S. No.	Head of Development	Chhattisgarh	%age of Total Budgetary Plan	Goa	%age of Total Budgetary Plan	Gujarat	%age of Total Budgetary Plan	Haryana	%age of Total Budgetary Plan
1	2	7		8		9		10	
I	Agriculture and Allied Activities	8,283.74	6.97	1,045.52	3.87	19,711.80	7.79	6,287.97	5.36
II	Rural Development	3,668.52	3.09	881.04	3.26	10,919.49	4.32	8,086.95	6.90
III	Special Area Programmes	3,313.50	2.79	83.50	0.31	1,276.30	0.50	263.14	0.22
IV	Irrigation and Flood Control	11,952.26	10.06	1,586.05	5.88	51,502.27	20.35	10,030.53	8.56
V	Energy	7,337.03	6.17	2,235.14	8.28	7,890.21	3.12	9,661.88	8.24
VI	Industry and Minerals	1,972.32	1.66	403.96	1.50	8,926.81	3.53	842.83	0.72
VII	Transport	13,017.31	10.95	2,341.05	8.67	29,064.04	11.49	12,844.29	10.96
VIII	Communication	0.00	—	0.00	—	0.00	—	0.00	—
IX	Science, Technology and Environment	2,840.14	2.39	727.98	2.70	2,268.98	0.90	1,528.03	1.30
X	General Economic Services	5,206.92	4.38	1,685.53	6.24	9,075.94	3.59	2,286.18	1.95
XI	Social Services	61,260.26	51.54	13,377.88	49.56	1,12,103.55	44.31	64,448.52	54.97
1	Education	30,013.19	25.25	3,842.29	14.23	15,201.10	6.01	19,581.16	16.70
2	Medical and Public Health	5,948.67	5.01	1,042.33	3.86	16,706.00	6.60	4,868.07	4.15
3	Water Supply and Sanitation	2,376.07	2.00	1,264.96	4.69	14,435.90	5.71	6,773.87	5.78
4	Housing	786.88	0.66	224.60	0.83	9,448.61	3.73	1,094.24	0.93
5	Urban Development	10,442.26	8.79	2,320.38	8.60	31,906.01	12.61	10,291.07	8.78
6	Others Social Services	11,693.19	9.84	4,683.32	17.35	24,405.99	9.65	21,840.12	18.63
XII	General Services	0.00	0.00	2,624.35	9.72	283.62	0.11	959.67	0.82
XIII	**Total Budgetary Plan (I to XII)**	**1,18,852.00**	**100.00**	**26,992.00**	**100.00**	**2,53,023.00**	**100.00**	**1,17,240.00**	**100.00**
XIV	Local Bodies Resources	4,421.00	—	540.00	—	0.00	—	13,190.00	—
XV	PSEs Resources	8,455.00	—	1,067.00	—	30,600.00	—	73,570.00	—
XVI	**Total Plan Outlay (XIII + XIV + XV)**	**1,31,728.00**	—	**28,599.00**	—	**2,83,623.00**	—	**2,04,000.00**	—

Note: Sectoral allocations in respect of some States/UTs are provisional and may undergo changes in consultation with concerned States/UTs.

S. No. | Head of Development | Proposed Sectoral Allocations for States and Union Territories in the Twelfth Plan (Current Prices) (₹ in Crore)

S. No.	Head of Development	Himachal Pradesh	%age of Total Budgetary Plan	Jammu and Kashmir	%age of Total Budgetary Plan	Jharkhand	%age of Total Budgetary Plan	Karnataka	%age of Total Budgetary Plan
1	2	11		12		13		14	
I	Agriculture and Allied Activities	2,173.83	9.68	2,843.09	6.45	4,157.42	3.77	19,824.01	8.94
II	Rural Development	1,084.93	4.83	1,541.78	3.50	10,657.89	9.67	7,170.73	3.23
III	Special Area Programmes	153.36	0.68	1,959.49	4.45	5,507.82	5.00	29,66.35	1.34
IV	Irrigation and Flood Control	1,661.50	7.40	1,914.33	4.35	13,620.18	12.36	39,430.95	17.78
V	Energy	3,549.83	15.81	11,195.82	25.41	8,372.10	7.59	23,165.55	10.45
VI	Industry and Minerals	227.34	1.01	1,066.82	2.42	1,346.77	1.22	3,649.23	1.65
VII	Transport	4,734.45	21.09	4,428.87	10.05	17,281.89	15.68	28,426.51	12.82
VIII	Communication	0.00	—	0.00	—	0.00	—	0.00	—
IX	Science, Technology and Environment	841.38	3.75	268.39	0.61	1,285.66	1.17	2,296.95	1.04
X	General Economic Services	585.20	2.61	3,216.63	7.30	9,610.32	8.72	5,971.63	2.69
XI	Social Services	7,088.23	31.57	13,196.14	29.95	36,293.06	32.92	85,428.94	38.52
1	Education	2,905.73	12.94	6,434.76	14.61	10,709.36	9.71	17,331.06	7.82
2	Medical and Public Health	131.79	0.59	2,991.54	6.79	3,816.28	3.46	7,899.31	3.56
3	Water Supply and Sanitation	1,777.52	7.92	1,473.40	3.34	2,093.32	1.90	12,606.59	5.68
4	Housing	339.78	1.51	71.81	0.16	147.38	0.13	7,031.07	3.17
5	Urban Development	395.30	1.76	600.09	1.36	6,586.83	5.97	16,620.80	7.49
6	Others Social Services	1,538.11	6.85	1,624.55	3.69	12,939.89	11.74	23,940.11	10.80
XII	General Services	349.96	1.56	2,423.63	5.50	2,106.89	1.91	3,433.15	1.55
XIII	**Total Budgetary Plan (I to XII)**	**22,450.00**	**100.00**	**44,055.00**	**100.00**	**1,10,240.00**	**100.00**	**2,21,764.00**	**100.00**
XIV	Local Bodies Resources	0.00	—	0.00	—	0.00	—	0.00	—
XV	PSEs Resources	350.00	—	0.00	—	0.00	—	33,486.00	—
XVI	**Total Plan Outlay (XIII + XIV + XV)**	**22,800.00**	—	**44,055.00**	—	**1,10,240.00**	—	**2,55,250.00**	—

Note: Sectoral allocations in respect of some States/UTs are provisional and may undergo changes in consultation with concerned States/UTs.

Proposed Sectoral Allocations for States and Union Territories in the Twelfth Plan
(Current Prices) (₹ in Crore)

S. No.	Head of Development	Kerala	%age of Total Budgetary Plan	Madhya Pradesh	%age of Total Budgetary Plan	Maharashtra	%age of Total Budgetary Plan	Manipur	%age of Total Budgetary Plan
1	2	15		16		17		18	
I	Agriculture and Allied Activities	8,831.00	11.47	17,076.50	8.46	19,324.87	7.03	642.98	3.08
II	Rural Development	3,339.00	4.34	12,946.70	6.41	9,089.07	3.31	946.89	4.54
III	Special Area Programmes	2,031.00	2.64	8,356.90	4.14	1,140.70	0.41	338.58	1.62
IV	Irrigation and Flood Control	3,327.00	4.32	27,313.50	13.53	47,990.34	17.45	3,219.66	15.44
V	Energy	8,323.00	10.81	20,941.90	10.37	20,694.87	7.53	1,563.00	7.50
VI	Industry and Minerals	3,912.00	5.08	5,839.70	2.89	2,174.94	0.79	435.31	2.09
VII	Transport	8,540.00	11.09	24,641.00	12.21	33,854.78	12.31	1,126.12	5.40
VIII	Communication	0.00	—	0.00	—	0.00	—	0.00	—
IX	Science, Technology and Environment	3,189.00	4.14	569.00	0.28	2,761.04	1.00	1,148.29	5.51
X	General Economic Services	1,975.00	2.56	3,501.49	1.73	3,351.45	1.22	401.97	1.93
XI	Social Services	33,207.00	43.13	79,820.22	39.54	1,19,699.61	43.53	10,755.50	51.59
1	Education	4,731.00	6.14	20,217.00	10.02	14,612.18	5.31	754.73	3.62
2	Medical and Public Health	3,534.00	4.59	6,314.20	3.13	10,200.86	3.71	1,301.04	6.24
3	Water Supply and Sanitation	4,656.00	6.05	3,116.40	1.54	6,073.25	2.21	3,664.02	17.57
4	Housing	412.00	0.54	2,002.30	0.99	9,376.97	3.41	248.45	1.19
5	Urban Development	6,920.00	8.99	8,767.30	4.34	23,960.91	8.71	620.98	2.98
6	Others Social Services	12,954.00	16.82	39,403.02	19.52	55,475.44	20.17	4,166.29	19.98
XII	General Services	326.00	0.42	855.09	0.42	14,918.34	5.42	269.72	1.29
XIII	**Total Budgetary Plan (I to XII)**	**77,000.00**	**100.00**	**2,01,862.00**	**100.00**	**2,75,000.00**	**100.00**	**20,848.00**	**100.00**
XIV	Local Bodies Resources	25,000.00	—	0.00	—	0.00	—	0.00	—
XV	PSEs Resources	0.00	—	8,291.00	—	0.00	—	0.00	—
XVI	**Total Plan Outlay (XIII + XIV + XV)**	**1,02,000.00**	—	**2,10,153.00**	—	**2,75,000.00**	—	**20,848.00**	—

Note: Sectoral allocations in respect of some States/UTs are provisional and may undergo changes in consultation with concerned States/UTs.

Proposed Sectoral Allocations for States and Union Territories in the Twelfth Plan (Current Prices) (₹ in Crore)

S.No.	Head of Development	Meghalaya	%age of Total Budgetary Plan	Mizoram	%age of Total Budgetary Plan	Nagaland	%age of Total Budgetary Plan	Odisha	%age of Total Budgetary Plan
1	2	19		20		21		22	
I	Agriculture and Allied Activities	2,114.47	10.74	346.35	2.85	1,795.13	13.81	8,387.40	7.40
II	Rural Development	1,116.94	5.68	178.69	1.47	492.07	3.79	2,214.07	1.95
III	Special Area Programmes	101.94	0.52	238.06	1.96	834.18	6.42	9,964.07	8.79
IV	Irrigation and Flood Control	755.79	3.84	460.20	3.78	1,142.08	8.79	17,597.77	15.53
V	Energy	2,679.50	13.62	656.20	5.40	748.89	5.76	14,086.59	12.43
VI	Industry and Minerals	213.34	1.08	1,817.44	14.95	341.70	2.63	478.96	0.42
VII	Transport	1,489.01	7.57	3,658.71	30.09	1,271.74	9.78	14,139.76	12.48
VIII	Communication	0.00	—	0.00	—	0.00	—	0.00	—
IX	Science, Technology and Environment	335.67	1.71	162.70	1.34	83.39	0.64	2,283.38	2.01
X	General Economic Services	4,231.86	21.50	1,154.40	9.49	1,585.58	12.20	2,374.24	2.10
XI	Social Services	6,124.98	31.12	3,270.95	26.90	3,932.85	30.25	40,335.83	35.59
1	Education	2,512.03	12.77	1,379.61	11.35	831.32	6.39	15,107.90	13.33
2	Medical and Public Health	1,427.12	7.25	269.77	2.22	208.43	1.60	2,723.77	2.40
3	Water Supply and Sanitation	873.75	4.44	363.42	2.99	231.69	1.78	3,410.99	3.01
4	Housing	67.72	0.34	643.53	5.29	361.73	2.78	1,365.53	1.21
5	Urban Development	997.53	5.07	399.65	3.29	980.07	7.54	2,634.32	2.32
6	Others Social Services	246.83	1.25	214.96	1.77	1,319.61	10.15	15,093.32	13.32
XII	General Services	515.51	2.62	216.29	1.78	772.39	5.94	1,459.92	1.29
XIII	**Total Budgetary Plan (I to XII)**	**19,679.00**	**100.00**	**12,160.00**	**100.00**	**13,000.00**	**100.00**	**1,13,322.00**	**100.00**
XIV	Local Bodies Resources	0.00	—	0.00	—	0.00	—	0.00	—
XV	PSEs Resources	2,321.00	—	0.00	—	0.00	—	11,051.00	—
XVI	**Total Plan Outlay (XIII + XIV + XV)**	**22,000.00**	—	**12,160.00**	—	**13,000.00**	—	**1,24,373.00**	—

Note: Sectoral allocations in respect of some States/UTs are provisional and may undergo changes in consultation with concerned States/UTs.

Proposed Sectoral Allocations for States and Union Territories in the Twelfth Plan
(Current Prices) (₹ in Crore)

S. No.	Head of Development	Punjab	%age of Total Budgetary Plan	Rajasthan	%age of Total Budgetary Plan	Sikkim	%age of Total Budgetary Plan	Tamil Nadu	%age of Total Budgetary Plan
1	2	23		24		25		26	
I	Agriculture and Allied Activities	1,524.19	2.92	7,254.82	5.58	469.30	4.14	20,680.00	10.04
II	Rural Development	4,733.82	9.08	10,436.99	8.02	1,302.98	11.51	23,870.00	11.59
III	Special Area Programmes	0.00	0.00	2,891.62	2.22	161.02	1.42	0.00	0.00
IV	Irrigation and Flood Control	2,985.06	5.73	4,097.46	3.15	912.50	8.06	8,700.00	4.22
V	Energy	13,850.09	26.57	48,692.80	37.43	681.27	6.02	24,258.00	11.78
VI	Industry and Minerals	1,437.62	2.76	665.22	0.51	412.63	3.64	5,470.00	2.66
VII	Transport	5,215.42	10.00	7,042.65	5.41	65.29	0.58	20,850.00	10.12
VIII	Communication	0.00	—	0.00	—	0.00	—	0.00	—
IX	Science, Technology and Environment	259.95	0.50	1,245.18	0.96	455.02	4.02	410.00	0.20
X	General Economic Services	829.16	1.59	2,467.21	1.90	681.53	6.02	3,880.00	1.88
XI	Social Services	20,529.21	39.38	44,126.56	33.92	5,241.30	46.28	97,400.00	47.28
1	Education	6,647.36	12.75	9,886.80	7.60	2,014.56	17.79	18,090.00	8.78
2	Medical and Public Health	1,598.75	3.07	4,999.62	3.84	812.43	7.17	10,830.00	5.26
3	Water Supply and Sanitation	3,671.84	7.04	9,786.27	7.52	1,319.69	11.65	11,310.00	5.49
4	Housing	34.47	0.07	1,588.22	1.22	93.25	0.82	3,380.00	1.64
5	Urban Development	1,192.42	2.29	10,469.87	8.05	978.45	8.64	10,690.00	5.19
6	Others Social Services	7,384.36	14.16	7,395.77	5.69	22.93	0.20	43,100.00	20.92
XII	General Services	769.47	1.48	1,164.48	0.90	942.16	8.32	470.00	0.23
XIII	**Total Budgetary Plan (I to XII)**	**52,134.00**	**100.00**	**1,30,085.00**	**100.00**	**11,325.00**	**100.00**	**2,05,988.00**	**100.00**
XIV	Local Bodies Resources	5,863.00	—	5,978.00	—	0.00	—	2,000.00	—
XV	PSEs Resources	27,362.00	—	60,929.00	—	0.00	—	3,262.00	—
XVI	**Total Plan Outlay (XIII + XIV + XV)**	**85,359.00**	—	**1,96,992.00**	—	**11,325.00**	—	**2,11,250.00**	—

Note: Sectoral allocations in respect of some States/UTs are provisional and may undergo changes in consultation with concerned States/UTs.

S. No. Head of Development   Proposed Sectoral Allocations for States and Union Territories in the Twelfth Plan
(Current Prices) (₹ in Crore)

S. No.	Head of Development	Tripura	%age of Total Budgetary Plan	Uttar Pradesh	%age of Total Budgetary Plan	Uttarakhand	%age of Total Budgetary Plan	West Bengal	%age of Total Budgetary Plan
1	2	27		28		29		30	
I	Agriculture and Allied Activities	980.78	6.84	24,354.83	8.51	2,672.88	5.93	8,582.90	5.52
II	Rural Development	425.67	2.97	8,322.73	2.91	3,082.42	6.84	11,142.45	7.16
III	Special Area Programmes	899.49	6.27	7,753.24	2.71	68.11	0.15	10,849.50	6.97
IV	Irrigation and Flood Control	583.54	4.07	30,080.39	10.51	3,604.40	8.00	13,385.80	8.60
V	Energy	398.28	2.78	39,532.33	13.81	6,036.17	13.39	4,513.00	2.90
VI	Industry and Minerals	197.25	1.38	20,520.35	7.17	177.99	0.39	5,934.70	3.81
VII	Transport	732.03	5.10	30,197.92	10.55	6,923.99	15.36	10,484.10	6.74
VIII	Communication	0.00	—	0.00	—	0.00	—	0.00	—
IX	Science, Technology and Environment	317.49	2.21	2,603.71	0.91	1,615.59	3.58	1,859.80	1.20
X	General Economic Services	4,921.19	34.32	6,644.83	2.32	1,207.22	2.68	1,079.60	0.69
XI	Social Services	4,658.13	32.48	11,4863.17	40.11	18,522.50	41.09	84,511.75	54.31
1	Education	848.83	5.92	36,876.85	12.88	4,973.78	11.03	22,353.60	14.37
2	Medical and Public Health	1,048.22	7.31	16,647.76	5.81	3,132.16	6.95	6,925.45	4.45
3	Water Supply and Sanitation	278.45	1.94	7,390.37	2.58	3,093.75	6.86	5,183.00	3.33
4	Housing	176.55	1.23	4,529.59	1.58	0.00	0.00	5,534.25	3.56
5	Urban Development	680.69	4.75	15,326.69	5.35	3,278.18	7.27	20,425.25	13.13
6	Others Social Services	1,625.39	11.33	34,091.92	11.91	4,044.62	8.97	24,090.20	15.48
XII	General Services	226.15	1.58	1,466.50	0.51	1,168.74	2.59	3,257.40	2.09
XIII	**Total Budgetary Plan (I to XII)**	**14,340.00**	**100.00**	**2,86,340.00**	**100.00**	**45,080.00**	**100.00**	**1,55,601.00**	**100.00**
XIV	Local Bodies Resources	0.00	—	0.00	—	100.00	—	0.00	—
XV	PSEs Resources	0.00	—	40,613.00	—	1,400.00	—	16,194.00	—
XVI	**Total Plan Outlay (XIII + XIV + XV)**	**14,340.00**	—	**3,26,953.00**	—	**46,580.00**	—	**1,71,795.00**	—

Note: Sectoral allocations in respect of some States/UTs are provisional and may undergo changes in consultation with concerned States/UTs.

Proposed Sectoral Allocations for States and Union Territories in the Twelfth Plan
(Current Prices) (₹ in Crore)

S. No.	Head of Development	Andaman and Nicobar Islands	%age of Total Budgetary Plan	Chandigarh	%age of Total Budgetary Plan	Dadra and Nagar Haveli	%age of Total Budgetary Plan	Daman and Diu	%age of Total Budgetary Plan
1	2	31		32		33		34	
I	Agriculture and Allied Activities	331.80	2.68	7.01	0.13	45.88	1.04	205.49	4.97
II	Rural Development	497.42	4.02	27.26	0.51	160.95	3.64	298.27	7.21
III	Special Area Programmes	0.00	0.00	0.00	0.00	0.00	0.00	0.00	0.00
IV	Irrigation and Flood Control	145.26	1.17	1.60	0.03	356.51	8.05	93.82	2.27
V	Energy	296.67	2.40	420.26	7.81	893.11	20.18	325.25	7.87
VI	Industry and Minerals	40.05	0.32	4.77	0.09	8.86	0.20	100.75	2.44
VII	Transport	5,093.78	41.16	454.42	8.44	660.32	14.92	937.77	22.68
VIII	Communication	0.00	—	0.00	—	0.00	—	0.00	—
IX	Science, Technology and Environment	900.96	7.28	95.98	1.78	94.34	2.13	182.69	4.42
X	General Economic Services	277.55	2.24	35.22	0.65	168.49	3.81	103.92	2.51
XI	Social Services	3,967.65	32.06	4,287.80	79.64	1,921.02	43.40	1,741.28	42.11
1	Education	1,357.25	10.97	1,026.11	19.06	481.79	10.89	413.88	10.01
2	Medical and Public Health	672.92	5.44	660.33	12.26	653.35	14.76	850.41	20.57
3	Water Supply and Sanitation	508.04	4.11	199.96	3.71	224.48	5.07	211.55	5.12
4	Housing	251.59	2.03	276.50	5.14	240.89	5.44	14.46	0.35
5	Urban Development	796.17	6.43	2,007.89	37.29	263.67	5.96	170.19	4.12
6	Others Social Services	381.69	3.08	117.01	2.17	56.83	1.28	80.80	1.95
XII	General Services	823.86	6.66	49.69	0.92	116.53	2.63	145.75	3.52
XIII	**Total Budgetary Plan (I to XII)**	**12,375.00**	**100.00**	**5,384.00**	**100.00**	**4,426.00**	**100.00**	**4,135.00**	**100.00**
XIV	Local Bodies Resources	0.00	—	0.00	—	0.00	—	0.00	—
XV	PSEs Resources	0.00	—	0.00	—	0.00	—	0.00	—
XVI	**Total Plan Outlay (XIII + XIV + XV)**	**12,375.00**	—	**5,384.00**	—	**4,426.00**	—	**4,135.00**	—

Note: Sectoral allocations in respect of some States/UTs are provisional and may undergo changes in consultation with concerned States/UTs.

Proposed Sectoral Allocations for States and Union Territories in the Twelfth Plan (Current Prices) (₹ in Crore)

S. No.	Head of Development	Delhi	%age of Total Budgetary Plan	Lakshadweep	%age of Total Budgetary Plan	Puducherry	%age of Total Budgetary Plan	Total All States and UTs
1	2	35		36		37		
I	Agriculture and Allied Activities	0.00	0.00	227.91	7.84	1,316.07	6.40	2,28,636.99
II	Rural Development	882.00	0.98	48.84	1.68	491.22	2.39	1,90,416.89
III	Special Area Programmes	0.00	0.00	0.00	0.00	0.00	0.00	80,370.15
IV	Irrigation and Flood Control	400.00	0.44	37.21	1.28	532.29	2.59	4,04,799.79
V	Energy	4,820.20	5.36	130.23	4.48	1,397.47	6.80	3,52,468.37
VI	Industry and Minerals	199.00	0.22	26.74	0.92	1,015.14	4.94	85,212.39
VII	Transport	21,954.62	24.39	777.91	26.76	1,853.20	9.01	3,84,689.75
VIII	Communication	0.00	—	0.00	—	0.00	—	0.00
IX	Science, Technology and Environment	546.50	0.61	238.37	8.20	164.99	0.80	37,295.98
X	General Economic Services	992.50	1.10	118.61	4.08	791.94	3.85	1,24,136.27
XI	Social Services	57,185.50	63.54	1,223.27	42.08	11,680.82	56.82	13,90,581.23
1	Education	12,240.50	13.60	422.10	14.52	2,674.40	13.01	3,45,178.28
2	Medical and Public Health	13,500.00	15.00	186.05	6.40	2,052.44	9.98	1,52,481.29
3	Water Supply and Sanitation	11,000.00	12.22	86.05	2.96	1,100.55	5.35	1,32,760.24
4	Housing	2,700.00	3.00	284.89	9.80	1,169.13	5.69	76,127.87
5	Urban Development	8,700.00	9.67	143.02	4.92	2,308.37	11.23	2,53,977.19
6	Others Social Services	9,045.00	10.05	101.16	3.48	2,375.93	11.56	4,30,056.38
XII	General Services	3,019.68	3.36	77.91	2.68	1,315.86	6.40	57,458.63
XIII	**Total Budgetary Plan (I to XII)**	**90,000.00**	**100.00**	**2,907.00**	**100.00**	**20,559.00**	**100.00**	**33,36,066.44**
XIV	Local Bodies Resources	0.00	—	0.00	—	0.00	—	57,092.00
XV	PSEs Resources	4,275.52	—	0.00	—	0.00	—	3,23,226.52
XVI	**Total Plan Outlay (XIII + XIV + XV)**	**94,275.52**	**—**	**2,907.00**	**—**	**20,559.00**	**—**	**37,16,384.96**

Note: Sectoral allocations in respect of some States/UTs are provisional and may undergo changes in consultation with concerned States/UTs.

4

Sustainable Development

INTRODUCTION

4.1. Sustainable Development, as defined by the Brundtland Commission in 1987, '*is development that meets the needs of the present without compromising the ability of future generations to meet their own needs*'. Economic growth and development have to be guided by the compulsion of sustainability, because none of us has the luxury, any longer, of ignoring the economic as well as the environmental threat, that a fast-deteriorating ecosystem poses to our fragile planet. None of us is immune to the reality of climate change, ecological degradation, depletion of the ozone layer and contamination of our freshwater.

4.2. India has been actively involved in international fora relating to environmental protection, and has been part of 94 Multilaterals Environmental Agreements such as the Ramsar Convention on Wetlands, Convention on International Trade in Endangered Species of Fauna and Flora (CITES), Convention on Biological Diversity (CBD), among many others. India has also signed the United Nations Framework Convention on Climate Change, and has acceded to the Kyoto Protocol in 2002. Despite not having binding mitigation commitments as per the United Nations Framework Convention on Climate Change (UNFCCC), India has communicated its voluntary mitigation goal of reducing the emissions intensity of its Gross Domestic Product (GDP) by 20–25 per cent, over 2005 levels, by 2020. The Indian Government is committed to the UNFCCC principle of *Common but Differentiated Responsibility* (CBDR). The Government has also formulated the National Action Plan on Climate Change that provides for eight missions to help the country adapt to the effects of climate variability and change.

SUSTAINABLE ECONOMIC GROWTH

4.3. It is often said that Gross Domestic Product is not the best way of measuring the true well-being of nations, because the pursuit of growth can be at the cost of the environment. There is obviously a two-way relationship between environment and economic growth. Natural resources and raw materials such as water, timber and minerals directly provide inputs for the production of goods and services. However, Industrial growth, which plays a major role in boosting the GDP, can cause some environmental damage. Manufacturing sector can lead to environmental degradation during all stages of production cycle, namely, (*i*) procurement and use of natural resources, (*ii*) industrial processes and activities and (*iii*) product use and disposal. Another important sector of the economy—agriculture—also has certain practices which harm the environment. For instance, activities like the use of chemical fertilisers result in both water pollution and soil deterioration. Unregulated withdrawal of ground water plays havoc with water balance in the ecosystem.

4.4. Conventional ways of measuring GDP in terms of production do not take into account the environmental damage caused by production of goods and services. Only after GDP is adjusted for environmental costs that growth of adjusted GDP can be called a measure of the increase in total production in the economy. Recognising this problem, the Planning Commission has commissioned an Expert Group under Professor Partha Dasgupta to prepare a template for estimating green national accounts, which would measure national production while allowing for the negative effects on national resources.

4.5. Environment is a public good that is rival and non-excludable. It is not owned by any one individual, and one person's consumption affects its quality available for others. Several economic activities generate negative externalities through the environment. Pricing natural resources properly, making pollution more costly and removing fossil fuel subsidies should be good for preservation of environment, and for sustaining growth in the long run. Better regulation can help protect human health and environment, support green technologies, and boost green private investment and jobs. This section first makes a business case for sustainable development, and then deals with financial and non-monetary incentives.

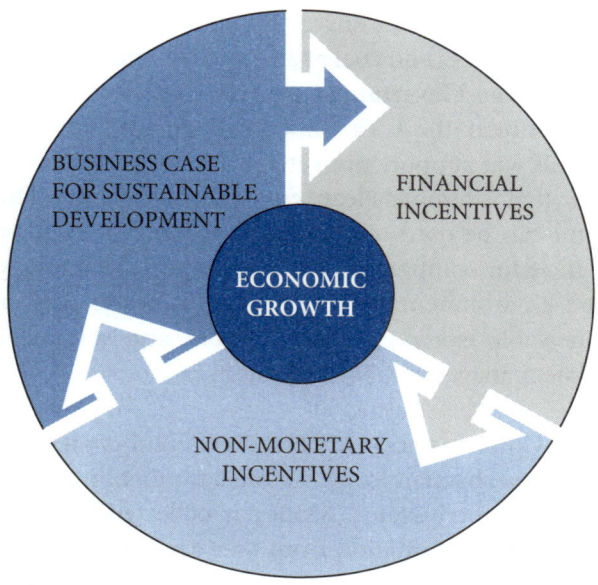

FIGURE 4.1: Policy Alternatives for Sustainable Growth

A Business Model for Sustainable Development

4.6. While in the mid 1990s, local authorities were probably the most active players trying to achieve sustainable development, the focus has recently shifted to business as a major actor. Many responsible business managers and their firms have opted for eco-efficiency as their guiding principle. Eco-efficiency is the economic value added by a firm in relation to its aggregated ecological impact. The World Business Council for Sustainable Development (WBCSD) has defined eco-efficiency as follows:

'Eco-efficiency is achieved by the delivery of competitively priced goods and services that satisfy human needs and bring quality of life, while progressively reducing ecological impacts and resource intensity throughout the life-cycle, to a level at least in line with the earth's carrying capacity.'

4.7. Similar to the concept of eco-efficiency, but so far less explored in corporate sustainability is the concept of socio-efficiency, that is, the relation between a firm's value added and its social impact. While it can be assumed that corporate impact on environment is usually negative, this may not be true for the social impact. Depending on the type of socio-efficiency, one can either try to minimize the negative social impact, or maximize the positive social impact while pursuing the value-added activity. Both eco-efficiency and socio-efficiency promote economic sustainability of the businesses in the long run.

Financial Incentives

4.8. The role of economic instruments in financing and promoting sustainable development is well recognised. The following economic instruments can help achieve sustainable development through their influence on behavioural patterns leading to sustainable consumption and production in the economy:

Environmental Taxes

4.9. An 'environment' or 'green' tax is imposed on a product (or a complementary product) that damages the environment, in an attempt to reduce its production or consumption. Well-designed environmental taxes and other economic instruments can play an important role in ensuring that prices reflect environmental costs, in line with the 'polluter pays principle'. Environmental taxes can be simple and efficient financial instruments for improving the productivity of natural resources. Environmental taxes on water and fossil fuels need not be part of the general revenues of the Government; rather they should be directly ploughed back into environmentally sustainable action on these fronts. Coal Cess is a good example of environment tax imposed by Government of India in recent times, whose proceeds are channelled to the National Clean Energy Fund. Some benefits of environment taxation are enumerated below:

- They provide incentives for measures that protect the environment, and deter actions that lead to environmental damage.
- Economic instruments such as taxes can enable environmental goals to be achieved at the lowest cost, and in the most efficient way.
- By internalizing environmental costs into prices, they help signal the structural economic changes needed to move to a more sustainable economy.
- They can encourage innovation and development of new technology.
- The revenue raised by environmental taxes can be used to reduce the level of other taxes. This could help reduce distortions, while raising the efficiency with which resources are used in the economy.

Subsidies

4.10. There has been a growing recognition of fiscal and environmental implications of the subsidy policies in energy, water and agriculture sectors. Most of these subsidies pose a threat to the environment. In the energy sector, for example, with the dismantling of the Administered Pricing Mechanism (APM) in April 2002, subsidies on all oil products were removed, barring liquid petroleum gas and kerosene, which are used by households. However, the policy has subsequently been reversed leading to a large and regressive subsidy on diesel that has distorted the use of energy in transport and industrial sectors, and worsened the problem of hazardous air pollution.

Similarly, excessive use of nitrogenous fertilizers and over-drawing of water, backed by subsidies at both Centre and State levels, is playing havoc with the sustainability of soil and water ecosystem.

Funds and Technology Transfers

4.11. A major stumbling block in making green business widespread is the lack of financial resources. The primary objective of developing green technology is to replace the obsolete and inefficient systems with more energy-efficient and clean technologies. Research & Development (R&D) funding assistance paves the way for leveraging the knowledge of educational and research institutions to create technologies that can be viewed as cutting-edge and advanced. Micro, Small and Medium Enterprises (MSMEs) have limited financial resources, and therefore tend to employ cheap, yet inefficient, technologies that invariably lead to non-compliance with regulations. Funds need to be made available to assist the industry adopt green technologies within their own premises, and also for building common environmental protection infrastructure within the industrial clusters. Funds need to be allocated in a manner that both existing and infant institutions can be continuously upgraded.

4.12. The Government of India (GoI) has already set up a National Clean Energy Fund (NCEF) in 2010 by imposing a cess on coal at an effective rate of ₹50 per tonne. The Government expects to collect ₹10,000 crore under the Clean Energy Fund by 2015. The NCEF will support projects, programmes and policies that promote clean energy technologies. This fund can be used to establish a focused investment vehicle for companies investing in green technology, and environmentally supportive businesses such as renewable energy, green transport, and water and waste management among others.

4.13. Compensatory Afforestation Fund is an innovative mechanism for attracting additional resources to the forestry sector. Money is collected for compensatory afforestation from user agencies in lieu of the land granted for non-forestry purpose, presently at the rate of ₹0.8 million per hectare.

4.14. Another fund, the National Gene Fund, has been established, which will be used to build capacity at Panchayat level for in situ conservation of genetic diversity of indigenous crop varieties. The Twelfth Plan should facilitate such initiatives.

Certificates and Obligations

4.15. The mounting pressure on conventional energy sources has made energy conservation a focus area for the Government. The Perform, Achieve and Trade (PAT) scheme is an example of a certificate based trading scheme promoting energy efficiency. Similarly, Renewable Energy Certificate (REC) mechanism is a market-based instrument introduced to promote renewable energy, and facilitate renewable purchase obligations, which legally mandate a percentage of electricity to be procured by distribution companies from renewable energy sources. REC mechanism aims to address the mismatch between availability of renewable energy resources in a State and the requirement of the obligated entities to meet their renewable purchase obligations.

Non-monetary Incentives

4.16. Non-monetary incentives are policy instruments that typically do not have a monetary value, but definitely have a financial impact that promotes sustainability. These incentives can be used as a bargaining tool by the Government to encourage conservation of resources in an economy. Activities such as those encouraging judicious use of water, planting trees, car pooling and avoiding use of plastic bags can be rewarded so that it encourages the practice, and acts as an example for others. Through the initiation of innovative policies and awards, the Government can provide recognition, which will encourage sustainable development amongst the citizens and the firms.

Setting an Agenda for Sustainable Development

4.17. There is a general impression that India is consuming more than what its ecosystem can sustain, and hence there is a need for programmatic inter-disciplinary planning and inter-agency efforts at all levels. A number of national strategies and policies, which inculcate the principle of sustainability, have already been put into place. The National Environmental Policy (NEP), 2006 articulates that only such development is sustainable which respects ecological constraints and the imperatives of social justice. The National Policy for farmers focuses on sustainable development of agriculture, by promoting technically sound, economically viable, environmentally non-degrading and socially acceptable use of the country's natural resources. The Policy also states that improving the quality of land and soil, its rational utilisation, conservation of water and sensitising the farming community to environmental concerns should receive high priority. The National Electricity Policy (NEP) underscores the use of renewable sources of energy, as does the Integrated Energy Policy (IEP) of 2010. The National Urban Sanitation Policy, 2008 seeks to generate awareness, eliminate open defecation, promote integrated city-wide sanitation, safe disposal and efficient operation of all sanitary installations. However, we need to tackle upfront the looming water crisis, made worse by the supply of free water and electricity; and the health and environmental hazards posed by excessive use of very cheap nitrogenous fertiliser. Some important perspectives for achieving sustainable development in our country are listed below:

Greenhouse Gas Emissions

4.18. India's sustained efforts towards reducing the emission intensity of its GDP will ensure that country's per capita emissions will continue to be lower than developed countries. It is estimated that India's per capita emission in 2031 will still be lower than the global per capita emission in 2005 (in 2031, India's per capita GHG emissions will be under 4 tonnes of Carbon Dioxide equivalent (CO_2eq.) which is lower than the global per capita emission of 4.22 tonnes of CO_2eq. in 2005). Even then India has taken upon itself the voluntary target of reducing the emission intensity of its GDP by 20–25 per cent, over the 2005 levels, by 2020.

Sustainable Agriculture Development

4.19. The major thrust of the agricultural development programmes is on improving the efficiency of use of scarce natural resources, namely, land, water and energy. This can be achieved through improved productivity, which in turn will improve the welfare of farmers and agricultural labour, and help eradicate rural poverty. Conservation of land resources can promote a sound land use, matching the land capabilities with development alternatives. Pricing water and electricity appropriately will help recharge the depleting aquifers. Shifting urea to a nutrient-based subsidy regime is also the need of the hour, which cannot be neglected any longer.

Industrial Development and Urbanisation

4.20. Industry plays a critical role in technology innovations, which are crucial for economic and social development of the country. It is also important to facilitate diffusion and transfer of environmentally sound technologies and management techniques, which are a key element of any sustainable development strategy.

4.21. A major environmental concern in urbanising India relates to high levels of water pollution due to poor waste disposal, inadequate sewerage and drainage, and improper disposal of industrial effluents. The dumping of solid waste in low-lying areas contributes to both land and groundwater pollution. The Jawaharlal Nehru National Urban Renewal Mission (JNNURM) needs a more focused approach over the Twelfth Plan period so that we resolve these issues at the earliest.

Eco-Industrial Hubs

4.22. An eco-industrial park (EIP) or estate is a community of manufacturing and service businesses located together on a common property. Member businesses seek enhanced environmental, economic and social performance through collaboration in managing environmental and resource issues. By working together, the community of businesses seeks a collective benefit that is greater than the sum of individual benefits each company would realise by only optimizing its individual performance.[1]

4.23. The goal of an EIP is to improve the economic performance of the participating companies while minimizing their environmental impacts. Components of this approach include green design of the park infrastructure (new or retrofitted); cleaner production; prevention of pollution; energy efficiency and inter-company partnering. An EIP also seeks benefits for neighbouring communities to assure the net impact of its development is positive. In particular, we should consider converting our Special Economic Zones (SEZ) and townships along the Mumbai–Delhi Industrial Corridor into Eco-industrial hubs as outlined above.

Sustainable Management of Himalayan Ecosystem and Western Ghats

4.24. The Hill Area Development Programme (HADP) and the Western Ghats Development Programme (WGDP) need to be continued in the Twelfth Plan with renewed vigour so that natural resources of these fragile areas can be preserved and used in a more sustainable manner. These programmes also need to be continued because most of the hill areas lack infrastructure, particularly roads, power, educational institutions and health care centres. These areas deserve high priority under the flagship programmes, particularly Sarva Shiksha Abhiyan (SSA) and the National Health Mission (NHM). It has also been observed that many nationwide programmes are not suitable for hilly areas, for example, wages should be higher than the wages prescribed under wage employment programmes. This also holds true for the norms set out for some other programmes, as settlements are often small hamlets, which do not qualify for coverage or are too expensive to cover. Local solutions and people's participation in decision-making need to be encouraged. The ecological and biodiversity issues should be dealt with on high priority. The programme should therefore have a twofold objective of preserving ecological balance and creating sustainable livelihood opportunities for the local communities. Further, most of these areas lack political power and consequently adequate funding. The highly fragile and backward pockets of the Western Ghats should be allocated more funds by the respective State Governments.

4.25. The Bill to include the Darjeeling Gorkha Hill Council Area in the Sixth Schedule needs to be expeditiously considered. Moreover, the G.B. Pant Institute for Himalayan Environment and Development (GBPIHED) should reorient its activities to evolve as a centre of excellence and as a resource base for advice on sustainable development of the Himalayan States. The focus of research should include socio-economic development of the mountain habitations. An Indian Alpine Initiative should also be started for tracking the dynamics of alpine biomes in the context of climate change.

Coastal Zone Management

4.26. The Coastal Regulation Zone notification regulates activities based on vulnerability of coastal areas to human activity. Coastal areas are currently classified into four categories (CZ 1 to 4) with different levels of permissivity for development activities. Category 1 includes ecologically sensitive areas, category 4 includes islands, while categories 2 and 3 permit construction activities based on vulnerability.

4.27. The Swaminathan Committee has recommended that local circumstances and vulnerabilities should be the basis of coastal zone management and regulations. For this purpose, scientific and local information should be used in preparation of environmental plans for coastal areas. Conservation of life forms (and their habitats such as nesting/ spawning sites), and integration of their environment with human well-being is important. Participation of civil society and local fishing/coastal communities in the coastal zone management committees should be ensured for building a better consensus for coastal zone environment regulation issues.

Public Participation for Sustainable Development

4.28. Effective management of resources requires participation by all stakeholders. As part of the national sustainable development agenda, the Indian Government has taken measures to develop policy instruments that encourage the active participation of stakeholders and environmental NGOs in national development programmes at the grass-roots level. The engagement of multi-stakeholder platforms such as Green Rating for Integrated Habitat Assessment (GRIHA), Joint Forest Management (JFM), women empowerment under Integrated Infrastructure Development (IID), National Knowledge Network (NKN) and Waste Minimization Circles (WMC) have led to innovations in the areas of poverty eradication, green city development initiatives, entrepreneurship development, empowerment of women and management of forest and water resources. Common-pool natural resources must be managed rationally to improve availability and to ensure equity in access and benefit-sharing. At the local level, strengthening democratic institutions will lead to better and more sustained management of natural resources.

4.29. Biodiversity and ecosystem services are freely available public goods and all of humankind, particularly the poor, depend on them for their livelihood. Environmental education and awareness programmes can be used to influence economic behaviour and encourage the formation of voluntary agreements between firms and local authorities/communities. Public disclosure of information on polluting activities of industries can promote environmental/green labelling of products, which can create pressure in the market to manufacture environment-friendly products. The GoI launched the eco-labelling scheme known as Ecomark in 1991 for easy identification of environment-friendly products. The Ecomark label is awarded to consumer goods which meet the specified environmental criteria and the quality requirements of Indian Standards.

LOW CARBON STRATEGIES FOR INCLUSIVE GROWTH

4.30. India needs to adopt low carbon strategy for inclusive growth in order to improve the sustainability of its growth process, while carbon mitigation will be an important co-benefit. Any such strategy must ensure that the focus is not just on low carbon development, but on increasing productivity that effectively lowers the use of fossil fuels.

4.31. An Expert Group on Low Carbon Strategies for Inclusive Growth was appointed by the Planning Commission. It has submitted its interim report, which outlines the low carbon strategy for major carbon emitting sectors, namely, Power, Transport, Industry, Buildings and Forestry. It has also computed the emission reduction numbers bottoms-up using the inventory building approach in a way similar to the official greenhouse gas (GHG) inventory building system. The 'determined effort' scenario assumes effective implementation of mitigation policies that require continuous upgradation of technology as well as finance from both public and private sources. The 'aggressive effort' scenario requires, in addition to the 'determined effort scenario', design and implementation of new policies that need to be supported through technology and finance from international sources.

4.32. The final report of the Expert Group will include an economy-wide modelling, and an analysis of co-benefits in a cross-cutting framework. It will spell out the policy actions required to implement low carbon strategies up to 2030, and also suggest some finance strategies for the same. To evaluate the alternative policy instruments, a four-pronged strategy of 'growth, inclusion, carbon mitigation and local environment benefits' has been formulated. Taken together, the economy-wide modelling and co-benefits analysis will provide the analytic tools for formulating the low carbon strategies for sustainable and inclusive growth.

The Expert Group has identified twelve focus areas for the Twelfth Plan:

> **Box 4.1**
> **Twelve Focus Areas for the Twelfth Plan**
>
> 1. Advanced Coal Technologies
> 2. National Wind Energy Mission
> 3. National Solar Mission
> 4. Technology Improvement in Iron and Steel Industry
> 5. Technology Improvement in Cement Industry
> 6. Energy Efficiency Programmes in the Industry
> 7. Vehicle Fuel Efficiency Programme
> 8. Improving the Efficiency of Freight Transport
> 9. Better Urban Public and Non-motorized Transport
> 10. Lighting, Labelling and Super-efficient Equipment Programme
> 11. Faster Adoption of Green Building Codes
> 12. Improving the Stock of Forest and Tree Cover

Co-benefits Framework

4.33. Annex 4.2 provides an indicative and qualitative analysis of the co-benefits that may be associated with each of the twelve policy thrust areas identified by the Expert Group. This initial analysis only examines the direct effects. In the final report, a more detailed analysis will assess the direct as well as indirect effects, the pathways through which policy actions operate, and the interactions among them which will lead to a more informed analysis of synergies and trade-offs.

The focus areas identified by the Expert Group are discussed sector-wise below:

Power

4.34. In the business-as-usual scenario, India would rely heavily on coal to meet its surging power demand. However, this poses an enormous environmental and natural resource challenge, as the Power Sector is the highest contributor (38 per cent) to India's GHG emissions. There are several initiatives which would improve efficiency, and reduce pollution and carbon footprints from this sector. These are discussed in greater detail in the chapter on energy, and therefore, only the main points are summarised here:

Advanced Coal Technologies

4.35. It has already been announced that 50 per cent of the Twelfth Plan target and the coal-based capacity addition in the Thirteenth Plan would be through super-critical units, which reduce the use of coal per unit of electricity produced. Super-critical (SC) power plants, which operate at steam conditions 560°C/250 bars, can achieve a heat rate of 2,235 kCal/kWh as against a heat rate of 2,450 kCal/kWh for sub-critical power plants. The specific CO_2 emission for super-critical plants is 0.83 kg/kWh as against 0.93 kg/kWh for sub-critical plants. Super-critical technology is now mature and is only marginally more expensive than sub-critical power plants. Determined efforts are needed to achieve these results, and prioritisation of coal linkages will be necessary to incentivise adoption of super-critical technology.

4.36. It is also necessary to invest in research and development of ultra-supercritical (USC) units (Box 4.2). These operate at USC steam conditions (620°C/300 bars) and can achieve a much lower heat rate of 1,986 kCal/kWh, while the specific CO_2 emissions are only 0.74 kg/kWh. This technology

> **Box 4.2**
> **Importance of Clean Coal Technology: Ultra-super Critical Power Plants**
>
> An Ultra Super Critical (USC) coal-based power plant has an efficiency of 46 per cent compared with 34 per cent for a sub critical plant and 40 per cent for a Super Critical (SC) plant. Thus, with an USC or SC plant, the savings in coal consumption and reduction in CO_2 emission can be substantial. A 10,000 MW power plant will generate 60 billion units of electricity per year at around 70 per cent load factor. It has a specific heat of 1,870 kcal/kwh compared to 2,530 kcal/kwh for a sub-critical plant. Thus, every unit generated with USC will save 0.165 kg [(2,530-1,870)/4,000] coal of 4,000 kcal/kg; and 60 billion units will save 9.9 million tonnes of coal per year.
>
> When we substitute a sub-critical coal plant with solar plants, for every kwh generated we save 0.63 kg of coal (2,530/4,000). Thus, 15.6 billion units (1,000*9.9/0.63) will have to be generated by solar plants to save the equivalent 9.9 million tonnes of coal. Since a solar plant generates 1,500 units per KW of installed capacity, the matching installed capacity needed will be nearly 100,000 MW (15.6*1,000/15,000). *To put it simply, faster adoption of USC and SC technology can save as much coal as would be saved by installation of ten times the solar power capacity.* While from a long term perspective we need the solar option, from a medium term perspective, development of USC and SC technology should be pursued vigorously.

also requires the development of special materials that can withstand very high temperature and pressure. The government should support research and development to promote indigenous manufacturing of USC units. The first USC plant, which is a joint effort of BHEL, NTPC and IGCAR, is expected to be operational in 2017. Deployment of USC plants may be suitably incentivised and targeted during the Thirteenth Plan period.

4.37. Coal gasification provides opportunities for higher efficiency. However, Indian coal has a very high ash content and initial results suggest that efficiency gain over sub-critical units is only marginal. Underground coal gasification is an important technology that will enable utilisation of deep coal deposits, which cannot be mined using conventional means, or because they are located in environmentally fragile regions. It also allows the possibility of in situ carbon capture. Given India's coal shortage, there should be greater research in this technology, including execution of a few pilot projects. Another potentially promising technology is coal bed methane and it may be desirable to undertake some pilot projects in this regard.

Wind Power

4.38. India has a potentially large capacity for adding generation capacity based on wind power. Since the power generated by a wind turbine is highly sensitive to wind speeds, the global practice is now to build towers in the range of 80–120 m, which significantly increases the power generation potential. At the same time, the size of wind turbines has increased—while the earlier turbines were typically less than 1 MW, the recent designs go up to over 5 MW. Taking these into consideration, the wind potential in India is now estimated at about 1,03,000 MW for 80 m hub height. This is based on meso-scale weather models and a land utilization rate at 2 per cent thought to be reasonable for Indian conditions. Some recent studies have estimated India's wind potential to be over 5,00,000 MW based on still higher hub heights and more land availability. However, this assessment is yet to be validated by experts working under Indian conditions.

4.39. Recent technological innovations, including raising the height of the tower, could make wind a major renewable source of power generation for India and we could safely target a wind capacity addition of 30,000 MW by 2020. However, as noted in Chapter 12, wind potential is unevenly distributed across the country; only Karnataka, Tamil Nadu, Andhra Pradesh, Maharashtra and Gujarat have significant potential. Therefore, realisation of wind potential requires careful regional level planning and coordination.

4.40. Wind power has significant seasonal and even intra-day variations. Therefore, setting targets for wind power capacity addition, without making a careful assessment of the capacity of the regional grid to balance its intermittency with alternative sources, may lead to a situation where either the wind generation cannot be utilised, or when the wind suddenly dies down, the loss of generation could impact grid stability and operation. Wind capacity addition needs to be complemented by other energy sources, which have a quick ramp-up time. There are several possible options to handle this intermittency—pumped storage hydro, open-cycle gas turbines, compressed air and high power density batteries. Till recently, these were not considered necessary since total wind capacity was only about 13,000 MW. However, if wind power has to reach 1,00,000 MW and more, the balancing issues will be critical. These variations are a result of technical factors associated with the wind resource, as well as non-technical factors including land policy among others. It will become increasingly necessary to address these factors, if the resource potential of wind energy is to be realised.

4.41. To summarise, achieving ambitious wind generation targets requires careful coordination between multiple Central and State agencies, particularly transmission and distribution utilities, financial institutions and so on. We need to set up a National Wind Energy Mission, similar to the National Solar Mission for effective formulation and implementation of policies both at the National and State levels. The objectives of the Mission should also include, but not be limited to the following:

- Incentivising the industry to invest in indigenous design and manufacture of turbines suited for India's low wind speed regimes. Presently, Indian wind farms use turbines that are designed for global markets.
- Land tenure policies that will encourage mixed land use for wind generation and agriculture (without having to pay commercial rents that will increase the cost of wind power). These powers must be delegated to the local sub-divisional officer.
- The bidding models currently being pursued need to be revisited, so that farmers, wherever willing, are able to benefit from mixed land use and a cost-plus approach can be used to determine feed-in tariffs provided it is done through an independent regulator.
- Mechanisms for using the National Clean Energy Fund (NCEF) to finance development of local grids by state distribution companies that will help evacuate wind power and solve the load curve problems on the supply side.
- Prioritise the development of pumped hydro storage, which may be suitable for complementing wind power.
- Invest in R&D in energy storage options that can provide backup for longer durations, like compressed air and high power density batteries among others.

4.42. India also has considerable off-shore wind potential, particularly in Tamil Nadu and Andhra Pradesh. It is also important to undertake studies to examine the economic viability and risks associated with off-shore wind in the Indian conditions.

Solar Power

4.43. The Jawaharlal Nehru National Solar Mission (JNNSM) envisages grid parity for solar power by 2022 and sets an ambitious target of setting up 20,000 MW for solar power with phased scale-up of capacity, coupled with technological innovation. Solar photovoltaic and solar thermal are each expected to contribute 50 per cent of the above target, in addition to a 2,000 MW target for off-grid solar power. The Government has facilitated generous financial incentives for grid-connected solar plants in the form of feed-in tariffs valid for 25 years. The Government has also incentivized state-level utilities to accelerate solar capacity addition by mandating a three per cent solar power target by 2022 (under the National Tariff Policy) and by providing opportunity for additional revenue streams through instruments such as Renewable Energy Certificates (RECs).

4.44. The feed-in tariff is determined through a competitive (bidding) process. In the two rounds of bidding so far, developers have bid at prices substantially lower than the nominal tariffs specified by Central Electricity Regulatory Commission (CERC). There are indications that the cost of solar cells could reduce further. Solar photovoltaic technologies have several advantages: they can provide distributed power, enable quick capacity addition and work with diffused solar radiation. Solar thermal technologies are conducive for utility-scale power generation, and have the advantage of energy storage and hybridization with biomass/gas to achieve greater capacity-utilisation. This can be used to provide base load power. However, solar thermal technologies only work on direct beam radiation and utility-scale plants require large amount of land and water, which could be potential impediments in scaling it up.

4.45. Amongst all the power generation sources, solar presents a unique opportunity for inclusive growth by providing clean off-grid electricity to the rural communities. The NSM has targeted 2,000 MW of off-grid solar power by 2022. Current guidelines limit a solar micro-grid to 100 kW per site and provide a capital subsidy of 30 per cent. The concept of micro-grid, even though attractive, has so far not been effective in augmenting rural power generation. This is mainly because the developers have found it difficult to get reasonable returns on their investments and they are unable to collect adequate revenues to cover operating expenses despite the initial capital subsidy.

4.46. Since the capital subsidy mechanism is not sufficient to incentivise developers to take the risk of setting up micro-grids, there is a need to examine other options given that rural electricity supply causes loss to the power utilities and it could take several years before reliable grid power reaches all the villages. First, there is a need for relaxing the cap on total and site-based project capacity. This could help rural industrial consumers who have high load requirements, but are constrained by guideline restrictions. Second, there is merit in providing a generation-based incentive, similar to that provided for grid-connected systems. This would make the off-grid solar projects bankable and assure the developers of steady revenue stream.

4.47. The rapidly growing telecom sector provides an excellent synergy for augmenting solar power in rural areas. At present there are close to 0.2 million telecom towers and about 40 per cent of these are in the rural areas. This number is expected to double in the next few years. The electricity supply being erratic in the rural areas, most of them rely on diesel for back-up power. Rural micro-grids can not only be used to meet the requirements of the telecom towers, but also to provide power to the rural communities for lighting and irrigation water pumping.

4.48. Currently, several national and state level agencies are involved with implementation of solar power projects, and it is difficult to coordinate and align their efforts. The solar industry is likely to attract large investments in the coming decade, and it is important that a single nodal agency is made responsible for the overall monitoring and implementation of the JNNSM.

4.49. The off-grid and even grid-connected solar power projects under National Solar Mission have taken a long time for financial closure. This is because of the reluctance of local banks to provide financing, due to lack of stability of policies and possibility of default by the utilities. The government should immediately classify solar power projects as 'priority lending' so that banks start giving it due importance in their credit plans.

4.50. Further discussion is needed in designing the institutional structures for ownership and operation of decentralised off-grid solar power systems. For example, enabling local panchayats with a stake in ownership could ensure local maintenance and operation, as also community-ownership leading to improved payment collection. An alternative model would be to have entrepreneurs bid for setting up of a cluster of such plants in a contiguous area, and then maintain and operate them on cluster basis.

4.51. In order to encourage indigenous manufacturing of components used in solar power generation, GoI has mandated for all the projects allotted in 2010–11 that 100 per cent PV modules should be manufactured in India. It has been further mandated that from 2011–12 onwards, 100 per cent of cells used in indigenous modules should be manufactured in India.

4.52. There is a need to review these policies. Crystalline silicon and thin films are the two proven technologies for solar photovoltaic systems. Of these, crystalline silicon dominates the global market; however, there is considerable interest in thin-film systems, given the potential for lower costs. The global manufacturing capacity is several times that of India, and several institutions around the world are pursuing cutting-edge research leading to a rapid decrease in solar cell costs. India needs easy access to the best available global technology to ensure rapid adoption of solar power. At the same time, developing domestic industry for manufacturing solar cells is important. The manufacturing policy should strike a balance between these two objectives, and mandate a more gradual indigenisation of cell and module manufacture. The following steps need to be taken:

1. Our customs duty structure should not be inverted along solar industry's value chain (basic and intermediate inputs should not attract higher tariffs than finished products).
2. The electricity tariff policy of the Government should be neutral to the type of solar technology being deployed in the approved projects.
3. Export subsidies (explicit and implicit) available to foreign manufacturers must be matched by tariff/domestic policy to the extent it provides a level playing field to the domestic solar manufacturers.
4. R&D efforts for indigenous manufacturers should be incentivised by permitting them to compete with government laboratories for research funding through the budgetary sources.

4.53. **Nuclear and hydro power** are also important for emissions reduction, but they face some critical challenges, which are briefly summarised below:

4.54. Nuclear power is considered an important source for low carbon and base-load power generation. India has ambitious plans in nuclear power through a combination of Light Water Reactors, Heavy Water Reactors and Fast Breeder Reactors. However, global concerns regarding safety of nuclear power following the Fukushima nuclear accident in 2011 have slowed down nuclear power capacity addition. Future growth will require addressing public concerns about safety of nuclear power, and consensus-building at the national and local levels. It is unlikely that large nuclear capacity could be added over the Twelfth Plan period.

4.55. Accelerated development of hydro-power potential is critical for our economy. Apart from the need to harness the country's water resources for irrigation and flood control, the motivation for accelerated development of hydro power is two-fold: first, it is required for meeting India's peak power demand; and second, it is vital for large-scale integration of solar and wind capacity into the grid. Storage hydro power has a multiplier effect in facilitating renewable energy as it provides the flexibility necessary to respond to fluctuations caused by intermittent sources of renewable power, particularly wind and solar. Prioritised development of this resource, along with close monitoring of a few carefully selected hydro-projects is important during the Twelfth and the Thirteenth Five Year Plans.

Industry

4.56. Indian industry is among the largest in the world and has some of the most advanced plants and technologies available globally. This sector is also one of the largest consumers of energy, and improving the efficiency of energy use is critical for energy security, improving industry profitability and competitiveness, and reducing the sector's overall impact on climate change. Since this sector is growing rapidly, the opportunities to introduce more efficient technologies are quite large as the capital stock will more than double in the next 10 years.

Industrial Energy Consumption Overview

4.57. In 2007, the industrial use of energy in India stood at 150 million tonnes of oil equivalent (Mtoe), accounting for 38 per cent of the country's total energy use. Though India is the fourth largest consumer of global industrial energy, surpassed only by China, the United States and Russia, its share is only 5 per cent of the total. In 2007, total final energy use in industry across the globe amounted to 3,019 Mtoe leading to direct emissions[2] of 7.6 gigatonnes of CO_2 (Gt CO_2) and indirect emissions[3] of 3.9 GtCO_2. Analysis by International Energy Agency (IEA) suggests that the industry worldwide needs to reduce its direct emissions by about 24 per cent of the 2007 levels to halve global emissions, from the 2005 levels, by 2050.

4.58. Industrial Energy and Emissions Intensity: Iron and Steel, Cement, Chemicals and Petrochemicals, Pulp and Paper and Aluminium are the five most energy-intensive industrial sectors in India. These accounted for 56 per cent of India's industrial energy consumption in 2007. The Compound Annual Growth Rate (CAGR) of the energy consumption of manufacturing industries in India from 1990 to 2008 was 9.8 per cent. The energy intensity of Indian industries has shown a decreasing trend; however, this trend needs to be accelerated and policy interventions may be required to overcome challenges the industry faces as a result of global energy and emission linked constraints. iron and steel, and cement sectors accounted for nearly 60 per cent of the total industrial GHG emissions in India in 2007. We deal with these in greater detail below.

Iron and Steel Sector

4.59. India's iron and steel sector is the largest user of industrial energy in India, consuming 38 million tonnes of oil equivalent (Mtoe) in 2007. India produced 53 million tonnes (Mt) of steel in 2007, an increase of over 10 per cent per year since 2000. India is now the fifth largest producer of steel in the world. Considering a steel consumption of 200 kg per capita per year (up from 48 kg per capita in 2008) to achieve a level of economic development comparable to global standards, India will need approximately 280 Mt of steel per year.[4] Most of this will be produced domestically, as India has comparative advantage in steel production.

Energy and Emissions

4.60. The Iron and Steel industry was estimated to have a Specific Energy Consumption[5] (SEC) of about 29.2 GJ/tonne of crude steel (tcs) and emission intensity of 2.78 tCO$_2$/tcs in 2007.[6] We find that although steel production in India has expanded rapidly, the energy intensity and specific emission ratios have declined considerably. Figure 4.2 depicts this trend over the last two decades.

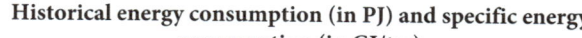

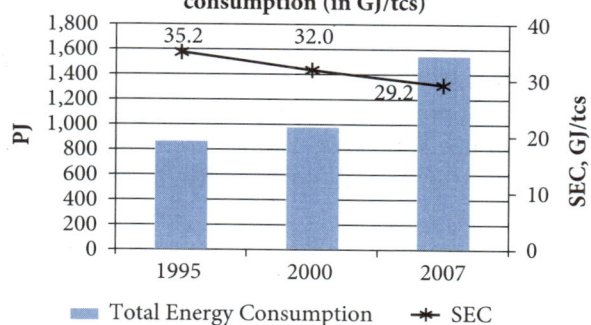

Source: Ray and Reddy, 2008; Singhal, 2009.

FIGURE 4.2: Iron and Steel Industry

Steel Production Processes

4.61. Energy intensity reduction comes from change in technology as well as from increase in efficiency of a particular process. In India there are four main process routes for manufacturing of steel.

1. BF–BOF: The blast furnace and basic oxygen furnace route.
2. DRI–EAF: Coal or gas based direct reduced iron (sponge iron) and electric arc furnace route.
3. COREX–BOF : The Corex process followed by basic oxygen furnace for conversion of iron into steel,
4. Induction Furnace : The induction furnace route for melting and production of steel.

Future Projections

4.62. In 2007, 47 per cent of the steel was manufactured using BF-BOF process; 27 per cent using IF; 20 per cent from COREX/FINEX–BOF and the remaining 6 per cent from DRI–EAF. DRI–EAF is the most energy efficient process, but it depends on the availability of scrap (India is the largest producer of DRI steel in the world). It is expected that BF–BOF will continue to dominate Indian steel production till 2020, while the share of COREX–BOF is expected to increase.

4.63. By 2020, the total steel production could reach 200 MT assuming an average economic growth rate of 8 per cent. The Expert Group has estimated that emission intensity of the iron and steel industry could further reduce by 14 to 17 per cent, over 2007 levels, by 2020.

Policy Measures

4.64. From a policy planning perspective, there are a number of measures that could provide the pathway for reduction of emissions intensity in the iron and steel sector:

1. A shift in the process mix of the iron and steel sector towards more efficient processes
2. Diffusion of energy efficient technologies into the sub-processes of various process routes mentioned above
3. Waste heat recovery systems for moisture reduction and power generation
4. Utilization of renewable energy in specific process/plant/colony applications
5. Increased use of waste as alternate fuels
6. Increased scrap utilisation
7. Improving quality of coke and coal before its use in the industry
8. Low carbon captive power generation

Ministry of Steel and Department of Industrial Policy and Promotion need to work together and evolve a suitable policy framework so that progress along the above dimensions is incentivised to improve the efficiency of iron and steel industry in our country.

Cement Sector

4.65. India is the second largest cement producer in the world, second only to China.[7] Its per capita consumption in 2008 was approximately 150 kg, which is almost a third of the world average. As of March 2009, Indian cement industry comprised of 148 large cement plants and 365 mini-cement plants, with installed capacities of 219 Mt and 11 Mt respectively. India's cement industry is the largest consumer of power among all industries, but it has managed to attain efficiencies comparable to the best in the world.

Energy and Emissions

4.66. The production of cement has increased by 146 per cent from 67 Mt in 1995 to 165 Mt in 2007, while over the same period, Specific Energy Consumption (SEC) has reduced from 3.89 GJ/t in 1995 to 3.3 GJ/t in 2007, which implies energy intensity reduction by about 1.5 per cent every year.[8] Figure 4.3 depicts this historical trend for the cement sector.

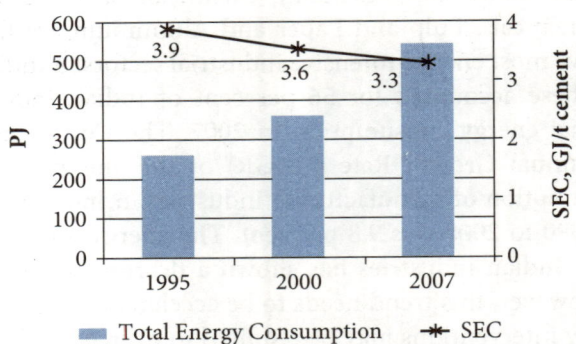

Source: PCRA, 2009; CMA, 2006.

FIGURE 4.3: Cement Industry: Historical Trends of Total Energy (in PJ) and Specific Energy Consumption (GJ/tonne)

Cement Production Processes

4.67. The cement industry comprises mostly of dry suspension preheater and dry precalciner plants, and a few old wet process and semi-dry process plants. The average installed capacity per plant in India is about 1.2 million tonnes per annum (MTPA) as against more than 2.1 MTPA in advanced countries like Japan. Production from large plants (with capacity above 1 MTPA) accounts for 88 per cent of the total production.

4.68. Three types of cements are produced in India: the Portland Pozzolana Cement (PPC), which has the maximum share of the total production (67 per cent), followed by Ordinary Portland Cement (25 per cent) and Portland Slag Cement (8 per cent). Blended cement[9] is another form of cement which is popular in India.

4.69. The production mix in the Indian cement industry is characterized by a large proportion of blended cement (which consumes less energy and is less emissions-intensive than ordinary Portland cement). Although the market share of blended cement in India (75 per cent) is much higher than the US (4 per cent), China (40 per cent) and Japan

(25 per cent) (2005 data), the percentage of blending material could improve further. Most PPC cement plants use fly ash to the extent of 20–30 per cent even though the Bureau of Indian Standards permits usage of up to 35 per cent.[10]

Future Projections

4.70. By 2020, the total cement production could reach 500 mT assuming an average economic growth rate of 8 per cent. In this sector, reduction in energy consumption is primarily attributed to reduction in the energy intensity of production processes. The Expert Group has estimated that emission intensity of cement industry could further reduce by 13 to 16 per cent, over 2007 levels, by 2020.

Policy Measures

4.71. From a policy planning perspective, there are a number of measures that could provide the pathways for further reduction in emissions intensity in the cement sector:

1. Diffusion of energy-efficient technologies in various sub processes of cement manufacture.
2. Waste heat recovery systems for moisture reduction in coal and raw materials and for power generation.
3. Utilisation of renewable energy in specific process/plant/colony applications.
4. Increased use of waste as alternate fuels, rationalizing the various policies that regulate this activity.
5. Increased blending using fly ash from thermal power plants and granulated blast furnace slag from steel plants, and the increased use of composite cements.
6. Improving quality of coal before its use in the industry.
7. Low carbon captive power generation.
8. Increase of blended cements in the public procurement process.

Department of Industrial Policy and Promotion needs to evolve a suitable policy framework to incentivise full realisation of the potential offered by the above measures in the cement industry.

Energy Efficiency Interventions in the Industry

PAT Mechanism Overview

4.72. Perform-Achieve-Trade (PAT) is a market-based mechanism under the National Mission for Enhanced Energy Efficiency (NMEEE), under the Prime Minister's National Action Plan for Climate Change (NAPCC). The aim of PAT, as mandated by NMEEE, is to improve cost-effectiveness and enhance energy efficiency in energy-intensive large industries through certification of energy savings, which could be traded. The Ministry of Power (MoP) has in March 2007 notified industrial units and other establishments consuming energy more than the prescribed threshold in nine industrial sectors, namely Thermal Power Plants, Iron & Steel, Cement, Pulp and Paper, Textiles, Fertiliser, Chlor-alkali, Aluminium and Railways. The industries notified are referred to as Designated Consumers (DCs). Table 4.1 gives the details.

PAT Framework

4.73. The PAT framework has been developed as per the legal requirement under the Energy Conservation Act 2001 and situation analysis of the designated

TABLE 4.1
Sector-wise Annual Energy Consumption of Designated Consumers

Sector	Minimum Annual Energy Consumption for the DC (Tonnes of Oil Equivalent)	Number of Probable DCs
Aluminium	7,500	11
Cement	30,000	83
Chlor-alkali	12,000	20
Fertiliser	30,000	23
Iron and Steel	30,000	101
Pulp and Paper	30,000	51
Railways[11] (diesel loco workshops)	–	8
Textiles	3,000	128
Thermal power plants	30,000	146

Source: BEE, 2011.

consumers. The PAT framework includes the following elements:

1. Methodology for setting specific energy consumption (SEC[12]) for each DC in the baseline year.
2. Methodology for setting the target to reduce the Specific Energy Consumption (SEC) by the target year from the baseline year.
3. The process to verify the SEC of each DC in the baseline year and in the target year by an accredited verification agency.
4. The process to issue energy savings certificates (ESCerts) to those DCs who achieve SEC lower than the specified value.
5. Trading of ESCerts.
6. Compliance and reconciliation of ESCerts.
7. Cross-sectoral use of ESCerts and their possible synergy with renewable energy certificates.

4.74. The first PAT cycle will be covered in 3 years (2012–15). In the first phase, the energy-intensive DCs (as depicted in Table 4.1) are assigned individual SEC targets and are allotted a 3-year time period to accomplish it. The Monitoring and Verification (M&V) is carried out from the second year onwards. After the completion of M&V, energy saving certificates will be issued and trading will be permitted.[13]

4.75. In the next cycle(s) of PAT scheme (post 2015–16), the number of DCs may get revised as more plants and sectors could be added. Petroleum refineries, petrochemicals, gas crackers/naphtha crackers, sugar, chemicals, port trusts, transport (industries and services), electricity transmission and distribution companies, and commercial buildings and establishments are some of the probable DCs that could be added in the second PAT cycle.

Rationale and Target Setting

4.76. The DCs of the 8 sectors account for about 231 mMtoe (million metric tonnes of oil equivalent) of energy consumption annually (as per the 2007–08 data), which is about 54 per cent of the total commercial energy consumed in the country. The target under the scheme will be defined in terms of the percentage reduction of Specific Energy Consumption (SEC) from the baseline value.

4.77. The methodology of establishing SEC reduction for each Designated Consumer is on a gate-to-gate basis. The targeted energy saving in the first commitment period of 3 years (2012–2015) is estimated at 10 million metric tonnes of oil equivalent (mMtoe), which will amount to 4.2 per cent energy intensity reduction over three years. Further, the overall target reduction of 10 mMtoe would be apportioned amongst identified sectors in proportion to their relative energy use. The break-up of energy consumption and the apportioned energy reduction of each sector is depicted in Table 4.2.

TABLE 4.2
Initial Estimate of Energy Consumption and Energy Reduction Targets

Sector	Energy Consumption in 2007 (mMtoe)	Share of Consumption in 2007 (%)	Apportioned energy reduction by 2015 (mMtoe) over 2007 levels	Number of probable DCs
Aluminium	2.42	1.05	0.11	11
Cement	14.47	6.25	0.6	83
Chlor-alkali	0.43	0.19	0.02	20
Fertiliser	11.95	5.16	0.51	23
Iron and Steel	36.08	15.58	1.56	101
Pulp and Paper	1.38	0.60	0.06	51
Textiles	4.5	1.94	0.2	128
Thermal power plants	160.3	69.24	6.92	146
Total	**231.53**	**100**	**10.00**	**563**

Source: BEE, 2011.

4.78. The PAT scheme is an energy intensity type of cap-and-trade scheme as it does not place an absolute cap on the total energy consumption in the industry. Some people argue that a simpler alternative for achieving energy efficiency and for mobilizing finances with greater certainty, would be to implement a carbon tax scheme. Both approaches have their own advantages and disadvantages. These are compared in the section below.

Cap-and-Trade vs Carbon Tax

4.79. Cap-and-trade programmes are often designed to achieve greater reductions over time, so the cap may be lowered in subsequent years to enable market participants achieve emission reductions gradually. To achieve compliance with the capped emission level, market participants are allocated allowances to emit (1 tonne per allowance) with the total number of allowances summing to the level of the cap. Market participants can purchase allowances from other participants to cover excess emissions, or sell allowances, if they reduce emissions below their allocation. Such trading increases economic efficiency.

4.80. A carbon tax is an alternative to a cap-and-trade (see Table 4.3). It can be given other names like cess, surcharge and levy among others. Although both policies generate a carbon price signal, there is a fundamental difference in the way in which the level of carbon price signal is determined under the two regimes. A carbon tax fixes the price of carbon and allows the quantity of emissions to adjust in response to the level of tax. In contrast, a cap-and-trade system fixes the quantity of aggregate emissions, and allows the price of CO_2 emissions to adjust to ensure the emissions cap is met.[14] UK's Climate Change Levy (CCL) and Australia's Clean Energy Package are examples of carbon tax.

Foundations of a New Policy Initiative for the Indian Industry

4.81. Global trends in energy and environment are likely to have a major impact on the profitability of Indian industry, as also on the larger goal of energy and strategic security. The existing National Mission on Enhanced Energy Efficiency (NMEEE) has been designed to deal with energy efficiency and emission reduction issues of a relatively small number of large industries, which contribute significantly to emissions. Many of the provisions of NMEEE such as strong baseline, monitoring & verification, penalty and trading mechanisms are not easily extendable to a large number of small and medium units. Some recent studies[15] have emphasised the need for developing a strong framework for increasing awareness and facilitating upgradation of technology in small and medium enterprises.

4.82. India is experimenting with both cap-and-trade in the form of the PAT scheme and a carbon tax in the form of a cess on coal (₹50 per tonne). Both are in early stages of implementation. While the cap-and-trade mechanisms have a greater certainty in emissions reduction, as a tool for financing they face greater uncertainty. Carbon tax mechanisms, on the other hand, can provide greater certainty as a source of financing, while uncertainty on emissions reduction can be brought down by using energy or emission intensity benchmarks.

4.83. Studies on the demand side of energy consumption have shown that pay-back periods for energy efficiency measures are in the range of two to eight years. Yet firms do not take up such measures on their own. The major barriers are perceived risk, uncertainty about technology, costs of disruption and initial financing. What is needed is a mechanism to insure risk and assure finance on reasonable terms. The need of the hour is to set up a special fund with seed capital that will be managed at an arm's length from the Government, with the participation of the private industry.

4.84. While the PAT should continue to evolve, it would be useful to envisage a combined Energy Efficiency Package—consisting of the PAT scheme and an Energy Conservation Fund, to be implemented by a unified Central Government agency, namely the Bureau of Energy Efficiency (BEE). The legal provision for this already exists in the Energy Conservation Act 2001, wherein under Section 13, the BEE is empowered to levy fees for services provided for promoting efficient use of energy and it conservation. These services, like capacity building,

TABLE 4.3
Cap-and-Trade vs Carbon Tax

Cap-and-Trade	Carbon Tax
It sets a steadily declining ceiling on carbon emissions, and by creating a market that rewards companies for slashing CO_2 (corporations that reduce emissions below their allotment can sell them on the open market), it uses the free enterprise system to achieve emissions reduction.	Uncertainty about how much will it reduce carbon emissions. However, tax linked to benchmarks of energy or emissions intensity can help improve certainty with respect to mitigation.
It does not provide cost certainty as price of permits fluctuates and could be highly volatile in the spot market.	Carbon tax provides cost certainty by setting a clear price on carbon emissions for many years ahead.
It needs a market monitoring agency to examine issues such as rent seeking, cornering the market and so on.	It is simple to understand and implement.
The design leaves out many small and medium organizations (who together may release significant portion of the emissions).	Carbon tax covers the entire economy, including automobiles, households and other units impossible to reach in a cap-and-trade.
The revenues are likely to be bargained away well before the first trade ever takes place.	Carbon tax raises a clear amount of revenue, which can be used for targeted purposes or rebated to the public.
It can be more easily manipulated to allow additional emissions; if the permits become too pricey, regulators would likely sell or distribute more permits to keep the price 'reasonable'.	The chances of manipulation are remote. The structure of the tax does not allow periodic regulator intervention.
The long-term signals from cap-and-trade are less powerful, and the behavioural changes (for example, choice of the type of power plant) could turn out to be far fewer.	Clear signals and impetus for behavioural changes.
Political pressures could lead to different allocations of allowances, which affect distribution, but not environmental effectiveness and cost-effectiveness	Political pressures could lead to exemptions of sectors and firms, which reduces environmental effectiveness and drives up costs.
It will be a difficult process to adopt different international allowances and make it at par with the domestic allowance.	Carbon-taxing nations can easily offset import price differences with a 'border tax adjustment'.
The setting of the price (in an open market) could be very opaque.	The process is more transparent and trustworthy.
One of the immediate consequences is the design of financial and legal instruments	This directly rewards innovation in engineering.

Source: Yale Environment 360. (2009). Putting a price on carbon: An emissions cap or a tax? Opinion.

preparation of detailed project reports and finance for adoption of energy-efficient technologies, are particularly important for non-PAT industrial units, which are smaller in size and cannot arrange such help on their own.

4.85. Unlike the coal cess which is deposited in the Government account, the energy efficiency fee will be deposited in the Central Energy Conservation Fund managed by the BEE (Section 20 of the Energy Conservation Act). The collections from the fee could be supplemented by international funding, as well as block grants from the Central Government through the NCEF.

4.86. Energy Conservation Fund could be used to leverage and/or finance energy-efficient technology upgradation of the domestic industry, particularly non-PAT industry, on terms softer than commercial borrowing. While participation under the scheme would be compulsory for non-PAT industry, industrial units participating in the PAT scheme could be permitted after one or two PAT cycles are over, but in a manner that does not crowd out the smaller non-PAT industry.

4.87. The UK Carbon Trust Fund could be a workable model for such an effort. An integrated Energy Efficiency Package of the kind suggested above, which covers both PAT and non-PAT industry, needs to be carefully evolved over the Twelfth Plan period. The Expert Group on Low Carbon Strategies should also delve into greater detail on this.

Transport

Vehicle Fuel Efficiency Programme
4.88. The number of motor vehicles in India has been growing at about 10 per cent per annum, while passenger and freight activity by road increased 15 and 6 per cent per annum respectively between 2001–02 and 2005–06, the last year for which data is available.[16] In turn, the fuel consumption has also increased, with petrol and diesel consumption increasing 10 and 8 percent respectively over the Eleventh Plan period. GHG emissions from the transport sector have also grown at 4.5 per cent per anum between 1994 and 2007.[17] Therefore, in addition to ensuring that automobiles pay for their full externalities such as congestion, pollution and reduced safety, India needs to urgently introduce fuel efficiency norms for the automobile industry to address both energy and environmentchallenges. Countries such as the US, Canada, Japan and the EU have already enacted such fuel economy legislations.

Framework of Fuel Efficiency Norms
4.89. Fuel efficiency norms can be defined within a 'standards and labelling' framework. Vehicle labelling is a demand side measure to enable consumers to take an informed decision while purchasing a vehicle, whereas fuel efficiency standards are supply side measures for manufacturers to adhere to.

Vehicle Labelling
4.90. Vehicles should carry prominent labels similar to those made popular by the appliance labelling scheme introduced by the BEE. These labels should give the consumer sufficient information about the relative efficiency of the vehicle to enable him to make an informed choice. It must contain the following:

- The fuel efficiency of the vehicle (in litres/100 km) as determined by an approved test mechanism.
- Its star rating, on a 1 to 5 scale, as compared to other vehicles of the same type and in the same (weight) category.
- A pointer on a band indicating the fuel efficiency position of this vehicle among all vehicles of the same category.

Fuel Efficiency Standards
4.91. Given the relatively smaller size of the average Indian vehicle, the Indian vehicle fleet is among the most fuel-efficient in the world. The fuel efficiency standards should ensure that this characteristic of Indian vehicles is encouraged and preserved. Some measures are suggested below:

- The standards should be applicable to all vehicles sold in India—whether manufactured domestically or imported.
- Ambitious efficiency improvement programmes, such as Japan's 'top runner' programme define efficiency standards based on the best performers in the industry[18]. However, given the efficiency levels of the Indian fleet; Indian standards may be derived considering the average efficiency of the global vehicle fleet of a given type, the best performer and the average efficiency of Indian fleet.
- The standards must ensure that Indian vehicles retain their global fuel efficiency advantage and remain among the most fuel-efficient in their class. It should be noted that the average efficiency of passenger cars in India improved by 3 per cent per annum between 2006–07 and 2009–10, in spite of an increase of 2 per cent per annum in average kerb weight of cars sold in that period.[19] This is comparable to the rate of efficiency improvement proposed in the European Union and South Korea.[20]
- There has been a tendency for vehicles to get heavier without a corresponding increase in capacity, as seen in the 2 per cent per annum increase in average kerb weight of cars sold in India. This is not a desirable trend as it leads to increased fuel consumption without additional benefits. Therefore, standards must contain an explicit disincentive against up-weighting of vehicles. This can be achieved by making the standards not linear, but a sub-linear function of the vehicle weight. In the

sub-linear case, the permitted fuel efficiency loss for a given increase in vehicle weight is lower at a higher weight as compared to the permitted loss at lower weight levels.
- The BEE has already proposed a fuel efficiency scheme for passenger cars, and sought feedback on the scheme at a public consultation held on 1 November 2011. Given the rapid rate of growth of vehicles in the country, this process needs to be expedited. Some suggestions on further course of action are as follows:
  - BEE is in the process of publishing an alternative proposal based on the inputs received. This should be followed by another round of public consultations to ensure that significant concerns are addressed. It should then notify the norms, say, by September 2012.
  - Consumption of diesel by heavy commercial vehicles (buses and trucks) is considerably more than the fuel consumption of cars and two wheelers. Therefore, norms must be defined for these vehicles also at the earliest—say, by the end of 2012.
  - Two wheelers account for about 70 per cent of the vehicle sales as well as vehicle fleet in the country. Therefore, norms must soon be defined for them also.
  - The definition of fuel efficiency norms must not only be expedited, but also be based on public consultations with all stakeholders including the citizens groups and the automobile industry.
  - A clear-cut policy should be put into place for encouraging electric vehicles, including facilities for recharging.

Improving the Efficiency of Freight Transport

4.92. India's growing economy has resulted in increased demand for movement of freight in the country, with freight movement increasing roughly in proportion to the GDP. This has resulted in a corresponding increase in energy consumption and GHG emissions from freight transport. In order to improve the efficiency of freight movement, it is necessary to devise policy instruments to incentivize modal shift to the more efficient modes of freight transport, namely the railways. Rail freight is significantly more energy-efficient than road freight, with the energy intensity of rail freight being 0.18 MJ/tonne-km, while the intensity for road freight being 1.6 MJ / tonne-km , that is a nine-fold difference.

4.93. However, the share of rail in total freight carried has steadily deteriorated from about 88 per cent at Independence to about 40 per cent at present, and the share of road freight has increased correspondingly. Figure 4.4 shows the historical trends in modal shares of freight transport. Such a change in freight modal share has not only increased the emissions, but has had other adverse effects listed below:

1. It has hurt the country's energy security as road freight is powered by diesel, and India imports over 80 per cent of its petroleum requirements.
2. It has worsened the balance of payments situation due to increased oil imports.
3. It has worsened the fiscal deficit given that diesel is a subsidized fuel in India.
4. It has worsened local air pollution in the form of tail-pipe emissions from diesel-powered commercial vehicles, which have been shown to have serious health effects in the form of respiratory problems, cancers and so on.

Increasing the Share of Rail Freight in India

4.94. As a principle, railways (which are more capital-intensive) should be the major freight mode along the major corridors, while road (with its greater reach and flexibility) should be the preferred mode from the 'spine' to the interior parts of the country. India's Integrated Energy Policy of 2006 also recognizes that there should be an increased role for railways in carrying freight in the country. GoI initiated the DFC project by setting up a special purpose vehicle called Dedicated Freight Corridor Corporation of India (DFCCIL) in 2006. The DFC project is expected to result in over 10,000 km of dedicated rail routes over six key corridors connecting India's four largest cities. The first phase of two corridors is expected to be complete by 2016–17. These corridors would be built with modern technology supporting higher axle loads, greater train lengths and speeds, thus further improving efficiency and reducing GHG emissions. However, work on these corridors is behind

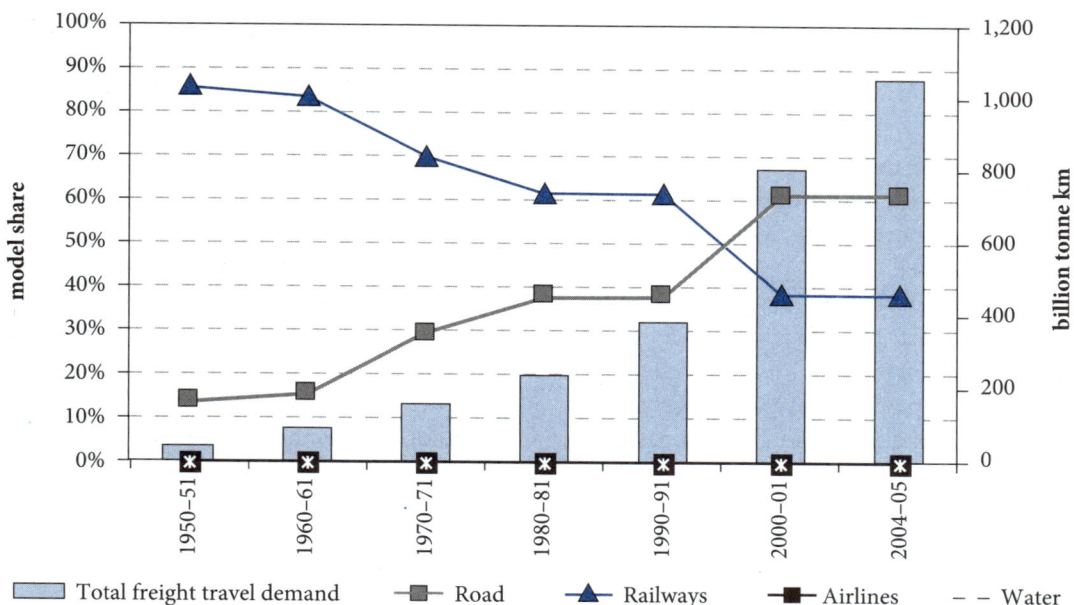

FIGURE 4.4: Modal share of freight transport in India[27]

schedule. The Government needs to use all its energies to ensure this is completed as soon as possible. For details of the dedicated freight corridor project see Chapter 13.

Improving the Efficiency of Road Freight
4.95. Road is expected to play an important part in freight movement even after a modal shift to railways. Therefore, there is a need to ensure that road freight performs as efficiently as possible. There is a perception that current road freight is inefficient because of reasons such as sub-optimal utilization of trucks, inefficient border crossing, toll regimes, insufficient use of multi-axle and tractor-trailer trucks, and lack of hub-and-spoke like arrangements for efficient dispersal of heavy loads onto smaller trucks for last mile connectivity. The Transport Policy Committee needs to further investigate these bottlenecks and suggest solutions to overcome them.

Water-Borne Freight
4.96. Freight carriage by waterways—both inland and coastal—is the most efficient form of freight transport. Though India has a long coastline and about 15,000 km of inland waterways, the share of water in freight transport is negligible at about 0.3 per cent. In contrast, water transport occupies about 6 per cent of the freight modal share in Europe. There is considerable room for improvement in this regard, and the GoI must initiate a serious study of how this potential can be maximized without affecting other uses of the water or waterways.

Improving Urban Public and Non-Motorized Transport
4.97. Our need for mobility has been growing rapidly. Official data indicates that passenger-km travelled by Indians is increasing at a rate of about 15 per cent per annum.[22] Consistent with this, automobile sales in the country are increasing around 10 per cent per annum. From an emissions perspective, this indicates rapid growth of emissions from the passenger transport sector, since most of the transport is powered by petroleum products. Further, such an increase of transport activity has also results in increased imports, since India's net import dependence for petroleum products is about 80 per cent. Given India's energy insecurity and balance of payment problems, there is a need to move transport in a more efficient direction so that mobility needs of our citizens are met with a lower consumption of fossil fuels.

4.98. Figure 4.5 depicts passenger transport activity and emissions in 2007. The important points to note are:

1. Only 4 per cent of the total passenger transport activity is by private automobiles in cities, but they contribute about 20 per cent of passenger transport emissions.
2. Air transport supports only 0.4 per cent of total passenger transport, but contributes 15 per cent to emissions from it.
3. Rail supports 11 per cent of passenger activity, and contributes just 5 per cent of the passenger transport emissions.
4. Non-motorized transport supports 4 per cent of passenger transport activity in the country without causing any emissions at all.

4.99. The way forward therefore is to promote public and non-motorized transport in cities, and rail for intercity passenger travel, while discouraging the use of private vehicles in cities, as well as intercity transport by air. This will have important co-benefits, such as:

1. Making mobility more inclusive as the promoted modes are typically more affordable.
2. Improving the country's energy security.
3. Reduce air pollution in the country's cities, towns and villages.
4. Reducing congestion on our city roads.
5. Improving road safety since studies show that public transport modes have lower per passenger-km fatality rates than private transport modes.

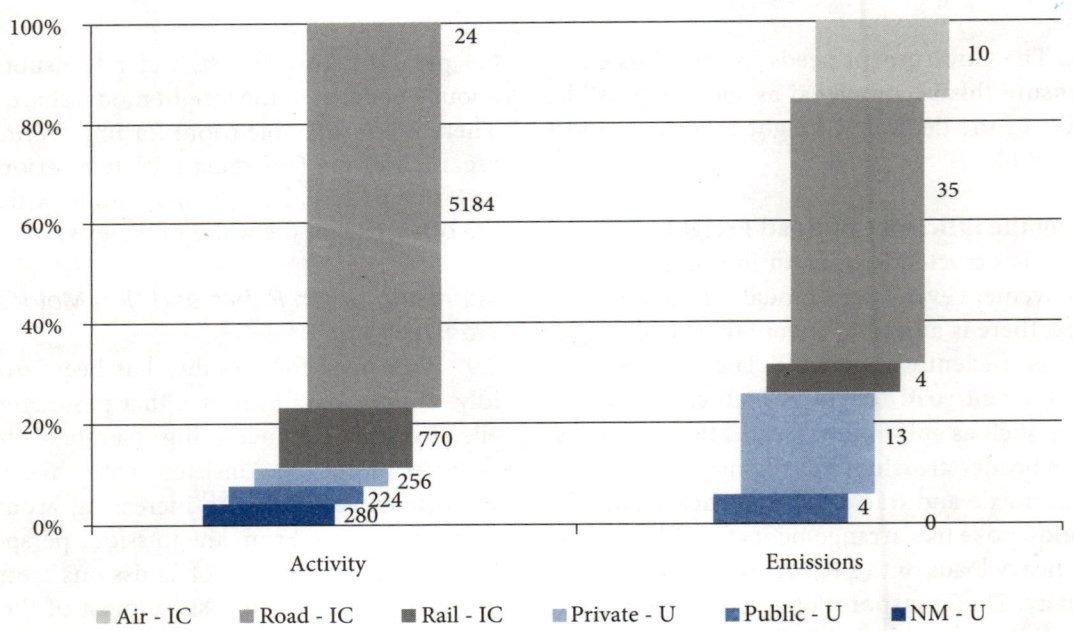

Sources: Ministry of Road Transport and Highways, Year book 2006-07, Directorate General of Civil Aviation, Indian Railways, Ministry of Petroleum and Natural Gas and *Study on traffic and transportation policies and strategies in urban areas in India,* Ministry of Urban Development, May 2008.
Note: NM-U: Non-motorised transport (Urban), Public-U: Public transport (urban), Private-U: Private transport (Urban), Road-IC: Road transport (inter-city), Rail-IC: Rail transport (inter-city), Air-IC: Air transport.

FIGURE 4.5: Passenger Transport Activity and Emissions in 2007

We should focus on policy instruments to encourage greater use of public and non-motorized transport in India's cities and towns, while discouraging the use of private motor vehicles. Official projections show that the current trend is exactly the opposite, as public and non-motorized transport is losing its share to private motorized vehicles. However, since urban transport is a State subject, the levers available with the Union Government are limited; and it is the State Governments and Urban Local Bodies which have an important role to play in realizing the transformation objective described above. The GoI can, however, leverage the funding under the Jawaharlal Nehru National Urban Renewal Mission (JnNURM) to further these objectives.

Supporting Public Transport

4.100. Most urban bus utilities in the country are financially unviable, and a significant part of their financial burden is due to capital expenditure (to buy buses) and taxes. Some studies[23] suggest that these expenses—including various taxes on fuel form about 20 per cent of the total expenditure of a bus utility, and that these are comparable to or higher than taxes on private vehicles. Such taxation policy is clearly contrary to the objective of promoting public transport and discouraging private transport. Government needs to revisit its taxation policy of vehicles and ensure that tax burden on bus utilities is considerably lowered. It could also consider refunding fuel taxes collected from the bus utilities.

Urban Planning and Governance

4.101. Urban Local Bodies (ULBs) in India currently do not have the capacity to deal with the challenges posed by rapid urbanization. As a result, presently, the urban planning in the country does not go beyond provision of basic services to a chaotic urban sprawl, and simply does not take an integrated view of the modern urban requirements, including transport. This needs to be addressed urgently and capacities of ULBs need to be strengthened to enable mixed land use planning and preparation of an integrated transport plan for each city in the country.[24]

Lighting, Labelling and Super-efficient Equipment Programme

4.102. Lighting and appliances (such as refrigerators, air conditioners, water heaters, fans and so on) account for about 10 per cent of the total electricity consumption in India, which was estimated to be 68 billion kWh in 2010–11. With rising incomes and increasing penetration of appliances in households, the demand for electricity for lighting and appliances is expected to rise to 155 billion units by 2016–17. Over the Eleventh Plan period, the standards and labelling programme of the Bureau of Energy Efficiency BEE has enabled consumers to identify and purchase more energy-efficient appliances. Labels have already been introduced for 13 appliances[25]. They have been made mandatory for four appliances, namely, frost-free refrigerators, room air conditioners, tube lights and distribution transformers. As a result of this programme, the average energy efficiency ratio (EER) of air conditioners sold in India increased from 2.2 in 2006–07 to 2.8 in 2011–12; and the average consumption of a 300 litre frost free refrigerator declined from 547 kWh per day in 2006–07 to 368 kWh per day in 2011–12. Overall, savings due to the standards and labelling programme avoided an installed capacity of over 7,500 MW during the Eleventh Plan period.

4.103. The BEE has tightened the labelling norms for refrigerators and air conditioners w.e.f. 1 January 2012, and has notified a second tightening of norms to come into effect from 1 January 2014. As a result of these interventions, a further 30 per cent reduction in the average energy consumption of refrigerators and air conditioners is expected by 2016–17, as compared to those sold in 2011–12.

4.104. Annexure 4.1 provides an estimation of the electricity savings from various appliances in the market. While the actual savings may be different due to changes in assumptions underlying sales projections, the list of the top five appliances that contribute about 85 per cent of the total savings will not change. Of the five appliances, while refrigerators and air conditioners have already effectively adopted the BEE's standards and labelling programme; a greater emphasis is needed for enhancing the efficiency of lighting appliances, motors and fans.

4.105. In the area of lighting, a major shift has taken place during the last 10 years due to large scale replacement of incandescent bulbs by Compact Fluorescent Lamps (CFLs), which consume only 20 per cent as much electricity as incandescent bulbs to produce the same amount of light. During 2011–12, the sales of CFLs in India exceeded 300 million; a 15 times increase as compared to the sales in 2002. However, incandescent bulbs continue to be used primarily in households where the higher first-cost of CFLs continues to be a barrier. The Bachat Lamp Yojana (BLY) provided an innovative business model to sell CFLs to households at the same price as incandescent bulbs, the balance being recovered as carbon credits. However, a sharp decline in the price of carbon credits has effectively made this business model non-viable.

4.106. At the same time, the emergence of solid state lighting, based on Light Emitting Diode (LED), presents an opportunity for another quantum jump in lighting energy efficiency. LED-based lighting appliances (bulbs and tube-lights) are 'super-efficient lights' in as much as they use only half as much electricity as fluorescent devices (CFLs and tube lights) to produce the same amount of light. However, their price is still much higher than those of CFLs; even though the price of a 5 W LED bulb (equivalent to a 10W CFL or a 50W incandescent bulb) declined from about ₹.1,200 in June 2010 to ₹.550 in December 2011. Further price decreases are possible with increased sales volume. During the Twelfth Plan period, enhanced procurement of LED bulbs and LED tube lights could create the sales volume necessary to bring down prices to levels where large scale penetration of LED lights in India would become a reality.

4.107. In a similar manner, 'super-efficient fans', which use half as much electricity as conventional fans, could be of great help in reducing electricity demand from this widely used appliance in the country. The current sales of ceiling fans in India is about 30 million per year and most of them are rated at 70W. The penetration of five-star fans (which are rated at 50W) has been only 2 per cent, reflecting the price-sensitive nature of this market. During the Twelfth Plan period, development, introduction and market penetration of super-efficient fans, which are rated at 35 or less, will be promoted in a manner that boosts their sales volume, while also making them affordable.

4.108. Motors are the fifth application where market transformation towards more energy-efficient motors could lead to large scale savings. Most of the motors are, however, sold to businesses (rather to end-consumers), who incorporate them into other products, such as pumps, fans, air conditioners and so on. Consequently, direct sales incentives for efficient motors may not be the most appropriate or efficient way of promoting their uptake. A more aggressive labelling programme that will help in selection of energy-efficient motors may be more effective. Branding of products containing efficient motors (for example, 'energy efficient motor inside') could help inform the end-consumers about the energy efficiency of products they are buying.

4.109. During the Twelfth Plan period, the Super-Efficient Equipment Programme (SEEP) for super-efficient fans, LED bulbs and tube lights, seeks to incentivize the sale of these products to increase their volumes and bring down their prices for large-scale adoption. This 'virtuous cycle' could be jump-started though provision of a financial incentive for each super-efficient fan or light that is sold, that would help lower the price for end-consumers and enhance sales volume. This will provide confidence to manufacturers to invest in the development, manufacture and marketing of these products, which would otherwise find limited markets because of their higher price. The incentive should decrease with increasing volumes and reducing prices, till it is no longer needed. In terms of the transaction costs, it would be cost-effective to provide the incentive directly to the manufacturers, once third-party verification of sales volume has been carried out. However, performance standards for each of the super-efficient devices need to be put into place before the start of the programme, and periodic check-testing of the super-efficient products that are being sold needs to be carried out to the check conformance to these standards. The SEEP for lights and fans could result in savings of 6.06 billion units per year by 2016–17, and help avoid an installed capacity of 1,500 MW during the Twelfth Plan period.

Green Building Codes

Introduction

4.110. We define the building sector to include residential and non-industrial buildings. The latter are called commercial buildings, which include offices, hospitals, hotels, retail outlets, educational buildings, government offices and so on. Here we only deal with energy consumed in using these buildings. The energy embodied in construction of these buildings and structures is not considered.

4.111. Energy consumption in buildings offers a large scope for improving efficiency. The potential to reduce energy consumption through improvement in efficiency of appliances and equipment is already accounted for above. However, apart from this, buildings can be made more energy efficient by designs that reduce the need for lighting, heating, ventilation and air conditioning. We concentrate on savings in energy intensity that can be realized over and above what is possible through improvement in appliances and equipment.

4.112. The sector-wise electricity consumption in India is shown in Figure 4.6. The residential and commercial buildings account for 29 per cent of the total electricity consumption and this is rising at a rate of 8 per cent per annum (CWF, 2010). Significant part of this goes into heating, cooling and lighting. In order to work out the likely opportunities to reduce emission intensity, we need to first project the likely growth in buildings of different categories. The energy demand by buildings will continue to grow with the growth of IT enabled services (ITES) and the hospitality sectors.

4.113. The major growth in constructed area up to 2030 will be seen by residential and commercial sectors, as much as 4 to 5 times the constructed area in

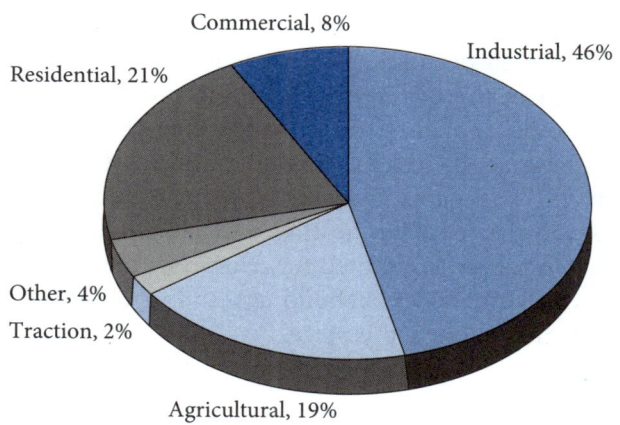

Source: IEA, 2008.

FIGURE 4.6: Sector-wise Electricity Consumption in India

2005 (CWF, 2010). The growth rates in hospitality and retail sectors may be even higher, though their shares are relatively small. While the residential area is projected to increase from 16,300 m sq.ft. in 2005 to 70,000 m sq.ft. by 2030, the commercial build up area is projected to increase from 2,900 m sq.ft. in 2005 to 20,000 m sq.ft. by 2030.

Residential Sector

4.114. Indian residential sector has witnessed phenomenal growth over the last fifteen years, primarily due to population increase, rise in income levels, growing urbanization, change in lifestyles and favourable public policies.

4.115. In 1961, the urban population of India was 78.9 million, that is, 18 per cent of the total population. By 2011 it has reached 377.1 million, which is 31.2 per cent of the total population. The urban populations are predicted to rise to over 600 million by 2031 (High Powered Expert Committee on Urban Infrastructure, 2011). This urban growth, combined with rapid growth in the economy, has put enormous pressure on housing requirements, urban infrastructure and other services. The residential sector accounts for 21 per cent of the total energy consumption[26] in India.

4.116. Ceiling fans and lighting constitute major energy use (62 per cent) in residential buildings.

Refrigeration and air-conditioning constitute another 20 per cent. The efficiency gains from the launch of the BEE energy labelling programme for domestic appliances to enhance energy efficiency of these appliances has already been accounted for above. The gains from redesigning buildings, to reduce the load for heating and air conditioning, have not been accounted for. However, these would be small for residential buildings, and we do not estimate them here at this stage.

Commercial Sector

4.117. The major energy-consuming equipments in the commercial sector are lighting (59 per cent); heating, ventilation and air conditioning (HVAC) (32 per cent), and other office related equipment (9 per cent). Commercial buildings also use window air conditioners and the gains in efficiency of these have been accounted for in the appliance efficiency programme. However, many of the commercial buildings have central air conditioning and chillers, whose efficiencies can be greatly improved. Architectural designs that increase daylight and reduce need for daytime lighting have not been accounted for above; nor have been the gains from better insulation, plugging of leaks and use of natural ventilation for geothermal energy. The gains from Energy Conservation Building Codes (ECBC) are mainly of these types and we estimate the potential for efficiency gains on this basis.

Present Codes and Standards

4.118. Codes and standards as determined by policy can significantly enable the reduction of CO_2 emissions in the building sector. The country has done well in developing various standards like National Building Code (NBC), Energy Conservation Building Codes ECBC and BEE rating programmes for appliances, and the more recent energy rating programme for the existing buildings. The market-driven voluntary Green Building Rating Programmes have significantly transformed the way buildings are designed. Green buildings have the potential to save 40 to 50 per cent energy vis-à-vis the conventional practices. Some of the widely used building codes in India are discussed below.

Energy Conservation Building Code

4.119. Energy Conservation Building Codes, formally launched in May 2007, specifies the energy performance requirements of commercial buildings in India. ECBC has been developed by the BEE under the provisions of the Energy Conservation Act, 2001. The code is applicable to all commercial buildings having a connected electrical load of 100 kW or more (or a contract demand of 120kVA or more).

4.120. The purpose of this code is to provide minimum requirements for the energy-efficient design and construction of buildings. The code is presently in the voluntary phase of implementation and is expected to become mandatory during the Twelfth Plan. However, some States have already moved ahead and notified it within their jurisdiction. The BEE is the primary body responsible for implementing the ECBC; and it works towards policy formulation as well as technical support for the development of these codes and standards, as well as in supporting compliance tools and procedures. States where ECBC has been made mandatory include Rajasthan, Orissa, Karnataka, Uttar Pradesh and Uttarakhand. Other States where ECBC is ready for implementation include Andhra Pradesh, Chhattisgarh, Gujarat, Haryana, Kerala, Maharashtra and Punjab.

Green Building Rating Systems

4.121. One of the major green building rating systems currently operating in India is the Indian Green Building Council (IGBC) programme. The ratings depend on a number of factors including energy consumption. The number of green buildings indicating their aggregate area by rating categories is given in Table 4.4:

4.122. Building sector provides tremendous opportunities for maximizing energy efficiency, and thereby reducing the GHG emissions. The large percentage of buildings (95 percent) that do not comply with the ECBC codes and the large savings that some of the rated buildings have achieved, indicate a large potential for energy savings in the building sector. These opportunities are available in both existing (for example, retrofitting of Bombay House) and new stock, covering both commercial and residential buildings. The projected area of commercial buildings is likely to increase from 4,580 million sq. ft. in 2005 to 15,200 Million sq. ft. by 2020. The existing consumption pattern in conventional buildings (data from BEE), and the consumption trends in some of the recently constructed energy efficient buildings which would be ECBC compliant, have been analyzed. The ECBC compliant buildings are estimated to be 20 to 30 per cent more efficient than conventional buildings. These buildings have many energy conservation measures such as the use of flash blocks, wall and roof insulation, high performance glass, high SRI paints, vegetated roofs, LPD's (<1w/sq.ft.), high performance chillers, economizers, variable frequency drives, cooling towers and so on. The current baseline for CO_2 emissions for conventional buildings is estimated at 40,000 tonnes of CO_2 per million sq. ft. or 430,570 tonnes of CO_2 per million sq. m of building area. The estimated abatement potential will be worked out by the Expert Group in its final report.

Policy Measures

4.123. Since approval plans for buildings lie within the domain of ULBsand/or Urban Development Authorities created by the State Government, the scope for Central intervention is limited, the only real legal backing being the Energy Conservation Act, 2001. However, JnNURM and Finance Commissions are now a major source of finance for the ULBs. *To hasten the adoption of Green Building Codes across the country, implementation of these codes should be made one of the important conditionalties under the revamped JnNURM in the 12th Five Year Plan. The next Finance Commission should also be given the task of linking financial devolution to urban local bodies to the implementation of Green Building Codes within their jurisdiction.*

Forest and Tree Cover

4.124. Enhancing forest and tree cover mitigates climate change by absorbing CO_2 from the atmosphere and turning it into biomass. This section attempts to bring out the present and the future potential that forestry sector of India can offer in mitigating the climate change, by directly increasing the forest and tree carbon sink on one hand, and by promoting efficiency of fuel-wood use, replacement of energy intensive building and household products with wood substitutes on the other. Needless to say, actions aimed at sustainable supply of domestic wood products would also aid mitigation and adaptation efforts, as sustained supplies would not be possible unless forests and tree vegetation themselves are first secured at reasonable levels.

4.125. With regard to the contribution to mitigation and adaptation actions, the forestry sector helps in mitigation by sequestering carbon, and helps in adaptation by increasing resilience of the system through ecological services of water retention, reduction in soil erosion, enhanced provision of renewable resources and so on. The forestry sector can make a positive contribution both in the numerator and the denominator—one, by increasing the forest carbon sink, and two, by increasing the GDP. Local livelihoods depending on forests are most likely to be impacted adversely not only because of climate change, but also due to continued pressure of land use change for development and other purposes. The national strategy aims at enhancing and improving the quality of forest and tree cover, which in turn will

TABLE 4.4
Coverage of Green Building Rating System up to October 2012

Green Building Rating Level	Energy Saving vis-à-vis Conventional Buildings (%)	Number of Buildings rated	Built-up area (in sq.m)
Platinum	40–50	85	19,76,800
Gold	30–40	163	72,06,544
Silver	20–30	48	10,52,107
Certified	15–20	8	82,190

enhance the quantum of forest ecosystem services that flow to the local communities.

4.126. Strategy proposed to realize enhanced potential of forestry sector in mitigation and adaptation should therefore be two pronged—first, focus on actions that promote carbon sequestration; and second, focus on actions that improve and enhance ecosystem goods and services. Some options in the forestry sector for saving, maintaining and increasing forest carbon stocks are enumerated below:

- Conservation and Sustainable Management of Forests:
  - Conservation and sustainable management of protected areas.
  - Sustainable management of native forests.
  - Natural forests and
  - Dissemination of improved and efficient wood-burning cook-stoves.

- Afforestation:
  - National Mission for a Green India.
  - Agro-forestry practices including pulpwood plantations.
  - Energy plantations, that is use of forestry products as bioenergy to replace fossil fuel.

- Wood Products Use Management:
  - Initiate part replacement of energy intensive building materials like cement, iron and steel with lumber.
  - Initiate part replacement of office and domestic furniture made with metals by commercial wood based furniture.

4.127. Our present initiatives like National Afforestation Programme (NAP), together with programmes in sectors like agriculture and rural development, are adding or improving about 1 mha of forest and tree cover annually in our country. This combined with the accretion of biomass in our managed forests, protected areas and in tree cover outside the government forests, the total carbon service at present has been estimated at 138 mt CO_2eq every year.[27] The cost of this business-as-usual reforestation and afforestation activities is estimated at about ₹5,000 crore annually.

4.128. **National Mission for a Green India**: The business-as-usual scenario will however, not suffice. In the Twelfth Plan, the national afforestation programme needs to be re-organized into a more comprehensive 'National Mission for a Green India' (for details see Chapter 7). The Mission is still being finalized, but the realistic aim would to double the present reforestation and afforestation efforts to about 2 mha of forest and tree cover annually. Over a ten-year period, this could increase or improve the quality of forest and tree cover over 20 mha of land area; which includes regeneration of 4.0 mha of degraded forests, improving canopy cover over 2.0 mha of moderately dense forests, restoration of 2.0 mha of degraded scrub/grasslands, and agro-forestry over another 2.0 mha of degraded/fallow agriculture lands, in addition to eco-restoration of mangroves and wetlands. The Green India Mission also proposes to improve the fuel-wood use efficiency (through the improved cook-stoves initiative) in 10 million rural households. It must also lay emphasis on liberalization of felling and transit rules for identified commercial species so that, on one hand, farmers get the right incentives to undertake agro-forestry in a big way, on the other, harvested wood products can replace building materials in house construction, while metal and plastic based furniture can be replaced with wood based substitutes.

4.129. According to preliminary estimates, the cost of this mitigation service would be double the amount currently being spent on afforestation activities—about ₹10,000 crore annually in the Twelfth Plan. It was estimated by the Expert Group that if implemented properly, the Green India Mission would help neutralize an additional 1.5 per cent of India's GHG emissions annually, bringing the total GHG removal by India's forests to 6 per cent by 2020. It will, however, not be possible to mobilize resources of this magnitude from gross budgetary support alone. CAMPA (Compensatory Afforestation Fund Management and Planning Authority) funds, already accumulated, could be used to supplement this resource. The REDD-plus funds (United Nations Collaborative Programme on Reducing Emissions from Deforestation and Forest Degradation in Developing Countries), as and when received, could also be channelized to supplement the available financial resources.

4.130. More resources could be mobilized using the 'Emitter Pays Principle'. Possible mechanism for implementing this could be a system of compulsory carbon credits purchased by emitting entities, equal to their emissions over and above the permissible limit, or a carbon tax regime with proceeds going to the carbon service providers, including the State Forest Departments, in proportion to the quantum of carbon service provided.

AN OVERVIEW

4.131. Human activities result in significant environmental changes that cause damage to species, ecosystems and ecological processes. Preservation of the integrity of these ecological components is critical, considering they provide the bio-physical base necessary for human life, such as water, land, air, forests, biodiversity and so on. Issues related to these will be discussed in detail in the succeeding chapters.

4.132. India needs to adopt low carbon strategies in order to improve the sustainability of its growth process, while carbon mitigation will be an important co-benefit. The focus areas outlined in this chapter deserve special attention, and physical achievement targets need to be fixed and monitored at the highest level. We need to sustain over 7 per cent growth for the next twenty years, if we are to meet the rising aspirations of our people and become a genuine middle income country that provides a decent standard of living to all its citizens. To achieve this dream, pursuit of low carbon strategies is essential, as otherwise, sustainability and energy insecurity would itself become a constraint on our growth process.

4.133. Globally, India's policy goal of achieving sustainable development is guided by the principle of 'common but differentiated responsibility' (CBDR). India is one of the countries that prefer an 'aspirational' rather than a mandatory or 'prescriptive' approach. India feels the issue of sustainable development should be approached with a sense of equity; and the development aspirations of the developing countries should be built into the green economy principles being evolved at the international level.

4.134. If development has to be sustainable, we need to innovate, invest and improve our planning processes at the national, state and local levels. India's opportunity has come in 2012, as we formulate the Twelfth Five Year Plan. To remind what Peter Drucker said, 'Management is doing things right; leadership is doing the right things'. Let us be good leaders first and then managers!

ANNEXURE 4.1
Estimated Energy Savings due to Electrical Appliances Programme in the Twelfth Plan

	Current Market Size (2007)	Expected Annual Growth Rate (2007–2020, in % terms)	Units Sold Cumulatively (between 2014–2020, both included)	Post 2014 Stock Surviving in 2020	Average power consumption (W)	Total Annual Electricity Consumption (in MWh)	Energy Saving Potential (in % terms)	Total Energy Savings Potential (in GWh)
Refrigerators	51,50,000	10.0	9,52,12,234	9,24,44,456	300	12,42,08,520	30	37,263
Motors	20,00,000	10.0	3,69,75,625	3,59,00,760	7,500	67,31,39,244	5	33,657
Air Conditioners	22,53,000	15.0	6,63,23,602	6,45,79,520	1,641	15,26,03,989	15	22,891
Colour Televisions (CTVs)	1,35,00,000	15.0	39,74,11,730	32,84,31,475	120	8,63,11,792	25	21,578
Lighting * (LEDs)	13,04,00,000	12.0	2,90,83,88,221	71,39,96,050	29	3,62,35,300	40	14,494
Lighting* (CFLs+TFLs)	19,56,00,000	12.0	4,36,25,82,331	1,07,09,94,074	29	5,43,52,949	15	8,153
Chillers	7,182	15.0	2,11,423	2,05,863	98,000	4,03,49,215	30	12,105
Ceiling Fans# (super-efficient)	40,00,000	11.0	8,12,46,576	8,03,87,618	65	1,56,75,586	50	7,838
Ceiling Fans# (higher-efficiency)	60,00,000	11.0	12,18,69,863	12,05,81,427	65	2,35,13,378	20	4,703
Central AC and Heat Pump	86,953	10.0	16,07,571	15,60,839	8,400	2,62,22,102	20	5,244
UPS	19,37,817	13.0	4,74,33,986	4,38,65,644	140	4,29,88,331	10	4,299
Computer Servers	2,93,233	20.0	1,35,70,829	1,14,50,034	350	3,36,63,100	10	3,366

* It is assumed that of supper-efficient lighting appliance sales, 40 per cent would be LED's and 60 per cent higher efficiency CFLs plus TFLs.
# It is assumed that of the total ceiling fan sales, 40 per cent would be super-efficient fans and 60 per cent would be higher efficiency fans.

ANNEXURE 4.2
Co-Benefits Framework for Low Carbon Strategies

S. No.	Thrust Area	Co-Benefit Sought	Brief Qualitative Assessment of Co-Benefit Potential
		Power	
1.	Advanced Coal Technologies	Growth	Positive—although costs are marginally higher, coal is used more efficiently. Energy security and reduced import dependence.
		Inclusion	Neutral or mildly negative if power costs increase and are passed on to low income consumers.
		Local Environment	Positive—reduced emission of SOx, NOx and particulate matter.
		Carbon Mitigation	Positive—10 GW of Ultra Supercritical coal plants can reduce emissions by ~ 15 per cent compared to current plants.
2.	National Wind Energy Mission	Growth	Positive—can substitute for fossil fuel imports and provide energy security. Indigenous manufacturing for large capacities can lead to job creation and growth.
		Inclusion	Neutral—Can be mildly negative if average electricity costs increase. Could also be mildly positive through creation of a decentralized energy industry.
		Local Environment	Positive—although land is required for wind installations, policy can enable mixed land use. Noise pollution could be a concern.
		Carbon Mitigation	Positive—zero emissions power.
3.	National Solar Mission	Growth	Mildly positive—can substitute for fossil fuel imports, decrease import bill and providing energy security.
		Inclusion	Neutral—Can be negative at present costs, which are higher than other sources. Could also be mildly positive through creation of a decentralized energy industry.
		Local Environment	Positive—decentralized rural applications substitute diesel, kerosene and firewood. For large projects, dedicated land and water requirement may be a concern due to competing uses. However, solar power does not emit local air pollutants.
		Carbon Mitigation	Positive—zero emissions power.
		Industry	
4.	Technology improvement in Iron and Steel Industry	Growth	Positive—Less fossil fuel consumption, reduction in import of fossil fuels; Improved domestic and global competitiveness.
		Inclusion	Neutral—Mildly positive, if MSME also benefits esp. the sponge iron industry; mildly negative, if cost of output increases.
		Local Environment	Positive—Usually, improved technologies provide increased environmental performance such as reduction in noise, particulate matter, SO_x, NO_x; reduction in slag and other waste.
		Carbon Mitigation	Positive—Reduced emissions per unit of iron and steel produced.
5.	Technology improvement in Cement Industry	Growth	Positive—Less fossil fuel consumption; Reduction in consumption of raw material per unit of cement produced;
		Inclusion	Neutral—Mildly positive if price of cement reduces with higher clinker substitution; mildly negative, if cost of output increases due to technology costs.
		Local Environment	Positive—Usually, improved technologies provide increased environmental performance such as reduction in noise, particulate matter, SO_x, NO_x, and so on; reduction in fly ash, slag and other waste and reduction in landfill;
		Carbon Mitigation	Positive—Reduced emissions per unit of cement produced.
6.	Energy Efficiency Programmes in the Industry	Growth	Positive—Less fossil fuel consumption, reduction in import of fossil fuels; Improved domestic and global competitiveness.
		Inclusion	Positive—Potential price reduction over a longer term due to increased efficiency; Lower consumption could reduce peak power or energy deficit.

S. No.	Thrust Area	Co-Benefit Sought	Brief Qualitative Assessment of Co-Benefit Potential
		Local Environment	Positive—improved technologies provide increased environmental performance such as reduction in noise, particulate matter, SO_x, NO_x, and so on; reduced waste as by-products of energy feedstock are utilized.
		Carbon Mitigation	Positive—reduced production intensity of fossil fuels.
		Transport	
7.	Vehicle Fuel Efficiency Programme	Growth	Mildly positive—reduced fuel imports, enhanced energy security. Savings on fuel expenditure could be invested domestically.
		Inclusion	Neutral, unless it results in significant improvement in bus efficiencies which could lower fares.
		Local Environment	Reduced Air Pollution—as tail-pipe emissions decrease.
		Carbon mitigation	Moderately positive—fuel consumption would reduce, unless undermined by increased driving patterns.
8.	Improving the Efficiency of Freight Transport	Growth	Positive—savings on fuel expenditure, reduced fuel imports. May facilitate enhanced trade.
		Inclusion	Mildly positive—transport cost of goods would reduce, thus impacting overall prices.
		Local Environment	Positive—decreased emissions either through modal shift or improvements in efficiency of road transport.
		Carbon Mitigation	Improving freight transport efficiency will have a positive impact on carbon mitigation.
9.	Better Urban Public and non-motorized Transport	Growth	Mildly positive—reduced fuel imports and savings on fuel expenditure could get invested domestically.
		Inclusion	Positive—mobility for the poor would improve significantly.
		Local Environment	Positive—reduced local emissions
		Carbon Mitigation	Positive—reduced consumption of fossil fuels.
		Others	
10.	Lighting, Labelling and Super-Efficient Equipment Programme	Growth	Mildly positive—energy efficiency is typically cheaper than new power generation, bringing down average cost of electricity.
		Inclusion	Neutral—positive, if appliances supported are used by relatively poor populations; negative, if predominantly used by the rich.
		Local Environment	Positive—energy efficiency substitutes for thermal power generation and brings down local air pollution.
		Carbon Mitigation	Positive—carbon mitigation as energy efficient appliances substitute for thermal power generation.
11.	Faster Adoption of Green Building Codes	Growth	Neutral or mildly positive—decreased energy costs lead to lower investments in higher cost power infrastructure.
		Inclusion	Neutral—negative if green building codes raise costs.
		Local Environment	Positive—energy efficiency substitutes for thermal power generation and brings down local air pollution.
		Carbon Mitigation	Positive—carbon mitigation occurs as energy efficient appliances substitute for thermal power generation.
12.	Improving the Stock of Forest and Tree Cover	Growth	Neutral or mildly positive—forest enhancement can increase ecosystem services.
		Inclusion	Neutral or negative—depends on the existing use of land; and whether afforestation causes displacement and loss of livelihood.
		Local Environment	Positive or negative—depending on the type of forest cover.
		Carbon Mitigation	Positive—forests sequester carbon.

NOTES

1. Lowe, 2001: ADB Publication.
2. Direct emissions include fuel combustion and process-related CO_2 emissions from within the industry.
3. Indirect emissions are emissions from the power generation sector due to electricity use in industry.
4. CCI, 2011; CSE, 2010.
5. Specific Energy Consumption is defined as the ratio of energy consumed to the total quantity of output produced.
6. Centre Study of Science Technology and Policy (CSTEP) estimates.
7. Assocham and Ernst & Young, 2011.
8. IEA, 2011; CSTEP estimates.
9. Clinker mixed with fly ash or slag is termed as blended cement.
10. Assocham and E&Y, 2011.
11. Railways have 8 DCs as per the notification of MoP. As the sectoral energy scenario and energy usage pattern is under study by BEE, these DCs have been excluded from the first cycle of the PAT scheme.
12. Specific Energy Consumption is defined as the ratio of energy consumed to the total quantity of output produced.
13. Bureau of Energy Efficiency (BEE), 2011.
14. Stavins, R.N., 2008. A meaningful U.S cap-and-trade system to address climate change. Harvard Environmental Law Review 32, pp. 293–371.
15. CSTEP 2012. Discussion on low carbon growth for SMEs.
16. Road Transport Year Book 2006–07 and 2007–09, Ministry of Road Transport and Highways.
17. India Greenhouse Gas Emissions 2007, Ministry of Environment and Forests.
18. Top runner program: Developing the world's best energy efficient appliances, Ministry of Economy, Trade and Industry, Government of Japan.
19. Consultation paper on proposed fuel efficiency norms published by Bureau of Energy Efficiency, Ministry of Power.
20. The International Council for Clean Transportation.
21. S. Sundar and C. Dhingra, *Transport and Energy: The Challenge of Climate Change*, International Transport Forum workshop on transport CO2 in emerging economies, Leipzig, May 2008
22. Ministry of Road Transport and Highways, *Year Book* 2006–07.
23. P. S. Kharola and Geetam Tiwari 'Urban public transport systems: Are the taxation policies congenial for their survival and growth', *Economic and Political Weekly* (11 October 2008).
24. For example, High Powered Expert Committee set up by the Government of India, *Report on Urban Infrastructure and Services*.
25. Labels have been introduced for TFLs, Room Air Conditioner, Frost Free Refrigerators, Distribution Transformers, Direct Cool Refrigerators, CTV, Storage Water Heaters, Agriculture Pumps, Induction Motors, Washing Machines, LPG Stoves, Laptops and Ceiling Fans.
26. Cooking is not included. This includes only electricity consumption in households.
27. Jagdish Kishwan, Rajiv Pandey and VK Dadhwal. (2011) Emission Removal Capability of India's Forest and Tree Cover. *Small Scale Forestry*. DOI: 10.1007/s11842-011-9168-9.

5
Water

5.1. The Indian economy and society face daunting challenges in the water sector. The demands of a rapidly industrialising economy and urbanising society come at a time when the potential for augmenting supply is limited, water tables are falling and water quality issues have increasingly come to the fore. As we drill deeper for water, our groundwater gets contaminated with fluoride and arsenic. Both our rivers and our groundwater are polluted by untreated effluents and sewage continuing to be dumped into them. Climate change poses fresh challenges with its impacts on the hydrologic cycle. More extreme rates of precipitation and evapo-transpiration will exacerbate impacts of floods and droughts. It is no wonder then that conflicts across competing uses and users of water are growing by the day. Meanwhile, water use efficiency in agriculture, which consumes around 80 per cent of our water resources is only around 38 per cent, which compares poorly with 45 per cent in Malaysia and Morocco and 50–60 per cent in Israel, Japan, China and Taiwan.

DEMAND AND SUPPLY OF WATER IN INDIA

5.2. Estimates of the annual flow of water available for human use after allowing for evapo-transpiration and minimum required ecological flow vary considerably. The water budget based on Ministry of Water Resources estimates shows utilisable water of 1,123 billion cubic metres (BCM) against current water demand of 710 BCM, suggesting more than adequate availability at the aggregate level given current requirements.[1] The Standing Subcommittee of the Ministry of Water Resources estimates total water demand rising to 1,093 BCM in 2025, which reaffirms a comfortable scenario at the aggregate level even in 2025.

5.3. However, more recent calculations, based on more realistic estimates of the amount of water lost to the atmosphere by evapo-transpiration, are less reassuring. Since the amount of water available is more or less constant, rising demands due to increasing population and economic growth will strain the demand–supply balance. The 2030 Water Resources Group (2009)[2] estimates that if the current pattern of demand continues, about half of the demand for water will be unmet by 2030.

5.4. We must also recognise that water balances for the country as a whole are of limited value since they hide the existence of areas of acute water shortage, to say nothing of problems of quality. What is required is a much more disaggregated picture, accurately reflecting the challenge faced by each region. The exact level at which regions need to be defined would depend on the purposes of the exercise, as also unifying features of the region, such as basin and aquifer boundaries.

NEED FOR A PARADIGM SHIFT

5.5. These challenges can only be met through a paradigm shift in the management of water resources in India. This shift comprises the following elements:

- A move away from a narrowly engineering-construction-centric approach to a more multi-disciplinary, participatory management approach to our major and medium irrigation projects,

with central emphasis on command area development and a sustained effort at *improving water use efficiency.*
- Since groundwater accounts for nearly two-thirds of India's irrigation and 80 per cent of domestic water needs, we need a *participatory approach to sustainable management of groundwater* based on a new programme of *aquifer mapping.*
- A massive programme for *watershed restoration and groundwater recharge* must be launched by transforming Mahatma Gandhi National Rural Employment Guarantee Act (MGNREGA) into our largest watershed programme,[3] giving renewed energy to the reformed Integrated Watershed Management Programme launched in the Eleventh Five Year Plan and launching a completely revamped programme on Repair, Renovation and Restoration (RRR) of Water Bodies.
- A *new approach to rural drinking water and sanitation.*[4]
- All *urban water supply projects to necessarily integrate sewage systems* within them.
- Definite targets for *recycling and reuse of water by Indian industry* to move in conformity with international standards.
- Renewed focus on *non-structural mechanisms for flood management.*
- Vastly *improved systems of water-related data collection and management* as also transparency in availability of data.
- Adaptation strategies to mitigate the likely impact of climate change to be pursued under the National Water Mission (NWM).
- Perennial rivers with sufficient draft through the year could be the focal point of a renewed thrust to inland waterways transport as an environment-friendly economical mode of transport compared to road and rail.[5]
- A *new legal and institutional framework for water* based on broader consensus among the States.

5.6. This chapter provides full details of each of these initiatives in the backdrop of a review of the experience so far and lays out the approach to be followed in the Twelfth Plan period, spelling out the programmes and allocations within which this is to be embodied.

Limits to Large Irrigation Projects

5.7. Traditionally, large dam projects have been the mainstay of the irrigation effort in the country. However, it is now recognised that there are definite limits to the role they can play in providing economically viable additional large water storage.[6] A World Bank study has pointed out that 'there is little value to additional storage in most of the peninsular river basins (the Kaveri, Krishna and Godavari) and in the Narmada and Tapti'.[7] Similarly, a study by the International Water Management Institute (IWMI).[8] shows that Krishna and Kaveri have reached full or partial closure. Another IWMI study shows that in the Krishna river basin, the storage capacity of major and medium reservoirs has reached total water yield,[9] with virtually no water reaching the sea in low rainfall years. Concern has also been expressed that the capture of so much water within the basin and the evaporation of an additional 36 BCM of water has changed the regional climate, increasing humidity and changing temperature regimes, aggravating saline ground water intrusion, and putting at risk the delicate wetland and estuarine ecology which is important not only for aquatic habitats and fisheries, but also for preventing shore erosion. The lack of adequate environmental flows in the Krishna River has significantly aggravated water pollution problems from cities, since domestic and industrial effluents can no longer be sufficiently diluted by flowing water.[10]

5.8. Given these constraints, the trend increasingly is to locate new projects in relatively flat topography that multiplies disproportionately the areas to be flooded and the people to be evicted. It also tends to aggravate already contentious relations between States, as witnessed in the Polavaram dam in Andhra Pradesh, strongly opposed by both Orissa and Chhattisgarh.

5.9. Water flow in the Himalayan Rivers, particularly the Ganga, is of course, far greater than in Peninsular Rivers but here there are other constraints. In the Ganga Plains, the topography is completely flat and storages cannot be located here. In a study for the Asian Development Bank, Blackmore[11] has argued that surface irrigation through dams in the Ganga river basin is of low value since water tables are already high. Similarly for the Indus, Blackmore shows that 'the next major dam (at a cost of US$ 12 billion) will yield less than 1.5 per cent increase in regulated flow'.[12]

5.10. There is also the problem that further up in the Himalayas we confront one of the most fragile ecosystems in the world. The Himalayas are comparatively young mountains with high rates of erosion. Their upper catchments have little vegetation to bind soil. Deforestation has aggravated the problem. Rivers descending from the Himalayas tend, therefore, to have high sediment loads. A 1986 study found that 40 per cent of hydro-dams built in Tibet in the 1940s had become unusable due to siltation of reservoirs.[13] Studies by engineering geologists with the Geological Survey of India record many cases of power turbines becoming dysfunctional following massive siltation in run-of-the-river schemes. Climate change is making predictability of river flows extremely uncertain. This will rise exponentially as more and more dams are built in the region. Diverting rivers will also create large dry regions with adverse impact on local livelihoods (fisheries and agriculture). Rapid rise of the Himalayas (from 500 to 8,000 metres) gives rise to an unmatched range of ecosystems, a biodiversity that is both enormous and fragile.

5.11. The north-east of India is one of just 25 biodiversity hotspots in the world.[14] According to Valdiya[15] as also Goswami and Das,[16] the neo-tectonism of the Brahmaputra valley and its surrounding highlands in the eastern Himalayas means that modifying topography by excavation or creating water and sediment loads in river impoundments can be dangerous. Quake-induced changes in the river system can adversely impact the viability of dams as several basic parameters of the regime of rivers and the morphology and behaviour of channels may change.

The last two major earthquakes in the region (1897 and 1950) caused landslides on the hill slopes and led to the blockage of river courses, flash floods due to sudden bursting of landslide induced temporary dams, raising of riverbeds due to heavy siltation, fissuring and sand venting, subsidence or elevation of existing river and lake bottoms and margins and the creation of new water bodies and waterfalls due to faulting.[17]

5.12. Even more recent research published in *Science*[18] on Zipingpu reservoir-induced seismicity as a trigger for the massive Sichuan earthquake in 2008 raises doubts about the wisdom of extensive dam-building in a seismically active region.

5.13. The ambitious scheme for interlinking of rivers also presents major problems. While detailed project reports (DPRs) have been prepared for a few of the links, many concerns have already been expressed about how far the initiative can be taken. The comprehensive proposal to link Himalayan with the Peninsular rivers for inter-basin transfer of water is estimated to cost around ₹5,60,000 crores. Land submergence and R&R packages would be additional to this cost. There are no firm estimates available for running costs of the scheme, such as the cost of power required to lift water. There is also the problem that because of our dependence on the monsoons, the periods when rivers have 'surplus' water are generally synchronous across the subcontinent.

5.14. A major problem in planning inter-basin transfers is how to take into account the reasonable needs of the basin states, which will grow over time. Further, given the topography of India and the way links are envisaged, it might totally bypass the core dryland areas of Central and Western India, which are located on elevations of more than 300 metres above mean sea level. It is also feared that linking rivers could affect the natural supply of nutrients through curtailing flooding of the downstream areas. Along the east coast of India, all major peninsular rivers have extensive deltas. Damming the rivers for linking will cut down the sediment supply and cause coastal and delta erosion, destroying the fragile coastal ecosystems.

5.15. It has also been pointed out that the scheme could affect the monsoon system significantly.[19] The presence of a low salinity layer of water with low density is a reason for maintenance of high sea-surface temperatures (greater than 28 degrees C) in the Bay of Bengal, creating low-pressure areas and intensification of monsoon activity. Rainfall over much of the subcontinent is controlled by this layer of low saline water. A disruption in this layer could have serious long-term consequences for climate and rainfall in the subcontinent, endangering the livelihoods of a vast population. It is, therefore, imperative that great caution is exercised in moving forward on this proposal.

5.16. The problems listed above provide a clear indication that further large-scale irrigation development in India will not be an easy option. This does not mean that the Twelfth Plan should reduce allocations to this vitally important sector of the Indian economy on which livelihoods of millions of our people depend. The only implication is that we need to seriously reconsider our priorities here. Over the last six decades since independence we have built up huge irrigation capacities. Improved utilisation of these capacities can dramatically add to irrigated area and also lead to a major improvement in water-use efficiency in our large irrigation sector. We also have many large projects underway that need to be expeditiously completed.

5.17. In order to fully understand the scale of the potential that exists in this direction, it would be useful to undertake an overview of the performance of this sector thus far.

Review of Major and Medium Irrigation (MMI) Projects in India

5.18. There has been a massive increase in plan expenditure on irrigation and flood control over the last 60 years. As can be seen from Annexure 5.1, MMI outlays rose from ₹376 crore in the First Plan to a projected outlay of more than ₹1,65,000 crore in the Eleventh Plan, amounting to a total expenditure of around ₹3,51,000 crore over this period.

5.19. At the same time, it is clear that these projects have suffered from massive time and cost overruns. A study carried out by the Twelfth Plan MMI Working Group on cost overruns reveals that the worst offenders are the major irrigation projects where the average cost overrun is as high as 1,382 per cent. 28 out of the 151 major projects analysed witnessed cost overruns of over 1,000 per cent. Of these, nine had cost overruns of over 5,000 per cent. The cost overruns were relatively lower for medium projects but still unacceptably high, the average being 325 per cent. 23 out of 132 medium projects had cost overruns of over 500 per cent and 10 had cost overruns of over 1,000 per cent. The data on time overruns compiled by the Working Group is in Annexure 5.2. A graphic overview is presented in Figure 5.1.

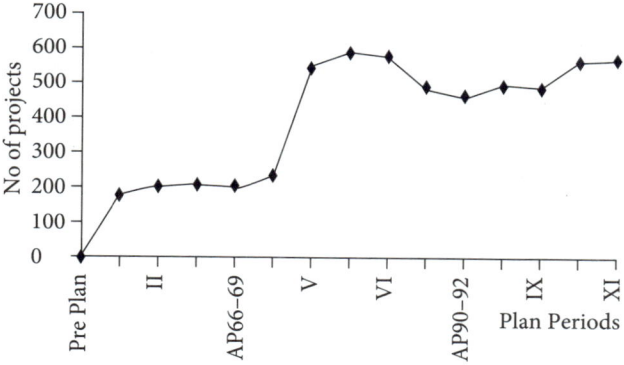

Source: Report of the Twelfth Plan Working Group on Major and Medium Irrigation and Command Area Development.

FIGURE 5.1: Incomplete MMI Projects across Plan Periods

5.20. It can be seen that the number of projects awaiting completion peaked in 1980 to 600; then there was decline till 1992 (460), after which it has again risen to 571, almost touching the 1980 figure again. Major irrigation projects are expected to have a gestation period of 15–20 years while medium projects should take 5–10 years for completion. Against these norms, a large number of major as well as medium projects are continuing for 30–40 years or even more. This reflects poor project preparation and implementation as well as thin spreading of available resources. As can be seen from Annexure 5.3, there is a spillover of 337 projects—154 major, 148 medium and 35 Extension, Renovation, Modernisation (ERM) projects into the Twelfth Plan from previous Plan periods.[20]

5.21. The Twelfth Plan, therefore, proposes that completion of ongoing projects be given the highest priority and new projects be taken up only where there is a demonstrated need of an outstanding character. The reversal since 1992 is also indicative of the declining capacities of individual State Governments in this regard. While financial capacities are being taken care of through programmes such as the Accelerated Irrigation Benefits Programme (AIBP), lack of capacities in terms of human resources and other 'soft' aspects have emerged as major new challenges, which are proposed to be addressed during the Twelfth Plan. The capability of a State to take up new projects in the light of the backlog of ongoing projects will be assessed before sanctioning a new project for the State.

5.22. To check these huge time-overruns, the Twelfth Plan proposes to put in place a systematic mechanism to monitor progress achieved and suggest measures needed to restore time schedules and link it to the annual allocation of plan resources to the States.

The AIBP Experience

5.23. The AIBP was launched in 1996 to fast-track the implementation of ongoing major and medium irrigation projects which were in an advanced stage of completion. Central assistance worth ₹54,251 crores has been provided to the States between 1996 and 2012 under AIBP. The AIBP has been successful in accelerating the rate of creation of additional irrigation potential in the MMI sector, which increased from 2.2 mha per Plan till the Eighth Plan to 4.10 mha during the Ninth Plan following the introduction of AIBP and further rose to 5.30 mha during the Tenth Plan and 4.28 mha during the Eleventh Plan. The real difficulty is that while we have done well in creating additional irrigation capacities, their utilisation has been less than satisfactory (Annexure 5.4). Please refer to Box 5.1.

5.24. The huge investments over the last 60 years have meant that the irrigation potential created through MMI projects has increased nearly fivefold from 9.72 mha in the pre-Plan period to around 46 mha by the Eleventh Plan. However, during the same period, the utilisation of this potential has failed to keep pace. From being almost equal to the potential created in the pre-Plan period (9.70 mha), it is now well short of it, reaching only about 35 mha during the Eleventh Plan. The plan-wise data for irrigation potential created (IPC) and irrigation potential utilised (IPU) is provided in Annexure 5.5. A graphic presentation of the increasing gap between the two is presented in Figure 5.2.

Box 5.1
IIM Lucknow Evaluates AIBP for Planning Commission

To assess the impact of the Accelerated Irrigation Benefits Programme (AIBP), the Programme Evaluation Organisation of the Planning Commission initiated an evaluation of the AIBP. This exercise, conducted by the Indian Institute of Management, Lucknow, carried out sample surveys in 10 different states covering 10 irrigation projects (4 Major, 4 Medium and 2 ERM). The study completed in late 2011 reveals that the gap between the irrigation potential created and utilised in these projects is substantial and growing. Major reasons are low water discharge, insufficient water distribution mechanism, unequal water distribution across farmers located at different points, loss of water during distribution, incorrect recording of irrigated area and diversion of cultivable land to other purposes within the command area.

State Governments are finding it difficult to finance recurring costs of irrigation and to collect economic water charges from the farmers. Majority of the farmers do not pay irrigation charges on time in major irrigation projects of UP, Karnataka, and Assam. These financial constraints not only affect the maintenance of assets under AIBP, that is, water outlets and distribution channels, which was found to be inadequate, but also the sustainability of these irrigation systems with adverse impact on water use efficiency and equity. Importantly, more than 50 per cent of the farmers in major irrigation projects are willing to pay extra charge for assured water supply indicating that access to water is more important than its cost.

If irrigation performance is to improve a wide range of mutually supporting interventions will be needed. Adequate funds should be allocated for timely repair and maintenance of the canals. High priority should be given to the task of lining of the whole canal system and lift irrigation system should be installed on the banks of canals. Farmers should be persuaded to adopt appropriate cropping pattern for optimum use of water. AIBP assistance should be extended even for construction of Field Irrigation Canal networks. Land acquisition needs to be completed before the project proposals are approved under AIBP. Institutional reforms such as restructuring of irrigation agencies including WUAs, irrigation management transfer to the farmers and promotion of self-financing of irrigation schemes is also required.

Source: Planning Commission, PEO, Report No. 214, November, 2010.

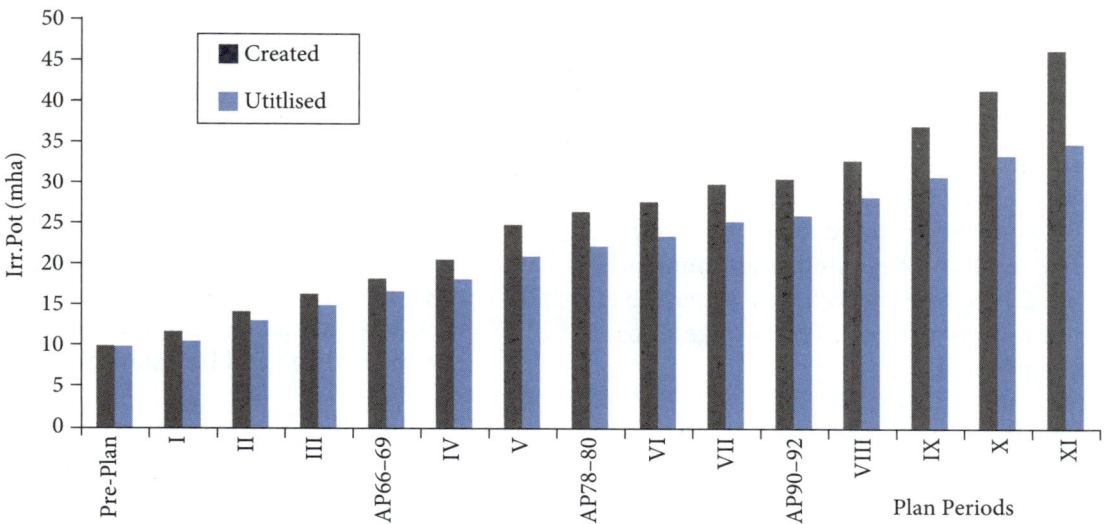

Source: Report of the Twelfth Plan Working Group on Major and Medium Irrigation and Command Area Development.

FIGURE 5.2: Increasing Gap between Irrigation Potential Created and Utilised

5.25. Studies by four Indian Institutes of Management (Ahmedabad, Bangalore, Kolkata and Lucknow) of 34 states and Union Territories (UTs) completed in 2009 show that the IPC–IPU gap reflects implementation issues such as faulty project designs, poor lining and desilting and shoddy maintenance of distribution channels. Another reason is that irrigation potential is defined on the basis of a certain volume of water expected in the reservoir which is divided by a presumed depth of irrigation required for a presumed cropping pattern. However, the actual values of these variables differ from their presumed values because of a switch to water-intensive crops at the upper end of the command. Institutional weaknesses are also important. There is lack of coordination between concerned department officials (resulting in delays in implementation and implementation without proper technical assessment) as also inadequate technical and managerial capacity of irrigation department staff. The absence or ineffectiveness of Water Users Associations (WUAs), is also mentioned as a significant contributor to the IPC–IPU gap.

5.26. The most important initiative for bridging the gap between IPC and IPU is the Command Area Development Programme (CADP) that has been running since 1974–75. Annexure 5.6 summarises the performance of the programme over the last four decades.

5.27. The difficulty is that the CADP has been both divorced from the AIBP and not received the emphasis it deserves. The mode of implementation of the CADP has also left much to be desired in terms of the complement of human resources provided for the programme as also an inadequate understanding of participatory and devolutionary approaches. At times the supporting legal framework in the form of Participatory Irrigation Management (PIM) Acts has been lacking. Only 15 States have enacted PIM Acts and/or amended the existing Irrigation Acts. As many as 13 States are yet to do so. Although a large number of WUAs are reported to have been formed in various States, only a few have actually been handed over the system. Successful functioning of WUAs is reported only in a few projects in Maharashtra, Gujarat, Andhra Pradesh and Orissa. The Twelfth Plan proposes major changes to strengthen these initiatives.

5.28. Perhaps the most important of the five goals of the NWM is to increase water use efficiency by 20 per cent. Given that nearly 80 per cent of our water resources are consumed by irrigation, an increase in water use efficiency of irrigation projects by 20 per cent will have a major impact on the overall availability of water not only for agriculture but also for other sectors of the economy. The Central Water Commission (CWC) has studied the water use efficiency in 30 completed major and medium irrigation projects. The results of these studies are summarised in Annexure 5.7. Nine projects have a water use efficiency of less than 30 per cent. The average across 30 projects is 38 per cent

5.29. Among the factors explaining the low water use efficiency levels identified by the CWC are poor maintenance of canal and distribution network resulting in growth of weeds and vegetation within them, siltation of canals, damage of lining in lined canals, distortion of canal sections due to siltation or collapse of slopes, leakages in gates and shutters. Non-provision of lining in canals, field channels and water courses passing through permeable soil strata has resulted in high seepage losses. No regulation gates on head regulators of minors has led to uneven distribution of water. Cases of over-irrigation due to non-availability of control structures in the distribution system have also been reported. Poor management practices and lack of awareness among farmers have contributed to an adverse performance overall.

MMI Reform: The Twelfth Plan Agenda

5.30. Learning from past experience, the Twelfth Plan proposes a major break from the past by focusing on four main thrust areas in the MMI sector:

1. Complete, as far as possible, the huge backlog of ongoing MMI projects by prioritising the allocation of investible funds to ongoing projects while taking up new only as a matter of exception; completing ongoing projects will help create new MMI irrigation potential of 7.9 million ha during the plan period;
2. Close the gap between IPC and IPU by at least 10 million ha by prioritising investments in Command Area Development and Management (CAD&M) projects and restore an additional 2.2 million ha of lost irrigated potential through ERM works in old MMI projects;
3. Catalyse, support and incentivise deep reform in irrigation departments by strengthening and broad-basing their human resources, by building capacities of civil engineers to move from a narrow construction-orientation to management roles (as being done by their counterparts throughout the world), capacitating Water and Land Managment Institutes (WALMIs) and other irrigation training and research institutions and strengthening incentives in irrigation service provision and Irrigation Service Fee (ISF) collection;
4. Redesign the information architecture of the MMI sector to promote and support strong Management Information System at the MMI level and for improved water resources management at various levels.

5.31. Reflecting the above objectives, the proposed outlays for the MMI sector in the Twelfth Five Year Plan will be subdivided as follows:

- Sixty-five per cent of total outlays will be earmarked for completing the backlog of ongoing projects.
- Fifteen per cent will be earmarked for CAD&M and ERM projects that are likely to quickly add to the irrigation potential. To encourage and support States in taking up CAD&WM works on a priority basis, central assistance to such works will be enhanced from present 50 per cent to 75 per cent of the project costs.
- The remaining 20 per cent will be for new projects, especially in States where irrigation infrastructure is underdeveloped and where great potential remains to be created.

5.32. The Twelfth Five Year Plan proposes the setting up of a National Irrigation Management Fund (NIMF) to catalyse and support demand for irrigation management and institutional reform. This is a departure from the past practice. All along, institutional and management reforms have been pushed through supply-side mechanisms. Thus, many state governments have passed PIM Acts assuming that these per se will make PIM work. Earlier Plans have provided funds for training and research in irrigation management but without notable success.

5.33. The MMI sector has been stuck in a low-level equilibrium during recent decades. It must be recognised that in addition to plan outlays for expanding the system, it is necessary to put maintenance on a viable trajectory. Even as MMI investments are growing, capacities of irrigation departments in many States to deliver quality services are getting depleted. States compete for capital investments in new MMI projects but do little to manage them efficiently. Even farmers in MMI command areas have given up on demanding better services from MMI managers and have increasingly fallen back on private wells. With electricity offered free or at subsidised rates, tubewell irrigation has boomed even in command areas causing widespread groundwater depletion. In many States, ISF to be collected from irrigators has been abolished; where it is not, actual collection of ISF is 2–8 per cent of dues. Because ISF collected has no relation with area irrigated or irrigation service provided, there is total lack of information needed for effective management of the MMI systems. This implies that the accountability loop between farmers and Irrigation Departments is broken. PIM has failed to take off in many States because in the current scenario, WUAs have all obligations but no rights nor secure access to irrigation.

5.34. The starting point in breaking out of this low-level equilibrium has to be increasing resources available with MMI systems managers for proper operation and maintenance (O&M) of systems. In 2005, the World Bank estimated that to minimise deferred maintenance on Indian MMI systems, we need to spend ₹19,000 crore on annual maintenance, which is nearly 20 times more than what States actually spend. State Irrigation Departments are content to generate enough revenue to meet their establishment costs, which many do from the water charges they recover by selling a small proportion of MMI water to industries. But this just covers salaries and leaves little or nothing for regular maintenance and upkeep of systems—especially canals and distribution systems—which affect irrigation more than industrial or municipal customers.

5.35. A related issue has to do with the accountability mechanism built into the ISF. Wherever ISF gets regularly collected, irrigation staff shows greater accountability and responsiveness to farmers. There is greater contact between the two; there is greater oversight of water distribution; and in general, farmers expect at least a minimal level of service if an ISF is demanded of them. When governments abolish ISF or fix it at a token rate or fail to undertake regular collection, farmers forfeit their right to demand service and irrigation staff can afford to neglect service provision.

5.36. Rationalising ISF and its full collection is, therefore, the key to management reform in the MMI sector. The Thirteenth Finance Commission took note of this aspect and recommended a grant of ₹5,000 crore over four years for providing central assistance to each State, linked to outcomes in terms of ISF collection, MMI performance and impacts. However, this incentive grant appears too small to nudge States to take up an aggressive irrigation reform agenda. Moreover, the formula of allocating incentive grants in proportion to Gross Receipts recovered and IPU of different States at the end of the Tenth Five Year Plan is not designed to reward improved irrigation outcomes in future. This is particularly so because many industrially developed States such as Maharashtra, Gujarat and Tamil Nadu can collect significant amounts of revenue by selling small portion of MMI water to industries. But this should not be the reason to ignore ISF collection which needs to be incentivised.

NATIONAL IRRIGATION MANAGEMENT FUND

5.37. Government of India should establish a non-lapsable NIMF, which will reimburse to each State Irrigation Department a matching contribution to its own ISF collection from irrigators on a 1:1 ratio. This will require that:

1. States desiring to avail of this matching grant maintain their own non-plan allocations to Irrigation Departments at the normal rate of growth of the aggregate non-plan budget of the State; that is, ensure that the Government of India (GoI)'s matching support is additional to the

State's non-plan budget for MMI systems which will now have more resources for regular maintenance and upkeep;
2. States allocate central grant to various MMI systems in proportion to the ISF collection of each MMI system; this would incentivise ISF collection among MMI staff and generate competition in augmenting GoI incentive;
3. At the end of the financial year, States desiring to avail of this matching grant will—through their regulator—present a certified, audited statement furnishing detailed data on the actual ISF collected from irrigators from different MMI systems preferably through Independent Water Regulator (or comparable independent agency). The Central Government will have an independent verification undertaken of the claims on ISF collection (including a scrutiny of a sample of vouchers), based on which central matching grant will be released each year.
4. To give strong encouragement to PIM, the NIMF will provide a bonus on that portion of each State's ISF collection which has been collected through WUAs, as certified by the State's Water Regulator and verified by an independent agency designated by the Central Government. This bonus will be allowable only if WUAs are allowed to keep 50 per cent of the ISF collected by them and their federations at the distributary level are allowed to keep 20 per cent of the ISF paid by irrigators. This will expand resources with WUAs and their federations to undertake proper repair and maintenance of distribution systems; and increase their stakes in water management.
5. Similarly, to encourage volumetric water deliveries and ISF collection, NIMF will provide an additional bonus on that portion of a State's ISF collection which accrues through volumetric water supply to WUAs at the outlet level under an irrigation service contract with each WUA.
6. Overall, NIMF will act as a catalyst to undertake reforms in the water sector such as improving water use efficiency, participatory community based managment of aquifers, regulation of groundwater, revamping irrigation/water resource departments and so on.

5.38. It is expected that such an Irrigation Management Fund which incentivises ISF collection, with proper implementation, will produce myriad beneficial impacts. In particular, it will: (*i*) enhance resources available with the MMI system managers to augment and broad-base their staff and their competencies; (*ii*) improve the ISF collection ratio; (*iii*) generate more accurate data on irrigation potential utilised; (*iv*) give strong fillip to PIM; (*v*) speed up CAD & WM; (*vi*) encourage rationalisation of ISF levels; (*vii*) encourage volumetric water supply and pricing; (*viii*) foster partnership between irrigation agencies and WUAs; and (*ix*) in general help reduce the gap between IPC and IPU.

5.39. The Union Ministry of Water Resources is instituting a study to evolve benchmarks for water sector reforms and gradation of States on their reform-friendliness. Based on this study, it should be possible to evolve a 'reform framework' laying down an objective system of benchmarks for assessing the reform-friendliness of the States based on which the incentive system can be operationalised.

5.40. To support institutional and management reform in the MMI sector, resources have also to be earmarked for redesigning the information architecture for the sector. The Ministry of Water Resources has initiated the process of development of a Water Resources Information System (WRIS). This will be completed at the earliest and made fully operational in public domain. Implementation of the NIMF will necessitate compilation of accurate statistics on area irrigated by MMI systems as well as ISF collected from farmers. This will create a reliable database on IPC and IPU, with third party verification. Such a data base will be the foundation of an information, planning and control system for improved management of MMI systems.

5.41. Institutional and management reform will also require major initiatives in training and research. The availability of real-time data on irrigated area, ISF collection and so on will facilitate benchmarking of MMI system performance and level of irrigation service received by users. To stimulate practical problem-solving research on MMI management improvements, the GoI will provide a core grant of up to ₹20 crore to interested national institutes of eminence such as Indian Institutes of Technology, Indian Institutes of Management, National Institutes of Technology, Indian School of Business, and so on to establish centres of excellence in irrigation management to undertake research, education and training for senior MMI managers. Leading management institutes will be invited to develop and offer practical management training to senior MMI managers, with focus on performance management through planning, budgeting and monitoring systems. To support such activities, provision is being made to involve leading players of the Information Technology enabled services of the country to work with State Governments to develop management information systems for MMI schemes with the specific purpose of generating real-time information on the working and performance of these systems to enable their benchmarking.

5.42. To improve the quality as well as amount of training to ground-level functionaries of Irrigation Departments as well as farmers, the GoI will provide each of the 14 WALMIs a grant-in-aid of ₹5 crore over the five-year period to strengthen their training, research and extension work provided: (*i*) they induct trainers in social science, extension, agriculture, environment and other disciplines, (*ii*) undertake regular evaluation of their training programmes, (*iii*) offer a certain minimum number of training programmes for farmers and irrigation staff every year, and (*iv*) submit an independent, third party evaluation report of their work at the end of every year.

MODIFIED AIBP

5.43. To support the objectives and priorities outlined above, central assistance to States under the AIBP will be modified as follows:

1. Central assistance at the rate of 90 per cent will continue for the projects in special category States, projects in KBK (undivided Kalahandi, Bolangir and Koraput) districts of Orissa and projects benefiting tribal areas, drought prone and flood prone areas, as well as in areas included under Desert Development Programme.
2. For general category States, the rate of central assistance under AIBP will be increased to 50 per cent in place of 25 per cent for all ongoing projects, provided the States initiate necessary actions and fully implement the reform agenda set out under the NIMF within the first two years of the Twelfth Plan, that is, during 2012–13 and 2013–14.
3. New MMI projects of general category States will be included for support under AIBP only in exceptional cases and such projects would be eligible for central assistance at the rate of 25 per cent only.
4. Lift irrigation schemes will be taken up for AIBP support only on the condition of implementing micro-irrigation (drip and sprinkler) in the command area of the project. Innovations may be tried in setting up micro irrigation systems (MIS) in clusters through Public–Private Partnership (PPP). Irrigation efficiencies are expected to increase to 90 per cent in case of Drip MIS and 80 per cent in case of Sprinkler MIS.
5. Monitoring of all schemes under central assistance should include a specific mention of the progress made in respect of implementation of the reform agenda of the NIMF.

5.44. To emphasise the centrality of Command Area Development (CAD) to all irrigations projects, the following steps will be initiated:

- All irrigation project proposals (major, medium or minor) will include CAD works from the very beginning. Thus, each proposal will plan for irrigation water from the reservoir to the farm gate and not just the outlet as at present.
- All DPRs will include CAD works and the estimated project cost and Benefit-Cost (BC) ratio will be worked out accordingly.
- No investment clearance will be provided to any irrigation project devoid of CAD integration.
- There will be parallel action in each irrigation command wherein works in the distributary network and software activities of CAD will be undertaken simultaneously with head works and

- main canal work, leading to a seamless integration of work in the head-reaches and tail-end of the command.
- Recognition of potential creation at the outlet of distributary will be discontinued. Potential creation will be recognised only after complete hydraulic connectivity is achieved from reservoir to farm-gate.
- CAD will concentrate on field channels and drainage. The system correction and waterlogging components will be removed as they dilute the programme objective.
- Pipeline-based field channels will be allowed, if necessary, especially in desert and drought-prone areas.
- In order that progress on CAD can be clearly monitored, each investment clearance will distinctly list these works along with head works, canals and distributaries.
- Whenever projects come up for revised investment clearance, they will need to incorporate a CAD component. This will apply even to completed projects that come up with proposals for rehabilitation/modernisation.
- No projects with part components (for example, left bank canal or right bank canal) will be entertained. This has led to a proliferation of projects without corresponding outcomes because the holistic overview of the project has been missing.
- Currently, the CAD wing of the Ministry of Water Resources operates separately from the Water Planning and Projects Wing of the CWC. Beginning with the Twelfth Plan, a Chief Engineer CAD) will work under the Member (Water Planning and Projects) of the CWC so that a more integrated view can be taken of AIBP and CAD.
- The CWC itself will be strengthened to also include agronomists, hydrogeologists and social scientists such as sociologists/anthropologists and social workers who understand the dynamics of engagement with civil society organisations for mobilising farmers in the command areas.

GROUNDWATER: AN EMERGING CRISIS

5.45. While public investments since Independence have focused largely on surface water, over the last three decades, groundwater has emerged as the main source of both drinking water and irrigation, based almost entirely on private investments by millions of atomistic decision-makers. The relative ease and convenience of its decentralised access has meant that groundwater is the backbone of India's agriculture and drinking water security. Groundwater is a common-pool resource (CPR), used by millions of farmers across the country. It remains the only drinking water source in most of India's rural households and many industries depend upon groundwater. Over the last four decades, around 84 per cent of the total addition to the net irrigated area has come from groundwater. India is by far the largest and fastest growing consumer of groundwater in the world. But groundwater is being exploited beyond sustainable levels and with an estimated 30 million groundwater structures in play, India may be hurtling towards a serious crisis of groundwater overextraction and quality deterioration. Please refer to Table 5.1 and Figure 5.3.

5.46. The report of the Expert Group on Groundwater Management and Ownership of the Planning Commission (2007), had reported that in 2004, 28 per cent of India's blocks were showing alarmingly high levels of groundwater use. A recent assessment by NASA showed that during 2002 to 2008, India lost about 109 cu.km. of water leading to a decline in water table to the extent of 0.33 metres per annum.[21] According to the Central Ground Water Board's latest assessment,[22] at the all India level, the stage of groundwater development is now 61 per cent. In Punjab, Haryana, Rajasthan and Delhi, this level has crossed 100 per cent, closely followed by Tamil Nadu (80 per cent) and UP (71 per cent). In addition to depletion, many parts of India report severe water quality problems, causing drinking water vulnerability. Nearly 60 per cent of all districts in India have problems related to either the quantitative availability or quality of groundwater or both. This is a serious situation warranting immediate attention.

5.47. There is no dedicated national programme on groundwater management. While groundwater resources are perceived as a part of a specific cadastre—watersheds, landscapes, river basins, villages, blocks, districts, states—aquifers are seldom

TABLE 5.1
Top 10 Groundwater-Abstracting Countries as of 2010

Rank	Country	Abstraction (km³/year)
1	India	251
2	China	112
3	United States of America	112
4	Pakistan	64
5	Iran	60
6	Bangladesh	35
7	Mexico	29
8	Saudi Arabia	23
9	Indonesia	14
10	Italy	14

Source: 'Managing Water Under Risk and Uncertainty', The United Nations World Water Development Report 4, Volume 1 (2012).

Note: About 72 per cent of the global groundwater abstraction takes place in these 10 countries.

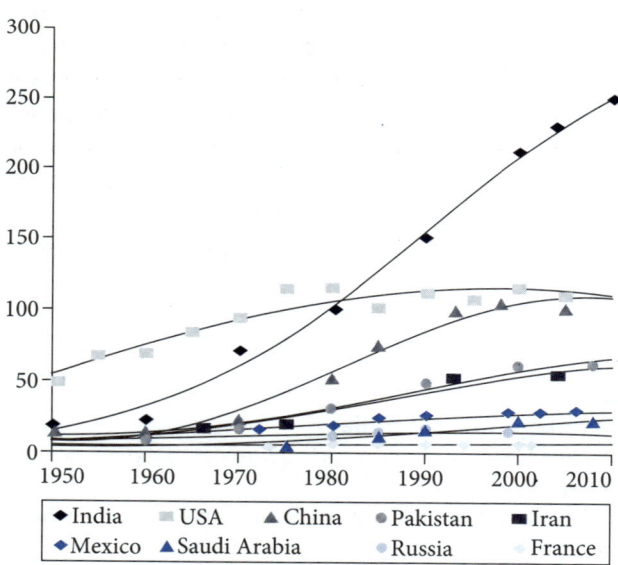

Source: 'Managing Water Under Risk and Uncertainty', The United Nations World Water Development Report 4, Volume 1 (2012).

FIGURE 5.3: Groundwater Abstraction Trends in Selected Countries (in km3/year)

considered. Aquifers are rock formations capable of storing and transmitting groundwater. A complete understanding of groundwater resources is possible only through a proper understanding of such aquifers. The current approach also tends to ignore the common-pool nature of groundwater. As the work of Nobel Prize winning economist Elinor Ostrom shows, the first design principle in management of CPRs is the clear delineation and demarcation of its boundaries. And an understanding of its essential features, which in the case of groundwater includes its storage and transmission characteristics.

Mapping India's Aquifers

5.48. The Twelfth Plan proposes to initiate a comprehensive programme for the mapping of India's aquifers as a prerequisite and a precursor to the National Groundwater Management Programme, which will also be started during the Twelfth Plan period. It is imperative that the design of the aquifer mapping programme has a clear-cut groundwater management purpose. This will ensure that aquifer mapping does not remain an academic exercise and that it will seamlessly flow into a participatory groundwater management programme.

5.49. Implementation of an integrated aquifer mapping and groundwater management programme is possible only through strong partnerships between Government Departments, research institutes, gram panchayats/urban local bodies, industrial units, civil society organisations and the local community. Such partnerships will break down the institutional silos that often constrain focused work on groundwater management. The Central Ground Water Board (CGWB) will lead this effort and State Agencies for groundwater will be constituted or reformed, to bring about organisational parity across the country. Most importantly, the interface of civil society and research institutes with government will be encouraged across all aspects of the programme, ranging from mapping India's aquifers, large-scale capacity building of professionals at different levels, action-research interface with implementation programme and development of social-regulation norms around groundwater, norms that can hold forward linkages to the overarching legislative and governance frameworks (elaborated later in this chapter).

5.50. Groundwater management responses would be most effective when a tractable aquifer typology is developed for the country. Each 'type' within the aquifer typology is a function of the hydrogeological setting, which defines the socio-ecology of groundwater and the level of groundwater development of the specific area. This typology will become the starting point for planning aquifer mapping and designing interventions with regard to groundwater management, including work on recharging aquifers.

National Groundwater Management Programme

5.51. The challenge of groundwater management arises from the fact that a fugitive, common-pool resource is currently being extracted by individuals, millions of farmers in particular, with no effective mechanism to ensure that the rate of extraction is sustainable. The good news is that over the last few years innovative approaches have been tried out across countries, which have blazed a trail in how this paradox might be resolved. Please refer to Box 5.2.

5.52. The Twelfth Plan will launch a National Groundwater Management Programme building upon these diverse experiences and carrying them to scale. The exercise of aquifer mapping will provide a foundation to this effort by enabling local planners to gain an understanding of the following aspects and make plans accordingly:

- Relationship between surface hydrologic units (watersheds and river basins) and hydrogeologic units, that is, aquifers;
- The broad lithological setup constituting the aquifer with some idea about the geometry of the aquifer—extent and thickness;
- Identification of groundwater recharge areas, resulting in protection and augmentation strategies;
- Groundwater balance and crop-water budgeting at the scale of a village or watershed.
- Groundwater assessment at the level of each individual aquifer in terms of groundwater storage and transmission characteristics, including the aquifer storage capacity.
- Regulatory options at community level, including the appropriate regulatory mechanisms at the panchayat level. These may include drilling depth (or whether to drill tube wells or bore wells at all), distances between wells (especially with regard to drinking water sources), cropping pattern that ensures sustainability of the resource (aquifer) and not just the source (well/tubewell), comprehensive plan for participatory groundwater management based on aquifer understanding—domestic water security, food and livelihood security and eco-system security, bearing in mind principles of equitable distribution of groundwater across all stakeholders and inputs to the use of

---

Box 5.2
Participatory Groundwater Management in India

- The FAO-supported APFAMGS programme in Andhra Pradesh aimed at involving farmers in hydrologic data generation, analysis and decision-making, particularly around crop-water budgeting.
- Social regulation in groundwater sharing under the AP Drought Adaptation Initiative (APDAI) involving Watershed Support Services and Activities Network (WASSAN), in parts of AP.
- Experiences from Barefoot College, Tilonia, with a water budgeting tool known as Jal Chitra.
- Foundation for Ecological Security (FES) taking a micro-watershed unit for water balance and planning groundwater use along with communities in Rajasthan, MP and AP.
- Experiences of Advanced Centre for Water Resources Development and Management (ACWADAM) with Samaj Pragati Sahayog in MP and with the Pani Panchayats in Maharashtra on knowledge-based, typology-driven aquifer-management strategies.
- Training programmes and drinking water initiatives by ACT in Kutch training local youth as para-professionals in their quest for improved groundwater management.
- Research on documenting local groundwater knowledge in Saurashtra and Bihar by INREM Foundation.
- The Hivre Bazar model of watershed development and social regulation to manage water resources in Maharashtra.

indirect instruments of regulation, mainly power rationing and/or metering based on aquifer characteristics and degree of exploitation.

Central Ground Water Board (CGWB) Reforms

5.53. Effective management of groundwater requires changes in the nature of coordination among the government ministries related to groundwater (water resources/irrigation, drinking water, rural development, agriculture, environment and forests, urban development, pollution control and industrial effluent). These agencies must be required to assess the impact of their decisions on groundwater and report to CGWB, on issues concerning groundwater. For this to be effective, the institutional mandate of CGWB should be strengthened to enable it to perform its role as the manager of groundwater resource, including hiring from the fields of community institutions, participatory management of resource, political economy and economics, water markets, regulatory systems, alternative uses, opportunity cost of groundwater extraction, energy management and so on.

5.54. The Environmental Impact Appraisal conducted by the Ministry of Environment and Forests needs to include impact on groundwater based on inputs from CGWB. MoEF must be required to seek the opinion of CGWB in all groundwater stressed regions as well as in cases where a negative impact on water quality is anticipated. CGWB may develop protocols for conducting assessment of impact of major (industrial/urban/hydrological) interventions on groundwater and strengthen its own internal capacities to widen its scope of work.

Breaking the Groundwater–Energy Nexus

5.55. The current regime of power subsidies for agriculture has had a major role to play in deteriorating water tables in most parts of India. These very same power subsidies fuelled the Green Revolution, which was driven by groundwater but given the emerging stresses on groundwater, an imaginative way needs to be found, which breaks the groundwater-energy nexus, without hurting farmer interests. Many States have found solutions that are producing very positive results.

5.56. The single most effective solution has been the physical segregation of power feeders to provide 24 × 7 electricity to rural habitations and non-farm users and separate feeders to give 3-phase predictable supply to agriculture, which is rationed in terms of total time, at a flat tariff. This provides requisite power to schools, hospitals and the non-farm economy, while allowing rationed supply of power to agriculture, which can be at off-peak hours. For example, the Government of Gujarat invested US$1,250 million during 2003–06 to separate 8,00,000 tubewells from other rural connections and imposed an 8 hour/day power ration but of high quality and full voltage. This was combined with a massive watershed development programme for groundwater recharge. The net result has been: (*i*) halving of the power subsidy; (*ii*) stabilised groundwater draft and (*iii*) improved power supply in the rural economy.

5.57. Combined with other measures such as High Voltage Distribution System (HVDS), specially designed transformers and energy-efficient pumpsets, this could be a better way of delivering power subsidies that cuts energy losses and stabilises the water table at the same time. Major investments will be required in this direction in the Twelfth Plan.

Promoting Groundwater Development in Eastern India

5.58. It is ironic that while much of India suffers from falling water tables due to overexploitation of groundwater, eastern India is broadly characterised by under-utilisation of this precious resource. During the Twelfth Plan sustainable groundwater irrigation development will be promoted in 11 Eastern Sates including the seven North-Eastern States,[23] in order to more fully realise the potential of this region to contribute to the needs of national food security, even while ensuring that this intensification of groundwater use does not lead to the same deterioration in water table and water quality that has been experienced in other parts of India.

5.59. To ensure sustainability, detailed aquifer mapping exercises at a scale 1:50000 will be conducted to delineate aquifers to be tapped, assess their storage and transmission potential, seasonal fluctuations in water levels, extent of natural monsoon recharge and the quantum of base-flow or rejected recharge. Such surveys would also address the question of water quality, to avoid problems of potential groundwater pollution. Proper hydrogeological survey is the primary requirement to be fulfilled before the scheme is implemented. The number of structures to be taken up will be based on norms for spacing of wells, based on an assessment of the groundwater potential of the aquifers. The subsidy will not be admissible for tubewell/borewell in over-exploited, critical and semi-critical areas in these States. Special care will be taken to ensure safe distance of these tubewells from drinking water sources, so as not to adversely impact the sustainability of these sources. Aquifers affected by arsenic or fluoride contamination will also be avoided. Given the relatively small size of holdings, Water User Groups (WUGs) will be formed around each new tubewell, which would federate into larger Aquifer Management Associations (AMA). The AMA would help facilitate sustainable and equitable ground water management.

5.60. A Steering Committee under the aegis of the Planning Commission and the Ministry of Water Resources, headed by an experienced and renowned professional in the field, will be responsible for preparing the detailed Operational Guidelines and sanctioning projects under the scheme.

INTEGRATED WATERSHED MANAGEMENT PROGRAMME (IWMP)

5.61. The Eleventh Plan saw several path-breaking initiatives in the watershed sector. The outlays of ₹15,359 crore for IWMP and ₹3,095 crore (at 2006–07 prices) for the Rainfed Areas Development Programme of the Ministry of Agriculture were unprecedented. But even more than the outlays a radically new approach was proposed for implementation of watershed programmes in the Eleventh Plan.

5.62. The Technical Committee on Watershed Programmes in India (Parthasarathy Committee) set up by the Ministry of Rural Development submitted its report in January 2006. Drawing upon the lessons of the last two decades, the Parthasarathy Committee proposed key reforms in the watershed programme. These include a dedicated full-time implementation structure run by professionals, especially at the district level and below; a 3-phase programme, which includes an initial preparatory phase of two years focused on building local capacities and institutions; central emphasis on capacity building, involving the best available expertise from the voluntary sector; much greater emphasis on monitoring, evaluation, learning and social audit; building a livelihoods perspective into the programme; enhancing the per hectare norm to ₹12,000 from the prevailing ₹6,000; watershed works to be carried out on clusters of micro-watersheds from 4,000 to 10,000 ha rather than the earlier 500 ha micro-watershed.

5.63. The National Rainfed Areas Authority (NRAA) was set up in November 2006. The NRAA, in coordination with the Planning Commission, issued a new set of Common Guidelines for Watershed Development Projects in February 2008, which are applicable to all watershed development projects in all Departments/Ministries of the government. The Desert Development Programme (DDP), Drought Prone Areas Programme (DPAP) and Integrated Wastelands Development Programme (IWDP) were merged into a single Integrated Watershed Management Programme (IWMP).

5.64. However, a major part of the Eleventh Plan was occupied in completion of a large number of ongoing projects under DDP, DPAP and IWDP, although no new projects were sanctioned under these programmes. Out of 45,062, 41,812 projects were either closed or completed by the end of the Eleventh Plan. The remaining older projects are to be completed by the end of 2012–13 (refer Table 5.2).

5.65. Sanctioning of new IWMP projects commenced towards the latter half of 2009–10 and an area of 15.13 million hectare has been sanctioned across 23 States in the country as given in Table 5.2. Overall, however, against an approved outlay of

TABLE 5.2
Physical and Financial Progress in Watershed Projects of DOLR

Year	Area to be Taken Up for Development (mha)		Finances (₹ in Crore)	
	Target	Achievement	Target	Achievement
2007–08		–	11,14.50	1,164.54
2008–09		–	15,45.00	1,594.40
2009–10	5.41	6.31	17,62.98	1,762.65
2010–11	8.5	8.82	24,58.00	2,456.73
2011–12	8.74	–	25,49.20	–
Total	22.65	15.13	94,29.68	6,978.32
In %	100	67	100	74

₹15,359 crore in the Eleventh Plan, the actual expenditure was only ₹9,430 crore.

5.66. The Ministry of Rural Development constituted a Committee under the Chairmanship of Dr. Mihir Shah, Member Planning Commission to revisit the Common Guidelines for Watershed Development Projects to provide necessary flexibility within the Guidelines and to ensure momentum to IWMP, even while strengthening its innovative features. The key features of the new Guidelines proposed by the Mihir Shah Committee to be applied to watershed projects wef 1st of April 2013 may be summarised as follows:

- Duration: In order to provide greater momentum to the programme and avoid thin spreading of resources, it has been decided to make the IWMP a five-year programme. The division into three phases will continue.
- Professionalisation: One of the key deficiencies of the programme was found to be the shortage of funds to deploy high-quality professional human resources for both social and technical aspects. Hence a special allocation of 10 per cent of the total project cost has been proposed for deployment of professional human resources.
- Capacity Building: A new national strategy for capacity building has been unveiled, since this was a key requirement of the programme that needed much greater direction and momentum.
- Institution Building: This crucial element required to ensure sustainability of benefits under the programme continues to be neglected. Hence, a special provision has been made for this activity and guidelines issued to facilitate the same.
- Role of Civil Society: All reviews of the watershed programme show that the best work has been done by civil society organisations. The new Guidelines seek to provide further scope and facilitation for civil society participation in the programme.
- Ridge to Valley Approach: A watershed programme must follow the ridge-to-valley principle since the ridge is the catchment of streams and water bodies in the lower reaches. If we do not treat these catchments, the capacities of dams in the valley are likely to be impaired. However, it is also to be recognised that this is a participatory programme that needs buy-in from the community. Hence, some work may initially be done in the lower reaches nearer the village settlements so that the people can understand the benefits of the programme and feel a sense of ownership over it. However, it must be ensured that the ridges/catchments of each water body are fully treated soon thereafter.
- Size of Watershed: Experience has shown that both from the point of view of economies of scale and proper planning, the ideal size of a watershed project should be between 3,000 and 7,000 hectares. Wherever possible, additional watersheds in contiguous areas may be taken up so as to form larger clusters. However, smaller size projects may be sanctioned in the hilly/difficult terrain areas.
- Smoother Fund Release Procedures: To overcome avoidable delays in the progress of work, a new set of expeditious fund release procedures are outlined in these Guidelines.
- Setting Up a Central Level Nodal Agency (CLNA): Many States have expressed the need for more intensive support from the Centre. A strong professionally managed CLNA is now being set up with major facilitating responsibilities elaborated in these Guidelines. The role of the NRAA is also being suitably redefined in line with the recommendations of the Working Group for the Twelfth Five Year Plan so that the synergy and

complementarity between CLNA and NRAA can provide requisite support to the watershed programme.
- Convergence: Based on the experience of several States, a new framework is proposed for convergence of IWMP with allied programmes such as MGNREGA, NRLM, RKVY and so on.
- Work on Forest Land: A major concern emerging especially in tribal areas has been the procedural complexities of work in ridge areas that fall within forest lands. These Guidelines proffer a framework within which this work can be facilitated.
- Focus on Physical Outcomes and Monitorable Indicators: These Guidelines provide a clear list of monitorable indicators and green metrics that will be tracked on a regular basis to ensure that the massive outlays are converted into enduring outcomes on the ground.

REPAIR, RENOVATION AND RESTORATION (RRR) OF WATER BODIES

5.67. There is a rich historical tradition of local water harvesting in India from the ahar-pyne system in Bihar, the tankas of Rajasthan, the Himalayan dharas, the talabs in Bundelkhand to the eries of Tamil Nadu. According to the fourth Minor Irrigation Census (2006–07), there are 5.56 lakh water bodies in the country, out of which 3.02 lakh are publicly owned. Tragically, many of these water bodies have been languishing in a state of disrepair and disuse.

5.68. A scheme for the repair, renovation and restoration of these water bodies was launched in 2005. With the aim of covering water bodies that are larger than those covered under schemes such as IWMP and MGNREGA but smaller than those created under medium and major irrigation projects, the Twelfth Plan proposes a major overhaul of this scheme based on the lessons learnt so far as also drawing upon exemplary work done in some parts of the county by civil society organisations such as the DHAN Foundation in Tamil Nadu.

5.69. The major change is to place greater emphasis on not merely the physical repair and desilting of the water body itself but to address the two major challenges that limit their potential benefits to users:

- restoring the health of their catchment areas that would reduce the rate of siltation of the water bodies and prolong their life and
- developing the command areas that are served by these water bodies

5.70. To realise its full potential, the RRR scheme must combine work that is generally done in separate silos of watershed treatment and command area development. It needs also to absorb the central lesson of both these schemes, that it is not merely engineering but institution-building that must equally take centre-stage. This would enable stakeholders to fully participate in the planning and implementation of the scheme and feel a full sense of ownership over the work done and assets created/restored. Without such participation and ownership, the outcomes will be necessarily short-lived and unsustainable.

5.71. The objective must be to converge all RRR projects with the IWMP in such a way that the treatment of the catchment of the water bodies to be restored occurs *paripassu* with, if not prior to, the repair and renovation of the water body itself. This calls for a well-defined 3-tier structure of nested institutions:

1. Water Users' Association (WUA) at the Gram Panchayat Level, which would plan and participate in the implementation of renovation, pisciculture, tree planting and command area development works, as also maintenance and management, including water distribution and conflict-resolution across uses and users. The WUA would also earn revenues by charging for its services from its members and build up a corpus for maintaining and managing the water bodies over time.
2. Cascade Association (CA), wherever water bodies within a milli-watershed are interlinked in a cascade through a network of channels. The CAs will be responsible for renovation, cleaning and excavation of feeder channels and repairs to diversion weirs/regulators on feeder channels. They will also help resolve conflicts across WUAs within the cascade on water sharing and maintenance responsibilities.

3. WUA Federations at the Block level, which will help mobilise funds for rehabilitation of water bodies from various sources, organise training programmes for WUAs, monitor O&M of rehabilitated systems as also the performance of WUAs and CAs.

5.72. During the Twelfth Plan, RRR will cover all water bodies with ayacuts of 20 ha to 2000 ha. A total of ₹5,000 crores is being allocated for the scheme during the Twelfth Plan period. For districts with Gross Irrigated Area less than or equal to 40 per cent of the Gross Sown Area or blocks with SC + ST per cent ≥ 30 per cent, 90 per cent Central assistance will be provided. For all other areas, Central assistance will be 50 per cent. The remaining part is to be mobilised by States from their own resources or through other schemes of the GoI (such as IWMP, MGNREGA, National Lake Conservation Plan, National Wetland Conservation Plan, JNNURM) or through external assistance or through loans from other agencies. Each RRR project will mandatorily include a 10 per cent contribution from stakeholders. Each project will be eligible for assistance of ₹70,000–1,40,000 per ha.

5.73. The typical cost composition of an RRR project will be as follows:

- Physical Works: 80 per cent
- Social Mobilisation and Institution Building: 8 per cent
- Capacity Building: 7 per cent
- Sustainable Livelihoods: 3 per cent
- Monitoring and Evaluation: 1 per cent
- DPR Preparation: 1 per cent

5.74. A Steering Committee under the aegis of the Planning Commission and the Ministry of Water Resources, headed by an experienced and renowned professional in the field, will be responsible for preparing the detailed Operational Guidelines and sanctioning projects under the RRR scheme.

URBAN WATER AND WASTE MANAGEMENT

5.75. Public health implications of unclean water are enormous and unacceptable. It is unacceptable that diarrhoea and other water borne diseases are one of the most common causes of death among children under age five. The Twelfth Plan will focus on the need to invest in water and waste management in human settlements based on a strategy that is both affordable and sustainable.

5.76. The growth of cities and industries is inevitable and this growth will have massive implications on the use of water and discharge of waste. In the industrialised world, water use is primarily in the industrial and urban sectors and the demand from these sectors is also bound to grow in India. This necessitates a 're-allocation' of water from agriculture to industrial/urban use. Unless this is managed in an equitable manner, it is likely to lead to conflict with traditional users in rural areas, especially farmers. Such tensions are already in evidence in certain parts of the country. Indian cities and industries will have to reinvent their water trajectory to both secure the water they need and do so in a way that minimises the scope for conflict. Indian cities and industries need to find ways to grow with minimal water and minimal waste.

5.77. Effective policy intervention requires data on the usage of water. The present system of estimating demand and supply of water in cities is rudimentary and leads to poor accounting and poorer planning. Indian cities compute demand by simply multiplying the population (as known) by an estimate of water demand per capita (as understood). This leads to huge variations between cities in terms of how much water needs to be supplied. The guidelines provided by the Central Public Health and Environmental Engineering Organisation (CPHEEO) are used at times by city planners, but these often fail to provide clarity about how much water is needed.[24]

Management and Equitable Supply of Water

5.78. As important as the quantum of water to be supplied, is the problem of its management and equitable supply to all. In most cities, water supply is sourced from long distances and the length of the pipeline determines the costs, including costs of pumping. In the current water supply system, there are enormous losses in the distribution system because of leakages and bad management.

But equally, there are huge challenges, for water is divided very unequally within cities. As per the NSS 65th round, only 47 per cent urban households have individual water connections.

5.79. Currently, it is estimated that as much as 40–50 per cent of the water is 'lost' in the distribution system. Even this is a guesstimate, as most cities do not have real accounts for the water that is actually supplied to consumers. Nagpur has prepared a water-loss balance sheet. According to this calculation, of the 765 mld the city sources from the Pench forest and tiger reserve—some 40 km away—it finally collects money for a mere 200 mld or 32 per cent of what is sourced. The revenue loss because of this leakage wipes out its entire budget. Please refer to Table 5.3.

5.80. The cost of delivering water is generally not computed or even understood when cities map out the current and future water scenario. City development plans submitted to JNNURM for funding typically emphasise the need to augment supply, without estimating what it will cost, in physical and financial terms. Data suggests that most cities spend anywhere between 30 and 50 per cent of their water supply accounts for electricity to pump water. As the distance increases, the cost of building and then maintaining the water pipeline and its distribution network increases. And if the network is not maintained then water losses also increase. The end result is that the government finds it impossible to subsidise the supply of water to all and, therefore, does not deliver water as needed. The poor are typically the worst-affected as they have to spend a great deal of time and money to obtain water since they do not have house connections.

Groundwater: Missing Link in City Water Accounts

5.81. City water agencies only provide estimates of the groundwater that they 'officially' source and 'officially' supply. They have no records of the amount of groundwater, which is privately extracted in the city, through private wells or supplied through tankers. The Central Ground Water Board's network of observation wells is marginal in cities. The state groundwater board's monitoring data, if available, is not factored into the city water agencies own assessment of water supply and usage in the city. It is clear that parts of the city that remain un-served by official water supply will depend increasingly on groundwater. Cities should, therefore, plan simultaneously for strategies that work to recharge aquifers. Without an assessment of groundwater usage, a city cannot estimate its wastewater discharge accurately, which then leads to flawed planning in terms of sewage and results in pollution.

5.82. The lack of recognition of the existing role of groundwater in city water supply leads cities to discount the need to provide for recharge and the role of local water bodies in this respect. These water bodies and their catchment are often encroached, reducing their supply potential. The essential role of water bodies as sources of local water supply and even potential spaces for sewage water treatment needs urgent consideration.

The Water–Waste Connection

5.83. Even as cities worry about water, they need to focus on the waste this water will generate. Sewage invariably goes into streams, ponds, lakes and rivers of the town, polluting the waterworks so that health is compromised. Alternatively, it goes into the ground, contaminating the same water, which will be used by people for drinking. It is no surprise then that surveys of groundwater are finding higher and higher levels of microbiological contamination—a sign of

TABLE 5.3
Nagpur's Water Highway: Losing as It Travels

Nagpur	Losses	Balance
Journey begins: water is sourced	–	765 mld
Losses in canal	140 mld	625 mld
Measurement losses in raw water purchase	125 mld	500 mld
Treatment	20 mld	480 mld
Distribution/commercial losses in theft/metre error	235 mld	245 mld
Collection losses	45 mld	200 mld

Source: S.S. Hastak, 24×7 Water supply project of Nagpur, NESL, presentation made to Ministry of Urban Development, New Delhi, April, mimeo.

sewage contamination. This compounds the deadly and costly spiral. As surface water or groundwater gets contaminated, the city has no option but to hunt for newer sources of its supply. Its search becomes more extensive and as the distance increases, the cost of pumping and supply increases.

5.84. We have no official accounts for the excreta we generate or the excreta we treat or do not treat. The fact is that we have no way of really estimating the load of sewage in our cities, because of the different ways in which people source water and the different ways in which people dispose sewage. Currently, we measure sewage in the most rudimentary of ways: we assume that 80 per cent of the water officially supplied by municipalities is returned as sewage.

5.85. The imperative is to provide sanitation to all and to ensure that the facility is hygienic and does not add to pollution. Currently, people living in cities greatly vary as to their sanitation status. At the bottom are those with no access to sanitation facilities and at the top are those connected to a flush toilet, which in turn is connected to the official underground sewage network. The 2001 Census found 74 per cent of urban India had access to sanitation and 46 per cent urban Indians had water closets. But it did not specify whether these flush toilets were connected to septic tanks or underground networks or open drains. The 2011 Census has corrected this anomaly as its data sheet differentiates between toilets and disposal systems. Census 2011 shows that only 32.7 per cent urban Indians are connected to a piped sewer system and 12.6 per cent—roughly 50 million urban Indians—still defecate in the open. The challenge is enormous and needs urgent intervention, which provides both sanitation facility and disposal. Please refer to Table 5.4.

5.86. Large parts of the modern cities remain unconnected to the sewage system as they live in unauthorised or illegal areas or slums, where the state services do not reach. In this situation, it is critical, we invest in sewage systems, but it is equally and even more critical that we invest in building affordable and scalable sewage networks, which requires a fresh look at the current technology for sewage and its treatment. Please refer to Box 5.3.

TABLE 5.4
Sanitation Facilities in Urban India

No.	Facility	%
1	**Flush/pour toilet latrine of which connected to**	**72.6**
A	Piped sewer system	32.7
B	Septic system	38.2
C	Other system	1.7
2	**Pit latrine of which**	**8.3**
A	With slab/ventilated improved pit	6.4
B	Without slab/open pit	0.7
C	Night soil disposed into open drain	1.2
3	**Service latrine of which**	**0.5**
A	Night soil removed by human	0.3
B	Night soil serviced by animals	0.2
4	**No latrine within premises of which**	**18.6**
A	Public latrine	6.0
B	Open	12.6
	Total	**100.0**

Source: Census of India 2011, Houses, Household Amenities and Assets: Latrine Facility, Office of the Registrar General and Census Commissioner, India.

Waste–Pollution Connection

5.87. If sewage systems are not comprehensively spread across the city to collect, convey and intercept waste of all, then pollution will not be under control. Currently, according to estimates of the Central Pollution Control Board, the country has installed capacity to treat only about 30 per cent of the excreta it generates. Please refer to Table 5.5 and Box 5.4.

TABLE 5.5
Waste Treatment Capacity in Indian Cities

	Class I (0.1–1 million)	Class II city (50,000–99,999)	Total
Wastewater generated (mld)	35,558	2,697	38,255
Waste treatment capacity (mld)	11,554	234	11,788
Missing capacity (mld)	24,004	2,463	26,467
Untreated Waste (%)	68	92	70

Source: CPCB 2009, Status of Water Supply, Wastewater Generation and Treatment in Class-I cities and Class-II towns of India, Central Pollution Control Board, Delhi.

> **Box 5.3**
> **Bengaluru: The Best?**
>
> No Indian city is in a position to boast of a complete sewerage system. Most Indian cities have a massive backlog of incomplete sewage systems or systems in serious need for refurbishment and repair. The most advanced city is Bengalaru with 3,610 km of sewage lines and 14 sewage treatment plants. The rough estimation is that the city generates some 800–1,000 mld of sewage and the installed capacity to treat it is roughly equivalent—some 721 mld. It also has high tariff, 100 per cent metered supply, high recovery of its dues, 100 per cent water supply and substantial investment in sewage infrastructure. However, there is a significant underutilisation of treatment capacity because Bengalaru's sewage treatment plants only receive some 300 mld of sewage. In other words, less than half the sewage is trapped and half is treated. It is no wonder then that its waterways—rivers and lakes remain polluted and nitrate levels in groundwater are increasing, which is dangerous for health.
>
> *Source:* Report of the Twelfth Plan Working Group on Urban and Industrial Water Supply and Sanitation.

> **Box 5.4**
> **A 'Wave' of Change in Tiruchirapally**
>
> Tiruchirapally (Trichy) in Tamil Nadu has a population of just over a million—of which 25 per cent live in slums. Until the end of the 1990s the slums of Trichy, with their sanitation and toilet facilities in an appalling state, were no different from the rest of the country. But things began to change about 10 years ago, and Trichy has not looked back since. The city was ranked 6th in the sanitation ranking of Indian cities by the Ministry of Urban Development in 2009–10.
>
> It all started with a major initiative launched by the NGO Gramalaya in 2000, mobilising women in the slums in self-help groups (SHGs) and launching an awareness campaign on sanitation through training and building/renovation of community toilets and child-friendly toilets in the slums, which would be managed by the women of the community on a pay-and-use basis. Sanitation health education teams were set up by the SHGs to propagate the message of sanitation, monitor the behaviour of residents, and supervise the maintenance of the toilets. Each toilet has a tap which supplies 24×7 water. Some have graduated to 'sanitary complexes' with room for bathing and washing. The Trichy City Corporation (TCC) waives the electricity charge for the pumping of water for the first few years of operating the toilets. Afterwards, the tariff for community toilets is levied at the lower domestic rate and not commercial rate. Most of these toilets are connected to the sewerage system or function through a septic tank.
>
> At the community toilets run by SHGs, sanitary health education team members take turns to sit at a table placed outside the toilet complex with tokens to sell as people come to use the toilet. They engage cleaners who clean the complex two to three times a day. I found that the toilets were cleaner than what we may typically find in cinema halls in Delhi.
>
> It is clear from the systems they have put in place to manage and maintain these toilets that these women understand the economics of it all. The collection from user charges is used to pay their electricity bills, the cleaner, the guard who keeps the watch, and expenses of minor repairs. The typical user charge varies from 50 paise to ₹1 per use, while children, the elderly and the physically challenged have free access. The accounts are meticulously-kept and are audited by the TCC.
>
> All teams make a small subscription to come together under Women's Action for Village Empowerment (WAVE) which is a registered society. Monthly meetings of WAVE allow them to discuss their problems and learn from each other in finding solutions. A member of the TCC is also invited to these meetings. They are now extending their sphere to cover solid waste management and better delivery of other public services.
>
> Together, the city corporation, the NGOs and the communities from the slums of Trichy have transformed the sanitation scenario.
>
> *Source:* 'SHE creates a WAVE of change in Trichy', Isher Judge Ahluwalia, *Indian Express*, 27 April 2011.

5.88. Just two cities, Delhi and Mumbai, which generate around 17 per cent of the country's sewage, have nearly 40 per cent of the country's installed capacity. What is worse, some of these plants do not function because of high recurring costs—electricity and chemicals and others because they do not have the sewage to treat. In most cities, only a small (unestimated) proportion of sewage is transported for treatment. And if the treated sewage transported in official drains is allowed to be mixed with the untreated sewage transported in unofficial and open drains, then the net result is pollution.

5.89. The added problem is that the location of the hardware—the sewage treatment plant—is not designed to dispose off the treated effluent so that it actually cleans the water body. Most cities don't seem to think of this factor when they build their infrastructure for sewage. They build a sewage treatment plant where there is land. The treated sewage is then disposed off, as conveniently as possible, invariably into a drain. But as this drain collects the untreated waste of large numbers of people, the end result is pollution.

Investment in Water and Sanitation

5.90. The scale of investment needed in this sector is substantial. In the past five years, JNNURM has been an important game-changer in this sector, providing much needed public funding to build and refurbish assets. Under JNNURM the bulk of the projects are for water and sewerage—some 70 per cent of the sanctioned cost of ₹60,000 crore. Please refer to Table 5.6.

5.91. Between 2005 and 2011, roughly ₹42,000 crore worth of water, drainage and sewage projects were sanctioned under these schemes. This needs to be compared to the ₹3,700 crore sanctioned for the same purpose in the 25 years before and the ₹5,000 crore sanctioned under the river conservation programmes. The High Powered Expert Committee Report on Indian Urban Infrastructure and Services pegs the total capital investment needed for infrastructure in the water, sewerage and storm-water sector at ₹7,54,627 crore over the next 20 years.

5.92. The average cost of a comprehensive water supply scheme under JNNURM is roughly ₹3 crore per mld. The average cost of a sewage project is ₹3.33 crore per mld. However, the cost of building sewage treatment systems and networks under the Union government's revamped Ganga programme averages over ₹5 crore per mld, with small cities like Munger in Bihar getting as much as ₹7 crore per mld. It is clear that the huge backlog of provisioning of water and waste services will require public investment. This investment must be carefully planned to provide affordable services that can then be sustained.

Reform Agenda for the Twelfth Five Year Plan

5.93. Nothing less than a paradigm shift is required in the Twelfth Plan if we are to move towards sustainable solutions to urban water and waste management. First, we will have to reduce the length of the pipeline to bring water to homes, thus reducing costs, including electricity and pumping costs and 'leakage'. This means giving higher priority to reviving local water bodies and recharging groundwater, so that we can source water from as close as possible. Secondly, we must use less, not more water in our homes, so that we have less to treat and less to dispose off. Thirdly, we must also cut the costs and transportation of sewage—use decentralised networks and use a variety of technologies to treat sewage as locally as possible. Finally, we must begin to learn that we will have to reuse every drop of our sewage. It is even technically possible to turn it into drinking water but at the very least we should plan to recycle and reuse it in our gardens, in our industries or use it (after treatment) to rejuvenate natural water bodies. This would require change of standards so that groundwater pollution boards incentivise the reuse of wastewater for recharge. This water-waste

TABLE 5.6
Sector-wise allocation of JNNURM Funds (as on 21.9.2011) 100th CSMC

Sector	₹ Crore	Per Cent of Total Cost Allocated
Water supply projects	19,233	32.09
Sewerage projects	14,624	24.40
Drainage	8,208	13.69
Preservation of water bodies	116	0.19
Total water sector	42,181	70.39
Other urban sectors	17,748	29.61
Total sanctioned	59,929	100.00

Source: JNNURM 2011, Sector-wise release of funds under submission for urban infrastructure and government, Ministry of Urban Development, 2011.

agenda needs to be incorporated deliberately into city plans.

5.94. Planning for urban water and sanitation must be made into essential pre-conditions for any support to urban projects under JNNURM. This should include:

1. Plan to supply water at affordable costs to all
2. Invest in protection and management of local water systems
3. Reduce water demand and intra-city inequity in water supply and sanitation
4. Invest on sewage first and water supply next
5. Reduce costs on sewage systems so that investment can reach all
6. Reinvent sewage management and treatment systems for sustainability
7. Plan to recycle and reuse every drop of water and waste

5.95. The reform agenda for the Twelfth Plan will have five major thrust areas:

Agenda 1: Investments in Water Supply Will Focus on Demand Management, Reducing Intra-City Inequity and on Quality of Water Supplied

5.96. The single biggest charge on municipal water supply today is the distance water needs to travel. The water supply programme of each city must provide for demand management and reduction in costs of supply. This will require cities to plan for local water bodies as well as plan to cut distribution losses through bulk water meters and efficiency drives.

5.97. User charges should plan to cover increasing proportions of O&M costs, while building in equity by providing 'lifeline' amount of water free of charge, with higher tariffs for increasing levels of use.

Agenda 2: Protection of Water Bodies

5.98. Each city must consider, as first source of supply its local water bodies. Therefore, cities must only get funds for water projects, when they have accounted for the water supply from local water bodies and have protected local water bodies and their catchments. This pre-condition will force protection and will build the infrastructure, which will supply locally and then take back sewage—the water's waste connection—also locally. It will cut the length of the pipeline twice over, once to supply and the other to take back the waste.

Agenda 3: No Water Scheme Will be Sanctioned without a Sewage Component, Which Joins the Dots with Pollution of Rivers and Waterways

5.99. Investment in sewage must match the investment in water supply. It is also important to note that pollution control is not possible without investment in an extensive sewage system to reach all people and intercept the waste of all for treatment. Cities must plan carefully keeping in mind the backlog of sewage facilities and the need for sewage infrastructure in new growth areas. This planning for 'full coverage and costs' will lead cities to look for unconventional methods of treating waste.

5.100. For instance, cities would then consider treatment of sewage in open drains and treatment using alternative biological methods of wastewater treatment. Biological methods of wastewater treatment introduce contact with bacteria (cells), which feed on the organic materials in the wastewater, thereby reducing its BOD content. Through their metabolism, the organic material is transformed into cellular mass, which is no longer in solution but can be precipitated at the bottom of a settling tank or retained as slime on solid surfaces or vegetation in the system. The water exiting the system is much clearer than the one that entered it. The principle has to be to cut the cost of building the sewage system, cut the length of the sewage network and then to treat the waste as a resource—turn sewage into water for irrigation or use in industry.

5.101. Indian cities have the opportunity to leapfrog into new ways of dealing with excreta, which are affordable and sustainable, simply because they have not yet built the infrastructure.

Agenda 4: Plan Deliberately for Recycling and Reuse of Treated Wastewater

5.102. Cities must plan for reuse and recycling of waste at the very beginning of their water and waste plan and not as an after-thought. It is also clear that cities must think through the plan for reuse for affordability and sustainability. The diverse options for reuse must be factored in—use in agriculture, for recharge of water bodies, for gardening and for industrial and domestic use. In each case, treatment plan will be different. But in all cases, the treated effluent will improve the hydrological cycle. It will return water and not waste to the environment. While a larger sewage treatment plant affords economies of scale in operation, a plant fitted to size—collecting the waste of a group of houses, an institution or even colonies—may have higher costs of operations but there are substantial savings in the piping and pumping cost.

Agenda 5: Plan on a Regional Scale

5.103. Drinking Water and Sanitation issues are inter-linked in urban, peri-urban and rural areas and increasingly impact each other as development upscales. Thus, a regional planning approach for provision of drinking water supply and wastewater treatment and disposal is necessary to meet needs of both rural and urban areas and avoid duplication of schemes.

Industrial Water and Waste Management[25]

5.104. As the economy industrialises, it is extremely important that industry adopts the best international practices to improve water use efficiency. This can be broadly done in two ways:

- reducing the consumption of fresh water through alternative water-efficient technologies or processes in various manufacturing activities; and
- reusing and recycling the waste water from such water intensive activities and making the reclaimed water available for use in the secondary activities within or outside the industry.

5.105. Such an approach is extremely important to reduce the water footprint of Indian industry, both in terms of fresh water used, as also polluted wastewater released untreated into the environment. The urgency of this issue is because water conflicts are increasingly arising across the length and breadth of India between competing users and uses. And industry, as a relatively new user of water, needs to recognise that economising on the use of water is now an essential ingredient in ensuring sustainability of its operations and may be in its own enlightened self-interest.

5.106. The first step in this direction during the Twelfth Plan period will be to make comprehensive water audits a recurring feature of industrial activity so that we know what is being used by the industrial sector at present and so that changes can be monitored and the most cost-effective basket of water efficiency technologies and processes designed and implemented to reduce water demand and increase industrial value added per unit of water consumed. The water audit will consider both quantity and quality aspects as the need to reduce polluting discharges to the aquatic environment or to sewage systems is often the key driver to water saving. The starting point will be large units in water-intensive industries such as paper and pulp, textiles, food, leather (tanning), metal (surface treatment), chemical/ pharmaceutical, oil/gas and mining.

5.107. The Planning Commission is working with leading representatives of Indian industry, as also the Ministry of Corporate Affairs, to make it mandatory for companies to include every year in their annual report, details of their water footprint for the year. This would include:

- the volume of fresh water (source-wise) used by them in their various production activities (activity-wise)
- the volume of water used by them that was reused or recycled (again activity-wise)
- a commitment with a time-line that the company would reduce its water footprint by a definite amount (to be specified) within a definite period of time (to be specified).

5.108. Simultaneously, the Planning Commission, working with concerned government institutions, would develop benchmarks for specific water use in different industries and would ensure their application in the grant of clearances for industrial projects.

As part of National Water Mission, Ministry of Water Resources has constituted a Committee with Industry Associations to carry out base line studies and to increase water use efficiency through water auditing, water footprints, and so on, including amendment in the Companies Act.

5.109. The second step would be to examine the measures to levy charges for water use and incentives for water conservation. Currently, the Water (Prevention and Control of Pollution) Cess Act 1977 is the only instrument to impose cess on discharge of effluent water from industrial units. This charge is based on the quantum of discharge from the industry and is used to augment the resources of the Central and State Pollution Boards. The charges imposed through the Water Cess are not enough of a disincentive for industries to reduce their water footprint. It is important to examine this Act and other provisions and options to increase the charges imposed on water use and effluents substantially. This is particularly important where industries use groundwater and do not pay municipalities, water utilities or even irrigation departments for water use. The importance of water pricing as an instrument for change is critical and must be actively used to incentivise industry.

5.110. The third step would be to publicly validate the water audit of industries so that this builds experience and confidence on the best practices. This water reduction commitment of each industry will be tracked for compliance and enforcement through environmental regulatory institutions.

5.111. The water audit would also help identify training requirements and the best way of achieving behavioural change within the business. The maximum water saving will be delivered when both behavioural change and hard measures are successfully adopted by the end user.

5.112. In order to more credibly move industry along this path, central and state governments need to set an example by undertaking their own audits of water use in their premises and setting targets for ensuring less water use and changes in technology and behaviour that will reduce waste.

5.113. It is also be very important to develop a forum which would:

- provide information on industry-specific good practices in wise water use;
- undertake to develop expertise in water audits and water use advisory services;
- provide details of 'exemplar' case studies that are relevant to the different industrial sectors operating in India;
- provide a 'gateway' for accessing information about water saving and water efficiency technologies in rain-water harvesting, recycling and reuse, water conserving devices and support to helping behaviour change. Please refer to Box 5.5.

5.114. Once such systems are in place, there is enough experience from across the world to show that significant economies can be effected in water use. Reported water savings range from 15 per cent to 90 per cent of current water use, depending on the industrial sub-sector considered, the individual process investigated or the combination of water saving measures analysed with the most commonly found figures being within the 30–70 per cent range. A study carried out by ICAEN for the Catalonia region in Spain between 1992 and 1997 shows potential water savings for different industrial sectors of 25–50 per cent (see Figure 5.4). The same study stressed that around 35 per cent of cost-saving measures were implemented in areas of management and control, 32 per cent in the process and 18 per cent in the reuse of effluents.

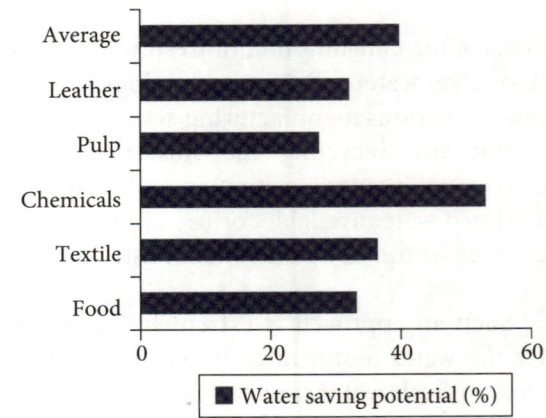

FIGURE 5.4: Water Saving Potential in Industry

Box 5.5
Water Use Efficiency in UK Industry

In the UK, water companies have a statutory duty to promote the efficient use of water and as a result, water companies (in England and Wales) carry out a range of water efficiency activities with the purpose of promoting water efficiency to their customers. This water efficiency activity has been a duty under the Water Industry Act (WIA91 Section 93a) since 1996. To date targets for water savings have been set by water companies themselves. However, as of 1 April 2010 water companies will be working within a regime of mandatory water efficiency targets set by Ofwat (Office of Water, Regulator) for all water companies to achieve. These targets can be achieved by either targeting domestic or industrial customers, but the targets must be met year on year. The water efficiency targets comprise three key elements:

- An annual target to save an estimated one litre of water per property per day through water efficiency activity, during the period 2010–11 to 2014–15.
- A requirement to provide a minimum level of information to consumers on how to use water more wisely.
- A requirement that each company actively helps to improve the evidence base for water efficiency.

In addition to target setting, the water industry set up and funded an organisation called Waterwise to make the case for large-scale water conservation. Waterwise is a UK NGO focused on decreasing water consumption in the UK and is central authority on water efficiency information and guidance in the UK (http://www.waterwise.org.uk/).

Another NGO operating in the UK is Envirowise which offers free and independent support to businesses to help them become more resource efficient and for them to save money. Since 1994, Envirowise has helped UK industry save more than £1 billion by reducing waste early on in their organisation processes. A part of this waste minimisation strategy includes water (http://envirowise.wrap.org.uk/uk/Topics-and-Issues/Water.html).

The National Symbiosis Programme is a UK-based organisation which promotes the efficient use of resources in industry and has previously worked in water. The UK Government publish a Water Technology list covering water using devices which contribute to water efficiency. Envirowise publish a range of information on industrial water use, water using devices and water conservation. The Watermark project published water use and water efficiency benchmarks in 2003 for 17 categories of building. Industry Trade Associations such as the Food and Drink industries group provide information and guidance on best practice in water use.

5.115. Possible water savings (average values) for different types of actions are presented in Table 5.7.

5.116. The regulatory system for water usage in industries also needs to be strengthened. Currently, the environmental regulations require industries seeking clearances to provide information about water sources, which in turn is provided by the state government irrigation departments or groundwater boards. This permission for water does not take into account availability, especially in water-stressed regions. The Planning Commission will work with the regulatory institutions to ensure that the system of water assessment is strengthened for enforcement.

Flood Management

5.117. The Twelfth Plan Working Group on Flood Management estimates that in the period 1953–2010, on an average, an area of 7.208 mha and a population

TABLE 5.7
Potential Water Saving from Various Measures in Industry

Efficiency Measure	Percentage of Water Saved (%)
Closed loop recycling	90
Closed loop recycling with treatment	60
Automatic shut-off	15
Counter current rinsing	40
Spray/jet upgrades	20
Reuse of wash water	50
Scrapers	30
Cleaning in place (CiP)	60
Pressure Reduction	Variable
Cooling tower heat load reduction	Variable

Source: Envirowise (2005): Cost-effective Water Saving Devices and Practices for Industrial Uses, United Kingdom.

of 3.19 million were affected by floods every year. The average annual flood damage to crops, houses and public utilities at constant (2010–11) prices works out to about ₹6,976 crores. This is excluding damage to private investments for which no estimate is available. Expenditure incurred by both the Central and State Governments in various Plans (at 2010–11 prices) is estimated to be about ₹1,26,000 crore. On an average this is an investment of ₹2,100 crores per annum, although allocation has increased in later Plan periods compared to earlier years. The States falling within Brahmaputra-Meghna, Ganga and Indus river basins are the most affected by floods. The current estimate of the flood-prone area in the country is 49.815 mha, which is higher than the assessment made by the Rashtriya Barh Aayog (RBA) in 1980 (40 mha). Overall, 39 districts in India have been identified as chronically flood-prone. Indiscriminate development and encroachment of flood plain areas, improper planning in construction of roads and railways, inadequate and ineffective drainage in urban areas, and so on, have contributed to increase in flood damage.

5.118. Broadly, three kinds of flood management strategies have been adopted:

1. Engineering/structural measures, including construction of reservoirs for impounding monsoon flow and its release after peak flows have passed (attenuation) and providing river embankments/flood walls;
2. Non-structural measures, including flood plain zoning, flood forecasting, flood warning and flood proofing;
3. Catchment area treatment, including watershed management and restoring the health of natural drainages.

5.119. The central focus has been on engineering/structural solutions. Apart from the massive investments in large dams, India has already constructed over 35,000 km of embankments. But these are rapidly reaching their limits. Recent studies show, for example, that the existing storage infrastructure in Peninsular rivers is mostly designed to smooth out the southwest monsoon flows in, say, 9 out of 10 years. There may still be the 1 in 10 year flood, for which, however, there is no economic justification to invest in substantial additional infrastructure. Instead, better weather and flood forecasting is required, along with flood insurance and possibly the designation of flood diversion areas, whereby farmers are asked to temporarily (and against compensation) set aside embanked land to accommodate flood overflow for the Ganges system, out of 250 BCM of potentially utilisable water, about 37 BCM are presently captured, and a total of at most 50 BCM would be captured if all possible dams under consideration were to be built. These would add little in the way of irrigation or flood prevention benefits. Tributaries at risk are already fully embanked, and floods have occurred not because water has flown over the embankments, but because embankments have been repeatedly breached as a result of poor maintenance (e.g., Kosi in Bihar) or inappropriate dam management (for example, Hirakud in Orissa).[26]

5.120. Evidence from floods in the Ghaggar river basin, both in 1993 and 2010, clearly shows the damage caused in Punjab and Haryana by breaches in embankments and unused, poorly designed and maintained canals, as also because settlements have been encouraged on flood plains and drainage lines. In 2008, a breach in an upstream embankment of the Kosi led to the nearly thousand deaths and the displacement of around 3.35 million people.[27] In North Bihar, despite the continued construction of embankments, the flood-prone area has increased 200 per cent since independence, at times because embankments end up obstructing natural drainages and impede the natural building up of river deltas and flood plains.[28]

5.121. In acknowledgement of the limits to further possibilities of building large storages and embankments, some State governments (such as Bihar) have decided to broaden their strategy of tackling floods by placing greater emphasis on rehabilitation of traditional, natural drainage systems, leveraging the funds available under MGNREGA. Since this involves a process of complex social mobilisation and social engineering, civil society organisations will work in close partnership with the State government in this endeavour. The Twelfth Plan strongly endorses such a paradigm shift in flood management.

5.122. Indeed, an attempt will be made to, as far as practicable, convert adversity into opportunity. Part of the waterlogged area could be used for construction of small multi-purpose farm ponds. The mud of the ponds would be raised on the side as embankments on which crops like banana, papaya, mango, pigeon pea and cashew nut can be grown. The pond water will be used to irrigate the non-waterlogged, upland area. Experiments have shown that in waterlogged areas, cultivation of water chestnut (Trapabispinosa) can be quite profitable. Research and field level trials have identified extra-tall varieties of paddy that can grow fast and can tolerate waterlogging. Waterlogging is often aggravated by the mismanagement of rainwater in the upper catchment. In situ rainwater conservation in the upper catchment and intensification of the use of groundwater through shallow tubewells are possible interventions to mitigate the problem. Through integrated management of land, water and nutrients, agricultural productivity of these uplands could be stabilised and enhanced, which would, in turn, have a positive impact on the waterlogged lowlands.

5.123. In addition, far greater priority will be given to non-structural measures such as the efficient management of flood plains, flood plain zoning, disaster preparedness and response planning, flood forecasting and warning, along with disaster relief, flood fighting including public health measures and flood insurance.

5.124. Many reservoirs were initially constructed without any flood cushion but with development and population growth, habitations have come up very close to the downstream of these reservoirs and operation of such reservoirs needs to be done carefully. The existing flood forecasting network of Central Water Commission (CWC) is not sufficient to cover the entire country adequately. The Twelfth Plan will draw up a concrete plan for extension of CWC's flood forecasting network in consultation with the State Governments and IMD to cover A, B-1, B-2 and C-class Cities located near rivers under the network of automatic data collection, transmission and flood information dissemination. At present, the CWC provides inflow forecast to 28 reservoirs in the country. In the Twelfth Plan this will be extended to an additional 160 reservoirs, which will cover 80–90 per cent of the total live storage capacity.

5.125. Moreover, a majority of the flood warning systems in India are not timely, primarily due to poor transmission. Delays cause enormous damage to property and lives every year. Models used for flood forecasting and its influence zones are not rigorous enough due to lack of integration of hydrology and the weather forecasting systems. The lead time for flood forecasting can be improved through the use of hydraulic and hydrologic models which are linked to the weather forecasting system, the real time data acquisition system, and the reservoir operation system. It is possible to improve the current forecasting methods by using satellite based information for better estimates of rainfall and snowmelt.

5.126. Adequate flood cushion needs to be provided in all water storage projects, wherever feasible, to facilitate better flood management. In highly flood prone areas, flood moderation will be given overriding consideration in reservoir regulation policy, even at the cost of sacrificing some irrigation or power benefits. As a policy minimum, flood cushion of 10 per cent of live storage will be provided in all new dams and if affordable with respect to other purposes, the flood cushion could be considered up to 20 per cent. A portion of the capital cost of the reservoir allocated to flood control could be shared by all beneficiary States.

5.127. Given the large network embankments that already exist, great emphasis will be placed on their proper upkeep and surveillance during the monsoon season, centrally involving primary stakeholders in this process.

5.128. The Ministry of Water Resources has prepared a Model Bill on Flood Plain Zoning. State Governments have reported difficulties in enactment of necessary legislation and enforcement of laws in this regard due to constraints of evacuation of people who are already occupying the flood plains and their settlement elsewhere due to constraints of land. However, demarcation of the flood plain zones by the concerned States in accordance with criteria suggested by CWC in the Model Flood Plain Zoning Bill and zone-specific strategies about the use of flood plains (including schemes of incentives and disincentives) need to be implemented. The States should also bring out standard norms for types of buildings which can be constructed in different zones of flood plains so that required water way is available for passage of the flood discharge.

5.129. A system of scientifically designed raised platforms, community housing with livestock units, health units where people can be accommodated during the four months of floods will be adopted. The National Disaster Management Agency (NDMA) will make adequate provision for development of model multipurpose flood shelters under the National Flood Risk Mitigation Project or other related programmes.

5.130. The Working Group has suggested a number of steps for strengthening the institutions dealing with flood management. Integrated water resources management, including integrated flood management, demands setting up of River Basin Authorities with requisite managerial skills and appropriate delegation of powers. The CWC, GFCC and Brahmaputra Board under the Ministry of Water Resources are required to play vital roles in the preparation of master plans for specific river basins. The strengthening of CWC is required in view of the proposed expansion of its hydrological and flood data collection network, flood data transmission and management of floods. The National Water Academy (NWA) located at Pune is presently involved in providing training to the engineers/officers of the Central/State Governments. During the Twelfth Plan, the NWA will be developed as a Centre of Excellence for international training programmes on matters pertaining to flood mitigation so that up-to-date globally available know-how could be shared under such training programmes. The NWA, Pune will also be suitably strengthened to meet the requirement of the NDMA for conducting trainings on disaster risk reduction programmes. Project-specific planning and implementation is to be ensured by the State Governments. The present structure of the State flood control departments needs to be revamped so that they can discharge their role as prime flood managers in the State. The specific needs of human resources and their skill development need to be addressed.

5.131. Digital Elevation Models (DEM) along major river systems including area falling in the flood affected zone in the range of 0.5–1 m will be prepared for all river basins. Use of NRSC's flood hazard zonation maps, close contour information, river configuration & bank erosion studies, geo-spatial tools and flood mapping and flood damage assessment will be encouraged. The Disaster Management Support Programme will be expanded to include more river basins and the NDMA will provide necessary support to NRSC in this regard. Basin-wise flood management models including ALTM technology based Digital Elevation Models, Inundation Forecast Models, Bathymetric Surveys and Cubature Study Models will be undertaken jointly by NRSC, CWC and concerned States. Development of integrated mathematical models will be undertaken jointly by IMD and CWC for flood/runoff forecasting using weather parameters, rainfall observed and rainfall forecast.

Water Database Development and Management

5.132. Keeping these challenges in mind, as part of the preparation for the Twelfth Plan, the Planning Commission decided to constitute, for the first time, a Working Group headed by Prof. A. Vaidyanathan (former Member, Planning Commission) to carry out a comprehensive and critical review of the present system for collection and dissemination of water related data, identify deficiencies in the data being generated and used for planning and policy, and to suggest a programme of action to overcome them. The Working Group highlights serious gaps and inadequacies in the scope, coverage and quality of data currently used for assessing India's potential and utilisable water resources from different sources, their actual utilisation for, and impact on, various end uses:

- Collection of data is fragmented between different agencies. The agencies responsible for collection of the 'physical data' (to use precipitation and stream gauging as examples) are administered by differing Ministries, while the user data come under such diverse classifications as public health and sanitation, irrigation and urban planning. There is a consequential absence of a coherent and internally consistent conceptual framework and protocols for data collection and validation.
- The fact that 'water' is a 'State' subject leaves the Central Government agencies that are responsible for the national data with little choice but to rely on the State agencies for such data. Agencies of the Central Government—India Meteorological Department (IMD), Central Water Commission (CWC), (CGWB), Central Pollution Control Board (CPCB)—do collect a considerable amount of data, but most of the information at the regional and project levels is collected by the State agencies. As a result, much of the data are not readily accessible even within and between Government agencies concerned with water resources development, leave aside in the public domain.
- The Hydrology Project that has now completed its first phase has expanded the physical infrastructure and equipped it with improved measuring and recording devices. The idea was to collate them into a national data network (called HIS) to facilitate easier access to users. But accomplishments have fallen far short of expectations because of the reluctance of the States to send all the information they collect fully and promptly to the national data pool.

5.133. The Working Group spells out a concrete programme for phased action to improve physical facilities, methodologies and mechanisms to generate more comprehensive, detailed and reliable data in each of these respects and outlines changes needed in institutional arrangements for collection validation and dissemination of data and for facilitating intensive analysis through research. These recommendations are summarised in Annexure 5.8. The Working Group's recommendations will begin to get implemented during the Twelfth Plan period.

5.134. Data improvement is a national effort of the Central and the State government agencies that requires active involvement of specialised government agencies and scholars in universities, research institutions and non-governmental organisations in a way that fragmentation of focus and effort is minimised. This calls for a common agreed framework of concepts. It is, therefore, suggested by the Working Group that the Central Government take the lead in creating appropriate institutional arrangements to ensure independent and professional conduct of the surveys, providing financial and technical support to the States and ensuring that all agencies follow prescribed protocols and transmit the data to the central pool. For this purpose the Working Group suggests the constitution of a Steering Committee chaired by Member (Water Resources), Planning Commission, with knowledgeable and reputed experts on water related issues from relevant disciplines within and outside government to work out

- the strategy, modalities and funding for building a comprehensive, technical and scientific data base on potential and utilisable water from different sources;
- details of the scope, content. methodology and mechanisms of the surveys to assess performance and impact of programmes through sample surveys of users and specific projects; and
- the design of an integrated and digitised National Water Resources Information System by suitably expanding, reorganising and equipping the existing WRIS in the CWC.

5.135. The bulk of the expenditure on the programmes for data improvement in the Twelfth Plan will be for expanding and upgrading facilities for assessment of resource potential and utilisation.. Sample surveys to assess actual performance and impact of schemes at the ground level will be a small but critical component. Altogether this investment in improving information on knowledge will be a small fraction of total outlays on water resource development but the returns in terms of improving efficiency and sustainability of water use will be huge.

NEW INSTITUTIONAL FRAMEWORK FOR WATER

National Water Commission
5.136. During the Twelfth Plan, there is also a proposal to set up a National Water Commission (NWC) to monitor compliance with conditionalities of investment and environment clearances given to irrigation projects. At present, there is no appropriate body that can provide rigorous, credible and timely feedback to sanctioning authorities about compliance with the conditionalities they impose at the time of sanction. A multi-disciplinary, professionally capable and independent NWC to oversee water reform would have credibility with both Centre and States and would function on the lines of what has been attempted, for example, in Australia and become a guide for further water resource development in India. A decision on the NWC will be taken after thoroughgoing consultations with the States by the Union Ministry of Water Resources.

Water Regulatory Authorities in Each State
5.137. We need to evolve an institutional framework backed by a legal regime that facilitates setting up of regulatory bodies that would enable resolution of water conflicts. To protect the right to drinking water for all, there is no alternative to entitlements and appropriate pricing of water. This demands a transparent and participatory process of determination of entitlements and prices. Again to ensure sustainability and meet environmental needs, a regulatory authority is a must in each State.

5.138. Since the water sector is a natural monopoly, international experience clearly indicates that it is regulators who provide the cutting-edge that is otherwise missing in a non-competitive environment. Regulators have contributed to major improvements in water-use efficiency, water quality and provision of environmental services. Thus, for example, while Scottish Water is a state monopoly, the legal and regulatory framework within which it functions, ensures that efficiencies are achieved, quality standards adhered to and expectations of consumers satisfied. And given the impact that their operations can have on public health and the environment, the water and wastewater industry have to be highly regulated. Being undertakers of a natural monopoly, there is a need to protect the customer's interests.

5.139. The water quality, environment and health standards set by the regulator have a bearing on tariffs. The final call on tariffs would, of course, be a political one but the regulators have a crucial role in advising governments on the objective basis for tariff determination (somewhat akin to what the CACP does for agriculture pricing).

5.140. The basic requirements of drinking water and of the environment need to be determined and ensured in a transparent manner and kept as a 'Reserve' (as it is called, for example, in South Africa). In South Africa, the Reserve constitutes an attempt to quantify an amount of minimum flow in the country's rivers and impoundments reserved for the maintenance of basic ecological functions (such as habitat for fish and plants) and to ensure that the South African population is guaranteed a minimum of 25 litres per capita per day for domestic purposes. Thus categories of use that are perhaps not sufficiently defended vocally are nevertheless declared to be non-negotiably in the public interest. The Reserve is an attempt to decide what level of loss is acceptable rather than an attempt to determine what 'the environment' needs. The determination of this level requires an independent regulator who can transparently, accountably, and in a participatory manner conduct the processes and procedures required for this determination.

5.141. As part of the work leading up to the Twelfth Plan, a Sub-Group under Prof. Subodh Wagle of the Tata Institute of Social Sciences (as part of the Working Group on Water Governance) has drafted a Model Bill for State Water Regulatory System.[29] This draft is based on a thorough study of latest international thinking on regulation as also the experience of the Maharashtra Water Resources Regulatory Authority (MWRRA). The draft bill tries to resolve the conflicting demands of autonomy and accountability brought into sharp relief by the Maharashtra experience. It does so by proposing a regulatory system with interrelated but separate institutions that handle distinct governance functions. The bill proposes a separation of the authority to make 'political' or 'normative' decisions and the authority to make 'technical' or 'predominantly non-normative' decisions. Thus, the State Water Regulatory and Development Council (SC) is expected to ensure accountability by providing the 'normative' or 'political' framework for the techno-economic regulatory decisions of the State Independent Water Expert Authority (SIWEA). The SIWEA will, in turn, be accountable to technical experts through the mechanism of regular peer reviews.

5.142. The SIWEA will be a multi-disciplinary body of independent professionals from civil engineering, ecology/environmental science, economics, accounts and auditing, sociology/political science and geology/hydrogeology. The SIWEA will prepare the Action Plan for Preparation of Regulations, CBRs and Criteria (APPRC), discharge specific regulatory functions, issue orders to the corresponding agencies, to enforce compliance with the guidelines, principles, rules, regulations, and criteria in a transparent, accountable, and participatory manner. The SIWEA will also be empowered to penalise defaulting agencies and issue orders on petitions, applications or proposals from governing agencies, stakeholders and citizens.

5.143. Chaired by the State Minister for Water Resources, the SC will comprise elected representatives from the State Legislature, PRI representatives from districts, blocks, GPs and ULBs as also stakeholder groups, including farmers, industry and civil society organisations. The SC will deliberate on the drafts of the APPRC prepared by SIWEA and provide considered comments and suggestions, which will be incorporated by SIWEA and re-presented to SC for final approval. The SC will undertake periodic review of orders and decisions of the SIWEA through deliberations in the general body of the SC in order to assess the compliance of the decisions and orders of SIWEA to the normative framework provided by the SC.

5.144. The areas of regulation to be covered include:

- *Water Access, Extraction and Use*, including criteria for allotment of entitlements, priority of water use, norms for maximum water use for various activities, norms for effluent treatment, criteria for limits of extraction from unregulated, local water sources;
- *Execution of Projects and Programmes*, including techno-economic, socio-cultural, environmental and ecological aspects of project and programme design, including adherence to the integrated state water plan;
- *Water Service Provisioning*, including quantity and quality of water, also with special reference to the disadvantaged and ensuring good financial health of the water provisioning system;
- *Allocation of Financial and other Resources*, including norms and standards for reducing losses and theft, increasing tariff for non-poor, criteria for equitable distribution of resources including priority for drought-prone and backward regions, criteria for prioritising competing demands and so on;
- *Environmental Sustainability*;
- *Disaster Management*;
- *Private Sector Participation*, including criteria determining the details of tariff recovery in case of private water provisioning, norms for project-level purchases related to equipment, establishment, and other aspects of project management, specification of sectoral responsibilities to be handed over to private parties and so on;
- *Preparation of Integrated State Water Plan (ISWP)*;
- *Addressing Climate Change Issues*.

5.145. The Model Bill incorporates the principle of subsidiarity by laying out water governance at four levels: (*i*) State (*ii*) River Basin (*iii*) Sub-Basin and (*iv*) Local. At all these four levels of governance, institutions with different structure, compositions, functions, authorities, and roles are provided for in the bill. The apprehension that such decentralisation might prove dysfunctional or sub-optimal, especially because of the lack of capabilities and understanding at lower levels of the institutional ladder is sought to be taken care of through the concept of phased institutional transition by providing step-wise, gate-protected processes for gradual introduction of the decentralised institutional structure.

5.146. The Bill also builds in enough flexibility in its design to take care of differences across States through a modular structure, from which modules based on the state-specific situation, requirements, priorities of water sector governance, and other factors could be selected by the state government while preparing and enacting their final draft of the Bill.

NEW GROUNDWATER LAW[30]

5.147. Since sustainable and equitable management of groundwater based on aquifer management is going to occupy centre-stage, this requires a new legal framework to support efforts in this direction.

Limitations of the Present Legal Framework for Groundwater

5.148. As early as the 1970s, the GoI put forward a model bill to regulate groundwater use for adoption by the States. This model bill has been revised several times (1992, 1996 and 2005) but the basic scheme adopted in the 1970s has been retained to date. The Model Bill to Regulate and Control the Development and Management of Ground Water, 2005 only introduces a limited regulatory framework to address groundwater depletion and pollution and amounts to little more than 'grandfathering' existing uses.

5.149. Rules concerning access to and use of groundwater in India have been progressively developed through judicial decisions. What is remarkable is that some of the most important legal principles governing groundwater even today were laid down in British common law as early as the middle of the nineteenth century and have not been updated since. These legal principles are:

- *Landowners given full control of groundwater*: Existing rules of access to and control over groundwater are still based on the common law doctrine of absolute dominion. This gives the landowner the right to take substantially as much groundwater as she or he desires from wells dug on own land. Landowners do not own groundwater but enjoy access as part and parcel of their ownership rights to the land above:

   > The person who owns the surface may dig therein, and apply all that is there found to his own purposes at his free will and pleasure; and that if, in the exercise of such right, he intercepts or drains off the water collected from underground springs in his neighbour's well, this inconvenience to his neighbour falls within the description of *damnumabsqueinjuria* [damage without injury], which cannot become the ground of an action.[31]

- *Defined vs Undefined channels*: 'Groundwater that percolates through underground strata, which has no certain course, no defined limits, but which oozes through the soil in every direction in which the rain penetrates is not subject to the same rules as flowing water in streams or rivers.'[32] On the other hand, where groundwater was found to flow in defined channels, case law says that rules applicable to surface water would also apply. This has been interpreted[33] to mean that the right of the landowner would then be limited to use and consumption for household and drinking purpose, for watering their cattle and even for irrigating their land or for purposes of manufacture provided that

   - the use is reasonable;
   - it is required for their purposes as owners of the land and
   - it does not destroy or render useless or materially diminish or affect the application of the water by riparian owners below the stream in the exercise either of their natural right or right of easement, if any.

5.150. A lot of legal hermeneutics was devoted over the years to clearly spelling out the distinction between defined and undefined channels of groundwater.[34] The difficulty, of course, is that this differentiation is completely meaningless in scientific hydrogeological terms since groundwater occurs in aquifers, which are not necessarily in the form of 'channels' like streams and rivers are. Aquifers are rocks or rock material possessing the capacity to store water in different openings and transmit water from one point in the aquifer to another, due to the interconnectedness between these openings. Hence, the question of water flowing through streams generally does not arise (except in case of carbonate rocks which have large openings on account of the phenomenon called *karst*).

5.151. Natural groundwater flow (under static or non-pumping condition), follows certain directions defined by groundwater contours (flow lines representing direction or movement of groundwater but not necessarily in the form of channels, defined or undefined). This also means that water flowing underneath any parcel of land may or may not be generated as recharge on that specific parcel. As a matter of fact, recharge areas for most aquifers are only a part of the land that overlies the entire aquifer. Hence, in many cases, water flowing underneath any parcel of land will have infiltrated the land and recharged the aquifer from another parcel, often lying at a distance. When many users simultaneously pump groundwater, complex interference results between different foci of pumping, which is a common feature in many parts of India, where wells are located quite close to one another. In such situations, natural groundwater flow is changed and groundwater moves depending upon the distribution of pumped water levels in different parts of the aquifer, again making it difficult to create rules based on defined streams of water akin to surface water movement.

- *Indian Easements Act*: It must also be noted that while the Indian Easements Act, 1882 does directly address groundwater, it cannot be invoked in trying to determine the rights of landowners over the groundwater found below their own land. This is due to the fact that an easement right involves by definition a (dominant) owner claiming the easementary right and a (servient) owner on whose land the easementary right is exercised. Consequently, 'ownership and easement are inconsistent and cannot coexist in the same person'.[35]

5.152. Apart from the absence of an understanding of aquifers in the present legal framework and the inability to separate the ownership of land from access to groundwater, there is the further problem that it only considers the interests of landowners, completely overlooking the hugely important fact that groundwater serves the basic needs of life of so many people who do not own land.

The Way Forward: A New Legal Framework for Groundwater

5.153. New developments in jurisprudence have created both the basis and the necessity to redefine the legal framework for groundwater. These include:

- new water law principles (for instance, the Public Trust Doctrine enunciated by the Supreme Court)[36]
- environmental law principles (for instance, the precautionary principle)
- decentralisation principles embodied in the 73rd and 74th amendments to the Constitution
- changes in irrigation law focusing on participatory irrigation management over for the past fifteen years and implemented in a number of States[37]
- the fundamental right to water that has been a part of Indian law for the past two decades[38]

5.154. The Twelfth Plan Sub-Group on Legal Issues related to Groundwater Management and Regulation (as part of the Working Group on Water Governance), has drafted a new *Model Bill for the Protection, Conservation, Management and Regulation of Groundwater*.[39] This model bill has been drafted keeping in mind all the considerations spelt out above. It is based on the idea that while protection of groundwater is key to the long-term sustainability of the resource, this must be considered in a framework in which livelihoods and basic drinking water needs are of central importance. The overall objectives of the Model Bill are to:

- Regulate and control iniquitous groundwater use and distribution, based on priority of allocation

to ensure in particular that the safe and secure drinking water/domestic needs of every person and irrigation needs of small and marginal farmers can be met;
- Regulate the over-extraction of groundwater in order to ensure the sustainability of groundwater resources, equity of their use and distribution, and to ensure fulfilment of ecosystem needs;
- Promote and protect community-based, participatory mechanisms of groundwater management that are adapted to specific locations;
- Prevent and mitigate contamination of groundwater resources;
- Promote and protect good conservation, augmentation (recharge) and management practices; and
- Protect areas of land that are crucial for the sustainable management of groundwater resources and ensure that high groundwater consuming activities are not located in areas unable to support them.

5.155. The Model Bill draws on the various developments that have taken place in the legal framework since the GoI proposed the first model bill in the 1970s. In particular, it reflects the following:

- The principle that water, and groundwater specifically, is a public trust as put forward by the Supreme Court. This implies that the state at all levels (from the panchayat to the state government) is the custodian of the resource. This applies to groundwater as a resource (aquifer) and not to mechanisms (wells/tubewells) for abstracting it;[40]
- The recognition of the fundamental right to water by the Supreme Court;
- The principle of subsidiarity, as explicated in the 73rd and 74th amendments to the Constitution (Articles 243G and 243W);
- Protection principles, such as the prevention and precautionary principles, most recently statutorily recognised in the National Green Tribunal Act, 2010 (Section 20);
- *Proposed* Andhra Pradesh Community Management of Groundwater Systems in Rural Areas Act, 2011;
- *Proposed* Maharashtra Groundwater (Development and Management) Act, 2009.

5.156. The Model Bill also builds on existing laws and schemes and contextualises them to groundwater, including

- The Right to Information Act, 2005;
- *The Environmental Impact Assessment Notification, 2006 under the Environment (Protection) Act, 1986;*
- *Social* audits called for under various schemes and policies of the Government.

NATIONAL WATER FRAMEWORK LAW (NWFL)

Need for a National Water Framework Law

5.157. In formulating the Twelfth Plan, a Sub-Group (as part of the Working Group on Water Governance) was set up under the former Secretary, Water Resources, Prof. Ramaswamy R. Iyer to draft a National Water Framework Law.[41] The Sub-Group has articulated the case for drafting such a law in the following terms:

5.158. Under the Indian Constitution water is primarily a State subject, but it is an increasingly important national concern in the context of:

- the right to water being a part of the fundamental right to life;
- the emergence of a water crisis because of the mounting pressure on a finite resource;
- the inter-use and inter-State conflicts that this leads to, and the need for a national consensus on water-sharing principles, and on the arrangements for minimising conflicts and settling them quickly without resort to adjudication to the extent possible;
- the threat to this vital resource by the massive generation of waste by various uses of water and the severe pollution and contamination caused by it;
- the long-term environmental, ecological and social implications of efforts to augment the availability of water for human use;

- the equity implications of the distribution, use and control of water: equity as between uses, users, areas, sectors, States, countries and generations;
- the international dimensions of some of India's rivers; and
- the emerging concerns about the impact of climate change on water and the need for appropriate responses at local, national, regional, and global levels.

5.159. The above considerations cast several responsibilities on the Central Government. Some of these can be dealt with only partially under existing laws such as the Environment (Protection) Act 1986, the Water (Prevention and Control of Pollution) Act 1974, and others. On inter-State rivers there are (*i*) Entry 56 in the Union List which enables the Central Government to act if Parliament legislates for the purpose, (*ii*) the River Boards Act 1956 enacted under it (which has remained inoperative), and (*iii*) the Inter-State Water Disputes Act 1956 (ISWD) enacted under article 262 of the Constitution and amended in 2002. However, inter-State rivers and river valleys are not the same thing as 'water' per se, and adjudication is not the only thing that needs to be provided for.

5.160. Given the concerns set forth above, the need for a national water law becomes imperative. Such a law will not preclude the further use of Entry 56, or the re-activation of the River Boards Act, or amendments and improvements to the ISWD Act. Several States are enacting laws on water and related issues. These can be quite divergent in their perceptions of water. Again, under a number of projects and programmes different States are undertaking 'water sector reforms', and as a part of this they have formulated or are formulating State Water Policies. Here again, significant divergences are possible. Some divergences of policy and law may be inevitable and acceptable, but they have to be within reasonable limits set by a broad national consensus on certain basics.

5.161. Different State Governments tend to adopt different positions on the rights of different States over the waters of a river basin that straddles more than one State. Such legal divergences tend to render the resolution of inter-State river-water conflicts even more difficult than they already are. A national statement of the general legal position and principles that should govern such cases seems desirable.

5.162. Water, like air, is one of the most basic requirements for life. If a national law is considered necessary on subjects such as the environment, forests, wildlife, biological diversity, and so on, a national law on water is even more necessary. Water is as basic as (if not more) than those subjects.

5.163. Finally, the idea of a national water law is not something unusual or unprecedented. Many countries in the world have national water laws or codes, and some of them (for instance, the South African National Water Act of 1998) are widely regarded as very enlightened. There is also the well-known European Water Framework Directive of 2000. The considerations behind those national or supra-national documents are relevant to India as well, although the form of a water law for India will clearly have to be guided by the nature of the Indian Constitution and our own specific needs and circumstances.

5.164. It is this recognition of the need for a minimal national consensus on certain basic perceptions, concepts and principles that led to the adoption of the National Water Policy (NWP) of 1987 and 2002. However, a national water policy has no legal status. A national water law is, therefore, necessary to make the tenets of such a consensual statement justiciable. The NWP 2012 recognises the need for a NWFL.

Nature and Scope of the NWFL

5.165. Having thus stated the case for drafting a national water framework law, it is important to clarify the nature and scope of this law:

- The proposed national water law is not intended to either centralise water management, or to change Centre–State relations or to alter the Constitutional position on water in any way. What is proposed is not a Central water management law or a command-and-control law, but a

framework law, that is, an umbrella statement of general principles governing the exercise of legislative and/or executive (or devolved) powers by the Centre, the States and the local governance institutions.
- No administrative machinery or institutional structure (except for a national water information system) is envisaged at the Centre under this framework law, and consequently no penal provisions are envisaged. This, of course, does not exclude the necessary administrative machinery, institutional structure and penal provisions in State laws within this framework.
- But the law is intended to be justiciable in the sense that the laws passed and the executive actions taken by the Central and State Governments and the devolved functions exercised by PRIs will have to conform to the general principles and priorities laid down in the framework law, and that deviations can be challenged in a court of law.
- The law will incorporate all major legal pronouncements by the Supreme Court with reference to water such as the Public Trust Doctrine and the recognition of the fundamental right to water as also the principle of subsidiarity, as explicated in the 73rd and 74th Constitutional amendments, the prevention and precautionary principles, most recently statutorily recognised in the National Green Tribunal Act, 2010 and the transparency principles of The Right to Information Act, 2005.

How the Law Is Proposed to be Enacted

5.166. According to the Twelfth Plan Working Group on Water Governance, given the present constitutional division of legislative powers between the Union and the States, the only way a national water framework law can be legislated is to follow the procedure laid out in Article 252(1) of the Constitution. Thus, if two or more State assemblies pass resolutions in support of Parliament enacting such a law, Parliament can also accordingly enact it. This was the procedure adopted in the case of the Water (Control and Prevention of Pollution) Act 1974 and more recently for the Dam Safety Act 2010. An Act so passed will be applicable to the States that had passed the resolution and to other States that adopt the Act.

5.167. In July 2012, the Ministry of Water Resources constituted a Committee under the Chairmanship of Dr. Y.K. Alagh, former Member, Planning Commission to draft a National Water Framework Law. Once drafted, this Framework Law would be finalised after evolving a consensus involving intensive deliberations with States, to be initiated by the Union Minister of Water Resources through meetings with the States.

OUTLAYS FOR THE TWELFTH PLAN

5.168. The Central Sector Outlay for Twelfth Five Year Plan for Ministry of Water Resources (MoWR) is ₹18,118 crore, which envisages schemes like Irrigation Management Programme, Development of Water Resources Information System, Ground Water Management and Regulation (including aquifer mapping) and so on. The indicative outlays for the Twelfth Five Year Plan under the Water Resources sector (irrigation, flood management and command area development) would be about ₹4,22,012 crore. The realisation of this outlay is dependent upon the resource position of the States and their priority to the sector.

ANNEXURE 5.1
Plan-wise Expenditure on Irrigation and Flood Control

(₹ Crores)

Plan Period	Major & Medium Irrigation	MI & CAD	Total Irrigation	Flood Control	Total Plan Outlay for all Sectors
I Plan (1951–56)	376	66	442	13	1,960
II Plan (1956–61)	380	162	542	48	4,672
III Plan (1961–66)	576	443	1,019	82	8,577
Annual Plans (1966–69)	430	561	991	42	6,625
IV Plan (1969–74)	1,242	1,173	2,416	162	15,779
V Plan (1974–78)	2,516	1,410	3,926	299	28,653
Annual Plans (1978–80)	2,079	1,345	3,424	330	22,950
VI Plan (1980–85)	7,369	4,160	11,529	787	1,09,292
VII Plan (1985–90)	11,107	7,627	18,734	942	2,18,730
Annual Plans (1990–92)	5,459	3,650	9,109	461	1,23,120
VIII Plan (1992–97)	21,072	13,885	34,957	1,692	4,83,060
IX Plan (1997–02)	49,289	13,760	83,049	3,038	9,41,041
X Plan (2002–07)	83,647	16,459	1,00,106	4,344	16,18,460
XI Plan (2007–12) (Projection)	1,65,350	46,350	2,11,700	20,100	36,44,718
Total	**3,50,892**	**1,11,051**	**4,81,944**	**32,340**	**72, 27,637**

ANNEXURE 5.2
Plan-wise Proliferation of Schemes in MMI Sector

	Major Projects		Medium Projects		ERM Projects		Total Projects	
	Taken Up	Completed	Taken Up	Completed	Taken Up	Completed	Taken Up	Completed
Pre Plan	74	74	143	143	0	0	217	217
I Plan	44	5	165	34	12	3	221	42
II Plan	33	20	102	85	5	5	140	110
III Plan	32	11	44	61	7	7	83	79
Annual Plans (1966–69)	11	5	27	43	1	3	39	51
IV Plan	33	15	74	62	7	4	114	81
V Plan	68	6	303	70	20	1	391	77
Annual Plans (1978–80)	11	2	55	18	3	2	69	22
VI Plan	31	30	89	138	37	4	157	172
VII Plan	11	14	36	137	24	15	71	166
Annual Plans (1990–92)	2	7	0	12	0	8	2	27
VIII Plan	19	9	72	48	30	22	121	79
IX Plan	32	30	38	66	27	13	97	109
X Plan	49	32	84	40	46	30	179	102
XI Plan	38	45	50	66	42	5	130	116

ANNEXURE 5.3
Spillover of Major, Medium and ERM Projects into the Twelfth Plan

Plan of Start of Project	Major	Medium	ERM	Total
I Plan	0	0	0	0
II Plan	0	0	0	0
III Plan	0	0	0	0
Annual Plans (1966–69)	2	0	0	2
IV Plan	7	2	0	9
V Plan	11	1	1	13
Annual Plans (1978–80)	10	2	0	12
VI Plan	14	13	0	27
VII Plan	6	9	0	15
Annual Plans (1990–92)	1	2	0	3
VIII Plan	13	17	0	30
IX Plan	28	28	3	59
X Plan	30	22	1	53
XI Plan	32	52	30	114
Total	**154**	**148**	**35**	**337**

ANNEXURE 5.4
CLA/Grant and Irrigation Potential Created through AIBP, 1996–2012

Year	Amount of CLA/ Grant Released (₹ Crore)*	Irrigation Potential Created (in '000 ha)
1996–97	500	72
1997–98	952	200
1998–99	1,119	257
1999–2000	1,440	220
2000–01	1,821	531
2001–02	2,595	443
2002–03	3,062	272
2003–04	3,129	357
2004–05	2,867	409
2005–06	1,900	703
2006–07	2,302	938
2007–08	5,399	544
2008–09	7,598	538
2009–10	6,946	Target 1,050.00 Actuals Under Assessment
2010–11	6,837	Target 950.00 Actuals Under Assessment
2011–12	5,784	Target 1,050.00 Actuals Under Assessment
Total	**54,251**	**5,485**

*Only for Accelerated Irrigation Benefits Programme Major and Medium Irrigation and Minor Irrigation. Others like CAD, FMP, RRR are not included.

ANNEXURE 5.5
Plan-Wise Irrigation Potential Created and Utilised

(in million hectares)

Plan		Potential Created				Potential Utilised			
		Major & Medium	Minor		Total	Major & Medium	Minor		Total
			S.W.	G.W.	Total		S.W.	G.W.	Total
Upto 1951 (Pre-Plan)	Cumulative	9.70	6.40	6.50	12.90	22.6	9.70	6.40	6.50	12.90	22.60
I Plan (1951–56)	During	2.50	0.03	1.13	1.16	3.66	1.28	0.03	1.13	1.16	2.44
	Cumulative	12.20	6.43	7.63	14.06	26.26	10.98	6.43	7.63	14.06	25.04
II Plan (1956–61)	During	2.13	0.02	0.67	0.69	2.82	2.07	0.02	0.67	0.69	2.76
	Cumulative	14.33	6.45	8.30	14.75	29.08	13.05	6.45	8.30	14.75	27.80
III Plan (1961–66)	During	2.24	0.03	2.22	2.25	4.49	2.12	3.03	2.22	2.25	4.37
	Cumulative	16.57	6.48	10.52	17.00	33.57	15.17	6.48	10.52	17.00	32.17
Annual Plans (1966–69)	During	1.53	0.02	1.98	2.00	3.53	1.58	0.02	1.98	2.00	3.58
	Cumulative	18.10	6.50	12.50	19.00	37.10	16.75	6.50	12.50	19.00	35.75
IV Plan (1969–74)	During	2.60	0.50	4.00	4.50	7.10	1.64	0.50	4.00	4.50	6.14
	Cumulative	20.70	7.00	16.50	23.50	44.20	18.39	7.00	16.50	23.50	41.89
V Plan (1974–78)	During	4.02	0.50	3.30	3.80	7.82	2.70	0.50	3.30	3.80	6.50
	Cumulative	24.72	7.50	19.80	27.30	52.02	21.16	7.50	19.80	27.30	48.46
Annual Plans (1978–80)	During	1.89	0.50	2.20	2.70	1.59	1.48	0.50	2.20	2.70	4.18
	Cumulative	26.61	8.00	22.00	30.00	56.61	22.64	8.00	22.00	30.00	52.64
VI Plan (1980–85)	During	1.09	1.70	5.82	7.52	8.61	0.93	1.01	4.24	5.25	6.18
	Cumulative	27.70	9.70	27.82	37.52	65.22	23.57	9.01	26.24	35.25	58.82
VII Plan (1985–90)	During	2.22	1.29	7.80	9.09	11.31	1.90	0.96	6.91	7.87	9.77
	Cumulative	29.92	10.90	35.62	46.52	76.44	25.47	9.97	33.15	43.12	68.59
Annual Plans (1990–92)	During	0.82	0.47	3.27	3.74	4.56	0.85	0.32	3.10	3.42	4.27
	Cumulative	30.74	11.46	38.89	50.35	81.09	26.31	10.29	36.25	46.54	72.85
VIII Plan (1992–97)	During	2.21	1.05	1.91	2.96	5.17	2.13	0.78	1.45	2.23	4.36
	Cumulative	32.95	12.51	40.80	53.31	86.26	28.44	11.07	37.7	48.77	77.21
IX Plan (1997–2002)	During	4.10	1.09	2.50	3.59	7.69	2.57	0.37	0.85	1.22	3.79
	Cumulative	37.05	13.60	43.30	56.90	93.95	31.01	11.44	38.55	49.99	81.00
X Plan (2002–07)	During	4.59	0.71	2.81	3.52	8.82	2.73	0.56	2.26	2.82	6.23
	Cumulative	41.64	14.31	46.11	60.42	102.77	33.74	12.00	40.81	52.81	87.23
XI Plan* (2007–12)	During	5.77	1.41	3.29	4.70	10.47	1.27	0.43	1.01	1.44	2.71
	Cumulative	47.41	15.72	49.40	65.12	113.24	35.01	12.43	41.82	54.25	89.94

*Anticipated.

ANNEXURE 5.6
Physical and Financial Achievements of CAD Programme

Period	Central Assistance Released (in ₹ Crores)	Achievement (in million hectares)	
		Field Channels	Field Drains
1974–75 to 1996–97	1,688.11	13.95	0.77
IX Plan	751.66	1.80	0.35
X Plan	818.57	2.31	0.64
XI Plan			
2007–08	277.14	0.39	0.07
2008–09	324.29	0.43	0.13
2009–10	413.70	0.38*	0.09*
2010–11	456.40	0.41*	0.06*
2011–12	205.00**	0.35 $	0.14 $
Total	**4,934.87**	**20.02**	**2.25**

*Provisional; **Released till 15 January 2012 $ Target for the year 2011–12.

ANNEXURE 5.7
Water Use Efficiency of Completed Major/Medium Irrigation Projects Based on Field Measurements of Losses

Sl. No.	Name of Project	Culturable Command Area (Hectares)	Conveyance Efficiency (per cent)	On Farm Application Efficiency (per cent)	Overall Project Water Use Efficiency (per cent)
(1)	(2)	(3)	(4)	(5)	(6)
1.	Bhairavanithippa Project	4,856	86	67	58
2.	Gajuladinne (Sanjeevaiah Sagar Project)	10,300	57	45	26
3.	Gandipalem Project	6,478	73	38	28
4.	Godavari Delta System (Sir Arthur Cotton Barrage)	4,10,108	83	54	45
5.	Kurnool – Cuddapah Canal System	65,465	62	45	28
6.	Kaddam Project	27,519	51	36	18
7.	KoilSagar Project	11,700	83	75	62
8.	Krishna Delta System (Prakasam Barrage)	5,29,000	87	46	40
9.	Nagarjuna Sagar Project	8,89,000	56	39	22
10.	Narayanapuram Project	15,855	47	32	15
11.	Nizamsagar Project	93,659	87	45	39
12.	Srisailam Project	59,900	50	34	17
13.	Rajolibanda Diversion Scheme	35,410	82	51	42
14.	Somasila Project	54,650	56	32	18
15.	Sri Ram Sagar Project	3,71,054	78	57	45
16.	Tungabhadra High Level Canal	45,800	81	58	47
17.	Tungabhadra Low Level Canal	61,163	72	45	32
18.	Vamsadhara Project	82,087	91	58	53
19.	Yeleru Project	27,240	50	28	14
20.	Augmentation Canal Project	85,443	79	72	57
21.	Dholabaha Dam Project	2,600	74	71	53
22.	Ranjit Sagar Dam Project	3,00,000	51	65	33
23.	Ahraura Dam Irrigation Project	14,964	70	70	49
24.	Matatila Dam Project	1,79,880	68	80	54
25.	Naugarh Dam Irrigation Project	64,221	71	70	50
26.	Pili Dam Project	4,044	58	65	38
27.	Walmiki Sarovar Project	6,271	62	62	38
28.	East Baigul Reservoir Project	16,605	64	65	42
Average			69	52	38

ANNEXURE 5.8
Water Data Base Development and Management in the Twelfth Plan

The major recommendations of the Twelfth Plan Working Group on Water Data Base Development and Management are summarised below:

1. Agro-Meteorological Data

In order to improve the coverage and quality of agro-meteorological data, the following steps will be initiated during the Twelfth Plan period:

- Setting up of a real-time, standardised rainfall data monitoring network geared to an automated data archiving and retrieval system, which will be relatively free from human errors. Modern technology makes it possible to achieve this goal through a hybrid system of Doppler Weather Radars (DWRs) which have a perception radius of about 200 km, supplemented with an adequate number of Tele-metred Automatic Rain Gauges (TRGs) required for calibration, ideally one per 50 sq km.
- A reliable set of real-time precipitation data covering the entire country can be generated in a standardised manner through an optimal network of ~60 DWRs with a radius of perception equal to ~200 km, provided they are meticulously supported and calibrated by ~40,000 automatic tele-metring rain gauges. Their standardised formats and calibrations would also enable countrywide consistent rainfall data and their user friendly retrieval and dissemination to bonafide users.
- The proposed network of 40,000 ARGs can be accomplished by setting up an additional 30,000 of them during the Twelfth Plan through a cooperative effort between IMD and the States. An example of such a network is already envisaged in Karnataka.
- To incentivise the process, the Centre will finance the capital and operating cost of upgrading State networks and arrange for the training of personnel with professional skills to operate them, subject to the condition that the States should observe the protocols prescribed by IMD, be open to inspection by its officials and undertake to transmit all the data to the national database.
- The current evapotranspiration and soil moisture measurement network is highly inadequate. Estimates based on direct observation derived in the past are most likely invalid now because of the considerable change in land-use patterns and meteorological conditions. As extant lysimeters have become very old, an adequate set of lysimeters equipped with digital/load cells, and data logger and GPRS transmission facility needs to be installed, and data collected and analysed to enhance the reliability of agro-met advisories on irrigation scheduling. The density required to get sufficiently disaggregated estimates for different agro-climatic regions, and to provide information for management of water in major projects and phased programmes covering design and costs, to achieve optimum density over the next 10 years needs to be worked out. Here again, a conscious effort will be made to build a national network in collaboration with the States, with financial support conditional on their being supervised by IMD.
- Direct measurements of PET in the 219 centres will be compared with empirical estimates in contiguous centres to establish the degree of confidence with which the latter can be used for operational purposes. If this exercise establishes the empirical formulae to be reasonably accurate, empirical methods can be used to get PET estimates for a much larger number of centres which are equipped to provide data on the relevant climatic variables.
- There are protocols by which estimates of daily PET estimates taken together with precipitation data can be converted to assess the soil moisture conditions in different seasons. Soil moisture status can also be estimated through remote sensing techniques, which needs to be corroborated/validated through actual measured ground data. In a similar pattern of gridded rainfall data, PET data will also be made available on 1° × 1° grid. This would greatly enhance the value of these datasets for assessing crop prospects in each season.
- These estimates will be validated by actual measurements on the ground in agricultural research stations that have experimental plots which are monitored by scientists, who have the necessary equipment with which to make the needed measurements.
- The efforts undertaken by various agricultural universities and the agro-met divisions of the State remote sensing applications centres (including the NRSC Agro-met Division) in terms of soil moisture monitoring need to be made inclusive and not limited to the 'research' domain.
- To assess agricultural needs of soil moisture a monthly average is suitable and the corresponding linear density is of the order of around 100 km. On the other hand when estimating run off, every event counts and the linear density should be 5–10 km. At the same time evaporation and Evapotranspiration are less variable than the rainfall itself thereby necessitating a linear density of around 50 km.

- Weather forecast models aided by cloud diagnostic support from satellites and radars are the tools for Quantitative Precipitation Forecast. But conventional methods, as were deployed till recently, essentially depend on climatological analogues of past events and weather pattern matching. Three major studies have been recently done for the river basins of Yamuna, Mahanadi and Narmada using the conventional methods. The Twelfth Plan augmentation in observational and predictive capabilities will make the ensuing studies for other river basins more accurate and reliable.

2. Water Resources Potential

The current estimate of utilisable surface flows for the country (690 bcm) as well as those for major basins is substantially the same as earlier ones (made in 1976, 1988 and 2001). The Working Group was unable to locate any document explaining the basis for these estimates. Given the present state of knowledge on these aspects, the data and assumptions underlying the estimates are impossible to verify or validate. The following proposals have been made by the CWC for the Twelfth Plan to improve estimates of overall and utilisable surface water resources potential:

- Expansion and up-gradation of the existing 878 hydrological observation (HO) stations and supporting infrastructure in site offices for repair and maintenance.
- 1917 additional HO stations will be opened in order to meet the minimum requirement of HO stations for achieving various goals such as assessment of basin wise water availability, study of climate change, better flood forecasting, flood mitigation, reservoir inflow forecasting, water quality and sediment assessment, morphological studies, planning and design of water resources projects, assessment of navigational potential for inland waterways, and so on.
- Eight hundred and ten of such sites shall be equipped with measuring systems to monitor silt load and water quality.
- Facilities for monitoring glacial lakes/water bodies and snow-melt forecasting in the Himalayan region.
- Expansion in the number of reservoirs equipped for telemetric monitoring of reservoir water level and live storage.
- Creating a Coastal Management Information System (CMIS) for collecting data on various natural phenomena occurring in coastal regions, and for appraisal and monitoring of projects for their protection.
- Setting up a new organisation, namely National Water Resources Information Centre (NWR-IC), comprising professionals with specialised expertise in water resources, GIS, remote sensing, computer science and other related disciplines to manage the large volume of data on water resources and allied fields generated under India-WRIS project and also to update periodically for proper decision-making.
- Strengthening in-house facilities for upgrading capacity for digitised management and dissemination of data.

3. Water Utilisation by Source and Use

Planning of water resource development policy and programmes requires reliable data on all potentially usable resources and also on how much each of these are being used from which source, where, for what purposes and with what effect; and how these are changing over time. The current state of data and knowledge on these aspects is extremely unsatisfactory for several reasons:

- Published estimates focus only on surface flows and groundwater. Very little attention is given to the contribution of rainfall, which is the sole source of water for all uses in un-irrigated areas and a significant source even in irrigated areas. More effective use of rainfall for increasing productivity of rainfed agriculture and supply of water supply for domestic use in rain fed areas is in fact the rationale for the integrated watershed management programme. Even with irrigation, the extent of improvement in soil moisture regime varies across agro climatic regions depending on the ability to adjust irrigation supplies according to rainfall across seasons;
- Estimates of utilisation of surface and ground water are available only for a few years and for major basins. They are not based on measurements of actual utilisation in particular years but are estimates of utilisation in an unspecified 'normal' or 'average' year, based on inadequate, unverified data and assumptions;
- Even for major and medium irrigation systems, which are supposed to maintain continuous records of water delivered into their canal networks the coverage and quality of recorded data are not known; nor are they compiled and collated by any agency;
- Estimates of groundwater extraction are also not based on any systematic measurements of actual draft per well of different types and in different regions;
- There are no data on overall utilisation of water from minor surface works;
- Estimates do not cover water extracted from private wells and tube wells used for non agricultural uses, and un-authorised diversion/pumping of water from rivers and streams;

- Available utilisation data do not cover canal water used outside the command area, water lifted from flowing water in rivers and streams, and underground water from river beds. Much of this is unauthorised and likely to go unrecorded by official statistics.

Concerted and sustained action to address these deficiencies is therefore of critical importance. For this purpose the Working Group suggests:

- Commission properly planned and scientifically rigorous studies of current utilisation of local rainfall and potential for its fuller, more effective use in selected watershed in different agro-climatic regimes.
- More effective use existing data sources including especially the records of water delivery being maintained by managers of major and medium surface systems and the detailed data on minor irrigation works of all kinds and the area/crops reported to be irrigated by them. It is essential to persuade/incentivise state agencies to collate both current and past series data from their records and make them available to the national data pool for scientific analysis and policy oriented research.
- Upgrade physical infrastructure for measuring water deliveries in all major public water supply systems.
- Rationalise the system for recording and validation of these data and reporting them to a central pool.
- Systematic field studies in selected systems of different types to assess technical efficiency of water use.
- Selectively assess the extent to which seasonal pattern of water deliveries relative to evapo-transpiration of crops being actually grown in the command may be a source of inefficiency.
- Monitored measurement of actual water pumped in a sample of wells/tubewells from different regions.

4. End Uses of Water

The basis of available estimates of both current levels of actual water consumption and projected future requirements are quite unsatisfactory in the absence of surveys of actual total and source-wise consumption by households and commercial establishments. Projections are based on norms regarding desirable levels of use per capita in rural and urban areas, assuming that this should be provided from public systems. Estimates for industries and power are again based on patchy data on requirements per unit of current and projected output in their different segments. In the case of agriculture, the system for compiling data on area of different crops irrigated by different sources based on village level records and estimating yields of major irrigated crops at the state level through sample crop cutting surveys has become unmanageable for a variety of reasons and the reliability of estimates based on them is in serious question.

The following steps are needed to redress these deficiencies:

- The recommendations of a recent Expert Group of the Ministry of Agriculture will vastly improve the quality of data needed to assess the impact of irrigation.
- This needs to be supplemented by more detailed and in-depth surveys of both rainfed lands and irrigated areas to collect comprehensive data on all important technical and operational aspects of water utilisation and socio-economic and environmental impact from different types of projects in different regions and river basins.
- The only way to get reliable estimates of actual groundwater extraction and use, is through sample surveys of all types of wells in rural and urban areas, distinguishing between wells which are primarily for irrigation as a sole source and used conjunctively with surface water, and those which are used primarily as a sources of domestic, commercial and different non-agricultural uses.
- Since the physical condition, water availability and use from all man made systems are prone to significant and rapid change over time, it is essential to repeat such surveys periodically.

These surveys will be entrusted to a consortium of government and non-governmental research institutions with experience in such studies who will use well-defined common concepts and methodologies to ensure comparability across regions and over time.

NOTES

1. This is based on the Central Water Commission's estimate of India's water resource potential as 1869 BCM.
2. The 2030 Water Resources Group (2009): *Charting Our Water Future*.
3. See full details of this initiative in Chapter 17 on Rural Development.
4. See full details of this initiative in Chapter 17 on Rural Development.
5. See full details of this initiative in Chapter 15 on 'Transport'.
6. R. Ackerman (2011): *New Directions for Water Management in Indian Agriculture*.
7. J. Briscoe and R.P.S. Malik (2006): *India's Water Economy: Bracing for a Turbulent Future*, The World Bank.
8. U.A. Amarasinghe et al. (2007): *India's Water Future to 2025–2050: Business-as-usual Scenario and Deviations*, IWMI.
9. J.P. Venot et al. (2007): *Shifting Waterscapes: Explaining Basin Closure in the Lower Krishna Basin*, IWMI.
10. R. Ackerman (2011): *New Directions for Water Management in Indian Agriculture*.
11. D. Blackmore (2010): *River Basin Management: Opportunities and Risks*, Asian Development Bank.
12. D. Blackmore (2010): *River Basin Management: Opportunities and Risks*, Asian Development Bank.
13. K. Pomeranz (2009): 'The Great Himalayan Watershed: Agrarian Crisis, Mega-Dams and the Environment', *New Left Review*, No. 58, July–August 2009.
14. N. Myers et al. (2000): 'Biodiversity Hotspots for Conservation Priorities', *Nature*, 403.
15. K.S. Valdiya (1999): 'A Geodynamic Perspective of Arunachal Pradesh', Keynote Address at Workshop organised by the GB Pant Institute of Himalayan Environment and Development.
16. D.C. Goswami and P.J. Das (2002): 'Hydrological Impact of Earthquakes on the BrahmaputraRiver Regime', Proceedings of the 18th National Convention of Civil Engineers, Guwahati.
17. M. Menon et al. (2003): 'Large Dams in the Northeast: A Bright Future?' *The Ecologist Asia*, Vol. 11, No. 1.
18. R.A. Kerr and R. Stone (2009): 'A Human Trigger for the Great Quake of Sichuan?', *Science*, 16 January 2009, Vol. 323, No. 5912.
19. V. Rajamani, U.C. Mohanty, R. Ramesh, G.S. Bhat, P.N. Vinayachandran, D. Sengupta, Prasanna Kumar and R.K. Kolli (2006): 'Linking Indian Rivers vs Bay of Bengal Monsoon Activity', *Current Science*, Vol. 90, 12–13.
20. Around 56 per cent of these 337 projects have not been approved by the Planning Commission and are not eligible for central assistance.
21. V.M. Tiwari et al. (2009): 'Dwindling groundwater resources in northern Indian region, from satellite gravity observations', *Geoph. Res. Lett.*, 36, L18401, doi:10.1029/2009GL039401.
22. Central Ground Water Board (2009): *Dynamic Ground Water Resources of India*.
23. The States are Assam, Tripura, Manipur, Meghalaya, Mizoram, Nagaland, Arunachal Pradesh, Chhattisgarh, Jharkhand, Orissa and West Bengal.
24. For instance, the guidelines differentiate between cities with and without sewerage (70 lpcd to without and 135 lpcd to cities with sewerage system). But these do not indicate how much area must be under a sewerage system before a city qualifies for higher water norms. The guidelines are also imprecise—they provide that cities could provide additional water if hospitals, schools, airports and institutions require 'considerable quantities'.
25. This section partly draws upon a working paper *Developing a Water Conservation Strategy for Industry* prepared by the Centre for Energy, Environment and Water for the Planning Commission.
26. R. Ackerman (2011): *New Directions for Water Management in Indian Agriculture*.
27. Government of Bihar (2008): *Kosi Flood: Assessment Report*, World Bank, Global Facility for Disaster Reduction and Recovery.
28. Samaj Pragati Sahayog and Megh-Pyne Abhiyan (2012): *Leveraging MGNREGA for Flood Control—A Case for Policy Reform in Bihar*, National Consortium of Civil Society Organizations on MGNREGA.
29. The draft model bill is available on the website of the Planning Commission.
30. This section is based on the work done by the Twelfth Plan Sub-Group on Legal Issues related to Groundwater Management and Regulation as part of the Working Group on Water Governance.
31. *Acton v Blundell* (1843) 12 Meeson and Welsby 324 (Court of Exchequer Chamber, 1 January 1843). This was confirmed in *Chasemore v Richards* (footnote 21), which found that the right of the owner of a mill using spring water had no action against other landowners abstracting groundwater to the extent of affecting his own use of the water. This was because the judges determined that such a right would 'interfere with, if not prevent, the draining of land by the owner'.
32. *George Chasemore v Henry Richards* (1859) VII House of Lords Cases 349 (House of Lords, 27 July 1859).
33. B.B. Katiyar, *Law of Easements and Licences* (New Delhi: Universal Law Publishing, 13th ed 2010).
34. Thus, for example, in the words of Justice Seshagiri Aiyar 'It must have a fairly defined course. It must mo.ve. Its water must be capable of identification. It need not always be confined within banks. It need not have a continuous flow. Its width need not be of particular dimensions' *Unde Rajah Raja Sri Raja Velugoti Sri Rajagopala Krishna Yachendrala Varu Bahadur, K.C.I.E. Maharajah of Venkatagiri v Secretary of State for India in Council* (1915) 28 MLJ 98 (High Court of Madras, 19 October 1914).
35. M.S. Vani, 'Groundwater Law in India: A New Approach', in Ramaswamy Iyer ed., *Water and the Laws in India* 435, 444 (New Delhi: Sage, 2009).

36. *MC Mehta v Kamal Nath* (1997) 1 SCC 388 (Supreme Court, 1996); *State of West Bengal v Kesoram Industries* (2004) 10 SCC 201 (Supreme Court, 2004).
37. For example, the Andhra Pradesh Farmers' Management of Irrigation Systems Act, 1997; Gujarat Water Users' Participatory Irrigation Management Act, 2007; Maharashtra Management of Irrigation Systems by the Farmers Act, 2005 and Tamil Nadu Farmers Management of Irrigation Systems Act, 2000.
38. For example, *Subhash Kumar v State of Bihar* AIR 1991 SC 420 (Supreme Court, 1991).
39. The draft is available on the website of the Planning Commission.
40. The Model Bill is built around the need to regulate unreasonable use of sources of groundwater that threaten the aquifer to ensure that the resource (aquifer) itself is protected and can provide a sustainable basis for meeting the basic needs of every person for decades to come.
41. This draft is available on the website of the Planning Commission.

6

Land Issues

6.1. India has had a long history of social discrimination, closely linked with denial of access to land. Specific land tenure systems prevailing at the time of independence also created their own set of problems. The deteriorating quality of land records administration over the last four decades has compounded the hardships of the poor. And in the recent past, the drive to acquire land for development has posed fresh challenges, most especially for the scheduled tribes. The last few years have witnessed a number of new government initiatives, including the Hindu Succession (Amendment) Act, 2005 and the Scheduled Tribes and Other Traditional Forest Dwellers (Recognition of Forest Rights) Act, 2006, which are a response to both historical injustices and recent challenges. In January 2008, the Prime Minister approved the constitution of two High Level bodies—the National Council for Land Reforms under the Chairmanship of the Prime Minister and a Committee on State Agrarian Relations and the Unfinished Tasks in Land Reforms under the Chairmanship of the Union Minister for Rural Development. The Union Government has drafted *The Right to Fair Compensation, Resettlement, Rehabilitation and Transparency in Land Acquisition Bill.*

6.2. The constraint posed by land is emerging as a key challenge in ensuring both inclusiveness and sustainability of the growth process. There is a constraint faced by the landless, small and marginal farmers within agriculture, as also the constraint faced by the growing need for land for the processes of urbanisation and industrialisation.

LAND FOR AGRICULTURE

Land Reforms: The Unfinished Agenda

6.3. Ever since independence, land reforms have been a major instrument of state policy to promote both equity and agricultural investment. Unfortunately, progress on land reforms has been slow, reflecting the resilience of structures of power that gave rise to the problem in the first place.

6.4. The main instrument for realising more equitable distribution of land are the land ceiling laws. These laws were enacted by several states during the late 1950s and 1960s, and the early 1970s saw more stringent amendments in the laws to plug loopholes in the earlier laws. But the record of implementation has not been satisfactory. Around 3 million hectares of land has been declared surplus so far, which is hardly 2 per cent of net sown area in India. About 30 per cent of this land has not yet been distributed as it is caught up in litigations. Besides, a number of benami and clandestine transactions have resulted in illegal possession of significant amounts of land above ceiling limits. There are widespread reports of allotment of inferior unproductive, barren and wasteland to landless households, many of whom have been forced to sell it off, in the absence of resources to make it productive. In many instances lands allotted to the rural poor under the ceiling laws are not in their possession. In some cases, pattas were issued to the beneficiaries, but possession of land shown in the pattas was not given, or corresponding changes were not made in the records of rights.

6.5. The balance of power in rural India is so heavily weighed against the landless and the poor that implementing land ceiling laws is difficult. It is clear that without massive mobilisation of the rural poor and a deepening of democratic governance in rural India, very little can be achieved in this direction. West Bengal, with more than half of India's ceiling surplus land beneficiaries, provides an example of what could be achieved.

6.6. Although half of India's population continues to depend on agriculture as its primary source of livelihood, 83 per cent of farmers operate holdings of less than 2 ha in size, and the average holding size is only 1.23 ha. This is often in fragments and unirrigated. There are also those who are entirely landless, although agriculture is their main source of livelihood. They have inadequate financial resources to purchase and often depend on leasing in small plots, on insecure terms, for short periods, sometimes only for one season. Hence many face insecurity of tenure and the growing threat of land alienation and pressures from urbanisation, industrialisation and powerful interests.

6.7. They are unable to take advantage of the economies of scale, or invest in lumpy inputs such as irrigation, technology or machinery. They have limited access to formal credit. Hence they have few resources for land improvement or crop insurance or adequate inputs (seeds, fertilisers, and so on). They are often ignored by extension agencies and seldom receive information on new technologies or training in skill-intensive agricultural practices.

6.8. Legally, land leasing laws in most states either prevent marginal and small farmers from increasing the area they cultivate by leasing in land, or create tenurial insecurity for informal tenants/sharecroppers. Unrecorded tenancies are mostly held by small and marginal farmers. At the same time, absentee landlordism is high in some regions (especially the hill states and rainfed areas), causing huge tracts of cultivable fallows to lie idle. Unfortunately, most tenancy laws have driven tenancy underground or made it even more informal. Micro-studies from different states show that the proportion of leased-in land is significantly higher than reported by both the NSS and Census. In some cases, it is as high as 20–25 per cent of the gross cultivated area. Tenancy contracts are oral and for a short period. The proportion of leased-in land is higher in agriculturally developed regions compared to backward regions. All classes of households participate in the lease market both as lessors and lessees. However, while in backward agricultural regions, the traditional pattern is more common wherein the small and marginal farmers dominate the lease market as lessees and large and medium farmers as lessors, in agriculturally advanced regions, the lease market is in a state of transition where all classes of households participate. The trend towards reverse tenancy is more pronounced in these regions.

6.9. There is, therefore, a strong case for legalising tenancy and allowing leasing-in and leasing-out land with adequate safeguards to protect the interests of small and marginal farmers. Liberalisation of the lease market does not mean abrogation of existing tenancy legislations. These must be suitably amended to permit leasing-in and leasing-out of land, while making ownership rights non-alienable and secure, fixing tenure, recording of lease and allowing landowners to resume land for cultivation after expiry of lease.

6.10. Reforming tenancy laws would allow all sections to appropriately participate in the lease market depending upon their resource endowment. Studies have shown that in states like Punjab and Haryana, large and medium farmers who lease in land from small and marginal farmers invest in modern inputs, reap economies of scale and raise farm productivity. The small and marginal farmers who lease out their land also gain in terms of occupational mobility and higher incomes. In other states like Bihar and Orissa, with low wages and fewer employment opportunities, small and marginal farmers lease in land, enlarge their holding size and thus afford a reasonable level of living with all attendant benefits of tenancy like borrowing from financial institutions. The medium and large farmers in these states migrate to urban areas to take non-farm employment opportunities without any risk of losing their land. When their livelihoods become secure in the non-farm sector, they could sell their land. Liberalising tenancy also helps in consolidation of holdings as farmers prefer to lease out rather than sell the piece of land that is inconveniently located. Long-term tenancy contracts would also help raise agricultural productivity.

6.11. These constraints are further compounded for tribal and women farmers. Increasingly, as more men than women move out of agriculture, there is a shift toward the feminisation of agriculture. Many women also serve as de-facto household heads. However, women farmers typically have little direct access to land and highly unequal access to inputs and other services.

6.12. Environmental factors further disadvantage poor farmers. Water tables have been falling and soils depleting. All this is happening against the backdrop of climate change. The key question is: *how can these constraints be transformed into opportunities?* Can the disadvantaged farmers attain sustainable livelihoods and become India's advantage for both higher growth and more inclusive development?

The Way Forward

6.13. The Twelfth Plan Working Group on Disadvantaged Farmers, including Women has proposed several mechanisms for easing the land constraint faced by the landless and land-poor:

Land Transfers by Government to Disadvantaged and Women (D&W) Farmers

6.14. There should be a comprehensive assessment of all land available with the government, including ceiling surplus land, uncultivated wasteland, and so on. Unofficial estimates by organisations such as Ekta Parishad suggest much more land is available for distribution than reflected in official estimates.

6.15. All such available land should be distributed to groups of D&W farmers rather than to individual families. The land so distributed could either be registered in the group's name, or it could be given to them under a very long-term lease arrangement.

6.16. The recommendation of the Eleventh Plan that all rural families without homesteads be allotted land in the woman's name, needs to be implemented in all States, to be used for shelter and supplementary livelihoods, although the amount allotted could be subject to availability. Some States have taken important initiatives in this direction. Kerala has had a longstanding programme of giving ownership rights on land on which a homestead stands, in its land reform programme. Some 4.46 lakh agricultural labour households benefited from this: the percentage of landless families declined from 15.7 per cent in 1971–72 to 4.8 per cent in 2002–03. These schemes provided land for shelter and also for supplementary livelihoods (for example kitchen gardens, goat and poultry rearing). The West Bengal and Orissa governments have also allotted homestead plots to landless families. Orissa has been allotting 4 to 10 cents and West Bengal has allotted up to 16 cents.

Facilitating Land Purchase

6.17. Apart from distributing all surplus land available with the government to D&W farmers, schemes could be instituted to enable the landless and land-poor to themselves purchase land. The Twelfth Plan Working Group on Disadvantaged Farmers, including Women recommends a loan-cum-grant scheme with 50 per cent being given as a low interest loan and 50 per cent being given as a grant, to help groups of landless or near landless women and men purchase land collectively. The land purchased can be registered in equal parts in each group member's name, but support is needed to help the group improve the land, and even cultivate it as a group.

6.18. A case in point is a scheme started in the 1980s by the Government of Andhra Pradesh, under which poor dalit women formed small groups to buy land collectively for joint farming, with support from the NGO Deccan Development Society. Many women's groups in Medak District took advantage of the scheme. The land was equally divided and registered in the names of individual women. But they are cultivating jointly by pooling it. However, experience has shown that government should not purchase land for leasing to D&W farmers, as attempted in Andhra Pradesh. Government entry in the land market tends to hike up prices, making the scheme unsustainable. It also adversely affects poor farmers who are outside the scheme when they seek to buy or lease in land on their own.

Facilitating Land Leasing

6.19. Land leasing is a significant mechanism for bringing in fallow or little used land under cultivation, and providing land access to the land-poor. This will need both legal changes and institutional innovation.

6.20. *Legal changes:* Tenancy should be legalised and regulated to provide security to the tenant while also protecting the landowner's rights. The contractual period should be long enough to encourage investment in land. Legalisation should also protect the landowner's rights so that s/he has an incentive to lease out the land which might otherwise remain underutilised. A group approach to leasing in and use of the land should be built into the system, as also financial and institutional support for such cultivation. In other words, leasing by women's Self Help Groups (SHGs), or groups constituted of male or female headed disadvantaged farmer families, or production cooperatives, or other forms of group farms should be permitted. Sub-leasing within the group to individual members should be banned. Financial and institutional support should also be provided for group cultivation.

6.21. In 2009 Andhra Pradesh introduced a bill in the Assembly (Self-Help Group Tenancy Bill 2009), which would legally permit leasing by women's Self-help Groups. Landowners are assured that their titles will not be in jeopardy. However, a flaw in AP 2009 Bill is that the land will be leased collectively by the group, but can be sub-leased to group members, with the group bearing liability for the lease. This is retrogressive since default by one member would make the entire group indebted. Also subleasing will fragment the holdings and undermine potential economies of scale. Also reports indicate that even the news of this potential legalisation has frozen the land lease market.

6.22. *Public Land Banks*: Even legal guarantee may be insufficient to mitigate the landowner's fear of losing his/her title, especially since many of the lessors are themselves small and marginal farmers. Enacting a law to recognise tenancies could freeze the informal land lease market in the short run. To guard against this, the Twelfth Plan Working Group on Disadvantaged Farmers, including Women proposes the creation of a *Public Land Bank* (PLB) at the panchayat level. This would regulate and rationalise land demand and supply. The PLB would take 'deposits' of land from landowners wanting to lease out their land, with the surety that they could withdraw their deposit when they wanted. The deposit could be for one season, one year, or three years and more. On deposit the farmers would get a small payment as incentive, the amount varying by the period of deposit (analogous to a current account, savings account, and fixed account in a financial bank). The incentive amount could be calibrated to a percentage of the prevailing average land rent in the panchayat. The landowner would receive an additional fee when the land is leased out.

6.23. The PLB would lease out the land under its command to specially designated categories of disadvantaged farmers, such as marginal farmers, women, dalits, and tribals, whether leasing as individuals or in groups. These lessees would get a guaranteed lease, fixed after assessing land quality, and in a consolidated plot where possible. Institutional finance and other support could also be provided.

6.24. There can be several incentives for farmers to deposit their land in the PLB: (*i*) a minimum rent from the PLB even for fallow land; (*ii*) an additional 'topping up' rent for land that gets leased out; (*iii*) development of the land in terms of soil conservation and so on, via MGNREGA or other means. (*iv*) government guarantee to protect the owner, with owners being free to withdraw their land from the Bank with due notice. For the lessees, it would provide D&W farmers access to land for which they cannot always compete in the open market. The PLB should provide a guaranteed lease and, where possible, a consolidated plot of reasonable size. This would, in itself, improve their ability to move up the value chain and taking advantage of new opportunities.

6.25. The PLB should be provided initial seed capital from the central and the state governments in a ratio of say, 80:20, or even 100 per cent by the Centre in the pilot stage for three years. The PLB would be registered as a Society.

Group Farming: An Integrated Approach to Ease Multiple Constraints

6.26. To ease the constraints D&W farmers face in access to land and other inputs, and to enable them to take advantage of new market opportunities, we need an integrated approach to problem resolution. The most comprehensive solution would be group farming with individual land ownership. There are several successful examples of group cultivation in India from which lessons can be learnt and the programme expanded to other states. The best known example is of the Kudumbashree project launched in 2007 by the Kerala Government; but initiatives in Andhra Pradesh are also of note.

6.27. The Kudumbashree project initially facilitated land leasing by small groups of women, typically women's SHGs. In March 2010, an additional step was taken under which SHGs undertaking group farming can be registered as Joint Liability Groups (JLGs)—a National Bank for Agriculture and Rural Development (NABARD) scheme—and given financial and technical support. The state government also provides support for land preparation and reclamation (linking it with MGNREGS in some districts). There are some 38,000 JLGs in Kerala today, covering 2.5 lakh women. Such collective/group farming is carried out in all 14 districts of Kerala, covering around 24,000 ha in 2010–11. Of this, 30 per cent is fallow land which is about 9 per cent of the total current fallow land in the state. Each JLG has 4–10 women members from poor families, who lease in land, and also pool small plots owned by members. Leases range between 1 and 3 years. Rent on fallow land is low. The main crops cultivated are paddy (almost one-third the acreage), tapioca, vegetables, banana and pineapple. Group farming through joint leasing has brought substantial uncultivated land under farming, revived agriculture and created employment.

6.28. The *Andhra Pradesh Mahila Samatha Society (APMSS)* is another significant case of successful group farming by women. In 2001, APMSS begun implementing a five-year GoI–UNDP supported Dry Land Agriculture Project by mahila sanghams in five districts. The project covered 500 villages, with women farming in groups on jointly leased in or pooled personal land. In 2005, **United Nations Development Programme (UNDP) involvement ended but the programme continued** under APMSS. Many of these groups survive today. There are about 175 women's groups in five districts, involving 4,376 women farmers, belonging to small and marginal farmers and landless labourers. The groups mainly cultivate paddy with little irrigation and use non-chemical farming practices. All farm operations are shared and the output is distributed among the women.

6.29. Group farming has greatly increased food security among the participating households, which would not have been possible on an individual basis. However, the groups need sustained technical support at the field level which had been provided during the project period with UNDP funding.

6.30. The Kudumbshree and APMSS models could be tried on a pilot basis in other States, adapted to local contexts. The group enterprise model should also be replicated for other agricultural sectors, such as fisheries (for example, group pisciculture), poultry or livestock management. Group farming could also be integrated with MGNREGS for improving agricultural land. For instance, MGNREGS has been used productively for land preparation or reclamation to support group farming in Kerala (under the Kudumbshree project). Such efforts to integrate group farming with MGNREGS need to be encouraged to leverage such schemes better for improving land resources for agriculture.

6.31. Setting up of group enterprises takes time and resources. Funding for five years could be provided to all organisations willing to help form and mentor groups until they become self-sustaining. NGOs or other agencies could play this role.

LAND ACQUISITION FOR NON-AGRICULTURAL USE

6.32. Faster industrialisation is both desirable and inevitable; so is faster urbanisation. Land is an essential requirement for these structural changes to proceed unimpeded. Government also needs to acquire land for a variety of public purposes, including human development and infrastructure projects. Recognising that all the land needed for development cannot be obtained in a purely voluntary manner, there is need for a fair land acquisition law which resorts to compulsory acquisition only where it is unavoidable and in a manner that seeks assessment of social impact as participatory as possible, while also ensuring that both fair compensation and Resettlement and Rehabilitation of the dislocated persons.

6.33. Independent estimates place the number of people displaced following development projects in India over the last sixty years at 60 million, and only a third of these are estimated to have been resettled in a planned manner. Most of these people are the asset-less rural poor, marginal farmers, poor fisherfolk and quarry workers. Around 40 per cent of those displaced belonged to Adivasis and 20 per cent to Dalits. Given that 90 per cent of our coal, more than 50 per cent of most minerals and most prospective dam sites are in Adivasi regions, there is likely to be continuing tension over issues of land acquisition in these areas.

6.34. These problems have arisen in large part because the legal framework under which land has been acquired is outdated. It is based on the principle of 'eminent domain'[1] under which the State can forcibly acquire land for a public purpose at prices which do not reflect the market price nor provide any premium to reflect the fact that the acquisition is forcible.

6.35. The way forward is to move away from the colonial perspective of treating people as 'subjects', which is inherent in the doctrine of eminent domain, towards a vision of citizens, whose rights are guaranteed under the Constitution. Ultimately, we have to go beyond narrow legality to seek broader legitimacy.

6.36. Resettlement & Rehabilitation (R&R) provisions must be made mandatory and not reduced to what they have generally tended to become—conditionalities without consequences. We also require an unequivocal commitment to imaginatively explore ways of rebuilding the livelihoods of those adversely affected by development projects.

6.37. Not addressing these issues has meant that even when the purposes for which land is to be acquired are in the legitimate national interest and/or subserve a vital public purpose, there have been fractious and irresolvable conflicts over land acquisition.

6.38. On the other hand, given the huge asymmetries of information and power in the land market, there are innumerable instances of distress sales by farmers to more powerful entities at throwaway prices. In many instances, these sales have been followed by use of the land in ways that run completely contrary to the original stated purpose and have yielded windfall profits to land and real estate mafias. That is why there has to be a role for the government—to put in place, a transparent and flexible set of rules and regulations, and to ensure its enforcement.

6.39. Government is in the final stages of formulating *The Right to Fair Compensation, Resettlement, Rehabilitation and Transparency in Land Acquisition Bill*. The Bill seeks to balance the need for facilitating land acquisition for various public purposes, including infrastructure development, industrialisation and urbanisation, while at the same time meaningfully addressing the concerns of farmers, and those whose livelihoods depend on the land being acquired.

6.40. The reason for combining the two into a single legislation is that land acquisition and R&R are two sides of the same coin. R&R must always, in each instance, necessarily follow upon significant acquisition of land. Not combining the two within one law, risks neglect of R&R which has been the experience so far.

6.41. Even as it protects the interests of the land and livelihood losers by ensuring them fair compensation and adequate R&R, the Bill also seeks to ensure that land acquisition for vital public purposes happens in a manner that is judicious, transparent and time-bound, so that public purposes can be served in an expeditious and efficient manner.

6.42. The Bill is a milestone in legislation that should lead to a reduction in instances of perceived injustices that have played a major role in fuelling Maoism. On the other hand, by improving the functioning of the land market, it should lead to an upgrading of the overall investment climate in the country.

6.43. The Bill lists eight categories of public purpose for which government can acquire land:

1. Land for strategic purposes relating to armed forces of the Union, national security or defence, police, safety of the people;
2. Land for railways, highways, ports, power and irrigation purposes for use by Government and public sector companies or corporations;
3. Land for the project affected people;
4. Land for Planned development or improvement of village or urban sites or for residential purpose to weaker sections in rural or urban areas;
5. Land for Government administered educational, agricultural, health and research schemes or institutions;
6. Land for persons residing in areas affected by natural calamities;
7. Land acquired by the Government for

    (a) use by government itself for purposes other than those above
    (b) public sector companies; or
    (c) PPP projects for the production of public goods or the provision of public services for physical infrastructure, social infrastructure and human development projects including those involving the production of intermediate goods and services for these purposes.

8. Land for private companies for the production of public goods or provision of public services for physical infrastructure, social infrastructure and human development projects including those involving the production of intermediate goods and services for these purposes.

6.44. Under categories (7) and (8), consent of at least 80 per cent of the landowning Project Affected Families (PAFs) is sought to be obtained through an informed process as outlined in the Bill. Under PPP projects, ownership of land will continue to vest with Government so that the PPP framework can apply.

6.45. In each case of land acquisition, fair compensation and R&R provisions as laid out in the Bill will apply. The compensation will be two times the market rate (including solatium) in urban areas and 2–4 times the market rate (including solatium) in rural areas (based on a sliding scale reflecting the distance of project from urban area). The sliding scale will be determined by State government or State Land Pricing Commission/Authority.[2] The land compensation calculated will not be taken as the base to determine the circle rate for subsequent acquisitions, in order to ensure there is no speculative price spiral.

6.46. In the interests of food security, reasonable restrictions have been placed on acquisition of multi cropped agricultural land, with the limits of these being in each case left to the States to decide. These restrictions shall not apply in the case of linear projects (such as railways, highways, major district roads, power and telegraph lines and irrigation canals)

6.47. The comprehensive R&R package for landowners and livelihood losers[3] includes:

1. Subsistence allowance at ₹3,000 per month per family for 12 months
2. The affected families shall be entitled to:
   (i) Where jobs are created through the project, mandatory employment for one member per affected family or (ii) ₹5 lakhs per family or (iii) ₹2,000 per month per family as annuity for 20 years, with appropriate index for inflation. The option of availing (i) or (ii) or (iii) shall be that of the affected family
3. If a house is lost in rural areas, a constructed house shall be provided as per the Indira Awas Yojana specifications. If a house is lost in urban areas, a constructed house shall be provided, which will be not less than 50 sq mts in plinth

area. In either case the equivalent cost of the house may also be provided in lieu of the house as per the preference of the project affected family
4. *One acre of land* to each family in the command area, if land is acquired for an irrigation project
5. ₹50,000 for transportation
6. A one-time 'Resettlement Allowance' of ₹50,000

6.48. Additional benefits have been provided for SC/ST families. The Bill also seeks to provide the same R&R package to affected families on sale/purchase of land where sale/purchase exceeds a certain threshold. This threshold shall be fixed by respective States keeping in view the availability of the land and density of the population.

6.49. 25 infrastructural amenities are to be provided in the resettlement area, including schools and playgrounds, health centres, roads and electric connections, assured sources of safe drinking water for each family, panchayat ghars, Anganwadis, places of worship and burial and/or cremation ground, village level post offices, as appropriate, with facilities for opening saving accounts, Fair Price shops and seed-cum-fertiliser storage facilities and so on.

6.50. In order to avoid delays, stringent time-lines have been set. Compensation will be given within a period of three months from the date of the award. Monetary R&R entitlements will be provided within a period of six months from the date of the award. Infrastructure R&R entitlements will be provided within a period of eighteen months from the date of the award. No involuntary displacement will take place without completion of R&R. In irrigation or hydel projects, R&R shall be completed six months prior to submergence.

INNOVATIONS IN LAND FOR URBANISATION

6.51. Work on issues related to urbanisation during the preparation of the Twelfth Plan has thrown up a number of innovative ideas to ease the land constraint in this sector:

6.52. Land Readjustment (LR) is gaining acceptance as an alternative to land acquisition as it has many advantages for land assembly. Under this process, a compact area is selected in consultation with the land owners for urban expansion/renewal. The municipal authorities provide infrastructure which is funded by exploiting a part of land. The remaining land, whose value has increased due to provision of infrastructure, is reallocated back to participating private landowners. In essence a participatory tool, LR avoids public discontent and protests to a great extent. It also reduces the need for raising large amounts of money for acquiring land.

6.53. India has already been experimenting with a variant of LR in Gujarat's Town Planning Schemes (TPSs). Another ongoing experiment is the improvement of the C ward in Mumbai that showcases the promises of participatory processes in urban renewal. There is need for scaling such experiments. However, successful LR is grounded in three main enablers:

- Fairly well-defined property rights
- Streamlined, independent, and transparent evaluation processes
- Strong judicial system to address public concerns

6.54. Adopting mixed land–use and subsequently modifying regulations governing land-use, and removing deficiencies in the urban land market need to be given high priority. In many parts of the country, urban land planning limits redevelopment, modernisation and repurposing of older inefficient areas. Weak institutional and information foundations still govern land markets. In many cases, urban plans seek to preserve status quo by limiting land assembly and freezing the density of developments by using very low Floor Space Indexes (FSI), and limited coordination with infrastructure development. Under the Eleventh Plan, JNNURM sought to address these issues by incentivising several urban reforms. Completion of reforms mandated by JNNURM must be given priority.

6.55. Simplification of procedures for conversion of land-use and change in building bye laws have been mandated under JNNURM. These reforms should be completed urgently.

6.56. Rights of Slum Dwellers: Phase-II of the Rajiv Awas Yojana (RAY) is to be launched during the Twelfth Plan. RAY mandates giving 'property rights' to slum dwellers by suitable enactment within a year of the project being sanctioned. Besides, during this period it also mandates enactment of legislations to earmark 10–15 per cent of land or 20–25 per cent dwelling units for housing projects for economically weaker sections/LIG category and earmarking of at least 25 per cent of municipal budget for urban poor. It also requires the participating states to draw specific timelines for legislations like modification of the Rent Control Act.

MODERNISATION OF LAND RECORDS

6.57. The deteriorating quality of land records administration over the last four decades has been a major cause for concern. Accurate and updated land records are a veritable lifeline for millions of small and marginal farmers in India. They secure them against a range of vulnerabilities and allow them to access credit and agricultural inputs, as also the benefits of various anti-poverty programmes. Unambiguously recorded land rights, firm in law, are the foundation for investments in higher farm productivity. On the other hand, chaotic land management results in sporadic encroachments and fratricidal litigation, at great cost to the poor. It also creates a governance regime within which rent-seeking and exploitation of the weak flourish unchecked.

6.58. Once land revenue began to decline in significance as an element in state income, especially in the 1970s, land record administration underwent great neglect. The most important activity for updating land records—original survey for cadastral mapping—has been neglected by many States. In many areas, especially the tribal hinterlands, land records have not been updated for decades. Mutation of names in the records does not happen (invariably as it should) upon transfer of possession and ownership of land. Millions of cases of mutation and measurement remain pending across the country.

6.59. In most states a multitude of departments are involved in land record management. People need to approach several agencies to obtain complete land records—Revenue Department for textual records and mutations; Survey and Settlement (or Consolidation) Department for maps; Registration Department for verification of encumbrances and registration of transfer, mortgage and so on. and panchayats for mutation. The harassment they potentially suffer can be imagined. Also because these departments work in relative isolation from each other, updation by any one of them makes the records of others outdated. Absence of integration of textual and spatial records makes it hard to get maps-to-scale with the records of rights (RoRs).

6.60. The current system of land registration in India is based on the Registration Act, 1908, which provides for registration of deeds and documents, and not titles. Only the transaction is recorded. The transfer of ownership title remains merely presumptive. The massive time-lag between registration and mutation gives space for fraudulent transactions in land, litigation and so on.

6.61. An alternative and more direct system used in many other countries (such as the US, UK, Australia, New Zealand, Canada, Switzerland, Singapore, Kenya and Malaysia) is that of 'conclusive titles' (Torrens System) which confers a legal indefeasible title to the holder of the land. The system of conclusive titles is based on four fundamental principles: *(i)* a single agency to handle land records to ensure consistency and reduce conflicts between different sources; *(ii)* the 'mirror' principle, whereby the cadastral records mirror the reality on the ground; *(iii)* the 'curtain' principle, which indicates that the record of the title is a true depiction of ownership status, so that mutation is automatic following registration, referring to past transactions is not necessary and the title is a conclusive, rather than a mere presumptive proof of ownership; *(iv)* title insurance, which guarantees the title for its correctness and indemnifies the title holder against loss arising on account of any inaccuracy in this regard. At present, land records in India do not reflect any of these principles.

6.62. In order to move decisively in the direction of a Torrens System of land records in India, the National

Land Records Modernization Programme (NLRMP) was launched in 2008. The NLRMP was formed by the merger of two pre-existing CSSs—Strengthening of Revenue Administration and Updating of Land Records (started in 1987–88) and Computerization of Land Records (launched in 1988–89). The main aims of NLRMP are:

- To usher in real-time land records
- Automated and automatic mutation
- Integration between textual and spatial records
- To ultimately replace the present deeds registration and presumptive title system with that of conclusive titling with title guarantee

6.63. Real-time records will be available, which will be tamper-proof. Automatic and automated mutations will significantly reduce scope for fraudulent deals. Since records will be placed on the website with proper security IDs, landowners will have free access to their records while maintaining confidentiality. Single window service or web-enabled any-time-anywhere access will save time and effort. Due to IT interlinkages, time for obtaining RoRs and maps will reduce drastically. Free access will decrease interface with officials, thereby reducing corruption and harassment.

6.64. Abolition of stamp papers and payment of stamp duty and registration fees through banks will also reduce interface with the registration bureaucracy.

6.65. Conclusive titling will reduce land disputes and litigation. E-linkages to credit facilities will become possible. Certificates based on land data (domicile, caste, income, and so on) will become available through the web. Issue of land passbooks will become easier.

6.66. A district will be taken as the unit of implementation, where all activities under the programme will converge. The NLRMP is to be implemented in a time-bound manner and all the districts in the country are expected to be covered by the end of the Twelfth Plan. The country could move into a Torrens System during the Thirteenth Five Year Plan.

6.67. The manual distribution of RoRs has stopped in 16 states. In 21 states legal sanctity to computerised copies of RoRs has been accorded. In 16 states, RoRs have been placed on websites. 26 states have taken up digitisation of cadastral maps, while 18 have begun effecting mutations using computers. Computer centres have been set up in 4,434 tehsils/taluks, 1,045 sub-divisions, 392 districts, and 17 state headquarter monitoring cells. Sixteen states have completed the construction of about 1,366 land record rooms, while 15 states have completed the construction of about 4,311 patwari/talathi office-cum-residences. In 20 states revenue/survey training institutes have been strengthened through construction, renovation, upgradation, and providing modern equipment.

6.68. There are several challenges that will need to be tackled in the coming years. As much as 2.16 million sq. km of cultivable area has to be surveyed. The survey and settlements have to be done for 140 million landowners with 430 million records. There are 92 million ownership holdings each with 4–6 parcels of land. Around 42 million field measurement blocks and around 1 million village maps have to be digitised.

6.69. Establishing Ground Control Points (GCPs) across India over 3.29 million sq. km will be a major challenge. So far, 300 GCPs (satellite) have been established at a spacing of 200–300 km; 2,220 points at a distance of 30 to 40 km (aerial) have to be undertaken in the second phase; the third phase will have GCPs at a spacing of 8 to 10 km (cadastral). Further, 42 million field measurement books and 1 million village maps will have to be digitised.

6.70. Of the 4,018 registration offices in the country, 1,896 are yet to be computerised. Nearly all of them have to be interlinked with the state revenue departments. As many as 1.5 lakh patwaris, the staff of 5,000 tehsils, 4,000 registration offices, and 50,000 survey staff need to be trained.

6.71. These challenges demand a greatly stepped up order of preparation on the part of the Department of Land Resources and the states. The most critical bottleneck that is likely to arise is in the capacity building of human resources. There is need to both strengthen the profile of the personnel deployed, as also to train those currently in service, whose skill sets are currently completely out of sync with the demands posed by the radically new architecture visualised for NLRMP.

NOTES

1. The Supreme Court traces the doctrine to Hugo Grotius (De Jure Belli et Pacis, 1625): 'The property of the subject is under the eminent domain of the state, so that the state or he who acts for it may use and even alienate and destroy such property... for ends of public utility, to which ends, private ends should give way... the state is bound to make good the loss to those who lose their property.'
2. This multiplier factor is the multiple of the market value as determined based on the average registered sale transactions in the last 3 years.
3. Their precise numbers will in each project be determined through a rigorous, transparent and participatory Social Impact Assessment.

7

Environment, Forestry and Wildlife

INTRODUCTION

7.1. Globally, environment has emerged as a major area of governance—bringing the scientific, socio-economic and political dimensions in a single crucible. Sustainability of economic development itself crucially hinges on the protection of environment. For India, challenges of arresting the pace of degradation of environment are formidable due to the imperatives of maintaining high economic growth, increasing trends of urbanisation, population growth, industrialisation, unmet basic needs, life style changes and biotic pressures. While these challenges are formidable, there are also positive factors such as our strong base in science and technology, our institutional infrastructure that can drive the new paradigms and a holistic approach demanded by the environmental governance today. Impacts on environment are an amalgam of the roles of multiple stakeholders such as government, industries and citizens. To respond to a diverse range of dynamic challenges, environmental governance should now be founded on adaptive and agile systems that optimise and strengthen the roles of all stakeholders.

The Twelfth Plan aims to transition the environmental governance system towards such holistic approach (refer to Box 7.1).

7.2. Global interfaces are gaining increasing importance in the field of environment. Environment is characterised by interconnectedness that transcends national/international boundaries and hence international cooperation and national efforts are seminally important to achieve the objectives of equitable access to clean air and water, adaptation and mitigation of climate change, conservation of biodiversity, sustainable forest management, safety in the management of chemicals, wastes and other hazardous substances.

7.3. Resource constraints had also limited the effectiveness of managing our environmental and forest resources. Currently, the annual budget of Ministry of Environment and Forests (MoEF) is around ₹2,000 crore, which is merely 0.012 per cent of Gross Domestic Product (GDP) and less than 0.25 per cent of the annual national budget. The situation in the

---

Box 7.1
Vision

Managing Environment, Forests, Wildlife and challenges due to Climate Change for faster and equitable growth, where ecological security for sustainability and inclusiveness is restored, equity in access to all environmental goods and ecosystem services is assured through institutionalisation of people's participation;

AND

A future in which the nation takes pride in the quality of its environment, forests, richness of its biodiversity, and efforts by the State and its people to protect, expand and enrich it, for intra and inter-generational equity and welfare of the local and global community.

States and at the city level is a real cause for concern. There is a need for significant increase in the investment towards environment protection and sustainable management of natural resources.

7.4. Constitutionally, Environment is a residual subject, with both the Central and the State Government responsible for regulation and enforcement. Thus, there is a need to include 'environment' as a concurrent subject in the constitution. This will help the State Governments and the local authorities enact and notify their own enforcement laws and rules to ensure compliance of relevant environmental norms. This issue, which was highlighted in the previous plan as well, not only remains relevant but needs to be pursued on priority. This initiative will also be important for integrating environmental concerns into planning and developmental activities across all the sectors. The MoEF is concerned with protection and management of the environment in the country. It is mandated with the responsibility of planning, promotion, cooperation and overseeing the implementation of various environmental and forestry schemes/programmes. The main objectives of the MoEF include protection of the environment; conservation and survey of flora, fauna, forests and wildlife; prevention and control of pollution; afforestation and regeneration of degraded areas; ensuring welfare of animals; and international cooperation in forestry and environment. The MoEF is also concerned with environmental management: to promote health considerations; to focus on poverty alleviation by enhancing access to poor of natural resources for livelihood; and to enhance the awareness regarding environmentally sound living process by focusing on nature–man synergy. MoEF is also designated as the nodal agency for the United Nations Environment Programme (UNEP) and the International Centre for Integrated Mountain Development and looks after the follow-up of the United Nations Conference on Environment and Development (UNCED).

7.5. Several Ministries, notably the Ministry of Urban Development (MoUD) run major programmes like Jawaharlal Nehru National Urban Renewal Mission (JNNURM) and Urban Infrastructure Development Scheme for Small and Medium Towns (UIDSSMT), which have a direct impact on the objectives of MoEF. Programmes such as the JNNURM and National River Conservation Programme (NRCP) need to be effectively combined to achieve the target of rivers cleaning. The MoUD should also ensure creation of required waste management system in all urban local bodies. Similarly, afforestation work including rehabilitation and livelihood improvement activities can be taken up under the schemes of Ministries of Rural Development (MoRD), Agriculture, Tribal Affairs, Panchayat Raj, Renewable Energy and so on. There is thus, considerable potential for dovetailing of resources with the schemes of several Ministries and an attempt could also be made for earmarking of resources under these Ministries for investment in environment and greening of the country.

7.6. Besides programmes, legislative initiatives of a number of Ministries also have a bearing and impact on the working of environment related laws. International commitments in various sectors and their compliance through new laws, institutions of enforcement and programmes of action also impact environmental governance. Further, the National Environmental Policy has the object of ensuring that all developmental decisions duly recognise and take into account the environmental imperatives of conservation and sustainable development.

REVIEW OF THE ELEVENTH PLAN

7.7. The Eleventh Plan laid emphasis on environmental sustainability while pursuing development by incorporating environmental concerns in development planning at all levels. A number of schemes on pollution abatement, conservation of biodiversity and habitat management were implemented.

Progress Achieved

7.8. The Eleventh Plan emphasised on four environment related targets and the progress achieved against these is summarised below:

Increase Forest and Tree Cover by 5 Percentage Points

7.9. The Forest and Tree Cover (FTC), as reported in the State of Forest Report 2009 is 23.84 per cent. To achieve the plan target of 5 per cent increase,

> **Box 7.2**
> **Waste Disposal in PPP Mode**
>
> The state of solid waste management in Kanpur was no different from most other Indian cities until only a few years ago. Kanpur Nagar Nigam (KNN) had the responsibility for collecting, transporting and disposing of the solid waste generated in the city, estimated at about 1,500 tonnes per day.
>
> In June 2008, KNN gave a BOOT (build, own, operate, transfer) contract for processing, disposing, collection and transportation of solid waste to A2Z Infrastructure, a private company, which was selected through a process of competitive bidding. Land (46 acres) was given free on a long lease of 30 years for the project. The plant to process 1,500 tonnes per day capacity of solid waste was set up with a tipping platform, a pre-segregation unit, a composting unit, an RDF (Refuse Derived Fuel) unit, a plastic segregating unit, a briquette manufacturing unit, and a secured landfill in place. Of the total project cost of ₹110 crore, ₹56.6 crore came from JNNURM and the rest from the private partner.
>
> Door-to-door collection of garbage is being done in bins attached to rickshaws by safaimitras using hand gloves and protective masks. The garbage is compressed while being transported. Garbage transport vehicle is equipped with Global Positioning System (GPS) and every incidence of the compactor halt to collect garbage is monitored and recorded. Rag-pickers have been given the opportunity of starting a new life. Some of the former rag-pickers (130, to be precise) now earn a regular salary as safaimitras, sport a bank ATM card, enjoy social security and health benefits, and their young kids have started going to schools.
>
> The garbage is taken to a central site where it is sorted, segregated, transformed into a number of products of value, for example, premium quality compost, refuse derived fuel (RDF), interlocking tiles from construction debris for use in footpath paving, and so on. Kanpur Waste Management Plant is the largest producer of compost from organic waste. The plant is not able to meet the growing demand for organic fertiliser.
>
> In 2010, A2Z Infrastructure, the private company, set up a waste-to-energy plant, creating the largest integrated project in solid waste management in Asia, which produces 15 MW of electricity, using RDF produced in house. The plant has been registered with United Nations Framework Convention on Climate Change (UNFCCC) for carbon credits claiming certified carbon reductions achieved by Clean Development Mechanism (CDM) projects under the Kyoto protocol. The KNN received best city award (JNNURM) for improvement in solid waste management from Prime Minister in 2011. Dr. Isher Judge Ahluwalia—a leading columnist after her visit and discussion published this article in print and electronic media which is widely acclaimed. Ahmedabad and Surat Municipal Corporations have also set up integrated Municipal Solid Waste collection and disposal mechanism. In the Twelfth Five Year Plan, every attempt will be made to replicate the similar model in maximum number of cities in the country.

an additional 16 million ha FTC was required by 2012. The tree planting during the Plan period has been around 1.5 million ha per year, but the actual increase in green cover is not likely to be more than 5.0 million ha during the entire Plan period.

Treat All Urban Waste Water by 2011–12 to Clean River Waters

7.10. Deterioration in river waters is largely due to discharge of raw/partially treated sewage into the rivers. Cleaning of rivers is a mammoth task requiring the involvement of all the stakeholders. As per the Central Pollution Control Board (CPCB), the estimated wastewater generation in 498 Class I cities and 410 Class II towns is estimated to be about 38,000 million litres per day (MLD), against which treatment capacity of only 12,000 MLD exists at present. Sewage treatment capacity of about 4,418 MLD has been created under NRCP and Ganga Action Plan-I (GAP-I). Given the large gap between sewage generation and treatment capacity available, substantial increase in allocations is required to be made in the Twelfth Plan period. (Also refer to Box 7.2 for waste disposal in PPP mode)

Attain World Health Organisation (WHO) Standards of Air Quality in All Major Cities by 2011–12

7.11. The MoEF feels that the notified National Ambient Air Quality Standards (NAAQS), instead of the WHO guidelines, would serve as a more realistic and appropriate goal for achieving better air quality in India. The NAAQS were revised in the Eleventh Plan, and limits for 12 pollutants, including new parameters such as Ozone, Arsenic, Nickel, Benzene and Benzo(a)Pyrene were notified.

Increase Energy Efficiency by 20 Percentage Points by 2016–17 in the Environment and Forests Sector

7.12. A National Mission on Enhanced Energy Efficiency (NMEEE) has been launched under National Action Plan on Climate Change (NAPCC) by the Ministry of Power in order to achieve fuel savings of 23 MTOE (against 24 MTOE consumed in nine sectors); avoid capacity addition of over 19,000 MW; and reduce 98.55 MTs of Carbon Dioxide (CO_2) equivalent annually over a five-year period. India has also announced its domestic mitigation goal of reducing emissions intensity of GDP by 20–25 per cent by 2020 compared with 2005. An Expert Group constituted by the Planning Commission is in the process of drafting a low carbon inclusive growth strategy for India for the Twelfth Five Year Plan.

Major Policy Developments

7.13. Besides the progress achieved in four monitorable targets, a number of major policies were formulated during the Eleventh Plan.

- The National Environment Policy was unveiled in 2006 to help realise sustainable development goals by mainstreaming environmental concerns in all development activities.
- The Environmental Impact Assessment (EIA) process has been made more efficient, decentralised and transparent, based on a comprehensive review of the existing environmental process and its re-engineering through the EIA Notification, 2006, and its amendments thereafter. A system of mandatory accreditation of EIA/Environmental Management Plan (EMP) consultants has also been introduced to improve the quality of impact assessment reports submitted by project proponents.
- Re-engineering of Coastal Regulation ZONE (CRZ) Notification 2011 was done to ensure livelihood security to fishing and other local communities, to conserve and protect coastal stretches and to promote development based on scientific principles. Another Notification on Island Protection Zone was issued for similar purposes for the islands of Andaman & Nicobar and the Lakshadweep.
- An NAPCC was released in June 2008 to outline India's strategy to meet the challenge of climate change. The Indian Network for Climate Change Assessment (INCCA), a network-based programme to make science the essence of our policymaking in the climate change space, was also launched.
- Towards conservation of biodiversity, a National Biodiversity Action Plan was released in November 2008. The Plan identifies major threats and constraints facing biodiversity and lists out action points for addressing/conserving the same.
- A National Ganga River Basin Authority (NGRBA) has been set up to ensure effective abatement of pollution and conservation of the river Ganga by adopting a holistic approach with the river basin as the unit of planning.
- The NAAQS have been revised and limits for 12 pollutants are notified. The revised standards are based on global best practices, local Indian conditions and in keeping with the advancement in technology and research.
- National Green Tribunal (NGT) was set up on 18 October 2010 for effective and expeditious disposal of cases relating to environmental protection and conservation of forests and other natural resources.
- Towards further environmental regulatory reforms and improving environmental governance, an exercise has been initiated to conceptualise and constitute a National Environment Assessment & Monitoring Authority (NEAMA).
- To resolve the deadlock of Compensatory Afforestation Fund Management and Planning Authority (CAMPA), State Level CAMPAs have been created, providing an integrated framework for utilisation of multiple sources of funding and activities relating to afforestation, regeneration, conservation and protection of forests.
- Interventions have been undertaken to increase forest cover. The Green India Mission under NAPCC is going to be operationalised in 2012–13.
- Wildlife (Protection) Act, 1972 was amended to enable Constitution of the National Tiger Conservation Authority and the Tiger and other Endangered Species Crime Control Bureau.

7.14. A number of externally aided projects also became operational in the Eleventh Plan including National Coastal Management Programme, Capacity Building for Industrial Pollution Management project (CBIPM) under Pollution Abatement scheme, and Biodiversity Conservation and Rural Livelihood Improvement Project. The aforementioned NGRBA for effective abatement of pollution and conservation of river Ganga, was funded under both budgetary support and external aid from the World Bank.

Rationalisation of Schemes during Eleventh Plan

7.15. Plan schemes of the MoEF were rationalised by suitably merging/clubbing its 68 smaller schemes into 22 thematic schemes, for implementation in the Eleventh Five Year Plan. Of these 22 approved thematic schemes, the scheme of Muli Bamboo was successfully completed in 2008–09. The new scheme of Afforestation through Panchayati Raj Institutions (PRIs), which proposes large scale intervention in non-forest areas, has been dropped following the formulation of National Mission for Green India with similar objective on a much higher scale. The scheme of Taj Protection had been put on hold pending an evaluation of the scheme by National Environmental Engineering Research Institute (NEERI), Nagpur. The Evaluation Report has since been accepted and it is proposed to revive the scheme in the Twelfth Five Year Plan. Thus, there are 20 thematic schemes under implementation at the end of the Eleventh Plan (refer to Table 7.1) with each scheme having further components/ programmes. Among the 20 thematic heads, there are 12 Central Sector (CS)

TABLE 7.1
Thematic Schemes under Implementation at the End of the Eleventh Plan

Environment and Ecology	Scheme Type
Environment Monitoring and Governance	CS
Pollution abatement	CS
Research and Development (R&D) for Conservation and Development	CS
Environmental Info, Education and Awareness	CS
International Cooperation Activities	CS
National Coastal Management Programme	CS
National River Conservation Plan	CSS
Conservation of Natural Resources and Ecosystems	CSS
Environment Management in Heritage including Taj Protection	CSS
Forestry	**Scheme Type**
Grants-in-aid to forestry and Wildlife institutions	CS
National Afforestation and Eco Development Board (NAEB)	CS
Capacity building in forestry sector	CS
Strengthening of Forestry Division	CS
Afforestation and Forest Management	CSS
National Afforestation Programme	CSS
Afforestation through PRIs (Panchayat Van Yojana)—being dropped	CSS
Wildlife	**Scheme Type**
Strengthening of Wildlife Divisions	CS
Animal Welfare	CS
Integrated Development of Wildlife Habitats	CSS
Project Tiger	CSS
Project Elephant	CSS

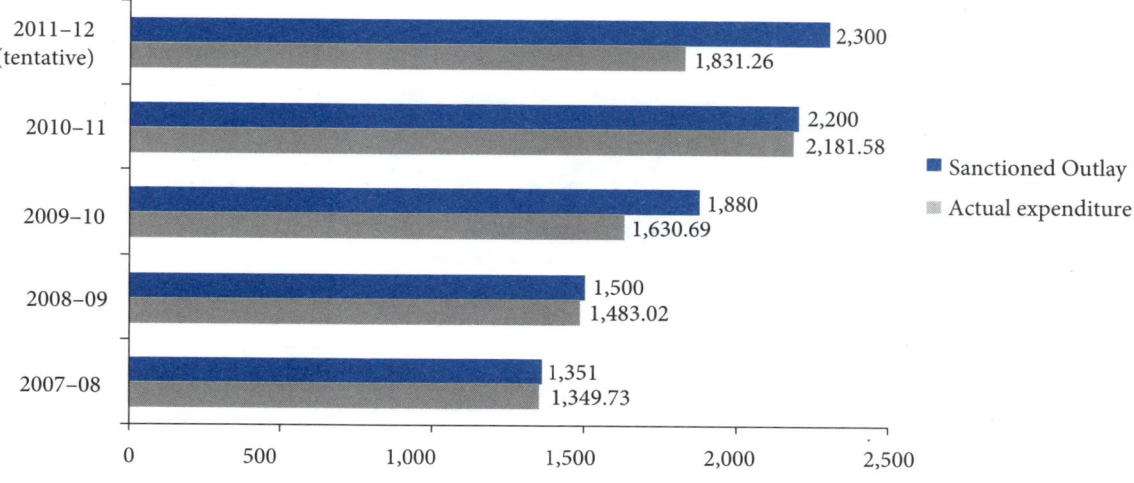

FIGURE 7.1: Sanctioned Outlay vs Actual Expenditure in the Eleventh Plan (₹ Crore)

schemes and the remaining are Centrally Sponsored Schemes (CSS).

7.16. Other developments during the Plan so far include transfer of the 'civil construction unit' component under International Cooperation Activities scheme to non-plan budget; merger of the 'state of environment' component with Environmental Information System (ENVIS) component under the Environmental Information, Education and Awareness scheme; and addition of a new externally aided component on Capacity Building for Forest Management and Training of Personnel under the scheme of Capacity Building for Forestry Sector.

Financial Performance of Eleventh Plan

7.17. MoEF had an approved outlay of ₹10,000 crore for the Eleventh Five Year Plan, 2007-12. Figure 7.1 provides the sanctioned outlay along with the actual expenditure for each year of the Eleventh Plan.

7.18. For the current financial year 2011–12, MoEF has been allocated an outlay of ₹2,300 crore, against which likely expenditure is tentatively placed at ₹1,831.26 crore.

7.19. Thus, a total outlay of ₹9,231.00 crore has been allocated to MoEF in the Eleventh Plan as budgeted expenditure (BE), against which its likely expenditure is ₹8,476.28 crore which implies a utilisation ratio of around 95 per cent during this period. Total allocations made in the Eleventh Plan amounted to around 92 per cent of MoEF's sanctioned/approved outlay.

7.20. The sector-wise position of allocations/expenditure during the Eleventh Plan is summarised in Figure 7.2.

7.21. During the Eleventh Plan the country pursued its development agenda considering environmental protection at the core of all policy formulation. In the Twelfth Plan it has been felt that the country needs more focused efforts not only to preserve and maintain natural resources but also to provide equitable access to those who are denied this currently.

TARGETS AND ACTION FOR THE TWELFTH PLAN

7.22. After an in-depth analysis of the policies and programmes in the Environment, Forestry, Biodiversity, Wildlife and Animal Welfare sectors, 12 monitorable targets (Box 7.3) have been set for the Twelfth Plan. These include three targets in the areas of Environment and Climate Change, four targets in Forestry, three targets under Wildlife, Ecotourism and Animal Welfare, and two under Ecosystems and Biodiversity.

7.23. Further, 15 areas which should receive special attention have been identified for the Twelfth Plan (presented in Box 7.4).

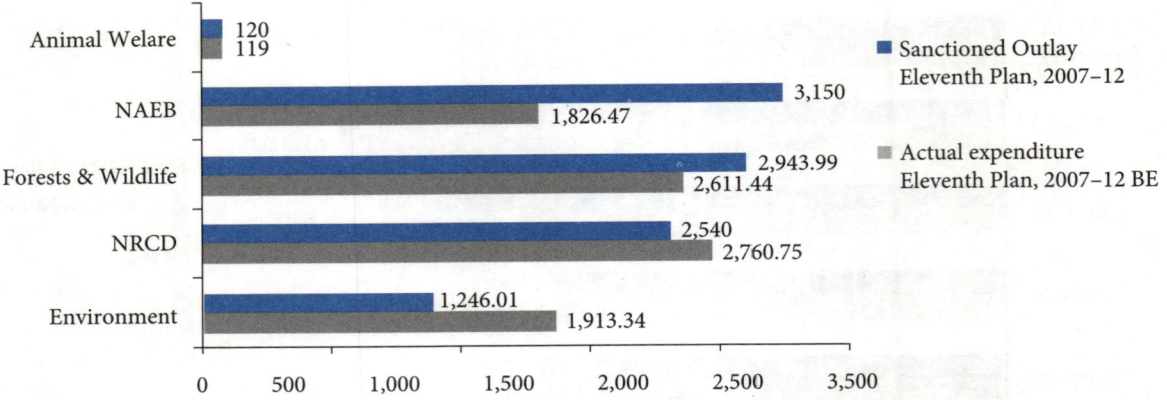

FIGURE 7.2: Sector-wise Allocations/Expenditure during the Eleventh Plan (₹ Crore)

Strategy for the Twelfth Plan

7.24. Due to its cross-cutting nature, and wide local and global stakeholder base, environmental governance needs to be strategic. An ideal framework should be anticipative, technically oriented, cognizant of legal issues, geo-politically relevant and forward-looking, capable of maximising national interests and progressive enough to make a social impact. Most importantly, management of the environment should include progressively adapting/changing actions that rely on sound scientific, technological, human-cognitive and collaborative principles. Thus, environmental management should be based on:

- Data and facts (founded on a sound measurement regime of key environmental parameters).
- Analytics and modelling (founded on scientific and predictive data integration/modelling)
- Indexing and thresholding (founded on scientific assimilation of time-profile data to determine constantly changing indices of environment status).
- Collectively powering the management and conservation of environment and also formulation of national policy and legal foundations.

7.25. The Twelfth Plan is thus oriented towards such strategic directions for managing environment in India. The following sections provide details on programmatic, institutional, regulatory, research and capacity building elements that weave into such an overall strategy, taking into account past experience as well as overall objectives of the plan.

Programmatic Strategies

7.26. The Approach Paper for the Twelfth Plan for environment, forests, wildlife and climate change focused strategic attention on the following:

- Securing ecology of watersheds and catchments;
- Cumulative environmental impact assessments for vulnerable regions;
- Carrying capacity studies in selected river basins;
- Maintaining acceptable water quality and quantity through pollution control of water resources;
- Restoration of wetlands/lakes; and
- Management of waste water discharge from industrial and commercial establishments into major water bodies.

7.27. It also emphasised in situ conservation and sustainable use of biodiversity to enhance livelihood security, promotion and evaluation of ecosystem services in the national planning process. This includes the study of the economics of ecosystem and biodiversity; abatement of marine pollution and prevention of traffic in marine resources; the need for safe storage and disposal facilities for hazardous

Box 7.3
Monitorable Targets for the Twelfth Plan

ENVIRONMENT AND CLIMATE CHANGE
1. Assess and remediate 12 identified contaminated sites (hazardous chemicals and wastes) with potential for ground water contamination by 2017.
2. Clean 80 per cent of critically polluted stretches in rivers by 2017 and 100 per cent by 2020.
3. States to meet NAAQS in urban areas by 2017.
4. To reduce emission intensity of our GDP in line with the target of 20 to 25 percent reduction over 2005 levels by 2020.

FORESTS AND LIVELIHOOD
5. Greening 5 million ha under Green India Mission including 1.5 million ha of degraded lands, afforestation and eco-restoration of 0.9 million ha of ecologically sensitive areas.
6. Technology-based monitoring of forest cover, biodiversity and growing stock including change-monitoring on periodical basis through dedicated satellite by 2017 and establishment of open web-based National Forestry and Environmental Information system for research and public accessibility by 2015.
7. Engagement of Village Green Guards/Community Foresters for every Joint Forest Management (JFM) village by 2016.
8. Establish forestry seed bank in forest circles and Model Nursery in every district with information on public portal by 2014.

WILDLIFE, ECOTOURISM AND ANIMAL WELFARE
9. Twenty per cent of veterinary professionals in the country will be trained in treating wildlife.
10. Integrated Ecotourism District Plans covering 10 per cent of all potential Protected Areas (PAs) by 2017.
11. Promoting participation of private sector, civil societies, NGOs and philanthropists in animal welfare.

ECOSYSTEM AND BIODIVERSITY
12. Restore 0.1 million ha of wetlands/inland lakes/water bodies by 2017.
13. Mapping and preparation of biodiversity management plans for deserts (both cold and arid), coastal areas, important coral zones, wetlands, mangroves and so on to be completed by 2017.

Box 7.4
Goals

ENVIRONMENT
1. Epidemiological studies to assess improvement in health status due to better management of environment and ecology.
2. Promotion and adoption of cleaner technology, strengthening and initiation of reforms in regulations, policy making and enforcement institutions for environmental governance.
3. Move towards cumulative and strategic EIA.
4. Ensure ecological flows in all rivers by regulating abstractions so as to allow conservation of riverine ecosystems through developing a legal framework and management strategy for conservation of river basins.
5. Promotion of recycling and reuse of treated sewage in urban projects such as sanitation, landscaping, central air conditioning and so on.

FORESTS AND LIVELIHOOD
6. Improve forest productivity, production and sustainable management of biodiversity (equity in access to benefit sharing with local people).
7. Restoration and intensification of forest-rangelands/grazing-land management and establish community grazing land around forest fringe villages.
8. Build capacity of Village Forest Committees/Joint Forestry Management Committees for management of forest resources including ecotourism.
9. Revive seed orchards and silviculture plots for various forest types of the country, as well as, for enlisted species under Minor Forest Produce/Non Timber Forest Produce (MFP/NTFP) including genetic improvement of and establishment of clonal orchards.

WILDLIFE, ECOTOURISM AND ANIMAL WELFARE
10. Reducing and managing human–wildlife conflict.
11. Commercialisation of permissible marine products rich in poly unsaturated fatty acids (PUFAs), vitamins and so on.
12. Promotion of ecotourism and participatory eco-development support livelihood of local population.

ECOSYSTEM AND BIODIVERSITY
13. Develop national targets and indicators related to biodiversity and support actions to strengthen implementation of Biological Diversity Act, 2002 and ensure bio-safety for economic and social development of local communities.
14. Assess coastal biodiversity resources, ensure sustainable management, restoration of mangroves, coral reefs and wetlands and support livelihood.

waste and its possible use as source of energy and raw materials; improvement in forest cover; management of invasive weeds; urban solid waste management; restoration of mined areas; community rights and NTFPs; achieving air quality to the level of NAAQS for urban environments; and community participation in forest management and climate change issues.

7.28. Taking these aspects as well as the progress made in the Eleventh Plan into account, the vision, the goals, the targets, the strategy and the action for Twelfth Plan have been formulated.

7.29. The Twelfth Five Year Plan adopts specific strategies to meet emerging challenges concerning conservation and assessment of flora, fauna, forests and wildlife; prevention and control of pollution; afforestation and regeneration of degraded areas; protection of the environment; and issues related to the welfare of animals (refer to Figure 7.3).

Organisational Strategies

7.30. In the Twelfth Plan, institutional mechanisms like establishment of a Department of Environment in the States for environmental management to resolve inter-sectoral issues needs to be addressed on priority. Inter-ministerial Standing Committees and Working Groups in specific domains within broad areas like air quality management and waste management need to be established both at the Central and State Government levels

7.31. It is proposed to set up a high powered body called the National Environment and Forestry Council (NEFC) with the Prime Minister as Chairperson, the Minister of Environment and Forests as Vice Chairperson, aided and advised by a group of experts. This body would have the representation from the Ministries of External Affairs, Science & Technology, Agriculture, Commerce, Urban and Rural Development, Tribal Affairs and so on. Its primary function would be to bring in harmony in the functioning of different Ministries and to ensure that the evolution of all policies, laws and their implementation concerning development, of every kind, are in conformity with the objectives outlined in the National Environmental Policy (NEP), 2006.

7.32. On similar lines as the NEFC, a high-powered body called State Environment and Forest Council (SEFC) needs to be constituted to align the working of the other Departments with that of the Department of Environment and Forests in each State. Additionally, Environment Cells have to be constituted in the related Ministries and Departments at the Central and State levels so as to mainstream environmental concerns in their activities and programmes.

Regulatory Strategies

7.33. A comprehensive review and reform of laws concerning Environment, Forests, Wildlife and Biodiversity will be undertaken in the Twelfth Plan in order to make them more effective, work in harmony with each other and address new challenges. This would particularly be carried out in the following areas:

1. Pollution control and waste management regime: Reforms would be carried out against the backdrop of the exponential expansion of the powers and functions of the existing authorities. Among other objectives, reforms would aim at dealing with non-point source pollution issues (like agricultural run offs and so on) and alarming increase in nutrient loading of soil and other natural resources. A National Environment Protection Authority (NEPA) is also proposed to be set up fully empowered to restructure the existing environmental management regime.
2. EPA and notifications under it such as EIA and CRZ: Reforms would be attempted to make the system more effective and to evolve better proactive legislative and administrative measures for:

   - Switching over from a carbon-intensive economy to a carbon neutral one;
   - Promoting alternative energy options;
   - Dealing with challenges arising out of creation of SEZs;

- Strengthening the Impact Assessment Law and coastal laws by making local authorities more responsible and accountable;
- Plugging the loopholes that weaken and dilute the system's effectiveness;
- Giving effect to the new Liability Regime to which India has committed itself (2010 UNEP Guidelines on Liability, Response Action and Compensation for Environmentally Harmful Activities—a new legal regime that will have far-reaching implications on all perceivable development activities and the actors engaged in them, without exception); and
- Foregrounding the idea of 'Commons' at the domestic level and securing it.

3. Forest, wildlife and biodiversity regime: Reforms would be undertaken, in the light of legislative developments in related areas initiated by other Ministries (like Protection of Plant Varieties and Farmers' Rights Act, Scheduled Tribes and Other Traditional Forest Dwellers (Recognition of Forest Rights) Act, Seeds Amendment Bill, Biotechnology Regulatory Authority Bill and so on) towards:

- Evolving effective and robust legal safeguards for addressing the issue of 'bio-safety';
- Internalising the international commitment concerning the access and benefit sharing regime (Nagoya Protocol);
- Providing sufficient and effective safeguards for the protection of traditional knowledge (TK) and folk art concerning biodiversity;
- Ensuring that India receives international recognition as the president of the CoP of the Convention on Biological Diversity (CBD) starting from 2012 in compliance with its international commitments over biodiversity issues (primarily over bio-safety, conservation of TK, equity, benefit-sharing and so on); and
- Developing harmony in the working of laws in the sector with the Panchayat Extension to Scheduled Areas Act, 1996.

7.34. A multi-pronged approach to environmental regulation in terms of capacity building of existing institutions, improved database management, professionalisation of environmental clearance system

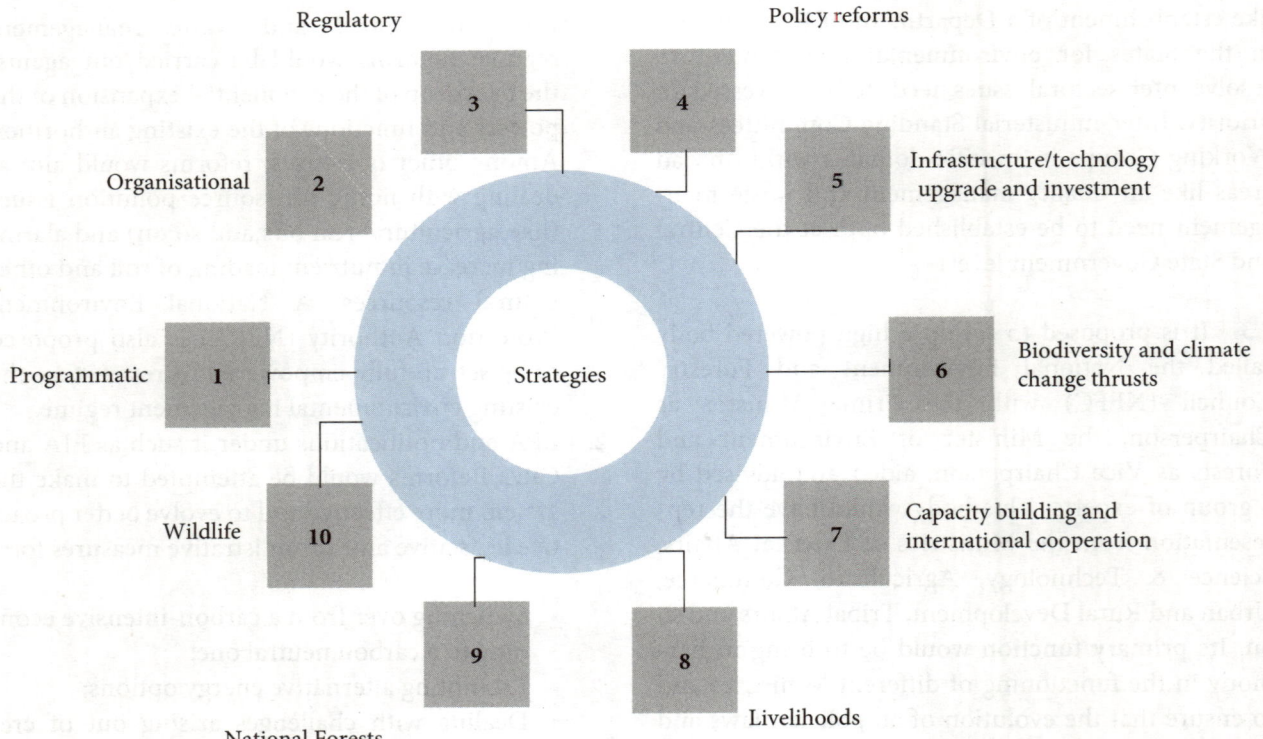

FIGURE 7.3: Strategies for the Twelfth Plan

and introduction of alternative system of regulation needs to be developed.

7.35. For effective regulation on environmental pollution it is suggested that the Environment (Protection) Act, 1986 may be amended for an upward revision in the quantum of penalties and also to include an enabling provision for civil administrative adjudication to fast-track levy of penalty.

Policy Reforms and Metrics-based Management

7.36. A number of initiatives need to be undertaken to promote:

- Implementation of load-based standards to facilitate carrying capacity based cumulative EIAs, particularly for areas having concentration of developmental activities such as mines and thermal power plants;
- Effective enforcement of the application of 'polluter pays' principle;
- Development and deployment of cleaner technologies in the Micro, Small and Medium Enterprises (MSMEs) sector, particularly for the 17 categories of highly polluting industries;
- Strengthening of the National Water Quality Monitoring Network;
- Collection and monitoring of basic data on coastal water quality, oxygen zone in the sea, transport of nitrogen and phosphorous in the rivers from agriculture;
- Review of existing policies to enable drafting of mitigation strategies and introduction of new effluent standards; and
- Implementation of continuous effluent monitoring systems at industries as well as CETPs.

7.37. It is proposed to setup a National Environmental Monitoring Programme (NEMP) for monitoring forests, air and water quality, river and ocean pollution, noise and so on with sharing of real-time data from local to national levels which will also help in monitoring change.

7.38. A multi-disciplinary autonomous body namely National Environment Assessment and Monitoring Authority (NEAMA) is proposed to be set up for strengthening the processes for grant of environmental clearances and monitoring thereof. NEAMA is also envisaged to grant clearances under the Environment (Protection) Act, 1986 including the coastal zone regulations and marine fisheries regulations.

7.39. In the Twelfth Five Year Plan, the Central and State Governments also need to invest in strengthening the mechanisms for implementing rules notified under the Environment (Protection) Act, 1986 including the CRZ Notification and the Marine Fishing Regulation Act.

Infrastructure/Technology Upgrade and Investment Strategies

7.40. A number of initiatives can be undertaken towards achieving infrastructure/technology upgradation and directing investment in the environment, forest and wildlife sectors. These include:

- Promotion of continuous 24 × 7 online air quality monitoring which includes Continuous Ambient Air Quality Monitoring Stations (CAAQMS) and Continuous Emission Monitoring System (CEMS);
- Introduction of cost-effective technologies such as bioremediation to address the pollution of water bodies is proposed;
- Encouragement of use of hazardous waste of high calorific value in cement kilns, power or steel plants as a safe alternative to conventional incineration;
- Integration of environmental attributes into cost-benefit analysis while making public investment decisions, to encourage more efficient allocation of resources;
- Amendment to the environmental laws to introduce pollution charges and other economic instruments to enable creation of fund in order to augment allocation to the sector. This fund can be utilised for incentivising good environmental performance;
- Creation of a National Environment Restoration Fund (NERF) from voluntary contributions and the net proceeds of proposed economic instruments such as user fees for access to specified natural resources. The Fund may be used for

- restoration of environmental resources and clean-up of sites contaminated with toxic and hazardous waste;
- Strengthening of Botanical Survey of India (BSI) and Zoological Survey of India (ZSI) in terms of manpower and infrastructure to scale up their mandated task of inventorisation of flora and fauna of the country needs to be achieved;
- Validation and updation of the Indian Biodiversity Information System (IBIS), the Indian Bio-resource Information System (IBIN), India Biodiversity Portal (IBP) and the Indian Ocean Census of Marine Life (IOCoML) needs to be undertaken, for which a consortium of research organisations needs to be created;
- An effort to digitise and make available existing collections of taxonomic collections should be piloted;
- The mandate of different institutes engaged in forestry, biodiversity and wildlife research requires to be broadened to accommodate emerging needs for collaborative multidisciplinary research.

Biodiversity

7.41. Ecological processes that generate ecosystem goods and services are central for ecological sustainability. It is proposed to establish an Ecosystem Research Institute (ERI) under MoEF for undertaking research in ecosystems, biodiversity and sustainable development.

7.42. The Biological Diversity Act 2002 has to be implemented at all levels throughout the country. Immediate steps need to be taken to constitute Biodiversity Management Committees (BMCs) at *Gram Panchayats*, *Taluka Panchayats*, *Zilla Panchayats*, as well as *Nagarpalikas* and *Mahanagarpalikas*. Further, the BMCs need to be obligated to levy 'collection charges' as provided in the Biological Diversity Act.

7.43. It is proposed to develop a national information grid for biodiversity, ecology and environment data for monitoring and management of natural resources. This should be an open, transparent and comprehensive web-based information system that covers various landscapes such as forests, coastal stretches and territorial waters of the country's Exclusive Economic Zones (EEZ), mountains and deserts regions.

Capacity Building and International Cooperation Strategies

7.44. In the area of international cooperation in the Twelfth Plan, the MoEF would take the lead in setting up an institutional mechanism for a regional alliance of South Asian Association for Regional Cooperation (SAARC) for developing and implementing policies, laws and action plans. Further, the mechanism could also promote strengthening of capacity by linking scientific and research institutions and Centres of Excellence (CoE) concerning forestry, wildlife and biodiversity. This could include a variety of measures such as strengthening the South Asia Co-operative Environment Programme (SACEP), technical cooperation, management practices for conservation and sustainable use of bio-resources, strengthening legal capacity in administration, information sharing and its dissemination and building capacity in justice-delivery.

Livelihoods

7.45. To develop the NTFP sector in a holistic way and coordinate the various activities for sustainable management and livelihood, an autonomous agency needs to be set up with branches in all states. For the overall management of NTFP resource including conservation and development of an estimated 6 lakh ha as well as value addition and marketing support, a new scheme for sustainable livelihoods through NTFP management including bamboo needs to be formulated.

7.46. There is an urgent need to focus on pasture management and formulation of grazing policy at the national level which will enhance the livelihood, nutrition and quality of life of all fringe forest dwellers. A new scheme on rangeland and silvi-pasture management for rehabilitation and productivity enhancement of rangelands, traditional grasslands on common/revenue lands around forest areas is required. Infrastructural and institutional mechanism for fodder storage, value addition facilities, maintenance of germ-plasm banks and nurseries is required to be developed during the Twelfth Plan period.

Forest Management Strategy

7.47. A proposed scheme on Satellite-based Forest Resource Assessment will put in place a system for technology-based collection of baseline data and evaluation of forestry schemes with **Geographic information system** (GIS) mapping of areas under the Scheduled Tribes and Other Traditional Forest Dwellers (Recognition of Forest Rights) Act, 2006.

7.48. To evolve a national consensus on forestry matters and meet new challenges, it is proposed that the Central Board of Forestry (CBF) be revived with Prime Minister as Chairperson and Minister of Environment & Forests as Vice Chairperson, on the lines of National Board for Wildlife. This could be the apex body for policy development and consultation in the country.

7.49. Reorientation of the Indian Council of Forestry Research and Education (ICFRE) on the lines of Indian Council of Agricultural Research (ICAR) with augmentation of funding also needs to be taken up during the Twelfth Five Year Plan.

7.50. The Working Plan Code based on which forest working plans are prepared and adhered to needs to be amended to incorporate new dimensions along with assigning specific responsibility to the cutting-edge level workers and for transferring the rights in the field with proper documentation.

7.51. There is a need for creation of a 'Green fund' for forestry activities by imposing forest development tax on sale of forest produce and forest conservation tax/cess on sale of petroleum products and coal mining. Further, other similar taxes such as Eco-tax in Himachal Pradesh, Uttarakhand and other States may also be pooled in for this purpose.

Wildlife and Animal Welfare

7.52. Integrated Development of Wildlife Habitats (IDWH) will continue to be the umbrella scheme for conservation and management of wildlife with focus on all species other than the tiger. Tiger conservation, as led by the National Tiger Conservation Authority, needs to be continued as a flagship programme of the MoEF. Based on past experience, several new thrust areas have been identified for implementation. This includes strengthening the protection and furthering the coexistence agenda in the buffer areas of tiger reserves and voluntary relocation along with regular monitoring of tiger population and their habitat.

7.53. Project Elephant needs a new focus under the plan through the creation of the National Elephant Conservation Authority (NECA) and notification of critical areas of Elephant Reserves as Ecologically Sensitive Areas under the Environment (Protection) Act 1986. Special focus is required for mitigation of human–elephant conflict through strengthening the existing Project Elephant Scheme.

7.54. The plan will specifically focus on following areas of concern:

- Scientific and socio-economic issues related to wildlife conservation including strengthening of veterinary care for wild animals;
- Scientific management of PAs and wildlife-rich areas outside PAs as well as mitigation of human–wildlife conflict;
- Operationalisation of ecotourism linked to livelihood enhancement of local communities and;
- Coordinated approach for rejuvenating the animal welfare structure in the country.

7.55. Strengthening of IDWH and Project Elephant schemes is necessary to achieve the above objectives. In addition, two new schemes, namely, Operationalisation and Strengthening of Ecotourism for Local Livelihoods and Promoting Participation of Private Sector and Philanthropists in Animal Welfare are also proposed to be taken up.

7.56. Animal Welfare Boards need to be setup in all the States, including Society for Prevention of Cruelty to Animals (SPCAs) under the Prevention of Cruelty (Establishment of Societies for the Prevention of Cruelty to Animals) Rules, in all districts within all States.

7.57. Significant increase in investment for better protection and conservation of wildlife, strengthening of institutional mechanism, improvement in livelihoods of forest fringe dwellers, capacity building of local level management committees needs to be the focus.

Rationalisation of Schemes

7.58. Pursuant to the recommendations of the B.K. Chaturvedi Report (September 2011) on CSS, MoEF has rationalised the eight schemes existing in the Eleventh Five Year Plan to five in the Twelfth Five Year Plan by suitable merger/clubbing as shown in Figure 7.4.

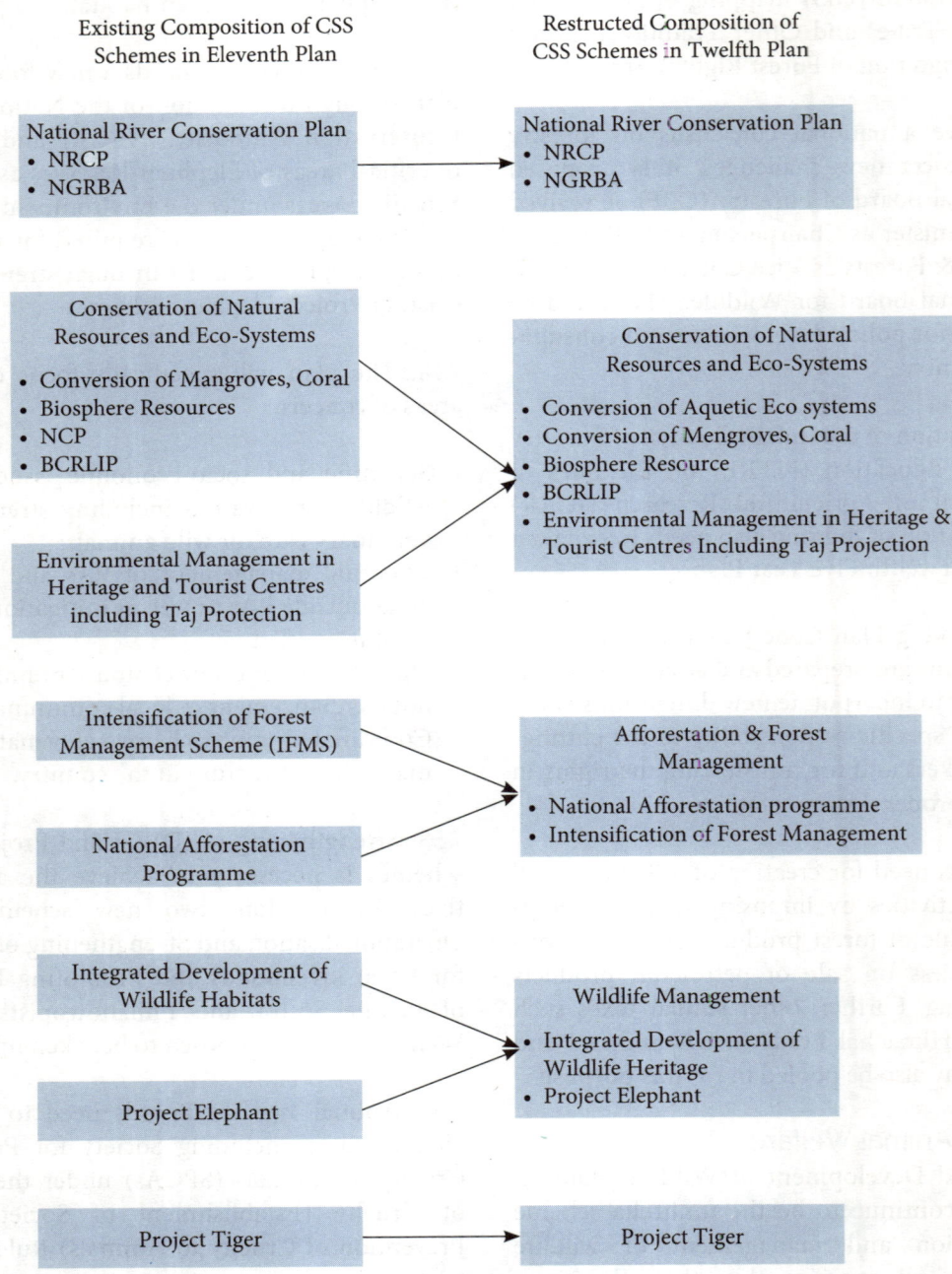

FIGURE 7.4: Rationalisation of Schemes from the Eleventh to the Twelfth Five Year Plan

7.59. The total number of thematic schemes in the Twelfth Plan has been reduced to 18 comprising of 5 CSS and 13 CS schemes, including one on Climate Change which has been approved by the Planning Commission. Amongst sub-schemes, the schemes of Industrial Pollution abatement through preventive strategies and Clean Technologies have been merged into a single scheme under the Pollution Abatement Scheme. Similarly, the schemes of National Lake Conservation Plan (NLCP) and Wetlands have been merged into a single scheme, namely, National Plan for Conservation of Aquatic Ecosystems under the thematic scheme of Conservation of Natural Resources and Ecosystems. The scheme of Taj Protection has also been clubbed under this scheme. Under the thematic scheme of International Cooperation Activities, a new sub-scheme on Desertification Cell has been proposed. The Civil Construction Unit scheme is a non-Plan scheme and has been shown to account for Plan expenditure on construction of new building of MoEF, which is likely to be completed in 2012–13.

New Initiatives for the Twelfth Plan

Recasting the Scheme of CETPS

7.60. In light of the operational deficiencies in the existing scheme of CETPs, the extant guidelines of CETPs are proposed to be revised for enforcement during the Twelfth Plan period. CPCB has initiated a study for 'Inventorization of industrial clusters in the country and assessment of the unmet demand for CETPs'. Based on the recommendations of the study, a prioritised list of required CETPs will be prepared and a strategy will be formulated for recasting of the existing scheme. A sub-scheme for Environment Protection was introduced for upgradation of CETPs in leather complexes in the Eleventh Plan by Department of Industrial Policy and Promotion (DIPP) which is to be strengthened during the Twelfth Plan.

Enhancement of Sewage Treatment Capacity

7.61. Concerted efforts would be made to complete the ongoing work of the Eleventh Plan under National River Conservation Plan (NRCP)/National Ganga River Basin Authority (NGRBA)/National Lake Conservation Plan (NLCP). Requirement of additional fund for enhancement of sewage treatment capacity need to be made available either under the JNNURM/UIDSSMT and/or under NRCP. Technical and financial capacity of ULBs will also have to be suitably augmented for meeting both the capital and Operations & Maintenance (O&M) requirements of Sewage Treatment Plants (STPs). States are also required to earmark allocations and mobilise necessary resources for funding sewerage infrastructure and their maintenance.

National Plan for Conservation of Aquatic Eco-Systems (NPCA)

7.62. Merger of National Wetland Conservation Programme (NWCP) and NLCP schemes into one integrated scheme entitled NPCA recommended by Expenditure Finance Committee is proposed with effect from Twelfth Plan period. This merger has been recommended with the objective of conserving aquatic ecosystems, namely, lakes and wetlands through implementation of sustainable conservation plans. The merged scheme is proposed to be implemented by National River Conservation Directorate in the MoEF in a mission mode with target oriented implementation.

7.63. Ganga River which has been declared as the national river supports the economic activity of the large part of the country. The NGRBA has proposed a river basin treatment strategy which includes augmentation and sustenance of ecological flow of the river and its tributaries. This needs to include initiatives on zero discharge and control of non-point source of pollution with people participation and public–private partnerships.

7.64. In river basins, recycle and reuse of sewage is not feasible when STPs are centralised systems to which sewage is conveyed over long distances involving intermediate pumping stations and outfall sewers. A decentralised sewage system offers opportunities to efficiently use the treated sewage and hence is recommended.

National Environmental Monitoring Programme

7.65. There is a need to set up a unified National Environmental Monitoring Programme NEMP focusing on tracking status and change in socially relevant biophysical parameters and their impact. This will enable real-time sharing of data on environmental parameters making the information widely accessible for monitoring and evaluation.

National Forestry Information System

7.66. The National Forestry Information System should enable networking with States for tracking changes in forest development, harvesting, trade and utilisation scenario with particular focus on issues of ownership and rights under Scheduled Tribes and Other Traditional Forest Dwellers (Recognition of Forest Rights) Act.

Invasive Species Management

7.67. A national programme specific to invasive species needs to be launched. One of its aims could be to compile a national inventory of invasive species. A standardised protocol needs to be developed for the identification of invasive species using GIS and remote sensing technology. Invasive species identification should not be limited to invasion in forests—it should also include invasion in aquatic and marine ecosystems, grasslands, wetlands and so on. A national invasive species monitoring system to track the introduction and spread of invasive is needed. Such a system should be linked to the state forest departments, and field staff should be trained to collect information on invasive species.

Coastal and Marine Conservation

7.68. Conservation of coastal and marine conservation in India requires to be scaled up and managed under CRZ guidelines. Effective management of these habitats needs integration of science with traditional knowledge systems and facilitation of greater involvement of communities/community based organisations in monitoring resource use, status, history and on-going changes. This will lead to better information flow within and between target groups to ensure that the communities/resource managers are empowered to play their roles effectively in conservation. Information on the following activities necessitates concerted efforts:

- Creation of vital information on spatio-temporal trends of responses of ecosystem/species to human and climate induced variations by initiating long-term monitoring of ecosystems and to develop valuable baseline information that will be critical in taking informed management decisions.
- Understanding critical ecosystem processes, identifying and bolstering the inherent resilience of ecosystems to climate and manmade perturbations.
- Evaluating impacts of resource exploitation (especially fisheries) on the functionality of coastal and marine ecosystems and evaluate efficacy of different management practices.
- Continuous monitoring of coastal biodiversity and digitisation for sustainable utilisation of marine bio-resources which calls for identification of institutions for implementing a national coordinated project through concerned Ministry for assessing the coastal and marine biodiversity resources so as to plan sustainable use of the same.
- Quantify Eleventh Plan accomplishments on the success of mangrove plantations and the difficulties encountered including steps taken by states for both conservation and enhancement of corals and its biodiversity and fix targets for the same during Twelfth plan.
- The potential of marine bio-resources towards commercialisation of PUFAs, vitamins, essential amino acids needs to be popularised and commercialised. Drug development from marine bio-resources need to be intensified by studying potential marine organism like sea snakes. There is significant potential for offering additional and alternative livelihood options by promoting marine cage cultures, marine ornamental fish culture such as clown and damsel, culture of algae and seaweeds towards organic fertilisers and growth promoters, micro-algae towards biofuels and so on.

Valuation of Ecosystem Services and Biodiversity

7.69. Successful and efficient ecosystem evaluation depends on development of appropriate institutional mechanism preferably by the Finance Commission, Planning Commission, Centre of Excellence in Environmental Economics and the MoEF. This institutional mechanism should allow for effective implementation of compensation and green bonus schemes which aim to fix, monitor, negotiate and share payments. Payments made to any state or organisation against green bonus should be based on negotiations between stakeholders. Institutional mechanism for research on ecosystems, bio-diversity and sustainable development is vital for ensuring sustainability of ecosystem services and biodiversity maintenance and hence an institution for achieving this is a necessity.

Environmental Performance Index (EPI)

7.70. The Planning Commission is in the process of developing an EPI to incentivise states for environmental performance through budgetary allocations. The Planning Commission's EPI may be a positive incentive for efforts by the States and UT's towards pollution abatement, conservation and sustainable management of natural resources and tackling climate change. The proposed EPI criteria and indicators are presented in Table 7.2.

Rangeland and Silvi-Pasture Development Scheme

7.71. A new scheme has been proposed for rangeland and silvi-pasture development. The scheme will take care of the grazing needs for cattle of local population. Major focus of the scheme will be rehabilitation and productivity enhancement of existing rangelands and potential grasslands in common/revenue lands around forest areas, fodder bank and storage, value addition technologies and facilities, establishing linkages with existing institutes/Centre of Excellence on fodder and pasture management, conducting fodder research, developing rangeland and silvi-pasture models, germ-plasm banks, fodder nurseries and so on. (Refer to Box 7.6 for Bundelkhand model of farmland productivity enhancement.)

Satellite Based Forest Resource Assessment

7.72. Remote sensing-based forest cover monitoring in close collaboration with Forest Survey of India, National Remote Sensing Agency and Indian Institute of Remote Sensing has been proposed. This initiative will be taken for developing a countrywide mosaic of high resolution satellite images (LISS IV, Cartosat) and overlaying polygons/grids of areas to be taken up for interventions. This centralised spatial data base in the GIS domain can be used as a policy tool for mid-course correction. In order to achieve higher level of accuracy in the monitoring and evaluation system, a dedicated

TABLE 7.2
Categories along with indicators selected for Planning Commission's EPI

S. No.	Criteria	Indicators	No. of Variables
1	Air Pollution	• Nitrogen Oxide (NOx)	
		• Sulphur Oxide SOx	3
		• Suspended Particulate Matter (SPM)/Respiratory Suspended Particulate Matter (RSPM)	
2	Forests	• TFC as a percentage of State GA and contribution to national average	
		• Increase/decrease in forest cover	4
		• Growing stock	
		• Afforestation efforts	
3	Water-quality	• Percentage of waste water (DOM)	
		• Surface water quality [Dissolved Oxygen (DO), Biochemical Oxygen Demand (BOD), TFC)]	3
		• Percentage ground water extraction	
4	Waste Management	• Municipal solid waste	
		• Bio-medical waste	3
		• Industrial waste—hazardous	
5	Climate Change	• Preparation of State Action Plan on Climate Change (SAPCC)	
		• RE growth rate including mini hydro	3
		• Electricity intensity of SGDP	
	Total		16

> **Box 7.5**
> **Tribal Families Jointly Manage 'Yepuru' Forests, Nellore District, Andhra Pradesh for One and Half Decade, for Sustainable Livelihood**
>
> Yepuru *Van Samrakshana Samithi* (Forest Protection Committee) was formed on 12 March 1997 in Rapur Range of Nellore Forest Division. The *Van Samrakshana Samithi* (VSS) formed by 37 tribal families consisting 64 tribal members. An extent of 310 ha has been allotted to the VSS in compartment nunber 300 and 301 of Nellepalli Reserve Forests in Yepuru Section (Tumaya Beat) of the Nellore Division. Out of 310 ha allotted to VSS, an extent of 198 ha has been raised with plantation of eucalyptus and NTFP up to 2010-11. Out of 198 ha, Eucalyptus clonal plantations were raised over an extent of 110 ha and the balance 88 ha was treated with NTFP species.
>
> In the year 2010-11, 80 ha Eucalyptus clonal plantations have been finally harvested as per the prescriptions of the Forestry Working Plan of the Division. A net revenue of ₹29,48,562 per has been realised up to the year 2010 from the intermittent and final harvests of the Eucalyptus plantations by the VSS.
>
> Fifty per cent of the net revenue, that is, ₹14,74,281 has been distributed to VSS members among 37 families at the rate of ₹39,845 per family. The balance 50 per cent amount was used to constitute a Reinvestment Fund. Reinvestment Fund was also utilised for post-harvest operations and regeneration works up by the VSS members. Out of ₹14,74,281, an amount of ₹12,75,946 has been spent towards Raising of 35 ha. Eucalyptus plantation and post-harvest operations while the balance amount ₹1,98,335 has been earmarked for maintenance works of plantations to be carried out in future.
>
> The uniqueness of *Yepuru*'s experience is the demonstration of willingness of the community to reinvest revenues from forest management to continue sustainable forest management. This is an example of a 'potential natural resource management tool' for economic inclusion of tribal hamlets through joint forest management. Almost 60 per cent of forest cover in the country lies in tribal districts where mainstreaming of participatory afforestation with definite usufruct sharing, holds the key for achieving inclusive development in the Twelfth Plan.

forest satellite for monitoring forest cover, NTFP resource, bio-diversity on periodical basis along with change monitoring has been proposed. The improved real-time, web-based monitoring system under this scheme would be extended to other schemes by strengthening the Forest Survey of India (FSI) and Remote Sensing/Geomatics Units in the states.

Green India Mission

7.73. The Government of India has taken initiatives by formulating National Mission for a Green India (GIM) as one of the 8 missions under the National Action Plan on Climate Change (NAPCC). The mission has been approved by the Prime Minister's Council on Climate Change with a proposed cost of ₹46,000 crore over 10 years starting from 2012-13. The GIM has been conceived as a multi-stakeholder, multi-sectoral and multi-departmental mission, recognising that climate change phenomena will seriously affect and alter the distribution, type and quality of natural resources of the country and the associated livelihoods of the people. GIM puts the 'greening' in the context of climate change adaptation and mitigation and is meant to enhance ecosystem services like carbon sequestration and storage (in forests and other ecosystems), hydrological services and biodiversity; along with provisioning services like fuel, fodder, small timber through agro and farm forestry, and NTFPs. During the Twelfth Five Year Plan, provisions have been kept for the GIM for increasing forest and tree cover on 2.5 mha area (non forest through agro/social/farm forestry), improving quality of forest cover on another 2.5 mha area, improving ecosystems services, and increasing forest based livelihood income and enhanced annual CO_2 sequestration. (Refer to Box 7.5 for the example of Andhra Pradesh.)

Plan Outlay

7.74. An indicative plan outlay of ₹17,899 crore at current prices for the Twelfth Five Year Plan has been made for the Ministry of Environment and Forests.

Box 7.6
Bundelkhand Model for Farmland Productivity Enhancement in Rain-fed Areas of the Country through Water Harvesting

The project area under Bundelkhand Special Package for Madhya Pradesh was marked by acute shortage of water, forage and low agricultural productivity. Lack of irrigation facilities coupled with scanty rainfall has resulted in low productivity and uncertainty in food grain production. During 2009-10 and 2010-11, 150 check dams, 192 contour trenches, 177 percolation tanks, 53 pond were constructed and other Soil Moisture Conservation (SMC) activities were carried out in 49,678 ha forest land. The catchment areas have since been regenerated with vegetation by artificial seeding of *Mahua, Ber, Stylosantus hamata, Thimida quadriwalivis, Cenchrus ciliaris, Guner and Deenanath* grass. Increased vegetative cover has enhanced the interception and percolation of rainwater facilitating groundwater recharge.

A study of the progress based on field observations indicate that people have started shifting from rain-fed maize to soyabean crop (high protein and nutrition crop) in the project area of Chatarpur and Tikamgrah districts. Similarly, SMC works such as staggered contour trenching, gully plugs, earthen check dams, banding. and plantation activities carried out in Banda, Chitrakoot, Jhansi and Mahoba districts of Uttar Pradesh has resulted in recharging of ground water in adjoining non-forestland, particularly agricultural land.

As a result of water retention in the higher reaches, mostly forest areas of the locality, and consequential increase in water table, there has been a marked increase in extent of Kharif and Rabi Crop coverage as well as in productivity. The coverage area under six districts of Bundelkhand region of MP has registered an increase from 23.39 lakh ha in 2007-08 to 27.61 ha in 2009-10. Similarly, the productivity has gone up from 15.51 lakh tonne to 26.7 lakh tonne and yield from 743.65 kg/ha to 996.52 kg/ha in 2009-10.

This project was implemented by the Forest Departments of the States and was funded under the Bundelkhand Special Package. This has not only improved the food security of the region but also the socio-economic condition of the farmers. Bundelkhand Model of MSC activities can be replicated in most of the rainfed areas as a strategy to combat desertification, practice resilient agriculture and climate change adaptation.

CLIMATE CHANGE

7.75. The threat of climate change is a serious global concern. There is near consensus among scientists that climate change is unequivocal. Increase in anthropogenic activities, since the advent of industrialisation in the mid-eighteenth century, has built upconcentration of Greenhouse Gases (such as Carbon Dioxide, Methane, Nitrous Oxides and so on) in the Earth's atmosphere. Greenhouse Gases (GHGs) trap infra-red radiations reflected by Earth, leading to global warming; which, in turn, could lead to changes in rainfall patterns, disruption in hydrological cycles, melting of ice caps and glaciers, rise in sea levels, and increase in frequency and intensity of extreme events such as heavy precipitation or cyclones. These developments can have a serious impact on sustainability of water resources, agriculture, forests and ecosystems, affecting the well-being of billions of people on Earth. Climate Change can slow down the pace of development either through its adverse impact on natural eco-systems, or through erosion of adaptive capacity of the people, particularly those who are socially and economically vulnerable. Projections of temperature change as estimated by the IPCC are given in Table 7.3 and Figure 7.5.

7.76. India is highly vulnerable to climate change. As per recorded observations, India has seen an increase of 0.4 degree Centigrade, in the mean surface air temperature over the past century (1901-2000). Change in mean temperature and precipitation will require change in cropping patterns. It has been estimated that a 2.0 to 3.5 degree Centigrade increase in temperature, and the associated increase in precipitation, can lower agricultural GDP by 9 to 28 per cent. Yields of most crops will fall in the long run. The impact in the short run may be small, but the heat stress will affect the productivity of animals and milk production may even decrease over the present levels. Agriculture technology can adapt to these changes to partially offset the adverse impact by adoption of water conservation practices, by changing cropping patterns and practices, and by developing new varieties that can withstand short term variability in weather patterns.

TABLE 7.3
Different Levels of Global Mean Temperature Increase above Pre-industrial Levels

Category	CO$_2$ Concentration (ppm)	CO$_2$ eq. Concentration (ppm)	Global Mean Temperature Increase Above Pre-industrial Levels (Deg C)	Peaking Year for CO$_2$ Emissions	Change in Global Emissions in 2050 (per cent of 2000 Emissions)
I	350–400	445–490	2.0–2.4	2000–2015	−85 to −50
II	400–440	490–535	2.4–2.8	2000–2020	−60 to −30
III	440–485	535–590	2.8–3.2	2010–2030	−30 to +5
IV	485–570	590–710	3.2–4.0	2020–2060	+10 to +60
V	570–660	710–855	4.0–4.9	2050–2080	+25 to +85
VI	660–790	855–1,130	4.9–6.1	2060–2090	+90 to +140

7.77. Climate Change will also affect the water balance, particularly the amount of runoff and recharge, which determines the overall water resources available in the ecosystem. This will change vegetative cover, affect availability of fodder, fuel-wood and minor forest produce. Climate change is also expected to raise sea levels, which could submerge coastal lands in some areas, thereby threatening coastal cities and habitations. Apart from the loss of land and property, millions may be displaced. Increase in sea and river water temperatures is likely to affect fish breeding, migration and harvest. We need to understand these threats and take action well in advance.

7.78. India is, and has been, on per-capita basis, one of the lowest GHG emitters in the world. Its emission of 1.18 tonnes of CO$_2$ equivalent per person in 2008, was nearly one-fourth of the global average of 4.38 tonnes (one-tenth that of Europe and one-eighteenth that of US). Since it is cumulative emissions that affect climate variability, it is the historical emissions of developed countries that have been the major contributor to climate change. However, India remains vulnerable to the adverse effects of both climate variability and change. Global action is urgently required to minimise the threat and damage that climate change can inflict on us.

7.79. As a responsible nation, India has already shown its commitment to help address the global climate challenge. It is determined to work, both at domestic and international levels, in accordance with the principle of common but differentiated

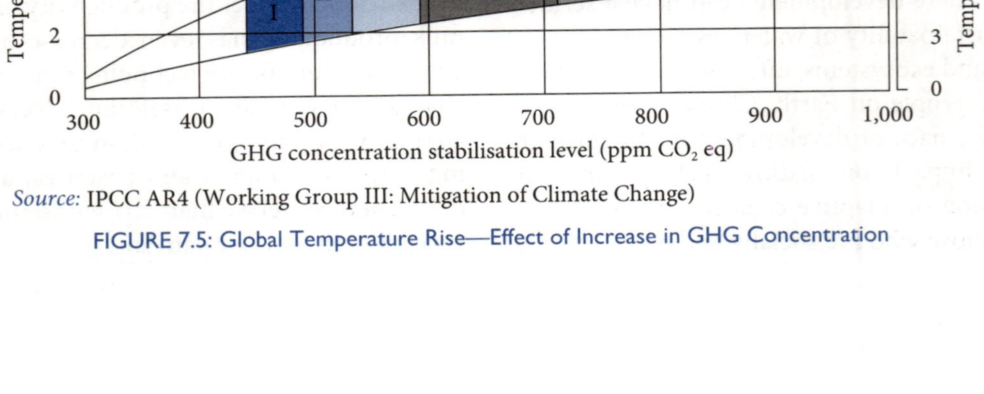

Source: IPCC AR4 (Working Group III: Mitigation of Climate Change)

FIGURE 7.5: Global Temperature Rise—Effect of Increase in GHG Concentration

responsibility under the United Nations Framework Convention on Climate Change. Prime Minister has already expressed on June 8, 2007, at the Heiligendamm meeting of G8+5, India's determination to see that her per capita emissions levels will never exceed the average per capita emissions levels of the developed countries in the world (Singh Convergence Principle). India is an active participant in the Clean Development Mechanism (CDM) under the Kyoto Protocol, with the second highest number of projects registered for any country; and these have the potential to offset almost 10 percent of India's total emissions per year. Furthermore, in December 2009, India announced that it would aim to reduce the emissions intensity of its GDP by 20–25 per cent over the 2005 levels by 2020. India's voluntary actions will hopefully lead other nations to reduce their emissions, and to arrive at an effective and just global agreement.

7.80. India has also formulated a NAPCC which has a mix of mitigation and adaptation actions. The plan formulated under the aegis of the Prime Minister's Council on Climate Change has outlined eight missions and several other initiatives. Four of these missions address adaptation to climate change, while three of them address mitigation and one relates to knowledge.

7.81. Since global warming depends upon the total concentration of GHGs, minimisation of the threat of climate change requires concerted action by all the countries. However, whatever the world community does, some effects of climate change seem unavoidable at this stage. It is, therefore, important for India to minimise the vulnerability of various sectors, and make its economy, society and environment adapt to climate change, even as it takes strong actions to enhance sustainability of its development path.

7.82. The Twelfth Plan adopts a three-pronged approach to realise this objective. First, it elaborates and articulates the objective of the NAPCC through various sectors of the Plan. It ensures that plans of all sectors contain an assessment of their vulnerability to climate change, and specific adaptation measures are identified and implemented over the longer term.

Second, a nationally agreed strategy will be implemented to achieve lower carbon inclusive growth and to realise the domestic goal of reduction in the emissions intensity of our GDP. The strategy will outline a potential for such reduction, as well as the required policy measures to achieve this objective in various sectors. The required financial outlays and the relevant delivery mechanisms will be part of this strategy. Lastly, the Twelfth Plan will take scientific and institutional initiatives for regular climate change assessments, GHG measurement, capacity building for technical analysis, monitoring and management of such complex systems at various levels.

India's Emission Structure

7.83. In 2007, India's GHG emissions, by sources and removal by sinks, were 1,727.71 million tonnes of CO_2 equivalents (or 1,904.73 million tonnes of CO_2 equivalents without land use, land use change and forestry), with the largest shares coming from electricity generation (38 per cent), agriculture (18 per cent) and other energy industries (12 per cent). However, India's CO_2 emissions from fuel use in 2007 were less than 5 per cent of the world total (International Energy Agency, 2009). In recent years, India has taken substantial initiatives to reduce energy intensity of its GDP, through measure such as energy efficiency standards, labelling of equipment and appliances, building codes, and introduction of market mechanisms for energy intensive industries. However, economic growth, increasing urbanisation, rise in per capita consumption and spread of energy access, are likely to substantially increase India's energy demand in the long run.

Vulnerability Assessment and Adaptation

Agriculture

7.84. Agriculture is the provider of livelihood for nearly half of our working population. Studies done at the Indian Agricultural Research Institute indicate the possibility of loss of 4–5 million tonnes in wheat production for every $1°C$ rise in temperature throughout the growing period. Losses for other crops are uncertain, but are expected to be smaller for the kharif crops. Agriculture sector contributes 18 per cent of the total GHG emissions from India. The emissions are primarily due to methane from the rice paddies, enteric fermentation in ruminant animals, and nitrous oxides from the application of manures and fertilisers. Although relative proportion of emissions from agriculture in India is likely to show considerable reduction in future because of the larger emission growth in other sectors, adaptation for agricultural communities will remain a major concern.

7.85. Some policy and programmatic interventions can help farmers and other stakeholders adapt to climate change and reduce the losses. Change in cropping patterns, for example, can help adjustment to changes in mean temperature and precipitation. Amongst the key actions for adapting Indian agriculture to climate change are improved land management practices, development of resource conserving technologies, development of crop varieties that can withstand climate-stress, effective risk management through early warning, credit-insurance support to farmers and nutritional strategies for managing heat stress in dairy animals. Complementary actions in terms of identification of cost-effective opportunities for reducing methane generation, emissions in ruminants by modification of diet, and in rice paddies by water and nutrient management will help make adaptation measures sustainable. New policies should support the new land use arrangements, enhance investment in water harvesting, promote small-farm mechanisation and efficient water use technologies. A package of financial incentives for improved land management, including resource conservation (water, carbon, energy) and balanced fertiliser use may facilitate quicker adoption of these measures.

Water

7.86. Given the stress on glaciers and snow covers, and the threat of reduced summer and autumn flows in the Himalayan river systems, a comprehensive analysis of the possible impact of climate change on water resources is necessary. Such an assessment should include the assessment of the likely impacts of climate change on the constituents of the hydrological cycle at the basin/sub-basin level.

7.87. The National Water Mission launched in 2008 partly addresses this need by aiming at *(i)* development of a comprehensive water database and assessment of the impact of climate change on water resources, *(ii)* promotion of citizen and state actions for water conservation, augmentation and preservation, *(iii)* focused attention on vulnerable areas including over-exploited areas, *(iv)* increasing water use efficiency by 20 per cent, and *(v)* promotion of basin level integrated water resources management.

7.88. During the Twelfth Plan, it should be our effort to create a framework which enables the mapping of hydrological units with the hierarchy of river basin at the highest level to catchment at the intermediate and watershed at the lowest level. Formulation of such framework including development of present and future scenarios can be undertaken by line Department(s) in consultation with the academic and research organisations working in this area. Assessment of water utilisation for various purposes linked to sources is a basic necessity for working out the adaptation measures. Such an exercise is also essential for addressing the issues of inter-sectoral competition for water. During the Twelfth Plan the National Water Mission would be revamped to ensure an integrated management of ground and surface water resources.

Forests and Other Natural Ecosystems

7.89. Climate is one of the most important determinants of forest vegetation patterns. However, climate change is expected to occur more rapidly than the rate at which ecosystems can adapt and re-establish themselves. Projected impacts for India indicate that 40 to 70 per cent of the forested grids in different states are likely to experience climate change, resulting in forest die back and loss of biodiversity.

7.90. Given the vulnerability of forests, the GIM launched during the Eleventh Plan period envisages a combination of adaptation and mitigation measures aimed at *(i)* enhancing carbon sinks in sustainably managed forests and other ecosystems, *(ii)* adaptation of vulnerable species/ecosystems to the changing climate patterns and *(iii)* adaptation of the forest-dependent communities. The specific target adopted by the Mission is to increase the forest and tree cover by 10 mha of forest/non-forest lands through *(i)* qualitative improvement of forest cover/ecosystem in moderately dense forests (1.5 mha), open degraded forests (3 mha), degraded grassland (0.4 mha) and wetlands 0.1 mha; *(ii)* eco-restoration/afforestation of scrub, shifting cultivation areas, cold deserts, mangroves, ravines and abandoned mining areas (2 m ha); *(iii)* bringing urban/ peri-urban lands under forest and tree cover (0.20 mha); and d) agro-forestry/social forestry (3 mha).

7.91. The incremental annual mitigation potential of the Mission interventions is estimated to be about 55 $MtCO_2$ in the year 2020, using moderate to conservative carbon accumulation rates. The GIM should also aim at implementing a programme of Reduced Emissions from Deforestation and Forest Degradation (REDD+) that ensures sustainable management of forests.

7.92. Current central assistance for afforestation programmes is only around ₹350 crore per year. While budgetary support needs to be enhanced, one of the keys to success of this Mission will be its ability to establish convergence with other flagship programmes like MGNREGA, Compensatory Afforestation Fund Management and Planning Authority (CAMPA) and National Action Plan (NAP); and effecting regulatory improvements that help local communities access and benefit from local forest resources. Synchronised implementation of MGNREGA and GIM, and unlocking of CAMPA funds for this purpose will not only enhance the availability of resources, but also achieve stronger inter-sectoral linkages. MoEF and the MoRD have already developed guidelines for convergence between NREGS and NAP. These need to be operationalised at the state level without any further delay.

Coastal Areas

7.93. Indian coast line is prone to increased frequency of climatically induced extreme events like cyclones, storm surge, high tides and rise in sea levels. Large portion of the population along the coastline derives livelihood from climate dependent activities such as marine fisheries and agriculture. Sensitive ecosystems such as the mangroves are also threatened by climate change. Identification of coastal vulnerability and assessment of the consequence of coastal inundation should, therefore, receive high priority during Twelfth Five Year Plan.

7.94. Protection and management of coastal areas is not specifically covered under any of existing programmes. During the Twelfth Plan, this gap needs to be filled by according priority to the Integrated Coastal Zone Management (ICZM). The ICZM policies should be designed to afford protection against coastal vulnerabilities. Coastal zone regulations concerning construction activities have recently been modified to take into account the likely prospect of long-term rise in sea-levels. Infrastructure development near the coast also needs to take these risks into account. Climate Change Impact Assessment needs to be integrated into the existing practice of cumulative impact assessment of the environment. Comprehensive modelling of the coastal processes incorporating all necessary parameters is essential for planning mitigation and adaptation strategies. To enable this, existing capabilities of MoES and Indian Space Research Organization (ISRO) (Remote Sensing) may also need to be strengthened during the Twelfth Five Year Plan.

Health

7.95. There is a growing concern in both medical and climatological communities that global climate change is likely to affect human health. Climate change may adversely affect mortality and morbidity rates through general warming. Diseases such as malaria, yellow fever, dengue and cholera are all sensitive to climate change. Many are spread by insects like mosquitoes, which prefer a wetter, warmer world. Deaths from heart diseases and respiratory illness during heat waves add to the toll. In a developing country like India, population growth, industrialisation, increased energy consumption, and degrading air and water quality may worsen the health impacts of climate change.

7.96. The Indian Council of Medical Research (ICMR) has identified four areas of risks arising from climate change such as *(i)* Climate Change and vector borne diseases, *(ii)* aerosols and respiratory diseases, *(iii)* UV-A and UV-B corneal damage and cataract and *(iv)* environment and heart diseases. Following this assessment, the ICMR has constituted Task Force Groups such as *(i)* Vector Borne Diseases and Climate Change *(ii)* Respiratory Diseases and Air Pollutants and *(iii)* Eye Health and Environment.

7.97. During the Twelfth Plan period, additional priority areas of research need to be taken up in the areas of climate variability, and its effect on diarrhoeal and viral diseases, heat stress and certain types of cancer such as skin cancer. Other multi-disciplinary long term studies would also be initiated in partnership with Indian Meteorological Department, Central Pollution Control Board and ISRO.

Infrastructure

7.98. Infrastructure plays a pivotal role in development. Hence, the large investments planned for future have to be protected against climate-change induced risks. This includes the infrastructure related to energy resources. An integrated climate change risks management framework for infrastructures should include market and policy induced enforcements and adaptation strategies. The key to manage risks lies in identifying them and initiating appropriate risk management and adaptation initiatives.

7.99. Some early assessments for specific sectors and locations suggest that adaptation costs for new infrastructure could be in the range of 3–10 per cent of the total investment, although for certain sectors and locations this may be higher. This, however, does not cover the cost of likely future damages due to climate change. For existing assets, the adaptation costs could be as much as 25 per cent of present costs of creating similar assets.

7.100. During the Twelfth Plan, detailed sectoral, regional and integrated studies need to be commissioned for assessment of risks to Indian infrastructure due to climate change, especially to establish the damage functions and costs. Assessments by neutral third parties may be conducted for all such upcoming infrastructure projects. Environmental Impacts Assessment of new infrastructure projects should also include impacts of climate change on the project in near, medium and long-terms.

Industry

7.101. Industry has recently taken several voluntary initiatives to adapt itself to the emerging international challenges from climate change. These include both the manufacturing and service sectors. Some corporate units have adopted the practice of making voluntary public disclosure of information relating to sustainability performance. In such cases, the units prepare sustainability reports using the guidelines followed by private corporate or civil society bodies. Some of them have even adopted voluntary practices for carbon foot-printing, using ISO 14,064, WRI-WBCSD GHG Protocol or IPCC Guidelines and so on. However, the relevance of such private actions for the national policy goals is not fully evident.

7.102. Transition of industries to a more energy efficient and lower carbon energy based operation is a more fundamental issue that is key to sustainable growth. However, this needs to be supported by availability of technological and financial resources. The key issue in this regard is the adoption of appropriate technologies that may help the industrial units in saving energy, improving energy efficiency and conserving natural resources without affecting their competitiveness. This will need to be addressed through a well thought out lower carbon strategy for inclusive growth.

National Action Plan on Climate Change

7.103. Eight national missions were launched in the Eleventh Plan covering the areas of solar energy, energy efficiency, habitat, agriculture, water, Himalayan ecosystems, forestry and strategic knowledge. The mission documents have been finalised by the Prime Minister's Council on Climate Change and are at various stages of implementation. Although the nodal Ministries entrusted with implementation of the missions are yet to fully assess the likely costs, the preliminary estimates indicate a sum of ₹2,30,000 crore may be needed to fulfil the Mission objectives. Funds of this magnitude cannot be mobilised through budgetary resources alone.

7.104. The Solar Mission aims at making solar electricity cost competitive to coal power and increasing the share of solar energy in the total energy mix through development of new solar technologies, both photovoltaic and solar thermal. The Mission recommends implementation in three stages leading up to an installed capacity of 20,000 MW by the end of the Thirteenth Five Year Plan in 2022. The total financial outlay during Phase 1 is estimated as ₹4,337 crore. Requirement for second phase will be assessed after review of phase 1.

7.105. The Energy Efficiency Mission seeks to upscale efforts to create a market for energy efficiency. It comprises of four initiatives, namely, Perform, Achieve and Trade (PAT), Market Transformation for Energy Efficiency (MTEE), Energy Efficiency Financing Platform (EEFP) and Framework for Energy Efficient Economic Development (FEEED). As a result of implementation of this mission over the next five years, it is estimated that by about 2015, about 23 million tonnes of oil-equivalent of fuel saving—in coal, gas, and petroleum products, will be achieved every year along with an avoided capacity addition of over 19,000 MW. While the initial cost of starting the Mission during the Eleventh Plan was about ₹425 crore (excluding the investment made by private investors) the costs for implementing the Mission during the Twelfth Plan period is estimated to be ₹3,400 crore (excluding the investment made by private sector). The cost for subsequent periods is yet to be estimated.

7.106. The Sustainable Habitat Mission attempts to promote energy efficiency in buildings, management of solid waste, and modal shift to public transport including transport options based on bio-diesel and hydrogen. Main components of the mission are *(i)* development of National Sustainable Habitat Standards (legal/regulatory) measures *(ii)* incorporation of principles of sustainable habitat in city development and planning and *(iii)* complementary action such as support for building green demonstration projects and outreach programme for creating consumer awareness. The total cost estimate projected in the Mission Document is ₹1,000 crore. During Eleventh Plan, expenditure of ₹50 crore is to be incurred and remaining ₹950 crore is to be incurred during the Twelfth Five Year Plan.

7.107. The Sustainable Agriculture Mission aims at making Indian agriculture more resilient to climate change through development of new varieties of climate-stress resistant crops, new credit and insurance mechanisms, and improving productivity of rain-fed agriculture. The main focus of the mission is ensuring food security and protecting land, water, biodiversity and genetic resources for sustainable production of food. An outlay of ₹12 to 15 thousand crore is likely to be available for this mission during the Twelfth Five Year Plan.

7.108. The Water Mission aims at conservation of water, minimising wastage and ensuring more equitable distribution both across and within states. The mission focuses on *(i)* intensive rain water harvesting and ground water charging to meet the demand of 1,120 critical blocks during the Eleventh Plan and remaining blocks in the Twelfth Plan (March 2017), and *(ii)* increasing water use efficiency at least by 20 per cent by 2012. Water has been identified as a major challenge of sustainable development for the Twelfth Five Year Plan. A new national program will be launched for sustainable management of water resources in the country. Since this issue is larger than climate change, it is better to subsume this into the larger mission to be launched for the Twelfth Five Year Plan.

7.109. The Mission on Sustainable Himalayan Eco-systems aims at evolving management measures for sustaining and safeguarding the Himalayan glacier and mountain eco-system. The four key issues to be addressed by the mission are *(i)* Himalayan glaciers and the associated hydrological consequences, *(ii)* biodiversity conservation and protection, *(iii)* wildlife conservation and protection, and *(iv)* traditional knowledge societies and their livelihood. For implementing its activities, a total provision of ₹900 crore needs to be made during the Twelfth Five Year Plan.

7.110. The Green India Mission focuses on enhancing eco-system services and carbon sinks through afforestation on degraded forest land, in line with the national policy of expanding the forest and tree cover in the country and improving the quality of forests. A total expenditure of ₹46,000 crore is projected under this mission for coverage of 10 mha over the next *ten years*. An outlay of ₹12,500 crore is likely to be available for this mission during the Twelfth Five Year Plan.

7.111. The Strategic Knowledge Mission intends to identify the challenges of, and the responses to, climate change through research and technology development and ensure funding of high quality and focused research into various aspects of climate change.

7.112. *For a Mission to succeed it must have separable objectives, dedicated implementation machinery and adequate funding.* For objectives which lie within the domain of other flagship programmes, or are completely cross-sectoral, it is better to identify a few policy thrust areas, which would still be part of the NAPCC and be regularly monitored by the Prime Minister's Council.

7.113. To achieve effective results, the missions stated above need to be reorganised in accordance with the updated priorities. We should aim at a short list of reorganised missions and a few policy thrust are as under the NAPCC, that will be achieve more focused and tangible results over the Twelfth Plan period. Some suggestions for reorganising the NAPCC are as follows:

1. The Water Mission here needs to be merged with the new *National Water Mission* that is being formulated for the Twelfth Five Year Plan. This will ensure water related issues are dealt with in a more holistic manner, as climate change is also an important subject under the new National Water Policy being put up for approval. However, critical actions like treatment of all sewage being released into water bodies, which have a bearing on our adaptive capacity to climate change, should be monitored as a separate policy thrust area under the Prime Minister's Council on Climate Change.
2. Strategic Knowledge Mission is also likely to remain peripheral and is not likely to attract adequate funding through this window. It is better to mainstream development of green technology and research into various aspects of climate change into the main programmes of ourscientific departments, like earth sciences, space, science & technology, agriculture, health, biotechnology and others, as these are likely to attract substantial funding during the Twelfth Five Year Plan. It can be monitored as a policy thrust area under the Prime Minister's Council on Climate Change.
3. Sustainable Habitat Mission presently has overarching objectives, some of which are out of proportion to the limited funding that is available. Solid Waste Management is an area that is funded through a separate central programme, namely the JNNURM. This subject, being of immense importance, should be monitored as a policy thrust area through the PM's Council; while the Habitat Mission under NAPCC should focus on critical areas like evolution, adoption and implementation of green building codes, urban habitat planning and development, so on.
4. Our efforts to develop wind energy meet the requirements of a separate mission like the solar mission. To accelerate progress in this area, and to meet the steep targets set for the Twelfth Plan, a new National Wind Power Mission needs to be launched under the NAPCC. India has already built up sufficient technological capability in this area, which needs to be harnessed to maximise utilisation of wind power potential in the country.
5. The Energy Efficiency in Industry is an important policy thrust area. PAT scheme is only suitable for certain large industries (called 'designated consumers' under the Energy Conservation Act). To facilitate efficiency improving technology interventions in the industry at large, an Energy Conservation Fund needs to set up under the aegis of the Bureau of Energy Efficiency. Similarly, Advanced Coal Technologies, Dedicated Freight Corridors and Improved Urban Public Transport are the critical policy thrust areas that can go a long way in saving the scarce fossil fuels for the country, and therefore, need a focused attention at the highest level.

7.114. Accordingly, a reorganised framework for the National Action Plan for Climate Change is suggested in Box 7.7. *These suggestions will be placed*

> **Box 7.7**
> **Suggested Re-organisation of the National Action Plan for Climate Change**
>
> A) NATIONAL MISSIONS
> 1. National Solar Mission
> 2. National Wind Energy Mission
> 3. The Energy Efficiency Mission
> 4. Sustainable Habitat Mission
> 5. Sustainable Agriculture Mission
> 6. Mission on Sustainable Himalayan Eco-systems
> 7. National Mission for a Green India
>
> B) POLICY THRUST AREAS
> 1. Advanced Coal Technologies
> 2. Energy Efficiency Improvements in Major Industries
> 3. Solid Waste Management Systems in Towns and Cities
> 4. Treatment of all Sewage before Release into the Water Bodies
> 5. Improved Urban Public Transport
> 6. Dedicated Freight Corridors along Major Routes
> 7. Climate Related Research through Scientific Departments

before the Prime Minister's Council on Climate Change and discussed before a formal decision is taken.

State Action Plans on Climate Change

7.115. Involvement of States is critical in building capacity at local levels to address climate change and to protect local communities that are vulnerable. During the Twelfth Plan period, attempt will be made to create capacity at the state level, and to provide some resources to incentivise state action in the area of adaptation and mitigation. MoEF has already initiated the process of preparing State Action Plans on Climate Change (SAPCC). The SAPCCs are to be finalised with assistance of experts and through a process of consultations. It will identify vulnerable areas and communities that need to be insulated against the adverse effects of climate change. Some of the effective adaptation strategies are listed below:

1. Agriculture: Change in land use management, development of resource conserving technologies, development of crop varieties that can withstand climate stress, effective risk management through early warning, credit insurance support to farmers and better nutritional management of dairy animals.
2. Water: Framework for mapping hydrological units, assessment of water utilisation to address inter-sectoral competition, research to support policy improvements in water use management and to improve understanding of linkages within the ecosystem.
3. Forests: Forest planning and development of programmes that will minimise the adverse impact of climate vulnerability and change, implement REDD+ activities programme.
4. Coastal Zone: Scientific evaluation of potential changes in the coastal zone, estimation of inundation of vulnerable zones, planning for infrastructure and large scale displacement of people in coastal areas.
5. Health: R&D and clinical management of vector borne respiratory, heart and corneal diseases.

7.116. The State Action Plans will include a strategy and a list of possible sectoral actions that would help the States achieve their adaptation and mitigation objectives. Most of the States have already started working on a template provided by the Central Government. An expert committee in the MoEF has been set up to examine the draft action plans from a technical point of view. A National Steering Committee has also been formed to endorse the SAPCCs, as well as strategies and outlays presented by the State Governments.

7.117. Most of the resources required for sectoral actions under the State Action Plans will need to be provided by the State Governments through their respective plan outlays. However, some resources may be mobilised as Central Assistance to State Plans through the Gross Budgetary Support. Towards this end, an umbrella scheme on Climate Change Action Programme is proposed to be launched during the Twelfth Plan. Support to State Governments could be based on a set of transparent and objective criteria to be monitored by a Steering Committee in the MoEF. In addition, State Government may earmark provisions for implementing activities under the SAPCC.

Thirteenth Finance Commission has recommended grants to the State Governments for environment action, which also cover some of the activities under the NAPCC. Even then, resources are likely to fall far short of what is required, and international assistance will need to be mobilised through bilateral and multilateral channels.

Climate Change Science and Assessment

7.118. Existing institutions in different Ministries have studied the patterns and behaviour of climate from a scientific angle. However, the science of study and assessment of climate change has acquired added importance in the recent years. There has been a significant leap in the understanding of the 'science' of climate change and its impacts on socio-economic systems, which is evident from the work done by the IPCC in its Third Assessment Report.

7.119. The Ministry of Environment and Forests has been engaged in the last two decades in assessing climate change and presenting its findings. It prepared the first National Communication in 2004. The Second National Communication based on the data of 2007 has been prepared and presented to the international community in 2012. To provide a systematic basis to the research in the area of climate change, the Ministry has set up an Indian Network for Climate Change Assessment (INCCA) as a network-based scientific programme. The INCCA is visualised as a mechanism to create new institutions as well as engage existing knowledge institutions working with the Government.

7.120. Considering the importance of scientific assistance to policymaking, we need to create a more systematic and credible institutional arrangement that would enable us to continuously enhance the understanding of the 'science' of climate change. It should make a regular assessment of the impacts due to changes in the climate system, and also assess the extent and nature of key vulnerabilities. It should include systematic preparation and publication of GHG inventory, preparation of National Communications (NATCOMs) as per international obligations, and facilitate mainstreaming of climate change related studies. Towards this end, it is proposed that new research programmes may be launched to strengthen scientific research, assessment, planning and management capability particularly in the following areas of Climate Change:

1. A specific programme aimed at Climate Change Assessment Studies (CCAS) and institutionalising the obligatory and scientific work of the Ministry is urgently called for. The programme is required to build capacity in modelling of climate change effects, which can be done with the help of technological, economic and scientific data collected in a systematic manner. This programme may initially be conceptualised within the MoEF with a Director and at least 10 scientists and experts from different fields and associated support staff. In the long run, a dedicated Centre for Studies and Research in Climate Change should be set up as an autonomous institution attached for budgetary purposes to the MoEF. The Centre should plan, collate and coordinate the assessment work for National Communication, which is a regular and mandatory international obligation performed by the Ministry. The Twelfth Plan should support provision of at least ₹25 crore over a period of five years to this Centre with an appropriate institutional arrangement.

2. GHG Inventory Management System (GHG-IMS) needs to be institutionalised as India is required to publish its Greenhouse Gases (GHG) inventory every two years. The programme can initially be planned in the same manner as the Climate Change Assessment Centre, to be housed under INCCA and operationalised at the MoEF. The programme should coordinate with network agencies for estimation and regular publication of GHG inventory. The nodal centre at MoEF would also act as a data repository for GHG inventory and conduct analysis to support policy making. The budgetary support required for this activity would be ₹20 crore per year for the initial five years, followed thereafter by regular budgetary support to ensure its continuity.

Strategies for Financing

7.121. Assessment of the costs of adaptation and mitigation is a difficult task, although it is clear that these costs are significant, and will likely rise in future as initiatives are taken to achieve the mitigation and adaptation goals outlined in our national policies. Though no ready estimates are available, several studies[1] suggest that incremental economic or investment costs incurred for adaptation and mitigation of emissions will be sizeable and may divert resources from other critical sectors of our economy.

7.122. During the Twelfth Plan, financing of climate change related actions will be a major challenge. Low carbon strategies will particularly require enhanced deployment of renewable and clean energy technologies, and capital finance for improvements in technology. Some of these objectives may be met through regulatory interventions and use of market mechanisms, in which case the required budgetary support may be small, but indirect and unquantified costs for economy may be large. In other cases, adequate financial outlays will be needed to implement policies and measures that can achieve specific mitigation outcomes in the individual sectors. A framework for understanding finance strategies is outlined in Box 7.8.

7.123. Before deciding on the optimal strategy it is important to answer questions like whether the incentive will actually be passed on to the consumer, whether the income transfer to the consumer would result in increased demand, what will be the impact on risk-sharing, information asymmetry, moral hazard and so on. Where markets exist, signals could be delivered through either price or quantities. Where they do not exist, and externalities are paramount; markets may need to be created as well as deepened. In this context, the relevance of regulatory measures as appropriate instruments to reflect externalities and trading as a possible way of minimising the economic costs will need to be examined.

7.124. Given that energy supply and end-use technologies are evolving rapidly, policy instruments should reflect the contemporary state of technology. Whether a technology will be viable and adopted widely depends on the private discount rate, the social discount rate and monetisation of net co-benefits. An example of what policy intervention will be optimal for what technology is explained with examples in Table 7.4.

Domestic Resources

7.125. The most obvious source of financing for climate change action is the government budgetary support. Most of it would come as sectoral finance since some of the resources for adaptation and mitigation are built into the on-going schemes and programmes of the respective Ministries. Although carbon mitigation is sometimes an important co-benefit, the deployment of resources for such purposes is largely guided by the overall availability of resources with the respective Ministries. Some prominent examples are budgetary support for super-critical thermal power plants, for dedicated freight corridor, for urban public transport, so on. This is supplemented by internal and extra-budgetary resources of public enterprises like NTPC, Ministry of Railways, Metro-Rail Corporations, so on. Additional allocations are available as grants from the Central Government on the recommendation of the 13th Finance Commission. Three grants of ₹5,000 crore each, namely for forest cover, renewable energy and water sector, have been recommended for the State Governments.

7.126. While the budgetary resources indicated above flow through the Consolidated Fund, Government of India has created another window for climate action through the Public Account. With a view to generate additional resources, a cess at the rate of ₹50 per

---

Box 7.8
Framework for Understanding Finance Strategies

A. Changing the Cost Curves (Producer Side Strategies)
   - Capital Costs: capital subsidy, interest subsidy, depreciation rules
   - Variable Costs: output based incentive (Feed-in-tariffs, rebate/drawback of commodity taxes)

B. Changing the Demand Curves (Consumer Side Strategies)
   - Purchase Based Incentives (purchaser rebates)
   - Purchase Quotas (Renewable Purchase Obligations)
   - Guaranteed Procurement (public procurement policy)

TABLE 7.4
Policy Interventions Optimal for Various Technologies

Technology Examples	Viability Using Private Discount Rates	Viability Using Social Discount Rates	Social Discount Rates + Monetised Mitigation Benefits	Policy Approach
ECBC, CFL, Supercritical Coal Tech.	Viable	Viable	Viable	Mandatory Standards + Information labelling
Super-efficient Appliances	Unviable	Viable	Viable	Incentive to Manufacturer and/or incentive to Consumer
LED's & Ultra-supercritical Coal Tech.	Unviable	Unviable	Viable	Domestic or International Carbon Finance (grant/loan)
Carbon Capture & Storage	Unviable	Unviable	Unviable	Pilot Project on 100 per cent grant basis

tonne of coal was levied in the budget of 2009. The cess has become operational and its revenue (of the order of about ₹3,000 crore every year) will go to a newly created National Clean Energy Fund (NECF), which will be used to finance innovative projects in clean energy technologies and to harness renewable energy sources to reduce dependence on fossil fuels. From the Fund, allocation of ₹200 crore has already been proposed for environment remediation programmes and another ₹200 crore for the Green India Mission.

7.127. Funds can also be established outside the Government. This is particularly important for private sector industry, even more so small and medium enterprises, who will find it difficult to access the National Clean Energy Fund in the Government Public Account. It would be simpler and more useful to set up a 'Carbon Trust' or a 'Low Carbon Fund' managed by an autonomous body like the Bureau of Energy Efficiency, into which collections from an 'Energy Efficiency Surcharge or Levy', as suggested in the industry section, could be deposited. The collections, even though small, could be supplemented by block grants from the National Clean Energy Fund under the Government, and indeed some international sources of finance. This could go a long way in meeting the demands of the private industry.

7.128. Given the importance of supporting the development of clean energy technologies, a separate window could be opened in the Fund to support development of early stage technologies and/or supporting diffusion, deployment and adoption of commercially available but high cost climate friendly technologies. Such measures could be taken in the mode of public–private partnerships. We could also create a 'priority' credit facility through the scheduled commercial banks to help finance their low carbon efforts, while interest subvention could be dovetailed with the Trust fund suggested above. To summarise, a clearly planned strategy and mechanism for supporting diffusion, deployment and adoption of climate friendly technologies should be launched during the Twelfth Plan.

International Sources

7.129. The intensity of domestic mitigation response depends rather significantly on the multilateral response to climate change. According to the UNFCCC, international financial support is to be provided to developing countries to enable them to take voluntary actions for mitigation and adaptation. Even though resources are scarce, India has been making specific budgetary outlays to address the challenge of climate change. However, domestic resources fall far short of the actual requirements. Expert Group on Low Carbon Strategies has explicitly stated in its Interim Report that aggressive mitigation cannot be achieved unless substantial international help, both in terms of financial resources and transfer of technology, is forthcoming.

7.130. A major channel for mobilising funds to the developing countries is likely to be the Green Climate Fund that is still under construction. At the same time, the World Bank (Climate Investment Fund) and other multilateral agencies are offering their funds to be used for climate action on the basis of agreed terms and conditions. The expected funds flow through the Green Climate Fund, and other bilateral and multilateral channels, will enhance India's capacity to address the climate challenge. It is important to ensure funds flows through these sources are indeed 'new and additional resources', and their terms of finance are in accordance with the multilateral rules of climate change. Unfortunately, the promises made through the Conference of Parties and recommendations of the High Level Panel on Climate Change Finance are yet to be implemented.

7.131. One way of differentiating between domestic and international sources of finance is the co-benefits framework mentioned above. Policy measures that generate adequate development co-benefits should be funded domestically, while those which primarily provide climate benefits should be funded by international sources. Even measures with adequate co-benefits may require international financing, if the initial investment is very large. Thus, actions which generate climate benefits along with development co-benefits should be the ones that should be categorised as the Nationally Appropriate Mitigation Actions (NAMAs).

Carbon Markets and Clean Development Mechanism

7.132. CDM is an international mechanism for emissions trading that helps developing countries gain some financial resources through sale of emission reduction certificates to developed countries, while enabling them to meet their emission reduction targets. The market for such trading is either compliance-based such as the one created under Kyoto Protocol, or voluntary in nature. India has been an active player in the Clean Development Mechanism and the National CDM Authority (NCDMA) in the Ministry of Environment & Forest has so far accorded Host Country Approval to over 2000 projects. These projects have the potential of facilitating an overall inflow of approximately US $ 7.07 billion in the year 2012, provided all of them get registered. Interestingly, most of the projects in India are unilateral in nature, wherein the project entity itself undertakes the initial investment, and aims to sell the Certified Emission Reduction (CER) units in the spot market rather than selling them in the forward markets.

7.133. Efforts are being made to increase participation of financial institutions/banks in financing voluntary projects, including the bundling of small projects which may reduce transaction costs and increase the average project size. A programme for capacity building to help industry adopt new and more efficient methodologies, such as programmatic CDM projects, is also being considered. However, the ability of international carbon markets to act as a stable source of adequate finance for domestic mitigation actions in developing countries is limited, because of the uncertainties about the scale of emissions reduction in the 2nd commitment period under the Kyoto Protocol. Further, in some of the key markets such as that of the Europen Union, unilateral restrictions are being imposed on sale of CERs from major developing countries in terms of eligibility, additionality criteria, sectoral caps, so on. In brief, the contribution of CDM to real technology transfer is limited, and as market prices remain depressed and volatile, considerable uncertainty prevails over its future.

7.134. Innovative domestic markets mechanisms are being evolved under the Perform, Achieve & Trade (PAT) Scheme that is being implemented by the Bureau of Energy Efficiency for designated industries under the provision of Energy Conservation Act 2010. Efforts are being made to support this scheme by creating a Partial Risk Guarantee Fund with help from the Global Environmental Facility. However, this scheme is not suitable for the small and medium industry, for which new forms of financial support and capacity building are needed.

7.135. Renewable Energy Certificates is another attempt at creating domestic markets through regulatory interventions at the state level. It may, however, be easier to deepen the existing quasi-markets in the power sector so that renewable power achieves grid parity faster.

7.136. The potential for these domestic measures to link with global carbon markets remains unclear, largely due to lack of clarity in the international negotiation process. Until such clarity emerges, the most that can be expected are loosely linked regional markets. We must be prepared to link with them, though we cannot expect substantial resource flow from this source in the short term. India's actions for climate change will, therefore, need to be financed from a pool of resources consisting of the domestic resources, international carbon finance and multilateral funds available to India in accordance with the agreed multilateral rules of the UNFCCC.

Way Forward

7.137. India faces the twin challenges of adaptation and mitigation. As a country with many critical sectors and regions that are highly climate-sensitive, there are significant costs in addressing the impact of climate variability and change. At the same time, as a signatory to the UNFCCC, India is expected to undertake mitigation actions consistent with the multilateral framework.

7.138. India has already taken decisive steps in this regard. Over the Eleventh Plan Period, it initiated the National Action Plan on Climate Change, which is monitored by a body no less than the Prime Minister's Council for Climate Change. It has voluntarily announced a domestic goal for reducing the emission intensity of its GDP. It has set up an Indian Network for Climate Change Assessment for making periodic assessment of climate variability and change. It has also set up an Expert Group to evolve Low Carbon Strategies for Inclusive Growth, which has made important recommendations for power, industry, transport, buildings and forestry sectors.

7.139. As adaptation is the urgent need of communities that are vulnerable to climate change, regular and periodical assessment of vulnerability in different sectors and preparation of adaptation strategies should be part of sectoral plans of the relevant Ministries. Climate change concern should permeate all processes of planning in the long term, and certain sectors where the needs are urgent, such assessments should be mounted urgently and integrated into the sectoral strategy.

7.140. As we embark on the Twelfth Plan, the NAPCC, like all major flagship programmes, needs to be reorganised in accordance with the updated priorities. As already mentioned, for any mission to succeed, it must have separable objectives, dedicated implementation machinery and adequate funding. For objectives which fail to meet this test, it is better to identify a short list of 'policy thrust areas', which could be separately listed under the NAPCC, and yet, be regularly monitored by the Prime Minister's Council. Accordingly, a reorganised framework for the NAPCC has been presented in Box 7.7.

NOTE
1. 'Energy and Environmental Sustainability: An Approach for India', Mckinsey & Co., New Delhi, 2009; 'National Energy Map for India, Technology Vision 2030', The Energy Resources Institute, New Delhi, 2006.

8

Science and Technology

INTRODUCTION

8.1. India's development plans have consistently emphasised the need for sustained investment in research and related activities leading to creation of substantial capacity and capabilities in science and technology (S&T). The fruits of this effort are evident in India's nuclear and space programmes, information and communication technology services, automotive and pharmaceuticals industries and other areas. As the Indian economy continues on the path of rapid, more inclusive and sustainable growth, it will be necessary to ensure that India's capabilities in S&T grow in strength. This is especially important if India is to become one of the major economies of the world over the next 20 years.

8.2. Many positive steps have been taken in recent years to give a boost to S&T efforts and these are having a steady, incremental effect. The Indian science sector has gained growth momentum during the last three years. Relative position of India with respect to scientific publications has improved from 15th in 2003 to 9th in 2010. Our science output has reached 3 per cent of the global output in 2010. While this is heartening, the current rate of improvement is slow and falls short of global standards in many areas. This is indicated by the fact that India's share of top 1 per cent publications is only 0.5 per cent, as of 2006, less than those of other Asian countries like China and South Korea.[1] Inventiveness in our basic science, as indicated by creation of intellectual property, is low and India's innovation system ranking varies between 50 and 60 among the nations. The country has major challenges to address in health, food, energy and environment and these can be met by doing quality science, showing greater inventiveness and achieving quality in product innovation. The challenges of a robust economy can be met by investing adequately in knowledge systems and achieving global leadership positions in some areas in the next two decades.

8.3. For a country of the size of India, with a robust scientific infrastructure and a vast pool of trained scientific manpower, productivity gains from a hike in research and development (R&D) spending could be huge. The country needs to move up from investing 1 per cent of gross domestic product (GDP) in the R&D sector to 2 per cent of GDP and more, as has been the case with several developed and emerging economies for quite some time now. This must be achieved through an additional government effort, but also a much increased private sector effort.

APPROACH TO THE TWELFTH PLAN

8.4. India made substantial investments in the R&D sector during the Eleventh Plan period laying a strong foundation for building a vibrant and dynamic S&T sector in the country. Average growth rate of publications from India in scientific journals is about 14 per cent during the last three years of the Eleventh Plan period. This is against the global average of 4.1 per cent during the same period. The share of scientific publications emanating from universities increased from 15 per cent in 2003 to 31 per cent in 2012. These are welcome changes as far as expanding the R&D base of the country is concerned. However, these remain incremental changes. What the country really needs at this point of time is a quantum jump, to position itself at par with the developed economies in the next two decades.

8.5. To face up to the increasing challenges in the new world order, the Indian S&T landscape needs to undergo a paradigm shift. It needs to evolve new delivery mechanisms for innovative deployment of technologies and business models for financing deployment of innovations. This calls for a well-enunciated Science, Technology and Innovation policy. The Twelfth Plan should therefore work to develop an ecosystem that addresses the national priority for sustainable, inclusive and accelerated growth taking along the education, research and corporate sectors. The corporate sector, in particular, must play a much larger role in building research capability as happens in other countries.

8.6. A competitive knowledge economy must be built on the pillars of: (*i*) an educational system that produces human resources which are employable and globally benchmarked; (*ii*) S&T pursued on an enormous scale to generate knowledge for long-term use and (*iii*) strategic translational research inspired by national needs and global opportunities. In pursuit of these objectives the Twelfth Plan should be geared to achieve the following:

- Evolve a new Science, Technology and Innovation policy to bring in more resources from both public and private sector for R&D for socially and strategically relevant projects and mainstream innovation-related activities with a focus on affordable and sustainable innovations;
- Catalyse a radical but participative transformation of the Indian S&T system by refocusing the efforts of the designated Departments/Agencies at:
  - National Focus—build partnership with identified players of the National Innovation System to build the scientific, technological and human resource niches for the country;
  - Organisational Focus—address the needs of each Department/Agency for achieving the goals in national focus and rigorously review the ongoing projects/programmes to phase out those which have by and large fulfilled their goals; and
  - Leadership Focus—stimulate the Department/Agency's leadership in identified domains of science, technology and human resource development.

- Ensure that S&T becomes an integral component of the national developmental processes by interconnecting competencies and research resources and strengthening interconnections with the weakly connected stakeholders to the R&D outputs;
- Increase the number of full-time researchers/scientists from the current level of 1.54 lakh to 2.50 lakh; the volume of publication outputs in basic research from a global share of 3 per cent to, say, 5 per cent; improve the global ranking from 9th to 6th by the end of the Twelfth Plan; focus on doubling the number of patents and increase the commercialisation of patent portfolio to 5–6 per cent from a level of less than 2 per cent;
- Increase R&D expenditure to 2 per cent of GDP and significantly enhance corporate sector R&D expenditure to at least 1 per cent of GDP by attracting investments and engaging the corporate sector in R&D through policy and reforms processes; earmark 10–15 per cent of public investment exclusively for public–private partnership (PPP) R&D to private sector through the competitive grant process with a stipulation that comparable provisions would be made by the private sector under PPP model;
- Provide more flexibility to the younger generation of scientists to pursue their ideas and greater mobility between industry, academia and R&D institutions; strengthen gender parity in R&D by way of mobility and women re-entry programmes; consolidate on the gains achieved during the Eleventh Plan in nurturing students to pursue science as a career;
- Build technology partnerships with States through new models of technological solutions, design, development and delivery;
- Initiate Grand Challenge Programmes and launch PAN-India missions to address national priorities

in various developmental sectors through bottom-up approach, particularly in the areas of Health, Water, Energy and Food through consortia of institutions and agencies cutting across public and private sectors; two major areas which require immediate focus during Twelfth Five Year Plan are Energy and Water;
- Encourage large Indian industries to establish globally benchmarked R&D centres on the lines of R&D centres set up by multinational companies (MNCs);
- Leverage the large-scale innovative component of strategic research spin-offs from defence, space and atomic energy for civilian benefits in a much larger segment.
- Create new Inter-University Centres (IUCs) and Inter-Institutional Centres (IICs) in chosen areas of Science and Engineering, which will provide access to state-of-the-art facilities and academic ambience for researchers in universities and academic institutions;
- Create new R&D institutions in trans-disciplinary science and engineering to achieve leadership positions;
- Create Peta-scale supercomputing facilities and provide high-performance computing for various applications such as climate modelling, weather prediction, aerospace engineering, computational biology, nuclear applications, earthquake simulations, animation in movies, national security and finance;
- Create an independent institutional arrangement for Technology Assessment capability.
- Bring in structural reforms in the S&T sector by creating new financial appraisal and audit mechanisms and a new personnel policy based on best global practices coupled with seamless mobility of S&T personnel;
- Partner with high-value global mega projects in the areas of contemporary scientific interest and technological relevance and enhance India's role in global mega projects such as India-based Neutrino Observatory, Thirty Meter Telescope, Square Kilometer Array, Next Generation Synchrotron and so on; and
- Enhance collaboration with reputed foreign universities/agencies towards addressing the scientific aspects of common interest and global in nature.

SPECIFIC FOCUS AREAS FOR THE TWELFTH PLAN

Enrichment of Knowledge Base

8.7. In 1985, the number of PhDs produced in India was in the range of 4,500 and the country figured among the top in the league of developing nations in the science sector. Since 1985, however, other emerging Asian economies invested heavily in R&D, blunting India's competitiveness in the S&T sector. None of the Indian institutions figure among the top 100 in the world. The full-time equivalent (FTE) R&D professionals in India have stagnated for long; India ranks 9th as far as FTE of R&D professionals are concerned. In scientific publications as well, India ranks 9th. The global share of Indian publications in most cited papers has also remained low.

8.8. The last few years show an improvement as far as some of these parameters are concerned, but if the country has to aim at positioning its R&D institutions among the top 50, or gaining the top three slots with respect to scientific publications or target a ranking of even 6th with respect to FTE, it will have to aim at quadrupling its R&D base, stimulate research where R&D productivity is relatively lower, provide challenges to institutions for global positioning including in intellectual property (IP) generation, establish new academies and institutions, build up large publicly funded and privately managed facilities to help researchers and adopt aggressive mechanisms to attract the Indian diaspora for R&D positions. Emphasis should also be given on strengthening linkages between universities, R&D institutions, science academies and industry.

8.9. India's established research centres from which R&D outputs are generated need to expand their personnel strength to give a boost to R&D outputs. Expanding the strength of R&D personnel in the established centres of R&D by about 10,000 within the Twelfth Plan period should be considered feasible. It is also imperative that the large latent potential in colleges, universities and some academic centres is tapped. Adequate measures for ensuring quality of research output should also be looked at.

8.10. Basic research in India should aim at cutting-edge science leading to impact-making discoveries. Investments in basic research may be sized to meet the aspirational goals of the research community during the Twelfth Plan period. Basic research supporting group and interdisciplinary efforts on grand challenges would require a new paradigm of R&D funding. Approaches for spotting, nurturing and encouraging sparks and talent in scientific research have to form one of the established strategies for promotion of basic research. In addition to support for emerging areas in various disciplines of science, there should also be a parallel effort to identify areas of national interest and gaps and promote basic research in such areas. Some orientation to basic research to combine relevance with excellence may be in order. Focus on the research areas of national relevance such as energy and food security, affordable health care and water-related areas needs to be accorded high priority.

S&T Human Resource Development and University Interaction

8.11. There is a close relationship between human resources in S&T and economic growth. Although the country has a vast network of schools, colleges and universities apart from national institutes and Indian Institutes of Technology (IITs), which have produced one of the largest pools of scientific manpower in the world, the global competitiveness of the S&T sector can only be achieved through much better quality. For this, the science education system, as it stands today, needs radical transformation.

8.12. Science teaching as a profession needs to be incentivised, accorded the respect it deserves and once again placed on a high pedestal. Equally important would be exposing these teachers at all levels in the country to the best global practices and pedagogy innovations to enable them to practise and spread superior methods of teaching and research. A scheme needs to be designed and developed jointly by the Ministry of Human Resource Development and the Ministry of S&T.

8.13. The quality of S&T education and research at the college and university levels needs to be improved to give an edge to the scientific task force coming out of these places of learning. There is now adequate evidence for significant gain in scientific outputs and citation frequencies when the university sector engages in S&T cooperation within the country and abroad. As one of the strategies, international cooperation for deployment needs to be scaled up manifold, for enriching quality of research in the university sector. IUCs have shown a positive impact on the university system. Several new IUCs in carefully chosen areas should be set up during the Twelfth Plan in newer areas such as Biodiversity and Genetic Epidemiology; Mathematical Modelling; Computer Science and Cyber Security; Cognitive Sciences; Advanced Materials, Manufacturing and Fabrication; Technology Management; and Interdisciplinary Approaches in Humanities, Social Science and Natural Sciences.

Aligning S&T to Developmental Needs

8.14. In addition to R&D in high science and strategic technology areas that would enable the country to position itself at the world level, there are several areas that require significant S&T inputs to generate solutions for issues that are significant for the country's development goals, in the context of both industrial development and rural development. These include energy, water and sanitation, farm production, health care, waste disposal, computing and communications, e-infrastructure, cyber security and so on.

8.15. A strategy needs to be evolved for implementation of R&D programmes focused on social and public goods for: (*i*) connecting competencies and research resources for scaling and impact; (*ii*) mounting Grand Challenge programmes on topics of national interest; (*iii*) adopting different funding strategies for basic and translational research under Extra Mural Research models; (*iv*) strengthening Intra Mural Research mechanisms for public and social goods in agencies like Council of Scientific and Industrial Research (CSIR); (*v*) forging State–Centre technology partnerships and technology coalitions among R&D agencies and (*vi*) promoting PPPs for public and social good by developing new models.

8.16. The Twelfth Plan must find ways of connecting States and socio-economic Ministries with R&D outputs leading to public and social goods as a priority. For deployment of readily available technologies in States, the following need to be evolved: (*i*) a synergy among the S&T and socio-economic sector, (*ii*) a policy decision by socio-economic Ministries to allocate a certain minimum percentage (say 1–2 per cent) of their overall budget for supporting R&D, (*iii*) setting up of joint centres by the socio-economic Ministries in R&D institutions and universities, (*iv*) participation of socio-economic Ministries in PPP projects supported by the science sector and (*v*) involving enterprises for effective implementation of R&D solutions arising out of synergies among science sector and socio-economic Ministries. Focus should also be on creating start-ups and utilising the cutting-edge knowledge base.

8.17. The involvement of States in R&D in the country is at present relatively low. Most States have not established suitable mechanisms for full utilisation of technologies emanating from public-funded research in the country. State Councils for S&T in many States remain as weak links between the national science sector and the State Governments. Allocation of States in their own budgets for S&T remains relatively insignificant. Special mechanisms need to be developed to promote the technology relationships between the Centre and the States. Establishment of special competitive fund for States for absorption of indigenous technologies could form one of the strategies for creating demand pull for technologies in the States. Emphasis should be given for connecting the State Councils for S&T to R&D organisations like CSIR, Indian Council of Medical Research (ICMR) and Defence Research and Development Organisation (DRDO) and so on.

8.18. The Indian R&D system is predominantly government funded. It is important that the corporate sector (both public and the private) come forward to fund R&D programmes directed towards national developmental goals. The target of total expenditure in R&D increasing to 2 per cent of GDP by the end of the Twelfth Plan could be achieved by about 1 per cent in the public sector and 1 per cent in the corporate sector, including public sector undertakings (PSUs). At present, the resources devoted to R&D by large public sector organisations are pitiably small. They need to be incentivised to make larger provisions for both in-house R&D as well as R&D in research institutions and universities, both public and private. The step taken during the Eleventh Plan by Bureau of Public Enterprises to include R&D in the memorandum of understanding (MoU) of a PSU with the government is a move in the right direction. These sectors should spend 2–3 per cent of their sales turnover on R&D contracting out research to institutions and universities. The current levels of coupling between the R&D and manufacturing sectors are weak. High priority to PPPs that would ensure flow of innovation into industrial manufacturing leading to wealth creation, thus, has to be accorded. Industry needs to identify critical technology areas where through the partnership with publicly funded R&D system they can become global leaders.

8.19. The corporate sector both from public and private sectors too needs to be encouraged and incentivised to set up R&D centres just as the R&D centres set up in India by some of the world's leading research institutions, as R&D activities by MNCs have created enclaves for world-class technological development and have helped the creation of a pool of highly skilled scientists and technologists through setting up of their R&D centres in India. Thus, it is crucial to evolve new strategies and mechanisms to propel investment by industry if 1 per cent of GDP investment on R&D is to be targeted by this sector.

8.20. The strategic research sector could play an effective role in meeting the national developmental goals in non-strategic areas, whether it is space technology, nuclear technology or defence research. Several technologies developed by the strategic sector could trigger successful spin-offs for social and industrial sectors. A suitable mechanism to provide thrust to utilising outputs of strategic research for the social and industrial sectors needs to be worked out and created.

Implementation of National Missions

8.21. Realising that national challenges cannot be tackled without nationally coordinated mission mode programmes involving interdepartmental and inter-ministerial collaborations, PAN-India S&T missions in select areas such as (i) Agriculture, (ii) Water, (iii) Energy, (iv) Environment and (v) Health need to be given priority.

Agriculture Sector

8.22. The Department of Biotechnology (DBT) proposes to support 10 agricultural universities through long-term R&D grants for promoting R&D on agriculture for public and social good. Synergy and connecting competencies of institutions under Indian Council of Agricultural Research (ICAR) with the research programmes supported by the six science departments form the selected approach for R&D on agriculture. As an example, synthesising R&D outputs from agro-metrological services of Ministry of Earth Sciences (MoES), advisory services of State remote sensing centres and State-based Spatial Data Infrastructure initiatives of Department of Space (DOS), National Spatial Data Infrastructure and National Geographic Information Systems (NGIS), fertiliser and other agrochemical technology solutions from CSIR, food processing technologies from both CSIR and Department of Atomic Energy (DAE), translation research in molecular breeding emanating from the efforts of DBT and technology deployment support to States for implementation of technologies and services by Department of Science & Technology (DST) would form a strong impact. Secondary agriculture, climate-resilient agriculture, water-saving agriculture, technologies for reducing food wastages as well as indigenous manufacture of fertilisers, precision agriculture for water-starved agro-climatic zones and international S&T cooperation for enhancing water and land productivity would form the priority areas of the six departments. The regulatory aspects for genetically modified (GM)-related crops will also be given due emphasis. Biotechnology Regulatory Authority of India (BRAI) Bill is considered as essential for streamlining regulation of all modern biotechnology products.

Water Sector

8.23. R&D for development of technologies for managing water-related challenges is being undertaken by almost all the six science departments in association with the line departments of Central and State Governments. While the DoS is engaged in resource mapping of water, MoES has developed and demonstrated technologies for Low Temperature Thermal Desalination (LTTD) and DAE has been developing and demonstrating a range of technologies including reverse osmosis (RO) and multi-stage flash for sea water desalination. CSIR has developed significant knowledge base on water, ranging from source finding to mapping of water resources, from quality assessment to enhancing potability of water and from recycling to waste water treatment. The technologies on flocculation and chlorination currently in vogue do not remove trace organics, metals and pathogens in treated drinking water and, therefore, R&D in ion exchange technique and nano-filtration processes need to be taken up. The DST is implementing a technology mission on Winning, Augmentation and Renovation of water where solutions to water-related challenges are being implemented and demonstrated in several locations. Therefore, in the design, development and delivery of the Twelfth Plan programmes, end-to-end solutions of water-related challenges by integrating R&D efforts of the six science departments with the line departments of both centre and State are to be given thrust.

Energy Sector

8.24. For achieving the full objectives of the National Solar Energy Mission, technology breakthroughs are required to increase the conversion efficiencies and to lower the costs of delivered power, for which it would be necessary to engage mainstream scientists drawn from the entire S&T sector of the country with expertise in relevant areas. R&D for clean energy systems is of paramount importance. On energy R&D, almost all six science departments are engaged in either performing research or supporting R&D or both. Similarly, clean coal technology, fuel cells, hydrogen energy, materials for harvesting both light and heat, new inorganic chemistry for converting coal into liquid fuels, bio-inspired inorganic materials for artificial photosynthesis and bio-refinery for agro-wastes as energy sources also need focus. Since energy sector works in regulated environments, it is necessary for the R&D sector to develop adequate synergies with Bureau of Energy Efficiency and the concerned departments. The MoES is engaged in the assessment of wind, wave and tidal energy potential as a part of tapping renewal energy, including gas hydrate exploration. Thus, collaboration and cooperation in areas of technology leads where synergies could benefit the R&D systems need to be promoted, including that from the defence research system during the Twelfth Plan period.

Environment Sector
8.25. R&D for controlling pollution of the local environments and emission of green house gases for mitigating global climate change demands different approaches. Whereas the R&D for mitigating pollution is promoted best through intramural research in domain area organisations, national capacity on climate change science needs to be developed over wider cross section of scientists and R&D professionals. Accordingly, under the National Action Plan for Climate Change, DST shall coordinate two missions under which formation of knowledge networks and thematic centres has been proposed by DST. These actions are focused on stimulating the latent and inherent capacities of the universities and research institutions. PPP for R&D for adaptation and mitigation of climate change will be another tool to be used. R&D sector may need to develop technology plans for solving the environment-related challenges of such sectors in association with the relevant line Ministry, and accordingly efforts of all the players need to be significantly synergised in the area of R&D on environment during the Twelfth Plan period. The MoES has been monitoring the health of coastal waters of India which would be of immense importance to UN endeavour on global assessment of marine environment.

Health Sector
8.26. Affordable human health care is an area of high priority to the country. There are several parallel efforts of high significance. Indian Council of Medical Research is the important national agency for R&D on human health care. The focus of the agency is generally on delivery of human health-care tools and public health–related R&D at this time. The agency is also well poised for delivery of R&D outputs. DBT is aggressively promoting research in human health care sector through both intra- and extramural mechanisms, as well as PPP models. CSIR has launched a major initiative on Open Source Drug Discovery (OSDD) and large number of programmes relating to R&D on human health care. In view of the high relevance of the R&D efforts for the country, some of these initiatives of the six science departments might have to be fostered as strategy for the Twelfth Plan. Human health care is an area where regulatory processes require advanced scientific knowledge and technical expertise. Speed in regulatory processes without sacrifice to the correctness of decisions demands applications of many modern technologies and R&D outputs and tools. Current mechanisms of regulation require a revisit. Biomedical Regulatory Authority Bill is considered essential if the indigenous manufacture of biomedical devices were to gain momentum and access to affordable health care system were to be enlarged. There is a strong case for promotion of PPPs for R&D on Drug and pharmaceuticals. Particularly, investment requirements for drug discovery are large. Special schemes for promotion of drug discovery and support for phase III clinical trials may be required in diseases of national interest. India could engage in basic research on disease biology for gaining new insights for discovering drugs including from marine organisms.

8.27. For building programme synergies and implementation on the above socially relevant missions, a special task force needs to be created. A separate PAN-India Mission Fund needs to be built-in in every department so that this fund could be deployed for building synergies among the programmes proposed by various departments and address gap areas. The Twelfth Plan emphasises that PAN-India mission mode projects addressing national needs and priorities may be launched through extensive participation of stakeholders to achieve the goals and targets in a defined time frame.

Mega Science Projects

8.28. While PAN-India missions could bring about synergies in R&D programmes at the national level, the efforts need to be made to position Indian researchers at the global level. This involves participation at the international level in exciting experiments like in European Organization for Nuclear Research (CERN) and International Thermonuclear Experimental Reactor (ITER). During the Twelfth Plan period, India needs to invest into developing following major Mega facilities: (*i*) Laser Interferometer Gravitational Wave Observatory (LIGO) Experiments; (*ii*) India-based Neutrino Observatory (INO); (*iii*) Thirty Meter Telescope (TMT); (*iv*) Square Kilometre Array (SKA); (*v*) National Large Solar Telescope and (*vi*) Next Generation Synchrotron.

8.29. These mega science projects would be coordinated by DAE and DST through appropriate funding sharing mechanism. Besides, the above mega science projects, each department will also have mega projects already built in their budget.

8.30. Besides providing a quantum leap for scientific research, many of the above international collaborations will open up possibilities of creating technological capabilities for India. It is also time to embark upon indigenous efforts to build Peta-scale supercomputer capacities and capabilities for the country's requirements that will place India among the top five supercomputing power in the world.

8.31. While Box 8.1 gives a glimpse of collaborative research through which India's competency to deliver good on global research agenda has been demonstrated, Box 8.3 provides a novel path to launch National Biodesign alliance through collaborative technology innovation for leveraging international collaboration, thereby strengthening national programmes.

Strategies for Transformational Changes

8.32. In order to promote transformational changes within the S&T sector and gain global competiveness with respect to S&T output indicators, it is necessary

---

Box 8.1
Discovery of Higgs Boson—Indian Contribution

During the Tenth and Eleventh Five Year Plan, India has taken major initiatives relating to mega science programmes by collaborating with international partners. These include themes related to High Energy Physics, Astronomy, Thermonuclear Fusion and Synchrotron supported material science research. This model is turning out to be very beneficial in the context of India's involvement in frontier science research, development of capabilities in high technology and facilitating the creation of new generation of scientists working for PhD as well as postdoctoral scientific research. The most recent example of this strategy of science collaboration relates to the Indian participation in the Large Hadron Collider (LHC). Indian Institutions joined the large LHC experiments at a pretty early stage, starting from 1994.

India contributed high technology items for Compact Muon Solenoid (CMS) experiment, which was a key detector facilitating the discovery of possibly the most important particle in High Energy Physics, the Higgs Boson. Further, India also contributed to the design and development of A Large Ion Collider Experiment (ALICE) looking for quark-gluon plasma which is important to answer some key questions in fundamental Physics beyond standard model. Both these experiments produced large amounts of data which need to be processed quickly. This called for creating a distributed computer environment and opened up a new computing regime called Grid computing. Indians not only contributed in the development of this field by developing the software but also set up a CMS computing centre resulting in the overall computing infrastructure for the experiments. The scientific team that participated in the CMS experiment included 33 PhD physicists from India. Further, the ALICE experiment has participation from several Indian universities and other institutions with 36 faculty, 22 engineers and 30 students. Together, the two experiments, CMS and ALICE, involved a total expenditure of about ₹150 crore besides kind contribution of about ₹300 crore involving many high-technology items from India.

This example of a collaborative research has demonstrated India's competency to deliver on global research agenda and provides an opportunity to work on similar model in the Twelfth Five Year Plan. Some of the mega science projects being considered in the Twelfth Plan are Laser Interferometer Gravitational Wave Observatory, National Large Solar Telescope and India-based Neutrino Observatory, besides the ongoing International Thermonuclear Experimental Reactor (ITER). These envisage adopting similar models to keep India in the forefront of scientific research, development of high technology capability, innovative computing techniques and creation of specialised human resource base.

to make strategic interventions during the Twelfth Plan period. These include: (*i*) increasing density of scientists by about 60 per cent, (*ii*) interconnecting competencies, (*iii*) synergy development of research resources, (*iv*) establishment of performance–reward relationships, (*v*) engaging in rewarding and mutual international partnerships, (*vi*) investing larger resources into performing individuals through grant model of funding, (*vii*) deploying more effectively the tool of PPP for R&D and (*viii*) creating an enabling policy environment for sustainable innovation ecosystem.

8.33. To this end, SAC to PM under National Vision for Science has suggested the development of a new, expansive personnel policy for R&D sector, based on global best practices. The National Vision also recommends re-engineering and rationalisation of processes for the science sector to increase the speed of decision-making, without compromising rules and processes, for accelerated and transformational changes and enabling youthful leadership opportunities. The SAC-PM has also suggested that the audit discipline needs to be modified from procedure- or process-based to performance- and objective-based system. In the Twelfth Plan, the suggested structural reforms for S&T sector need to be pursued so as to derive the best out of it. More recently, SAC to PM has also prepared outlines of an agenda for action on the S&T inputs to pressing national problems which will be pursued for implementation.

Performance Measurement Systems

8.34. For Indian science to gain global competitiveness in all its dimensions, it is essential to develop suitable measurement systems for the science, technology and innovation output indicators for India. Appropriate measurement systems and comparative analysis of India vis-à-vis other emerging economies needs to form a basis for outcome-based performance. It may accordingly be desirable to adopt strategic planning for positioning India in niche positions in areas of comparative strength rather than to invest through a broad spectrum approach.

Review of the Eleventh Plan Programmes

8.35. High priority was accorded by the government during the Eleventh Plan period for investments into S&T for deriving maximum benefits for the society and knowledge generation for capacity building. Major priorities of the Eleventh Plan for S&T sector have been:

- Setting up national-level mechanism for evolving policies and providing direction to basic research
- Enlarging the pool of scientific manpower and strengthening the S&T infrastructure and attracting and retaining young people to careers in science
- Implementing selected national flagship programmes that have direct bearing on the technological competitiveness of the country in a mission mode
- Establishing globally competitive research facilities and centres of excellence
- Developing new models of PPPs in higher education, particularly for research in universities and high technology areas
- New ways and means of catalysing industry–academy collaborations
- Promoting strong collaborations with advanced countries including participation in mega international science.

8.36. Significant initiatives/contributions have been made for each of these priority areas. Detailed account of these is provided in the respective section of the S&T departments.

STRATEGY FOR THE TWELFTH PLAN

8.37. In spite of some positive signs, India's performance in science is yet to match her potential. The emphasis during the Twelfth Plan by the six science departments and agencies is to consolidate the gains of the Eleventh Plan period and propose new initiatives with the objective of enhancing global competitiveness of the Indian R&D system. All departments and agencies have developed programmes based on their own niche and position in the mind-to-market chain.

8.38. All the six departments of science sector must make elaborate efforts to meet the aspirations of their stakeholders. This section below presents the summaries of the proposals of each department for Twelfth Plan programmes. The deliverables and targets from the S&T sector as a whole and those from the departments are provided in Annexure 8.1 given at the end of the chapter.

Department of Science & Technology

Twelfth Plan Objectives/Thrust

8.39. The DST, engaged in the formulation of S&T related policies and promotion of R&D through Extra Mural Research Schemes has mounted a large number of proactive schemes and measures during the Eleventh Plan period. There are some incremental improvements in the S&T outputs of the Indian science sector. The department is committed to align its Twelfth Plan programmes and initiatives to support the overall plan of the Indian Science, Technology and Innovation sector towards global leadership. One of the strategies evolved for implementation of Twelfth Plan proposals of the Indian science sector is connecting competencies and research resources. Several new initiatives of DST for the Twelfth Plan period have been prepared taking into account national needs and likely impact. However, such initiatives should be preceded by a careful and critical review of all ongoing programmes and consolidation of successful schemes as well as the new Eleventh Plan initiatives. While formulating the Twelfth Plan programmes, the department has adopted an output-directed development path and related inputs to expected and targeted goals as well as likely impacts.

8.40. The significant achievements of Department of Science & Technology during Eleventh Plan are given in Box 8.2.

Box 8.2
Significant Achievements/Development of DST during Eleventh Plan Period

ORGANISATIONAL
- National Science and Engineering Research Board (SERB) has been established as an autonomous funding body and has assumed the major role from the erstwhile Science and Engineering Research Council (SERC).
- DST has also established new institutions, namely, National Innovation Foundation (NIF), Ahmedabad; Institute for Advanced Studies in Science and Technology, Guwahati; National Center of Molecular Materials, Thiruvananthapuram; and Institute of Nano Science and Technology, Mohali.

PROMOTIONAL
- The SERC, one of the largest schemes for promoting basic research in the country supported about 1800–2000 new projects annually, which has resulted in more than 7500 scientific publications. Five hundred departments were supported under the fund for improvement of S&T infrastructure in the form of the state-of-the-art R&D facilities in universities and higher educational institutes.
- Promotion of University Research and Scientific Excellence (PURSE) and Consolidation of University Research, Innovation and Excellence (CURIE) have been launched to improve and support the R&D in the universities.
- Two hundred and seven JC Bose National Fellowships, 155 Ramanujan Fellowships and 323 Boyscast Fellowships were awarded to support excellence in research. A major scheme known as INSPIRE for attracting talent in science and for nurturing students right from the school level has been initiated and around 14000 students have been awarded SHE Scholarships; more than 6 lakh awards for students in classes ranging from Class VI to X and 1200 INSPIRE Fellowships for pursuing doctoral degrees have been granted, and INSPIRE faculty awards have been made to 74 postdoctoral scholars.

S&T HIGHLIGHTS

- Several technologies aimed at specific end use have been developed, which include: atmospheric plasma processing system for angora wool, arsenic removal technology using microbial-cum-adsorbent route and ceramic membrane–reverse osmosis based iron removal plant for removal of iron and salinity in drinking water; development of large chemical vapour deposition (CVD)-coated silicon carbide substrates for space optics applications.
- Sree Chitra Tirunal Institute for Medical Sciences and Technology, Thiruvananthapuram, has successfully commercialised indigenous technologies like Chitra Heart Valve, Bioceramic Bone Graft, Opthalmic Sponge and so on. International Advanced Research Centre for Powder Metallurgy and New Materials (ARCI), Hyderabad, has developed and supplies IR transparent ZnS domes to DRDO for the missile programme, light-weighted SiC substrates for satellite mirrors for Indian Space Research Organisation (ISRO) and oxide dispersion strengthened (ODS) steel for Fast Breeder Reactor (FBR) clad tubes. Raman Research Institute (RRI), Bangalore, studied re-ionisation era of early universe and also published papers on generation of Nano Scale heat conductors which has practical application in minimising heat dissipation in computer connectors.
- Under Drugs and Pharmaceutical Research Programme, 25 collaborative R&D projects and 15 new facilities like the clinical research facility to develop stem cell technologies and regenerative medicine have been implemented with leading industries. The programme has resulted in filing of 10 product patents. Some of the important products that have been developed include: (*i*) BONISTA for osteoporosis; (*ii*) RECEPTOL for the management of HIV/AIDS and (*iii*) RHOCLONE for Hemolytic disease of the new born (HDN). Several industrial leads on psoriasis, migraine, malaria and anti-glaucoma are being taken up for different phases (Phase I, II and III) of clinical trial. A drug for fighting malaria developed through PPP.

MAJOR FACILITIES

- Several high-end R&D facilities have been established. Some of the notable ones are Clean room facilities at IISc, Bangalore; Ultra High Resolution Aberration Corrected Transmission Electron Microscope (TEM) at Jawaharlal Nehru Centre for Advanced Scientific Research (JNCASR), Bangalore; and Centre for Knowledge Management of Nano Science and Technology (CKMNT) at ARCI, Hyderabad. Three accelerator-based research facilities have also been established at IIT, Kharagpur, Kurukhestra University and University of Allahabad. In addition, an India–Japan beam line was established for nano materials research at the photon at KEK, Tsukuba, Japan. India has also leased 13 beam lines equivalent times at the PETRA-III synchrotron radiation facility at DESY-Nano sized X-ray source for access by Indian scientists.
- The following major atmospheric observatory facilities have been established/being created: (*i*)1.3 m Optical Telescope; (*ii*)3.6 m Devasthal Optical Telescope; (*iii*) high-energy pulse LIDA system; (*iv*) fabrication and development of an Ultraviolet Imaging Telescope (UVIT) as a payload for the dedicated Indian astronomy mission ASTROSTAT; (*v*) design, development and execution of experiments for studying the solar corona through total solar eclipses; (*vi*) High Altitude Gamma Ray (HAGAR) telescope system at the Indian Astronomical Observatory, Hanle.

Twelfth Five Year Plan Programmes

8.41. Basic research in frontier areas of S&T will remain a priority of the R&D sector. Since basic research is expected to give rise to applications in the long-term horizon, investments into basic research are generally made on the basis of competitive grant model employing concepts of Extra Mural Research funding. Among the various departments and arms of the government, the DST has emerged as the major source of Extra Mural

Research funding in the country. In recent times, the department has also established Science and Engineering Research Board as an autonomous agency and alternative mechanism for supporting basic research in India.

Scenario in Basic Research—Strategies for Global Positioning of India

8.42. The DST has adapted, to the extent possible, evidence-based approaches to make its proposals for investments during the Twelfth Plan for supporting basic research. DST has made an attempt to compare the per capita outputs of Indian scientists in basic research in terms of scientific publications and developed national strategies for improving the relative position of India in global ranking. The current rate of growth of scientific publications is more than 14 per cent during the last three years. If Indian rank were to improve from the current 9th to 6th during the Twelfth Plan period in basic research-based on volume, the total number of scientific publications should increase from the current levels to at least 62,500 per year.

8.43. The SERB scheme would be strengthened during the Twelfth Plan. In addition to current models of project funding, SERB proposes to invest into researchers of proven record and establish about 200–250 centres based on Grant Model with fixed budgets and reward–performance relationships. 'Centres of Excellence' around a group of individuals would also be established. Advanced centres in scientific research around performing scientists in the cutting-edge areas of science of relevance within the country are proposed.

8.44. *Rejuvenation of Research in the University Sector*: During the last three years, DST has been investing into university sector through PURSE based on volume of scientific publications and h-indices of these universities. The success of the PURSE scheme is evident from the growth of number of universities eligible for support increasing from 14 in 2008 to 44 in 2010. The collective share of publications of the universities receiving support through PURSE has improved from less than 15 per cent to 25 per cent as of 2010. Analysis of data has shown that among the top 50 Indian institutions engaged in scientific publications, 23 are from the university sector. Further analysis of citations per paper for publications emanating from the university sector indicates that as many as seven universities register citations per paper for the data corresponding to the period 2004–09 above the national average of 3.47 per paper. All the 23 universities seem to gain in citations per paper when they collaborate with other international R&D centres. New schemes to promote the international S&T cooperation for the performing universities are proposed during the Twelfth Plan.

8.45. *Performance Observation in Science Sector*: Overall, the percentage share of scientific publications emanating from individuals and various institutions receiving support from DST (without discounting contributions from funding by other sources to the same researchers and institutions) could be assessed as high as 40–42 per cent of India's publications in Science Citation Index (SCI)-indexed journals currently. However, the R&D outputs of the individuals and institutions could not be entirely attributed to the support extended by DST for basic research. DST proposes to establish Science Observatory as well as Technology Observatory for monitoring the S&T output indicators of the Indian R&D system without cause attributions. Such measures are considered necessary as planning tools and decision support systems.

8.46. *National SERB—New Vehicle of Funding Basic Research*: SERB is emerging as a new body and mechanism for promoting basic research in the country. SERC is a national flagship for Extra Mural Research support. Ongoing programmes of SERC for investigator-based research grant models and investments into individual scientists based on track records will be dealt by SERB. The new body is expected to offer the benefits of (*i*) re-engineering and rationalisation of governance processes to suit the nature and efficiency of funding agencies, (*ii*) enrolling other arms of the government and private sector into R&D funding and (*iii*) flexibility and speed in research funding. Some of the new initiatives proposed by DST for investing into individuals would be delivered through SERB. DST proposes to invest up to 35 per cent of its budgetary resources through SERB during the Twelfth Plan period for supporting the ongoing and some new initiatives of DST.

8.47. *Strategic Interventions for India Emerging as One of the Top Six Global Powers in S&T Sector*: Indian aspiration to emerge as one of the top six scientific powers in basic research would call for twin strategies. For increasing the volume share of scientific publications from India to reach the top six nations in the world, the FTE of R&D personnel may need to be increased to about 2,50,000. This could be partially accomplished by (*i*) increasing the density of scientists in performing institutions and (*ii*) unleashing the latent potentials available in the academic sector in colleges and universities. DST has proposed schemes for increasing the volume and density of R&D professionals by enlisting researchers from the university sector.

Approaches for Strengthening and Expanding R&D Base

8.48. *Programmatic Approaches*: During the Twelfth Plan period, DST has proposed a number of new initiatives. They are: (*i*) 1,000 overseas doctoral scholarships, (*ii*) 250 overseas postdoctoral fellowships, (*iii*) women mobility scheme for employed scientists, (*iv*) Enlarging the PI base to include about 500 teachers from colleges and universities, (*v*) Start-up research grant for Indian diaspora undertaking faculty assignments in Indian academia, (*vi*) 'Disha' for women in science programme, (*vii*) building educators for science teaching, (*viii*) challenge awards for institutions for global positioning and (*ix*) National Centres for Advanced Research.

8.49. Technology Development and Deployment: The DST has responded to the changing stakeholder aspirations with respect to Technology Development and Deployment programmes. Whereas the programmes of the DST under Technology Development and Deployment in the previous plans were generally focused on demonstrating the viabilities of technologies developed by public-funded institutions, proposals for the Twelfth Plan under this objective have been developed under a different paradigm. User needs for technologies have been accorded high priority in selection of technology goals. Technology platform for solving real-life challenges is a novel approach proposed. Technology platforms are expected to enlarge the scope of work of DST in the technology arena. The department has proposed a total of eight platforms. Climate change programmes, modernisation of Survey of India (SoI) and National Atlas and Thematic Organization (NATMO), and district-level technology interventions for increases in per capita incomes are new objectives of the Twelfth Plan programmes. Promoting technology deployment will receive as much focus as technology development. Technology solutions for agricultural, chemicals, water, energy requirement, environmental sustainability and affordable human health care would form areas of thrust. Technology Mission for biomedical devices engineering and technology is proposed for implementation during the Twelfth Plan period.

8.50. *Partnerships and Alliances Involving DST and Programmes for Serving the Social Contract of S&T*: Partnerships and alliances for technology development and deployment form essential linkage capitals. Objectives of the programmes under partnerships and alliances are generally based on reciprocity and parity principle for international cooperation and for value generation of R&D outputs from public-funded research under national linkages. New mechanisms have been proposed for PPPs and Centre–State Technology partnerships. Established mechanisms are proposed to be employed for bilateral and multi-lateral S&T cooperation. Contributions to PAN-India missions, like Joint (Virtual) centres and North East Centre for Technology Applications and Reach form new schemes. Social contract of S&T has remained an important programme of the department. DST has recently constituted a Council for Science and Technology for Rural India (CSTRI) providing new mechanisms for delivering technologies to the rural India. Special schemes for vulnerable sections of the society will be taken through CSTRI.

8.51. *Building Capability and Capacity in Supercomputing*: A national programme on creating supercomputing capabilities and scaling capacities to Peta scale is being envisaged for which DST has been assigned the coordinating responsibility. Alliance and partnership programmes with Ministry of Human Resource Development for enhancement of quality to science teaching and with DAE for the creation of large R&D office structure for Mega Science would be further developed during the Twelfth Plan Period.

8.52. *Strengthening Existing Autonomous Grant-in-Aid Research Institutions*: DST extends Grant-in-Aid to a total of 13 research institutions across the country. These institutions have been established by eminent scientists and citizens. Some of these institutions, although small in size with respect to the number of scientific personnel employed there, have emerged as major sources of scientific outputs with contributions to the national share of high-impact-making publications. Some of these institutions lend themselves to playing important roles in increasing the share of India in high-impact-making publications. During the Twelfth Plan, a strategic funding support to these institutions based on their contributions to national share of high-impact-making scientific publications and citation frequencies is proposed to be implemented. It is proposed to commission performance review of these existing Grant-in-Aid institutions by international or national experts during the Twelfth Plan Period. The Terms of Reference to the proposed Review teams would include as suggestions for directional changes and recommendations for governance model, if required.

8.53. *Strengthening of R&D Support and Knowledge Service Organisations under DST*: DST would continue to support the governance of Technology Development Board (TDB), Technology Information, Forecasting and Assessment Council (TIFAC), Vigyan Prasar (VP), National Accreditation Board for Testing Laboratories (NABL), Good Laboratory Practice (GLP), SoI and NATMO and National Spatial Data Infrastructure. These organisations serve special and niche needs in their own domain. The role of TDB in promoting PPP for R&D is proposed to be expanded significantly during the Twelfth Plan. TIFAC proposes to refocus its programmes and meet the mandated goals better and participate in developing a technology vision 2035 for India. Vigyan Prasar is working in unique space in science communication, particularly with respect to development of content and new communication tools and techniques. Alliances and partnerships for larger outreach of R&D outputs of VP are proposed. NABL has emerged as a major national accreditation body in the world platform. The body does not receive government grants and is engaged in a special space. This organisation proposed to expand its reach by establishing regional centres and expanding its scope of business. It is proposed to modernise SoI and new administrative governance systems for SoI and NATMO is proposed to be introduced.

8.54. *National Geographical Information System (NGIS)*: To meet the rapid growth of the country and developmental activities, it is proposed to establish a robust information and decision support system as envisaged through setting up an Indian Geographical Organisation (INGO) under the programme NGIS. The endeavour will be implemented through a network of agencies such as ISRO, DIT, NIC, DST, SoI and MoES, so on. The process would give a boost to various developmental activities for government, industry, academia and citizens including sectors like education and research.

8.55. An indicative plan outlay of ₹*21,596 crore* at current prices for the Twelfth Five Year has been made for the DST.

Department of Biotechnology

Twelfth Plan Objectives/Thrust

8.56. The overall strategy for DBT for the sector during the Twelfth Plan is to 'accelerate the pace of research, innovation and development to advance biotechnology as strategic area by taking India's strengths in foundational sciences to globally competitive levels and expanding the application of

> **Box 8.3**
> **Leveraging International Collaboration for Strengthening National Programmes**
> **Journey From Stanford–India Biodesign Programme—A Novel Collaborative Technology Innovation to Launching National Biodesign Alliance**
>
> Bioengineering and biodesign integrates physical, chemical or mathematical sciences and engineering principles for the study of biology, medicine, behaviour or health. It advances fundamental concepts, creates knowledge for the molecular to the organ systems levels and develops innovative biologics, materials, processes, implants, devices and informatics approaches for the prevention, diagnosis and treatment of disease, for patient rehabilitation and for improving health.
>
> Recognizing the need for capacity building in terms of human resources as well as biodesign and medical technology development, Department of Biotechnology sponsored the program "Stanford India Biodesign Internship" in the year 2008–09 as a collaborative venture with Stanford University, USA, for a period of five years. In India, this programme is centred at All India Institute for Medical Sciences (AIIMS) and Indian Institute of Technology (IIT), Delhi, with a focus to develop implants, medical devices and bioinstrumentation matching national priorities.
>
> Achievements so far include (*i*) training of a total 20 fellows and 28 interns; (*ii*) formation of a start-up company 'Consure' by the fellows of the first batch (2008) of this programme; (*iii*) development of several other technologies/prototypes such as: Intraosseous device—useful for intraosseous infusion in any emergency that overcomes the limitation of resource constrained environment; patient transfer device—to transfer patient from one surface to another surface; limb immobilisation device—to immobilise and support an injured body part; and (*iv*) technology transfer of a low-cost disposable device to manage fecal incontinence in non-ambulatory patients across all care facilities.
>
> Phase II of this programme has been initiated for refinement, validation, testing developing business model for commercialisation of developed prototypes/technologies.
>
> Scale up at national level: During the Twelfth Plan, a programme "National Biodesign Alliance" has been established with various partners such as Regional Centre for Biotechnology, Gurgaon; Translational Health Science and Technology Institute, Gurgaon; International Centre for Genetic Engineering & Biotechnology, Delhi; IIT, Delhi; AIIMS, Delhi; and Christian Medical College, Vellore. A Centre for Biodesign and In vitro Diagnostics has been established at Translational Health Science and Technology Institute, NCR region. Efforts are being made to expand the concept of biodesign at other IITs, medical schools and other related institutions.

biotechnologies for overall growth of bio-economy within the framework of inclusive development'.

8.57. The significant achievements of DBT during Eleventh Plan are given in Box 8.4.

Twelfth Five Year Plan Programmes

8.58. The strategy of the Twelfth Plan complementing the foundations laid during the Eleventh Plan shall be achieved through focused investments, policy support, reforms in governance and management of projects around the following strategic goals:

1. *Expand available pool of research scholars and scientists at all levels (PhD, PDFs, young faculty) in biological and interdisciplinary space by three to five folds*: A major programme-based support will be provided for expanding biological/life science departments and clusters in universities, IITs, medical, veterinary and agriculture and pharmaceutical universities/departments, centres of excellence. This would involve important interdisciplinary bio-based science linking to quantitative sciences (chemistry, engineering, and physics) and expanding biological and interdisciplinary sciences in human, animal and plant science systems to achieve greater translatability of knowledge with feasible model system.

2. *Connecting and augmenting existing competences across institutions and universities for bio-economy and social impact*: Interdepartmental and institutional centres and extramural centres of DBT institutions supported with a novel contractual career path for faculty and scalability to connect existing competencies will improve interdisciplinary science, using inspired and

> **Box 8.4**
> **Significant Achievements/Development of DBT during the Eleventh Plan Period**
>
> - Under Human Resource Development efforts, a total of 5,887 research personnel were supported in R&D projects which include 1,768 Junior Research Fellows, 1,844 Senior Research Fellows, 1,060 Research Associate and 70 professorships. In addition, about 2,142 postgraduate students in life sciences and biotechnology were given biotechnology industry training fellowships involving 200 industries. About 2,410 projects have been implemented under various R&D schemes costing about ₹1,600 crore, of which 26 per cent (535) of the projects in the area of medical biotechnology and allied areas, 22 per cent in agriculture and allied areas of biotechnology, 21 per cent in basic research and emerging areas, 19 per cent bio resources and bioprospecting and 12 per cent in capacity building.
> - Through DBT support, a total 1,104 publications of impact factor 5 and above published; 312 patents (national/international) were filed and 110 patents have been granted; and 105 technologies developed, 21 transferred to industry and 5 commercialised. A large number of technology transfers are in process. Health care technologies dominated in technology development compared to agriculture.
> - Under Centres of Excellence activities around innovative leaders and institutions, 35 programme supports and 11 individual projects resulted in 200 publications with impact factor >5 published; 33 national patents filed and 24 granted; 37 international patents filed and 26 granted; 10 research leads obtained and 1 technology transferred.
> - Ten translational research centres and platforms established for clinical development service, GM crops translational research, energy biosciences, bio-design for implants and medical devices, stem cell research, drug discovery, Primate Research and veterinary biologicals. Major translational research initiatives through Grand Challenge schemes and network programmes in the areas of agriculture and health care resulted in several technological developments. Vaccines for malaria, dengue, cholera, and rotavirus are at various phases of clinical trials. Rota viral vaccine is in phase III trials and may be commercialised soon.
> - Seven new autonomous R&D institutions, namely (*i*) Translational Health Science and Technology Institute, Faridabad; (*ii*) Regional Centre for Biotechnology, Faridabad; (*iii*) National Agrifood Biotechnology Institute, Mohali; (*iv*) National Institute of Biomedical Genomics, Kalyani; (*v*) Institute of Stem Cell Biology and Regenerative Medicine, Bangalore; and (*vi*) National Institute of Animal Biotechnology, Hyderabad were set up.
> - Under Small Business Innovative Research Initiative (SBIRI) and Biotechnology Industry Partnership Programme (BIPP), 100 PPP projects have been launched so far which has resulted in 6 Indian patents and development of 16 technologies in agriculture, health care and instrumentation. Sixty projects supported under BIPP scheme benefitted 51 companies (27 small, 12 medium and 12 large companies).
> - Public sector–developed GM crops such as insect-resistant chickpea, rice, brinjal; drought-tolerant groundnut, sunflower and mustard with hybrid vigour are in regulatory pipeline. Accelerated molecular breeding programmes in rice, wheat, corn and mustard have been launched, and protein-rich maize is already commercialised.

translational research. Some such connectivities proposed are: Biosciences with chemical sciences and synthetic biology for next-generation biofuels; Nano science; chemical sciences and pharmaceutical sciences with clinical research for novel drug delivery, novel diagnostic and medical imaging; engineering–medicine–biology and medical science for implants and devices, chemical biology and physical biology.

3. *Expanding, diversifying career paths with a linkage to high-end interdisciplinary sciences, innovation, translation and entrepreneurship*: Involving

support to centres of excellence, incubators, programmes for expanding existing research and human resource capacity by threefolds through increase in current areas of relative strength such as molecular and cell biology, structural biology, immunology, neurobiology, bioengineering and promoting career paths in clinical and translational research, regulatory sciences, Intellectual Property (IP) technology transfer and knowledge management, entrepreneurship and education, and so on, are proposed. It is also proposed to expand, redesign and create extramural and inter-institutional centres as a cost-efficient process of scale up, utilising the existing best people with some additional younger people. The IIT system offers a unique opportunity over a substantially large interconnected and effective bioscience, interdisciplinary science, bio and other engineering science linked to technology innovation in almost all areas of biotechnology relevant to the country. This would receive high priority and use the instruments defined above for connectivity and for conversion of early leads to meaningful solutions and products.

4. *Strengthening regulatory science and infrastructure*: Involves establishment of BRAI; central agency for regulatory testing and certification laboratories with some core activities and network of testing facilities in public sector laboratories; promotion of regulatory science research units; and human resource development.

5. *Expanding existing autonomous R&D institutions*: The expansion aims at expanding current strengths of researchers and scientists by threefolds at all levels through on-site expansion or establishment of second research campus; setting up of Extra Mural Research centres on or off site to promote translational science, launch mission programmes or to advance interdisciplinary science area and expanding physical infrastructure including technology platforms. It is proposed to adopt a system of intramural institutes and extramural centres for each of the 13 autonomous institutes of DBT. These extramural centres would be located in medical schools, State agricultural universities, engineering schools with about 10–12 Principal Investigators at each extramural centre. About 500 scientists additionally can be supported with existing leadership and anchor role by the autonomous institutes.

6. *Expansion and commissioning of bio clusters at Faridabad, Mohali, Kalyani and Hyderabad*: This would involve adding new programme-based centres at each cluster: academic centres, medical centres, bioengineering centre, contract labs, Genetically Modified Products (GMP) units, animal model resources, novel platforms for therapeutics for sharing by SMEs, technology incubators and parks of entrepreneurship training centres and offices for technology transfer and management and to provide connectivity for innovation.

7. *Establish DBT Grant-in-Aid or partnership research and translational centres through long-term support* in 10 best universities/institutions in at least 10 areas of interest, for example: Agriculture sciences and innovation for pre-breeding, genetic modification (GM) technology and molecular breeding; veterinary S&T for animal productivity and health; biopharmaceutical sciences and health technology; chemical biology and synthetic biology.

8. *Reorient 'Grand Challenge Programme' scheme of the Eleventh Plan to address national priorities* in various developmental sectors through bottom-up approach and also encourage discovery-led innovative ideas: These are eight mission mode programmes with separate governance, management, milestones with inter-departmental participation and global partnerships and bottom-up idea-based competitive grants for R&D and innovation or network projects with several partners along the biotechnology value chain.

9. *Rejuvenate existing and establish new research resources, facilities and services*: A National Life Sciences Resource Centre (NLSRC) with specialised research staff, informatics support and databases to network all research resources, training for skill development activities and organise a systematic information access management facilitating biology research community proposed to set up. New facilities and resources proposed include: low-end virtual supplies for

small organisations such as micro array, knockout mice; validation and prototyping, safety testing technology platforms/centre for implants, devices, cell therapies; large animal resource centre; viral testing facilities; genomic and proteomic facilities; new generation sequencing service units and so on.

10. *Leverage international collaboration for partnerships in cutting-edge areas of research, education and technology development, access and acquisition*: The experience with existing global partnerships with countries and international agencies will be leveraged to bring about directional change in partnership strategies. Towards this objective, focus shall be on establishing joint centres of excellence; graduate schools across universities; forging 2×2 international partnership involving industry and academia on either side, 1×1 partnership among SMEs; projects linking DBT autonomous institutions with international institutions and universities; joint development of industrial biotechnologies with global organisations. Global consortia of industries and public institutions will be promoted on the lines of the Indo-US Bioenergy initiative in other areas, such as molecular breeding, cell therapy and regenerative medicine and so on.

11. *Continued and sustained support to PPPs with new innovative funding schemes*: Besides continuing with some reforms in SBIRI and BIPP schemes operations innovative funding schemes such as: Ignition Grant Scheme available to individuals or a team of individuals–in partnership with private investment agencies; schemes for creating and nurturing start-up for early-stage technologies; provision of 'bridge funding' firms to function between successive private equity funding or planning for IPOs; funding for technology access and acquisition and licensing and special investment incentives to industry for building more biotechnology/pharma special economic zones (SEZs). Biotechnology Industry Research Assistance Council (BIRAC) would be made fully operational in Twelfth Plan to assess and facilitate bio industry as per its mandate and manage funding through PPP schemes. The affordable health technology initiative with Welcome Trust will be launched. It will have a pro-poor bias, focus on mass health impact and enhance our abilities to access technology from overseas in addition to from within the country.

12. *Promoting discovery-led innovation and strategic investments in priority sectors*: The department has been funding investigator-driven R&D projects across areas of basic agriculture, health care, environment, animal health and reproduction, bio resource utilisation and food S&T and so on. During the Twelfth Plan, it is proposed to redesign sectoral strategy in such a way that every sector utilises more than one mechanism or modality, linkages, partnerships and alliances and platforms that are required for successful development of both S&T.

13. *Promoting new-generation biotech industries*: Innovative funding schemes and incentives within the framework of existing mechanisms shall be extended to develop capacity for setting up of new bio industries such as bulk/specialty chemicals/biochemicals; food and nutrition technologies; biotech-led/biotech-enabled services engineering, components and equipment manufacture; nano–bio industries and so on. Efforts would also be made for reengineering the economic model for biotechnology product/industry development.

14. *Technology acquisition, transfer and licensing for product development*: Major initiatives will be taken in Twelfth Plan such as establishment of Intelligence Innovation and Idea units to serve as 'think tanks' in life sciences and biotechnology to imagine the future and prepare for the future to analyse needs and opportunities and create product profile for products that will be usable and marketable; technology acquisition fund with legal process and mechanism technology and IP management centres, particularly DBT partner universities and institutions.

15. *Communication platform/system for creating awareness and public understanding of biotechnology*: To address this issue, it is proposed to set up Centre for Biotechnology Communication for content creation and coordination; communication units in universities and institutions; commissioning regular programmes

and publications in electronic and print media and constitution of authorised communication expert groups for crisis management and response.
16. *Expedite legal framework and legislations*: BRAI Bill has been tabled in parliament for introduction. It is proposed to bring other bills dealing with public sector–funded IP management; DNA profiling and Regional Centre for Biotechnology.
17. *Strengthening and consolidation of the major Eleventh Plan initiatives*: Keeping in view zero-based budgeting (ZBB) exercise, certain projects and programmes that have outlived their relevance will be phased out. At the same time, successful schemes shall be strengthened through stringent project management and scale up. Schemes in this category belong to promotion of innovation and excellence; PPPs; research resources specialised centres, translation platforms and service facilities; innovative human resources development programmes and major R&D programmes and networks for technology development.
18. *Promote policy research and analysis in biotechnology*: Policy research and analysis has become an essential ingredient of biotechnology development due to IPR, regulations, public concerns and technology options/alternatives, affordability, access and trade issues. Besides general capacity building through workshops, training and research, centres/units for health and agriculture biotechnology policy research will be supported along regular policy dialogue among stakeholders through special meetings and seminars.
19. *Establishment of new autonomous national research centres/institutions in emerging areas*: It is proposed to establish few institutes/research centres in emerging areas of translational research such as Bioinformatics and Computational Biology; Marine and Microbial Biotechnology; Biodesign, Bioscience and Bioengineering; Chronic Disease Science and Biotechnology and Infectious Science and Biotechnology Institute in North East (linking to Translational Health Science and Technology Institute [THSTI] as partner for Training and Education).

8.59. An indicative plan outlay of ₹*11,804 crore* at current prices for the Twelfth Five Year has been made for the DBT.

Ministry of Earth Sciences

Twelfth Plan Objectives/Thrust

8.60. The MoES/Earth System Science Organisation (ESSO) was established by the Government of India in 2006 to address holistically various aspects relating to earth processes for understanding the variability of earth system and for improving forecast of the weather, climate and hazards. The programs of the Ministry has been reinforced and restructured with a view to provide best possible services relating to earth system science towards socio-economic benefit of the Indian sub-continent and in the Indian Ocean region. The various services being rendered by the Ministry caters to over 25 sectors and the estimated economic benefits appear to be contributing significantly to GDP of the country. The major focus of the Twelfth Plan proposals has been to carry out research on discovering new phenomena; exploring unchartered areas, especially sea-bed and Antarctica; understanding earth processes and developing new services as well as improving existing services for societal, environmental and economic benefits. The programmes of MoES/ESSO have been grouped into major schemes which are as follows: (*i*) Observation System, (*ii*) Atmospheric Processes, Modelling and Services, (*iii*) Climate Change Research, (*iv*) Airborne Platforms for Atmospheric Research, (*v*) Ocean Observations, (*vi*) Ocean Science and Services, (*vii*) Ocean Survey and Mineral Resources, (*viii*) Ocean Technology, (*ix*) Ocean Research Vessels, (*x*) Polar Science and Cryosphere, (*xi*) Marine Geoscientific studies, (*xii*) Seismological Research, (*xiii*) High Performance Computing (HPC) for Earth System Science Research, (*xiv*) Research, Education, Training & Outreach, and (*xv*) Earth Enterprises.

8.61. The significant achievements of ESSO during the Eleventh Plan are given in Box 8.5.

Twelfth Five Year Plan Programmes

8.62. *Atmospheric Observation Systems Network*: The modernisation plan aims at commissioning of

Box 8.5
Significant Achievements/Development of MoES/ESSO during the Eleventh Plan Period

- Under the first phase of modernisation of the India Meteorological Department (IMD), accomplishments include: (i) commissioning of 10 global positioning system (GPS) stations; (ii) installation of nine Doppler Weather Radars (DWRs) one each in Delhi, Nagpur, Patna, Patiala, Agartala, Lucknow, Hyderabad besides the existing five DWRs which have improved now casting services; (iii) installation of integrated Airport Meteorological Instruments (AMIs) at Mumbai, Hyderabad, Bangalore, Jaipur and Delhi airports; (iv) installation of 550 Automatic Weather Stations (AWSs) apart from the existing 125 AWSs, in addition to installation of 689 Automatic Rain Gauges (ARGs); (v) commissioning of a set of four HPCs with a total installed capacity of 124 Teraflops for global data processing and Numerical Weather Prediction (NWP) for weather forecasting services. A district-level agro-meteorological advisory service along with a five days in advance district-level weather forecast system, covering all the 555 districts, was launched for farmers in partnership with a number of Central Government ministries and organisations, state-level institutions, private agencies, non-governmental organizations (NGOs), progressive farmers and the media. Over 3 million farmers have subscribed for receiving this information through mobile phones.
- A programme on 'National Monsoon Mission' was launched which will be equipped with the state-of-the-art infrastructure, namely, high-end computers, radars and scientific manpower to generate more detailed and accurate forecasts.
- In atmospheric modelling, there has been remarkable improvement in capability by running a wide range of high-resolution global circulation models. By introduction of these models like T574, the spatial resolution of the models has been increased sustainably from 50 km to around 22 sq km.
- Under Ocean Science and Services, an integrated unique system of fisheries advisories based on identification of Potential Fishing Zones (PFZs), using remote sensing technology, has been made operational. A tuna fishery forecast specifically for deep sea fish industry has also been made operational.
- A high resolution Indian Ocean forecast for the Indian Ocean on various parameters, namely, currents, sea surface temperature and mixed layer depth was also launched using a suite of ocean models. Towards strengthening ocean observation systems, a ground station for Ocean Sat-2, Ocean Colour Monitor (OCM) data has been established. Over 160 Argo floats (10 floats with oxygen sensors), and 66 drifting buoys were deployed in the Indian Ocean. Besides, a 16-moored buoy network has been made operational for continuous acquisition of data from the seas around India for operational weather forecast. In addition, over 25 tide gauge stations and 10 Coastal Radars were also installed to improve ocean information services.
- The first Indian scientific expedition to the South Pole was conducted in December 2010 which significantly improved India's scientific capability in the Antarctic. A scientific expedition using the international research facility at Ny-Alesund in the Spitsbergen island of Norway has been undertaken for Arctic research. India has successfully commissioned 3rd Permanent Antarctic Station 'Bharati' in the Larsemann Hills with state-of-the-art facilities for conducting Antarctic Research.
- Two Low Temperature Thermal Desalination (LTTD) technology-based desalination Plants with 1 lakh litre capacity have been established, one each at Minicoy, Agatti islands of Lakshadweep. Using waste heat from power Plants, a 1 lakh litre per day LTTD Plant was demonstrated which has been operational at the North Chennai Power Plant.
- With climate change science getting special attention and focus, a dedicated Centre for Climate Change Research at Pune has been set up to address scientific issues relating to climate change, including impact on sectors like health, agriculture and water.

- For activities under ocean resources, an instrument, along with complete hardware and software has been developed in collaboration with Russia to measure seabed soil properties in situ, at a depth of 5,200 metres. A prototype for a remotely operated vehicle has also been developed and tested successfully at a depth of over 5,284 metres. India has become one among a handful of nations that have the capacity for deep sea mining. Further, survey and exploration of polymetallic nodules has been carried out at a closer grid of 6.25 km for selected blocks, along with developing and testing the artificial nodule laying system.
- Under disaster support activities, the state-of-the-art Tsunami Warning System with the world's best infrastructure and communication system was made fully operational on 24×7 basis at INCOIS, Hyderabad. A set of 17 broadband seismic observational networks in peninsular India and six bottom pressure recorders in the Arabian Sea and Bay of Bengal were also upgraded. Towards this, an Earthquake Risk Evaluation Centre was created in New Delhi to evaluate seismic hazards at a very high resolution. The Indian Tsunami warning centre, which has been recognised the best centres in the Indian Ocean, is capable of issuing bulletins within 10 minutes of occurrence of earthquakes in the Indian Ocean.

state-of-the-art observing systems throughout the country. It is proposed to undertake phase II of the modernisation, focusing on the augmentation of the existing infrastructure established during the phase I of the modernisation in terms of observing systems and integrating the same with the rest of the network, namely, ground-based radiometers providing temperature and humidity profiles and complementing the sonde observations to be developed with priority. A Centre for Atmospheric Technology (CAT) is also planned to coordinate development of instruments, calibrate instruments including satellite-based and provide overall technology support to atmospheric sciences, besides validation of satellite data. It is proposed to set up a dedicated forecasting system for the entire Himalayan region with a much focused objective of integrating and improving the weather related services.

8.63. *Atmospheric Processes and Modelling and Service*: The sole purpose of the programme is to develop a wide range of atmospheric models for providing weather and climate forecasting services to various sectors by integrating all the process studies and models. The major sectors would be agriculture, aviation, metro cities, mountain regions, defence, sports and disasters. The existing district-level Agromet Advisory Services (AAS) to deliver crop and location-specific AAS to farmers will be graduated to the block level with village-level advisory. The upgradation of facilities of about 100 airports in the country will be taken up. Metropolitan air quality and weather service providing real-time weather, as well as now casting of weather and air quality in all metro cities as well, are proposed. It is essential to work out a modelling framework and put it in use to predict monsoon weather and climate in India on different time scales ranging from short and medium range to seasonal mean. National Monsoon Mission will be set up with the state-of-the-art weather infrastructures, namely, high-end computers, radars and scientific manpower to generate more detailed and accurate forecasts. Other deliverables are Cloud Physics and severe weather warning system.

8.64. *Climate Change Research*: It is proposed to develop long-term (multi-decadal) simulations of monsoon using coupled ocean–atmospheric models upon the commissioning of the HPC system upgrade for climate change research. The development of seasonal and intra-seasonal prediction of monsoon through coupled model is to be taken up. The utility of geo-engineering schemes to mitigate global warming has to be explored. There is need to develop expertise in India to evaluate the benefits and risks of these schemes. The research projects would be taken up to enhance our understanding of the changing water cycle. Besides, paleoclimatic studies will be conducted to understand the past variations of climate for possible projections of climate scenarios.

8.65. *Airborne Platforms*: A wealth of atmospheric, aerosol and cloud microphysics data will be generated using airborne platforms which will be useful to validate the convection and cloud schemes, and for improving the model physics. The proposed programme will be useful in air pollution assessment and associated impacts over India (health, visibility, climate), hydrological and water resources studies, and enhancement of research infrastructure.

8.66. *Ocean Observation System (OOS)*: The objective is to acquire time-series data from the seas around India and to develop a wide range of ocean atmospheric models towards augmentation of services. The data acquired through Argo floats, Drifters, Current Meter Arrays are being used for various operational and research purposes including forecasting of cyclones and understanding the climate variability.

8.67. *Ocean Science and Services (OSS)*: The OSS have been reoriented into a major programme during the Twelfth plan by integrating all the service-oriented ocean-related projects under one umbrella. These are providing a suite of Ocean Information services, assessment of marine Living Resources, periodical monitoring of health of the coastal waters of India, Management of Coastal Marine Area and operation of Tsunami Warning system on 24×7 basis for issue of bulletins for India and to the countries of the Indian Ocean region. In the Twelfth Plan, an International Centre for Operational Oceanography has been planned. The major deliverables under the scheme are high-resolution ocean modelling and microbial oceanography.

8.68. *Ocean Survey and Mineral Resources*: This programme is primarily aimed at conducting surveys for harnessing the marine nonliving resources in a sustainable way, available in exclusive economic zone (EEZ) and deep sea region of the Indian Ocean. These include gas hydrates, polymetallic nodules, hydrothermal sulphide minerals and cobalt crust. Apart from continuing some of the activities of ongoing schemes like gas hydrate and polymetallic manganese nodule (PMN), the major emphasis would be on research activities relating to Hydrothermal.

8.69. *Ocean Technology*: The Ocean Technology programme of India encompasses four core missions as Ocean Energy, Deep Sea Mining, Coastal end Environmental Engineering and Marine Instrumentation. National Institute of Ocean Technology plays a key role in undertaking ocean-related activities, Ocean Science & Technology and enhancement of marine living resources, development for breeding, rearing and fattening of lobsters, to begin with, for Andaman and Nicobar Islands. Consolidation of deep sea mining technology such as integrated deep sea mining system, soil tester, Remotely Operated Vehicle (ROV) and manned submersible would be carried out, besides developing Marine Sensors and underwater equipment. Under ocean technology, a set of eight in-house R&D programmes like Energy, Ocean Acoustics, Marine Sensor, offshore structures, Inter-institutional R&D of National Institute of Ocean Technology (NIOT) would be carried out. Desalination plants would be established in all major islands of Lakshadweep.

8.70. *Ocean Research Vessels*: Two new vessels are proposed which will be greater than 100m, Ice class, with speed of 20 knots and fitted with winches and systems for exploration of deep sea living resources. *Sagar Sampada* had the limitation of undertaking these studies only up to 1,000m to 1,500m depths. These vessels will give a considerable boost to mineral surveys and ocean research in the Indian Ocean Region.

8.71. *Polar Sciences and Cryosphere*: The Polar Science and Cryosphere programme entails the study of the Antarctic, Arctic and Glaciers of Himalayas that are important to understand the climate change and climate variability in the Indian region. The deliverable under the scheme would be replacement of Maitri station.

8.72. *Seismological Research*: It is proposed to provide thrust to the earthquake-related studies and to generate inputs for earthquake disaster mitigation. The primary activities would include: (*i*) Deep crustal studies across the Indian continental margin and the interior, (*ii*) Paleo seismological studies and kinematics of the Himalayan region, (*iii*) Andaman subduction zone and (*iv*) Active faults of India. Besides, this programme also envisages reconciling the constraints from available geophysical and geological data along a series of transects across the Indian peninsula into a consistent model of the Indian lithosphere to conduct studies on deep bore holes investigations in Koyna, Warna region and Marine Geoscientific Studies. To address these issues relating to earthquake in a holistic manner, a National Centre for Seismology (NCS) is being set up.

8.73. *Geoscience*: Deep sea drilling in the Arabian Sea basin through the Integrated Ocean Drilling Programme is proposed to be undertaken. The scientific proposal of deep sea drilling in the Arabian Sea for discovering the tectonic climatic unknowns will be taken up. An institute for Geo Technologies, integrating all the scientific and operational bodies and taking new initiatives on merit like finding geo technology solutions to serious problems like global warming is proposed to be established. The deliverables under the scheme would be exploring the origin of the largest Geoid low on the earth and origin of monsoon and evolution of Himalayas. For advanced research in isotope geochemistry and geochronology pertaining to earth, atmospheric and oceanic sciences, high-resolution Secondary Ionization Mass Spectrometry studies would be carried out.

8.74. *High Performance Computing System*: Towards catering to the demand of computing facility for Centre for Climate Change Research (CCCR), Seasonal Prediction of Monsoon, Extended Range Prediction of Active Break Spells, National Monsoon Mission, Programme for Advanced Training in Earth System Science and Climate, and activities of CCCR, it is proposed to augment computing power from existing 124 Terra-flops to 2.5 Peta-flop during the Twelfth Five Year Plan.

8.75. *Research Education, Training and Outreach*: Facilities will be created to provide necessary infrastructure. The other main activities would be setting up a Centre for Operational Meteorology and an International Training Centre for Operational Oceanography as part of UNESCO's endeavour for training and capacity building and Indo-African Centre for Medium Range Weather Forecast for extending weather forecasting services in the African region. It is proposed to support Human Resource Development through establishment of MoES Chair Professorship in IITs and IISERs and initiation of academic programmes at IITs and IISERs.

8.76. *Earth Enterprise*: There has been a phenomenal increase in the sectoral applications of weather and climate products as well as ocean technologies and related products, resulting in an unprecedented demand for reliable and timely supply of products and information. A PSU, the Earth Systems Enterprise, would be set up under the Companies Act under the administrative control of the Ministry for providing data/technologies on commercial basis developed by the autonomous bodies/attached and subordinate offices.

8.77. An indicative plan outlay of ₹*9,506 crore* at current prices for the Twelfth Five Year has been made for the MoES.

Department of Scientific & Industrial Research (Including CSIR)

Twelfth Plan Objectives/Thrust

8.78. The thrust of the Department of Scientific & Industrial Research (DSIR) is to promote industrial research, technology development and transfer to enable India to emerge as a global industrial research and innovation hub. Emphasis is on attracting industrial research in the country through industry and institution-centric motivational measures and incentives, creating an enabling environment for development of new innovations to channelise benefits to the people.

8.79. CSIR has conceptualised and developed a document entitled 'CSIR@80: Vision and Strategy 2022', which is a road map for 2022. The document is based on the motivation that the year 2022 would bring us to India@75—the platinum jubilee of Indian independence. The India@75 will coincide with CSIR@80, a unique stage in the life of any R&D

organisation. By that time, as per the various projections, India would have changed its image as a third world country to the third most powerful country in the world. CSIR, as India's largest and most diverse S&T organisation is aspiring to help India in achieving this goal. In view of the building scenario by 2022, CSIR's vision would be to build a new CSIR for new India and CSIR's mission would be: 'Pursue science which strives for global impact, technology that enables innovation-driven industry and nurture trans-disciplinary leadership thereby catalysing inclusive economic development for the people of India.' The people and nation-centric thrust to science, technology and societal pursuits would remain the cornerstone of CSIR's mission.

8.80. The Twelfth Five Year Plan of CSIR focuses on achieving science and engineering leadership; developing innovative technological solutions; practising open innovation initiatives; developing and nurturing human resource in trans-disciplinary areas; facilitating science-based entrepreneurship; and enabling socio-economic transformation through appropriate S&T intervention. In view of attaining the above focus, CSIR proposes many new initiatives and envisages adopting strategies that are goal focused—attaining the identified goals; process focused—building and streamlining organisational processes; growth focused—achieving organisational growth; and competitive advantage focused—achieving competitive advantage over peers.

8.81. The significant achievements of DSIR including CSIR during the Eleventh Plan are given in Box 8.6.

Twelfth Five Year Plan Programmes

8.82. *Programmes of DSIR*: The major Plans and Programmes of DSIR for the Twelfth Five Year Plan include: (*i*) *Promoting Innovations in Individuals, Start-ups and MSMEs (PRISM)*—wherein innovative proposals of MSMEs shall be supported; CSIR—Cluster Innovation Centres (CICs) promoted by National Innovation Council shall be supported for providing innovative solutions; existing network of TePP Outreach Centres shall be expanded; proposals from individual innovators/incubates shall be supported and support shall be extended to approved Technopreneur Promotion Programme (TePP) projects, spilling over from the Eleventh Five Year Plan; (*ii*) *Scheme on Patent Acquisition and Collaborative Research and Technology Development (PACE)*—wherein support shall be provided to Indian industries to acquire Intellectual Property at early stage from overseas or within the country and add value to the acquired IP; and focus shall be on PPPs to create enabling environment for collaborative research between Industry and Universities/Public Funded Research Institutions; (*iii*) *Building Industrial R&D and Common Research Facilities* (*BIRD*)—wherein R&D in Industry shall be encouraged and supported; and support shall be provided for creation of Common Research Facilities for Small and Micro Industries; (*iv*) *Access to Knowledge for Technology Development and Dissemination (A2K+)*—wherein science-, technology- and innovation-related international journals from major publishers shall be made accessible to 1,500 in-house R&D units of industry and 600 Scientific & Industrial Research Organisations (SIROs) and techno-entrepreneurs, besides conducting studies/conferences on industrial status in the country; support shall be provided for Technological Empowerment of Women projects, including projects spilling over from the Eleventh Five Year Plan; and support shall be extended to Technology Development and Demonstration Programme (TDDP) projects, spilling over from the Eleventh Five Year Plan.

Consultancy Development Centre

8.83. The important activities envisaged during the Twelfth Five Year Plan period would include Consultancy Promotion, Services, Research and Analysis, National Programme for Competency Development in strategic focus areas, Technology Delivery Transfer and Commercialisation, National Knowledge Depository, Training and Development, Export promotion and International Collaborations.

Central Electronics Ltd. (CEL)

8.84. During the Twelfth Five Year Plan period, leveraging on its technology prowess, CEL plans to develop capabilities for the manufacture of Dye Sensitized Solar Cells (DSSCs or Grätzel cells), which

Box 8.6
Significant Achievements of DSIR/CSIR during the Eleventh Plan Period

- CSIR has enabled India excel in high science and has been the pioneer of the country's intellectual property movement. It has been contributing on an average 12 per cent of the national SCI publications with an average impact factor per paper of more than two. It has published 16,664 research papers in SCI journals of national and international repute during 2007–10. It has also contributed towards the development of highly qualified S&T manpower in diverse areas and has supported over 8,396 research scholars; 4,000 students are pursuing PhD in various CSIR laboratories. It produces 500 PhDs and 2,000 postgraduate degree holders and research trainees every year. Being in the forefront of generating intellectual property, it was granted 1,282 foreign and 1,507 Indian patents, and it has 3,250 foreign and 2,350 Indian patents in force and 222 patents licensed as on date. The percentage utilisation of patents is 8.67 per cent, which is much above the world average of 3–5 per cent. CSIR's per patent cost is the lowest in the world amongst state-funded R&D organisations.

- CSIR designed and developed, through a PPP, the CNM5, a five-seater all-metal civil aircraft that had been successfully test flown. The carbon fibre technology was licensed to M/s Kemrock. The technology for recovery of Sulphate of Potash (SOP), developed by CSIR-Central Salt and Marine Chemicals Research Institute (CSIR-CSMCRI) from bittern has been transferred to M/s Arcana Chemical Industries. Technology for Head Up Display (HUD) for Light Combat Aircraft (LCA) was transferred to Bharat Electronics Limited (BEL), Panchkula. The ATBS process developed by CSIR-NCL has been commercialised by M/s Vinati Organics Limited (VOL) at MIDC, Lote Parsuram, Chiplun.

- CSIR has licensed to Nostrum Pharmaceuticals for worldwide commercialisation of new generation thrombolytic molecules and will receive over 150 million US$. A new-generation clot-specific protein that displays plasminogen activation property was transferred to M/s Nostrum Pharmaceuticals, USA at ₹19.60 crore plus 5 per cent royalty. Technology for Caerulomycin A, and its proprietary derivatives and analogues for their novel indication of immuno-suppression—a discovery of immense importance in tissue transplantation like in kidney and heart—was licensed to M/s Nostrum Pharmaceuticals, USA at ₹14.70 crore plus 2 per cent royalty. Recombinant streptokinase produced from *Escherichia coli* was launched by M/s Shasun Drugs & Chemicals through M/s Lupin Pharmaceuticals and M/s Alembic Chemicals, at a cost of ₹1 crore plus 3.5 per cent royalty. This would bring down the prices of clot busters significantly. A new anti-ulcer drug—CSIR's patented know-how on a natural agent for treatment of symptoms associated with gastrointestinal toxicity and ulcer—was licensed to M/s IPCA Laboratories Ltd., Mumbai, at ₹2.5 crore plus royalty.

- CSIR developed a 10hp tractor named 'Krishi Shakti' which is low in cost (₹1 Lakh) and is suitable for small and marginal farmers. A facile process for Heptafluropropane (FM 200), a halon substitute used in fire-fighting systems was transferred to M/s Mechvac Fabricators Ltd., Mumbai, for commercial production. A 3,000 TPA Plant from Aditya Birla Group for the manufacture of epichlorohydrin from allyl chloride, based on an improved and patented catalytic process, went on stream at Ryong, Thailand. Process technology for sugarcane bagasse for the recovery of cellulose, hemi-cellulose and lignin was licensed to M/s Godavari Sugars at ₹6.5 crore plus 3 per cent royalty.

- CSIR laboratories have developed significant knowledge base on water and water-related technologies. CSIR has developed a high-flux hollow-fibre membrane based technology for disinfection and purification of water. Refined and portable device called the Terafil water filter has been developed which provides drinking water without the use of chemicals. This coupled with a technology for RO desalination has been used extensively to provide fresh drinking water in disaster-affected areas. RO plants are further being exported to Afghanistan and Kenya.

- A novel variety of Ashwagandha with a high root yield developed and released to farmers. The plant has useful anti-inflammatory, anti-stroke and anti-arthritic applications.
- In the area of affordable health care, the first-ever large-scale comprehensive study of the genetic structure of the Indian population has been completed, thereby creating an Indian Genome Variation database (IGVdb). This has opened up new vistas for developing predictive medicine using repeats and single nucleotide polymorphisms. India's footprint in the genomic world, a CSIR initiative along with others, led to reconstructing Indian population history. CSIR with Cadila Pharmaceuticals has developed for the first time a novel therapy named as 'RISORINE' for the treatment of tuberculosis. Lead for this novel therapy is obtained from Ayurveda. Commercialisation of Risorine has reduced the cost of formulation containing Rifampicin–Isoniazide by 23 per cent. Prostalyn, an anti-cancer drug, a herbal molecule obtained from *Murraya koenigii* and *Tribulus terrestis* for treatment of prostate cancer was released in the market. CSIR has also developed bacosides-enriched standardised extract of *Bacopa*—Bacosides Enriched Standardized Extract of Bacopa (BESEB)—a single plant–based unique natural memory enhancer formulation, and patented the development. The BESEB is successfully commercialised.
- A high-yielding cultivar of Lavender developed by CSIR has proved to be an excellent alternate crop for cultivation by farmers in the state of Jammu & Kashmir. CSIR has set up post-harvest centres in Mizoram (Aizawl) and Arunachal Pradesh (Pashighat). More than 10,000 farmers of the North-East would be able to sell their produce at 20–25 per cent higher price to these processing centres.
- CSIR has launched an ambitious, socially relevant programme named CSIR 800. This programme aims at developing and providing innovative R&D-based products and processes which would be affordable by the common masses. These would come in handy not only for removing drudgery but also for adding to economic upliftment of the Indian populace by successfully launching small scale enterprises. CSIR has designed and developed an eco-friendly dual-powered rickshaw named 'Soleckshaw'. The soleckshaw is in commercial production.
- CSIR launched Open Source Drug Discovery (OSDD) programme has emerged as a new platform for innovation in the domain of health care. This CSIR-led 'Team India' consortium with global partnership has more than 4,500 researchers from over 100 countries as registered participants.
- CSIR's Traditional Knowledge Digital Library (TKDL) in collaboration with Department of Ayurveda, Yoga & Naturopathy, Unani, Siddha and Homoeopathy (AYUSH) has emerged as a unique resource for protecting Indian traditional knowledge from exploitation through IP filings. TKDL has signed access agreements with European Patent Office (EPO), United States Patent and Trademark Office (USPTO), German Patent Office, Japan Patent Office and so on.
- CSIR has established an Academy of Scientific and Innovative Research (AcSIR) through a gazette notification by the government which would aim at innovative curricula, pedagogy and evaluation for creating high-quality personnel in trans-disciplinary areas.
- CSIR has set up the CSIR Tech Private Limited, registered at Pune, to catalyse the valorisation of its technologies. The main purpose of CSIR Tech is to hold equity and give feedback loop of technology creation and transfer.
- DSIR has granted or renewed recognition to over 1,600 in-house R&D units of industry. Over ₹10,000 crore of R&D investment by in-house R&D units were reported to Directorate General of Income Tax (Exemptions) for weighted tax deduction under Section 35(2AB) of Income Tax (IT) Act. Support was also extended to 400 innovator's projects (TePP projects), 34 TePP outreach centres and 70 new technology development and demonstration projects.

are emerging as one of the highly creditable alternatives to silicon photovoltaic and to the more recently developed thin film technologies. CEL has proposed to develop the design of systems for a relatively new approach for optimising solar system efficiency and improving reliability with the design and manufacture of micro-inverters that connect to individual solar panels. CEL will establish an R&D Division to cater to the needs for design, development, testing and validation of a range of improved strategic electronic, special purpose vehicle (SPV), surveillance, safety/security products. Harnessing technology advancements and improvement of manufacturing techniques as also the need to enhance manufacturing capacity commensurate with active marketing efforts and business expansion, steps are being taken up by CEL to ensure that the present plan capacity of 10 MW for SPV products is increased to 80 MW. CEL has also proposed through a joint venture to set up a National Silicon Wafer production facility for producing silicon wafers of 1,000 MW/year capacity to reduce the nations' reliance on availability of this critical resource of silicon materials through import from other countries.

National Research Development Corporation (NRDC)

8.85. NRDC was assigned more than 270 technologies by various R&D institutions in the country, and it signed more than 175 license agreements with industry for commercialisation during the Eleventh Five Year Plan period. The focus of NRDC during the Twelfth Five Year Plan period will be on launching (*i*) Programme for Inspiring Inventors and Innovators (PIII) and (*ii*) Programme for Development of Technologies for Commercialisation.

Council of Scientific and Industrial Research

8.86. CSIR proposes to pursue 10 schemes during the Twelfth Plan. The initiatives are summarised below:

8.87. *Setting Up of New Institutions*: CSIR envisages setting up five new institutes during the Twelfth Five Year Plan, in both physical and virtual mode. These institutes include: CSIR-Institute of Synthetic and Systems Biology (CSIR-ISSB); CSIR-Fourth Paradigm Institute (CSIR-4PI); CSIR-Institute of Bio-Mimetic Materials (CSIR-IBMM); CSIR-Network Institute of Solar Energy (CSIR-NISE) and CSIR-Network Institute of Manufacturing Technology (CSIR-NIMT).

8.88. *R&D in Clusters through National Laboratories*: During the Eleventh Plan, CSIR has categorised its R&D programmes across seven clusters. The Twelfth Plan envisages strengthening and streamlining the cluster approach substantially. Programmes of the National Laboratories in the Twelfth Five Year Plan would be undertaken across five clusters which are as follows: Biological Science, Chemical Science, Engineering Science, Information Science and Physical Science. There is a specific focus on Human Resource Development in cluster mode. The projects have been formulated to encompass intra-cluster, inter-cluster and trans-cluster entities covering the domains of mega projects, large mission projects, supra-institutional network projects, cross-cluster projects, facility creation/augmentation projects and other small projects.

8.89. *CSIR Outreach Centres*: CSIR during the Twelfth Five Year Plan envisages setting up CSIR Outreach Centres that would essentially function in partnership with stakeholders. The focus is on new States and other such States where CSIR has no presence. CSIR Outreach Centres are envisaged to be operated and managed through CSIR–people partnership mode (CPP), and implemented either through mobile kiosks or pre-fabricated self-inclusive containers placed at identified locations. The centres would also have close coordination and networking with the CICs of the NInC-CSIR initiative.

8.90. *Initiative for Scale-up and Validation of Leads*: In order to ensure that the various leads developed as a result of R&D in CSIR labs attain fruition, CSIR has proposed to upgrade an activity for scale-up and validation of leads towards product/process development into an independent initiative.

8.91. *CSIR Special Centres for North-Eastern States, Lakshadweep and Andaman and Nicobar Islands*: In its endeavour to align with the national approach to achieve faster, sustainable and more inclusive growth of the country, CSIR during the Twelfth Plan would focus on special eco-regions of the country and facilitate their sustainable development through S&T intervention. The North-East region and the islands of Lakshadweep, Andaman and Nicobar have been chosen in this regard. CSIR's efforts would include promoting innovation and CSIR technologies for the north-eastern States and undertake S&T intervention towards disaster mitigation and sustainable development of the coral reefs in the Lakshadweep, Andaman and Nicobar Islands.

8.92. *R&D Infrastructure Creation and Refurbishment*: Increase in the number of research programmes and the number of scientist calls for a corresponding increase in R&D infrastructure. This includes building new facilities; advanced workplace design; building ancillary facilities such as animal house, test range, fab-labs and so on.

8.93. *Energy Efficient Green Campus Development*: During the Twelfth Plan, it is proposed to continue with this initiative so as to spruce up CSIR laboratories to substantially high standards such as green building. The building of civil infrastructure would also cover increasing the number of staff quarters, student hostels, guest houses and other fringe facilities. Initiatives would be undertaken to renovate and improve the existing staff quarters, hostels, guest houses and so on.

8.94. *Building Excellence*: CSIR during the Twelfth Plan envisages building excellence. Well-focused initiative to pursue innovative ideas and embark upon high-risk, high-impact projects, thus, would be pursued to travel traversed paths and open up newer vistas. Programmes under this category include EMPOWER (Encouraging and Motivating Pursuit of World Class Exploratory Research), RISK (Research Initiative to Scale New Knowledgebase) and U-Excel (Unit for Excellence), targeted at early career scientists, mid-career scientists and late-career scientists, respectively.

8.95. *Innovation Complexes*: CSIR during the Mid Term Appraisal of the Eleventh Five Year Plan had resolved to bolster its translational research capability through establishment of Innovation Complexes at identified locations across the country. The Innovation Complexes are envisaged to consolidate and sustain the value chain of R&D within the CSIR; consolidate the CSIR brand and make CSIR R&D accessible to society at large; catalyse regionally balanced economic development and promote entrepreneurial culture among the scientific community. During the Twelfth Plan period, CSIR would endeavour to operationalise twelve such complexes all over the country including the three complexes that are initiated during the Eleventh Plan.

8.96. *CSIR 800*: The programme on CSIR 800 that was launched during the Eleventh Five Year Plan for improving the quality of life and augmenting livelihood for the people at the base of the economic pyramid is being expanded during the Twelfth Five Year Plan. As a part of the programme, CSIR would address the needs of rural communities also through implementation of 24 identified CSIR Technology Enabled Villages (TECHVILS) across the country. The programme would be implemented in the following three stages: the REACH-TECH (to be transferred immediately), DEMO-TECH (to be transferred mid-way into the Plan) and INNO-TECH (to be transferred by the end of the Plan period).

8.97. *Open Innovation*: CSIR is building up open innovation as a key vehicle for delivering S&T output to the public at large. CSIR during the Eleventh Plan has achieved significant success through its OSDD initiative. Open Innovation has been identified as a major platform during the Twelfth Plan. It shall cover an expanded version of the OSDD programme (encompassing OSDD, Open Source Drug Delivery, Open Source Drug Development and Open Source Disease Diagnostics), and the Distributed Organic Chemical Synthesis (DOCS) programme that envisages building a national repository of 4,00,000 small molecules by the end of the Plan through open source. Apart from these, Science 3.0, an initiative for open innovation and knowledge-ware development through crowd sourcing would endeavour to engage a large number of engineering institutions to identify the most vexing problems, and attempt to provide solutions on issues like attaining energy efficiency, reduction in materials use, minimising waste generation and developing business and financial models to increase productivity and profitability of the units.

8.98. *CSIR Initiative on Inclusive, Participative and Collaborative R&D*: This new initiative for CSIR during the Twelfth Plan would comprise the following four sub-components: Grand Challenge Initiative, Inverted Innovation, Participative Science and Participatory Technology Development, and Centres for Collaborative Research.

- *The Grand Challenge Initiative*—would focus on solving unsolved problems or providing a comprehensive solution to an enduring national problem. It will help in creating new core competence in the CSIR system; or create leadership in a new domain in trans-disciplinary/interdisciplinary science that would position CSIR globally;
- *The CSIR Initiative for Inverted Innovation*—a unique paradigm where children/young engineers invent, CSIR laboratories mentor and industries commercialise;
- *CSIR Initiative on Participative Science and Participatory Technology Development*—an initiative to pursue R&D that would provide mutual benefits to all the stakeholders participating in the scheme; inclusive innovation can be achieved, translational research can be carried out, a fluid team with like-minded people can be involved and the scientific outcome can be effectively leveraged.
- *Centres for Collaborative Research—CSIR-Academia, CSIR-R&D Institutes and CSIR-Industry*: The centres would focus on collaborative R&D in the identified domains through desired networking. They would be state-of-the-art set-ups and work in a fluid networked organisation mode. The R&D in such centres would be in domains such as health care, secondary agriculture, civil aviation and green transportation, sustainable energy and infrastructure engineering. It is envisaged that these centres would help develop seamless linkages between CSIR and Academic institutions, CSIR and R&D institutions, and CSIR and industry.

8.99. *National S&T Human Resource Development*: CSIR envisages continuing its endeavour of strengthening S&T human resources in the country through fellowships at various levels. In addition, during the Twelfth Plan, it is envisaged to introduce novel fellowship programmes such as hand-holding support to dyslexic children; provision of analytical ability–based fellowships; and also introduce the PC Ray Innovation Postdoctoral Fellowship.

8.100. *Intellectual Property and Technology Management*: CSIR continues to remain at the fountainhead of innovation through ownership of a large number of patents. During the Twelfth Plan period, the efforts to consolidate this IP portfolio further would be continued.

8.101. *R&D Management Support*: The programme on R&D Management Support comprises the following four components: International Collaboration, Planning and R&D Management, collaborative activities with the National Innovation Foundation, and Science Dissemination. The entire programme is proposed to be strengthened considerably during the Twelfth Plan period and taken to new heights.

8.102. *New Millennium Indian Technology Leadership Initiative (NMITLI)*: The NMITLI has been among one of the successful programmes of CSIR during the Eleventh Plan. The programme is envisaged to be strengthened and broadened further during the Twelfth Plan by the following approach:

- Post-NMITLI projects
- Funding with industry (50:50 initiative)
- Co-financing with Venture Capital funds
- NMITLI innovation centres
- Acquisition of early-stage relevant knowledge/IP for portfolio building.

8.103. *National Civil Aircraft Development Programme*: CSIR also envisages being a part of the National Civil Aircraft Development (NCAD) programme to develop the first civil aircraft in the country.

8.104. An indicative plan outlay of ₹17,896 crore at current prices for the Twelfth Five Year has been made for the DSIR including CSIR.

Department of Space

Twelfth Plan Objectives/Thrust

8.105. The space programmes are driven through a decade profile and directions for 2025. The broad directions for the space programme for the next decade would include: (*i*) Strengthening/Expanding of operational services in communications and navigation; (*ii*) developing enhanced imaging capability for natural resource management, weather and climate change studies; (*iii*) space science missions for better understanding of the solar system and the universe; (*iv*) planetary exploratory missions; (*v*) development of heavy lift launcher, reusable launch vehicles and (*vi*) the human space flight programme. Innovations in space-based communications and earth observations (EOs) will be pursued to achieve faster delivery of information to remote areas and finer observations of the earth. Overall, 58 missions are planned for realisation during the Twelfth Plan period which includes 33 Satellite missions and 25 Launch Vehicle missions.

8.106. The significant achievements of DOS during the Eleventh Plan are given in Box 8.7.

Twelfth Five Year Plan Programmes

8.107. *Satellite Communications Programme*: In the area of Satellite Communications, it is proposed to augment the Indian National Satellite System (INSAT) capacity to bridge the gap between the demand and supply of the transponders for meeting all the requirements of the country and also to maintain sufficient spares capacity to meet contingencies. Development of state-of-the-art technologies and latest applications areas shall also be

---

Box 8.7
Significant Achievements/Development of DOS during the Eleventh Plan Period

- During the Eleventh Plan period, 29 major space missions were successfully accomplished, which included 13 launch vehicle missions with the Polar Satellite Launch Vehicle (PSLV) and the Geosynchronous Satellite Launch Vehicle (GSLV) and 16 satellite missions. The most significant achievement of the Eleventh Plan period was the successful launch of India's first unmanned moon mission Chandrayaan-1 on 22 October 2008, thereby achieving the historic feat of placing the Indian tricolour on 14 November 2008 on the moon's surface. The deep space network with two large antennae (18-metre and 32-metre diameter) with associated ground segment was established in Byalalu, near Bangalore to provide Telemetry, Tracking and Command (TTC) support for the mission. High-resolution data of excellent quality from Indian scientific instruments on board Chandrayaan-1 has led to the identification of new lunar features and characteristics around the moon. Analysis of scientific data jointly with international agencies has led to the detection of water molecules on the lunar surface.
- The other important achievements include the launch of (*i*) 10 satellites including Cartosat-2A and IMS-1 in a single launch of PSLV-C9; (*ii*) Microwave Radar Satellite RISAT-2 and Mini Satellite Anna University Satellite (ANUSAT) on board PSLV-C12; (*iii*) high-power satellite INSAT-4CR on board GSLV-F04; (*iv*) Oceansat-2 satellite along with six Nano satellites (commercial) on board India's PSLV-C14; (*v*) Cartosat-2B along with three Nano satellites and Student Satellite (STUDSAT) on board PSLV-C15; (*vi*) Resourcesat-2, Youthsat and Singaporean Satellite, X-Sat, on board PSLV-C16; (*vii*) GSAT-12 on board PSLV-C17; (*viii*) Indo-French joint mission Megha-Tropiques on board PSLV-C18; (*ix*) GSAT-8 through procured launch services; (*x*) conducting a qualification test of indigenously developed cryogenic stage; (*xi*) building two state-of-the-art communication satellites (W2M and Hylas) for international customers; (*xii*) providing launch services for two satellites for international customers (AGILE and TECSAR) on commercial basis by PSLV-C8 and PSLV-C10 and (*xiii*) establishing GEO and GPS Augmented Navigation System (GAGAN).

- Significant progress has been made towards developing GSLV Mk III, the next-generation advanced launch vehicle. A world-class solid propellant plant has been successfully commissioned at the Satish Dhawan Space Centre SHAR (SDSC-SHAR), Sriharikota, for manufacturing large solid stage booster segments (S-200) for GSLV Mk III vehicles. Two static tests of Solid propellant Rocket Booster stage (S-200), the third largest booster in the world, was successfully conducted to demonstrate the repeatability of S200 motor performance within the specified limits and has reconfirmed its design adequacy. As a part of C25 cryogenic stage development, realisation of thrust chamber test article and its trial suiting at the thrust chamber test facility has been successfully completed. The second static test of L110 stage of the GSLV Mk III vehicle was successfully conducted for its flight duration of 200 seconds.
- During the Eleventh Plan, there were failures of 2 GSLV flights, namely, GSLV-D3 with Indigenous Cryogenic Stage during April, 2010, and GSLV-F06 with Russian Cryogenic Stage during December 2010. The GSLV-D3 mission failed as the Indigenous Cryogenic engine after its ignition couldn't sustain the combustion beyond 1 second. The corrective steps based on Failure Analysis Committee are being effected for future launches.
- A new Remote Sensing Data Policy (RSDP 2011) containing modalities for managing and/or permitting acquisition/dissemination of remote sensing data in support of developmental activities has been approved which will enable the department to provide high-resolution data in time to concerned users.
- An Indian Institute of Space Science and Technology (IIST) was established for developing critical human resources for space S&T and the first batch of fresh graduates from the institute to the ISRO system have been inducted.
- Significant developments have taken place in the area of societal applications of space technology. Some of the important ones are: (*i*) expansion of tele-education network to over 55,000 classrooms; (*ii*) telemedicine facility in 382 hospitals; (*iii*) setting up of 473 Village Resource Centres (VRCs); (*iv*) location of drinking water sources using Indian Remote Sensing (IRS) satellite images covering more than 2 lakh habitations in 10 states; (*v*) wasteland mapping and monitoring of the whole country using IRS data; (*vi*) space-based Potential Fish Zone mapping benefitting the fishermen community of coastal areas (*vii*) biodiversity characterisation of bio-rich areas of the country; (*viii*) wetland mapping of entire country and (*ix*) operationalisation of Earth Observation Data Visualisation portal BHUVAN.

pursued. The operational transponder capacity from INSAT/GSAT satellites at the end of Eleventh Five Year Plan is satisfying a demand of around 198 transponders.

8.108. Based on the demand, about 400 transponders are planned to be realised by end of the Twelfth Plan period. Towards this, 14 communication satellites are planned to (*i*) increase the transponder capacity, (*ii*) introduce new-generation broadband very small aperture terminal (VSAT) systems, (*iii*) introduce Ka-band systems, (*iv*) build high-power S-band satellite mobile communications and (*v*) introduce new-generation geo-imaging satellite.

8.109. In terms of spacecraft platforms, it is planned to adopt I-2K, I-3K and I-4K buses for the communication satellites. I-3K and I-4K buses are planned to be launched using procured foreign launcher. It is also planned to initiate development of High throughput I-6K–12KW bus in higher frequency bands like Ka/Ku and the technologies associated with it.

8.110. Maintaining and securing sufficient orbit-spectrum resources for country's Satcom activities will be a thrust area of the Twelfth Plan. It has been planned to pursue rigorously to secure spectrum for 100 additional Ku-band transponders and around 50 C-band/Ext C-band transponders in newer orbital locations.

8.111. *Satellite Based Navigation*: Satellite-based Navigation service is an emerging satellite based system with commercial applications. To meet the Civil Aviation requirements, ISRO is working jointly with Airport Authority of India (AAI) in establishing the GAGAN system. To meet the user requirements of the positioning, navigation and timing, ISRO is establishing a regional satellite navigation system called Indian Regional Navigational Satellite System (IRNSS).

8.112. The Satellite Navigation Programme (SNP) has the primary objective of establishing a space-based infrastructure, Ground Segment for satellite-based position, navigation and timing services. The SNP also has an objective for the user segment, the task of developing the receivers for IRNSS including Global Navigation Satellite System (GNSS) indigenously through participation of Indian industry.

8.113. The Major Programmatic Targets of the Twelfth Plan are:

1. Implement the final operational phase for satellite-based augmentation system (SBAS) GAGAN over the Indian Airspace jointly with AAI and providing position, navigation and timing services through an integrated receiver.
2. Implement an independent IRNSS over Indian region and encourage the growth of user segment in Indian Market.
3. Develop indigenous expertise in applications of GNSS for critical National applications, identify specific application software development areas and work towards development of receivers for IRNSS including GNSS through participation of Indian industry.
4. Secure sufficient orbit-spectrum resources for country's Sat-Nav Programme activities.
5. There is a need to formulate the Indian Satellite Navigation Policy as ISRO is implementing and going to provide satellite-based navigation services in India.

8.114. *IRNSS* is an independent and indigenously developed Indian satellite-based positioning system for critical national applications. The main objective is to provide reliable Position, Navigation and Timing services over India and its neighbourhood; to provide fairly good accuracy to the user and to provide Integrity and Ionosphere correction messages to the user. The IRNSS will basically provide the following two types of services: (*i*) Standard Positioning Service (SPS); (*ii*) Restricted Service (RS). Space Segment consists of seven satellites, three satellites in geosynchronous earth orbit (GEO) and four satellites in geostationary earth orbit (GSO). The three GEOs will be located at suitable orbit slots, and the four GSOs have their longitude crossings at two suitable orbit slots (two in each plane). All the satellites will be visible at all times in the Indian region. Ground Segment is responsible for the maintenance and operation of the IRNSS constellation. It provides the monitoring of the constellation status, computation of the orbital and clock parameters and navigation data uploading. The Ground Segment comprises TTC and Up-linking Stations, Spacecraft Control Centre, IRNSS Timing Centre, Code Division Multiple Access (CDMA) Ranging Stations, Navigation Control Centre and Data Communication Links. User segment mainly consists of a single frequency receiver for SPS, dual-frequency IRNSS receiver for both SPS and RS service and a multi-mode receiver compatible with other GNSS providers. The first IRNSS satellite is planned for launch in 2012–13. Thereafter, it is planned to launch two satellites each year and complete the constellation by 2015–16.

8.115. *EO Systems and Atmospheric Science Programme*: The thrust areas of EO for the Twelfth Five Year Plan have been identified based on extensive interactions with users under the aegis of National Natural Resources Management System (NNRMS) as well as after detailed deliberations in the inter-centre committee of ISRO. In terms of spacecraft missions, there are eight EO missions planned for Twelfth Five Year Plan (including special projects) that cover observation in the area of natural resources, ocean and atmosphere, climate and environment, all weather and high resolution imaging. With the realisation of these missions, there would be significant improvements in the areas of short-term weather and ocean state forecasting, natural resources management, high-resolution cartography, large-scale mapping, space-based Essential Climate Variables (ECVs) with enhanced spatial, spectral, radiometric and temporal resolution. In the area of applications, the focus will be to ensure continuity of services in the areas of Natural Resources Census (1:50000 and 1:250000 scale), groundwater potential mapping, snow and glacier studies, coastal zone management, PFZ, Ocean State forecasting, weather forecast, Space-based Information Support for Decentralized Planning (SIS-DP), Accelerated Irrigation Benefit Programme (AIBP), India-Water Resource Information System (India-WRIS), National Urban Information System (NUIS), including the initiative to help user Ministries in the institutionalisation process for remote sensing–based services (with MoEF, MoES, Ministry of Agriculture [MoA], Ministry of Water Resources [MoWR], already in the forefront).

8.116. *Disaster Management Support (DMS)*: The DMS Programme of ISRO is intended to provide near-real-time support and services from imaging and communication satellites towards efficient management of disasters in the country. The major programmatic targets of DMS programme in Twelfth Five Year Plan are:

1. Operationalisation of National Database for Emergency Management (NDEM)
2. Continue impact mapping and monitoring of natural disasters with improved turnaround time and with newer capabilities
3. Risk evaluation and reduction
4. Acquisition of close contour data through Airborne Laser Terrain Mapper (ALTM)
5. Extension of the communication network to the District Emergency Operation centres
6. Geolocation-based services such as Search and Rescue and distress alerts
7. Operational dissemination of the information and products directly to the affected areas
8. Operational utilisation of early warning systems
9. Extension of the Hydro-meteorological network
10. Key areas of R&D
11. Continued participation in international initiatives

8.117. *Space Transportation System*: The main focus of the Space Transportation Systems during the Twelfth Plan period will be towards achieving self-sufficiency in launching our satellites, developing launch vehicles for enhanced payload capability, adopting appropriate outsourcing strategies for assuring productionisation of launch vehicles, enhancement of infrastructure for launch vehicles and developing technologies for the future programmes of ISRO. The major thrust areas of Space Transportation System during the Twelfth Plan period would include:

1. Enhanced level of production of PSLV systems with vigorous industry participation to meet the projected launch requirements.
2. Complete the development flights and operationalise GSLV MKII with indigenous Cryogenic Upper Stage
3. Complete development and qualification of C25 Engine and Stage
4. Complete the development flights of GSLV MkIII with 4.0 T geostationary transfer orbit (GTO) capability
5. Progress in the development of Semi-cryogenic engine with the establishment of test facilities.
6. Enhancement of infrastructure to meet the launch vehicle requirements and advanced mission requirements.
7. Demonstrate critical technology related to reusable launch vehicle (RLV) and dual-mode ramjet (DMRJ) through technology demonstration
8. Develop the critical technology and subsystems related to Human Space flight programme
9. Develop and demonstrate the critical technologies that will make ISRO's launch vehicle more cost-effective and more capable.
10. Continue the technology development efforts to improve the present capabilities and to contribute for long-term Space Research.
11. The mission profile for meeting the satellite launch demand includes 17 PSLV missions, 6 GSLV MK-II missions and 2 GSLV MK-III missions (this also includes one experimental mission). This demands increased stage and system production rates, expanding human infrastructure and test facilities and substantial technological achievements in cryogenic stage elements.

8.118. *Space Sciences and Planetary Exploration*: Space Sciences and Planetary Exploratory missions contribute significantly towards understanding the mysteries of the universe, our existence, and provide an opportunity towards development of cutting-edge technologies. Through space science investigations, we seek to understand the processes governing solar radiation, evolution of planetary systems, formation of galaxies, evolution of stellar systems and the universe. Successful launch and realisation of Chandrayaan-1, India's first Mission to Moon in 2008, has been a landmark achievement in Indian Space Programme. The major contributions of Chandrayaan-1 were the discovery of water on the lunar surface and exosphere, clear evidence for the production of energetic neutral atoms and the development of detailed Digital Elevation Model of regions mapped by its stereographic camera. The work on Chandrayaan-2, Astrosat-1 and Aditya-1, initiated during the Eleventh Plan, is in progress and all these missions will be realised in the Twelfth Plan. Besides the spillover missions of Chandrayaan-2, Astrosat-1 and Aditya-1, the newer mission that is planned during the Twelfth Plan is Mars mission. In addition, POLIX (to study the X-ray polarisation from bright X-ray–emitting objects) shall also be persued.

8.119. *Mission to Mars (during November 2013 launch opportunity)*: Mars with its many similarities to earth is an important planet to understand the origin and evolution of the solar system. India certainly cannot afford to be behind in its independent exploration of the red planet. India's first Mission to Mars during 2013 would be important more from the technological perspective, namely, entire mission design, planning, management and operations, and communication from a distance of nearly 400 million km. This mission will demonstrate ISRO's capability to undertake deep-space planetary mission where the travel time from earth to Mars is nearly 300 days. The Indian Mission to Mars would also provide an opportunity to the scientific community, to further understand the Martian Science. The present plan is to launch a Mars-orbiter using PSLV-XL during the November 2013 launch opportunity. Mars-orbiter will be placed in an orbit of 500×80,000 km around Mars and will have a provision for carrying nearly 25 kg of scientific payloads on board.

8.120. An indicative plan outlay of ₹*39,750 crore* at current prices for the Twelfth Five Year has been made for the DOS.

Department of Atomic Energy

8.121. The DAE has been pursuing R&D in nuclear science and engineering and also in advanced mathematics. The Department comprises several multidisciplinary R&D centres, aided institutions and closely linked industrial units that contribute towards basic R&D of technologies so as to harness nuclear science for the growth of the country. R&D by the R&D units of DAE provide valuable support to expand the indigenous Indian nuclear power programme and also to develop non-power applications of nuclear technology for use in industry, agriculture, health care and research. The DAE programmes also support collaborative research, establishment of centres of excellence as a part of efforts to establish linkages with academia.

8.122. *Programmatic Activities of DAE*: The mandate of the Department is to develop and deploy technologies for the production of nuclear power and to harness applications of radiation and isotope technologies for societal benefits. To fulfil this mandate, several technologies need to be developed and it is necessary to carry out basic research to provide a strong foundation to ongoing developments and to spur new developments. To meet all these objectives, human resource development is the most important requirement. Categorisation of the DAE's R&D activities into seven major programmes MP1 to MP7 followed during the previous two Plan periods will be maintained in the Twelfth Plan. Major programmes MP1–MP3 address R&D support to the three-stage Indian nuclear power programmes; MP4 addresses the development of advanced technologies such as accelerators, lasers and so on, and radiation technologies and their applications; MP5 incorporates the basic research in all the relevant branches of science; MP6 facilitates strengthening the research-education linkages and MP7 aims to development of the infrastructure for all the R&D activities.

Twelfth Plan Objectives/Thrust

8.123. Right from its inception, the Indian nuclear power deployment is based on a three-stage programme. The first stage is well established and is already in the commercial domain. The second stage is also geared to take off in a big way with the Prototype Fast Breeder Reactor (PFBR) going operational soon. The third stage of nuclear programme is in the R&D phase. The main emphasis of the DAE in the Twelfth plan includes ageing management and safety upgrades of all nuclear plants in operation, and incorporating enhanced safety features in the upcoming plants. Another thrust area, metallic fuel deployment with its associated fuel cycle in the fast reactor, is the key to reducing doubling time, thus accelerating the pace of nuclear power deployment. In short, the thrust areas address pursuit of multiple reactor technologies, safety upgrades to address beyond-design-basis external events, increased emphasis on development of applications of nuclear technology for societal benefits, outreach programmes to enhance public awareness and acceptance, and strengthening of linkages with universities and national laboratories.

8.124. The significant achievements of DAE under R&D sector during the Eleventh Plan are given in Box 8.8.

Twelfth Five Year Plan Programmes

8.125. The details of the projects and programmes planned to be pursued are given below. Programme under MP1–MP3 include experimental verification of safety-related issues, ageing and degradation studies, life-extension assessment and investigation of new safety concepts for incorporation in nuclear power plants to address extreme external events. Thrust would be given to the development of new techniques for further exploration of uranium with a view to augmenting installed nuclear power capacity.

Box 8.8
Significant Achievements/Development of DAE during the Eleventh Plan Period

- Bhabha Atomic Research Centre (BARC) and Indira Gandhi Centre for Atomic Research (IGCAR) have developed indigenous Time Domain Electromagnetic (TDEM) systems for airborne survey to locate deep-seated uranium deposits. Other achievements include: development of BARC Containment Model (BARCOM) of 540 MWe Pressurised Heavy Water Reactor (PHWR) at Tarapur, the largest nuclear containment model in the world for ultimate load capacity assessment; installation and commissioning of thermal denitration pilot plant; development of prototype magnetic crawler robot for in-service inspection of boiler tubes at thermal power plants; and establishment of country-wide Indian Environmental Radiation Monitoring Network (IERMON) Stations at 115 new locations to provide online information about the radiation levels.
- Construction of Prototype Fast Breeder Reactor of 500 MWe capacity at Kalpakkam is nearing completion. Other activities for the fast reactor programme include production of mixed oxide fuel pins for PFBR at Advanced Fuel Fabrication facility; alloy characterisation facility for fast reactor fuels, pyrochemical reprocessing and sodium fire facilities, fuel cell and argon glove box for sodium chemistry studies and ultra filtration units for separation of strontium, cesium, lanthanides and actinides from simulated wastes. Robotic device for in-service inspection and indigenous spider-robot for steam generator tube inspection have also been developed.
- Under R&D for future reactors that use thorium-based fuel, $(ThO_2\text{-}1\%PuO_2)$ and $(ThO_2\text{-}1\%^{235}UO_2)$ Mixed oxide (MOX) fuel pins have been fabricated to be used for experiments in the AHWR Critical Facility. The AHWR fuelling machine has been manufactured, assembled and tested. An AHWR calandria test facility has been commissioned. A scaled semi-transparent experimental set-up of the calandria has been designed, fabricated and installed in house. For U-233 clean-up project, copper vapour laser systems and the tuneable lasers have been fabricated indigenously.

- Starting from raw materials, technologies and processes leading to the fabrication of long lengths of niobium-titanium–based superconducting cable-in-conduit-conductor (CICC) have been realised. These cables are capable of carrying 30 kA current at 5 tesla. These indigenously manufactured cables have applications in accelerator program and also in Steady-state Superconducting Tokamak.
- The Indian synchrotron Indus-2 became operational and the beam life time in Indus-2 has reached 22 hours at 2 GeV and 100 mA. Six beam lines were made operational, and are being used by researchers from the Department as well as other universities in the country. On 6 December 2011, Indus-2 reached a major milestone of 100mA current at the design energy of 2.5 GeV. Raja Ramanna Centre for Advanced Technology (RRCAT) has developed a new technique of laser welding of niobium superconducting radio frequency (RF) cavities, which offers advantages of low-energy deposition and, therefore, less shrinkage and distortion, and is of a much lower capital cost.
- Research in nuclear agriculture has resulted in development of 10 new mutant crop varieties. One hundred and twenty Nisargruna biogas Plants have been installed in various parts of the country. Cancer research in Tata Memorial Hospital has resulted in cost-effective screening method (costing less than ₹100) in breast cancer.
- High-power Nd:YAG lasers along with fibre optic delivery systems and remote control operation developed by RRCAT were commissioned in different units of PHWRs for cutting and welding operations and for cutting of 612 bellow lip weld joints during the En-masse Coolant Channel Replacement (EMCCR). Besides the large savings in time, this technique also reduces the occupational radiation exposure to the workers by a factor of about 40 as compared to the conventional technique.
- The Board of Research in Nuclear Sciences (BRNS) and University Grants Commission–Department of Atomic Energy (UGC–DAE) Consortium for Scientific Research stand out as important initiatives of DAE in the direction of linking research with education. The Homi Bhabha National Institute (HBNI) is fully functional and plays an important role in conducting academic programmes under its own umbrella as well as in linking DAE with other academic institutes in the country and abroad.
- Large experimental facilities that were set up by DAE during the Eleventh Plan period to facilitate basic research include commissioning of High Altitude GAmma-Ray (HAGAR) array, which consists of seven telescopes, at the high-altitude (4,300 m) station Hanle (in Ladakh) for ground-based gamma ray astronomy, and a high-resolution spectrometer Indian Gamma Ray Array consisting of Germanium clover detectors at the Pelletron Linac Facility at the Tata Institute of Fundamental Research (TIFR). The first phase of parallel supercomputer (Anupam Adhya), delivering 47 terraflop of sustained linpack computational performance, has been developed and released to the users. New campus of TIFR at Hyderabad and two major new centres for basic research—International Centre for Theoretical Sciences at Bengaluru and the TIFR Centre for Interdisciplinary Sciences at Hyderabad are being established. Under ITER-India, design activities of in-kind contribution to ITER, namely, neutron-shielding plates, cryostat, RF and neutral beam systems, and so on, have been completed. Other areas of basic research leading to important findings include radiation biology towards understanding of mechanism of processes involved in response to radiation and other abiotic stresses, utilisation of microbes for bioremediation of radioactive waste, development of stress-resistant crop plants, diagnosis, treatment and research in cancer, establishing the lack of deleterious health and biological effects in people living in high-level natural background radiation areas (HLNRA).
- A total of 11,206 journal papers were published by 13 major DAE institutions during 2007–10. These publications received a total of 49,578 citations during the period. The average number of publications published per year was 2,801.50 and the number of citations per publication during the period was 4.42.
- The first batch of Integrated MSc students joined the National Institute of Science Education Research (NISER) in September 2007. NISER also initiated PhD programmes from 2009 onwards.

For Light Water Reactor (LWR) programme, R&D to develop, design and verify indigenous LWR concepts and development of equipment is planned. The civil construction of the PFBR is in an advanced stage and is expected to be completed by 2012–13. Two 500 MWe MOX-fuelled fast reactors are planned to be set up. For validating the design of the fuel sub-assembly and to gain large-scale experience in the fabrication and irradiation testing of metallic fuels, a 120 MWe metal-fuelled fast reactor will be designed at IGCAR in the Twelfth Plan, with construction proposed in the Thirteenth Plan.

8.126. *R&D related to Thorium-based Reactors*: The development and demonstration of thorium-fuelled Advanced Heavy Water Reactor (AHWR) is an important initiative for thorium utilisation and for the third stage of nuclear power programme. This reactor also already embodies several innovative passive safety features that have now assumed added significance internationally following the Fukushima-Daiichi events. A major programme to experimentally demonstrate the available margins to extreme internal and external events will be carried forward in the Twelfth Plan period to further add to validation of these advanced safety features, many of which are generic in nature.

8.127. *Compact High Temperature Reactor (CHTR) Technologies*: In addition to AHWR, planning for a CHTR is an important step towards the development of advanced reactor technologies required for hydrogen generation. For designing CHTR, consideration of material behaviour as well as technologies for utilisation of high temperature heat warrant investigations for assessing the performance of structural material in corrosive environment of liquid metal and molten salt coolants. Molten salt is a promising coolant for high-temperature application as it also offers the possibility of a thorium-based thermal breeder reactor design suitable in the Indian context with a high level of passive safety. The advanced reactor systems including fusion reactor systems require appropriate materials to be specially developed, characterised, and compatibility issues resolved. Furthermore, special instruments and sensors also need to be developed for measurement of process parameters in such harsh environment. All necessary studies will be taken up in the Twelfth Plan.

8.128. *Research Reactors*: Cirus reactor was permanently shut down in December 2010 and presently only Dhruva reactor, which is in operation for more than 25 years, is available for providing the research reactor–based facilities. Further, the requirement of medical isotopes is expected to increase. To meet the increasing requirement of various radioisotopes for use in the field of medicine, industry and agriculture, needs of special materials, and various facilities for basic and applied research, a 125 MW(th) Research Reactor and a 30 MW High Flux Research Reactor (HFRR) are proposed in the Twelfth plan at BARC Campus Vizag. These new reactors will also provide advanced facilities for basic research in frontier areas of science and for applied research related to development and testing of nuclear fuels and reactor materials. An associated isotope processing laboratory is also proposed.

8.129. *Development of Applications of Radiation Technology*: Radioisotopes and their formulations (radio chemicals, labelled compounds and radio-pharmaceuticals) and radiation sources (isotope sources, gamma plants and electron accelerators) are required for nuclear applications in health care, industry, food security, agriculture, water resources management and research. A national hadron therapy facility for cancer treatment at Advanced Centre for Treatment, Research and Education in Cancer at Tata Memorial Centre (ACTREC-TMC) will be set up. Accelerators and lasers are very powerful tools for basic as well as applied research. Several new beam lines will be installed at INDUS 2 and the existing ones will be upgraded with modern equipment for supporting high-quality research.

8.130. *International Cooperation in Accelerator Physics and Astronomy*: DAE continues to increasingly participate in international collaborative ventures. Participation in activities at LHC, CERN, Geneva, has led India to get the status of an 'observer state'. Indian participation in the seven-member ITER project will continue during the Twelfth Plan. The test blanket module (TBM) development for testing in ITER will be another major activity. India's participation in ITER has demonstrated our scientific and technological strength to be a partner in mega science projects. India has joined the multinational, multi-organisational project Facility for Anti-proton and Ion Research (FAIR) being set up in Germany.

8.131. *Participation in Mega Science Projects*: DAE is participating in several Mega Science Projects. The S&T expertise in the Department will be leveraged in order to contribute to these projects. The FAIR and India-based Neutrino Observatory (INO) are the other ongoing projects. Several new projects are proposed, such as LIGO, Thirty Metre Telescope and Square Kilometre Array. Apart from these, setting up of an Indian Synchrotron for Materials and Energy Research is also proposed. These projects will involve several DAE Institutions including BARC, IGCAR, RRCAT, Variable Energy Cyclotron Centre (VECC), TIFR, IPR as well as universities, and the research facilities built will be available for utilisation by the research community of the nation.

8.132. *DAE in Human Resource and Expertise Building*: The research centres and aided institutions lay strong emphasis on frontline research and human resource development for their personnel and also contribute towards human resource development requirement of the country. Units of the Department also maintain strong linkage with the academic and research community in the country. The initiative of the Department to set up HBNI as a deemed-to-be university is another step towards strengthening the linkage between the institutions of the DAE and also with the academic and research community in the country. It will also help DAE in utilising its vast research infrastructure and faculty towards human research development for the country. Similarly, TIFR has increased intake of research students after having been declared a deemed-to-be university. The present methods of collaboration through BRNS and MOUs with select academic institutes will continue to be supported and further strengthened. The Department of Atomic Energy–Science Research Council (DAE–SRC) award scheme, providing incentive to competent professionals within and outside DAE, will be continued. Increasing linkages with the national higher education institutions (universities, IITs and NITs and so on.) will be continued so as to ensure availability of quality manpower for DAE programmes and projects.

8.133. The Global Centre for Nuclear Energy Partnership (GCNEP), the sixth R&D centre of DAE, is being set up in Haryana near Delhi. The main objective of setting up GCNEP is to enable India in establishing the leadership in the field of nuclear energy through research and training and organise workshops, schools and seminars by Indian and international scientists/experts on topical issues. Under GCNEP, the following schools are being set up:

- School for Studies on Applications of Radioisotopes and Radiation Technologies
- School of Advanced Nuclear Energy System Studies
- School of Nuclear Security Studies
- School of Radiological Safety Studies
- School of Nuclear Material Characterisation Studies

8.134. *Strengthening R&D infrastructure*: In order to meet the growing number of programmes and projects, including in greenfield locations, it is necessary to strengthen and expand the investments in infrastructure. The ongoing projects towards strengthening and upgrading existing security systems need to be also continued. New campuses coming up, for example of BARC in Vizag and of TIFR in Hyderabad, would involve considerable efforts and resources. The TIFR Centre for Interdisciplinary Sciences (TCIS), Hyderabad, has started functioning at the transit premises from mid-June 2011. Laboratories for research in chemistry, biology, lasers and optics, magnetic resonance and condensed matter will be set up in this transit campus during the twelfth plan. Development of the new TIFR Hyderabad campus will be given priority. The newly formed International Centre for Theoretical Sciences (ICTS, TIFR) in Bengaluru is a multi- and interdisciplinary effort with a strong component of human resource development. Emphasis will be on research areas such as biophysics, computational science, complex systems, fluids, the interface between cosmology, particle physics and string theory, new emergent areas of mathematics with applications to biology, and so on.

8.135. An indicative plan outlay of ₹*19,878 crore* at current prices for the Twelfth Five Year has been made for the DAE under R&D sector.

PLAN OUTLAY

8.136. A total Plan outlay of ₹*1,20,430 Crore* has been approved for Six Scientific Departments/Agencies for the Twelfth Five Year Plan. Table 8.1 provides Department-wise allocation and expenditure for the Eleventh Five Year Plan and the break-up of Outlay for Twelfth Five Year Plan.

TABLE 8.1
Plan Outlays and Expenditure of Central Scientific Ministries/Departments/Agencies During Eleventh Five Year Plan and Indicative Outlay for Twelfth Five Year Plan

(₹ in Crore)

Sl. No.	S&T Department/Agencies	Eleventh Plan (2007–12)		Twelfth Plan (2012–17)
		Outlay	Anti. Expdr	Outlay
1	DAE (R&D sector)	11,000.00	8,068.26	19,878
2	MoES	7,004.00	3,202.30	9,506
3	DST	11,028.00	8,636.61	21,596
4	DBT	6,389.00	4,832.24	11,804
5	DSIR including CSIR	9,000.00	6,940.61	17,896
6	DOS	30,883.00	15,834.79	39,750
	Grand Total	75,304.00	47,514.81	1,20,430

ANNEXURE 8.1
National Targets for S&T Sector for the Twelfth Plan

National Targets for S&T Sector for the Twelfth Plan

Global Share of Publications	:	>5 per cent
Global Ranking in SCI publications	:	better than sixth
Global Ranking in Number Patent Cooperation Treaties (PCTs)	:	better than tenth
FTEs in R&D Personnel	:	2,50,000
PhDs Outputs in Whole Science Sector	:	12,500 per year
Public–Private Sharing of Investments		50:50
Gender Parity in EMR Funding (PI Ratios)	:	better than 60:40
The Relative Global Rank in Patent Portfolio	:	better than ninth
Commercialisation of Patents	:	better than 5 per cent levels
Share of High Technology Content in Exports	:	better than 20 per cent
Global Ranking in Innovation Index	:	better than 25th
Establishment of Section 25 Companies	:	in select sectors

DEPARTMENT-BASED DELIVERABLES AND TARGETS FOR THE TWELFTH PLAN

DST

- To strengthen Human Capacities, 30,000 new scholars for Scholarship for Higher Education targeted, Award of Overseas Doctoral scholarships—3,000 man years, Overseas postdoctoral fellowships—500 man years, Women mobility scheme for employed scientists—1,000 positions, Start-up research grant for Indian diaspora undertaking faculty assignments in Indian academia—1,000 man years, enlarging the Principal Investigator base—1,500 man years, INSPIRE Award scheme—2 million awards.
- Support under Fund for improvement of S&T Infrastructure (FIST)-1200-1500 departments and 500 colleges, PURSE—50 Universities, CURIE—6 Universities and 50 Women colleges, IRHPA—15 research areas, SAIF—25 new centres and 10 select centres. Autonomous Institutions focused on Institutional Capacities, Water Technology Solutions—20 implementable solutions to be demonstrated in at least 15 clusters, 20 centres to be created for Nano S&T Mission, 5 National Centres in Advanced Research.
- Centre–State Technology partnerships—At least five viable partnerships through programme support, PPP for R&D. One mega PPP for national challenge area, five PPPs for large-scale challenge, 25 PPPs for proof of concepts for technology solutions.
- Technology Development and Transfer, IDP, IS-STAC through the ongoing programmes, 200 technologies demonstrations, 150 proof of concepts, and 25 cooperative investments with other socio-economic Ministries have been targetted.
- Five product designs and prototypes under security technology R&D.
- Solar Energy Research Initiative—Support 250 doctoral-level researchers from 10 institutions.
- Under Natural Resources Data Management System (NRDMS) and National Spatial Data Infrastructure (NSDI), State Spatial Data Infrastructure has been targeted.
- Technology Platforms for four Identified Areas.
- Under Modernisation of SoI and NATMO, 1:10000 scale map has been targeted.

- Under Nano S&T Mission—25 start-up companies under PPP models would be created.
- PPP for R&D—One mega PPP for national challenge areas and five PPPs for large-scale challenge and also 25 PPPs for proof of concepts for technology solutions.
- Hundred projects for Science for Equity, Employment and Development and 50 Model Demonstration Projects.
- To commission 15 Study Reports, 10 Policy Research Studies, 3 Development of STI indicators for India, 5 Inter-country policy comparison studies, 12 External consultations and inter-country and 10 Technology and Innovation (STI) indicator reports have been planned.

DBT

- Under Human Resource Development, it is proposed to establish 100 Star Undergraduate Colleges, 100 Ramalingaswami fellowships for returning scientists from abroad, 10 finishing schools for industry-ready graduates, award 200 Welcome trust-DBT biomedical fellowships, junior research fellows and 250 postdoctoral fellowships in life sciences.
- Under Promotion of Excellence and Innovation, the targets are to create 25 Centres of excellence in plant sciences, animal sciences, human biology systems and industrial research;10 new centres for translational science education and innovative research in Medical Schools, 20 IICs connecting basic sciences with translational R&D and 2 centres for policy research in agriculture and health care biotechnology.
- For Biotech Facilities and Research Resources the targets are to establish five research resources and service facilities, upgrade and redesign life science research and education in 38 universities.
- Launching of eight Grand Challenge programmes in health care and agriculture on a mission mode around national priorities in development sectors through bottom-up approach and discovery-led innovation, interdepartmental participation and separate government and management structure.
- Establishment and commissioning of three ongoing bio-clusters at Faridabad, Mohali and Bengaluru and two new bio-clusters with clusters boards to govern, and establish incubators, common technology platforms, contract labs for SMEs, genetically modified products (GMP) facilities, research hospital and so on.
- Establish five national research centres/institutions in the areas of Bioinformatics and Computational Biology; Marine and Microbial Biotechnology; Bio-design; Bioscience and Bioengineering; Chronic Disease Science and Biotechnology; and Infectious Science and Biotechnology Institute in the North-East.
- Strengthening of regulatory system for biotechnology through establishment of BRAI, under the act of Parliament and establishment/strengthening of 10 regulatory testing laboratories with good laboratory practice (GLP) standard.
- Expanding existing AIs threefold in terms of human resource, setting up of Extra Mural Research centres on or off site to promote translational science; starting of number of disease-specific network programmes; and physical infrastructure.
- Establishment and operationalisation of BIRAC and launching of two to three new PPP schemes such as ignition grants, start-up grants, shared technology incubators and bio-parks.
- For translational and strategic research in agriculture, health care and environment, about 50 projects/networks shall be launched in system biology, synthetic biology, computational sciences, nano-biology, pre-breeding of crops, photonics, molecular imaging and tissue engineering, biopharmaceuticals and drug development and other emerging areas.

MoES

- Augmentation of Agrometeorological Advisory Services (AAS) from the existing district level to the block level. Plan to reach 30–40 per cent (10 million) farmers for providing the agro-met services from the current level of 10 per cent (2.5 million).
- Strengthen HPC facility from the existing 124 T flops to 2.5 P flops.

- Upgradation of facilities of about 100 airports in the country.
- Setting up of an International Training Centre for Operational Oceanography.
- Development of high resolution model of 13 km to provide a credible, integrated ocean information services.
- Development and demonstration of higher-scale offshore desalination of 10 MLD
- Acquisition of three state-of-the art ocean research vessels.
- Commissioning of third station at Antarctic to strengthen research activities in the Polar Regions.
- Drilling a deep bore hole in Koyna–Warna region for better understanding of stable continental region earthquakes and Reservoir Triggered Seismicity.

DSIR
- Establishment of 40 CICs; support to 1,200 plus innovative proposals from MSME Clusters; acquisition of around 20 Globally Patented Technologies by Indian Industries and value addition.
- Establishment of R&D Facilities for Solar Photovoltaic (SPV) and Solar Thermal (ST) at CEL.

CSIR
- Development of five game-changing technologies that impact lives of millions.
- Thirty exceptional publications of global impact.
- Development and transfer of 50 advanced products/technologies.
- Setting up 15 spin-off companies.
- Training of 3,000 PhDs in trans-disciplinary areas of science and engineering through AcSIR.
- Establishment of the following five new institutes: CSIR Institute of Synthetic and Systems Biology; CSIR Fourth Paradigm Institute; CSIR Institute of Bio-mimetic Materials; CSIR Network Institute for Solar Energy and CSIR Network Institute for Manufacturing Technology.
- Setting up of 10 CSIR Outreach Centres.
- 1,000 patent applications to be filed in India, 1,000 patent applications to be filed abroad and 75–150 non-patent IPRs to be secured and prosecuted.
- To award 15,000 fellowships under the JRF-NET, 1,000 Syamaprasad Mookherjee Fellowships to be awarded, 100 awards under Trans-Disciplinary Fellowship Scheme yearly, 100 awards under CSIR Nehru Science Post-Doctoral Fellowship Scheme yearly, 250 scholarships for dyslexic students.
- Establish 24 CSIR TECHVILS across the country. Showcase TECHVIL to enroll 1 million citizens in adjoining communities to the benefits of technology.
- Setting up CSIR offshore Joint Centres of Excellence in Malaysia, Sweden and USA. Setting up of 12 world-class Innovation Complexes in identified locations across India.
- Under NMITLI, the target is to launch five to seven new projects per year; launch some unique products such as Micro PCR (a platform technology for diagnostic applications), dental implants benefiting Indian masses, next generation clutch plates and so on.
- Expand OSDD to OS drug discovery, OS drug development, OS drug delivery and OS disease diagnostics for MTb.
- Extending OSDD programme to malaria.
- Launching of three Grand Challenge–driven projects with global participation. Develop at least five technologies in participatory mode and transfer the same to stakeholders. Set up at least five CSIR Centres for Collaborative Research with academia, R&D institutions and industry.

DOS
- Realisation of total 25 launch vehicle flights—17 PSLVs + 6 GSLVs + 2 GSLV Mk III including one Experimental Mission (as against 14 flights of the Eleventh plan). First Developmental Flights of GSLV Mk III—the next generation launch vehicle.

- Establishment of Indian Regional Navigational Satellite System (IRNSS) with a constellation of seven satellites.
- Implementation of fully operational base of GAGAN.
- Augment the INSAT/GSAT capacity to ~500 Transponders in C, Ku, Ka, MSS and BSS bands.
- Realisation of GSAT-11—Advanced Communication Satellite.
- Realisation of Advanced Remote Sensing Technology for 0.25m resolution.
- Realisation of Geo Imaging Satellite (GISAT) for Disaster Management Support.
- Implementation of Space based Information Support for Decentralised Planning.
- Multi-wavelength Astronomy Observational Satellite—ASTROSAT.
- Undertaking challenging Mars Orbiter Mission.
- Realisation of Chandrayaan-2 with Rover and Lander. Operationalisation of NDEM with multi-thematic, multi-scale database and relevant Decision Support systems.

DAE
- Apsara Reactor upgradation with indigenously developed fuel.
- Construction and commissioning of AHWR Thermal Hydraulics Test Facility (ATTF) and AHWR Fuelling Machine Test Facility (FMTF).
- Technology development and commissioning of a low energy (20 MeV) linear proton accelerator (LEHIPA) as a part of front end of ADS driver.
- Setting up additional 500 IERMONs (Radiation monitoring stations).
- Setting up an experimental Solar Test Facility (SOTEF).
- Technology development for Electron and Ion Accelerators.
- Augmentation of facilities for Fast Reactor Fuel Reprocessing.
- Establishment of 30 MeV Medical Cyclotron.
- Commissioning of the MACE at Hanle.
- 3m scale optical interferometer as prototype gravitational wave detector.
- Enhancement of INDUS synchrotron user facility.

NOTE
1. SAC-PM (Scientific Advisory Council to the Prime Minister), *India as a Global leader in Science*, 2010.

9

Innovation

9.1. India is the second fastest growing economy in the world, but as the pace of development increases rapidly, the country faces an increasing challenge to ensure that future growth is sustainable and inclusive. Innovation can play a key role in not only driving growth and competitive advantage, but also ensuring that this development includes a larger cross section of people and is socially, economically and environmentally sustainable. Realising that innovation is the engine for national and global growth, employment, competitiveness and sharing of opportunities in the 21st century, the Government of India has declared 2010—20 as the 'Decade of Innovation'.

9.2. India has unique challenges and large unmet needs across diverse areas such as health, education, skills, agriculture, urban and rural development, energy and so on. We also have significant challenges of exclusion and inequitable access due to multiple deprivations of class, caste and gender—all of which require innovative approaches and solutions, and looking beyond the conventional way of doing things. Innovation is going to be central to providing answers to the most pressing challenges and for creating opportunity structures for sharing the benefits of the emerging knowledge economy. Affordable solutions, innovative business models or processes which ease delivery of services to citizens can enable more people to join the development process.

9.3. In this context, there is a need for an Indian Model of Innovation that focuses on affordability and inclusive growth which can be a model for emulation for countries across the globe facing similar challenges of sustainable development. Indian entrepreneurs and policymakers are already moving towards this inclusive model of innovation, and three distinctions of this emerging Indian approach to innovation are worth noting. First, it focuses on finding affordable solutions for the needs of people—for health, water, transport, so on—without compromising quality. For instance, extremely low-cost eye surgeries which do not compromise on surgical standards at US$50 compared to US$1,650 in the US. Second, in this Indian approach to innovation, desired outcomes are produced by innovations in organisational and process models that deliver to people the benefits of technologies that may be developed in scientific laboratories. An example is the delivery models of mobile telephony services that have expanded the reach of telephony with the cheapest call services in the world. Third, there are innovations in the process of innovation itself to reduce the cost of developing the innovations. An example is the Open Source Drug Discovery (OSDD) process being applied by the Council of Scientific and Industrial Research (CSIR) to develop drugs for treatment of tuberculosis, based on a semantic-search, web-based platform for collaboration developed by Infosys, an innovative approach that has cut down the costs and reduced the time for drug development.

9.4. This new paradigm of innovation, focused on producing 'frugal' cost solutions with 'frugal' costs of innovation, in which India may be emerging as a global leader, contrasts sharply with the conventional approach, mostly focused on increasing inputs of Science and Technology (S&T) and R&D and measurement of the numbers of papers and patents produced. Frugal innovation is focused on the efficiency of innovation and on outcomes that benefit people, especially the poor. Industrially advanced countries too are examining their innovation policies to incorporate this broader concept of innovation that moves beyond the R&D paradigm.

9.5. India is also uniquely poised to reap the advantages provided by a nation of a billion connected people, with over 800 million mobile phones, and global leadership in Information and Communication Technology (ICT) and software. This connectivity as well as ICT talent is changing the nature of processes, business, industry, governance, education and delivery systems: and our innovation thinking also has to leverage the unprecedented advantages provided by this changing landscape of connectivity and collaboration.

Towards an Innovation Ecosystem: The Role of NInC

9.6. Conversion of R&D to results for people requires an ecosystem of enterprises working in conjunction: entrepreneurs, researchers, finance providers, business enterprises, and policymakers. Therefore, the national strategies for innovation need to focus on various types of institutions in the ecosystem and aim for more effective collaboration amongst them. This must be India's agenda too if India is to accelerate inclusive growth through innovation.

9.7. Government has a critical role to play in strengthening the innovation ecosystem. It must provide the enabling policy interventions, strengthen knowledge infrastructure, improve inter-institutional collaborations, provide a mechanism for funding business innovations at all levels especially small and medium scale enterprises (SMEs) and provide vision through a national-level road map for innovations. Recognising this need, the Prime Minister has set up a NInC with the mandate to formulate a Road Map for Innovations for 2010–20 with a focus on inclusive growth.

9.8. NInC is focused on encouraging and facilitating the creation of an *Indian Model of Innovation* by looking at five key parameters: Platform, Inclusion, Ecosystem, Drivers and Discourse. The aim is to redefine innovations to go beyond formal R&D parameters and look at innovation as a broader concept that breaks sectoral silos and moves beyond a high-tech, product-based approach to include organisational, process and service innovation where many players can plug into this platform. The core idea is to innovate to produce affordable and qualitative solutions that address the needs of people at the Bottom of the Pyramid, eliminate disparity and focus on an inclusive growth model. NInC's initiatives are also aimed at fostering an innovation ecosystem across domains and sectors to strengthen entrepreneurship and growth, and to facilitate the birth of new ideas. While conceptualising these initiatives, the key drivers are going to be parameters of sustainability, affordability, durability, quality, global competitiveness and local needs. Finally, through its various initiatives, NInC will aim to expand the space for disruptive thinking, dialogue and discourse on innovation.

9.9. Principal initiatives already undertaken by the Council to drive innovation and create an innovation ecosystem in the country are mentioned below.

Supporting Financial System and Mentoring: India Inclusive Innovation Fund (IIIF)

9.10. Innovators need financial support at an early stage to develop and test their ideas in the marketplace. Venture funds are recognised globally as the most suitable form of providing risk capital for the growth of innovative technology and breakthrough ideas. While India is amongst the top recipients in Asia for venture funds and Private Equity Funds, these investments are so far focused on relatively large and 'safer' investments. Thus, despite the growth in the venture capital industry in India and some government schemes for supporting entrepreneurs, the seed funding stage in the innovation pipeline, where amounts required may be small but risks high, is severely constricted.

9.11. To plug this gap and to promote inclusive innovation and entrepreneurship focusing on the needs of people in the lower echelons of society, NInC is creating an India Inclusive Innovation Fund (IIIF). The Fund seeks to promote enterprises engaged in developing solutions in key areas such as health, education, agriculture, handloom, handicrafts and other small business enterprises. The Fund will combine commercial and social returns. The Fund will be capitalised to an eventual target size of ₹5,000 crores to be achieved in phases. It will be kick-started with seed investment from the government and bilateral/multilateral institutions and go to scale with private capital. The Fund will be an autonomous, professionally managed entity with a social investment focus. Government of India has committed seed capital of ₹100 crore to kick-start the Fund and NInC will aim to operationalise this Fund by the year 2013 with an initial close of ₹500 crore.

Increasing Skills, Productivity and Competitiveness of Micro, Small and Medium Enterprises (MSMEs) through Innovation

9.12. MSMEs are among the largest job creators in the country. They contribute to 40 per cent of export and are recognised as engines of economic growth. However, to keep up the pace of strong economic growth and to stay globally competitive, MSMEs need to innovate in all aspects of business. Recognising this need, NInC has envisioned the Industry Innovation Cluster initiative.

9.13. The focal point of this initiative would be the creation of a Cluster Innovation Centre (CIC). The CIC will actively seek relationships to address the needs of the cluster and establish frameworks for knowledge and best practice sharing. By connecting and creating local ecosystem encompassing actors and stakeholders who can bring in technology, financing, skills and mentors, the CIC will help enhance productivity, growth and employability. The Pilot Phase of the Innovation Cluster Initiative has been launched and nine clusters (seven industry and two university) have been chosen to be part of this phase. Pilot activities have commenced at the Ayurveda cluster in Thrissur, Kerala; Food Processing cluster in Krishnagiri, Tamil Nadu; Bamboo cluster at Agartala, Tripura; Auto Components cluster at Faridabad, Haryana; Brassware cluster at Moradabad; Furniture cluster at Ernakulam, Kerala; Life Sciences cluster at Ahmedabad, Gujarat; Delhi University, Delhi; and Maharaja Sayajirao University, Baroda, Gujarat. NInC has been collaborating with State Governments, Ministry of MSME and the Department of Scientific and Industrial Research in this effort.

Nurturing Innovation through Education

9.14. Schools are the best places to inculcate a spirit of innovation. To promote creativity and nurture innovations in the education system, NInC has made the following proposals to the Ministry of Human Resource Development (MHRD), including:

1. Creation of a separate scholarship stream of National Innovation Scholarships analogous to the National Talent Search Scheme. This will help identify talented children at the school level who think creatively, laterally and innovatively on issues that they perceive as important in their local environment. It is expected to have a multiplier effect of valuing creativity and innovation by parents, teachers and the learning system.
2. Setting up an Innovation Centre in each DIET (District Institute of Education and Training) to enhance teacher training and enable them to become facilitators of creativity and innovative thinking.
3. Mapping of local history, ecology and cultural heritage by each high School in the country to create critical thinking on their local environment by students.
4. Creation of a National Innovation Promotion Service to replace/add to National Service Scheme in colleges to use college students to identify local innovations. This is a scheme of the Ministry of Youth Affairs and Sports which along with Ministry of Human Resource Development (HRD) has been requested to examine its feasibility.
5. Setting up a Meta University, as a redefinition of the university model in the 21st century by leveraging India's National Knowledge Network to enable multidisciplinary learning and collaborative knowledge creation.

6. Setting up 20 Design Innovation Centres co-located in Institutes of National Importance. Co-location in campuses of national repute like Indian Institutes of Technology (IITs)/National Institutes of Technology (NITs) will help leveraging of academic and industry resources and give a boost to design capacity in the country. Also, setting up an Open Design School; creating an institute for facilitating training of trainers in design and introducing design thinking at the school level.

7. Identifying and facilitating the development of 20 University Innovation Clusters across the country where innovation would be seeded through CICs, as mentioned earlier. The CIC will provide a platform for the university and its partners to forge linkages between various stakeholders from industry and academia, initiate and assist innovation activities, encourage innovations in curricula and act as a catalyst and facilitator. It will also work closely with other industry clusters in its region. As mentioned earlier, initial pilot with University of Delhi and Maharaja Sayajirao University in Baroda have commenced and have received overwhelming response from the student community.

9.15. The Ministry of Human Resource Development has green-lighted the proposals relating to the award of 1,000 Innovation Fellowships at the school level (Classes 9–12); introducing the Mapping of Local History, Local Ecology and Local Culture and Heritage by all high schools and setting up the first Meta University of the world for multi-disciplinary learning and collaborative learning. MHRD has also incorporated steps on re-positioning DIETS in the country in the new Guidelines for the Centrally Sponsored Scheme on Teacher's Training. MHRD is also working on a concept note on design education in consultation with the Council and Planning Commission.

Connecting India for Innovation: Rural Broadband and Applications

9.16. Government approved the proposal to connect all panchayats through optic fibre and the rural broadband plan on 25 October 2011. NInC is currently working on applications for rural broadband in collaboration with Ministries of Rural Development, Panchayati Raj, HRD, Health and the Prime Minister's National Council on Skill Development so that even as hardware connectivity is under progress, applications also get addressed. The vision is to transform governance, service delivery in areas such as health, education and agriculture, and unleash local innovation capacity through rural broadband.

Platform for Best Practices and Innovations

9.17. Currently, there are many enterprises across the country which are delivering benefits to citizens and meeting challenges of inclusion in areas such as health, education energy, low-cost housing and sanitation, through innovative solutions. It is often said that India is a country with many successful experiments that do not achieve scale. Scaling up the impact of such innovations requires that such ideas be spread around rapidly so that others could emulate them. And it also requires that larger business organisations and venture funds become aware of them and support them. We have instances of documentation of these practices in the form of the Honey Bee Network, but no virtual platform exists for the same. Therefore, the strengthening of the innovation ecosystem requires a platform for information sharing and dissemination. While some knowledge portals for innovations in specific areas already exist, the NInC has developed the India Innovation Portal to enable easy access to these as well as to become a wider information repository on innovation and a platform for collaboration as well. (www.innovation.gov.in)

Developing Institutional Framework for Innovation

9.18. An extensive innovation ecosystem requires many lateral connections, often at local levels, between producers, sellers and financiers, and the facilitating government machinery. Sweden has a region-wise process of participation of citizens and enterprises in formulating the innovation agenda. In a much larger and more diverse country, as India is, development of the innovation ecosystem must be even more widely devolved.

9.19. To create a cross-cutting system to boost innovation performance in the country, NInC is facilitating the setting up of State Innovation Councils in each State. These Councils would enlist non-government expertise and are expected to drive the innovation agenda in the States. Using the broad templates suggested by NIC, they will develop interventions to suit their State's specific needs. In this way, the national innovation agenda will combine with other thrusts for improvement of governance and service delivery described elsewhere in the Plan to introduce more flexibility and innovation in centrally sponsored schemes and, thus, improve the efficiency and inclusiveness of the growth process. Currently, 22 States have constituted State Innovation Councils.

9.20. NInC is also encouraging the setting up of Sectoral Innovation Councils aligned to Union Government Ministries to promote innovation ecosystems across sectors and domains. Currently, 24 Ministries have set up Sectoral Innovation Councils.

Challenge Funds for Innovation

9.21. To induce a culture of innovation in the country, there is a need to offer encouragement through awards and challenges which mobilise people to engage and respond creatively and bring focus on neglected societal challenges. Internationally, examples range from the X Prize to the DARPA Grand Challenges and the World Bank's Development Marketplace. The NInC is also seeking to set challenges for the Indian imagination to incentivise the citizens to come up with solutions, especially those that relate to inclusive innovation. NInC has already announced awards for its challenge to improve work tools, innovate on products and processes that reduce drudgery of the working-class population.

Partnering for Innovation: Collaboration and Networks

9.22. In an increasingly global world, partnerships and knowledge sharing are critical and can lead to mutual growth and development. NInC is also focused on facilitating and leveraging platforms for international collaboration for driving innovation and multidisciplinary research. To exchange ideas on fostering international collaborations for innovation, NInC hosted a Global Roundtable on Innovation on 14th–15th November 2011 in New Delhi where heads of innovation policy from 15 governments across the world came together to share cross-country experiences and best practices. This was followed by a Second Global Roundtable on Innovation in 2012 where several collaborative initiatives were outlined.

Bringing Innovation into Science Museums

9.23. Science Museums and Centres in the country can be an important resource for nurturing creativity and encouraging a spirit of innovation in the country, but their potential remains underutilised. The NInC is partnering with the National Council of Science Museums (NCSM), National Museum of Natural History (NMNH) and others to enhance the impact of existing Science Centres in the country and use them as channels for innovation outreach. NInC will aim to invigorate the existing Science Centres in the country through more interactive exhibits, while leveraging locally available resources to showcase science in a hands-on manner. It will also use the Science Centres for showcasing innovations on a regular basis and improving outreach.

9.24. NIC is currently working on seven pilots of Innovation Spaces at Science Centres/Museums in Ahmedabad, Bangalore, Delhi, Kolkata, Mumbai, Sawai Madhopur and one in the North-East.

9.25. Apart from these initiatives, NInC is also working on several other ideas such as announcing 10 Grand Challenge Awards to leverage public imagination for innovative solutions in critical areas. It is also looking at promotion of projects that create an innovation dividend like the setting up a Knowledge City in Kerala. NInC is also working on the 'Courts of Tomorrow' initiative to give effect to the extensive computerisation plan as laid down by the e-courts Mission Mode Project. This initiative will put the best ICT tools in the hands of judges and the registrars, to aid them in the speedy dispensation of justice. Further, NInC is also working towards creating draft policies on innovation and entrepreneurship to institutionalise innovation thinking into policymaking for providing the requisite stimulus from the Central Government.

9.26. The efforts of NInC are just a starting point for creating an innovation ecosystem in the country. Apart from the earlier mentioned efforts on stimulating finance for innovation, driving innovation at industry clusters or institutionalising innovation by liaising with States and Central Ministries, focus also has to be on stimulating new models of enterprise where producers are also the owners so that they can not only earn incomes but also share in the wealth created by the enterprise. Organisations like Self Employed Women's Association (SEWA), and companies formed by the Chanderi weavers in Madhya Pradesh, are such examples. Such enterprises require innovations in organisational and legal forms. The Planning Commission is examining changes that would facilitate the multiplication of more such enterprises. Through such innovations, businesses that are of the people (owned by them), and businesses by the people (in which people are a principal resource in production and distribution) can cost-effectively produce products and services for people at the bottom of the pyramid.

9.27. Creating a robust innovation ecosystem will also require focus on Intellectual Property Rights (IPR) issues. Management of IPR has become extremely important in the new knowledge economy with global competition. Adequate rights on the intellectual property produced by an innovator enable innovators to recoup their investments and make profits: thus IPR spurs innovation. Good national IPR systems also enable knowledge of technological advances to be accessible through the patent system to others who can build on them. To obtain both these benefits, India must improve its management of IPR. The administrative machinery for IPR management must be considerably strengthened and professionalised and Department of Industrial Policy and Promotion (DIPP) has taken up this task.

9.28. Holders of IPR have incentives to strengthen and extend their monopolies. However, monopolies can restrain competition and further innovation, and thus tend to increase costs for customers. This is the fear even in the West, with respect to pharmaceuticals, for example. The concept of monopolising knowledge, albeit for a limited period, that underlies prevalent models of IPR can have perverse effects when it is extended to areas of traditional knowledge, preventing poorer people from continuing to use their own knowledge without payments to those who have 'patented' it under IPR. Also new models of collaborative innovation are emerging, such as OSDD, mentioned before. Concepts of IPR will have to be developed to suit such new models of innovation in which, incidentally, India has great stakes because of their potential to produce 'frugal' innovations for inclusive growth. Therefore, as India aims to become amongst the global leaders in innovation, it will also have to be amongst the leaders in efficient management of IPR and innovations in IPR concepts and policies.

Technology Innovations in the Government

9.29. Apart from the effort of the NInC to strengthen innovation and provide a policy direction for fostering innovation within the system, there are also several innovative efforts underway within the government structures that aim to improve processes and service delivery, enhance collaboration and generate greater transparency and accountability.

9.30. The *Aadhaar* or Unique Identity Programme is the first 'online' identity system anywhere in the world wherein resident's identity can be authenticated 'in real-time', even on a mobile network, anywhere in India. This programme will create a foundation for more transparent and efficient public service delivery and is internationally considered as a game-changing approach to inclusion. By providing a clear proof of identity, *Aadhaar* will empower India's poorer citizens in accessing services such as the formal banking system and give them the opportunity to easily avail various other services provided by the government and the private sector. It seeks to cover 60 crore residents in India by 2014 and eventually cover the entire country. Twenty crore residents have been enrolled into the system as on March 2012.

9.31. Going forward, the *Aadhaar*-enabled bank account and payment infrastructure will enable e-payments to the beneficiaries' bank accounts for government's social welfare schemes such as Mahatma Gandhi National Rural Employment Guarantee Act (MGNREGA) and mitigate delays and losses. For trying out the *Aadhaar*-enabled payments for various government schemes, a list of 50 districts in the country for initiation of the programme has been proposed to the Ministry of Finance. The government is also looking at using the *Aadhaar* platform for PDS and achieving substantial economies in subsidy outgo in areas such as Fertiliser, Liquefied Petroleum Gas (LPG) and Kerosene by enabling direct transfer of subsidies. Pilot projects on the above are currently ongoing. Collectively, this will have a transformational impact on the delivery of public services in the country.

9.32. Government is also leveraging ICT to reduce pendency in the legal system, encourage a move towards e-governance, e-procurement, e-tendering and e-office. It is also undertaking an ambitious initiative to connect 2,50,000 panchayats with fiber-based broadband to improve governance and service delivery at the last mile. A national geographic information system (NGIS) organisation is also being thought of to map information, assets and data accurately, which will assist in policy and works planning and improve delivery of services in urban and rural areas.

9.33. The National Knowledge Network (NKN) of the Government of India which is a high-speed multi-gigagibit network is not only connecting educational and research institutes in the country, but is getting connected to global research networks to enable real-time collaboration and research. The NKN is allowing students and researchers to move towards a new paradigm of education and research based on a virtual platform that breaks silos of geography and boundaries.

9.34. Other innovations are in the management of performance of government Ministries. The government has initiated a performance management system which requires every ministry and department to undertake a stakeholder consultation to assess the gaps between its stakeholders' expectations and its actual delivery. Ministries must develop innovative strategies to bridge these gaps, and must accordingly specify the measures of its performance by which it should be judged. After initial trial runs and adjustments in its design, this system, generally called the Results Framework Document (RFD), is now adopted by almost all Ministries at the Centre. Some State Governments such as Kerala and Himachal Pradesh have also begun to adopt this approach.

9.35. There are also other complementary actions by multiple agencies of the government to facilitate innovation in the public systems. For instance, on the initiative of the Office of the Prime Minister, the Cabinet Secretariat issued orders to have the agenda of innovation embedded in all proposals to the Cabinet where action on innovation is reported specifically in each proposal to the Cabinet. The 13th Finance Commission which predated NInC provided for ₹1 crore (₹10 million) for each of the over 600 districts as a District Innovation Fund in the country to promote innovation. Further, on the suggestion of the 13th Finance Commission, a new institution to create a 'climate and nurture a culture of accelerating and diffusing innovation in public systems' has been set up in the Administrative Staff College of India (ASCI) in Hyderabad called the Centre for Innovations in Public Services. Also, as mentioned above, an initiative of the CSIR, the portal for OSDD, has been created as a platform for global partnership to provide affordable health care to poorer people afflicted by diseases.

9.36. Apart from the above, the Department of Science & Technology has launched an INSPIRE programme to identify and reward young talent in science, and it covers students from high schools, Bachelor of Science and Master of Science levels. Finally, to encourage local responses to local problems and encourage local problem solving, flexi-funds have become an integral part of major flagship programmes like Sarva Shiksha Abhiyan (Elementary Education) and the National Rural Health Mission (Basic Health). The National Rural Employment Guarantee Act (NREGA), the largest flagship programme, promotes local innovation by providing for comprehensive planning with funds directly given to panchayats.

9.37. *To summarise*, innovation can play a very important role in the development discourse, because it can offer a new approach to a system that is currently over-burdened by the multiple demands and has limited resources at its disposal. Enhanced focus on innovation can have an impact much beyond the realm of S&T in diverse areas such as health and education delivery, governance, enterprise development and much more. Collectively, this can herald a generational change in the country and can lay out a chart for a more sustainable and inclusive growth paradigm.

10

Governance

10.1. Good governance is increasingly viewed as an essential element of any well-functioning society. It ensures effective use of resources and deliverance of services to citizens and also provides social legitimacy to the system. Rising income levels in a democracy also bring with them rising expectations and a demand for good governance, both at the level of the Centre and the States, and also lower down in the third tier of government.

10.2. Good governance is critical to translating Plan outlays into significant outcomes on the ground. It is critical because without good governance, resources that are allocated are not efficiently utilised; management of public service delivery is sub-optimal; efficiency of public expenditure is affected; and finally, it impacts the effective management of natural resources which are sovereign wealth under sovereign ownership.

10.3. The problem of governance that has to be tackled surfaces in three different ways. The first relates to systemic improvements, which increase the effectiveness of government plan expenditure on new programmes. The second relates to improvements in customer satisfaction on the delivery of services by government agencies. The third relates to the perception of corruption and what we can do to tackle it.

IMPROVING THE EFFECTIVENESS OF PLAN PROGRAMMES

10.4. The pace of public expenditure in the last few years has increased dramatically and a large part of this expenditure is aimed at promoting the welfare of the weaker and more vulnerable sections of the population. Nearly ₹7 lakh crore have been spent on the 15 major Flagship programmes during the Eleventh Plan period. This sharp rate of increase is unprecedented. A number of legislative steps have also been taken at securing rights to the people, like the Right to Information Act, the Mahatma Gandhi National Rural Employment Guarantee Act, the Forest Rights and the Right to Education Act. Nevertheless, questions remain on whether these programmes which involve a large volume of resources are actually delivering benefits as expected. In other words, the funds are in place, the rights constitutionally guaranteed, and many achievements have also been recorded but much more work needs to be done to translate the immense promise of these initiatives into reality.

10.5. There is a need for an in-depth review of administrative processes at various levels to ensure expeditious decisions that can advance development priorities of the nation. The administrative system must promote and encourage decision making without delay to promote efficiencies in governance, and to prevent cost overrun where major development projects are concerned. An essential requirement for this is to ensure that the administrative system and ethos protects civil servants, who act *bona fide*, and in good faith.

10.6. A key lacuna is that implementation continues to be in a business-as-usual mode, while these new programmes demand a new architecture based on innovative breaks with the past in significant respects. A number of changes are being instituted in the architecture of implementation of Plan programmes in the Twelfth Plan to overcome the universalization without quality ('U without Q') syndrome.

Strengthening Local Institutions

10.7. A key diagnostic conclusion regarding the relative lack of success of Plan programmes is that these are designed in a top down manner and do not effectively articulate the needs and aspirations of the local people, especially the most vulnerable. With the 73rd Constitutional Amendment, several functions were transferred to Panchayati Raj Institutions (PRIs). Since 2004, there has also been massive transfer of funds, especially after the enactment of the Mahatma Gandhi National Rural Employment Guarantee Act (MGNREGA). But institutionally, the PRIs remain weak and they do not have the capacity to plan or implement programmes effectively. Many studies show that the impressive figures on the formation of self-help groups (SHG) under Swarnjayanti Gram Swarojgar Yojana (SGSY) hide a lot of poor quality work. The potential power of the National Rural Livelihoods Mission (NRLM) lies in the economies of scale created by SHG Federations (comprising 150–200 SHGs each). This is evident, for example, in bulk purchase of inputs (seeds, fertilisers and so on) and marketing of outputs (crops, vegetables, milk, NTFPs and so on). They can also provide larger loans for housing and health facilities to their members by tying up with large service or loan providers. A variety of insurance services can be made available through this route, including life, health, livestock and weather insurance. It has also been shown how doing business with SHG Federations can help public sector bank branches in remote rural areas becoming viable entities. However, for all this to happen, consistent efforts are needed to strengthen these institutions. Watershed Committees and Water Users Associations need strengthening, as do the Forest Protection Committees. When these local institutions are stronger, the sustained impact of Plan programmes can be ensured with careful maintenance and upkeep of the assets created with their active involvement. These institutions also strengthen the fabric of Indian democracy at the grass-roots. Only strong PRIs can ensure effective implementation of Panchayats (Extension to the Scheduled Areas) Act 1996 (PESA) and Scheduled Tribes and Other Traditional Forest Dwellers (Recognition of Forest Rights) Act.

10.8. The Twelfth Plan, therefore, proposes a complete break from the past and provides sizeable resources to the Ministry of Panchayati Raj. From an Eleventh Plan allocation of ₹636 crore to a Twelfth Plan outlay of ₹6,437 crore, the increase from the second year of the Twelfth Plan, the first year being devoted to strengthening the capacities of the States and the Ministry to absorb these additional funds will be deployed for the Rajiv Gandhi Panchayat Sashaktikaran Abhiyan meant for strengthening human resource and systems capacities of PRIs.

Social Mobilisation

10.9. The experience with Plan programmes has clearly established the central role of a socially mobilised and aware community as a decisive determinant of success. However, it is also clear that romanticizing community action and presuming that this will happen automatically, is to perpetuate a myth that actually hurts the poor. Local communities, left to themselves, will not necessarily allow the poor, Dalits, Adivasis and women, to express themselves. The States that have emphasised the role played by social mobilisers and have made specific financial and human resource provisions have, invariably, succeeded. It is the participation of users in planning, implementation and social audit of these programmes has proved critical to their success. It is only when we recognise the key role of social mobilisers in raising awareness and engendering active participation of local people, especially women, that the true potential of demand-driven and bottom-up programmes such as MGNREGA, TSC and NRLM are effectively realised.

10.10. In this background, specific provisions are being made during the Twelfth Plan in each flagship programme for dedicated time and human and financial resources for social mobilisation, awareness generation and social audit. The new Operational Guidelines for MGNREGA, for example, provide that those blocks of the country where either scheduled castes plus scheduled tribes form ≥30 per cent of the population or the annual MGNREGA expenditure was more than ₹12 crore in any year since the programme started, will mandatorily have at least three Cluster Facilitation Teams (CFT). Each CFT will service a cluster of Gram Panchayats (CGP), being accountable to each GP within their Cluster. Each CGP will cover around 15,000 job cards or an area of about 15,000 ha, broadly corresponding to the boundaries of a mini-watershed and local aquifer. The CFT will comprise a fully dedicated, three-member professional support team for MGNREGA. The CFT will be a multidisciplinary team led by an Assistant Programme Officer and will comprise specialists in earthen engineering, community mobilization, hydrogeology, agriculture/allied livelihoods.

10.11. Civil Society has a crucial role to play in social mobilisation and capacity building to help PRIs to take up the tasks assigned to them. Government must strongly encourage partnerships with civil society including not only NGOs but also academic institutions, local colleges and universities. Students and teachers play a significant role in supporting development programmes by providing vital inputs that are scarce, particularly in the remote areas. The precise institutional arrangements within which these are embodied could vary, depending on the requirement and context but these spaces do need to be mandated. For instance, they could, as considered appropriate, be either in-sourcing or out-sourcing types of relationships, so that the synergy of state and civil society can truly be harnessed. Both types of relationships have already been tried out with great success as, for example, the network of volunteers mobilised under the National Service Scheme (NSS). These examples must be built upon and taken to scale.

10.12. The Twelfth Plan proposes setting up of a dedicated institution meant to foster state-civil society partnerships. The Bharat Rural Livelihoods Foundation (BRLF) is proposed to be set up to foster and facilitate civil society action in partnership with government for transforming the livelihoods and lives of people in areas such as the Central Indian Adivasi belt. Initial BRLF support will be provided to civil society partners as 'trigger funding', that is, to develop proposals that reflect this partnership with State Governments/PRIs/banks. BRLF will assist its civil society partners in ensuring that the design of their proposals incorporates a collaborative mode of functioning with governments/PRIs/banks. The aim is to support grassroots level action towards empowerment of people, particularly the Adivasis and scaling up of approaches that are innovative both in terms of programme content and strategy. Innovation can be in many directions—technology, social mobilisational approaches, local institution building, architecture of partnerships, management techniques and so on. Each project supported by BRLF will attempt to leverage the vast resources being made available by both banks and government for a large number of programmes, such as MGNREGA, NRLM, IWMP, BRGF, IAP, RKVY, RADP, NHM, IAY, NRDWP, TSC and so on. The aim is to provide support through the BRLF to projects that largely seek to leverage government programmes and funding already available on the ground.

10.13. Beginning with an initial amount of ₹200 crore, the Government of India (GOI) will provide a Corpus of ₹500 crore in three tranches over the next three years to BRLF, against achievement of well-defined milestones. Funds would also be sourced from concerned State Governments and philanthropic foundations in India and abroad as also high net worth individuals and the Indian diaspora.

Voluntary Sector

10.14. To strengthen governance at the panchayat, block, district, State and Central levels with special focus at the critical level of the district planning board, it is essential to build mechanisms that institutionalise consultative planning to enable greater representation of the stakeholders. One way of achieving the same is through institutionalised consultations with the voluntary sector. The Voluntary Sector can help build a self-reliant, motivated and harmonious social order by enabling people and people's groups to access democratic processes and entitlements that lead to empowerment. It can also present a critique of public functioning and provide alternatives. Its inherent objective being to ensure enhanced participation of people and articulation of agreement or dissent against use of excessive power by State and failure of the market institutions to reach the poor. The Voluntary Sector thus contributes to:

1. strengthening democracy and governance through improved participatory representation. awareness of rights and capacity building of local institutions;
2. advancing rural and urban development through grass-roots–level innovation and human resource and talent management;
3. transforming inter-personal, familial and community spaces through awareness generation and sensitisation;
4. providing platforms for dialogue and dissent for appreciation of and respect for differences in opinions and affiliations; and
5. promoting art, culture, environment protection and other forms of public enquiry; alternatively, it may be said that the sector should cover the spaces of social defence, social security, social service and social change.

10.15. The Twelfth Plan should institutionalise the Joint Consultative Groups/Forums/Joint Machineries recommended by the National Policy on the Voluntary Sector in all forms of planning, right from the grass-roots levels up to the level of Central Government Ministries. Within the Joint Consultative Groups/Forums/Joint Machineries structure, members of civil society, including the voluntary sector would be made partners in the debates that precede designing and development of policies/schemes/programmes, and also be involved in mid-course corrective measures to create a window for improvements as well as incorporation of regional/cultural specificities. Further, mechanisms would be set up to identify and up-scale innovations that have made visible changes in the lives of beneficiary communities. Experiments in health, women's empowerment and watershed management have yielded particularly impressive returns. This approach should now be extended to other domains of governance.

10.16. States would be encouraged to formulate state voluntary sector policies on the lines of the national policy on the voluntary sector to enable and empower an independent, creative and effective voluntary sector in each state, which can contribute to the social, cultural and economic advancement of its people.

Financing the Sector

10.17. In keeping with the letter and spirit of the National Policy on the Voluntary Sector, there is a need to facilitate funding to voluntary organisations in order to enable them to mobilise people as agents of social transformation.

Strengthening Data Collection and Management Systems

10.18. With increase of voluntary organisations in India, there is an urgent need to identify and list organisations based on their registration, expertise, size, activities and so on. A national data bank that lists VOs on the basis of the registration (trust/society/non-profit company), thematic area of expertise (women's empowerment/health/environment and so on) and nature of work (research/implementation/evaluation/designing and so on) would be developed to make the present system of engagement more rewarding and efficient.

Accreditation and Certification

10.19. Accreditation and certification of voluntary agencies to enhance their credibility, transparency and accountability, and also ensure their capability in performing certain activities will help improve standards. A system that is acceptable to all VOs and other stakeholders would be set up to bring in certain minimum standards for the VOs. A national accreditation authority and its mechanisms would be designed.

Partnership between Public, Private and Voluntary Sectors

10.20. While expected roles of the Voluntary, Public and Private Sectors are well understood, each has contributed to the domain of the other. Many evolved, multinational Indian companies are increasingly participating in allocating both financial and human resources support to VOs over and above self-managed initiatives of Corporate Social Responsibility (CSR).

CSR initiatives and Corporate–VO Partnerships should also include affirmative action to ensure equity, reduce ethnic and social conflicts and make public/private spaces more sensitive to diversity and social justice. There is also a need to create a cadre of professionals who can deal with governance issues within the voluntary sector. Capacity building of people involved in voluntary action is necessary to improve governance at all levels.

Restructuring of Centrally Sponsored Schemes

10.21. Over a period of several Plans, the number of Centrally Sponsored Schemes (CSSs) has been growing. Large funds are being transferred to States under these Schemes. In view of the large diversity of physical and economic infrastructure in the States, their potential for development and investment requirements, the Schemes need to provide greater flexibility in their design. The Planning Commission had appointed a Committee under Shri B.K. Chaturvedi, Member, Planning Commission to suggest measures and identify changes required in the restructuring of the CSSs. The Committee has suggested:

1. The number of CSS should be limited and only those schemes which are required as a part of the convergence process as a broader scheme have large outlays so as to make impact across the states to be implemented, the rest to be weeded out and to be converged with other schemes.
2. The existing CSS should be categorised into Flagship schemes that have large outlays and address major national issues; major sub-sectoral schemes to address developmental problems of major sectors like agriculture, education and health and Sector-umbrella schemes which deal with the range of problems of concerned sector.
3. Distribution of CSS funds among States should be based on transparent notified guidelines which should be put on the website of the concerned Ministries. The State may be incentivised to provide larger outlay in certain sectors like health, education, skill development and rural infrastructure. The incentives could be by provisions of additional funds based on the State's own efforts to increase outlays for the sector.
4. The physical and financial norms for the Schemes may be varied depending on the requirement of the State. A mechanism for developing flexibility in such norms as against the normal CSS prescription has been suggested. This should take care of large variation often requested by North East States or States like Kerala, Rajasthan, Uttarakhand and Himachal Pradesh which have special needs.
5. All CSS must have 20 per cent flexi funds (10 per cent for Flagship schemes). These should be utilised by the States to prepare schemes which are especially suited for the requirement of that State.
6. Each flagship programme will provide a flexible pool of financial resources to be used to facilitate and incentivise innovative practices that blaze a trail for others to follow during the Twelfth Plan period.
7. There should be a concurrent monitoring and evaluation of the CSS. This should be done by independent monitors and put on the website of the concerned Ministry and the Planning Commission. This assessment could be done by professional institutions, visit of experts to major project-implementing States or assessment by individual experts by visits to the field.

10.22. The Twelfth Plan will restructure the CSSs and provide flexibility in the light of the recommendations of the BKC Committee.

Convergence

10.23. A key deficiency of Plan programmes is that they continue to function within the confines of departmental silos without requisite convergence and with a high degree of duplication of effort. The Twelfth Plan visualises a convergence of implementation across programmes to pool financial and physical resources across sectors to attain synergy to benefit the target group. For example, rural drinking water and sanitation programmes should be converged so that the two objectives are attained in a mutually consistent manner. Similarly, it is proposed that under the JNNURM, every water supply project will necessarily also be a sewage treatment project and green buildings will require linkages with the energy sector. Creating common sanctioning authorities within districts for the IWMP and RKVY programmes so that the IWMP has a livelihoods focus and the RKVY based on watershed principles is another step in this direction. Similarly convergence is required between Women and Child Development programmes, Public Health and Drinking Water; nutrition, mid day meals (MDMs) and physical education in schools; and skill development programmes that will call for backward linkages with school programmes and forward linkages with industry and other service sectors who will be potential employers of skilled manpower.

Effective Design and Implementation

10.24. While formulating schemes, it is important to ensure that they are well-designed for the objective at hand and also that the guidelines and procedures help in effective implementation. Some of the areas which will need focus in ensuring good architecture of the schemes will be:

1. While preparing the schemes, the central ministries role would be to act as a knowledge partner and enabler to the project implementation, which will be typically in the states. For this ministries will prepare capabilities in preparing for scheme design and creation of learning systems and networks from which the states and local implementers can learn.
2. These schemes would have specific strategic outcomes. For example, it could result in improved number of patents, employment generation, providing learning support to the disabled or improved energy efficiency.
3. While, capabilities are prepared in the ministries, time should be devoted to preparation of good scheme, as mentioned earlier. The Ministry would use funds to design schemes which might require higher consultation experts/expertise or reaching out to numerous stake holders. There has been so far very little investment made in this area. Often, not enough time and energy is devoted to this. The schemes after a proposed design have a good chance of delivering the desired outcomes.
4. The consultation with the stakeholders is one of the key requirements for ensuing that the architecture of these schemes meet the objectives. Often, the consultation process is not mandatory. The schemes which may require formulation of laws or guidelines would need to have extensive consultative machinery. Resources would need to be provided to improve the quality of consultations.
5. The architecture of this scheme must have evaluation and feedback mechanisms. It is important to evaluate the schemes against the strategic outcomes to ensure effective use of money being spent. Not enough attention is devoted to this aspect. Often this is left to the audit function. It is not a good use of public money and resources. An effective evaluation can lead to improved versions of these schemes, leading to better outcomes and more efficient use of public resources.

10.25. Some of the areas which will need to be kept in mind for effective implementation are:

1. Developing flexibility and its effective use during the implementation of these schemes for improving their outcomes would need collective action. It is important to have learning and feedback mechanisms in place to ensure that implementation effectiveness improves. This would help in diagnosis of issues during implementation and rectifying problems identified, using flexibility components of the scheme.
2. It is important to prioritise, sequence and create momentum through results. Often it takes time for results of policy recommendation to become visible. To ensure that the implementation process does not lose momentum, it is important to have some early wins. These would help build confidence and commitment to the policy.
3. Public programmes must have clear outcomes. It is imperative that time is spent upfront to find outcomes in consultation with stakeholders. Failure to do this causes the system to adopt simplistic measures of performance against the targets.

Capacity Building for Implementation

10.26. The Twelfth Plan must address capacity building at the local level as a key instrument for improving outcomes. Some of the specific measures required are:

1. While, functions have been devolved to PRIs/ULBs, there has not been a commensurable devolution of functionaries and funds or effort to build human capacity at the lower level. Unless PRIs/ULBs get good quality personnel, they cannot perform the functions devolved upon them. A pooled fund across programmes should be created from which resources could be drawn for capacity building. Given the considerable overlap in both the people to be trained and the issues their capacities need to be built for across programmes.
2. Government institutions charged with capacity building have, by and large, under-performed and are in urgent need of reform. They need to be thoroughly professionalised and also need to develop powerful partnerships with carefully selected civil society organisations which have a commendable track-record in this sphere. A number of institutes of the government, which have otherwise limited staff can be upgraded by entering into public–private partnership (PPP) and thus, strengthen the excellence of the faculty as well as, the quality of training imparted. This will improve the capacity building capability across the States.
3. To meet shortage of personnel in the short to medium term, recruitment from the private sector and hiring of external consultants through a fast track process needs to be enabled by an appropriate hiring policy. A list of empanelled professional institutions to streamline the recruitment process and enable PRIs/ULBs to access external talent in a timely manner.

10.27. Keeping the needs of the capacity building both for ULBs/PRIs, the Twelfth Plan would make adequate provisions in each Plan programme that would serve the requirements of capacity building at the cutting-edge level of implementation.

10.28. The Eleventh Plan period has seen many examples of the use of modern technology to improve transparency, access and efficiency of Plan programmes. The transfer of funds in an unmediated and timely manner to the target beneficiaries has seen great improvement. However, the spread of such good practices remains uneven across States. The Twelfth Plan will see the roll-out of the unique identification (UID) platform across the country that will enable efficient and expeditious transfer for funds to ultimate beneficiaries without leakage.

Independent Evaluation Office

10.29. Government programmes can benefit enormously from independent evaluation. At present concurrent evaluation is done by the Ministry concerned on a on-going parallel process. Expert evaluation of programmes that have been in operation is done by the Programme Evaluation Organisation (PEO) of the Planning Commission. This evaluation function is being strengthened by setting up an Independent Evaluation Office (IEO), under the aegis of Planning Commission. The new IEO would be an important instrument in evaluating some of these programmes and could come up with recommendations which would highlight need for reforms and programmes which were successful.

IMPROVING PUBLIC SERVICE DELIVERY

10.30. A number of services are today provided by the State Governments and Central Ministries. These include ration cards, caste certificates, income certificates, certificates for proof of residence, passports and similar other services. It is important that these are available within a prescribed time line. Failures and deficiencies in delivery of public services lead to dissatisfaction and public anger against the government.

10.31. A number of States have taken the initiative to notify services and time-limits within which these are to be available to the citizens. Simultaneously, necessary simplified procedures should be put in place within the government to enable these services to be available. Failure to deliver the service must result in swift punitive action. The legislations which have been passed by Bihar, Madhya Pradesh, Delhi and number of other States are excellent examples of efforts to provide public services expeditiously.

10.32. An important aid to delivery of services can be the use of e-governance and technology. A number of areas had been taken up in the Eleventh Plan for e-governance. These included reforms in the Ministry of Corporate Affairs and 27 areas for introduction of e-technology and reforms. The experience in the Railways earlier for reservation, and in refund of customs duty by the Department of Customs have been very positive. By the end of Eleventh Plan, 60,000 common service centres are in place to provide delivery of public services across the country. It is also planned now to expand the optical fibre network and expand broadband connectivity to each panchayat levels. This would help in providing all services which are available at the panchayat level through e-mode to the citizens.

10.33. Another area which has been thrown open for use of technology is development of unique ID numbers with biometrics to establish proof of identity. The expansion of UID in the Twelfth Plan, along with the National population register should result in a UID Number by the end of Twelfth Plan to every resident. This would help in providing services to various users and results in controlling fake cards and thereby bring enormous savings. The financial inclusion services are also feasible by using UID and the telecom services. It is also possible to use technology for expanding banking correspondence and thereby expand the extent of banking services. The use of technology in delivery of public services will need to be expanded rapidly to reduce delays and discretion used to the advantage of the citizen.

Dissemination of Information

10.34. Government needs to communicate more effectively with the citizens. Citizens are not aware of many schemes set up by central and state governments for their benefit. Stakeholders, who will be affected by new government policies, realise only after the policies are announced, that they have great concerns whereas government departments claim that the policies were posted on their websites and views had been invited. Further, dissemination of information on existing policies, on availability of documents, written communications in the electronic media as well as newspapers can help citizens avail of benefits of governments schemes. Governance can be much more interactive if extensive use is made of all channels of communication including print and electronic media, social media, electronic boards in public places, written materials, website, an internet and other methods that have a wide reach and are able to convey messaging directly and swiftly.

10.35. Government must become much more effective in communicating with the public. Citizens are not aware of many schemes set up by Central and State Governments for their benefit. Stakeholders, who will be affected by new government policies, realise only after the policies are announced, that they have great concerns whereas Government Departments claim that the policies were posted on their websites and views had been invited. Moreover, with the ubiquity of electronic communications, including 24×7 TV news and the advent of social media, government's communication processes must be modernised, become more proactive, and reach out to citizens more effectively.

Combating Corruption

10.36. The third major area of concern in achieving good governance is the elimination of corruption. Corruption is a problem which arises in all countries, developed or developing, and it is self evident that corruption is not only morally objectionable, but also that it leads to serious economic distortions. No country can afford to ignore the problem of corruption and all must find ways of combating it. Governance reform aims at improving the working efficiency of government departments, providing mechanisms to ensure efficient delivery of public services, transparency and accountability of public officials, and an efficient civil service. Public service delivery is the window through which government is viewed, and deficient tardy and defective delivery breeds corruption.

10.37. The concern with corruption is inevitably greater in a democracy committed to open government and transparency, and it is not surprising that concern about the extent of corruption in our society has increased. The indices of corruption produced by the World Bank and the Transparency International do not support the view that corruption has increased. According to both these indices the corruption level in the last decade has been high, but has remained almost at the same level. The fact that perception of corruption has increased is a different issue and reflects the consequence of greater transparency and awareness. The point that is indisputable is that whatever be the indices, strong measures need to be taken to combat corruption.

10.38. The best way to prevent corruption is to have procedures, which provide minimum scope for such malpractices. This would require large use of e-governance and other technologies. It will also simultaneously need an extensive review of procedures so that the rules are simple, and do not provide scope for interpretations. Simultaneously, if the delivery of a public service is through an e-mode and automaticity is brought in decision-taking based on facts furnished, the scope for illegal gratification reduces substantially. During the Plan, it is proposed to further expand e-governance. Already a scheme for expanding connectivity up to the village panchayat level is being implemented. Earlier, common service centres had been opened to provide e-services. These efforts will have to continue.

10.39. The other aspect of corruption is development of transparent procedures in award of government contracts, government procurement and award of licences for permitting various activities including mining or the use of other natural resources. It is important that the use of e-tendering, mandatory posting of all major procurements on the websites and other transparent procedures are adopted for all major procurements. Similarly, in awarding of contracts, transparency in selection of contractors and the bids is must. This can be strengthened by using e-technology more extensively. In award of natural resources to private players, while transparency is a must, public policy must simultaneously ensure the pricing policies do not lead to exorbitant rise in the price of services which benefit the ordinary consumers. It has to be appreciated that communication, power and water are today basic necessities for all citizens. The allocation award procedures for these natural resources must keep these factors in mind.

10.40. The economic reforms successfully eliminated discretionary decision making in areas such as industrial licences and import licences. With the lowering of tariffs and abolition of license and permits, the transaction costs went down dramatically and this led to an enormous reduction in corruption. With the growth of the economy at a rapid rate, new areas have emerged. It is important that the corruption is controlled by ensuring that services, which are to be given by the government are also available from a number of other competing suppliers.

10.41. While steps to reduce the likelihood of corruption are extremely important, it is necessary to put in place a system that will investigate allegations of corruption and also punish the guilty expeditiously. The existing methods of enquiry have often been long drawn and delays in the delivery of justice only encourage corruption further. Special courts may need to be set up to expeditiously try such cases. The government has also recently introduced a legislation to create Lokpal as an institution to enquire into corruption at higher levels.

Civil Services' Reforms

10.42. The Civil Services over a period of years have acquired a very large role covering both development and regulatory functions. Reforms are necessary to enable them to perform these roles better. There has also been recent criticism of the civil service for its inability to deliver public services satisfactorily. The Second Administrative Reforms Commission (ARC) in its Report has given a number of recommendations. While these need to be implemented, three specific areas need special focus. First, the service should be young and the recruitment should, therefore, take place around 21 years of age. Second, the training for enabling the services to handle the vast variety of economic and management problems should be extensive and done periodically. Third, the officers must have long tenures to enable them to understand the intricacies of an assignment and make effective contribution. Unfortunately, over a period of years, the services that were expected to perform their responsibilities in a very unbiased manner, have often failed to do so. These values of uprightness, integrity and fairness need to be strengthened both in the Civil Services and by the political executive, respecting and supporting these values.

10.43. The Second Administrative Reforms Commission has made several important recommendations that have expressed need for extensive measures for reforming the Civil Service. It has recommended (ARC Report on *Refurbishing of Personnel Administration—Sealing New Heights*) changes in the career structure of the administrative services that will ensure that senior postings have adequate tenure. It has also recommended an 'up or out' evaluation system so that only the better officers will stay in service and move to postings at the top. It has, also, provided for lateral entry from outside Government, of suitably qualified personnel for such top positions. These are important areas and need to be implemented expeditiously.

10.44. An important area of Reform is the need for developing greater accountability, improved management, effective service delivery and empowerment of the front line staff. With this objective, the ARC has in its report (organisational structure of Government of India), suggested that policymaking functions of Government and execution functions be separated and organized in appropriate structures. For 'execution' functions, the 'agency' structure has been strongly recommended. The concept of 'agencification' is to carve out of government departments, 'executive agencies' to carry out, specific executive functions within a framework of policy and resources. Each such agency is institutionalised in a framework document which spells out its mandate, mission and objectives, structure, accountability, standards and targets, financial arrangements and so on, and is mandated to release an annual performance report and accounts. The agency has the freedom to mould its management style, strategy, operations, systems, workforce and so on within broad government guidelines. The advantage of the 'agency' structure is that it leads to clarity about outcomes. It also allows for an inculcated culture of service delivery, empowerment of frontline staff, greater accountability and openness, improved management, transparency and so on. Once this policy is adopted, it will be necessary for ministries, both in the Central and State Government to scrutinize their functions and keep only those with them which relate to policy analysis, strategy decisions and other key areas which have to be performed by them only. The executive arm can then be empowered to execute the policies effectively. Right balance between autonomy and accountability needs to be struck while designing the framework of institutional agencies.

Accountability

10.45. It is widely accepted that government's accountability is a primary concern that needs to be addressed on an urgent basis in India. We need to move from goals of meeting expenditure targets in government programmes to goals of meeting physical targets and, even more, towards increasing satisfaction of the range of stakeholders of government policy.

10.46. It may be useful to look at the difference between the accountability related to government and that related to private organizations. Private, profit-motivated organisations have a narrower set of stakeholders to whom they are accountable, principally their shareholders and customers of their specific products or services and their performance is directly reflected in their profits. On the other hand, governments are compelled to account to citizens at large and a much broader set of stakeholders and poor performance does not trigger internal financial penalties. In other words, private organisations are characterised by 'intensive accountability', that is, being answerable to a narrower set of masters in a far more focused way; governments require 'extensive accountability'.

10.47. Because governments' accountability is broader, management of public programmes require much more attention to the definition and measurement of the accountability. In a recent reform initiative, a number of central ministries have adopted a Results Framework Document, which provides a summary of the most important results that the concerned departments and ministries expect to achieve in the year. The main purpose of this is to move the focus of the department from the current resource-allocation mode to result orientation, and to provide an objective and fair basis to evaluate the departments' or ministries' overall performance. In the first round, the RFD targets had emphasised financial and physical targets. It was observed that 'outcomes' from the citizens' and stakeholders' perspectives were generally missing. Therefore in the later round, stakeholder consultation and feedback has been built into the RFD framework. By ensuring a broad range of well-managed consultations to determine goals, 'extensive accountability' can be brought about.

10.48. While the above system of accountability under RFDs has led to some very interesting results and has been an important development for improving accountability, the physical targets often tend to be kept at a very moderate level by the concerned ministries while framing the annual plans. This defeats the very purpose of developing a document which can ensure physical progress consistent with the needs of the economy. Unless, the targets are kept at a challenging level, the document is likely to give a wrong picture of departments, and its accountability. There is a clear need to guard against this while RFDs are prepared.

10.49. Many, and often the most important outcomes that citizens and the economy need are not within the ambit of any single ministry. Collaboration is required among several departments and ministries. The roles of departments and ministries to achieve these outcomes requires a systemic analysis of the issues from which the actions required of the various departments/ministries can be determined and their goals developed. This critical "system's input" to the RFD process can be provided by the Planning Commission.

Regulatory Structures

10.50. Regulatory authorities have been set up in several areas including power, oil and gas, airports, telecom and warehousing where public services are being provided by private players and competition is not viewed as a sufficient discipline. Regulators are also proposed in the field of water in a number of states. Although regulators have proliferated, there is no clear assessment of the functioning of individual regulators. It is also not very clear as to what extent they are answerable and accountable and to whom. Regulatory authorities without any accountability would in the long run lead to functioning of government arms not responsible to any one and, therefore, may not meet the overall objective of government policy. It is necessary that these regulatory authorities are made accountable and assessed for their performance. Necessary legislation in this regard needs to be finalised quickly.

GETTING THINGS DONE

10.51. Research on success of countries that built effective systems for improving the quality and timelines of implementation of policies and projects in multiple sectors provides some principles for a robust implementation process.

- *Build an implementation system, don't just do the task*: Explicit attention to the process of policy development and implementation has been lacking to a large extent in the Indian context. An effective implementation system is not limited to the success of a single initiative. It builds broad-based capabilities across several industries.
- *Systemic experimentation and learning help to progressively, and rapidly improve implementation*: Even carefully designed programmes are likely to face challenges from unforeseen changes in the environment. Therefore, it is important to have learning and feedback mechanisms in place to ensure that implementation effectiveness improves through successive cycles. Good policy development (and implementation) should follow the PDCA cycle (Plan—develop strategy; Do—implement strategy; Check—diagnose issues in strategy and its implementation; Act—rectify issues identified).

- *Prioritize, sequence and create momentum through results*: Often it takes time for results of policy recommendations to become visible. When results are not visible, the implementation process may lose momentum. Therefore, to build momentum, some early wins must be targeted. They build confidence and commitment to the process.
- *Performance measures for government programmes have to be defined consultatively*: The old management adage—'you can't manage what you don't measure'—is especially true with regards to complex government programmes. The need for performance measures is well accepted. However, it is also very important to define these measures appropriately. A key difference between public sector and private sector programmes is that the value required to be produced by public programmes is generally more intangible than in private programmes where shareholder value and profit may be good measures. Outcomes of public programmes must deliver against expectations of diverse public stakeholders.

  Therefore, it is imperative that time is spent, up front, to define outcomes in consultation with key stakeholders. Failure to do this causes the system to adopt simplistic measures of performance against expenditure targets, which are not good indicators of the outcomes that were desired.
- *Co-ordination between government departments is critical*: Given the complexity of policy issues relating to manufacturing, most solutions are likely to require co-ordinated actions between a number of government departments. While the default solution is to create another agency/committee to oversee this co-ordination, this is not always the optimal solution. Before setting up such an agency/committee, the tasks required to be performed by such an agency/committee must be analysed and the existing system of agency/committees must be mapped to eliminate any overlaps and redundancies.

  Additional agencies/committees can increase the clutter in the system rather than improve its performance. Since co-ordination is an essential function to improve system performance, co-ordination/oversight should be accountable for performing its task and its performance must be measured too in terms of decisions taken which are then implemented.
- *Stakeholder consultations are key to improve the quality of policy development and implementation*: Rather than seeking to a priori design a detailed plan in an unpredictable environment, it is better to create effective forums to identify problems, and for joint teams to be formed to tackle them. These forums should be broad-based and inclusive to ensure that all stakeholders can contribute to the process.

Collaboration and Implementation

10.52. Poor implementation has been the root cause for India's poor performance in building its infrastructure and growing its manufacturing sector too. In China, Japan and Germany—countries that have developed very competitive manufacturing sectors and good infrastructures—things get done. In contrast, things do not get done as seamlessly in India. Two root causes identified for poor implementation are: inadequate consensus amongst stakeholders for policy changes, and very poor co-ordination amongst agencies in execution. These challenges are not restricted only to the infrastructure and manufacturing sectors in India. They exist in almost all sectors. Therefore solutions to these root cause problems, can improve outcomes in many sectors.

10.53. The traditional approach to address co-ordination and implementation failures is to (*i*) appoint committees to co-ordinate, and (*ii*) set up monitoring agencies. Thus, the system has become cluttered with committees for co-ordination, and co-ordination amongst them has become another problem! Monitoring can point out that things are not happening—which is useful information. But more useful is the ability to get things done.

10.54. Broad based consensus-building processes, therefore, need to be institutionalised to ensure successful implementation of plans. This is true for many sectors. Institutions for representation, such as employee unions, employer associations, and civil society organisations (CSOs), must become more professional, more democratic, and more competent in arriving at agreements that ensure fairness to all stakeholders. It is worth noting that the strength of such organisations of representation and the processes of consultation amongst them can explain the continuing competitive strengths of the German and Japanese manufacturing ecosystems, even though wages in these countries are amongst the highest in the world, and their currencies are very strong too. In other words, low wages and cheap currencies need not be the only sources of competitive advantage in manufacturing. The ability of people to work together is a more sustainable, and a more satisfying, source of national competitive advantage.

10.55. There are examples internationally of successful implementation of similarly ambitious and complex transformation plans in a democratic context—and these illustrate processes created with deliberate intent to improve multi-stakeholder collaboration and implementation. In economies as diverse as Malaysia and Brazil, this role has been played by often small organisations that: facilitate a common vision; act as a disinterested party in finding solutions to common problems; maintain momentum through transparent monitoring and evaluation; store and distribute learning and induce effective stakeholder consultation. Such a role is often modest and unobtrusive, but can be the key to implementation and growth.

10.56. In a highly diverse as well as democratic country, such as India, a broad consensus is required for all stakeholders to move together, forward and faster. This consensus cannot be commanded. We need another mechanism specifically designed to bring people with different perspectives together: to listen to each other, to distil the essence of their shared aspiration for the country and the critical principles they will adhere to in the work they have to do together as partners in progress.

10.57. An ongoing process of public reasoning, conducted with good techniques of dialogue, in which people from many walks of life participate, and people with different ideologies listen to each other, could provide the glue we need. The all-round development of India will not happen in spite of our being a democracy. It will happen because we are a democracy, provided we improve our abilities to deliberate and decide democratically and effectively.

10.58. Hence, there is a need to establish an effective 'backbone' capability which will provide strength to multi-stakeholder policy and implementation processes. Cohesion can be brought about through more effective co-ordination amongst agencies, and more effective consultation amongst stakeholders. The common feature of successful cases of new policy implementation in countries, especially democratic countries which provide freedom for independent actions to multiple agencies, has been the creation of a web of institutions, processes and other mechanisms. For this web to be effective, it must have strong 'backbone' capabilities to give it coherence and direction. For this, the government will require specialised skills such as consensus building and programme management to manage this process.

10.59. The 'backbone' capability does not require an organisation with a large amount of resources and manpower; nor one with the power to command top-down. The term 'organisation' may connote the creation of a new unit that would do the job itself. However, there are too many projects and implementation challenges all over the country. Therefore the 'backbone' capability must essentially comprise of small catalytic units located in many parts of the system, which can provide the 'tools and techniques' to the various states and ministries to effectively co-ordinate, design and implement their programmes.

10.60. We must take advantage of the political set-up in the country which has put in place many institutions to govern and to manage these challenges, and which are given authority and financial resources for their responsibilities. The 'backbone' capability must enable these institutions to fulfil their co-ordination and implementation roles more effectively, rather than aim to be a master co-ordinator over them. If the backbone organisation was set up as a new, over-arching authority, which is a tempting idea, it would start competing with existing authorities and that would make the co-ordination problems even more complicated.

10.61. The backbone capabilities must be delivered by a network of backbone units spread across the country. The backbone units must not be positioned as higher authorities positioned over other agencies. Instead, they must enable the ministries and departments to unlock the constraints that are impeding them from successfully planning, co-ordinating and implementing.

A 'Movement' of Learning and Improvement

10.62. The distinction between creating yet another 'organisation' and stimulating a 'movement' is crucial. For widespread acquisition of capabilities, across a large, diverse, and democratic system, a movement of learning and change is required.

10.63. The improvement of quality across Japan in the 1970s provides a good example of a successful national movement that transformed a nation's economy. Japan, in the 1950s and 1960s had the reputation of being a producer of low quality, cheap, goods. By the 1980s, Japan had become the hall-mark of quality across many industries, and its infrastructure of rail and road transportation had become a benchmark for efficiency and punctuality. The widespread improvement of quality was brought about through Total Quality Management (TQM), whereby seven simple tools of quality and other techniques were widely disseminated throughout Japan. The dissemination was done by multiple agencies. The Japanese Union of Scientists and Engineers was one of the leaders, and several business associations, government agencies and voluntary organisations came together to promote quality across the country. A variety of channels including public radio, daily newspapers and professional journals were used to infect the country with the challenge to improve quality everywhere and to disseminate useful techniques.

10.64. The subject of the TQM movement in Japan was 'quality'. Relevant principles, techniques and tools were provided by many persons and organisations, notable amongst them were Professors Deming and Ishikawa, and Taichi Ohno of Toyota. These principles and tools were deployed by the movement. The need for democratic management of multi-stakeholder collaboration processes has been felt in many countries. In response to this, many initiatives have been taken over the past three decades, in several countries, to facilitate such processes. Experience has been gained from these interventions, and a body of practice, with established principles, and tools has emerged. These principles and tools, with case studies, have been recorded by several organisations. A 'movement' to disseminate and use such tools and processes will accelerate implementation and growth.

DISASTER MANAGEMENT

10.65. A development strategy under the planning process has risk management as one of its key components. Globally, there is an increasing recognition that disasters affect growth and the poorer sections of society gets a major share of the impact. Therefore, there is a consensus that investing in prevention and mitigation is economically and socially more beneficial than expenditure in relief and rehabilitation. In a recent World Bank Study, it has been established that one dollar spent on prevention is ten times more valuable than a dollar spent on relief in net present value.

10.66. The large size of the Indian continent, varied geography, national features, climate, and effects of economic development and growth process results in number of risks. These are clearly both due to natural hazards and effect of human development process on nature. The human and economic losses from disaster are economically high in the country as compared to the other development nation of the world. According to a World Bank study titled 'National Hazards, Unnatural Disasters', India faces losses up to 2 per cent of its GDP due to natural disasters. Disasters impact growth particularly of the poor and vulnerable sections of society. Table 10.1 gives details of the losses caused due to natural disasters in the decade of 2001–10.

TABLE 10.1
Year-Wise Damage Caused Due to Floods, Cyclonic Storms, Landslides and so on during Last 10 Years in India

Year	Live Last Human (In No.)	Cattle Lost (In No.)	Houses Damaged (in No.)	Cropped Areas Affected (in Lakh ha)
2001–02	834	21,269	3,46,878	18.72
2002–03	898	3,729	4,62,700	21.00
2003–04	1,992	25,393	6,82,209	31.98
2004–05	1,995	12,393	16,03,300	32.53
2005–06	2,698	1,10,997	21,20,012	35.52
2006–07	2,402	4,55,619	19,34,680	70.87
2007–08	3,764	1,19,218	35,27,041	85.13
2008–09	3,405	53,833	16,46,905	35.56
2009–10	1,677	1,28,452	13,59,726	47.13
2010–11	2,310	48,778	13,38,619	46.25

Source: Ministry of Home Affairs (MHA).

10.67. The strategy in the initial years of the planning process has been to handle only some of the natural hazards, like floods and water proofing against drought. It has, however, been gradually realised that a more comprehensive approach is called for. This must lead to mitigation of ill-effects of disasters, and a development process which encompasses within itself, a strategy for mitigation of human misery and adverse consequences of the disaster.

10.68. The Tenth Five Year Plan initiated the process of shift from relief and response centric disaster management to prevention, mitigation, and preparedness as means to revert or more effective handling of the disasters. The Plan prescribed a strategy of disaster management which included three important components: first, policy guidelines on preparation of developmental plans across sectors for integrating disaster management into developmental plans and a specific scheme; second, a multi-pronged strategy for the total risk management and third, recognition of a need for plan expenditure on disaster management and preventive measures in addition to calamity relief fund. In pursuance of this strategy, the National Disaster Management Authority was proposed under National Disaster Management Act 2005. The process of strengthening disaster preparedness was further strengthened in the Eleventh Plan. The disaster management authority was set up at the national level. It formulated extensive guidelines and a national policy on disaster management. Similar to above, state and district level authorities were also set up gradually.

10.69. The Twelfth Plan will further build on the developments of the last few years and specifically undertake programmes in several areas. First, setting up of early warning systems in all hazards prone areas of the country would need a special focus. Specifically, we will need to utilise our science and technology in disaster risk and warning communities well in advance to save life and property. Effective communication systems have to be set up in all the levels to ensure timely and accurate dissemination of warning signals to vulnerable communities. It is proposed that disaster risk reduction in respect of earthquake, flood, drought, Tsunami, cyclones, forest fire, chemical nuclear and biological disasters be set up. Necessary innovative technologies and their application would need to be accordingly taken up in the plan.

10.70. Second, mainstreaming disaster risk reduction in all major schemes would need to be an important area of focus. The development programmes and policies would need specifically to keep the disaster risk reduction in mind. These would, therefore, have to while, preparing programmes, focus on its impact on increasing disaster risks and how its mitigation is proposed in the concerned schemes. Disaster risk reduction will need to be thus incorporated in all major schemes, specifically the flagship schemes, for reducing the vulnerability in the hazards prone areas of the country. For example, safety of the school buildings, especially in earthquake prone areas has to be ensured.

10.71. Capacity building would be an important area proposed for development during the plan. The current experience has been with authorities primarily on handling national disasters after these have occurred. It is important that community awareness and capacity building within the community and government is undertaken at all the three levels: National, State and Districts including villages. These would need to cover education and research, public sensitisation and awareness and institutional strengthening and development.

10.72. The indicative Gross Budgetary Support for the Twelfth five Year Plan for the Ministries/Departments dealing with governance issues is given in Table 10.2.

TABLE 10.2
Gross Budgetary Support for the Twelfth Five Year Plan

S. No.	Ministry/Department	₹ Crore
1	Ministry of Home Affairs	52,839
2	Ministry of Panchayati Raj	6,437
3	Ministry of Law, Justice and Company Affairs	5,802
4	Ministry of Personnel, Public Grievance and Pensions	1,385

Source: Planning Commission.

11

Regional Equality

INTRODUCTION

11.1. With its wide diversities in physiography, history, demography and sociology, India has been characterised by regional disparities in socio-economic development not only between States but also between districts of a State and between areas and social groups within districts. Therefore, an important objective of the Five Year Plans has been to address the problem of regional imbalances. The main instruments have been the formula for distribution of Central Assistance to the States, Special Area Programmes and various Centrally Sponsored Schemes (CSS) for poverty alleviation.

11.2. Prior to the Tenth Plan, the general approach was that planning and development of an area and allocation of funds for the purpose were primarily the responsibility of the respective State Governments. Government of India (GOI) merely supplemented the efforts of State Governments with Special Area Programmes targeted at areas with certain geographic characteristics that called for additional funding. Examples of such supplemental programmes are the Hill Areas Development Programme (HADP), Western Ghats Development Programme (WGDP) and the Border Area Development Programme (BADP).

11.3. During the Tenth Plan for the first time the GOI introduced an area development scheme targeted at backward areas. The Rashtriya Sam Vikas Yojana (RSVY) was initiated in 2003–04 for putting in place activities for backward areas covering 147 districts which would help reduce imbalances and speed up development. In 2006–07, this programme was replaced by the Backward Regions Grant Fund (BRGF). The BRGF enlarged the Districts Component to cover 250 districts. In 2010–11, a new component was added, namely, the Integrated Action Plan (IAP) for Selected Tribal and Backward Districts. This covers 82 districts of which 76 districts are already part of BRGF.

11.4. This chapter summarises the latest available evidence on inter-regional disparities in India, reviews the performance of the various programmes aimed at promoting inter-regional equity and describes the changes being proposed to these programmes in the Twelfth Plan.

INTER-STATE INEQUALITIES

11.5. The inter-State inequalities in PCIs have been a cause of concern. These have been rising in the last three decades for two reasons. First, the rates of growth of State Domestic Product (SDP) of many of the States in the south, west and northern regions, like Punjab, Himachal Pradesh, Gujarat, Karnataka and Tripura, have been quite high as compared to some of the other States, like Uttar Pradesh (UP), Bihar and Rajasthan. Second, the rate of growth of population in some of the low PCI States has been fairly high. This has resulted in widening of PCIs and consumption in different States.

11.6. The second nature of inequality has been within the States themselves. A number of these States of the Indian Union have large areas and growth in them is uneven. Even in some of the States with comparatively small geographical area, the levels of development are very uneven, especially in the Himalayan region of Nagaland, Mizoram, Arunachal Pradesh, Jammu & Kashmir (J&K), Himachal Pradesh and Uttarakhand. The unequal levels of development in the larger States, including several regions like Vidarbha region of Maharashtra; Koraput, Bolangir and Kalahandi (popularly known as KBK districts) of Orissa; Bundelkhand region, Eastern UP and parts of Central UP, northern Bihar, tribal areas of Jharkhand and Chhattisgarh, Andhra Pradesh, Maharashtra, UP and north Karnataka are a few examples.

11.7. The third nature of inequality is between the rural and the urban and within the rural societies and the urban societies themselves. While the development strategy for the last-mentioned inequality is being separately addressed in the Plan, this chapter deals with the inter-State and intra-State regional inequalities and strategies to deal with these during the Plan.

11.8. Regional inequalities, both between States and within States, present a serious development challenge to the Indian economy. Existing literature attributes the growing regional disparities in India to inequities in access to social and physical infrastructure. Recent scholarly works also suggest that private sector investment tends to move to places where the enabling environment, that is, investment climate is better (infrastructure availability and good regulations facilitate growth). Purfield[1] estimates the impact of several policy variables on PCIs over a 30-year period and finds that investment climate variables, measured by days lost in industrial disputes, the relative size of government expenditures, and the predominance of the share of agriculture in the economy and lower investment—all adversely affect growth rates. Another factor which explains regional disparity is the quality of human capital, which in turn depends on the level of education and health of the population. Finally, institutions matter, and regions with better law and order and governance benefit in the form of higher and sustained growth. Kochar et al.[2] find that States with weaker institutions and poorer infrastructure did worse in terms of industrial and Gross Domestic Product (GDP) growth. Besley et al.[3] find that variables such as property rights (defined primarily as land rights); access to credit; labour market flexibility; presence of media that holds governments accountable and literacy and human capital are significant in explaining inter-State disparities.

11.9. An important objective in the Eleventh Plan was to reduce the inter-State inequalities in PCIs. This is feasible if the growth rate growth rates accelerate but the growth rate of population and related indicators, including Total Fertility Rate, show a decline. The experience in the last two decades has been that number of these States which have low growth rates, like UP, Bihar, Rajasthan, Orissa and Madhya Pradesh (MP), had high growth rates of population, too. However, the GDP growth trend has been reversed during the Eleventh Plan. During the Eighth, Ninth and Tenth Plans, States with lowest average PCI, along with the growth rates are given in the Table 11.1.

11.10. The above indicates clear trends. Five States, namely, Bihar, Orissa, UP, MP and Rajasthan, had the lowest PCI in the Eighth Plan. All of these gradually improved their growth rates, particularly in the Eleventh Plan. The average GDP growth rate of these States increased from 5.16 per cent in the Eighth Plan to 6.38 per cent in the Tenth Plan and 8.80 per cent in the Eleventh Plan. Also, individually, several of them recorded excellent growth. Bihar, which was for quite some time a cause of worry for planners, has been able to record growth rate of 9.9 per cent in the Eleventh Plan. Similarly, MP, UP and Rajasthan have all recorded growth rates of 7 per cent or more in the Eleventh Plan. This is an encouraging and positive trend. Please refer to Figure 11.1 and Table 11.3.

11.11. Table 11.2 indicates the growth rates of the SDPs of different States.

11.12. The growth rates of SDP show several interesting convergence trends. First, the average GDP growth rate of States with lowest PCI over the last three Plans is increasing continuously and during the Eleventh Plan, it exceeded the average growth rates of general category States. Second, these also exceeded the growth rates of all States (including special category) during the Eleventh Plan. Third,

TABLE 11.1
Comparative Growth Rates in GSDP for Selected Low-Income States

Eighth Plan 1992–97	Ninth Plan 1997–2002	Tenth Plan 2002–07	Eleventh Plan 2007–12
Bihar (3.9)	Bihar (3.7)	Bihar (6.9)	Bihar (9.9)
Odisha (2.3)	UP (2.5)	UP (5.8)	UP (7.1)
UP (5.0)	Odisha (5.1)	MP (5.0)	MP (9.2)
MP (6.6)	MP (4.5)	Jharkhand (5.0)	Jharkhand (9.3)
Rajasthan (8.0)	Rajasthan (5.3)	Odisha (9.2)	Rajasthan (8.5)
Average (5.16)[a]	Average (4.22)[a]	Average (6.38)[a]	Average (8.80)[a]

Source: Planning Commission.
Note: [a]Average GDP growth rates of five States with lowest PCI, amongst General Category States.

the ratio of average growth rates of States with lowest PCI, as against those of five highest PCI States, increased from 49 per cent (Eighth Plan) to 76 per cent (Eleventh Plan). Fourth, the coefficient of variation indicating the extent of inequality in growth rates amongst different States also shown increasing convergence (assuming Sikkim an outlier with growth of 22.8 per cent during the Eleventh Plan) of Gross State Domestic Product (GSDP) growth rates over successive Plan periods.

Disparities in Per Capita Income

11.13. While the acceleration of SDP growth rates is a very positive trend, the PCI does not show any significant improvement in income disparities. Regional differences in PCI levels are further reflected in a study of per capita State GDP figures from 1981 to 2008, which enabled the computation of the Gini coefficient,[4] which has been updated to include Gini coefficient computations up to year 2010–11. Figure 11.2 shows a continuing upward march of the coefficient and inter-State inequality.[5] The average Gini coefficient during 1981–90 is 0.15 which increased to 0.19 during 1991–2000. The average Gini coefficient for the period of 2000–10 is 0.224, which remains stagnant for the year 2010–11. This indicates the growing income disparity in India. The inter-State Gini for 2005 which is, 0.22 is far lower

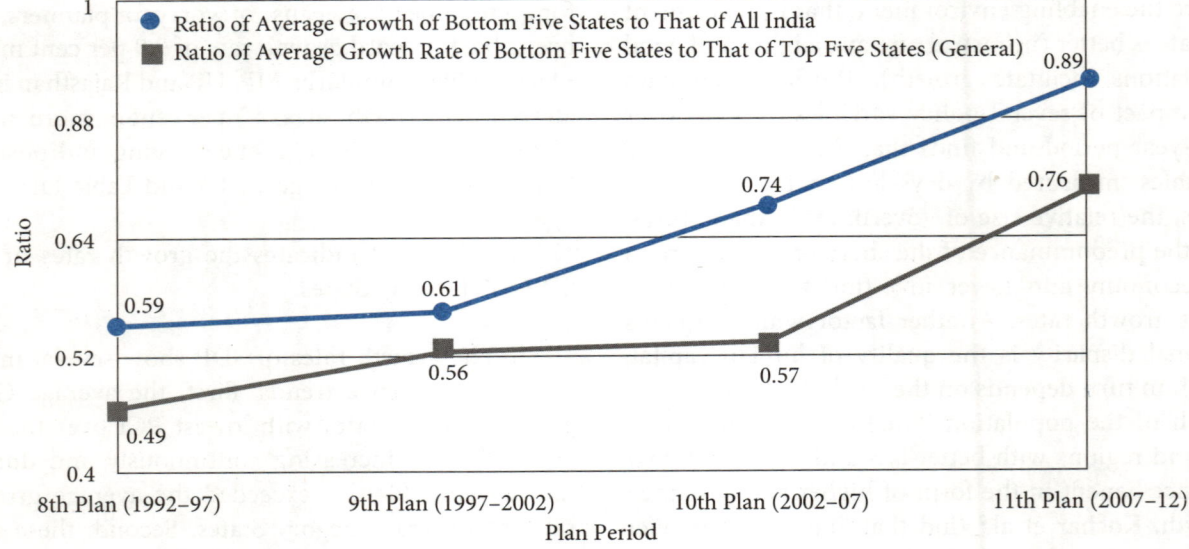

FIGURE 11.1: Convergence of GDP Growth Rates during Successive Plans

TABLE 11.2
Growth Rates in SDP in Different States

Sl. No.	States/UTs	Averages for Plan Periods (% per annum)			
		Eighth Plan 1992–97	Ninth Plan 1997–2002	Tenth Plan 2002–07	Eleventh Plan 2007–12
1.	Andhra Pradesh	5.4	5.5	8.2	8.2
2.	Bihar	3.9	3.7	6.9	9.9
3.	Chhattisgarh*	….	….	8.8	7.7
4.	Goa	9.0	5.7	8.5	9.1
5.	Gujarat	12.9	2.8	11.0	9.5
6.	Haryana	5.2	6.1	9.0	9.0
7.	Jharkhand*	….	….	5.0	9.3
8.	Karnataka	6.2	5.8	7.7	7.2
9.	Kerala	6.5	5.2	8.3	8.2
10.	Madhya Pradesh	6.6	4.5	5.0	9.2
11.	Maharashtra	8.9	4.1	10.1	8.6
12.	Odisha	2.3	5.1	9.2	7.1
13.	Punjab	4.8	4.0	6.0	6.7
14.	Rajasthan	8.0	5.3	7.1	8.5
15.	Tamil Nadu	7.0	4.7	9.7	7.7
16.	Uttar Pradesh	5.0	2.5	5.8	7.1
17.	West Bengal	6.3	6.5	6.2	7.3
	Special Category States				
18.	Arunachal Pr.	5.0	6.6	6.2	8.5
19.	Assam	2.8	1.8	5.0	6.8
20.	Himachal Pr.	6.5	6.3	7.6	8.0
21.	Jammu & Kashmir	5.0	4.2	5.5	5.9
22.	Manipur	3.7	4.7	5.7	6.2
23.	Meghalaya	4.0	7.2	6.7	7.8
24.	Mizoram	….	5.7	5.9	10.8
25.	Nagaland	7.2	6.5	7.4	6.2
26.	Sikkim	4.6	6.6	7.7	22.8
27.	Tripura	6.7	9.4	6.9	8.9
28.	Uttarakhand*	….	….	11.7	12.8

Sources: 1. Eighth, Ninth and Tenth Plan achievement from most recent base year series (CSO).
2. Eleventh Plan achievement from 2004–05 series (CSO).
*These States have been formed recently.

than the Gini for India as a whole (0.36 for the year 2005 from HDR of United Nations Development Programme [UNDP]) revealing that the geographic disparity of income is much lower than the social disparity between the richest and poorest people in the country.

11.14. Table 11.4, however, indicates the disparities in PCI since 2004–05.

11.15. The variation in PCIs amongst various States has been worsening in the last two decades. The

TABLE 11.3
Convergence of GDP Growth Rates in Successive Plans

	Eighth Plan 1992–97	Ninth Plan 1997–2002	Tenth Plan 2002–07	Eleventh Plan 2007–12
Average GDP Growth of top five States, amongst General Category States	9.03	5.96	9.98	9.42
Ratio of Average Growth of Bottom five States to that of All India	0.59	0.61	0.74	0.89
Ratio of Average Growth of Bottom five States to that of non-special category States	0.67	0.75	0.72	0.88
Ratio of Average Growth rate of Bottom five States with that of Top five States (General Category States)	0.49	0.56	0.57	0.76

Source: Planning Commission.

coefficient of variation had increased from 34 per cent (1993–94) to 36 per cent (2004–05) and further to 42 per cent in 2011–12 as mentioned in Table 11.4 and the following graph. The ratio of lowest to highest PCI has changed marginally from 21 per cent in the year 2004–05 to 20 per cent in the year 2011–12.

11.16. The widening disparities in PCIs across States show that convergence in growth rates does not appear to have resulted in convergence in income levels across States. Figure 11.4 plots the growth rate of the States for the period 2001–10 against the log of income per capita in 2001. If there was convergence in income levels, the relationship would

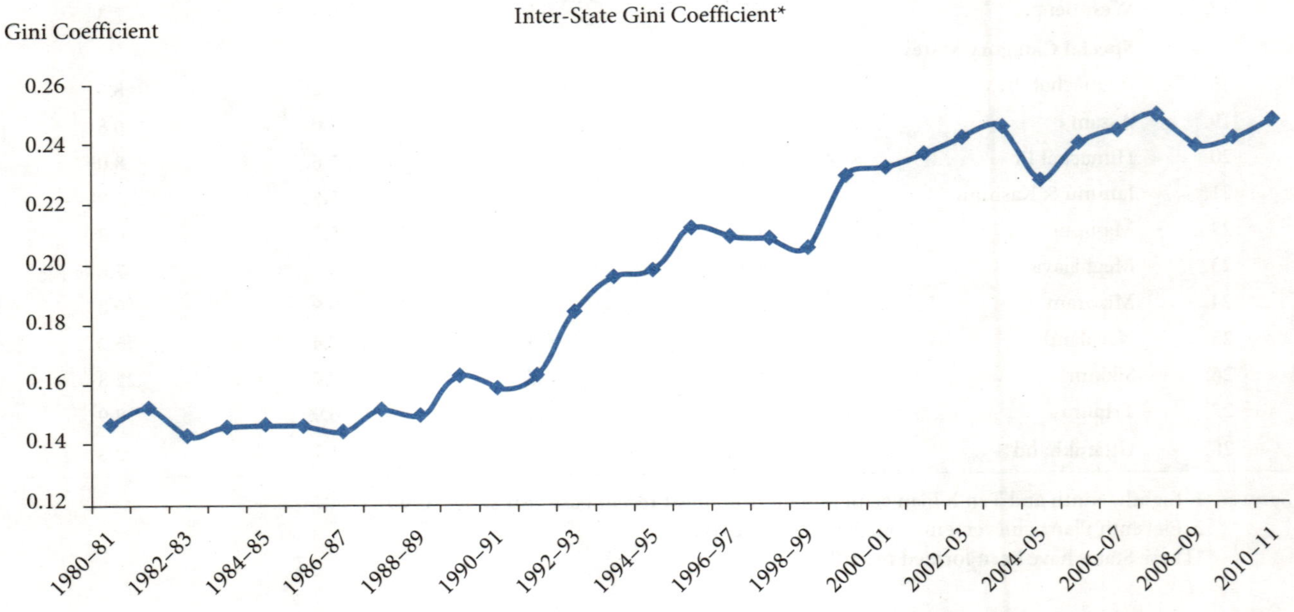

The Gini coefficient is calculated assuming that all individuals withing each state have gross income equal to per capita GSDP. This method ignores the inequality arising out of the unequal distribution withing each state, and focuses only on inequality arising from interstate differences in per capita GSDP.

Source: MS Ahluwalia, 'Prospects and Policy Challenges in the Twelfth Plan', *Economic and Political Weekly of India* XLVI, no. 21 (21 May 2011).

FIGURE 11.2: Trends in Inter-State Inequality

Regional Equality

TABLE 11.4
Disparity in PCI (Per Capita NSDP) at 2004–05 Prices

Year	State with Lowest PCI	PCI (₹)	State with Highest PCI	PCI (₹)	Ratio of Lowest to Highest PCI (%)	Coefficient of Variation in PCI across Major States (%)
2004–05	Bihar	7,914	Haryana	37,972	21	36
2005–06	Bihar	7,749	Maharashtra	40,671	19	39
2006–07	Bihar	8,900	Maharashtra	45,582	20	40
2007–08	Bihar	9,233	Maharashtra	50,138	18	40
2008–09	Bihar	10,241	Maharashtra	50,183	20	40
2009–10	Bihar	10,771	Haryana	55,044	20	41
2010–11	Bihar	11,792	Maharashtra	59,735	20	42
2011–12	Bihar	13,178	Maharashtra	64,951	20	42

Source: Directorate of Economics and Statistics of respective State Governments.

be downward sloping. But, as Figure 11.4 indicates, the relationship is upward sloping. States with higher initial income (per capita Net State Domestic Product [NSDP]) on average grew faster, suggesting that the inequality across States is actually increasing. Thus, despite the strong growth performance of the hitherto laggard States (Bihar, Madhya Pradesh, Rajasthan and Uttar Pradesh [BIMARU] States), we do not see the phenomenon of convergence across Indian States, whereby the poorer States, by virtue of growing faster than the richer States, start catching up with the level of income of the latter. Of course, it is important to clarify that although we see no unconditional convergence (reducing dispersion of income), there still might be conditional convergence. Conditional convergence can be consistent with divergence in PCIs over a certain period of time. It is possible that Indian States are converging to increasingly divergent steady States.[6]

11.17. There are some positive trends recently. The gap between the highest and lowest PCI States is declining in recent years, as evident from the above figure. This trend was not so evident during the

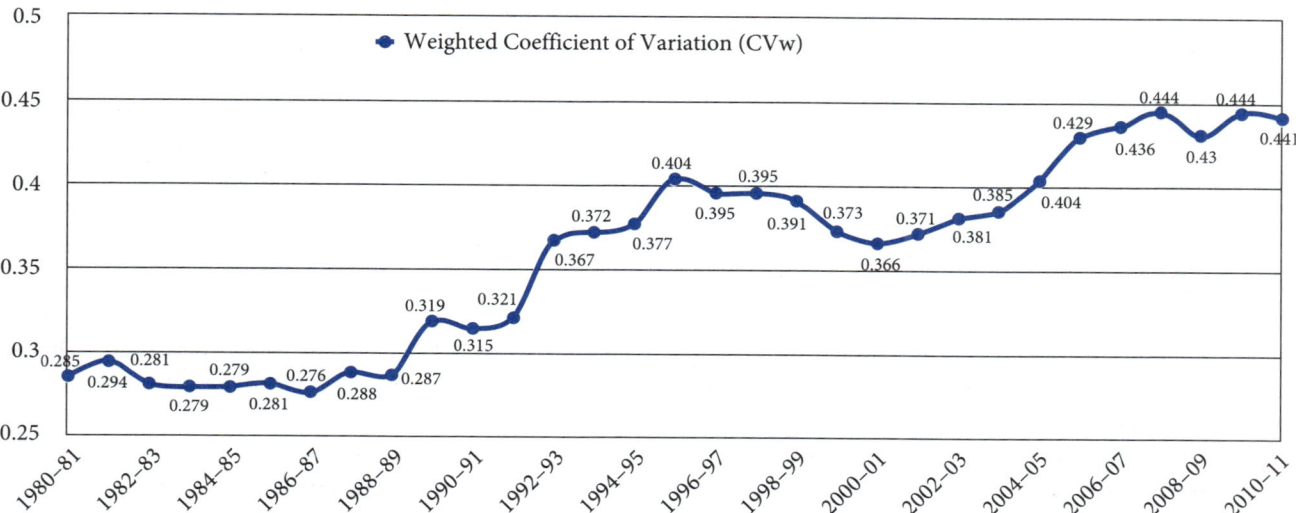

FIGURE 11.3: Inter-State Income Inequalities (Bases on States' GSDP Per Capita on Current Price)

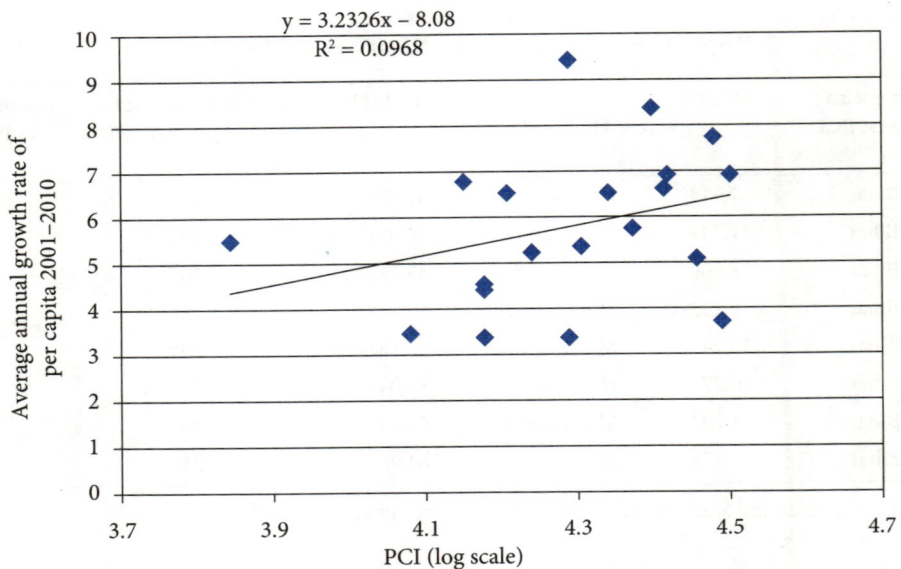

FIGURE 11.4: Growth during 2001–10 and Income in 2001

Tenth Plan. The income of lowest PCI State was 27.586 per cent of the highest PCI State in 1996–97. It deteriorated to 21 per cent in 2004–05. In recent years, however, with the growth rates picking up, especially in the low income States, as mentioned above, the trend of disparity between the lowest and the highest PCI States has been somewhat arrested as in the year 2011–12 the corresponding figure was 20 per cent. Two factors have contributed to this recent improvement. First, the growth rates of GDP of low PCI States have accelerated. Second, the rate of growth of population has gradually decelerated and getting closer to that of high PCI States. These two trends, if continued in the next two Plans, will lead to much higher degree of convergence and further reduce inter-State inequalities in the next decade.

Performance on Human Development Indicators

11.18. Disparities in regional performance are a matter of concern not just in terms of income indicators, but also human development indicators. State-wise data on human development indicators[7] display considerable variation in performance across States. Kerala was the best performer, witnessing a literacy rate of 93.91 per cent, sex ratio of 1,084 and infant mortality rate of 12 per thousand. At the other end of the spectrum, the worst performance on these indicators was displayed by Bihar (lowest literacy rate of 63.82 per cent), Haryana (sex ratio of 877) and MP (infant mortality rate [IMR] of 67). Importantly, the BIMARU States, despite witnessing impressive growth rates, continued to remain at the bottom of the distribution in terms of performance on human development indicators. However, the richer States too were not immune from poor performance on these indicators. The below-average performance of Haryana and Punjab, two of India's richest States, on indicators such as sex ratio and female literacy rates points to the inadequacy of PCIs in measuring the economic and social progress in society.

11.19. The India Human Development Report 2011 (IHDR-2011), which estimates the Human Development Index (HDI) for States at beginning of the decade and for the year 2007–08, allows us to compare HDI across States and over time. The top five ranks in HDI in both years are occupied by Kerala, Delhi, Himachal Pradesh, Goa and Punjab. At the other end of the spectrum are States such as Chhattisgarh, Orissa, Bihar, MP, Jharkhand, UP and Rajasthan. These States have over time shown tremendous improvement in their HDI and its component indices over time, leading to a convergence in HDI across States[8]. The coefficient of variation of the HDI for States in 2000 was 0.313 and this had fallen

TABLE 11.5
Disparities in Human Development Indicators

State	Literacy Rate (2011)	Female Literacy (2011)	Sex Ratio (2011)	IMR (2009)
Andhra Pradesh	67.66	59.74	992	49
Assam	73.18	67.27	954	61
Bihar	63.82	53.33	916	52
Jharkhand	67.63	56.21	947	44
Gujarat	79.31	70.73	918	48
Haryana	76.64	66.77	877	51
Himachal Pradesh	83.78	76.6	974	45
J&K	68.74	58.01	883	45
Karnataka	75.6	68.13	968	41
Kerala	93.91	91.98	1084	12
MP	70.63	60.02	930	67
Chhattisgarh	71.04	60.59	991	54
Maharashtra	82.91	75.48	925	31
Orissa	73.45	64.36	978	65
Punjab	76.68	71.34	893	38
Rajasthan	67.06	52.66	926	59
Tamil Nadu	80.33	73.86	995	28
UP	69.72	59.26	908	63
Uttarakhand	79.63	70.7	963	41
West Bengal	77.08	71.16	947	33

Source: Literacy data and sex ratio are from Census of India, 2011; IMR data are from *SRS Bulletin*, January 2011.

sharply to 0.235 in 2008. Furthermore, the IHDR-2011 finds that the absolute improvements in health and education indices for low PCI States such as Chhattisgarh, Jharkhand, MP and Orissa have been better than for all India, with their gaps with the all-India average narrowing over time. In six of the low HDI States—Bihar, Andhra Pradesh, Chhattisgarh, MP, Orissa and Assam—the improvement in HDI (in absolute terms) is considerably more than the national average. In fact, if we look at absolute changes in HDI over the decade (Table 11.6), the conclusion that the poorer States are catching up with the national average is strengthened. For instance, in Uttarakhand, the increase in HDI has been 0.151 points between 1999–2000 and 2007–08 compared to the national average of 0.080 points. Other relatively poor States that have seen an improvement in HDI greater than the all-India average are Assam (0.108 points), Jharkhand (0.108 points), MP (0.090 points) and Orissa (0.087 points). Chhattisgarh with an improvement of 0.080 points has performed as well as the national average in terms of HDI. However, among the relatively poor States, the increase in HDI in Bihar (0.075 points) and UP (0.064 points) was less than the national average. But the relative improvement (that is, percentage change) in HDI is greater in Bihar than the national average. As Table 11.6 shows, the percentage change in HDI is greater for the majority of low PCI States than the HDI improvement for India as a whole. In the backdrop of widening regional disparities in terms of per capita NSDP in the first decade of the 21st century, it is encouraging to observe convergence in HDI.

DISTRICT-LEVEL ANALYSIS

11.20. There are considerable regional disparities in socio-economic development not only between

TABLE 11.6
Human Development Index (1999–2000 and 2007–08)

State	HDI (2007–08)	HDI (1999–2000)	Change in HDI	Percentage Change
Uttarakhand	0.49	0.339	0.151	44.54
Kerala	0.79	0.677	0.113	16.69
Assam	0.444	0.336	0.108	32.14
Jharkhand	0.376	0.268	0.108	32.14
Andhra Pradesh	0.473	0.368	0.105	28.53
North-East (excluding Assam)	0.573	0.473	0.100	21.14
MP	0.375	0.285	0.090	31.58
Tamil Nadu	0.57	0.48	0.090	18.75
Karnataka	0.519	0.432	0.087	31.64
Orissa	0.362	0.275	0.087	31.64
All India	0.467	0.387	0.080	20.72
Chhattisgarh	0.358	0.278	0.080	28.78
Bihar	0.367	0.292	0.075	25.68
Himachal Pradesh	0.652	0.581	0.071	12.22
Maharashtra	0.572	0.501	0.071	14.17
West Bengal	0.492	0.422	0.070	16.59
J&K	0.529	0.465	0.064	13.76
UP	0.38	0.316	0.064	20.25
Punjab	0.605	0.543	0.062	11.42
Gujarat	0.527	0.466	0.061	13.09
Haryana	0.552	0.501	0.051	10.18
Rajasthan	0.434	0.387	0.047	12.14
Goa	0.617	0.595	0.022	3.70
Delhi	0.75	0.783	−0.033	−4.21

Source: IHDR, 2011.

States but also within States. The fallacy of taking the State as a unit for judging economic advancement/laggardness has been well known for years. Human development reports (HDRs) of various States bring out starkly the extent to which intra-regional disparity prevails within the very advanced States. For example, though Maharashtra, Karnataka and Andhra Pradesh are regarded as rapidly developing States, the fact of the matter is that there are a few pockets within these States which, due to their better physical and social infrastructure, have been able to attract large investments and register a faster rate of economic growth. State-level analysis does not reveal anything about what might be taking place in different regions within States. In fact, intra-State disparities are as much a cause of concern as inter-State disparities.

Disparities in Gross District Domestic Product (GDDP)

11.21. We begin our analysis at the district level by examining GDDP. Data for this are available starting 1999. Table 11.7 calculates the coefficient of variation of per capita GDDP for 1999–2000 and for the most recent time period, till which data are available. It is interesting to note that while some States witnessed an increase in the dispersion of per capita GDDP, others witnessed a decline. The coefficient of variation of per capita GDDP increased in several States, with the largest increase being in Bihar from 0.671 in 1999–2000 to 0.823 in 2004–05. Karnataka, Orissa and West Bengal also witnessed increases in dispersions of per capita GDDP. Barring Rajasthan, all the other BIMARU States witnessed an increase in the dispersion of per capita GDDP. It appears even though the BIMARU States are being lauded for their impressive growth rates in the 2000s, disparities within these States are increasing, suggesting that development and growth are being concentrated in a few pockets. Importantly, States such as Maharashtra, Assam and Chhattisgarh witnessed a decrease in dispersion of per capita GDDP.

11.22. We can also get a measure of the extent of intra-State disparities by comparing the ratios of per capita GDDP of the richest district to the poorest district in the State (Table 11.8). Bihar is suffering from growing intra-State disparity. The per capita GDDP for Patna district is by far the highest among the State's districts. The difference has increased in recent years with the ratio of per capita GDDP in Patna district to that of Sheohar district, which has the lowest income in Bihar, increasing from 6.68 in 1999–2000 to 8.65 in 2006–07. In UP the ratio of per capita GDDP in Gautambudhnagar district to that of Shravasti district has increased from 6.80 in 1999–2000 to 9.20 in 2005–06. The rise in intra-State disparities is particularly stark in the case of Haryana, where the ratio of per capita GDDP in the richest district in the State (Gurgaon) to the poorest district (Mahindergarh in 1999–2000 and Mewat in 2005–06) has increased from 3.47 in 1999–2000 to 9.87 in 2005–06. In Karnataka, the ratio of per capita GDDP in the richest district in the State to the poorest

TABLE 11.7
Weighted Coefficient of Variation in District-level Domestic Product

State	1999–2000	Most Recent Time Period for Which Data Are Available
Andhra Pradesh	0.239	0.235 (2005–06)
Assam	0.444	0.357 (2007–08)
Bihar	0.671	0.823 (2004–05)
Jharkhand	0.283	0.296 (2005–06)
Haryana	0.326	0.764 (2005–06)
Himachal Pradesh	0.358	0.321 (2005–06)
Karnataka	0.359	0.539 (2005–06)
Kerala	0.181	0.211 (2006–07)
MP	0.380	0.426 (2007–08)
Chhattisgarh	0.622	0.521 (2006–07)
Maharashtra	0.434	0.396 (2006–07)
Orissa	0.377	0.434 (2004–05)
Punjab	0.100	0.149 (2005–06)
Rajasthan	0.251	0.232 (2005–06)
Tamil Nadu	0.229	0.239 (2005–06)
UP	0.414	0.452 (2005–06)
Uttaranchal	0.218	0.238 (2008–09)
West Bengal	0.197	0.302 (2006–07)

Source: Directorate of Economics and Statistics, Respective State Governments.

TABLE 11.8
Ratio of Per Capita GDDP in Richest District to Poorest District

State	1999–2000	Most Recent Time Period for Which Data Are Available
Andhra Pradesh	2.33	2.23 (2005–06)
Assam	3.37	3.66 (2007–08)
Bihar	6.68	8.65 (2004–05)
Jharkhand	2.72	2.83 (2005–06)
Haryana	3.47	9.87 (2005–06)
Himachal Pradesh	3.72	3.10 (2005–06)
Karnataka	2.76	4.42 (2005–06)
Kerala	1.97	2.23 (2006–07)
MP	4.17	3.92 (2007–08)
Chhattisgarh	5.42	5.20 (2006–07)
Maharashtra	4.31	3.41 (2006–07)
Orissa	4.02	4.55 (2004–05)
Punjab	1.51	1.59 (2005–06)
Rajasthan	2.48	2.22 (2005–06)
Tamil Nadu	2.31	3.30 (2005–06)
UP	6.8	9.20 (2005–06)
Uttaranchal	1.91	2.27 (2008–09)
West Bengal	2.37	3.27 (2006–07)

Source: Directorate of Economics and Statistics, Respective State Governments.

district increased from 2.76 in 1999–2000 to 4.42 in 2005–06. In Orissa, too, the income of richest district has continued to remain more than four times that of the poorest district. It is also worth noting that though the ratio of per capita GDDP of the richest district to the poorest district has declined over time in some States, the disparity continues to remain large. For instance, in the case of Maharashtra despite a decline in this ratio, the richest district (Mumbai) still has a per capita GDDP which is 3.4 times that of the poorest district. Similar is the case of MP and Chhattisgarh, where the income of the richest district is still almost four to five times that of the poorest district.

11.23. This then leads us to the question of which of these States witnessed convergence (or divergence) in PCIs across districts during the first decade of the 21st century. This exercise is important to understand if districts with higher initial incomes were also the ones that grew relatively faster, and continued to enjoy a cumulative advantage causing some districts in the States to be left behind. But, district-level analysis of convergence is difficult as there are serious data limitations at the district level. We, therefore, attempt to provide an initial answer to this question by plotting the average growth rates during the time period under study against the (log of) initial PCI.

11.24. Recent studies for growth in incomes since 1999 to recent periods (for which data are available) indicate interesting trends in the States of Bihar, Karnataka, West Bengal, Haryana, Jharkhand and Kerala; the relationship is upward sloping. This suggests divergence in growth performance across districts, that is, districts which were richer to begin with grew faster, suggesting that inequality between districts in these States was increasing. Each of these States witnessed very high growth rates in the first decade of the 21st century, and the fact that they also observed rising intra-State disparities indicates that growth was concentrated in a few pockets. This, in turn, may have contributed to overall inequality in the State, which explains why States such as Bihar did not perform well in terms of poverty reduction despite recording impressive growth rates.

11.25. In the States of MP, UP, Tamil Nadu, Orissa and Uttarakhand, the relationship is upward sloping, but the trend lines are quite flat and no clear pattern emerges in terms of divergence. Interestingly, in Maharashtra, Rajasthan, Himachal Pradesh and Andhra Pradesh, the relationship is downward sloping, indicating that districts with lower initial income were indeed growing faster.

Disparities in Poverty Ratios and Human Development Indicators

11.26. A remarkable characteristic of regional disparities in India is the presence of backward areas even within States that have grown faster and are at relatively high income levels on average. Debroy and Bhandari,[9] in a study that identifies India's most deprived districts, identify those districts that fall in the bottom 25 per cent under various categories such as head count ratio (HCR), food sufficiency, IMR and literacy rate.[10] On examining this dataset, we find that the most backward districts in terms of these parameters lie not just in the undivided BIMARU States, but also in States that have grown faster and are at a relatively high income level on average. This reveals the extent of intra-State disparities. For instance, district-level poverty estimates show that the poorest districts in India lie not only in undivided BIMARU States and Orissa, but also in rich States such as Maharashtra, Karnataka and Tamil Nadu. The disparity across district-level HCR is stark in the case of Maharashtra. At one end of the spectrum, there are districts with poverty HCR exceeding 40 per cent such as Wardha (44.9 per cent), Washim (43.1 per cent), Akola (43.1 per cent), Amravati (47.6 per cent), Bhandara (44.7 per cent), Buldana (46.6 per cent), Dhule (40 per cent), Gondiya (44.7 per cent), Nanded (43.9 per cent) and Nandurbar (40 per cent). While at the other end of the spectrum, there are districts such as Mumbai and Pune with HCR of 11.3 per cent and 14.1 per cent, respectively. Similarly in the case of Karnataka, there are districts with extremely high poverty HCRs, such as Bellary (43.3 per cent), Gulbarga (42.2 per cent), Koppal (48.8 per cent) and Raichur (48.8 per cent); while there are also districts with extremely low percentage of poor such as Kodagu (6.7 per cent) and Bangalore (8.6 per cent). In Tamil Nadu, too, we find the range in district-level HCR is wide with Tiruvanamalai, having an HCR of 60.2 per cent and Toothkudi, having an HCR of 3.3 per cent. The fact that these three States have lower poverty HCRs than the national average and yet have the poorest districts in India is an indicator of the extent of intra-State inequalities.

11.27. On further examination of this dataset, we find that disparities are not just in terms of income, but also non-income indicators. Importantly, non-income indicators, such as hunger (defined in National Sample Survey (NSS) terms) exhibit a spatial distribution too. Even the rich States with their higher levels of PCI have some of the most hungry districts in the country. These include Andhra Pradesh (East Godavari, Khammam, Mahbubnagar), Haryana (Fatehbad, Hisar), Karnataka (Gulbarga) Kerala (Malappuram, Palakkad, Thiruvananthapuram, Thrissur), Maharashtra (Kolhapur, Ratnagiri, Satara, Sindhudurg). In terms of infant mortality, the worst districts are located not just in the BIMARU States of UP, Orissa, MP, Chhatisgarh and Rajasthan, but also a few neighbouring districts of Karnataka and Andhra Pradesh. Also, even though Maharashtra's IMR is near the best in the country, its worst districts have IMRs that are higher than those of States with lower ranks. Districts identified as backward under the literacy criterion while concentrated in Orissa, undivided BIMARU, are also present in richer States such as Karnataka (Gulbarga, Koppal, Raichur, Chamarajanagar) Andhra Pradesh (Adilabad, Karimnagar, Kurnool, Mahbubnagar, Medak, Nizamabad, Srikakulam, Vizianagaram), Gujarat (Banas Katha, Dohad, Kachchh), Himachal Pradesh (Kinnaur) and Punjab (Mansa). Importantly, all these States, barring Andhra Pradesh, had a literacy rate higher than the national average. The fact that such States would include those districts that fall in the category of the lowest 25 per cent in terms of literacy highlights the extent of intra-State disparities. In addition to revealing the extent of disparities between districts in a State, the fact that the richest States in India have districts with the highest poverty, highest IMR and lowest literacy rates also highlights the limitations of PCIs in measuring the economic and social progress in society.

INTRA-DISTRICT INEQUALITIES

11.28. A discussion on regional disparities in India would be incomplete without mentioning that there is considerable intra-district inequality too, with some blocks in a district better off than others. An analysis at the block level is severely constrained by data availability. An India Development Foundation study,[11] which estimates poverty headcount ratios at the block level, allows us to get a sense of intra-district disparities. For instance, in the Madhepura district of Bihar, poverty HCR varies from 19.83 per cent in Bihariganj block to 71.01 per cent in Puraini block. In the Darbhanga district, poverty HCR varies across blocks from 42.63 per cent to 88.16 per cent. In the Osmanabad district of Maharashtra, poverty HCR ranges from 36 per cent to 62 per cent. Of the 4,869 blocks covered in this study, 2,445 (50 per cent) blocks have a poverty HCR exceeding 50 per cent. Another interesting observation that emerges from this dataset is that the poorer blocks in a district sometimes tend to be the ones populated by a greater percentage of Scheduled Tribes (STs). For instance, in the Yavatmal district of Maharashtra, poverty HCR ranges from 38.37 per cent in the Ner block to 73.79 per cent to Kelapur block. The former has a tribal population of 7.19 per cent while the latter has a tribal population of 36.88 per cent. In the Kalahandi district of Orissa, poverty HCR ranges from 38.1 per cent in Kokasara (which has a tribal population of 32.59 per cent) to 99.99 per cent Thuamul Rampur (which has tribal population of 57.55 per cent). Similarly, in the Kendujhar district, poverty in the Nandipada block, which has a 5 per cent tribal population, stands at 32.31 per cent, while poverty in the Kanjipani block, which has 84.69 per cent tribal population, stands at 89.84 per cent. In the Betul district of MP, too, we find that the poorest block, Shahpur (poverty HCR of 97.49 per cent) has a tribal population of 64.4 per cent while the Multai block (poverty HCR of 64.5 per cent) has a tribal population of 17.14 per cent. In this dataset, 897 blocks can be classified as tribal blocks, that is, having a tribal population exceeding 20 per cent. Of these 897 tribal blocks, 649 blocks (72 per cent) have poverty HCR exceeding 50 per cent and 577 tribal blocks (64 per cent) are rainfed. It appears, therefore, that there is a high correlation between tribals, rainfed areas and incidence of high poverty. The fact that the blocks inhabited by greater percentage of tribals tend to be the poorest blocks is a matter of serious concern. When spatial inequalities align with differences in group identity, they pose a great threat to national unity and peace and could be regarded as a contributory factor to Maoist violence.

INFRASTRUCTURE DEVELOPMENT

11.29. One of the key strategies for growth has been development of infrastructure. As low-income States invest in infrastructure supported by Central investments and private investments, the growth potential improves significantly. During the Eleventh Plan, this process was strongly emphasised. This was specially supported by investment under Public–Private Partnerships (PPP). This helped increase the level of investment in Infrastructure Sector from 5.6 per cent (2006–07) to 7.27 per cent (2011–12). The States have also invested in development of agriculture, communication, energy and transport. An inter-State Infrastructure Index was developed earlier by the Eleventh Finance Commission. The index developed by the Commission was composite index of social and economic infrastructure. It classified physical infrastructure into five sectors: agriculture,

TABLE 11.9
Index of Infrastructure

Sl. No.	States	1999–2000 (FC)		2008–09 (Working Group of PC)	
		Index	Rank (PCI)	Index	Rank
1	Andhra Pradesh	103.3	11	112.84	11
2	Arunachal Pradesh	69.71	13	NA	NA
3	Assam	77.72	16	62.02	19
4	Bihar	81.33	19	78.79	20
5	Chhattisgarh	NA	NA	70.14	18
6	Goa	200.57	1	215.11	1
7	Gujarat	124.31	8	124.72	7
8	Haryana	137.54	4	136.43	6
9	Himachal Pradesh	95.03	5	164.20	4
10	Jharkhand	NA	NA	52.09	21
11	J&K	NA	NA	81.40	16
12	Karnataka	104.88	9	124.35	8
13	Kerala	178.68	7	197.36	2
14	MP	76.79	15	78.91	17
15	Maharashtra	112.80	3	115.56	10
16	Orissa	81.00	17	81.83	15
17	Punjab	187.57	2	175.81	3
18	Rajasthan	75.86	14	84.11	14
19	Sikkim	108.99	12	NA	NA
20	Tamil Nadu	149.1	6	152.24	5
21	UP	101.23	18	86.99	13
22	Uttarakhand	NA	NA	118.38	9
23	West Bengal	111.23	10	97.01	12

Source: Eleventh Finance Commission Report, PCI of States—CSO.
Note: FC = Finance Commission; PC = Planning Commission; PCI = Per Capita Income.

communications, banking, electricity and transport. Each one of these different variables was studied and the index was developed. Centre for Monitoring of Indian Economy (CMIE) had developed 'CMIE, 2000', an Infrastructure Development Index based on 13 indicators, covering seven major infrastructure sectors. These included transport, energy, irrigation, banking, communications, education and health facilities. Subsequently, efforts have been made by other analysts to develop an Index based on Principal Component Analysis. All these indices have indicated a strong correlationship between infrastructure, PCIs and poverty ratios.

11.30. Based on the earlier studies, a slightly more comprehensive index has been developed by the Working Group constituted by the Planning Commission. It identified 6 sectors and took into account 12 indicators to develop Infrastructure Index. The broad areas included agriculture, communications, banking, electricity, road transport and railways. It used four alternative methodologies and recommended use of Principal Component Analysis for developing the Infrastructure Index. Table 11.9 indicates the comparative picture.

11.31. The correlation of Infrastructure Index with PCI and poverty is quite strong (Table 11.10).

11.32. There exists a direct negative relationship between infrastructure development and levels of poverty and the relative strength of this correlation suggests that infrastructure affects poverty primarily due to increased economic activity resulting in higher PCIs. An analysis of the States in this context indicates that Kerala has improved its ranking from 7 (Finance Commision) to 2. This is primarily due to improved efforts in road, rail density, power and tele-density. UP has also recorded an improvement in the ranking from 18 (Finance Commision) to 13, primarily due to surface roads, railways, rural electrification and, most importantly, irrigation. Gujarat, Himachal Pradesh, Karnataka and Tamil Nadu had shown marginal improvement.

11.33. Maharashtra, however, had a deceleration with the ranking declining from 3 (Finance Commision) to 10, primarily because of poor road-density, railway route length as well as irrigation. Haryana, too, performed badly. Bihar, MP and West Bengal, however, improved their ranking.

TARGETED TWELFTH PLAN GROWTH RATES

11.34. The Twelfth Plan growth rates of GSDP have been worked out for different States. National growth rates of GDP and State-wise break-up of specific economic performance since 2004–05, the potentialities and constraints present in each State and scope for growth based on an assessment within the Planning Commission have been taken into account in computing this. For this purpose, the aggregate performance of each State has been broken into sectoral components. The distribution of the national growth rates among the three major sectors of the economy—agriculture, industry and services—has been done keeping the sectoral consistency across the projected growth rate of the States in mind. The State-specific growth rates for each sector have been pro-rated to the

TABLE 11.10
Rank Correlation between Infrastructure Index, Poverty Ratio and Per Capita Income of States

	1999–2000	2007–08[a]	2008–09[b]
Between Infra Index and PCI	0.7895	0.8623	0.8506
Between Infra Index and Poverty Ratio	0.6386	0.8727	0.8208
Between PCI and Poverty Ratio	0.8193	0.7390	0.7481

Source: Planning Commission, Report of the Working Group on 'Issues Relating to Growth and Development at Sub-national Level'.
Note: PCI = Per Capita Income.
[a] Poverty Ratio (2009–10) and PCI of States (2007–08).
[b] PCI (2008–09) and Poverty Ratio (2009–10).

TABLE 11.11
State-wise and Sector-wise Expected Growth Rates for the Twelfth Five Year Plan (2012–17)

(in percentage)

Sl. No.	States/UTs	Sector-wise Growth Rates Expected by Planning Commission				Growth Targets Proposed by State Govt.
		Agriculture	Industry	Services	Total	
1.	Andhra Pradesh	5.0	8.3	9.4	8.3	10.0
2.	Bihar	6.0	12.0	11.0	10.0	13.0
3.	Chhattisgarh	6.0	7.5	9.5	8.0	10.0
4.	Goa	0.5	7.2	9.9	8.5	15.0
5.	Gujarat	4.0	9.2	10.5	9.2	10.8
6.	Haryana	4.2	7.3	11.5	9.0	10.2
7.	Jharkhand	6.0	7.0	10.5	8.5	10.0
8.	Karnataka	5.0	5.5	9.2	7.5	8.0
9.	Kerala	1.0	6.0	9.6	8.0	9.0
10.	Madhya Pradesh	6.5	9.3	9.6	8.8	12.0
11.	Maharashtra	3.0	8.2	9.5	8.6	10.5
12.	Odisha	3.2	8.2	9.5	8.0	9.0
13.	Punjab	1.6	8.0	8.0	6.5	6.5
14.	Rajasthan	5.5	5.5	9.0	7.2	7.7
15.	Tamil Nadu	3.4	7.4	8.5	7.7	11.0
16.	Uttar Pradesh	3.2	5.8	9.6	7.2	8.5
17.	West Bengal	2.5	5.5	8.8	7.0	8.0
Special Category States						
18.	Arunachal Pradesh	5.7	10.3	9.0	8.5	9.02
19.	Assam	4.8	4.6	8.9	7.0	8.33
20.	Himachal Pradesh	2.0	8.2	10.0	8.0	8.2
21.	Jammu & Kashmir	1.5	4.3	9.5	6.5	7.5
22.	Manipur	6.0	4.5	8.4	6.5	6.6
23.	Meghalaya	2.8	8.5	9.2	8.0	11.0
24.	Mizoram	6.9	9.3	9.8	9.0	11.0
25.	Nagaland	4.8	9.0	7.5	7.0	8.0
26.	Sikkim	4.0	8.3	9.8	8.5	8.5
27.	Tripura	5.0	8.0	9.7	8.2	8.5
28.	Uttarakhand	3.0	9.0	11.2	9.5	10.5
	All India	**4.0**	**7.6**	**9.0**	**8.0**	

Source: Planning Commission.

National growth rate so that contribution of each State to all-India level in sector-specific growth is maintained at the levels achieved during 2004–05 to 2009–10. This has then been adjusted for the Twelfth Plan keeping in view the potentialities and constraints present in each State and the need for improvement so that the erstwhile slow-growing States realise their full potential. GSDP growth rates arrived on the basis of above methodology are indicated in Table 11.11.

TABLE 11.12
Financial Transfers under Normal Central Assistance (Plan) and Thirteenth Finance Commission

Sl. No.	States	Per Capita GSDP 2011–12 at 2004–05 Price (₹)	Population (2011 Census)	Share in NCA[a] during Eleventh Plan (2007–12)	Share % as per 13th FC
Non-special Category States				**Within Group (%)**	
1	Andhra Pradesh	47,547	7.60	6.260	7.642
2	Bihar	14,647	9.30	11.320	11.578
3	Chhattisgarh	33,206	2.30	2.832	2.812
4	Goa	1,28,917	0.13	0.475	0.293
5	Gujarat	67,056	5.43	3.918	3.601
6	Haryana	69,726	2.28	1.848	1.303
7	Jharkhand	28,815	2.84	3.409	3.205
8	Karnataka	47,911	5.42	4.386	4.979
9	Kerala	60,535	3.00	3.217	2.699
10	MP	27,620	6.56	7.131	7.806
11	Maharashtra	70,885	10.10	6.883	6.139
12	Orissa	30,946	3.78	5.983	5.287
13	Punjab	52,908	2.48	2.238	1.719
14	Rajasthan	33,274	6.18	5.936	6.550
15	Tamil Nadu	61,530	6.48	5.885	5.586
16	UP	20,868	17.89	20.134	20.897
17	West Bengal	37,765	8.23	8.144	7.899
			100	100	100
Special Category States				**Within Group (%)**	
1	Arunachal Pradesh	40,556	1.84	7.929	4.274
2	Assam	26,037	41.49	19.535	27.153
3	Himachal Pradesh	60,772	9.13	9.659	10.184
4	J&K	34,533	16.72	19.137	18.986
5	Manipur	26,687	3.63	5.840	6.370
6	Meghalaya	42,003	3.94	4.852	4.621
7	Mizoram	43,187	1.45	5.590	4.134
8	Nagaland	46,548	2.63	5.910	6.453
9	Sikkim	83,568	0.82	3.770	2.125
10	Tripura	42,970	4.88	8.244	6.164
11	Uttarakhand	58,404	13.47	9.536	9.535
			100	100	100

Source: Planning Commission.
Note: FC = Finance Commision; NCA = Normal Central Assistance.
[a] Calculation including a notional loan component.

TABLE 11.13
Criteria and Weights for Tax Devolution

Sl. No.	Criteria	Weight (%)
1	Population (1971)	25.0
2	Area	10.0
3	Fiscal Capacity Distance	47.5
4	Fiscal Discipline	17.5

Source: Thirteenth Finance Commission Report, December 2009.

TABLE 11.14
Criteria and Weights under Gadgil-Mukherjee Formula

Sl. No.	Criteria	Weight (%)
1	Population (1971)	60
2	PCI	
	1. For States with Lower than National Average	20
	2. For all States	5
3	Performance (Tax Effort, Fiscal Management, National Objectives)	7.5
4	Special Problems	7.5

Source: Planning Commission.
Note: PCI = Per Capita Income.

STRATEGY TO ADDRESS REGIONAL INEQUALITY

11.35. The inter-State and intra-State disparities are a major source of concern for faster and more inclusive development at national level. Different States of the country, if are not able to access the fruits of development equitably so that the levels of services and benefits to them are fair and just, the overall stress in the national polity is increased. This gets reflected in the handling of various national issues and acts as a drag on overall economic growth of the country.

11.36. There are, therefore, several policy instruments within the government for addressing these problems, apart from Constitutional transfers of Finance Commission. The two major sources of financial transfers to the States have been transfers under the Finance Commission awards and Plan transfers. The successive Finance Commissions have tried to make these more equitable. Specifically, the formula for Plan transfers has been based on consideration of PCIs, population, geographical areas and similar other factors which are reflective of low PCI States. Thirteenth Finance Commission award indicates transfers as mentioned in Table 11.12.

11.37. The principle of criterion for horizontal sharing in Thirteenth Finance Commission has been indicated in Table 11.13.

11.38. The above incorporates major disability of States, namely low PCI, resulting in poor investment capability, which in turn results in slow growth rates. In the other criterion for horizontal transfers too, similar progressive approach has been used. This has resulted in more equitable sharing of resources by the Centre. Since, of the total transfers to the States, the major share is that of the Finance Commission, the above horizontal transfer formula has helped the States to meet their expenditure requirements and have more equitable growth strategy.

11.39. The second strategy for transfers is that of the Planning Commission, which is based on Plan transfers. These again are clearly progressive in nature and support low income States. The total transfers consist of Normal Central Assistance (NCA), transfers under the CSS and transfers under Additional Central Assistance (ACA) under special scheme. The NCA transfers are under the Gadgil-Mukherjee Formula, as depicted in Table 11.14.

11.40. The share of NCA in the overall transfers to the States is, however, comparatively small. During 2011–12 it was estimated at 4.5 per cent of the total Plan transfers to States.

11.41. The transfers under CSS have been fairly large and focused on major areas of social and economic development. In the Eleventh Plan, the focus was on 14 Flagship Schemes, which covered the areas of agriculture, education, health, employment, urban development, rural and urban infrastructure and energy. This has led to substantial transfers to the States, which has impacted both the overall development and infrastructure levels. The Central Plan transfers under these Flagship Schemes are given in Table 11.15.

TABLE 11.15
Statewise Central Releases under Important Flagship Schemes as Per Cent of Total

State	Population 2011 (% share)	SSA	NRHM	ICDS	PMGSY	NREGS	MDM	BRGF	Total
Non-special Category States									
Andhra Pradesh	7.11	8.87	6.35	6.56	3.87	5.07	8.69	9.36	6.48
Bihar	8.72	8.94	5.35	5.78	21.27	4.46	8.35	10.431	8.62
Chhattisgarh	2.15	3.38	2.87	2.72	5.11	5.62	4.84	6.64	4.33
Goa	0.12	0.05	0.14	0.09	0	0.01	0.08	0	0.05
Gujarat	5.07	4.25	4.22	5.70	0.42	1.11	3.60	2.80	2.92
Haryana	2.13	1.96	2.02	1.61	0.38	0.94	1.71	0.48	1.34
Jharkhand	2.77	2.80	3.18	2.31	5.37	4.24	5.33	4.69	3.85
Karnataka	5.14	3.03	4.57	5.42	0	2.27	5.77	2.37	3.13
Kerala	2.81	0.82	3.96	2.62	1.28	3.26	1.46	0.88	2.27
MP	6.10	9.20	6.53	6.56	7.26	10.18	7.83	10.3	8.39
Maharashtra	9.44	5.70	8.90	10.10	5.04	3.57	7.07	6.51	6.19
Orissa	3.53	4.48	4.72	4.83	12.53	3.35	3.79	8.32	5.50
Punjab	2.33	2.32	2.29	1.85	1.05	0.39	1.79	0.40	1.43
Rajasthan	5.77	7.18	7.11	4.18	4.26	5.55	5.40	7.31	5.76
Tamil Nadu	6.06	3.29	5.27	3.83	1.02	9.65	4.12	2.71	5.07
UP	16.77	12.74	12.67	15.66	1.30	14.54	10.98	13.81	11.82
West Bengal	7.68	8.58	6.33	8.20	5.25	8.90	7.88	5.23	7.65
Special Category States									
Arunachal Pradesh	0.12	1.15	0.52	0.69	1.36	0.21	0.21	0.27	0.66
Assam	2.62	5.17	5.97	4.85	10.73	1.46	5.43	1.52	4.93
Himachal Pradesh	0.58	0.69	1.34	1.04	1.95	1.07	0.75	0.60	1.11
J&K	1.05	1.45	1.72	1.20	4.83	2.68	1.37	0.78	2.24
Manipur	0.23	0.19	0.42	0.58	1.12	2.14	0.19	0.82	0.96
Meghalaya	0.25	0.70	0.42	0.67	0.24	0.98	0.36	0.63	0.63
Mizoram	0.09	0.52	0.46	0.32	0.60	1.13	0.34	0.64	0.65
Nagaland	0.17	0.47	0.60	0.76	0.06	2.31	0.25	1.06	0.96
Sikkim	0.05	0.19	0.18	0.09	0.51	0.35	0.11	0.36	0.26
Tripura	0.03	0.85	0.47	0.93	1.32	3.29	0.86	0.35	1.52
Uttarakhand	0.85	1.01	1.42	0.83	1.88	1.28	1.45	0.75	1.27
Total (crore) (% share)	119 (100)	29,171 (100)	20,695 (100)	9,801 (100)	15,685 (100)	14,703 (100)	3,917 (100)	14,159.80	1,08,133 (100)

Source: Planning Commission.
Note: SSA=Sarva Shiksha Abhiyan; NRHM=National Rural Health Mission; ICDS=Integrated Child Development Services; NREGA=National Rural Health Mission; NREGS=National Rural Employment Guarantee Scheme; PMGSY=Pradhan Mantri Gram Sadak Yojana; MDM=Mid Day Meal Scheme; BRGF=Backward Regions Grant Fund; UT=Union Territories.

SPECIAL AREA PROGRAMMES

11.42. Interventions to tackle regional disparities being taken up by the Union Government fall into two categories. The first is to direct investments into less developed States under CSS through more favourable norms for distribution of assistance. For instance, under the Indira Awas Yojana, funds are allocated State-wise based upon the housing shortage and population below the poverty line. Consequently in 2010–11, Bihar received about 25 per cent of the allocation under the programme. Similarly, in the case of the National Rural Health Mission (NRHM), 17 States have been identified for focused attention. However, the most important intervention of the Central Government are the special area development programmes that have a clear focus on some aspect of development in identified backward areas. These programmes are:

1. The BRGF
   a. The District Component
   b. The IAP for Selected Tribal and Backward Districts
   c. The special package for Bundelkhand region
   d. The Special Plan for Bihar
   e. The Special Plan for West Bengal
   f. The Special Plan for the KBK Districts of Orissa
2. The HADP/WGDP
3. The Border Areas Development Programme (BADP)

BRGF

11.43. The BRGF, launched in late 2006 at the end of the Tenth Plan, was designed to redress regional imbalances in development. It aimed at catalysing development in backward areas by converging, through supplementary infrastructure and capacity building, the substantial existing development inflows into these districts as part of a well-conceived, participatory district plan.

District Component of the BRGF

11.44. The BRGF District Component provides financial resources for supplementing and converging existing developmental inflows into identified districts, so as to:

1. bridge critical gaps in local infrastructure and other development requirements that are not being adequately met through existing inflows;
2. strengthen, to this end Panchayat- and Municipality-level governance with more appropriate capacity building, to facilitate participatory planning, decision-making, implementation and monitoring, to reflect local felt needs;
3. provide professional support to local bodies for planning, implementation and monitoring their plans; and
4. improve the performance and delivery of critical functions assigned to Panchayats, and counter possible efficiency and equity losses on account of inadequate local capacity.

11.45. The BRGF District Component subsumed the ongoing RSVY. The management of the scheme was also shifted from the Planning Commission to the Ministry of Panchayati Raj (MoPR), given that planning was to be through Panchayati Raj Institutions (PRIs), culminating in a Draft Development Plan prepared by the District Planning Committee (DPC). It was hoped that the focus on decentralised participative planning in the implementation framework for the scheme would catalyse the formation and functioning of constitutionally mandated DPCs, an arrangement that had hitherto been neglected in most States.

11.46. All funds sanctioned by MoPR under the Programme are transferred to the Consolidated Funds of the concerned State Governments. The funds are required to be transferred to the Panchayats, the Municipalities and other implementing authorities such as the State Institutes of Rural Development, and so on, by the State Governments within 15 days of the release of funds to the Consolidated Fund following the same approach as mandated in the case of transfer of Twelfth Finance Commission Grants. States were requested to adopt the mechanism of bank transfer to local governments through core banking arrangements.

11.47. Under the BRGF, for bridging identified critical gaps in infrastructure, participative plans are required to be prepared by each Panchayat and

Municipality for its functional domain. These plans, which should take into account all development inflows into the area, including those other than BRGF, are then to be consolidated into district plans by the DPCs. The funds provided under BRGF are untied and can be used to meet any development gap identified by the community in its interaction with the Panchayats and Municipalities.

Physical Performance

11.48. As far as physical achievements under the programme are concerned, the analysis of the District Plans and Progress Reports received in the Ministry so far from the various States indicates that the untied fund allocated to the districts are generally being used for filling infrastructure gaps in drinking water, health, education, social sectors, electrification, and so on. The basket of works taken up includes construction of school buildings/classrooms, toilets, playgrounds, health sub-centre, bore wells, drinking water facility, sanitation facilities, anganwadi buildings, Panchayat buildings, irrigation tanks/channels, agriculture and animal husbandry facilities, electrification, street lights, link roads, market yards, Haat Bazaars, flood control structures, soil and water conservation measures, cremation/burial grounds, houses for below poverty line (BPL) families, training and marketing facilities for self-help groups (SHGs), culverts, suspension bridges, and so on.

11.49. The Ministry has adopted the principle of 'Rolling Plans and Revolving Funds' under which incomplete works of a year are to be included in Action Plan for the next year.

Financial Performance

11.50. The details of achievement of the financial targets for the Eleventh Plan, up to 2010–11, are given below (Table 11.16).

Evaluation of the Programme

11.51. The programme has been evaluated by a World Bank Mission on the request of the MoPR in 2009, which visited two districts each in eight States in July 2009. The MoPR also constituted a National Advisory cum Review Committee for BRGF. Among the strengths of the programme, the evaluations have identified the fact that the programme has pioneered implementation through the Panchayats, Municipalities and the DPCs, making decentralised planning more meaningful. It is also found that focus on capacity building of local bodies has enhanced the confidence, awareness and performance of their elected representatives and officials. The discretionary nature of the BRGF development funds has been appreciated by the Local Bodies as the most significant feature of the programme.

11.52. The major weaknesses identified include the criteria for identification of BRGF districts, the very low quantum of grant per Panchayat, which averages to ₹2 to 3 lakh per year and is regarded as too small to have any significant impact, cumbersome procedures for release of funds and the fact that PRIs/Urban Local Bodies (ULBs) still suffer from inadequate quality of human resource and infrastructure support.

TABLE 11.16
Eleventh Plan Expenditure

Financial Year	Allocation (₹ Cr.)		Expenditure Achievement		
	BE	RE	₹ Cr.	% of BE	% of RE
2007–08	4,670.00	3,600.00	3,600.00	77.09	100.00
2008–09	4,670.00	3,890.00	3,889.75	83.29	99.99
2009–10	4,670.00	3,670.00	3,669.97	78.59	100.00
2010–11	5,050.00	5,050.00	5,050.00	100.00	100.00
2011–12	5,050.00	3,717.00	3,917.00	77.56	105.38

Source: Planning Commission.
Note: Expenditure are till 2010–11 and do not cover the last year of the Plan.

11.53. Based on the insights drawn from the reviews of the BRGF and many other considerations, we are proposing a completely new architecture from the second year of the Twelfth Plan (see below).

Special Plan for Bihar

11.54. The Special Plan for Bihar is one of the components of the BRGF, designed to reduce regional imbalance more holistically in the region. The Special Plan has been formulated to bring about improvement in sectors such as power, road connectivity, irrigation, forestry and watershed development.

11.55. An allocation of ₹1,000 crore per annum was being made for the Special Plan during the Tenth Plan period. The same allocation was approved for the Eleventh Plan period. However, this allocation has been enhanced to ₹2,000 crore for 2010–11 and ₹1,468 crore for 2011–12. The Planning Commission is administering the Special Plan and funds are being released on a 100 per cent grant basis.

11.56. Most of the projects started under the Plan are still incomplete and would require funding in the Twelfth Plan period. Further, revised cost estimates have been received for the State Highways Project and the Rail Road Bridge at Digha near Patna. Special Plan for Bihar needs to continue as infrastructure and development gap is still quite high between Bihar and other States, and there is some obligation arising from the preamble to the Bihar Re-organization Act. Further the Inter-Ministerial Group (IMG) to consider a Memorandum for Special Category status to Bihar has also recommended continuation of Special Plan for Bihar in the Twelfth Plan.

Special Plan for the KBK Districts of Orissa

11.57. The undivided districts of Koraput, Bolangir and Kalahandi (later reorganised into eight districts since 1992–93) cover 47,646 sq km area and comprise 14 Sub-divisions, 37 Tehsils, 80 CD Blocks, 1,437 Gram Panchayats and 12,293 Villages. The KBK districts, with population of 72.87 lakh (19.80 per cent of the State's population) have 89.95 per cent rural and 54.66 per cent ST (38.41 per cent) and Schedule Caste (SC) (16.25 per cent) population as per 2001 Census. Demographically, tribal communities dominate this region.

11.58. The backwardness of the KBK region is rooted in its history. Recurrent droughts and floods have adversely affected lives of the people and their economies in these districts. Hostile agro-climatic conditions, poor connectivity and infrastructure and physical isolation characterise this region.

11.59. More than 50 per cent of forest area of these districts has been considerably degraded. These are mostly revenue forests on hill slopes which have not been surveyed. Whereas the total area of forest under KBK districts on record is 15,957 sq km (that is, 33.5 per cent), actual forest cover is only 12,690 sq km. This includes 5,703 sq km of dense forests, 6,987 sq km open forests and 3,267 sq km barren forests. The continuous process of forest degradation adversely affects livelihoods options of the poor.

11.60. The KBK districts have been the focus of attention since the 1980s. A Long-term Action Plan for a period of seven years was launched in 1995–96. This plan was further revised in 1998–99 and the Revised Long Term Action Plan (RLTAP) was put in place for a period of nine years. This RLTAP was actually a sum total of the allocations made by various Central Ministries for CSS and the ACA allocated by the Planning Commission to fill critical gaps. This ACA was released in the form of 70 per cent loan and 30 per cent grant.

11.61. On the advice of the Planning Commission, the State Government started preparing the Special Plan for the KBK districts from 2002–03 onwards. An allocation of ₹200 crore was made for the Special Plan for the year 2002–03, which was later enhanced to ₹250 crore after approval to the scheme in 2003–04. Thus, an allocation of ₹250 crore was made for the Special Plan during the Tenth Five Year Plan period, from 2003–04 to 2006–07, under the RSVY on 100 per cent grant basis. The RSVY was replaced by the BRGF from 2006–07. The Districts Component of the BRGF covers 19 districts of Orissa. All the eight KBK districts are included in the 19 districts of Orissa covered under the Districts component.

11.62. In 2006–07, it was decided that the eight KBK districts will be funded under the BRGF district norms, with the balance being provided under the KBK Special Plan. Accordingly, an annual allocation of ₹120 crore is being made under the Districts Component of the BRGF for the eight KBK districts and the remaining allocation of ₹130 crore is being made through the Special Plan for the KBK districts from 2007–08. In all, funds to the order of ₹3,080.06 per head have flowed to this region under the aforesaid programmes since 1995–96 to 2010–11. In addition, this region has been recently receiving development funds under Mahatma Gandhi National Rural Employment Guarantee Scheme (MGNREGS), Pradhan Mantri Gram Sadak Yojana (PMGSY), SSA, NRHM and other development programme. With improvement in the fiscal conditions of the State, flow of the State funds to this region has also improved in recent years.

11.63. Impacts:

- A preliminary analysis of NSS data has indicated that poverty reduced by 24.6 percentage points from 87.1 per cent in 1999–2000 to 62.5 per cent in 2004–05 as per MRP Methodology.
- Enrolment rate in primary schools in KBK districts has gone up from 75.89 per cent in 1996–97 to 94.11 per cent in 2008–09. Similarly, the enrolment rate in upper-primary schools in KBK districts has gone up from 56.39 per cent in 1996–97 to 95.29 per cent in 2008–09.
- Dropout rate in primary schools in KBK districts has been reduced from 57.13 in 1996–97 to 6.79 in 2008–09.
- Female literacy rate has increased from 15.87 in 1991 to 29.10 in 2001. At the same time, the overall literacy rate has increased from 29.24 in 1991 to 43.30 in 2001. Literacy levels in 2011 have significantly improved to 57.56 per cent (that is, male literacy—69.5 per cent, and female literacy—45.9 per cent).

11.64. There are several reasons as to why the Special Plan for the KBK region should be extended beyond the Eleventh Five Year Plan with increased Special Central Assistance (SCA). Briefly these are:

- *Geographic and Demographic Characteristics Have Meant Slower Development*: The demographic and geographic characteristics of the region indicate that the inter-habitation and inter-village connectivity in the region is still poor. Public infrastructure such as schools, Anganwadi centres and health institutions are still not available in sufficient numbers. The implementation of national Flagship Schemes, such as PMGSY, to improve connectivity has not yet been able to close the gap, because of the scattered habitations in the region.
- *Human Development Gaps Still Exist*: While there has been improvement in human development indicators, they are still far below the desirable levels. For instance, literacy is still below the State average of 73.4 per cent (male literacy—82.4 per cent, and female literacy—64.3 per cent). Female tribal literacy rates are much lower than the State averages. Though poverty came down to 62.5 per cent in 2004–05, that still is a high and perturbing level of incidence.
- *Flow of Development Funds Has Not Yet Closed the Gap of Insufficient Funding in the Past*: Though the flow of public investments has considerably improved in recent times, the region was grossly neglected in the past and did not receive any appreciable flow of development funds.

IAP for Selected Tribal and Backward Districts

11.65. An IAP for 60 selected tribal and backward districts in 9 States was approved by the government on 25 November 2010 with a block grant of ₹25 crore and ₹30 crore per district for 2010–11 and 2011–12, respectively.

11.66. The main principles which underline the IAP are flexibility and local autonomy, clear-cut accountability, frequent communication and monitoring, interaction for problem solving and horizontal learning through video conferences/meetings and early audit. In furtherance of these principles, the funds under the scheme are placed at the disposal of a committee headed by the District Collector and consisting of the Superintendent of Police of the district and the District Forest Officer. The district-level committee has the flexibility to spend the amount for development schemes according to need, as assessed by it. The State Governments and the District Collectors/District Magistrates have also been advised to ensure a suitable form of consultation with the local Member of Parliament on the schemes to be taken up under IAP. The district-level committee has to draw up a Plan consisting of concrete proposals for public infrastructure and services such as School Buildings, Anganwadi Centres, Primary Health Centres (PHCs), Drinking Water Supply, Village Roads, Electric Lights in public places such as PHCs and schools, and so on. The Development Commissioner/equivalent officer in charge of development in the State is responsible for scrutiny of expenditure and monitoring of the IAP. Total releases under IAP have been ₹5,100 crore.

11.67. An online MIS system has been set up to facilitate reviews and special reviews. In addition, the Review Group headed by the Cabinet Secretary also reviewed the progress of implementation of IAP with the Chief Secretaries of nine States through Video Conferences on 21 March and 8 September 2011.

11.68. Apart from special schemes as above, the GOI has also been focusing on channelising funds from existing programmes, coupled with better monitoring, to ensure the effective implementation of all-India schemes in the IAP districts. One of the recent initiatives in this regard is the setting up of an Empowered Group of Officers for this purpose with Member-Secretary, Planning Commission, as chairperson; Secretary, Ministry of Rural Development, Secretary, MoPR and Secretary, Ministry of Tribal Welfare, as Members; and Special Secretary, Ministry of Home affairs as Member-Secretary. The Empowered Group, inter alia, has overriding powers to modify existing norms/guidelines of various development programmes and Flagship Schemes in consultation with the Ministries/Departments concerned. As decided by the Empowered Group, following relaxations of norms have been effected for the 60 IAP districts:

1. Under the PMGSY, the norms for maximum length of bridges has been relaxed from 50 m to 75 m and the population norm of 500 for habitations coverage has been relaxed to 250. The minimum tender package amount under PMGSY has been reduced to ₹50 lakh.
2. Under the Indira Awaas Yojana (IAY), the ceiling of per unit cost of IAY house has been increased from ₹45,000 to ₹48,500.
3. The Empowered Group recommended to the Ministry of Environment and Forests that the grant of general approval under section 2 of the Forest (Conservation) Act, 1980, for diversion of forest land for activities like schools, dispensaries/hospitals, electrical and telecommunication lines, drinking water, water/rain water harvesting structures, minor irrigation canal, non-conventional sources of energy, skill up gradation/vocational training centre, power sub-stations, rural roads, communication posts; and police establishments like police stations/outposts/border outposts/watch towers in sensitive areas and underground laying of optical fibre cables, telephone lines and drinking water supply lines should be relaxed. This was agreed to by the Ministry of Environment and Forests. Ministry of Environment and Forests have also agreed that no compensatory afforestation in lieu of the forest land diverted in accordance with the above-said general approval shall be insisted upon for 60 IAP districts.
4. The stipulation of 80 per cent utilisation of funds for further release of funds under BRGF has been revised to 60 per cent utilisation of funds. Changes have been made to ensure quick release of fund from State to the local bodies under BRGF. Also DPCs have been given power to approve the district Plans under BRGF and the High Powered Committee (HPC) will act not as approval granting bodies but as oversight committees and issue broad guidelines.
5. For effective implementation of electrification projects in 60 IAP districts, Empowered Group had approached the Ministry of Power to relax the conditions in the Decentralized Distributed Generation (DDG) guidelines relating to non-availability of grid for implementation of the scheme. This has been agreed to by the Ministry of Power.
6. The Empowered Group raised the subsidy limit for a scheme for providing solar charging stations from 30 per cent to 90 per cent. Accordingly,

Ministry of New and Renewable Energy proposes to provide solar charging station consisting of 50 LED solar lanterns with solar panels, and so on, in villages/habitations of the 60 IAP districts.

11.69. The Twelfth Plan Working Group on Special Area Programmes has remarked that although

> the Planning Commission has been espousing the cause of decentralised planning at the level of each Panchayat, the IAP has put in place exactly the opposite approach. The schemes/works to be taken up under this programme are decided by a Three Member Committee headed by the District Collector and consisting of the Superintendent of Police of the District and the District Forest Officer. This system is totally against the letter and spirit of the 73rd & 74th Amendments and considerably dilutes the stand of the Planning Commission in favour of decentralised participative planning. We suggest strongly that the implementation mechanism under the scheme should not in any way differ from that prescribed by the Planning Commission in its own Decentralised Planning Guidelines.

11.70. The IAP is being recast from the second year of the Twelfth Plan accordingly.

The Bundelkhand Region

11.71. The Bundelkhand region comprises seven districts of UP—Banda, Chitrakoot, Hamirpur, Jalaun, Jhansi, Lalitpur and Mahoba and six districts of MP—Chhatarpur, Damoh, Datia, Panna, Sagar and Tikamgarh. Keeping in view the consecutive deficient rainfall experienced in this region since 2004–05, on 19 November 2009, the Union Government approved a special package for implementing drought mitigation strategies in Bundelkhand region at a cost of ₹7,266 crore comprising ₹3,506 crore for UP and ₹3,760 crore for MP, to be implemented over a period of three years starting 2009–10. Of the entire package, ₹3,650 crore (₹1,696 crore for UP and ₹1,954 crore for MP) are additional allocations through an ACA (including ₹100 crore each for UP and MP to provide drinking water in the region, approved on 19 May 2011). The balance of the funds is to be met by converging resources from the Central sector and CSS by dedicating specified amounts. The responsibility for implementation of projects under the special package rests with the State Governments of UP and MP. It is reported that activities under the package are at different stages of implementation. A total of ₹1,921.43 crore has been released as ACA so far. With expenditure being ₹630.81 crore, the activities have taken time to settle down and pick up pace.

11.72. The progress of implementation is monitored by the Planning Commission and National Rainfed Area Authority (NRAA). The Planning Commission has set up a Monitoring Committee with Members of Planning Commission in charge of UP and MP as Chairman and Co-chairman, respectively; the Chief Secretaries of both States and the Secretaries of the Departments concerned as Members. An Advisory Committee under the Chairmanship of the Deputy Chairman, Planning Commission, with all Members of the Lok Sabha from Bundelkhand as its Members, also reviews the progress of the implementation of the projects.

11.73. In view of the short period, the project is yet to give full results. There is need to continue this and step up flow of ACA.

Special Plan for West Bengal

11.74. Additional Central Assistance is being provided for the Special Plan for West Bengal to address the development needs of the backward regions of the State through focused projects in the year 2011–2012 and during the Twelfth Plan period. The Special Plan for West Bengal was approved on 7 December 2011 with an allocation of ₹8,750 crore. Schemes with allocation of ₹8,791.97 crore have been approved in sectors such as power, health, road connectivity, water supply and sanitation, education, micro- and small-scale enterprises, irrigation, rural housing, skill development and so on. An amount of ₹2,903.66 crore has been released to the State Government.

Hill Areas Development Programme/Western Ghats Development Programme (HADP/WGDP)

11.75. The HADP/WGDP has been in operation since the Fifth Five Year Plan in identified hill areas. Its main objective is to ensure ecologically sustainable socio-economic development of hill areas, keeping in view the basic needs of the people there. The main objectives of both programmes are eco-preservation and eco-restoration with a focus on sustainable use of biodiversity. They also focus on the needs and aspirations of local communities, particularly their participation in the design and implementation of the strategies for conservation of bio-diversity and sustainable livelihoods.

11.76. The Designated Hill Areas covered under HADP were identified in 1965 by a Committee of the National Development Council (NDC). These included eight (later bifurcated into 12) districts of UP. However, consequent on the formation of Uttarakhand as a separate State, HADP is no longer in operation in the hill districts of erstwhile UP. Presently, the designated Hill Areas covered under HADP include two hill districts of Assam—North Cachar and Karbi Anglong, the major part of Darjeeling district of West Bengal and the Nilgiris district of Tamil Nadu.

11.77. Out of the total SCA outlay under the programme, 90 per cent is a grant and the remaining 10 per cent is State share. These funds are allocated to identified hill areas under HADP and blocks/talukas under the WGDP. Funds under the SCA are apportioned between the HADP and WGDP in the ratio of 60:40. Under HADP, funds are distributed to States implementing the programme on the basis of equal weightage to area and population. Under the WGDP, the weightage for allocation is 75 per cent to area and 25 per cent to population. The 1981 Census is taken as the baseline for calculation.

11.78. The schemes being implemented under HADP/WGDP are mainly in the sectors of Agriculture and Soil Conservation, Forestry, Social Forestry, Animal Husbandry, Horticulture, Sericulture, Apiculture, Minor Irrigation, Veterinary, Fisheries, Link Roads and Foot Bridges, Livelihood Activities, Small Scale Industries, Watershed Development, Welfare of SCs/STs, Rural Energy Conservation, Administration and Training.

Western Ghats Development Programme (WGDP)

11.79. The main problems of Western Ghats region are the pressure of increasing population on land and vegetation. These factors have contributed to the ecological and environmental problems in the region. The fragile ecosystem of the hills has come under severe pressure because of submergence of large areas under river valley projects, damage to area due to mining, denudation of forests, clear felling of natural forest for raising commercial plantation, soil erosion leading to silting of reservoirs and reduction in their lifespan and the adverse effects of floods and landslides, encroachment of forest land and poaching of wildlife.

11.80. The WGDP was launched in 1974–75 to cover contiguous talukas/blocks along the Ghats that have at least 20 per cent of their area above an elevation of 600 m above mean sea level (MSL). Currently, the programme is being implemented in 175 talukas (Maharashtra—63, Karnataka—40, Kerala—36, Tamil Nadu—33 and Goa—3). Allocation during the Eleventh Plan under this programme is ₹594 crore, including ₹59.60-crore State share.

11.81. At present, the main emphasis has been on watershed development with small gap-filling infrastructure. The SCA may be used for livelihood schemes which preserve and even increase productivity without disturbing the environment such as, minor forest produce, afforestation, horticulture, pisciculture, and so on. In the case of watershed schemes, the cost norms of the guidelines of the NRAA/Ministry of Rural Development may be followed.

11.82. Given the great longevity of these programmes and lack of tangible outcomes on the ground, it is proposed that the HADP and WGDP be restructured.

Border Area Development Programme (BADP)

11.83. The BADP is a 100 per cent Centrally Funded Programme initiated in the border areas of the western region during the Seventh Five Year Plan period for ensuring balanced development through development of infrastructure and promotion of sense of security among the border population. Since then the BADP has been implemented by the GOI together with State Governments as part of a comprehensive approach to border management. The programme now covers 358 border blocks of 94 border districts of 17 States located along the international land border (Arunachal Pradesh, Assam, Bihar, Himachal Pradesh, J&K, Manipur, Meghalaya, Mizoram, Nagaland, Punjab, Rajasthan, Sikkim, Tripura, UP, Uttarakhand and West Bengal). Under the BADP, priorities are given to the areas closer to the border. Works under BADP are taken up by the States under various sectors such as strengthening of social and economic infrastructure; filling up of critical gaps in the road network, especially link roads, bridges, culverts, and so on; schemes for employment generation, education, health, agriculture and allied sector and schemes which provide for critical inputs in the social sector.

11.84. As per the Report of the Working Group on BADP for the Twelfth Five Year Plan, BADP has contributed towards creating a conducive environment for undertaking normal economic activities in border areas and has potential to bring about an improvement in the quality of life of the people living there. Furthermore, the programme has created confidence amongst the people and helped security forces in obtaining the cooperation of the local population in carrying out their functioning smoothly and peacefully.

11.85. The weaknesses reported in the programme are that the level of assistance is supplemental nature and it does not permit undertaking major infrastructure projects. Thus, funds are utilised for small schemes and programmes. The allocations under the programme are too small to address the livelihood and other socio-economic issues. Fragmentation of the programme leads to it not receiving focused attention of the implementing agencies. Difficulties are also experienced in converging various Central/State schemes with the BADP.

11.86. To address these issues, flexibility in implementation has been supported by the revised guidelines, which enable the involvement of local governments, communities, non-governmental organisations (NGOs) and SHGs that do not receiving foreign aid assistance, for executing schemes. These measures can be adopted by the State-level Screening Committees under intimation to the Ministry of Home Affairs. Projects not exceeding ₹5.00 lakh are to be strictly implemented through local governments alone. State Governments are encouraged to involve the community in sharing of 10 per cent to 15 per cent of the cost of social infrastructure wherever possible. Security-related works can also be taken up under BADP to the extent of 10 per cent of the total allocation in a particular year.

11.87. Border areas should have a high standard of living so that they serve as a demographic buffer. Infrastructure should not only cater to the current needs of these areas but also include scope for further expansion. Participatory plans for border villages and blocks should be prepared based on the instructions of the Planning Commission on the formulation of district plans. These village-/block-level plans will be a part of the comprehensive district plan. The preparation of plans will be preceded by baseline surveys in all villages in the border blocks to assess gaps in physical and social infrastructure. The district plans would help ensure convergence/dovetailing of CSS with BADP. It is also important that the Stats ensure earmarking of due share of resourc4s from Centrally Sponsored and State Plan Schemes to the Border Areas.

11.88. While the BADP has helped in supplementing infrastructure development in border areas and addressing livelihood and other socio-economic issues of the border areas, the allocation under the programme has been relatively too small to ensure a focused attention of the State Governments. A much larger effort is, therefore, required to develop these areas not only in terms of funds for creation of infrastructure but also to have a re-look at the policies which distort the development process and increase the sense of alienation of the border population.

11.89. The current level of funding for BADP is inadequate. An outlay of ₹7,230 crore is proposed for the Twelfth Plan.

New Approach to BRGF in the Twelfth Plan

11.90. The experience of Special Area Programmes has made it abundantly clear that the persistence of backwardness is not a problem that can be solved merely with a generous infusion of funds. It is increasingly clear that overcoming underdevelopment is critically dependent upon the robustness of the institutional structure of governance in these areas. This is the key binding constraint on their very capacity to absorb more development funds.

11.91. The principle of subsidiarity is now well established in development literature across the world.[12] The role of local governments in ensuring efficient and accountable delivery of basic services is now well understood. The instrumentality of participative planning, as the thin end of the wedge to energise local governments, has been repeatedly endorsed by the Planning Commission. Development experience within India's States shows that the best examples of implementation are where people feel a sense of ownership over the programmes. Involving people in the monitoring of performance also ensures greater accountability in the programme. This is the experience, for example, of midday meals in Tamil Nadu; health in Maharashtra; watershed development and MGNREGA in MP, drinking water and sanitation in Haryana; public distribution system (PDS) in Chhattisgarh; groundwater management, social audit and Girijan Co-operative Corporation for Minor Forest Produce in Andhra Pradesh; participatory irrigation management (PIM) in Karnataka; power reforms and agricultural extension in Gujarat; Kudumbashree in Kerala and IAP in Orissa. However, these examples also show that participatory approaches work only when the necessary conditions for their success are in place. The new approach to the BRGF during the Twelfth Plan seeks to incorporate these key lessons so that real potential of devolution can be realised.

11.92. The support being provided in the Twelfth Plan through this BRGF window for these districts would be used in building capacities and developing and implementing Plans in a bottom-up and participatory manner. The Centre will not specify anything beyond this about the heads on which this money would be spent, so long as the districts adhere to this decentralised process of formulating the programmes in convergent manner. The Twelfth Plan Working Group on Special Area Programmes illustrates the dangers of non-convergence in Box 11.1.

Box 11.1
From the Report of the Twelfth Plan Working Group on Special Area Programmes

Currently, the KBK districts receive funding under three components of the BRGF—₹130 crore under the Special Plan, ₹120 crore under the District Component and ₹240 crore under the IAP. However, the mode of utilisation is different and the authorities choosing the schemes are different! The State Government decides the schemes to be taken up under the Special Plan, the PRIs the schemes under the District Component and the three-member committee comprising of the Collector, the SP and the DFO, under the IAP. Needless to say, a lot of money swirls around in the district, but there is no district plan, only a health plan, an education plan, a BRGF plan and an IAP plan!

11.93. It is in view of this understanding that the Approach Paper to the Twelfth Plan proposed to address these issues by creating a 'Plan within a Plan'. The Approach Paper suggested a special arrangement whereby in the next two years of the Twelfth Plan, funds would be unconditionally released for Special Area Programmes to facilitate:

- capacity building of PRIs, in terms of both human resources capacities and systems of implementation;
- improved implementation of flagship programmes;
- speedy implementation of Panchayat (Extension to the Scheduled Areas) Act (PESA) in tribal areas; and
- speedy implementation of Scheduled Tribes and Other Traditional Forest Dwellers (Recognition of Forest Rights) Act in tribal areas.[13]

11.94. This would improve the absorptive capacities of these districts for outlays provided under various schemes and also for the use of additional funds to be provided to those districts that are able to move in the direction specified in the next two years of the Plan. This progress would be monitored against the list of indicators developed by the Planning Commission and additional funds provided in the next two years to those districts which show progress against these indicators.

11.95. The restructured BRGF will be based on the following formulation:

1. *Focus on all three levels: district, sub-district and supra-district*: Among the major lessons of the experience of BRGF implementation, as emphasised by the Union Ministries of Panchayati Raj, Tribal Affairs and Rural Development, as also several State Governments, is that there is a need to focus on the sub-district level for effective realisation of outcomes. The restructured BRGF, therefore, seeks to make a special emphasis on the sub-district level. However, it is also the experience of the BRGF and other Special Area Programmes, that there are many activities that require a district-level focus, and some even require a supra-district thrust, especially when we consider important infrastructure projects.

   Thus, the restructured BRGF will focus on all three levels: district, sub-district and supra-district. Bihar and West Bengal Special Plans, as also the Supra-district Components of the KBK and Bundelkhand packages, will continue to be overseen by the Planning Commission. The district-level programmes like the IAP and the District Component of existing BRGF will be reorganised into a new programme, where some flexi-funds would be made available to the district administration (more in Left Wing Extremism [LWE] districts) to fill in the critical gaps, while the bulk of the programme will be implemented through PRIs.

2. *Criteria for Selection*: The criteria for selection of areas under BRGF have also come in for criticism. The Twelfth Plan proposes that we rely only on the relatively unimpeachable data made available through Census, 2011, for selection of districts and sub-districts. The criteria of inclusion of districts and sub-districts under the new BRGF would be:

   a. Percentage of agriculture workers/total workers (economic backwardness)
   b. Percentage of SC + ST population (social backwardness)
   c. Female literacy rate (educational backwardness)
   d. Percentage of households without electricity (infrastructure backwardness)

   Based on these criteria, it is proposed to include the 200 most backward districts and 1,500 most backward sub-districts[14] under the restructured BRGF.

3. *Financial Allocations*: We propose to substantially raise the financial allocations to overcome the criticism that BRGF is inadequately funded and lacks the critical mass to make a significant difference on the ground. What is more, the greater the intensity of deprivation of a district or sub-district, the higher the allocation it will receive. Thus, a rainfed district will get a higher allocation and sub-districts with a significant proportion of STs will also receive more. This is because rainfed areas and tribal populations have been highly correlated with poverty and backwardness in various dimensions.

4. *Plan Outlay*: The indicative allocation for the Supra-district (State) Component in the Twelfth Plan is likely to be ₹30,000 crore, which will include the Bihar and West Bengal Special Plans, as also the KBK and Bundelkhand Packages. The allocation for the revamped District/Sub-district Component is likely to be around ₹46,500 crore. Thus, the total indicative allocation for BRGF during the Twelfth Plan is ₹76,500 crore, which includes both State and District Components.

Rajiv Gandhi Panchayat Sashaktikaran Abhiyan (RGPSA)

11.96. Even as we restructure the BRGF, a concomitant initiative critical for the success of the new BRGF, as shown by all evaluations of the programme, is also being launched by the MoPR in the Twelfth Plan. This is the RGPSA, which not only amalgamates the existing small schemes of the MoPR, but also empowers PRIs. The RGPSA is backed by a tenfold increase in resources for MoPR in the Twelfth Plan as compared to the Eleventh Plan. The RGPSA will be a decisive move in favour of empowering PRIs, which will greatly strengthen the implementation of BRGF and many other flagship programmes. The RGPSA seeks to enhance capacities and effectiveness of Gram Panchayats and the Gram Sabhas by strengthening the institutional structure for knowledge creation and capacity building and by providing them necessary human resource and infrastructure support. RGPSA will provide performance-linked funds from 2014–15 onwards. Twenty per cent scheme funds will be tied to State performance on identified deliverables in the State Plan. Strengthening the Panchayati Raj system involves not just provision of capital and human resource such as buildings, training, technical expertise, and so on, but also adequate devolution, bottom-up planning, convergence, accountability and free and fair elections. Under RGPSA, States are expected to show progress on these fronts as a condition for accessing funds under this scheme.

11.97. The indicative allocation for BRGF during the Twelfth Plan is ₹76,500 crore which includes both State and District Components.

NORTH-EASTERN REGION DEVELOPMENT

11.98. NER comprises of eight States of the North-East (NE), including Assam, Arunachal Pradesh, Manipur, Meghalaya, Mizoram, Nagaland, Tripura and Sikkim. Special requirements of the NER and the need for significant levels of investment are now well recognised. Accordingly, efforts have been made since inception of the planning process to address the problems in the critical areas of development with special programmes and funding arrangements. There has also been continuous attempt to supplement development efforts of the Special Category States of NER by the Centre by providing Central Plan Assistance. Some of the programmes, like BADP, HADP, grants under Article 275(1) and BRGF are attempts to address some of the area-specific problems in a limited way. Setting up of the North-Eastern Council (NEC) under NEC Act, 1971, as regional planning body has been another sincere step for balanced development of the region. In the latter part of the Ninth Plan, the announcement of 'New Initiatives for the North Eastern Region' in October 1996 gave further boost to the development process. Earmarking of at least 10 per cent of the Plan Budget of the Central Ministries/Departments for NER and creation of Non-lapsable Central Pool of Resources (NLCPR) were the outcome of this announcement. Both of these helped transfer of resources to the region.

Plan Expenditure

11.99. In terms of flow of development fund, a positive impact is visible after the policy decision of earmarking 10 per cent of Gross Budgetary Support (GBS) of the Departments for the NE. At present, more than 50 Non-exempted Central Ministries/Departments earmark 10 per cent of the GBS for the NER. Seventeen Ministries/Departments are exempted from 10 per cent mandatory earmarking due to nature of their functions. According to the assessment made by Ministry of Development of North Eastern Region (M/o DoNER), the Central Ministries/Departments spent ₹44,909.36 crore out of total earmarked fund of ₹53,293.86 crore since 1998–99 till the end of the Tenth Plan (2002–07). During the Eleventh Plan, the expenditure incurred by the Central Ministries in the NER was ₹59,072.95 crore (March 2010–11). By the end of the Plan, it is likely to be ₹75,000 crore. This is against total earmarked outlay of ₹87,502.97 crore for the Plan.

11.100. The utilisation of the 10 per cent mandatory earmarked funds by the Central Ministries has gone up from 80.8 per cent till the Tenth Plan to 89.7 per cent in the first four years of the Eleventh Plan. An amount of ₹19,364.03 crore had accrued to the NLCPR till 2010–11; out of this, an amount of ₹9,595.11 crore has also been released to the States under the NLCPR scheme of M/o DoNER for specific projects in the States of NER.

11.101. The total Plan expenditure by the Centre and the States of NE, including NEC, had been approximately ₹1,23,756 crore during the four years of the Eleventh Plan (March 2011) through various windows of funding (including Central assistance provided to the States under their plan, NLCPR and NEC, CSS, and so on). However, this does not include the investments made by the public sector undertakings. (Please refer to Table 11.17.)

TABLE 11.17

Total Plan Expenditure by the Centre and States of NE, Including NEC

	Source of Fund Flow	₹ Crore
1	State Plan	57,258.84
2	Central Ministries	59,072.95
3	M/o DONER, NEC	7,424.71
	Total	1,23,756.50

Source: Planning Commission.

11.102. This is likely to go up to ₹1.50 lakh crore by the end of the Plan.

Major Developments in the Field of Infrastructure

11.103. During the latter part of the Ninth Plan, action for identification of infrastructure deficit in the key areas and funding arrangement for the major infrastructure resulted in prioritisation of projects of connectivity (Road, Rail, Air), development of power, investment in Human Resource Development, expansion of Skill Development, and so on. Survey and investigation, forest and environment clearance, detailed project report (DPR) preparation, land acquisition of many projects were initiated and impletion of some of the major projects started on ground during the Tenth Plan. This has accelerated in the Eleventh Plan. Some of the major projects under implementation are:

Roads
1. East–West Corridor (670 km in Assam) by National Highways Authority of India (NHAI) stated in 2005–06,
2. Special Accelerated Road Development Programme for the North-Eastern Region (SARDP-NE) connecting State Capitals, District Headquarters and strategic border roads by 2/4 lane roads (approved in 2005–06)—to be implemented in Phase-A and Phase-B—10,141 km (NH 4,798 km and State Road 343 km), including important bridges like Dhola–Sadia over Brahmaputra.
3. Trans-Arunachal Highway with district connectivity (added subsequently in the SARDP programme)—total length 2,319 km.

Railways
1. Broad Gauge (BG) line conversion—connecting Guwahati–Dibrughar–Tinsukia, Rangia–Murkongselek Bridge (rail-cum-road) across Brahmaputra at Bogibeel
2. Alternative BG line—New Jalpaiguri–Guwahati via Jogighopa–Goalpara–Dudhnoi (commissioned)
3. Third alternative BG route from New Moinaguri to Jogighopa
4. BG route from Lumding–Silchar and Kumarghat–Agartala–Samboom
5. New lines: Agartala–Akhura, Tetelia–Byrnihat–Shillong, Harmuti–Itanagar, Silchar–Jiribam–Imphal (Tupul).

Airways
11.104. Major works under implementation for upgradation of airports are:

- Guwahati (works in progress to be continued during the Twelfth Plan), Dibrugarh, Silchar, Agartala, Shillong, Imphal and Dimapur;
- New airports at Itanagar, Ceithu (Kohima), Pakyong (Gangtok);
- Up-gradation of smaller airports and Advanced Landing Grounds (ALGs) in Arunachal Pradesh.

Power
1. Major Hydro project—Lower Subansiri (2,000 MW), Pare, Kameng, Dibang.
2. Thermal Power Palatana gas-based (726 MW), Bongaigaon (750 MW) coal-based.
3. There is also number of identified projects for transmission lines for evacuation/connecting to the grid.

11.105. Apart from the above projects under the Central sector, Telecom connectivity also improved considerably. States' role in the development of the priority areas in their respective States was very encouraging during the Eleventh Plan period.

Growth in SDP

11.106. Larger Plan investments and focus on infrastructure development has helped growth in this region. It is encouraging to note that there has been substantial improvement in the growth rate in the NE States, particularly in the Eleventh Plan. The growth rate of 6.1 per cent in the Ninth Plan improved to 6.4 per cent in the Tenth Plan, though less than the National Average of 7.8 per cent. The average GSDP growth of these States during Eleventh Plan improved to 9.8 per cent against 8 per cent at the national level. Average growth of NE States exceeded the National average in the Eleventh Plan. If the exceptional growth of Sikkim is excluded, the average of seven States was 7.9 per cent. This improvement in the growth is due to concerted efforts of the Centre and the State. The following table indicates growth achievements from the Eighth Plan to the Eleventh Plan.

11.107. The major contributors of growth in the Eleventh Plan in Assam have been Agriculture and Allied and the Services sectors. The growth of Industry sector has picked up momentum in the fourth and fifth year. The good performance in the areas like Transport and Communication, Banking and Insurance, Trade and Commerce, Hotel and Restaurant, Real estate and Business Services has been able to generate employment both in the public and private sector. In the State of Meghalaya, Industry sector performance was remarkable. However, this improvement was primarily due to commissioning of two units of the Myntdu Leshka Hydel Project (MLHEP) under the State sector. The Services sector has also done quite well. Tripura has done well in agriculture, followed by Services. Manipur also had very good growth in agriculture. But, Industry and Service sectors were below par.

11.108. Mizoram achieved a remarkable growth of 10.8 per cent. This is a huge improvement over the Tenth Plan growth of 5.9 per cent. The major contributors in the growth have been Agriculture & Allied sector, Business Services and Construction.

TABLE 11.18
Growth Rate in SDP in the NE States

(in percentage)

Sl. No.	State\UT	Eighth Plan Achievement	Ninth Plan Achievement	Tenth Plan Achievement	Eleventh Plan Target	Eleventh Plan Achievement
1.	Arunachal Pr.	5.0	6.6	6.2	6.4	8.5
2.	Assam	2.8	1.8	5.0	6.5	6.8
3.	Manipur	3.7	4.7	5.7	5.9	6.2
4.	Meghalaya	4.0	7.2	6.7	7.3	7.8
5.	Mizoram	N.A	5.7	5.9	7.1	10.8
6.	Nagaland	7.2	6.5	7.4	9.3	6.2
7.	Sikkim	4.6	6.6	7.7	6.7	22.8
8.	Tripura	6.7	9.4	6.9	6.9	8.9
	Average NE	4.9[a]	6.1	6.4	7.0[b]	9.8[c]
	All India GDP	7.5	5.5	7.8	9.0	8.0

Sources: 1. Eighth, Ninth and Tenth Plan achievement from most recent base year series (CSO).
2. Eleventh Plan achievement from 2004–05 series (CSO).

Notes: [a]Seven NE States' average for Eighth Plan.
[b]Only indicative (arithmetic) average as there is no separate growth target for the NE region.
[c]It is on the higher side as Sikkim's growth (22.8 per cent) is an outlier.

State's Flagship Programme of New Land Use Policy (NLUP) appears to have started making some impact.

11.109. Among the North-Eastern States, Nagaland could not achieve the targeted growth of 9.3 per cent. The achievement was 6.2 per cent. Compared to the Tenth Plan agriculture performance was subdued.

11.110. The impressive growth of Sikkim is attributed to commissioning of power projects during the Eleventh Plan period. The Agriculture Sector, particularly floriculture and horticulture has also performed relatively well during the Plan period. In Arunachal Pradesh, higher growth in the Industry sector can be attributed to construction activity. In the Service sector, there had been increase in the activities of banking and insurance, trade and commerce.

Development Concerns

11.111. The States of NE has been suggesting expeditious completion of most of the incomplete ongoing Central projects works listed above. The States have emphasised on the flexibility of CSS, specifically under schemes like PMGSY for coverage of villages below 250 population and modification in the length of bridges, under SSA to accommodate hostel facilities and reconsider distance norm in view of sparse habitations and improving the Telecom connectivity. General concern in the region has been that many of the projects are under implementation for a long time. While projects are also being reviewed at the apex level, this progress is still slow. It is important to note that during the Eleventh Plan, there has been a general feeling of improvement in the security scenario. Area-specific problems have been also addressed through negotiations/peace talks. For the first time, the much-awaited elections of the hill district councils could be held in Manipur. Economic activities generated in the region have created a positive environment, especially in the minds of the young.

11.112. Some of the other important issues needing attention of the Centre are erosion due to flood and rehabilitation of affected people, disadvantaged groups/areas (District Councils, Tribe-specific Autonomous Councils, Tea-tribe Inhabited Areas, Minority Areas), early operationalisation of road connectivity with Myanmar, special package for the eastern Nagaland, items of intervention as per Indo-Bangladesh Joint Communique (flight between Agartala and Dhaka, access to sea through Chittagong Port, Agartala–Dhaka–Kolkata direct bus service, access to Ashuganj Inland Port, construction of bridge over river Feni, connecting Sabroom–Chittagong), Kaladan Multi-modal Transit Transport Project linking Mizoram and Myanmar up to Sittwe port.

Problem of Low Financial Resources

11.113. The States of the region have a weak financial base and also limited scope to raise additional resources. Although expenditure control measures and initiatives in fiscal reforms did yield some marginal improvement in the fiscal management, the impact of growing expenditure due to revision in the salaries of the State Government employees has gone much beyond the means and has affected the availability of resources for Plan programmes. While Planning Commission has supplemented the resource requirement by providing SCA, particularly during the last two years of the Eleventh Plan, this continues to be an area of concern.

Investment Opportunities

11.114. Despite having large investment opportunities in sectors like hydropower, infrastructure and natural gas, health care, textile and handicrafts, tourism, horticulture and agro-based industries, minerals, and so on, the NE States are yet to witness any major investments in these sectors by private investors. Special fiscal package under North East Industrial Policy (NEIP) has so far failed to trigger major investment flow in the region in the manner as it was conceived. NEIP did lead to some investment in industrial units in and around Guwahati in tea, coal, plastics, cement, cosmetics, metallurgy, and so on, but could not attract investors in other parts of the region. According to an assessment based on the financial investment intentions by private/public sector enterprises during the Eleventh Plan period, 336 units expressed intention for investment in the North-East involving ₹38,892 crore (approximately). However, this does not necessarily reflect the actual flow of investment during the period. Majority of them were in Assam (133 units), Sikkim (70 units), Meghalaya (62 units). Number of units in the rest of the States was less than 10. It may be mentioned that the indicative investment flow is inclusive of Gas Cracker Project (Bharat Petroleum Corporation Limited [BPCL]) in Assam, expansion of Guwahati and Digboi Refinery of Indian Oil Corporation (IOC), who have the largest share. The share of investment (based on letter of Intent) in the NE was, however, only 0.58 per cent of the total intended investment at the national level.

Financial Institutions and Credit Availability

11.115. Availability of credit is one of the critical weaknesses in the development of economic activities in the NER. Various indicators for NER show that despite improvement in the banking facilities in last five years, the level of financial outreach is low. The main impediment for banking and financial development are topography of the region, sparse population settlements, infrastructural bottlenecks, smaller size of the market, lack of entrepreneurship, law and order conditions in some parts of the NER, land tenure system, especially in hilly areas, and so on. The penetration of banking in the NER, particularly in the rural areas, has been very low. The Credit–Deposit (CD) ratio of the NER as a whole as also the individual States is far below the national average.

11.116. According to the available information, CD ratio in the NER in March 2011 was 33.8 per cent (as per sanction) and 36.3 per cent as per utilisation. At the all-India level, the CD ratio as per sanction and utilisation is 75.6 per cent.

Critical Areas for Intervention in the Twelfth Plan

11.117. From the performance analysis of the States, suggestions made by the States of NER in the regional consultation, discussions in the Planning Commission and in the NEC meeting, it emerges that continued emphasis on the development of physical and social infrastructure must continue so that the region can become strong, confident and capable of engaging with external market. Following are some of the areas requiring special attention during the Twelfth Plan:

Roads

1. East–West Corridor (670 KM in Assam) by NHAI.
2. All stretches of SARDP-NE connecting State Capitals/District Headquarters, (including National Highway-39 and National Highway-53 in Manipur, NH-31A in Sikkim).
3. Strategic border roads,
4. Trans-Arunachal Highway along with identified district connectivity.
5. Roads connecting Kaladan Multi-modal Transit Transport Project,
6. Important bridges include Dhola–Sadia over Brahmaputra and all other crucial bridges on the major road projects.
7. Four-lane highway from Tizit in the north to Dimapur via Tuli–Jalukie–Khelma (proposed by the State Government for survey in investigation and DPR preparation, and so on).

Railway

1. Broad Gauge (line conversion)—connecting Guwahati–Dibrughar–Tinsukia, Rangia–Murkongselek Bridge (rail-cum-road) across Brahmaputra at Bogibeel.
2. BG route from New Moinaguri to Jogighopa.
3. BG route from Lumding–Silchar and Kumarghat–Agartala–Samboom.
4. New lines: Agartala–Akhura, Tetelia–Byrnihat–Shillong, Harmuti–Itanagar, Silchar–Jiribam–Imphal (Tupul).

Airways

11.118. Major works for upgradation of airports are:

- Guwahati, Dibrugarh, Silchar, Agartala, Shillong, Imphal and Dimapur; and
- New airports at Itanagar, Ceithu (Kohima), Pakyong (Gangtok). In addition, there are smaller airports, ALGs to be upgraded in Arunachal Pradesh.

Inland Water Transport (IWT)

11.119. IWT development in the Brahmaputra and Barak National Waterway.

Power

1. Long-term health of power sector seriously undermined (losses ₹70,000 crore per year). However, aggregate technical and commercial (AT&C) losses are slowly coming down. State Governments must push distribution reform.
2. Hydropower development seriously hindered by forest and environment clearance procedures. Need to look at special dispensation for these States, especially Arunachal Pradesh.
3. A time-bound plan to operationalise development and evacuation of hydropower from NER required. Road connectivity an issue for expeditious project completion.
4. Given limited connectivity of NER with other parts of the country (through Siliguri corridor), access through Bangladesh needs to be explored.
5. Electricity tariffs not being revised to reflect rising costs. Regulators are being held back from allowing justified tariff increases.

Agriculture/Horticulture/Allied Sector

1. The growth has to be more rapid and inclusive; the focus has to be on better performance in agriculture, irrigation, drinking water health services, better education in the rural and remote areas, rural connectivity, improved delivery system and governance. Farm-based economic activities—Horticulture, Animal Husbandry, Fisheries, Poultry, and so on, have to be the prime drivers.
2. Post-harvest management and marketing infrastructure required to be attended to by dovetailing of programmes/schemes between Central Ministries and the State Governments for filling up gaps in infrastructure.
3. There has to be continued emphasis on creation of employment opportunities. During the Eleventh Plan, there is a general feeling of improvement in the security and law and order scenario. Efforts have to continue to further improve the scenario. The initiatives so far have created some momentum of development as may be seen from the above analysis. This has to continue with all possible support from the Centre.

Encouraging Private Investment

11.120. The impact so far under the Industrial Policy for the North-East has not been impressive. There are many reasons including the issue of connectivity, power and pocket specific disturbance in the region. However, there is also a demand for a review of the incentive package under the policy which may be looked into during the Twelfth plan for creating enabling environment for investors and rational use of local resources. In this context, Department of Industrial Policy and Promotion initiated some action. Meetings between Industry associations and banks would be of helpful in understanding the associated problems related to industries for suitable incorporation in the modified policy.

Water Management/Flood Moderation

11.121. The issue of creation of the North East Water Resource Authority for flood moderation is pending for a long time. Erosion particularly in the Brahmaputra Valley and Barak Valley is a major concern expressed by the State of Assam in various forums. It has to be recognised as a national issue. There is no scheme to take care of the impact of large-scale erosion which is a recurring feature in the State. This needs to be attended to with all seriousness.

Education/Skill Development/Health

1. Focus on quality of education. Investment in teachers' training and evaluation. Use distance education infrastructure for quick completion in the North-East.
2. Social, gender and regional gaps in education need special attention. Special emphasis on capacity building and skill development with focus on curriculum is needed. State-specific approach for creation of opportunities for employment generation may be taken up. Reforms in vocational education to ensure employability in the changing market would help.
3. Development and operationalisation of PPP models in school and higher education and focus on increase in seats in medical colleges, nursing colleges and other licensed health professionals require special attention.

4. Improvement in the quality of NRHM services, rationalisation in the manpower requirement and involvement of PRIs/communities in improving health services is important. Special focus required for development of infrastructure and availability of doctors, paramedics and nurses. Role of PPP in secondary and tertiary health care required to be encouraged.

Look East

1. Focus on strong relationship with Bangladesh to ensure effective connectivity by different transport modes. Access to Chittagong port, declaring Ashuganj (Bangladesh) as port of call, Kolkata–Agartala–Dhaka bus service.
2. Connecting the NE by road to south-east (SE) Asia through Tri-lateral Highway–Moreh (Manipur)–Mandalay/Bagan (Myanmar)–Mae Sot/Chiang Mai (Thailand).
3. Focus on development of all Land Customs Stations (LCS) for strengthening border trade and business communication.
4. Expeditious implementation of multi-modal transport using Kaladan River as alternate connectivity to the North-East.

Asset Management

11.122. Maintenance of assets, especially roads, is an important aspect and needs a separate financial arrangement. Even maintenance of roads developed under PMGSY is likely to be a major problem.

Need for Continued Support

11.123. NER witnessed encouraging growth during last two Plan periods. This is primarily due to the investments in the major projects by the Centre and the developmental programmes taken up by the States. As already discussed above, the major connectivity projects are yet to be completed and the NEIP incentive package has not been able to attract investment. Completion of all the major projects is likely to take more time (10–15 years). Success of Look East policy will also depend on the cooperation from the neighbouring countries. There are still some remote areas deprived of development opportunities. Requirement of these areas will need to be addressed by special plan investments.

11.124. The indicative Gross Budgetary Support for the Twelfth Five Year Plan for the Ministry of development of North-Eastern Region (NER) is ₹955 crore excluding NEC, NLCPR, BTC and Central assistance for State plan.

NOTES

1. C. Purfield, 'Mind the Gap: Is Economic Growth in India Leaving the Poor States Behind?' IMF Working Paper No. WP/06/103, Washington, DC, 2006.
2. K. Kochar, U. Kumar, R. Rajan, and A. Subramanian. 'India's Patterns of Development: What Happened, What Follows', NBER Working Paper No. 12023, National Bureau of Economic Research, Cambridge, MA, 2006.
3. T. Besley, R. Burgess and B. Esteve-Volart, 'Operationalizing Pro-poor Growth: India Case Study', Department of Economics, London School of Economics, 2005.
4. MS Ahluwalia, 'Prospects and Policy Challenges in the Twelfth Plan', *Economic and Political Weekly of India*–XLVI, no. 21 (21 May 2011).
5. This Gini coefficient was calculated assuming that all individuals within each state have income equal to per capita GSDP. It ignores inequality arising out of unequal distribution within each state.
6. At this point, we do not have state-level data on capital and other relevant variables to estimate the growth equation to take this analysis forward.
7. Provisional Census Data, 2011.
8. S. Mehrotra and A. Gandhi 'India's Human Development in the 2000s: Towards Social Inclusion', *Economic and Political Weekly* XLVIL, no. 14 (7 April 2012).
9. B. Debroy and L. Bhandari, 'District Level Deprivation in the New Millennium', RGICS and Indicus Analytics, 2003.
10. Data used are estimates for 2001.
11. India Development Foundation, 'Poverty Mapping in India Using the Small Area Estimation Method', 2010.
12. Hans P. Binswanger-Mkhize, Jacomina P. de Regt and Stephen Spector, *Scaling Up Local & Community Driven Development (LCDD): A Real World Guide to Its Theory and Practice* (The World Bank, 2009).
13. The issues concerning PESA and FRA are discussed at length in the Chapter 24.
14. Sub-district is the category used in the census that helps us overcome the ambiguities created by varying categories of block, taluka, tehsil, mandal, and so on, used by different States.

Twelfth Five Year Plan (2012–2017)

Economic Sectors

Volume II

Copyright © Planning Commission (Government of India) 2013

All rights reserved. No part of this book may be reproduced or utilised in any form or by any means, electronic or mechanical, including photocopying, recording or by any information storage or retrieval system, without permission in writing from the Planning Commission, Government of India.

First published in 2013 by

SAGE Publications India Pvt Ltd
B1/I-1 Mohan Cooperative Industrial Area
Mathura Road, New Delhi 110 044, India
www.sagepub.in

SAGE Publications Inc
2455 Teller Road
Thousand Oaks, California 91320, USA

SAGE Publications Ltd
1 Oliver's Yard, 55 City Road
London EC1Y 1SP, United Kingdom

SAGE Publications Asia-Pacific Pte Ltd
33 Pekin Street
#02-01 Far East Square
Singapore 048763

Second Printing 2014

Published by Vivek Mehra for SAGE Publications India Pvt Ltd, Phototypeset in 11/13pt Minion Pro by RECTO Graphics, Delhi and printed at Saurabh Printers, New Delhi.

Library of Congress Cataloging-in-Publication Data
India. Planning Commission
    Twelfth five year plan (2012/2017)/Planning Commission, Government of India.
        Volumes cm
    1. India—Economic Policy—1991–92. Finance, Public—India. I. Title.
HC435.3.I39   338.954009'0512—dc23   2013   2013009870

ISBN: 978-81-321-1368-3 (PB)

The SAGE Team: Rudra Narayan, Archita Mandal, Rajib Chatterjee and Dally Verghese

Twelfth Five Year Plan (2012–2017)
Economic Sectors

Volume II

**Planning Commission
Government of India**

Thank you for choosing a SAGE product! If you have any comment, observation or feedback, I would like to personally hear from you. Please write to me at contactceo@sagepub.in

—Vivek Mehra, Managing Director and CEO,
SAGE Publications India Pvt Ltd, New Delhi

Bulk Sales

SAGE India offers special discounts for purchase of books in bulk. We also make available special imprints and excerpts from our books on demand.

For orders and enquiries, write to us at

Marketing Department
SAGE Publications India Pvt Ltd
B1/I-1, Mohan Cooperative Industrial Area
Mathura Road, Post Bag 7
New Delhi 110044, India
E-mail us at marketing@sagepub.in

Get to know more about SAGE, be invited to SAGE events, get on our mailing list. Write today to marketing@sagepub.in

This book is also available as an e-book.

Contents

List of Figures — vii
List of Tables — viii
List of Boxes — xii
List of Acronyms — xiv
List of Annexures — xxv

12. Agriculture — 1
13. Industry — 51
14. Energy — 130
15. Transport — 195
16. Communication — 258
17. Rural Development — 286
18. Urban Development — 318
19. Other Priority Sectors — 362

Figures

12.1	Growth and Fluctuations in GDP Agriculture and Allied	2
12.2	All India Average Real Daily Wage Rate at 2011–12 Prices (₹ Per Day)	9
13.1	Contribution of Manufacturing to GDP Very Low in India	52
13.2	India and Global Manufacturing States	52
13.3	New Approach to Industrial Policy	55
13.4	Focus on Sectors as well as Cross-cutting Issues	59
13.5	Strategy for Land Issues	81
13.6	Description of Land Acquisition Process	83
13.7	Two Connected 'Tracks' for Implementation and Systems' Improvement	101
13.8	Capability Map	102
14.1	Exploration Blocks awarded in NELP Rounds	172
14.2	Renewable Power Capacities, Top Five Countries, 2010	183
14.3	Cost of Renewable Energy Technologies Per MW	185
15.1	Existing and Proposed Thermal Power Plants on National Waterways	232
15.2	National Waterway-2	234
15.3	Kaladan Multimodal Transit Transport Project	234
16.1	Telephone Subscribers Growth during 2007–12	259
16.2	Distribution of Urban and Rural Subscribers	260
16.3	Number of Telephone and Broadband Connections	260
16.4	Mobile Tariff Trends V/s Growth in Mobile Subscribers in India (1999–2012)	261
17.1	Access to Household Amenities in Rural India (2001 to 2011)	303
17.2	Households by Type of Latrine Facility in Rural India in 2001	304
17.3	Households by Type of Latrine Facility in Rural India in 2011	304
17.4	PURA Transaction Structure	312
17.5	Institutional Structure for PURA	314
18.1	Sources of Increase in Urban Population	319
18.2	Key Constitutes of India's Urban Future	324

Tables

12.1	Growth Rate of Agricultural and Allied Sectors	1
12.2	Some Weather Details	3
12.3	Averages and Standard Deviations of Annual Growth Rates of GSDP from Agriculture and Allied Sectors	4
12.4	Growth of Output, Inputs and Productivity	6
12.5	Gross Capital Formation (GCF) in Agriculture, Forestry and Fishing (2004–05 prices)	8
12.6	Average Annual Growth Rates in Yields Per Hectare	10
12.7	Public Sector Capital Formation and Subsidies to Agriculture (Centre and States)	13
12.8	Real Prices of Agricultural Produce	17
12.9	Demand and Supply of Food Commodities during the Twelfth Plan	18
12.10	Expenditure on Agricultural Research and Education	30
12.11	Outlays and Expenditure of MoA and Its Three Departments (DAC, DAHDF and DARE)	47
12.12	Gross Budgetary Support (Department-wise)	50
12.13	Comparison of States Outlay and Expenditure for Eleventh and Twelfth Plan	50
13.1	Rate of Growth of GDP at Factor Cost at 2004–05 Prices (Per cent)	53
13.2	GCF in Industry	53
13.3	Employment by Sector	54
13.4	Processes that Enable Learning	62
13.5	Manufacturing Ecosystem Infrastructure	62
13.6	Registered MSMEs—Manufacturing	85
13.7	Definition of MSME	85
13.8	Manufacturing GDP by Sector and Employment Projections	96
13.9	Key Variables and Assumptions	105
13.10	Ministry/Department-wise Twelfth Five Year Plan (2012–17) Outlays Industry Sector	129
14.1	Energy Intensity for Total Primary Energy*	130
14.2	Energy Intensity	131
14.3	Household Access (%)	132
14.4	Trends in Supply of Primary Commercial Energy	133
14.5	Share of Each Fuel in Total Energy Production and Consumption	134
14.6	Installed Capacity Addition during the Eleventh Plan (in MW)	136
14.7	Mode-wise/Sector-wise Break-up of Generation	137
14.8	All-India Cumulative Generating Capacity (as on 31 March 2012) (in MW)	137
14.9	Planned Manufacturing Capacity MW Per Annum	139
14.10	Cumulative Achievement of Transmission Lines at the End of the Eleventh Plan	140
14.11	Aggregate Technical and Commercial Losses of State Power Utilities (within State)	141
14.12	Viability of Major State Utilities Not Improving (Excluding Delhi and Odisha)	142
14.13	Details of Year-wise Progress Achieved on Restructured APDRP (as on 31 March 2012)	142

14.14	Status on RGGVY Progress during the Tenth and the Eleventh Plan	143
14.15	Outlay/Expenditure: Centre, States and UTs (₹ Crore)	146
14.16	Sector-wise and Mode-wise Capacity Addition (Provisional) during the Twelfth Plan (MW)	146
14.17	Changing Structure of Fuel for Electricity	147
14.18	Status of Hydro Electric Potential Development	148
14.19	Fuel Requirement during 2016–17	149
14.20	Transmission Line at the End of the Twelfth Plan Period	150
14.21	Inter-Regional Flow of Power at the End of Twelfth Plan Period	151
14.22	Details of Coal and Lignite Production	160
14.23	Inventory of Coal and Lignite Reserves as on 1 April 2012	160
14.24	Accretion of Coal Reserves	161
14.25	Coal Washing Capacity by the end of Eleventh Plan Period	162
14.26	Financial Performance of the Coal Sector	165
14.27	Coal Demand during the Twelfth Plan	165
14.28	Coal Production	166
14.29	Share of Underground Production in Total Production	167
14.30	Price Comparison of Domestic Coal with other Countries	167
14.31	Consumption of Petroleum Products	171
14.32	Physical Performance of Petroleum and Natural Gas Sector	172
14.33	Share of Overseas Hydrocarbon Production	173
14.34	Under-Recoveries on Petroleum Products	174
14.35	Demand of Petroleum Products	176
14.36	Projection of Crude Oil Production in the Twelfth Plan	176
14.37	Natural Gas Demand for Twelfth Five Year Plan	176
14.38	Projection of Natural gas production in Twelfth Plan (BCM)	177
14.39	Breakup of the Exploration Programme for the Twelfth Plan	177
14.40	Likely Under-Recoveries on Petroleum* Products	178
14.41	Projected Refining Capacity during Twelfth Plan (MMTPA)	178
14.42	R&D Expenditure by Major Oil and Gas Companies	180
14.43	Eleventh Plan Power Capacity Addition through Grid Interactive Renewable Power	185
14.44	Cost of Power for Various Renewable Energy Sources	186
14.45	Power Capacity Addition through Off Grid Renewable Power	186
14.46	Eleventh Plan Financial Allocations and Expenditure: MNRE	187
14.47	Indicative Twelfth Five Year Plan Outlay for the Various Ministries/Departments in the Energy Sector	190
15.1	CO_2 Emissions from Various Transport Modes	196
15.2	Overview of Financial Position of the Indian Railways	199
15.3	Investment in Railways during Eleventh Plan	200
15.4	Performance of Freight Business during Eleventh Five Year Plan	201
15.5	Performance of Passenger Business during Eleventh Five Year Plan	201
15.6	Losses in Passenger Services	201
15.7	Capacity Creation during Eleventh Plan	202
15.8	Throw Forward of Infrastructure Projects as on 1 April 2012	202
15.9	Rolling Stock Performance during Eleventh Plan	203
15.10	Productivity Performance	203
15.11	Benchmarking Indian Railways with Chinese and Russian Railways	204
15.12	Traffic Projections	206

15.13	Passenger Traffic Projections for Twelfth Plan	207
15.14	Projection of Originating PKM for Twelfth Plan	207
15.15	Creation of Fixed Assets during the Twelfth Plan	209
15.16	Rolling Stock Requirement during the Twelfth Plan	210
15.17	Passenger Service Yields in some Major Economies	213
15.18	Freight Yields in some Major Economies	213
15.19	Physical Achievements under NHDP during the Eleventh Five Year Plan	215
15.20	Progress of NHDP up to 30 April 2012	216
15.21	Physical Progress of Non-NHDP NHs during Eleventh Five Year Plan	217
15.22	State Roads Progress during the Eleventh Plan	218
15.23	Physical Progress–PMGSY (as on 31 March 2012)	219
15.24	Financial Progress (as on 31st March, 2012)	219
15.25	Habitation Coverage–Bharat Nirman (as on 31 March 2012)	220
15.26	Cumulative Physical Progress under Bharat Nirman (up to March 2012)	220
15.27	Targets for the Twelfth Plan	223
15.28	Projected Road Freight and Passenger Traffic	225
15.29	Financial Performance of the Shipping Sector in the Eleventh Plan	227
15.30	Estimated Requirements of Additional Vessels and Investment	228
15.31	Eleventh Plan Projection and Achievements of Traffic and Capacity by Major Ports	237
15.32	Commodity Wise Capacity Creation by Major Ports during Eleventh Plan	237
15.33	Traffic Handled at Major and Non-Major Ports during Eleventh Plan	238
15.34	Trend of the Productivity Parameters during Eleventh Plan	238
15.35	Year-wise Awards during Eleventh Plan under PPP	238
15.37	Commodity wise Capacity by the end of Twelfth Plan	239
15.36	Major Ports wise Traffic/Capacity Projections by End of Twelfth Plan	239
15.38	Commodity Wise Traffic by the End of Twelfth Plan (2016–17)	240
15.39	Growth Projections for the Twelfth Five Year Plan: Passenger and Cargo Traffic Forecasts	243
15.40	Investment Requirements during the Twelfth Plan	243
15.41	Comparison of ATF Prices in India with Competing Hubs	245
15.42	Flights/Week	247
15.43	Ministry/Department–wise Twelfth Five Year Plan (2012–17) Outlays for Transport Sectors	251
16.1	Targets and Achievements	267
16.2	Key Targets for the Twelfth Plan for the Electronics and IT-ITeS Industry	268
17.1	Overview of MGNREGA Performance, 2006–12	287
17.2 (A)	Average Daily Wage Rates for Agricultural Labour: Male	289
17.2 (B)	Seasonality of MGNREGA Employment Provided during 2010–11	290
17.3	Additional List of Permissible Works Under MGNREGA	291
17.4	Wage Payment Cycle under MGNREGA	294
17.5	Accountability Matrix for Delays in Wage Payments under MGNREGA	295
17.6	Phasing of the National Rural Livelihoods Mission	299
17.7	Investments in Rural Drinking Water, 1951–2012	300
17.8	Access to Household Amenities in Worst Performing States in Terms of Toilet Facilities in Rural India, 2011 (Percentage of Rural Households)	303
17.9	Percentage of Households with No Latrine Facilities in Rural India, 2011	304
17.10	Total Sanitation Campaign, Physical Progress, Eleventh Plan	305
17.11	Total Sanitation Campaign, Financial Progress, Eleventh Plan	305
17.12	Major Increase in Unit Cost Support for IHHLs during the Twelfth Plan	305
17.13	IAY-Financial Performance during Eleventh Plan (2007–08 to 2011–12)	307

17.14	Physical Performance of IAY During Eleventh Plan (2007–08 to 2011–12)	307
17.15	Convergence of IAY with other Rural Infrastructure	308
17.16	Scheme for Purchase of Home Site and Incentive for Additional Target under IAY	308
17.17	Infrastructure and Amenities to be Provided, Operated and Maintained under PURA Project by Private Developer in the Twelfth Plan	313
17.18	NSAP Progress in the Eleventh Plan	314
17.19	Physical and Financial Progress of NSAP Components, Eleventh Plan	315
18.1	Physical and Financial Progress under JNNURM (March 2012)	323
18.2	Estimates of Urban Transport Investments by HPEC	344
18.3	Requirement of CAPEX	344
18.4	Investments under JNNURM	349
18.5	Investment Requirement Estimates by HPEC	350
18.6	Requirement of CAPEX as per Working Group	350
19.1	Construction Sector-Macro Aggregates	362
19.2	Flow of Bank Credit to Construction Sector	371
19.3	Flow of FDI in Construction Activities (including Roads and Highways)	371
19.4	Alternative growth scenarios of tourism	376
19.5	Performance of Handloom Sector during the Eleventh Plan Period	397
19.6	Performance of Handicrafts Sector during the Eleventh Plan Period	402

Boxes

13.1	Examples of Weak Domestic Standards Leading to Influx of Sub-standard Products in the Country	61
13.2	Dwindling Indian Capital Goods Industry	68
13.3	Strategies for Highest Overall Impact	98
13.4	Key Recommendations for Manufacturing	99
13.5	Key Recommendations	122
13.6	Key Recommendations	125
14.1	Achievements in Power Sector during the Eleventh Plan	136
14.2	Recommendations of Task Force on Open Access	145
14.3	Perform, Achieve and Trade Mechanism	157
15.1	Containerisation In Railways	207
15.2	Business Models for Passenger and Rail Freight Logistics: The JR East and Deutsche Bahn Ways	208
15.3	Dedicated Freight Corridors (DFCs) – A Game Change for the Indian Rail Sector	209
15.4	New Generation Locomotives	210
15.5	Public-Private Partnership (PPP) in Railways	212
15.6	Key Message from Reports on Railways: The Need for Organisational Reforms	214
15.7	Financing of National Highway Development Programme (NHDP)	216
15.8	Engineering, Procurement, Construction (EPC) Contract	217
15.9	Innovations by some State Governments	223
15.10	Introduction of Electronic Toll Collection (ETC)	225
15.11	Coal Transport to Farakka through Power Station – A Break through for IWT	233
15.12	Development of Airports During the Eleventh Plan	242
15.13	GAGAN—The Indian Satellite Based Augmentation System (SBAS) for Air Navigation Services (ANS)	244
16.1	Spectrum Trading	263
16.2	Twelfth Plan Targets for the Telecommunication Sector	264
16.3	Key Achievements (as on 31 March 2012)	267
17.1	New Guidelines Strengthen Demand-driven Character of MGNREGA	293
17.2	Limitations of SGSY	298
18.1	Vision of Our Cities	320
18.2	State of Service Delivery—Key Indicators	321
18.3	Transforming Public Transport in Cities	324
18.4	Harmonising the Role of Parastatals with Elected Municipal Bodies	326
18.5	Strategic Densification—International Examples	330
18.6	Recommendation of Isher Ahluwalia Committee on Financial Devolution to ULBs	332
18.7	PPP in Urban Sector under JNNURM	333

18.8	FSI and Coverage Areas Can be Combined to Increase Densities	338
18.9	Metro—A Transformational Approach to Public Transport	341
18.10	Reforms and Desired Outcomes Related to Water Supply and Sanitation	348
18.11	Reforms under JNNURM Comprehensive List of Reforms in Urban Sector	355
18.12	Major Schemes for Urban Renewal at a Glance	358
19.1	Financing Instruments for Affordable Housing	374
19.2	Popular Choice by Design!	399
19.3	Twelfth Plan Interventions for Handlooms	401
19.4	Twelfth Plan Schemes for Handicrafts	404
19.5	Upturn in India's Sporting Performance	410

Acronyms

2G/3G/4G	Second Generation/Third Generation/Fourth Generation	ASSOCHAM	Associated Chamber of Commerce
AAI	Airport Authority of India	ATC	Air Traffic Control
AAY	Antodaya Anna Yojana	ATF	Automatic Transmission Fluid
ACA	Additional Central Assistance	ATFC	Agriculture Technology Forecast Centre
ACC	Artisan Credit Card	ATIs	Administrative Training Institutes
ACS	Average Cost of Supply	ATMAs	Agriculture Technology Management Agency
ADB	Asian Development Bank		
ADC	Access Deficit Charges	ATS	Apprentice Training Scheme
ADDA	Asansol Durgapur Development Authority	B.P.Ed.	Bachelor of Physical Education
		BAF	Batch Annealing Furnace
AES	Acute Encephalitis Syndrome	BC	Business Correspondent
AI	Artificial Insemination	BCM	Billion cubic metres
AIBP	Accelerated Agriculture Benefit Programme	BDOs	Block Development Officers
		BE	Budgetary Estimate
AIC	Agricultural Insurance Corporation	BEE	Bureau of Energy Efficiency
AIR	All India Radio	BEML	Bharat Earth Movers Ltd.
AIU	Association of Indian Universities	BFDAs	Brackish water Farmers Development Agencies
AL	Arable Land		
AML	Anti-Money Laundering	BFO	Business Facilitation Officer
AMM	Abandoned mine methane	BHEL	Bharat Heavy Electricals Ltd.
AMPC	Automated Mail Processing Centre	BIPP	Biotechnology Industry Partnership Programme
ANM	Auxiliary Nurse Midwife		
AnSI	Anthropological Survey of India	BIRAP	Biotechnology Industry Research Assistance Programme
AOC	Agreement of Collaboration		
APL	Above Poverty Line	BIS	Bureau of Indian Standards
APMC	Agriculture Produce Marketing Committee	BLY	Bachat Lamp Yojana
		BMPTC	Building Material and Technology Promotion Council
APMSS	Andhara Pradesh Mahila Samakhya		
APO	Assistant Programme Officer	BORL–Bina	Bharat Oman Refineries Limited
ARPU	Average Revenue Per User	BOT	Build-Operate-Transfer
ARR	Average Revenue Realised	BPCL	Bharat Petroleum Corporation Limited
ARYA	Attracting & Retaining Youth in Agriculture		
		BPL	Below Poverty Line
ASHA	Accredited Social Health Activist	BPO	Branch Post Office/ Business Process Outsourcing
ASI	Archaeological Survey of India		
ASPIRE	Agriculture Science Pursuit for Inspired Research Excellence	BPR	Business Process Re-engineering
		BRCs	Block Resource Centres

BRO	Border Roads Organisation	CGP	Cluster of Gram Panchayats
BRT	Bus Rapid Transit	CGRF	Consumer Grievance Redressal Forum
BSUP	Basic Services to the Urban Poor		
BTKM	Billion Tonne Kilometre	CH4. CO	Methane, Carbon Monoxide
BU	Billion Unit	CHPs	Coal Handling Plants
BWA	Broadband Wireless Access	CIDC	Construction Industry Development Council
C&AG	Comptroller & Auditor General		
CA	Conservation Agriculture	CII	Confederation of Indian Industry
CACP	Commission for Agriculture Costs & Prices	CLCSS	Credit Linked Capital Subsidy Scheme
CAG	Comptroller and Auditor General	CM	Confederation of Indian Industries
CAGR	Compound Annual Growth Rate	CMA	Counter Magnet Area
Cal/Kg	Calorie/ kilogramme	CMM	Coal mine methane
capex	Capital expenditure	CMPDIL	Central Mine Planning and Design Institute
CBDT	Central Board of Direct Taxation		
CBM	Coal bed Methane	CMSA	Community Managed Sustainable Agriculture
CBOs	Community Based Organisations		
CBRM	Capacity Building and Reform Management	CNG	Compressed natural gas
		CPCB	Central Pollution Control Board
CCDA	Coal Conservation and Development Act	CPCL	Chennai Petroleum Corporation Limited
CCL	Central Coalfields Limited	CPE	Customer Premises Equipment
CCRF	Code of Conduct for Responsible Fisheries	CPIAL or CPIIW	Consumer Price Index for Agricultural Labour/Consumer Price Index for Industrial Workers
C-DAP	Comprehensive District Agriculture Plants		
		CPIS	Coconut Palm Insurance Scheme
C-DOT	Centre for Development of Telematics	CPMG	Chief Post Master General
		CPPs	Captive power plants
CDP	City Development Plans	CPWD	Central Public Works Department
CEA	Central Electricity Authority	CREDAI	Confederation of Real Estate Developers' Associations of India
CEF	Citizen Engagement Framework		
CEIG	Chief Electrical Inspectorate to Govt. of India	CRPs	Community Resource Persons
		CRRI	Central Road Research Institute
CERC	Central Electricity Regulatory Commission	CRRI-In	Indian Computer Emergency Response Team
CERT	Computer Emergency Response Team	CSC	Cluster Stimulation Cell/Common Services Centre
CERT–In	Indian Computer Emergency Response Team	CSIR	Council for Scientific and Industrial Research
CETP	Common Affluent Treatment Plan	CSO	Central Statistical Office/Civil Society Organisation
CeWiT	Centre for Excellence in Wireless Technology		
		CSR	Corporate Social Responsibility
CFI	Construction Federation of India	CSS	Centrally Sponsored Scheme
CFSI	Children Film Society of India	CST	Central Sales Tax/Concentrating Solar Technology
CFT	Cluster Facilitation Team/ Combating of Financing of Terrorism		
		CTL	Coal to liquid
		CUF	Capacity Utilisation Factor
CGD	City Gas Distribution	CVO	Chief Vigilance Officer

C-WET	Centre for Wind Energy Technology	DWDM	Dense Wavelength Division Multiplexing
CWG	Common Wealth Games	E&P companies	Exploration and Production Companies
DAC	Department of Agriculture & Cooperation	EBP Programme	Ethanol Blended Petrol Programme
DAE	Department of Atomic Energy	ECB	External Commercial Borrowing
DAHDF	Department of Animal Husbandry, Dairying & Fisheries	ECBC	Energy Conservation Building Code
DALY	Disability Adjusted Life Years	ECO	Local Cable Operators
DAP	Diammonium Phosphate	EDGE	Enhanced Data for Global Evolution
DARE	Department of Agricultural Research & Education	EDMC	Electronic Design and Manufacturing Cluster
DAS	Digital Addressable System	EDS	Electronics Delivery of Services
DAVP	Directorate of Advertisement and Visual Publicity	EEZ	Exclusive Economic Zone
DBT	Department of Bio-technology	EFC	Expenditure Finance Committee
DCI	Dredging Corporation of India	eFMS	Electronic Fund Management System
DD	Doordarshan	EIAs	End Implementing Agencies
DeitY	Department of Electronics and Information Technology	EIL	Engineers India Limited
DEMU/ MEMU	Diesel-Electric Multiple Unit/ Mainline Electric Multiple Unit	EM	Entrepreneur's Memorandum
		EMC	Electronics Manufacturing Cluster
DFC	Dedicated Freight Corridor	EMMC	Electronic Media Monitoring Centre
DFP	Directorate of Field Publicity		
DGCA	Directorate General of Civil Aviation	EMSC	Environmental Measures and Subsidence Control scheme
DGH	Director General of Hydrocarbons		
DGPS	Differential Global Positioning System	EMU	Electric Multiple Unit
		EOL	Essar Oil Ltd
DIPP	Department of Industrial Policy and Promotion	EPC	Engineering Procurement and Construction
DIPP	Department of Industrial Policy and Promotion	ERP	Enterprise resource planning
		ESDM	Electronics System Design & Manufacturing
DoP	Department of Posts		
DoT	Department of Telecommunication	ETP	Effluent Treatment Plant
DP	Development Plan	EWS	Economically Weaker Sections
DPC	District Programme Coordinator	EXIM	Export Import
DPRs	Detailed Project Reports	FAB	Fabrication Unit
DPSU	Defence Public Sector Undertaking	FAO	Food and Agriculture Organisation
DRDA	District Rural Development Agency	FAR	Floor Area Ratio
DRDO	Defence Research & Development Organisation	FDI	Foreign Direct investment
		FFDAs	Fish Farmers Development Agencies
DRI	Differential Rate of Interest		
DRM	Digital Radio Mondiale	FICCl	Federation of Indian Chamber of Commerce & Industry
DSM	Demand side management		
DSS	Decision Support System	FM	Frequency Modulation
DST	Department of Science & Technology	FMD	Foot & Mouth Disease
		FO/LSHS	Furnace oil/Low Sulphur Heavy Stock
DTC	Direct Tax Code		
DTH	Direct to Home	FOLD	Forum of Load Dispatchers

FoR	Forum of Regulators	HMCP	Hardware Manufacturing Cluster Park
FPOs	Farmer Producer Organisation	HMEL	Hindustan Mittal Energy Limited
FPS	Fair Price Shop	HMT	Hindustan Machine Tools
FRBM	Fiscal Responsibility and Budget Management Rules	HPCL	Hindustan Petroleum Corporation Limited
FSA	Fuel Supply Agreement	HPEC	High Powered Expert Committee
FSI	Floor Space Index	HPOs	Head Post Offices
FSRU	Floating Storage & Regasification units	HPT	High Power Transmitter
FTA	Free Trade Agreement	HRD	Human Resource Development
FTII	Films and Television Institute of India	HRSS	High Resolution Seismic Survey
		HS	Herorrhagic Septicemia
FYP	Five Year Plan	HSIL	High Surge Impedance Loading
GAIL	Gas Authority of India Ltd	HTLS	High Temp. Low Sag
GBI support	Generation based incentive support	HTREL	High-tech Reconnaissance & Exploration Licences
GBS	Gross Budgetary Support	HUDCO	Housing and Urban Development Corporation
GCF	Gross Capital Formation		
GCV	Gross calorific value	HUMS	Indian Institutes of Urban Management
GDP	Gross Domestic Product		
GIPCL	Gujarat Industries Power Company Ltd	I&B	Information & Broadcasting
		IAAS	Integrated Agro-Meteorological Advisory Service
GIS	Geographical Information System		
GKMS	Gramin Krishi Mausam Seva	IAASTD	International Assessment of Agricultural Knowledge, Science & Technology for Development
GMO	Genetically Modified Organisms		
GOI	Government of India		
GoI-UNDP	Government of India-United Nations Development Programme	IAP	Integrated Action Plan
		IAY	Indira Awaas Yojana
GPR	Ground Penetrating Radar	IBF	Indian Broadcasting Foundation
GPS	Global Positioning System	IBIN	India Backbone Implementation Network
GPs	Gram Panchayats		
GQ	Golden Quadrilateral		
GRIHA	Green Rating for Integrated Habitat Assessment	IBM	Indian Bureau of Mines
		IBP	Indian Broadcasting Foundation
GSDP	Gross State Domestic Product	IBS	In Building Solutions
GSI	Geological Survey of India	IC	Integrated Circuit
GSM	Global System for Mobile Communication	ICAR	Indian Council of Agricultural Research
GST	Goods and Services Tax	ICD	Inland Container Depot
GT	Gross Tonne	ICF	Integrated Coach Factory
GTO/IGBT	Gate Turn Off (Thyrister)/Insulated Gate Bipolar Transistor	ICMR	Indian Council of Medical Research
		ICRIS	Integrated Coal Resource Information System
GW	GigaWatt		
HD	High Definition	ICT	Information and Communication Technology
HDTV	High Definition Television		
HEC	Heavy Engineering Corporation	ICTE	Information, Communication Technology and Electronics
HEIs	Higher Educational Institutions		
HEMM	Heavy earth moving machinery	IDA	International Development Association
HITS	Headend In The Sky		

IEBR	Internal and Extra Budgetary Resources	IPR	Intellectual Property Rights
IEC	Information Education and Communication	IPTV	Internet Protocol Television
		IPV 4/IPV 6	Internet Protocol version 4/Internet Protocol version 6
IFFI	International Film Festival of India	IRDA	Insurance Regulatory Development Authority
IGNDPS	Indira Gandhi National Disability Pension Scheme	IRDP	Integrated Rural Development Programme
IGNOAPS	Indira Gandhi National Old Age Pension Scheme	ISO	Indian Standard Organisation
IGNWPS	Indira Gandhi National Widow Pension Scheme	ISPRL	Indian Strategic Petroleum Reserve Ltd
IHHL	Individual Household Latrine	ISRO	Indian Space Research Organisation
IHSDP	Integrated Housing & Slum Development Programme	ISSHUP	Interest Subsidy Scheme for Housing the Urban Poor
IIDS	Integrated Infrastructural Development Scheme	IT	Information Technology
		ITA-1	Information Technology Agreement-1
IIFCL	India Infrastructure Finance Company Limited	ITI	Indian Telephone Industries
IIHT	Indian Institute of Handloom Technology	ITIs	Industrial Training Institutes
		IT-ITeS	Information Technology-and Information Technology enabled Service
IIIT	Indian Institute of Information Technology		
IIPA	Indian Institute of Public Administration	IVRS	Interactive Voice Response System
		IWAI	Inland Waterways Authority of India
IISc	Indian Institute of Science		
IIT	Indian Institute of Technology	IWT	Inland Waterways Transport
IIUMs	Indian Institutes of Urban Managements	JE	Japanese Encephalitis
		JLGs	Joint Liability Groups
ILCS	Integrated Low Cost Sanitation Scheme	JMP	Joint Monitoring Programme
		JNNURM	Jawaharlal Nehru National Urban Renewal Mission
ILRIS	Integrated Lignite Resource Information System	JNNUSM	Jawaharlal Nehru National Solar Mission
IMD	Indian Meteorological Department		
IMEI	International Mobile Equipment Identity	JRDA	Jharia Rehabilitation and Development Authority
IMIS	Integrated Management Information System	JV	Joint Venture
		JWGs	Joint Working Groups
IMPCC	Inter Media Publicity Coordination Committee	KCC	Kisan Credit Card
		Kgoe/US$	Kilograms of Oil Equivalent/US Dollar
IMT	International Mobile Telecommunications	KVIC	Khadi & Village Industries Corporation
INDIPEX	India International Philatelic Exhibition	KVK	Krishi Vigayan Kendra
IOCL	Indian Oil Corporation Limited	KVs	Kendriya Vidyalayas
IP	Intellectual Property/Internet Protocol	kW	Kilo Watt
		Kwh	Kilowatt hour
IPM	Integrated Pest Management	L. km	Line kilometre

LAD	Least Assured Depth	MM-III	Mini Mission III
LARR	Land Acquisition and Rehabilitation and Resettlement Bill, 2011	MMP	Mission Mode Project
		MMSCMD	Million Metric Standard Cubic Metre Per Day
LBFL	Local Bodies Finance List		
LCO	Local Cable Operators	MMT	Million Metric Tonnes
LDBs	Livestock Development Boards	MMTOE	Million tones oil equivalent
LDC	Land Development Corporation	MMTPA	Million Metric Tonne Per Annum
LDO	Light Diesel Oil	MNAIS	Modified National Agricultural Insurance Scheme
LEED	Leadership in Energy & Environmental Design		
		MNRE	Ministry of New and Renewable Energy
LHB	Linke Holfmann Busch		
LIGs	Low Income Group	MoA	Ministry of Agriculture
LNCPE	Laxmibai National College of Physical Education	MoC	Ministry of Coal
		MoHUPA	Ministry of Housing and Urban Poverty Alleviation
LNG	Liquefied natural gas		
LPG	Liquefied Petroleum Gas	MoP	Ministry of Power
LPT	Low Power Transmitter	MoP&NG	Ministry of Petroleum and Natural Gas
LR	Land Readjustment		
LTCCS	Long Term Cooperative Credit Structure	MoRD	Ministry of Rural Development
		MoRTH	Ministry of Roads Transport & Highways
LTE	Long Term Evolution		
LWE	Left Wing Extremism	MoSPI	Ministry of Statistics & Programme Implementation
M&A	Mergers and Acquisitions		
M.P.Ed.	Master of Physical Education	MOT	Multi-organisation Team/ Muriate of Potash
MA	Moving Average		
MANAGE	National Institute for Agriculture Extension and Management	MoU	Memorandum of Understanding
		MoUD	Ministry of Urban development
MAT	Minimum Alternative Tax	MPCs	Metropolitan Planning Committees
Mbps	Megabits per second	MRP	Maximum Retail Price
MCCL	Mahanadi Coalfields Limited	MRPL	Mangalore Refinery and Petrochemicals Limited
MCS	Monitoring, Control and Surveillance		
		MS	Motor spirit
MDI	Management Devolution Index	MSE-CDP	Cluster Development Programme of the M/o MSME
MDRR	Mines and Minerals (Development and Regulation) Bill, 2011		
		MSEFC	Micro & Small Enterprise Facilitation Councils
MEA	Ministry of External Affairs		
MES	Minimum Economic Size	MSIPS	Modified Special Incentive Programme Scheme
MFIs	Microfinance Institutions		
MGNREGA	Mahatma Gandhi National Rural Employment Guarantee Act	MSME	Micro, Small & Medium Enterprise
		MSMED Act	MSME Development Act, 2006
MGNREGS	Mahatma Gandhi National Rural Employment Guarantee Scheme	MSP	Minimum Support Price
		MT	Million Tonnes
MGR	Merry-Go-Round	MTA	Mid-term Appraisal
MHz/GHz	Mega Hertz/Giga Hertz	MTEE	Market Transformation for Energy Efficiency
MIS	Management Information System		
MITI	Ministry of International Trade and Industry, Japan	MTOE	Million tons of oil equivalent
		MW	Medium Wave/Megawatt
MMBTU	Million Metric British Thermal Unit	MWe	Megawatt electrical

MWp.	Megawatt Peak	NGRCA	National Gender Resources Centre in Agriculture
NABARD	National Bank for Agriculture and Rural Development	NGRI	National Geophysical Research Institute
NABFINS	NABARD Financial Services	NHAI	National Highway Authority of India
NAC	Non Agricultural use of Land	NHB	National Horticulture Board/ National Housing Bank
NADA	National Anti-Doping Agency		
NAIS	National Agricultural Insurance Scheme	NHDP	National Highway Development Programme
NAPCC	National Action Plan on Climate Change	NHM	National Horticulture Mission
		NIA	Net irrigated area
NARS	National Agriculture Research System	NICRA	National Initiative on Climate Resilient Agriculture
NATRIP	National Automotive Testing and R&D Infrastructure Project	NIMZ	National Investment and Manufacturing Zone
NAVA	National Audio-Visual Archives		
NBA	News Broadcasters Association/ Nirmal Bharat Abhiyan	NIPER	National Institute of Pharmaceutical Education & Research
NBECI	National Bio Energy Corporation of India	NIS	National Institute of Sports
		NISC	National Institute of Sports Coaching
NBFCs	Non-Banking Finance Companies		
NBS	Nutrient Based Subsidy	NISSM	National Institute of Sports Science and Sports Medicine
NCC	National Cadet Corps		
NCP	National Competition Policy	NIUA	National Institute of Urban Affairs
NCR	National Capital Region	NKN	National Knowledge Network
NCTE	National Council of Teacher Education	NLCPR	Non-Lapsable Central Pool of Resources
NDDB	National Dairy Development Boards		
NDP	National Dairy Plant	NLP	Natural Language Processing
NDTL	National Dope Test Laboratory	NMCC	National Manufacturing Competitiveness Council
NE	North East		
NEF	National Electricity Fund	NMCP	National Manufacturing Competitiveness Programme
NEGP	National e-Governance Plan		
NERUDP	North Eastern Region Urban Development Programme	NMEEE	National Mission for Enhanced Energy Efficiency
NELP	New Exploration Licensing Policy	NMSA	National Mission for Sustainable Agriculture
NER	North Eastern Region		
NFAP	National Frequency Allocation Plan	NMSH	National Mission on Sustainable Habitat
NFBS	National Family Benefit Scheme		
NFDB	National Fisheries Development Board	NMT	Non-Motorised Transport
		NOCL	Nagarjuna Oil Corporation Limited
NFDC	National Film Development Corporation	NOFN	National Optical Fibre Network
		NPBB	National Programme for Bovine Breeding
NFSA	National Food Security Act		
NFSB	National Food Security Bill	NPBBD	National Programme for Bovine Breeding and Dairy
NFSM	National Food Security Mission		
NGN	Next Generation Network	NPCBB	National Project for Cattle & Buffalo Breeding
NGO	Non-Governmental Organisation		
NGP	Nirmal Gram Puraskar	NPFAI	National Playfields Association of India

NPFP	National Physical Fitness Programme	NVG	National Voluntary Guidelines on Soc., Env., & Eco Responsibility for Business
NPK	Nitrogen Phosphorous & Potash		
NPM	Non-Pesticidal Management of Pests	NVs	Navodaya Vidyalayas
		NYC	National Youth Corps
NPMSH&F	National Project on Management of Soil Health & Fertility	NYKs	Nehru Yuva Kendras
		O&M	Operation & Maintenance
NPS	New Pension Scheme/ New Pricing Scheme	O+OEG	Oil and oil equivalent gas
		OBCs	Other Backward Classes
NPYAD	National Programme for Youth and Adolescent Development	ODF	Open Defecation Free
		OFB	Ordinance Factory Board
NRAA	National Rained Area Authority	OIL	Oil India Limited
NRDWP	National Rural Drinking Water Programme	OMCs	Oil Marketing Companies
		OMS	Output per man shift
NREGS	National Rural Employment Guarantee Scheme	OMT	Operate-Maintain-Transfer
		ONGC	Oil and Natural Gas Corporation Limited
NRL	Numaligarh Refinery Limited		
NRLM	National Rural Livelihood Mission	OVL	ONGC Videsh Ltd
NSAP	National Social Assistance Programme	oya	Year on Year Average
		PACS	Primary Agriculture Cooperative Society
NSD	National School of Drama		
NSDC	National Skill Development Corporation	PAPU	Pan African Postal Union
		PAT	Perform, Achieve & Trade
NSDF	National Skill Development Fund	PATM	Perform, Achieve and Trade Mechanism
NSF	National Sports Federation		
NSIC	National Small Industry Corporation	PCB	Pollution Control Board
NSNIS	Netaji Subhas National Institute of Sports	PCU	Policy Coherence Unit
		PDAs	Pension Distribution Agencies
		PEARL	Peer Experience and Reflective Learning
NSS	National Sample Survey/National Service Scheme		
		PHPDT	Peak Hour Peak Direction Traffic
NSSO	National Sample Survey Office/ National Sample Survey Organisation	PIB	Public Information Bureau
		PIC	Public Information Campaign
		PKM	Passenger Kilometre
NTDPC	National Transport Development Policy Committee	PLB	Public Land Banks
		PLI	Postal Life Insurance
NTKM	Net Tonne Kilometre	PMEGP	Pradhan Mantri Employment Guarantee Programme
NTP	National Telecom Policy		
NTPC	National Thermal Power Corporation	PMGSY	Pradhan Mantri Grameen Sadak Yojna
NTS	National Institute of Sports	PNG	Piped natural gas
NUHHP	National Urban Housing and Habitat Policy	PNGRB	Petroleum and Natural Gas Regulatory Board
NULM	National Urban Livelihoods Mission	POL	Petroleum, Oil and Lubricants
		POLIF	Post Office Life Insurance Fund
NURTA	National Urban Rail Transit Authority	POs	Post Offices
		POSOCO	Power System Operation Corporation Limited
NUSP	National Urban Sanitation Policy		

PPAC	Petroleum Planning and Analysis Cell	RGNIYD	Rajiv Gandhi National Institute of Youth Development
PPAs	Power purchase agreement	RHF	Rural Housing Fund
PPP	Public–Private Partnership	RIA	Regulatory Impact Analysis
PPPP	People Private–Public Partnership	RIDF	Rural Infrastructure Development Fund
PPPIAD	Public–Private Partnership for Integrated Agricultural Development	RIL	Reliance Industries Limited
		RIL-KG	Reliance Industries Limited-Krishna Godavari Basin
PPVFRA	Protection of Plant Variety & Farmers Rights Authority	RIS	River Information System
PRGF	Partial Risk Guarantee Fund	RITES	Rail India Techno Economic Services
PRIs	Panchayati Raj Institutions		
Provi.	Provisional	RKVY	Rashtriya Krishi Vikas Yojana
PSB	Public Service Broadcaster	RMSA	Rashtriya Madhyamik Shiksha Abhiyan
PSCs	Production Sharing Contracts		
PSUs	Public Sector Undertakings	ROB/RUB	Road Over Bridge/ Road Under Bridge
PTA	Preferential Trade Agreement		
PURA	Provision of Urban Amenities in Rural Areas	RoW	Right of Way
		RPLI	Rural Postal Life Insurance
PWD	Public Works Department	RPO	Renewable Purchase Obligation
PWSS	Piped Water Supply System	RPOLIF	Rural Post Office Life Insurance Fund
PYD	Programme for Youth Development		
PYKKA	Panchayati Yuva Khel aur Krida Abhiyan	RRTS	Regional Rapid Transit System
		RTE	Right to Education
R&D	Research and Development	RUDSETIs	Rural Development and Self-Employment Training Institutes
R&M AND LE	Renovation & Modernisation and Life Extension		
		S&DD	Song and Drama Division
R&R	Rehabilitation and Resettlement	S&L	Standards and Labelling
R/P ratios	Reserves-to-Production ratio	SAD	Special Additional Duty
R–APDRP	Restructured Accelerated Power Development and Reforms Programme	SAGES	Goaf edge supports
		SAMETIs	State Agriculture Management Extension & Training Institutions
RAY	Rajiv Awas Yojana	SARDP-NE	Special Accelerated Road Development Programme for the North East
RBCs	Rural Building Centres		
RCUES	Regional Centres of Urban and Environment Studies		
		SAT	Sports Authority of India
RDF	Rural Development Flexi-fund	SAU/SAUs	Social Audit Unit/State Agricultural Universities
RDSO	Research Design and Standards Organisation		
		SBD	Standard bid documents
RE bonds	Renewable Energy bonds	SCCL	Singareni Collieries Company Limited
RE	Revised Expenditure		
READY	Rural Entrepreneurship & Awareness Development Yojana	SCs	Scheduled Castes
		SCSP	Scheduled Castes Sub-Plan
REC	Renewable Energy Certificate	SDO	Standard Developing Organisations
RFD	Result Framework Document	SDTV	Standard Definition Television
RFID	Radio Frequency Identification	SEB	State Electricity Board
RGGVY	Rajiv Gandhi Grameen Vidyutikaran Yojana	SEBI	Securities & Exchange Board of India
		SECC	Socio-Economic and Caste Census

SECF	Contribution to State Energy Conservation Fund	TMNE (NE)	Technology Mission for North Eastern Region
SFAC	Small Farmers Agribusiness Consortium	TNUDF	Tamil Nadu Urban Development Fund
SFCs	State Finance Commissions	TOD	Time of Day
SGSY	Swarnajayanti Gram Swarozgar Yojana	TOPS	Terrestrial Observation & Prediction System
SHBs	State Housing Boards	TPDS	Targeted Public Distribution System
SHGs	Self-Help Groups	TPSs	Town Planning Schemes
SIBRI	Small Industry Business Research Initiatives	TQM	Total Quality Management
		TSC	Total Sanitation Campaign
SITP	Scheme for Integrated Textile Park	TSDO	Telecom Standards Development Organisation
SJSRY	Swarna Jayanti Sahari Rozgaar Yojana	TSP	Telecom Service Provider/Tribal Sub-Plan
SKO	Superior Kerosene Oil	TUFS	Technology Upgradation Fund Scheme
SLNA	State-Level Nodal Agency		
SLSC	State Level Sanctioning Committee	UC	Utilization Certificate
SME	Small and Medium Enterprise	UCG	Underground Coal Gasification
SOC	Soil Organic Carbon	UGC	University Grants Commission
SOE	State Owned Enterprise	UHV	Useful heat value
SOP	Standard Operating Producer	UID	Unique Identification
SoRs	Schedule of Rates	UID	Unique Identification—AADHAR
SPTLs	State Pesticide Testing Laboratory	UIDSSMT	Urban Infrastructure Development for Small & Medium Towns
SPV	Special Purpose Vehicle		
SRFTI	Satyajit Ray Film and Television Institute	UIG	Urban Infrastructure and Governance
SRI	System of Rice Intensification	UK	United Kingdom
SSA	Sarva Shiksha Abhiyan	ULBs	Urban Local Bodies
STB	Set Top Box	ULIP	Unit Linked Insurance Plan
STL	Short term liabilities	UMPPs	Ultra Mega Power Projects
STOA	Short-Term Open Access	UMTA	Unified Metropolitan Transport Authority
STs	Scheduled Tribes		
STU/CTU	State Transmission Utilities/Central Transmission Utility	UNICEF	United Nations Children's Fund
		UPU	Universal Postal Union
SW	Short Wave	USA	United States of America
SWAN	State Wide Area Network	USEPA	United States Environment Protection Agency
TCF	Trillion cubic feet		
TCIL	Telecommunications Consultants India Ltd	USHA	Urban Statistics for HR and Assessments
TCoE	Telecom Centres of Excellence	USIS	Urban Sport Infrastructure
TDB	Technology Development Board	USOF	Universal Service Obligation Fund
TDR	Transfer of Development Rights	UT	Urban Transport
TDRs	Tradable Development Rights	VAS	Value Added Services
TDSAT	Telecom Disputes Settlement Appellate Tribunal	VAT	Value Added Tax
		VCFEE	Venture Capital Fund for Energy Efficiency
TEC	Telecom Engineering Centre		
TFP	Total Factor Productivity	VFX	Visual Effects
TISCO	Tata Iron and Steel Company Limited	VGF	Viability Gap Funding

VLFM	Visionary Leadership for Manufacturing	WHO	World Health Organisation
VLPT	Very Low Power Transmitter	WiPS	Wireless Intrusion Prevention System
VoIP	Voice Over Internet Protocol	WRDA	Warehouse Regulatory & Development Authority
VUs	Vehicle Units		
VWSC	Village Water and Sanitation Committee	WSCs	Weavers' Service Centres
		WTO	World Trade Organisation
WBCIS	Weather Based Crop Insurance Scheme	XGPON	Next Generation Gigabit Passive Optical Network
WDM-PON	Wavelength Division Multiplexed Passive Optical Network		

Annexures

13.1	Manufacturing GDP by Sector and Employment Projections	105
13.2	Sector-wise Recommendations	106
13.3	Twelfth Five Year Plan (2012–17) Outlays (GBS) for Industry Sector	129
14.1	Eleventh Plan Physical Progress of RGGVY Projects under Implementation	191
14.2	Sectoral Coal Demand/Off-take for Annual Plan 2012–13	192
14.3	Annual Plan 2012–13—Company-wise Production—Ministry of Coal	193
14.4	Physical Targets of Renewable Programme for the Twelfth Plan	194
15.1	Central Road Sector Outlay and Expenditure-At Current Price for Eleventh Plan	252
15.2	Plan-wise Addition to NH Length	254
15.3	Achievement on National Highways	254
15.4	National Highways Development Project Phase I to VII	255
15.5	Physical Performance of Air India Limited during Eleventh Plan Period	256
15.6	Financial Performance of Air India Ltd. during the Eleventh Plan Period	256
15.7	Financial Performance of Airports Authority of India during Eleventh Plan Period	257
15.8	Financial Performance of Pawan Hans Helicopters Ltd. during Eleventh Plan Period	257
16.1	Twelfth Five Year Plan (2012–17) Outlays for the Ministry of Communications and IT and Ministry of Information and Broadcasting	285

12

Agriculture

INTRODUCTION

12.1. Although agriculture now accounts for only 14 per cent of Gross Domestic Product (GDP), it is still the main source of livelihood for the majority of the rural population. As such rapid growth of agriculture is critical for inclusiveness. Important structural changes are taking place within the sector and there are definite signs of improved performance. Agricultural growth has accelerated compared to the Tenth Plan and diversification is proceeding (Table 12.1). The National Sample Survey Organisation (NSSO) data brings out that rural labourers are shifting to non-agricultural work, tightening the labour market in agriculture and putting pressure on farm wages. However, dependence on agriculture remains unchanged among the rural self-employed whose average farm size continues to decline with population growth. This is also an ageing, more feminised population, whose educated young members are less likely to want to stay in farming. The viability of farm enterprise, mostly small farms, must therefore be a special area of Plan focus in the Twelfth Plan. The Plan must also focus on other priorities such as resource-use efficiency and technology to ensure sustainability of natural resources, adaptation to climate change and improvements in total factor productivity.

RECENT TRENDS: PERFORMANCE AND POINTERS

GDP Growth

12.2. The average of annual growth rates of GDP in agriculture and allied sectors during the Eleventh

TABLE 12.1
Growth Rate of Agricultural and Allied Sectors

(in percentage)

Plan	Share of Agriculture in the Economy	Growth Rate of Agriculture and Allied Sectors	Growth Rate of Total Economy
	(All Figures based on 2004–05 prices)		
Ninth Five Year Plan	23.4	2.5	5.7
Tenth Five Year Plan	19.0	2.4	7.6
Eleventh Plan (2007–08 to 2011–12)			
2007–08	16.8	5.8	9.3
2008–09	15.8	0.1	6.7
2009–10	14.6	0.8	8.6
2010–11 (2nd RE)	14.5	7.9	9.3
2011–12 (Rev Est.)	14.1	3.6	6.2
Eleventh Plan Average	15.2	3.7	8.0

Source: Central Statistical Office, New Delhi Press Release dated 7th Feb, 2013.

Five Year Plan is now placed at 3.7 per cent. This is short of the target of 4 per cent but is significantly better than the achievement of 2.4 per cent in the Tenth Plan. Failure to reach the target growth is one reason for the high inflation in prices of food and other primary commodities that persist despite the recent slowdown in overall GDP growth. Consequently, although the overall GDP growth target of the Twelfth Plan has been revised down since the Approach Paper, the growth target for agriculture is maintained at 4 per cent.

12.3. A natural question which arises is whether the target of 4 per cent is attainable in view of past shortfalls. Although growth trends and targets are subject to high errors due to weather variability (for example, the Eleventh Plan average was pulled down by two successive bad harvests in 2008–09 and 2009–10), there is reason for cautious optimism because the turn-around that began after 2004 appears to be maintaining its momentum. Figure 12.1 plots averages and standard deviations of annual growth rates over moving five-year periods, a trend of the growth averages and also annualised five-year growth rates based on five-year moving averages. All these show growth still trending up and variability reducing. The Eleventh Plan growth rate based on five-year moving averages is at 3.6 per cent, the highest for any five-year period ever and, significantly, growth variability has also reduced to lowest ever.

12.4. The reduction in variability is important since claims of acceleration or deceleration make sense only when variability is low. Also, it is a measure of how well the system is able to cope with inevitable bouts of aberrant weather and yet maintain the growth momentum. It should be noted that agricultural growth was positive in 2009–10 despite the worst drought in nearly 40 years. More generally, whereas earlier periods saw at least one and normally two years of negative growth in every five year, there has not been a single year of negative growth of agriculture and allied sectors after 2002–03.

12.5. The magnitude of secular decline in growth variability over the last 30 years is also important. This is now less than a third of its peak. A major role must have been played by the increase in irrigation from about 20 per cent of arable area in 1981 to 35 per cent today, based mainly on groundwater. However, since water tables have fallen and temperatures risen, the extent of variability decline is surprisingly large. Even assuming zero variability on irrigated land, this implies that variability on rain-fed land must have reduced very substantially. Clearly factors such as a more diversified agriculture,

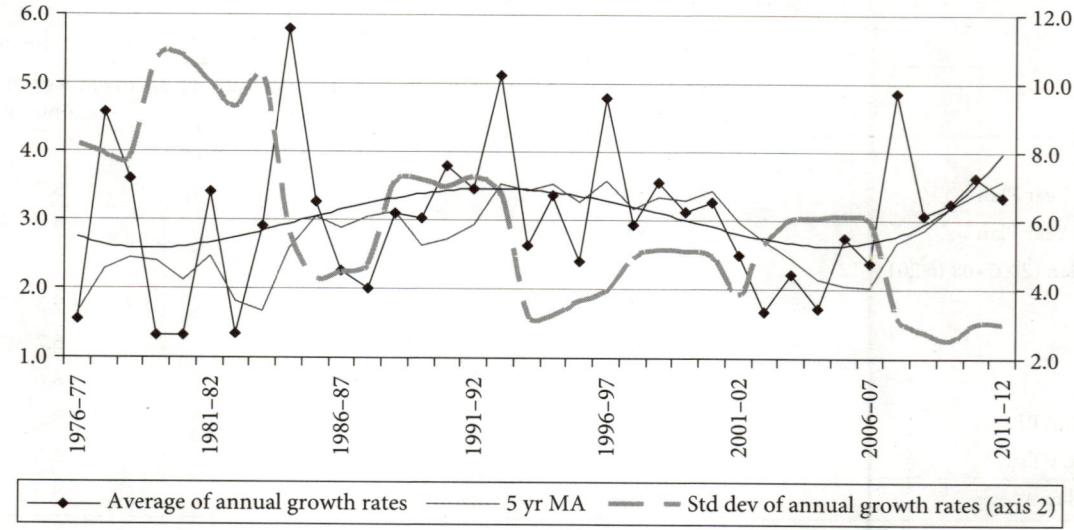

FIGURE 12.1: Growth and Fluctuations in GDP Agriculture and Allied

extended information reach and investments both on-farm and in watershed development, appear to have enabled better responses to depleting natural resources and weather risk. Although there is considerable scope to improve each of these factors further, it is a matter of satisfaction that developments in these areas are having a positive effect.

The Climate Challenge

12.6. The climate challenge facing agriculture needs to be taken seriously. Table 12.2 shows a distinct trend towards both drier and warmer weather, particularly during the last three Plan periods. Rainfall in context of agriculture has traditionally been discussed in terms of the monsoon (that is, June–September) but annual precipitation is probably much more relevant now since the dominance of Kharif crops has reduced. Viewed in this perspective, it is noteworthy that each of the last three Plan periods has recorded lower mean rainfall and higher rainfall variability compared to the immediately previous period. Three (2008, 2009 and 2011) of the five Eleventh Plan years had annual rainfall below 95 per cent of long period average, as compared to only five in the previous 15 years. Temperature conditions have deteriorated even more. Periods prior to 1997 can be considered normal, but warming has increased at an accelerating pace since then. The Eleventh Plan period contained the two warmest years (2010 and 2009) ever recorded since 1900. Even the coolest year (2008) during these five years was the thirteenth warmest in the last 110 years.

State-wise performance

12.7. The Mid-term Appraisal of the Eleventh Plan (MTA) had noted that the recovery in agriculture after 2004 was associated with clear signs of renewed dynamism in rain-fed areas. Table 12.3, presents state-wise averages and standard deviations of annual growth rates of Gross State Domestic Product (GSDP) from agriculture and allied activities for four separate periods since 1981–82. It clearly shows the following:

1. The all-States average and median growth rates of GSDP recovered beyond levels before mid-1990s, to reach near 4 per cent in the period after 2004–05, this also happened individually in many states, particularly those with large rain-fed areas. The states with best performance were Jharkhand, Chhattisgarh, Manipur, Tripura, Mizoram, Rajasthan, Gujarat, Maharashtra, Karnataka and Andhra Pradesh, all with above 5 per cent growth.
2. Despite more difficult weather conditions, all except few hill states managed substantial reduction of growth variability (measured by standard deviation of annual growth rates) during 2005–12 as compared to the past.

TABLE 12.2
Some Weather Details

	1951/52 to 1967/68	1968/69 to 1980/81	1981/82 to 1990/91	1991/92 to 1996/97	1997/98 to 2001/02	2002/03 to 2006/07	2007/08 to 2011/12
Annual Rainfall (cm)							
Mean	122.5	118.7	120.1	121.0	118.5	113.7	111.7
Standard Deviation	12.5	10.2	11.5	7.2	8.3	9.4	10.0
Monsoon Rainfall (cm)							
Mean	91.9	88.8	88.8	90.0	87.8	83.9	86.6
Standard Deviation	10.1	9.6	11.0	6.5	5.5	7.9	9.7
Annual Temperature anomaly from normal (°C)							
Mean	0.04	−0.03	0.09	0.19	0.34	0.56	0.65
Standard Deviation	0.28	0.24	0.03	0.10	0.22	0.11	0.26

Source: Climate bulletins and other publications of the India Meteorological Department.

TABLE 12.3
Averages and Standard Deviations of Annual Growth Rates of GSDP from Agriculture and Allied Sectors

	Average of Annual Growth Rates				Standard Deviation of Annual Growth Rates			
	1981–82 to 1993–94	1994–95 to 1999–2000	2000–01 to 2004–05	2005–06 to 2011–12	1981–82 to 1993–94	1994–95 to 1999–2000	2000–01 to 2004–05	2005–06 to 2011–12
Andhra Pradesh	3.9	2.8	4.7	5.0	10.0	13.8	9.7	6.5
Arunachal Pradesh	9.3	−0.8	1.6	5.0	9.7	8.5	7.2	7.8
Assam	2.5	0.2	−0.1	4.1	4.8	2.7	1.4	2.2
Bihar	1.1	3.1	7.4	3.3	12.9	22.7	24.1	11.9
Chhattisgarh	4.9	−2.1	4.6	7.3	10.5	10.5	35.3	9.1
Gujarat	8.8	5.2	9.1	5.5	53.5	27.0	24.2	10.4
Haryana	4.5	2.1	2.7	4.2	12.2	7.0	3.5	5.7
Himachal Pradesh	2.8	0.3	8.0	1.5	12.4	2.1	6.2	9.7
Jammu & Kashmir	1.3	5.2	3.6	0.7	11.2	5.7	3.8	2.9
Jharkhand	1.1	4.3	5.0	8.0	12.9	7.2	19.6	5.1
Karnataka	4.5	4.1	−2.9	5.1	8.7	5.7	15.1	6.8
Kerala	3.2	1.9	1.7	−0.2	6.4	4.9	2.4	3.4
Madhya Pradesh	4.9	1.6	2.2	4.4	10.5	3.4	27.1	4.7
Maharashtra	5.7	3.1	1.6	5.3	17.3	10.1	6.9	11.5
Manipur	2.8	2.1	5.8	5.9	3.6	6.2	6.9	4.4
Meghalaya	1.1	7.2	4.8	3.3	11.2	6.2	2.1	2.2
Mizoram			0.1	5.7			4.8	5.9
Nagaland			14.1	2.5			9.7	2.3
Odisha	2.6	0.0	3.5	3.1	18.6	11.0	16.4	2.5
Punjab	4.9	2.5	1.8	1.8	4.6	4.4	2.6	1.6
Rajasthan	5.9	5.5	10.9	5.5	26.5	14.4	44.9	10.1
Sikkim		−1.2	6.5	3.4		11.1	1.0	2.4
Tamilnadu	5.8	1.8	−0.5	4.6	12.7	9.6	14.0	7.0
Tripura	2.5	3.7	4.0	5.7	7.1	5.7	11.4	5.6
Uttar Pradesh	2.8	3.5	1.0	2.8	3.2	5.2	1.8	1.4
Uttarakhand	2.8	2.4	3.3	2.0	3.2	3.5	4.9	4.3
West Bengal	5.3	4.1	2.4	2.6	9.2	4.3	4.0	3.4
Sum of GSDP of:	3.4	2.5	2.1	3.8	5.8	5.2	6.5	2.8
All above states	(3.4)	(3.3)	(1.7)	(3.7)	(5.1)	(4.6)	(6.1)	(2.5)
High irrigation states	3.8	3.2	1.7	2.7	3.1	3.8	2.1	0.9
Medium irrigation states	2.9	1.8	3.1	4.2	9.8	9.1	8.5	3.0
Low irrigation states	3.6	2.8	1.5	4.5	5.6	4.7	9.1	5.3
High productivity states	4.1	2.9	2.5	2.1	3.9	3.1	2.2	0.8
Mid productivity states	3.0	2.4	2.1	3.7	4.0	6.6	4.5	2.3
Low productivity states	3.6	2.6	2.5	5.1	11.0	6.4	16.7	5.4
Across States:								
Median	3.6	2.5	3.5	4.2	10.5	6.2	6.9	5.1
Standard deviation	2.2	2.3	3.7	1.9				

Note: Figures in brackets use corresponding national GDP agriculture and allied (2004–05 prices) data. High irrigation refers to the GSDP sum over Haryana, Punjab, Uttar Pradesh and West Bengal (Net irrigated area (NIA)/Arable land (AL) > 55 per cent in 2008–09). Low irrigation (NIA/AL < 30 per cent) refers to Assam and North-East, Chhattisgarh, Himachal Pradesh, Jharkhand, Karnataka, Kerala, Maharashtra, Rajasthan and Uttarakhand. Medium refers to the rest. High productivity states (present GSDP/AL > ₹70,000/hectare at 2004–05 prices) are Tripura, West Bengal, Kerala, Himachal Pradesh, Punjab, J&K and Haryana. Low productivity (GSDP/AL < ₹35,000) states are Rajasthan, Meghalaya, Madhya Pradesh, Chhattisgarh, Maharashtra, Odisha, Jharkhand, Karnataka and Gujarat. The rest are Middle productivity. The 1980–81 series gives data only for undivided Bihar, MP and UP; these have been split using 1993–94 ratios to get GSDP for new States.

3. The variation in performance across States suggests that State-level responses and implementation play a very significant role in determining agricultural performance. However, to the extent that available technology limits potential growth, it will be difficult to maintain high growth rates where productivity has increased close to potential levels. This is relevant because the Eleventh Plan strategy gave much greater flexibility to States and focused more on yield gaps within existing technology, rather than emphasising new technologies and supporting these. The growth acceleration since 2005 has therefore been much stronger in states with lower productivity and less irrigation. This suggests that the strategy may be correcting the past relative neglect which caused rain-fed farming, covering over 60 per cent of arable land, to perform well below potential.

12.8. It is a matter of concern that the recent growth revival has been weak in areas with high land productivity, not only in relatively more irrigated states such as Punjab, Haryana, Uttar Pradesh and West Bengal that had green revolution success, but also in less irrigated states such as Kerala, Himachal Pradesh and Jammu & Kashmir where high productivity reflects a high-value cropping pattern based on horticulture. These States together contribute about 35 per cent of national agricultural output from 20 per cent of arable land, but none of them have been able to surpass growth rates achieved in the past. Even Gujarat, a low productivity state that sustained near 10 per cent growth for almost a decade through better water use and rapid adoption of Bt cotton hybrids, slowed down perceptibly in the Eleventh Plan as Bt adoption saturated and yields reached a plateau. Clearly, growth is more difficult to accelerate at higher productivity levels without new technology, particularly if past patterns of growth have taken a toll on natural resources.

OUTPUTS, INPUTS AND PRODUCTIVITY

12.9. The Eleventh Plan had made four conscious choices. First, with technology fatigue evident, it funded research better but emphasised on getting more from existing technology. Second, since one size does not fit all, it decentralised plan funds to encourage initiatives at State and lower levels. Third, aware of low public investment and food security needs, it increased Centre's spending on these, particularly in disadvantaged regions. Fourth, noting farmer distress, it tried to focus not just on production but also on farm incomes, stressing service delivery and suggesting encouragement of group activity with land and tenancy reforms put back on the agenda. Compared to the original green revolution that built on the best, this strategy sought to deliver faster growth, that is, more inclusive, more stable and less concentrated spatially. Nonetheless, there is a wide demand for a 'second green revolution' with more irrigation and better crop-specific technologies, with some even claiming that Bt cotton has been the only recent success. The Twelfth Plan accepts the proposition that a greater technical thrust is needed, and the strategy for agriculture should take this into account

12.10. In order to provide a snapshot of the Eleventh Plan performance and give indication of what the Twelfth Plan should do differently, long-run data on growth of output by sub-sector and also rates of growth of input use and productivity are presented in Table 12.4. Since performance is almost invariably discussed in the context of well-defined policy periods, those chosen for this table are same as in the Eleventh Plan document: (*i*) Pre-Green Revolution (1951–52 to 1967–68); (*ii*) Green Revolution proper (1968–69 to 1980–81); (*iii*) Wider technology coverage (1981–82 to 1990–91) when focus shifted from intensification of Green Revolution in best areas to its spread to new areas; (*iv*) Early liberalisation period (1991–92 to 1996–97) when relative prices became an additional focus, both because agriculture was expected to gain from reduced trade protection to industry and also with Minimum Support Prices (MSP) used for active growth promotion rather than just passive price support. The other three periods in the table are subsequent Plan periods: (*v*) Ninth Plan (1997–98 to 2001–02); (*vi*) Tenth Plan (2002–03 to 2006–07) and (*vii*) Eleventh Plan (2007–08 to 2011–12). For each of these periods, the average of annual growth rates is presented for each variable chosen.

12.11. As noted above, growth of agricultural GDP at 3.3 per cent was short of the 4 per cent target for

TABLE 12.4
Growth of Output, Inputs and Productivity

(period averages of annual growth rates)

	Pre-Green Revolution	Green Revolution	Wider Coverage	Early Liberalisation	Ninth Plan	Tenth Plan	Eleventh Plan
	1951/52 to 1967/68	1968/69 to 1980/81	1981/82 to 1990/91	1991/92 to 1996/97	1997/98 to 2001/02	2002/03 to 2006/07	2007/08 to 2011/12
I. Value of Output (2004–05 prices)							
Cereals	4.2	3.4	3.5	2.4	1.5	1.0	3.0
Pulses	3.0	0.7	3.4	0.8	0.3	1.8	4.2
Oilseeds	3.2	1.8	7.4	4.4	−2.5	7.4	4.5
Sugars	3.3	4.1	4.2	2.4	9.4	1.7	2.2
Fibres	4.4	2.5	5.3	6.5	−5.6	15.1	10.7
Non-horticulture crops	3.2	2.7	3.0	2.1	1.7	2.1	2.8
Horticulture	2.6	4.2	3.1	5.7	3.8	2.6	4.7
All Crops	3.0	3.0	3.0	3.1	2.3	2.1	3.4
Livestock	1.0	3.3	4.8	4.0	3.6	3.6	4.8
Crops and Livestock	2.5	3.0	3.3	3.3	2.6	2.5	3.8
Fishing	4.7	3.1	5.7	7.1	2.7	3.3	3.6
Forestry	1.7	−0.2	0.3	0.3	2.7	1.3	2.3
Agriculture and allied	2.3	2.4	3.0	3.1	2.6	2.4	3.6
II. Value of Intermediate Inputs (2004–05 prices)							
Seed	1.5	1.1	2.3	1.6	−0.6	1.4	4.1
Feed of livestock	1.9	4.0	0.1	0.9	3.9	0.7	3.3
Organic manure	0.0	1.3	0.7	0.5	1.6	2.9	3.3
Fertilisers and pesticides	18.2	9.3	8.7	2.0	3.9	4.8	6.7
Diesel oil	26.0	13.1	8.7	4.3	5.1	5.1	5.8
Electricity	18.5	15.2	12.9	14.4	−4.1	2.6	8.0
All inputs crops and livestock	2.4	4.5	2.2	1.9	3.0	2.5	4.4
Inputs for fishing	4.6	3.3	5.4	6.5	2.7	1.5	3.5
Inputs for forestry	1.7	−0.2	0.1	0.3	2.6	1.3	2.3
All inputs Agriculture and allied	2.3	3.9	2.1	1.9	3.0	2.4	4.3
III. Gross Value Added (2004–05 prices)							
Crops and Livestock	2.7	2.7	3.7	3.7	2.5	2.5	3.5
Fishing	4.7	3.0	5.8	7.2	2.7	3.6	3.7
Forestry	1.7	−0.2	0.4	0.3	2.8	1.3	2.3
Agriculture and allied	2.5	2.4	3.5	3.7	2.5	2.4	3.3
IV. Factor Inputs into Agriculture							
Land (Gross cropped area)	1.3	0.4	0.8	0.3	−0.1	0.6	0.3
Labour	1.8	1.1	0.5	2.3	0.3	0.5	−1.5
Net Fixed Capital Stock	2.3	3.6	2.8	3.1	3.4	4.7	6.0
Of which: Public			3.9	2.0	1.4	2.3	3.6
Private			1.4	4.3	5.1	6.6	7.5
V. Partial Factor Productivities (2004–05 prices)							
Land productivity	1.2	2.0	2.7	3.3	2.6	1.8	3.1
Labour productivity	0.7	1.4	3.0	1.4	2.2	1.8	4.8
Capital productivity	0.2	−1.1	0.7	0.6	−0.9	−2.4	−2.7

Note: Cropped Area from Ministry of Agriculture, Land use statistics; Labour is agricultural employment from Census till 1971 and NSSO (weekly status) from 1972–73; all other data are from Central Statistical Office (CSO): National Accounts 2004–05 prices.

agricultural GDP but was faster than that in the Tenth or the Ninth Plan, though lower than the period from 1981–82 to 1996–97. The growth rates for individual crops shown in Table 12.4 are for gross value of output and not value added, but they present a valid basis for inter-period comparisons.

1. Growth of total value of output in agriculture proper (crops and livestock) during the Eleventh Plan averaged 3.8 per cent per year which was the highest among all seven periods considered.
2. Total non-horticulture crop output grew marginally faster than target (2.8 per cent against 2.7 per cent target) mainly because of foodgrains (3.1 per cent actual against 2.3 per cent target), oilseeds (4.5 per cent against 4 per cent) and fibres (10.7 per cent against 5 per cent).
3. Horticulture at 4.7 per cent was only marginally short of the 5 per cent target.
4. Growth of output from livestock (4.8 per cent) was again highest amongst all the periods considered but this performance, and even more, so for fishing (3.6 per cent), fell short of the ambitious 6 per cent target set for these two sub-sectors.
5. Growth of forestry was expectedly slower, pulling down the growth of total value of output in agriculture and allied to 3.6 per cent, but this too was the highest among all the seven periods considered.

12.12. Growth in intermediate inputs has accelerated steadily reaching 4.3 per cent per annum during the Eleventh Plan, which was much higher than growth of output and over twice the growth rate of intermediate input use during 1981–97. The more rapid growth in input use explains why despite the faster growth of the gross value of output during the Eleventh Plan at 3.6 per cent than in the period 1981–82 to 1996–97 (about 3.0 per cent), GDP in agriculture (which is a value added concept) grew more slowly. In other words, agricultural growth became more input intensive in the Eleventh Plan. This suggests the need to re-look policies relating to inputs, especially fertiliser and power.

12.13. Policies towards input use need to distinguish between traditional inputs such as seed, feed and organic manure and modern inputs such as chemical fertiliser, pesticides and farm power. With low seed replacement, underfed farm animals and soils short of organic carbon, projections by working groups for the Twelfth Plan suggest that past growth of these traditional inputs should be improved upon. However, these working groups also project lower growth of 'modern' inputs than observed during the Eleventh Plan. For example, 2016–17 requirements of chemical fertiliser and farm power are placed at levels that imply annual growth for both fertilisers and 'modern' energy at about 4.5 per cent. These exceed corresponding the Eleventh Plan projections but are much less than the Eleventh Plan actual. Reduced fertiliser and fuel subsidies would be consistent with the desired moderation in trend of these inputs. Restraint is also needed on pesticides use which rose sharply in the Eleventh Plan after years of being subdued.

12.14. In parallel with high growth of intermediate inputs, there was acceleration in growth of the net capital stock in agriculture and allied sectors during the Eleventh Plan. As shown in Table 12.4 (item IV), Net Fixed Capital Stock in agriculture expanded at 6.0 per cent per year, much faster than in the previous two Plans. The public component of capital stock increased by 3.6 per cent while the private component increased at 7.5 per cent per year, both showing acceleration compared to the previous two Plans. However, public investment in agriculture, which was stepped up very substantially in the last three years of the Tenth Plan, stagnated in the Eleventh Plan (Table 12.5). This was mainly because of a large shortfall in planned investment in irrigation. As a result a key part of the Eleventh Plan strategy to achieve 4 per cent agricultural growth which was to increase public investment in agriculture to 4 per cent of agricultural GDP and thereby achieve growth of public sector capital stock in agriculture at least equal to the required 4 per cent growth of total capital stock has not fructified. Clearly, to attain 4 per cent agricultural growth in the Twelfth Plan will require firmer commitment to ensure realisation of this unattained the Eleventh Plan objective.

12.15. Private investment in agriculture has accelerated over the past three Plans. Private investment

TABLE 12.5
Gross Capital Formation (GCF) in Agriculture, Forestry and Fishing (2004–05 prices)

Year	GDP from Agriculture and Allied 2004–05 Prices	GCF in Agriculture and Allied at 2004–05 Prices			GCF in Agriculture as Per Cent of GDP from Agriculture		
		Public Sector	Private Sector	Total	Public Sector	Private Sector	Total
1	2	3	4	5	6	7	8
Tenth Plan							
2002–03	5,17,559	10,299	63,215	73,514	2.0	12.2	14.2
2003–04	5,64,391	12,683	57,238	69,921	2.3	10.1	12.4
2004–05	5,65,426	16,187	59,909	76,096	2.9	10.6	13.4
2005–06	5,94,487	19,940	66,664	86,604	3.5	11.2	14.6
2006–07	6,19,190	22,987	69,070	92,057	3.7	11.2	14.9
Eleventh Plan							
2007–08	6,55,080	23,257	82,484	1,05,741	3.6	12.6	16.1
2008–09	6,55,689	20,572	1,06,555	1,27,127	3.1	16.3	19.4
2009–10	6,62,509	22,719	1,08,420	1,31,139	3.4	16.4	19.8
2010–11	7,09,103	21,500	1,20,754	1,42,254	3.0	17.0	20.1

Source: Central Statistical Office National Accounts Division.

averaged 15.6 per cent of agricultural GDP in the first four years of the Eleventh Plan as against expected 12 per cent. The main driver of this was a large relative price shift in favour of agriculture, showing that farmers respond to price incentives. If calculated in current price terms rather than constant, private investment averaged 13 per cent of agricultural GDP—only slightly higher than expected. Nonetheless, total capital stock in agriculture grew more than expected. While private investment in irrigation and water-saving devices did increase, the largest increase was in labour-saving mechanisation. This was a natural response to growing labour scarcity which is reflected in rising wages.

12.16. Table 12.4 also shows growth rates of the two other factors of production in agriculture: land and labour. Not unexpectedly, while capital stock has grown quite rapidly throughout, the other two factors have not. As far as labour is concerned, the measure shown is employment in agriculture by usual status estimates of the National Sample Survey (NSS), which is available almost annually since 1987–88 but requires interpolation for earlier years. Combined with Census data, these show continuous increase of agricultural employment till 1994, although at varying rates of growth and at a particularly sharp rise in early 1990s when there was slow-down in rural non-agricultural employment. Agricultural employment fluctuated in the next decade, but has clearly declined after 2004–05. NSS employment data for 2007–08 and 2009–10 show clear evidence of an accelerated shift of rural labourers to non-agricultural work, which in itself is not an undesirable development. For land, the measure shown is gross cropped area which, despite the loss of nearly 3 million hectares of arable land to non-agricultural uses since 1990–91, has increased in all periods excepting a slight dip in the Ninth Plan. This is because cropping intensity has increased almost continuously. However, cropped area growth which averaged 0.9 per cent per annum till 1990–91 has averaged only 0.2 per cent subsequently.

12.17. Table 12.4 also shows growth rates of partial productivity of land, labour and capital taking GDP agriculture and allied as numerator. Labour productivity growth has historically been low, averaging 2 per cent per annum or less except during 1981–90 when it reached 3 per cent. Labour productivity

FIGURE 12.2: All India Average Real Daily Wage Rate at 2011–12 Prices (₹ Per Day)

jumped to nearly 5 per cent during the Eleventh Plan. The accelerated shift of rural labour to non-agriculture caused real wages to rise at about 5 per cent annually between 2004–05 and 2009–10, according to the NSS, and latest reports of the Commission of Agricultural Costs and Prices (CACP) suggest even faster growth of real wages in the last three years of the Eleventh Plan at almost 8 per cent per year. The trend in real wages in 2011–12 prices, as estimated by CACP, is shown in Figure 12.2.

12.18. Labour saving mechanisation, a significant contributor to the sharp increase of private investment in the Eleventh Plan period, was a natural response to tighter labour markets and rising wages. But, while mechanisation helped farmers to cope with labour scarcity, it exacerbated a decline in capital productivity. Private capital stock in agriculture has increased twice as fast as agricultural GDP since the Ninth Plan and, although mitigated by terms of trade gains and a debt write-off, continued investment with declining capital productivity may not be sustainable.

12.19. While greater private investment in farming is desirable where it reflects both an ability to invest and a desire to increase farm productivity, the same phenomenon can become a source of distress if farmers keep investing to cope with shrinking natural resources, more frequent adverse weather and less assured labour supply, and do not get adequate returns for this investment. The Eleventh Plan had tried to address this in two ways: first, increase public investment to lessen the private burden and add economies of scale; and second, rework architecture of the Plan spending on agriculture to make it more decentralised and flexible but also more coordinated locally to improve total productivity of private resources by better service delivery in all areas from extension to input supply and marketing. However, as noted earlier, public investment did not increase. And, although combined Plan expenditure of Centre and States in agriculture did increase from 1.9 per cent of agricultural GDP in the Tenth Plan to 2.9 per cent in the Eleventh, this was relatively small and left research, education and extension under-funded, leaving much to be desired in the quality of service delivery.

12.20. Nonetheless, growth of land productivity did increase significantly (Tables 12.4 and 12.6). Having climbed from about 1 per cent per annum before Green Revolution to over 3 per cent during 1991–97, land productivity growth had decelerated to below 2 per cent. This rebounded to over 3 per cent during the Eleventh Plan.

12.21. Total factor productivity (TFP) improved during the Eleventh Plan. Individual factor productivity data in Table 12.4, weighted by a range of factor shares suggest that TFP growth during the Eleventh Plan was back to around 1980s level. For example, applying factor shares of 30 per cent land, 40 per cent labour and 30 per cent capital give the following averages of annual TFP growth: 0.7 per cent in pre-Green Revolution period, 0.8 per cent during Green Revolution period, 2.2 per cent during the wider coverage period, 1.8 per cent during early liberalisation, 1.4 per cent during the Ninth Plan, 0.6 per cent during the Tenth Plan and 2.0 per cent in the Eleventh Plan. Although these estimates must be treated as tentative since data on factor shares is not robust, it does suggest that the deceleration of TFP in agriculture observed in the previous two Plans, which had caused widespread apprehension, may have been reversed in the Eleventh Plan. In other words, the Eleventh Plan architecture, with the Rashtriya Krishi Vikas Yojana (RKVY) as core, appears to have delivered despite adverse weather, a public investment shortfall and implementation gaps. The strategy of spreading known technology wider had paid.

SUB-SECTOR-WISE PERFORMANCE AND ISSUES

Crop Sector

12.22. In addition to above, two indicators worth highlighting in the crop sector are the pace and pattern of crop area diversification and trends in yields/hectare of important individual crops. There has been gradual but sustained shift in cropping pattern away from coarse cereals and pulses towards other crops over the last four decades. Area under coarse cereals had declined by 18 million hectares and that under pulses by nearly 2 million hectares from earlier peaks to end of the Tenth Plan. During the Eleventh Plan, there was further decline of 2 million hectares in area under coarse cereals but area under pulses reversed earlier decline to reach a new peak in 2010–11. Noting, that technology and price policy had neglected pulses earlier despite their importance as source of protein, special attention was given to pulses in both the National Food Security Mission (NFSM) and RKVY, the two major schemes launched during the Eleventh Plan. Cotton gained most area, followed by fruits and vegetables, with rice area steady, an increase in wheat area and decline in area under oilseeds and sugarcane.

12.23. Although area under coarse cereals and oilseeds declined during the Eleventh Plan, both these crop groups averaged over 4 per cent output growth. This was because growth of yields per hectare accelerated across almost all crop groups, especially those mainly rain-fed (Table 12.6). Not only did coarse cereals and oilseeds yields increase faster during the

TABLE 12.6
Average Annual Growth Rates in Yields Per Hectare

	Pre-Green Revolution	Green Revolution	Wider Coverage	Early Liberalisation	Ninth Plan	Tenth Plan	Eleventh Plan
	1951/52 to 1967/68	1968/69 to 1980/81	1981/82 to 1990/91	1991/92 to 1996/97	1997/98 to 2001/02	2002/03 to 2006/07	2007/08 to 2011/12
Wheat	3.7	3.3	3.6	2.8	0.7	−0.3	3.0
Rice	3.2	2.7	3.0	1.4	2.1	1.2	2.2
Jowar	3.4	2.9	3.2	1.3	0.2	2.1	3.1
Bajra	2.6	6.3	8.8	6.2	4.9	7.3	8.4
Maize	4.8	1.7	4.1	2.6	3.1	−0.2	6.5
Coarse cereals	2.6	1.5	3.1	4.3	1.3	1.7	7.3
Pulses	2.3	−0.2	2.3	1.9	−0.3	0.6	2.7
Oilseeds	1.3	0.8	4.8	3.3	0.4	3.5	5.4
Cotton	3.0	2.6	5.3	3.1	−6.2	19.4	3.9
Sugarcane	1.6	3.1	1.3	0.4	0.3	0.7	0.5

Note: Data is up to fourth advance estimate for 2011–12, Ministry of Agriculture.

Eleventh Plan than in any of the earlier periods, so did pulses yields. Apart from hybrids in case of maize, and to less extent in bajra, these yield increases came mainly from better seed quality, higher seed replacement and better practice rather than from new crop technology or more irrigation.

12.24. Yield growth of cotton, another largely rainfed crop, was also respectable although it was down sharply from a spectacular performance during the Tenth Plan following adoption of Bt hybrids. With more than 90 per cent of cotton area now under Bt hybrids, and cotton yields more than doubling over the last decade, there is no doubt either about general farmer acceptance or its being a clear case of technological transformation unlike other rain-fed crops. But disagreements continue about the extent to which Bt contributed to this yield increase and on wisdom of India's total dependence on Bt hybrids rather than the Bt varieties used in the rest of the world. There are also legitimate complaints of non-availability of non-Bt seeds, for example in Vidharbha. Genetically modified organisms (GMOs) therefore remain controversial, as was evident in case of Bt Brinjal. Nonetheless, since significant breakthroughs in production technologies are required to cope with increasing stress, particularly for rain-fed crops, it is necessary to remain abreast with latest advances in biotechnology. It is, therefore, time to put in place scientifically impeccable operational protocols and a regulatory mechanism to permit GMOs when they meet rigorous tests that can outweigh misgivings, while simultaneously noting that many feasible advances in biotechnology do not in fact involve GMOs.

12.25. Moreover, the Eleventh Plan experience is that continuous less-visible efforts by farmers to adapt and improve can be made effective. The NFSM, which aimed to reduce gaps between potential and actual yields, was designed to aid farmers in their own efforts by demonstrating and supporting a wide range of interventions. This seems to have worked. For example, growth in wheat yields nationally was negligible during the Ninth and the Tenth Plans but increased to 3 per cent in the Eleventh Plan. Even in Punjab, where it was believed that wheat yields had reached a plateau below 4.5 tonnes per hectare, yields increased steadily during the Eleventh Plan to reach 4.9 tonnes, accompanied by wider use of conservation practices such as laser levelling, zero tillage and raised beds. Rice yield growth was also higher in the Eleventh Plan than in any period after 1991, with Assam, Bihar, Chhattisgarh, East Uttar Pradesh and West Bengal contributing 80 per cent of this, again with growing awareness of conservation practices. For example, many States are now using RKVY to mainstream the System of Rice Intensification (SRI) that was not officially accepted till 2004 and was only small part of NFSM.

Livestock and Fishery

12.26. Livestock contributes 25 per cent of gross value added in the agriculture sector and provides self-employment to about 21 million people. Rapid growth of this sector can be even more egalitarian and inclusive than growth of the crop sector because those engaged in it are mainly small holders and the landless. Growth of livestock output averaged 4.8 per cent per annum during the Eleventh Plan recovering from an average of 3.6 per cent in the Ninth and the Tenth Plans.

12.27. Growth, of dairying, which is the main constituent of livestock sector though slightly higher than the 4 per cent averaged since 1990, was short of demand. With over 75 per cent of cattle located in rain-fed areas, the major issue is access to feed, fodder and drinking water which is becoming increasingly scarce. The problems of the sector are compounded by growing numbers of unproductive male cattle. Developing a strong fodder base needs intensive effort and innovation in institutional aspects of pasture protection and management and usufruct sharing. There is little concerted effort in this area at present as it is too fragmented across various departments to be able to provide the technical inputs, institutional designs and adequate investments to make a meaningful impact. Richer farmers with access to groundwater irrigation can grow irrigated fodder and increase herd size. Poorer livestock owners, dependent mainly on commons and agriculture residues, end up underfeeding the animals. This problem raises questions about the present breeding strategy that focuses almost exclusively on induction of breeds that are high yielding, but are much less tolerant to adverse conditions in extensive livestock systems.

12.28. These issues, which also affect owners of small ruminants, poultry and even those involved in inland fishery, came to the fore during the Eleventh Plan following the drought of 2009. The consequent high inflation in feed and fodder, that also led to high inflation in prices of livestock products, revealed a need for much greater coordination not only between agencies responsible for livestock and those responsible for crops that sustain livestock, but also with other policies, for example, trade policies that influence feed and livestock product prices. RKVY provided a window which cut across departments to allow States to focus on fodder shortages and restored growth of livestock output much quicker than in earlier droughts. Nonetheless, underlying problems remain, as does so called protein inflation. The Twelfth Plan must address these problems by involving dairy cooperatives in breed and feed issues, revisit breeding strategies and make fodder development higher priority in both animal husbandry and crop programmes.

12.29. India produces about 65 billion eggs annually and production growth has accelerated from around 4 per cent per annum during the 1990s to over 5 per cent during the Tenth and the Eleventh Plan. This acceleration has been achieved despite new challenges such as periodic outbreaks of avian influenza and the biofuels effect on international prices of maize, the main poultry feed, which has now transmit into the domestic economy. One reason for this vitality has been the growth of a large and vibrant commercial poultry sector with adequate economies of scale and fairly good backward and forward linkages. Besides eggs, this commercial poultry sector also produces over 2 million tonnes of broiler meat which is an increasing part of total meat production of about 5 million tonnes. Meat, with production growth at over 5.5 per cent per annum during the Eleventh Plan, is the fastest growing segment in the livestock sector.

12.30. The performance of the fisheries sub-sector has been impressive on the whole, with growth more than 5 per cent per annum during the 1980s and 1990s, but growth in this sub-sector has been decelerating since mid-1990s. The main reason for this has been stagnation of marine fishery, a phenomenon which is expected to continue. The major growth in fisheries in recent years has come from the inland fisheries, with particularly rapid development of brackish water aquaculture. This has been linked to prawn cultivation for export, although there is also strongly growing domestic demand for fresh water fish. Fish prices more than doubled during the Eleventh Plan, a higher inflation than either crops or any other livestock segment, despite a small acceleration in production growth compared to the Tenth Plan. A problem in this sector is that although a National Fisheries Development Board was set up, responsibilities are still not clearly defined between this and the Department of Animal Husbandry, Dairying and Fisheries. This has in particular meant an inability to realise the vast potential of inland fresh water fishery. Fish production can be enhanced 2 to 4 times in rain-fed water bodies, whether irrigation reservoirs, natural wetlands or ponds and tanks created by watershed development or Mahatma Gandhi National Rural Employment Guarantee Scheme (MGNREGS). If fully harnessed, these can secure over 6 per cent fishery growth in the Twelfth Plan.

EMERGING IMBALANCES

12.31. Although the discussion so far suggests that agricultural performance did improve during the Eleventh Plan, experience of the Eleventh Plan also points to emerging imbalances in agriculture which call for a long-term strategic reorientation.

Subsidies vs Public Investment

12.32. The Eleventh Plan document had highlighted that public investment in agriculture as per cent of agricultural GDP had halved between the 1980s and in the end of the Ninth Plan while, simultaneously, budgetary subsidies to agriculture had doubled as proportion of agricultural GDP. The tendency for subsidies to increase much faster than public investment was checked to some extent during the Tenth Plan, but it reappeared again during the Eleventh Plan (Table 12.7). Budgetary subsidies to agriculture (excluding food subsidy, which should be treated as a consumer subsidy) increased from an average of 4.1 per cent of agricultural GDP during the Tenth Plan to average 8.2 per cent in the first four years of the Eleventh Plan. Actual subsidies to agriculture were higher in both periods since CSO books budgeted subsidy on domestic urea manufacture entirely to industry and because part of the power subsidy received by agriculture is not budgeted but borne by utilities. Compared to these numbers, public investment in agriculture averaged only about 3 per cent of agricultural GDP during both Plan periods.

12.33. The imbalance between subsidy expenditure and expenditure on public investment raises the issue whether a shift away from subsidies and towards greater public investment would not be beneficial. The usual argument for reducing subsidies is that it will improve the fiscal deficit, but that is not the relevant point in this context, there is a need to shift from subsidies to public investment aimed at increasing land productivity on the grounds that this would produce better agricultural outcomes and would also be more inclusive. This is particularly important in the context of strategies for combating the effect of climate change where public investment in conservation and management of water resources will be crucial.

12.34. There are also other uses of resources in agriculture which could be promoted if agricultural subsidies are restrained. The Eleventh Plan document had pointed to trade-offs that subsidies might have with other non-Plan revenue expenditures, particularly staffing of essential farm support systems such as extension. Moreover, capacity and skill shortages have made upgrading agricultural universities an urgent need. The Eleventh Plan had aimed to increase spending on agricultural education and research from 0.6 to 1 per cent of agricultural GDP, but this remains less than 0.7 per cent—a large gap in a very important area that is miniscule in relation to subsidies.

TABLE 12.7
Public Sector Capital Formation and Subsidies to Agriculture (Centre and States)

(in ₹ crore and as per cent to GDP from agriculture and allied at current prices)

	Public GCF Agriculture and Allied		Budgetary Subsidies (CSO)		Food Subsidy		Total Fertiliser Subsidy		Subsidy on Indigenous Urea		All other Agriculture Subsidies	
Tenth Plan												
2002–03	9,563	2.0	43,597	9.0	24,176	5.0	11,015	2.3	7,790	1.6	16,196	3.3
2003–04	12,218	2.2	43,765	8.0	25,181	4.6	11,847	2.2	8,521	1.6	15,258	2.8
2004–05	16,187	2.9	47,655	8.4	25,798	4.6	15,879	2.8	10,243	1.8	16,221	2.9
2005–06	20,739	3.3	51,065	8.0	23,077	3.6	18,460	2.9	10,653	1.7	20,181	3.2
2006–07	25,606	3.5	59,510	8.2	24,014	3.3	26,222	3.6	12,650	1.7	21,924	3.0
Eleventh Plan												
2007–08	27,638	3.3	85,698	10.2	31,328	3.7	32,490	3.9	12,950	1.5	34,830	4.2
2008–09	26,692	2.8	1,56,823	16.6	43,751	4.6	76,603	8.1	17,969	1.9	54,438	5.8
2009–10	33,237	3.1	1,39,248	12.9	58,443	5.4	61,264	5.7	17,580	1.6	37,121	3.4
2010–11	34,548	2.7	1,50,170	11.8	63,844	5.0	62,301	4.9	15,081	1.2	39,106	3.1

Note: Public sector agricultural GCF and GDP are from CSO, National Accounts Division; budgetary subsidies, are also from CSO and are based on the economic and purpose classification of Government expenditure. Food and Fertiliser subsidies are from budget documents of the Central Government. 'All other agriculture subsidies' in the table are defined as budgetary subsidies (CSO) *plus* subsidy on indigenous urea *minus* food subsidy. This is because CSO classifies food subsidy as subsidy to agriculture but classifies subsidies on indigenous urea as subsidy to industry.

12.35. Another, very important reason why subsidies should be rationalised and restrained is that some of these subsidies could actually be doing harm. A case for subsidies exists if there is clear evidence that some input is being underused. Conversely, when with there is clear evidence of overuse of a subsidised input, there is a case to reduce or even eliminate the subsidy. Today, there is clear evidence of overuse. Data from all over India, especially from the prime green revolution areas, show that high use of chemical fertilisers and power is causing excessive mining of other soil nutrients and of groundwater, and that this is also leading to loss of quality of both soil and water. There is of course about 20–25 per cent of the country's arable area, located largely in North-East, East and Central India, where use of these inputs is so low that further intensification is desirable *per se*. But with nearly 90 per cent of fertilisers and 95 per cent of farm electricity currently being used outside this area, there can be no doubt that the present subsidies are actually encouraging practices that need to be discouraged.

12.36. Any proposal for reducing subsidies will be opposed by farmers on the grounds that output will fall if the subsidy cut reduces input use. This is true unless other investments are made simultaneously but such investments would indeed be facilitated by the resources released. Efforts were made in the Eleventh Plan to encourage more efficient practices without actually reducing the quantum of subsidy. For example, many States have undertaken separation of feeders so that electricity supply for agricultural use can be treated differently from that for rural non-agricultural use, and stricter scheduling imposed on the former while maintaining its lower price. Similarly, the Centre introduced a new scheme, the 'National Project on Management of Soil Health & Fertility' (NPMSH&F) to promote soil testing and issue of soil health cards to farmers, aimed particularly to spread awareness of micronutrient deficiencies resulting from excessive and unbalanced fertiliser use and to encourage balanced and judicious use of chemical fertilisers in conjunction with organic manures to maintain soil health and fertility. Moreover, in order to rationalise fertiliser subsidies, a nutrient-based subsidy (NBS) system was adopted to subsidise fertiliser products uniformly on basis of nutrient content, rather than set product-wise subsidies and separate maximum retail prices (MRPs) for each product. The objective was to reduce dead-weight of the fertiliser control order, set nutrient-specific subsidies that maintain desirable NPK balance, and evolve a subsidy protocol to encourage both development of new complex fertiliser products (including micronutrients) and more investment in the sector.

12.37. These initiatives have had some success in particular regions, but they do not as yet show up in national data in terms of higher additional output per unit additional use of these inputs. Moreover, NBS roll-out was seriously flawed since urea was kept out of its ambit. Urea prices remain controlled with only a 10 per cent rise at the time of adoption of the NBS in 2010. Meanwhile prices of decontrolled products doubled. The fixity of the urea price naturally worsened the NPK balance. Also, there has been very little product innovation. The subsidy bill has increased because resulting higher urea demand has been met entirely by imports at a unit subsidy twice that on domestic output, with little incentive to expand domestic capacity. The NBS as rolled out has been counterproductive because urea has not been included.

12.38. As may be seen from Table 12.6, the fertiliser subsidy is now much higher than all other subsidies to agriculture put together. While this is partly because fertiliser consumption rose over 30 per cent during the Eleventh Plan, the main reason is that world prices of all fertilisers and feedstock have doubled since 2006. With world fertiliser prices very sensitive to demand from India, which is not only the world's largest importer of fertilisers but also dependent almost entirely on imports for feedstock, improving efficiency of fertiliser use must be a the Twelfth Plan focus, almost as important as the issue of water use efficiency taken up in another chapter.

A New Road Map for Fertiliser Policy

12.39. A broad idea of what is necessary is evident from a few key indicators about the price of urea, the most important and politically sensitive fertiliser in India. At the world level, urea prices had averaged about 80 per cent of world wheat price during the 25 years before 2005. Since then, they have been fluctuating wildly at much higher levels and world urea prices are now over 150 per cent of world wheat price. In comparison, the price of urea in India has been declining continuously in relation to wheat MSP—from over 150 per cent during the 1980s, to 75 per cent in 2005, to only 41 per cent currently. While MSP of wheat for 2012 was 90 per cent of April–June average of world reference price of wheat, the MRP for urea was only 21 per cent of world reference price of urea.

12.40. Similarly, achieving the recommended national 4:2:1 NPK balance has proved elusive, again partly because urea (main source of N) is priced cheap relative to other fertilisers. World prices of DAP (main source of P) and MOP (main source of K) have fluctuated around 150 per cent and 100 per cent of world urea price over the last 30 years with no obvious trend. Relative prices of P to N were similar in India as globally, and K much cheaper, till decontrol in 1992 made these more expensive. The MRP for DAP and MOP in India were 194 per cent and 92 per cent of urea MRP before NBS, after which these have risen sharply again. Voluntary MRP for these are now 380 per cent and 230 per cent of urea MRP. Unless corrected soon, this large distortion in NPK prices is bound to reduce crop productivity.

12.41. One way out of the present conundrum is to bring urea into NBS and decontrol its prices. But this has not been possible so far and fertiliser decontrol both in 1992 and again in 2010 excluded urea with counterproductive effect. The reason for this is not just opposition to rise in urea prices, but also issues related to domestic urea industry. For example, subsidy provided to N for decontrolled fertilisers in the present NBS formula is based on the weighted average of subsidies on imported (around $320/tonne) and indigenous (around $160/tonne) urea. Three consequences would follow if urea prices were decontrolled fully with the subsidy on both imported and domestic urea equated to this (around $200/tonne). First, the domestic urea industry as a whole would get a windfall gain, and there may be consequent audit objections, since average unit subsidy on domestic urea is presently half that on imported. Second, notwithstanding this, that part of urea industry which uses feedstock other than gas would complain that they could become unviable since their present subsidy is more than the weighted subsidy. Third, since post-subsidy price of urea would tend to settle at import cost less the weighted subsidy; this would, with world urea prices now about $420/tonne, not only double from the present MRP of ₹5,310 per tonne but also be subject to the very large fluctuations in world urea prices that have been evident since 2005.

12.42. Although political opposition to decontrol is mainly on the third point above, the other points, which relate to differences in costs of production between different Indian producers and between Indian costs and world prices, have historically been at least equally important impediments to reform in this sector. This is unfortunate since India's fertiliser industry, although at disadvantage on feedstock, is largely efficient and can play a key role both in ensuring future nutrient supply and in the effort to increase fertiliser-use efficiency. However, with more than half of its revenues coming from subsidies and with Government also allocating scarce feedstock cheaply, industry effort currently is more to meet pre-set requirements and lobby, rather than to either secure long-term feedstock sources or develop new products and services for its customer base. This needs to change, and one way that this can be done is by reducing industry's dependence on Central subsidies, allowing greater space for it to set prices. The industry's present cost structure is such that no subsidy would be required on over 70 per cent of domestic urea production if urea MRP was allowed to rise to MSP for wheat or paddy. This level of urea MRP would reduce subsidy by about ₹15,000 crore annually and bring domestic NPK price parities in line with corresponding world parities while still leaving absolute fertiliser prices in India at about half international levels.

12.43. Of course, if this were all, urea prices would more than double with all its negative consequences. It would be politically unpopular even with the

5–10 per cent extra increase in MSP that would be required to compensate increases in cost of production. There would definitely be some loss of output as result of lower urea use and farmers unable to avail MSP increase would suffer loss of income. But these negatives can be neutralised and a win-win outcome ensured if the saving in subsidy is ploughed back to develop suitable location and crop-specific packages with adequate price incentives so that farmers do not suffer income loss and yet are encouraged to use appropriate combinations not only of NPK but also organic matter and required micronutrients.

12.44. However, for this, the architecture for public intervention will need to go well beyond NBS. Designing and contracting suitable packages will require stability in prices of basic NPK in relation to crop MSPs and also considerable location-specific input, both scientific and operational. The Centre will need to ensure some insulation of domestic prices of straight fertilisers from their large world price fluctuations and devolve many functions and most of the savings from reduced urea subsidy to States. States, in turn, will need to involve universities and local bodies to design suitable local packages of products and subsidies and then contract directly with industry.

Cereals Production and Build up of Stocks

12.45. Another major imbalance that emerged during the Eleventh Plan was between production and consumption of cereals, particularly rice and wheat on the one hand which led to rising stocks and rising consumption of edible oils and pulses which led to imports. Cereals production increased by 37 million tonnes (8 million tonnes coarse cereals, 11 million tonnes rice and 18 million tonnes wheat) between 2006–07 and 2011–12. This was the result of several factors, including the NFSM, an Eleventh Plan initiative to increase production, combined with remunerative prices and an expanding and effective procurement machinery in Madhya Pradesh for wheat and Chhattisgarh for paddy. However, although NFSM exceeded targets and per capita production has bounced back beyond earlier highs, much of the increase has been absorbed by increase in Government stocks. There are lessons that need to be learnt from this for the Twelfth Plan.

12.46. The rapid accretion of stocks between 2006–07 and 2008–09 was because cereals output responded quickly to policy, both NFSM and MSP, rising from 203 million tonnes in 2006–07 to 220 million tonnes, accompanied by even larger increase in procurement, from 36 million tonnes to 59 million tonnes, while off-take from public stocks rose only from 37 to 39 million tonnes. Consequently, market availability declined during this period, increasing grain prices, the dominant source of food inflation till 2009–10 (Table 12.8). Availability contracted further in 2009–10 because of drought which caused output to fall back to 203 million tonnes. Rice and wheat relative prices eased somewhat in the subsequent two years because output increased even more rapidly than during 2006–09 to reach 240 million tonnes in 2011–12 and because this time rise in procurement (to nearly 73 million tonnes) was less than output and off-take increase (to 56 million tonne) was relatively much more. Nonetheless, procurement exceeded off-take throughout the Eleventh Plan, even during 2009 drought, and present stocks are clearly too high. Costing about ₹5 per kg per year to store, these are tying up huge resources that could have been put to better use.

12.47. One important point to emerge is that although food inflation is usually ascribed to production shortfalls, policy decisions on MSP and on pricing and quantum of PDS and open market sales can be even more important. This is of course true of rice and wheat prices that are directly affected by such policies, but there are indirect effects as well. For example, milk, eggs, fish and meat had almost no effect on food inflation from 2004–05 till 2008–09, but have contributed most to food inflation subsequently (Table 12.8). As discussed earlier, much of this was due to feed and fodder shortages that the 2009 drought exacerbated. But the high build-up of rice and wheat stocks may in this context have contributed additionally. Substitution effects from lower availability of rice and wheat appear to have pushed up real prices of coarse grain to levels that compare with and most likely influenced inflation in livestock products. To maintain rapid agricultural growth, it will be necessary to continuously assess both MSP and trade policy in light of domestic production

TABLE 12.8
Real Prices of Agricultural Produce

(WPI commodity/WPI all commodities, 2004–05 base)

	2004–05	2005–06	2006–07	2007–08	2008–09	2009–10	2010–11	2011–12
Rice	100	101	99	105	112	121	117	110
Wheat	100	101	112	115	117	127	120	108
Coarse Cereals	100	107	110	115	113	123	122	136
Pulses	100	108	134	124	124	146	137	129
Vegetables	100	109	103	118	113	124	128	115
Fruits	100	99	99	98	102	104	114	119
Milk	100	97	98	98	98	112	123	124
Eggs, Fish and Meat	100	102	101	100	99	116	133	137
Oilseeds	100	86	85	97	104	103	99	102
Sugarcane	100	96	91	87	80	81	109	107
Fibres	100	92	91	96	109	107	138	140
All Agriculture	100	99	101	104	106	115	123	122

Note: All agriculture comprises food and non-food primary articles.

trends, paying attention to such wider linkages, so as to minimise undue production imbalance and the inflationary pressures resulting from these.

12.48. Another important and related issue is the likely future demand for food. The Twelfth Plan Working Group on Crop Husbandry, Demand and Supply Projections, Agricultural Inputs and Agricultural Statistics has made projections for foodgrains and other food items by the terminal year of the Twelfth Plan, that is, 2016–17 (Table 12.9) which would suggest that present levels of cereals production already exceed likely demand at the end of the Twelfth Plan. These projections are based on actual past patterns of observed demand and the fact that cereals consumption per capita has declined since at least mid-1990s. However, it is also the case that India has very high levels of malnutrition and, although there are many reasons for this, deficiencies in calorie intake remain one of the most important. With cereals supplying over 50 per cent of total calorie intake even now, falling cereals consumption is the main reason why per capita calorie intake has not increased despite rising incomes. It is not just that the share of cereals in total food expenditure is falling; even poor people are reducing the share of income spent on all foods in order to meet other non-food needs. In such a situation, where there is a disjunction between such a basic element of human development as nutrition and other demands in an increasingly consumerist society, there is need to ensure that minimum nutrition requirements are actually met. This is the goal of the proposed National Food Security Act (NFSA) under which a majority of the population will be entitled to some very cheap cereals. This is likely to increase cereals demand from those projected in Table 12.9, but nonetheless cereals demand is unlikely to rise much faster than population.

12.49. This means that agricultural production must diversify during Twelfth Plan so as to satisfy both tastes and nutrition. In particular, MSP policy should be more restrained for rice and wheat and made more effective in case of pulses and oilseeds where India is a net importer. Although MSP for pulses and oilseeds have been increased substantially in recent years, farmers are still not encouraged enough to put in the effort and resources required to substitute for current imports of these commodities. This is primarily because procurement efforts in these commodities, which are currently not part of Public Distribution, simply do not offer farmers the certainty that they have from procurement effort in rice and wheat.

TABLE 12.9
Demand and Supply of Food Commodities during the Twelfth Plan

(in million tonnes)

Crop/Group of Crops	Projected Demand (million tonnes)		Projected Supply (million tonnes)	Actual Production (million tonnes)	
	2016–17	2020–21	2016–17	2006–07	2011–12
Rice	110	117	98–106	93	104*
Wheat	89	98	93–104	76	94*
Maize	19	22		15	22*
Coarse Cereals	36	38	42–48	34	42*
Cereals	235	253	240–251	203	240*
Pulses	22	25	18–21	14	17*
Foodgrains	257	277	258–272	217	257*
Oilseeds/Edible oils	59	71	33–41	24	30*
Sugarcane/Sugar	279	312	365–411	355	358*
Vegetables	161	189		116	147**
Fruits	97	124		59	75**
Milk	141	173		103	122**
Fish	11	14		6.9	8.3**
Meat, other than poultry	3.7	5.0		2.3	2.7**
Poultry Meat	3.3	4.3			2.2@

Source: Twelfth Plan Working Group on Crop Husbandry, Demand and Supply Projections, Agricultural Inputs and Agricultural Statistics; *4th advance estimate for 2011–12; **Production for the year 2010–11; @Production 2010–11 for only commercial poultry meat.

Public Distribution System

12.50. The Eleventh Plan period witnessed significant improvements in administration of the Targeted Public Distribution System (TPDS). A nine-point action plan has been useful in elimination of large number of ghost ration cards, reduction in leakages and greater transparency in the conduct of TPDS operations. While carrying forward these initiatives with greater vigour, there is a need for rejuvenated approach towards the TPDS during the Twelfth Plan period. The foremost amongst those is the move towards facilitating rights-based approach under TPDS by enacting the National Food Security Bill (NFSB). The Bill has been introduced in the Parliament and is expected to provide food and nutritional security, in human life-cycle approach, by ensuring access to adequate quantity of quality food at affordable prices to people to live a life with dignity. This would require strengthening of existing infrastructure and taking up new initiatives and schemes. Reforms in the TPDS would be crucial as it would bring about more efficiency in the system with enhanced transparency and accountability. Entitlements of foodgrains are expected to shift from per household basis to per capita basis. One of the important challenges for implementation of NFSB would be proper identification of beneficiaries which may be based on the ongoing Socio-economic and Caste Census. Another important initiative required during the Twelfth Plan is the end-to-end computerisation of the TPDS operations with the help of a comprehensive Plan scheme. This shouldnot only address current challenges but also facilitate proper tracking foodgrains and lifting by consumers using Aadhaar numbers or adopting innovative methods like smart cards.

12.51. The up-scaling of the TPDS for proper implementation of NFSA is an opportunity to expand PDS coverage to include coarse cereals, pulses and edible oils and thereby bring scale and certainty to their procurement. However, given that consumption and production patterns vary greatly from state to state, this is probably something that can be done better by the States themselves than by any Central agency. Nonetheless, as part of PDS reform, the Central Government could moot the idea not only of decentralised procurement but also the innovative methods of transferring food subsidy. One option could be that, while the Centre continues to bear responsibility for delivering adequate quantities of cereals to every State, these may be priced close to market and food subsidy transferred to the States as recommended by the High Level Committee on Long Term Grain policy in 2002. Alternatively, subsidy could be credited directly to the bank accounts of the beneficiaries or the FPS dealers using authentication mechanism of Aadhaar numbers. Other option could be to have a comprehensive electronic benefit transfer system whereby subsidy is loaded on to a smart card and consumers have a choice of commodities or fair price shops. These initiatives are expected to bring down leakages significantly as there would be little incentive left for intermediaries to divert the PDS foodgrains into the open market. While implementing these measures, it would be pertinent to address the issue of viability of FPS and improve their functioning. The Gross Budgetary Support for the Department of Food and Public Distribution is ₹1,523 crore for the Twelfth Five Year Plan.

Consumer Welfare and Protection

12.52. Consumer welfare has been one of the core concerns of the Government since the post-Independence period. Policies have been designed and legislations enacted to protect the interests of consumers and grant them the rights of choice, safety, information and redressal. For the Twelfth Plan period, it would be apposite to expedite formulation of a comprehensive National Consumer Policy in conformity with the UN guidelines on consumer protection. Secondly, there would be a need to revisit existing legislations administered by the Department of Consumer Affairs so as to bring the provisions in line with the changes in the economy, trade, business and consumer expectations. This, inter alia, includes amendments in Bureau of Indian Standards Act and Forward Contracts (Regulation) Act. There is also a need to conceptualise a National Policy for Quality Infrastructure covering standardisation, testing and legal metrology so as to provide the infrastructure for development of definitive standards, systems of legal metrology and conformity assessment. The commodity futures markets need to be strengthened to enable it to serve the dual purpose of price discovery and risk management. Besides, a structured system of information, counselling and mediation need to be put in place with emphasis on rural consumers. The data analysis and price monitoring also need to be more comprehensive and structured so as to make informed decisions on market intervention. The Gross Budgetary Support for the Department of Consumer Affairs is ₹1,260 crore for the Twelfth Five Year Plan.

MAJOR CHALLENGES AND PRIORITIES DURING THE TWELFTH PLAN

12.53. The main lesson from the performance in the Eleventh Plan is that while there has been a welcome turn-around from the deceleration that was evident in the decade to 2005, and while several indicators have shown marked improvement and potential to build upon, several policy imbalances exist that can prove to be major handicaps. There are also other formidable challenges, for example, a shrinking land base, dwindling water resources, the adverse impact of climate change, shortage of farm labour, and increasing costs and uncertainties associated with volatility in international markets. The Twelfth Plan will need to face these challenges boldly.

12.54. The key drivers of growth will remain:

1. viability of farm enterprise and returns to investment that depend on scale, market access, prices and risk;
2. availability and dissemination of appropriate technologies that depend on quality of research and extent of skill development;
3. Plan expenditure on agriculture and in infrastructure which together with policy must aim to improve functioning of markets and more efficient use of natural resources; and

4. governance in terms of institutions that make possible better delivery of services like credit, animal health and of quality inputs like seeds, fertilisers, pesticides and farm machinery.

12.55. In addition, certain regional imbalances must be clearly addressed. A national priority from view of both food security and sustainability is to fully extend Green Revolution to areas of low productivity in the eastern region where there is ample ground water, and thereby help reduce water stress elsewhere. Rain-fed areas continue to be at a disadvantage, and their development still requires some mindset changes.

FARM VIABILITY: SECURING ECONOMIES OF SCALE AND BETTER MARKET ACCESS AND RETURNS

12.56. Farm profitability is central to achieving rapid and inclusive agricultural growth. Improved agricultural prices (Table 12.8) were an important driver in success of the Eleventh Plan. But slower growth of demand in some major sub-sectors (Table 12.9), combined with higher input costs due to world price trends, could cause this driver to be more muted in Twelfth Plan unless offset by increase in productivity. The reports of the Commission on Agricultural Costs and Prices show low net farm revenue for many crops, particularly rain-fed. Diversification towards higher value crops and livestock remains the best way not only to improve farm incomes and accelerate growth, but also to reduce stress on natural resources which form farmers' production base. This needs better infrastructure and emphasis on integrated farming systems, combining crops and livestock, including small ruminants, for different location-specific endowments. This also requires innovative institutional and contractual arrangements so that smallholders have the requisite technology and market access.

(A) The Centrality of Smallholdings

12.57. Small farms typify Indian agriculture and this predominance continues to increase. Agriculture Census 2005–06 reported the average size of an operational holding at only 1.23 hectare, with farms less than 2 hectares comprising 83 per cent of all holdings and 41 per cent of area. No agricultural development Plan can be credible unless it is relevant to this vast majority of farmers. Also, 12 per cent of rural households are now female headed with even smaller holding, and the feminisation of agriculture poses special problem.

12.58. An important step that would help small and marginal farmers is to reform the tenancy laws. These were originally meant to help small and marginal farmers but now operate against them. Even limited legalisation of agricultural tenancy and freeing the land lease market with proper record of ownership and tenancy status will help such farmers. Some small farmers may lease out land to shift to other occupations, provided they were assured that they could resume the land if they wished. Some large farms may lease in land and even employ the small owner on his own farm to grow specific crops under supervision. Moreover, a stark reality of India's farm situation today is that while land hunger continues unabated amongst the poor and uneducated, especially female, educated young men in richer households are leaving agriculture. The rapid rise of wages for rural casual labour during the Eleventh Plan period has further increased the relative cost of cultivating with hired labour. Many large and absentee owners are leaving land under-cultivated which could be leased out if they were assured of retaining ownership.

12.59. The Eleventh Plan had set out in detail the key elements necessary to make land policy effective for equity and efficiency. These are:

1. Modernisation of land records must be both time-bound and comprehensive. Full digitisation of land records, including GIS maps, should be completed with required survey/settlement by end of the Twelfth Plan, during which pilots should also be initiated to enable movement towards a Torrens system in the Thirteenth Plan.
2. Although there is no strong case to change existing ceiling laws, there are several pending implementation issues that can and should be addressed as land records are modernised.
3. Land issues in tribal areas require urgent and special attention.

4. Although no major new redistribution of agricultural land is likely, it is possible to ensure that all rural households have at least homestead-cum-garden plots.
5. Tenancy should be legalised in a 'limited' manner. Prescribed rents, if any, should allow a band wide enough for rents to be contracted mutually over contract periods long enough to encourage investment by tenants while protecting ownership rights so that landowners have incentive to lease out land rather than keep this underutilised or fallow.
6. Small and marginal farmers, particularly women, lack adequate access to credit, extension, insurance and markets. While every effort should be made to strengthen delivery of public services in their favour, the intervention likely to be most potent is support to group action by farmers themselves. It was suggested that subsidies in Government schemes give preference to group activity.

12.60. Most of these issues, as well as the associated matter of consolidating fragmented holdings in course of survey/settlement, are in the State domain and progress is uneven. Ongoing efforts of Ministry of Rural Development (particularly, Department of Land Resources) and Ministry of Tribal Affairs also address some of these issues, although not necessarily related directly to agriculture. However, there was little progress during the Eleventh Plan on the suggestion to redesign schemes so that subsidies favour group activity among small and marginal farmers. In fact, a criticism of the Eleventh Plan schemes has been that these diluted earlier specific support for such farmers.

12.61. Almost all the Twelfth Plan working groups set up by the Agriculture Division of Planning Commission have strongly recommended that the Twelfth Plan should put special focus on building capacity that encourages group formation and collective effort by small, marginal and women farmers, rather than simply provide additional subsidy to individuals in these categories. Existing group activity takes many forms depending on purpose. From lower tiers of formal cooperative structures in credit, marketing, dairy and fishery, extending to self-help groups (SHGs), farmer clubs, joint liability groups (JLGs) and, more recently, to producer companies. For simplicity, these can all be termed Farmer Producer Organisations (FPOs).

12.62. The Twelfth Plan Working Group on Disadvantaged Farmers, including women has provided evidence-based assessment of the ground situation. New insecurities of tenure from urbanisation and industrialisation are impacting small farms which are efficient but lack adequate access. Its main recommendation is that a collective approach should be promoted in agriculture for small and women farmers at all points of the value chain. It cites many successful examples that stretch from the Gambhira farmer's collective in Gujarat, initiated in 1953 and still going strong, to several initiatives of women's group farming in Andhra Pradesh such as one initiated by Deccan Development Society in 1989 and another initiated by a UNDP-GoI project in 2001 and sustained since 2005 by the Andhra Pradesh Mahila Samakhya (APMSS). The most recent success story is the collective farming initiative launched in 2007 under Kudumbashree jointly by Kerala Government and NABARD. Success of these in increasing production and empowering women point to a need for States to experiment with (*i*) channelising NGO strength in mobilising people to encourage small holders to shift from an individual to a group-oriented approach; and (*ii*) facilitating land access by groups of disadvantaged farmers with appropriate arrangement for provision of inputs, including credit. Financing such experiments should be permissible under RKVY.

12.63. Since land access was the most difficult part in all the above efforts, the Working Group has suggested that, except distribution of homesteads to the homeless which should have the highest priority, future Government land distribution should be to groups of landless and women farmers rather than to individuals. This could take the form of long-term lease which would expire if the group broke down, for which it would be necessary to legalise tenancy at least for this purpose. Moreover, an innovative suggestion of both this Working Group and the

Working Group on Marketing is to set up Public Land Banks (PLB) at Panchayat level. Landowners could 'deposit' uncultivated land and receive regular payments from the PLB varying by period of deposit and rents actually obtained with the guarantee that this 'deposit' can be withdrawn with suitable notice. The PLB could then lease out to small and women farmers or their collectives. A form of 'limited' tenancy aimed at fuller agricultural use of available farm land and to slow down speculation in such land for future non-agricultural use, this idea excludes leasing to corporate entities. However, to set up PLBs will require some initial seed capital and a clear legal framework. If States provide the legal framework and the necessary guarantees, the seed capital could also be permissible under RKVY.

12.64. Access to finance, especially by small holders, is crucial for improved agricultural performance. Credit flow doubled in the Eleventh Plan but mainly by credit deepening, with little increase in farmer coverage and still leaving 60 per cent of farmers without institutional credit. There are several ways in which credit access can be widened. Primary Agricultural Co-operative Societies (PACS) still have the widest coverage and must be made more member-driven and less dependent on higher tiers. Joint Liability Groups (JLGs) are still the most appropriate mechanisms for farmers and livestock owners who have productive assets but cannot access credit because they have no land records, are located too far from banks or have last mile problems. The SHG-Bank Linkage programme is still the most appropriate financial mechanism to extend credit to marginal and dry land farmers as this allows better income smoothing since SHGs provide space for diversity in loan purposes and sizes, enabling financing of a variety of activities that such families select as part of livelihood strategies when income from agriculture is low.

12.65. Commercial banks have not supported JLGs or SHGs as much as they could have, preferring instead to comply with priority sector requirements by offering bulk finance through Non-Banking Financial Companies (NBFC) and Micro-Finance Institutions (MFI). However, NBFC–MFI lending is mainly individual and based on standard products imposing short repayment schedules which did not dovetail with cash flows from agriculture. This caused multiple borrowings, increased risk to borrowers and led to a backlash. The solution is to restore the principle of group decisions by borrowers both in the borrowing process and in use of borrowed resources. This need not exclude NBFC–MFI so long as shortcuts are avoided. For example, NABFINS, a NBFC promoted by NABARD, lends only to groups and uses a Business Correspondent (BC) Model that also provides working capital to second level institutions like cooperatives and producer companies which aggregate, add value and market commodities. The SHGs have a stake in these second level institutions which help expand their livelihood base.

12.66. Small and marginal farmers face problems not only with shrinking land assets and with credit; they have difficulty in accessing critical inputs for agriculture such as quality seeds and timely technical assistance. In this situation, FPOs offer a form of aggregation that leaves land titles with individual producers and uses the strength of collective planning for production, procurement and marketing to add value to members' produce through pooled resources of land and labour, shared storage space, transportation and marketing facilities. These also improve bargaining power of small farmers and, most importantly, reduce transactions costs of banks and buyers to deal them. Investing in such group efforts has strong externalities.

12.67. The Twelfth Plan Working Group on Agricultural Marketing, Infrastructure, Secondary Agriculture and Policy for Internal and External Trade has in fact suggested that an institutional development component, along lines of NABARD's farmer club scheme, be introduced in all Centrally sponsored schemes to specifically target FPO formation among small producers, especially tribals, *dalits* and women. It notes that a majority of FPOs that are likely to emerge as a result of such an intervention will remain focused on addressing issues of crop planning, technology infusion, input supply and primary marketing. But, with adequate support for business development, about one fourth to a third would seek to leverage presence further up the value chain, most likely at the lower end (for example, setting up pack houses, grading centres, small cold stores, drying or quick freezing plants). Larger FPOs, for example, existing cooperatives could provide this support and in fact could aim bigger, but issues may be different. For example, the National Dairy Development Board's SAFAL has had only limited success although the wide network and logistics of milk cooperatives make these obvious incubators for village-level aggregation of other perishable products. Therefore, the Twelfth Plan must try to mainstream support for FPO formation and capacity building using all credible agencies for the purpose: existing cooperatives, NABARD and the Small Farmers' Agribusiness Consortium (SFAC).

(B) Issues in Expanding Agricultural Marketing and Processing

12.68. A major problem facing cultivators is that they do not get remunerative prices because of uncertainties caused by inadequate market information, unnecessary controls, lack of physical infrastructure and price volatility—both domestic and global. In order to provide adequate incentives to farmers, the Twelfth Plan will have to focus on leveraging the required private investment and also policies that make markets more efficient and competitive.

12.69. Reforming the Agricultural Produce Marketing Committee (APMC) Acts should therefore have priority as emphasised in the Eleventh Plan and the Mid-term Appraisal. The introduction of the Model Act in 2003 was directed towards allowing private market yards, direct buying and selling, and also to promote and regulate contract farming in high-value agriculture with a view to boost private sector investment in developing new regularised markets, logistics and warehouse receipt systems, and in infrastructure (such as cold storage facilities). This is particularly relevant for the high-value segment that is currently hostage to high post-harvest losses and weak farm-firm linkages. While many States have moved towards adoption of the Model Act, actual progress has been limited. Often the permissions given are subject to unacceptable restrictions which make them ineffective. Vested interests in maintaining the existing *mandi* system intact are very strong. In view of the slow progress, the Ministry of Agriculture set up a Committee of State Ministers in-charge of agricultural marketing. The Committee submitted a 'First Report' in September 2011 which has been circulated to all States and UTs. The report calls for 'speedy reforms' of Agricultural Produce Market Committees (APMC) Act across different States along with 'time-bound development' of marketing infrastructure. Calling for a ten-year perspective plan to improve infrastructure of backward and forward linkages for agriculture production and marketing, the report has suggested that agricultural marketing be given access to priority sector lending. Thus, the process to secure necessary amendments in APMC Acts and thus create the enabling legal environment is still ongoing. The Twelfth Plan will need to fast-track modernisation of *mandi* infrastructure, with adequate provision of communication and transportation, and also empower small producers through their organisations and marketing extension.

12.70. Post-harvest losses, probably average 10 to 25 per cent, being particularly high in horticulture, livestock and fisheries. Very large investments are required in developing agricultural markets, grading and standardisation, quality certification, warehouses, cold storages and other post-harvest management of produce to address this problem. Such large investments are possible only with the participation of the private sector which, in turn, require freedom from controls on sales/purchase of agricultural produce, its movement, storage and processing. Many new initiatives were taken up during the Eleventh Plan, including both terminal markets under Public–Private Partnership (PPP) mode in the National Horticulture Mission (NHM) and a model of public sector investment combined with professional management by stakeholders as exemplified by NDDB's fruit and vegetable wholesale market at Bengaluru and APEDA's Modern Flower Auction Houses.

12.71. The Twelfth Plan Working Group on Horticulture and Plantations which studied the matter in detail has observed that participation by traders, wholesale buyers, exporters and processors has actually been very low in all these new initiatives because of reluctance to be subject to transparent operating procedures. It has come to the conclusion that the present model of Market Sector Reforms which is trying to create space for a new set of modern markets in coexistence with much less transparent procedures in APMC regulated markets is unlikely to result in any major private investment in modern marketing infrastructure. In its view, to break the barrier of reluctance to participate in business of modern markets it is necessary as part of marketing reforms to define and introduce a common Standard Operating Procedure (SOP) for all markets: both the new modern markets envisaged as well as existing regulated markets under APMC Acts. Therefore, it proposes that managements of existing regulated markets must be made to adopt the modern marketing model: that is, undertake the auction function themselves and all payments to sellers ensured by the Market Committee through a system of bank credit limits of the buyers. This would involve redefining the role of APMC management with introduction of SOP and an open policy of registering buyers; permitting setting up of private markets in APMC areas; removal of interstate barriers to allow an unified national market, either by using entry 42 of the union list or at least for sealed container cargo; and single point levy at first point of sale.

12.72. While this entire area of regulation of agricultural product markets is thus in some flux and movement is still slow, an important initiative in the Eleventh Plan involved setting up a Warehouse Regulatory and Development Authority (WRDA) to set standards and modernise warehousing. The aim is enlarged use of negotiable warehouse receipts that can be linked to e-trading, both spot and future, so that farmers have an alternative to *mandi*s. However, so far less than 300 warehouses have been registered and there is yet no effective coverage of perishable products. Cold storages have recently been brought under WRDA but minimum standards are yet to be set. This may be as difficult as meeting the requirement of cold storage additional capacity estimated at around 32 million tonnes over the next decade. Present cold storages are of inadequate quality, most domestic component manufacturers do not have certified performance ratings, BIS standards do not exist for many critical components of cold chain infrastructure and critical storage conditions prescribed internationally for cold chain structures have yet to be validated for many Indian agro-climatic conditions or cultivars.

12.73. Although India ranks second in world production of fruits and vegetables, only 6–7 per cent of this is processed, compared to 65 per cent in US and 23 per cent in China. A well-developed food processing industry is expected to increase farm-gate prices, reduce wastage, ensure value addition, promote crop diversification, generate employment opportunities and boost exports. Further, issues concerning food processing industry are dealt with in Chapter 9.

12.74. The private sector needs to invest much more in creation of warehousing capacity, cold storages and supply chains. In this context, the Planning Commission had also set up a Committee on Encouraging Investments in Supply Chains including provision for cold storages for more efficient distribution of farm produce, which submitted its report in May 2012. The Committee has indicated that with regard to foodgrains, the Department of Food and Public Distribution has initiated steps for creation of 17 million tonnes of additional storage capacity including 2 million tonnes in the form of silos. This additional capacity is expected to take care of public sector's warehousing requirement during the Twelfth Plan. The Committee has recommended to exempt perishables from the purview of APMC, provide freedom to farmers and make direct sales to aggregators and processors, introduce electronic auction platforms for all the *mandi*s where daily transaction is above ₹10 crore, and replace licensees of APMC markets with open registration backed by bank guarantees to ensure wider choice to growers and to prevent cartelisation by traders. The Committee has recommended encouraging large-scale private investments in the cold chain sector using PPP Model with Viability Gap Funding besides providing budgetary support and capitalising on schemes such as Rural Infrastructure Development Fund (RIDF). An Inter-Ministerial Group on Cold

Chain Infrastructure and Allied Sectors has been set up by the Government to facilitate implementation of these recommendations.

12.75. There is merit in planning part of such investment as infrastructure to reduce waste and enlarge markets rather than wait for corporate investment in processing or retail. The extent of wastage is not easily ascertainable and new research suggests that some of the older estimates were quite likely exaggerated, especially if quality loss leading to lower prices is not counted as waste. Also, the experience so far is that corporate entrants have not fared very well in the competition with incumbent traders since existing trading margins, although high, are in fact much less than, for example, in the USA. However, there is no doubt that modern storage and logistics do reduce waste. If such infrastructure also improves farm shares, social returns could exceed the private and justify subsidies. Subsidy rates, increased recently to 25–50 per cent, are now quite high and policy should be clear on whether the goal is just capacity targets or wider market access and improved marketing efficiency. If the latter, eligibility criteria need to be specified and also linked clearly with marketing reform. Social returns to subsidy will be more if access to both the infrastructure and to markets is more open. The real test is whether these can spawn and sustain enterprise in aggregation, grading and processing at the bottom, preferably by FPOs, but also by lead farmers and even by existing commission agents.

12.76. The recent decision to open up debate on FDI in retail must be seen in this context. With multi-brand retail already open to the domestic corporate sector, FDI in retail should not be viewed as an entirely new disruptive factor affecting traditional retail. It will only add depth and competition to the present situation. Deeper pockets and technology, and the compulsions to invest in supply chain development which is not there for domestic modern retail may accelerate investment in logistics, quicken consolidation of retail trade and create new proprietary supply chains. It must be emphasised that FDI alone will not resolve back-end issues related to modernising agricultural markets that have so far muted the domestic corporate effort and investment. FDI has an added potential to link farmers to wider markets by expanding exports. However, the Eleventh Plan had also noted the legitimate concern that if front-end investment outpaces backward linkage, the outcome could instead be more imports and lower farm prices. The introduction of FDI will increase, not lessen, the importance of priorities identified above: marketing reforms, aggregation at the bottom and public funding of stand-alone infrastructure.

12.77. With less than 40 per cent of farm produce presently consumed in urban areas and much less processed, use of public funds to improve market efficiency will have a positive effect on farm growth. There are benefits in coordinating this effort with other steps to encourage corporate investment in this area. For example, the NHM was designed based on a concept of adequately sized area clusters so that processors could plan capacities based on anticipated future fruit production that would in turn ensure markets for farmers when trees finally bore fruit. But processors have preferred to wait and watch while farmers, not sure of adequate market for any single crop, have usually chosen to diversify their production basket. Most clusters have therefore not developed in the manner intended. A larger thrust to modernise processing and retail will require bringing more synergy between corporate actors and farmers, particularly in infusion of technology and capital at the farm end.

12.78. The Ministry of Agriculture has proposed a RKVY window for Public–Private Partnership for Integrated Agricultural Development (PPPIAD) for States to facilitate 'large scale integrated projects led by private sector players with a view to aggregating farmers and integrating agricultural supply chains.' The idea is to leverage corporate interest and marketing solutions to part-finance mobilisation of expertise to form FPOs and infuse technology and capital to enhance farm production and value addition. This is in line with views of various working groups, and needs to be piloted. But since this will in effect be public subsidy to contract farming, it is necessary to be clear on what should and should not be subsidised. First, project selection should go beyond where contract farming would normally occur; that is, give priority to proposals involving FPOs composed mainly of small and marginal farmers in less accessible and rain-fed locations. Second, tangible assets that are property of the corporate partner cannot be subsidised by RKVY. Only stand-alone assets of farmers or their FPOs should be subsidised. Third, a transparent project selection mechanism will be required to rank proposals, for example, by assigning marks based on States' priorities to deliverables offered, with outcome indicators for subsequent monitoring. If this works, it might be a game changer, not only to form FPOs and widen farm-industry linkage but also to fast-track desirable changes in cropping patterns.

(C) Credit and Cooperatives

12.79. The Twelfth Plan Working Group on Institutional Finance, Cooperatives and Risk Management has projected the demand for credit during Twelfth Plan at between ₹31,24,624 crore and ₹42,08,454 crore, depending on the methodology used. At the higher end of these estimates, that is, assuming agriculture growth at 4 per cent and ICOR at 4.5, the size of the credit requirement in the Twelfth Plan period translates into about double the flow during the Eleventh Plan, that is, ₹8 lakh crore per year, as against the level of ₹4.68 lakh crore achieved during 2010–11.

12.80. This projected level of credit appears feasible in view of the Eleventh Plan achievement. As against credit flow of ₹2,29,401 crore in agriculture during 2006–07, the total institutional credit flow to agriculture in 2011–12 was ₹5,11,029 crore. But despite this very robust growth, many issues continue to confront agricultural credit, particularly in the area of financial inclusion necessary for ensuring inclusive growth. Agricultural credit continues to neglect certain sub-sectors, the flow of term lending is dwindling and there is inordinate increase in the share of indirect finance. Credit dispensation by institutions to small and marginal farmers has been disappointing, including by the Cooperative Credit Structure (CCS) which has traditionally catered to relatively smaller farmers.

12.81. On these issues, the working group has pointed to the need for more objective assessment of credit requirements for direct and indirect financing of agriculture and also to redefine the priority lending sectors. It has suggested updating of KCC databases with priority analysis of KCC percentage provided to the small and marginal farmers and more intensive use of ICT applications to track the flow of credit and transmission losses, with reference to such farmers.

12.82. Some ongoing and emerging changes appear to hold promise of triggering off better financial inclusion for banking activity:

1. The Core Banking Platform provides seamless connectivity which, with the telecom infrastructure, brings a new architecture to access financial services.
2. The BC model, together with mobile phones, can along with post offices provide significant last-mile connectivity.
3. Mandating payments (for example, of wages under the National Rural Employment Guarantee Act, pension dues and so on) through formal channels, including post offices, is helping to reach financial services to those so far not reached.
4. The enormous economies of scale generated by SHG Federations (each of 150–200 SHGs) is enabling banks to give larger loans for housing and health facilities for their members. A variety of insurance services are also being made available, including life, health, livestock and weather insurance.
5. The UID project of the GoI with biometric identity may facilitate easier opening of bank accounts, although this has yet to happen.

12.83. The financial health of the Long-term Cooperative Credit Structure (LTCCS) continues to deteriorate with accumulated losses of ₹5,275 crore by March 2010, resulting in erosion of 59 per cent in owned funds. A quick decision is warranted on the implementation of the revival package for the LTCCS too on the lines of the Short-term Cooperative Credit Structure (STCCS).

12.84. Notwithstanding, the relatively improved financial health of the STCCS following implementation of the revival package, its share in total institutional credit continues to show a declining trend. The package for STCCS was conditional to radical restructuring of coops into autonomous, democratic and self reliant institutions without intrusion of politics and bureaucracy. The States have not implemented these recommendations with full seriousness. Therefore, Cooperative Sector Reforms should continue to be insisted upon during the Twelfth Plan.

12.85. In the interest of strengthening of the ground level tier, there is also need for considering disciplined refinancing of PACS as stand-alone institutions, provided that these are member driven. PACS still have the widest coverage and the recent development of financing PACS through commercial banks needs to be widened, deepened and strengthened, especially in cases where higher tiers of the STCCS are weak and not in a position to fund them.

(D) Farm Income Variability: Managing World Price Volatility and Climate Risk

12.86. The Eleventh Plan document had noted that farmers are now subject to much greater risk than what Indian farmers have been used to in the past. The frequency and severity of risks in agriculture have increased on account of climate variability and this has been accompanied by much greater variability of world prices and their quicker transmission into the domestic economy. On price variability, it had recommended much greater co-ordination between MSP and trade policies and for putting in place a system whereby tariffs on imports and exports of farm products could be varied quickly in response to world price movements rather than having to take recourse to outright bans which hurt both farmers and trade. On climate variability, it had recommended going beyond current insurance measures and to put in place a tertiary mechanism for management and assessment through climate forecasting and mapping of agricultural losses.

12.87. World agricultural prices rose sharply during the Eleventh plan period, with inflation about 9 per cent per annum in US dollar terms and price volatility much higher than before, accompanied by even higher world inflation in fuels and fertiliser. It is now generally agreed that among the several factors that contributed to this were more frequent weather shocks, policies to promote biofuels and increased demand on commodity future markets as a result of speculation and portfolio diversification. There is also consensus that linkage between agricultural prices and price of oil is now very strong and may cause high volatility to persist. As compared to this, domestic Indian agricultural prices were much less volatile and domestic prices of fuel and fertiliser were increased much less than corresponding international prices. Indian farmers were thus relatively better protected against both higher price volatility and higher costs. However, this has involved repressing inflation in fuel and fertiliser and required bans on exports during world-price spikes. Co-ordination between MSP and tariff policy is still very weak. For example, while other aspects of a recent CACP suggestion for oil palm development can be met by ongoing schemes, the proactive tariff support required is a sticking point. These will need to be addressed during the Twelfth plan.

12.88. On the climate side, a number of initiatives taken by the Indian Space Research Organisation (ISRO) and the India Meteorological Department (IMD) during the Eleventh Plan have significantly improved the scope and quality both of climate data and of other remote sensing tools. Although IMD's long-range forecasts of the monsoon still have a very large margin of error, its shorter-range products not only have greater accuracy but cover an array of agro-meteorological variables with fairly high resolution. There is also much better co-ordination today between ISRO and IMD on one hand and the Ministry of Agriculture, corresponding State departments and NARS on the other. For example, Department of Agriculture and Cooperation (DAC) has set up a Mahalanobis National Crop Forecasting Centre with ISRO collaboration to augment present crop forecasts and assessment with regular remote sensing, GIS and Global positioning System (GPS) data.

12.89. With better satellite products, an Eleventh Plan innovation was the Integrated Agro-Meteorological Advisory Service (IAAS) which now issues regular weekly Agro-Met Advisory Bulletins up to district level on field crops, horticulture and livestock. This involves agricultural universities to collect and organise soil, crop, pest and disease information and amalgamate this with weather forecasts to assist farmers in their decisions. Though still of very variable quality from district to district, and limited since district is too big a unit for useful advisory, a 2009–10 NCAER study concluded that this brought large savings to farmers. In the Twelfth Plan, a Gramin Krishi Mausam Seva (GKMS) will be launched to extend IAAS to block level, initially on experimental basis. Also, IMD will implement the Monsoon Mission aimed at generating better seasonal monsoon rainfall forecasts in different spatial ranges.

12.90. In a parallel Eleventh Plan initiative, that took advantage of IMD experience with Automatic Weather Stations technology, Government launched a Weather Based Crop Insurance Scheme (WBCIS) through the Agricultural Insurance Corporation (AIC). Initiated as a pilot in Kharif 2007 in 70 hoblis of Karnataka for 8 rain-fed crops, by 2010–11 the Scheme was being implemented in 17 States and covered more than 67 lakh farmers growing crops on 95 lakh hectares spread over 1,010 blocks in 118 districts.

12.91. At present WBCIS has about one-third the coverage of the National Agricultural Insurance Scheme (NAIS), the main crop-insurance vehicle. Based on results of crop-cutting experiments, this has been in operation since 1999–2000. Although a useful device, especially for farmers growing relatively risky crops, the main problem with NAIS is that it is not actuarial insurance. Premiums for most important crops are fixed at all-India level irrespective of risk and Central and State Governments pay for the entire excess of claims over premium received. Moreover, being compulsory for all borrowers from banks in States where it is in force, and with relatively few non-loanee farmers involved, it mainly insures banks against default following poor harvest. Further, its popularity with farmers is limited since crop-cutting experiments delay claims/payments until well after harvest and risk covered is only of yield shortfalls at the block level.

12.92. For these reasons AIC is also piloting a Modified National Agricultural Insurance Scheme (MNAIS) since 2010 that aims to (*i*) reduce the insurance unit from block to village panchayat with higher indemnity as proportion of threshold yield, (*ii*) move to actuarial premiums supported by upfront subsidies instead of NAIS practice of Government paying the entire excess of claims over premium, and (*iii*) extend insurance cover to situations such as failed sowing, cyclonic rains and localised calamities, such as hailstorms and landslides. The main problem is lowering insurance unit which although good for farmers increases the cost and effort on crop-cutting experiments exponentially.

12.93. As a result, the Government of India is currently implementing four schemes, that is, NAIS, MNAIS, WBCIS and another pilot Coconut Palm Insurance Scheme (CPIS). Only NAIS is being implemented as a full-fledged scheme and the other three are being implemented on pilot basis. The pilot programmes will be evaluated early in the Twelfth Plan for future revisions/modifications to evolve a *National Agricultural Insurance Programme*. For this, the following will be necessary. First, define what should be the core programme which Government should set up and what should be left to companies to devise their own insurance products. Second, to examine the trade-off between competition and benefits of risk pooling, that is, a centralised reinsurance system. Third, arrive at an optimum mix between weather-based insurance and those dependent on yield measurements whether by crop-cutting experiments or remote sensing.

12.94. Some suggestions, based mainly on the Twelfth Plan Working Group on Institutional Finance, Cooperatives and Risk Management, are:

1. Taking as core the ongoing NAIS, modifications being made through the pilot MNAIS should be continued. The high cost of lowering the insurance unit should be dealt with progressively in

consultation with States. Centre may share part of the cost of crop-cutting experiments in the short-run but should shift to new technologies such as satellite imagery in the long run.

2. The issue of private-sector involvement in agricultural insurance can be creatively addressed, for example, through a system of co-insurance under which the AIC is lead insurer (with underwriting responsibilities and contacts with multiple agencies).

3. Weather-based insurance should continue, again focused on customisation and innovation such as double trigger (weather and yield) and index-plus products, with State Governments choosing what to subsidise. Roll-out of AWS can be demand-led and private sector also involved but with mandatory accreditation from a competent third-party designated by Government to ensure consistent and high-quality weather data. Further, Terrestrial Observation and Prediction Systems (TOPS) platforms need to be pilot tested.

4. Other innovative products such as community-based mutual insurance, savings-linked insurance, a properly designed product fort contract farming arrangement and so on can help establish insurance culture, especially if linked to FPO formation.

5. Agriculture insurance, being specialty insurance with huge Governmental intervention should be seen more as a social instrument of the Government rather than a commercial instrument, hence is unlikely to be effectively administered unless backed by a statute.

6. To protect non-insured farmers from extreme financial distress, Government may consider 'Catastrophe Protection.' A blanket Life Insurance cover could be devised for at least small/marginal farmers (including tenant farmers) to meet liabilities to banks or other RFIs in the unfortunate eventuality of death and to secure some financial support to families of the deceased. Premia on such group/blanket insurance could be funded by Central/State Governments and financing banks, in full or in part.

7. Crop losses arising out of natural calamities are presently compensated by Government funding or concessions like loan/interest waivers/deferments. This practice is fraught with inefficiency, besides crippling repayment ethics. It is, therefore, necessary that dealing with loan losses should be internalised within the banking system through the constitution of Relief and Guarantee Funds and Stabilisation Funds (set up partly with Government funding, by diversion of subsidies for loan repayments and so on).

AGRICULTURE RESEARCH AND EDUCATION

12.95. Agricultural research has played a vital role in agricultural transformation and in reducing hunger and poverty and its role in the Twelfth Plan will be crucial. The Eleventh Five Year Plan had noted that research in the past had tended to focus mostly on increasing yield potential by more intensive use of water and biochemical inputs, paying less attention to either the long-term environmental impact of this approach or to methods and practices for efficient use of inputs and natural resources (Table 12.10). But now that limitations of this approach were evident, there appeared to be lack of any clear agricultural research strategy or to assign definite responsibilities and prioritise the research agenda rationally. It had proposed that ICAR institutes undertake basic, strategic and anticipative research, focusing particularly on problems of rain-fed agriculture, while SAUs concentrate on generating required manpower and on applied and adaptive research to address local problems. It had emphasised that research should shift from a commodity based approach to a farming systems approach through convergent efforts of R&D agencies within each agro-climatic region to address local problems identified by stakeholders, including development agencies. It had also stressed the need to enhance spending on NARS and proposed to raise this to 1 per cent of agriculture GDP by end of the Plan period.

12.96. As it turns out, research spending at 2006–07 prices, although reaching nearly 0.9 per cent in 2010–11, averaged only 0.7 per cent during the Eleventh Plan. At current prices, it was even less, averaging only 0.64 per cent during the Eleventh Plan. Part of the reason was a shortfall of about 20 per cent in the

TABLE 12.10
Expenditure on Agricultural Research and Education

(₹ crore at 2006–07 prices)

		Tenth Plan	2007–08	2008–09	2009–10	2010–11	2011–12	Eleventh Plan
States	Plan	4,151	694	965	1,070	1,289	1,382	5,401
	Non-Plan	6,477	1,464	1,315	1,497	1,755	1,599	7,629
	Total	10,629	2,158	2,279	2,567	3,044	2,981	13,030
Centre	Plan	4,977	1,210	1,418	1,402	1,909	1,998	7,938
	Non-Plan	4,125	852	1,040	1,235	2,168	1,512	6,808
	Total	9,102	2,063	2,458	2,636	4,077	3,510	14,745
RKVY	Plan		55	197	63	100	160	576
Centre and States	Plan	9,128	1,961	2,580	2,534	3,298	3,540	13,914
	Non-Plan	10,603	2,316	2,355	2,732	3,923	3,111	14,437
	Total	19,732	4,277	4,935	5,266	7,221	6,652	28,351
GDP Agriculture and Allied (2006–07 prices)		33,40,648	7,64,890	7,65,601	7,73,565	8,27,969	8,50,812	39,82,837
Research/Education as % GDP Ag		0.59%	0.55%	0.61%	0.67%	0.86%	0.76%	0.70%

Centre's Plan expenditure from that originally targeted, but the main reason was inadequate spending by States. While Centre's expenditure (non-Plan and Plan, including RKVY) increased 68 per cent in real terms between the Tenth and the Eleventh Plan periods, corresponding States expenditures increased only 22 per cent. In particular, non-Plan spending on SAUs increased less than 17 per cent, less than required to meet the pay commission awards in most States. Consequently, most SAUs are understaffed and underfinanced. This is undoubtedly the most serious problem confronting NARS.

12.97. Nonetheless, new SAUs continue to be created, especially in animal husbandry, which lack adequate staff, have little infrastructure and are grossly underfunded. Emphasis has to be laid on arresting proliferation and improvement, especially in core disciplines like modern biology, to ensure a steady supply of quality human resources. ICAR should specify minimum standards, and meeting these standards could be an eligibility condition for States to get RKVY funding.

12.98. Significant contributions of public-sector research during the last decade have included breakthroughs in basmati varieties, improved wheat varieties resistant to rust including race ug99, improved varieties of soybean, Bengal gram, mustard, chickpea and single cross hybrid maize; which have led to higher growth in these crops. Similarly, although most Bt cotton hybrids that are commercially successful are from private producers, these are based mostly on public material. With respect to natural resource management, public research claims significant contribution in developing resource conservation technologies like integrated farming, micro-irrigation, laser levelling, zero tillage and agricultural practices to improve efficiency of nutrients and water, including in situ rain water harvesting. In fruits and vegetables, better varieties and hybrids, disease management and multiplication of planting material and in livestock and fisheries, disease management technologies (vaccines and diagnostics), feed and fodder management, improving reproductive health and production of fisheries seed.

12.99. Broadly, although NARS has yet to respond to changes suggested in the Eleventh Plan, there are signs of some new research priorities and agendas. As example of new collaborative research, ICAR launched the 'National Initiative on Climate Resilient

Agriculture (NICRA)' in February 2011 as a network project with several collaborating institutions with a view to enhance resilience of Indian agriculture to climate vulnerability through strategic research and technology demonstration. The research on adaptation and mitigation covers crops, livestock, fisheries and natural resource management. The project aims to enhance resilience through development and application of improved production and risk-management technologies. It plans to demonstrate site-specific technology packages on farmers' fields for adapting to current climate risks and to enhance the capacity of scientists and other stakeholders in climate resilient agricultural research and its application. This will be continued during the Twelfth Plan.

12.100. For the Twelfth Five Year Plan, the ICAR has proposed a number of new initiatives in its manner of functioning, such as extramural funding for research, creation of funds for agri-innovations and agri-incubation and setting up of an Agriculture Technology Forecast Centre (ATFC). To improve staff strength and quality it has proposed an Adjunct Professor Scheme, Agriculture Sciences Pursuit for Inspired Research Excellence (ASPIRE), e-courses and more post-doctoral fellowships. Modernisation of SAU farms is also contemplated. In particular, it has proposed the following new thrusts:

- *Conceived Research Platforms*: Research consortia platforms are proposed for focused, time bound multi-disciplinary research in areas of 'Agro Biodiversity Management; Genomics; Seed; Hybrids; GM Foods; Biofortification; Plant Borers; High Value Compounds/Phytochemicals; Nanotechnology; Diagnostics and Vaccines; Conservation Agriculture; Waste Management; Water Management; Natural Fibre; Health Foods; Precision Farming, Farm Mechanisation and Energy; Secondary Agriculture and Agri-incubators.' These will involve partnership of ICAR with R&D organisations inside and outside NARS. Inter-departmental platforms for research in these priority areas and also capacity building in basic sciences, remote sensing and medium range agri-advisory services will be fostered involving CSIR, DBT, ICMR, DRDO, DST research institutes as well as general universities and Ministries of Environment, Space and Earth Sciences.
- *National Agricultural Education Project*: A National Agricultural Education Project for Systemic Improvement in Higher Agricultural Education and Institution Development is proposed to be undertaken as an externally-funded project to improve education quality in State Agricultural Universities.
- *National Agriculture Entrepreneurship Project*: Another externally-funded project is proposed in order to build an ecosystem for nurturing entrepreneurship development through translational research for technology commercialisation, management of technologies for commercialisation, research for breakthrough technologies for accelerated growth and higher-economic impact.
- *Farmer FIRST*: In order to make technology delivery process more effective through the existing 630 Krishi Vigyan Kendras, this new initiative will enhance farmers–scientist contact through multi-stakeholders' participation to move beyond production and productivity to privilege the complex, diverse and risk prone reality faced by most farmers.
- *Student READY*: A one-year composite programme, the Rural Entrepreneurship and Awareness Development Yojana (READY) is proposed with the objective to develop professional skills for entrepreneurship: knowledge through meaningful hands-on experience in project mode; confidence through end to end approach in product development; and enterprise management capabilities including skills for project development and execution, accountancy and national/international marketing.
- *Attracting and Retaining Youth in Agriculture (ARYA)*: This initiative will be implemented with a youth-centric approach, targeting areas of agriculture research which can be converted into viable economic enterprises and build capacities to attract rural youth to agriculture.

12.101. The Twelfth Plan allocation for ICAR is of a size that will allow spending on NARS to reach 1 per cent of agriculture GDP by end of the Plan provided

States fund SAUs similarly. The above ICAR proposals can have priority if defined in terms of deliverables, rather than areas. Also, NARS should address the following issues on priority basis during the Twelfth Five Year Plan:

- Strengthening soil organic carbon (SOC) research, particularly on the quality of organic matter and microbial activity, physical properties of SOC, validation and refinement of models and SOC dynamics under different land uses and management regimes.
- Developing Models and technology interventions on rational use of inputs, especially nutrients and irrigation water, under diverse agro-ecologies through interdisciplinary and farmer participatory mode in order to enhance their use efficiency, as also farm profits.
- The Expert Group on Pulses has been critical of NARS. Efforts to enhance the yield potential of pulses, by analysing physiological and biochemical limitations of the current crop and designing more efficient types, is a priority which should also involve improving the nutritional quality of pulses and reducing various anti-nutritional factors.
- Another priority continues to be the development of heat resistant varieties of wheat.
- Greater thrust needs to be given to post-harvest management, secondary agriculture and value addition, along with by-products and waste management. The agricultural technologies which have been developed and matured in the Eleventh Plan should be taken for commercialisation in the Twelfth Plan. Accordingly, the human resource development including para-technicians should be emphasised.
- Private agriculture input and seed companies use the research products of public system to generate profits. The public research system should seek a share in such profits which is possible if the public research system takes due care in protecting its intellectual property rights under the Protection of Plant Variety and Farmers' Rights Authority (PPVFRA). This requires development of an appropriate pricing mechanism and preparing a suitable licensing system.

NATIONAL MISSION ON EXTENSION AND TECHNOLOGY MANAGEMENT

12.102. The extension system of State agricultural departments is the weakest link in the chain between research and the farmer. Large number of vacancies of extension workers in the State Agriculture Department was one of the gravest concerns expressed by the Eleventh Plan document. During the Eleventh Plan, efforts were initiated to improve extension services by extending Central support to State extension reforms. This has resulted in 604 Agriculture Technology Management Agencies (ATMAs) to be established across the country with 21,000 new posts sanctioned with Central assistance at State, district and block levels. Also, since a continuous problem plaguing extension has been lack of organic link between the research system and the extension machinery, R&D linkage guidelines were jointly brought out by the DAC and ICAR and sent to all States and SAUs. The basic thrust of these guidelines were to get ATMAs and KVKs to work together at the district level and below, keeping in view the priorities reflected in Comprehensive District Plans. Although neither has delivered full results, there is now much greater acceptance that things must be done together.

12.103. Seed is also an area where NARS made much greater effort than in previous recent Plan periods.

12.104. Along with seeds, farm mechanisation was also highlighted earlier as a source of the Eleventh Plan labour productivity gains. In view of emerging labour shortages in many states, there is demand to expand custom hiring services, as well as for new implements. During the Twelfth Five Year Plan it is proposed to give a co-ordinated thrust on seeds, farm mechanisation and extension through a new *Mission on Extension and Technology Management*. This should also have a component to fund ICAR research platforms to find solutions to problems thrown up by extension and requiring expertise beyond SAU.

(A) Seeds and Planting Material

12.105. Three major yield successes during the last decade relate to cotton, maize and basmati rice.

These were driven by new seeds of which cotton and maize hybrids were mainly from private sector while basmati rice varieties were almost entirely public. Increased adoption of hybrids in cross-pollinated crops like cotton, maize, pearl millet and sorghum has been led largely by the private sector, which accounts for three-fourths of hybrids developed so far in the country. But there is discernable change in role of public sector in development of hybrids after 2001–02. Till 2001–02, private sector developed 150 hybrids of cotton compared to 15 by public sector; 67 hybrids of maize compared to three in public sector. In the next seven years, public sector increased its share from 8 per cent to 19 per cent in cotton, from 4 per cent to 40 per cent in maize and from 25 per cent to 58 per cent in rice, with similar changes in other crops. In parallel, public production of quality seeds of varieties have increased rapidly in recent years, expanding the public share in total seed use. Production of quality seed doubled from 140 lakh quintals in 2004–05 to 280 lakh quintals in 2009–10, contributing significantly to the Eleventh Plan yield performance. Private sector accounted for 39 per cent of this seed production. Nonetheless, the ratio of quality seed to total seed use by farmers is still much lower than norm and there is considerable scope to raise crop productivity by raising this ratio.

12.106. There are several pending issues regarding seeds. For example, at present there is no regulatory mechanism to protect farmers against non-performance, say poor seed germination rate. The Seeds Bill, 2004, introduced in Parliament in 2004, is still under consideration of the Parliamentary Standing Committee on Agriculture. It aims to regulate the quality of seeds and planting material of all agricultural, horticultural and plantation crops to ensure availability of true to type seeds to Indian farmers; curb the sale of spurious, poor quality seeds; protect the rights of farmers; increase private participation in seed production, distribution and seed testing; liberalise import of seeds and planting materials while aligning with World Trade Organization (WTO) commitments and international standards. Comprehensive and authentic databases on seed production and trade in India by public and private sectors as required under the seed and plant variety laws need to be built up. The seed chain and the norms for quality control should be followed without any compromises or shortcuts.

12.107. At present, the public sector is responsible for most valuable germplasm while private seed agencies concentrate on more remunerative high value seed segment. Under the circumstances, clear protocols need to be developed for sharing precious germplasm with the private sector on payment of royalty, while ensuring their conservation and preventing possible erosion of the national interest in the context of international agreements on plant variety and intellectual property rights. If this can be done, there is vast scope to expand linkages between the private seed industry and public research institutions to take advantage of the positive aspects of both the segments for the benefit of farmers.

12.108. ICAR needs to revisit procedures for variety identification, release and notification to cover private and farmers' varieties and also to avoid bias in favour of varieties evolved by the testing institutions. The number of seed testing centres in the country should be expanded rapidly, if necessary in PPP mode and with third party oversight, to reduce the time taken in assessment and refinement of varieties and hybrids and technologies for production and protection of crops. There is also a need for 'Phytosanitary' certification, especially for export/import of seeds. The State Seed Corporations may establish at least one such certification centre in each major State.

12.109. The DAC made the present assessment of seed requirement during the Twelfth Plan for its proposed Seed Mission with respect to some of the major crops which brings out that even excluding requirements arising from possible shift to hybrids, seed production of varieties will need to increase by about a third to meet the projected increase in seed replacement rates. Since seed-production planning should be done with a long-term perspective (considering the viability of the seed) and also to keep buffer stock of seed to meet eventualities of natural calamities that require replanting, the actual production requirements may be higher. To meet the seed demand for 45 major crops produced within the country and required under diverse conditions, seed hubs need to be identified to produce seed and supply the same to the farmers in each area. This will save cost of transportation. Public agencies will also need to strengthen infrastructure for seed processing, storage, transportation and distribution.

12.110. Adequate availability of quality seeds is a particular challenge for farmers in rain-fed areas where rainfall risks are high and productivity depends crucially on timely sowing within a short rainfall window. The seed system must be capable of providing seeds of contingency or alternative crops during prolonged dry spells. With protection of crop diversity important in rain-fed areas, strengthening and improving local-seed systems and linking these to NARS is a necessity for productivity enhancement.

12.111. An important part of the new Mission will therefore be to better integrate farmers with production and distribution of quality seeds through, for example, seed village programmes and by encouraging NGOs to help FPOs take up seed production. Therefore, capacity building will be vital to success. Fodder seeds that are presently neglected and scarce will need to be emphasised. Equally, the Mission must be enabled to convey to NARS accurate feedback from farmers on seed suitability.

(B) Farm Machinery

12.112. Wages have increased significantly in recent years and with labour accounting for more than 40 per cent of variable cost, many farm organisations report that shortage of labour is obstructing operational efficiency. Animal power is also declining, with commercial banks reluctant to extend loans for bullocks. This has naturally led to an increase in farm mechanisation. However, farm mechanisation has so far been biased in favour of tractors and been concentrated in irrigated-command areas paying little attention to the needs of farmers in dryland areas and the scope for introducing small machines that might be useful to meet their needs.

12.113. Considering the farm sizes and prevailing skills, farm mechanisation penetration would have to be enhanced through promotion of custom hiring models as well as individual ownership. While draft animal power based implements and manual tools should be owned by individual farmers (with appropriate financial incentives, for example, off season employment for animal power by integrating some services such as 'manure transport' with MGNREGS), expensive machinery should be promoted thorough custom hiring. This could be done by promoting machinery service centres involving existing FPOs or by groups of farm youth trained in machinery operation and maintenance.

12.114. Greater impetus is needed to develop need-based and regionally differentiated farm machinery. Ongoing efforts by NARS need to be suitably strengthened with appropriate participation of commercial agricultural machinery manufacturers. Financial incentives could be linked to requirements thrown up by extension experience from different locations or from FPO demand. The Mission should identify and convey to NARS the critical mechanisation gaps and, in particular, specific local requirements related to machinery for soil and water conservation and gender-friendly implements.

(C) Strengthening Extension

12.115. During the Eleventh Plan, the task of strengthening and restructuring agricultural extension was approached through a wide mix of different initiatives. The context for this was that while public sector extension arrangements have weakened, the number and diversity of private extension service providers have increased in the last two decades. These include the media, NGOs, producers associations, input agencies and agri-business companies. Many provide better and improved services to farmers, but their effective reach is limited and most poor producers are served neither by public nor private sector in many distant and remote areas. Notwithstanding the important role being played by private sector extension, there are also concerns with regard to wholesomeness of information, given equity and long-term implications.

12.116. Although setting up ATMAs in almost all districts was the single most important achievement, this went hand-in-hand with efforts to enhance quality through domain experts and regular capacity building. Other efforts included interactive ways of information dissemination, public–private partnerships and pervasive and innovative use of ICT/Mass Media. Efforts were also made to involve agri-entrepreneurs, agri-business companies and NGO experts to bolster public extension. Most of these efforts will have to continue in the Twelfth Plan since extension is a continuous process. But, in view of the initial broken down condition, there are considerable gaps even after the subsequent effort. For example, an evaluation of ATMAs by the Agricultural Finance Corporation in 2009–10 found that although 52 per cent of respondent farmers said that they gained knowledge of new practices and technologies from this, only 25 per cent felt that this had helped to increase production. It is perhaps time to conduct a country-wide extension census to identify extension resources (manpower, infrastructure, expertise) available in public and private sectors.

12.117. It is also necessary to continue with experimentation. There are number of models which have been successfully implemented in several States and countries which can be tried as pilots by ATMA and then expanded. Many civil society organisations have successfully experimented with community managed extension systems with members of the local community acting as agents of agricultural extension. In the Community Managed Sustainable Agriculture (CMSA) model of Andhra Pradesh, members of the village community have been trained and developed as Community Resource Persons (CRPs). CRPs adopt elements of sustainable and eco-friendly agricultural practices in their own farms and are in a better position to motivate and convince other farmers than normal extension workers. Working with agricultural scientists and extension personnel under the broad ATMA umbrella, CRPs can help technology transfer and diffusion.

12.118. Agricultural extension covering crops and allied sectors is primarily the responsibility of the States and it is expected that States should drive the extension reforms process. Any national effort in this regard can only support States' efforts. Moreover, as noted by the Twelfth Plan Working Group on Agricultural Extension, while public policy in agriculture increasingly recognises importance of public–private partnership in extension, the experience so far is that PPPs have been the exception rather than the rule. States must adopt PPP, but this is not substitute for strengthening the public extension system. Future collaboration between public and private players will have to focus more on the public sector's ability to set standards and monitor progress so that these standards are enforced on all players, including public extension agents, while providing institutional training and support.

12.119. An important task of the new Mission should therefore be to consult with States so as to evolve a standards and regulatory framework for certifying and validating extension activities by all players, including public extension agents. MANAGE and SAMETIs should take the leading role in driving extension reforms at the National and State levels respectively. The corporate sector should be encouraged to involve itself in this effort and in agricultural extension in general, if only as part of their Corporate Social Responsibility (CSR). Even more important than funding under CSR, the corporate sector can support by providing adequate extension training to their extensive promotion network of distributors and dealers so as to meet required standards.

12.120. The Twelfth Plan Working Group on Agricultural Extension has noted that although ATMAs exceeded targets on training, demonstrations and exposure visits, the number of farm schools set up was well below target and that matters were lagging also on strengthening and extending Farmer Advisory Committees at every level. Since active involvement of farmers in planning and executing extension reforms was a key ATMA goal, the new Mission must concentrate on this and on feedback, particularly on technology and on agricultural plans at district and lower levels. A critical aspect of this will be ATMA–KVK coordination and more intensive ICT use.

12.121. Extension services must also be gender-sensitised, and this will require joint efforts, involving the

Mahila Kisan Sashaktikaran Pariyojana component of the National Rural Livelihood Mission (NRLM) under MoRD, the Project Directorate for Women in Agriculture of ICAR and National Gender Resource Centre in Agriculture (NGRCA) of Ministry of Agriculture (MoA). Further, since the present extension system does not pay adequate attention to livestock, fishery and fodder and separate extension machinery for animal husbandry and fishery is not feasible in many states, this function will need to be integrated with ATMA with suitable KVK and NGO backstopping. Indeed, convergence should be a basic goal of the new Mission, both on the side of technology dissemination and feedback as well as for planning integrated agricultural development.

12.122. The ultimate objective of the Mission should be to upgrade ATMA from a society operating as an adjunct to line agricultural departments to an independent entity with technical capability to offer local solutions and deliver feedback to NARS on location-specific technology needs. The larger trends of public policy point towards decentralised governance of natural resources and the promotion of growth with increasing emphasis on district (and lower) level planning. It is necessary to see decentralised planning as an iterative planning—doing—learning—planning cycle rather than as simply a one-time activity. The challenge is to institutionalise this process and ensure that the agency facilitating planning also has accountability in the overall outcome. ATMAs are a natural choice for such an agency in the present context.

SPECIFIC PLANS AND OBJECTIVES FOR THE MAJOR SUB-SECTORS

(A) Livestock

12.123. For achieving growth rate of 5–6 per cent per annum the animal husbandry sector would need to address important challenges during the Twelfth Plan. These include delivery of services, shortage of feed and fodder and frequent occurrence of deadly diseases. Compared to its contribution in the economy livestock sector has received much less resources and institutional support. Livestock extension remains grossly neglected. The country still lacks adequate facilities and the infrastructure for disease diagnosis, reporting, epidemiology, surveillance and forecasting. Livestock markets are underdeveloped, which is a significant barrier to commercialisation of livestock production. Besides, the sector is also coming under significant pressure of increasing globalisation of agri-food markets. Although there is demand for Indian meat products in international markets, lack of international processing standards is a hindrance. Unfortunately, schemes on modernisation of slaughterhouses and by-product utilisation have not been effectively implemented. In the animal husbandry sector, the major priority areas during Twelfth Five Year Plan will be breed improvement, enhancing availability of feed and fodder and provision of better health services, including proper breeding management. Conservation and perpetuation of diverse local germplasm, which are adaptable to Indian climate conditions and resistant to various endemic diseases, will be another important area, with clearer focus on sub-sectors such as small ruminants that have so far been neglected.

12.124. An important Twelfth Plan initiative is the National Dairy Plan (NDP), which has already been launched as a central sector scheme with credit support from the International Development Association (IDA). To be implemented by the National Dairy Development Board (NDDB) through a network of End Implementing Agencies (EIAs), mainly dairy cooperatives and producer companies, this aims to (*i*) increase productivity of milch animals and thereby increase milk production and (*ii*) provide rural milk producers with greater access to the organised milk-processing sector. These objectives would be pursued through adoption of focused scientific and systematic processes in provision of technical inputs, supported by appropriate policy and regulatory measures.

12.125. An important sub-component of (*i*) above will be scientific progeny testing and pedigree selection of bulls for semen required in artificial insemination (AI) services. It is planned to make available about 900 high genetic merit bulls for replacement of bulls maintained at all 'A' and 'B' graded semen stations and thereby achieve 100 per cent high genetic merit bull replacement at these semen stations by end of the Twelfth Plan. It is estimated that this would produce some 100 million high-quality disease-free semen doses annually.

12.126. Taking NDP into account and, with RKVY incentives for States to substantially enhance public sector investment in agriculture and allied sector during the Eleventh Plan, the Department of Animal Husbandry, Dairying and Fisheries (DAHDF) has also decided to redesign its schemes. It aims to provide more flexibility to States while reducing the number of Centrally Sponsored Schemes (CSS) and reorientating these to secure better programmatic focus.

12.127. On genetic improvement in bovines, the current major programme is the 'National Project for Cattle and Buffalo Breeding (NPCBB)' which is being implemented since October 2000. Unlike NDP, which aims to provide breeding services from the dairy side, NPCBB is administered as part of States' veterinary services. DAHDF proposes to continue NPCBB in this present form since the DAHDF target is to expand the artificial insemination programme from present coverage of about 25 per cent of breedable population to 50 per cent, which will require an expansion of AI services beyond the about 35 per cent coverage planned for under NDP. This is because NDP will not cover all States and there are likely to be farmers not covered by dairy-led breeding services even in States covered by NDP. Moreover, States have already established Livestock Development Boards (LDBs) in the present format to implement bovine breeding programmes with a stated focus on development and conservation of important indigenous breeds. The critical requirement is that NPCBB and States' efforts through LDBs share common standards and protocols with NDP in progeny testing, pedigree selection and to improve conception rates. If so, resources are sufficient to achieve 5 per cent growth of milk production in the Twelfth Plan

12.128. Since standards and protocols will be the key to success on the breeding side and basic commonality will have to be brought between NDP, LDBs and NPCBB, there is need for some architectural redesign during the Twelfth Plan. Therefore, although NPCBB will continue, this will be as a component of a new *National Programme for Bovine Breeding and Dairy (NPBBD)* which will subsume all DADF existing schemes on dairy development. Thus, NPBBD will have two main components, namely National Programme for Bovine Breeding (NPBB) and Dairy Development. The component for Dairy Development will mainly focus on States/areas not covered under NDP and, in addition to existing support areas, convergence will be attempted in a phased manner so that dairy cooperatives which are not part of NDP also offer breeding and extension services. It is hoped that such combined activities in respect of dairying with breeding will be more effective in extension of artificial insemination services, feed management and marketing of good quality of milk which are essential for improving productivity and income of farmers. In the meantime, NPBB will continue existing NPCBB functions through LDBs and the veterinary side with two areas of focus: first, to harmonise breeding standards and protocols; and, second, to achieve the so far unrealised stated focus on development and conservation of important indigenous breeds.

12.129. The main programme on the veterinary side will be an expanded scheme for *Livestock Health and Disease Control*. Such an expansion is necessary because occurrence of diseases like foot and mouth disease (FMD), hemorrhagic septicemia (HS), brucellosis, mastitis, blood protozoon and so on, have been accentuated with introduction of exotic breeds. Taking into account the economic losses from these diseases, and also those of small ruminants (PPR or peste-des-petits ruminants), particularly to small, marginal and landless farmers including women farmers, it is necessary to have a strong focus on national control programmes for all major animal diseases, backed by epidemiological analysis and assessment of the animal diseases in different agro-climatic regions. Unrestricted movement of livestock, as well import of germplasm, and changes in ecosystems due to climate change are adding to occurrence of diseases. The availability of improved, potent and efficacious vaccines meeting international standards against major prevalent diseases can enable better management, containment and control of the diseases. The new programme will associate all ICAR institutes specialising in animal diseases and, in consultation with the State Governments, formulate and implement more effective strategies for control of different diseases.

12.130. The third major programme of DADF will be the *National Livestock Mission (NLM)*. Apart from bovine breeding, dairying and livestock health schemes, DADF runs a plethora of other schemes relating small ruminants, poultry, piggery and fodder development which although of extreme importance, especially to small, marginal, landless and women farmers, have so far not received focused attention. The multiplicity of small schemes in these livestock sectors has been a major constraint since this limits the capability of states to effectively access funding under various schemes. In order to provide greater flexibility to states in formulating and implementing various projects, it is proposed to merge these schemes with the main objective of achieving sustainable development and growth of the livestock sector.

12.131. The NLM will have an important mini-mission of feed and fodder, with an objective to substantially reduce the gap between availability and demand. The deficit of dry fodder (10 per cent), concentrates (33 per cent) and green fodder (35 per cent) continues to be high, although availability of feed resources has improved somewhat. The forage and fodder seed need varietal and quality improvement alongside better availability. The NLM will encourage seed companies and SAUs to take up forage seed production on a priority basis. Developing common property resources, including grazing land and wasteland, and better utilisation and enrichment of crop residues/agricultural by-products is the other priority. Ration balancing, which is being promoted under NDP, will also be promoted under this mini-mission on feed and fodder.

12.132. The NLM will also have an additional mini-mission relating particularly to development of small ruminants, but also covering poultry, piggery and other minor livestock species. While subsuming some of the existing Central Sector Schemes for poultry, small animals and fodder development, the objective will be fuller development of the animal biodiversity available in our country, which is a rich treasure of germplasm. NLM will also focus on predominantly non-descript pig populations, concentrated in NE region and eastern region there have poor productivity. Indian poultry industry is well equipped and organised to achieve target growth rate of 11 per cent for commercial broilers and 7 per cent for layers although it failed to diversify in favour of duck, quail, turkey and emu production. Need-based import of grandparent stock of reputed international brands may be continued with strict enforcement of bio-security measures. Rural poultry sector however, needs financial, infrastructure and technological support to raise the present 2 per cent growth rate to 3 per cent. All these, including the conservation of threatened breeds, will be covered by NLM in a flexible but more focused programmatic manner.

12.133. Other issues that NLM will address include livestock insurance and extension and any innovative initiative proposed by states for development of the livestock sector, for example, to deal with unhygienic slaughtering and processing. If State Governments notify minor veterinary services accordingly, shortage of human resources of veterinary staff could also be supplemented by recruitment of para-vets, similar to that of ASHA, to provide minor veterinary services and supplement the livestock-extension activity in the States. In this context, it might be noted that as public-sector spending is enhanced for development of livestock, there is need for continuous assessment of the efficacy of AI and of animal health programmes in terms of success rates, lactating efficiency and of potential and actual yield per animal.

(B) Fisheries

12.134. Potential of fisheries sector in providing quality food and nutrition, creating rural livelihoods, advancing socio-economic development in the rural and far flung areas is widely demonstrated and globally recognised as a powerful tool for poverty reduction and fostering rural development. Annual fish production has reached to the level of 8.30 million tonnes during 2010–11 (P). Annual export earning has also touched record US$2.9 billion mark contributing about 17 per cent to national agricultural export. About 14.5 million people are engaged in fishing, aquaculture and other allied activities of which about 75 per cent are in inland fisheries and the remaining in marine fisheries.

12.135. In marine fisheries, uncontrolled fishing capacity has led to over-exploitation of the coastal resources. The estimated potential of the offshore waters offers opportunities which calls for upgradation of the fleet as well as skills and capacities of the fishers and incentives to promote diversified fishing in the offshore waters. Implementation of Monitoring, Control and Surveillance (MCS) as a new programme in the ensuing Plan is expected to bring more discipline and regulate the activities so as to maintain the growth rate in a sustainable manner. There is a need of additional infrastructure and also upgradation of facilities infrastructure for landing and berthing facilities of marine fishing fleet and for domestic marketing that have been the main reasons for post-harvest losses.

12.136. Freshwater aquaculture, which contributed to the 'Blue Revolution' in the country in late 1970s, is now almost stagnating in terms of species diversification and yield rates due to less focus on sustainable development of inland capture fisheries in past Plans; increasing pressure on the resources, including habitat degradation; and multiple use of inland water bodies with least priority to fishery requirements. Average yield rates are around 1,000 kg/ha/yr, against potential of 3–4 thousand kg/ha/yr. The efforts to raise productivity should, however, be accompanied by formulating guidelines and regulatory measures for the judicious use of critical inputs keeping in view the principles of the FAO Code of Conduct for Responsible Fisheries.

12.137. Quality fish seed is the most critical input to enhance the productivity and production of fishes. But, there are no organised brood-stock production and management facilities in the country. Therefore, there is need to set up brood banks in each State with one at the Central level. There is need to promote commercial fish feed mills and indigenously formulated fish feeds with locally available ingredients by supporting the private players with enhanced capital subsidy especially in the States where there are no feed mills.

12.138. Adequate infrastructure is not available for disease diagnosis and treatment for fish disease management. There is a strong need for capital investment as well as support for the State Governments in capacity building and managing the disease diagnostic laboratories. There is also a need for creating a disease surveillance and communication agency/mechanism at National level along with its wings at suitable regional locations to build awareness and send alerts to the stakeholders. This agency shall have adequate regulatory powers to ensure the disease control.

12.139. The gradual decline of Freshwater Fish Farmer's Development Agencies (FFDAs) and Brackish water Farmer's Development Agencies (BFDAs) and their resultant poor performance coupled with weak extension services has impacted the overall growth of aquaculture in the country. Rejuvenation and consolidation of the two field-level agencies (FFDA and BFDA) into a single agency—Fisheries and Aquaculture Development Agency or can undertake extension of technologies, promote networking of farmers and fishers (mainly from reservoirs) and provide effective liaison between the farmers and developmental and other extension agencies such as the Krishi Vigyan Kendras and the ATMAs as well as sourcing the public finance for fishers.

12.140. An important initiative of Government of India for development of fisheries sub-sector has been to launch 'National Fisheries Development Board' (NFDB) as a Special Purpose Vehicle (SPV) in the year 2006 for implementing fishery developmental schemes in an integrated manner. The scope of NFDB would be expanded to include management of fish diseases and creation of related infrastructure which is a gap in the present scenario. During the Twelfth Plan, the existing CSS on inland and marine fisheries (except welfare of fishers) will be merged with NFDB to facilitate expansion of fisheries through integration of a wide array of activities, but with its main focus on inland fresh water fishery. The schemes will be implemented under the aegis of NFDB removing any duplication or overlap of efforts. This clear demarcation of work, it is hoped will enable the growth rate of the sector to rise to 6 per cent during the Twelfth Plan.

12.141. DADF would focus its efforts on policy, regulation and welfare of fishers, and will implement the scheme relating to welfare of inland and marine fishers. The DADF will also handle the strengthening of fisheries data base, implementation of the proposed scheme on Monitoring, Control and Surveillance (MCS), all fisheries policy and legal matters, coordination with the sister Ministries/Departments at the Centre and the States to make the sector's foundation more robust and sustainable and build stronger linkages between research and development. Future course of fisheries management will have to work at two fronts—sustainable utilisation of healthy resources and rehabilitation of threatened resources by habitat restoration and appropriate conservation measures. Climate change and its possible impact on fisheries and fishers is again an additional challenge. Thus, the future course of management will require highest level of compliance of acts and regulations, extensive adoption of BMP and implementation of CCRF (Code of Conduct for Responsible Fisheries introduced by FAO) which would be possible only through the cooperation and active participation of resource user communities as partner in the development and management process.

(C) Horticulture

12.142. With increasing per capita income, Indians are consuming more of fresh and processed horticultural products indicating growing scope of horticulture by improving crop productivity and efficiency in the value chains. The initiatives taken in the horticulture sector during the Tenth Five Year Plan have helped in achieving high growth in production. During the Eleventh Five Year Plan, the growth rate of horticulture is expected to be 4.7 per annum, slightly short of the projected 5 per cent. There has been a marked push to the expansion in area under horticulture crops since taking up of a number of initiatives for horticulture development through NHB, TMNE (NE) and then NHM in 2005–06.

12.143. However, in quest for area-expansion efforts, the states have neglected due thrust on increasing productivity of existing orchards through technology infusion or by capital investment in fertigation, input management, plant protection and farm mechanisation. The area expansion programmes have also lacked the proper backward linkage with supply of quality seed and planting material. Even where Nursery Act exists, it has not been enforced effectively. A proper system of accreditation and rating of nurseries, with clearly defined protocols, is the most important priority and will have to be put in place during the Twelfth Plan.

12.144. Adequate attention to post-harvest management and market development and processing has yet to pick up and is the weakest aspect of diversification towards high-value products resulting in frequent and sharp fluctuations in prices of fruits and vegetables in domestic market. As discussed earlier, marketing sector reforms implemented by States have so far not resulted in efficient marketing of perishables, or put in place transparent system of auction and price discovery. There are huge logistic gaps between production clusters and marketing centres, often at long distance, and private sector investment in post-harvest management and in marketing infrastructure has not come forward to the desired extent. There is also lack of proactive steps to enhance export competitiveness for high-end export destinations. The availability of adequate regular, uninterrupted, affordable power supply for setting up infrastructure like tissue culture labs, seed processing plants, bio control labs and post-harvest management units like cold storages, ripening chambers and so on is a constraint which needs to be addressed at least in and around horticulture clusters. Since horticulture operations are cost intensive and hi-tech, horticulture growers need to be provided affordable credit with higher ceiling and insurance against risk.

12.145. The horticulture development missions depend on a loose set-up of Technology Support

Groups for technology inputs. This has proved inadequate. Many States do not have adequate technical trained manpower to implement programmes. Unless State Governments fill up vacant posts and create additional posts to provide necessary technical input, it should be deemed that they are uninterested and the mission wound up in those States.

12.146. During the Twelfth Five Year Plan the National Horticulture Mission will integrate the several existing schemes in this sector and aim at holistic growth of horticulture sector, including bamboo, through area-based regionally differentiated strategies, which include research, technology promotion, extension, post-harvest management, processing and marketing, in consonance with comparative advantage of each State/region and its diverse agro-climatic features. The Mission will also facilitate marketing reforms discouraging payment of unnecessary market levies and encouraging private investment for setting up horticulture produce markets. While continuing existing efforts, and aiming at 5 per cent growth of horticulture production during the Twelfth Plan, the main objective will be to build required capacities at State level, and assess their seriousness, so that the horticulture development related activities can be transferred fully to States by end of the Twelfth Plan.

12.147. Another objective will be to improve horticulture statistics which continue to be weak, lacking both a validated methodology for data collection of horticulture crops and adequate machinery to collect such data. Generation and dissemination of quality data can also help in averting frequent situations of gluts and shortages and exploitation of such situations by the middlemen and speculators. DAC needs to take up a one-time horticulture census with the objective of generating reliable base line data. Further, as recommended by NSSO committee on improvement horticulture statistics, there is need to set up an extensive network of Horticulture Information Systems (HIS) with proper data units in all relevant districts and at State and Centre level covering all relevant aspects. To facilitate this, at least 3 per cent of Mission funds should be earmarked for this purpose.

(D) Food Grains and Oil Seeds

12.148. Since cultivated land is limited, with potential for only marginal future increase through higher cropping intensity or development of cultivable wasteland, future increase in production will have to come mainly from yield improvement. Declining average annual growth of food grains yields from 3.2 per cent in 1980s to 1.6 per cent in 1990s and further to only 0.6 per cent during the Tenth Plan, taking this well below population growth, had led to widespread concern about future food security. The issue was, therefore, analysed fully with several alternatives considered and the *National Food Security Mission (NFSM)* was formulated for the Eleventh Plan. This was based on an assessment of yield gap data then available, and was focused on increasing yields in low-yield districts using a variety of known interventions, with particular attention to availability of quality seeds. Although this has paid off, with food grains yield growth increasing to 3.3 per cent during the Eleventh Plan, a valid question regards continuation of NFSM is whether yield gaps are still large?

12.149. A committee set up under Chairmanship of Chief Minister of Haryana has recently examined the issue and suggested continuing with the strategy to bridge the gap between real and potential yields. The analysis of gap between potential and achieved yields presented to this committee suggests that there is considerable potential of increasing yields even in high productivity irrigated areas with the current technology. For these areas, the strategies will need to concentrate on propagation of balanced use of fertilisers and application of micro-nutrients, water and soil-saving technology. In case of wheat, however, there is need to step up research to develop varieties resistant to temperature. The major yield gaps are due to management practices. Other reasons for this gap need to be ascertained through specific studies and addressed through appropriate interventions.

12.150. In addition to enhancing productivity of food grains in the low productivity areas, it is equally important to stabilise the productivity gains in these areas as well as in areas where productivity levels are comparatively high. With these issues in mind, the *National Food Security Mission (NFSM)* will be revamped during the Twelfth Plan. While the Eleventh Plan approach of focused attention on identified districts and crops in a location specific, target-oriented manner will continue, greater attention will be put in most areas to shift from exclusive focus on individual crops to the cropping system/farming system approach. In particular, the Mission will be extended to cover coarse cereals and fodder, in addition to wheat, rice and pulses as at present. The Mission contemplates that promotion of package of practices in compact blocks in a hand holding approach would not only help in enhancing the production and productivity of a region but also help in changing mindsets of farmers due to its positive large-scale impact. This approach will ensure inclusion of all farmers in the compact block irrespective of their size of holding or social status and will be compatible with other efforts that encourage strengthening of institutions, including building of farmers organisations and FPOs. The Mission will also build upon the Eleventh Plan experience regarding conservation agriculture.

12.151. However, the main way in which NFSM will be extended during the Twelfth Plan is through greater emphasis on strategic-area development. The two programmes that were started as RKVY sub-components in the Eleventh Plan namely, the 60,000 pulses village programme and the intensive millets production programme will largely be shifted into NFSM. On another sub-component of RKVY—Bringing Green Revolution in Eastern India (BGREI)—a view will be taken by DAC in consultation with States regarding format of its continuation during the Twelfth Plan. Also, some additional districts in Himachal Pradesh, Uttarakhand and the north-eastern region will be included to provide a specific thrust on foodgrains cultivation in hill areas.

12.152. Such restructuring of RKVY and NFSM will address the problem of bridging the existing large gap between potential and realised rice yields in eastern States and the challenge of increasing pulses production. Since BGREI allows components which are not part of NFSM, and since development of the eastern region requires significant investments in power and marketing infrastructure, the final design of how to proceed on the relative contributions of RKVY and NFSM will need to be decided in consultation with the States. Also, since a counterpart of expanding rice production in eastern States is to reduce rice area and resulting groundwater stress in the North-West, a decision will have to be taken on what components of the latter effort should be stressed in NFSM/RKVY.

12.153. Preliminary targets under the NFSM for the Twelfth Plan are enhancing production by additional 25 million tonnes of foodgrains consisting of 10 million tonnes of rice, 10 million tonnes of wheat, 3 million tonnes of pulses and 2 million tonnes of millet. Also it aims to expand fodder production to meet the demand both of green and dry fodder. In all probability, the requirement of sufficient quantity of dual purpose feed and fodder will require raising this target to 30 million tonnes, with additional production of coarse cereals put at 7 million tonnes. All these targets are less than was actually achieved during the Eleventh Plan and are consistent with demand forecasts. This would amount to targeting 2–2.5 per cent increase in foodgrains production in the Twelfth Plan.

12.154. Another consequence of the expanded scope of NFSM will be to absorb the pulses and maize components presently in the Integrated Scheme for Oilseeds, Oil palm, Pulses and Maize Development. During Twelfth Five Year Plan, it is proposed to replace this scheme with a new *Mission on Oilseeds and Oil Palm* which will be launched with a preliminary target to increase the production of oilseeds by at least 4.5 per cent per annum, that is, the same rate of growth as actually achieved during the Eleventh Plan. The core of this Mission will therefore be to continue past efforts with a clearer focus on oilseeds. However, since production of oilseeds has not been able to match the increasing demand of edible oils, resulting in persistence of a huge gap between demand and production of edible oils in the country, the Mission will also aim to expand area under oil palm to realise the latent potential of the oil palm in the country. This part of the Mission will fully consider a proposal made recently by CACP and incorporate whatever is feasible.

NATURAL RESOURCES

(A) Water

12.155. The water resource potential of India is assessed as 186.9 million hectare meter, mostly from rainfall. With annual availability still more than utilisation and with its uneven spatial and temporal distribution leading to floods/droughts in some or other parts of the country every year, there is a strong demand to fully utilise this potential as soon as possible. The total States proposals on investment in Irrigation and Flood Control for the Twelfth plan add up to about ₹4,00,000 crore, which alone would amount to over the 4 per cent of cumulative GDP from agriculture and allied sectors being targeted as total public investment in this sector during the plan. Recognising both the criticality of irrigation for agricultural growth and the potential available, the Centre's Twelfth plan gross budgetary support for development of water resources (including on AIBP) is being stepped up to ₹1,09,552 crore from the Eleventh plan actual expenditure of ₹41,427 crore.

12.156. However, the performance in respect of creation and utilisation of irrigation facilities during the Eleventh Five Year Plan was not satisfactory. The original Eleventh Five Year Plan target for creating irrigation potential was 16 million ha. This was subsequently revised to 9.5 million ha, which has been achieved. However, utilisation out of the created potential is expected to be only 2.7 million ha. The ever increasing gap between created potential and its utilisation is an issue that is a Twelfth Plan priority, steps to address which are discussed in another chapter.

12.157. In recent decades irrigation facilities have increasingly been created through exploitation of groundwater deployment. However, non-judicious exploitation of groundwater for irrigation purposes in India is already showing signs of crisis in many parts of country. Studies report that more than 26 cubic miles of groundwater has already disappeared from underground aquifers in large areas of Haryana, Punjab, Rajasthan and Delhi, between 2002 and 2008 (NASA 2009). Global Runoff Data Centre, University of Hampshire and International Earth Science Information Networks have projected that around 30 per cent area of India falls in the extreme water scarce zone having less than 500 m^3/person/year supply of renewable fresh water. The information from the Central Ground Water Board reveals that situation has worsened in most of the states since 2004. The groundwater level has been declining annually by about 4 cm during the past decade, often resulting in drying of rivers and wetlands and contamination with arsenic, fluoride and other toxic substances. This requires effective regulatory framework and participatory watershed development, especially because groundwater extraction is often highly unfavourable to the small farmers who cannot keep investing to tap deeper aquifers. Apart from developing appropriate regulatory framework, and people's participation, the need of water saving devices and crop planning cannot be overemphasised. Micro-irrigation coverage will be given priority both in irrigated and rain-fed areas, as part of comprehensive local planning.

(B) Watershed Development

12.158. Watershed development has long been one of the major channels directing public investment to natural resource base and production systems in rain-fed agriculture. From their earlier emphasis on soil and water conservation, the focus in case of watershed projects is shifting towards livelihood security and income generation. It is also now generally accepted that to be effective, the watershed development and soil conservation investments have to be complemented with farming systems investments in a watershed-plus framework that takes into account the diversity of rain-fed agriculture.

12.159. However, despite considerable emphasis on this in the Eleventh Plan design and development of common guidelines, actual performance in regard to watershed development was poor during the Eleventh Plan. The details of the Eleventh Plan had target and achievement may be seen in the Chapter on Water. Since all watershed development programmes have been transferred to the Department of Land Resources, the Ministry of Agriculture has to redefine its initiatives for rain-fed farming and sustainable agriculture.

12.160. The National Rainfed Area Authority was constituted with the specific objective of integrating schemes/programmes and activities of various Departments of the Centre and the State Governments with regard to dryland farming as well as providing technical back stopping for watershed development in a comprehensive manner. The authority was expected to play a major role in training of the officials associated with the watershed development projects and also take a lead role in social mobilisation which is critical in the success of the watershed development programmes. It was also expected to take up studies for evaluation of the implementation of projects by the States. So far Departments both at the Central and State level has not taken much interest in associating NRAA either in evaluation of the programmes or for providing technical input for these. NRAA expertise will be better utilised during the Twelfth Plan.

(C) Land and Soil Health Management

12.161. Land is the prime natural resource of which 140.02 million hectares are net sown area. Since 1990–91 there is gradual but sustained decrease in net sown area from 143 million hectare to 140 million hectares with corresponding increase in fallow land. The demand from non-agricultural uses like industrial and urban requirement as well as speculative demand on account of rising land value is putting pressure on availability of land for agricultural use. There is an urgent need for State Governments to lay out clear policies to protect productive agricultural land and provide specific guidelines on preservation of commons and their protection. There are also other important institutional and policy issues concerning land: proper recording of land titles, easing tenancy rigidities, computerisation of land records as well as addressing declining size of holdings.

12.162. An important aspect of land is its degradation in terms of mechanical, chemical and biological. Widespread and continuing erosion of country's natural resource base is threatening the sustenance of agriculture sector's growth rate. Over 120 million ha have been declared degraded or problem soils (NAAS 2010). Conservation agriculture (CA), integrated nutrient management, carbon sequestration, erosion control, saline and alkaline soils management, legislation for soil protection, development of remote sensing and GPS-based Decision Support System (DSS) and amelioration of polluted soil are required to rejuvenate deteriorated soils.

(D) Use of Fertilisers and Pesticides

12.163. Fertiliser consumption in the country has been increasing over the years and now India is the second largest consumer of fertilisers in the world, after China, consuming about 26.5 million tonnes of NPK. However, imbalanced nutrient use coupled with neglect of organic matter has resulted in multi-nutrient deficiencies in Indian soils. These deficiencies are becoming more critical for sulphur, zinc and boron. As nutrient additions do not keep pace with nutrient removal by crops, the fertility status of Indian soils has been declining rapidly under intensive agriculture and is now showing signs of fatigue, especially in the Indo-Gangetic plain. Potassium is the most mined nutrient. Sulphur deficiencies are also showing up in all parts of the country especially in the southern region. In a comprehensive study carried out by ICAR through their Coordinated Research Project on Micronutrients, Toxic and Heavy metals, based on an analysis of 2,51,547 soil samples from different states, it was found that 48 per cent of these samples were deficient in zinc, 33 per cent in boron, 13 per cent in molybdenum, 12 per cent in iron, 5 per cent in manganese and 3 per cent in copper. The micronutrient deficiency is a limiting factor lowering fertiliser response and crop productivity. As a result of over-emphasis on chemical fertilisers and imbalanced fertiliser use, efficiencies have become abysmally low: hardly 35 per cent for N, 15–20 per cent for P and only 3–5 per cent for micronutrients like zinc, resulting not only in high cost of production but also causing serious environmental hazards. At this rate, the National Academy of Agricultural Sciences has estimated that for meeting the food needs of the country by 2025, India may have to increase NPK supply to over 45 million tonnes from the current level of 26.5 million tonnes and of organic manures from 4 to 6 million tonnes. The Twelfth Plan envisages NPK demand at 34–36 million tonnes by 2016–17, but the more important priority should be to give much greater emphasis than hitherto on fertiliser use efficiency and soil health.

12.164. Restoration of soil health requires initiatives for continuous monitoring of soil health, measures to arrest decline of soil health, creating adequate facilities for soil testing, fertilisers testing, developing and upgrading testing protocols, ensuring judicious and efficient use of fertilisers and pesticides. Judicious use of fertiliser requires adequate soil testing facilities. By 2010–11 there were 1,049 soil tests labs in the country with a soil analysis capacity of 106 lakh soil samples per annum. The State Governments have issued 40.8 million soil health cards to the farmers by October 2011. Although a massive achievement in fairly short time, this remains far below the requirement of soil testing capacity. To augment the capacity the State Governments need to utilise resources from Rashtriya Krishi Vikas Yojana and also engage State Agricultural Universities, Agricultural Produce Marketing Committee and other institutions. There is need for widespread awareness creation for soil-test–based fertiliser use by involving State Agricultural Universities and KVKs and NGO and other stakeholders.

12.165. Measures to soil health improvement need to be comprehensively centred on addition of soil organic matter in substantial quantities over time. The efforts for production and use of available biological sources of nutrients like bio-fertilisers, organic manure, bio-compost for sustained soil health and fertility and improving soil organic carbon and so on as alternative inputs have been inadequate so far. For promotion of these inputs in conjunctive use with chemical fertlisers, and to promote organic farming we need to formulate and define standards for unregulated organic and biological inputs and bring them under quality control mechanism and define/upgrade standards and testing protocols.

12.166. Similarly, use and availability of safe and efficacious pesticides and their judicious use by the farming community is critical to a sustained increase in agricultural production and productivity. Quality of pesticides is monitored by the Central and State insecticide inspectors who draw samples of insecticides from the market for analysis in the 68 State Pesticide Testing Laboratories (SPTLs) that have a total annual capacity of 68,110 samples in 23 States and one Union Territory. However, sale of low quality/spurious pesticides by dealers is widespread and is an issue that States need to handle with seriousness. Further, since use of synthetic pesticides needs to be confined to target control in the right quantity and at the right time, presence of pesticides residue in food commodities is becoming a serious food safety matter. DAC implements a scheme for monitoring pesticide residues and sharing outcomes of the sample analysis with State Governments as well as advising States to take necessary action including promotion of the Integrated Pest Management (IPM) approach, which emphasises a safe and judicious use of pesticides. Many NGOs, however, represent that sporadic promotion of IPM is not helping in establishment of sustainable agriculture practices and that Non-Pesticidal Management (NPM) of pests is the only sustainable answer.

NATIONAL MISSION FOR SUSTAINABLE AGRICULTURE

12.167. A major new mission that will be launched during the Twelfth Plan is the National Mission for Sustainable Agriculture (NMSA). Conceived originally as part of the National Action Plan on Climate Change (NAPCC), this aims at transforming Indian Agriculture into a climate-resilient production system through adoption and mitigation of appropriate measures in the domains of both crops and animal husbandry. Since a number activities relating to sustainable agriculture are already parts of other proposed missions, NMSA as programmatic intervention, will primarily focus on synergising resource conservation, improved farm practices and integrated farming for enhancing agricultural productivity especially in rain-fed areas. Key deliverables under this mission will be developing rain-fed agriculture, natural resource management, enhancing water and nutrient use efficiency, improving soil health and promoting conservation agriculture.

12.168. Nonetheless, since sustaining agricultural productivity through climate and other challenges to the natural resources base is the focus of this mission, it will have to go beyond its programmatic interventions to bring mind-set changes required in transiting from the past focus on irrigated, chemical intensive agriculture. The recent ICAR network project on National Initiative on Climate Resilient Agriculture (NICRA) provides some insights on requirements of adaptation. NMSA can collaborate with ICAR on specific matters regarding adaptation to climate change. The key to this is a paradigm shift that moves towards a knowledge-based, farmer centric and institutionally supported system where the Government is prime mover and facilitator to demonstrate at scale the overall strength and impact of rain-fed agriculture packages that have slowly emerged through several years of grass-roots work by Government and civil society organisations and have shown the strength of combining water and other interventions at a micro-level. The starting point of NMSA must be an accurate assessment of the natural resource, comprising water, land, climate and biodiversity, which determine the opportunities for livelihoods of the people.

(E) Design of NMSA

12.169. While the decision to launch the National Mission for Sustainable Agriculture (NMSA) is quite historical, there are design issues both in view of the fact that the Ministry of Agriculture no longer has a watershed development component in its programmes and because there are strong differences on the matter of fertiliser and pesticides use. While the current National Mission on Micro-Irrigation, the National Project on Management of Soil Health and Fertility and the Rainfed Areas Development Programme (RADP) window in RKVY can be merged with NMSA, none of these address fully the issues that have been raised by the Twelfth Plan Working Group on Natural Resources Management and Rainfed Farming. Its main recommendation is to observe the following:

1. Focus on stabilising and securing diverse cropping by bringing a focus on 'Rainfall Use Efficiency' as central to policy as against mere use efficiency of applied water. This shift calls for two major focal areas:

    a. Promote measures for in-situ conservation and efficient use of rainwater
    b. Invest in shared and protective/supportive irrigation

2. Harness the inclusive growth potential in the so far untapped Agronomic and Management Innovations that are aligned to enhancing sustainability of natural resources, reducing costs, increasing efficiency of resource use and improving total factor productivity. System of Rice Intensification and non-pesticidal management (NPM) of pests as mentioned in the Approach Paper and options evolving in conservation agriculture are some examples.

3. Strengthen the extensive livestock systems depending wholly or partly on commons and agriculture residues through intensive efforts in improving health care, feed, fodder, drinking water, shelter, institutions and so on. The domain of public policy and intervention must shift to these from the present almost exclusive focus on high yielding breeds.

4. Invest in decentralised and local institutional capacities that enable a shift away from one-time Planning to 'iterative Planning—implementation—learning cycles' anchored by local institutions.

5. Enhance institutional capacities in local governance and resource management, particularly related to Commons and strengthen Panchayat Raj, cooperatives and other stakeholder institutions. Such institutional base is a prerequisite for evolving location and agro-ecology specific mechanisms of programme designing, credit access, filling in infrastructure gaps, marketing and so on.

12.170. The specific recommendations of this working group, including the setting up of a National programme on rain-fed farming, could be another component of NMSA, financed by resources currently expended under the scheme of Macro-management in agriculture which housed the watershed development schemes of DAC and will now have to be wound up. This component could mainstream the learning that has emerged from the International Assessment of Agricultural Knowledge, Science and Technology for Development (IAASTD) along with ICAR's National Initiative on Climate Resilient Agriculture (NICRA).

PLAN FINANCING

Expenditure on Agriculture and Allied Sectors

12.171. During the Eleventh Five Year Plan, a combined Plan outlay of ₹1,36,381 crore (at 2006–07 prices) by the Centre, States and UTs was envisaged for the agriculture and allied sectors. The realisation is estimated to be ₹1,30,076 crore at 2006–07 prices, that is, 95 per cent of projected Plan. The priority to agriculture and allied sectors in allocation of resources in the combined Plan of Centre, States and UTs has been around 5.6 per cent in the Eleventh Plan, an improvement over 3.6 per cent during the Tenth Plan. At present about 50 per cent of the agriculture and allied sectors plan in the country is being financed by the Centre, including expenditure on Rashtriya Krishi Vikas Yojana (RKVY).

FINANCIAL PERFORMANCE OF THE MINISTRY OF AGRICULTURE

12.172. Table 12.11 gives the outlay and expenditures of the MoA and its three departments, DAC, DAHDF) and Department of Agricultural Research and Education (DARE), which implement plans and programmes for development of agriculture and allied sectors. The Ministry is likely to realise 88 per cent of the outlay at current prices. A noticeable feature is that RKVY, which was initiated in 2007–08, accounted for 38 per cent of MoA's total plan expenditure in 2011–12(RE).

12.173. DAC with utilisation of around 94 per cent of projected outlay for Eleventh Plan at current prices has shown a better performance. The NHM fell short of targets mainly on account of below par performance in grounding the Terminal Market Complexes. The NFSM and horticultural programmes except NHM have achieved the envisaged financial targets and expenditure on agricultural insurance exceeded the Eleventh Plan projection because of demands arising from the drought of 2009. DAHDF incurred major shortfall in the Plan expenditure. One of the reasons for this was the attempt to introduce a large number of schemes with small outlays during Eleventh Plan which faced problems in their conceptualisation, formulation and approval at various stages. Inadequate staff in the State implementing Departments and resulting limitations on absorption capacity of the States to implement the programmes has also been responsible for the shortfall. Both DAC and DAHDF also transferred increasing amounts through State/District level autonomous bodies, which will need to be avoided in future since this limits the capacity of States to plan comprehensively for agriculture development. Plan realisation is expected to be around 77 per cent in the case of DARE.

TABLE 12.11
Outlays and Expenditure of MoA and Its Three Departments (DAC, DAHDF and DARE)

	DAC	DAHDF	DARE	RKVY	WDPSCA	Total
Eleventh Plan proposed (Current Prices)	41,337	8,174	12,588	25,000	240	87,339
2007–08 Actual	5,769	782	1,280	1,247	40	9,118
2008–09 Actual	6,545	865	1,630	2,887	39	11,966
2009–10 Actual	6,827	871	1,707	3,761	40	13,206
2010–11 Actual	10,208	1,096	2,522	6,720	40	20,585
2011–12(RE)	8,654	1,357	2,850	7,811	50	20,722
Total Eleventh Plan Actual	38,003	4,970	9,989	22,426	209	75,597
% utilisation during Eleventh Plan	92	61	79	90	87	87

RASHTRIYA KRISHI VIKAS YOJANA

12.174. The National Development Council (NDC), in its meeting held on 29 May 2007 resolved to initiate a special Additional Central Assistance Scheme viz. Rashtriya Krishi Vikas Yojana (RKVY). The purpose behind this programme was to encourage States to draw up District and State agricultural plans and also increase their own spending on the sector so as to reorient agricultural development strategies for rejuvenating Indian agriculture during the Eleventh Plan (2007–12). RKVY is preferred by States for its inbuilt flexibility in selecting interventions and setting State specific targets.

12.175. One objective of RKVY during the Eleventh Five Year Plan was incentivising States to increase expenditure on agriculture and allied sectors. State plan expenditures (excluding RKVY receipts) as percentage of GDP in agricultural and allied increased from 1.0 per cent in the Tenth Plan to 1.4 per cent in the Eleventh Plan. State plan expenditures on agriculture and allied sectors (excluding RKVY) have also increased as percentage total plan spending by States, from about 5 per cent during the Tenth Plan to over 6 per cent during the Eleventh Plan. RKVY was therefore successful in motivating States to pay greater attention to agriculture, besides providing increased Central assistance for the sector.

12.176. RKVY as assistance was particularly useful for the funds-starved animal husbandry, dairying and fisheries sectors. Projects amounting to over ₹5,000 crore were sanctioned under RKVY for these sectors during the Eleventh Plan, about 20 per cent of the total sanctioned RKVY projects, and more than spending on DAHDF's schemes. This has provided a substantial push to these sectors which account for a significant contribution to the agricultural GDP.

12.177. However, preparation of Comprehensive District Agriculture Plans (C-DAPs) has been a weak area in many states, partly due to lack of capacity at District/State level. Although there are reservations regarding quality and effective capability of district level planning and project design, this was an original NDC intention and must be fully implemented during the Twelfth Plan. At least 25 per cent of projects sanctioned by SLSCs should originate from the district level, preferably approved by District Planning Committees. For the purpose, suitable units will have to be formed involving ATMA/KVK/SAU and any other technical support unit that States may specify. As mentioned earlier, it is necessary to see decentralised planning as an iterative planning—doing—learning—planning cycle rather than simply a one-time activity. The challenge is to institutionalise this process and ensure that the agency facilitating planning is also accountable for the outcome.

12.178. Further, while there is very strong anecdotal evidence of the early success of RKVY, a detailed impact assessment of the scheme is needed for further experience and learning. Moreover, two modifications are desirable in the present practice. First, there should be a proper committee to examine and vet all projects proposed to the SLSC. Second, that at least this vetting committee or even the SLSC work closely with, and preferably be coterminous with, State level bodies that select MoRD projects, particularly for watershed development. This would permit better convergence and better project selection.

12.179. Many States have requested changes in the allocation criteria of RKVY and some have objected to opening of new windows within the RKVY. A decision has been taken that no more than 20 per cent of RKVY funding will be in such windows of national importance. A decision has also been taken that at least 40 per cent of RKVY spending should be on hard infrastructure spending. A meeting of all States will be held to discuss proposals for changes in allocation criteria.

12.180. Finally, future RKVY design needs to be seen in the context of many pending key reforms. Despite efforts by the Central Government, progress in agricultural marketing, extension and cooperative reforms continue to be sluggish. Delivery of services has not been efficient due to lack of staff at various levels. State Agricultural Universities (SAUs) need greater funding support from the State Governments. Inadequacy of agricultural infrastructure hampers achievement of growth potential of the agriculture sector. During the Twelfth Plan RKVY will need to be reoriented to facilitate such market reforms, higher expenditure on SAUs and for infrastructure development, besides emphasising effective formulation and implementation of District Agriculture Plans. These could be incorporated by changing the current eligibility conditions and allocation formula for RKVY. The proposed meeting of all States as mentioned above will need to be held before these changes in RKVY are proposed to Cabinet.

AGRICULTURAL STATISTICS

12.181. Statistics are the hard input into planning. There are numerous gaps in agricultural statistics hampering the agricultural development planning some of which include reliable and timely availability of forecasts of agricultural crops especially foodgrains, reliable statistics for small areas like blocks and Panchayats, estimates of agricultural production losses due to pests, diseases, floods and drought, good estimates of production of minor crops including spices, condiments, medicinal plants, floriculture and so on, estimates of requirement of foodgrains for seed, feed and industrial use, harvest and post-harvest losses in agricultural production and estimates of meat production. Further, the available estimates generated through sample surveys suffer from organisational and operational problems bringing in inconsistency in these surveys.

12.182. The Vaidyanathan Committee has recommended setting up a National Centre for Crop Statistics, independent of the present system, for providing reliable quick estimates at the National and State level. This should have high priority since not only are there strong doubts about quality of present data among experts, the large increase in number of crop-cutting experiments for insurance purposes may further vitiate the system. An independent source of high-quality data is vital for improving the quality of agricultural statistics in India.

12.183. The existing database relating to horticulture sector needs to be strengthened as mentioned earlier in the horticulture section. Cost of production data for animal husbandry products also needs improvement. Development of appropriate methodology for estimation of feed consumed by livestock will help in updating ratios currently used by the National Accounts Division. Similarly, the existing methodology for generation of fishery statistics needs fine tuning.

12.184. For ascertaining the reliability of land use statistics in the context of diversion of agriculture land to other uses for residential, industrial, urbanisation, roads and so on, there is a need for conducting a study for checking the land records through khasra registers/other records of those villages where the area have come under diversion of agriculture land to non-agriculture uses particularly in the vicinity of the metropolitan cities.

12.185. Pilot studies need to be undertaken for perfecting remote sensing techniques and GIS/GPS tools to develop reliable estimates of area under agro-forestry area under crop production, land-use planning, land development and precision farming and so on.

12.186. All in all, the Twelfth Plan objective is to continue with the decentralisation thrust of RKVY, while reducing number of Centrally Sponsored Schemes. As discussed in relevant sections above, this vision on decentralisation could extend to fertiliser and food subsidies also. While doing this, the main Twelfth plan foci are:

- Bringing scale through development of Farmer Producer Organisations
- Emphasising technology, both on the research and development sides
- Stressing standards and protocols and standard operating procedures in every scheme
- Improving statistics and evaluation
- Initiating a shift towards sustainable and climate-resilient agriculture, not only through NMSA but more generally by laying emphasis on rain-fed areas and bringing about shifts of water-intensive rice cultivation from water-stressed North-West India to Eastern India.
- Preparing for faster growth through a more diversified agriculture, with investment in the necessary modern infrastructure required for perishable products.

12.187. As shown in Table 12.13, States have indicated that they will more than double their plan expenditure on agriculture and allied sectors from ₹1,11,824 crore during the Eleventh plan to ₹2,26,500 crore during the Twelfth Plan. The Centre shall also more than double its plan expenditure. The allocation for RKVY is being raised to ₹63,246 crore for the Twelfth Plan from actual expenditure of ₹22,426 during the Eleventh Plan. The indicative Twelfth Plan Gross Budgetary Support (GBS) for all other schemes of the MoA is ₹1,11,232 crore. This is against corresponding the Eleventh Plan actual expenditure of ₹53,171 crore. Refer to Table 12.12 for department-wise break-up, excluding RKVY:

TABLE 12.12
Gross Budgetary Support (Department-wise)

Department	Gross Budgetary Support (GBS) (₹ Crore)
Department of Agriculture and Cooperation (DAC)	71,500
Department of Agriculture and Research Education (DARE)	25,553
Department of Animal Husbandry, Dairying and Fisheries (DAHDF)	14,179

TABLE 12.13
Comparison of States Outlay and Expenditure for Eleventh and Twelfth Plan

(₹ in crore at current prices)

Name of Sate	Eleventh Plan Outlay		Eleventh Plan Expenditure		Twelfth Plan Outlay		Increase in Twelfth Plan over Eleventh Plan Expdr. (%)
	Agriculture and Allied Sector	% of Total Plan	Agriculture and Allied Sector	% of Total Plan	Agriculture and Allied Sector	% of Total Plan	
Andhra Pradesh	3,487.44	2.4	9,510.46	6.0	17,138	5.0	80
Arunachal Pradesh	752	9.5	617.71	5.7	1,114	5.3	80
Assam	877.86	2.1	2,335.56	7.8	3,272	5.9	40
Bihar	3,672.73	4.8	4,805.33	6.3	15,613	6.0	225
Chhattisgarh	4,613	8.6	5,637	12.7	8,284	6.9	47
Goa	211.76	2.5	325.39	3.6	1,046	3.9	221
Gujarat	9,092.94	0.7	8,879.8	6.9	19,712	7.8	122
Haryana	1,638.82	4.7	2,733.02	5.7	6,288	5.4	130
Himachal Pradesh	1,470.08	10.7	1,642.82	12.1	2,174	9.7	32
Jammu & Kashmir	1,818.21	7.0	892.98	3.5	2,843	9.7	218
Jharkhand	3,130.53	7.8	2,319.85	5.9	4,157	3.8	79
Karnataka	8,426.85	8.3	10,484.4	7.7	19,824	8.9	89
Kerala	2,649.11	7.8	2,931.54	7.6	8,831	11.5	201
Madhya Pradesh	3,408.18	4.8	6,057.09	7.3	17,076	8.5	182
Maharashtra	9,507.64	5.9	10,636.4	7.3	19,325	7.03	82
Manipur	386.55	4.7	234.04	3.2	643	3.1	175
Meghalaya	735.52	8.0	845.2	9.8	2,114	10.7	150
Mizoram	536.31	9.6	387.86	7.1	346	2.8	
Orissa	1,230.29	3.8	3,580.37	8.2	8,387	7.4	134
Nagaland	434.31	8.3	725.08	11.3	1,795	13.8	148
Punjab	1,309.13	4.5	1,410.77	4.0	1,524	2.9	8
Rajasthan	2,919.07	4.1	5,990.67	6.2	7,255	5.6	21
Sikkim	260.43	6.9	228.27	6.4	469	4.1	106
Tamil Nadu	7,831.57	9.2	8,170.01	8.8	20,680	10.0	153
Tripura	798.51	9.0	858.79	11.3	980	6.8	14
Uttar Pradesh	19,146.37	10.6	14,164.8	7.8	24,354	8.5	72
Uttarakhand	2,478.5	8.4	2,079.25	10.0	2,673	5.9	29
West Bengal	1,846.50	2.9	3,339.26	5.1	8,583	5.5	157
Total States	94,670.21	3.6	1,11,824	7.2	2,26,500	7.1	103

13
Industry

13.1. India has become one of the fastest growing economies in the world over the last two decades, undoubtedly aided in this performance by economic reforms. The striking aspect of India's recent growth has been the dynamism of the service sector, while, in contrast, manufacturing has been much less robust, contrary to the experience in other emerging market countries, where manufacturing has grown much faster than GDP; this has not happened in India. Consequently, manufacturing sector's contribution to the GDP has stagnated at 16 per cent, raising questions about India's development strategy, especially its implications for generating adequate employment. Additionally, employment in manufacturing declined in absolute terms from 55mn to 50mn between 2004 and 2005 and 2009–10, after having grown by 25 per cent between 1999 and 2000 (44mn) to 2004–05 (55mn).

13.2. The Eleventh Plan period was marked by unfavourable global economic conditions brought on by the financial sector crisis of 2007–09 followed by the risks of sovereign debt crisis mid-2011 onwards. While this led to slackening demand, exchange-rate volatility and economic uncertainty, domestic difficulties such as poor implementation and delayed reforms also slowed the growth of the Indian manufacturing sector. The year 2009–10 witnessed a fleeting return of manufacturing buoyancy largely on account of a few sectors such as the automotive sector along with a revival in cotton textiles, leather and food products. This brief spurt, however, has now moderated. The net result is that the share of the manufacturing sector in the country's GDP continued to be stagnant, a trend now observed for nearly three decades and remained relatively lower than other emerging and developed economies (refer to Figure 13.1).

13.3. Further, India was not able to fully leverage the opportunities provided by the dynamics of globalisation that resulted in a dramatic shift of manufacturing to developing countries over the last decade. The increasing gap in both, the sectoral share of manufacturing and the competitiveness of the manufacturing sector in India, compared with countries, such as China, is testimony of that (Figure 13.2).

13.4. This shift of manufacturing capacities from developed nations to rapidly developing economies (RDEs) is likely to continue. It is estimated that by 2025 RDE production will account for over 55 per cent of global production compared to 36 per cent presently. Hence, India's ability to capitalise on this by capturing a disproportionate share of such a shift in global economic setting through an accelerated growth rate will be imperative.

PERFORMANCE REVIEW OF THE MANUFACTURING SECTOR

Growth Rate
13.5. The manufacturing sector averaged a growth of 7.7 per cent (till 2009–10) during the Eleventh Plan (refer to Table 13.1). Growth peaked at 14.3 per cent in 2007–08 and then started decelerating. The decline in manufacturing growth was primarily responsible for the slowdown in GDP in 2011–12.

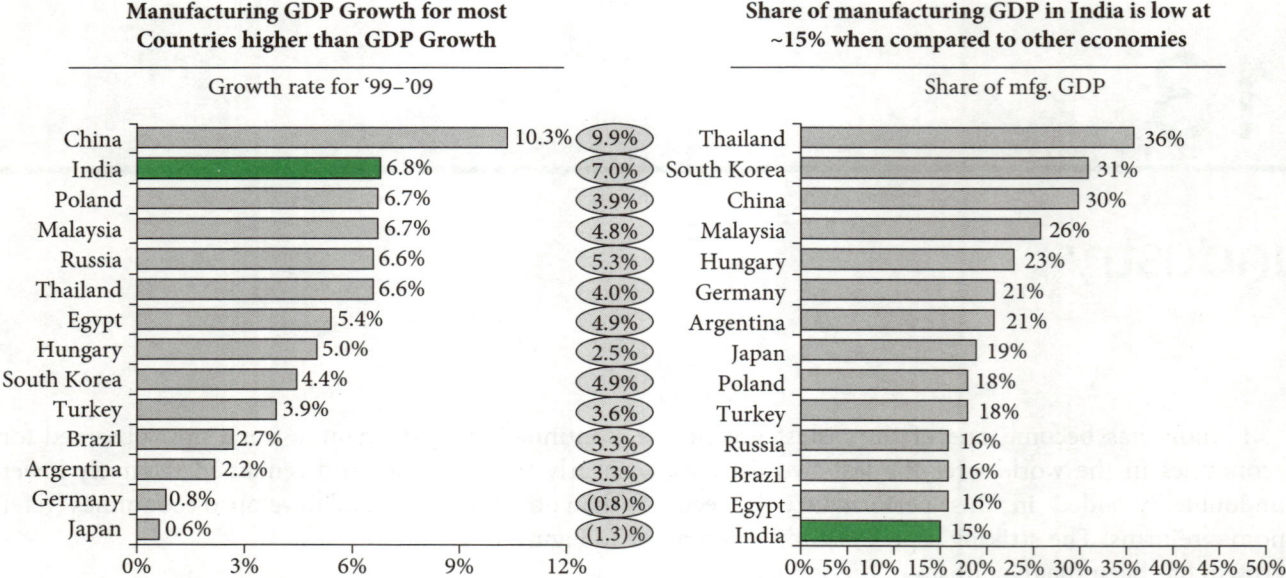

FIGURE 13.1: Contribution of Manufacturing to GDP Very Low in India

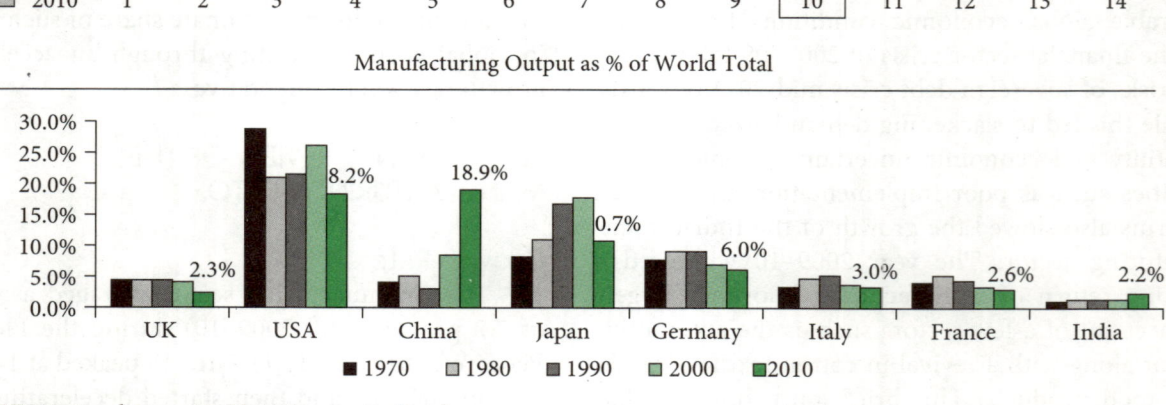

FIGURE 13.2: India and Global Manufacturing States

Initial deceleration in industrial growth was largely on account of the global economic meltdown. Fragile economic recovery in US and European countries, and subdued business sentiments affected the growth of the manufacturing sector. Rising interest rates and appreciation of the rupee during the Eleventh Plan period also contributed to this slow down. It is significant to note though, that volatility of manufacturing growth has become more pronounced over the last five years. An important implication of this is the need for greater flexibility both in policy and non-policy factors which have a bearing on the manufacturing sector.

Investment

13.6. Investment and capacity additions are critical for sustained industrial growth. National accounts data clearly indicate a moderation in the growth of gross capital formation (GCF) in industry (Table 13.2). The rate of growth of GCF in four broad sectors of industry comprising mining, manufacturing, electricity and construction averaged 10.9 per cent during 2004–11, almost the same as the rate of growth of GCF in the economy as a whole. For manufacturing to grow faster than other sectors in the economy, rate of GCF in manufacturing will have to be higher.

Employment

13.7. Employment in manufacturing increased from 44 million to nearly 56 million between 2000–01 and 2004–05. However, employment in manufacturing reduced by 5 million between 2004–05 and 2009–10 (Table 13.3). The net increase in employment over the decade 2000–01 to 2009–10 was around 6 million, that is, a 13 per cent increase over 10 years. Manufacturing in India contributes to only ~11 per cent of total employment. This compares unfavourably to other emerging economies where the share of employment in manufacturing range from 15 per cent to 30 per cent.

TABLE 13.1
Rate of Growth of GDP at Factor Cost at 2004–05 Prices (Per cent)

	2007–08	2008–09	2009–10PE	2010–11 QE	2011–12 AE
Agriculture, Forestry and Fishing	5.8	0.1	1	7	2.5
Industry	9.7	4.4	8.4	7.2	3.9
Mining and Quarrying	3.7	2.1	6.3	5	−2.2
Manufacturing	10.3	4.3	9.7	7.6	3.9
Electricity, Gas and Water Supply	8.3	4.6	6.3	3	8.3
Construction	10.8	5.3	7	8	4.8
Services	10.3	10	10.5	9.3	9.4
GDP at Factor Cost	9.3	6.7	8.4	8.4	6.9

Source: CSO.

TABLE 13.2
GCF in Industry

(₹ Crore at 2004–05 Prices)

	2004–05	2005–06	2006–07	2007–08	2008–09	2009–10	2010–11	CAGR (Eleventh Plan*)
Mining	37,322	52,259	60,456	68,372	57,045	65,984	70,389	3.9%
Manufacturing	3,44,517	4,04,928	4,74,405	6,11,928	4,20,506	5,98,445	6,40,982	7.8%
Construction	54,445	57,531	95,799	1,15,157	88,523	86,290	98,426	0.68%
Total Industry	4,89,584	5,79,391	7,07,029	8,81,464	6,65,067	8,52,999	9,13,051	6.6%
Share of GCF in Industry as % to Total GCF	48.4	49	51.8	54.9	42.5	49.6	48.3	

Source: Economic Survey 2011–12; *CAGR has been calculated for a period of four years.

TABLE 13.3
Employment by Sector

(in Millions)

Sectors	1999–2000	2004–05	2009–10
Agriculture	237.67	258.93	244.85
Manufacturing	44.05	55.77	50.74
Mining	2.17	2.64	2.95
Electricity, Gas and Water Supply	1.13	1.3	1.25
Construction	17.54	26.02	44.04
Services	94.2	112.81	116.34
Total	396.76	457.46	460.22

Source: Planning Commission.

13.8. One hundred and eighty-three million additional income seekers are expected to join the workforce over the next 15 years. Agriculture cannot be expected to provide more jobs. Manufacturing must provide a large portion of the additional employment opportunities required for India's increasing number of job seekers. Unless manufacturing becomes an engine of growth, providing at least 70 million additional jobs, it will be difficult for India's growth to be inclusive. Since the pattern of development of the manufacturing sector so far has not delivered the desired growth in output and employment, a change in strategy is required. This Plan is a description of the strategy, and the process for its implementation, without which the national objectives cannot be achieved.

OBJECTIVES FOR THE TWELFTH PLAN AND BEYOND

13.9. In order to create a paradigm shift in the manufacturing sector, it is essential to consider the objectives over a longer timeframe, such as 15 years. The National Manufacturing Policy, which was introduced in 2011, states these objectives and these are the underlying objectives that the Plan aims to achieve as well. These objectives are:

1. Increase manufacturing sector growth to 12–14 per cent over the medium term to make it the engine of growth for the economy. The 2 to 4 per cent differential over the medium term growth rate of the overall economy will enable manufacturing to contribute at least 25 per cent of the national GDP by 2025.
2. Increase the rate of job creation in manufacturing to create 100 million additional jobs by 2025. Emphasis should be given to creation of appropriate skill sets among the rural migrant and urban poor to make growth inclusive.
3. Increase 'depth' in manufacturing, with focus on the level of domestic value addition, to address the national strategic requirements.
4. Enhance global competitiveness of Indian manufacturing through appropriate policy support.
5. Ensure sustainability of growth, particularly with regard to the environment.

REALISATION OF OBJECTIVES NEEDS A PARADIGM SHIFT

13.10. The Eleventh Five Year Plan as well as Plans that preceded it aimed at establishing a strong manufacturing sector but this has not happened. This suggests that a radical change in the policy approach is needed.

13.11. Comparison with the performance of other countries shows that the countries that managed to catch up with the earlier industrialised, high-income countries were the ones whose governments proactively promoted structural change. Industrial policy, and with a special focus on manufacturing, is back on the national agendas of many countries and we need to consider what lesson we can draw given our particular circumstances. In other words, the critical question now is not whether there should be an industrial policy but what should be the architecture of the industrial policy.

13.12. Industrial policies, where they have succeeded, have generally not been an outcome of Centrally planned economies but of economies that have had the active involvement of private enterprises and other non-governmental stakeholders. Successful strategies evolve from ongoing productive interactions between government and producers. Therefore, the government must improve the process of interaction, collaboration and learning amongst producers and itself. This is very different from the paradigm of Indian industrial policy prior to India's economic reforms commencing in the 1980s. In that era, industrial planning was a top-down control activity with Government determining who should produce what, where and how much and also what technology they should use. The roadmap for the Twelfth Plan and beyond can definitely not be a return to this type of planning.

Nature of Industrial Policy

The Question of 'Industrial Policy'

13.13. The Government of India needs a strategy to accelerate the growth of the country's manufacturing and industrial sectors to meet the goals and obtain the outcomes mentioned. The concept of 'industrial policy' has varied across countries and also over time. In India, industrial policy becomes assaulted under a stifling system of bureaucratic controls through licenses and quotas for industrial production. There is no doubt that these controls were highly dysfunctional and needed to be dismantled but the mere removal of these controls and reliance on markets alone was not sufficient. The collapse of the Soviet Union and the ascendancy of Western free-market approaches to economic growth which was fashionable for a time in the 1990s implied abandonment of any concept of 'industrial policy' altogether. However, this is not the recipe which delivered rapid industrial growth for many of the post-war success stories, whether we think of Japan or Korea or, more recently, China. In planning a strategy for rapid growth of industry in India we need to learn from these success stories and apply them suitably to our circumstances.

Paradigms of Industrial Policy

13.14. Countries that have succeeded in growing the competitiveness and scale of their manufacturing sectors have adopted different policy approaches. However, a common element in their approaches has been a close coordination between producers and government policymakers, with Governments playing an active role in providing incentives for domestic industrial growth and in relieving constraints on industrial competitiveness. The process by which this coordination has been achieved has differed according to the political structure of each country's economy (Figure 13.3). In Japan the coordination between Government and industry (and within Government) was very successfully orchestrated by MITI in partnership with Japanese industrial associations. In South Korea, the Chaebol and the Government collaborated to create world-class and world-scale winners. In Singapore, the Government identified industries to be developed and created ecosystems (skilled human resources, tax regime, Government incentives and so on) to support growth of competitive enterprises in the country. In China,

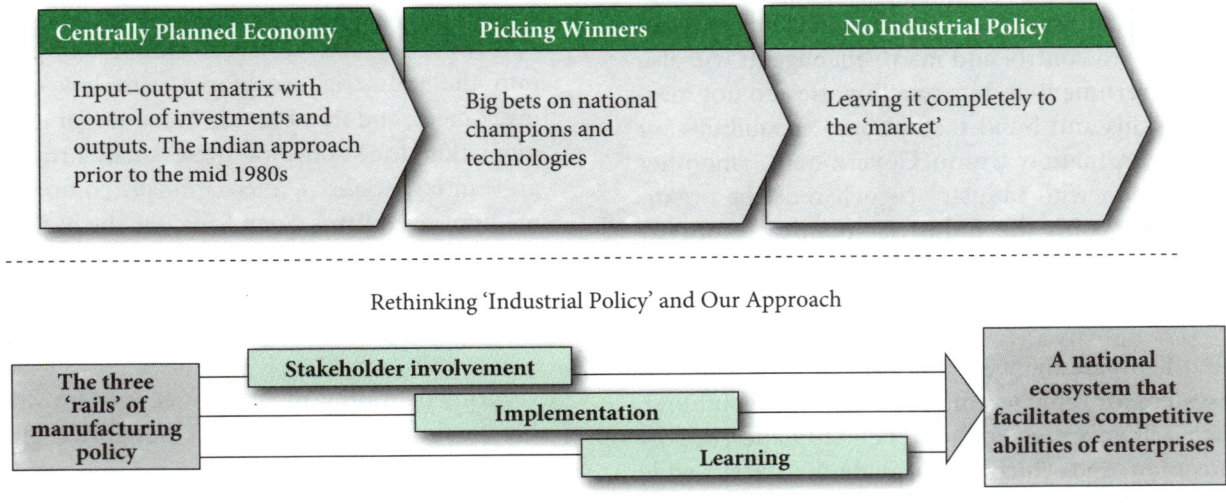

FIGURE 13.3: New Approach to Industrial Policy

the large State Owned Enterprise (SOE) sector has enabled the Chinese Government to adopt a very muscular 'industrial policy'. Along with preferential treatment to domestic companies, large investments in technology development/acquisition, massive investments in infrastructure and restraints on its exchange rate, China's industrial policy has been remarkably successful. Germany's manufacturing sector remains very successful in spite of high labour costs and a strong currency because collaboration between stakeholders in the German industrial system is deeply embedded in policymaking processes and also within industrial enterprises.

13.15. A deeper analysis of such successes (Japan, Korea, China and Germany) of 'industrial policy' and also of its failures (India, the Soviet Union and some instances in Latin America) reveals the essence of successful industrial policy. Firstly, 'industrial policy' is a web of ongoing changes that facilitates the growth of a competitive industrial/manufacturing ecosystem in the country. Secondly, Governments have a key role in facilitating the process of learning and collaboration between producers and policymakers. Thirdly, and this is key, it is the quality of this process of collaboration and the speed of learning and execution in the system that enables the system to improve its competitiveness faster than other countries' systems. Government policymakers must have the skills and orientation to facilitate and coordinate, rather than to control. Industrial policy will not produce a competitive manufacturing ecosystem if the orientation of the Government and its functionaries is to control and micro-manage. It will also fail if Government and its functionaries do not master the skills and build institutional capabilities for better coordination within Government, smoother collaboration with industry (which must be organised in line with the industrial–political economy of the country, as mentioned before) and, above all, faster learning.

13.16. The paradigm we must adopt is to build an ecosystem for rapid learning and capability building, which will encourage entrepreneurship and support innovation, and which will provide the system-wide processes to support collaboration and build stronger value chains with depth. This paradigm requires a change in the mindset of Government functionaries from being 'controllers' to 'facilitators', from 'resource allocators' to 'knowledge managers' and from 'scheme managers' to 'continuous learners'.

Essential Features of a Manufacturing Ecosystem that Learns

13.17. A dynamic manufacturing ecosystem has three features that enable it to learn and grow.

1. Firstly, it must have depth (value addition) in manufacturing processes. A manufacturing sector, no matter how large, that is composed mostly of low value addition assembly industries, cannot create new technological capabilities. It may compete on low costs on account of scale and low labour costs, but it can easily lose these advantages to other countries which have even lower labour costs. Also, merely having R&D capabilities, without the wherewithal around them to convert ideas into manufactured products will not enable the growth of manufacturing industries.
2. Second, it must combine four capabilities: human skills, embodied technology in hardware, knowledge (intellectual property) and a large and demanding customer base. All four components grow together to create a productive and competitive industry.
3. Third, it must have a range of different sized firms, especially small and medium sized ones. Small firms provide the first stages for skill development. They take up larger numbers of people into the industrial workforce with less capital investment, and they provide nurseries for experimentation too. Some of these small firms can grow into specialised, internationally competitive, medium sized firms. Such firms are the backbone of the German industry, and also the strength of India's internationally recognised automotive component, pharmaceutical and IT sectors.

13.18. Firms operating in such an ecosystem would be able to flourish in an open competitive global economy. While there is a case for special support for strategically chosen industries for a limited period, the only way the industry can demonstrate competitiveness is to be able to export to global markets within a defined period.

13.19. In addition to the three features described above, there are five processes that enable the ecosystem to learn.

- Firstly, learning is accelerated through *the interaction of the diverse components of the system*: R&D with producers, both with customers, producers with institutes for skill development, and interactions amongst adjacent sectors and technologies that spur new combinations and innovations. Thus complexity breeds further technological development and growth. This requirement translates into the strategies for building clusters, and linking research and development institutes with *producers*.
- Second is the process of Innovation. Innovation can be spurred by several enablers that create 'safe-failing' spaces for experimentation. These enablers include early stage risk capital, incubators and quick exit/bankruptcy laws. Analysis reveals that the Indian industrial ecosystem has inadequate support systems for experimentation and innovation.
- Third is a regime of Standards. Standards are an embodied learning of the ecosystem. They enable firms, small ones in particular, with a base of knowledge, and also act as means to reduce transaction costs with their customers and suppliers, domestically and globally.
- Fourth is an IP regime. Like Standards, a good IP regime provides a base of knowledge for researchers and producers to develop upon further without having to reinvent the wheel. An IP regime also provides incentives for taking risks by assuring rewards.
- The fifth category of processes that enable system-wide learning and continuing improvement are a class of processes such as total quality management, total productive maintenance, business excellence and so on. In fact, such processes have been the foundations for the rapid, country-wide growth of productivity and competitiveness of the Japanese and Korean industry. The power of such processes has been realised by some sectors of Indian industry too, such as the auto industry, steel industry and so on.

The Architecture of a Strategy to Accelerate Growth of Manufacturing

13.20. Manufacturing enterprises, unlike IT and financial services enterprises, involve the production and movement of material goods. They, therefore, require good physical infrastructure to be competitive and this means improving transportation, uninterrupted power and adequate land to build. Moreover, the materiality of manufacturing activities also results in more regulations—of safety, pollution, factory inspections, labour conditions—and hence a more complex administration structure too. The quality and efficiency of the physical and administrative infrastructure is a basic requirement for productive manufacturing enterprises. This is a major weakness in India at present. The thrust in Government's New Manufacturing Policy (2011) to create good infrastructure for manufacturing enterprises along transportation corridors is, therefore, overdue.

13.21. Good physical infrastructure and smoothly functioning administrative infrastructure are threshold requirements for Twenty-first century manufacturing enterprises to compete in the international arena. However, these will not be sufficient. Competitive manufacturing, requires the development of complex capabilities—technologies, skills and management abilities to coordinate diverse interactions and processes of learning. Such capabilities can be learned and improved. Continuous improvement in these capabilities is the key to sustainable competitive advantage, even absent advantages from raw materials required for manufacturing, as Japan and Korea have demonstrated. Therefore, the thrust of Government strategy must be on the enrichment of the composition of these capabilities in the country's manufacturing ecosystem.

Three Components of India's Manufacturing Strategy and Plan

13.22. India's Manufacturing Plan strategy in the Twelfth Plan must be built around three components. The first are **capabilities and processes** that go across many, if not all sectors of manufacturing, and that build into the ecosystem the processes for rapid learning and building of capabilities.

13.23. The second component has to be the plans to **strengthen the performance of selected sectors**. The selection of these sectors is done by a combination of top-down and bottom-up analysis. From the top, certain sectors appear more important to meet the goals of the Plan for more employment, for example, to produce goods that India needs for its strategic security. On the other hand, the capabilities created by Indian entrepreneurs in some sectors provide potential for more growth, and they should be supported. For example, the pharmaceutical and auto parts sectors. Thus the Plan, at present, has identified 18 such sectors.

13.24. India's sectoral strategy has to be broad-based, covering many sectors, to achieve the large-scale growth that India needs in manufacturing. India cannot achieve its goals by 'picking winners'. In each of these sectors, a sector strategy is required to grow capabilities and relieve constraints. Such sector strategies should be formulated jointly by the associations of producers in the sector (and other principal stakeholders too) and the relevant Government department. They should describe the opportunity for the sector and the actions required from the producers themselves, along with support from Government policies.

13.25. The third, vital, component of the Strategy is the **institutional ability for effective consultation and collaboration** between producers and public policymakers and implementers and the systemic reform of existing systems and processes within the Government. The strength of this process has been found to be the common factor in the success stories of all countries that have built large, competitive manufacturing sectors.

13.26. Lack of co ordination amongst government ministries, and the relatively poor quality of interaction between business associations and government—which is constrained by the competition amongst associations, and the orientation, by and large, towards lobbying and financial sops—prevents improvement in the process of collaborative learning and capability building that India needs to grow its manufacturing sector.

13.27. The challenges to developing and implementing a cohesive manufacturing strategy in democratic India are many. Cohesion can be brought about through more effective coordination amongst agencies, and more effective consultation amongst stakeholders. Apart from this, the Government will also require specialised skills such as consensus building and programme management to manage this process. Government should consider a 'Backbone Organisation (BBO)' to facilitate this process.

ISSUE IDENTIFICATION AND STRATEGIES TO ADDRESS THE VARIOUS CROSS-CUTTING ISSUES

13.28. The focus of this Plan has specifically been on transforming the approach to align the varied stakeholders to a common national goal, instead of having silo-limited views on individual sectors and individual goals (Figure 13.4). In order to achieve this coordination between the various sectors, and to identify the underlying causes of the slow progress of manufacturing, a set of thematic 'cross-cutting' issues were identified in addition to the major sectors of manufacturing. The 'cross-cutting' issues affect the growth of manufacturing across sectors. They fall into two categories: one category is those issues that 'industry' ministries and industrial enterprises have responsibility to address, albeit in collaboration with other stakeholders; and the other category is those broader issues that affect the economy overall in which the responsibility primarily lies with other ministries.

13.29. In the first category is the weak development of human resources, of which a vast quantum is essential to achieve our goals. Another key issue, common to all sectors, is depth within the country of technology in the sector's supply chain. Yet another is a set of the infrastructural challenges, both physical and administrative, related to acquisition of land and water management, and the business regulatory framework, in which industry has a key role to play in developing and implementing solutions in consultation with other stakeholders. These cross-cutting issues have been identified in the National Manufacturing Policy recently approved by the Cabinet. This Plan describes the actions to be taken in all these areas and a process for their implementation and monitoring.

13.30. The second category, that of external inputs to industry that affect the economy as a whole too, and which are managed outside industry, includes four principal constraints on the growth of manufacturing: transport infrastructure, power, cost and availability of credit, and the exchange rate. Transport infrastructure and power have a direct bearing on the competitiveness of manufacturing. Energy and logistics are critical requirements for competitive manufacturing operations. While significant investment were made in transportation infrastructure in the Eleventh Plan, Indian industries continue to suffer from severe infrastructure handicaps compared with the infrastructure available to manufacturers in other countries. Ports are already close to full-capacity utilisation resulting in extremely inefficient turnaround times and similarly roads suffer from congestion resulting in heightened costs. Unreliable and inadequate power supply continues to be a serious impediment in India in spite of the considerable efforts made to enhance power generation capacity in the country. Improving the supply and quality of both transport infrastructure and power are essential requirements for attaining the targeted growth rates for manufacturing in the Twelfth Plan and beyond.

13.31. Adequate availability of low-cost credit is a vital requirement for sustainable manufacturing growth. Continued monetary tightening due to the recent turn of global events has resulted in a high cost of capital, adversely impacting manufacturing investment and growth in India. Cost of capital is key for ensuring competitiveness, especially of exports, of the manufacturing sector and needs to be carefully managed through a more balanced blend of fiscal and monetary measures. Specifically for MSME's, access to credit continues to remain a challenge and besides a host of measures to facilitate greater flow of credit to this segment detailed in Section 5, the overall pool of available capital needs to be enlarged to include alternate sources of capital such as private equity, venture capital and so on.

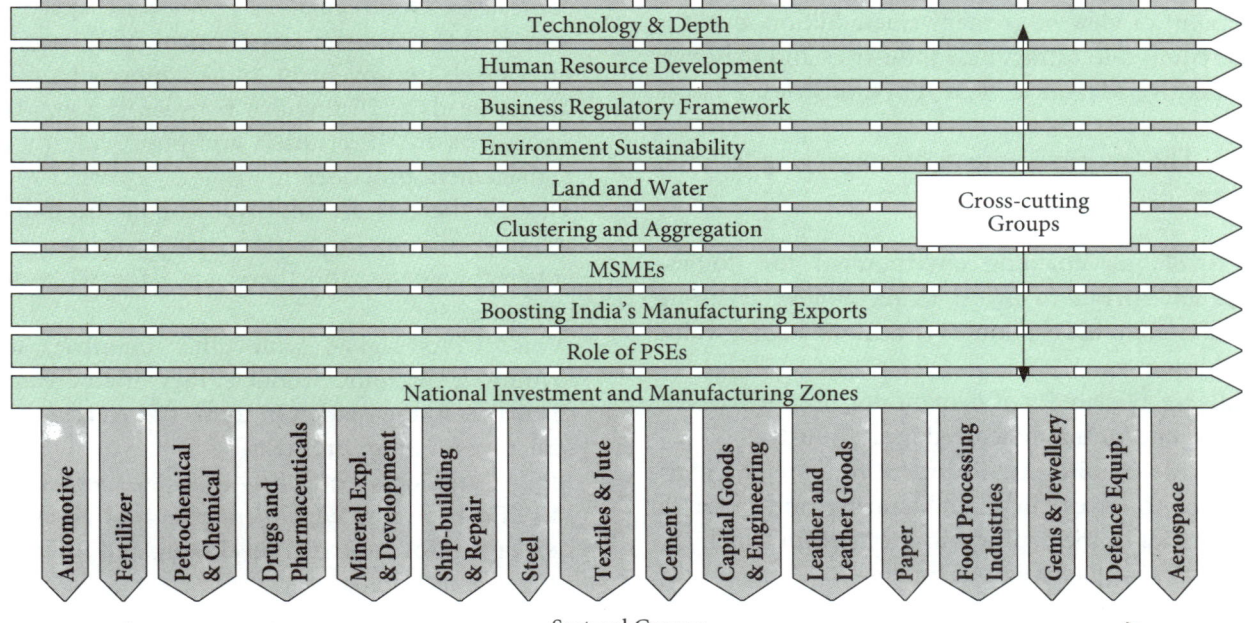

FIGURE 13.4: Focus on Sectors as well as Cross-cutting Issues

13.32. Finally, the exchange rate is an enormously important factor affecting the international competitiveness of a country's manufacturing sector. Large fluctuations in exchange rates can disrupt the management of supply chains. Monetary and fiscal authorities need to be cognisant of the impact that such fluctuations have on the growth of manufacturing.

TECHNOLOGY AND DEPTH

13.33. A principal objective of the Twelfth Plan must be to increase 'depth' in manufacturing, to increase domestic value addition, and meet national strategic requirements. The technological depth of the country's manufacturing sector goes up when it becomes an active player in more parts of the manufacturing value chain (research, development and production). Depth defined in these terms increases synergies across the value chain and also strengthens the overall trade position. It may be noted that depth is not necessarily required in all sectors. There is merit in being part of a global value chain but substantial part of industry must have technological depth.

13.34. Depth in technology is extremely important for a country to sustain its competitive advantage in a global economy. It is not only important from the point of view of greater value addition, but it is also required to attract new industries and maintain competitive advantage of current industries.

13.35. The key requirements for improving technology and depth are to:

- Provide an enabling environment for domestic enterprises to invest in technology creation, technology absorption and achieve higher value addition
- Ensure availability of demand for products developed and/or manufactured indigenously
- Provide enabling environment for foreign enterprises to invest in manufacturing and research activities in the country, in the areas in which the country needs foreign technology
- Mitigate the risks of MSMEs investing in technology development and technology upgradation

Status and Key Challenges

13.36. Lack of depth in technology is one of the foremost issues affecting the growth of manufacturing sector in the country. India's R&D spend is 0.9 per cent of GDP, whereas China, UK and Israel spent about 1.2 per cent, 1.7 per cent and 4.3 per cent, respectively. India needs to increase its R&D expenditure to improve its depth. The private sector finances 70 per cent of the total R&D spending of China, 65 per cent in United States and 75 per cent in Korea and Japan, while Indian private sector funds only 25 per cent of the total R&D spend. As majority of private sector funding of other countries is towards industrial R&D, Indian corporate sector needs to increase its spending on industrial R&D (see chapter on Science and Technology).

13.37. The key challenges faced by Indian industries are:

- The Indian Industry has not given sufficient importance to the documentation of knowledge and creation of IP. As a result, not only were opportunities lost to create IP, but we lost IPs to other countries, such as in traditional agricultural products (IPs filed by western countries on neem, turmeric and basmati rice, which India has contested). Our regulatory framework, speed of award of IPs and the enforcement of IP regulations needs improvement. India's approach on IP, hence, needs to distinguish between shaping the framework for IP creation and improving its IP management processes.
- Though there is an improvement in the industry-academia collaboration in creating patents/technologies, still there is a large scope for improvement.
- While FTAs signed with other countries are favourable for some products, they often create a distortion in the market in terms of inverted duty structure for other products.
- Many segments of the industry, especially MSMEs, have limited information and access to risk capital for sourcing/developing and internalising new technologies.
- The weak attention to standards not only invites dumping of sub-standard products by other

Box 13.1
Examples of Weak Domestic Standards Leading to Influx of Sub-standard Products in the Country

A) Absence of standards

In the absence of technical standards, it becomes easy to import poor-quality products into the country. This hurts the domestic industry as the domestic industry is unable to match the price of these poor-quality products; it also exposes consumers to the harmful effects of spurious products. In the absence of such standards, it would not be possible to make such technical regulations which would curb import of poor-quality products. Some of the examples include mobile telephones, batteries for the mobile telephones, digital blood pressure measuring equipment, decorative lights (imported from China during Diwali festival), medical equipment and so on.

Mobile telephones: Lack of manufacturing standards and testing/sampling labs are prompting dumping by foreign manufacturers. For example, till 2009, there was no standard mandating all imported mobile phones to have an IMEI number. As a result, Chinese handsets without IMEI numbers had a market share of about 13 per cent at that time.

B) Lack of a clear framework for voluntary and mandatory compliances

In some situations, where Indian Standards exist for products or processes, the Central Government has not notified them for mandatory compliance.

Toys: Standards have been laid out for safety of toys such as quality of plastics and paints, electrical and mechanical hazards, migration of heavy elements (Lead, Cadmium) and so on. However it is not mandatory to comply with, and hence toys from other countries are being dumped in the Indian market.

Structural steel: This is used in building damns, bridges and so on. Standards in the manufacturing of structural steel are voluntary and lack the need to specify end use. The lack of compliance to such voluntary guidelines and the absence of the need for requisite certification lead to dumping of poor grade structural steel.

---

countries (refer to Box 13.1), but also makes it difficult for the industry participants to benefit from each other's learning and improve their technology depth.
- Absence of national agenda and policy framework to support innovation.

A Systems Improvement Framework

13.38. It is essential to set the context before moving to the recommendations. Government support is essential to enable a country's industrial ecosystem to gain depth because technological learning takes a long time, requires large investments and is risky. Support to the enterprises should be in such a way that it motivates and enables enterprises to learn and develop complex capabilities and not become complacent and inefficient, which was the outcome of the industrial policy adopted by India until the 1980s.

13.39. Table 13.4 and Table 13.5 capture the generic policy levers that should be moved for faster growth of manufacturing over the next five years. The specific policy interventions must be tailored to fit the requirements of sectors by a process of industry—Government consultation which, as has been emphasised before, will be the key to 'get it right'. MSMEs and large enterprises will require different kind of interventions from Government.

13.40. MSMEs play a critical role in innovation, thanks to their nimbleness and their ability to experiment with new technologies on small scales. However, they often suffer from lack of funds, inability to take risks associated with technology developments and the difficulty of attracting skilled manpower. Policy interventions for MSMEs must be tailored to their conditions. Government policies for MSMEs should therefore help them improve their technological capabilities by focusing on:

- Providing access to risk capital
- Setting up of standards for the industry
- Improving Industry/research institute/academia interaction, mostly in clusters
- Stimulating demand/providing scale through preferential treatment in government purchases

TABLE 13.4
Processes That Enable Learning

Process that Enables Learning	Policy Levers
1. Interaction between diverse components of the system—R&D, producers, customers, Government, institutes of skill development and so on.	• Cluster development • FDI and JVs • Industry/research institute/academia partnership • Higher education in the country
2. Creating 'safe-failing' spaces for experimentation by firms	• Access to risk capital, technology funds • Subsidy on interest costs • PPP model of funding
3. Creating a regime of 'Standards'	• Setting up a system of National Standards benchmarked to International Standards
4. IP regime, which helps firms to build on each other's innovation	• Effective 'IP' regime • Improving awareness of IP
5. System-wide improvement: Processes such as 'Total Quality Management'	• Mainly the firm's role to adopt such tools and increase organisational learning • Nation-wide, and State-wide campaigns to improve 'Total Quality' in all enterprises, including MSMEs, should be sponsored by Government through institutions such as Quality Council of India

Source: Planning Commission.

TABLE 13.5
Manufacturing Ecosystem Infrastructure

Ecosystem Infrastructure	Policy levers
1. Physical infrastructure	• Cluster development • Special manufacturing zones (NIMZ)
2. Improving capabilities	• Skill development • Total quality management • JV, Technology transfer, FDI
3. Creating the manufacturing ecosystem	• Developing MSMEs • Common facilities through clusters • Developing Standards • Availability of quality human resources • Demand availability for manufactured products

Source: Planning Commission.

- Modular industrial estates/laboratories near premier technical institutions with the required plug and play facilities.

Setting Up of a Technology Acquisition and Support Fund

13.41. On the other hand, large enterprises handle complex technologies and manufacture globally competitive products for domestic as well as global customers. They compete with global manufacturers in local as well as in global markets. The Government policies for large enterprises can focus on:

- Improving IP regime
- Ensuring human resource availability by establishing institutions for technology education and research, educational institutions and so on
- Ensuring access to critical raw materials

Strategies for Change

13.42. Some high impact strategies for India at this time to accelerate the development of technological depth in the manufacturing sector have been analysed. These should receive special attention in policymaking and implementation.

13.43. Creation of coherence amongst existing institutional agencies towards developing national priorities for indigenous technology development.

13.44. Several countries like China and Singapore have followed a comprehensive approach to identify critical technologies to be developed indigenously and have formulated mechanisms to ensure that these technologies were funded and incubated.

13.45. In India, we have various agencies like the Department of Science and Technology, NMCC and the Planning Commission working in this area. Connections between these agencies remain weak as they continue to function in silos, resulting in a cluttered approach to technology development. To make this process more robust and comprehensive (including funding and incubating projects), the present process/institutional arrangements should be reviewed and fine-tuned/restructured. The industry, as key stakeholders, should be involved and consulted in the design of new arrangements.

Create 'Safe-failing' Spaces for Companies to Engage in Innovation

13.46. Government participation in funding of research through a 'Technology Fund' or 'Technology Upgradation Fund' is an important instrument for reducing the risk for firms in investment in research. The structure of the 'Technology Fund/ Technology Upgradation Fund' has to evolve over a period of time. Traditionally such funds have been operated in the form of Government grants or schemes. However, they can be more effective in producing outcomes if they were managed by professionally managed investment entities.

13.47. The ways in which the Government could provide/redesign fiscal incentives for R&D activities are:

- *Tax credit instead of tax incentives*: With the imposition of Minimum Alternate Tax (MAT) of 20 per cent, companies are unable to avail full benefit of weighted deduction. Equivalent benefits of weighted deduction on R&D spend should be treated as tax credit and be allowed to be set off against Tax and/or MAT payable.
- *Credit on inputs/capital goods used for R&D outside the factory premises*: The Cenvat Rules provide that credit can be availed on inputs and capital goods if they are used in the factory of the manufacturer. Enterprises having R&D facility separately from manufacturing facility will not be able to claim Cenvat benefits on inputs and capital goods used for R&D. This anomaly should be removed and the Cenvat benefits to be available for inputs and capital goods used in R&D, even if the R&D is carried out in a different premises, as long as linkage between manufacturing and R&D activities can be established. Due to this lacuna, assesses with sizeable investments in R&D facilities outside their factory of manufacture will not be entitled to avail Cenvat credit on investments and certain operating expenses. Consequently, this forms a disincentive to setting up of R&D centres by increasing the costs of setting up such centres.

13.48. The tax incentives should be provided in such a way that they do not penalise existing enterprises that do not operate in special economic zones or particular locations/States. To ensure a 'level playing field' to all domestic manufacturers and to provide a wider stimulus by the incentives, the tax incentives should be available for all enterprises involved in a specific activity rather than for a few enterprises operating in some specific locations. Knowledge sharing should be improved between the industrial and financial sectors.

13.49. The financial sector works with many industrial sectors and thus can see patterns and, with its perspective, obtain insights that are not available to people within industrial institutions. There are several programmes like Small Industry Business Research Initiatives (SIBRI), Technology Development Board (TBD), Biotechnology Industry Partnership Programme (BIPP) and Biotechnology Industry Research Assistance Programme (BIRAP) which promote early stage innovations and PPPs. These institutes should work more often and closely with financial sector institutions to share knowledge that can improve policies for the manufacturing sector.

Strengthen the IP Regime and Systems to Leverage IP

13.50. A strong intellectual property regime is a prerequisite for creation of global IP from India. It has also become a requirement under WTO. While the importance of IP for creation of innovations in the industry is well understood, the question is whether developing countries will get penalised given that they are starting with a low base compared to developed countries. Various alternatives like 'utility model' of patents (as China has) to manage this need to be examined to put in place an efficient model that can help generation and protection of incremental innovations in Indian manufacturing.

13.51. Given the need for a strong IP regime from a long-term point of view, the following steps need to be taken:

- Improve IP management and protection mechanisms.
- Develop global information database on IPs accorded.
- Strengthen and modernise the process of patent examination and according patents.

13.52. Also, in order to leverage the benefits of IP:

- Build awareness about IP through education and training.
- Create national IP mission to continually evolve the IP strategy of the nation.
- Encourage joint IP filings by industry/academia/research institutes.
- Encourage the formation of companies specialising in IPs (through tax incentives).
- Exempt income tax for the income generated from domestic IPs.

Strengthen Partnership between Industry and Academia/Other Research Institutes to Create IPs Domestically

13.53. Industry–academia partnerships are relatively weak in India compared to many other countries. The partnership should aim for building an ecosystem which can create a virtuous cycle of education and research leading to IP creation and its subsequent commercialisation. Such aspect in turn will incentivise and inspire further innovation. Some of the policy measures that Government can use to accelerate the development of industry–academia partnership are:

- Joint ownership of IP arising out of these collaborations.
- Align the goals and annual planning processes of central research institutions with that of industries through industry associations.
- Incentivise Central/State Research institutes to create joint IPs with Industry.
- Tying up a certain percentage of their budget to the number of collaborative IPs created.
- Incentivise university and industry for forging successful partnerships in university's governance, infrastructure, course curriculum design, faculty/students development and research.
- Create cluster innovation centres at universities with the aim to foster a favourable ecosystem and enforce industry–academia linkage.
- Provide an institutional framework for active interface between funding agencies, academia and industry.

Clusters (and NIMZ) Can Provide Enabling Infrastructure to Improve Technological Depth

13.54. Clusters play a critical role in propagating technological depth by facilitating technological learning and manufacturing through the presence of the entire ecosystem in the same geographical location. The National Manufacturing Policy, which outlines creation of NIMZs, was cleared by the Cabinet in November 2011. It ensures that business is provided with the ecosystem required for growth, not only in manufacturing, but also for investments in research and development. The attractiveness of NIMZs will be even higher for new high-technology industries, which will benefit from the localised presence of the entire value chain of participants. Also, the benefits of industrial clusters to MSME participants are also well understood, and the MSME Ministry is using the cluster approach to drive the growth and depth of MSME industries.

Improve Technical Standards, Voluntary Compliance and Conformity Assessment

13.55. Standards are a form of embodied technical knowledge accessible to all types of business that enables more effective product and process development. They promote and enable the diffusion of technology in a form that is readily assimilated by firms with the complementary capabilities to take up and use the new methods. Standards, therefore, constitute one of the important foundations for the technological depth in manufacturing, and are accorded high importance by the policy planners in the developed world.

13.56. During the Twelfth Five Year Plan, the focus on technical regulations should be on:

- Developing a policy on technical regulations.
- Capacity building of regulators (BIS).
- Review of technical regulations to identify the gap vis-à-vis national standards.
- Sensitising the industry regarding the need to provide scientific data to regulators to formulate effective technical regulations.
- Setting up of helpdesks in industry bodies and export promotion councils for information dissemination.

13.57. In addition, voluntary compliance initiatives must be strengthened:

- Promoting and funding a 'Standards Cell' in industry associations and Standards Developing Organisations (SDO).
- Capacity building of SDOs.
- Capacity-building programmes for the training of technical staff in the industry for writing company- and industry-level standards.

13.58. Government should also create a database-based/software-based system to track the changes in technical standards/voluntary compliances globally and alert Indian manufacturers of development.

13.59. While the Standard-setting process sets the standards to be followed, conformity to the standards is assessed by conformity assessment agencies. While many conformity assessment agencies have sprung up in the last few years, it is important that these conformity assessment agencies are of world class and their certificates are acceptable across the world.

13.60. To achieve these, the following steps are envisaged during the Twelfth Five Year Plan period:

- Promoting the acceptance of Indian conformity assessment globally
- Capacity building for inspection bodies/certification bodies
- Developing regulation on conformity assessment

13.61. Quality Council of India, set up jointly by the Government of India and the top industry associations—CII, FICCI and ASSOCHAM, has been working to

- Establish and maintain an accreditation structure in the country
- Help representing India's interest in International forums
- Spread the quality movement through the country

13.62. The Twelfth Plan will focus on strengthening the capabilities and role of the QCI.

Removing Anomalies in Duty Structure

- *Remove special schemes that allow import of finished goods at concessional custom duty*: In almost all promotional schemes where import duties are reduced (nil duty project imports, certain defence purchases, SAD exemption under ITA Agreement for IT products and so on), imports get the benefit of reduced duties/nil duty. This erodes the level of protection which would have otherwise been available, thereby, creating a systemic disadvantage for local manufacturers. It is therefore recommended that import of finished goods at concessional custom duty under special schemes be discontinued.
- *Inverted duty structures (Higher duty on intermediate products vs. final products)*: For specified purposes, presently there is higher duty on

intermediate goods (used by the domestic manufacturer for assembly/manufacture of goods), as compared to duty on finished goods. This in turn leads to higher input cost for the domestic manufacturer. It is therefore recommended that duty on intermediate goods be brought in line or set lower than applicable for final products.

13.63. The Government has corrected, as best possible, the issues related to inverted duty structures (illustrated above) raised by industry. It must review any new case that is brought to its notice and must undertake a study of effective rate of protection across sectors.

13.64. Some issues regarding CST/VAT retention and VAT/SAD were also analysed:

- *CST/VAT Retention:* Interstate movement of goods by domestic manufacturers carries added cost in the form of central sales tax (on interstate sales)/retention of input VAT credits (on interstate stock transfers). This can be avoided in case of imports by executing sales in the course of import or through directly consigning the goods to the customer's state. This creates disadvantage to domestic manufacturers. Therefore, CST on interstate sales and provisions with respect to retention of input VAT on interstate stock transfers should be abolished.
- *VAT vs. SAD*: VAT rates have been increased from 4 per cent to 5 per cent, however there has been no consequential increase in the rate of SAD on imported products which is levied in lieu of VAT. Therefore, SAD should be increased to 5 per cent to reflect the pan-India based trend of revision of the VAT/CST rate bracket of 4 per cent to 5 per cent.

13.65. In order to resolve the aforesaid issues, it is necessary for the Central and State Governments to quickly build consensus on the design of a comprehensive GST and implement the same at the earliest.

Encouraging FDI and Joint Ventures

13.66. FDI (investments by foreign companies in Indian ventures) and Joint Ventures of Indian companies with foreign partners can provide access to technology in areas in which domestic expertise is inadequate. The Government must identify the areas, in consultation with the industry, in which FDI and Joint Ventures can help to bring technology. Several problems that are impeding FDI/JVs need to be addressed. Some these are:

- The ambiguity in the characterisation of income arising to foreign investor on transfer of technology from the perspective of direct-tax obligations. This leads to uncertainty with regards to its taxability in the hands of foreign investor thereby discouraging the flow of technology from outside India. The foreign investor is required to obtain PAN to enable the payer to withhold taxes at appropriate rates. Also, the foreign investor is required to file its annual return of income before the tax authorities in India for the purpose of claiming credit with respect to the taxes withheld by the payer in India. Such additional compliances could become quite cumbersome for the foreign investor in India especially where the foreign investor does not have any operations in India.
- The R&D cess paid by the importer cannot be adjusted against any output taxes paid by the importer, resulting in additional cost of 5 per cent for the technology importer.
- Service tax paid on import of technology cannot be adjusted against taxes paid on output, if the manufacturing is outsourced.
- Limitation on technology cost as percentage of total investment available for state tax exemptions.

Preference for Domestic Products in Government Procurement

13.67. The cost of any manufacturing activity (excluding raw materials and utilities) depends on the maturity of manufacturing technology used and the magnitude of the demand. For a matured technology, the cost of manufacturing will be relatively low, due to the learning curve effects. Similarly, due to scale effects, the unit cost of manufacturing goes down with the increasing demand. Therefore, a domestic enterprise using new indigenous technology will have a cost disadvantage compared to a global enterprise that has the benefits of matured technology. Unless there is some incentive provided to domestic enterprises to offset this handicap, developing indigenous technology will be difficult.

13.68. Therefore, Governments in many countries, developing as well as developed, provide preference in Government procurement to domestic enterprises. However, to ensure that this policy measure does not lead to development of substandard quality products or create inefficiencies in the domestic enterprises, the preference in procurement can be made applicable with minimum quality standards; a cap on the permissible price differential between domestic and imported products, and also a sunset clause.

13.69. Some ways in which the preference for indigenous products can be provided in Government purchases are:

- In sectors of strategic importance, procurement should be done only from those vendors, who have locally established manufacturing base.
- A multi-tier tax structure can be introduced, which offers concessional tax rates for products with higher local value addition.
- A certain percentage of Government procurement to be reserved for enterprises using domestic manufacturing/domestic IP; and a certain percentage of it can be reserved for firms in MSME Sector.

13.70. However, as a prerequisite to implementing this procurement strategy, streamlining of procurement functions is essential. Public procurement organisations must be clear about how national policy goals should be translated into procurement practices without compromising quality. 'Least cost' is not always the right strategy and needs to be balanced by other guidelines (life-cycle costs such as service agreements, continuous improvement contracts and so on). A balanced approach should be taken to determine the weight assigned to price versus other qualifying criteria.

Aligning Investment Obligations Under 'Offset Policy'

13.71. Offsets as a policy tool should be encouraged for public procurement in sectors where the Indian industry does not have existing technology or capability. The obligations of investments of foreign companies under 'Offset Policy' should be targeted towards investment in industries in which the country needs to improve technological depth. Articulation of clear objectives for an offset programme, not just for defence industry but also for the economy as a whole can become an instrumental lever to further investment and growth of the country's manufacturing sector.

Encouragement of Local Value Addition in Critical Natural Resources

13.72. Some natural resources like good-quality coal and iron ore are becoming short in supply in the global economy with growing demand from developing economies especially China and now India. Domestic availability of some of these raw materials provides us a competitive advantage which we should leverage to build domestic industries that add value to these resources, thus creating additional jobs and improving our trade balance. Going further up the value change Government policies and duty structure should be designed in a way to incentivise value addition of steel rather than exporting steel in raw material form.

13.73. In general the trade-off between export of inputs which are in demand elsewhere in the world, and use of those inputs for improving the competitive position of domestic user industries is a tricky one, while promoting entrepreneurial freedom and free trade. These trade-offs must be understood and sensitively managed to ensure competitive and sustainable growth of domestic manufacturing. Examples of vulnerabilities that have developed for Indian industries, when longer term consequences of policies have not been foreseen, are the virtual disappearance of production of intermediaries for generic drugs which China is now dominating, and also the dwindling of Indian capital goods industries (refer to Box 13.2), where too Chinese industry is becoming a big international supplier. Chinese industrial policy

> **Box 13.2**
> **Dwindling Indian Capital Goods Industry**
>
> The capital goods industry can be considered as the 'mother' of all manufacturing industry and is of strategic importance to national security and economic independence. It is in the interest of User Sectors that the capital goods industry be strengthened since it is well established that the presence of a strong domestic industry increases competition and helps in reducing the capital cost of projects. And most importantly, in economical maintenance of plant and machinery. Imported plants come at lower cost but the foreign suppliers make up for that in their high priced spares and maintenance contracts.
>
> However, Indian capital goods industry is facing severe competition from Chinese companies over the last few years. In the case of machine tools, imports account for about two-thirds of the domestic requirements and is increasing further. The import of power-generation equipment from China at much lower cost is also making the domestic industry uncompetitive.
>
> The major factors responsible for increasing Chinese competitiveness are:
>
> - Artificially depreciated Chinese currency
> - Tax advantages and Government subsidies given by the Government
> - Much lower interest rates
> - Simpler labour laws
> - Better infrastructure leading to lower cost of power, transportation and cluster approach helping specialisation of labour and engineering skills
>
> This is further complicated by the absence of level playing field for Indian manufacturers:
>
> - All domestic manufacturers of capital goods are rendered uncompetitive due to additional burden of sales tax, entry tax, octroi, VAT and other local duties and levies.
> - For specified projects (Oil and Gas, mega nuclear/hydel power, fertiliser, refinery and so on) zero/5 per cent customs duty applies on capital goods.
>
> While it may be preferable from user industry point of view to allow the import of capital goods at lower costs in order to improve their competitiveness, this will result in over reliance of Indian industry on other countries for key strategic inputs, exposing itself to vagaries to the policies of these countries. Also, this does not help in building technological depth of the Indian industry and manufacturing ecosystem.

has evidently done far better than India's in building depth in China's industries.

HUMAN RESOURCE DEVELOPMENT, JOB CREATION AND SOCIAL PROTECTION

13.74. One of the primary objectives of the plan is to increase the competitiveness of Indian manufacturing. Human resources are of critical importance for the growth of knowledge and technology, value addition and improvement of competitiveness in manufacturing through processes of continuous improvement. In fact, the human resource is the only 'appreciating resource' in a manufacturing system. It is the only resource that has the motivation and ability to increase its value if suitable conditions are provided, whereas all other resources—machines, building, materials and so on—depreciate in value with time. The best enterprises view their people as their prime asset and the source of their competitive advantage. Nations that have achieved sustainable competitiveness in manufacturing even when they do not have raw materials required, such as Germany, Japan and South Korea, have created systems for the continuous improvement of the capabilities of their human resources.

13.75. India must invest in and build its human resource capabilities to catch up with other countries that have moved ahead and thereafter sustain competitive advantages in manufacturing. Indeed the contentious debate of 'labour' versus 'capital' in the enterprise, as well as disputes between the institutions that represent the people working in the enterprise and owners of the capital could be reframed if employees were seen as assets, with value that can appreciate, rather than as labour costs.

13.76. The purpose of this section is to propose a set of holistic changes in key areas that require close involvement and buy-in from various stakeholders.

Consensus about these holistic changes is more likely to be achieved if, as mentioned before, the primary challenge was reframed as the development of human assets to build India's manufacturing ecosystem and strengthen India's manufacturing enterprises, rather than merely management of costs of labour.

13.77. Challenges in meeting the objectives lie broadly in three areas:

- From a skill development perspective, there is a significant gap between the existing training capacity and people entering the workforce. A very small proportion of total manufacturing workforce is currently skilled.
  Moreover, less than 25 per cent of the total number of graduates are estimated to be employable[1] in manufacturing.
- The total training capacity in the country is about 4.3 million for all sectors including manufacturing.[2] The Apprentice Training Scheme (ATS), which is supposed to provide a bridge from education to employment, has very low penetration and is suffering from significant administrative issues.
- For entrepreneurs and other employers, the perceived lack of flexibility of changing the size and nature of the workforce can act as a retardant in making investments that could lead to greater employment opportunities. Furthermore, the complexity of labour laws and the administrative mechanism of the laws make it harder to do business in the country.
- By 2025, an additional 8 million management workers[3] (supervisors and above) are estimated to be required. Well-trained management/supervisory staff are critical for improving the productivity and industrial relations in large as well as small manufacturing enterprises.

Strategy and Key Recommendations

13.78. Human resources should be managed as a source of sustainable competitive advantage. Government policy changes should induce and support such firm level strategies. The key stakeholders who will need to work together to make the necessary changes to the system in key areas mentioned above are: Government (at the Centre and State level), Industrial organisations and the unions.

13.79. The strategies for meeting the objectives are in the following categories:

- Inducing job creation by reducing the cost of generating employment.
- Developing a supply of qualified human resources to meet the demand from additional job creation.
- Enhancing skill levels of current workforce to improve productivity.
- Improving the state of manufacturing management in the country.
- Providing social protection to low-income workforce.
- Improving industry–workforce relationships.

Inducing Job Creation by Reducing the Cost of Generating Employment

13.80. There are two major barriers to employment generation: limited flexibility in managing the workforce and cost of complying with labour regulations. Both these barriers must be removed in order for jobs to be created at a much faster rate.

Limited Flexibility in Managing the Workforce

13.81. The recommendations to increase the level of flexibility while ensuring fairness are:

- Companies should be allowed to retrench employees (except categories such as 'protected workmen' and so on) as long as a fair severance benefit is paid to retrenched employees. This severance benefit should be higher than what is currently mandated—and the value should be arrived at through tripartite dialogue between Government, employers' associations and employees' associations.
- In order to ensure that there is sufficient liquidity to pay the severance benefit to the retrenched employees, a mandatory loss-of-job insurance programme could be put in place. This will especially be useful in situations where the retrenchment is due to bankruptcy or exit of the employer and will reduce the justification for requiring prior permission to shut down businesses.

- The threshold level of employment for the Chapter VB of the Industrial Disputes Act and the threshold for applicability of the Factories Act should be raised to at least 300 which was the level in 1983.
- The process of engaging contract labour should be reformed—employers should be allowed freer use of contract labour while ensuring that the rights of contract workers are protected, which is not the case at present.

Cost of Complying with Labour Regulations

13.82. The traditional enforcement approach which is based on inspection—prosecution—conviction creates incentives for rent-seeking behaviour, especially if the laws are complex or have provisions that are contradictory. The complexity of compliance impacts smaller enterprises much more. They cannot bear the high administrative costs.

13.83. Recommendations to improve compliance and also contain the cost of complying with labour regulations are:

- Simplification of labour laws: The implications of labour laws should be detailed through a series of ready reckoners that are easily available and regularly updated so that inspectors and employers have a common set of rules to look at.
- Improvement of administration: Higher investment should be made in the training of inspectors to ensure that they are able to efficiently identify incidences of actual non-compliance rather than harass employers.
- Facilitating easier filing: Filing of reports should be made a once a year activity with an online option. As far as possible, the interface between enterprises and Government should be computerised to increase transparency and efficiency and remove scope for rent seeking.
- Developing a self-certification model: While ensuring that regulations governing labour welfare must be complied with, a self-certification model should be developed where appropriate.
- Additionally, fiscal incentives to encourage permanent job creation should also be considered, after evaluating their implications and potential impact. For example, skill building and training costs of permanent employees can be considered for accelerated tax benefits (subject to a ceiling on percentage of salary paid to permanent employees).

Developing a Supply of Qualified Human Resources to Meet Demand from Additional Job Creation

13.84. The manufacturing sector may need more than 90 million people by 2022. However, the current capacity for skill development is ill equipped to meet this demand.

13.85. *Role of industry*: To enable the industry to play its role in defining the requirement of manpower both in terms of quality and quantity, Sector Skills Councils envisaged in the National Skills Policy are being set up. These councils will identify skill development needs in their sector, evaluate the gaps, create plans for skill development and improve the quality of the training system. The councils are also expected to establish sector specific Labour Market Information Systems (LMIS) to assist in planning and delivery of training.

13.86. *Private sector participation in skill development*: For the private sector to play a role in augmenting the skill-development capacity in the country, effective PPP models are needed. Existing ITIs should be clustered together in projects with total training capacity of at least 1,00,000 each to allow private sector service providers to leverage scale benefits leading to long term financial sustainability. For inducing the private sector to participate in creation of additional capacity, scalable and sustainable business models with direct linkages to employment should be deployed. The NSDC has created such models. They should be implemented across 20–30 projects specific to manufacturing in partnership with industry associations and from funding through NSDF.

13.87. *Improving ITIs*: We need to improve private-sector involvement in upgrading existing ITIs and also improve their curriculum and content through the sector-skills councils.

13.88. *Attracting students*: As a long-term strategy, it is important to make acquisition and improvement of skills an aspiration for people, especially youth. This could be achieved by recognising high-skill persons at the national and State levels along with recognition of other worthy citizens. For example, an unsecured loan scheme should be created for those who aspire to undertake vocational training. Large enterprises could also provide special incentives and recognition for acquisition of high skills.

13.89. *Overall coordination*: A number of initiatives have already been taken by various Government ministries to tackle issues related to skill development both at the Central and the State level. Coordination between these initiatives should be improved. The role and performance of the National Skill Development Coordination Board should be assessed. To ensure that skill-development activities are aimed towards areas of maximum impact, it is important to put in place an information system that provides data on availability and requirement of skilled resources.

Enhancing Skill Levels of Current Workforce to Improve Productivity

13.90. Training and skill building of the existing workforce is an important element of the strategy for increasing productivity of manufacturing in India. Training of employees can be incentivised by allowing tax deductions for expenditure incurred on training. Currently, skill building is predominantly achieved by in-house training of workers by each enterprise. However, clusters and NIMZs provide opportunities for shared infrastructure to provide training for skilled and semi-skilled workers.

13.91. A number of existing initiatives are focused on setting up tool rooms which are necessary for SMEs. These tool rooms can be made more effective by periodic performance audits by independent agencies and also by operating them on a PPP model in collaboration with industry associations. Just as tax incentives are provided for investments in critically required infrastructure assets, fiscal measures including tax benefits on training expenditure may also be considered for investment in critical human assets. MSME Sector alone needs to skill 42 lakh persons in the Twelfth Plan period, thus, requires to increase its current training capacity from 4 lakh person per year to at least 17 lakh persons per year by 2017.

13.92. Apprenticeships can be an effective way of ensuring that entry-level workers have the skills required to join the formal workforce. While there should be no obligation to employ apprentices, the current apprenticeship model needs to be reformed by simplifying workflow for engagement of apprentices by employers, inclusion of new trades and recording compliance through e-filing, removing NOC requirement for out-of-region candidates. Further, it is proposed to make all graduates eligible for apprenticeships and the duration of courses should be reduced to a minimum of three months and should be converged with MES. Outdated curriculum needs to be updated and outsourcing of classroom trainings should be allowed.

13.93. Changes in the Apprenticeship Act may have to be made. In the meantime, a new model of in-company training should be deployed. In this model, companies should be allowed to take trainees for a period of up to six months.

Improving the State of Manufacturing Management in the Country

13.94. There were a total of approximately 5 million managers in the manufacturing sector in 2008. If the manufacturing sector grows at the targeted 12–13 per cent, 8 million more managers will be needed by 2025. Well-trained managers are extremely important for improving the productivity of manufacturing enterprises and maintaining harmonious industrial relations. Currently, only a very small portion of graduates from engineering and management institutes take up careers in manufacturing. Consequently, there is a significant gap between supply and demand.

13.95. The quantity and the quality of management in the manufacturing sector can be improved by the following initiatives:

- Increasing collaboration between manufacturing companies and engineering/management institutes for joint projects in which staff and

students of the institutes can get some hands-on experience.
- Encouraging enterprises (especially larger ones) to run good graduate engineering programmes which can be a source of management talent for themselves as well as the manufacturing sector generally.
- Scaling up programmes such as Visionary Leadership for Manufacturing (VLFM) at the national level.
- Setting up centres of excellence for manufacturing management through MoUs between institutes, government bodies and industry partners. Business schools that focus only on manufacturing management should also be encouraged.
- Creating a PPP model for engineering and management colleges with partnership with industry associations and employers with focus on manufacturing management.
- Launching a campaign focused on attracting management talent to the manufacturing sector.
- A large source of potential managerial/supervisory staff is the current workforce. Support should be provided to enable deserving members of the workforce to be promoted to management positions.

13.96. Recent reviews with many sectors of industry reveal a crying need for better supervisors and foremen—the first and second levels of supervision—who are the backbone of productive and harmonious manufacturing enterprises. Development of supervisors and foremen, through suitable programmes, collaboratively designed and managed by industry and educational and training institutions must be ensured along with the emphasis on development of skilled workmen and good managers.

Providing Social Protection to Low-income Workforce

13.97. Formal sector workers can leverage collective bargaining to obtain social security; however, the informal workforce is dependent on government actions to improve social protection for them. A number of social security schemes have been launched in the recent past. However, the existing coverage represents a very low percentage of the total number of workers in the manufacturing sector. For example, the New Pension Scheme (NPS) that was launched in May 2009 to increase pension coverage, particularly to the informal sector, has less than 2,00,000 voluntary subscribers—this is far less than the total intended coverage for such a scheme. Limited access to social security is exacerbated for those with low or uncertain incomes.

13.98. *Unemployment benefits*: Low income workers in transitional phases of unemployment are particularly vulnerable as they are unlikely to have significant savings. To help overcome the problems associated with social protection for temporarily unemployed workers, which include contract workers at the end of their contracts, a solution could be for these workers to be part of a 'sump' as permanent employees of contract agencies that are provided with Government support to ensure skill upgradation of these workers. The focus should be on creating a pool of workers who can be available to employers and ensuring that those that are unemployed have avenues for training as well as financial assistance. For example, the Automotive Mission Plan has recommended the formation of a Supplementary Unemployment Benefits Fund to be created by automotive companies for providing compensation to laid-off workers. Such funds in other sectors too can be utilised to finance the creations and sustenance of the 'sumps' that could be the 'win-win' solution out of the 'fairness–flexibility' dilemma.

13.99. *Increasing penetration of existing schemes*: To ensure that existing schemes reach the entire workforce, it is important to increase awareness of these schemes through communication programmes. The distribution channels for these schemes should be evaluated and measured regularly and private sector participation should be encouraged too. Financial literacy of the workers in the informal sector should also be improved so that they make better informed decisions about participating in social-security schemes.

Improving Industry Workforce Relationships

13.100. Strong and effective industry relations can enable managements of enterprises and their workers to collaborate in increasing the productivity and competitiveness of the manufacturing sector. Unions have a critical role to play in ensuring inclusive growth of the manufacturing sector, especially by working towards social protection for the workforce. They can also play valuable roles in other areas such as skill development. The National Skill Development Policy has recommended that trade unions contribute in areas such as developing competency standards, course design, improving awareness of and promoting participation in skill development among the workforce. To ensure that unions can play a broader and more effective role, it is important to invest in capacity development of unions through training of their leadership.

13.101. The multiplicity of unions in the same enterprise for the same type of workers can lead to inter-union rivalries and can weaken collective bargaining. Therefore, legislation that enables one union per enterprise is strongly recommended. The union leadership should also be held accountable for any illegal behaviour by union members during negotiations. The practice of withholding recognition of unions should be discouraged. Strong gain-sharing systems can help to improve productivity.

13.102. The Government has a crucial role in enabling good industrial relations by providing platforms for the industry and the workforce to participate in policy development and implementation. Since labour figures in the concurrent list in India, both the Central and State Government's role in such platforms should be that of an impartial facilitator focused on creating consensus amongst employers and employees around solutions. In especially contentious areas such as changes in labour laws, the Government should enable the development of consensus positions between the various interested parties. The 'backbone organisation' described in the Way Forward Chapter should have the capabilities to effectively assist in such a process of consensus creation.

BUSINESS REGULATORY FRAMEWORK

13.103. Countries that have performed better than the others in terms of thriving business have, to a great extent, done so on account of the quality of the business regulatory environment, which is an important factor distinguishing better performing countries from others. The key objectives of streamlining of business activities through the regulatory framework should be:

- Low compliance cost for doing business in India
- Simple regulatory environment, saving time and energy for the businesses; and
- Ensuring fair competition

13.104. The country must improve regulations and implementation in many subjects to make India generally a more attractive country for doing business. These include land and environmental regulations, labour laws and their administration and so on. It should be noted that, in the context of India's federal structure, the ability to mandate specific reforms to the regulatory framework from any centralised apex body is fairly constrained. Therefore, while nodal agencies may be set up to focus attention on matters that must be attended to across the country, and this section and others mention some, it is imperative that the role of such agencies in the process of making improvements across the country fits the country's federal and decentralised political structure. Such agencies cannot and must not usurp local authority.

Status and Key Challenges

13.105. The present regulatory environment is seriously deficient for the reasons enumerated below:

- Weak institutional architecture for business regulations in the country
    - Despite that high priority of the business regulatory reform agenda in the country, there is no dedicated authority that can guide the whole process of reform in a structured, planned, cogent and systematic manner, which could mandate the respective departments of the Union, State and Local Governments to comply in a timely, result oriented and predictable way.
- Ambiguous nature and vast scope of business regulations: there are vast numbers of business regulations at different levels of Government in existence in the country. There are instances of

contradictory as well as overlapping business regulations on account of these being administered by the different tiers as well as layers of Government.
- Absence of national repository of business regulations: despite the advancements in Information and Communication Technology (ICT) and its ever-growing applications and usage, there is no dedicated online repository to track all the business regulations and procedures.
- Lack of coherence in business regulatory governance across country; business facilitation is often mentioned as part of the agenda at the national as well as State levels. But there is lack of coherence in all such efforts. There are wide variations in Government-business transactions taking place in different locations of the country. It has also been found that there is a lack of predictability and standardisation in terms of timelines as well as process adopted by different State Governments when it comes to facilitating business.
- Lack of defined mechanism for consultation between Government and industry: the interface between Government and the industry is also not well defined. There are periodic consultations among various industry collectives and specific Government departments located at different levels, but such consultations are not structured enough to be guided by a well-defined and outcome-oriented process.
- Inherent limitations of regulatory system in country: lack of periodic-review clauses in regulations and Lack of Regulatory Impact Analysis (RIA).
- There have been recommendations for regulatory reforms earlier as well, but due to absence of any one dedicated agency accountable for the reforms, they could not be implemented.

Strategy and Key Recommendations

Follow-up Over Previous Administrative and Regulatory Reform Endeavours

13.106. Lack of implementation of earlier recommendations on regulatory reforms has contributed to the current situation of business-regulatory framework in the country, both at the Central and State level. All these recommendations need to be reviewed and a repository of all these documents needs to be created. After this an enquiry can be taken up to check the extent to which these recommendations have been implemented or are pending by the public authority or department.

13.107. There is a need for a process for responding to the existing recommendations. In such a system once a certain expert group or commission of enquiry has submitted its report, the respective departments are required to prepare a response. That response is put up in the public domain along with the original recommendations. This makes it easier for various stakeholders to understand the extent to which the recommendations have been accepted along with the reasons for non-acceptance, if any.

Establishing Enabling Institutional Architecture
- Formulating national policy on business development and regulation
  - The policy should also provide the principles of optimal business regulatory governance. It is recognised that there will be a special role of the Prime Minister and Chief Ministers in the aforementioned policy making process because in the final analysis, the actual adoption of the policy will entirely be dependent on the political leadership.
- Drafting and enacting 'National Business Development and Regulation Bill'.
- Building institutional architecture for looking after the business-regulatory reforms in the country: a dedicated institution can be set up for this purpose. The institution should be set up at the national level as well as at State level.
- Enabling institutional architecture for ensuring competitiveness in manufacturing. The same is required in both, Central as well as State level.
  - At the Central level the National Manufacturing Competitiveness Council (NMCC) has been entrusted with this responsibility.
  - Similar institutions may be set up at State level; to be called State Council on Manufacturing Competitiveness and Competition Reforms.
- In June 2011, the Ministry of Corporate Affairs has set up a Committee to draft National

Competition Policy (NCP). In February 2012, the Drafting Committee submitted a Draft National Competition Policy and comments of all stakeholders have been invited. Once this policy is approved by the Union Cabinet, further steps are required:
- Building consensus on the policy
- Creating institutional framework for operationalising the policy, as recommended by the Committee
- Creating incentive and disincentive mechanisms for States to implement NCP
• Operationalisation of National Manufacturing Policy and development of State manufacturing plans in line with National Manufacturing Plan.

Systematisation of Business Regulatory Governance
• Mapping and classification of all existing business regulations and procedures and providing an online one-stop shop—'National Business Facilitation Grid' for all information related to business regulations and procedures in India. Design principles of this on line portal can be finalised through a consultative process. The Department of Industrial Policy and Promotion is the nodal agency for the NBFG repository.
• A system of mandatory reviews of existing regulations at periodic intervals should be established and operationalised. This will achieve the desired goal of making the regulatory system intrinsically strong and up to date.
• A decentralised Single Window System should be established with appropriate geographical spread. The Single Window System, governed by a common minimum standard, should, rather than being a coordination office, be endowed with access to relevant information and sufficient delegation of powers from all concerned regulators, including Central, State, Local and Sector regulators. This would help reduce the start-up time for businesses by providing all requisite approvals and licenses, if any, through the Single Window System.
  - Recognising the wide variations with business procedures at the country level, it is recommended to benchmark the execution timelines and processes that are undertaken by different Government entities to facilitate business requirements.
  - A team of Business Facilitiation Officers (BFOs), in each of the partcipating regulatory authorities, may be asked to aid the Single Window System, and the BFOs could be made accountable for defaults or deviations resulting in aggravated costs of compliance to businesses. The desirability and feasibility of such a Single Window System should be determined through a consultative process.

eBiz Mission Mode Project
13.108. The eBiz Mission Mode Project, under the National e-Governance Plan, aims to create a business and investor-friendly ecosystem in India by making all business and investment related regulatory services across Central, State and Local governments available on a single portal, obviating the need for the investors or the business to visit multiple offices or a plethora of websites. It in envisaged that the services offered on eBiz will eventually cover the entire life cycle of a business—right from its establishment, through its ongoing operations, to even its possible closure. Once operational, this project will also create a platform for multiple Government agencies to cross validate their information.

13.109. The project is being implemented as a 10-year PPP with M/S Infosys. The first-year pilot includes 8 Central Departments and States (Andhra Pradesh, Haryana, Maharashtra, Tamil Nadu and Delhi) covering 29 core services. Five more states (Punjab, Uttar Pradesh, Odisha, West Bengal and Rajasthan) and 21 more services will be added during the next two years of the pilot phase. An end-to-end solution providing the services under the Andhra Pradesh Single Window Act will also be provisioned on the eBiz platform by September 2013 along with the payment solution gateway.

Adopting Regulatory Impact Assessment (RIA)
• Tool of RIA should be developed for Indian context through a consultative process and due research reflecting upon global experiences with its adoption and usage.

- The parameters of RIA should be clearly spelt out for evaluation (which should gradually be expanded to include the following eight elements: policy coherence; cost of doing business; competition; innovation; SMEs; consumers; labour; environment and commons).
- Process of doing RIA should involve a wide stakeholder consultation.
- RIA has be to be mandated in the country in ex ante as well as ex post manner.
- It is recommended that Policy Coherence Units (PCUs), for conducting RIA, be established under the respective State Planning Boards and at the national level. Such policy analysis functions can be connected with the capabilities of the proposed backbone organisation.

Making Businesses More Responsible Towards Society

- Considering the importance of the subject, 'business responsibility' should be included as a separate subject under the Government of India (Allocation of Business) Rules 1961, and Ministry of Corporate Affairs can be entrusted with the responsibility of carrying out these activities.
- Redefining the contract of business and society and developing new rules of the game for corporate conduct.
  - Needs to be done through a widespread consultative process.
- Stronger role of business associations in responsible business.
  - Business associations should be encouraged to develop and impose rules of conduct on their own members.
  - Business associations should be entrusted with the responsibility of overseeing the compliance to rules of corporate conduct.
  - Such associations should provide their members a process for debating and agreeing on voluntary imposed norms, assistance to members to develop capabilities to conform to these norms and, very necessarily for such associations to become trusted by stakeholders as effective institutions for self-governance, internal governance that disciplines errant members.
- Disclosures on the adoption of 'National Voluntary Guidelines on Social, Environmental and Economic Responsibilities on Business' (NVG) principles should be made mandatory for businesses. Adoption of NVG principles can be made mandatory for all public–private partnership projects by the relevant authority at the time of project inception. This will help in mainstreaming these principles.
- Establishing the required institutional architecture for facilitating adoption of NVG principles. Awareness and implementation of NVG principles is currently the responsibility of the Indian Institute of Corporate Affairs. The IICA's abilities in this respect should be further strengthened.

Developing an Ongoing Process of Stakeholder Consultation

13.110. For achieving the objectives of a stakeholder consultation, it is imperative to have capacity, building both ends: at the Government side as well as at the industries. A process of productive consultations, and the roles of representative institutions of employers and unions in these consultations, in improving the productivity of the country's manufacturing ecosystem, and its sustainable competitiveness, cannot be overemphasised. The competitiveness of German and Japanese manufacturing industries, in spite of high-wage costs and expensive currencies, in contrast to the relative decline of US and UK manufacturing industries, is attributed to the better collaborative processes in the former countries. The following actions must be taken to achieve this objective:

- Passing a legislation mandating stakeholder consultation and also defining the process that needs to be followed.
- Measures to strengthen industry associations and their structure to enable them to convey the view of industry in a constructive manner.
- Similar capacity building for stakeholders, such as labour unions.

13.111. *Developing a Business Regulatory Governance Mechanism* to choose appropriate regulatory alternatives among self-regulation, co-regulation and public regulation.

- Currently there is no structured modality exploring various alternatives for achieving regulatory objectives.
- Detailed analysis should be undertaken to determine which alternatives to regulations are feasible as well as beneficial for Indian context.
- As each form of regulation has merits and demerits, a desirable combination of all three regulatory alternatives may be evolved gradually.
- Such mechanism will serve as a ready reference one-stop shop for the policymakers as well as the business community while arriving at the choice of appropriate mode of regulation.

Capacity Building for Carrying Out Regulatory Reforms

13.112. Since carrying out the aforementioned regulatory reforms requires a tremendous effort, capacity needs to be built in order to implement them. The capacity-building framework needs to incorporate the following:

- Developing resources such as modules, guidelines, methodologies, reference manuals, checklists, case studies and so on as reference material for regulators.
  - These resources should also be available through an online-knowledge portal.
- Training programmes for regulators need to be arranged.
- A review may be initiated to determine the feasibility of expanding the roles of institutions functioning under the aegis of the Ministry of Corporate Affairs, namely, Indian Institute of Corporate Affairs, Competition Commission of India, Institute of Chartered Accountants of India, Institute of Company Secretaries of India and Institute of Cost Accountants of India.

ENSURING ENVIRONMENTAL SUSTAINABILITY WITH INDUSTRIAL GROWTH

13.113. The rise in growth in the resource intensive manufacturing sector is enabled and facilitated by an ever-increasing rate of material use leading to manifold impacts to the environment. The contribution of the manufacturing sector to environmental degradation primarily occurs during the following stages:

- Procurement and use of natural resources
- Industrial processes and activities
- Product use and disposal

13.114. The air, water and land are affected through the environmental impacts created through the operations of manufacturing units.

Key Objectives

13.115. Rapid ecologically sustainable industrial growth with focus on

- Mainstreaming and promoting green business: an environment has to be created wherein being green is not viewed as just an obligatory expectation of a company, but as an area of primary focus for the company to develop further and be recognised as a leader.
- Protecting natural resources: natural resources have to be prolonged to their fullest use to maintain the aim for continual economic growth and lessen environmental impacts.
- Addressing funding issues: which act as a constraint for movement towards a more sustainable industrial model.

Status and Key Challenges

13.116. The Central Pollution Control Board has identified 17 highly polluting industries, the majority of which are manufacturing industries. MSMEs, in particular, can have a significant impact on the environment as they are generally liable to be equipped with obsolete, inefficient and polluting technologies and processes. Seventy per cent of the total industrial pollution load of India is attributed to MSMEs.

13.117. New technologies leading to cleaner processes and operations are not being developed at a fast enough pace to address the urgent need for environmental protection.

13.118. The current ecosystem does not encourage and facilitate the mainstreaming and scaling up of new technologies for widespread use, mainly due to a lack of financial support, resources and Government assistance.

13.119. The waste management and recycling industry in India is currently vast but largely unorganised. In this space, it is necessary to mainstream the industry and ensure that the livelihoods of all people dependant on this industry are supported and upgraded.

Strategy and Key Recommendations

Organised Waste Management and Recycling
- Development of a National Waste Management and Recycling Programme
  - This is an overarching framework to create and mainstream the organised waste management and recycling industry.
  - Structured frameworks and guidelines for recycling industry to be developed to integrate it with the existing waste management rules and guidelines.
  - Development of industry and sector specific recycling standards.
- Promotion of PPP model for waste management and recycling
  - Establish facilities for reuse, recycling and reprocessing of wastes from various sectors should be encouraged by providing incentives and ensuring the process for setting up PPP facilities.
- R&D funding
  - Promoting new technologies and processes for waste management and recycling.
  - This should be aligned with the overall technology fund as discussed earlier.
- Building institutional capacity
  - Local institutional bodies must have their capacity built on recycling and waste management.

Creation of a Green Technology Fund
- For usage in three key areas: technology upgradation, promotion of green entrepreneurs and funding for R&D.
- This could be disbursed in the form of concessional loans, grants and so on.
- This fund should be a part of the overall technology fund proposed for improving depth in manufacturing and must ensure focus on commercialisation of new technology areas.

Promotion of Green Products
- Development of a framework and guidelines for promotion of green products
  - Definition of the specifications
  - Creation of/assignment of a new/existing entity to perform this task on a regular basis
  - Identification of top 100 green products (based on assessment of maximum environmental impact) and setting of standards for the same
- Promoting green public procurement through price incentives on Government tenders
- Encourage and develop voluntary rating programmes
- Creation of centres of excellence to promote green products and processes
- Incentive programmes for creation of Life Cycle Inventories
- Incentives for export of green products

Environmental Regulatory Reforms and Market Based Instruments
- Strengthening regulatory institutions together with bringing institutional reforms
  - Moving towards load-based standards from concentration based regime.
- Implementing polluters-pay principle, with specific pollution loads beyond a defined benchmark should be priced and paid for by industry.
  - Reforming the existing environmental clearance process.
  - Institutionalise the concept of cumulative impact assessment of the region.
  - Introducing technology assessment while appraising new projects.
  - Process for administering the clearances needs to be streamlined—should include considerations of decentralisation, requirements and tenure of clearances.
- Establishing integrated chemical-management policy and regulatory regime
  - Set up a regulatory process to assess all chemicals, register and phase-out toxic chemical products and replace them with non-toxic/less-toxic substitutes.
- Market-based instruments and emission trading
  - Initial pilot Emissions Trading System to limit particulate matter emissions.

- Scale up the emissions market to address additional pollution problems at the State and national levels.
- Monitoring technology for all types of pollutants be made as affordable as possible for industry; waiving of applicable taxes and excise duties, as well as direct subsidies to monitoring technology wherever their installation is mandated by the State pollution boards.

Sustainable Environment Management in MSMEs
- Reconstitution of regulatory bodies
  - Inclusion of stakeholders/associations.
  - Sector-wise product sub-groups need to be formed as part of PCBs.
  - Grievance Redressal Mechanism should be established at each PCB.
- Creation of common infrastructure for MSMEs in clusters
  - Central Grant Scheme for soft infrastructure, unit level technology upgradation assistance, portion of project cost for Common Effluent Treatment Plants.
  - State Grant Scheme with provision for arranging land for CETPs, time-bound speedy legal clearances, provision for equity participation in SPVs by SPCBs/State agencies.

Disclosure on Performance
- Short-term action to increase voluntary disclosure of environmental sustainability performance.
  - Development of reporting standard-based on several existing sustainability reporting initiatives.
  - Incentives for voluntary disclosure.
- Long-term steps to compare environmental sustainability performance of organisations with industry-specific benchmarks.

Development of Environment Sustainability Benchmark Index, Especially for Identified Highly Polluting Sectors

Organised Waste Management and Recycling
- As covered in the chapter on Environment, the development of a National Waste Management and Recycling Programme and the promotion of PPP model for waste management and recycling are required.

WATER ISSUES

13.120. With its increasing population and industrial activity, India is moving towards perennial water shortages. The current per-capita water availability is estimated at around 1,720.29 m3 per capita according to data from the Central Water Commission and as per the World Water Development Report—one of the United Nations, India has been ranked 133 (Out of total of 182 countries) in terms of total renewable per capita water resources.

13.121. The total water demand is projected to increase by 22 per cent by 2025, and 32 per cent by 2050. A major part of the additional water demand will come from the domestic and industrial sectors. The water demands of the domestic and industrial sectors will account for 8 per cent and 11 per cent of the total water demand by 2025.

Key Objectives
- Improve the governance and management of water in order to ensure availability of water for all purposes.
- Improve the management of water by industry, in particular in terms of utilisation and pollution.

Status and Key Challenges
- Inadequate storage capacity
- Governance deficit and fragmented institutional framework
- Inadequate water management by and for industry
  - Water intensity high as compared to global benchmarks—to the extent of ~30–50 per cent.
  - Recycling water in industry is not common and its proliferation is not happening at the scale as required.

Strategy and Key Recommendations

13.122. Strategy on improving overall governance and management of water has been covered in detail in the section on Water Resources. The proposed draft National Water Framework Bill will provide the broad overarching national legal framework of general principles on water which will necessitate the requisite administrative frameworks needed for greater clarity on demand management, protection of water resources, improving efficiency of water use and so on.

13.123. Specifically, strategic measures to ensure availability for and efficient utilisation of water by industry have been outlined below.

Water Management in Industry

- Create equity-based and efficiency-based Water Pricing Regime for industries
  - Overcome lack of a clear policy framework based on cost-recovery principles.
- Current pricing regime is undervalued for all users.
- This would overcome wide variations in tariff structure due to current determination by various States.
- All Indian cities currently operate a mix of measured/metered or unmeasured/unmetered tariffs.
  - Potentially two different pricing regimes in two-tier tariff system/IBT tariff system.
- Enforce 'Water returns'
  - Annual return to be filed by water users on similar lines of tax returns—should include key measures like water utilisation per unit produce, effluent discharge details, rain water harvested, water reuse details, fresh water consumption and so on.
  - Mandatory for major water using industries and businesses.
- Promote reuse and recycle of wastewater in industry
  - Regulations and incentives through national frameworks and a system of water returns
- Industry specific standards
  - Promoting rain-water harvesting in industry, both within and beyond the fence through incentives and regulation.

LAND ISSUES

13.124. Among all the traditional factors of production for any economic activity, land being natural, immovable and non-renewable, is a distinct resource. It needs to be looked at from Industry's perspective as a tangible resource with supply and demand issues and the linkage in the form of land acquisition for industrial demand.

13.125. Land in India has a special significance because it carries a huge tangible and emotional value for owners and also for those whose livelihoods depend on it. This makes it very important to consider the land acquisition process in a critical manner.

Key Objectives

13.126. The key objectives with regard to solving the various issues and challenges related to land pertain to:

- Improving the management of land as an asset in India.
- Setting up a more transparent, fair and efficient process of land acquisition for industry development.

13.127. By achieving these key objectives, we would be able to ensure a more productive utilisation of land, and in particular, be able to spur industrial development, which has in many instances been hindered as a result of poor land management and land acquisition processes.

Status and Key Challenges

13.128. India has sufficient land for all uses—agriculture, industry, human dwelling, infrastructure and other uses—as long as it is used with prudence and productivity. Currently industry utilises only about 2–4 per cent of all land in India. Even at heightened industrial activity in the future, it is expected that there would be sufficient land for all users, including industry. However, there are some critical issues that need resolution in order for land to become a well-managed resource, especially from the point of view of Industry.

13.129. Land is inherently an imperfect market, because land is an immobile asset. Hence, no two pieces of land are alike and can be differentiated. This gives rise to a monopolistic power with the landowners. Furthermore, the value of a piece of land effectively changes when we change its usage and due to development of surrounding areas. In addition, the owner is often emotionally attached to his land. In India, land is considered a very important asset from an emotional perspective.

13.130. A major characteristic of land ownership in India is that the land holdings are typically small. Typical industrial usage requires development of large tracts of land. Consequently, industrial development has as a prerequisite need to acquire land from a large number of owners in order to develop a contiguous piece of land for industrial use.

13.131. Another problem in the land market is the incomplete, outdated and inaccurate land records, which give rise to disputes and litigation. Since industrial projects require large amounts of land and land holding in India is fragmented, industrialists have to deal with a large number of landowners and consequently face substantial risk of litigation.

13.132. In addition, there are some restrictions on usage of agricultural land for non-agricultural purposes. Non-Agricultural Use Clearance (NAC) from the local/State Government is necessary before agricultural land can be considered for other uses.

Strategy and Key Recommendations

13.133. A three-pronged approach should be undertaken for tackling the land issues. This includes the development of an institutional framework to support the various actions, a drive to create Land Use Policies to manage land better, and a reformed process of land acquisition (Figure 13.5).

13.134. *A National Land Use Policy should be developed* to take care of the growing requirements of land for sectors other than agriculture. *State Governments should formulate appropriate Land Use Policy* in alignment with the National Land Use Policy. The main features of this policy should be *Land Mapping* (record of types and quanta of land available), *Land zoning and Digitisation of Land Records*. The Land

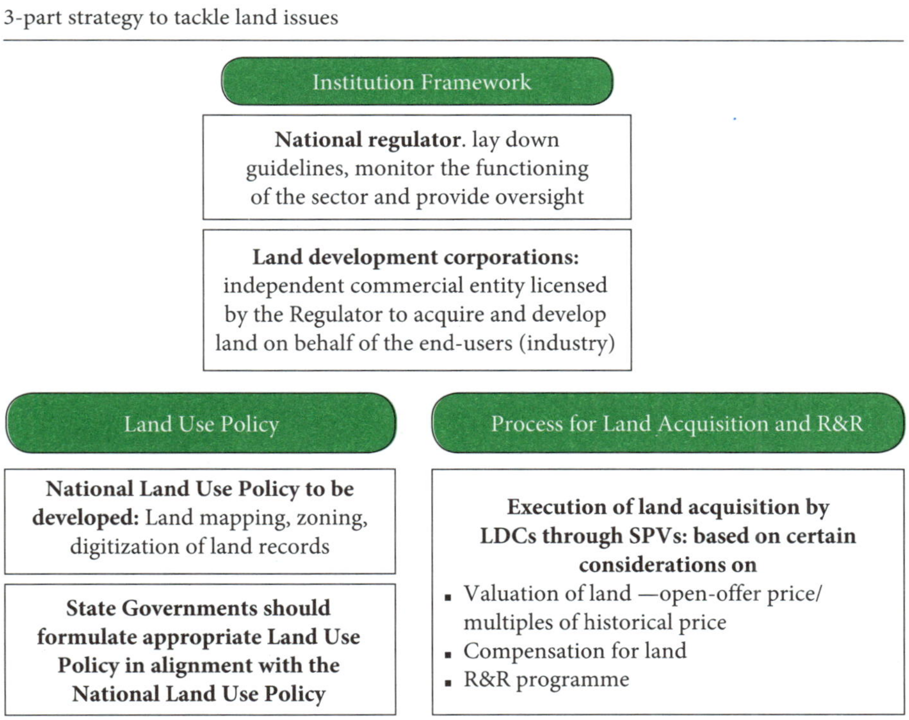

3-part strategy to tackle land issues

Institution Framework

National regulator: lay down guidelines, monitor the functioning of the sector and provide oversight

Land development corporations: independent commercial entity licensed by the Regulator to acquire and develop land on behalf of the end-users (industry)

Land Use Policy

National Land Use Policy to be developed: Land mapping, zoning, digitization of land records

State Governments should formulate appropriate Land Use Policy in alignment with the National Land Use Policy

Process for Land Acquisition and R&R

Execution of land acquisition by LDCs through SPVs: based on certain considerations on
- Valuation of land —open-offer price/ multiples of historical price
- Compensation for land
- R&R programme

FIGURE 13.5: Strategy for Land Issues

Use Policy should also look at measures to optimise utilisation of land by benchmarking current utilisation efficiency with global benchmarks, and setting standards and incentives for more efficient utilisation.

- There is a need to establish an independent and autonomous regulator which can lay down guidelines, monitor the functioning of the sector and provide oversight. The regulator should
  - encourage State and local Governments to define zoning of land, ear-marking them for different uses, and encourage digital land records
  - define guidelines for valuing various types of land for different uses
  - Establish norms for setting up and operating Land Development Corporations (LDCs) and monitor adherence to the norms by these institutions
  - lay down the guidelines for acquiring land by a corporate body
  - establish norms for process of land acquisition, compensation and relocation and rehabilitation of various stakeholders for different project characteristics
- *Value of land* can be determined, as per the guidelines laid down by the regulator, in the following ways:
  - *Open-offer price*: Land owners will be asked to submit their application for sale of land in a reverse-auction process.
  - *Multiple of historical price*: The regulator can set a price based on a multiple of the historical land prices, as mentioned in the land records of the government.
- The acquiring agent for land should be an independent commercial entity—Land Development Corporation— that has been licensed by the regulator to acquire land. The role of LDC would be to acquire and develop the land on behalf of its clients (end users) in exchange of the process and maintenance fee. A State can have multiple LDCs and each LDC will execute projects through SPVs. The operations of the LDC will be under the purview of the regulator.
- The *process of land acquisition* will be guided by the regulatory framework applicable for the project characteristics as defined by the LDC in its SPV. The role of local/State Government authorities in supporting the acquisition process should be laid out clearly by the regulator based on project characteristics. The acquisition process may vary depending upon
  - minimum per cent that the SPV needs to acquire from individual landholders before regulation mandates compulsory acquisition of land from other owners
  - nature of consent required from different stakeholders
- *Compensation for land* needs to factor the following:
  - upfront payment
  - annuity income stream
  - participation in the future appreciation due to growth as a result of land development

  In addition to the above factors, the land owner needs to have the flexibility to choose a compensation package
  - an owner can choose to take the full value in upfront compensation or take a part of it as annuity payouts (determined by prevailing financial indicators of the time)
  - however, every land owner will necessarily have the component of 'participation in future appreciation' as part of the compensation
- The *LDC has to operate a rehabilitation and resettlement programme* with combination of different elements which have been defined by the regulator based on the project characteristics; these include elements like.
  - alternative dwelling, if displaced
  - skill development
  - assistance in employment/income-generating opportunities
  - community development
- The *Industry* must be *responsible for payment of cost of land acquisition*, including market price, share of the appreciating value and cost of the comprehensive R&R.
- There should be a *timeframe defined for land acquisition*, and the LDCs must *interface*

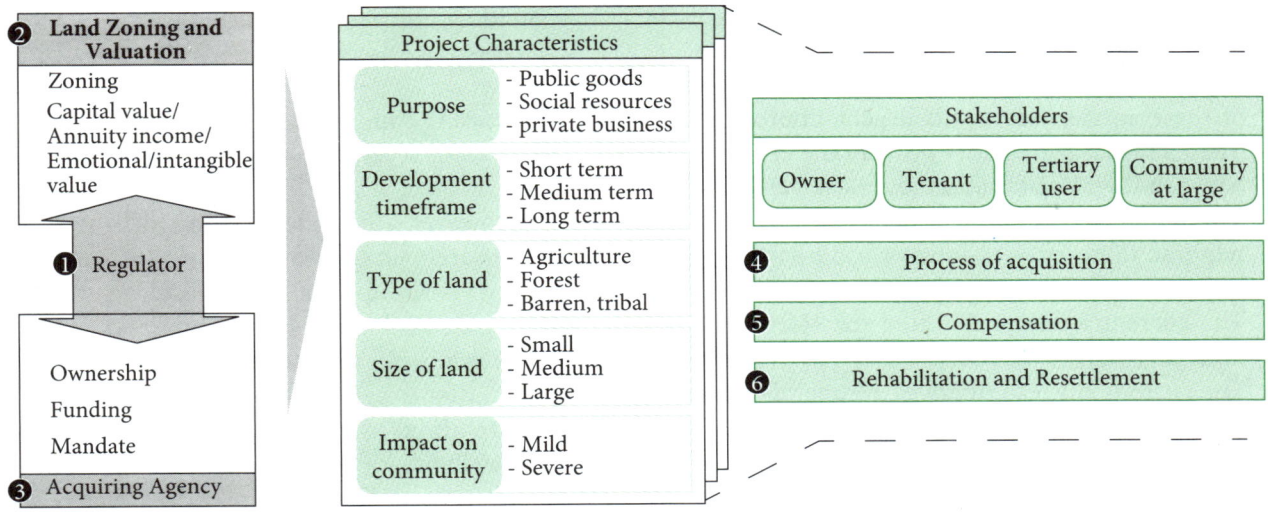

FIGURE 13.6: Description of Land Acquisition Process

appropriately not only with the local self-governance bodies, but also other grass-root level organisations in order to *build awareness about the land acquisition process.*

13.135. A description of the process of land acquisition, the role of the institutional framework and the other modalities related to land acquisition is provided in Figure 13.6.

CLUSTERING AND AGGREGATION

Introduction

13.136. Industrial clusters are increasingly recognised as an effective means of industrial development and promotion of small and medium-sized enterprises.

Status and Key Challenges

- For MSME participants, clusters play an important role in their inclusiveness, technology absorption, efficiency improvement and availability of common resources. Ministries dealing with MSME enterprises have been using Cluster programme as one of the key policy tools in administering Industrial Policy. There are around 7,000 clusters in traditional handloom, handicrafts and modern SME industry segments.

- The Ministry of Micro, Small and Medium Enterprises (MSMEs) adopted the cluster approach as a key strategy for enhancing the productivity and competitiveness as well as capacity building of small enterprises (including small scale industries and small scale service and business entities) and their collectives in the country. The Ministries have been administering hard and soft interventions to help the cluster participants. While hard interventions will include investments in infrastructure like common facilities, common testing centres, roads, the soft intervention will include training, capacity building, skill improvement, marketing inputs, product design and development and so on.

- In order to assess the level of intervention required, MSME Ministry has carried out a diagnostic study of about 471 clusters. However, the follow-up on these studies have been weak.

- Today, the cluster programmes are administered by various ministries (textiles, leather, food, MSME, heavy industry [auto]) under various names with different terms and conditions. This apart from putting the cluster participants through procedural hurdles also makes it very tough to learn from each other and improve the efficiency of these schemes.

- Though many of the cluster schemes make it mandatory to have an SPV, a Project Management Agency and Cluster Associations, the capacity of these aggregators needs urgent improvement. These cluster aggregators provide the crucial link between the Ministry and the cluster participants. The cluster aggregators also need to have soft skills required to impart a vision to cluster participants, and see beyond their immediate requirement.
- The current amount allocated for soft interventions is grossly inadequate.
- The current cluster initiatives are mainly focused towards MSME Sector. Other industries can also benefit from cluster programmes as demonstrated by the automotive industry clusters.
- There is a deficit of trust between the various participants in clusters today, which needs to be addressed.

Strategy and Key Recommendations

- It may be desirable to set up a Cluster Stimulation Cell (CSC) at apex level (to be located in DIPP/NMCC) to monitor the performance of clusters and share best practices across them. The CSC should also develop a cluster manual which may define clusters, development strategies adopted across the clusters, share best practices and develop a communication channel. The constitution of a CSC will considerably reduce the coordination problems across the clusters and within clusters across different sectors. The CSC should.
- Undertake mapping of clusters to identify the key bottlenecks and the means for overcoming the same. It would also enable devising an appropriate strategy and support mechanisms for including the clusters in the growth trajectory.
- Maintain information about all the clusters along with the cluster participant profile, employment generated and so on.
- Evaluate the performance of these clusters on predetermined range of various performance parameters.
- Identify best practices and ensure sharing the best practices across clusters, in areas like
  - Building trust among participants
  - Cluster branding
  - Building innovation at cluster level
  - Suggesting fiscal incentives to provide to clusters
  - Increasing competitiveness of cluster players
  - Effectively leveraging the common facilities

13.137. However, the effectiveness of the CSCs depends entirely on the way they are structured and run. If CSC is set up as a hierarchical organisation controlling clusters, it will lead to suboptimal results as the line ministries are the best agencies for implementing cluster programmes. On the other hand, If CSC is structured as knowledge organisation, with the responsibility of enabling clusters to improve their performance, CSCs can play an effective role in improving the performance of clusters across the country.

13.138. Today there are several agencies playing critical roles in developing and supporting clusters:

- Implementing ministries like MSME, Textiles, Leather, Food Processing and Heavy Industries
- State Governments
- Department of Science and Technology and National Innovation Council in the areas of technology upgradation and innovation

13.139. Normally, clusters, especially for MSMEs, develop on their own and Government may play a facilitating role to accelerate their growth. However, going forward the State Governments should have devolved powers to create clusters while the Central Government's role should be to stimulate learning across the system. Hence, the CSC is envisaged as knowledge partner to these agencies. The roles of CSC will complete a crucial missing link in the cluster support ecosystem.

- Provide assistance to State Governments in the cluster formation through strengthened DICs at district level besides NGOs and reputed institutions that have capacity to undertake this type of work.
- Develop strategies for growing different types of clusters (for example, hub-and-spoke, MSME, high tech and so on) for the different sectors.

- The CSC should undertake this exercise and include details on the approach to be employed for each type of cluster and sector.
- The scope of soft interventions should be expanded to include capacity building of Cluster associations, initiatives aimed at improving market linkages, improving product quality, improving access to credit, encouraging innovation, skill development and so on.
- The allocation of funds for soft interventions should be increased accordingly.

PROMOTING MSMEs

13.140. The Micro, Small and Medium Enterprises (MSME) sector has emerged as a highly vibrant and dynamic sector of the Indian economy over the last few decades. It is estimated that this sector contributes about 45 per cent of manufacturing output and 40 per cent of total exports of the country and employs about 69 million persons in over 29 million units throughout the country. Within the MSME Sector there is a significant concentration of Micro Enterprises, both in terms of working enterprises and employment (refer to Table 13.6). There are over 6,000 products ranging from traditional to high-tech items manufactured by the MSMEs. The sector also covers the enterprises established in khadi and village industries and coir sector (plans for these sectors are detailed in Annexure 13.3).

TABLE 13.6
Registered MSMEs—Manufacturing

	Micro	Small	Medium
Working Enterprises	94.9%	4.9%	0.2%
Employment	69.2%	26%	4.8%

13.141. Recognising the contribution and potential of the sector, the definitions and coverage of MSE Sector have been broadened significantly under Micro Small and Medium Enterprises Development (MSMED) Act, 2006 (refer to Table 13.7). Service sector, an important emerging sector, has also been included under this Act, depending on its category into Micro, Small and Medium Enterprises. The criteria of investment limit in plant and machinery is the only parameter, used to categorise the enterprises in the sector in the country.

TABLE 13.7
Definition of MSME

Nomenclature and Classification of MSME (Manufacturing)	Ceiling on Investment in Plant and Machinery (in INR)
Micro	25 lacs
Small	5 crore
Medium	10 crore

13.142. It is important to recognise though that a broad band of differentiation exists within the MSME Sector across indicators such as turnover, employment and so on. Further discussion on MSMEs also needs to specifically address organised and unorganised segments. Classification based on investment in plant and machinery only superficially institutes a numeric threshold for describing a funnel of growth. Schemes and interventions based on such concretised classifications, however, may not be able to necessitate real growth as such definitions create perverse incentive structures that might thwart firms from graduating from small to medium, such as service tax exemptions for firms with less than 10 lac revenue, exemption from central excise duty for firms with an annual turnover of less than ₹1.5 crore and so on.

Key Objectives

13.143. The objectives for the MSME Sector are:

- Promoting competitiveness and productivity in the MSME space
- Making the MSME Sector innovative, improving technology and depth
- Enabling environment for promotion and development of MSMEs
- Strong presence in exports
- Improved managerial processes in MSMEs

Status and Key Challenges

13.144. MSME Sector has been consistently registering a higher growth rate than the overall growth of the industrial sector. During the first four years of the Eleventh Plan, MSME Sector exhibited a growth rate of 13 per cent on an average. There are some inherent challenges faced by the sector which have a strong impact on its growth. These relate to (*i*) availability of credit and institutional finance (*ii*) outdated technology and innovation, (*iii*) need for skill development and training, (*iv*) inadequate industrial infrastructure, (*v*) marketing and procurement.

13.145. The Plan explores various aspects of MSME Sector, relating to the growth of the sector. These may be classified under six important verticals to provide theme-based focus, while devising any strategy for the sector. These are (*i*) finance and credit (*ii*) technology (*iii*) infrastructure (*iv*) marketing and procurement (*v*) skill development and training (*vi*) institutional structure, however, keeping in view of the unique status of the khadi and village industries and coir sector in the Indian economy, it was decided that there will be separate recommendations for these sectors. Similarly, concerns of unorganised sector and special areas and groups would be given due consideration while formulating any programmes/schemes under the aforementioned six major verticals.

Strategy and Key Recommendations

Credit and Finance

13.146. Credit is a crucial input for promoting growth of MSME Sector, particularly the MSE Sector, in view of its limited access to alternative sources of finance. Access to information, simplification of loan procedures and interest subvention for micro enterprises are enabling features for timely and affordable credit to MSMEs. The Plan should provision resources for promoting e-platforms for information flow and simplification of procedures. To address the risk perception of banks, particularly for lending to MSEs, the Credit Guarantee Scheme needs to be strengthened, with enhanced budgetary support. There should be substantial increase in the number of MSEs covered under the Performance and Credit Rating Scheme which is a facilitating factor for easy access to credit with liberal terms.

13.147. The reach of the MSEs to the banking network has to be substantially enhanced through setting up of branches near clusters. While there has been an effort to facilitate credit to clusters by financial institutions such as SIDBI, reach and thereby coverage needs to be increased. In fact, a cluster-centric approach is the best bet for addressing the credit needs of the MSME Sector because of reasons of operational convenience and trust building.

13.148. Access to finance needs to be enlarged through alternative sources of capital such as private equity, venture capital and angel funds. This is crucial for facilitating the growth of knowledge-based enterprises which have high potential in the Indian context. Further, prospective enterprises in emerging areas such as nanotechnology, biotechnology, aerospace and defence applications would also require such alternative sources of finance since traditional channels are unable to meet their needs.

13.149. There has to be aggressive market intervention, such as promoting companies for market making and ensuring scaling up of operations of SME exchange. The Plan has to provide resources for such market interventions.

Technology Upgradation and Support for Emerging Sectors

13.150. Technology will be the foremost factor for enhancing the global competitiveness of Indian MSME Sector. The Prime Minister's Task Force on MSMEs has identified low technology, generally used by the MSME Sector, as a major cause for poor competitiveness of the sector. Strategies for improving technological capability of MSMEs have been previously discussed in the section on improving technology and depth in domestic manufacturing.

13.151. The main focus needs to be on developing appropriate technologies for various manufacturing processes to bring down cost, develop collaborations between private and public sector on boosting R&D, and facilitate absorption of globally competitive technologies. Also, separate schemes of the ministry for installation of plants and equipment's with advanced technologies viz. CLCSS and NMCP components may be merged into one scheme, skill development and capacity building.

13.152. Lack of skilled manpower and information as well as lack of reach to modern technology are affecting the growth of the MSME Sector. Among its major recommendations, the Prime Minister's Task Force has identified lack of skilled manpower as a road block for the growth of the MSME Sector. The Ministry of MSME has been mandated to provide skill to 42 lakh persons during the Twelfth Plan period. Strategies for this, including enhancing training capacities for skilling and industry-led skilling and training programmes have been covered previously in the Human Resources Development Section.

Infrastructure Development

13.153. Cluster-based intervention has been acknowledged as one of the key strategies for comprehensive development of Indian industries, particularly the Micro and Small Enterprises (MSEs). The Ministry of MSME has adopted the cluster approach as a key strategy for enhancing the technical and physical infrastructure as well as capacity-building of micro and small enterprises and their collectives in the country. Since 1994, Ministry had also been supporting creation and upgradation of industrial infrastructure in the States under Integrated Infrastructural Development (IID) Scheme, which was subsumed under MSE-CDP in October 2007.

13.154. Land and infrastructure constraints are a major problem, particularly in metros and bigger cities. As production processes of majority of MSEs can be accomplished in flatted factories, flatted factory complexes may be encouraged by providing financial support likewise. Accommodation problem of industrial workers may be addressed to a great extent by supporting dormitories (in or around industrial estates/areas). SPVs may run the dormitories on sustainable basis.

13.155. Maintenance of industrial estates (mainly maintenance of roads, drainage, sewage, power distribution and captive power generation, water supply, dormitories for workers, common effluent treatment plants, common facilities, security and so on) is a critical component for successful functioning of the industrial enterprises in any industrial estate/industrial area. It would be appropriate to handover maintenance of industrial estates to the industry associations, local bodies, State Government agencies, SPVs on self-sustaining basis. World over high-tech and innovative enterprises start in Modular Industrial Estates. To encourage such ventures, modular industrial estates are proposed to be set up near centres of excellence like IITs.

13.156. The Cluster Development Programme of the Ministry of MSME (MSE-CDP) may be continued in the Twelfth Plan period with streamlining of interventions and also ensuring the sustainability of clusters developed. The Programme should also address the requirements of the large unorganised manufacturing sector.

Marketing and Procurement

13.157. Marketing and procurement are the other areas where MSMEs face more challenges than opportunities. The challenges range from procurement of raw materials to lack of market information. MSMEs face several constraints in the marketing and procurement front due to their limited manoeuvrability in such wide ranging activities either on account of lack of finance or on account of lack of awareness. While marketing of products of MSMEs mostly depends upon the market forces and individual efforts of the enterprises, Government and its organisations can play the role of a facilitator to help MSME Sector in these endeavours.

13.158. There are multiplicity of market development assistance programmes to support MSMEs, like participation in domestic and international trade fairs, bar coding, packaging and standardisation within the Ministry. There is a need for rationalisation and consolidation of such programmes under different broad heads.

13.159. However, schemes especially in areas of use of ICT for creating cluster-level, State-level and national-level B2B portals with connectivity to international markets and marketing infrastructure may be required in the Twelfth Plan such as setting up of testing facilities and establishment of information dissemination centres and display-cum-exhibition centres.

13.160. The plan allocation for such schemes can be made under the infrastructure vertical and technology vertical (ICT Scheme), respectively. The vacant land available in the premises of MSME DIs and DICs can be put to use for construction of display-cum-exhibition centres and establishment of information dissemination centres.

13.161. Setting up of marketing organisations in clusters in PPP mode through formation of SPVs, which would form the focal point at the cluster level for all marketing-related activities, such as e-marketing, branding, advertising, barcoding and so on could be considered in the Twelfth Plan.

13.162. National Small Industries Corporation (NSIC), the autonomous outfit of Ministry of MSME may be the apex organisation to coordinate market development activities under different schemes.

13.163. The Government has recently introduced a Public Procurement Policy for the MSME Sector. Further, there is also need for inclusion of private sector in the procurement policy for the MSME Sector. An offset under defence purchases has vast potential for MSME Sector. There is need for setting up a mechanism in the Ministry of Defence to ensure that the offsets under defence purchases are suitably focused to support SMEs in upgrading their capacities.

13.164. All new and existing schemes should be merged into one scheme, namely Marketing Development Assistance Scheme.

Institutional Structure

13.165. The Institutional and legal framework for promotion and development of Micro, Small and Medium Enterprise (MSME) Sector of India is spread both at the National and State level. The primary responsibility for the development of MSMEs lies with the State Governments and Government of India supplements their efforts through a range of initiatives. The Prime Minister's Task Force in its report have made significant recommendations on liberalising the policy regime for the MSME Sector, viz. introduction of insolvency act, liberalisation of labour laws, liberalisation of apprenticeship act, strengthening of district industry centre and so on.

13.166. The following issues need to be immediately addressed to unshackle the growth of the MSME Sector (*i*) environmental issues, (*ii*) labour issues, (*iii*) exit policy, (*iv*) amendment of MSMED Act (*v*) restructuring of the DICs and MSME-DIs.

13.167. On the environmental issues, it is recommended that policies be made uniform pan-India with appropriate relaxation of the controls for the MSMEs. Regarding the labour issues, the immediate need is to consolidate the plethora of labour laws and acts into one user-friendly law. The enactment of Micro, Small and Medium Enterprises Development (MSMED) Act, 2006 is a harbinger for the growth of the MSME Sector. However, there is an urgent need to strengthen the various provisions of the Act along with enactment of the rules under the various sections.[4]

13.168. However, the implementation of the process of filing of Entrepreneurs' Memorandum is still very tardy. Application of e-governance for streamlining of the procedures and for that purpose setting up of an information and database network among the DICs, MSME-DIs and the Ministry may be considered.

13.169. The provision regarding the delayed payment under the MSMED Act was another facilitator for ensuring regular cash flow to the micro and small enterprises against the supplies made. The Micro and Small Enterprises Facilitation Councils (MSEFC) stipulated under the Act to be set up at the State level where foreseen as facilitators to the MSEs.

13.170. However, most of these MSEFCs are not operating efficiently. In fact, in some States they are yet to be constituted. The group recommends immediate action for upscaling the activities of these MSEFCs and introduction of an information and communication network for operation and monitoring of these MSEFCs. A budget of ₹100 crore may be allotted for ICT enabled upscaling of the EM filing and MSEFC operations.

THE UNORGANISED SECTOR

13.171. The Prime Minister's Task Force on MSMEs have stated that no discussion on MSME can be completed without a full treatment of the unorganised sector. More than 94 per cent of MSMEs are unregistered with most of them being in the informal/unorganised sector. The Task Force has commented that in addition to the growth potential of the sector and its critical role in the manufacturing and value chains, the heterogeneity and the unorganised nature of the Indian MSMEs are important aspects that need to be factored into policy making and programme implementation.

13.172. Policies/programmes for the larger sized MSMEs need to address issues relating to growth, marketing, access to raw material, credit, development and technology upgradation. Programmes for the micro and small enterprises in the unorganised sector need to address similar issues for improving their productivity and competitiveness. In addition, they must address requirements of social safety nets for workers in these, more vulnerable enterprises. The future strategy should focus on providing social security to the unorganised workers in the MSME Sector in terms of the mandate under Unorganised Workers Social Security Act (UWSSA).[5]

13.173. The policies for the MSME Sector would have to be devised especially in the areas of skill formation and credit and technology upgradation, and should meet the special needs of the informal sector. Instead of consigning these responsibilities to other departments, the Ministry of MSME will have to actively provide an enabling environment for the unorganised sector to flourish and integrate with the organised sector. Towards this, it is suggested that separate approaches/schemes for the unorganised sector be built into the broad verticals—credit, technology, skill formation and so on. For example, some of the important suggestions can be incorporated into the flagship MSE-CDP Scheme as these can be done on a cluster basis. Apart from this, the Ministry may work out the modalities of how enterprises in the sector can be registered.

BOOSTING MANUFACTURING EXPORTS

13.174. In order to achieve the desired growth rate for the manufacturing sector, it is necessary to have a high growth rate for the country's exports as well. Considering this, the Department of Commerce has come up with a strategy paper on doubling India's exports.

13.175. The recent spiral of exchange rate depreciation of Rupee, while has exerted pressure on imports, has made Indian goods more competitive in international markets. However, this has not materialised into a much needed spurt in exports, largely due to falling global orders and declining domestic demand on account of rising prices, especially of fuel. Over time, repricing of Rupee, if sustained, will incentivise domestic manufacturing. However, it is important to consider that demand for two of India's biggest imports, oil and gold, is not as sensitive to prices. Exchange rate depreciation will therefore have to be supported and balanced by fundamental changes in the ecosystem that can sustainably boost Indian exports and also overall domestic manufacturing.

Key Objectives
- Accelerating the rate of growth of manufacturing exports
- Building a brand image for Indian products
- Increasing technology intensity of products being exported from India

Status and Key Challenges
- Low level of production
  - Output is the most important determinant of exports. Therefore, quantum, quality and competitiveness of domestic manufacturing is very important for export performance of the manufacturing sector. Unfortunately, India's manufacturing is growing at a very low rate as compared to other developing countries.
- Very low share of high tech exports
  - High-tech products have better terms of trade due to high income elasticity. However, India's share in the global trade of high tech products is very low, and has been between 5–8 per cent during 2003–09.

- Non-tariff barriers being placed by countries
  - There is a lack of information and clarity on procedural norms and regulations of various countries regarding specification as well as methods of sampling, inspection and testing. Several conformity assessment issues also have the effect of restricting trade.

Strategy and Key Recommendations

13.176. For achieving the above mentioned objectives, a stable and comprehensive policy for promotion of exports is required. Following specific action points can be considered for achieving the above mentioned objectives:

Accelerating Rate of Growth of Indian Exports

- Providing world-class infrastructure at ports and airports. For promoting exports, adequate infrastructure at all major ports and air ports is required. Further, deepening of draughts at berths, anytime working in ports, deployment of shore mobile cranes for cargo, LPG and CNG connection through pipes, and making them available in every town are also required.
- Dedicated export berths for automobile industry at Chennai port and one more port on west coach, equipped with facilities to handle ~5l vehicles by 2010 and space for parking are required.
- Ranipat, Gurgaon and Unmao should be notified as town of export excellence as this would enhance infrastructure development there.
- Providing an enabling mechanism for facilitating exports is required.
- Reduction of transaction cost for exporters
  - Export procedure to be simplified and human interface with exporters to be reduced
- Addressing non-tariff barriers to ensure fairness to exporters
  - Indian standards need to be in line with international standards and technical regulations
  - Review of our existing standards and their benchmarking with international standards is required
  - More improved labs with international accreditation
- Reform of the FTA process to include improved consultative process with stakeholders
  - Include better input taking mechanism from industries and associations
- Improving fiscal incentives to exporters
- Attracting FDI in country
  - Linking FDI investment with market access and giving preferential incentives for investment in areas where Indian domestic market is non-existent
  - Reduction of threshold limit for offset obligation should be considered
- Ensuring availability of funds to exporters
  - For example, reduction in ECGC premium, availability of pre-shipment and post-shipment credit
- Market strategy to capture unexplored markets and products
- Move to higher value-added products exported to traditional markets
- Focus on Asian and African countries
  - Market access through quota system should be negotiated with competing countries
  - Conducive trade agreements need to be put in place
- Focus on globally dynamic products
  - Products which are gaining significant share in global trade

Building a Brand Promotion Strategy to Coalesce the Brand Values of the Indian Manufacturing Sector

- Initial survey of existing product-promotion strategy and product perception—through IBEF
- Initiate study to benchmark Indian products with competitors in terms of quality and price; all stakeholders should be consulted in this exercise
- A logo and a standard brand kit should be developed
- Focus required on strong PR initiative
  - Participation of Government and industry should be ensured at major national and international trade fairs, seminars and exhibitions

Focus on Moving Towards 'High-tech' Exports from Current Low Tech Exports

- Identify the sectors having high technology and high export growth potential

- Frequent consultations among export promotion councils, industry associations and major technology agencies required
- CII is already in partnership with many agencies for development of technology. Department of Commerce may partner with these efforts to assist R&D for manufacturing exports
- Need to focus on measures to promote these identified sectors

REFORMING THE ROLE AND MANAGEMENT OF PSEs

13.177. Public-sector enterprises occupy an important space in manufacturing. While PSEs like SAIL and BHEL have performed very well in competition with private-sector enterprises, there are also many PSEs that have performed very poorly. In an economic environment that has changed considerably since the early days of India's post- Independence development journey, the need for PSEs as well as the systems for their governance and management should be re-evaluated. Considering this, the Roongta Committee was set up to examine a range of issues of the PSEs and suggest a roadmap for reforms and further development of these enterprises.

13.178. Major recommendations of the Roongta Committee are given below

Strategy and Key Recommendations

13.179. A fundamental problem facing CPSEs which inevitably affect their performance is that they are expected to compete in the market with private-sector companies while having much less freedom of manoeuvre. To deal with this problem it is necessary to consider some fundamental changes as outlined below:

Change in Corporate Governance Structure in CPSEs

- Setting up a strategy and business development committee by every CPSE Board. The committee needs to set direction for the company towards diversification, acquisition, joint ventures, new business entry and review of organisational structure and so on.
- Introduce a system of annual self-evaluation for board of CPSEs.
- Changing the board composition to have 50 per cent board members as independent directors.
- Role of Government director should be equivalent to independent directors on matters where Government has no views as Government. These directors should be paid sitting fees for attending board committee meetings. Their evaluation should also be based on their performance as Directors of board of CPSEs.
- Reform the process of selection of independent directors to make the process more efficient. For this DPE/PSEB can formulate a panel of approved names, out of which independent directors can be appointed for CPSEs. Full-time CEOs of successful enterprises should also be eligible to be appointed as independent directors provided there is no conflict of interest.
- Streamlining the process of appointment of CMDs and full-time directors, in particular the mechanism of obtaining vigilance clearance Process of selection of CMDs/CEOs of Maharatna and Navratna Companies to be different from current process. A separate body may be constituted within PSEB and the selection criteria should be more focussed on leadership quality, strategic thinking, capability to manage external environment and so on, apart from domain/sectoral expertise. Selection of CMD should be made three months before the term of incumbent CMD. Vigilance-clearance process also needs to be reformed in line with the previous point.
- Tenure of CMD/Functional director should be minimum made three years irrespective of the age of the person.
- Reforming vigilance function in CPSEs.

Change in Human Resource Strategy for CPSEs

- All CPSEs should undertake a comprehensive manpower planning exercise to identify key skill and talent requirement across all levels within an organisation from a medium term and a long term perspective.
- CPSEs should develop a leadership pipeline for its key positions and a leadership development strategy.
- To fill the immediate gaps at the higher level in CPSEs, an extension of two years may be allowed

at DGM and above level, subject to certain conditions.
- Autonomy in recruitment policy.
- Autonomy in compensation policy.

Review of Memorandum of Understanding for CPSEs
- Current MOU System to be modified and greatly linked to the organisation's approach towards diversification, acquisition, formation of JVs, new/strategic business, usage of ICT, R&D initiative, HR development and organisational changes.
- Physical performance parameters, if included in MOU should be benchmarked with industry parameters including those in private sectors. CPSEs should be encouraged to reach to these standards within a defined timeframe.

Joint Ventures, Public–Private Partnership and Procurement
- CPSE board should be empowered to select the partner for JV and companies for acquisition.
- Process of entering into partnership and JVs need to be simplified. Current restriction of minimum ownership of 51 per cent in case of JV to be done away with.
- Disinvestment through privatisation of loss making CPSEs may be considered.
- Creation of a Public Sector Land Development Authority for the purpose of developing surplus lands with CPSEs and unlocking their real value.

Technology Mapping for CPSEs
- Every CPSE to have a technology policy, clearly indicating the commitment of the enterprise in using/sourcing/developing type of technology as per needs of the organisation.
- A technology committee may be set up in every CPSE to identify the technology needs and finding alternative ways of developing or finding such technology.

13.180. There is a need for changing the governance model for CPSEs in sectors in which private-sector investments are not forthcoming. Government should be able to enter or exit from any such investment in good time. Otherwise, the benefit of Government investment in the industry is missed or Government's investments, when they have outlived their necessity, become a drag on the performance of the units and a drain on the public exchequer too.

- For this purpose, a Single Holding Structure (SHS) for all new government-owned companies can be established.
  - The SHS can be in the form of holding company owning different stakes in different Government companies.
  - The management can be a mix of senior incumbent bureaucrats and members chosen for their integrity, expertise and domain knowledge in industry, economic or commerce.
  - The SHS can be self-managed like a mutual fund. The board of the SHS would appoint the board of the company it has invested into to the extent of its investment.
  - SHS would earn income through dividends from entities it invested into or through divestiture of its stake.
  - The performance of the SHS entity could be monitored by an empowered group of ministers to whom it would be accountable.

13.181. The above mentioned model can be used to fill gaps where there is not enough Indian presence in sectors and which the Government considers strategic and vital to India's future.

NATIONAL INVESTMENT AND MANUFACTURING ZONES (NIMZs)
13.182. NIMZ is a new concept which is an integral part of the recently approved National Manufacturing Policy of DIPP. The NMP is a policy solution for a number of challenges discussed in this document, and is a policy tool to be applied to select zones designated for promoting manufacturing.

Key Objectives
13.183. Creation of dedicated zones for manufacturing in the nation to

- Promote investments in manufacturing
- Make the country a hub for both domestic and international markets

- Promoting ease of development of manufacturing units

Concept and Approved Strategy

13.184. The National Investment and Manufacturing Zones (NIMZs) will be developed as integrated industrial townships with state-of-the art infrastructure and land use on the basis of zoning; clean and energy-efficient technology; necessary social infrastructure; skill development facilities, and so on to provide a productive environment to persons transitioning from the primary sector to the secondary and tertiary sectors. These NIMZs would be managed by SPVs which would ensure master planning of the zone; pre-clearances for setting up the industrial units to be located within the zone and undertake such other functions as specified in the various sections of this policy.

13.185. To enable the NIMZ to function as a self-governing and autonomous body, it will be declared by the State Government as an industrial township under Art 243 Q1(c) of the Constitution. In sum, the NIMZs would be large areas of developed land, with the requisite ecosystem for promoting world class manufacturing activity. They would be different from SEZs in terms of size, level of infrastructure planning, and governance structures related to regulatory procedures and exit policies.

13.186. The administrative structure of NIMZ will comprise of a Special Purpose Vehicle, a developer, State Government and the Central Government. The Central Government shall, by notification in the Official Gazette, notify an NIMZ. An SPV will be constituted to exercise the powers conferred on, and discharge the functions assigned to it under this Policy to manage the affairs of the NIMZ. Every SPV shall be a legal entity by the name of the NIMZ. This SPV can be a company, including a Section 25 company depending upon the MOU between stakeholders.

Role of Central Government

- Expenditure on master planning for the NIMZ.
- Improve/provide external physical infrastructure linkages to the NIMZs including—rail, road (national highways), ports, airports and telecom.
- Viability gap funding through existing schemes will be provided for internal infrastructure development in the zone including infrastructure for skill development.
- The Central Government, through its institutions and schemes, will provide institutional infrastructure for productivity, quality (testing facilities and so on) and design capabilities, encouraging innovation and skill development within the NIMZ.
- The Central Government will be responsible for the technology acquisition and development interventions in the policy.
- The Central Government will put in place a job-loss policy for units in the NIMZ.
- The Central Government will undertake, along with the State Government concerned, the promotion of domestic as well as global investments in NIMZs.

Role of State Governments

13.187. The State Governments would play the lead role in setting up of the NIMZs. In particular, the State Government would be responsible for providing/facilitating the following infrastructure:

- Land
- Power connectivity
- Provision of bulk requirements of water
- Road connectivity (State roads)
- Sewerage and effluent treatment linkages, from edge of NIMZ, to the final disposal sites
- Appropriate infrastructure to address the health, safety and environmental concerns

Institutional Framework for Implementing NIMZs

- The Department of Industry Policy and Promotion (DIPP) will be the nodal department of the Government of India for the NIMZs.
- Board of Approval constituted by DIPP will scrutinise applications for setting up the NIMZ, and subsequently monitor and expedite the progress of implementation.
- The administrative structure of NIMZ will comprise of a Special Purpose Vehicle, a developer, State Government and the Central Government.

- The SPV would be constituted for each NIMZ and will be responsible for its development and management. It will also be empowered to issue/expedite approvals and pre-approvals.

The Major Benefits for Units within NIMZ
- Job-loss policy will enable units to pay suitable worker compensation in the eventuality of business losses/closures through insurance and thereby eliminate the charge on the assets.
- The transfer of assets belonging to a firm which has been declared sick will be facilitated by the SPV of the concerned NIMZ.
- Exemption from capital gains tax.
- Skill up gradation programmes for new employees as well as for the existing employees in coordination with NSDC.
- Soft loans from multilateral institutions will be explored for funding infrastructure development.
- The developers of NIMZs will be allowed to raise ECBs for developing the internal infrastructure.

Special Incentives for Green Technologies in NIMZs
- Environmental audit will be mandatory
- Water audit will be mandatory
- Exemption from water cess
- Ten per cent one-time capital subsidy for units practicing zero water discharge
- Rainwater harvesting will be compulsory
- Under renewable energy appropriate incentives under existing schemes will be available
- Incentive to obtain green rating for buildings

Delhi–Mumbai Industrial Corridor Project

13.188. The DMIC is proposed to be developed on either side along the alignment of the 1,483 km long Western Dedicated Rail Freight Corridor between Dadri (UP) and JNPT (Navi Mumbai). Running across the six States of Uttar Pradesh, Haryana, Madhya Pradesh, Rajasthan, Gujarat and Maharashtra, the project seeks to create a strong economic base with a globally competitive environment and state-of-the-art infrastructure to activate local commerce, enhance investments and attain sustainable development.

13.189. Initially, seven investment nodes/cities have been taken up for development:

13.190. DMIC is conceived as a model industrial corridor comprising global manufacturing and commercial hubs, that is, self-contained, state-of-the-art, industrial cities. These cities will have world-class physical infrastructure like high speed road and rail connectivity for freight movement between the ports and production/consumption centres, logistics hubs, international air connectivity, reliable power and water, waste management and recycling.

13.191. With the view to taking the project forward to the implementation stage, the Cabinet in its meeting held on 15 September 2011 has approved the financial and institutional structure and financial assistance for the development of industrial cities in the DMIC. This inter alia includes creation of the 'DMIC Project Implementation Fund' of ₹17,500 crore over the next five years for the development of industrial. The Government of Japan has also announced their financial support for the DMIC project to an extent of US$ 4.5 billion for projects with Japanese participation in the first phase of the project.

STRATEGIES FOR THE VARIOUS MANUFACTURING SECTORS

13.192. The objectives of the Plan will be met by the performance of enterprises in select sectors. The selection of the sectors that are included in the Plan has been on a 'bottom-up–cum–top-down' process. India's New Manufacturing Plan is not made on a blank slate. Manufacturing enterprises are operating in the country in a large variety of sectors. They are competing with one another and with enterprises from abroad too. They understand the constraints in India on their competitiveness and growth, as well as opportunities before them. Therefore, associations of enterprises in various sectors were encouraged to prepare plans for their sector's growth, along with the central Government ministry/department responsible for the sector. They have indicated what the enterprises (and their associations) will themselves be responsible for and the support required from Government.

Sector Coverage

13.193. Some sectors have been identified as critical in achieving the overall manufacturing goals. The key characteristics of these sectors are:

Sectors of Strategic Importance

13.194. It is essential for the country to develop domestic manufacturing capabilities in certain sectors for ensuring national security and self-reliance. Industries such as *Defence Equipment, Aerospace, Capital Goods, Electronics Systems Design and Manufacturing (ESDM) and Shipbuilding and Ship Repair* are sectors where greater focus is required to increase indigenisation in production.

Sectors for Basic Inputs

13.195. Availability of high-quality raw material and production inputs is essential for ensuring sustained growth of the manufacturing sector. Industries which are engaged in the production of *steel, cement, fertilisers,* and in the *exploration and development of Minerals*, underpin this growth. Significant impetus is required towards developing production capacities in these sectors.

Sectors for Depth and Value Addition

13.196. These are knowledge-intensive and technology-intensive industries with high growth potential. Developing competitive advantage in them through increasing depth and value addition in domestic manufacturing will contribute to long-term sustained economic growth. While India has developed good technological capability in certain sectors in this category (*automobiles, pharmaceuticals and petrochemicals*), it lags behind significantly in others (*electronics, chemicals and paper*).

Sectors for Employment Generation

13.197. Industries such as *textiles, food processing, leather goods, and gems and jewellery* are less capital intensive and more labour absorptive in nature. These are high employment generating industries that are currently dominated by MSMEs. They lack the deployment of sophisticated technologies in their manufacturing processes and instead rely heavily on manpower. Maximum growth in employment is likely to come from these industries and hence their success is imperative for the country to achieve its job-creation goals.

13.198. The definition of the sectors was influenced by the way the ministries are organised. However, most of the growth and employment data available under NIC classification does not follow this sector definition. Therefore, we have attempted to correlate the Plans for the sectors (in the way we have defined in this Plan) to the industrial segments as per NIC classification to arrive at the likely scenarios for manufacturing growth rate and employment that will be achieved if the recommendations suggested in this Plan are implemented. The Table 13.8 provides the likely growth rate and employment figures that would be achieved on a 'business as is' basis with the manufacturing sector growing as per its historical growth rate (Scenario 1).

13.199. Under Scenario 2, we consider the manufacturing growth rate provided the manufacturing strategy is implemented. Targets for sectoral growth rates[6] in manufacturing were derived by the respective working groups. This then provided the starting point towards identifying the supporting and enabling conditions that would need to be effected to realise the requisite outcomes. One such condition is that capital investment in the economy needs to be labour supplementing and not labour displacing; to reflect this we have deflated the growth rate of labour productivity in Scenario 2. As can be seen from the following table, in Scenario 2, the creation of 70 million additional jobs is a possibility, provided the manufacturing strategy recommendations are implemented, while a 'business as usual' approach will not create the requisite additional employment opportunities.

13.200. The Plan is a living process to shape and to strengthen the productivity and competitiveness of a large industrial ecosystem so that much faster growth of industrial output and more employment can be created across the country. Actions will be required in all States, and in many industrial sectors, to meet the ambitious national goals for the country's industrial sector that this Plan has laid out. This Plan cannot be 'the last word' on all that

TABLE 13.8
Manufacturing GDP by Sector and Employment Projections

Manufacturing Sectors (Excluding Mining)	Eleventh Plan*			Scenario 1: Manufacturing Growth as per Historical Growth Rates		Scenario 2: Growth rate as per Manufacturing Plan		
	Contribution to Manufacturing GDP	GDP CAGR 11th Plan	Employment 2009–10	Employment 2016–17	Employment 2024–25	GDP CAGR as per Manufacturing Plan	Employment 2016–17	Employment 2024–25
Food products and beverages	8.7%	7.3%	5.5	6.46	6.94	8.8%	7.29	9.50
Tobacco products	1.7%	4.7%	4.1	4.12	3.61	4.7%	4.35	4.17
Textiles	9.2%	3.8%	8.4	8.00	6.56	11.5%	12.07	19.14
Wearing apparel	3.9%	7.3%	7.3	8.57	9.20	11.5%	10.94	17.34
Leather products and others	1.3%	4.6%	0.9	0.90	0.79	24.0%	2.22	8.25
Wood and others	2.2%	12.0%	3.6	5.52	8.34	12.0%	5.82	9.57
Paper, publishing and others	2.7%	5.8%	1.6	1.72	1.64	8.7%	2.08	2.69
Coke, petroleum products, and nuclear fuel, rubber and plastics	10.6%	7.5%	0.8	0.95	1.03	10.7%	1.16	1.73
Chemicals and chemical products	12.2%	9.0%	1.7	2.20	2.66	12.0%	2.66	4.36
Other non-metallic mineral products	6.8%	13.6%	4.3	7.22	12.22	13.6%	7.61	14.03
Basic metals	9.7%	1.9%	1.4	1.19	0.84	10.3%	1.86	2.71
Machinery and equipment and others	11.1%	8.1%	3.8	4.68	5.33	16.8%	7.25	16.67
Electrical machinery and apparatus, telecom and others	6.0%	12.8%	1.3	2.09	3.34	12.8%	2.20	3.82
Motor vehicles and other transport equipment	7.7%	6.0%	1.5	1.63	1.59	13.0%	2.37	4.18
Furniture and other manufacturing	6.3%	6.3%	4.3	4.76	4.47	6.3%	5.02	5.43
Total			**50.5**	**60.01**	**68.83**		**74.91**	**123.59**

Note: *Contribution to Manufacturing GDP as per GDP Data series provided by CSO—2009–10. Basis of GDP CAGR Eleventh Plan estimates provided in the Annexure. Employment figures are in millions. Employment for 2009–10 does not include employment of 0.20 million for recycling and medical, precision and optical instruments, watches and clocks.
^ The key variables and assumptions are part of Annexure 13.1.

is required to be done. Just as many stakeholders, many sectors and many industry ministries have come together to start this comprehensive, collaborative process, others are expected to join too. Thus, the snowball will grow into a larger and faster movement. Indeed, the preparation of this Plan has already brought forth demands from sectors that did not join the first wave to come on board too. In the directions set by the Plan, they see opportunities for their growth too. For instance, biotechnology, which focuses on industrial enzymes, alternate energy, seed manufacturing, diagnostics, vaccines, discovery research and clinical services and biotech drugs, is emerging as an important focus area for the country.

13.201. While we have not included this as a separate section (this is included in the Drugs and Pharmaceuticals Section), the policies needed for the sector would be given due importance in the ongoing planning process. More such sectors are likely to join the planning process as we go along.

13.202. With this in mind, the process of planning has been designed as an ongoing activity with periodic reviews to ensure that right policies are provided to encourage new emerging industrial sectors and reviewing policies of existing sectors based on the changing global and domestic economic and industrial environment.

13.203. While there are certain common challenges and underlying solutions across sectors, which have been articulated in the previous section, each sector also has its unique constraints that need to be addressed. These sector-wise recommendations have been attached as an annexure to this document (Annexure 13.2).

STRATEGIES FOR HIGHEST IMPACT

13.204. The overall manufacturing strategy outlined in the chapter details many initiatives and actions that address the key challenges in each sector as well as focuses on capitalising on the opportunities that lie within. Also, recommendations have been formulated to relieve the cross-cutting constraints across sectors. A few high-impact strategies emerge, which would serve well to further the overall growth of manufacturing in India (Box 13.3).

13.205. The Central and the State Governments are responsible for implementing the various policy-related and institution-related recommendations. This categorisation can be seen in Box 13.4.

WAY FORWARD

Principles of Policy Implementation

13.206. Research on success of countries that built effective implementation systems to create sustained competitive advantage across multiple manufacturing sectors provides some principles for a robust implementation process.

- *Build an implementation system, don't just do the task*: Explicit attention to the process of policy development and implementation has been lacking to a large extent in the Indian context. An effective implementation system is not limited to the success of a single initiative. It builds broad-based capabilities across several industries.
- *Systemic experimentation and learning help to progressively and rapidly improve implementation*: Even carefully designed programmes are likely to face challenges from unforeseen changes in the environment. Therefore, it is important to have learning and feedback mechanisms in place to ensure that implementation effectiveness improves through successive cycles. Good policy development (and implementation) should follow the PDCA cycle (Plan—develop strategy; Do—implement strategy; Check—diagnose issues in strategy and its implementation; Act—rectify issues identified).
- *Prioritise, sequence and create momentum through results*: Often it takes time for results of policy recommendations to become visible. When results are not visible, the implementation process may lose momentum. Therefore, to build momentum, some early wins must be targeted. They build confidence and commitment to the process.
- *Performance measures for government programmes have to be defined consultatively*: The old

> **Box 13.3**
> **Strategies for Highest Overall Impact**
>
> **Policy and Process Interventions**
> - Align stakeholders in the process of development and implementation of industrial policies.
> - Simplify processes for doing business in India by mandating a 'Regulatory Impact Assessment' and operationalising single window clearance across the country.
> - Create a level-playing field for Indian manufacturers through fiscal measures by correcting anomalies in duty structures.
> - Boost demand for domestic manufacturing, regardless of ownership of enterprises, through public procurement backed by minimum threshold quality parameters.
> - Bring down the cost of finance.
>
> **Technology Upgradation Measures**
> - Improve Government–industry and industry–academic collaboration.
> - Encourage technology transfers through FDI/JVs.
> - Improve technical standards and voluntary compliance, across the industry.
> - Encourage adoption of 'green technology'.
> - Modernise MSMEs through technology adoption and adequate access to finance.
>
> **Infrastructure Creation**
> - Improve transport and power infrastructure.
> - Set up NIMZs (National Investment and Manufacturing Zones).
> - Make industrial clusters more effective by creating both, the 'hard' physical infrastructure as well as the 'soft' infrastructure for knowledge creation and sharing.
> - Design an effective land-acquisition process for industrial development.
>
> **Human Capital Formation**
> - Modernise labour regulations and institutions.
> - Improve skill availability through Skill Councils.
> - Ensure social protection to all employees in the manufacturing sector by creating 'sump institutions' for workers in transitory phase and develop innovative insurance systems for the informal sector.
> - Improve 'industrial relations' through streamlining of consultative processes and representative institutions.
> - Improve the quality of manufacturing managers/supervisors.

management adage—'you can't manage what you don't measure'—is especially true with regards to complex Government programmes. The need for performance measures is well accepted. However, it is also very important to define these measures appropriately. A key difference between public sector and private sector programmes is that the value required to be produced by public programmes is generally more intangible than in private programmes where shareholder value and profit may be good measures. Outcomes of public programmes must deliver against expectations of diverse public stakeholders.

Therefore, it is imperative that time is spent, upfront, to define outcomes in consultation with key stakeholders. Failure to do this causes the system to adopt simplistic measures of performance against expenditure targets, which are not good indicators of the outcomes that were desired.

- *Coordination between Government departments is critical*: Given the complexity of policy issues relating to manufacturing, most solutions are likely to require coordinated actions between a number of Government departments. While the default solution is to create another agency/committee to oversee this coordination, this is not always the optimal solution. Before setting up such an agency/committee, the tasks required to be performed by such an agency/committee must be analysed and the existing system of agency/committees must be mapped to eliminate any overlaps and redundancies.

Otherwise additional agencies/committees can increase the clutter in the system rather than

Box 13.4
Key Recommendations for Manufacturing

Category	Central Governments	State Governments
Policy recommendations	• Develop National Land Use policy • Reform the existing environmental clearance processes • Initiate Reforms in labour laws • Create a 'Sump' for transitory workers and 'job loss insurance • Mandate Regulatory Impact Assessment (RIA) for all regulatory changes in the country • Develop functional National Business facilitation and development policy • Develop functional competition Act • Evolve a Single Holding Structure for all PSEs • Create a National IP Mission • Develop Policy on technical regulations • Mandate minimum 30% local value addition for capital goods • Provide preference to local content in PSE purchases of capital goods • Rationalise the import of second hand capital goods • Make changes in ECB and FDI policy and removal of sectoral cap for banking sector (Steel) • Accord 'deemed exports' status to Steel Industry • Prepare policy on fuel usage in Transport sector • Evolve National Policy on Vehicle Retirement and End-of-life solution • Develop integrated chemical management policy and regime • Passing of MMDR bill	• Reforming the existing environmental clearance processes • Developing State Land Use policy • Initiate reforms in labour laws • Developing State business facilitation and development policy • Developing State Competition Act • Mandate Regulatory Impact Assessment (RIA) for all regulatory changes in the State • Mandate minimum 30% local value addition for capital goods • Provide preference to local content in PSE purchases of capital goods • Improve the performance of power generating and distributing companies in the States • Streamlining the administration of sales tax, VAT and so on
Institution-related recommendations (new institutions)	• Create RBOs mandated and empowered for integrated Water Resource Management • Establish an independent and autonomous regulator for Land • Establish functional National-State Business Facilitation and Development Commissions • Establish functional national state institutions for promoting business responsibilities, competitiveness and competition reforms • Establish cluster stimulation cells • Establish speciality chemical forum • Constitute domestic council for leather industry • Create National Aeronautics Commission • Create National Discovery and Development Center for Pharma Industry • Develop institutional mechanisms enabling expert study of techno-economic policy issues relating to national raw materials security	• Development of State maritime policies and boards • Strengthen land management at State level • Establish/strengthen State-level cluster stimulation cells

Strengthening of existing institutions	• Strengthen capabilities of
	  – Local bodies for recycling and waste management
	  – Standard developing organisations
	  – Inspection bodies/certification agencies/regulators in the areas of Technical Standards
	  – Scale up of operations of SME exchange
		• Strengthen capabilities of micro and small enterprises facilitation centers in States

improve its performance. Since coordination is an essential function to improve system performance, coordination/oversight should be accountable for performing its task and its performance must be measured too.

- *Stakeholder consultations are key to improve the quality of policy development and implementation*: Rather than seeking to a priori design a detailed plan in an unpredictable environment, it is better to create effective forums to identify problems, and for joint teams to be formed to tackle them. These forums should be broad-based and inclusive to ensure that all stakeholders can contribute to the process.

A Two Track Process of Implementation

13.207. The Manufacturing Plan makes many recommendations developed through a managed, participative process with structured involvement from a diverse set of stakeholders (Figure 13.7). Previous experiences of implementation in India have shown that the inability of various stakeholders to work together is a root cause of failure of policies.

13.208. The conventional response to this has been to try and create a structure with a chain of command. However, this becomes untenable when there are many stakeholders and owners who cannot all be included within such a structure. The recommended approach for policy implementation, based on the principles enunciated before, is characterised by three 'L's: enable *local* action, create *lateral* connections; and focus on *learning*. Local actions and lateral connections require a process of implementation that coordinates multiple entities in a consultative manner. Learning requires a process that systematically distils lessons from experience to improve the ongoing evolution of policies and their implementation.

13.209. Therefore, a two-track approach for implementation and learning is recommended: the first track delineates the steps required to convert the recommendations of the Plan to implementation and the second track concentrates on the systemic changes that need to be undertaken to strengthen the process of consultation, learning, policy making and ongoing implementation.

13.210. The 'third rail' that provides the power to accelerate learning and institutional capacity improvement is an ongoing process of evaluation and learning, which must be proactively facilitated through the creation of a 'backbone' organisation and other means. This approach is schematically represented in Figure 13.7.

Collaboration and Implementation

13.211. Two root causes identified for poor implementation are: inadequate consensus amongst stakeholders for policy changes and very poor coordination amongst agencies in execution.

13.212. Wide-spread consensus-building processes, therefore, need to be institutionalised within the Indian manufacturing system to ensure successful implementation of plans.

13.213. This consensus cannot be commanded. We need another mechanism specifically designed to bring people with different perspectives together: to listen to each other, to distil the essence of their shared aspiration for the country and the critical principles they will adhere to in the work they have to do together as partners in progress.

13.214. Hence, there is a need to establish an effective 'backbone' capability which will provide strength to multi-stakeholder policy and implementation processes.

13.215. The 'backbone' capability neither requires an organisation with large amounts of resources and manpower nor one with the power to command top-down. The 'backbone' capability must essentially comprise of small catalytic units located in many parts of the system, which can provide the 'tools and techniques' to the various States and ministries to effectively coordinate, design and implement their programmes. The backbone network (and its units) must rely on 'learning by doing' to enhance its own capacity and to transfer knowledge to other stakeholders tackling specific systemic issues.

13.216. The India Backbone Implementation Network will provide these institutions with tools

Implementation Tracks

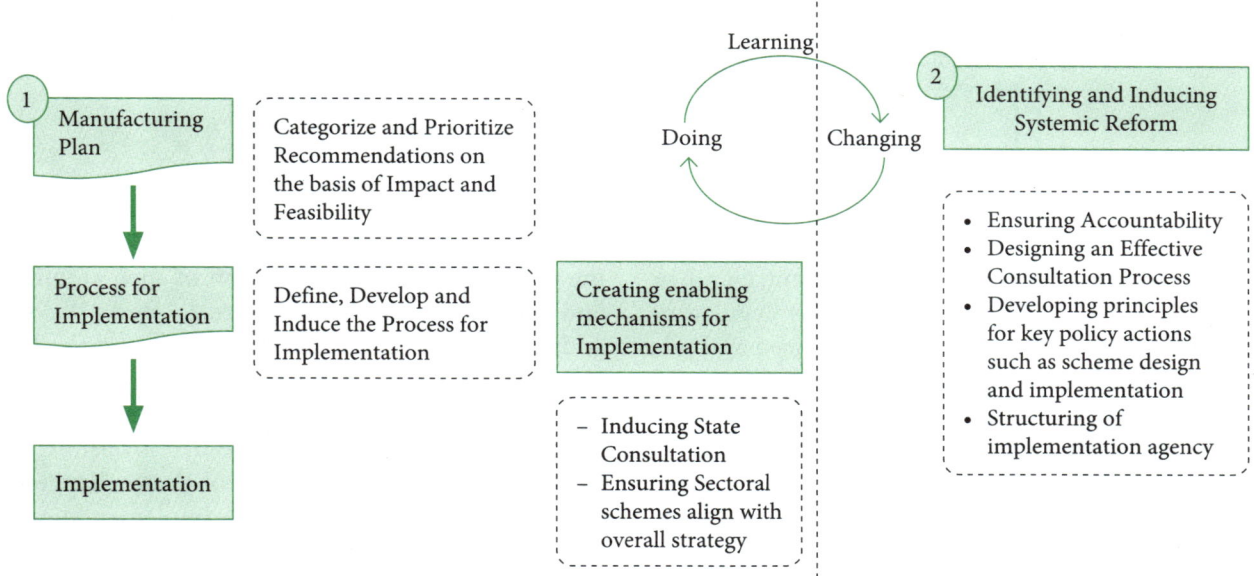

FIGURE 13.7: Two Connected 'Tracks' for Implementation and Systems' Improvement

and assistance to fulfil their coordination functions more effectively. This has been discussed in detail in Volume I of the Plan document, in the section on Collaboration and Implementation, under the chapter on Governance.

A 'Movement' of Learning and Improvement

13.217. The distinction between creating yet another 'organisation' and stimulating a 'movement' is crucial. For widespread acquisition of capabilities, across a large, diverse, and democratic system, a movement of learning and change is required.

13.218. Japan was able to improve the quality of all is enterprises, in the public and private sectors, through the TQM movement. Relevant principles, techniques and tools were provided by many persons and organisations, notable amongst them were Professors Deming and Ishikawa, and Taichi Ohno of Toyota. These principles and tools were deployed by the movement. The subjects of the IBIN Movement are stakeholder collaboration and implementation. IBIN must play a catalytic role, and it must be designed for it. Strategic functions such as high-stake partnership brokering and project management are capabilities that should rest within IBIN and can be managed with a compact team. Some amount of time will have to be invested in identifying staff and partners with the appropriate skills and character required for the work of IBIN and its units. Given that India has never quite had an organisation like the proposed IBIN, the enrolment process of partners will need to be very deliberate about selecting the right individuals and organisations for the job, keeping in mind how these selections will impact stakeholder perceptions of IBIN and, therefore, willingness to solicit services of IBIN and its units. Empanelment of partner organisations should be based on established guidelines/principles with a rigorous selection process whereby partners should expect to be challenged and evaluated, even being dropped from IBIN's panels if deemed necessary.

13.219. Further to develop project management and stakeholder-alignment skills, IBIN needs the support of quality *policy analysis* to ensure consistency in implementation in the present federal structure (refer to Figure 13.8). Thus, IBIN could be well positioned to drive policy coherence at the central level and ensure nation-wide consistency in actions and

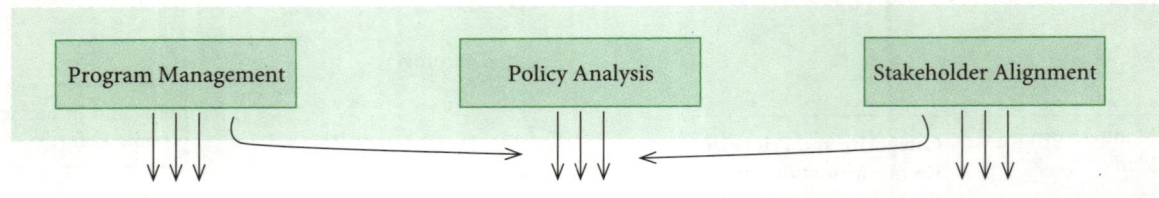

FIGURE 13.8: Capability Map

policies. For this IBIN's units at the Centre and in the States will use tools such as Business Regulatory Impact Analysis (BRIA) to analyse the need and relevance of existing as well as new regulations on the basis of set criteria, developed though a consultative process, and relevant to the Indian context.

13.220. As mentioned 'backbone' units should form at several nodal points in the institutional structures of governance in the country where coordination and management of implementation are key responsibilities. These will be in State Governments and they will be within national missions that bring together several agencies to produce integrated outcomes. In each of these, the three modules of capabilities described above may be required. Of these, stakeholder-alignment and programme management would be required invariably. The third capability, policy analysis, may be required in some units, not all. For example, it would be most likely required in State level units, but perhaps not in units supporting missions.

13.221. A decision will have to be made about where the central node of the 'backbone' capability (which as mentioned before must grow and be distributed across the country) will reside, taking into consideration how its location will impact stakeholder perceptions of its purpose, neutrality and capabilities, and therefore the willingness of stakeholders to solicit 'backbone' services or take part in IBIN interventions.

Make Systemic Reforms

13.222. In the course of developing the Plan for manufacturing, through intensive discussions with stakeholders, 'root causes' for present problems in the country with implementation of such ambitious and complex programmes were located. Ways to address some of these have been built into the Way Forward for the Manufacturing Plan. However, some root causes require broader institutional changes. Efforts are being made by Government to address these. Implementation of those changes by Government will accelerate the implementation of the many actions required to achieve the country's ambitious goals for its manufacturing sector. These broader institutional changes, the benefits of which will be in all sectors of the economy, are described below.

Improve Architecture of Government Programmes and Schemes

13.223. Schemes, especially those that aim to provide financial incentives to encourage specific behaviours from the private sector, are popular instruments of manufacturing policy in the country. However, significant reforms are required in the architecture of schemes to ensure that they effectively and efficiently help to fulfil policy goals:

1. *Change the role of the central Government ministry from micro-manager to scheme designer and facilitator*: The ministry's role should be to act as a knowledge partner and enabler to the project implementers (which will typically be in the States). In order to be able to play this role effectively, the ministry will need to develop capabilities which are focused on scheme design and creation of learning systems and networks from which the States and other local implementers can learn.

2. *Establish strategic alignment of schemes*: Schemes should have strategic outcomes defined (such

as employment generation, number of patents, output generation and so on) so that measures of schemes' performance are not limited to expenditures against targets.
3. *Invest in good scheme design*: While the Planning Commission includes schemes in principle during the five-year plan process based on the strategic logic supporting them, the actual monies should be released only when the scheme design meets well-defined quality considerations. The ministry should be provided funds to design the scheme—which might require hiring consultants/experts or reaching out to numerous stakeholders—after which they should be provided funds for the schemes only if the design can demonstrate that the scheme will deliver on the desired outcomes.
4. *Establish an evaluation and feedback mechanism*: Schemes should be measured on productivity of the money being spent—this allows various schemes to be compared with each other. Also, the ministry should demonstrate how learning from implementing a scheme is being used in improving it.

Reform Government Institutions

13.224. The Second Administrative Reforms Commission has made several important recommendations that will improve the performance of Government generally and that will substantially improve Government effectiveness in growing the country's manufacturing sector. Since the recommendations are very well developed and explained in the ARC's reports, they will not be elaborated here; however, the following may be highlighted:

- In its Report No. 10, the ARC has recommended changes in the career structure of the administrative services that will ensure that senior postings have adequate tenure. It has also recommended an 'up or out' evaluation system so that only the better officers will stay in service and move to postings at the top. And it has provided for lateral entry from outside Government, of suitably qualified personnel for such top positions.
- In its Report No. 13, the ARC has recommended that policymaking functions of Government and execution functions be separated and organised in appropriate structures. For 'execution' functions, the 'agency' structure has been strongly recommended. 'Agency' structures have enabled several countries—UK, Sweden, Japan, Australia and Thailand, to name a few—to substantially improve Government's performance.

13.225. The concept of 'agencification' is to carve out of Government departments, 'executive agencies' to carry out, under competitively selected professional managers on fixed tenures, specific executive functions within a framework of policy and resources. Each such agency is institutionalised in a framework document which spells out its mandate, mission and objectives, structure, accountability, standards and targets, financial arrangements and so on and is mandated to release an annual performance report and accounts. The agency has the freedom to mould its management style, strategy, operations, systems, workforce and so on within broad Government guidelines.

13.226. The advantage of the 'agency' structure is that it leads to clarity about outcomes. It also allows for an inculcated culture of service delivery, empowerment of frontline staff, greater accountability and openness, improved management, transparency and so on.

Role of Industry Associations

13.227. Industry associations have a vital role to play in the evolution and implementation of the Manufacturing Plan at the Centre and in the States. They provide platforms for their members to come together to analyse the constraints in the environment that must be addressed. Good-quality associations, that are democratic in their governance, transparent in their functioning and represent their industrial sector, or perhaps all industry, satisfactorily (that is, have large membership) can be invaluable partners of Government in the development and implementation of plans for manufacturing growth. Associations can also arrange platforms for consultations with Government and other stakeholders on the lines described above and thus can facilitate the achievement of the country's goals for its manufacturing sector.

Involve Commercial Banks in the Analysis Process

13.228. Commercial banks, who provide finance to manufacturing enterprises, large as well as small ones, are a valuable (and neutral) source of insight into constraints of different sectors. They should be involved, more systematically, in the processes of evaluation of sectoral performance and for developing solutions, along with other stakeholders.

Disseminate Information to Public Effectively

13.229. Government must become much more effective in communicating with the public. Citizens are not aware of many schemes set up by Central and State Governments for their benefit. Stakeholders, who will be affected by new Government policies, realise only after the policies are announced, that they have great concerns whereas Government departments claim that the policies were posted on their websites and views had been invited. Moreover, with the ubiquity of electronic communications, including 24 × 7 TV news, and the advent of social media, Government's communication processes must be modernised, become more proactive, and reach out to citizens more effectively.

NEXT STEPS

13.230. The immediate next steps for implementing the Plan are:

- Take the Plan to the States: Much of the implementation of the Manufacturing Plan will be in the States. Therefore, State Governments and stakeholders in the States must be engaged.
- Put the implementation system in place: The implementation system described in this section will need to be instituted through the collaboration of various National and State agencies as well industry associations. The DIPP, NMCC and the Planning Commission will need to collaborate to delineate their roles in the implementation process.
- Ensure sectoral schemes align with overall strategy: The financial outlay of the Plan should be aligned with the strategies identified in the Plan. Rather than following the process where budgets are determined as variances to previous year's outlays, allocations should be designed and reviewed in accordance to the strategies identified.
- Communicate the Plan to a broader audience: Communication is critical to the successful implementation of any major change programme. Communications must be designed to suit the audiences for which they are intended. Some can be delivered in the form of documents or presentations. Others should be delivered through interactive discussions where clarifications can be given and even suggestions obtained. Industry associations can play a very important role in these. The Planning Commission, DIPP and NMCC would have to provide leadership and play a major role in the communications outreach.

ANNEXURE 13.1
Manufacturing GDP by Sector and Employment Projections

TABLE 13.9
Key Variables and Assumptions

Variable	Assumption(s)
GDP by Sector (Excluding Mining)	National Accounts Statistics published by CSO provides GDP data series till 2009–10 for the manufacturing sector. This data was then extrapolated basis the projected growth rates in the economic survey report 2010–11 and adjusted for the slowdown in 2011–12 to estimate the overall growth rate for the Eleventh Plan. The growth rate thus arrived at, has then been used to project GDP for Scenario 1.
	For Scenario 2, growth rates as per sectoral working-group reports have been considered. It is important to note that NIC classification at the two digit level for capturing data related to individual sectors under manufacturing does not correspond to the classification of sub-sectors (eighteen) in the manufacturing strategy. Projected growth rates for the individual sectors as per the respective working groups have been mapped on a best information basis. The outcome of this approach is an average growth rate of 12 per cent for manufacturing sector as a whole during the Twelfth Five Year Plan and till 2025.
GDP	GDP growth rate for the country is assumed to be at 9% for the model.
Employment by Sector (Excluding Mining)	Employment data is quinquennial as published by NSSO. Employment data last available is for 2009–10. This has been used to calculate labour productivity, (GDP_t/$Employment_t$) for 2009–10 for each sector which is a key input variable towards projecting employment.
	Reflecting recent trends in productivity, the labour productivity growth rate has been assumed to be 6% p.a. under Scenario 1 and 5% p.a. under Scenario 2. Employment in manufacturing declined between 2004–05 and 2009–10 despite an increase in output. Hence, it is important to consider a long run view of the trend in labour productivity. As per Papola and Sahu (2012), labour productivity in India grew by 3.8% p.a. between 1993–94 and 2004–05 and by 6% between 1993–94 and 2009–10. It is important to note that in the unorganised segment which employs more than 80% of the workforce, manufacturing sector productivity per worker was estimated to be almost one-twentieth of that in the organised sector in 2006–07 (Papola et. al., 2011). Hence, a 6% growth rate has been an outcome of declining employment combined with a concentration of manufacturing output in the organised sector. This trend is not likely to be sustainable for the Indian economy, especially if the objective of inclusive growth needs to be realised. The manufacturing strategy for the Twelfth Five Year Plan aims to address systemic deficiencies in the economy with a clear focus on accelerating both growth and employment. Hence historical labour productivity growth rates cannot be relied on to project the likely impact of manufacturing strategy during the Twelfth Five Year Plan and beyond. The moderate adjustment in labor productivity growth rate from 6% in Scenario 1 to 5% Scenario 2 reflects the assumption that with increased focus on employment generation, capital investment will supplement labour rather than displace it (contrary to the trend that has been observed historically).

ANNEXURE 13.2
Sector-wise Recommendations

1. As indicated earlier, we have included Plans for 17 different industrial sectors, under four categories—sectors of strategic importance, sectors of basic inputs, sectors of depth and value addition and sectors of employment generation. It is these sectors, which will have to achieve the Plan objectives, that is, growth and employment objectives. Following are the sector-wise recommendations.

(A) SECTORS OF STRATEGIC IMPORTANCE

DEFENCE EQUIPMENT

Introduction
2. India has been rapidly enhancing its spending on defence. It is expected that India would become the third largest defence spender after the US and China by 2014. Equipment spending by Ministry of Defence has increased by 15–20 per cent over the last five years. With several large equipment and modernisation programmes in the pipeline, analysts are projecting an overall spend of USD 80–100 billion in the next five years. This makes India one of the world's most lucrative markets for military products, and defence suppliers are gearing up to compete.

3. The Indian defence equipment market can be divided into four large areas:
- Land Systems
- Naval Systems
- Electronics Systems
- Aerospace

Key Objectives Under the Twelfth Plan
- Progressive increase share of domestic procurement from 30 to 75 per cent in next 10 years.
- Ensure that 8–10 largest weapons programmes in the country have a targeted large percentage of locally manufactured content.
- Build local IP in critical defence areas.
- Promote and track civilian applications of technologies and material developed during defence research.
- Support local defence manufacturers in building export capabilities.
- Enable creation of one million new direct and indirect jobs in the defence manufacturing space.
- Monitor implementation of Government's offset policy in letter and spirit for large contracts.

Strategy and Key Recommendations
- Set up a National Defence Manufacturing Council.
- Set up a national defence manufacturing council under the aegis of the Prime Minister's office to ensure that domestic manufacturing gets due focus.
- Pass an Executive Order with decision to use Make/Buy and Make (Indian) mandatory for flagship large programmes with appropriate funding to enforce Make or Buy and Make (Indian) classification for all flagship defence contracts and mandate that the prime contractor be an Indian entity, which can be a JV between a local entity and relevant global vendors.
- Decide the right financial model for Indian entities working with the Government on these flagship programmes.
- Streamline the defence procurement infrastructure
  - Need to streamline at the level of offset implementation, DPSU and OFB procurement and Ministry of Defence cantered capital procurement.
  - Centralisation of procurement systems and infrastructure for DPSU and OFB, creation of a centralised list of defence vendors and providing guidance to new entrant in the system.
  - Provide standardised contractual frameworks and clauses that can be accessed by the multiple contracting agencies to reduce contract variation and complexity across the system.

- Adopt more professional and specialised approach to enhance the offset facilitation process.
- Increase the FDI limit for foreign participation
  - The current upper cap of 26 per cent on FDI in defence production needs to be relaxed to 49 per cent on case to case basis. Specific technology transfer should be specified and post-contract technology should reside in the JV/country.
- Support for SMEs
  - SME-specific support structure for upgradation of defence manufacturing facilities for deeper capability building, achieve manufacturing certifications like ISO, developing IPs and in establishment of licensed defence units.
- Create enabling infrastructure for capability building
  - Mechanisms to provide access to critical technologies available with research agencies or obtained through Transfer of Technology (TOT) arrangements.
  - Creation of a Centre of Excellence for Defence Electronics: to be modelled on a PPP model aimed at generation of indigenous IP.
- Vendor development
  - Continuous development of vendor base by DPSU.

AEROSPACE

Introduction
4. Aerospace manufacturing is a high-technology industry that produces 'aircraft, space vehicles, aircraft engines, propulsion units, and related parts.' Its value chain is characterised by a long project life cycle spanning R&D, engineering design, manufacturing, assembly, maintenance, repair and overhaul. India is one of the fastest growing aerospace markets.

5. The three segments of the Industry are:

- Defence
- Civil Aviation
- Space

Key Objectives Under the Twelfth Plan
- Develop greater design and manufacturing capabilities in the defence space.
- Become a global player in supplying advanced technology in space sector at a fair price in the global space market.
- Drive dedicated technology development for civil aviation, develop greater manufacturing capabilities.
- Become the international hub for maintenance, repair and overhaul needs.

Strategy and Key Recommendations
- *Strengthening institutional architecture* through a National Aeronautics Commission, if required
  - All the knowledge residing in entities like aeronautics organisations, colleges, labs and so on should be synergistically harnessed.
  - Map indigenous capabilities, identify knowledge gaps, direct resources efficiently to address critical technology gaps.
  - Formulate a national aeronautics policy to strengthen the aerospace industry.
- *Strengthening of certification organisations*
  - Given the expected increase in the work in the sector, CEMILAC and DGCA must be strengthened.
  - The government should facilitate certification of SMEs.
- *Promotion of PPP model*
  - PPP model by forming JVs should be encouraged in order to fully exploit the knowledge base of the government and the entrepreneurship of the private sector.
- *Earmarking special aerospace economic zones may be considered*
  - Creating clusters to certify and quality test aircraft and system components.
  - The growth in offsets could be efficiently utilised in the creation of such SEZs.

SHIP BUILDING AND SHIP REPAIR

Introduction
6. Nearly 95 per cent of India's foreign trade in terms of volume and more than 65 per cent in terms of value is through sea routes. Currently, about 10 per cent of our trade is carried by ships with an Indian flag while the ships manufactured in India carry even less cargo. India's emergence as a major economic power would mean greater integration in terms of trade with the rest of the world, requiring huge shipping tonnage. To ensure the safety of our vast coast line, the naval requirement of sophisticated and modern vessels is also growing rapidly. Therefore, shipbuilding is very important from a civilian as well as defence perspective.

7. While the Indian seaborne trade has been growing rapidly, Indian shipping and shipbuilding sector has been lagging behind despite their development potential. Indian registered ships form just about 1.1 per cent of the global shipping stock. Indian EXIM trade is being increasingly serviced by foreign flagged vessels whose share in the Indian shipping market has increased from 60 per cent in 1980s to about 92 per cent by 2009–2010. This is both a cause of concern and a huge opportunity for India's shipping and shipbuilding sector.

Key Objectives Under the Twelfth Plan
- Medium and long term goals have been set for the Indian shipbuilding and ship repair industry. These are:
- To achieve 5 per cent share of the global shipbuilding market and 10 per cent share in the global ship repair industry by 2020.
- To be self-sufficient in ship repair requirements of the country and to emerge as a dominant ship repair centre displacing Colombo, Dubai, Singapore and Bahrain.
- To develop a strong ancillary base for shipbuilding/ship repair in the country by 2020.
- To generate additional employment for 2.5 million persons (0.5 million direct and 2.0 million indirect) by 2020 in the core shipbuilding as well as the ancillary and supporting industry sector.
- To develop strong R&D facilities and design capabilities for commercial shipbuilding.

Strategy and Key Recommendations
8. The key recommendations to enable the shipbuilding and ship repair sector to meet its mid-term and long-term goals are:

1. Incentives: In the line of the erstwhile Shipbuilding Subsidy Scheme, some form of adequate financial/fiscal incentive would need to be considered in order to facilitate the industries to achieve critical mass.
2. Infrastructure status to shipbuilding: Granting infrastructure status would enable the indigenous shipbuilding industry to enjoy tax benefits and lower interest rates for investment in the technological development and modernisation.
3. Purchase preference for Indian built, Indian flagged vessels and Indian shipyards in Government/Defence purchase: On the lines of global practice, promotion of the use of locally build vessels by local shipping companies would help To develop domestic shipbuilding capabilities.
4. Offset scheme for Government procurement: In order to provide impetus to the ancillary industry in India, it should be mandated that during the purchase of any ship from a foreign yard, the foreign yard would have to source a certain amount of marine engineering goods from India. This can create a steady stream of orders for domestic marine engineering companies and help develop capabilities in the sector.
5. To examine the issue of incidence of taxes that disadvantages the domestic shipbuilding industry.

CAPITAL GOODS AND ENGINEERING

Introduction
9. The Prime Minister's Group constituted under Chairman, National Manufacturing Competitiveness Council in its Report (Prime Minister's Group Report—PMGR) identified capital goods as one of the sectors that is strategic for strengthening national capabilities for the long term. The PMGR has recommended support for the following sub-sectors within the capital goods sector: (*i*) machine tools, (*ii*) heavy electrical equipment's, (*iii*) heavy transport, earth moving and mining equipment's, and (*iv*) high technology equipment's like IT, telecommunications and electronics hardware. The PMGR has recommended that a time-bound action plan should be prepared in each of these areas for building high class modern capacities with R&D facilities, appropriate programme to encourage growth and development of these areas in the private sector together with

strengthening of the existing public sector and revisiting the existing policies to protect and promote selected capital goods industries.

10. PMGR has also recommended enunciation of a clear policy to provide incentives for acquisition of advanced technologies strengthening the country's technological capabilities in the long term. Need for a dedicated fund for acquiring technology for tier-2 suppliers of priority sectors and an 'offset policy' as one of the means to boost domestic content in the total equipment imported has been underlined. A review of the current FDI policy from the point of view of transfer of technology as well as considerations of national security was also recommended. This can be done by giving preference to JVs instead of 100 per cent foreign-owned companies.

Key Objectives

11. The Plan focuses on the following sectors: machine tools, earth moving, heavy electrical, metallurgical, textile, process plant, mining, power plant and other industrial machinery and engineering sectors. The key objectives were to make the capital goods sector globally competitive, reduce overseas dependence in strategic sectors, increase depth in manufacturing and enhance production levels, employment, exports and contribution to the national exchequer.

Strategy and Key Recommendations

I. *Investment inducement through clusters*: Apart from common facilities for product development, design and testing, clusters should include enterprise management development through a common training centre promoted through SPVs.

II. *Skill development support*: Problem of skill deficit impacting the machine tools, electrical machinery and earth moving equipment segments should be remedied through a two-pronged approach comprising skill development through public agencies as well as with the help of private sector on a Public–Private Partnership mode.
The action steps suggested in the different sub-sectors of capital goods include upgradation of selected ITIs, polytechnic institutions and engineering colleges and to establish centre of excellence for executive development.

III. *Fund for Expansion/Modernisation of existing units; fund for technology transfer, acquisition of firms abroad*: The industry is considered high risk and not considered a preferred borrower. Therefore, low-cost funds are required to stimulate creation of additional capacity and for technology upgradation.

The following major *recommendations for policy initiatives* are proposed for the capital goods and engineering sector:
- Support for incentivising technology development/transfer and value addition in India
  - Modify FDI policy to ensure transfer of technology by giving preference to JVs instead of 100 per cent foreign-owned companies
  - Develop indigenous facilities for design, development and testing of equipment
  - Incentivise/mandate foreign players to increase value addition in India
  - Preference in PSE/Government purchases for products having higher local content
- Substitute Imports: Calibration of duties and taxes to remove disadvantages for domestic players
  - Regulate/ban import of second-hand machinery
  - Address adverse tax structure for local manufacturers in India
  - Modify Government tender terms to remove disadvantages to Indian firms against imports
- Promote exports by facilitating dedicated line of credit and brand development

12. Though many of the issues constraining the growth of the capital goods sector are common, there are specific sub-sector issues that would require to be addressed with specific measures. The issues specific to machine tool, heavy electrical and power plant equipment, earth moving and mining equipment and associated recommendations are as follows:

Machine Tools Industry

13. India's share of machine tool production is at present only 0.8 per cent of world production. At present, about 70 per cent of the requirement of machine tools is met through imports. There are 8–10 large companies (turnover above ₹100 crores), 10–15 medium companies (50–100 crores) and rest are small. HEC and HMT are two CPSEs in the machine tools sector. New investments have been few, due to low returns on investments. However, the machine tool industry has the potential to grow from about 12 per cent per annum to 15–20 per cent. To achieve a market share of about 50 per cent by 2020, the industry will require a set of policy, investment and technology development measures.

14. The recommended measures, in addition to policy support, include Government support for capacity expansion. The measures include support for technology transfer, common facilities, R&D/incubation centres, business and market development and cluster parks. Some of the major recommendations are as follows:

1. Define a National Mission for Machine Tools
2. Introduce immediate fiscal incentives
3. Mission to indigenise critical mechanical elements and machine tool electronics
4. Measures to attract investment are a priority
5. Creation of modern state of the art capacities
6. Realise full potential of PSU capacities—currently, capacity in PSUs such as HMT and HEC not optimally utilised
7. Fillip to R&D and technology development is essential
8. Industry–academia–R&D linkages

Heavy Electrical and Power Plant Equipment

15. Heavy electrical and power plant equipment sector is growing at about 14 per cent. Its growth in two distinct segments, that is, power plant equipment and electrical equipment for power transmission and distribution are being driven by the major power addition programmes namely, Restructured Accelerated Power Development and Reforms Programme (R-APDRP) and Rajiv Gandhi Vidyutikaran Yojana (RGGVY) and transmission projects.

16. With increase in the requirements for meeting the planned additions and a shift towards setting up higher efficiency super critical power plants in the country, the Indian domestic manufacturers have formed joint ventures (JVs) with foreign companies and are focusing on manufacturing higher efficiency equipment's. The domestic industry has expressed concern about contract with Chinese suppliers and the lack of capacity utilisation in BTG segment. The 'Electrical Equipment Manufacturing Industry'—Industry Report 2010 by IEEMA has highlighted concerns of limited high-voltage testing facilities, varied procurement guidelines of state utilities, persisting gap between Indian and international standards. Threat of rising imports issues of inverted duty structure, critical raw material constraints and absence of appropriate clause to allow preference in domestic procurement on the lines of procurement guidelines of World Bank and ADB. Following are the sector-specific policy recommendations:

1. Ensuring utilisation of domestic capacity
    a. Ensuring sufficient investment in power generation through appropriate Government policies to create adequate demand potential for heavy electrical and power plant equipment
    b. Creation of appropriate conditions enabling full capacity utilisation of domestic manufacturers of heavy electrical and power plant equipment
    c. Constituting a special vehicle for State Electricity Boards (SEB) facilitating replacement of old and ageing power plants
    d. Facilitating availability of critical raw materials
2. Standardisation: Adoption of uniform ratings by Central Electricity Authority (CEA)/Ministry of Power (MoP) as standard ratings to be adopted for the Indian grid.
3. Testing facilities: Strengthening of R&D Infrastructure at national level for type testing of prototypes with a view to minimise development/commercialisation cycle.

Earth Moving and Mining Equipment Sector

17. The earth moving and mining equipment as well as the construction equipment industry (CEI) in India enjoys a positive long-term outlook. Planned investment in infrastructure (more than US$1 trillion) and growing urbanisation will drive the construction industry to grow at 16–17 per cent CAGR over the next 10 years. The growth opportunities are accompanied by increasing competition from equipment's from countries like Brazil and China.

18. The sector has evolved over the years and is at present in an intermediate stage of development. Some products manufactured in India by some of the MNC's who have set up assembly plants in India are meeting the global standards. It is estimated that the domestic content is nearly 35 per cent in standard equipment whereas the domestic content is about 78 per cent in high technology equipment's. Over the years three Chinese companies have emerged as leading construction equipment

manufacturers and have cornered a 12 per cent share of the market. Competition is likely to intensify as many Chinese players have improved their distribution and after-sale networks in India.

19. Like its global counterpart, the domestic mining sector is now graduating into high-end technology products and is in demand of transfer of such technology. A recent Industry Report by CII on the Indian Construction Equipment Industry emphasises for (*i*) rationalisation of taxes to mitigate impediments for interstate movement of earth moving and construction equipment, (*ii*) bridging skill gaps, (*iii*) prohibiting unregulated import of used equipment, and (*iv*) removal of ambiguity about emission and safety standards.

Following are the major recommendations:

- Emission standards must be made applicable to earthmoving equipment's and so on.
- Initiatives for indigenous development of certain equipments like dredgers are to be taken to achieve self-reliance in this area
- The existing competence and capability of Bharat Earth Movers Ltd (BEML) need to be, inter alia, strengthened by providing support for transfer of technology

ELECTRONICS SYSTEMS DESIGN AND MANUFACTURING

Introduction
20. Electronics Systems Design and Manufacturing (ESDM) comprises semiconductor design; high-tech manufacturing; electronics components; electronics systems design telecom products and equipment's; IT systems and hardware and other segments. Electronics, along with Information and Communications Technology (ICT), is considered a meta-resource: the competitiveness of various industries often depends on their ability to integrate ICTE in their business processes. Electronics is the largest and the fastest growing manufacturing industry in the world. It is expected to reach US$ 2.4 trillion by 2020.

Key Objectives Under the Twelfth Plan
The key objectives for the ESDM Sector are:

- To achieve domestic production of USD 122 Billion by 2017 (growth of 30 per cent)
- To ramp up domestic value addition in ESDM manufacturing

Strategy and Key Recommendations
The strategies and key recommendations are:

Creating a level playing field
- Introduce Modified Special Incentive Package Scheme for improved value-addition
- Provide preferential market access to domestic industry in the ESDM sector and remove trade barriers through effective negotiations in WTO
- Mandate Indian standards for ESDM to safeguard against substandard items
- Introduce reforms in Government procurement procedure for electronics hardware

Creating an enabling environment
- Set up a national electronics mission
- Promote exports of ESDM by providing appropriate incentives and brand development
- Promote sustainable growth through waste management practices

Providing support across the value chain
- Set up semiconductor fabs in India and encourage innovation, R&D and Indian IP by setting up of Electronics Development Fund
- Promote the semiconductor chip design, electronics components and strategic electronics industry

STEEL

Introduction

21. Indian iron and steel industry, with its strong forward and backward linkages contributes significantly to the overall growth and development of the economy. The industry today directly contributes 2 per cent to India's Gross Domestic Product and its weightage in the official Index of Industrial Production is 6.2 per cent. India has become the world's fourth largest producer of crude steel, preceded only by China, Japan and USA. However, India has been lagging behind other major steel producing countries in terms of techno-economic efficiency of operations and hence Indian steel industries are not very globally competitive.

22. There is an urgent need to address its basic constraints irrespective of equity size and nature of operations. In 2010, our per capita consumption of steel was only 51.7 kg, as against the world average of 202.70 kg. There is tremendous potential for improvement in the domestic steel consumption given the economy's large untapped markets, especially in rural areas. With a GDP growth of ~9 per cent, the sector is expected to grow by ~10.3 per cent in terms of steel consumption. This translates to a need an installed capacity addition of 142.3 MT of steel in the Twelfth Plan.

Key Objectives Under the Twelfth Plan

- Increase capacities to ~142.3 MT in accordance with demand projections
- Ensure raw material security, especially in terms of iron ore and coking/non-coking coal

Strategy and Key Recommendations

Raw Materials

23. Iron ore is the basic raw material used in steel making. Though iron ore is abundantly available in the country, large scale exports of iron ore have raised serious concerns about the future availability. Side by side, there is an urgent need to address the problems of degradation of the environment, displaced population, transportation bottleneck and so on.

24. The domestic availability of coking coal, a critical raw material required by steel industry is limited and therefore the Indian steel industry has to depend heavily on imported coking coal to meet its needs. To ensure raw material security and minimise the impact of volatility in coal prices, it is desirable to acquire overseas coking coal assets and to increase the domestic production of coking coal and upgrade its quality.

Infrastructure

25. Given the rising demand anticipated in the Twelfth Plan period, the already overburdened domestic infrastructure and more particularly in mineral rich states requires immediate attention. Apart from ensuring adequate rail–road connectivity, National Investment and Manufacturing Zones (NMIZs) proposed in the National Manufacturing Policy may provide an excellent option for future location for new steel plants due to close proximity to consumers. However, for this to happen, the perspective planning for NMIZs has to consider some of the NMIZs in the eastern region of mineral-rich states.

Financial Resources

26. The requirement of financial resources to create an additional capacity during the Twelfth Plan at reasonable costs will be a challenging task. Softening of norms for external borrowings and having a special purpose long-term financing facility may ease the situation.

Technology and Research and Development

27. Indian Steel Plants are less efficient in terms of specific consumption of raw material/consumables, energy/power consumption, environmental and pollution norms than those in advanced countries. It is essential to build up indigenous capacity to develop technologies to suit indigenous raw materials, improve energy inputs norms and meet national emission and comply with global standards on emissions and carbon foot print and so on. Several small units engaged in manufacturing iron and steel products need to focus on domestic R&D to improve their technology and performance standards.

28. Improvement in raw materials is to be achieved through selection of appropriate beneficiation process and improvement in operational practices of ore beneficiation/coal-washing circuit. Coal gasification of non-coking coals and recovery and

utilisation of CBM, are the important steps to address the issues such as coal coke shortage and CO_2 emission. To alleviate the shortages of iron, there is a need to put up pellet plants. Due to increasing demand for high-strength steel, current Batch Annealing Furnace (BAF) technology may get replaced with Continuous Annealing Technology.

29. The strategies for development of steel sector should not only focus on volume growth but also on quality of growth. It is necessary to evolve an approximate sustainable development framework which balances the need for rapid growth of the steel industry and also addresses the concerns on environment and climate change. There is a consensus that there exists a lot of scope for the Indian steel industry to contribute to the National Mission on Enhanced Energy Efficiency (NMEEE) as well as National Action Plan on Climate Change (NAPCC) of 2008, which basically aims to reduce the emission intensity. Existing plants need to evolve short-term and long-term action plan to phase out the old and obsolete facilities by State-of-art, clean and green technologies with an aim not only to achieve higher standards of productivity but also to harness all waste energy.

30. The Steel Industry needs policy support from the States to achieve the object of the National Steel Policy to make India a global producer.

Plan Assistance/Allocation for the Steel Industry
31. The Twelfth Plan's new projects essentially focus promotion of beneficiation and agglomeration of low grade iron ore and iron-ore fines and improvement of energy efficiency in secondary steel sector.

MINERAL EXPLORATION AND DEVELOPMENT

Introduction
32. India is endowed with ample resources of a number of minerals and has the geological environment for many others. The metals and minerals sector has a direct bearing on the growth, development, depth and sustainability of the manufacturing and infrastructure sectors. Hence, its extraction and management have to be integrated into the overall strategy for the country's development. Raw material security and the ability to provide the range of metal-based mineral required in terms of quality, standards and prices are keys to the process.

Key Objectives Under the Twelfth Plan
33. The mining sector is strategically very important for India. The key goals that need to be met for this space are:

- Raw material security: for all the user industries
- Enhanced co-production of by-product metals for Technology Metals and Energy Critical Metals and Rare Earths Elements
- Ensuring sustainability of the environment

Strategy and Key Recommendations
34. The core function of the state in mining needs to be the facilitation and regulation of exploration and mining activities of investors and entrepreneurs, provision of infrastructure and royalty and tax collection. In order for the State to achieve the key objectives associated with the sector, a select set of reforms are essential. The major recommendations are as under.

Strengthening of Institutions
- Equip and position public agencies like the Mineral Exploration Corporation Limited, Atomic Minerals Directorate for Exploration and Research, Indian Rare Earths Limited, Directorates of States and other organisations to conduct detailed exploration at the State's expense to enable the State Government to adopt a bidding route for exploration to a larger extent.
- Position GSI to emphasise on geospatial and multi-disciplinary work for the benefit of science, society and the nation, by placing emphasis. An overarching mechanism to provide policy direction for geosciences is a must.

Encouraging R&D and Technology Development
- Engage IBM to drive process of giving special focus in select areas of mining.
- Strengthen the Mineral Process Laboratories of IBM and other research organisations must before the development of processes for beneficiation, elemental analysis of ores and so on.
- Inspire concessionaires to undertake deposit-specific process R&D.

35. Develop an institutional mechanism for the direct lab scale research to commercialisation for the production of materials of high purity,

- Reorient focus of organisations like Non-Ferrous Technology Development Centre, Jawaharlal Nehru Aluminium Research Development and Design Centre on process R&D for Technology and Energy Critical Metals.

Creation of Infrastructure
- Special emphasis needs to be given to linking infrastructure in mineral bearing areas.

Skill Development
- Review and upgrade existing training facilities for manpower to meet the requirements of the mining industry.

Ensuring Full and Productive Coverage of Survey and Exploration
- GSI needs to ensure that its regional surveys cover all major geo-scientific datasets
    - All pre-competitive data must be available to facilitate entrepreneurs to take investment decisions.
- India's Exclusive Economic Zone (EEZ) needs to be fully explored and exploited. This requires sea-bed exploration and mining, and the Ministry of Earth Sciences and GSI need to cooperate at an institutionalised level to expedite and complete this task.
- There is need to address all important aspects of Rare Earths including Mapping the potential sources, enhancing survey and exploration indigenously as well as in joint collaboration overseas, scaling up R&D in extraction, re-cycling and research for increase use in other alternative materials in place of Rare Earths.

A Database of Mineral Resources Needs to be Developed
- Consider an efficient IT system in GSI, IBM and State Directorates to ensure availability of a comprehensive and up-to-date review of exploration data.
- For this purpose, create a National Geophysical Data Repository and a National Drill Core Library.
- Implement the National Tenement Registry and integrated it with the cadastral maps being digitised under the National Land Records Computerisation Scheme.

Ensuring Availability of Financial Resources
- Access to "risk funds" from capital markets and venture funds needs to be facilitated since prospecting is a high risk venture.
- A suitable scheme for taking full advantage of the HTREL licence must be completed in consultation with the major financial institutions in India, including SEBI, RBI, CBDT and IVCA.

Ensuring Environmental Sustainability of Mining
- Promote a scientific and efficient process of small scale mining of small deposits
    - Regulations related to safeguarding the ecology must be ensured and their compliance strengthened.
    - A cluster approach must be adopted with a single lease model for multiple small deposits within a defined area
- Undertake all mining undertaken within the parameters of a comprehensive Sustainable Development Framework
    - Under such a framework, no mining lease should be granted without a proper mining plan including an approved environment management plan.
    - For this purpose, the IBM must acquire the expertise to approve Environment Management Plans and conduct Environmental Impact Assessments. Thus, the IBM should be able to position itself as the internal environmental regulator as well as the official mining regulator for the sector.

Select Policy Changes in Line with the Overall Strategy
- Adopt an open-sky policy of non-exclusivity for reconnaissance work
- Introduce a new instrument called the High Technology Reconnaissance and Exploration License (HTREL) to attract large investment and better technology
- Ensure higher value addition in the sector and curb non value-added exports
    - Encourage mineral value addition through techniques of beneficiation, pelletisation, agglomeration and processing making use of fine.
    - Incentivise export of minerals in value added form and develop is a coherent long-term strategy for this

- In line with this, forge long-term relationships with countries with complementary resources, in terms of minerals and technologies.
- Encourage the user industries to develop long-term linkages with mineral producing units.
• A fair and transparent process for land acquisition must be ensured. This is already under way through the LARR bill

36. The MMDR bill aims at enabling some of these key recommendations, and must be pushed for implementation at the earliest.

FERTILISER

Introduction

37. The Indian fertiliser industry, given its strategic importance in ensuring the food security in the country has remained under Government control. Through its impact on agricultural productivity, fertiliser usage directly impacts food security of the country. Government has been consistently pursuing policies conducive to availability of adequate quantity of quality fertilisers throughout the country and their appropriate use. The annual consumption of nutrients (N + P + K), has increased by 62 per cent, from 17.4 million tonne in 2001–02 to 28.1 million tonne in 2010–11. The nutrients N, P and K accounted for 16.6, 8.0 and 3.5 million tonne respectively in 2010–11.

38. In recent years, there has been a significant increase in imports of urea and DAP because there has been hardly any investment for major capacity additions. Fertiliser consumption in India is highly skewed, with wide inter-regional, interstate, inter-district and inter-crop variations. The average intensity of fertiliser use in India is much lower than most countries in the world.

39. Government introduced Nutrient Based Subsidy (NBS) for Phosphatic and Potassic (P and K) fertilisers with effect from 1 April 2010 with broad objectives of ensuring balance use of nutrients, introduction, and promotion of innovative and efficient fertiliser products and allowing market dynamics in pricing of products.

Key Objectives Under the Twelfth Plan

40. The key objective for the fertiliser sector is to ensure national food security by generating sustainable rapid growth in fertiliser use to increase agricultural production and productivity at the desired rate. In order to meet the growth targets in fertiliser use, the following measures are needed:

- Ensuring adequate and timely availability of quality fertilisers to the farmers at fair prices
- Creating an attractive environment for improving indigenous fertiliser
- Rationalisation of the level of fertiliser subsidy disbursed

Strategy and Key Recommendations

Improving Fertiliser Use

41. For continuous rapid growth in fertiliser use to increase agricultural production and productivity, the Fertilisers Monitoring System (FMS) should be strengthened. There is a need to produce and promote right kind of efficient fertilisers like customised, water-soluble and fortified fertilisers.

Attracting Investment in the Sector

42. With rising demand and no major domestic capacity addition during the last few years, the industry has been exposed to volatility of world markets. There is an urgent need to create a conducive environment for new investments in the sector. Investment for revival of closed units of Fertiliser Corporation of India Ltd (FCIL) and Hindustan Fertiliser Corporation Ltd (HFCL) will significantly bridge the demand–supply gap of urea.

Availability of Feedstock

43. The Government needs to ensure long-term supply of natural gas at reasonable prices with pipeline connectivity to attract fresh investment in urea sector. For this, part of future gas finds need to be committed for the new investment in urea units and incentivising alternative feedstock like coal, CBM and so on to enlarge the choice of raw materials. There is a need to explore the possibility of investment in R&D for extracting potash from other resources in the country.

Rationalising Subsidy

44. The burden of fertiliser subsidy has increased substantially during the last few years mainly owing to increase in international prices of inputs as well as finished fertilisers. A phased approach towards reforming the subsidy disbursement mechanism needs to be developed as under:

- Phase 1: Create information visibility of the movement of fertilisers along the supply chain
- Phase 2: Release subsidy to the retailer through transfer of subsidy directly to the retailer's bank account on receipt of fertiliser from the wholesaler
- Phase 3: In the long run once Aadhaar enabled payments are operational, subsidy disbursement to the farmer can be made directly into the bank accounts of the intended beneficiary

Joint Ventures Abroad

45. Rising imports of fertilisers are a cause of concern and require urgent attention. India, being one of the largest consumer of fertilisers in the world, has significant impact in world trade and prices and is exposed to high volatility in prices. There is a need to ensure long-term supplies of raw materials/intermediates to fertiliser sector by promoting investment and setting up JVs in mining capacities of the countries with rich reserves of natural gas, rock phosphate and potash with appropriate buy-back arrangement or long term off-take arrangements.

Setting up R&D Centre

46. R&D centres need to be encouraged especially in the area of catalyst efficiency, retrieval of elements from spent catalyst, new fertiliser development, improving fertiliser use efficiency and so on.

Fertiliser Prices Regulatory Authority

47. With the implementation of Nutrient Based Subsidy (NBS) regime in non-urea sector and likelihood of extension to urea sector, the fertiliser sector moved towards a free market system. Therefore, it may be necessary to consider a fertiliser prices regulatory authority to oversee and regulate fertiliser prices in the interest of the agriculture sector.

Road Map for Sick CPSUs

48. Despite the overall health being fairly satisfactory. Three of the central CPSUs, three units BVFCL, MFL and FACT are incurring losses due to outdated technology and, high energy consumption. There is a need to explore various possibilities for their revival and sustainable operation to come up with a holistic revival plan for the sick CPSUs.

CEMENT

Introduction

Key Features of Cement Industry

- Cement production is one of the world's most energy-intensive industries. Cement industry is in a way a scavenging industry and has been burning alternative fuels such as, residue derived fuel, municipal sewage wastes, agro wastes, plastic and polythene wastes, paint sludge, shredded tyres and so on in the kiln and conserves fossil fuels.
- Because of low-value high-density product, cement movement is normally restricted to nearby markets and has very limited international trade.
- Initial investment of setting up a plant is very high.

Production Trends

49. Global cement production has continued to be expanding at an average rate of 6.4 per cent in last five years from 2,568 million tonnes in 2006 to 3,294 million tonnes in 2010. Around 56 per cent of production originates in China. China (with an average annual growth of 11.4 per cent) and India (with an average annual growth of 9.8 per cent) have been the drivers of the growth in global cement output, with increase in production in rest of countries remaining virtually stable. Production of cement in India has increased from 100.1 million tonnes in 2000–01 to 228.3 million tonnes in 2010–11. The demand for the cement in India has been influenced mainly by the housing, infrastructure and irrigation and so on.

Key Objectives Under the Twelfth Plan
- Reducing environmental impact of industry and encouraging use of fly ash
- Modernisation of plants based on older technology and further improvement of plants

Strategy and Key Recommendations

Measures to Maintain Existing Capabilities
- Allocation of coal of better quality and consistency to cement plants and also speeding up privatisation of collieries for captive consumption of cement plants should be considered
- To ensure availability of limestone process of limestone mining lease approval/renewal need to be streamlined and simplified as well as encourage mining of limestone at remote areas
- Rationalising duty structure
    - Simplification of excise duty to have specific rate or percentage of sale price with appropriate abatements
    - Rationalisation of inverted duty structure to address any inversions

Reducing Environmental Impact of the Industry
- Incentivise non-polluting cement plants adopting newer technologies
- Grant cogeneration of power through waste heat recovery status of renewable energy
- Cement plants should be permitted to move waste from other states with minimum restrictions if they are following standing guidelines
    - Encouraging use of fly ash by ensuring availability of comprehensive data on fly ash generation, disposal, stock and its pricing, setting standards for making composite cement and so on.

Upgradation of Existing Plants and Research in Further Developed Technologies
- Funding from corpus of clean energy fund for cement sector for development of processes for using alternate fuel and municipal and solid waste and energy efficient technologies.
- NCCBM, which is primarily an R&D organisation would need support for development of infrastructure.

Development and Adoption of Nanotechnology
- Promoting collaborative research involving national and international laboratories on technologies to produce nanoparticles and the latest characterisation techniques Establishing a well-equipped Centre of Excellence for development and adoption of nanotechnology practices to cement and concrete through PPP mode.

Improving the Transportation Facilities for Cement Industry
- Rail transport: Railway should try and attain a share of 50 per cent in total dispatches of cement and clinker.
- Road transport: Load carrying capacity of trucks may be increased to 1 tonne.
- Inland waterways: Sufficient infrastructure need to be provided at IWT terminals/jetties to integrate with other modes of transportation.

SECTORS FOR DEPTH AND VALUE ADDITION:

AUTOMOTIVE

Introduction
50. The automotive industry is also a key sector for the Indian economy. Owing to its deep forward and backward linkages, it has a strong multiplier effect and acts as one of the drivers of economic growth. With the gradual liberalisation of the automotive sector in India since 1991, the numbers of manufacturing facilities have grown progressively. It produces a wide variety of vehicles ranging from passenger cars to heavy commercial vehicles to tractors and other agricultural equipments and so on.

51. The competitive paradigm for the automobile sector world over is rapidly undergoing complete transformation on account of environmental and energy security concerns. It is estimated that by 2020, electric vehicle (EV) and other green cars will

represent up to one third of total global sales in developed markets and up to 20 per cent in urban areas of emerging markets. The Indian auto sector which has close linkages with international auto industries will be deeply impacted by the evolving trends.

Key Objectives Under the Twelfth Plan

52. The Auto Policy of the Government had the following objectives:

1. Exalt the sector as a lever of industrial growth and employment and to achieve a high degree of value addition in the country
2. Promote a globally competitive automotive industry and emerge as a global source for auto components
3. Establish an international hub for manufacturing small, affordable passenger cars and a key centre for manufacturing tractors and two-wheelers;
4. Ensure a balanced transition to open trade at minimal risk to the Indian economy and local industry
5. Conduce incessant modernisation of the industry and facilitate indigenous design, research and development
6. Steer India's software industry into automotive technology
7. Assist development of vehicles propelled by alternate energy sources
8. Development of domestic safety and environmental standards at par with international standards

53. The Automotive Mission Plan 2006–16 laid down a 10 year road map for the industry The specific targets set up AMP are as follows:

- To continue to be the world's largest tractor and three-wheeler manufacturer in the world.
- To continue as the world's second largest two-wheeler manufacturers.
- To emerge as the world's fifth largest car producer (as compared to the seventh largest currently).
- To become world's fifth largest commercial vehicle manufacturer.
- Automotive sector would double its turnover ratio to India's GDP in 10 years.
- To export USD 35 billion by 2016.

54. The industry is planning to take a mid-term review of the AMP in 2013 and come up with objectives and targets for beyond 2016.

Government Initiatives

55. Government has also decided to constitute National Council for Electric Mobility (NCEM) and National Board for Electric Mobility (NBEM) for fast policy and decision making at the apex level for promoting electric mobility and for encouraging manufacture of electric vehicles in the country. Deliberations at the level of NBEM have been initiated to define short-term and long-term objectives and to develop short-term/long-term plans.

56. To address the issue of lack of testing infrastructure, a Plan scheme—National Automotive Testing and R&D Infrastructure Project (NATRIP) was initiated in the Tenth Plan. With the coming up of NATRIP facilities (in the first year of the Twelfth Plan), the industry would be in a position to adopt higher safety standards. NATRIP implementation Society (NATIS) is overseeing the implementation of NATRIP.

Strategy and Key Recommendations

- Providing an enabling environment to the industry to encourage growth, promote domestic competition and stimulate innovation to achieve operational efficiency.
- Removal of taxation on interstate movement of goods to make the Indian market a genuine 'free trade area' domestically.
- A stable import tariff structure consonant with the AMP that encourages investments rather than trade in fully built vehicles.
- Continuation of lower excise duty (in future GST) for manufacture of vehicle types that are a national priority for the country.
- Ensuring that the Free Trade Agreements being entered into with other countries do not distort markets for Indian automobile and auto component manufacturers.

- Inadequate availability of skilled labour—to be addressed with partnership with NSDC.
- Government to prepare a strategy paper on utilisation of different fuels in the transport sector to meet our national priorities of emission control, energy security as well as fuel efficiency
- Evolving the emissions and fuel availability road map beyond 2010
- Deepening competence in manufacturing of fuel efficient cars and electric vehicles including the hybrid segment.
- User incentives for adoption of EVs.
- Auto component industry needs to be supported by the Government by easing access to capital, logistic and infrastructure development in auto component hubs and so on.
- To address the issue of road safety, an appropriate regulatory body would be required.

DRUGS AND PHARMACEUTICALS

Introduction

57. Indian pharmaceutical industry is one of the high performing knowledge-based segments of the Domestic Manufacturing Sector. The soft patent regime prior to 2005 provided opportunity for this industry to consolidate its position and witness significant growth in generic production and exports. Indian pharmaceutical Industry has entered an era in which it has to play a pivotal role in providing generic medicines to the world and also become a global hub for R&D activities. Despite our success, we are still at the periphery of a vast unexplored opportunity. At this juncture, it is all the more important to recognise the challenges and opportunities and realign our strategies along with appropriate policy and institutional frameworks for shaping the future of the Indian pharmaceutical industry.

Key Objectives Under the Twelfth Plan

- The Indian pharmaceutical sector should grow to US$ 60 billion size in 2017 (CAGR of 18 per cent) and have a 5 per cent share of the global pharmaceutical industry by the end of the Twelfth Five Year Plan. By 2020, the sector should be at US$ 100 billion.
- Exports should be at INR 1,30,000 crores by the end of the Twelfth Five Year Plan.
- The sector should employ 1.5 million people by 2015, 1.898 million people by 2018 and 2.464 million people by 2022.
- Domestic R&D should be internationally competitive.
- Universal access of quality medicine at affordable prices.
- Improve domestic content in medical devices.
- Make all the CPSUs self-sustaining by 2020.

Strategy and Key Recommendations

58. The recommendations are summarised below:

- Capacity building of private sector to meet WHO–GMP standards and other international manufacturing standards.
- Enabling the Indian pharmaceutical industry to develop competence in advanced areas of drug manufacturing like dedicated research facility in bulk drugs, improving processes of manufacturing generics and new APIs.
- Developing common infrastructure in drug discovery and development, such as, manufacturing, distribution, exports, medical devices and so on.
- Appropriate coordination between relevant ministries/departments and stakeholders to build a coordinated strategy s to tackle non-tariff barriers through counter measures and during signing of FTAs.
- Develop competencies for 2D Bar-coding for SMEs.
- Developing capacity of Central Drug Standards and Control Organisation to ensure timely clearance for new drug trials, pharmaco-vigilance, and assistance to the willing industry members to shore up their technical capacities for better regulatory compliances and adequate number of labour inspectors.
- Developing, evolving and rationalising regulatory frameworks for biosimilar drugs, fixed-drug combinations, clinical trials and early drug development.
- Developing the ecosystem to take advantage of the opportunity in clinical research and development of Clinical Research Centres for high-risk trials such as Phase-I.
- Create a level-playing field for domestic manufacturers in the bulk drugs industry.

59. Induce higher levels of research and development:

- Strengthening the NIPERs to boost patent filing from these institutes.
- Improving industry–academia linkages by creating a strong platform for incentivising innovation in producing safe, affordable medicine, arranging public–private partnerships with industry and leading academic partners.
- Providing incentives for New Drug Development.

60. Review the regulatory system including expanding tax deduction (to cover activities such as international patenting costs, regulatory consultants, outsourced R&D services and patent litigation expenses), reducing approval timelines and so on.

- Improving access to quality healthcare promotion of unbranded generics through Jan Aushadhi Stores (JAS) Ministry of Health needs to bring out legislation for prescription of medicines in generics nomenclature by the doctors on a mandatory basis.
- Inducing greater level of domestic manufacture of medical devices by creating infrastructure and parks for setting up greenfield medical devices and equipment units and setting up a National Centre for Medical Devices.
- Enabling CPSUs to be self-sustainable by upgrading the existing manufacturing facilities to WHO–GMP compliance.

61. India, with its significant advantage of low cost of innovation, low capital requirements and lower costs in running facilities, well-established manufacturing processes, R&D infrastructure, is strategically well positioned to emerge as a major force to reckon with in the pharmaceuticals sector.

62. Moving to a higher growth trajectory will require focussed institutional support and incentivise the clusters to foster innovation, encouragement to maximise investments in enhancing manufacturing capacities and aggressive drive for creation of 'Brand India' image in select segments including biopharmaceuticals/biosimilars and Indian systems of medicines.

CHEMICAL

Introduction

63. The domestic chemical industry is heterogeneous in nature comprising organic, inorganic, petrochemicals, dyes, paints, pesticides and specialty chemicals manufactured in the small scale and large units (including MNCs). In the global context, the industry is increasingly moving eastwards in line with the shift of its key consumer industries (for example, automotive, electronics and so on) to leverage greater manufacturing competitiveness and share of Asia in the global chemical industry has risen from 31 per cent in 1999 to 45 per cent in 2009. With the current size of $108 billion, the Indian chemical industry accounts for ~3 per cent of the global chemical industry.

Key Objectives Under the Twelfth Plan
- Ensuring optimal allocation of resources for adequate feed stock (coal, natural gas, naphtha and refinery cuts) to industry.
- Developing new and more energy efficient and environment-friendly/green technologies and processes.
- Clustering and providing common infrastructure to units.

Strategy and Key Recommendations

Ensuring Availability of Feed Stock
- Refinery configuration to focus on optimisation of availability feedstock and source feedstock from feedstock rich countries through , long term contracts.
- NCL and IICT to take initiative towards development of processes to use bio-based raw material instead of crude-based ones.

Development of Common Infrastructure
- Set up Greenfield PCPIRs and R&D parks through public private partnership.
- Establish a site operator, with the right functional expertise, to market and manage each PCPIR.

Focus on R&D
- Establish chemical sector specific council having representation of stakeholders to develop the innovation road map for chemical industry.
- Develop dedicated innovation centres in universities for chemical industry.

Focus on Green Technology and Consolidation of Environmental Regulations
- Consolidation of rules governing environment protection for chemical industry.
- Development of green technologies—implementation of the related provisions and fiscal measures of the National Manufacturing Policy.
- Central and State Government to work together to ensure more rigorous and transparent enforcement of pollution-related and environment-related regulations in chemical units.

Human Resource Development
- Setting up specialised vocational training centres in the clusters for chemical industry.

Other Strategies
- Fiscal incentives to the chemical sector for tackling the threat from cheap imports.
- Simplifying the process of registration of pesticides to boost export possibilities.
- Better testing mechanisms for tackling the problem of spurious pesticides.

PETROCHEMICALS

Introduction
64. Petrochemicals are chemicals derived from petroleum or natural gas and they form an essential part of the chemical industry today. Due to its very nature, Petrochemicals is an 'enabler' industry playing a vital role in the functioning of virtually all key sectors in the economy including packaging, agriculture, infrastructure, healthcare, textile and consumer goods. Petrochemicals provide critical inputs which enable other sectors to grow. Even though this industry is capital and technology intensive, the downstream sector is a major avenue for large-scale employment. The downstream plastic processing industry employs over 3.53 million people who derive their livelihood from this sector.

Key Objectives Under the Twelfth Plan
- Developing new technologies
- Reducing the environmental impact of the sector
- Development of clusters

Strategy and Key Recommendations

Technology Upgradation
- Setting up a petroleum research and development fund under PPP model.
- Augmenting existing testing centres to act as certifying agencies for testing plastic products and raw materials to meet international as well as BIS standards.

Ensuring Sustainable Growth of the Sector
- Setting up a code of conduct for the industry and permitting certain types of industries, beyond a particular size only if they can ensure zero discharge.
- Fiscal incentive to encourage use of renewable feedstock, adoption of green processes and build energy-efficient housing.
- Focus on recycling industry.

Creating Infrastructure
- Formation of industrial clusters/plastic parks—benchmarking with similar clusters in China, Singapore, Taiwan and so on, and other areas which have successfully built such facilities over the years to serve as a blueprint on policy actions.

Human Resource Development
- Specialised programmes for technical training, which can address the specific requirements of plastic industry.

Other Policy Initiatives for Promoting the Sector
- Branding 'made in India' products for increasing export competitiveness of the sector.
- Ensure strict and effective enforcement of the 'Edible Oil Packaging (Regulation) Order', 1998 by all State Governments.
- Encourage use of plastic packaging in key applications, for example, milk packaging.
- Encourage the use of plastic components in housing to reduce energy requirements.

PAPER

Introduction

65. The Indian Paper industry produces 10.11 million tons of paper per annum and accounts for 2.6 per cent of total world production. The annual turnover of the Indian paper industry is nearly ₹30,000 crores and it employs about 3.70 lakh people. Per capital consumption of paper in India is also very low. Most of the paper mills are in existence for a long time and hence technologies used by them fall in a wide spectrum ranging from oldest to the modern.

66. As many as 30 large integrated paper mills, accounting for about 31 per cent of total domestic production, use wood-based/bamboo-based pulp. One hundred and fifty paper mills, contributing 22 per cent of domestic production, use agro-based (bagasse and straws) and about 473 mills, accounting for 47 per cent of total production, use recycled fibre or waste paper for paper production.

Key Objectives Under the Twelfth Plan
- Developing new technologies
- Improving availability of raw material
- Development to be environmentally sustainable

Strategy and Key Recommendations

67. The deliberations of the woking group on Pulp and Paper Sector have shown that expected increase in demand of paper in the country will require considerable increase in the indigenous production base of the paper sector in the next 15 years. Clearly, this would require in-depth planning to address critical issues like non-availability of fibrous resources, technological obsolescence and lack of economies of scale. The group has come out with a set of recommendations in respect of areas requiring improvement and focus. The key recommendations are given in the Box 13.5.

Box 13.5
Key Recommendations

- Ensuring availability of basic raw material and power
  - Wood: Large scale promotion of agro based plantation and substantial improvement in productivity of agro based plantation activity; Restoration of degraded forest land
- Bagasse: Review of incentives policy for use of bagasse in sugar mills,
- Identification and promotion of alternate lingo-cellulosic raw materials
- Setting up waste paper collection centres and creation of awareness
- Modernising entire RCF/WP bases industry to adopt state of the art technology
- Technology improvements for better energy efficiency and reduced environmental impact
  - Improving energy efficiency of existing and designing of incentives for technology upgradation for paper industry
  - Development of indigenous technologies to make agro-based industries competitive and environmentally sustainable
  - Development of energy efficient technologies
  - R&D institutes like CPPRI to be strengthened with appropriate funding support
- Support for indigenous manufacturing facility for capacity expansion.
- Fiscal measures to support the sector
- Rationalisation of duty structure to address inversions, if any
- Assistance to forestry/plantation

68. The Indian paper and pulp industry has potential and also capabilities to service the growing demand in domestic and international market. It can also create huge employment avenues in rural India through agro-forestry and can provide direct employment in production at mills through capacity addition/expansion, provided the competitiveness of the value chain is ensured. This warrants an enabling policy environment to gear up productive capacity, ensure varied raw material options, induce new technologies and promote local innovation.

(B) SECTORS FOR EMPLOYMENT GENERATION

TEXTILES

Introduction
69. The strength of the Indian textiles and clothing industry lies in its strong raw-material base, indigenous design capabilities, presence in the entire value chain, large and growing domestic demand, and the availability of trained manpower at internationally competitive rates. The Indian Textiles and Clothing Industry consumes a diverse range of fibres and yarns but is predominantly cotton based.

70. The sector plays a pivotal role in the economy, contributing about 12 per cent of the manufacturing output, 11 per cent of merchandise exports and employs about 45 million people. It has a major presence in the unorganised sector as compared to the organised sector, both in terms of the workforce and number of enterprises.

Key Objectives Under the Twelfth Plan
71. The growth of this Sector is crucial to the realisation of targets relating to total output and employment growth. The key objectives of the Textile sector for the 12th plan period are:

- Achieve an annual average growth rate of 11.5 per cent in volume terms in cloth production and 15 per cent in value of exports by increasing domestic value addition and technological 'depth' and by enhancing the global competitiveness.
- It is expected that training to 35 lakh persons would be provided.
- Additional employment to the tune of 15.81 million by 2016–17 would be created.

Strategy and Key Recommendations
72. Based on the lessons learnt in the Eleventh Plan and continuing with the thrust on technology up gradation and modernisation, the Twelfth Plan envisages critical interventions in the weaker segments of the textile value chain such as processing and garmenting. The main elements of the strategy for the Textiles Sector would be as under:

Technology with Focus on Weaving and Processing Sectors
73. The benefits of the Technology Up gradation Fund Scheme (TUFS), have mainly been availed by the Spinning and Composite Sectors. While investments in the spinning sector may be required to ensure yarn availability and domestic value addition of cotton, it is also important to promote forward integration. A study by CRISIL has recommended that the interest subsidy for spinning should be allowed only when it is accompanied by matching investments in weaving or knitting. Investment for technology up gradation in the downstream segments of weaving and processing is necessary to ensure that maximum quantity of yarn produced in the country is converted into spinning products domestically.

Infrastructure
74. The Scheme for Integrated Textile Parks (SITP) was launched in 2005 to neutralise the weakness of fragmentation in the various sub-sectors of textiles value chain, and the non-availability of quality infrastructure, with only 9 projects completed of 40 projects sanctioned in the 11th Plan, impact of these Parks is yet to emerge.

75. There is little evidence of vertical integration in these parks, which specifically encourages both forward and backward linkages in the entire textile value chain. It would be prudent to focus on consolidation of the gains for existing Parks. The proposed new scheme of setting up of Integrated Apparel Clusters, activities laid down in the Technology Mission for Knitwear and Wovenwear should be subsumed in SITP.

Cotton Sector

76. As per the evaluation study carried out by ICRA Management Consultancy Services Limited, trash content in Indian cotton has reduced from high levels of 4–8 per cent during the pre-TMC period to 1.5–3 per cent post modernisation under Mini Mission-IV of the Technology Mission on cotton. Under Mini Mission-III, up-gradation/improvement in the Market Yards has arrested the level of contamination. Based on the estimated cotton production of 438 lakh bales by the end of the terminal year of the Twelfth Five year Plan, MM-III and IV should make efforts for modernisation of G&P factories and Market Yards.

Environmental Concerns

77. The major challenges faced by the textiles processing are availability of water, effluent treatment and disposal of the treated water and solid effluents. A scheme for Common Effluent Treatment with Marine Outfall for the existing textile processing clusters on a PPP mode needs consideration.

Jute

78. Dependence of Jute Mills on Government orders the Jute Mandatory Packaging Act is one of the major barriers to modernisation and product diversification within the industry. The Jute Sector must plan for a gradual phasing out of this order and achieve more self-reliance through modernisation and diversification.

79. The major focus of interventions during the Twelfth Plan would be on aggressive implementation of Technology Mission on Technical Textiles which would include implementation of regulatory framework in specified areas, encouraging indigenous production of specialty fibres and yarns, encouraging investment in high end technical textiles products, including FDI, encouraging R&D in technical textiles, formulation and notifications of standards by BIS and ensuring availability of data base.

Silk

80. India is the second largest producer of silk in the world, a distant second to China, with 15.50 per cent share of the world production.

81. The objectives in the Twelfth Plan would be to facilitate and create conducive conditions for achieving the targeted silk production of 32,000 M.T. at a CAGR of 7.14 per cent by the terminal year of the Twelfth Plan. This would be done through intensive efforts in R&D, technology transfer and enterprise development, creating an inbuilt pyramid structure of federated farmers and farmer associations to synergise and synchronise the production processes. Also, efforts will be directed to develop 3rd Generation multivoltine crossbreeds to increase production and matching quality parameters of bivoltine silk and accelerate the growth in vanya silk production and explore better value realisation in domestic and international markets.

Powerlooms

82. The decentralised powerloom sector plays an important role in the textile economy in terms of fabric production and employment generation. It contributes 62 per cent to the total fabric production in the country and provides employment to the tune of 57.2 lakh persons.

83. The interventions required for Powerloom Sector development during Twelfth Plan period include Powerloom Cluster Development Programme, setting up of Common Facility Centres, Yarn Bank, setting up of Design Development Centres in the clusters, conducting awareness programmes/seminars/workshops/pilot activities and Distress Relief Fund Scheme for powerloom weavers. An exclusive provision for Powerloom Sector under TUFS for its modernisation and creation of an office of the Powerloom Commissioner need to be considered.

Wool and Woollens Textiles

84. The woollen industry in the country is of the size of ₹10,000 crore and broadly divided and scattered between the organised and decentralised sectors. India has the third largest sheep population in the world, having 6.40 crore sheep producing 43.30 million kgs of raw wool, out of which, about 85 per cent is carpet grade wool,

85. It has been estimated that the raw wool production and imports would double from 114.2 million kg in 2008–09 to 260.8 million kg by 2019–20. During the period 2009–10 and 2014–15, exports of woollen yarn fabrics and made-ups are expected to record a CAGR of 11.6 per cent.

86. There is a need to have proper data base and action plan to reduce mortality rate of sheep, increasing coverage of shepherds as well as sheep under insurance, faster development of CFCs, improvement in productivity in wool production. Thrust of the scheme/programmes has to be oriented accordingly.

Human Resource Development

87. As per the study conducted by National Skill Development Corporation, with the overall growth of 9.5 per cent in the Textiles and Clothing Sector, its incremental human resource requirement would be about 17.8 million by the end of Twelfth Plan.

FOOD PROCESSING INDUSTRIES

Introduction

88. As a leading producer of food grains, milk, fruits and vegetables, India has the advantage of adequate food at the farm gate to ensure food security for the nation and to even have a surplus for exports. Food processing industry in India has immense potential for boosting the rural economy as it brings about synergy between consumers, industry and agriculture. A well-developed food processing industry is expected to increase farm-gate prices, reduce wastages, ensure value addition, promote crop diversification, generate employment opportunities and boost export earnings.

Key Objectives Under the Twelfth Plan

89. Following are the main objectives for the Twelfth Plan:
- Develop the food processing sector to enable containment of food inflation and food wastage
- Create 1 million additional jobs during the Twelfth plan period

Strategy and Key Recommendations

90. Based on lessons learnt during Eleventh Plan and keeping in view the priorities of the proposed Manufacturing Plan, the strategy for 12th Plan has been devised based on three basic principles. Firstly, greater emphasis would be laid on decentralised process of implementation with greater involvement of states in selection of projects vis-à-vis beneficiaries and monitoring their implementation.

91. Secondly, instead of project implementation, focus would be on policy making and coordination so as to address critical issues impacting the value chain in the sector. Lastly, the existing focus on infrastructure development will be continued with expansion of scope and depth so as to ensure sustainability of the value chains. The major recommendations in regard to Twelfth Plan activities are in Box 13.6.

92. Adoption of a decentralised approach to instil greater involvement of states and appropriate coordination between states and stakeholders is a well-conceived idea for development of Food Processing Sector. Launching a National Mission on Food Processing (NMFP) will be appropriate vehicle to carry forward the idea of decentralisation.

Box 13.6
Key Recommendations

- Setting up of National Mission on Food Processing to improve coordination and implementation of schemes and to enable greater involvement of state governments.
- Expanding and modifying existing infrastructure development schemes
  - Mega Food Parks Scheme, Integrated Cold Chain Scheme
- Setting up and Modernisation of Abattoirs—Establishment of new abattoirs and modernisation of existing abattoirs
- Develop and strengthening of existing and new institutions
- Taking up a nation-wide skill development programme along the lines of special projects for skill development of rural youths under SGSY of MoRD.
- Putting in place a network of food testing labs (Government/Private) through providing incentives.
- Encouragement for larger participation in Codex deliberations and setting up/strengthening of Codex Cell in FSSAI to promote, coordinate and monitor related initiatives at the level of stakeholders
- Setting up of an Innovation Fund and Venture Capital Fund for Food Processing to promote innovations and technology development

93. Likewise shift of focus of the Ministry from project implementation to policy initiative is in right direction towards holistic development of the sector. The policy to be effective will have to be comprehensive and should evolve through consultation with the states and the industry.

94. While basic agricultural research has strong and large institutional network in the country, there is inadequate focus on the food processing sector. There is an urgent need for building a bridge between agricultural universities, premiere technological and industrial research institute and the private sector to actively undertake collaborative strategic research in this important sector.

95. Apart from National Institute of Food Technology Entrepreneurship and Management (NIFTEM), the Central Food Technology Research Institute (CFTRI) should play a more central, pro-active role to strengthen knowledge base of the industry through greater public and private partnership in technology development.

96. Another critical objective should be for the industry to reach international standards of food safety and quality. All efforts should be made to harmonise Indian Food Standards with Codex. Enactment of the comprehensive legislation, the Food Safety and Standards Act, 2006 in the recent past has already provided an enabling vista for taking the above aspects forward.

97. Last but not the least; it is required to recalibrate the existing schemes of MFPI for greater effectiveness. The proposed Centrally Sponsored Scheme of NMFP has to be structured in such a manner so that it is efficiently managed. It may also be worthwhile for new mega food parks to explore options of identifying one or more anchor industry(ies) to speed up their pace of implementation.

LEATHER AND LEATHER GOODS

Introduction

98. The leather and leather products industry occupies an important position in the Indian economy in view of its massive potential for employment generation, potential for growth both in domestic and export markets. The leather industry is spread in different segments, namely, tanning and finishing, footwear and footwear components, leather garments, leather goods including saddlery and harness and so on.

Key Objectives Under the Twelfth Plan
- To increase the number of employed in the industry–ensuring the availability of trained/skilled labour
- To improve the export competitiveness of our products and facilitating exports
- Improving the scale of businesses in the sector
- Ensuring clean processes (environmental pollution)
- Improving the social conditions

Strategy and Key Recommendations

Attracting Large Scale Investments through FDI and Domestic Companies
- Promoting the model adopted China and Vietnam to build a strong leather industry, Promotional activities in foreign countries to be carried out in various formats, print campaign, investment meet, missions for collaborations on raw materials and so on.

Skill Development Initiatives
- Establishment of new Footwear Design and Development Institutes (FDDI) to skill deficit in the sector.
- Support to Artisans' scheme—360 degree intervention plan.
- Placement linked Skill Development Programme and Training of Trainers—For providing employment opportunity and to fill the demand of operators in the footwear sector and improving the quality of training.

Ensuring Environmental Sustainability
- Animal Husbandry Measures, Slaughter and Skin Collection Improvement Measures and Rural Tanning Improvement Measures.
- Technology Upgradation and Modernisation, environmental impact upgradation and technology benchmarking of Tanneries.

Improving Export Competitiveness
- Brand Building and Indian Leather Mark
- Constitution of Domestic Council—Footwear and Leather Products Development and Promotion Council (FLPDPC)

Others
- Improving the availability of raw-materials

GEMS AND JEWELLERY

Introduction

99. India's Gem and Jewellery (G&J) industry is an important foundation of the country's export-led growth. It is a leading foreign exchange earner and one of the fastest growing sectors accounting for 16.67 per cent of India's total merchandise exports during FY 2010-11. India now accounts for nearly 55 per cent of world net exports of cut and polished diamonds in value terms, 90 per cent in terms of pieces and 80 per cent by cartage. The industry employs about 2 million highly skilled workforce out of which one million are exclusively engaged in export production.

100. India is known to be the largest consumer of gold in the world. It is estimated that the current annual demand for gold in the country is well over 800 tonnes. Naturally India is also the largest fabricator of gold.

101. In the diamond segment, the industry is importing rough diamond from countries such as Belgium, UK, UAE, Israel, Hong Kong, Switzerland and other mining countries. The polished diamond is exported to countries such as UAE, Hong Kong, USA, Belgium and Israel.

Key Objectives Under the Twelfth Plan
- To ensure access and availability of raw material to the industry
- To make Indian products attractive at global markets

Strategy and Key Recommendations

Secure Raw Material Sources:
1. Diamond
   - Restrict the export of rough diamonds from domestic mines and invest in diamond reserves abroad through PPP to ensure the sustained availability.

2. Gold
   - Explore possibility of free import of precious metal gold for manufacturing exports.
   - Examine option of permitting import of gold as per international practice in place of current practice of import by canalising agencies to erratic supply and frequent shortages.

3. Coloured Gem Stones
   - Commissioning exploration programmes and surveys to ascertain availability of coloured gemstones in India.

Training and Development
- Create Sector Skill Council, under the aegis of NSDC, GJEPC and other critical stakeholders. Develop and administer 'Train the Trainer' programmes, create training infrastructure and roll out the training programmes.

Research and Development and Technological Upgradation
- Documentation of existing tacit knowledge of traditional artists.
- Develop a Design Centre of Excellence and Product Development at Mumbai.

Infrastructure Facilities
- Setting up Gem Bourses, jewellery parks/clusters, Gem trading centres and G&J training centres in some key cities across the country.

Marketing and Brand Promotion
- Creation of a fund with contribution of industry to promote 'Made in India' brand image across the globe.
- Appropriate measures by Government of India to have access in the untapped market for G&J products.
- Government should encourage the participation of the industry in international trade forums.

Regulatory and Fiscal
- Introduction of Turnover based taxation system for Indian Gem and Jewellery industry.
- Relaxation in EPC norms for import of machineries from Italy.
- Allowance of External Commercial Borrowings for working capital as well.
- RBI to allow financing for retail jewellery business abroad.
- Create dollar fund to refinance banks to finance industry at competitive international rate.
- Introduction of adequate credit guarantee mechanism for Gem and Jewellery Sector.
- Decrease of transaction cost—Introduction of regulatory control like IRDA to monitor the different transaction charges that an exporter pays to the different government agencies and financing institutions.

KHADI AND VILLAGE INDUSTRIES

102. The broad targets for development of Khadi and Village industries sector during the 12th Plan period are to achieve at least 11 per cent growth in Khadi sector and 13 per cent growth in Village Industries. The strategy for achieving targets are to develop product-wise clusters of Khadi and Village Industries products and develop their domestic as well as export market, introduce innovations in design and technology, creation of entrepreneurship and growth in manufacturing in rural non-farm sector to prevent migration by enhanced allocation for PMEGP. The Khadi Reform Programme has been taken up in the 11th Plan for up scaling marketing of Khadi Products and improving earning of Khadi artisans. The reform also includes introduction of Khadi mark, strengthening Khadi Institutions, market promotion of Khadi products and participation of private party in the form of partnership in the existing establishment of Central Silver plants. The process has been slow and needs to be stepped up in the 12th Plan. Also, outcomes need to be clearly defined.

103. Although the PMEGP is the flagship Programme under KVIC, it is yet to be evaluated in terms of its efficacy. A quick evaluation is warranted before any major up-scaling. Likewise an evaluation of the cluster based initiative by the name of SFURTI is also necessary to evaluate how shortcomings can be overcome while taking up the proposed expansion and introduction of Heritage Clusters. Since the Textile Ministry has been implementing such clusters in Handloom and Handicrafts sectors it would be desirable to ensure convergence whenever possible and avoid duplication.

COIR INDUSTRY

104. Coir Industry is mostly confined in Southern states namely, Kerala, Tamil Nadu and Karnataka. Enterprises in this sector are usually in Micro and Small sector. At present, products manufactured in the Coir Sector are for limited uses. R&D initiatives have been made by the Central Coir Research Institute in Kalavoor and the Central Institute of Technology in Bangalore to develop innovative products for diverse uses. Under the Prime Minister's Gram Sadak Yojana (Bharat Nirman), it has already been decided to use Coir geo-textiles for construction of rural roads in nine States. In future, the project is likely to be extended to all the 28 States of the country. The coir industry is likely to face problems in catering to the huge requirements. Hence it may be required to infuse appropriate technology to improve quality and up-scaling manufacturing capacity in the Twelfth Plan to meet the requirements.

The Twelfth Five Year Plan (2012–17) outlays (GBS) for the sectors discussed above are given in Annexure 13.3.

ANNEXURE 13.3
Twelfth Five Year Plan (2012–17) Outlays (GBS) for Industry Sector

TABLE 13.10
Ministry/Department-wise Twelfth Five Year Plan (2012–17) Outlays Industry Sector

(₹ Crore)

S. No.	S. No. of Annex. 3.2	Ministry/Department	Budgetary Support	IEBR	Outlay
1	34	Department of Chemicals and Petrochemicals	2,890	3.00	2,893.00
2	35	Department of Pharmaceuticals	2,968	127.00	3,095.00
3	36	Department of Fertilisers	1,484	15,437.00	16,921.00
4	40	Department of Industrial Policy and Promotion	12,601	0.00	12,601.00
5	43	Ministry of Corporate Affairs	233	0.00	233.00
6	52	Ministry of Food Processing Industries	5,990	0.00	5,990.00
7	53	Department of Heavy Industry	4,680	17,543.00	22,223.00
8	54	Department of Public Enterprises	50	0.00	50.00
9	27	Ministry of MSME	24,124	1,890.00	26,014.00
10	56	Ministry of Mines	2,332	18,221.00	20,553.00
11	64	Ministry of Steel	200	90,975.00	91,175.00
12	65	Ministry of Textiles	25,931	0.00	25,931.00

NOTES

1. According to NASSCOM—for all graduates (not only related to manufacturing).
2. Aon Hewitt Survey.
3. ASI 2008–09 data shows ~9 per cent of workforce at supervisory and above levels. Assumption of 9 per cent continued for calculating managerial staff requirement in 2025 (organised and unorganised).
4. Recommended changes include (*i*) Defined limit of investment in plant and machinery for classifying the micro, small and medium enterprises may be deleted from the MSMED Act, 2006 and should be announced through Notifications. (*ii*) The monetary limit of penal provisions of MSMED Act, 2006 should be provided in Rules instead of in the Act. (*iii*) Delayed payment of earnest money/security money should be included for payment of penal interest in case of MSEs as per provision in Chapter 5 of MSMED Act, 2006. (*iv*) Amount of award given by Micro and Small Enterprises Facilitation Council should be realizable as arrear of land revenue.
5. The UWSSA provides for a National Social Security Board at the Central level and for welfare schemes to be formulated by the Central Government on matters relating to (*i*) health and disability cover, (*ii*) health and maternity benefits, (*iii*) old age protection, and (*iv*) any other benefits as may be determined by the scheme (Indira Gandhi National Old Age Pension Scheme, National Family Benefit Scheme, Janshri Bima Yojana, Rashtriya Swasthya Bima Yojana and so on. are among the welfare schemes notified in Schedule 1 of the Act under the Central Government). The Act provides a State Social Security Board at the state level to recommend suitable schemes in the State sector and monitor social welfare schemes for unorganized workers. Schemes relating to (*i*) Provident Fund (*ii*) Employment Injury Benefit (*iii*) housing (*iv*) educational schemes for children (*v*) skill up gradation of workers, (*vi*) funeral assistance and (*v*) old age homes, is to be formulated and administered by the State Governments.
6. It is important to note though that the overall condition of the economy will be a key driver of sectoral growth rates. And emerging economic realities, especially globally, are likely to create some restraints in the growth of domestic manufacturing. Hence, deliberate effort is needed to implement the manufacturing strategy to boost the Indian manufacturing sector.

14

Energy

INTRODUCTION

14.1. India is the fourth largest consumer of energy in the world after USA, China and Russia but it is not endowed with abundant energy resources. It must, therefore, meet its development needs by using all available domestic resources of coal, uranium, oil, hydro and other renewable resources, and supplementing domestic production by imports. High reliance on imported energy is costly given the prevailing energy prices which are not likely to soften; it also impinges adversely on energy security. Meeting the energy needs of achieving 8 per cent– 9 per cent economic growth while also meeting energy requirements of the population at affordable prices therefore presents a major challenge. It calls for a sustained effort at increasing energy efficiency to contain the growth in demand for energy while increasing domestic production as much as possible to keep import dependence at a reasonable level.

ENERGY INTENSITY OF GDP

14.2. Energy intensity, defined as the energy input associated with a unit of gross domestic product (GDP), is a measure of the energy efficiency of a nation's economy. India's energy intensity has been declining over the years (See Table 14.1) and is expected to decline further.

14.3. Falling energy intensity implies that the growth in energy used is less than the growth of GDP, which in turn implies that energy elasticity, that is, the ratio of the growth of energy to the growth of GDP is less than unity. In fact, this elasticity has been declining over the years. Total primary energy–GDP elasticity was around 0.73 during the period 1980–81 to 2000–01 and it declined to 0.66 in the period 1981–81 to 2010–11. The elasticity of commercial energy is higher than that of total primary energy because of the ongoing shift from non-commercial to commercial energy. However, even this elasticity declined from a level of 1.09 in the period 1980–81 to 2000–01 and to 0.91 during 2000–01 to 2010–11. The decline in share of non-commercial energy could be attributed to increased availability of clean fuels and replacing traditional fuels such as wood and cow dung cakes to meet household energy needs. The Twelfth Plan continues to focus on enhancing household access to cleaner forms of energy with an aim to promote sustainable development.

TABLE 14.1
Energy Intensity for Total Primary Energy*

Period	Energy Intensity (Kgoe/US$)**
1981	1.09
1991	0.99
2001	0.85
2011	0.62

* Energy intensity indicated is energy required to produce a unit of GDP.
** kgoe: Kilograms of oil equivalent.
Source: Planning Commission.

14.4. A National Mission on Energy Efficiency (NMEE) has been launched to improve energy efficiency in all areas of the economy including power, transport, urban housing, consumer goods and industries. As a part of Clean Energy Mechanism, which is a global initiative, a number of measures are being planned for improving efficiency in lighting by use of light-emitting diodes (LEDs) and super-efficient appliances. A strategy has also been devised to improve the share of energy-efficient modes of transport. This improvement in efficiency will lead to reduced energy intensity of GDP and lower elasticity of energy against GDP. It is estimated that during the Plan, the elasticity may further improve by about 10 per cent by the end of the Plan.

14.5. Table 14.2 shows energy intensity of some select countries for the year 2010, with GDP measured in terms of 2010 USD purchasing power parity (PPP). India's energy intensity using PPP GDP is 0.191, which is on par with the world average but higher than most of the European countries. China's energy intensity is roughly 1.5 times that of India.

TABLE 14.2
Energy Intensity

S. No	Country	Energy Intensity (Kgoe/US$)
1	United Kingdom	0.102
2	Germany	0.121
3	Japan	0.125
4	Brazil	0.134
5	USA	0.173
6	China	0.283
7	South Korea	0.189
8	India	0.191

Source: World Energy Outlook 2011.

EXPANDING ACCESS TO ENERGY

14.6. Higher levels of GDP will obviously require higher levels of energy as an input but in addition to this requirement India's energy planning must allow for the need to expand access to clean energy at affordable prices for the bulk of the population. Village electrification and connection of rural households to electric supply under Rajiv Gandhi Grameen Vidyutikaran Yojana (RGGVY) is a critical instrument. The supply of kerosene/liquefied petroleum gas (LPG) at affordable prices is equally important.

14.7. There is ample evidence of unmet demand in rural areas indicating the need to expand access even as we expand total supply. The NSS 66th Round Survey conducted by National Sample Survey Organisation (NSSO) for 2009–10 shows improvement in access to cleaner forms of energy by households for cooking and lighting purposes as compared to the NSS 61st Round Survey for 2004–05. Access to electricity in this period increased from 92 per cent of urban households to 94 per cent and from 55 per cent of rural households to 67.3 per cent. Since 2009–10, 1.40 crore below poverty line (BPL) households have been provided electricity connection under RGGVY. If we add only the number of BPL households connected during last three years to the NSSO data, the estimated household electrification level as on 31 March 2012 would be of the order of 75 per cent. However, the availability of electricity supply continues to remain an area of concern, particularly in rural areas, where consumers get supplies for less than eight hours a day in certain states. Though 67 per cent of the rural households are reported to have access to electricity in 2009–10, their per capita consumption of electricity is only around 8 units per month, which is just one-third of reported consumption of 24 units in urban areas. This is because of poor quality of electricity supplies and reflects significant unmet demand.

14.8. Achieving universal access to electricity is one of the most important goals and the Government plans to provide electricity to each and every household in the country in the next five years by extending RGGVY programme to every habitation irrespective of the size of the population. Sub-transmission, distribution network and renewable sources will need to be expanded suitably in consultation with the State Governments to realise this objective. Adequate investments in the distribution networks will improve the quality of electricity supply for the existing consumers as well as the targeted consumers in the next five years

14.9. The percentage of all households using LPG as cooking fuel increased from 57 per cent of the households in 2004–05 to around 66 per cent in 2009–10. Access to LPG supplies in rural areas increased from

TABLE 14.3
Household Access (%)

Energy Source	61st Round 2004–05			66th Round 2009–10		
	Rural	Urban	Total	Rural	Urban	Total
Electricity	54.9	92.3	65.2	67.3	93.9	75.5
LPG	8.6	57.1	21.9	15.5	66.2	31.2

Note: Access to energy data for Census 2011 shows primary energy sources for lighting in 2011 as 55.3 per cent rural, 92.7 per cent urban and 67.2 per cent overall, as against 43.5 per cent rural, 87.6 per cent urban and 55.8 per cent overall in 2001. The difference in NSSO and Census data is possibly due to differences in questionnaire. It will need to be further looked into.

8.6 per cent in 2004–05 to around 15.5 per cent in the year 2009–10. Besides, per capita consumption reported in rural areas was just 0.3 kg per month as compared to 1.8 kg in urban areas. Since the disparity between urban and rural per capita total consumption is much lower it is reasonable to assume that potential in rural areas is much higher, but is left unsatisfied because of insufficient access. Women being the main energy users and primary energy suppliers are worst affected by restricted LPG supply. This poses one of the most difficult barriers to the empowerment of women. Table 14.3 shows the access levels in 2004-05 and 2009–10.

ENERGY DEMAND AND SUPPLY

14.10. The demand for energy during the Plan will increase as the economy grows and as access in rural areas expands. Table 14.4 presents estimates of the total primary energy demand projected to the end of the Thirteenth Plan. The annual average growth rate of the total energy requirement is expected to accelerate from 5.1 per cent per year in the Eleventh Plan to 5.7 per cent per year in the Twelfth Plan and 5.4 per cent per year in the Thirteenth Plan. The faster growth in supply in the Twelfth Plan is in part a reflection of the need to meet suppressed demand.

14.11. The demand for non-commercial energy is expected to decline with increasing expansion of the network and access to commercial energy. As shown in Table 14.4, whereas commercial energy is expected to grow at 6.91 per cent in the five years up to 2011–12, non-commercial energy is projected to grow at only 2.6 per cent in the same period. The growth of non-commercial energy is projected to decline to around 1.5 per cent in the next 10 years.

14.12. Table 14.5 shows the share of each energy source in total domestic production and also its share (including imports) in the total commercial energy consumption. The most important point to note is that coal remains the dominant source of primary energy. Domestic production of coal and lignite account for two-third of total production of commercial energy in 2000–01 and is projected to be about the same in 2021–22. As a percentage of total consumption of commercial energy, the share of coal and lignite is projected to increase to 57 per cent, from a level of 50 per cent in 2000–01. While share of oil in total commercial energy consumption is expected to decline from 37.5 per cent in 2000–01 to 23.3 per cent in 2021–22, the share of natural gas and liquefied natural gas (LNG) is projected to rise from 8.5 per cent to 13 per cent in the same period. The combined share of oil and natural gas in energy consumption was 24.7 per cent in 2011–12 and is expected to be about the same in 2021–22.

14.13. The supply from renewables is expected to increase rapidly from 24,503 MW by the end of the Eleventh Plan to 54,503 MW by the end of the Twelfth and 99,617 MW by the end of theThirteenth. This fourfold increase in the next 10 years is expected to continue in subsequent years as policies provide a strong incentive for the renewables. Nevertheless the base is small and the share of renewables in total commercial energy used will remain small. It is expected to rise from about 1 per cent in 2011–12 to 1.43 per cent in 2016–17 and just under 2 per cent in 2021–22. Though small, the share of renewable energy in India is comparable with that in many other countries: USA (1.7 per cent), Indonesia (1.4 per cent), Thailand (1.0 per cent) and China

TABLE 14.4
Trends in Supply of Primary Commercial Energy

(in mtoe)*

	2000–01 (Actual)	2006–07 (Actual)	2011–12 (Provisional)	2016–17 (Projected)	2021–22 (Projected)
DOMESTIC PRODUCTION					
Coal	130.61	177.24	222.16	308.55	400
Lignite	6.43	8.76	10.64	16.80	29
Crude Oil	33.40	33.99	39.23	42.75	43
Natural Gas	25.07	27.71	42.79	76.13	103
Hydro Power	6.40	9.78	11.22	12.90	17
Nuclear Power	4.41	4.91	8.43	16.97	30
Renewable Energy	0.13	0.87	5.25	10.74	20
Total Domestic commercial Energy	206.45	263.28	339.72	481.84	642.00
Non-commercial Energy 1	136.64	153.28 (1.93)	174.20 (2.6 %)	187.66 (1.5 %)	202.16 (1.5 %)
Total	343.09	416.56	513.92	669.50	844.16
IMPORTS					
Coal	11.76	24.92	54.00	90.00	150.00
Petroleum Products	77.25	98.41	129.86	152.44	194.00
LNG	0	8.45	12.56	24.80	31.00
Hydro power	0	0.26	0.45	0.52	0.60
Total Net Imports	89.01	132.04	196.87	267.76	375.60
Total Commercial Energy (growth over the previous five years)	295.46	396.32 (5.01 %)	536.59 (6.25 %)	749.60 (6.91 %)	1017.60 (6.30 %)
Total Primary Energy	432.01	549.60 (4.09 %)	710.79 (5.28 %)	937.26 (5.69 %)	1219.76 (5.41 %)

*mtoe: million tons of oil equivalent.
Source: Planning Commission.
Note: Figures in brackets are annual average growth rates over the previous five years' period.

(0.5 per cent). Brazil at (3.1 per cent) is significantly higher. We have made a good start but there is need to do more.

14.14. Even though domestic production of energy resources is projected to increase, import dependence will continue at a high level. The main area of import will be crude oil, where nearly 78 per cent of the demand will have to be met from imports by the end of the Twelfth Plan. However, import dependence for coal is also estimated to increase from 18.8 per cent in 2011–12 to 22.4 per cent by the end of the Twelfth Plan and 25.9 per cent by the end of the Thirteenth Plan. It is estimated that the import dependence for coal, LNG and crude oil taken together in the terminal year of the Twelfth Plan is likely to remain at the Eleventh Plan level of 36 per cent. However, this assumes that we are able to realise projected domestic production levels of coal, petroleum and natural gas. If this is not achieved, the level of import dependence would increase further if the GDP growth rates projected are to be maintained.

ENERGY PRICING

14.15. Energy pricing is an economically important but also politically sensitive issue, which will pose major challenges in the Twelfth Plan. While the political sensitivity of energy prices is self-evident,

TABLE 14.5
Share of Each Fuel in Total Energy Production and Consumption

(in percentage)

	2000–01 Actual	2006–07 Actual	2011–12 (Provisional)	2016–17 (Projected)	2021–22 (Projected)
Share in Commercial Energy Production					
Coal and Lignite	66.38	70.65	68.53	67.52	66.82
Crude Oil	16.18	12.91	11.55	8.87	6.70
Natural Gas	12.14	10.52	12.60	15.80	16.04
Hydro Power	3.10	3.71	3.30	2.68	2.65
Nuclear Power	2.14	1.86	2.48	3.52	4.67
Renewable Energy	0.06	0.33	1.55	2.23	3.12
Share in Total Commercial Energy Supply					
Coal and Lignite	50.36	53.22	53.45	55.41	56.90
Crude Oil	37.45	33.41	31.51	26.04	23.29
Natural Gas	8.49	6.99	10.32	13.46	13.17
Hydro Power	2.17	2.53	2.17	1.79	1.73
Nuclear Power	1.49	1.24	1.57	2.26	2.95
Renewable Energy	0.04	0.22	0.98	1.43	1.97

the economic role of rational energy pricing is not adequately appreciated. Rational energy prices help to balance consumer energy demand with producer supply, providing incentives to reduce consumption on the one hand and to stimulate production on the other. As a general rule, energy prices should be aligned with the global energy prices, especially when large imports are involved.

14.16. Misalignment of energy prices poses both microeconomic and macroeconomic problems. At the microeconomic level, underpricing energy to the consumer reduces the incentive to be energy-efficient and also promotes leakage of subsidised products for sale in open market and also (in case of kerosene) adulteration. Underpricing to the producer reduces both the incentive and also the ability to invest in the sector, depressing production and increasing reliance on imports. This obviously undermines energy security. At the macroeconomic level, misalignment either hits producers as stated above, leading to excessive import dependence with implications for the balance of payments, or if producers are sought to be insulated, it necessitates a subsidy, which places a burden on the budget.

14.17. Over the years, India's energy prices have become misaligned, and are now much lower than global prices for many products. The extent of misalignment is substantial, leading to large un-targeted subsidies. The implications of price misalignment are discussed in the individual sections relating to different sources of energy.

ENERGY SECURITY

14.18. Energy security involves ensuring uninterrupted supply of energy to support the economic and commercial activities necessary for sustained economic growth. Energy security is obviously more difficult to ensure if there is large dependence on imported energy. This calls for action in several areas.

1. First, and most importantly, the domestic production of coal, oil and gas and other energy sources has to be stepped up. Some of the recent issues in this regard have been availability of land, clearances for environment and forest and implementation of the Scheduled Tribes and Other Traditional Forest Dwellers (Recognition of Forest Rights) Act, 2006. Uncertainty about

production sharing contracts has also posed problems. Management strategies and procedures will have to be devised for ensuring effective implementation of fuel development projects while meeting the requirements of above policies and legislations.

2. Second, a stable and attractive policy regime has to be provided to ensure substantial private investment including foreign investment in oil and natural gas blocks and new capacities for renewable energy. Producers must have clarity in the price they will receive and an assurance of a stable tax regime. Since oil exploration is a global industry the terms India offers must be comparable with those offered elsewhere. In this context the entire structure of New Exploration Licensing Policy (NELP) contracts for oil and gas need to be reviewed.

3. Third, investments in renewable energies need to be strongly emphasised. By present projections, the share of renewable energy in total energy consumption will only reach 2 per cent by 2021.

4. Fourth, investments in energy assets in foreign countries, especially for coal, oil and gas and uranium should be stepped up.

5. Fifth, to meet any possible disruption in oil supplies, on which we are import-dependent to the extent of more than 80 per cent, storage capacities need to be created. The Organisation for Economic Cooperation and Development (OECD) countries have generally created these capacities to the extent of 90 days of their domestic demand. We have created the capacity for 5 million tonnes. It has, however, not been fully utilised so far. There will be a need to increase this gradually and utilise it fully. Innovative ways will have to be found to fill up these tankages.

3.2. POWER SECTOR

14.19. The electric power sector consists of a mix of plants depending on different primary fuels, including conventional sources like coal, lignite, natural gas, oil, hydro and nuclear power; and non-conventional sources like wind and solar power, and agricultural and domestic waste. However, coal remains the dominant primary energy source used in power generation accounting for 67 per cent of total generation. The power sector is currently at a crucial juncture of its evolution from a dominantly public sector environment to a more competitive power sector, with many private producers and greater reliance on markets, subject to regulation. The performance of the power sector shows many positive features, especially relating to the pace of addition to power generation but there are numerous problems relating to fuel supply which need to be resolved as also problems relating to the financial viability of the operation of the distribution companies (Discoms).

REVIEW OF THE ELEVENTH PLAN

14.20. The Eleventh Plan was the period in which the Electricity Act of 2003, which was enacted during the Tenth Plan period was to be fully operationalised. The objectives of the Act are "to consolidate the laws related to generation, transmission, distribution, trading and use of electricity, and taking measures conducive for the development of electrical industry, protecting interests of consumers and supply of electricity to all areas, rationalisation of electricity tariff, ensuring transparent policies regarding subsidies, promotion of efficient and environmentally benign policies, constitution of regulatory commission and establishment of Appellate Tribunals". While substantial progress was made in setting up the institutional structure, there are several important areas where reforms have yet to take place. These are:

1. Open access to consumers, which is mandated under the Electricity Act, remains ineffective due to reluctance of state utilities to comply.

2. Trading of power at very high rates and its purchase by utilities even though not willing to pass on the higher cost in the form of consumer tariffs. This has a distortionary effect and threatens to jeopardise the financial viability of the Discoms.

3. Energy audit of power utilities has not been undertaken.

4. Electricity retail tariffs have remained static for many years because of political pressure, widening the gap between the average tariff and average cost of supply.

5. The distribution companies suffer from serious financial stress. Losses of the distribution utilities remain high. The annual loss of the State power utilities (without subsidy) was ₹33,698 crore during 2007–08 and increased to ₹59,891 crore in the year 2009–10 (provisional). The State Discoms cannot sustain such high losses indefinitely.

Physical Achievements

14.21. An important gain in the Eleventh Plan was the ramping up of the pace of addition to generation capacity. The Eleventh Plan aimed at a substantial increase with a target for additional capacity of 78,700 MW. Actual achievement in the Eleventh Plan was 54,964 MW. Sector-wise and mode-wise capacity addition achievements are given in Table 14.6. This is 30 per cent lower than the original target, but it is more than twice the addition achieved in the Tenth Plan. More importantly, the pace of capacity creation picked up in the Eleventh Plan, and there is at present about 90,000 MW of generation capacity currently under construction which would achieve commercial production in the Twelfth Plan. If these projects proceed to completion as scheduled, and a strong effort is made to initiate new projects in the first year of the Twelfth Plan, we could reasonably expect to achieve addition to capacity in the Twelfth Plan of the order of 80,000–1,00,000 MW.

14.22. While the pace of addition to generating capacity is commendable, there has not been comparable progress in delivering fuel and the availability of both coal and gas to the new power plants is not assured. Resolution of this problem must have high priority in the Twelfth Plan.

14.23. The main physical milestones achieved in the power sector during the Eleventh Plan are summarised in Box 14.1.

TABLE 14.6
Installed Capacity Addition during the Eleventh Plan (in MW)

Type	Target				Actual			
	Central	State	Private	Total	Central	State	Private	Total
Hydro	8,654	3,482	3,491	15,627	1,550	2,702	1,292	5,544
Thermal	24,840	23,301	11,552	59,693	12,790	14,030	21,720	48,540
Nuclear	3,380	–	–	3,380	880	–	–	880
Total	36,874	26,783	15,043	78,700	15,220	16,732	23,012	54,964

Source: Central Electricity Authority (CEA).

Box 14.1
Achievements in Power Sector during the Eleventh Plan

- Capacity addition during the Eleventh Plan period has been at 54,964 MW which is 69.8 per cent of the original target and 88.1 per cent of the reduced target of 62,374 MW set in the Mid-term Appraisal (MTA). It is more than 2.5 times that of any of the earlier Plans.
- Total installed capacity as on 31 March 2012, including renewable energy sources of the country is 1,99,877 MW. The share of renewable energy capacity is about 12.2 per cent
- Approximately 69,926 circuit km (ckm) of transmission line. 1,50,362 MVA capacity of alternating current (AC) substations and 1,750 MW capacity of high-voltage, direct current (HVDC) substations were added to the existing transmission systems.
- Total number of villages electrified till March 2012 was about 5.6 lakhs, indicating that more than 93 per cent village electrification has been achieved. However, a large number of small habitations still remain unconnected.
- Various activities under different schemes of Bureau of Energy Efficiency (BEE) and Ministry of Power (MoP) have resulted in saving in avoided power capacity of 11,000 MW.
- Works relating to 18 units for life extension aggregating to 1,931 MW and 69 units for repair and maintenance (R&M) aggregating to 17,435 MW have been completed during the Eleventh Plan.

Electricity Generation

14.24. The Eleventh Plan estimated a terminal year (2011–12) requirement of electricity generation from utilities at 1,038 billion units (BU), implying growth rate of 9.1 per cent (CAGR) per annum over the gross generation level of 670.65 BU in 2006–07 (the terminal year of the Tenth Plan). As against the above, the actual generation from utilities in 2011–12 was 876.88 BU, a shortfall of about 16 per cent, implying an annual growth rate of only 5.51 per cent for power from the utilities. The mode-wise and sector-wise energy generation for 2011–12 is given in Table 14.7. After allowing for captive generation of about 110 BU in 2011–12, the growth rate in total power generation is likely to be 5.7 per cent (CAGR) over the Eleventh Plan period, against the Plan target of 9.5 per cent. This has resulted in a demand–supply gap. On 31 March 2012, it was estimated that the peak deficit gap was 11.1 per cent and energy deficit was 8.5 per cent. These deficits are lower than the corresponding deficits of 13.8 per cent and 9.6 per cent respectively at the end of the Tenth Plan, but there is a clear need to step up capacities and energy availability as the economy grows.

14.25. The actual cumulative capacity as on 31 March 2012 was 1,99,877 MW, including 24,503 MW of renewable sources of energy, the details of which are given in Table 14.8.

14.26. The Eleventh Plan has clearly succeeded in creating the precondition for achieving much larger addition to capacity in future. The performance of the private sector exceeded targets (see Table 14.6) whereas the Government sector fell short, with the shortfall being the generation in the Central sector. The share of the private sector in the total installed capacity has risen to about 42 per cent

TABLE 14.7
Mode-wise/Sector-wise Break-up of Generation

(in Billion Units)

Type	Central	State	Private	Total
Hydro	55.97	71.02	8.81	135.80
(Incl. Bhutan Import)	(5.28)			(5.28)
Thermal	281.04	296.93	130.84	708.81
(a) Coal	225.18	271.98	87.63	584.79
(b) Lignite	18.76	2.88	6.45	28.09
(c) Gas	37.09	21.27	35.10	93.46
Nuclear	32.29	–	–	32.29
Total	369.28	367.95	139.65	876.88
(Incl. Bhutan Import)	(5.28)			(5.28)

Source: CEA.

TABLE 14.8
All-India Cumulative Generating Capacity (as on 31 March 2012) (in MW)

	Hydro	Thermal	Nuclear	RES (MNRE)*	Total
Centre	9,085.40	45,817.23	4,780.00	0.00	59,682.63
State/UTs	27,380.00	55,024.93	–	3,513.72	85,918.65
Private	2,525.00	30,761.02	–	20,989.73	54,275.75
Total	38,990.40	1,31,603.18	4,780.00	24,503.45	1,99,877.03

* MNRE: Ministry of New and Renewable Energy.
Source: CEA.

of the incremental capacity in the Eleventh Plan. The capacity addition program has benefited from increase in the potential of the domestic equipment suppliers like Bharat Heavy Electricals Limited (BHEL), and also increased imports. BHEL has now the potential to deliver about 15,000–20,000 MW of new capacity per year as against 6,000 MW per year a few years ago. Further, more private-sector equipment manufacturers are also entering the market and the total capacity may increase to about 40,000 MW per year by 2016–17.

Ultra-Mega Power Projects

14.27. The Ultra Mega Power Projects (UMPPs) Programme, which brings in private investment into power generation, was a major initiative of the Eleventh Plan. So far power purchase agreements have been signed for four UMPPs of 4,000 MW each on the basis of competitive tariff-based bidding. They are based in Sasan (Madhya Pradesh), Mundra (Gujarat), Krishnapatnam (Andhra Pradesh) and Tilaiya (Jharkhand). Out of these, one unit of 800 MW of Mundra by Tata Power has been commissioned in March 2012. 12 more supercritical UMPPs are being planned covering Chhattisgarh, Gujarat, Tamil Nadu, Andhra Pradesh, Odisha, Maharashtra and Karnataka. An important element of this programme is the induction of supercritical technology, which is an important shift towards energy efficiency. Unfortunately, some of these projects are plagued with uncertainties regarding fuel supply because they were based on imported coal and changes in government policies in the countries where the coal mines were located have raised the cost of coal whereas the power tariff is based on a competitive bid which does not contain a provision for passing on such increases.

Super Critical Projects under Construction

14.28. Thermal power stations based on present-day subcritical technology have efficiency of about 38 per cent. To improve energy efficiency further, it was decided that new thermal power plants should be based on supercritical technology. Already, eleven supercritical units with a total capacity of 7,400 MW have been installed. Large number of supercritical units are under construction and about 50 per cent of coal-based capacity addition in the Twelfth Plan is expected be based on supercritical technology. For the Thirteenth Plan, it has been decided that all coal-fired capacity addition shall be through supercritical units. Higher stream parameters of 565/593 degree centigrade are being adopted for supercritical units which would lead to design efficiency of over 40 per cent and lower CO_2 emissions by about 5 per cent as compared to a typical 500 MW subcritical unit.

14.29. Initiatives have been taken by the Government for developing indigenous capacity/capability for manufacturing of supercritical boilers and turbine generators as indigenous manufacturing capacity is considered vital to support large-scale induction of supercritical units envisaged. BHEL has entered into a technology collaboration with M/s Alstom and Siemens for supercritical technology for boilers and turbine generators respectively. BHEL has intimated that it had augmented its manufacturing capacity to 20,000 MW per year by March 2012. Further, setting up of joint ventures (JVs)/subsidiary companies by international manufactures of supercritical boilers and turbine generators was encouraged. As a result, several JVs have come up in the country for setting up manufacturing facilities for supercritical boilers and turbines generators. Manufacturing capacities which may come up are indicated in Table 14.9. The Government of India has also approved the policy of encouraging domestic production of supercritical plants by bulk-tendering of such units. Two bulk orders—11 × 660 MW supercritical units for National Thermal Power Corporation (NTPC) and Damodar Valley Corporation (DVC) and 9 × 800 MW supercritical units for NTPC—were approved and being implemented.

Transmission

14.30. A programme for construction of 88,515 ckm transmission lines for evacuation of power from generating stations was envisaged at the beginning of the Eleventh Plan based on the target for capacity addition that was planned. When the capacity target was scaled down to 62,374 MW at the time of the Mid-Term Appraisal (MTA), the target for transmission was scaled down to 68,673 ckm. Details of

TABLE 14.9
Planned Manufacturing Capacity MW Per Annum

Joint Venture	Boilers	Turbine-Generators	Remarks
L&T–MHI	4,000 MW	4,000 MW	Production for boiler and turbine commenced
Alstom–Bharat Forge	–	5,000 MW	All manufacturing facilities for manufacture of turbines to be completed by June 2013
Toshiba–JSW		3,000 MW	All manufacturing facilities to be completed by April 2013
Gammon–Ansaldo	4,000 MW	–	Probable date of completion of facilities—December 2012 (2,000 MW) and December 2014 (additional 2,000 MW)
Thermax–Babcock and Wilcox	3,000 MW		All manufacturing facilities to be completed by September 2012
BGR–Hitachi Boilers Private Limited	5 Boilers per annum (~3,000 MW)		All manufacturing facilities to be completed by January 2013
BGR–Hitachi Turbine Generator Private Limited		5 Turbine Generators per annum (~3,000 MW)	All manufacturing facilities to be completed by July 2014
Doosan Chennai Works Private Limited	2,200 MW (Both subcritical and Supercritical)		DCW Pvt. Ltd. is 100 per cent subsidiary of Doosan Korea. Company incorporated in India on 20 July 2000. Existing facility–Chennai Additional facility acquired at Mannur village, Kancheepuram district. Production from additional facilities to start by Sept-2012.

the achievement of transmission lines at the end of the Eleventh Plan are given in Table 14.10. The addition achieved during the Eleventh Plan is 69,926 ckm which is greater than the scaled-down target.

Distribution

14.31. Distribution is the weakest link in the power system with large losses leading to financial unviability. The cash losses of utilities selling power directly to consumers, after accounting for subsidy from the State Governments, increased from ₹17,620 crore in year 2007–08 to ₹42,415 crore in year 2009–10. The cumulative book losses (on accrual basis) of State Discoms have increased from ₹79,339 crore as on 31 March 2009 to ₹1,06,247 crore at the end of year 2009–10. The net worth of the Discoms has decreased from ₹31,972 crore to ₹14,786 crore as on 31 March 2010. While some of the States have shown improvements in the financial health of their utilities, others are yet to demonstrate the impact of the policy initiatives.

14.32. Distribution companies have not been able to recover the cost of supply through tariff, and the gap between Average Cost of Supply (ACS) and Average Revenue Realised (ARR) has widened and the same has been increasing over the years. This gap is partly a reflection of lower tariff, but it also reflects high aggregate technical and commercial (AT&C) losses which reduce the average revenue realised. The trends in AT&C for all States are shown in Table 14.11. The position is especially serious in the special category states, which have losses (2010–11, Provisional) varying between 29.17 per cent in the case of Uttarakhand to 74.30 per cent in Jammu & Kashmir. Himachal Pradesh with AT&C loss of 13.53 per cent is an exception. The non-special category states have generally performed better, though the losses are still unacceptably high in several of these, for example, Jharkhand (45.11 per cent), Bihar (49.99 per cent), Chhattisgarh (36.41 per cent), Uttar Pradesh (37.86 per cent), Odisha (44.35 per cent)

TABLE 14.10
Cumulative Achievement of Transmission Lines at the End of the Eleventh Plan

Transmission System Type/Voltage Class	Unit	At the End of the Tenth Plan (March 2007)	Addition during the Eleventh Plan	At the End of the Eleventh Plan (March 2012)
Transmission Lines				
765 kV	ckm	1,704	3,546	5,250
HVDC + 500 kV Bi-pole	ckm	5,872	3,560	9,432
400 kV	ckm	69,174	37,645	1,06,819
230/220 kV	ckm	1,10,805	25,175	1,35,980
Total	ckm	1,87,555	69,926	2,57,481
Substations				
765 kV	MVA	0	25,000	25,000
400 kV	MVA	92,942	58,085	1,51,027
230/220 kV	MVA	1,56,497	67,277	2,23,774
Total	MVA	2,49,439	1,50,362	3,99,801
HVDC				
Bi-pole link capacity	MW	5,000	1,750	6,750
Back-to-back capacity	MW	3,000	0	3,000
Total	MW	8,000	1,750	9,750

Source: CEA.

and Madhya Pradesh (41.10 per cent). In contrast, Andhra Pradesh, Gujarat, Punjab, Delhi and Tamil Nadu show relatively good performance in containing AT&C losses.

14.33. Due to unsustainable levels of AT&C losses and other inefficiencies in metering, billing and collection, the utilities are not able recover the cost of supply resulting in widening of gap between average cost of supply and tariff. Table 14.12 shows recent trends in financial parameters of major States.

14.34. The Comptroller and Auditor General (CAG) of India has carried out a study involving 24 utilities on issues impacting financial health of power distribution utilities in India and has pointed out the need for rationalisation of tariffs charged for various consumers. Unless the measures to contain these inefficiencies are taken, the Discoms will not be able to break even. Further, default in payments, non-metering of consumers, inadequate energy auditing, inadequate investments in upgradation of the distribution system are some of the other issues that need to be addressed. This situation is a cause of serious concern and remedial steps need to be taken on priority basis in the Twelfth Plan to ensure that utilities generate adequate surpluses to support their ongoing projects.

Restructured Accelerated Power Development and Reform Programme (R-APDRP)

14.35. To address the problems of distribution losses, the Central Government had launched the APDRP scheme in 2002–03 as an Additional Central Assistance (ACA) scheme to finance the modernisation of sub-transmission and distribution networks with the objective to reduce AT&C losses to 15 per cent. This programme was not effective in reducing losses. A Re-structured APDRP was approved as a Central scheme in 2008 with a total outlay of ₹51,577 crore over the Eleventh Plan period. The focus of the programme is on actual, demonstrable performance in terms of AT&C loss reduction. The coverage of the programme is for the urban areas—towns and cities with a population of more than 30,000 (10,000 for

TABLE 14.11
Aggregate Technical and Commercial Losses of State Power Utilities (within State)

(in Percentage)

S. No	State	2007–08 (Actual)	2008–09 (Actual)	2009–10 (Actual)	2010–11 (Provisional)
	Special Category States				
1	Arunachal Pradesh	78.31	74.27	63.14	65.48
2	Assam	36.77	35.37	38.24	45.13
3	Himachal Pradesh	19.52	16.20	17.39	13.53
4	Jammu & Kashmir	73.43	70.69	72.03	74.30
5	Manipur	86.75	83.55	69.23	67.74
6	Meghalaya	39.74	35.27	43.19	37.93
7	Mizoram	38.38	46.43	42.89	42.08
8	Nagaland	51.20	55.85	58.02	55.98
9	Sikkim	46.87	46.81	51.37	46.81
10	Tripura	41.44	40.08	37.52	41.19
11	Uttarakhand	35.37	29.35	28.61	29.17
	Non-Special Category States				
1	Andhra Pradesh	20.61	19.39	18.32	16.78
2	Bihar	47.60	41.66	42.39	49.99
3	Chhattisgarh	35.17	37.78	46.62	36.41
4	Goa	17.69	17.81	16.18	15.57
5	Gujarat	26.43	25.46	26.87	18.25
6	Haryana	29.01	28.43	29.50	26.72
7	Jharkhand	54.18	54.23	49.07	45.11
8	Karnataka	31.63	24.79	23.69	23.64
9	Kerala	44.80	34.98	28.81	29.72
10	Madhya Pradesh	46.64	45.78	42.93	41.10
11	Maharashtra	30.67	28.75	27.44	23.47
12	Orissa	41.68	42.20	39.71	44.35
13	Punjab	22.36	19.76	19.97	18.35
14	Rajasthan	40.18	32.99	33.06	25.60
15	Tamil Nadu	19.25	20.19	19.11	18.27
16	Uttar Pradesh	38.89	35.29	36.69	37.86
17	West Bengal	20.67	28.81	26.13	28.87
18	Delhi	34.58	17.92	20.78	15.76

special category States). Private distribution utilities are not covered under the programme which has been a point of criticism by some States. Projects under the R-APDRP scheme were to be taken up in two parts. Part A focused on establishing reliable and automated system for sustained collection of accurate baseline data, and the adoption of IT in the areas of energy accounting and auditing and consumer-based services. Part B includes projects to strengthen the distribution system, including activities like automation

TABLE 14.12
Viability of Major State Utilities Not Improving
(Excluding Delhi and Odisha)

	2007–08 Actual	2008–09 Actual	2009–10 Provisional	2010–11 RE
Energy sold/energy available (%)	72.86	74.55	74.33	76.21
Revenue from sale of electricity (₹ crore)	1,31,220	1,48,605	1,63,475	1,92,827
Total cost of electricity sold (₹ crore)	1,74,452	2,12,292	2,35,701	2,61,467
Commercial losses without subsidy (₹ crore)	33,290	52,452	60,172	59,050
Average cost of supply (paise/kWh)	405.86	464.48	480.37	485.67
Average tariff (paise/kWh)	305.29	325.13	333.17	358.18
Gap between the cost of supply and tariff (paise)	100.57	139.35	147.20	127.49

Source: Power Utilities of various States and UTs.

and validation of baseline system, project evaluations, capacity-building and development of franchisees in the distribution sector and consumer attitude surveys. Projects under Part B would be taken up after the baseline data is established (Table 14.13).

14.36. The status of R-APDRP at the end of the Eleventh Plan is as follows:

- Under Part A of R-APDRP, 1,402 projects at an estimated cost of ₹5,196.50 crore have been approved for 29 States/UTs.
- Part A SCADA projects for 63 towns of 15 States have also been sanctioned at an estimated cost of ₹1,443.48 crore.
- Under Part-B of R-APDRP, 1,086 projects at an estimated cost of ₹24,776.17 crore have been approved for 20 States.
- All Part A projects have been awarded except in one State. These are under implementation and at a stage of advanced progress in several States.
- Part A of R-APDRP is to be completed by utilities in three years after its approval. Presently, there are no projects which have completed three years' time since they were sanctioned. However, it has been observed that State procurement policy and procedures have delayed the appointment of IT consultants in some of the States.

Rajiv Gandhi Grameen Vidyutikaran Yojana (RGGVY)

14.37. RGGVY was launched by the Government of India in April 2005 as a comprehensive scheme for providing access of electricity to all rural households. The scheme involved electrification of all un-electrified villages plus a free connection for

TABLE 14.13
Details of Year-wise Progress Achieved on Restructured APDRP (as on 31 March 2012)

(₹ Crore)

Year	Project Sanctioned			Budget Allocation			Actual Releases		
	Part A	Part B	Total	Loan	Grant	Total	Loan	Grant	Total
2008–09	1,947.70	0.00	1,947.70	0	1	1	0.00	350.00	350.00
2009–10	3,183.00	3,059.28	6,242.28	1,650	80	1,730	1,331.46	1.26	1,332.72
2010–11	715.40	12,915.31	13,630.71	3,600	100	3,700	2,246.42	100.00	2,346.42
2011–12	793.88	8,801.58	9,595.46	1,959	75	2,034	1,600.00	67.87	1,667.87
Total	6,639.98	24,776.17	31,416.15	7,209	256	7,465	5,177.88	519.13	5,697.01

Source: Ministry of Power.

TABLE 14.14
Status on RGGVY Progress during the Tenth and the Eleventh Plan

Year	Un-electrified Villages (No.)			BPL Households (lakh)		
	Target	Achieved	% Achieved	Target	Achieved	%Achieved
Tenth Plan						
2005–06	10,000	9,819	98.2	3	0.17	5.7
2006–07	40,000	28,706	71.8	40	6.55	16.4
Eleventh Plan						
2007–08	10,500	9,301	88.6	16	16.21	101.3
2008–09	19,000	12,056	63.5	35	30.85	61.7
2009–10	17,500	18,374	105.0	47	47.18	100.4
2010–11	17,500	18,306	104.6	47	58.84	125.1
2011–12	14,500	7,934	54.7	52	34.45	66.2
Cumulative (as on 31 March 2012)	1,12,795*	1,04,496	92.6	275*	194.25	70.6

* Revised coverage including Phase II projects.
Source: Ministry of Power.

BPL households. The scheme provided a subsidy of 90 per cent of the total project cost and balance 10 per cent of the project cost was to be provided by the Rural Electrification Corporation (REC) as loan. Initially, Phase I of the RGGVY scheme was approved for implementation with a capital subsidy of ₹5,000 crore during the remainder of the Tenth Plan period. Subsequently, the scheme was approved to be continued in the Eleventh Plan with a capital subsidy of ₹28,000 crore. As on 31 March 2012, out of the total of 1,12,795 villages to be covered under RGGVY (including Phase II projects), works in 1,04,496 villages have been completed and only 8,299 un-electrified villages remain; 6,000 villages are targeted to be electrified during 2012–13. In addition, about 10,000 remote villages are to be covered by the MNRE through non-conventional sources. Overall, by the end of Eleventh Plan, out of the total 5,93,732 villages in India (Census 2001), 5,56,633 villages (93.8 per cent) have been electrified as per CEA report. Some of the villages which have been electrified, that is, connected to the grid, have not yet been energised. The gap is primarily in the States of Bihar, Jharkhand, Odisha and Assam. Most of the projects are expected to be completed during 2012 except in the north-eastern region and in areas involving difficult terrain.

14.38. The year-wise targets and achievements for RGGVY during the Tenth and the Eleventh Five Year Plan are given in Table 14.14.

14.39. Studies were carried out to evaluate the socio-economic impact of electrification in Odisha. Other such studies are also underway. The key findings of the studies are:

1. Electrification has altered the household energy mix through substitution of traditional kerosene-based lighting source by electric light. This has resulted in energy and financial savings of households as families would no longer be subject to exorbitant price of kerosene.
2. Security within the villages as well as the quality of living of masses have improved.
3. Electrification has enhanced livelihood generation in the field of agriculture and related activities, small shops and other entrepreneurial activities.
4. Availability of electricity during post-sunset time allowed for extension of study hours for students.
5. Increased mobility and overall comfort, especially for women, have enhanced safe spaces and reduced the drudgery of household chores.

14.40. The RGGVY programme has several deficiencies in implementation. Firstly, nearly 6,000 villages electrified till December 2011 were still not energised due to lack of supporting network or other resources. Secondly, access to electricity in rural areas is still limited, especially in smaller hamlets. The traditional approach to policy and planning in power has assumed gender neutrality, thus failing to recognise that the needs of men and women can differ. Attention needs to be paid to livelihood activities of women and to their concerns of safety, security such as street lighting, healthcare, education and so on. Thirdly, poor financial health of utilities and high cost of power act as a disincentive for States to give new connections. Fourthly, some States do not have supporting network and are unable to provide energisation. Fifthly, a viable revenue model is yet to emerge. This has hindered larger access to new consumers.

14.41. Some of the other areas of concern are:

1. In certain States, even the minimum required hours of supply of six hours to eight hours could not be met.
2. There is a need to upgrade transformer capacity as the current average demand of BPL and above poverty line (APL) consumers is in the range of 300 to 500 watts and 0.5 to 1.15 KW, respectively. There have been several complaints of frequent burning of transformers.
3. The progress of release of APL connections is slow on account of poor supply of electricity, long delays in processing of applications and inadequate transformer capacity.
4. In many States, the distribution company takes a long time for issuing the first bill which can be anywhere between three to six months. Because of this delay, the total bill comes to around ₹1,000 to ₹1,500 which a rural household finds difficult to pay. This leads to a permanent high level of outstanding bills.
5. In most of the operating States, no franchisee was found in any of the surveyed villages and the Discoms had their own mechanism of meter reading, billing and so on.
6. As far as project preparation is concerned, it has been observed that in most cases, the detailed project reports (DPRs) were prepared in a hurried manner and quality was compromised.
7. As far as the socio-economic impact is concerned, it is found that electrification has so far not generated substantial employment opportunities or economic development in the rural areas except in a few cases.
8. The number of actual BPL families in the villages in many cases has been higher than the number indicated in the DPR.

Status on Open Access

14.42. The Electricity Act, 2003, mandates that non-discriminatory open access for interstate as well as intra-state transmission and distribution networks be provided by the utilities. Effective implementation of open access is crucial for opening up consumer choices as well as encouraging a healthy trading function in the country. The open access at interstate level is fully operational. Starting from 17 BUs of energy transacted through Short-Term Open Access (STOA) at the interstate level in 2004–05, the volume has grown to 55 BUs in 2010–11. While carriage and content separation at interstate level has been largely addressed by design, a point of concern has been the adequacy of carriage. Therefore, adequacy issues with respect to carriage need to be specified. Little progress has been made in the implementing of open access at intra-state transmission and distribution network level.

14.43. An inter-Ministerial Task was constituted under the chairmanship of Member (Energy), Planning Commission in February 2008 to examine the status and make recommendations on the measures for operationalising the provisions of the Electricity Act, 2003 in respect of open access. The Forum of Regulators (FoR) has issued model regulations for intra-state open access in September 2010. Adoption of these model regulations by State Electricity Regulatory Commissions (SERCs) would go a long way in successful implementations of intra-state open access. Further, a Second Task Force was constituted in February, 2010 to review the progress made on the recommendations of the previous

Task Force and suggest further course of action on the issues upon which there was no consensus in the First Task Force. The report of the second task force has been received and States have been asked to take necessary action to implement the recommendations. Recommendations of the Task forces on open access are given in Box 14.2.

14.44. At the State level, Discoms need to create distribution control centres and empower them so that open access at the distribution level becomes a reality. The request for open access is given at the State level to the State distribution control centres. If these can be empowered to take a quick decision in accordance with the prescribed guidelines and norms for providing open access, the decisions will not be delayed. Such an empowerment of the State distribution centres is, therefore, is important for the open access.

Financial Performance

14.45. The approved Eleventh Plan power sector budgetary outlay for the public sector (Central and State sectors) was ₹5,72,648 crore which was 15.71 per cent of the total Plan outlay. Summary of the year-wise investment made during the Eleventh Plan is shown in Table 14.15.

14.46. The Table indicates major shortfalls in case of central power sectors. This is primarily because the pace of capacity addition of NTPC and National Hydroelectric Power Corporation (NHPC) has been lower than the expected. The internal and

---

Box 14.2
Recommendations of Task Force on Open Access

REGULATORY AND SYSTEM CHANGES

1. SERCs to regulate the tariffs of all consumers of 1 MW and above in accordance with the provisions of Sections 42, 49 and 86 of the Act and fix only the wheeling charges (in conformity with section 42, read with section 62 of the Act) and open access surcharge.
2. Tariff to be charged by the discoms for providing standby supply should not exceed the maximum UI rate for the applicable hours plus a 5 per cent administrative charge thereon or alternatively, the bulk consumers may directly handle the UI supplies with the respective State Load Dispatch Centres (SLDCs) and to act as independent entities with financial and operational autonomy.
3. SLDCs should be upgraded in a time bound manner to enable open access, under section 42.
4. SERCs should ensure enabling arrangements such as metering and settlement.
5. Regulators should meet bulk consumers to take proactive action for encouraging open access. Timelines should be provided for the same.
6. The trading margin fixed by the Central Electricity Regulatory Commission (CERC) should apply in a seamless manner in any one transaction emanating from a generating company and terminating with a discom through multiple traders and should not exceed the maximum margin allowed to a single trader.

CENTRAL GOVERNMENT

7. To earmark a specified proportion, say, 25 per cent of the Centre's discretionary allocation of 15 per cent of central public sector undertakings' (CPSUs') generating capacity which may be made available for direct sale by CPSUs to open access consumers. As for new and upcoming capacity of CPSUs, 75 per cent of the discretionary quota may be reserved for sale to open access consumers and the sale price should determine by bidding. 75 per cent of the profits made by the CPSUs on this account may be transferred to the respective states where open access consumers are located.
8. Scheme of UI charges should be reviewed to ensure that UI does not become a vehicle for gaming in scheduling. For this a mechanism should be evolved to facilitate corrective measures against gaming including stiff penalties.
9. Commencing from the Twelfth Five Year Plan, the Central Government should release Accelerated Power Development and Reforms Programme (APDRP) assistance only to States that comply with the above and enable consumers to exercise their statutory right to open access. A package of incentives and disincentives should also be formulated by Power Finance Corporation (PFC) and REC for States to operationalise open access.

TABLE 14.15
Outlay/Expenditure: Centre, States and UTs (₹ Crore)

Sector	Eleventh Plan Approved Outlay	2007–08 (Actual)	2008–09 (Actual)	2009–10 (Actual)	2010–11 (RE)	2011–12 (RE)	Eleventh Plan Likely Expenditure	Per cent Utilisation
States and UTs	2,25,385	27,243	31,577	34,059	43,749	48,068	1,84,696	81.95
Central Sector	3,47,263	29,596	42,242	44,528	46,746	70,390	2,33,501	67.24
All India	5,72,648	56,839	73,819	78,587	90,495	1,18,458	4,18,197	73.03

Source: Planning Commission.

extra budgetary resource (IEBR) of the power sector CPSUs was 63 per cent of the original Plan targets.

TWELFTH PLAN PROGRAMME

Addition to Generation Capacity

14.47. The Working Group on Power has estimated a capacity addition requirement of 75,785 MW corresponding to 9 per cent GDP growth during the Twelfth Plan period. However, in order to bridge the gap between peak demand and peak deficit, and provide for faster retirement of the old energy-inefficient plants, the target for the Twelfth Plan has been fixed at 88,537 MW. As shown in Table 14.16, the share of the private sector in the additional capacity will be 53 per cent, compared to a target of 19 per cent in the Eleventh Plan. Since the growth rate of GDP for the Twelfth Plan is likely to be 8.2 per cent and not 9 per cent, the target for capacity addition contain an element of slack of about 10 per cent.

14.48. The share of power based on non-fossil fuel plants is very low at present and should be increased over time to promote low carbon growth strategy. The share of coal and lignite in the additional capacity being created during the Twelfth Plan is 79 per cent, up from 76 per cent in the target from the Eleventh Plan which actually ended up at 79 per cent. The projected capacity addition in non-fossil fuel plants covers addition of hydro capacity of 1,0897 MW and nuclear capacity of 5,300 MW. Besides this, 1,200 MW import of hydro power from Bhutan has also been considered. In addition, it is planned to add a grid interactive renewable capacity addition of about 30,000 MW comprising of 15,000 MW wind, 10,000 MW solar, 2,100 small hydro, and the balance primarily from bio mass planned. Details of the projected Twelfth Plan capacity addition, sector-wise and mode-wise, are given in Table 14.16.

Power Generation

14.49. The Working Group for the Twelfth Plan has estimated a requirement of 1,403 BU by the year 2016–17, after taking into account energy conservation measures and demand–supply management.

TABLE 14.16
Sector-wise and Mode-wise Capacity Addition (Provisional) during the Twelfth Plan (MW)

Sector	Hydro	Total Thermal	Thermal Breakup			Nuclear	Total
			Coal	Lignite	Gas/Lng*		
Central	6,004	14,878	13,800	250	827.6	5,300	26,181.6
State	1,608	13,922	12,210	0	1,712.0	0	15,530.0
Private	3,285	43,540	43,270	270	0.0	0	46,825.0
Total (Excluding RES)	10,897	72,340	69,280	520	2,539.6	5,300	88,536.6
Renewables	–	–	–	–	–	–	30,000
Total (Including RES)	10,897	72,340	69,280	520	2,539.6	5,300	1,18,536.6

* Addition of gas capacity is provisional and will depend upon the availability of gas. This will be reviewed during the MTA.

Without such measures, the generation requirement is projected at 1,463 BU. Even if the moderate level of 1,403 BU is taken as the Twelfth Plan target, the projected growth rate in power generation will be 9.8 per cent.

14.50. The projected change in the mix of generation by fuel supply by the end of 2030 is given in Table 14.17. The share of renewables in electricity generated is expected to rise from around 6 per cent in 2012 to 9 per cent in 2017 and 16 per cent in 2030. However, the share of hydro electricity is expected to fall from 15 per cent in 2012 to 11 per cent in 2030. The share of nuclear power, another clean source from a carbon emission perspective is expected to rise from 3 per cent in 2012 to 5 per cent in 2017 and to 12 per cent in 2030. Taking all these clean energy sources together, the share of hydro, renewables plus nuclear energy is expected to rise from 26 per cent in 2012 to 39 per cent by 2030.

Renovation and Modernisation and Life Extension of Thermal Power Plants (R&M and LE)

14.51. Coal-based thermal plants are the backbone of the Indian power sector. Most of the old and smaller size non-reheat type units are on the verge of retirement. R&M and LE is an economical option to supplement the capacity addition programme which was initiated in 1984 as a Centrally Sponsored Programme during the Seventh Plan. It continued till the Eleventh Plan and CEA has recommended for its continuance during the Twelfth Plan also.

R&M of Hydro Plants

14.52. The normal life expectancy of hydro plants is about 30–35 years after which they need life extension. Many of the existing hydro power stations could be modernised to generate reliable and higher yield by restoration and modernisation schemes. These involve adopting modern equipments like static excitation, microprocessor-based controls, electric microprocessor, high speed static or numerical relays, data logger, optical instrumentation for monitoring vibrations, air gaps, and silt contained in water and so on. These measures would improve availability of hydro power stations and minimise outages. Routine maintenance activities are not included in these schemes. Only activities which aim at increasing the efficiency of the unit and improve availability or steps required to meet environmental norms, or aimed at renovating obsolete equipment controls and instrumentation, are included in R&M scheme.

Exploitation of Hydro Electric Potential

14.53. Hydro power plants, particularly storage-based, are generally planned for their ability to meet peak power demand. Estimated hydro potential in India is about 149 GW including the plants of less than 25 MW capacity. The total capacity developed and under development put together so far is about 32 per cent of this potential. A major part of the unexploited potential is in North-East and Himalayan regions. With the deployment of latest technologies we can harness the remaining potential without damaging the ecology. Table 14.18 shows

TABLE 14.17
Changing Structure of Fuel for Electricity

		Capacity (%)			Generation (%)		
		2012	2017	2030	2012	2017	2030
1.	Coal	56	57	42	70	69	58
2.	Oil	1	1	0	0	0	0
3.	Gas	9	6	3	7	5	3
4.	Hydro	20	15	13	14	12	11
5.	Renewables	12	17	33	6	9	16
6.	Nuclear	2	4	9	3	5	12
	Total Clean Energy (4 + 5 + 6)				23	26	39

TABLE 14.18
Status of Hydro Electric Potential Development

(In terms of Installed capacity—above 25 MW)

Region	Total potential	Capacity developed	Capacity Under development	Total Developed+ Under development (%)	Capacity yet to be developed (%)
Northern	52,263	15,479	5,416	20,895 (40)	31,368 (60)
Western	8,131	5,552	400	5,952 (73)	2,179 (27)
Southern	15,890	9,367	570	9,937 (62.5)	5,953 (37.5)
Eastern	10,680	2,908	2,713	5,621 (52.6)	5,059 (47.4)
North Eastern	58,356	1,200	2,852	4,052 (7)	54,304 (93)
All India	1,45,320	34,506	11,951	46,457 (32)	98,863 (68)

the status of hydro potential development in the country (above 25 MW).

Peaking Power and Reserve Plants

14.54. The generation system must be designed to meet base load as well as peak load of the power system and have the ability to respond dynamically and efficiently to variations in demand within a short time. Since our system has wide variation in demand during peak and off-peak periods there is a need for peaking support with very high ramping rate. Peaking power can be provided by reservoir-based hydro plants or gas-based generation. Apart from the above, an optimal power system should have adequate reserves to meet the contingency of outage of certain operating generation capacity. It is important to set up these capacities to meet peaking power demand. It will be necessary to start up 2,000 MW of peaking gas-based plants, despite the limitations on availability of gas improvement.

14.55. Since it is expensive to carry unutilised capacity, and power from gas is likely to be especially expensive, the ability to meet peak loads is critically dependent on introducing time of day metering with a sufficient difference between peak and off-peak tariffs.

Pollution and Ash Utilisation

14.56. An important positive development in the power sector is that the utilisation of ash has increased impressively from 9.63 per cent in 1996–97 to 56 per cent in 2010–11. This is the consequence of deliberative planning to reduce adverse environmental impact as the coal-based capacity expanded. There are 13 thermal power stations in the country which have achieved 100 per cent or more ash utilisation during the year 2010–11. The ash generation by coal/lignite-based thermal power stations is estimated to increase to 170 million tons per year by the end of 2010–11 and reach to a level of about 300 million tonnes per year by the end of the Twelfth Plan. The Ministry of Environment and Forests (MoEF) has issued notifications for achieving 100 per cent utilisation of fly ash. The quantity of fly ash which has to be disposed off in ash ponds shall be reduced significantly which will help in addressing problems of pollution. All project developers will have to meet the stringent requirement of environmental norms for setting up thermal power plants to minimise air and water pollution.

Captive Power Plants

14.57. A number of captive power plants (CPPs), including coal-based power plants of varied type and size, exist in the country. These are either used in process industries or for in-house power consumption for large units. Capacity addition of around 13,000 MW of captive power is likely to be commissioned during the Twelfth Plan. Surplus power, if any, from CPPs is fed into the grid. The tariff for the surplus power is regulated. The captive power capacity generators find it profitable to supply electricity to the grid as the fixed cost has already been recovered by them from the power supplied for their captive use. The variable costs plus additional margins which is provided by the utility is found attractive by them for supplying power surplus to their use.

14.58. The installed capacity of CPPs has increased from 22,335 MW at the beginning of the Eleventh Plan to 36,511 MW (provisional) in March 2012, adding a total of around 14,000 MW addition of captive capacity during the Plan period.

Fuel Supply Problems

14.59. Although the pace of creation of generation capacity has picked up considerably, the fuel supply capability has not kept pace and serious fuel supply problems have arisen in the last year of the Eleventh Plan. Since 80 per cent of the additional generating capacity will be coal-based, resolution of coal supply to the power plants coming on stream will be crucial. With 50 per cent of the new capacity being created in the private sector fuel supply agreements have to be legally binding with credible penalties to reassure bankers and other financiers financing the establishment of capacity. The problems of coal supply are discussed in coal sector.

14.60. Availability of gas is also a problem as gas has yet to be ensured for 5,156 MW of gas-based projects commissioned during the Eleventh Plan period which are currently stranded/operating at a very low plant load factor (PLF) due to non-supply of gas. In addition to these projects, at least 2,538 MW of additional gas based capacity is expected to come up during the Twelfth Plan and as mentioned above, there is need for 2,000 MW of gas-based capacity to deal with peaking requirements. The requirement for coal, lignite and gas/LNG for power sector at the end of the

TABLE 14.19
Fuel Requirement during 2016–17

Fuel	Requirement	Availability
Coal	730 Million Tonnes	550 Million Tonnes
Lignite	46 Million Tonnes	46 Million Tonnes
Gas/LNG	207 MMSCMD*	102 MMSCMD*

Source: Planning Commission estimates based on Working Group Reports on Power and Petroleum and Natural Gas.
*In addition, about 17,500 MW gas-based capacity is under various stages of construction for which additional gas requirement is about 84 MMSCMD.

Twelfth Plan period has been shown in Table 14.19. Clearly domestic supply of both coal and gas needs to be augmented by imports. Since imports will be at much higher prices, some method must be found to make the higher priced fuel acceptable to generators. If domestic prices cannot be fully aligned with import prices, some resort to price pooling will be necessary and the scope for such price pooling must be urgently explored.

Expansion in Transmission System and Capacity

14.61. The large expansion in production and consumption of electricity has to be supported by a significant expansion and strengthening of the transmission network. Technological developments for transmission lines of 765 KV and 1,000–1,200 KV are of great relevance to reduce land requirement and transmission losses. Greater reliance will have to be placed on gas insulated substations which need about 20 per cent of the space required for conventional stations. This is an area where public investment can be supplemented by private investment and a good start has been made in the Eleventh Plan. It is important to build a policy framework within which more private sector investments will be forthcoming in the Twelfth Plan. A policy framework for public–private partnership (PPP) and a standardised documentation is being prepared for use by the States.

14.62. A total of about 1,07,440 ckm of transmission lines; 2,70,000 MVA of AC transformer capacity and 12,750 MW of HVDC systems are estimated as needed during the Twelfth Plan. Table 14.20 gives

TABLE 14.20
Transmission Line at the End of the Twelfth Plan Period

Transmission System Type/ Voltage Class	Unit	At the end of Eleventh Plan	Expected addition during Twelfth Plan	Expected by end of Twelfth Plan
Transmission Line				
HVDC Bipole lines	ckm	9,432	7,440	16,872
765 kV	ckm	5,250	27,000	32,250
400 kV	ckm	1,06,819	38,000	1,44,819
220 kV	ckm	1,35,980	35,000	1,70,980
Total	ckm	2,57,481	1,07,440	3,64,921
Sub-Station				
765 kV	MVA	2,5000	1,49,000	1,74,000
400 kV	MVA	1,51,027	45,000	1,96,027
230/220 kV	MVA	2,23,774	76,000	2,99,774
Total	MVA	3,99,801	2,70,000	6,69,801
HVDC				
Bi-pole link capacity	MW	6,750	12,750	19,500
Back-to-back capacity	MW	3,000	0	3,000
Total	MW	9,750	12,750	22,500

the transmission programme to be taken up during the Twelfth Plan period and also gives the anticipated cumulative achievement at the end the year 2016–17.

Creation of a National Grid

14.63. The power system in the country is demarcated into five regions. Four regional grids have been operating in synchronous mode as a single system for the past few years. Only the southern grid is yet to be connected to the rest of the system. The high voltage link to connect southern grid is under construction and likely to be completed by January 2014. Once this is achieved, all the five regional grids will operate as a single system in synchronous mode. This will be the largest single such system in the world, both in terms of the grid size and system capacity of around 2,00,000 MW, though, at a given point of time, actual power flow may be lower than this level.

14.64. The capacity for transfer of power across regions at the end of the Eleventh Plan is shown in Table 14.21. The total capacity to transfer power which is currently about 27,750 MW and this is expected to increase by 136 per cent to 65,550 MW by the end of Twelfth Plan. The specific line which is under construction for connecting the southern region is the Raichur–Sholapur 765 KV line. In fact, these are two single circuit lines and the total transmission capacity of these two lines would be about 4,200 MW. Three HVDC systems and a number of 765 KV lines and substations shall be implemented during Twelfth Plan. The Aurangabad–Wardha 400 KV QUAD DC, line which is part of the transmission system for evacuation of power from Mundra Ultra Mega Power Project (UMPP) has been planned and designed in such a way that the lines would be converted into a 1,200 KV S/C lines by a later date.

14.65. There is a three-tier structure for load dispatch, namely, State Load Dispatch Centre, Regional Load Dispatch Centre and the National Load Dispatch Centre. The Government of India notified Power System Operation Corporation Limited (POSOCO) as the designated entity to operate RLDC/NLDC with effect from 1 October 2010. A Forum of Load Dispatchers (FOLD) has been

TABLE 14.21
Inter-Regional Flow of Power at the End of Twelfth Plan Period

Region	End of Eleventh Plan	End of Twelfth Plan (Tentative)
Eastern/Southern	3,630	3,630
Eastern/Northern	12,130	17,930
Eastern/Western	4,390	12,790
Eastern/North Eastern	1,260	2,860
Northern/Western	4,220	14,420
Western/Southern	1,520	7,920
132/110 KV Lines	600	–
North Eastern/Eastern–Northern/Western	–	6,000
Total	27,750	65,550

constituted as approved by the Forum of Regulators (FOR) in January 2009 for harmonising practices across different load dispatch centres.

Evacuation of Power from the North-East

14.66. The North-East has very large potential for producing hydro power—close to 50,000 MW—but the pace of implementation has been poor. The evacuation of power from the North-East poses a major challenge for several reasons. First, the entire capacity has to be evacuated through a narrow strip of about 25 km in West Bengal. Although no forest clearance is needed, land acquisition issues could pose problems, which need to be tackled. Second, the number of hydro power plants coming up in the region, especially in Arunachal Pradesh, is expected to be spread over the Twelfth and Thirteenth Plans but the transmission system has to be devised as a onetime operation and may therefore have redundancy initially. This will increase the costs of transmission. Thirdly, a number of States including Arunachal Pradesh, Tripura and Manipur do not have adequate 132/220/400 KV systems and this may cause problems in evacuation of power. Fourthly, the distribution system is inadequate and consequently leads to large power losses.

14.67. The road map for the development of power sector, strengthening of overall transmission system and sub-transmission system of North-East Region (NER) and Sikkim was brought out in Pasighat Summit of North Eastern Council on 17 January 2007. As a follow-up to the recommendations of the summit, a subgroup under the chairmanship of Member (Power Systems), CEA was constituted to suggest the road map for strengthening the transmission system in the region. Subsequently a comprehensive review was taken at the Member (Energy), Planning Commission level to find out the modalities and source of funding to realise the objective.

14.68. Based on the recommendation of CEA and in consultation with each State of NER and Sikkim, Power Grid has prepared detailed project reports for comprehensive schemes for strengthening of transmission, sub-transmission and distribution system in each state of NER and Sikkim and also for interstate transmission system in NER in June 2010. The estimated cost of the above schemes is about ₹11,348.50 crore. The schemes were to be implemented in two phases by 2015–16. Considering the strategic importance of Arunachal Pradesh and Sikkim, a separate scheme for strengthening of transmission system for these two has been formulated at an estimated cost of about ₹3,014 crore. The Planning Commission has conveyed its in-principle approval to this scheme recently. Funding for this project will be provided jointly by the Ministry of Development of North Eastern Region (DoNER) and from the Non-Lapsable Central Pool of Resources (NLCPR). For the strengthening of transmission systems in the remaining six states, Ministry of Power is exploring the possibility of tying up funds from the World Bank.

14.69. Integration of Indian electricity grid with countries such as Bhutan and Nepal would result in optimisation of electricity resources on a large scale and provision of additional benefits and opportunities to the selling and buying countries. This will enhance hydro-thermal mix in generation, and reduce carbon emission and dependence on fossil fuels. An electric grid interconnection between India and Bangladesh through a Berhampur (India)–Bheramara (Bangladesh) 400 KV DC, 125 km line along with 1 × 500 MW HVDC back to back asynchronous link at Bheramara is being developed for facilitating exchange of power up to 500 MW between the two countries. The capacity of this interconnection can be upgraded in future. The asynchronous link ensures that any fluctuations or disturbances on one side would not affect the other side.

Challenges in Transmission Sector

14.70. The proposed rapid expansion of the capacity to transfer capacity poses some serious challenges, viz. right of way, flexibility in line loading and regulation of power and improvement of operational efficiency. Following measures may be implemented to meet the above challenges:

- Upgradation of transmission lines
- High capacity 400 KV multi, circuit/bundle conductor line
- High Surge Impedance Loading(HSIL) line
- Compact towers
- Increase in current: High Temperature Low Sag (HTLS)
- Reduction in land for substation
- Regulation in power flow/FACATS devices
- Improvement of operational efficiency with condition based monitoring and private maintenance
- Development of 1,200 KV AC system
- Creating adequate evacuation and transmission facilities for renewable power including construction/strengthening of interstate transmission.

The Distribution System

14.71. The distribution segment plays a crucial role in the overall functioning of the power sector because it is the part of the system which generates the revenues needed to pay generation and transmission utilities. The viability of the power sector as a whole is therefore critically dependent on the health of the distribution sector. Unfortunately, as the Eleventh Plan experience amply demonstrates, the financial viability of the system is under severe strain. Poor financial health of utilities has resulted in underinvestment in the distribution network causing poor upkeep and maintenance. Consequently the quality of supply is hampered, leading to customer dissatisfaction and poor recovery. This, in turn, leads to further deterioration of financial health of utilities. This vicious cycle needs to be broken.

14.72. It is absolutely vital that the distribution system is made financially viable during the Twelfth Plan. The key focus of the Twelfth Plan must be to strengthen the performance of the distribution system to achieve improved financial viability of Discoms and to expand access to power in rural areas. This calls for concerted attempts at AT&C loss reduction, introduction of smart grid to allow effective demand side management (DSM), greater private sector participation to achieve management efficiency and so on. Since distribution is entirely the domain of States, the responsibility for improving distribution lies almost entirely with State Governments. The Central Government can incentivise action in a manner which allows the States leeway for experimenting with different ways of obtaining better results.

14.73. The Government had constituted the Shunglu Committee in July 2010 to study issues relating to the financial viability of the Ds and give recommendations on how to improve the situation. The Committee has since given its recommendations. In order to examine these recommendations, and suggest a strategy for the turnaround of the distribution sector in the Twelfth Plan, an Expert Group under the chairmanship of Member (Energy), Planning Commission was set up to look into the problems being faced by the State Discoms.

Debt Restructuring Policy

14.74. The Expert Group gave extensive recommendations for improving the financial health of the discoms during the Twelfth Plan. Based on the recommendations of the Expert Group, the Cabinet has approved a debt restructuring plan which can be summarised as follows:

1. a. 50 per cent of the outstanding short term liabilities (STL) as of 31 March 2012 to be taken over by State Governments by way of bonds to participating lenders shall be first converted into bonds to be issued by Discoms duly backed by the State Government guarantee. The State Government will take over the liability during the next two to five years by issuance of special securities in favour of participating lenders in a phased manner keeping in view the fiscal space available till the entire loan (50 per cent of STL) is taken over by the State Government.
   b. The State Government would provide full support to the Discoms for repayment of interest and principal.

2. Balance 50 per cent of the STL will be rescheduled by lenders and serviced by the Discoms with a moratorium of three years on principal and would be backed by a State Government guarantee. The best possible terms are to be extended for the rescheduled loans to improve viability of Discoms' operations.

3. The restructuring/reschedulement of loan is to be accompanied by concrete and measurable action by the Discoms/States to improve the operational performance of the distribution utilities. In order to make the effort meaningful, the State Government/Discoms have to commit themselves and carry out certain mandatory and recommendatory conditions contained in part (c) of the Scheme.

4. To set up a Transitional Finance Mechanism in support of the restructuring effort of the State Government for their distribution utilities having the following features:

   a. For providing liquidity support by way of a grant equal to the value of the additional energy saved by way of accelerated AT&C loss reduction beyond the loss trajectory specified under Restructured Accelerated Power Development and Reform Programme (RAPDRP).
   b. The eligibility of grant would arise only if the gap between ARR and ACS for the year has been reduced by at least 25 per cent during the year judged against the benchmark for the year 2010–11.
   c. This scheme would be available only for three years beginning 2012–13.
   d. Incentive by way of capital reimbursement support of 25 per cent of principal repayment by the State Government on the liability taken over by the State Government under the scheme. The amount to be reimbursed only in case the State Government takes over the entire 50 per cent of the short-term liabilities corresponding to the accumulated losses outstanding as on 31 March 2012. Detailed guidelines for the Transitional Finance Mechanism as outlined above would be worked out by the Ministry of Power in consultation with Ministry of Finance.

5. The Scheme would be applicable to all State Discoms having accumulated losses and facing difficulties in financing operational losses.

6. For removal of difficulties in interpreting or implementing the Scheme, Ministry of Power may be authorised to issue clarification, after inter-ministerial consultations, wherever required, with the approval of the competent authority.

14.75. Effective implementation of the restructuring package during the Twelfth Plan would send a powerful signal that the power sector is on the path of financial viability.

Restructured APDRP

14.76. The challenge of providing power to all involves considerable investment in distribution. The Working Group for the Twelfth Plan has assessed a total investment requirement for the distribution sector at ₹3.06 lakh crore. Some of the key initiatives proposed during the Twelfth Plan are:

1. The population norms under R-APDRP for including a city under R-APDRP may be relaxed

by lowering the existing population threshold. More extensive coverage will bring uniformity in billing and customer service of the utility across all its service areas. R-APDRP may also cover assistance to private distribution companies.

2. A National Electricity Fund (NEF) had been set up. This will now be operationalised. It will provide interest relief to the distribution utilities to cover loans taken from financial institutions for development of the distribution sector.

3. Utilities and regulators shall make an action plan to eliminate the gap between the average cost of supply and average tariff realised through improved tariff implementation and adoption of multi-year tariff framework.

4. Time of Day (TOD) metering shall be taken up by all the utilities for effective demand side management (DSM).

5. Load shifting arrangement by regulators and improvement in energy efficiency and its measurement by BEE in the agriculture sector shall contribute towards DSM and ease out the pressure on utilities.

6. Open Access shall be provided to consumers with more than 1 MW load in accordance with the Electricity Act, 2003. This was mandatory with effect from 1 January 1 2009 but it has not been operationalised due to reluctance of State Governments and the utilities to give the necessary freedom to large customers to choose their own sources of supply. In fact, under the law, the State electricity regulator should not set tariffs for large customers leaving them to be determined through negotiations.

7. To improve safety, counter theft and improve aesthetics, underground cabling work shall be taken up by the utilities for towns under R-APDRP in selected areas.

8. Moving towards a smart grid in a manner relevant to our needs will be a key focus area in the distribution sector in the Twelfth Plan. A number of pilot projects will be taken up.

9. Phased installation of smart metres, extending SCADA system to 100 more towns, and integration of renewable into the grid.

The Role of Private Investment and Participation in Distribution

14.77. The experience of privatisation in Delhi, Kolkata, Mumbai, Ahmedabad, and Surat shows that transmission and distribution losses can be reduced, network efficiency increased, and service levels improved. The experiences in Bhiwandi, Maharashtra of franchising have also indicated positive gains with network losses going down from 63 per cent to 19 per cent in Bhiwandi and service levels improving. The Franchise model is now being expanded to Nagpur, Aurangabad, Jalgaon in Maharashtra and Agra in Uttar Pradesh. An alternative model is public–private partnership (PPP) in the distribution segment for which necessary concession agreements are being designed. The Twelfth Plan will have to place a major emphasis on expansion of Franchise or PPP or privatisation in different utilities as a strategy to reduce network losses and improve efficiency of service and consumer satisfaction.

Separation of Rural Feeders

14.78. An important initiative to improve the availability of power in the rural areas and have more effective management of power for the agriculture sectors where the requirements may be for limited hours, has been to separate rural feeders for lighting and agriculture loads. This was initiated by Gujarat utilities and has subsequently been taken up by Rajasthan, Andhra Pradesh, Haryana, Uttar Pradesh, Chhattisgarh, Madhya Pradesh, Karnataka, Maharashtra and a number of other States. A World Bank study on the efficacy of these reforms is underway. According to the initial indications, the benefits have been found to be more in the field of improved lighting in the villages with varying degree of success on reducing T&D losses.

Universal Electrification

14.79. The RGGVY was started with an aim to provide electricity connections to all villages and free connections to BPL families (Annexure 14.1). It has certainly provided increased access of power to a large number of households as indicated in paragraph 3.1.8. Clearly, there is still a large population which is not using electricity either because of lack of network in the villages or absence of connectivity to the household. There are also a large number of habitations left uncovered. To provide power to all during the Twelfth Plan would require dealing with the large backlog in the States of Uttar Pradesh, Bihar, Odisha, Assam and some of the North Eastern States.

14.80. Connectivity by itself is only a part of the programme. In many States there is also a real shortage of power. Besides, RGGVY focuses only on household supply and does not address the needs for providing electricity for small industries and agriculture, which need three-phase supply. This, in turn, requires strengthening of the rural network and not just the last mile connectivity to households, which is what RGGVY covers. States are often unable to invest in this. For effective universal access, the RGGVY programme will be restructured.

Human Resource Development and Capacity Building

14.81. The present power scenario demands a very comprehensive and pragmatic approach to attract, use, develop and conserve valuable human resources. Technically trained work force comprising of skilled engineers, supervisors, artisans, managers and so on are required in every sphere of the power supply industry. A growing concern over environmental degradation and depletion of the conventional energy sources has made the task of electricity generation even more challenging and therefore, quality standards of the staff are becoming increasingly vital.

14.82. For a capacity addition of about 1,00,000 MW (including renewables) in the Twelfth Plan, the additional work force requirement shall be of the order of 4 lakh out of which nearly 3 lakh will be technical. Therefore, all Central sector utilities, State sector utilities, and IPPs would need to create required training infrastructure for providing O&M training. Additional training infrastructure shall be created by organisations like NPTI and training institutes of other utilities. These should augment their existing training institutes for meeting the increased training requirement of the power sector.

R&D in Power Sector

14.83. The power sector being highly technology-intensive, R&D plays a major role in its developmental plans. In the present scenario, R&D initiatives are particularly required in four different conventional sectors, viz. generation, transmission, distribution and environment.

14.84. Thermal, hydro, renewable energy and distributed generation are the key areas in the generation sector. Design and development of the equipment, real-time simulators and controllers, creation of data bank, automation pilot plant demonstration, development of alternative materials, equipment performance, biological efforts and exploratory studies are required in the transmission sector. R&D initiatives in smart grid and distributed generation are required for improvement of distribution sector. Major PSUs involved should be encouraged to do the necessary R&D. Further clean development mechanism for bulk utilisation of fly ash, control of SOx, NOx and mercury in coal-based thermal power plants need immediate attention for clean and green energy.

14.85. R&D in distribution and rural electrification needs more thrust. The key research areas may be AC/DC micro-grid demonstration for improving reliability and power quality, energy storage scheme for improving the reliability of sensitive loads, development of intra-operable standards and protocol for energy metering, load research, I.T. applications in distribution and smart grid and so on. R&D initiatives are also required for enhancing material strength and durability and for standardisation on their specifications. A key initiative for R&D in the Twelfth Plan may include setting up of a technical cell in CEA, which will focus on best practices, R&D in data collection and specific projects and technical support to States for consultancy and implementation. The research projects will include support to universities.

Project Implementation

14.86. Land is increasingly becoming a scarce resource and availability of land is posing a serious challenge for future power plants. The optimum utilisation of land is therefore crucial. Design changes are required to reduce land requirement. Similarly, availability of water has become scarce. To meet future water demand of thermal power, technical measures for reducing water consumption, creation of large reservoirs/dams of potential rivers to retain flood water and encouraging coastal power plants will be undertaken.

14.87. Achievement of the generation capacity targets depends critically on supporting infrastructure in different transport sectors like railway, highways and roads, inland waterways and gas pipelines. Railways need to enhance their capacity for coal evacuation from coal fields by expanding proposed dedicated freight corridors and also ensure rail connectivity to all ports having coal unloading facilities. Roads and highways need to be augmented for transportation of over dimensional consignments and changes in Motor Vehicle Act may be required to accommodate consignments, with safeguards, of above 49 million tonnes and also include hydraulic axle trailers. Accordingly, load classification for roads and bridges may be reviewed and toll plaza building on highways may be designed keeping these requirements in view.

14.88. Coal handling arrangements at ports must be expanded to handle the larger quantities of imported coal required for power stations. Increase of draft, creation of roll-on/roll-off berths and mechanisation shall improve the load handling capabilities of ports. All these ports must be given priority in effective road/rail connectivity.

14.89. Adequate manufacturing capacities of main plant equipment including that for large supercritical thermal sets shall be available indigenously to meet the capacity addition requirement of the country during the Twelfth Plan. Regarding balance of plants construction agencies and construction equipment/techniques, the capacities and capabilities have to be further developed and enhanced. There is no shortage of key material except Cold Rolled Grain Oriented Steel, higher grade Cold Rolled Non Grain Oriented Steel and thick boiler steel plates. There is a need to set up plants to produce Cold Rolled Grain Oriented Steel, augment indigenous capacity for tubes and pipes, create short circuit testing facilities for transformers, augment manufacturing facilities for gas-insulated substations and create indigenous capacity for thicker boiler water plates. It should be possible to set up domestic capacity in these areas which is internationally competitive.

Management of Energy Demand and Energy Efficiency

14.90. Improving energy efficiency is an important instrument for containing the demand for energy and several initiatives are possible in this area. The Bureau of Energy Efficiency (BEE) and the Ministry of Power (MoP) had introduced a number of schemes during Eleventh Plan for promotion of energy efficiency in India. The schemes of BEE include Standards and Labelling (S&L), Energy Conservation Building Code (ECBC), Energy Efficiency in Existing Buildings, Bachat Lamp Yojana (BLY), SDA strengthening, Energy Efficiency in Small and Medium Enterprises (SMEs), Agriculture and Municipal Demand Side Management (DSM) and Contribution to State Energy Conservation Fund (SECF). Schemes implemented by the Ministry of Power include Energy Conservation Awards and National Mission for Enhanced Energy Efficiency (NMEEE). These schemes are estimated to have achieved savings equivalent to 11,000 MW of avoided power capacity during the Plan. Details of savings projected to be realised through various measures are given below, along with Plan for the period 2012–17.

Energy Efficiency in Equipment and Appliances

14.91. Large energy inefficiencies exist in consumer and industrial appliances. The S&L Programme was quite successful during the Eleventh Plan period and it is anticipated that by the end of the Eleventh Plan, total savings in avoided capacity addition would be 7,315 MW. Under this scheme, a large number of appliances were covered initially under the voluntary labelling categories, out of which four appliances/equipment are under the mandatory labelling program. The Eleventh Plan has already envisaged coverage of 21 appliances under S&L. This programme will be continued and expanded during the Twelfth Plan.

Efficiency in Transport

14.92. As on 2010–11, there were a total of 13.3 million passenger cars in India which consumed about

9 mtoe. An additional 1.1 million passenger cars are added every year. In the transport sector, a labelling scheme is envisaged which is aimed at achieving energy efficiency. This will cover:

- Introduction of fuel economy norms effective from the first year of the Twelfth Plan. This will be mandatory from 2015 under the Energy Conservation Act.
- Technical study for two- and three-wheelers and commercial vehicles (Trucks and Buses) to finalise additional S&L Programme. Norms for these will be modified.

14.93. The targeted energy saving by the end of the Twelfth Five Year Plan is 4.3 mtoe in the sector.

Energy Efficiency in Industries

14.94. The total commercial energy consumed by industry including SMEs stands at about 40–50 per cent of the total commercial energy consumption in the country. Hence energy efficiency measures would yield substantial benefits in this sector. The projected energy saving potential in the Twelfth Plan is 13.18 mtoe which consists of a saving of 6.2 mtoe from the seven energy-intensive industries (DCs), 1.75 mtoe from SME sector and 5.23 mtoe from thermal power stations sector.

National Mission for Enhanced Energy Efficiency (NMEEE)

14.95. NMEEE is one of the eight Missions created by India's National Action Plan for Climate Change and is based on the Energy Conservation Act, 2001.

The Mission will enable transactions in energy efficiency. Specific initiatives envisaged by the NMEEE include:

- Perform Achieve and Trade scheme—a market-based mechanism to enhance energy efficiency (see Box 14.3 for details). The scheme is expecting an energy saving of 3.5 million tons of oil equivalent (mtoe) in seven selective industrial sectors and 3.1 million tons of oil equivalents in thermal power stations by 2014–15;
- Market Transformation for Energy Efficiency (MTEE)—CDM roadmap, Standards and Labelling, ESCO promotion, capacity-building;
- Financing Energy Efficiency—tax exemptions, revolving fund, Partial Risk Guarantee Fund; and
- Promotion of performance contracting business model—enabling upgradation of existing buildings, streetlights, municipal pumping and so on through Energy Service Companies which invest in the upgradation and are paid through sharing of the resultant savings in the energy bill.

14.96. Fans and Lights are the major users of electricity in homes and offices across the country. Energy consumption by fans and lights is expected to occur rapidly because of increasing incomes and enhanced access to electricity. During the Twelfth Plan period the introduction of 'super-efficient' lights and fans will be incentivised so as to accelerate their development and adoption to enable lower the rate of growth of electricity demand while enhancing services to households.

Box 14.3
Perform, Achieve and Trade Mechanism

The Perform, Achieve and Trade (PAT) mechanism is a market-based mechanism to incentivise improvements in energy efficiency in eight energy-intensive industries (including TPS) by setting up standards and certification of energy saving achieved which can be traded. The vision for PAT scheme during Twelfth Plan covers the following points:

- While implementation of the first cycle of PAT is to achieve the set target of 6.6 mtoe by 2014–15, widening and deepening the scope of PAT during the second cycle of PAT envisages including other energy-intensive sectors like efineries, Chemicals, Petrochemicals, Automobile Manufacturing, Sugar, Glass and so on to reduce the threshold energy consumption limit;
- Fiscal instruments like Partial Risk Guarantee Fund (PRGF) and Venture Capital Fund for Energy Efficiency (VCFEE) which have been proposed in NMEEE for successful implementation of PAT scheme will be expanded in order to provide confidence to the financial institutions and to equity investors to invest in energy efficiency products and companies.

14.97. Major R&D programmes may be initiated in selective areas and selective sectors for developing new customised energy-efficient technology through indigenous development of applications of already available energy efficient technologies/concepts.

14.98. The total projected saving in the year 2016–17, that is, end of the Twelfth Five Year Plan is of the tune of 11.43 mtoe in which 10.41 mtoe is contributed by thermal energy. The rest, which is equivalent to 11.96 BU of electricity saving is estimated at bus-bar in 2016–17.

Policy Reforms in the Power Sector

14.99. The Twelfth Plan must push for policy reforms in several areas, the most important of which are listed below:

1. Resolution of fuel supply problems related to availability of coal and gas for the plants expected to come on stream in the Twelfth Plan will be critical. These are discussed in the section on Coal and Gas in this Chapter.
2. The introduction of open access must have top priority. State Governments, SERCs and Discoms need to conform to the Electricity Act, which prohibits tariff regulation for consumers of 1 MW and above. These consumers must be free to purchase electricity through open access in a competitive market. Where cross-subsidy is required, an open access surcharge may be levied. The Act requires phased implementation of open access to all consumers. By the end of the Twelfth Plan, all consumers up to 0.25 MW may be covered.
3. There is a need to develop ancillary power markets and CERC should come out with a framework for implementation of such market. To facilitate further development of power market, jurisdiction issues regarding forward and future market products may be clarified in the policy/Act. Development of markets can be expanded further by permitting short-term procurement for three months in advance by the Discoms. Also, long-term procurement and medium-term procurement by the Discoms may be encouraged and impediments, if any, may be identified and removed.
4. Strengthening of NLDC/RLDCs/SLDCs is vital for effective grid management and for implementation of open access. It is necessary to separate the management of POSOCO from PGCIL. The State Governments must take steps to upgrade and modernise the SLDCs which must be made functional and financially independent in accordance with the Electricity Act.
5. Spinning reserves need to be facilitated for grid stability at the regional level to accommodate infirm renewable energy injection into the grid. The State Governments need to contract additional capacity for this purpose.
6. Suitable incentives for low-cost transmission, linking the renewable energy generation sources, development of smart grid for evacuation and transmission of renewable power and creation of spinning reserves may be done through the National Clean Energy Fund.
7. There is a need to strengthen measures for increasing share of renewable energy over time. SERCs should provide long-term trajectory for renewable purchase obligations and issue relevant regulations within a specified timeframe. Further, for the procurement of renewable power, demand of more than one distribution licensee may be pooled at the State level or jointly among States and procurement through competitive bidding route under section 63(a) of Electricity Act 2003/National Tariff Policy should be made permissible.
8. Power procurement and allocation of power must be done in line with the Tariff Policy and the guidelines/standard bid documents (SBD) issued by Government of India under the Electricity Act, 2003. The National Electricity Policy (2005) may need to be suitably amended to ensure State Governments abide by these provisions.
9. Consumer Grievance Redressal Forum (CGRF) should be made a multi-member set-up comprising representation from all stakeholders. The office of Ombudsman should be funded by the SERCs.
10. Reforms in the distribution sector should include:

    a. Prepaid metres to those categories of consumers who are chronic defaulters, 100 per cent spot billing, spot collection, semi or fully automatic meter reading and standardisation of metering protocols for extensive use of automated meter readings.

b. Institution of Chief Electrical Inspectorate to Government of India/State Government (CEIG) to be strengthened and to work out a scheme for delegation of authority of mandatory inspection including self-certification to the CEIG to liberalise it from unnecessary controls.

c. Separation of rural feeders to control losses and improve power availability. Dedicated feeders may be extended to energy-intensive consumers at their cost.

11. The State Government should clear all the outstanding dues to the utilities, and ensure timely payment of subsidy. State Governments with financially strained Discoms should be encouraged to undertake restructuring of the debt as per the package recently approved by the Cabinet. This includes restructuring of short-term loans of Discoms with poor financial health, sharing by concerned State Governments of the burden of the utilities to the extent of 50 per cent of such short-term loans, provision of special market bonds and relaxation of FRBM norms for the State Governments. Financial restructuring should be supported by regular revision of tariff through adoption of regulations suggested by Forum of Regulators, including automatic tariff adjustment with change in fuel prices and other reform measures to ensure regular revision of tariff and simultaneous investments in reducing AT&C losses.

12. There is a need for an independent oversight over programmes like RGGVY and R-APDRP on a concurrent basis. These should be incorporated in these schemes for the Twelfth Plan.

3.3. COAL AND LIGNITE SECTOR

14.100. Coal is the mainstay of India's energy sector accounting for over 50 per cent of primary commercial energy supply in 2010–11. This share will actually increase to 57 per cent over the next 10 years. The gap between the demand and the domestic supply of coal has made it imperative to augment domestic production both from the public sector and the private sector and to expedite the reform process for realising efficiency gains through increased competition in the sector during the Twelfth Plan. An important feature of the Eleventh Plan was the attempt to augment domestic coal production from captive mines. However, the programme has slipped and expected production from captive blocks fell well short of the projected target of 104 million tonnes in the terminal year of the Plan because only 29 captive blocks could start production out of the 195 blocks allocated so far. The main impediments in the progress of captive mining are reported to be similar to those in other PSU-held blocks like delays in forest and environmental clearances, problems of land acquisition and R&R, allocation of a block to more than one user and so on. CIL will continue to play a major role in meeting the coal requirements of the country but the growth in CIL production will not be enough to meet the rising demand. Hence, efforts need to be made to ensure that additional captive coal blocks start producing in Twelfth Plan to meet the rising coal demand. It is also necessary to plan for larger imports of coal.

REVIEW OF THE ELEVENTH PLAN

Coal Demand and Production

14.101. The target for coal production at the end of the Eleventh Plan was initially set at 680 million tonnes and revised downwards to 630 million tonnes at the time of the MTA. The actual achievement was only 540 million tonnes. Since demand in the terminal year (2011–12) of the Eleventh Plan was around 640 million tonnes there was a large demand–supply gap of 100 million tonnes which was only partially met by imports. This has adversely affected the coal supplies to end consumers, particularly the power sector. It is estimated that out of capacity addition of 41,894 MW, around 25,000 MW of coal-based capacity commissioned is being sub-optimally utilised because of inadequate availability of domestic coal.

14.102. The widening gap between demand and supply has to be met by imports because of which the share of imports in the total coal demand is likely to

TABLE 14.22
Details of Coal and Lignite Production

Sl. No.	Parameter	Tenth Plan 2006–07	Eleventh Plan (2011–12)			Eleventh Plan % CAGR		
			Initial	MTA	Latest	Initial	MTA	Latest
0	1		2	3	4	7	8	9
1	Coal Demand (million tonnes)	474.18	731.10	713.24	640.00	9.53	8.98	6.98
2	Coal Production (million tonnes)	430.84	680.72	629.91	539.99	9.58	7.89	4.62
3	Imports	43.08	51.00	83.33	90.00	3.43	14.11	15.88
4	Imports as per centage of total demand	9.00	6.98	11.68	14.06			
5	Lignite Production (million tonnes)	31.28	54.96	42.59	41.64	12.04	12.04	6.72

Source: Ministry of Coal.

increase to around 14.06 per cent in 2011–12 as compared to just 9 per cent in the year 2006–07. Details of coal imports in Eleventh Plan are given in Table 14.22.

Lignite Production and Demand

14.103. The Eleventh Plan envisaged lignite production to reach 54.96 million tonnes in the terminal year of the Plan (2011–12) from 31.13 million tonnes in 2006–07 yielding a growth rate of 12 per cent. The projected production of 54.96 million tonnes was expected to come from lignite mines spread in three contributing States with their respective share as 24.23 million tonnes from Tamil Nadu, 22.26 million tonnes from Gujarat and 8.47 million tonnes from Rajasthan. However, actual production in 2011–12 was 43.10 million tonnes combined from all the three states. This shortfall is mainly due to non-starting of several mines under Private and State Sector and due to delay in commissioning of lignite-based power plants and certain mines under the Central Sector. As far as NLC is concerned, thinning of lignite seam thickness and the washout zone encountered in Mine I is the main reason for the shortfall of 2.42 million tonnes in Tamil Nadu. Similarly, in Barsingsar Mine under NLC at Rajasthan, though the mine is ready in all respects to give full production, it was warranted to limit its production to cope with the demand of its linked TPS which has certain teething problems. The lignite based capacity addition in the Eleventh Plan is 1,490 MW against the target of 2,280 MW.

Coal and Lignite Reserves

14.104. The inventory of geological resources of India's coal and lignite reserves as on 1 April 2010 has been shown in Table 14.23. This is 15.09 per cent higher than the reported reserves level of 255 billion tonnes in January 2007. Corresponding increase in lignite reserves level is 9.6 per cent from 38.27 billion tonnes reported level in 2007. The accretion of coal resources over the years has been shown in Table 14.24.

Review of the Central Sector Schemes

14.105. The schemes implemented with budgetary support from the Ministry's plan covered regional/promotional exploration, detailed drilling in non-CIL blocks, Environmental Measures and

TABLE 14.23
Inventory of Coal and Lignite Reserves as on 1 April 2012

(billion tonnes)

	Proved	Indicated	Inferred	Total
Coal	118.145	142.169	33.183	293.497
Lignite	6.18	25.76	10.02	41.96

Source: Ministry of Coal.

TABLE 14.24
Accretion of Coal Reserves

(million tonnes)

Reserves as on	Proved Category	Accretion in Proved Category	Inferred Category	Indicated Category	Total Reserves	Reserves Accretion
1 January 2005	92,960	–	1,17,090	37,797	2,47,847	–
1 January 2007	97,920	4,960	1,18,992	38,260	2,55,172	7,325
1 April 2008	1,01,829	3,909	1,24,216	38,490	2,64,535	9,363
1 April 2009	1,05,720	3,891	1,23,570	37,921	2,67,211	2,676
1 April 2010	1,09,798	4,078	1,30,654	36,359	2,76,810	9,599
1 April 2011	1,14,002	4,204	1,37,471	34,390	2,85,862	9,051

Source: Coal Directory of India.

Subsidence Control scheme (EMSC), R&D schemes, Conservation and Safety measures and development of transport infrastructure in the coal fields and so on.

Regional/Promotional Exploration

14.106. Exploration for coal and lignite in the country is taken up in stages. In preliminary exploration, geological surveys are undertaken by the Geological Survey of India (GSI) to identify potential coal and lignite areas. Regional promotional exploration aims at widespread drilling to establish broad framework of the deposits to facilitate planning for detailed exploration and subsequent projectisation and mine development. While regional exploration drilling target for Eleventh Plan was 1.94 lakh metres which was revised to 1.47 lakh metres, promotional drilling target was 4 lakh metres. Against the envisaged targets, achievement will be 1.14 lakh metres (about 78 per cent) in case of regional drilling, establishing 7.07 Bt of coal and 2.95 lakh metres (74 per cent) in case of promotional drilling, establishing 20.05 Bt of coal resources.

14.107. In case of lignite, regional exploration drilling achievement is likely to be 1.32 lakh metres against a target of 1.48 lakh metres during Eleventh Plan mainly by NLC and by other agencies, viz. GMDC and RSMML establishing 1.85 Bt of lignite resources. Achievement in promotional exploration is likely to be 2.74 lakh metres (78 per cent) against a target of 3.50 lakh metres establishing 3.22 Bt of lignite resources.

14.108. 2D HRSS surveys were not a part of the exploration programme of Eleventh Plan. However, in view of trends worldwide, these surveys were considered as a part of regional (promotional) exploration by Subcommittee on Energy Minerals. The National Geophysical Research Institute (NGRI), a premier organisation for geophysical studies in the country, was therefore, inducted to carry out these surveys in coal and lignite bearing areas. It is expected that a total of 31 Line kilometre (L.km) in coal areas and 94 L.km in lignite areas HRSS survey will have been carried out during the Eleventh Plan.

Detailed Drilling in Non-CIL Blocks

14.109. Detailed exploration surveys focus on establishing adequate geological resources data for projectisation and mine development. The blocks outside the purview of CIL have been proposed to be explored in detail for reducing the time lag between offering the blocks to potential entrepreneurs and starting of the operation by them through budgetary support. The cost of exploration, in turn, will be recovered from entrepreneurs who have been allotted the blocks. CMPDI and its contractual agencies including MECL have been able to progress well in detailed exploration activities and are expected to achieve 8.09 lakh metres against a target of 13.50 lakh metres in non-CIL blocks establishing 5.2 Bt of private coal reserves.

14.110. Regarding detailed exploration in CIL blocks as against a target of 5 lakh metres, the actual achievement has been 11.2 lakh metres (224 per cent) of exploratory drilling achieved by CMPDIL and by contractual agencies including MCCL and 9.01 billion tonnes of coal reserves were proved during the Eleventh Plan. SCCL has achieved 2.99 lakh metres of actual drilling against a target of 3.39 lakh metres and estimated 0.91 billion tonnes of coal reserve through detailed exploration.

Productivity and Benchmarking

14.111. Traditionally, the output per man shift (OMS) has been measured as tonnes in coal mines and it has improved significantly for all the three PSUs operating in coal and lignite mining. While overall OMS in case of CIL improved from 3.54 in year 2006–07 to 4.92 in year 2011–12 this was still lower than the target of 5.54 in the terminal year of the Eleventh Plan. In case of SCCL this has improved from a level of 2.39 to 3.80 over the same period, which is significantly higher than the target of 2.67. This significant improvement in overall OMS level is for both opencast and underground mining operations. This could be due to the outsourcing of some of the activities, particularly in the opencast mining operations. In case of NLC, the improvement is marginal because lignite production level could not increase due to delays in the completion of lignite-based power plants. One of the important areas to improve productivity is benchmarking of operations and equipment productivity. Productivity of equipment and machinery used in opencast and underground mining has significantly improved during the Eleventh Plan period.

Clean Coal Technologies

14.112. Coal beneficiation is one of the prime clean coal technologies aimed at supplying washed coal to the pulverised coal combustion boilers of power plants. The MoEF's directive aimed at restricting the use of coal of not more than 34 per cent ash content at thermal power stations located far away from pit heads and load centres and critically polluted areas, has also contributed to improvement in economics of operations of such power stations. The CIL envisaged building 20 new washeries with a capacity of 111 mt in the Eleventh Plan. However, coal washing capacity did not grow as planned due to delays in awarding of contracts to set up washeries by the CIL. The coal washing capacity at the end of the Eleventh Plan is as indicated in Table 14.25.

TABLE 14.25
Coal Washing Capacity by the end of Eleventh Plan Period

	Coking Coal	Non-coking coal
	(in million tonnes)	
Public	24.22	17.22
Private	5.66	78.74
Total	29.88	95.96
Washed Coal Production	7.18	40.95

Coal Bed Methane

14.113. The potential of Coal Bed Methane/Coal Mine Methane was recognised in a new policy of Government of India in 1997. The Ministry of Coal (MoC) and the Ministry of Petroleum and Natural Gas (MoP&NG) are working together for the development of Coal Bed Methane and the Government has offered 33 blocks in four rounds of bidding for CBM covering 17,416 sq. km of area. One block in Raniganj coalfield has commenced commercial production in 2007 and two blocks are in advanced stage of commencing production. The Director General of Hydrocarbons (DGH) is the regulator for CBM activities in the country. The CBM/CMM clearance house has been established in CMPDIL, Ranchi, in collaboration with United States Environment Protection Agency (USEPA) which will provide information for development of CBM/CMM in India. The current level of production, being only 0.2 mmscmd, is confined mostly to the private sector. There is no separate pricing regime for CBM and the gas prices are determined by the developer, subject to Government approval.

Research and Development

14.114. A total of 29 R&D projects were implemented during the Eleventh Plan. Out of these, 16 projects have already been completed by September 2012. Remaining 13 projects are likely to slip into the Twelfth Plan period. Some of the major projects under implementation are:

- Development of CMPDI capacity for delineation of viable coal mine methane (CMM)/abandoned mine methane (AMM) blocks in the existing and potential mining areas having partly de-stressed coal in virgin coal seams.
- Recovery and utilisation of coal methane in Jharia and Raniganj coalfields.
- Development of immediate roof fall prediction system in underground mines using wireless network.
- Demonstration of cost-effective technology for dry beneficiation of coal by all airjig.
- Demonstration of coal dry beneficiation system using radiometric technique.
- Assessment of prospect of shale gas in Gondwana basin with special reference to CIL areas.
- Development of indigenous catalyst through pilot-scale studies of coal to liquid (CTL) conversion technology.
- High resolution seismic monitoring for early detection and slope failures in opencast mines.
- Application of Ground Penetrating Radar (GPR).
- Integrated communication system to locate trapped miners in underground mines.
- Development of self-advancing (mobile) goaf edge supports (SAGES) for de-pillaring operations in underground coal mines.

Conservation and Safety in Coal Mines

14.115. Safety of miners and safe mining operations are of paramount importance in coal mining. These two schemes are under the statutory provisions of Coal Conservation and Development Act (CCDA) and were being implemented as a part of non-Plan scheme during the Tenth Five Year Plan through reimbursement of cess collected under CCDA. The Ministry of Finance has taken a view that cess collected under CCDA is a revenue of the Government of India, which is reimbursed back to coal companies for implementation of these schemes. Therefore, these schemes are treated as Plan schemes during the Eleventh Plan.

Development of Transport Infrastructure in Coal Field Areas

14.116. Development of infrastructure in coalfields is essential to ensure the timely evacuation of coal produced in mines to the rail heads or railway yards. Also substantial time is taken by Railways to build the critical rail links and that is affecting the movement of coal to the end users. Four critical rail links that have been pending for years are the Tori–Shivpur–Katholia rail link in North Karanpura coalfield (CCL command area), the Bupdevpur Baroud rail link connecting coal blocks in Mand Raigarh coalfield, the Jharsuguda–Barpalli railway line in IB valley coalfield and the Sattapalli–Bhadrachalam rail link (SCCL command area). Commissioning of these lines would facilitate movement of around 125–130 million tonnes of coal to end users. Construction of Tori–Shivpuri line was delayed due to delays in getting forest clearance. Railways have changed the alignment of the line to bring down the forest land involved and MoE&F has cleared the project recently with certain conditions. Railway Board is yet to approve the implementation of the Bupdevpur Baround rail link. CIL, State Government and Railways are in discussion to implement other critical links in Mand–Raigarh area in joint venture to facilitate coal movement from the upcoming mines. The SCCL and Railways were not able to sort out the differences in the implementation of Sattapalli–Bhadrachalam link project but this issue has been resolved recently and SCCL has agreed to provide funds to the Railways to implement the project on turnkey basis.

Environmental Measures And Subsidence Control

14.117. The purpose of this scheme is to improve environmental conditions in old mined-out areas, particularly Jharia and Raniganj coalfields through implementation of a number of schemes for mitigating the damage caused by unscientific mining, carried out before nationalisation of coal mines. Under the scheme, a Master Plan proposal for Jharia–Raniganj coalfields with a total outlay of ₹9,773.84 crore was taken up to deal with fire, rehabilitation of uncontrollable subsidence-prone inhabited areas and diversification of roads/railway lines within command area of BCCL and ECL. Recently, the Cabinet has approved the scheme. For implementation of the Master Plan, Jharia Rehabilitation and Development Authority (JRDA) for BCCL areas and Asansol Durgapur Development Authority (ADDA) areas have been notified as implementing agencies by the respective State Governments of Jharkhand and West Bengal. A High Powered Central Committee under the Chairmanship of Secretary (Coal) with representatives from other Ministries/Departments, State Governments of Jharkhand and West Bengal and concerned coal companies, has been monitoring the implementation of the Master Plan. Demographic surveys and land acquisition by JRDA and ADDA are in progress.

Integrated Coal and Lignite Resource Information System (ICRIS and ILRIS)

14.118. ICRIiS and ILRIS are coal and lignite resources structured on the UNFC pattern approved in October 2004 and are under progress at different data centres in CMPDI/Singareni and NLC. These projects need to be continued during the Twelfth Plan with enhanced outlays for successful completion, maintenance and regular updating.

Application of Information Technology

14.119. Information Technology (IT) has been used by the coal industry in India for improving productivity and decision making. Some of the applications already in use are:

- Enterprise resource planning (ERP).
- Real-time trip counting system at opencast mines with latest technologies like GPS, GIS, GSM, RFID, Wi-Fi and so on.
- Proximity warning system for HEMM at opencast mines.
- Truck movement monitoring system at weighbridges and coal handling plants mines with latest technologies like GPS, GIS, GSM, RFID, Wi-Fi, and so on.
- Online underground air and gas monitoring systems (CH_4, CO, Temperature).
- UG communication system and miners' tracking with warning system for the miners entering the unsafe areas.

14.120. An SAP-ERP system in coal mines in the country has been introduced by SCCL with effect from July 2008 covering business processes related to Purchase and Stores, Marketing and Dispatches, Quality Management, Human Capital Management, Finance and Accounts, and Costing. The CIL is also in the process of adopting such a system in the near future.

Financial Performance of Coal Sector

14.121. The approved Eleventh Plan outlay of ₹37,100 crore for MoC was planned to be financed through an IEBR of ₹35,774.37 crore, and a GBS of ₹1,326.00 crore. The budgetary support sought for the Ministry's plan schemes covered regional/promotion exploration, detailed drilling in non-CIL blocks, Environmental Measures and Subsidence Control Scheme (EMSC), R&D schemes, conservation and safety measures and development of transport infrastructure in the coal fields. These schemes were proposed to be funded by subsidence excise duty collected under CCDA, IEBR of CIL and budgetary support. Actual expenditure during the Eleventh Plan is ₹26,337.62 crore which is only 63 per cent of the approved outlay. This comprises ₹26,374.20 crore of IEBR of three PSUs namely CIL, SCCL and NLC and balance ₹1,500 crore GBS for Ministry of Coal funded schemes. The major shortfalls are in the reported expenditure of CIL and NLC whereas SCCL is expected to spend ₹3,707.59 crore against the approved IEBR of ₹3,340 crore. The financial performance of the coal sector is summarised in Table 14.26.

THE TWELFTH PLAN

Coal Demand

14.122. Total demand for coal grew by around 6.6 per cent during the Eleventh Plan against domestic production growth of only 4.61 per cent, and the gap was filled from higher imports. The projected GDP growth targeted during the Twelfth Plan will lead to a high demand for coal in the next five years on a business-as-usual basis. However, increased efficiency measures, including introduction of supercritical technology in power plants will reduce the demand for coal. The trend growth for coal demand during the Twelfth Plan is therefore likely to be similar to that in the Eleventh Plan.

14.123. Ministry of Coal has projected two scenarios of coal demand during the Twelfth Plan. Scenario I

TABLE 14.26
Financial Performance of the Coal Sector

(in ₹ Crore)

Sl. No.	Sector	The Eleventh Plan Outlay		
		Approved	MTA	Anticipated
1	CIL	17,390.07	16,090.68	13,460.78
2	SCCL	3,340.00	3,802.07	3,707.59
3	NLC–Power	12,051.41	6,140.61	6,246.36
4	NLC–Mines	2,826.00	2,334.39	1,483.67
5	Total NLC	14,877.41	8,475.00	7,730.30
	Total IEBR	35,607.48	28,367.75	24,898.40
6	Central Sector Schemes	1,326.01	4,225.80	1,416.19
	Total MOC	36,933.49	32,623.55	26,314.59

projects a demand of 1,204 mt in the terminal year of the Twelfth Plan and Scenario II projects 980.5 mt. Scenario I implies 13.5 per cent CAGR and Scenario II implies a growth rate of 8.9 per cent. Scenario II is considered realistic, based on specific consumption in each consuming sector observed in the past few years. From this scenario, total coal demand will reach 980.50 million tones, an increase of 186 million tonnes over the Twelfth Plan period as shown in Table 14.27.

TABLE 14.27
Coal Demand during the Twelfth Plan

(in million tonnes)

Sector	Eleventh Plan (2011–12) Annual Plan Demand Projection	Twelfth Plan (2016–17) Demand Projection Scenario II
Coking Coal	46.67	67.20
Power Utility	412.00	682.08
Power Captive	40.00	56.36
Cement	28.89	47.31
Sponge Iron	30.47	50.33
Others*	81.97	77.22
Total non-coking	593.33	913.30
Grand Total	640.00 (6.6 %)	980.50 (8.9 %)*

* Annual average growth rate during the Twelfth Plan period.
Source: Working Group on Coal and Lignite.

14.124. The total demand by the power sector including that from captive power plants is expected to be 75 per cent of the total coal demand during the terminal year of the Twelfth Plan. The share of the steel sector is expected to be 6.85 per cent of the projected demand and the shares of cement and sponge iron sectors are expected to be 4.8 per cent and 5.1 per cent respectively and balance 7.9 per cent is estimated to be consumed by the brick and others sectors. Cumulative annual growth rate of coal demand during the Twelfth Plan is projected to be around 8.9 per cent. Coal demand for Eleventh Plan and Twelfth Plan is given in Annexure 14.2.

14.125. The total addition to electric generation capacity in the Twelfth Plan is targeted at 88,536.6 MW, which includes 69,280 MW of coal-based capacity. The estimates for coal requirements of the power sector have been computed considering the fact that 40,000 MW of capacity based on Supercritical technology will be added in the Twelfth Plan and efficiency measures are also being taken. Further, power generation capacities were running at very high PLF so far, in view of high demand–supply gap. With the planned increase of new capacities and the pace of setting up new power capacities getting accelerated, the PLF of the power plants is likely to go down. Taking all these factors together, it is estimated that the total demand for coal from the power sector may be 738.44 mt in the terminal year of the Twelfth Plan 2016–17. Taking into account the requirements of steel, cement and other sectors of the economy, the total coal demand is estimated at 980.50 mt. The quality of coal available from the MCL and IB valley mines has been poor and a large portion of coal during the Twelfth Plan will be provided by these mines. If the overall quality of coal available from domestic mines deteriorates, the total coal demand may go up.

Coal Production

14.126. The initial years of the Twelfth Plan are likely to see continuing constraints on coal availability reflecting the difficulties experienced in increasing production in the last two years of the Eleventh Plan. Delays in obtaining E&F clearances, land acquisition and R&R issues continue to plague coal production and remedial action is urgently needed. There is an urgent need to take effective measures to step up coal production. The Working Group on Coal in the most optimistic scenario (Scenario II) has suggested domestic production for the Twelfth Plan period from various sources as shown in Table 14.28.

TABLE 14.28
Coal Production

(in million tonnes)

Sector	Eleventh Plan (2011–12)	Twelfth Plan (2016–17) Projection Scenario II
CIL	435.84	615.00
SCCL	52.21	57.00
Captive Blocks	36.04	100.00
Others	15.91	23.00
Grand Total	540.00	795.00

Source: Ministry of Coal.

14.127. The incremental production envisaged in the optimistic Scenario of the Twelfth Plan works out to 255 million tonnes over the production level of 540 million tonnes during the Eleventh Plan. Major contribution has to come from the CIL, which is expected to add incremental production of 185.5 million tonnes yielding a cumulative annual growth rate in coal production of 8 per cent. This is much higher than the actual growth rate of 4.6 per cent achieved in the Eleventh Plan. Details of coal production in the Eleventh Plan and envisaged production during the Twelfth Plan period are given in Annexure 14.3.

14.128. A number of initiatives are being taken to promote faster extraction of coal. The policy on competitive bidding for allocations of captive blocks has been finalised by the Ministry of Coal and is expected be made operational during 2012–13. This should result in allocation of new coal blocks.

Import Requirements

14.129. The level of imports at the end of the Twelfth Plan is projected to increase from 137 million tonnes of Indian quality coal at the end of the Eleventh Plan to 185 million tonnes at the end of the Twelfth Plan based on total coal demand of 980 million tonnes and domestic supply of 795 MT. If domestic supply does not match the target growth rate of 8 per cent per year, the import demand will be higher. The projected level of imports of around 185 million tonnes is large keeping in mind that international trading in coal is only around 900–1,000 million tonnes (15–16 per cent) of the total consumption of over 6,000 million tonnes world over, and there are competing requirements from other countries like China who have large coal-based capacities. The international availability of coal is going to be restricted due to concerns on climate change. International prices of coal are also likely to remain high because of taxes which are being imposed by several coal-producing countries including Australia and Indonesia.

Underground Mining

14.130. Only 15 per cent of India's coal production is from underground mines. The industry aims to reach a total coal production of 30 per cent from underground mines by 2030. There is a clear trend towards underground mines as this has positive implications for the environment. However, the extraction of coal from the underground mines is lower than that from the opencast mines. In forest areas, underground mining is clearly feasible and will sharply reduce the impact of ecological degradation. It is, however, feasible only if the pool reserves and the seam thickness permits its exploitation accordingly. The share of coal production for underground mines in major coal producing countries is given in Table 14.29.

TABLE 14.29
Share of Underground Production in Total Production

Sl. No.	Country	Percentage (%)
1	China	90
2	USA	33
3	Australia	20
4	India	10

14.131. Considering the emerging hurdles in forest clearance and land acquisition in future, serious efforts need to be made to increase the share of underground production considerably by the end of the Twelfth Plan by focusing on long wall technology and productivity in underground mines. Indian coal companies must accept the challenge of transplanting the international best practices with more effective management. CIL can have joint ventures or formulate PPP projects with appropriate terms with renowned international players to shore up the underground production level in the Twelfth and the Thirteenth Plans.

Lignite Demand and Production

14.132. The Twelfth Plan envisages lignite demand of 68.60 million tonnes in the terminal year 2016–17 of the Plan which includes production from Tamil Nadu, Gujarat and Rajasthan—27.20, 21.60 and 19.80 million tonnes respectively. The additional lignite-based power generation capacity during the Twelfth Plan is envisaged as 2,280 MW. It is stated that projected lignite production of 68.60 million tonnes would almost be adequate to meet the growing demand for various sectors consuming lignite. The projected shortfall would be around 10 million tonnes which needs to be met by either taking up new mines or improving the production levels from the existing mines.

Coal Pricing

14.133. Globally, pricing of coal is based on gross calorific value (GCV) of coal. The Integrated Energy Policy which was based on the Integrated Energy Policy Report of the Planning Commission, and was approved by the Cabinet in December 2010, had proposed adoption of this pricing system. This was finally implemented in January 2012 with the Ministry of Coal issuing a notification for pricing of coal on GCV basis with effect from 31 January 2012, replacing the earlier system of pricing on the basis of useful heat value (UHV) which takes into account the heat trapped in ash content also, besides the heat value of carbon content. The revised GCV system has 17 bands of calorific values with a bandwidth of 3,000 kilo calorie each instead of the existing seven grades of A, B, C, D, E, F and G. The revision to GCV is likely to increase the prices of domestic coal to some extent. This is desirable adjustment because domestic thermal coal continues to be underpriced compared to internationally traded coal prices. International coal prices of thermal coal are currently about three to four times higher than domestic coal but this reflects the fact that imported coal is of higher calorific value and better quality. After adjusting for these differences, international coal prices are a little over twice the domestic prices as shown in Table 14.30. It must also be noted that the volume of coal traded is small compared to international production which makes international prices a less reliable guide. Table 14.30 compares domestic coal prices of thermal coal in India with the domestic sale price of thermal coal in other countries. The comparison shows that Indian coal is underpriced even on this basis. It is necessary to plan for a steady upward price adjustment over the Twelfth Plan period.

TABLE 14.30
Price Comparison of Domestic Coal with other Countries

Country	Calorific Value K (Cal/Kg)	Price (US $ per tonne)	Price (in ₹/Mk Cal)
China	5,000–6,000	70	636
USA	5,000–6,000	40	363
India	3,500–4,000	26	342

14.134. The price differential between domestic and imported coal creates distortions in the power sector. Since Coal India is not in a position to provide domestic coal to meet the demand of all power generating units expected to come on stream in the Twelfth Plan, increased reliance on coal imports is necessary. However, power generators supplying power with PPAs at a regulated tariff will not be able to pass on the higher cost of imported coal. There is a need to consider a mechanism of price pooling under which Coal India undertakes to meet the full FSA requirement using a combination of domestic and imported supplies, pooling the price of its imports with its domestically produced coal to give coal to power generators at a uniform price.

Coal Movement Constraints

14.135. Currently the share of rail in movement of coal in the country is around 52 per cent. The share of other modes of transportation is 15 per cent by merry-go-round (MGR), 7 per cent by belt/rope and 27 per cent by road. Against this, the coal movement matrix in the terminal year of the Twelfth plan (2016–17) is envisaged to show a 58 per cent share of rail, 25 per cent share of road, 11 per cent of MGR and 6 per cent of belt/rope. This includes planning for movement of 800 million tonnes of indigenous coal and coal products and 166 million tonnes of imported coal which is equivalent to about 250 million tones of domestic coal. To realise this objective, average wagon requirement is envisaged at 446.4 rakes per day out of which 165.6 rakes per day will be required for imported coal. The annualised growth in rail loading is expected to be 7.1 per cent.

14.136. Some of the important identified railway infrastructure projects are at North Karanpura, Mand–Raigarh and at Ib Valley coalfields. These projects were initially proposed during the Eleventh Plan but could not be implemented due to delays in land acquisition and clearance from Environment Ministry. The current status of these projects is given in paragraph 14.116. In addition to these, a few more feeder lines have been suggested for improving rail movement during the Twelfth Plan in potential coalfields. Completion of these projects should have top priority in Railway Planning.

Coal Quality and Beneficiation

14.137. Coal washing is one of the practices being promoted as a measure to encourage implementation of clean coal technologies. While coking coal washing has been in practice for quite some time in the country, washing of non-coking coal, particularly for power generation, has come into focus only recently. Use of washed non-coking coal has increased manyfold over the last 10 years. Currently coking coal washing capacity is around 29.88 million tonnes comprising of washery capacity of 22.18 million tonnes of CIL, 2.04 million tonnes of SAIL and 5.66 million tonnes of TISCO. However, the actual total washed coal production from all these washeries is much below the capacity at 7.03 million tonnes, with an approximate raw coal feed of 15.5 million tonnes. It has been observed that performance of CIL managed washeries is not satisfactory and the output of washed coal from CIL washeries is only 3.89 million tonnes.

14.138. Non-coking coal washing capacity in the country is around 96 million tonnes, comprising of 17 million tonnes of CIL and 79 million tonnes of others. In this case also, the output of washed coal is below capacity at around 36 million tonnes, with a raw coal feed of around 52 million tonnes. Thus, utilisation of existing washery capacity is suboptimal and suitable measures need to be taken to optimally use existing capacity. The CIL proposes to set up 20 more washeries with an aggregate capacity of around 111 million tonnes in the Twelfth Plan.

14.139. Considering the need to increase the level of washed coal, it is proposed to enhance washeries capacity in Twelfth Plan period. Coking coal washing capacity is likely to increase from the existing level of around 30 million tonnes in 2011–12 to 49 million tonnes by the end of 2016–17. Similarly the non-coking coal washing capacity is planned to increase from about 96 million tonnes by the end of the Eleventh Plan to around 175 million tonnes by the end of the Twelfth Plan.

14.140. There has been some progress in dealing with the problems of oversized coal. Coal companies are establishing Coal Handling Plants (CHPs) and feeder breakers. Coal India Ltd. is now supplying almost 99 per cent of crushed coal to the power sector. Further, deployment of surface miners in different projects is also helping in producing sized coal for supply to the consumers. A total of 212 CHPs (74 major CHPs and 138 mini CHPs/Feeder Breakers) with a total capacity of about 277 million tonnes per annum are operating in different subsidiary companies of the CIL. Further, 50 surface miners deployed at CCL, SECL and MCL produced about 103 million tonnes of sized coal in the year 2010–11, which has helped augment supply of sized coal.

Exploration for Coal and Lignite

14.141. Coal and lignite exploration efforts should not only aim at expanding the resource base through regional exploration but also at upgrading the known resources remaining under 'Indicated' and 'Inferred' categories through detailed exploration to facilitate their projectisation for mining. Significant accretion of resource in coming years is envisaged in the intermediate and deeper levels (beyond 300m of depth). As such there is also an emerging need to fully bring out the potential of coal resources which are at greater depths, for other forms of exploitation like CBM, underground gasification (UCG) and so on to augment the coal resources.

14.142. With ever increasing demand of steel in the country the requirement of coking coal is projected to increase from 69.47 million tonnes to 85.06 million tonnes at the end of the Twelfth and the Thirteenth Plans. There is a need to focus exploration efforts on the prime coking coal resources available beyond 300 m of depth to bring them to 'Proved' category.

14.143. Against a target of 1.94 lakh metres for regional exploration during the Eleventh Plan, 1.14 lakh metres (78 per cent) of drilling will be achieved and 7.07 billion tonnes of coal resources are likely to be established. In promotional exploration, against a target of 4 lakh metres of exploratory drilling, 2.72 lakh metres (68 per cent) are expected to be achieved, establishing 20.05 Bt of coal resources. The Twelfth Plan envisages taking up 1.05 lakh metre regional explorations drilling to establish resource base of around 6.8 billion tonnes. The corresponding programme under promotional exploration envisages promotional drilling of 4.80 lakh metre covering an area of 1,204 Sq. Km. to establish resources of 16.64 billion tonnes. Similarly a drilling target of 54.46 lakh metres is envisaged for detailed drilling in the Twelfth Plan which includes 19.03 lakh metres in non-CIL blocks. The envisaged coal resource establishment under detailed drilling is 76.80 billion tonnes including 16.22 billion tonnes under detailed drilling in non-CIL blocks.

Royalty on Coal and Lignite

14.144. According to a decision taken by the Government, royalty rates have to be revised periodically once in every three years. Based on the above decision, Ministry of Coal had set up a Committee to suggest revision in royalty rates in 2009. The Committee suggested ad-valorem royalty on coal and lignite instead of the earlier system of combination of specific and ad-valorem duty on various grades of coal. The Government has accepted the suggestion and approved the suggested royalty regime based on ad-valorem basis with effective royalty rates of 14 per cent on raw coal prices and 6 per cent on lignite with effect from April 2012.

Amendment to the Coal Mines Act

14.145. The Coal Mines (Nationalisation) Act, 1973 does not allow private companies to mine coal for sale to third parties though captive mining is allowed for specified end use sectors. This is a limited opening which is helpful but unlikely to attract big investment. Unless large investment and technology in the sector comes in, mining coal by a host of small players would not increase production to desired levels.

14.146. Development of large coal blocks holds the key to rapidly increase production. There are political sensitivities in opening up the coal sector to private investment, but it is simply not logical to keep private investment out of coal, when it is allowed in petroleum and natural gas. Besides, the energy security of the country needs full involvement of all concerned in producing coal. Hence, amendment to the Coal Mines (Nationalisation) Act is needed. A Bill to amend the Act for this purpose was introduced in Parliament in 2001 but has not been pursued. Allowing private sector mining does not involve privatisation of Coal India but only entry of new mining companies. This issue needs to be considered in the interest of energy security.

New Initiatives to Expand Coal Availability

14.147. Given the importance of coal to India's energy security, it is necessary to give priority to a number of policy initiatives in the Twelfth Plan which can address obvious weaknesses:

1. Coal exploration must be stepped up to ensure availability of more coal mining blocks for both private and public sectors. Either CMPDIL ought to be made an independent organisation, or a new independent organisation should be created to develop and maintain the repository of all geological information in the country on the lines of CEA for power sector, or the DGH for petroleum and natural gas sector.
2. To expedite clearances, a coordination committee at the Centre and State level may be set up (single window concept), involving senior representation from the concerned departments for quick environment clearances. Even if statutory clearances can only be given by the relevant agency, the establishment of a coordinative mechanism will expedite the decision-making.
3. Enactment of a central legislation to ensure uniform R&R policy and speedy land acquisition on appropriate terms is absolutely necessary.
4. There is a need to incentivise coal availability from captive coal mining blocks. The decision to allocate all future coal blocks on the basis of transparent bidding should be implemented in the first year of the Twelfth Plan. Further, we must create an institutional mechanism for planning and development of common infrastructural facilities with participation of coal mining companies and the respective State Governments.
5. In several cases, development of captive coal may be in a position to produce coal in excess of their requirement. At present the terms of allocation of coal blocks do not permit sale to a third party except with permission. If they could be encouraged to produce more than their consumptive use it would avoid the need to import much more expensive imported coal. This will be done by making surplus coal available to CIL subsidiaries at a price which provides adequate incentive for the captive block owners. The principle on which such coal should be priced can be approved by the Cabinet.
6. Coal companies should develop a comprehensive plan for increasing the share of production from underground mines and suitable policy initiatives such as cost plus pricing, fiscal incentives and so on need to be introduced to improve the potential returns currently available from underground mining activities. It is suggested that the share of underground mining be increased from the existing 10 per cent to a considerable level by the end of the Twelfth Plan in the next five years.
7. In view of the availability of increased coal imports for the Twelfth Plan period the Ministry must ensure that mechanisms are in place which will be up and appropriate mix of long-term and sport contracts.
8. A coal sector regulator should be set up on a priority basis.
9. Finally it is not clear whether the present structure on which the operating coal companies are subsidiaries of CIL as the holding company is desirable. The industry would be better served if the subsidiaries were spun off as separate public sector companies encouraged to develop their own strategies of coal development including joint venture activity and acquisition of assets abroad. A High Level Committee should be appointed to examine this option and submit a report within six months.

Benchmarking of Productivity

14.148. The Twelfth Plan envisages an improvement in productivity per person from 4.92 tonnes per person in CIL to 7 tonnes per person and from 3.8 tonnes per person in SCCL to 4.93 tonnes per person. This will still leave India well below other producers, as countries like USA, Australia and China have productivity levels of about 14 tonnes per person for combined underground and opencast mines. The targets set to realise the productivity level mentioned above envisage productivity levels of 14.0 tonnes per person for CIL and 14.83 tonnes per person in SCCL in the terminal year of the Plan for opencast operations, and only 1.10 and 1.83 tonnes per person for CIL and SCCL, respectively for underground operations. Thrust would be given on improvement of operational efficiency of the coal mining companies by establishing benchmarks for different mining operations and work force productivity comparable with international standard. The productivity norms of different heavy earth moving machinery (HEMM) benchmarked earlier for both availability and utilisation in different coal companies would be examined so that these become comparable with international standards.

3.4. PETROLEUM AND NATURAL GAS SECTOR

14.149. Managing the petroleum and natural gas sector will present critical challenges in the Twelfth Plan. The demand for petroleum products is expected to expand while the scope for increasing domestic production is limited. Oil prices in world markets are expected to be volatile but generally high. The oil and gas import bill is likely to be around 6–7 per cent of GDP during the year 2011–12. Unfortunately, domestic prices of certain petroleum products have not been adjusted in line with world prices, with the result that there is large 'under-recovery' by the oil sector. Important steps were taken in 2012 to adjust diesel prices and to put a limit on highly subsidised LPG, but even after these adjustments, under-recoveries remain large and the subsidy provided in the budget covers only a fraction of this. Continuing this scale of under-recovery is simply not viable. Prices of sensitive petroleum products like diesel, kerosene and LPG will therefore have to be adjusted periodically to reduce the under-recoveries which are currently borne by the Government and upstream oil companies. This is not consistent with developing a healthy petroleum sector capable of investing in exploration and production.

REVIEW OF THE ELEVENTH PLAN

Demand for Petroleum Products

14.150. Demand for petroleum products grew at an annual rate of 4.15 per cent during the Eleventh Plan period which is close to the upper-case scenario that was envisaged at the start of the Eleventh Plan as shown in Table 14.31. The elasticity of POL demand with GDP growth during the Eleventh Plan has been 0.53 which is slightly higher than 0.49 for the Tenth Plan. The use of FO/LSHS and LDO in power, fertiliser and general trade has declined. Also, increased availability of natural gas has replaced naphtha that was extensively used in the fertiliser industry. LPG consumption in India has increased from 10.85 million tonnes in the year 2006–07 to 15.36 million tonnes in the year 2011–12, growing at a rate of 7.21 per cent per annum CAGR.

Exploration, Production and Refining Sector

14.151. Both oil and gas production targets have slipped by large percentages during the Eleventh Plan period. Against the crude oil production target of 206.73 MMT in the Eleventh Plan, the actual achievement is only 177 MMT, that is, 14 per cent below the target. The actual natural gas production was 212.54 BCM as against the production target of 255.76 BCM, with a shortfall of about 17 per cent of the Eleventh Plan targets. The balance recoverable reserve position as on 1 April 2011 of O + OEG was about 2015 million tonnes, which has increased by 10.5 per cent from 1,847 million tonnes as on 1 April 2007.

14.152. In contrast to the large slippage in oil exploration and production, addition to refining capacity is likely to be 88.42 per cent of the target. Some of the refinery projects like MRPL expansion and Paradip refinery projects have also slipped into the Twelfth

TABLE 14.31
Consumption of Petroleum Products

Consumption		2007–08	2008–09	2009–10	2010–11	2011–12	CAGR (%)
Actual		128.95	133.6	137.81	141.75	147.98	4.15
Working Group Eleventh Plan	Base	116.35	119.1	121.99	126.97	131.77	2.93
	Upper	117.56	121.95	127.79	136.59	141.79	4.45

TABLE 14.32
Physical Performance of Petroleum and Natural Gas Sector

Sl. No.	Item	Eleventh Plan Target	Actual 2007–08	Actual 2008–09	Actual 2009–10	Actual 2010–11	Actual 2011–12	Total in the Eleventh Plan
1	Crude Oil Production (MMT)	206.73	34.12	33.51	33.69	37.68	38.09	177.09
2	ONGC	140.06	25.94	25.37	24.86	24.42	23.72	124.30
3	OIL	18.99	3.10	3.47	3.57	3.58	3.85	17.57
4	PVT. JVC	47.71	5.08	4.67	5.26	9.68	10.53	35.22
5	Gas Production (BCM)	255.76	32.42	32.85	47.50	52.22	47.56	212.54
6	ONGC	112.39	22.33	22.49	23.10	23.10	23.32	114.33
7	OIL	16.42	2.34	2.27	2.42	2.35	2.63	12.01
8	PVT. JVC	126.95	7.74	8.09	21.99	26.77	21.61	86.20
9	Refining Capacity (MMTPA)	240.96	148.97	177.97	185.39	193.39	213.07	213.07*
10	Hydrocarbon Reserve Accretion (O + OEG)	1,847	–	–	–	–	–	2,014.81#

* Refining Capacity estimate as on 1 April 2012. # HCRA as on 1 April 2011.

Plan due to delays in providing captive power equipment by BHEL to these refineries. Table 14.32 gives the target and achievements of various physical parameters during the Eleventh Plan period.

New Exploration Licensing Policy (NELP) Programme

14.153. The NELP programme is a major initiative aimed at attracting private investment into oil and natural gas. There have been nine rounds of bidding, starting with a first in 1998, and a total investment of US$ 15.88 billion has been made by various operators in E&P sector till 2010–11. Out of 235 Production Sharing Contracts (PSCs), 73 were signed during the Eleventh Plan period. To step up the pace of exploration, in the ninth round of NELP (NELP-IX), 34 exploration blocks were offered in October 2010, of which 18 PSCs have already been signed with the awardees. Details of blocks awarded under the nine NELP rounds are shown in Figure 14.1.

Equity Oil, Gas from Overseas Assets

14.154. Oil PSUs (OVL OIL, GAIL, IOCL, BPCL and HPCL) have invested ₹59,108 crore (US$ 13 billion) up to 31 March 2011 on acquisition of assets abroad, mainly in oil producing assets. There are nine major production assets in Russia, Sudan, Brazil, Syria, Vietnam, Venezuela and Colombia. Production from overseas oil and gas blocks is presently about 10.22 per cent of India's domestic production. The

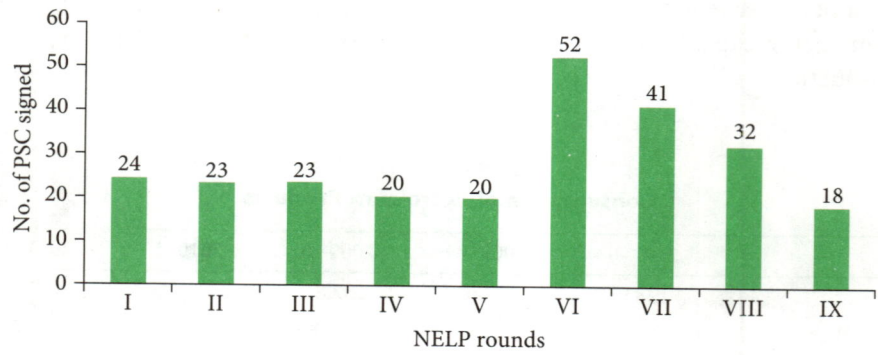

FIGURE 14.1: Exploration Blocks awarded in NELP Rounds

TABLE 14.33
Share of Overseas Hydrocarbon Production

Year	2007–08	2008–09	2009–10	2010–11	2011–12 #
Total Domestic oil and gas (MMTOE)	66.53	66.35	81.19	89.93	85.64
Overseas production of OVL (MMTOE)	8.8	8.78	8.87	9.43	8.75
Overseas production as a percentage of Domestic (%)	13.23	13.23	10.93	10.49	10.22

Source: Ministry of Petroleum and Natural Gas/ONGC Videsh Ltd. (#) Prov.

share of overseas vis-à-vis indigenous production of oil and gas is given in Table 14.33.

Policy Initiatives during the Eleventh Plan

14.155. Various policy initiatives were taken to address the issues relating to attaining hydrocarbon energy security. Major policy initiatives taken by the Government during the Eleventh Plan are as follows.

Regulatory Measures

14.156. The Government has set up Petroleum and Natural Gas Regulatory Board with effect from 1 October 2007 to regulate downstream activities of oil and gas sector under the PNGRB Act, 2006. However, the mandate of PNGRB is fairly narrow and deals largely with pipelines. PNGRB is currently empowered to give authorisation to entities for laying, building, operating and expanding any pipeline as common or contract carrier and expanding city gas distribution projects.

Allocation of Natural Gas

14.157. Natural gas produced from NELP blocks is subject to Government-prescribed allocation to different uses and also Government approval of the pricing formula. The Government has prioritised allocation of gas produced from NELP blocks in the following order:

- Fertiliser plants producing subsidised fertilisers
- LPG plants
- Power plants
- City Gas Distribution (CGD) for CNG and domestic PNG
- Steel, petrochemicals, refinery, captive power plants and CGD for industrial and commercial customers

14.158. An Empowered Group of Ministers has allocated 93.336 MMSCMD of gas on a combination of firm and fallback basis from the blocks producing gas under NELP.

Strategic Storage of Crude Oil

14.159. The Government is in the process of creating strategic crude oil storage capacity for 15 days at Vishakhapatnam (1.33 million tonnes), Mangalore (1.50 million tonnes) and Padur (2.5 million tonnes) through a Special Purpose Vehicle, namely, Indian Strategic Petroleum Reserve Ltd. (ISPRL). The storage would be further upgraded at other suitable locations by an incremental capacity of 12.5 million tonnes during the Twelfth Plan period.

Promoting Bio-Fuels

14.160. A programme of 5 per cent blending of ethanol with petrol is already underway with effect from November 2006 targeting 20 States and 4 UTs. Subject to availability, the percentage of blend can be enhanced to 10 per cent as specification for petrol with 10 per cent ethanol blend is already given by the BIS. At present, the EBP Programme is successfully running in 14 States and three UTs; OMCs have been able to contract 55.87 crore litres of ethanol against the requirement of 105 crore litres of ethanol for 5 per cent blending in the entire notified area.

Pricing of Petroleum Products

14.161. In 2002, the Government dismantled the Administered Pricing Mechanism, and announced that prices of all petroleum products would be deregulated. This decision, however, was not fully implemented after the prices of crude oil in international market rose sharply leading to increase in international prices of petrol, diesel, LPG and kerosene.

On 25 June 2010 the Government announced that the price of petrol was fully deregulated and the oil companies were free to fix it periodically. However, diesel price deregulation was deferred to be implemented later. Prices of LPG and kerosene remained under price regulation by the Government. The continuance of price control reflects the political sensitivity of the issue despite the evident economic desirability of implementing the Integrated Energy Policy.

14.162. The under-recovery by oil companies because of the inability to adjust oil prices is shown in Table 14.34. The amount of under-recoveries on sensitive petroleum products was ₹1,38,541 crores (excluding the under-recoveries of ₹4,890 crores incurred by OMCs on sale of petrol) in the year 2011–12 including the under-recoveries incurred by OMCs on petrol. The total under-recoveries by the Government and oil PSUs amount to ₹4,43,197 crore during the Eleventh Plan period. That has seriously affected the profitability and viability of the oil marketing companies. The under-recoveries of the oil companies in 2012–13 will rise to ₹1,52,937 crore as per Refinery Gate price effective from 1 July 2012 if prices are not adjusted.

Pricing of Natural Gas

14.163. Gas price for NELP Blocks is supposed to be determined through an arm's length process by contractor, and is subject to approval by the Government. Accordingly the price of RIL KG Basin gas was fixed at $4.2/MMBTU ex-Kakinada in 2007 by EGoM and the price was expected to be valid till March 2014. The purchase price of long-term LNG imported from Qatar for Petronet LNG has been linked to Japanese Crude Cocktail (JCC) and varies on a monthly basis. It is sold at prices fixed by resellers. Spot RLNG prices are based on market conditions, which are currently hovering around US$12–13/MMBTU. Following the fixation of the KG basin gas price at US$4.2 per MMBTU, the administered price of gas from nominated fields awarded earlier to ONGC/OIL, which varied depending on the field, were raised to US$4.2 per MMBTU, except for the North-East where it is US$2.52 per MMBTU.

14.164. The NELP of the Government of India provides freedom to price the gas by the operator at a market-determined price for gas produced from the NELP blocks, subject to the Government approving the pricing formula. However, questions have arisen regarding the interpretation of various clauses in the existing contracts. There is a need to review the provision of pricing under PSC to clarify the extent to which producers will have the freedom to market the gas. Clarity is obviously essential if we are to attract private investment into exploration and production. Legally, gas as a resource belongs to the Government and the Government has the right to fix an appropriate price. However, if the intention is to attract private investment into this sector, the Government should state clearly what degree of pricing freedom will be given. Ideally, private investors would expect freedom to price the gas at a level at which there are willing buyers, which in turn will be determined by the price at which consumers can import. On the other hand, the CBM policy envisages a different contractual regime. In order to encourage this

TABLE 14.34
Under-Recoveries on Petroleum Products

(₹ crores)

Petroleum Products	2006–07	2007–08	2008–09	2009–10	2010–11	2011–12
Petrol	2,027	7,332	5,181	5,151	2,227	–
Diesel	18,776	35,166	52,286	9,279	34,706	81,192
Domestic LPG	10,701	15,523	17,600	14,257	21,772	29,997
PDS Kerosene	17,883	19,102	28,225	17,364	19,484	27,352
Total	49,387	77,123	1,03,292	46,051	78,190	1,38,541

Source: PPAC.

emerging source of gas, its pricing should be left to the market without the need for Government approval.

14.165. There are a number of other issues regarding existing PSC. First, questions have been raised regarding investment multiple which determines the profit share of Government and the investor after allowing recovery of investment cost. It has been argued that this incentivises greater capital intensiveness, and a stronger profit share based on production would be better. This assessment needs to be weighed against the argument that the IM enables Government to insulate the contractor at higher levels of investment, which increases the possibility of oil/gas being discovered. There are also concerns on the need to improve the provisions under the PSC to make them more transparent and also fully safeguard the interests of the stakeholders. Second, the existing management system has not led to an effective supervision over the projects. There is a need to consider alternate mechanisms. Several other issues have been raised also. Government has, therefore, appointed a Committee under the chairmanship of Dr. C. Rangarajan, Chairman, Economic Advisory Council to the Prime Minister to review existing PSCs and recommend changes for the future.

14.166. Finally, the Twelfth Plan is likely to see a continuation of high oil and gas prices in the world markets and our dependence on imports for both oil and gas is also likely to increase. There is an urgent need to align domestic oil and gas price to market price for sound development of the sector and to send the right signals to consumers and producers. This would also enable the oil PSUs to generate internal resources to fund new projects and create growth momentum. Price reform along these lines would also permit entry of private companies for marketing of petroleum products which would help expand competition. Price adjustment in the petroleum sector has to be carried out keeping in mind the need for ensuring affordability for the poor and vulnerable sections. This can be done in various ways. It does not require generalised subsidies.

TWELFTH PLAN STRATEGY

Demand of Petroleum Products

14.167. Demand of petroleum products is projected to increase at an annual rate of 4.7 per cent during the Twelfth Five Year Plan. This will increase consumption of POL products from 147.98 MMT in 2011–12 to 186.21 MMT by 2016–17. The demand for diesel will continue to be dominant followed by MS and LPG. The demand estimates of petroleum products in Twelfth Plan period are given in Table 14.35.

Supply of Petroleum Products

14.168. Oil production during Twelfth Plan is likely to increase marginally and then decline by 3.26 per cent by the end of the Plan. As a result, import dependence in petroleum products is expected to increase from 76.6 per cent at the end of the Eleventh Plan to 77.8 per cent by the end of the Twelfth Plan. The crude oil production profile for the Twelfth Plan, based on established reserves, present status of different fields, input implementation schedules and the health of reservoirs is as given in Table 14.36.

Natural Gas Demand

14.169. The demand of natural gas during the Twelfth Plan is likely to grow by about 19.2 per cent to meet the incremental requirement of power, fertiliser and other industries. The CNG and city gas sector will also see a quantum growth in natural gas use. It is expected that by the end of the Twelfth Plan about 300 cities are likely to be covered under city gas distribution. Yearly estimates of natural gas demand are given in Table 14.37.

Natural Gas Production

14.170. Domestic production of natural gas during the Twelfth Plan will depend upon the output from gas fields discovered under NELP by various operators. As majority of new gas prospects are in deep water, the investments, technology and pricing of gas for developing these fields would be important. The estimated gas production by different operators has been given in Table 14.38. However, the projected production from Private/JV producers may need to be reviewed during the Plan period, as

TABLE 14.35
Demand of Petroleum Products

Products	2011–12	2012–13	2013–14	2014–15	2015–16	2016–17	CAGR (%)
1. Petroleum Products ('000MT)							
LPG	15,358	16,986	18,363	19,675	20,857	21,831	7.3
MS	14,993	16,091	17,527	19,083	20,766	22,588	8.5
NAPHTHA/NGL	11,105	12,353	11,417	11,417	11,022	11,022	−0.1
ATF	5,536	6,009	6,587	7,202	7,849	8,540	9.1
SKO	8,229	7,949	7,631	7,326	7,033	6,751	−3.9
HSDO	64,742	65,040	68,654	72,589	76,904	81,599	4.7
LDO	415	400	400	400	400	400	−0.7
LUBES	2,745	2,691	2,772	2,857	2,945	3,036	2.0
FO/LSHS	9,232	7,954	7,902	7,899	7,872	7,872	−3.1
BITUMEN	4,628	5,254	5,541	5,732	5,971	6,114	5.7
PET COKE	6,145	6,765	7,514	8,345	9,268	10,294	10.9
OTHERS	4,869	5,445	6,127	6,109	6,085	6,162	4.8
Total POL	1,47,997	1,52,937	1,60,436	1,68,635	1,76,972	1,86,209	4.7

Source: Ministry of Petroleum and Natural Gas.

TABLE 14.36
Projection of Crude Oil Production in the Twelfth Plan

(in MMTPA)

	2012–13	2013–14	2014–15	2015–16	2016–17	Total
ONGC	25.045	28.27	28.002	26.286	25.456	133.059
OIL	3.92	4.00	4.06	4.16	4.20	20.34
Pvt./JV	13.34	13.30	12.70	12.10	11.50	62.94
Total	42.305	45.57	44.762	42.546	41.156	216.339

Source: Ministry of Petroleum and Natural Gas.

TABLE 14.37
Natural Gas Demand for Twelfth Five Year Plan

(in MMSCMD)

Sector	2011–12	2012–13	2013–14	2014–15	2015–16	2016–17	CAGR (%)
Power*	91	135	153	171	189	207	17.9
Fertiliser**	43	55	61	106	106	106	19.8
Demand(Price Elastic) – Sub Total	134	190	214	277	295	313	18.5
City Gas	13	15	19	24	39	46	28.8
Industrial	16	20	20	22	25	27	11.0
Petrochemicals / Refineries/Internal Consumption	25	54	61	67	72	72	23.6
Sponge Iron/Steel	6	7	8	8	8	8	5.9
Demand (Relatively price Inelastic) – Sub Total	60	96	108	121	144	153	20.6
Grand Total Demand	194	286	322	398	439	466	19.2

Source: *Ministry of Power, **Ministry of Fertilizers.

TABLE 14.38
Projection of Natural gas production in Twelfth Plan (BCM)

	2012–13	2013–14	2014–15	2015–16	2016–17	Total
ONGC	25.266	25.472	26.669	28.215	38.676	144.298
OIL	3.30	3.80	4.00	4.27	4.45	19.82
Pvt./JV	23.71	32.38	39.4	40.43	41.46	177.38
Total	52.276	61.652	70.069	72.915	84.586	341.498
Total MMSCMD	143.22	168.91	191.97	199.77	231.74	187.12 (Average)

Source: Ministry of Petroleum and Natural Gas.

the production profile from their exploration acreage gets approved by the Directorate General of Hydrocarbons.

Exploration Activities

14.171. During the Twelfth Plan period, 13,8974 kilometres of 2D seismic and 82,488 square km of 3D seismic are likely to be acquired by ONGC, OIL and private/JV companies. Also, 1,310 exploratory wells are likely to be drilled during the Twelfth Plan period. These exploratory efforts are likely to result in hydrocarbon reserve accretion of about 727 million metric tonnes of oil and oil equivalent gas in the country. The break-up of exploration programme by ONGC, OIL and Private/Joint Venture companies is given in Table 14.39. The role of DGH as the upstream advisor and supervisor for the Government is very important. Efforts will be made to increase the capacity of the DGH, as also efficiency in decision-making. It can play an important role in obtaining various clearances for the upstream operators from multiple agencies of the Government. This has to be viewed particularly in the light of the fact that a large number of discoveries made under NELP are yet to be appraised and developed. The DGH needs to monitor their evaluation and development quickly.

Pricing and Under Recoveries of Petroleum Products

14.172. Although important steps have been taken in the first year of the Twelfth Plan to adjust diesel prices and to cap the subsidy on LPG, this has not eliminated the under-recovery of oil companies. The increase in under-recoveries of OMCs is adversely affecting the financial position of OMCs and may affect mobilisation of funds for new projects during the Twelfth Plan period. Currently, the under-recoveries of OMCs are compensated by the Government from fiscal budget, discount on crude and products by upstream oil companies and part absorption by OMCs. The OMCs are expected to incur under-recoveries of ₹8,32,737 crore during Twelfth Plan period. If no further adjustment occurs, and if global prices stay at present level, the total under-recovery in the Twelfth Plan period will be over ₹8.32 lakh crore which is simply not viable (Table 14.40)

TABLE 14.39
Breakup of the Exploration Programme for the Twelfth Plan

Activity	Unit	ONGC	OIL	Private/JV	Total
Seismic Surveys 2D	km	28,170	6,850	1,03,954	1,38,974
Seismic Surveys 3D	Sq Km	24,163	8,364	49,961	82,488
Exploratory Wells	Nos	611	174	525	1,310
Reserves Accretion IIH	MMTOE	1,080	78.14	728	1,886.14
Ultimate Hydrocarbon Reserve Accretion	MMTOE	360	26	341	727

Source: Ministry of Petroleum and Natural Gas.

TABLE 14.40
Likely Under-Recoveries on Petroleum* Products

(₹ Crore)

Sensitive Petroleum Products	2012–13	2013–14	2014–15	2015–16	2016–17	Total
Diesel	86,910	90,820	95,053	99,673	1,04,664	4,77,120
PDS Kerosene	28,880	27,725	26,617	25,552	24,528	1,33,301
Domestic LPG	38,182	42,054	44,931	47,531	49,618	2,22,316
Total	1,53,973	1,60,598	1,66,601	1,72,756	1,78,810	8,32,737

* Price of Petrol is made market determined. It assumes oil prices at US$ 100 per barrel with exchange rate of US$ = ₹55.

Addition to Refining Capacity

14.173. With grass-roots refineries at Bhatinda (9 MMTPA), Paradip (15 MMTPA) and expansion of some of the existing refineries, the total refining capacity is projected to be around 218.37 MMTPA by the year 2012–13 and is expected to touch 313.57 MMTPA by the end of the Twelfth Plan as shown in Table 14.41. Majority of new refining capacity would be added from expansion of existing refineries at low costs.

Alternate Sources of Hydrocarbons

14.174. The development of alternate sources of hydrocarbons such as coal bed methane, gas hydrate, shale gas, oil shale and so on are some of the areas which require greater attention. Oil companies would also need to focus on development of renewable energy sources including biodiesel, ethanol, wind, solar, biomass and so on to make the hydrocarbon use for various activities carbon neutral by the companies.

TABLE 14.41
Projected Refining Capacity during Twelfth Plan (MMTPA)

	2012–13	2013–14	2014–15	2015–16	2016–17
IOC	54.2	69.2	69.2	74.0	77.0
BPC (Mumbai)	12.0	12.0	13.5	13.5	13.5
Kochi	9.5	9.5	9.5	15.5	15.5
BORL–Bina	6.0	6.0	7.2	7.2	9.0
HPC (MR + VR)	16.5	17.2	17.2	17.2	23.2
Maharashtra Refinery	0.0	0.0	0.0	0.0	9.0
HMEL (GGSRL)	9	9	9	9	9
MRPL	15	15.5	16	16.5	18
ONGC (Tatipaka)	0.066	0.066	0.066	0.066	0.066
CPCL	12.1	12.1	12.1	12.1	18.3
NRL	3	3	3	3	8
Sub Total PSU	137.4	153.6	156.8	168.1	200.6
RIL-DTA and SEZ, Jamnagar	60	60	60	60	60
EOL, Jamnagar	19	20	20	30.8	38
NOCL, Cuddalore	2	6	6	6.1	15
Sub Total Private	81	86	86	96.9	113
Total	218.4	239.6	242.8	265.0	313.6

Source: Ministry of Petroleum and Natural Gas.

Coal Bed Methane (CBM)

14.175. The prognosticated CBM resources in the country are about 92 trillion cubic feet (TCF), out of which only 8.92 TCF has so far been established. The Government of India has awarded 33 CBM exploration blocks. Commercial production of CBM has already commenced in Raniganj (South) in West Bengal. CBM production by the year 2016–17 is expected to be around 4 MMSCMD. This is quite low compared with the resource potential estimated by the DGH. In spite of the fact that more than a decade has lapsed since the award of CBM blocks, the evaluation and development continues to be behind schedule. Efforts are required to enhance the production of CBM through suitable policy measures. There are also delays in approving prices for CBM projects shortly to go into production. This needs to be expedited.

Simultaneous Operations of Coal Bed Methane (CBM) and Oil and Gas

14.176. At present there is no mechanism to work together simultaneously for the exploration and exploitation of coal, coal bed methane, shale gas and oil and gas production in same block/ acreages due to the fact that both coal and oil and gas sectors are governed by different administrative ministries. Regulations and Acts do create conflict of interest for the simultaneous exploration and exploitation of coal, CBM, coal mine methane and also underground Coal gasification along with coal and oil and gas. There is a need for the operators to work under similar contractual regime for simultaneous operations of CBM, Coal and shale gas and CBM, oil and gas and shale gas in the same area. A policy framework for this will need to be developed expeditiously in the year 2012–13 itself.

Shale Gas Exploration

14.177. The Government has initiated steps for development of shale oil and shale gas from on land sedimentary basins. MoU has been signed between Ministry of Petroleum and Natural Gas and Department of State, USA on 6 December 2010 for cooperation in resource assessment, regulatory framework, training and so on. A multi-organisation team (MOT) has been constituted involving DGH, ONGC, OIL and GAIL for collection of required G&G, geochemical and petro-physical data for assessment of shale oil and shale gas prospects in Indian on land sedimentary basins. The involvement of private sector in this initiative will be enhanced as well. A policy of regulatory framework is to be put in place for shale oil and shale gas development.

Underground Coal Gasification (UCG)

14.178. ONGC has signed an Agreement of Collaboration (AOC) with Skochinsky Institute of Mining, Russia on 25 November 2004 for implementation of Underground Coal Gasification (UCG) project in India. The Vastan Mine block belonging to GIPCL in Surat district, Gujarat has been selected for UCG Pilot project. The total financial implication of the project is about US$ 15.32 million. ONGC will be asked to complete this pilot at the earliest.

National Gas Hydrate Programme

14.179. An MoU was recently signed in the area of marine gas hydrate research and technology development between the Leibniz Institute of Marine Sciences, Germany and DGH for research on methane production from gas hydrate by carbon dioxide sequestration. The NGHP programme has also been going on for a long time, with no tangible results so far. Efforts will be made for better monitoring and conclusion of this programme at the earliest.

Flaring of Natural Gas

14.180. Currently about 3 per cent of gas produced is flared by the ONGC and Oil India Limited. The total volume of gas flared is estimated to be around 3.5–4.0 MMSCMD. There is a need to stop such flaring through use of this gas by the local industry and/or gathering it either through compression or by liquefaction mode and then re-injecting the gas into pipeline. A separate mechanism to reach a zero flaring of gas and its commercialisation can be developed to stop such wasteful flaring of gas.

Focus on Research and Development

14.181. The need to develop domestic capability in the exploration, production, refining and processing of oil and natural gas has led to the creation of R&D

institutes by oil sector organisations. While in-house institutions can make a significant contribution to the activities of their parent PSUs, they are not subjected to any peer review. They have also been unable to attract private sector business and have remained dependent on captive assignments. On the other hand, the existence of in-house institutions has restrained the PSUs from outsourcing their assignments to outside institutions/niche area experts. The objective should be to ensure that R&D centres of the oil sector PSUs develop into world class institutions, with induction of fresh capital and top scientific personnel.

14.182. Efforts will be intensified to obtain the latest technology from global centres of excellence while at the same time strengthening our own capability. Several alliances were signed with international organisations and Governments during the Tenth and the Eleventh Plan periods. Diplomatic efforts were also made through JWGs and other forms of MEA assistance to increase interaction between Indian and foreign experts. These efforts will be renewed, and fresh initiatives taken. Some of the key areas for R&D development to strengthen domestic capability are in exploration, geo-data processing and interpretation, drilling technology, reservoir studies, ocean technology, oil and gas production technology, well logging technology, biotechnology and geotectonic, quality improvements of the products, improving energy efficiencies of various processes, and yield maximisation of distillation. The experience of Brazil in having developed scientific and technical know-how as well as manpower domestically, tailor-made to suit their geological requirements is a good example to follow.

14.183. Various oil and gas sector organisations plan to invest ₹6,326 crore during the Twelfth Plan period as R&D of oil and gas sector activities as indicated in Table 14.42. Some of the focus areas in oil and gas sector are:

1. Producing waxy crude
2. Smart horizontal well completions
3. 4D Seismic mapping
4. Long heated insulated pipeline for crude evacuation
5. Improving energy efficiency in refineries
6. Product yield maximisation
7. Exploration of unconventional energy resources, viz. shale gas, CBM, UCG and so on
8. Oil shale and study of gas hydrates in eastern and western offshore areas of India

TABLE 14.42
R&D Expenditure by Major Oil and Gas Companies

Company	2009–10 (Actual)		Eleventh Plan (Actual)	Twelfth Plan (Estimated)
	Expenditure ₹ crore	per cent of R&D expenditure/Revenues	Expenditure ₹ crore	Expenditure ₹ crore
Indian Oil	89.65	0.04	317.83	955
BPCL	26	0.02	155.38	429
HPCL	2.1	0	24.5	315
CPCL	0.3	0	7.4	14
RIL	41	0.02	1,640	2,000
EOL	–		12	25
ONGC	219.95	0.34	1,289.32	2,156
OIL	22.49	0.27	108.63	257
GAIL	16.17	0.06	17.23	71
EIL	11	0.54	46	104
Total	428.66	0.06	3,618.29	6,326

Source: Ministry of Petroleum and Natural Gas.

Infrastructure and Capacity Building

- The unlicensed offshore areas and Deccan basins are technologically challenging due to higher water depths and sub-basalt sediments, respectively. It is important to access latest technology from global centres of excellence to address the specific needs of these balance areas. The Government would endeavour to encourage technology alliances with our upstream companies, and also attract service industries to set up base in India.
- Strengthen and empower technical and scientific manpower for better decision-making and capacity-building in oil sector specifically the E&P companies. Deployment of large qualified workforce will be necessary during the Twelfth Plan for exploration and production sector.
- Both ONGC and OIL would step up efforts, to raise oil and gas production from the near stagnant levels of the past one decade or so. These companies ought to enhance production by reducing their R/P ratios. They would also be encouraged to quickly appraise their entire licensed areas to enhance reserves. In the offshore nominated areas, technology is likely to play an important role. The Government would also encourage them to induct cutting-edge technology in these acreages, often available only as in-house with global players, on risk–reward basis.
- The Integrated Energy Policy had laid down that there is a need for an independent upstream regulator. The Government needs to distance itself from routine contract administration, as well as capex/pricing decisions. As long as the Government itself is the upstream regulator, the reasoning that the DGH provides it technical advice does not lend it independence. Audit issues and contractor–Government conflicts may get much reduced if an independent regulator were to be put in place. Further, in order to make marginal offshore oil and gas discoveries viable, offshore infrastructure needs to be shared between operators. The DGH would issue regulations to encourage operators to collaborate on mutually beneficial terms.
- Development of strategic and commercial gas storages by the E&P and marketing companies to address price volatility, balancing of seasonal gas requirement by various sectors at different locations in the country.
- Development of strategic crude oil storage beyond 5 MMTPA capacity. The Government would be open to private sector involvement in building and operating strategic storage, on the condition of the crude being available for release, at its discretion.
- Strategy for refining capacity additions considering current market situation
- Marketing and distribution infrastructure facilities for the petroleum products
- Additional development of new LNG import and regasification capacity both on the East and the West coasts of India.
- Gas Pipeline transportation infrastructure both on the East and the West coasts and also in southern and northern parts of the country for supply of gas throughout the country.
- Facilitating development of city gas distribution in about 300 identified cities in the country.
- Improving efficiency of operations of various oil and gas sector installations. Benchmarks for refineries, pipelines process plants, buildings and any other installations to be developed by all the organisations and to be monitored periodically.
- Develop capacity building for 5 MMTOE per year of energy from renewables and unconventional hydrocarbon resources. This is with an aim to become carbon neutral for oil sector companies.
- Developing LNG import capacity based on Floating Storage and Regasification units (FSRU) in coastal cities of the country which are not connected to gas pipelines to expedite the city gas supply.
- Deploy the CSR resources for creating health and education infrastructure. Help communities in creating opportunities for clean and sustainable energy supplies for cooking and lighting for better quality of life in areas of operations from CSR funds.

Reforms Required in the Oil and Gas Sector

14.184. Given the challenges in managing the oil and gas sector, it is necessary to focus on the agenda of critical reforms needed in this sector in the Twelfth Plan period. They are listed below:

- Eliminate the uncertainty that has arisen regarding gas pricing from NELP production sharing contracts by implementing a new design of contracts. The recommendations of the Rangarajan Committee may be an important input in finalising this policy. Appropriate steps should be taken to resolve conflicts in existing contracts where interpretation of the contract terms is open to multiple options.
- Operationalise a road map to move petroleum product prices received by marketing companies to prices aligned with global prices. This may not be possible immediately, but it can be achieved by the end of the Twelfth Plan for diesel and petrol.
- Phasing out subsidies on domestic LPG and PDS kerosene. Subsidised LPG is now capped at nine cylinders per household with the rest being available at market price. Consideration should be given to converting the subsidised supply to an equivalent cash transfer targeted to those who need it.
- Kerosene supplies can be progressively reduced considering improved electricity access provided under RGGVY and LPG connections provided in rural areas.
- Rationalise tax structure in sales of petroleum products considering thermal value for its use in transport, industry, power, households and other sectors. Unified State taxes and removal of tax anomalies for efficient use of petroleum products.
- Incentivise exploration and production of domestic non-conventional fuels like shale gas, CBM, coal mine methane, underground coal gasification and so on.
- Promote development and production of bio-fuels by the oil sector E&P and marketing companies at commercial level. Appropriate policy and integration issues facilitating bio-fuels development be provided by both the State and the Central Governments.
- Expand exploration and production of domestic oil and gas sources for which quick decision-making for awarding and development of NELP blocks is necessary.
- In order to attract efficient E&P companies globally to bid for our acreages, it is vital to provide seismic and other technical data of the acreages on offer. It is proposed that the entire unlicensed sedimentary area be surveyed, so that 100 per cent exploration coverage may be achieved during the Plan period.
- NELP was launched as a stopgap arrangement until a National Data Repository was ready to facilitate an all-year round acreage award policy. The Government will introduce an Open Acreage Licensing Policy so that the target of full exploration coverage by the end of Plan period may be achieved.
- Provide 'Declared Goods Status' for natural gas/LNG so that it is available at uniform price in most of the States.
- Natural gas prices charged to producers must also be determined by market forces. There is a need for clarity on fiscal incentives on exploration of natural gas under NELP. The concept of uniform gas price across consuming sectors also needs to be examined afresh as the desire to keep prices low for certain sectors tends to distort pricing; it is inconsistent with the principle that the price of gas will be determined by market forces.
- Develop a policy framework to exploit shale gas. It is proposed that a new policy for exploration and production of shale gas be launched, and acreage be speedily awarded during the Plan period.
- Coal mining leases acreages often have methane or even oil/gas deposits. Similarly, oil and gas lease/PSC acreages have the possibility of coal/methane production. The Government should put in place a policy for simultaneous exploitation of CBM, coal, coal mine methane, oil and gas in a unified manner wherever such resources are available.
- Acquisition of equity oil and gas abroad including conventional and shale gas assets.
- Contracting LNG imports both on long- and short-term basis considering market price affordability.

3.5. NEW AND RENEWABLE ENERGY

14.185. The need to increase total domestic energy production in order to reduce import dependence, combined with the need to move away from fossil fuels in the longer run in view of climate change considerations, points to the need for stronger efforts to increase the supply of energy from renewables.

All over the world, investment in renewable power sources has been increasing. India has been a late entrant into the field of renewable energy, but it is beginning to make rapid strides in this sector with an annual growth rate of 33 per cent in 2010 against the global growth rate of 26 per cent during the same period. It must be emphasised however that these increases are from a very low base since renewables at present account for about 1 per cent of the total commercial energy used. Nevertheless, it is important to make a start and to gain significant experience in this important sector keeping in mind its potential over the longer term.

14.186. An important limitation on the extent to which we can shift to renewables is the high unit cost at present, compared with other conventional sources. However, unit costs of renewable energy, especially solar energy, are coming down and the marginal cost of conventional energy based on fossil fuels is likely to remain high and rise. These trends suggest that over the next 7 years the unit cost of energy from renewable sources such as wind and solar may come close to the unsubsidised cost of conventional energy. Since India has a large potential of both wind and solar energy, the exploitation of this potential should form an important part of our long-term energy strategy.

14.187. The potential for renewable power has been revised upward over time. In the early 80s, India was estimated to have renewable energy potential of about 85 GW from commercially exploitable sources, viz. (*i*) Wind: 50 GW (at 50 m mast height) (*ii*) Small Hydro:15 GW (*iii*) Bio-energy: 20 GW and (*iv*) solar radiation sufficient to generate 50 MW/sq. km using solar photovoltaic and solar thermal energy. These estimates have since been revised to reflect technological advancements. Initial estimates from Centre for Wind Energy Technology (C-WET) suggest that wind energy potential at 80 metres height (with 2 per cent land availability) would be over 100 GW. Some studies have estimated even higher potential ranges up to 300 GW. The MNRE has initiated an exercise for realistic reassessment of the wind power potential, whose results are expected by the end of 2013.

14.188. Some of the key issues facing renewable power generations are:

1. **Regional Concentration of Renewable Energy Potential:** Because renewable energy

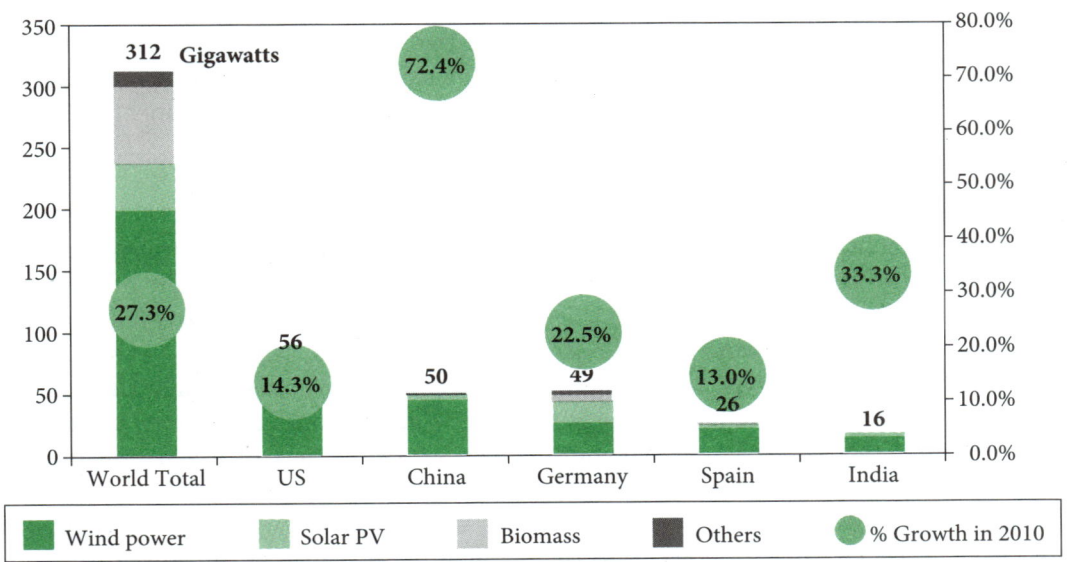

* Excludes Hydro.
Source: REN21, Global Status Report, 2011.

FIGURE 14.2: Renewable Power Capacities, Top Five Countries, 2010

is location-specific and not evenly distributed there are problems on scaling up grid connected renewable power. For instance, wind potential is mainly confined to the wind resource rich States of Tamil Nadu, Maharashtra, Gujarat, Karnataka, Rajasthan, Andhra Pradesh and Madhya Pradesh. The States of Gujarat and Rajasthan have excellent solar radiation and the other suitable states for solar power are Andhra Pradesh, Tamil Nadu, Karnataka, Madhya Pradesh, Maharashtra, Orissa and so on. Similarly, small hydro power potential is mainly available with the Himalayan States and north-eastern States. The intermittent nature of Solar and Wind Power in the absence of an adequate balancing mechanism limits the flexibility of the State grid to absorb this power.

2. **Insufficiency and High Cost of Evacuation Infrastructure:** Utilisation of variable renewable energy requires a robust transmission infrastructure from remotely located generating plants to the load centres. Further, combining geographically dispersed renewable energy sources to reduce variability requires much larger, smarter and upgraded transmission network. A recent study conducted by the Power Grid Corporation Ltd. has identified the requirement for strengthening of both intra-state and interstate transmission system for facilitating transfer of renewable energy from renewable-energy–rich potential States to other States as well as for absorption within the host States. The study has estimated that for capacity addition plans for the Twelfth Five Year Plan period, an investment of around ₹30,000 crore would be required for creating renewable power transmission infrastructure.

3. **Regulatory Issues**: Renewable power, especially solar, is significantly costlier than conventional power, thus making its adoption by the cash-starved utilities difficult unless it is incentivised through Renewable Purchase Obligation (RPO) and introduction of Renewable Energy Certificate (REC). This would enable States to procure a fixed percentage of their power portfolio from renewable power.

4. **Financial Barriers**: Renewable energy technologies require large initial capital investments, making the levelised cost of generation higher than it is for many conventional sources. These technologies need to be supported until technology breakthroughs and market volumes generated are able to bring the tariff down at the grid parity level. Moreover, high technology and project risks perceived by financers for renewable projects make access to low-cost and long-term funding difficult. Thus, there is a need to generate instruments for low-cost and long-term financing of such projects from both domestic as well as overseas resources and also banks to adopt separate exposure limits for renewable energy sector.

5. **Low Penetration of Renewables for Urban and Industrial Applications**: Solar applications for heating water in urban, industrial and commercial applications is one of the most mature and viable renewable energy technologies available worldwide. Better market penetration of such technologies can lead to better demand side management for commercial as well as household usage. With already matured technology and rapidly growing industry, solar water heater installations have witnessed a massive growth throughout the world but the installations in India have remained low on account of poor adoption due to high upfront cost and poor quality standards of collectors. Moreover, the binding regulation in building codes that encourage adoption of such technologies are seldom implemented and only few States have such regulations.

REVIEW OF ELEVENTH PLAN

14.189. Progress in grid interactive renewable power generation capacity, especially of wind-based power was broadly in line with the targets of the Eleventh Plan. However, actual renewable energy generation has been substantially lower. Wind-based power generation has suffered the most partly also because of the lack of evacuation infrastructure in the resource rich States and partly because of lack of enforcing mechanisms and incentives for operational performance of the wind turbines. Incentives such as Accelerated Depreciation have not yielded the desired results and the recommendation now is to enforce generation-based incentive. Achievement

TABLE 14.43
Eleventh Plan Power Capacity Addition through Grid Interactive Renewable Power

Source	Target (MW)	Actual (MW) as on 31st March '2012
Wind	9,000	10,260.00
Small Hydro	1,400	1,419.17
Biomass Power	500	626.00
Waste to Energy	80	46.20
Bagasse Cogeneration	1,200	1,369.70
Solar Power	50	939.74
Total	12,230	14,660.81

Source: MNRE, GoI.

in capacity addition has been satisfactory for most sectors except in waste to power. The details of targets and achievements during the Eleventh Plan for grid interactive renewable power have been given in Table 14.43.

14.190. Solar and wind sectors have been facing following key challenges:

1. Globally, development of storage technologies has not been in line with the technology developments in wind and solar, due to which capacity utilisation of grid connected solar and wind has been relatively poor.

2. Though most of the States have come up with the RPO obligation, proper enforcement and monitoring is an issue.

14.191. Although private investments in wind power have increased, technological improvements and economies of scale have not reduced the costs in the industry. On the contrary, the cost per MW of wind power has increased from ₹4.3 crore/MW in FY 2003–04 to ₹5.7 crore/MW in FY 2010–11 (Figure 14.3). Rising land acquisition costs and turnkey project approach has resulted in the increase of project cost. Small hydro power, in spite of using mature and indigenous technology, has witnessed

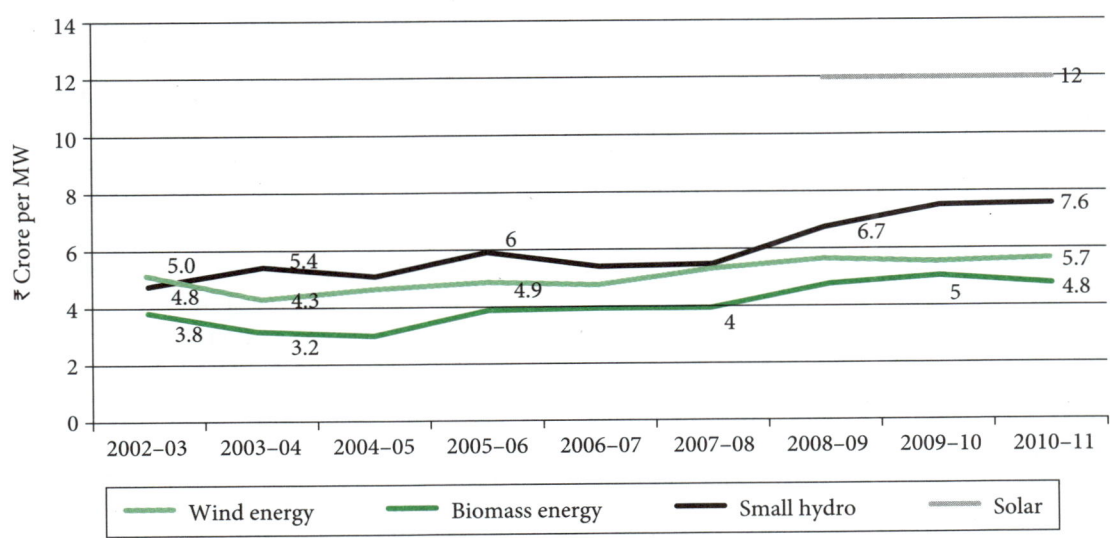

Source: MNRE.

FIGURE 14.3: Cost of Renewable Energy Technologies Per MW

the same trend partly because of the rise in land costs and partly because of costs associated with delays for obtaining clearances for the sites where project development is difficult.

14.192. The cost of renewable power as against various sources of renewable energy is given in Table 14.44. The cost of wind power is already quite competitive. Solar power is much more expensive but costs are coming down. At the time of selection of the first batch in the Jawaharlal Nehru National Solar Mission (JNNUSM) the tariff for solar P.V. was ₹17.91 per Kwh and for solar thermal it was ₹15.31 per unit. In Batch II the tariff has come down to ₹8.77 per unit for solar P.V. Thus, although renewable power sources are significantly costlier than conventional power, the costs are clearly declining and over the next 5–10 years renewable energy may well be fully in line with the cost of new electricity capacity based on conventional energy sources if no subsidy is involved.

TABLE 14.44
Cost of Power for Various Renewable Energy Sources

Source	Estimated initial capital cost (₹ in crore/MW)	Estimated cost of electricity generation (Financial) (₹/kWh)
Small Hydro Power	5.50–7.70	3.54–4.88
Wind Power	5.75	3.73–5.96
Biomass Power	4.0–4.45	5.12–5.83
Bagasse Cogeneration	4.20	4.61–5.73
Solar Power	10.00–13.00	10.39–12.46

Source: CERC (Terms and Conditions for Tariff Determination from Renewable Energy Sources) Regulations, 2012 dated 27 March 2012.

Off-Grid Renewable Power

14.193. Off-grid renewable sector has the advantage that it is potentially much more competitive with conventional power because it avoids the investment in transmission to remote locations. Off-grid renewable power has made progress during the Eleventh Plan, but lack of scalable business models and non-availability of institutional finances have stalled the pace of its progress. Policy interventions are required to incentivise creation of financeable business models like rice husk gasifiers based electricity generation. The issue of unwillingness of public sector banks to finance small scale off grid renewable based business models need to be addressed. The detailed overview of targets and achievements for the Eleventh Plan for off-grid renewable power has been given in Table 14.45.

TABLE 14.45
Power Capacity Addition through Off Grid Renewable Power

Source	Target (MW)	Actual (MW)
Waste to Power (Urban + Industrial)	58.00	85.15
Non-bag Cogen	255.00	336.59
Gasifiers	67.00	63.23
Acro-Gens/Hybrid Systems	1.75	1.14
SPV Systems	20	46.64
Total	401.75	532.75

Source: MNRE.

14.194. Progress of the scheme for electrification of remote villages/hamlets through renewable generation has not been satisfactory. Only 57 per cent of the targeted villages have been electrified so far. Initially no target was fixed for the grid solar photovoltaic system during the Eleventh Plan. Under National Action Plan on Climate Change, Jawaharlal Nehru National Solar Mission was launched which aims to install 20GW solar power, 2 GW of off-grid Solar, 20 million sq. metre of solar thermal collector area and 20 million rural households to have solar lighting by 2022. Under off grid solar application scheme of Jawaharlal Nehru National solar Mission, a total target of 100 MW of solar photovoltaic system and power plants for sanctioning was fixed for 2010–11 and 2011–12. Against this the ministry sanctioned projects aggregating to 118.07 MWp. During the Eleventh Plan SPV systems of standalone power projects aggregating to 46.64 MWp capacity were installed against a target of 20 MWp.

14.195. Another thrust area for the Eleventh Plan was 'optimizing energy plantations by raising plants on degraded forest and community land'. A detailed analysis for availability of wasteland in India was carried out based on the information available. IISc,

TABLE 14.46
Eleventh Plan Financial Allocations and Expenditure: MNRE

(₹ in crores)

Programme Component	BE	Expenditure
Grid-connected and Distributed Renewable Power	1,779	1,839.82
Renewable Energy for Rural Applications	910	910.95
Renewable Energy for Urban, Industrial and Commercial Applications	216	147.28
Research, Design and Development in Renewable Energy	481	340.33
Supporting Programmes	682	559.98
Total	4,068	3,798.36

Bangalore has estimated the waste land available in the country. Suitability of those areas for high yielding plantation and for Juliflora plantation has been estimated but policy models along with implementation guidelines to promote energy plantations have to be worked out.

14.196. The approved outlay for the Eleventh Plan for New and Renewable Energy programmes was ₹10,598.31 crore comprising of GBS of ₹4,068 crore and ₹6,530.13 crore of IEBR. The likely expenditure at the end of Eleventh Plan is ₹3,798.36 crore (Table 14.46).

TWELFTH PLAN STRATEGY

14.197. Renewable energy has to play an expanding role in achieving energy security and access in the years ahead. The areas on which attention should be focussed during the Twelfth Plan are:

- Grid interactive and ff-Grid/Distributed Renewable Power
- Renewable Energy for Rural Application
- Renewable Energy for Urban, Industrial and Commercial Applications
- Research, Design and Development for New and Renewable Energy
- Strengthening of Institutional Mechanism for enhanced deployment and creation of public awareness.

14.198. The National Action Plan for Climate Change (NAPCC) norms envisage that the share of renewable electricity in the electricity mix which was 7 per cent in 2011–12 should reach 12 per cent by 2016–17. For this the corresponding renewable power requirement would be 132 BU or 52,000 MW considering the conservative average capacity utilisation factor of 30 per cent. The present installed capacity of renewable power is around 25,000 MW and, consequently, the renewable power capacity addition required for the Twelfth plan would be about 30,000 MW. The component wise break up of physical targets for the Twelfth Plan is given in Annexure 14.4.

14.199. For the Twelfth Five Year Plan, in addition to reorienting various existing policy initiatives, several new measures have been identified that are deemed essential to accelerate the pace of deployment of renewable energy in the country.

Schemes Spilling from the Eleventh Plan

Grid Connected Renewable Power

14.200. A capacity addition of 30,000 MW of Grid connected renewable power is proposed of which 15,000 MW is envisaged to come from wind power, 10,000 MW from solar capacity and 5,000 MW from other types of renewable sources. Institutional mechanisms to accelerate adoption of Renewable Power by States in the form of RPOs are sought to be enforced by bringing in an amendment into the Electricity Act, 2003. Accelerated depreciation benefit for wind power projects will come to an end at the end of the Eleventh five year plan. Tariff for Solar power under JNNSM is expected to continue falling due to enhanced indigenisation and local manufacturing. Further, to ensure volumes GBI support will be continued in the Twelfth Five Year Plan. It is also proposed to restrict the upfront subsidy support for Small Hydro plants to 10 MW size of hydro plants from an existing size of 25 MW.

Off-Grid Distributed Renewable Power

14.201. An ambitious capacity addition target of 3,400 MW has been proposed, which is almost five times the targets of the Eleventh Plan for off-grid renewables. Cogeneration in non-bagasse industry is supposed to contribute maximum (2,000 MW) of the overall ambitious targets proposed by MNRE. 1,000 MW of off-grid solar capacity addition has been proposed in line with the targets of phase-2 of Jawaharlal Nehru Solar Mission. The financing for incentives for such projects would be sourced from a pool of funds originating out of National Clean Energy Fund, CSR activities and tax-free donations.

Renewable Energy for Rural Applications for Cooking

14.202. The biogas technology has now reached a stage of becoming robust and mature enough for meeting cooking energy needs with additional advantages of meeting good organic fertiliser needs for sustaining crop yield and productivity and soil health. It is recommended to continue biogas and solar cooker program. Additionally solar cooking could be promoted under mid-day meal programme.

Renewable Energy for Rural Electricity Access

14.203. Some of the existing models for providing off grid electrification have shown notable response. Consequently, models like Solar home lighting systems through banking system, entrepreneur based biomass gasifier models for providing electricity for lighting, and mini micro hydro systems would continue to be supported.

14.204. Renewable energy has to be seen as a complementary option to the current conventional power generation and it has special characteristics in terms of variability in availability. Solar power is available only during the day and the availability of wind power varies depending upon the time of the year and also intra-day depending on wind conditions. These characteristics imply some special efforts at balancing with other sources to ensure a reliable supply to the grid. Fortunately solar power is at its peak precisely when demand is highest. However, that may not be the case with wind power. Effective utilisation of such power will require focused efforts towards balancing wind power with other power capacity which can be moderated to stabilise supply and also the development of efficient storage technologies. For this reason, special emphasis needs to be given on pumped water storage hydro plants. Central Government may consider providing assistance to the states for creating spinning reserve at the regional level by setting up of storage technologies. In the long term, other hybrid technology options such as gas with solar/wind, which are at a nascent stage, need to be developed. As the cost of power through conventional generation rise in the long term and technological developments in future increase the commercial viability of hybrid options, the cumulative financial benefits realised from using these options to meet peak demand requirements would outweigh the financial push provided to them in the present scenario.

Off Grid Solution for Industrial, Commercial and Buildings Applications

14.205. Existing scheme on solar water heaters will continue with a review of capital subsidy. Additionally green building programme and solar city initiative will be expanded to add new cities.

Major New Initiatives

14.206. The following are some of the new initiatives in the area of renewable energy:

1. **National Institute of Solar Energy**: The existing Solar Energy Centre would be converted into an autonomous institution for undertaking applied research, demonstration and development in solar energy including solar hybrid areas.
2. **National Bioenergy Corporation of India:** National Bio Energy Corporation of India (NBECI) will be set up to implement bioenergy mission including cook stove programme.
3. **Renewable Energy Development Fund:** In order to address the financing constraints for the grid connected as well as the off-grid applications of renewables, it is proposed to create a Renewable Energy Development fund. The fund will plug the gap between the sector financing needs and

the amount that falls short of the banks' obligations to their lending to this priority sector.
4. **National Bioenergy Mission**: Biomass energy for electricity generation has turned out to be one of the most attractive source of power which is scalable, has the largest potential for improving energy access and which can be linked to generating additional rural income. In view of the success of such biomass-based off-grid renewable models in rural areas of Bihar, it is proposed to launch the Biomass Mission with an objective to create a policy framework for attracting investment and to facilitate rapid development of commercial biomass energy market based on utilisation of surplus agro-residues and development of energy plantations.
5. **Renewable Power Evacuation Infrastructure**: Special emphasis will be placed on creating evacuation infrastructure and transmission facilities for renewable power in a time-bound manner to support the large expansion in consumption and production of renewable power. Judicious planning of transmission system, that is, creating pooling substation for cluster of renewable power generators and connecting them with receiving station of STU/CTU at appropriate voltage level, will lead to optimal utilisation of transmission system.
6. **National Biomass Cook Stove Programme**: The proposed initiative plans to universalise access of improved biomass cook stoves by providing assistance in exploring a range of technology deployments, biomass processing and delivery models leveraging public-private partnerships.

Policy Approach

14.207. The logic of subsidising new initiatives is that once they gain criticality of mass in terms of manufacturing capacity they should be able to survive without receiving any subsidy or fiscal incentives from the government. In keeping with this approach the objective should be to move away to the extent possible from capital subsidies and fiscal incentives to performance based incentives. Attaining the proposed higher deployment levels for wind energy, GBI support will require to be continued during the Twelfth Plan period.

14.208. To ensure lowest cost procurement of renewable energy, particularly wind and solar power should be through an open competitive bidding process. This has proved successful and in line with the ultimate objective of reaching grid parity earlier. This is particularly true of solar, which is at present costly, however it is expected to achieve grid parity in the Thirteenth Plan period in conjunction with the objectives of JNNSM. The competitive bidding process adopted for selection of projects has already resulted in significant reductions in base tariffs notified by CERC. The tariff for solar energy is expected to continue falling due to technological development and focus on indigenisation and local manufacturing for future projects, thus paving way to grid parity in due course of time.

14.209. There is a need to create a special sectoral exposure limit for the renewable energy sector by the banks. Additionally, creation of special instruments like tax-free RE bonds on the line of infrastructure bonds would facilitate low cost and long term lending to the renewable sector. Priority-sector status may also be granted to the renewable sector in view of the social and environmental benefits of the projects. This will act as a major policy push for the off-grid applications, which face maximum barriers in receiving low cost finances.

14.210. India's strategic focus would need to be augmenting of decentralised renewable energy capacity in the rural areas where it is having large social impact. Off-grid renewable energy applications have significant potential of reducing furnace oil/diesel/kerosene consumption in the country and can significantly contribute to oil import substitution. A cluster based approach for village electrification needs to be adopted. Under this approach, tariff-based bidding mechanism for such clusters inviting participation from business models would bring down the tariff by a significant amount. The difference that the consumers in the clusters are willing to pay and tariff discovered through the bidding mechanism can be financed through annual viability gap funding. The choice of technology can be left to the entrepreneurs, which would encourage entrepreneurs to constantly innovate their products and services to bring down the cost of producing electricity. Such projects would also be encouraged in the areas with grid availability but with lack of reliable supply so that power can be fed into the grid when the grid is energised and can be supplied to households when the grid is down. However, proper regulatory framework needs to be developed which can be adopted at state level, and has clear cut guidelines on monitoring, evaluation, multi-year operation and maintenance and ensures grid compatibility for such projects. Moreover, a sufficient financing mechanism for meeting out the viability gap requirement and an institutional mechanism to create an ecosystem for deployment of such projects needs to be put into place.

14.211. India is the second largest wind turbine manufacturer next to China. The installed manufacturing capacity in India ranges around 6,000 MW per year, with large export potential. The manufacturing base for wind turbines and its components has expanded to 16 manufacturers with 43 models of varying technologies and capacities. Till the year 2000, most of the machines were of 500 kW or lower capacity. Today, there are about 14 models from 5 different manufacturers of capacity 2 MW and above, the largest capacity being 2.5 MW. Larger machines have resulted in a steady increase in the Capacity Utilisation Factor (CUF) from 10 per cent–12 per cent in 1998 to 22 per cent–25 per cent in 2012. Technology is moving towards better aerodynamic design, use of lighter blades, direct drives, permanent magnet technology, and variable speed gearless operation using advanced power electronics. The health monitoring of wind turbines is now computer-controlled and on real-time basis.

14.212. Improvements in wind turbine technology and its installations at higher hub heights are working towards induction of higher capacity turbines. At the higher hub heights, wind potential is estimated to be substantially higher compared to the normal wind turbines at 40–60 metres hub heights. It is estimated that average capacity factor in USA has grown by about 25–30 per cent over the last decade. Even in India, the low capacity, older machines at highly favourable locations, need to be replaced by newer, and high capacity ones. Higher hub heights will enhance wind energy outputs, and will also be cost efficient.

PLAN OUTLAY

14.213. The indicative Twelfth Five Year Plan outlay for the various Ministries/Department in the energy sector is given in the Table 14.47 below:

TABLE 14.47
Indicative Twelfth Five Year Plan Outlay for the various Ministries/Departments in the Energy Sector

Sl. No.	Name of the Ministry/Department	Twelfth Plan (2012–17) Projections		
		GBS	IEBR	Total Outlay
1.	Ministry of Power	54,279	3,86,517	4,40,796
2.	Ministry of Coal	4,617	1,08,244	1,12,861
3.	Ministry of Petroleum and NG	5,147	4,36,541	4,41,688
4.	Ministry of Renewable Sources of Energy	19,113	13,890	33,003
	Sub-Total 1-4	83,156	9,45,192	10,28,348
5.	Department of Atomic Energy			
	(Power, Industry and Minerals Sectors)	21,737		
	R&D	19,878		
	Sub-Total DAE	41,615	65,572	1,07,187
	TOTAL (Energy)	1,24,771	10,10,764	11,35,535

ANNEXURE 14.1
Eleventh Plan Physical Progress of RGGVY Projects under Implementation

Sl. No	State/UT Name (Number of Districts)	Electrification of Un/De-Electrified Villages (Achievement)	Intensive Electrification of Electrified Villages (Achievement)	No. of Connections to BPL Households (Achievement)
1	Andhra Pradesh (22)	0	25,562	27,02,273
2	Arunachal Pradesh (16)	1,313	825	21,646
3	Assam (23)	7,829	11,672	8,07,290
4	Bihar (38)	22,029	4,267	21,49,834
5	Chhattisgarh (14)	857	10,512	9,15,407
6	Gujarat (25)	0	14,457	8,02,818
7	Haryana (18)	0	2,744	1,94,442
8	Himachal Pradesh (12)	78	1,059	10,078
9	Jammu & Kashmir (14)	148	2,380	44,014
10	Jharkhand (22)	1,7905	5,505	12,72,755
11	Karnataka (25)	61	24,575	8,34,196
12	Kerala (7)	0	37	17,238
13	Madhya Pradesh (32)	504	17,942	7,17,394
14	Maharashtra (34)	0	32,528	11,60,732
15	Manipur (9)	616	401	28,814
16	Meghalaya (7)	1,172	1,537	62,768
17	Mizoram (8)	89	338	14,743
18	Nagaland (11)	79	725	28,514
19	Orissa (30)	14,226	21,207	27,48,137
20	Punjab (17)	0	0	53,925
21	Rajasthan (33)	3,999	29,083	10,43,522
22	Sikkim (4)	25	375	9,366
23	Tamil Naidu (26)	0	9,992	5,02,956
24	Tripura (4)	127	463	80,986
25	Uttar Pradesh (65)	27,759	2,982	10,44,494
26	Uttarakhand (13)	1,511	9,028	2,30,558
27	West Bengal (17)	4,169	18,357	19,26,383
	Total (546)	1,04,496	2,48,553	1,94,25,283

ANNEXURE 14.2
Sectoral Coal Demand/Off-take for Annual Plan 2012–13

(In Million Tonnes)

Sl. No.	Sector	2006-07 Actual	2007-08 Actual	2008-09 Actual.	2009-10 Actual	2010-11 Actuals	2011-12 BE	2011-12 Provi.	2012-13 BE	2016-17
I	Coking Coal									
1	Steel/Coke Oven (indigenous)	17.37	16.99	16.58	15.92	16.80	17.23	16.05	22.00	31.70
2	Import	17.88	22.03	21.08	23.47	23.20	29.44	30.62	30.00	35.50
	Sub-Total Coking:	35.17	39.02	37.66	39.39	40.00	46.67	46.67	52.30	67.20
II	Non Coking									
3	(i) Power Utilities (Gen. Req.)	307.92	332.40	362.08	380.13	405.00	460.00	412.00	512.00	682.08
4	Cement	19.74	21.27	20.09	20.80	25.98	28.89	28.89	30.24	47.31
5	Steel DRI	17.47	20.92	19.78	22.89	28.80	30.47	30.47	35.30	50.33
7	Fertilisers	2.96	2.94	3.09	2.63	85.00	90.00	81.97	100.00	77.22
8	LTC/Soft Coke*	51.49	57.50	72.54	77.18					
9	Cokeries/Coke oven (NLW)*									
10	BRK and Others									
11	Captive Power	28.13	29.31	32.94	38.47	40.00	40.00	40.00	43.00	56.36
12	Colly.Consumpt.	0.99	0.93	0.85	0.76			0.73		
	Sub Total Non-Coking:	428.70	465.27	511.37	542.86	584.78	649.36	593.33	720.54	913.30
	Grand Total(I + II): including middlings	463.87	504.29	549.03	582.25	624.78	696.03	640.00	772.84	980.50
	Middlings	3.25	3.18	2.61	2.21					

Note: (i) *Included in BRK and Others.

ANNEXURE 14.3
Annual Plan 2012–13—Company-wise Production—Ministry of Coal

Company	2006–07 Actual	2007–08 Actual	2008–09 Actual	2009–10 Actual	2010–11 Actual	2011–12 Target	2011–12 Provi.	2012–13 Target	2016–17 Target
ECL	30.47	24.06	28.14	30.06	30.81	33.00	31.00	33.00	45.00
BCCL	24.21	25.22	25.51	27.51	29.04	30.00	30.20	31.00	37.00
CCL	41.32	44.15	43.24	47.08	47.52	51.00	49.00	55.00	92.00
NCL	52.16	59.62	63.65	67.67	66.25	68.50	64.50	70.00	82.00
WCL	43.21	43.51	44.70	45.74	43.65	45.50	43.80	45.00	45.00
SECL	88.50	93.79	101.15	108.01	112.71	112.00	113.75	117.00	145.00
MCL	80.00	88.01	96.34	104.08	100.28	106.00	103.00	112.00	167.00
NEC	1.05	1.10	1.01	1.11	1.06	1.00	0.75	1.10	2.00
CIL	360.92	379.46	403.74	431.26	431.32	447.00	436.00	464.10	615.00
SCCL	37.71	40.60	44.54	50.43	51.33	51.00	51.00	53.10	57.00
Other Public Sector	1.77	2.02	1.84	3.30	1.81	3.55		18.00	23.00
Private–TIOSCO	7.04	7.21	7.28	7.21	7.03	8.40	17.75		
Captive	17.61	21.17	29.87	35.03	34.60	38.25	36.15	39.80	100.00
Meghalaya	5.79	6.54	5.49	5.77	6.97	5.80			
Grand Total	430.84	457.00	492.76	533.00	533.06	554.00	540.00	575.00	795.00

ANNEXURE 14.4
Physical Targets of Renewable Programme for the Twelfth Plan

	Programme	Proposed Twelfth Plan Targets
1.	Grid-interactive Renewable Power(MW)	30,000
	Grid Interactive Solar	10,000
	Grid Connected Wind	15,000
	Other Renewable Sources	5,000
2.	Off-grid/Distributed Renewable Power (MWe)	3,400
	Cogeneration from bagasse	2,000
	Solar Off-Grid Applications	1,000
	Waste to Energy	200
	Bio Gas Based Decentralised Power	50
	Others (Biomass Gasifiers, Micro-hydel)	150
3.	Renewables for Rural applications (Cooking)	
	Biogas Plants (million)	0.7
	National Biomass Cook stoves Programme (million)	3.5
	Solar Cookers (Box type + Dish type)	3.5
	Solar Cooking in schools for mid-day scheme (Schools in lakhs)	5.0
4.	Renewable Energy for Urban, Industrial and Commercial Applications	
	Solar Water Heating Systems (million sq.m of collector area)	6
	Solar Air Heating System (sq m.)	
	CST based systems for community cooking (sq.m.)	50,000
	CST based system for air-conditioning	40,000
	(125 systems, 30TR)	37,000
	CST based systems for process heat	
	(225 systems, 250 sq.m. area each)	53,750
5.	Solar Cities	
	New Solar Cities in addition to existing target of 60 cities and pending liabilities.	15
	Model and Pilot Solar Cities.	
	Green Townships.	25
	Tourist/Religious/ Important Places	150
		100
6.	Alternate Fuel Vehicles (in numbers)	2,75,000
7.	Power Generation from Hydrogen	
	Stationery Power Generation (KW)	4,000
	Hydrogen/H-CNG Stations (nos)	10
	Demonstration projects for Hydrogen/H-CNG vehicles	500
8.	Power Generation from Fuel Cell	10.0
	Stationery Power Generation (KW)	10/2,000
	Back- up units for telecom towers (MW/nos)	
	Fuel cell Vehicles	100

Source: MNRE.

15

Transport

INTRODUCTION

Issues and Challenges

15.1. India's transport sector is grossly overstretched. The pace of economic development after the economic reforms has imposed a heavy burden on this sector. To meet the requirements of the economy during the Twelfth Plan it will have to address several challenges.

15.2. First, capacity needs are expected to double every decade in the medium term. It will consequently require large step-up in investments for capacity creation. The congestion and shortage of capacity is exhibited in all transport sectors. The National Highway network and the rail links along the North-South East-West corridors have very high traffic. In spite of expansion of ports capacity to more than a billion metric tonne by the end of the Eleventh Plan, a number of major ports have very high dwell time and are running at more than 90 per cent capacity. Of India's National Highways, less than one-third are two- or four-lane and a very large length of these are not able to support the 10.2 tonne permissible load per axle trucks are allowed to carry. While airport capacities have expanded significantly and kept pace with passenger demand, there is a need to expand the freight capacities to meet the growing requirements of the economy. Transportation of key commodities such as coal, iron ore, iron and steel and POL put heavy demands on transport system. Over the next 20 years, the demand for transport (both domestic and import) of these commodities could well increase by a factor of four to six which would require investment in rail capacity and other modes. Apart from transport, there is severe lack of capacity in the allied activity of warehousing.

15.3. Second, the transport efficiency is low. The cost of rail and coastal shipping in the country is higher than many economies. Even the road costs and transit time across different modes are large. Partly, it is because the average speeds of movement of all the modes: Rail, Road, Coastal Ships is lower than those in more efficient economies. The average speed of freight trains is 25 km per hour which is nearly half that of the U.S. The other nature of inefficiencies relate to poor handling equipments at the ports, inadequate rail infrastructure, absence of modern technologies in several areas and high handling costs resulting from a variety of factors including thefts.

15.4. Third, there is an important distortion in the overall transport movement of goods. A study conducted by RITES indicates that there is a discernible gap between the way in which the traffic is actually moving today and the way in which it should move. A comparative assessment of the impact arising out of the two different scenarios of modal mix, that is, Actual and Optimal (applying break-even distances based on resource cost) on the transport system during the base year (2007–08) in terms of flows, cost and throughput reveals that there is a significant scope for modal switch from Road to Rail in the case of miscellaneous/other commodities up to the extent of 78 per cent.

15.5. The country transports nearly 57 per cent of the total goods by road, as compared to 22 per cent in China and 37 per cent in the U.S. In contrast, the share of rail is only 36 per cent compared to 48 per cent for the U.S. and 47 per cent for China. Despite the fact that a large part of India's freight traffic comprises bulk materials and moves over long distances that can be served efficiently by rail and waterways, the share of shipping through waterways is nearly 6 per cent as compared to 14 per cent in U.S and 30 per cent in China. This is imposing high cost on the economy by way of much higher dependence on fossil fuels and high level of green house gas emissions. On the basis of mode-wise share of originating loadings in 2007–08, the indicative CO_2 emissions from the major modes are given in Table 15.1.

TABLE 15.1
CO_2 Emissions from Various Transport Modes

Freight Transport (gm/tkm)		Passenger Transport (gm/pkm)	
Road	160	Passenger Cars	175
Rail	29	Rail	75
Shipping	31	Airways	229

15.6. On environmental considerations, hence, there is a need to encourage rail and shipping. Added to this is the lower cost of accidents associated with rail transport compared with road.

15.7. Fourth, there is a need to provide transport access to large unserved areas of the country. A number of States in the North-East have very little rail network. A number of airstrips in the NE region are not in use. While there have been efforts to expand the airlines network and the number of flights to the North East Region, its intra-regional connectivity is still low. A programme for development of roads in the northeast including Trans-Arunachal Highway has been taken up to improve road connectivity. It requires large financial and physical resources and management expertise to complete the projected network. Similarly, the expansion of rail network in the North East and several other parts of the country has been limited in the last six decades. Large areas of Jharkhand, Orissa, Madhya Pradesh, and Rajasthan have no access to rail network. In the Himalayan States of Uttarakhand and Jammu & Kashmir, the network, particularly in the Hilly areas, is nonexistent. These areas require extensive road and rail network for their integration with the markets.

15.8. Fifth, safety is a major area of concern especially in the road transport. Over 1.3 lakh people are known to die annually in road accidents alone and their number is rising. This is about 10 per cent of the world figure, though India's share in number of vehicles in the world is only 1 per cent. The World Health Organisation has forecasted road traffic injuries to rise and become the fifth leading cause of death by 2030. Safety levels in railways are also in need of urgent improvement.

15.9. Sixth, there is a near absence of an integrated regulatory regime for overseeing tariff setting, cost of operations, anti-competitive practices and accountability to consumers. There is a division of power between the Central Government and the State Governments. Some areas are reserved exclusively for Central Governance, while there are a few sectors that are subject to joint governance. An examination of the existing laws, policies and regulations indicate that they are a result of an ad hoc approach, which is exacerbated by the overlapping power of the Central and State Governments. The regulatory framework in different sectors has been developed without proper coordination among the sectors. Sometimes only a set of laws and/or policies govern a particular sector without a regulatory body to oversee the development and operations. The absence of a sectoral authority in the transport sector as a whole has led to fragmented and ineffective centres of governance.

Strategy

15.10. The challenges in the transport sector need to be addressed in a comprehensive manner with a set of policies, laws and regulations. This requires transport reforms. Some of the major initiatives required are mentioned below.

15.11. First, a more integrated approach is required to be taken of transport as a whole. Our vision for transport should be guided by a modal mix that will lead to an efficient, sustainable, economical, safe, reliable, environmentally friendly and regionally balanced transportation system. Choices will need to be made on the priorities to be placed on different investments. Decisions on road expressways, dedicated rail freight corridors (DFCs), high speed trains and movement through inland waterways or coastal shipping must be taken holistically so that the objective of speed and efficient energy usage is achieved. Policy decisions should be based on life cycle energy costs of different transport modes.

15.12. While, pursuing the above objectives, two important initiatives could be taken:

1. Transportation by containerisation would need rapid expansion. While a number of initiatives in this regard have been taken earlier, the share of container transport is still low. Considering the international experience, major efforts are required to expand container traffic including expansion of the network of dry prots (ICDs).
2. Intermodal connectivity to be given thrust during the Twelfth Plan, by developing India's Inland Waterways which totals about 14,500 kilometers in length along with coastal shipping. Strategies, such as setting up coastal terminals at major ports, providing adequate road and rail connectivity to inland water and coastal terminals and non-major coastal ports, lowering the manning scales and vehicle specifications for coastal ships and other measures would be taken during the Twelfth Plan.

15.13. Second, the sector requires large increase in investments. Larger and focused investments will be able to address the two key issues of rapid increase in capacity and improvement in efficiency of infrastructure. The Interim Report of the National Transport Development Policy Committee (NTDPC) has strongly focused on need for capacity expansion of the railways over the next 20 years. All projections for the growth in demand for both freight and long distance passenger services suggest that overall economic growth could be stymied if appropriate strategic choices are not made now to facilitate significant capacity expansion of the railways, as has been done in China over the past decade or so. Such an expansion will not take place in a business as usual scenario. If consistent economic growth of 7–10 per cent per annum is to be achieved over the next 20 years, there is a pressing need for unprecedented capacity expansion of the Railways for both freight and passenger traffic in a manner that has not taken place since independence. It is of utmost importance that a vision similar to that of NHDP is laid down for the Railways now so that we may expect a transformed railway network by 2030.

15.14. It is estimated that the infrastructure sector will need investment of one trillion dollars in the Twelfth Plan. Of this, major share will be in the transport sector. Given the limitation of public resource, private investments will have to be emphasised and expanded. A Public–Private Partnership (PPP) regime has already been put into operation in road sector very successfully. While in Ports, Airports, Railways and Inland Waterways, there have been efforts in private investments in varying degrees, there is a need to step up an investment particularly in the railways. There will be a special focus required for increased investment in the railways from public resources, as well for safety, modernisation and expansion. It is estimated that the share of private investments, of the total infrastructure investments in the economy was nearly 40 per cent by the end of the Eleventh Plan, the rest being public investments. This needs to be increased to 50 per cent to 60 per cent during the Plan.

15.15. Third, transport reforms are needed in pricing and fiscal areas. In several sectors, the transport pricing policies are unsustainable. The Railways have not revised their passenger tariffs for several years, despite sharp increase in fuel prices and other operating costs. They are further making investments in uneconomic lines, despite lack of resources. This thin spreading of the financial resources has delayed completion of viable projects and thus, led to further deterioration of their finances. There is an urgent need to undertake a review of projects and prioritise them as well as to abandon or not to commence work on the many unremunerative projects which have not made substantial progress till now. Similarly, the taxation policies on aviation fuel have led to uneconomic operations of the airlines. For coastal shipping lines, similarly, benefits as available in other major economies to the coastal shipping lines need to be provided.

15.16. Fourth, transport safety has been a neglected area in the past and credible institutional framework to address these issues at Centre, States and city level is required. The entire transport system must be designed to accommodate the individual who has the worst protection and lowest tolerance of violence. The Twelfth Plan period would be used to setting appropriate institutional structures that create a demand for scientific work in safety issues; have proper legislation and regulation; monitoring and measurement by setting up national databases of relevant information to monitor and assess various aspects of safety policies, technologies and knowledge needs. The National Transport Policy Development Committee (NTDPC) has recommended setting up institutes for road, railway, water and air safety to ensure the safety professionals are abreast of international knowledge and findings as well as provision for funding and establishment of multidisciplinary safety research centres at academic institutions. It has also recommended establishing National Boards for Road, Railway, Water/Marine and Air Safety. There is a strong need to put into action the recommendations of the Sundar Committee on Roads and the Kakodkar Committee on Railways.

15.17. Fifth, transport access is critical for inclusive growth, economic development, access to markets and participation in the political process. Development of rural roads, expansion of rail infrastructure in large unserved areas will, therefore, need special emphasis during the Twelfth Plan. Every minute a woman dies in child birth, but many of these deaths could be avoided with timely access to transport. Gender responsive infrastructure interventions can free up women's time by lowering their transaction costs. This, in turn, will increase girls' school enrollment and facilitate women's participation in income generation and decision making activities.

15.18. Social inclusion requires that needs of the differently abled are kept in mind while developing the economy. It will be, therefore, important that the transport sector makes special arrangements for their needs, so that they are able to access it conveniently and thus fully participate in our social and economic process and contribute to it.

15.19. Sixth, human resource development would be a key factor in achieving the objective of creating a well-developed and efficient transport system in the country. The NTPDC report has pointed to a severe lack of expertise in the country in almost every sphere of transportation which makes it necessary for a quantum jump in capacity augmentation for all modes. The quantitative improvements to infrastructure need to be made in the context of more qualitative considerations of safety, emissions, energy efficiency, climate change impact and social equity. The Committee has recommended setting up national institutes for research and statistics, multi-disciplinary research institutions, State and city level institutions and centres of excellence in existing academic institutions. These suggestions will need to be implemented during the Plan.

15.20. Seventh, connectivity of the North-East, both within the region and with the far eastern region, including Myanmar, Bangladesh and Thailand, would be one of the focus areas for economic development of the region and expanding economic activities including trade and commerce. Inland Water Transport connectivity with Bangladesh will need to be specially emphasised. Simultaneously, connectivity of the North East region through rail, road, air with the neighboring countries and its rapid expansion within the region would also need special focus during the Plan.

RAILWAYS

15.21. Indian Railways is the fourth largest railway network in the world in terms of route kilometers. As on 31 March 2011, it has a total route length of 64,460 km of which 21,034 km is electrified. The total track length is 1,13,994 km of which 1,02,680 km is broad gauge, 8,561 km is meter gauge and 2,753 km is narrow gauge. Considering the requirements of the economy and size of the country, the expansion of the railway network has been inadequate. Indian Railways have added 11,864 km of new lines since independence.

It has not been able to cover major areas in many states and has very little presence in the North-East States and the Himalayan region. However, during the same period the length of broad gauge route kilometer has been doubled from 25,258 km to 55,188 km through new lines as well as gauge conversion of 21,658 km from meter and narrow gauges to broad gauge. Gauge Conversion has been instrumental in adding capacity in the system despite a relatively low addition of new lines. The network needs extensive modernisation, increase of speeds, improvement in safety and modernisation of rolling stock to meet the needs of a rapidly growing economy.

Review of the Eleventh Plan

Financial Performance

15.22. The Eleventh Plan period has seen steady deterioration in Railway's financial position (Table 15.2) which is in sharp contrast with the Tenth Plan performance when the Railways had achieved a remarkable turnaround in financial performance. The Revenue (gross traffic receipts) have gone up by 7.7 per cent (CAGR) during the period 2007–08 to 2011–12 whereas the Total Working Expenses has gone up by 12.6 per cent (CAGR) during the same period leading to decline in the net revenue which has shown a negative growth rate of –17.9 per cent (CAGR) during the above period. After accounting for dividend, the net excess has reduced from ₹13,431 crore in the first year of the Plan to only ₹1,201 crore in the terminal year of the Plan. In 2009–10, the balance had reduced to a token figure of less than a crore. One of the major reasons for increase in the working expenses during the Eleventh Plan period has been the increase in wage bills by nearly ₹73,000 crore due to the implementation of the Sixth Pay Commission. However, in the first year of the Twelfth Plan (2012–13) Indian Railways have targeted a revenue surplus of ₹15,557 crore and operating ratio of 85 per cent.

Investments in Eleventh Plan

15.23. Lack of surplus has impacted the capacity to generate resources for investment in the system (Table 15.3).

15.24. During the Eleventh Plan period (2007–12), the Ministry of Railways had an investment target of ₹2,33,289 crores comprising of ₹63,635 crore as GBS, ₹90,000 crore as internal generation and ₹79,654 crore as Extra Budgetary Resources (EBR) through

TABLE 15.2
Overview of Financial Position of the Indian Railways

(in ₹ Crores at current prices)

Sl. No.	Description	Terminal Year of Tenth 2006–07	2007–08	2008–09	2009–10	2010–11	2011-12 (RE)	Twelfth 2012–13 (BE)
1	Gross Traffic Receipts	62,731	71,720	79,862	86,964	94,536	1,03,917	1,32,552
2	Net Ordinary Working Expenses	37,432	41,033	54,349	65,810	68,139	75,650	84,400
3	Appropriation to Pension Fund	7,416	7,979	10,490	14,918	15,820	16,800	18,500
4	Appropriation to Depreciation Reserve Fund	4,198	5,450	7,000	2,187	5,515	6,160	9,500
5	Total Working Expenses	49,047	54,462	71,839	82,195	89,474	98,610	1,12,400
6	Net Revenue	14,453	18,334	9,714	5,544	6,346	7,144	22,233
7	Total Dividend Payable	4,247	4,903	4,718	5,543	4,941	5,652	6,676
8	Excess/Shortfall	10,206	13,431	4,456.78	0.75	1,405	1,492	15,557
9	Operating Ratio (per cent)	78.7	75.9	90.50	95.30	94.60	95	85
10	Ratio of Net Revenue to capital at charge and investment from capital fund (per cent)	19.0	20.71	8.80	4.51	4.40	4.43	12.10

Source: Explanatory Memorandum to the Railway Budget for Various Years.

TABLE 15.3
Investment in Railways during Eleventh Plan

(In ₹ Crore at current prices)

Eleventh Plan	Approved Outlay	2007–08	2008–09	2009–10	2010–11	2011–12 (RE)	Total for Eleventh Plan	Excess/ Shortfall	2012–13 (BE)
Gross Budgetary Support	63,635*	8,668	10,110	17,716	19,485	21,060	77,039	13,404	24,000
	27.3 %	29.9 %	27.8 %	44.7 %	47.9 %	45.3 %	40.1 %	21.1 %	41.8 %
Internal Generation	90,000	14,948	18,941	12,196	11,528	9,091	66,704	(–)23,296	18,948
	38.6 %	51.6 %	52.1 %	30.7 %	28.3 %	19.4 %	34.7 %	(–)25.9 %	31.5 %
Extra Budgetary Resources	79,654	5,364	7,284	9,760	9,680	16,316	48,404	(–)31,250	16,050
	34.1 %	18.5 %	20.0 %	24.6 %	23.8 %	35.1 %	25.2 %	(–)39.2 %	26.7 %
Total	2,33,289	28,980	36,336	39,672	40,693	46,467	1,92,147	41,142	60,100

*Includes 13572 crore as additional budgetary support for national projects

market borrowings. The actual expenditure against this originally approved outlay for the Eleventh Plan period comes to ₹1,92,147 crore—comprising of GBS of ₹77,039 crore, internal generation of ₹66,704 crore and EBR of ₹48,404 crore. Thus there was a shortfall of ₹41,142 crore (17.6 per cent). The anticipated utilisation under GBS would be ₹77,039 crore against the projected outlay of ₹63,635 crore which is an increase of 21 per cent over the estimate whereas internal generation and EBR components were lower by 25.9 per cent and 39.2 per cent respectively. It is evident that the internal generation and borrowings have not kept pace with the investment requirement.

Physical Targets and Achievements

15.25. The Eleventh Plan targets and achievements for freight and passenger business are summarised in Tables 15.4 and 15.5. It will be seen from Table 15.4 that as against the original target of 1,100 MT for the terminal year of the Eleventh Plan, the actual achievement is 970 million tonnes which is 11.8 per cent lower than the original target and 5 per cent lower than the revised target of 1,020 MT. In NTKM terms, the achievement has been 639.77 billion which is 8.9 per cent lower than the original target of 702 billion and 5.1 per cent lower than the revised target of 674 billion. In terms of growth rates of traffic, as against the projected growth in originating freight traffic of 8.6 per cent, the actual growth was only 5.8 per cent (CAGR) and in NTKM terms, it was 6.1 per cent as against a target of 7.8 per cent. The performance in NTKM is better because of marginal increase in lead.

Growth rate of freight traffic is lower than the growth rate in GDP during this period. This was contributed by a sharp drop in exports of iron ore, problems in mining of iron ore leading to inadequate domestic movement and poor growth in coal movement due to slowdown in coal production, particularly in the last two years of the Plan. The freight basket of railways needs diversification to include manufactured goods through containerisation so that slow down in the core sector of the economy (coal, steel and so on) can be compensated.

Passenger Business

15.26. The originating passenger traffic achieved in the terminal year of the Eleventh Plan is 8,139 million which is 3.2 per cent lower than the original Eleventh Plan target of 8,400 million but 0.75 per cent higher than the revised target of the Eleventh Plan. In terms of growth rates, against the targeted CAGR of 6.2 per cent, originating passenger traffic grew at the rate of 5.5 per cent (Table 15.5). In terms of Passenger Kilometers (PKM), the volume achieved is 1,062 billion which is higher than the original target but lower than the revised target. The CAGR of PKM was 8.8 per cent which was much higher than the original target of 5.9 per cent. This indicated a very significant expansion due to higher leads of non-suburban traffic. It increased from 215.5 km in year 2006–07 to 229.3 km in year 2008–09 and has maintained the higher level. Railways are making large revenue losses in passenger traffic both in suburban as well as non-suburban segments (Table 15.6). Non-revision

TABLE 15.4
Performance of Freight Business during Eleventh Five Year Plan

Item	Tenth Plan Actuals in Terminal Year 2006–07	Eleventh Plan Targets for Terminal Year 2011–12	Eleventh Plan Revised Targets in Mid-Term Review for Terminal Year 2011–12	2007–08	2008–09	2009–10	2010–11	2011–12	CAGR
Originating Tonnage (Million Tonnes)	728.4	1 100	1 020	794.21	833.31	887.99	921.5	970	
Growth (%)		8.6	7	9.03	4.92	6.56	3.77	5.26	5.8
NTKM (Billion)	475	702	674	511.8	538.23	584.76	605.99	639.77	
Growth (%)		7.8	7	7.7	5.16	8.65	3.63	8.67	6.1

of tariff for several years has led to poor financial health of this segment.

Infrastructure Capacity Creation—Targets and Achievements

15.27. The Eleventh Plan attempted a paradigm shift from the earlier incremental approaches to one of significant infrastructure capacity addition to handle the quantum increase in traffic levels and to sustain mobility on the network by setting ambitious targets as compared to the performance during the Tenth Plan. The targets in respect of new lines and electrification have been exceeded (Table 15.7). However, in respect of doubling of lines which is a major component for improving Railways' capacity, there has been a shortfall as compared to original targets and in case of gauge conversion there has been a shortfall as compared to the revised targets.

Throw-Forward of Infrastructure Projects

15.28. One of the major problems in the Railways has been excessive sanctioning of new projects annually, much beyond the resources available which only increases the throw-forward (number of projects under implementation) (Table 15.8). There is an urgent need for a policy to limit the throw-forward to a certain proportion of their annual expenditure on these projects.

TABLE 15.5
Performance of Passenger Business during Eleventh Five Year Plan

Item	Tenth Plan Actuals in Terminal Year 2006–07	Eleventh Plan Targets for Terminal Year 2011–12	Eleventh Plan Revised Targets in Mid-Term Review for Terminal Year 2011–12	2007–08	2008–09	2009–10	2010–11	2011–12	CAGR
Originating Passengers (Million)	6,219	8,400 (CAGR = 6.2 %)	8,200	6,524	6,920	7,246	7,651	8,139	5.5 %
Passenger KM (Billion)	695	924 (CAGR = 5.9 %)	1,100	770	838	903	979	1,062	8.8 %

TABLE 15.6
Losses in Passenger Services

Year	2004–05	2005–06	2006–07	2007–08	2008–09	2009–10	2010–11
Losses (₹crore)	6,159.41	6,022.66	6,449.22	7,067.67	13,901.22	18,960.67	19,964.03

TABLE 15.7
Capacity Creation during Eleventh Plan

Item	Tenth Plan Achievement (km)	Eleventh Plan Original Target (km)	Revised Target for Eleventh Plan during Mid Term Appraisal (km)	Eleventh Plan Achievement (km)	Improvement over Tenth Plan (%)
New Lines	920	2,000	2,000	2,205	139.6
Gauge Conversion	4,289	10,000	6,000	5,290	23.4
Doubling	1,300	6,000	2,500	2,756	112
Railway Electrification	1,810	3,500	4,500	4,501	148.7

Rolling Stock Procurement and Production

15.29. During the Plan, acquisition of wagons has exceeded the target but fallen short in coaches while in diesel locomotives and electric locomotives the revised targets have been achieved. The performance, however, represents a large jump over the Tenth Plan achievements (Table 15.9).

15.30. The emphasis in the Eleventh Plan period has been on manufacturing high horse power electric and diesel locomotives, EMUs/MEMUs and Metro coaches based on GTO/IGBT technology.

Track Renewal

15.31. Arrears of track renewal have been brought down from 6,200 km in the beginning of the Eleventh Plan to 3,500 km at the end of the Eleventh Plan. Around 18,000 km of track renewals have been carried out in the Eleventh Plan period.

Productivity

15.32. Table 15.10 gives an assessment of the performance of Railways and productivity improvements during the first four years of the Eleventh Plan. The improvement in productivity during the Plan indicates increased congestion on the Railway track system.

15.33. The productivity of employees and of the network is important for assessing the operational efficiency. Table 15.11 gives an international comparison. It is clear that the network productivity of Indian network is good in passengers traffic. In terms of employees' productivity in freight Indian Railways is 1/3rd that of China and about 1/4th that of Russia

Initiatives Taken During Eleventh Plan

Freight and Passenger Business

15.34. Railways have taken several initiatives during the Plan for expanding the share of freight traffic. These include introduction of freight marketing of select commodities by third parties, introduction of liberalised wagon investment schemes to attract private investment in special purpose and

TABLE 15.8
Throw Forward of Infrastructure Projects as on 1 April 2012

Infrastructure	Number of Works in Progress	Length in km	Cost (₹ crore)	Throw Forward 1 April 2012 (₹ crore)
New Lines	132	14,212	1,23,767	89,792
Gauge conversion	42	9,880	35,051	18,659
Doubling	174	9,015	49,295	38,766
Electrification	39	4,700	4,100	6,229
DFC Project	2	3,338	95,860	93,860
Total	389	41,145	3,08,073	2,47,306

TABLE 15.9
Rolling Stock Performance during Eleventh Plan

Item	Tenth Plan Achievement	Eleventh Plan Original Target	Revised Target for Eleventh Plan during Mid Term Appraisal	Achievement in the Eleventh Plan	Improvement over Tenth Plan (%)
Wagons	36,222	62,000	62,000	63,481	75
Coaches (including EMU/MEMU/DEMU)	12,202	22,500	19,863	17,085	40
Diesel Loco	622	1,800	1,019	1,288	107
Electric Loco	524	1,800	1,205	1,218	132

Note: This includes acquisition, as well as, railways' own production.

high capacity wagons, freight incentives policies including dynamic pricing concept and so on. On the passenger front, during the Eleventh Plan, 323 pairs of new trains have been introduced, services of 111 trains have been extended and frequency of 63 trains increased. 2,813 coaches have been added for expanding passenger carrying capacity. High capacity, air-conditioned double-decker coaches, low-priced, fast train services such as Garib Rath and facilities in trains services for ladies, students and marginalised groups have been introduced.

Traffic Facility Works, Strengthening of High Density Network (HDN), Augmentation of Terminal Capacity and Development of Logistics Parks

15.35. A substantial amount of traffic of Indian Railways moves on the route connecting four metropolitan cities—Delhi, Mumbai, Chennai and Kolkata. These 7 main routes along with feeder routes totalling 17,383 Route km have been identified as high density network (HDN). A total of 124 works costing about ₹14,000 crore including doubling, third and fourth lines, bye passes, flyovers, crossing stations,

TABLE 15.10
Productivity Performance

Productivity indicator	Tenth Plan (2006–07)	Eleventh Plan			
		2007–08	2008–09	2009–10	2010–11
Wagon Utilisation					
NTKM/VU/Day (Broad Gauge (BG)	3,238	3,539	8,687	9,022	9,247
Wagon Km/Wagon/Day (BG)	230	248.9	253.7	256.2	262.1
Wagon turnaround in days) (BG)	5.49	5.23	5.19	4.98	4.97
Track Utilisation					
NTKM/route Km (million)	9.67	10.19	10.43	11.07	11.34
Passenger Km/route Km (million)	13.47	14.63	15.53	16.35	17.36
NTKM/Engine Day Online (goods-BG)					
Diesel	2,68,410	2,64,137	2,70,912	2,85,008	3,02,245
Electric	3,61,543	3,84,981	4,25,329	4,43,386	4,53,960
Human Resources Productivity					
NTKM/employee (million)	0.34	0.37	0.39	0.44	0.47
PKM/employee (million)	0.49	0.55	0.60	0.66	0.73

TABLE 15.11
Benchmarking Indian Railways with Chinese and Russian Railways

Railways	Employee Productivity (Annual)		Network Productivity		Wagon Productivity (Annual)
	NTKM (million)/ Employee	PKM (million)/ Employee	NTKM (million)/ Network Length	PKM (million)/ NetworkLength	NTKM (million)/ Wagon holding
Russia	1.81	0.15	21.87	1.80	5.52
China	1.23	0.38	39.66	12.38	4.31
India	0.44	0.66	9.39	14.12	2.73

Source: UIC Statistics 2009–10.

intermediate block stations, automatic signalling works, yard remodelling and so on were planned to augment capacity on the HDN. A total of 128 works for development and modernisation of freight terminals have been sanctioned since the year 2007–08 and are in progress at different locations.

Information Technology Initiatives

15.36. The Eleventh Plan emphasised the need to 'use IT for improved customer services'. More than 5,071 locations have been provided with Unreserved Ticketing System (UTS). The Passenger Reservation System (PRS) is now available at more than 2,438 locations and is planned further to be expanded to facilitate the passengers to buy tickets closer to their homes and work places. Proliferation of e-ticketing has helped in reducing queue lengths at reservation offices. To facilitate dispersal of tickets, PRS counters have been provided at 151 Post Offices. Complete roll out of Rake Management System (RMS) module has enabled online monitoring of freight train operations and improved intra and inter-zonal coordination. Terminal management system has been introduced at 1,653 terminals. The e-payment facility is being availed by 440 freight customers and accounts for more than 40 per cent of freight earnings. Other IT initiatives undertaken to improve operational efficiency are Crew Management System, Control Office Application, e-Procurement and so on.

Energy Management, Energy Efficiency and Measures to Improve Environmental Friendliness

15.37. Reduction in empty wagon movement by adopting a new maintenance regime of premium examination and rationalisation of coaching links for increased maintenance intervention of 3,500 km (from the earlier limit of 2,500 km) are some of the important operational improvements. On fuel efficiency front, increased production of 3 phase electric locos with 14 per cent to 15 per cent energy regeneration feature during braking, fuel efficient 3 phase diesel locos with 10 per cent higher fuel efficiency than conventional locos and adoption of 3 phase EMUs regenerating about 25 per cent to 30 per cent of energy during braking are some of the important initiatives taken up during the Plan period. A 10.5 MW capacity wind farm has been commissioned to provide captive power to Integral Coach Factory at Chennai and more wind farms are planned in other states 2.6 million incandescent lamps are being replaced with CFLs in households to conserve energy.

15.38. For availing electric power at lower tariff, Indian Railways has set up a 1,000 MW power plant at Nabi Nagar through a JV with NTPC. It is expected to be operational by the beginning of the Twelfth Five Year Plan. This plant will supply 90 per cent of generated power to 164 substations of Indian Railways located in Eastern and Western regions and will result in a saving of ₹400–600 crores per year to the Railways due to lower tariffs. Another 1,000 MW captive power plant is being set up at Adra through a JV with NTPC.

15.39. To improve sanitation and to prevent discharge from toilets while the train is in Railway Station premises, speed actuated discharge toilets have been provided in all LHB type coaches and a select number of ICF coaches. Field trials for biodegradable and environment friendly toilets (in collaboration with IIT/Kanpur and DRDO) are on. On successful completion of these trials toilets would be introduced in passenger coaches in a phased manner.

The Twelfth Plan

Strategies

15.40. The Twelfth Plan aims at faster, more inclusive and sustainable growth. This will require continued work in several areas and a change in strategy in others. The expanding requirements of the economy will need much faster expansion of the freight network along with its ability to carry larger freight per wagon, improve efficiency of the Rail system to deliver it faster and expand the network. There will also be need to improve the share of the Railways in the overall national freight market. With increasing incomes, passenger traffic will increase but plan for expansion must factor in the fact that demand will be for better quality services for which passengers will be willing to pay.

15.41. The rail network will have to develop a strategy to be part of an effective multi-modal transport system to ensure environmental-friendly and economically efficient transport movement. The Twelfth Plan will strive towards achieving a gender equal Railway Transport System designed to meet the needs of both men and women. Priority will be accorded to women's safety and security. Simultaneously, the network will have to be expanded to other areas where so far there has been little presence, especially in the Himalayan region and some of the tribal areas. One of the most important components of this strategy will be stepping up private investments in the Railways.

15.42. Investment needs to be prioritised in the important areas, viz. Dedicated Freight Corridors, high capacity rolling stock, last mile rail linkages and port connectivity. Development of logistic parks would also need to be taken up on priority basis to create matching terminal and handling capacity, and facilitate integration of rail with other modes of transportation. Enhancing project execution capabilities would be critical for speedy capacity creation and improved returns on investments. Along with new capacity addition, improving productivity of existing network and assets would also be crucial to increase transportation output.

15.43. It has to be clearly realised that the modernisation of Indian Railways cannot be achieved by simply relying on additional General Budgetary Support (GBS). Even the norms and methodology of GBS allotment should be clearly defined. There is a case for larger GBS but the requirements are so large that the Railways have to plan for much stronger revenue growth. Clear Strategies would need to be formulated and executed to identify segments where it can play low-cost strategy by playing on volumes, taking advantage of economies of scale and segments where it can play differentiation strategy by providing high quality services and command premium prices.

Physical Targets for the Twelfth Plan

Freight Traffic Projections

15.44. Traffic projections for the Twelfth Plan are given in Table 15.12. It is targeted that during the Twelfth Plan, the rail share in freight should go up by at least 2 per cent. The targets for originating freight tonnage may need to be reviewed on an annual basis or during the mid-term review to ensure the target of 2 per cent increase in originating tonnage. Given that the level of traffic growth achieved in the last Plan has been 5.8 per cent for originating traffic and 6.1 per cent for NTKM, it will require a major increase in efforts and a conscious strategy to move the road traffic over to the rail. This is going to be a challenging task.

Technological and Logistical Measures for Improving Freight Movement Efficiency

15.45. An important component of the strategy for increasing the freight movement efficiency will be introduction of new technologies aimed at

TABLE 15.12
Traffic Projections

Loading	2012–13	2013–14	2014–15	2015–16	2016–17
MT (million)	1,038	1,119	1,206	1,300	1,405
CAGR			7.8 per cent		
NTKM (billion)	690	737	795	857	927
CAGR			7.7 per cent		
Lead	665	664	663	661	660

improving axle load of wagons, expansion of long haul, use of GPS and RFID technology for tracking purposes and technological innovations to improve efficiency of operations.

1. *Proliferation of 25 tonnes axle load running*: Along with this, feasibility of 30 tonnes axle load running and induction of 30 tonnes axle load wagon needs to be planned.
2. *Raising the current axle load regime from 22.82 tonnes to 23.5 tonnes on selected routes*: It is observed that 98 per cent of Indian Railways loading comes within a gross weight of wagons being equivalent to 94 tonnes which translates to 23.5 tonnes of axle load. The new BOXNHL wagons primarily designed for coal have sufficient volumetric capacities for loading additional 2 tonnes of coal.
3. *Expansion of Long Haul*
4. *Use of GPS technology and RFID technology* for tracking purposes and use of Distributed Power Systems.
4. There is also a need to create multimodal logistics parks to reduce the cost of interfacing and costs of intermodal transfer and overall production. Logistics parks are network hubs, critical for efficient multimodal transport as they allow transshipment between modes and consolidation of freight. Earmarking land for logistics parks at about 15 to 20 key interchange points around major key urban and industrial centres, ideally on the proposed rail Dedicated Freight Corridor (DFC) routes; and providing infrastructure such as power, utilities, road/DFC linkages and rail sidings.
5. Containerisation would be a major strategy to gain share of the freight market (Box 15.1).

Passenger Traffic Projections

15.46. The CAGR of passenger traffic during the Eleventh Plan has averaged around 5.5 per cent. The number of passengers travelling annually will thus increase from 8.9 billion in the first year of the Plan to 11.7 billion by the end of the Plan (Table 15.13). The projections for Passenger Kilometers have also been made based on past trends (Table 15.14). The growth in PKM is expected to be 10.8 per cent per annum with an increase to 1,760.4 billion PKM (2016–17) from 1,195 billion PKM (2012–13).

Measures to Upgrade Quality of Passenger Services

15.47. To meet the requirements of passenger services a number of steps are planned in the Twelfth Plan. Some of the important areas proposed to be taken up are mentioned below:

1. *Enhancing accommodation in trains*: Augmenting the load of existing services with popular timings and on popular routes to 24/26 coaches would help generating additional capacity and availability of additional berths/seats for the traveling public.
2. *Enhancing speed of trains*: At present, speed of Mail/Express trains is below 55 kmph. Segregation of freight and passenger traffic, enhancing the sectional speeds, and rationalisation of stoppages are important measures for speed enhancement. The speed of passenger trains is quite low at present primarily because of the coaching stock in use and due to multiplicity of stoppages en-route. There is scope for speeding up of these services by replacing trains with conventional stock by fast moving EMUs/MEMUs/DEMUs. Enhancing the sectional

Box 15.1
Containerisation In Railways

Due to the economic and technological attributes of the railways, it has always been a challenge to attract consignments which are less than at least a thousand tonnes. Container trains combine the operational efficiency of unit trains with the commercial flexibility of booking 20 tonnes or even less at a time.. According to the Total Transportation Study (TTS) conducted by RITES for the Planning Commission, the volume of non-bulk traffic in 2006–07 was 227.17 million tonnes out of the total traffic of 2,386.97 million tonnes.

Indian Railways set up Container Corporation of India (Concor) in 1988 as a public sector company to spear head containerisation. It commenced operations in 1989 at which stage Indian Railways transferred all Inland Container Depots (ICDs) and container related business to Concor. From the 7 ICDs it took over from Indian Railways at inception, Concor has now expanded the network to more than 44 ICDs and 14 domestic and port side terminals and has 213 rakes of flat wagons. Using IR's network and haulage, it has pioneered the concept of multi-modalism through its core activities as a carrier of rail borne container traffic and terminal operation.

Anticipating higher container traffic at Indian ports, Railways liberalised the entry of private players in the area of rail-based haulage of containers in 2005. The response has been quite good with 15 new entrants. These 15 new operators have procured 132 rakes and developed 9 new terminals. Sizeable on-track competition has emerged in some of the exim sectors as well as the domestic sector. Competition also led to an increase in the growth of rail based intermodal traffic at a rate of 15.5 per cent in the period 2007–08 till 2011–2012 although there has been a negative growth rate in the domestic sector during 2011–12 due to introduction of container class rate for some of the commodities moved normally by conventional wagons. There is a need to expand containerisation business and improve Railways share in transport sector. Policies in the Twelfth Plan will aim at this.

TABLE 15.13
Passenger Traffic Projections for Twelfth Plan

Year	Projected Passengers Originating (Million)				
	Suburban		Non-Suburban		
	Nos.	Ratio	Nos.	Ratio	Total
2012–13	4,545	51.25	4,323	48.75	8,868
2013–14	4,855	51.07	4,651	48.93	9,506
2014–15	5,186	50.89	5,005	49.11	10,191
2015–16	5,540	50.71	5,385	49.29	10,925
2016–17	5,917	50.53	5,793	49.47	11,710

Note: Originating passenger traffic projections have been made based on average correlation with GDP calculated for the preceding 5 years.

TABLE 15.14
Projection of Originating PKM for Twelfth Plan

Year	Projected PKMs Originating (Billion)				
	Suburban		Non-Suburban		
	Nos.	Ratio	Nos.	Ratio	Total
2012–13	159	13.32	1,036	86.68	1,195
2013–14	170	12.97	1,146	87.07	1,316
2014–15	182	12.54	1,268	87.46	1,450
2015–16	194	12.15	1,404	87.85	1,598
2016–17	207	11.76	1,553	88.24	1,760

speeds is another enabling factor in speeding them.

4. *Introduction of tailored services*: The travelling requirements of various sectors and various classes of passengers differ. Between major cities and metros, fast services with very limited stoppages are preferred. Introduction of non-stop services and services with higher accommodation between popular destinations would better serve passengers' requirements.

15.48. Strategies for decongesting major passenger terminals: This would be done through development of alternative terminals in suburban areas of major cities and expeditious operationalisation of the Dedicated Freight Corridors resulting in segregation of passenger and freight traffic. Spin off effects in the form of larger number of passenger services, faster passenger services, quicker freight movement, and help in decongesting major terminals would be achieved. There are international examples of efficient passenger and freight operations which have relevance for Indian Railways (Box 15.2).

> **Box 15.2**
> **Business Models for Passenger and Rail Freight Logistics: The JR East and Deutsche Bahn Ways**
>
> JR East is the largest among the four Japanese railway companies and amongst the most successful operators of rail passenger business in the world. It operates urban, high speed and regional railways. On a daily basis, JR East handles 17 million passengers, runs 12,761 trains which cover 7,10,600 Km. per day. Its average delay is less than 1 minute including all kinds of delays, even those due to snow and typhoons. JR East runs the famous Shinkansen high speed trains. Out of a total operating Km. of 7,512.6, Shinkasen lines cover 1,134.7 Km. and conventional lines cover 6,377.9 Km. An important aspect of JR East business is that it earns 30 per cent of its revenues from non-transportation business. This translates to nearly 8.13 billion dollars from non-transportation business out of its total business of 27.7 billion dollars. Non-transportation business includes station space utilisation (15.4 per cent), shopping centres and office buildings (8.3 per cent) and other services (8.4 per cent). The non-transportation business, also called the life-style business is aimed at maximising the values of JR East's tangible and non-tangible assets such as railway network and stations. It has renovated a large number of stations in the past two years including the iconic Tokyo station which is being modernised. It includes building two towers of more than 4,30,000 sq.m of office buildings and hotels, 1,500 sq.m of shopping floors and development of pedestrian decks and restoration and conservation of the old Tokyo station.
>
> An alternative model of earning revenues and running the business profitably is that of Deutsche Bahn (DB) of Germany. It consists of 3 divisions and 9 business units including passenger transport which covers long distance, regional and urban passenger transport; infrastructure which includes track, station and electrification and the third Division being Schenker, world's leading logistics service company covering areas of rail freight transport, global logistics services and rail technology and services. In 2011–12, the total revenue of DB was 37.9 billion Euros with an EBIT of 2.3 billion Euros. Like JR East, substantial part that is 48 per cent of the revenues of DB comes from non-rail business. DB is increasingly becoming active in markets outside Germany with 41 per cent of the revenues coming from international operations. It runs 26,000 passenger trains per day which carry 2.7 billion passengers per year in trains and buses. It is also the fifth largest provider of energy in Germany. As part of its freight and logistics business, DB is spread to more than 2,000 locations in over 130 countries with 412 million tonnes of freight transported by rail per year, 96 million shipments sent per year via European land transport and more than 5 million sq.m. of storage space around the world (figures as in December 2011). It is interesting to note that Germany has 33,600 Km. long rail network which is three times as long as the German Autobahn (Highway) network.

Parcel Business

15.49. One of the important areas to be taken up for rationalisation and expansion will be the parcel business. The annual earnings from parcel services were ₹1,377.38 crore (2010–11). These are projected to grow at a rate of 12.8 per cent during the Plan. The strategy to expand this will include innovative pricing. Escalation in freight rate for parcel traffic should be based on the Wholesale Price Index and increase in the cost of fuel. Concessional pricing based on marginal costing principle can be tried out for parcel express trains in empty flow direction. Differential pricing is needed for different types of parcel services, especially for use of passenger trains using parcel vans. This will help Railways to shift parcel traffic from passenger trains to exclusive Parcel Express trains.

15.50. The Parcel business will be expanded apart from the other initiatives, with the help of capacity augmentation. This will involve the following: Increase in rake loading; Introduction of High Capacity Parcel Vans; Development of dedicated parcel terminals; Mechanisation of handling; Provision of end logistics with value added services; Introduction of premium super fast parcel express services between major production and consumption centres with guaranteed transit and assured supply on the nominated day of loading; and Computerisation of Parcel Management System

Expansion of Fixed Assets

15.51. The targets for creation of fixed assets during the Twelfth Plan have been shown in Table 15.15. Upgradation of balance 1,575 RKM of Iron Ore route for 25 tonnes of axle load (5,425 km done in the Eleventh Plan) and upgradation of Feeder Routes of DFC to run 25 tonnes of axle load will be the areas of focus.

15.52. It is planned to undertake 19,000 km of track renewals including 1,500 km renewal for replacement

TABLE 15.15
Creation of Fixed Assets during the Twelfth Plan

	Eleventh Plan Actuals (Km)	Twelfth Plan Physical Target (Km)
New Line	2,205	4,000
Eastern and Western Dedicated Freight Corridor	Work in Progress	3,338 (Double line except 400 km)
Gauge Conversion	5,290	5,500
Doubling	2,756	7,653
Railway Electrification	4,501	6,500

of 52 kg rails with 60 kg rails on Group A routes. During the Plan, 17,500 km of renewal will become due apart from 3,500 km which is due at the beginning of the Plan.

Dedicated Freight Corridors (DFCs)

15.53. Two Dedicated Freight Corridors (Box 15.3) are expected to be commissioned by March 2017.

Rolling Stock Requirement

15.54. With the expansion of the freight network and passengers demand, the requirement of rolling stock will increase substantially (Table 15.16).

15.55. A range of technological solutions are being implemented for improving the quality of wagons, coaches and locomotives. Some of the measures planned in this regard include transfer of technology from USA for track-friendly bogies of advanced technology capable of carrying enhanced axle loads of 25 tonnes and higher axle loads while exerting lesser forces on the track. Keeping the huge demand for passenger travel in mind, it has been planned to have a complete switchover to new manufacture of only LHB design coaches by the end of Twelfth Plan. This will help in introduction of AC/non-AC trains at speeds more than 130 kmph by induction of LHB design coaches and raise the crash worth quotient of coaching stock on Indian Railways through larger deployment of LHB coaches and incremental

---

Box 15.3
Dedicated Freight Corridors (DFCs) – A Game Change for the Indian Rail Sector

The Dedicated Freight Corridors on the Western and the Eastern routes is a strategic capacity augmentation initiative taken by Railways and involves construction of 3,338 kms of dedicated freight lines to carry predominantly coal and steel on the Eastern corridor and containers on the estern corridor. The ports in the Western region covering Maharashtra and Gujarat would be efficiently linked to the Northern hinterland and similarly on the Eastern side, coal would move to the power plants in the North. The Project completion cost is estimated at ₹95,860 crore. A major part of the project is being financed through multilateral/bilateral debt. World Bank funding of part of Eastern DFC is estimated at US $2.73 billion (₹13,625 crore) and JICA funding of 504 billion Yen (₹31,486 crore). Dankuni–Sonnagar section of Eastern DFC (₹10,022 crore) is to be implemented through PPP. The balance requirement would need to be met through Budgetary Support. Both Eastern and Western DFCs are targeted for completion in the terminal year of the Twelfth Plan.

Dedicated Freight Corridor can be justifiably called an innovation in rail transport in India because of a number of reasons. The average speed of freight trains will go up from 25 kmph to 70 kmph which will reduce the transit time by less than half from the present leves.

Railway technology would get a major up-gradation with the help of heavy hauled freight trains of 15,000 tonnes capacity and 1,500 meters length. The axle loads of DFC routes will also go up from 25 tonnes to 32.5 tonnes which would enhance the track loading capacity from 8.67 tonnes per meter to 12 tonnes per meter. Wagons with much better pay load to tare ratio would also get introduced through this technology. Newer technology in signaling, train communication, track-maintenance and operations would get introduced in the Indian Railways system. The capacity released by freight trains can be used for running more passenger trains at higher speeds after upgrading the existing mixed corridors of Indian Railways.

In addition, this initiative is expected to offer significant reduction of Green House Gas (GHG) emissions in transport sector of India.

Pre-feasibility studies have also been completed on the four new Freight Corridors, *viz.* North-South, East-West, East-South and Southern corridors and Preliminary Engineering cum Traffic Survey is being undertaken by RITES. Based on the outcome of the PETS a beginning would be made in the Twelfth Plan in implementation of the new corridors in a phased manner.

TABLE 15.16
Rolling Stock Requirement during the Twelfth Plan

Type of Stock	Requirement* on Additional Account (2012–13 to 2016–17)	Requirement** on Replacement Account (2012–13 to 2016–17)	Total Requirement (2012–13 to 2016–17)	Anticipated Acquisition 2012–2017
Coaches	25,440	7,626	33,066	24,000
Diesel Locos	1,500	500	2,000	2,000
Electric Locos	1,800	210	2,010	2010
Wagons (in Vehicle Units)	76,396	29,263	1,05,659	1,05,659

* Requirement of coaches includes EMUs, MEMUs and DEMUs.
** Requirements on replacement account for all rolling stocks are based on actual over age arising and the trend of average condemnation.

enhancement in ICF coaches. In case of locomotives higher horsepower capacities and more fuel efficient technologies are being inducted (see Box 15.4).

15.56. With new sections in BG coming on the Indian Railways network either due to gauge conversion or due to new lines, need for branch line operations of passenger trains is increasing. This is best addressed by DEMUs since they are low cost, do not require massive infrastructural investments and they release locos for freight and passenger operations on main line. With a new factory coming up at Haldia which is slated to manufacture up to 400 DEMU coaches per annum, there would be possibility of large scale deployment of DEMU services in the North East, North Bihar, Eastern and North Eastern UP, Gujarat, J&K and many other far-flung areas of the country. Similarly for the electrified sections, EMU/MEMU services would be enhanced with enhancement of technology. A factory is being set up at Kachrapara for manufacturing EMUs/MEMUs and Kolkata Metro coaches which will be operational during the Twelfth Plan.

Signalling and Telecom

15.57. Initiatives in Signalling and Telecom will include deployment of proven and reliable on-board train protection system, isolation of run-through line and provision of complete track circuiting of station sections, and computerised real time monitoring of assets and use of conditions based productive maintenance system. It is also envisaged to increase Line Capacity through use of suitable technology options, viz. Automatic Block Signalling, Intermittent Block Signalling, Automatic Train Control with Cab Signalling, Integrating Train Controlling and

---

Box 15.4
New Generation Locomotives

Ministry of Railways is planning to set up a factory with a foreign partner selected through international competitive bidding for supply of 12,000 HP Electric Locomotives. This will be a major jump over the current 6,000 HP locomotives. During the ten-year period of supply programme, the proposed factory at Madhepura will supply 800 electric locomotives with performance guarantees based on international best practices. This locomotive will have very high energy efficiency and will constitute a part of India's response towards mitigation of the emission of green-house gases. Successful execution of this project by the JV route will usher Indian Railways into a new era of reforms and will provide impetus to PPP funding of railway projects.

Ministry of Railways is also procuring 200 number, 9,000 HP electric locomotives under the JICA loan for Western DFC. These locomotives would be mainly used forcontainer train operations on the Western DFC.

A factory is also planned at Marowhra for manufacture of diesel locomotives with a capacity of 5,000 HP as against current usage of 4,000–4,500 HP by the Indian Railways. The Madhepura and Marowhra factories are likely to be awarded during 2012–13.

Signalling System; and switch over to systems and equipment of higher reliability and safety levels and built in design redundancy.

New and Renewable Energy Projects

15.58. It is proposed to develop renewable energy projects and have strategies for more clean energy in the total consumption basket. Some of the strategies in this regard will include: Grid connected Solar Panels at major stations; Provision of roof top Solar Panels on passenger coaches running in Close Circuits; Provision of solar Panels, Solar Water heaters, Solar Pumps and so on. in Hospitals, Running Rooms, Rest Houses; and LED based lighting and Display Systems. In addition to above, it is also proposed to develop wind energy for meeting the above requirements.

Safety Performance

15.59. There are 14,896 unmanned and 17,839 manned level crossings on Indian Railways network as on 1 April 2011. These level crossings contribute to 30 per cent of fatalities in Railway mishap and statistically contribute to about 40 per cent of accidents of Indian Railways. Accordingly, Indian Railways Vision: 2020 envisage elimination of all unmanned level crossings by provision of subway, diverting road traffic from unmanned level crossing gates to existing ROB/RUB and manned gates by constructing diversion road, closure of very low Train Vehicle Units (TVU) gates, manning of unmanned level crossing gates; upgradation of infrastructure, provision of interlocking of gates, lifting barrier and so on, in the next five years. Railways also envisage provision of ROB/RUB in lieu of manned level crossings with heavy traffic density (high Train Vehicle Units that is above one lakh in about 2122 in number and those level crossings located in station yard/limits about 842 in number). Railways have also planned to eliminate level crossings along the Eastern and Western DFC network. It has been decided to replace level crossings with TVU>50,000 with ROBs and TVUs<50,000 with RUBs. Elimination of level crossings will require General Budgetary Support to Railways for this work. Above works will help in achieving zero accidents at level crossings, minimum detention to road and punctual train operation.

15.60. Railways have prepared a Corporate Safety Plan, 2003–13. Railways have also appointed a High Level Safety Review Committee (Kakodkar Committee) for suggesting measures on Railways safety which has submitted its report. Their recommendations will also be considered during the Plan for strengthening overall safety environment of the Railways. According to this report, the present safety environment on Indian Railways is inadequate largely due to poor infrastructure, paucity of resources and lack of empowerment at the functional level. The committee has recommended setting up of a statutory Railway Safety Authority. The Committee has also recommended adoption of Advance Signaling System based on continuous track circuiting and cab signaling similar to European Train Controlling System Level-II and total elimination of all level crossings within five years. Following key areas related to safety will need to be taken up during the Plan:

1. Development of Train protection and Warning System (TPWS) and Anti Collision Device (ACD)/Train Collision Avoidance systems (TCAS).
2. Provision of improved safety systems with audio visual warning to road users in advance of approaching trains.
3. For moving towards a fault tolerant zero defect regime, computerised real time monitoring of assets and use of condition based in predictive maintenance systems shall be necessary.
4. Development of 'crashworthy' structural design capable of absorbing high impact loads in unfortunate case of collision/accidents.
5. All the furnishing materials in the coaches to have superior fire retardant properties in line with international norms.
6. Mobile Communication and Train Radio Communication (MCTRC).
7. Replacement of 2,000 km of overhead alignment which is an outdated technology for block and control working.

8. Provision of Biometric VCD (Driver's Vigilance Telemetry Control System).
9. Provision of Intelligent fire surveillance and Extinguishing system of locos.
10. Provision of GPS-based fog safe device

Developing High Speed Rail Corridors and Upgradation of Speeds

15.61. Ministry of Railways has selected following six corridors for conducting pre-feasibility studies for development of High Speed Rail Corridors: Delhi–Chandigarh–Amritsar (450 km); Pune–Mumbai–Ahmedabad (650 km); Hyderabad–Dornakal–Vijaywada–Chennai (664 km); Chennai–Bangalore–Coimbatore–Ernakulam–Thiruvananthapuram (849 km); Howrah–Haldia (135 km); and Delhi–Agra–Lucknow–Varanasi–Patna (991 km). The viability of each corridor identified for pre-feasibility study is being examined by consultants. Efforts are being made to complete all such studies, undertake at least two Detailed Projects Reports and develop one corridor of about 500 km for construction.

15.62. It is also proposed to set up a National High Speed Rail Authority (NHSRA), an autonomous body through a Bill in Parliament for implementation of High Speed Rail Corridor projects of Indian Railways. This authority will be entrusted with the work of planning, standard setting, implementing and monitoring these projects.

15.63. It is planned to undertake civil and signaling works to support faster movement of trains on few selected routes. This will enable increase in speed to 130–140 kmph in certain routes and 160 kmph in Delhi–Mumbai and Delhi–Howrah to be further upgraded to 200 kmph.

Public Private Partnerships (PPP)

15.64. Investments in Railways can be stepped up with the help of PPP. So far, such investments have been extremely small. Private investment mobilisation in the Eleventh Plan is likely to be to the tune of 4 per cent of the Plan Outlay. This is far less compared to the Private Capital share in other sectors like Ports – 80 per cent, Telecom 82 per cent, Electricity 44 per cent, Airports 64 per cent and Roads 16 per cent. PPP Projects related to rolling stock manufacturing units, modernisation of railway stations, multifunctional complexes, logistics parks, private freight terminal, freight train operators, liberalised wagon investment schemes, Dedicate Freight Corridors and so on which are in pipeline offer excellent opportunities for private investment. These need to be speedily executed in the Twelfth Plan (Box 15.5).

Tariff and Prices

Tariff Structure

15.65. The tariff structure in Railways is seriously distorted because passenger fares are kept very low and freight fares are increased to cross-subsidise the low level of passenger tariff. Table 15.17 below indicates Indian passenger fares compared with other countries and Table 15.18 compares the freight rates.

15.66. Indian passenger tariffs are one-fourth of China and are one-ninth of Russia. They are nearly one-twentieth of Japan. Even in Purchase Price

---

Box 15.5
Public-Private Partnership (PPP) in Railways

As on date, the Indian Railways have a large shelf of on-going projects whose completion would require about ₹2,25,000 crore. The magnitude of the task is huge and any neglect of the same is bound to lead to severe capacity limitations adversely affecting the competitiveness and growth of the Indian Railways.

It is estimated that the Indian Railways would not be able to generate sufficient funds internally, through borrowings and from budgetary support for meeting the investment requirements of the Twelfth Five Year Plan. The shortfall would be met through private investments in PPP projects. Additional investment from private sector is also expected through their investments in manufacturing facilities created as a consequence of partnerships with IR. Together it is expected that investments of about ₹1 lakh crore would be made by the private sector during the Twelfth Five Year Plan on traffic facilities, other electrical works; workshops including PSUs, passenger amenities; investment in PSUs/JVs/SPVs, and so on.

TABLE 15.17
Passenger Service Yields in some Major Economies

Country	Passenger Service Yield US Cents/ Passenger-KM at nominal prices	Passenger Service Yield US Cents/Passenger-KM adjusted for PPP (India=1)
India	0.6	1.0
China	2.4	2.7
Russia	5.2	6.7
Japan	19.0	9.4
Germany	12.6	6.2

Source: World Bank (2012): Railways International Overview: Issues for India.

TABLE 15.18
Freight Yields in some Major Economies

Country	Freight Yield US Cents/Total Tonne-KM at nominal prices	Freight Yield US Cents/Total Tonne-KM adjusted for PPP (India=1)
India	2.11	1.00
China	1.49	0.58
Russia	2.20	0.75
USA	2.28	0.51

Source: World Bank (2012): Railways International Overview: Issues for India.

Parity terms, the tariffs bear no comparison. In terms of freight rates, however, the Indian freight rates are the highest whereas those of China, Russia and the USA are 58 per cent, 75 per cent and 51 per cent of the Indian rates adjusted for PPP. Even in nominal terms, Chinese freight rates are only around 72 per cent of the Indian fright rates.

15.67. The low passenger fares, which have not been revised for several years, have led to huge losses in passenger traffic operations estimated at ₹22,000 crore in 2011–12. Unless the trend is arrested by rationally linking passenger fare to input costs, the Railways will be out priced in the freight market and would find it unsustainable to run the Railway operations.

15.68. In the passenger service segment, suburban services contribute almost 54 per cent in number of passengers over the IR's total passenger traffic. Their earning share is, however, only 7.13 per cent (2009–10). The losses suffered in the segment during 2008–09 and 2009–10 were ₹1,651.19 crore and ₹2,214.06 crore respectively. In view of the rising input costs, the suburban fares need to be revised and the level of subsidies gradually reduced in line with the proposed indexation of lower class fares.

Tariff Regulatory Authority and other reforms
15.69. In the earlier Plans, it had been suggested that a Tariff Regulatory Authority may be set up to fix up tariffs both for passenger and freight. It has, however, so far not been possible. It has to be realised that with the coming up of more PPP projects, the need has become more pressing. The Tariff Regulatory Authority like the regulators in the other sectors will recommend the tariff structures consistent with the level of cross-subsidies feasible.

15.70. Numerous reports have mentioned the need to undertake organisational reforms in the Railways (see Box 15.6). The current departmental organisation of the Railways is not conducive to the running of railways as an economic and business enterprise, and towards executing the necessary changes to overhaul the service. The Railway Board should be re-organised along business lines, in contrast with the current division between the various disciplines, electrical, mechanical, traffic and so on. This view has also been strongly endorsed by the Kakodkar and Pitroda Committees. Early adoption of standard business accounting policies will necessitate adequate appropriations to depreciation reserves on a predictable, systematic and transparent basis.

Financing of the Twelfth Plan
15.71. The Plan will require large investments to achieve its objectives. The estimated resources required are ₹5,19,221 crore including GBS of ₹1,94,221 crore, IEBR of ₹2,25,000 crore and private sector investment of ₹1,00,000 crore.

> **Box 15.6**
> **Key Message from Reports on Railways: The Need for Organisational Reforms**
>
> In the past decade or so, a number of reports have been presented related to the rail sector. The Indian Railways Expert Committee Report (2001) recommended significant organisational changes including corporatisation of the Indian Railways and a new investment programme to achieve high traffic and revenue growth along with improvement in safety performance. Indian Railway's Vision 2020 (2009) is an aspirational plan which charts out a growth of 10 per cent for the Railways over the next 10 years by developing a sharper commercial focus with strong social commitment. Recently in February 2012, two more reports have been submitted. The Expert Group on modernisation of Indian Railways (Pitroda Committee) has unequivocally stated that Indian Railways are in urgent need of modernisation and generational change to ensure safety, improve productivity, take advantage of advances in technology and respond to ever increasing demand in order to meet the inclusive growth aspirations of the country. The High Level Safety Review Committee (Kakodkar Committee) was also presented in February 2012. All these reports have recommended organisational reforms in the Railways.

15.72. Some major initiatives in the Twelfth Plan are:

- Twelfth Plan would target to enhance rail share in freight traffic by at least 2 per cent.
- The Eastern and Western Dedicated Freight Corridors would be completed during the Twelfth Plan period and planning for other DFCs—North-South, East-South, East-West and South-West may be firmed up during the Twelfth Plan period.
- The Twelfth Plan would focus on five areas—track, bridges, signalling and telecom, rolling stock and station and freight terminals which would lead to safety, decongestion, capacity augmentation and modernisation of system creating more efficient, faster and safer railways.
- Signalling system would be modernised with provision of advanced technological features and development of Train Protection and Warning System (TPWS), Anti Collision Device (ACD), Trains Collision Avoidance System (TCAS), GPS-based Fog Safety Device and Biometric Drivers Vigilance Elementary Control System.
- Phased elimination of all unmanned level crossings by provision of subway, ROBs/RUBs, constructing diversion roads, and so on.
- Expansion of Long Haul trains using distributed power system.
- Improvement in the design and technology of wagons, coaches and locos through acquisition as well as investment in R&D along with induction of latest technology in rolling stock by encouraging expansion in capacity of manufacturing units through PPP.
- Developing High Speed Rail corridors and Setting up National High Speed Rail Authority (NHSRA) as an autonomous body for planning, standard setting, implementation and monitoring of high speed corridors.
- Promoting private investment in special purpose high capacity wagons under the Liberalised Wagon Investment Scheme (LWIS) and Encouraging private freight operators to transport select commodities where railway modal share is low, that is automobile, un-bagged cement and fertiliser, fly ash, edible oils, and so on.
- Activity Based Accounting to facilitate managerial decision making and to establish profit/loss making routes/activities.
- Correcting the imbalance between passenger and freight traffic by setting up a Tariff Regulatory Authority to suggest tariff structures consistent with the level of feasible cross-subsidies.
- Resolution of regulatory issues regarding CONCOR and private players and further expansion of containerisation.
- Reorganisation of Indian Railways on business lines, hiving off non-transportation tasks and separation of policy making and operational responsibilities of the Railway Board.

ROADS

15.73. India has one of the largest road networks in the world, consisting of (*i*) national highways (NHs), (*ii*) state highways (SHs), (*iii*) major district roads (MDRs) and (*iv*) rural roads (RRs) that include other district roads and village roads. The NHs with a length of 76,818 km comprises only 2.0 per cent of the road network but carry 40 per cent of the road-based traffic. The SHs and the MDRs together constitute the secondary system of road transportation which contribute significantly to the development of the rural economy and industrial growth of the country. The secondary system also carries about 40 per cent of the total road traffic, although it constitutes about 13 per cent of the total road length. At the tertiary level are the Other District Roads (ODRs) and the Rural Roads (RRs). These, once adequately developed and maintained, hold the potential to provide rural connectivity vital for generating higher agricultural incomes and productive employment opportunities besides promoting access to economic and social services.

15.74. In recent years special efforts have been made by the central government to strengthen the National Highway and also to improve rural road connectivity. Despite this, the road network remains grossly inadequate in various respects. It is unable to handle high traffic density and high speeds at many places and has poor riding quality. It is necessary to accelerate completion of ongoing projects, including expressways besides speedy implementation of the Golden Quadrilateral (GQ) and the North-South and East-West (NS-EW) corridors and also to address the deterioration of large stretches of the NHs.

Review of the Eleventh Plan

15.75. Against an outlay of ₹1,92,428 crore in the Eleventh Plan for the road sector, the anticipated expenditure was ₹1,58,077 crore (at current prices). The scheme-wise and year-wise outlay and expenditure are given in Annexure 15.1.

National Highways (NHs)

15.76. At present, out of 76,818 kms of National Highways about 23 per cent length is of 4-lane (and above standard), 54 per cent length is of 2-lane standard and 23 per cent length is of single and intermediate standard. As on March 2012, 30,537 km length of NHs was entrusted to NHAI, 42,483 km to State PWDs and 3,798 km to BRO. Plan-wise details of increase in the NHs network are enclosed (Annexure 15.2). An overview of the physical targets and achievements of normal NH works, Border Roads Development Board (BRDB) works, and works by the NHAI during the Eleventh Plan period is enclosed (Annexure 15.3)

15.77. Despite the progress in NHs, only 23 per cent of their total length is wider than two lanes, leading to heavy congestion. Shortfall in construction of bypasses, inadequate capacity, insufficient pavement thickness, and weak, narrow, and distressed bridges/culverts as well as ROBs are some of the other deficiencies.

National Highway Development Programme (NHDP)

15.78. India's road network has benefited greatly from the NHDP programme which envisages an investment of about ₹2,36,247 crore during the period 2005–12. Although NHDP envisaged award of concessions/contracts by the year 2012, the actual completion of the programme was expected to be accomplished only by the end of the Twelfth Plan. Phase-wise progress of NHDP during the Eleventh Plan is given in Table 15.19 and details of various phases are given in (Table 15.20). A map showing these details is given at Annexure 15.4.

Financing of National Highway Development Programme (NHDP)

15.79. Development and maintenance of National Highways is financed through various sources. Details are given in Box 15.7.

TABLE 15.19
Physical Achievements under NHDP during the Eleventh Five Year Plan

NHDP	Total length completed (km)*
NHDP Phase I	639
NHDP Phase II	5,210
NHDP Phase III	3,599
NHDP Phase V	913
NHDP Phase VII	13
Other Projects	235
Total	10,609

* Up to 31 March 2012 (Provisional).

TABLE 15.20
Progress of NHDP up to 30 April 2012

Total length (km)	GQ 5,846	NS&EW 7,142	NHDP Ph.-III 12,109	NHDP Ph.-IV 14,799	NHDP Ph.-V 6,500	NHDP Ph.-VII 700	Other NHs 1,383
Completed Total till date (km)	5,840	6,018	3,798	–	940	14	961
Under Implementation							
Length (km)	6	691	2,802	3,318	1,181	27	409
Contracts (Nos.)	8	66	56	23	15	2	5
Letter of Award issued/Agreement signed and Work to be started							
Length (km)	12	3,669		1,866			0
Contracts (Nos.)	1	36		12			0
Total							
Length (km)	6	703	6,471	3,318	30,47	27	409
Contracts (Nos.)	8	67	92	23	27	2	5
Length to be awarded							
Length (km)	0	421	1,840	1,1481	2,513	659	20

Box 15.7
Financing of National Highway Development Programme (NHDP)

- Gross Budgetary Support (GBS) and Additional Budgetary Support (ABS).
- Dedicated accruals under the Central Road Fund. Present rate of cess is ₹2.00 per litre on both petrol and diesel. A part of this cess is allocated to NHAI to fund the NHDP.
- External Assistance through World Bank, ADB, JBIC, and so on.
- Ploughing back of toll revenue including toll collection, negative grant, premium and revenue share deposited by NHAI into Consolidated Fund of India and equivalent amount to be released to NHAI for ploughing back in its projects.
- Private Sector Investment under Public Private Partnership(PPP) frameworks that is BOT-(Toll) BOT(Annuity), Special Purpose Vehicle (SPV)- with Equity participation by NHAI.
- Market Borrowings by NHAI as authorised by GOI to bridge the gap between the available resources and funds requirement.

Roads Under SARDP-NE

15.80. To promote the development of road network in the North-East, a Special Accelerated Programme for Road Development in North-East (SARDP-NE) was taken up in two phases. Under Phase 'A' of SARDP-NE approved by the Government, improvement of about 4,099 km length of roads (2,041 km NHs and 2,058 km State roads) is envisaged. The SARDP-NE Phase-A was targeted for completion by March 2014. However, it is expected to be completed by March, 2015. Under Phase 'B' of SARDP-NE Programme, covering 3,723 km (1,285 km NH and 2,438 km State road), have been approved for DPR preparation. So far DPRs of about 450 km has been completed. About 892 km (21.8 per cent) length has been completed under SARDP-NE Phase-A till end March 2012.

15.81. Part of SARDP-NE is the Arunachal Pradesh Package for Road and Highways involving development of about 2,319 km length of road (1,472 km is NHs and 847 km is State/General Staff/Strategic roads) has also been approved by the Government. Projects for 776 km are to be taken up on BOT (Annuity) mode and the balance 1,543 km is to be developed on EPC basis. The entire Arunachal Pradesh Package is targeted for completion by June 2016. Out of the BOT (Annuity) Projects, 3 Projects have been awarded for 369 km costing ₹3,126 crore; balance 407 km costing ₹1,985 crore is in the process of award. In case of EPC Projects, out of the sanctioned 359 km, 143 km is under process for sanction andDPRs are under preparation for balance 928 km. Target for award of all civil works is March, 2012. So far during 2011–12, 10 km of road has been completed.

Roads for LWE Districts

15.82. A programme for development of about 1,202 km of National Highways and 4,362 km of State Roads in Left Wing Extremism (LWE) affected areas as a special project costing about ₹7,300 crore has been taken up. The programme is slated for completion by March, 2015. The projects cover 34 districts in eight States, namely Andhra Pradesh, Bihar, Chhattisgarh, Jharkhand, Madhya Pradesh, Maharashtra, Orissa and Uttar Pradesh. So far, 178 number of works containing a road length of 4,967 km costing ₹6,637 crore have been sanctioned. Out of these, 157 number of works containing a road length of 4,181 km estimated to cost ₹5,270 crore have been awarded and remaining are at various stages.

National Highways Outside NHDP Programme

15.83. Physical progress of Non-NHDP National Highways during Eleventh Plan is given in Table 15.21.

15.84. Procurement of public funded projects has witnessed a paradigm shift and now there is a shift towards EPC mode of procurement instead of the traditional mode of item rate contract (Box 15.8).

> **Box 15.8**
> **Engineering, Procurement, Construction (EPC) Contract**
>
> The conventional item-rate contracts are generally prone to time and cost overruns, particularly in the National Highway sector, resulting in enhanced cost to the exchequer, as also considerable delays in the completion of projects. Developed countries have moved to Engineering, Procurement and Construction (EPC) contracts where the contractor is responsible for design and construction on a turnkey basis and for a fixed price. The Planning Commission has published a model Engineering, Procurement and Construction (EPC) contract for Highways. It is expected that about 20,000 km of 2 lane National Highways would be developed under this model. A similar document is also being prepared for Dedicated Freight Corridor of the Indian Railways.

State Highways (SHs) and Major District Roads (MDRs)

15.85. Investments including PPP under VGF programme of central government have been made by the State Governments to expand the networks of roads, especially state highways, which are part of the secondary and territory network. This has resulted in expansion of the road network as shown in Table 15.22.

15.86. It has been found that many State roads suffer from low investment, inadequate width of carriageway to meet traffic demand, weak pavement and bridges, congested stretches passing through

TABLE 15.21
Physical Progress of Non-NHDP NHs during Eleventh Five Year Plan

Sl. No	Category	Total Completion of Works from 2007–08 to 2010–11		2011–12 (Provisional)	
		Target	Achv.	Target	Achv. (Up to March 2012)
1	Missing Link (km)	59.4	55.3	—	—
2	Widening to 2-lanes (km)	4,533	4,379	1,070	727
3	Strengthening (km)	3,554	3,950	1,080	672
4	Improvement of Riding Quality (km)	7,769	9,321	1,672	2,367
5	Widening to 4-lanes (km)	301.5	267	104	74
6	Bypasses (No.)	32	13	7	7
7	Bridges /ROBs (No.)	518	388	129	87

TABLE 15.22
State Roads Progress during the Eleventh Plan

	Lane wise Length of SH in 2007 (km)				Lane wise Length of SH in 2011 (km)			
	Total Length	SL/IL	2 Lane	4 Lane and above	Total Length	SL/IL	2 Lane	4 Lane and above
States	1,50,492	1,11,850	36,349	2,293	1,65,724	1,00,819	60,747	4,157
UTs	221	145	56	20	405	230	63	112
Total	1,50,713	11,995	36,405	2,313	1,66,129	1,01,049	60,811	4,269

cities/towns, poor safety features and road geometrics, and inadequate formation width in hilly and mountainous regions, missing links and bridges and several railway level crossings requiring urgent replacement with ROB/road under bridge (RUB) to improve safety and faster traffic movement. A broad assessment shows that over 50 per cent of SHs and MDRs network have poor riding quality. According to one assessment, annual losses due to poor condition of these roads would be around ₹6,000 crore. Many policy and implementation deficiencies have to be redressed. These include: thin spreading of resources; delay in pre-construction activities due to delay in land acquisition; delay in environmental clearance and shifting/removal of utilities; weak management by contractors due to improper deployment of human resources and equipment; and poor implementation capacities of the state Public Works Departments (PWDs).

Road Maintenance

15.87. The road network built at a huge cost needs to be maintained properly to prevent disintegration and deterioration, ensuring its continuous utilisation in an optimum manner and road safety of its users. However, maintenance of roads, is treated as a non-Plan activity and has, therefore, tended to be neglected because of financial resources constraints. The maintenance requirement of the high density corridors of NHs under construction and post-implementation is provided by the NHAI. However, the non-NHDP NH sections, which are maintained by State PWDs, are poorly managed, primarily because funds made available to them for maintenance are well short of the requirement as per norms. According to an estimate, the NHs get only 50 per cent of the total funds required for proper maintenance of NHs. Maintenance of SHs and MDRs has also been suffering from paucity of resources made available for the purpose. For rural roads under PMGSY, there is provision for maintenance for five years following the completion of a project but the long-term issue of maintenance beyond the initial five year period has not been addressed so far. Besides inadequacy of resources, management of roads is unsystematic and inspections are irregular. There is weak accountability and poor monitoring of the maintenance activities.

Public–Private Partnership (PPP) Projects

15.88. During the Eleventh Plan, total private-sector investment on NHDP has been ₹62,629 crore against a target of ₹86,792.00 crore, which is a substantial jump over the achievement in the Tenth Plan of ₹11,032 crore (2011–12 prices) Appropriate policy and regulatory framework for the PPPs, including institutional mechanisms are put in place such as the Model Concession Agreement (MCA) for BOT projects.

Pradhan Mantri Gram Sadak Yojana (PMGSY)

15.89. Empowering rural India through the strategic provision of all-season road access has emerged as one of the key priorities for the Government of India. The Eleventh Five Year Plan (2007–12), and the Tenth Plan before it, recognised that rural connectivity is a key component of rural development and poverty alleviation in India. The main mechanism for enhancing rural connectivity in a more systematic way has been the Pradhan Mantri Gram Sadak Yojana (PMGSY), a Centrally Sponsored Scheme (CSS), launched on the 25 December 2000. The programme seeks to connect all habitations with a population of 500 persons and above in plain areas and 250 persons and above in Hill States, Tribal (Schedule V) areas, the Desert Areas (as identified in Desert Development Programme) and in the 82 Selected and Tribal Backward districts (under IAP) as identified by the Ministry of Home Affairs/Planning Commission. The Government of India has also identified 'rural roads' as one of the six components of 'Bharat Nirman' with a goal to provide connectivity to all habitations with a population of 1,000 persons and above in plain areas and 500 persons and above in hilly or tribal areas with an all-weather road.

15.90. The physical and financial progress of PMGSY upto the end of Eleventh Plan is presented in Tables 15.23 and 15.24. Although the PMGSY has achieved only 53 percent of its initial targets—mainly due to limited implementation capacity—its achievements have been significant. The length of the new and improved rural road network under the program to date has reached 2,09,500 km and as a result 84,414 habitations have been connected. The main strength of the PMGSY programme has been its ability to develop a strong national focus for rural roads development through the National Rural Roads Development Agency (NRRDA). The NRRDA has developed a common set of operating procedures that are applied nationwide through the dedicated State Rural Roads Development Agencies (SRRDAs) and their Program Implementation Units (PIUs). These operating procedures are set out in a series of PMGSY manuals covering overall operations, technical design, quality control and accounting. There is a systematic planning process in place which has included the prioritisation of a 1.5 million km core rural road network, of which about 750,000 km are eligible for new connectivity and upgrading under the PMGSY programme. The programme has also developed a web-based On-line Monitoring Management and Accounting System (OMMAS) which is accessible to the public.

15.91. Evidence from several impact evaluation exercises on PMGSY indicates the multiple benefits generated in the rural economy in both commercial and social spheres by improving road connectivity. A study by Bell (2012)[1] examines the contribution

TABLE 15.23
Physical Progress–PMGSY (as on 31 March 2012)

	Total Eligible	Sanctioned	Completed
Habitations (in Nos.)	1,58,891	1,14,963 (72%)	84,414 (53% of eligible)
New Connectivity length (km.)	3,67,673	2,79,811 (76%)	2,09,570 (57% of eligible)
Upgradation length (UG) (km.)	3,74,844 2,25,111–UG 1,49,733–Renewal	1,64,096 (73%) (UG)	1,40,930 (62% of eligible) (UG)

TABLE 15.24
Financial Progress (as on 31st March, 2012)

(₹ crore)

Value of Proposals Sanctioned	Funds Released	Expenditure Incurred
127786	1,00,417	91,498

of PMGSY in drawing India's villages into the mainstream, in three ways. First, with improved connections to markets, villagers should face more favourable prices for inputs and outputs. Second, by reducing the time spent travelling to school and the days lost due to bad weather, an all-weather road should improve the attendance, not only of pupils, but also of their teachers, thus promoting the formation of human capital and the growth of productivity over the long run. Third, by improving the villagers' access to timely treatment, especially in emergencies, the connection should lower mortality and morbidity.

15.92. Bell (2012) attempts to estimate the relative sizes of each of these respective contributions to total benefits from PMGSY. The author finds that providing backward rural areas with all-weather roads promotes not only production and trade in what can be called the 'commercial' sphere of life, but also the formation of human capital and health in the 'non-commercial' one. In a further analysis[2], he along with his co-author undertakes a cross section comparison of 30 villages (nine of which benefited from PMGSY) and 'before and after' comparisons in these nine villages. The authors find that net output prices were 5 per cent or higher; substantially fewer days of schooling were lost due to bad weather, largely because teachers had fewer absences. The improvement in the accessibility to education resulted in increased school enrolment and school attendance. Importantly, there was an increase in the number of girls going to schools. The acutely sick received more timely treatment and were more likely to be treated in a hospital than in the nearest primary health clinic in villages connected by PMGSY. Better management of infectious diseases and attending to emergencies due to faster access to health facilities and increase infrequency of visits by health workers were the other outcomes. Moreover, there was an increase in the number of institutional deliveries in hospitals outside the village, improvement in ante-natal and post-natal care and a decline in infant and child mortality.

15.93. Several independent impact evaluation exercises commissioned by the Ministry of Rural Development have also revealed the huge benefits in terms of agricultural growth, income and employment generation, access to healthcare and education, and poverty reduction generated by PMGSY. Better connectivity resulting in easier access to markets and improved flow of information led to improvements in agricultural production and incomes of the farmers inhabiting the connected area. Considerable change in cropping pattern was observed, with a shift from food crops to cash crops. Non-farm opportunities like opening of shops, small business, cottage industries increased and more avenues for self-employment emerged. Besides, road connectivity led to expansion of local industries, which in turn generated employment opportunities. The construction of the PMGSY road also led to an increase in frequency of visits by Government officials. This is likely to result in better implementation of various Government schemes and programmes.

Bharat Nirman

15.94. Under Rural Connectivity component of Bharat Nirman, all habitations having population of 1,000 or more persons (500 or more in hilly and tribal areas) are to be provided connectivity with all-weather roads. Accordingly, the programme envisages to provide connectivity to 63,940 habitations under above category. Projects to connect 58,387 habitations have been sanctioned and 44,089 habitations connected by constructing 1,41,095 km of new roads up to 31 March 2012. Also 1,03,471 km of roads were upgraded (excluding renewals by States) (Tables 15.25 and 15.26).

TABLE 15.25
Habitation Coverage – Bharat Nirman (as on 31 March 2012)

	Total Eligible	Projects Cleared (Sanctioned)	Completed
Habitations (in numbers)	63,940	58,387 (91%)	44,089 (69% of eligible)

TABLE 15.26
Cumulative Physical Progress under Bharat Nirman (up to March 2012)

Activity	Target (2005–12)	Achievement
New Connectivity (Length in km.)	1,89,897	1,41,096 (74%)
Up-gradation including renewal (in kms)	1,94,131	2,35,903 (122%)

The Twelfth Plan

15.95. The Twelfth Plan will have to continue the thrust of upgrading the road infrastructure, with the objective of improving mobility and accessibility while reducing the cost of transportation. The main targets of the Twelfth Plan will be as follows:

1. Completion of on-going works on Golden Quadrilateral and North–South and East–West corridors taken up in NHDP Phases I and II of the programme. The balance works remaining are marginal and will get completed in the first two years of the Plan.
2. In respect of the remaining phases of NHDP, namely NHDP-III for inter-district roads and other roads taken up under the programme and NHDP-IV which aims to convert single-lane roads to double-lane roads, the programmes will be taken up for completion in the Twelfth Plan.
3. Similarly, NHDP-V which involves conversion of the GQ to six-lane roads now will be

continued in the Twelfth Plan and specific targets set for completion.
4. National and State Highways would be upgraded to minimum two lane standard by the end of the Plan.
5. All villages will be connected with all-weather roads by the end of the Plan.
6. Work on access controlled expressways has moved at a slow pace. A comprehensive master plan for development of 15,600 km of expressways would be developed, the alignment determined and work taken up in phases. It is hoped that 1,000 km of expressways would be completed during the Twelfth Plan, while land for another 6,000 km would be acquired to initiate work.
7. The Plan will aim to prioritise special links for feeder roads to important railway routes and ports which are essential for development of domestic and international trade. The overall effort will be to integrate with the road development programme with the other modes of transport so as to have an integrated transport movement. Such links which connect important minor and major ports and developed with minimum two/four-lane National Highways or State Highways. Important areas of focus will be development of way-side amenities and improving capacities of implementing agencies, including State Public Works Departments. While undertaking construction of roads, modern technologies which can help in improvement of energy conservation and environmental protection will be taken up. The National Highways had added 10,000 km in the Eleventh Plan. Another 10,000 kms will be added during the Twelfth Plan so that the total length of the highways becomes 91,200 km. This will require additional resources for maintenance and improving riding quality. These will be adequately funded.

Road Development in the North-East

15.96. The development of roads in the North-East had been taken up by special programme under Special Accelerated Road Development Programme for North-East (SARDP-NE). It is proposed that the balance works under these programmes, which includes connectivity of all State capitals of North-East with two or four-lane NHs with paved shoulders and connecting all district headquarters with two-lane NHs will be taken up for completion. SARDP-NE Phase-B for which work has been taken up to prepare DPRs would get completed. It is planned to develop and complete the Trans-Arunachal Pradesh Highway during the Plan.

15.97. The construction of roads on PPP basis has gained momentum in the Eleventh Plan and most of the roads are getting constructed on BOT (Toll) basis. It is proposed to continue with this policy in the Twelfth Plan. Simultaneously, a Model Concession Agreement (MCA) for organisation and maintenance (OMT) for tollable roads will be taken up to ensure effective maintenance. The strengthening and restructuring of the roads in the North East will be taken up for non-tollable roads. These are assets which need to be effectively maintained. To ensure this, modern management techniques and scientific assessment of maintenance strategies will be taken up. The capacities of NHAI and BRO would be further developed for this purpose.

Non-NHDP Road

15.98. The Twelfth Plan will also aim at development of roads not covered under the NHDP, which have been taken up by NHAI. It is proposed that 19,200 km of roads will be taken up for conversion of two-lane roads, including 10,000 km of NHs so declared during the Eleventh Plan. It is proposed to develop 3,770 km of roads with the help of the World Bank assistance and another 6,350 km through BOT (Toll) route. 1,000 km of expressways are planned, in addition to the NHDP programme. In addition, some of the other developments, including strengthening and improvement of riding quality, construction of bridges/ROBs will be taken up.

Roads in LWE Areas

15.99. The programme for development of roads in the Left-Wing Extremism (LWE) affected districts will be continued and works taken up earlier in the Eleventh Plan be completed during the Plan. It is expected that 4,426 km of work will get completed by March 2015 and another 9,615 km by March 2017.

New Schemes During Twelfth Plan

15.100. New Schemes during the Twelfth Plan are as under:

1. Special Package for development of roads in the Schedule Areas (under Fifth Schedule) under Tribal Sub-Plan—1,000 km for total GBS requirement of ₹5,000 crore.
2. Development of road corridors in Delhi–Mumbai industrial corridor project.
3. Special package for development of State roads in the State of J&K from strategic considerations—complete about 700 km out of total length of about 1,000 km for total GBS requirement of ₹700 crore.
4. Special package for development of road connectivity for about 50 minor ports—1,000 km for total GBS requirement of ₹5,000 crore.
5. Special package for development of road connectivity for 24 Airports—360 km for total GBS requirement of ₹1,800 crore.

Rural Roads

15.101. The Twelfth Plan will, aim to connect remaining these habitations by constructing about 1,58,000 km of new roads. 84,181 km of existing roads are planned to be upgraded during the Twelfth Plan.

15.102. In addition, the funds are required for following activities:

1. NABARD Loan (Principal) and interest repayment.
2. Provision for left-out bridges on already sanctioned roads.
3. Inclusion of left out habitations due to revision of core-network permitting to take habitations (as per guidelines) instead of revenue villages as units of connectivity in Core-Network.
4. Coverage of new habitations of 250+ in 78 IAP districts
5. Providing bridges of 75 m length in 78 IAP districts
6. Additional provisions due to snow fall/landslides in Hill States
7. For providing connectivity to left-out habitations (as per 2001 census) in core-network and for up gradation of some selected roads in 78 IAP districts
8. For launching of PMGSY-II during Twelfth Five Year Plan on sharing basis

15.103. During the Tenth and Eleventh Plan periods, huge investments of over ₹1,00,000 crore have been made in expanding the rural roads network. Hence, it has been proposed to launch PMGSY-II, to consolidate the existing rural road network. It would cover up gradation of existing selected rural roads based on a criterion to make the road network vibrant, on sharing basis with the States. The selection of routes would be with the objective of identification of rural growth centres and other critical rural hubs.

State Highways

15.104. A programme similar to the NHDP for the state highways is needed. The States will be encouraged to develop a core network. The development of four-lanes and two-lanes will accordingly be taken up as part of this Plan. The resources required for the State's programme of the above are estimated at ₹4.9 lakh crore, of which 20 per cent is expected to be private sector investment. For this purpose, PPP would be encouraged through Viability Gap Funding (VGF) window available with the Central Government. Targets for Twelfth Plan are mentioned in Table 15.27.

Public-Private Partnerships (PPP) and Other Initiatives

15.105. The NHDP programme will be funded primarily through PPP, a policy which had been initiated in the Eleventh Plan. For this purpose, a VGF of 40 per cent is provided in the Road Sector, including 20 per cent from the cess on petrol and diesel, which is available with the NHAI. It is proposed to continue and further strengthen the PPP construction and build BOT (Toll) roads. It is also proposed to strengthen and improve the existing framework, specifically these will be further expanded for construction of roads by the State Governments. Some of the innovations undertaken by the State Government are given in the (Box 15.9).

15.106. Roads are a major user of construction material especially of bitumen and asphalt which

TABLE 15.27
Targets for the Twelfth Plan

	State Highways		Major District Roads	
	Kilometres	% of Existing/Total Lengths	Kilometres	% of Existing/Total Lengths
2–Laning	30,000	30	20,000	8.5
4–Laning	5,000	8	1,000	4
Strengthening	41,500	25	66,500	25
IRQP	50,000	30	80,000	30

are known to emit gases into the atmosphere. Use of green bitumen materials and specific R&D schemes for possible adaptation of state-of-the-art innovative technologies and materials in highway development and maintenance would be encouraged during the Twelfth Plan.

15.107. The rapid pace of development of the road sector has resulted in skill deficit especially among the technical and engineering staff. Involvement of contractors and developers in creating skilled resource pool and encouraging Engineering and Technical Institutions to attract students in Highway Engineering profession would be some initiatives for bridging the skill gap. National Academy of Construction could be an institution worth emulation by other states.

Regulator for Roads

15.108. There is no independent regulatory authority for India's Roads and Highways sector. Current arrangement both at Centre and States (MORTH, NHAI, MPRDC, PWDs and so on) results in a potential conflict as the rule making body is also the implementing body and there is no independent assessment of its performance across various parameters. There is, therefore, a need for a regulator whose key functions should include tariff setting, regulation of service quality, assessment of concessionaire claims, collection and dissemination of sector information, service-level benchmarks and monitoring compliance of concession agreements.

Some Major Initiatives in the Twelfth Plan

15.109. Major initiatives in the Twelfth Plan Period are:

- Earmarking of Plan funds for IRQP and strengthening/maintenance of non-tollable roads.
- Development of capacities of NHAI, BRO and other implementing agencies.

Box 15.9
Innovations by some State Governments

- Crucial role being played by Madhya Pradesh Road Development Corporation and Gujarat State Road Development Corporation (GSRDC) in upgrading SRs using Central Government's VGF which extends subsidy of up to 20 per cent of total project cost and an additional up to 20 per cent financed by State Government. Contribution to GSRDC is also kept to defray expenditure on pre-construction activities.
- PPP (Annuity) model adopted by Gujarat since strengthening/widening of SRs does generate a commercially viable return despite 40 per cent upfront subsidy.
- Adoption of a plan scheme for land acquisition for identified corridors by Punjab to reduce traffic congestion on major highways, with funds proposed to be released on the condition that these shall be recovered by PWD by imposing a cess on sale/purchase and any development activity carried out by the private parties on lands adjoining PWD roads.
- Creation of a Rajasthan State Road Development Fund, through a cess on sale of petrol and high speed diesel, towards extending interest free loan and share capital to the Road Infrastructure Development Company of Rajasthan for projects to upgrade SHs.

- Prioritisation of special links for feeder roads to important railway points, ports and areas where rail link is not possible.
- Special focus on development of roads for Delhi–Mumbai industrial corridor.
- States to be encouraged to develop core network for rural connectivity.
- Providing universal connectivity in rural areas under PMGSY, launch of PMGSY-II and pilots on PPP in some selected PMGSY roads.
- Focus on implementation of rural road projects in the LWE districts through the Integrated Action Plan (IAP).
- Investment in R&D, green technology and design for better and safer roads.

Road Transport

Issues

15.110. Road transport has emerged as the dominant segment in India's transportation sector with a share of 4.7 per cent in India's GDP in 2009–10 which is higher than Railways that has a 1 per cent share. Road transport has gained importance over the years despite significant barriers to inter-state freight and passenger movement compared to inland waterways, railways and air which do not face rigorous en route checks/barriers. Despite the performance of the road transport sector, it is beset with slow technological development, low energy efficiency, pollution and slow movement of freight and passenger traffic.

Eleventh Plan Review

15.111. The Road Transport policies cover efficient road movement, road safety and related areas. The approved outlay for the Eleventh Five Year Plan for the Transport Sector was ₹1,131 crore for Road Safety, National Database Network, Inspection and Maintenance Centre, Strengthening of Public Transport, Creation of National Road Safety Board.

Approach to Twelfth Plan

15.112. With the sustained high rates of economic growth, the growth of passenger and commercial traffic will be high. An estimate of this was made by working group making assumptions for various scenarios (Table 15.28). The Plan will aim at several policy interventions to ensure efficient development of transport of passenger and freight across the country.

Development of Database in Road Sector

15.113. The availability of relevant data depends primarily on the efforts of States. Currently, the database on road transport is restricted to number of registered motor vehicles category-wise as required by the Motor Vehicle (MV) Act, 1988. There are serious gaps in Road Transport data such as decentralised generation of data, multiplicity of agencies, time lag, no data on movement of people, goods and vehicles, passenger and freight flows measured in a variety of ways and so on. These issues can be resolved by a national consensus on data generation using IT extensively. A group will be set up during the Plan to resolve the above issues and improve the national database

Efficiency of Road Transport

15.114. Measures need to be taken to improve road transport efficiency. Some of the areas which will be taken up in the Plan include: Integration of tax administration with inter-state road freight and passenger movement through online communication network system at National, Regional and Local level; Reforms in tax administration including replacing various road transport related taxes/levies (road tax, goods tax, passenger tax) and so on by a single composite tax; Reforms in Motor Vehicles Act to simplify inter-State movement with simplified procedures; Automate and Use of IT for Cross Border Road Freight Transport Management.

Electronic Tolling System

15.115. The Road Transport System needs to be modernised. For this, there is need to introduce Electronic Toll Collection (ETC) system in (Box 15.10). At present, there are very few truck terminals in cities. There is need to create a number of truck terminals in almost all 'A', 'B' and 'C' class cities and towns. These truck terminals will ease the traffic congestion in the city and decrease pollution, facilitate emergence of hub spoke system for distribution of goods and greatly improve the turnaround time

TABLE 15.28
Projected Road Freight and Passenger Traffic

Years of Twelfth Plan	Billion Tonne Kilometre (BTKM)					Billion Passenger Kilometre (BPKM)	
	S I (BAU)	S II	S III	S IV	S V	S A (BAU)	S B
2012–13	1,315	1,337	1,351	1,366	1,381	8,150	8,483
2013–14	1,429	1,465	1,489	1,513	1,538	8,868	9,111
2014–15	1,553	1,605	1,641	1,677	1,714	9,648	9,762
2015–16	1,688	1,760	1,808	1,858	1,909	10,497	10,438
2016–17	1,835	1,928	1,993	2,059	2,126	11,421	11,140

Note: BAU: Business as Usual; S-Scenario; SI-freight traffic assumed to grow at 8.7 per cent per annum in line with the past trend; SII-GDP growth 8 per cent per annum and elasticity 1.2; SIII-GDP growth 8.5 per cent per annum and elasticity 1.2; SIV-GDP growth 9 per cent per annum and elasticity 1.2; SV GDP growth 9.5 per cent per annum and elasticity 1.2; SA-passenger traffic assumed to grow at 8.8 per cent per annum; SB-BPKM derived through regression analysis as a function of population growth, urbanisation and per capita income.

Box 15.10
Introduction of Electronic Toll Collection (ETC)

- A Committee was set up under the Chairmanship of Shri Nandan Nilekani, Chairman, Unique Identification Authority of India.
- Recommendations of the Committee have been accepted and notified by the Ministry of Road Transport and Highways for the use of National Highways.
- In the first phase, a pilot project on ETC was inaugurated on 19 April 2012 on a section of NH-5 between Delhi and Parwanoo. Three Toll Plazas with ETC have been operationalised by the concessionaires at Panipat, DeraBassi and Parwanoo.
- A second pilot project on the Mumbai and Ahmedabad section of the National Highways has also been initiated. Progress on the project is being monitored continuously for early completion of the same.
- The other stretches of the NHs on which pilot projects have been undertaken are – Bengaluru–Chennai (State Bank of India); Kolkata–Dhanbad (IDFC Infra) and Gurgaon–Jaipur–Beawar (Feedback Infra Ltd.).
- The work of implementation of ETC on all stretches of the NHs in the country has been entrusted to NHAI. All the toll plazas across the country are proposed to be completed by January 2014.

of goods carriages. In these truck terminals there could be medical facilities, rest room, restaurant and equipment handling facilities. It is suggested that while planning SEZ or SER or Industrial Park at least 10 per cent of the area should be embarked for logistics and warehousing to support industrial activities efficiently.

Seamless Passenger Movement

15.116. There is need for promoting seamless passenger across the country. Unfortunately, there are difficulties in having inter-State agreements particularly on issue of passenger tax. There is a clear need to resolve these issues and provide the mechanism for issues arising day to day basis. During the Plan, efforts will be made to evolve a system for a smooth interstate passenger transport movement.

Transport Safety

15.117. Transport Safety is an important area, especially for Road Transport. Annually 1.3 lakh people die in road accidents. To strengthen the data, there is need to set minimal road death and injury data reporting requirements in accordance with standards set by the International Accident Database Group (IRTAD) for national level data. Web based data systems should be established and be made operational in the Twelfth Plan period. There is need to implement on an urgent basis the key recommendation of the Sundar Committee Report regarding the creation of National Road Safety and Traffic Management Board.

Awareness, Education and Driver Training

15.118. High level of awareness is required so that systemic problems get rectified. Awareness should be spread using all modes of communication: TV, Newspapers and Radio. ITIs need to be involved in driver training. MoRTH provides a scheme for setting up IDTR/DTI at state level. Before they start imparting driving training in driving schools, they should attend 'Trainers Training' in IDTRs/RSIs. To ensure that the needs are met, driver training schools should be encouraged to come up in the PPP mode.

Vehicle Safety

15.119. At present, the introduction of new safety standards is dependent on testing facilities available in the country including those at NATRIP. Since the vehicles produced in the next few years will be present on the road for about two decades, it is essential that the provision of testing facilities and introduction of new standards should be expedited. Impact standards for vehicles should be implemented on an early basis. Since a vast majority of those injured and killed in road accidents comprise of pedestrians, bicyclists, and motorcyclists, India should take the lead in introduction of pedestrian impact standards for all vehicles. India should set up a NCAP India Programme. In the first phase, cities with significant transport vehicles (Metros) should introduce a modern Inspection and Certification regime.

Some Major Initiatives in the Twelfth Plan

15.120. Some major initiatives during the Twelfth Plan Period are:

- Investment in R&D, technology and design of better and safer roads.
- Reforms in Motor Vehicles Act to simplify inter-State movement with simplified procedures.
- Integration of tax administration with interstate road freight and passenger movement through online communication network system at National, Regional and Local level.
- Reforms in tax administration (road tax, goods tax, passenger tax) to reduce collection cost and compliance cost of vehicle owners/operators.
- Creation of truck terminals to ease traffic congestion, decrease pollution, facilitate emergence of hub spoke system for distribution of goods and improvement in turnaround time of goods carriages.
- Creation of National Road Safety and Traffic Management Board to promote and sustain improved road safety in India, reflect international good practice and provide an informed basis for effective action.

Outlay for the Twelfth Plan

15.121. The Twelfth Plan budgetary support for Central Sector Roads is ₹1,44,769 crore. In addition, the sector is expected to generate IEBR amounting to ₹64,834 crore and private-sector investment of ₹2,14,186 crore during this period.

15.122. The Twelfth Plan budgetary support for Rural Roads (PMGSY) is ₹1,26,491 crore.

SHIPPING

15.123. There has been a consistent decline in the share of Indian ships in the carriage of India's overseas trade from 31.5 per cent in 1999–2000 to 13.7 per cent in 2004–05 and further to 7.95 per cent in 2010–11. There is a need for policy intervention to arrest this declining trend. Indian shipping fleet is characterised by the predominance of oil tankers and bulk carriers. While as on 31.03.12, oil tankers account for 63.76 per cent of the Deadweight Tonnage (DWT), bulk carriers account for 28.77 per cent, with all other vessel types such as liner vessels, OSVs and so on accounting for a mere 7.47 per cent.

Review of the Eleventh Plan

15.124. During the Eleventh Plan, three scenarios were set with first having a target of 10 million Gross Tonne (GT). It was further envisaged that with supportive policy measures, acquisition of vessels might go up to 12 million GT and 15 million GT. During the Eleventh Plan, shipping tonnage witnessed a rise from 787 vessels carrying about 8.6 million GT to 1,135 vessels amounting to 11.03 million GT. A total of 348 vessels of 2.43 million GT were added to the fleet as against a target of 279 vessels of 4.16 million GT. The Eleventh Plan is likely to witness a growth of 6.36 per cent in DWT.

15.125. An outlay of ₹15,026 crore, including IEBR of ₹13,135 crore was provided in the Eleventh Plan for the Shipping sector. Against this, expenditure was ₹9,788.39 crore, accounting for 65.00 per cent of the total outlay. The scheme-wise details are given in Table 15.29.

15.126. Ministry of shipping has a number of organisations. This includes Director General of Shipping (DG (S)), Director General of light houses and light ships (DGLL) and Shipping Corporation of India. During the Eleventh Plan, DG Shipping which is a statutory authority under the Merchant Shipping Act, 1958 and is responsible for implementing the Act and thus perform regulatory functions, invested ₹230.68 crore for strengthening of mercantile marine department, procuring modern survey instruments for minor port survey organisations and setting up of Indian Maritime University (IMU).

15.127. The DGLL provided Marine aids to navigation along the Indian Ports and managed 180 light houses, one light ship, 22 different ships global system and 21 deep seas lighted buoys for maritime navigation. It was able to earn ₹768.02 crore and spend ₹147.98 crore (98.65 per cent) of its outlay.

15.128. The Shipping Corporation of India had planned for ₹13,135 crore (IEBR) against which ₹8,537.85 crore (65 per cent) has been spent. It ordered 39 vessels against the acquisition targets of 67 vessels and inducted 20 vessels. The pace of vessel acquisition is slow during 2011–12, due to fall in the markets. The SCI profits decreased during the Plan from ₹813.9 crore in 2007–08 to a loss of ₹428 crore in 2011–12. Its fixed assets increased from ₹7,086.3 crore to ₹13,057.3 crore.

Strategies for the Twelfth Plan

15.129. A national shipping fleet commensurate with our overseas cargo needs would help in reducing the freight costs of Indian cargo. There is need to develop our freight policies consistent with efficiency of transport. A thriving shipping sector encourages the growth of associated industry and services providers required for servicing this industry, accounting to over 75 per cent of the shipping sector's national contribution. Most importantly, national tonnage is decisive in maintaining the supply line of essential cargo during international emergencies.

15.130. In order to enhance its reach, Director General of Lighthouses and Lightships plans to extend the facility for Coastal Surveillance and avoid environmental pollution under the National Maritime Domain scheme awareness by providing Vessel Traffic Service to Non-major Ports.

Increase in Tonnage

15.131. As on 30 June 2012, Indian tonnage stands at 11.03 million GT and ranks sixteenth in the world. During the Twelfth Plan it is planned to increase it to a target of 12.4 million GT if Indian shipping tonnage share of 1.16 per cent of global fleet remains constant in the Plan. However, with more supportive

TABLE 15.29
Financial Performance of the Shipping Sector in the Eleventh Plan

(in ₹ crore)

Sl. No.	Scheme/Programme	Financial Performance-Eleventh Plan		
		Approved Eleventh Plan Outlays	Approved Annual Plan Outlays	Actual Expenditure
1.	SCI	13,135.00	14,283.00	8,537.00
2.	DG (Shipping)	366.00	230.68	191.27
3.	DG (LL)	150.00	243.60	147.98
4.	IWT	615.00	693.00	537.25
	Total	15,026.00	16,108.84	9,788.39

policies this could increase to 26.6 Million GT or even to 53.3 MGT. These scenarios along are given in the Table 15.30 along with their required investments. An environment conducive to the growth of Indian shipping can be fostered by fiscal rationalisation, strengthening of regulatory mechanism, and increased focus on maritime training. Supportive policy measures as detailed below need to be taken to enable acquisition of vessels up to 26.6M GT.

TABLE 15.30
Estimated Requirements of Additional Vessels and Investment

	Tonnage Target	Investment (₹ in crore)
Scenario 1	11.2—12.4 m GT	2,500
Scenario 2	11.2—26.6 m GT	32,000
Scenario 3	11.2—53.3 m GT	80,000

Fiscal Regime Rationalisation

15.132. The Government had provided Indian shipping a level playing field by introducing tonnage tax in April 2004. Although tonnage tax regime provided temporary relief, some changes in direct and indirect taxation subsequently diluted these benefits. According to industry estimation, Indian shipping as against its counterparts is currently subjected to 12 types of taxes. Another aspect which translates itself into a tax-related disadvantage for the ships with Indian flags is that national manning is compulsory for them. The shipping company has to make withholding tax payments for Indian seafarers since they are not exempt from income tax. As this obligation does not devolve on ships registered in other jurisdictions employing Indian seafarers, the result is that the Indian ships have to pay a higher salary. It is critical for the growth of shipping in India that a level playing field is created as compared to other regimes in respect of taxes.

Cargo Support

15.133. The continuation of the policy with respect to Government owned and controlled cargo to be imported on FOB basis and shipping arrangements to be channelised through the Ministry of Shipping's Chartering Wing, Trans-chart would be advisable. Measures to promote use of Indian Flag Ships can significantly boost the growth of Indian shipping fleet during the Twelfth Plan. It has been suggested that a portion of the EXIM trade say, one-third of the POL and dry bulk cargo can be reserved for Indian Flag Ships as a condition for availing benefits from the government for export schemes. This would enhance cargo availability for Indian ships, and be a major catalyst to boost the growth of Indian fleet. This suggestion would need to be examined and an incentive policy to promote Indian Flag Ships should be developed.

Maritime Human Resource Development and Training

15.134. India has positioned herself as a major human resources–supplying nation to the maritime industry. As a result of the initiatives taken by the government in encouraging private participation in maritime training, the number of maritime training institutes under the assurance of quality training by the Directorate General of Shipping DG(S) rose from 128 in 2005 to 138 in 2012 including seven Government institutes.

15.135. Global demand for seafarers is estimated to reach 6,70,000 Officers and 7,20,000 Ratings by 2015. This will imply an incremental demand of 1,20,000 Officers and 1,25,000 Ratings. Seafarer supplying countries (for example China, Philippines, Turkey and Ukraine) are expected to compete for capturing this incremental demand to increase their global share. Shortage of officers is expected to aggravate due to high fleet growth. India has an opportunity to supply more officers in the international maritime sector.

15.136. The target for the maritime training programme for the Twelfth Plan is to increase the share of Indian officers from 6.3 per cent to about 9 per cent by 2017, whereas for ratings from 7.5 per cent to about 9 per cent by 2017. Policy initiatives are required to retain and build talent. Initiatives for this could include the co-option of the member lines of the INSA into allocating 10–15 per cent of each ship's manning scales exclusively for sea training berths.

15.137. With the objective of providing world class training opportunity for the shipping sector, the

Government has established an Indian Maritime University (IMU) in Chennai with campuses in Kolkata, Mumbai, Visakhapatnam, Kochi, Chennai and Kandla. The IMU aims to play the role of a centralised nodal agency to facilitate Maritime studies and research in emerging areas such as marine science and technology and marine environment. The Indian Maritime University should play the role of a centralised university in controlling higher maritime education through academic support processes in its campuses throughout India.

15.138. There is a need to strengthen the IMU through induction of high quality faculty. The important role presently being played by the Regional Academic Councils under the Directorate General of Shipping should be further strengthened by reconstituting them to form an Advisory Group.

15.139. There should be a strong emphasis on the need for improving quality of Indian seafarers to keep up the reputation and credibility of Indian certifications. For this, not only the number of training institutes but the quality of such training, examination and certification of seafarers is to be emphasised. To achieve this, there is an urgent need of modernising the examination system and strengthening the pool of qualified examiners.

15.140. It is proposed to form a Research Support Group to effectively monitor, support and coordinate the activities of Maritime Training Institutes and to develop proper monitoring and reporting systems and conduct systems audit on a continuous and sustainable basis. The Research Support Group would identify the difficulties experienced by institutes in implementing the quality standards prescribed by Indian Maritime Administration and IMU and would serve as a watch dog. The Support Group will work under the control of the Director General of Shipping and assisted by technical administrative officers/Staff meant specifically for this function.

15.141. For effective implementation of a regulatory regime as per the requirements of International Maritime Organisation (IMO), it is necessary to strengthen Directorate General of Shipping. A data base of seafarers should be built. Biometric identity cum smart card, capable of storing individual's professional record in electronic form must be issued to every seafarer. There is also a need for capacity building of the DG(S), with greater technological tools, training, human resources availability and greater autonomy for authorising surveyor movement to Indian ships on foreign shores, and in deciding the delegation of powers to Mercantile Marine Departments. Every port regardless whether it is private or non-major, but having target of more than 110 ships a year, (which works out to two ships a week) should have an office of MMO.

15.142. In order to prevent poor quality foreign flag ships operating in our waters, Port State Control inspections have to be strengthened in the years ahead. The main constraint in the implementation is the availability of manpower. It is therefore proposed to create separate divisions in the DG (Shipping office) and to recruit more surveyors to achieve 10 per cent Port Security Control (PSC) inspections by the year 2015 as mandated by the IMO. It is also proposed to carry out 100 per cent FSI inspections of Indian ships by the year 2020.

15.143. Very often a seafarer's job is perceived to be arduous, monotonous, risky and unsafe. This calls for critical welfare and safety measures. Welfare measures for seafarers should include a free or subsidized health and insurance policy.

15.144. Indian ships have to mandatorily employ Indian seafarers, and cannot employ foreign seafarers as per the Merchant Shipping Act. In view of the increasing worldwide shortages of senior officers, there is inherent disadvantage to the Indian ship owner as employers. On account of the extra burden of income tax on Indian seafarers' income, employment on a foreign flag is the first choice of an Indian seafarer, thereby denying the best talent to the local shipping industry. A positive approach on this issue for granting freedom for the Indian shipping industry by permitting them to employ foreign seafarers could be explored.

Other Policy Initiatives

Establishing P&I Club

15.145. In present day scenario, maritime insurance of ships, wreck removal, dealing with maritime both for the ship and seafarers are organised by P&I Clubs of foreign origin. Establishing P&I Club in India should not only increase trade but would also augment foreign exchange earnings when these clubs are used by foreign companies. It is therefore proposed to establish one P&I Club in Indian League by the year 2015 and one more in the IG League by the year 2020.

Strengthening Participation in IMO

15.146. The increasing number of International Codes and Conventions, emanating from the International Maritime Organisation (IMO), have changed the maritime trade relationships between nations and also created a whole new statutory structure for maritime countries.

Navigational Safety In Port Committee (NSPC)

15.147. The scope of NSPC may be extended to major as well as non-major ports and the duties should include port navigational safety issues, cargo related safety aspects, oversight function of oil pollution response mechanism, reception facilities in the ports, and so on. For the protection of the environment, it may be necessary to develop a 'Ballast Water Management System' in accordance with the requirements of International Convention for the Control and Management of Ships as adopted by the IMO in 2004, along with the development of waste disposal facilities in ports.

Coastal Shipping

15.148. Out of the total traffic at major ports of 560.90 million tons (MT) in 2009–10, coastal traffic was 107.94 MT. During 2006–10, the total traffic at the major ports grew at 7.20 per cent (CAGR) and that at the non-major ports at 17.20 per cent (CAGR). However, during 2006–10, coastal traffic at the major ports grew at 4.5 per cent (CAGR) and the percentage share of coastal traffic in the total traffic handled at the major ports was constant between 19 per cent to 21 per cent. During Eleventh Plan period there was a net increase of about 15 per cent in the total volume of cargo carried per year meant for coastal shipping. Coastal shipping in the country is still in its infancy, with the coastal fleet of 764 vessels accounting for merely over a million GT as on 31 March 2012. This period witnessed a remarkable growth in the number of smaller size vessels (Liner, Passenger-cum-Cargo and other types viz., Tugs, Ro-Ros, Dredgers and Pilot/Survey Launches), with the number of coastal bulk carriers and tanker fleets declining.

15.149. In view of the positive externalities of coastal shipping, a number of policy interventions would be required during the Plan. There is a need to consider fiscal incentives for registered multi-modal transport operators, shippers, trade/industries that prefer transporting sizeable domestic cargos through coastal shipping. Unfortunately, despite having the lowest unit transportation cost for the sea leg, the overall end-to-end cost of coastal shipping escalates due to inadequate port and land side infrastructure (capacity and connectivity), resulting in a preference for the road/rail modes by the industry and trade. The burden of customs duties and the perceived cumbersome customs/other procedures, low port productivity and high tariffs, aggravates the problem. There is a need to remove these bottlenecks.

15.150. Adequate incentives and a level playing field are required to encourage the growth of the Indian coastal shipping companies in the face of stiff competition from the foreign lines. The scope of coastal shipping needs to be enhanced in the Indian Merchant Shipping Act, 1958. There is a need to create dry-docks and ship repair yards at existing/new non-major ports to accommodate smaller coastal vessels. The connectivity for the ports with rail/road transport needs to be enhanced. Further, the government may also consider following incentives for the development of Coastal Shipping: (*i*) Grant infrastructure status to Coastal Shipping Industry for taxation purposes (*ii*) Allow tax exemption for the building of coastal ships in India (*iii*) Confer 'Declared Goods' status for the bunker used by coastal ships (*iv*) Establish a 'Coastal Development Fund'. A separate tariff matrix should be formulated for coastal vessels.

15.151. To reduce greenhouse gases (GHGs) emissions, the conversion of Indian coastal vessels to compressed natural gas (CNG) fuel powered, as an alternate to the extant fossil fuel diesel, in a phased manner, is necessary.

Promoting Fishing Activity In Indian Seas
15.152. There is a need to promote decent working conditions for fishermen. The provisions of the International Labour Organisation Fishing Convention, 2007 may be implemented for the Indian fishing boats above 15 meters in length. The number of such Indian fishing vessels is approximately 55,000. These improvements would contribute to the decent working conditions of the fishermen working on these boats.

Multimodal Transportation
15.153. Multimodal transportation system is the chain that interconnects different links or modes of transport air, sea, and land into one complete process that ensures an efficient and cost-effective door-to-door movement of goods under the responsibility of a single transport operator, known as a Multimodal Transport Operator (MTO), on one transport document. The multi-modal transportation in India is governed by the Multimodal Transportation of Goods Act 1993 which needs to be strengthened to address issues such as liability regime, setting of service standards and registration of service providers, to provide transparency in operations. In view of the overall efficiencies associated with this system, Government would develop policy interventions encouraging companies to use this.

Strategies for the Twelfth Plan
- Increase in tonnage to meet the growing requirements of the Indian Trade and Commerce.
- Fiscal regime rationalisation and cargo support to expand Indian flag vessels.
- Maritime Human Resource Development for larger utilisation of Indian technical personnel in national and international shipping.
- Expansion of Coastal shipping and policies to promote infrastructure and economic operations.
- Development of strategies for expansion of multimodal transport.

INLAND WATERWAYS TRANSPORT (IWT)

Introduction
15.154. With a meager share of 0.4 per cent in the total cargo handled in the country Inland Waterways is an under developed mode of transportation in India. India has a potential of 14,500 km of navigable waterways but so far only 2,716 km have been developed for commercial transportation. The share of IWT in transport sector in other countries is far more significant than that of India. For example, the shares of IWT as proportion of total tonne-km in EU, China and the US for the year 2006 were 5.6 per cent, 8.7 per cent and 8.3 per cent respectively.

15.155. The potential for development of this mode of transportation is very promising. IWT mode is best-suited for movement of bulk cargo, over dimensional cargo and hazardous goods. IWT also offers an environment-friendly economic mode of transport compared to road and rail. According to recent studies, the total external costs of inland navigation after accounting for all externalities, including accidents, congestion, noise emissions, air pollution and other environmental impacts are seven times lower than that of road transport.

15.156. On Ganga (NW-1) alone there are 10 thermal power plants and at least 10 more are slated to come up in near future (See Figure 15.1). The transportation of coal to these power plants is considered to be one of the most challenging tasks. IWT can be effectively used for this purpose, particularly for the imported coal since most of these plants would be importing 10–20 per cent of their coal which can be transported through NW-1.

Review of the Eleventh Plan
15.157. At present the traffic of IWT is only 5 billion tonne km (btkm). The target for Eleventh Plan has been largely achieved, not so much by utilising NW1, 2 and 3 but by increased IWT movement of iron ore in Goa waterways. In the Eleventh Plan IWAI reached expenditure level of about ₹560 crore during the five years (2007–12) with an average of ₹112 crore.

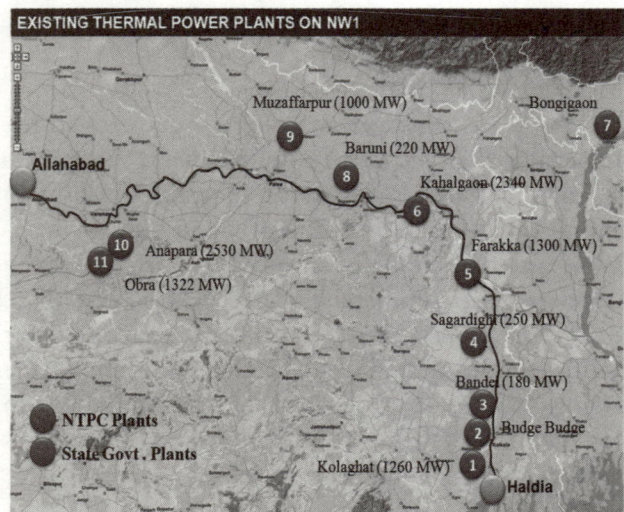
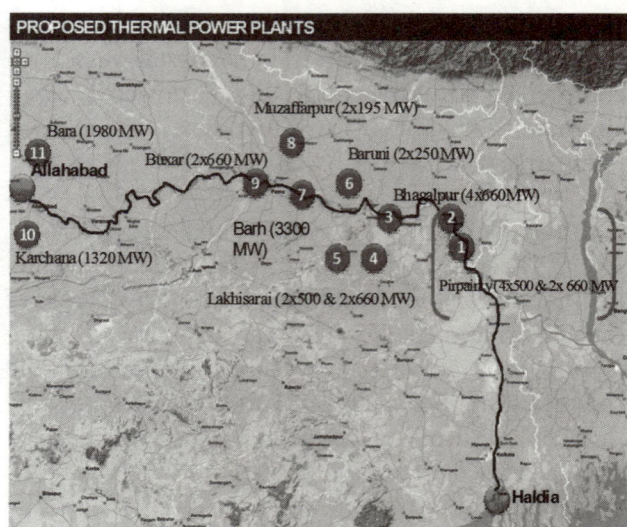

FIGURE 15.1: Existing and Proposed Thermal Power Plants on National Waterways

15.158. The main developments during the Eleventh Plan were:

1. Two additional waterways were declared as National Waterways in November 2008. These were NW-4 and NW-5. As a result of this, the following waterways totaling 43,82 km have been declared as National Water Ways (NWWs):
    a. Ganga–Bhagirathi–Hoogly river system (Allahabad Haldia-1,620 km) in the States of Uttar Pradesh, Bihar, Jharkhand and West Bengal as NW-1, declared in 1986.
    b. River Brahmaputra (Dhubri–Sadiya—891 km) in the State of Assam as NW-2 declared in 1988.
    c. West Coast Canal (Kottapuram–Kollam) along with Udyogmandal and Champakara Canals—(205 km) in the State of Kerala as NW-3 declared in 1993.
    d. Kakinada–Puducherry canals along with Godavari and Krishna rivers (1,078 km)—in the States of Andhra Pradesh, Tamil Nadu and Union Territory of Puducherry as NW-4 declared in 2008.
    e. East Coast Canal integrated with Brahmani river and Mahanadi delta rivers (588 km) in the states of West Bengal and Odisha as NW-5 declared in 2008.

2. A major project has been finalised involving a private agency for developing infrastructure and transportation of 3 million tonnes per year of imported coal from Sagar/Sandheads to Farakka power plant of NTPC Ltd. through NW-1 for a period of 7 years. A number of Over Dimentional Cargoes (ODCs) have also been transported on NW-1 from Haldia/Kolkata to Barauni, Barh, Ballia, Jamania, and so on for Barauni refinery, NTPC, BHEL, Power Grid Corporation, Relianace (Sasan), Tori power plant, Reghunathpur power project and so on. ODC also moved from Kolkata to Jogighopa on NW-2 and to Silchar on Barak river. This became possible due to enhanced level of infrastructure on waterways in respect of depth, navigation aids and intermodal terminals.
3. Pandu port in Guwahati is being developed as an IWT based inter modal hub in the North East region with broad gauge railway connectivity.
4. Besides 8 terminals at various locations on NW-3, IWT Ro-Ro/Lo-Lo jetties at Bolghatty and Willingdon islands in Kochi on NW-3 are to provide IWT linkage to Vallarpadam Port.

Transportation of Project Cargo for Palatana Power Project in Tripura

15.159. Another important development in IWT has been Palatana project. The commissioning of a gas based power project of ONGC at Palatana in Tripura was getting delayed due to serious problems in transporting project material from Kolkata/Haldia to the site by road and railways. However, declaration of Ashuganj in Bangladesh as a port of call under Indo Bangladesh Inland Water Transit and Trade Protocol during the year 2010 opened a new route. With this route having become operational the new possibilities of transporting other cargo including food grains to Tripura and Mizoram by IWT mode have emerged.

Strategic Importance of IWT For North East: Brahmaputra-Barak Route

15.160. Only in case of IWT there is transit treaty between India and Bangladesh. All weather IWT route therefore has strategic significance in the North East as it helps to avoid the congested West Bengal–Sikkim narrow corridor. Several North Eastern States can be reached through IWT routes (Brahmaputra and Barak). Distance to Tripura, Mizoram and Southern Assam is also much less through IWT (Figure 15.2).

Kaladan Multimodal Transport Project

15.161. This project was conceptualised by the Ministry of External Affairs to provide alternative connectivity from Mizoram to Haldia/Kolkata ports through River Kaladan in Myanmar. The project envisages Coastal Shipping/Maritime Shipping from Haldia to Sittwe, IWT from Sittwe to Paletwa (in Myanmar) and thereafter by road from Paletwa to Mizoram. An Indian contractor has been appointed for construction of port and IWT components at a cost ₹342 crore with a completion period of 3 years. The construction work of Sittwe port has commenced and is in progress (Figure 15.3).

Strategies for the Twelfth Plan

Navigation-Based Infrastructure

15.162. Large parts of Indian Waterways have inadequate Least Assured Depth (LAD) for commercial movement of cargo. Many shippers have expressed that there is no dearth of cargo if the waterway with assured depth and 24 hours navigation facility is provided and there is an adequate number of cargo vessels.

1. Efforts should be made to develop deeper stretches of the rivers for IWT/navigational purposes (at least 2.5 m, preferably 3.0 m. LAD for round the year navigation).
2. Several rivers in India meander resulting in increase in distance to be travelled on waterways as compared to road and rail. Technical feasibility of reducing the IWT route length by strengthening the waterway (wherever feasible) to avoid bends could be studied.
3. There are bridges with low vertical clearance which impede passage of bigger IWT vessels on the waterways such as NW-3. Raising these bridges to at least 5 m or some other technical solution to make these canal systems navigable for commercial cargo carriers could be considered. Alternatively vessels with lower masts can be used to negotiate the already constructed major bridges.
4. Lack of IWT terminals including those with intermodal connectivity of inland waterways inhibits door to door connectivity to end user. There are IWT terminals on NW-1, NW-2 and NW-3 but many of these terminals require better linkage with road/rail. IWT terminals must have

---

Box 15.11
Coal Transport to Farakka through Power Station – A Break through for IWT

NTPC's power plant at Farakka had been facing shortage of coal mainly on account of limitation in transportation capacity of railways and low draft at Haldia dock. Since, the power plant having been located on the bank of Ganga (the National Waterway-1), it was felt that transportation of imported coal from Haldia/Sagar/Sandheads to Farakka by inland water transport (IWT) mode would be feasible. In August 2010, NTPC decided for transportation of 3 million tonnes per year (MMTPA) imported coal for seven years. IWAI and NTPC then developed a project envisaging an investment of about ₹650 crore for setting up (*i*) trans-shipment facility at Sagar/Sandheads (*ii*) barges for 3 MMTPA coal transportation (*iii*) inland water terminal at Farakka and (*iv*) conveyor system from the terminal to the coal stack yard of Farakka power plant. IWAI has now guaranteed Least Available Depth (LAD) of 2.5 m to Farakka along with other navigational aids for safe 24×7 navigation. A private company is developing facilities and will maintain these for seven years.

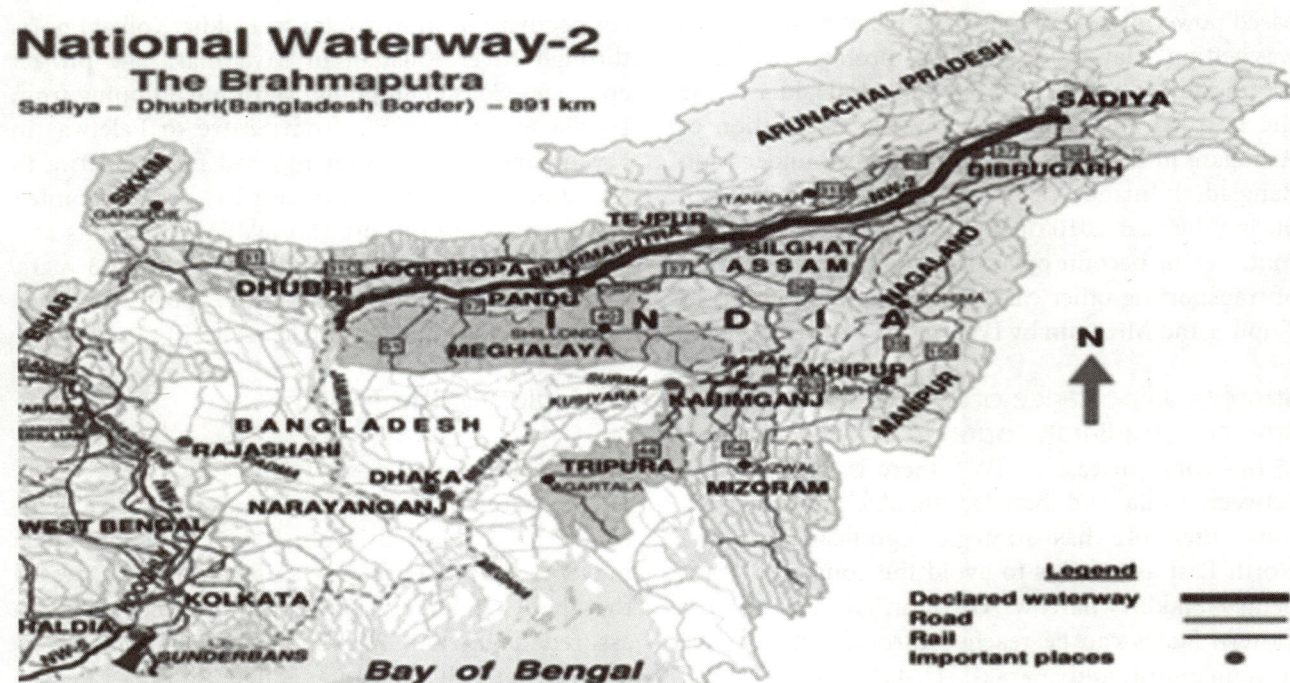

FIGURE 15.2: National Waterway-2

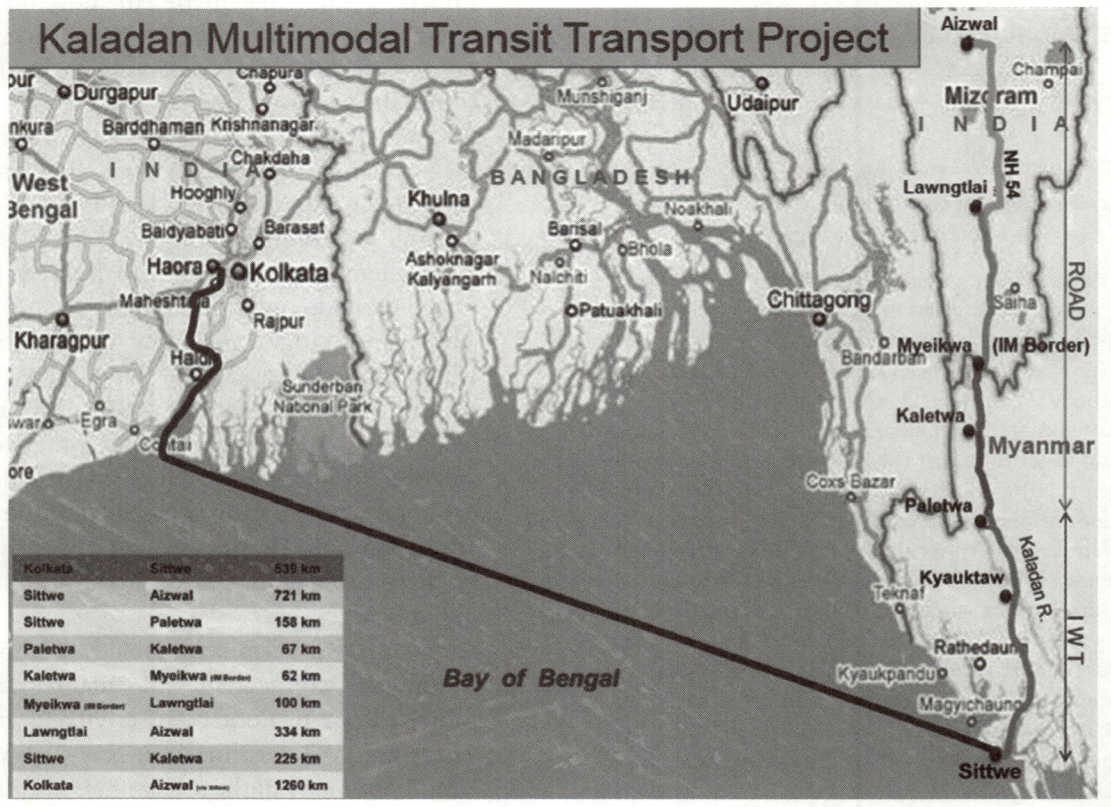

FIGURE 15.3: Kaladan Multimodal Transit Transport Project

good connectivity with road and preferably with rail for last mile connectivity on lines of bimodal and tri-modal concept of developed waterways of other countries. Similar terminal development is required in NW-4, 5 and proposed NW- 6.
5. Private sector is reluctant to make investment in barges unless long term cargo commitments for onward/return trips are made available from user industry. Eligibility of IWT Vessel building "Infrastructure Status" could be considered to help obtain easier credit availability.
6. Developing night navigation infrastructure with DGPS and RIS in a time bound manner could help 24 hour navigability.
7. MRO (Maintenance, Repair and Overhaul) facilities which are presently in short supply could also catalyse the sector.

15.163. Shortage of vessels is perceived to be the most important factor inhibiting faster growth in IWT cargo movement. The fleet requirement for 15 btkm of IWT traffic is about 2,500 vessels of average 1,000 tonne capacity each. At present, there are just about 600 IWT vessels in the entire country with nearly 80 per cent vessels being located in Goa alone. This would call for an investment of ₹13,000 crore. There is need to incentivise these investments and develop a policy framework so that private sector investments are attracted to vessel building.

Level Playing Field

15.164. There is a transport subsidy for movement of raw materials and finished goods for the new industries of NER but this is applicable only for rail and road modes and not to IWT. Similarly, the transport subsidy available for movement of fertilisers is also meant for rail and road modes. The service tax applicable to IWT is more than rail and roads. There is need for a level playing field and removal of distortions resulting from such policies.

15.165. Development of inland waterways is an eligible sector for Viability Gap Funding and India Infrastructure Project Development Fund. The usage of the IWT network for 'water tourism' theme has potential to generate considerable income for the local economies and additional income from tourist/luxury taxes for regional and state governments. For example, in Kerala, over 2,000 people are employed in houseboats and other motorboats that cruise the inland waterways filled with tourists. Expanding the usage of IWT for tourism can be included as one of the objectives to improve waterways for economic development.

Human Resource Development
15.166. To meet trained manpower requirements of the sector, it is necessary that National Inland Navigation Institute (NINI) is strengthened and networked with Indian Maritime University and at the same time, a few Regional Crew Training Centres are also set up. The training should be benchmarked to the best available standards.

Strengthening of IWT Institutional Set Up in Riverine States
15.167. In every IWT developed region the importance of trunk waterways gets significantly enhanced with development of feeder waterways which are smaller in length but provide vital 'last mile connectivity'. In India too, every big waterway has a number of tributaries which if developed can effectively serve as feeder routes to the main waterways. But these waterways will have to be developed by respective State Governments which do not have the organisation, the expertise and the resources to even consider this aspect in their planning. Hence IWT institutions set up in the States need to be strengthened in a big way including for checking the safety of vessels to prevent accidents.

Target for the Twelfth Plan
15.168. At present the share of IWT in terms of tonne-km is about 5 btkm which is less than 0.5 per cent of total inland cargo transportation. Given the distinct advantages of promoting IWT, Twelfth Plan target to at least triple the tonne-km to 15 btkm and increase the share of IWT in transport to 1–1.5 per cent of total inland cargo transportation from the current level of less than 0.5 per cent.

Strategy For Development of Inland Water Transport

- Increased public and private investments in infrastructure of notified Inland Waterways.
- New policies to promote manufacture of Inland Waterways Vessels for cargo movement by private sector.
- Development of National Waterway 4 and 5.
- Development of night infrastructure facilities to help 24 hours navigation.
- Promoting connectivity with Bangladesh and strengthening IWT infrastructure.
- Hinterland connectivity through IWT with ports, both major and non-major having this facility.

PORTS

15.169. Ports constitute inter-modal interface between maritime and road and rail transport. India has a coast line of around 7,517 km with 12 major ports and over 200 non-major ports along the coast line and sea islands. Almost 95 per cent by volume and 70 per cent by value of India's global merchandise trade is carried through the sea route. In 2011–12 the 12 major ports handled about 60 per cent of the maritime cargo of the country. The balance 40 per cent was handled by the non-major ports. Of the 12 major ports, 11 are administered by the respective Port Trusts and Ennore Port, the twelfth major port, which started functioning in February 2001, is corporatised.

Review of the Eleventh Plan

Capacity Creation in the Eleventh Plan

15.170. The projected capacity creation was 1,001.80 million tonnes for the major port sector but the achievement was 689.83 MT (Table 15.31) as compared to 504.75 MT in 2006–07 registering a growth of 37 per cent but below the target by 31 per cent. Cargo-wise capacity creation details for major ports are shown in Table 15.32. Capacity of non-major and Private Ports was envisaged to increase from 228.31 MT to 575 MT. The actual achievement was 544.65 MT, thus registering a growth of 139 per cent.

Traffic Handled by Major and Non-Major Ports

15.171. During the Eleventh Plan, traffic handled by major ports (Table 15.31) increased from 463.78 MT in the year 2006–07 to 560.15 MT in the year 2011–12 against a projection of 708.09 MT, thus registering a growth of 29.48 but 26.55 per cent lower than the projection. However, non-major ports registered a cargo growth of 98.81 per cent during the same period, that is, from 186.11 MT in the year 2006–07 to 370.00 MT in the year 2011–12 which is 23.26 per cent higher than the projection of 300.86 MT. Commodity wise details are shown in Table 15.33.

Productivity in Major Ports

15.172. The average turnaround time and average pre-berthing time at major ports have worsened during the Eleventh Plan (Table 15.34). There is an improvement of average output per ship berth day from 9,745 MT in year 2006–07 to 10,967 MT in year 2011–12. Ports-wise performance shows that the average turnaround time declined mainly due to good performance by Paradip, Mormugao, Chennai and Kolkata ports. Commodity-wise it declined for other liquid bulk, Iron Ore, FRM and Coal. It is estimated that 57 per cent of turnaround time of ships at Indian Ports is caused by delays due to port related inefficiency. The Pre-berthing detention during the Eleventh Plan period has shown an increasing trend. Among the ports, healthy improvement has been observed in Visakhapatnam, Ennore, New Mangalore and Mormugao ports, whereas in other ports the improvement has not been significant primarily due to non-availability of berths meant for the cargoes like Iron Ore, Coal and Other Miscellaneous and General Cargo continuously for a long period.

Private Sector Participation

15.173. During the Eleventh Plan, award of PPP projects commenced only in the year 2009–10 as first two years of the Plan were spent in finalising MCA documents. There were, however, projects awarded to private players based on earlier contracts. Upto 2011–12, 30 PPPs involving an investment of 9,447.40 crore and capacity addition of 204.65 MT were completed. During Eleventh Plan, PPP projects with capacity addition of 154.5 MT were awarded with an investment of ₹13,195.85 crore. The details of year wise awards during the Eleventh Plan are given in Table 15.35.

TABLE 15.31
Eleventh Plan Projection and Achievements of Traffic and Capacity by Major Ports

Port	Traffic in Eleventh Plan (MT) (2011–12)			Total Capacity in Eleventh Plan (MT) (2011–12)		
	Project	Achievement	per cent	Project	Achievement	per cent
Kolkata	13.43	12.23	91	31.45	16.35	51
Haldia	44.50	31.01	70	63.40	50.70	79
Paradeep	76.40	54.25	71	106.4	76.50	71
Visakhapatnam	82.20	67.42	82	108.1	72.93	67
Ennore	47.00	14.96	32	64.20	31.00	48
Chennai	57.50	55.71	97	72.30	79.72	110
Tuticorin	31.72	28.10	89	63.98	33.34	52
Cochin	38.17	20.10	53	54.75	40.98	74
NMPT	48.81	32.94	68	60.50	50.97	84
Mormugao	44.55	39.00	88	66.90	41.90	62
Mumbai	71.05	56.18	79	91.91	44.53	48
JNPT	66.04	65.75	100	95.60	64.00	66
Kandla	86.72	82.50	95	122.20	86.91	71
Total	708.09	560.15	79	1,001.80	689.83	69

TABLE 15.32
Commodity Wise Capacity Creation by Major Ports during Eleventh Plan

(Million Metric Tonnes)

Sl. No.	Capacity	2006–07	2011–12	Increase (per cent)
1.	POL	174.70	228.76	30.94
2.	Iron Ore	57.50	79.50	38.26
3.	Coal	46.25	65.95	42.59
4.	Container	88.08	137.53	56.14
5.	Other Cargo	138.22	178.09	28.84
6.	Total	504.75	689.83	36.67

Dredging

15.174. The requirement of capital dredging in the Eleventh Plan was envisaged to increase more than two-fold, to 298.28 million cubic meters (MCuM) for major ports and 368.59MCuM for non-major ports, besides maintenance dredging of 380.06 MCuM and 46.41MCuM, respectively. To enable this, a more liberal dredging policy was brought into force which allows ports to charter foreign flag dredgers after granting the Indian companies the 'first right of refusal'. Against the targeted Plan, only 40.02 per cent and 67.92 per cent have been achieved under the capital and maintenance dredging respectively.

15.175. The capacity of the DCI, established in 1976, to provide integrated dredging services to major and minor ports was 73.60 MCuM of Trailer Suction Dredgers (TSDs) and 6.25 MCuM of Cutter Suction Dredgers (CSDs) at the start of the Tenth Plan. During the Eleventh Plan, DCI was envisaged to acquire 10 TSDs of 5,000–9,000 CuM hopper capacity and 5 CSDs of 2,000–3,000 CuM hopper capacity in addition to other auxiliary equipment. However, against outlay of ₹2,292 crore, DCI's anticipated expenditure by the end of Eleventh Plan is only ₹828.35 crore.

Port Connectivity

15.176. The Eleventh Plan envisaged that each major port should have at least four-lane road and double lane rail connectivity. At present, 13 road projects with combined road length of 360 km at a total cost of ₹4,149.66 crore and rail projects at a cost of ₹3,903.00 crore are under implementation.

TABLE 15.33
Traffic Handled at Major and Non-Major Ports during Eleventh Plan

Traffic	Major Ports			Non-Major Ports			Major and Non-Major Ports		
	2006–07	2011–12	% increase	2006–07	2011–12	% Increase	2006–07	2011–12	% Increase
POL	154.34	179.28	16.16	80.37	188.00	133.92	234.71	367.28	56.48
Iron Ore	80.59	60.60	(–)24.80	34.33	51.00	48.56	114.92	111.60	(–)2.89
Fert. and FRM*	14.12	20.42	44.62	4.67	11.00	135.55	18.79	31.42	67.22
Coal	59.98	78.74	31.28	12.92	77.00	495.98	72.90	155.74	113.64
Container	73.44	120.22	63.70	7.87	19.00	141.42	81.31	139.22	71.22
Other Cargo	81.31	100.89	24.08	45.95	24.00	(–)47.77	127.26	124.89	(–)1.86
Total	463.78	560.15	20.78	186.11	370	98.81	649.89	930.15	43.12

* Fertiliser and Fertiliser Raw Material (FRM).

TABLE 15.34
Trend of the Productivity Parameters during Eleventh Plan

Year	Average Output Per Ship Berth Day (Tonnes)	Average Turnaround Time (Days)	Average Pre-berthing Detention Time (Hours)
2006–07	9,745	3.62	10.05
2007–08	10,071	3.93	11.40
2008–09	10,473	3.87	9.55
2009–10	10,482	4.42	11.75
2010–11	10,735	4.67	11.76
2011–12	10,967	4.44	11.14

TABLE 15.35
Year-wise Awards during Eleventh Plan under PPP

Years	Investment/Awards (₹ in crore)	Capacity Addition (in MMT)
2007–08	703.34	7.50
2008–09	749.43	18.00
2009–10	618.95	19.50
2010–11	3,147.13	30.50
2011–12	7,977.00	79.00
Total	13,195.85	154.50

Eleventh Plan Outlay and Expenditure

15.177. An outlay of ₹30,323.11 crore (at 2006–07 prices) had been approved for the port sector, comprising ₹3,315.00 crore as GBS and ₹26,574.11 crore through IEBR of which ₹17,684.61 crore or 59.62 per cent is expected to be utilised. In addition, private sector investment of ₹36,868.00 crore and a public investment of ₹3,627.00 crores is expected in the state sector.

Twelfth Plan

Traffic and Capacity Augmentation

15.178. To meet the overall projected traffic of 1,758.26 million tonnes by 2016–17, the total capacity of the port sector is envisaged to be 2,289.04 million tonnes. The traffic forecast by the end of Twelfth Plan would be 943.06 million tonnes and 815.20 million tonnes for the major ports and non-major ports respectively with the corresponding ports capacities of 1,229.24 million tonnes and 1,059.80 million tonnes respectively.

15.179. The details of the traffic/capacity projections (port wise and commodity wise as well as major and non-major ports wise) by the end of Twelfth Plan are given in Tables 15.36, 15.37 and 15.38 respectively.

Issues and Strategies for the Twelfth Plan

Committee on Ports

15.180. The Plan will need to ensure adequate investments in the Port Sector to meet the growing capacity needs of our international and coastal trade, improve efficiency by reducing dwell time and turnaround time and introduce legislative and institutional reforms to support these. The Committee on Ports headed by Shri B.K. Chaturvedi, Member (Transport), Planning Commission has suggested a series of reforms to attain the above objectives and these will need to be taken up. To support capacity expansion in port sector, necessary measures for efficient environment clearance and land acquisition will be taken up. An area, which will need special attention, is security clearance. The policy on this needs to be revised and made efficient.

Tariff Regulation

15.181. With the key objective of determining tariffs for the major ports and also specify the conditionality governing these tariffs, TAMP was established in 1997 by an amendment in the Major Port Trust's Act, 1963. With the increase in port capacities, it is necessary that in the next five years, the ports move gradually to a competitive mode of tariff. Already all non-Major Ports are doing so. A task force under the Chairmanship of Shri B.K. Chaturvedi to review the draft Port Regulatory Bill was formed which has finalised its report which will be of use to review the policy in this area.

Electronic Data Interchange

15.182. Efficient electronic data interchange is required to improve the efficiency of Ports. It is necessary for Port Community System (PCS) to integrate the electronic flow of document/information and function as centralised hub for all the major Ports of India and also stakeholders like shipping lines/agents, surveyors, stevedores, banks, container freight stations, custom house agents, importers and customs. Further, non-major ports should also gradually integrate with the centralised port community.

TABLE 15.36
Major Ports wise Traffic/Capacity Projections by End of Twelfth Plan

(Million Tonnes)

Port	Traffic		Capacity	
	Existing (2011–12)	Forecast (2016–17)	Existing (2011–12)	Forecast (2016–17)
Kolkata	12.23	22.87	16.35	32.85
Haldia Dock Complex	31.01	53.20	50.70	71.10
Paradip	54.25	87.70	70.50	125.50
Visakhapatnam	67.42	80.00	72.93	130.23
Ennore	14.96	82.45	31.00	78.00
Chennai	55.71	69.74	79.72	114.72
V.O. Chidambaranar	28.01	48.84	33.34	81.54
Cochin	20.10	45.50	40.98	57.83
New Mangalore	32.94	53.50	50.97	84.89
Mormugao	39.00	58.25	41.90	72.71
Mumbai	56.18	67.40	44.53	79.13
JNPT	65.75	140.21	64.00	155.61
Kandla	82.50	130.90	86.91	145.13
Port Blair		2.50		
Total	560.15	943.06	689.93	1,229.24

Dredging

15.183. Drafts at Indian Ports both in the channel and at berths need to be improved. It should be a major objective of the Twelfth Plan that ports in India

TABLE 15.37
Commodity wise Capacity by the end of Twelfth Plan

(Million Tonnes)

Commodity	Major ports		Non-major ports		Total	
	Existing (2011–12)	Forecast (2016–17)	Existing (2011–12)	Forecast (2016–17)	Existing (2011–12)	Forecast (2016–17)
POL (incl. LNG)	228.76	299.66	276.74	299.90	505.50	599.56
Iron Ore	79.50	143.55	75.07	101.40	154.57	244.95
Coal	65.95	178.65	113.35	365.20	179.30	543.85
Containers	137.53	306.19	27.97	130.00	165.50	436.19
Others including Fert and FRM	178.09	301.19	51.52	163.30	229.61	464.49
Total	689.83	1,229.24	544.65	1,059.80	1,234.48	2,289.04

TABLE 15.38
Commodity Wise Traffic by the End of Twelfth Plan (2016–17)

(Million Tonnes)

Commodity	Major Ports	Non-Major Ports	Total
POL (incl. LNG)	249.49	230.70	480.19
Iron Ore	112.00	78.00	190.00
Fert and FRM	22.57	8.60	31.17
Coal	158.10	280.90	439.00
Containers	268.50	100.00	368.50
Others	132.40	117.00	249.40
Total	943.06	815.20	1,758.26

increase the draft to at least 14 meters in all Ports by the end of Twelfth Plan period and achieve 17 meters in Hub-Ports according to the potential of bigger size ships calling at these ports. In the Twelfth Plan, the requirement of capital dredging has been estimated at 221.11 MCuM for major ports and 418.03 MCuM for non-major ports, besides maintenance dredging of 404.25 MCuM and 125.58 MCuM, respectively.

15.184. The dredging capability of DCI is limited which needs to be enhanced substantially. The All India Dredging Cadre scheme needs to be strengthened and suitable measures have to be taken to retain the trained personnel. Suitable measures will need to be taken to overcome the time overrun experienced in dry docking of the existing dredgers. Long-term contracts with ports, which have continuous maintenance dredging needs to be developed. Financing of such ventures could help DCI to acquire new dredgers with equity support from such ports. Technological developments and innovations taking place in this area should be kept in mind and DCI should go for the latest technology in procuring the dredgers and in the execution of dredging.

Productivity and Dwell Time
15.185. To improve port efficiency and labour productivity, broad strategies like, creation of adequate port capacity with a gap of 30 per cent between the installed capacity and the traffic consistent with international norms, and the drafts of at least 14 meters up to 17 meters according to the potential of bigger size vessels calling at particular port is essential. Several Indian ports are unattractive due to high dwell time on account of customs and port side constraints like inadequate infrastructure (PH offer/test laboratories/testing procedures), absence of seamless connectivity with other modes, and various IT related bottlenecks.

Containerisation and Hinterland Connectivity
15.186. Containerised traffic is growing at a faster pace than other forms of traffic. In India too container cargo which formed only 15.8 per cent of total cargo handled in Major Ports in 2006–07 increased to 21.5 per cent per cent in 2011–12. The CAGR of container traffic was 5.2 per cent during the Eleventh Five Year Plan which was much higher than the overall growth of traffic of 1.5 per cent for Major Ports during the same period. The Twelfth Plan will therefore give due focus on increasing the share of containerised cargo in ports with a view to capturing a higher share of international trade. The projects for rail/road connectivity need to be taken up and monitored closely both for Major and non-Major Ports. For all these, ports, rail and road investments will be prioritised. Port traffic within India is carried largely by railways and road transport, with pipelines carrying crude oil and petroleum products. Railways are presently carrying considerably less than their optimal share of port traffic and road transport has made up the deficit partly with many negative externalities.

Private Sector Participation
15.187. The Private Sector participation will play a major role in realising the anticipated capacity augmentation in the ports during the Twelfth Plan. It is, therefore, imperative that PPP model is worked successfully and impediments removed. Specially, the system for security clearance for ports needs to be streamlined and made faster. There is also a need to expand existing framework to attract participation from the private sector for development of infrastructure facilities other than container terminals and berths such as are dredging, road infrastructure, creation of SEZ and development of integrated parking zones in the port area.

Non-Major Ports

15.188. An important component of the capacity creation is the development of non-major ports. The Indian Ports Association has information on a regular basis only about major ports, but has less details about progress of works in non-major ports. Considering the fact that nearly 1/3rd of the traffic is handled by them and it is likely to increase significantly during Twelfth Plan, this gap in the system needs to be rectified quickly.

Institutional Reforms and Corporatisation

15.189. Presently, Indian Ports Act, 1908 extends uniformly to all the ports in the country whereas, the Major Port Trusts Act, 1963 applies only to major ports. Though both the Acts have undergone piecemeal revisions to accommodate necessary changes from time to time, no comprehensive review of the various provisions of the Act was carried out so far. There is a need for reform to ensure growth and meet the international competitive environment.

15.190. The present institutional and regulatory arrangements are inadequate and deficient to meet the challenge of efficiency and bringing port services to world class standards. The ports management needs to be strengthened so that they work on commercial basis. Corporatisation is one way of achieving this by conversion of major ports trusts into truly commercial organisation. It is the process by which a port trust is converted into legally and financially independent entity with its own Board of Directors and governed by the provisions of the Companies Act. It is equally important that they are given full autonomy to respond quickly to the requirements of port development which are very large. We need to shift to landlord port organisational model quickly. The role of the state must be confined to setting policies and evolving strategies. Necessary reforms will be carried out during the Plan on the above approach.

Outlay for Shipping Sector in Twelfth Plan

15.191. The outlay for Shipping Sector in Twelfth Plan includes ₹6,960 crore as GBS and ₹21,990 crore as IEBR. In addition the private sector is expressed to invest nearly 1,70,000 crore in the Port Sector.

Some Major Initiatives in the Twelfth Plan

15.192. Some of the major initiatives for the Ports Sector is indicated below:

- Re-look at MCA to promote PPP in port sector
- Re-look at port regulation and tariff setting by TAMP by adopting practices consistent with the Landlord Port model.
- Capital Dredging to increase the draft of ports to at least 14 meters in all ports by the end of the Twelfth Plan and to achieve 17 meters in sub-ports according to the potential of trade.
- Investment in land infrastructure including modern cranes, silos/ warehouses, ICDs, connectivity and so on.
- Move towards greater flexibility for decision making by Port Trusts through greater delegation of powers.
- Landlord port model.
- Corporatisation of major ports in the long run.

CIVIL AVIATION

Overview

15.193. The Civil Aviation services have expanded rapidly with the opening up of domestic skies to private carriers in the second half of the Tenth Plan through PPP investment in the airport infrastructure. The sector contributes significantly to development by generating employment opportunities directly and indirectly besides facilitating enhancement of productivity and efficiency in the movement of goods and services.

Review of the Eleventh Plan

15.194. The Eleventh Plan aimed to provide world class infrastructure for safe, reliable, and affordable air services so as to encourage growth in passenger and cargo traffic, and air connectivity to remote and inaccessible areas with special reference to North-Eastern part of the country.

15.195. Against an investment target of ₹49,267.00 crore comprising of ₹1,900.00 crore as budgetary support and ₹47,367.00 crore as IEBR, the anticipated expenditure during Eleventh Plan period is

₹44,124.00 crore comprising of IEBR of ₹39,571.11 crore and budgetary support of ₹4,552.89 crore. Thus there would be a shortfall of ₹5,143.00 crore (10.44 per cent) in utilisation of the approved outlay. The anticipated utilisation under budgetary support would be 239.63 per cent and 83.54 per cent under IEBR.

15.196. The Indian civil aviation industry managed to exhibit resilience in face of the recent global economic slowdown. Both passenger and cargo traffic have shown robust growth and there has been modernisation and augmentation of capacities, in a major way, at various metro and non-metro airports. Some of the key developments during last five years include the following:

- India has become the ninth largest civil aviation market in the world;
- Passenger handling capacity has risen three-folds from 72 million (FY 06) to over 220 million (FY 11);
- Cargo handling capacity has risen from 0.5 million MT (FY 06) to 3.3 million MT (FY 11);
- Connectivity to North Eastern region has risen from 87 flights per week to 286 flights per week;
- Four international airport projects were successfully completed through the public-private partnership (PPP) mode, viz. greenfield development of Hyderabad and Bengaluru international airports and modernisation of Delhi and Mumbai international airports (Box 15.12);
- The Airport Economic Regulatory Authority (AERA) was established to safeguard the interests of users and service providers at Indian airports; and
- As of now five Indian carriers are operating on international routes.

Twelfth Plan

Objectives

15.197. The Plan aims to propel India among the top five civil aviation markets in the world by providing access to safe, secure and affordable air services to everyone through an appropriate regulatory framework and by developing world class infrastructure facilities (Table 15.39).

Box 15.12
Development of Airports During the Eleventh Plan

The Private sector played an unprecedented role during the Eleventh Plan in the area of airport development. Five international airport projects were successfully completed through the public–private partnership (PPP) mode, viz. greenfield development of Hyderabad and Bengaluru international airports and modernisation of Kochi, Delhi and Mumbai international airports. Total investment made by private airport operators in the last five years was to the tune of ₹30,000 crore. Along with the private sector, Airport Authority of India (AAI) has continued to create airport infrastructure at a rapid pace incurring an expenditure of ₹12,500 crores during the Eleventh Plan. AAI is upgrading and modernising 35 non-metro airports in the country including those at Agra, Ahmedabad, Amritsar, Bhopal, Jaipur, Pune and Goa, at an estimated cost of around ₹4,500 crore. Of these 35 airports, 26 have already been developed, while the remaining are likely to be completed by end of 2012. AAI is also enhancing air connectivity in the North-East by way of Greenfield airport at Pakyong (Sikkim).

The Delhi, Mumbai, Bengaluru, Hyderabad and Cochin now have airports that compare very well internationally. A major achievement during the Eleventh Plan was the commissioning of terminal 3 (T3) and associated infrastructure at Delhi international airport in a record period of 37 months. The Chennai and Kolkata airports are also being modernised and expanded by the Airports Authority of India (AAI). These airports handle 60 per cent of the air traffic in the country. The passenger handling capacity has increased from 13.83 to 60 million at Delhi; 18.50 to 25 million at Mumbai; 3.25 to 9.78 million at Bengaluru; 3.60 to 12 million at Hyderabad; 3.46 to 5 million at Kochi; 7.74 to 23 million at Chennai and 4.06 to 24.06 million at Kolkata during the Eleventh Plan period. Airport capacity in these cities is therefore considered adequate till the end of the Twelfth Plan period except for the city of Mumbai where the total capacity required at the end of Twelfth Plan would be 50.27 million against the total capacity creation of 40 million by the end of Twelfth Plan. Since, the capacity required and the capacity created would not match, there is need for developing another airport at Mumbai.

Traffic Projections

TABLE 15.39
Growth Projections for the Twelfth Five Year Plan: Passenger and Cargo Traffic Forecasts

Passenger/Freight	2011	2016–17	Average Annual Rate of Growth
Passenger (Million)			
(i) Domestic	106	209	12 %
(ii) International	38	60	8 %
Cargo (MMTPA)			
(i) Domestic	0.9	1.7	12 %
(ii) International	1.5	2.7	10 %

Strategies

15.198. To realise objectives of the Twelfth Plan, (*i*) aircraft and airport capacities would be increased, (*ii*) airports to be modernised and upgraded to increase passenger facilities and to speed up cargo clearance, strengthen security and safety measures for safe and reliable air services, (*iii*) improve air connectivity to NE Region, other remote areas and tourist destinations, create right infrastructure for the rapid growth of helicopter operations, (*iv*) introduce seaplane operations, (*v*) to generate employment and to provide better infrastructure for training to make available qualified human resources, and (*vi*) strengthening of regulatory framework on safety and economic regulatory aspects of Civil Aviation, by setting up Civil Aviation Authority.

Airport Infrastructure

15.199. Passenger terminal capacity in all airports put together is expected to be 230-240 million by 2012 and by 2017 it would be about 370 million as per the investment plans of the operators. Cargo growth presently being witnessed will necessitate investment in specialised cargo terminal and equipment. Independent estimates suggest an additional requirement of 30 functional airports by 2017 and about 180 functional airports in all over the next 10 years. Thus, growth in the passenger and cargo traffic requires significant investments for construction of new airports, expansion and modernisation of existing airports, improvement in connecting infrastructure (road, metro, sea link, and so on.) and better airspace management.

15.200. Budgetary support from Government for investment in development of airports in remote areas and regions which need special consideration from socio economic and connectivity point of view would be taken care by the AAI. Regional airport development to cater to the emerging air traffic in Tier II and Tier III towns may initially require budgetary support during the initial period of its operations and until such time the operations become viable. Even at present, there are only 12–13 airports of AAI that are making profit at current level of operations.

15.201. Indian airports would require to meet the traffic growth projections an investment of about ₹67,500 crores during the Twelfth Plan, of which around ₹50,000 crore is likely to be contributed by the Private Sector (Table 15.40).

TABLE 15.40
Investment Requirements during the Twelfth Plan

Investor	Investment Category	₹ in crore
AAI	Airport projects	17,500
Private Investments	By Airport Operator	40,000
By Others (Concessionaires, Third Party, and so on.)		10,000
TOTAL		67,500

Air Navigation Services (ANS)

15.202. Air Space and Air Traffic Management infrastructure assumes critical importance in the context of the Indian Air Transport sector transitioning to the next growth phase. Broadly, it involves deployment of equipment relating to CNS (Communication Navigation and Surveillance) and Air Traffic Management Systems. Presently air navigation services in India are provided by the Airport Authority of India. An important initiative that needs to be pursued and implemented is separation of Air traffic control (ATC) from airport authority of India (AAI) in line with the best practices in the world. It has been suggested that in addition to adequate investment proposed in ANS infrastructure during

> **Box 15.13**
> **GAGAN—The Indian Satellite Based Augmentation System (SBAS) for**
> **Air Navigation Services (ANS)**
>
> GAGAN, the Indian SBAS (Satellite Based Augmentation System) is a project jointly undertaken by the Airport Authority of India and ISRO to achieve smooth transition to satellite based navigation and seamless air traffic management across continents. GAGAN is designed to provide additional accuracy, availability, and integrity necessary to enable user to rely on GPS for all phases of flight, form en route through approach, for all qualified airports within the GAGAN service volume.
>
> GAGAN will provide the capability for increased accuracy in position reporting, thereby making possible high-quality Air Traffic Management (ATM). GAGAN will provide benefits beyond aviation to all modes of transportation, including maritime, highways, railways and public services such as defense services, security agencies, and disaster recovery management by aiding in search and rescue to locate the disaster zone accurately, telecom industry and personal users of position location applications.
>
> After USA, Japan and Europe, India has taken up the challenge of establishing the regional SBAS that will redefine the navigation in India and in adjacent regions. The footprint of GAGAN will cover huge area beyond Indian Territory, from Africa to Australia and can support seamless navigation across the globe. The system is also interoperable with other such systems of WAAS of USA, EGNOSS of Europe and MSAT of Japan.
>
> The lead taken by the Ministry of Civil Aviation in implementing GAGAN and possible certification by 2014 will propel India as the only fourth country to have this facility in the world.

the Twelfth Plan, an independent Air Navigation Services Corporation should be set up to manage capacity, safety, congestion and efficiency issues of air transport.

15.203. The Ministry of Civil Aviation has constituted a Committee for formulating the next generation ANS master plan to enhance capacity and safety levels in the face of higher air traffic movements in future. The ANS infrastructure would move towards greater integration and automation with implementation of state-of-the-art technologies. The system would include a centralised Air Traffic Flow Management with networked VHF and Radars capable of providing dynamic sectors, which permits alignment with traffic pattern. Existing software and hardware infrastructure would be upgraded or replaced. It is estimated that an investment of ₹4,400 crore will be made into this sector during the Twelfth Plan of which ₹3,700 crore would be in ANS infrastructure and air safety and ₹700 crore in the GAGAN (see Box 15.13) project.

Air Lines

15.204. Anticipating significant growth in traffic, most Indian carriers have placed orders to augment their aircraft fleet. According to an estimate, airlines in India are expected to add around 370 aircrafts worth ₹1,50,000 crores to their fleet by 2017. Fleet expansion at this scale would require airlines to explore multiple funding options including capital markets, long-term borrowings and leasing, and so on.

Aviation Turbine Fuel

15.205. A major difficulty being faced by airlines is the high cost of Aviation Turbine Fuel (ATF), which is further aggravated by taxes. Viewed in inter-modal context, it is desirable to rationalise ATF pricing and to review the tax structure so that Airline operation becomes viable. The cost of ATF constitutes 40–50 per cent of the total operating cost and thus is a formidable challenge for the financial health of airlines. This has been a long standing issue that requires an immediate resolution. ATF prices in India are distorted because it is subjected to a multitude of cascading taxes by different government entities despite being an input fuel (similar to coal and gas); it is subjected to sales tax as high as 30 per cent. It is nearly 60 per cent costlier than competing hubs like Dubai, Singapore and Kuala Lumpur and hurts India's competitiveness. The comparison of ATF prices in India with competing hubs has been detailed below (Table 15.41)

TABLE 15.41
Comparison of ATF Prices in India with Competing Hubs

Location	Price/Kilolitre (USD)
India	1,400
Singapore	825
Bangkok	880
Kuala Lumpur	810
Dubai	840

15.206. Due to the distortion in the price structure caused by the taxation policies, the financial viability of airlines is getting strongly affected. Either ATF should be included in the unified Goods and Services Tax or ATF should be accorded the status of "Declared Good" that carries lower and uniform tax rate.

Multi-Modal Connectivity

15.207. The major airports in India are mostly at a considerable distance from the city centre. Apart from causing inconvenience to the passengers, this also adversely affects the comparative advantage in terms of saving in time otherwise enjoyed by other modes of transport. These airports need to be connected to cities by metros and expressways to get full advantage of air transportation by reducing the total travel time, as has been done in the case of IGI Airport, New Delhi.

Foreign Equity Participation

15.208. The Domestic Air Transport Policy approved by the government provides for foreign equity participation up to 49 per cent and investment by non-resident Indians (NRIs) up to 100 per cent in the domestic air transport services. With a view to attracting new technology and management expertise, government has permitted up to 49 per cent Foreign Direct Investment (FDI) by foreign airlines in Indian airline companies.

Air Cargo

15.209. The current share of air-cargo compared to other modes of cargo-transportation is fairly low in India. The potential for air-cargo growth in India can be gauged from the fact that some of the global airports such as Hong Kong, Dubai and Incheon (Seoul) handle cargo volumes which are much more than at Indian airports. The present operating parameters (daily throughput, dwell times) at most air-cargo terminals of the country are far from international best-practices. The following key enablers would be imperative for growth of India's air-cargo industry:

1. Higher Automation: Poor cargo handling infrastructure at airports leads to spoilage and pilferage, increased turnaround times and degradation in the quality of items causing perception issues for Indian exports. There is an urgent need to facilitate efficiency in air-cargo through IT tools and automated material handling.
2. India as a Trans-shipment Cargo Hub: Given its geographic location, India can aspire to become an international cargo hub. To begin with, India needs to facilitate trans-shipment of cargo to and from our neighboring countries, many of whom do not have regular air services to key markets in Europe and America.
3. Trans-shipment at Indian airports is currently negligible. Major bottlenecks are absence of dedicated trans-shipment infrastructure at airports and lack of clarity on the trans-shipment procedures. Conservative estimates by KPMG indicate that the Indian subcontinent alone can offer trans-shipment opportunity of 80,000-1,00,000 MT per annum.
4. Dwell Time Reduction: Cargo dwell times for large Indian airports currently range from 3 to 5 days as compared to an average of 4 to 12 hours at leading global airports. Reduction in dwell time and faster clearance of cargo are extremely critical for India.
5. 24×7 Customs Operation: A review of the current customs clearance procedures is extremely important. There is also a serious need for Indian Customs to operate in a 24×7 environment. This would require close and regular interaction between MoCA, Central Board of Customs and Excise (CBEC) and the industry.
6. Establishment of Air-Freight Stations (AFS) in the hinterland: A significant amount of congestion, damage and pilferage is caused by the

current practice of cargo being brought to terminal in loose units which is then unitised into pallets or containers before being loaded onto aircrafts. This problem can be alleviated by setting up AFSs' in the hinterland. Customs check, X-ray screening and palletisation can take place at the AFS and airport terminals would only act as a 'processing gateway' between airlines and cargo carriers. Success of Containers Freight Stations (CFS) for marine cargo is a clear indication of the need for a similar concept in the air-cargo industry.

Maintenance, Repair and Overhaul (MRO)

15.210. Indian MRO industry is expected to triple in size from ₹2,250 crore in 2010 to ₹7,000 crore by 2020. However, this may still be small compared to the present MRO industry size of other countries such as UAE (₹8,000 crore per annum) and China (₹10,000 crore per annum). India has the potential to be an MRO hub due to the growing aircraft fleet, locational advantage and availability of talent. Given the growth of Indian aviation, it is logical to encourage MRO infrastructure to support the growth in the sector.

Ground Handling

15.211. By 2017, ground handling market is expected to double from present ₹2,000 crore to ₹3,900 crore. A number of global ground-handling players have aggressive expansion plans in India. This would, however, depend significantly on supportive policies and requisite airport infrastructure development.

Regional Airlines

15.212. To tap the vast potential of growth of traffic and to encourage balanced growth of civil aviation, regional airlines need to be promoted. The promotion of regional airlines would, however, be through more liberal policy and provision of better infrastructure facilities. The rules and procedures governing the entry may also be simplified.

Other Challenges

Route Dispersal Guidelines (RDG)

15.213. In accordance with the Route Dispersal Guidelines, all routes were divided into three categories, viz. Category I, II and III. Route categorisation was based on traditionally surplus generating routes (Category I), loss making routes (Category II) and the remaining routes (Category III). The Category I routes were largely inter-metro routes and generated surplus that cross-subsidised losses largely on Category II routes which served regions of difficult terrain and destinations in remote areas. Implementation of Route dispersal guidelines aimed at ensuring that all players in the liberalised era would deploy capacity to destinations in remote areas and would participate equitably in providing air transportation to remote areas.

Air Connectvity in North Eastern Region and Other Remote Areas

15.214. North-East Region of India comprises of eight states viz. Assam, Arunachal Pradesh, Manipur, Meghalaya, Mizoram, Nagaland, Tripura and Sikkim. Most of the places in the North-Eastern states are inaccessible due to inadequate road/rail facilities. Only viable means of transportation in the region is by air. At present, air services are available to/from 11 airports in the North Eastern Region. During last five years from 2006–2011, total number of flights operated on domestic network vis-à-vis flights in North-Eastern Region, Jammu & Kashmir Region, Andaman & Nicobar Island and Lakshadweep Island are indicated in Table 15.42.

15.215. The connectivity to NER, J&K, A&N Islands and Lakshadweep has grown at 43 per cent, 72 per cent, 75 per cent and 67 per cent respectively which are higher than growth in total domestic Network of 39 per cent during the period from 2006 to 2011. In addition to scheduled air services, non-scheduled air services are being provided by North East Shuttle (a non-scheduled operator) with small aircraft. Pawan Hans Helicopters Ltd is also providing helicopter services in Arunachal Pradesh, Meghalaya, Tripura and Sikkim with subsidy from Government for carriage of passengers, emergency/medical evacuation. A private Helicopter operator also operates passenger services in Arunachal Pradesh.

15.216. Despite some degree of success of Route Dispersal Guidelines in ensuring air connectivity to

TABLE 15.42
Flights/Week

Flight Details	2006	2007	2008	2009	2010	2011
Total on Domestic Network	8,724	10,624	11,048	1,063	11,315	12,107
North-Eastern Region	259	285	298	286	347	370
Jammu & Kashmir	104	116	110	113	120	179
Andaman & Nicobar Island	24	42	42	35	40	42
Lakshadweep Island	06	13	10	07	13	10

North-Eastern Region, Jammu & Kashmir and other places, air connectivity has largely been confined to few airports in these regions. The air connectivity is largely concentrated on routes connecting state capitals. Air connectivity has not increased proportionately on routes connecting Island airports. Although all the scheduled domestic airlines are complying with mandatory capacity deployment requirements contained in Route Dispersal Guidelines, however, some parts of the country still remain unconnected by air services or partly connected. A sustainable and durable solution in the long run could be found only in direct intervention by way of development of small low cost 'no-frill' airports and regional airlines through providing direct subsidies in a transparent manner both for airport operator and for the carrier. As of now there are 22 airports and civil enclaves in the NER. Amongst these there are seven fully operational AAI airports at Agartala, Barapani, Dibrugarh, Guwahati, Imphal and Lilabari. Besides there are four civil enclaves at Jorhat, Bagdogra, Silchar and Tejpur. AAI has plans to develop Guwahati as a inter-regional hub and Dibrugarh, Imphal and Agartala as intra-regional hub. As a low cost airport, to begin with, AAI would be developing Daparizo Airport in Arunchal Pradesh for 20 seater aircraft in phase I. Similarly the other airports in the region could be identified for developing as small airports suitable for small carriers keeping in view the strategic and socio-economic development needs of the areas.

Safety

15.217. With the advancement and growth in aviation activities in India, the challenges to keep the skies safe need to be met appropriately. Safety is of paramount importance. As the number of operations increase, it is a challenging task to keep the rate of accident and incident in check. The congestion in the skies also poses a threat of near-misses and collision warnings. The increase in number of movements affects runway safety, ramp safety, incursions and excursions, ramp congestion, precautionary landings, aborted take offs, and other serious situations affecting safety. The implementation of Safety Programme by DGCA and safety management systems by all stake holders needs to be ensured. It is proposed to further strengthen DGCA during the Plan. Dedicated staff for the training academy has already been sanctioned. As a joint venture with AAI, the training academy will ensure technical capability of the highest level to enhance the skills of officials in various fields

Human Resource Development

15.218. It has been estimated that total manpower requirement of airlines will rise from 62,000 in FY 2011 to 1,17,000 by FY 2017. This includes number of pilots, cabin crew, aircrafts engineers and technicians (MRO), ground handling staff, cargo handling staff, administrative and sales staff. India currently has over 4,500 pilots, including 400 expatriates. With the doubling of fleet size expected by 2017, India will require a total of around 9,000 pilots by 2017. This implies an average addition of at least 800 pilots per year for the next five years, not accounting for attrition and replacements of expatriate pilots (about 400), required to be phased out by end of 2013. Currently 23 out of 40 institutes for pilot training are non-operational. The remaining 17 institutes offer training facilities for commercial pilots with an annual turnover of over 100 pilots. There is acute shortage of trained pilots/commanders in India. In addition, many courses of some of the pilot training institutes are not recognised by DGCA, leading to high rejection rates. Exams are conducted every three months compared to weekly exams in developed countries. It is necessary to meet these gaps in the Twelfth Plan and increase facilities for human resource development.

Current Regulatory Environment in Civil Aviation Sector

15.219. In order to regulate tariff and other charges for the aeronautical services rendered at airports and to monitor performance of airports, Airports Economic Regulatory Authority of India was set up in 2008 through an Act of Parliament. DGCA performs safety oversight functions of airline industry, and limited Economic Regulation covering fares, rates, services affecting such fares and rates.

15.220. Globally, Civil Aviation sector is regulated by independent regulators. Therefore, creation of a Civil Aviation Authority as a unified regulator covering both safety and economic aspects of airline industry is the need of the hour. Existing Directorate General of Civil Aviation could be subsumed in the proposed Civil Aviation Authority as an enforcement wing. CAA will be the regulatory policy making body which will also have administrative control over the enforcement wing (the present DGCA) to ensure the implementation of its regulatory decisions. Setting up of independent and autonomous regulatory body is not only consistent with international best practices but also essential to meet the challenges of a growing industry with multiple players from both India and abroad. Independent Regulators are mandated to adopt transparent process in decision making, which is necessary to impart regulatory certainty to investors current and potential.

National Aviation University

15.221. A skilled and competent workforce is essential to create a safe and efficient aviation industry. Without this India cannot join the ranks of the leading aviation nations. A vibrant, world class education and training sector is therefore essential to meet the rising demand for skilled workforce at all levels. It is found that there is a near absence of qualitative and duly recognised formal Educational programme leading to award of Diploma/Degree/Post Graduate Degree in the field of Civil Aviation in the country. As a result of this, all major as well as minor agencies/organisations in the sector have to mostly recruit persons and invest considerable resources in post recruitment training. It is therefore necessary to establish National Aviation University to cater to the growing educational and training requirements of the Civil Aviation Sector on the pattern of National Maritime University which has been established under the Ministry of Shipping, Government of India for the purpose of development of Human Resources for Shipping and Ports sector

Development of Areospace Industry

15.222. Considering the growth prospects of Air Traffic in the country, the potential for large scale acquisition of aircrafts by the carriers in India, and the competitive advantages arising out of growing pool of scientific and technical manpower in the country it is felt necessary to consider initiating activities towards development of aerospace industry. Independent traffic forecasts suggest that by 2020 or so, the number of aircraft required in the Indian market would exceed one thousand. Most of the requirements would be in the narrow body segment to cater to the needs of Tier II and Tier III towns. Also India could capture the pie of Aerospace outsourcing due to significant cost advantages. Skilled labour costs are currently far less than USA and Europe. Therefore, there is a need to take up Aerospace development programmes in the country for meeting the needs of Civilian aircraft.

Establishment of Civil Aviation Museum

15.223. The Civil Aviation Museum shall enshrine the evolution and development of aviation and spaceflight in India, and so seek to educate and inspire the nation by preserving and displaying aeronautical and spaceflight material and data of technical and historical interest and significance to national programmes; developing educational material and conducting programmes to enhance public understanding of and involvement in, the development of aviation and spaceflight and conducting and disseminating new knowledge on aviation and spaceflight and their related technologies. The aim is to archive the development of aviation in India, collect, preserve and display aeronautical equipment and provide educational material for the study of aviation and spaceflight sciences.

MOCA Institutions

Air India Limited

15.224. Against the Eleventh Plan approved outlay of ₹32,730.71 crore, the anticipated expenditure of Air India Ltd during Eleventh Plan period would be ₹28,203.04 crore including the budgetary support of ₹3,200.05 crore in the form of equity infusion. Air India Ltd ordered 93 aircraft comprising of 50 Boeing and 43 Airbus aircrafts. Out of these 93 aircrafts, 85 aircrafts were projected to be received during the Eleventh Plan period. The physical and financial performances of Air India Limited are given at Annexures 15.5 and 15.6.

Airport Authority of India

15.225. The approved Eleventh Plan outlay of Airports Authority of India was ₹12,964.21 crore, including budgetary support of ₹1,461.68 crore. Out of ₹12,964.21 crore, ₹6,973.40 crore was provided for non-metro airports and the balance of ₹5,990.81 crore for metro airports. The anticipated expenditure of Airports Authority of India during Eleventh Plan period would be ₹12,547.56 crore including budgetary support of ₹850.61 crore. The financial performance of Airports Authority of India during Eleventh Plan period is given in Annexure 15.7.

Pawan Hans Helicopters Limited

15.226. The approved Eleventh Plan outlay of Pawan Hans Helicopters Limited was ₹603.50 crore including budgetary support of ₹20.00 crore against which the anticipated expenditure during Eleventh Plan period would be ₹797.26 crore including budgetary support of ₹58.00 crore. Major portion of the Eleventh Plan outlay was earmarked for acquisition of helicopters. Details of performance is enclosed in Annexure 15.8.

Hotel Corporation of India Limited

15.227. The Eleventh Plan approved outlay of Hotel Corporation of India Limited is ₹75.00 crore, against which the anticipated expenditure is ₹43.75 crore.

Directorate General of Civil Aviation

15.228. The anticipated expenditure of Directorate General of Civil Aviation during Eleventh Plan period is ₹210.19 crores against the approved outlay of ₹258.80 crores. The major scheme of the Directorate envisaged for implementation during Eleventh Five Year Plan period is 'New Flying training Academy in Gondia' for training of pilots.

15.229. The endeavor of Directorate General of Civil Aviation (DGCA) during Twelfth Plan period will be to promote safe and efficient Air Transportation through regulation and proactive safety oversight system. Schemes proposed under the Twelfth Plan are aimed at DGCA's capacity building.

Bureau of Civil Aviation Security

15.230. During Eleventh Plan period, the Bureau of Civil Aviation Security (BCAS) is likely to spend ₹73.31 crore as against actual allocation of ₹222 crore. One of the major schemes, namely, setting up of Civil Aviation Security Training Academy is at approval stage. Implementation of the restructuring and strengthening of BCAS which includes creation of infrastructure of office building, acquisition of some modern equipment including enhancing the manpower requirement at both the BCAS Headquarters and regional level is going slowly. The Bureau of Civil Aviation Security is working out its future plans of strengthening organisationally and technologically vis-à-vis the current security scenario.

Indira Gandhi Rashtriya Uran Akademi

15.231. Indira Gandhi Rashtriya Uran Akademi (IGRUA) is an autonomous body. A management contract was signed with CAE Flight Training (India) Private Limited, a wholly owned subsidiary of CAE Inc, Canada on 7.2.2008 for an initial period of 10 years without affecting the legal entity of IGRUA. IGRUA is provided grants-in-aid to pursue its plan projects. Against the approved outlay of ₹42.00 crore, the anticipated expenditure of IGRUA during Eleventh Plan period is ₹41.00 crore. Facilities at IGRUA have been upgraded to impart training to 100 pilots per year. IGRUA has projected an outlay of ₹95.00 crore for Twelfth Plan period for purchase of additional 14 aircrafts, setting up of MRO hub and AME school at IGRUA and extension of tarmac at Sultanpur for parking IGRUA aircraft.

Aero Club of India
15.232. Aero Club of India is granted grants-in-aid for its plan projects. The anticipated expenditure of Aero Club of India is ₹31.65 crores against the Eleventh Plan approved outlay of ₹35.32 crores.

Major Initiatives to be Taken by Moca in the Twelfth Plan

- Doubling of passenger handling capacity of Airports primarily through private investments (PPP).
- Setting up of Unified Regulatory Agents.
- Up gradation of Air Navigation Services (ANS) using the latest technology.
- Encouraging emergence of regional airlines to cater to air transport needs of Tier II and Tier III towns and promoting low cost carriers for this purpose.
- New Policy for ATF to improve Airline competitiveness.
- Policy on increased foreign direct investments, including by foreign airlines in domestic airlines.
- Policy on MRO to encourage establishment of dedicated MRO hubs through joint ventures with MRO service providers and airport companies. This would also encourage mechanisation and modern ground handling processes for greater efficiency.
- Revised policy on Route Dispersal Guidelines to improve services to far flung and inaccessible areas.
- Setting up of National Aviation University to meet critical skill development needs of the aviation Sector.

Investments During Twelfth Five Year Plan for Civil Aviation

15.233. The projected investment during Twelfth Five Year Plan from Central sector is expected to be ₹33,198 crore of which ₹16,983 crore is from GBS and ₹16,215 crore from IEBR. Out of the GBS of ₹16,983 crore, ₹15,096 crore is earmarked for Air India and ₹1,887 crore for all other plan schemes/programmes for the Ministry. Besides, an investment of ₹50,000 crore comprising ₹40,000 crore from private investment and ₹10,000 crore by others including concessioners, third party and so on have been projected to be made in airport projects during the Twelfth Five Year Plan.

NORTH EAST REGION

15.234. The North East region has a number of characteristics that make it imperative for more organised inter-sectoral planning to be done for transportation in the region: it is remote from the rest of India; several areas feature difficult hilly terrain; it also has many rivers, which can permit significant inland water transport options, but also contribute to difficulties in engineering transport infrastructure; it has a long border with neighbouring countries which increases the importance of transport infrastructure from a strategic and security viewpoint; and it consists of 8 states, each of which have their own requirements and priorities. A region-wide transport planning for the four transport sectors – roads, civil aviation, rail, and inland waterways – in an integrated framework is therefore required.

Railways
15.235. A decision has already been taken to connect all the state capitals in the North East with the rest of the country. The state capitals of Assam and Tripura are already connected. New lines for connecting state capitals of Arunachal Pradesh, Manipur, Nagaland, Mizoram and Meghalaya have been sanctioned and works are in progress. In the Twelfth Five Year Plan, the work on these railway lines will be expedited so that all state capitals in the North East Region are on the rail map by 2020.

Roads

15.236. A number of programmes such as the SARDP-NE have been launched for the development of National Highways, State Highways and other roads in the North East Region. As a result of these programmes investments have been increasing. As a matter of fact, the implementing agencies are unable to spend the allocated amount and complete the projects in time. Hence there is a great need for capacity augmentation and institutional strengthening in the areas related to evolving of projects, preparation of project reports, implementation, monitoring and management of projects in the North East region as a whole.

Air Connectivity

15.237. Considering the importance of civil aviation to the development of the NER, a new policy centred around small aircrafts is required to implement a hub-and-spoke model. With more frequent flights in and out of this geographically difficult region, there may be considerable reduction in the physical exclusion of the region. The development of existing airports and operationalisation of non-operational airports would not only make air links feasible between the state capitals but also with neighbouring countries. Multi-utility based air services which enable the movement of high value cargo can also be instrumental in improving the economic vitality of the region. However, in order to achieve the objective of uninterrupted and reliable air services and to prevent accidents, there is a need to develop state of the art weather and navigation information systems and human resources together with the actual physical airport infrastructure. Guwahati Airport should also be developed as a potential major gateway to South East Asia, both for passenger and freight traffic.

Inland Water Transport

15.238. IWT has a natural fit with the bulk commodities that the North East Region imports from the rest of India. Tea, oil, cement and coal are exported, while food grains, fertilisers and petroleum products are imported. All these items are non-perishable and transported in high volumes, making them suitable for transportation by IWT. Major development of IWT requires participation by Bangladesh. The Indo-Bangladesh Protocol on Inland Water Transit and Trade already exists. Efforts would be made to extend the validity of this protocol for at least 20 years. This would provide stability to the trading environment and hence enable appropriate investment planning in both the public and private sectors. It would also clear the way for the development of public private partnerships in the development, management and operation of inland water transport in the region.

TWELFTH PLAN OUTLAY

15.239. The indicative Gross Budgetary Support and IEBR for Twelfth Five Year Plan for various Ministries in the Transport Sector is Given below (Table 15.43):

TABLE 15.43
Ministry/Department – wise Twelfth Five Year Plan (2012–17) Outlays for Transport Sectors

(in ₹ crore)

Sl. No.	Ministry	Twelfth Plan (2012–17) GBS Outlays	IEBR
1.	Ministry of Road Transport and Highways	1,44,769	64,834
2.	Ministry of Civil Aviation	16,983	16,215
3.	Ministry of Railways	1,94,221	2,25,000
4.	Ministry of Shipping	6,960	21,990
5.	PMGSY (part of Rural Development Allocation)	1,26,491	–

ANNEXURE 15.1
Central Road Sector Outlay and Expenditure-At Current Price for Eleventh Plan

(₹ Crore)

S No	Schemes/Programmes	Eleventh Plan (2007–12) Outlay	2007–08 BE	2007–08 Exp.	2008–09 BE	2008–09 Exp.	2009–10 BE	2009–10 Exp.	2010–11 BE	2010–11 Exp.	2011–12 BE	2011–12 Exp. (Prov.)	Total Outlay for the Eleventh Plan (BE)	Total Expenditure at Current Prices (prov. for 2011–12)
1	2	3	4	6	7	9	10	12	13	15	16	18	19	20
1	External aided projects													
	(i) External aided (RW)	0.00											0.00	0.00
	(ii) Counterpart funds (RW)	0.00											0.00	0.00
	EAP Ministry	0.00											0.00	0.00
	(iii) Externally aided (NHAI)	3,563.20	1,788.80	1,776.00	1,515.00	1,515.00	272.00	272.00	320.00	320.00			3,895.80	3,883.00
	(iv) Counterpart funds (NHAI)	0.00									20.00	0.00	20.00	0.00
	(v) Loan to NHAI	890.80	447.20	444.00	379.00	379.00	68.00	68.00	80.00	80.00			974.20	971.00
	(vi) EAP under RW								100.00		80.00	0.00	180.00	0.00
	EAP-NHAI	4,454.00	2,236.00	2,220.00	1,894.00	1,894.00	340.00	340.00	500.00	400.00	100.00	0.00	5,070.00	4,854.00
	(vii) Strengthening of PIC	0.00											0.00	0.00
2	Other Schemes-NH (O)	16,500.00	2,079.25	2,011.07	2,142.79	2,852.70	3,342.55	4,298.12	3,958.10	4,496.35	4,964.34	4,519.58	16,487.03	18,177.82
3	Rail cum Road Bridge, Munger, Bihar	392.00			40.00	40.00	60.00	60.00	100.00	100.00	180.00	72.00	380.00	272.00
4	Development of roads in LWE affected area						500.00	5.00	1,000.00	718.05	825.00	792.47	2,325.00	1,515.52
5	Development of Vijawada-Ranchi Road						200.00	0.00	100.00	0.00	100.00	67.25	400.00	67.25
6	Tribal Sub Plan										375.00	374.96	375.00	374.96
7	Mughal Road in Jammu & Kashmir	127.50			30.00	0.00	20.00	0.00					50.00	0.00
8	Improvement of Duburi-Brahmanipal-Harichandanpur-Naranpur State Road in Orissa (POSCO)	140.85			40.00	40.00	30.00	0.00	20.00	0.00	33.02	33.02	123.02	73.02

#	Item	C1	C2	C3	C4	C5	C6	C7	C8	C9	C10	C11	C12	C13
9	Works under BRDB	2,500.00	499.76	623.93	650.00	645.80	600.00	723.49	700.00	693.00	700.00	515.00	3,149.76	3,201.22
10	Travel expenses (domestic)				2.00	1.24	2.00	1.20	2.00	1.31	2.00	1.22	8.00	4.97
11	Other charges		0.50	0.50	0.50	0.13	0.50	0.00	0.50	0.03	0.50	0.00	2.50	0.66
12	Development of Information Technology	64.00	9.50	0.32	3.50	0.71	3.50	3.05	3.50	1.10	3.50	1.74	23.50	6.92
13	Strategic roads under Roads Wing	0.00	7.00	6.35					5.00	0.00			12.00	6.35
14	Strategic roads under BRDB	500.00	67.00	61.45	78.00	76.96	60.00	82.17	100.00	72.66	105.00	53.00	410.00	346.24
15	R&D Planning studies	100.00	8.50	0.20	8.50	0.71	5.50	3.84	6.00	0.92	5.50	0.48	34.00	6.15
16	Training		1.50	0.35	1.50	0.16	1.50	0.39	1.50	0.00	1.50	0.11	7.50	1.01
17	Machinery and equipments				10.00	3.07	15.00	0.53	15.00	0.01	5.00	0.00	45.00	3.61
18	Charged expenditure	36.00	6.00	5.93	6.00	2.07	6.00	5.32	6.00	0.21	7.00	0.00	31.00	13.53
19	NHAI (investment)	36,238.00	6,541.06	6,541.06	6,972.47	6,972.47	8,578.45	7,404.70	7,848.98	8,440.94	8,250.00	6,187.00	38,190.96	35,546.17
20	E&I for States from CRF	900.00	264.93	169.70	180.74	175.65	216.97	104.35	195.75	208.23	232.27	173.74	1,090.66	831.67
21	E&I for UTs from CRF		9.00	1.60	10.00	0.00	16.03	0.00	14.67	0.00	17.48	2.04	67.18	3.64
22	NHDP-III, two-laning expressways and six-laning												0.00	0.00
23	SARDP-NE	9,877.65	710.00	698.02	1,200.00	643.72	1,200.00	658.55	1,500.00	1,044.49	1,600.00	1,939.98	6,210.00	4,984.76
24	Strategic roads in Arunachal Pradesh under Ministry of Defense												0.00	0.00
25	NHAI(Toll Remittance)								1,623.00	1,623.00	2,092.89	2,692.89	3,715.89	4,315.89
	Total (GBS)	71,830.00	12,440.00	12,340.48	13,270.00	13,349.39	15,198.00	13,690.71	17,700.00	17,800.30	19,600.00	17,426.48	78,158.00	74,607.36
26	IEBR	34,829.00	2,090.00	305.18	4,100.00	1,630.74	5,000.00	1,273.26	7,455.00	2,100.00	17,500.00	12,500.00	36,145.00	17,809.18
	Total GBS + IEBR	1,06,659.00	14,530.00	12,645.66	17,370.00	14,980.13	20,198.00	14,963.97	25,155.00	19,900.30	37,100.00	29,926.48	1,14,303.00	92,416.54
	Private Sector Investment	86,792.00	7,325.00	7,057.38	13,938.00	8,179.75	16,071.66	8,944.61	21,256.00	15,354.37	23,301.68	25,749.38	81,892.34	65,285.49
	Pvt Sec (non-NHDP)			60.00		43.68		142.33		129.49		0.00		375.50
	Total Pvt Sect	7,325.00	7,325.00	7,117.38	13,938.00	8,223.43	16,071.66	9,086.94	21,256.00	15,483.86	23,301.68	25,749.38	81,892.34	65,660.99
	Total Central Roads Sector	21,855.00	21,855.00	19,763.04	31,308.00	23,203.56	36,269.66	24,050.91	46,411.00	35,384.16	60,401.68	55,675.86	1,96,195.34	1,58,077.53

ANNEXURE 15.2

Plan-wise Addition to NH Length

Plan	Length Added (in km)	Total Length (in km)
As on 1 April 1947		21,440
Pre First Plan (1947–51)	815	22,255
First Plan (1951–56)		22,255
Second Plan (1956–61)	1,514	23,769
Third Plan (1961–66)	179	23,948
Interregnum (1966–69)	52	24,000
Fourth Plan (1969–74)	4,819	28,819
Fifth Plan (1974–78)	158	28,977
Interregnum (1978–80)	46	29,023
Sixth Plan (1980–85)	2,687	31,710
Seventh Plan (1985–90)	1,902	33,612
Interregnum (1990–92)	77	33,689
Eighth Plan (1992–97)	609	34,298
Ninth Plan (1997–2002)	23,814	58,112
Tenth Plan (2002–07)	9,008	66,590*
Eleventh Plan (2007–12)	10,228	76,818
Eleventh Plan (2007–12)		
2007–08	164	66,754
2008–09	3,794	70,548
2009–10	386	70,934
2010–11	0	70,934
2011–12	5,884	76,818**

* 530 km length of National Highways of Madhya Pradesh has been de-notified.
** Includes 1,388 km under notification at present

ANNEXURE 15.3

Achievement on National Highways

Period	Total Length# (km)	Widening to Two Lanes (km)	Widening to Four Lanes (km)	Strengthening of Pavement (km)	Major Bridges (Nos)
1947–69	24,000	14,000*	Nil	Nil	169
1969–90	33,612	16,000	267	9,000	302
1990–2002	58,112	3,457	1,276	7,000	87
Tenth Plan (2002–07)	66,590	4,177	6,769**	8,377	611***
Eleventh Plan (2007–12)	75,430	4,892	10,165	4,417	121
Total	75,430	42,526	18,477	28,794	1,290

Note: # Length at the end of the period.
* Includes 6,000 km which were already two-lane at the time of designation as NHs.
** Includes 216.62 km which have been six or eight laned up to Tenth plan.

NHAI AND MORTH

S. No.	Schemes/Programmes	Physical Performance Eleventh Plan	
		Targets	Achievements
1	Widening to two-lanes (km)	5,603	5,161
2	Widening to four-lanes (km)	14,975	10,947
3	Strengthening of weak two-lanes (km)	4,634	4,625
4	Bypasses (nos)	99	29
5	Major bridges /minor bridges including ROBs (nos)	660	483
6	IRQP (km)	9,441	11,831

BRDB

S. No.	Schemes/Programmes (Normal NH Works)	Physical Performance Eleventh Plan	
		Targets	Achievements (Up to Jan 2012)
1	Widening to two-lanes (km)	1,111	915
2	Widening to four-lanes (km)	6	3
3	Strengthening of weak two-lanes (km)	135	133
4	Bypasses (nos)	18	6
5	Major bridges /minor bridges including ROBs (nos)	188	127
6	IRQP	911	811

ANNEXURE 15.4

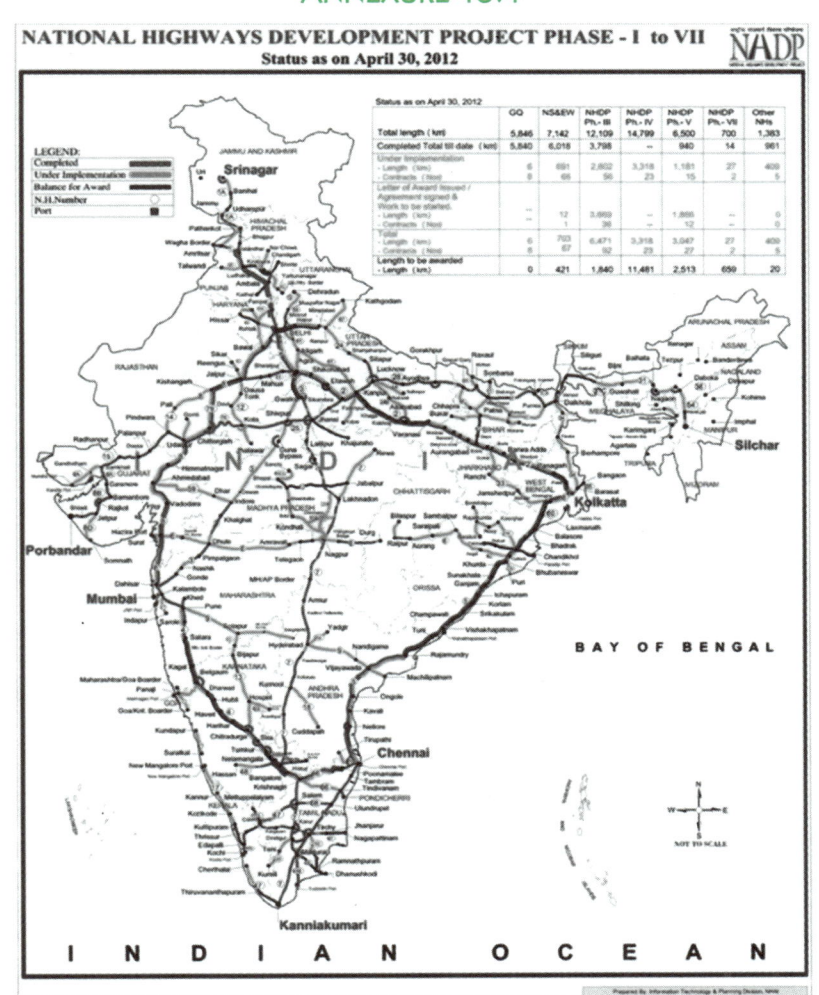

NATIONAL HIGHWAYS DEVELOPMENT PROJECT PHASE – I to VII
Status as on April 30, 2012

ANNEXURE 15.5

Physical Performance of Air India Limited during Eleventh Plan Period

Particulars	Eleventh Plan	2007–08		2008–09		2009–10		2010–11		2011–12	
	Targets	Targets	Ach.	Targets	Ach.	Targets	Ach.	Targets	Ach.	Targets	Ach.
1	2	3	4	5	6	7	8	9	10	11	12
Available TonneKms (mill.)	54,114	7,180	6,168	8,474	5,602	10,927	6,053	12,811	6,365	14,722	6,482
Revenue TonneKms (mill.)	38,217	5,160	3,688	6,169	3,191	7,782	3,533	8,921	3,726	10,185	3,620
Overall Load Factor (per cent)	71	72	60	73	57	71	58	70	58	69	56
Available Seats km (mill.)	3,74,639	53,411	48,393	61,072	43,591	75,534	44,723	86,230	45,845	98,392	45,803
Rev. Passengers km (mill)	2,74,075	38,795	30,891	44,691	25,950	55,529	28,965	63,252	30,556	71,808	31,456
Passenger Load Factor (per cent)	73	73	64	73	60	74	65	73	67	73	69

Source: Air India Limited.
Note: Ach. – Achievement

ANNEXURE 15.6

Financial Performance of Air India Ltd. during the Eleventh Plan Period

Particulars	Eleventh Plan	2007–08		2008–09		2009–10		2010–11		2011–12	
	Targets	Targets	Ach.	Targets	Ach.	Targets	Ach.	Targets	Ach.	Targets	Ach.
1	2	3	4	5	6	7	8	9	10	11	12
Total Revenue	1,13,367	16,541	15,257	19,096	13,479	23,050	13,485	25,682	14,166	28,998	15,383
Total Expenses	1,11,926	16,423	18,556	18,926	20,668	22,839	19,036	25,345	21,160	28,393	23,237
Profit/(Loss) After Tax	1,441	118	(2,226)	170	(5,548)	211	(5,552)	336	(6,994)	605	(7,854)

Source: Air India Limited.
Note: Ach. – Achievement

ANNEXURE 15.7

Financial Performance of Airports Authority of India during Eleventh Plan Period

Particulars	Eleventh Plan	2007–08		2008–09		2009–10		2010–11		2011–12	
	Targets	Targets	Ach.	Targets	Ach.	Targets	Ach.	Targets	Ach.	Targets	Ach.
1	2	3	4	5	6	7	8	9	10	11	12
Total Revenue	23,783	3,425	4,289	4,117	4,186	4,045	4,615	4,919	5,139	5,382	5,878.66
Total Expenses	14,419	2,187	2,550	2,715	3,070	3,161	3,387	3,758	3,793	4,030	4,514.53
Profit/(Loss) before Tax											
Profit/(Loss) after Tax	5,150	743	1,082	842	687	530	712	720	846	810	859.01

Note: Ach. – Achievement

ANNEXURE 15.8

Financial Performance of Pawan Hans Helicopters Ltd. during Eleventh Plan Period

Particulars	Eleventh Plan	2007–08		2008–09		2009–10		2010–11		2011–12	
	Targets	Targets	Ach.	Targets	Ach.	Targets	Ach.	Targets	Ach.	Targets	Ach.
1	2	3	4	5	6	7	8	9	10	11	12
Total Revenue	1,810	243	243	239	329	311	396	364	424	446	438.15
Total Expenses	1,602	219	214	226	291	283	349	334	384	419	437.05
Profit/(Loss) after Tax	210	22	23	14	25	20	36	20	9	2	(10.35)

Note: Ach. – Achievement

NOTES

1. Clive Bell (2012), 'The Benefits of India's Rural Roads Program in the Spheres of Goods, Education and Health- Joint Estimation and Decomposition', World Bank Policy Research Working Paper 6169, August 2012.
2. Clive Bell and Susanne van Dillen (2012), 'How Does India's Rural Roads Program Affect the Grassroots? Findings from a Survey in Orissa', World Bank Policy Research Working Paper 6167, August 2012.

16

Communication

INTRODUCTION

16.1. Democratisation of information makes it possible for ideas, opinions, knowledge and education to be accessible to everyone, anywhere, anytime. This is the key to innovation and empowerment of citizens. In order to enhance access to information emphasis is laid on building platforms that can leverage broadband and create public information infrastructure and move towards the next generation of governance to ensure accountability, transparency, information sharing and collaboration. The key challenge now is to build and integrate national platforms for the Unique Identification (UID-AADHAR), Geographical Information System (GIS), Cyber Security and Payment Gateway. Finally, leveraging the Fourth Screen i.e., the Mobile Phone for reaching out to citizens is desirable, as it allows a much wider reach and in a language people can understand.

16.2. The ICT sector is predominantly a service sector and has redefined service delivery and the way business houses and common man interact with Government. Rapid technological developments over the years have made it possible to provide services on a single platform due to convergence. During the Twelfth Plan period, this sector is poised for substantial growth both in terms of expansion of carriage (networks) and content (voice, data and multimedia). Since, ICT infrastructure and services encompasses all sectors of economy, the next five years offer a unique opportunity to leverage upon our strength in all facets of ICT. This chapter deals with the Telecommunications, Information Technology, Postal and Information and Broadcasting sectors.

TELECOMMUNICATIONS

Overview

16.3. The telecommunications sector has witnessed phenomenal growth during the last decade. Growth of mobile telephony has been the most visible indicator and catalyst to economic growth. Coverage in terms of number of subscribers has reached 951.34 million in March 2012. The most encouraging feature has been the growth in coverage and increase in the number of subscribers in rural areas powered by low tariffs. More than 5,55,000 villages out of more than 6,00,000 villages in the country have the benefit of mobile coverage and the remaining villages are likely to be covered very soon, either by the Telecom Service Providers (TSPs) on their own, or with support from the Universal Service Obligation Fund (USOF). A worrying feature, however, has been the slow growth in broadband penetration and usage. Broadband subscription was only about 14 million in March 2012, much below what is needed.

16.4. The growth of world-class telecommunication infrastructure in the country has been driven by proactive policy initiatives. The National Telecom Policy (NTP)-1999 recognised that access to telecommunications is of utmost importance for achieving the social and economic goals and help in addressing the developmental challenges of the country. Availability of affordable and effective communications for the citizens was at the core of the vision and goal of the policy makers. Another important objective was to provide a balance between the provision of universal service to all uncovered areas, including the rural areas, and the provision of high-level services capable of meeting the needs of the country's economy.

16.5. The sector has shown great resilience during a period of global downturn and has registered an annual growth rate of more than 35 per cent during 2008–11. However, the growth has been predominantly propelled through voice based services. The Twelfth Plan period needs to leverage the new technological developments in the sector and provide affordable value added services.

16.6. Important gains have been made in the R&D sector and India is being seen as the global destination for R&D, engineering design and prototype development, as well as a manufacturing hub for high tech products. Generation of Intellectual Property (IP) and products has, however, been limited, even though there are numerous instances of IP and products being registered outside India where the bulk of R&D has been carried out in India. Now the aim must be to translate resident R&D capability into products, patents and IPRs that drive the next generation of technology innovation. The need to channelise the capability that exists in the academia into applied R&D for the Telecom sector cannot be overemphasised.

REVIEW OF THE ELEVENTH PLAN (2007–12)

16.7. The Eleventh Five Year Plan saw an impressive four and half fold increase in total telephone connections from 205.86 million in March 2007 to 951.34 million in March 2012 (Figure 16.1). The Eleventh Plan had envisaged a target of 600 million connections by March 2012. However, during 2009–10 the total telephone connections had already increased to 621.25 million.

16.8. The overall teledensity has also increased from 18.31 per cent to 78.66 per cent during the Eleventh Plan period. However, the subscriber base for telecom services in India is skewed in favour of urban areas. Urban teledensity is around 4.4 times that of rural teledensity (Figure 16.2).

16.9. The sector has been dominated by a preference for wireless phones, as confirmed from the rising share of wireless phones, which increased from 80.19 per cent (165.09 million) in March 2007 to 96.62 per cent (919.17 million) in March 2012. On the other hand, there had been continuous decline in the number of wireline telephones in the country from 40.77 million in March 2007 to 32.17 million in March 2012 (Figure 16.3). The service providers need to leverage the wireline infrastructure, and build services in new and innovative segments, to address this decline and salvage the investments made so far.

16.10. While the wireless led penetration appears impressive, it is dominated by private sector players and voice telephony services. The mobile broadband services also need to keep pace with the voice telephony growth with the launch of 3G/BWA services. The growth of the economy is highly dependent on data services as opposed to voice telephony. Therefore, a significant challenge remains in making the Indian telecom infrastructure accessible and responsive to this basic requirement.

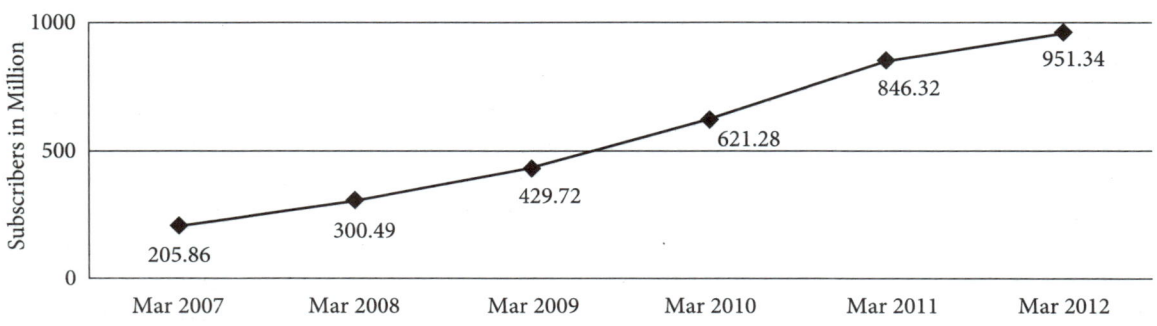

Source: TRAI.

FIGURE 16.1: Telephone Subscribers Growth during 2007–12

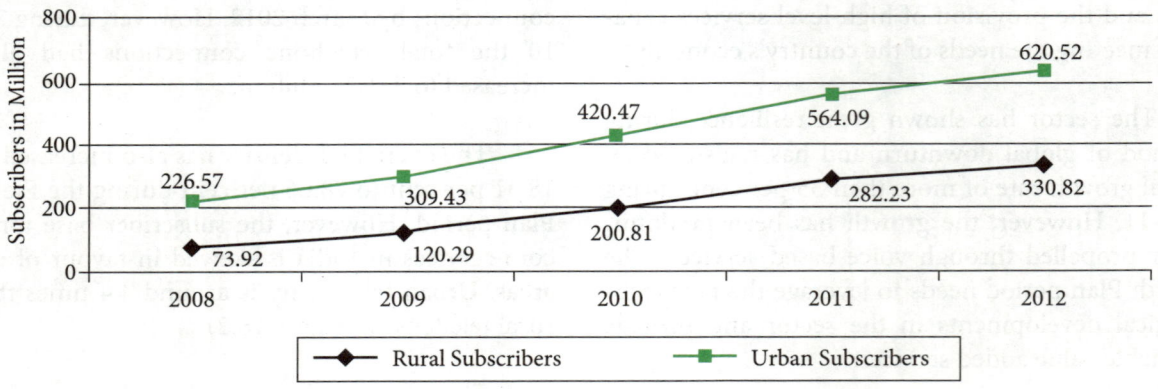

Source: TRAI.

FIGURE 16.2: Distribution of Urban and Rural Subscribers

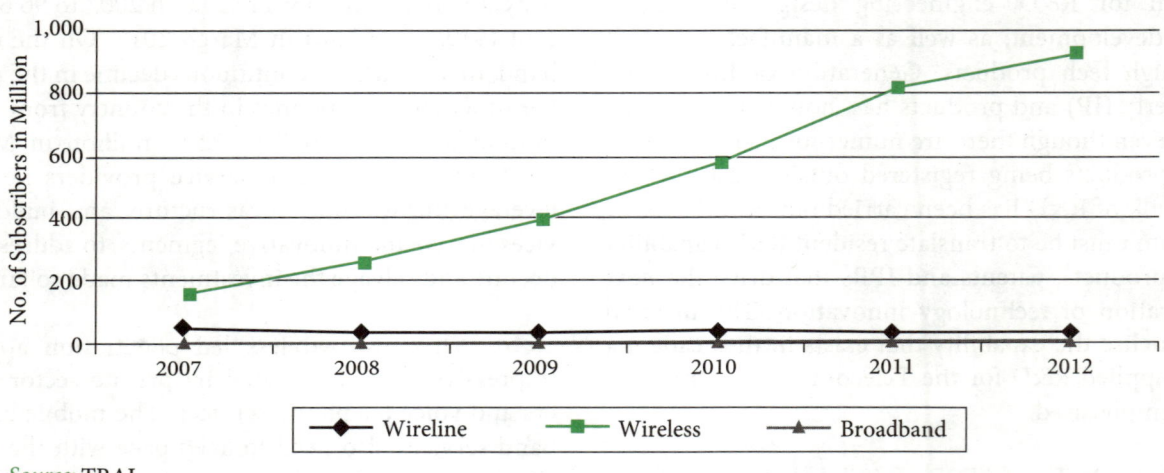

Source: TRAI.

FIGURE 16.3: Number of Telephone and Broadband Connections

16.11. The first wave of initiatives leading to tariff reduction started with the introduction of the Telecom Tariff Order in 2000 bringing down call charges to 50 per cent and the introduction of the 3rd and 4th cellular operator. The 'Calling Party Pays' regime further brought down call charges. During the Eleventh Plan period, further steps were taken to encourage competition. These include reduction in tariff for national roaming services; abolition of Access Deficit Charges (ADC); reduction of interconnect usage charges and country wide mobile number portability. These led to a huge boost to the subscriber base and the average tariff also came down sharply. Falling tariffs coupled with the increased number of mobile subscribers, resulted in increase in overall industry revenues. The sector is characterized by high subscriber base and low average tariff per outgoing call as indicated in Figure 16.4.

Auction of 3G and BWA Spectrum

16.12. The unprecedented growth of voice based mobile telephony in the country has led to demand for other value added services that include data communication, video, mobile TV and so on. With a view to extend the benefit of new technology and for providing a variety of services to the customers, the government decided to introduce the Third Generation (3G) systems, which represent the next step in the evolution of mobile cellular communication. 2G systems focus on voice communication, while 3G systems support increased data communication. Subsequently, the auction of 3G and BWA Spectrum was successfully conducted in 2010 and garnered

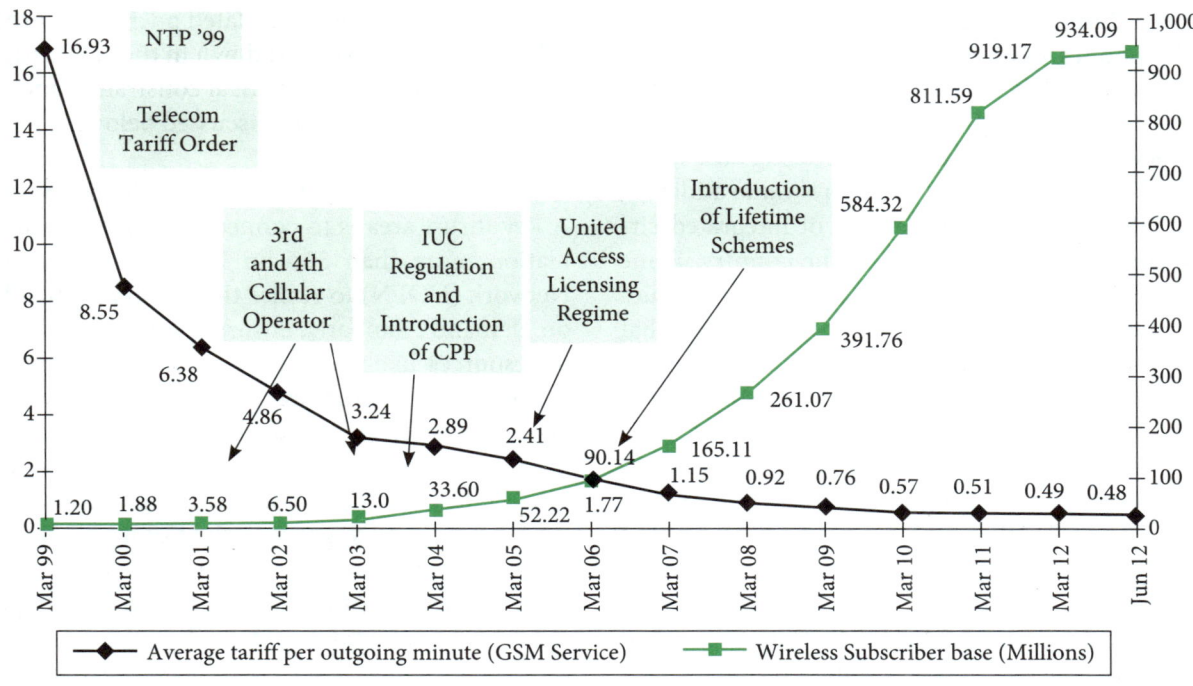

FIGURE 16.4: Mobile Tariff Trends V/s Growth in Mobile Subscribers in India (1999–2012)

₹1,06,262 crore. Now, the operators have started rolling out wireless broadband networks in the country and very soon these services are likely to be available in the entire country.

Controversies Arising Out of Decisions Taken in 2008 and Its Fallout

16.13. The policy measures taken so far have paid rich dividends in terms of expansion and provision of affordable telecom services. However, problems arose in the implementation of the First Come First Served (FCFS) policy framework in 2008. These led to a legal challenge, and subsequently, in 2012, quashing of 122 licences by the Supreme Court and a direction by the Court that the Spectrum thus released be auctioned. This is being done. With the completion of the auction in the later months of 2012 it is hoped that there will be a revival of investment in this important sector.

16.14. During this period, the downturn in the economy coupled with the financial stress being faced in the sector, dampened the growth potential of the sector. The unprecedented expansion during the initial phase (1994–2003) followed by years of optimism in an environment of increasing competition and more choices in technology and services to consumers had led the industry into an ambitious asset acquisition mode. The over-leveraging has, partly on account of the exuberant bidding for 3G spectrum in the auction held in 2010, led to a downward pressure on revenues and earning capacities. The cut throat price competition for adding customers, without adequate emphasis on provision of value added services, have further decelerated the industry's growth and put a brake on plans for network expansion as well as provisioning for new services.

TELECOM EQUIPMENT MANUFACTURING, R&D, PRODUCT DEVELOPMENT AND IPR

16.15. The Indian telecommunication industry has now matured and has started venturing outside the country and investing abroad. However, the telecom manufacturing in India is yet to attract investment on a sustained basis. During the Eleventh Plan period, it was projected that 75 per cent of telecom equipment demand would be met from indigenous sources; however the actual production was much lower. During this period, mobile handset manufacturing began, but the production as well as value addition has been limited. Some of the indigenous brands of mobile phones have also made their mark, though their design and manufacturing are still being done outside India. A number of world renowned manufacturers have set up their manufacturing base in the country. There is concern about low value addition, lack of R&D and IPR, availability of integrated circuits, components/piece-parts in the country. Some indigenous R&D and manufacturing companies have emerged in the country and demonstrated that world-class products can indeed be developed indigenously. At the same time, some key IPRs have been created in futuristic wireless technologies by R&D centers such as Centre for Excellence in Wireless Technology (CeWiT) and premier academic institutions such as IITs, IISc, IIITs. It is critical to develop an ecosystem that maintains a sustainable supply chain from thought to action; from ideas to products; from development to production and actual deployment to achieve higher value addition.

THE TWELFTH FIVE YEAR PLAN (2012–17): CHALLENGES AHEAD

16.16. The sector stands at the cross roads of opportunities as well as challenges at the beginning of the Twelfth Plan. On the one hand, recent developments in the sector arising out of aberrations in the licensing and policy implementation have provided an opportunity for introspection. On the other, there is a need to sustain the growth momentum in the sector achieved during the Eleventh Plan to realise the objective of inclusive growth. The National Telecom Policy-2012 has been adopted against this backdrop to address all the key challenges before the sector in a holistic manner. NTP-2012 seeks to achieve Broadband on Demand and envisages leveraging telecom infrastructure to enable all citizens and businesses, both in rural and urban areas, to participate in the Internet and web economy thereby, ensuring equitable and inclusive development. The objective is to transform the country into an empowered and inclusive knowledge-based society, using telecommunications as a platform. It provides the enabling framework for enhancing India's competitiveness in all spheres of the economy. NTP-2012 envisions support to platform neutral services in e-governance and m-governance in key social sectors such as health, education and agriculture that are at present limited to a few organisations in isolated pockets. In order to achieve the objectives laid down in the NTP 2012, we need to address certain critical constraints and challenges. Some of these are discussed below.

16.17. **Expansion of Reach—Broadband Services:** A key thrust area is to connect all villages with population more than 500 on National Optical Fiber Network (NOFN) to realise the vision of 'Broadband on Demand'. Similarly, ensuring sufficient allocation of resources like spectrum, 'Right of Way' management and infrastructure sharing for broadband is essential. There is a need for national level effort to harmonise the policies of various state governments/local bodies to address issues relating to allocation of land, power supply, grant of right of way and policy/by-laws for erection of towers and so on. In addition, there is a need to provide incentives to encourage the uptake of broadband in sectors like education, healthcare, public safety, government operations, and so on.

16.18. **Rollout of 3G/4G:** Though the 3G spectrum was acquired by the Telecom Service Providers (TSPs) during 2010, the rollout of 3G services is yet to reach out across the country at affordable rates. This has affected the introduction of value added services requiring higher bandwidth. India being a price sensitive market, one of the main reasons for poor rollout of 3G/4G services is the high cost of smart phones. There is an urgent need to encourage technologies and R&D initiatives to pave way for the introduction of cost effective smart phones for expanding penetration and out-reach. Provision of funding and support to encourage the rollout of mobile broadband on 3G/4G/LTE/BWA spectrum in rural and remote areas will be crucial for broadband expansion.

16.19. The fulcrum in the sector is the issues surrounding spectrum, its availability, management and pricing. Telecommunications is characterised by rapid changes in technology and introduction of new technologies like Long Term Evolution (LTE), high bandwidth applications and the demands of an ever increasing user base requiring additions to the spectrum available for non-strategic uses. Since spectrum is a scarce resource, priority will be on its vacation from lesser efficient uses and shift to more efficient use. This will involve intensive policy intervention to have Government agencies like the Defence and Railways vacate spectrum bands and reforms in spectrum management practices. It has already been decided to allow a liberalised use of spectrum in any band for any technology. In addition sharing spectrum and thereby pooling resources and eventually move towards a regime that permits spectrum trading on a trading platform and creating a market driven mechanism towards its efficient use. Box 16.1 gives the historical perspective of spectrum trading.

> **Box 16.1**
> **Spectrum Trading**
>
> Historically, in most countries, the Regulator has used a command and control mechanism to decide allocation of spectrum. But in the last decade, a number of countries have adopted market mechanisms for spectrum assignment. However, it is being increasingly felt that this system does not allow the spectrum licence holders the flexibility to respond quickly to changes in market demand and technology, resulting in chunks of spectrum lying underutilised, thereby creating an artificial scarcity. Therefore, some countries like Australia, Canada, New Zealand, and some EU countries have permitted spectrum trading in the secondary market as an additional means of spectrum distribution. This is likely to improve spectrum efficiency, boost market competition and provide incentives to innovation to service providers. On the other hand it could lead to situations wherein service providers of less profitable services would prefer to sell their spectrum instead of continuing to provide services and which may increase the risk of possibility of concentration of spectrum and market power. Spectrum Trading requires implementation of a successful trading platform in the form of a secondary market requiring creation of an extensive automated infrastructure in the form of an exchange/online registry which entails considerable regulatory costs.

16.20. **Consolidation in Industry:** Presently, there are six or more TSPs in most of the service areas and are grappling with reduced ARPUs and high competitive pressures. The future development of cellular markets is likely to witness consolidation between the Service Providers to become financially viable. The revised TRAI recommendations with the relaxation of M&A norms are expected to act as enablers for further consolidation in the telecom industry.

16.21. **Financial Health of the Sector:** The aggressive bidding in 3G/BWA spectrum auction held in 2010 left the industry financially weak. In addition, expansion into overseas markets, coupled with the global meltdown and non-availability of funds has restricted the industry's expansion plans. This to a large extent has decelerated network expansion as well as introduction of new technologies such as 4G/LTE and value added services.

16.22. **Licensing Reforms:** For facilitating orderly growth of the telecom sector, steps such as introduction of Unified Licensing regime, de-linking license and spectrum, license renewal terms, technology neutrality, rationalisation of licensing regime and enabling convergence need to be taken on priority basis. In addition, there is a need to encourage deployment of Low Power In-Building Solutions (IBS)/In-Campus/Remote Townships and so on, in tune with the provisions contained in NFAP 2011 and NTP 2012 through de-licensing of small chunks of spectrum.

16.23. **Regulatory Issues:** TRAI was established in 1997 after the sector was thrown open to private players. Since then there has been far reaching changes including number of operators, subscriber base and range of services being offered. There is a need to revisit the TRAI Act and revise its provisions to address the emerging issues. There is also a need to review the regulatory and executive functions for instance, the Department of Telecommunication is involved in activities which are mandatory in nature such as spectrum allocation, management, auditing and monitoring. For effective and transparent Spectrum allocation and management and to facilitate better coordination amongst various government and non-government agencies, the National Radio Regulatory Authority namely, the Wireless Planning and Coordination (WPC) wing of DOT, needs to be repositioned with greater autonomy and fuller authority.

16.24. **Network Security:** With rapid expansion of telecom and IT networks and increased dependence on the networks for delivery of services and operation of physical and financial infrastructures has given rise to security concerns. There is an absolute necessity to ensure security of networks at all times and adopt effective measures to deal with cyber threats. For ensuring telecom network security there is a need to strengthen the Centre for Communication Security Research and Monitoring and Telecom Testing and Security Certification

Centre. Similarly, developing and deploying a Pan India secure network and network-based services such as email, VoIP, mobile communication through survivable and available network architecture for Government use is also essential.

16.25. **Convergence:** Convergence of technologies has thrown open many new challenges and opportunities. This calls for establishment of a proactive and suitable regulatory framework which would address issues related to both content and carriage, there by leading to eventual convergence of IT, Broadcasting and Telecom.

16.26. **Future of PSUs:** The poor health of the PSUs under DOT is a matter of concern. The Department has under its administration control, not only MTNL and BSNL, but also the Indian Telephone Industries (ITI) and Telecom Consultants of India Ltd. (TCIL). Urgent steps are required to be taken to turn them around by leveraging upon their strengths and assets as well as financial reengineering. For ensuring DOT organisations to effectively flourish in the competitive telecom market there is a need to exploit individual strengths of these organisations for their mutual benefit. Efforts should be made by all the PSUs to reduce their dependence on government support and become competitive by shedding obsolete technological and non-profitable product lines and moving on to more remunerative activities and services. There is also a need to look for newer markets and alliances. Government support should be restricted only for initiatives which address and meet the social obligations of the government and in areas where the market is not fully developed.

16.27. **Issues of Transition:** The telecom sector faces rapid technological change and concomitantly issues relating to transition to new technologies and obsolescence. The phasing out of technologies where eco-systems are dying, has attendant economic difficulties. There is therefore, a compelling need for ensuring minimum quantum of spectrum allocation for effective harnessing of technology and paving the way for the entry of new technologies, calling for an appropriate policy response which helps in the adoption of new technologies and creating appropriate eco systems for ensuring a smooth transition.

Box 16.2
Twelfth Plan Targets for the Telecommunication Sector

- Provision of 1,200 million connections by 2017.
- Mobile access to all villages and increase rural tele-density to 70 per cent by 2017.
- Broadband connection of 175 million by 2017.
- Commissioning of National Optical Fibre Network (NOFN)
- Make available additional 300 MHz of spectrum for IMT services
- Making India a hub for telecom equipment manufacturing by incentivising domestic manufacturers with thrust on IPR, product development and commercialisation.
- Provide preferential market access for indigenously manufactured products.
- To increase domestic manufactured products in telecom network to the extent of 60 per cent with value addition of 45 per cent by 2017.
- Adoption of green policy in Telecom and incentivise use of renewable energy sources.

THE PATH AHEAD

16.28. The Twelfth Plan Programmes for the telecom sector are guided by the NTP-2012. The thrust of NTP 2012 is on raising the competitiveness of Indian telecom sector, to make it a world leader, while at the same time making available a variety of services on a single platform utilising the technological advancements taking place in the sector. Spectrum, which is an important input has been a limited and reusable resource. With the introduction of new technologies, high bandwidth applications and increasing user base, there will be a requirement of significant amount of additional spectrum. While effective spectrum planning in this regard needs to be carried out, the requirement of spectrum in 60 GHz and above bands for backhaul purposes, audit of spectrum usage and re-farming of spectrum to ensure the efficient utilisation should also be taken into account during the Twelfth Plan Period. Twelfth Plan targets for Telecommunication Sector is given in Box 16.2.

16.29. In view of the situation analysis and the identified needs of the key stakeholders, the following approach is suggested for Twelfth Plan period.

(a) **USOF Activities:** USO fund needs to be leveraged for providing incentives for pilot projects, fixed wireline/wireless phones, use of renewable energy sources, telecom infrastructure and for wireline broadband in rural difficult terrain and LWE areas.

(b) **Applications, Value Added Services (VAS) and Devices:** Development of new applications, VAS and devices would be triggered by e-Governance projects and growth of Broadband in Rural Areas. Developing synergies between DoT, DeitY and I&B to tap the Cable TV segment for proliferation of broadband and broadband access to all schools for promoting literacy through e-learning programs will also propel the introduction of VAS and development of low cost devices.

(c) **Telecom Equipment Manufacturing:** The large and growing domestic market for telecom equipment provides an opportunity to leverage this potential to stimulate domestic manufacturing without financial impact to the government. Provision has been made to require India manufactured products in procurement by the government and also in projects funded by government or under Universal Service Obligation. The preference is for products which have a specified domestic manufactured content and the requirement is only of manufacture/value addition in India. Foreign companies manufacturing in India would be eligible. Telecom Operators also need to be encouraged to participate in trials of newly created Indian products and nurture them. Funding R&D and supporting Indian IPR creation and driving standards are equally important aspects of the promotion of the telecom equipment manufacturing. Creation of National Investment and Manufacturing Zones (NIMZs) as proposed by DIPP and incentivising manufacturers in line with Modified Special Incentive Programme scheme (MSIPs) and Electronic Design and Manufacturing Cluster (EDMC) of DeitY are other initiatives that need to be taken forward for the growth of telecom equipment manufacturing in India. Setting up of Mega Fabrication Units (FAB) facility for the manufacture of Integrated Circuits (IC), Development of Hardware Manufacturing Cluster Parks (HMCPs), Stable fiscal policies, tax structure that encourages manufacturing, Market pull for domestic manufacturers, R&D facilities, access to low cost funds, testing and certification and so on, also need to be taken up to make India a telecom equipment manufacturing hub.

(d) **R&D, IPR and Standardisation:** There is a need to create a mechanism for Technology and Product development forecast and to carryout periodic updates of the national five year rolling programme of technology/product development and its field absorption. The current functioning and strengthening of public R&D institutions such as C-DOT also needs to be reviewed to enable them to collaborate with public as well as private industry and academia for technology development. In order to enable creation of IPRs and progressively mature them into standards, Telecom Standards Development Organisation (TSDO) may be established with participation from industry, telecom service providers, academia, R&D centres and government. Academic R&D, R&D centres and Telecom Centre of Excellence (TCoEs) need to be repositioned towards IPR generation and creation of telecom standards, development and commercialisation of Indian Products. Some of the other major initiatives include Strengthening Telecom Engineering Center; setting up of accredited test facilities for conformance, performance, inter-operability and security of the products; creation of live testbeds for Next Generation technologies; reserving certain spectrum for indigenous R&D, product development and field trials (pilots); developing safety and aesthetic standards for wireless towers; and ensuring compliance against existing Electromagnetic (EM) emission standards.

(e) **Disaster Management:** A Rapidly Deployable Multi-Protocol Wireless Communication system, interoperable across all the services engaged in disaster management needs to be developed. A dedicated communication link needs to be given to disaster management agencies by every service provider to receive guaranteed service during disasters.

(f) **Capacity Building in Telecom Sector:** For evolving a strategy for capacity building in telecom sector there is a need for a comprehensive repository of all telecom related information/ standards/benchmarks/resources/programme curriculum, besides setting up of state-of-the-art telecom labs in all high-end technology areas and inclusion of Electronics and Telecom as part of the curriculum at the polytechnic level and in Industrial Training Institutes for trades specific to telecom.

(g) **Financing of Telecom Sector:** The sector should be allowed to access funding from Indian Infrastructure Finance Company Ltd. (IIFCL). Telecom Finance Corporation may be created as a vehicle to access funds at competitive rates to facilitate the funding needs of this sector on requirement. Rationalisation of levies and taxes in the sector may also be reviewed from time to time to ensure affordable delivery of services to the consumers.

(h) Besides the above, several new programmes like Telecom Promotion Fund, Telecom Entrepreneurship Promotion Fund, Research Development Fund and Human Resource Development and Skill Development are proposed to be taken up during the Twelfth Five Year Plan. C-DOT would take programmes on Next Generation Mobile Technology, R&D for emerging Wireless Technologies; Optical Technologies—XGPON-1/2, WDM-PON, DWDM; Development for a Secure Mobile Communication Network namely WiPS based GSM technologies like EDGE and 3G, BWA; Satellite based Technology; R&D for converged NMS, Software intensive Applications for new services, service delivery platform to support multiple applications and Value Added Services; Power efficient and Green Technologies for Rural areas and Next Generation security for Telecom and Data Networks. Major Investment would be required during the Twelfth Five Year Plan in the area of network expansion in the rural and remote areas, network upgradation in customer demand cycles, 3G subscriber base, NGN and IPV6, rural telephony, broadband expansion, National Optical Fiber Network (NOFN), convergence of technology, Value Added Services and manufacturing and R&D.

INFORMATION TECHNOLOGY

Overview of the Sector

16.30. The Information Technology sector has made remarkable progress in the last decade. It has transformed the world, enabling innovation and enhancing productivity, connecting people and communities, and improving standards of living and providing opportunities across the globe. While changing the way individuals live, interact, and work, IT has also proven to be a key enabler for enhanced competitiveness and economic and societal modernisation, as well as an important instrument for bridging economic and social divides and reducing poverty.

16.31. The pace of technological advance is accelerating and Electronics and ICT is increasingly becoming a ubiquitous and intrinsic part of people's behaviours and social networks as well as of business practices and government activities and service provision. These transformations will continue to guide human progress forward by further leveraging IT's positive social, political, and economic impact on government, enterprise, and civil society alike.

Review of Eleventh Plan

16.32. The following five thrust areas were identified for the Eleventh Five Year Plan:

- Electronics/IT Hardware Manufacturing
- Exports of Computer Software and Services
- Domestic Computer Software and Services
- Enhancing Cyber Security Capabilities
- Human Resource Development and R&D

16.33. The key targets and achievements with respect to Electronics/IT Hardware Manufacturing, Exports of Computer Software and Services and employment are given in Box 16.3 and Table 16.1.

Broad Objectives, Targets and Thrust Areas for the Twelfth Five Year Plan

16.34. The vision and mission for Electronics and IT Sector for the Twelfth Five Year Plan is e-Development of India through a multi-pronged strategy. This includes promotion of e-Infrastructure creation to facilitate and fast track e-governance, promotion of software (IT-ITeS) Industry, building knowledge network and securing India's cyber space. While India's software strengths are recognised globally, we have not focused on building indigenous hardware, research and manufacturing capabilities. The

> **Box 16.3**
> **Key Achievements (as on 31 March 2012)**
>
> *E-Governance*
> - SWANs rolled out in 30 States/UTs.
> - 1,00,086 Common Services Centres rolled out in 33 States/UTs.
> - 16 State Data Centres are operational.
> - The National Data Centres at Delhi, Pune and Hyderabad are operational.
>
> *National Knowledge Network*
> - 681 links to institutions commissioned and made operational.
> - 52 virtual classrooms set up.
>
> *Enterprise*
> - Open Source Software (BOSS) released.
> - Param 'Yuva' Super computing system commissioned.
>
> *E-Security*
> - The Information Technology (Amendment) Act, 2008 enforced and rules of important sections notified.
> - Security Assurance frame work for Govt. developed and validated in Customs Department.
> - Resource Centre for Cyber Forensics established.
> - CERT-In operates a 24 × 7 Incident Response Help Desk.
>
> *Empowerment*
> - Software tools and fonts for all 22 constitutionally recognised Indian languages released in public domain.
> - Various IT projects initiated for empowerment of gender and SC/ST and development of North Eastern region.
>
> Draft National Policy on Electronics—2011 and Draft National Policy on Information Technology, 2011 released.
>
> Policy for Preference to Domestically Manufactured Electronic Goods issued on 10 February 2012.

TABLE 16.1
Targets and Achievements

Targets	Achievements (Estimated) upto 2011–12	Percentage Achievement (%)
Electronics Hardware		
• Electronics production—US$ 67 Billion @ 32 per cent growth	US$ 33.0 Billion	49
• Exports—US$ 6.7 Billion	US$ 7 Billion	104
Software Services		
IT-ITES Exports—US$ 86 Billion	US$ 69 Billion	80
Employment		
• Direct Employment in IT-ITES Exports—3.4 Million	2.8 Million	82

Electronics and ICT strategy for the Twelfth Plan should aim to focus on promoting domestic manufacturing, including hardware design, building Semiconductor Wafer Fab manufacturing facilities and strengthening R&D capabilities.

16.35. Appropriate application of ICT has the potential to vastly improve productivity and efficiency. Therefore, there is a need to promote the use of ICT platforms and convergence of technologies to ensure better delivery of public services, increased efficiency in the implementation of the Government's flagship programmes and the overall competitiveness of the economy, since ICT applications will have a pervasive effect on the resilience and dynamism of all sectors of the economy.

16.36. India is home to millions of persons with disabilities who are living on the fringes of society due to their inability to participate in the information age. There is a need to redefine important areas for intervention with emphasis on improving the accessibility of ICT to the differently-abled people of the society as well as promoting its use as an assistive technology to improve their quality of life.

16.37. In order to achieve the objectives of the Twelfth Five Year Plan, the following themes have been identified:

- e-Government
- e-Learning
- e-Security
- e-Industry (Electronics System Design and Manufacturing)
- e-Industry (IT-ITeS)
- e-Innovation/R&D
- e-Inclusion

16.38. The overall strategy for the sector is to plan action/programmes/projects for each of these themes in the Twelfth Five Year Plan, with innovation and inclusion as the fundamental paradigm in each one of them. The Sub-strategies under each of these areas have been designed to address suitably the major challenges facing the sector in the next five years. The key targets for the Twelfth Plan for the Electronics and IT-ITeS Industry are given in Table 16.2.

Policy Issues, Programme Reforms and New Initiatives in the Twelfth Plan

16.39. Some of the Policy issues and new initiatives proposed in the Twelfth Five Year Plan are given below:

Policy Issues

- Several new policies have been approved by Government relating to promotion and development of the ESDM sector. A Governance mechanism which would ensure that the benefit of these and other policies envisaged for the sector reach the targets in a speedy, fair and transparent manner also needs to be developed. Necessary policy to mandate standards in electronic goods also need to be put in place. Policies to induce greater participation of private sector in human resource development also need to be ensured.
- Finalisation and implementation of National policies on Electronics and Information Technology, spanning the entire spectrum from science to

TABLE 16.2
Key Targets for the Twelfth Plan for the Electronics and IT-ITeS Industry

(Values in USD Billion)

I. Production and Export Targets (Electronics Hardware)		
A. High Manufacturing Growth Scenario (Optimistic)		
Description	FY 2011–12 (E)	Target FY 2016–17
Exports (Growth Rate: 22 per cent)	7	20
Production (Growth rate 30 per cent)	33	122
B. Natural Manufacturing Growth Scenario		
Exports (Growth Rate: 22 per cent)	7	20
Production (Growth rate 16 per cent)	33	69
II. Revenue and Employment Targets of IT-ITeS Industry		
IT-ITES Exports	69	130
IT-ITES Domestic Revenue	19	40
Direct Employment	2.8 million	4.2 million

(E): Estimated.

technology to products, eventually resulting in mass scale deployment.
- Establish 'National Electronics Mission' to help in synchronised functioning of the industry through effective coordination across ministries and government departments at the Centre and the States.
- Removing barriers of cost, language and accessibility and provide equitable access to Internet and its benefits to all. Formulate and implement a national digitisation plan and a digital information literacy campaign for enabling the common man to use ICT optimally.
- Create a comprehensive national IT standards framework for current and emerging paradigms like bio-metrics, cloud computing, Green IT and so on.
- Formulate specific policies to enable public Cloud Computing for citizens, business verticals and for government.
- Formulation of governing principles for allocation, management and sharing of Critical Internet resources namely Internet Protocol addresses and Domain Names.
- Bring out Best Practices and Public Policy on Internet openness, security and privacy in cyberspace.
- Promote development and deployment of security standard and practices, which are internationally accepted for ensuring a secure cyber space.
- Participate globally in standard setting exercise on Electronics and ICT for business and consumer applications to ensure competitiveness of Indian industry.
- Develop strong capabilities in encryption, forensics and establish test labs for testing products for security and quality; early detection and mitigating capabilities of newer threats and vulnerabilities, which have potential to disrupt the ICT infrastructure.
- Creation of a separate Electronics Development Fund with Govt. and Industry bodies as stakeholders to incentivise R&D in this field.
- Promotion of indigenous R&D and product development coupled with progressive induction into strategic defense and civilian space.
- Develop a holistic approach for funding socially relevant R&D projects in Public Private Partnership (PPP) modes.
- Define 'R&D in Services' specially, R&D in Electronics and ICT Services to make it broad based. The present definition of R&D as accepted by DSIR and Income Tax Department appears weak to accept R&D in Services.
- Initiation of a comprehensive IPR promotion programme covering education, awareness creation, IP exchange, related technology development and support to SMEs and start-ups.
- Revamping the procurement cycle for Electronics and ICT products and services to keep them in tune with the technology obsolescence and shelf life of products. Also there is a need to relook at the 100 per cent pre-dispatch acceptance testing clause.
- Ensure flexibility in policy to support and adopt new and emerging technology paradigms in Electronics and ICT

New Initiatives

- *Modified Special Incentive Package Scheme for improved value addition*: Manufacturing base of electronic products in the country is grossly inadequate in comparison to demand of such goods. Even in cases where products are manufactured in India, the extent of domestic value addition is low. This scheme (M-SIPS) has been introduced to promote large scale manufacturing in the Electronics System Design Manufacturing (ESDM) sector by providing a special incentive package. The incentives would partially offset the disabilities faced by domestic ESDM industry due to factors like higher cost of power, finance, logistics, fragmented location of industry and so on, and thereby reduce the viability gap faced by the manufacturing units in India.
- *Promotion of Electronics Manufacturing Clusters (EMC)*: The growth of the Electronics System Design and Manufacturing (ESDM) industry in the country is constrained by infrastructure, power and finance, the three elements of operating environment which needs to be addressed. The scheme envisages financial support for development of EMCs as they are expected to aid the

- growth of ESDM sector, help development of entrepreneurial ecosystem, drive innovation and catalyse economic growth. The scheme would support setting up of both Greenfield (in undeveloped/underdeveloped geographical area) and Brownfield EMCs (where a significant number of existing ESDM units are located). The focus is on upgrading infrastructure and providing common facilities for the ESDM units.
- *Semiconductor Fabs*: Semiconductor is at the heart of any electronic system and constitutes at least 25 per cent of the total value. In case of high-end equipment and mobile handsets, this content goes as high as 60 per cent. Presently, while this is imported, in order to enable manufacturing of electronic equipment and also push up the value addition in India, setting up of Semiconductor wafer fab (full scale as well as proto type) is a prerequisite and critical requirement for enhancing domestic manufacturing capabilities in India.
- *Cyber Security R&D and Human Resource Coordination*: The focus would be on supporting and facilitating basic research, technology demonstration, proof of concept and test bed projects in thrust areas of cyber security through sponsored projects at recognised R&D institutions. Proactive and collaborative actions in PPP aimed at cyber security incidents prevention, prediction, response and recovery actions and cyber security assurance will be the cornerstone for the cyber security R&D and human resource coordination.
- *Cyber Security Preparedness*: In order to ensure the cyber security preparedness, an improved interaction and engagement with various key stakeholders such as Govt., critical infrastructure sectors, sectorial CERTs, International CERTs, service providers including ISPs, product and security vendors, security and law enforcement agencies, academia, media, NGOs and cyber user community is essential. Carrying out periodic cyber security mock drills to assess the preparedness of critical sector organisations to resist cyber-attacks and improve the security posture are some other important steps in this regard.
- *Green IT*: Enhanced deployment and usage of Green IT in both computing and non-computing infrastructure (for example, buildings) would be promoted. Procurement policy needs to incorporate guidelines for preference for energy efficient products and to drive Green rating and stricter regulation and implementation of e-waste disposal.
- *Promote E-Governance cloud*: Cloud computing as a technology paradigm has a tremendous potential to reduce cost, implementation timelines and increase reusability. There should be an increased focus on cloud computing as a mainstream delivery model by establishing an 'e-Gov Cloud' which can be accessed by various tiers of government to implement digital public services.
- *Promotion of use of ICT by domestic industry for enhancing productivity in priority sectors like agriculture, health, education, retail, automotive, textile*: With the emergence of country-wide high bandwidth broadband networks, there is a need to build HR centric applications such as virtual labs, country wide virtual classrooms, and so on to ride on these platforms for improving the quality of students, faculty as well as research. There is also a need to continue with the programme on development of suitable technology/products for mass applications in these sectors.
- *Promote development of SMEs in ICT Sector*: The Software Technology Park scheme has played a stellar role in the growth story of the IT-ITeS/BPO sector in the country. To provide competitive edge to small and start-up companies and to attract investments beyond Metro cities (that is Tier II and Tier III cities), there is a need for similar enabling environment.
- *Enhancing Supercomputing Capacity in India*: Supercomputing plays an important role in both scientific advancement and economic competitiveness of a nation. In order to keep pace with supercomputing developments globally, it is important that we focus on building supercomputing systems of different sizes matching with the demands of HPC user applications, Supercomputing applications development, manpower development and R&D for Exascale computing by leveraging the already built HPC capabilities in the country.
- *Citizen Engagement Framework for e-Governance Projects*: As the government is incorporating ICT

into delivery of G2C services, there are hardly any embedded mechanisms to facilitate the voice and space for citizen participation in e-governance. It is with this vision that Citizen Engagement Framework (CEF) for e-Governance projects has been conceptualised. In addition, Social Media Framework for the Government of India has been created to enable government agencies to use blogs, forums and online social networks more effectively and reach out to their stakeholders and understand their concerns and hear their voices.

- *HR Policy Framework for e-Governance*: There is an urgent need not only to augment the HR pool but to create suitable organisational structures with clear roles and responsibilities for implementation of e-Governance projects. To supplement the resource pool within the Government, competencies outside the Government ought to be leveraged and an enabling framework for attracting, retaining and optimally utilising such skilled persons need to be put in place. Setting up of an e-Governance Academy as a Centre of Excellence and think tank in this area is also desirable.

Key Constraints and Challenges

16.40. The sector is facing numerous constraints and challenges. A list of these constraints and challenges theme wise is given below:

- e-Government

  - *Business process re-engineering (BPR)*: Implementation of BPR as an integral part of e-government programmes on the national and local levels, especially for those involving the transition to single-window electronic services' delivery based on integration of information systems operated by multiple agencies.
  - Fast tracking of the Mission Mode Projects identified under the National e-Governance Plan for electronic service delivery is a formidable challenge in view of the fact that a number of actors covering central, State and local governments are involved.
  - Constraint of internal capacity to manage large e-Governance Projects and resourcing of Skilled, experienced manpower across all stage of Life Cycle.
  - *Mobile Governance*: Providing adequate financial and institutional support to various agencies to foster creativity and innovation in developing appropriate applications for mobile based delivery of public services is very important with the involvement of all stakeholders in the supply chain.
  - *E-waste management*: IT can be a strong enabler for realising the objectives of India's National Action Plan for Climate Change. Sustainable and environment friendly E-wastage management should be a part of these objectives.
  - *Government procurement*: Adoption of standardised RFPs, Model Contracts, developed by DeitY, to reduce procurement cycles.

- E-Learning

  - Create and leverage Government e-Learning platform to aid training and skills development of Government Staff, especially end-users at junior level for driving adoption of e-Governance systems.
  - *Natural Language Processing (NLP)* is a complex technology area. Building any language technology product requires large resources. There are very few researchers working in the NLP area and constant efforts are required to expand the team all over India to address requirement of all 22 constitutionally recognised languages. Issues related to e-Pedagogy for content and its delivery on the e platform, establishment of e-classrooms for delivery of e-content and e-learning are very important and the corner stone for the successful implementation of e-learning module.

- E-Security

  - *Cyber security:* In addition to land, sea and air, cyber space is a new dimension without any borders affecting each individual. There is increasing evidence of espionage, targeted attacks and lack of traceability in the cyber world as state and non-state actors are compromising, stealing, changing or destroying information and therefore potentially causing risk to national security, economic growth, public safety and competitiveness. Therefore, it is essential to focus on R&D, Human Resource, Security Standards and Certification and Cyber Security coordination in order to overcome such challenges during the Twelfth Plan.

- *E-Industry (Electronics Hardware and IT-ITeS)*

    – *Competition and strong pull from other countries*: China, Philippines, Vietnam, Poland, Hungary, Mexico, Brazil, Egypt are an indicative list of countries that are emerging as competitive locations for IT-ITeS sector. These are fast increasing to almost 50 locations which presents a huge challenge to India's success story. India's biggest competition in the Electronics Hardware sector is from China, which has achieved high economies of scale and has highly subsidised operating environment which is largely opaque.
    – *Reduced competitiveness of the industry*: India's competitiveness in IT-ITeS Sector is declining due to high cost of doing business due to inefficiencies of power, transport, security, concentration in metros due to inadequate infrastructure in other towns and so on.
    – *'Made in India' procurement*: Indian firms particularly the SME firms who develop products find it difficult to sell to the Government as they lack the sales capacity or they fail to meet the qualifying procurement criteria, for example, annual revenue, number of customer and so on. As a result the 'Made in India' IT products find it difficult to scale up.
    – *Lack of research capacity*: A key weakness of the Indian IT industry including Government agencies is the lack of original technology development. Majority of IT deployed in India is either imported or IPR resides with non-Indian entities. Innovation ecosystems in places like Silicon Valley, which lead in technology development, have demonstrated that a key lever for technology development is the maturity of the post-graduate and doctoral research programmes. In India, the number of computer science doctoral research programmes is very low—both qualitatively and quantitatively.
    – *ITA and the WTO*: Electronics was the first sector to be opened up and which accepted zero duty regime for large number of products. As a signatory to the Information Technology Agreement-1 (ITA-1) of the World Trade Organisation (WTO), India has implemented zero duty regime on 217 product lines. Under the Free Trade Agreements (FTAs) and Preferential Trade Agreements (PTAs) with various countries, the import of electronics hardware from these countries is allowed at a duty which is lower than the normal duty rate.
    – *Disability Costs in local Manufacturing*: The three elements of operating environment which pose significant challenges to Indian manufacturers are: infrastructure, power and finance.
    – *Lack of support for industry led innovation*: Electronics Sector constituted one of the largest IP wealth in the world. These IPRs have been created by industry competing with each other. However, our efforts have not led to industry led innovation in the sector. During the Twelfth Five Year Plan efforts would be to stimulate provision of risk capital to seed new ideas and startups in Electronics System Design and Manufacturing. An Electronic Development fund is proposed to be set up with industry/financial institutes' participation.

Path Ahead

16.41. Widening of R&D base, promoting R&D for manufacturing and creation/augmentation of R&D infrastructure in the field of Electronics and IT is essential for maintaining the competitive edge.

16.42. The Information, Communication Technology and Electronics (ICTE) has come to be accepted as a key enabler in development and is globally being accepted as a 'Meta-Resource'. The demand for electronics hardware is increasing and demand supply gap is widening. Moreover, since the value-addition in domestically produced electronic goods is very small. Therefore, there is a need to offset the debility and attract Investments in ESDM Sector by providing suitable incentives to the sector.

16.43. To realise the vision of NEGP, there is a need to reorient the activities for maximising outcome to the citizens. Electronics Delivery of Services (EDS) Act needs to be put in place at the earliest in order to mandate provisioning of all public services compulsorily through electronics means from a specified date. Electronics and ICT are all pervasive today and there is a dire need to synergise with the important initiatives and capabilities in the strategic departments.

INDIA POSTS

Overview of the Sector

16.44. India Posts has been the backbone of India's communication and at the core of the country's social-economic development for the last 150 years. It has touched the lives of every citizen. A network of 1.55 lakh (approx.) Post Offices (POs) in the country with more than 1.39 lakh POs in rural areas is indicative of the commitment of the department towards its customers. The core activity of the department is processing, transmission and delivery of mails. The department has undertaken Mail Network Optimisation Project to improve the quality and efficiency of mail processing, transmission and delivery. Considering the vital need for providing benefits of technology to the customers, the counter operations are now being progressively computerised.

16.45. The Post Office Savings Bank provides financial inclusion to people all over the country through various saving schemes, as its reach and services are unparalleled by any other banking agency in the country. Postal Life Insurance (PLI), one of the oldest life insurance schemes initially meant only for the Postal employees, now caters to employees of the Civil and Military Personnel of the Central and State Governments, local bodies, government aided educational institutions and so on. Following the recommendation of Malhotra Committee on Insurance Sector Reforms, the Department of Posts (DoP) started the Rural Postal Life Insurance (RPLI) Scheme for insuring the rural populace with special emphasis on women and weaker sections of Society.

16.46. The department is facing twin challenges posed by increasing competition and continuing advances in communication technologies. The department has therefore initiated an end to end IT modernisation project to connect all the 1.55 lakh post offices. The benefits and impact of this IT project will flow into all the Twelfth Five Year Plan schemes and activities and the next five year Plan period will be extensively a period for consolidation and implementation of the IT project.

Review of the Eleventh Five Year Plan

16.47. The Eleventh Five Year Plan witnessed the continued drive of computerisation of the post offices, administrative offices and accounts offices and completion of the supply of hardware to departmental post offices. Establishment of a strong IT base has enabled Department of Posts to provide several value added services, besides providing the platform for anywhere anytime banking. Mail Network Optimisation Project and setting up of Automated Mail Processing Centres were undertaken to improve the quality of mail operations. Postal Life Insurance is being transformed into a commercial business entity with the development and operationalisation of software modules for reporting daily net accretions of POLIF and RPOLIF by Head Post Offices. The Department of Posts has steadily expanded the insurance business during the Eleventh Five Year Plan. As on 31 March 2012, Postal Life Insurance had 5.6 million policies and Rural Postal Life Insurance had 19.63 million policies with a total sum assured of ₹79,183.44 crore and ₹82,540.86 crore respectively.

16.48. The department in last few years has also computerised 24,969 post offices and networked 22,177 post offices (as on 30 June 2012) in urban and rural areas. The department has also taken up Project Arrow for modernisation of post offices, as a part of which, 1,736 post offices have been modernised. India Post, 2012 Project aims to roll out integrated software for Postal Banking, Postal Life Insurance, e-commerce and retailing. In addition, it will also provide rural ICT solution to more than 1,30,000 POs. With the introduction of 'One India One Rate' scheme, speed Post was expanded to cover more than 1,200 towns. The department has also completed construction of 95 post offices, 13 administrative offices and 15 staff quarters projects, besides organising the 6th World Philatelic Exhibition INDIPEX. Some of the other achievements include introduction of e-Post Office, opening of 1,008 franchisee outlets and providing necessary infrastructural equipment to more than 1 lakh branch post offices (BPOs).

Mails (Including International Mails and Global Business)

16.49. Department of Posts initiated a number of projects during the Eleventh Five Year Plan for modernisation of mails network, which include: Mail network optimisation; setting up of automated mail processing centres; deployment of dedicated freighter aircraft for carriage of mail in North East as well as metro routes; National Address Database Management project for building and managing the address database across the country along with postal Geographic Information System (GIS) mapping of the country; and Mail Motor Vehicles project for monitoring the movement of mail vans for their effective management and route optimisation.

Rural Business and Access to Postal Network

16.50. During the Eleventh Five Year Plan, 'Access to the Postal Network' scheme was implemented for improving access to postal network. Major components under the scheme include: opening of new BPOs in Rural Areas, opening of BPOs by redeployment, opening of sub post offices by redeployment, opening of franchise outlets in urban areas, rationalisation of postal network by relocation of branch post offices and sub post offices and provision of Infrastructural equipment for extra departmental branch post offices.

Computerisation and Modernisation of Postal Network

16.51. The department has initiated the programme of Computerisation of Post Offices, Mail Offices, Administrative and other offices, establishment of IT infrastructure and development of software applications. As a part of this programme, DoP has engaged M/s. Accenture for providing professional consultancy to develop a technology strategy and action plan for process re-engineering total networking and computerisation of post offices, administrative offices and offices of the accounts wing. A comprehensive IT roadmap has been developed for network architecture, integrated software, proper data management including strengthening/establishment of National Data Centre(s) and Disaster Recovery Centre. In addition, the DoP has initiated projects for (i) Computerisation and Networking of Departmental Post Offices, and (ii) Upgradation and modernisation of Postal Accounts Offices and Postal Accounts Wing of Postal Directorate. Under the Human Resource Management programme, multiple training programmes, covering all the cadres of employees including Business Orientation Programmes, Capacity Building, Technology Training, Standardisation of Training and departmental training for the officers, Postmasters and new entrants, were conducted.

Vision and Strategy for the Twelfth Five Year Plan

- To make the Department of Post's products and services customer's first choice and serve its customers with a human touch.
- To sustain its position as the largest postal network in the world touching the lives of every citizen in the country.
- To provide mail, parcel, money transfer, banking, insurance and retail services with speed and reliability.
- To provide services to the customers on value for money basis.
- To continue to deliver social security services and to enable last mile connectivity as a Government of India platform.

Objectives

16.52. To fulfil the mandate, the department needs to reinvent itself for providing best in class customer service and growing its existing businesses by developing a professional workforce and modernising and consolidating the network. The department also needs to come up with new services including financial Services.

Policy Issues, Programme Reforms and New Initiatives in the Twelfth Plan

16.53. The India Post has more than 1,50,000 post offices and its reach in the rural India is unmatched. This network spread should be leveraged to provide services to the residents. The department needs to reinvent itself by embracing technology and redefining its role by taking up e-commerce, banking and financial services especially in the rural areas. The Indian Postal Office Act 1898 needs to be replaced with a new act keeping in line with the latest trends.

16.54. *IT Induction and Modernisation*: The major thrust of the Twelfth Five Year Plan would on implementing the IT Induction and Modernisation programme. Implementation of new and improved processes, enterprise resource planning, integration and interlinking of applications, greater access, enhanced productivity, improved functionality and efficient and cost effective services would be the hallmark of this programme. The main features of the project include Supply of mail office hardware, Development and deployment of rural ICT, Banking and PLI solutions, Establishment of Data Centre and Disaster Recovery System, Network Integration, Development and deployment of Integrated Scalable Software and change management activities. The DoP also needs to implement 'Sevottam'—a Service Delivery Excellence Model and Quality Certification as per the corresponding standard IS 15700: 2005 during the Twelfth Five Year Plan. It is also proposed to attain ISO 9001 Certification for all Head Post Offices.

16.55. *Project Arrow*: The Project Arrow envisages upgradation of POs in urban and rural areas both in terms of upgrading and enhancing the quality of service in 'core areas' and improving the 'look and feel'. So far 1,736 POs have been covered under the project. This activity has won the Prime Minister Excellence Award during the year 2009–10. It is proposed to cover more than 2,500 POs under Project Arrow in a phased manner. It is also proposed to undertake audit of 1,000 post offices.

16.56. *Mails Sector*: The Twelfth Five Year Plan aims at ensuring readiness of the department not only for the anticipated mail volumes but also to meet rising customer expectations and competition from electronic channels of communication and private couriers. The main focus shall be on the Express mail segment, bulk mail and parcels which is presently the most competitive as well as profitable sector worldwide, as well as in India covering Speed Post, International Mail, First class mail and second class mail. While continuing with the Automated Mail Processing Centre (AMPC) project at Mumbai, Chennai, Hyderabad and Bangalore, AMPCs would be established at Ahmedabad, Jaipur, Kochi, Patna, Lucknow, Bhubaneshwar, Ludhiana and Vashi (Navi Mumbai). Under the National Address Database Management Project, GIS maps for the entire country and address database for 300 million households is proposed to be developed. The department has also proposed to replace the existing bag sealing system with a new single use self-locking plastic seals and tag labels to improve environmental conditions in the POs.

16.57. The department is incurring heavy expenditure on account of payment of haulage charges to Railways for conveyance of mails and has become uneconomical as the Railways charges passenger displacement fares for RMS wagons instead of freight charges. Non-availability of adequate capacity of wagons also adds to abnormal delay in transmission of mails and adverse public reaction. The dynamics of new type of mail flow makes it imperative for the department to rethink its operational strategy in mail process and transmission. It is therefore proposed to replace rail based transportation on short hauls with road transport network by outsourced/departmental vehicles wherever feasible. It is also proposed to upgrade Mail Motor Service vehicles and containerised transportation of mail and procure 4-wheeled vehicles (one tonner), for mechanisation of Business Mail and Speed Post, two wheeler vehicles for delivery and collection at Mail Hubs/POs during Twelfth Five Year Plan. Postman is the key person, in the postal network and ensuring his mobility is essential for last mile delivery of mail.

16.58. *International Mails, Global Business and e-Commerce*: Quality and efficiency improvement for Express Mail Service (International) will be one of the priority programmes during the Twelfth Five Year Plan. Business process enhancements that improve the ease of doing business, reduce operating expenses and improve customer services would be reinforced. DoP also needs to revamp its mail/parcel delivery capabilities. Postal operators across the world are playing an important role in the development of e-Commerce. In the first phase, the entire range of postal products will be made available to customers online. In the final phase, the e-Commerce business of DoP will evolve into a best-in-class portal with e-market place functionality. It will be an online market place selling a variety of non-postal products.

16.59. A Centre of Excellence for promoting cooperation between India Posts and other designated postal operators of the world is proposed to be established with focus on evolving modern postal operations and practices through experience sharing. The proposed Centre of Excellence could take over all deliberations with member countries of UPU, PAPU, African Union and the Asia Pacific on matters of cooperation in consultancy, Human Resource and allied areas.

16.60. *Financial Services (Savings Bank and Remittances)*: During the Twelfth Five Year Plan, the DoP has envisaged the setting up Post Bank of India with expansion of IT infrastructure along with Processing centres and Customer Call centres. Automatic Teller Machine network of the PO will be expanded to semi urban and block level POs. Integrated remittance services, including Mobile based remittance services will be introduced in order to exploit the penetration of mobile phones all over the country. In addition, an Anti-Money Laundering (AML)/Combating of Financing of Terrorism (CFT) Compliance Structure will be put in place.

16.61. *Postal Life Insurance (PLI)*: During the Twelfth Plan period, it is proposed to increase the coverage of PLI beyond the Government and Semi Government employees and digitise the records of PLI/RPLI with the objective to insure 15 million more lives. Several new products such as ULIPS and Group policies which will benefit the masses especially in rural areas will also be introduced. This will go a long way in providing financial inclusion and risk coverage to rural population with special emphasis on women workers and economically weaker sections of the society. It is also proposed to undertake technology upgradation to facilitate payment of online premium of policies through electronic clearance service facility and use of hand held devices by PLI/RPLI Sales force and operators.

16.62. *Rural Business and Access to Postal Network*: Improving the access to postal network and rationalisation of the existing network are important Plan objectives of the department during the Twelfth Five Year Plan. As the Panchayats are increasingly becoming hubs of various kinds of activities in the villages, it is important that the rural Branch Post Offices are co-located with Panchayats so that they are able to provide the required infrastructural support to all activities of Panchayats in the interest of rural population and also increase the revenues of the department. It is recommended that BPOs should be established at all the Panchayat headquarters to ensure efficient delivery of various services to the people in such areas and also to improve financial inclusion of the currently excluded people. Efforts would also be made to link different local and community institutions such as Aanganwadis and people's collectives including SHGs with the POs.

16.63. *Engagement with Social Protection Programmes*: Department of Posts is considered as the first choice as a delivery channel for various social protection programmes. Availability of an extensive postal network with vast experience of delivering financial and other services offers an opportunity to the Central/State Governments in India to address the constraints associated with delivery of various social protection programmes. The postal network can also be substantially engaged towards achieving financial inclusion in rural India. The department should collaborate with other Government and non-Government agencies to implement their schemes and programmes on financial inclusion.

The BPOs can also be leveraged to transmit information like weather, prices, transfer of knowledge on farm management and facilitate sale/distribution of farm inputs to the farmer right at his doorstep. This would call for building capabilities of rural postal personnel by imparting knowledge and skills on various Government programmes, banking, insurance, accounts and finance, entrepreneurship and usage of computers to Gramin Dak Sewaks in the country.

16.64. *Business Development*: It is essential for the department to include logistics as one of its core activities as development of logistics sector is of paramount importance for the economic development of the country and it offers excellent opportunity for the department to improve its revenues. The department also needs to take a leap forward in express parcel post service in view of the overall volume of business being transacted across the country, and improve the overall efficiency of speed post service delivery due to increased technological capabilities. Human resource development and management is of paramount importance for achieving the goal of reaching out to all sections of society and providing efficient services.

16.65. *Estates Management*: Building requirements of the DoP have undergone significant changes with large scale induction of technology. Thrust during the Twelfth Five Year Plan will be to provide functionally useful modern space for post office operations; improve the general ambience and aesthetics of postal buildings and provide modern facilities and amenities to the users of India Post.

16.66. *Philately Operations*: Indian philately is respected internationally for its theme and design and adherence to good international practices. Several initiatives are proposed to be taken up during the Twelfth Five Year Plan to promote the philately operations, right down to the district level, including establishment of research wing and consultancy for marketing.

16.67. *Postal Accounts and Finance*: As per the decision of Ministry of Finance, all Government departments have to migrate to accrual based accounting system. The department has already initiated action on this line.

Key Constraints and Challenges

16.68. In the rapidly transforming communications and financial services sectors and emerging socio-economic trends within the country and globally, the DoP is facing challenges posed by globalisation, entry of the private sector, growth of telephony, focus on inclusive growth, higher level of delivery standards, developments in other Postal Administrations and so on in its quest of becoming self-sustaining. The DoP also has to address issues relating to multiplicity of application software, co-existence of manual and computerised processes and raising productivity norms and demand for greater accountability and transparency. In the area of financial services, challenge is to achieve the projected financial inclusion and rural empowerment. In addition, enhancing skills and faster generation of employment in the sector, decentralisation, empowerment, dissemination of information and rural transformation with credit facilities by the postal sector are some of the other challenges faced by the department.

The Path Ahead

16.69. The total revenue of the DoP increased by 6.6 per cent from 2007–08 to 2008–09, by 11.1 per cent in 2009–10 to 2010–11 and by 13.75 per cent in 2010–11 to 2011–12. This trend is indicative of the fact that incremental improvements in infrastructure, IT support and quality monitoring during Eleventh Plan has taken effect and with the roll out of all IT induction dependent activities like Core Banking, Rural ICT, Mail Network Optimisation and Modernisation, the upward trend will not only be sustained but will also register a higher percentage growth. The objective is to achieve the challenges with the help of ongoing as well as new schemes like expansion of Automatic Teller Machine network; expansion of Mail Processing Centres and Customer Call centres; Setting up Post Bank of India; e-commerce; Integrated remittance services and Mobile remittance service; and creation of an Anti-Money Laundering (AML)/Combating of Financing of Terrorism (CFT) Compliance Structure. Induction of IT in all post offices will also help in revenue generation due to the speed and accuracy in transactions, transparency, improved customer grievance redressal and provision of greater range of services over a secured network.

INFORMATION AND BROADCASTING

Overview of the Sector

16.70. The Indian Media and Entertainment Industry has evolved as fastest growing sectors of the economy over the last few years and it is expected to grow at an annual average rate on 13.2 per cent in the next five years to reach ₹1.19 trillion in 2015. Television, Radio and Films are projected to grow at Compound Annual Growth Rate (CAGR) of 14.5 per cent, 19.2 per cent and 10 per cent respectively by 2015. Digitalisation, enhanced number of channels, increased number of private stakeholder, momentum in crossover movies and crossover audience, increasing share in the global market, domestic demand for animation and special effect are some of the salient features of this sector. India today has a large broadcasting and distribution sector comprising around 800 plus satellite TV channels, 100 Multi System Operators (MSO), 6,000 Independent Cable operators, around 60,000 Local Cable Operators (LCO), 7 DTH operators and several IPTV service providers. As per industry reports, out of a total of 138 million TV homes, about 30 million are dependent on Doordarshan's terrestrial broadcast services and 74 million are covered by cable services and the rest by Direct to Home (DTH) and Internet Protocol Television Services (IPTV) services. Television industry is more and more getting localised in nature with the spurt of regional channels over the last few years. Doordarshan (DD) is the world's largest terrestrial broadcaster with over 1,400 terrestrial TV transmitters. The reach provided by this route is phenomenal with DD covering 88 per cent of India's geographical areas and these transmitters provide coverage to about 92 per cent population of the country. It is estimated that Direct to Home (DTH) subscriber base could reach 70 million by 2015. With the widespread adoption of broadband in the country and the growing techno savvy population, Internet Protocol Television (IPTV) has a potential to become a huge success in India. Appropriate policy guidelines have been adopted in respect of IPTV, Headend in The Sky (HITS), expansion of FM radio network (Phase III), and Community Radio Services, and so on FM Phase-III will extend radio's reach to 294 towns and 839 stations.

16.71. With convergence of technologies, it is now possible to provide multiple services on a single platform and on single device. To take full advantage of the technology, digitisation of broadcasting network needs to be given priority along with archiving of content and complete switch over to digital transmission. This would help usher in new value added services like Internet Protocol TV, Mobile TV and HDTV. This also calls for a policy to review the existing regulatory institutions and enactment for the establishment of a common regulator for content as well as for carriage.

16.72. The film and entertainment sector needs to be holistically reviewed in the light of technological interventions which have redefined entertainment today. The Cinematographic Act needs to be relooked to address issues relating to digital cinemas, piracy concerns. There is also a need to establish low cost cinema exhibition houses across the country to make cinema affordable. The film festivals needs to be more attractive and should be projected as a platform for encouraging film distribution, exhibition and other related activities.

16.73. There are various issues that revolve around this sector, these inter-alia include foreign investments, content regulation, intellectual property rights, content enrichment, restructuring of PrasarBharati, digitalisation of network and, content for archival and dissemination, issues of piracy, spectrum allocation and maintaining archives of the entire spectrum of Information and Broadcasting media unit.

Review of Eleventh Five Year Plan

Doordarshan

16.74. Eight new High Power Transmitters (HPTs) were set up at Port Blair (A&N), Kokrajhar

(Assam), Bikaner (Rajasthan), Dharamshala (H.P.), Chattarpur (M.P.), Saharsa (Bihar) and Bilaspur (Chattisgarh), thereby providing coverage especially to remote, hilly and border areas hitherto uncovered. Six high power transmitters were also commissioned at Kupwara (J&K), Jalgaon (Maharashtra), Vaodara (Gujarat), Barrmer (Rajasthan), Balurghat (W.B.) and Kharagpur (West Bengal), which enabled Doordarshan to provide reliable and extended service to the people. Two high power ageing and obsolete transmitters were also replaced with new transmitters at Chennai for DD1 and DD News thereby helping to improve the transmission quality. In addition, 56 Low Power Transmitters (LPTs) were also installed during the Plan period. This has increased the reach as well as quality of the TV services in the targeted areas. Also during the Plan, 34 new Very Low Power Transmitters (VLPTs) were installed. Capacity of Doordarshan's Direct To Home (DTH) platform 'DD Direct plus' was upgraded from 50 to 59 Standard Definition Television (SDTV) channels and 65,000 Set Top Boxes (STBs) along with 35,000 TV sets were distributed in remote and border areas. DTH Service in C-Band especially for Andaman and Nicobar (A&N) Islands was commissioned by setting up of a 10 Channel C-Band Earth Station at Delhi. This has enabled the people of A&N island territory to access 10 channels of Doordarshan.

16.75. Doordarshan as a Host Broadcaster of Commonwealth Games—2010, successfully provided coverage of Commonwealth Games Delhi—2010 in High Definition (HD) format. On the eve of Commonwealth Games, a new High Definition DD channel was launched by Doordarshan. Necessary HD uplinking facility in 'C' and 'Ku' bands was commissioned. There has been some setback in the physical and financial targets during Eleventh Five Year Plan period. The main reasons were litigation relating to procurement of transmitters, delay in approval of new schemes specially digitalisation scheme of Doordarshan, lengthy procurement procedure for machinery and equipment and re-tendering of work due to non-compliance of the specifications by bidders.

16.76. *Digitalisation of Transmitters and Studios in DD Network*: The Doordarshan network presently has 1,415 analog transmitters of varying powers providing coverage to 92 per cent of the population and 81.6 per cent by Area. Doordarshan network also comprises of 67 studio centres spread all across the country. Eleventh Five Year Plan scheme of digitalisation, which inter alia includes establishment of 40 digital transmitters and full digitalisation of 39 Studio centres, was approved at a cost of ₹620.12 crore in April, 2010. Digitalisation of Doordarshan network is targeted to be completed by December 2017. For digitalisation of its terrestrial Network, Doordarshan has planned to establish a total of 630 digital transmitters (HPTs-230 and LPTs-400) for providing the present level of coverage as is being provided by 1,415 analog transmitters.

All India Radio (AIR)

16.77. AIR launched digital transmission in DRM from a 250 kW Short Wave (SW) transmitter in Delhi. AIR programmes in digital quality are now available in UK, West Europe, Nepal, Mauritius, East Africa, Sri Lanka, Russia and NE Asia. Obsolete 1,000 kW Medium Wave (MW) transmitters at Rajkot and Kolkata (Chinsurah) have been replaced with state-of-the-art digital (DRM) transmitters. In addition to the western and eastern parts of India, AIR programmes to Afghanistan, Iran and Pakistan from the Rajkot transmitter and to Bangladesh, China and Nepal from the Kolkata transmitter would now be available in digital format. Establishment of permanent studios in Leh (J&K) and Tawang (AP) have been initiated and the studio facilities at Mysore (Karnataka) have been upgraded. New Studios are also getting ready at Jaipur and Dehradun, which will have digital production and transmission facilities. AIR has also commissioned satellite earth stations at Leh (J&K) and Rohtak (Haryana), enabling these areas to distribute news and other important programmes to other AIR stations in the regions. News-on-Phone Service has been introduced from 5 more stations—Lucknow, Imphal, Simla, Guwahati and Raipur, making a total of 14 such stations. Strengthening of radio coverage in the border areas and Jammu & Kashmir is of strategic importance for India. Therefore, a programme for strengthening

AIR and Doordarshan coverage in the J&K was taken.

16.78. *Digitalisation Plan*: The Eleven Five Year Plans have given impetus to the growth of broadcasting in India resulting in a phenomenal expansion. From the six radio stations at the time of independence, the network has now grown to 279 stations with 436 transmitters providing coverage to 99.18 per cent of the population and 91.85 per cent area of the country. AIR FM, which is increasingly becoming popular, provides coverage to about 37 per cent of population at present. Digitalisation of AIR production, transmission and networking infrastructure is to be completed by December 2017. But it has to be ensured that till that time, the listeners are not deprived of the programmes on the existing analogue receivers. During the Eleventh Five Year Plan a scheme for digitalisation of Transmitters (70 MW and 9 SW), Studios (98 nos) and Connectivity as well as augmentation of Training and R&D facilities was taken up.

Film Sector

16.79. There is a gradual increase in the number of countries and films participating in the International Film Festival of India (IFFI). During the 42nd IFFI which was recently concluded, 255 films from 67 countries participated. IFFI now attracts entries from all over the world. The participation by Indian films in various film festivals and in various film markets has also increased. During the Eleventh Five Year Plan, National Film Development Corporation (NFDC) has produced 11 films in different languages and 8 films are under production. Films Division has completed production of 183 documentaries and Children Film Society of India (CFSI) produced 11 feature films during this period. A programme was also taken up for digitisation and restoration of old films. Considerable progress has been made towards setting up of National Museum of Indian Cinema and is likely to be completed by 2013 to coincide with the Centenary year of Indian Cinema.

Information Sector

16.80. Directorate of Advertisement and Visual Publicity (DAVP) is the nodal multi-media advertising agency of the Government which carries information on policies, programmes and achievements of various Ministries and Departments to masses through various media. It focused on the technological upgradation of its communication equipment and modernisation of its programme designs. In order to disseminate information on flagship programmes of the Government, Public Information Campaigns (PICs) is the most crucial and important component of the Media Outreach Strategy organised by Public Information Bureau (PIB) in joint collaboration with fellow media units of Ministry of Information and Broadcasting to raise awareness on flagship programmes of the Government. Song and Drama Division (S&DD) mounted a new Sound and Light Programme titled 'Jamunia' based on a Multi Media Theatrical format, which was well received by the people.

Broad Objectives, Targets and Thrust Areas during the Twelfth Five Year Plan

16.81. The growth potential of Media and Entertainment sector needs to be harnessed in order to place Broadcasting sector on a higher growth trajectory by taking advantage accrued due to convergence of technologies. In the liberalised economy, the role of Government has undergone a phenomenal change from a services provider to facilitator and there is a need for creating supportive policy environment for different stakeholders in the media and entertainment sector in order to step up the growth trend. There is a need to promote and facilitate the Broadcasting, Films and Print media industry in India to ensure its growth and development and to generate employment. Media Units need to be strengthened further to ensure dissemination of public messages in a more purposeful and efficient manner. Keeping in view the present day realities and emerging scenarios, their individual roles also need to be clearly redefined so as to achieve complete synergy in delivery mechanism among the media units. There is a need to ensure free flow of information to the public and safeguarding freedom of the media in general. The Government's role in making information available to people in strategic and inaccessible areas of the country should continue to remain paramount. Last but not the least, the potential of software in film and broadcasting needs to be exploited internationally to make India a global soft power and there is a need to review the Acts, Rules and Regulation as per the contemporary needs of this sector. During the Twelfth Five Year Plan thrust would be on the following major programmes:

Broadcasting Sector
1. Digitalisation needs to be given thrust with special emphasis on convergence technology. The digitalisation of AIR, Doordarshan, Cable sector should be completed as per schedule.
2. Digital content needs to be given push during Twelfth Plan along with comprehensive programme audit of DD and AIR and to improve the content being telecast by DD/AIR.
3. Restructuring and strengthening of Prasar Bharati with the twin objectives of (i) enabling it to perform its primary role of Public Service Broadcaster (PSB) more purposefully and efficiently; (ii) making the non-PSB component self-financing within Twelfth Plan period.
4. Enhancing broadcast coverage in boarder areas and North Eastern areas through expansion of broadcasting infrastructure and services in the border areas.
5. Earmarking of some frequencies/channels of DD and AIR for niche programmes.
6. Expansion of FM coverage in the Twelfth Plan and dedicating one channel for nationwide news and current affairs FM channel.
7. Strengthening the capacity of Electronic Media Monitoring Centre (EMMC) for monitoring broadcast content including Private FM channels and Community Radio services.
8. Notification of policy and guidelines for Mobile TV services.
9. Supporting Community Radio Movement and Information, Entertainment and Communication (IEC) activities.
10. Installation of DRM+ transmitters at 50 locations including all state capitals and some other major cities in the country.
11. Replacement of 28 MW transmitters by FM and installation of 330 new FM transmitters (150 at the locations where private FM is coming in phase III [but AIR does not have FM set up there], 25 at the locations for which demands from a number of VIPs are pending, 5 for additional channels and 150 in the uncovered areas).
12. Broadcasting Infrastructure Network Development.
13. Special Projects like Auditorium, Global Coverage of DD International Channel and Broadcast Museum.
14. IEC activities for promoting Digitalisation, Automation of Broadcasting wing and Capacity building of Cable TV industry in Digital wire line Broadcasting.

Film Sector
1. To devise appropriate policy initiatives for creating an enabling environment conducive to the growth and development of film sector including preservation and sustenance of the film heritage of India.
2. To devise appropriate policy for simplifying the procedure for clearance for setting up of film theatres.
3. To preserve and enhance public access to the archival wealth of films, video and audio resources.
4. To devise single window clearance system for film shooting in India, for both domestic and international film production houses.
5. To promote India as a film destination in film market and film festivals.
6. To aggressively pursue for entertainment tax and services tax to be subsumed in Goods and Services Tax (GST).
7. Establishment of a National Museum of Indian Cinema at Mumbai to coincide with the centenary year of Indian cinema in 2013.
8. Infrastructure Development Programme relating to Film Sector.
9. Development Communication and Dissemination of Film Content.
10. Anti-Piracy initiatives.
11. Setting up of National Film Heritage Mission.
12. Setting up of National Centre for Animation, Gaming and VFX.

Information Sector
1. To encourage information dissemination in traditional media through PPP mode for intensive campaign at village fairs, festivals and social gatherings.
2. To create awareness on social issues through inter-personal and live performance.
3. Media Infrastructure Development Programme.
4. Development Communication and Dissemination.
5. Human Resource Development.

Key Constraints and Challenges

16.82. Information and Broadcasting sector in the country will undergo a major facelift Twelfth Five Year Plan making it comparable with that of developed world. Some of the game changers and challenges for the sector are as follows:

1. *Going digital in TV and Radio*

   a. The Government is committed to adhere to the date-line already notified for Cable TV digitalisation. HITS is an alternate platform to the cable sector.
   b. Digitalisation of terrestrial transmission, adding to the digital network capacity in the country.
   c. Digitalisation of All India Radio, particularly MW, SW and FM is another challenge. PrasarBharati has designed a plan of action to go digital to replace analogue MW and SW transmission through adoption of DRM+ technology.
   d. Ensuring that PrasarBharati re-gains its lost position as public service broadcasting agency and becoming self-financing for non-PSB component.

2. *Community Radio Expansion and Community Empowerment*

   a. Provision for adequate availability of fund for NGOs to initially set up Community Radio stations and judicious decision in terms of policy intervention for increasing commercial airtime.
   b. Making this sector a vibrant medium of IEC, spurring content innovation and carrying message from the Government to the local people.

3. *Film Heritage Mission*

   a. Film Heritage Mission will not only consolidate and add value to the cultural assets but also will act as a game changer in converting thousands of films to digital format. This Mission will help propagate India's cultural values to different countries.

Policy Issues and Recent Initiatives

16.83. The Ministry has taken a number of initiatives in the recent past with the objective to create an enabling environment in the information and broadcasting sector. These include:

1. *Broadcasting Sector*

   a. *Policy on Headend in the Sky (HITS)*: HITS would provide greater channel capacity and is capable of bringing down the investments required at the level of the last mile operator, thereby enabling deeper penetration of cable services into rural areas. However, there is some constraint with regard to availability of transponder capacities for HITS services. The implementation of Digital Addressable System (DAS) in the cable TV sector would have a great positive impact on HITS services as it would enable HITS to penetrate and capture greater market share, particularly in rural areas.
   b. *Policy on IPTV Service*: IPTV platform is promising due to its superior quality and interactive service but the reach is limited to households having broadband connections. Once broadband penetration in rural India improves, IPTV would stand a better chance of success. However, it is likely to take some time before the service makes inroads in the market.

c. *Digital Addressable System (DAS) in the Cable TV Sector*: The Ministry has taken a major decision at reforming the present analogue cable television networks by digitalising the same to address the inherent drawbacks in the analogue networks. DAS will be implemented in a phased time bound manner with the complete switch off of analog cable TV service in the country by 31 December 2014. The implementation of DAS will be a game changer for the television sector and will take growth of broadcasting sector to new heights. It will benefit all stakeholders including cable operators, broadcasters, customers and the government.

d. *Enhancement of FDI Limits in the Broadcasting Sector*: Rationalisation of Foreign Investments (FI) limits in various segments of broadcasting sector needs to be addressed. There is need for a holistic review of the existing FI limits for different segments of broadcasting sector.

e. *Content Regulation and Broadcasting Regulator*: Regulation of content of Television channels and setting up an independent regulator for the broadcasting sector has been a much debated issue. Within the industry, the preponderant view is that self-regulation is the best way to regulate the media and no purpose would be served by introducing any other measures to regulate content. The Indian Broadcasting Foundation (IBF), taking a cue from NBA's self-regulation and in consultation with the Ministry, has set up a mechanism for self-regulation in case of general entertainment channels. As part of this, IBF has laid down Content Code and Certification Rules 2011 covering an entire gamut of content-related principles and criterion for television broadcast. The self-regulation mechanism put in place by the broadcasters will, however, not replace the existing regulatory functions of the Government, arising out of the extant statute, namely, Cable Television Networks (Regulation) Act, 1995 and Rules framed thereunder.

f. *Amendment to the Guidelines on Uplinking/Downlinking of Channels*: There is need to make changes with respect to existing policy on uplinking/downlinking of Channels and teleports which, inter-alia, includes uniform permission period of 10 years for uplinking/downlinking of channels and teleports, stipulating time frame for operationalisation, enhancement of permission fee, mandatory submission of performance Bank Guarantee for fulfilling the roll out obligations. The proposed policy also provides for transfer of permission in case of merger/demerger/amalgamation with the approval of the Government.

g. *Interoperability of DTH Set-Top-Boxes (STB)*: Interoperability of the STBs has been a long pending issue. Technical interoperability essentially protects the interest of the subscribers by enabling them to shift from one operator to another without having to buy a new STB.

h. *License Fee Computation in DTH Sector*: Presently, the license fee collected by the Ministry of Information and Broadcasting from DTH operators is based on the Gross Revenue, as defined in the Article 3 of the Schedule to the DTH License Agreement. As per this definition, taxes revenue earned from the sale of Set Top Box, installation, commissions, content cost, subscription and service are required to be included for the purpose of calculation of annual license fee. The TDSAT has, however, in its orders dated 26 August 2008 and 28 May 2010, applied the principle of Adjusted Gross Revenue (AGR) for determination of annual license fee, removing majority of components such as installation charges, taxes, commissions, content cost, sale of STBs and so on. The Government has filed an appeal in the Supreme Court against these TDSAT orders. As of now, the DTH operators are paying license fee as per adjusted gross revenue which is less than according to gross revenue computation.

i. *Rationalisation of Taxes in Broadcasting Sector*: A long standing demand of the broadcasting sector has been for DTH, Cable Services, IPTV services, HITS services and for similar content distribution services, the Service Tax, Entertainment Tax and VAT be subsumed under the proposed Goods and Services Tax regime (GST) and only a single/unified GST rate be notified for these services.

j. *Music royalty in FM Radio:* Music royalty issue is a major bone of contention between radio and music players and the royalty rates have been one of the problems affecting the viability of the private FM industry. The Copyright Board, which was given powers by the Supreme Court of India to decide in the matter of radio companies versus music rights owners on the issue of royalty payment, has decided to reduce the royalty payment to two per cent of their net advertising revenues. This matter is still not settled as music companies have challenged this order in court and the industry will need to wait for a final decision; however no stay has yet been granted.

k. *Promotion of Indigenous Manufacturing Capacity:* A concern has been raised in various quarters that there is a lack of indigenous manufacturing capacities for broadcasting equipment in India. With digitalisation being one of the priority agenda for all the stakeholders, there is a need to enhance domestic manufacturing capabilities for production of STBs and other digital equipments.

2. *Film Sector*

a. The Government has initiated steps for setting up of a mechanism for single window clearance for film shooting in India.
b. The Ministry has taken up the matter with the Ministry of Finance for adoption of GST subsuming all service tax and entertainment tax under it.
c. To enable expansion of the exhibition sector, the issue of simplification of regulatory clearances for setting up exhibition outlets needs to be addressed. State Governments will need to be asked to explore possibility for granting exemption from entertainment tax to low cost theatres for Indian and world award winning cinema.
d. Revision of the Cinematograph Act, 1952.
e. Declaring SRFTI, FTII as national centres of excellence enabled by an Act of the Parliament.
f. There is a need to resolve issues with respect to high rates of entertainment tax and lack of uniformity in tax structure, across States.
g. There are issues which need to be addressed as digital technology and broadband infrastructure include:

   i. Establishment of uniform standards of technology for theatres;
   ii. An effective preservation and archiving of films in digital formats vis-à-vis traditional forms of storage; and
   iii. internet and web-based piracy of films.

h. *Countering Piracy*: The film sector faces the massive challenge of grappling with pirated software on web-based platforms in the current Indian environment. Further, mechanisms for regulation of content on the Internet are non-existent. Appropriate policy framework needs to be designed.

3. *Information Sector*

a. In DAVP, on-line billing has been introduced. This has substantially raised the transparency level of its functioning. There is a need to take the matter forward by making DAVP's operation entirely online.
b. There is a need to periodically review the pricing of the Government spot in various channels in order to ensure that Government spots reach the maximum viewers and particularly at the regional channels catering to niche viewers.
c. While the Government has been spending a large sum of its publicity budget through DAVP, there is a need for periodical evaluation of the campaigns to ascertain their impact.

d. There is a need to cover all districts of the country though Public Information Campaigns (PICs) during the Plan period and support for expansion of 'Jamunia' in all regional languages of the country.
e. There is a need to take appropriate steps to make DFP (Directorate of Field Publicity) effective.
f. There is need for an integrated approach by combining all the media units such as PIB, DAVP, DFP and S&DD engaged in information dissemination to ensure maximum impact of the Government information campaign on the people.
g. Inter Media Publicity Coordination Committee (IMPCC), at the State capital level duly constituted by the Ministry needs to be strengthened and rejuvenated through appropriate policy direction to regularly meet, assess and refocus its media campaign.
h. IIMC (Indian Institute of Mass Communication) needs to be upgraded to an institute of excellence in media education and research.

Path Ahead

16.84. The Twelfth Five Year Plan would aim at transforming the information, film and broadcasting sector into a modern, efficient, responsive and vibrant sector. To achieve this objective, necessary policy intervention, suitable infrastructure, investment in traditional as well as modern media unit, participation of private sector in PPP model, viable policy environment for facilitating and sustaining growth and development of media and entertainment sector need to be created. Apart from these, barriers in the way of investment in infrastructure, reaching out to rural, remote and inaccessible and strategic area need to be tackled effectively and efficiently. For optimal and efficient utilisation of resources, both manpower and capital, synergy between various media units of media and entertainment sector is required. Suitable plan/policies/programmes are needed in this direction.

16.85. The Twelfth Five Year Plan (2012–17) outlays (GBS) for the Ministry of Communications and IT and Ministry of Information and Broadcasting are given in Annexure 16.1.

ANNEXURE 16.1

Twelfth Five Year Plan (2012–17) Outlays for the Ministry of Communications and IT and Ministry of Information and Broadcasting

₹ in crore

Ministry/Department	GBS	IEBR	Twelfth Plan Outlay
1. Ministry of Communications and IT			
• Department of Telecommunications	20,825.00	51,285.40	72,110.40
• Department of Electronics and IT	36,078.00	3,944.29	40,022.29
• Department of Posts	5,527.00	0.00	5,527.00
2. Ministry of I&B	7,583.00	1,000.00	8,583.00
Total	70,013.00	56,229.69	1,26,242.69

17
Rural Development

17.1. The Eleventh Plan period saw major new initiatives towards inclusive growth in rural India. The total budgetary allocation for all rural development programmes by the Government of India in the Eleventh Plan was ₹2,91,682 crores which accounted for 25 per cent of the total Central Budget Plan provision. Rural development programmes cover employment through the Mahatma Gandhi National Rural Employment Guarantee Act and the National Rural Livelihoods Mission, housing via the Indira Awaas Yojana and other State schemes and bank support, sanitation through the Total Sanitation Campaign, provision of drinking water via the National Rural Drinking Water Programme, social security through the National Social Assistance Programme, watershed development via the Integrated Watershed Management Programme (covered in Chapter 5 of Volume 1), road connectivity through the Pradhan Mantri Gram Sadak Yojana (described in Chapter 15 of Volume 2) and electrification via the Rajiv Gandhi Grameen Vidyutikaran Yojana (described in Chapter 14 of Volume 2).

17.2. Based on a critical review of these programmes and their performance in the Eleventh Plan, this chapter outlines the major new initiatives proposed during the Twelfth Plan period.

MAHATMA GANDHI NATIONAL RURAL EMPLOYMENT GUARANTEE ACT (MGNREGA)

The Experience So Far

17.3. The most significant rural development initiative of the Eleventh Plan period was the Mahatma Gandhi National Rural Employment Guarantee Act (MGNREGA). Over the last six years, MGNREGA has delivered the largest employment programme in human history, which is unlike any other in its scale, architecture and thrust. Its bottom-up, people-centred, demand-driven, self-selecting, rights-based design is new and unprecedented. Never have in such a short period so many crores of poor people benefited from a Government programme.

17.4. In 2011–12, nearly 5.00 crore families were provided over 211 crore person-days of work under the programme. Over the last six years, MGNREGA has generated more than 1,200 crore person-days of work at a total expenditure of over ₹1,66,760 crores. The share of SC/ST families in the work provided under MGNREGA has been 55 per cent and 45 per cent of workers are women. Average wages of workers have gone up by 54 per cent over the last five years and wages have now been so indexed that workers will be protected from the ravages of inflation. Nearly 10 crore bank/post office accounts of our poorest people have been opened and around 80 per cent of MGNREGA payments are made through this route, an unprecedented step in the direction of financial inclusion. An overview of MGNREGA performance from 2006–07 to 2011–12 is given in Table 17.1.

17.5. In many parts of the country, spectacular successes have been recorded in water harvesting. Distress migration has been arrested in several areas. Some State Governments have been leaders in this and the National Consortium of Civil Society Organisations on MGNREGA has also set up examples of excellent work.

TABLE 17.1
Overview of MGNREGA Performance, 2006–12

	2006–07 (200 Districts)	2007–08 (330 Districts)	2008–09 (All Districts Hereon)	2009–10	2010–11	2011–12
Households Employed (crore)	2.10	3.39	4.51	5.26	5.49	4.99
Person-days of Employment generated (crore)	90.5	143.59	216.32	283.59	257.15	211.41
Work Provided per year to Households who worked (days)	43	42	48	54	47	42
Central Release (₹ crore)	8,640.85	12,610.39	30,000.19	33,506.61	35,768.95	29,184.85
Total Funds Available (including Opening Balance) (₹ crore)	12,073.55	19,305.81	37,397.06	49,579.19	54,172.14	43,273.58
Budget Outlay (₹ crore)	11,300	12,000	30,000	39,100	40,100	40,100
Expenditure (₹ crore)	8,823.35	15,856.89	27,250.10	37,905.23	39,377.27	37,548.79
Average Wage per day (₹)	65	75	84	90	100	117
Total Works taken up (lakhs)	8.35	17.88	27.75	46.17	50.99	74.13
Works completed (lakhs)	3.87	8.22	12.14	22.59	25.90	15.01

Source: Ministry of Rural Development, GoI.

17.6. Many critics and sceptics of MGNREGA who were extremely vocal during the years leading up to its passage by Parliament and in the early years of its implementation have been silenced, especially after it was recognised that the purchasing power the programme created in rural areas and the operation of the Keynesian multiplier played a crucial role in generating demand for industry during the dark days of the recession and assisted in our comparatively faster emergence out of it.

17.7. However, there is no denying the fact that the true potential of MGNREGA as an instrument of rural transformation is yet to be fully realised. Since the programme marks a radical departure from earlier efforts of a similar kind, there have been many problems in infusing the system with the new culture of demand-driven, rights-based, decentralised decision-making. The MGNREGA provides a historic opportunity for strengthening Panchayati Raj in India but the experience so far also alerts us to the need for doing much more in this direction.

17.8. There are problems that arise from the sheer scale of the programme. At the same time, new opportunities have arisen because of advances in Information Technology that allow us to get rid of inefficiencies and corruption in a manner quite inconceivable in the past. The MIS currently used by MGNREGA is already the best we have ever had. More than 8 crore muster rolls and over 12 crore job cards have been placed online. But there is huge scope for further improvement in overcoming systemic delays as shown by the software being used, for example, in Andhra Pradesh.

17.9. We also need to view MGNREGA as a programme whose success will, in itself, pave the way for its downscaling. A large proportion of MGNREGA workers are small and marginal farmers, the productivity of whose lands has been so decimated over the years, that they have been compelled to work under MGNREGA. The real success of MGNREGA will lie in raising the agricultural productivity of millions of these farmers who will then be able to return once again to farming and will no longer need to depend on MGNREGA for their survival. Urgent measures are required to convert MGNREGA into a productivity-enhancing instrument that will also allay the falsely perceived conflict between MGNREGA and agriculture—for MGNREGA is the foundation for solving the problems of the poorest farmers of our country.

Relationship with Agriculture and Rural Livelihoods

17.10. Ever since work on MGNREGA was launched in 2006 there have been two divergent perceptions about its relationship with agriculture—one, as a relationship of positive synergy and the other, of a potential source of conflict. The sources of synergy are many:

17.11. The MGNREGA has led to major increases in wages of rural workers and when we recognise the fact (attested by NSSO data on 'landed labourers') that the majority of MGNREGA workers are impoverished small and marginal farmers, especially in our tribal areas, we can see the direct impact MGNREGA has made on raising incomes of our small and marginal farmers.

17.12. A comprehensive time series of rural wage data—both agricultural and non-agricultural—put together by the Ministry of Statistics and Programme Implementation indicates that the advent of MGNREGA has resulted in a significant structural break in rural wage increases.[1] Between 1999 and 2005, pre-MGNREGA, nominal wages in the rural economy grew at an average annual rate of 2.7 per cent (year on year average). Post-MGNREGA, the rate of average wage increases almost quadrupled to 9.7 per cent between 2006 and 2009. And between January 2010 and May 2011 (the last date for which this data is available), annual nominal wage growth averaged almost 18.8 per cent. Since January 2010, agricultural wages rose 20.2 per cent over year ago while non-agricultural rural wages increased 16.7 per cent over year ago. Wage growth for men in the agricultural sector averaged 19.7 per cent over year ago while that for women 20.8 per cent over year ago. The average daily wage rates for male agricultural labour are given in Table 17.2 (A).

17.13. State-wise trends in the wages of casual workers in rural areas compiled by the Labour Bureau, Shimla indicate that agricultural wages are booming at the fastest rate ever. The Labour Bureau's data, compiled on a monthly basis, are based on primary information collected from 600 sample villages over 20 States. They cover wage payments both in cash as well as kind, with the latter valued at the prevailing local retail prices.

17.14. The tightening of the labour market post-MGNREGA is a positive indicator of poverty alleviation and also signals a pressure for technological advances that raise farm productivity in areas of relative labour shortage. This is the process of agrarian transformation the world over.

17.15. What is more, since a very large proportion (80 per cent) of the works under MGNREGA are also focused on soil and water conservation on the lands of the small and marginal farmers, it is clear that MGNREGA is making a potential contribution to raising their incomes through improved agricultural productivity, and also reducing the need for small and marginal farmers to continue to work on MGNREGA sites. Studies conducted by Indian Institute of Science (IISc), Bangalore; Indian Institute of Forest Management, Bhopal; Administrative Staff College of India, Hyderabad and University of Agricultural Sciences, Bangalore have all concluded that MGNREGA works have had a positive impact on agricultural productivity. In one of the studies conducted in Chitradurga district of Karnataka, IISc found that MGNREGA works, besides enhancing agricultural productivity, successfully reduced water, soil and agricultural vulnerability.

17.16. As far as the perception of conflict between MGNREGA and agriculture is concerned, this is based on a number of misconceptions and exaggerations.

17.17. Let us first remember that the average annual person-days of work generated under MGNREGA since inception has never exceeded 54 days. Surely this in itself indicates the critical but still small and supplementary nature of this employment for our self-selecting poorest people. And if we closely examine the question of seasonality of this work, an analysis of the quantum of MGNREGA works provided across the year indicates a powerful seasonal fluctuation, with a disproportionately higher share of works

TABLE 17.2 (A)
Average Daily Wage Rates for Agricultural Labour: Male

(in ₹)

State	December			% Increase	
	2008	2009	2010	Dec 09/Dec 08	Dec 10/ Dec 09
Andhra Pradesh	98.31	137.95	176.29	40.32	27.79
Assam	81.19	96.40	114.10	18.73	18.36
Bihar	71.42	86.55	101.85	21.18	17.68
Gujarat	78.72	82.76	91.36	5.13	10.39
Haryana	132.64	168.22	195.02	26.82	15.93
Himachal Pradesh	164.72	180.42	195.22	9.53	8.20
Karnataka	72.90	87.54	111.76	20.08	27.67
Kerala	220.27	250.79	319.13	13.86	27.25
Madhya Pradesh	61.33	69.79	84.43	13.79	20.98
Maharashtra	82.61	95.10	119.36	15.12	25.51
Orissa	68.05	86.70	123.96	27.41	42.98
Punjab	130.63	133.49	176.21	2.19	32.00
Rajasthan	109.84	113.65	145.69	3.47	28.19
Tamil Nadu	113.28	137.98	174.08	21.80	26.16
Uttar Pradesh	81.14	94.89	116.53	16.95	22.81
West Bengal	87.40	99.94	118.47	14.35	18.54

Note: Average rate for five operations (ploughing, sowing, weeding, transplanting and harvesting) has been considered.

being done during the off-season in agriculture. The month-wise employment data under MGNREGA during FY 2010–11 (Table 17.2 B) indicates that it is in the lean agricultural season (January–June), that around 70 per cent of person-days of work were generated. And if we were to correct for the fact that in major MGNREGA States like Tamil Nadu this is actually not the lean season, the proportion of MGNREGA work provided in the off-season in agriculture would be even higher.

Expanded List of Works

17.18. During the Twelfth Plan we propose to allow the largest possible number of works which help strengthen the synergy between MGNREGA and agriculture without compromising on the fundamental features of the Act or its architecture, which have been celebrated across the globe. The more rural people feel a sense of resultant ownership and a stake in the programme, the more efficiency and transparency we will be able to achieve. The list of works has also been expanded in response to demands of the States for greater location-specific flexibility in permissible works, as also to help improve the ecological balance in rural India and provide a cleaner, healthier environment to its people (Table 17.3). In response to each of these demands, Schedule I of the Act has been modified to provide an additional list of permissible works under MGNREGA. Some of these works are new but many of them come within the category of works already permitted under MGNREGA. This is being provided in response to demands from States for more elaborate, specific and unambiguous list of works that could be taken up under the categories currently permissible.

17.19. Each work indicates the unit cost as also the labour–material ratio. These unit cost estimates are indicative and provide a broad order of magnitude. They may vary depending on local conditions and more updated SoRs. However, the labour–material ratio specified for each work must be strictly adhered

TABLE 17.2 (B)
Seasonality of MGNREGA Employment Provided during 2010–11

State	April %	May %	June %	July %	Aug %	Sep %	Oct %	Nov %	Dec %	Jan %	Feb %	March %	Total %
Andhra Pradesh	23.5	33.3	22.5	6.9	2.5	1.1	1.0	0.7	0.7	0.8	1.8	5.2	100.0
Assam	9.8	6.6	4.2	3.3	4.9	6.5	6.7	9.6	13.7	11.8	11.1	11.7	100.0
Bihar	11.2	13.7	11.4	6.2	5.6	6.8	5.4	5.7	8.9	9.5	9.3	6.3	100.0
Chhattisgarh	19.6	27.1	14.2	1.3	0.7	1.0	2.0	1.8	3.2	9.7	10.8	8.7	100.0
Goa	6.9	7.7	7.3	6.8	7.4	4.8	6.5	5.8	10.1	14.5	12.8	9.4	100.0
Gujarat	18.1	26.8	10.7	4.0	2.8	2.3	3.1	4.3	6.3	8.4	7.2	5.9	100.0
Haryana	3.8	3.5	3.1	3.4	5.1	6.0	8.1	10.3	13.5	16.3	13.8	13.2	100.0
Himachal Pradesh	9.7	12.9	12.0	10.1	9.5	9.4	7.2	8.2	5.4	1.9	4.2	9.4	100.0
Jammu And Kashmir	3.7	3.3	3.0	5.6	7.0	8.8	11.2	12.7	14.9	12.4	9.3	8.0	100.0
Jharkhand	11.9	13.2	11.3	7.6	6.8	8.6	6.2	4.8	5.9	7.7	8.6	7.5	100.0
Karnataka	0.5	0.6	1.3	1.6	2.2	3.2	4.7	5.4	7.5	13.3	26.9	32.8	100.0
Kerala	3.0	6.0	7.6	9.8	8.0	10.1	7.1	7.2	8.8	11.3	11.2	9.9	100.0
Madhya Pradesh	15.7	18.0	16.6	7.5	3.8	3.2	3.4	3.8	6.7	8.1	7.6	5.4	100.0
Maharashtra	28.8	25.1	12.9	3.4	1.7	1.3	1.5	1.3	3.4	4.7	7.3	8.6	100.0
Manipur	3.3	11.8	4.7	11.5	13.0	10.9	10.2	5.0	4.3	12.7	8.8	3.9	100.0
Meghalaya	8.7	7.2	8.7	9.1	10.4	11.6	10.2	9.2	6.8	6.6	6.1	5.5	100.0
Mizoram	6.7	6.4	9.8	7.0	7.1	8.9	8.1	8.2	6.3	7.2	14.0	10.4	100.0
Nagaland	14.0	11.6	8.9	7.1	8.6	5.9	7.0	11.1	7.8	7.0	5.5	5.6	100.0
Odisha	16.8	24.6	12.7	3.1	2.8	3.3	4.0	4.7	5.9	6.8	8.2	7.2	100.0
Punjab	7.8	9.6	10.4	6.8	7.4	7.9	7.5	5.7	5.7	5.5	8.2	17.5	100.0
Rajasthan	12.4	22.9	26.5	9.4	2.7	1.5	1.1	1.2	2.9	6.0	7.2	6.1	100.0
Sikkim	6.5	9.0	9.5	8.9	5.0	6.6	3.3	5.9	11.1	15.6	11.5	7.0	100.0
Tamil Nadu	12.4	12.6	12.1	15.9	10.7	7.6	7.7	3.2	3.8	3.6	5.2	5.2	100.0
Tripura	3.7	7.7	9.4	9.5	11.9	13.2	7.2	5.7	5.2	8.6	8.0	9.9	100.0
Uttar Pradesh	8.8	9.8	10.5	9.6	5.9	2.9	1.9	4.5	11.1	13.5	12.2	9.3	100.0
Uttarakhand	8.2	6.0	6.3	6.8	7.7	6.1	6.2	7.6	11.3	14.5	11.3	7.8	100.0
West Bengal	17.0	16.3	14.6	7.4	4.1	4.0	3.2	2.9	4.8	8.3	9.9	7.4	100.0
Andaman and Nicobar	23.7	9.7	11.7	3.7	1.5	0.0	0.8	1.3	1.3	25.3	16.8	4.0	100.0
Lakshadweep	4.5	1.9	11.1	24.0	11.2	10.7	4.8	11.7	9.1	6.5	4.3	0.3	100.0
Puducherry	4.1	12.0	19.6	24.0	16.7	13.6	9.9	0.0	0.0	0.0	0.1	0.0	100.0
All India	13.5	17.3	14.4	8.0	5.0	4.1	3.7	3.7	5.7	7.6	8.7	8.3	100.0

to. Many of these activities entail a higher material component but it must be ensured that in the final mix of activities chosen by the Gram Panchayat, the overall labour–material ratio in each Gram Panchayat is maintained at 60:40. The selection of more material-intensive works and their number must be done within this overall constraint. While taking up works under MGNREGA, the following conditions will need to be followed:

- Only those works to be taken up that result in creation of durable assets
- The order of priority of works will be determined within the GP

TABLE 17.3
Additional List of Permissible Works Under MGNREGA

No	Work	Standard Dimensions	Unit Cost	Wage: Material Cost Ratio
A. WATERSHED RELATED WORKS				
1.	Contour Trenches	Cross section 0.5m*0.5m	₹11,300 per hectare	100:0
2.	Contour Bunds	height 0.6m, base width 2.0m and cross-sectional area of 0.66 sq.m	₹13,637 per hectare	100:0
3.	Boulder Checks	7m length, maximum height 1m, upstream and downstream slopes 1:1 and 3:1, top width of 0.5m	₹1,600	100:0
4.	Farm Bunding	height 0.6m, base width 1.7m and cross-section area 0.57 sq.m	₹7,729 per hectare	100:0
5.	Gabion Structures	2m height, 1m top width and 12m length	₹45,000	30:70
6.	Underground Dykes	12m length, 6m maximum depth and 2m top width	₹43,000	70:30
7.	Earthen Dams	65m length, maximum height 4.65m, upstream and downstream slopes 2:1 and 2.5:1, top width 2m	₹2.63 lakhs	95:5
8.	Dugout Farm Ponds	25m*20m*2m	₹98,470	100:0
9.	Stop Dams	length 20m, maximum height 2.7m, top width 1.5m and side slopes 1:1	₹5.32 lakhs	25:75
B. WATERSHED RELATED WORKS IN MOUNTAIN REGIONS				
10.	Springshed Development	Various watershed interventions	₹18,000–₹38,000 per hectare	90:10–60:40
C. AGRICULTURE RELATED WORKS				
11.	NADEP Composting	3.6m*1.5m*0.9m	₹8,000	25:75
12.	Vermi-Composting	3.6m*1m*0.75m	₹9,000	25:75
13.	BioLiquid Manure	Sanjeevak Pit 1m*1m*1m	₹2,000	30:70
D. LIVESTOCK RELATED WORKS				
14.	Poultry Shelter	7.5 sq m for 100 birds	₹40,000	20:80
15.	Goat Shelter	7.5 sq m for 10 animals	₹35,000	25:75
16.	Pucca Floor, Urine Tank and Fodder Trough for Cattle	Cattle shed floor 26.95 sq.m, 1 cu.m fodder trough and cattle urine collection tank 250 litres	₹35,000	30:70
17.	Azolla Cattle-Feed	Azolla pit 2m x 2m x 0.2 m	₹2,000	15:85
E. FISHERIES RELATED WORKS				
18.	Fisheries in Water Bodies on Public Land	500 cu.m fish nursery pond, excavation of 15000 cu.m in tank bed, fish drying platform 30 sq.m	₹11 lakhs (₹75 per cubic metre)	80:20
F. WORKS IN COASTAL AREAS				
19.	Fish Drying Yards	10m*10m, 15 cm thick plain cement concrete, brick protection work 20 cm thickness	₹75,000	15:85
20.	Belt Vegetation	Plant	₹20	80:20
21.	Storm Water Drains	100 m long storm water drain	₹2.3 lakhs	15:85
G. RURAL DRINKING WATER RELATED WORKS				
22.	Soak Pits	NRDWP specifications	₹2,000	50:50
23.	Recharge Pits	NRDWP specifications	₹5,000	50:50

(Contd.)

(Table 17.3 Contd.)

No	Work	Standard Dimensions	Unit Cost	Wage: Material Cost Ratio
H. RURAL SANITATION RELATED WORKS				
24.	Household Toilets	TSC specifications	₹4,500	60:40
25.	School Toilets	TSC specifications	₹35,000	25:75
26.	Anganwadi Toilets	TSC specifications	₹8,000	25:75
27.	Solid Liquid Waste Management	TSC specifications for 1000 people	₹5 lakhs	35:65
I. FLOOD RELATED WORKS				
28.	Deepening and Repair of Flood Channels		main channels: ₹180/metre	100:0
			field channels: ₹30/metre	100:0
29.	Chaur Renovation		₹4,76,000 per hectare	100:0
J. IRRIGATION COMMAND RELATED WORKS				
30	Rehabilitation of Minors, Sub-Minors and Field Channels		₹3,000 per hectare	60:40

Source: Mihir Shah Committee (2012): MGNREGA Operational Guidelines, MoRD, GoI.

- 60:40 ratio for labour:material costs should be maintained at the GP level
- No contractors/labour-displacing machinery to be used

Strengthening the Demand-driven Character of MGNREGA

17.20. The single most important distinguishing feature of MGNREGA from employment programmes of the past is that provision of work is triggered by the demand for work by wage-seekers and provided as their legal right. All previous employment programmes provided work when governments decided to provide work, not when people demanded work. MGNREGA is to change that. The old practice of *jab kaam khulega, tab kaam milega* has to be changed to *jab kaam maangege, tab kaam khulega*. This requires that we pay very close attention to generating awareness among potential wage-seekers and set up systems that facilitate and rigorously record registration for work, issuance of job cards and application for work.

17.21. The major weakness so far has been that States have not set up effective systems of recording demand. The new MGNREGA Guidelines in operation from the Twelfth Plan (Box 17.1) take major steps to overcome this weakness.

Labour Budget

17.22. A unique feature of Mahatma Gandhi NREGA is its demand-driven character. But before we begin to record demand we need to make a prior assessment of the quantum of work likely to be demanded as also ascertain the timing of this demand. Concomitantly, we need to prepare a shelf of projects that would allow us to meet this demand. This matching of demand and supply of work is the process of planning under MGNREGA and this is to be achieved through the preparation of a Labour Budget, which has two sides—one, assessment of quantum and timing of demand for work and two, preparing a shelf of projects to meet this demand in a timely manner.

17.23. A Labour Budget must, therefore, reflect
1. Anticipated quantum of demand for work
2. Precise timing of the demand for work, and also
3. A plan that outlines the quantum and schedule of work to be provided to those who demand work

17.24. This is the only way work-providers can open work in a manner that is synchronised with the pattern of migration in that area so as to pre-empt distress migration. It must also be incumbent upon work-providers to proactively inform

> **Box 17.1**
> **New Guidelines to Strengthen Demand-driven Character of MGNREGA**
>
> 1. The Gram Panchayat or Programme Officer, as the case may be, shall be bound to accept valid applications and to issue a dated receipt to the applicant.
> 2. Refusal to accept applications and provide dated receipts will be treated as a contravention under Section 25 of MGNREGA.
> 3. The provision for submitting applications for work must be kept available on a continuous basis through multiple channels so designated by Gram Panchayats who may empower ward members, anganwadi workers, school teachers, self-help groups, village-level revenue functionaries, common service centres and Mahatma Gandhi NREGA Labour Groups to receive applications for work and issue dated receipts on their behalf.
> 4. Provision must also be made (wherever feasible) for workers to register applications for work through mobile telephones in addition to the MGNREGA website and this should feed in directly into the MIS. In case of mobile telephones, the system must be made convenient to illiterate workers and may include Interactive Voice Response System (IVRS) and voice-enabled interactions. This option must automatically issue dated receipts.
> 5. State Governments will ensure that the MGNREGA MIS will record the demand for work. It will track (for each GP) the gap between date of application for work and date of opening of work.
> 6. MGNREGA software will automatically generate the pay order for payment of unemployment allowance to such wage seekers whose demand for work is not met within 15 days of demand. Reports prepared on this will have to be part of the essential set of reports to be tracked at the State level.
>
> *Source:* Mihir Shah Committee (2012): MGNREGA Operational Guidelines, MoRD, GoI.

work-demanders well in advance about the schedule of work to be provided so that they do not need to migrate in distress.

17.25. These plans are currently supposed to be presented for approval only at the Gram Sabha on 2nd October each year. This is far too late to prevent distress migration of households because decisions on migration are normally taken in the monsoon season. In the absence of a timely work guarantee, many are likely to migrate after the harvest of the kharif crop. It is important, therefore, for the GP to inform potential workers of available employment and the timing of this employment well in advance of the kharif harvest. With effect from the Twelfth Plan, annual plans will be presented by the Gram Panchayat at a Gram Sabha meeting to be held on the 15 August.

Planning for an Adequate Shelf of Projects

17.26. As demand gets better recorded, there needs to be a corresponding increase in supply of work. This requires strengthening of capacities at the cutting-edge level of implementation. Unfortunately, the main implementing agency under MGNREGA, the Gram Panchayat, is badly lacking in capacities to plan and implement high quality works under MGNREGA. This is also the missing 'F' (functionaries) which could galvanise PRIs, especially Gram Panchayats, as the bedrock of Indian democracy.

17.27. Beginning with the Twelfth Plan, each Block will appoint a full-time Programme Officer for Mahatma Gandhi NREGA. It will not be good enough for BDOs or other block officers to be given 'additional charge' for the programme. It has also been decided that blocks, where either scheduled castes plus scheduled tribes form greater than or equal to 30 per cent of the population or the annual MGNREGA expenditure was more than ₹12 crores in any year since the programme started, will mandatorily have at least three Cluster Facilitation Teams (CFT), each of which will service a Cluster of Gram Panchayats (CGP), being accountable to each GP within their Cluster. Each CGP will cover around 15,000 job cards or an area of about 15,000 ha, broadly corresponding to the boundaries of a milli-watershed and local aquifer. The CFT will comprise a fully dedicated, three-member professional support team for MGNREGA. The CFT will be a multidisciplinary team led by an Assistant Programme Officer (APO) and will comprise specialists in earthen engineering, community mobilisation, hydrogeology, agriculture/allied livelihoods. This will enable more professional planning based on the watershed approach aimed at improved land and water productivity.

Reducing Delays in Wage Payments

17.28. Delays in wage payments have emerged as one of the main weaknesses of MGNREGA over the last six years. According to section 3(3) MGNREGA, 'It is essential to ensure that wages are paid on time. Workers are entitled to being paid on a weekly basis, and in any case within a fortnight of the date on which work was done.' Thus, MGNREGA 2.0 specifies a payments schedule that will need to be followed and tracked using a transactions-based MIS.

17.29. States must effectively track delays in payment so that effective remedial action can be expeditiously taken when delays are spotted. For this States must develop a customised MIS that enables better tracking of delays. The best example before us is the transaction-based MIS along the lines implemented in Andhra Pradesh. The tightly integrated, end-to-end computer network in Andhra Pradesh identifies delay in execution of any work registered online and takes corrective action immediately. The measurement sheets and muster rolls of the week's work are compiled on the sixth day of that week and transmitted to the Mandal (sub-block) computer centre. The next day, the muster data is fed into the computer and on the eighth day pay orders generated and cheques prepared. By the tenth day, cheques are deposited into post office accounts of workers. By the thirteenth day, workers are able to access wages from their accounts (Table 17.4). Free availability of payment information facilitates public scrutiny and transparency.

17.30. Use of such real-time technologies to enable online updation of critical data at each stage of the MGNREGA workflow is now being facilitated by the Centre for each State. States need to urgently identify the connectivity and hardware bottlenecks so that these can be removed. State Governments should undertake business process re-engineering of all activities starting from capturing attendance to the end-point payment of wages in order to improve efficiency of implementation of MGNREGA. States should do away with redundant processes/records which contribute to delay in payments. States should closely monitor all the critical activities: closure of muster roll, capturing measurements, generating pay-order, issuance of cheque and pay-order to paying agency, transfer of cash to sub-agency (Branch Post Office/ Business correspondent) and wage disbursement to workers. Timelines for each activity should be clearly laid out against the concerned

TABLE 17.4
Wage Payment Cycle under MGNREGA

Activity	Day 1	Day 2	Day 3	Day 4	Day 5	Day 6	Day 7	Day 8	Day 9	Day 10	Day 11	Day 12	Day 13	Day 14	Day 15
Executing works	■	■	■	■	■	■									
Making and Checking Measurement						■	■								
Data Entry at Computer Centre							■	■							
Pay Order generation and Preparation of Cheques								■	■						
Handing Over Cheques to SPO/Banks									■	■					
Conveyance of Cash to Paying Agency at GP Level										■	■				
Disbursement of Wages by Paying Agency												■	■	■	■

TABLE 17.5
Accountability Matrix for Delays in Wage Payments under MGNREGA

Reasons for Delay in Wages	Enter the Designation of Personnel/Officer Responsible for Delay in Wage Payments and Number of Days of Delay					
	Centre	State	District	Block	GP	Paying Agency
Delay in making available the MGNREGA funds						
Delay in closing of muster rolls						
Delay in measurement						
Delay in data-entry, generation of pay order						
Delay in issuing cheque for wage-payments						
Delay in transfer of cash to sub-agency						
Delay in end-point wage disbursement						

MGNREGA staff/agency responsible for meeting the timelines. Non-adherence to stipulated timelines should be penalised and the states should levy penalties on MGNREGA staff or agency responsible for any delay in wage payments. An accountability matrix (Table 17.5) will be used to track the inefficiencies in delay in wage payments and disciplinary/punitive actions shall be initiated accordingly.

17.31. An important cause for delay of wage payments is also non-availability of sufficient funds at district/block/GP level. In some districts/blocks/GPs there is shortage of MGNREGA funds, while in others there is a surplus. Once the MGNREGA fund is allotted to a district/block/GP, it is very difficult to perform transfers of the fund across district/block/GP. Fund allocation hence becomes an arduous task in implementation of MGNREGA. To tackle this problem, MGNREGA 2.0 proposes an integrated fund management system called e-FMS (Electronic Fund Management System) which ensures that the MGNREGA fund is not excess or deficient at any level. Under e-FMS, the MGNREGA fund is a centrally pooled fund managed at state level. The users, that is, GP at village level or Programme Officer at Block level or DPC at district level, all across the State, are the users of this centralised fund and will have access to this pooled fund (with certain restrictions). The users can now undertake only electronic transactions through the centralised fund, for the purpose of wage/material/administrative payments as per the actuals (with certain ceilings). All electronic transfers are realised in a span of 24 hours. Based on this principle of centralised fund and decentralised utility, the e-FMS ensures timely availability of funds at all levels and transparent usage of MGNREGA funds. This improves efficiency of the programme on the whole and also has a multiplier effect on timely delivery of wage payments.

Strengthening Banks and Post Offices

17.32. Another inadvertent source of delays has been the decision by Government for MGNREGA payments to be made through banks and post offices. While this has led to a palpable reduction in leakages, the lack of sufficient density of banks/POs and lack of adequate personnel manning them, has emerged as a major bottleneck, especially in remote, tribal areas, contributing to delays in wage payments. The Business Correspondent (BC) model is one way to overcome these problems. In order to strengthen the viability of the BC model, the Ministry of Rural Development (MoRD) has written to all States asking them to appoint BCs through a transparent process of selection with ₹80 per active account per year to be absorbed under the 6 per cent administrative expenditure head of MGNREGA. This is an interim measure that will help BCs overcome teething problems before they mature to self-sustaining viability as their business expands. A major point of delay has been the crediting of workers' bank accounts as this involves physical movement of cheques and wage lists from the GP to the bank after which banks are required to feed in details of the bank accounts of wage earners once again. To make this transaction seamless, MoRD has worked with five banks in four States (Orissa, Gujarat, Rajasthan and Karnataka) to successfully develop electronic transfer of data files to banks. This solution is now being taken up in other States also and should be in place by the second year of the Twelfth Plan in all States. This will reduce the time taken in crediting accounts of workers.

17.33. A similar solution is being developed for transmitting data to Head Post Offices (HPOs) which will cut down the time required for documents to travel from Branch Post Offices (BPOs) to HPOs via Sub-Post Offices. This is being already tried out in Rajasthan. A major problem faced by BPOs is that their cash and line limit is very low. States need to raise the cash and line limit for their BPOs so that they are not strapped for funds while making payments to MGNREGA workers. A provision is being made that, in consultation with the Chief Post Master General for the circle, an amount equal to one month's wages will be mandatorily required to be kept with the HPO to avoid delays on account of clearance of cheques and so on.

Better Social Audits, Vigilance and Grievance Redressal

17.34. Given the large number of complaints of corruption, MGNREGA 2.0 pays great attention to strengthening both preventive and ameliorative measures to address the issue. Whereas in Andhra Pradesh, social audits have been institutionalised by State Governments, they have worked very well. They have proved a great check on corruption and large recoveries have also been made. Under MGNREGA 2.0, the MoRD has notified Social Audit Rules that mandate the establishment of a Social Audit Unit (SAU) to facilitate conduct of social audit by Gram Sabhas. This Social Audit Unit can be either a Society or a Directorate, in each case independent of the implementing departments/agencies. The Social Audit Unit shall be responsible for building capacities of Gram Sabhas for conducting social audit by identifying, training and deploying suitable resource persons at village, block, district and State-level drawing from primary stakeholders and other civil society organisations having knowledge and experience of working for the rights of the people. The SAU will create awareness amongst the labourers about their rights and entitlements under the Act and facilitate verification of records with primary stakeholders and work sites. All States have agreed that they will immediately initiate this process and social audit will first be completed in all Gram Panchayats in one selected block in every State.

17.35. States are now required to upload photographs of works at different stages of execution through the Ministry's software NREGASoft. A pilot has been launched in the Ramgarh district in Jharkhand for use of the Aadhaar number for biometric based authentication of payments to MGNREGA workers. The Aadhaar number along with the job card number will be now part of the MIS to help eliminate non-genuine and duplicate job cards.

17.36. Complementing social audit will be audit by the Comptroller and Auditor General (CAG). All expenditure on all schemes of the Ministries of Rural Development and Drinking Water Supply and Sanitation have now been opened up to audit by the C&AG both at the Centre and in the States. This will be irrespective of the implementing agency and will include not only financial audit and compliance audit but also performance audits with regard to these schemes. To begin with performance audits of MGNREGA will be taken up in 12 States—Assam, Andhra Pradesh, Bihar, Chhattisgarh, West Bengal, Jharkhand, Madhya Pradesh, Rajasthan, Gujarat, Maharashtra, Orissa and Uttar Pradesh.

17.37. All States will also make an arrangement for a three-tier vigilance mechanism to proactively detect irregularities in the implementation of the Act and to follow up detected irregularities and malfeasance, including those identified during social audit, and ensure that the guilty are punished and recoveries of misspent funds duly made. At the State level there will be a Vigilance Cell consisting of a Chief Vigilance Officer who could be either a senior Government officer or a retired officer supported by at least two senior officials (serving or retired), one engineer and an auditor.

17.38. Elaborate steps to institute transparency, proactive disclosure and grievance redressal have also been put into place under MGNREGA 2.0. It has also been decided that the following will be considered offences punishable under Section 25 of the Act:

- Job cards found in the possession of any Panchayat or MGNREGA functionary
- Missing entries or delay in entries in the Job Card
- Refusal to accept applications and provide dated receipts
- Unreasonable delays in measurement of works
- Unreasonable delays in payment of wages
- Failure to dispose of complaints within seven days

17.39. Limitations have also been imposed on administrative expenses, which form a maximum of 6 per cent of expenses under MGNREGA. At least two-thirds of the expenses admissible under this head will be spent at the block level and below. The following items shall under no condition be booked under the administrative costs of MGNREGA:

- New vehicles
- New buildings
- Air-conditioners
- Salaries/remuneration/honoraria of functionaries who are not exclusively or wholly dedicated to MGNREGA work

NATIONAL RURAL LIVELIHOODS MISSION (NRLM-AAJEEVIKA)

17.40. Even as a reformed MGNREGA 2.0 gets underway, during the Twelfth Plan it is the NRLM that will emerge as the centrepiece of India's battle against rural poverty. NRLM has been designed to overcome the limitations of SGSY (Box 17.2). The foundation of water infrastructure and agrarian stability provided by MGNREGA will be harnessed to generate sustainable livelihoods for the poor through the NRLM, which will work simultaneously on five critical dimensions of rural livelihoods and human development:

- Strengthening the package of credit-cum-technology support to strengthen rural livelihoods
- Empowering institutions of the poor that will fundamentally alter the balance of power in rural India
- Facilitating the poor to compete on more equal terms in the market so that they can derive real benefits from the new opportunities opening up in rural India (rather than being at their receiving end)
- Improving the quality of human development programmes such as drinking water, sanitation and housing by making higher private investments possible through a credit component being added to the subsidies being currently provided
- Imparting the much needed skills to the rural population to meet the demands of both the growing rural and urban economies and ensuring placement of skilled workers in appropriate jobs

NRLM: New Directions

17.41. Phased Implementation: The SGSY experience is yet another instance of the 'universalisation without quality' syndrome that has plagued many rural development initiatives in the recent past. The NRLM has been designed to be implemented in a phased manner (Table 17.6) specifically keeping this experience in mind to ensure quality of outcomes and to avoid spreading resources too thin, too quickly.

17.42. In each phase, select districts and blocks will be identified by each state for intensive implementation of NRLM activities. The 'intensive blocks' that are taken up for NRLM implementation would be provided a full complement of trained professional staff to undertake a whole range of activities under the key components of the Mission:

- Building institutions of the poor
- Promotion of financial inclusion
- Diversification and strengthening of the livelihoods of the poor
- Promotion of convergence and partnerships between institutions of the poor and the government and non-government agencies
- Promotion of skills and placement support
- Support for livelihoods and social innovations

> **Box 17.2**
> **Limitations of SGSY**
>
> The SGSY was launched in 1999 by restructuring the Integrated Rural Development Program (IRDP). The cornerstone of the SGSY strategy was that the poor need to be organised and their capacities built up systematically so that they can access self-employment opportunities. In the 10 years of implementing SGSY, there is a widespread acceptance in the country of the need for poor to be organised into SHGs and SHG federations as a prerequisite for their poverty reduction.
>
> A major problem identified by the Radhakrishna Committee on Credit Related Issues under SGSY (2009) is that most of the SHGs remain crowded in low productivity, primary sector activities. The success of the programme depended on raising their abilities to diversify into other high productive activities. Even in the better performing state of Andhra Pradesh, the income gain to a swarozgari from enterprise activities under SGSY was a mere ₹1,228 per month. The small income gain was due to low productive, traditional activities in which they were engaged and due to low absorption of technology.
>
> The Committee argued that nearly two thirds of the total funds were given out as subsidy, thus making the whole programme subsidy-driven. The subsidy disbursed under SGSY was ₹12,900 crore, while credit mobilised was ₹27,800 crore, that is a credit-subsidy ratio of only 2.15:1, much below the target ratio of 3:1. This was partly due to the failure to strengthen the demand side by improving the capacity of the poor to absorb credit for income generating activities. But it was also due to supply side failures. Financial services did not have the systems and procedures suited to the poor.
>
> Only 6 per cent of the total SGSY funds were utilised for training and capacity building during the past decade. Ill-trained groups under SGSY were a severe handicap in moving towards the Eleventh Plan goal of inclusive growth. Training is of vital importance in the management aspects of running both SHGs and their federations, as well as in improving existing livelihood options and also adopting new ones. It is very important to recognise as argued by the Radhakrishna Committee 'that prior to SHG-Bank Linkage, substantial preparatory work needs to be done for bringing the poor together through a process of social mobilisation, formation of sustainable SHGs and training them to pool their individual savings into a common pool for lending it among the needy. It also includes equipping them with skills to manage corpus fund created with their own savings, interest earned from lending and revolving fund contributed by the government'.
>
> Another defining feature of SGSY was the very uneven distribution of SHGs across regions, with the southern states, which account for 11 per cent of the rural poor having 33 per cent of the SHGs, while the northern and north-eastern States, which account for more than 60 per cent of the rural poor having only about 39 per cent SHGs.
>
> It was in the backdrop of these limitations of the SGSY that the Government of India approved restructuring of SGSY as the National Rural Livelihoods Mission (NRLM) and launched the same in June 2011.

17.43. The rationale behind adopting a phased, intensive approach is as follows:

- Building sustainable institutions of the poor, promotion of financial literacy and inclusion through bank linkage and provision of livelihood support services, skill development and placement, involves intensive social mobilisation effort and capacity building.
- All these activities also require a good deal of professional support. While the NRLM envisages hiring of services of competent professionals, most of the States do not have the required capacity, which can only be built in a phased manner.
- In the long run, institutions of the poor can be sustained only if leaders from the poor communities are identified, trained and prepared for undertaking larger leadership roles. The process of building local community leaders and resource persons is by its very nature time-consuming.
- Promotion of livelihoods of the rural poor does not afford a simple linear solution which all States and districts can equally adopt. What works in one state/district may not work equally effectively in another. It is only from learning by doing and innovating that appropriate solutions can emerge, as amply demonstrated by the successful phased expansion adopted in the states of Andhra Pradesh, Kerala and Tamil Nadu.
- The phased expansion approach will also facilitate early piloting of key strategies in certain 'resource blocks' which can then provide the 'proof of concept' required on the ground for others to adopt and replicate.

TABLE 17.6
Phasing of the National Rural Livelihoods Mission

	2012–13	2013–14	2014–15	2015–16	2016–17	Total Twelfth Plan	Total 13th Plan	Total
Intensive Districts	150	0	150	0	300	600	0	600
Cumulative Intensive Districts	150	150	300	300	600	600	600	600
Intensive Blocks	600	0	1,500	0	2,100	4,200	1,800	6,000
Cumulative Intensive Blocks	600	600	2100	2,100	4,200	4,200	6,000	6,000
Households Covered in Lakh	45	23	60	75	128	330	570	900
Cumulative Households Covered in Lakh	45	68	128	203	330	330	900	900
SHGs in '000	360	180	480	600	1,020	2,640	4,560	7,200
Cumulative SHGs in '000	360	540	1,020	1,620	2,640	2,640	7,200	7,200
Youth Skilled for and Placed in Jobs in Lakh	5	10	25	30	30	100	150	250
Cumulative Youth Skilled for and Placed in Jobs in Lakh	5	15	40	70	100	100	250	250
Self-employed in Lakh	2	4	6	8	10	30	60	90
Cumulative Self-employed in Lakh	2	6	12	20	30	30	90	90

Note: The figures for 2012–13 include figures of already existing SHGs.

- The community-based institutions also require certain amount of time to internalise new learning, practices and innovative experiments, before expanding and scaling up.
- Simultaneous implementation of the intensive strategy in all blocks and districts would imply a thin distribution of available resources leading to sub-optimal and non-sustainable outcomes. The phased approach will enable States to apply scarce resources to their priority districts and blocks, where strong civil society support may also be available.

Block Level Professional Support

17.44. The lack of quality in SGSY outcomes had a great deal to do with absence of high quality professional support at the block and sub-block level for undertaking intensive social mobilisation, institution building, capacity building, financial inclusion and promotion of multiple livelihoods of the poor. Under NRLM a special provision will be made for this and the professional support costs incurred at the block/sub-block levels will be treated as costs of institution and capacity building and not as administrative costs. In the phased approach adopted under NRLM, the block-level professionals will move from one block to another after promoting and nurturing community institutions of the poor for a certain period. Gradually, the trained community resource persons (CRPs) would take over the responsibility of the institutions from the professional staff, whose costs would be progressively absorbed by the institutions as they grow financially stronger. The professional support costs of NRLM will progressively diminish with the increase in the use of CRPs.

Skill Development and Placement in Jobs

17.45. A major focus of the NRLM is skilling rural poor youth. This is both for self-employment in microenterprises and job placement given emerging widespread employment opportunities at the entry level in high growth sectors like textiles, construction, hospitality, retail, security, automobile, health, services and so on. The services provided by NRLM in the 'jobs' sub-component will include:

- Mapping the demand for jobs;
- Skill development/training;

- Counselling youth by matching their aspirations and existing skill set with demand;
- Placement and post-placement support.

17.46. NRLM will aim at supporting 1 crore youth in the Twelfth Plan in this manner. The focus will be on youth from IAP districts, J&K, North Eastern States, districts/blocks with high SC population and minority concentrated districts. The initiative will also aim at enrolling as many girls as possible.

17.47. The self-employment and microenterprises sub-component would pursue multiple streams:

- Micro-entrepreneurs and enterprises directly nurtured by Rural Development and Self-Employment Training Institutes (RUDSETIs)
- Micro-entrepreneurs through apprenticeship and nurturing by practicing micro-entrepreneurs (as under Kudumbasree in Kerala)
- Working with other training partners, including CBOs, CSOs and so on

17.48. These models envisage transforming unemployed youth into confident self-employed entrepreneurs through a short duration experiential learning program followed by systematic long duration hand holding support/ apprenticeship. In the Twelfth Plan it is proposed to nurture 30 lakh entrepreneurs from among the poor to set up micro-enterprises.

RURAL DRINKING WATER AND SANITATION

Review of National Rural Drinking Water Programme (NRDWP)

17.49. As against the target of 7,98,967 habitations for coverage under NRDWP during the Eleventh Plan, the coverage up to 31 March 2012 was 6,65,034 (83 per cent). States of Jharkhand, Chhattisgarh, Nagaland, Madhya Pradesh, Odisha, Himachal Pradesh and Tamil Nadu have exceeded their targets, whereas Sikkim, Punjab, Assam, Arunachal Pradesh and Jammu & Kashmir have reported low (less than 50 per cent) achievement against targets. As against the planned Central outlay of ₹39,300 crore in the Eleventh Plan the anticipated expenditure is ₹39,211 crore. In addition, the States are expected to spend ₹49,000 crore. The investments in rural drinking water (1951–2012) are given in Table 17.7.

TABLE 17.7
Investments in Rural Drinking Water, 1951–2012

Plan Period	Investment made (₹crore)	
	Centre	State
First (1951–56)	0	3
Second (1956–61)	0	30
Third (1961–66)	0	48
Fourth (1969–74)	34	208
Fifth (1974–79)	157	348
Sixth (1980–85)	895	1,530
Seventh (1985–90)	1,906	2,471
Eighth (1992–97)	4,140	5,084
Ninth (1997–2002)	8,455	10,773
Tenth (2002–07)	16,254	15,102
Eleventh (2007–12)	39,211	49,000

17.50. The difficulty has been that even as coverage becomes universal, there is a growing problem of 'slipback', with habitations suffering a fall in the water table and water quality, especially given the growing dependence on groundwater. Water quality has emerged as a growing concern, chemically due to geogenic leaching (arsenic and fluoride) and biologically due to bacteriological contamination. The fact that the same aquifer is being tapped for both irrigation and drinking water, without any coordinated management of the resource, has greatly aggravated availability of drinking water. Lack of convergence with sanitation, on the other hand, compromises water quality, even as it makes provision of improved sanitation difficult.

17.51. Poor operation and maintenance has resulted in high rates of attrition and dilapidated facilities. This has happened mainly because primary stakeholders do not feel a sense of ownership over the facility created and in the absence of sufficient support structures and professional capacities, upkeep suffers. On the other hand, where people have been centrally involved, they have both paid for the service provided and felt a stake in maintaining the assets, garnering adequate support for the same through the revenues generated. There are also disturbing reports about social exclusion, with SCs, STs and minorities being discriminated against. Keeping this in mind, from 2011–12, earmarking of funds for expenditure under the SCSP (22 per cent) and the TSP (10 per cent) has been made mandatory under NRDWP. Appropriate use of IMIS and GIS maps in the planning process is being promoted to prevent social exclusion. Provision of drinking water in minority concentrated districts is one of the activities monitored under the Prime Minister's New 15 Point Programme. Implementation of rural water supply schemes is being closely monitored in the 90 minority concentrated districts.

NRDWP in the Twelfth Plan

17.52. Based on this analysis of what is going wrong with NRDWP and drawing upon some successes, the Twelfth Plan envisages a major change in the way NRDWP projects are to be run:

- While the ultimate goal is to provide households with safe piped drinking water supply at the rate of 70 lpcd, considering that 40 lpcd has been the norm over the last 40 years and there is still a large population uncovered with this level, as an interim measure the goal has been kept at 55 lpcd for the Twelfth Plan.
- By 2017, it is targeted that at least 50 per cent of rural population in the country (as against 35 per cent today) will have access to 40 lpcd piped water supply within their household premises or within 100 metres radius (and within 10 metres elevation in hilly areas) from their households without barriers of social or financial discrimination. Individual States can adopt higher quantity norms.
- By 2017, it is targeted that at least 35 per cent of rural population have individual household connections (as against 13 per cent today).
- Convergence between drinking water supply and sanitation will be strengthened taking up villages covered with piped water supply to get open defecation free (ODF) status on priority and vice versa.
- A part of NRDWP outlay will be set apart for integrated Habitat Improvement Projects to provide housing, water and sanitation facilities in rural areas at par with urban areas.
- Participation of the beneficiaries, especially women, in water supply schemes will be ensured right from the conceptualisation and planning stage, spanning construction and post-scheme completion management stages. Capacity building of members of the Village Water and Sanitation Committees is of critical importance here.
- The subsidiarity principle will be followed and decisions made at the lowest level possible especially on issues like location, implementation, sustainability, O&M and management of water supply schemes, while retaining an umbrella role for the Gram Panchayats for effective implementation.
- The Ministry of Drinking Water and Sanitation has devised a Management Devolution Index (MDI) to track and incentivise more substantive devolution of functions, funds and functionaries to the Gram Panchayats. While allocating resources across States, 10 per cent weight is given to the population of GPs to whom drinking water supply schemes have been devolved weighted by the MDI for the State.
- The weakest aspect of rural water supply is Operation and Maintenance. Allocation for O&M has been increased from 10 per cent of NRDWP allocation at present to 15 per cent in the Twelfth Plan.
- All new drinking water supply schemes will be designed, estimated and implemented to take into account life cycle costs and not just per capita capital costs.
- All Government schools and anganwadis (in Government or community buildings) will be provided with water supply for drinking and for toilets as per relevant quantity norms by convergence of NRDWP for existing schools and SSA for new schools set up under SSA. For private schools, supply of water will be ensured by enforcement of the provisions of the Right to Education Act by the Education Department.
- All community toilets built with public funds and maintained for public use will be provided with running water supply under NRDWP.
- Solar powered pumps will be provided for implementation in remote, small habitations and those with irregular power supply, especially in IAP

districts, by converging subsidy available under Ministry of New and Renewable Energy.
- Waste water treatment and recycling will be an integral part of every water supply plan or project. Management of liquid and solid waste will be promoted together with recycling and reuse of grey water for agriculture and groundwater recharge and pollution control. This will be done on priority in NGP villages.
- A holistic aquifer and surface water management approach with active community and PRI participation will converge in a District Water Vision that includes monitoring and recording of groundwater levels and rainfall at sub-block level and Aquifer Management Plans to protect and recharge drinking water sources.
- Care will be taken to ensure that minimum distance is maintained between the toilet systems and water sources, to alleviate the problem of nitrate contamination.
- Mining activity should only be carried out at a safe distance from major drinking water sources to protect the quality and sustainability of the source.
- A progressive tariff with different pricing tiers for different uses and different classes of consumers can be considered at various administrative levels, that is, the Gram Panchayat, district and State as appropriate. Incentives may be provided to the GPs for collecting user charges from the beneficiaries. A minimum collection of 50 per cent of O&M cost (including electricity charges) through user charges will be the target.
- Given the growing importance of water quality issues, dedicated funding will be provided to States with quality affected habitations, over and above the normal NRDWP allocation to the State. Within this dedicated funding highest priority will be given to arsenic and fluoride affected habitations. Part of the funding would also be made available to tackle bacteriological contamination in the priority districts with high incidence of JE/AES cases as identified by the Ministry of Health and Family Welfare.

REVIEW OF TOTAL SANITATION CAMPAIGN (TSC)

17.53. The TSC was launched in 1999 as a demand-driven, community-led programme with major IEC inputs to make sanitation a felt need of the people. The TSC has been able to accelerate sanitation coverage from 22 per cent as per the 2001 Census to 31 per cent in 2011, with over 28,000 PRIs becoming 'Open Defecation Free' (ODF). TSC received a major boost during the later half of the decade, with the introduction of the Nirmal Gram Puraskar (NGP) in 2005, an innovative incentive scheme for Gram Panchayats, blocks and districts, that have attained 100 per cent sanitation coverage.

17.54. However, progress remains far from satisfactory. Open defecation by around 600 million people is our biggest national shame. Since drinking water and sanitation continue to be treated in separate silos, both the quality of drinking water and that of sanitation gets compromised. Latest Census data reveals that the percentage of households having access to television and telephones in rural India in 2011 exceeds the percentage of households having access to toilet facilities and tap water (Figure 17.1).

17.55. Access to household amenities in ten worst performing States in terms of toilet facilities in rural India in the year 2011 (percentage of rural households) is given in Table 17.8.

17.56. The households by type of latrine facility in rural India as per Census 2001 and Census 2011 are given in Figures 17.2 and 17.3, respectively. The percentage of households with no latrine facilities in rural India in 2011; physical progress and financial progress during the Eleventh Plan of Total Sanitation Campaign are given in Table 17.9, Table 17.10 and Table 17.11, respectively.

17.57. Several independent assessments signal the need for a radical change in approach. The WHO/UNICEF Joint Monitoring Programme (JMP) for Water Supply and Sanitation estimates that in 2008 around 638 million people in India still defecated in the open and the reported usage of sanitation facilities at 30.7 per cent against the TSC sanitation coverage figure of 57 per cent for the same year. The JMP also revealed that 58 per cent of the world's population defecating in the open in 2008 was in India. A recent impact study by the World Bank's Water

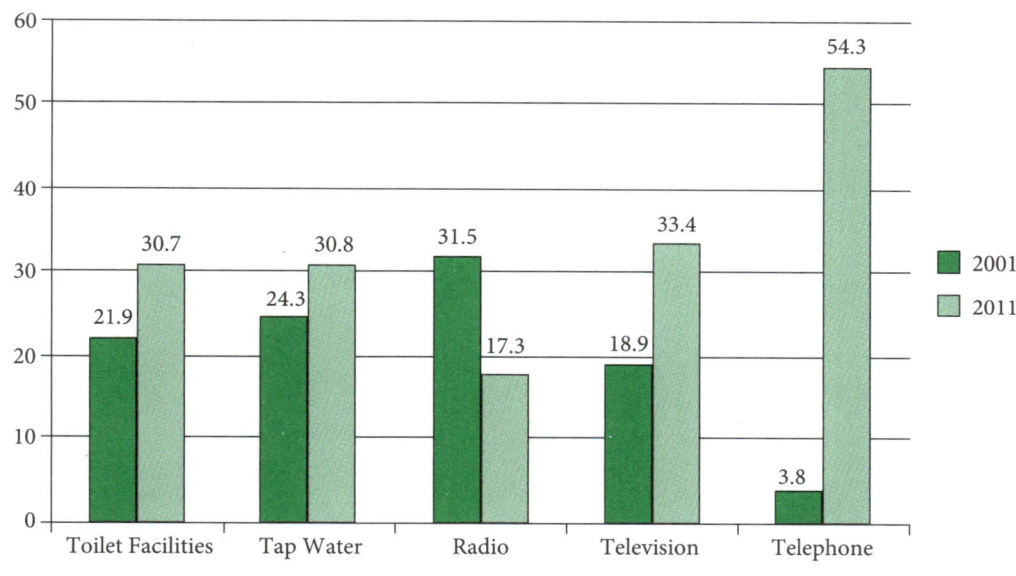

Source: Census of India, 2001 and 2011.

FIGURE 17.1: Access to Household Amenities in Rural India (2001 to 2011)

TABLE 17.8
Access to Household Amenities in Worst Performing States in Terms of Toilet Facilities in Rural India, 2011
(Percentage of Rural Households)

Rank (worst as 1)	State	Toilet Facilities	Tap Water	Radio	Television	Telephone
1	Jharkhand	7.6	3.7	17.3	13.7	38.7
2	Madhya Pradesh	13.1	9.9	13	18.6	36.4
3	Odisha	14.1	7.5	10.6	19.4	33.6
4	Chhattisgarh	14.5	8.8	9.5	21.1	21.2
5	Bihar	17.6	2.6	25.8	10.2	53.5
6	Rajasthan	19.6	26.9	13.9	25.6	66.2
7	Uttar Pradesh	21.8	20.2	25	23.5	63.6
8	Tamil Nadu	23.2	79.3	18.7	85.3	66.3
9	Karnataka	28.4	56.4	17.6	46.3	62.6
10	Andhra Pradesh	32.2	63.4	6.1	49.3	54.8

Source: Census of India, 2011.

and Sanitation Programme in five States reveals that only 67 per cent of the toilets even in NGP villages were being used, while this percentage fell to just 46 per cent in non-NGP villages. A study, supported by UNICEF in 2008 revealed that in 56 per cent of NGP Gram Panchayats 70 per cent families were still defecating in the open and only 6 of the 162 NGPs had been able to sustain the NGP status. In a study for the Ministry of Drinking Water and Sanitation, the Centre for Media Studies (2010) found that the key factors explaining the gap between access to and usage of sanitation facilities were poor quality of construction and unfinished toilets, a major reason for which was the very low incentive provided under the TSC.

17.58. The Twelfth Plan Working Group is of the clear view that the APL–BPL distinction and the very low incentive under the TSC have played havoc with the programme. Many slip-backs in the NGP villages have been attributed to non-availability of water, clearly indicating need to synergise the drinking

TABLE 17.9
Percentage of Households with No Latrine Facilities in Rural India, 2011

State	2011	2001
Jharkhand	92.4	93.4
Madhya Pradesh	86.9	91.1
Odisha	85.9	92.3
Chhattisgarh	85.5	94.8
Bihar	82.4	86.1
Rajasthan	80.4	85.4
UP	78.2	80.8
Tamil Nadu	76.8	85.6
D&N Haveli	73.5	82.7
Karnataka	71.6	82.6
Andhra Pradesh	67.8	81.9
Gujarat	67	78.3
Maharashtra	62	81.8
J&K	61.4	58.2
Puducherry	61	78.6
West Bengal	53.3	73.1
Daman & Diu	48.6	68
Arunachal Pradesh	47.3	52.7
Meghalaya	46.2	59.9
Uttarakhand	45.9	68.4
Haryana	43.9	71.3
Assam	40.5	40.4
A&N Islands	39.8	57.7
HP	33.4	72.3
Nagaland	30.8	35.4
Punjab	29.6	59.1
Goa	29.1	51.8
NCT of Delhi	23.7	37.1
Tripura	18.5	22.1
Sikkim	15.9	40.6
Mizoram	15.4	20.3
Manipur	14	22.5
Chandigarh	12	31.5
Kerala	6.8	18.7
Lakshadweep	2	6.9
India	69.2	78.1

Source: Census of India, 2011.

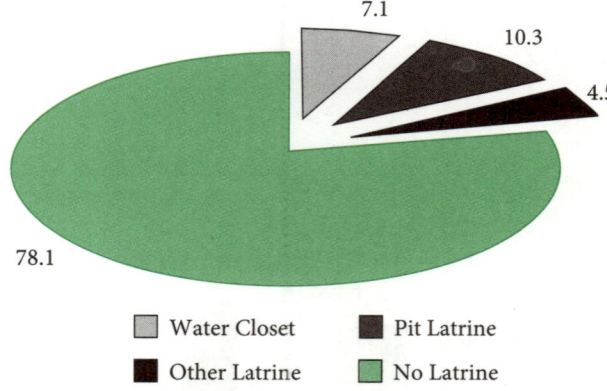

Source: Census of India, 2001.

FIGURE 17.2: Households by Type of Latrine Facility in Rural India in 2001

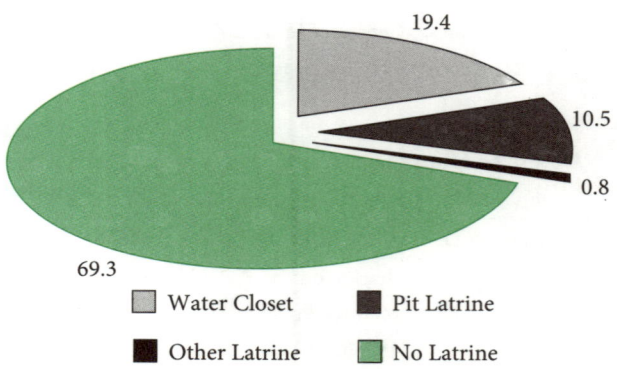

Source: Census of India, 2011.

FIGURE 17.3: Households by Type of Latrine Facility in Rural India in 2011

water and sanitation programmes. One of the limitations of the TSC is the narrow range of technology options offered in a country with such immensely diverse geographic, hydrologic, climatic and socio-economic conditions (high water table, flood prone, rocky ground, desert/water scarce areas and extreme low temperatures). This has led to many problems, including non-acceptance by local communities, water pollution especially in shallow water table regions, and waste of public funds. There is need to broaden the ranges of models permissible under TSC. Finally, the absence of a dedicated implementation agency at either the State/district or GP level, to implement TSC has emerged as a major bottleneck affecting quality of outcomes.

TABLE 17.10
Total Sanitation Campaign, Physical Progress, Eleventh Plan

Financial Year	IHHL BPL	IHHL APL	Total IHHL	School Toilets	Sanitary Complexes	Anganwadi Toilets
2007–2008	57,63,430	57,64,460	1,15,27,890	2,36,259	3,006	86,489
2008–2009	55,70,899	56,94,983	1,12,65,882	2,53,004	3,245	68,995
2009–2010	58,69,608	65,38,170	1,24,07,778	1,44,480	2,230	66,227
2010–2011	61,55,933	60,87,798	1,22,43,731	1,05,509	3,377	50,823
2011–2012	47,34,816	40,64,048	87,98,864	1,22,471	2,547	28,409

TABLE 17.11
Total Sanitation Campaign, Financial Progress, Eleventh Plan

Financial year	Total outlay (₹ in crore)	Total expenditure (₹ in crore)
2007–08	1,060	996
2008–09	1,200	1,193
2009–10	1,200	1,200
2010–11	1,580	1,580
2011–12	1,500	1,500
Total (in crore)	6,540	6,469

Total Sanitation Campaign in the Twelfth Plan

17.59. The Twelfth Plan visualises a major break from the past under TSC:

- The goal of the Twelfth Plan will be that 50 per cent of the Gram Panchayats attain Nirmal Gram status by the year 2017.
- The APL–BPL distinction and the focus on individual toilets are to be replaced by a habitation saturation approach. Rechristened the Nirmal Bharat Abhiyan (NBA), the programme will cover SC, ST, physically handicapped, small and marginal farmers and woman-headed households in each habitation.
- The idea is not to sacrifice quality and sustainability of outcomes in the mad rush to attain targets, even if this means moving somewhat slower in reaching universal coverage.
- Through a convergence with MGNREGA, the unit cost of individual household latrines will rise to ₹10,000 as described in Table 17.12.
- Toilet designs will be fine-tuned in accordance with local social and ecological considerations.
- There will be a specific provision for capacity building at a rate not exceeding 2 per cent of district project outlay.
- In order to focus more centrally on sustainability of outcomes, the programme shall be taken up in a phased manner wherein GPs shall be identified, based on defined criteria of conjoint approach to sanitation and water supply, for achievement of NGP status. This would progressively lead to Nirmal blocks, Nirmal districts and eventually Nirmal States. The pattern of fund release will be tweaked with flexibility to the districts to prioritise funding to GPs identified for Nirmal Grams. Thus, Nirmal Grams with full access and usage of toilets, water availability and systems of

TABLE 17.12
Major Increase in Unit Cost Support for IHHLs during the Twelfth Plan

IHHL	Centre	State	Beneficiary	Total TSC	MGNREGA	Total
Total Cost (₹)	3,200	1,400	900	5,500	4,500	10,000
Labour Cost (₹)				0	2,700	2,700
Material Cost (₹)				5,500	1,800	7,300
Labour: Material Cost				0:100	60:40	27:73

waste disposal and drainage, shall be the outcome of NBA.
- A new strategy will be devised to facilitate convergence between drinking water and sanitation projects. NBA will give priority to coverage of areas with functional piped water supply systems (PWSS), followed by areas with ongoing PWSS that are nearest to completion. Next, new PWSS will be taken up in GPs of districts where IHHL coverage has reached higher milestones of coverage in a descending order. In all such new and ongoing PWSS, NBA should be implemented simultaneously with the planning and execution of PWSS to ensure that behavioural change for usage of toilets is generated. Care will be taken that PWSS are planned and executed covering entire habitations on a saturation basis, so that health and other impacts of safe water and sanitation are clearly discernable.
- Running water availability must also be ensured in all Government school toilets, anganwadi toilets and Community Sanitary Complexes under NRDWP.
- Child-friendly toilets will be developed in anganwadis and schools. This will be accompanied by capacity building of school teachers, ASHA and anganwadi workers and ANMs among others on hygiene and sanitation. Sanitation will be made a part of the school curriculum so that safe sanitation practices are ingrained in the minds of children who would be the torch bearers of sanitation in their households and the community.
- In order to ensure smooth O&M of toilets, a massive training campaign will be launched in convergence with the National Rural Livelihoods Mission in skills such as masonry work, brick-making, toilet pan making and plumbing. 'Nirmiti Kendras' will be set up for development and manufacture of cost-effective construction materials. The existing Production Centres and Rural Sanitary Marts will also be revitalised and appropriate SHGs entrusted with this task.
- Effective hand-holding with adequate IEC must continue for a period of time even after construction to ensure sustainability of outcomes. Comprehensive region-specific communication and information strategy will be deployed for demand generation and sustainability. Office-bearers and members of GPs, VWSCs, BRCs, SHGs, Swachhata doots, women and youth groups, school committees, and so on will be involved in dissemination of information and effective communication. NGOs and CBOs of repute may be engaged for maximum results for individual contact, motivation and implementation. Key Resource Centres must also be identified within State/district for training of State/district level functionaries in IEC.
- NBA will be implemented at the GP level through VWSCs who could receive technical support from NGOs/CBOs identified by the District authorities. The VWSC must be mandatorily made a Standing Committee of the GP to ensure community participation in planning, construction, operation and management with the GP providing overall guidance to the VWSCs. A sense of ownership will be created through owner-driven construction through self labour and hiring of skilled labour.
- Solid and liquid waste management will be taken up in Nirmal Grams on a priority basis for which an assistance of ₹5,00,000 will be additionally available per 1,000 people from the redesigned MGNREGA 2.0.

17.60. Justification for the huge jump in outlays for sanitation and drinking water is provided by recent scholarly work on the relationship between sanitation and health. A recent article in *Lancet*[2] suggests that the impact of sanitation and hygiene interventions on child under-nutrition has been seriously undervalued in the existing research as this effect has been modelled entirely through diarrhoea. The study argues that a key cause of child under-nutrition is a subclinical disorder of the small intestine known as tropical enteropathy. This is caused by faecal bacteria ingested in large quantities by young children living in conditions of poor sanitation and hygiene. The study finds that provision of toilets and promotion of hand-washing after faecal contact could reduce or prevent tropical enteropathy and its adverse effects on growth; and that the primary causal pathway from poor sanitation and hygiene to under-nutrition is tropical enteropathy and not diarrhoea. Though based on field studies conducted in Africa, This study has important policy implications for India. Accelerating provision of toilets and improved drinking water quality will prevent tropical enteropathy, which in turn will yield improvements in child growth, health and survival.

17.61. A study of the TSC completed in July 2012,[3] finds that at mean program intensity, infant mortality decreased by four per thousand and children's height increased by 0.2 standard deviations. Relative to other children born in the same districts or in the same years, rural children exposed to better sanitation in their first year of life were more likely to survive infancy. Districts in which more latrines were constructed over this period saw a greater decline in rural infant mortality rates, controlling for other changes. Rural children born in years and districts with more TSC latrines available in the first year of their lives are taller than children born in other years or districts.

RURAL HOUSING

17.62. Allied to these initiatives on rural livelihoods, are significant steps towards improving basic amenities in rural India, the most important of which is housing. Under the Indira Awaas Yojana (IAY), since 1985, nearly 285 lakh houses have been constructed with an expenditure of about ₹84,234 crore.

IAY during the Eleventh Plan Period

17.63. The summary of the financial and physical progress of IAY during the Eleventh Plan period is given in Tables 17.13 and 17.14.

TABLE 17.13
IAY-Financial Performance during Eleventh Plan (2007–08 to 2011–12)

Year	Total Available Fund* (₹crore)	Utilisation (₹crore)
2007–2008	6,527.17	5,464.54 (83.72)
2008–2009	14,460.35	8,348.34 (57.73)
2009–2010	15,852.35	13,292.46 (83.85)
2010–2011	17,956.54	13,465.73 (74.99)
2011–2012	18,982.69	12,451.12 (65.59)

Notes: (i) *Includes Opening Balance and Centre and State Releases.
(ii) Figures in the parentheses are per cent utilisation to total available fund.

TABLE 17.14
Physical Performance of IAY During Eleventh Plan (2007–08 to 2011–12)

Year	IAY Houses (in lakh)	
	Target	Constructed
2007–2008	21.27	19.92 (93.66)
2008–2009	21.27	21.34 (100.32)
2009–2010	40.52	33.85 (83.55)
2010–2011	29.09	27.15 (93.36)
2011–2012	27.27	22.30 (81.80)

Note: Figures in the parentheses are per cent achievement of total target.

17.64. Over the years, there have been important revisions in the scheme and related institutional processes for making IAY accessible to the poorest in rural India:

1. IAY waitlists have been prepared Gram Panchayat–wise by the States/UTs on the basis of their housing and poverty status as per the BPL list. In order to introduce transparency in the selection of beneficiaries, permanent waitlists are supposed to be displayed in all Gram Panchayats.
2. IAY houses are allotted (in this order of preference) in the name of the woman or jointly between the husband and the wife.
3. Financial assistance provided under IAY was raised twice during the Eleventh Plan, on 1 April 2008 from ₹25,000 in plain areas and ₹27,500 for hilly/difficult areas to ₹35,000 and ₹37,500 respectively and to ₹45,000 in plain areas and ₹48,500 in hilly/difficult areas on 1 April 2010. The higher assistance is also provided to districts under the Integrated Action Plan (IAP) for select backward and tribal districts. IAY beneficiaries are also covered under the Differential Rate of Interest (DRI) scheme for lending up to ₹20,000 per housing unit at 4 per cent interest.
4. Sanitary latrine and smokeless chullah are required to be constructed along with each IAY house. For construction of the sanitary latrine, financial assistance is made available from the Total Sanitation Campaign (TSC) funds in addition to IAY assistance.
5. There is a provision for making available homestead sites to those rural BPL households whose

names are included in the permanent IAY waitlists but do not have a house site. ₹10,000 per homestead site is currently provided, this funding being equally shared by the Centre and the States. States are also incentivised by allocating additional IAY houses equal to the number of homestead sites provided through any of the stipulated means—regularisation of existing occupied land, allotment of government land or purchase/acquisition of land. If the amount per beneficiary falls short, the balance amount is contributed by the State Government. BPL families allotted land through purchase are, to the extent feasible, provided assistance for house construction in the same year.

17.65. Progress on some of these innovative features has been slow. For instance, Table 17.15 shows that the drive towards convergence with other rural infrastructure schemes has not been up to the mark.

17.66. Again, only a few States such as Bihar, Karnataka, Kerala, Rajasthan, Andhra Pradesh, Maharashtra, UP and Sikkim have so far requested for funds for purchase of homestead land under this scheme. Progress is summarised in Table 17.16.

TABLE 17.15
Convergence of IAY with other Rural Infrastructure

S. No.		Convergence (per cent of IAY houses)						
	Period	TSC	Smokeless Chullahs	Bio-Gas Plant	RGGVY	Kitchen Garden	Life Insurance Scheme	Health Insurance Scheme
1	2008–09	5.91	5.17	0.00	0.11	0.29	0.74	0.29
2	2009–10	26.50	22.70	0.12	0.65	0.64	4.21	1.00
3	2010–11	26.85	24.05	0.07	1.10	0.95	6.18	2.07

TABLE 17.16
Scheme for Purchase of Home Site and Incentive for Additional Target under IAY

S. No.	State/UT	2009–10			2010–11		
		Purchase of Homesite		Incentive	Purchase of Homesite		Incentive
		Amount Released (₹ Lakh)	No. of Sites to be Purchased	Additional Houses Sanctioned	Amount Released (₹ Lakh)	No. of Sites to be Purchased	Additional Houses Sanctioned
1	Andhra Pradesh				10,228	2,04,568	
2	Bihar	5,334	1,06,674				
3	Gujarat			33,154			18,342
4	Karnataka	5,400	1,08,000		6,082	1,21,634	31,806
5	Kerala	3,209	64,189				
6	Madhya Pradesh						1,05,200
7	Maharashtra				2,500	50,000	
8	Rajasthan	1,721	34,412				95,702
9	Sikkim	83	1,666				
10	Tripura						15,050
11	Uttar Pradesh				190	3,790	
	Total	15,747	3,14,941	33,154	19,000	3,79,992	2,66,100

Rural Housing through other Sources

17.67. During the Eleventh Plan period, rural housing was also facilitated by assistance from State Governments and financial institutions/banks. This has been through both supplementing IAY grant assistance as well as via State-level schemes for rural housing. For instance, Government of Kerala provides additional resources to enhance the unit cost to ₹75,000 for general category households, ₹1,00,000 for SC households as well physically and mentally handicapped persons and ₹1,25,000 for ST households and destitute families. Government of Andhra Pradesh provides additional ₹20,000 to SC/ST beneficiaries of IAY. Around 15 States/UTs have their own schemes. During the Eleventh Plan, about 30 lakh houses were constructed under various rural housing schemes of State Governments.

17.68. National Housing Bank (NHB), National Bank for Agriculture and Rural Development (NABARD) and Housing and Urban Development Corporation (HUDCO) also provide support for rural housing. The NHB is the apex financial institution for housing in the country. It runs schemes such as the Rural Housing Fund (RHF), Golden Jubilee Rural Housing Refinance Scheme (GJRHFS) and Productive Housing in Rural Areas (PHIRA). NABARD made refinancing for rural housing as an eligible activity in the year 2001–02. Under the Rural Housing Scheme, NABARD extends refinance to banks for provision of loans to individuals/cooperative housing societies. HUDCO has been supporting Housing Boards, Panchayati Raj Institutions (PRIs), Development Authorities and other para-statals by extending loan assistance for weaker sections at 8 per cent to 8.5 per cent against its borrowing rate of 10.25 per cent. Of the total 1.5 crore housing units supported by HUDCO till date, over 89 lakh units (60 per cent) have been constructed in rural areas.

Rural Housing in the Twelfth Plan

Need for Greater Financial Support

17.69. One of the major reasons for continued shelterlessness in rural India is shortage of financial resources. According to the NSSO, about 66 per cent financing of new construction in rural areas in 2010–11 was done by rural families with their own resources; about 27 per cent construction had some amount financed from non-institutional agencies such as moneylenders, family and friends while only 9 per cent of new construction was financed by institutional channels such as Government schemes, banks and so on. A Committee constituted by the Ministry of Rural Development for formulation of Concrete Bankable Schemes for Rural Housing (2011) found that although credit flow to the housing sector witnessed a growth of about 30 per cent over the last five years, lending to rural areas grew only about 10 per cent.

17.70. Quality of housing has also suffered due to inadequate financial support. It is, therefore, proposed to increase the unit assistance for house construction under IAY to ₹65,000 in plain areas and to ₹70,000 in hilly/difficult areas during the Twelfth Plan, with an increase each year to absorb rising cost of material and labour'. Given the overall financial constraint this may lead to a slowing down of achievement of targets but a conscious decision is being taken to ensure that good quality housing becomes possible through an increase in unit cost assistance provided. At the same time, DRI loans for IAY families will be enhanced up to ₹50,000 at 4 per cent rate of interest, along with extended repayment tenure up to 15 years. Provision of DRI loans for IAY beneficiaries will be made obligatory on the part of the banks given the investment that the government commits when sanctioning an IAY house. Approval of DRI loans will be included as an indicator of financial inclusion by the banks. Banks will develop standard processes that are simple and hassle-free to enable easier access to DRI loans by beneficiaries.

Smoother Transfer of Funds

17.71. The process of fund transfer from the Centre to the States is being simplified to facilitate convergence as well as enhance effectiveness and efficiency in the implementation of various rural habitat schemes. Funds will now be released to the States through a fund to be created by the State on the lines of MGNREGA or TSC. Central releases as well as State contribution will be credited to the State

Fund and the States are expected to release funds to DRDAs on the basis of predetermined criteria as defined in the guidelines. It is expected that these modifications in the administration of the scheme would help in reaching out to the targeted population effectively and in a manner that facilitates smooth functioning across departments.

Abolition of the APL–BPL Distinction

17.72. The Socio-economic and Caste Census (SECC) will be complete in time for the Twelfth Plan implementation. This Census will provide lists of households that are homeless as well as those who live in poor quality houses. There will be no reference made to any BPL list. Assistance under IAY will be provided to these households in order of priority to be determined on the basis of the other indicators of deprivation thrown up by the SECC.

Enhancing Access of the Poor to Land

17.73. The unit cost for purchase of homestead plots under IAY will be increased to ₹20,000 on IAY assistance pattern, that is, 75:25 contributions by the Centre and the State, respectively. A dedicated officer at the district level will be designated by the state government to address various bottlenecks faced by the beneficiaries in accessing homestead sites. A cluster approach will be adopted for developing homestead lands for groups of homeless families.

Improving Quality of IAY Houses

17.74. The most important change the Twelfth Plan seeks to bring is an improvement in quality of housing. Raising the financial assistance is certainly a necessary condition for improved quality but it is not sufficient in itself. IAY guidelines recommend that State Government and implementing agencies should facilitate access to information on innovative technologies, materials, designs and methods, but most States do not have any mechanism to do so. There is a clear need for developing and popularising appropriate technology through a network of institutions, which could result in low-cost, environment-friendly and disaster-resistant houses as per local cultural preferences. Developing a menu of specific designs and technology options for each region reflecting variations in environmental and cultural conditions would be the way to go forward.

Rural Building Centres (RBCs)

17.75. RBCs at the district level could play an important role as a single window solution for guidance on quality construction, supply of alternative materials, skill building of artisans and development and dissemination of innovative, location-appropriate technologies that minimise the use of high-energy construction materials. They could also carry out special skill upgradation programmes intended to impart both skills and organisational abilities, effective monitoring of housing construction, knowledge building and awareness creation on quality and safety features

17.76. The RBCs would provide a platform for developing comprehensive knowledge and experience of application of common alternative technologies for various geo-climatic zones of India needs to be developed. A network of RBCs would serve to link research institutions with rural habitat practitioners for dissemination of technical know-how. It would also facilitate further development of knowledge on alternate materials and technologies for different geo-climatic zones.

17.77. Proven alternative technologies that are cost-effective and environment-friendly need to be included in the State Schedule of Rates. Towards this end, partnerships need to be forged by the States with specialised research and development institutions, academic institutions and NGOs that have worked on alternate technologies. For instance, the National Mission on Bamboo Applications can provide advice on treatment, use and costing of bamboo based building elements for use in areas that have bamboo in abundance and have used the material traditionally due to its appropriateness in the specific geo-climatic context.

Emphasis on Disaster Risk Reduction

17.78. Along with concerted efforts to demystify and enable access to technical knowledge and skills for good quality construction, it is important that disaster risk in various locations be considered and analysed. Technical guidelines for house construction need to be modified suitably. Under the GoI–UNDP Disaster Risk Management Programme, the Ministry of Home Affairs has developed 'Guidelines for Development and Building Construction including Safety Provisions for Natural Hazards in Rural Areas'. The guidelines provide detailed understanding of the role and responsibility of various institutions including PRIs for addressing disaster risk of buildings in rural areas. In addition, there is detailed guidance on construction details that can make a difference to the safety of a building. There is a need to include such considerations for reducing disaster risk of housing stock in rural India irrespective of the source of funding. There is a need to pay special attention to 'multi-hazard'–prone areas spelt out in the Vulnerability Atlas of India through incorporation of disaster resistant designs in house construction. These areas will be designated as 'difficult areas' and provided higher unit assistance under IAY. In addition, all new houses will be insured through group insurance to spread the risk of losses due to natural disasters and other calamities such as fires.

Training of Masons, Artisans and Others

17.79. A large pool of skilled workers like masons, bar benders, plumbers, carpenters and other construction-related artisans trained in safe and sustainable construction practices needs to be developed for all construction activity in the future. Five per cent of the IAY budget in the Twelfth Plan is being dedicated to capacity building of these personnel

Partnerships with Civil Society and PRIs

17.80. Given the scale of shelterlessness and the need for improving quality, it is important that local stakeholders are able to effectively participate in housing delivery. PRIs are central to effective habitat development in rural areas. They need to take a lead in micro-planning and prioritising habitat development needs. Services of trained local groups and enterprises to take up innovative implementation of housing and habitat schemes should be made available to PRIs by the State Governments. SHGs could be an important vehicle for production of building materials and provision of construction services. NGOs have been playing an important role in facilitating rural housing through promotion of innovations in architectural design, housing finance, alternative technology, supervision of construction and promotion of an eco-habitat approach. NGOs could be professionally engaged to support PRIs to facilitate safe and sustainable habitat development.

PROVISION OF URBAN AMENITIES IN RURAL AREAS (PURA)

17.81. PURA aims to provide urban amenities and livelihood opportunities in rural areas to bridge the rural–urban divide in the Indian society. The pilot phase of PURA was implemented from 2004–05 to 2006–07, with a total budget of ₹30 crores. There were seven clusters selected in seven States, with budgets of ₹4–5 crores per cluster. The implementation of the pilot phase did not yield the desired results as it faced the following issues:

- The pilot projects lacked a detailed business plan and there was limited participation by the private sector.
- The pilot projects were predominantly infrastructure-oriented projects, with limited attention being given to the implementation of economic activities.
- The criteria for selection of the clusters did not factor the growth potential for that area.
- There was no ownership at the State Government level and the entire implementation lacked an appropriate institutional structure with dedicated professional support.
- There was no convergence with other schemes of rural development or other departments.

17.82. Given the experience of the pilot projects, a restructured PURA was launched in the Eleventh Plan as a demand-driven programme through Public–Private Partnership (PPP) between Gram Panchayats and private sector partners. Core funding is sourced from the convergence of Central Government schemes and complemented by additional support through the PURA Scheme. The private sector brings on board its share of investment besides operational expertise. The PURA Scheme is implemented and managed by the private sector on considerations of economic viability but designed in a manner whereby it is fully aligned with the overall objective of rural development. To attract the private sector, the Scheme has a 'project based' design

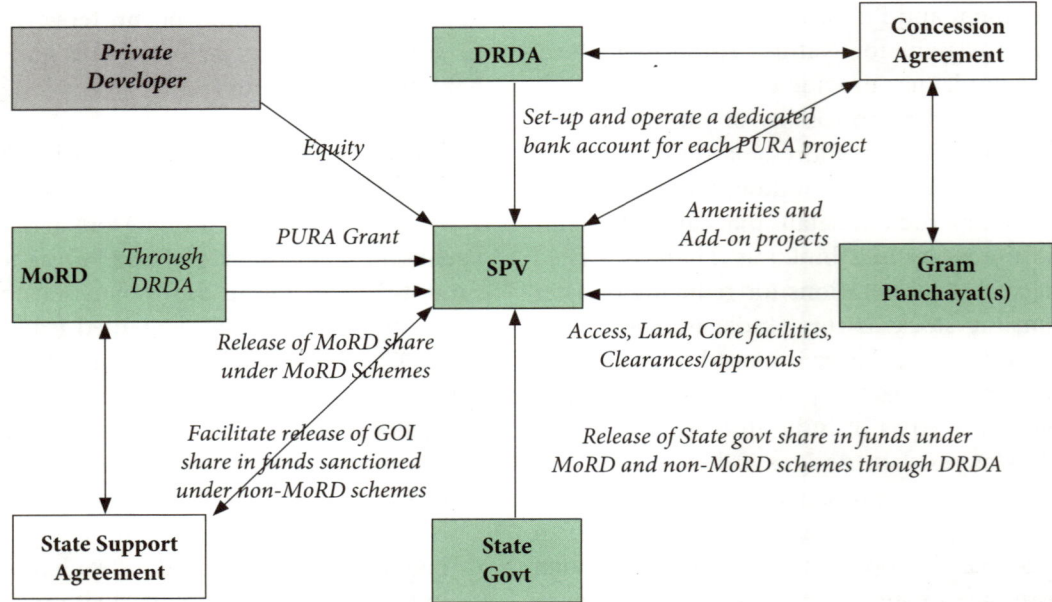

FIGURE 17.4: PURA Transaction Structure

with well-defined risks, identified measures for risk mitigation and risks sharing among the sponsoring authority (Gram Panchayat), Central Government, State Government and the selected bidder.

17.83. The transaction structure conceived to implement the project is shown in Figure 17.4.

17.84. MoRD issues Letters of Award to only those projects whose DPRs have been approved by an Inter-Ministerial Empowered Committee (EC) constituted for PURA. Post the issue of the Letter of Award, the concession and State support agreements are executed. Based on an understanding of challenges that have emerged through the brief experience of these pilot projects, the following improvements will be made in PURA going into the Twelfth Plan:

- There will be a better coordination procedure for granting the approvals to projects under non-MoRD schemes to ensure a single window clearance for the bidders. Guidelines will be issued to future bidders regarding the potential non-MoRD schemes that could be integrated within PURA projects, which could act as a useful databank for bidders.

- In many PURA projects it became evident that bidders had not adopted a consensus-building process and hence failed to incorporate many of the demands of the villagers. A proactive consensus building approach will be a basic guideline to the bidders with each step being documented. Each demand should be documented and if the same is not accommodated by the bidder, then this should be transparently shared with the primary stakeholders.
- Due to the multiple activities involved in a PURA project, the selected concessionaire is required to approach various departments within the State Government. This process can be time-consuming. Hence a project-level coordination committee must be constituted at the State Government level to grant various approvals or take decisions on the implementation challenges associated with PURA projects. An example is the committee constituted by the Government of Kerala to address issues relating to PURA projects.
- A Project Implementation Unit also needs to be established at MoRD to undertake the monitoring role for all PURA projects within the country.
- There is an imperative need for undertaking capacity-building activities for officials of Gram Panchayats and the District Administration. This

capacity-building would be aimed at providing officials with necessary skill sets to meet their obligations under the Concession Agreement and State Support Agreement. Handholding by the MoRD in the pilot phase would be required to achieve smooth implementation of the projects.

- An accurate baseline survey is crucial in determining the PURA grant for the project. The broad contents of the baseline survey needs to be provided to bidders as a standard document.
- Given the diverse backgrounds of the bidders, standard technical solutions (like sample designs of various structures) may be provided as a manual to the bidders. Such a reference document would enable standardisation of the DPRs and enable a smoother approval process for MoRD.
- A manual of various innovative cost-effective technologies may also be provided that could be adopted by the bidders in their projects.

17.85. Table 17.17 shows the infrastructure and amenities to be provided, operated and maintained under a PURA project by the private developer during the Twelfth Plan.

17.86. In order to ensure scaling of the PURA Scheme, it would necessary for State Governments to lead the entire process of managing PURA projects. The key activities would involve undertaking the procurement process for selection of private developers, facilitating/interacting with the private players in the course of preparation of Concept Plans and DPRs and undertaking its obligations under the Concession and State Support Agreements. Further the State Governments would need to identify their nodal departments and build capacities of these nodal departments to handle PURA Projects. In addition, a funding pattern for PURA Grant in the ratio of 80:20, with 80 per cent of the funding for PURA Grant coming from MoRD and 20 per cent from the concerned State Government will be adopted. The role of MoRD will be that of a facilitator and the final approving and monitoring authority of the PURA Projects. An institutional structure on the lines of the PMGSY Scheme of the MoRD is suggested for upscaling PURA (Figure 17.5).

NATIONAL SOCIAL ASSISTANCE PROGRAMME (NSAP)

17.87. An integral element of India's battle with poverty and distress is to provide succour to senior citizens, differently abled people and others who have suffered due to mishaps in life through unconditional cash transfers. The NSAP refers to a basket of welfare schemes that provide social assistance to a wide range of people in need in both rural and urban India. At the beginning of the Eleventh Plan, the NSAP comprised the Indira Gandhi National Old Age Pension Scheme (IGNOAPS), the Annapurna Scheme and National Family Benefit Scheme (NFBS). In February 2009, two more schemes were added under NSAP—the Indira Gandhi National Widow Pension Scheme (IGNWPS) and the Indira Gandhi National Disability Pension Scheme (IGNDPS). Although they are small, these pensions have been described as a veritable lifeline for the millions of widows,

TABLE 17.17

Infrastructure and Amenities to be Provided, Operated and Maintained under PURA Project by Private Developer in the Twelfth Plan

Mandatory-under MoRD schemes	Under non-MoRD schemes as local conditions permit (Illustrative list)	Add-on projects to generate economic and livelihood opportunities* (Illustrative list)
- Water and sewerage - Village streets - Drainage - Solid waste management - Skill development - Development of economic activities	- Village street lighting - Telecom - Electricity generation, and so on	- Village linked tourism - Integrated rural hub, Rural market - Agri—common service centre and warehousing - Any other rural economy based project

*At least one such activity would be included in the project.

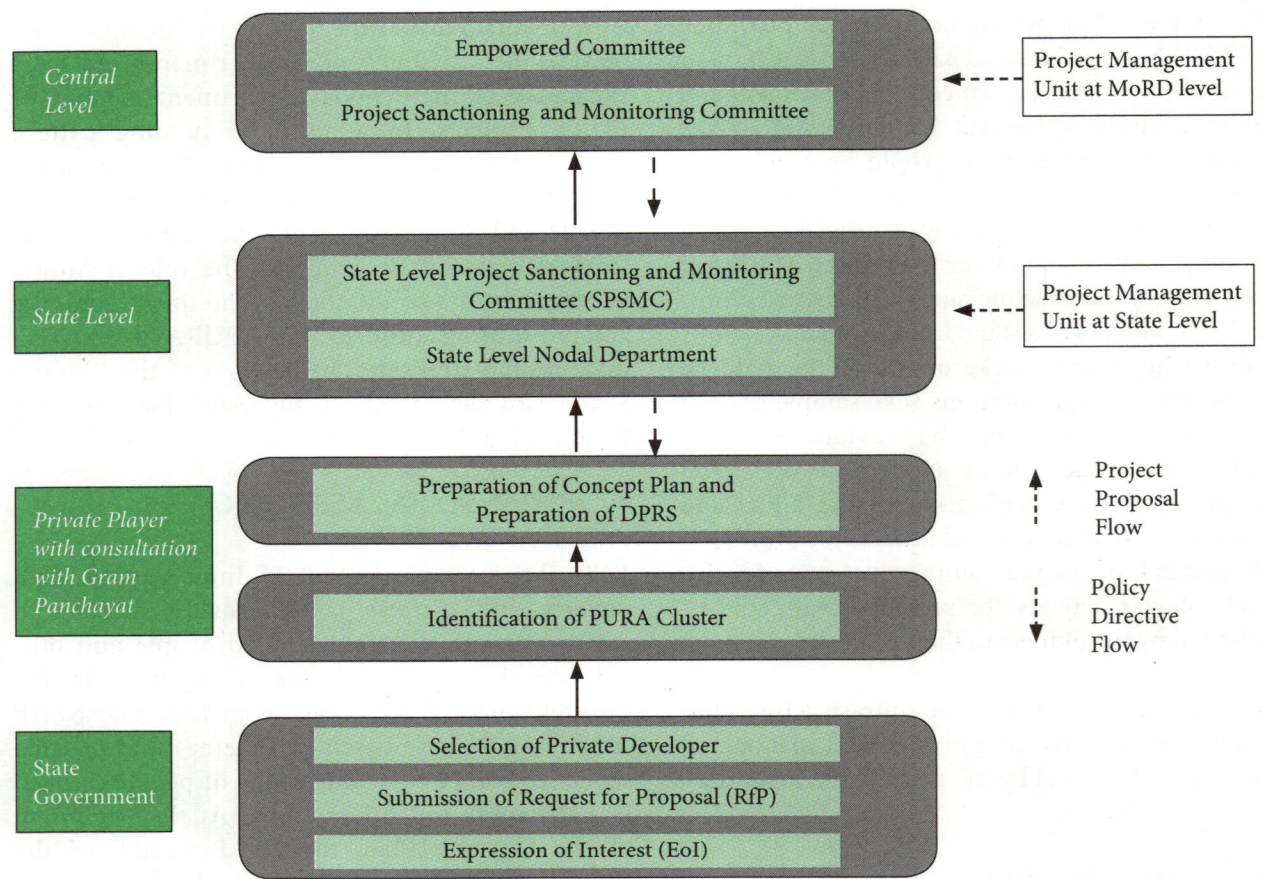

FIGURE 17.5: Institutional Structure for PURA

elderly and disabled people who receive them.[4] NSAP allocation has increased eight-fold since 2002–03. IGNOAPS is the largest scheme within NSAP. In 2011–12, 82 per cent of the total NSAP expenditure was on IGNOAPS followed by the IGNWPS at 9.7 per cent. The physical and financial progress of NSAP during the Eleventh Plan is given in Table 17.18.

TABLE 17.18
NSAP Progress in the Eleventh Plan

Year	Expenditure Reported (₹ crore)	Beneficiaries (in lakh)
2007–08	3,110.99	128.89
2008–09	3,875.31	167.63
2009–10	4,718.83	216.06
2010–11	5,480.60	231.12
2011–12	5,121.95	253.64

17.88. While NSAP started as a Centrally Sponsored Scheme (CSS) in 1995, it was transferred to State Plans in 2002–03 and funds are now released as Additional Central Assistance to the States. Guidelines are issued by the MoRD at the Centre and the MoRD monitors expenditures under the ACA, but it is the responsibility of State Governments to identify beneficiaries, sanction benefits and disburse payments.

17.89. Under IGNOAPS, since 2006–07, old age pension of ₹200 per month was being provided to persons of 65 years and above who are destitute (BPL with effect from 19 November 2007). With effect from 1 April 2011, the age limit has been lowered to 60 years and for persons above 80 years, the pension has been enhanced to ₹500 per month. It is estimated that this change will benefit an additional 7.2 million persons in the age group of 60–64 years and 2.6 million persons above the age of 80 years.

Currently, 19 States/UTs are providing an additionality of ₹200 to ₹800 per month. Another 11 States/UTs are providing additional pension of between ₹50 to ₹200.

17.90. The NFBS provides a lump sum family benefit of ₹10,000 to the bereaved household in case of the death (natural or accidental) of the primary breadwinner (male or female) whose earnings contribute substantially to the total household income. This scheme is applicable to all the eligible persons in the age group 18 to 64. The bereaved household should belong to BPL families to qualify for this benefit. This sum has been raised to ₹20,000 with effect from 18 October 2012 with eligibility criteria of age group 18 to 59 years.

17.91. In February 2009, the IGNWPS was started to provide pension to BPL widows in the age group 40–64 years at the rate of ₹200 pm per beneficiary. The estimated number of beneficiaries under Indira Gandhi National Widow Pension Scheme (IGNWPS) is 45 lakhs. IGNDPS was also started in the same month for BPL persons with severe or multiple disabilities[5] (in the age group of 18–64 years) at the rate of ₹200 per month per beneficiary. It is estimated that 15 lakh beneficiaries will be covered under IGNDPS. As a result of change in the eligibility criteria for receiving old age pension in April 2011, eligibility criteria for widow pension under IGNWPS and disability pension under IGNDPS got revised from 40–64 years to 40–59 years and from 18–64 years to 18–59 years, respectively. 36.05 lakh beneficiaries have been covered so far under IGNWPS and 7.69 lakh under IGNDPS. With effect from 1 October 2012, the widow and disability pensions have been raised to ₹300 per month and eligibility criteria to age group 40–79 years for IGNWPS and 18–79 years for IGNDPS. The component-wise physical and financial progress of NSAP during the Eleventh Plan is given in Table 17.19.

17.92. NSAP faces several types of implementation challenges: logistical (application and sanctioning process, funds flow management), bureaucratic (low incentives, weak capacity), and management (MIS, reporting systems, verification). In the execution of NSAP, greater professional support is needed for ensuring quality, delivery and for suitable monitoring and evaluation, both at the Centre and State levels. Technical support groups comprising professionals and voluntary organisations will be set up at Central, State and district levels for continuous review of policy and performance of NSAP during the Twelfth Plan. Documentary requirements for proving eligibility and identity have proved extremely onerous for the beneficiaries who are among the most vulnerable. It is hoped that the use of UID (once available) will ease some of these pressures. Many States have devised somewhat arbitrary and harsh exclusion criteria which have been applied in a mechanical manner that discriminate against some of the most vulnerable. Even having a living adult son has meant exclusion in some cases. Such practices must be stopped. Shifting to payment through post offices or banks is a significant step in ensuring transparency. But as under MGNREGA, where density of banks/POs is low or because of lack of adequate staff, people have had to suffer great hardships in the transition period. Aged and disabled people may not be able to reach the POs or banks. The banking correspondent model with UID biometrics could be a way out as it would provide payments at the doorstep in a transparent manner.

TABLE 17.19
Physical and Financial Progress of NSAP Components, Eleventh Plan

Year	IGNOAPS		IGNWPS		IGNDPS		NFBS		Annapurna	
	₹Crore	Lakh	₹Crore	Lakh	₹Crore	Lakh	₹Crore	Lakh	₹Crore	Lakh
2007–08	2,896	115.14					176	3.34	40	10.76
2008–09	3,422	150.21					329	4.23	47	10.41
2009–10	4,354	163.34	152	32.13	29	7.00	154	3.44	30	10.16
2010–11	3,528	170.60	524	34.25	134	7.28	324	3.35	45	9.58
2011–12	4,214	199.55	496	36.55	105	7.77	282	2.48	25	7.28

17.93. IT solutions need to be seen as central to scheme implementation and not just as a peripheral MIS system. Use of IT can help reduce discretion, stem leakages through duplication, enhance efficiency by reducing time taken between steps, reduce the need for reporting at multiple levels, and facilitate accounting, particularly in States with lower human resources capacity. To be most effective, IT needs to be an end-to-end solution. This means not only that the solution encompasses the entire process cycle—from application to pension payment—but that it links each of the functional processes to each other. The solution needs to be transaction-based in the sense that it must involve no or extremely limited opportunity for original transaction data entry. An electronic registry of beneficiaries will require digitisation of legacy data and continuous entry of new beneficiaries. Digitisation will need a robust data migration process (for example, minimise duplicates, reduce risk of missing records) to ensure accuracy. Mechanisms should be built in to cross-check the registry with other databases such as the SECC, UID or ration cards for verification. A robust electronic registry is the base on which application management can be built to record, acknowledge and check compliance with eligibility norms while minimising the burden of proof of documentation that is presently placed on the applicant.

17.94. In order to streamline the processes of communication of information of actual transfers to programme managers at the State level, an electronic fund management system (as described for MGNREGA above) could make a big difference. The NSAP guidelines do not require any formal fiduciary assurance from the States in terms of end-use of funds other than the annual utilisation certificate (UC). The basis for recognition of programme expenditure for the purpose of the UC is not clear, which may result in States adopting varying yardsticks for what is expenditure. Third party review of the payment processes and enforcement of ploughback of unspent balances with pension distribution agencies (PDAs) must be introduced so that the possibility of 'ghost beneficiaries' and unspent balances lying with PDAs is reduced.

17.95. At present, there is no mechanism for systematic revision of pension payments in line with inflation. A case can be made during the Twelfth Plan to adopt an approach similar to that adopted for MGNREGA wages, whereby an index such as the CPIAL or CPIIW could be adopted to tie pension payments to inflation, allowing for cost of living differences across States. The periodicity of revision could be aligned with preparation of annual budget estimates.

17.96. The use of BPL lists has led to large errors of inclusion and exclusion. Eligibility and coverage rates will need to be reassessed after the SECC process is completed.

FLEXI-FUND FOR RURAL DEVELOPMENT

17.97. There is an increasing demand to give States much greater flexibility in spending decisions with respect to Government schemes. The demand is justified on the basis that States have differing needs, priorities and levels of development and the 'one size fits all' model of Centrally Sponsored Schemes (CSS) does not allow these interstate variations to be adequately reflected. The BK Chaturvedi Committee has addressed this issue and proposed a new framework for introducing much greater flexibility as described in Chapter 10 of Volume 1 on Governance.

17.98. The Ministry of Rural Development has proposed going even further by setting up a Rural Development Flexi-fund (RDF) of ₹40,000 crores (of which 70 per cent would be the Central share of ₹28,000 crore) with the intent to devolve a significant share of Central funds related to Rural Development to the States over the Twelfth Plan period directly though this Fund. This would ensure better targeting and focused projects on state-specific priorities. It would also send a powerful signal about the Central Government's deep commitment to cooperative federalism.

17.99. The RDF will be a separate line item in the Budget of the Ministry of Rural Development (MoRD). It would be available as an additional amount that can be spent either on existing Centrally Sponsored Schemes of the MoRD and Ministry of

Drinking Water and Sanitation, or on new projects proposed by the respective States. Thus the RDF would provide inter-scheme flexibility to States among the Centrally Sponsored Schemes of the Ministry of Rural Development and Ministry of Drinking Water and Sanitation.[6] This will be in addition to the *intra-scheme flexibility* made possible by the BK Chaturvedi Committee for all Centrally Sponsored Schemes. The MoRD will lay out broad guidelines on what the RDF can be used for. In order to avoid inter-district distortions, the flexi-fund will be essentially a fund to incentivise: (*i*) innovation in service delivery, (*ii*) building sustainable rural infrastructure (*iii*) 'Greening' of rural development and (*iv*) devolution to and empowerment of PRIs.

17.100. With these provisos the RDF will be available for use under any CSS and even for work not currently covered under any of the CSS. In order to be eligible to use the fund, States will have to propose projects that merit support based on the above four criteria. The project reports (DPRs) prepared by the States will be discussed and approved by a Central Committee under the Chairmanship of Member (RD) Planning Commission, and comprising Secretary (RD), GoI and 2–3 eminent Rural Development experts.

PLAN OUTLAY

17.101. The tentative Gross Budgetary Support (GBS) for the Ministry of Rural Development for the Twelfth Five Year Plan (2012–17) is ₹4,43,261 crore. Out of this, about 85 per cent is for the flagship programmess implemented by the Department of Rural Development, that is, Mahatma Gandhi National Rural Employment Guarantee Act (₹1,65,500 crore), Indira Awas Yojana (₹59,585 crore), Pradhan Mantri Gram Sadak Yojana (₹1,24,013 crore) and National Rural Livelihood Mission (₹29,006 crore).

17.102. The Twelfth Plan Central Sector Tentative Gross Budgetary Support for Rural Drinking Water Supply and Sanitation is ₹98,015 crore. 100 per cent of this outlay is for flagship programmes, namely National Rural Drinking Water Programme and Nirmal Bharat Abhiyan, administered by Ministry of Drinking Water and Sanitation. This provision will draw matching provisions from the States to the tune of ₹1,32,393 crore. Thus, the total outlays in the Twelfth Five Year Plan for Rural Drinking Water Supply and Sanitation sector would be about ₹2,30,408 crore.

NOTES

1. JP Morgan (2011): *India: Rural Wages Surge*, India Equity Research Reports.
2. Jean H Humphrey (2009): 'Child Undernutrition, Tropical Enteropathy, Toilets and Hand Washing', *Lancet*, 374: 1032–35.
3. Dean Spears (2012): *Effects of Rural Sanitation on Infant Mortality and Human Capital: Evidence from India's Total Sanitation Campaign*. This study uses administrative records on implementation of TSC and data from the third round of the District Level Household Survey (DLHS-3) and bulletins of the 2010–11 Annual Household Survey.
4. Dutta, P., S. Howes, and R. Murgai (2010): 'Small but Effective: India's Targeted Unconditional Cash Transfers.' *Economic and Political Weekly*, XLV(52) pp. 63–70.
5. Disability is legally defined as (i) blindness, (ii) low vision, (iii) leprosy cured, (iv) hearing impaired, (v) loco motor disability, (vi) mental retardation and (vii) mental illness. Persons with disability are persons suffering from not less than 40 per cent of any of the above disabilities as certified by a medical authority. Persons with severe disability are persons with 80 per cent or more of one or more disabilities. Multiple disabilities are combination of two or more disabilities.
6. Mahatma Gandhi NREGA is excluded from this list as it a special demand driven scheme based on a legal entitlement under the MGNREGA Act, 2005.

18

Urban Development

INTRODUCTION

18.1. About 377 million Indians comprising of about 31 per cent of the country's population, live in urban areas according to Census 2011. This is a smaller proportion compared to other large developing countries, for example, 45 per cent in China, 54 per cent in Indonesia, 78 per cent in Mexico and 87 per cent in Brazil. With the more rapid growth of the Indian economy in recent years, which is expected to continue, the rate of urbanisation will increase. Projections are that by 2031, about 600 million Indians will reside in urban areas, an increase of over 200 million in just 20 years.

18.2. Urban areas are engines of economic growth. Data on the urban share of the gross domestic product (GDP) for the Indian economy is not available on a regular and consistent basis but estimates by the Central Statistical Office (CSO), available for a few years, indicate that this share increased from 37.7 per cent in 1970–71 to 52 per cent in 2004–05. The mid term appraisal of the Eleventh Plan projected the urban share of GDP at 62–63 per cent in 2009–10.

18.3. Urbanisation will be central to India's strategy of achieving faster and more inclusive growth because agglomeration and densification of economic activities (and habitations) in urban conglomerations stimulates economic efficiencies and provides more opportunities for earning livelihoods. Thus urbanisation increases avenues for entrepreneurship and employment compared to what is possible in dispersed rural areas. It, thereby, enables faster inclusion of more people in the process of economic growth.

18.4. Although the theme of a 'rural–urban divide' still colours some policy discourse in India, there is a growing recognition that urbanisation is necessary to realise India's growth potential, and that rural–urban linkages must be strengthened. Indeed this will accelerate growth of the rural sector also.

18.5. The High Powered Expert Committee (HPEC) under the chairpersonship of Dr. Isher Judge Ahluwalia that was constituted by the Ministry of Urban Development for estimating the investment requirements for urban infrastructure services has observed that the fortunes of the agricultural sector are crucially linked to the manner in which growth in the industry and services sectors unfolds. People living in rural areas typically tap the opportunities that cities provide for employment, entrepreneurial avenues, and education. As urbanisation grows, demand for food items other than food-grains, that is, vegetables, lentils, milk, eggs and so on, also grows. This leads to investments in infrastructure, logistics, processing and packaging in rural and peri-urban areas. Such investments and other economic inter-linkages connect and build synergy between rural and urban centres. Thus the rural sector also benefits from good management of neighbouring urban conglomerations.

Urbanisation Trends and Their Implications

18.6. As mentioned above, the degree of urbanisation at 31 per cent of the population is one of the lowest in the world though it is accelerating. The share of persons living in urban areas rose by 3.35 per cent in the decade 2001 to 2011 while it had risen by only 2.10 per cent in the decade 1991 to 2001. The sources of increase in urban population are shown in Figure 18.1.

18.7. About 60 per cent of the growth in the urban population is due to natural increase. Rural–urban migration has contributed to only about 20 per cent of increase in urban population. In this regard, the Isher Ahluwalia HPEC has observed that notwithstanding three decades of rapid economic growth, rural urban migration has remained relatively low as industrialisation has been capital intensive and the services boom fuelled by the knowledge economy has also been skill intensive. This has prevented Indian cities from realising their full potential of generating employment opportunities and consequently making the development process more inclusive.

18.8. There is a concentration of the urban population in large cities and existing urban agglomerations. As per census 2011, there are 53 million plus cities accounting for about 43 per cent of India's urban population. Class-I cities with population over 3 lakh accounted for about 56 per cent of the urban population and with a population ranging from 1 lakh to 3 lakh accounted for another 14 per cent. This pattern of population concentration in large cities reflects spatial polarisation of the employment opportunities. While it is expected that gains from an agglomeration economy would lead to some polarisation of economic activities, there is a need for developing an optimal portfolio of cities by drawing regional development plans and promoting growth centres that are employment intensive and consistent with the economic potential including the natural endowment of cities and regions. The availability of water to provide for the needs of a large urban population must be a critical factor in plans for urban development.

18.9. Though the proportion of urban population concentrated in larger cities continue to remain high, there is some evidence that other urban growth nodes are emerging underscoring the need for adequate policy attention to smaller cities and peri-urban areas as against the narrow focus of concentrating on large 'Mission Cities' as was followed in the Eleventh Plan period. Census 2011 notes that the number of towns in India increased from 5,161 in 2001 to as many as 7935 in 2011. It points out that almost all of this increase was in the growth of 'census' towns (which increased by 2,532) rather than 'statutory' towns (which increased by only 242).

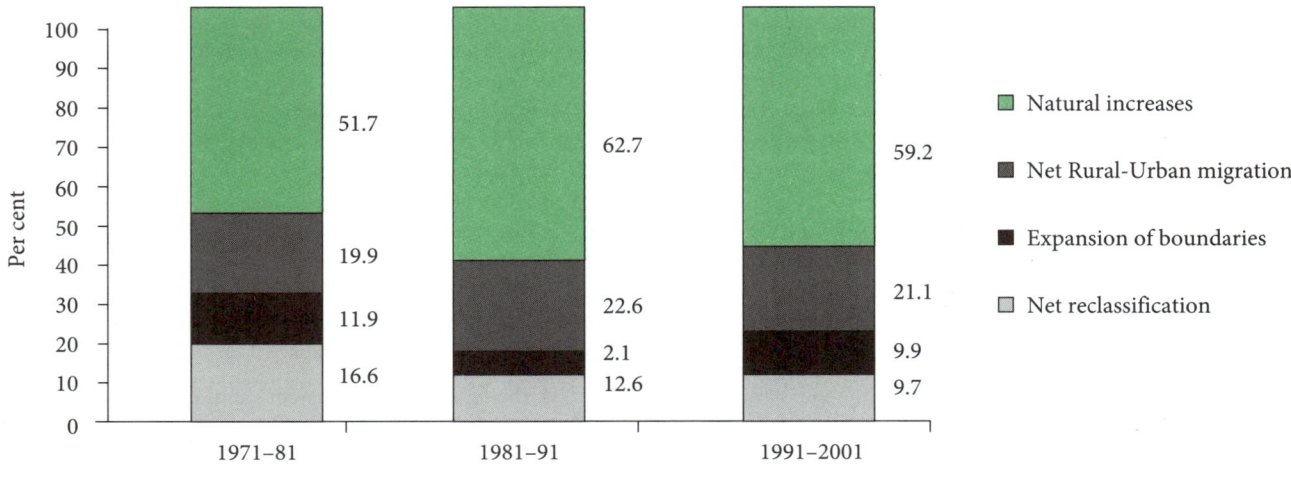

Source: Reproduced from Isher Ahluwalia Hpec Report (2011).

FIGURE 18.1: Sources of Increase in Urban Population

'Statutory' towns are towns with municipalities or corporations. Whereas, 'census' towns are agglomerations that grow in rural and peri-urban areas, with densification of population that do not have an effective urban governance structure or requisite urban infrastructure, for example, sanitation, roads and so on in place.

18.10. An accelerated pace of urbanisation would imply significant spill over of existing cities into peri-urban areas. As borne out by a recent study by the World Bank—*India Urbanisation Review: Urbanisation beyond Municipalities* (2012) already there are evidences that peri-urban areas in the vicinity of large cities are centres of intense economic activities. A large number of new towns are 'born' in the vicinity of existing cities with million plus population. If these trends are any indication of how the future will unfold, much of India's urbanisation challenge will be to transform land-use and expand infrastructure in its largest cities and neighbouring suburbs—places that are not pristine or green field, but already support 9 per cent of the country's population and provide 18 per cent of the employment on 1 per cent of the country's land area. Jobs and people are flowing from metropolitan cores to nearby settlements—regardless of whether they are classified as urban or rural often giving rise to haphazard urbanisation in the peri-urban areas. The challenge is to ensure that new cities and existing metropolises are connected and land-use change is coordinated with infrastructure development to accommodate urban redevelopment and urban spatial expansion (refer to Box 18.1). Failure to do so would eventually necessitate expensive 'retrofits' in future.

The Country's Urban Conditions and Challenges

18.11. Broadly, the urban sector in India faces two distinct but mutually linked sets of challenges. Based on NSSO Report No. 508 (2004–05) it is estimated that the number of urban poor had increased by

---

Box 18.1
Vision of Our Cities

The objective of the Twelfth Plan is faster, more inclusive and more sustainable growth. The vision of India's urban growth must be aligned with the objectives of inclusion and sustainability.

Urbanisation should be guided towards inclusive, equitable and sustainable growth of towns and cities with proper civic amenities. Good urbanisation would ensure that towns and cities are free from slums and provides adequate opportunities for productive employment and a decent quality of life to all their inhabitants including the poor.

The smart cities of our vision would be engines of growth as they would increasingly compete for investments nationally and internationally too. Therefore, cities must provide world class infrastructure and services at affordable costs to give a competitive edge to the economic activities they host. Besides, cities should be able to provide basic services to migrant workers, their families and other vulnerable sections of society including women and children. The future renewal of our cities should facilitate transition from 'informality' of large number of workers towards more formal livelihoods in line with their aspirations. They should address various vulnerabilities including residential, occupational and social vulnerabilities, associated with urban poverty. As an overriding principle, 'people' should be brought to the heart of the urban agenda, for both, deciding the vision of their city and for choosing the process of reaching that goal. This implies that all citizens have access to basic services of clean water, sanitation, sewage, solid waste management, urban roads, safe and affordable public transport systems, affordable housing, and a clean and healthy environment. Besides creating avenues for gainful employment, Indian cities should also meet the rising aspirations of people for a better quality of life. Citizens should be proud of their towns and cities and take responsibility for their cleanliness, safety and hospitality.

Environmental sustainability of Indian cities is another integral part of the vision. Future growth should be consistent with cities' natural endowments and the economic potential of the region in which they are situated. All cities should be efficient in using available resources particularly energy, water and land.

Our cities must also preserve and foster their cultural and historical heritage and benefit from the tourism potential of their heritage and natural endowments.

34.4 per cent from 1973 to 2004. The NSSO (66th round) has estimated that during the period 2004–05 and 2009–10, the unemployment rate in terms of the usual status decrease by 1 percentage point for both, urban male and females notwithstanding an impressive growth registered by the economy in this period. Hence, the first challenge is to significantly step up the rate of creation of jobs in the urban sector

18.12. The second set of challenges before the Government is to guide the process of urbanisation and ensure that basic services, for example, sanitation, water supply, and basic housing are provided to urban citizens expected to be around 600 million within 20 years. If these challenges are not tackled expressly, not only would India's cities get increasingly chaotic and choked, rural poverty will be converted to urban poverty with no gains to improvement of livelihoods of India's burgeoning population.

18.13. Already, cities and towns of India are visibly deficient in the quality of services they provide, even to the existing population. A recent compilation of key indicators of the present state of urban service delivery is given in Box 18.2.

18.14. The high coping cost of deficient infrastructure especially to the urban poor has been reported in several studies. For example, due to the intermittent and inadequate supply of water, it has been estimated that the urban poor pays significantly more than the average price for water, often tenfold higher. In a city sanitation study, conducted by the MoUD (2010) none of the 423 cities where the study was conducted were found to be 'healthy and clean'. The Water and Sanitation Programme of the World Bank, using data for 2006, suggested that per capita economic cost of inadequate sanitation in India is ₹2,180. The cost in terms of Disability Adjusted Life Years (DALY) of

---

Box 18.2
State of Service Delivery—Key Indicators

Water supply: As per 2011 census 70.6 per cent of urban population is covered by individual connections, compared with 91 per cent in China, 86 per cent in South Africa and 80 per cent in Brazil. Duration of water supply in Indian cities ranges from 1 hour to 6 hours, compared with 24 hours in Brazil and China and 22 hours in Vietnam. Per capita supply of water in Indian cities ranges from 37 lpcpd to 298 lpcpd for a limited duration, while Paris supplies 150 lpcpd continuously and Mexico 171 lpcpd for 21 hours a day. Most Indian cities do not have metering for residential water connections. Seventy per cent of water leakages occur from consumer connections and due to malfunctioning of water meters. Non-revenue water (NRW) accounts for 50 per cent of water production compared with 5 per cent in Singapore.

Sanitation: Even a partial sewerage network is absent in 4861 cities and towns in India. Almost 50 per cent of households in cities like Bangalore and Hyderabad do not have sewerage connections. As per 2011 census, about 13 per cent of urban households do not have access to any form of latrine facility and defecate in the open. Census 2011 also revealed that about 37 per cent of urban households are connected with open drainage and another 18 per cent are not connected at all. Less than 20 per cent of the road network is covered by storm water drains. As per the report of the Central Pollution Control Board (CPCB) 2009, only about 20 per cent sewage generated was treated before disposal in Class I cities and Class II towns (as per 2001 census). As per CPCB report brought out in 2005, about 1,15,000 MT of Municipal Solid Waste is generated daily in the country. However, scientific disposal of the waste generated is almost non-existent.

Public transport: Public transport accounts for only 27 per cent of urban transport in India. Share of the public transport fleet has decreased from 11 per cent in 1951 to 1.1 per cent in 2001. In 2009, only 20 out of 85 Indian cities with a population of 0.5 million had bus services.

Source: As compiled in Isher Ahluwalia HPEC report (2011) and Census of India and MoUD

Affordable housing: The Technical Group on the Estimation of Housing Shortage projects the total shortage of dwelling units in urban areas in 2012 to be 18.78 million units. The projected slum population in India is 94.98 million in 2012. As against this, the number of dwelling units sanctioned under JNNURM in 7 year Mission period was 1.6 million units. The supply of decent affordable housing by private sector has remained woefully inadequate.

Source: Ministry of Housing and Urban Poverty Alleviation and Report of the Pronab Sen Committee on Slum Statistics (2010).

diarrhoeal disease for children from poor sanitation is estimated at ₹500 crore (HPEC 2011).

18.15. Many studies have demonstrated that there is considerable positive impact on health status after having adequate access to water and sanitation, both in terms of hygiene related behaviour as well as reduction in water borne diseases and skin diseases. There is a very strong gender dimension to safe water and sanitation. Women bear the maximum brunt in their absence. They are forced to spend time and energy collecting water for the household use and by that are forced to give up on income generating opportunities and leisure time. There are severe health consequences of such work on women. In absence of sanitation they have to go out in dark only for defecation which has adverse health consequences on them besides increasing risks of sexual violence. Higher morbidity rates within the families because of lack of these services forces them to spend time on caring for the sick within the family and thereby increasing their burden. This also leads to poor health status of women and lower incomes in their hands.

18.16. The scenario in urban transport is equally alarming. Current urban transport trends in Indian cities are leading to broader sustainability challenges for people and the environment in terms of lost man-hours due to long commute times, greater reliance on expensive private transport, increasing emissions and road fatalities. A MoUD study in 2010 based on sample of 87 cities estimated than under a business-as-usual scenario, in about 20 years time, the expected average journey speeds on major corridors in many cities would fall from 26–17 kmph to 8–6 kmph.

18.17. Air quality has also deteriorated sharply carrying with it concomitant health costs. For instance, per capita emission levels in India's seven largest cities have been estimated (Palanivel 2002) to be at least three times higher than the WHO standards. Air pollution levels were low in only three cities of the 127 cities monitored by the Central Pollution Control Board under the National Air Quality Monitoring Programme (2009).

18.18. To conclude, urbanisation is increasing at a faster rate than earlier. Since urbanisation is 'efficient' and could be job-creating, it must be planned and properly guided. An accelerated pace of urbanisation would also result in significant spill over in peri-urban areas and therefore, these areas need to be included in urban planning and provided for. While India needs to plan for its urban expansion, the conditions of delivery of services in existing cities and decent housing even for the current level of urban population is highly deficient. There is a pressing requirement to address the problem of urban poverty. The task enumerated above calls for a renewed thrust towards improvement in governance structure especially at the level of urban local bodies and a major improvement in delivery of urban services in cities.

REVIEW OF MAJOR INITIATIVES TAKEN UNDER THE ELEVENTH PLAN

JNNURM

18.19. The Jawaharlal Nehru National Urban Renewal Mission (JNNURM) was launched in December 2005 for a period of seven years with an outlay of ₹66,085 crore. The objectives of the scheme included empowerment of Urban Local Bodies (ULBs), planned and holistic development of cities and making them inclusive. The scheme mandated preparation of City Development Plans (CDP) and a set of urban reforms at State and Municipal levels.

18.20. JNNURM renewed the focus on urban renewal and gave impetus to many urban reforms. Central allocation of ₹66,085 crore led to overall commitment of investment of ₹1,23,711 crore under the scheme (refer to Table 18.1).

18.21. Some of the key inadequacies noted during implementation of the programme included failure to mainstream urban planning, incomplete reforms and slow progress in project implementation. Delay in securing land for projects and obtaining approval from various regulatory authorities also led to delay in implementation of some of the projects.

18.22. Despite the stress on urban planning, in many cities the planning process is yet to be strengthened

TABLE 18.1
Physical and Financial Progress under JNNURM (March 2012)

	UIG	UIDSSMT	BSUP	IHSDP	Total
7 year Allocation (in ₹ crore)	31,500	11,400	16,357	6,828	66,085
No. of Projects sanctioned	559	808	528	1,078	2,973
Total cost of project (in ₹ crore)	67,275	14,039	30,416	11,981	1,23,711
Total ACA Committed (in ₹ crore)	30,971	11,372	15,092	7,704	65,139
Total ACA released (in ₹ crore)	18,479	8,469	8,642	4,905	40,495
Per cent of ACA released to ACA sanctioned	60%	74%	57%	64%	62%
No. of DU approved in lakh (BSUP and IHSDP)			10.3	5.7	16.0
No. of projects completed (UIG and UIDSSMT)	127	142			269
No. of Dwelling units completed (in lakh) (BSUP and IHSDP)			4.4	1.8	6.2

and made participatory. Invariably peri–urban areas around cities' limits have grown haphazardly. Lack of participatory planning has resulted in programmes suffering from 'lack of ownership'.

18.23. A significant interstate variation in completion of reform underscores the need for their careful calibration on the basis of city size and capabilities. In many States, incomplete governance and financial reforms prevented emergence of the municipal entities as viable and financially sustainable entities. Lack of capacity has further emerged as a serious constraint. Thus, despite some good examples in some cities, the overall progress in improving service delivery standards has been unsatisfactory. Another major shortcoming was the limited success in leveraging of JNNURM fund by locating non-budgetary financial resources including funds under PPP framework.

Other Initiatives in the Urban Sector in the Eleventh Plan

18.24. Swarna Jayanti Sahari Rozgaar Yojana (SJSRY) is designed to enable urban poor to get gainful employment. Under this scheme 3,941 towns have been covered and an assistance of ₹3,360 crore has been released. Since inception, about 12.3 lakh persons have been imparted training under the scheme. For making India slum free, pilot phase of Rajiv Awas Yojana was launched in 2011. The scheme has a progressive architecture which includes in-situ rehabilitation of slums and legislation to provide property rights to slum dwellers. Another thrust has been implementation of the Employment of Manual Scavengers and Construction of Dry Latrines (prohibition) Act 1993. Under the Integrated Low Cost Sanitation Scheme (ILCS) 2.5 lakh dry latrines have been converted into sanitary ones and about 1.55 lakh new toilets have been sanctioned.

Urban Transport

18.25. A major achievement leading to transformational change in public transport has been a significant extension of Metro rail network in large cities. Delhi metro phase-II has been successfully completed and phase-III involving an investment of ₹35,242 crore is under implementation. Metro rail projects in Bangalore, Chennai and Kolkata involving an investment of ₹31,084 crore are under implementation In addition, metro projects in Hyderabad and Mumbai involving investment of more than ₹22,000 crore are being developed on a Public–Private Partnership basis. Under JNNURM, 21 projects including Bus Rapid Transit (BRT) System with an approved cost of ₹5,211 crore were sanctioned. Besides, purchase of 15,260 buses gave a major boost to public transport. Another 123 projects like roads, flyovers, ROBs and parking projects with an approved cost of ₹10,162 crore were sanctioned for traffic improvement and parking (refer Box 18.3).

> **Box 18.3**
> **Transforming Public Transport in Cities**
>
> Under UIG component of JNNURM, 15,260 low-floor and semi–low-floor buses enabled with intelligent transport system were sanctioned to 65 Mission cities with admissible central assistance of ₹2,089 crore. As a result of the scheme, 34 cities across India have organised city bus services for the first time.

Conclusion

18.26. JNNURM has led to a significant step up in investment in urban sector. However, urban sector continues to suffer from low-level of service delivery, structural problems, grossly inadequate availability of resources and lack of capacity at different levels of the government. Successful management of India's urbanisation would not only require a significant step up in investments for urban improvements under the Twelfth Plan period, but also emphasis on measures to address the glaring weaknesses in urban governance and management. In addition, reducing urban poverty has emerged as a major thrust area in managing our cities.

THE STRATEGY FOR URBANISATION

Enablers for effective urbanisation

18.27. The strategy for the Twelfth Five Year Plan will be focused on strengthening the five enablers for urbanisation—governance, planning, financing, capacity building and innovation (Figure 18.2).

Strengthen Urban Governance

18.28. Despite the 74th Constitutional Amendment, which required States to transfer eighteen functions to the ULBs, there is significant variation in devolution of functions, functionaries and funds across the States. City mayors lack the powers and tenure to be truly accountable for delivery of urban services. At the metropolitan level, Metropolitan Planning Committees (MPCs) are yet to evolve and District Planning Committees must function not only in letter but in the intended spirit too. In most States either State agencies or parastatals are in-charge of urban service delivery rather than ULBs. This maze-like structure of management and accountability hampers good urban management.

18.29. To strengthen the urban governance framework, it is proposed to adopt the following strategies during the Twelfth Five Year Plan period:

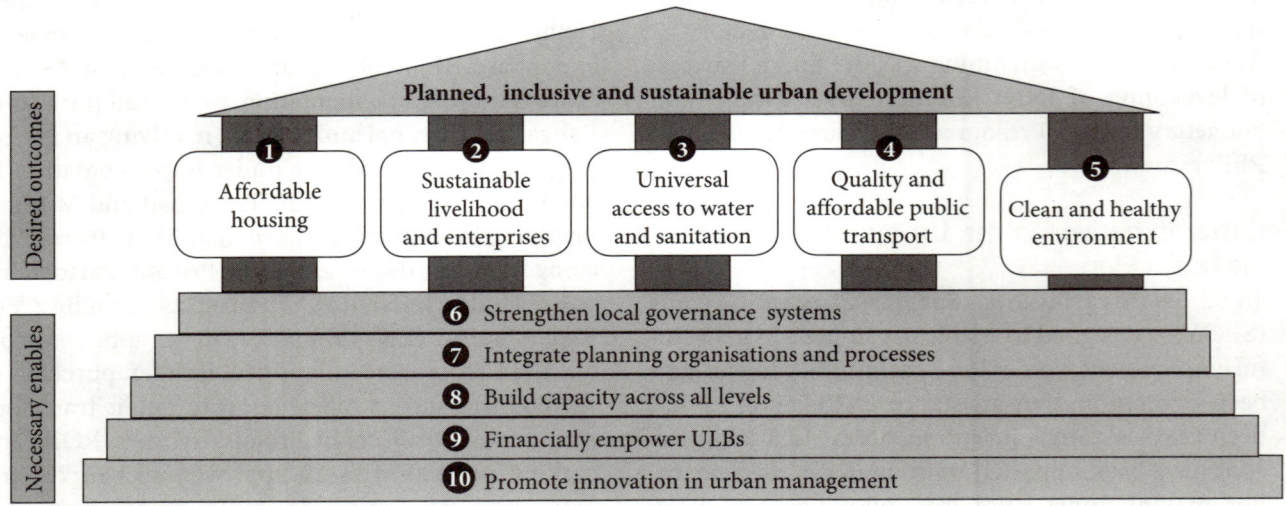

FIGURE 18.2: Key Constitutes of India's Urban Future

Achieve Convergence at the Central Government Level

18.30. Urban development, housing and poverty alleviation are inter-related subjects. Various expert bodies including Isher Ahluwalia led HPEC have recommended the merger of the Ministry of Urban Development with that of the Housing and Urban Poverty Alleviation. Their merger would improve the effectiveness and the efficiency of urban management in India. Till this is achieved, a concerted effort must be made for convergence of the programmes and initiatives of both the Ministries and merger of both the Ministries deserves a careful consideration. Ultimately all schemes run by different Ministries of the States and the Central Government must converge on ground at the municipal level. This must be an overarching guiding principle for the Twelfth Plan.

Set Up Municipal Services Regulators

18.31. An independent utility regulator should be set up at the State level to monitor service levels and adjudicate disputes related to delivery and pricing of services. The regulator would facilitate transparency by regular publication of service level benchmarks, and help set the vision for ULBs. Therefore, setting up of a suitable urban regulator at the State level must be a priority.

Empower and Extend the Term of the Mayor

18.32. Eminence of elected bodies in decision making is a prerequisite for participatory development processes. JNNURM pushed for elections to municipal bodies. The stage has come where the heads of such elected bodies should be adequately empowered. With the objective of establishing single point accountability the Mayor should be the executive head of the city. Also the Mayor should be vested with appropriate authority, for example, in a Metropolitan Area the Mayor of the largest ULB should be the Chair of the Metropolitan Planning Committee. While local conditions should determine whether cities should adopt a Mayor-in-Council or an Executive Mayor system, in either scenario, the Mayor's term should be extended to five years. The Isher Ahluwalia HPEC has also recommended that the executive head of the city will need to be empowered to run an efficient system of delivering urban services in a manner which harnesses agglomeration economies, minimises congestion diseconomies and creates a socio-economic environment that attracts investment and generates livelihoods whilst adhering to the constitutional requirements of a duly elected legislative body, the third-tier of Government. Hence suitable empowerment of mayors should be mandated as a key governance reform under JNNURM.

Strengthen the Unified Metropolitan Transport Authority (UMTA)

18.33. As recommended by the Second Administrative Reforms Commission, all the million plus metropolitan areas should set up an UMTA to develop and implement city level transportation plans. These must be integrated with spatial and land use plans of cities.

Introduce Citizen Charters

18.34. Every municipality should publish a citizen's charter. The charter should contain comprehensive information on service levels for all urban services, including the same for basic services for the urban poor at ward level and specification of time limits for approvals relating to regulatory services such as licenses and permits. The charter should also specify the relief available to the citizens in case of non-adherence as prescribed in the report of the Second Administrative Reforms Commission.

Increase Adoption of Information Technology at the ULB Level

18.35. Information Technology (IT) can play an important role in improving governance. With municipal administration becoming increasingly complex, the benefits of IT adoption are becoming more visible across several municipalities. E-governance must be a mandatory reform under the renewed JNNURM and its implementation should be required in all cities receiving assistance under the capacity building component of the Mission. A major constraint in full fledged transition to e-governance is lack of a suitable national level architecture. This has led to States and ULBs independently developing e-governance platforms which are often mutually incompatible. This has also prevented

States from replicating successful architecture developed in other States leading to avoidable expenditure. To address this problem, the Ministry of Urban Development should finalise a suitable national level architecture with sufficient flexibility for customisation at the State and ULB level within the first year of the Twelfth Plan.

Clarification of Roles of ULBs and Parastatals

18.36. In large metropolitan areas and cities, dedicated Government agencies with operational autonomy should be carved out to provide services like water supply, solid waste management, sewerage, sanitation, primary health services, primary education, roads and urban transport. The elected municipal bodies may procure services from these agencies by entering into suitable MoUs with them with clearly specified and mutually agreed upon output parameters/deliverables. This arrangement would make delivery of services more accountable to people while the expert knowledge available with parastatals will be available in conceptualisation and implementation of projects (refer Box 18.4).

Set Up Area Sabhas and Ward Committees to Decentralise Urban Governance

18.37. Ward Committees and Area Sabhas should be set up for institutionalising participatory development process for effectively carrying out the functions devolved to ULBs under the Twelfth schedule of the Constitution. For this purpose, Area Sabhas would be constituted by comprising all citizens in one or two polling station areas who should elect, once in a five year, a small Committee of representatives. Further, Ward Committees should be set up in every electoral ward of Municipalities and Panchayats by drawing representatives from Area Sabhas. Together, these institutions will ensure that executive power is located at the ULB level, while the deliberative powers are vested with the Ward Committee. These structures will institutionalise participatory and accountability mechanisms. These structures should be further empowered through enactment of Community Participation Act and Public Disclosure Law. Enactment of these laws would be part of the mandatory reforms under the renewed JNNURM.

Box 18.4
Harmonising the Role of Parastatals with Elected Municipal Bodies

A frequently expressed criticism of JNNURM has been that large numbers of projects were executed through parastatals. As a result, ULBs, which are the main institution under the constitutions for participatory governance at ground level, have remained marginalised. Lack of participatory process has reduced ownership of programmes by people. At the same time, planning and execution of urban service delivery like water supply, sanitation, urban transport and so on are highly interdependent and complex in nature and require technical inputs. Thus, a key challenge is harmonising the role of experts dominated parastatals with the elected municipal bodies representing people for whom the Plan is drawn.

The roles and responsibilities of different institutions in such situations should be clarified along five principal dimensions:

- **Unique Purpose:** Each institution should have a clearly defined 'unique' purpose for itself, in line with people's aspirations. Typically it should not overlap with any other institution at the same federal level
- **Measure of Effectiveness:** In line with the unique purpose, relevant measures of effectiveness should be put in place. These will not only help in creating external accountability for the institution as a whole, but will also provide guidance to the individual employees to discharge their duties.
- **Exclusive Decision Rights:** The decisions which the institution is empowered to take and which others are required to follow must be specified. These decisions rights must be reconciled with decision rights granted to other institutions.
- **Expertise and Capabilities:** Empowering any institution with certain decision rights alone is not enough. The critically necessary capabilities/expertise required by the institution to perform its functions and fulfil its purpose must be defined, along with processes for ensuring it will have these capabilities.
- **Inter-linkages within the Ecosystem:** Lastly, it is critical to understand the inter-linkages with other institutions in a complex, multi-institutional environment. A particular institution may have different types of relationships with other institutions. These could range from being a regulator, to having a contractual arrangement or serving as a technical advisor.

Put In Place a Fiscal Responsibility Framework for ULBs

18.38. Adoption and monitoring of prudent financial management in ULBs should be institutionalised through appropriate legislation. ULBs should prepare a medium term (10 years) fiscal Plan, fix a ceiling for revenue expenditures and perform regular audits.

Adopt an Outcome Based Approach and Put Up a Robust Monitoring Mechanism

18.39. A significant change would be to shift to outcome-based monitorable milestones as a measure of performance instead of exclusively relying on expenditure. The implementing ministries should suitably draw their Result Framework Document (RFD) for better implementation of programmes aligned to the needs of people. For instance, Ministry of Housing and Urban Poverty Alleviation may draw a quantitative target of reduction of households staying in slum. Ministry of Urban development may draw target of increase in share of public transport; coverage of access to water and sanitation and so on. This robust system of monitoring of the implementation of the Plan would also require frequent consultations with all stakeholders including elected representatives, citizens groups, civil societies and experts. All the schemes drawn under the Twelfth Plan must contain these provisions for monitoring and for receiving feedback so that plans are owned by the people for whom and progressively by whom, they are made.

Set up Lokayuktas/Ombudsman at State and City Level

18.40. In line with the recommendations of the Thirteenth Finance Commission, it is essential to bring local office bearers, councillors and other office bearers under the purview of an Ombudsman or the Lokayukta. The role of the Ombudsman would be to mediate conflicts between citizens and various urban authorities.

Urban Planning

18.41. A key weakness of India's urbanisation efforts is that the agenda is being implemented through disjointed projects/activities with inadequate or no planning for the urban area as a whole. The 'Master Plan' approach generally focuses on only the core area of the city, has little linkages to any financial and operating strategy and, in many cases has been used as a regulatory tool instead of being a blue print for development of dynamic and smart cities. A master plan typically freezes the land use pattern and building bye-laws and so on determines the permissible limits of Floor Space Index (FSI) and minimum setback areas. Often these provisions do not take into account the potential of the city to grow, especially where trunk infrastructure has been laid. This results in sub-optimal use of land as well as the infrastructure. Though JNNURM mandated preparation of City Development Plans (CDP) before taking up any projects, in many cases, the CDPs became hastily put-up documents with limited consideration of socio-economic aspects. Exclusion of peri-urban areas where fast growth is taking place has further limited the adequacy of such planning for guiding the emergent needs of a city.

18.42. Absence of any long-term plan prevents development of 'good cities' in which all the parts of the system—urban services, transportation, housing, commercial activities—fit together harmoniously. Planning must be holistic before it is detailed, for example, urban housing and urban poverty issues cannot be separated from other aspects of urban planning. A whole-city–approach is required and, therefore, there is a need for both Central Ministries which provide assistance under JNNURM for urban renewal to work very closely together. Holistic planning, even if not detailed, is required at the local urban level, at the metropolitan level and at State and national levels too.

18.43. The concept of 'Master Plan' to guide a city's long-term development has evolved in many countries to increase the quality of participation of all sections of citizenry in the preparation and endorsement of the plan. Earlier master plans used to be prepared mostly by experts in urban planning to engineer the physical layout of the city which often excluded the needs of citizens, especially the poorest whose requirements thus became peripheral to the Plan. Best practice master planning today is a core participatory process and addresses the needs of citizens more holistically.

City Development Plan and Financial Plan

18.44. Every city/town should mandatorily draw a *Development Plan (DP)* by taking at least a 10-years perspective. The plan should take into account a city's natural endowment, and its economic potential and should promote clean and green city It should specifically provide for the following:

1. Strategic densification especially along mass transit corridors with mixed land use
2. City mobility plan with special emphasis of making cities safe for vulnerable groups including women and children, pedestrian and cyclists
3. City sewerage and sanitation plan
4. City water plan
5. Economic and commercial activity plan
6. Infrastructure plan
7. Affordable housing plan
8. Environment conservation plan
9. Urban poverty reduction strategy and inclusionary zoning (old age homes, orphanages, working hostels, night shelters and so on)
10. Plan for peri-urban area

18.45. Financial plans that indicate the sources of funds required for the holistic urban development of a city must also be prepared. Performance against the agreed upon targets indicated in the Financial Plan should not only be used to monitor the efficacy of financial reforms being implemented across the State and city but also form the criteria of release of central assistance to the ULBs.

18.46. Drawing of DP and FP should be a necessary precondition for receiving assistance under the renewed JNNURM.

18.47. To ensure planned development of cities, a series of policy and institutional strategies should be adopted during the Plan period:

Ensuring Citizens' Participation at the Planning Stage

18.48. Success of any Plan depends on the extent it is owned by the people. This in turn would depend on what the Plan does for a common person. Since, in an emerging economy, every sector makes a claim for available resources, it is necessary that scarce resources made available for the urban sector are utilised efficiently and spent in the manner that is relevant for the people. Therefore, in accordance with the spirit of the 74th CAA, it is necessary that 'people' should be brought to the heart of the urban agenda, both, for deciding the vision of their city and for choosing the process of reaching the goal. Thus, involvement of people through Area Sabha and Ward Committees in the Planning Stage must be a necessary prerequisite for implementation of all schemes for urban development including schemes for slum improvement.

Constitute/Strengthen the Metropolitan Planning Committees (MPC) and District Planning Committees and Restructure the Role of the Metropolitan Development Authority

18.49. As per the 73rd and 74th CAA, a minimum of 2/3rd of the MPC shall be constituted of elected representatives from the metropolitan region, and a minimum of 4/5th of the DPC shall be elected by, and from amongst, the elected members of the District Panchayat and Municipalities in the district in proportion to the ratio between the population of the rural areas and of the urban areas in the district. Currently, DPCs are dysfunctional in most States.

18.50. Once constituted, the MPC/DPC should create the spatial development Plan for the region including any rural areas that may lie within the district boundary but outside the municipal limits of an urban area. Such Plans should take a longer 20+ year perspective with a formal review every 5 years. The broad Spatial Development Plan should then be used by the ULBs as a guiding framework to create the second level detailed plans for the city. The timeline of the Metropolitan Development Plans and the District Development Plans should be synchronised with ULB Spatial Plans.

18.51. The Metropolitan Development Authority under the aegis of the Metropolitan Planning Committee should be vested with the responsibility of enforcing and regulating the metropolitan development Plan. It should be the appellate authority for conflict resolutions on spatial plans for all Local Planning Authorities in the metro region, in keeping with the letter and spirit of the Constitutional Amendment Act.

18.52. Given the revised mandate of the Development Authority it should be relieved from responsibilities related to project implementation and land development so as to avoid any conflict of interest between the roles of planner/regulator, and that of project implementer or developer. Finally, it is recommended that the Chief Planning Officer and his establishment in the district ought to become part of the technical support system of the DPC.

ULBs must Prepare Municipal Plans while Utilities, Environmental Bodies and Parastatals should Provide Technical Inputs

18.53. Each municipality must mandatorily fulfil its obligation to produce a spatial plan within a specified time period. The Spatial Development Plans prepared by a municipality should be submitted to the MPC/DPC. Any directions given by the MPC/DPC from the point of view of ensuring the fulfilment of requirements and imperatives of the notified Metropolitan/District SDP should be complied with and these should be binding on the municipality. The spatial plan which fully complies with such directions (if any) shall be approved by the concerned municipal corporation/council. This will not only ensure compliance with the requirements of regional planning, but will also safeguard the power of the individual ULBs to approve the SDPs prepared by them without submitting it to the State Government for final approval.

Modify State Town Planning Acts, Municipal Laws, Building Byelaws and Land-Use Conversion Norms

18.54. These legislations need to be reviewed and revised to address the current challenges of urbanisation as well as to reflect recent policy recommendations to allow regional decentralisation and citizen participation. Metropolitan plans should be binding on municipal plans and should integrate top-down and bottom-up plans, reinforcing the concept of 'urban development regions' around the municipal boundaries.

Provide Incentives for Strategic Densification of Cities/New Towns on Growth Corridors

18.55. Strategic densification as a planning strategy should be pursued to accommodate future urbanisation needs. In addition, mandating inclusionary zoning and providing higher FSI to make the economics of affordable housing viable should be considered. Similarly, new cities may be planned to nurture emerging growth nodes in the urban landscape. However, as international experience indicates, the success of new cities is dependent on factors like their proximity to, as well as connectivity linkages with an existing metropolitan city. An effective regulatory regime which allows ease in conversion of land use while cities and their peri-urban areas are developing is critical. As a long-term strategy, the Ministry of Urban Development should identify such corridors and nodes with urban growth potential and facilitate their development (refer Box 18.5).

Consider Land Readjustment

18.56. Land readjustment (LR) is gaining acceptance as an alternative to land acquisition as it has many advantages for land assembly. Under this process, a compact area is selected in consultation with the land owners for urban expansion/renewal. The municipal authorities provide infrastructure which is funded by exploiting a part of land. The remaining land, whose value has increased due to provision of infrastructure, is reallocated back to participating private landowners. In essence a participatory tool, LR avoids public discontent and protests to a great extent. It also reduces the need for raising large amounts of money for acquiring land. However, successful LR is grounded in three main enablers:

- Fairly well-defined property rights
- Streamlined, independent and transparent evaluation processes
- Strong judicial system to address public concerns

Financing Urban Infrastructure

18.57. The Isher Ahluwalia Committee on Urban Infrastructure and Services (2011) estimated the

Box 18.5
Strategic Densification—International Examples

Large Indian cities have high population density. However, FSI in these cities are low compared to many smart cities in the world. This results in low per capita availability of urban space. Strategic densification of cities through higher FSI has numerous advantages: it makes the cities compact and efficient and frees space for accommodating more people as well as for providing urban amenities. Pricing of higher FSI also generates resources for funding urban infrastructure projects.

In Manhattan, as well as in other international best practice examples, FSIs vary by location and land use Density zones are typically small and are determined by street width and capacity as well as land use patterns. Commercial and office districts typically have higher FSIs than residential districts FSIs are set in conjunction with the formulation of development and strategic plans. Optimising infrastructure and density is a central element of urban planning.

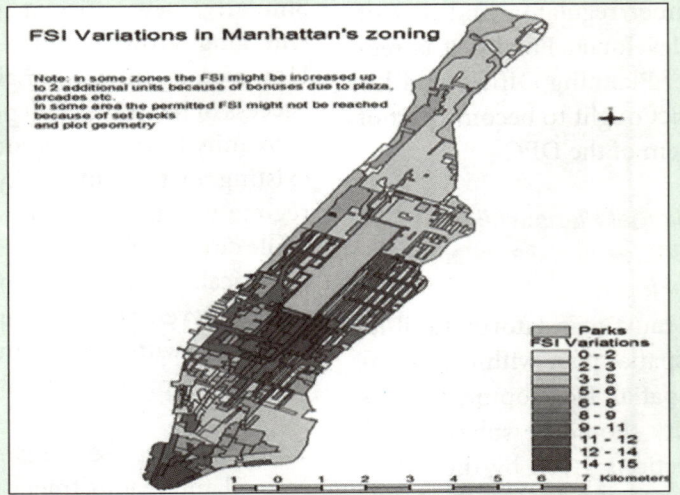

Singapore makes highly effective use of FSI with variations by location and type of use. FAR is higher near metro stations because transport system can accommodate increased density. As higher FSIs will require more infrastructure investments, they can be financed by suitable instruments like development fees or pricing of Tradeable Development Rights (TDRs) and so on.

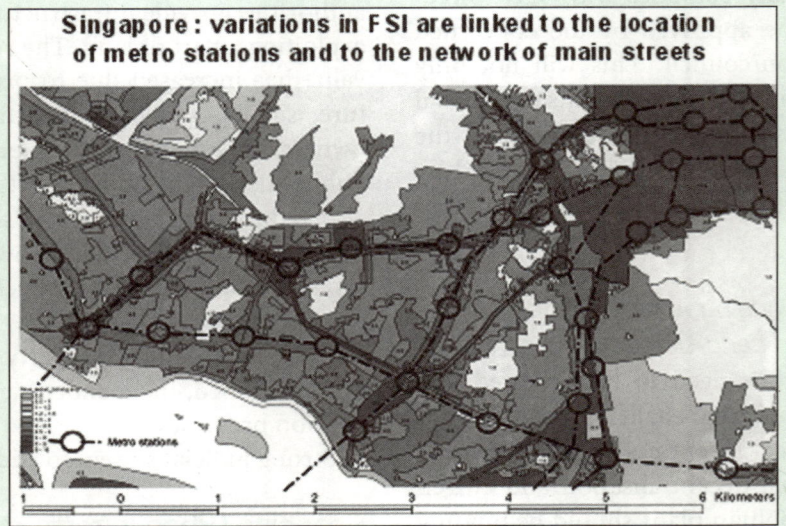

Source: India Urbanisation Review: Urbanisation beyond Municipalities (2012), World Bank.

total capital investments in urban infrastructure at about ₹39 lakh crores over the next 20 years. To meet this requirement, ULBs will need to identify robust revenue streams. In addition, both central and State Governments will also have to increase their commitment to the urban sector.

18.58. Working on the 20 year estimate provided by the Ahluwalia Committee, three alternative scenarios of covering the backlog of service deficits in 10 year, 15 years and 20 years respectively were developed for projecting investment. The aforesaid 15-years scenario up-fronted investment in water and sanitation sectors as well as investment in capacity building in view of the huge externalities and also moderated its projection on the basis of capacity constraint. Unless stated otherwise, the estimates so derived have been used in the chapter.

18.59. The share of ULBs' own revenues has declined significantly from 63 per cent in 2002–03 to 53 per cent in 2007–08. Property Tax collection is hampered by poor assessment methods, limited coverage, weak collection efficiency, loss on account of exemptions and poor enforcement. User charges also remain low, most often lower than the operational costs for ULBs. Most States have also not fully implemented the recommendations of State Finance Commissions, leaving ULBs with unpredictable funds' transfers from State Governments.

18.60. During the Twelfth Plan period, the finances of ULBs should be strengthened with a three-pronged approach

- create robust tax and non-tax based revenue streams for ULBs;
- attract private capital to the urban sector; and
- systematically monetise land.

18.61. A major strategy under the Twelfth Plan would be to strengthen the municipal finances and make them predictable through suitable reforms under JNNURM. This is necessary for attracting private funds for urban infrastructure. To this end, the following initiatives must be undertaken by the central and State Governments.

Institutionalise the Revenue Streams for ULBs

18.62. The Ministry of Urban Development should facilitate the process of making a Constitutional Amendment that clearly outlines the various tax and non-tax revenue streams for ULBs through the incorporation of a Local Bodies Finance List in the Constitution. In addition to property, entertainment, professional, motor vehicle, advertising tax and stamp duty, the amendment should also entitle the ULBs to collect appropriate user charges, trade license fees and use land-based instruments to augment their revenues. It must ensure that all taxes are regularly revised using scientific principles such that they serve as relevant sources of funds for ULBs.

Ensure Revenue Sharing from States to ULBs

18.63. According to HPEC, States should share 25 per cent of the GST equivalent with urban and rural local bodies, and this should be enforced through an appropriate constitutional mechanism. HPEC's recommendations in this regard are given in the Box 18.6.

Ensure Generation of Non-budgetary Revenues through Innovative Measures Including Monetisation of Land

18.64. Additional FSI that is given beyond what is normally prescribed should be charged for adequately. Such charges should be a part of the balanced strategy for expanding the effective supply of prime land going hand-in-hand with the strategy for creating 'virtual land' in the required location by building tall. The charges for additional FSI and land-use conversions should be determined professionally and should be at least 50 per cent of the actual land value in the concerned area. Apart from FSI, ULBs should also use various other land value-based instruments like betterment fee, land use conversion charges, impact fees and development charges that should be parked in a ring fenced city development fund and used for developing the required urban infrastructure in the city.

18.65. To enable land monetisation, a comprehensive and transparent framework should be put in place with the following features:

> **Box 18.6**
> **Recommendation of Isher Ahluwalia Committee on Financial Devolution to ULBs**
>
> The Committee recommends more broad-based revenue sharing by States with ULBs through appropriate amendments of the Constitution/other measures so as to:
>
> - Insert a 'Local Bodies Finance List' (LBFL) along the lines of the Union and State Lists
> - Empower ULBs to exclusively levy property tax, profession tax, entertainment tax and advertisement tax and retain the whole of their proceeds (hereinafter referred to as 'exclusive taxes'). In case States continue to levy and collect profession tax or entertainment tax, then the entire revenues, net of collection cost, should be passed on to the ULBs
> - Constitutionally ensure sharing of a pre-specified percentage of revenues from all taxes on goods and services (including motor vehicle tax and stamp duty) which are levied by States to enable ULBs to meet their functional responsibilities assigned to them by the 74th Amendment (hereinafter collectively referred to as 'revenue-shared taxes')
> - Provide for formula-based sharing of the divisible pool with the ULBs and also grants-in-aid to ULBs from the divisible pool for bridging, wherever necessary, horizontal fiscal imbalance;
> - Provide that the devolution in (c) above shall be on the basis of a formula designed by the SFC, taking into account the level of economic activity, population levels, extent of poverty, capacity to mobilise resources and other factors as may be necessary over time.
>
> The Committee also recommends that States should strengthen SFCs by improving their capacity, following the recommendations of the thirteenth CFC. They must also ensure that the recommendations of SFCs are given the same level of consideration as the recommendations of the CFC to the Government of India.
>
> *Source:* HPEC Report (2011).

- Development Plans should be prepared using a standardised approach on a regular basis
- Land-use patterns must be maintained as per approved Master Plans
- The process of land development should be strategically sequenced to generate resources for infrastructure creation
- Roles and responsibilities of Urban Development Authorities and ULBs in the land management process must be clearly delineated

Increase User Charge Collection

18.66. ULBs should levy user charges for all measurable services where beneficiaries are easily identifiable. Appropriate level of user charges should be determined based on actual service use, and regulated by the proposed municipal services regulator. These charges should not only cover the O&M costs, debt servicing costs and depreciation, but also provide a minimal profit to the ULBs to facilitate creation of an equity base for ULBs over time. Also, there should be a tiered structure of user charges, where higher levels of consumption should be charged a higher tariff.

Establish a Comprehensive Approach to Facilitate PPPPs

18.67. As much as 13–23 per cent of investments in urban infrastructure in the Twelfth FYP can be raised through public private and people partnerships. This should be done under an extended '4P' framework—*People–Private–Public Partnerships* as experience across the world indicates that in urban renewal and management, the role of 'People' in design of projects and partnerships is crucial, much more so than in large infrastructure projects such as highways, airports, power, power plants and so on, in which 'People' have a relatively limited role in the ongoing governance of the projects and their outcomes. Therefore, best practices and model documents for 'PPPP' must be evolved and deployed for India's urban management agenda to succeed. This would improve the ownership of these projects and would facilitate an effective R&R component of the project. These PPPP projects may become more viable if a subvention from property and other urban taxes is imaginatively used to meet any financial gap in the projects where felt necessary (refer Box 18.7).

Box 18.7
PPP in Urban Sector under JNNURM

It has been estimated that about 13–23 per cent of the total investment requirement in urban sector can potentially come through PPPs including annuity model. This would roughly translate to about 250–300 PPP projects in urban sector each year.

JNNURM-I was the first major initiative which encouraged PPP in urban sector. Forty-nine projects involving total project cost of about ₹5,458 cr were taken up under PPP framework in sectors likes solid waste, water supply, sewage and urban transport in which private concessionaire brought in investment of ₹1,066 crore.

A major factor that has prevented mainstreaming of PPP framework in urban sector is that given low user charges, very few projects are financially free standing and sustainable on the basis of user fee alone. PPP projects in urban sector would require relatively higher degree of government support and may be broadly classified as follows:

- Projects which are free standing, usually based on user charges, sometimes combined with Viability Gap Funding (VGF) or revenue streams from real estate
- Revenue linked to a performance based unitary charge (tipping fee for instance) with a minimum throughput assurance
- Revenue linked to a performance based periodical payment (annuity payment)
- Projects having little or no capital investment from private sector but designed to bring in efficiency improvements: for instance management contracts

Experience in other infrastructure sectors especially highways have shown that beside enabling environment, standardisation of bidding documents is key to encourage PPP projects. Such standardisation leads to greater certainty, broad public acceptability, reduction in transaction costs and time besides addressing the issue of capacity constraint.

Under the Twelfth Plan, there is need to develop such model documents for PPP projects in urban sector including:

- Water supply
- Urban waste management including solid waste and sewerage
- Urban transport
- Social sectors like Health care and education
- Affordable housing

Another important aspect in designing a PPP project is to ensure participation of people so that the project has the requisite ownership.

Set up a 'Ring-Fenced' City/State-level Development Fund

18.68. **Set up a city/State-level development fund**: Proceeds accruing to ULBs from innovative sources like land monetisation and other land based instruments should be pooled into a 'ring fenced' city development fund and then used only for urban infrastructure projects and projects for providing shelters to the urban poor in respective cities and not for any other purpose. In view of the capital intensity of transport projects, it is suggested that the fund may have two parts—(i) Fund marked for urban transport projects and (ii) fund for other infrastructure and shelter related projects. To start with, such funds may be created in metropolitan cities. To meet the demands of smaller ULBs, each State should set up a State Financial Intermediary, on the lines of Tamil Nadu Urban Development Fund (TNUDF), which can then pool funding requirements of the ULBs in the State and provide economies of scale.

Empower ULBs to Leverage Municipal Bonds Including Pooled Financing

18.69. A handbook should be created based on consultation with key stakeholders that specifies regulations relating to lenders and lending instruments, mixed or shared authority and responsibility between the Central and State Government and the ex ante borrowing activities of municipalities and ex post procedures relating to municipal default and insolvency.

Bolster State Finance Commissions

18.70. The State Finance Commissions (SFCs) need to be further strengthened for financial devolution and imparting predictability to the municipal finances. For efficient functioning of the SFCs, there is a need for revamping MIS at municipal level. Suitable assistance for strengthening of SFCs and creation of municipal level MIS should be admissible under capacity building component of JNNURM.

Building Capacity for Managing India's Urbanisation

18.71. Lack of sufficient capacity across all levels of Government is a root cause of India's urban development challenges. The Mid-term Appraisal of the Eleventh Plan highlighted that many States have lagged in programme utilisation due to inadequate capabilities of governance and management. Traditionally, capacity building, though critical, has been given low priority, which is evident in the absence of dedicated municipal cadres and robust urban management structures. Substantial skill gaps exist across almost all areas of urban management. This is driven as much by the lack of credible and specialised supply side institutions as it is by poor demand from those responsible for urban management in cities. Addressing the capacity deficit must be a key endeavour during the Twelfth FYP and the following strategies should be adopted to achieve this:

Create a Comprehensive Capacity Building Strategy

18.72. The Central Government should create a comprehensive framework that addresses issues such as staffing, training and skill development and finances. This framework should then be used by the States to evolve a capacity building strategy for all their ULBs detailing staffing norms, cadre rules that reflect service delivery and governance norms to be met by ULBs. This strategy should dynamically meet future needs, incentivise knowledge and skill development and provide an environment for using the acquired skills. State strategies should translate into ULB level implementation plans for capacity building. In view of its centrality to India's urban agenda, a separate sub-mission for capacity building, with 10 per cent of the overall funds should be created under the renewed JNNURM.

18.73. The wide-spread need and extreme urgency for urban management capabilities to catch up with the relentless process of India's urbanisation, makes a 'Just-in-Time and Task-Aligned' approach imperative to build capabilities. In a 'Just-in-Time and Task-Aligned' approach, functionaries are provided requisite tools and skills as they get to do the tasks, rather than acquiring these only through 'remote' training programmes not synchronised with action requirements. Therefore, the training process must be flexible and accessible. IT-based training systems enable this.

18.74. Key elements of capacity building could be as follows:

Institutionalisation and Professionalisation of Municipal Cadre

18.75. Every State should institutionalise a dedicated municipal cadre with necessary technical skills. The cadre should cover the key areas of urban governance and be equipped for increasing complexities of modern city management. State Governments should suitably frame the recruitment rules including norms for direct recruitment to ensure that the cadre attracts top-quality talent. A career path should also be put in place by allowing functionaries to move to higher levels of local bodies based on their experience and should ensure that employees are continuously motivated and recognised.

Leverage Private Sector Expertise

18.76. To meet the skill deficit in the short to medium term, policies should enable recruitment from the private sector and hiring of external consultants through a fast-track process. States can consider creating a list of 'empanelled urban practice professional institutions' to streamline the procurement process and enable ULBs to access external talent in a timely manner.

Establish a Reforms and Performance Cell at the Central Level

18.77. A dedicated unit to address issues such as implementation of reforms, dissemination of best practices across urban issues should be set up under the Capacity Building Mission structure of JNNURM. This unit should comprise urban planners, municipal finance experts, IT personnel, public health engineers' and others from required disciplines in addition to programme managers.

Launch Five Indian Institutes of Urban Management (IIUMs)

18.78. The Government of India in partnership with State Governments and the private sector should set up five Indian Institutes of Urban Management (IIUMs) over next two Plan periods and at least two in the Twelfth Plan to help prepare future generation of urban managers/regulators with world-class training in urban issues. It is also of utmost importance that these institutions are professionally managed by a joint board of stakeholders having required autonomy.

Facilitate Information Sharing Between Urban Managers

18.79. Strengthen the Urban Resource Link Project, designed by the Administrative Staff College of India in partnership with the World Bank Institute, to provide timely, relevant and quality information related to urban issues to urban managers across cities. Existing city manager associations should also be strengthened and networking opportunities should be created for urban managers to interact and learn.

Use ICT and e-Governance

18.80. e-governance initiatives including Online Project Management Information System should be implemented across all ULBs. There should be a State level nodal agency for implementation and monitoring of all e-governance initiatives within the State. It should also identify the training needs and coordinate with relevant agencies to conduct trainings.

Strengthen Institutions to Cater to Dynamic Urban Needs

18.81. The Ministry of Urban Development and Ministry of Housing and Urban Poverty Alleviation should bolster existing institutions and set up new ones to assist with policy research, design, and implementation as well as to train municipal officials, and elected representatives. Of these at least one to two institutions should have investments and involvement of the private sector.

Reorient the Activities of Existing Organisations namely IIPA, NIUA, RCUES

18.82. The Indian Institute of Public Administration (IIPA) along with the Administrative Training Institutes (ATIs) should be tasked with the preparation of standardised training modules and testing of training modules before they are circulated across the country to ensure they are in synchronisation with current requirements. The National Institute of Urban Affairs (NIUA) focus should be renewed such that it is capable of assisting the MoUD with policy formulation, providing advisory services to States on a variety of urban governance dimensions, and implementing high end capacity building activities for policymakers. The Regional Centres of Urban and Environment Studies (RCUES) should conduct active research related to policy support to cities and also disseminate various policies and programmes of Government of India and State Governments. These centres should carry out capacity building programmes in respect of new initiatives and priorities identified by the MoUD.

Enter into PPP Arrangements for Capacity Building

18.83. The Government's network of 1,817 Industrial Training Institutes (ITIs) and the 3,338 Industrial Training Centres run by the private sector could be roped in to up-skill and re-skill ULB personnel.

18.84. In conclusion, it must be reiterated that a modern 'Just-in-Time and Task-Aligned' approach is required to ensure that supply-side capability building institutions meet the demand side needs rapidly and effectively. India's urbanisation is unstoppable. Urban managers will have to learn while doing.

Leveraging Innovation to Solve the Challenges of Urbanisation

18.85. Managing India's ongoing urbanisation will place huge requirements on financial as well as human resources in the country. Given the scarcity of resources in the medium term, innovation will have a significant role to play. In the Twelfth Five Year Plan period, it is critical to promote innovation and research in several ways :

Provide Support and Incentives for Innovation

18.86. Given the huge requirement of funds, it is critical to incentivise cost reducing innovations in the fields of materials and processes. The support can be in the form of incubation assistance and low cost funds. Incentives could be in the form of recognition and rewards.

Use Technology Extensively in Urban Management

18.87.. Technology can unlock significant potential in building capacity across the ULBs. Innovative uses like, self learning packages which simulate real life situations relating to operations and maintenance can be developed in areas like water supply and sanitation, solid waste management and urban planning.

Recognise and Replicate Innovation

18.88. Creating innovative solutions is not enough. These solutions need to be spread across the country to maximise impact. Various approaches to identify, and spread the use of innovations should be institutionalised. These would include 'innovation and best practices' portals. The portals created by the national Innovation Commission can provide a platform. The Peer Experience and Reflective Learning (PEARL), platform created by the Ministry of Urban Development under JNNURM whereby cities can learn from each other, will also propagate solutions and its use and coverage should be dramatically scaled up.

SECTOR SPECIFIC APPROACH

Affordable Housing

18.89. The Technical Group on the Estimation of Urban Housing Shortage has estimated the current shortage of 18.78 million dwelling units. Further, the Group has also estimated that 73 per cent of the shortage in self occupied housing is in bottom 40 per cent of the urban households. The proportion of slum dwellers in large metropolitan areas is higher.

18.90. As against this huge requirement, during the seven years of implementation of the BSUP and the IHSDP component of JNNURM, only about 1.6 million dwelling units have been sanctioned. Given the huge investment required to bridge the gap between demand for affordable housing and its availability, all the costs cannot be borne by the Government and hence the key would be to attract private investment and to enable the beneficiary to increase his/her contribution. A multi-pronged strategy is required to meet the need for housing of the urban poor. First, a facilitative environment must be created by reviewing the regulatory processes governing land use to augment the supply of affordable housing with private capital. Second, encouraging contributions from beneficiaries of the slum—rehabilitation schemes are required for increasing the ownership of the programme. For this, the flow of institutional credit to the urban poor should be ensured. Third, they should be organised in suitable societies and self-help groups. These measures would improve the capacity of urban poor to afford a decent shelter either through incremental improvement of their existing dwelling units or take up shelter on rental basis or new units on ownership basis. Fourth, the Government should continue to undertake and expand the slum rehabilitation programme under the overall umbrella scheme of Rajiv Awas Yojana. Fifth, innovative approaches to facilitate the creation and maintenance of rental housing stock including dormitories should be expressly undertaken to serve the needs of the floating and migrant urban poor. And lastly innovations aimed at low cost housing must be encouraged.

18.91. Availability of land for affordable housing is perhaps the most crucial issue. Progress in implementation of BSUP and IHSDP and now RAY has been hampered by non-availability of suitable land for in-situ slum rehabilitation. The scarcity of land is the result of sub-optimal land-use patterns largely induced by the regulatory regime in place, lack of long term urban planning and lack of participatory planning process to determine the most efficient use of a parcel of land.

18.92. Several strategies can improve land availability for affordable housing and monetise land values for infrastructure. They are as follows:

1. Instead of relying on public land acquisition using the power of eminent domain under the current 1894 Law, which often give rise to discontent, the use of Land Readjustment methods must be extended for land assembly and infrastructure development to the extent possible. India has already been experimenting with a variant of LR in Gujarat's Town Planning Schemes (TPSs). Another ongoing experiment is the improvement of the C-ward in Mumbai that showcases the promises of participatory processes in urban renewal. There is need for scaling such experiments.
2. Adopting mixed land use and subsequently modifying regulations governing land use and removing deficiencies in the urban land market need to be given high priority. In many parts of the country, urban land planning limits redevelopment, modernisation and the repurposing of older inefficient areas. Weak institutional and information foundations still govern land markets. In many cases, urban plans seek to preserve status quo by limiting land assembly and freezing the density of developments by using very low Floor Space Indexes (FSI), and limited coordination with infrastructure development. Under the Eleventh Plan, JNNURM sought to address these issues by incentivising several urban reforms. Completion of reforms mandated by JNNURM must be given priority.
3. Simplification of procedures for conversion of land use and change in building bye-laws have been mandated under JNNURM. These reforms should be completed.
4. JNNURM mandated earmarking at least 20–25 per cent of developed land for housing projects for EWS/LIG category with a system of cross subsidisation. This reform should be completed on priority.
5. As mentioned in paragraph 18.55 above, there is an urgent need for strategic densification of our cities, especially along trunk transport networks and around zones of intense economic activities. Densification would make space available for affordable housing and generate resources for affordable housing. An argument in favour of keeping the densities low is that the existing infrastructure systems in cities would collapse if urban densities were increased. While cities do have severe infrastructure limitations, these arguments ignore the opportunities of using increases in land values by strategic densification to finance higher-capacity and higher-quality infrastructure networks and also affordable housing for low-income and moderate-income groups. In addition, compact development fosters increase in agglomeration economies and increased productivity which in turn leads to additional livelihood opportunities. However, care should be taken that the valuation of FARs required for strategic densification is not 'given away'. It has been observed that high FARs are 'given away' in the name of densification, cluster development and redevelopment. These 'giveaways' should be properly valued and put in a dedicated City Development Fund.

18.93. Since land and housing are State subjects, both JNNURM-II and RAY should continue to provide incentives to States to professionalise urban planning and undertake tenuous land-related reforms that reduce distortions in land markets.

Estimation of Budgetary Support for Slum Rehabilitation Programme

18.94. The Isher Ahluwalia HPEC has estimated a requirement of about ₹4.1 lakh crore over the 20 years for the purpose of slum rehabilitation. In addition, noting that about 25 per cent of urban population live in slum, the HPEC recommended that for inclusive growth, out of the estimated CAPEX of 34.1 lakh crore over a period of 20 years, 25 per cent, that is, about ₹8.5 lakh crore should be for slum population, assuming universal standards for all as well as universal provision for access and mobility. However, an objective estimation of the budgetary requirement from Central Government for the Twelfth Plan is difficult because this is crucially linked to the extent of innovation in low cost housing, the flow of private capital for such dwelling units and the extent of contribution from other stakeholders like the State Government, ULBs and the beneficiaries.

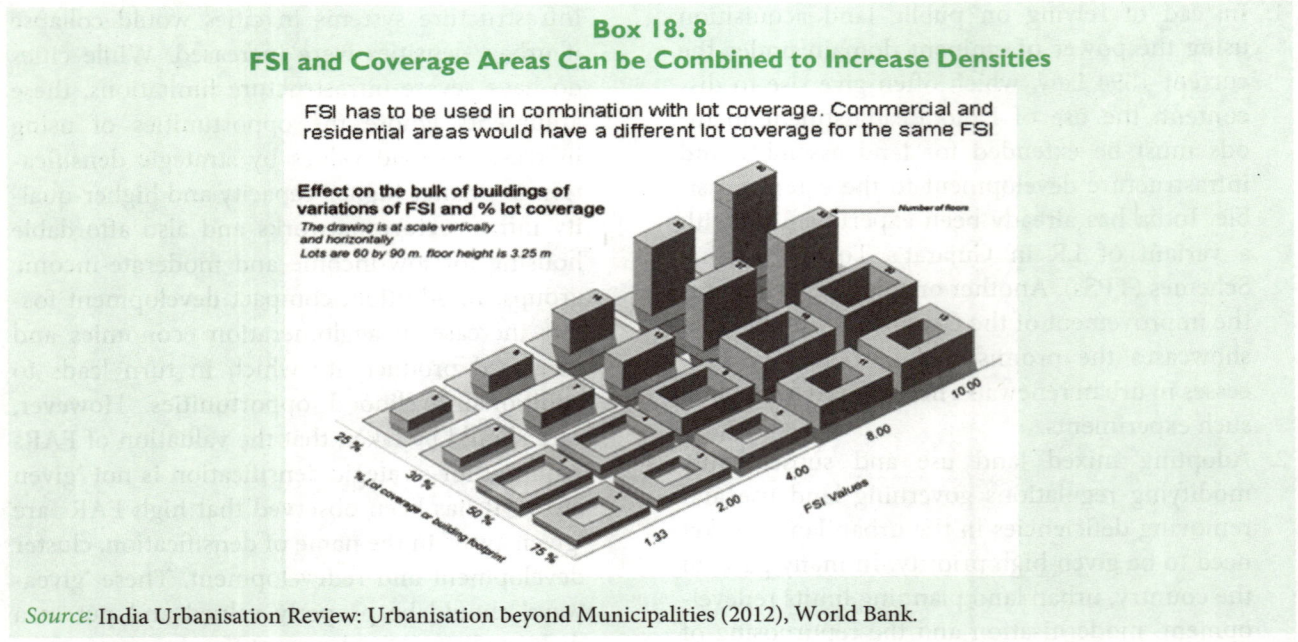

Box 18.8
FSI and Coverage Areas Can be Combined to Increase Densities

Source: India Urbanisation Review: Urbanisation beyond Municipalities (2012), World Bank.

18.95. Besides availability of resources, an important element that determines provision of central budget is the capacity available with different level of governments to undertake the activities required. Under the BSUP and IHSDP components of JNNURM, the cumulative expenditure across seven years has been approximately ₹13,000 crore. Despite its superior architecture, RAY has not evoked immediate response from the ULBs or the State Governments.

Schemes for Slum Rehabilitation and Affordable Housing in the Twelfth Plan Period

18.96. The schemes under the Twelfth Plan would be as follows:

1. Rajiv Awas Yojana: Phase-II of the Rajiv Awas Yojana would be launched. Ministry of Housing and Urban Poverty Alleviation should constitute a suitable committee to recommend the design of second phase of RAY by incorporating the learnings from the pilot phase. Phase II of the scheme should retain the principal architectural feature of phase-I of Rajiv Awas Yojana which are as follows:

    a. It is based on a *holistic approach*: Before seeking assistance under the scheme, all participating cities are required to make a city wide plan for rehabilitation of 'all' slums.

    b. It mandates *in-situ rehabilitation* of slums so that the livelihood opportunities of their dwellers are not disrupted. In case such slums have to be relocated because the sites at which they are situated are 'untenable', this should be done through a transparent process and the rehabilitations should be planned in close vicinity of the existing slum.

    c. It mandates *giving 'property rights' to slum dwellers* by suitable enactment within a year of the project being sanctioned. Besides, during this period it also mandates enactment of legislations to earmark 20–25 per cent of developed land for housing projects for EWS/LIG category and earmarking of at least 25 per cent of budget of municipal and other such body which provide basic urban services for urban poor. It also requires the participating States to draw specific timelines for legislations like modification of the Rent Control Act.

    d. Central assistance is up to 50 per cent of the project cost.

    e. The scheme provides for measures to improve the flow of institutional credit to the beneficiary. These measures are expected to incentivise banks and other lending institutions to provide credit to slum dwellers.

2. Phase-II of RAY would also emphasise following:

   a. *Creation of social/rental housing*: The focus of RAY on provision of rental/social housing stock for the migrant population is a critical element of a long-term preventive strategy. Of the total stock created under RAY, at least 30 per cent should be rental, and 5 per cent should be dormitories. Dormitories can be set up in industrial and commercial areas that see a significant influx of migrant workers.
   b. *Slum-upgradation as the solution of choice and transparent process for determining the tenability of slum rehabilitation*: Resettlement or relocation should be seen as an alternative option only in exceptional situations. A clear policy for in-situ slum upgradation including redevelopment and resettlement/relocation should be evolved by the GoI and implemented in the State as broad guidelines with State-specific amendments as per individual contexts. While evaluating the city wide slum rehabilitation plan, tenability of slums should be clearly identified by the Central Government in consultation with the State Government.
   c. *Building affordable housing stock in peri-urban areas*: RAY should also make provisions for affordable housing for the urban poor in peri-urban areas. The provision of affordable housing in peri-urban areas must be accompanied by the provision of basic services as well as functional transport linkages into the city.
   d. *Encouraging community participation to develop customised approaches for slum rehabilitation related to local needs*: Since a large number of slums are located on prime urban land which has multiple socially productive uses, every effort should be made to economise on land use through higher FSI. But in doing so it is vital to involve the community in designing slum rehabilitation plans. This should include the involvement of the community in planning, execution, and analysis/feedback of various schemes. Schemes should encourage the creation of Community Based Organisations in slums, federated at a higher level into an association/federation, eventually working to the administrative level of the ULBs with clear-cut, institutionalised frameworks mandating dialogue between ULB level functionaries and the community. The involvement of NGOs in programmes and schemes may be encouraged wherever appropriate to the aims of the scheme. Community-based organisations should be accredited and enabled to play a meaningful role in initiatives such as RAY. This will help such organisations to build on the community mobilisation, participation and social audit, and evaluations guidelines provided for in RAY. Guiding principles for designing slum improvement could include exploring the possibility of channelising community savings, reuse of building materials and other innovative method of reducing the cost of new dwelling units. In those cases where slums are not on prime urban land, incremental improvement in existing dwelling units along with provision of basic services like water supply, sanitation, power connection and so on may be adopted.

   For ensuring convergence with other schemes in the urban sector, RAY should be implemented within the overall umbrella of JNNURM-II. However, the funding pattern of RAY may be different. It should be run in project mode as project-wise involvement of centre in slum rehabilitation is desirable.
   e. *Slum rehabilitation scheme for smaller towns under JNNURM-II*: For the cities not covered under RAY, slum rehabilitation would be taken up under JNNURM-II. This scheme should have the flexibility to undertake new

construction while its thrust should be on *incremental slum rehabilitation* though new constructions as in the case of IHSDP of JNNURM-I would also be an admissible component. The budgetary provision for the scheme would come from the overall allocation made under JNNURM-II.

f. *Affordable Housing in Partnership*: While under the Twelfth Plan, this scheme may continue to remain dovetailed with RAY, it needs to be completely revamped. Its thrust should be to incentivise the private sector to augment supply of affordable housing in line with the strategy envisaged under the National Urban Housing and Habitat Policy (NUHHP) of 2007.

3. In addition to launching of the aforesaid schemes, following activities should also be undertaken to augment provision of affordable housing:

   a. *Revitalise and reorient the role of State Housing Boards*: Efforts should be made to reorient the role of State Housing Boards (SHBs) and Development Authorities. They should be encouraged to develop multiple partnerships with the private sector for construction of affordable housing. State Governments should provide the necessary impetus by preparing State housing plans that are integrated into the overall metropolitan/city master plan and outline the roles of the SHBs. They should provide a larger quantum of guarantee to social housing programmes to enable SHBs to access a larger quantum of loan assistance from Housing Finance Institutions. SHBs should also work with the State Governments to acquire land at appropriate locations that can be used for the creation of affordable housing stock. The activities of SHBs can be broad based so that cross-subsidisation opportunities may be made available to them.

   b. *Promote a corporatised agency for delivery of affordable housing under the Metropolitan Development Authority*: At the metropolitan level there is no specific agency that is responsible for the delivery of affordable housing stock. The State Government may constitute a corporatised agency that functions with an empowered board and steers the development and delivery of such stock in the top 20 to 30 metropolitan areas.

   c. *Accredit community-based organisations*: Community-based organisations should be accredited and enabled to play a meaningful role in initiatives such as RAY. This will help such organisations to build on the community mobilisation, participation and social audit, and evaluations guidelines provided for in RAY.

   d. *Promote PPPP for affordable housing*: Further measures to facilitate private sector participation should be introduced. This should include capacity building and legislative arrangement for rolling out PPP projects for providing affordable housing. Additional FAR grant and the provision of using some part of the developed area for commercial purposes could be provided to developers interested in slum redevelopment projects targeted at the EWS and LIG segments. The ISSHUP scheme which provides interest subsidy on housing loans to EWS sections should also be reoriented to facilitate PPP models.

   e. *Increase the corpus of the Credit Risk Guarantee Fund*: The credit mortgage fund launched under RAY should also be extended to cover any slum rehabilitation schemes undertaken by the Central Government. The corpus should be suitably enhanced and the policy should be fine-tuned such that allocated funds are used to underwrite similar funds created for this purpose by the private sector. This will generate significant additional capital for the sector and stimulate on-the-ground demand for affordable housing stock.

   f. *Simplification of the process of approval for projects of affordable housing*: Delay in approval process not only acts as a disincentive for the flow of private capital, it makes assembly of land more difficult besides time and cost overrun.

Urban Transport

18.97. Importance of an efficient urban transport system which is cheap, safe and reliable can hardly be overemphasised. The National Urban Transport Policy 2006 calls for increasing the share of public transport in our cities from 22 per cent to 60 per cent. The achievements under the Eleventh Plan especially in terms of an extension of metro rail network and provision of projects as well as buses under JNNURM to improve public transport need to be further built up under the Twelfth Plan (refer Box 18.9).

Box 18.9
Metro—A Transformational Approach to Public Transport

High capacity Metro rails are already in use in India and are proving to be successful in addressing the issues of public transport. However, it is a highly capital intensive mode of transport and hence should be first deployed in large metropolitan areas.

When to Deploy a Metro Based System?

Given the high capital costs, high ridership is a must for a metro system to become economically viable. Ridership is a multi-determinant variant that includes population, disposable income per capita, city densification, availability and opportunity cost of land, morphology of the city, and more importantly, the aspirations of people revealed through political demand.

A metro rail project is recommended in cities which ordinarily have:

- Peak hour peak direction traffic (PHPDT) of more than 20,000 for at least 5 kms of continuous length by 2021
- Total population of more than 2 million as per 2011 census
- Average trip length of more than 7–8 kms for motorised trips
- At least 1 million ridership per day on organised public transport

These criteria are in the nature of guidelines and are not to be construed as entitlement for a metro project. As huge public money is involved in construction of these projects, in all such cases, in the first instance, feasibility of relatively cheaper options should be examined.

However, it is recognised that in some cases, especially along busy corridors, difficulty and cost involved in acquisition of land may make metro rail projects a better option. In addition, surface vehicular transport system in general are less energy efficient and cause pollution especially along busy corridors where rail based systems are the best option. Hence, there is a need for a thorough cost-benefit analysis to choose an optimum mode of transport to ensure value-for-money.

Funding the Investments for Metro Systems

Global experiences suggest that metro rail transit systems have largely been developed by the public sector (an analysis of 132 cities worldwide shows that 113 cities (~88 per cent) have metros which are developed and operated in public sector mode). As MRTS alignment usually result in a significant rise in value of the real estate along its zone of influence, Government entities promoting metro rail have used this resource to fund other urban infrastructure. The efficiency gains through PPP have been brought in at the O&M stage. However, given the huge requirement of capital and willingness as well as capability of the private capital to undertake such projects, in high-density corridors, projects which are viable on their own (with admissible Viability Gap Funding and commercial utilisation of land ordinarily required for the project) may be encouraged under PPP mode. However, projects which are financially unviable without providing additional real-estate development rights and so on, should primarily be funded by Government. The central Government may suitably contribute in funding such projects preferably by way of making grants. Appropriate arrangements however need to be placed for densification across such corridors and use of the enhanced value of the real estate for funding other infrastructure projects. Wherever projects are to be developed under public sector, apart from grant, long-tenured debt financing should be facilitated through Government guarantee.

Quality and Affordable Public Transport

18.98. A study (2008) conducted by Ministry of Urban Development estimated that public transport had accounted for only 27 per cent of urban transport in India. The same study also estimated that in cities having population more than 1 million, the share of public transport is even lower. Promoting public transport in a big way with an approach of transporting people rather than vehicles is therefore not an option but is central to any strategy to make cities sustainable and efficient. Hence under the Twelfth Plan, the aim must be to raise the share of public transport to at least 50 per cent of all motorised trips.

18.99. This would require appropriate legislative, institutional and financial arrangements under the plan. Besides incentives for promoting public transport, effective measures are needed to disincentivise the use of private transport, along with creation of an affordable and efficient public transport network.

18.100. The measures recommended for the urban transport sector are:

1. Strengthen UT Wing in MoUD

18.101. Being capital intensive by nature, urban transport will attract the highest share of investment in the urban sector in the coming years. A key challenge is to generate non-budgetary resources to fund these projects, especially through land-based instruments. To manage this scale and complexity, it is recommended that the UT wing of the MoUD is appropriately strengthened with a full time Additional Secretary in-charge to exclusively focus on urban transport issues and drive its implementation across the country. MoUD should suitably initiate a proposal in this regard.

2. Constitution of National Urban Rail Transit Authority

18.102. Currently the Metro Act 1978 provides for formations of a Metro Advisory Board for every Metro project to assist the Government in implementation and running the project. In view of the growing importance of rail-based mass urban transit, there is a requirement of a national level organisation for research, drawing of specifications and standards, developing appropriate financing model of MRTS projects and so on. The Ministry of Urban Development should initiate a proposal for setting up an apex institution namely the National Urban Rail Transit Authority (NURTA) to promote rail-based mass urban transport in the country. The major functions of the Authority would include:

a. Advisory services to centre, States and Urban local bodies by emerging as the knowledge and resource centre for rail-based urban transport excluding the sub-urban railways which are under the Ministry of Railways

b. To draw specification and standards for rail-based mass transport system and determine the service level benchmarks for these systems

c. To develop alternative financial models for funding the rail-based projects

d. To develop capacity across different levels of government to roll out rail-based urban transport project on PPP basis. In this regard, to develop model bid documents

e. To promote research and innovation in rail based urban transport system

3. Setting up of a Research Centre for Rail-based Urban Mass Transport System

18.103. The Ministry of Urban development should initiate a proposal for setting up a Centre of excellence for rail based mass transit system which should promote research in all the major components of such system viz. civil network, rolling stock, tracks and signalling. Fostering innovation in such capital intensive systems would reduce dependence on imports for projects in the country and would help India emerge as an exporter of these equipments. The aforesaid research centre may also become a resource centre for the proposed National Urban Rail Transit Authority.

4. Promote High Speed Urban Rail and the Regional Rapid Transit System

18.104. Linking the core of large cities with their periphery through a fast and efficient transport system has the potential to unlock significant gains and reduce the transport related bottlenecks. As the disposable income rises, citizens value their time and are likely to be willing to pay higher fare. This also offers the opportunity for transit oriented development and promotes efficient land use. Besides inducing growth in satellite towns and peri-urban areas which are zones of intense economic activities, this also reduces congestion in the core of the city. As the experience of metro rail in India has shown, such transport networks are safe and have enabled the citizenry, especially women to participate more effectively in the economic activities of a city. The Ministry of Urban Development should explore such possibilities of developing rapid transport system and develop financial models for funding these projects through capture of value of the real estate along the alignment with an aim to reduce budgetary requirements.

5. Intelligent Transport System and Seamless Integration of Different Modes through Smart Card

18.105. Use of IT based applications for making public transport more efficient should be an integral part of any urban transport project. Already, in the Eleventh Plan, significant progress has been made in drawing City Mobility Plans and integrating various modes of transport. This initiative should be expanded in the Twelfth Plan to have a Common Mobility Card across all operators and all modes including parking.

6. Policy to Disincentivise Usage of Private Vehicles

18.106. Based on the 'polluter pays principle' it is recommended that an additional urban transport tax may be considered on private vehicles. This tax can be levied on an annual basis and can be collected through insurance companies for existing vehicles and directly on the purchase of new private vehicles. As the coverage of public transport improves in Indian cities, suitable disincentive to private cars may be introduced. Congestion pricing may also be explored as a means to reduce or stagger traffic on busy corridors and generate revenue for further expansion of public transport.

7. Social and Gender Auditing of Transport Projects

18.107. It is necessary that the benefits of urban transport projects are shared by all. Hence, choice of alignment and timing of running the trains or buses should be carefully done so that poorer sections of the society and workers in the informal sector are given priority as these sections are wholly dependent on public transport unlike the relatively richer sections which have other options. Besides, the safety and security of public transport is of prime importance. The Ministry of Urban development would issue detail guidelines for social and gender auditing of the outcomes of urban transport project.

8. Promote Non-motorised Transport (NMT)

18.108. NMT such as bicycles, pedal rickshaws and pedestrianism are affordable, environment friendly and promote healthy living. They are particularly suitable for short trips, especially for last mile connectivity. Despite these obvious advantages, these modes have suffered from policy neglect. Urban planning in many cities has not made any provision for dedicated tracks for these modes. Consequently, safety concerns have prevented many citizens from switching over to NMT. MoUD should bring out a comprehensive set of guidelines to incentivise NMT under JNNURM-II. For instance, while renovating arterial roads or new road projects, it should be ensured that the project provides for pedestrian path and bicycle lanes, wherever the space permits. Innovations in improving designs of NMT like pedal rickshaw should be suitably incentivised.

9. Create New Departments of UT in State Urban Development Ministries

18.109. States should institute a dedicated department for urban transport within the Municipal Administration and Urban Development ministry. This will help bring focus on the urban transport agenda for the State at large and key cities in particular. Ministry of Urban Development could suitably take up the matter with State Governments.

10. Institute a Safety Commission for Rail/ Guided and Road Transport

18.110. Safety is a critical issue in urban transport. For rail based mass rapid system, the Central Safety Commission should be appropriately strengthened. For road based system, State-level commissions may be set up for performing safety audits.

11. Promote PPP Arrangements, where Appropriate

18.111. Given the huge requirement of capital and willingness as well as capability of the private capital to undertake urban transport project, promoting PPP could be a key priority. All metro projects which are in high density corridors, and are viable on their own (with admissible Viability Gap Funding and real estate development on land ordinarily required for the project) may be encouraged under PPP mode. However, projects which are financially not viable without providing additional real-estate development rights and so on, should primarily be funded by Government. The central Government may suitably contribute in funding such projects preferably by way of grants. Similarly PPP arrangements in bus transport systems based on a gross cost model should be encouraged. The O&M of metro rail projects as well as BRT projects should also be entrusted to the PPP concessionaire to bring in the efficiency gain. For successful implementation of the PPP projects, specification of the service standards, outcomes and its monitoring would be the necessary prerequisite to ensure value for money.

Schemes and Projects for Urban Transport in the Twelfth Plan Period

Requirement of overall Capex Investment

18.112. For 20 years period beginning the first year of the Twelfth Plan, the requirement of Capex (at 2009–10 prices) estimated by the Isher Ahluwalia HPEC for urban transport from all sources are given in the Table 18.2.

18.113. For the Twelfth Plan period, the working group constituted by the Planning Commission on financing urbanisation worked out the requirement of investment for the urban transport sectors (refer to Table 18.3).

Schemes/Projects

18.114. In view of the importance of the urban transport, schemes/projects under the Twelfth Plan would be as follows:

1. *JNNURM-II*: as described in para 18.143 to 18.167, the assistance under JNNURM would be released to the city through concerned State

TABLE 18.2
Estimates of Urban Transport Investments by HPEC

Sector	Investment from all sources (in ₹ Cr) over 20 year period	% share in investment in urban sector
Urban Roads	17,28,941	55.8%
Urban Transport	449,426	14.5%
Traffic support infrastructure	97,985	3.2%
Street lighting	18,580	0.6%
Total	22,94,932	74.1

TABLE 18.3
Requirement of CAPEX

Annual Cap Ex (₹ Crore)	Requirement of CAPEX across different sectors in urban area					
	2012	2013	2014	2015	2016	Total
Urban Roads	29,842	35,214	41,552	49,032	57,858	2,13,498
Mass Transit	7,757	9,154	10,801	12,745	15,040	55,497
Traffic Managements Systems	1,691	1,996	2,355	2,779	3,279	12,100
Street Lighting	321	378	447	527	622	2,294
Capacity Building (urban transport)	1,000	1,000	1,000	1,000	1,000	5,000
Total	40,611	47,742	56,155	66,083	77,799	2,88,389

Governments as long as they adhere to the approved development plans, meet the reform related conditionality as well as mutually agreed financial parameters. Hence all urban transport projects and related activities including provision of buses, which improves public transport are admissible components under JNNURM-II.

2. *Urban road projects*: Of the overall capex estimation for 20 years for the urban sector, HPEC estimated that about 55.8 per cent would be required for urban roads. Since assistance under JNNURM is proposed to be fungible, urban road projects should be admissible under the scheme.

3. *Provision for metro rail projects and RRTS*: Success of the Delhi metro in transforming the public transport system in NCR region has led to demand of metro rail projects from many cities. Considering the long gestation period of conceptualising a metro rail project and arranging funds for it, following is recommended as a guideline for making a city eligible to receive central assistance for metro rail project:

- Peak hour peak direction traffic (PHPDT) of more than 20,000 for at least 5 kms of continuous length by 2021
- Total population of more than 2 million as per 2011 census
- Average trip length of more than 7–8 kms for motorised trips
- At least 1 million ridership per day on organised public transport

18.115. These criteria are in the nature of guidelines and are not to be construed as entitlement for a metro rail project. As huge public money is involved in construction of these projects, a thorough cost-benefit analysis across available mode of transport is to be ensured in case of every project.

Water Supply, Sewerage, Storm Water Drainage, Solid Waste Management and Environment Sustainability of the Cities

18.116. Safe water and sanitation are public goods as they have very large positive externalities. While access to water supply and sanitation is important for all the urban residents, for the poor, it becomes a question of basic survival. Lack of safe water and sanitation cause outbreaks of epidemics and Indian cities are every year affected by this. The impact of epidemics on the poor is much larger than on the non-poor for many reasons; firstly epidemics break out in areas where the poor live, their access to safe water and sanitation is far lower than non-poor and their nutritional status being poor they easily succumb to the epidemics than the non-poor. Thus, lack of safe water and sanitation cause health disorders and keep the mortality rates high in general and among the poor in particular. On the other hand, it has been estimated that access to water increases the productive working hours of the urban poor in general and the poor women in particular by 1.5 to 2 hours. Access to water and sanitation has positive impact on overall health and decline in disease burden reduces household expenditure on health and that itself has positive impact on household income. It is well known that higher incidence of morbidity pushes low income households below the poverty line.

18.117. The central assistance to States and ULBs for improving these services would be within the overall umbrella scheme of JNNURM-II. Besides, the focus of the Plan should be to bring about structural and governance change at ULB levels and to build capacity so that these services are provided on a sustained basis. This would be incentivised through a set of reforms related to water and sanitation and providing assistance to the cities conditional to progress in achieving reforms.

Water Supply

18.118. Following should be the target for the Twelfth Plan period:

1. *Universalisation of water and sanitation to urban areas*: This involves the universal coverage of all urban population for the minimum levels of safe drinking and household-use water along with a clean toilet, sewerage, storm water drainage and solid waste management. The provisioning of basic water and sanitation should be de-linked from issues of land tenure and legal status. These services should be provided on the clear understanding that this provision does not

automatically translate into legal entitlements in other spheres, especially as regards legal rights to the land and/or dwelling space. Further any decisions as to whether the slums are to be legalised or not should be made irrespective of the provision of basic services.

2. *Reduction in unaccounted for water*: A systematic approach for identification and reduction of leakage and preventive maintenance would be promoted as an integral part of the operation and maintenance of the water supply system on a regular basis. This would help save precious quantities of treated water and increase revenues to make systems self-sustaining. Such measures can often obviate the need for immediate augmentation of capacities of the existing schemes, which are very often quite capital intensive, while triggering significant improvements in service delivery.

3. *Hundred per cent metering of water supply*: Metering is essential for recovery of reasonable user charges and conservation. It acts as an incentive for those who wish to conserve water and a disincentive to those who waste water. Metering helps increasing the total quantum of water available and consequently increases the quantum of water available for supply and increases the overall revenue. Metering also leads to reduction of wasteful use of water and increases efficiency and sustainability of the water supply system that is an important O&M function.

4. *Ensure 24 × 7 water supply*: Yet another priority is to move towards continuous water supply. Intermittent supply leads to sucking of external pollution into the system during non-supply hours due to inadequate pressure, causing health hazards.

5. *Address structural dysfunctionalities through reforms mentioned in Box 18.10*: For meeting the aforesaid target, it is necessary that structural issues facing the sectors are addressed through completion of reforms mandated under JNNURM. These issues include high levels of non-revenue water, low level of metering, intermittent supply, inadequate quality, low sustainability and so on. The poor, particularly those living in slums and squatter settlements, are generally deprived of potable water. The implementing Ministry would work with States and ULBs to introduce operational, financial and institutional reforms related to water sector and these reforms under JNNURM-II.

18.119. Water is an extremely valuable but scarce resource and should be treated as such. In this connection following are recommended:

1. *The issue of allocation of water resource between rural and urban India needs to be addressed in ways that reduce intra-national tension*: In many instances, growth of urban and industrial sectors increases consumption of water which may give rise to conflicting claims on allocation of water across different sectors. It is imperative that while all efforts are made to conserve water for augmenting its availability, Indian cities and industries reinvent their water strategy with an aim to grow with minimal water and minimal waste generation.

2. *To cut the costs of water supply and distribution losses, focus on building, renewing and replenishing local water sources, including groundwater*: As cities expand their water footprint which implies sourcing water from distance sources, the cost of water supply as well as transportation losses and leakages rise. Committing a larger capital investment in creating such infrastructure also leaves utilities with very little money to maintain these networks which further compounds the problem. It is necessary therefore that all efforts should be made to develop a source of water close to where people need supply. The city sources are it water bodies, which capture rain or floodwaters from rivers as well as its underground water aquifers. There is an urgent need to protect and nurture these sources. Such measures may include bringing specific legislations apart from taking up specific projects under JNNURM-II.

3. *Include ground water in water supply calculations*: While preservation and recharging of ground water are increasingly receiving attention of city planners, there is a tendency to exclude this source from urban water planning.

In absence of universal access to piped water supply, people are forced to rely on ground water extraction. Another problem is perverse incentivisation for substitution of piped water supply by ground water extraction in case the water tariff is perceived to be high. There is therefore an urgent need to map groundwater and include this resource in water planning of a city for its sustainable utilisation.

4. *Take an integrated view of water supply and sanitation*: Investment in sewage should be a function of investment in water supply as any augmentation of water supply also leads to increase in sewage generation. It is, therefore, necessary that planning of a water supply project should also include provision for treatment of sewage. Discharge of untreated sewage, besides making cities and our water bodies unhygienic also significantly raises the cost of treatment of water. The guiding principle should be to incentivise cost saving innovations in building sewage network, reducing the length of sewage network and treating waste water as resource by turning it into water for irrigation or use in the industry.

5. *Set real and hard targets for affordable recycling and reuse of treated waste water*: Recycling and reuse of waste water is already in practice. This is required to be scaled up in a planned way. Reuse of waste water after its treatment in agriculture and other sectors should be properly planned for optimal utilisation of this scarce resource (refer Box 18.10).

Sewerage, Drainage and Solid Waste Management

18.120. The Ministry of Urban Development should work towards the implementation of the National Urban Sanitation Policy. Cities should be encouraged to formulate city-wide sanitation plans and all the States shall be encouraged to adopt State Sanitation Strategies. These activities should be supported under JNNURM-II.

Reuse Treated Sewage for Industrial Applications

18.121. Cities should be encouraged to meet part of their water supply, at least for industrial use, by reusing/recycling waste water. Incentives may be provided to users (through water tariff, property tax and so on) to recycle and reuse treated wastewater. These should also be incorporated in building bye-laws for new constructions.

18.122. Ministry of Urban Development should support these activities through financial and policy support through various schemes. While the major intervention would be under the JNNURM-II for preventing manual handling of human excreta, a separate sub-scheme for achieving the goals of the National Urban Sanitation Policy (NUSP) shall be formulated in the Twelfth Plan.

Solid Waste Management

18.123. Some of the major issues concerning solid waste management are:

1. Absence of segregation of waste at source
2. Lack of funds for waste management at ULBs
3. Lack of technical expertise and appropriate institutional arrangement
4. Unwillingness of ULBs to introduce proper collection, segregation, transportation and treatment/disposal systems
5. Indifference of citizens towards waste management due to lack of awareness
6. Lack of community participation towards waste management and hygienic conditions

18.124. As a general approach, Ministry of Urban Development should work with the States to explore the following strategies:

- The recovery of recyclables is presently being done in an unorganised manner. This needs to be replaced with informal arrangements of rag pickers and NGOs/CBOs who could also be involved for facilitating effective door-to-door collection.
- Acquisition/earmarking of land required for the project should be facilitated by proactive guidelines/direction from the State. A Master Plan process should actively address this requirement.
- The concept of regional solid waste management solutions needs to be encouraged. This has been taken up in Gujarat with a view to achieving economies of scale.

> **Box 18.10**
> **Reforms and Desired Outcomes Related to Water Supply and Sanitation**
>
> *Reforms (water and sanitation sector)*
> - Enact bylaws for reuse of recycled water
> - ULBs to ensure accountability of the water supply utility by drawing service level agreements with them
> - Have road map for bringing down wastage
> - Prepare a detailed database for the city relating to water supply and regularly update it
> - Draw up a roadmap, that is, city sanitation plan in accordance with the Urban Sanitation Policy
> - Prepare a sewage master plan for the city
> - Draw-up a roadmap for achieving Service Level Benchmark
> - Set tariffs on a scientific basis with cross subsidised* tariffs for the economically weaker sections
> - Have an effective grievance redressal mechanism
> - Draw-up demand management measures
> - Formulate ground water use by laws and enforce effectivelyenergy conservation measures especially in pumping
>
> * In general, since the charge can be only for water and one time sanitation connection charge, the charge for water must therefore cover O&M + Capex for water and sanitation for all categories. For both water and sewerage, subsidy can be in terms of low charges for the first x litres of water and higher than normal for the rest.
>
> *State level reforms*
> - Set up a regulator for the sector
> - Introduce policies to augment bulk water and resource allocation plans in alignment with the basic requirements of the city
> - Transfer the water supply function fully to the cities
> - Follow the three 'Rs'—*Reuse, Reduce, Recycle* policy for waste management based on the quantum generated
> - Provide incentives for waste water recycling policy incentives
> - Increase resource provision for augmentation of sewage system/toilets for weaker sections
> - Prepare a regional solid waste management arrangements (to have larger aggregation and economies of scale)
> - Prepare implementable PPP policy for cities
>
> *Desired outcome*
> - Universal Access to Water and Sanitation
> - Hundred per cent Metering of water supply
> - Opt for 24 × 7 water supply wherever possible and feasible
> - Provide for step by step improvement in the operations of the water utility
> - Steadily bring down distribution inefficiencies by bring down wastage of water closer to international best practice. Successful examples of utilities such as Phnom Penh, Manila (East Zone) demonstrate that reduction in NRW levels to below 20 per cent is possible even in developing country contexts
> - Commit to given hours of supply and be accountable for it through citizen charters
> - Commit to quality of water to be supplied
> - Ensure that the cities are free from open defecation and measures for providing toilets
> - Community toilets especially in areas that are home to the economically weaker section
> - Provide sufficient no of public toilets/urinals in city
> - Hundred per cent collection of garbage from houses/establishments and straight transportation for disposal
> - Conversion of waste to energy/other forms

- Waste characterisation has to be done properly taking representative samples from the city for various types of wastes and the treatment process should be selected accordingly.
- Appropriate technology options for treatment of the organic content of the wastes should be chosen based on the physical and chemical characteristics of the wastes and local conditions and so on.

- IEC (Information, Education and Communication) in order to educate households, municipal staff as well as personnel engaged in collection and management of waste about need for segregation at source and improved sanitation is the most important element in success of a SWM project. This must be accorded due and adequate priority.
- Polluter Pay Principle should be implemented in a calibrated manner in order to instil a sense of discipline with respect to throwing of litter by people without any concern for cleanliness.
- In the area of solid waste management, a general approach should be to pursue the concept of 'waste to wealth'. PPP may also be explored/introduced for functions such as door-to-door collection, street sweeping, transportation, treatment and so on.

Storm Water Drainage

18.125. Lack of storm water drainage often exacerbates the sanitation problem in many Indian cities especially during the monsoon months. The problem has its genesis in illegal, unplanned development and encroachment often on natural areas and drainage systems/ways. As the cities develop and grow, benefits from important environmental functions (natural water ways/areas) are often ignored and overlooked as a result of which natural areas are degraded and damaged. This along with the increase in built-up area results in increased incidences of flooding and accompanied ill effects. The densification of cities is leading to construction of roads, buildings which has resulted in increase in impermeable areas. As a result often permanent changes to the catchment are caused, leading to changes in runoff patterns, which affect the magnitude, frequency and occurrence of flooding.

18.126. Lack of storm water drains lead to water logging every monsoon and outbreak of vector diseases such as malaria, dengue and so on, that afflict the poor the most as the poor live in settlements that are in low-lying and un-serviced areas. However, such epidemics rarely remain confined and easily spread throughout the city.

18.127. The core of sustainable storm water management is to consider storm water as a potential resource rather than as a liability or a waste product. This shift can only be initiated by a visionary storm water management approach which combines the preventive measures with the traditional curative and reactive measures in appropriate sum so as to minimise negative impacts on human, property and environmental health. In this respect, environmental health would include preserving and maintaining the natural hydrological cycle, groundwater recharge, natural drainage system and so on.

18.128. Urban water supply, sanitation and storm water drainage were accorded priority under the Eleventh Plan. Number of projects sanctioned and level of investment in these services under JNNURM are given in Table 18.4.

18.129. At present, a large number of these projects are under various sages of implementation hence their full benefit are yet to be felt. However, given the level of deficit in these essential services and their importance in making a city liveable, they would

TABLE 18.4
Investments under JNNURM

Particulars	UIG		UIDSSMT		Total	
	No. of projects	Cost (in ₹ cr)	No. of projects	Cost (in ₹ cr)	No. of projects	Cost (in ₹ cr)
Water supply	158	20,562	453	8,901	611	29,463
Sewerage	112	14,992	89	2,833	201	17,826
Drainage	73	8,404	67	790	140	9,193
Solid waste management	45	2,091	56	342	101	2,433
Total	388	46,050	665	12,865	1,053	58,915

continue to receive top most priority under the Twelfth Plan.

National Urban Sanitation Policy

18.130. This policy aims at creating cities free from open defecation practices. Under the policy, annual ratings of cities on select sanitation-related parameters shall be carried out and the best performing cities will be recognised. The policy seeks to improve the status of sanitation in the country through formulation of State sanitation strategies, city sanitation plans, and a national awareness generation campaign. The Ministry of Urban Development and the Ministries of Housing and Urban Poverty Alleviation should continue to operationalise the policy under the Twelfth Plan period.

Projected Requirement of Investment

18.131. The Isher Ahluwalia Committee estimated the 20 years investment requirement from different sources as given in Table 18.5.

18.132. The requirement of Capex from all sources for these sectors under the Twelfth Plan as estimated by the Working Group on financing urbanisation is as given in Table 18.6.

18.133. Adopting mixed land use and subsequently modifying regulations governing land use and removing deficiencies in the urban land market need to be given high priority. In many parts of the country, urban land planning limits redevelopment, modernisation and the repurposing of older inefficient areas. Weak institutional and information foundations still govern land markets. In many cases, urban plans seek to preserve status quo by limiting land assembly and freezing the density of developments by using very low Floor Space Indexes (FSI), and limited coordination with infrastructure development. Under the Eleventh Plan, JNNURM sought to address these issues by incentivising several urban reforms. Completion of reforms mandated by JNNURM must be given priority.

TABLE 18.5
Investment Requirement Estimates by HPEC

Sector	Requirement of investment from all sources (in ₹ cr)	per cent share in required investment in urban sector
Water supply	3,20,908	10.4%
Sewerage	2,42,688	7.8%
Solid waste management	48,582	1.6%
Storm water drains	1,91,031	6.2%

Schemes

18.134. Following schemes should be launched under the Twelfth Plan for assisting the States and ULBs to improve service delivery:

1. *JNNURM-II*: The broad principle on which the scheme is to be launched is given in paragraph 18.143 to 18.167.
2. *National Mission on Sustainable Habitat (NMSH)*: The National Mission on Sustainable Habitat (2010) is one of the eight missions under the National Climate Change Action Plan. The Mission should be implemented in the Twelfth

TABLE 18.6
Requirement of CAPEX as per Working Group

Annual CAPEx (₹ Crores)	Requirement of CAPEX					
	2012	2013	2014	2015	2016	Total
Water Supply	5,539	6,536	7,713	9,101	10,739	39,628
Sewerage	4,189	4,943	5,833	6,883	8,121	29,969
Solid Waste	839	989	1,168	1,378	1,626	6,000
Storm Water Drains	3,297	3,891	4,591	5,418	6,393	23,590
Total	13,864	16,359	19,305	22,780	26,879	99,187

Plan period with the aim to make cities sustainable through improvements in energy efficiency of buildings, management of solid waste, and shift to public transport.

The Mission should broadly cover:

a. Extension of the energy conservation building code, which addresses the design of new and large commercial buildings to optimise their energy demands
b. Better urban planning and modal shift to public transport, that is, making long-term transport plans to facilitate the growth of medium and small cities in such a way that ensures efficient and convenient public transport. These plans should be in sync with the city's overall development plan and be a part of it
c. Recycling of material and urban waste management, a special area of focus being the development of technology for producing power from waste
d. The National Mission will include a major R&D programme, focusing on biochemical conversion, waste-water use, sewage utilisation, and recycling options, wherever possible
e. As JNNURM-II would be launched as an umbrella scheme for urban renewal and as environment sustainability is an important feature, many of the activities envisaged under the NMSH should be taken under JNNURM-II to ensure convergence. Hence, NMSH should essentially be a scheme for taking up pilot and demonstration projects in cities to promote environmental sustainability. Close involvement of the Central Ministry in such projects is desirable. Hence, the scheme would be run on project mode

3. *Scheme for mechanical cleaning of septic tanks and so on*:
Implementation of Employment of Manual Scavengers and Construction of Dry Latrines (Prohibition) Act 1993 is required to be attached priority as this addresses the age old abominable practice of manually handling the human excreta. The Ministry of Urban Development should take up this activity within the overall framework of JNNURM in which one-time procurement of the equipments for the purpose is supported.

Alleviating Urban Poverty: Creating Sustainable Livelihoods and Enterprises

18.135. Based on NSSO Report No. 508 (2004–05), it is estimated that the number of urban poor had increased by 34.4 per cent from 1973 to 2004. Approximately 81 million, that is, 26 per cent of the estimated 310 million urban dwellers were below the monthly consumption of ₹539 in 2004–05.

18.136. An important feature of urbanisation in India during the period 1981–2001 was the relatively small contribution of migration to the increase in urban population in India. The HPEC has noted that the evidence in India suggests that the rural–urban differentials in productivity have widened since 1993–94, indicating that there is considerable scope for migrants to take advantage of the higher-productivity non-agricultural sectors if they can be equipped with the skills and education relevant for employment in urban areas.

18.137. At the same time, the poor who are already living in cities are largely employed in the informal sector. Even though they contribute significantly to the economy of the cities, they suffer from multiple deprivations and vulnerabilities that include lack of access to basic amenities such as water supply, sanitation, health care, education, social security and decent housing.

18.138. If cities have to emerge as engines of inclusive growth, the country is required to address the basic needs of the urban poor by equipping them with necessary skills to take advantage of the growth process and at the same time reducing institutional dysfunctionalities which have been pointed to earlier that hamper inclusive and sustainable development of our urban conglomerations. A multi-pronged strategy is required to meet the following objectives:

1. Accelerate the rate of job creation in urban areas

2. Impart relevant skills to urban poor
3. Facilitate self-employment for urban poor wherever this viable
4. Proactive and mandatory creation/allocation of spaces within city boundaries to ensure livelihood opportunities to the urban poor.
5. Provide basic services to the urban poor, especially through rehabilitation of slums
6. Ensure financial inclusion of urban poor
7. Ensure legislative inclusion of urban poor
8. Facilitate the transition of the urban poor from the informal sector to the formal one and extend the provisions of social security

18.139. For making our cities engines of inclusive growth, in addition to launching of an improved JNNURM-II and RAY, the following schemes would be taken up under the Twelfth Plan:

18.140. The National Urban Livelihood Mission (NULM). This entails revamping the guidelines of SJSRY and enhancing its scope. Its basic thrust would be to build capacities and skills in sectors that have growing employment opportunities and are relevant to local socio-economic conditions. In its design NULM should deal with important issues like financial exclusion, policy and legal exclusion, and lack of access to information and technology, raw materials and markets. It should also develop linkages with the organisations like the National Skills Development Corporation and other private sector organisations including vocational training institutions that can actually train and hire the urban poor to meet their growing capacity needs.

18.141. In addition, within the umbrella of NULM, following two sub-components would be launched.

1. Sub-component for National scheme for support to street vendors
2. Sub-component for assistance to the States for provision of shelters

18.142. To make the scheme more effective, the Ministry of Housing and Urban Poverty Alleviation should initiate proposals to undertake following policy changes:

a. *Enactment and implementation of a suitable Act on livelihood promotion of street vendors and adoption of a no-eviction strategy by State Governments*: This will enable the creation of physical legal spaces for the informal economy and recognise and support natural markets of street vendors with a non-eviction guarantee. For this, a no-eviction policy should be put in place in combination with a land policy aiming at the provision of developed lands for the urban poor. This strategy should be implemented with the caveat that evictions for the purpose of the common social good may occur, but with provisions for resettlement and rehabilitation of project affected persons. The strategy should also cover Central Government and private lands.

1. *Formalisation of participation of informal workers in the economy*: Informal sector workers should be organised as associations or federations such as trade unions, cooperatives, and must be formally recognised. Similarly workers guilds and self-help groups should be recognised as fee paying organisations and must have the capacity to negotiate with utilities like DISCOMs and water supply boards to provide services at specified locations by paying user charges.
2. *Design of new financial strategies and products to meet the needs of the urban poor*: Typically poor cash flow hinders the success of micro-enterprises, women, children and also those belonging to minorities or SC/ST caste groups. Thus, innovative products and services that help meet the needs of the informal economy, for example, branchless banking, business correspondents and micro-finance should be created. Workers guilds and self help groups should be provided with a package of financial services including micro-credit for working capital and assets, micro-insurance for life, health and livelihoods.
3. *Convergence of schemes for social protection of the urban poor*: A large number of programmes are being implemented by the Government to help uplift poor in the

country. At present, multiple ministries (for example, health and education) are driving separate initiatives aimed at the poor across rural and urban areas. To increase their effectiveness, convergence across these efforts is essential. In addition, ULBs have the potential to emerge as an interface between the citizenry on one hand and the State and national Government on the other for ensuring better outcomes of these initiatives.

JNNURM UNDER THE TWELFTH FIVE YEAR PLAN

18.143. JNNURM which was launched in December 2005 is co-terminus with the Eleventh Plan. Under the Twelfth Plan period, JNNURM-II would be launched as a State sector ACA scheme. The scheme will have a focused approach on urban reforms, capacity building and helping achieve fiscal prudence across ULBs. The salient feature of the scheme and budgetary provisions under the Twelfth Plan period would be as follows:

Objective

18.144. The objectives of JNNURM-II would be as follows:

- Alleviating urban poverty
- Improving service delivery standards in urban areas including basic services for urban poor
- Empowering urban local bodies
- Facilitating participatory governance
- Effectively managing land resources
- Fostering sustainable, inclusive and faster growth

Strategies of JNNURM-II

18.145. To realise these objectives, the key strategies of the programme would be as follows:

- Build adequate capacity including dedicated municipal cadre
- Planned urbanisation by preparing a Development Plan through a participatory process
- Remove distortions in land market
- Establish efficient governance structures
- Promote financial sustainability and accountability of ULBs
- Attract more private investment, in particular, through PPPP
- Adoption of service level benchmarks and social and gender audit of the outcomes of programme
- Slum rehabilitation and creation of affordable housing
- Planned development of smaller towns and peri-urban areas
- Incentivising innovation and rapid learnings across urban systems

Components of JNNURM

18.146. The programme should have following components:

1. Urban Infrastructure and Governance (UIG)
2. Rajiv Awas Yojana (RAY)
3. Slum rehabilitation in cities not covered under RAY
4. Capacity building

18.147. The scheme for Urban Infrastructure Development in Satellite Towns should be merged with the sub-mission on UIG under JNNURM-II. Further, while BSUP and IHSDP should be discontinued, RAY should be a sub-mission under JNNURM-II for the purposes of achieving convergence.

Coverage of JNNURM-II

18.148. Under JNNURM-I, a 'Mission city' approach was followed. About 70 per cent of the central assistance was provided to 65 Mission cities. In the Twelfth Plan, adequate attention should also be paid to encourage the medium and small town to realise their full economic potential. Hence under JNNURM-II, the limiting concept of 'Mission cities' should be dispensed with and while all cities should be eligible to participate, a fair system of selection of cities to be covered under the programme should be put in place.

Outlay for JNNURM-II and its Division

18.149. The five year budgetary outlay for JNNURM-II is given in paragraph 18.184. This outlay should be divided between the following:

- Base Fund (80 per cent of the total outlay of JNNURM-II)

- Capacity Building Fund (10 per cent of the total outlay of JNNURM-II)
- Incentive Fund (10 per cent of the total outlay of JNNURM-II)

Capacity Building under JNNURM-II

18.150. Capacity building at different levels of government would be a key focus area under the programme. For this purpose:

- A separate Mission Directorate for Capacity Building and Reform Management should be established.
- Ten per cent of the overall JNNURM fund should be earmarked for capacity building.
- MoUD and MoHUPA should prepare a road map for operationalising the recommendations made by HPEC and the Working Group on capacity building.
- All capacity building efforts currently undertaken by the MoUD and MoHUPA in urban sector may be brought under the umbrella of JNNURM-II. However, capacity building efforts for highly specialised sectors like urban transport (Metro Rail) or for proposed National Urban Livelihood Mission could be run independently though the Ministries should ensure their convergence with the efforts taken under JNNURM-II.

18.151. The main thrust of capacity-building activities would be:

- Creation and professionalisation of the Municipal Cadre
- Identifying the gap in capacity at different levels to establish the demand
- Strengthening the supply side of capacity building
- Opening of suitable institutions in case the existing ones are unable to meet current requirements
- Support to opening of a apex level institutions that have involvement from the private sector and centres of excellence in specific sectors like water supply and sanitation, housing and so on
- Creation of a dedicated PPPP cell for developing model bid documents
- Creation of cell on municipal finance and framework for land monetisation and other innovative method of generating finances and so on
- Dissemination of national and international best practices in urban governance
- Conducting annual reform audits to monitor the progress of reforms across participating States and cities

Planned and Holistic Development of Cities under JNNURM-II

18.152. Every town and city participating in the programme would prepare a Development and Financial Plan as provided in paragraph 18.44 and 18.45.

Reforms under JNNURM-II

18.153. Since the engagement of Government of India in the urban sector is largely to incentivise the State Governments and ULBs to bring about structural transformation in cities, reforms must remain at the heart of the JNNURM. In addition a robust system of evaluation of reforms should be put in place.

18.154. JNNURM-I has set the stage for attempting second generation reforms. Secondly, since JNNURM-II takes a relatively longer time horizon of 10 years, it provides sufficient opportunity to achieve reforms to even those States which have struggled to make any significant progress.

18.155. All pending reforms under JNNURM-I should become base reforms for JNNURM-II. A few second generation reforms including reforms in water and sanitation sector should be introduced and made mandatory. In view of different level of preparedness for achieving the reforms across cities of different sizes, the required milestones to be achieved in a particular reform should be calibrated according to the size of cities. Besides, since some of the reforms mentioned in the comprehensive list are difficult ones but are transformational in nature, it is desirable to introduce additional incentives for fast tracking such difficult reforms. Their completion should entitle States/ULBs to get additional allocation from the Incentive Fund which is proposed to be 10 per cent of the outlay of JNNURM-II (refer to Box 18.11).

Box 18.11
Reforms under JNNURM Comprehensive List of Reforms in Urban Sector

ULB Level Reforms (cities having population more than 5 lakh)
1. Introduce and enhance e-governance system
2. Adoption of accrual based double entry system of accounting
3. Collection of property tax
4. Rationalisation of user charges collection
5. Create a ring-fenced development fund
6. Put in place transparent FAR policies and market value based FAR charges
7. Earmarking of 20–25 per cent of developed land for housing projects for EWS/LIG category with a system of cross subsidisation
8. Internal earmarking within local body budgets for basic service to the urban poor
9. Sector specific reforms of water and sanitation that includes:

    - Enact bylaws for reuse of recycled water
    - Ensure accountability of the water supply utility through service level agreements with ULBs
    - Draw road map for bringing down wastage
    - Prepare a detailed database for the city relating to water supply and regularly update it
    - Draw up a roadmap, that is, City sanitation plan in accordance with the Urban Sanitation Policy
    - Prepare a sewage master plan for the city
    - Draw-up a roadmap for achieving Service Level Benchmark
    - Have an effective grievance redressal mechanism
    - Draw-up demand management measures

Reforms for Metropolitan Areas
1. Institute the Metropolitan Planning Committee (MPC)
2. All metropolitan areas (UAs) with population above 4 million, should set up an UMTA to facilitate integration of multi-modal transport systems and ensure it works with the MPC and has the MDA as the secretariat

State Level Reforms
1. Create and establish the Municipal Cadre
2. Set up a Municipal Regulator at the State/city level to

    - advise and monitor the service delivery levels;
    - regulate the pricing of services; and
    - ensure equitable access to all urban citizens, including urban poor.

3. Revise town planning act, development control regulations, municipal laws and building bye-laws with a view to promote strategic densification, single window clearance process, to promote conservation of environment and so on
4. Simplification of legal and procedural frameworks for conversion of agricultural land for non-agricultural purposes within a time bound period
5. Repeal of Urban land Ceiling and Regulation Act
6. Amendment of Rent Control Laws
7. Rationalisation of Stamp Duty to bring it down to 5 per cent or lower
8. Introduction of computerised process of registration of land and property
9. Provide security of tenure at affordable prices to urban poor
10. To facilitate public–private partnerships, and market borrowing (through provisions in the Municipal Act)
11. Transfer 18 functions to ULB as per 74th CAA
12. Strengthen the State Finance Commissions and act on the existing recommendations of previous SFCs
13. Set up a State Property Tax Board
14. Extending the term of Mayor to five years and adopt a Mayor-in-Council or Executive Mayor system
15. Enactment of community participation law
16. Enactment of Public Disclosure Law

17. State-level reforms pertaining to water and sanitation sector which includes:
    - Prepare a regional water supply, sanitation and solid waste management plan. (to have larger aggregation, development of watershed and economies of scale)
    - Transfer the water supply function (distribution within the city) fully to the cities
    - Introduce policies to augment bulk water and resource allocation plans in alignment with the basic requirements of the city
    - Follow the three 'Rs'—*Reuse, Reduce, Recycle* policy for waste management based on the quantum generated
    - Provide incentives for waste water recycling policy incentives.
    - Increase resource provision for augmentation of sewage system/toilets for weaker sections
    - Prepare implementable PPP policy for cities
    - Formulate ground-water use by laws and enforce effectively energy conservation measures especially in pumping

Incentive Reforms and Conditionalities
- Create and establish the Municipal Cadre
- Set up a Municipal Regulator at the State/city level
- Extending the term of Mayor to 5 years and adopt a Mayor–in–Council or Executive Mayor system
- Revise Town Planning Act and so on
- Simplification of legal and procedural frameworks for conversion of agricultural land for non-agricultural purposes
- Amendment of Rent Control Laws
- Provide Security of Tenure at affordable prices to urban poor
- Amend Municipal Laws to include Fiscal Responsibility and Budget Management principles for ULBs
- Release the land under ULCRA for development of affordable housing
- Introduction of Property Title Certification System in ULBs
- Transfer 18 functions to ULB as per 74th CAA
- Any substantial innovation in the area of urban governance or financing
- Take up projects under PPPP
- Leverage fund through non-budgetary resources

Incentive Reforms for Metropolitan areas
- Adoption of an agency model, for example, BEST model of service
- Exceptional performance in the area of service delivery, collection of user charges and property tax.

Addressing Operational and Organisational Issues through JNNURM-II

18.156. The need to adopt a unified approach to achieve planned, inclusive and sustainable urban development has long been recognised. Hence one of the objectives of JNNURM-II which has been envisaged as the umbrella programme should be to facilitate convergence of the initiatives at central and State-level for guided urbanisation.

18.157. To this end, at the central level it is proposed that the reform agenda for the Urban Infrastructure and Governance (UIG) sub-mission and Ray Awas Yojana (RAY) and the programme on slum rehabilitation for others cities outside of RAY is strengthened. Similarly to effectively assist States with reform management and implementation, and capacity building initiatives it is proposed that a separate sub-mission, that is, Capacity Building and Reform Management (CBRM) is launched under JNNURM-II. This approach would facilitate convergence across the two ministries at the centre, and enable the Central Government to collectively provide State and city Governments with adequate support to implement reforms and projects. In addition, it would also systematically monitor the progress on reform implementation across States and assist them with strategic capacity-building initiatives, for example, revitalising existing institutions, setting up a municipal cadre and so on.

18.158. To facilitate convergence at the State-level, a single State-level nodal agency (SLNA) should be set up for implementing all centrally sponsored urban programmes in the State. This agency would have project management and implementation units for UIG, RAY, National Urban Livelihoods Mission (NULM), other housing programmes and capacity building, and the would be led by either the Secretary Urban Development or Housing depending on their seniority.

18.159. The SLNA could be the nodal contact for all participating ULBs. It would also help strengthen the District Urban Development Authorities to assist smaller cities with project development and finance and reform implementation. In addition, it would technically appraise projects submitted by ULBs, and forward them onto the competent authority for sanction, transfer money to ULBs as per the project implementation phase and provide ULBs with the requisite technical support, and enable pooled finance development through the setting up of State-level financial intermediaries, in order to provide financial assistance to smaller ULBs.

Providing Operational Flexibility

18.160. In keeping with the recommendations of the Second Administrative Reforms Commission, JNNURM-II should encourage agencification to provide operational flexibility, essential for the missions to discharge their duties effectively.

18.161. In line with this, all the four sub-missions envisaged under JNNURM-II could be set up as agencies, that is, organisation with a board, and the board could be chaired by the Secretary of the respective ministries at the central level. Other board members could include senior representatives from the Department of Expenditure, Urban Transport, Mission Director—RAY, Planning Commission, Mission Director—Capacity Building and Mission Director of the programme for slum rehabilitation in smaller cities. In addition, to further the spirit of participatory governance, a few eminent individuals should also be co-opted as board members. The board of the sub-mission, CBRM could be chaired by eminent individual as it seeks to facilitate convergence across the two ministries.

18.162. It is important to note that all decisions with regard to capacity building should ultimately be approved by the CBRM board after gathering muster with the Council on Capacity Building, that is, a three-member council chaired by the Additional Secretary heading this unit with Mission Director, JNNURM-I and Mission Director—RAY as members. Similarly, the SLNA should also be set up as an agency whose board should chaired by the nominee of the Chief Secretary of the State and include senior representatives from the State Government's department on finance, housing, parastatals, for example, housing Boards, transport and local self-government, depending on the governance structure of the State. In addition it should have also co-opt a few eminent civil society representatives.

Preparing for JNNURM-II

18.163. Significant preparatory work is required to be undertaken by the centre and States in the areas of planning, capacity building and preparation of model legislations, and policies. During the initial two years of JNNURM-II the following should be accomplished:

- The projects sanctioned under JNNURM-I and pending reforms should be completed
- The implementing ministries through CSMC may sanction projects based on the allocation provided for basic services
- The Centre, State and the ULBs should undertake extensive capacity building programme and formulate State-level strategies for a 10-year horizon
- Municipal cadres should be established and professionalised in States in which they have been established. This would include clear guidelines on roles, career progression, and recruitment rules to ensure these cadres fructify into high quality capacity on the ground.
- DP and FP should be prepared based on the guidelines proposed by the MOUD

Fund Flow Mechanism

18.164. The cities receiving assistance under the programme would be selected as per the mechanism designed for the programme.

- Once the DP and the FP are approved, the annual allocation of the city are recommended to be released in two instalments by the Ministry of Finance, that is, in April and October of the year. The release should be made to the ULBs by Ministry of Finance through the State Government.
- In the second year, the Mission Directorate should examine the financial and reform related parameters made in the DP, FP and RFD. In the initial year of Plans, while releasing funds, progress in approved project would be taken into account. As projects would start maturing, by the Thirteenth Plan the release should be linked to the outcome of the projects in terms of service delivery. As long as these parameters are met, the annual allocation for the second year should be released in two instalments. In the subsequent years, the Mission Directorate will follow the same procedure for release of funds.
- Under this arrangement, JNNURM funds should be fungible across various approved projects in a city.
- The fund flow mechanism of Rajiv Awas Yojana should continue to be governed by the current approved mechanism and may be reviewed at the time of review of RAY.

Leveraging Funds under JNNURM-II

18.165. As brought out by the HPEC Report and the Report of the Working Group on Financing Urbanisation, there is a huge gap between the funds required for successful urbanisation and the funds available with ULBs. In view of the severe budgetary constraint, this gap can only be partly filled by contribution from the Centre and States. Therefore, the ULBs must leverage such contributions from the Centre and States to attract private investment besides generating their own revenues through comprehensive reforms. One of the key focus areas of the scheme would be to leverage central assistance under JNNURM so that investment in urban sector is augmented.

Share of the State Government

18.166. JNNURM-II would incentivise the State Governments for financial devolution to ULBs for improving their financial sustainability. Till this is done, the State should contribute 50 per cent of the amount of grant provided to a ULB by the Centre under JNNURM-II or the amount recommended by the State Finance Commission, whichever is higher.

Incentive Fund

18.167. For incentivising completion of second generation urban reforms 10 per cent of JNNURM funds would be earmarked as Incentive Funds. These funds are envisaged to be disbursed to States and metropolitan cities once the CRBM certifies that the reforms have been implemented in letter and spirit (refer to Box 18.12).

MISCELLANEOUS SCHEMES

18.168. In accordance with the recommendations of the Chaturvedi Committee, a guiding principle in the Twelfth pan is to run umbrella schemes having different components. In the preceding sections, major scheme for urban renewal for the Twelfth Plan period have been described. In addition, following schemes/projects would also continue in the Twelfth Plan period.

General Pool Accommodation (Residential and Non-residential)

18.169. This scheme provides for office and residential accommodation for Central Government

---

Box 18.12
Major Schemes for Urban Renewal at a Glance

State sector ACA scheme: Jawaharlal Nehru National Urban Renewal Mission (JNNURM) having following components:
- Urban Infrastructure and Governance (UIG)
- Rajiv Awas Yojana (RAY)
- Slum rehabilitation in cities not covered under RAY
- Capacity building

Centrally Sponsored Schemes
National Urban Livelihood Mission having two additional components:
- Scheme for support to street vendors
- Scheme for assistance to the States for provision of shelters.

1) **National Mission on sustainable Habitat**

departments and employees through CPWD. As land parcels available with the Ministry are mostly in prime locations they have significant potential to generate resources, embarking on PPPs towards this end would be an effective route to pursue, given the thrust of the Twelfth Plan on such arrangements.

North Eastern Region Urban Development Programme (NERUDP)

18.170. Launched with the assistance of the Asian Development Bank (ADB) to encourage development in the North Eastern Region as well as increase support through multilateral agencies, the programme provides support for priority urban services viz. (i) Water Supply, (ii) Sewerage and Sanitation and (iii) Solid Waste Management in the capital cities of five North-Eastern States viz. Agartala (Tripura), Aizawl (Mizoram), Gangtok (Sikkim), Kohima (Nagaland) and Shillong (Meghalaya). Under the Twelfth Plan, this programme would be recast and taken under the overall framework of JNNURM.

National Capital Region Planning Board

18.171. The NCR Planning Board is providing financial assistance to create civic amenities in the National Capital Region (NCR). The assistance is in the form of soft long-term loans to the participating State Governments and other parastatals for infrastructure development projects in the constituent NCR States and identified Counter Magnet Area (CMA) towns. The activities of the NCRPB would be expanded in the Twelfth Plan period.

Other Schemes/Projects

Ministry of Urban Development

Urban Transport Planning and Capacity Building in Urban Sector

18.172. The scheme provides assistance upto 80 per cent of cost of city specific comprehensive traffic and transportation studies and builds capability to undertake comprehensive urban transport planning. The scheme should be subsumed under the renewed JNNURM in the Twelfth Plan period.

Research and Capacity Building in Urban and Regional Planning

18.173. The scheme was launched to build capacity building for urban regional planning at the ULB level. While capacity building for regional planning is a prerequisite for sound urban development, the scheme should be subsumed under the renewed JNNURM.

Capacity Building Scheme for Urban Local Bodies

18.174. A scheme for capacity building for ULBs was initiated for supporting implementation of various reforms. This was supported by the creation of nine Centres of Excellence in reputed institutes like IIT Chennai, IIT Guwahati, IIM Bangalore, ASCI Hyderabad, Centre for Science and Environment, Lal Bahadur Shastri National Academy of Administration, Mussoorie and so on. Under the Twelfth Plan, the scheme should be subsumed under the Capacity Building sub-component of JNNURM.

National Mission Mode Project for E-Governance in Municipalities

18.175. This scheme was launched under the UIG component of JNNURM for providing 'single window' services to the citizens. Since e-governance is not only a reform in itself, it is an enabler for other reforms, a major emphasis has been recommended under the improved JNNURM. Hence, the scheme would be subsumed under the capacity building submission of JNNURM under the Twelfth Plan.

Scheme for Urban Infrastructure Development in Satellite Towns/Counter Magnets of Million Plus Cities

18.176. Under the renewed JNNURM, special emphasis has been laid on development of satellite towns, especially by developing their transport and communication linkages with the mega city. Hence the scheme would be subsumed under the JNNURM.

Pooled Finance Development Fund

18.177. The Pooled Finance Development Fund was approved in 2006 to help ULBs to raise funds from capital markets for urban infrastructure projects. An amount of ₹2,500 crore was provided for the

Eleventh Plan. However, the scheme could not pick up during the Eleventh Plan period. Since raising finances at municipal level is one of the main thrust under JNNURM, for which several interconnected recommendations have been made to boost investors' confidence, the scheme would be subsumed under the new JNNURM.

Ministry of Housing and Urban Poverty Alleviation

Interest Subsidy Scheme for Housing the Urban Poor (ISSHUP)

18.178. The scheme was launched to provide interest subsidy of 5 per cent per annum for housing purpose for lending to the EWS and LIG segments of urban areas. Since slum rehabilitation requires a holistic approach the scheme has been subsumed under the Rajiv Awas Yojana.

Grant to Building Material and Technology Promotion Council (BMPTC)

18.179. Under the Eleventh Plan, grant has been provided to the BMPTC to meet multiple objectives of promoting innovation in building material, mainstreaming disaster management and to work as a resource centre for capacity building and skill development. As these objectives are critical to success of any housing related scheme, there is a need for their continuation as well as convergence with the other programmes being implemented by the Government in housing sector. Encouragement to the innovative practices should be funded under the overall umbrella scheme of the Rajiv Awas Yojana rather than taking up these activities on stand alone basis. Hence, the assistance to BMPTC should be done under the capacity building component of the Rajiv Awas Yojana.

Urban Statistics for HR and Assessment (USHA) Scheme

18.180. The scheme has been launched to develop and maintain a data base, MIS and knowledge repository relating to urban poverty, slums housing, construction and other urbanisation related statistics. Creation of a Municipal level MIS system has been recommended under the new JNNURM. Hence the scheme should be subsumed under the renewed JNNURM.

Externally Aided Capacity Building Schemes

MOUD

1. Capacity building for urban development (JNNURM)—assistance from the World Bank:
2. Capacity building for Urban Transport—Assistance from the World Bank

MOHUPA

1. World Bank Capacity Building Project for urban development
2. Technical assistance from DFID for support to National Policies for urban poor

18.181. It is recommended that all Capacity Building activities should be taken under the overall framework of JNNURM.

EXPECTED OUTCOMES IN IMPROVEMENT IN SERVICE DELIVERY

18.182. The urban sector is predominantly a State subject. The nature of engagement by the Central Government would be to primarily incentivise urban reforms and assist the States/ULBs in improving the delivery of urban services at affordable costs. Such measures would not only improve the financial health of ULBs, but also dismantle structural barriers and in turn make cities more inclusive. These would constitute broad outcomes of the schemes under the Twelfth Plan period.

18.183. As regard specific outcomes in terms of improvement in service delivery, the Ministry of Urban Development has developed detailed service level benchmarks for a number of urban services. Such benchmarks include 24×7 water supply, water consumption norms of 135 lpcd for all cities, 100 per cent individual piped water supply, 100 per cent collection and treatment of solid and liquid waste, underground sewerage system for all cities. Similarly, benchmarks have also been developed for storm water drainage, urban transport, urban roads, traffic support infrastructure, urban transport and street lighting. As observed by the Isher Ahluwalia Committee, these benchmark norms are consistent with the economic and social aspirations arising from India's GDP growth target of 8 to 9 per cent per annum. Since different States and cities are at different stage of development, it will be essential for the Central Government to undertake an audit during the preparatory phase of JNNURM-II to determine the service levels across States and set outcome-based targets for services admissible under JNNURM-II for individual states. In the longer term, all state and cities should aspire to achieve the aforesaid service-level norms.

OVERALL BUDGETARY OUTLAYS FOR URBAN SECTOR

18.184. An indicative outlay of ₹1,20,557 crore for Ministry of Urban Development (MoUD) and ₹43,521 crore for Ministry of Housing and Urban Poverty Alleviation (MoHUPA) has been made. This includes provision of ₹1,01,917 crore for the Flagship Scheme of JNNURM which is a State sector ACA scheme and is implemented jointly by both the aforesaid Ministries. The share of MoUD in JNNURM is ₹66,246 crore and of MoHUPA is ₹35,671 crore.

19

Other Priority Sectors

CONSTRUCTION SECTOR

BACKGROUND

19.1. Construction activity creates physical assets in a number of sectors of the economy. Construction sector has two key segments: (*i*) Buildings, falling into one of the following categories: residential, commercial, institutional and industrial; and (*ii*) Infrastructure such as road, rail, dams, canals, airports, power systems, telecommunication systems, urban infrastructure including water supply, sewerage, and drainage and rural infrastructure. Assets once created also need to be maintained. Many upstream economic activities depend upon the construction sector. It is roughly estimated that 40–45 per cent of steel; 85 per cent of paint; 65–70 per cent of glass and significant portions of the output from automotive, mining and excavation equipment industries are used in the construction industry.

19.2. Construction accounts for nearly 60–80 per cent of the of project cost of roads and housing and a significant portion in case of other infrastructure sectors. Construction materials such as cement and steel, bricks and tiles, sands and aggregates, fixtures and fittings, paints and chemicals, petrol and other petro-products, timber, minerals, aluminium, glass and plastics account for nearly two-third of the construction costs. The forward and backward multiplier impact of the construction industry is significant.

CONSTRUCTION SECTOR AND THE INDIAN ECONOMY

19.3. The Construction sector has been contributing around 8 per cent to the nation's GDP (at constant prices) in the last five years (2006–07 to 2010–11). As indicated by Table 19.1, GDP from Construction at factor cost (at constant prices) increased to ₹3.85 lakh crore (7.9 per cent of the total GDP) in 2010–11 from ₹2.85 lakh crore (8 per cent of the total GDP) in 2006–07. The growth in construction sector in GDP has primarily been on account of increased spending on physical infrastructure in the last few years through programmes such as National Highway Development (NHDP) and PMGSY/Bharat Nirman.

EMPLOYMENT IN THE CONSTRUCTION INDUSTRY

19.4. With around 31,000 enterprises involved in the construction industry in 2011, the industry is the

TABLE 19.1
Construction Sector-Macro Aggregates

Macro-variable	2006–07	2007–08	2008–09	2009–10	2010–11
GDP from Construction (lakh crore)	2.85	3.15	3.33	3.56	3.85
Share of GDP (%)	8.0	8.1	8.0	7.9	7.9
Growth rate for GDP in Construction (%)	10.3	10.7	5.4	7.0	8.1

Source: Handbook of Statistics, RBI 2010–11.

second largest employer in the country after agriculture. Over 95 per cent of the enterprises numbering around 29,600 employ less than 200 persons; over 3 per cent or around 1,050 enterprises employ between 200 and 500 persons and only a little over 1 per cent or 350 enterprises have more than 500 employees. The employment figures have shown a steady rise from 14.5 million in 1995, 31.5 million in 2005 to 41 million in 2011. Between 1995 and 2005, there was a substantial drop in the proportion of skilled engineers in the workforce from 4.71 per cent to 2.65 per cent. This trend seems to have been arrested if not reversed with the number of engineers in 2011 at 2.56 per cent, that is, 1.05 million. The number of technicians and foremen is 1.12 million which represents 2.74 per cent of the workforce which shows an improvement over the 2005 when their proportion was 1.85 per cent. The number of skilled workers at 3.73 million constitutes 9.1 per cent of the total workforce which is marginally lower than their proportion of 10.57 per cent in 2005. Apart from clerical staff of 0.93 million, that is, 2.26 per cent, the rest of the workforce of 41 million in 2011 is comprised of unskilled workers whose number stood at 34.2 million representing 83.3 per cent which is almost at par with the proportion of 82.45 per cent in 2005. A large part of the industry remains unorganised which negatively impacts on the quality of delivery. Amongst the workforce, there is predominance of migrant labour which increases their vulnerabilities. There is a need to go in for state-centric surveys to capture the flow and pattern of migration rather than depending upon macro level data.

DEVELOPMENTS DURING THE TENTH AND ELEVENTH PLANS

19.5. Some notable achievements during the previous plan periods have been:

- Construction Sector was declared as an industrial concern under the IDBI Act in March 2000 in order to increase the flow of institutional credit to the sector.
- Implementation of national Human Resource Development (HRD) initiatives in the non-formal sector, including the workers' level to the upper levels of engineering and managerial categories
- Setting up of the Arbitral Institutions for resolution of business disputes in construction industry
- Setting up of disaster identification and mitigation centres which helped in development of a cadre of professionals well-trained to take disaster mitigation activities
- Development of institutions and implementation plans for safety and quality related issues
- Obtaining state-of-the-art global technology through strategic association between industry, government and international bodies
- Effective dissemination of information, regarding good work practices, and development of an action frame work for quality and safety audits, assessment and certification as well as training of man-power both for practice and research
- Improvement in procurement practices for the public sector, and also development of regulatory manuals to ensure quick and effective procurement procedures
- Electronic tendering process, online publishing of tender notices and related procedures are becoming more and more common.
- Setting up of models of public-private partnership in construction activity
- Development of consultancy and advisory services in the areas of project and construction management, procurement services, regulatory issues, and technology. Institutional Arbitration has taken firm root with the operationalisation of Construction Industry Arbitration Council. Nineteen cases have been undertaken so far.
- Specialised institution (Construction Industry Vocational Training Council) was set up at the national level to provide training to vocational and supervisory trades of the construction industry.
- Safety record of the industry has shown improvement. The accident frequency rate in 2011 declined to 0.006 accidents per million man-hours worked from 0.009 in 2007. This is due to professionalisation of big contractors.
- On account of better training opportunities and enhanced mechanisation, productivity per person

in the industry has increased from ₹78,440 in 2007 to ₹98,620 in 2011.
- A national level comprehensive Green Rating Initiative has been made ready and is ready to be launched.
- National level awards (Vishwakarma Awards) instituted by Construction Industry Development Council (CIDC) for outstanding performance have received good response. The awards cover all levels from artisans to life-time achievement awards for industry captains. Awards are also given for projects, with categories including Safety, Health, Environment, Special Features and so on.
- Construction cost indices, sponsored by MOSPI have received good response from project owners.

CONSTRAINTS IN THE CONSTRUCTION INDUSTRY

19.6. Despite the achievements during the previous plans, construction industry faces many constraints. Although 41 million people are employed in this sector, less than 6 per cent has the benefit of structured training and skill building. Skill upgradation schemes launched by the state and Central Governments are not adequate and only a handful of large firms organise training programmes. Construction firms are regulated under multiple laws and there is no unified regulatory framework. There is lack of efficient and stable regime for dispute resolution in contracts leading to costly and time-consuming disputes between the promoters of the project and contractors. Although the flow of bank credit has improved to the construction industry, institutional finance still remains inadequate. High cost of finance translates into high costs for the industry and the economy. Presently construction industry suffers from poor state of technology leading to inefficiencies, wastage and low value added. Investment in R&D is 0.03–0.05 per cent of the investment in construction as against 1.5–2 per cent in South East Asian countries and 4–6 per cent in developed economies. These and other constraints require to be redressed during the Twelfth Plan period.

STRATEGIES FOR THE TWELFTH PLAN PERIOD

Key drivers of growth of construction industry

19.7. Forecasts for the market size of construction industry for the Twelfth Plan period indicate that that the aggregate output of the industry during the period 2012–13 to 2016–2017 is likely to be 52.31 lakh crores increasing from 7.67 lakh crores in 2012–13 to 13.59 lakh crores in 2016–17. As noted earlier, growth in construction industry is linked to the growth in the infrastructure sector and the building industry. The output of the industry is likely to be contributed almost equally by the buildings and infrastructure segments respectively. The thrust on capacity expansion in the infrastructure sector will continue in the Twelfth Plan. Apart from steady growth in construction related to industrial buildings, the industry catering to commercial real estate in the non-residential sector is likely to grow at an accelerated pace due to a vibrant and growing service industry such as IT and related sectors, hospitality and tourism industry and logistics services. The real estate sector faces challenges despite strong growth in the past. The current trend in real estate market is that after making investments in land, the project construction is mainly retail financed, that is, through advances or milestone based payments from owners. In affordable housing projects retail financing would be a challenge as the ability of the retail investors would be very limited. This issue becomes more significant in the category of affordable housing for low income group and economically and weaker segments of the society.

HUMAN RESOURCE STRATEGIES FOR THE TWELFTH PLAN

19.8. Construction industry faces acute shortage of skilled workers especially in mechanised trades. Even in the case of engineers, there is reduction of share of new trainees in Construction Engineering Streams (Civil, Electrical, and Mechanical Engineering). This is due to reduced intake by colleges following the lack of placement opportunities for civil engineers. The trend has started reversing but needs stepping up considerably. On account of natural attrition and the need of skills of contemporary trades, Construction Industry needs infusion of at least 6 million persons per year. The total training capacity is woefully inadequate. Against a requirement of over 3.5 million trained tested and certified workers, the capacity available is about 0.5 million per annum. The ITIs, both in private and public sector are not able to offer many trades relevant to construction Industry. Schemes such as NREGS have further reduced the state of fresh entrants since the unskilled or semi-skilled workforce is no more desirous of migrating as they are able to source employment locally. Skill upgradation schemes launched by the Governments both at State and Central Government level are inadequate and industry sponsored apprenticeship is not easily available. Only a handful of large firms organise training programmes. NSKDF (National Skill Development Fund) schemes are not attractive since the funds are provided to training providers as loan which have to be recovered from recipients who are generally too poor to be able to pay for training. Apart from shortage of workers, the industry is facing shortage of contractors, especially in specialised areas. Most of the construction materials continue to be manufactured in the informal sector which makes it difficult to induct modern technology.

19.9. Construction Industry Development Council (CIDC)—an industry association formed with the initiative of the Planning Commission—is actively involved in imparting training and skill up-gradation of the workers in the industry. It has taken steps in association with a few states such as Madhya Pradesh, Rajasthan, Bihar and Haryana for training and certification of construction workers. These states have made available the physical infrastructure of the ITIs situated in their States, where training in self-financing mode is being conducted by CIDC and skill certification is given by CIDC. This scheme needs to be extended to other states after auditing the scheme and removing any deficiencies. Ministry of Labour and DG (ET), NCVT (National Council of Vocational Training), have taken measures to launch skill certification initiatives through CIDC and also under MES/SDI schemes. Resources from the SDI (Skill Development Initiative) Scheme can be used for training the workers in construction industry. Some firms in the construction industry such as L&T have undertaken their captive training programmes. More firms should be encouraged to do so. These efforts need to be up-scaled and accelerated. One source of funds for doing this can come from The Building and other Construction Workers Welfare Cess Act, 1996 which aims to garner resources, through a cess but does not lay down specific norms for expenditure of the sums, thus collected. It is proposed that a portion of this fund could be utilised to meet the financing requirements of workers training through a nominated and authorised nodal agency. A dedicated fund for human resource development in the construction industry could be set up for taking these ideas forward. This fund known as Construction Skill Development Fund (CSDF) could be set up with ₹200 crores per year from above source and a matching amount from the industry to facilitate training of at least 2,00,000 workers per year.

19.10. The next major issue needing attention is continuous skill upgradation and reversing the attrition of engineers from the Construction Industry. Engineering Council of India, the apex body, having representation of several engineering professional organisations has made several proposals to the Government of India, in this context, which may be studied and acted upon. It is proposed that an Engineers Bill be enacted to look into issues of professional development of practicing engineers and Industry be encouraged through some tax incentives, which could be availed for HRD initiatives launched by them. Curriculum for Construction should be developed and harmonised. Steps must be taken to establish Department of Construction Engineering in Colleges and Universities. As per a CIDC survey, nearly 85 per cent of engineering graduates are unemployable on graduation. This position can be improved by internship after or during graduation. A pilot project undertaken by CIDC with an Engineering University saw employability going up significantly. A continuing programme for industry orientation and experience for teachers is essential for improving employability further. Workshops are needed at every state capital in collaboration with engineering institutions to evolve a mechanism to improve the engineering curricula and also introduce apprenticeship. A structured interface is required between the industry bodies and the Ministry of HRD, UGC and AICTE on these issues.

SAFETY AND RELATED ISSUES OF CONSTRUCTION WORKERS

19.11. Apart from training, welfare for workers should be a major area of action during the Twelfth Plan. Workers in the construction industry are vulnerable to inherent risks to their life and limbs. Temporary relationships between employer and employee, uncertain working hours, lack of basic amenities and inadequacy of welfare facilities are some of the difficulties faced by the employees. The Building and other Construction Workers (Regulation of Employment and Conditions of Service) Act 1996 was enacted recognising the need for a comprehensive Central legislation for regulating the safety, health, welfare, and other conditions of service for construction workers. However, only a few states have implemented the provisions of the Act, such as setting up welfare boards. Twelfth Plan will aim at accelerating this process of implementation of the provisions of the Act. As a substantial segment of the construction industry workforce, women workers need to be accorded special focus in both skill training as well as stipulated social benefits.

19.12. A major issue concerns with the Provident Fund for Construction Workers. It has been pointed out by the industry representatives that although large sums of monies are being deposited with the PF Trust every year, use and withdrawal of these monies by the beneficiaries, is near absent. Proceeds of this deposit are estimated at about ₹25,000 crores by industry bodies but would require official authentication. Such unutilised funds need to be distributed amongst the beneficiaries and used for the welfare of the workers. Industry representatives have suggested that a sub-trust for construction industry should be created. Another source of funds is The Building and other Construction Workers Welfare Cess Act, 1996 through which since 1996, a cess amounting to 2 per cent of the contract value being executed by any contractor is being deducted as the mandatory workers welfare cess. It is believed by industry bodies that sums with various State Governments now aggregate to ₹22,500 crores and are reportedly lying unutilised. These funds could be used for skill upgradation and improving the living conditions of the workers.

REGULATORY FRAMEWORK IN THE CONSTRUCTION INDUSTRY

19.13. Construction has been declared as an industry but has presently no regulatory framework on an all India basis. For example, although the National Building Code and Common General Conditions of Contract have been evolved, they have not been mandated as applicable either by the Central Government or any of the states. Presently no common construction law exists and the construction activities are administered through 32 different laws, rules and statutes. For example, there are 27 different statutes dealing with labour alone, starting with the Children (Pledging of Labour) Act, 1938 to the Employees Provident Fund and going to the Miscellaneous Provisions (Amendment) Act, 1996. To deal with the multiplicity of laws, it has been suggested by the construction industry to have a Common Construction Law which would harmonise the existing statutes related to construction sector. It has also been suggested that a nodal regulatory authority in the shape of Central Construction Authority at the national level and State Authorities at the state levels should be formed to administer and monitor the Construction Law. The proposed authority could act as a nodal agency of the Government on all issues related to the construction sector. It has also been suggested that the related statutes of Japan and Singapore could be studied for adoption in India. These suggestions would need to be discussed widely and debated before a firm view could be taken on them. This exercise would be taken up during the Twelfth Plan period.

19.14. Apart from the actions to be taken by the Government, the Industry itself should adhere to the principles of self-regulation with the help of industry associations such as Builders Association of India, CREDAI, CFI and others. The focus of self-regulation should be labour welfare measures, adherence to environment norms, ethical work practices, joint apprenticeship programmes.

CONTRACTING SYSTEMS AND DISPUTE RESOLUTION

19.15. There are shortcomings in the present contracting procedures as pointed out by various industry bodies. The procedures are costly and cumbersome for both the project owners as well as the contractors. It has been estimated that the total cost of procuring, supervising and monitoring incurred by the project owner comes to about 22 per cent of the cost of asset created. Lack of standardisation of contract procedures and evaluation criteria is another difficulty associated with contracting process. Whereas the special conditions could vary, core conditions could be standardised to avoid subjective interpretation of clauses leading to disputes. In this connection, it would be useful to study the Uniform Contract Conditions and a model bidding document for domestic contracts finalised by the Ministry of Statistics and Programme Implementation, Government of India and promote a wider adoption of the same. There is also a prevailing view that the contract conditions are not equitable. Elements such as performance guarantees and other requirements lead to an increase in the cost of the project. Time and cost over-runs are often caused by ambiguities in conditions governing damages to contractors due to delays by project owners, resource mobilisation through advances and cost escalations. In case of PPP contracts for the road sector, Planning Commission has come out with standardised model concession agreements which have facilitated the implementation of these projects.

19.16. It has been suggested that the criteria of awarding works to the lowest cost bidder adopted by the procuring agencies in the public sector hinders in the process of adoption of better technology, best practices and quality. It might result in cost cutting practices by contractors and preventing passing on the benefits to the workers. In this respect, it has been suggested that 'Effective Lowest Price' rather than the 'Lowest Price' as adopted by the Ministry of National Development, Government of Singapore may be considered for adoption. Technology capacity of contractors should be made part of contract requirement for different categories of projects—based on their value and it should also be part of pre-qualification process. Efforts could be made to include contractors' proposals as part of contract conditions. Availability of some minimum percentage of skilled and certified manpower with Contractors should be made part of contract requirement for different categories of projects based on value. Incentive for better efficiency should be made part of the contract requirements. A system of incentives for timely completion and better performance needs to be integrated in procurement procedures by all public agencies. Instead of pre-qualifying the agencies time and again, departments desirous of engaging the contractors can resort to choosing contractors on the basis of their grading, followed by a periodical surveillance. Intensification and universalisation of the e-tendering system is also required to be undertaken.

ARBITRATION AND DISPUTE RESOLUTION

19.17. The enactment of Arbitration and Conciliation Act 1996 provided for an effective framework for resolution of disputes without depending on the overburdened judicial system of the country. Despite these improvements, the arbitration process continues to be predominantly ad-hoc leading to a situation where according to a CIDC survey, ₹1,35,000 crores remains blocked in the construction sector over disputes. There is an increasing tendency to appeal on grounds of 'misconduct' on the part of arbitrators particularly taking the view that they are not being approved by any responsible organisation. There is no provision for a neutral body to administer and supervise arbitration. Besides, there is no quality control of arbitrator's qualifications and expertise, no assistance is available in managing arbitrator's fees and there is lack of close supervision of arbitrator's progress. A solution to the above problems is to use the Institutional Arbitration system according to which appointment of arbitrators is done from international, national or regional panels. Other features of this system are: having a code of ethics which binds the arbitrators and a pre-determined level of fees. This system is hoped to improve the quality of arbitrators, manage arbitral fees and maintain close supervision and monitoring of arbitrator's progress. During the Twelfth Plan, steps would be taken to operationalise these recommendations.

ENVIRONMENT AND ENERGY

19.18. Construction sector is one of the highest consumers of natural resources and energy amongst the various industries. The industry needs to give particular attention to the following aspects: management of water resources and amelioration of water pollution; efficient use of materials and energy and environmental management during implementation phase and post completion phase. All construction projects undertake mandatory Environment Impact Assessment as per the guidelines of Ministry of Environment and Forest and the concerned State Governments. It is now being increasingly realised in the construction industry that sustainable development concepts, applied to the design, construction and operation of buildings, can enhance both the economic well-being and environmental health of communities. If sustainable design principles are incorporated into building projects, benefits include resource and energy efficiency, healthy buildings and materials, ecologically and socially sensitive land use, transportation efficiency, and strengthened local economics and communities. Under National Bankers Mission, for example, the Government is funding establishment of bamboo mat-making centres and giving training to local women workers in bamboo growing areas of the North-eastern States of India. These centres will supply the bamboo mats for further processing at industrial units for production of bamboo mat corrugated sheets for roofing of buildings. With a view to promote green building materials, the Government of India in their successive budgets after 1993 have been providing excise duty concessions on the materials manufactured from recycling of agro-industrial wastes and by-products. It has also set up an inter-disciplinary organisation. Building Materials and Technology Promotion Council was set up in the Urban Development Ministry to address the issues of environment friendly and energy efficient building materials and technologies.

19.19. Construction Industry needs to work in unison with Bureau of Energy Efficiency to develop Green Building Guidelines based on energy efficiency and use of renewable energy; direct and indirect environmental impact; resource conservation and recycling; minimisation of waste; water-harvesting; indoor environmental quality and community and site related issues. Construction industry should develop typical green building guidelines for different geo-climatic regions. Energy Consumption Indices should be developed for different types of building occupancies, site conditions, and climatic zones. Governments at Central, State and Local levels should also encourage use of green construction. CIDC is now taking an initiative along with a few states to facilitate development of technologies and building guidelines and promoting practice of green construction. CIDC is also interacting with international agencies which have expertise in concepts and technologies relating to green building materials and construction systems. CIDC is collaborating with Building Construction Authority of Singapore to evolve a Green Mark for Buildings. This aims at assessing buildings in five key areas of environment energy efficiency, water efficiency, site development and building management, indoor environmental quality and environmental innovations. Green Marking will provide a meaningful differentiation of buildings in the real estate market. The Government may also consider giving fiscal incentives for use of building materials produced from recycling of wastes and by-products from agricultural, forestry and industrial operations. Concrete steps will be taken during the Twelfth Plan period to promote the concept of green building.

TECHNOLOGY AND PRODUCTIVITY

19.20. Bulk of the construction industry suffers from poor state of technology. Inefficiency, wastage and low value added arise at two fronts: first, due to low technology used in the manufacturing of construction material and second due to low technology used during construction itself. It is important that productivity enhancement of construction industry is driven both by a demand for high quality as well as supply for the same. In order to reduce cost of works in rural roads sector, it is important to develop and use 'marginal materials' instead of traditional costly materials. As part of technology up gradation, there is need to enhance the use of IT and IT-based solutions for the construction industry. It is proposed that a

National Construction Research and Development Fund be created with a grant from the Government and matching contribution from the industry.

19.21. The productivity of the industry has shown a positive trend in recent years as seen from Table 19.3 earlier on account of better training and higher mechanisation. However, compared to other countries, for example, China, US, Europe, on an average, it is 35–45 per cent lower after factoring in purchase power parity. With rapid advances in technology and much better training especially at the lower and middle levels, productivity is expected to rise substantially.

QUALITY AND STANDARDS

19.22. Quality of construction has been recognised by the industry as a weakness. In recent years, some companies by actively supporting training and certification of workers, supervisors and managers have tried to improve on the quality dimension. The skill upgradation programme by CIDC is also a sustained effort in that direction. Use of technology like Ready Mixed Concrete and pre-fab techniques along with more intensive use of information technology has also helped. Many construction companies are working to obtain ISO 9000 series certification. Bureau of Indian Standards has started formulating performance standards which will gradually supercede prescriptive standards. There are two good global examples for quality certification in the construction sector from Singapore and UK respectively. Singapore has introduced a scheme called The Construction Quality Assessment System or CONQUAS which was developed by the Building and Construction Authority (BCA) in co-operation with major public sector agencies and various leading industry professional bodies to measure workmanship quality in a completed building. Since the launch of CONQUAS in 1989, more than 1,500 public and private building projects have been assessed by BCA. The contract value of these projects exceeded US$50 billion. The scheme covers three main aspects of the general building works: structural, architectural and mechanical and electrical. Developers are using CONQUAS increasingly to promote and market their property developments. For instance, it is common for promoters to specify target CONQUAS Score in the tender contracts as targets for contractors. Similarly, contractors that are capable of delivering a consistently high CONQUAS Score would be in demand and command a higher premium. The other international scheme is the Agreement Certificates which is a Quality Appraisal Scheme of the British Board of Agreement (BBA). BBA's Agreement Certificate Scheme provides authoritative and independent information on performance of building products. The main focus of the Agreement process is the evaluation of the extent to which the product allows compliance with relevant Building Regulations and other statutory requirements. These two examples are very relevant for the industry in India to consider and adopt. During the Twelfth Plan period steps would be initiated to launch such schemes.

19.23. In the area of standards, Bureau of Indian Standards (BIS), is the statutory and apex organisation for laying down of standards and their adherence, but does not having any mandate for enforcement. Even the standards are recommendatory in nature, which prevent stake holders to strictly conform and follow. BIS needs to be granted necessary authority and powers to ensure serious adherence to Indian standards. The issue of shifting from Prescriptive to Performance Standards as well as formulation of standards on green and intelligent building design should be given high priority

R&D IN CONSTRUCTION SECTOR

19.24. R&D in construction sector needs to be built around a vision of delivering inclusive growth supported by collaboration between the research providers and the research users. In the field of construction sector in India the principal institutions involved in research include Central Building Research Institute (CBRI), Building Materials and Technology Promotion Council (BMTPC), Institute of Steel Development and Growth (INSDAG), Central Institute of Plastics Engineering and Technology (CIPET), National Council for Cement and Building Materials (NCB), Central Road Research

Institute (CRRI) and Research Designs and Standards Organisation (RDSO). The challenge for the construction industry in the coming years is to establish a framework which supports innovation, research, development, demonstration and use of knowledge for benefits to society at large. Such a framework would be built around integration of various technologies into viable assets; develop designs and practices for meeting the needs of climate control; develop new materials and construction techniques; asset management deploying ICT right from conceptualisation to construction; automation in design, construction and operation and risk mitigation. Apart from R&D in construction technology, adequate focus is required on construction materials to help answer questions like: which alternatives have the lowest resource inputs and environmental emissions and wastes throughout their life cycle?

19.25. R&D vision shall motivate towards an innovative sustainable and productive construction industry and shall ensure collaboration and alignment amongst policymakers and all sections of the construction industry supply chain. A clear objective and identification of well-defined research projects would accelerate development of an innovative mind-set and in time should cause users to demand change. Since the country has a variety of geophysical conditions with varying materials available locally, technology should be adaptable to local conditions. To enable that, regional technology centres with autonomous functioning coupled with accountability are required under a national level umbrella organisation which in turn should also be accountable. One of the aforementioned organisations, along with the participation of policymakers, associations, academic institutions and industry be mandated to spearhead the collaborative effort needed to drive the R&D initiatives in Construction Industry. Industrially advanced countries too depend on collaboration amongst all stakeholders to decide on policies and their implementation framework. It is also suggested that spending on research for construction industry, require special incentives (for example, 150 per cent tax exemption) to encourage such research.

CONSTRUCTION MACHINERY AND TECHNIQUES

19.26. Construction equipment accounts for 21–23 per cent of the total project cost and as such, variations in equipment pricing have a huge impact on the project costs. The prices of construction equipment vary according to the product. As per estimates by Off-Highway research, the sale of construction equipment is expected to reach 84,000 units by 2014, of which infrastructure and real estate sectors will account for 70 per cent. This translates into a CAGR of about 20 per cent over the next five years (2009–14) in sales of construction equipment. Over the years, the equipment used in construction has improved significantly to provide better productivity, safety and accuracy. Mechanisation ensures greater efficiency and reduces the need for skilled labour. It also enables access to hazardous areas where manual intervention is not possible. Developments in this area include: evolving sustainable construction practices; enhanced usage of precast products; close proximity radiography; concrete production and placement; earth moving and mining; automation to enhance productivity and safety; facilitate availability and deployment of construction equipment through incentives and penetration of good practices into rural construction sector and low cost housing.

PROJECT EXPORT IN CONSTRUCTION INDUSTRY

19.27. Indian Construction Industry had been very active in the overseas market, especially the Gulf in the decades of seventies and eighties, when Indian companies ventured out to fill the demand for construction activities, fuelled by oil boom. Between 1975 and 1980, Indian companies handled construction work worth nearly US$ 5 billion. Out of this nearly US$ 1.5 billion was repatriated back to India, mainly in the form of profits, wages and construction material exported abroad. But this trend did not last, and by mid and late 1980s the volume of contracts secured, fell down sharply. From US$443 million in 1986–87 the contracts came down to just US$98 million in 1995–96. Though this was mostly due to the prevalent political situation in the Gulf region, even then it was a major drop for the industry. There is a strong need to reverse this trend through strong government support in aggressively marketing Indian products and services in construction in the overseas market. In order to boost export of both services and goods from Indian Construction Sector it is important to evolve and set up an institutional mechanism for maintaining operational and effective linkages with Indian Missions abroad. In selected countries with a high potential for project export the commercial sections of the missions may be strengthened by placing a representative of the Construction Industry to create awareness and provide strengthening of Indian Construction Industry and to facilitate industry constituents from India to participate in bidding process of selected projects and also explore possibilities of promoting joint ventures in India and abroad. This would also attract greater FDI and new technologies in the domestic construction sector.

FINANCE AND RELATED ISSUES IN THE CONSTRUCTION SECTOR

Flow of Funds into the Construction Sector

19.28. Even though the construction sector is attracting both domestic (gross bank credit) as well as foreign direct investment, more resources are needed for the sector to fulfil the ever rising pressures of enhancing the housing and infrastructure sectors in the country. Institutional financing of construction sector still remains an underdeveloped area. Table 19.2 shows the flow of bank credit to construction sector during 2006–07 to 2010–11. In the year, 2010–11, around ₹50,135 were lent by banks to the construction industry which was 1.4 per cent of the gross bank non-food credit disbursed during the year. Table 19.3 depicts the year wise and cumulative FDI flows into construction activities including roads and highways sector. The cumulative FDI inflows from April 2000 to August 2011 into construction activities stood at around US$ 9,417 million or ₹42,072 crore, which is nearly 6 per cent of the total cumulative FDI inflow into the country during same period.

EXISTING SHORTCOMINGS IN INSTITUTIONAL FINANCING FOR CONSTRUCTION INDUSTRY

19.29. The Indian construction industry is faced with high operation, maintenance, and financial costs. As the magnitude of housing shortage in the country is huge requiring substantial investments in housing and related infrastructure, the Banks, Financial Institutions and Housing Finance Companies have not lent to the poorer segments of the population for affordable housing segments. The priority sector lending by Banks for affordable housing loans up to ₹5 lakh constitutes only 22.75 per cent, of the total lending to housing sector according to the housing loan data received from the 26 leading public sector banks including SBI for the year 2010–11. Further,

TABLE 19.2
Flow of Bank Credit to Construction Sector

(in ₹ '000 Crore)

	2006–07	2007–08	2008–09	2009–10	2010–11
Gross Bank Non-Food Credit	1,801	2,205	2,602	3,040	3,667
Bank Credit to Construction Industry	20	28	39	44	50
Percentage share (%)	1.1.	1.3	1.5	1.5	1.4

Source: Annual Reports, RBI.

TABLE 19.3
Flow of FDI in Construction Activities (including Roads and Highways)

	2007–08	2008–09	2009–10	2010–11	Cumulative(April 2000–August 2011)
In ₹ Crore	6,989	8,792	13,469	4,979	42,072
In USD million	1,743	2,028	2,852	1,103	9,417 (6% of total FDI inflows)

Source: DIPP, MoC&I.

as per latest BSR report of RBI for the period ended March 2010, loan sizes up to ₹5 lakh constitutes 24.16 per cent of the total outstanding housing loans of ₹3,06,307 crore. It can thus be safely concluded that a very low proportion of the low ticket loans have actually gone to the EWS/LIG individuals. Mortgage penetration is already low in India and mechanisms are only now developing to maintain credit histories. Informal sector workers in particular have variable income streams and in some cases, might not have access to a bank account.

19.30. Key reasons for the reluctance on the part of banks/FIs to lend to the construction industry include: (*i*) lenders do not understand the working dynamics of the construction industry; (*ii*) lack of adequate safeguarding mechanisms to assure the banks about the credibility of the industry and (*iii*) banks have better options to lend their precious money to sectors with assured returns at much lower risks. There is no appropriate institutional set up to absorb the flow of funds to the construction sector. Apart from non-availability of credit for the sector, non-availability of bankable DPRs in the construction sector and huge time and cost overruns of the construction projects are some of the reasons for projects in the construction sector not taking off in a sustainable manner. Another shortcoming in the construction sector in India is that the State Governments do not make funds available after they approve the projects. There is no law to ensure that a contract cannot be awarded unless finances are arranged. A programmatic approach for large construction programmes at the State level requiring a planned approach with resources tied up needs to be encouraged.

STRATEGIES TO IMPROVE FLOW OF FUNDS TO CONSTRUCTION INDUSTRY

19.31. Although the industry is not fixed capital intensive, it is working capital-intensive in terms of gross working capital requirements with high payment receivable risk. Five types of financing requirements can be identified in respect of the Construction Industry: (*i*) working capital requirements; (*ii*) Capital requirements for modernisation of equipments and/or expansion of industry; (*iii*) Project specific bridge loans; (*iv*) Loans for BOT projects; and (*v*) Equity for BOT and real estate project. The funds requirement of the construction industry is approximately USD 1 trillion with the modernisation requirements of the construction industry estimated to be to the tune of US$150–200 billion. Further, as per the High Powered Expert Committee (HPEC) Report for estimating the investment requirement for urban infrastructure services, the investment requirement for urban infrastructure over the 20-year period (2012–31) is estimated at ₹39.2 lakh crore at 2009–10 prices.

19.32. The construction sector remains in need of financial support while sizable funds available with Banks and Financial Institutions remain unutilised. Lenders do not have a reasonably sound and reliable system for risk assessment in the construction sector. In order to have a sustained and enhanced flow of credit to the construction sector, greater transparency, better corporate governance, sharing of experiences and specific regulations are required. Innovative financing methods or instruments are required to enhance the flow of funds and institutional credit to the construction sector. Various strategies for this are:

- Enhancing flow of finance through grading of construction companies
- Construction industry-specific lending norms
- Credit enhancement product or agency which would provide bridge finance to the construction sector on lines of the ₹300 crores partial guarantee facility launched recently by IIFCL for the infrastructure sector
- Setting up of a Mortgage Refinance Company which would be a financial institution owned by the banks with the sole purpose of supporting banks to do construction mortgage lending by refinancing banks' mortgage portfolios
- Setting up of a Construction Bank especially dedicated to suit the sector's financial needs on lines of countries like China, Singapore and Ethiopia
- Indian Infrastructure Equipment Bank which would make use of construction equipment owned by Companies by putting them to productive use when they are unutilised

- Compulsory Escrow accounting for Construction Projects in order to provide credit cushion to the investors
- Letter of Credit may be opened in the name of the contractor at the time of award of project by the Client to ensure that the payment is made as soon as the project milestone approval is received
- Working capital advance may be provided to contractors in order to kick-start the construction project
- 'Delayed Payment Act' for Construction Projects which would make it mandatory for the clients or big contractors to pay the small contractors the money along with the prevailing interest rate, the cases where contractors are not paid by the clients in time
- Lending and Non-Performing Assets (NPA) norms for construction sector may be reviewed and reformed
- Sector-specific (for example, housing, real estate, Power, Roads, Ports, and so on) innovative financing instruments may be developed to enhance the flow of funds to the specific sectors
- Innovative financing instruments/products like 'Insurance Product', 'Housing Warranty' and 'green construction finance' (and green rating other than LEED and GRIHA) may be explored for enhanced and orderly flow of institutional credit to the construction sector
- The possible credit enablement mechanisms/ financial instruments for affordable housing are given the Box 19.1
- Developing Housing Warranty Scheme as being offered to the consumers in the Developed Countries, (for example, Japan, North America and so on) could be a potent instrument for covering risk elements at micro level for houses and buildings/ structures
- Developing Insurance Products to mitigate construction business risks to cover the risk elements Bidding Indemnity Policy (BIP); Delay in meeting obligation by client policy (DIMO Policy); Settlement of Claims Policy (SOC Policy); Loss of Profit Policy (LOP Policy); Transit Insurance Policy (TI Policy); Loss of Performance of Construction Equipment (LOPCE Policy); Force Majeure Loss Policy (FML Policy); Financial Risk Coverage Policy (FRC Policy)
- Fiscal incentives such as allowing resource mobilisation through tax-free bonds
- Accessing International Financial Markets through External Commercial Borrowings (ECB), Infrastructure Debt Funds (IDFs), Global Depository Ratios (GDR) and other debt instruments
- Infrastructure Debt Funds (IDFs) to deepen the corporate bond market to make it attractive for these investors
- Foreign Private Equity and Venture Capital Funds
- Regulatory reforms required for PE and VC for fulfilling their role as growth enablers a host of regulatory changes
- Builders and Real Estate Developers involved in construction sector may be incentivised to take up affordable housing construction through grant of additional FAR/FSI/TDR and appropriate fiscal incentives
- State Plan Document should have a Chapter on construction sector which would clearly mention the construction financing requirements in the state
- Single Window Clearance to reduce the hassles and delays in the approval process resulting in delay in completion of projects

19.33. Obviously, such a vast financial requirement cannot be addressed by a single enterprise or institution. Government initiatives must be in coordination with all the constituents of the construction industry for dedicated flow of credit to the sector. Workable Action Plans incorporating the above suggestions would be made during the Twelfth Plan period.

TOURISM

TOURISM AS A MEANS TO FASTER, MORE INCLUSIVE AND SUSTAINABLE GROWTH

19.34. The tourism sector has a major role to play to promote faster, sustainable and more inclusive economic growth—the goal of the Twelfth Five Year Plan. It has better prospects for promoting pro-poor growth than many other sectors. This is because tourism involves a collection of activities, services and industries comprising transportation,

> **Box 19.1**
> **Financing Instruments for Affordable Housing**
>
> 1. Credit enhancement mechanisms like Setting up of *'Credit Risk Guarantee Fund'* need to be expedited.
> 2. A city level dedicated fund for financing urban infrastructure/amenities including affordable housing need to be created which may finance affordable housing including slum housing programmes. Resources can be pooled to this Fund through land monetisation and other innovative sources of funds, contributions from Federal/State/Local Governments, HFCs, Banks, Financial Institutions/Corporate Bodies, levy of labour cess/slum upgradation cess/service tax on construction; and Multi-lateral/bi-lateral bodies. There is a need to look at workable models for Social Rental housing which can be driven through private sector with conducive legal/regulatory environment. In this context, the options of issuing *'Rental Housing Voucher'* may be explored.
> 3. Set up Apex Institution by Government of India for Financing/re-financing *Housing Micro finance* by MFIs. Development of a robust micro-mortgage market for mitigating risk of providing institutional credit in EWS/LIG segment may be explored.
> 4. Banks lending for affordable housing upto certain limit should be provided *with 1 per cent of the loan amount as incentive for covering their operational costs.*
> 5. Banks/HFCs may be permitted to *float tax-free infrastructure bonds* to raise cheaper funds and reserve for affordable housing so that they can reduce the lending rates for EWS/LIG housing loans.
> 6. Interest Subsidy may be enhanced and targeted for affordable housing. Other Subsidy methods like interest-cum-capital subsidy may also be worked out Incentives to private builders for creation of affordable/ rental housing stock through appropriate tax incentives, low cost credit and other incentives like *additional FAR/FSI/TDR* and so on may be provided.
> 7. *Pre-finance and start-up capital* may be provided to NGOs/CBOs for taking up affordable housing programme for the poor.
> 8. Substantial enhancement of *transfer of funds from Federal/State Govts to Local Governments.* To avoid time and cost over runs, there should be no delay in transferring Land required for projects of affordable housing and slum rehabilitation programme to ULBs.
> 9. Enable Municipal Bodies to raise resources through tax-free bonds and transfer of Government land.
> 10. Municipal Governments should be given a part of the profit earned by the Development Authorities/Improvement Trusts as suggested by the 2nd Administrative Reforms Commission and Thirteenth Finance Commission to create a revolving fund for affordable housing.
> 11. Specific dispensation for affordable housing at municipal level should be considered in the forthcoming Goods and Services Tax (GST).
> 12. Initiatives under service level benchmark for water, sanitation and solid waste, as per Thirteenth CFC recommendations, should include specific coverage of affordable housing.
> 13. Short-term construction finance should be made available to municipal bodies to meet the immediate shortfall of funds due to delayed transfer of funds and receipt of beneficiary contribution.

accommodation, eating and drinking establishments, retail shops, entertainment businesses and other hospitality services provided to individuals or groups traveling away from home for leisure, business or other purposes. The broad scope of economic activities involved enables wide participation in its growth, including participation by the informal sector. Tourism is also highly dependent upon natural capital (for example, forest, wildlife) and culture and these are assets that some of the poor have, even if they have no financial resources. For all these reasons, across the world, the tourism industry is one of the largest generators of employment. In India, the travel and tourism sector is estimated to create 78 jobs per million rupees of investment as compared to 45 in the manufacturing sector. The role of tourism in promoting inclusive growth was also recognised in the meeting of Heads of States of G-20 countries held in June 2012 in Mexico.[1]

19.35. While Tourism is important for both growth and employment generation, it must also be sustainable. The World Tourism Organization (WTO) has defined sustainable tourism as 'leading to management of all resources in such a way that economic, social and aesthetic needs can be fulfilled while maintaining cultural integrity, essential ecological processes, biological diversity and life support systems.' In 1992, the 'Earth Summit' in Rio established the triple principles of environmental, economic and social sustainability. Since then, the principles of sustainable tourism have been adopted by the tourism industry worldwide. In India, the tourism sector is based on exploiting its unique endowments of biodiversity, forests, rivers, and its rich culture and heritage. The challenges in this sector lie in successfully preserving these in their original form, and making them accessible to domestic and international travellers. Tourism in India has the potential to create economic interest of local communities in the protection of its natural and cultural endowments leading to a more *sustainable growth*.

19.36. The Twelfth Plan envisages a growth rate of 4 per cent in the agricultural sector, 8 per cent in the manufacturing sector and 9.1 per cent in the services sector. The annual growth of the Tourism sector is estimated to be 8.1 per cent during the last five years, which is marginally higher than the overall economic growth of 7.9 per cent expected to be achieved during the Eleventh Five Year Plan. Under the *business-as-usual* scenario, the tourism sector is forecasted to grow by 8.8 per cent per annum during the period 2011–21 even though, according to the World Travel and Tourism Council (WTTC), tourism in India has the highest 10-year growth potential in the World during 2009–18. The expected growth of the tourism sector is, therefore, inadequate both in terms of its contribution to the overall economic growth and its potential. The approach to tourism in the Twelfth Plan must focus on achieving a substantially higher growth rate than the aggregate growth rate envisaged so as to provide a cushion against any shortfall in other sectors.

19.37. In view of the above, the Twelfth Plan must evolve a strategy based on the ability of tourism to promote a more inclusive, sustainable and faster growth in the face of resource constraints. Tourism should be accorded a priority status to enable the Government to achieve its planned growth and employment objectives and foster national integration.

REVIEW OF ELEVENTH PLAN

19.38. For the Eleventh Five Year Plan (FYP), the vision for the tourism sector was 'to achieve a superior quality of life through development and promotion of tourism through a multi-pronged strategy, that is, (*i*) *Position and maintain tourism development as a national priority*. In spite of this, the global ranking of India in respect of 'Government Prioritization of the Travel and Tourism Industry' *declined* from 59 in 2006 to 80 in 2010.[2] (*ii*) *Improve and expand the development of product and infrastructure for destination/circuits*. This was sought to be achieved through the centrally-sponsored scheme *'Product/Infrastructure Development for Destination and Circuits' (PIDDC)*. In spite of these initiatives, the global ranking of the level of tourism infrastructure in India (measured by the number of hotel rooms, number of ATMs accepting visa cards and the presence of major car rental companies) *improved* only marginally from 96 in 2006 to 89 in 2010.[3] (*iii*) *Develop and implement an effective programme for marketing of brand 'Incredible India'*. While both central and State Governments allocated a significantly large proportion of their plan outlay on tourism on marketing and social awareness campaigns, the effectiveness of the marketing strategy is questionable. The global ranking of India in respect of 'Effectiveness of Marketing and Branding' *declined* from 59 in 2006 to 63 in 2010.[4] (*iv*) *Build capacity of service providers in the tourism sector*. The Central Government launched a scheme to create and upgrade adequate institutional infrastructure for training and certification of manpower resources; and (*v*) *To enhance and maintain India's competitiveness as a tourism destination*. During the Eleventh Plan period, the global ranking of India in the Travel and Tourism Competitiveness Index improved from 65 in 2006 to 62 in 2008 and thereafter fell to 68 in 2010 due to increase in out-bound Indian tourists from 8.34 million in 2006 to 12.07 million in 2010.

TARGET FOR TWELFTH PLAN

19.39. Under the business-as-usual scenario, the tourism sector is forecasted to grow by 8.1 per cent per annum only during the period 2011–21 even though, according to the World Travel and Tourism

Council (WTTC), tourism in India has the highest ten-year growth potential in the World during 2009–18. The currently projected growth of the tourism sector is, therefore, inadequate both in terms of its contribution to the overall economic growth and its potential, and the Twelfth Plan must target a significant improvement.

19.40. The direct employment in the tourism sector has registered an annual growth rate of 2.04 per cent during the six-year period 2004–05 to 2010–11. The employment elasticity with respect to value-addition in the tourism sector is estimated to be 0.28 during the same period. This is substantially lower than the estimated world-wide employment elasticity of 0.65 in the tourism sector. Therefore, there is significant potential for the tourism sector in India to absorb a substantially larger workforce.

19.41. In the aforesaid context, three alternative scenarios are presented in Table 19.4.

TABLE 19.4
Alternative growth scenarios of tourism

Scenario	Growth in Value-addition	Growth in employment	Creation of New Jobs over Plan period
Scenario—I	10 per cent	4.0 per cent	5.5 million
Scenario—II	11 per cent	4.4 per cent	6.1 million
Scenario—III	12 per cent	4.8 per cent	6.7 million

19.42. The growth in direct employment is estimated on the assumption that in the medium term it may not be feasible to sharply raise the employment elasticity to the international level but will increase to 0.4 during the Twelfth Five Year Plan.

19.43. The T&T Competitiveness Report[5] ranks India at 12th in the Asia Pacific region and 68th overall, out of 139 countries in the Travel and Tourism Competitiveness Index for 2011 down six places since the Index of 2009. India is well assessed for its natural resources (ranked 8th) and cultural resources (24th), with many World Heritage sites, both natural and cultural, rich fauna, many fairs and exhibitions, and strong creative industries. India also has quite good air transport (ranked 39th), particularly given the country's stage of development, and reasonable ground transport infrastructure (ranked 43rd). However, some aspects of its tourism infrastructure remain underdeveloped (ranked 89th), with very few hotel rooms per capita by international comparison and low ATM penetration. Another area of concern is the policy environment, which is now ranked 128th, with much time and cost for starting a business, bilateral Air Service Agreements that are not assessed as open, and visas required for most visitors. Other areas requiring attention are health and hygiene standards (112th) and the country's human resources base (96th). It is imperative to point out that India has the advantage of a strong domestic tourism base which is likely to further grow on the back of a rapidly rising middle class with increased disposable incomes and awareness. However, much of the domestic tourism is 'low end' and the challenge is to persuade 'high end' domestic tourists to substitute domestic tourism for foreign tourism by upgrading the tourism related infrastructure and the quality of tourism services.

19.44. In spite of low rankings on the Competitiveness scale, India can leverage its higher ranking in certain categories to exploit its tourism potential over the next decade with proper planning. This potential, exploited in an intelligent and sustainable manner, can prove to be the proverbial engine of growth for India. This can be achieved only with active cooperation from the States/UTs.

19.45. The approach to tourism in the Twelfth Plan must focus on achieving a substantially higher annual growth rate of 12 per cent in the value addition in the tourism sector during the Twelfth Five Year Plan. The strategy for promoting tourism should be re-oriented to increase the employment elasticity in the tourism sector to the international level. Further, India should strive to be amongst the top 50 countries in the Travel and Tourism Competitiveness Rankings by the terminal year of the Twelfth Five Year Plan and increase the share of India to *1 per cent* in Global foreign tourist arrivals.

STRATEGY FOR DEVELOPMENT OF TOURISM DURING TWELFTH PLAN

19.46. Tourism in India has the potential to promote faster, sustainable and more inclusive growth. However, during the Eleventh Plan period this potential could only be partially realised. In the Twelfth Five Year Plan period, it is necessary to re-orient the strategy so as to achieve the targets set-out in the earlier section.

19.47. The traditional approach to tourism development is a direct result of an extremely open and deregulated world economic environment. This approach is characterised by inequity in redistribution of economic benefits. Over the last two decades, new non-traditional approaches like eco-tourism[6] which are concerned more with ecological and cultural conservation than poverty reduction have become popular. The aim is more on minimising costs on people's lives rather than bringing benefits to them. The approach for development of tourism in the Twelfth Five Year Plan should be re-oriented to eliminate poverty.

19.48. The *Approach Paper* to the Twelfth Plan released by the Planning Commission lays down the overall strategy for enabling tourism to realise its potential. It emphasises the need to adopt a 'pro-poor tourism' approach aimed at increasing the net benefits to the poor from tourism and ensure that tourism growth contributes to poverty reduction. The benefits may be economic, social, environmental or cultural. For this purpose, the Approach Paper identified the need for developing a comprehensive set of strategies for a diversity of actions, from micro to macro level, including product and infrastructure development, marketing, branding and promotion, planning, policy and investment and increasing the spread of benefits to the weaker sections. It also prescribes that the 'principal strategy' to realise the tourism potential of India's enormous assets, namely historical sites, places of religious significance, and its vast range of national attractions, must be to focus on developing clusters or circuits around such assets. The development of these clusters/circuits requires collaboration between many agencies at the local level to create an attractive and safe transit experience. Therefore, development of tourism requires that States take a leading role in developing their own tourism potential to obtain growth in employment as well as State Domestic Product.

19.49. Pro-poor tourism is increasingly becoming popular but there are not many places in the world where this initiative has been effectively implemented in line with pro-poor tourism principles. In 2006, the Kerala Department of Tourism proactively decided to make the state tourism policies more '*pro-poor*' through the framework of Responsible Tourism (RT) Initiative. Under this initiative, development of tourism in Kumarakom was taken up as a pilot destination. The initial phase was characterised by local farm land being converted into tourism infrastructure, reduction in agricultural production and increase in wage income of the local workers from the hectic pace of construction activity. However, it soon became apparent that the gap between the tourism industry and the local population was rapidly widening. Most villagers eventually got into financial difficulties after losing their land and no meaningful skills with which to operate tourism activities.

19.50. Eventually it became apparent that the local people in Kumarakom were not benefitting from the new tourism businesses. While many job opportunities were created with the opening of hotels and restaurants, they could not be availed by the local people since the local wages were substantially higher than those in other parts of the country. Over 80 per cent of the hotels' staff was recruited from outside Kumarakom; a significant number of them were from Northeast India, the poorest part of the country. Further, the working conditions in the tourism sector were very poor: workers had no job security, there were many cases of broken contracts without sufficient reasons and employees were poorly paid.

19.51. Besides, the locals in Kumarakom became victims of the tourism industry in many other different ways. Villagers' lifestyle and occupations were closely related to the canals, bays, lakes and shores in the area that have been using for fishing, collecting shells, or as a mean of transportation. However, many resort-owners closed the access to lakes and canals for the local community in order to satisfy the tourists' need for privacy and tranquillity. In addition, resorts increasingly operated tourist cruises in the backwaters by motorboats, which have considerably damaged the fishing nets used by local fishermen. A survey conducted by Equations in 2002 among 140 households in the village shows that tourism expansion has not meaningfully contributed to infrastructure development and improvement of the living standards of people of the community. Responding to the query whether development of tourism in Kumarakom has improved the overall development of the region, 62 households responded that tourism had not made any significant contribution to improving roads or transportation system. Similarly, 87 households responded in the negative regarding the supply and quality of water, 90 households responded in the negative for the electricity, and 99 responded in the negative on the possibility of getting an employment.

19.52. The Department of Tourism of Kerala declared the place as a pilot destination for Responsible Tourism in 2007 but it was extremely difficult to commence work on the project due to local resistance. It was possible to start the implementation of the initiative only after the Panchayat representatives and officials from the Kerala Department of Tourism organised a mass meeting in May 2007 to explain the schedule, the means, aims and objectives of the RT initiative and the key players involved.

19.53. The first objective was to revive the agricultural sector in Kumarakom. The Department of Tourism sought the help of Kudumbashree, the Panchayat and Kerala Institute of Travel and Tourism Studies (KITTS) to conduct a survey and analysis of the possibility of linking the local population with the tourism businesses and market. For this purpose, first, KITTS identified the most vulnerable groups, that is, families of farmers living below the poverty line and the local producers who had difficulty in accessing the market to sell their produce. In addition, KITTS researchers conducted a survey of the hotels and restaurants to establish their exact requirement for fruits and vegetables. Based on the survey results, the Destination Level Responsible Tourism Committee (DLRTC) cell prepared an agricultural calendar for the supply of produce to the hotels, that is, what should be cultivated and when, and the overall amount that will be needed by the hotels. This process made it possible for the local self-government to establish the link between the local farmers and the hotels. Consequently, 18 hotels and resorts agreed to purchase their vegetables, fruits, and so on, exclusively from local producers.

19.54. In spite of the agreement, the hotels and resorts refused to buy the local produce when all the crops were ready for harvest in February 2008. Most of them argued that Kumarakom produce were too expensive relative to neighbouring Tamil Nadu. The crisis was averted only with the firm intervention of the State Government; the hoteliers and resort owners were firmly requested to co-operate with the initiative and respect the agreement. Two weeks later, 15 hotels, among them the luxury Taj Resort and Lake Resort, made a written and formal agreement with DLRTC and the Panchayat to purchase the produce from the local farmers. The first sales of the produce were made to the hotels and resorts on 18 March 2008. The farmers and tourism business owners now enjoy a healthy working relation. The RT initiative in Kumarakom has reached 1,350 direct beneficiaries through this agricultural project.

19.55. The RT initiative has produced several real and quantifiable results within one year of its implementation. Some of the important outcomes are significant increase in local agricultural production, creation of a cultivation calendar, creation of systems for steady prices to avoid inflation and market fluctuations, creation of 10 Karshakasamity (farmers groups), with a total of 460 people, creation of 20 Kudumbashree units, with a total of 250 women, creation of five Micro Enterprises focused on women, one women fish processing unit, one women chicken processing unit; one women Chapathy (local bread) processing unit and two coconut supply units.

19.56. One year after the initiation of the RT in Kumarakom, new projects were developed to enable local people to access the tourism market and benefit from it. A link between several tourist hotels and some local artists was established whereby, the hotels agreed to buy products, services or performances from two handicraft units, one women's cultural group performing Thiruvathirakaly (traditional Kerala dance art), and one women's painting group. Besides providing additional income for the art performers, this project also enables the promotion and conservation of the traditional art forms from Kerala, and avoids the usual cultural breakdown that happens when tourism is developing in a destination.

19.57. In July, 2009, a new initiative called the 'Village Life Experience @ Kumarakom' was launched. Under this initiative, the tourists are taken around villages to have a real experience of the village life where they can enjoy a visit to a fish farm; vegetables and fruits farm, duck farm, paddy fields, and can also learn a bit about the traditional fishing techniques. The cost for a half-day trip is about ₹1,000 and the amount of money earned is equally divided among the villagers who participate in the tour.

19.58. Further, there is also a very special role for women in the Responsible Tourism initiatives and projects. In co-operation with Kudumbashree, 760 women are included in the cultivation programme, 35 in retail activities, 30 in art and cultural groups, and 45 in the village tour group. This is an important step toward women empowerment in Kumarakom; these groups of women are now participants in decision making for the programme. In such a way, a carefully managed tourism industry can help the poor rural women to become increasingly empowered, improve their status in their families and within the society.

19.59. The learning experience from the implementation of the pilot project in Kumarakom, Kerala provides a successful pro-poor tourism model for replication across the country with such localisation as may be necessary.

19.60. In view of the above, a 'pro-poor tourism' approach should be adopted for development of tourism and furthering the objectives of the Twelfth Plan. The goal of 'pro-poor tourism' is to bring net benefit to the poor and marginalised through tourism activities thereby, eliminating poverty. The means to achieve this goal is to expand the opportunities for them through capacity building and transfer of skills in close co-operation with the education and training sector and microfinance institutions. 'Pro-poor tourism' has a holistic notion of poverty alleviation. Non-economic benefits are as important as economic gains. An improved management approach of the tourism industry can provide new skills, better access to education and health care, improving access to clean water and transportation networks. Intangible benefits may also be provided such as access to information, opportunities to communicate with the outside world, increased access to market opportunities, strengthening the community institutions and structures, and enhancing community pride.

19.61. 'Pro-poor Tourism' is essentially about redistribution of resources and opportunities and not just the creation of a new tourism product. Therefore, a proactive interventionist approach is needed from the governments in order to effectively realise the objective of the concept. Since the poor and marginalised communities do not have the avenues to negotiate with tourism companies, the authorities have the responsibility to advocate for and promote their interests. Governments need to change their policies and create new ones that cater for the needs of the marginalised within the tourism industry framework. Without such actions at the macro level, 'pro-poor tourism' may remain a niche market without addressing the larger picture of poverty reduction objective.

19.62. The 'pro-poor tourism' approach comprises of practical strategies based on the principles underlying the approach. These practical strategies essentially focus on three core areas: increased economic benefits, positive non-economic impacts, and policy/process reform. In each area three distinct (but often overlapping) methods can be identified.

19.63. The *increased economic benefits* can be achieved by (*i*) expanding business opportunities for the poor; (*ii*) expanding employment opportunities for the poor; and (*iii*) enhancing collective benefits.

Business opportunities for the poor can be expanded by enabling them to set up small enterprises, particularly in the informal sector. The main activities in this area should be enterprise support, expansion of markets and development of complementary tourism enterprises, such as craft initiatives and cultural displays. Local enterprises need to be developed to supply the tourism industry itself (for example, with accommodation, food and materials). A wide range of measures will have to be used to overcome the multiple barriers to economic participation (such as lack of credit, inappropriate social organisation, insecure tenure and remote location). Since local entrepreneurs generally lack entrepreneurial skills to engage with private operators in the formal tourism sector, training will need to be a key intervention. Further, there is a need to combine supply side measures (developing products and skills directly with the poor) with measures to expand demand for the products and services of the poor amongst tourists and operators. Supportive NGO-type organisations dedicated to supporting small enterprises need to be encouraged to assist them. *The employment opportunities for the poor* can be expanded by ensuring that the investors and operators in the formal tourism sector are committed to source employment locally thereby, also benefitting from low staff turnover. However, the jobs should not be concentrated among few families and the better off in the local community. Further, focus must also be placed on pursuing skills development to enable local community to take up skilled jobs which may be created. The *collective community income* can be enhanced, inter alia, through levies on tourists and operators; equity partnerships in which the community holds a stake; lease fees paid by private operators; and donations from tourists. However, it is necessary to develop strong, accountable and transparent community organisations to ensure that the collective income is not misused. The enhanced collective benefits can spread benefits well beyond the direct earners.

19.64. The *non-economic benefits* can be increased by (*i*) Capacity building, training and empowerment; (*ii*) Mitigating the environmental impact of tourism on the poor; and (*iii*) Addressing social and cultural impact of tourism. *Capacity building* is central to the strategy in increasing non-economic benefits since the poor often lack the skills and knowledge to take advantage of opportunities in tourism. Investment in capacity building is essential but a long-term process. The main focus should be on increasing poor people's basic understanding of tourists and the tourism industry; training in business skills; and local institutional capacity building for empowerment. *Environmental sustainability* is an important element of 'pro-poor tourism' since tourism can lead to displacement of the poor from their land and/or degradation of the natural resources on which the poor depend. Therefore, tourism should be integrated with broader rural development work that includes natural resource management activity. The *social and cultural impact of tourism* can be addressed by promoting cultural tourism which allows for capitalising on cultural assets which are predominantly owned by the poor. Similarly strategies should be designed to improve local infrastructure, health care and access to information and communication.

19.65. The *policy/process reform* should focus on (*i*) promoting participation; (*ii*) bringing the private sector in the formal tourism sector into business partnerships with small local entrepreneurs; and (*iii*) building a more supportive policy and planning framework. *Participation* can be promoted by enhancing the participation of the local community[7] in decision-making. Tourism should be integrated into the participatory district planning process as one of a range of opportunities for local economic development. The *private sector in the formal tourism sector should promote business partnerships* by acting as an important market for the products of small entrepreneurs (for example, goods and services purchased for a lodge). Private companies, particularly tour operators and agents, should also channelise their own clients to small enterprises of the local community. The formal tourism sector will need to take responsibility for developing local, skills marketing links, and commercial expertise of locally driven tourism enterprises. The *policy and planning framework* can be a strong enabler of 'pro-poor tourism'. Therefore, there is a strong case for reform. Some of the most influencing strategies include promoting participatory planning; increasing communication with Government and establishing a voice for small producers; lobbying government for supportive policies and legislation—both within tourism and in other sectors (for example, land tenure, infrastructure, local planning); lobbying the local conservation authority to invest in destination marketing and infrastructural development and to lift restrictions on development; promoting inter-departmental initiatives and coordination; linking with the national tourism authority; and using Government's power to allocate concessions to influence investors.

19.66. In general, *tourism provides better opportunities for women's participation* in the workforce, women's entrepreneurship, and women's leadership than other sectors of the economy. Women in tourism are still underpaid, under-utilised, under-educated, and under-represented; tourism offers pathways to success. The 'pro-poor tourism' approach should be a vehicle for furthering the advancement and empowerment of women who constitute a large proportion of the most vulnerable in the local community. The Global Report on Women in Tourism 2010 has made a set of recommendations for increasing the participation of women in tourism which should form the agenda for increasing participation of women in tourism. These recommendations need to be integrated into the 'pro-poor tourism' approach to enhance the 'inclusive' agenda for the Twelfth Plan.

19.67. The implementation of various strategies for development of tourism would involve developing formal and informal links between all stakeholders and coordination across all levels of Government. It would be necessary to establish a 'whole government' agenda for tourism development between departments at national level and between national and local government so as to create convergence and synergy across programmes. This requires that awareness is created amongst all stakeholders and across Government about the contribution of tourism to local livelihoods and engage them in joint initiatives to increase the local economic development and impact on poverty reduction. *The National Tourism Policy should reflect clear progress in 'tilting' tourism to unlock more opportunities for the poor.*

It should form an integral part of the poverty reduction strategy during the Twelfth Five Year Plan.

19.68. The realisation of the country's huge, barely tapped, tourism potential is contingent upon simultaneously addressing the multiple challenges thrown up by capacity constraints and inadequate policies. These constraints include inadequate transportation infrastructure; accommodation; land; multiple taxes and an overall high tax burden; inadequate financial resources for enterprises; skills; safety and hygiene conditions around tourist attractions; and convergence of actions by multiple agencies. The challenges are further magnified in the context of a federal structure where the responsibilities for policymaking and implementation fragmented across levels of government and co-ordination between them is often lacking.

DEVELOPMENT OF TOURISM INFRASTRUCTURE

19.69. Availability of good infrastructure is one of the essential requirements at selected tourist destinations. The infrastructure for tourism includes travel infrastructure networks like airports, railways, roads, waterways, telecommunications; amenities like electricity, water supply, drainage sewerage, solid waste disposal systems and tourism facilities, services and amenities like accommodation, restaurants, recreational facilities and shopping facilities. The operation of tourism facilities, services and amenities are often dependent on a number of travel infrastructure networks. The most usual case in tourism development is for infrastructure development to precede the completion of the tourism facilities. This means that the installation of the infrastructure becomes a public sector responsibility. The case for infrastructure services being a public sector responsibility is based on the consideration that the network of services is available to both tourists and residents of the area *and* the construction of an integrated system would also facilitate non-tourism development within the region.

19.70. In terms of the federal framework of the Constitution, the responsibilities of the Union Government and the State/UT Governments are elaborated in separate schedules to the Constitution.

The Central Government is responsible for matters such as external affairs, visa regulations, foreign exchange regulations and import/export procedures, while the State/UT Governments are responsible, inter alia, for law and order, land use, civic amenities, shops and establishments. These Governments have separate agencies for dealing with specific subjects and regulations. For example, the Ministry of Tourism in the Union Government is concerned with the over-all coordination and planning of tourism development in the country and for undertaking tourism promotion and publicity in the international market. However, the State/UT Governments control all factors of production including land in their territories. Further, there is empirical evidence to suggest that a significant proportion of their tax revenues is attributable to consumption by tourists. Therefore, the State/UT Governments have the responsibility and the incentive for facilitating the creation of infrastructure for tourism. The role of the Union Government is restricted to establishing a policy and regulatory framework, creating the appropriate incentive structure and synergising the activities of different infrastructure sectors across levels of government and supplementing these efforts by financial assistance.

19.71. The strategy for development of tourism infrastructure should essentially focus on identifying clusters of habitations/destinations having unique craft, ethnic art form, culture and heritage, natural spots for development as tourism products and develop tourist circuits/destinations around them on a Mission Mode with the active participation of local communities. As part of this strategy, State Governments should be expected to identify at least *one integrated tourist circuit*, map all the tangible and intangible natural and cultural assets along the circuit, estimate the sustainable destination carrying capacity and undertake a gap analysis of the travel infrastructure network and tourism facilities, services and amenities. Based on this, a comprehensive integrated physical and financial plan should be prepared through a community participatory process. The Plan should identify, inter alia, the winners and losers, agencies responsible for executing the sub-components of the plan and the timelines for achieving the milestones. The integrated plan should be approved and monitored by the Ministry of Tourism as part of the Product/Infrastructure Development of Destination and Circuits Scheme (PIDDCS). To the extent there is shortfall in the financing of the plan, the same may be considered for financing under the PIDDC subject to a ceiling there under. The PIDDC scheme should also be modified along the lines recommended in the Report of the Steering Committee to the extent they are not inconsistent with the recommendations in this Chapter.

19.72. Easy access to tourism destinations in terms of international transport and facilities for easy movement within the destinations are prerequisites for the development of tourism. India ranks 39th and 43rd in the Travel and Tourism Competitiveness Index 2011 for Air Transport Infrastructure and Ground Transport Infrastructure respectively. However, its rank in respect of Airport density is as low as 135 from amongst 139 countries and 90 in respect of quality of roads. India's ability to open up new areas and properly service emerging tourism resorts, while also providing access to natural tourism attractions and circuits for tours will significantly depend upon its ability to quickly improve the airport density and quality of rail and roads. The existing Pradhan Mantri Gram Sadak Yojana (PMGSY) and other schemes of the Central Government could be used to improve the quality of transport infrastructure.

19.73. In terms of investment, especially private investment, tourist accommodation represents the most expensive facility in tourist resorts. In the past few decades, the character and composition of tourist accommodation has undergone considerable change. New types of accommodation, such as self-catering units, home stay, budget hotel accommodation and camping sites, have evolved to meet market demands for increased levels of independence, self-sufficiency, informality, economy and convenience. Such changes have been influenced by the emergence of the new types of travellers and the tourists who invest in a holiday home or unit in a preferred tourism destination. As the spectrum of travellers has undergone transformation, there have also been changes in the requirements for traditional hotel accommodation.

19.74. The availability of hotel rooms in India is extremely limited; it ranks 136th from amongst 139 countries ranked on the basis of the number of hotel rooms. Further, there is acute shortage of land in urban areas particularly in cities due to land market distortions discussed separately in Chapter 4. Therefore, the prospect of large-scale new traditional hotel accommodation is extremely limited. It is imperative to expand the number of registrations under the home stay scheme in various stays so as to significantly augment hotel room capacity in India. This will open up new livelihood opportunities for local people.

HUMAN RESOURCE DEVELOPMENT AND CAPACITY BUILDING

19.75. Tourism is a labour-intensive industry and a major source of employment. Therefore, issues of human resources development and capacity building are extremely important. The problem of human resource is identified as a shortage of trained labour; lack of trainers; inadequate training materials and lack of tourism education strategies as part of national tourism planning. Other issues concerning human resources development in the tourism industry include: working conditions, availability of education and training, policy issues, information and technology and cultural issues.

19.76. Developing human resources in the tourism sector faces unique challenges because customer preferences, travel patterns, information technology and conditions at destinations are changing rapidly. As a result, strong and flexible human resources development strategies are needed. The strategy should mirror human resources needs and the corresponding recruitment, employment and training requirements.

19.77. Training programmes need to articulate well with employment creation, for maximum synergy. Training should be strictly need-based and demand-led. Thus, it is necessary to establish linkages with various labour market institutions and processes: labour market information, employment services, public works, credit and other support to small enterprises, unemployment and social support services and so on. Training services for existing enterprises to upgrade and re-orient technical skills or develop management capacity can help stimulate their labour absorption, avoid retrenchments and facilitate redeployment of retrenched workers. Therefore, the tourism training strategy should focus on employability, sustainability and promotion of decent work culture especially to safeguard foreign tourists. In the light of the above, the following initiatives need to be undertaken during the Twelfth Plan period to expand the tourism related human resource base:

a. *Setting up new SIHMs:* Government will need to accord permission to set-up new SIHMs which will also implement the craft courses, short duration skill development courses and skill certification programme.

b. *Setting up of new Food Crafts Institutes (FCIs):* Government will need to sanction new FCIs to increase the number of turn-outs with hospitality skills and ensuring sustainable operations.

c. *Setting up of a Hospitality University:* Presently, an IHM affiliated to the NCHMCT awards a B.Sc. (Hotel and Hospitality Administration) degree of Indira Gandhi National Open University (IGNOU). It is felt that hospitality education course will be pursued as part of the mainstream academic effort only if it is part of a regular University. Accordingly, IHMs will be affiliated to local or Central Universities for awarding a B.Sc. (Hotel and Hospitality Administration).

d. *Revamping NCHMCT:* Hospitality education, especially at the degree level, needs to be positioned as a mainstream discipline

e. *Preserving and promoting Indian Cuisine— Setting up of a Indian Culinary Institute (ICI):* The proposed Indian Culinary Institute (ICI), would be set up with headquarters in the National Capital Region, and six regional centres located in four metropolitan cities, one in Central India and one in the North East. The Institute should be set-up under a PPP mode so that industry expertise from the private sector could be used to build quality and brand value.

f. *Expansion of Indian Institute of Tourism and Travel Management (IITTM):* This initiative will include setting up of a North-Eastern Centre of the IITTM; seeking Deemed University/Institute of National Importance status for the IITTM; and developing Simulation Labs at IITTM Centres for hands on training.
g. *Reorganising the Indian Institute of Skiing and Mountaineering, Gulmarg:* IISM is presently a subordinate office of the MOT. The possibility of its being incorporated in the IITTM as a centre would be explored. The financial assistance for infrastructure upgradation of IISM under the Plan Scheme may also be extended.
h. *Modifications in the Scheme of Assistance to IHM/FCI:* The Scheme of Assistance to IHMs/FCIs and so on, under the Ministry of Tourism, introduced in 2008, enables the Central Government to establish institutional infrastructure necessary for supporting hospitality and tourism related training and education. Based on the experience, appropriate amendments to the Scheme should be made to enhance its effectiveness and impact.
i. Expand the scope and size of the *Hunar-se-Rozgar program.*
j. *Promotion of excellence in institutes:* promotion of research and specialisation in tourism; academic audit of the hospitality institutes; curricula review; faculty development; students' exchange programme; and attached applied training centres/training hotels.
k. *Merits-cum-scholarships:* Introduce a scheme to provide financial support to meritorious students on merit-cum-means scholarship to encourage students to opt for tourism-related courses.

19.78. Market Pulse has estimated a total additional requirement of 77,000 trainers during the Eleventh Plan period. Train-the-trainers strategies can often ensure that a critical mass of experts and experience is made available on a larger scale. A significant positive impact can be created over time on the industry as a whole if a small number of participants are equipped with the skills to train, educate, and service workshops. As of now, there is no dedicated teachers' training institute. Therefore, the following measures are recommended to meet the gap:

a. *Setting up of dedicated teachers' training institutes:* The MOT will set up need based autonomous training institutes catering to the needs of the hospitality and tourism sectors both at skill and diploma/degree levels.
b. *Designating some IHMs as teachers' training institutes* with need-based infrastructural and faculty strengthening.
c. *Setting up of Training Institutes in Rural Areas:* In collaboration with Ministry of Rural Development, attempts would be made to explore the possibilities of setting up of training institutes in rural areas to conduct training for forest guards, handicraft workers and so on.

19.79. In 2011, Ministry of Tourism commissioned a study by Market Pulse, which estimated a requirement of 36.18 lakh skilled manpower in the hospitality sector. However the Institutional capacities (including the National Skill Development Corporation) created by the end of Eleventh Plan would be able to fulfil only 10 per cent of the estimated additional requirement of manpower in hospitality and tourism sector (inclusive of supply from Non-MOT sources). Thus, there is need to give a major boost to the initiatives through convergence with the other ministries of GOI, States/UT administration and the Private Sector. In governments, it is essential to involve all relevant ministries and agencies, not only in environment but also tourism/economy, education, foreign affairs, planning, regional affairs and finance/budgeting. At times, it may be important to institutionalise these multi-stakeholder and inter-institutional boards by establishing a national committee or council for tourism education and training, so that initiatives can survive beyond short political mandates and/or circumstances. Such a committee or council could be advisory and consultative and should bring together the various ministries; workers' organisations (unions); professional and trade associations (employers), the national association of hotel and tourism schools and all other parts of the tourism sector. Similarly, since almost all tourism employment will be in the private sector, it is crucial that the private sector participates, provides support and resources and gives consultation. The private sector must ensure that it benefits from national objectives, strategies and policies for human resources development in the tourism industry. Trade associations need to play an important role to encourage the private sector's direct contribution to tourism human resources development.

19.80. With a view to ensuring the successful implementation of the various initiatives relating to human resource development, it is necessary to establish separate institutional structures for developing, implementing, monitoring and evaluating the programmes. For this purpose, it is recommended that:

a. Separate divisions should be established in the Ministry of Tourism to deal with degree and higher level tourism education *and* skill training programmes.
b. The institutional infrastructure envisaged in the Twelfth Plan, and the carry over work from the Eleventh Plan, is a means to providing trained manpower to the Industry. Timely completion of the projects sanctioned is, therefore, of paramount importance. A Programme Monitoring Unit (PMU) with adequate staffing should be set-up for projects sanctioned under the Scheme of Assistance to IHMs and so on.
c. The various initiatives relating to human resource development for the tourism sector will enable the Ministry of Tourism to annually train 2.5 lakh persons for employment in the tourism sector and partially meet the human resource gap.

CAMPAIGN CLEAN INDIA

19.81. A study conducted by MoT at important tourist destinations revealed that cleanliness and hygiene at these places was much below the acceptable level. This not only inconvenienced the tourists, both domestic and foreign, but also had a pull-down impact on image-India. Government should launch a Clean India Campaign by adopting a multi-pronged strategy comprising of persuasion, education, sensitisation, training, demonstration and regulation. The Campaign should involve every strata of the society, the NGOs and the Corporate Sector. For steering and monitoring the Campaign, a dedicated Cell in the MoT should be set up. As a first step, top 50 most popular monuments and tourist sites may be identified for setting-up pay toilets with separate facilities for women and the physically challenged.

PUBLICITY, PROMOTION AND MARKETING

19.82. In order to promote and market brand India and increase India's share in global tourists' arrival to 1 per cent, it is imperative to adopt a multi-pronged tourism marketing strategy. Some of the important elements of the strategy are discussed below:

a. *Establish overseas tourism offices/information centres in the target markets*

19.83. Ministry of Tourism should enhance the reach of brand 'Incredible India' and increase inbound tourism from established source markets and new potential markets which increasingly contribute to global traffic like Spain, Russia, South America, and Scandinavian nations, Thailand, Malaysia and Korea and so on. The existing scheme of opening tourist marketing offices of the Ministry of Tourism should be supplemented by appointing 'India Tourism Marketing Representatives (ITMR)'. The ITMRs would be private firms and companies who would represent and undertake required promotional activities in the desired markets in the local language on behalf of the Ministry of Tourism. They will have the necessary market intelligence to work with the local trade in their language on increasing awareness, undertaking publicity and branding, facilitating travel trade, printing of collaterals and so on. The ITMRs will be paid performance related charges for the services rendered by them.

b. *Produce effective marketing and promotional materials*

19.84. The medium of 'Cinema and TV' is a powerful tool for the development and promotion of destinations. Several destinations have indeed gained by being the venue/location of popular cinema and TV. Ministry of Tourism should extend support for the production of films (international and domestic) showcasing tourism destinations in the country. Details of the scheme for extending such support may be worked out in collaboration with the stakeholders. To further leverage the medium of cinema and TV, the Ministry may also partner with major cinema and TV-related events.

c. *Promote travel festivals*

19.85. An annual National Travel Mart under the title 'Global Travel Mart, India' should be organised every year with the main objective of attracting buyers to an event which offers them the entire range of Travel and Tourism products and services in India, in one location. The scope of the fair should include Travel trade. Government should also organise 'India Festivals' in important overseas markets to showcase and promote the tourism destinations, culture, cuisine, handicrafts, textiles and costumes, and so on, of the country. These events should be organised by the Indian tourist industry in collaboration with all the stakeholders but the cost should be borne by the Central and State Governments. Similarly, business meetings may be organised between tour operators from India and the Festivals hosting country.

d. *Develop a specialised website for tourism products*

19.86. During the Eleventh Plan, there was a greater focus on print, television and outdoor advertising. However, with the growing importance of information technology and internet as a powerful tool for communication, greater emphasis need to be placed on online campaigns, interactive/social media and other modern and innovative technology spheres (for example, i-pad). E-learning online programmes like 'Know India' with video walk-in and multiple languages may be undertaken in overseas markets to educate and equip the tour operators.

e. *Arrange more familiarisation trips for travel agencies abroad*

19.87. Road Shows should be organised in overseas markets, in collaboration with all stakeholders for promoting tourism destinations, products and tour packages in the country. These Road Shows may include business meetings. Government may also host 'Mega Familiarization Tours' inviting tour operators, travel agents, trade partners and famous travel writers to India to obtain first-hand knowledge of Indian tourism products. Similarly, sub-national governments should be encouraged to organise road shows in other States/Union Territories to promote their tourist destinations and products.

f. *Arrange international meetings in the region where delegates can be exposed to tourist attractions and activities*

19.88. International Buddhist Conclave should be organised every two years with the objective of promoting Buddhist circuits and sites in the country. The conclaves may host eminent scholars, tour operators, media and opinion makers from India and abroad. Similarly, conclaves could be held for other religious and cultural groups.

g. *Advertorial campaigns to promote and provide information about new and niche tourism products and destinations*

19.89. The Incredible India campaigns have been generic in nature and have effectively generated general awareness about India as a tourism destination. The campaigns should be more focused and niche tourism products of the country like Heritage Home Tourism, Religious Tourism, Rural Tourism, Wellness and Medical Tourism, MICE Tourism, Adventure Tourism, Golf, Polo, and so on, should be promoted aggressively through the Campaigns. Specific Road Shows focusing on these Niche Products may also be organised overseas, in association with stakeholders from the relevant fields. The Himalayas and the Sayadhris can be promoted aggressively as destinations for adventure tourism, wildlife and indigenous culture and heritage. Similarly, other physical features of the country need to be exploited.

h. *Undertake social awareness campaigns*

19.90. The 'Atithidevo Bhava' campaign should be re-enforced to generate wide-spread awareness on issues related to good behaviour towards tourists, civic responsibilities, security and comfort of tourists and so on. It will also help to train local policemen to bring about an attitudinal change towards tourists.

i. *Public–Private Co-operation*

19.91. Cooperation among public and private sectors is essential in the development of hospitality and tourism marketing mix. The NTO and the private sector should put more efforts in searching and sharing tourism promotional funds, product development, raising awareness of the destination.

PROMOTING SUSTAINABLE TOURISM

19.92. India provides enormous experiential opportunities for tourists based on the wide variety of all-season attractions available throughout the country. It is imperative that these attractions get developed for the socio-economic benefit of the local communities, especially in order to strengthen inclusive economic growth. It is equally important to ensure that increased socio-economic well-being does not cause permanent or long-term damage to the country's physical, cultural and environmental heritage. The use of existing resources, both tangible and intangible, has to be undertaken judiciously for the well-being of the present generation but not at the cost of depriving future generations of any part of our inheritance. Promoting sustainable tourism will enable the country to take full advantage of the potential of tourism for inclusive growth with livelihoods support to the poor, most disadvantaged, women and youth. Therefore, growth of tourism needs to be sustainable to meet the overall objective of the Twelfth Plan.

19.93. Against this background, it is necessary to define the *Sustainable Tourism Criteria for India (STCI)* and the indicators. The STCI system should be evolved to address the issues relating to the modus operandi of the STCI certification mechanism; incentivising STCI certification; capacity building in industry and the Government; creating governance coefficients using contemporary technology; grievance redressal and review of the certification process.

19.94. STCI needs to be immediately operationalised. In the initial years, the adoption of STCI by individual tourism establishments will have to be voluntary. For implementation of STCI, a system of rating/certification of establishments would have to be evolved. Such a system would need to address key issues like type of rating; incentive for rated/certified establishments; logo for rated/certified establishments; process and institutional mechanism for certification, validity of certification; audit and capacity building.

19.95. The Working Group on Tourism set-up by the Planning Commission has made a number of recommendations on promotion of sustainable tourism which should be fully implemented. Similarly, the recommendations on eco-tourism, rural tourism and heritage tourism by the Working Group also needs to be implemented to provide an impetus to such form of tourism.

'NICHE' TOURISM PRODUCTS

19.96. During the Eleventh Plan period, the Government took the initiative of identifying, diversifying, developing and promoting the nascent/upcoming 'niche' products of the tourism industry so as to overcome 'seasonality' and promote India as a 365 days destination, attract tourists with specific interests *and* ensure repeat visits for the unique products in which India has comparative advantage. This endeavour of the Government needs to be pursued with greater vigour during the Twelfth Plan period. Some of the 'niche' tourism products identified for development and promotion include Adventure; Meetings Incentives Conferences and Exhibitions (MICE); Cruise; Medical; Wellness; Golf; Polo; Pilgrimage/spiritual travel; Film; Tea/Coffee; Wild Life; and Caravan. Identifying niche products is a dynamic exercise wherein new products may be added in due course. Further, the recommendations on various 'niche' tourism products in Chapter 8 of the Report of the Working Group on Tourism in the Twelfth Plan should be implemented to provide an impetus to 'niche' products.

VERTICAL AND HORIZONTAL CO-ORDINATION

19.97. Tourism is a multi-sectoral activity transcending multiple services provided by a range of suppliers. The related sectors include airlines, surface transport, hotels, basic infrastructure and facilitation systems, external affairs, sanitation, health, internal security and so on. Growth of tourism cannot be attained unless policy and implementation issues across all the sectors are coordinated and addressed simultaneously. For its development, active involvement of all vertically and horizontally placed agencies is required. Since the tourism projects are implemented at the State/UT level, convergence among various Ministries/Organisations is required at Central and State level.

19.98. At present, there is a lack of horizontal and vertical coordination among the many actors that intervene, directly or indirectly, in the tourism development process. This lack of coordination is observed at the national level, firstly among different government departments that make decisions on tourism related issues, for instance concerning transport infrastructure, or natural protected areas, or education, without considering the implications these decisions may have on the tourism sector. The lack of coordination results in dispersed sector-specific policy orientations and concomitant difficulties in trying to harmonise diverse national, local and sectoral interests. Secondly, there is often a lack of cooperation and coordination between the public institutions concerned with tourism and the traditional tourism private sector for establishing the requirements for tourism investments and operations

19.99. Therefore, it is necessary to establish a mechanism to facilitate horizontal and vertical coordination to optimise tourism induced outcome. In order to achieve this goal, a Tourism Development Authority under the chairmanship of the Prime Minister may be created with multi-sectoral representation from Government (both Centre and States) and other stakeholders to ensure that different interests and viewpoints are considered before a given policy is designed to accomplish national goals and build consensus on differences between stakeholders. The Authority would need to be supported by a Standing Committee.

TAXATION

19.100. Basically, the tourism sector can be taxed either by taxing the businesses in the tourism sector or by taxing the tourists directly. In practice, tourism can be taxed in two ways: through the general tax system, particularly profits and sales taxes, and through special taxes imposed on 'tourist' activities, particularly entry and exit taxes and taxes on hotels. Most important taxes on tourism in almost every developing country are taxes on hotel services, whether levied as part of a general sales tax or as special 'excise' taxes.

19.101. In general, developing countries do not seem to obtain much revenue from levying income and profits taxes on the tourist industry. In principle, there are no special problems in applying the normal income tax system to the tourist industry. Corporations engaged in providing tourist services should be taxed like any other corporations. The case for any exemption from income tax is extremely weak with the caveat that there should be no bias against the tourism industry under the income tax. Similarly, the individuals they employ and the self-employed tourist operators should be subject to income tax in the same manner as any other employed individual and any other self-employed persons, respectively.

19.102. In countries with general sales taxes, particularly value-added taxes, these taxes are usually extended to hotel accommodation and other tourist activities, although sometimes at reduced rates for competitive reasons. In developing countries, however, as a rule only a limited range of services are subjected to so-called 'general' sales taxes. Instead, special taxes (also referred to as 'tourist' taxes) tend to be applied to such services as those provided by tourist hotels. Since the special taxes applied to tourist services as hotel *accommodation*, *rental cars*, *entertainment* and restaurants may often be intended to approximate to the general level of sales taxation/VAT, they do not, in substance, really constitute industry-specific taxation.

19.103. The most important tourist tax is invariably that on accommodation (and related catering). Hotel accommodation in India is subject to luxury tax by the States at rates ranging from 4 per cent to 20 per cent of the tariff above a threshold limit. With a view to preventing mis-declaration of actual tariff, the levy is imposed on printed tariff with a low threshold limit. Since the actual tariff in lean seasons is substantially lower than the printed tariff, the effective tax rate increases to 30 per cent. Further, the disparity in the rates of luxury tax across states adds to the dissatisfaction of tourists and compliance cost by tour operators. In addition, the Central Government has, in the Union Budget 2011–12, introduced service tax on the tariff value of hotel accommodation with an abatement of 50 per cent. *Similarly, food and beverages is also subject to State-VAT at varying rates.* VAT on food items range from 5 per cent to 16.84 per cent and on liquor from 13 per cent to 58 per cent. In addition, service tax on air conditioned restaurants has been imposed in the Union Budget 2011–12, with an abatement of 70 per cent.

19.104. Many of the popular tourist circuits require inter-state movements. Tourist coaches/cars moving along inter-state circuits are liable to road and passenger taxes. To illustrate, the golden triangle circuit of Agra-Delhi-Jaipur cover four states of Delhi, Haryana, Uttar Pradesh and Rajasthan. While moving across these states, tourist vehicles are liable to pay road and passenger taxes which varies across states. According to estimates made by Indian Tourist Transport Association (ITTA), for a three day package between Delhi, Agra and Jaipur, the total road and passenger tax paid accounts for 23 per cent of the cost of a three-day package for the Delhi-Agra-Jaipur circuit. In the absence of a centralised tax payment facility, the problem is further aggravated by collection of the tax at each entry/state border. This causes harassment, undue delay in itinerary resulting in dissatisfaction of the tourists and encourages rent seeking behaviour.

19.105. Air travel in India is subject to the multiple levies, thereby undermining the competitiveness of Indian destinations. These are fuel surcharge varying from ₹1,850 to ₹2,500/-; transaction charge varying across sector; new service tax of ₹185/-; passenger service tax; Airport Tax/User development fee which varied from ₹200 to ₹400/- depending on port of departure; Service tax (0.62 per cent of basic fare charged from the travel agents/tour operator services); and Tax on Air Turbine Fuel (ATF) (ranging from 20 per cent to 38 per cent across States).

19.106. Some of the levies are in the nature of user charges and need to be continued. However those in the nature of taxes are cascading in nature thereby substantially increasing the incidence of tax. Further, there is lack of transparency in collection of these taxes since they vary across airlines. This leads to dissatisfaction amongst the customers.

19.107. The Central Government has introduced a constitutional amendment to enable the introduction of a comprehensive, dual, harmonised and a VAT-type Goods and Services Tax (GST) at the Central and State Government levels. The final contours of the GST regime are under discussion and the new regime is expected to be operationalised from 1 April 2013. The new regime is expected to subsume all Central taxes on goods and services and a number of taxes levied on goods and services at the State level.[8] The rationalisation of the multiple levies on goods and services consumed in the course of tourism should be consistent with the GST regime. Towards this objective, the tax regime for goods and services relating to the tourism industry should be restructured in the following manner:

a. The taxes on hotel accommodation, food and beverages levied both by the Centre and the States should be subsumed in the GST. Since GST rates will be uniform across states, the tax incidence will be transparent and reduce compliance burden for tour operators. It will also resolve disputes regarding taxation of self-supply. However, liquor being a 'sin' good, should continue to be subject to a non-vatable type 'excise'.

b. The goods and passengers tax levied by the States should be subsumed in the GST and the revenue loss may be recouped by suitably adjusting the revenue neutral rate for State GST.

c. Since the purpose of collecting taxes is to enable the Government to provide public goods like roads, the case for a separate levy like the motor vehicle tax which is in the nature of a user charge for use of roads, is extremely weak. Therefore, Motor vehicles tax/road tax should be subsumed in the GST and the rates adjusted suitable to recoup the revenue loss. The State level registration charges for vehicles should be replaced by an annual Central registration fee for all vehicles so as to enable them to move unhindered across inter-state borders. It will help establish seamless movement of people across States and eliminate the requirement for tourist permits. The collection from registration charges may be fully devolved to the States in the ratio of their road density.

d. The aviation sector, like the road transport sector, should be brought under the GST regime and the ATF, fuel surcharge, and service tax should be subsumed. This will ensure that the tax on ATF is fully vatable and therefore do not add to the tax incidence on aviation services.[9] The other levies like transaction charge, new service tax, airport tax, user development fee, and passenger service tax are in the nature of user charges and therefore may be rationalised to reflect the level and quality of service.

e. As GST stabilises, consumption of goods and services by foreign tourists should be treated as exports and GST paid by them refunded when they leave the country, in line with best international practice.

VISA FACILITATION

19.108. Smooth and speedy issue of *Visa* is catalytic to the growth of tourism to any destination. The prompt delivery of visas to inbound tourists is one of the key contributors to sustainable development of tourism. As a policy, Ministry of External Affairs is committed to issuing visas within three days of the receipt of an application. However, in practice, there are inordinate delays.

19.109. The Government should, therefore, set-up a High-Powered Committee comprising of officers from the Ministries of Home, External Affairs, Tourism, and Planning Commission and trade representatives to re-engineer the procedure for issuing of visa within 48 hours of receipt of the application, enabling the online filling of visa applications in local language in the non-English speaking countries (especially in Europe); a single window clearance system for conference and medical visa applications *and* extending the facility for issuing visa on Tatkal (emergency) basis on the payment of higher fee as in the case of passports. Similarly, the fee for Medical Visa needs to be rationalised and the facility of collective landing permit should be introduced.

19.110. Another aspect of visa which needs to be reviewed relates to issuance of Tourist Visa on Arrival (TVOA). An evaluation conducted by Ministry of Tourism shows that the decision to travel to India is significantly influenced by TVOA. Hence, it is necessary to further extend the TVOA facility to European countries (for example, Germany, France, Spain) for which multiple entry visa is allowed; CIS countries like Russia, Kazakhstan, and so on; ASEAN countries—Thailand, Malaysia, Brunei; and other International Airports of the country like Panaji, Bengaluru, Bodh Gaya, Trivandrum, Kochi and Hyderabad. Further, in order to enrich the experience of tourists with the TVOA facility, immigration Officials dealing with TVOA facility need to be trained to create an awareness of the tourism industry among the immigration officers.

19.111. A number of grievances arising from implementation of the visa system can be resolved through inter-ministerial coordination. A permanent task force of Joint Secretary level officers from Ministries of Tourism, Home and External Affairs may be formed under the chairmanship of Joint Secretary from Ministry of Home Affairs to expeditiously resolve visa related problems brought to their notice.

SAFETY AND SECURITY

19.112. Safety and the security of the tourists is a worldwide concern. Any adverse perception about safety and security of the tourists has serious implications for tourist arrivals to the country and its tourist destinations. Accordingly, based on experience, the scheme for constitution of Tourist Facilitation and Security Organization(s) (TFSOs) in States/UTs employing ex-servicemen introduced during the Eleventh Plan may be extended during the Twelfth Plan. Similarly, the Government should undertake awareness campaigns for spreading a message for adoption of Code of Conduct for 'Safe and Honourable Tourism' among the stakeholders, service providers and State level Tourism Departments. The Code is a set of guidelines primarily intended to encourage tourism activities to be undertaken without compromising the basic rights like dignity, safety and freedom from exploitation of both tourists and local residents, in particular, women and children.

MARKET RESEARCH AND TOURISM STATISTICS

19.113. Tourism statistics are extremely vital for policy formulation on demand and supply of tourism services at national, regional and local levels. The key tourism statistics which need to be compiled on a regular basis should relate to visitor arrival information; tourism expenditure estimates; visitor surveys (expenditure, motivation, satisfaction and so on); accommodation and tourism establishment surveys and tourism satellite account (TSA). Effort should be to establish an internationally consistent system of tourism statistics and harmonise the method and conceptual basis of collection, collation and dissemination of tourism related information at all levels in the country. In this regard, the recommendations made by the Working Group on Tourism should be fully implemented.

CONCLUSION

19.114. Tourism has the potential to help achieve the objectives of the Twelfth Plan for faster, more inclusive, and sustainable growth. More importantly, it is a powerful antidote to poverty. It eliminates the disadvantage of market inaccessibility suffered by the poor in respect of their goods and services by bringing the consumer to their doorstep. This reduces the need for intermediation thereby improving recovery. However, the potential can be fully realised only if the international competitiveness of the Indian tourism sector improves significantly by removing both the supply and demand constraints.

19.115. India has a large domestic tourism market too, in addition to international travellers. A variety of products and price points required to realise the country's large domestic tourism potential must be developed. Standard, international products will not be able to open up this market. Indeed even foreign tourists to India come for a variety of experiences, from the luxurious to the simple and spiritual. This would require innovations in products. Therefore, on the supply side, it is necessary to identify new tourism products and create destinations and circuits around them through a comprehensive physical and financial plan through a community participatory process. This would have to be complemented by building the necessary human resource skills for servicing the tourist. Similarly, on the demand side, a multi-pronged effective tourism marketing strategy would need to be adopted to eliminate information asymmetry and create brand India. Since pricing is an important determinant in the choice of an international destination, the tourists cannot be excessively burdened with statutory levies and taxes. Therefore, taxation of tourism should be rationalised in conformity with best international practice.

19.116. The responsibilities for implementing the comprehensive plan for development of tourist circuits and building brand India is fragmented vertically across levels of governments and horizontally across the private and public sector. Hence, it is imperative to establish a transparent and effective policy and regulatory framework; create the appropriate incentive structure; and institute a coordination mechanism to synergise the activities of different stakeholders.

19.117. The Gross Budgetary Support for the Twelfth Five Year Plan (2012–17) for the Ministry of Tourism is ₹*15,190 crores* that excludes IEBR of 155 crore.

ARTS AND CULTURE

19.118. India has a long, rich and diverse cultural heritage that is deeply rooted in its pluralistic ethos providing a creative expression to thousands of communities that make contemporary Indian society. The expression of this rich cultural tradition by individuals and groups not only creates a vibrant society but also provides livelihood to a large section of people contributing to the country's economy. With its rich cultural tradition, India occupies an important place on the cultural map of the world. This is also an expression of its 'soft power'. A variety of cultural traditions and diverse historical legacies of different regions join together to provide India its unique identity as a 'nation state'. Thus, culture should not be seen as a mere 'fringe' activity, but is now at the 'core' of the holistic development strategy of the country and its people.

19.119. The Government through its network of institutions and a slew of grants-in-aid schemes has been supporting preservation, popularisation and promotion of the rich cultural heritage of the country. Different activities create a link between the past and present and lay the foundation for future development of the country's tangible and intangible cultural heritage. This is done through museums, archives, libraries, the performing arts and so on and by organising a variety of events and festivals. Government efforts create an environment and sensitivity for sustenance of the country's cultural heritage and promotion of cultural activities in all its variety. Thus, activities and institutions under the Ministry of Culture are important pillars for inclusive development of the country.

STRATEGIC SHIFT IN THE TWELFTH PLAN

19.120. During the Twelfth Plan, we need to adopt a new approach and appropriate policies which are less dependent on Government financing and catalyse local partnerships. The programmes must be integrated into strategies for sustainable development at every level and take into account the needs and aspirations of the community where cultural assets are found. Sustainable heritage conservation depends upon the commitment and involvement of local communities. Conservation policies, to be successful, need to promote local community stewardship of the heritage as well as provide socio-economic benefits for local communities. Therefore, a direct link must be made between safeguarding the heritage and socio-economic development. This calls for the deliberate recasting of heritage conservation as a development activity that brings economic opportunities, creates jobs, and generates income based on traditional technologies and knowhow. This new programme is aimed at complementing and extending those efforts by moving heritage conservation beyond the exclusive sphere of high technology and elite specialisation and to become the concern and responsibility of every citizen and transform heritage conservation into a grassroots movement which will return the heritage to the communities that created it and who rely on it as the foundation for their future development.

19.121. While ongoing professional and institutional efforts at heritage conservation would be strengthened, participatory approach would be used to catalyse engagement of local community and various interest groups. They would assess the unique characteristics, strengths and economic potential of the elements making up their physical as well as intangible cultural heritage, and then design a community action plan to self-develop these elements in a way which is both profitable and sustainable. Through the programme assistance should be provided in the form of practical, technical, and small "start-up" grants to the local communities and NGOs. At least some part of the annual plan outlay for culture should be used for these "local" grants.

TANGIBLE CULTURAL HERITAGE

19.122. The Archaeological Survey of India (ASI) would be strengthened during the Twelfth Plan for proper conservation, preservation and maintenance of the built heritage of the country. For this, it would be necessary to prepare a comprehensive coordinated plan for conservation and development of monuments and archaeological sites by the Central and State governments and academic and research institutions. They could also be involved in archaeological exploration and excavation. UNESCO Category-2 Regional Centres would be established. Efforts would be stepped up for conservation of unprotected heritage buildings, monuments, archaeological sites, and historic buildings. Fellowships for visiting scholars would be instituted. Cultural Heritage Management Council would be created. And, finally, mapping of cultural heritage resources would be taken up. Schools would be engaged in mapping of local history, ecology and cultural heritage of the area where they are located.

19.123. Museums play an important role in society. They preserve and promote art, culture and scientific learning. They are the learning centres for children during their formative years. They help in building public awareness of the wealth of the nation as well as scientific temper in the population. Compared to its size and vast heritage, the country has a small number of museums and these are not all properly managed. There is a need to set up modern museums of arts and science all over the country that use advanced technology to showcase Indian art, culture and science (including science cities and science centres) as used in day-to-day life. The museums should be interactive and help in learning. These should provide an experience for children and public at large and should also provide information in the local and regional languages. A large number of Science museums in partnership with the Ministry of Science and Technology and Ministry of HRD also be established. These could have three parts—pedagogy centre for school/college teachers, science activity centre for students, and science Exploratorium for general public.

19.124. During the Eleventh Plan, various measures were taken for up-gradation/modernisation, and improvement in functioning, of the national-level museums directly funded by the Government of India and a large number of local-level museums run by State Governments, trusts, foundations and so on. Academic and research institutions should be supported to set up more museums across the country. These measures have helped in furthering the cause of the 'museum movement' and the pace of modernisation should be accelerated during the Twelfth Plan period. For this purpose, it is imperative to adopt a multi-pronged strategy comprising the provision of financial assistance for establishment and up-gradation of local and regional museums through the revision of the existing scheme; modernising of State and national level museums; establishing larger scale museums in State capitals through partnership with State Governments/Civil Society; digitisation of collections in all museums to facilitate accessibility through a virtual museum portals including 3D exhibits and virtual 3D tours; making museum websites more dynamic, interactive and social-media enabled to attract online participation; creation of innovation spaces in museums based on framework provided by the National Innovation Council and capacity building and training of existing staff of Museums. Role of museums in education, informal as well as formal learning aligned to curriculum would be strengthened in the Twelfth Plan.

INTANGIBLE CULTURAL HERITAGE

19.125. At present, Anthropological Survey of India (AnSI) is involved in collaborating scientific work relating to anthropology with scientific institutions. However, there is no scheme for providing financial assistance for such scientific work. Therefore, a mechanism should be established to enable AnSI to provide financial assistance to projects proposed by the scientific organisations of State Governments, departments of anthropology in universities, NGOs involved in anthropological studies and similar bodies. Further, assistance to State Governments, institutions and organisations should also be provided for documentation and dissemination of research results in the field of anthropology.

19.126. A large amount of cultural wealth is stored in the form of audio-visual materials available with various government and non-governmental institutions and private individuals. In the absence of a systematic organisation and periodic up-gradation, these materials are fast deteriorating. To digitise them and to provide the wider public an easy access to these and to the new audio-visual resources being constantly generated, appropriate technological and institutional framework is urgently required.

19.127. For this purpose, a separate National Audio-Visual Archives (NAVA) should be established as a virtual network of cultural resources in audio-visual form. NAVA will be engaged in instituting state-of-the-art digitisation and storage system for independent repositories of audio-visual resources; setting up a virtual network of these repositories and offering interactive online access to their resources; and standardising and periodically upgrading the methods and technologies used in production, storage and retrieval of audio-visual resources. The design of data-retrieval systems, being the point-of-access for users of the database, must be given adequate attention and must provide for relevant interactive tools to be used. The genres to be covered will include oral traditions, traditional crafts and textiles, dance, music and theatrical practices, cultural practices and traditional knowledge.

19.128. Dissemination of India's traditional and contemporary cultural expressions is an important means for preservation of culture. For this, high quality programmes on art and culture could be supported. Such programmes may be telecast on all public and private channels. All this video content could also be made available in the public domain. Competitions can be launched inviting short films, documentaries and short videos on specified themes to capture the cultural diversity and expressions across the country.

19.129. Unlike most capital cities of the world, Delhi does not have a world class integrated infrastructural facility for culture and performing arts. This gap needs to be filled up by setting up a National Centre of Performing Arts at New Delhi. The Centre will be a state-of-the-art "cultural multiplex" housing a set of auditoria/performance spaces of varying sizes and specifications and present, round the year, world class productions of India's varied arts from across the country. It will also develop its own repertoire and be a vibrant cultural hub. This would require about 15–20 acre land in Central Delhi. Similar centres may also be set-up in Kolkata, Chennai and other major cities in due course. In Kolkata, the area encompassing Rabindra Sadan Cultural Complex and Central Cultural Institute has a potential to be developed into such a Centre. New and innovative institutional arrangements and partnerships may be needed to create and manage such integrated complexes.

19.130. National School of Drama (NSD) has emerged as a foremost theatre training institution in the world and the only one of its kind in India. It has played an important role in shaping contemporary theatre in all its variety in the country. Need for more such schools were recognised in the Eleventh Plan. During the Twelfth Plan, five Regional Schools of Drama at Bengaluru, Kolkata, Maharashtra/Goa, J&K, and the North-East region will be set up by the Ministry of Culture as independent, autonomous Schools of Drama having their own repertory companies. These Schools will be free to draw upon the experience of NSD, New Delhi and grow on their own. In addition, the States will be encouraged to set-up their own language-based versions of NSD.

KNOWLEDGE RESOURCE HERITAGE

19.131. During the Twelfth Plan, public library system in the country should be rejuvenated by taking advantage of the technological developments that have transformative potential to change the public libraries. Existing public libraries must modernise their collections, services and facilities and become pro-active in resource sharing, professional development of staff, extending library facilities right up to the grassroots through the Panchayats. Based on the recommendation of the National Knowledge Commission, a National Mission on Libraries has already been established. The mission should now be enabled to undertake specific activities as per NKC recommendations and could pave way for setting up of an independent and financially autonomous National Commission on Libraries.

19.132. Archival system including National Archives would also be strengthened. The process of acquisition and accession of public and private records at the National Archives of India would be stepped up. Digitisation and security microfilm making would also be done expeditiously. Old public institutions including academic and research institutions and private archives should be supported to conserve, preserve, digitise and archive valuable Indian heritage.

19.133. India has unique and unparalleled living and diverse cultural traditions of an unimaginable magnitude. To provide sustenance to, and showcase the richness of living and diverse cultural traditions of India, an overarching mechanism in the form of a National Network Centre on India's Intangible Cultural Heritage should be set up for mapping and documenting India's valuable tangible and intangible cultural assets in different eco-cultural zones. It should provide for coordinated identification, documentation and preservation of the extensive and diverse range of India's traditional knowledge system and integrate its various dimensions. For this purpose, Government may seek international technical assistance for designing a system based on best international practice.

19.134. Ideas, ideals and values promoted by Mahatma Gandhi have become more relevant today than before—not only for India but for the entire world. Thus, a Gandhi Heritage Mission would be taken up to conserve, preserve and promote Gandhi's physical and the intellectual heritage. Further, his ideas and values would be promoted across the world through conference and seminars on Gandhi's intellectual heritage.

19.135. Indian writing is unique in its pluralistic, multilingual traditions and has an incredible heritage of rich literary diversity. During the Eleventh Plan, the Government had initiated a pilot project, 'Indian Literature Abroad', to promote and showcase Indian literature to a larger international audience. This was meant to support and facilitate translation and promotion of literary heritage and contemporary literature of various Indian languages into major foreign languages. This project has been widely appreciated and would be continued during the Twelfth Plan.

EDUCATION, RESEARCH AND INTERNATIONAL CULTURAL RELATIONS

19.136. The existing schemes under the Education and Research Section should be modified to be more effective. With a view to preserving and promoting Buddhist Culture the setting up of Bodh Darshan Higher Study School, Tabo (Himachal Pradesh) will get priority during the Twelfth Plan period. Similarly, the existing schemes for promoting international cultural relations need to be rationalised to effectively foster friendly relations and project Indian culture in the countries concerned.

19.137. Further, it is also necessary to put in place a mechanism for providing financial assistance for artists and cultural professionals going abroad for seminars, festivals and exhibitions on cultural subjects and for providing financial assistance to foreign artists desiring to study and/or learn Indian culture in any form like dance, music and drama for supporting Indian artistes to go abroad or foreign artistes to take up study in the field of Indian culture. This assistance does not have to be entirely through Government support, but should bring together private donors and corporate entities. The Government should provide matching grants.

19.138. During the Twelfth Plan, India should explore the possibility of having a permanent presence at the prestigious Venice Biennale of Art. The space could be used not only for the Art Biennale but also for the equally prestigious Venice Biennale of Architecture and in the lean months for any other cultural activities.

GOVERNANCE AND PARTNERSHIPS

19.139. India's traditional and contemporary cultural expressions are extremely diverse and spread out and therefore no centralised academy or agency can do full justice with the demands of the sector. For various reasons, many of the State Academies set up by various State Governments are in disarray. Central Government needs to partner with the State Governments in making the State Academies play an important role in preserving and promoting performing, visual and literary arts of each State. For this purposes, Ministry of Culture will introduce scheme for rejuvenating both central and the State Academies working in the field of performing, visual and literary arts by providing financial assistance subject to professionalisation of the management of these bodies.

19.140. In order to leverage professional expertise and capacity from outside in specific disciplines, Government could enter into partnership with selected universities, institutions of national importance, research institutions and cultural organisations to undertake a mutually agreed programme and function as Centre of Excellence in the specified fields. While autonomy of these organisations will be respected, deliverables will be closely monitored. This partnership could be with well-established theatre groups and professional repertory companies with high standard of excellence, cultural research centres and repositories of archives on a particular subject, and centres of excellence in cultural texts, stagecraft, cross translations, interactive documentation, teaching and learning of traditional arts, conservation and preservation of both tangible and intangible heritage of the country.

19.141. Ministry of Culture and its autonomous organisations have a large number of grants-in-aid schemes meant to provide financial support to individuals and organisations in the area of culture. Several steps like electronic payments, online applications and minutes of expert committees available online have been introduced to bring about transparency. During the Twelfth Plan, greater objectivity and transparency would be infused by developing a comprehensive management information system with online filing and tracking of all applications and IT solutions for back-end operations in a seamless manner.

19.142. Capacity-building and training of personnel to work in various Cultural Organisations is a critical requirement. Presently, some training is being imparted, but in a limited and distributed manner with various institutes under the aegis of the Government. Coordination and expansion of training research should be undertaken through an apex institutional mechanism or a Central Cultural University for the purpose.

CONCLUSION

19.143. The conservation of culture is extremely vital for inclusive growth. In general, cultural assets are owned by the relatively poorer section of the society. Any erosion in these assets will further aggravate the asset ownership pattern to the detriment of the poor. The problem is further aggravated by the fact that often these assets are also income generating. These assets cannot be protected by individuals and therefore Government must step in to provide technical and financial support. Such efforts should essentially complement the new programme for conservation, which should usher a paradigm shift in our hitherto conservation efforts, by integrating it into the overall development strategy for local communities.

19.144. The Plan allocation for the Twelfth Five Year Plan (2012–17) for Ministry of Culture is ₹*7,275 crores*.

HANDLOOMS AND HANDICRAFTS

INTRODUCTION

19.145. The handloom and handicrafts sectors have their roots in the rich traditional, historical and cultural diversity that distinguishes India from the rest of the world. The two sectors are also particularly significant as they provide low-cost and green livelihood opportunities to lakhs of families, besides supplementing incomes in times of agrarian distress, checking migration and preserving the traditional economic relationships between different sections of the society. As on June 2011, the handloom and handicraft sectors employed 43.32 lakh weavers/workers and 68.86 lakh craftspersons respectively, resulting in total employment of 112.18 lakh persons. With women contributing a majority (85 per cent) of the pre- and post-loom labour and accounting for over 50 per cent of weavers/artisans in the country, and a significant mass of weavers/artisans consisting of Scheduled Castes (SCs), Scheduled Tribes (STs), other backward classes (OBCs) and religious minorities, these two sectors also represent the economic lifeline of the most vulnerable sections of the population. Owing to their cultural and economic importance in India's development process, various policies along with programmatic interventions, are proposed to be implemented in the Twelfth Plan, aimed at generating sustained and productive employment with suitable working conditions for the entire weaver, artisanal and ancillary worker population, and also to ensure that the crafts and their products continue to flourish across the country as well as abroad.

HANDLOOMS

19.146. Indian handlooms are characterised by an infinite variety of weaves, textures and designs spun on the handloom, ranging from the finest muslins to heavy bedspreads, from delicate pastels to earthy hues, and from appealingly simple to amazingly intricate compositions, which are known throughout the world since ancient times. This sector can meet every need, from exquisite fabrics, which take months to weave, to popular items of mass production for daily use. Handloom, being a State subject, its development is primarily the responsibility of the State Governments. However, the Government of India has been supplementing the efforts of the States with its policy of promoting and encouraging the sector through suitable interventions.

Current Situation

19.147. As per the latest (3rd) Handloom Census of 2009–10, there are 23.77 lakh handlooms in the country, providing employment to 43.32 lakh handloom weavers and ancillary workers which include 38.47 lakh adult handloom weavers and ancillary workers. Of the latter, 77.90 per cent are women, 10.13 per cent belong to the SCs, 18.12 per cent to the STs and 45.18 per cent to OBCs. A total of 27.83 lakh handloom households are engaged in weaving and allied activities, of which 87 per cent are located in rural areas and remaining 13 per cent in urban areas. Most of the handloom households live in kutcha (54 per cent) or semi-pucca (31 per cent) houses; only 15 per cent households live in pucca houses. However, 53 per cent of the handloom households weave only for commercial purposes, and nearly 16 per cent households undertake a mix of domestic and commercial production. In the North Eastern Region (NER), 90 per cent of handloom worker households are weaver households and account for 63.4 per cent of total handloom worker households in the country. The Approach Paper for the Twelfth Plan has identified handlooms as one of the priority sectors that will create large scale employment opportunities.

19.148. The performance of the handloom sector during the Eleventh Plan period is indicated in *Table 19.5* which shows that total handloom cloth production was 6,947 million square meters during the first year of the Eleventh Plan (2007–08), but it declined by 3.89 per cent in the following year (2008–09) which was marked by global recession. However, since then, production has consistently risen in the third and fourth years of the Eleventh Plan, to reach a production level of 6,930 million square meters during 2011–12, which accounts for over 14 per cent of total cloth/textile production, comprising handloom, mill-made and powerloom, in the country. Exports rose by 26 per cent in 2010–11 to ₹1,574.95 crore as compared to the previous year and further to ₹2,653.95 crore, registering a growth of 68 per cent over the previous year.

Challenges for the Twelfth Plan for Handlooms

19.149. While considerable progress has been made in the handloom sector during the Eleventh Plan as depicted in Table 19.5, a lot still remains to be done as the sector continues to face several daunting challenges and uncertainties.

Welfare and Livelihood of Weavers

19.150. Nearly 47 per cent of all handloom weavers belong to BPL families and 10 per cent fall in the Antodaya Anna Yojana (AAY) category. About 29.4 per cent of all handloom workers have never attended school and 12.7 per cent are educated only up to the primary school level. Poverty and illiteracy among weaver families is accompanied by poor access to basic necessities including health, water, sanitation, housing and livelihood facilities. The contribution of women is largely unacknowledged, although women constitute nearly 70 per cent of total handloom weavers/workers.

TABLE 19.5
Performance of Handloom Sector during the Eleventh Plan Period

Item	2007–08	2008–09	2009–10	2010–11	2011–12	CAGR (%)
Cloth Production (million square meters)	6,947	6,677	6,806	6,903	6,930 (Prov.)	1.25 (base: '08–'09)
Employment (lakh persons)	NA	NA	43.32	43.32	43.32	–
Export (₹crore)	NA*	NA*	1,252.81	1,574.95	2,653.95	45.55

Source: Office of Development Commissioner (Handlooms), Ministry of Textiles.
Note: *Not available due to absence of ITC (HS) codes for handloom products.

Rising Input Costs

19.151. Despite more than 700 yarn depots being operated, the issue of easy sourcing of raw materials, both yarn and dyes and chemicals, at reasonable prices has been a key problem across centres of handloom production, particularly in the NER, as in recent period, there has been a sharp rise in yarn prices. The problem is more acute for individual weavers who need smaller quantities of yarn which are not readily available.

Sparse Credit Coverage and High Cost

19.152. Weavers are prone to diverting credit towards consumption needs, and lack of even rudimentary financial literacy aggravates the existing credit-related obstacles faced by them. Further, a majority of the weavers continue to operate outside the fold of institutionalised financing, with nearly 44.6 per cent being dependent on Master Weavers, 13.4 per cent on moneylenders and only 14.8 per cent having access to institutionalised sources of credit. For rural households, access to institutional financing was far lower at 7.7 per cent revealing the extent to which weavers are trapped in the vicious cycle of debt and resultant poverty.

Marketing Bottlenecks and Lack of Opportunities

19.153. Dearth of innovation and limited dynamism in the handloom sector, particularly in the field of marketing, is a matter of concern, which is impeding its expansion and growth. As 61.1 per cent of the total weaver workforce (24 per cent for non-North Eastern States) comprise of independent workers, a majority of the weavers necessarily bear all the risks associated with the business of procurement, marketing and sale, with obvious consequences. Certain State Governments have undertaken innovative measures to popularise the use of handloom products (Box 19.2). Such innovative measures for promoting handloom products need to be replicated by other States.

Poor Institutional Coverage and Management

19.154. About 85 per cent of weavers are outside the cooperative fold, as they either work under Master Weavers/traders or independently. Further, several Apex/Handloom Corporations have become dormant due to a host of reasons such as financial losses, lack of professional management, over-staffing and poor marketing and distribution channels, which have, in turn, affected the health of about 50 per cent of the Primary Weavers' Cooperative Societies.

Poor Policy Dissemination and Information Gaps

19.155. Lack of information to weavers regarding various Government policies/schemes under implementation, is a significant cause for deteriorating conditions of the weavers. Sometimes even the implementing agencies may not possess complete information, resulting in critical gaps in implementation. Also, major institutions providing critical inputs like credit, research, technology, management, and market development, are largely centralised and hence unable to reach the dispersed and largely home-based weavers.

Infrastructure Gaps

19.156. Infrastructure in the handloom sector continues to be inadequate, with substantial gaps, particularly in the NER. Facilities such as clean drinking water, sanitation, effluent treatment plants and electricity, are yet to be universally provided in all hubs of handloom production. Systems that ensure efficient supply chain management from the stage of availability of raw materials up to sale of finished goods are yet to be set up.

Monitoring and Evaluation

19.157. There is a need for a strong Web-based monitoring and evaluation system to promote transparency and accountability and facilitate regular tracking of physical and financial performance of individual programmes/projects, particularly the ongoing clusters.

Education, Skills, Research and Training

19.158. The formal education system, including research institutes, has not included teaching, training and skill development for handlooms into its mainstream curricula. Hence, the onus of introducing innovation in design and techniques, and passing the traditions to younger generations, is left to

> **Box 19.2**
> **Popular Choice by Design!**
>
> - The Jharkand Silk, Textile and Handicraft Development Corporation (Jharcraft) has adopted an innovative method to implement the weavers' credit card scheme, involving a tripartite agreement between the weaver, Jharcraft and Dena Bank, under which three different accounts are maintained by the Bank—savings account of weaver, loan account of weaver and Jharcraft's account. The price of raw material issued to the weaver is deducted from loan account of the weaver and deposited into Jharcraft's account. When the latter gets the finished product, weaver's dues are credited into savings account of weaver. After the finished product is sold, the sale proceeds are deposited into the loan account of the weaver. In view of the success of this pilot, it is now being scaled up by the State. Jharcraft has also, after making sustained efforts, revived two unique tribal paint forms—Jadopatia of Dumka and Pyathar of Singhbhum which had almost become extinct. Under a project named 'HARSH', more than 50,000 Self-Help Groups have been organised, mainly consisting of women. In addition, bamboo-based low cost houses and toilets are being developed for weavers and artisans. Jharcraft is now operating 25 emporia across the country, with its initiatives having resulted in an incredible jump in turnover from ₹50 lakh in 2007–08 to ₹70 crore in 2011–12!
> - For creating sustainable jobs for weavers/artisans, upgrading skills/product quality, raising earnings and creating market linkages, Government of Odisha has signed an MOU with a subsidiary of Fabindia under which a Community Owned Company was set up in October 2010. In 2011–12, the Company has inducted 300 artisans as shareholders; total sale of products during this period was ₹1.4 crore; another project by Boyanika (Orissa State Handloom Weavers' Cooperative Society) is aimed at improving designs and creating a market for the State's handloom and textile products; leading designers such as Rta Kapur Chishti, Bibhu Mohapatra, Rajesh Pratap Singh, and Rakesh Thakore are associated with it.
> - Lepakshi of Andhra Pradesh has launched a major ICT initiative through a web-based service for online sale of craft items produced in the State. Now, markets are just a click away, besides keeping the intermediaries away!
> - In Madhya Pradesh, handloom angvastrams/stoles are, inter alia, presented to dignitaries and guests at State functions, providing visibility to the products both domestically and internationally, besides creating a growing, captive market for such products. Presentation of 'Chanderi' angvastrams was a major highlight at the Commonwealth Games!

weaver families who usually have no resources to devote to this critical field.

Limited Role of Private Enterprise

19.159. The success of project interventions is limited by the capacity of NGOs/implementing agencies which often have weak linkages with the market, thereby limiting the sustainability of their operations. Also, implementing agencies are often unable to sustain operations after funding support under the concerned Schemes has stopped. Greater private participation for promoting professional management and handholding support, inter alia, through adoption of the PPP model, is required to supplement Government resources and bring about greater efficiencies and ensure attainment of project targets.

Consolidation

19.160. The existing clusters need consolidation for converting the Self-Help Groups (SHGs) into self-sustainable community-based enterprises. Hence, adequate measures are necessary to ensure consolidation of all existing clusters introduced in the earlier Plans. At the same time, for equitable growth of the sector, the remaining clusters/areas also need coverage in a phased manner. As such, cluster development needs to be given continued emphasis for achieving integrated and holistic development of the weavers. Consolidation of all efforts introduced in the earlier Plans is a big challenge for the Twelfth Plan.

The Vision and Strategies for the Twelfth Plan for Handlooms

19.161. The vision for the handloom sector for the Twelfth Plan is to develop a strong, competitive and vibrant sector in order to provide sustainable employment to the weavers and ancillary workers, particularly belonging to the disadvantaged sections of the population and to ensure faster, more inclusive growth of the sector. To achieve the vision, the emphasis in the Twelfth Plan will be on consolidation of past gains and strengthening of marketing systems. Effort will continue over the next five years to promote supply of yarn/dyes and chemicals in smaller quantities/sachets and allocation of more depots; achieving universal financial inclusion of weavers/ancillary workers with margin money and credit guarantee support, interest subvention, greater coverage of Weaver Credit Cards and linking SHGs with banks, Microfinance Institutions (MFIs) and others for greater access to credit; expanding coverage under weaver welfare programmes; restructuring the cluster development approach for more efficient management and increased sustainability of existing clusters and taking up new clusters where none have been assisted so far; broadening the eligibility of implementing agencies to include NGOs, associations, design institutes, management institutes and other institutions of repute which have local and regional experience and relevant expertise; enumerating women's contribution in mapping/diagnostic exercises; and establishing robust monitoring and evaluation systems, along with defined goalposts.

19.162. The Twelfth Plan will also encourage greater environmental compliance and occupational health and safety by adoption of measures such as quantifying environmental impact in planning for cluster development, mandatorily installing effluent treatment plant (ETP) in all the dyeing units in PPP mode, promoting solar lighting and supporting adoption of improved looms with better ergonomics to reduce drudgery of weavers. To overcome the exiting training and skill gaps, the Weavers' Service Centres (WSCs) and Indian Institutes of Handloom Technology (IIHTs) will be strengthened and further consolidated. Formal crafts education will be introduced through establishment of Textiles chairs in leading regional and national universities to inspire and draw young people into joining the sector. A Textile Museum/Observatory/Resource centre/Hastkala Academy to support preservation, revival, archiving and documentation of languishing handloom crafts (including handicrafts) will also be set up under PPP. Design and product diversity, including development of niche products will be directed towards strengthening marketing and brand building. The brand of 'Handmade in India' will be promoted domestically as well as abroad, and since the handlooms, handicrafts, and khadi and the village industry sectors are distinct but have threads of commonality, greater synergy will be encouraged between them to achieve more efficient utilisation of resources. The coverage of 'Handloom Mark' is proposed to be enlarged to cover all handloom products within a definite time frame. States will be encouraged to leverage the rich tradition of the handloom sector to develop tourism potential by showcasing the unique skills/products by setting up permanent establishments where live demonstration of the crafts along with sales counters could be provided for, at strategic locations, which could serve as captive marketing channels for weavers. To boost exports, besides participation in fairs and exhibitions abroad, 'India Weaves Week' will be organised at the Indian Embassies/High Commissions.

19.163. Special Assistance to NER will be extended through focus on up gradation of looms, dye houses and work-sheds after in-depth evaluation and review of existing infrastructure. SHGs will be formed and training facilities upgraded to arrive at 100 per cent coverage of handloom workers. An Apparel Designing and Training Institute is proposed to be set up, linked with one Special Weavers' Service Centre. A new umbrella scheme that gives space for framing projects for NER within the objectives for the handloom sector with flexibilities in guidelines to suit their peculiar difficulties is proposed. One of the projects within the scheme would be conversion of domestic handloom units into Minimum Economic Size (MES) commercial units aimed at creating commercial areas with infrastructure including worksheds, equipment and common facility centres for making the handloom industry in NER more market responsive and professionally oriented.

19.164. Major interventions proposed for the handloom sector during the Twelfth Plan are given in Box 19.3.

HANDICRAFTS

19.165. Handicrafts are items made by hand with the use of simple tools, generally artistic and/or traditional in nature, which are used for decorative purposes, including as gifts and souvenirs as well as for utility purposes. Handicrafts activity is predominantly carried out in the unorganised household

> **Box 19.3**
> **Twelfth Plan Interventions for Handlooms**
>
> *Marketing, Exports, Brand Building and Promotion of Handloom Products*—Marketing Events; Urban Haats; Retail Outlets; Strengthening of Handloom Organisations; Marketing Incentive Component; International Fairs and Exhibitions; and Export Projects.
>
> *Infrastructure and Cluster Model*—Consolidation of existing Clusters; New Clusters/Projects; Will include Group Projects/State-specific Projects and Innovative ideas; New component of Margin Money support.
>
> *Raw Material Availability*—Yarn to be supplied, including supplies under 10 per cent Hank Yarn Price Subsidy and increased freight/depot charges for NE States; Depots to take up distribution of dyes and chemicals also; Depot-cum-Warehouse for supply of smaller quantities of yarn.
>
> *Credit Availability*—Credit Guarantee and Interest Subvention to weavers against targeted credit.
>
> *Social Welfare Measures/Environmental Compliance*—Health Insurance Scheme and Mahatma Gandhi Bunkar Bima Yojana; Environmental Compliance Projects; Solar lighting; Looms improvement and better ergonomics.
>
> *Training, HRD, R&D and Technical Processes*—Improvement in infrastructure and machinery in existing WSCs and IIHTs; Introduction of degree courses; R&D Projects; Revival and documentation of languishing handloom crafts.
>
> *North Eastern Region*—Umbrella scheme for greater flexibility; conversion of domestic handloom units into Minimum Economic Size (MES) commercial units

sector, and in India as well as in many other regions of the world, the handicrafts sector is identified as the largest sector of rural employment after agriculture. As in the case of handlooms, the handicrafts industry has also been identified in the Approach Paper for the Twelfth Plan as one of the priority sectors that will create large-scale employment opportunities.

Current Situation

19.166. The Handicrafts Census is yet to be completed, which will indicate the precise extent and nature of the sector. As per latest available estimates, employment in this sector has risen from 47.61 lakh in 2005–06 to 68.86 lakh crafts persons in 2010–11; 20.80 per cent belong to the SCs, 7.50 per cent to the STs, 52.40 per cent to OBCs and 56.0 per cent are women. It is proposed to include Handicrafts in the Sixth Economic Census scheduled to be conducted during 2012–13.

19.167. The performance of the handicrafts sector during the Eleventh Plan period is given in Table 19.6. It is to be noted that towards the beginning of the Eleventh Plan, exports of handicrafts (inclusive of carpets) suffered a severe setback due to the global economic recession in 2008. Thus, exports declined by 37.89 per cent in the second year of the Eleventh Plan (2008–09) to ₹10,891.85 crore. However, steps taken by the Government led to total handicraft exports increasing by 3.05 per cent in 2009–10, followed by a 20.51 per cent increase during 2010–11 and further by 24.58 per cent during the last year (2011–12) of the Eleventh Plan, to reach a level of ₹16,851.27 crore. The revival of the industry has now led to the return of many artisans who had left the sector earlier. However, India's share in total world handicrafts exports is estimated to be less than 2 per cent, indicating the potential for raising handicrafts exports in the largely unexplored international market.

Challenges for the Twelfth Plan for Handicrafts

19.168. Like handlooms, the handicrafts sector, being a State subject, is also primarily the responsibility of the State Governments, and assistance is provided by Government of India to supplement the States' resources. However, while measures taken in the Eleventh Plan have helped in the revival of the sector, it remains beset with several constraints, many of which are common to the handloom sector already brought out in the previous section. Other challenges specifically faced by the handicrafts sector are indicated below.

TABLE 19.6
Performance of Handicrafts Sector during the Eleventh Plan Period

Item	2007–08	2008–09	2009–10	2010–11	2011–12	CAGR (%) (base: '08–'09)
Production (₹ crore)	31,940.36	19,375.88	20,221.58	24,393.14	30,257.18	16.01
Employment (lakh persons)	NA	58.50	62.60	68.86	72.30	7.3
Export (₹ crore)	17,536.78	10,891.85	11,224.27	13,526.66	16,851.27	15.70

Source: Office of Development Commissioner (Handicrafts), Ministry of Textiles.

Resource Mapping and Data Base

19.169. Several crafts are languishing and slowly dying due to prolonged neglect and lack of awareness, and inadequate appreciation of the intricacies and skills involved. Lack of proper processes and systems for identification, documentation and mapping of all crafts in India is still a major challenge. Data on craftspersons, including their socio-economic status, livelihood and family details, and scientific mapping of market trends and consumer profiles is also inadequate.

Infrastructural and Technological Gaps

19.170. The availability of infrastructure, including formal institutions/organisations for production, marketing and distribution of handicrafts in an organised manner is lacking and often non-functioning. Artisans do not have direct access to markets within the country and abroad. Lack of technological up gradation has aggravated the situation as age-old technology/methods of production are utilised, leading to inefficient operations and low quality of output.

Technical Resource Gaps

19.171. There is a lack of comprehensive data on equipments used by various crafts, apart from lack of concentrated efforts to develop good quality, low-cost tools for artisans. Several design banks are outdated and redundant, as they fail to undertake continuous revision through, inter alia, use of internet. Designers often lack requisite knowledge on practical application of crafts, and training programmes introduced to upgrade skills of artisans are treated as a one-time activity, with no mechanism to institutionalise learning.

Regional Imbalances

19.172. Regional imbalances continue to prevail with visible gaps in production and consumption (sales), as the northern and central regions account for bulk of the exports.

Programmatic Issues

19.173. Various programmatic issues, such as eligibility criteria, financial aspects and fund release pattern need to be reviewed to facilitate greater efficiency in implementation.

The Vision and Strategies for THE Twelfth plan for Handicrafts

19.174. The vision for the handicrafts sector for the Twelfth Plan is to create an equitable, world-class globally competitive and enabling environment, and provide sustainable livelihood opportunities to the artisans through innovative product designs, improvement in product quality, introduction of appropriate technology including modern technology, wherever required, and preserving traditions, thereby resulting in balanced socio-economic development and inclusive growth of the sector. In line with the vision, focus will be on consolidation of existing infrastructure including measures to ensure sustainability; institutionalisation of systems of implementation and scientific evaluation and continuous monitoring of all existing programmes; and compulsory scientific mapping of crafts, artisanal communities, market trends and consumer profiles and using this as basis for introducing new schemes or programmes, where necessary. For this purpose, the existing programmes/schemes in the Eleventh Plan will be continued with suitable modifications and consolidation and, in addition, some new initiatives will be introduced. Existing clusters will be consolidated through design development efforts, intensifying forward and backward linkages, and fostering compliance and quality control, so that they become sustainable, vibrant and resourceful centres of craftsmanship. Core issues of water and energy management, sanitation facilities for workers, and crèche facilities for women artisans will be included mainly through convergence with other programmes, and details on raw material availability and related information will be placed in public domain. New clusters will be demand and need-driven, and set up under the PPP mode wherever possible. MFIs and Non-Banking Finance Companies (NBFCs) will be tapped as additional sources of credit, and banks will be encouraged to ensure that lending to artisans which falls under priority lending, is at least 10 per cent of such lending, and give due thrust to the Scheme of Artisan Credit Card (ACC). Technological interventions will be promoted to enhance competitiveness of handicraft products. Awards/scholarships will be introduced to encourage young generation craftspersons, and Shilp Gurus/National Awardees will be conferred honours at par with other National honours.

19.175. The marketing strategy will involve sustained focus on brand building and promotion of 'Handcrafted in India' brand through a dedicated campaign to promote domestic sales as well as exports, including a new consumer awareness scheme for domestic markets, introduction of national level events on the lines of National Handlooms Expo, and greater involvement of the private sector including the civil society. PPP mode will be encouraged at all levels in marketing promotion. Steps will be taken for adherence to compliance issues so that products meet the acceptable international quality standards and also convey their historical, cultural and traditional significance. As proposed for handlooms, States will be encouraged to leverage the unique skills and products of the handicrafts sector to develop tourism potential in individual States through suitable linkages with the tourism industry. Efforts will be made to conceive or upgrade craft training programmes to cover core areas such as craft design, technology, marketing and management through recognised institutions and universities. Social welfare measures will be modified to provide for improved delivery, monitoring and grievance redressal mechanisms. A new Scheme called the 'Infrastructure and Technology Development Scheme' will be introduced by shifting the infrastructure components of existing schemes for developing infrastructure with focus on technology. Emphasis will also be placed on establishment of Handicrafts Museums/Conservatories/Resource Centres for preservation, revival, archiving and documentation of languishing crafts. Another new initiative called the 'North Eastern Regional Development Scheme' is proposed, to tap the potential of handicrafts in NER, by facilitating access to markets, providing infrastructure support for improved quality and productivity and introducing an institutional framework of development.

19.176. Major interventions proposed for the handicrafts sector during the Twelfth Plan are given in Box 19.4.

THE WAY FORWARD

19.177. In the Twelfth Plan, the overall policy framework for the handloom and handicrafts sectors will be to focus on consolidation of gains achieved from the existing schemes/programmes, along with impact evaluation and suitable modifications in the schemes to improve their efficacy and delivery. Special focus will be placed on promoting a unified 'Handmade in India' brand for Indian hand-crafted products and encouraging greater synergy between handlooms, handicrafts and khadi and village industry sectors to achieve more efficient utilisation of resources and improved performance of the sectors, with as much emphasis on domestic markets as for exports. There will also be a focus on supporting private entrepreneurship and professionalism along with institutionalisation of e-governance and leveraging of innovations for achieving sustainable growth of the sectors. Special efforts will be made towards preservation, revival and documentation of languishing crafts, and harnessing the rich tradition of handlooms and handicrafts in the country to develop tourism potential. State Governments will be encouraged to adopt innovative measures to popularise handlooms

> **Box 19.4**
> **Twelfth Plan Schemes for Handicrafts**
>
> *Babasheb Ambedker Hastshilp Vikas Yojna:* Consolidation of clusters by strengthening existing skills, harnessing design development efforts; New clusters preferably in PPP mode.
>
> *Design and Technology Up-gradation Scheme:* Introduction and dissemination of new Designs; Development of Innovative Technologies/Technical Processes; Showcasing of Prototypes in Exhibitions as well as online.
>
> *Marketing Support and Services Scheme:* Initiation of new consumer awareness scheme for increasing domestic sales; Introduction of national level events; Brand promotion; Domestic Exhibitions and International Exhibitions/events.
>
> *Human Resource Development Scheme:* Introduction of Craft Training Programmes in design, technology, marketing and management through recognised institutions and universities.
>
> *Handicrafts Artisans Comprehensive Welfare Scheme:* Modified Rajiv Gandhi Shilpi Swasthya Bima and Janashree Bima Yojana; Credit Guarantee/Interest Subvention; Cards to new Artisans.
>
> *Research and Development Scheme:* Completion of Handicrafts Census; Studies on languishing crafts; Occupational Health and Safety Issues; Special advocacy efforts for benefit of artisans.
>
> *Infrastructure and Technology Development Scheme (New):* Strengthening of Raw Material Depots/CFCs as well as opening of new ones; establishment of Mini Haats/Urban Haats; Construction of warehouses; Handicraft Museums.
>
> *Special Package for NER (New):* Capacity development; Setting up State Initiative Design Centre/International Craft Complex; Raw Material and Design Banks; Marketing Extension activities.

and handicrafts within their States as well as in other parts of the country. Policy will also focus on promotion of financial inclusion and financial literacy support programmes, addressing environmental and occupational health and safety concerns, recognising the contribution of women in their own individual capacities, and giving arts and crafts education its due place in mainstream educational systems. Mechanisms will be put in place to define goalposts and provide for periodic reviews to ensure compliance of policy directives. The proposals included in the Twelfth Plan, spanning institutional, financial, administrative and strategic reforms, are aimed at raising the production and productivity of the handloom and handicrafts sectors, so as to provide better prospects for the crafts and the crafts persons as well as to fully tap the potential inherent in the two sectors to contribute towards national development through higher production and exports. The outlay for these sectors is included in the overall outlay of the Ministry of Textiles.

YOUTH AFFAIRS AND SPORTS

19.178. The youth play a crucial role in shaping a country's destiny. The Twelfth Plan would focus on all round development of youth by empowering them with attitudes, skills and competencies so that they can fulfil their legitimate aspirations and engage more effectively in the process of nation building. In the area of sports, the vision is to broad base participation in sports and games, particularly participation of students in schools and institutions of higher education and to excel in national and international competitive sports to bring glory and pride to the nation. With a view to provide special focus to the activities of youth affairs and sports, these were bifurcated into two Departments in 2008. These are discussed below one after the other.

19.179. Even though public spending on youth affairs and sports has risen from a meagre ₹1,146 crore in the Eighth Plan to ₹14,764 crore during the Eleventh Plan, it remains very small, just about 2 per cent of the public spending on education. This should progressively be increased to 5 per cent over the years. More so, the relative share of the States has continuously gone down from 62 per cent in the Eighth Plan to 43 per cent during the Eleventh Plan. This needs to be enhanced.

YOUTH AFFAIRS

19.180. The total youth population (10–35 years) in the country was 563 million as per Census 2011 with about 70 per cent living in the rural areas. With a view to bring greater focus and better targeting, youth is being redefined to cover people in the age group of 15 to 30 years in place of 15 to 35 years. A youth development index to serve as a ready reckoner for educators and policymakers is proposed. There would be focus on developing qualities of good citizenship and community service amongst the youth and inculcating in them the spirit of volunteerism. They would be provided training and research support and encouraged to take up sports and adventure activities. Youth travel would be promoted and initiatives would be taken to create an international perspective amongst them. All this would be done by building on synergies with the activities of other ministries, departments and agencies. Special focus would be on the rural youth. These efforts would aim at channelising youth energy in productive activities and engaging them in nation-building activities. Aligned with this thinking, a National Youth Policy would be formulated through a consultative process.

19.181. The above objectives are currently being met by implementing various schemes such as National Service Scheme (NSS) in collaboration with State/UT Governments and expansion of activities of Nehru Yuva Kendra(s), National Youth Corps, scheme of youth hostels and so on. In addition, several ministries and departments like Health, Women and Child Development, Education, and Rural Development are also implementing various programmes for youth.

REVIEW OF THE ELEVENTH PLAN

19.182. Currently, there are 12 schemes/programmes that either support youth-based organisations and/or support youth development activities. The progress under these various schemes during the Eleventh Plan has been uneven. The NSS has not been able to keep pace with the expansion of the university, college and +2 school networks. The NYKs could extend its activities much beyond the districts already covered. Linkages between NYKs and grass-roots youth organisations such as youth clubs, sports clubs, Mahila Mandals continues to be weak. Although NYKs have about 3 lakh youth clubs with membership of over 80 lakh, only about 1 lakh youth clubs were active at the grass root level as per recent survey. Female participation in youth development activities has been low. In States with large youth population the visibility of National Schemes like NYKs and NSS is poor. Coordination of the NYKs with the schemes run by other ministries/agencies continues to be a challenge.

TWELFTH PLAN STRATEGY AND INITIATIVES

19.183. The Twelfth Plan would look *de novo* at the existing policies, instruments and institutions, and suggest innovative policies, efficient and effective instruments and creative ways to rejuvenate institutions in order to utilise and channelise the youth energy in nation-building and economic development of society. Convergence in approach and synergy in action would be the key elements. NSS/NCC may be treated as compulsory co-curricular activity in educational institutions. Popular Village adoption activities for health and literacy should be expanded and training component for NSS volunteers strengthened and volunteers' services should be recognised with certification. The NYKs should set target for female membership and achievement should have weightage in grading of youth clubs. The NYKs should be evaluated before expansion. Convergence for optimal utilisation of NYKs/National Youth Corps is possible only with proper coordination between Centre and States in implementing various youth development programmes. A new National Youth Policy with focus on youth empowerment and employability will be unveiled.

19.184. Although most of these activities are funded under various schemes and programmes, there is a need for coordination and synergy for supplementing their efforts towards the development of youth in the following areas:

1. Utilising extensive youth network for implementation of programmes and for monitoring, oversight, social audit and so on.
2. Using the youth network for extension and awareness campaign for issues relating to girls' nutrition, dowry, female foeticide, voter

awareness, drug abuse, alcoholism and so on; Capacity building of youth clubs for social empowerment under MGNREGA.
3. Training of youth leaders and formation of supervisory committees at village level under Pradhan Mantri Grameen Sadak Yojana (PMGSY).
4. Prevention, education and awareness generation programme against Alcoholism and Substance Abuse in the States under Ministry of Social Justice and Empowerment.
5. Promoting youth employability through provision of a variety of skill based training courses.

TWELFTH PLAN INITIATIVES

Rajiv Gandhi National Institute of Youth Development (RGNIYD)

19.185. During the Twelfth Plan, RGNIYD would be upgraded as an 'Institute of National Importance' and ultimately become an international institute of repute, meeting the requirement of youth development/leadership programmes of South East Asian and South Asian countries. The Institute would have strong research support by creating several self-sustaining Centres of Excellence in the areas of adolescent and youth development with knowledge capital infusion. The Institute would establish linkages with other national, State and regional institutions, including open university system, and create a network of institutions for carrying out its activities. The Institute would lay special focus on youth leaders from PRIs and on issues relating to youth and local governance.

National Programme for Youth Development

19.186. During the Twelfth Plan, an umbrella programme for youth development would be launched. It will bring activities under the ongoing programmes under one umbrella for better coordination. This would include:

a. Strengthening of the network of Nehru Yuva Kendra(s)
b. Expansion of National Youth Corps
c. Support to organisations for activities related to youth development
d. International youth exchange programmes

Nehru Yuva Kendra(s)

19.187. In the Twelfth Plan, the thrust of the Nehru Yuva Kendra(s)—NYKs—would be on consolidating, expanding and energising the youth club movement for engaging the rural youth in various socio-economic and community activities. NYKs services would be utilised for fostering national unity and secular values and stemming the tide of extremism, essentially through programmes like national integration camps, inter-state youth exchange, culture and sports activities and celebration of days and weeks of national importance. The reach of NYKs would be extended from existing 501 to all districts in the country with emphasis on increasing female membership. NYKs in collaboration with National Skill Development Corporation (NSDC) have taken up the initiative for providing young people with knowledge, new skills, insight and ideas to raise employability in the North East Region through 'Train the Trainers' Centres. Such activities would be replicated in other disadvantaged areas including left-wing extremist areas. Success of NYKs depends upon quality of coordinators and volunteers and 80 per cent of the operational cost is on salaries. Thus, it is necessary that the process of selecting District Youth Coordinators should be reviewed with a view to attract better talent.

National Youth Corps (NYC)

19.188. The NYC envisaged enrolment of 20,000 volunteers in the 18–25 age group to serve up to two years in nation building activities in lieu of fixed honorarium. In 2011–12, the enrolment strength was 18,808 and about 12,300 volunteers have been deployed in various Kendras across the country @ 2 volunteers per Block. However, keeping in view special circumstances in LWE districts and NER, there is a need to deploy additional volunteers. Expansion should be considered on evaluation of the scheme, both in terms of process and impact. The monthly honorarium of NYC volunteers would be enhanced to cover mobility and connectivity expenses. The NYC volunteers would be provided training in two phases, namely 15 days induction training and 5 days refresher training.

Support for Activities for Youth Development

19.189. The guidelines for National Programme for Youth and Adolescent Development (NPYAD) has been revised enabling financial assistance to State Governments, NYKs, NSS, and NGOs to participate in youth development activities such as vocational training, entrepreneurship development, national and state level exhibitions, camps and festivals, life-skills education, counselling and career guidance and so on. In the Twelfth Plan, the NPYAD would be modified and renamed as Programme for Youth Development (PYD). Promotion of Scouting and Guiding would be continued with expansion in membership and a renewed focus on inculcating in the youth a spirit of patriotism, social service and communal harmony. The membership would expand from 50 lakh to 55 lakh during the Twelfth Plan. Integration and coordination among NSS, NCC, and Scouts and Guides is also desired. Since the programme is centred on students, it is preferable to implement it in close coordination with the Ministry of HRD.

National Service Scheme (NSS)

19.190. The NSS would be revamped and strengthened with its coverage expanding from the existing 33 lakh by 5 lakh per annum over the next five years. The special focus would be on areas where the enrolment of volunteers so far has been low. It is planned to train about 10,000 programme officers, per annum, so that about 30,000 of them get training in a cycle of three years. Priority would be accorded to extend NSS to uncovered Universities, Colleges, Technical Institutes and +2 Schools under Higher Secondary Councils/Boards, particularly in low representation States like Bihar, Jharkhand, Chhattisgarh, J&K and all NE states. Enrolment of women volunteers would be encouraged through a targeted special drive. Village adoption activities such as under the Samarth Bharat Abhiyaan of University of Pune have been most successful in solving problems of sanitation, water management, tree planting and so on. Similarly, Soft-Skills Development Programme and 'Each One Teach One' literacy programme of Pune University are also success stories that could be replicated. NSS should have training programmes for disaster management and crowd management. The existing funding pattern between the Centre and the States would be revised to 75:25 with special dispensation to NE states in the ratio of 90:10.

Youth Hostels and Youth Resource Centres

19.191. These would be strengthened by developing them as youth resource centres and making them vibrant with a lot of activities. The construction/operations of new hostels could be in franchising/PPP mode for addressing issues of site selection, construction, occupancy for other purposes and so on. Some existing hostels in tourist locations deserve one time grant for upgradation of facilities and infrastructure. Part of hostel could be run on competitive market rates so as to cross-subsidise and meet operation and maintenance expenses.

19.192. During the Twelfth Plan, a National Youth Centre at Delhi and five regional centres including one for the North Eastern Region would be established. These could be co-located with the existing youth hostels with additional investment for infrastructure and capacity building. The National and Regional Centres would become the hub of youth camp activities.

SPORTS AND PHYSICAL EDUCATION

19.193. After India hosted the Ninth Asian Games in 1982, Sports began to receive attention. This led to the creation of the Sports Authority of India (SAI) and the formulation of the National Sports Policy. This helped in generating awareness about the multidimensional character of sports and emphasised the need for making sports and physical education an integral part of the educational curriculum.

19.194. In 2010, the country successfully hosted the Commonwealth Games and created a world class sports infrastructure, achieving an impressive medals tally in swimming, gymnastics and athletics by overshadowing major sporting nations like South Africa and Australia. Also, the performance of Indians in recent Olympics has been quite good. A good beginning has also been made in strengthening and creating of sports competition structures at Sub-State levels. Broad basing of sports and mass participation is being pursued through Panchayat Yuva Khel aur

Krida Abhiyan (PYKKA) in a decentralised manner. Further, an opening has been made for development of school sports and in many States school playgrounds are being developed with assistance from PYKKA. The RTE Act 2009 mandates school sports facilities and provision of sports instructors. The Rashtriya Madhyamik Shiksha Abhiyan (RMSA) too provides for physical education instructors in every secondary school.

19.195. The conduct of National Games has been gaining importance and States are showing keen interest in developing sports infrastructure. National Playfields Association of India has been formed at National level and Sports Playfields Associations have been formed at state level in some of the States. Draft National Sports Development Bill has been formulated, which includes aspects such as participation of athletes in the management/decision making of the concerned National Sports Federations and the Indian Olympic Association through the Athletes Advisory Council, ensuring fair and transparent functioning of autonomous sports bodies and promotion of welfare measures for sportspersons and ethical practices in sports and games.

REVIEW OF THE ELEVENTH PLAN

19.196. There was twofold thrust in the Eleventh Plan. One was to broad base games and sports through PYKKA and secondly to promote excellence in national and international competitions. Under the PYKKA, 51,759 villages and 1,538 block panchayats were covered during the Eleventh Plan in the rural areas. This is however only 21 per cent of the total number of village and block panchayats. For the urban areas, a scheme of assistance for creation of Urban Sports Infrastructure (USIS) on pilot basis was started in the year 2010–11. This aimed at addressing the entire 'sports eco-system' in a holistic manner and included players' training, coaching and developmental needs and sports infrastructure.

19.197. The Sports Authority of India (SAI) continued its activities of promoting sports excellence, broad basing sports, talent identification and development through Netaji Subhas National Institute of Sports (NSNIS), Patiala and LNCPE, Thiruvanthapuram, and its Training centres. In order to create a dope-free sports environment in the country, two separate autonomous entities, namely National Anti-Doping Agency (NADA) and National Dope Test Laboratory (NDTL) were established.

TWELFTH PLAN STRATEGY

19.198. The twin planks of Government policy of broad-basing of sports and achieving excellence in sports will continue to be pursued in the Twelfth Plan. While the primary responsibility for promoting sports culture will remain with the State Governments with active support from the Central Government through various schemes and programmes, achieving excellence in competitive events at the national and international levels will be the responsibility of various autonomous National Sports Federations. The role of the Government would be to create basic infrastructure as well as build capacity through training and resource support that will enable sportspersons to excel in various national and international sporting events.

19.199. Setting up of State Sports Authorities will be encouraged and Sports Complex Stadia, playfields and so on will be treated as 'Infrastructure' enabling viability gap funding (VGF) for encouraging investment through public private partnership and linkages with corporate social responsibility (CSR) of the corporate houses for Sports Infrastructure development at State and Sub-State levels.

TWELFTH PLAN INITIATIVES

19.200. Nurturing and promoting excellence in sports requires a long-term strategy. During the Twelfth Plan, a long-term plan would be drawn up by building on initiatives already underway and taking into consideration the shortcomings of the actions taken so far.

Sarva Krida Abhiyan

19.201. For broad basing sports and games and connecting them to the schools and colleges on one hand and local bodies on the other, Sarva Krida Abhiyan would be launched during the Twelfth Plan. This would bring all ongoing programmes under one umbrella for better coordination. This would include:

1. Panchayat Yuva Krida aur Khel Abhiyan (PYKKA)
2. National physical fitness programme
3. Support for sports in institutions of higher education
4. Support for sports infrastructure

Panchayat Yuva Krida Aur Khel Abhiyan

19.202. Under the Panchayat Yuva Krida aur Khel Abhiyan (PYKKA), the need now is to capitalise on the enthusiastic response that the scheme has evoked in the States and to enhance its coverage to all village and block panchayats during the Twelfth Plan period, as originally envisaged. School playgrounds will be developed by converging PYKKA with MGNREGA and State schemes. The NVs and KVs will also open up their playgrounds for neighbourhood schools. Local bodies will be persuaded to earmark open spaces and community parks for neighbourhood schools in urban areas. School adoption by national/international sports stars and corporate bodies will be promoted along with tax incentives for investment in school sports infrastructure. In consultation with all stakeholders, a national sporting calendar would be developed so that sports become an integral part of the annual calendar and parents do not view it as distraction from studies. Holding of state-level age group specific 'low-cost' sports would be promoted with a view to encourage continued excellence from school to higher education level. School-based investment as a part of SSA/RMSA will strengthen school sports and games. A full time sports teacher will be made available under RMSA and SSA will provide part-time sports instructor. Scholarships/stipends would be introduced for students excelling in sports.

National Physical Fitness Programme

19.203. Recognising physical fitness as crucial for social and economic well-being of the nation, a National Physical Fitness Programme (NPFP) for school children would be launched in the Twelfth Plan. Physical education, games and sports will be made an integral part of school curriculum. To be implemented along with the Ministry of HRD and the State governments, the scheme would encourage school children to be physically fit and concurrently evaluate their fitness. This would be motivational. Students' scores/grades for physical fitness would be given adequate weightage and added to their academic scores/grades. Under this programme, all students of class 5 and above would be evaluated on six parameters of physical fitness, namely (i) cardio respiratory endurance, (ii) muscular strength, (iii) muscular endurance, (iv) flexibility, (v) explosive strength, and (vii) body composition (percentage of body fat).

Support for Sports in Institutions of Higher Education

19.204. An initiative to promote sports and wellness in the higher education institutions (HEIs) would be taken up in partnership with the Ministry of HRD and the Association of Indian Universities (AIU). Activities under this initiative would include—start fitness and wellness programme for all students, encourage HEIs to include physical education as general institutional requirement, raise participation in competitive sports from current 2 per cent students to 10 per cent, create and support departments and units for physical education in all HEIs with adequate staff, support creation of adequate sports infrastructure, encourage sports club system in HEIs, establish inter-disciplinary research centres on sports technology, sports medicine and sports management, and finally create an information network on sports. In view of increased demand for physical education teachers/Instructors, there is a need for expansion of Physical Education in universities/colleges in Western, Northern and Eastern Zones and NCTE should relax restrictions on B.P.Ed./M.P.Ed to expand intake capacity.

Sports Infrastructure

19.205. The Urban Sports Infrastructure Scheme (USIS) would be dovetailed with JNNURM project funds to benefit from synergy in the urban areas. Due to pressures of urbanisation, playfields are under serious threat. They need to be protected. All States should establish State Playing Fields Associations and take necessary steps for preservation, protection and development of playfields. The National Play Fields Association of India (NPFAI), as an apex body, would provide requisite support to the State

Associations with financial assistance provided by the Central and State Governments.

19.206. State-of-the-art sports infrastructure for competition and training for mega sporting events is created at various locations at considerable costs. Such sports infrastructure should be put to optimal use after the main events are over. For this, the concerned agencies would be encouraged to have viable plans for utilisation. Such sports infrastructure should be made available to District/State Sports Federations for preparation and training of sub-junior and junior level athletes as well as to the local community/schools. Possibility for setting up a separate company (possibly under the Sports Authority of India) for this purpose could also be explored. This could tentatively be called Sports Asset Management Ltd., whose job would be to develop plans for each asset and then to bid them out under transparent criteria. There should be efforts for intense use of sports infrastructure, particularly the expensive ones, in the evenings and night. Finally, public-private partnerships (PPP) in creation and operation of expensive sports facilities could be explored.

Promotion of Excellence in Sports

19.207. The country's performance in mega sporting events such as Olympic Games, Asian Games and Commonwealth Games has consistently improved over the years (see Box 19.5). Focused attention and improved funding along with better sports infrastructure and facilities and coaching through 'Operation Excellence' launched in April 2011 has helped in achieving this. As a matter of strategy, besides providing generalised training through national camps, individualised training was also provided to the players, tailor-made to their specific needs, including training in foreign training institutes. The country should aim to get at least 20 Medals in Olympics 2016 and 30 Medals in Olympics 2020 and be amongst the top 10 sporting countries. In the Asian Games 2014, the country could aim to get 75 Medals and then 100 medals in Asian Games 2019 and be amongst the top 3 countries. With a view to achieve these targets, there would be a clear and well-funded strategy to build on past performance and further improve country's performance in international events during the Twelfth Plan.

19.208. 'Operation Excellence' so far is structured with short-term objectives. In order to build on this, a long-term vision for identification and nurturing of talent would be needed. The pool from which the elite sports persons are drawn has to be significantly enlarged. The skill sets of our sports persons has to be augmented through better coaching, more dependent sports medicines, better sports services and enhanced participation in competitions of higher standards, both in India and abroad. Focused attention is required in respect of 10 Olympic sports disciplines, namely athletics, wrestling, shooting, weightlifting, boxing, archery, badminton, field hockey, judo and taekwondo, rowing, sailing, kayaking and canoeing, in which India has greater potential for excellence and winning medals. For enlarging the pool, there is a need for identifying talent through grass-root competition, particularly in rural areas and nurturing sports talents through special sports schools, separate from mainstream schools with greater emphasis on sports training and coaching support. Early identification of skill sets of individual sports persons on a scientific basis—at least partly based on bio-medical and other scientific evidence—would be helpful.

Box 19.5
Upturn in India's Sporting Performance

The Country had won a total of 50 medals in the Commonwealth Games—2006 and the tally went up to 101 in the Commonwealth Games—2010. Similarly, India had won 53 medals in Asian Games—2006 that improved to 64 medals in the Asian Games—2010. India's performance in the London Olympics—2012 has been the best ever performance by the Indian contingent in the Olympic Games with six medals, up from three medals in Beijing Olympics—2008. In addition, 12 of the country's athletes secured 4th to 12th positions, while until then only 5 Indian athletes had secured such positions in all previous Olympic Games taken together. This shows the growing sporting potential of the country. India also had the largest contingent of 81 sports persons that qualified for participation in London Olympics.

Preparation of Teams/Athletes

19.209. The scheme for preparation of Indian team for mega sporting events with clearly defined roles/responsibilities for each agency/authority will be continued and supported with adequate budget during the Twelfth Plan. This would be linked to the scheme to support identified sportspersons who have attained a certain level of achievement. There is a need for greater convergence of all such initiative including support through National Sports Development Fund. Corpus for this fund would also be enhanced. There is a need for further enhancing the award money for these championships as well as introducing, during the Twelfth Plan, a system of giving cash awards to personal coaches, who may not fulfil the eligibility criteria of imparting 240 days training preceding the medal winning performance of their trainees, but who have trained the athletes for a substantial period of time.

Assistance to National Championships and National Games

19.210. The Scheme of Assistance to NSFs should be recast to provide financial assistance for conduct of National Games and national championships at senior, junior and sub-junior levels for both men and women. The level of financial assistance for conduct of national championships would also be raised substantially. The Twelfth Plan will encourage each State Government to have its own State-level games every four years—with teams from each district. This would be in parallel to the national games. State Games will spread the spirit of competitive sports to each district.

Pension to Meritorious Sportspersons

19.211. As regards meritorious sportspersons from Para-sports category, winners of gold, silver and bronze medals in Para-Olympics alone are eligible for pension. Now, since physically challenged sportspersons are taking part in CWG and Para-Asian Games, they should also be included in the scheme of Pension to Meritorious Sportspersons and given pension at par with able-bodied sportspersons. The scheme should be transferred to SAI and its funding could be included in the block grant of SAI.

Coaching Upgradation

19.212. The availability of well qualified coaches is a critical area for the promotion of sports excellence and requires focused attention in the Indian context. There is a need for producing quality coaches of international standards and developing a holistic system for imparting coaching within the country. Therefore, it has been decided to de-merge National Institute of Sports (NIS, Patiala) from SAI to form a new society, the National Institute of Sports Coaching (NISC). The establishment of NISC would go a long way in producing quality coaches of international standards to meet the requirements of our athletes and teams. There is also a need for keeping our coaches updated with latest techniques and methods of coaching in competitive sports and, for this, they should be sent abroad for short and medium-term courses in specific disciplines. Institutes and Sports Universities offering such courses in countries such as Cuba, Hungary, Belarus, UK, Australia, China, New Zealand and so on, would be identified.

Establishment of Network of Sports Training/Advanced Training Centres

19.213. With a view to nurture sports talent, a network of district sports centres and advanced training centres at the regional level would be established. To begin with, districts having high potential for sports talent would be identified and taken up. This would enable identification of sports talent from the grassroots level and nurture them over a long period of time and create bench strength of sports persons in various disciplines. These fully residential training centres catering to sports talent in age group of 8 to 17 years would preferably be co-located with Navodaya Vidyalayas, Kendriya Vidyalayas, Sarvodaya Vidyalayas, Schools under the armed forces or even well-established State Government schools. Possibility of setting up such schools even with the private schools subject to proper checks and balances could also be explored. These centres would have high quality sports infrastructure.

Sports Authority of India (SAI)

19.214. The SAI, as the apex body for promotion of excellence in sports, would be strengthened during the Twelfth Plan. Existing twelve (12) centres of excellence catering to training requirements of national level athletes preparing for participation in international events would continue to be supported and more such centres with state-of-the-art facilities and international standard equipment would be established, particularly in sports disciplines where India has a higher medal potential. These centres should be given flexibility to engage the best National/International coaches and technical support staff to provide their services to National Teams and other players. The SAI would set up National level Institutes in their five major sports complexes in Delhi, such as National Institute of Hockey at Dhyan Chand National Stadium. These would become centres of excellence, training and research for these specific sports.

Sports Science and Sports Medicine

19.215. During the Twelfth Plan, existing sports science and medicine facilities at SAI Centres would be upgraded to prepare the country for the Commonwealth Games and the Asian Games in 2014. In addition, a National Institute of Sports Science and Sports Medicine (NISSM) would be set up to provide integrated and quality-assured testing services and for training and capacity building of leading experts to drive innovation and share knowledge that will have positive impact on sporting performance.

19.216. In order to address the fundamental weakness in the sports sector in the country, there is a need for focused and coordinated approach. There has to be a space for sports in the overall economic activity in the country. This would entail providing better employment opportunities to promising sports persons including better opportunities for career progression, commercialising and developing certain aspects of sports development and marketing so as to attract private sector participation and capital investment in sports.

19.217. The indicative Gross Budgetary Support for the Twelfth Five Year Plan for the Ministry of Youth Affairs and Sports is ₹6,648 *crore*.

NOTES

1. The resolution read as:

    We recognize the role of travel and tourism as a vehicle for job creation, economic growth and development, and, while recognizing the sovereign right of States to control the entry of foreign nationals, we will work towards developing travel facilitation initiatives in support of job creation, quality work, poverty reduction and global growth.

2. Travel and Tourism Competitiveness Reports for various years published by World Economic Forum which ranks 139 countries on various parameters which effect travel and tourism competitiveness. The global ranking of India in respect of 'Government Prioritization of the Travel and Tourism Industry' is a reflection on the priority accorded by the Government and not on the actual performance.
3. Travel and Tourism Competitiveness Reports for various years published by World Economic Forum.
4. Ibid.
5. The Travel and Tourism Competitiveness Report 2011, World Economic Forum.
6. Eco-tourism is a comprehensive idea encompassing numerous concepts such as *Nature Tourism*, which aims at discovering natural wonders by minimising the impacts of people on the environment; *Adventure Tourism* and *Ethnic Tourism*, which takes the tourists into a cultural immersion within local indigenous communities.
7. The emphasis should be on decision making through the gram sabha rather than through the gram panchayat.
8. The electricity duty, tax on goods and passengers, motor vehicle tax and stamp duty levied by the States will not be subsumed in the GST at the time of its introduction.
9. In the case of the transport sector, credit for input tax is allowed by way of abatement on a presumptive basis. However, in the case of aviation services, credit for input tax including tax on ATF should be allowed on actual basis.
10. Travel and Tourism Competitiveness Reports for various years published by World Economic Forum which ranks 139 countries on various parameters which effect travel and tourism competitiveness. The global ranking of India in respect of 'Government Prioritization of the Travel and Tourism Industry' is a reflection on the priority accorded by the Government and not on the actual performance.
11. Travel and Tourism Competitiveness Reports for various years published by World Economic Forum.
12. Ibid.

Twelfth Five Year Plan (2012–2017)

Social Sectors

Volume III

Copyright © Planning Commission (Government of India) 2013

All rights reserved. No part of this book may be reproduced or utilised in any form or by any means, electronic or mechanical, including photocopying, recording or by any information storage or retrieval system, without permission in writing from the Planning Commission, Government of India.

First published in 2013 by

SAGE Publications India Pvt Ltd
B1/I-1 Mohan Cooperative Industrial Area
Mathura Road, New Delhi 110 044, India
www.sagepub.in

SAGE Publications Inc
2455 Teller Road
Thousand Oaks, California 91320, USA

SAGE Publications Ltd
1 Oliver's Yard, 55 City Road
London EC1Y 1SP, United Kingdom

SAGE Publications Asia-Pacific Pte Ltd
33 Pekin Street
#02-01 Far East Square
Singapore 048763

Second Printing 2014

Published by Vivek Mehra for SAGE Publications India Pvt Ltd, Phototypeset in 11/13pt Minion Pro by RECTO Graphics, Delhi and printed at Saurabh Printers, New Delhi.

Library of Congress Cataloging-in-Publication Data
India. Planning Commission
   Twelfth five year plan (2012/2017)/Planning Commission, Government of India.
     Volumes cm
   1. India—Economic Policy—1991–92. Finance, Public—India. I. Title.
HC435.3.I39   338.954009'0512—dc23   2013   2013009870

ISBN: 978-81-321-1368-3 (PB)

The SAGE Team: Rudra Narayan, Archita Mandal, Rajib Chatterjee and Dally Verghese

Twelfth Five Year Plan (2012–2017)
Social Sectors

Volume III

Planning Commission
Government of India

Thank you for choosing a SAGE product! If you have any comment, observation or feedback, I would like to personally hear from you. Please write to me at contactceo@sagepub.in

—Vivek Mehra, Managing Director and CEO,
SAGE Publications India Pvt Ltd, New Delhi

Bulk Sales

SAGE India offers special discounts for purchase of books in bulk. We also make available special imprints and excerpts from our books on demand.

For orders and enquiries, write to us at

Marketing Department
SAGE Publications India Pvt Ltd
B1/I-1, Mohan Cooperative Industrial Area
Mathura Road, Post Bag 7
New Delhi 110044, India
E-mail us at marketing@sagepub.in

Get to know more about SAGE, be invited to SAGE events, get on our mailing list. Write today to marketing@sagepub.in

This book is also available as an e-book.

Contents

List of Figures — vii
List of Tables — viii
List of Boxes — x
List of Acronyms — xi
List of Annexures — xviii

20. Health — 1

21. Education — 47

22. Employment and Skill Development — 124

23. Women's Agency and Child Rights — 164

24. Social Inclusion — 221

Figures

20.1	Disease Burden of India, 2008 (Estimated number of deaths by cause)	2
20.2	Disability Adjusted Life Years in India, 2009 (Estimated percentage of DALY by cause)	2
20.3	Strategies to Prevent Pre-Term Births and Manage Pre-Term Babies	30
20.4	Projected HRH Capacity Expansion in the Twelfth Plan	37
21.1	GER for Secondary Education: By States/Select Countries	69
21.2	Improvements in Literacy Levels, 1981–2011 (%)	87
21.3	Strategic Framework	91
21.4	Enrolments in Higher Education (in lakh): 2006–07 to 2016–17	97
21.5	Gross Attendance Ratio, 2007–08	102
22.1	Trend in Unemployment Rate	126
22.2	Unemployment Rate among Youth	133
23.1	Child Sex Ratio 0–6 Years and Overall Sex Ratio India: 1961–2011	182
23.2	Nutrition Status of Children under 3 Years (%)	197
23.3	Inadequate Exclusive Breastfeeding in India (0–6 Months)	198
23.4	Children Aged 6–35 Months who Received a Vitamin A Dose During Last Six Months (%) (AHS 2010–11)	199

Tables

20.1	Eleventh Plan Monitorable Goals and Achievements	4
20.2	Allocation and Spending by Ministry of Health in Eleventh Plan	5
20.3	Funding for Health in Eleventh Plan: Core and Broad Health Components	5
20.4	State-Wise Targets on IMR and MMR in Twelfth Plan	16
20.5	National Health Goals for Communicable Diseases	17
20.6	Budget Support for Departments of MoHFW in Twelfth Plan (2012–17)	18
20.7	Interventions to Combat Non-Communicable Diseases (NCDs)	32
20.8	Availability of HR during Eleventh Plan and Projections for Twelfth Plan	36
20.9	Illustrative List of Health Systems Strengthening in States	39
21.1	Cumulative Progress under SSA up to 2011–12	54
21.2	Civil Works under SSA in the Twelfth Plan	63
21.3	GER for Secondary Education by Social Groups (2009–10)	68
21.4	RMSA: Achievement in the Eleventh Plan	71
21.5	Centrally Sponsored Schemes for Secondary Education	71
21.6	Roles in System Improvement	86
21.7	Growth of Enrolment in the Eleventh Plan	93
21.8	Growth of Enrolment in ODL Programmes in the Eleventh Plan	93
21.9	Growth of Enrolment by Field of Study during the Eleventh Plan (in lakh)	94
21.10	Growth of Institutions in the Eleventh Plan	94
21.11	Growth of Central Institutions during the Eleventh Plan	95
21.12	Enrolment Targets by Level/Type for the Twelfth Plan	96
21.13	Funding Responsibility for Universities and Colleges	118
21.14	Gross Budgetary Support for the Twelfth Plan	122
22.1	LFPR and WFPR by Usual Principal and Subsidiary Status, 1993–94, 2004–05 and 2009–10 (%) Persons	125
22.2	Estimated Number of Persons in Millions	125
22.3	Unemployment, Wages and Consumption Expenditure, 1993–4 to 2009–10	126
22.4	Proportionate Share of Sectors in Employment	127
22.5	Formal and Informal Employment in Organized and Unorganised Sector (millions)	131
22.6	Number of Workers by Size of Enterprise in Industry and Services	132
22.7	Number of Workers According to Usual Status (PS+SS) Approach by Broad Employment Status (Million Workers)	132
22.8	LFPR by Usual Principal and Subsidiary Status, 1993–94, 2004–05 and 2009–10 (%) by Gender	133
22.9	WPR by Usual Principal and Subsidiary Status, 1993–94, 2004–05 and 2009–10 (%) by Gender	133
22.10	Child Workforce Participation Rate by UPSS (Percentage), 1993–94, 2004–05 and 2009–10	133

22.11	Workforce Participation Rate by Usual Principal and Subsidiary Status, by Social Group, 1993–94, 2004–05 and 2009–10 (%)	134
22.12	Unemployment Rate by Usual Principal and Subsidiary Status, by Social Group, 2004–05 and 2009–10 (%)	134
22.13	Population and Labour Force Projections	135
22.14	Employment Elasticity from Past Data	136
22.15	Sectoral Growth Rates: Business-as-usual Scenario	136
22.16	Sectoral Employment (in million): Business-as-usual Scenario	137
22.17	Sectoral Growth Rates—Twelfth Plan Scenario	137
22.18	Sectoral EMPLOYMENTS (in million): Twelfth Plan Scenario	138
22.19	General Education Level of Labour Force (PS+SS) in the Age Group 15–59	140
22.20	Estimated Number of Workers (PS+SS in the age group of 15–59) by Level of Education by Sector (millions), 2009–10	141
22.21	Distribution of Formally and Informally Vocationally Trained Workers (PS+SS in the age group of 15–59) Within Primary, Secondary and Tertiary Sectors (%) in 2009–10	142
22.22	Apprentices in India (Under the Apprenticeship Training Act, 1961)	144
22.23	A Typology of Training Funds	156
23.1	Ministry-Wise Incorporation of Gender Concerns (under RFD)	180
23.2	Monitorable Targets of Eleventh Plan and Its Achievements	201
23.3	Existing Programmes/Schemes	204
24.1	Incidence of Poverty across Social Groups	221
24.2	Eleventh Plan Allocation and Expenditure for Special Schemes for SCs	222
24.3	Rural Population Living Below Poverty Line (1993–94, 1999–2000 and 2004–05) (in %)	229
24.4	Literacy Rates of STs and Total Population (in %)	229
24.5	Female Literacy Rates of STs and Total Population (in %)	229
24.6	Mortality and Undernutrition	230
24.7	Eleventh Plan Allocation and Expenditure for Special Schemes for STs	230
24.8	Literacy Rate among Religious Communities, SCs and STs	250
24.9	Educational Levels among Different Communities	251
24.10	Percentage Distribution of Workers by Category	252

Boxes

20.1	Recommendations of High Level Expert Group on Universal Health Coverage	12
20.2	Illustrative List of Preventive and Public Health Interventions Funded and Provided by Government	14
20.3	Public–Private Partnerships (PPP) in Health Sector	20
20.4	Institute of Liver and Biliary Sciences, Delhi: A Model of Autonomy and Sustainable Financing	24
20.5	Flexibility and Decentralised Planning: Key Elements of National Health Mission	28
20.6	Suggested Items in Model HR Guidelines	35
20.7	Convergence: Village Health and Nutrition Day in North Tripura	45
21.1	Targets for the Twelfth Plan	51
21.2	Twelfth Plan Strategy for Elementary Education	56
21.3	School Excellence Programme—Mumbai	62
21.4	Secondary Education: Twelfth Plan Goals	72
21.5	CBSE Examination Reforms	75
21.6	Pilot Project on Vocational Education under NVEQF	79
21.7	Enrolment Target for the Twelfth Plan	91
21.8	TISS: A Multi-Location Networked University	99
21.9	Strategic Shift in Central Funding for State Higher Education	100
21.10	Concept and Framework for Establishing Community Colleges	101
21.11	Student Financial Aid Programme (SFAP)	104
22.1	Conceptual Framework of Key Employment and Unemployment Indicators	127
22.2	Skill Policy for Promoting India's Competitiveness in the Global Market	143
22.3	Priority Sectors Identified in the Twelfth Plan	148
22.4	Strategies for Expanding and Scaling up the Skill Development in Twelfth Plan	151
22.5	Major Functions of Proposed National Skill Development Authority	151
22.6	Good Performers in Financing—Chile, Australia, South Africa, Singapore	157
22.7	Equity Implications of User Fees	158
23.1	Women Friendly Infrastructure Development in Kerala	171
23.2	Declining Child Sex Ratio—A Call for Urgent Action	183
23.3	Making the Difference—ICDS Restructuring	189
23.4	Learning by Doing—SNEHA SHIVIRs	190
23.5	Early Joyful Learning-Chilli Pilli	193
24.1	Eleventh Five Year Plan Schemes	253
24.2	Vision for the Twelfth Five Year Plan	255
24.3	Specific Interventions under PM's 15 PP	256
24.4	The Jaipur Foot Story	264
24.5	Possible Actions by Central Government Ministries to Benefit Those with Disabilities	269

Acronyms

AAY	Antodaya Anna Yojana	BRGF	Backward Regions Grant Fund
ABL	Activity-Based Learning	CABE	Central Advisory Board of Education
AESDCs	Adult Education & Skill Development Centres	CAGR	Compounded Annual Growth Rate
		CAL	Computer Aided Learning
AHS	Annual Health Survey	CAT	Common Admission Test
AICTE	All India Council for Technical Education	CBM	Community Based Monitoring
		CBSE	Central Board of Secondary Education
AIDS	Acquired Immuno Deficiency Syndrome	CBUs	Community Based Organisations
AIEEE	All India Entrance Exam for Engineering	CCD	Conservation cum Development
		CCE	Continuous and Comprehensive Evaluation
AITT	All India Trade Test		
ALIs	AIIMS like Institutions	CDS	Current Daily Status
ALMSC	Anganwadi Level Monitoring and Support Committee	CES	Coverage Evaluation Survey
		CFR	Community Forest Rights
ANM	Auxiliary Nurse & Midwife	CGHS	Central Government Health Scheme
ARUNIM	Association of Rehabilitation under National Trust Initiative of Marketing	CHC	Community Health Centre
		CHEB	Central Health Education Bureau
		CIHEC	Council for Industry and Higher Education Collaboration
ARWU	Academic Ranking of World Universities	CII	Confederation of Indian Industries
ASC	Academic Staff College	CLAT	Common Law Admission Test
ASER	Annual Status of Education Report	CMB	Conditional Maternity Benefit Scheme
ASHA	Accredited Social Health Activist		
ASSOCHAM	Associated Chambers of Commerce & Industry	COBSE	Council of Boards of School Education
ATS	Apprenticeship Training Scheme	CoE	Centre of Excellence
AVI	Accredited Vocational Institutes	CPI	Consumer Price Index
AWTC	Anganwadi Training Centre	CPL	Commercial Pilot Licence
AWW	Anganwadi Worker	CPMT	Combined Pre Medical Entrace Test
BESU	Bengal Engineering and Science University	CPPE	Council for People's Participation in Education
BJRCY	Babu Jagjivan Ram Chatarvas Yojana	CRC	Cluster Resource Centre
BMI	Body Mass Index	CSC	Common Service Centre
BPL	Below Poverty Line	CSIR	Council of Scientific and Industrial Research
BPO	Business Process Outsourcing		
BRC	Block Resource Centre	CSO	Civil Society Organisations

CSR	Corporate Social Responsibility	ER	Elected Representatives
CSS	Centrally Sponsored Scheme	ERP	Enterprise Resource Planning
CTA	Criminal Tribes Act	FDC	Fixed Dose Combination
CTC	Central Tripatite Committee	FICCI	Federation of Indian Chamber of Commerce & Industry
CTE	College of Teacher Education		
CTET	Central Teacher Eligibility Test	FRA	Forest Rights Act
CUE	Centre for Universal Education	FRU	First Referral Unit
CVD	Cardio-Vascular Diseases	FSSA	Food Safety and Standards Act
CWSN	Children With Special Needs	FSSAI	Food Safety and Standards Authority of India
DALY	Disability Life Adjusted Year		
DAPCU	District AIDS Prevention & Control Unit	GAR	Gross Attendance Ratio
		GBPS	Gigabit Per Second
DEC	Distance Education Council	GBS	Gross Budgetary Support
DEI	Distance Education Institution	GDP	Gross Domestic Product
DFS	Double Fortified Salt	GER	Gross Enrolment Ratio
DGET	Directorate General of Employment & Training	GNM	General Nursing and Midwifery
		GP	Gram Panchayats
DHR	Department of Health Research	GPI	Gender Parity Index
DIC	Design Innovation Centre	GPS	Global Positioning System
DIET	District Institute of Education and Training	GS	Gram Sabhas
		GVA	Gross Value Added
DISE	District Information System of Education	HCR	Head Count Ratio
		HEI	Higher Education Institution
DLHS	District Level Health Survey	HFW	Health and Family Welfare
DNB	Diplomats of National Board	HH	House Holds
DNT	De-notified Tribes	HIS	Health Information System
DONER	Department of North Eastern Region	HIV	Human Immunodeficiency Virus
DOTS	Directly Observed Treatment – Short Course	HLEG	High Level Expert Group
		HMIS	Health Management Information Systems
DPC	District Planning Committees		
DPEP	District Primary Education Programme	IAP	Indian Academy of Pediatrics/ Integrated Action Plan
DRG	Diagnostic Related Group	IASE	Institute of Advanced Studies in Education
DSLL	Department of Skills and Lifelong Learning		
		IAY	Indira Awas Yojana
DTH	Direct-to-Home	IBA	Indian Banks' Association
DWS	Drinking Water Supply	ICAI	Institute of Cost Accounts of India
EAG	Empowered Action Group	ICDS	Integrated Child Development Services
EBB	Educationally Backward Blocks		
ECCE	Early Childhood Care and Education	ICMR	Indian Council of Medical Research
EESC	Essential and Emergency Surgical Care	ICT	Information and Communication Technology
EGS	Education Guarantee Scheme	IDD	Iron Deficiency Disorder
EHP	Essential Health Package	IDMI	Infrastructure Development in Minority Institutions
ELM	Elementary (Classes I–VIII)		
EMR	Electronic Medical Record	IEC	Information, Education and Communication
EPC	Engineering, Procurement and Construction		

IEDSS	Inclusive Education for the Disabled at Secondary Stage	JIPMER	Jawaharlal Institute of Post Graduate Medical Education and Research
IFA	Iron Folic Acid	JKGBV	Kasturba Gandhi Balika Vidyalay
IFR	Individual Forest Rights	JNNURM	Jawaharlal Nehru National Urban Renewal Mission
IGMSY	Indira Gandhi Matritva Sahyog Yojana	JNV	Jawahar Navodaya Vidyalaya
IGNOU	Indira Gandhi National Open University	JPC	Joint Parliamentary Committee
		JRF	Junior Research Fellowship
IIC	Inter Institutional Centre	JSS	Jan Shiksha Sansthans
IIIT	International Institute of Information Technology	JSY	Janani Suraksha Yojana
		KGBV	Kasturba Gandhi Balika Vidyalaya
IIM	Indian Institute of Management	KV	Kendriya Vidyalaya
IISER	Indian Institute of Science Education and Research	KVKs	Krishi Vigyan Kendras
		KVY	Kaushal Vikas Yojana
IIT	Indian Institute of Technology	LEP	Learning Enhancement Programme
IMCs	Institute Management Committees	LFPR	Labour Force Participation Rate
IMNCI	Integrated Management of Neonatal and Childhood Illness	LLIN	Long Lasting Insecticide Net
		LMIS	Labour Market Information System
IMR	Infant Mortality Rate	LMS	Learning Management System
IMRB	International Marketing and Research Bureau	LWE	Left Wing Extremism
		MAEF	Maulana Azad Education Foundation
IMS Act	Infant Milk Substitutes Act		
IMS	Infant Milk Substitute	MCDs	Minority Concentration Districts
INC	Indian Nursing Council	MCS	Model Cluster Schools
INN	International Non-proprietary Name	MDG	Millennium Development Goal
INT	Indian Institute of Information Technology	MDM	Mid-Day Meal
		MDMS	Mid-Day Meals in Schools
IPC	Indian Penal Code	MES	Modular Employable Skills
IPERPO	Intellectual Property Education, Research and Public Outreach	MFP	Minor Forest Produce
		MGHN	Merry Gold Health Network
IPHS	Indian Public Health Standard	MGNREGA	Mahatma Gandhi National Rural Employment Guarantee Act
IPOP	Integrated Programme for Older Persons		
		MGNREGS	Mahatma Gandhi National Rural Employment Guarantee Scheme
IPR	Intellectual Property Rights		
IRCAs	Integrated Rehabilitation Centre for Addicts	MHFW	Ministry of Health and Family Welfare
ISCED	International Standard Classification of Education	MHRD	Ministry of Human Resource Development
		MIB	Ministry of Information and Broadcasting
ISM	Indian School of Mines		
IT	Information Technology	MIS	Management Information System
ITCs	Industrial Training Centres	MITI	Model Industrial Training Institute
ITIs	Industrial Training Institutes	MLA	Member of Legislative Assembly
ITPA	Immoral Trafficking Prevention Act	MMER	Management, Monitoring, Evaluation and Research
IUC	Inter University Centre		
IVRS	Interactive Voice Response System	MMP	Mission Mode Project
IYCF	Infant and Young Child Feeding		
JE	Japanese Encephalitis	MMR	Maternal Mortality Ratio
JEE	Joint Entrance Exam	MMU	Mobile Medical Unit

Acronym	Expansion
MoHFW	Ministry of Health & Family Welfare
MoLE	Ministry of Labour & Employment
MoMA	Ministry of Minority Affairs
MOOC	Massive Open Online Course
MoSJE	Ministry of Social Justice and Empowerment
MoTA	Ministry of Tribal Affairs
MoU	Memorandum of Understanding
MoWCD	Ministry of Woman & Child Development
MP	Madhya Pradesh
MPCE	Monthly Per-capita Consumption Expenditure
M.Phil	Master of Philosophy
MPLADS	Member of Parliament Local Area Development Scheme
MPR	Ministry of Panchayati Raj
MS	Manila Samakhya
MSDP	Multi Sectoral Development Plan
MSDP	Multi Sectoral Development Programme
MSJE	Ministry of Social Justice and Empowerment
MSME	Ministry of Micro, Small and Medium Enterprises
MTP	Medical Termination of Pregnancy
MVA	Manual Vacuum Aspiration
MYA	Ministry of Youth Affairs
MYA&S	Ministry of Youth Affairs & Sports
NAAC	National Assessment and Accreditation Council
NAC	National Advisory Council
NACP	National AIDS Control Programme
NAS	National Assessment Survey
NBA	National Board of Accreditation
NBCFDC	National Backward Classes Finance and Development Corporation
NBHE	National Board for Health Education
NBT	National Book Trust
NBTTC	National Board for Trade Testing and Certification
NCD	Non Communicable Disease
NCERT	National Council of Educational Research & Training
NCF	National Curriculum Framework
NCFTE	National Curriculum Framework for Teacher Education
NCHER	National Commission for Higher Education and Research
NCHRH	National Commission for Human Resources in Health
NCHS	National Centre for Health Statistics
NCLSE	National Centre for Leadership in School Education
NCRB	National Crime Records Bureau
NCSC	National Commission for Scheduled Castes
NCST	National Commission for Scheduled Tribes
NCTE	National Council for Teacher Education
NCVT	National Council of Vocational Training
NDDB	National Dairy Development Board
NDIN	National Design Innovation Network
NDRDA	National Drug Regulatory and Development Authority
NE	North East
NEAC	National Evaluation and Assessment Committee
NEGP	National e-Governance Plan
NER	North Eastern Region
NFHS	National Family Health Survey
NFIDA	National Fund for Innovative Development Activities
NFSB	National Food Security Bill
NGO	Non-Governmental Organisation
NHA	National Health Accounts
NHFDC	National Handicapped Finance Development Corporation
NHM	National Health Mission
NHPPT	National Health Promotion and Protection Trust
NHRDA	National Health Regulatory and Development Authority
NHSRC	National Health System Resource Centre
NICE	National Institute of Clinical Excellence
NIDDCP	National Iodine Deficiency Disorders Control Programme
NIFFT	National Institute of Foundry and Forge Technology

NIHFW	National Institute of Health arid Family Welfare	NSFDC	National Scheduled Castes Finance and Development Corporation
NIN	National Institute of Nutrition	NSIGSE	National Scheme of Incentive to Girls for Secondary Education
NIOS	National Institute of Open Schooling		
NIPPCD	National Institute of Public Cooperation and Child Development	NSKFDC	National Safai Karamcharis Finance and Development Corporation
NIRD	National Institute for Rural Development	NSQF	National Skills Qualification Framework
NISD	National Institute of Social Defence	NSS	National Sample Survey/Nutrition Surveillance System
NIT	National Institute of Technology	NSSO	National Sample Survey Organisation
NKC	National Knowledge Commission		
NLM	National Literacy Mission	NSTFDC	National Scheduled Tribes Finance and Development Corporation
NMDFC	National Minorities Finance and Development Corporation	NT	Nomadic Tribe
NME-ICT	National Mission on Education through Information and Communication Technology	NTFs	National Training Funds
		NTFP	Non Timber Forest Product
		NUEPA	National University of Educational Planning and Administration
NMMS	National Merit-cum-Means Scholarships	NV	Navodaya Vidyalaya
NNMB	National Nutrition Monitoring Bureau	NVEQF	National Vocational Education Qualifications Framework
NNP	National Nutrition Plan	OBCs	Other Backward Classes
NOSS	National Overseas Scholarship Scheme	ODL	Open and Distance Learning
		ODS	Open Design School
NPAN	National Plan of Action on Nutrition	OECD	Organisation for Economic Co-operation & Development
NPCC	National Programme Coordination Committee	OOP	Out of Pocket
NPCDCS	National Programme for the Prevention and Control of Cancer, Diabetes, Cardiovascular Diseases and Stroke	OoSC	Out of School Children
		ORS	Oral Rehydration Solution
		PCR Act	Protection of Civil Rights Act
		PDS	Public Distribution System
NPEGEL	National Programme for Education of Girls at Elementary Level	PEC	Punjab Engineering College
		PESA Act	Panchayat Extension to Scheduled Areas Act
NP-NSPE	National Programme for Nutritional Support to Primary Education	PET	Physical Education Teacher
NRDWP	National Rural Drinking Water Programme	PG	Postgraduate
		PGIMER	Post Graduate Institute of Medical Education and Research
NREGA	National Rural Employment Guarantee Act	PHC	Primary Health Centre
NRHM	National Rural Health Mission	Ph.D	Doctor of Philosophy
NRLM	National Rural Livelihoods Mission	PIP	Project Implementation Plan
NSDC	National Skill Development Corporation	PISA	Programme for International Student Assessment
		PLHA	People living with HIV/AIDS
NSDCB	National Skill Development Coordination Board	PMAGY	Pradhan Mantri Adarsh Gram Yojana

PMDT	Programmatic Management of Drug-resistant Tuberculosis	SCDC	Scheduled Caste Development Corporation
PMGSY	Pradhan Mantri Gram Sadak Yojana	SCERT	State Council of Educational Research & Training
PMS	Post Matric Scholarship	SCP	Special Component Plan
PMSSY	Pradhan Mantri Swasthya Suraksha Yojana	SCR	Student Classroom Ratio
POA Act	Prevention of Atrocities Act	SCSP	Scheduled Caste Sub Plan
PPP	Public–Private Partnership	SDCs	Skill Development Centres
PRI	Pahchayati Raj Institution	SEMIS	Secondary Education Management Information System
PS	Primary School	SFAP	Student Financial Aid Programme
PSL	Priority Sector Lending	SGSY-SP	Swarnajayanti Gram Swarozgar Yojana–Special Projects
PSSCIVE	Pandit Sunder Lal Sharma Central Institute of Vocational Education	SHGs	Self Help Groups
PSUs	Public Sector Undertakings	SHSRC	State Health System Resource Centre
PTA	Parent Teacher Association	SIA	Supplemental Immunization Activity
PTG	Primitive Tribal Groups	SIE	State Institute of Education
PTR	Pupil Teacher Ratio	SIEMAT	State Institute of Educational Management & Training
PVTGs	Particularly Vulnerable Tribal Groups	SIHFW	State Institute of Health and Family Welfare
PYKKA	Panchayat Yuva Krida Khel Abhiyan	SII J&K	Special Industry Initiative for Jammu & Kashmir
QMT	Quality Monitoring Tools	SJE	Social Justice and Empowerment
R&D	Research and Development	SKA	Sarva Krida Abhiyan
RCH	Reproductive and Child Health	SKP	Skill Knowledge Providers
RDA	Recommended Dietary Allowance	SMC	School Management Committee
RDK	Rapid Diagnostic Kits	SMEPWD	State Mission for Empowerment of Persons with Disabilities
RGI	Registrar General of India	SNT	Semi Nomadic Tribe
RGNCS	Rajiv Gandhi National Crèche Scheme	SOS	State Open School
RGNFS	Rajiv Gandhi National Fellowships Scheme	SPO	State Project Office
RGSEAG	Rajiv Gandhi Scheme for Empowerment of Adolescent Girls	SPQEM	Scheme for Providing Quality Education in Madarasas
RKS	Rogi Kalyan Samitis	SRCs	Socio Religious Communities
RMP	Registered Medical Practitioner	SRF	Senior Research Fellowship
RMSA	Rashtriya Madhyamik Shiksha Abhiyan	SRI	Social and Rural Institute
R&R	Rehabilitation and Re-settlement	SRMS	Scheme for Rehabilitation of Manual Scavengers
RRTCs	Regional Resource and Training Centres	SRS	Sample Registration System
RSBY	Rashtriya Swasthya Bima Yojana	SSA	Sarva Shiksha Abhiyan
RSC	Residential School Complex	SSCs	Sector Skill Councils
RTE	Right to Education	ST	Scheduled Tribe
RUDSETI	Rural Development and Self Employment Training Institute	STDCs	State Tribal Development Corporations
SBA	Skilled Birth Attendants	STEP	Support to Training and Employment Programme for Women
SC	Scheduled Caste		
SCA	Special Central Assistance		
SCAs	State Channelizing Agencies		

STET	State Teacher Eligibility Test	UGC	University Grants Commission
STI	Sexually Transmitted Infection	UHC	Universal Health Coverage
TB	Tuberculosis	UID	Unique Identification
TBA	Traditional Birth Attendant	ULB	Urban Local Bodies
TEI	Teacher Education Index	UMDT	Uniform Multi-Drug Therapy Regimen
TEQIP	Technical Education Quality Improvement Programme	UNCRPD	United Nations Conventions on the Rights of Persons with Disabilities
TET	Teacher Eligibility Test		
TFR	Total Fertility Rate	UNESCO	United Nations Educational, Scientific & Cultural Organisation
THE	Times Higher Education		
TISS	Tata Institute of Social Sciences	UNICEF	United Nations International Children Emergency Fund
TLC	Teaching and Learning Centre		
TLE	Teaching Learning Equipment	UP	Uttar Pradesh
TLM	Teaching Learning Material	UPS	Upper Primary School
TNTFP	Traditional Non Timber Forest Product	UPSS	Usual Principal Subsidiary Status
		USA	United States of America
TPDS	Targeted Public Distribution System	UT	Union Territory
TREAD	Trade Related Entrepreneurship Assistance and Development	VEC	Village Education Committee
		VET	Vocational Education & Training
TRI	Tribal Research Institute	VHND	Village Health and Nutrition Day
TRIFED	Tribal Cooperative Marketing Development Federation of India Limited	VHNSC	Village Health Nutrition Sanitation Committee
		VHSND	Village Health, Sanitation and Nutrition Day
TRIPs	Trade-Related Aspects of Intellectual Property Rights		
		VO	Volunteer Organisations
TSC	Total Sanitation Campaign	VRCs	Vocational Rehabilitation Centres
TSP	Tribal Sub-Plan	VTPs	Vocational Training Providers
TVET	Technical and Vocational Education & Training	WCD	Women and Child Development
		WCP	Women and Child Programmes
UEE	Universalisation of Elementary Education	WFPR	Work Force Participation Rate
		WHO	World Health Organization
UG	Undergraduate	WTO	World Trade Organisation

Annexures

22.1	Employment Across Various Sectors (in millions) 1999–2000, 2004–05, 2009–10—on UPSS basis	160
22.2	Absolute Increase/Decrease Employments Across Various Sectors (in millions) in Manufacturing, 1999–2000, 2004–05, 2009–10	161
22.3	Incidence of Unemployment for 15 Years and Above Age Group, by Level of Education, 2004–05 and 2009–10 (UPSS) in Percentage	162
22.4	Dependency Ratio Across India States, Census 2001	163

20

Health

20.1. Health should be viewed as not merely the absence of disease but as a state of complete physical, mental and social well-being. The determinants of good health are: access to various types of health services and an individual's lifestyle choices, personal, family and social relationships. The latter are outside the scope of this Chapter. The focus in this Chapter is on the strategy to deliver preventive, curative and public health services. Other sectors that impact on good health, such as clean drinking water and sanitation are dealt with in other Chapters of the Plan.

AN OVERVIEW

20.2. At present, India's health care system consists of a mix of public and private sector providers of health services. Networks of health care facilities at the primary, secondary and tertiary level, run mainly by State Governments, provide free or very low cost medical services. There is also an extensive private health care sector, covering the entire spectrum from individual doctors and their clinics, to general hospitals and super speciality hospitals.

20.3. The system suffers from the following weaknesses:

1. *Availability* of health care services from the public and private sectors taken together is quantitatively inadequate. This is starkly evident from the data on doctors or nurses per lakh of the population. At the start of the Eleventh Plan, the number of doctors per lakh of population was only 45, whereas, the desirable number is 85 per lakh population. Similarly, the number of Nurses and Auxiliary Nurse and Midwifes (ANMs) available was only 75 per lakh population whereas the desirable number is 255. The overall shortage is exacerbated by a wide geographical variation in availability across the country. Rural areas are especially poorly served.

2. *Quality* of healthcare services varies considerably in both the public and private sector. Many practitioners in the private sector are actually not qualified doctors. Regulatory standards for public and private hospitals are not adequately defined and, in any case, are ineffectively enforced.

3. *Affordability* of health care is a serious problem for the vast majority of the population, especially in tertiary care. The lack of extensive and adequately funded public health services pushes large numbers of people to incur heavy out of pocket expenditures on services purchased from the private sector. Out of pocket expenditures arise even in public sector hospitals, since lack of medicines means that patients have to buy them. This results in a very high financial burden on families in case of severe illness. A large fraction of the out of pocket expenditure arises from outpatient care and purchase of medicines, which are mostly not covered even by the existing insurance schemes. In any case, the percentage of population covered by health insurance is small.

4. The problems outlined above are likely to worsen in future. Health care costs are expected to rise because, with rising life expectancy, a larger proportion of our population will become vulnerable to chronic Non Communicable Diseases (NCDs), which typically require expensive

treatment. The public awareness of treatment possibilities is also increasing and which, in turn, increases the demand for medical care. In the years ahead, India will have to cope with health problems reflecting the dual burden of disease, that is, dealing with the rising cost of managing NCDs and injuries while still battling communicable diseases that still remain a major public health challenge, both in terms of mortality and disability (Figures 20.1 and 20.2).

5. The total expenditure on health care in India, taking both public, private and household out-of-pocket (OOP) expenditure was about 4.1 per cent of GDP in 2008–09 (National Health Accounts [NHA] 2009), which is broadly comparable to other developing countries, at similar

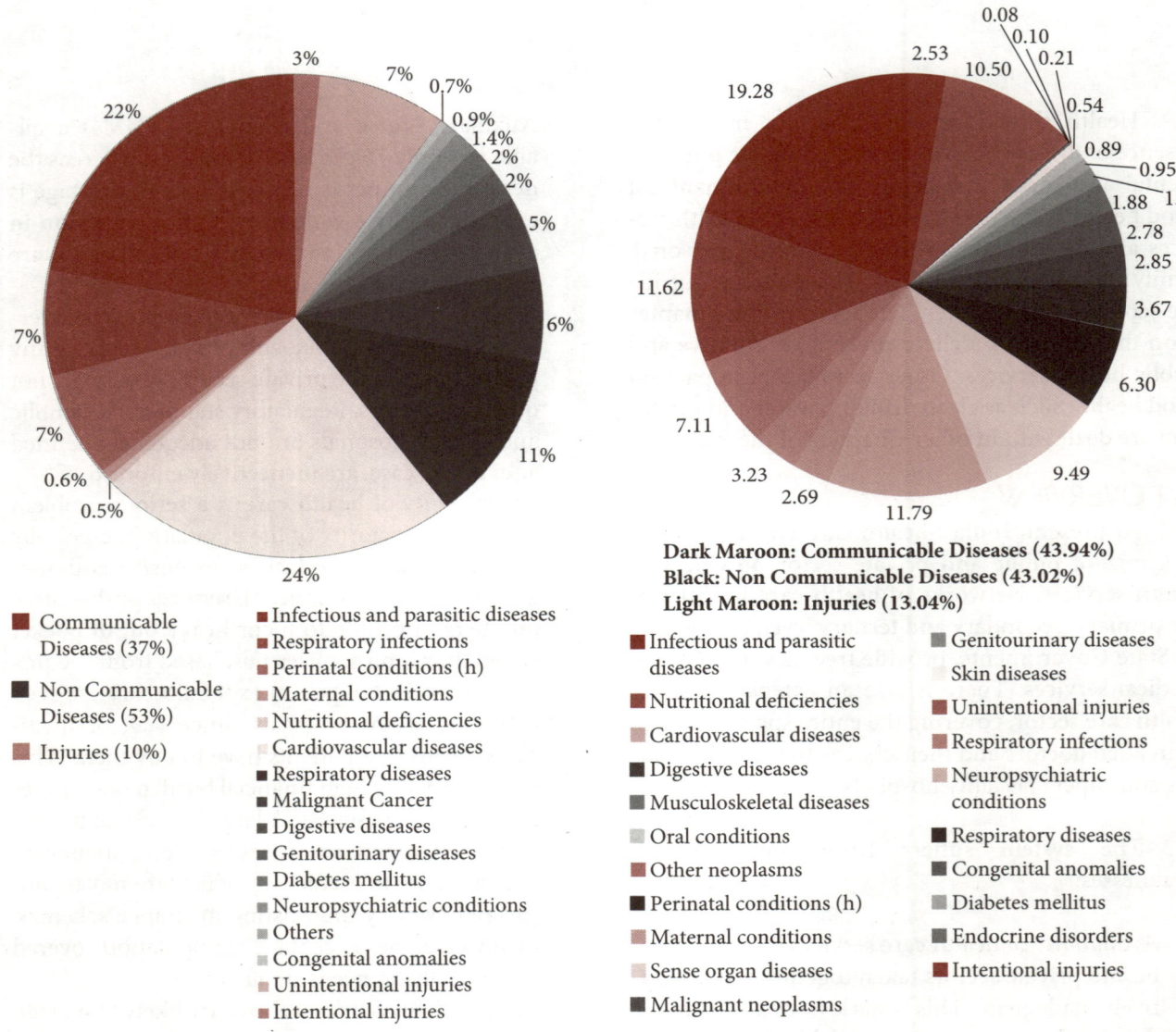

Source: Mortality and Burden of Disease Estimates for WHO Member States in 2008.

FIGURE 20.1: Disease Burden of India, 2008
(Estimated number of deaths by cause)

Source: Global Burden of Disease Estimates for WHO Member States 2009.

FIGURE 20.2: Disability Adjusted Life Years in India, 2009
(Estimated percentage of DALY by cause)

levels of per capita income. However, the public expenditure on health was only about 27 per cent of the total in 2008–09 (NHA, 2009), which is very low by any standard. Public expenditure on Core Health (both plan and non-plan and taking the Centre and States together) was about 0.93 per cent of GDP in 2007–08. It has increased to about 1.04 per cent during 2011–12. It needs to increase much more over the next decade.

20.4. The enormity of the challenge in health was realised when the Eleventh Plan was formulated and an effort was made to increase Central Plan expenditures on health. The increase in Central expenditures has not been fully matched by a comparable increase in State Government expenditures (Table 20.3). The Twelfth Plan proposes to take corrective action by incentivising States.

20.5. As an input into formulating the Twelfth Plan strategy, it has relied on the High Level Expert Group (HLEG) set up by the Planning Commission to define a comprehensive strategy for health for the Twelfth Five Year Plan. The Group's report is accessible on the web site of the Planning Commission. In addition, wide consultations have been held with stakeholders and through Working Groups and Steering Groups. Based on the HLEG report and after extensive consultations within and outside the Government, as well as a close review of the actual performance of the sector during the Eleventh Plan period, a new strategy for health is being spelt out in the Twelfth Plan towards rolling out Universal Health Coverage—a process that will span several years. The consensus among stakeholders is that the magnitude of the challenge is such that a viable and longer term architecture for health can be put in place only over two or even three Plan periods. However, a start must be made towards achieving the long term goal immediately.

REVIEW OF ELEVENTH PLAN PERFORMANCE

20.6. A review of the health outcome of the Eleventh Plan and of NRHM is constrained by lack of end-line data on most indicators. Analysis of available data reveals that though there has been progress, except on child-sex ratio, the goals have not been fully met. Despite efforts through the flagship of NRHM, wide disparity in attainments across states outlines the need for contextual strategies.

1. *Maternal Mortality Ratio (MMR)* which measures number of women of reproductive age (15–49 years) dying due to maternal causes per 1,00,000 live births, is a sensitive indicator of the quality of the health care system. The decline in MMR during the 2004–06 to 2007–09 of 5.8 per cent per year (that is, 254 to 212) has been comparable to that in the preceding period (a fall of 5.5 per cent per year from 301, over 2001–03 to 2004–06). MMR of 212 (2007–09) is well short of the Eleventh Plan goal of 100. Besides Kerala (81), two more States namely Tamil Nadu (97) and Maharashtra (104) have realised MDG target of 109 in 2007–09, while Andhra Pradesh (134), West Bengal (145), Gujarat (148) and Haryana (153) are in closer proximity. A major burden of MMR is in EAG states, where the average MMR was 308 in 2007–09 (SRS), and continues to remain high as per the recent Annual Health Survey (2010–11). These are Assam (381), Bihar (305), Jharkhand (278), MP (310), Chhattisgarh (275), Odisha (277), Rajasthan (331), Uttar Pradesh (345) and Uttarakhand (188). Suboptimal performance in EAG states points to gaps in Ante-Natal Care, skilled birth attendance and Emergency Obstetrical care and to draw lessons from maternal death reviews.

2. *Infant Mortality Rate (IMR)*, death of children before the age of one year per 1,000 live births, is a sensitive indicator of the health and nutritional status of population. IMR fell by 5 per cent per year over the 2006–11 period, an improvement over the 3 per cent decline per year in the preceding five years, but short of the target of 28. The decline in IMR has accelerated, but is short of the required pace. While seven states have achieved the target, IMR is still high in MP, Odisha, UP, Assam, and Rajasthan.

3. *Total Fertility Rate (TFR)*, which measures the number of children born to a woman during her entire reproductive period, fell by 2.8 per cent per annum over the 2006–10 period from 2.8 to

2.5, which is faster than the decline of 2 per cent per year in the preceding five years, but short of the Eleventh Plan goal of 2.1. Replacement level TFR, namely 2.1, has been attained by nine states. High fertility remains a problem in seven States, namely Bihar (CBR 2011 27.7; TFR 2010 3.7), Uttar Pradesh (27.8; 3.5), Madhya Pradesh (26.9; 3.2), Rajasthan (26.2; 3.1), Jharkhand (25.0; 3.0), Chhattisgarh (24.9; 2.8) and Assam (22.8; 2.5). Reasons are early marriage, close spacing of births, high unmet need and lack of skilled contraceptive services. Low couple protection rate (40.4 per cent Family Welfare Statistics in India, 2011) and a high unmet need for contraception (20.5 per cent) in 2007–08 point to gaps in service delivery.

4. On the goal of raising *child sex ratio*, there has been a reversal. All States and UTs except Punjab, Haryana, Himachal Pradesh, Gujarat, Tamil Nadu, Mizoram, Andaman and Nicobar Islands and Chandigarh have witnessed a decrease in the child sex ratio (0–6 years) in the 2001–11 decade.
5. Progress on goals on reducing *malnutrition* and *anaemia* cannot be assessed for want of updated data, but localised surveys indicated that the status has not improved.

FINANCING FOR HEALTH

20.7. During the Eleventh Plan funding for health by Central Government has increased to 2.5 times and of States to 2.14 times that in Tenth Plan, to add up to 1.04 per cent of GDP in 2011–12. When broader determinants of health (drinking water and sanitation, ICDS and Mid-Day Meal) are added, the total public spending on health in Eleventh Plan comes to 1.97 per cent of GDP (Tables 20.2 and 20.3).

20.8. An analysis of performance reveals achievements and gaps. These follow.

INFRASTRUCTURE

20.9. There has been an increase in number of public health facilities over the 2007–11 period—Sub-Centres by 2 per cent, PHC by 6 per cent, CHC by 16 per cent and District Hospitals by 45 per cent. Yet shortfalls remain, 20 per cent for Sub-Centres, 24 per cent for PHCs and 37 per cent for CHCs, particularly in Bihar, Jharkhand, Madhya Pradesh and Uttar Pradesh. Though most CHCs and 34 per cent Primary Health Centres (PHCs) have been upgraded and operationalised as 24 × 7 facilities and First Referral Units (FRU) have doubled, yet the commitment of Eleventh Plan to make all public facilities meet IPHS norms, and to provide Emergency Obstetric Care at all CHCs have not been achieved. Access to safe abortion services is not available in all CHCs, a gap which is contributing to maternal mortality. Though Mobile Medical Units (MMUs) have been deployed in 449 districts of the country, their outreach medical services are not adequate for the need.

TABLE 20.1
Eleventh Plan Monitorable Goals and Achievements

S. No.	Eleventh Plan Monitorable Target	Baseline Level	Recent Status
1	Reducing Maternal Mortality Ratio (MMR) to 100 per 100000 live births.	254 (SRS, 2004–06)	212 (SRS, 2007–09)
2	Reducing Infant Mortality Rate (IMR) to 28 per 1000 live births.	57 (SRS, 2006)	44 (SRS, 2011)
3	Reducing Total Fertility Rate (TFR) to 2.1.	2.8 (SRS, 2006)	2.5 (SRS, 2010)
4	Reducing malnutrition among children of age group 0–3 to half its level.	40.4 (NFHS, 2005–06)	No recent data available
5	Reducing anaemia among women and girls by 50%.	55.3 (NFHS, 2005–06)	No recent data available
6	Raising the sex ratio for age group 0–6 to 935	927 (Census, 2001)	914 (census, 2011)

TABLE 20.2
Allocation and Spending by Ministry of Health in Eleventh Plan

(Figures in ₹ Crore)

Department	Eleventh Plan Allocation	Eleventh Plan release	Eleventh Plan Expenditure	% Expenditure to Release
HFW	1,25,923	87,460	83,407	95.4%
Of which under NRHM	89,478	68,064	66,127	97.2%
AYUSH	3,988	3,083	2,994	97.1%
DHR	4,496	1,938	1,870	96.5%
AIDS Control	5,728	1,500	1,305	87.0%
Total	**1,40,135**	**93,981**	**89,576**	**95.3%**

Note: Outlay for the new departments of DHR and AIDS Control was transferred from Department of HFW.

TABLE 20.3
Funding for Health in Eleventh Plan: Core and Broad Health Components

(Figures in ₹ Crore)

Year	Centre Core Health	States Core Health	% GDP Core Health			% GDP (Broad Health)		
			Centre	States	Total	Centre	States	Total
X Plan	47,077	1,07,046	0.29%	0.65%	0.94%	0.56%	1.18%	1.74%
2007–08	16,055	30,536	0.32%	0.61%	0.93%	0.71%	1.17%	1.89%
2008–09	19,604	36,346	0.35%	0.65%	0.99%	0.75%	1.22%	1.98%
2009–10	25,652	44,748	0.40%	0.69%	1.09%	0.78%	1.24%	2.02%
2010–11	27,466	55,955	0.36%	0.73%	1.09%	0.75%	1.27%	2.02%
2011–12	30,587	62,343	0.34%	0.70%	1.04%	0.74%	1.19%	1.94%
XI Plan	1,19,364	2,29,928	0.35%	0.68%	1.04%	0.75%	1.22%	1.97%

Note: Core health includes health care expenditure of central ministries (MoHFW, Labour on RSBY and so on) on health; Broad health includes Drinking Water and Sanitation, Mid-Day Meal and ICDS (Plan and non-Plan).

HEALTH PERSONNEL

20.10. ASHAs positioned under NRHM have been successful in promoting awareness of obstetric and child care services in the community. Better training for ASHA and timely payment of incentive have come out as gaps in evaluations. Despite considerable improvement in health personnel in position (ANM 27 per cent, nurses 119 per cent, doctors 16 per cent, specialists 36 per cent, pharmacists 38 per cent), gap between staff in position and staff required at the end of the Plan was 52 per cent for ANM and nurses, 76 per cent for doctors, 88 per cent for specialists and 58 per cent for pharmacists. These shortages are attributed to delays in recruitment and to postings not being based on work-load or sanctions. Public health cadre as envisioned in the Eleventh Plan to manage NRHM is not yet in place. Similarly, lack of sound HR management policies results in irrational distribution of available human resource and sub-optimal motivation.

TRAINING CAPACITY

20.11. Setting up of 6 AIIMS like institutes and upgradation of 13 medical colleges has been taken up under Pradhan Mantri Swasthya Suraksha Yojana (PMSSY). Seventy-two State Government medical colleges have been taken up for strengthening to enhance their capacity for PG training. Huge gaps, however, remain in training capacity for all category of health personnel.

COMMUNITY INVOLVEMENT

20.12. Though Rogi Kalyan Samitis (RKS) are in position in most public facilities, monthly Village

Health and Nutrition Days are held in most villages, Jan Sunwais (public hearings) and Common Review Missions have been held yet, their potential in terms of empowering communities, improving accountability and responsiveness of public health facilities is yet to be fully realised.

SERVICE DELIVERY

1. To reduce maternal and infant mortality, institutional deliveries are being promoted by providing cash assistance to pregnant women under Janani Suraksha Yojana (JSY). Though institutional deliveries have increased in rural (39.7 to 68 per cent) and urban areas (79 per cent to 85 per cent) over the 2005–09 period, low levels of full Ante-Natal care (22.8 in rural, and 26.1 in urban in 2009, CES) and quality of care are areas of concern.
2. Full immunisation in children has improved from 54.5 per cent in 2005 (CES) to 61 per cent in 2009 (CES) during the Eleventh Plan. Additions to the Universal Immunization Program include Hepatitis B, Japanese Encephalitis (JE) vaccine in endemic districts, and Pentavalent vaccine, which is a combination vaccine against Diphtheria, Pertussis, Tetanus, Hepatitis B and Haemophilus influenza B. There has been no reported case of polio during 2011. Immunisation cover is far from universal as envisioned in Eleventh Plan, and remains particularly low in UP (41 per cent), MP (43 per cent), Bihar (49 per cent), Rajasthan (54 per cent), Gujarat (57 per cent) and Chhattisgarh (57 per cent), Assam (59 per cent) and Jharkhand (60 per cent). In contrast, some States like Goa (88 per cent), Sikkim (85 per cent), Punjab (84 per cent) and Kerala (82 per cent) have achieved high level of immunisation coverage. Home Based Neonatal Care (HBNC) through ASHAs has been promoted to improve new born care practices in the community and to enable early detection and referral. Continued high rates of child mortality suggest that the public health system has not been very effective in promoting healthy practices as breastfeeding, use of ORS and preventive and care seeking behaviours.
3. Despite improvements in infrastructure, and personnel deployed, evaluation has reported that utilisation of public facilities for chronic disease remains low in UP (45 per cent), MP (63 per cent) and Jharkhand (70 per cent) as compared to Tamil Nadu (94 per cent) reflecting poor quality of service.
4. To reduce fertility, increasing age of marriage, spacing of births, access to a basket of contraceptive services are some of the possible innovations that need to be tried.
5. The Eleventh Plan commitment of providing access to essential drugs at public facilities has not been realised. This reflects in continued high out-of-pocket expenditure on health care, as suggested by some local surveys.

GOVERNANCE OF PUBLIC HEALTH SYSTEM

20.13. The *Eleventh Plan* had suggested Governance reforms in public health system, such as performance linked incentives, devolution of powers and functions to local health care institutions and making them responsible for the health of the people living in a defined geographical area. NRHM's strategy of decentralisation, PRI involvement, integration of vertical programmes, inter-sectoral convergence and Health Systems Strengthening have been partially achieved. Despite efforts, lack of capacity and adequate flexibility in programmes forestall effective local level planning and execution based on local disease priorities. Professional procurement agencies on the lines of Tamil Nadu are still not in place at the Centre and most States making the process fragmented, with little forecasting or use of the power of monopsony. Wide variation in the performance of health facilities across states have been reported with Tamil Nadu topping and UP and MP at the bottom, pointing to the need for learning from best practices within the country through state level initiatives.

DISEASE CONTROL PROGRAMMES

1. National Vector Borne Disease Control Programme encourages states to take measures, as disease management, integrated vector management and supportive interventions like behaviour change communication, for the prevention and control of diseases like Malaria, Dengue, Chikungunya, Japanese Encephalitis (JE), Lymphatic Filariasis and Kala-azar. India bears

a high proportion of the global burden of TB (21 per cent), leprosy (56 per cent) and lymphatic filariasis (40 per cent). Though there has been progress in the Eleventh Plan in reducing rate of new infections, case load and death from these diseases, a robust surveillance system at the community level is lacking and considerable hidden and residual disease burden remains. Multi-drug resistance to TB is being increasingly recognised. Gaps in infectious disease control programmes relate to testing services in all PHCs, active engagement with private providers, prescribing standard treatment, restricting over-the-counter sale of anti TB drugs, and timely referral through a continuum of care.

2. Among the NCDs, Cardiovascular Diseases (CVD) account for 24 per cent of mortality followed by Respiratory Disease, and malignant cancers. During the Eleventh Five Year Plan National Programme for the Prevention and Control of Cancer, Diabetes, Cardiovascular Diseases and Stroke (NPCDCS) was initiated in 100 selected districts in 21 states. So far, 87 lakh people have been screened for diabetes and hypertension, out of which 6.5 per cent are suspected to be diabetic and 7.7 per cent are suspected to be suffering from hypertension. Despite enhanced allocations for the National Mental Health Programme, it has lagged behind due to non-availability of qualified mental health professionals at district and sub-district levels. Training of non-physician mental health professionals and implementation of community based mental health programmes are needed to reduce the rising burden of mental health disorders. NCD programmes need to be integrated within NRHM to provide preventive, testing, care and referral services.

REGULATION

20.14. The Food Safety and Standards Act (FSSA), 2006 came into force from 5.8.2011 and replaced multiple food laws, standard setting bodies and enforcement agencies with one integrated food law. The Government of India has enacted the Clinical Establishments (Registration and Regulation) Act, 2010 for Registration and Regulation of Clinical Establishments. The Government of India has notified important amendments in rules under the Pre-Conception and Pre-Natal Diagnostic Techniques (Prohibition of Sex Selection) Act, 1994, including amendment to Rule 11 (2) of the PC and PNDT Rules, 1996 to provide for confiscation of unregistered machines and regulating the use of portable ultrasound equipment and services offered by mobile clinics. The Transplantation of Human Organs Act, 1994 has been amended to make the process of organ donation and reception more streamlined and malpractice free. Quality and reach of regulation are major issues.

HMIS

20.15. During the Eleventh Plan, a web based Health Management Information System (HMIS) application software has been developed and made operational for online data capture at district and sub-district levels on RCH service delivery indicators. The data captured is scanty, restricted to public facilities and is not always used for programme planning or monitoring.

AIDS CONTROL

20.16. Against a target to halt and reverse the HIV/AIDS epidemic in India, there has been a reduction of new HIV infections in the country by 57 per cent. Still, an estimated 20.9 lakh people were living with HIV/AIDS (PLHA) in 2011. The programme includes Targeted Interventions focused on High Risk Groups and Bridge populations, Link Workers Scheme, Integrated Counselling and Testing Services, Community Care, Support and Treatment Centres, Information, Education, and Communication (IEC) and condom promotion. Gaps in the programme include low rate of coverage of Anti-Retroviral Therapy among infected adults and children, low levels of opioid substitution therapy among injection drug users (3 per cent), testing of pregnant women for HIV and Syphilis (23 per cent) and low Anti-Retroviral coverage for preventing mother to child transmission. There is scope for greater integration with NRHM to avoid duplication of efforts, as in reaching non-high risk groups and distribution of condoms.

INDIAN SYSTEMS OF MEDICINE AND HOMOEOPATHY (AYUSH)

20.17. Against the Eleventh Plan objective of 'mainstreaming AYUSH systems to actively supplement the efforts of the allopathic system', 40 per cent PHCs, 65 per cent CHCs and 69 per cent District hospitals have co-located AYUSH facilities. Though considerable progress has been made in documenting identity and quality standards of herbal medicines, scientific validation of AYUSH principles, remedies and therapies has not progressed. Similarly, though the National Medicinal Plants Board has supported many projects for conservation, cultivation and storage of medicinal plants, only 20 per cent of the 178 major medicinal plant species traded as raw drugs are largely sourced from cultivation. Nine AYUSH industry clusters through Special Purpose Vehicle having common facility centres for manufacture and testing of AYUSH medicines are being set up in eight States. While AYUSH sector has considerable infrastructure, it remains under-utilised.

HEALTH RESEARCH

20.18. The newly established department of Health Research, and Indian Council of Medical Research (ICMR) have piloted several innovations, including an on-line Clinical Trials Registry, Uniform Multidrug Therapy Regimen (UMDT) for Leprosy, and lymphatic filariasis, kits for improved diagnosis of malaria, dengue fever, TB (including drug resistant), cholera, Chlamydia infection. Leptospirosis; and development of indigenous H1N1 vaccine. Yet, health research in India has yet to make a major impact on the health challenges facing the country. The reasons are that ICMR has focused on biomedical research, especially in communicable diseases, while gaps in health attainments are largely due to behavioural factors, inadequate attention to prevention and fragile health systems.

TWELFTH PLAN STRATEGY

20.19. The Twelfth Plan seeks to strengthen initiatives taken in the Eleventh Plan to expand the reach of health care and work towards the long term objective of establishing a system of Universal Health Coverage (UHC) in the country. This means that each individual would have assured access to a defined essential range of medicines and treatment at an affordable price, which should be entirely free for a large percentage of the population. Inevitably, the list of assured services will have to be limited by budgetary constraints. But the objective should be to expand coverage steadily over time.

20.20. Based on the recommendations of the HLEG and other stakeholder consultations, it is possible to outline the key elements of the strategy that should be followed in the Twelfth Plan. These elements should be seen as a part of a longer term plan to move towards UHC, which is a process that will unfold over two or three Plan periods.

1. There must be substantial expansion and strengthening of the public sector health care system if we are to meet the health needs of rural and even urban areas. The bulk of the population today relies upon private sector health providers, paying amounts which they cannot afford, because of the inadequate reach of the public sector. While the private sector can continue to operate for those who can afford it, an expansion of good quality affordable public sector care is essential. As supply in the public sector increases, it will cause a shift towards public sector providers freeing the vulnerable population from dependence on high cost and often unreachable private sector health care.
2. Health sector expenditure by the Centre and States, both Plan and Non Plan, will have to be substantially increased by the end of the Twelfth Plan. It has already increased from 0.94 per cent of GDP in the Tenth Plan to 1.04 per cent in the Eleventh Plan (Table 20.3). The provision of clean drinking water and sanitation as one of the principal factors in the control of diseases is well established from the history of industrialised countries and it should have high priority in health related resource allocation. The percentage for this broader definition of health sector related resources needs to be increased to 2.5 per cent by the end of the Twelfth Plan. Since expenditure on health by the State Governments is about twice the expenditures by the Centre,

the overall targets for public sector health expenditure can only be achieved if, along with the Centre, State Governments expand their health budgets appropriately. A suitable mechanism should therefore be designed to incentivise an increase in State Government spending.

3. Financial and managerial systems will be redesigned to ensure more efficient utilisation of available resources, and to achieve better health outcomes. Coordinated delivery of services within and across sectors, delegation matched with accountability, fostering a spirit of innovation are some of the measures proposed to ensure that 'more can be done from less for more' for better health outcomes.

4. Efforts would be made to find a workable way of encouraging cooperation between the public and private sector in achieving health goals. This would include contracting in of services for gap filling, and also various forms of effectively regulated and managed PPP, while also ensuring that there is no compromise in terms of standards of delivery and that the incentive structure does not undermine health care objectives.

5. The present Rashtriya Swasthya Bima Yojana (RSBY) which provides 'cash less' in-patient treatment for eligible beneficiaries through an insurance based system will need to be reformed to enable access to a continuum of comprehensive primary, secondary and tertiary care. The coverage of RSBY was initially limited to the BPL population but, was subsequently expanded to other categories. It should be the objective of the Twelfth Plan to use the platform and existing mechanisms of RSBY to cover the entire population below the poverty line. In planning health care structures for the future, it is desirable to move away from a 'fee-for-service' mechanism for the reasons outlined by the HLEG, to address the issue of fragmentation of services that works to the detriment of preventive and primary care and also to reduce the scope for fraud and induced demand.

6. Availability of skilled human resources remains a key constraint in expanding health service delivery. A mere expansion of financial resources devoted to health will not deliver results if health personnel are not available. A large expansion of medical schools, nursing colleges, and so on, is therefore necessary and public sector medical schools must play a major role in the process. Since the present distribution of such colleges is geographically very uneven, a special effort will be made to expand medical education in States which are at present under-served. In addition, a massive effort will be made to recruit and train paramedical and community level health workers.

7. An important lesson from the Eleventh Plan is that the multiplicity of Central Sector and Centrally Sponsored Schemes addressing individual diseases, or funding activities or institutions, prevents a holistic health-systems-approach, leads to duplication and redundancies, and makes coordinated delivery difficult. This multiplicity also constrains the flexibility of States to make need based plans or deploy their resources in the most efficient manner. As a result, new programmes cannot take off and old ones do not reach their maximum potential. The way forward is to focus on strengthening the pillars of the health system, so that it can prevent, detect and manage each of the unique challenges that different parts of the country face.

8. A series of prescription drugs reforms, promotion of essential, generic medicines, and making these universally available free of cost to all patients in public facilities as a part of the Essential Health Package will be a priority.

9. Effective regulation in medical practice, public health, food and drugs is essential to safeguard people against risks, and unethical practices. This is especially so given the information gaps in the health sector which make is difficult for individuals to make reasoned choices.

10. The health system in the Twelfth Plan will continue to have a mix of public and private service providers. The public sector health services need to be strengthened to deliver both public health related and clinical services. The public and private sectors also need to coordinate for delivery of a continuum of care. A strong regulatory

system would supervise the quality of services delivered. Standard treatment guidelines should form the basis of clinical care across public and private sectors, with adequate monitoring by the regulatory bodies to improve quality and control the cost of care.

INCLUSIVE AGENDA FOR HEALTH

20.21. In order to ensure that all the services in the Twelfth Plan are provided with special attention to the needs of marginalised sections of the population the following will be emphasised in the Twelfth Plan.

20.22. *Access to services*: Barriers to access would be recognised and overcome especially for the disadvantaged and people located far from facilities. Medical and public health facilities would be accessible to the differently-abled. They would be gender sensitive and child friendly. Information on health would be accessible to the visually impaired and to all caregivers; especially to those who look after autistic and mentally challenged persons. Hospitals would have facilities for the hearing impaired. Among marginalised groups, the SC and ST populations, and minorities, the doubly disadvantaged such as the Particularly Vulnerable Tribal Groups (PVTGs), the De-notified and Nomadic Tribes, the Musahars and the internally displaced must be given special attention while making provisions for, setting up and renovating Sub-Centres and Anganwadis.

20.23. *Special services*: Special services should be made available for the vulnerable and disadvantaged groups. For example, counselling of victims of mental trauma in areas of conflict, or the supply and fitting of aids for the differently-abled are some examples of special services for certain categories of users. As there are other segments of the population which are also vulnerable, the list should be open-ended.

20.24. *Monitoring and evaluation systems*: Routine monitoring and concurrent impact evaluations should collect disaggregated information on disadvantaged segments of the population. This is to assess the ease with which they access services and their impact, as also to understand how they compare to the general population.

20.25. *Representation in community fora*: Wherever community-level fora exist or are being planned for, such as Rogi Kalyan Samitis, VHSNC, representation of the marginalised should be mandatory. Also, every Village Health Sanitation and Nutrition Committee would strive to have 50 per cent representation of women.

20.26. *Training of health and rehabilitation professionals* should incorporate knowledge of disability rights, as also the skills to deal with differences in perspectives and expectations between members of disadvantaged segments and the general population that may arise out of different experiences. All health related training institutes must have a comprehensive policy to make their educational programmes friendly for the differently-abled. This should also include sensitisation of faculty, staff and trainees.

TOWARDS UNIVERSAL HEALTH COVERAGE

20.27. The Twelfth Plan strategy outlined is a first step in moving toward Universal Health Care (UHC). All over the world, the provision of some form of universal health coverage is regarded as a basic component of social security. There are different ways of achieving this objective and country experiences vary. We need to ensure much broader coverage of health services to provide essential health care and we need to do it through a system which is appropriate to our needs and within our financial capability.

HLEG'S RECOMMENDATIONS

20.28. The High Level Expert Group has defined UHC as follows: 'Ensuring equitable access for all Indian citizens in any part of the country, regardless of income level, social status, gender, caste or religion, to affordable, accountable and appropriate, assured quality health services (promotive, preventive, curative and rehabilitative) as well as services addressing wider determinants of health delivered to individuals and populations, with the Government being the guarantor and enabler, although not necessarily the only provider of health and related services.'

20.29. This definition affirms that the system must be available for all who want it, though some, typically the upper income groups, may opt out. For operational purposes, it is necessary to define with greater precision, the coverage of assured services, especially in terms of entitlement for in-patient treatment and to define the specific mechanism through which the service will be delivered. The extent of the coverage offered in terms of the range of treatments covered will obviously be constrained by finances available, though it can be expected to expand over time. The HLEG has recommended the prioritisation of primary health care, while ensuring that the Essential Health Package (EHP) includes essential services at all levels of care.

20.30. The HLEG has examined different ways in which UHC could be delivered without any cash payment by the beneficiaries. At one end, we can have a purely public delivery of services from public sector service providers using private sector only to supplement critical gaps, and whose costs are covered by budgetary funds. At the other end, we can have a system where defined services are delivered by service providers charging a fee for service, with payment to the providers being made by State funded medical insurance, with no payment to be made by the patient. The HLEG has also recommended: 'State governments should consider experimenting with arrangements where the state and district purchase care from an integrated network of combined primary, secondary and tertiary care providers. These provider networks should be regulated by the government so that they meet the rules and requirements for delivering cost effective, accountable and quality health care. Such an integrated provider entity should receive funds to achieve negotiated predetermined health outcomes for the population being covered. This entity would bear financial risks and rewards and be required to deliver on health care and wellness objectives. Ideally, the strengthened District Hospital should be the leader of this provider network' (Recommendation 3.1.10).

20.31. The main recommendations of the HLEG are outlined in Box 20.1.

UHC MODELS AROUND THE WORLD

20.32. While many countries subscribe to the objective of UHC there is a great deal of variety in how this objective is achieved. Many countries have adopted a tax-financed model, while others have adopted an insurance based model. Some countries deliver care through salaried public providers; others have adopted capitation as the preferred model for payment for out-patient care, and fee-for-service for in-patient care. A summary of the UHC models in some countries follows.

Canada

20.33. *Medicare* is a regionally administered universal public insurance programme, publicly financed through Federal and Provincial tax revenue. Out-patient services are provided through private providers. All Secondary and Tertiary care services are provided by private and non-profit providers. Primary care payment is mostly 'Fee for Service' with some alternatives (for example, capitation). In-patient service payment is through global budget (case-based payment in some provinces) which does not include physician's cost.

New Zealand

20.34. *National Health Service* is publicly financed through general tax revenue. Outpatient services are provided through private providers. Secondary and Tertiary care services are mostly provided by public, some private providers. Primary care payment is a mix of 'Capitation' and 'Fee for Service'. In-patient service payment is through global budget and case-based payment, which includes physician's cost.

Germany

20.35. *Statutory Health Insurance* is funded by 180 'sickness funds'. Outpatient services are provided through private providers. Secondary and Tertiary care services are provided by public (50 per cent), private non-profit (33 per cent) and private for-profit (17 per cent) providers. Primary care payment is 'Fee for Service'. In-patient service payment is through global budget and case-based payment, which includes physician's cost.

> **Box 20.1**
> **Recommendations of High Level Expert Group on Universal Health Coverage**
>
> 1. *Health Financing and Financial Protection*: Government should increase public expenditure on health from the current level of 1.2 per cent of GDP to at least 2.5 per cent by the end of the Twelfth Plan, and to at least 3 per cent of GDP by 2022. General taxation should be used as the principal source of healthcare financing, not levying sector specific taxes. Specific purpose transfers should be introduced to equalise the levels of per capita public spending on health across different states. Expenditures on primary healthcare should account for at least 70 per cent of all healthcare expenditure. The technical and other capacities developed by the Ministry of Labour for the RSBY should be leveraged as the core of UHC operations—and transferred to the Ministry of Health and Family Welfare.
> 2. *Access to Medicines, Vaccines and Technology*: Price controls and price regulation, especially on essential drugs, should be enforced. The Essential Drugs List should be revised and expanded, and rational use of drugs ensured. Public sector should be strengthened to protect the capacity of domestic drug and vaccines industry to meet national needs. Safeguards provided by Indian patents law and the TRIPS Agreement against the country's ability to produce essential drugs should be protected. MoHFW should be empowered to strengthen the drug regulatory system.
> 3. *Human Resources for Health*: Institutes of Family Welfare should be strengthened and Regional Faculty Development Centres should be selectively developed to enhance the availability of adequately trained faculty and faculty-sharing across institutions. District Health Knowledge Institutes, a dedicated training system for Community Health Workers, State Health Science Universities and a National Council for Human Resources in Health (NCHRH) should be established.
> 4. *Health Service Norms*: A National Health Package should be developed that offers, as part of the entitlement of every citizen, essential health services at different levels of the healthcare delivery system. There should be equitable access to health facilities in urban areas by rationalising services and focusing particularly on the health needs of the urban poor.
> 5. *Management and Institutional Reforms*: All India and State level Public Health Service Cadres and a specialised State level Health Systems Management Cadre should be introduced in order to give greater attention to Public Health and also to strengthen the management of the UHC system. The establishment of a National Health Regulatory and Development Authority (NHRDA) a, National Drug Regulatory and Development Authority (NDRDA) and a, National Health Promotion and Protection Trust (NHPPT) is also recommended.
> 6. *Community Participation and Citizen Engagement*: Existing Village Health Committees should be transformed into participatory Health Councils.
> 7. *Gender and Health*: There is a need to improve access to health services for women, girls and other vulnerable genders (going beyond maternal and child health).

England
20.36. *National Health Service* is publicly financed through general tax revenue. Outpatient services are provided through both public and private providers. Secondary and Tertiary care services are mostly provided by public, some private providers. Primary care payment is mostly a mix of capitation and pay for performance for private providers, and salaries for public providers. In-patient service payment is through global budget and case-based payment, which includes physician's cost.

Thailand
20.37. *Universal Health Coverage Scheme* is financed through general tax revenues paid to local contracting units on the basis of population size. Outpatient services are provided through both public and private providers. Secondary and Tertiary care services are provided by public and private providers. Primary care payment is by risk-adjusted capitation. In-patient service payment is through Diagnostic Related Group (DRG) based capped global budget, and fixed rate fees for some services.

Sri Lanka
20.38. *Universal Health Coverage Scheme* is tax-financed and Government operated. Outpatient services are provided through public providers. Secondary and Tertiary care services are provided by both public and private providers. Primary care payment is by Fee for Service. In-patient service payment is through Fee for Service for Public Hospital and Capitation for Private Hospitals.

Mexico

20.39. *Seguro Popular Insurance Scheme* is financed through Federal and State general tax revenues and member's contributions through premiums from informal sector, and progressive contribution from enrolled families. Outpatient services are provided through both public and limited contracting in of private providers. Secondary and Tertiary care services are usually provided by private providers. Primary care payment is a mix of 'Capitation' and 'Fee for Service'. In-patient service payment is through DRG although such payments take place on an ad-hoc, non-systematic basis.

20.40. The evidence from countries that have attempted to move towards UHC points to the critical importance of initial conditions in terms of both what is necessary and what is feasible, in attempting to meet the objectives of improving coverage, expanding access, controlling cost, raising quality, and strengthening accountability.

20.41. In our system, the initial conditions include a large but severely underfunded public sector, a growing but high cost private sector, with serious issues of inadequate quality and coverage in both, and an ineffective regulation.

20.42. In moving forward, there are two key questions:

1. How to combine public and private providers effectively for meeting UHC goals in a manner that avoids perverse incentives, reduces provider induced demand, and that meets the key objectives specified above?
2. How to integrate different types and levels of services—public health and clinical; preventive and promotive interventions along with primary, secondary, and tertiary clinical care—so that continuum of care is assured? Inadequate prevention and inappropriate utilisation of secondary or tertiary care, when primary care should suffice, would result in much higher cost of care.

20.43. Global evidence from different countries' experiences gives us some pointers to answering these questions:

1. A mix of public and private services is the reality of most countries. In order to make this mix work, a strong regulatory framework is essential to ensure that the UHC programme is most effective in controlling cost, reducing provider-induced demand, and ensuring quality.
2. Provider payment mechanisms, in themselves, are not magic bullets, and there are limits to what they can do. Capitation-based networks can reduce disincentives to continuity of care, but by themselves, they will not guarantee it. For this, there have to be, in addition, improvements in service delivery, improvements in human resources and related regulatory development and enforcement.
3. Further, there is a need to build up institutions of citizens' participation, in order to strengthen accountability and complement what the regulatory architecture seeks to do.

20.44. It must be noted that even developed countries have taken decades to evolve networks that can implement alternative models of UHC. Many countries are opting for 'coordinated care' models where primary, secondary and tertiary care is delivered as an integrated framework with the participation of both public and private sector. The need is first to strengthen our public health infrastructure at all levels. It could be supplemented by private service providers as well as Public Private Partnerships (PPPs). Our endeavour, in the long run, is to move towards an organised system of UHC. We should also learn from the service contracting arrangements initiated through RSBY and other State level initiatives.

20.45. In order to achieve health goals, UHC must build on universal access to services that are determinants of health, such as safe drinking water and sanitation, wholesome nutrition, basic education, safe housing and hygienic environment. To aim at achieving UHC without ensuring access to the determinants of health would be a strategic mistake, and plainly unworkable. Therefore, it may be necessary to realise the goal of UHC in two parallel steps: the first, would be clinical services at different levels, defined in an Essential Health Package (EHP), which the Government would finance and ensure provision through the public health system, supplemented by contracted-in private providers whenever required to fill in critical gaps; second the universal provision of high impact, preventive and public health interventions which the Government would universally provide within the Twelfth Five Year plan (Box 20.2). The UHC would take two plan periods for realisation, but a move in terms of pilots and incremental coverage can begin in the Twelfth Plan itself.

20.46. *Roadmap*: The present health care delivery system needs reform to ensure better utilisation of resources and health outcomes. The building blocks of the reform in the Twelfth Plan would be as follows. Health Services will be delivered with seamless integration between Primary, Secondary and Tertiary sectors. The Primary Health Care will be strengthened to deliver both preventive, public health and curative, clinical services. Publicly funded health care would predominantly be delivered by public providers. The primary health care providers within the network will act as the gateway to secondary and tertiary care facilities in the network. Private sector will be contracted in only for critical gap filling. In areas where both public and private contracted in providers co-exist, patients shall have a choice in selecting their provider. Networks of such integrated facilities at different levels will be encouraged to provide a continuum of care, universally accessible and affordable services with the District Hospital as the nodal point. No fee of any kind would be levied on primary health care services with the primary source of financing being from general taxation/public exchequer. Details of the roadmap shall be worked out by the States through UHC pilots after considering global experience and current local structures.

20.47. *UHC Models*: Various options for financing and organisation of delivery of services need to be carefully explored. Cashless delivery of an Essential Health Package (EHP) to all ought to be the basic deliverable in all models. Since out-patient care and medicines are major elements of household's out-of-pocket and catastrophic expenditure on health,

---

Box 20.2
Illustrative List of Preventive and Public Health Interventions Funded and Provided by Government

1. Full Immunisation among children under three years of age, and pregnant women
2. Full antenatal, natal and post natal care
3. Skilled birth attendance with a facility for meeting need for emergency obstetric care
4. Iron and Folic acid supplementation for children, adolescent girls and pregnant women
5. Regular treatment of intestinal worms, especially in children and reproductive age women
6. Universal use of iodine and iron fortified salt
7. Vitamin A supplementation for children aged 9 to 59 months
8. Access to a basket of contraceptives, and safe abortion services
9. Preventive and promotive health educational services, including information on hygiene, hand-washing, dental hygiene, use of potable drinking water, avoidance of tobacco, alcohol, high calorie diet and obesity, need for regular physical exercise, use of helmets on two-wheelers and seat belts; advice on initiation of breastfeeding within one hour of birth and exclusively up to six months of age, and complimentary feeding thereafter, adolescent sexual health, awareness about RTI/STI; need for screening for NCDs and common cancers for those at risk
10. Home based newborn care, and encouragement for exclusive breastfeeding till six months of age
11. Community based care for sick children, with referral of cases requiring higher levels of care
12. HIV testing and counselling during antenatal care
13. Free drugs to pregnant HIV positive mothers to prevent mother to child transmission of HIV
14. Malaria prophylaxis, using Long Lasting Insecticide Treated Nets (LLIN), diagnosis using Rapid Diagnostic Kits (RDK) and appropriate treatment
15. School check-up of health and wellness, followed by advice, and treatment if necessary
16. Management of diarrhoea, especially in children, using Oral Rehydration Solution (ORS)
17. Diagnosis and treatment of Tuberculosis, Leprosy including Drug and Multi-Drug Resistant cases.
18. Vaccines for hepatitis B and C for high risk groups
19. Patient transport systems including emergency response ambulance services of the 'dial 108' model

ambulatory EHP would be a priority and every UHC model would include systems for full and free access to essential generic medicines, through linkages with Government pharmacies (for public providers) and Jan Aushadhi outlets (for all). Since the frequency of use of services, nature of service delivery and cost of services are fundamentally different for out-patient (ambulatory) and in-patient care, and to obviate the possibility of substitution of primary care by secondary and tertiary care, cost of ambulatory care would need to be earmarked in each UHC pilot. An effective health information network that could be accessed by all service providers and patients (for their own records) would enable the continuum of care. All models could learn from the platform developed by RSBY in terms of beneficiary coverage, facility enrolment and prevention of fraud.

20.48. States may be encouraged and partially funded to run at least one, but up to three UHC pilots in districts through the 'Incentive Pool' under NHM. Individual States, in consultation with the MoHFW, expert groups and institutions may finalise the details of the pilot models before roll out. The pilots could explore different models for providing universal access to an EHP, including those by using public facilities in that area after being suitably strengthened, empowered and networked, and a combination of public and private facility networks. The pilot models must demonstrate the comparative advantages and costs of different approaches to UHC that would be appropriate for the level of development and the socio economic context of that state. Medical colleges can be asked to devise rigorous evaluation designs for testing the cost-effectiveness, patient's satisfaction and change in household's out-of-pocket expenses.

20.49. However, before rolling out UHC on pilot mode, preparations for the following items need to be initiated:

1. Frame a national, core Essential Health Package for out-patient and in-patient care for uniform adoption in pilots. It is possible to expand the package of services under RSBY into an EHP, with the vision of replacing an insurance based system with a tax funded UHC system, over a period of time.
2. The State Health Society should be empowered with requisite resources and its capacity built to administer the coverage.
3. Prepare the UHC Plan as a part of the District Health Action Plan of NHM for the pilot districts and identify the additional items to be covered for EHP.
4. Frame and ensure compliance with Standard Treatment and Referral Guidelines.
5. Strengthen the State and District programme management units to implement the EHP.
6. A robust and effective Health Management Information System which, in the best case scenario, tracks every health encounter and would enable assessment of performance and help in allocating resources to facilities.
7. Register all resident families in the area covered.
8. Build an effective system of community involvement in planning, management, oversight and accountability.
9. Build an effective community oversight and grievance redressal system through active involvement of Local Self-Government Agencies and Civil Society.
10. Develop and strengthen Monitoring and Independent Evaluation Mechanisms.

OUTCOME INDICATORS FOR TWELFTH PLAN

20.50. The Twelfth Plan must work towards national health outcome goals, which target health indicators. The national health goals, which would be aggregates of State wise goals (Table 20.4), are the following:

1. *Reduction of Infant Mortality Rate (IMR) to 25*: At the recent rate of decline of 5 per cent per year, India is projected to have an IMR of 36 by 2015 and 32 by 2017. An achievement of the MDG of reducing IMR to 27 by 2015 would require further acceleration of this historical rate of decline. If this accelerated rate is sustained, the country can achieve an IMR of 25 by 2017.
2. *Reduction of Maternal Mortality Ratio (MMR) to 100*: At the recent rate of decline of 5.8 per cent per annum India is projected to have an MMR

TABLE 20.4
State-Wise Targets on IMR and MMR in Twelfth Plan

Sl. No	Name of the States/UTs	Recent Status			Target for Twelfth Plan		
		IMR	MMR	Anaemia	IMR	MMR	Anaemia
	India	**44**	**212**	**55.3**	**25**	**100**	**28**
1	Andhra Pradesh	43	134	62.9	25	61	31
2	Arunachal Pradesh	32	NA	50.6	19	–	25
3	Assam	55	390	69.5	32	177	35
4	Bihar	44	261	67.4	26	119	34
5	Chhattisgarh	48	269	57.5	28	122	28
6	Goa	11	NA	38	6	–	19
7	Gujarat	41	148	55.3	24	67	28
8	Haryana	44	153	56.1	26	65	28
9	Himachal Pradesh	38	NA	43.3	22	–	22
10	Jammu & Kashmir	41	NA	52.1	24	–	26
11	Jharkhand	39	261	69.5	23	109	35
12	Karnataka	35	178	51.5	15	80	26
13	Kerala	12	81	32.8	6	37	16
14	Madhya Pradesh	59	269	56	34	122	28
15	Manipur	11	NA	35.7	6	–	18
16	Maharashtra	25	104	48.4	15	47	24
17	Meghalaya	52	NA	47.2	30	–	24
18	Mizoram	34	NA	38.6	20	–	19
19	Nagaland	21	NA	NA	12	–	–
20	Odisha	57	258	61.2	33	117	31
21	Punjab	30	172	38	16	78	19
22	Rajasthan	52	318	53.1	30	145	27
23	Sikkim	26	NA	60	15	–	28
24	Tamil Nadu	22	97	53.2	13	44	27
25	Tripura	29	NA	65.1	17	–	33
26	Uttar Pradesh	57	359	49.9	32	163	20
27	Uttarakhand	36	359	55.2	21	163	28
28	West Bengal	32	145	63.2	11	66	32
29	Andaman & Nicobar Islands	23	NA	NA	12	–	–
30	Delhi	28	NA	44.3	15	–	22
31	Chandigarh	20	NA	NA	12	–	–
32	Dadra & Nagar Haweli	35	NA	NA	20	–	–
33	Daman & Diu	22	NA	NA	13	–	–
34	Lakshadweep	24	NA	NA	14	–	–
35	Puducherry	19	NA	NA	11	–	–

Note: States which have opted for targets more ambitious than on pro-rate basis are coloured maroon.

of 139 by 2015 and 123 by 2017. An achievement of the Millennium Development Goal (MDG) of reducing MMR to 109 by 2015 would require an acceleration of this historical rate of decline. At this accelerated rate of decline, the country can achieve an MMR of 100 by 2017.

3. *Reduction of Total Fertility Rate (TFR) to 2.1*: India is on track for the achievement of a TFR target of 2.1 by 2017, which is necessary to achieve net replacement level of unity, and realise the long cherished goal of the National Health Policy, 1983 and National Population Policy of 2000.

4. *Prevention, and reduction of under-nutrition in children under 3 years* to half of NFHS-3 (2005–06) levels: Underweight children are at an increased risk of mortality and morbidity. At the current rate of decline, the prevalence of underweight children is expected to be 29 per cent by 2015, and 27 per cent by 2017. An achievement of the MDG of reducing undernourished children under 3 years to 26 per cent by 2015 would require an acceleration of this historical rate of decline. The country needs to achieve a reduction in below 3 year child under-nutrition to half of 2005–06 (NFHS) levels by 2017. This particular health outcome has a very direct bearing on the broader commitment to security of life, as do MMR, IMR, anaemia and child sex ratio.

5. *Prevention and reduction of anaemia among women aged 15–49 years* to 28 per cent: Anaemia, an underlying determinant of maternal mortality and low birth weight, is preventable and treatable by a very simple intervention. The prevalence of anaemia needs to be steeply reduced to 28 per cent by the end of the Twelfth Plan.

6. *Raising child sex ratio in the 0–6 year age group from 914 to 950*: Like anaemia, child sex ratio is another important indicator which has been showing a deteriorating trend, and needs to be targeted for priority attention.

7. *Prevention and reduction of burden of Communicable and Non-Communicable diseases (including mental illnesses) and injuries*: State wise and national targets for each of these conditions will be set by the Ministry of Health and Family Welfare (MoHFW) as robust systems are put in place to measure their burden. Broadly, the goals of communicable diseases shall be as indicated in Table 20.5.

8. *Reduction of poor households' out-of-pocket expenditure*: Out-of-pocket expenditure on health care is a burden on poor families, leads to impoverishment and is a regressive system of financing. Increase in public health spending to 1.87 per cent of GDP by the end of the Twelfth Plan, cost-free access to essential medicines in public facilities, regulatory measures proposed in the Twelfth Plan are likely to lead to increase in share of public spending. The Twelfth Plan measures will also aim to reduce out-of-pocket spending as a proportion of private spending on health.

FINANCING FOR HEALTH

20.51. In the Twelfth Plan, general tax revenues would be the principle source of finance for publicly delivered health services supplemented by partnerships with the private sector and, contribution by corporates as a part of their Corporate Social Responsibility. A designated sin tax to finance a part

TABLE 20.5
National Health Goals for Communicable Diseases

Disease	Twelfth Plan Goal
Tuberculosis	Reduce annual incidence and mortality by half
Leprosy	Reduce prevalence to <1/10000 population and incidence to zero in all districts
Malaria	Annual Malaria Incidence of <1/1000
Filariasis	<1 per cent microfilaria prevalence in all districts
Dengue	Sustaining case fatality rate of <1 per cent
Chikungunya	Containment of outbreaks
Japanese Encephalitis	Reduction in mortality by 30 per cent
Kala-azar	Elimination by 2015, that is, <1 case per 10000 population in all blocks
HIV/AIDS	Reduce new infections to zero and provide comprehensive care and support to all persons living with HIV/AIDS and treatment services for all those who require it.

TABLE 20.6
Budget Support for Departments of MoHFW in Twelfth Plan (2012–17)

(Figures in ₹ Crores)

Budget Support for Central Departments in Eleventh Plan (2007–12) and Twelfth Plan (2012–17) Projections (₹ Crores)

Department of MoHFW	Eleventh Plan Expenditure	Twelfth Plan Outlay	% Increase
Department of Health and Family Welfare	83,407	2,68,551	322%
Department of Ayurveda, Yoga and Naturopathy, Unani, Siddha and Homoeopathy (AYUSH)	2,994	10,044	335%
Department of Health Research	1,870	10,029	536%
Aids Control	1,305	11,394	873%
Total MoHFW	89,576	3,00,018	335%

of the health budget can lead to reduced consumption of these harmful items (as tobacco and alcohol) and could be considered.

20.52. For financing the Twelfth Plan the projections envisage increasing total public funding, plan and non-plan, on core health from 1.04 per cent of GDP in 2011–12 to 1.87 per cent of GDP by the end of the Twelfth Plan. In such an event, the funding in the Central Plan would increase to 3 times the Eleventh Plan levels involving an annual increase by 34 per cent (Table 20.6). With the incentive measures proposed, States' total funding, Plan and Non-plan, on Health is expected to increase to three times the Eleventh Plan levels involving a similar annual increase. The Central and State funding for Health, as a proportion of total public sector health funding will remain at 2011–12 levels of 33 per cent and 67 per cent respectively.

20.53. When viewed in the perspective of the broader health sector, which includes schemes of Ministries other than Health aimed at improving the health status of people, namely Drinking Water and Sanitation, Mid-day Meal and Integrated Child Development Services Scheme the total Government expenditure as a proportion of GDP in the Twelfth Plan is likely to increase from 1.94 per cent of GDP in the last year of the Eleventh Plan to 3.04 per cent in the corresponding year of the Twelfth Plan.

FUNDING AS AN INSTRUMENT OF INCENTIVE AND REFORM

20.54. In the Twelfth Plan, a paradigm shift is envisaged in Central Government funding to ensure that sufficient amounts are made available and, further that they leverage a comparable effort from the States. In the Approach Paper to the Twelfth Plan, it was stated that we should aim at raising the total expenditure on health in the Centre and the States (including both Plan and Non-Plan) to 2.5 per cent of GDP by the end of the Twelfth Plan period. Accordingly, the allocations proposed for the Twelfth Plan makes Health a priority and will allow Central Plan expenditure to expand by about 34 per cent per year. Since the expenditure by the States is double the expenditure by the Centre, it is necessary to ensure that the States match the effort. If this is achieved, the total expenditure of the Centre and the States on Core Health would rise to about 1.87 per cent of GDP at the end of the Twelfth Plan period.

20.55. A key objective is to ensure that the States increase their expenditure on health at the same rate as the Centre. This may become possible if the transfer to the States is made conditional upon a higher expenditure by the States on health. States would be eligible to receive assistance through an incentive grant on the lines being recommended for all Centrally Sponsored Schemes. They would be eligible if they maintain their health expenditure (Plan and Non-Plan) as a proportion of their budget at the base level (average of last three years) at the minimum, and also prepare a State wide health sector plan based on District Health plans. The incentive grant could be operated as an instrument of equity between states, where both performance and need is recognised in making allocative decisions. The details of the proposed arrangement will be worked out by the Ministry of Health and Family Welfare in consultation with Planning Commission.

20.56. Flexibility in Central funding for States may be built in so that States take the lead in devising plans suited to their health needs. The proposal for a flexi fund to the States is being recommended for all Centrally Sponsored Schemes in the Twelfth Plan. Accordingly, in the health sector, within the broad national parameters, States would have the flexibility to plan and implement their own Health Action Plans. A fixed portion of National Health Mission funds could be earmarked to States and UTs, using an objective formula based on the total population and health lag of the State; these baseline funds would be allotted and made known to the States. A sector-wide Memorandum of Understanding (MoU) between the State and Central Government may formalise mutual commitments and provide strategic direction for health sector reforms.

OTHER MODELS OF FINANCING

20.57. *Public–Private Partnerships*: PPPs offer an opportunity to tap the material, human and managerial resources of the private sector for public good. But experience with PPP has shown that Government's capacity to negotiate and manage it is not effective. Without effective regulatory mechanisms, fulfillment of contractual obligations suffers from weak oversight and monitoring. It is necessary, as the HLEG has argued, to move away from ad hoc PPPs to well negotiated and managed contracts that are regulated effectively keeping foremost the health of the '*aam-admi*'. Health has been included with other infrastructure sectors which are eligible for Viability Gap Funding up to a ceiling of 20 per cent of total project costs under a PPP scheme. As a result, private sector could propose and commission projects, such as hospitals and medical colleges outside metropolitan areas, which are not remunerative per se, and claim up to 20 per cent of the project cost as grant from the Government. Some models of PPP in healthcare covering Primary Health Care, Diagnostic services, Hospitals which are currently being implemented in the States are illustrated in Box 20.3. These can be considered wherever appropriate for replication and upscaling.

20.58. PPP arrangements should address issues of compliance with regulatory requirements, observance of Standard Treatment Guidelines and delivery of affordable care. An additional model for consideration is the Not-for-profit Public Private Partnership (NPPP) being followed in the International Institute of Information Technology (IIIT), which have been set up as fully autonomous institutions, with partnership of the Ministry of Human Resource Development, Governments of respective States and industry members. PPP and Not-for-Profit PPP models can be considered in order to expand capacities for tertiary care in the Twelfth Plan.

20.59. *Resource generation by facilities and Colleges*: Given the gap in need and availability of tertiary care facilities and to ensure maximisation of benefits from limited public funds, public facilities should be encouraged to part-finance their recurring costs by mobilising contributions (including under Corporate Social Responsibility) and Internal Extra-Budgetary Resources. Under the recently drafted Companies Bill, the Government has proposed that companies should earmark 2 per cent of their average profits of the preceding three years for Corporate Social Responsibility (CSR) activities. CSR is mandatory for Central Public Sector Enterprises, the guidelines of which issued by the Department of Public Enterprises include health service as one of the eligible components. To avail of this opportunity, all publicly funded health care facilities would be allowed to receive donations, and funding from companies under their Corporate Social Responsibility head. Adequate safeguards have to be built in so as to ensure 'no-frills funding' and that donations are not used to influence the policies or practices of healthcare facilities in any way. All medical colleges should be encouraged to develop their own corpus to attain financial flexibility over a period of time. Tamil Nadu has issued guidelines to authorise Medical Officers in charge of particular healthcare facilities to enter into MoUs with interested persons to receive contributions for capital or recurrent expenditure in the provision and maintenance of facilities. On available models for self-generation of revenues, the option for cross-subsidy in line with the Aravind eye care system based in Tamil Nadu could also be explored. Tertiary care

> **Box 20.3**
> **Public–Private Partnerships (PPP) in Health Sector**
>
> *Tertiary Care: Rajiv Gandhi Super-speciality Hospital, Raichur, Karnataka*
> Contracting Arrangements: Government of Karnataka and Apollo Hospitals
> Type of Partnership: Joint Venture (Management Contract)
> Services: Provides super-speciality clinical care services and management of Hospital. Free Out-patient services for BPL patients.
>
> *Rural Health Care Delivery and management of PHCs*
> Contracting Arrangements: Karuna Trust and Government of Arunachal Pradesh
> Type of Partnership: Contracting in
> Services: Manages 11 PHC's, provides health care facilities to the local population.
>
> *Labs, Drug Supply and Diagnostic Services: Hindlabs*
> Contracting Arrangements: MoHFW and HLL Life Care Ltd
> Type of Partnership: Contracting in
> Services: A novel initiative, delivers high end diagnostic services at CGHS rates
>
> *Health Insurance: Community Health Insurance Scheme*
> Contracting Arrangements: Karuna Trust, National Insurance Co. and Government of Karnataka
> Type of Partnership: Joint Venture
> Services: A community health insurance scheme to improve the access and utilisation of health services
>
> *Outreach/Health Delivery: Mobile Health Service in Sunderban, W. Bengal*
> Contracting Arrangements: Government of West Bengal and Non-profit NGO
> Type of Partnership: Contracting in (Joint Venture)
> Services: Mobile boat based health services and access to health services in remote areas
>
> *RCH Services: Merry Gold Health Network (MGHN) and SAMBHAV Voucher Scheme in UP*
> Contracting Arrangements: Joint endeavour of Government of India and USAID through UP SIFPSA
> Type of Partnership: Social Franchising network and Voucher system
> Services: Provide FP/RCH services through accredited private providers

facilities would have an incentive to generate revenues if they are allowed flexibility in the utilisation of self-generated resources within broad policy parameters laid down by the Government.

RASHTRIYA SWASTHYA BIMA YOJANA (RSBY)

20.60. Health insurance is a common form of medical protection all over the world and until the Eleventh Plan, it was available only to government employees, workers in the organised sector; private health insurance has been in operation for several years, but its coverage has been limited. The percentage of the total population estimated to be covered under these schemes was only 16 per cent. The poor did not have any insurance for in-patient care. The 'Rashtriya Swasthya Bima Yojana' (RSBY), introduced in 2007, was designed to meet the health insurance needs of the poor.

20.61. RSBY provides for 'cash-less', smart card based health insurance cover of ₹30,000 per annum to each enrolled family, comprising up to five individuals. The beneficiary family pays only ₹30 per annum as registration/renewal fee. The scheme covers hospitalisation expenses (Out-patient expenses are not covered), including maternity benefit, and pre-existing diseases. A transportation cost of ₹100 per visit is also paid. The premium payable to insurance agencies is funded by Central and State Governments in a 75:25 ratio, which is relaxed to 90:10 for the

North-East region and Jammu and Kashmir. The maximum premium by the Central Government is limited to ₹750 per insured family per year.

20.62. RSBY was originally limited to Below Poverty Line (BPL) families but was later extended to building and other construction workers, MGNREGA beneficiaries, street vendors, beedi workers, and domestic workers. The scheme is currently being implemented in 24 States/UTs. About 3.3 crore families have been covered as on date and 43 lakh persons have availed hospitalisation under the scheme till November 2012.

20.63. Key feature of RSBY is that it provides for private health service providers to be included in the system, if they meet certain standards and agree to provide cash-less treatment which is reimbursed by the insurance company. This has the advantage of giving patients a choice between alternative service providers where such alternatives are available. Several State Governments (such as those of Andhra Pradesh and Tamil Nadu) have introduced their own health insurance schemes, which often have a more generous total cover.

20.64. A general problem with any 'fee for service' payment system financed by an insurance mechanism is that it creates an incentive for unnecessary treatment, which in due course raises costs and premiums. There is some evidence that this is happening and it is necessary to devise corrective steps to minimise it. Some groups oppose insurance schemes per se on these grounds, but that is not realistic. The beneficiary is able to choose from alternative care givers covered by a common insurance scheme. Experience with the RSBY, and with the other State-specific insurance schemes, needs to be thoroughly studied so that suitable corrective measures can be introduced before integrating these schemes into a framework of Universal Health Coverage (UHC). The shortcomings of RSBY noted so far include high transaction costs due to insurance intermediaries, inability to control provider induced demand, and lack of coverage for primary health and out patient care. Fragmentation of different levels of care can lead to an upward escalation towards the secondary level of patients who should preferably be handled at the primary or even preventive stages. The RSBY also does not take into account state specific variations in disease profiles and health needs.

Innovative Payment Methods to Improve Outcomes

20.65. The weakness of line item budget payment methods for public facilities is well documented. More responsive resource allocation is a challenge for the Government. Investments in public facilities will translate into better access, coverage, quality of care and superior health outcomes only if these facilities and their personnel perform their expected tasks in a responsive manner. Payment methods could be used as one of the instruments to improve public sector performance. For example, managers and health personnel in public sector facilities could be paid bonus for achieving higher coverage of services as measured by reduction in the use of private sector services in the coverage area (unless these are contracted in by the Government); they can be paid further incentives for delivering preventive care services effectively and achieving measurable health outcomes in their respective areas. UHC pilots to be rolled out by States could experiment with different methods of organisation and delivery of services, and payment systems so that resources allocated are able to generate better health outcomes.

Health Care for Government Employees

20.66. There is a proposal for introduction of a health insurance scheme for the Central Government employees and pensioners on a pan-India basis, with special focus on pensioners living in non-CGHS areas. The proposal is to make this scheme voluntary cum contributory for serving employees and pensioners. However, it is proposed to be made compulsory for the new entrants in Government service.

HEALTH AND MEDICAL REGULATION

20.67. Regulations for food, drugs and the medical profession requires lead action by the Central Government not only because these subjects fall under the Concurrent List in the Constitution, but also because the lack of consistency and well enforced standards hugely impacts the common citizen and diminishes health outcomes. Keeping in view the need to place authority and accountability together, the proposed Public Heath Cadre in States would be expected to be the single point for enforcement of all health related regulations.

20.68. There is also an urgent need to strengthen the regulatory systems in the States, where most of the implementation rests. This would entail the strengthening of and establishment of testing labs and capacity building of functionaries. Such proposals will be part-funded under the National Health Mission (NHM). Regulation can be made affordable and effective by encouraging self-regulation, and entrusting responsibility to Public Health officers.

DRUG REGULATION

20.69. E-governance systems that inter-connect all licensing and registration offices and laboratories, GPS based sample collection systems and online applications for licensing would be introduced. A repository of approved formulations at both State and national levels would be developed. The drug administration system would build capacity in training, and encourage self regulation.

20.70. The MoHFW would ensure that irrational Fixed Dose Combinations (FDCs) and hazardous drugs are weeded out in a time bound manner.

20.71. Pharmaco-vigilance, post-marketing surveillance, Adverse Drug Response Monitoring, quality control, testing and re-evaluation of registered products would be accorded priority under drug regulation.

20.72. Use of generic names or the International Non-proprietary Name (INN) would be made compulsory and encouraged at all stages of Government procurement, distribution, prescription and use, as it contributes to a sound system of procurement and distribution, drug information and rational use at every level of the health care system. Established brand manufacturers would be encouraged to bid for Government procurement, but should provide medicines in non-propriety names.

20.73. The Drugs and Cosmetics Act would be amended to include medical devices incorporating provisions for their risk-based classification, clinical trials, conformity assessments and penalties. As recommended by the Mashelkar Committee, a Central Drug Authority needs to be set up. This authority would review the issuance of licenses for manufacture and sale of drugs. Once this Authority is in place, suitable strengthening of its infrastructure and laboratories would be done. The Government would mandate that labels on drugs and food fully disclose all its ingredients.

20.74. Strengthening of existing, and creation of new drug testing laboratories is essential to ensure the quality of drugs being produced in India, whether they are used for domestic distribution or for export to other countries.

20.75. A National List of Essential Medicines would be made operational with the introduction of Standard Treatment Guidelines, including for AYUSH. It would be printed and supplied to all facilities at regular intervals. These guidelines would incorporate generic prescriptions. Implementation of Standard Treatment Guidelines in the public and private sectors is a priority to address drug resistance, promote rational prescriptions and use of drugs, and contain health care costs.

20.76. Pharmaceutical marketing and aggressive promotion also contributes to irrational use. There is a need for a mandatory code for identifying and penalising unethical promotion on the part of Pharma companies. Mandated disclosure by Pharmaceutical companies of the expenditure incurred on drug promotion, ghost writing in promotion of pharma products to attract disqualification of the author and penalty on the company, and vetting of drug related material in Continuing Medical Education would be considered. To avoid medical conflicts of interest, legislation requiring drug companies to disclose payments made to doctors for research, consulting, lectures, travel and entertainment would also be considered.

20.77. MoHFW would encourage public and patient education in the appropriate use of drugs, particularly antibiotics and antimicrobials, since it would benefit individual patients and public health.

20.78. Institutional frameworks for regulation of clinical research and trials to ensure safety of research subjects will be a priority. In addition, efficient assessment and approval of new technologies, drugs and devices would also be done. The process of approval and introduction of new medical technologies, and devices, would be notified. India still has to safeguard itself from TRIPS plus provisions which will evergreen patents for more than 20 years. Safeguards like compulsory licensing, parallel imports, and so on, need to be adopted to protect nation's public health.

FOOD REGULATION

20.79. The newly established Food Safety and Standards Authority of India (FSSAI) would strive to improve transparency in its functioning and decision making. Bio-safety would be an integral part of any risk assessment being undertaken by FSSAI.

20.80. Food surveys would be carried out regularly and their results made public. An annual report on state of food safety would be published.

20.81. Policies to promote production and consumption of healthy food would be developed. Sale and consumption of unhealthy food would be discouraged in general and in schools in particular. Public information campaigns to create awareness on food safety matters will be launched.

20.82. An appropriate module on food safety and bio-safety will be introduced in the Medical and Nursing curriculum.

REGULATION OF MEDICAL PRACTICE

20.83. The provisions for registration and regulation of clinical establishments would be implemented effectively; all clinical establishments would also be networked on the Health Information System, and mandated to share data on nationally required parameters. The Government would consider mandating evidence based and cost-effective clinical protocols of care, which all providers would be obliged to follow. It would endeavour to gradually move towards a regime where clinical decision-making would be routinely subjected to prescription audits to confirm compliance. The rights of patients to obtain rational treatment of good quality at reasonable cost would be protected. Professional councils and faculty in medical colleges shall be encouraged to undertake prescription audits to assess extent of compliance with Standard Treatment Guidelines for identifying violations of guidelines and taking appropriate action. There is a need to revise and strengthen the existing regulatory mechanism for medical practice to prevent wilful negligence and malpractice. Grievance redressal mechanisms would be put in place.

20.84. Since there are no legislations on registration of clinical establishments in many States, and the ones existing (as in States of Andhra Pradesh, Maharashtra, Delhi, Madhya Pradesh, Manipur, Nagaland, Odisha, Punjab and West Bengal) have major gaps, all States will be persuaded to adopt the Central Act under Clause (1) of Article 252 of the Constitution.

20.85. An appropriate regulatory mechanism would be considered to ensure compulsory rural service by medical graduates. Concurrently, a set of monetary and non-monetary incentives would be built up to encourage doctors and allied health cadres to serve in rural areas.

20.86. Effective enforcement of the provisions of Pre-Conception and Pre-Natal Diagnostic Techniques (Prohibition of Sex Selection) Act and relentless public awareness measures would be put in place. A concerted societal conscientisation and communication campaign would be launched to create value for the girl child and women, along with affirmative action for girls. Local Self Government Institutions, specially the newly elected women panchayat and urban local body members, would be mobilised to change deeply entrenched behaviours and mindsets about the girl child. Panchayats and urban local bodies which are able to achieve a reversal of the falling trend in child sex ratio would be recognised and awarded, along the lines of the Nirmal Gram Puraskar.

NATIONAL LEVEL TERTIARY CARE INSTITUTIONS

20.87. A single Central Sector Scheme on 'National Level Tertiary Care Institutions' will fund up-gradation of existing medical colleges and converting tertiary care facilities of the Central Government across different departments into teaching institutions.

20.88. In the Twelfth Five Year Plan a concerted effort needs to be made to confer greater autonomy to the existing Tertiary Care Institution and Hospitals. They need to be delegated greater administrative and financial powers and need to be empowered to function as effective Board managed entities (see Box 20.4).

20.89. In the Central Government sector, more AIIMS like Institutions (ALIs) will be established during the Twelfth Plan period in addition to the eight already approved. These would be completed and made operational during the Plan period. They will serve as composite centres for continued professional education, and multi-skilling of health workers.

20.90. The existing teaching institutions will be strengthened to provide leadership in research and practice on different medical conditions, and research themes. Priorities include Cancer, Arthritis and musculo-skeletal diseases, Child Health, Diabetes, Mental Health and Neuro Sciences, Geriatrics, Biomedical and Bioengineering, Hospital and Health Care Administration, Nursing Education and Research, Information Technology and Tele-Medicine and Complementary Medicine.

20.91. Centres of Excellence need to be created for training public health professionals in epidemiology, entomology and microbiology for effective disease surveillance and disease outbreak investigations and for effectively responding to outbreaks, epidemics and disasters, and also for AYUSH.

20.92. A continuous stream of qualified teachers would be required for serving in the new teaching institutions proposed. Apex institutions of learning like AIIMS, Post Graduate Institute of Medical Education and Research (PGIMER) and Jawaharlal Institute of Post Graduate Medical Education and Research (JIPMER) will be geared to build capacity in regional and State teaching institutions for training of trainers.

20.93. A new category of mid-level health-workers named Community Health Officers, could be developed for primary health care. These workers would be trained after Class XII for a three year period to become competent to provide essential preventive and primary care and implement public health activities at sub-centre level. Details of their functions, qualifications, designations, placement and career tracks within the health system need to be worked out. This new category offers an opportunity to break through professional silos, develop competencies that draw upon different but complementary streams of knowledge and help generate employment while meeting health needs of under-served populations. These Community Health Officers would be groomed to discharge public health functions.

20.94. Simultaneously, programmes for Continuing Medical Education would be strengthened and expanded. Agencies such as the National Academy

---

Box 20.4
Institute of Liver and Biliary Sciences, Delhi: A Model of Autonomy and Sustainable Financing

The Institute is a super specialty medical institute under Government of NCT Delhi that seeks to provide quality tertiary health care. Its services: are free for BPL card holders of Delhi, and charges for other classes are competitive. Its business model aims at attaining efficiency and self sustenance.

The Institute is governed by a Society in an autonomus manner, which aims to combine the skills and structure of academic Universities, clinical and research acumen of the super-specialists and the managerial skills of the corporate world.

of Medical Sciences can play a useful role in providing good quality teaching material and also help in its dissemination, by using the National Knowledge Network.

20.95. Good health planning requires high quality data on estimates of supply and demand of various categories of health workers. Accurate data on the number, specialisation, distribution, status of practice of health professionals in the country is, however, not available. Professional Councils in respective States and at the national level should therefore, continually update their records on Human Resources, trying to take into account the extent of internal and international migration The MoHFW would exercise due vigilance to ensure this.

20.96. Licensing of medical professionals with a view to control the entry of unqualified persons into the market is governed by various laws. The National Commission for Human Resources and Health (NCHRH) would be created as an overarching regulatory body for medical education and allied health sciences with the dual purpose of reforming the current regulatory framework and enhancing the supply of skilled human resource in the health sector. The proposed Commission would subsume many functions of the existing councils, namely Medical Council of India, Dental Council of India, Nursing Council of India and Pharmacy Council of India. The proposed NCHRH would also constitute a National Board for Health Education (NBHE) and a National Evaluation and Assessment Committee (NEAC) with a mandate to prescribe minimum standards for health education, and developing and maintaining a system of accreditation of health educational institutes respectively. Apart from this, a National Council has also been proposed to be set up under NCHRH to inter alia ensure ethical standards among medical professionals. The NCHRH is expected to assess the demand and availability to plan for the creation of the right mix of human resource in health.

INFORMATION TECHNOLOGY IN HEALTH

20.97. Information Technology can be used in at least four different ways to improve health care and systems:

1. Support public health decision making for better management of health programmes and health systems at all levels
2. Support to service providers for better quality of care and follow up
3. Provision of quality services in remote locations through Tele-medicine
4. Supporting education, and continued learning in medicine and health

20.98. A composite HIS, when fully operational, would incorporate the following:

1. Universal registration of births, deaths and cause of death. Maternal and infant death reviews.
2. Nutritional surveillance, particularly among women in the reproductive age group and children under six years of age.
3. Disease surveillance based on reporting by service providers and clinical laboratories (public and private) to detect and act on disease outbreaks and epidemics.
4. Out-patient and in-patient information through Electronic Medical Records (EMR) to reduce response time in emergencies and improve general hospital administration.
5. Data on Human Resource within the public and private health system
6. Financial management in the public health system to streamline resource allocation and transfers, and accounting and payments to facilities, providers and beneficiaries. Ultimately, it would enable timely compilation of the National Health Accounts on an annual basis.
7. A national repository of teaching modules, case records for different medical conditions in textual and audio-visual formats for use by teaching faculty, students and practitioners for Continuing Medical Education.

8. Tele-medicine and consultation support to doctors at primary and secondary facilities from specialists at tertiary centres.
9. Nation-wide registries of clinical establishments, manufacturing units, drug-testing laboratories, licensed drugs and approved clinical trials to support regulatory functions of Government.
10. Access of public to their own health information and medical records, while preserving confidentiality of data.
11. Programme Monitoring support for National Health Programmes to help identify programme gaps.

20.99. To achieve these goals, computer with internet connectivity would be ensured in every PHC and all higher level health facilities in this Plan period. Connectivity can be extended to sub-centres either through computers or through cell phones, depending on their state of readiness and the skill-set of their functionaries. All District hospitals would be linked by tele-medicine channels to leading tertiary care centres, and all intra-District hospitals would be linked to the District hospital and optionally to higher centres.

20.100. The role of the MoHFW would be to lay IT system standards, and define indicators which would be openly shared. States will be funded for their initiatives in this field at primary or secondary levels through the National Health Mission. Health surveys would be annually conducted to generate district level information on health status, which will also serve to verify the accuracy of routine health information system

NATIONAL HEALTH MISSION (NHM)

20.101. The Prime Minister in his Independence Day speech, 2012 had declared: 'After the success of the National Rural health Mission, we now want to expand the scope of health services in our towns also. The National Rural Health Mission will be converted into a National Health Mission (NHM) which would cover all villages and towns in the country.'

20.102. The gains of the flagship programme of NRHM will be strengthened under the umbrella of NHM which will have universal coverage. The focus on covering rural areas and rural population will continue.

20.103. A major component of NHM is proposed to be a Scheme for providing primary health care to the urban poor, particularly those residing in slums. Modalities and institutional mechanisms for roll-out of this scheme are being worked out by the Ministry of Health and Family Welfare in consultation with Planning Commission. NHM would give the States greater flexibility to make multi-year plans for systems strengthening, and addressing threats to health in both rural and urban areas through interventions at Primary, Secondary and Tertiary levels of care. The roles and responsibilities of the Centre and States in the health sector would be made operational through instruments such as State specific and Sector-wide Memoranda of Understanding (MoU). The MoU mechanism is a tool for collective priority setting, involves agreement on measurable outcomes and their relative weight, allows flexibility in implementation and accountability based on objective assessment and incentivisation of performance.

20.104. The targets in the MoU would be finalised through a consultative process so that there is a consensus. The MoU will cover the entire health sector, be subject to rigorous monitoring, and linked to a performance based appraisal and incentive system. The MoU would include important policy reforms, which may not necessarily have budgetary implications such as regulation, HR policies, inter-sectoral convergence, use of generic medicines. The MoU can have a set of obligatory parameters, state specific optional parameters and reform parameters. The MoU will follow the log frame approach in setting inputs, outputs, outcomes and impact goals for the districts and States. System-wide MoUs between Centre and States would allow a lot of flexibility to the latter to develop their own strategies and plans for delivery of services, while committing the States to quantitative, verifiable and mutually agreed upon outputs and outcomes.

20.105. In addition to the Common Review Mission, a methodology of external concurrent evaluation would be finalised and put in place to assess the progress in MoU goals. These reports will be placed before the Mission Steering Group at the national level and before the Governing Body of the State and district health societies. All major programme components would be evaluated as part of operational research and programme evaluation.

20.106. The National Health Mission will incorporate the following core principles.

CORE PRINCIPLES

Universal Coverage

20.107. The NHM shall extend all over the country, both in urban and rural areas and promote universal access to a continuum of cashless, health services from primary to tertiary care. Separate strategies shall be followed for the urban areas, using opportunities such as easier access to secondary and tertiary facilities, and better transport and telecommunication services. There is greater scope for contracting arrangements with the private sector in urban areas, to fill gaps in strengthened public facilities. Area specific NHM plans shall address the challenges unique to their areas such as overcrowding, poor sanitation, pollution, traffic injuries, higher rates of crime and risky personal behaviour in urban areas.

Achieving Quality Standards

20.108. The IPHS standards will be revised to incorporate standards of care and service to be offered at each level of health care facility. Standards would include the complete range of conditions, covering emergency, RCH, prevention and management of Communicable and Non-Communicable diseases incorporating essential medicines, and Essential and Emergency Surgical Care (EESC).

20.109. All government and publicly financed private health care facilities would be expected to achieve and maintain these standards. An in-house quality management system will be built into the design of each facility, which will regularly measure its quality achievements. Facilities will be provided with an incentive, which they can share with their teams, to achieve and improve their quality rating. The service and quality standards shall be defined, made consistent with requirements under the Clinical Establishments Act, and performance of each registered facility made public, and periodically ranked. The work of quality monitoring will be suitably institutionalised.

20.110. To enable access to quality diagnostic facilities, pooling of resources available with different agencies, their up-gradation wherever needed, outsourcing and in-sourcing strategies would be adopted.

20.111. The objective would be to achieve a minimum norm of 500 beds per 10 lakh population in an average district. Approximately 300 beds could be at the level of District Hospitals and the remaining distributed judiciously at the CHC level. Where needed, private sector services also may be contracted in to supplement the services provided by the public sector. The sanction of new facilities other than sub-centres should be undertaken only when mapping of access demonstrates the need for new facilities to improve accessibility.

20.112. States would be encouraged to put in place systems for Emergency Medical Referral to bridge the gaps in access to health facilities and need for transport in the event of an emergency. Standards for these services will specify the time taken to transport patients from the location to designated health facilities, and these standards shall be evaluated and followed. The possibility of positioning such referral with the response teams of Fire-Fighting Departments, as is the practice in many developed nations, should be explored. These facilities, once operational, would also help in managing disasters, in terms of early response, search and rescue, emergency care and rehabilitation.

20.113. For ensuring access to health care among under-served populations, the existing Mobile Medical units would be expanded to have a presence in each CHC. Mobile Medical Units may also be dedicated to certain areas, which have moving populations. For example, boat clinics of C-NES in Assam provide curative and emergency care for the population residing in islands and flood plains of the State.

Continuum of Care

20.114. A continuum of care across health facilities helps manage health problems more effectively at the lowest level. For example, if medical colleges, district hospitals, CHCs, PHCs and sub-centres in an area are networked, then the most common disease conditions can be assessed, prevented and managed at appropriate levels. It will avoid fragmentation of care, strengthen primary health care, reduce unnecessary load on secondary and tertiary facilities and assure efficient referral and follow up services. Continuum of care can lead to improvements in quality and patient satisfaction. Such linkages would be built in the Twelfth Plan so that all health care facilities in a region are organically linked with each other, with medical colleges providing the broad vision, leadership and opportunities for skill up-gradation. The potential offered by tele-medicine for remote diagnostics, monitoring and case management needs to be fully realised. Appropriate faculty at the medical college can be given responsibility for training, advising and monitoring the delivery of services in facilities within their allotted jurisdiction. The resources saved in avoiding duplication could be used to universalise the upgrading of standards of health facilities and teaching colleges.

Decentralised Planning

20.115. A key element of the new NHM is that it would provide considerable flexibility to States and Districts to plan for measures to promote health and address the health problems that they face (Box 20.5). The NHM guidelines could provide flexibility to States and districts to plan for results.

20.116. New health facilities would not be set up on a rigid, population based norm, but would aim to be accessible to populations in remote locations and within a defined time period. The need for new facilities of each category would thus be assessed by the districts and States using a 'time to care' approach. This will be done based on a host of contributing factors, including geographic spread of population, nature of terrain, availability of health care facility in the vicinity and availability of transport network. For example, a travel time of 30 minutes to reach a primary healthcare facility, and a total of two hours to reach a FRU could be a reasonable goal. As for staffing, the healthcare facilities should have a basic core staff, with provisions for additional hands in response to an increase in case load, or the range of services

---

Box 20.5
Flexibility and Decentralised Planning: Key Elements of National Health Mission

1. The guidelines of NHM would be indicative and within broad parameters leave the decision on prioritisation of requirements to the best judgement of the States and Districts. Each District would develop, through effective public participation, a multi-year Health Action Plan for prevention, service delivery and systems management. These plans would become the basis for resource allocation and be made public to enable social audits of the progress made towards the goals. The implementation of these plans would involve the local community. The outcomes of these plans would be subject to Community Based Monitoring (CBM).
2. Health Action Plans at District level and below will aim at convergent delivery of services in an integrated manner to the last beneficiary. The District Health Plans would factor in all determinants of health, and assign roles to each agency for achieving convergence. For instance, these plans can leverage the mid-day meal programme for addressing issues of school child malnutrition and anaemia. Joint training of AWWs and ASHAs would be promoted to build camaraderie and clarity on mutual roles and responsibilities. Anganwadi Centres could be used as base stations for ASHAs, and upgraded into health posts for the delivery of essential health services.
3. Innovations in service delivery to improve coverage, quality of care, health outcomes and reduce costs would be encouraged, and recognised.
4. The sector-wide health plans prepared by the States should incorporate all dispensations of health and health care, and all sources of funding. For instance, medical education, AYUSH, AIDS control, Health Research, convergence with ICDS and Drinking Water and Sanitation would find space in the state health plans.

provided. Indian Public Health Standards (IPHS) would be revised accordingly. Individual States can choose from a range of staffing options, including those suggested by the Working Group on NRHM and by the HLEG, both options will be included in the Central funding envelop. Such flexibility to States in location, size and staffing of the health care facilities would ensure optimum utilisation of existing resources, and infrastructure. Every Panchayat and urban municipal ward should have at least one sub-centre. The sub-centre's package of assured services, and consequent staffing will vary according to the epidemiological and health systems contexts.

PRIORITY SERVICES

Access to Essential Medicines in All Public Facilities

20.117. Availability of essential medicines in public sector health facilities free of cost is critical to achieve affordable health care for the bulk of the population. This is the area which provides the speediest scope for improved service delivery in return for allocation of sufficient resources. A set of measures including revision and expansion of the Essential Drugs List, ensuring the rational use of drugs, strengthening the drug regulatory system, and supporting the setting up of national and state drug supply logistics corporations is being recommended as core components. States would be encouraged to plan and partially fund universal access to essential drugs and diagnostic services in all government health care facilities. Drug supply would be linked to centralised procurement at state level to ensure uniform drug quality and cost minimisation by removing intermediaries.

20.118. The provision of essential medicines free of cost must be backed by logistic arrangements to procure generic medicines from suppliers of repute that match pre-qualifying standards. The MoU instrument shall be used to encourage States to adopt the TNMSC model, for professional management of procurement, storage and logistics. Support to rational and generic drug prescription for the private sector requires a different approach. This can be achieved through expansion of the existing Jan Aushadhi stores in all sub-divisions and blocks. These stores could be linked to centralised procurement at state level.

Strategy for Maternal and Child Health

20.119. Maternal and child health care will continue to be a major focus, especially given the inadequate progress in reducing IMR and MMR. Programme monitoring needs to track experiences and outcomes of women rather than only disbursement of cash. Training being provided to the Skilled Birth Attendants (SBA) needs to be evaluated independently. Plans need to be made for rational posting of those SBAs who have received this training, so as to reach the maximum population with skilled attendance at birth. Appropriate area-specific interventions will be made such as equipping Traditional Birth Attendants (TBAs)/dais for safe deliveries, (especially in remote and inaccessible areas) universalising access to the SBA over a period of time, and prioritising better access to emergency obstetric care (both public and private) within a two-hour travel time in cases of complications. The quality of care being provided in routine institutional deliveries needs to be carefully monitored and accessible grievance redressal mechanisms put in place.

20.120. Simple strategies for prevention of pre-term births, and reducing deaths among pre-term babies can make a difference in survival and health of children during the critical first month of life. These will be built into protocols for health workers and standards for health facilities (Figure 20.3).

20.121. Home-based newborn care, drawing on validated models, such as that of Gadchiroli in Maharashtra, and focused efforts to encourage breastfeeding and safe infant and child feeding practices will be promoted. While emphasis on early breastfeeding is a part of Accredited Social Health Activists' (ASHAs) training, special training on neonatal care for community and facility-level health functionaries will result in a faster reduction in IMR. The findings of Maternal Death Reviews and Infant death audits will be used to fill gaps in health systems, in skills and service provision. Control and management of diseases like malaria, TB and HIV/AIDS, and conditions like hypertension and gestational

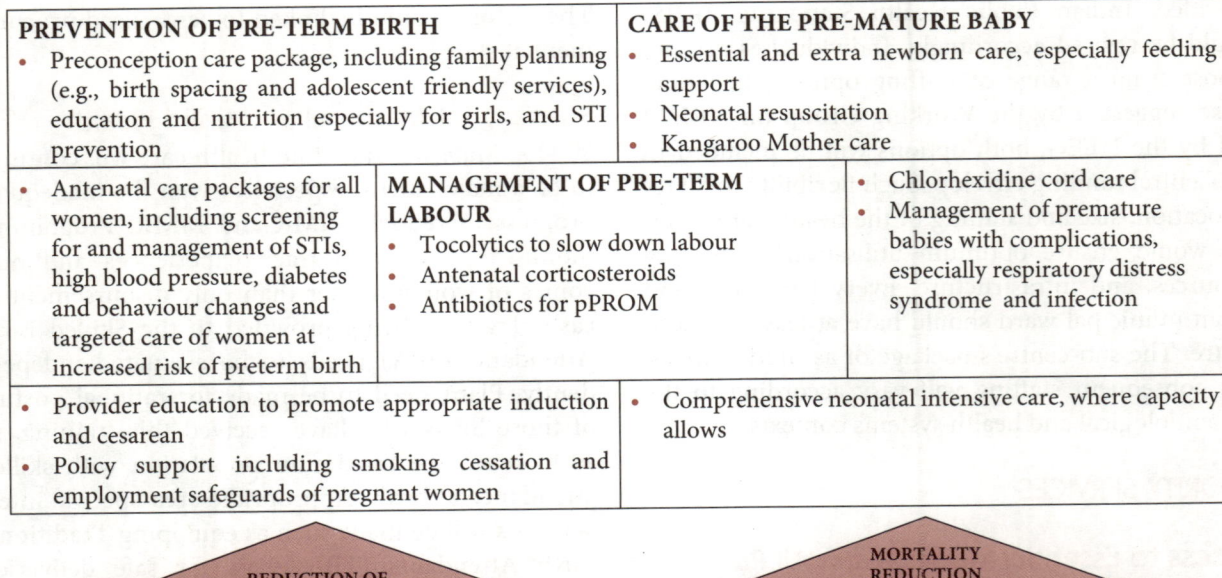

Source: Born too Soon: Global Action Report on Pre-term births, WHO 2012; pPROM: Premature Rupture of Membrane.

FIGURE 20.3: Strategies to Prevent Pre-Term Births and Manage Pre-Term Babies

diabetes which are directly related to maternal mortality would be integrated with RCH service delivery.

20.122. AYUSH doctors, wherever feasible, would to be given SBA, RCH and IMNCI training and their services will be used in meeting unmet needs. This will increase the availability of trained human resource for better outreach of child and maternal health services.

Universal Immunisation Coverage

20.123. The goal of ensuring universal coverage of routine immunisation through campaigns in districts throughout the country is now within reach and will be achieved by the end of the Twelfth Plan. Registered Medical Practitioners (RMPs) will be used in this effort, wherever feasible. There is need for expanding the use of available vaccines for various preventable diseases through an evidence based approach. The existing alternate vaccine delivery mechanism through mobile immunisation services for outreach work will be upgraded. Other disease specific recommended strategies will also be adopted; such as, in the case of measles, periodic Supplemental Immunization Activities (SIAs), that is, mass vaccination campaigns aimed at immunising 100 per cent of a predefined population within several days or weeks, introduction of a routine second dose in high prevalence states, laboratory-supported surveillance, and appropriate management of measles cases. Public awareness of the benefits of immunisation will be built, so that they demand the services. Effective implementation of the Mother and Child Tracking system and Mother and Child Protection Card jointly issued by the MoHFW and the MoWCD would be used in capturing immunisation data better. Electricity supply will be ensured, especially at places where cold chains are maintained.

Family Welfare

20.124. The experience of Indonesia and Japan shows that, as compared to limiting methods, emphasis on family spacing methods like IUCD and male condoms has had a better impact in meeting the unmet needs of couples. A recent study has estimated that meeting unmet contraception needs could cut maternal deaths by one-third. There is, therefore, a need for much more attention to spacing methods such as, long term IUCD. IUCD insertion on fixed days by ANMs (under supervision of LHV for new ANMs) would be encouraged. Availability of MTP by Manual Vacuum Aspiration (MVA) technique and medical abortions will be ensured at fixed points where Mini-Laparotomy is planned to be provided. Services and contraceptive devices would be made easily accessible. This would be achieved through strategies including social marketing, contracting and engaging private providers. Post-partum contraception methods like insertion of IUD which are popular in countries like China, Mexico, and Egypt and male sterilisation would be promoted while ensuring adherence to internationally accepted safety standards.

Communicable Disease Control

20.125. State and District specific action plans will incorporate status and strategies for TB control, with universal and assured access to quality DOTS services. PMDT services will be included in the standards of care and made available in all districts for comprehensively tackling the challenge of drug-resistant TB.

20.126. An increasing incidence of vector borne diseases like malaria, dengue and chikungunya in urban, peri-urban and rural areas because of expanding urbanisation, deficient water and solid waste management has been reported. To control this, the emphasis would be on avoidance of mosquito breeding conditions in homes and workplaces and minimising human–mosquito contact. The spread of zoonotic diseases will also be prevented by strengthening integrated surveillance of transmission between wildlife, close bred veterinary populations and human communities.

20.127. Improved entomological surveillance for source reduction, strengthening and expanding diagnostic services, strengthening case management through standard guidelines, enhanced community participation and inter-sectoral collaboration, enactment and enforcement of civic and building by-laws would be encouraged. Anti-microbial resistance will be closely monitored through effective surveillance, and enforcement of guidelines on the sale and prescription of antibiotics.

20.128. There would also be a thrust on identified geographic areas where the problems are most severe. The strategies employed would be disease management including early case detection and prompt treatment, strengthening of referral services, integrated vector management, use of Long Lasting Insecticidal Nets (LLIN) and larvivorous fishes. Other interventions including behaviour change communication will also be undertaken.

Prevention and Control of Non-Communicable Diseases

20.129. For the escalating threat of NCDs like cardiovascular diseases, diabetes, cancers and chronic respiratory diseases which are emerging as major killers, a package of policy interventions would be taken up. These include raising taxes on tobacco, enforcing bans on tobacco consumption in electronic media, counselling for quitting tobacco, early detection and effective control of high blood pressure and diabetes, screening for common and treatable cancers; and salt reduction in processed foods (Table 20.7).

20.130. Care for the elderly would focus on promoting healthy lifestyles, encouraging care within families, linking strengths of Indian Systems of Medicine with Modern Systems of Medicine in rejuvenation therapies, and preferential attention in all public facilities.

20.131. Problems relating to mental health, especially in conflict zones would be managed with sensitivity at the community level, through better training of community workers and primary care teams, and through education of care givers.

Focus on Public Health

20.132. Insufficient focus on public health is a major weakness of the system and must be urgently corrected. Effective public health management requires a certain degree of expertise. There is an urgent real need for a dedicated Public Health cadre (with support teams comprising of epidemiologists, entomologists, public health nurses, inspectors and male Multi-Purpose Workers) backed by appropriate regulation at the state level. At present, only Tamil Nadu has a dedicated public health cadre. In other

TABLE 20.7
Interventions to Combat Non-Communicable Diseases (NCDs)

Non-Communicable Disease (NCD)	Interventions
1. Tobacco control	Raise taxes on tobacco Clean indoor air legislation Tobacco advertising ban • Information and labelling • Brief advice to help quit tobacco • Counselling to quit
2. CVD prevention	Salt reduction in processed food via voluntary agreement with industry, and/or via legislation Health education through mass media Treatment for high Blood pressure, cholesterol and education
3. Diabetes and complications	Health education on diet and physical activity Diabetes detection and management in primary health care Intensive glycaemic control Retinopathy screening and photocoagulation Neuropathy screening and preventive foot care
4. Cancer	Screening for cervical, breast and oral cancer Strengthening of cancer therapy in District Hospitals
5. Dental Caries	Education on oral health and hygiene; reducing dietary sugars; water fluoridation
6. General measures	• Promote physical activity in schools and society • Restrict marketing of and access to food products high in salt, sugar or unhealthy fats • Targeted early detection and diagnosis using inexpensive technologies

Note: The list is illustrative only.

States, the erstwhile Public Health cadre has been merged with the regular medical cadre. The choice of having a separate Directorate of Public Health on the lines of Tamil Nadu or incorporating it suitably in the existing set-up will be left to the judgement of States.

20.133. A centrally recruited, professionally trained and constitutionally protected service on the lines of All-India services would be the preferred model for the Public Health Service. A second option would be to have separate public health cadres at Centre and States.

20.134. The Centre and States would develop good quality training programmes for public health functionaries, including the suggested new cadre of public health officers.

20.135. Public health officials should be made responsible for the health of all people residing in their assigned areas or jurisdictions, including migrants. Their responsibilities would, thus, not be limited to only those who visit or use the health facilities, but would require them to actively reach out and impact health outcomes in their respective catchment areas. An implication of such an approach would be that all data generated in the facility would be analysed in terms of the denominator, that is, the total population at risk in the jurisdiction of that facility. Public health officials should also be deployed in Municipal areas to assist the Urban Local Bodies in maintaining public health.

20.136. The National Centre for Disease Control (formerly National Institute of Communicable Diseases) shall function as the apex public health institute for providing surveillance, prevention and control of all diseases of public health importance. The upgradation of NCDC covers physical infrastructure including public health labs and additional trained human resource. It is also proposed that NCDC branches will be opened/strengthened in State Headquarters to provide timely technical assistance to the State health authorities in routine disease surveillance and in addressing epidemic-prone diseases.

20.137. Even though the subject of Public Health falls in the State list, a draft Model Public Health legislation has been prepared by the MoHFW, which could serve as a useful reference for States in framing their own Public Health Acts. The experience of Tamil Nadu in prevention of diseases and promotion of health through a Public Health Cadre, and the regulatory mechanism using Public Health Legislation deserve emulation. Also required are systems to implement those Acts, and mechanisms to motivate and involve the community in ensuring that provisions are complied with. One aspect of community-based monitoring could be to conduct public health audits in States, including in major cities and publicise the results to help build public pressure to improve conditions and bridge capacity gaps where needed. The indicators for such audits could include faecal contamination of water, vector density, food safety and safe disposal of solid and liquid wastes.

20.138. While safety measures at the workplace are necessary for the safety of workers and adjoining residents, and must be enforced, the workplace also presents an opportunity to introduce and practice promotive behaviour, such as a healthy diet and exercise. Ban on consumption of tobacco in public places is a progressive legislation, but it needs effective enforcement. Regular screening of workers for occupational diseases should be introduced. The regulations relating to workplace safety can be enforced more effectively if there is greater coordination between District health and labour authorities.

20.139. Institutions like schools, workplaces and prisons provide opportunities for preventive health check-ups, regular and group exercises, early detection of disease and for dissemination of information on lifestyle choices, yoga, exercise and healthy living. Thus, regular health status and competency check-ups, including laboratory investigations, of children in schools, employees in workplaces and prisoners in jails would be done, with the Government health machinery taking responsibility for public institutions. Age old principles of healthy living and prevention, including those documented in AYUSH texts would be popularised during such health check-ups. Employees and workers will be informed of the ill-effects of sedentary lifestyle, and encouraged to increase physical activity.

20.140. Employees and their families, in large and medium industries of the organised sector can also form an excellent sentinel surveillance system, especially for risk factors of NCDs, incidence of diseases and health care costs as they are linked to organised intra-mural health services or reimbursement systems which maintain regular records. An 'organised sector' surveillance system (such as one involving the Indian Railways network and PSUs) can be established, at relatively low cost and also support work-site based programmes, health promotion and early care seeking.

Behaviour Change Communication

20.141. The state of peoples' health is dependent on living habits that are partly determined by individual behaviour choices. The existing campaigns urging the avoidance of harmful behaviours such as use of tobacco, alcohol and drugs, advocating the use of helmets and seat belts, valuing the girl child, shunning of sex-selective abortions, adoption of the small family norm would be further strengthened. Home-based newborn care, exclusive and continued breastfeeding are time tested and proven strategies to promote child health and survival, and need to be encouraged on a priority basis. Mass media campaigns on mental illness should be launched, to reduce the stigma, promote early care seeking and encourage family members to be supportive and sensitive.

20.142. Electronic (including 'new' media) and print media can play a critical role in informing and empowering communities and individuals on issues relating to health and quality of life. This includes using mobile telephones, multimedia tools as well as Community Radio Stations to achieve this objective. While regulation of the media falls outside the domain of the MoHFW, there is a need to encourage the media to carry messages that make healthy living popular, and to avoid the display of unhealthy behaviour like smoking. Since there are several media-dark areas where the NCD disease burden is increasing, innovative state specific Behaviour

Change Communication strategies would also be required apart from electronic and print media.

20.143. The MoHFW would also champion measures like legislation, regulation and fiscal measures to reduce the exposure of citizens to health risks. An existing agency of the MoHFW, Central Health Education Bureau (CHEB), shall be assigned the responsibility of undertaking and guiding Health Promotion all over the country. In this task, it will use the health promotion Portal for dissemination of information. The CHEB shall involve multi-sectoral actors, conduct health impact assessment and will be developed as the Institute of Health Promotion.

20.144. Teaching self-care to patients and care givers of chronic diseases not only empowers them to manage their condition, but can also make a significant difference to long term health outcomes. NGOs can play a very active role in such campaigns, as the success of BRAC, Bangladesh in reducing infant mortality by promoting use of Oral Rehydration Solution has shown.

INSTRUMENTS FOR SERVICE DELIVERY

Effective Governance Structures

20.145. The broad and flexible governance structure of the National Health Mission would be used to seek willing participation of all sectoral agencies, and civil society in identifying risks and planning for their mitigation, and integrated delivery of quality services. States would be advised to converge the existing governance structures for social sector programmes, such as drinking water and sanitation, ICDS, AIDS control and NRHM at all levels, pool financial and human resource under the leadership of local PRI bodies and make multi-sectoral social plans to collectively address the challenges.

20.146. The existing National Programme Coordination Committee (NPCC) of NRHM will be expanded to serve the National Health Mission. It will be made more representative of all social sectors, sub-sectors within the health sector, and include expertise on monitoring and independent evaluation. All the four Secretaries of the MoHFW will be on this committee, which will be chaired by Secretary Health, and can also serve as a forum for coordination within the Ministry.

20.147. Gaps in the management capacity at the state level need to be addressed. States will be encouraged to set up efficiently functioning agencies/cells for procurement and logistics, recruitment and placement of human resource, human resource management, design, construction and upkeep of health care buildings, use of Information Technology, Financial management, transport systems, standards setting and quality control, monitoring and evaluation of process and outcomes. States shall be advised to expand the roles and responsibilities of Medical Officers in charge of public health facilities to cover all determinants of health, with a focus on improving national health outcome indicators. Their territorial jurisdiction should be made co-terminus with the developmental machinery, as Rural Development Blocks.

20.148. States can empower facility managers with more financial and hiring powers so that they can take quick decisions on service related local issues. The Rogi Kalyan Samiti model of facility autonomy launched under NRHM would be expanded to enable investment in facility upkeep and expansion, or even filling temporary HR gaps. Enhanced autonomy would have to be matched by greater accountability for the management of the facility for timely and quality care, and availability of essential drugs. This will also need stringent regulation to ensure that mismanagement of funds, drugs and equipments does not happen.

20.149. In order to promote sound HR management policies across the states, the Central Government would design model management systems incorporating improved methods for recruitment, retention and performance, incentive-based structures, career tracks for professional advancement based on competence. These guidelines could include strategies suggested in Box 20.6.

Accountability for Outcomes

20.150. In order to ensure that plans and pronouncements do not remain on paper, a system of accountability shall be built at all levels, namely Central Government reporting to the Parliament on items which are its business, States reporting on service delivery and system reforms commitments undertaken through the MoU system, district health societies reporting to States, facility managers reporting on health outcomes of those seeking care, and territorial health managers reporting on health outcomes in their area. Accountability shall be matched with authority and delegation; the MoHFW shall frame model accountability guidelines which will suggest a framework for accountability to the local community, requirement for documentation of unit cost of care, transparency in operations and sharing of information with all stakeholders.

Health Delivery Systems

20.151. Trained and competent human capital is the foundation of an effective health system. Without adequate human resources, additional expenditure on health will not lead to additional services and will only bid up wages. In this context it is important for the Twelfth Plan to embark on a clear strategy to expand the supply of appropriately trained health workers to support health care objectives being targeted.

20.152. Effectively functioning health systems depend on human resource, which range from medical, AYUSH and dental graduates and specialists, graduate and auxiliary nurses, pharmacists to other allied health professionals. The production of human resource in health is a time consuming process, taking as long as nine years for a specialist, to eighteen months for an ANM. The current availability of health personnel in the country (Table 20.8) is below the minimum requirement of 250 per lakh of population (*Human Resources for Health: Overcoming the Crisis*, 2004, Joint Learning Initiative, page 23). Given the existing production capacity, we can expect an availability of 354 health workers by 2017. It is generally accepted that the doctor to nurse ratio should be at least 1:3 for the team to perform optimally. This ratio is currently 1:1.6 and is expected to improve to 1:2.4 by end of Twelfth Plan if no new colleges are started. These numbers regarding total availability mask the fact that there is substantial regional variation in the distribution of doctors and nurses, because of which we should plan for a total availability which is significantly higher than the recommended minimum. The basic data on the availability and rate of new additions is summarised in Table 20.8.

20.153. We need to take up a large scale expansion in teaching capacity in this plan so the situation improves towards the end of this plan, and reaches

---

Box 20.6
Suggested Items in Model HR Guidelines

- Quality standards for facilities should be taken as guiding principle for sanctioning posts, which would indicate the maximum staff that can be posted. In case a facility does not attract expected case-loads, the staff may be rationalised.
- Recruitment should be decentralised with a quicker turnaround time and preference must be given to residents of the region of proposed deployment.
- Fair and transparent system of postings and timely promotions.
- Financial and non-financial incentives (like preferential eligibility for post graduate courses, promotions, subsequent choice of postings, reimbursement of children's school fee) would be suggested to States for adoption, for performance and service in remote areas.
- Measures to reduce professional isolation by preferential access to continuing medical education and skill up-gradation programmes, as well as back-up support on tele-medicine (Internet or mobile based) and by networking of professionals working in similar circumstances.
- Measures to reduce social isolation by investing in processes that bring community and providers closer together.
- Completion of training of ASHAs and retraining of the existing cadre of workers as Male Multi-Purpose Workers, AWW and ANMs, to make them relevant to local needs, and for their own upward mobility.

optimal levels by the end of Thirteenth Plan. If we adopt a goal of 500 health workers per lakh population by the end of Thirteenth Plan, we would need an additional 240 medical colleges, 500 General Nursing and Midwifery (GNM)/nursing colleges and 970 ANMs training institutes. If work on these new teaching institutions begins from the 2013–14 annual plan, and is completed by the end of the Twelfth Plan, the flow of nurses and ANMs would begin within this plan, while doctors from these institutions would be available only from the beginning of the Thirteenth Plan. The ratio of doctors to nurses will then rise from 1:1.6 in 2012 to 1:2.8 in 2017 and reach 1:3 in 2022.

20.154. The projected availability of HR in health during the Twelfth Plan is given in Figure 20.4. A density of 398 workers per lakh would be well achieved by 2017, and 509 by 2021.

Expansion of Teaching Facilities

20.155. The Government shall take the lead role in creating teaching capacity in health, while private sector colleges would also be allowed. Initiatives would be taken to upgrade existing District hospitals and CHCs into knowledge centres, where medical, nursing and para-medical teaching and refresher courses can be held side-by-side with patient care. States shall be encouraged to take this up through the incentive fund of the NHM. The existing state level teaching institutions such as the State Institutes of Health and Family Welfare would also be strengthened. Simultaneously, the existing Government medical colleges and central Government institutions would be strengthened so that the seats could be increased to the maximum level of 250. Efforts to support the existing institutions to create more Post-graduate seats would continue. The long term goal would be to build at least one training centre in

TABLE 20.8
Availability of HR during Eleventh Plan and Projections for Twelfth Plan

Category	Enrolled and Available (2011–12)			Annual Capacity	Expected Availability by 2017		Desirable Density	Colleges Required	Available if Colleges Created	
	Enrolled	Available	Density	Nos.	Total	Density			2017	2021
Physicians	9,22,177	6,91,633	57	42,570	8,48,616	65	85	240	67	85
AYUSH	7,12,121	5,34,091	44	30,000	6,42,386	49	49	0	51	54
Dentists	1,17,827	88,370	7	24,410	1,93,797	15	15	0	16	21
Nurses/GNM	12,38,874	7,43,324	61	1,78,339	15,08,684	115	170	500	129	170
ANM	6,03,131	3,61,879	30	38,290	5,16,090	39	85	970	60	85
Pharmacist	6,57,230	4,92,923	41	1,00,000	9,18,276	70	70	0	76	95
Total			**241**			**354**	**474**		**398**	**509**
Nurse/ANM: Doctor Ratio			1.6			2.4	3.0		2.8	3.0

Notes: Density: Per Lakh Population
Current availability based on attrition @ 25 per cent (Physicians, AYUSH, Pharmacists and Dentists), 40 per cent for Nurses and ANM.
Except for New ANM schools all other colleges will be phased as follows: 50 per cent by 2013, 40 per cent by 2014 and 10 per cent by 2015. ANM schools will be phased as follows 50 per cent by 2014 and 50 per cent by 2015.
New colleges have been assumed to have a capacity of 250 (physicians), 100 (AYUSH, Dentist, Nurses/GN, Pharmacist) and 80 (ANM, bi-annual batch of 40).

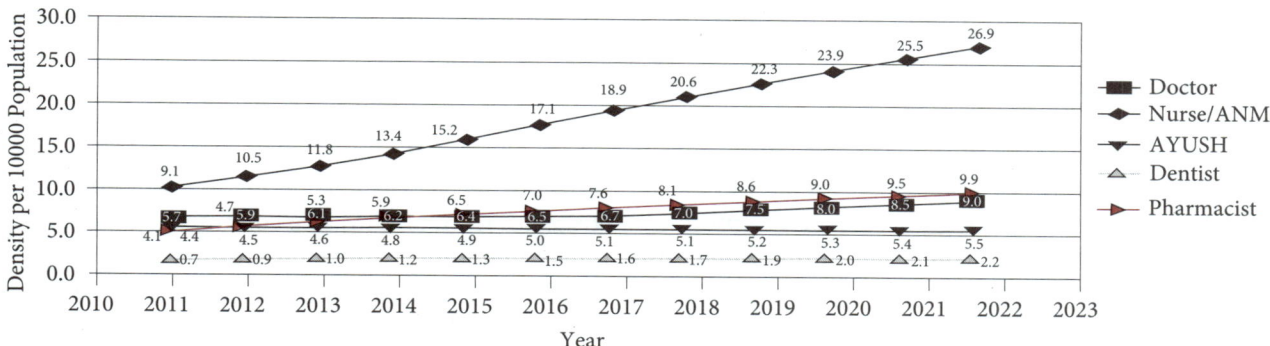

FIGURE 20.4: Projected HRH Capacity Expansion in the Twelfth Plan

each District, and one para-medical training centre in each sub-division/block.

20.156. District hospitals which cannot be converted to teaching institutions, can be accredited with the National Board of Examinations for training Post-Graduate candidates in the Diplomate of National Board (DNB) programme, in courses such as Family Medicine. This is a low cost measure which will help increase production of specialists, bring professionalism and also help improve standards of patient care in district hospitals.

20.157. Centres of Excellence for Nursing and Allied Health Sciences also need to be established in every State. These Centres would impart higher education in specialised fields, offer continued professional education and have provisions for faculty development and research. Centres for paramedical education would to be set up in 149 Government medical colleges, in addition to initiating paramedical institutions in 26 States. Initiatives already taken to upgrade and strengthen the existing Nursing Schools into Colleges of Nursing would continue. Establishment of ANM/GNM schools in under-served areas would also be accorded priority. A road-map would be prepared for strengthening of pre-service, mid-wifery training and career development.

20.158. In the Pharmacy sector, strengthening and up-gradation of Pharmacy Colleges and setting up of Colleges of pharmacy attached to Government medical colleges would be initiated, wherever possible.

20.159. There are other categories of skilled health-workers, such as Physician assistants, who increase the productivity of the medical team, and should be encouraged. In the context of hospitals, a survey by FICCI in June 2011 has identified five skill-sets that need immediate attention, namely Dialysis Technician, Operation Theatre/Anaesthesia Technician, Paramedic, Lab Technician, Patient Care Coordinator cum Medical Transcriptionist. The profession of midwifery will be revived, and provided training and legal authority to serve as autonomous medical practitioners for primary maternity care, such as in the Netherlands, so that skilled birth attendance is universalised. The proposed District knowledge Centres would create sufficient teaching capacity for such newer categories of health workers.

20.160. A peculiar feature of India's healthcare system is the presence of a large number of non-qualified practitioners, such as traditional birth attendants (dais), compounders and RMPs. As per law, they are neither authorised to practice Medicine, nor to prescribe drugs. Nonetheless, they work everywhere in the country and address a huge unfulfilled demand for ambulatory care, particularly in rural areas. The challenge is to get them into the formal system. The plan recommends giving these practitioners, depending on their qualifications and experience, an opportunity to get trained and integrate them into the health work-force in suitable capacities by mutual consent.

20.161. Another opportunity lies in utilising the services of AYUSH graduates for providing primary care. There are two pre-requisites before this can be done—first by amendment of the legal framework to authorise the practice of modern medicine for primary care by practitioners of Indian Systems of Medicine; and secondly by supplementing skills of AYUSH graduates by imparting training in modern Medicine through bridge courses. High professional standards of eligibility for, and qualifying in the bridge courses should be laid down so that the quality of such primary care integrated physicians remains high. States like Tamil Nadu and recently Maharashtra have shown the lead in this regard. Associations of allopathic practitioners are generally opposed to AYUSH practitioners being allowed to prescribe allopathic medicines; they will have to be persuaded to yield in the national interest of serving the masses, particularly the rural population and the urban poor. Suitably trained, AYUSH graduates can provide primary health care, and help fill in the human resource gaps in rural areas.

20.162. The NHM will encourage the States to modify the designation and job profiles of human resource created under various central and externally funded programmes into generic, multi-functional categories whose services can be used as per local need.

Community Participation and PRI Involvement

20.163. Government health facilities at the level of blocks and below can become more responsive to population needs if funds are devolved to the Panchayati Raj Institutions (Village Council or its equivalent in the Scheduled Areas), and these institutions made responsible for improving public health outcomes in their area. States should formalise the roles and authority of Local Self-Government bodies in securing convergence so that these bodies become stakeholders for sustainable improvements in health standards. The States would be advised to make Village Health, Sanitation and Nutrition Committees as the guiding and operational arms of the Panchayats in advancing the social agenda.

20.164. Health Action Plan for service delivery, systems management and prevention would be formulated through effective public participation to ensure relevance to local needs and to enable enhanced accountability and public oversight.

20.165. Greater efforts at community involvement in planning, delivery, monitoring and evaluation of health services would be made using established strategies from NRHM like community based monitoring, citizens' charters, patients' rights, social audits, public hearings and grievance redressal mechanisms. Newly elected members of PRIs, especially women members, need support as they grow into their new roles. NGOs have an important role in strengthening capacity. An integrated curriculum will be drawn up to facilitate this process. NGOs can play a key role in providing support to VHSNCs and PRIs in capacity building, planning for convergent service delivery and more effective community based monitoring. Recognition and instituting awards for achievers along the lines of Nirmal Gram Puraskar under the Total Sanitation Campaign will be one way of incentivisation.

Strengthening Health Systems

20.166. A major objective of enhanced funding, flexibility to and incentivisation of States is to build health systems. Some of the components of health systems strengthening for which States shall be encouraged are listed in Table 20.9.

NATIONAL AIDS CONTROL ORGANISATION

20.167. The programme strategy would be two-pronged: intensification of interventions for high risk groups and bridge populations, and integration of prevention (including mother to child transmission), testing, counselling and treatment services among the general population, including pregnant women, with the routine RCH programme. To achieve mainstreaming of services, the State AIDS Control Societies and District AIDS Prevention and Control Unit (DAPCU) will be linked with the National Health Mission structure at these levels. To build a multi-dimensional reporting system, the information systems on health systems, and AIDS control shall be synergised.

TABLE 20.9
Illustrative List of Health Systems Strengthening in States

Health System Elements	Suggested Health System Strengthening Activities by States
1. Effective Public Health Administration	Enact and Enforce Public Health Act Put in place a *Public Health cadre*, whose members shall be responsible for detecting public health problems within their jurisdiction, framing strategy for its correction and implementing it Develop and deploy a *Health Management Cadre*, for providing management support to public health programmes and hospital administration Mandatory practice of Clinical Treatment Guidelines and prescription of generic medicines listed in the National List of Essential Medicines in all Government facilities Mandatory test audit of medical prescriptions by faculty of medical colleges Improve governance through stronger oversight mechanisms that include citizen participation, social audit and greater transparency Develop an effective and responsive grievance redress system Frame policies for, and provide services so as to achieve the goals of the National Population Policy (2000).
2. Health Financing	Increased expenditure on Health Sector Prioritise strengthening of Primary Health Care in state budgets
3. Health Regulation	Extend and enforce Central Clinical Establishment Act Empower Public Health functionaries under relevant laws namely Pre-conception and Pre-natal Diagnostic Techniques Act, Food Safety Standard Act, and Drugs and Cosmetics Acts
4. Develop Human Resource for Health	Develop District Hospitals and Community Health Centres (CHCs) into Medical and para-medical training institutions with improved quality of training Organise bridge Courses for AYUSH graduates and legally empower them to practice as Primary Health care physicians Encourage career progression of ASHA and AWW into ANM, and assure career tracks for competency-based professional advancement of nurses
5. Health Information Systems	Build a Health Information System by networking of all health service providers, establishing state level disease surveillance systems, universal registration of births and deaths to give accurate picture of health of the population
6. Convergence and Stewardship	Assess Health impact of policies and activities of departments other than health Main-streaming of AYUSH into NHM Main-streaming of STI and HIV prevention and treatment up to district levels into NHM Main-streaming of all disease control programmes into NHM Empower Panchayats with funds, functions and functionaries to play a meaningful role in bringing convergence in the social sector Achieve inter-sectoral coordination at Block, District and State levels by using the mission structure of NHM Create and support systems for grievance redressal Synergise the working of ASHA and AWW by declaring AWC as the convergence station for all village level NHM and ICDS personnel, and Sub-centre as the HQ of ICDS supervisors Ensure that only double fortified salt (Iron-Iodine) is used in ICDS Scheme, Mid-Day Meal and sold through Public Distribution System
7. Health Services	Master plan for ensuring each district is able to provide assured set of services to all its residents Road-map for achieving Indian Public Health Standards at all facilities Public health care facilities are provided financial and administrative autonomy Develop an effective grievance redress system
8. Ensure access to Medicines, Vaccines and Diagnostics	Create a Special Purpose Vehicle to procure, store and distribute medicines, vaccines and diagnostics through an open, tender based procurement Mandate availability of drugs under the National List of Essential Medicines in all health facilities Strengthen state level drug regulation Ensure Jan Aushadhi stores in all Block Headquarters

20.168. The primary goal of NACP during Twelfth Plan will be to accelerate the process of reversal and further strengthen the epidemic response in India through a well-defined, integration process. The programme will be further strengthened and programme management capacities decentralised to state and district levels. NACP-IV will remain a prevention oriented plan with adequate coverage of HIV care in the context of the concentrated epidemic situation in India. NACP will synergise with other national programmes and align with the overall Twelfth Five Year Plan goals of inclusive growth and development. The key priorities of NACP-IV will be as follows:

- Preventing new infections by sustaining the reach of current interventions and effectively addressing emerging epidemics.
- Preventing Patent-to-Child Transmission
- Focusing on IEC strategies for behaviour change, demand-generation for HIV services among those at risk and awareness among general population
- Providing comprehensive care, support and treatment to people with infection
- Reducing stigma and discrimination through greater involvement of HIV affected persons
- Ensuring effective use of strategic information at all levels
- Building capacities of NGO and civil society partners, especially in states of emerging epidemics
- Integrating HIV services with the health system in a phased manner
- Mainstreaming HIV/AIDS activities with all key central and state level Ministries/departments and leveraging resources of the respective departments
- Leveraging social protection and insurance mechanisms

STRATEGIES FOR NACP-IV

1. Intensifying and consolidating prevention services with a focus on (*i*) high-risk groups and vulnerable population and (*ii*) general population;
2. Expanding IEC services for (*i*) general population and (*ii*) high-risk groups with a focus on behaviour change and demand generation;
3. Increasing access and promoting comprehensive care, support and treatment;
4. Building capacities at national stage, district and facility levels and
5. Strengthening Strategic Information Management Systems

INDIAN SYSTEMS OF MEDICINE AND HOMOEOPATHY SERVICES (AYUSH)

20.169. Practice and promotion of AYUSH in the States would be carried out under the broad umbrella of the National Health Mission. A revamped National Programme Coordination Committee of the National Health Mission with Secretaries of all the departments under the MoHFW, and chaired by Secretary Health, would provide the funding and programme guidance for convergence and mainstreaming of AYUSH in the health care system.

20.170. States would be encouraged to integrate AYUSH facilities, and provide AYUSH services in all facilities offering treatment in modern systems of medicine. The goal is to ensure that all Government health care facilities offer suitable AYUSH services as per laid down standards.

20.171. In addition, the concept of AYUSH Gram will be promoted, wherein one village per block will be selected for implementation of integrated primary care protocols of AYUSH and modern system of medicine. In these villages, herbal medicinal gardens will be supported, regular Yoga camps will be organised, preferably through PRI institutions and youth clubs, and the community provided basic knowledge on hygiene, promotion of health and prevention of diseases.

STRENGTHENING AYUSH

20.172. The strengths of Indian Systems of Medicine and Homoeopathy, if suitably used, can help advance the goals of the Twelfth Plan. AYUSH systems would be main-streamed using their areas of strengths namely in preventive and promotive health care, diseases and health conditions relating to women and children, older persons, NCDs, mental ailments, stress management, palliative care, rehabilitation and health promotion.

20.173. Every element of health system strengthening and development, particularly use of IT, is equally applicable to AYUSH systems and institutional capacity development and would be pursued. What follows are additional measures and institutional capacity development tailored to unique opportunities and requirements of AYUSH systems.

RESEARCH

20.174. The National Health Policy of 2002 set an objective, which involved a re-orientation and prioritisation of research to validate AYUSH therapies and drugs that address chronic and life style-related emerging diseases. Cross-disciplinary research and practice requires standardisation of terminologies of classical therapies, and development of Standard and Integrated Treatment Protocols. These would be developed based on core competencies and inherent strengths of each system, and comparative efficacy studies. National Health Programmes shall use such composite protocols.

20.175. To take this ambitious research agenda forward, all five Research Councils of AYUSH will pool resources, particularly human resource, clinical facilities and information, to avoid duplication. For this to happen on an institutionalised basis, a common governance structure for the five Research Councils would be put in place.

20.176. The documentation of traditional knowledge associated with medicinal plants is very important not only to preserve it for posterity but also to contest bio-piracy and bio-prospecting. This will be continued.

HUMAN RESOURCES DEVELOPMENT

20:177. Cross-disciplinary learning between modern and AYUSH systems at the post-graduate level would be encouraged. Details of modification in syllabi that would be required at the undergraduate level, in order to make such cross-disciplinary learning possible, would be worked out by a team of experts from the different Professional Councils. Collaboration between AYUSH teaching colleges and with medical colleges for mutual learning would be encouraged. AYUSH Chairs in Medical Colleges of the country would be encouraged to provide the necessary technical expertise to jointly take up research, teaching and patient care. Orientation of medical students and doctors about basic concepts, applications and scientific developments of AYUSH in order to dispel ignorance and foster cross-system referral would be encouraged. Relevant AYUSH modules would therefore be incorporated into medical, nursing and pharmacy course curricula and in the CME programme for medical practitioners.

PRACTICE AND PROMOTION OF AYUSH

20.178. The Department of AYUSH would develop standards for facilities at the primary, secondary and tertiary levels as a part of IPHS; Standard Treatment Guidelines and a Model Drugs List of AYUSH drugs for community health workers will be developed. All primary, secondary and tertiary care institutions under the MoHFW, State Health Departments and other Ministries like Railways, Labour, Home Affairs and so on, would create facilities to provide AYUSH services of appropriate standards.

20.179. As longevity increases, geriatrics as a discipline would need greater attention. AYUSH therapies have strengths in restoration and rejuvenation. To bring together the best of care for the elderly that AYUSH systems have to offer, and to develop it further using modern scientific methods, a National Institute on Geriatrics (through AYUSH) will be set up.

20.180. In view of the growing incidence of metabolic and lifestyle diseases like diabetes and hypertension and considering the strengths of AYUSH systems in their prevention and treatment, a National Institute on Metabolic and Lifestyle Diseases will be established.

20.181. In view of the growing problem of drug abuse, and increase in use of tobacco, and the potential of AYUSH therapies and practices, particularly of Yoga, for disease prevention and health promotion, a National Institute for Drug and Tobacco De-addiction will be established. Each of the three national institutes would be equipped with post-graduate education and research facilities and house advanced hospital facilities in all disciplines of medicine. These institutes would conduct and promote interdisciplinary research in their area, advance frontiers of knowledge on prevention and condition management, teach and promote evidence-based use of AYUSH systems, and are expected to emerge over time as global centres of research, care and education.

Regulation and Quality Control

20.182. Systems for quality certification of raw materials, accreditation of educational programmes, health services and manufacturing units and products would be promoted in the Twelfth Plan. This would achieve both minimum standards through regulations and laws, as well as, excellence through a voluntary scheme of accreditation. The existing practice of a common legislation, and regulatory systems for AYUSH and modern medicines would be further strengthened, with mandated representation of AYUSH experts at all levels. Modernisation of pharmaceutical technology, in order to standardise the use of natural resources and production processes that are used by AYUSH, will be taken up as a priority in the Twelfth Plan period.

HEALTH RESEARCH

20.183. Given the lag in progress on health indicators in the country, need for accelerated progress and optimal use of limited resources, DHR should strategically move in a direction which brings forth actionable evidence in a time bound manner for quick translation to address national health needs. In setting its priority areas, DHR would be guided by the disease profile in the country, burden of disease, and the possibility of cost-effective intervention.

20.184. The strategy for health research in the Twelfth Plan would be the following:

20.185. *Address national health priorities*: The key outcome of the efforts of DHR would be to generate intellectual capital, which may have a public health impact. DHR would, therefore, prioritise its research to find cost-effective solutions for health priorities and health system issues facing the country, namely:

1. Maternal and child nutrition, health and survival;
2. High fertility in parts of the country;
3. Low child sex ratio and discrimination against the girl child;
4. Prevention, early detection, treatment, rehabilitation to reduce burden of diseases—communicable, non-communicable (including mental illnesses) and injuries (especially road traffic related), congenital malformation and disorders of sex development;
5. Sustainable health financing aimed at reducing household's out-of-pocket expenditure;
6. HIS covering universal vital registration, community based monitoring, disease surveillance and hospital based information systems for prevention, treatment and teaching;
7. Measures to address social determinants of health and inequity, particularly among marginalised populations;
8. Suggest and regularly update Standard Treatment Guidelines which are both necessary and cost-effective for wider adoption;
9. Public Health systems and their strengthening; and
10. Health regulation, particularly on ethical issues in research.

20.186. Existing institutes of ICMR will be re-organised, strengthened and new centres set up in deficit areas to achieve the above listed goals.

20.187. *Build Research Coordination Framework*: Though DHR is the empowered Department on medical and health research, many organisations are engaged in research on related topics, namely the Ministry of Environment and Forest, Departments of Health and Family Welfare, AYUSH, AIDS control, Space, Science and Technology, Biotechnology, Agricultural Research; agencies like ICAR, DSIR, CSIR, NDMA, DRDO and the National Knowledge Network. DHR would play a lead role in research involving human health, bringing all the concerned organisations on one platform to facilitate mutual discussion, resource pooling and prioritisation, and avoid duplication, to find innovative solutions to national priorities in a timely manner. It would also take the lead in suggesting institutional structures, like mutual representation in each others' decision-making and scientific bodies, and 'coordinating structures' so that consultation and collaboration become a norm rather than an exception. Efficient mechanisms for selection, promotion, development, assessment and evaluation of affordable technologies would be established. DHR would bring together basic, translational and clinical investigators, networks, professional societies and industry to facilitate development of programmes and research projects. DHR would establish a mechanism for coordination between academia and the industry, with a preference for multidisciplinary approaches.

20.188. To address the need for operations research on impediments in delivery of services, DHR will explore the possibility of stationing multi-disciplinary research teams within the NHM structure at different levels, so that practical, relevant and area specific solutions to problems are suggested to programme managers. To address the gaps in critical areas such as Health Information Systems, National Health Accounts and Public Health delivery DHR will dedicate national centres to these needs, and position specialised teams alongside operational managers.

20.189. *Autonomy coupled with accountability in research*: The elements of an efficient research system are clear enunciation of goals, sufficient resources with flexibility to raise extra-budgetary funds, functional autonomy, accountability and incentives for performance. DHR would work to observe these principles in its research institutes so that each one of them develops into a centre of excellence in its allotted field.

20.190. *Efficient research governance, regulatory and evaluation framework*: DHR would also put in place appropriate regulations, guidelines, authorities and structures to strengthen ethics-based research governance and to protect the interests of research subjects especially, in clinical trials. DHR would prepare guidelines on, among others, Stem Cell Research and Therapy, Assisted Reproductive Technologies incorporating rights of egg donors; Ethical Guidelines for Biomedical Research involving human subjects, Ethical Guidelines for Conducting Research on Mental Illness or Cognitive Impairment, Compensation to Participants for Research Related Injury in India and Bio-banking. DHR would also develop mechanisms to evaluate health research undertaken by various scientific departments including ICMR. DHR would put in place mechanisms for benchmarking and accreditation of health research institutions. The criteria for accreditation of research institutes would be based on the intellectual capital generated and its public health impact.

20.191. *Nurture development of research centres and labs*: In addition to the development of centres in deficit and strategic areas, DHR would identify and fund the development of existing medical colleges and research centres into specialised subject areas, which may become capable of conducting cross-cutting, multidisciplinary and translational researches. Similarly, DHR would fund up-gradations of existing Government labs to increase the capacity for diagnosis of viral and other infectious diseases at the national, regional and District levels. A national list of diagnostic facilities shall be centrally maintained to help guide decisions on creation of and up gradation of laboratory facilities. DHR would also build capacity of States and other institutions on the periphery for solving various clinical and public health problems.

20.192. *Utilise available research capacity by promoting extra-mural research*: Extramural programmes, under which grants are competitively awarded on selected topics, would be expanded to help tap talent in medical colleges, tertiary hospitals, health universities and public health institutions. DHR would aim to increase the share of extramural funding in its research budget from the current 33 per cent to 50 per cent by the end of Twelfth Plan. It may also commission 'problem-solving research', following the Open Source Drug Discovery model of CSIR, but would need to subject it to strict scrutiny for outcomes. Translational Research would be promoted so that research findings can be translated into better health status in the country.

20.193. *Human Resource Development*: Investments would be made in producing qualified researchers, by improving career opportunities for young researchers and providing good initial support in the form of start-up grants. Additionally, fellowships for training researchers in identified advanced fields, scholarships at the PG level, Young Researcher Programmes to encourage young students, mid-career research fellowships for faculty development at medical colleges are some ways to ensure a steady flow of committed researchers. DHR will explore, in consultation with concerned regulatory authorities, the possibility of introducing a stream of research professionals in medical colleges who would have avenues for professional advancement equal to those of teaching faculty. DHR will utilise the potential of Information Technology to standardise research methodology courses, and train students in academic institutions through distance learning.

20.194. *Cost-effectiveness studies to frame Clinical Treatment Guidelines*: On the lines of the UK's National Institute of Clinical Excellence (NICE), DHR would develop expertise to assess available therapies and technologies for their cost-effectiveness and essentiality, and formulate and update, on a regular basis, the Standard Treatment Guidelines, and suggest inclusion of new drugs and vaccines into the public health system. The formulation of the Guidelines must, of course, incorporate the best available evidence, including in AYUSH systems, and prevalence of anti-microbial drug-resistance in order to suggest treatment protocols for regular clinical practice. Standard Treatment Guidelines developed by Army Medical Corps can also be referred to. The justification for housing the proposed institute outside the Department of Health, but within the Ministry, is to provide it an element of objectivity and independence from practitioners, and to avoid conflict of interest.

CONVERGENCE ACROSS SECTORS FOR BETTER OUTCOMES

20.195. The impact of policies and programmes of non-health sectors on health remains invisible for long periods. It is, therefore, necessary to take proactive steps to determine the health impact of existing and new policies in sectors which have a bearing on the health of population. The MoHFW would constitute a dedicated 'Health Impact Cell' to conduct such an analysis, and its views would be taken into consideration before framing or modifying policies of non-health Ministries which can potentially impact public health. The proposed 'Health Impact Cell' in the MoHFW would also perform Monitoring and Surveillance functions in order to continuously gather information on health impacts of policies and programmes of key non-health Departments. It can harmonise the programme data obtained from the sectors/non-health Ministries with the health impact reports received from the field, such as on water and sanitation related disease outbreaks, and determine gaps in policies as well as in programme implementation. Various sectors would share data, particularly those that are relevant to health outcomes, with the proposed cell. The proposed cell would also be equipped to serve early warnings and coordinate responses to health related emergencies and natural disasters.

CONVERGENT ACTION ON NUTRITION

20.196. The Ministry of health would build institutional arrangements with the Ministry of Women and Child development so that convergent delivery of services under ICDS becomes the norm. A national policy on promoting healthy diets, and regulating extent of salts, and trans fats in foods is required. Double fortification of salt with iron and iodine presents a cost-effective and feasible strategy to prevent two of the key nutritional deficiencies in our country. While the Food and Nutrition Board under the Ministry of Women and Child Development is expected to take the lead, all health workers would be sensitised so that they are able to disseminate knowledge on nutrition and healthy living.

ANGANWADI CENTRE AS THE CONVERGENCE HUB

20.197. Nutritional issues call for multi-stakeholder strategies, including informing communities on how to maximise nutritional benefits from locally available foods, food fortification and micro-nutrient supplementation. States shall be encouraged through the sector-wide MoUs to observe Village Health and Nutrition Days in complete convergence mode (Box 20.7) and ensure that Anganwadi Centres become the hub for all health related services.

> **Box 20.7**
> **Convergence: Village Health and Nutrition Day in North Tripura**
>
> The Village Health and Nutrition Day (VHND) organised in North Tripura district in a complete convergence mode secured it the Prime Minister's award for excellence in Public administration for 2010–11.
>
> A monthly VHND is to be organised in every village through inter-sectoral convergence and community involvement with the Anganwadi Centre as the hub for service provision. It is an effective platform for providing first-contact primary health care. The Village Health, Sanitation and Nutrition Committees are expected to be the organiser with participation of ASHA, ANM, AWW and the PRI representatives.
>
> As per *NRHM guidelines*, the services to be provided on VHND include registration of all pregnant women, Ante-Natal Checkup, Vitamin A administration and vaccination of all eligible children, weighing of children, plotting of weights on cards and suitable management, administration of drugs to TB patients, provision of contraceptives (condoms and oral) to all eligible couples as per their choice, supplementary nutrition to underweight children, community awareness generation, identification of cases needing special attention.
>
> Special and *additional features* in North Tripura were the following:
>
> - Organisation of a health mela in a transparent and participative manner; extensive publicity through sign-boards and in-person contact for the event
> - Pooling of funds from different departments, and clear delineation of roles
> - Leadership role of headmasters of schools in training and health education
> - Convergence of service providers of health, ICDS, rural development, panchayat, drinking water,, district disability rehabilitation centre, education and adult literacy
> - Additional services provided include disability certificates, wheel chairs to the disabled, medicines and water purification tablets. doctor's consultation, testing of eye, dental and for HIV, Strong cultural orientation to the event by including local songs, dances, drama, quizzes, sports events, healthy baby shows
> - The mid-day meal and ICDS were served together; with a community meal
> - Intense training of functionaries
> - Effective monitoring, record keeping and display of data on web site
>
> *Outcomes:* A quantum jump in detection of cases of various diseases and health problems, fewer deaths due to fever, malaria, diarrhoea, lowering of MMR and IMR while immunisation coverage improved, identification of malnourished children, initiation of their treatment and periodical monitoring.
>
> *Lesson:* Effectively organised VHSND can lead to awareness in the community on health issues, effective utilisation of services on health, and its determinants.

MAIN-STREAMING DISASTER MANAGEMENT

20.198. The Ministry of Health shall in its policies and programmes give due consideration to the elements of disaster management, namely Mitigation, Preparedness, Response and Recovery. At all stages of disaster management, active engagement of local communities shall be the ensured.

CONVERGENCE WITHIN DEPARTMENTS OF MINISTRY OF HEALTH

20.199. Given the fact that many health conditions often co-exist and exacerbate each other with poor nutritional status as the underlying factor, therapies under different systems of medicine can synergistically improve health status, and need for evidence based decision making and practice, all the four departments of health which are engaged in their allocated domains can act synergistically to address the key national health needs. A coordinated delivery of national programmes at the grass-root level can increase outreach and help better manage programmes. Frontline health workers, and Government health facilities for primary care can be developed as single points of contact for all local residents in meeting their entire range of health care needs.

CONCLUSION

20.200. The Twelfth Plan faces a colossal task of putting in place a basic architecture for health security for the nation. It must build on what has been achieved through the NRHM and expand it into a comprehensive NHM. Since the primary responsibility for health care rests with the States, the strategy needs to effectively incentivise State Governments to do what is needed to improve the public health care system while regulating the private health care system, so that together they can work towards addressing the management of delivery of preventive, promotive, curative and rehabilitatory health interventions. This is not a task that can be completed within one Plan period. It will certainly span two or three Plan periods, to put the basic health infrastructure in place.

21

Education

INTRODUCTION

21.1. Education is the most important lever for social, economic and political transformation. A well-educated population, equipped with the relevant knowledge, attitudes and skills is essential for economic and social development in the twenty-first century. Education is the most potent tool for socio-economic mobility and a key instrument for building an equitable and just society. Education provides skills and competencies for economic well-being. Education strengthens democracy by imparting to citizens the tools needed to fully participate in the governance process. Education also acts as an integrative force in society, imparting values that foster social cohesion and national identity. Recognising the importance of education in national development, the Twelfth Plan places an unprecedented focus on the expansion of education, on significantly improving the quality of education imparted and on ensuring that educational opportunities are available to all segments of the society.

21.2. Recognising the importance of education, public spending on education increased rapidly during the Eleventh Plan period. Education expenditure as a percentage of gross domestic product (GDP) rose from 3.3 per cent in 2004–05 to over 4 per cent in 2011–12. Per capita public expenditure on education increased from ₹888 in 2004–05 to ₹2,985 in 2011–12. The bulk of public spending on education is incurred by the State Governments and their spending grew at a robust rate of 19.6 per cent per year during the Eleventh Plan. Central spending on education increased even faster at 25 per cent per year during the same period. Aggregate public spending on education during the Eleventh Plan period is estimated at ₹12,44,797 crore for both the Centre and States taken together. Of this, 35 per cent was accounted for by Plan expenditure and 65 per cent by non-Plan expenditure. About 43 per cent of the public expenditure on education was incurred for elementary education, 25 per cent for secondary education and the balance 32 per cent for higher education. About half of the Central Government's expenditure was incurred for higher education and the remaining for elementary (39 per cent) and secondary (12 per cent) education. In the State sector, about 75 per cent of education expenditure is for school education, of which 44 per cent is on elementary education and 30 per cent on secondary education.

21.3. The following sections of this chapter provide details of the strategy and initiatives for school education and literacy and then for higher education. Issues related to skill development that have close linkages to education are dealt with in Chapter 3 along with a discussion on employment.

SCHOOL EDUCATION AND LITERACY

21.4. The country has made significant progress in improving access to education in recent years. The mean years of schooling of the working population (those over 15 years old) increased from 4.19 years in 2000 to 5.12 years in 2010. Enrolment of children at the primary education stage has now reached near-universal levels. The growth of enrolment in secondary education accelerated from 4.3 per cent per year during the 1990s to 6.27 per cent per year in the decade ending 2009–10. Youth literacy increased from 60 per cent in 1983 to 91 per cent in 2009–10 and adult literacy improved from 64.8 per cent in 2001 to 74 per cent in 2011.

21.5. A good progress has also been made in bridging the equity gap in education. India's educational inequality, measured in terms of the *Gini co-efficient*[1] for number of years of education, has decreased from 0.71 in 1983 to 0.49 in 2010, indicating a large reduction in inequality. The gender gap in elementary education has declined with the female/male ratio for years of education and literacy reaching over 90 per cent in 2009–10. A significant reduction in socio-economic inequality in access to education and a narrowing of the gap between SCs/STs and other social groups has been achieved.

Challenges

21.6. Despite many gains during the Eleventh Plan, education in India faces several challenges. The country's mean years of schooling at 5.12 years is well below the other emerging market economies such as China (8.17 years) and Brazil (7.54 years) and significantly below the average for all developing countries (7.09 years). A matter of particular concern is the steep dropout rate after the elementary level. The sharp drop-off in enrolment at the middle school level and the increasing enrolment gap from elementary to higher secondary suggests that the gains at the elementary level have not yet impacted the school sector as a whole. Disadvantaged groups are worse off with the dropout rates for SCs and STs higher than the national average.

21.7. While enrolment levels at the elementary level are generally high, studies of student attendance show that there is considerable variation across States in the percentage of enrolled students who are attending school on any given day during the school year. Of particular concern is that some of the most educationally backward States (Uttar Pradesh [UP], Bihar, Madhya Pradesh [MP] and Jharkhand) have the lowest student attendance rates (below 60 per cent). In the Twelfth Plan, there is a need for a clear shift in strategy from a focus on inputs and increasing access and enrolment to teaching–learning process and its improvement in order to ensure adequate appropriate learning outcomes. In this context, States need to set up transparent and reliable systems for tracking attendance in a meaningful way and work on effective strategies for boosting attendance and sustaining high levels of attendance throughout the school year.

21.8. While there has been a decline in the percentage of out-of-school children (OoSC) across gender and social categories, Muslim, scheduled caste (SC) and scheduled tribe (ST) children need greater and focused attention. The number of OoSC who are physically or mentally challenged remains a cause for concern. The proportion of disabled out-of-school children in 2005 was 34.19 per cent and remained unchanged at 34.12 per cent in 2009. It is important to note that the maximum number of OoSC are those with mental disabilities (48 per cent), followed by children with speech disabilities (37 per cent). Neither the school system nor any other institutional mechanism is equipped to address the challenging needs of mentally disabled children who are most disadvantaged both socially and educationally in the system.

21.9. There has been a substantial increase in the availability of teachers at elementary level during the past few years and if all the teacher posts sanctioned under both Sarva Shiksha Abhiyan (SSA) and State budgets are filled, the pupil–teacher ratio (PTR) at the national level will almost be 27:1. The challenge, however, lies in correcting the imbalance in teacher deployment. The number of schools that do not comply with the Right to Education (RTE) norms for the required PTR is fairly high. School-wise analysis based on District Information System for Education (DISE) 2009–10 indicates that 46 per cent of primary and 34 per cent of upper primary schools have poor PTRs. Another serious challenge is the presence of teachers without professional qualifications approved by the National Council of Teacher Education (NCTE), as is required under the RTE Act. There are about 8.1 lakh untrained teachers in the country with four States—Bihar, UP, Jharkhand and West Bengal—accounting for 72 per cent of them.

21.10. Under SSA, the country has seen massive infrastructure development at the school level. Apart from opening over 3 lakh new schools, SSA has also provided basic facilities in existing schools. The average student–classroom ratio (SCR) which was 39 in 2005–06 has come down to 32 in 2009–10. There are still a large number of schools which do not have these minimum facilities. Only 4.8 per cent government schools have all nine facilities stipulated in the RTE Act, approximately one-third of the total schools have up to seven facilities, and about 30 per cent schools do not have even five of these facilities. Keeping in view the RTE stipulations, these facilities have to be provided in all schools in a time-bound manner.

21.11. The biggest concern in elementary education is the poor level of student learning—both scholastic and co-scholastic/non-cognitive. Evidence suggests that learning outcomes for children in Indian schools are far below corresponding class levels in other countries, and that the learning trajectories for children who remain in school are almost flat. Clearly, the additional time spent by students in school as they move from one class to another is not translating into much improvement in learning levels.

21.12. At the heart of the issue of quality are the weak teaching processes and transactions between teachers and learners that are neither child-friendly nor adopt child-centred approach to curriculum. The capacity, motivation and accountability of teachers to deliver quality education with significant and measurable improvements in learning outcomes of students need to be critically and urgently addressed. Similar challenges of quality of learning also exist at the secondary and higher education levels. Dropout rates in secondary and higher education continue to be high, especially for socially excluded and economically marginalised groups of learners.

21.13. Despite higher levels of enrolment at all levels of education, and a massive increase in physical infrastructure, the value added by formal education is still weak. Poor quality of education resulting in weak learning outcomes at each stage of education is the central challenge facing the Indian education sector today. This is particularly disturbing since both macro- and micro-level evidence suggests that what matters for both national economic growth as well as individuals' ability to participate in this growth process is not the total years of education as much as the quality of education and value-addition for each successive year in school as represented by continuously improving learning outcomes and skills. Improving learning outcomes is crucial for inclusive growth and, therefore, a major focus of the Twelfth Plan will be on measuring and improving learning outcomes for all children, with a clear recognition that increasing inputs (number of schools, classrooms, teachers and so on) will by themselves not be enough to ensure quality education for all children.

Strategies

21.14. The Twelfth Plan needs to address these challenges in an integrated and holistic manner. The focus needs to be on meeting the residual needs of access with sharper focus on the needs of the disadvantaged social groups and the difficult-to-reach areas; improving the school infrastructure in keeping with the RTE stipulations; increasing enrolment at the upper primary and secondary school levels; lowering dropout rates across the board; and, broad-based improvement in the quality of education with special emphasis on improving *learning outcomes*. The four main priorities for education policy have been access, equity, quality and governance. The Twelfth Plan will continue to prioritise these four areas, but will place the greatest emphasis on improving learning outcomes at all levels.

21.15. It is critical for the country to make secondary education much more job-relevant through skills training within the schools. For this, higher investments will need to be made to equip secondary schools with teachers/trainers who have technical skills, and equipment (such as workshops, machines, computer equipment) that can be used to impart technical and vocational skills. In countries such as South Korea and Australia, 25–40 per cent of high school students opt for vocational courses, making them job-ready once they finish Grade 12. The vocational credits they earn in secondary schools are recognised by the general education system and a high proportion of these students return to universities to pursue a college degree at a later stage.

Access

21.16. The challenge of access is no longer one of enrolments at the primary level, but one of increasing attendance, reducing dropouts and increasing enrolments at the secondary level. These challenges will have to be tackled through a multi-pronged strategy that should include: (*i*) a realistic assessment of the problems of the most vulnerable categories of children; (*ii*) measures to help schools meet the required PTR, classroom and other infrastructure norms (since they impact the retention of children); (*iii*) improving management systems for better tracking and monitoring of school functioning; (*iv*) a focus on improvements in teaching–learning processes; and (*v*) on developing schools as inclusive learning spaces. Improving learning outcomes at the upper primary level is a critical requirement for improving enrolment levels in secondary schools. A big part of the increase in secondary enrolment has to come from students who are better prepared to benefit from secondary education and, therefore, are able to continue their education rather than drop out. This will require increasing the effectiveness of teaching models at both the primary and the secondary levels.

Equity

21.17. While discussing the issue of social access and equity, the tendency is to confine it to broad categories like SC, ST, Muslims, girls and so on. But these are not homogenous groups. Social realities are far too complex and there are groups within these groups, which for different reasons are more disadvantaged than the category as a whole. In order to fully meet the goal of universal access, the Twelfth Plan will need to remove barriers to access arising out of such social and economic realities. Special focus would be to ensure educational access in civil strife–affected areas and in context of rising urbanisation. While the gaps in average enrolments between disadvantaged groups and the general population have decreased, there is still a considerably large gap in learning levels with historically disadvantaged and economically weaker children having significantly lower learning outcomes. These gaps exist at the point of entry into the school system and continue to grow over time. Large and growing learning gaps threaten the equity gains achieved on the enrolment front because children with lower levels of learning are more likely to drop out. Therefore, it is essential to bridge gaps in learning levels at an early stage if the equity goals of the Twelfth Plan are to be met effectively.

21.18. Given the complex and chronic nature of inequality and exclusion, the strategies adopted so far have tended to be somewhat isolated, fragmented and devoid of institutional support. As a result, the many forms that exclusion takes, and the different ways in which it is manifested, have not been sufficiently addressed across the landscape of access, participation, retention, achievement and completion of elementary education. This makes exclusion the single most important challenge in universalising elementary education. The Twelfth Plan will, therefore, address the issue of equity as integral to the whole gamut of elementary education, moving away from an incentives-and-provisions-based approach to a rights and entitlements approach.

Quality

21.19. Improvement of the quality of education is strongly linked to the quality of physical space, textual materials, classroom processes, academic support to the teachers, assessment procedures and community involvement. All these areas will continue to receive support during the Twelfth Plan period. While adequate inputs and infrastructure are necessary for the proper functioning of schools, inputs will not automatically translate into effective teaching–learning processes or satisfactory learning outcomes. Therefore, the Twelfth Plan will treat improving school inputs as just the starting point in improving educational quality, and will take a more comprehensive view for building a strong systemic focus on teacher capacity, improving school leadership/management, strengthening academic support system, better community and parents' participation, measuring and improving learning outcomes in a continuous manner. Focus would be on provision for child-friendly schools and systems in teaching and learning processes as well as in improved water, sanitation, hygiene and midday meal practices. Considerable resources will be invested to not only provide high-quality independent measures of student learning levels and trajectories over time, but also resources for large-scale instructional changes that will lead to improvement in classroom transactions leading to better learning outcomes.

Governance

21.20. Several studies have reported the challenges in education governance exemplified by teacher absence, delayed fund flows to schools and administrative capabilities at the school level. Studies have also found that improved measurement and management of teacher performance has a significant positive impact on student learning outcomes. Specific and targeted measures of student learning along with measures to hold teachers, schools and school systems accountable for these learning outcomes will go a long way in improving governance by orienting the education system towards outcomes. The Twelfth Plan will prioritise and invest in improving educational leadership and management at the district, block and school levels, with a focus on making better use of data and governing the education system with the objective of improving learning outcomes at all levels of schooling.

21.21. While there is a broad range of challenges facing education in the country, a focus on learning outcomes is a unifying theme of the Twelfth Plan. Addressing the problem of quality will simultaneously address many of the other challenges. This is not to say that inputs and resources do not matter, but focusing on learning outcomes will also help to ensure that these inputs and resources are provided and utilised in a manner where they have the greatest impact. Research from around the world highlights the importance of early childhood education, and suggests that high-quality early childhood education may have the highest long-term returns in terms of improved human development. The Twelfth Plan will therefore place a high priority on universalising pre-school education and improving school preparedness—especially for historically and economically disadvantaged children. More broadly, the approach of the Twelfth Plan for school education will be to define and measure outcomes, and allocate resources in ways that maximise progress towards achieving these outcomes.

21.22. The Twelfth Plan strategies need to respond to these challenges and drive towards achieving the outcome targets laid out for the Plan (see Box 21.1). The six core elements of the driving principles and strategy for the Twelfth Plan are:

1. All stages of education need to be viewed in an integrated manner, through the perspective of lifelong learning and education;

Box 21.1
Targets for the Twelfth Plan

1. Ensure universal access and, in keeping with letter and spirit of the RTE Act, provide good-quality free and compulsory education to all children in the age group of 6 to 14 years;
2. Improve attendance and reduce dropout rates at the elementary level to below 10 per cent and lower the percentage of OoSC at the elementary level to below 2 per cent for all socio-economic and minority groups and in all States;
3. Increase enrolments at higher levels of education and raise the Gross Enrolment Ratio (GER) at the secondary level to over 90 per cent, at the Senior Secondary level to over 65 per cent;
4. Raise the overall literacy rate to over 80 per cent and reduce the gender gap in literacy to less than 10 per cent;
5. Provide at least one year of well-supported/well-resourced pre-school education in primary schools to all children, particularly those in educationally backward blocks (EBBs); and
6. Improve learning outcomes that are measured, monitored and reported independently at all levels of school education with a special focus on ensuring that all children master basic reading and numeracy skills by class 2 and skills of critical thinking, expression and problem solving by class 5.

2. Strengthening the quality of teaching–learning processes requires comprehensive concerted large-scale efforts with simultaneous attention to how these processes translate into better outcomes;
3. Motivation, capacity and accountability of teachers for improving learning outcomes at all levels must be focused upon;
4. Governance of educational institutions requires an institutional focus on quality based on principles of autonomy, accountability and performance; this may involve fundamentally re-defining the recruitment criteria, eligibility of teachers and merit-based processes of recruitment in these institutions;
5. Within a common national legal and policy framework, innovations and diversity of approaches will be encouraged in matters of curricula, pedagogies and community engagements in order to respond to the diversity of learner groups, regional/social contexts and various stages/forms of institutional and human development in the educational sector; and
6. It is imperative to strengthen the monitoring and accountability mechanisms of stakeholders in school education including community and parents as envisaged under the RTE Act.

21.23. The following subsections provide details of strategy and initiatives for elementary education and then secondary education. This is followed by a section on issues that cut across school education such as the use of technology, teacher education, governance and school leadership, followed by a section on adult education.

ELEMENTARY EDUCATION

21.24. Elementary Education comprising primary (Class I–V) and upper primary (Class VI–VIII) forms the foundation of the education pyramid. Unless this foundation is strengthened, it will not be feasible to achieve the goal of universal access to *quality education* for all. A major achievement in recent years has been the establishment of Constitutional and legal underpinnings for achieving universal elementary education. The *Right of Children to Free and Compulsory Education (RTE) Act*, 2009, became operative on 1 April 2010.

REVIEW OF THE ELEVENTH PLAN

21.25. With the RTE Act, 2009, becoming operational from 1 April 2010, the vision and strategies of the ongoing SSA were harmonised with the RTE mandate and the programme norms were revised accordingly. Financial outlays were enhanced and the changes approved to the annual work plans to enable government schools to become RTE Act compliant.

Enrolments

21.26. Against an estimated child population of 192 million in the 6–14 age group, 195 million children were enrolled at the elementary stage in 2009–10. The GER[2] increased from 111.2 per cent in 2006–07 to 115 per cent in 2009–10 and the Net Enrolment Ratio (NER)[3] improved significantly from 92.7 per cent to 98 per cent during this period. The GERs for SCs and STs range between 130 per cent and 140 per cent at the national level and, in some States, these are nearly double that of eligible age group children. GER in excess of 100 per cent at the primary stage indicates presence of overage and underage children in the schools, and reflects the delayed provision of access to schooling and lack of pre-schooling facilities, particularly in rural areas.

21.27. Girls account for the majority (5.3 million) of the additional enrolment of 7.21 million children between 2006–07 and 2009–10. More than half of them (53 per cent) belong to SCs and STs. Three initiatives of the Eleventh Plan helped to increase the enrolment of girls. These included (*i*) setting up of 3,600 Kasturba Gandhi Balika Vidyalayas in 27 States and Union Territories (UTs), (*ii*) establishment of 7,000 Early Childhood Care Centres in EBBs and (*iii*) implementation of Mahila Samakhya programme in ten States.

21.28. The GER at upper primary level is low, even though it improved by 11.8 per cent in the four years between 2006–07 and 2009–10. At 62 per cent the NER at upper primary level is also a cause for concern. This varies from 47 per cent in UP and 53.1 per cent in Bihar to 91 per cent in Tamil Nadu and 83 per cent in Himachal Pradesh.[4] It is evident that although a larger number of children are entering the educational system, all of them are not progressing through the system and this progression is uneven across the States.

21.29. A large number of children are still OoS. Of the 8.1 million OoSC in the country in 2009, UP (34 per cent), Bihar (17 per cent), Rajasthan (12 per cent) and West Bengal (9 per cent) account for 72 per cent.[5] Although surveys have reported a decline in the proportion of OoSC to the corresponding child population of various communities such as SCs, STs and Muslims,[6] these estimates need to be taken with caution, keeping in mind the steep decline in absolute numbers of OoSC reported in the corresponding period. A recent study for rural India places the proportion of children not enrolled in schools at 3.5 per cent.[7] However, in a few States like Rajasthan and UP, the percentage of OoS girls in the age group of 11–14 years is as high as 8.9 per cent and 9.7 per cent, respectively.[8]

21.30. The Eleventh Plan had targeted a reduction in dropout rates from 50 per cent to 20 per cent at the elementary stage. Even though there has been some reduction, progress has not been satisfactory and the national average is still as high as 42.39 per cent. The dropout rates for SC and ST children at 51.25 per cent and 57.58 per cent, respectively, are much higher than that for non-SC/ST children at 37.22 per cent. This clearly suggests the challenge of school retention of children from vulnerable communities.

21.31. Having achieved near-universal enrolment at the lower primary level, it is critical to turn the focus on the poor levels of learning outcomes achieved by children who complete five years of primary schooling. Several independently conducted national studies including the ASER (2005 to 2011) and the School Learning Study (2010) have reported very low levels of learning among Indian school children. The ASER 2011 findings illustrate that over half the children in class V are unable to read even at class II level. In the recent Organisation for Economic Co-operation and Development–Programme for International Student Assessment (OECD–PISA) study, India has been placed at the tail-end in international comparisons rating (PISA-2009+). These results underscore the fact that quality of education should be the key focus of attention in the Twelfth Plan. Improving learning outcomes, with a focus on supplemental instruction for disadvantaged children, will directly contribute to the objective of reducing dropouts, because evidence suggests that children who fall behind grade-appropriate learning levels are significantly more likely to drop out. The structure of enrolments in elementary education shows that about 80 per cent of children are enrolled in government and government-aided institutions; therefore, the focus on quality improvement in elementary education has to be on government institutions.

21.32. Some progress has been made in preparing children better for primary education. Pre-school enrolment has more than doubled from 21 per cent in 2005 to 47 per cent in 2010.[9] More recent ASER data (2010) indicates that 83.6 per cent of 3- to 6-year-olds in rural areas are enrolled in some preschool programme mostly in Integrated Child Development Services (ICDS) centres, including those in private pre-schools. The quality issues of pre-primary education in Anganwadi need serious review.

21.33. During the Eleventh Plan, the Sarva Shiksha Abhiyan (SSA) was the flagship programme for impacting elementary education, but the following major Central Government schemes and programmes were also implemented: National Programme of Nutritional Support to Primary Education (NP-NSPE; commonly known as the Mid-Day Meal Scheme), Teacher Education Scheme; Mahila Samakhya; Schemes for Providing Quality Education in Madrasas (SPQEM) and Infrastructure Development in Minority Institutions (IDMI).

SARVA SHIKSHA ABHIYAN (SSA)

21.34. The SSA is implemented as India's main programme for universalisation of elementary education (UEE). Its overall goals include universal access and retention, bridging of gender and social gaps in enrolment levels and enhancement of learning levels of all children. The SSA has merged components of the National Programme for Education of Girls at Elementary Level (NPEGEL) and the residential school scheme, Kasturba Gandhi Balika Vidyalaya

(KGBV), that have focus on girls' education. The *approved outlay for* SSA in the Eleventh Plan was ₹71,000 crore. Against this, an amount of ₹77,586 crore was released to the States. Details of cumulative progress made under the SSA up to 2011–12 are given in Table 21.1.

TABLE 21.1
Cumulative Progress under SSA up to 2011–12

S. No.	Item	Sanctions
1	Opening of New Schools	2,09,914
2	Opening of New Upper Primary Schools	1,73,969
3	Construction of Primary Schools	1,92,392
4	Construction of Upper Primary Schools	1,05,562
5	Construction of Additional Classrooms	16,03,789
6	Toilets	5,83,529
7	Drinking Water facilities	2,23,086
8	Teachers	19,65,207

Source: Ministry of HRD.

21.35. Though there was notable success in expanding capacity and enrolments during the Eleventh Plan, the challenge of raising quality standards still remains. Although the number of elementary schools has increased to 13.04 lakh, many schools lack the basic infrastructure facilities required under the RTE Act. For example, the retention of girls in school remains difficult given that over 63 per cent of rural schools have no usable toilet facilities for them.[10] If the envisaged convergence of the Mahatma Gandhi National Rural Employment Guarantee Scheme (MGNREGS), Total Sanitation Programme (TSP) and Drinking Water Supply (DWS) Mission materialises, some of these infrastructural shortcomings could be mitigated. While bridging infrastructure gaps may be achievable, it will be far more challenging to bridge learning gaps.

TWELFTH PLAN STRATEGY

21.36. The overarching goal of the Twelfth Plan is to enrol OoSC, reduce dropouts and improve learning outcomes across the elementary school years. In order to enrol OoSC, strengthening of institutional capacity, developing an appropriate statistical base, harmonising the definition of OoSC and finally identification and mainstreaming of all children into age-appropriate class would be needed. Reduction in dropout rates is closely linked to quality. There is a need for a system-wide effort to move the focus of all activity in elementary education from schooling to learning. This entails a shift at every level, macro and micro, whether in planning, resource allocation and implementation or measurement of processes and practices that is designed to achieve significant, substantial and continuous improvement in children's learning outcomes. The entire process of education should be firmly anchored to the notion that every child must be in school and learning well.

21.37. A major focus of the Twelfth Plan will be on implementing the objectives of the RTE Act and aligning the government policies and practices with the overall goal of providing quality schooling for all children until the age of 14 years. The States that have seven-year elementary education cycle (four years of primary education and three years of upper primary education) have begun to realign to eight-year cycle. During the Twelfth Plan this would be implemented throughout the country. All the States have notified State-specific rules under the Act. Pursuant to the RTE Act, notifications of teacher qualifications under section 23 of the RTE Act and the prescription of a Teacher Eligibility Test (TET) by the NCTE have also been issued.

21.38. Clear articulation of learning goals is the critical first step in this process. National learning standards must be developed on the basis of which States should be encouraged to define, in simple terms, meaningful learning goals to be achieved at the end of each class or set of classes. Resources will have to be devoted to developing concrete, achievable measures of student learning at the State and national level. Articulation and expression, team work, critical thinking and problem solving are important skills to be learned, alongside basic literacy and numeracy. The meaning of literacy and numeracy should not be traditional, but keep in mind, reading, and math literacy as defined by PISA/OECD countries contextualised for Indian conditions. Teachers and administrators should be reoriented to ensure that they understand and imbibe the values of critical thinking, problem solving and expression. The National Curriculum Framework 2005 (NCF-2005) and its accompanying 22 focus group reports form the basis for curriculum revival and improved learning outcomes in the country. The formulations of NCF-2005 need to be converted into tangible teaching–learning materials, classroom transactions and assessment systems in every State of the country. The creation of improved textbooks by the National Council of Educational Research and Training (NCERT) after NCF-2005, used mostly by schools affiliated with the Central Board of Secondary Education (CBSE), needs to be emulated in every State to cover all the children of the country.

21.39. Once basic goals are clearly articulated, all aspects of the elementary education system (such as methods of teaching–learning, use of materials, grouping for effective instruction, optimal use of time, daily instructional time and number of days of teaching, measurement of progress, capacity building and ongoing support for teachers and administrators) will need to be strongly aligned to the achievement of the learning goals. System-level administrators at various levels need to ensure that the activities of the system at every level are aligned to the stated goals. Periodic reviews (at least annually) need to be conducted to track progress and refine and rework strategies to reach the stated goals.

21.40. The elementary education system needs to focus on two major tasks. First, children entering school should be prepared and should learn basics by the time they complete class 2 or 3. Second, the proportion of children who are lagging behind in higher grades (class 3, 4 and 5 and also in upper primary) acquire required levels of competencies. There is strong evidence that for children whose home language is different from the textbook language with no supplemental parental guidance at home, problems of 'coping' eliminate them from the system earlier on by class 3. A great deal of attention needs to be paid to such linguistically determined barriers in the passage of children from lower to higher classes. There is a need to develop primers for bridging the home language to the school language from pre-school to class 1 and 2, which is a very effective mechanism to ensure child motivation and 'coping' ability to deal with school texts. Besides, a strong foundational learning support needs to be immediately given to children in class 3–5, and 6–8 who have not even achieved basic skills to negotiate the curriculum of upper primary or secondary schooling to which they will transit. The methodology of Comprehensive and Continuous Evaluation (CCE) mandated by the RTE Act once properly implemented can go a long way in tackling this issue.

21.41. To make sure that all the children make progress towards the learning goals, new and innovative strategies will have to be tried in terms of teaching–learning and consequently in preparing and supporting teachers. The overall strategy for elementary education in the Twelfth Plan is summarised in Box 21.2.

TWELFTH PLAN INITIATIVES

21.42. SSA will continue to be the *flagship* programme for developing elementary education during the Twelfth Plan for realising the rights to elementary education for each and every child. There would be four strategic areas under SSA during the Twelfth Plan. These are: (*i*) strong focus on learning outcomes; (*ii*) addressing residual access and equity gaps; (*iii*) focus on teacher and education leadership; (*iv*) linkages with other sectors and programmes. These are described in the following sections.

I. Strong Focus on Learning Outcomes

21.43. Quality in education is inherently dependent on the following six aspects: (*i*) curriculum and learning objectives, (*ii*) learning materials, (*iii*) pedagogic processes, (*iv*) classroom assessment frameworks, (*v*) teacher support in the classrooms, and (*vi*) school leadership and management development. A new framework for curriculum is needed at regular intervals in order to take cognizance of the developing issues in society and how to address them. A variety of learning packages should be developed at State and district levels, with adequate provision for cluster- and school-level modifications to aid the teacher and provide increased choice. As

> **Box 21.2**
> **Twelfth Plan Strategy for Elementary Education**
>
> 1. Shift from a project-based approach of SSA to a unified RTE-based governance system for UEE;
> 2. Address residual access and equity gaps in elementary education by adopting special measures to ensure regular attendance of children in schools and devising special strategy to tackle the problem of dropping out before completing the full cycle of elementary schooling;
> 3. Integrate pre-school education with primary schooling in order to lay a strong foundation for learning during primary school;
> 4. Prioritise education quality with a system-wide focus on learning outcomes that are assessed through classroom-based CCE independently measured, monitored and reported at the block/district/State levels;
> 5. Focus on early grade supplemental instruction to ensure that all children achieve the defined age-/class-specific learning levels by the end of class 2;
> 6. Articulate clear learning goals that have to be achieved by the end of each class or set of classes. These goals should be understood by parents and teachers;
> 7. Improve teacher training with an emphasis on effective pedagogy given the realities of Indian classrooms such as multi-age, multi-grade and multi-level contexts. Also, make teachers' professional development a needs-driven process as opposed to top-down decision wherein curriculum design and delivery is centrally driven;
> 8. Invest in both top-down administrative oversight and bottom-up community-driven monitoring of schools;
> 9. Focus on strengthening practices of good governance in all schools and related institutions that ensure performance-based internal and external accountability for teachers and administrators at all levels and also ensure holistic assessment-driven development of schools;
> 10. Invest in strengthening ongoing and continuous field-based systems of academic support to schools and teachers and in strengthening district and block-level capacity for better management and leadership;
> 11. Support States to set learning goals and invest in independent monitoring of outcomes, but provide States with substantial autonomy in how to achieve these goals, and provide additional results-based financing to States who show the most improvement in educational outcomes;
> 12. Provide a supportive environment for evaluation of innovative practices, and sharing of best practices across States and districts;
> 13. Support States towards motivation, capacity development and accountability of community and parents for ensuring regular attendance and quality education; and
> 14. Ensure convergence with panchayats, Community-Based Organisations (CBOs) and other sectors at school level.

education is concerned with all-round development of the child (physical, socio-emotional along with cognitive), all aspects need to be assessed rather than only academic achievement. During the Twelfth Plan, however, there will be a system-wide focus on holistic development of children by improving learning outcomes and other non-scholastic areas. Learning enhancement programme (LEP) under the SSA would be continued in the Twelfth Plan, for which specific zones of operation should be identified by the concerned State/District authorities. Every year, States need to articulate the learning goals that are being targeted and the strategies (methods, materials, models and measurement) that will be used to reach those goals. Institutional assessment/accreditation of the elementary schools will be introduced in the Twelfth Plan, and possibly made mandatory from the Thirteenth Plan onwards.

(A) Strong Focus on Early Years in School

21.44. Research on the impact of PTR on student learning suggests that a low PTR matters most at younger ages, when children are being socialised into the process of learning, and less so in older classes. Thus, it may make sense to supplement the requirements under the RTE, for communities to hire multiple community-based teachers on contract to focus on improving school preparedness and basic literacy and numeracy for pre-school children. In addition, class I should receive special attention in the Twelfth Plan period. Ideally, the strongest or most experienced teacher in the school should be assigned to this class. States must develop a process to identify specialist teachers of early/initial primary education and design specific professional development and academic support programmes for them. If the foundations are strong and solid in class I, many of the later problems that children encounter—both academically and non-academically—would be reduced. Special training needs to be provided each year to the teachers who will work with class I. Countries like Finland, Sweden and Denmark, who top the PISA tests have demonstrated that equity can considerably help to improve overall learning outcomes, through mixed and inclusive classrooms, that do not segregate the so-called 'bright' and 'slow learners', or children from different social, ethnic or other differences. Students who had attended pre-primary tend to perform better than those who have not. These approaches need to be emulated in our classrooms too so that the classrooms of the country resonate with the diversity of our country, and help improve learning outcomes as the Scandinavian school systems have shown.

(B) Review of School Textbooks

21.45. School textbooks should be reviewed by NCERT/State Council of Educational Research and Training (SCERT) to be made more engaging yet simple and interesting. Review of textbooks must always be accompanied by special development of teachers to use these books effectively. Learning levels expected of children as seen in textbooks should be aligned to the overall learning goals—keeping in mind that the goals and standards should be achievable by majority of the children. Work-books should accompany textbooks for mathematics, science and languages. The textbook should be supplemented by learning facilitation manuals for teachers for improving classroom transaction. All government schools should be provided with electricity and facilities for computer-aided learning on a large scale. Private sector resources should also be enlisted for content development based on curriculum and syllabi.

(C) Enhancing Facilities in Schools

21.46. A programme for Information and Communication Technology (ICT) in elementary schools will replace the erstwhile Computer-Aided Learning (CAL) under SSA. This would include provision of networked computers, accessories and an Internet connection in a phased manner. A variety of software tools and pedagogically appropriate e-content in local languages will be sourced or developed to serve the school curriculum. The focus will be to enable students and teachers to access wide variety of resources available in the digital format, and digital resources that are seamlessly integrated in classroom processes. Efforts will be made to adopt energy-efficient, cost-effective ICT solutions, which increase the number of access points in each school enabling more and more children to use the facility more frequently. Appropriate mechanisms to maintain the infrastructure and protect it from breakdowns will be ensured. ICT should also be used to network teachers and schools in a specific geography—this would enhance collaborative teaching and learning. The RTE Act mandates provision of laboratory and library facilities in schools. SSA funding would be made available for this purpose particularly to cater to children from the disadvantaged groups.

(D) Research for Quality Improvement

21.47. Priority will be given to research projects concerned with quality-related issues, including, for example, assessing States' curriculum in the light of NCF-2005, students' learning outcomes, students' and teachers' attendance rates, effectiveness of teacher training, efficacy of textbooks and other TLMs, quality of academic supervision provided by Block Resource Centres (BRCs)/Cluster Resource Centres (CRCs)/District Institutes of Education and Training (DIETs), discriminatory practices in schools, teaching–learning in classrooms, implementation of CCE in schools, role of School Management Committees (SMCs) in school management; estimating OoSC; status and effectiveness of Special training centres, completion rate/dropout rate and transition rate; and so on.

(E) Pre-Primary Education

21.48. Every primary school would be facilitated to have a pre-primary section to provide pre-primary education with a school readiness programme for at least one year for children in the age group of four to six years. The concept of 'early learning units' would be introduced which would bring together the pre-primary and early primary grades into an integrated unit. The implementation would be phased out and by the end of the Twelfth Plan, about 50 per cent of the schools would have pre-primary classes. Educationally lagging States/Districts/Blocks should be covered on priority basis. For this, pre-school education would be included under SSA/RTE as a separate component with a specific budget line. NCTE would lay down standard qualifications and adapt its TET guidelines to accommodate teachers of this Early Learning Stage, that is, pre-primary and Grades 1 and 2. A few States have planned Anganwadi in primary schools. Pre-service teacher preparation curriculum needs to be enhanced to address needs of pre-primary children. Pre-Service Teacher Education in the area of Early Childhood Education must be significantly strengthened. Selected universities and institutions must be specifically encouraged to run rigorous exemplar Early Childhood Teacher Education programmes. There is a huge dearth of other specialists in this area—developmental psychologists, curriculum developers for early childhood education and so on. Similar programmes in these areas too need to be designed and implemented. Short-term certified refresher programmes for in-service early childhood teachers and Anganwadi workers (this could also include teachers of early primary classes) must be designed and implemented by identified organisations.

21.49. The RTE Act has provided for pre-primary education for underprivileged children enrolled in private schools in 25 per cent earmarked seats. States should also be free to obtain services from reputed private-aided and unaided institutions/NGOs and to compensate them on a cost recovery basis for these services. Communities can also be empowered and provided the financial resources to hire one or more educated local young men and women (meeting minimum qualifications) on a contractual basis for dedicated pre-school instruction. Broadly, from planning to implementation, this pre-school year should be well resourced and supported. Currently, there is an overlap with ICDS in so far as pre-primary education is concerned. A strategy could be developed for gradual shift of the pre-primary year from the purview of ICDS to the primary schools. The nutrition component of ICDS in any case gets addressed through midday meal. Thus, in the third and fourth year, children go to the Anganwadi centres for early childhood education and in the fifth year, children attend pre-primary classes in regular schools that would have adequate provision for the same. This would help to improve retention at the primary stage.

(F) Moving From Grade-Level to Ability-Level Teaching–Learning

21.50. Recent research in the country and abroad underlines the need for teaching children from the level that they are and taking them to the level that they need to be. This requires a substantial rethinking of the age–grade instructional pattern by which the education system is organised. In the last decade there have been several promising approaches to break away from this mould in order to enhance and accelerate children's learning. Such approaches have been tried on scale in the government and also by non-governmental organisations (NGOs). However, barring the effort of some NGOs, none others have been rigorously evaluated. The main government effort in this direction is activity-based learning (ABL) or multi-grade multi-level learning (MGML) that is reaching more than 3 million children. Three States—Andhra Pradesh, Karnataka and Tamil Nadu—have expanded the programme to all schools in their States. This method promotes child-friendly learning and assessment methods that enable children to be 'free from fear and anxiety' and in promoting social inclusion among children in the classroom situations. Systemic reforms are needed to ensure its sustainability, including its integration with curriculum/textbooks, pre-service teacher education, sustainability across leadership changes. There is a need for an objective evaluation of these efforts along with other initiatives that are child friendly, effective in multi-grade, multi-ability situations before scaling up in the country.

(G) Promote State-Level/Local-Level Innovation

21.51. Across the country, there are several promising approaches to improve teaching–learning at the elementary stage. These need to be explored in greater depth to understand the basic elements of their functioning and their impact on learning outcomes. Among others, these include ABL initiated by the Government of Tamil Nadu, Gujarat government's innovative Gunotsav programme, and Punjab government's Purrho Punjab initiative. Among efforts initiated by non-government bodies (often working in collaboration with State Governments), among others, there is the Pratham Read India programme, the Hoshangabad Science Teaching Programme and Prashika of Eklavya, and other initiatives undertaken by UNICEF, Azim Premji Foundation, Tata Institute of Social Sciences and Shiv Nadar Foundation. These are all promising interventions that can be scaled up further during the Twelfth Plan in order to achieve explicit focus on learning outcomes.

(H) Child-Friendly Assessment

21.52. The RTE Act mandates that a system of Continuous and Comprehensive Evaluation should be put in place to enable the teacher to be continuously guided by the child's response and participation in classroom activities. Support will, therefore, be provided to enable teachers to maintain child-wise portfolios, incorporating a record of children's work and progress—as an integral part of their teaching–learning process. Teacher Training programme will include training on systems for CCE. Since a majority of children in Indian schools are not at grade level, adequate flexibility needs to be provided in the CCE framework and in its implementation to identify and to address the needs of such children. In fact, teacher education institutes must be mandated to use (not just teach) CCE during the pre-service teacher preparation programmes.

21.53. Regular and accurate reports of student learning and progress should be provided to parents, along with encouragement and guidance for parents on how to support their child's educational progress. It is important to de-stigmatise falling behind ('failing'). Every child (and parent) needs to be assured that learning basic skills is well within his/her reach, and if he/she is not learning, it is a failure of the system rather than that of the child. 'Assessment of learning' and 'assessment for learning' are two aspects of education representing accountability and improvement. One cannot be emphasised over the other and neither can be sacrificed in favour of the other. While the teacher needs to 'assess for learning', the administrators and the parents of the children need 'assessment of learning'. In the spirit of these aspects, teachers must be supported to use these 'learning reports' to modify their classroom/teaching–learning approaches.

(I) Measuring Learning

21.54. Considerable efforts and resources are needed to develop independent and objective and achievable measures of student learning at the school, block, district and State levels that approach the issue with an understanding of the linguistic complexities while formulating their testing methods. It is expected that better measurement and reporting of outcomes will play a strong catalysing role in making State, district and block-level education administrators focus more on improving education quality as measured by student mastery of achieving the defined grade-wise learning outcomes. States should be encouraged to define transparent, meaningful and simple learning levels to be achieved at the end of class 2, 5 and 8. Mechanisms must be put in place to ensure that schools neither 'teach these external tests' nor use these for punitive measures.

(J) Learning from International Experience

21.55. There are also several international initiatives that have recognised the centrality of moving from focus on enrolment to learning outcomes. United Nations Educational, Scientific and Cultural Organization (UNESCO) and the Centre for Universal Education (CUE) at the Brookings Institution have recently set up a 'Learning Metrics Task Force' to investigate the feasibility of identifying common learning goals to improve learning opportunities and outcomes for children and youth. India should both learn from these international efforts, where possible, and more importantly, play a leading role in defining and implementing these standards, since it has the largest primary school education system in the world and also has the world's largest number of children who do not meet basic learning levels.

II. Address Residual Access and Equity Gaps

21.56. Special efforts are needed in the Twelfth Plan for those children who are still not in school or who need sustained attention for remaining linked to school. Here the focus has to be on every child in school and learning well. So efforts must include strategies for effective and sustained mainstreaming with accelerated learning strategies built in as part of the mainstreaming strategy. Special focus would be on targeting OoSC, girls and socially excluded groups in specific locations.

(A) Targeting Out-of-School Children

21.57. In order to achieve universal elementary education in a planned and time-bound manner, better targeting of uncovered and under-covered children is necessary. Concerted and flexible efforts are needed to reach out to all OoSC, including children with special needs (CWSN) and street children. Bridging the social and gender gaps in enrolment with regard to SCs, STs and minority girls should receive special attention. Residential programmes for the 11–14 age group need continued support as do the efforts to ensure sustained mainstreaming into the regular school system. The option of open schooling needs to be strengthened so that rural labour, artisans and others in petty jobs in villages and urban slums achieve some learning equivalency in order to enable them to continue in community polytechnics, part-time community colleges, Jan Shikshan Sansthan (JSS) and accredited Skill Knowledge Providers (SKPs) to pursue secondary education and acquire upgraded vocational skills. Those who have dropped out before completing the elementary stage need opportunities for education and certification in a flexible manner. Helping such children (those who have been left out or left behind) to accelerate to the learning levels of their counterparts in school has to be an important part of the strategy for mainstreaming. Hence, the identification of OoSC should include an assessment of current ability to read and to do arithmetic, comprehension, critical thinking, problem solving as well as their ability to express themselves. Teachers would require special training for 'accelerated learning' of OoSC to be mainstreamed into age-appropriate class. States would need guidance for this.

(B) Provision of Residential Schools

21.58. Residential schools are particularly useful to reach out to children from vulnerable sections of society. The RTE-enabled SSA envisages the provision of residential schools for children in areas of civil strife, children of migrating populations and tribal children. Special thrust is needed for children at risk that include orphans, run-away platform children, Human Immunodeficiency Virus/Acquired Immunodeficiency Syndrome (HIV/AIDS) patients, children of sex workers, and so on. It also requires that transport/escorts be provided for children in areas of civil strife, for children with disabilities, and for children of the most marginalised ST and SC groups. Residential schooling opportunities are also excellent for accelerating learning among children. Residential facilities for children should be provided by: (*i*) redeploying existing government/local body buildings and underutilised schools, (*ii*) constructing new buildings where redeploying existing buildings is not possible. New buildings will be as per KGBV norms and school playgrounds will be developed in convergence with Sarva Krida Abhiyan (SKA).

(C) Focus on SC/ST Children

21.59. At least 5 per cent of existing Government elementary schools in all EBBs with more than 50 per cent tribal population would be converted into residential school complexes (RSCs) having provisions for pre-school (non-residential), primary and middle schools. There should be provision of seasonal hostel facilities for children of migrating families both at the place of origin and of migration in urban and rural areas. These hostels will follow norms set out in the KGBV scheme. In EBBs with over 50 per cent tribal population, government schools would be converted into RSCs and seasonal hostels for migrating tribal children. A few State Governments, such as that of Andhra Pradesh, have integrated *Ashram* schools (regular residential schools) under the RTE-harmonised SSA. Other States should follow the same approach. Further, convergence with the Ministry of Tribal Affairs for all *Ashram shala*s should be forged to achieve adequate PTR and infrastructure/facilities/Teaching–Learning Equipment (TLE) *as per* the RTE norms. Special support would be needed to ensure retention and improved learning for children from SC communities that are socially, economically and educationally deprived and discriminated. These efforts need to converge with the programmes of the Ministry of Social Justice and Empowerment (MSJ&E). There is a need to review and revise curriculum addressing caste-based exclusion and promoting inclusion. Interventions for SCs include (*i*) process-based interventions such as curricular review to include discussion on caste-based discrimination in textual material; (*ii*) residential schools run with assistance from the MSJ&E to conform to the RTE norms; (*iii*) convergence on pre-matric scholarships and incentives provided by MSJ&E; (*iv*) partnerships with Dalit Civil Society Organisations (CSOs) for support of Dalit children. As discussed in the previous sections, it is important to plan for improvement of learning of children from disadvantaged backgrounds. It is only when the special efforts and provisions translate into learning gains that such children have a real chance to complete and go beyond elementary education.

(D) Special Provision for Children with Special Needs (CWSN)

21.60. For CWSN, efforts will include identification, educational placement in general schools, school readiness programmes, provision of aids and appliances, development and production of Braille books and construction of ramps and disabled-friendly toilets. Considering the complexities and enormity of the work involved in developing appropriate curricula, NGOs and competent private entities with relevant experience and ability to work in this area should become natural partners in implementation of this aspect of the RTE Act. Such children would need individualised educational plan, for which community mobilisation, parental training and peer sensitisation would be necessary. Engagement of resource teachers and volunteers/caregivers to cater to their needs would also be needed. States must work closely with the Rehabilitation Council of India on this—it is important not to duplicate efforts especially where teacher development in this area is concerned.

(E) Special Focus for Education of Girls

21.61. Promoting girl's education is a critical issue. During the Twelfth Plan not only efforts will be made to enable girls to keep pace with boys, but girls' education will be viewed from the perspective spelt out in the National Policy on Education 1986/92 which states that education should be a transformative force, build women's self-confidence and improve their position in society. Interventions in the Twelfth Plan will be guided by the principle that gender equality in elementary education is both a quality issue and an equity issue. Special focus needs to be placed on developing gender-sensitive curricula, pedagogical practices, teacher training and evaluation. Schools should be developed to be inclusive and safe places. Specific modules on issues such as sexual harassment and violence will need to be developed and integrated into the teacher training design. Other specific initiatives to improve girls' education include:

1. Strengthening and expansion of KGBVs to provide one more KGBV in EBBs, with special focus on wards with high migration rates in urban and semi-urban areas, and EBBs with a high concentration of SC, ST and Muslim populations.
2. NPEGEL programme to include running Bridging Centres, developing MCS as Model Schools for gender, equity and quality integration, development of MCS library to include digital content, including audio visual resources, development of bridging modules and manuals and training of SMCs on gender and equity issues.
3. Mahila Samakhya would be continued as an independent programme with full operational and programme autonomy and a National Resource Centre, with strong State-level or regional units would be set up to strengthen this programme (see 21.84 and 21.85 for details).

21.62. Overall, the interventions with regard to girls' education would be aligned to the 'National Vision for Girls' Education in India: Road-map to 2015' which was developed last year at State and national level through partnership between SSA, Mahila Samakhya and civil society with the support of UNICEF with the aim of ensuring increased and more targeted investments for girls' education through strengthened systems for local service delivery which ensure gender equality in basic education.

(G) Focus on Educationally Backward Minorities

21.63. Even though there has been significant improvement in enrolment and retention of Muslim children in elementary education, the gap between Muslims and non-Muslims continues to be high.

During the Twelfth Plan, the unit of earmarking, targeting and monitoring of interventions for Muslim children would be changed from District to Block. SPQEM and IDMI could be merged. Urdu would be offered as an optional language in schools located in Muslim-dominated areas, along with its attendant requirements like teacher training, TLMs and so on. There seems to be some overlapping activities with the Multi-Sectoral Development Plan (MSDP) of the Ministry of Minorities Affairs and the support extended on a 'first come first serve' basis by the Ministry of Human Resources Development (MHRD). The specific activities of minority institutions supported under the MHRD schemes should be part of the larger district plan prepared for minorities, particularly with regard to the convergent infrastructure approach which is recommended.

21.64. The Central Government has been implementing the *SPQEM* to encourage traditional institutions like madrasas and *maktab*s to modernise their curriculum by giving financial assistance to introduce science, mathematics, social studies, Hindi and English in their curriculum so that academic proficiency for classes I–XII is attainable for children studying in these institutions. This has enabled Muslim children to transit to higher studies and also ensured quality standards similar to the national education system. The States of UP, MP, Andhra Pradesh, Tripura and Jharkhand have been supported with teachers, book banks, science kits, computer laboratories and teacher training for madrasa teachers teaching modern subjects in about 1,000 madrasas. The *Scheme for Infrastructure Development of Private Aided/Unaided Minority Institutions (IDMI)* facilitates education of minorities by augmenting and strengthening of infrastructure in minority schools and expanding facilities for formal education of minority children. Over 100 minority institutions have been assisted during the Eleventh Plan Period. Both these schemes need to be continued in the Twelfth Plan with larger outlays and wider coverage of minority institutions. There is a need to ensure that all efforts for inclusion also result in improved learning outcomes for children from educationally backward communities which is essential for sustained mainstreaming of such children and their continued progress through the education system.

(H) Focused Efforts in Urban Areas

21.65. Along with growth in urban population, urban poverty has increased, as large numbers of families migrate to urban habitations in search of livelihoods. Greater attention needs to be paid to enhancing the access to elementary education by children of urban poor families. Innovative partnerships with urban local bodies are the key to enhancing access and improving learning outcomes (see Box 21.3). Allotment of land and buildings for new schools and extension of existing schools needs to be facilitated. The requirement that schools earmark 25 per cent of their admission for children from disadvantaged groups and weaker sections will require support for related costs: uniforms, bags, books and bridging and supplementary support. SSA norms would need to be revised to provide for financial support to the State for reimbursement of cost to private unaided schools against such admissions and also for other costs mentioned above. In order to cater to the high population density in urban areas, the norms for establishment of new schools in urban areas with high population density should be based on number of children being served per school rather

---

Box 21.3
School Excellence Programme—Mumbai

1. Programme taken up by the Mumbai municipal authorities with technical support of UNICEF to enhance learning outcomes of urban slum children in Mumbai municipal schools targeting 5,00,000 children across 1,327 schools.
2. Involved systematic tracking of school and children, baseline assessment of learning levels of children, development of pedagogy and training of teachers in more inclusive and interactive teaching and learning process, training of headmasters on school leadership and partnership development.
3. Multiple partners involved included the State Bank of India, Tata Consultancy Services, McKinsey as well as several reputed CSOs including Naandi Foundation and Rishi Valley.

than distance. Migration brings huge challenges for children—regular/typical school programmes will not work. States must be encouraged to use specific approaches which have been tried and established as useful.

III. Focus on Teachers and Education Leadership

21.66. Competence of teachers and their motivation is crucial for improving the quality. This would require a number of initiatives towards (i) addressing teacher shortages, particularly through new and rigorous approaches to imparting teaching certifications, (ii) improving the quality of pre-service teacher education, (iii) improving the quality of in-service teacher professional development and options for their upward career mobility with special attention to para-teachers in many States, (iv) enhancing the status of teaching as a profession and improving teachers' motivation to teach well and their accountability for ensuring learning outcomes, (v) improving the quality of teacher educators. It is important to align all ongoing teacher capacity and capability building exercises to the achievement of improved learning outcomes.

21.67. Teachers need to be adequately prepared to deal with the realities of their schools. In many areas, particularly rural areas, there are multi-age, multi-grade and multi-ability classrooms. This would require special competencies amongst teachers to not only have the necessary subject knowledge, but a repertoire of pedagogical approaches and techniques that help them to teach effectively to improve learning outcomes for a diverse group of children. For improving teacher competence, quality of teacher training and the rigor of teaching certification have to be considerably enhanced. Motivating teachers is more difficult. Teachers usually get motivated when they are supported to achieve attainable learning goals for their students, and are recognised and rewarded for the same. The issue of teachers is critical and needs focus; hence, it is discussed separately later in the chapter after secondary education. Similarly, the issues of governance and leadership development, building community partnership and parental engagement, educational leadership and institutionalising a system of school mentoring are common in elementary and secondary education sectors and are dealt later in the chapter.

IV. Linkages with Other Sectors

21.68. In order to achieve targeted outcomes for elementary education, there is a need to bring in resources and knowledge from related sectors. Several States, particularly those that have acute school infrastructure gaps, will face limitation of funds to implement the RTE Act. A pragmatic approach to meet the goals with limited resources is through convergence with schemes like Mahatma Gandhi National Rural Employment Guarantee Scheme (MGNREGS). Appropriate revision in the MGNREGA guidelines would be required to bring about such convergence. Decentralised implementation would ensure that local bodies take up these works on a priority basis and ensure full access to elementary education in a convergent manner.

21.69. The Twelfth Plan target for civil works is given in Table 21.2. School buildings being meaningful assets, particularly in rural areas, additional support could come from Member of Parliament Local Area Development Scheme (MPLADS) and Member of the Legislative Assembly (MLA) funds as well. A few States are already utilising funds under Integrated Action Plan (IAP) and Backward Regions Grant Fund (BRGF) for strengthening school infrastructure. Besides, there is a need to tap funds from philanthropy for accelerated infrastructure building. One creative way is to allow donors to name

TABLE 21.2
Civil Works under SSA in the Twelfth Plan

Items	Number	Estimated Cost (₹ in Cr)
1. New School Buildings	67,010	7,685
2. Residential Schools	10,500	10,500
3. Additional Classrooms	4,98,560	19,942
4. DWS	62,366	468
5. Toilets	3,43,013	2,884
6. KGBVs and so on	3,598	3,692
Total		45,171

Source: Ministry of HRD.

buildings or rooms or install plaques, or other such commemorative features (such as naming a scholarship scheme after a benefactor).

Develop Partnerships with the Community-Based Organisations (CBOs)

21.70. A Council for People's Participation in Education (CPPE) will be set up as a registered autonomous body for institutionalising the partnership through well-defined structures involving both government and voluntary agencies on a regular basis. In addition to processing proposals for funding support for educational projects, such partnerships will provide technical support, facilitate peer interaction amongst practising groups and provide resources and technical persons on a continuous basis. CPPE will be a permanent structure, funded by the government, with functional autonomy but working in consultation with the Central and State Governments.

Integration of Sports and Physical Education

21.71. Physical education, games and sports should be made an integral part of the curriculum and daily routine in schools for the holistic development of children. Provision of infrastructure for these activities should also be made in the Twelfth Plan in convergence with SKA, the principal scheme for broad basing of sports and developing a sports culture in the country. The Schedule to the RTE Act mandates that all schools shall be provided play material, games and sports equipment. Since many urban schools have inadequate facilities of sports on their own, other neighbourhood schools with such facilities in the public and private sectors and also municipal parks and public play fields should be opened up for children of such schools during school hours on nominal maintenance costs. Building on innovative approaches undertaken during the Eleventh Plan, teachers must also be trained to lead quality and inclusive physical education sessions as part of both their pre-service and in-service training.

Integration of Arts in Education

21.72. Visual and performing arts are a critical part of school education and also provide space for children with different abilities. Arts are a powerful tool in the teaching learning process. It enables children to express ideas, emotions and thoughts freely, to comprehend and build perspectives. Children experience joy, sense of freedom in the process of learning when they have the opportunity to explore, to imagine, visualise, observe through their senses, to participate and communicate. It enhances interest as children connect arts with all subjects and with their daily lives. Art also has a cognitive component; it makes us think, reflect, hypothesise, perceive, comprehend and create. Institutions like the National Centre for Performing Arts and the National School of Drama along with the Central academies should contribute significantly to the inclusion of arts in the school curriculum and its implementation.

Increased Role of the Private Sector

21.73. Private providers (including NGOs and non-profits) can play an important role in elementary education. Their legitimate role in expanding elementary education needs to be recognised and a flexible approach needs to be adopted to encourage them to invest in the sector. The current licensing and regulatory restrictions in the sector could be eased and a single window approach should be adopted so that the process of opening new schools by private providers is streamlined. It is also important that the regulations be flexible and context-dependent—care needs to be taken so that schools that are serving disadvantaged populations effectively do not get shut down. A few States have already adopted a more flexible approach in this regard in framing State rules. In all, private players would be encouraged to set up more schools, provided they are committed to, and held accountable for, providing high-quality education and are transparent in their operations.

FUNDING PATTERN

21.74. Government has revised the fund-sharing pattern between the Central and State Governments for implementation of the modified SSA programme, which is now fixed in the 65:35 ratio. The fund-sharing pattern for the States in the NER, however, continues to be in the ratio of 90:10. While the revised fund-sharing pattern may be adequate for most States, some States that are educationally disadvantaged with low levels of literacy, grossly inadequate school infrastructure and difficult terrain face a heavy financial burden to meet the RTE mandate and norms. A big push is called for to enable these States to come at par with other States. This is crucial to achieve national and international goals under the Millennium Development Goals (MDG). Over time, financing of SSA has to be made more sustainable. Since the grants available based on the Thirteenth Finance Commission recommendations for elementary education for the States would extend up to 2015, the new funding pattern (50:50) would be deferred until the beginning of the Thirteenth Plan. Central assistance to the States in terms of per child norms and performance-based financing would gradually be built in along with results-based management. States and institutions which perform well should be incentivised with untied funds. Educational spending should be equitable and more efficient. More pragmatic tax concessions should be devised to encourage private investment in education.

IMPLEMENTATION, MONITORING AND EVALUATION

21.75. The focus in the Twelfth Pan is to address the weaknesses in implementation that have been a major constraint in achieving the goals of previous Plans. Implementation needs to take into account local conditions, it would therefore be desirable to give States (and even districts) a lot of autonomy. Consequently, the approach in this Plan would be to provide clear goals and direction to States and education departments, provide considerable operational autonomy to States on how to achieve these goals, and invest in strong and independent monitoring of outcomes by the Central Government.

21.76. In implementation, equal emphasis would be placed on provision of inputs for quality education (infrastructure, teachers, training, enrolment and other inputs) as well as ensuring that these inputs translate into improved processes (attendance, instructional time) and outcomes (retention, learning outcomes, equity). States will be encouraged to innovate and experiment with ways of achieving these outcomes effectively. Innovations can cover a very broad range of areas—some of which may include methods for systematic assessment of student learning, improved teacher training, innovative pedagogies in the classroom including those that leverage technology in the classroom, supplemental instruction for first-generation learners, methods for improving teacher motivation and effectiveness, and methods for leveraging resources from third parties for improving education. States may also become partners with appropriate third parties to provide key capabilities that may help these goals. States will be encouraged to carefully document and evaluate these initiatives and to share best practices with other States and with the Centre.

21.77. To encourage innovation and sharing of best practices, the Plan will provide a certain amount of untied 'flexi' funds to the States and also provide additional amounts of 'results-based' financing. States in turn will be encouraged to invest in district-level leadership and provide autonomy and resources to districts and encourage capacity building at the district level to monitor and improve education outcomes. To support this endeavour, the Plan will also dedicate resources to high-quality independent measurement and monitoring of learning outcomes (along the lines of the Annual Health Survey). The annual reporting of learning outcomes at State, district and block levels can in turn be used to encourage a mission-like focus on improving education outcomes in the Twelfth Plan.

21.78. A key challenge for e-monitoring is the absence of high-quality data that is updated on a frequent and reliable basis. Infrastructure such as the Unique Identification (UID) could be deployed to keep track of student enrolment, attendance, and dropouts, and biometric authentication could also be deployed to improve teacher attendance. Modern cell phone–based technologies may prove to be a promising way of empowering communities to report real-time data on school performance metrics such as teacher attendance, student attendance, availability of midday meals and so on. Technology platforms such as mobile phones and tablet personal computers (PCs) can also be used for rapid diagnostic testing of student learning, analysis of common mistakes and areas of misunderstanding, and dynamic testing based on performance on initial questions. Several non-profit and third-party organisations are working on building such applications, and States/districts will be encouraged to experiment with such methods for improved real-time data collection on the performance of the education system.

21.79. Finally, it is worth noting that the evidence base for effective policymaking in elementary education is quite limited—especially in crucial areas such as the effectiveness of different types of pedagogy, the effectiveness of using technology within the classroom, the optimal ways to organise children of different initial learning levels in a classroom, and handling multi-grade teaching more generally. The Twelfth Plan will place a high priority on improving research and the evidence base for policymaking, and will provide both funds as well as strong encouragement to States to take up high-quality research studies on primary education in India in partnership with universities and reputed individual researchers. Each State should be encouraged to earmark and spend adequate funds for independent measurement of learning outcomes. While each State may adopt different ways of doing it, some broad central guidelines may be desirable.

MID-DAY MEAL SCHEME (MDMS)

21.80. In keeping with the Constitutional provisions to raise the level of nutrition of children and enable them to develop in a healthy manner, the NP-NSPE was launched as a Centrally sponsored scheme in 1995. Commonly referred to as MDMS, this was expected to enhance enrolment, retention, attendance of children in schools apart from improving their nutritional levels. This was extended to upper primary (classes VI to VIII) children in 3,479 EBBs in 2007 and then universalised at the elementary level in the year 2008. The scheme is implemented through the States/UTs. MDMS is managed and implemented by School Management/Village Education Committees, Panchayati Raj Institutions, and Self-Help Groups. MDMS now includes madrasas and *maktab*s supported under the SSA as well as children under the National Child Labour Projects. A detailed survey of implementation of intended nutritional values including calorific value, protein inclusion, additional nutritional supplements and vitamins, as detailed in the scheme, needs to be carried out to ensure that the nutrition scheme is implemented in both spirit and letter.

Coverage

21.81. MDMS covered 7.18 crore primary school children and 3.36 crore upper primary school children in 2010–11. The coverage of children in the States of Bihar (43 per cent), UP (57 per cent) and Jharkhand (58 per cent) is below the national average of 72 per cent, whereas it is well above the national average in Chhattisgarh (83 per cent) and Odisha (82 per cent). Based on the Annual Work Plan and Budget of the States/UTs for the year 2012–13, the district-wise performance of the MDMS in all the States/UTs has been analysed and the poor performing districts (144) have been identified for focused attention. Of the poor performing districts, 17 are in areas affected by the Left Wing Extremism (LWE); 11 in the North Eastern States (Tripura—3, Meghalaya—4, Assam—4); 17 in tribal districts, and 13 in the hilly areas (Uttarakhand—4, J&K—9).

21.82. During the Twelfth Plan, MDMS will be expanded to cover pre-primary schooling in a progressive manner, private unaided schools, particularly in the SC/ST and minority-concentrated areas, and poor children admitted in neighbourhood private schools against the 25 per cent earmarked seats as per provisions of the RTE Act. While expanding the coverage, fiscal incentives like tax exemptions may be considered to encourage private participation in the scheme. Partnerships with panchayats and municipalities, as well as with other NGOs and government agencies may be developed to ensure good-quality, nutritious and regular supply of food to all children. The guidelines revised in 2009 require supply of cooked food. For this, funding for construction of kitchen-cum-store for proper storage of foodgrains and preparation of meal in hygienic environment is being provided. This would be implemented throughout the country and capacity-building initiatives would be taken up for this. Full convergence of the MDMS with the school health programme would be ensured during the Twelfth Plan to benefit from synergy in two programmes. Over a period of time, this will provide good longitudinal data on the impact of MDMS.

Monitoring and Evaluation

21.83. There are several concerns in implementation of the MDMS, namely, wide variations in enrolment, attendance and actual coverage of children, mismatch of foodgrains and cash fund utilisation, lack of controls over the quantity and quality of meals, irregular and uncertain supply of meals, and poor quality of grains in certain States. In order to address these concerns, the monitoring system under MDMS would be made more effective during the Twelfth Plan. An MIS portal for monitoring of the scheme has already been launched. All the States/UTs are now feeding data into the portal and annual data for 2.7 lakh schools have already been fed into the portal. The MIS would be integrated with Interactive Voice Response System to capture the information on daily basis and monitor the Scheme on real time basis. The MIS would enable the States/UTs and Central Government to plan the visits to the poorly performing area of the respective States. It will also be used as a mechanism for social audit as the data fed into the system through the IVRS would also be sent back to SMC members for verification. This will enhance transparency and accountability in the implementation of the MDMS and enhance the overall effectiveness of the Scheme. Such independent evaluations would be strengthened during the Twelfth Plan.

MAHILA SAMAKHYA (MS)

21.84. Mahila Samakhya (MS) launched in 1988–89 is being implemented in 10 States across 105 districts, 495 blocks (including 233 EBBs) and 33,577 villages and has special focus on the EBBs. Successive evaluations have acknowledged Mahila Samakhya as a unique process-oriented programme which has demonstrated ways of empowering rural poor and marginalised women and thereby enabling their effective participation in the public domain and in educational and learning processes. Through sustained perspective building and training of field staff, it has been possible to keep the focus of MS programme on most marginalised women. Of the 10.5 lakh women that were covered until the end of the Eleventh Plan, 36.74 per cent are SC, 16.33 per cent ST, 27.47 per cent OBC, 9.13 per cent Muslim and only 10.38 per cent are women from the general categories.

21.85. Continuance of Mahila Samakhya during the Twelfth Plan is crucial due to current thrust on inclusive education through the RTE-SSA. The large pool of trained women associated with MS would be used to achieve goals of the RTE, namely, equity and equality in and through education. Once the external funding is completely utilised, the programme would be brought under RTE-harmonised SSA with 100 per cent internal funding. A National Resource Centre with strong State level or regional units would be set up to bring MS programme's varied insights on women's empowerment, learning, agency, girls' education and institution-building to address gender barriers into the mainstream. The programme itself would be strengthened and expanded both in its coverage as well as scope/role during the Twelfth Plan.

SECONDARY AND HIGHER SECONDARY EDUCATION

21.86. With a dramatic growth in elementary education enrolments and improvements in retention and transition rates in recent years, particularly amongst the more disadvantaged groups, there is an increasing pressure on the secondary schools to admit more students. With the enforcement of RTE Act and further improvement in retention and transition rates, demand for secondary schooling will grow rapidly in the coming years. Meeting this demand is critical for three reasons. First, the secondary education fulfils large manpower needs of the semi-organised and the organised sectors of the economy. Second, it is the supply chain for higher education. And, finally, it caters to the needs of teachers for primary schooling. Low participation rates and poor quality at the secondary stage are a bottleneck in improving both the higher education participation and the schooling at the elementary stage.

21.87. Further, there are both social and economic benefits of secondary schooling. While there are clear improvements in health, gender equality and living conditions with secondary education, investments in secondary schooling have high marginal rates of return. Thus, the country needs to move towards universalisation of opportunity to attend secondary schooling of adequate quality. With enrolment in elementary education reaching near universal levels, there would be an opportunity to move towards universal access to secondary education. The current GER for the combined secondary and senior secondary stages (Classes IX–XII) in 2009–10 at about 50 per cent is woefully low. Thus, the capacity of the secondary schooling system has to be expanded significantly. There are very large inequalities in access to secondary education, by income, gender, social group and geography. The average quality of secondary education is very low. Thus, urgent efforts are needed to improve its quality. The challenge is to dramatically improve access, equity and quality of secondary education simultaneously.

21.88. India has a long tradition of partnership between the public and private sectors in secondary education. There are four types of schools: (*i*) government—established by State Governments (as well as some Centrally established institutions); (*ii*) local body—established by elected local government bodies; (*iii*) aided schools—private schools that receive State Government grants-in-aid; and (*iv*) private unaided schools. Most of the growth of secondary schools in the private sector in the last two decades has occurred among unaided schools (25 per cent of schools). About 60 per cent of schools are now aided or unaided. It is essential, therefore, that the private sector's capabilities and potential are tapped through innovative public–private partnerships, while concurrently stepping up public investment by the Central and State Governments at the secondary level. And given that the presence of private schools varies considerably across States, context-specific solutions need to be promoted.

21.89. While private provision in secondary education should be fostered wherever feasible, the government will have to take the prime responsibility to provide access to disadvantaged sections and to bridge the rural/urban, regional, gender and social group gaps. Simultaneously, government must invest in teacher education and accountability, curriculum reform, quality assurance, examinations reform, national assessment capabilities and management information systems, which will require time and significant institutional capacity building to succeed at a national scale.

ENROLMENTS

21.90. GERs at the secondary (Class IX–X) and senior secondary (Class XI–XII) levels are 62.7 per cent and 35.9 per cent, respectively, leading to a combined GER for Class IX–XII at a considerably low 49.3 per cent (see Table 21.3). The significant dip in GERs from secondary to senior secondary level for all categories is driven by a number of factors including

TABLE 21.3
GER for Secondary Education by Social Groups (2009–10)

	SCs	STs	Non-SCs/STs	Overall
Secondary Level				
Boys	71.19	54.24	67.02	66.65
Girls	63.50	44.22	58.97	58.45
Total	67.58	49.41	63.13	62.71
Senior Secondary Level				
Boys	37.42	31.36	39.17	38.31
Girls	33.48	22.32	34.39	33.31
Total	35.60	26.91	36.88	35.92
Both Secondary and Senior Secondary Level				
Boys	54.52	43.45	52.86	52.39
Girls	48.86	33.68	46.54	45.86
Total	51.88	38.70	49.82	49.26

Source: Selected Education Statistics, Ministry of HRD, 2009–10.

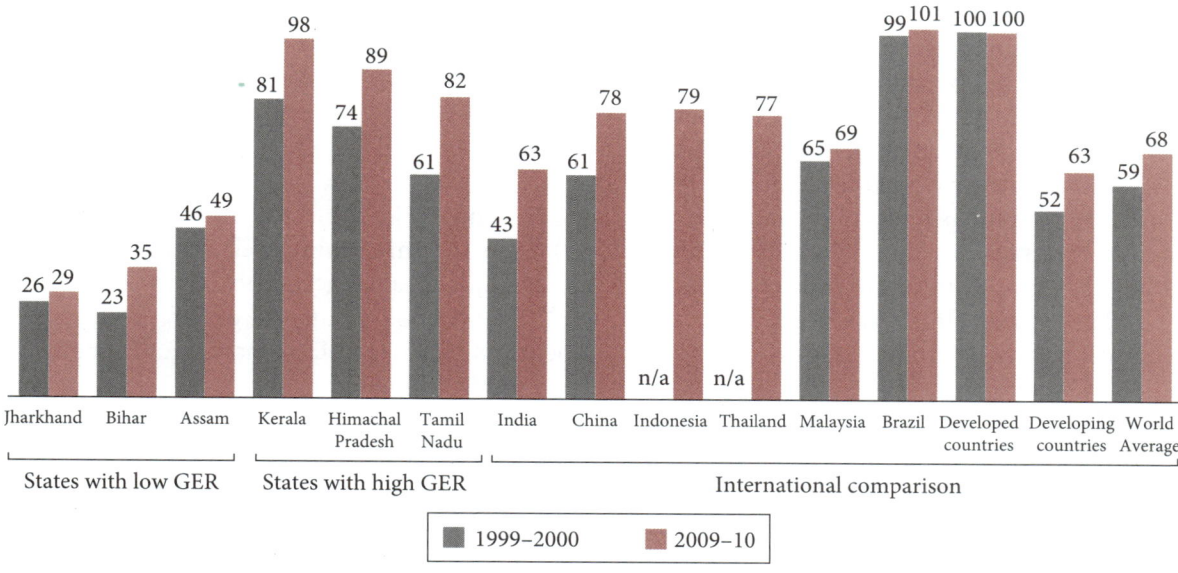

Source: Selected Education Statistics, Ministry of HRD, 2009–10, EFA-GMR-2011 and UIS.

FIGURE 21.1: GER for Secondary Education: By States/Select Countries
(High/Low GER States and International Comparisons)

general lack of access, paucity of public schools, high cost of private senior secondary education and poor quality of education, along with the very important factor of high opportunity cost of deferred entry into the workforce. India's GER at the secondary level is close to that of the average for all developing countries (63 per cent), but substantially lower than that of emerging economies like China, Indonesia, Thailand and Brazil (see Figure 21.1).

21.91. Enrolments of the SCs—both boys and girls—have improved significantly in recent years and now compares favourably with the non-SC/scheduled tribe categories. This has been possible with government support for hostels, scholarships and other forms of financial aid combined with increased access to secondary education, particularly in urban and semi-urban slum areas. However, despite similar efforts, the GER for STs continues to be significantly low at the secondary level. This may be attributed to low transition rates from the elementary to the secondary level as well as access related challenges in disadvantaged locations—both of which are accentuated for girls.

21.92. Within the relatively low GER at the secondary level, there are wide regional and inter-State variations. Among the major States, secondary-level GERs are as low as 29 per cent in Jharkhand and 35 per cent in Bihar and as high as 89 per cent in Himachal Pradesh and 98 per cent in Kerala, as compared to the national level (62.7 per cent). At the Senior Secondary level, the GER ranges from being very low at 6.5 per cent in Jharkhand and 13 per cent in Assam and quite high at 60 per cent in Haryana and 69 per cent in Himachal Pradesh. In addition, in some States like Rajasthan and MP, the gender gap in GER is as wide as 20 per cent.

21.93. In India, only 5 per cent of the population of 19–24 age group has acquired some sort of skills through vocational education, while the corresponding figure for Korea is as high as 96 per cent. The National Knowledge Commission has recommended expansion and re-designing of vocational education and improvement of its quality. The mid-term appraisal of the Eleventh Plan emphasised the need for curriculum revision in vocational education, appropriate certification by accrediting agencies, horizontal and vertical mobility with multiple entry/exit possibilities and linkage with industry for employment opportunities. The National Skill Development Mission has also recognised the demand for employment-oriented vocational education programmes with provision for hands-on training. In order to reap the benefits of the demographic dividend, it is critical to align vocational education within the composite framework of secondary schooling. Thus, more efforts are needed for vocational education at the secondary stage.

GOVERNMENT SPENDING

21.94. Public expenditure on secondary education has increased from ₹35,806 crore in 2007–08 to ₹94,183 crore in 2011–12, leading to an increase in its share as a percentage of GDP from 0.78 per cent to 1.05 per cent. Per capita expenditure on secondary education has gone up from ₹315 to ₹784 during this period. The Central Government's expenditure has gone up from ₹2,578 crore in 2007–08 to ₹13,278 crore in 2011–12, a five-fold increase. There is significant private expenditure as well. The average private expenditure on secondary education in private schools is as high as ₹893 per month as compared to only ₹275 per month in Government Schools.[11] This difference is primarily due to high tuition fees in private schools.

21.95. During the Eleventh Plan, the Central Plan outlay for secondary education was ₹54,945 crore. Against this, an amount of ₹17,723 crore (or 32.26 per cent of the outlay) was actually spent. Elaborate consultation process with stakeholders including the State Governments preceded launch of the new schemes, resulting in sub-optimal utilisation of planned resources in the first three years of implementation. However, in the last two years of the Eleventh Plan period, the Ministry was fully geared to implement schemes rapidly, but only limited resources were made available.

REVIEW OF THE ELEVENTH PLAN

Rashtriya Madhyamik Shiksha Abhiyan (RMSA)

21.96. Secondary schooling received a major thrust during the Eleventh Plan with the Central Government support for it increasing several fold. The Rashtriya Madhyamik Shiksha Abhiyan, a Centrally sponsored scheme with a funding pattern of 75:25 between Centre and States (90:10 for Special Category and NE States), was launched in 2009–10.

21.97. The major objectives of the RMSA are to (i) raise the minimum level of education to class X and universalise access to secondary education; (ii) ensure good-quality secondary education with focus on Science, Mathematics and English; and (iii) reduce the gender, social and regional gaps in enrolments, dropouts and improving retention. The interventions supported under RMSA included (i) upgrading of upper primary schools to secondary schools; (ii) strengthening of existing secondary schools; (iii) providing additional classrooms, science laboratories, libraries, computer rooms, art, craft and culture rooms, toilet blocks and water facilities in schools; (iv) providing in-service training of teachers; and (v) providing for major repairs of school buildings and residential quarters for teachers. Despite being launched in the third year of Plan, there was good progress under the RMSA during the Eleventh Plan (see Table 21.4). Against a target of enrolling an additional 3.2 million students, 2.4 million additional students were enrolled in secondary schools during the Eleventh Plan period.

Other Schemes

21.98. In addition to the RMSA, the following five Centrally sponsored schemes were launched during the Eleventh Plan: (i) setting up of model schools; (ii) setting up girls' hostels in secondary and senior secondary schools; (iii) National Scheme of Incentive to Girls for Secondary Education (NSIGSE); (iv) Inclusive Education for the Disabled at the Secondary Stage (IEDSS); and (v) National Merit-cum-Means Scholarship scheme (NMMS). In addition, the ongoing scheme of ICT in Schools was revised. The targets and achievements under these schemes are given in Table 21.5. In addition, the scheme of vocational stream at the +2 stage that was launched in 1988 and revised in 1992–93 was continued after further revision as approved in 2011. Despite massive infrastructure of 21,000 Sections in over 10,000 schools for vocational streams catering

TABLE 21.4
RMSA: Achievement in the Eleventh Plan

Sl. No.	Items	Target	Achievement (Approved)
1	Sanction of New Schools	11,188	9,636
2	Strengthening of existing Schools	44,000	34,311
3	Additional Classrooms	88,500	49,356
4.	Additional Teachers	1,79,000	59,000
5.	In-Service Training for All Teachers	100 per cent	100 per cent
6.	Annual Grants to Schools	Full coverage	75,394
7.	Minor Repair to Schools	Full coverage	62,221

Source: Department of School Education and Literacy, Govt. of India.

TABLE 21.5
Centrally Sponsored Schemes for Secondary Education
Target/Achievements in the Eleventh Plan

Sl. No.	Schemes	Start Year	Target	Achievement
1.	Model Schools			
	(a) EBB (KV Template)	2009–10	3,500	1,940
	(b) Non-EBB (PPP Mode)	2012–13	2,500	–
2.	Girls' hostels	2008–09	3,479	958
3.	Inclusive Education for Disabled at the Secondary Stage			
	(a) Beneficiaries (in lakh)	2009–10	–	10.76
	(b) School Covered (in lakh)	2009–10	–	2.18
4.	NSIGSE (in lakh)	2008–09	–	12.60
5.	NMMS (in lakh)	2008–09	4.0	1.04
6.	ICT in Schools			
	(a) School covered (nos.)	2009–10 (Revised)	–	90,209
	(b) Smart Schools (nos.)	2009–10 (Revised)	150	63

Source: Department of School Education and Literacy, MHRD. Govt. of India.

to over 1 million students, only about 4.8 per cent of all students are enrolled in the vocational streams against a target of covering 25 per cent of such students.

21.99. There are 1,740 schools (Kendriya Vidyalayas—1,092, Jawahar Navodaya Vidyalayas—586 and Central Tibetan Schools—62) with an enrolment of about 13 lakh students that are directly under the Central Government. These schools usually outperform other schools both academically and otherwise and hence there is demand for more such schools all over the country. During the Eleventh Plan, over 100 new schools were set up. In addition, there are Sainik Schools and Eklavya Residential Schools under Ministry of Defence and Ministry of Tribal Welfare under the Central Government, respectively.

21.100. The apex bodies in school education, National University of Educational Planning and Administration (NEUPA) for policy, planning and data collection, National Council of Education Research and Training (NCERT) for curriculum design, and developing textbooks and teaching–learning materials for school education, Central Board of Secondary Education (CBSE) for affiliation, examination and assessment and National Institute for Open Schooling (NIOS) were very active during the Eleventh Plan and played a key role in school education reforms.

TWELFTH PLAN STRATEGY

21.101. The Twelfth Plan's objective for secondary education is to make quality education available, accessible and affordable to the target population in the age group of 14–18 years. Given this general objective, the following targets (see Box 21.4 below) will need to be achieved during the Plan period:

> **Box 21.4**
> **Secondary Education: Twelfth Plan Goals**
>
> 1. Achieve near-universal enrolment in secondary education, with the GER exceeding 90 per cent by 2017;
> 2. Raise the GER at the higher secondary level to 65 per cent by 2017;
> 3. Reduce Dropout rate to less than 25 per cent by 2017;
> 4. Ensure quality secondary education with relevant skills including basic competency in mathematics, science, languages and communication;
> 5. Implement common curricula and syllabi of nationally acceptable standards for Science, Maths and English in all schools in the country.
> 6. Develop life skills including skills of critical and constructive thinking, use of ICT, organisation and leadership, and community services.

21.102. Key elements of the strategy to achieve these objectives include: (*i*) consolidation and optimum use of existing resources; (*ii*) facilitating private growth, (*iii*) improving quality, (*iv*) focus on teacher availability and teacher training, (*v*) ICT integration in education and (*vi*) renewed focus on vocational education at the secondary level. Each of these elements is briefly described below.

Consolidation and Expansion

21.103. Strategies for universal secondary education must be based on population projection of the secondary education age group. There have been some projection exercises for some States on secondary age group population and demand for secondary education depending upon population growth rate and rate of transition from elementary to secondary education corrected by dropout factor. Some States are already stagnating, some will reach the peak by 2016–17, some will stabilise only by 2025. Micro-planning for secondary education is hence necessary with proper future projections. Each State may devise a 10-year perspective plan for school education that would cover the period till the end of the Fourteenth Plan.

21.104. Enrolment in more than one-third of the secondary schools in the country is less than 80 students per school. The numbers of such schools are about 40,000 and 16,000 in rural and urban areas, respectively. About one-half of the rural schools are government funded. Secondary and higher secondary schools must be viable and large enough to benefit from investment on quality. The fact is that it is much harder to have good-quality education in very small schools with few teachers. The consolidation in secondary education will be achieved by (*i*) creating more and more composite schools from grades 1 to 12; (*ii*) upgrading primary schools into elementary schools in phases to fulfil the commitments of RTE-universal elementary education; (*iii*) upgrading every third elementary school to a secondary school; (*iv*) upgrading every fourth Secondary School to a Higher Secondary School by adding additional classrooms, laboratories, strengthening libraries and sports and games facilities and teachers. The cost of additional classrooms and facilities will be far less than establishing new schools. New schools will be set up only in un-served areas. Provision of transport, especially in rural areas, will be made for schools to avoid school dropout, especially among girls and economically weaker sections due to non-availability of schools within 'walking distance'. The transport facility will be more cost-effective and socially acceptable than setting up hostels. Nonetheless, hostel facilities would be provided in these schools on a priority basis in order to make them operationally viable in terms of teacher deployment and provision of other infrastructure facilities. In the unaided private sector, there are about 25,000 schools operating with enrolments of less than 80 pupils, per school. Efforts are required to utilise the surplus intake capacity in these schools to meet additional demand for secondary education. There are about 14,000 such schools located in rural areas. These schools may also be incentivised to cater to the educational needs of disadvantaged groups in their neighbourhoods.

21.105. Several institutions of higher education have vast tracts of unutilised or underutilised land. Model schools/JNVs/KVs could be set up in such places. The public sector should also concentrate on opening new secondary schools in un-served and difficult areas where availability of land is not a major constraint. Second shift operations in schools in thickly populated areas and urban slums should also be evaluated. Overall, the strategy should be on consolidation by better use of existing land, infrastructure and physical facilities through resource-mapping and leveraging private and non-governmental expertise and resources to improve the quality of education.

Facilitating Private Growth

21.106. The role of the private sector in secondary schooling can be further strengthened through right policies, proper regulation, innovative public–private partnerships and a variety of demand-side financing measures that improve accountability and enhance parental choice, thereby achieving all three objectives of access, quality and equity in secondary education. This would require easing of entry barriers with dismantling of multiple licensing systems and procedures and the State Governments should revisit norms including requirement of land for setting up institutions. Many States have school land norms laid down in the 1960s and 1970s which need to be immediately revisited. A single window approach needs to be adopted to facilitate barrier free entry of private institutions including online monitoring of application status for setting up of new schools. Suitable taxation and land policies are needed to encourage expansion of secondary schools in the private sector, along with concessional loans for NGOs, trusts and registered societies for building new schools or improving the infrastructure of existing schools. Most of the publicly funded schools that have been in existence for some time have large open spaces, particularly those in rural areas. Most of these old school buildings require repair and upgradation and, in several cases, reconstruction. SSA and RMSA do not fund the reconstruction of old schools. Some portion of the land area could be evaluated to be leased out to private schools under contractual obligation of the lessor for reconstruction of existing government school building. The contractual agreement should provide for access of government school children to laboratory, library and common playfield facilities of the private partner in the same campus.

21.107. Many schools in the country that were initially started as private schools through local initiatives have become government grant-in-aid schools. This system encourages local participation and fills the gap that exists in interior areas. Devising a good regulatory mechanism designed to ensure quality will be a preferable option over governments setting up their own schools and operating with very low levels of enrolments. Encouraging private unaided schools would cater only to the population which can pay, unless there is a policy of cross subsidisation of fees so that certain percentage of children from the poorer sections of the society can also be accommodated for free or at subsidised tuition fees. There is no ceiling on their intake capacity but resource constraints could come in the way of expansion. Institutional funding for expansion of school infrastructure is essential for accelerated growth of secondary education. This is also an important opportunity which should be seized to link new funding to the performance of institutions in achieving certain objectives, such as graduation of students, academic improvement and retention of disadvantaged groups.

21.108. There is an urgent need to focus on Economically Backward Blocks (EBB) to reach the learning population from marginalised groups and provide them access to secondary education. Public Private Partnerships in secondary education should be fostered wherever feasible. In private schools, a mechanism could be devised to fund enrolment of disadvantaged children with reasonable cost per child norms. For this to happen, three elements are essential: (*i*) funding facilities for investible resources for additional infrastructure development of recognised schools; (*ii*) proper accreditation of schools for ensuring quality education; (*iii*) revisiting of rules and regulations infringing upon autonomy of schools, including prescription of teachers' salary for private schools. If minimum prescribed standards and norms are met for school infrastructure and qualified teachers with CTET/STET eligibility are deployed, the market should be left to determine the compensation structure for the faculty and staff.

Improving Quality

21.109. No recent, reliable, large-scale learning assessments at the secondary level exist. However, small-scale standardised assessments of student achievement in mathematics at the secondary and senior secondary level in two States (Rajasthan and Odisha) suggest that the quality of instruction and learning is very low at the secondary level. There are multiple factors for low levels of learning. Schools play a very important role in determining nearly half of student achievement. Thus, in the Twelfth Plan, all secondary and higher secondary schools would be made to conform to minimum standards in facilities and quality. This will require a greater role for the Central Government in supporting the States, particularly those lagging in secondary education. The focus should be on building the capacity of schools in terms of knowledge and skills, autonomy and accountability structures, and allocation of untied grants for undertaking school improvement measures for imparting quality education. Local capacities would be strengthened at the school level giving them the ability to 'think and innovate'.

21.110. In secondary schooling, there is too much emphasis on rote learning and insufficient development of conceptual understanding and higher order thinking skills. There is insufficient quality assurance and accountability mechanisms in place, while capacity and quality of pre-service and in-service training of teachers is low. The issues of curriculum, examinations reforms, school leadership, assessment and accreditation would also have to be addressed.

Curriculum Renewal

21.111. The outdated curricula and syllabi in the educational system need a complete overhaul. There is a need for periodic revision of curricula and for reforms in the examination system. Directorates of School Education, State Boards of Secondary Education, Resource Institutions like NCERT, SCERTs, SIEs and such other institutions should be strengthened as part of RMSA/Teacher Education schemes so that these institutions lend credible support services and undertake effective periodic monitoring and concurrent evaluations. While the rate of funding for MMER (Management, Monitoring, Evaluation and Research) will be suitably raised under RMSA, its current skewed distribution across the States should be revised with minimum funding ensured for smaller States/UTs. National programmes on curriculum renewal, school-based Continuous and Comprehensive Evaluation (CCE), innovation and related institution-building would be launched during the Twelfth Plan. Each State has multiple agencies, that is, SCERTs, SIEs, Education Boards, SPOs, Directorates and so on, which have more or less the same objective of imparting quality education to all and improving the education system but they lack synergy. There is an urgent need to establish effective linkages amongst them for achieving the desired results.

Examination Reforms

21.112. Examination reforms that would focus on problem-solving, critical thinking and reasoning skills and decrease the emphasis on rote memorisation are critical to improving quality at the secondary level. Such reforms have the potential to change the teaching–learning processes inside the classrooms and have direct relation to improving learning outcomes. In recent years, CBSE has introduced wide-ranging examination reforms in 13,000 schools affiliated to it (see Box 21.5). During the Twelfth Plan, other Boards would be facilitated to emulate these reforms.

SCHOOL BOARDS FOR ACADEMIC TRANSFORMATION

21.113. Exceptions apart, currently, all School Boards function exclusively as examining bodies. During the Twelfth Plan, the School Boards should be enabled to take up leadership for reforms in the school system. They must remodel themselves in such a way that they have strong academic and IT divisions closely coordinating with examination

> **Box 21.5**
> **CBSE Examination Reforms**
>
> Class X Board Examination has been made optional from the year 2011 for students studying in CBSE's Secondary Schools and who do not wish to move out of the CBSE system after Class X.
>
> Continuous and Comprehensive Evaluation (CCE) has been strengthened in all CBSE-affiliated schools from October 2009 onwards in Class IX, wherein both scholastic and co-scholastic areas, including life skills of the students, are assessed on an ongoing basis for their holistic development.
>
> In order to bring greater objectivity in reporting of performance and to reduce stress and undesirable competition, a system of grading in place of marks has been introduced.

and administration divisions for academic transformation and capacity building. They should take upon themselves the role of capacity building of the school principals, headmasters, teachers and even parents. Quality initiatives taken up by some School Boards like the CBSE should be promoted as national programmes. Among the important initiatives are producing quality-assured digital content in local language and encouraging teachers to create their own content and upload on a common web portal, provisioning affordable ICT facilities in classrooms, ICT-integrated education supported by LMS, Continuous and Comprehensive Evaluation for reducing stress on students through adopting scientific techniques of evaluation, School Quality Assessment and Accreditation for Social Accountability, and such others. All State boards must be encouraged and supported wherever necessary for implementing these quality interventions. CoBSE shall catalyse this development. The voluntary association of School Boards and CoBSE needs to be strengthened and made much more effective. Most School Boards are financially sound and may not need additional funding.

Development of School Leadership

21.114. Programme of Leadership Development in School Education will act as the vehicle to empower and drive critical education reforms through intensive and interdisciplinary curricular experiences, active exchange of ideas, adoption of an interactive pedagogical approach that promotes team work and collaboration; creation of opportunities for professional development of leaders in school education; identification and nurturing of talent within and outside the school system to take up leadership; and establishment of a network of institutions to impart leadership education. The programme will have two-tier institutional arrangement with a National Centre for Leadership in School Education and Leadership Academies in selected Institutions of Higher Learning. NUEPA through the National Centre for Leadership in School Education (NCLSE) will be entrusted with the responsibility of coordinating the work of the Leadership Academies located in different Institutes of Higher Learning.

School Quality Assessment and Accreditation

21.115. A School Quality Assessment and Accreditation System would be established to cover all aspects of school functioning, including scholastic and co-scholastic domains, physical infrastructure, faculty management, school leadership, learning outcomes and satisfaction of pupils and their parents/guardians. This system should be in sync with similar accreditation systems in advanced countries and in CBSE-affiliated schools. Examination reforms are needed to promote the acquisition of analytical and thinking skills amongst students rather than emphasising rote learning. The Government is already committed to developing a national assessment survey at grade X, which could lead the way to new forms of learning assessment, and which will enable cross-State comparisons of performance to be made. Schools should be encouraged to work towards achieving average international standards and this effort should be led by the Centrally funded KVs and JNVs, which would function as exemplars. There are half-a-dozen States with GERs above the world average.

21.116. Orientation and capacity-building programmes need to be organised for officials of school boards, teachers, principals and school administrators on a massive scale for effective implementation of NCF and RTE. Close collaboration is needed between SCERTs and school boards for organising workshops for teachers and educators for strengthening skills in teaching–learning and assessments. Involvement of grass-roots teachers drawn from schools including KVs and JNVs for preparation or adaptation of NCERT textbooks should also be promoted. Continued benchmarking against international performance is essential to measure India's progress. The outcomes for this system of assessment and accreditation must be made public so as to promote greater accountability of secondary schools.

School Mentoring

21.117. The Government will reach out to private schools with a reputation for quality and standards to ask them to support government schools in their neighbourhoods to improve quality. Partnerships will be forged for sharing their infrastructure and academic facilities with neighbourhood schools for teacher training and empanelment of certified resource persons. The Centrally funded KVs and NVs could become hubs for inter-school activities so as to catalyse improvement in other publicly funded schools in the area. This is especially true in the case of science and mathematics education, organising joint school seminars and educational exhibitions and running bridge courses in English. Well-functioning schools under the State Governments and private schools could also become hubs for inter-school activities.

Teacher and Training

21.118. Teacher training for secondary education was launched in the Eleventh Plan but the approach so far has been mechanical and limited to training teachers to help students score high marks in national board exams so as to raise school averages with very little focus on developing thinking, application skills, attitudes and values. The Twelfth Plan will promote professional cadre development in education and will empower educators to develop effective tools for promoting and gauging creative problem solving and ideation in the classroom setting. Research scholars in the field of education in Universities/Colleges should be brought in to conduct seminars, classes and tutorials and should be compensated over and above their fellowships.

21.119. Significant shortages of secondary school teachers exist, especially in the critical subjects of mathematics, science and foreign languages. A major recruitment effort is needed. Curricular reform can also promote more efficient use of teachers. Moreover, new and flexible ways of encouraging people to come into or return to the teaching profession are needed; with an emphasis on identifying those with relevant competencies rather than those who have certain qualifications. National Mission on Teachers and Teaching should address issues of teachers at the secondary stage in a comprehensive manner.

Renewed Focus on Vocational Education

21.120. Recognising the fact that younger children learn and acquire skills faster, skills training of elementary nature, for example, manipulating simple instruments at the elementary level, and pre-vocational courses as an alternative to work education would be offered in Class IX and X. Students who take these pre-vocational options could be encouraged and facilitated to take up advanced vocational subjects at the higher secondary level. In addition, vertical mobility options for students taking vocational courses should be available at the undergraduate and postgraduate level. For high-quality vocational education at school level to evolve and grow in the country, there is a need to train and equip teachers on a continuous basis with the latest skills and pedagogy techniques in vocational education.

21.121. The vocational curriculum needs to be integrated and closely aligned with the academic curriculum and should contain modules on various generic and specific vocational skills for which industry should be involved. There should be an emphasis on development of generic and multiple skills so that trainees/students may respond to changes in technology and market demands. The revised scheme of vocationalisation of secondary education should be revisited based on the pilots that have been undertaken to test and to ensure that it is aligned with the new qualifications framework and industry-led sector skill councils, so that vocationalisation does not become an expensive dead end for students. Given the different economic contexts across the country, system of monitoring and evaluation of the scheme must be strengthened.

TWELFTH PLAN INITIATIVES

Rashtriya Madhyamik Shiksha Abhiyan (RMSA)

21.122. During the Twelfth Plan, RMSA will be made a single comprehensive scheme to address issues of coverage and quality in secondary education. This should be gradually extended to the higher secondary stage and should cover all government and government-aided schools. There are several Centrally sponsored schemes that benefit secondary school students of different categories and background. These are:

1. Rashtriya Madhyamik Shiksha Abhiyan (RMSA)
2. Model Schools Scheme
3. Girls Hostel Scheme
4. ICT @ Schools
5. Inclusive Education for Disabled at Secondary Stage
6. Scheme of Vocational Education
7. National Means-cum Merit Scholarship Scheme
8. National Incentive to Girls
9. Appointment of Language Teachers

21.123. While the RMSA is a large scheme, others are comparatively smaller schemes. For convergence and improved efficiency, the smaller schemes shall be merged into RMSA. This should be done without losing focus on the objectives, goals and targets of any of the existing schemes. In following the example of RTE, RMSA shall develop and/or adopt/adapt national norms of secondary schooling for universalisation of secondary education. This will be required to ensure minimum quality of schooling. Significant issues to be addressed within the RMSA framework include construction of residential facilities for boys and girls, revising civil works norms to State schedule of rates, review of school infrastructure, coverage of aided schools and higher secondary schools, provision of untied funds for innovation and so on. In addition, the RMSA framework should focus on promoting better-quality education against clear-cut benchmarks and enable States, districts and schools to respond flexibly to their specific needs.

21.124. The RMSA should continue with the current funding pattern in the Twelfth Plan period. RMSA should have inter-State allocation criteria for equitable distribution of Central assistance so that educationally backward States are not denied their legitimate share, while advanced States take additional advantage due to prior preparation. The RMSA should gradually move towards funding States on per child cost basis/norms which would incentivise enrolment, retention and completion, and thus move away from inputs-based funding to outcome-based decision-making.

21.125. The RMSA will make provisions for residential schools/hostels for boys and girls in existing schools to enhance access and participation of children from hilly and sparsely populated areas and from districts afflicted with civil strife as well as support OoSC as per guidelines developed by NIOS. It would include provision for schools without buildings and relax ceiling on civil works for infrastructure-deficient States with adoption of State Schedule of Rates for civil works. Provision should be made for ramps and at least one toilet for CWSN.

21.126. Science and Maths education would need special attention during the Twelfth Plan. Poor science and maths education (and English) accounts for 80 per cent of total students who fail in Tenth Board Examination. The transition rate from X to XI in Science is very small as indicated by less than 12 per cent share of students in UG Science stream. This low enrolment in science stream at higher secondary level and poor-quality education is a constraint in development of scientific manpower in the country. Under RMSA, a special component will be created to identify scientific talents at the secondary level and to strengthen science and mathematics education; teachers will be trained and retrained on modern methods of science education.

21.127. Physical education and games and sports would be made an integral part of the curriculum in schools for the holistic development of youth. Minimum infrastructure and consumables will be made available under RMSA in convergence with MYA&S (Ministry of Youth Affairs and Sports) schemes to all government and government-aided schools. School playgrounds of NVs and KVs will be opened up to neighbourhood schools. Local bodies would be impressed upon to extend support in earmarking open fields, sports stadia and community playgrounds for neighbourhood schools in urban areas, as many private schools and even some publicly funded schools do not have playgrounds within school campuses in many cities and towns. Such schools will be encouraged to adopt alternative sports and games activities that support physical development and nurturing of kinaesthetic intelligence. Appointment of additional Physical Education Teachers (PETs) would be funded under RMSA.

21.128. In an effort to ensure coordination and efficient implementation across a range of secondary education programmes, RMSA will become the umbrella programme and four other schemes would be subsumed under it during the Twelfth Plan. These are:

1. ICT@Schools will be integrated with RMSA to provide greater flexibility, enable optimal utilisation of resources and yield better results.
2. Inclusive Education for Disabled at Secondary Stage (IEDSS) scheme will be subsumed under RMSA and will cover children with blindness, low vision, leprosy cured, hearing impairment, locomotor disabilities, mental retardation, mental illness, autism and cerebral palsy. Coordination of the scheme with other programmes will be emphasised.
3. Girls' Hostel for Students of Secondary and Higher Secondary Schools will be subsumed under RMSA. The scheme also provides for a PG teacher as warden to support residents in scholastic assignments and boost their confidence.
4. The Scheme of Vocational Education will be subsumed under RMSA without any modification in the existing fund-sharing pattern and will be implemented from the secondary stage onward.

21.129. The National Scheme of Incentive to Girls for Secondary Education will be continued as separate scheme. Schemes that are based on specific proposals from the States could easily be integrated within the composite RMSA. MHRD could provide financial assistance to the State/UTs for (*i*) appointment and training of Hindi teachers in non–Hindi-speaking States/UTs; (*ii*) appointment of Urdu teachers and grant of honorarium for teaching Urdu; (*iii*) appointment of teachers of Modern Indian Language (other than Hindi) in Hindi-speaking States/UTs; (*iv*) appointment of Urdu Teachers in any locality where more than 25 per cent are from Urdu language–speaking group.

Vocational Education

21.130. Vocational education at the secondary stage provides for diversification of educational opportunities so as to enhance individual employability, reduce the mismatch between demand and supply of skilled manpower and provides an alternative for those pursuing higher education. Hence, it is important and would be implemented from class IX onwards, unlike the present provision for its implementation from class XI, and would be subsumed under RMSA. Vocational Education courses will be based on national occupation standard brought out by the Sector Skill Councils (SSCs) that determine the minimum levels of competencies for various vocations. Academic qualifications would be assessed and certified by educational bodies and vocational skills would be assessed and certified by respective SSCs.

21.131. In the Twelfth Plan, a mechanism would be created for convergence of vocational courses offered by various ministries, private initiatives and vocational education institutions, and use schools as the outlet for vocational education of young people. A comprehensive repertoire of vocational courses, duration of each course, equipment and facilities, costs and agencies will be developed. Like Germany and many other industrialised countries, the repertoire should have modular courses, which allow exit and entry into the job market and further.

21.132. The process for revamping of the scheme of vocational education at the higher secondary stage has already been initiated. This is now aligned with NVEQF (National Vocational Education Qualifications Framework) to create clear educational pathways from school to higher education level and provide more options to students to choose vocational modules depending on their aptitude and economic requirements. The revised scheme has been designed to address the weaknesses identified in the current system of vocational education. The salient components of the revised scheme include (*i*) strengthening of existing schools imparting vocational education; (*ii*) establishing new schools; (*iii*) in-service teacher training of seven days for existing teachers; (*iv*) 30-day induction course for new teachers and (*v*) support to private schools in PPP mode and support to NGOs for carrying out innovative practices. Competency-based modules will be developed for each individual vocational course. It will be mandatory for schools to revise their curricula every three years to ensure that it is guided by the needs of the industry. A separate Pilot programme within the National Vocational Education Qualifications Framework has been launched in Haryana. Assam, West Bengal and Karnataka are also in the process of launching a pilot. Based on the learning from the pilot, this would be scaled up in the Twelfth Plan. An MIS and web portal on vocational education will be set up to share best practices and experiences. Haryana has launched a pilot for introducing vocational education under NVEQF in 40 pilot schools in eight districts (see Box 21.6).

21.133. Based on the learning from the pilot(s), a possible road map could be to expand the coverage of vocational education from 2013–14 to about 400 schools in Haryana. The number of courses offered could be increased from 8 to 10 and pilots be started during 2013–14 in all States which show interest. States which manage the pilot successfully could expand the coverage in year 2014–15 to about ten times the number of schools covered under pilot. A nodal resource centre could be created at the national level to support the State Governments.

21.134. Students pursuing vocational courses at +2 level would be provided facilities for apprenticeship training under the Apprenticeship Act. While skill formation has to be mainstreamed in the formal education system right from class IX onwards, skill creation outside the formal education system needs coordinated action and innovative approaches. A VE cell has been established within the CBSE. The States would also be encouraged and supported to set up similar cells in the State Boards and encourage students to take vocational courses along with academic courses either as combination subjects or additional subjects, and allow credit accumulation and transfer on the pattern of CBSE-NIOS collaboration. The National and State Boards would draw up a detailed scheme of evaluation with respective SSCs to enable competency-based assessment of students. As the course design and TLM development get decentralised, PSSCIVE, the expert central institution, should be elevated for quality assurance in vocational education.

Box 21.6
Pilot Project on Vocational Education under NVEQF

- Each of the pilot schools offers two vocational subjects out of IT/ITes, Retail, Automobile and Security. These would be started from Class 9 and Class 11.
- The Curriculum has been designed by the respective Sector Skills Councils (SSCs) under NSDC. The content has been created by PSSCIVE, CBSE and Wadhwani foundation.
- Teachers have been recruited on contract basis, and have undergone training in pedagogy and domain skills. Principals of schools have undergone orientation.
- Each school has a vocational coordinator to create and nurture linkages of local industry and business with the school and its students. They will also facilitate guest lectures, industry visits and placements.
- Assessment will be done by Board of School Education Haryana and assessors of respective SSCs.

21.135. PSSCIVE in collaboration and partnership with State Boards/CBSE/Experts will develop exemplar competency-based curricula with inputs from industry, business organisation, agricultural initiatives for contextualisation and localisation of content by States. Competency-based curricula will be adopted/adapted by Central/State Boards of Education. Each curriculum will have to meet national standards for competencies and other applicable norms set by SSCs.

21.136. Vocational education at the secondary level would be aligned with skills training under the Ministry of Labour through Industrial Training Centres and modular training programmes as well as short-term training provided through National Skills Development Corporation (NSDC). Skills training under the JSS and NGO schemes of Adult Education programmes would be aligned with the framework for vocational education at the secondary level. In order to roll out these skills programmes, a massive effort would be needed for professional development of school leadership, master faculty trainers, inspectors, test evaluators and counsellors. Appropriate institutional arrangements with linkage to NSDC for capacity development for professional certification and accreditation systems for institutions should also be put in place.

Model Schools

21.137. During the first three years of the Twelfth Plan, 2,500 Model Schools in PPP mode would be rolled out in non-EBBs in a phased manner. Instead of setting up of a new organisation to oversee implementation of Model Schools, it is preferable that the additional responsibility is given to KV Sangathan so that the new schools can benchmark the format of KVs. However, the number of Model Schools being substantially large, as compared to existing KVs, the Sangathan needs to be considerably strengthened with resources and their role with regard to Model Schools should be clearly defined. It should also be ensured that these Model Schools indeed serve as exemplars in their blocks and carry out specific activities to share their best practices with other government schools in their vicinity.

National Means-Cum-Merit Scholarship

21.138. This scheme will be continued in the Twelfth Plan to award 1,00,000 scholarships each year, at class IX stage. The scheme should have reached a targeted coverage of 4 lakh scholarship by 2011–12. Reasons for poor performance of the scheme should be studied and remedial action taken. The States in which the number of candidates selected is low in comparison with the quota allotted to them may require remedial classes for students. There is a need for wider publicity for the scheme to generate awareness. There are several NGOs, Foundations and Corporate organisations which offer merit-cum-means scholarship to students in schools. To avoid duplication and avoidable waste of resources, a database of all such agencies will be developed; similarly, a database of all beneficiaries will be created so that scholars can be traced for evaluation of the scheme and for improving its effectiveness.

Schools under the Central Government

21.139. During the Twelfth Plan, an additional 500 KVs and 378 JNVs, including 27 for uncovered districts and 2 special NVs in Manipur, will be set up. The intake capacity will be expanded from 80 to 160 students per class and 10 Science Magnet schools will be set up within or in close proximity to the institutions of higher education and other scientific research institutions. The charter of KVs and NVs will be revisited and their scope expanded including provisions for economically weaker section enrolments. About one-third of enrolments could be allowed for wards of non–Central Government employees.

21.140. The Twelfth Plan will work towards shaping KVs and JNVs into pace setting schools with specific activities such as acting as Smart Schools. To begin with, about 500 KVs and 500 NVs covering all States will commence pace setting activities by extending their facilities after school hours to students of neighbouring State/UT Government schools. The KVs/NVs could use outsourcing model for innovative programmes including training of students for participation in international assessments and allow the use of their premises for the purpose. Arts Departments will be established in KVs to achieve excellence in co-scholastic areas such as visual and performing arts.

21.141. The KVs/NVs will also be able to avail funding for additional sports activities from the schemes of Urban Sports Infrastructure/PYKKA under the Ministry of Youth Affairs and Sports. Rural KV/NVs will allow rural youths to utilise their facilities after school hours. Neighbouring school children will be allowed enrolment in NCC/NSS/Scouts and Guides/Judo/Karate/Yoga/Archery and so on in KVs/NVs. These schools will be hubs for the National Physical Fitness Programme to be launched during the Twelfth Plan with 100 per cent Central Assistance. These new initiatives of KVs/NVs, including hiring of personnel for providing coaching and other recurring expenses, will be supported with budgetary provisions to cover about 20,000 children per year.

21.142. All facilities, provisions, and quality initiatives stipulated for JNVs shall be made available to Eklavya and Sainik Schools, which are residential schools. The respective Ministries would be required to provide financial resources for these initiatives. MHRD will coordinate with other ministries and wherever necessary shall provide academic inputs. Similar coordination would also be required with Atomic Energy Education Society.

21.143. The Twelfth Plan will strengthen the infrastructure facilities for NIOS and 16 State Open Schools (SOS) under RMSA in order to improve the outreach of open schooling programmes with special focus on skill development and vocationalisation, particularly in the educationally backward districts of the country. An enrolment target of 25 lakh students has been set for NIOS/SOS. The Accredited Vocational Institutes (AVIs) under NIOS will be evaluated and rated before expansion. Examination reforms will be carried out so that year-round facilities are made available for open schooling.

RESEARCH, MONITORING AND EVALUATION

21.144. There are three areas that require urgent attention with regard to secondary education, namely, Curriculum Reform, Reform in Assessment and Examination and Reform in Pre-service and In-service teacher education. These three areas require in-depth studies, impact studies as well as action researches. A proper system of documentation for researches and best and innovative practices in secondary education needs to be evolved at various levels. Moreover, researches must not be limited to only providing research reports; there is also a need to evolve a mechanism for sharing of these researches with various stakeholders including curriculum developers and policymakers.

21.145. A panel of agencies both at the national and State levels will be put in place to carry out third-party appraisals and evaluations of ongoing schemes by identifying sectors/sub-sectors and developing appropriate tools for evaluation. There is a need to involve national-level institutions to build the capacity of teacher educators and resource persons in States/UTs and help them to evolve a mechanism for monitoring the introduction of the interventions in the classroom process which have been provided during the training programmes. Resource and Responsibility centres at national, State, district and sub-district levels for enhancing the quality of secondary education would be put in place.

21.146. A school-based Annual Information System, called SEMIS, is already in place to collect data on physical infrastructure and facilities, availability of teachers, enrolment and academic performance of students, professional development of teachers, and so on. This needs to be strengthened. A number of quality indicators could be generated for different levels that will reflect the wholesome educational scenario of the respective State. This will also promote micro-planning and the preparation of annual work plans for a district/State. Unified System of Data Collection for School Education Statistics would be put in place in the Twelfth Plan.

USE OF TECHNOLOGY IN EDUCATION

21.147. Most of the secondary schools have limited availability of computer facilities. This constrains the students from acquiring ICT-related skills essential in the knowledge economy and limits teachers' ability to upgrade their subject-matter knowledge and students' ability to access essential learning materials. ICT can potentially make significant difference in improving quality. The National Policy of ICT in School Education envisions and provides for the development of a holistic framework of ICT support in the school system. Mission Mode Project (MMP) on School Education is now under the National e-Governance Plan (NeGP). This would enable comprehensive technology enablement of the school education sector. More specifically, this would cover:

1. Developing ICT skills of all heads of schools, teachers, non-teaching staff and students;
2. Creating a repository of quality-assured digital contents in English, Hindi and regional languages in all subjects especially in science and mathematics;
3. Training and encouraging teachers to develop and use e-content;
4. Creating provisions for ICT in classrooms or portable facilities like a netbook/laptop/iPad and a projector with rechargeable battery, and implement ICT-integrated education;
5. Enabling provision of ICT-integrated examination and e-governance at the institutional and systemic level including setting up of education portal(s).

21.148. The MMP also envisions extensive use of technology to ensure delivery of services to students, teachers, autonomous institutions and partners on an 'anytime-anywhere' basis by leveraging the Common Service Centres (CSC) established up to the village level across the country. This along with the policy on ICT in School Education will enable a holistic and coordinated attempt to optimally use and leverage technology to achieve quality and efficiency in all of the interventions under various schemes.

21.149. There would be special focus on Aadhaar linkage of teachers and students databases with a view to remove ghosts, fakes, duplicates and cleaning up databases. This linkage coupled with effective analytics can help in addressing accountability, traceability and measurement-related challenges. It could also be used for tracking students and teachers attendance, tracking deployment, training programme attended by teachers, their skills/capability areas and so on. Using this targeted deployment plan, skill development programme could be developed. Tagging records of students with those of teachers can help build accountability of teachers. In long run, this may also provide pointers to interventions (made at teachers' improvement areas) that have had a higher impact on improving learning outcomes. Aadhaar seeding would be used in tackling scholarship funds misuse. Recently, Andhra Pradesh has used it to identify fake student enrolments, same student enrolments in multiple colleges/courses, same faculty teaching in a large number of institutions. Aadhaar-enabled payment system could be used for transferring and managing scholarship payments.

TEACHER EDUCATION

21.150. There is a large number of teacher vacancies in the school system. An estimated 12.58 lakh (5.64 lakh old and 6.94 lakh newly sanctioned under *SSA*) vacancies exist at the elementary level. These are mainly accounted for by six States: UP (3.12 lakh), Bihar (2.62 lakh), West Bengal (1.81 lakh), MP (0.89 lakh), Chhattisgarh (0.62 lakh) and Rajasthan (0.51 lakh). Several States in the North, East and North-Eastern regions have an acute problem of untrained teachers. Therefore, pre-service and in-service training of teachers needs to be mounted on a mission mode during the Twelfth Plan. In particular, modular teacher training programmes should be developed so that para-teachers can attend training courses during the summer and winter vacations and get formally qualified over a three- to five-year period. In-service training using technology and innovative delivery methods could address the problem of poor quality of existing teachers.

21.151. In order to address the issue of availability and quality of teachers for the school system, each State must maintain a detailed district-wise database of teachers, teacher educators and teacher education institutions. National professional standards for teachers and teacher educators must be evolved. These must be used as a basis for designing pre-service and in-service training programmes and their performance assessment processes for professional development. A system of teacher performance appraisal and feedback needs to be put in place as a tool for their development and empowerment and not as punitive measures. These systems are directly linked to improved classroom teaching and student learning. Rational deployment of teachers and objective and transparent policies for their transfers and placements would help in mitigating teacher shortages. Innovative ways need to be found to attract talent from other streams into the teaching profession. Superannuated qualified teachers may be re-employed in subject areas that have severe shortages. This strategy would be particularly useful in States like Kerala and Andhra Pradesh that have a relatively low retirement age for teachers in the government schools.

21.152. Upward career mobility options for teachers should be developed within each stage of education rather than across the stages, and should be linked with achievement of specific in-service certifications and experience criteria. High-quality teachers who wish to remain in active teaching as opposed to taking up administrative roles should have opportunities for career progression. A system of teacher evaluation based on objective measures of performance can be used as a basis for career ladders for teachers for bonuses, increments and promotions. These efforts along with continued professional development of teachers will ensure the teachers are motivated and lead to improving learning outcomes of the children.

Revamp Pre-Service Teacher Education

21.153. In view of large gaps in both quantity and quality of teachers, pre-service teacher education would be revamped. A revised scheme for teacher education would be implemented during the Twelfth Plan. The Scheme would strengthen institutional structures of DIETs, CTEs, IASEs and SCERTs. For their regular monitoring, elaborate process and performance indicators would be developed. In order to ensure adequate representation of teachers from the SC/ST/Minority communities, Block Institutes of Teacher Education in 196 SC/ST/Minority concentration districts would be set up.

21.154. The content and pedagogy of teacher education would be gradually aligned with the National Curriculum Framework for Teacher Education, 2009, which, inter alia, recommends a shift to a four-year integrated degree programme with concurrent study of a subject discipline and education after Class XII or two-year Bachelors in Education degree after graduation. Diploma in Education programmes for teachers for the elementary stage currently imparted by DIETs and other independent institutes should be progressively upgraded to degree programmes and these institutions could be upgraded as undergraduate colleges affiliated to the universities.

21.155. Distance-cum-contact degree programmes, increased use of ICT in regular programmes and adopting learn-work-learn cycles as an alternative to one-shot training would also be promoted. The professionals and BRCs/CRCs should be organically linked with DIETs under SCERT with knowledge capital infusion. It is essential that all these institutions are headed by professionals with appropriate qualification, experience, competence and vision. A large number of institutions and individuals must be identified to develop material for teachers and teacher educators in Indian languages based on curricular needs of pre-service programmes to begin with.

21.156. Linkages of teacher education institutes with each other, for example, of DIETs with CTEs and IASEs, and with the field, for example, the school system and NGOs operating in the sector need to be strengthened across the country such that academics and practitioners can work together towards the improvement of teacher education and school education more broadly. There should be effective use of technology as a tool for teacher education where special modules could be imparted to candidates across different geographical locations. These modules should integrate video lectures of professionals and highly reputed facilitators with careful selection of content. This can be combined with practical 'hands on' training in school environments in identified schools. Videos of best practices in teaching and pedagogy in Indian languages should be made available at these centres. Innovative alternate paths that would also allow lateral entry of talent from various other streams into the teaching profession by choice should be explored and appropriate policy and regulatory structures put in place to support their adoption.

21.157. Regulatory arrangements for teacher education require overhaul with proper oversight in each State. Accreditation arrangements need to be strengthened and new credible agencies could be roped in for the purpose. There is an immediate need to lay down performance standards and benchmarks for teacher education institutions with clear accountability. This needs to be balanced with greater flexibility and rational norms and standards around infrastructure, faculty, curricula and entry eligibility from regulatory and governing bodies and Boards, in particular the National Council for Teacher Education (NCTE). Importantly, innovative programmes should be recognised by NCTE promptly so that these programmes can begin developing teachers in a short period of time. The recently introduced *Teacher Education Index* would be widely used to measure the quality of teacher education institutions. This third-party assessment by approved entities to avoid malpractice should be done periodically every five years and made public to ensure transparency.

Develop Teacher Educators

21.158. Availability of adequate number of quality teacher educators will receive high priority during the Twelfth Plan. A large number of teacher educators would be developed by identifying potential teacher educators through a transparent competency-based process. They will then undergo full-time capacity programmes at selected institutions. For this purpose, credible institutions in both the public and private sectors would be involved. Voluntary professional networks of teacher educators must be facilitated and strengthened to provide forums for professional interaction and development.

21.159. New programmes would be conceptualised for teacher educators. Curriculum, duration and structure of the M.Ed. programme would be revamped based on NCFTE 2009 and the new model curricula proposed by NCTE. At least 100 institutions across all States in the country would be identified and prepared to deliver such programmes. Selected multi-disciplinary public and private universities must be facilitated to establish departments/schools of education with direct links to good schools which can serve as a practice ground for honing practical teaching skills. Universities can also provide special courses which could be designed to combine specialised subject knowledge with educational courses and practical learning in an integrated manner, so that the problem of shortage of subject teachers is also addressed.

Ensure Continued Professional Development

21.160. The system of continued professional development of in-service teachers would be strengthened during the Twelfth Plan. For this, training needs would be systematically identified and programmes designed to meet their local requirements so that the teachers are engaged and find the programmes useful. Capacity-building programmes of short duration as well as relatively longer full-time or distance-cum-contact degree programmes should be encouraged. These programmes should develop in teachers the necessary orientations and expose them to the range of skills/activities which impact upon quality classroom transactions. Use of technology and innovative delivery methods would be important components. Along with specific training programmes, exposure visits or action research projects to be conducted with field organisations and academia should be organised. Appropriate enablers in the form of long-leave options or a significant number of mandated required days of in-service training along with appropriate budgetary support per-day/per-practitioner should be provided to the schools.

21.161. Untrained teachers and para teachers would require special attention. Modular courses to be delivered in distance-cum-contact mode could be developed and delivered so that these teachers can obtain formal qualifications over a three- to five-year period. Partnerships between teacher education institutes and colleges, both public and private, and National and State Open Universities to develop and deliver these programmes at an accelerated pace should be actively encouraged.

Quality and Certification Issues

21.162. In order to assess the quality of teachers, TETs would be institutionalised and made mandatory for teacher hiring. This would ensure that despite alternate pathways open to become teachers, standards of teaching are maintained. Teachers could be required to renew their certifications periodically so that they continue to invest in their own development. With focus on outcome, teacher education institutions could be rated on the basis of the scores in the eligibility tests. While focusing on eligibility tests as objective and transparent outcome measure for performance of teacher and teacher education institutions, care is needed that such eligibility tests do not become an end in themselves.

21.163. Thus, in addition to TETs, national performance standards for teachers, teacher educators and teacher education institutions must be developed. A well-defined system of teacher performance appraisal (based on teacher competencies, teacher performance, efforts made by the teachers to transact learning-related processes in the classroom and learning levels) would be introduced in stages. These could include (*i*) possibilities for internship for three years before getting a 'license', (*ii*) introducing a system of teacher evaluation based on attendance, effective teaching, evaluation of classroom work and so on, (*iii*) teachers once appointed could come up for evaluation and renewal of license every 5 years, (*iv*) teachers should have avenues open for retraining for other jobs they may want to take, and (*v*) lateral and vertical mobility for professional growth of teachers.

National Mission on Teachers and Teaching

21.164. During the Twelfth Plan, a National Mission on Teachers and Teaching would be launched so that issues of teacher education are dealt with in a holistic manner. This would also strengthen institutional mechanisms for strengthening vertical and lateral linkages. This would consolidate and strengthen ongoing programmes related to teachers and teaching through effective coordination and synergy by significantly enhancing the investment. Under the proposed mission, 30 Schools of Education will be established in the selected universities that will conduct research into curriculum, pedagogy, and assessment and evaluation issues and offer degree programmes and conduct training for teacher educators. While CTEs that offer B.Ed. degrees are undergraduate colleges, these and organisations like the NCERT and the SCERTs lack any meaningful linkages with the university system.

GOVERNANCE AND EDUCATION LEADERSHIP

21.165. Performance-based innovative practices like social audits, linkages with panchayats and municipalities, energising and empowering village education committees, public reporting of expenditures linked to outcomes and results, and multi-stakeholder dialogues would be used to improve governance in the school system. Most important would be to empower local communities so that they have better oversight over schools and teachers. Local community could be given authority to hire, pay, and renew the contracts of community-based contract teachers (hired over and above the stipulated number of regular teachers), who can focus on supplemental and remedial instruction after school hours or during summer camps.

21.166. Overall strategy in governance reforms would be to strike a right balance between mandating and persuading. While efforts should be made to listen to stakeholders and embrace their concerns, a line must be drawn when it came to pushing through a reform or in ensuring commonality across the system. At the initial stage, the reforms are almost always driven from the Central agencies. Later, as the system improves, the locus for improvement shifts to instructional practices and primarily driven by the teachers and the schools by themselves.

21.167. A system of regular assessment of schools for both managerial and pedagogical aspects is needed. This would set the stage for formal accreditation of schools. In addition, there is a need to establish a vibrant teacher support system closer to the school setting. Block Resource Centres and Cluster Resource Centres that were conceptualised under DPEP and continued under the SSA would be revamped and repositioned so that these can work effectively for improving teacher performance. Their role could be extended to the secondary schools. Finally, systemic improvement requires integration and coordination across different levels as can be seen in Table 21.6. The Twelfth Plan would focus on such integration and ordination.

21.168. Seven specific interventions are proposed in the Twelfth Plan. First is to improve functioning and strengthening of existing institutions such as the SCERT, SIEMAT, and DIETs. These entities would develop and disseminate best practices for effective classroom instruction, support teachers in effective pedagogy and efficient organisation of resources at school level (that is, people, teachers and students, space and time) so as to optimise learning opportunities for all children. A key goal will be to identify highly effective teachers for positions of educational leadership and mentoring, and to identify less-effective teachers for coaching and support.

21.169. Second would be on training of district and block-level education officers as well as head teachers for better management practices, on using data to better monitor and support school performance, and to mobilise community resources and efforts to improve school performance. Good performance of schools and teachers should be recognised and rewarded to motivate teachers and administrators to achieve excellence. This recognition can be either financial or non-monetary, but the system as a whole should show that effort and performance is valued and rewarded. Third is to ensure full functioning of the already established National Centre for School Leadership and setting up of four Regional Centres of Educational Management co-located in existing institutions.

21.170. Fourth, the parents have to be more effectively engaged so that they demand better quality education and result-oriented teaching–learning process. For this, effective functioning of SMCs and Parent Teacher Associations (PTAs) is essential. These are central to the formation of School Development Plans and effective working of the schools. Special efforts and innovative approaches would be needed to enable illiterate, semi-literate or less-educated parents to partner with schools in their children's learning process. Fifth is focus on the role of community-based structures and the complementary and mutually reinforcing nature of their responsibilities in support of government machinery in monitoring of schools. Given the technical requirements, while the government can go deeper into the issue of inclusive classroom, some simple indicators

TABLE 21.6
Roles in System Improvement

Stakeholder	Key Role
Teachers	Deliver classroom instruction Collaborate with peers to develop, and share pedagogical practices that raise learning outcomes Engage parents as needed to advance student performance
School Administrators	Define and drive school improvement strategy, consistent with direction from district/State headquarters Provide instructional and administrative leadership for the school Involve school community to achieve school improvement goals
District/Sub-district School Leadership	Provide targeted support to schools and monitors compliance Facilitate communication between schools and the State Encourage inter-school collaboration Buffer community resistance to change
State Leadership	Set system strategy for improvement Create support and accountability mechanisms to achieve system goals Establish decision rights across all system entities and levels Build up skills and leadership capacity at all system levels

Source: Adapted from 'Education: How the World's Most Improved Systems Keep Getting better' by Mona Mourshed, Chinezi Chijioke and Michael Barber.

could be developed for monitoring by community-based institutions.

21.171. Sixth, good schools could act as exemplars for neighbourhood schools and a system of mentoring of schools, particularly in educationally backward regions, would be institutionalised. A system of sharing of best practices would also be introduced. This means that schools should match the best practices from a variety of perspectives from other schools in the same region. All Kendriya Vidyalayas and Navodaya Vidyalayas, along with newly set up Model Schools, should undertake pace setting activities for neighbourhood schools.

21.172. Seventh, sensitisation and re-orientation programme for national, State and field-level functionaries of the education departments would be conducted to bring quality and learning outcome focus in their work. Quality indicators need to be included in the agenda of review meetings at all levels. This would include attendance of students and teachers, learning outcome, supportive supervision provided by the field functionaries, graduation/dropout rate and so on. Revamping MIS/reporting systems having specific provision for reporting on quality issues and active involvement of parents in the monitoring of quality of education imparted in the schools will also be ensured.

ADULT AND ADOLESCENT EDUCATION

21.173. As shown in Figure 21.2, in the decade from 2001 to 2011, literacy levels rose from 64.8 per cent to 74 per cent and the number of illiterates declined in absolute terms by 31 million with the number of literates rising by 218 million. The gap in literacy rates between urban and rural areas reduced by 5 percentage points. Female Literacy rate increased at a faster rate (11.79 per cent) than that for males (6.88 per cent), thus reducing gender gap from 21.59 per cent to 16.68 per cent. Gains in literacy levels are in part due to success of the adult education programmes and in part due to improvements in primary schooling. Relative contribution of each would be known once the age-wise disaggregated data for the 2011 Census is available. Despite these significant gains, large gender and regional disparities in literacy levels persist.

Saakshar Bharat

21.174. During the Eleventh Plan, *Saakshar Bharat*, a Centrally Sponsored Scheme that focused on women

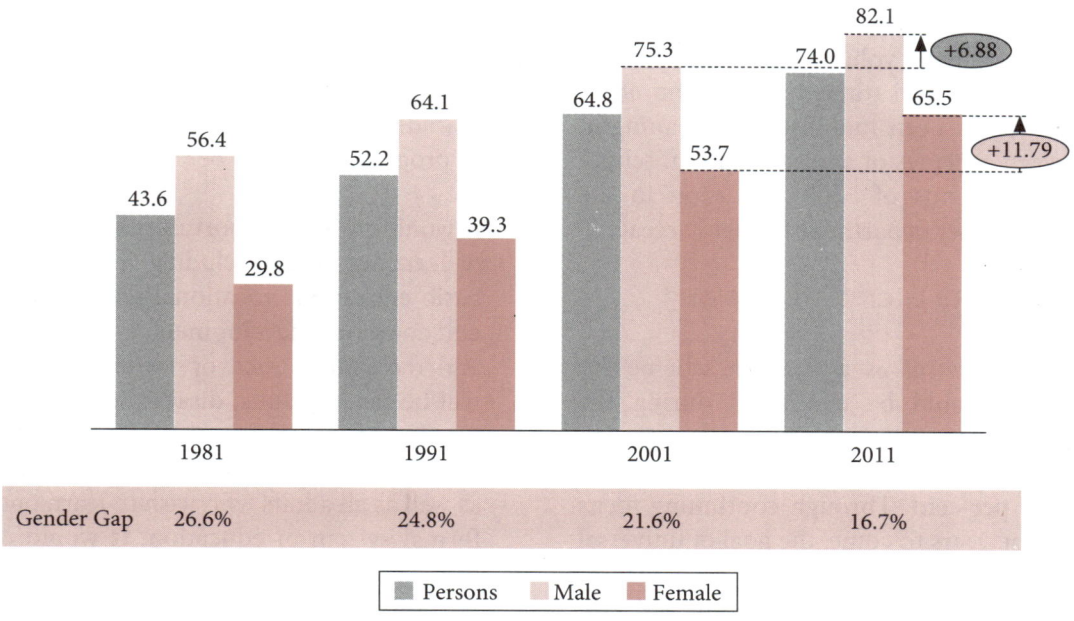

Source: Census of India, 2011.

FIGURE 21.2: Improvements in Literacy Levels, 1981–2011 (%)

in particular and the disadvantaged groups in general, was launched. *Saakshar Bharat* is currently in operation in 372 districts. Under this scheme, functional literacy would be provided to 70 million adults (60 million women and 10 million men) in the age group of 15 years and above. Besides 3 million adults, half of them under basic education programme and the other half under vocational education and skill development programme are aimed to be covered. The scheme is anchored with Panchayati Raj Institutions and local self-government bodies and adopts a targeted approach with focus on women, SC, ST, and minorities; gives emphasis on quality; user context and group specific approach; promotes convergence and partnership and effectively uses ICT in implementation. *Saakshar Bharat* is using the concept of total quality management and is developing core curriculum framework for adult literacy.

21.175. Though *Saakshar Bharat* is conceived as a variant of National Literacy Mission (NLM), yet due to hiatus during the Tenth Plan period, management structures under the NLM had become moribund. Thus, galvanising the implementation machinery for *Saakshar Bharat* was a huge challenge. Now that it is in third year of its operation, significant support for *Saakshar Bharat* has been mobilised. Through large scale countrywide environment building and mass mobilisation campaigns, voluntary teachers/*prerak*s have been motivated and trained in large numbers and community has been mobilised. A meaningful synergy between schemes of adult education, school education, departments of adult education in the universities, and other departments is being created.

Strategic Shift from Literacy to Lifelong Learning

21.176. *Saakshar Bharat* as a flagship scheme for adult education would be continued during the Twelfth Plan and, by 2017, it shall strive to raise the literacy rate to 80 per cent and reduce the gender gap to less than 10 per cent. Through continuing focus on literacy in the years to come, the goal of universal literacy by 2025 or even earlier would be achieved. During the Twelfth Plan, *Saakshar Bharat* will give special focus on young adults and OoS adolescents (15–19 years).

21.177. At the same, there is a need to redefine literacy and go for a paradigm shift from basic literacy to lifelong learning. In the present technology-driven knowledge-based competitive economy, even the basic ability to read and write with understanding is not enough; adults need to learn to manage information and knowledge in a critical and reasonable manner, learn to search, identify, evaluate, select, and use information and knowledge wherever they are available: print, mass media, or the Internet. Nevertheless, becoming literate can no longer be viewed as a specific and terminal period in the life of a person. In fact, literacy is the entry point to basic education and a stepping stone to lifelong education. Lifelong learning is today essential for survival and for enhancing people's quality of life, as well as for national, human, social and economic development. It should cover 'all learning activity undertaken throughout life-whether in formal, non-formal and informal settings with the aim of improving knowledge, skills and competence within personal, civic, social and for employment related perspective'. Under this new paradigm of lifelong learning and literacy, the focus is not only on non-formal education set up but on establishing strong linkages with the formal system with mechanism for recognising prior learning and accreditation.

21.178. Accordingly, *Saakshar Bharat* would be revamped during the Twelfth Plan and aligned to the new paradigm of lifelong learning. The key features of this programme would be:

1. It would provide opportunities to meet all types of learning needs including functional literacy, basic education, vocational education, physical and emotional development, arts, culture, sports and recreation. Such opportunities of learning will be for all adults, disadvantaged and advantaged, in the age group of 15 years and above, who missed the opportunity of formal education as well as all adults who wish to learn outside the formal system of education. It would continue to focus on inclusion with programmatic interventions in rural areas, urban slums, low literacy areas, tribal areas, SCs and minority concentrated areas. To facilitate more equitable access

and participation, the revamped programme would create appropriate infrastructure, especially in difficult, backward, tribal, and rural areas, and enhance culture of learning and education by eliminating barriers to participation through ICT, awareness, mobilisation, environment building and well-designed and targeted guidance, information and motivation.

2. At the Gram Panchayat level and at the equivalent levels in the urban areas, the existing well-equipped ICT-enabled multi-purpose Adult Education and Skill Development Centres (AESDCs) would be strengthened (or set up where these do not exist) to offer a range of adult learning and education programmes to meet local needs of the adults. For higher levels of adult education, secondary level institutions at the block and community colleges at the district level need to be set up.

3. Existing programme structures, including National Literacy Mission Authority at the apex level, the State Literacy Mission Authorities at the State level and the Lok Shiksha Samitis at the District, Block and the Gram Panchayat, as well as the resource support bodies, would be remodelled, strengthened and aligned to lifelong learning and literacy. Inter-sectoral and inter-ministerial cooperation would be obtained. In addition, active involvement of public authorities at all administrative levels, civil society, private sector, community and adult learners' organisations in the development, implementation and evaluation of adult learning and education programmes would be obtained. The revamped programme would need a permanent system with nationwide and multilevel network of institutions and structures that conform to these parameters. Additional resources should be allocated for building capacities of PRIs and other implementing agencies.

4. Objective criteria to assess learning outcomes, skill development, prior learning and equivalency should be developed based on which third party assessment and certification should be undertaken. For this, partnerships should be developed with accredited national and State-level agencies and open and distance learning systems. *Lifelong learning and literacy* under the revamped programme should be seamlessly integrated with formal education system for horizontal and vertical migration by establishing equivalency frameworks to facilitate credit transfer among formal, non-formal and informal education.

21.179. The revamped *Saakshar Bharat* would be a continuing programme as a lifelong learning and literacy support system for the country. To promote a systematic lifelong learning, the country might require comprehensive legislation to formally recognise forms of education other than formal, integrate formal, non-formal and informal learning and for recognition, validation and accreditation of learning obtained in non-formal ways. Need for enabling legislative measures would thus be examined to provide a robust framework for lifelong learning and literacy.

HIGHER EDUCATION

21.180. Higher education is critical for developing a modern economy, a just society and a vibrant polity. It equips young people with skills relevant for the labour market and the opportunity for social mobility. It provides people already in employment with skills to negotiate rapidly evolving career requirements. It prepares all to be responsible citizens who value a democratic and pluralistic society. Thus, the nation creates an intellectual repository of human capital to meet the country's needs and shapes its future. Indeed, higher education is the principal site at which our national goals, developmental priorities and civic values can be examined and refined.

21.181. It is estimated that developed economies and even China will face a shortage of about 40 million highly skilled workers by 2020, while, based on current projections of higher education, India is likely to see some surplus of graduates in 2020. Thus, India could capture a higher share of global knowledge-based work, for example by increasing its exports of knowledge-intensive goods and services, if there is focus on higher education and its quality is globally benchmarked. The country cannot afford to lose time. The demographic bulge evident in India's population pyramid is encountering lower fertility rates, leading to a rapid slowdown in population growth rates and a looming decline of the population in the prime educable age up to 25 years within the next couple of decades.

21.182. Despite considerable progress during the Eleventh Plan, less than one-fifth of the estimated 120 million potential students are enrolled in HEIs in India, well below the world average of 26 per cent. Wide disparities exist in enrolment percentages among the States and between urban and rural areas while disadvantaged sections of society and women have significantly lower enrolments than the national average. The pressure to increase access to affordable education is steadily increasing with the number of eligible students set to double by 2020. At the same time, significant problems exist in the quality of education provided. The sector is plagued by a shortage of well-trained faculty, poor infrastructure and outdated and irrelevant curricula. The use of technology in higher education remains limited and standards of research and teaching at Indian universities are far below international standards with no Indian university featured in any of the rankings of the top 200 institutions globally.

21.183. The key challenge is to find a path to achieve the divergent goals for the growth of higher education in India. Combining access with affordability and ensuring high-quality undergraduate and postgraduate education are vital for realising the potential of the country's 'demographic dividend'. Future expansion should be carefully planned so as to correct regional and social imbalances, reinvigorate institutions to improve standards and reach international benchmarks of excellence, match demand with supply by improving employability, and extend the frontiers of knowledge.

STRATEGIC AIMS OF THE TWELFTH PLAN

21.184. The Twelfth Plan will build on the momentum generated during the Eleventh Plan and continue the focus on the 'Three Es'—expansion, equity and excellence. However, the Plan proposes a paradigm change in the way we achieve such goals—through three new principles. First, an overriding emphasis will be given to quality—as further expansion without quality improvement would be counterproductive for the future of India, given the serious quality issues noted in the sector. Second, the Plan also strives to diversify higher education opportunities, not only to meet the needs of employers, but also to offer a wide range of paths to success for our youth. India must develop world-class research universities as well as have sophisticated teaching institutions to impart key vocational and generic skills in a timely manner to cope with the rapidly changing labour market needs. Third, this excellence in diversity will be implemented through governance reforms, to enable institutions to have the autonomy to develop distinctive strengths, while being held accountable for ensuring quality. Hence, the Twelfth Plan adopts a holistic approach to the issues of expansion, equity and excellence so that expansion is not just about accommodating ever larger number of students, but is also about providing diverse choices of subjects, levels and institutions while ensuring a minimum standard of academic quality and providing the opportunity to pursue higher education to all sections of society, particularly the disadvantaged.

21.185. These objectives must guide the development of all three segments of higher education: Central institutions, which account for 2.6 per cent of the total enrolment; State institutions which account for 38.5 per cent of enrolment; and private institutions that cater to the remaining students. All three segments have to be expanded to achieve enrolment target (see Box 21.7) by creating additional capacity and ensuring equal access opportunities, while being supported to improve the quality of teaching–learning, attain excellence in research, and contribute to economic development.

STRATEGIC FRAMEWORK OF THE TWELFTH PLAN

21.186. In the light of past experience and considering the inter-linkages between expansion, equity, and excellence, a new strategic framework (see Figure 21.3) is required to pursue the objectives of the Twelfth Plan. This would involve cultural, strategic and organisational changes impacting on all aspects of higher education ranging from access and equity to governance,

Box 21.7
Enrolment Target for the Twelfth Plan

Additional enrolment capacity of 10 million students including 1 million in open and distance learning would be created by the end of the Twelfth Plan. This would enable roughly 3 million more students in each age cohort to enter higher education and raise the country's GER from 17.9 per cent (estimated for 2011–12) to 25.2 per cent by 2017–18 and reach the target of 30 per cent GER by 2020–21 which would be broadly in line with world average.

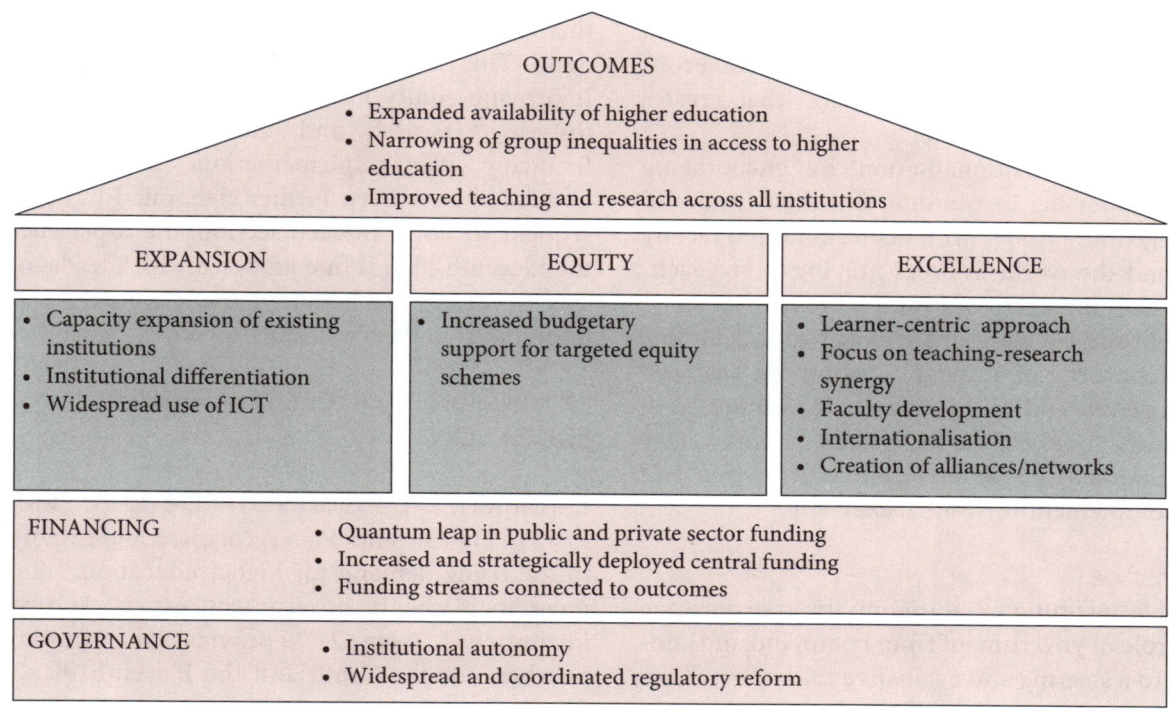

FIGURE 21.3: Strategic Framework

funding, monitoring and regulation, institutional structures, curricula and teaching–learning processes.

21.187. The strategic framework for the Twelfth Plan for higher education identifies such a paradigmatic shift in the following critical areas related to expansion, equity, excellence, governance and financing.

Expansion

1. Expand access by scaling up capacity in existing institutions rather than increasing the number of institutions, with the exception of new institutions needed to address critical regional and social gaps.
2. Create a system of institutional differentiation and distinctiveness to cater to a diverse body of students and the varied needs of employers.
3. Use the transformative potential of new technologies to improve quality, reduce costs, improve processes and efficiency and reach a larger body of students, while promoting efficient and transparent governance and raising the quality of teaching and research.

Equity

4. Provide significant increase in budgetary support for equity-related measures through targeted, integrated and effective equity-related schemes, which will replace the existing maze of multiple and diffused small outlay schemes.

Excellence

5. Foster a shift from an input-centric and credential-based pedagogical approach to a

learner-centric and learning-outcome based approach to improve the quality of teaching and research.
6. Ensure availability, recruitment and retention of qualified people to meet the growing need for quality faculty; upgrade the skills of existing faculty; and, build synergies between teaching and research to promote excellence in both.
7. Facilitate translation of academic research into innovations for practical use in society and economy and foster entrepreneurship that creates wealth and public goods.
8. Promote internationalisation by encouraging and supporting institutions and their faculty to engage more deeply with institutions and faculty around the world in areas ranging from teaching–learning to research and outreach.
9. Create and facilitate alliances, networks, clusters, and consortia of academic institutions amongst themselves and with research institutions and industry to accelerate the process of knowledge development by better resource utilisation and by complementing mutual expertise.

Governance
10. Enable institutional autonomy by transforming the role of government from command and control to a steering and evaluative role.
11. Enhance the capacity of the higher education system to govern itself by widespread and coordinated regulatory reform.
12. Increase transparency in both public and private institutions by requiring them to disclose important standardised information related to admissions, fees, faculty, programs, placements, governance, finance, business tie-ups and ownership.

Financing
13. Implement a quantum leap in both public and private sector investment in higher education to achieve the various goals set out for the Twelfth Plan.
14. Implement a significant increase in Central plan funds for higher education and strategically deploy these funds to improve the entire system of higher education, including State systems.
15. Directly connect funding streams to specific outcomes and desired impacts related to the Plan objectives through reforms in governance arrangements at the national, State and institutional levels with suitable implementation and monitoring mechanisms.

21.188. Figure 21.3 shows the various elements of the strategy framework and inter-linkages amongst them. The issues of expansion or widening access, improving equity in access, improving quality and fostering research and innovation, governance, financing, Plan implementation, monitoring and evaluation have been further elaborated in the subsequent sections. In each section, the experience of the Eleventh Plan is first analysed which leads to the specific strategy to be adopted and initiatives to be undertaken in the Twelfth Plan.

EXPANSION OF ACCESS TO HIGHER EDUCATION

Enrolment Expansion in the Eleventh Plan
21.189. The Eleventh Plan recognised and responded to the rising demand for higher education.[12] Enrolment increased in government as well as private institutions. Table 21.7 provides the enrolment numbers for the Tenth and the Eleventh Plan, the increase in enrolment and the compounded annual growth rate (CAGR).

21.190. Enrolment[13] in open and distance learning (ODL) programmes also grew rapidly during the Eleventh Plan from 27.41 lakh students in 2006–07 to 42.01 lakh students in 2011–12 (Table 21.8). Apart from the Indira Gandhi National Open University, there are 13 State Open Universities and 183 other Distance Education Institutions (DEIs) approved by the Distance Education Council. Enrolment in DEIs that includes at least 44 private institutions grew most rapidly over 10 per cent per year during the Eleventh Plan period.

21.191. GER is often used to measure the higher education access. GER is the total enrolment in higher education (both degree and diploma programmes) as a percentage of the population in the eligible age

TABLE 21.7
Growth of Enrolment in the Eleventh Plan

(Enrolment in lakh)

Category	2006–07		2011–12		Increase	Growth Rate (Per cent)
	Total	Per cent	Total	Per cent		
By type of institutions						
Government	63.38	45.8	89.63	41.1	26.25	7.2
Central	3.10	2.2	5.63	2.6	2.53	12.7
State	60.28	43.6	84.00	38.5	23.72	6.9
Private	75.12	54.2	128.23	58.9	53.11	11.3
By degree/diploma						
Degree	123.54	89.2	184.84	84.8	61.30	8.4
Diploma	14.96	10.8	33.02	15.2	18.06	10.8
Total	138.50	100.00	217.86	100.00	79.36	9.5

Source: University Grants Commission (UGC), All India Council for Technical Education (AICTE), NCTE, Indian Nursing Council (NCTE).
Note: Central institutions include Indian Institutes of Management even though they award PG diplomas in management.

TABLE 21.8
Growth of Enrolment in ODL Programmes in the Eleventh Plan

(Enrolment in lakh)

Enrolment	2006–2007	2011–2012	Increase	Growth Rate (per cent)
Indira Gandhi National Open University	4.68	6.97	2.29	8.3
State Open Universities (SOU)	7.77	10.80	3.03	6.8
Distance Education Institutions (DEI)	14.96	24.24	9.28	10.1
Total	27.41	42.01	14.60	8.9

Source: Distance Education Council.

cohort of 18–23 years. Using this definition, GER for higher education was 12.3 per cent in 2006–07 and increased to 17.9 per cent in 2011–12. In regular programmes alone, GER has increased from 10.4 per cent in 2006–07 to 15.2 per cent in 2011–12.

21.192. Increased enrolments in the Eleventh Plan enabled Indian higher education to cross the threshold of 15 per cent GER, moving the country from an 'elite' to a 'mass' higher education system. Despite this, the unmet demand for access to higher education remains significant, indicating that a further expansion is required. However, expansion during the Twelfth Plan must factor that the recent growth has been skewed in favour of certain regions, disciplines and sectors (see Table 21.9 for growth by field of study) and ensure further expansion has diversity in the provision of higher education including a focused emphasis on improving the quality of institutions, faculty and curricula.

INSTITUTIONAL EXPANSION IN THE ELEVENTH PLAN

21.193. Increase in higher education capacity during the Eleventh Plan was largely achieved through the setting up of new institutions by Central and State Governments and the private sector. The number of institutions grew by 58 per cent from 29,384 to 46,430. By the end of the Plan, the country had 645 degree awarding institutions, 33,023 colleges affiliated to

174 universities and over 12,748 diploma granting institutions. Table 21.10 provides a snapshot of this growth. With the growth rate of institutions matching that of enrolment, the problem of low enrolment per institution evident at the start of the Eleventh Plan remains. Combined with the skewed growth of engineering and technical disciplines, this indicates that further expansion should be undertaken in the context of also achieving disciplinary diversity and increasing capacity within existing institutions rather than creating new institutions.

TABLE 21.9
Growth of Enrolment by Field of Study during the Eleventh Plan (in lakh)

Faculty	2006–07		2011–12		Growth Rate (Per cent)
	Total	Per cent	Total	Per cent	
Arts	54.86	39.6	65.78	30.2	3.7
Science	25.43	18.4	30.57	14.0	3.8
Commerce and Management	22.87	16.5	34.34	15.8	8.5
Education	6.21	4.5	13.00	6.0	15.9
Engineering	18.06	13.0	54.68	25.0	24.8
Medicine, Nursing and Pharmacy	5.98	4.3	12.02	5.5	15.0
Agriculture and Veterinary Science	0.93	0.7	1.21	0.6	5.4
Law	3.00	2.2	3.48	1.6	3.0
Others	1.16	0.8	2.78	1.3	19.1
Total	**138.5**	**100**	**217.86**	**100**	**9.5**

Source: UGC, AICTE, NCTE and INC.

TABLE 21.10
Growth of Institutions in the Eleventh Plan

Category	2006–07	2011–12	Increase	Growth Rate (Per Cent)
Central Institutions				
Degree Awarding Institutions	87	152	65	11.8
Colleges	58	69	11	3.5
Sub total	145	221	76	8.8
State Institutions				
Degree Awarding Institutions	227	316	89	6.8
Colleges	9,000	13,024	4,024	7.7
Diploma Institutions	1,867	3,207	1,340	11.4
Sub total	11,094	16,547	5,453	8.3
Private Institutions				
Degree Awarding Institutions	73	191	118	21.2
Colleges	12,112	19,930	7,818	10.5
Diploma Institutions	5,960	9,541	3,581	9.9
Sub total	18,145	29,662	11,517	10.3
Total	**29,384**	**46,430**	**17,046**	**9.6**

Source: UGC, AICTE, NCTE and INC.
Note: Central degree institutions include Indian Institutes of Management even though they award PG diploma in management.

21.194. Growth in private institutions was significant during the Eleventh Plan period. Ninety-eight private State universities, 17 private deemed universities, 7,818 private colleges, and 3,581 private diploma institutions were set up during the Plan period. While a majority of them offer professional or vocational programmes almost exclusively, it's worth noting that a number of arts, commerce and science colleges and a few comprehensive multidisciplinary universities have also been established in the private sector in recent years.

21.195. The expansion of Central institutions during the Eleventh Plan was historic. The Central Government has never established so many institutions in a single Plan period. The Central Government established 65 new institutions during the Eleventh Plan period (see Table 21.11). Each State now has at least one Central university except Goa, where the State Government did not want one. Special financial assistance was provided by the Central Government to existing Central institutions to raise their intake capacity in order to provide 27 per cent reservation to OBCs without affecting the number of general seats. The Central Government also supported the States to set up 45 model degree colleges (as against the 374 proposed in low enrolment districts) and 279 government polytechnics (as against the 300 proposed) during the Plan period.

On their own, the State Governments added 89 universities, 4,024 colleges and 1,340 diploma institutions during the same period.

21.196. Expansion of HEIs by Central ministries and departments other than MHRD was also significant with 14 institutions being established by other Ministries/Departments. These include medical and agricultural universities, institutes of fashion technology, pharmaceutical education and research institutes and the South Asia and Nalanda universities. However, this does not include institutions for maritime education and for flying and aeronautical education approved by the Directorate General of Shipping and Directorate General of Civil Aviation.

21.197. Affiliated colleges, which enrol 86.7 per cent of all students, are the mainstay of the country's higher education system. They enrol over 90 per cent of undergraduate students, over 70 per cent of the postgraduates and about 17 per cent of doctoral students. They follow curricula and examination systems determined by the affiliating universities.

21.198. Despite the growth in number of institutions, their geographical spread remains highly skewed with a large concentration in big cities and towns. While overall institutional density increased from 10 to 14 institutions per 1,000 sq. km. during

TABLE 21.11
Growth of Central Institutions during the Eleventh Plan

Type of Institution	2006–07	2011–12	Increase
Central Universities	19	40	21
Indian Institute of Technology	7	15	8
Indian Institute of Management	6	13	7
Indian Institute of Science Education and Research	2	5	3
School of Planning and Architecture	1	3	2
National Institute of Technology	20	30	10
Other Technical Institutions	15	15	0
Other Universities/Institutions	17	31	14
Total	**87**	**152**	**65**

Source: Ministry of HRD, Other Ministries.
Note: Other universities/institutions include deemed universities fully funded by the Central Government (via UGC) and institutions under other ministries.

the Eleventh Plan, a large number of habitations and settlement clusters with a population of more than 10,000 and less than 1,00,000 are without any proximate institution of higher education.

21.199. Even though GER at the national level is 18 per cent, there are wide inter-State variations. Delhi, Chandigarh and Puducherry, which attract a large number of students from outside their States, have GERs exceeding 30 per cent while States like Bihar, Jharkhand, Assam, Rajasthan, Odisha and West Bengal have significantly lower GERs. This suggests a need for State-specific strategies in addressing issues of expansion of higher education during the Twelfth Plan period.

21.200. To support institutional expansion, Central Government spending on higher education has grown steadily over the years and increased over six-fold between 2006–07 and 2011–12. In contrast, State non-Plan funding grew at a modest pace even though institutions in the State sector have also expanded significantly. As a result, the quality of State institutions has continued to deteriorate over the years.

21.201. During the Eleventh Plan, enrolment in higher education (including enrolment in open and distance learning) grew by 9.3 million from 16.6 million (in 2006–07) to 25.9 million in 2011–12. Target for the Twelfth Plan is to increase enrolment capacity by another 10 million. Of this, 1 million will come from ODL, 3.3 million through large scale expansion of skill-granting diploma programmes and remaining 5.7 million will come from further expansion of degree programmes with accelerated expansion of postgraduate and doctoral programmes (see Table 21.12).

21.202. This additional enrolment capacity of 10 million students would enable roughly 3 million more students in each age cohort to enter higher education and raise the GER broadly in line with the current global average from 17.9 per cent (estimated for 2011–12) to 25.2 per cent by 2017. Enrolment capacity of Central institutions would be doubled from 0.6 million to 1.2 million. In the State institutions, it will increase from 8.4 million to 11 million. The bulk of growth would be in the private institutions. In private institutions, the enrolment capacity would increase from 12.7 million now to 18.5 million by the end of the Twelfth Plan period (see Figure 21.4).

21.203. Planning for expansion should be demand-driven. First, the national government would

TABLE 21.12
Enrolment Targets by Level/Type for the Twelfth Plan

(student numbers in lakh)

Level/Type	2011–12 (Estimates)	2016–17 (Targets)	Growth Rate (Per Cent)
PhD	1	3	24.6
PG General	17.3	33.2	13.9
PG Technical	5	12.2	19.5
UG General	116.6	128	1.9
UG Technical	45	66	8.0
Sub total	184.9	242.4	5.6
Diploma	33	65	14.5
Total	**217.9**	**307.4**	**7.1**
ODL	42	52	4.4
Grand Total	**259.9**	**359.4**	**6.7**
Population 18–23 years	1,451.2	1,427.4	–0.1
GER (%)	17.9	25.2	

Source: Planning Commission Estimates/Targets.

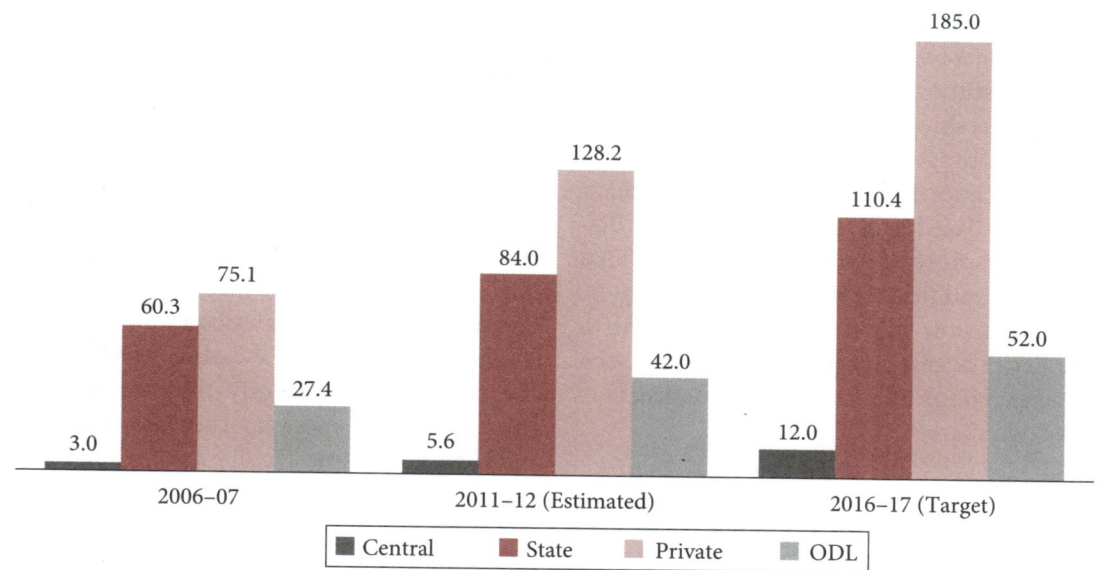

Source: Based on figures drawn from UGC, AICTE, NCTE, MHRD and INC.

FIGURE 21.4: Enrolments in Higher Education (in lakh): 2006–07 to 2016–17

prepare long-term occupational demand projections recognising that these must be updated periodically to meet the changing needs of the economy and society. For Central institutions, this would be followed through by developing institutional supply targets. For each State, the expansion plan should similarly be based on State-level demand projections. This would require coordinated efforts and enhancing the capacity for such planning both at the national and State levels.

TWELFTH PLAN EXPANSION STRATEGY

21.204. The expansion that took place in the Eleventh Plan was a logical response to the rising aspirations of young people, improved schooling, and the fact that jobs created through rapid economic growth and skill-based technical change require higher levels of education. During the Eleventh Plan, Indian higher education moved from 'elite' to 'mass' higher education (threshold of 15 per cent GER) and is now moving towards universal higher education (threshold of 50 per cent GER). This must be accompanied by offering a wider, diverse range of education—the student should be able to acquire skills in multiple disciplines while achieving a solid core set of skills and at a pace that is customised to individual's capacity to learn. With this in mind, further expansion will require a re-examination of the design, organisation, definition, and purpose of higher education. The Twelfth Plan strives to create diverse education opportunities to cater to the growing number of students passing out of higher secondary classes on the one hand and the diverse needs of the economy and society on the other. Therefore, the four key principles that will drive the strategy for higher education expansion in the Twelfth Plan are as follows:

1. Expansion must focus on locations, States, subject areas/disciplines, and types of institutions where current capacity is low, instead of creating additional capacity across the board.
2. Expansion must be aligned to the country's economy. Therefore, a variety of HEIs offering innovative and relevant curricula designed to serve different segments of the job market or provide avenues for self-employment must be developed. Specific emphasis must be given to the expansion of skill-based programmes in higher education.
3. The relative strengths of different types of institutions must be harnessed to serve different needs. Central institutions must be assisted to become quality-leading institutions. State institutions must be supported to expand further and simultaneously address equity issues and improve quality. The philanthropic sector should

be invited and incentivised to infuse more funds and build larger, sustainable and higher quality private institutions. New models of Public–Private Partnership (PPP) in higher education must be encouraged not only for technology intensive education but also for multidisciplinary and research-based education. Open and distance learning must be used to widen access in a cost-effective and flexible manner.

4. Overall, expansion will be carefully planned to provide better access to the poor and disadvantaged social groups and first generation learners from backward areas.

21.205. Expansion should not only mean having more institutions of the same kind, but also developing new kinds of institutions. First, the country must have some globally competitive research-intensive institutions which should: (*i*) keep India abreast of the international scientific frontier; (*ii*) ensure that educational content and curricula is of world standards and updated regularly; (*iii*) ensure that research is actively used to solve India's own problems; and (*iv*) engage the best researchers in the country in teaching the next generation of students both within and outside their institution.

21.206. Second, teaching-focused institutions must offer a wide range of good-quality educational options, from liberal arts to professional and technical education. Part-time programs should also be introduced for working professionals and adult learners conferring the same degrees that are awarded through traditional full-time programmes.

21.207. Third, there must be institutions offering credible short-duration programmes that provide skills for development opportunities as well as remedial education—to make sure that those coming out of variable quality secondary schools have the opportunity to succeed in the higher education environment. Fourth, geographical mapping of HEIs should be done to identify habitations and settlements that lack higher education facilities. Expansion at the State or district level should be planned to develop diverse types of institutions of higher education depending on the opportunities for employment and the size of the student body passing out at the higher secondary level.

21.208. While expanding capacity, costs have to be kept low while maintaining high quality. This can be achieved by ensuring that expansion primarily takes place by increasing the capacity of existing institutions. Several universities and colleges operate sub-optimally with just a few hundred students. Several specific strategies could be adopted for optimal operations. First, existing physical facilities can be used more efficiently through scheduling with multiple shifts and year-round operations. Second, high-cost full-time faculty can be engaged in high-value teaching while specially trained teaching assistants or adjunct faculty could be used for tutorials and online courses that are blended with face-to-face instruction.

21.209. Third, the land, which has become a binding constraint for setting up new campuses, should be efficiently used. Norms for land area requirement should be reviewed, keeping in mind energy and environmental impact, while affording adequate physical space for learning. The advent of new teaching technologies must be factored in the way, classrooms, laboratories and libraries are designed. Institutions, particularly in urban agglomerations, would be encouraged to consolidate capacity through mergers. The more reputed institutions would be encouraged to establish multiple campuses and benefit from the economies of scale and scope. And finally, there is benefit in co-locating institutions in large education or integrated hubs that would incubate and nurture talent, create innovation ecosystem and foster entrepreneurship. A few large education clusters would be established during the Twelfth Plan. These could be anchored by public and/or private universities with other higher education institutions and knowledge intensive industries in close proximity. This would facilitate and enhance interactions and collaborations across different higher education institutions and firms.

TWELFTH PLAN EXPANSION INITIATIVES

21.210. The Twelfth Plan initiatives would be designed to implement these strategic objectives through new and continuing initiatives. The specific major Twelfth Plan initiatives are as follows:

Develop Central Institutions as Quality-Leading Institutions

21.211. Enrolment in Central institutions will be increased from 6 lakh to 12 lakh students mainly within existing Central institutions. Only research and innovation based institutions or exemplar institutions would be established in the Central sector or supported by the Central Government (see Box 21.8). Older Central institutions will be financially supported to redevelop campuses to achieve scale and build state-of-the-art facilities. In some cases, multiple campuses would be encouraged to enable economies of scale and institutional efficiency. The campuses to be upgraded during the Twelfth Plan would include ISM Dhanbad to IIT-level, BESU Shibpur to an Indian Institute of Engineering, Science and Technology, and NIFFT Ranchi as a premier institution for forging and foundry technology. HEIs with potential in the UTs that come under the Central Government (through the Ministry of Home Affairs) and have potential like the PEC University of Technology and Chandigarh College of Architecture would also be upgraded.

21.212. Central institutions should become catalytic role models for other institutions in all aspects including governance, infrastructure, faculty and curricula. For instance, in infrastructural development, they can help define new building technologies, the use of fixed-cost and time EPC contracts and PPP models for the basic infrastructure. They will thus assist other institutions to improve standards, particularly in the States or regions where they are located. Co-location of State and private institutions and other enterprises with new Central institutions could build vibrant innovation clusters.

Strategic Support for State Higher Education

21.213. Central funding for State higher education is small; its reach is limited, and its impact insignificant. It is poorly coordinated and plagued by excessive bureaucracy, inefficiencies, low levels of monitoring and poor quality of outcomes. It therefore, provides little value for money. During the Twelfth Plan, State higher education would be provided significantly more Central funding. There will be a strategic shift in the manner in which State higher education systems are supported by the Central Government. Central funding for higher education will be done on a State-specific basis and allocated for the State's higher education system as a whole, even though it would flow to individual universities and colleges via the UGC as before. Details for allocation and flow of Central funds to State universities and colleges would be worked out through a consultative process. The UGC would play an important and more strategic role in allocation and disbursal of Central funds, particularly in funding strategic investment plans as proposed by institutions on a selective basis (see Box 21.9).

21.214. The goal of Central funding of State higher education should be to benefit from the synergies

---

Box 21.8
TISS: A Multi-Location Networked University

Tata Institute of Social Sciences has expanded rapidly since 2006 and emerged as a multi-location networked university for social sciences. It has enlarged its research base in social sciences and diversified its course offerings to provide access to a much larger body of students in various trans-disciplinary areas across the country. The capacity of its Mumbai Campus increased from 200 masters and 50 doctoral students in 2006 to 1,650 masters and 350 doctoral students in 2012; with a corresponding increase in the range of courses it offers. The Institute has established three campuses at Tuljapur (operational since 2004) and at Hyderabad and Guwahati, each of them will have about 1,000 students each by 2016. This expansion has been funded largely from resources mobilised through Indian trusts and foundations that have so far contributed about 130 crore with Central Government putting in another 26 cr. In addition, the Institute mobilised over ₹200 crore for research work and to set up new academic programs. Further, the Institute has collaborative research, faculty and student exchange programs with over 60 universities and institutions in the country—each of the collaboration is supported by competitive funding secured by the institute that enabled exchange at no extra cost to its students.

> **Box 21.9**
> **Strategic Shift in Central Funding for State Higher Education**
> - Enable a State system-wide planning perspective and benefit from the synergy in spending by the Central and State Government.
> - States to develop comprehensive State higher education plans that utilise an interconnected strategy to address issues of expansion, equity and excellence together.
> - Central funding to be linked to academic, administrative and financial reforms of State higher education.
> - Funding to be provided through a flagship programme: Rashtriya Uchcha Shiksha Abhiyan (RUSA).

between State and Central spending and to more effectively use Central funding to bring about administrative, academic and financial reforms in State systems, and as a powerful tool to address equity issues and improve quality at the State level.

Quality Private Growth

21.215. The Private sector has contributed significantly to higher education expansion during the Eleventh Plan and private higher education now accounts for 58.5 per cent of enrolments. The private sector will be encouraged to establish larger and higher quality institutions in the Twelfth Plan. Currently, for-profit entities are not permitted in higher education and the non-profit or philanthropy-driven institutions are unable to scale-up enough to bridge the demand–supply gap in higher education. Therefore, the 'not-for-profit' status in higher education should, perhaps, be re-examined for pragmatic considerations so as to allow the entry of for-profit institutions in select areas where acute shortages persist. This should, however, be subjected to the necessary oversight and accreditation arrangements to ensure quality and equity. For-profit private higher education can be taxed and the revenue from it can be channelled into large scale scholarship programme to promote equity as is practised in Brazil and China.

21.216. At the same time, innovative ways have to be found to encourage the infusion of more private capital in the traditional not-for-profit higher education. Some proposals that require serious consideration include: (*i*) enabling liberal financing options for the sector, like allowing private institutions to raise funds through public offerings of bonds or shares; (*ii*) changing the legal status of the sector to attract more investors, like allowing all types of institutions to be established under Section 25 of the companies Act and allowing existing trusts and societies to convert to institution under Section 25 of the companies Act; (*iii*) giving priority recognition to the sector, like providing it 'infrastructure' status with similar, financial and tax treatment.

21.217. The government could support non-profit private institutions in three ways—(*i*) access to public student financial aid would be extended to accredited private institutions; (*ii*) access to research funding will be on an equal footing with public institutions with suitable protection for intellectual property derived from such research; and (*iii*) private institutions would benefit from various long-term quality enhancement efforts like enhanced use of technology and faculty development initiatives. The corporate sector could be involved in higher education and their large in-house training capacities, particularly in skill development and management, could be leveraged to improve access to higher education.

21.218. Simultaneously, measures to ensure that private institutions are committed to quality, equity and transparency will be introduced through reform of regulatory oversight. The current regulatory framework needs to be revamped to: (*i*) encourage serious private philanthropy and investment to innovate and provide high-quality education; (*ii*) promote better availability of information on private institutions to the public; (*iii*) ensure that institutions that indulge in unfair practices are dealt with swiftly. Accreditation will be central to such reforms.

21.219. New models of Public–Private Partnerships (PPP) in higher education will be encouraged in the Twelfth Plan, particularly in the establishment of research and innovation institutions. Based on the Eleventh Plan experience of setting up Indian Institutes of Information Technology (IIITs) and polytechnics in PPP mode, a framework will be put in place to encourage the spread and growth of PPP models, increase and improve resource utilisation and enhance the quality of education in such institutions. In some cases, public institutions that are failing to meet standards could be assisted by the private partners to transform them through innovative PPP models.

Expansion of Skill-Based Programmes

21.220. Special emphasis will be placed on expansion of skill-based programmes in higher education during the Twelfth Plan. A framework for setting up community colleges based on the North American model is under development and has been endorsed in principle by the Central Advisory Body on Education (see Box 21.10).

21.221. Community Colleges can serve multiple needs, including (*i*) provide career oriented education and skills to students interested in directly entering the workforce; (*ii*) provide contracted training and education programmes for local employers; (*iii*) provide high-touch remedial education for secondary school graduates not ready to enrol in traditional colleges, giving them a path to transfer to three or four year institutions; (*iv*) offer general interest courses to the community for personal development and interest. Given these objectives, community colleges would be located to afford easy access to underprivileged students. Such colleges could either be established as affiliated colleges of universities governed, guided and managed through a 'Department of Skills and Lifelong Learning' (DSLL) or as entirely autonomous institutions linked to sector-skill councils.

21.222. Ongoing UGC initiative that supports career-oriented add-on courses in traditional universities and colleges and the IGNOU's scheme of community colleges would be reviewed. Technical support of Philanthropic Foundations and the Indian Centre for Research and Development of Community Education (which has 230 community colleges in its fold) would be taken to build on the current initiatives and create a robust framework for skill-based education within the higher education sector in the country. This could include institutional arrangements for recognition of prior learning.

Open and Distance Learning Initiatives

21.223. Open and Distance Learning (ODL) will be used to widen access and significantly expand capacity in a cost-effective and flexible manner. During the Twelfth Plan, support to IGNOU, State open universities and other institutions of distance education will be increased to expand access particularly for those beyond the normal schooling age. Such programmes will be regularly evaluated for learning

---

Box 21.10
Concept and Framework for Establishing Community Colleges

- Community Colleges will provide modular credit-based courses with entry and exit flexibility that conforms to the National Skills Qualifications Framework (NSQF).
- They will offer programmes leading to certificates (after one year), diplomas, advanced diplomas or associate degrees (after two years) with options to transfer to regular degree programmes.
- Their curricula will include an appropriate mix of academic and vocational skills and will be aligned to national occupational standards determined by employer-led sector skill councils.
- The assessment of vocational skills and training provided by Community Colleges will be done in accordance with assessment protocols developed by sector skill councils.
- Their faculty will typically consist of a permanent core, who will teach fundamentals (language, mathematics, science) and a large pool of adjunct or part-time faculty who will focus on specialisations.
- Well-designed online offerings would be integrated with face-to-face instruction to enhance and maintain quality.
- Community Colleges will be located in habitations with large potential student population.
- There will be local community involvement in their academic and administrative boards.
- They could be established in the premises of existing colleges, polytechnics, or even higher secondary schools and use online training and industry sites, wherever possible.

outcomes so that curricula and pedagogical changes can be made on an ongoing basis. In the face of growing concern about the quality of ODL programmes, regulatory oversight would be strengthened during the Twelfth Plan. Traditional institutions will be encouraged to offer part of their curriculum online to promote blended learning and provide students more choices while keeping costs low. This would also enable them to reach out to more students and non-traditional learners.

EQUITY IN ACCESS TO HIGHER EDUCATION

Multi-Dimensional Inequalities

21.224. Equitable access to quality higher education is an essential prerequisite for realising the Constitutional promise of 'Equality of Opportunity' as well as achieving the goal of inclusive development in the Twelfth Plan. However, many of these imbalances occur at the school level due to low enrolments and high dropouts amongst the deprived, underprivileged and marginalised sections. Thus, only a limited pool of such students is available for entry into higher education. As a result, a large proportion of seats in higher education reserved for SC, ST, OBC, and persons with disabilities remain unfilled (see Figure 21.5).

21.225. The data on Gross Attendance Ratio for 2007–08 confirms that higher education access for all disadvantaged social groups is well below the national average of 17.2 per cent. As Figure 21.5 shows, despite substantial overall improvement, the broad picture of inter-group inequality has changed only marginally. While access to higher education has improved for all social groups, including the disadvantaged, their relative disparities have not reduced substantially. These inequalities are not one dimensional: gender, disability, class, caste, religion, locality and region are some of the principal dimensions of inequality and when more than one of these conditions exist, their impact is compounded. Access to higher education, especially to prestigious programmes and institutions that are in demand, continues to reflect inherited social privileges.

21.226. The participation of SCs, STs and OBCs in higher education is significantly lower than the national average. The low percentage of students from the SC/ST and OBC categories in the domain of higher education is an acute problem that still persists and pulls the country backward. As per data of NSS 64th round, GER in the ST category is one-fourth that of general category students. It is less than half for the SC and more than half for the OBC

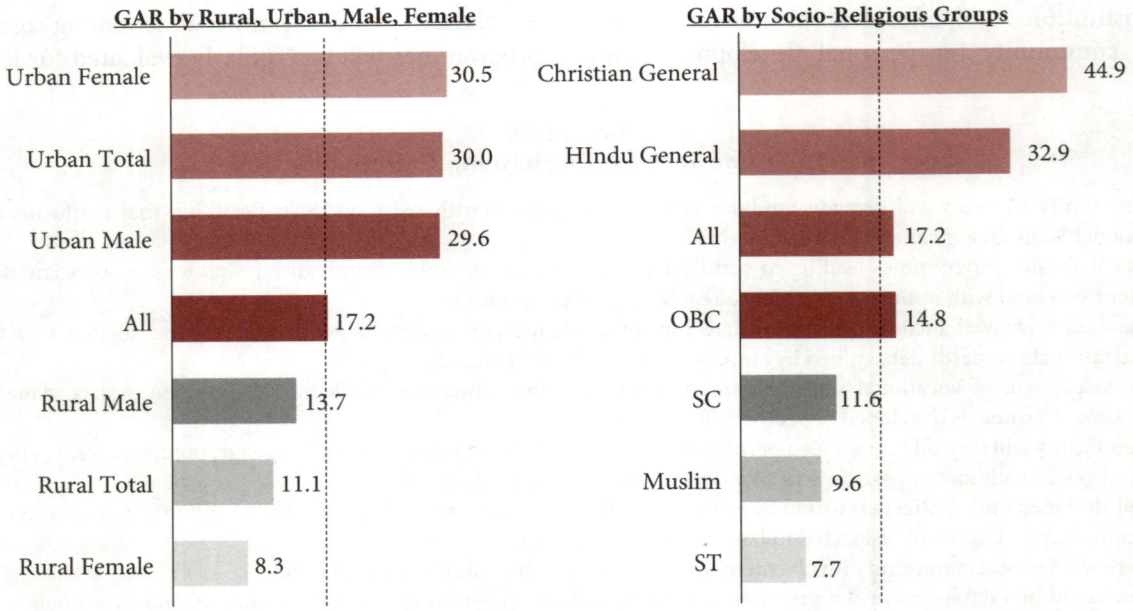

Source: Graph drawn from various sources like UGC, AICTE, NCTE, MHRD and INC.

FIGURE 21.5: Gross Attendance Ratio, 2007–08

students. When compared with the 2004–05 data, there is improvement in the educational levels of SC and the OBC groups, but a lowering of the figures for the ST group.

21.227. As higher education expands, more students will come from hitherto marginalised sections of society. HEIs must gear themselves to face the challenge of catering to the needs of such students to further reduce inequalities in access. The higher education system must:

1. Facilitate entry of the socially disadvantaged into HEIs and, in the case of some extremely disadvantaged communities, devise incentives that would allow 'over-drawing' from this currently small pool of eligible students.
2. Support retention of those disadvantaged students who enter higher education by ensuring that they do not drop out for lack of resources and inadequate academic preparation.
3. Enhance the quality of learning of disadvantaged students and provide guidance and support to improve their chances of entering disciplines that ensure decent employment opportunities or gaining admission to postgraduate degrees at top institutions.
4. Use the 'community college' as a key vehicle for entry into regular higher education by way of widely located, community-based institutions offering relevant education of high quality.

ELEVENTH PLAN EXPERIENCE

21.228. Several measures were initiated in the Eleventh Plan to achieve the goals of equity and inclusion. Centrally funded institutions received special financial assistance to increase the intake of disadvantaged groups and provide 27 per cent reservation for OBCs without affecting the number of general seats. Establishment of 374 colleges in low GER districts and setting up of 1,000 new polytechnics was taken up. Universities and colleges located in border, hilly, remote, small towns, and educationally backward areas and those with larger SC/ST/OBC/Minority/Persons with Disabilities student population were supported. Construction of a large number of girls' hostels was taken up to encourage girls to enrol in HEIs.

21.229. Merit-cum-means scholarships for students from families with annual incomes less than ₹4.5 lakh were started in 2008–09. Since 2009–10 the Central Government has provided 100 per cent interest subsidy during the moratorium period on educational loans taken by students with family income of less than ₹4.5 lakh per annum. A review of these initiatives and previous experience provides the following basic lessons:

- despite progress, relative disparities across various social groups and gender gaps in educational attainments continue to be high even today and area/beneficiary targeted approaches and specific interventions are necessary to narrow these inequalities;
- a substantial increase in funding is needed to achieve a quantum jump in the volume, range and amount of student support in the form of scholarships, stipends, assistantships and loans for disadvantaged students;
- the funding mechanisms for such aid should be structured in such a way that money follows the students for whom it is meant;
- it is necessary to have differentiated access strategies for different groups and in particular for those extremely disadvantaged communities/social groups that still remain largely excluded from the world of higher learning;
- special attention needs to be paid to measuring and redressing inequalities in high-end courses and institutions;
- special emphasis should be put on those schemes that recognise the intersectional nature of disadvantages to address all dimensions of inequality in a holistic manner;
- the delivery system for financial aid needs revamping to remove cumbersome processes and promote awareness of the schemes among the intended recipients;
- there is a need for mechanisms such as a 'Diversity Index' to monitor equity performance of institutions and to link it with monetary incentives.

TWELFTH PLAN STRATEGY

21.230. The thrust of the Twelfth Plan will be to achieve a quantum jump in the number, range and amount of student financial aid schemes in order to (*i*) significantly enhance funding for equity-related measures; (*ii*) evolve a differential response to the various dimensions of inequality; (*iii*) consolidate a range of schemes, especially those which address the intersection of more than one dimension of disadvantage.

21.231. The Plan will pay special attention to inter-State variations, the rural-urban divide, income inequality, gender disparities, persons with disabilities, marginal social groups such as SC, ST, Muslims, and the especially vulnerable sub-groups such as communities involved in scavenging, particularly vulnerable STs, most backward SEBCs and Nomadic/DNT communities. Muslim disadvantage has been highlighted by the Sachar Committee report and the needs of communities engaged in scavenging and DNT/Nomadic communities have also received a lot of attention in recent times. Inter-sectional dimensions of inequality shall be recognised by linking individual-oriented schemes to a multi-dimensional 'Index of Disadvantage'. HEIs would be encouraged to craft their admission policies to address intersectional dimensions of inequality as is practised by Jawaharlal Nehru University for over three decades now. The performance of institutions in increasing the participation of disadvantaged groups could be measured through a 'Diversity Index' and linked to budgetary incentives.

21.232. The reach of scholarships and student loans with government guarantees would be universalised so that no student is deprived of higher education opportunities for financial reasons. This will be complemented by schemes tailored to the specific needs of different groups. Attention to measures like improving the quality of teaching–learning in Indian languages should also be initiated in order to address the language-based dimension of inequality.

TWELFTH PLAN INITIATIVES

Creation of a Comprehensive Student Financial Aid Programme

21.233. Public spending on student financial aid would be enhanced considerably so as to increase the number and amount of scholarships. All student financial aid schemes under the Ministry of HRD would be consolidated under a single 'Student Financial Aid Programme' in order to rationalise and strengthen the administration of equity-related schemes by bringing them under a single umbrella initiative (see Box 21.11). An Empowered Committee would decide on guidelines for each of the scholarships keeping in mind the need for avoiding overlap and enhancing impact.

21.234. In addition to the Student Financial Aid Program, which focuses on scholarships, the Central Government will take significant steps to support student loan programs. A student loan guarantee corpus would be created under the management of a Credit Guarantee Trust to guarantee against default

---

Box 21.11
Student Financial Aid Programme (SFAP)

- Cover higher education at all levels—undergraduate, postgraduate, doctoral and post-doctoral research and include general as well as professional education;
- Cover significant costs of education in determining scholarship amounts and establish a mechanism to linking its revision to change in price index;
- Earmark a fixed proportion of these scholarships for SC, ST, SEBC, Minorities and Person with Disabilities as per the existing policy;
- Create a multi-dimensional 'Index of Disadvantage' that measures the inter-sectional dimensions of inequality that gives due weight to caste/community, gender, poverty and rural background and provide additional scholarships and individual-oriented financial aid schemes linked to such an Index;
- Simplify processes, self-certification and linkages to the unique identity numbers under the UID scheme; and
- Implement a single portal for delivery of all scholarships under the Central Government and explore the possibility of allowing States to join and integrate their student financial aid programmes with this single portal.

in repayment of student loans. This will substantially protect lending institutions from student default thereby encouraging them to make more student loans. In addition, the government guarantee should reduce the rate of interest on student loans (it should be only slightly more than the yield on comparable 10-year Government Securities) benefitting the student community at large.

National Initiative on Inclusion of Persons with Disabilities

21.235. All ongoing and several new initiatives for inclusion of persons with disabilities shall be covered under an umbrella National Initiative on Inclusion of Persons with Disabilities in higher education. This initiative would:

1. provide incentives and support to individual students and faculty with disabilities;
2. give support and policy direction to HEIs and services to make them disabled-friendly and create model universities and colleges at the State and district levels;
3. use new technologies effectively to address challenges of learning for persons with disabilities through various access devices and high quality learning materials;
4. create curricula, and provide research and training-related support to enhance awareness, knowledge and sensitivity about disability issues;
5. specify minimum standards of disability access that must be met by all physical infrastructures offering higher education.

National Initiative for Quality Higher Education in Indian Languages

21.236. The proposed national initiative (the 'Bhasha Initiative') recognises that language connects access and equity with quality of education and thus improving quality of teaching–learning in Indian languages is a cost-effective and sustainable intervention for reducing inequalities. This initiative is aimed at coordinating all the agencies that promote Indian languages with the aim of enhancing the teaching–learning process with Indian languages as the medium of instruction and promoting original research and publication in Indian languages in colleges and universities. This initiative would have effective linkages with the other ongoing and new activities for language development and book promotion. This decentralised, flexible, and user-driven initiative would include setting up of new centres within and across universities, creation of teaching–learning resources, use of technology to create e-books and other learning media in Indian languages, career incentives and support for teachers and support for quality Indian languages publications in academic disciplines.

Focus on Muslims, SC, ST and OBCs

21.237. Schemes for establishing model degree colleges, community colleges and new polytechnics in the low GER districts would be modified to cover districts that have concentration of Muslims. Setting up of Women's Colleges in small towns and quantum jump in the capacity as also number of hostels for women would be given high priority. All these schemes should be included within the ambit of the State strategic plans for higher education to take into account the local context of each State.

21.238. Targeted schemes will be launched to draw students from Muslims that have low participation in higher education. These schemes will have to combine special incentives to the very tiny pool of school pass-outs from these communities (for example, scholarship from first degree to doctorate) with a pro-active approach to identification of beneficiaries with the help of non-governmental organisations working among these communities. Special scheme will be devised to support those HEIs in districts that have Muslim concentration. Particular emphasis will be given to educational opportunities for girls.

21.239. Despite a number of initiatives in the previous Plan periods, there is a staggering difference among different groups. Hence, a targeted approach with focus on SC and ST dominated regions and convergence of various equity schemes in a composite manner to address the educational needs of the disadvantaged sections including the OBCs will be critical to enhancing their inclusion in the mainstream of higher education. Given the co-existence of educational backwardness in both social and locational factors, such as their greater presence in rural, hilly, geographically difficult to reach terrains, a synergy of efforts to address these multiple factors in a holistic manner will be significant.

Other Equity-Related Initiatives

21.240. Concerted efforts to increase the enrolment of students from disadvantaged communities will be supplemented by strengthening the current remedial teaching programmes with teaching/coaching modules, preparatory training and special coaching for entrance examinations to highly sought-after courses and institutions.

21.241. Schemes for establishing model colleges, community colleges and new polytechnics in low GER districts may be modified to cover minority concentrated districts and Fifth Schedule Districts with greater focus on States with low enrolment. Targeted schemes will be launched to draw students from especially vulnerable communities such as the most backward amongst the Muslim and the minority community. Given the negligible presence of such groups in higher education, these schemes will have to combine special incentives to the very tiny pool of school pass-outs from these communities with a pro-active approach to identification of beneficiaries with the help of non-governmental organisations working among these communities.

21.242. All equity-related schemes in higher education across different ministries under the Central Government would be brought under one umbrella, namely, 'Equal Opportunity for Higher Education Initiatives'. These would be coordinated by the Planning Commission to effectively monitor them and also take into account State-level initiatives.

EXCELLENCE AND IMPROVING ACADEMIC QUALITY

Criticality of Quality

21.243. Except at a few top-level institutions, quality is serious concern. The casual link between cognitive skills acquired through education and economic growth is now well-established. A major goal of the Twelfth Plan is, therefore, to improve the overall quality of higher education in the country by improving the quality of the 'average' institution in the system.

21.244. Notwithstanding the growth of technical higher education, over half of students will enrol in general (meaning arts, science and commerce) undergraduate programmes. If properly imparted, general education could be an excellent foundation for successful knowledge-based careers. Therefore, focus should be primarily on improving the quality of general education. Graduates should be able to acquire skills beyond the basics of reading, writing and arithmetic (the '3Rs'). Critical thinking, communication, collaboration and creativity (the '4Cs') are increasingly important now. Special emphasis on verbal and written communication skills, especially, but not limited to, English would go a long way in improving the employability of the large and growing mass of disempowered youth. 'Professional' education that currently focuses on technical skills alone should adopt integrated curriculum with greater flexibility in choice of subjects and innovative pedagogic practices to improve its quality and enable better learning outcomes.

ELEVENTH PLAN EXPERIENCE

21.245. Several initiatives to improve quality were taken up in the Eleventh Plan. These were related to faculty issues, use of technology, academic and governance reforms and accreditation.

Faculty Initiatives

21.246. Measures taken during the Eleventh Plan to address faculty shortages, included (*i*) raising the retirement age of faculty to 65 years with provision for further extension to 70 years; (*ii*) institution of several fellowship and scholarship schemes for MPhil and PhD programmes; (*iii*) a faculty re-charge scheme to enable increased availability of young faculty; (*iv*) an initiative to enlist professionals and experts from outside academic institutions as adjunct faculty or scholars-in-residence; (*v*) a programme for post-doctoral fellowships for Indian scholars to augment faculty resources which will begin operations during the Twelfth Plan.

Technology Initiatives

21.247. The National Mission on Education through Information and Communication Technologies (NME-ICT) was launched during the Eleventh Plan. Under this initiative, 392 universities and 18,374 colleges were provided broadband connectivity. Ongoing initiatives for creation of e-content were strengthened and new initiatives were taken up. Virtual labs were developed for science and engineering and are currently being rolled out. Enterprise resource planning software for administrative and financial management of institutes and learning management system, both using open source software have been developed and are being tested by a number of institutions. A low-cost computing-cum-access device 'Aakash' was developed and is being currently tested for large-scale deployment. Overall, an investment of ₹1,472 crore was made on this mission during the Eleventh Plan.

Quality Initiatives

21.248. The first phase of the three-phase 'Technical Education Quality Improvement Programme (TEQIP)' with World Bank support was conducted from 2002 to 2009. With an investment of ₹1,378 crore, the programme covered 127 engineering institutions. Phase-II of TEQIP (2010–14), which extends into the Twelfth Plan, would cover another 180–190 institutions. Evaluation of the first phase has clearly shown a marked improvement in placement of graduates, more capacity in postgraduate and doctoral programmes and improved research performance.

Governance, Regulatory and Financial Initiatives

21.249. Several measures were taken during the Eleventh Plan to rationalise governance to promote innovative programmes and ensure standards, particularly in the areas of academic structure, interdisciplinary teaching and research, and accreditation. In order to promote interdisciplinary teaching and research both at the UG and PG levels, 417 departments of universities/colleges were provided financial support of up to ₹60 lakh during the Eleventh Plan. A few States adopted the semester system for their institutions and several universities, most notably University of Delhi, have shifted to the semester system. While institutional accreditation through NAAC and programme accreditation through NBA gained momentum during the Eleventh Plan, the coverage is still small. Only about one-third (167 out of 516) eligible universities and about one-fifth (4,529 out of 22,500) eligible colleges have been accredited so far.

TWELFTH PLAN STRATEGY

21.250. Improving academic quality is a major objective of the Twelfth Plan. Higher education needs to prepare graduates not only for immediate employment but also for an economy in which most people will not only change jobs but also change careers several times in their lives. Hence, it requires inculcating the ability in students to think creatively, read critically, construct effective arguments using persuasive evidence, write clearly, remain flexible and look at issues with an open mind. This, in turn, requires the right curriculum, better teaching–learning processes, sharing of best practices nationally and internationally and the ability to impart a well-rounded and socially conscious education.

21.251. The Twelfth Plan strategy, therefore, includes a range of reforms aimed at improving the overall educational experience in HEIs. These include reforms in institutional organisation; reforms of pedagogy and curricula, particularly at the undergraduate level; and a focus on faculty and their work. These reforms would be supported by smarter use of technology, initiatives to promote internationalisation, the fostering of social responsibility in higher education, promotion of sports and wellness, increasing inter-institutional collaboration and coordination, and strengthening the accreditation system.

TWELFTH PLAN INITIATIVES

Reforming Institutional Organisation

21.252. During the Twelfth Plan, a five-pronged strategy will be adopted to reform the affiliating college system. First, large and reputed colleges with necessary capabilities and diverse learning streams will be converted into full-fledged universities. Second, college-cluster universities, under a new name, with each college working as a campus of the university or its constituent unit will be created. Third, some of the large and unwieldy affiliating universities will be bifurcated or trifurcated into manageable units. Fourth, colleges desiring to scale up to leverage existing infrastructure and to offer new programmes would be allowed to consolidate through merger under an autonomous framework. Finally, affiliating universities will be required to revamp their college development councils and give greater autonomy to their colleges in all academic, administrative and financial matters.

Deepening Academic Reforms

21.253. The institutional framework to deepen academic reforms would include introduction of choice-based credit system, CCE, and regular revision of curricula for making them up-to-date and relevant to contemporary and future needs. To help institutions reform their courses, subject-specific model curricula and packaged, re-usable digitised content (such as packaged lectures and open source textbooks) would be created by instructors with the requisite expertise. This can best be done by subject-based networks such as Network of Social Work Education led by the Tata Institute of Social Sciences and the mathematics initiative taken by Delhi University. Such networks across subject areas would be encouraged. An important goal of these reforms would be to create active learning environments in colleges and universities.

Re-Crafting Undergraduate Education

21.254. Reforming undergraduate curriculum through funding and institutional support will be emphasised in the Twelfth Plan. Undergraduate programmes should provide a holistic education and give students opportunities for intellectual exploration, hands-on research, job skilling, experiential learning, creative thinking, leadership, ethics education, community service and more. In place of three-year programs, several institutions have introduced four-year undergraduate programs to achieve these multiple objectives. During the Twelfth Plan, four-year undergraduate programmes would be promoted. UGC currently provides financial support for starting specialised programmes in interdisciplinary and emerging areas, which could be strengthened and could include support for four-year undergraduate programmes.

Focus on Teachers and Teaching

21.255. Due to rapid expansion, number of quality teachers in higher education is grossly inadequate. A doubling of faculty from the current 8 lakh to 16 lakh is envisaged during the Twelfth Plan. The large increase in capacity at the postgraduate and doctoral levels to enable this would require all institutions, whether Central, State or private to work in collaboration.

21.256. There is a common perception that higher education is a poorly paid profession in India. However, a recent survey[14] of academic salaries across 28 countries shows that median academic salaries in India (on a purchasing power parity basis) are amongst the highest in the world. It is important, therefore, to correct the misperceptions about teaching careers in India in order to attract talent.

21.257. A large portion of those teaching in HEIs are currently casual or part-time academic staff and this is likely to continue. To improve their performance, improvements in their hiring practices and working conditions, and engaging them in faculty development programmes, including using online technologies for faculty development are needed. Most of the sixty-six Academic Staff Colleges (ASCs) established for faculty development have unfortunately not delivered. These were recently reviewed by NAAC. Based on the review findings, institutional weaknesses in the ASCs should be removed and a qualitative change in their content and methodology of faculty development must be brought about.

21.258. In addition to the ASCs, 'Teaching and Learning Centres (TLCs)' must be established in the country within existing universities, preferably those that have a strong research culture as well as large undergraduate programmes. During the Twelfth Plan, 50 such centres will be set up. In some cases the Academic Staff Colleges could also serve as a TLC.

21.259. To provide global exposure and thus facilitate adoption of innovations and best practices in teaching and research, an International Faculty Development Programme would be launched. As part of this, Indian universities would be supported to organise 2–4 weeks summer workshops conducted by leading international teachers and researchers for select Indian post docs and faculty. Forty to fifty such workshops would be held annually on a range of topics and disciplines. Collaborations with foreign universities would be encouraged for organising such workshops. In addition, faculty in large numbers would be sent for three to six months to the best universities of the world for training and mentoring. An enabling policy framework would be put in place to attract faculty from abroad, particularly from amongst the overseas Indians teaching in universities abroad. Senior and tenured overseas faculty could be invited as international visiting professors by offering them attractive remuneration.

21.260. A programme to fund doctoral students to study at international institutions needs to be implemented, in return for commitments to join the faculty pool in India on completion of their studies. This could be supplemented by tapping the growing pool of retired experts. They could function as adjunct faculty and also enrol for doctoral degrees, for which current eligibility requirements could be waived.

21.261. Faculty motivation is crucial to improve academic quality. For faculty to be actively engaged in the teaching–learning process, they need control over their task, time, technique, and work environment, which is often not the case. Absence of basic amenities is one of the most de-motivating factors for a large section of faculty. The strategy for motivating faculty would focus on developing healthy work environment with high-quality minimum facilities and a flexible framework of accountability and performance evaluation. Consistent with international best practices, faculty selection, performance evaluation and promotion should be handled at the department level. New faculty may be kept under probation for a period of five years and confirmation could then be done on the basis of rigorous performance evaluation including peer review and student feedback.

21.262. Recognising the central role of teachers in improving academic quality, a 'National Mission on Teachers and Teaching' would be launched in the Twelfth Plan. This would address all the issues of teachers and teaching in a comprehensive manner and strengthen linkages between the school and higher education sectors. This would be organised under two sub-missions aimed at the school and the higher education sectors, respectively.

21.263. The sub-mission on higher education would pool all the ongoing initiatives and new initiatives on faculty development under one umbrella for their implementation and better monitoring. Under the sub-mission on school sector, the focus would be on expanding the capacity for preparation of teacher educators by setting up 30 Schools of Education in the university system. These schools of education would also conduct research and capacity building in curriculum, teaching–learning processes and assessment and evaluation systems. In addition, Schools of Academic Leadership will be established in select institutions.

21.264. The transformative potential of online learning is beginning to unfold now. From a few courses by a couple of elite universities, there are now global efforts to build massive online courseware by many of the world's best universities. Given the acute shortage of faculty and the unlikelihood of our ability to overcome this severe constraint, technology would be leveraged by using these massive online courses so that the Indian students are a part of global learning systems at very low cost. The country's efforts should be to contribute to this global repository, contextualise and perhaps translate these courses in the local languages to reach out to the maximum number of the students in the country.

National Mission on Use of ICT in Higher Education

21.265. During the Twelfth Plan various initiatives of the Eleventh Plan would be carried forward with an objective to make these programmes more effective, efficient and sustainable. These include:

1. Digital Infrastructure Initiatives: (*i*) upgrade connectivity for universities and colleges to 10GBPS and 1 GBPS, respectively; (*ii*) build computer labs in all institutions as required and increase availability of laptops and low-cost access devices for faculty and students; (*ii*) provide smart classrooms; (*iii*) set up classrooms with interactive video-conference facilities linking Meta-universities and affiliating universities; (*iv*) set up 100 server farms for cloud computing.
2. Content Initiatives: (*i*) develop virtual labs, to promote creation of user-generated content; (*ii*) establish a single national-level consortium for propriety content; (*iii*) create open access content repositories including interoperable institutional repositories; (*iv*) create platforms to facilitate user-generated content and related networks; (*iv*) create a single portal for access to all content; (*v*) continue current initiatives of DTH channels to telecast digital educational videos.
3. Governance Initiatives: (*i*) rollout institutional Enterprise Resource Planning (ERP); (*ii*) computerise examination wings of all universities; (*ii*) provide robust online linkage of all affiliating universities with their affiliated colleges; (*iii*) create online data collection system; (*iv*) library automation; (*v*) automation of grants management.
4. Training and Capacity-Building Initiatives: (*i*) train faculty in instructional design content creation; (*ii*) implement massive capacity-building efforts for adopting technology-mediated pedagogy in classrooms.

Technical Education Quality Improvement Programme

21.266. During the Twelfth Plan, the second phase of TEQIP would be continued and phase-3 of TEQIP would be launched. Under phase-3, focus would be on the 'eco-system' by supporting State Technical Universities introducing curriculum diversity and scaling up sector-wide programmes. This would ensure that the benefit of quality improvement interventions flow to all segments of technical education. The programme would also leverage synergy with other initiatives like the mission for teachers and teaching and mission for use of technology. Architecture and town planning would be included in phase-3 of TEQIP. Separate and independent initiatives should be taken up for improving quality in other fields like management education, pharmacy education, and hotel management.

Language and Book Promotion Programmes

21.267. Promotion and development of Indian languages, including classical languages, English, and foreign languages will receive focused attention during the Twelfth Plan. Particular thrust would be on preservation, promotion and development of endangered languages which have less than 10,000 speakers. The National Translation Mission will be strengthened. There will be a focus on developing specialised courses in translation technology and related areas and capacity building of translators through short-term training programmes and language teaching programmes. Recognising the growing use of technology in knowledge delivery, promotion of e-books and digitisation of National Book Trust (NBT) books and records will be taken up during the Twelfth Plan. Capacity of NBT would be strengthened to discharge its new responsibilities.

Strengthening Intellectual Property Rights

21.268. During the Twelfth Plan, existing programmes under the Scheme of Intellectual Property Education Research and Public Outreach (IPERPO) will be continued. New Plan initiatives include: the setting up of new IPR Chairs, modernising the Copyright Office, and establishing a Centre for IPR studies. The rise of new electronic methods of publishing and distribution has resulted in an expansion of the scope of copyright issues internationally. The Copyright Board would be strengthened with experts in new and emerging areas of Copyright law as per the new Copyright (Amendment) Act, 2010 that came into force in June 2012. Copyright offices would also be modernised on the lines of other IPR offices like the Trademark office and the Patent office.

Higher Education Internationalisation

21.269. A strategy for higher education internationalisation to be developed during the Twelfth Plan would include faculty and student exchange programmes, institutional collaborations for teaching and research, exposure to diverse teaching–learning models and enhanced use of ICTs. Globally compatible academic credit systems, curricula internationalisation and processes for mutual recognition of qualifications would be put in place. A professional national agency and on 'India International Education Centre' at New Delhi would be created to undertake internationalisation activities. It will support selected institutions to establish dedicated internationalisation units.

Fostering Social Responsibility in Higher Education

21.270. In the face of growing isolation of HEIs from society, there is a need for renewed effort for HEIs for genuinely engaging with community, conduct socially relevant research and education and foster social responsibility amongst students as part of their core mission. For this purpose, a National Initiative to Foster Social Responsibility in Higher Education would be launched. An Alliance for Community Engagement, an independent association of practitioners, academics and community leaders would be created to support its implementation.

Promoting Sports and Wellness

21.271. A National Initiative on Sports and Wellness would be launched in the Twelfth Plan. Activities under this initiative would include: (*i*) fitness and wellness programmes for all students; (*ii*) encouraging institutions to include physical education as a general institutional requirement; (*iii*) raising participation in competitive sports from the current 2 per cent of students to 10 per cent of students; (*iv*) creating and supporting departments and units for physical education in all institutions; (*v*) supporting creation of adequate sports infrastructure in institutions; (*vi*) encouraging development of a sports club system; (*vii*) establishing inter-disciplinary research centres on sports technology, sports medicine and sports management; (*viii*) creating an information network on sports.

Increase Inter-Institutional Collaboration and Coordination

21.272. In the Twelfth Plan, inter-institutional collaboration and coordination would be encouraged to reap the benefit from synergies in capabilities and capacities and to create shared visions and agendas for excellence in teaching and research.

21.273. With a view to expanding student choice and increasing the design of innovative interdisciplinary programmes, a Meta-university framework as a network of universities would be promoted in the Twelfth Plan. This would enable several universities to come together and offer courses across disciplines, treat faculty and students from all institutions alike, and provide all network members access to content, teaching, and the research support they need. Massively open online courses (MOOCs) would also be encouraged under this framework.

Strengthening Accreditation System

21.274. Accreditation will play a central role in the regulatory arrangements for higher education under the Twelfth Plan. Accreditation will be mandatory with clear incentives and consequences. In order to handle large-volume accreditation, multiple accreditation bodies (in addition to NAAC for institutional accreditation and NBA for programme accreditation) would be established. In order to facilitate student mobility and academic articulation, it is important to develop easily comparable, comprehensible and consistent qualifications throughout the system. A new accreditation law that provides for accreditation by independent non-profit agencies registered with a national accreditation authority is currently under consideration. While, the proper institutional structure would only emerge once the new law is enacted, capacities of existing agencies, NAAC and NBA should be enhanced in the interim. Indian institutions would also be encouraged to obtain programmatic accreditation from a select group of credible international accrediting bodies.

RESEARCH AND INNOVATION

21.275. Research and innovation are now vital functions of higher education worldwide. The value of interdisciplinary research is recognised globally, as innovation is now happening at the intersections of disciplines. Collaboration is now central to innovation. Entrepreneurship that leverages innovation is also an increasingly integral part of higher education systems. While all HEIs cannot be expected to become research-based institutions, it is vital that the country promote a research culture across all institutions while ensuring special support for those able to engage in state-of-the-art research.

21.276. The HEIs should contribute to the national innovation agenda, even when they are not research intensive—albeit in different ways. Teaching-focused institutions must train their students in the techniques of research so that the doors to research-based graduate education and employment are opened to them. Vocational institutions must enable the future workforce to engage at least in the 'development' component of R&D. It is essential that all institutions equip their graduates with core skills of critical thinking, communication, collaboration and creativity to enable the country to continuously innovate to adapt to new environments.

21.277. India's research performance turned around in the last two decades, after over a decade of stagnation. An improvement in scientific output is evident both in absolute terms and relative to the comparison group. During the past 10 years, India's overall share of publications in the world has risen from 2.8 per cent to 3.4 per cent, with a significant improvement in researcher productivity since 1999. India produces over twice as many scientific publications a year than it did a decade ago. Though dwarfed by China's achievements, India's output of publications has grown faster than that of Brazil and Russia.

21.278. There are indications that research quality has improved as well. India's publications have accumulated 16,10,511 citations with 5.77 citations per paper, better than China, but still low compared to the world average of 10.81 citations per paper. The relative impact rose from 0.48 to 0.66 (world average being one). In 2009, India stood eleventh in terms of the number of papers published, seventeenth in terms of the number of citations, and thirty-fourth in terms of number of citations per paper as per the ISI Web of Science.

21.279. Notwithstanding such achievements, Indian higher education continues to have limited research capacity. Low levels of funding and segregation of the country's R&D institutions from universities and colleges have been responsible for the weak research capacity of Indian universities. It is disappointing to note that even the country's top universities remain largely teaching-focused with limited research and doctoral education.

21.280. This lack of research orientation, even in the best of the Indian institutions, is reflected in their standing in global rankings, most of which rely heavily on measurable indices of research performance. No Indian university figured amongst the top 200 universities in the Times Higher Education (THE) Rankings or the Academic Ranking of World Universities (ARWU) for the year 2011. While it is neither necessary nor realistic to expect all institutions to achieve high levels of research excellence, a natural pyramid of quality excellence suggests that, if the average quality improves, then the best will enter the top leagues of research-intensive universities.

21.281. India's output in PhDs was small at 10,781 in 2008–09, when compared against international peers. The total number of PhDs in science and engineering at 4,500 is miniscule as compared to the approximately 30,000 and 25,000 for China and the USA, respectively. In terms of innovation and the creation of intellectual property, Indians file and receive only a small number of worldwide patent applications (merely 11,937 applications filed by Indians compared to 2,41,546 by Chinese in 2009) and no Indian academic institution figures in the list of top applicants for patent filing.

21.282. Output measures related to publications, patents/licensing and spinoffs can provide some indications of research and innovation performance for research intensive institutions though even for them, these would be too narrow for gauging overall research performance. For less research intensive institutions, their contributions to innovation and economic development could derive from much less visible activities such as faculty consulting or development projects or education to instil students with creativity and entrepreneurship.

ELEVENTH PLAN EXPERIENCE

21.283. During the Eleventh Plan, several schemes for promoting excellence in academic research were implemented. A major scheme was to promote Basic Scientific Research (BSR). This included grants to departments and colleges for improving basic infrastructure; fellowships both for doctoral and post-doctoral work, networking centres, summer and winter schools, faculty recharge scheme, and promotion of research at the undergraduate level.

21.284. In addition, several new Central institutions with research focus were established in the Eleventh Plan. However, these initiatives tended to spread resources thinly and raised concerns about 'relevance' to needs and to innovation and entrepreneurship in particular. While national research institutions play key roles in meeting national needs in some key areas, much more could be done.

TWELFTH PLAN STRATEGY

21.285. In the Twelfth Plan, research efforts need to be more directly linked to the national development agenda and better connected to the needs of industry and society. Public R&D institutions should be permanently and closely coupled—including in governance structures—to local institutions of higher education. HEIs must, in turn, be the doors to collaborating with industry. There is also a need to look beyond an institutional focus for research productivity to a faculty focus, so as to enable creative faculty to build teams that cross the boundaries of institutions.

21.286. The Twelfth Plan would focus on the development of faculty, institutions, departments and centres of excellence in research and research training. Overall, investments in research will need to increase gradually from the current low level of less than 1 per cent of GDP to over 2 per cent nationally, with HEIs receiving a much higher share of research investments than before.

21.287. Emphasis will be laid on creating a better research infrastructure and work environment to attract the top talent from within the country and also bring back India's brightest graduates who left the country to study abroad. Upper-tier institutions should be allowed to hire globally, including foreigners on permanent appointments, and provide compensatory benefits to those who relocate.

21.288. The governance and structure of doctoral education must be reviewed, as current programmes often sacrifice quality in the interests of rapid completion of the doctorate. Benchmarking doctoral programmes with global requirements on capacity to be developed is the key. Existing PhD programmes would be modernised, and new ones created, particularly in new institutions and those that require inter-disciplinary efforts.

21.289. There is a need for an overall increase in the level of research spending, more of which should be spent through HEIs which would provide multiple benefits. Concentrating significant resources in high-potential institutions and faculty through competition is necessary to create exemplars of global excellence. In funding research, social sciences require a greater boost given past neglect. The country must also put in place better mechanisms for university research capacity to lead to innovation, as has become the norm globally. This will require building university research capacity in areas of high potential, encouraging closer linkages between academia and industry, building institutional capacity to support academics to engage in innovation and commercialisation, and creating a dynamic ecosystem which can provide an enabling environment for innovation and entrepreneurship. There is a need for Indian institutions to build a range of institutional support mechanisms such as technology incubators, proof-of-concept centres, entrepreneurship programmes and technology transfer mechanisms within HEIs. Institutions should also be encouraged to build collaborative ties with private actors in the area of innovation and entrepreneurship including technology companies, venture capitalists, as well as national and international foundations.

21.290. During the Twelfth Plan, the country must develop objective and transparent research evaluation practices that are relevant to the national context and culture. To provide analytical underpinning for research evaluation at national and institutional levels, a Centre for Research Evaluation within a research-intensive university could be established.

TWELFTH PLAN INITIATIVES

21.291. In the Twelfth Plan, universities at the top of the quality hierarchy would be identified and generously supported so they can reach the global top league. Equally important, promising faculty in all tiers of institutions will be identified through peer review and supported. Similarly centres of excellence within existing universities would be created. High-calibre faculty would be attracted from around the world on non-permanent teaching assignments and, similarly, Indian faculty would be provided exposure to teaching and research practices in the best universities from across the world. All related initiatives would be pooled to benefit from synergy under an 'India Excellence Initiative' during the Twelfth Plan. This would include:

Multi-Disciplinary Research Universities

21.292. During the Twelfth Plan, research universities with the capacity to engage in research and teaching in multiple disciplines will be promoted. A legislative framework to set up such universities termed 'Universities for Research and Innovation' is currently under consideration, with a target of 20 institutions by the end of the Twelfth Plan. These could be public or private universities or they could be set up as Public–Private Partnerships and may include both the conversion of existing institutions and new universities. Some may be mentored by existing world-class universities. At the core of achieving excellence is the ability of institutions to attract and retain high-quality faculty from across the world.

Centres of Excellence (CoE)

21.293. The Twelfth Plan will aim to create 20 Centres of Excellence as world-class research centres within existing universities and institutions of national repute. In addition, fifty (50) centres for training and research in the frontier areas of science and technology, social science and humanities would be established. The goal is to build the competencies of the host institutions in selected disciplines of national importance. Collaborations with promising faculty across the nation will be encouraged.

NATIONAL INITIATIVES

21.294. A National Initiative for Excellence in Basic Sciences would cover the ongoing activities for promotion of basic scientific research that are being implemented by the UGC. A new National Initiative for Excellence in Social Sciences and Humanities would be launched to encourage bright students to choose programmes in the humanities and social sciences and improve the quality of teaching and research in these disciplines. An empowered committee may be constituted for revamping existing institutional funding and launching new schemes such as scholarships on the lines of INSPIRE scholarships for basic sciences, up-scaling doctoral and post-doctoral fellowships, flexible one-time support to existing centres of global excellence and creation of new Inter-University Centres.

21.295. A National Initiative for Innovation and Entrepreneurship will be launched. This initiative would (*i*) enable an environment that fosters innovation, value creation and technology transfer; (*ii*) aim at creating awareness and developing a culture for protection and management of IPRs in HEIs; (*iii*) help maximise benefits and returns from investments in research by developing partnerships amongst universities/institutes, R&D organisations and industry; (*v*) creation of national research parks. This initiative would pool all related activities under the MHRD, UGC and AICTE and build synergy with similar activities, schemes and programmes under the Ministry of Science and Technology.

21.296. Design-centred innovation is a force multiplier that can help the country move up the value chain, making Indian industry globally competitive. In this context, a National Initiative for Design Innovation would be launched in the Twelfth Plan. Under this initiative, 20 new Design Innovation Centres (DIC), one Open Design School (ODS) and a National Design Innovation Network (NDIN), linking together all these schools, would be set up. ODS would ensure maximum reach of design education and practice in the country through various collaborative education programmes (linking a broad spectrum of educational institutions), and free sharing of its courseware through the Internet. NDIN would be a network of design schools that work closely with other leading institutions of industry and academia, NGOs and government to further the reach and access of design education, to promote design innovation in all sectors, and to develop wide-ranging collaborative projects between institutions. ODS and NDIN would also raise the standards of design education and innovation in the country through various initiatives including the creation of fabrication labs and digital media zones across educational institutions on a large scale.

Promoting Collaborative Research

21.297. Driven by the success of the research-based Inter University Centres (IUCs) and their positive impact on the university system, several new research-based IUCs in different areas would be established in the Twelfth Plan. These areas would be broad, contemporary, inter-disciplinary and of strategic importance to the country, and would involve both basic and applied research. All research-based IUCs could be brought under an umbrella Governing Council, while each of them would have its own governing board.

21.298. In order to foster inter-disciplinary research, enhance research training and increase innovation capacity, about 10 Inter-Institutional Centres (IICs) would be established in the Twelfth Plan. These Centres could either emerge as broad partnership between multiple research-oriented institutions or programme-specific partnership between funding agencies and research institutions.

21.299. Excellence Clusters and Networks will be established by creating linkages between national laboratories/national research centres and the universities. During the Twelfth Plan, several of these cluster and networks would be supported through research funds earmarked for research teams involving two or more institutions.

21.300. Similarly, local alliances would be created in different cities and interaction across institutions in such hubs would be enhanced through a structured, highly interactive and collaborative framework. The institutions would be incentivised to collaborate and allow their courses to be available for students of other institutions.

21.301. Even though the collaboration between the academia and the industry is now growing, but this continues to be low-key and has significant room for improvement. A systematic approach to strengthen the scale and scope of these partnerships would be adopted during the Twelfth Plan. For this, a nodal agency—potentially called the Council for Industry and Higher Education Collaboration (CIHEC)—would be established to promote and facilitate industry-higher education collaboration. CIHEC will be an independent not-for-profit organisation founded by contributions from industry and government and will comprise business and higher education leaders. The goals of the CIHEC span the entire higher education and research landscape including framework development, capacity creation, research, training, and certification. The corporate sector could participate in existing institutions of higher education by setting up institutes offering degree/non-degree programmes in specific fields, creating centres of excellence for research and postgraduate teaching, establish teaching–learning centres to train faculty. In addition, the Indian Corporate Higher Education Scholarship Fund with contribution from the corporate sector and the Indian Corporate R&D Fund jointly funded by the government and the corporate sector could also be established.

21.302. Finally, international research collaborations now hold the key to competitiveness in the global knowledge economy. Only a few top Indian institutions are currently engaged in international research collaborations. In the Twelfth Plan, special efforts would be made to strengthen international research linkages and involve a larger number of Indian institutions in forging such links. Such collaborations would leverage the 22 million–strong Indian Diaspora which is recognised worldwide as a powerful asset for research, innovation and entrepreneurship.

GOVERNANCE

21.303. The government needs to play a sensitive and less intrusive role in the governance and regulation of higher education than it does at present. In place of a uniform regulatory role in respect of all institutions, the government's role could be calibrated according to the type of institution involved. While, the government could have a promotional and evaluative role for upper-tier institutions, it may play a steering role in mid-tier institutions, and should actively regulate the lower-tier institutions. The governance structure should also enable institutions to increasingly differentiate themselves through course diversity, multi-disciplinary programmes and other approaches. Enabling differentiation requires a new regulatory structure that encompasses all fields of education rather than the current structure that separates the regulation of technical fields from other fields. In this context, a paradigm shift in governance is needed. It should shift from inspection-based processes to autonomy and accountability through independent third-party validation, regulation by mandatory self-disclosures, and objective evaluation schemes. The overall approach is to allow institutions to make their own policies and decisions within a broadly defined memorandum of understanding on performance.

National-Level Governance

21.304. Based on the recommendations of the National Knowledge Commission (2005) and the Committee on Renovation and Rejuvenation of Higher Education (2009), steps were initiated during the Eleventh Plan to create a new legislative framework and provide a new governance structure for higher education in the country. For this purpose, several new laws are currently under consideration. These include (*i*) The Prohibition of Unfair Practices in Technical Educational Institutions, Medical Educational Institutions and Universities Bill aimed at checking unfair practices relating to capitation fees and misleading advertising through mandatory disclosures by academic institutions; (*ii*) The National Accreditation Regulatory Authority for Higher Educational Institutions Bill that seeks to make accreditation by independent accreditation agencies mandatory for all higher educational institutions; (*iii*) The Education Tribunals Bill to create a Central tribunal and State-level tribunals for expeditious resolution of disputes relating to institutions, faculty, students and regulatory authorities; (*iv*) Foreign Educational Institutions (Regulation of Entry and Operations) Bill to enable quality foreign education institutions to enter and operate in India and regulate operations of foreign education providers; (*v*) National Commission for Higher Education and Research (NCHER) Bill to create an umbrella regulatory authority subsuming the UGC, and current regulators, AICTE, NCTE and DEC; and (*vi*) The National Academic Depository Bill, 2011, to create a repository of all academic credentials in the country.

21.305. These new laws together reflect the Government's focus on quality, accountability, access, and inclusion and on preparing the country's higher education system for a more competitive globalising world. These reforms would enable and facilitate innovative and high-quality institutions to grow, while making it difficult for poor-quality institutions to operate. In the next few years, a new governance structure at the national-level consisting primarily of the NCHER, National- and State-level Tribunals and the National Authority for Accreditation would be in place.

21.306. In the meantime, the UGC and other regulatory agencies have an opportunity to revitalise themselves to ensure a smooth transition to the NCHER. In this context, a review of internal processes and staff capabilities is essential and agencies should draw up year-wise transformative action plans. In addition, the UGC could immediately implement a number of innovative financing schemes that could impact the state of higher education significantly. For example, (*i*) the UGC could shift from its current scheme-based approach to more effective programmatic interventions including norm-based financing of institutions; (*ii*) it could consider a move from historically determined detailed operational budgets to formula-based funding for general operations; (*iii*) it could start strategic funding of innovative programmes to promote certain activities/changes/investments based on institutional proposals evaluated selectively and competitively; (iv) finally, the UGC or some other Central agency could further play a leading role in longitudinal profiling of students as they transition through the higher educational cycle into the workplace and could also play a role in institutional benchmarking on a longitudinal basis.

State-Level Governance

21.307. The structure of governance of higher education and their legislative framework varies widely across the States. All States will be encouraged to undertake a review of their current legislative and governance arrangements with a view to preparing themselves for the unique challenges they face in higher education.

21.308. It would be desirable for each State (except small States) to set up a State Council for Higher Education to lead the planned and coordinated development of higher education in the State and to foster sharing of resources between universities, benefit from synergy across institutions, lead academic and governance reforms at the institution level, maintain databanks on higher education and conduct research and evaluation studies. In small States, the main affiliating university can perform this role. Private universities and colleges form a bulk of higher education in several States. States could also establish independent agencies to regulate private HEIs.

Institutional Level Governance

21.309. Academic institutions primarily rely on individual initiative and creativity to develop their unique institutional culture and tradition over a long period of time. Principles of academic freedom, shared governance, meritocratic selection, promotion of diversity and institutional accountability are defining features of a well-governed academic institution. Moreover, the oversight, governance and management of HEIs should be closely tied to their mission. For this the current practice of treating all institutions alike will need to be abandoned. There is a need to move away from enforcing standardisation of education and processes to allow for diversity in institutional types, missions, resources and privileges. This would require a categorisation of institutions of higher education, with each category of institutions being treated differently for purposes of academic regulation, governance and funding.

21.310. Empirical evidence suggests that better-run institutions are highly autonomous, especially when autonomy over academic matters vests with faculty. Autonomy in the areas of finance, organisational structure, operations and staffing is also important, but should be consistent with internal systems of evaluation and accountability and tied to the mission of the institution. Recently the Central Government has taken several measures to loosen its grip over institutions funded by it, as in the case of the Indian Institutes of Management, where the government no longer has any role in the selection of Board members. The Board plays the key role in the selection of the Director, though the final decision is still made by the government. The government has also explicitly promoted autonomy in State-funded institutions through programmes like the Technical Education Quality Improvement Programme. This process of freeing public institutions from government controls would be continued in the Twelfth Plan. This would be based on a framework for autonomy on all its five dimensions.

21.311. Institutional autonomy and external discipline arising from competitive grants and competition for students and faculty go hand in hand. For effective institutional governance, there is a need to shift towards smaller and more effective governing bodies that have several external experts that the universities select themselves, faculty representation and alumni that value the reputation of the institution. Given the potential positive contribution that the alumni can make in the growth of institutions, well-established institutions, with over 10 years in existence should have a fair representation of the alumni in their governing bodies. Overall, competition amongst institutions with nimble and professional governing boards responsive to external change would be encouraged in the Twelfth Plan.

Developing Academic Leadership

21.312. During the Twelfth Plan, an ecosystem for scholarship and development of professional academic leadership in higher education would be created. For this, an 'Institute for Academic Leadership in Higher Education' could be co-located within NUEPA or any other institution of higher education. This institute would function as a hub with university-based 'Academy for Leadership Development' as nodes. At least five such academies would be set up in the Twelfth Plan.

Student Services and Admissions

21.313. Student affairs and services receive scant attention and are plagued by lack of professionalism in Indian higher education. The Twelfth Plan focuses on supporting universities and colleges to address the basic personal needs of students by providing them a comprehensive set of out-of-classroom student services.

21.314. Since HEIs fall under multiple agencies, reliable and current information about institutions is not available in any one place and information provided by regulatory agencies is not in a student-friendly format. As a result, students and their parents often rely upon brokers/agents, and promotion materials in the selection of institutions. Such information is often unreliable. The Prohibition of Unfair Practices in Technical Educational Institutions, Medical Educational Institutions and Universities Bill has provisions that can take care of such admission-related unfair practices and maladies. The Bill is under consideration. However, until the law comes into force, a centralised portal may be created to provide accurate and current information about institutions and courses to students and parents in a way that helps them in the process of decision-making with respect to institutions and courses for admissions.

21.315. There is also a very obvious need to reform the overall admissions process in the country. The multiplicity of admissions tests has resulted in large-scale coaching, often at the cost of regular education. The country should move towards fewer admissions tests, each of which should be conducted in a transparent and objective manner. Universities should be provided the autonomy to set their own admissions criteria and utilise the results of the nationwide tests for their admissions process as appropriate to their academic mission and admissions philosophy. This would align students with the right institution, significantly reduce hardships on students and reduce admission-related unfair practices.

FINANCING STRATEGY

Review of Funding Trends

21.316. India faces a huge challenge to fund its rapidly growing higher education sector. Overall, the country spent about 1.22 per cent of its GDP on higher education in 2011–12. Household spending and investments by the private sector have grown more rapidly than government spending on higher education in recent years. Government spending, and particularly State Government spending, has fallen far short of the funding requirement in the face of a dramatic expansion of the system and the rising expectations of the people in terms of quality, equity and access. The Central and the State Governments jointly fund higher education. The Central Government's share is about 30 per cent, while the State Governments spend the balance 70 per cent mostly under the non-Plan head. Table 21.13 shows the funding responsibilities of Central and State Governments for the country's universities and colleges.

TABLE 21.13
Funding Responsibility for Universities and Colleges

Funding Responsibility	Universities	Colleges
Central govt. (both Plan and Non-Plan)	152	69
Central govt. (Plan only for State institutions via UGC)	144	6,285
State govt. (both Plan and Non-Plan)	316	13,024
No funding from Central or State Govt(s)	191	19,930

Source: Planning Commission.

21.317. Overall, Central funding of State institutions is meagre. Together the State systems enrolled 15 times more students than Central institutions, but received only one-third of the Plan grants during the Eleventh Plan. Half of the Central Plan funds (₹20,630 crore) went to Central institutions, with State universities, colleges and polytechnics receiving just about ₹10,446 crore. In addition, Central institutions received about ₹25,000 crore as non-Plan grants during the Eleventh Plan period, while the State institutions do not receive any non-Plan grants. Consequently, State universities and colleges face serious financial difficulties that often result in poor quality.

21.318. The government spending on higher education has grown steadily over the years. Central Plan spending grew most rapidly from ₹1,600 crore in 2005–06 to ₹13,100 crore (over eight times), while State Plan funding increased much less. On the non-Plan side, while Central spending increased two and a half times, State non-Plan funding just about doubled during the same period. Thus, State Government spending has been growing slower than Central spending and the rise in funding levels do not match the rapid expansion of the State higher education systems.

21.319. The share of education in total Plan outlay increased from mere 6.7 per cent in the Tenth Plan to 19.4 per cent for the Eleventh Plan, of which 30 per cent was earmarked for higher education. This was a nine-fold increase over the Tenth Plan—₹84,943 crore against ₹9,600 crore during the Tenth Plan. Actual expenditure during the Eleventh Plan has been ₹39,647 crore (45.6 per cent of the Plan outlay). This was mainly due to the fact that funds were not allocated as per the approved outlays. It may be worthwhile to note that there is a committed investment of over ₹53,200 crore for activities initiated in the Eleventh Plan. A large part of this would in new Central institutions established during the Eleventh Plan, where investment so far has been very small.

Twelfth Plan Strategy

21.320. Higher education requires significantly larger investments to deliver on the multiple objectives and to achieve the various goals set out in the Twelfth Plan. This investment has to come from both public and private sources and from both Central and State exchequers. The role of Central Plan funds for higher education is critical not only to revamp Central institutions so that they can play national leadership roles in delivering three Es, but also to leverage desired change in the entire system of higher education. This will include serious investments in building key institutions such as accreditation and funding bodies and mechanisms, so that they can take on the strategic central roles effectively. A continued and significant increase in Central Plan funds including investments to promote better implementation capacity is essential.

21.321. The Twelfth Plan advocates a paradigm shift in funding from demand-based grants and input-based budgeting to normative and entitlement-based grants and outcome-based budgeting. For example, block grants should replace line-item budgets and Plan allocations should be based on long-term strategic plans developed by the institutions. Consequently, annual funding should be linked to the performance of institutions against the milestones and targets laid down in their strategic plans. In turn, institutions need to provide complete transparency about their financial performance and use of funds by putting their financial statements online. All institutions should implement the recently finalised accounting standards developed by ICAI that lay down a common format for the reporting of financial statements.

Public Funding

21.322. Funding from both the Central and the State Governments has to be significantly increased and efficiency of its utilisation improved during the Twelfth Plan. The Plan should target public spending on higher education to reach 1.5 per cent of the GDP from the current 1.22 per cent. For this, the Central Government has to use its Plan funds strategically to encourage greater State funding and promote efficiency in expenditure.

21.323. During the Twelfth Plan, the States would be encouraged to draw up strategic plans for higher education. Such plans should be comprehensive and take a holistic view of increased demand pressure with improvements in the school system and greater need for more qualified people from the economy and the labour market. An institutional mechanism for joint funding of State plans by the Central and the State Governments would be evolved and there would be a joint review mechanism to ensure proper use of funds. Central funding would be linked to governance and academic reforms in the State system that would focus on building overall system capacity.

Institutional Fee Structure

21.324. While, about 60 per cent students are enrolled in private unaided institutions and pay full fees, the remaining 40 per cent are enrolled in public-funded institutions and usually pay very low fees. Central universities, particularly that are Delhi-based, have not raised the fees for decades, while several State universities have raised the fees to reasonable levels. Maintaining low levels of fees is not sustainable; in fact, it is regressive since it often tends to benefit the better-off students. With growing prosperity, rising household incomes and strong family values, more and more households are now willing to pay higher fees. Hence, the process of raising fees, which started with the elite Central institutions like the IIMs and IITs raising their fees in recent years, should be continued and brought to reasonable levels. This should eventually cover all Central institutions. Similarly, State Governments should also be encouraged to raise fees to reasonable and sustainable levels in State universities and colleges. Some flexibility should also be provided to private institutions in matters related to fee fixation, which should be accompanied with transparency and provision of credible information about quality and fee levels to potential students.

Revenue from Other Sources

21.325. Institutions should be encouraged to mobilise resources through alternative sources so that student fees do not form the only source of revenue. They should be encouraged to seek funding from diverse stakeholders through external contracts/grants for research, consulting and/or training projects. The profile of external funding would be different across institutional types, with some having revenues from patent licensing, with others having greater incomes from short courses or consulting or even training. There is also a need to develop conducive framework to encourage endowment and promote culture of philanthropy in education sector in the country. Worldwide, individual and corporate donations have been a significant source of revenue for educational institutions, a practice that should be encouraged and incentivised by the government. The focus can be on setting up empowered committees to devise and execute strategies to tap funds from individuals and corporates. Such funds can be targeted to be deployed for the purpose of specific projects like creating and running research centres for specialised subjects.

Twelfth Plan Outlay

21.326. During the Twelfth Plan, the focus will be on expansion by scaling up capacity of existing institutions, better targeting of equity initiatives and greater focus on improving quality and fostering excellence. Central institutions, in particular the new ones established in the Eleventh Plan, would require huge investments over the next few years for developing basic infrastructure and facilities to gain critical mass and make a meaningful impact. State universities and colleges that constitute the bulk of HEIs are poorly funded and suffer from acute quality deficit. A quantum jump in Central funding for State universities and colleges is envisaged. This funding would be strategically used to foster academic and administrative reforms, address challenges and fill in the gaps in the overall State plans for higher education. In addition, a separate outlay has been kept for creation of a large-scale ecosystem for skill-based higher education. A large outlay is needed for the revamped students' financial aid programme to significantly increase the reach of scholarships and education loans through government-backed guarantees as well as for various equity-related initiatives.

21.327. In addition, there are other ongoing schemes and initiatives of the Ministry of HRD, UGC and AICTE which require large outlays. These would also include the provision of flexi funds. Much of the focus is on consolidation and improving quality and focused interventions to address challenges of access, equity and excellence. Overall, an outlay ₹1,10,700 crore for higher education is proposed for the Twelfth Plan. This is merely 30 per cent more than the outlay in the Eleventh Plan, even though it is more than two and a half times the actual expenditure in the Eleventh Plan. Such a significant increase is justified because of the increasing demand for quality higher education driven by improved schooling coupled with the shortfall in spending during the Eleventh Plan. A detailed matrix for the outlay is provided in the appendix.

21.328. About two-thirds of the increase in the Twelfth Plan outlays over the actual expenditure in the Eleventh Plan is accounted for by the following four major areas: (*i*) State universities and colleges (including polytechnics); (*ii*) equity initiatives (including student financial support); (*iii*) Central universities and institutions; and (*iv*) research and innovation initiatives.

IMPLEMENTATION, MONITORING AND EVALUATION

Implementation Framework

21.329. Specific interventions taken up during the Twelfth Plan would be aligned to the broad strategy spelt out in the Plan document. To overcome procedural bottlenecks, a system of empowered committees would be deployed wherever necessary. New structures and institutional mechanisms would also be created for coordination across ministries and agencies.

21.330. The implementation framework for the Twelfth Plan aims to:

1. Interlink expansion, equity and excellence, and focus on those programmes that serve as the locus at which more than one objective is met.
2. Bring down the walls that separate higher education from technical education with a focus on interdisciplinary action points.
3. Recognise State education systems as the principal site for expansion and focus on improving the average quality of State institutions.
4. Recognise that diverse disadvantaged groups suffer from different kinds of disadvantages and need specifically targeted interventions.
5. Revamp student financial aid programmes as the main channel for individual-focused equity schemes.
6. Recognise that fostering excellence is a multi-dimensional challenge requiring simultaneous action on many fronts.
7. Provide greater flexibility to the implementing agencies by grouping schemes under umbrella national initiatives.

Monitoring and Evaluation

21.331. Based on the implementation framework, it would be necessary to develop strategic indicators against various goals that clearly identify what would be measured. Monitoring of achievement of Twelfth Plan targets, annual and cumulative, may be done on the baseline data at the beginning of the Twelfth Plan. Monitoring would not be confined to the flow of funds and their utilisation, but will also include evaluation of programmes and initiatives for outcomes and impact. Services of independent evaluation agencies and researchers could be used for the purpose. Data on institutional performance on various parameters would be collected, compiled and shared. It is important that the practice to assess learning outcomes, to conduct student experience surveys, and to undertake longitudinal studies of students as they transition through the educational cycle into the workplace should be initiated. In order to globally benchmark Indian higher education, India should proactively participate in various international surveys and evaluations.

Higher Education Database Management System

21.332. The country lacks current and comprehensive data for evidence-based policymaking and effective planning. It would be critical to publish a comprehensive data book on the landscape of higher education with complete facts, figures and trends. This could include data across time and geography and should contain both State-level break-up and also inter-temporal trends. Data collection on higher education should be aligned to the International Standards Classification of Educational Data finalised by UNESCO recently. A classification framework of HEIs will also be necessary for getting a better sense of the institutional landscape in the country.

21.333. The Central Government is conducting an All India Survey on Higher Education. This should provide useful insights and can be the first step towards creating a comprehensive higher education data management system. The onus of providing timely and reliable data on student enrolments and other strategic indicators/key metrics for a centralised web-based higher education data management system should rest with the educational institutions, whether public or private. The web-based higher education data management system should be used for tracking the progress of HEIs and for carrying out a variety of analysis leading to improved performance of HEIs. Also, the higher education data management system can be used for conducting surveys and generating additional data from educational institutions that could be used as inputs for higher education planning at the Central, State and institutional levels. Higher education database management system can also provide the desired data to various stakeholders such as national academic depository, planning bodies, research entities, students and other academic bodies.

Higher Education Policy Research

21.334. India does not have any major higher education research centre or a group of researchers focusing on this key subject. Higher education as an academic subject is not taught at Indian universities. As a result, there is a dearth of dependable, reliable, fact-based, unbiased, ideology-neutral policy information about Indian higher education. It is important for the country to create an ecosystem for higher quality policy research on higher education. In the Twelfth Plan, a network of centres for higher education research located at institutions that have the expertise for such research activity will be created.

21.335. In conclusion, it is imperative that during the Twelfth Plan period the country undertakes an overhaul of higher education and creates a robust, quality-driven system that is accessible to all segments of society. This is essential not only to ensure the continued economic growth of the country, but it is also necessary for social cohesion and to meet the rising aspirations of the country's young people. Building such a system of higher education requires clear articulation of the shortcomings and problems of the current system, a shared understanding of the solutions, and an alignment of the efforts of various stakeholders in higher education to implement these solutions. This chapter has outlined the widespread systemic changes needed to effect such a paradigm shift in the cultural, policy, strategic and operational environment of higher education in the country.

FINANCIAL RESOURCES

21.336. The indicative Twelfth Five Year Plan Gross Budgetary Support for Ministry of Human Resource development is ₹4,53,728 crore. The Department wise allocation is given Table 21.14 below:

TABLE 21.14
Gross Budgetary Support for the Twelfth Plan

	₹ Crore
Department of School and Secondary Education	**3,43,028**
Of which	
1. Sarva Siksha Abhiyan	1,92,726
2. Rashtriya Madhyamik Shiksha Abhiyan	27,466
3. Mid-day Meal Scheme	90,155
4. Others	32,681
Department of Higher Education	**1,10,700**
Of which	
1. Central Universities and Centrally funded institutions	35,750
2. State Universities and Colleges, including RUSA	25,000
3. Equity initiatives (including students financial support)	11,300
4. Technical education quality improvement programmes	2,500
5. Research and innovation initiatives	5,900
6. Expansion of skill-based higher education including polytechnics & community colleges	4,450
7. National mission in education through ICT (NMEICT)	4,000
8. National Mission for Teachers and Teaching including teaching quality improvement initiatives	1,200
9. Open and Distance Learning	700
10. UGC (multiple schemes including flexi-funds)	9,000
11. AICTE (multiple schemes including flexi-funds)	5,000
12. Other initiatives (including language development, book promotion & copyright, Internationalisation, Planning etc.)	5,900

Source: Planning Commission.

NOTES

1. Gini coefficient is a measure of inequality. Zero value shows perfect equality where all values are the same, while value of one shows maximal inequality.
2. Total enrolment as a percentage of the child population in specified age groups including under-age and over-age children.
3. Percentage of age-specific enrolment to the estimated child population in specified age-groups.
4. DISE, 2010–11.
5. IMRB, 2009.
6. IMRB, 2005, 2009; ASER-Rural, 2011.
7. ASER, 2011.
8. ASER, 2011.
9. UNESCO, 2010.
10. ASER, 2010.
11. NSS, 2007–08.
12. Globally, enrolment in the 18–22 age cohorts is used to measure the GER. Using the global definition GER increased from 15.2 per cent in 2007–08 to 20.2 per cent in 2011–12.
13. Students enrolled in ODL programmes might not register in each semester/year. They usually take longer than students enrolled in regular programmes to complete their studies, and a large proportion of ODL students are older than those in the traditional age cohort and some of them may also be enrolled in regular programmes.
14. This survey was conducted by the Centre for International Higher Education at Boston College and Laboratory of Institutional Analysis (LIA) at the Higher School of Economics (Russia). See http://acarem.hse.ru/.

22

Employment and Skill Development

EMPLOYMENT

22.1. Generation of productive and gainful employment with decent working conditions on a sufficient scale to absorb the growing labour force was a critical element in the Eleventh Plan strategy for achieving inclusive growth. The Eleventh Plan aimed at bringing the overall unemployment down by generating new work opportunities exceeding the projected addition to the labour force. The results of NSS 66th round (2009–10) indicate that 18 million new work opportunities were created on CDS basis between 2004–05 and 2009–10. The unemployment in absolute terms came down by 6.3 million and the unemployment rate declined to 6.6 per cent in 2009–10 for the first time since 1993–94, after increasing to 7.31 per cent in 1999–2000 and 8.28 per cent in 2004–05. On UPSS basis also, during the same period, the unemployment rate declined to 2 per cent in 2009–10 from 2.3 per cent in 2004–05. The overall labour force expanded by just 11.7 million. The increase in labour force was lower compared to previous years. This, however, is a positive development as it can be attributed to higher retention of the young in schools and colleges, and also lower distress labour participation by working age women as family incomes improved in both rural and urban areas.

22.2. The employment elasticity in India in the last decade declined from 0.44 in the first half of the decade 1999–2000 to 2004–05, to as low as 0.01 during second half of the decade 2004–05 to 2009–10. The similar trends have been witnessed at the sectoral level, namely agriculture, service, and manufacturing sectors. In agriculture and manufacturing employment elasticity in the latter half of the decade has been negative. The negative employment elasticity in agriculture indicates movement of people out of agriculture to other sectors where wage rates are higher. This migration of surplus workers to other sectors for productive and gainful employment is necessary for inclusive growth. However, the negative employment elasticity in manufacturing sector is a cause of concern particularly when the sector has achieved 6.8 per cent growth in output during Eleventh Plan.

TRENDS IN THE LABOUR FORCE AND WORK FORCE PARTICIPATION RATES

Quantitative Dimensions of Employment

22.3. The quantitative dimensions of employment captures the trends in Labour Force, Work force at rural–urban, Male Female and sectoral level. Table 22.1 provides the Labour Force (LFPR) and Work Force Participation Rates (WFPR) during the decade 1999–2000 and 2009–10. It emerges that the second half of the last decade witnessed the decline in LFPR in spite of increase in the population growth. Further it emerges that there has been decline in both rural and urban LFPRs and WFPRs during the second half of the decade. Female LFPR and WFPR show greater fluctuations particularly in rural India. The rise in female LFPR and WFPR during the first half of the decade might be the result of agricultural distress which depressed household income and pushed women into the labour force. Since all women entering the labour force did not get employment, the first half of the decade was also characterised by an increase

TABLE 22.1
LFPR and WFPR by Usual Principal and Subsidiary Status, 1999–2000, 2004–05 and 2009–10 (%) Persons

	LFPR, WFPR and Unemployment Rate of 1999–2000, 2004–05 and 2009–10 by UPSS								
	LFPR			WFPR			UR		
	1999–2000	2004–05	2009–10	1999–2000	2004–05	2009–10	1999–2000	2004–05	2009–10
Rural	42.3	44.6	41.4	41.7	43.9	40.8	1.5	1.7	1.6
Urban	35.4	38.2	36.2	33.7	36.5	35	4.7	4.5	3.4
All		43	40	39.7	42	39.2		2.3	2

Source: NSS 55th, 61st and 66th Rounds.

in unemployment rate. In absolute terms, the first half of the decade experienced an increase of 20 million workers (238 million to 258 million) in agriculture. The slow growth in the labour force and hence in work force in second half of the decade may be due to rising participation in education by both male and female after the enactment of the Right to Education for 6–14 years old.

22.4. There has been a substantial divergence in the directions of growth of labour force and workforce in rural and urban sectors. In the Rural sector, the labour force declined marginally by 6.8 million from 348.7 million in 2004–05 to 341.9 million in 2009–10. The size of the workforce also showed similar trends. The workforce declined from 342.9 million in 2004–05 to 336.4 million in 2009–10, in the rural sector, marking a decrease of 6.5 million. The decline in labour force and workforce in the rural sector are impacted by MGNREGA programme and other new opportunities in rural sector (Table 22.2).

22.5. In the Urban sector, the trends show a totally different picture. The size of the labour force went up by 6.6 million from 120.3 million in 2004–05 to touch 126.9 million in 2009–10. The workforce grew by 7.6 million from 115 million in 2004–05 to 122.6 million in 2009–10, in the urban sector. However the number of unemployed in the rural sector declined from 5.9 million in 2004–05 to 5.5 million in 2009–10 and in urban sector from 5.4 million to 4.3 million during the same period, indicating that the decline in urban sector was steeper than in the rural sector. The unemployment rates in rural sector have also seen a marginal fall from 1.7 per cent in 2004–05 to 1.6 per cent in 2009–10 and from 4.5 to 3.4 in the urban sector (Table 22.1 and Figure 22.1).

22.6. After rising from 6.06 per cent in 1993–94 to 7.31 per cent in 1999–2000 and further to 8.28 per cent in 2004–05 unemployment rate fell to 6.6 per cent in 2009–10. On the UPSS the unemployment rate has declined from 2.3 per cent in 2004–05 to 2 per cent in 2009–10. The decline in the LFPR for women and increase in the WFPR for men are suggestive of increase in the wages. Table 22.3 indicates that the wages for regular salaried male rural workers in real terms have increased by about 51 per cent and 56 per cent for casual workers. It also emerges from table below that increase in the wages have resulted

TABLE 22.2
Estimated Number of Persons in Millions

		61st Round of NSS (2004–05)		66th Round of NSS (2009–10)	
		Rural	Urban	Rural	Urban
Usual Status (ps+ss)	Labour Force	348.7	120.3	341.9	126.9
	work force	342.9	115	336.4	122.6
	unemployed	5.9	5.4	5.5	4.3

Source: NSS 61st and 66th Rounds.

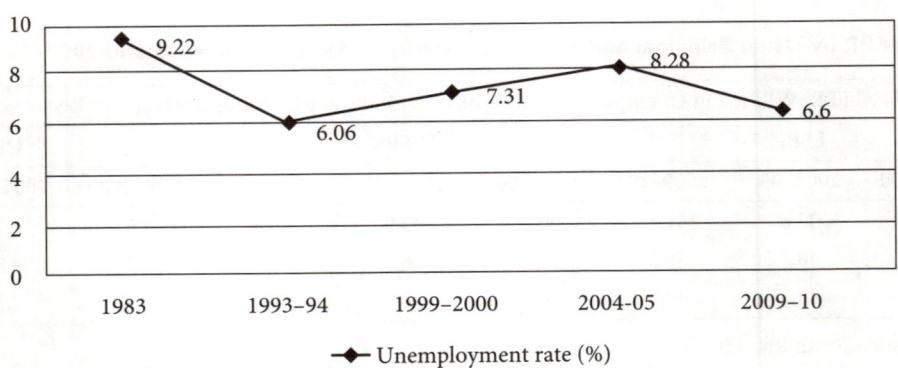

Source: NSS Rounds.

FIGURE 22.1: Trend in Unemployment Rate

TABLE 22.3
Unemployment, Wages and Consumption Expenditure, 1993–4 to 2009–10

	Unemployment Rate (%) (CDS)	Salaries and Wages		Consumption	
		Regular	Casual	Rural	Urban
		₹ Per day, for male rural workers		Monthly per capita (in ₹)	
1993–94	6.06	58.48 (33.23)	23.18 (13.17)	281.4 (159.9)	458.04 (264.8)
1999–2000	7.31	127.32 (46.98)	45.48 (16.78)		
2004–05	8.2	144.93 (45.43)	55.03 (17.25)	558.78 (175.2)	1,052.36 (311.3)
2009–10	6.6	249.15 (50.44)	101.53 (20.55)	927.7 (187.8)	1,785.81 (355.0)

Source: NSS Rounds.
Note: Figures in parentheses are at constant prices. For rural areas derived from CPI for agricultural labourers with base 1986–87 = 100, and for urban areas derived from CPI for urban non-manual employees with base 1984–85 = 100.

in increase in the consumption both in the rural and urban areas by 17.4 per cent and 34 per cent respectively during 1993–94 to 2009–10.

22.7. The rise in employment for males and wages has led to a sharp rise in consumption. As per NSSO data on consumption (NSS 66th Round) Monthly per capita consumption expenditure in rural areas in real terms increased to 1.4 per cent per year in the five years from 2004–05 to 2009–10 from 0.8 per cent per year in the 1993–94 to 2004–05 period. For urban areas, the real per capita expenditures grew faster during the same period from 1.47 per cent between 1993–94 and 2004–05 to 2.67 per cent between 2004–05 and 2009–10. The Conceptual framework of employment and unemployment indicators are presented in Box 22.1.

22.8. In terms of Sectoral shares in employment it emerges that the agriculture share in employment declined from 59.9 per cent at the beginning of decade to 53.2 per cent at the end of the decade. However, this is still very high compared with the share of agriculture in other countries in the region. The share of manufacturing in the total employment after increasing to 12.2 per cent in the first half of the decade declined to 11 per cent in the second half of the decade indicating usage of more capital intensive technology in the absence of skilled manpower. The share of services has increased from 23.7 per cent in

> **Box 22.1**
> **Conceptual Framework of Key Employment and Unemployment Indicators**
>
> Different approaches for determining activity status: On the basis of activities pursued by individuals during certain specified reference periods. There are three reference periods, namely (*i*) one year, (*ii*) one week and (*iii*) each day of the reference week. Based on these three periods, three different measures of activity status are arrived at. These are termed respectively as usual status, current weekly status and current daily status.
>
> *Usual activity status:* The activity status on which a person spent relatively longer time (major time criterion) during the 365 days preceding the date of survey is considered the usual principal activity status of the person.
>
> *Subsidiary economic activity status:* A person whose principal usual status is determined on the basis of the major time criterion may have pursued some economic activity for 30 days or more during the reference period of 365 days preceding the date of survey. The status in which such economic activity is pursued during the reference period of 365 days preceding the date of survey is the subsidiary economic activity status of the person.
>
> *Current weekly activity status:* The current weekly activity status of a person is the activity status obtaining for a person during a reference period of 7 days preceding the date of survey. It is decided on the basis of a certain priority cum major time criterion. A person is considered working (or employed)) if s/he, while pursuing any economic activity, had worked for at least one hour on at least one day during the 7 days preceding the date of survey. A person is considered 'seeking or available for work (or unemployed)' if during the reference week no economic activity was pursued by the person but s/he made efforts to get work or had been available for work any time during the reference week though not actively seeking work in the belief that no work was available.
>
> *Current daily activity status:* The current daily activity status for a person is determined on the basis of her/his activity status on each day of the reference week using a priority-cum-major time criterion (day to day labour time disposition).
>
> *Labour force participation rate (LFPR):* Labour force refers to the population which supplies or offers to supply labour for pursuing economic activities for the production of goods and services and, therefore, includes both 'employed' and 'unemployed' persons/person days. Labour-force participation rate (LFPR) is defined as the proportion of persons/person days in the labour-force to the total persons/person-days.
>
> *Worker Population Ratio (WPR):* The estimates of employed (or worker) according to the usual principal status gives the number of persons who worked for a relatively long part of the 365 days preceding the date of survey. The work force, considering both the usual principal status and the subsidiary status, includes the persons who (*i*) either worked for a relatively long part of the 365 days preceding the date of survey and (*ii*) also those persons from among the remaining population who had worked at least for 30 days during the reference period of 365 days preceding the date of survey.
>
> *Unemployment rate (UR):* Unemployment Rate (UR) is the ratio of number of unemployed persons/person-days to the number of persons/person-days in labour force (that is, number of employed and unemployed person/person-days). Estimates of UR are obtained by the three approaches used for classification of the activity statuses of the person.
>
> *Source:* NSS Reports.

the beginning of the decade in 1999–2000 to 25.3 per cent in the end of the decade. The non-manufacturing sector has seen a sharp increase in employment and this is mostly in the construction sector (Table 22.4).

Sector-wise Employment Generation

22.9. During the period between 2004–05 and 2009–10 a total of 18 million work opportunities on CDS basis and 2 million at UPSS basis have been created. The performance varied across different sectors. The mining, manufacturing, trade, electricity

TABLE 22.4
Proportionate Share of Sectors in Employment

Sectors	1999–2000	2004–5	2009–10
Agriculture	59.9	56.6	53.2
Manufacturing	11.1	12.2	11.0
Non-manufacturing	5.3	6.5	10.5
Services	23.7	24.7	25.3
Total	**100**	**100**	**100**

Source: NSS Various rounds.

related sectors witnessed a decline in employment opportunities in spite of good sectoral growth. In all the sectors the performance was slightly short of the projections at the beginning of the Plan. The data in respect of employment in different sectors is given in Annexure 22.1.

22.10. Agriculture witnessed an oscillating trend in the employment in the last decade. While in the first half of the decade there was an increase in employment from 237.67 million in 1999–2000 to nearly 258.93 million in 2004–05, an increase of 21.26 million, there was a substantial decline in the number of people employed in agriculture in the later half of the decade from 258.93 million to 244.85 million, a decline of about 14.08 millions. However, total agricultural employment at the end of the decade was still higher by 3 per cent than it was at its beginning (Annexure 22.1). This suggests that the process of structural change in employment that one would expect with a period of unprecedented growth in output in the economy outside of agriculture, is not occurring fast enough.

22.11. The manufacturing sector witnessed an absolute increase in employment in the first half of the decade from 44.05 million to nearly 55.77 million in 2004–05. However, the second half of the decade witnessed a decline by about 5 million to reach the employment level of 50.74 million. However, this was still 15 per cent higher than the employment in the beginning of the decade. This change in the trend in employment generation in manufacturing sector may perhaps be due to faster increase in the average annual increase in real wages in India driven by a greater shortage of skilled workers (use of capital intensive technologies) and unskilled casual workers. The employment elasticity for manufacturing sector has shown a downward trend from 0.76 in the first half of the decade to –0.31 in the second half of the decade. This suggests substitution of labour by capital intensive technology resulting in fall in total employment despite an increase in total manufacturing output.

22.12. A close look at the employment trend in the main manufacturing industries given in Annexure 22.2 reveals interesting results. It emerges that the industries that registered an increase in employment in the first half of the decade, more than 80 per cent of them registered decline in the employment during the latter half of the decade. This decline was observed in the labour intensive industries which accounted for 68 per cent of total manufacturing employment in 1999–2000. The decline may be due to fall in the international demand for these products such as textiles, food products; tobacco, wearing apparel, wood products, fabricated metal and so on. These six industries registered an increase of 8.7 million employment during the first half of the decade, and a decline of 7.6 million employment during the second half.

22.13. The employment in the non-manufacturing sector in the decade 1999–2009 has increased by 27.44 million to reach 48.28 million in 2009–10, an increase of 2.3 times relative to 1999–2000. In the first half of the decade non-manufacturing employment increased from 21 million in 1999–2000 to 30 million in 2004–05, nearly a 50 per cent increase from 1999–2000. The absolute size of employment in non-manufacturing by the end of the decade was 1.6 times compared to 2004–05, or 2.3 times relative to the level in 1999–2000. This is comparable to employment in manufacturing sector which is 50 million during the same period. The main increase has been contributed by construction sector where the employment in the decade increased by 26.6 million of which 8.5 million was in the first half and 18.1 million during the second half. The other important sectors, namely mining and quarrying, electricity, gas and water supply have witnessed a very marginal increase (Annexure 22.1).

22.14. The Services/Tertiary sector witnessed an increase in the employment in the decade to reach a level of 116.34 million in 2009–10, contributing about 25.3 per cent to total employment. The growth in employment in the services sector was lower in the second half of the decade than in the first half. Within services, trade was the most important contributor to employment and accounted for one third of total services and employment in the economy both at the beginning as well as at the end of the decade. It accounted for around 36 per cent (nearly 7 crore) of the increase in employment that occurred in the service sector in India in first half of the decade as compared to second half of the decade, when there was hardly any increase in employment. The second most important sector within services is transport, storage and communication whose contribution to total employment increased from 15.5 per cent at the beginning of the decade to 17.2 per cent at the end of the decade in 2009–10.

22.15. The employment in public sector services stagnated and there is, severe shortage in the public services of doctors, nurses, teachers, policemen, and judges. A rapidly growing economy cannot function without the simultaneous rapid expansion of such services. As this transition occurs in India in the next ten years a substantial improvement in higher quality jobs in public sector services may occur. The other services sector viz; banking and financial services and real estate have also witnessed an increase. The Employment in banking and insurance, which was 2.25 million in 1999–2000, had risen to 3.82 million in 2009–10 and in real estate from 2.7 million in 1999–2000 to 5.7 million at its end. The growth in real estate employment commensurate with increased focus of the government on both housing as well as infrastructure investment in the Eleventh Plan period.

22.16. Investment in infrastructure is expected to grow from $500 billion during the Eleventh Five Year Plan to 1 trillion dollars in the Twelfth Plan, that is, to nearly 10 per cent of GDP. NSS data on employment in health and education services show marginal increase in the second half of the decade although first half had witnessed an increase. However while the GVA for education sector increased to 8.4 per cent per annum in the latter half of the decade from 7.1 per cent in the first half, for health sector the growth rate of GVA in was robust (10.1 per cent per annum) in the first half of the decade and declined to 4.2 per cent per annum in the second half of the decade, which perhaps explains the rather small increase in employment in the health sector in the latter half of the decade. The greater thrust of the government on education, skill development and health in the Twelfth Plan will increase employment in the sector in the Twelfth Plan.

EMPLOYMENT SCENARIO IN THE STATES

22.17. The variation in population increase in different states and in turn working age population has implication for employment generation. The present analysis of trends in employment in different sectors in different States would highlight the sectors that are contributing and would contribute to employment in future.

Agriculture

22.18. In agriculture at the national level there has been increase in the absolute number of people employed in the last decade (1999–2000 to 2009–10) although in the second half of the decade the proportion has declined marginally. The vast majority of the states have also experienced a decline in employment in agriculture between 2004–05 and 2009–10. However, since the total fall in employment in agriculture in the latter half of the decade was only 14.08 million, the distribution of this decline among the states did not lead to a significant shift of workers out of agriculture to industry or services. This does not indicate that temporary migration from rural to urban areas was not occurring. In fact for the first time since the Census of 1921 within the last decade, that is, 2001 to 2011 Census, the increase in the urban population (91 million) has been greater than the increase in the rural population over the decade (90 million). This may be because workers do migrate from rural to urban but only for temporary periods during the lean season for agriculture and move back during the peak season. Therefore, this workforce is not available for work in manufacturing or modern services due to lack of appropriate skill set. Their migration reflects rural distress, driven by the fact that 84 per cent of India's farmers are small and marginal, tilling less than 2.5 acres of land.

22.19. In this context, it is important to mention that just two states alone accounted for nearly half of the decline in agricultural employment in the latter half of the decade. Thus, in Bihar employment in agriculture fell from 21.2 million in 2004–05 to

17.2 million at the end of the decade. Similarly, in U.P. employment in agriculture fell from 43.3 million in the middle of the decade to nearly 39.7 million at its end. On the contrary, the state of Maharashtra witnessed an increase in the employment in agriculture 3.97 million in the latter half of the decade. Another state which saw an increase in agriculture in the latter half of the decade was Punjab, from 3.6 to 4.7 million.

Manufacturing

22.20. The employment in manufacturing sector at All India level has fallen in the second half of the decade from 55.77 to 50.74 million. Most of this decline in employment was confined to states like Maharashtra (1.81 million) Tamil Nadu (0.98 million), Uttar Pradesh (0.85 million) and Jharkhand (0.25 million). The most distressing part was the fall in employment in the most industrialised states, namely Maharashtra, Tamil Nadu which accounted for 75 per cent of the decline in the manufacturing employment in the country in the second half of the decade.

22.21. In terms of state wise share of employment, it emerged that the national average for the share of manufacturing employment accounted for 11 per cent of total employment in 2009–10. There are 9 major states where this share is greater than the national average: Andhra Pradesh (11.9 per cent) Delhi (24.84 per cent), Gujarat (12.6 per cent), Haryana (12.2 per cent), Kerala (13.5 per cent), Punjab (15.9 per cent), Tamil Nadu (19.6 per cent), Uttar Pradesh (11.1 per cent) and West Bengal (18.4 per cent). Given the fact that there are advantages of agglomeration in the manufacturing sector it is likely that even in the future these states will continue to account for growth in manufacturing of GVA and employment. The state of Karnataka (9.4 per cent) also has similar proportion in employment as at national.

22.22. In terms of the share of manufacturing in state GVA, seven states have higher than the national average of manufacturing share in GDP (15.9 per cent) in 2009–10: Chhattisgarh, Gujarat, Haryana, Jharkhand, Karnataka, Maharashtra, and Tamil Nadu. These states could continue to grow fast during the Twelfth Plan period. But this depends to a larger extent on the manufacturing employment elasticity of output. While States of Chhattisgarh, Gujarat, Haryana, Delhi, Uttarakhand and West Bengal have positive employment elasticity, the states of Jharkhand, Maharashtra and Tamil Nadu have negative employment elasticity which implies usage of more capital intensive technology.

Non-Manufacturing

22.23. All the States experienced increase in non-manufacturing employment, mainly in construction sector in the second half of the decade.

Services

22.24. Services sector contributed about 25.3 per cent of total employment in 2009–10. Most of the states have shown a positive trend in the employment generation in the services sector in the latter half of the decade with exception of Andhra Pradesh, Madhya Pradesh, Maharashtra and Punjab which have shown decline in the service sector employment and negative employment elasticity. There is need for state governments to focus their attention on promotion of services for employment generation. 11 states share of services in total employment is greater than the national average namely Delhi (67.9 per cent), Haryana (25.2 per cent), Kerala (39.2 per cent), Maharashtra (29.8 per cent), Punjab (29.1 per cent), Tamil Nadu (27.0 per cent) and West Bengal (30.4 per cent).

QUALITATIVE DIMENSIONS IN EMPLOYMENT TRENDS

22.25. While the above analysis provide trends in creation of total employment both at the macro level and at state level as also the sectoral composition of the employment so created, it is necessary to look into the qualitative dimensions of employment in terms of equity, dignity, social security, status of employment and so on. This would help in formulating strategy for India's future challenges in generating productive employment, with decent working conditions.

Informalisation of Employment

22.26. A critical issue in assessing employment behavior of the economy is the growth of employment in the organised sector vis-à-vis the

TABLE 22.5
Formal and Informal Employment in Organized and Unorganised Sector (millions)

Sectors	Employment 2009–10		
	Informal	Formal	Total
Unorganised	385.08	2.26	387.34
Organised	42.14	30.74	72.88
Total	**427.22**	**33.00**	**460.22**
2004–05			
Unorganised	393.5	1.4	394.9
Organised	29.1	33.4	62.6
Total	**422.6**	**34.9**	**457.5**
1999–2000			
Unorganised	341.3	1.4	342.6
Organised	20.5	33.7	54.1
Total	**361.7**	**35.0**	**396.8**

Source: For 2009–10, computed from NSS 66th round, for other years taken from NCEUS, 2007.

unorganised sector and particularly in terms of formal and informal employments. It is generally opined that unorganised sector employment is of low quality compared to organised sector employment. Table 22.5 presents the employment in organised and unorganised sector in terms of formal and informal employment.

22.27. The above data shows a decline in the employment in the unorganised sector from 86 per cent in 2004–05 to 84 per cent in 2009–10. This means that the share of organised sector employment has increased to 16 per cent in 2009–10 from 14 per cent in both 1999–2000 and 2004–05. However, the increase in the organised sector employment is mainly in the informal category. The informal employment in the organised sector has increased from 46.4 per cent in 2004–05 to about 57.8 per cent in 2009–10. The informal employment in the unorganised sector remains the same. Nearly 93 per cent of the total workforce in 2009–10 is in informal employment, a rise from 91 per cent in 1999–2000. If agriculture is excluded from the workforce, the share of informal workers in the total non-agricultural workforce drops to 85.6 per cent from 93 per cent, which is still very high as compared to that in Brazil (51 per cent), Mexico (50 per cent), Indonesia (78 per cent), Philippines (72 per cent), and Thailand (49 per cent).

22.28. The above trend is indicative of movement of workers from informal agricultural sector employment to informal non-agricultural sectors. The transition from informal employment in the unorganised sectors to informal employment in the organised sectors is indicated by a decline of 8.4 million informal workers in unorganised sector along with an increase of 13 million informal workers in the organised sector. What is notable is that formal employment in the organised sector is not increasing. This shows that organised enterprises employers are increasingly hiring workers on contractual terms due to labour laws and other concerns. Small and medium size enterprises generally belong to the unorganised sector and employ informal workers. Hence analysing employment by size of enterprises would provide some insights on the qualitative dimensions of employment.

Size of Enterprises by Employment

22.29. The data in Table 22.6 on size class of enterprises by the number of workers that they employ shows an occurrence of shift in non-agricultural employment in the 2000s. The workers in the enterprises with less than six employees (that is, micro enterprises) show a remarkable decline both in absolute as well as in relative terms between 2004–05 and 2009–10. Such micro enterprises accounted for 152.5 million workers in the middle of the decade, or 75 per cent of all non-agricultural workers. By the end of the decade the number of workers in such enterprises had fallen by nearly 4 million, and the share of such micro enterprises in the total non-agricultural employment was down to 65.6 per cent. Correspondingly there was an increase in the number of workers employed in enterprises with 6 and above but less than 10 workers, from 15.2 million in the middle of the decade to nearly 24 million at its end, thus raising the share of workers in such enterprises from 7.5 per cent to 10.5 per cent of all non-agricultural employment in the country. It is better for workers since it reduces the fragmentation and enables them to organise.

TABLE 22.6
Number of Workers by Size of Enterprise in Industry and Services

Number of Workers in Enterprises	2004–05		2009–10	
	Number of Workers in Million	Share %	Number of Workers in Million	Share %
Less than 6	152.5	74.93	148.7	65.6
6 and above but less than 10	15.2	7.46	23.8	10.5
10 and above but less than 20	11.8	5.81	15.4	6.8
20 and above	24.0	11.8	38.8	17.1
Total		100		100

Source: Compiled from NSS, 2009–10 (66th Round) and NSS, 2004–05 (61st Round).

Category of Workers by Employment Status

22.30. In the labour market casual labour and self-employed are most vulnerable. Table 22.7 shows the annual increase in the work-force by category of employment in first half of the decade compared with second half of the decade. A notable feature is the increase in the number of jobs created at regular salaried wage and as casual worker. This may be due to increase in non manufacturing and service sector employment as discussed earlier.

TABLE 22.7
Number of Workers According to Usual Status (PS+SS) Approach by Broad Employment Status (Million Workers)

	1999–2000	2004–05	2009–10
Self employed	209.3 (52.6)	258.4 (56.4)	232.7 (50.7)
Regular/Salaried employee	58.2 (14.6)	69.7 (15.2)	75.1 (16.4)
Casual labour	130.3 (32.8)	129.7 (28.3)	151.3 (33.0)

Source: Compiled from NSS, 55th, 61st and 66th Rounds.

Unemployment among Young and the Educated

22.31. The data and the Figure 22.2 show that Unemployment is higher among the youth and the educated who are looking for better quality jobs. The figure shows that unemployment among the age group 15–29 years for both males and females and in urban and rural areas is significantly higher than the average level of unemployment of all persons.

22.32. The incidence of employment by level of education in India (by UPSS) in Annexure 22.3 indicates that illiterates have the lowest rate of unemployment, and the rate of unemployment tends to rise with every level of education, with the highest unemployment rate for those with diploma/certificates (or those with one or two years of post higher secondary education). The unemployment rate for Diploma/Certificate holders was 9.6 per cent at the end of the decade. The unemployment rate does decline for graduates and slightly again for postgraduates and above, but not significantly.

EMPLOYMENT TRENDS AMONG THE SOCIAL GROUPS

Women's Employment

22.33. Although there has been consistent decline in workforce participation rate (WPR) of women since 1980s but the decline seems to have accelerated in the later half of the decade, that is, between 2004–05 and 2009–10 pushing down the overall LFPR and WFPR to a low level. The decline in female labour force participation has occurred in both rural and urban areas, though the decline is much sharper in rural compared to urban areas. This points to the fact that that in both urban and rural areas girls over 14 years of age (that is, of working age) are either attending the educational institution or have withdrawn from work due to improvement in the family income. The most serious problem that women in the work force face is poor quality of work. For the vast majority of

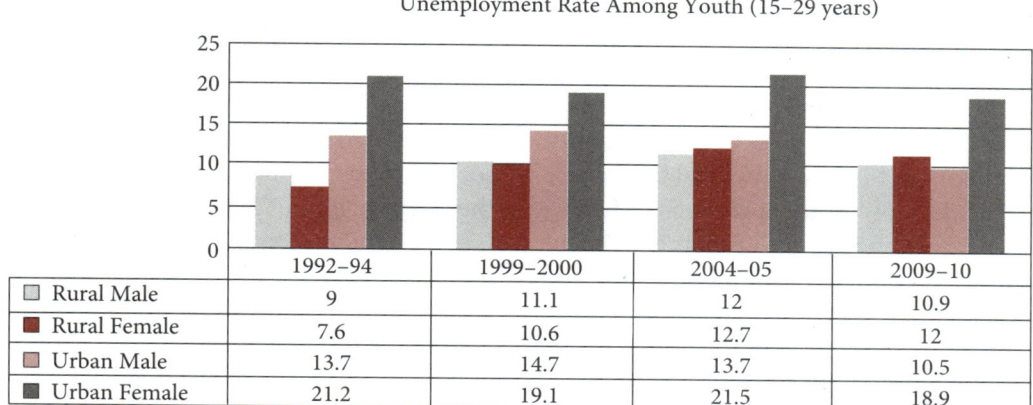

Source: NSS 55th, 61st and 66th rounds.

FIGURE 22.2: Unemployment Rate among Youth

women in non-agricultural employment they tend to work from home in home-based work, usually sub-contracted to them by male contractors in a variety of low-productivity work (for example, bidi-making, zari-making, and so on) or as helper in the construction industry. It is expected that attainment of the education would empower the women to join the labour market at a slightly later age better qualified and in quality employment though in unorganised sector (Tables 22.8 and 22.9).

22.34. At the policy level, there is need to give priority to Women in the National Rural Livelihood Mission (of the Ministry of Rural Development). NRLM will facilitate the creation of self-help groups of women at national scale and provide credit to SHGs to enable them to undertake self-sustaining economic activity.

Child Labour

22.35. Table 22.10 analyses incidence of Child labour since 1993–94. The incidence of child labour has declined since 1990s.

TABLE 22.8
LFPR by Usual Principal and Subsidiary Status, 1993–94, 2004–05 and 2009–10 (%) by Gender

Sector	Males			Females		
	1993–94	2004–05	2009–10	1993–94	2004–05	2009–10
Rural	87.6	85.9	82.5	49	49.4	37.8
Urban	80.1	79.2	76.2	23.8	24.4	19.4

TABLE 22.9
WPR by Usual Principal and Subsidiary Status, 1993–94, 2004–05 and 2009–10 (%) by Gender

	Male			Female		
	1993–94	2004–05	2009–10	1993–94	2004–05	2009–10
	86.4	84.6	81.2	48.7	48.5	37.2
	76.8	76.3	74	22.3	22.7	18.3

TABLE 22.10
Child Workforce Participation Rate by UPSS (Percentage), 1993–94, 2004–05 and 2009–10

Area	1993–94			2004–05			2009–10		
	Boys	Girls	Children	Boys	Girls	Children	Boys	Girls	Children
Rural	6.8	7.8	7.3	3.5	3.7	3.6	2.0	2.4	2.2
Urban	3.5	2.7	3.1	2.6	1.9	2.3	0.7	1.5	1.1
Combined	6.2	6.0	6.2	3.3	3.3	3.3	1.7	2.2	2.0

Source: NSSO 1993–04, 2004–05 and 2009–10.

22.36. It emerges that the active participation of both boys and girls in the labour market is falling. The decline in child labour commensurate with significant increase in school enrolment of both boys and girls. Since the proportion of girls who were out of school was higher than that for boys until the middle of the 2000s, the decrease in the incidence of female child labour is largely on account of their enrolment in schools. However, the NSS data for 1993–94 and 2007–08 reveals that girls are still being held back at home in order to perform household chores. In the proportion of children in the age of 5–14 who are categorised neither as child labourers nor as students enrolled in schools 11.4 per cent of girls belong to the category of nowhere girls in the 6–14 year old age group, while only 3.8 per cent of boys in the same age group belong to nowhere children. The education sector has a pre-eminent role in ensuring that all children in the age group 6–14 years are at school. The stricter implementation of SSA and Child labour regulations can ensure that the child labour is eradicated from the country.

Weaker Social Groups: The Scheduled Castes (SCs), Scheduled Tribes (STs)

22.37. In terms of most social indicators the Scheduled Castes (SCs) and the Scheduled Tribes (STs) among social groups are the most marginalised sections (Table 22.11). For instance, the work force participation rate (by usual principal and subsidiary status) for SCs in 1993–94 was 71 per cent and for STs it was 81 per cent, which were both much greater than the workforce participation rate (WFPR) for all social groups (68 per cent) in rural areas; similarly, they were higher in 2004–05. Although urban WFPR is consistently lower for all groups, SCs and STs have a much higher WFPR compared to all groups. This higher than average WFPR for SCs and STs is attributed to the fact that SCs and STs of working age (that is, 15 and above) have lower enrolment ratio in secondary school than other social groups. The vulnerability of SCs and STs in terms of the labour market is emphasised by the fact that by UPSS SCs and STs have much higher unemployment rates, by and large, at least in urban areas.

22.38. Table 22.12 gives the unemployment rates among various social groups including SCs and STs from National Sample Surveys from 1993–94 to 2009–10. It may be seen that between 2004–05 and 2009–10, the unemployment rates for SCs have declined by 2.1 percentage points in urban areas while it did not change for rural areas and remained at 1.6 per cent. The unemployment rates for all the social groups in both the rural and urban areas, however, witnessed a decline, 0.1 percentage point in rural areas and

TABLE 22.11
Workforce Participation Rate by Usual Principal and Subsidiary Status, by Social Group, 1993–94, 2004–05 and 2009–10 (%)

Sector	SCs			STs			All Groups		
	1993–94	2004–05	2009–10	1993–94	2004–05	2009–10	1993–94	2004–05	2009–10
Rural	71.1	68.7	61.4	81.4	79.1	68.9	67.8	66.6	59.5
Urban	56.8	54.1	51.8	57	54.9	49.2	50.9	50.6	47.2

Source: NSS rounds.

TABLE 22.12
Unemployment Rate by Usual Principal and Subsidiary Status, by Social Group, 2004–05 and 2009–10 (%)

Sector	SCs			STs			All		
	1993–94	2004–05	2009–10	1993–94	2004–05	2009–10	1993–94	2004–05	2009–10
Rural	1	1.6	1.6	0.6	0.8	1.4	1.2	1.7	1.6
Urban	4.4	5.3	3.2	3.9	3.1	4.4	4.5	4.4	3.4

Source: NSS rounds.

1.0 percentage points in urban areas. But the unemployment for STs has increased in both rural and urban areas during the period 2004–05 to 2009–10.

LABOUR FORCE AND WORKFORCE PROJECTIONS FOR THE TWELFTH PLAN

Labour Force Projections

22.39. The projections of labour force have been made using the latest population projections made by the NSSO and 2011 census data. The projected increase in labour force during the Twelfth Plan period for the 15 and above age group is now estimated to be around 24.5 million from 477.9 million in 2011 to 502.4 million by the end of 2017. This is calculated on the basis of age specific LFPRs and population distribution trend that has existed since 2004–05. India has seen deceleration in population growth rate (Census 1991, 2001 and 2011). The 66th Round has also shown a decline in the female participation rate, which could be the effect of increasing enrolment in educational institutions, as also the impact of rising incomes, where women do not want to do low quality jobs (backward bending labour supply curve). With the focus of the policy planners on raising the gross enrollment ratio in secondary and higher education, the number of people entering the labour force may not see a significant rise. Assuming the rate of decline in population growth rate to be in line with the past trend, and taking into account the effect of education and rising family income on female work participation, the LFPR is expected to decline further. The absolute increase in the labour force by the end of Twelfth plan is therefore expected to be small. Based on these assumptions, the population and labour force projections for the Twelfth Five Year Plan are shown in the Table 22.13.

22.40. With the enactment of Right to Education (RTE), introduction of the National Skills Qualification Framework (NSQF) and integration of vocational education with the secondary education, drop-out rates are likely to decrease. Creating non-farm employment opportunities for the educated youth will be a challenge for the country in near future. To meet the education targets of near full universalisation of secondary education (>90 per cent), GER of 65 per cent in higher secondary classes and expected increase of enrollment in universities and colleges from 200.3 lakhs in 2011–12 to 300.2 lakhs by 2016–17, about 28 million will be drawn out of the labor force (15–59 age group). Therefore, in order to ensure that the overall labor force participation rate does not fall much over the Plan period; efforts have to be made to raise the female work participation rates.

Work Force Projections: Total and Sectoral Employment Projections

22.41. The total employment over the period has been estimated on the basis of employment projections for individual sectors which are then aggregated for the economy as a whole. These sectoral employment projections are based on sectoral GDP growth rates combined with computed employment elasticities (1999–2000 to 2009–10). There are two plausible scenarios with respect to employment situation over the Twelfth Plan period. First is the business-as-usual scenario, where projections rely on an analysis of growth and employment trends

TABLE 22.13
Population and Labour Force Projections

Year	2011	2012	2013	2014	2015	2016	2017
Total population (0+)	1,210.2	1,227.1	1,244.0	1,260.6	1,277.1	1,293.5	1,309.7
15 and above population (%)	70.2	71.0	71.8	72.6	73.4	74.2	75.0
Population (15 and above) in millions	849.6	871.3	893.2	915.2	937.4	959.8	982.2
LFPR for 15 and above age group (%)	56.3	55.4	54.6	53.7	52.9	52.0	51.2
Labor force (15 and above) (in millions)	477.9	482.7	487.2	491.5	495.4	499.1	502.4

Source: NSS Round and Census 2011.

TABLE 22.14
Employment Elasticity from Past Data

	Agriculture	Mining and Quarrying	Manufacturing	Utilities	Construction	Trade, Transport and so on	Finance, Real Estate, and so on	Other Services	Total
Employment elasticity	0.04	0.52	0.09	0.04	1.13	0.19	0.66	0.08	0.19

for agriculture, manufacturing, non-manufacturing industry and services over the last Five Year Plan period. It is built on the assumption that the growth pattern of various sectors during the Twelfth Plan would be similar to what it was during the Eleventh Plan period. Second is the Twelfth Plan scenario, which takes into account the aim of the Twelfth Five Year Plan of creating quality and productive employment opportunities, with focus on acceleration of the rate of transition of labor out of low productivity agriculture to higher productivity industry and services sectors. If the manufacturing sector is able to reverse the declining trend of employment growth with focus on expanding the labor-intensive manufacturing, agriculture is able to grow at 4 per cent with improvements in productivity and diversification, and the contribution from the non-manufacturing sectors, particularly construction and services continues to increase, the planned scenario gives the alternative set of employment projections (Set 2). One of the main objectives of the growth strategy in the Twelfth Plan period must be to ensure that this process of structural change in terms of employment opportunities is accelerated.

Employment Elasticity

22.42. Sectoral employment elasticities have been calculated by running a log-log regression on observed sectoral GDP figures at constant prices from 1999–2000 to 2009–10 (independent variable) and employment figures for the same period, obtained by interpolating the series on the 1999–2000, 2004–05 and 2009–10 employment outcomes obtained from various NSSO rounds.

Business-as-Usual Scenario

22.43. If the economy and its sectors continue to grow at the rates with which they grew during the Eleventh Plan (Table 22.14), the projected employment (15 and above age group) on a pure demand side basis is about 508.9 million. This would lead to a reduction in unemployment rate, and when adjusted for labor force participation rates, the employment in agriculture is expected to decline. Even with business-as-usual growth rates, the farm sector share in employment is expected to drop from 51.8 per cent in 2011–12 to 47.3 per cent in 2016–17. This also shows that shift from the farm to non-farm sector would be small, if the skill up-gradation and expansion of employment opportunities in manufacturing and services does not take place (Tables 22.15 and 22.16).

Twelfth Plan Scenario

22.44. If the manufacturing sector becomes an engine of growth, by growing at the targeted two percentage points above the overall growth rate (11 per cent); and the agriculture sector grows at 4 per cent, the sectoral growth rates would be as given in the Table 22.17.

TABLE 22.15
Sectoral Growth Rates: Business-as-usual Scenario

Sector	Growth Rates
Agriculture	3.3
Mining and quarrying	3.2
Manufacturing	6.8
Utilities	6.0
Construction	7.3
Trade, transport, hotels, and so on	10.0
Finance, insurance, real estate and so on	10.7
Community, social and personal services	8.3
Total	**7.9**

TABLE 22.16
Sectoral Employment (in million): Business-as-usual Scenario

Year	Agriculture	Mining and Quarrying	Manufacturing	Utilities	Construction	Trade, Transport, Hotels, and so on	Finance, Banking, Real Estate, and so on	Community, Personal and Social Services	Total
2009–10	241.7	2.7	50.0	1.4	43.6	68.6	9.5	37.2	454.7
2011–12	242.3	2.8	50.6	1.4	51.1	71.2	10.9	37.7	468.0
2016–17 (pure demand side)	243.9	3.1	52.2	1.4	75.8	78.2	15.4	39.0	508.9
2016–17 (adjusted for labour force participation rates)	237.4	3.1	52.2	1.4	75.8	78.2	15.4	39.0	502.4
Projected Share of Employment in per cent									
2011–12	51.77	0.60	10.81	0.29	10.91	15.22	2.34	8.06	100.0
2016–17	47.25	0.61	10.38	0.28	15.09	15.57	3.06	7.77	100.0

TABLE 22.17
Sectoral Growth Rates—Twelfth Plan Scenario

	Agriculture	Mining and Quarrying	Manufacturing	Utilities	Construction	Trade, Transport, Hotels, and so on	Finance, Insurance, Real Estate and so on	Community, Social and Personal Services	Total
Growth Rates	4.0	3.2	11.0	6.0	7.3	10.0	10.7	8.3	9.0

22.45. The cornerstone of the manufacturing policy for the Twelfth Plan is to create 10 million additional jobs in the manufacturing sector by focusing on labor-intensive manufacturing and by suitable amendments to the labor regulatory framework, so that manufacturing becomes a genuine engine of employment growth in the country. If we focus on more productive and quality (organised and self-employed) employment in the manufacturing and services sector, additional 50 million job opportunities can be created in the non-farm sector. But this will need a huge effort in the form of skill development aligned to the market needs. In particular, manufacturing, construction, trade, transport, hospitality and financial services are the promising sectors where skill development can lead to a faster growth in employment opportunities.

22.46. As more skilled people coming back to the labor force after completing their education and training to join the work force, those under-employed in agriculture will be drawn out to fill the job opportunities created by the non-farm sector. This could, in the planned scenario, bring down the projected share of employment in farm sector to about 45 per cent of the total. The details are summarised in the Table 22.18.

22.47. To summarise, the Twelfth Plan should focus on demand aligned skill development, and aim at significantly stepping up growth in employment in manufacturing, so that under-employed labour force can speedily move from low-paid farm jobs to better paid, more productive manufacturing and services sectors. Simultaneously, we should improve

TABLE 22.18
Sectoral Employments (in million): Twelfth Plan Scenario

Year	Agriculture	Mining and Quarrying	Manufacturing	Utilities	Construction	Trade, Transport, Hotels, and so on	Finance, Banking, Real Estate, and so on	Community, Personal and Social Services	Total
2011–12	242.4	2.8	51.0	1.4	51.1	71.2	10.9	37.7	468.6
2011–12	Farm 242.4	Non Farm 226.1							
2016–17	226.0	3.1	63.5	1.4	75.8	78.2	15.4	39.0	502.4
2016–17	Farm 226.0	Non Farm 276.4							
Projected Share of Employment (in per cent)									
2011–12	51.74	0.60	10.88	0.29	10.90	15.20	2.33	8.06	100.00
2016–17	44.99	0.61	12.65	0.28	15.09	15.57	3.06	7.77	100.00

Note: The sectoral employment projections are based on the initial growth rate of 9 per cent and would undergo change if based on 8 per cent.

the working conditions for women to improve their work participation rates, and focus on greater organised sector jobs that will meet the aspirations of the rising number of educated and skilled youth in the country.

CHALLENGES FOR EMPLOYMENT POLICY

Expanding Employment Opportunities

22.48. The employment elasticity of the manufacturing sector has witnessed a decline in spite of increase in the gross value added in the sector. The usual structural transformation associated with high growth does not seem to have happened in India and more people continued to be employed in agriculture and other forms of informal employment. The Twelfth Plan hopes to make the manufacturing sector a genuine engine of growth, which could generate 100 million work opportunities by 2022. The employment contribution of labour intensive manufacturing, namely textile and garments, leather and footwear, gems and jewellery, food processing industries and so on can be greatly enhanced provided the Government puts supportive policies in place. Some of these are mentioned in the sub-section below.

22.49. Incentives will have to be improved for expanding employment in the organised sector. Services like information technology, finance and banking, tourism, trade and transport are going to be major generators of employment in the Twelfth Plan period and beyond. Sector specific strategies need to be adopted to ensure sustained expansion of employment opportunities in these areas.

Simplifying Regulatory Framework

22.50. The multiplicity of labour laws administered both by the Central and the State governments are not conducive for the congenial development of the factory sector. The 84 per cent of the unorganised sector is outside the purview of the labour laws, while the 16 per cent organised sector is overburdened with regulatory interference at all levels. There is need to simplify labour laws both at the Centre and the State level. In particular the following actions need to be taken on an urgent basis:

I. To ensure speedy resolution of industrial disputes, particularly the collective disputes which have a bearing on law and order, the District Collector or the Sub-Divisional Magistrate may be appointed as Conciliatory Officers under the Industrial disputes Act, 1947.

II. A comprehensive social security must be put into place for workers in the organised sector, which provides for pension, medical insurance and unemployment benefits that are seamlessly transferable across employers in all sectors of the economy. Suitable provisions need to be made for workers in the unorganised sector, where their own contributions can be supplemented by some support from the Government.

III. To generate greater overall employment, at least labour intensive manufacturing industries like textiles and garments, leather and footwear, gems and jewellery, food processing and so on must be permitted to adjust its labour force, in response to fluctuations in demand. The focus should be on promoting labour market flexibility without compromising fairness to labour.

Addressing the Problems of Specific Categories

22.51. NSS data shows that female employment has declined both in rural areas and urban areas in recent years. This is a major concern and needs to be addressed during the Twelfth Plan period. While this could be partly due to improved enrolment of girls and young women in secondary and higher education, the effect of increasing household income on female work participation rates is also being felt. As household incomes rise and budget constraints relax, women weigh the trade-offs between available employment opportunity and home making more carefully. The only way to slow down the declining female work participation rate is to make the work environment more conducive to women, and provide for the genuine needs of home-making and child care.

22.52. Unemployment among educated people is going to be a major issue during the Twelfth Plan period. India is one of the few countries which have educated unemployed in large numbers. The major reason is the dearth of vocational and technical education leading to skill mismatch in the job market. Similarly, the issue of promoting employment opportunities for minorities, SC/ST and disabled people assumes greater importance, and employment oriented education needs to be provided in a manner that ensures the needs of the vulnerable sections of the society are taken care of.

Bridging the Skill Gap

22.53. There is need for skilling and reskilling the persons entering the labour force to harness the demographic dividend that India enjoys. While the enrolment in technical higher education has grown, the employers continue to complain about non availability of requisite number of skilled persons. This challenge needs to be addressed at the All India as well as the State level in a mission mode manner, as otherwise the benefits of demographic dividend would be lost. The skill enhancement also leads to increased wages for the people and a positive growth outcome for the economy at large.

22.54. The employment challenges as reflected above needs to be addressed so as to meet the faster and inclusive growth agenda for the Twelfth Plan. Skill development should, therefore, occupy centre-stage in any employment strategy for the Twelfth Plan. The following paras will discuss the current status of skill development in India, the challenges emerging from thereon and the road map for skilling the requisite manpower so as to reap the demographic dividend on one hand and enhance the employability of the labour force for inclusive growth on the other.

SKILL DEVELOPMENT: THE CHALLENGE

22.55. Skill development is critical for achieving faster, sustainable and inclusive growth on the one hand and for providing decent employment opportunities to the growing young population on the other. The demographic window of opportunity available to India would make India the skill capital of world. India would be in position to meet the requirement of technically trained manpower not only for its growing economy but also of the aging advanced economies of the world. Hon'ble Prime Minister has rightly indicated that young population is an asset only if it is educated, skilled and finds productive employment. If this happens then our dream of realising India's potential to grow at 10 per cent or more per annum for a substantial period of time can become a reality. Boston Consultancy Group's study in 2007 had clearly indicated that by 2020 while India will have surplus of 56 million working people, the rest of the world will encounter a shortage of 47 million working people. However, skilling this large and growing young population from an exceedingly small base would be a big challenge for India. The skill strategy for the Twelfth Plan would have to accordingly model for these skill challenges in terms of outreach, quality, systemic/institutional setups, current status of skill development efforts and various economic policies proposed in the Twelfth Plan.

22.56. Structural shifts in the economy in terms of increase in contribution of secondary and territory sectors to GDP and demographic dividend have implications for skills development strategy. India will have about 63 per cent of its population in the working age group by 2022. China's demographic dividend would start tapering off by 2015, but India would continue to enjoy it till 2040. India needs to provide skills and training to its young workforce if this window of opportunity is not to be lost. However, the availability of demographic dividend varies across the country with wide variation in Northern and Southern states. While the Northern states would have young population the southern states have already started aging. It emerges from the Annexure 22.4 that the Dependency ratio in UP and Bihar at 1.05 and 1.08 respectively is lower than the dependency ratio in Tamil Nadu and Kerala at 1.74 and 1.79 respectively. This is also lower than the dependency ratio at All India Level at 1.33.

22.57. The rise in the share of the working-age population would lead to increase in demand for decent employment opportunities. However, the realisation of full potential of the demographic dividend depends on generation of adequate decent non-farm employment opportunities and up gradation of skills of existing as well as new entrants to the workforce.

The Level of Education of the Labour Force

22.58. As per the 66th round of NSS (Table 22.19) the general education level of over 50 per cent of India's labour force in the age group 15–59 remains extremely low. Of the total labour force of 431 million on UPSS basis about 29 per cent are not even literate and another about 24 per cent were having education up to primary level. Of the balance, about 29 per cent had education level up to secondary which included 17.6 per cent with middle level education. Only about 17 per cent have higher levels of education (including higher secondary, diploma/certificate, graduates, and higher than graduation).

22.59. As indicated earlier in the chapter the growth is expected to lead to transition of labour out of agriculture into industry and services sectors. However, the low education levels of the labour force, especially those engaged in agriculture would make transition to non-farm sector difficult except as low

TABLE 22.19
General Education Level of Labour Force (PS+SS) in the Age Group 15–59

	Numbers (mn.)	Share in Labour Force in Age Group 15–59 per cent	Share in Labour Force (470.1 million) per cent
Not literate	125.65	29.14	26.73
Literate without formal schooling	2.12	0.49	0.45
Below primary + Primary	102.38	23.74	21.78
Middle	76.08	17.64	16.18
Secondary	52.39	12.15	11.14
Higher secondary	29.19	6.77	6.21
Diploma/certificate course	6.02	1.40	1.28
Graduate	28.01	6.49	5.96
Graduate and above	9.40	2.18	2.00
Total	**431.23**	**100.00**	**91.73**

Source: NSS 66th Round 2009–10.

paid laborers in the construction industry. In other words, there is need to ensure basic skill, that is, at least functional literacy and numeracy among the labour force.

The Share of Vocationally Trained in the Labour Force

22.60. As per the 66th Round of NSS (2009–10), the vocationally trained in the age group 15–59 in the labour force are around 10 per cent of the Labour Force in that age group. The absolute number of those who are receiving formal vocational training is 1.9 mn in 2009–10. An additional 9 mn in the labour force have already received vocational training formally. Finally, an additional 32.7 mn have received non-formal vocational training. Thus, the total number of those received or receiving vocational training in the labour force (15–59) was 43 mn in 2009–10.

Educational Qualification and Vocational Training of Workers

22.61. A look at the profile of workers by economic sectors in Table 22.20 indicates that the proportion of illiterate workers is highest in agriculture and allied activities (about 40 per cent), followed by the non-manufacturing sector (33 per cent).

22.62. Overall 10 per cent of the workforce in the age group of 15–59 years received some form of vocational training. The proportion of workers who received vocational training was the highest in the services sector (33 per cent), followed by manufacturing (31 per cent), agriculture (27 per cent), and non-manufacturing and allied activities (9 per cent). But the important thing is that vast majority of workers received non-formal vocational training. The proportion of workers with non-formal vocational training was the highest in agriculture and it was primarily in the form of hereditary transfer of knowledge. In the non-agricultural sector, the non-formal vocational training was in the form of on the job learning. Dependence on non-formal vocational training to such an extent highlights the grossly inadequate system of vocational training that currently exists in the country. What is remarkable is that there is little difference between manufacturing and agriculture in the share of those with vocational training who only received non-formal training: 86 per cent in agriculture and 91.7 per cent in manufacturing. Only in services is the share of those informal training much lower at 56 per cent (Table 22.21).

THE SKILL TARGETS FOR TWELFTH PLAN

22.63. During the Twelfth Five Year Plan (2012–17), 50 million non-farm employment opportunities are proposed to be created and at least equivalent number of people would be provided skill certification.

TABLE 22.20
Estimated Number of Workers (PS+SS in the age group of 15–59) by Level of Education by Sector (millions), 2009–10

	Agriculture and Allied	Manufacture	Non-Manufacture	Service	Total
Not Literate	87.36	9.56	14.42	13.65	124.99
Literate without formal schooling	1.23	0.25	0.21	0.42	2.11
Below primary + Primary	57.62	12.69	12.47	18.32	101.10
Middle	36.20	10.27	8.67	18.98	74.12
Secondary	21.30	7.02	4.27	18.21	50.79
Higher secondary	10.36	3.21	1.45	12.43	27.45
Diploma/certificate course	0.58	1.16	0.53	3.12	5.39
Graduate	3.84	3.01	1.25	17.82	25.93
Graduate and above	0.74	0.73	0.24	7.00	8.70
Total	**219.23**	**47.90**	**43.50**	**109.96**	**420.59**

Source: Computed from NSS (66th Round), 2009–10.

TABLE 22.21
Distribution of Formally and Informally Vocationally Trained Workers (PS+SS in the age group of 15–59) Within Primary, Secondary and Tertiary Sectors (%) in 2009–10

	Agriculture and Allied	Manufacture	Non-Manufacture	Service	Total
Receiving formal vocational training	18.7	16.6	5.5	59.2	100
Received vocational training: Formal	7.8	19.8	8.1	64.4	100
Received vocational training non-formal, of which:	31.9	35.0	11.0	39.7	100
Received vocational training non-formal: Hereditary	56.9	26.3	4.1	12.6	100
Received vocational training non-formal: Self-learning	26.4	33.5	9.2	30.8	100
Received vocational training non-formal: Learning on the Job	11.1	45.1	14.5	29.3	100
Received vocational training non-formal: others	22.0	33.6	7.0	37.4	100
Total	**26.8**	**31.4**	**8.7**	**33.1**	**100**

Source: Computed from NSS (66th Round), 2009–10.

The existing annual training capacity in the country is 4.5 million. It needs to be more than doubled to achieve the target.

AN OVERVIEW OF THE ELEVENTH PLAN

22.64. The Eleventh Five Year Plan while focusing on utilisation of the human resources for economic growth, recognised that skill building is not a static process and that individual's skills needs to be upgraded continuously for workforce to remain relevant and employable. To realise this Coordinated Action on Skill Development was initiated in 2008 which provides for a three tier governance structure, namely Prime Minister's Council on Skill Development as apex body for policy direction to be supported by National Skill Development Coordination Board (NSDCB) in Planning Commission for coordinating and synergising the efforts of the various central ministries that are involved in the skill development and National Skill Development Corporation for catalysing private sector efforts in the skill development. During the Eleventh Plan most of the states have set up state skill development missions for focused and synergised approach for scaling up of skill efforts in respective states. A National Policy on Skill Development was also formulated in 2009 which focuses on policy coherence, inclusivity, improving the quality with emphasis on employment outcomes. The government has, therefore, put in place a governance structure for implementation of skill initiatives at highest level and the policy for providing an enabling environment and framework to address the challenges of skill development.

National Policy on Skill Development, 2009

22.65. The National Policy on Skill Development Policy formulated in 2009 envisions empowering all individuals through improved skills, knowledge, and nationally and internationally recognised qualification to gain access to decent employment and ensure India's competitiveness in the global market. The Key Features of the Policy for addressing the challenges in the skill space are given in Box 22.2.

Expansion of Training Capacity—Industrial Training Institutes, Modular Employable Skills (Vocational Training Providers) and Polytechnics

22.66. The training infrastructure in terms of Government Industrial Training institutes as well as Industrial Training Centers run by private sector saw a significant increase to reach a level of 9,447 in the Eleventh Plan from about 5,114 in the beginning of the Plan. The seating capacity also increased to 13.35

Box 22.2
Skill Policy for Promoting India's Competitiveness in the Global Market

Objectives
- Expanding the outreach by adopting established and innovative approaches to ensure equitable access to training to all irrespective of any gender, regional, social and sectoral divide.
- Promoting greater and active involvement of all stakeholders including social partners and forging a strong, symbiotic, private-public partnership in skill development.
- Develop a high-quality demand driven skilled workforce/entrepreneur relevant to current and emerging employment market needs.
- Enable the establishment of flexible delivery mechanisms that respond to the characteristics of a wide range of needs of stakeholders.
- Enable effective coordination between different ministries, the Centre and the States and public and private providers.
- Creating institutional mechanism for reaserch, development, quality assurance, examination and certification, affiliation and accreditation and coordination of skill development across the country.

Coverage
The National Skill Policy aims at promoting the following forms of delivery of skills: institution-based skill development including ITIs/Private ITIs/vocational schools/technical schools/polytechnics/professional colleges; learning initiatives of sectoral skill development organised by different ministries/departments; formal and informal apprenticeships and other types of training by enterprises; training for self-employment/entrepreneurial development; adult learning, retraining of retired or retiring employees and lifelong learning; non-formal training including training by civil society organisations; and e-learning, web-based learning and distance learning.

Finance
All stakeholders, the Government both at Centre and States, the enterprise—public and private, and the direct beneficiary—the individual, would share the burden of mobilising financial or in-kind resources for skill development.

lakhs from 7.42 lakhs in 2007. However, the geographic distribution of ITIs/ITCs remained skewed with South and West Zones accounting for 67 per cent of private and government ITIs catering to 51 per cent of the population with 60 per cent of seating capacity and North and East Zones accounted for 33 per cent of ITIs catering to 49 per cent of population with 40 per cent of seating capacity. Even within each zone, there are significant state-wise variations.

22.67. With the objective of expanding the outreach of the training facilities to school dropouts/and recognising need for prior learning of workers in the unorganised sector, 'Modular Employable Skills (MES)' programme has been initiated by Ministry of Labour and Employment wherein short duration courses are provided to prospective trainees using both government and private infrastructure. 1,402 modules covering more than 60 sectors have been developed, 36 Assessing Bodies empanelled for conducting assessment, 6,951 Vocational Training Providers (VTPs) registered and more than 13.53 lakh persons have been trained/tested up to 31.3.2012.

22.68. In addition the quality of training at ITIs has been improved through up gradation and creation of Centers of Excellence by introducing multi-skilling courses. This is done under public-private-partnership in the form of Institute Management Committees (IMCs) with representatives from industries, government, and academic organisations who play a major in terms of providing practical training and identification of emerging skill demands in the local industry. An interest free loan is provided to the IMC with 10 year moratorium and repayable in annual equal instalments over 20 year period. The evaluation of such training institutes indicates improvement in physical infrastructure. However, the shortage of quality trainers remains a cause of concern which needs to be addressed urgently by up grading facilities at Model Industrial Training Institutes (MITIs) and also by capacity enhancement for Training of Trainers under Directorate General of Employment and Training (DGET).

22.69. The Courses in Polytechnics have been diversified to address skilled manpower demand of the service sector besides conventional subjects. Women's polytechnics continued to offer courses in garment technology, beauty culture, textile design with modern techniques. The number of polytechnics have increased to 1,914 during the year 2009–10. In addition under the Coordinated Action on Skill Development, Ministry of Human Resource Development has taken initiatives to set up 300 polytechnics through PPP by the State Governments/Union Territories in consultation with CII, FICCI, ASSOCHAM and PHD Chamber of Commerce and 400 additional Polytechnics by the private sector.

22.70. For an effective vocational education system, it is not only necessary to increase the training capacity, but also maintain a minimum standard of training. For a mandatory accreditation system, appropriate institutional structure has to be created. The details about the increase in the capacities, accreditation bodies for technical education and for universities and so on is given in Education chapter.

Apprenticeship Training Scheme (ATS)

22.71. The Apprentice Training Scheme is implemented by Ministries of Labour and Employment and Human Resource Development under the Apprentices Act, 1961. About 254 groups of industries are covered under the Act and about 27,000 establishments engage apprentices. DGE&T is responsible for implementation of the Act in respect of Trade Apprentices in the Central Government Undertakings and Departments. It is done through six Regional Directorates of Apprenticeship Training located at Kolkata, Mumbai, Chennai, Hyderabad, Kanpur and Faridabad. It covers 15–18 year olds, who have completed at least eight years of schooling. Department of Secondary Education in the Ministry of Human Resource Development is responsible for implementation of the Act in respect of Graduate, Technician and Technician (Vocational) Apprentices. This is done through four Boards of Apprenticeship Training located at Kanpur, Kolkata, Mumbai and Chennai and is targeted at 19 to 22 year olds who are certificate or diploma or degree holders in engineering and management. The scheme has a focus on manufacturing or non-manufacturing industry and within that also only the organised sector leaving the unorganised sector completely dependent on informal system of apprenticeship. The progress under the scheme is given in Table 22.22.

Vocationalisation of School Education

22.72. The vocational education was started in schools in 1985 but the progress under the scheme remained very slow as in the beginning of the Eleventh Plan only 3 per cent were enrolled in Vocational courses at the secondary level. The Department of Secondary Education has revamped its existing scheme of Vocationalisation of Secondary School Education in 2011 which envisages strengthening of 10,000 existing secondary schools with vocational stream and establishment of 100 new vocational schools through State Governments. The scheme envisages provision of assistance to run 500 vocational schools under PPP mode. There is a provision for in-service training of 7 days for 2,000

TABLE 22.22
Apprentices in India (Under the Apprenticeship Training Act, 1961)

Year	Trade Apprentices (Mole)			Graduate, Technician and Technician (Vocational) Apprentices (MHRD)		
	Seat Available in Lakhs	Seat Utilised in Lakhs	Per Cent Utilised	Seat Available in Lakhs	Seat Utilised in Lakhs	Per Cent Utilised
Upto March 2011	3.37	2.21	65.57	1.02	0.65	63.74

Source: Ministry of Labour and Employment.

existing vocational education teachers and induction training of 30 days for 1,000 new vocational education teachers. 250 competency based modules are proposed to be developed for each individual vocational course. The revision in curriculum is mandatory once in three years to ensure that the curriculum is guided by needs of the industry. A separate vocational cell has been established within the Central Board of Secondary Education. There is also provision for assistance to reputed NGOs to run short duration innovative vocational education programmes. All the components and activities would be guided by the National Skills Qualifications Framework (NSQF).

22.73. The approach so far has been to create stand-alone vocational education facilities. The need of the hour is that secondary schools in every panchayat can be used for vocational training outside the school hours. A formal system of vocational education certification needs to be evolved to certify students and youths to acquire skills through this method. This would require adequate and suitable infrastructure to impart the vocational training.

Promoting Public Private Partnerships

22.74. The Eleventh Plan has seen a paradigm shift in skill development strategy wherein Public Private Partnership model has been encouraged in the skill development. Besides involving private sector in upgrading the capacity in the existing institutions both at the ITI and Polytechnic level, an institutional structure in the form of National Skill Development Corporation (NSDC) has been put in place to catalyse the private sector efforts. The NSDC provides soft loans to the private partners for undertaking skill activity. NSDC works in around 365 districts in 28 states and 2 Union Territories in both organised as well unorganised sectors. NSDC along with its partners have trained over 1.8 lakh people in the year 2011–12 with an aggregate placement record of around 79 per cent.

22.75. To bring together all stakeholders, namely industry, training providers and the academia. NSDC has been catalysing the setting up of industry led Sectoral Skill Councils (SSCs) for identified priority sectors. Till March 2012, 11 such SSCs have been approved. These SSCs are expected to lay down the National Occupational Standards for different levels of jobs in their respective sectors, formulate certification and accreditation norms, strive to create knowledge repository on current requirement of skill development in the industry, assess the supply of skilled workers, identify the demand and supply gap in each sector, and identify trends and future requirements.

Training Programme for the Poor and Vulnerable

22.76. Ministry of Rural Development has launched schemes for empowering young people from poor and the weaker sections of the society by imparting skills and providing gainful employment including 'Special Projects for Placement Linked Skill Development of Rural BPL Youth' under Swarna Jayanti Gram Swarozgar Yojana (SGSY-SP) and RUDSETI for setting up a dedicated Skills development infrastructure in each district in the country aimed towards entrepreneurial development. The SGSY has been restructured and called NRLM/Aajeevika which focusses on harnessing the innate capabilities of the poor and complements them with capacities (information, knowledge, skills, tools, finance and collectivisation) to participate in the growing economy of the country. Ministry has also initiated Himayat, a placement linked skill development scheme for youth from Jammu and Kashmir. Himayat scheme will cover 1 lakh youth from J&K in the next 5 years and will be implemented through competent training providers, from the private sector and non-profit Organisations. The training providers for placement linked skill training will give a 75 per cent placement guarantee for the trained youth. Placement for youth will be provided all over the country, within J&K and outside. Under SII J&K Scheme, different training strategies will be used for diverse groups of youth—school dropouts, dropouts of XII class level, and those who have had college education. Ministry has also initiated Parvaaz—a pilot programme on 'Comprehensive Skills and Education Program for Rural BPL Minority Youth' with the objective of mainstream the minority BPL youth of the country by empowering them with education, skills and employment. This would help in bridging social divide.

Skill Development in the Unorganised/Informal Sector

22.77. As per 66th NSSO round 2009–2010, 84 per cent of the total workforce was in the unorganised sector and 93 per cent in informal employment (Table 22.5). The sector is heterogeneous which cut across all economic activities in rural and urban areas. It contributes about 60 per cent of the GDP. The unorganised sector is dominated by workers in micro enterprises, unpaid family members, casual labourers, home based workers, migrant labourers, out of school youth and in need of skills, farmers and artisans in rural areas. These groups form a bottom of skill pyramid who have low skills, poor productivity and low income.

22.78. The skill profile among this labour force in young group is distressing. The key issues of skill development in unorganised sector include inadequacy of current training programme to meet the requirement of large workforce in the informal sector. The formal training system because of its entry requirement and urban buyers needs does not offer skills to people with limited education and when it does, it is not appropriate to those in the rural non-farm sectors. Most workers continue to learn on the job informally at their place of work from other low skilled qualified people. The Modular Employable Skill Programme of the Ministry of Labour; STEP of Women and Child Development; Himayat, Parvaaz and NRLM of Ministry Rural Development; Community Polytechnic Development Programme of Human Resource Development and Programmes of the Ministry of Micro Small and Medium Enterprises are some of the programmes that are benefitting this segment of the workforce. However, given the scale of the problem much more needs to be done in terms of up scaling the training capacities, recognition of prior learning, functional literacy and so on.

22.79. Besides these initiatives, sectoral Ministries of Textiles, Woman and Child Development, Tourism, Health and Family Welfare, Agriculture, MSME, Urban Development and so on have also initiated large number of programmes to address the training requirement of their sectors and groups.

ISSUES AND PRIORITIES FOR THE TWELFTH PLAN

22.80. There is an urgent need to mainstream skill formation in the formal education system and at the same time innovative approaches for the skill creation outside the formal education system. Although the Coordinated Action on Skill Development has brought about a paradigm shift in addressing the issues of relevance in skill development, the gaps in the skill development are to be identified so as to achieve the objectives in terms of quantity, quality, outreach and mobility while building on the foundation. The workforce not only needs to be trained to meet the requirement of all sectors and all kinds of jobs but also linking them to job opportunities and market realities. This would facilitate transformation of young population into a productive workforce engaged in economic activities and not unproductive activity. Some of the areas that merit attention are:

- Since over 90 per cent of India's labour force is engaged in the non-formal sector, the most important challenge would be to reach out to this sector. An approach would need to be worked out to cater to the skilling needs of this very large section of workforce. Innovative approaches of working through grass-root level organisations such as panchayati raj bodies would need to be considered.
- Putting in place a National Skills Qualification Framework which lays down different level of skills required by industry, which allows multiple points of entry and exit, which recognises prior learning, and which allows for mobility across different levels, as well as between vocational and technical training on the one hand, and general education on the other.
- To put in place a permanent institutional framework, entrusted with the requisite authority and resources, and which is responsible solely for skill development in the country.
- Students belonging to the economically weaker sections need to be supported in terms of access to bank loans on soft terms that are linked to their

placement as is the case in the higher education loans.
- To increase the training capacity in the country by adopting myriad approaches—such as facilitating capacity creation in public private partnerships as being done by NSDC, allowing available government infrastructure to be used for training by both the public and private sector, running training institutions in multiple shifts, increasing the number of trainers by adding to Teachers' Training capacity in the country, and by making it attractive for qualified persons to opt for becoming trainers. As part of this approach, the possibility of using the infrastructure, equipment and manpower of sick public sector units would also be explored.
- Further building on the potential of the Modular Employable Skill Programme by ensuring that combination of modules sufficient to guarantee employability are delivered to the trainees introducing more course modules and strengthening of assessment and certification systems for quick delivery.
- Developing a cogent and sustainable approach to provide for industry participation in skill development, particularly in the field of developing course content which is aligned to industry requirements. Similarly, accreditation and certification standards to be developed with industry's active participation through the medium of Sector Skill Councils.
- Developing the Labour Market Information System for real time information on sectoral basis to help trainees and make training relevant.
- Making necessary changes to the regulatory framework governing the employment of apprentices so that this avenue is able to contribute significantly to the skill development effort in the country. To achieve this, industry needs to be made an active partner, and a collaborative approach with industry would be adopted. Such an approach would permit using the potential offered by MSME units also. Through the use of policy and other tools, to encourage the creation of training capacity in a manner that dovetails with the population and sectoral requirements. The current lop-sided geographical distribution of training facilities and the concentration of training facilities in only a few sectors would be corrected so that training capacity is created in the areas of high population and in sectors which have been identified to offer skill gaps.
- Making Skills aspirational among youth, through advocacy campaigns aimed at social change. These efforts would be complemented by necessary changes in the regulatory framework to make it economically rewarding for persons to become skilled—such as through providing sufficient differential in the minimum wages for unskilled, semi-skilled and skilled workers.

22.81. The aim should be to increase the percentage of the workforce which has received formal skills through vocational education and training from 10.0 per cent at present to 25.0 per cent by the end of the Twelfth Plan. This would mean substantial increase in the skill training capacity in the next five years.

22.82. The approach to the Twelfth Five Year Plan has identified Priority sectors for employment generation and skill development (see Box 22.3 below).

22.83. The key challenges/areas requiring attention are discussed below.

Quality, Quantity, Equity and Systemic Reforms

22.84. The priorities/challenges in Skill Development and Training as indicated in the foregoing paragraphs can be grouped under the following: (*i*) quality and relevance, (*ii*) quantity, (*iii*) expansion of outreach and equity, and (*iv*) systemic reforms.

Quality Issues

22.85. Quality Issues: Quality and relevance of skill development are key to India's global competitiveness as well as improving an individual's access to decent employment. To increase the relevance with future labour market including promotion of self-employment, soft skills and entrepreneurship skills need to be made integral parts of skill development.

> **Box 22.3**
> **Priority Sectors Identified in the Twelfth Plan**
>
> Sectors that will create large employment; Textiles and Garments, Leather and Footwear, Gems and Jewellery, Food Processing Industries, Handlooms and Handicrafts.
>
> Sectors that will deepen technology capabilities in Manufacturing: Machine Tools, IT Hardware and Electronics.
>
> Sectors that will provide Strategic Security: Telecommunications equipment, Aerospace Shipping, Defence Equipment,
>
> Manufacturing Technology Sectors for Energy Security: Solar Energy, Clean Coal Technologies, Nuclear power generation,
>
> Capital equipment for India's Infrastructure Growth: Heavy electrical equipment, Heavy transport, earth moving and mining equipment
>
> Sectors where India has competitive advantage: Automotive Sectors, Pharmaceutical and Medical Equipment,
>
> Micro Small and Medium Enterprises Sector: The base for the Manufacturing Sector— employment and enterprise generation
>
> *Source:* Draft Approach Paper for Twelfth Five Year Plan.

22.86. Mismatch in demand and supply: The second major issue in skill development is mismatch between the demand and supply of skills. The problem has arisen due to supply driven skill delivery system. Presently the labour market is facing a strange situation, where on the one hand, an employer does not get manpower with requisite skills and on the other, millions of job seekers do not get employment. Such a mismatch compromises potential economic development. This requires:

- Establishing a mechanism for providing access to information on skill inventory and skill map on real time basis.
- National Qualification Framework to ensure both vertical and horizontal mobility and clarity of career choices, options and acceptability of the qualifications.
- Building skills training as a mainstream and inclusive programme to be promoted by creating a formal arrangement among the three key stakeholders in the delivery process: Government, Industry and Skills providers.
- Focus on International Collaborations to have better understanding of the fast changing skills demands and provide skills solutions that transpose the models and practices and Reverse transfer the best practices from India to world.

22.87. Industry participation and Setting up of Sector Skills Council: In order to make the skill development system relevant and driven by labour market signals, it is necessary to increase participation of industries through Sector Skill Councils. Functions of SSCs could include inter alia, identification of skill gaps, preparation of Skill Development Plans and establishment of well-structured sector specific Labour Market Information System to assist planning and delivery of training.

Quantity Issues

22.88. Limited capacity: The first major roadblock in expanding the outreach is our limited capacity to absorb all those joining the Labour Market. As per Twelfth Plan projections about 25 million new entrants would join the labour force in the next 5 years.

22.89. Shortage of Trainers: Training of trainers is a key component of the skill development. There is an acute shortage of trainers not only in the existing trades but also in the proposed new trades. There is an urgent need for improving the quality and size of trainer resource. Skill up-gradation of trainers, their quality assurance, and improvement of their status in society are important to improve the quality of training. It is the pedagogical expertise of the trainer which ensures that the learner gets a wholesome experience, understands the standards and is fully equipped to apply the concepts learnt during his employment. The Training of Trainers hence becomes a major challenge. As per the NSDC report on Education sector there is an incremental requirement of 86,64,000 teachers and trainers between 2008 and 2022. This fund support should not only allow the State Governments to retain the trainers for the schools and other institutions but also invite participation of many more people into the training industry.

Expansion of Outreach and Equity

22.90. India's large geographical territory comprising of 6,38,365 villages, 4,378 towns in 35 states/UTs and 640 districts with difficult terrain and varying socio-economic conditions make the implementation of standardised skill-training a huge challenge. 11 most populous States like Bihar, (with a population greater than that of Germany), Jharkhand, Uttar Pradesh, Chattisgarh comprising 80 per cent of India's population with little access to skills training and need to be taken up on priority. About 90 per cent of the 15–59 year olds have had no vocational training. Of the 10 per cent who received vocational training, only 2 per cent received formal vocational training. Therefore, access to skills programmes is a major challenge. Moreover, many emerging fields are coming up for which vocational training is needed (such as Nano Technology, Green Initiatives, and so on) so as to maintain relevance with recent changes. The need is to implement the customised training depending on the geographical differences, capacities of the local people and requirement of the industry. Providing opportunities of skill development to all sections of society irrespective of any economic, social, regional, gender, spatial and sectoral divide is necessary to achieve faster and inclusive growth and for development of a just and equitable society.

Systemic Reforms

22.91. National Skills Qualifications Framework: Currently there is no system in place which provides a framework to whole skill development and training sphere. There are no standards set in many areas creating problems for all the stakeholders. It is therefore needed to implement and run NSQF effectively.

22.92. Labour Market Information System: Dynamic and relevant inputs are important for taking informed decisions. Presently, there is no system where the stakeholders of employment and training, namely Government, Industry, Job seekers, private vocational training setups and so on can stream relevant information on a common ICT platform and benefit there from.

22.93. Testing Bodies: The number of Industrial Training Institutes (ITIs) and Polytechnics have increased significantly over the past years. Also, with the introduction of modular pattern of training, the number of examinations conducted has also increased. All these activities have increased the volume of the work involved, resulting in delay in certification. The successful trainees have to wait for months to obtain the certificates. The assessment and certification bodies could be separated for facilitating early employment outcomes.

LEARNING FROM OTHER COUNTRIES

22.94. As noted above, skill devlopment and vocational education is a critical area of concern in the Indian context. As far as enrolment in vocational education and training courses is concerned, India has net enrolment of 3.5 million per year, as compared to 90 million in China and 11 million in US. India can learn from the strengths of the vocational education and training systems of other countries, namely, active participation of industry and employers to map current and future skill needs; sharing of work benches by the Industry; creation of asset bank of infrastructure to be used both by the private and the public sector; capacity to effectively train its large young population in Apprenticeship programme through use of MSME clusters; Training of Trainers including testing and certification of vocational teachers may be adopted; Incentives for Industry in terms of tax exemptions in lieu of training and extensive use of ICT.

LEARNING FROM DIFFERENT STATES INITIATIVES

22.95. The skill development has been a priority area for government at the State level as well. The States are implementing Central as well as their own schemes which take into account the State issues. Some of the good practices in terms of Skill Voucher, multi skill development centres, addressing needs of non literates and dropouts and so on are addressing different challenges, namely expanding outreach, improving quality, ensuring mobility and flexibility can be replicated and scaled up to address the issues at national level. The key learning's from different States best practices are:

1. Emphasis on outcome and not infrastructure.
2. Government should ensure level playing field for private providers vis a vis public institutions.
3. Provide flexible schedule and multi skilling at own time.
4. Success through innovation in training and development.
5. Continuous linkage with industry.
6. Encourage Public Private Partnerships.
7. Enhance choice for trainees.
8. Create awareness among the prospective trainee and employers.

A ROADMAP FOR THE TWELFTH FIVE YEAR PLAN

22.96. It emerges from above that at present there is low penetration of vocational education and training in India and skills are yet to become aspirational among the youth. In order to realise the vision of the PM Council on Skill Development the need of the hour is to formulate appropriate policies and Programmes that lead to scaling up of skill efforts; improve quality and relevance of vocational education through active industry involvement; Promote Public Private Partnership in skill development; facilitate mobility between general and vocational stream; and creation of credible certification and assessment system with industry participation. The success of skill initiatives depends on creation of awareness among youth and adequate availability of financial resources.

22.97. In order to address the issues relating to quantity and quality improvement; expansion of outreach and equity and systemic and institutional reforms a time bound action plan in terms of well-defined implementation and operational strategies with focus on the delivery of the skill is the need of the hour. The key strategies that need to be followed are given in the Box 22.4.

Permanent Institutional Structure for Driving the Skill Development Agenda

22.98. There is need for an overarching institutional structure that has the authority and responsibility to coordinate the skill development activities of all the other agencies engaged in the same—both at the central and state levels, and to also engage with non-government players, including the corporate and NGO sectors. Accordingly, setting up of a National Skill Development Authority is being considered. The proposed Authority may discharge the functions outlined in Box 22.5.

National Skill Qualification Framework (NSQF)

22.99. The national policy on skill development mandates the necessity of qualification framework to address inter-alia the issues of the fragmentation in the skill system both at the central and the state level; lack of uniformity in nomenclature of courses, duration, curriculum design, content and examination system of various Technical Vocational Education & Training (TVET) courses alongwith recognition of prior learning; easy entry and exit for students between vocational and general education stream as well as to progression in vocational education like in the general education and facilitate mobility between programmes and institutions across the country. The system of multi-entry and multi-exit will enable students to acquire some skills after finishing compulsory general schooling, then enter the labour market and gain some work experience and return to the Vocational Education and Training system to continue their vocational education/training. The system would facilitate credit accumulation and transfer which would convert all forms of learning in higher certificate/diploma and degree. It would be particularly beneficial for relatively poor students, since it would enable them to continue in either the vocational education stream of the secondary system or the ITI system, rather than dropping out from the educational or vocational training space altogether.

22.100. It would facilitate the training system to be in sync with Industry demand and recognition of prior learning. The certification of prior learnt skills would improve the employability and raise the income and also dignity of such skilled workers.

Box 22.4
Strategies for Expanding and Scaling up the Skill Development in Twelfth Plan

Implementation Strategies:

- Expanding outreach to bridge all divides;
- Improving quality through better infrastructure, new machines and technology and trainers;
- Defining standards for outcome driven training programme and regular monitoring;
- Introducing flexibility by adopting global standards and dynamic processes to suit the requirement of both national and international users;
- Developing strong partnerships between all stake holders, encouraging private partners through incentives;
- Creating enabling environment and Monitoring the training Programme to achieve outcomes.

Operational Strategies:

- Replicability and scalability; Strengthening existing centers;
- Linking training with Outcome;
- Affordability across economic levels;
- Stress on Inclusivity and Technology and innovation;
- Flexibility in course content; Qualification standards; Quality trainers; and
- Focus on delivery.

Box 22.5
Major Functions of Proposed National Skill Development Authority

1. To launch a National Skill Development Mission to, inter alia, skill 5 crore persons during the Twelfth Plan through appropriate strategies, including support to State Governments/State Skill Missions, and for active engagement with the private sector, NGOs and so on.
2. To lay down strategies, financing and governance models to expedite skill development activities and coordinate standards of skill development working in close coordination with regulators concerned like NCVT, AICTE, Sector Skill Councils, and so on.
3. To assist Central Ministries in enhancing their skill development capacities.
4. To act as a nodal agency for guiding State Skill Development Missions and providing funds to them to increase level of skill development activities.
5. To act as the nodal agency for the launch and operations of National Skills Qualifications Framework (NSQF) and keeping the NSQF constantly updated and ensuring its implementation of the same.
6. To monitor, evaluate and analyse the outcomes of various schemes and programmes relating to skill development through a technology-enabled national monitoring system, and suggest/initiate mid-course corrections, additions and closure of parts or whole of any particular programme/scheme.
7. Promote greater use of Technology in the area of Skill Development.
8. To oversee the advocacy campaign to ensure that aspirational aspect and enrolment in skill development programmes continue to rise.
9. To advise as well as take required measures in various matters related to skill development like training of trainers, apprenticeship training, assessment, accreditation, certification systems and national occupational standards and so on.
10. Discharge any other functions and assume any other responsibility related to skill development as may be assigned to it by the Government of India.
11. Overseeing and supporting the on-going skill development efforts of Central and State/UTs Ministries and Departments and ensure that the estimated training target of 5 crore during the Twelfth Plan is achieved.

The assessment of competency and certification will enable informally trained workers currently in the workforce to either continue to acquire further certificates by entering the VET system, or alternatively, returning to the labour market with such recognition and certification. To conclude, the NSQF would address the issue of mobility both vertical and horizontal by establishing the equivalence in general and vocational education; reflect the labour market requirement for skill training through involvement of industry in curriculum development, certification and so on; encourage multi entry and multi exit and recognition of prior learning.

Skilling Workers in the Unorganised/Informal Sector

22.101. As indicated in para 22.77, 84 per cent of the workers are employed in the unorganised sector and 93 per cent are engaged in informal employment. Although different Ministries/Departments have taken initiatives however, the scale of problem in the heterogeneous sector dominated by workers in the micro enterprises, unpaid family members, farmers, artisans, out of school youths, casual, migrant and home based workers is huge and requires more concerted effort to improve their skills. It is estimated that there are about 7,000 clusters in the country of which more than 6,000 are classified as micro enterprise clusters and around 650 are manufacturing clusters. The skill up gradation can be undertaken in clusters which are providing informal employment. The Ministry of Micro, Small and Medium Enterprises is operating schemes to develop such clusters to become globally competitive as well as to develop entrepreneurs. There is need to adopt the district level programme with the clusters. The skill development in the unorganised sectors requires more. There are 2.6 crore MSMEs in the country which are providing employment to 6 crore persons and manufacture more than 6,000 products. It contributes about 45 per cent of the total manufacturing output, 40 per cent share in the exports and contributes 8 per cent to the GDP.

22.102. To promote skill development in unorganised sector following issues need to be addressed:

a) To upscale the training capacities from the present capacity of training,
b) Skill up-gradation and certification,
c) Recognition of prior learning,
d) Spreading skill development activities throughout the country, particularly in the backward areas and the areas affected by extremism and reach the weaker sections of the society through setting up of Skill Development Centres (SDCs),
e) Provision of literacy and basic education,
f) Replication of successful models,
g) Provision of mobile training vans for larger out reach,
h) Each MSME cluster can act a centre for apprenticeship training,
i) Developing an eco-system for improvement in the success rate of training in self-employment or job employment through the process of Train—Loan-Link—Support,
j) Developing a pool of certified trainers with adequate technical competency, and
k) Developing a transparent system for conduct of the programmes, registration of participants and so on and putting it in the public domain.

Fostering Public Private Partnerships

22.103. Governments have taken number of steps to catalyse the involvement of private sector in the skill development efforts which range from setting up of institutional framework of NSDC, setting up Industrial Management Committees for up gradation of infrastructure, adoption of institutes by industrial houses and so on. However, given the scale of the challenge to train 500 million skilled manpower by 2022, there is need for greater participation on the part of private sector both in terms of technology transfer and actual training both trainees and trainers. This may involve extension of financial support to the private industrial training institutions in modernisation of their infrastructure and expansion. The industries need to be involved in curriculum design to make it more relevant and also in assessment and certification. Permitting the private sector to use the unutilised/under-utilised capacity created within the government system would be another cost-effective way to foster the PPP approach. The NGOs can be effective partner for reaching out effectively in the remote and difficult areas.

Strengthening and Revamping the Institutional Structure

22.104. The introduction of skill framework would require re-engineering of existing institutions and the building of new ones. There is need for a permanent institutional structure as indicated in Para 22.98 which can act as focal point for coordinating the efforts of different Central Ministries/Departments and state governments in the field of skill development. The proposed new Authority would be responsible for policy formulation, assisting the skill development mission in capacity enhancement and promoting NGOs and Private sector involvement in the skill development.

22.105. Another critical set of new institutions that have to be built are the Sector Skill Councils. For identifying skills availability and for scaling up skill development efforts in different sectors. The Sector Skill Councils can act as a crucial means to promote industry ownership and acceptance of skill development standards. The role of existing institutions such as the National Council of Vocational Training (NCVT, currently part of the MoLE's Directorate-General of Employment and Training); the establishment of new Regional Directorates of Apprenticeship Training; expanding capacity for instructor training; and so on, need to be reviewed.

22.106. The National Policy on Skill Development has envisaged re-engineering of National Council of Vocational Training (NCVT) to play a greater role in the field of skill development. Presently NCVT is the apex advisory body looking after various functions like trade testing and certification, prescribing standards in respect of syllabi and so on for training provided by the ITIs (Government and Private). The NCVT needs to be given autonomy with its own secretariat through a bill in the Parliament. The Ministry of Labour and Employment has already initiated a process to this effect in the Eleventh Plan.

22.107. In addition there is need to have additional Trade Testing Capacity an independent—National Board of Trade Testing & Certification (NBTTC), to avoid inordinate delay in issuance of certificates to the students for speedy employment. This centre needs to be independent of the delivery system making assessment more relevant, transparent and swift. The center would design and conduct all India Trade Tests; after evaluation entered the results into the centralised 'Trade Testing Certification' system which would be developed by the NBTTC and accessible through intranet/VPN based internet by each centre. The NBTTC would ensure issuance of provisional certificate by the centre (Generated online by TTC system) to the candidate, printing of trade certificate by NBTTC and sending the same by courier in a pre-defined service level agreement with a logistics partner and provision of an electronic certificate and giving legal sanctity to it.

Expanding the Out Reach to Under-served Areas and North Eastern States through PPP

22.108. There is need to set up ITIs and Skill development centers in the under-served Blocks of the country. MOLE is proposing to set up these institutions under PPP mode in the Kaushal Vikas Yojana. The scheme when implemented would create 3,000 ITIs and 5,000 Skill Development Centers in the country. This would take skill development to the doorstep of the rural population. Skill Development Centers would provide training on short term modular basis course certification system. In addition women skill development would also be promoted through opening of new Regional Vocational Training Institutes which would enable them to earn decent employment and gain economic independence. There is also need to set up training institutes in SC/ST, minority and weaker section of the society dominated areas to facilitate their participation in skill development for enhancing their employability.

22.109. Youth from low-income families in rural and semi-urban areas are unable to access vocational training as they cannot afford to pay the fees normally charged by training institutes located primarily in urban centres. The existing framework, in both public and private sectors, currently provides formal skill development opportunities to about 1.4 million persons annually, which is far less than the projected requirement. Since the current policy and regulatory framework will not be able to attract the required investment into this sector, there is an urgent need to create an enabling framework that would attract private participation through Public Private Partnership (PPP).

22.110. As part of the Government's initiative to augment the programmes for skill development, the Prime Minister had announced setting up of 1,500 ITIs through Public Private Partnership (PPP) during the

Eleventh Plan. The scheme could not be launched in the Eleventh Plan and it is now proposed to take up 3,000 ITIs during the Twelfth Plan in blocks which are unserved, that is, no government approved ITI is operating in such blocks. For this purpose, the Central Government has prepared a scheme for private participation in ITIs under the Kaushal Vikas Yojana (KVY). The objective of the scheme is to set up 3,000 ITIs through (PPP) for skill development of about 30 lakh youth, of which 15 lakh would be from socially and economically disadvantaged categories.

22.111. This scheme aims at optimising on the respective strengths of the public and private sector entities engaged in skill development. Mobilising the requisite investments, setting up first-rate ITIs, ensuring efficiency in operations and management, and enabling post-training employment will be the primary responsibilities of private sector entities while the Government will provide the enabling framework and the requisite financial support especially in respect of students from socially and economically less privileged families. The proposed model would accelerate this much needed skill development programme and not only provide gainful opportunities to a large number of aspiring youth, but also meet the growing deficit of skilled personnel.

22.112. There is need to enhance the training infrastructure in the North East also to enhance employability and competencies and promotion of self-employment and entrepreneurship amongst youth. The existing programmes of MoLE and Ministry of DONER needs to be strengthened. Ministry of Labour and Employment proposes to initiate schemes to cater to this requirement.

Training of Trainers

22.113. The demand for trained instructors is huge as compared with the capacity of instructor training of DGE&T field institutes. Presently, the gross requirement of instructors is 79,000. The additional requirement of instructor per annum is about 20,000 whereas the present instructor training capacity of about 2,000 per annum which is inadequate to meet the demand. There is huge gap and in many institutes there are 60 to 70 per cent vacancies which would be a serious bottleneck in enhancing skill development target. To address this problem, the facilities of Model ITIs are proposed to be upgraded. This initiative would add further capacity to bridge the gap between the demand and the existing infrastructure in place. The output from such an initiative would be 1,200 trained instructors per year at the rate of 300 trained instructors/MITI every year. As of now there are 4 MITI. There is need for a setting up of dedicated trainers skill institute.

22.114. In addition the industry may be involved in training the trainers. This can be done through various fellowship programmes, industry exposure to faculty to match the emerging needs of the economy, flexible teaching and cross movement of faculty to industry and industry personnel to institutions to enhance quality of teaching learning process; active participation of industry in training programmes conducted in ITIs and other technical institutions; encouraging employment of retired trained manpower from the defense forces, employ skilled workers from the industry and also retired instructors. In addition there is need to strengthen the capacities of the line ministries and institutes involved in curriculum development.

Reforming the Apprenticeship System

22.115. The Apprenticeship system is in need of major reform in terms of enhancement in both physical and human infrastructure. There is a need to develop a centralised institutional mechanism at the RDATs and a matching Web Portal at the district/state/national level with transparency in the process of filing applications for apprentice training. The web-based Portal would enable the employers to publish their trade-wise requirements of apprentices and facilitate apprentices to apply online. These processes may be facilitated by the LMIS. The MoLE is proposing the Amendment in the Apprenticeship Act, 1961. The norms relating to engagement of skilled workers as apprentices under the Apprenticeship Act 1961 need to be made flexible. The stipend paid may be enhanced linked to minimum wages for the trade at the state level. Industry should be free to pay higher stipend to apprentices if it feels so. Given the need to train larger numbers as apprentices for eventual employment. The MSME may explore the avenues for engaging apprentices. Further modular courses can be brought under the purview of the Apprenticeship Act.

Credible Assessment and Certification System

22.116. Certification and assessment are one of the key drivers leading to quality assurance and enhanced employability which would result in industry engagement. Certification and assessment as a procedure and as an outcome are key aspects for collaboration.

Labour Market Information System (LMIS)

22.117. Currently there is no common platform where industry, job seekers and government can share information and take informed decisions. Prospective employees may acquire skills which have little or no demand or may take a career path which has little relevance in the market. The government does not have reliable data source of industry demand/available skills and the labour market conditions with the result effective policy decisions impacting training and enhancing employment potential of youth cannot be taken. This situation is disappointing for both prospective employers and employees resulting in job mismatch and low and inferior quality output. This necessitates the implementation of a Labour Market Information System (LMIS) which would pave the way for a shared platform providing quantitative and qualitative information and intelligence on the labour market to all the stakeholders for making informed plans, choices, and decisions related to their business requirements, career planning, education and training programmes, job search, recruitment, labour policies and workforce investment strategies. LMIS would facilitate formulation of effective policies for filling the skills gap; evaluating results of labour related policies and programmes; providing key indicators on demand and supply labour. It would assist the job seekers take informed decisions about their future career development by providing information on the needs of the labour market; identify current and future job market opportunities; provide analysis of the labour market based on the economic development and also enable employers take decisions about upgrading their employees' skills; access information on skills available in the labour market; different labour characteristics such as labour policies, labour costs and so on.

Making Skills Aspirational through Advocacy

22.118. There is great need of attaching prestige to Vocational Training and make it aspirational in the society. To improve the social acceptability, intensive awareness generation is necessary. At present there is lack of awareness about the type of courses, trades and institutions both Government and private and also about opportunities in the field of vocational education and training. The awareness generation requires sensitisation through various audio visual media, skill fair and competitions at District, State and National Level; public campaign about the significance of the vocational training in enhancing the employability for decent jobs and so on.

22.119. The information can be created and spread through key locations/centers where it is conveniently accessible to the target group. In addition to being repository of information these centers can also act as training/testing centers. Universities can facilitate creating a brand value of vocational education and training by setting up skill development centers with a good degree of autonomy.

22.120. The NSQF would also go a long way to attract students to vocational courses for better career prospects than going to a general education system. At present different ministries/departments are creating awareness generation through different medias but in a very limited way. The NSDC is doing advocacy to popularise vocational education and training in the country in a focused manner. The details of the skill development initiatives at the secondary school and higher education are discussed in the respective chapters in the Plan document.

FINANCING SKILL DEVELOPMENT

22.121. In India, currently the training programmes both at the Central and the State level are funded from the plan budget. However, the challenge of skilling the youth bulge requires a paradigm shift in the financing pattern of vocational training and skill development involving innovative solutions. Financing of the skill development involves both mobilisation of resources and allocating the same. The financing should involve public, private and PPP mode. A successful financing model for vocational education and training depends on factors such as demand driven skill system; sustainable funds; transparent and outcome based fund allocation; competition for funds among training providers and so on. This can be done when the ad-hoc allocation of funds is stopped and institutions are provided funds for training based on some transparent guidelines both at central and state level requiring placement as an end result (that is, as in the NSDC funding model). Creation of training funds are an increasingly common vehicle for financing training in many countries worldwide A typology of funds for training based on the purpose is given in Table 22.23.

22.122. The strategy for financing the skill development requires addressing both the aspects of financing, namely resource mobilisation and allocation of resources. The resource mobilisation requires that all the stakeholders, namely Government, students and employers share the burden. While government provides funds through budget, there is role for greater involvement of employers and students in the financing of the training. However, this will happen only if the outcomes of the training are improved in terms of availability of right skilled workers to employers and decent employment to skilled youth. As regards students sharing the cost of training it may be indicated that governmentt can offset the adverse impact on the poor students by providing the scholarships/loan on easy terms. In fact large number of Central Ministries/Departments and State governments are providing scholarships to students of poor and marginalised sections of the society. The private sector needs to take greater responsibility for skill development. In India, the employers do bear the cost through their own in-service training but the results are not very encouraging. Box 22.6 gives details of successful financing innovation in number of countries.

22.123. The experiences of other countries in terms of innovative financing solutions such as tax deductions; levy grant system; training funds; skill vouchers need to be considered. Across the globe and many of the South Asian and East Asian Countries, National Training Funds (NTFs) or Skill Development fund (Singapore) or Human Resource Development Fund in Malaysia levy reimbursement scheme have been created for financing training. The Training Fund provides an institutional framework for collecting and allocating funds to training providers. The fund has been responsible for massive growth in the training. The fund unifies and augments public funding and allocate resources in line with national priorities. The training funds need to be sustainable and used to provide budgets to institutions training for workers for the formal sector, incentives to formal sector enterprises to train their workers through some kind of levy grant scheme, training courses for the unemployed and the disadvantaged groups, training for micro enterprises and the informal sector.

22.124. As indicated above in India most of the training is funded by the public resources although in the Eleventh Plan, National Skill development

TABLE 22.23
A Typology of Training Funds

Type	Main Purpose	Financing Sources
Pre-employment Training Fund	Finance the expansion and delivery of initial training before employment	Payroll levy—revenue generating
Enterprise Training Fund	Provide incentives to increase in-service training of workers within enterprises	Payroll levy—incentive schemes
Equity Training Fund	Increase opportunities for skills acquisition by disadvantaged groups not covered by enterprise schemes	Public subsidy, levy or donors

Source: Johanson, R. (2009), A Review of National Training Funds—SP Discussion Paper No. 0922, World Bank, November 2009 (page 6).

> **Box 22.6**
> **Good Performers in Financing—Chile, Australia, South Africa, Singapore**
>
> - Tax Deductions and Credits (encourages private spending)
> - Performance budgeting for the public sector (encourages good use of public expenditure, focus on outcomes in financing formulas)
> - Vouchers and learning accounts (targeting special groups, use in lifelong learning, empowers demand side of market)
> - Training funds and competitive procurement (promotes competition, targets marginalised group)
> - Levy grant systems (promotes in service training, encourages enterprises to train, free-rider problem)
>
> *Source:* Arvil Van Adams, 2012.

Corporation has been set up to mobilise the efforts of the private sector and raise funds through private participation, multilateral and bilateral institutions. The scale of challenge of skill development requires huge resources and innovative ways to mobilise resources and allocate them in an efficient manner. Some of the innovative financing strategies that can be used for meeting the skill challenge are:

- A training fund for the mobilisation and allocation of resources can be set up by the appropriate authority. In South Asian countries the funds are mobilised through either payroll or Tax levies. To begin with the levies could be collected from medium and large enterprises in the organised sectors as it would be difficult to collect levies from highly fragmented widely spread unorganised sector. Both Organised and the Unorganised sector enterprises should be entitled to draw on the fund. But the exact share needs to be worked out through a process of consultation of stake-holders, so that organised sector enterprises feel that they have a stake in the system, while at the same time equity considerations are taken into account in deciding on disbursement of funds. In addition the resources can be allocated based on performance of institutions in either the public or private sector.
- There is need for India to adopt both revenue-raising and levy disbursement schemes. Given the wide variety of enterprises in terms of size, and in the form of organised/unorganised segments, it would be wise to adopt a variety of modalities to raise revenues. Exactly which modalities should be adopted for which segments of enterprises should be a matter of discussion between relevant stake-holders. For instance, while a combination of revenue raising and levy disbursement schemes may be applied to the large public enterprises, the medium enterprises may be encouraged to adopt levy disbursement schemes for provision of in service training.
- There should be considerable scope for demand side financing of training through payment of stipend. Training provision in India has historically been supply-driven while the demand for skills has been neglected. There is a very strong case for using training levy funds for financing students from poor backgrounds who are unable to bear the opportunity cost of undertaking training before entering the labour market. Students must earn in order to survive, and cannot 'afford' to be trained. If trainees are provided a stipend, it would partially offset the opportunity cost of not working, and the cost of training fees (Box 22.7).
- Schemes of demand side financing could be encouraged to pay for in service training. This would encourage not only the trainees to come forward and obtain training in various industries, but would also encourage companies to come forward and participate in such scheme so as to get labour paid by the fund directly. The key defining feature of a demand side subsidy is a direct link between the intended beneficiary, the subsidy and the desired output, that is, training in this case. Different techniques which could be used to fulfill these are stipend, targeted bursaries and vouchers. The skill vouchers allow the trainees to purchase their own training which can help to build the

> **Box 22.7**
> **Equity Implications of User Fees**
>
> The positive financial benefits from cost-recovery through user fees need to be weighed against the potentially adverse effects on equity. Here the tradeoff is clear. Higher, realistic fees may exclude from training those who cannot afford to pay, while low fees may not contribute enough for the provider to recover costs. Negative impacts on access to training opportunities for the poor, minorities, rural populations, and other disadvantaged groups are likely to ensue. Governments can offset the adverse impact of fees on equity by using some of the savings realised from fee income to provide targeted scholarships to low income groups. Theoretically, at least, increased fees could lead to increased equity of access because with the savings the government can afford to finance the enrollment of more low-income students. This, of course, presupposes that the relatively well-off students are willing to pay fees—they will only do so if they perceive the quality of education being provided is good and that they are likely to find employment after graduation. The equity implications of charging fees underscore the widely recognised need to introduce subsidies targeted to at-risk groups, in the form of scholarships and fee discounts. The challenge will lie in developing appropriate mechanisms which will effectively target the poor.
>
> *Source:* Johanson, R. and Adams A.V. (2004), Skills Development in Sub-Saharan Africa, cited in Skill Development in India—The Vocational Education & Training System, World Bank, January 2006 (page 74).

demand side of the training. They can stimulate competition among the training providers. The key element is competition for the funds.

- Incentivising institutions to generate income from the sale of products and service activities of trainees and to retain it for meeting the operating costs. As per estimates of DGET, 64 per cent of ITIs have started revenue generation activities. This needs to be institutionalised. This would not only facilitate generation of additional resources but would also give exposure to local market and help in market oriented training. This requires change in the training fee policy so that the funds becomes part of the institution's budget and does not flow back to the government revenues.
- A number of possibilities exist today to enhance financing for skill development. First, the Union government collects a cess upon construction companies with projects of value above a certain threshold. This Construction Workers Cess Fund has accumulated many thousands of crores, which have been lying unutilised for years. Part of these funds could be used for skilling construction workers, who are in the industry which has been expanding employment the fastest in any Indian industry in the last 10 years (as discussed earlier).
- In order to shift away from the existing practice of providing only plan funds for the training, the Indian Banks' Association (IBA) is working on vocational education loan scheme that would provide an impetus to the country's skill mission, part of a thrust to improve the efficiency of the labour force and boost the economy. The scheme will help not just students but also skill providers complaining of low enrolment due to financial reasons. No collateral security is contemplated and the interest rate would be linked to the base rate of banks. Simple interest will be charged during the study period and up to the commencement of repayment. The repayment schedule is proposed to be dependent on duration of a course. The skill loan amount may be in the range of ₹20,000 to ₹1.5 lakh. The modalities are being worked out between the NSDC and the IBA. A universal vocational loan scheme is expected to increase financial accessibility for poor students. Gujarat is experimenting with the Skill voucher scheme to provide choice to the trainees for training providers.
- Corporate Social Responsibility: This is another source of fund to finance the skill training. Both public sector and private sector companies need to invest in the skill training as part of their corporate social responsibility. As per law the PSUs with about ₹100 crore profit are to invest about 5 per cent in the training. The central government and state need to proactively involve with the PSUs to undertake this responsibility and spend the resources earmarked meaningfully.

TO SUMMARISE, THE TWELFTH PLAN NEEDS TO FOCUS ON

1. Improving the outreach of the skill development, both quantitatively and qualitatively to bridge the divides, namely spatial, sectoral, regional and gender and so on.
2. Putting in place an institutional mechanism that is focused solely on skill development.
3. Put in place necessary support mechanisms to enable the financial requirements/skill loans for poor students (Credit Guarantee Fund).
4. Development of National Skill Qualification Framework, incorporating the standards developed by Sector Skill Councils, and have in place a regulatory framework to oversee the functioning and ensure accountability of Sector Skill Councils.
5. Improving quality and quantity by focusing on Training of Trainers.
6. Promoting Public Private Partnership.
7. Greater interaction encouraged among industry, academia and skill providers to narrow the gap between the demand and supply of skilled manpower.
8. Focus on Informal sector by finding a model that reaches out to the people, as the livelihood promoting institutions, panchayati raj institutions and and NGOs are engaged effectively.
9. Developing ICT based real time labour market information system.
10. An outcome based approach which ensures that the employability created is manifested in immediate, measurable and tangible employment/self-employment of the trainees.
11. An online national register of the persons skilled, and their current engagement—to not only provide a national database to employers and all other stakeholders, but also to facilitate a transparent monitoring system.
12. Review labour laws which inhibit the hiring of short term interns and trainees.
13. All employment exchanges to come online, and act as pro-active counseling and placement centres.
14. Activating State Skill Missions and make them nodal points for receiving most of the skill related funding from Centre.
15. Setting up of National Skill Registry having facility to link various data bases across Ministries and states to work as a platform to link people seeking training to trainers/sponsoring organisations and people having skills to prospective employers.
16. Improving focus of Ministries like Social Justice and Empowerment (SJE), Tribal Affairs (TA), Minority Affairs, Women and Child Development (WCD), Development of North Eastern Region (DONER) and so on, working for disadvantaged sections on skill development programmes so that much larger funding for skill development through them may be ensured.

PLAN OUTLAYS FOR THE MINISTRY OF LABOUR AND EMPLOYMENT

22.125. An indicative outlay of ₹13,223 crore has been made for the Ministry of Labour and Employment to carry implement various schemes. Of this an amount of ₹7,316 crore is earmarked for Rashtriya Swastahya Bima Yojana and ₹5,907 crore for other schemes of the Ministry of Labour and Employment.

ANNEXURE 22.1
Employment Across Various Sectors (in millions) 1999–2000, 2004–05, 2009–10—on UPSS basis

Sectors	Employment Across Various Sectors (in millions)			Absolute Increase in Employment (in millions)	
	1999–2000	2004–05	2009–10	1999–2000 to 2004–05	2004–05 to 2009–10
Agriculture	237.67	258.93	244.85	21.25	−14.08
Manufacturing	44.05	55.77	50.74	11.72	−5.03
Non-manufacturing	20.84	29.96	48.28	9.11	18.32
Mining and quarrying	2.17	2.64	2.95	0.47	0.31
Electricity, gas and water supply	1.13	1.30	1.25	0.17	−0.05
Construction	17.54	26.02	44.08	8.48	18.06
Services	94.20	112.81	116.34	18.77	3.53
Trade	36.63	43.36	43.53	6.74	0.17
Hotels and restaurants	4.62	6.10	6.13	1.48	0.03
Transport, storage and communication	14.61	18.47	19.97	3.86	1.5
Banking (and insurance)	2.25	3.10	3.82	0.84	0.72
Real estate, Renting and Business Activities	2.67	4.65	5.75	1.98	1.12
Public administration and defence	10.48	8.84	9.46	−1.64	0.62
Education	8.47	11.43	11.85	2.96	0.42
Health	2.62	3.34	3.59	0.73	0.25
Other Services	11.85	13.51	12.24	1.66	−1.27
Total	**396.76**	**457.46**	**460.22**	**60.70**	**2.76**

Source: NSS Employment Unemployment Surveys.
Note: Based on different NSS Rounds.

ANNEXURE 22.2
Absolute Increase/Decrease Employments Across Various Sectors (in millions) in Manufacturing, 1999–2000, 2004–05, 2009–10

Sectors	1999–2000 to 2004–05 Increase/Decrease	2004–05 to 2009–10 Increase/Decrease
food products and beverages	−0.30 ↓	−0.15 ↓
tobacco products	0.25 ↑	−0.52 ↓
Textiles	2.25 ↑	−1.7 ↓
wearing apparel; dressing and dyeing of fur	5.26 ↑	−1.62 ↓
wood and of products of wood and cork, except furniture	0.70 ↑	−1.62 ↓
paper and paper products	0.36 ↑	−1.15 ↓
coke, refined petroleum products and nuclear fuel	−0.28 ↓	−0.84 ↓
chemicals and chemical products	0.24 ↑	−0.39 ↓
other non-metallic mineral products	1.07 ↑	−0.16 ↓
basic metals	−0.12 ↓	0.37 ↑
fabricated metal products, except machinery and equipment	0.53 ↑	−2.01 ↓
electrical machinery and apparatus, that is	−0.21 ↓	0.05 ↑
motor vehicles, trailers and semi-trailers; other transport equipment	0.50 ↑	−0.42 ↓
medical, precision and optical instruments, watches and clocks	.83 ↑	−3.14 ↑
Recycling	0.07 ↑	0.01 ↑
Furniture: manufacturing n.e.c.	0.6	2.89 ↑
Rubber and Plastic products	–	0.7 ↑
Office accounting and commuting machinery	–	0.1 ↑
Radio, television and communication equipment and apparatus	–	0.2 ↑
Publishing, printing and reproduction of recorded media	–	1.1 ↑
Other transport equipment	–	0.8 ↑
machinery and equipment n.e.c.	–	1.6 ↑
Total Manufacturing Employment change	11.7	−5.07

Source: NSSO Various Rounds.

ANNEXURE 22.3
Incidence of Unemployment for 15 Years and Above Age Group, by Level of Education, 2004–05 and 2009–10 (UPSS) in Percentage

Level of Education	2004–05	2009–10
Not Literate	0.3	0.3
Literate Without Formal Schooling	1.2	0.3
Below Primary	1.2	0.7
Primary	1.4	1.2
Middle	2.7	2.1
Secondary	4.8	2.7
Higher Secondary	6.4	5.2
Diploma/Certificate	10.4	9.6
Graduate	8.8	6.9
Post Graduate and Above	8.1	6.7
All Level of Education	2.3	2.0

Source: Calculated from NSS Database, Employment and Unemployment Survey (2004–05 and 2009–10).

ANNEXURE 22.4
Dependency Ratio Across India States, Census 2001

	Ratio—15–59:<15 Persons	Ratio—15–59:>59 Persons	Ratio—WA: Non-WA Persons
Bihar	1.22	7.72	1.05
Uttar Pradesh	1.26	7.37	1.08
Meghalaya	1.25	11.62	1.13
Rajasthan	1.32	7.84	1.13
Madhya Pradesh	1.40	7.63	1.19
Jharkhand	1.37	9.26	1.19
Arunachal Pradesh	1.36	12.10	1.23
Chhattisgarh	1.51	7.72	1.26
Uttaranchal	1.53	7.23	1.26
Haryana	1.57	7.51	1.30
Assam	1.51	9.67	1.31
Jammu and Kashmir	1.61	8.60	1.35
Orissa	1.76	7.07	1.41
Nagaland	1.60	12.92	1.42
Tripura	1.75	8.11	1.44
Maharashtra	1.84	6.77	1.45
Mizoram	1.67	10.71	1.45
Sikkim	1.70	11.05	1.47
Punjab	1.90	6.60	1.47
West Bengal	1.79	8.37	1.48
Lakshadweep	1.74	9.69	1.48
Himachal Pradesh	1.93	6.63	1.49
Gujarat	1.83	8.72	1.52
Andhra Pradesh	1.88	7.93	1.52
Karnataka	1.89	7.85	1.53
Manipur	1.85	9.01	1.54
Dadra and Nagar Haveli	1.72	15.18	1.55
Delhi	1.92	11.97	1.65
Kerala	2.43	6.05	1.74
Tamil Nadu	2.38	7.22	1.79
Pondicherry	2.40	7.77	1.83
Andaman and Nicobar Islands	2.23	13.39	1.91
Chandigarh	2.27	13.21	1.94
Goa	2.71	7.99	2.02
Daman and Diu	2.47	13.29	2.09
India	**1.61**	**7.64**	**1.33**

Note: WA: Working Age; NWA: Non- Working Age.

NOTE
1. Organised and unorganised sectors have been defined as per NCEUS definition.

23

Women's Agency and Child Rights

INTRODUCTION

23.1. The Twelfth Five Year Plan recognizes the primacy of India's Women and Children, who constitute over 70 per cent of India's people. This Chapter reflects their voices and aspirations, and the nation's commitment to translate this vision into a reality during the Plan period. The Twelfth Plan strategy of inclusion envisages the engendering of development planning and making it more child-centric. Structural transformation is called for—not only in the women and child related direct policy and programme interventions, but also more generally in the policies and programmes of the many sectors that impact upon women and children especially those from the weaker sections or whose individual circumstances make them the most vulnerable. High priority will be given to women and children from the poorest communities, from the most deprived socio-religious communities, such as Scheduled Castes, Scheduled Tribes, particularly vulnerable tribal communities, de-notified and nomadic groups, religious minorities, other backward classes, migrants, those living in inaccessible or scattered hamlets, those living in insecure environments and the urban poor, among others.

23.2. Since many of the programmes most relevant for children and women are implemented at the third level of government, that is, the Panchayati Raj Institutions (PRIs) and Urban Local Bodies (ULBs)—success in achieving these outcomes depends critically on women's participation in these levels of government and their empowerment with respect to programme implementation. We must move towards creating 'Women and Child Friendly Panchayats" and ULBs, complemented by Baal Panchayats, with child participation taking on a new dimension. With progressive devolution of powers to PRIs and an increasing number of states requiring 50 per cent reservation for women in PRIs, new opportunities are emerging for making development planning processes gender sensitive and child friendly at the grass roots level in the Twelfth Plan.

23.3. There are many faces of vulnerability and deprivation, which the Twelfth Plan strategy for Women and Children addresses. The intergenerational cycle of multiple deprivation and violence faced by girls and women is epitomized by the adverse child sex ratio in children under 6 years of age. The ending of gender based inequities, discrimination and violence is an overriding priority in the Twelfth Plan. Ending gender based violence against girls and women including improvement in the adverse and steeply declining child sex ratio, is therefore, recognized as an overarching monitorable target of the Twelfth Plan for Women and Children. The 12th Plan will endeavor to provide nurturing, protective and safe environment for women to facilitate their entry into public spaces.

23.4. Part I of this Chapter focuses on Women's Agency and engendering of development. The key strategies for women's agency in the Twelfth Plan have been identified as: (*i*) Economic Empowerment; (*ii*) Social and Physical Infrastructure; (*iii*) Enabling Legislations; (*iv*) Women's Participation in Governance; (*v*) Inclusiveness of all categories of vulnerable women, (*vi*) Engendering National Policies/Programmes. These strategies bring out the crucial challenges posed by traditional determinants of women's agency and empowerment such as asset ownership, skill development, financial inclusion, along with new and emerging challenges posed by urbanisation, climate change, energy insecurity, the role of the media and so on. Strategies for the inclusion of vulnerable women such as those belonging to the Scheduled Castes (SC), Scheduled Tribes (ST) and minorities; single women, differently abled women; migrant and trafficked women have also been identified. Specific initiatives for empowering women and engendering development in the Twelfth Plan have been outlined.

23.5. Part II of this Chapter highlights the Twelfth Plan strategy to fulfill the rights of children to survival, protection, participation and development. Based on an analysis of the current situation of children this chapter outlines the vision, key priorities, and monitorable targets of the Twelfth Plan strategy for children. This includes both child specific and child related policy and programme interventions that are multi-sectoral in nature. These relate to (*i*) Child Survival and Development—which includes ICDS Restructuring; (*ii*) Early Childhood Care and Education; (*iii*) Child Protection and Participation; (*iv*) The Girl Child and (*v*) Adolescents. Child specific initiatives and schemes for children are detailed in these sections, while related sectoral strategies such as Health and Education are provided in relevant sectoral chapters.

23.6. Part III highlights the Twelfth Plan Strategy towards achieving Nutrition Security For All, especially the most vulnerable children, adolescent girls and women who are locked into an intergenerational cycle of multiple deprivation. The monitorable targets for nutrition and key priorities evolve from a detailed situation analysis and evaluation of the progress made during the Eleventh Plan. The Nutrition Strategy in Part III outlines: (*i*) the evolving multisectoral interventions for nutrition, including introducing a strong nutrition focus to sectoral programmes, strengthening and re-activating Institutional Arrangements and the Multi-sectoral Nutrition Programme in 200 High Burden Districts; (*ii*) Promoting Optimal Maternal, Infant and Young Child Care and Feeding Practices; (*iii*) Combating Micronutrient Deficiencies in a holistic manner; (*iv*) Addressing the Dual Burden of Malnutrition; (*v*) Nutrition Capacity Development; (*vi*) Nutrition Education and Social Mobilization—including a societal campaign against malnutrition and (*vii*) Nutrition Monitoring and Surveillance Systems, to monitor and review nutrition outcomes.

WOMEN'S AGENCY AND THE ENGENDERING OF DEVELOPMENT

23.7. According to the 2011 census, women account for 586.47 million in absolute numbers and represent 48.46 per cent of the total population of the country. While there has been an appreciable gain in the overall sex ratio of 7 points from 933 in 2001 to 940 in 2011, the decline in child sex ratio (0–6 years) by 13 points from 927 in 2001 to 914 in 2011 is a matter of grave concern. On the health front, implementation of the National Rural Health Mission has resulted in an improvement on many indicators pertaining to gender. Fertility Rates have come down and have reached replacement levels in a number of states; Maternal Mortality Rate (MMR) is improving, from 301 per 100,000 live births in 2003 it has come down to 212 (SRS 2007–2009); Infant Mortality Rate, though still high, has reduced to 47 per 1,000 in 2010. Institutional deliveries have risen from 41 per cent in 2006 to 73 per cent in 2009. There are increasing concerns regarding the gap between male and female infant mortality rate 49 for girls as compared to 46 for boys. The under-five mortality rate for girls in India is very high at 64 per 1,000 live births as compared to 55 per 1,000 live births for boys. The decline in MMR has fallen behind and is less than the target of 100 in the Eleventh Plan.

23.8. There has been an increase in literacy amongst women from 53.67 per cent (Census 2001) to 65.46 per cent (Census 2011). The challenge however remains in bridging the gender gap which stands at 16.68 per cent. The gender differential in education is declining, particularly at the primary level. There is a need to address the issues of retention of girls' in school, quality of education and the provision of separate toilets, sibling care facilities, and so on. From 1993–94 to 2009–10 women's participation in the labour force has decreased substantially from 36.8 per cent to 26.1 per cent in rural areas and from 17 per cent to 13.8 per cent in urban areas as indicated by NSSO data. Another major concern is the gender gap in the educational level of the labour force. Whereas in 2004–05, 60 per cent of employed females were illiterate and 3.7 per cent were graduates for men it was 28 per cent and 8 per cent, respectively. Female hourly wage rates in agriculture vary from 50 per cent to 75 per cent of male rates, and are insufficient to overcome absolute poverty.

23.9. Addressing violence against women, in both public and private sphere, is a major challenge. Data from National Crime Records Bureau (NCRB) shows that the total number of crimes against women increased by 29.6 per cent between 2006 and 2010. What is equally disturbing is that conviction rates remained low, reflecting inter alia, that many of these cases are not being well prosecuted and inadequate proof is tendered before the courts. The 2005–06 National Family Health Survey (NFHS-3) also reported that one-third of women aged 15 to 49 had experienced physical violence, and approximately one in 10 had been a victim of sexual violence. Early marriage makes women more vulnerable to domestic violence. According to the NFHS 3 data, the median age of marriage for women in the 20–49 years age group ranges between 16.5 years to 18.3 years. Trafficking of women and children is a gross violation of human rights which needs to be addressed. Trafficked women and children are subjected to multiple conditions of exploitation such as commercial sexual exploitation and bonded labour.

BARRIERS TO WOMEN'S EMPOWERMENT

23.10. The barriers to women's empowerment are manifested in various ways. Deep-rooted ideologies of gender bias and discrimination like the confinement of women to the private domestic realm, restrictions on their mobility, poor access to health services, nutrition, education and employment, and exclusion from the public and political sphere continue to daunt women across the country. Other parameters that reflect the status and position of women in society are work participation rates, sex ratio in the age group of 0–6 years and gender based violence which remain heavily skewed against women. New challenges such as increased intra-country migration, changing labour markets that require new skill sets and rapidly changing technologies have also emerged.

23.11. The access of women to key social services such as health and education is a critical determinant of the status of women and their ability to participate in making society a better place. Details of access in each dimension are discussed in the relevant chapters (see especially Chapters on Health and Education). While the overall picture is one of progress in many dimensions, large gaps still remain. India's Gender Inequality Index value of 0.617 in 2011 placing the country at 129 among 149 countries globally is reflective of the high gender inequality that is prevalent. The lower attainments of women in key human development indicators are indicative of the sharp disparities in opportunities available to women and men. An exceptionally worrying factor is the deteriorating child sex ratio.

23.12. Hence, the key elements for Gender Equity to be addressed in the Twelfth Plan can be clubbed under the following:

1. Economic Empowerment
2. Social and Physical Infrastructure
3. Enabling Legislations
4. Women's Participation in Governance
5. Inclusiveness of all categories of vulnerable women
6. Engendering National Policies/Programmes
7. Mainstreaming gender through Gender Budgeting

ECONOMIC EMPOWERMENT

23.13. The Twelfth Plan will endeavour to increase women's employability in the formal sector as well as their asset base. It will improve the conditions of self employed women. Focus will be on women's workforce participation particularly in secondary and tertiary sectors, ensuring decent work for them, reaching out to women in agriculture and manufacturing, financial inclusion, and extending land and property rights to women.

EMPLOYMENT GENERATION WITH EQUITY IN WORK CONDITIONS

23.14. A significant increase is required in formal sector employment, that is work with reasonable pay and conditions, which would provide for the specific needs of women workers. Fortunately, the Twelfth Plan strategy focussing on health, education, sanitation and infrastructure development will create many productive jobs, a large proportion of which will be in the formal sector. This must be accompanied by measures to ensure that women have adequate access to these new job opportunities.

23.15. The Plan will strengthen the implementation of the Equal Remuneration Act and the Maternity Benefits Act. As a complement to the strategy for increasing women's employment in the formal sector, it is imperative that the Protection of Women from Sexual Harassment at Work Place Bill is made into law.

SKILL DEVELOPMENT

23.16. One of the major impediments affecting women's participation in the workforce, particularly in secondary and tertiary sectors, is the lack of skills. The Twelfth Plan envisages a major scaling up of skill development as outlined in the Chapter on Employment and Skill Development. This must be accompanied by special efforts to promote skill development of women from traditional skills to emerging skills, which help women break the gender stereotypes and move into employment requiring higher skill sets. Training of women as BPO employees, electronic technicians, electricians, plumbers, sales persons, auto drivers, taxi drivers, masons, and so on. will be incorporated in the skill development programmes. Skill development would be seen as a vehicle to improve lives and not just livelihoods of women. The curriculum should therefore include inputs that help women to assert themselves individually and collectively. Gender disaggregated data should be maintained by the National Skills Development Corporation on the number of women that receive training in the programmes supported by the corporates. This would allow for the assessment of whether the minimum reservation of 33 per cent of seats for women is being utilized and whether women are getting employment and spaces in the market economy after they are trained.

SPECIAL PROMOTION OF ENTERPRISES OF HOME-BASED WORKERS/SMALL PRODUCERS

23.17. The promotion of enterprises of home based workers, self employed workers and small producers is an essential component of the Twelfth Plan and is of particular relevance for women. The Twelfth Plan strategy would be to identify such workers and support their enterprises through setting up of common facility centres to ensure all important services including technology and skill training, entrepreneurship training, market information, access to institutionalised credit, power and other infrastructure and related facilities are readily provided.

23.18. Medical Insurance policies will be modified to recognise needs of women headed and single women households and encouraged to have uniform coverage norms. Policies on Pensions and Post-retirement benefits will be engendered to reflect the needs of single women and women headed households. Kisan Credit Cards should be issued to women farmers, with joint pattas as collateral. There will be provision of refinance loan for women entrepreneurs to extend their involvement in economic activities. Government loan guarantees to substitute for collateral to facilitate women's access to credit will also be provided. Efforts will be made to ensure that SHGs are classified under priority sector and given loans at concessional rates. Under the National Rural Livelihood Mission, the Government is extending an interest subsidy so that the SHG beneficiaries pay only 7 per cent interest on their loans. The scope for extending this benefit to SHGs under other schemes also must be considered. There is a need to review the SHG interventions and ground realities to determine how SHGs may better serve the interests of poor women, and suggest changes required in overall SHG policy frameworks.

WOMEN IN AGRICULTURE

23.19. Women's role as agricultural workers, especially their work on family farms is increasing thanks to the process of feminisation of agriculture (see Chapter on Agriculture). This process reflects the fact that small and fragmented holdings do not allow for the generation of sufficient household income leading to migration of male members into other sectors, leaving the family farms to be tended largely by women and children. The Twelfth Plan recognizes the need to increase awareness about the growing feminisation of agriculture through sensitisation of policy makers, so that the gender stereotype of farming being a solely male activity is adequately challenged.

23.20. Existing formal institutions must recognize women's roles and needs in various fields of agricultural activity and must ensure the participation of women farmers in designing programmes for technical training and research. The methodologies, time duration, location and other factors of programme design must be appropriate to the needs of women. Women must also be included in land and water management, *pani* panchayats, preservation of soil fertility and nutrition management, sustainable use of soil, water, livestock and fishery resources and in creating village level community seed banks, and so on.

23.21. Women's access to the various agriculture schemes being implemented by the government will be ensured. A quota for women will be incorporated by modifying the guidelines of agriculture related schemes like Rashtriya Krishi Vikas Yojana (RKVY). Further involvement of women can be ensured by providing financial and infrastructural support to SHGs for seed production, storage, preservation, and distribution.

23.22. Access to agricultural technology for women will improve by designing agricultural technology that is women friendly. Technology to reduce drudgery would, at the very least, lead to better health and productivity. Technology transfer to women would be prioritised in all aspects of farming and farm management, including dry land farming technologies, animal husbandry, forestry, sustainable natural resource management, enterprise development, financial management and leadership development. They would be provided training in pre and post-harvest technologies. To train women farmers in new technologies and practices, gain access to information on schemes and subsidies, training in crop planning and so on. Special Resource Centres would be provided. Women and young girls will be given training in the use and repair of bore wells with special focus on promoting low cost irrigation.

23.23. Endowing women with land is an important instrument for empowering them economically and strengthening their ability to challenge social and political gender inequities. There are three main sources of land for women: direct government transfers, purchase or lease from the market and inheritance. To enhance women's land access from all three sources, a range of initiatives are needed, including joint land titles in all government land transfers, credit support to poor women to purchase or lease land from the market, increase in legal awareness and legal support for women's inheritance rights, supportive government schemes and recording of women's inheritance shares, and so on. There is also need for reliable, fair and accessible mechanisms such as social audit with greater participation of women in the audit bodies for resolving disputes and providing remedies in matters related to tenure and security of lease.

23.24. States should also consider the adoption of a "group approach" in land cultivation and investment in productive assets. States could undertake an assessment of all uncultivated arable land presently with the Government and give women's groups long term usufruct rights to it for group cultivation. The group leasing rights will be recognised under government programmes for agricultural promotion to allow women to avail benefits of schemes such as agricultural extension services and crop insurance to mitigate risks. Women will also be helped to purchase land in groups for group cultivation by a loan-cum-grant scheme with 50 per cent of the loan as a low interest loan and the remaining 50 per cent as a grant. Incentives will be provided to women farmers/SHGs, for group farming on leased or owned land through financial support for group formation; tying credit subsidy, technology access, and so on. to group farming.

23.25. Where new land is being distributed or regularised, individual titles in women's names only rather than joint titles with husbands could be considered. States may also want to consider group titles to women's groups though this would require changes in tenancy laws to allow leasing of land to women's groups as well as recognise such groups as a valid category of landowners. As many states have already given joint pattas on government land in the past, and this trend may continue, such pattas would be made partitionable, so that the wives, if they so desire, can have half the share of land in their single names. The present reality is that after divorce or abandonment, wives are left without any share in such land.

23.26. The 2005 Hindu Succession Amendment Act (HSAA) brings all agricultural land on par with other property. This makes Hindu women's land inheritance rights legally equal to men's across states, overriding any inconsistent State laws. Various provisions need to be reviewed and strategically acted upon. This includes devolution of a woman's property in the same manner as a man's, restricting the right to will to prohibit disinheritance of wives and daughters, protecting women's right to property by eliminating forced coercion aimed at women relinquishing their shares, and ensuring that HSAA overrides State laws related to agricultural land. In addition, the Ministry of Women and Child Development in collaboration with the Department of Land Resources, should start intense monitoring of the progress in implementation of HSAA, and ensure its speedy implementation.

23.27. In irrigation projects, any new land arrangements (that is compensatory land given to displaced persons) must be in the joint names of the man and the woman, or exclusively in the name of the woman where she is the main economic provider. This would increase women's equity in property.

WOMEN IN MANUFACTURING

23.28. In order to promote the participation of women in the manufacturing sector, the plan supports the promotion of marketable manufacturing skills in production activities with special emphasis on skill development of women belonging to marginalized sections. For important traditional industries like leather, handlooms, handicrafts and sericulture, existing publicly funded institutions will be activated to identify the industry's market potential and existing skills. Bottlenecks for modern market-oriented production will be located, and incremental technological improvements including use of computerised technologies for coordination through a gendered analysis of the industrial climate will be introduced. State policies will be encouraged to publicise the opportunities in these industries among potential women entrepreneurs and give assistance to them in their ventures. The Twelfth Plan must also encourage social action and propaganda to change attitudes towards gender stereotyping of skills and removal of prejudice against caste-based activities and worker communities.

WOMEN IN THE UNORGANIZED SECTOR

23.29. Women in the unorganized sector require social security addressing issues of leave, wages, work conditions, pension, housing, childcare, health benefits, maternity benefits, safety and occupational health, and a complaints committee for sexual harassment. This can only be ensured by extending labour protection to these sectors in a manner that pays special attention to the needs of women workers.

SOCIAL AND PHYSICAL INFRASTRUCTURE

23.30. The strengthening of social and physical infrastructure especially health and education, sanitation, transportation, and so on is critical for inclusive growth. There are considerable gender differences in the needs of men and women in the various infrastructure development projects. So there is a need for a gender analysis of infrastructure policies to ensure women's needs are taken into account. Women should be consulted at the time of designing the project—its site selection, objective, operation and maintenance plans, and so on. They should also be involved in the social audit of these programmes.

HEALTH

23.31. It is vital to widen the emphasis hitherto laid on women's reproductive health to adopt a life cycle approach towards women's survival, overall health and well-being. The sex ratio and the decline in child sex ratio is clearly a major problem. High anaemia, unrecognised care burden, differentials in morbidity and mortality and access to care also need more attention. Sex disaggregated data on disease burden and access to treatment is inadequate and must be expanded in the Twelfth Plan. This data will be further disaggregated on the basis of socio-religious categorisation to identify the most vulnerable women. The Plan recognises the gender dimension of health problems and seeks to address issues of women's survival and health through a life cycle approach.

23.32. In view of the consistently higher female IMR figures, along with the increasingly disturbing dynamics of the declining child sex ratio, a separate target for lowering female IMR will be added under NRHM. An impact assessment of Janani Suraksha Yojana, Jansankhya Sthirata Kosh and equity implications of health insurance, user fees and other activities under the NRHM will also be undertaken.

23.33. Dovetailing of IGMSY (a pilot conditional maternity benefit scheme), National Food Security Bill (NFSB) and related State schemes with NRHM will be undertaken for an effective convergence of programmes relating to pregnant and lactating mothers. Successful State level schemes/initiatives for reducing MMR would be considered for replication.

EDUCATION

23.34. Under Sarva Shiksha Abhiyan (SSA), the number of women teachers, especially in rural schools and remote, inaccessible areas will be increased by providing enabling work conditions for women teachers including transportation facilities and housing. In the wake of RTE, a child tracking system would be adopted to achieve full inclusion and to address the issue of school drop-outs. Providing hostel facilities and scholarships for girls as well as including non-traditional vocational training as part of the overall education curriculum are the best instruments for engendering the education strategy. These issues are discussed in detail in the Chapter on Education.

SANITATION

23.35. Lack of sanitation, especially toilets, in rural areas is a major weakness in our system and one that impacts most adversely on women. The Twelfth Plan will undertake a gender impact assessment of the Total Sanitation Campaign to assess whether it has reduced women's workload, provided security, improved hygiene and reproductive health of women, decreased school dropout rates for girls, and so on. The Plan will also ensure the provision of toilets with water in all schools and anganwadi centres and the active involvement of women in determining the location of sanitation facilities. Implementation of eco-sanitation, non-flushing, self-composting toilets will go a long way towards success given the chronic water scarcity everywhere.

TRANSPORTATION

23.36. There are women-specific transport needs like transportation of primary products; inter- and intra-village roads/paths; non-motorised transport; dedicated bicycle lanes, pedestrian sidewalk use, passenger safety, and so on which should be included in any transport policy or plan. Every major transport project should undertake a Pre-project Rapid Gender Assessment Survey to ensure that women's needs are addressed right at the design and planning level. Project planning and implementation need to be participatory, including community infrastructure management and maintenance.

23.37. Design improvements are necessary to meet the specific needs of women, especially lower height of entry steps, length of straps, and so on in buses and trains, installation of handrails, ramps, and so on. Dedicated exclusive services such as ladies special buses and trains are also necessary in our social circumstances. Women's needs require better route planning. The provision of special buses, increased services for women travelling during off-peak hours or services on less-travelled routes all need more attention. Personal security risks at parking lots, buses, bus stops, airports, highways and so on, affect women's travel patterns. A Gender Audit of transport terminals must be undertaken

> **Box 23.1**
> **Women Friendly Infrastructure Development in Kerala**
>
> In **Kerala** it was decided that in the year, 2010–11, a major focus would be on women friendly infrastructure. This included interventions like construction of toilets in public buildings, bus stations, construction of night shelters for fisherwomen, energy efficient gas stoves within EGS schemes, cheaper rental flats for women who commute, creation of domestic violence Counselling Desks in public hospitals, and so on. These measures helped promote convergence and are also examples of Gender Budgeting in mainstream Departments like Kerala State Road Transport Corporation (KSRTC), Public Works Department (PWD), Ports and Housing. With these interventions, the number of Departments with women specific schemes has increased from 10 in 2009–10 to 16 in 2010–11. Further, there has been an increase in allocations for women from 5.5 percent in 2009–10 to 8.6 percent in 2010–11 and to approximately about 10 percent in 2011–12.

and safety measures for women introduced. The Plan will promote creation of night shelters and toilets for women at bus stations, and so on to facilitate travel. The Plan will also undertake a national level assessment of the transport requirements of women particularly those in the informal sector.

ENERGY AND NATURAL RESOURCES MANAGEMENT

23.38. Women are the primary stakeholders in energy and natural resources management, especially for domestic use. A comprehensive policy on domestic energy must be evolved to create a portfolio of energy options. Apart from electricity and biomass sources, non-biomass sources of energy, including solar, for small production units will be promoted. Women's groups will be encouraged to undertake smaller power production units and energy-based enterprises such as making charcoal, briquette making and gassifiers. Capacity building and seed-capital assistance will be provided to women to manage energy programs. Special trainings will be provided to women to develop their expertise in the renewable energy sector, including the repair of solar lanterns, improved cooking stoves, pumpsets and so on. Gender sensitive energy development will be promoted in the Twelfth Plan through the two pronged strategy of customizing technology to reflect the views and experiences of women and creating a large pool of trained female energy technocrats/energy entrepreneurs.

URBAN PLANNING AND LIVELIHOODS

23.39. Urban livelihoods are often overlooked and undermined by policies, regulations, and practices of municipalities and urban planners and are eroded by urban renewal schemes. With 85 per cent of all urban women being employed informally, women in urban India face threats to their livelihoods on a daily basis. Allocation of urban land/space and other resources will be made for livelihoods of the poor. Resettlement schemes must be evaluated by the affected communities, with a gendered assessment of repercussions on livelihoods of the evictees. The number of safe shelter homes, women friendly public toilets, public crèche facilities, and so on should be increased on a priority basis to reach saturation levels in all cities.

CLIMATE CHANGE

23.40. There are important gender perspectives in all aspects of climate change. Adaptation efforts must systematically and effectively address gender-specific impacts of climate change in the areas of energy, water, food security, agriculture and fisheries, biodiversity and ecosystem services, health, industry, human settlements, disaster management, and security. Gender inequalities in access to resources, including credit, extension services, information and technology, must be taken into account in developing mitigation activities. While National and State level Action Plans on Climate Change are being formulated, the Twelfth Plan will ensure a gender assessment of these plans including gender specific objectives, indicators, monitoring and evaluation dimensions, capacity building and so on, in order to make climate change mitigation and adaptation plans more responsive to women's concerns and needs. Gender and climate change adaptation strategies will be made a part of all ongoing poverty reduction and development policies, including Disaster Risk Reduction (DRR) planning and implementation at local, national and regional level, country's Nation Adaptation Programmes of Actions (NAPAs); and in the numerous climate change related funds that are in the process of being established.

ENGENDERING THE MEDIA

23.41. The visual and audio media, including television, films and radio shows are important channels of information dissemination. The Twelfth Plan is committed to engendering the different channels of the media including local media like Nukkad Nataks (Street Plays), Community Radio and so on. The Information and Broadcasting Ministry will encourage gender messaging in major programmes and shows across channels. This will entail substantive engagements with the executive producers, content writers and editors of all channels on critical gender concerns and issues. Recognition will be accorded to the programmes that air messages critical to the empowerment of women.

ENABLING LEGISLATIONS

23.42. **The Pre-Conception and Pre-Natal Diagnostic Techniques ACT (PC-PNDT Act):** Several laws were conceived to promote the objective of women's equality and gender balance in society. These must be effectively administered with the State taking primary responsibility. The practice of using technology for foetal sex determination to engage in female foeticide needs to be addressed stringently. The provisions of the PC-PNDT Act must be reviewed to make sex selection practices effectively punishable. This calls for strengthening the enforcement mechanisms for the Act and making penalties severe. Restrictions on sex detection and sex selection advertisements must be enforced. Registration/Regulation of sonography machines must be ensured. It must be mandatory for all registered centres to maintain all records, charts, forms, reports and consent letters for a period of two years or until permitted by the concerned Appropriate Authority. Decoy and sting operations must be an integral part of the strategy to catch the doctors/clinics indulging in the illegal practice of sex-determination and abortion of the female foetus.

23.43. **Maternity Benefit Act:** The Maternity Benefit Act 1961 will be reviewed to increase the length of leave women employed in factories, mines, plantations, shops and so on can take and to give her the choice of utilising the period of paid absence as per her convenience.

23.44. **Equal Remuneration Act, 1976 (ERA):** Discrimination against women workers in payment of wages, and so on exists in spite of the provisions of the Equal Remuneration Act, 1976 (ERA). The implementation and monitoring of the Act will be strictly enforced.

IMPROVING IMPLEMENTATION OF PROTECTION OF WOMEN FROM DOMESTIC VIOLENCE ACT (PWDVA) AND DOWRY PROHIBITION ACT (DPA)

23.45. Under the Protection of Women from Domestic Violence Act (PWDVA) the State Governments are required to appoint Protection Officers, register Service Providers and notify medical facilities. Most of the States/UTs have given additional charge to their existing officers to perform the duties of Protection Officer which is said to be affecting implementation of the Act. State governments must be encouraged to appoint personnel as needed and provide support for establishing Counselling Facilities or Family Counselling Centres as well as for capacity building of the officials and infrastructural support to Protection Officers. A Scheme to this effect will be introduced during the Twelfth Plan. Appointment of sufficient number of dedicated, full time Dowry Prohibition Officers to enforce the DPA Act will also be undertaken. Training and capacity building of law enforcement agencies and the Judiciary on issues concerning dowry related harassment of women and dowry deaths will also receive attention. Besides this new initiatives such as One Stop Crisis Centres for providing shelter, police desk, legal, medical and counseling services and Women's Helpline will be considered.

23.46. The Twelfth Plan recognises the need to partner with the corporate sector in its fight against gender discrimination by making gender equity an integral objective of corporate social responsibility. The corporate sector will be encouraged to take up projects that provide assistance and support services to women in situations of domestic violence and for rehabilitation of victims of trafficking.

WOMEN'S PARTICIPATION IN GOVERNANCE

23.47. Effective participation of women in institutions of governance is the only assured way of empowering women and bringing gender dimensions under focus.

WOMEN IN PANCHAYATS

23.48. The power of Elected Women Representatives (EWRs) must be harnessed as change agents for better governance and social change. They need to be equipped to ensure the efficient delivery of public services under the Integrated Child Development Services, the National Rural Health Mission, Sarva Shiksha Abhiyan, Mahatma Gandhi National Rural Employment Guarantee Scheme and so on. by overseeing the functioning of grassroots workers like Anganwadi Workers (AWW), Accredited Social Health Activists (ASHA), primary school teachers, and so on. Village level committees must be formed in which women workers at grassroots level that is members of the Panchayat and SHGs, AWWs, ASHAs, school teachers, and so on could collectively discuss and formulate work plans to address issues arising in the implementation of programmes, lead campaigns and highlight issues of importance in the gram sabha.

23.49. The role of panchayat must be increased in enforcing registration of births, deaths, marriages and migration so as to make an impact on issues of trafficking and child marriage and to equip EWRs to enable their panchayats to focus on elimination of violence against women and girls and achieve universal education.

23.50. The Ministry of Women and Child Development and the Ministry of Panchayati Raj in collaboration with other Ministries must promote several activities including especially, (*i*) capacity building and training modules on women's programmes for government functionaries and officers, (*ii*) pre-election preparation of women candidates and voters, intensive training of elected panchayat women representatives, and (*iii*) gender budgeting and gender audit in rural and urban local bodies.

23.51. The Gender Resource Centres (GRC) of Department of Women and Child Development, Government of Delhi are envisaged as instruments to bring social, economic and legal empowerment of women, particularly those belonging to the under privileged sections of society. The activities of GRC are to ensure (*i*) Social Empowerment (*ii*) Legal Rights (*iii*) Access to Healthcare (*iv*) Non-Formal functional Literacy (*v*) Economic initiatives-Skill building/Vocational Training in Conventional and Non-Conventional trades (*vi*) Micro enterprise and Entrepreneurship Development through Self-Help Groups, and (*vii*) Information-Cum-Facilitation Centre for information sharing and networking aspects. This experiment should be tried in other states.

WOMEN IN URBAN BODIES

23.52. Urban local bodies need (*a*) a gender focal point in each body, (*b*) citizen report cards with focus on meeting women's needs in urban services such as water and sanitation, widows' pensions and so on. The Plan would also lay more focus on capacity building and networking of women councillors to improve their participation in urban infrastructure planning. This will include training in planning, budgeting and resource mobilisation, ICT and networking, and so on.

SPECIAL PROBLEMS OF WOMEN IN VULNERABLE GROUPS

23.53. The Twelfth Plan pays special attention to the needs of vulnerable women, including the Scheduled Castes, Scheduled Tribes, OBCs and Minorities. The strategies towards these groups must be crafted to ensure effective engendering. The special provision for women in programmes for these groups are discussed in detail in the Chapter on Social Justice and Empowerment. An overarching fact of vulnerablilty is that women from every state and every community, dalits, adivasis, minorities and so on suffer due to the prevalence of alcoholism which eats its way into precious family income, leads to poverty, malnutrition and domestic violence, problems which the plan aims to tackle. This needs to be addressed with utmost urgency.

23.54. The groups of women that deserve special attention are discussed below.

SCHEDULED CASTE WOMEN

23.55. In view of the multiple vulnerabilities faced by SC women they should be provided with good quality house sites in the joint names of both the wife and husband. Under PDS, outlets should be opened in SC bastis which should be operated, as far as possible, by local SC women. In view of the particular vulnerability faced by SC women and children, migrant labour, special programmes and interventions should be drawn up for them, particularly in the fields of education and health. Special measures should be undertaken in the Twelfth Plan for better implementation of the Scheduled Castes and Tribes (Prevention of Atrocities) Act, 1989.

SCHEDULED TRIBE WOMEN

23.56. The Twelfth Plan must lay greater focus on awareness building among tribal women about policies, programmes, schemes and legislations meant for them by using various print and electronic media. The Twelfth Plan must focus on the implementation of the Scheduled Tribes and other Traditional Forest Dwellers Act and on the provision of adequate land development facilities and credit facilities on priority basis to all land allottees under the Scheduled Tribes and Other Traditional Forest Dwellers (Recognition of Forest Rights) Act, 2006. Representation of tribal women on Committees formed for fixation of Minimum Support Prices for Minor Forest Produce (MFP) will be considered. Within the Scheduled Tribes, a special category called PVTGs (Particular Vulnerable Tribal Groups) has been identified. A special scheme needs to be developed targeting women of these communities. Interventions are needed to ensure that during the 12th plan period their status is lifted to match that of the other tribal groups.

WOMEN OF RELIGIOUS MINORITIES

23.57. Muslim girls will be given additional support for education including provision of collective transportation facilities (not limited to cycles) which can largely improve their enrolment and attendance. This should be made a part of the SSA and also linked with KGBV Schools. Along with STs and SCs, OBCs from religious minorities should be included as a target group. For improving accessibility to health services, coverage of minority dominated blocks under NRHM will be specifically reviewed. Sanitation and health facilities, (including the construction of toilets) along with social education will be provided for in religious educational institutions including Madarasas. Women artisans from religious minorities who desire occupational diversification will be provided alternative training.

DIFFERENTLY ABLED WOMEN

23.58. Differently abled women suffer from being doubly disadvantaged as they are subjected to sociocultural restrictions as well as prevailing economic limitations, which impede their access to health care, education, vocational training and employment. The Twelfth Plan will endeavour to engender all programmes aimed at the differently-abled. Screening campaigns for early detection of children with different abilities in schools, especially girls' schools and KGBVs will be conducted Also provision of enabling infrastructure amenities in schools, KGBVs, Polytechnics and AWCs will be undertaken. Sensitisation and training of school teachers and AWWs, vocational training and assured employment for women with different abilities, and special rehabilitation services along with care provisions in existing MWCD run short stay homes and hostel facilities must be conducted.

SINGLE WOMEN AND WIDOWS

23.59. Special attention is needed on the issues of single women, particularly widows. The provision of rehabilitation and compensation, besides economic packages for widows, must be examined. Further, the widow's pension scheme should be extended to a larger pool of beneficiaries by reworking the age eligibility criteria as some States have done. Indexing of pension to inflation should be considered.

23.60. A separate quota under Indira Awas Yojana and Rajiv Awas Yojana for single women will be considered and their access to employment and equal wages through special job cards for single women under MGNREGA must be ensured. Separate entrepreneurship and leadership development schemes for single women will be promoted along with preferential selection in credit grants with flexible payment modalities and lower interest rates.

23.61. Single women must be made aware of their rights and entitlements within their maternal and matrimonial households. For this, special focus is needed on legal aid to single women as well as promotion of separate federations of single women at block and district levels.

ELDERLY WOMEN

23.62. The Twelfth Plan will give special attention to older women in order to address their health, nutrition and pension concerns. Focus will be upon creating awareness of various diseases that older women are more susceptible to such as osteoporosis, breast cancer and cervical cancer. Mental health issues among older women will be a key area of focus. The cost of medical procedures for single/poor senior citizens will be subsidised. Waiver of the income criteria for old age pensions to women above the age of 75 years in rural areas/urban slums/JJ colonies will be provided. A pension fund will be made for elderly women in the unorganised sector rendered jobless and without any savings when unable to work.

WOMEN AFFECTED WITH HIV/AIDS

23.63. The Twelfth Plan will reach out to women living with HIV/AIDS, especially those who have been deserted by their family, have lost their husbands, and are without any social or economic support. Access of women living with HIV/AIDS will be prioritised in the different livelihood programmes. HIV positive or affected women will be empowered through vocational training, including training to conduct HIV/AIDS awareness programmes. Legal services will be made a part of the process of rehabilitation. HIV/AIDS awareness will be integrated in the training programmes for government personnel. Caregivers of People Living with HIV (PLHIV) and AIDS will be trained in all aspects of the disease. The ICDS guidelines will integrate information on nutritional support to women and children on ARTs. Training programmes for crèche personnel will include information about the needs of children infected and affected with HIV. Transport and nutritional support will be extended to PLHIV and to children with HIV.

MIGRANT WORKERS

23.64. The Twelfth Plan will ensure provision of financial services to migrant women to enable promotion of savings and to facilitate secure transfer of remittances. To protect migrant domestic workers from exploitation by placement agencies, a system of registration, monitoring and accountability of placement agencies for domestic workers may be introduced. To prevent marginalisation of migrant labour, especially women migrants at their new destination, portability of entitlements such as ration cards based on the experience of the RSBY card will be ensured. Migrant Resource Centres/Assistance centres will be set up in major destination areas to provide information counselling for migrants including training and placement to ensure better integration in urban labour markets.

WOMEN IN DISTURBED AREAS

23.65. Women in disturbed areas face special issues including continuous army presence, suspended civil rights and lack of normal access to facilities/services due to continuous violence. They are most vulnerable to atrocities and need special attention in areas like health care measures, schools, free legal aid and so on. Gender sensitisation programs will be held for the authorities who implement specific legislations applicable to disturbed areas such as the Armed Forces Special Powers Act (AFSPA), and so on. The Twelfth plan will also initiate review of the Armed Forces Special Powers Act (AFSPA) using a gender lens. Documentation of the gendered dimension of violations and needs assessment of women in disturbed areas presently under AFSPA will be done.

23.66. Gender Resource Centres will be established by the State Departments for Women and Child Development in all pockets of disturbed areas on a priority basis in order to provide information and counselling for women, enable access to justice, benefit from all central government schemes, including social protection schemes and public services. District plans and funds will be directed towards providing sustainable livelihood opportunities, increased and equitable access to land, common property resources, improved social and physical infrastructure and governance institutions, greater coverage of MGNREGA and NRLM, and better credit opportunities for women in the disturbed areas.

TRAFFICKED WOMEN

23.67. Trafficking for commercial sexual exploitation is one of the worst forms of crimes against women and children as it exposes them to a life of humiliation and sexual abuse. Poverty, illiteracy, lack of livelihood options, natural/man made disasters and lack of social and family support, migration are among the factors which make women and children vulnerable to such trafficking. A study entitled 'Girls and Women in Prostitution in India' (2002–2004) by Gram Niyojan Kendra (GNK), sponsored by the Ministry of Women and Child Development, estimates that the primary means of entry into prostitution of about three fourths of the women and children is through trafficking and that there are about 2.8 million sex workers in the country of which 36 per cent are children. Cross-border trafficking from Bangladesh and Nepal to various cities in India is another area of concern.

23.68. The Government has ratified the United Nations Convention on Transnational Organized Crime (UNCTOC) and its Protocol to Prevent, Suppress and Punish Trafficking in Persons especially trafficking in Women and Children. The Protocol casts an obligation on the State Parties to undertake measures for prevention of trafficking as also for providing physical, psychological and social recovery of victims of trafficking in persons. The Government has also ratified the SAARC Convention on Preventing and Combating Trafficking of Women and Children for Prostitution.

23.69. During the Twelfth Plan the Government will intensify its efforts to prevent trafficking for commercial sexual exploitation and efforts at rehabilitation of the trafficked victims including those in prostitution who wish to leave the exploitative situation. Skills training for alternative livelihood opportunities will be provided for women in prostitution to enable them to move out and support their families. In order to break the vicious cycle of second generation prostitution and brothel related livelihood, the children of sex workers should be mainstreamed with proper education and an enabling, conducive environment including placement in suitable homes as well as enrollment in residential schools under Sarva Shiksha Abhiyan.

WOMEN IN PRISON

23.70. The prison population in India in 2010 was 36, 68,998 against an official capacity of only 3,20,450. About 4 per cent of prison population is female. Despite numerous attempts at prison reforms, problems such as overcrowding, prolonged detention of undertrial individuals, poor living conditions, and allegations of physical, sexual and mental abuse have featured repeatedly in the public domain. Women with children are rarely provided facilities for childcare and the lack of skills makes it difficult for them to find meaningful employment after serving their sentences. The All India Committee on Jail Reforms (1980–1983), the Supreme Court of India and the Committee of Empowerment of Women (2001–2002) have all highlighted the need for a comprehensive revision of the prison laws. This is an area where further action is needed.

TRANSGENDER COMMUNITIES

23.71. The Twelfth Plan proposes empowerment of the transgender community by advocating that line Ministries support their education, housing, access to healthcare, skill development, employment opportunities and financial assistance. Identification will be provided for transgendered persons in all Government and non-Government records by introducing a separate column to include the third gender. The Ministry of Social Justice and Empowerment along with the Ministry of Statistics and Programme Implementation will determine the number of transgendered persons in India, map their socio-economic status in order to create a law to protect interests of the community and improve their living conditions.

ENGENDERING FLAGSHIP PROGRAMMES

23.72. To ensure that the Twelfth Plan's thrust on faster, sustainable and more inclusive growth benefits both women and men, it is necessary to address gender concerns at all levels of policy especially in the operation of special programmes.

23.73. The Government of India is implementing a number of programmes, for improving access to employment, education, health, infrastructure development, urban development, and so on. Many of these programmes, although seemingly gender neutral, often have a differential impact on women in view of their different life experiences, requirements, socio-cultural drivers and priorities. These constraints must be identified and addressed.

23.74. A gender analysis of all flagship programmes will be undertaken at the design stage. This will include an activity profile of what women do and an access and control profile of women which can be used to build gender considerations into the project. Systems will be put in place to ensure that women are consulted at the time of designing the project—its location, objective and so on. Further there will be provisions put in place to undertake a social and gender audit of flagship programmes. A brief summary of issues is given below:

23.75. The Ministry of Women and Child Development/The Ministry of Statistics and Programme Implementation will monitor the gender dimensions of the flagship programmes.

BHARAT NIRMAN PROGRAMME

- Any new land arrangements (that is compensatory land given to displaced persons) must be in the joint names of the man and the woman or exclusively in the name of the woman. In particular, women will be trained in operation and maintenance work of drinking water projects.
- Women's participation in site selection will be ensured.

PRADHAN MANTRI GRAM SADAK YOJANA (PMGSY)

- The PMGSY will be engendered by incorporating gender differentials and women-specific needs especially in keeping with women's economic, domestic and community management roles.
- The ongoing process of convergence between PMGSY and MGNREGA will be strengthened by strategic coordination with NRLM aimed at the empowerment of women.

NATIONAL RURAL LIVELIHOOD MISSION (NRLM)

- More clusters and federations of women SHGs will be promoted to enable women to operate on a larger scale and avail benefits of aggregation.
- Women will be provided with information on marketing and business skills including pricing, budgeting, and access to pension and insurance products.

THE MAHATMA GANDHI NATIONAL RURAL EMPLOYMENT GUARANTEE SCHEME (MGNREGS)

- A day per month will be allocated as sensitisation day, devoted to sessions on raising awareness about the various components and rights under MGNREGS and on socially relevant legislations like Protection of Women from Domestic Violence Act, PC-PNDT Act, and Dowry Prohibition Act. Wages will be paid as on normal work days to those present in order to encourage attendance.
- The list of permissible work under MGNREGA will be expanded to allow for greater diversity of activities.
- Women's Groups will be included as implementing agencies of MGNREGS works.
- The existing provision for crèches at the work site will be implemented on a priority basis. The possibility of setting up crèches in collaboration with ICDS Anganwadis will be explored.
- The wages under MGNREGS will not be calculated on a piece-rate basis which often works to the detriment of women.

NATIONAL RURAL HEALTH MISSION

- Women from vulnerable communities, especially the scheduled castes, scheduled tribes, de-notified and primitive tribal groups, minorities, will be reached.
- Sex disaggregated data will be generated on disease burden and access to treatment.
- Focus will be extended to address ailments which women are especially prone to, such as post-menopausal problems, osteoporosis and breast and cervical cancer, and so on.
- Special measures will be undertaken on problems of those affected by HIV/AIDS.
- Dovetailing of NRHM with IGMSY (a pilot conditional maternity benefit scheme) and National Food Security Bill (NFSB) will be undertaken.

INTEGRATED CHILDHOOD DEVELOPMENT SCHEME

- Training component of Anganwadi and ASHA workers on issues relating to nutrition, counselling, child rights and gender discrimination will be strengthened.
- Area-based strategies of production/consumption based on local procurement will be encouraged. Use of PDS will also be encouraged.
- The work of ASHAs/AWWs, will be valued and recognised.

SARVA SHIKSHA ABHIYAN (SSA), KASTURBA GANDHI BALIKA VIDYALAYA AND THE RIGHT OF CHILDREN TO FREE AND COMPULSORY EDUCATION ACT

- Kasturba Gandhi Balika Vidyalayas would be upgraded up to secondary school level.
- Standards of quality of education will be adhered to at all levels with focus on availability of teachers, proper infrastructure and standardisation of learning levels.
- Gender sensitive educational system would be developed which would entail addressing sexual stereotyping, changing the attitudes and perceptions of school teachers, providing a safe and secure environment for the girl child, especially those belonging to the SC, ST and minority communities, provision of schools within easy reach, child care support to release girls from the burden of sibling care, transport and separate girl's toilets.

INDIRA AWAS YOJANA/RAJIV AWAS YOJANA

- Special provisions for housing for vulnerable women, especially single women and female headed households will be made.
- As a part of promoting economic opportunities for women in urban slum areas, particularly if the settlements are away from the city, space and buildings will be allotted for creation of work sheds for women in Rajiv Awas Yojana settlements.

NATIONAL RURAL DRINKING WATER PROGRAMME AND TOTAL SANITATION CAMPAIGN

- Women will be actively involved in determining the location of sanitation facilities.
- Targets will be set for providing toilets with water in all schools and anganwadi centres.

23.76. Difficulties in the usage of toilets will be addressed (eg. need for lighting, inappropriate location, and so on). This will be supported by IEC campaigns.

RAJIV GANDHI GRAMEEN VIDYUTIKARAN YOJANA (RGGVY)

- Some states have adopted policies for bifurcation of feeders for farms and homesteads. This allows regular flow of electricity to homesteads thereby facilitating women in accessing drinking water, studies of children and other household requirements. This model will be replicated in other states.

JAWAHARLAL NEHRU NATIONAL URBAN RENEWAL MISSION (JNNURM)

- Component on safe city planning will be added.
- Adequate resources will be allocated for undertaking safety audits and infrastructure creation for the same.
- New provisions for creating infrastructure, for example, market spaces for women hawkers, and so on will be introduced.
- Women water users groups, women councillors, a mohalla committee with women members will be included in decision making.

- Skill and capacity building amongst women will be undertaken to increase their employability in JNNURM projects.

GENDER BUDGETING (GB) INSTITUTIONALISING GB WITH GREATER VISIBILITY

23.77. The process of GB will be further strengthened in the Twelfth Plan and its reach extended to all Ministries, Departments and State Governments. Steps will be taken to further institutionalise the GB processes by strengthening and empowering the Gender Budget Cells (GBCs.). To ensure this, the suggested area of work in the Charter for GBC will be included in the quarterly/half yearly/annual plan of action. A comprehensive evaluation of GBC will also be undertaken.

23.78. The Gender Budgeting Statement (GBS) has emerged as an important advocacy tool which reflects on the flow of funds for women and encourages debate and discussions on Gender Budgeting. The scope of the GB Statement must be expanded to cover all Union Ministries and Departments by making it mandatory for all to report under the same. The new methodology and format of the GBS will promote *purposive gender planning*. To ensure better analysis, a review of the format and the methodology of the Gender Budget Statement will be undertaken in the Twelfth Plan. To further engender the union budget making process, formal pre-budget consultations must be undertaken by Ministry of Finance with women's groups as is the practice in several countries.

GB AT THE DESIGN STAGE FOR NEW PPS

23.79. In order to move from environment building and reporting to actual engendering of Policies/Programmes/Schemes (PPS), there is a pressing need to make the objectives, operational guidelines, financial norms and unit costs of the existing schemes across various Ministries/Departments more gender responsive. Planning and budget approval systems will need to be modified to make gender clearance and specific approvals of GBCs mandatory to ensure that PPS are engendered from the design stage itself.

23.80. The EFC formats must be modified to include questions to confirm that the scheme has been examined by the GBC of the Ministry. The Planning Commission at the Union Level and the State Planning Boards at the State level will ensure that proposals submitted by Ministries/Departments for any new Policy, Legislation, Programme or Scheme, includes an assessment of gender concerns/impacts on the same lines as is mandated for environmental clearance.

GENDER ANALYSIS AND AUDIT

23.81. Gender Audit as an integral part of Gender Budgeting will be promoted in the Twelfth Plan. Ministries/Departments will undertake gender audits of major programmes, schemes and policies. At the State level, mandatory gender audit of all Centrally Sponsored Schemes and Central Schemes would be undertaken. Building up the technical expertise to undertake gender audit would be integrated as part of the GB training programmes. A quantum leap in this direction will be achieved by gender perspective being incorporated within the Expenditure and Performance audits conducted by CAG.

GENDER APPRAISALS, MONITORING AND EVALUATION

23.82. Evaluation and impact assessment of schemes by an external agency are a mandatory requirement for the continuation of existing schemes beyond the plan period. It will be ensured that all impact assessment and evaluation of schemes would include a gender assessment/status of gender mainstreaming. The Ministry of Women and Child Development would ensure that the existing schemes are engendered.

GENERATION OF SEX-DISAGGREGATED DATA

23.83. Effective Gender Budgeting requires data. Hence, it is necessary to put mechanisms in place for mandatory collection of sex disaggregated data. To make this happen, all Ministries/Departments must ensure that all MIS data generated on number of users/beneficiaries is classified by sex.

CONTINUED EMPHASIS ON CAPACITY BUILDING

23.84. The current efforts of capacity building of policy makers, programme planners, budgeting and implementing officials on the tools and techniques of Gender Budgeting will be continued and expanded taking it further down to district and urban local bodies.

GENDER FOCAL POINTS

23.85. Gender Focal Points will be established within various organisations like the Ministries/Departments of the Central Government and Urban and Rural Local Bodies to enable all institutions to identify and respond to gender issues. The existing constraint of adequate and appropriately trained human resources will be addressed by drawing up a Comprehensive Human Resources Plan to make the gender architecture effective. A comprehensive evaluation of the entire gender architecture in our country will be undertaken in the Twelfth Plan.

TECHNICAL SUPPORT FOR GB

23.86. To provide technical back stopping to this process, officers dedicated to Gender Mainstreaming and Gender Responsive Budgeting must be placed within the Ministry of Women and Child Development. The GBCs will be supported by a gender expert or gender resource centre.

INCREASING ACCOUNTABILITY ON GB

23.87. Gender Budgeting will be used to mainstream gender into the existing accountability mechanisms of the Government. The Results Framework Document (RFD) is an accountability mechanism which must be gender mainstreamed by making gender outcomes a mandatory part of the RFD. For improving gender accountability a section on gender sensitivity and initiatives undertaken for gender equality could be added as part of the personnel appraisal systems of the Government.

23.88. To oversee the progress of the GB efforts, the Ministry of Women and Child Development must create a Gender Task Force with representation from the National Mission for the Empowerment of Women, Ministry of Finance as well as the Planning Commission to review the functioning of Gender Budget Cells. This Task Force would undertake a scan of all new laws, policies and programmes for

TABLE 23.1
Ministry-Wise Incorporation of Gender Concerns (under RFD)

Ministry/Department	Commitment under RFD
Science & Technology	Application of Science & Technology for weaker sections, women and other disadvantaged sections of society is one of the key functions of the Ministry. Among the key objectives, priority is being accorded to providing support to women for gender parity in Science & Technology.
Department of Bio-Technology	Under its objective of promotion of specialised human resource for frontier research the Department has accorded priority to participation of employed/unemployed women scientists.
Information Technology	Priority has been accorded to make Common Service Centre sustainable which includes e-literacy for women as success indicators.
Labour	Imparting vocational training to women has been accorded priority among the key objectives of Ministry of Labour.
Youth Affairs	Under the key objective of 'Engaging Rural Youth in Nation Building Activities', priority has been accorded to Skills Development Programmes for women in Jammu & Kashmir and border areas.
Panchayati Raj	Ministry of Panchayati Raj has incorporated enhancement of reservation for women in PRIs and also their leadership quality among its objectives.
Human Resource Development	The School Education and Literacy Department has reflected girls' education in the key objectives to meet its goal of equity and inclusion of disadvantaged groups and weaker sections by increasing enrolment in KGBVs and approval of girls hostels for secondary schools.
Health and Family Welfare	The Mission statement of the RFD document of Ministry of Health and Family Welfare includes bringing down Maternal Mortality Rate.
Rural Development	The RFD document of Rural Development Ministry has set gender disaggregated targets for employment generated under MNREGA.

gender inclusiveness. Similar mechanisms will be created at the state and district levels as well.

REFLECTING GENDER CONCERNS IN RESULTS FRAMEWORK DOCUMENT

23.89. Gender being a cross cutting issue, the RFD document of Ministries would explicitly reflect gender concerns in their vision, mission and objectives, especially those pertaining to equity, inclusiveness and empowerment and also gender disaggregated inter se priorities, targets/success indicators to make the gender outcome accountable and visible. Since the policies, programmes and schemes of these Ministries have a key role in social, political and economic empowerment, gender mainstreaming of their RFD is necessary for gender equity and inclusion.

23.90. An illustrative list of Ministries which have already incorporated gender concerns in their vision, objectives and indicators under RFD is outlined below as on Table 23.1.

TWELFTH PLAN SCHEMES

23.91. During the Twelfth Plan a number of initiatives will be undertaken for empowering women. To promote socio economic development existing schemes like the Support to Training and Employment Program (STEP) for skill development and income generation, Priyadarshini for improving sustainable livelihood opportunities and Working Women Hostels will be strengthened. The Swayamsiddha Phase II will ensure holistic empowerment of women in a sustainable manner through SHGs.

23.92. Ujjawala, a comprehensive scheme to prevent and combat trafficking with provisions for rescue, rehabilitation and reintegration of victims will integrate the victims back into society. The Swadhar Greh Scheme, based on the merger of two earlier schemes that is Swadhar and Short Stay Home will reach out to women who as victims of unfortunate circumstances are in need of institutional support for rehabilitation. A scheme for providing restorative justice to victims of rape through financial assistance as well as support services will be implemented in the Twelfth Plan in pursuance of the Supreme Court of India directives.

23.93. The Gender Budgeting Scheme which assesses gender differential impact of the budget will be continued in the Twelfth Plan Period.

NATIONAL MISSION FOR EMPOWERMENT OF WOMEN (NMEW)

23.94. With the specific objective of ensuring convergence and better coordination among the schemes/programmes of various Ministries/Departments, the Ministry launched the National Mission for Empowerment of Women (NMEW). The Mission would aim to strengthen the processes that promote all round development of women by focussing on a coordinated approach to implementation of schemes of participating Ministries/Departments. This would include generating awareness, building strategies to question prevalent "patriarchal" beliefs, establishing a convergence mechanism at multiple levels, creation of gender resource centres, formation of women's collectives and improving their capacity to access the benefits of government schemes, programmes, laws and policies and developing empowerment indicators relating to the survival, visibility, freedom and equality of women. The NMEW will also look at the inclusive development of women, including mapping vulnerabilities of women living in difficult circumstances—taking age, caste, different abilities, women headed households, ethnicity, education, income, minority status, religion, marital status, region, and so on as parameters. Collection of data on mortality of women, especially maternal mortality, deaths related to diseases, different abilities and violence based on the different socio-economic parameters is recommended.

AUTONOMOUS BODIES UNDER MWCD

23.95. **Central Social Welfare Board (CSWB)** will continue providing financial assistance to various voluntary organisations under its different schemes like Integrated Scheme for Women Empowerment for North East Region, Condensed Courses of Education for Women, Awareness Generation Projects for Rural and Poor Women, Family Counselling Centres, etc. It will also undertake a Vocational

Training Programme for Women of Weaker Section in order to provide qualitative training in traditional and non-traditional trades to women and to equip them with marketable skills.

23.96. Rashtriya Mahila Kosh (RMK) as the credit extending arm of the MWCD will be strengthened and restructured with an enlarged corpus of ₹500 crores. This will enable it to reach out to a larger number of poor, assetless and marginalised women for income generation, production, skill development and housing activities.

23.97. The National Commission for Women was set up in the year 1992 as a statutory body at the national level to protect and safeguard the rights of women. In the Twelfth Plan coordination between the National Commission and State Commissions will be strengthened. The National Commission for Women will also spread awareness of Women's Laws and Rights through various communication strategies. It will also ensure capacity building of Judicial and Police officials for proper implementation of Women related laws.

II. CHILD RIGHTS

23.98. More inclusive growth begins with Children. So the Twelfth Plan accords the highest priority to the needs of children of all classes of our society. It must ensure the fulfillment of the rights of children to survival, development, protection and participation as the foundation of human development and as a major driver of faster, more inclusive and sustainable growth.

MONITORABLE TARGETS

23.99. The Monitorable Targets of the Twelfth Plan for Children are-

- Improve the Child Sex Ratio from 914 in 2011 to 950 by 2017.
- Prevent and Reduce Child Under nutrition (percentage of underweight prevalence in children 0–3 years) by half (50 per cent) of the NFHS–3 levels.
- Reduce anaemia in girls and women by half (50 per cent).
- Ensure that all children receive a protective environment at family and community levels and through health and child care centres, schools and other facilities.
- Ensure that 80 per cent or more panchayats, districts and cities progressively become child friendly.

STATUS OF CHILDREN: AN OVERVIEW

23.100. India is home to the largest number of children in the world. Nearly every fifth child in the world lives in India. It is estimated that there are about 43 crore children in the age group of 0–18 years. It is estimated that a large proportion of these children are in very difficult circumstances or vulnerable. This includes children in poor households without family income, children denied education opportunities and forced into labour, abused/trafficked children, children on the streets, children affected by substance abuse, by armed conflict/civil unrest/natural calamity and so on. Survival, growth, development and protection of these children therefore need priority focus and attention.

23.101. The status of children in the dimensions of health, and education are discussed in detail in the Chapter on Health and the Chapter on Education. Further analysis of children of different socio-religious communities is also provided in the Chapter on Social Justice and Empowerment. Some important indicators of the situation of children are summarised below.

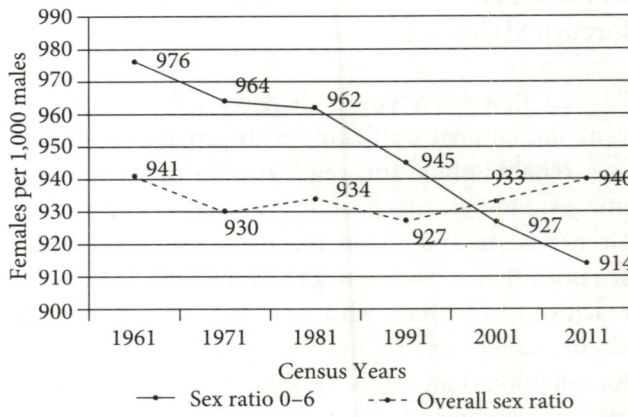

FIGURE 23.1: Child Sex Ratio 0–6 Years and Overall Sex Ratio India: 1961–2011

23.102. **Maternal Mortality Ratio** has improved and is 212 (2007–2009), as compared to 254 (2004–06).

23.103. **Infant Mortality Rate** has come down to 47 in 2010 from 58 in 2005, a decline of 11 points over the last 5 years and an annual average decline of about 2.2 points. Despite this decline, one in every 21 infants, one in every 20 infants in rural areas and one in every 32 infants in urban areas still die within one year of life in our country (SRS, 2010). Neonatal mortality in India is 33 per 1,000 live births (SRS 2010). This contributes to around 55 per cent of under five deaths. Three quarters of these deaths occur in the first week of life, 20 per cent take place within the first 24 hours of birth. This clearly highlights that reduction in early neonatal mortality (currently 25 per 1,000 live births) is critical for ensuring child survival.

23.104. **Child mortality** in children under 5 years was 59 in 2010, showing a decline of 5 points over 2009.

23.105. **The Child Sex Ratio** in the age group of children 0–6 years has declined from 927 girls per thousand boys in 2001 to 914 girls per thousand boys in 2011 (as shown in Figure 23.1). The decline is especially disturbing as it is occurring in spite of a strong legal and policy framework and various government initiatives, including cash transfers and incentive schemes, various media and messaging efforts. If not reversed, it will alter demography, erode gender justice, social cohesion and human development. The state wise position is summarised in Box 23.2.

23.106. **Sex Ratio at Birth** has shown marginal improvement from 901 in 2005–07 to 905 in 2008–2010. This is unacceptably low. Chhattisgarh has reported the highest Sex Ratio at Birth (985) while Punjab has reported the lowest (832).

23.107. **Gender differentials in Mortality Rates** continue to be discernible. The Infant Mortality Rate for girls is 49 as against 46 for boys, with differentials of over 5 points seen in states such as Gujarat, Chhattisgarh, Rajasthan, Uttar Pradesh and Himachal Pradesh in 2010. Significant gender differentials (9 points) are reflected in India's Child Mortality Rates (in children under 5 years) which were 64 for girls as against 55 for boys in 2010. Even sharper gender differentials of 10 points or more in Under Five Child Mortality Rates are seen in states such as Rajasthan (19), Uttar Pradesh (16), Jharkhand (14), Himachal Pradesh (14) and Punjab (10). This clearly highlights the need for a comprehensive strategy for care and protection of the girl child, rooted in long term interventions for gender equality (SRS Statistical Report 2010, RGI 2012).

23.108. **High levels of under nutrition in children:** India faces major nutrition challenges, with 22 per cent babies born with low birth weight, as many as 40.4 per cent of under three children underweight, 44.9 per cent stunted and 22.9 per cent wasted in 2005–07 according to the data provided by NHFS-3. It should be noted that this data indicates the position prior to the Eleventh Plan and it is likely that the position has improved since then because of initiatives taken in the Eleventh Plan. Unfortunately the relevant data will not be available for some time.

23.109. **An Inter-generational Cycle of Under nutrition:** About one-third of currently married women in the age-group 15–49 years have low Body Mass Index (BMI) (less than 18.5 kg/m2) and about 47 per cent girls in the age-group 15–19 years have low

---

Box 23.2
Declining Child Sex Ratio—A Call for Urgent Action

The lowest child sex ratio (0–6 years) has been observed in the States of Haryana (830), Punjab (846) and Jammu and Kashmir (859), with alarmingly low child sex ratios in districts such as Jhajjhar (774) and Mahendragarh (778).

Child sex ratio (0–6 years) has declined in 22 States and 5 UTs, which is a serious concern, highlighting both the increasing magnitude and spread of the problem. Jammu and Kashmir records the steepest fall of 82 points, with other states also registering sharp declines, such as Maharashtra (30) and Rajasthan (26). The number of States and UTs with child sex ratio 0–6 years below 915 has increased from nine in 2001 to fourteen in 2011 and the share of population in this category has doubled.

BMI. These factors, along with factors such as early marriage and early childbearing manifest in unfavourable outcomes for the mother and the neonate, including low birth weight. Around 43 per cent of currently married women in the age-group 20–24 years were married before attaining the age of 18 years (DLHS 3).

23.110. **The high prevalence of anaemia** amongst women, adolescent girls and children remains a major challenge. NFHS-3 (2005–06) indicates that about 55 per cent of women in the age group 15–49 years suffer from anaemia and about 79 per cent of children in the 6–35 months age group were found to be anaemic.

23.111. **Common neonatal and childhood illnesses** such as respiratory infections, diarrhoeal diseases, other infectious and parasitic diseases and malaria, account for about half of under-5 deaths in India. Respiratory infections and diarrhoeal diseases together contribute to around one-third of all deaths in children under-5 years of age. As per DLHS 3 (2007–08), the coverage rate of treatment of diarrhoea with only Oral Rehydration Solution (ORS) has been 34 per cent.

23.112. **Complete immunisation (all vaccinations)** remains a challenge, especially in some states, even though coverage rates for vaccinations have significantly improved in the recent past. A major milestone is that India has now become polio free. It is also seen that the current level of Vitamin A supplementation amongst children is low. The DLHS-3 (2007–08) reports that only 19 per cent of children aged 12–35 months had received 3–5 doses of Vitamin A.

23.113. **Children of vulnerable communities with multiple deprivations**: Wide disparities in social indicators relevant to children and their communities continue to exist across and within states, districts and diverse socio religious communities. Vulnerabilities such as poverty, exclusion, gender discrimination compound each other and their impact is often inter-generational.

23.114. **Children living in insecure environments**: Children living in insecure environments experience denial or disruption of access to health, childcare, education and other basic services which may create exposure and vulnerability to violence. A major initiative was effectively taken up addressing areas affected by Left Wing Extremism and other tribal and backward districts through an Integrated Action Plan launched in initially 60 and later 78 districts in 9 states. This has provided learning models for strengthening a protective environment in such areas—in families, communities, in health and childcare centres and schools—with an effective community based child tracking system, psychosocial care and support and special protection measures as needed. Similarly, enabling interventions are also needed in any other areas that may be affected by insecurities in the environment.

23.115. **Children of urban poor communities**: As pointed out in the Chapter on Urban Development, the size of the urban population is expected to increase rapidly and this will involve stress on children because urban basic facilities are not expanding as they should. Children of the poor in urban areas face multiple instances of deprivation and exclusion in rapidly increasing cities and towns—especially children of communities who live in unregistered/unrecognised slums or settlements. Children of urban poor communities living on or off the streets are often "invisible"—denied an identity and vulnerable to abuse, violence and exploitation—including sexual abuse. Increased vulnerability to substance abuse is another facet of these conditions. Despite various policy provisions, these children are not only denied a protective environment but also subjected to different forms of abuse, including in occupations such as domestic work, especially the girl child. This highlights the need to ensure that all children receive basic services, regardless of their location and the status of their settlements.

23.116. **Children at Work:** A large number of children are forced to work to earn money to contribute to families. According to the Census 2001, about 12.6 million child labourers in the age group of 5–14 years were engaged in hazardous occupations. Some of them are living on the streets or off the streets as well, which further results in them being exploited. A survey Conducted by National Sample Survey

Organisation (NSSO), showed 90.75 lakh working children in 2004–05 which came down to 49.84 lakh in 2009–10. As per NFHS-3 data, about 11.8 per cent children are engaged in work.

23.117. **Children in Conflict with Law** Incidents of juvenile crime reduced slightly in 2009—lower by about 2.5 per cent with reference to 2008. Under IPC crimes the highest numbers of apprehensions were for theft, followed by hurt, burglary and riots. These together contributed to 55.8 per cent of the reasons for children being in conflict with the law under the IPC.

23.118. **Child victims of Crime**: Crimes against children, increased by 18.57 per cent between 2007 and 2009 as reflected in Crimes in India 2009 published by the National Crime Records Bureau. The increase is attributed to an increase in kidnapping and abduction, infanticide, rape and murder during the period.

23.119. **Victims of Child Abuse**: The Study on Child Abuse conducted by MWCD in 2007 in thirteen states, also reported high incidence of sexual abuse of children. Sexual offences against children are inadequately addressed by earlier existing legislation. A large number of sexual offences are neither specifically provided for nor are they penalised, as a result of which offenders are tried under more lax and non-specific provisions of the Indian Penal Code (IPC).

23.120. **Children affected/infected by HIV/AIDS**: In the context of children affected/infected by HIV/AIDS, the greatest impediment is the denial of basic services. This is especially so in the sectors of health and education where stigma and discrimination weaken social support systems leading to social exclusion.

23.121. **Children with disabilities**: There are a multitude of challenges faced in the context of children with disabilities, which include the exclusion of certain types of disabilities, lack of awareness regarding issues of children with disabilities including those with learning difficulties and lack of information about the law and its specific entitlements.

PROGRESS DURING THE ELEVENTH PLAN

23.122. Progress during the Eleventh Plan in various government schemes aimed directly at benefiting children is summarised below.

CHILD SURVIVAL AND DEVELOPMENT UNIVERSALISATION OF ICDS

23.123. The Eleventh Plan witnessed the universalisation of ICDS in 2008–09 and a consequent expansion of anganwadis from 10.5 lakhs to 13.17 lakhs by the end of the Eleventh Plan, against a requirement of 14 lakhs. ICDS is a unique early childhood development programme aimed at addressing health, nutrition and development needs of young children, pregnant and breastfeeding mothers. ICDS began in 33 community development blocks selected in 1975 and covers almost all habitations across the country. However, the larger part of expansion (more than 50 per cent) has taken place post 2005. ICDS today reaches out to 7.9 crore children (6 months to 6 years) and 1.82 crore pregnant and lactating mothers through a network of 13. 17 lakh operational AWCs/Mini AWCs in 7005 operational projects. The early learning component of the programme benefits 3.5 crore children, 3–6 years old (As on 30.06.12). ICDS provides the critical link between communities and the primary health care and education systems.

23.124. Two new schemes were introduced from the platform of ICDS—Indira Gandhi Matritava Sahyog Yojana (IGMSY) and Rajiv Gandhi Scheme for Empowerment of Adolescent Girls (SABLA). They address the needs of the pregnant and lactating mothers and adolescent girls respectively, across the life cycle continuum. Indira Gandhi Matritva Sahyog Yojana (IGMSY) was introduced on a pilot basis in 53 districts in all States/UTs for providing cash directly to women during pregnancy and lactation to improve the health and nutrition status of pregnant, lactating women and infants, benefiting nearly 12.5 lakh mothers every year. SABLA, primarily for out of school adolescent girls (11–18 years) is being implemented in 200 districts on a pilot basis using the ICDS platform, to address their multi-dimensional needs. It is likely to cover nearly one crore adolescent girls annually.

23.125. **The Prime Minister's National Council on India's Nutrition Challenges** was constituted in end 2008 and in its first meeting in end 2010, it gave new policy directions which provide the road map for the Twelfth Plan. (Detailed in Part III).

EDUCATION

23.126. A critical milestone in education was the enactment of the Right of Children to Free and Compulsory Education Act, 2009. The RTE Act came into force on April 1, 2010, extending India's commitment to a rights-based system of development and translating the Constitutional provision for children's education to a justiciable right for children 6–14 years old. The impact on RTE on the lives of children, with respect to enabling them to realise full development potential and ensuring their safety and protection, is expected to be significant. The Act includes provisions against corporal punishment and makes 25 per cent reservation for disadvantaged children in private schools mandatory.

23.127. A core committee of Experts in Early Childhood Care and Education (ECCE) constituted by the Ministry of WCD has formulated a draft National ECCE Policy, National Curriculum Framework and Quality Standards for ECCE, which is likely to be finalised in the Twelfth Plan period.

CHILD PROTECTION AND CHILD RIGHTS

23.128. **Introduction of Integrated Child Protection Scheme to comprehensively address child protection**: To give a fillip to the implementation of the JJ Act and facilitate better implementation in the States/UTs, the centrally sponsored umbrella scheme 'Integrated Child Protection Scheme' (ICPS) was introduced in 2009–10. This was done by merging three Schemes of the Ministry, along with substantially enhanced infrastructural, staffing and financial norms, and introducing a range of new measures.

23.129. **Protection of Children from Sexual Offences Act 2012:** The Act was passed by Parliament in May 2012 and seeks to protect children from sexual offences. The Act regards the best interests and well-being of the child as of prime importance at every stage of the judicial process, and incorporates child friendly procedures for reporting of cases, recording of evidence, investigation and trial of offences. The Act is a step towards creating child-sensitive jurisprudence. This process will be further strengthened during the 12th Plan period by making further amendments in the Juvenile Justice Act, 2000.

23.130. **Child Rights:** The Eleventh Plan started several significant initiatives with regard to child rights such as the setting up of the National Commission for Protection of Child Rights (NCPCR) in 2007 as an independent statutory commission, with similar commissions envisaged at State level. Since then fifteen States have set-up State Commissions, and strengthening, empowering these SCPCRs, with mentoring support by NCPCR remains an issue that needs to be addressed.

23.131. **Review and Updation of the National Policy for Children (NPC) 1974** was initiated to reflect a paradigm shift from a 'needs-based' to a 'rights-based' approach, aligning this with the strategic directions of the Twelfth Plan.

STRATEGIES FOR PROMOTING CHILDREN'S RIGHTS: KEY PRIORITIES
STRENGTHENING POLICY AND LEGISLATIVE FRAMEWORKS

- Harmonisation of different child related legislative provisions and ensuring child-sensitive jurisprudence.
- Updation of the National Policy For Children in harmony with the Twelfth Plan.
- Development and implementation of National/State/District Plans of Action for Children, with monitorable outcomes, based on the updated policy, building on the Twelfth Plan.
- Focused interventions to improve the Child Sex Ratio, within an overall National Strategy for Care and Protection of the Girl Child.
- Designing a strategic approach to respond holistically to the emerging needs of children of excluded socio religious community groups such as SC, ST, particularly vulnerable tribal groups, Minorities, other disadvantaged communities, including urban poor communities.

- Development of National ECCE Policy, curricular framework and standards with National and State Early Child Development Councils.

PROGRAMME INTERVENTIONS
- ICDS strengthening and restructuring, in mission mode, with flexibility in implementation.
- Repositioning AWCs as vibrant child friendly ECD centres, owned by women and communities and with piloting of AWCs cum crèches, linked to ICDS restructuring. Models of MGNREGA/ICDS AWC cum crèche convergence are also envisaged.
- Redesign of the Rajiv Gandhi National Creche Scheme, with different models.
- Strengthening and progressive expansion of SABLA and IGMSY, with projected universalisation of maternity benefits under the Draft National Food Security Bill.
- Design and implementation of multi-sectoral initiatives to address maternal and child undernutrition (as detailed in Part III of this Chapter on Nutrition).
- Consolidation and enrichment of ICPS with strengthening of institutional capacity through a National Resource Centre.
- Strengthening the protective and nurturing environment for children in the family, community and in service institutions like crèches, Anganwadi centres, schools, health centres, and child care homes.
- Expansion of Childline and replication of this kind of partnership model to other thematic areas, such as IYCF, IMS Act and areas for attention to specific and concerted action such as learning disability in early childhood, in convergence with the Ministry of Social Justice and Empowerment.
- Harmonisation, design and coordination of interventions for adolescents—(girls and boys).
- Design of a new child participation intervention including "Baal Panchayats" which complement child friendly panchayats.

INSTITUTIONAL CAPACITY DEVELOPMENT
- Strengthening of institutional mechanisms and capacities at National, State and District levels for converging multi-sectoral action for children with reference to child specific and child related sectors.
- Strengthening of institutional mechanisms and capacities at National and State levels for the Protection of Child Rights, through empowered SCPCRs in states.
- Creating a multidisciplinary resource support network for children.
- Focus on enabling and recognising child friendly panchayats and urban local bodies where children's rights are respected, protected, facilitated and fulfilled.
- Guidelines for strengthening civil society engagement in children's issues and forums.
- Improving understanding and duty responses amongst prime care givers and service providers towards a full spectrum of care, protection and development.

TWELFTH PLAN STRATEGY
23.132. The strategy for child development in the Twelfth Plan will build on what has already been achieved in the Eleventh Plan. The fulfillment of child rights will constitute a sensitive lead indicator of national development, at national, state, district and local levels and be reflected in the Monitorable Targets for the Twelfth Plan. This will provide an overarching framework to which concerned ministries/departments that impact the lives of children, will be committed. Policies of concerned child specific and child related sectoral ministries will need to be aligned to the same. The Programme Implementation Plans of different flagship programmes will reflect child related outcomes and concomitant resources. These commitments will also be reflected in the Results Framework Documents and Five year Strategic Plans of concerned ministries and regularly reviewed.

MULTI-SECTORAL POLICY AND PLANNING FOR CHILDREN
23.133. **Key child related policies and legislations** need to be developed and/or strengthened to create the enabling policy environment needed to fulfil children's rights. This includes the *Development of a comprehensive Children's Code*, harmonising and updating different legal provisions for children, with

uniformity in the definition of "children," and creating more effective mechanisms for Child sensitive and child friendly Jurisprudence. The **Child Labour (Prohibition and Regulation) Act** will need to be amended in line with the RTE as it makes a distinction between hazardous and non-hazardous categories of work for children under 14 years. It will need to be amended to abolish all forms of child labour, as children cannot be both working and in school at the same time. Transition measures and support for families, enhanced opportunities for skill development, vocational training and rehabilitation for children will also be needed. Setting up of **State Commissions for Protection of Child Rights (SCPCRs)** needs to be made mandatory for all State Governments. The mentoring role of NCPCR needs to be strengthened and SCPCRs mandated to adopt normative guidelines for their constitution and functioning. The **Immoral Trafficking Prevention Act (ITPA)**, needs to be amended to clearly define trafficking and sexual exploitation, recognising different aspects of the same. **The Protection of Children from Sexual Offences Act 2012,** passed in Parliament will be taken forward in the Twelfth Plan. It also needs to be ensured that **the draft National Food Security Bill** protects children's rights and does not dilute earlier provisions for all six services of ICDS, mandated by earlier Supreme Court directives and also provides support for maternity protection.

23.134. **Review and Updation of the National Policy for Children 1974** to fulfil children's rights and harmonisation of State policy interventions is a critical initiative in the Twelfth Plan. Under the proposed renewed National Policy for Children, **National and State Plans of Action For Children (and progressively District Plans of Action For Children)** need to be developed, implemented and monitored, with accountability for achieving child related outcomes.

23.135. **Aligned to and building on the Twelfth Plan Monitorable Targets and strategies**, the Plans of Action For Children will have monitorable outcomes, measurable indicators, defined multisectoral commitments, enhanced resource allocation and specified time frames. The **National, State and District Plans of Action For Children** will also specifically highlight how concerns for the care and protection of the girl child are being addressed.

23.136. **Institutional Arrangements will also need to be strengthened** for improved formulation, regulation, implementation and monitoring of child rights related legislations, policies, plans, and interventions across child specific and child related sectors. The National Coordination Group will need to be revisited and redefined, linked to the PM's National Council on India's Nutrition Challenges and the possible constitution of a Standing Committee on Women and Children in the National Development Council. Similar multisectoral Coordination mechanisms are needed at State/District levels for effective implementation of the revised National Policy for Children and National, State/District Plans of Action For Children. States may also be encouraged to set up separate departments of WCD, distinct from Social Welfare, and clearly bifurcate responsibilities for Women and for Children, so that each group receives high priority.

23.137. **Capacity Development** is needed and human resources will need to be enriched, with continuity of technical support within the Ministry of Women and Child Development, at National and State levels, (progressively at district levels) to respond to emerging issues and initiatives related to children. This needs to be provided on a planned and sustained basis from government resources, reducing dependency on external aid for the same. A Technical Directorate for Child Development and Protection is needed for sustained technical support in view of the progressive universalisation/expansion and quality enrichment of major schemes. The role of NIPCCD in networking with other national institutions such as NCERT, NIN, NHSRC, NIHFW, NIUA and others working on child specific and child related themes needs to be enhanced. Institutional capacity development would need to include linking with and/or creating Centres for Child Development and Protection in Universities, Home Science/Medical Colleges in collaboration with UGC or others (as has been done for Gender Studies or as Ambedkar University and Jamia Millia Islamia have done for ECD) and establishing learning hubs and multi disciplinary training resource networks. A Child Web Portal needs to be created which includes a comprehensive data base on child survival, development, protection and participation, with supportive resources and links to similar state portals/networks of other sectors.

23.138. **Community Action:** This will be geared to creating child friendly panchayats and urban local bodies, with recognition and awards along the line of Nirmal Gram Puruskar, complemented by Baal Panchayats, where children's voices will be heard in assessing how their panchayat fares.

23.139. **Convergence:** For binding commitments of different sectors to multisectoral action, a matrix of the indicative contribution that can be made by different sectors for fulfilling children's rights will be finalised, based on the updated National Policy and National Plan of Action For Children, in consultation with child specific and child related sectors and states.

EDUCATION

23.140. The Twelfth Plan places special emphasis on education which is critical for child development. The detailed strategy for education, especially at the elementary and secondary level, is discussed in Chapter on Education. It is a key element in the strategy for equipping our children with the learning capacities and skills they need to ensure the realisation of their full development potential, without discrimination.

CHILD SURVIVAL AND DEVELOPMENT RESTRUCTURING THE ICDS

23.141. The ICDS is a unique national flagship programme for children. While it has been universalised there is much that needs to be done to improve the quality of delivery for achieving child development and nutrition outcomes. Based on the decisions of the Prime Minister's National Council on India's Nutrition Challenges and the recommendations of the Inter Ministerial Group on ICDS Restructuring, chaired by Member Planning Commission, a major strengthening and restructuring of the ICDS Scheme has recently been approved by the Cabinet. The restructured ICDS is a critical component in the Twelfth Plan strategy for child development. The reformed and strengthened ICDS embodies a genuinely integrated life cycle approach to early childhood care and development—transforming AWCs into vibrant, child friendly ECD centres, to be ultimately owned by women in the community.

23.142. **Repositioning the AWC as a vibrant, child friendly ECD centre** (Baal Vikas Kendra) which will ultimately be owned by women in the community. This will have expanded/redesigned services, extended duration (6 hours), with an additional AWW provided initially in 200 high burden districts and with piloting of crèche services in 5 per cent of AWCs. These would function as the first village outpost for health, nutrition, early learning and other women and child related services. This would include the provision of adequate infrastructure, facilities such as safe drinking water, toilets, hygienic SNP arrangements, wall painting, play space and a joyful early learning environment including provision for activity corners, and anchoring of other

---

Box 23.3
Making the Difference—ICDS Restructuring

- 'What is different'—the focus on the critical age group—pregnant and breastfeeding mothers and children under three years—for integrated early child development.
- The defining difference in 'How will things be done differently' is decentralisation, with flexibility in implementation.
- Panchayat led models which respond effectively to the needs of local communities—especially the most vulnerable communities—SCs, STs and minorities, among others.
- ICDS Restructuring seeks to empower states/districts/blocks and villages to contextualise the programme and find innovative solutions, building on local capacities and resources.

services for maternal, child and care for out of school adolescent girls through the Rajiv Gandhi Scheme for Empowerment of Adolescent Girls. Greater ownership by women and communities would also come with institutional reforms that include the establishment of Anganwadi Management Committees, which include mothers/mahila mandals/parents as members, empowered with untied funds for local action.

23.143. **Re-designing and reinforcing of the package of ICDS services**, including a new component of Child Care and Nutrition Counselling for mothers of children under three years. This will focus on regular and prioritised home visiting at critical contact points, improving key family care behaviours—Infant and Young Child Feeding, health, hygiene, psychosocial care, early learning and care of girls and women.

23.144. **Enhancing Nutritional Impact** with revised nutrition and feeding norms; ensuring provision for nutritious, freshly cooked, culturally appropriate meal, (morning) snack and Take Home Rations in harmony with Supreme Court directives and the IMS (and its Amendment) Act and greater involvement of women's SHGs. Piloting of community kitchens and joint kitchens with Mid Day Meals will also be undertaken. A focus on early preventive action in a public health perspective will be promoted by reaching pregnant and breastfeeding mothers and children under three years more effectively in the family and community.

23.145. **A continuum of care** will be promoted across the life cycle, extending from care in the family, in anganwadis and communities to health sub centres and health facilities. An innovative new component is SNEHA SHIVIRS (see Box 23.4) for promoting community based prevention and care of severely undernourished children, backed by stronger referral linkages with the health system (Nutrition Rehabilitation Centres under NRHM). Requisite safeguards will be ensured so that there is no "product driven" or commercial interference with infant and young child feeding practices.

23.146. **Strengthening Early Childhood Care and Education (ECCE)** by redefining ICDS non formal preschool education to ECCD, with additional and trained human resources, introduction of a developmentally appropriate curriculum framework with joyful learning methodologies. This will be supported by the use of local culturally relevant play/activity materials, AWC activity corners and local toy banks in child friendly AWC environments. Joyful early learning approaches will be promoted—for children 3–6 years of age, including school readiness interventions for children 5 plus years of age, either in AWCs or in schools (depending upon the state context). Co-location of ICDS AWCs with schools where locally decided, will enable resource sharing, mentoring of AWWs and better school readiness and transition. Children from different community groups, playing/learning together and eating together at AWCs will lay the foundation for more inclusive early socialisation and more inclusive and cohesive communities.

Box 23.4
Learning by Doing—SNEHA SHIVIRs

Building on learnings from the positive deviance approach initiated, SNEHA SHIVIRs will be introduced for community based care of undernourished children.

These include 12 day Nutrition Care and Counselling Sessions at AWCs, using positive role model mothers, whose children are growing well, for demonstrating positive care practices, cooking and feeding, (with mothers' contribution) to mothers of undernourished children in similar community environments.

This improves family care and feeding behaviours (Learning By Doing) through sustainable approaches, enhancing local caregiving capacities through peer counselling, demonstrating positive care practices and enabling change, using local resources—touching the lives of young children and their communities.

23.147. **Strengthening civil society partnerships to allow operating up to 10 per cent of the ICDS projects by CSOs.** These models will contribute to innovation, component enrichment, quality improvement, extending reach to unreached areas and better responsiveness to local contexts. Flexibility will be provided to States to decide upon this.

23.148. **Ensuring convergence with related sectors such as NRHM, TSC, NRDWP, SSA, MGNREGA** through joint planning, inclusion of young child related concerns in State/District Annual Programme Implementation Plans (APIPs) of relevant sectors, joint monitoring of key results and indicators and defined roles and accountabilities. Institutional mechanisms for convergence will be anchored in Panchayati Raj Institutions such as Village Health, Sanitation and Nutrition Committees at village level. These will be strengthened and platforms such as Fixed Monthly Village Days at AWCs (for Health, Nutrition and ECCE) will take this forward. Resources of other programmes will also be mobilised for AWC construction and upgradation.

23.149. **Institutional Reforms** aim at transforming ICDS into a "Mission Mode." decentralised programme, with a flexible implementation framework with monitorable outcomes for improved effectiveness, efficiency and accountability. The ICDS National Mission Steering Group would function for Nutrition coordination as well and report to the PM's National Council. A Policy Coordination Support Unit in Planning Commission would need to provide multi-sectoral policy coordination support to the same.

23.150. **ICDS Missions at National, State and District levels with structure and systems,** enhanced human and financial resources, empowered for action with clearly laid down systems for financial, human resource, logistics and procurement, programme and operations monitoring. The existing service delivery mechanisms will be strengthened through setting up of National/State ICDS Mission Directorates, Technical thematic groups State and District Child Development Societies with coordination and monitoring committees at block, village and anganwadi levels.

23.151. **Progressive devolution of powers to Panchayati Raj Institutions and Urban Local Bodies** is envisaged. The emphasis is on reinforcing the AWC as a village habitation level institution owned by the community, with the leadership and support of panchayati raj institutions. Training, capacity development of PRIs, especially women members and members of VHSNCs will be supported, with need based catalytic support from NGOs at field level.

23.152. **Strengthening of ICDS Management Information System (MIS)** This would be revamped to focus on real time data for assessment, analysis and action, closest to the level at which data is generated, using Information Communication Technology (ICT) and the reach of mobile telephones. The use of Mother and Child Protection Cards for the monitoring and promotion of young child growth and development is critical, with transparent community validation at Village Health and Nutrition Days and community owned accreditation processes, with the active involvement of VHSNCs and women's/community groups.

23.153. **Community owned ICDS accreditation system** will be introduced to ensure quality standards in child care service delivery at all levels, with grading of AWCs, sectors, block/projects, districts, based on child related outcomes, using a checklist based on service standards. This would be reinforced by community based recognition and awards for child friendly Anganwadi Centres, Panchayats, blocks and districts.

23.154. **Community ownership of ICDS** will be ensured through the common Village Health, Sanitation and Nutrition Committees and the AWC Management Committees. Involvement of Women SHGs, Mothers' Committees/women link volunteers will also be promoted in order to deepen community ownership of ICDS. Initiatives for extending and deepening the involvement of women's SHGs in ICDS, including in the Supplementary Nutrition component, will be promoted, in convergence with Rural Development.

23.155. **The IDA assisted Integrated Child Development Services Systems Strengthening and Nutrition Improvement Project** (ISSNIP) will also be implemented in 162 high burden districts of 8 states, reinforcing the strengthening and restructuring ICDS, and enhancing child nutrition and development outcomes.

23.156. **Indira Gandhi Matritva Sahyog Yojana (IGMSY)—the Conditional Maternity Benefit Scheme** will be expanded in the Twelfth Plan, building on learnings from the pilot in 53 districts. Promoting a life cycle approach, this will also be linked to the umbrella ICDS mission. This is also likely to be included as an entitlement for Maternity Protection under the proposed National Food Security Bill 2011.

23.157. **Rajiv Gandhi National Crèche Scheme** (RGNCS) needs a relook, with the universalisation of ICDS, which aims to cater to a similar target group of children, and provides a larger gamut of services. Appropriate linkages may be developed with the ICDS mission on pilot basis.

EARLY CHILDHOOD CARE AND EDUCATION (ECCE)

23.158. The approach would be to address areas of systemic reform in ECCE across all channels of services in the public, private and voluntary sectors, going beyond ICDS, and with stronger linkages with Education.

23.159. **National Policy on ECCE:** A National Policy on ECCE will be formulated accompanied by a comprehensive Plan of Action. It will address four main policy challenges that is Access, Inclusion, Quality and Institutional Capacity for ECCE.

23.160. **Ensuring Universal Access with Inclusion:** Universalisation of access with inclusion will imply that each and every child in the relevant age group from all social and economic categories is given access to ECCE of acceptable quality. For children below 3 years, the focus will be on home based early childhood development. Universal Access with Inclusion will call for greater flexibility and a move away from the current centralised, standard design towards more decentralised, habitation based and contextualised planning and interventions. The ECCE strategy includes (*a*) Restructuring of ICDS with flexibility and decentralisation; (*b*) Involvement of NGOs; (*c*) Community based models; (*d*) Demand driven models; (*e*) Innovations grant for New Schemes; (*f*) Promoting Public Private Partnerships; (*g*) Urban strategy; and (*h*) Convergence.

23.161. **Quality with Inclusion:** Strategies for ensuring quality with inclusion will include: (*a*) National Curriculum Framework for ECCE; (*b*) Quality Standards and a system of Accreditation; (*c*) Developmentally appropriate Curriculum; (*d*) Ensuring a child friendly joyful early learning environment; (*e*) Professionalisation of ECCE; (*f*) Training Framework; and (*g*) Advocacy and Communication.

23.162. **Institutional Capacity:** Strategies for strengthening institutional capacity for improved ECCE will include: (*i*) Establishing a reliable and efficient Management Information System; (*ii*) Research; and (*iii*) Capacity Strengthening through establishment of National/State ECD Resource Centres, linked to NIPCCD Regional Centres, NCERT/SCERTs and ECCE Units in DIETs. This would also be linked to a network of ECCE centres/study units in established universities, as has been demonstrated by ECCE centres in Ambedkar and Jamia Millia Islamia Universities.

23.163. **National/State ECD Councils:** A National Early Childhood Development (ECD) Council will be established to take on policy, curricular framework and standards regarding ECCE. Progressively similar Councils are envisaged at State levels for effective monitoring of the proposed ECCE policy.

> **Box 23.5**
> **Early Joyful Learning-Chilli Pilli**
>
> The Government of Karnataka introduced the concept of early joyful learning in anganwadis in Karnataka. Chilli Pilli, designed to address all interrelated development domains of the child-physical, cognitive, psycho social and language development.
>
> Chilli Pilli is a comprehensive package which adopts developmentally appropriate practices, through training of anganwadi workers and ICDS functionaries, use of a thematic activity bank relevant to the local cultural context. Stree Shakti groups are also involved in making these materials. Activities encourage children to explore their environment and learn while doing. The activities include stories, games-indoor and outdoors, art and craft related and concepts of colour, shape pre-number. Curiosity corners are set up and children clustered into two groups 3 to 4 years and 4 to 5 years to enable developmentally appropriate practices.
>
> By effective demonstration, Chilli Pilli has increased the participation of children and their active learning capacities, preparing them better for school. It has also reached out to parents, communities and panchayats in ICDS, who own this initiative.

23.164. **Strengthening NIPCCD:** NIPCCD will be strengthened to function as a global centre of excellence. It will have an expanded resource network of additional Regional Centres/State Institutes to reach out effectively, with clusters of States/UTs. New initiatives will be taken to expand and enrich the pool of core trainers to respond to training needs arising from ICDS Restructuring, likely universalisation of IGMSY under the Draft National Food Security Bill, strengthening of SABLA—especially the non nutrition component (life skills) and ICPS expansion, upcoming new ECCE policy and new thematic focus areas.

23.165. In view of the ICDS Restructuring recommendation that 10 per cent of ICDS projects be taken up in partnership with NGO's, NIPCCD and its regional and state centres need to redesign and strengthen their support for Voluntary Action as related to Women and Child Development. National and State NGO Forums for Children may be enabled, through networking, dialogue and a resource inventory created so that NGOs are able to access information and resources related to child care. Other new initiatives envisaged include setting up a National Nutrition Resource Centre and National/Regional Child Development Resource Centres; setting up Child Budgeting/Training Cell and collaboration with Breastfeeding Promotion Network of India and MWCD on the lines of ChildIine Foundation.

PROMOTING CHILD PROTECTION AND PARTICIPATION

INTEGRATED CHILD PROTECTION SERVICES

23.166. **Strengthening Implementation of Integrated Child Protection Scheme** as a vehicle for implementation of the JJ Act is a priority. Although ICPS is a comprehensive scheme on child care and protection, it does not adequately focus on restoration of children back to the families and rehabilitation. It requires consolidation as well as focused efforts to address implementation gaps. Emphasis will, therefore be placed on improved implementation by the states, reviewing norms and procedures and building capacities.

23.167. **Ensuring and Enhancing response for children in emergency situations:** Children separated from their families that is missing children, children being trafficked/abused or exploited, children on the streets needing immediate help can be assured of timely help through the 24 hr. telephone outreach CHILDLINE service currently available in 181 cities. Services will be expanded and improved through Strengthening and Expansion of Childline Services to all districts/cities through professionalising of the service, stronger partnerships and consultations with voluntary organisations, greater investment of resources and capacity building.

INCLUSIVE APPROACHES FOR REACHING THE MOST VULNERABLE
CHILDREN IN NEED OF CARE AND PROTECTION AND IN CONFLICT WITH LAW

23.168. **Amendment of JJ Act:** Since the last amendment to the Act in 2006, various issues have emerged such as the abuse and trafficking of children in Homes not registered under JJ Act. To establish and sustain a Justice System that is truly child centric, the next five years will seek to address the needs of all children (including vulnerable children) holistically.

23.169. **Other elements of the Child Protection Strategy** in the Twelfth Plan will include strengthening families and communities to care for and protect their children, interventions such as Open Shelters, community based foster care; Registration Rationalization and Up-gradation of Institutional services; professionalisation of Child Protection services and orientation/training of Police personnel. Creating a database of Children availing child protection services and a system for matching 'missing' and 'found' children, promoting adoption of children without parental support and strengthening of CARA/SARAs will be other elements of the strategy for Child Protection. Effective linkages with programmes such as SSA will bring children in need of care and protection back into the mainstream.

23.170. **Differently Abled Children:** The emphasis on primary prevention of childhood disability and early intervention through NRHM and ICDS will be strengthened in the Twelfth Plan along with community based management and inclusion of children with different abilities. Major relevant flagship programmes will include specific earmarked allocations for reaching out to and including children with special needs, as was initiated with Sarva Shiksha Abhiyan. Similarly the restructured ICDS will include specific resource provisions for mainstreaming prevention, early intervention, community based care and referral support for addressing disability in the very young child early on. The joint ICDS\NRHM mother-child card is a useful starting point and referral care linkages with the health system and with institutional support mechanisms such as District Rehabilitation Centres (DRCs) will also be strengthened for effective community based rehabilitation.

23.171. Major initiatives in the Twelfth Plan will be the constitution of a National Task Force on Childhood Disability, setting up of Childhood Disability Resource Centres in relevant National Institutes, in key national/state institutions responsible for training NRHM, ICDS and SSA personnel (such as NIHFW/SIHFWs, NCERT/SCERTs, NIPCCD/MLTCs/AWTCs) and the development of core training modules for integration in respective training programmes. Greater participation of civil society, including parent networks, will be a significant feature to develop and scale up innovative models and approaches.

CHILDREN OF MOST VULNERABLE COMMUNITIES WITH MULTIPLE DEPRIVATIONS

23.172. Reaching every child through universal approaches with normative standards and flexible, locally relevant and culturally appropriate strategies is a challenge that will be addressed not only in terms of the manifestations of social exclusion—but through structural transformation in its causal framework, along with affirmative action for disadvantaged groups. Recognising the need to anchor inclusion of children of socio-religious communities more firmly in relevant national flagship programmes and closely monitor the child related component of schemes taken up under targeted interventions such as Scheduled Castes Sub-Plan SCSP and the Tribal Sub Plan (TSP) and the MSDP for minorities, new linkages will also be established with the Assessment and Monitoring Authority for this purpose.

23.173. Relevant child related flagship programmes will also be enabled through capacity development, more inclusive institutional mechanisms (mission steering groups/programme committees/village committees and so on), greater representation of women of these communities as community workers (AWWs, ASHAs, link volunteers), and decentralised participatory planning processes, with leadership of PRIs. Disaggregated tracking and reporting of child related outcomes to monitor social inclusion of diverse socio religious communities will be a major initiative with community based monitoring and social audits.

23.174. There will also be incentivisation of sectors, States (through Additional Central Assistance) and panchayats where social inclusion indicators related to children of socio religious communities—including minorities—improve, with peer learning/motivation through sharing of best practices, within and across States/Districts.

ENDING DISCRIMINATION AGAINST THE GIRL CHILD

23.175. Advancing the rights of the girl child and ensuring gender equality is a critical development challenge. The recommendations for the 12th Five Year Plan centre around four main conceptual issues intended at addressing the underlying and root causes. These are: (*i*) Protection and advancement of rights of the Girl Child; (*ii*) Gender Equality; (*iii*) Empowerment and enhancement of Self Esteem; and (*iv*) Institutional arrangements.

23.176. **Girl Child Specific District Plan of Action:** An integrated approach focusing on the girl child is needed. It must be led by State Multi sectoral Task Forces for Care and Protection of the Girl Child, which bring together different departments of government and civil society, to improve the child sex ratio, especially in States where the child sex ratio is very adverse and/or the decline has been steep. The implementation of the Pre-Conception and Pre-Natal Diagnostic Techniques (Prohibition of Sex Selection) Act will be strengthened so as to prevent the misuse of medical technology for sex selection, supported by a concerted societal campaign to change societal norms to ensure equal value for the girl child. The Girl Child Specific District Plan of Action will be developed through decentralised planning processes, involvement of panchayati raj institutions and partnership with civil society organizations. These will also link with the proposed pilot interventions planned by the Ministry of Panchayati Raj to award panchayats that improve the child sex ratio and enhance care and protection of the girl child (proposed as Rashtriya Gaurav Gram Sabha Awards).

In the Twelfth Plan, a High Level Inter-Ministerial Committee will be set up on "Care and Protection of the Girl Child," which will constitute the institutional mechanism for mobilising and monitoring multi sectoral interventions for addressing the adverse child sex ratio, rooted in longer term interventions for gender equality. The time bound National Strategy will bring together government, sectors, states and civil society for urgent concerted action. The High Level Inter-Ministerial Committee will also link with and mentor State Task Forces which will develop State Programmes of Action across the country.

23.177. **Quality Education For Girls:** Increasing girls' access to and motivation for additional schooling can be a key intervention strategy for affirmative action for girls and women, as detailed in the Chapter on Education.

23.178. **Prohibiting Dowry and Child Marriage:** Effective enforcement of the Child Marriage Prohibition Act, Dowry Prohibition Act (DPA) and Protection of Women from Domestic Violence Act (PWDVA) needs to be encouraged through several actions, as detailed in Part I.

23.179. **Incentive Schemes For the Girl Child:** Review and Redesigning of Cash Incentive Schemes and Conditional Cash transfers for the Girl Child (including Dhanlakshmi) will be undertaken in the first half of the Twelfth Plan. The Government of India's pilot scheme on conditional cash transfer with insurance benefit, titled 'Dhanalakshmi' also will be revisited and the possibility of providing ownership of assets such as a house under Indira Awas Yojna rather than cash incentives will be explored.

23.180. **Interventions for improving the Self Esteem of Girls and Women:** For enabling girls to challenge the norms of a patriarchal and male-dominated society, they have to be empowered with high self-esteem, as detailed in Part I. Additionally, gender and girl child impact analysis based on disaggregated data focusing on gender, caste, minority status and geographic location, in benchmarking, designing, implementation and monitoring policies and programmes needs to be undertaken. Concerns of the girl child, which are unique, and which need special attention and provisions, should be focused upon in the National/State/District Plans of Action For Children that are envisaged.

ADOLESCENTS

23.181. **Strengthen Coordination Mechanisms:** The mandate for strengthening existing coordinating mechanisms is vested in the Ministry of Women and Child Development, in partnership with the Ministry of Youth Affairs and this may be linked to the reconstitution of the National Coordination Group in the Twelfth Plan.

23.182. **Uniformity in the age-group:** The age group for adolescents under various schemes varies and needs to be standardised. For adolescents, the age group 10 to 18 years may be taken and necessary harmonisation of guidelines undertaken accordingly.

23.183. **Abolition of all forms of Child labour:** The abolition of all forms of child labour for the effective implementation of RTE Act needs to be mandated. Child labour in any form is detrimental to the physical, mental and cognitive growth and development of the child. The RTE Act, guarantees the right to every child between the ages of 6 and 14 to free and compulsory elementary education whereas the Child Labour (Prohibition and Regulation) Act makes a distinction between hazardous and non-hazardous categories of work for children under 14 years. Children cannot be both working and in school at the same time.

23.184. **Extension of Right of Children to Free and Compulsory Education Act, 2009 (RTE Act) upto Senior Secondary:** The extension of RTE upto senior secondary level is proposed in the Twelfth Plan, for expanding the possibilities of the adolescents to realise their full learning rights and to address early marriages of girls, teenage pregnancy and juvenile delinquency.

23.185. **Strengthening of RGSEAG—SABLA scheme:** The pace of implementation of the SABLA scheme has been slow. The scheme components, especially the linkages with education and skill development, or the non nutrition component, requires strengthening and the scheme requires evaluation, before expansion is recommended.

CHILD PARTICIPATION

23.186. Involving children and encouraging their participation in all decisions related to programmes and policies meant for them, is the key to institutionalising a child rights framework within the country. Children must be provided with an environment wherein they are aware of their rights; possess the freedom and opportunity to fully and freely express their views in accordance with their age and maturity; and that their views, especially those of the girl child and of children from minority groups or marginalised communities, are respected. During the 12th Plan, making information on child rights, laws and policies available and accessible to all children in accordance with their age and maturity will be a priority. NCPCR will be the nodal agency to develop different models, undertake research to develop monitorable indicators of child participation and document best practices in child participation. The models will include building on the experience with Baal Panchayats and Baal Sabhas, complementing child friendly panchayats.

STRENGTHENING INSTITUTIONS AND PROCESSES FOR PROMOTING CHILD RIGHTS- NCPCR AND SCPCRs

23.187. During the 12th Plan period, the NCPCR will be strengthened in its role as an independent statutory Commission, with enabling provisions to expand its mentoring support to SCPCRs and with enhanced human and financial resources. As State Commissions have not been set up in all states, NCPCR will also consider setting up representative offices in some states, to cover all regions of the country, to ensure access to services to children across the country and to address cases of child rights violation. To encourage each State/UT to set-up the SCPCR with adequate infrastructure and human resources as envisaged under the Commissions for Protection of Child Rights Act, 2005, funding through Additional Central Assistance is also envisaged. Policy and programme recommendations for providing a protective environment for children, with child tracking mechanisms, especially in areas affected by conflict (such as Integrated Action Plan districts), will be a priority, building on learnings from the Baal Bandhu pilot programme.

Outcome Oriented Child Budgeting

23.188. Child Budgeting has received recognition in the 11th Five Year Plan. However, there is need for better targeting through child budgeting mechanisms to ensure that all child-related needs are not only adequately resourced and that outlays are increased, but also effectively utilised and translated into meaningful outcomes for children.

23.189. To institutionalise child budgeting procedures during the 12th plan, there will be focus on building capacities to analyse the central and state budgets and their impact on the outcomes for children. This assessment will then inform policy and programme formulation for children across ministries/departments. Outcome oriented Child Budgeting will be progressively institutionalized in the Twelfth Plan period, building on the experience with Gender Budgeting. A Child Development Index also needs to be developed on the lines of 'Women Development Index.'

23.190. An Impact Assessment of relevant sectoral policies and programmes on children will be made a mandatory part of the Mid Term Appraisal of the Twelfth Plan. This will provide the basis for mid course policy and programme redesign to ensure more inclusive growth, linked to similar initiatives for assessing the inclusion of different communities.

NUTRITION

23.191. The challenging state of nutrition in India, highlighted by high rates of child malnutrition has been a matter of grave concern and a legitimate focus of criticism. Nutrition constitutes the foundation for human development, by reducing susceptibility to infections, reducing the related morbidity, disability and mortality burden, enhancing cumulative lifelong learning capacities and adult productivity. There can be no doubt that improvement in the nutritional status of both children and adults must have high priority in any strategy for human development. Nutrition

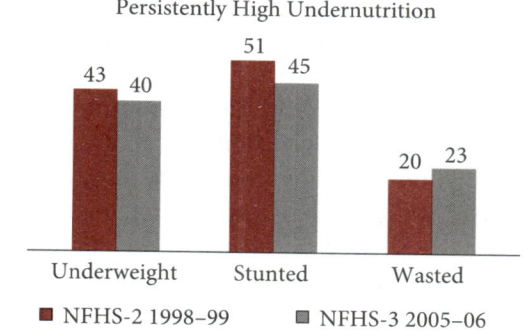

Note: Using WHO 2006 International Reference population.

FIGURE 23.2: Nutrition Status of Children under 3 Years (%)

status of the most vulnerable age group of children is both a sensitive proxy indicator of human development and also a key determinant of the effectiveness of national socio economic development strategies.

23.192. However, in designing strategies to improve nutrition, it must be recognised that nutrition is an outcome of multi-sectoral interventions that impact communities, especially women and children over the life cycle. Under-nutrition is the outcome of many factors. Insufficient dietary intake and absorption and inadequate prevention and management of disease/infections linked to the lack of access to health and child care services, lack of access to safe drinking water, environmental sanitation and hygiene, lack of access to household food security and livelihoods, and inadequate caring and feeding practices for children and women are key determinants. Basic determinants include income levels, agriculture, animal husbandry, public distribution systems, water and environmental resources, education and communication, control and use of resources (human, economic, natural), shaped by the macro socio-economic and political environment.

23.193. Part III of this Chapter focuses on addressing direct nutrition related interventions for maternal and child care, with different Chapters addressing other facets of multi-sectoral action for Nutrition. These include the Chapters relating to Health, Drinking Water and Sanitation, Food and Agriculture, Rural Development, Panchayati Raj Institutions and Education among others.

23.194. In India, undernutrition levels remain high—especially in utero and in the first two years of life, in adolescent girls and in women across the life cycle, in vulnerable/excluded community groups and those living in poverty and in areas or conditions of high nutritional vulnerability and where the disease load is high. The latest data for malnutrition in children measured in terms of weight for age, height for age or weight for height are for 2005–06 from NHFS 3. When these are compared with earlier NHFS data from NHFS 2 and 1 there is a moderate trend improvement over time (See Figure 23.2).

23.195. There are also large inter-state variations in the patterns and trends in underweight prevalence reported in NFHS 3—amongst children this was highest in Madhya Pradesh (60 per cent), followed by Jharkhand (57 per cent) and Bihar (56 per cent) and lowest in Mizoram, Sikkim, Manipur, and Kerala.

23.196. A recent HUNGAMA (Hunger and Malnutrition) Survey conducted in 2011 across 112 rural districts of India with especially challenging socio economic indicators, suggests that the prevalence of underweight in children under 5 years has decreased significantly from an estimated 53 per cent (as per DLHS 2 in 2002–04) to 42 per cent (2010–11) in this survey. This represents a 20.3 per cent decrease over a 7 year period (compared with DLHS 2) with an average annual rate of reduction of 2.9 per cent. The study however does not elaborate upon its assessment of wasting levels in children under five years (both severe and moderate) in these districts, at around half of what is estimated as the All India average by NFHS 3 (2005–06).

23.197. It is possible that malnutrition is being reduced more rapidly than earlier as in the case with poverty reduction. However this can only be validated by the Data from the Annual Health Survey and District Level Household Survey, which will be available by 2013.

23.198. **Infant and Young Child Feeding Practices:** Appropriate feeding practices in children under 2 years are crucial for their survival, healthy growth and intellectual and physical development. Early initiation of breastfeeding (within one hour of birth) and exclusive breastfeeding for the first six months of life provides optimal nutrition for growth and development. According to the Lancet 2004, universalisation of breastfeeding (including exclusive breastfeeding for the first six months and continued breastfeeding for the next six months) will reduce mortality of children under 5 years by 13 per cent globally and by around 16 per cent in India (India Analysis). Introduction of appropriate complementary feeding after six months also prevents undernutrition in children and growth faltering. The initiation of breastfeeding within one hour in India was only 24.5 per cent while the exclusive breastfeeding rate in children under six months was 46.4 per cent (NFHS 3), as seen in the Figure 23.3.

23.199. NFHS 3 data also indicated that around half (56 per cent) of children aged 6–9 months are provided with the recommended semi-solid complementary foods and breast milk.

23.200. However some improvement is visible in early initiation, as the rate of breastfeeding within one hour of birth increased from 27.8 per cent in DLHS 2 to 40.5 per cent in DLHS 3. Recently released AHS data 2010–11 for 9 states (UP, Rajasthan, Odisha, Bihar, MP, Uttarakhand, Assam, Jharkhand and Chhattisgarh) reveals that children exclusively breastfed (0–6 months) ranges from 17.7 per cent in UP to 47.5 per cent in Chhattisgarh, highlighting the challenges ahead, especially in these states.

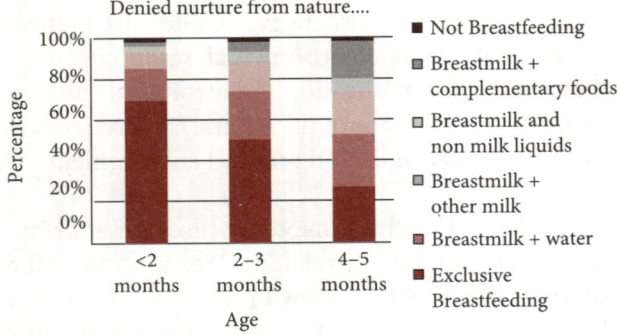

Source: NFHS 2005–06.

FIGURE 23.3: Inadequate Exclusive Breastfeeding in India (0–6 Months)

NUTRITIONAL STATUS OF WOMEN AND ADOLESCENT GIRLS

23.201. More than one third (36 per cent) of women aged 15–49 have a Body Mass Index (BMI) below 18.5, which indicates chronic energy deficiency. About 16 percent are moderately to severely thin. Bihar (45 per cent), Chhattisgarh (43 per cent), Madhya Pradesh (42 per cent) and Odisha (41 per cent) are the states with the highest proportion of undernourished women. Adolescent girls are also one of the vulnerable groups which require concerted attention. Adolescent Girls between 11–18 years constitute 16.75 per cent of female population (Approx. 8.32 crore). Among these, approximately 2.75 crore (33 per cent) are undernourished. Their health and nutrition status is further compromised by early marriage and early childbearing as reflected in DLHS 3 findings according to which around 43 per cent of currently married women in the age-group 20–24 years were married before attaining the age of 18 years.

MICRONUTRIENT DEFICIENCIES

23.202. Micronutrients are Vitamins and Minerals that humans need to consume in small amounts for optimal health and development. Micronutrient deficiencies often coexist with protein energy malnutrition and also have independent and interacting effects on health, growth and immuno competence. The groups most vulnerable are pregnant mothers, breastfeeding mothers and young children. Iron, Vitamin A and iodine deficiencies are major public health problems, among the range of Vitamin and Mineral Deficiencies.

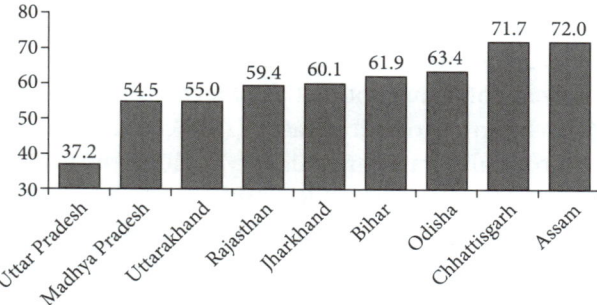

FIGURE 23.4: Children Aged 6–35 Months who Received a Vitamin A Dose During Last Six Months (%) (AHS 2010–11)

23.203. **Vitamin A**: Sub-clinical Vitamin A Deficiency (VAD) is a well-known cause of morbidity and mortality, especially among young children and pregnant women. Vitamin A deficiency limits the growth of young children, weakening their immunity and, in cases of acute deficiency, leading to blindness and to increased mortality. Vitamin A supplementation has proven successful in reducing the incidence and severity of illness. It has been associated with an overall reduction in child mortality, especially from diarrhoea, measles and malaria. As per NFHS-3, only one in four children aged 12–35 months received the six monthly Vitamin A supplement in the six months before the survey. This figure drops further, to only 18 per cent, among children aged 6–59 months. This data relates to 2005–06.

23.204. The later DLHS 3 survey for 2008–09 shows the 54.5 per cent Children (aged 9 months and above) received at least one dose of the Vitamin A supplement. The most recent Annual Health Survey 2010–11(Figure 23.4) showed that at least every 2nd child aged 6–35 months has received a Vitamin A supplement in AHS States in the last six months—except in Uttar Pradesh where it is every 3rd child. (AHS 2010–11 covered 9 states—UP, Rajasthan, Odisha, Bihar, MP, Uttarakhand, Assam, Jharkhand and Chhattisgarh). These surveys suggest that the challenge of achieving high coverage with completion of all six monthly Vitamin A doses (9 m-under 5 years), remains an unfinished agenda, especially in states with low coverage rates.

23.205. **Iron**: Iron deficiency anaemia (IDA) is common across all age groups, but highest among young children, adolescent girls, pregnant and lactating women. The consequences of IDA in pregnant women are increased risk of low birth weight or premature delivery, peri-natal and neonatal mortality, inadequate iron stores for the new-born, lowered physical activity, fatigue and increased risk of maternal morbidity. Iron deficiency impairs growth, cognitive development and immune function. It leads children to perform less well in school and adults to be less productive. Prevalence of anaemia among children 6–35 months has increased from 74 per cent in NFHS-2 to 79 per cent in NFHS-3.

23.206. AHS 2010–11 data shows that IFA (Iron Folic Acid) supplementation to children aged 6–35 months during last 3 months ranges from 9.4 per cent in Rajasthan to 37.7 per cent in Chhattisgarh. This merits attention across the 9 States covered by AHS, especially Rajasthan and Uttar Pradesh.

23.207. Amongst adolescent girls, anaemia levels continue to be high; 2.75 crore girls are found to be undernourished, and their health and nutrition status is further undermined by early marriage and early child bearing.

23.208. Anaemia is a major health problem for adults as well, affecting 55 per cent of women and 24 per cent of men. The prevalence of anaemia in ever-married women has increased from 52 per cent in NFHS-2 to 56 per cent in NFHS-3. This highlights the need to accelerate interventions for prophylaxis and control of nutritional anaemia across the life cycle.

23.209. **Iodine**: Iodine Deficiency is the most common cause of preventable mental retardation and brain damage in the world. Iodine deficiency during pregnancy is associated with low birth weight, increased likelihood of stillbirth, spontaneous abortion and congenital abnormalities such as cretinism and irreversible forms of mental impairment. During the childhood period, it impairs physical growth, causes goitre and decreases the probability of child survival. It has been estimated that 200 million people in India are exposed to the risk of iodine deficiency and more than 71 million suffer from goitre and other iodine deficiency disorders (MoHFW, 2005). As per the district level IDD survey conducted by Directorate General of Health Services, ICMR, AIIMS, NIN, Hyderabad, State Health Directorate and other Health institutions, out of 365 districts surveyed covering all States/UTs, 303 districts are endemic where the prevalence of iodine deficiency disorders is more than 10 per cent. Thus, no State/UT is free from IDD.

23.210. According to NFHS-3, among the households that had their salt tested, just over half (51 per cent) were using salt that was adequately iodized others were using salt that was either inadequately iodized or was not iodized at all. However, CES 2009 shows that the household consumption for iodised salt has increased to 71 per cent.

23.211. **Zinc** deficiency also results in the stunted growth of children. Zinc deficiency compromises the effectiveness of the immune system, increasing the incidence and severity of infections such as diarrhoeal disease and pneumonia. Therefore, as per MHFW guidelines, diarrhoea management is envisaged through ORS with zinc supplementation.

THE DUAL BURDEN OF MALNUTRITION: UNDER NUTRITION AND OBESITY

23.212. There is a small, but increasing percentage of overweight children who are at greater risk for non-communicable diseases such as diabetes and cardiovascular heart disease. These levels of overnutrition significantly compromise health and productivity. There was, however, a modest improvement in the situation during the 1990s (NFHS-3). The NNMB 2006 report shows an increase in the prevalence of overweight/obesity among rural men (6 per cent vs. 8 per cent) and women (8 per cent vs. 11 per cent) from the year 2000–01. On the other hand, NFHS-3 has reported that overweight/obesity has affected almost 15 per cent of women and 12 per cent of men, mostly in urban areas, in wealthier households, and among older adults.

MATERNAL AND CHILD HEALTH

23.213. **Maternal Mortality Ratio (MMR)** is estimated to have declined from 400 maternal deaths per 1,00,000 live births in 1997–98 to 254 in 2004–06 (SRS, 2009) to 212 (SRS, 2011). However, these achievements have not met the Eleventh Plan health goals. Infant Mortality Rates (IMR) and Under-5 child mortality rates are still very high that is IMR is 47 per 1,000 live births (SRS 2011 for the year 2010). During 2010, child mortality in children under 5 years was 59, showing a decline of 5 points over 2009, with a sharp gender differential, as this was 64 for girls as against 55 for boys in 2010 (SRS Statistical Report 2010, RGI 2012).

23.214. ***Maternal, neonatal, infant and child health*** is a critical determinant of nutrition status. In the causal matrix of under nutrition, important determinants include access to health care and hygienic environments and caring practices—health, hygiene and psychosocial care for girls and women. There is increasing awareness that cultural and behavioural practices with regard to child rearing practices influence child nutrition, survival and development. Health related interventions such as those related to antenatal care, institutional deliveries, prevention and management of common neonatal and childhood illnesses such as acute respiratory infections, diarrhoea, timely and complete immunisation, with requisite Vitamin A and IFA supplementation, deworming and regular monitoring and promotion of child growth and development contribute significantly to improving nutrition outcomes. There has been improvement in several health related indicators but this has not been adequate. (Details of this are provided in the Health Chapter).

23.215. ***Nutrient Intakes among Children (1–6 years):*** Projected data from the surveys carried out by NNMB on nutrient intake in pre-school children between 1975 and 2006 has not shown any substantial improvement in their dietary intake over the last two decades. There has not been a major change in energy and protein intake of the children. Time trends of the intra familial distribution of food

TABLE 23.2
Monitorable Targets of Eleventh Plan and Its Achievements

Sl. No.	Eleventh Plan Monitorable Targets/Strategies	Achievement
1.	Reduce malnutrition among children of age group 0–3 to half of 46 per cent.	Current data not yet available.
2.	Reducing anaemia among women and girls by 50 per cent by the end of 2012.	Recent data not yet available.
3.	Providing clean drinking water for all by 2009 and ensuring no slip-backs.	88 per cent have access to an improved source of drinking water (NFHS-3).
4.	IFA Supplementation Programmes under RCH (NRHM) to cover infant and young children, by providing IFA in syrup form, and weekly iron supplements to adolescent girls (10–19 years).	Policy in this regard has been worked out. No recent study with regards to extent of coverage. Scheme for adolescents being finalised.
5.	Vitamin A Supplementation Programme had to cover all children between 9 months to 5 years of age and existing low coverage to be brought to 90 per cent by 2009.	Current data not yet available.
6.	Promotion of breastfeeding, promotion of consumption and production of fruits and vegetables in the Community, Environmental sanitation and hygiene.	DLHS 3 data shows an improvement in the rates of initiation of breast feeding within an hour (was 24.5 per cent as per NFHS-3 and 40.2 per cent by DLHS-3).
7.	High priority to micro-nutrient malnutrition control, specifically to tackle anaemia.	Double Fortified Salt has been introduced and MHFW has come up with the scheme to provide weekly iron and folic acid supplementation to adolescent girls.
8.	DLHS of RCH Programme to monitor prevalence of micro-nutrient deficiencies on priority.	Limited progress in this regard.
9.	National Nutrition Monitoring Bureau (NNMB) of ICMR to be expanded to all States/UTs.	Limited progress in this regard.
10.	Studies undertaken for collecting evidence regarding interaction amongst micro-nutrients, regional variations in deficiency and so on.	Limited progress in this regard.
11.	Vigorous awareness campaign.	A vigorous IEC campaign against malnutrition is under active consideration.

indicate that the proportion of families where both the adults and preschool children have adequate food has declined from 30 per cent to 22 per cent over the last 30 years. The proportion of families where the preschool children receive inadequate intake while adults have adequate intake has increased to a greater extent. This data reinforces the need to strengthen infant and young child caring and feeding practices.

REVIEW OF ELEVENTH FIVE YEAR PLAN MONITORABLE TARGETS

23.216. During the 11th Five Year Plan, Nutrition assumed a central role with the constitution of the Prime Minister's National Council on India's Nutrition Challenges in 2008. The first meeting was convened on 24th November 2010. The decisions taken during the meeting of the Prime Minister's National Council included- (*i*) Strengthening and restructuring the ICDS Scheme; (*ii*) Introduction of a multi-sectoral programme to address maternal and child malnutrition in selected 200 high burden districts; (*iii*) Introducing a nation-wide information, education and communication campaign against malnutrition; and (*iv*) Bringing a strong Nutrition focus in sectoral programmes.

23.217. These decisions were informed by the Recommendations For Action that emerged from the Multi-stakeholder Retreat on Addressing India's Nutrition Challenges, anchored by the Planning Commission in August 2010.

23.218. The commitment of the 11th Plan to adopt a life cycle approach to reducing under-nutrition was realised by initiating the process of strengthening and restructuring ICDS in Mission Mode and by introducing two new schemes—IGMSY for pregnant and lactating mothers and SABLA for adolescent girls, as detailed in Part II of this Chapter.

23.219. Table 23.2 presents a summary assessment of what has been achieved in the Eleventh Plan compared with the monitorable targets that were set.

REVIEW OF IMPORTANT DEVELOPMENTS

23.220. Major developments during the 11th Five Year Plan that have significantly impacted upon the nutritional scenario include:

DRAFT NATIONAL FOOD SECURITY BILL, 2011

23.221. The Bill seeks to provide food and nutritional security, in a human life cycle approach, by ensuring access to adequate quantity of quality food at affordable prices, for people to live a life with dignity. The provisions related to Nutrition include Direct provisions; Indirect provisions and Other miscellaneous provisions. Direct provisions list specific entitlements for pregnant and lactating women, children between 0–6 years, destitute persons, homeless persons, migrants, emergency and disaster affected persons and persons living in starvation, among others. Support for exclusive breastfeeding of infants between 0–6 months is also a mandated entitlement.

REVISED RECOMMENDED DIETARY ALLOWANCES (RDA)

23.222. The ICMR Expert Committee has revised the RDA for Indians (Nutrient Requirements and Recommended Dietary Allowances for Indians: A Report of the Expert Group of the Indian Council of Medical Research, 2010). The recommendations take into account the fact that body weight and physical activity are major determinants of energy requirement. Similarly the Expert Committee has provided recommendations for energy requirements for reference children as well as energy requirements per kilogram, so that the gap between the energy requirement and energy intake can be computed on the basis of current stature. This is an important contribution, because the country has entered the dual nutrition burden era. In view of the revised RDAs, it may be noted that various food supplementation programs like SABLA, MDM and IGMSY will need to consider this while reviewing the nutritional norms of these programmes.

BRINGING STRONG NUTRITION FOCUS INTO DIFFERENT SECTORAL POLICIES AND PROGRAMMES

23.223. Another milestone was the institution of a regular multisectoral review mechanism for bringing a strong nutrition focus in relevant programmes, convened by the Planning Commission since mid 2010. Different Ministries have given their commitments for taking proactive measures. These will need to form the core of the renewed National Plan of Action for Nutrition in the Twelfth Plan, with specific sectoral outcomes and indicators.

23.224. An illustrative example is how this initiative has mobilized the leadership of Panchayati Raj Institutions for Nutrition and the Girl Child. Ministry of Panchayati Raj has asked States to mainstream Nutrition in the training of PRIs—especially Women panchayat members, for Malnutrition free panchayats, earmarking certain wards to them. A special gram sabha meeting dedicated to Nutrition is to be held in every gram panchayat in the month of August. Panchayati Raj Institutions are also being enabled to actively monitor the ICDS programme through the Anganwadi level Monitoring and Support Committees and key programmes (NRHM, ICDS, TSC) through Village Health, Sanitation and Nutrition Committees.

23.225. *Village level institutional mechanism established for nutrition convergence, anchored in Panchayati Raj Institutions*: NRHM Village Health and Sanitation Committees were expanded in July 2011 to include Nutrition and ICDS to become Village Health, Sanitation and Nutrition Committees, recognised as sub committees of Gram Panchayats. There are 4.97 lakh such Committees which will provide the village level institutional mechanism for the convergence of NRHM, Total Sanitation Campaign and ICDS and also Drinking Water. Linking these to similar mechanisms at block and district levels will be the next steps in the Twelfth Plan.

23.226. **The adoption of the WHO Growth Standards** was another policy development milestone, based on a national consensus evolved in early 2007. These were introduced in mid 2008 under ICDS as well as NRHM, for the monitoring and promotion of young child growth and development. The WHO Child Growth Standards are rights based and gender specific. These normative standards recognise the breastfed infant as the norm for healthy growth. They also link physical growth with development milestones and care for development. As anticipated, this change in the standards and classification used (from the NCHS standards—IAP classification to WHO standards 2006) has resulted in much higher estimates of severely undernourished children, and with higher under-nutrition prevalence in infants between 0–6 months.

23.227. It needs to be reiterated that the perceived increase in the reported percentage of severely undernourished children in programme data reflects the change in the standards/classifications used rather than deterioration in the situation of children. The change to WHO child growth standards from the NCHS standards used by earlier NFHS/other surveys and from the Harvard Standards (IAP Classification) used by ICDS earlier has also enabled both harmonisation and updating standards used across different systems. The refrain that ICDS figures do not match NFHS data needs to be understood in the perspective of the different growth standards/classifications used before this updation and harmonisation process.

THE NATIONWIDE INTRODUCTION OF THE JOINT MOTHER AND CHILD PROTECTION CARD

23.228. The introduction of the joint card by ICDS and NRHM in March 2010 was another landmark, signifying the strategic focus on reaching mothers and children under three years of age and a holistic approach to child health and development. The maternal and child care entitlement card which enables unreached groups to demand and access health (NRHM) and child care (ICDS) services, has currently been rolled out in more than 6,305 of the 7,076 ICDS projects so far. It is a counselling tool—improving family care behaviours, using critical contact points for strengthening the continuum of care and enabling mother—child cohort tracking. The card is unique in linking maternal, newborn and child care, in integrating health, nutrition and development, thereby reinforcing a rights based and integrated approach to the young child, that recognises the indivisibility of child rights and empowers families. The card promotes the use of the JSY registration number and birth registration number (with the potential for linking with UID in future). It also enables gender disaggregated tracking, to accelerate interventions for ensuring optimal care for the young girl child.

INFANT MILK SUBSTITUTES, FEEDING BOTTLES AND INFANT FOODS (REGULATION OF PRODUCTION, SUPPLY AND DISTRIBUTION) ACT 1992 AND ITS AMENDMENT ACT 2003

23.229. Popularly known as IMS Act, this is a globally well-recognized instrument to promote, protect and support breastfeeding and to ensure optimal infant and young child feeding practices. Following its amendment in 2003, direct advertisement for IMS has stopped. However, commercial interference with infant and young child feeding practices and growth related claims still continue surreptitiously. Besides, promotion in the name of symposia and sponsorships by companies in the health care and other education systems are being used as covert tools for promotion. The implementation of the Act suffers due to inadequate enforcement machinery, understanding and the knowledge of the Act, lack of adequate resources and commercial onslaughts. These would require appropriate regulation and supervision.

23.230. Enhanced resources, enforcement machinery and reactivation of institutional mechanisms such as National/State Breastfeeding and IYCF committees, with designated nodal officers at state/district levels in both the health and ICDS systems are required for effective compliance. Experience over the Eleventh Plan period highlights that requisite safeguards also need to be established to curb commercial interference with Infant and Young Child Feeding Practices.

NATIONAL NUTRITION POLICY AND NATIONAL PLAN OF ACTION ON NUTRITION (NPAN)

23.231. Like the National Nutrition Policy, the implementation of NPAN requires acceleration. State Nutrition Councils have been set up in a few states and some states had initiated state specific plans of action. In view of the changes that have taken place in the policy and programme environment, there is a need to review the NPAN and state initiatives and their linkages with other sectoral institutional arrangements such as NRHM mission societies or National/State Food Commissions if these are established when the draft NFSB is enacted. It also needs to be ensured that nutrition interventions are planned and implemented in consonance with the national policy framework.

TABLE 23.3
Existing Programmes/Schemes

Target Group	Schemes	Expansion
Pregnant and Lactating Mothers	ICDS, RCH-II, NRHM, JSY, Indira Gandhi Matritva Sahyog Yojana (IGMSY)—The CMB Scheme	NRHM (2005–06) JSY (2006–07) ICDS (2008–09)
Children 0–3	ICDS, RCH-II, NRHM, Rajiv Gandhi National Creche Scheme	RGNCS (2005–06) ICDS (2008–09)
Children 3–6	ICDS, RCH-II, NRHM, Rajiv Gandhi National Crèche Scheme, Total Sanitation Campaign (TSC), National Rural Drinking Water Programme (NRDWP)	TSC (2008–09)
School going children 6–14	Mid Day Meals (MDM), Sarva Shiksha Abhiyan (SSA)	SSA (2002/2005–06) MDM (2008–09)
Adolescent Girls 11–18	Rajiv Gandhi Scheme for the Empowerment of Adolescent Girls (RGSEAG), Kishori Shakti Yojana, Total Sanitation Campaign (TSC), National Rural Drinking Water Programme (NRDWP)	NRDWP (2010) RGSEAG (2010–11)
Adults and Communities	MGNREGS, Skill Development Mission, Adult Literacy Programme, TPDS, AAY, Old and Infirm Persons Annapurna, Rashtriya Krishi Vikas Yojana, Food Security Mission, Safe Drinking Water and Sanitation Programmes, National Horticulture Mission, National Iodine Deficiency Disorders Control Programme (NIDDCP), Nutrition Education and Extension, Bharat Nirman, Rashtriya Swasthya Bima Yojana	NHM (2005–06) MGNREGS (2005–06) NRLM (2010–11) NIDDCP (1992) RSBY (2007) Bharat Nirman (2005)

DOUBLE FORTIFIED SALT FOR REINFORCING ANAEMIA CONTROL

23.232. To reinforce interventions for prophylaxis and control of nutritional anaemia, the use of Double Fortified Salt (DFS) was mandated in government Food Supplementation programmes such as ICDS and MDM, among others, as a follow up of multi sectoral consultations.

REVIEW OF EXISTING PROGRAMMES/SCHEMES

23.233. The Government of India has been implementing a number of programmes, which have the potential to contribute to improving nutrition security, as they address immediate, underlying and basic causes of malnutrition—especially maternal and child under-nutrition. An indicative list of the programmes relevant for different groups across the life cycle is given in Table 23.3 with an indication of when they were expanded.

23.234. The major government interventions with the potential to address the nutrition challenges include interventions for maternal and child care and care of adolescent girls. These include the Integrated Child Development Services (ICDS), the Rajiv Gandhi Scheme for the Empowerment of Adolescent Girls (RGSEAG)—SABLA, the Indira Gandhi Matritva Sahyog Yojana IGMSY, which have been discussed earlier in Part II of this chapter. Also relevant are the programmes related to-

- Access to Maternal and Child Care such as ICDS, IGMSY, and SABLA for adolescent girls;
- Access to health care such as NRHM;
- Access to safe drinking water, hygiene and environmental sanitation such as the National Rural Drinking Water Programme and the Total Sanitation Campaign;
- Access to household food security and food supplementation programmes such as the National Food Security Mission, Targeted Public Distribution System, Mid Day Meals Scheme;
- Programmes related to Agriculture, Animal Husbandry and horticulture;
- Programmes related to poverty alleviation, livelihoods and skill development such as MGNREGA and NRLM;
- Access to Education, Information and Communication through Sarva Shiksha Abhiyan, Sakshar Bharat, initiatives for girls' education, women's literacy and empowerment and youth initiatives, information campaigns;
- Social and community mobilisation, including ownership of panchayati raj institutions/urban local bodies;
- Targeted development interventions for different vulnerable community groups such as Scheduled Castes, Scheduled Tribes, including particularly vulnerable tribal groups and minorities, among others.

These have been discussed in the relevant sectoral Chapters of the Twelfth Plan.

STRATEGIES FOR PROMOTING NUTRITION SECURITY IN THE TWELFTH PLAN

23.235. The decisions of the first meeting of the PM's National Council on India's Nutrition Challenges provide the road map for the Twelfth Plan and are as follows:

1. **The ICDS requires strengthening and restructuring**, with special focus on pregnant and lactating mothers and children under three years. The ICDS also needs to forge strong institutional convergence with the National Rural Health Mission and the Total Sanitation Campaign particularly at the district and village levels. It needs to provide flexibility for local action and empower mothers in particular and the community in general to have a stake in the programme.
2. **A multi-sectoral programme to address maternal and child malnutrition** in selected 200 high-burden districts would be prepared. This programme will bring together various national programmes through strong institutional and programmatic convergence at the State, District, Block and Village levels.
3. **A nation-wide information, education and communication campaign** will be launched against malnutrition.
4. The Ministries that deal with Health, Drinking Water Supply and Sanitation, School Education, Agriculture and Food and Public Distribution

will **bring strong nutrition focus** to their programmes.

23.236. Multi-sectoral interventions are envisaged because as outlined in the preceding section, different sectors address different determinants of malnutrition—directly or indirectly, thereby contributing to improving nutrition outcomes. This is by increasing access to maternal and child care services and improving caring practices, access to health care, water, sanitation and hygiene, household food security, TPDS, agriculture, poverty alleviation and livelihoods, education and communication and mobilisation of community support. The Twelfth Plan strategy therefore accords priority to multi-sectoral action, which is reflected in relevant sectoral chapters. This section focuses on outlining how such multisectoral interventions and direct nutrition interventions will converge for improving maternal and child related nutrition outcomes and achieving monitorable targets.

23.237. Based on these broad directions, the following are the areas on which policy planning must concentrate in the Twelfth Plan—

EVOLVING MULTI-SECTORAL INTERVENTIONS FOR NUTRITION

23.238. The National Nutrition Strategy in the Twelfth Plan will be based on the decisions of the PM's National Council on India's Nutrition Challenges; multi-sectoral commitments (emerging from the reviews convened by the Planning Commission); the Recommendations For Action of the Multi-stakeholder Nutrition Retreat, anchored by the Planning Commission (August 2010) and building on the joint strategy paper evolved through this process. It envisages Multi-sectoral State/District Nutrition Plans of Action which will be developed, implemented and monitored by National/State/District Nutrition Councils, especially in high burden/high focus States/Districts. Key commitments would be included as a part of State MOUs, binding all parties towards monitorable outcomes. Nutrition monitorable targets and outcomes would be reviewed regularly by National/State/District Nutrition Councils and also by a National Development Council Sub Committee periodically.

23.239. The monitorable targets, strategies and interventions of National Nutrition Policy NNP and National Plan of Action on Nutrition (NPAN) will be updated in the light of emerging policy directions. The updated National Plan of Action on Nutrition (NPAN) will be aligned with the Twelfth Plan. It will also aim to strengthen multi-sectoral interventions addressing maternal, neonatal, infant and child mortality and under-nutrition synergistically—especially in 200 high burden districts, linking with 264 high focus districts under NRHM.

BRINGING STRONG NUTRITION FOCUS TO SECTORAL PROGRAMMES

23.240. Building on multi-sectoral reviews anchored by the Planning Commission in 2010–2012, the Nutrition component will be prioritised in relevant social sector and flagship programmes through the Twelfth Plan sectoral strategies, sectoral Results Framework Documents, 5 year strategy plans and Programme Implementation Plans of relevant flagship programmes. The Nutrition component in National Rural Health Mission Programme Implementation Plans will especially be strengthened. Nutrition status of children under 3 years (Underweight prevalence) will be used as a lead proxy indicator in national/state/district level reviews and specifically for NRHM and ICDS.

23.241. To provide an illustrative example—National Rural Health Mission (NRHM) has achieved considerable progress in the Eleventh Plan in providing universal access to equitable, affordable and quality health care, which contributes to improved nutrition outcomes. There are many health services under NRHM and other health sector interventions that have relevance to preventing and reducing under-nutrition, including: (*i*) Immunisation Programme; (*ii*) newborn care; prevention and management of common neonatal and childhood illnesses including diarrhoea and Acute Respiratory Infections; (*iii*) Care of the sick child—at the community level through the ASHA and at the institutional level through primary health care facilities; (*vi*) Vitamin A administration; (*v*) Anaemia management and Paediatric De-worming; (*vi*) School health programmes with supervised weekly IFA supplementation and six monthly deworming; (*vii*) Nutrition Rehabilitation centres—for sick and severely malnourished children; (*viii*) Programmes of adolescent health which address nutrition counselling and anemia; (*ix*) National Maternity benefit scheme—now a component of JSY; and (*x*) State specific programmes of nutrition supplementation such as the Muthu Laxmi maternity benefit scheme of Tamil Nadu and the Velugu programme in Andhra Pradesh and (*xi*) Universal Salt Iodisation programme and the national goitre control programme. Details of these interventions are provided in the Health Chapter and similarly in respect of other sectors.

STRENGTHENING/RE-ACTIVATING INSTITUTIONAL ARRANGEMENTS

23.242. Nutrition is a complex issue which cuts across the sectors. There is a recognized need for institutional mechanisms as well as programme implementation platforms to effectively converge and monitor both direct and indirect multisectoral interventions for enhanced nutrition outcomes. The National Nutrition Policy provides for enabling institutional arrangements for addressing India's nutrition challenges. While some of these institutional arrangements have been functional in some States, these have not been fully operationalised, especially at district and sub district levels. Priority would be accorded to strengthening/re-activating comprehensive institutional mechanisms related to the National Nutrition Mission at all levels, and ensuring their synergistic linkages with the institutional arrangements envisaged under ICDS Restructuring. These are as follows:

23.243. **National Level**: Under the guidance and policy direction of the PM's National Council on Nutrition, the Executive Committee headed by the Minister for WCD [which will be the same as ICDS National Mission Steering Group] will oversee and coordinate the implementation of Nutrition related Programmes. This Executive Committee under the chairpersonship of Minster for WCD would have Member, Planning Commission (In Charge of WCD) as Vice Chairperson with representation of some State Ministers and Chief Secretaries, Secretaries of different Ministries, on rotation basis. At an operational level, in order to ensure multi-sectoral convergence, an Empowered Committee headed by the Secretary—MWCD and comprising of representatives from different Ministries will guide the implementation of multisectoral policies and programmes for nutrition. This Committee will also ensure convergence at the national level and will report to the Executive Committee (and thereby to the PM's Council) on the same. This Council would be technically supported by a Policy Coordination Support unit in the Planning Commission to bring in inter-sectoral nutrition focus and accountability and a strengthened Food and Nutrition Board (MWCD).

1. **State Level**: The CM's State Nutrition Council and the State Executive Committee headed by the Chief Secretary will guide the convergent actions at the state level.
2. **District Level**: The District Nutrition Council headed by the concerned District Magistrate/CEO Zila Parishad will be responsible for convergent action at the district level.
3. **Village Level**: The Village Health Sanitation and Nutrition Committees which are recognized as sub committees of the Gram Panchayat, will have representation from health, ICDS, TSC functionaries, user groups and PRIs. They will be responsible for reviewing the performance of individual programmes, as well as for enabling convergent multi-sectoral actions which impact upon nutrition outcomes, with reference to the Subjects allocated to Panchayats under the Eleventh Schedule of the Constitution and mandated by the 73rd Constitutional Amendment.
4. **Habitation level**: At the Anganwadi centre level, the anganwadi monitoring and support committee (ALMSC), including representation from mothers' groups/women's SHGs will monitor convergent actions and suggest actions for effective programme implementation.
5. **In the urban context**: similar institutional arrangements will be set up, depending on the category of the urban local body, with city/town/

ward and neighbourhood committees being constituted, with representation of elected representatives of ULBs.

23.244. The above framework has been deliberated and agreed upon in the Inter-Ministerial Group on ICDS Restructuring, chaired by Member, Planning Commission. In the context of institutional mechanisms for nutrition, similar arrangements, including at State, district and sub district levels will be correlated with the ICDS Mission and monitoring structures.

MULTI-SECTORAL APPROACH FOR ACCELERATING ACTION ON DETERMINANTS OF UNDERNUTRITION

23.245. As indicated earlier, the National Nutrition Policy advocated a comprehensive inter-sectoral strategy between 14 sectors (which directly or indirectly affect dietary intake, prevention and management of disease/infections and nutritional status of the population) for combating the multifaceted problem of under-nutrition. The number of sectors mobilized has now expanded to nearly twenty. The core strategy envisaged under NNP is to tackle the problem of nutrition through direct nutrition interventions for vulnerable groups, as well as through various development policy instruments which will improve access and create conditions for improved nutrition. Both the direct and indirect interventions cannot be undertaken by a single sector. There is need for a comprehensive response that addresses the multiple and inter related determinants of malnutrition and different dimensions of the nutrition challenges synergistically. In order to achieve this, the 12th Five Year Plan will focus on the following:

23.246. **Multi-sectoral Programme to address maternal and child malnutrition in selected 200 high burden districts:** As mandated by the PM's National Council on India's Nutrition Challenges, a Multi-sectoral Nutrition Programme is being finalised for 200 high burden districts. The Multi-sectoral Nutrition Programme is designed to (*i*) focus action on the critical age groups to prevent and reduce under-nutrition as early as possible, across the life cycle (pregnancy, lactation, infancy and early childhood, adolescence); (*ii*) address key inter related determinants of malnutrition together by facilitating convergence; (*iii*) provide local flexibility, support pilots and innovative panchayat led models of convergent action and (*iv*) to focus on districts with the highest burden of malnutrition, so that reduction in maternal and child under-nutrition is accelerated. This will also be linked to reducing maternal, neonatal, infant and young child mortality in NRHM high focus districts.

23.247. This will be designed and implemented to facilitate convergence of key services and stakeholders. The proposed programme would seek to ensure universal access to women and child care services, primary health care, safe drinking water and sanitation, nutrition counselling as a service, change caring and feeding practices in families and communities, link with initiatives for ensuring food security and livelihoods, and address the different determinants of under-nutrition in an integrated way, with effective institutional arrangements. This would synergise multisectoral interventions from ICDS, NRHM, Rajiv Gandhi Scheme for the Empowerment of Adolescent Girls, Indira Gandhi Matritva Sahyog Yojana, Mid-Day Meal Scheme, the proposed National Food Security Act, Public Distribution System, Total Sanitation Campaign, NRDWP, MGNREGS, NRLM and others. It would ensure a platform of coordinated nutrition relevant action at the State, District and grassroots levels for addressing maternal and child under-nutrition, with strong teamwork of AWWs, ASHAs, ANMs, ICDS and NRHM functionaries, involvement of women's/community groups and leadership of panchayati raj institutions.

23.248. The Multi-sectoral Programme to address maternal and child malnutrition would ensure that relevant nutrition outcomes are not only integrated into the concerned sectoral plans but also that appropriate resources are allocated for achieving those outcomes. Funds for local gap filling support would be provided as per the needs identified on the basis of the District/State Nutrition Plans and reviewed by the District/State Nutrition Councils. At the national level, an Empowered Committee headed by the Secretary, Ministry of WCD would be set up for approval and budget release, based on the annual State Nutrition Plans submitted by the concerned States/UTs.

23.249. **Operationalising Convergence through the multi sectoral programme:** There are several programmes and schemes aiming to directly and indirectly affect nutrition related outcomes. There is a need to bring more coherence among these programmes through processes of convergence at programmatic, thematic, operational and institutional levels.

MOBILISING A NATIONWIDE CAMPAIGN AGAINST MALNUTRITION

23.250. A concerted societal campaign against malnutrition will be initiated, which would create a mass movement for improved nutrition and development of children and women. A National Communication Strategy Framework (with contextualisation/adaptation at State/District levels) will be developed. This will include an advocacy strategy that creates the necessary priority and media environment for nutrition; a social mobilisation strategy that mobilises communities and resources for concerted action and a behavioral development strategy for changing key care behaviours at field level.

23.251. A nation-wide communication campaign coordinated by the Ministry of Women and Child Development, in consultation with the Planning Commission and Ministry of Health and Family Welfare, will be launched against malnutrition.

23.252. A social mobilisation or societal movement will be initiated, including strategic partnerships and linkages with civil society organisations, professional networks, Voluntary Action Groups, home science, medical and public health colleges, practitioners, community groups with voluntary action for sharing of technical knowledge, experiential learning, increasing nutrition awareness and community based monitoring.

23.253. Changing and sustaining positive care practices will be critical through skilled counseling support from the ICDS and NRHM team, using a common core counseling package, building on the joint ICDS NRHM Mother Child Protection Card. Positive role model mothers will be encouraged to demonstrate improved care and feeding practices to community/mothers' groups for peer learning through Sneha Shivirs. The strategy would cover different aspects of care behaviour such as health, hygiene, care for girls and women, psychosocial care and early learning, supporting for improved parenting, with shared responsibilities of both parents and family support.

23.254. National/State communication strategies would also improve the demand for, utilisation and monitoring of key health and child care services and be integrally linked with service quality improvement interventions under the Multi-sectoral Programme, ICDS Restructuring and NRHM. Behavioral outcomes of the communication strategy will be monitored through the institutional arrangements for Nutrition.

PROMOTING OPTIMAL MATERNAL, INFANT AND YOUNG CHILD CARE AND FEEDING PRACTICES

23.255. Optimal Infant and Young Child Feeding (IYCF) practices form the cornerstone of child care and development. Despite breastfeeding having numerous recognised advantages, and several initiatives to promote breastfeeding, early and exclusive breastfeeding rates in most states of India are low. The following actions will be taken urgently in the Twelfth Plan:

23.256. *Emphasis on IYCF and dissemination of National guidelines on IYCF:* A comprehensive National Policy on Infant and Young Child Feeding will be developed through consultative processes, linked to the updation of the National Policy on Nutrition and NPAN and within the legal framework provided by the IMS Act. Supporting National/State Plans of Action with monitorable outcomes will be developed and implemented, linking ICDS, NRHM and others, backed by adequate resource allocations to bridge various identified programmatic gaps.

23.257. Community initiatives for supporting women: Aggressive marketing of baby food by companies can easily mislead women who do not have access to accurate information. An empathetic and skilled health worker must support women at the time of birth to succeed in beginning breastfeeding within an hour of birth and providing prolonged skin-to-skin contact. They should also have access to counselling (one to one or group) and support to continue exclusive breastfeeding for the first 6 months, with counselling for adequate complementary feeding and continued breastfeeding at the completion of 6 months for two years or beyond.

23.258. Critically addressing infants under 6 months: The 0–6 months infant is often left out of initial weighing/child care counselling sessions. The Twelfth Plan accords high priority to promoting early and exclusive breastfeeding for the first six months of life and reaching these infants and mothers. Nutrition and breastfeeding support centres will be set up, with skilled counsellors initially in all district hospitals—and followed at CHC, PHC levels in a phased manner.

23.259. Strengthening ICDS: Nutritional and care counselling will be introduced as a service in ICDS in the Twelfth Plan, with provisions for an additional Anganwadi worker in 200 high burden districts, based on state requirements. This would focus on prioritised home visits for children under 3 years and mothers to promote infant and child care and feeding practices.

23.260. Enhancing capacity building of field level functionaries on IYCF practices. It is imperative to build knowledge and skills, capacity for behaviour change communication, counselling and develop problem solving skills for Anganwadi Workers (AWWs), Accredited Social Health Activists (ASHAs) and Auxiliary Nurse Midwives (ANMs) for improving IYCF practices. Resource provisions for capacity development for IYCF will be enhanced in ICDS and NRHM. A network of National/State Resource Centres on IYCF will be established, in partnership with professional networks/civil society organisations/medical colleges—functioning as "living universities" with decentralised and field based capacity development.

23.261. Pre-service curriculum strengthening for doctors and nurses will be undertaken systematically in the Twelfth Plan. This will reduce the need of in-service training and improve the knowledge and skills of doctors and nurses, which is a recognized need. Medical colleges must be involved for this purpose and "Centres of Excellence" in IYCF will also be identified, forming the hub of an institutional strengthening effort.

23.262. Behaviour change communication: An extensive and focused communication campaign on IYCF will be launched, integrally linked to the Nationwide IEC Campaign for Nutrition.

23.263. Skilled nutrition counselling: Skilled nutrition counselling will be recognized as a service with a support chain from village level to sub centre, PHC, CHC, subdivision, district and state levels, including mother and child cohort tracking and linking with referral services.

23.264. Protecting breastfeeding and compliance with the Infant Milk Substitutes Act (IMS Act): In the Twelfth Plan, the Infant Milk Substitutes, Feeding Bottles and Infant Foods (Regulation of Production, Supply and Distribution) Act 1992, and Amendment Act 2003, will be strengthened through effective implementation mechanisms and earmarked resources for ensuring and monitoring compliance. Monitoring the compliance of the IMS Act by companies will also be taken up for effective implementation of IMS Act, while ensuring that commercial influences and conflict of interest do not undermine optimal infant and young child feeding practices.

23.265. IYCF counselling centres in Health facilities: Through an IYCF component in NRHM PIPs, it will also be ensured that each health facility has skilled IYCF counselors—doctors and nurses trained in the skills to deal with infant and young child feeding counselling as well as on HIV and infant feeding.

23.266. **VHND:** The frontline workers' team comprising of ASHA, AWW, ANM, and the PRI representatives, will be fully involved in organising VHND to bring about changes in child caring practices and promote IYCF practices. A nodal person will be identified and trained to oversee convergence between the ANM and ASHA; and the network of Nutrition counsellors will serve as a link between ICDS and NRHM.

23.267. *IEC and Nutrition messages:* Mass Media campaigns will be designed that will enable families to adopt better maternal, child care and IYCF practices. A technical core group will be constituted as a part of the Nutrition institutional arrangements to ensure that the content of messages is updated, consistent with the national policy framework and IMS Act and is appropriately sensitive to local traditions, practices and needs. Convergence of MWCD, MHFW, MYA, MHRD, MIB and MPR especially will be strengthened.

23.268. *Introduce Village/Panchayat report cards:* VNSNCs will monitor and support the regularity of functioning of AWCs, ensuring coverage of all eligible beneficiaries as against the surveyed population. Community based accreditation system under ICDS Restructuring will be used to recognize villages, panchayats, blocks and districts for achieving targets of children growing well and preventing them from becoming undernourished. These could even spark and catalyse a community movement for other aspects contributing to "child friendly panchayats". Every village can prominently display these cards, depicting what progress the village has made. This will therefore link with the concept of baby and child friendly panchayats detailed in Part II on Child Rights.

23.269. *National IYCF/Nutrition Communication Campaign and the role of media:* A national nutrition communication strategy framework will be developed as outlined earlier, a campaign linking concerned sectors (e.g. gender related issues, health and hygiene practices) must be evolved. A national movement for promoting IYCF must be an integral part of the same.

23.270. **Strengthen National and State Coordination Mechanisms and Capacity for promoting Infant and Young Child Feeding and implementation of the IMS Act:** The National Breastfeeding Committee under the IMS Act will be rejuvenated and strengthened, and State Breastfeeding Committees constituted as envisaged, with identified State Nodal Officers within State WCD and Health Departments for IYCF, supported by technical teams at different levels. This will be appropriately linked to Nutrition institutional arrangements. A National Resource Centre will be established, in partnership with appropriate professional networks/voluntary agencies to enable capacity development for IYCF for both NRHM and ICDS, supporting both the Ministries of WCD and Health and Family Welfare, with State level Resource Units, linked to other training institutions. This could also be assigned to national level partner organizations or set up especially to focus on the issue.

23.271. *Conflict of Interest:* Policy guidelines and mechanisms will be developed to ensure that infant feeding practices are kept free from commercial influences and that nutrition programme implementation is free from conflict of interest, as mandated by the IMS Act.

COMBATING MICRO-NUTRIENT DEFICIENCIES IN A HOLISTIC MANNER

23.272. There are clear strategies to combat micro-nutrient deficiencies (Iron, Vitamin A and Iodine) in children, women and adolescent girls. A comprehensive approach should be adopted which includes complementary strategies to address micro-nutrient malnutrition including: (*i*) Infant and Young Child Feeding Practices; (*ii*) Dietary Diversification; (*iii*) Horticultural interventions; (*iv*) Nutrient Supplementation; (*v*) Food fortification; and (*vi*) Public Health Measures.

23.273. *Supplementation with micro-nutrients/food:* Micro-nutrient deficiencies, particularly Iron Deficiency Anemia, IDD and Vitamin A will be addressed through intensified actions focussing on: (*i*) Adopting a comprehensive approach involving improved IYCF practices, dietary diversification, food supplementation, food fortification and horticultural interventions, Iron and Folic Acid supplementation for young children, adolescent girls, pregnant and lactating women, also supported by the use of Double Fortified Salt; (*ii*) Periodic screening for anaemia; (*iii*) Strengthening Vitamin A supplementation Programme in convergence with NRHM for improved coverage; (*iv*) Supply of adequately Iodized salt through TPDS and also double fortified salt; (*v*) Public health measures—deworming, environmental sanitation, safe drinking water; and (*vi*) Micro-nutrient supplements and health check-up for school children through MDM programme.

23.274. *Food Fortification:* Micro-nutrient malnutrition control programmes in the country have focused on nutrient supplementation of some vulnerable groups. This will be complemented by addressing micro-nutrient malnutrition through a comprehensive strategy. Double fortified salt is a successful example, which has been introduced for government food supplementation programmes. Requisite safeguards against commercial interference and regulatory mechanisms for the above will also be developed.

23.275. *Improved health education and IEC:* This will carried out with the aim to disseminate knowledge on micro-nutrients and its prevention as well as advocacy for food diversification to include iron, vitamin A, and carotene rich food in regular dietary intake. Besides, it would also help in ensuring improved dietary intake to meet RDA, improved compliance of IFA and improved iodized salt consumption in every household.

23.276. *Monitoring and Surveillance:* Initiatives for monitoring the programme for preventing and controlling micro-nutrient deficiencies would include strengthening routine reporting under NRHM/RCH and ICDS programmes to include percentage of pregnant women, children, adolescent girls, anaemic women and girls, percentage given IFA tablets, compliance for IFA, Vitamin A supplementation for children as well as mobilising PRIs, Women Self Help Groups and Anganwadi Workers to monitor intake of IFA tablets.

23.277. Evaluation of the on-going process and impact is expected to be done as a part of the Annual Health survey/District Health Survey/National Health Survey including haemoglobin estimation, questions regarding IFA coverage and intake. In addition as and when large-scale surveys are done, information can be collected on prevalence of anaemia.

23.278. Wherever possible, (such as during school health check-up) attempts will be made to screen adolescent girls for anaemia. Special focus should be on those who are undernourished or have menstrual problems. Adolescents who are pregnant should receive very high priority for screening and management of anaemia.

Addressing the Dual Burden of Malnutrition

23.279. Increasingly, health systems in many developing countries are simultaneously confronting under- and over-nutrition—not only at the national level, but also within households. Both under-nutrition and over-nutrition are linked with a range of adverse health conditions. Importantly, however, underweight and overweight are both forms of malnutrition, a term that encompasses either a lack of or excess in energy and/or nutrients. The Dual burden of Malnutrition presents a unique challenge for public health. Programmes should promote nutritious foods and a healthy lifestyle to address both types of malnutrition at the same time. In the Twelfth Plan, the Health system will be responsible for screening persons for over-nutrition, while ICDS and health will be responsible for screening for under-nutrition. The Health system will also support personalized advice for early detection of overweight and diet counselling as well as monitoring the improvement and providing focused care to those who are facing problems in modifying their lifestyles. Nutrition and health education through all available modes of communication will emphasize the need for: (*i*) eating balanced diets; and (*ii*) adopting healthy lifestyles with adequate physical activity. Health interventions will be carried out by the health system including, (*i*) screening persons for over-nutrition whenever they access health care; (*ii*) using of BMI for adults and BMI-for-age in children and adolescents for early detection of over-nutrition; (*iii*) identification of over-nourished persons and personalised advice regarding modification of dietary intake and life style; and (*iv*) monitoring the improvement and providing focused care to those who are facing problems in modifying their lifestyles.

NUTRITION CAPACITY DEVELOPMENT

23.280. ***Capacity Development*** for Nutrition will need to include strengthening and networking of Nutrition resources within key National Institutions such as NIHFW, NHSRC, NIRD, strengthening the Food and Nutrition Board and NIPPCD and networking with Nutrition Resource Units in Agricultural Universities, Medical Colleges and Home Science Colleges. Appropriate training is needed at state, district and block management levels and service provider and supervision levels. A shared training space and team at the state, district and block levels would therefore be essential. A shared resource centre of WCD and health or State/District Resource Centres for Nutrition need to be progressively established—building on existing institutions such as SIHFWs/SHSRCs, Medical College Hospitals, Home Science Colleges, AWTCs—responding to the requirements of different sectors and stakeholders. This should be linked to State/District Nutrition Mission Councils, and will need to be set up in a phased manner, initially in high burden states/districts. This will also require mentoring support by voluntary agencies, resource teams at district/block//local levels, especially for strengthening community processes, decentralized planning and monitoring.

23.281. ***Nutrition Resource Platform*** In order to strengthen the knowledge base on nutrition education, national, regional and state level Nutrition Resource Centres and networks also need to be set up. A national Nutrition Resource Platform is envisaged as a web portal for easy access to information relating to nutrition and child development and as a repository of nutrition related resources including research, new publications, government policies, training materials and so on.

NUTRITION EDUCATION AND SOCIAL MOBILISATION

23.282. **Nutrition Education** will be integrated and appropriately/strengthened in the school education curriculum framework at national levels and linked to Mid Day Meals, so that children also promote nutrition relevant practices in the community and through the Child to Child approach. This will be incorporated in Sakshar Bharat. Similarly, the nutrition component in the medical and nursing education curriculum will also be strengthened, networking medical colleges, nursing colleges and councils.

23.283. **Education of girls and women's literacy** will be promoted, responding to their nutrition, development and protection needs. Their nutrition status will also improve by availing of MDM, health care, IFA supplementation and deworming interventions, increased duration of schooling, higher education and improved life skills and productivity. Education of girls and women's literacy will have multiple long term benefits.

23.284. **Community Mobilisation**: Improving community mobilisation levels will imply greater sensitization and involvement of Panchayati Raj Institutions and Village Health Sanitation and Nutrition Committees. Effective nutrition orientation for grass-root workers, PRIs, women's and youth groups would create an understanding about the importance of nutrition and their pivotal role in the prevention of malnutrition.

NUTRITION MONITORING AND SURVEILLANCE SYSTEMS

23.285. Effective monitoring of national nutrition programmes requires both monitoring and assessment of processes and outcomes. A responsive and dynamic Nutrition Surveillance System (NSS) will be put in place in order to capture nutrition related information. It would help assess the current situation, analyse the causes/reasons of the problem and based on the analysis and available resources, suggest solutions to improve the situation. It would provide information on nutritional practices of vulnerable groups including SCs, STs, and Minorities being reached under ICDS, NRHM and related programmes of different sectors, keeping in view the multi-factorial nature of nutrition. It would take the following measures in a synergistic manner to achieve optimal results:

- The critical indicators of maternal, infant and child care and nutrition will be constantly monitored to ensure better young child survival, nutrition and development, in case of each mother-child cohort tracked, with the aid of Mother and Child Protection Card, linked to the NSS network and to the NRHM Mother-Child Cohort Tracking System.
- The Kishori card being linked to the NSS database will ensure better health and nutrition among adolescent girls, through consistent data inputs on BMI and IFA intervention.
- Baseline Surveys of nutrition and health related indicators of children under six years of age, adolescent girls and women will be undertaken by all States/UTs before the commencement of XII Five Year Plan. The support of Technical Institutions like NIN, Medical Colleges and Home Science Colleges, to establish the benchmark of nutrition indicators for the National NSS and Database is crucial. This will complement planned AHS, DLHS and NHFS surveys.
- The Geographical Information System (GIS) Mapping will be used to generate data at the Anganwadi level for monitoring at Block/District levels. The National Nutrition Database for National Nutrition Surveillance and policy inputs will provide support.
- It will help in mapping of undernourished endemic zones of the country in terms of identifying districts and terming them as 'high risk and vulnerable districts". Special focus within National NSS will be on household food security in difficult survival environments like remote, hilly, tribal and drought prone areas, deserts, BPL populations, different socio religious groups, and so on.
- Central Monitoring Unit (CMU) set-up under ICDS will be utilized for NSS as well as for a comprehensive, non-repetitive assessment and correction of the field situation.

CONCLUSION

23.286. The Twelfth Plan seeks to make the fulfillment of women's rights an inalienable condition to achievement of rapid and sustainable economic growth. According the highest priority to ending gender based inequities, discrimination and violence faced by girls and women is the prerequisite to the objective of the Plan. Fulfilling children's rights to survival, development, protection and participation is a critical development imperative that must be realised in the Twelfth Plan. Linking with the approach to Universal Health Care, converging the health, child care and education systems, ensuring a continuum of care and development, the Twelfth Plan strategy for inclusive development is unique.

23.287. The Twelfth Plan reiterates that Nutrition is crucial for the fulfillment of human rights—especially those of the most vulnerable children, girls and women, locked in an inter-generational cycle of multiple deprivations. Critical priority is accorded to prevent under-nutrition as early as possible, across the life cycle, to avert irreversible cumulative growth and development deficits that compromise maternal, child and adolescent health and survival, achievement of optimal learning outcomes in education and gender equality. It is envisaged that this synergy of multi-sectoral action, led by panchayats in partnership with communities—will enable the Twelfth Plan to realise our vision of Nutrition Security for all for faster, more inclusive and sustainable growth.

23.288. Convergent action will make the defining difference to the lives of children and women-especially for reaching the most vulnerable among them. It will translate Twelfth Plan commitments into effective policies and programmes that touch the lives of women and children—in the families and communities, where they live, grow and develop.

23.289. The total outlay for the Women and Child Development Sector (including Nutrition) is ₹1,17,707 crore which includes an outlay of ₹1,08,503 crore for the ICDS flagship programme.

A Call for Multisectoral Action for Children and Women

Indicative Action

1. Ministry of Women and Child Development

- Lead and convene Multi-sectoral Action for Children, Women and Nutrition with multi-sectoral commitments to Children embodied in the Results Framework Documents and Five year Strategic Plans of concerned ministries, Programme Implementation Plans and reviewed.
- Mainstream the rights based approach and gender perspective in Policies and Programmes.
- Harmoniszation of child-related legislative provisions and child-sensitive jurisprudence.
- Updation of the National Policy For Children in harmony with the Twelfth Plan and National Policy for Nutrition.
- Development and implementation of National/State/District Plans of Action for Children, with monitorable outcomes, based on the updated policy, building on the Twelfth Plan.
- Focused interventions to improve the Child Sex Ratio, within an overall National Strategy for Care and Protection of the Girl Child and longer term interventions for gender equality.
- Designing a strategic approach to respond holistically to the emerging needs of children of excluded socio-religious community groups such as SC, ST, particularly vulnerable tribal groups, Minorities, other disadvantaged communities, including urban poor communities.
- Development of National ECCE Policy, curricular framework and standards.
- ICDS Restructuring as per framework evolved.
- Strengthening the early care, development and learning continuum.
- Strengthening the protective environment for all children—with a focus on prevention of vulnerability to abuse and exploitation, including in conflict and disturbed areas.
- Ensuring fulfillment of children's rights to achieve full development potential and quality education-including the one in ten differently-abled child.
- Institutionalizing child participation through incorporation of children's views into mainstream policy and programme formulation, implementation and monitoring processes.
- Valuing and recognizing the work of AWWs and AWHs—demonstrating the commitment to gender equality that is being advocated.
- Strengthening institutional capacity and partnerships between government sectors, civil society, panchayati raj institutions, families and communities for fulfilling children's rights.
- State and district level nutrition multi-sectoral action plan framework for 200 high burden districts, especially linking with NRHM 264 high focus districts.
- State and District level Nutrition Councils to be set up in the above, along with inter-departmental coordination committees, thematic working groups.
- Institute mechanisms to ensure that infant and young child feeding and nutritional support interventions are free from commercial influence and conflict of interest.
- Roll out of RGSEAG SABLA and IGMSY, with an evaluation framework, with likely scaling up of IGMSY, as linked to the Draft National Food Security Bill 2011.
- Mandating an Impact Assessment of relevant sectoral policies and programmes on children as a part of the Mid Term Appraisal of the Twelfth Plan.

2. Ministry of Health and Family Welfare

- Progressively move towards universal health and child care; enhancing efforts to address the persistently high levels of mortality, morbidity and under-nutrition across the life cycle, focusing on addressing maternal, neonatal, infant and child mortality and malnutrition.
- Reduce regional disparities; address the inter-generational cycle of poor health, under-nutrition and gender discrimination faced by girls and women.
- Ensure universality with quality and inclusion of the most vulnerable and deprived communities, women and children—such as SC, ST, particularly vulnerable tribal groups, minorities and others.
- Improve efficiency, effectiveness and accountability of health care, especially women and child care delivery systems, and increase community and women's ownership of delivery systems.
- Address adolescent health holistically—with skilled counseling support at drop-in clinics in identified health facilities. This will also affect issues related to mental health, substance abuse, living in insecure environments and preventing and addressing HIV/AIDs.

- Address the adverse and steeply declining child sex ratio through a multi-layered approach, responsive to different state/city/district contexts.
- Proactively address gender differentials in infant and under five child mortality rates—especially in states where this is high or increasing, using the Mother Child Tracking System.
- Set up necessary health infrastructure for ensuring maternal and child care, emergency obstetric care, sick newborn care, referral support and child care corners in health facilities and ensure that progressively all maternity facilities are "baby friendly".
- Position Nutrition Status of children under 3 years as a lead progress indicator of NRHM.
- Strengthen the Nutrition component of NRHM PIPs—especially in 264 NRHM high focus districts, in synergy with 200 high burden districts identified for multi-sectoral nutrition action.
- Utilise VHNDs, antenatal care, institutional delivery (JSY) and immunisation contact points with mothers and infants for strengthening nutrition interventions.
- Strengthen NRHM Village Health Sanitation and Nutrition Committees as sub committees of panchayats and strengthen such linkages similarly at block, district and state levels.
- Ensure timely and complete Universal Immunisation and improve the prevention and management of common neonatal and childhood illnesses such as diarrhoea and acute respiratory infections, which impact significantly on Child Nutrition.
- Strengthen the implementation of programmes addressing Micro-nutrient Malnutrition (including Vitamin A Deficiency, Anaemia and Iodine Deficiency Disorders) including the use of Double Fortified Salt in government feeding programmes.
- Create National/State Resource Centres or Centres for Excellence for Maternal and Child Health Nutrition within existing institutions and/or in partnership with professional networks.
- Ensure that Health Surveys provide timely quality national, state and district level data on nutrition status (anthropometric indices) and micro-nutrient status for the effective monitoring of key nutrition outcomes.

3. Ministry of Human Resource Development: Department of School Education and Literacy
- Provide free and compulsory education to all children at elementary level as envisaged under RTE Act 2009.
- Ensure Universal Access to quality school (elementary and secondary) and adult education.
- Ensure Equity—inclusion of disadvantaged and more vulnerable community groups such as SCs, STs, minorities and vulnerable child groups such as first generation learners, children with different abilities.
- Strengthen education infrastructure and institutional capacity in districts with a high concentration of vulnerable groups such as in Tribal sub plan areas, Minority concentrated districts linked to MSDP and so on.
- Strengthen initiatives focused on the girl child and women such as KGBV, NPGEL, linked to longer term interventions for gender equality.
- Ensure Quality and improve standards of education—also making it child friendly and gender sensitive.
- Strengthening the protective environment for all children—with a focus on prevention of vulnerability to abuse and exploitation.
- Introducing Child Tracking systems especially in left wing extremism affected areas—helping retain children in school and bringing them back to school.
- Linking with Ministry of Labour to address Child Labour holistically.
- Establish linkages with RGSEAG, for addressing under-nutrition and anaemia in both out-of-school and school going adolescent girls, also giving out-of-school girls a second chance.
- Strengthen ICDS convergence and linkages with primary schools for supporting the early care, development and learning continuum, synchronization of timings/location of AWCs, where feasible and appropriate. This will also provide child care support, releasing girls from the burden of sibling care to be retained in schools.
- Strengthen linkages of ICDS SNP with Midday Meals in schools and specific piloting of community kitchens in innovative models within the 200 high burden districts initiative.
- Strengthening of gender sensitive, child friendly concepts and nutrition education components in school curriculum and Sakshar Bharat.
- Mandate assessment of "inclusiveness of the most vulnerable child groups" in sectoral reviews and missions.

4. Ministry of Agriculture
- Strengthen improvement in food and nutrition security for children, women and their families through improved agricultural productivity, better cropping patterns, improved procurement and distribution, the National Food Security Mission, National Horticulture Mission (NHM) and Horticulture Mission for North East and Himalayan States (HMNEH).

- Strengthen convergence of Rashtriya Krishi Vikas Yojana with other schemes such as MGNREGA, BRGF, SGSY for improving livelihood and food security of nutritionally vulnerable groups to improve social protection of children and women.
- Support for kitchen gardens in AWCs as village demonstration sites.

5. Ministry of Consumer Affairs, Food and Public Distribution

- Expedite finalisation of draft National Food Security Act, with other sectors, thereby enhancing social protection to women and children of the families covered.
- Include universal maternity protection within the purview of the same—impacting directly upon maternal and infant nutrition and care.
- Ensure food and nutrition security at the household level by making the essential food grains (rice, wheat, and coarse grains), edible oils and sugar available through the Targeted Public Distribution System.
- Effective implementation of TPDS along with reform measures, tools/measures for strengthened monitoring, on an ongoing basis.
- Support for piloting of community grain banks in high burden districts, based on district plans in identified 200 high burden districts.

6. Ministry of Food Processing Industries

- Promote processing of locally available nutritious foods through training of women's SHGs/Federations (564 FPTCs in 2010–11) and use this for nutrition communication.
- Cater to cluster development for nutritious food preparation.
- Enable women's SHGs to become nutrition educators and change nutrition related behaviour within their own families and communities.

7. Ministry of Rural Development

- Engender major flagship programmes such as MGNREGA and make them more child friendly (as detailed earlier) for ensuring social protection. For example by increasing the participation of women, introduction of more women friendly activities, technologies and tools, ensuring equal remuneration for equal work, (with greater responsiveness to older women or those with challenging health conditions or during pregnancy and lactation.
- Improve livelihoods and strengthen social protection for families, their women and children through MGNREGA, SGSY/NRLM.
- Create institutional capacity for incorporating gender and child related concerns in training, programme management and monitoring—such as by creating Women and Child Resource Units in SIRDs.
- Provide social assistance to the elderly and widows with empathy and dignity.
- Strengthen implementation of the enabling provisions for women, maternal and child care under MGNREGA, with piloting of crèches cum AWCs in remote and tribal areas.
- Amendment of MGNREGA guidelines to include greater diversity of work and AWC construction as a permissible work.
- Encourage use of BRGF funds for strengthening nutrition interventions, AWC and HSC construction.
- Integrate concerns for gender, children and nutrition in the training of programme managers, functionaries and women's SHGs.
- Link Women's SHGs/NRLM with provision of SNP in ICDS where locally feasible.
- Mandate Gender assessment as an integral part of all programme reviews and fora.

8. Ministry of Drinking Water and Sanitation

- Progressively ensure provision of toilets and safe drinking water supply in all AWCs. HSCs and schools, including measures for ensuring water quality. Separate toilets for girls in schools with requisite facilities to be promoted.
- Ensure that women's work sites and sites used by adolescent girls are covered with appropriate facilities.
- Ensure involvement of women and Village Health Water Sanitation and Nutrition Committees in micro-planning and decision on location of facilities.
- Cover AWCs running in rented premises with toilets through TSC revolving fund or enhanced rent and for covering all AWCs in govt./community/public buildings with drinking water facilities, as facilitated also by new MGNREGA guidelines.
- Strengthen IEC component for both NRDWP and TSC to be more child friendly with children as protectors of the environment and change leaders in their communities. Hygiene improvement under TSC to be better integrated with other IEC campaigns.

- Training and IEC activities under TSC, NRDWP, NRHM and ICDS to be linked and coordinated, including training of Village Health Water Sanitation and Nutrition Committees.

9. Ministry of Panchayati Raj

- Support States in the effective devolution of powers to PRI s-funds, functions and functionaries, as Women and Child Development is a part of the Eleventh Schedule (Article 243 G) of the 73rd Constitutional Amendment.
- Enable States to implement 50 per cent reservation for women in PRIs, with requisite support for capacity development.
- Build on work initiated to recognize and incentivize panchayats that improve the Child Sex Ratio through additional flexible resources.
- Institute Rashtriya Gaurav Gram Sabha Awards for the above.
- Mainstream Nutrition in the training of PRIs—especially Women panchayat members for malnutrition free panchayats, earmarking certain wards to them.
- Support the development of innovative district models run by PRIs within the 200 high burden districts initiative.
- Share best practices to support the devolution of powers related to nutrition programmes—to PRIs in all states.
- Special Gram Sabha meetings dedicated to Nutrition and also to the Girl Child in every gram sabha and with Mahila Sabhas being constituted.
- Especially in disturbed and other special areas Gram panchayats should be the actual delivery agency for PDS of food grains; Ward Sabha and Ward members should take up issues of absentee school teachers, dropout children and missing children—including girls. Supervision and monitoring to be led by gram panchayat or its sub committee.
- States which do not have gram panchayats like bodies should constitute the same.
- Ensure that the proposed Rajiv Gandhi Panchayati Sashaktikaran Abhiyan integrates concerns for gender and children in the training curriculum/packages being envisaged and those institutions that train PRI members include faculty resources on Gender and Children.
- Move towards the concept of 'Women and Child Friendly Panchayats' where the rights of children and women are protected and end violence against children, girls and women.

10. Ministry of Housing and Urban Poverty Alleviation

- Allocation of land/building for AWC especially in urban poor settlements.
- Inclusion of nutrition safety nets in resettlement plans for migrant and unrecognized urban poor groups.
- Support the development of innovative city model/s run by ULBs within the 200 high burden districts initiative, linked to JNNURM.
- Piloting of community canteens for urban poor, based on plans.
- Actions to be effected through State Governments, as Urban Water Supply and Sanitation is a State Subject and a function of the Urban local bodies.

11. Ministry of Urban Development

- City planning to also be made child friendly—as a key indicator of good governance.
- Replicate with urban local bodies what the Ministry of Panchayati Raj has done with PRIs.
- Inclusion of child care as a 'basic service' which cannot be denied to communities living in unrecognized urban poor areas—with no legitimacy or security of tenure.
- Progressively ensure access to health care, education, skill development, livelihoods for urban poor families with social protection for women and children and physical amenities like potable water supply, sewerage, sanitation and drainage for all.
- Nutrition related concerns to be integrated in the second phase of JNURM with the incorporation of child-friendly criteria.

12. Ministry of Social Justice and Empowerment

- Ensure that priority is accorded to concerns for children and women of the specific community groups addressed (that is Scheduled Castes, OBCs) within the different schemes.
- Ensure gender disaggregated tracking of beneficiary oriented programmes for SCs, others.
- Constitute a multi-sectoral National Task Force on Childhood Disability—prevention, early detection, intervention, community-based management, rehabilitation and inclusion, including civil society and parent networks.
- Set up Childhood Disability Resource Centres in relevant National Institutes such as NIMH, NIHH, NIOH, NIVH, in key national/state institutions responsible for training NRHM, ICDS and SSA personnel and development of core training modules for integration in respective training programmes.

- Enable relevant flagship programmes to include specific earmarked allocations for reaching out to and including children with special needs, as was initiated with Sarva Shiksha Abhiyan.
- Special interventions to be taken up for children subjected to substance abuse and with multiple vulnerabilities to violence and exploitation.
- Strengthen nutrition interventions in existing MSJE schemes, with appropriate budgetary allocation MSJE may obtain technical advice and engage with technical institutions such as NIN, FNB on the quality and nutritional value of food being provided in institutions.
- Piloting of community destitute feeding centres, based on district plans.

13. Ministry of Labour and Employment

- Amend the Child Labour (Prohibition and Regulation) Act in line with the RTE.
- Ensure that provisions of relevant legislations are implemented for women.
- Address support for women working in the unrecognized sector and recognize 'unrecognized care economy'.
- Strengthen implementation of provisions for maternity protection and child care support.
- Undertake review relating to provisions for special target groups like women and children, seasonal/migrant labour to strengthen women and child care and nutrition related components.
- Strengthen implementation of Rashtriya Swasthya Beema Yojana and also use RSBY cards as an opportunity for nutrition education/IEC to BPL families.

14. Ministry of Information and Broadcasting

- Ensure normative standards are in place so that media and internet material/usage is gender and child sensitive.
- Facilitate a nationwide IEC and intensive media campaign along with MoWCD.
- Review of Up linking/Down linking guidelines 2005 to consider making it mandatory for the private satellite television channels to carry advertisements/public messages in the public interest.
- Allocate free time for communicating nutrition messages during the prime time on Doordarshan.
- Facilitate use of Community Radio Services for conveying important messages on health.

15. Ministry of Tribal Affairs

- Ensure that priority is accorded to concerns for children and women of the specific community groups addressed (that is Scheduled Tribes) within the different schemes.
- Nutrition interventions for Tribal Areas to be reflected as a part of Tribal Sub Plan—especially in selected high burden districts.
- Special focus to be given to PTGs (particularly vulnerable tribal groups).
- Construction of AWCs as a comprehensive mother and child care centre, and HSCs to be funded from Tribal Sub Plan—especially in LWE areas with large infrastructure gaps.
- Engage with technical institutions, such as NIN, FNB on the quality of food and their nutritional value being provided in institutions being run under the Ministry.

16. Ministry of Minority Affairs

- Ensure that priority is accorded to concerns for children and women of the specific community groups addressed (that is Minorities) within the different schemes.
- Incentivisation of sectors, States and panchayats where social inclusion indicators related to children of socio religious communities—including minorities—improve, with peer learning/motivation through sharing of best practices, within and across States/Districts.
- Specific interventions for girls education and skill development to be accelerated in MSDP, with study centres at community level—with inclusion.
- Ensure disaggregated tracking of beneficiary oriented flagship programmes by beneficiary group (Minorities) and gender so that multiple vulnerabilities are addressed.
- Construction of physical infrastructure for Anganwadi services and Health care services under MSDP.

17. Ministry of Environment and Forests

- Capacity Development (through schools, colleges) of children as protectors of the environment.
- Inclusion of nutrition safety nets in resettlement plans for displaced populations.
- Review and strengthen steps for enhancing nutritional security through improved forest/crop diversification and environmental security.

18. Ministry of Youth Affairs
- Mobilise youth groups for communication campaigns related to nutrition and the girl child.
- Strengthen youth groups for supporting malnutrition free panchayats/communities through training/orientation.

19. Ministry of Statistics and Programme Implementation
- Institutionalize disaggregated tracking of key monitorable targets and progress of beneficiary oriented flagship programmes by community groups and gender to ensure social inclusion.
- Share best practices/examples of the use of MPLADs funds for addressing the child sex ratio and for nutrition interventions, AWC construction and so on.
- Position nutrition status of children under 3 years as a lead progress indicator for reviews at national/state/division/district levels, for relevant sectors.

20. Ministry of Home Affairs
- To ensure a safe and secure environment for children, women and their communities, with the implementation of various provisions for security, and anti trafficking.
- Ensuring gender-sensitive and child-friendly law enforcement institutions and mechanisms.

24

Social Inclusion

INTRODUCTION

24.1. Planning has traditionally focused on the need to provide special support to historically disadvantaged groups. The Scheduled Castes (SCs) and Scheduled Tribes (STs), have a special status under the Constitution. Other disadvantaged groups needing special support are Other Backward Classes (OBCs), Minorities and also other marginalised and vulnerable groups which suffer from handicaps such as Persons with Disabilities, senior citizens, street children, beggars and victims of substance abuse.

24.2. Across social groups, the incidence of poverty has been most pronounced among the SCs and STs (Table 24.1). Even though the incidence of poverty among these groups has declined over the years, the headcount ratio (HCR) for SCs and STs remains higher than the national average. However, it is encouraging to note from recent poverty estimates that poverty has declined at an accelerated rate between 2004–05 and 2009–10 for SCs and STs. The annual rate of decline of HCR for SCs and STs in the period between 2004–05 and 2009–10 has been higher than the overall annual rate of decline of HCR. For SCs, the annual rate of decline accelerated sharply from 0.80 percentage points per annum in the period between 1993–94 and 2004–05 to 2.25 percentage points per annum in the period between 2004–05 and 2009–10. The annual pace of poverty reduction amongst STs was disappointingly low in the period between 1993–94 and 2004–05 (0.34 percentage points per annum). However, in the period between 2004–05 and 2009–10, the annual rate of decline increased steeply to 2.98 percentage points per annum, exceeding the pace of overall poverty reduction.

24.3. Over the years several steps have been taken to bridge the gap between these marginalised groups and the rest of the population. But gaps still persist and further efforts are needed. The social justice

TABLE 24.1
Incidence of Poverty across Social Groups

Social Group	RURAL					URBAN				
	Headcount Ratio			Annual Rate of Decline		Headcount Ratio			Annual Rate of Decline	
	1993–94	2004–05	2009–10	1993–94 to 2004–05	2004–05 to 2009–10	1993–94	2004–05	2009–10	1993–94 to 2004–05	2004–05 to 2009–10
SC	62.28	53.53	42.26	0.80	2.25	51.16	40.56	34.11	0.96	1.29
ST	66.02	62.28	47.37	0.34	2.98	39.46	35.52	30.38	0.36	1.03
All India	50.19	41.79	33.8	0.76	1.60	31.45	25.68	20.9	0.52	0.96

Source: Planning Commission.

objectives of the Twelfth Plan can be achieved with full participation in the benefits of development on the part of all these groups. This calls for an inclusive growth process which provides opportunities for all to participate in the growth process combined with schemes that would either deliver benefits directly or more importantly help these groups to benefit from the opportunities thrown up by the general development process.

24.4. This Chapter reviews the efforts made by the Government for the socio-economic development of each of these disadvantaged groups in the Eleventh Plan and presents the new initiatives that will be taken during the Twelfth Five Year Plan period (2012–17) towards their empowerment.

24.5. The Eleventh Five Year Plan (2007–12) adopted a three pronged strategy:

1. Social Empowerment—removing existing and persisting inequalities besides providing easy access to basic minimum services with a top priority assigned to education as the key factor in social development;
2. Economic Empowerment—promoting employment-cum-income generation activities with an ultimate objective of making them economically independent and self-reliant; and
3. Social Justice—striving to eliminate all types of discrimination with the strength of legislative support, affirmative action, awareness generation and change in the mind-set of the people.

24.6. The effectiveness of this strategy in terms of the results achieved and implications for the Twelfth Plan are discussed for each group in turn.

SCHEDULED CASTES (SCs)

24.7. The Scheduled Caste population constituted 16.2 per cent of the total population in census 2001 and has increased marginally around 16.9 per cent in census 2011. People belonging to SC communities, by and large, are spread all over the country, with about 80 per cent of them living in the rural areas. Around half of the SC population is concentrated in the five States of Uttar Pradesh, West Bengal, Tamil Nadu, Andhra Pradesh and Bihar. Recognising that the Scheduled Castes have historically suffered grave social disabilities and educational and economic deprivation, the Constitution provides special provision for advancement of their interests.

Scheduled Caste Development: An Overview

Education

24.8. Expansion in education in general was a major thrust of the Eleventh Plan and this was accompanied by several schemes aimed specifically at educational development among SCs especially women and girl children. The 7 individual scholarship type schemes are described below. The allocation and expenditure in each scheme in the Eleventh Plan is presented in Table 24.2.

TABLE 24.2
Eleventh Plan Allocation and Expenditure for Special Schemes for SCs

(₹ in crores)

		Allocation	Expenditure
1.	Post Matric Scholarship	4,082.00	7,344.93
2.	Pre-Matric Scholarship to those engaged in Unclean occupations	200.00	264.25
3.	Top Class Education for SC Students	204.00	44.36
4.	National Overseas Scholarship Scheme	125.00	18.32
5.	Rajiv Gandhi National Fellowship	574.70	518.98
6.	Upgradation of Merit	10.00	10.74
7.	Scheme of Free Coaching	43.00	27.09
8.	Total	5,238.70	8,228.67

Source: Ministry of Social Justice and Empowerment.

Post Matric Scholarship

24.9. This is the single largest intervention by the Government of India for educational empowerment of SCs. It provides scholarships to about 48 lakh SC students for pursuing higher education in various courses beyond matriculation. Under the scheme, 100 per cent Central assistance is provided to States/UTs over and above their committed liability except for North-East States where committed liability is not applicable to them. The Scheme was revised in December 2010. In addition to increasing the rate of scholarship the income ceiling of parents whose children would be eligible to avail the scholarship was raised from ₹1.00 lakh to ₹2.00 lakh per annum.

Pre-Matric Scholarship to Children of those engaged in Unclean Occupations
24.10. This scheme, being implemented since 1977–78, provides financial assistance to children of manual scavengers, tanners, flayers and sweepers who have traditional link with scavenging, to enable them to pursue pre-matric education. The scheme was revised in 2008 changing the Central share from 50 per cent to 100 per cent over and above the committed liability and increase in the rate of scholarships. Scholarship @ of ₹110 per month is provided under the scheme to children studying in classes I to X. In addition, ad-hoc grant of ₹750 per annum is also provided to these children. However, children studying in classes III to X and staying in hostels are provided scholarship @ of ₹700 per month and also ad-hoc grant of ₹1,000 per annum. About 7 lakh children benefit under the scheme annually.

Top Class Education for SC students
24.11. This scheme aims to promote quality education amongst SC students, by providing full financial support for pursuing studies beyond 12th class in premier institutions of the country. The maximum number of slots for new scholarships each year is 1,250. Scholarships are granted to the students studying in 205 premier institutions for pursuing 182 courses including Engineering, Medical/Dentistry, Law, Management and other Specialised Streams. SC students who secure admission in the notified institutions (according to the norms prescribed by the respective institutions) and whose total family income is ₹4.5 lakh (recently revised upwards from ₹2 lakh), are eligible for the scholarship.

National Overseas Scholarship Scheme (NOS)
24.12. Under the Scheme, scholarships are provided to selected students for pursuing higher studies for Master level courses and Ph.D programme in specified fields. Until 2009–10, this scheme was restricted to the fields of engineering, technology and science only but in 2010–11, the scope was broadened by including additional disciplines, including medicine, agricultural science and management. A total of 30 scholarships are awarded annually under the scheme, with 9 scholarships (30 per cent) earmarked for women candidates. The scheme provides for fees charged by institutions, monthly maintenance allowance, passage and visa fee, contingence allowance and so on The scholarship is awarded to those candidates who are not more than 35 years of age and whose parental/guardian's income is not more than ₹25,000 per month.

Rajiv Gandhi National Fellowships (RGNF)
24.13. The Scheme was launched in 2005–06 as a special incentive to extend scholarships to SC students to pursue higher studies and research degrees such as M. Phil and Ph.D. The scheme is implemented through University Grants Commission (UGC) and the benefits are comparable to Junior Research Fellowships (JRF) and Senior Research Fellowships (SRF) of UGC. The Scheme was revised in 2010–11 and the number of fellowships has been increased from 1,333 to 2,000 to benefit more SC students. The income ceiling for availing the Scholarship is ₹3.00 lakh per annum.

Upgradation of Merit
24.14. This scheme has been in operation since 1987–88 and provides funds to educational institutions for conducting remedial and special coaching to SC students in Class IX to XII so that their merit is upgraded into professional and technical courses.

Central Sector Scheme of Free Coaching
24.15. The scheme, being implemented since Sixth Five Year Plan, provides coaching to students belonging to Scheduled Castes and those coming from socially and economically disadvantaged sections to sit for competitive examinations. The examinations cover Group A and Group B categories in the Central/State Governments, Officers grade examinations for PSUs, Banks, and so on and soft skill development programmes for employment in private sector covering areas like call centres, BPO,

retail management, information technology, and so on. The income ceiling under the Scheme is ₹2.00 lakh per annum. The scheme was revised in April 2007. The outlay for the Scheme in Eleventh Plan was ₹43.00 crore and the likely expenditure is of the order of ₹27.09 crore benefitting around 19,500 individuals.

Babu Jagjivan Ram Chhatravas Yojana (BJRCY)
24.16. The objective of the Scheme launched in 1963–64 (and renamed subsequently as Babu Jagjivan Ram Chhatravas Yojana w.e.f 01.01.2008) is to reduce the high dropouts and to increase the retention rates amongst SC students. Facilities in the form of hostels for SC boys and girls are provided, to pursue studies from middle school to the university level. Central assistance is provided for construction of hostel buildings on matching basis (50:50) to States and 100 per cent to UTs and 100 per cent to States for SC Girls Hostels (since 2007–08). 98 girls' hostels were constructed covering 6,379 beneficiaries and 125 boys' hostels were constructed covering 9,603 beneficiaries during the period, 2008–09 to 2010–11.

Economic Development
24.17. Economic empowerment of SCs is an important mechanism for achieving inclusion and education is obviously a key element of economic empowerment, but in addition, this objective is achieved through various programmes for economic support for SCs with a focused attention on women, manual scavengers and most backward communities. Review of the implementation of major schemes for economic development of SCs is presented below:

National Scheduled Castes Finance and Development Corporation (NSFDC)
24.18. NSFDC was set up in 1989. It provides financial and other support to beneficiaries for taking up various income generating activities. The Corporation has introduced an Education Loan Scheme since December, 2009. The authorised share capital of NSFDC is ₹1,000 crore and cumulative share capital is ₹676.80 crore. As on 31.3.2012, the Corporation has disbursed ₹2,302.91 crore benefitting 7.95 lakh SCs.

State Scheduled Castes Development Corporations
24.19. The Scheme of State Scheduled Castes Development Corporation (SCDC) was launched in 1979 with an objective of participating in the equity share of the Scheduled Castes Development Corporation (SCDC) in the ratio of 49:51 (49 per cent by MSJE and 51 per cent by the respective State Governments). The main function of SCDC include identification of eligible SC families and motivating them to undertake economic development scheme, sponsoring the schemes to financial institutions for credit support, providing financial assistance in the form of margin money at low interest rates and subsidy in order to reduce repayment liability and providing necessary tie up with other poverty alleviation programmes. SCDCs finance employment-oriented schemes and cover agriculture and allied activities including minor irrigation; small scale industry; transport and trade and services.

24.20. The NSCFDC and NSKFDC continue to depend only upon governmental funding, whereas they are expected to work as independent financial supporting mechanism with a social mandate. This raises a question regarding the viability of economic activities identified by the Corporation. On the whole, there is a need to restructure the Scheme so that these Corporations become financially more viable and sustainable.

National Safai Karamcharis Finance and Development Corporation (NSKFDC)
24.21. NSKFDC was set up in 1997 with the aim to promote social and economic development of Safai Karamcharis by way of providing financial assistance at concessional rates of interest to promote self-employment in alternative occupations and scheme of skill development. The channelising agencies for identification of beneficiaries and disbursement of loans are the State Scheduled Caste Development Corporations (SCDC). No income ceiling is fixed under the Scheme for availing financial assistance. Priority is, however, accorded to economic development and rehabilitation of scavengers, whose income is below double the poverty line besides women and persons with disabilities among the target group.

Authorised share capital of the corporation was enhanced from ₹300 crore to ₹600 crore in January, 2012. Cumulative disbursements since incorporation of NSKFDC till 31.3.2012 are ₹724.24 crore which benefitted 2.31 lakh beneficiaries.

Pradhan Mantri Adarsh Gram Yojana (PMAGY)
24.22. This Centrally Sponsored Scheme was launched in March 2010 as a pilot scheme for integrated development of 1,000 SC majority villages. The scheme is presently being implemented in five States viz. Assam (100 villages), Bihar, Himachal Pradesh, Rajasthan and Tamil Nadu (225 villages each). The objective of the Scheme is to ensure integrated development of the selected 1,000 villages with more than 50 per cent SC population into 'model villages'. Integrated development of selected villages is to be achieved primarily through implementation of existing schemes of the Central and State Governments. Each village covered was provided with ₹10 lakh as the Central assistance which was raised to ₹20 lakh in 2011–12.

Other Important Schemes Benefiting SCs
24.23. Besides the programmes of the Ministry of Social Justice and Empowerment, there are various other programmes of the Government that are not targeted exclusively for the SCs but which benefit the SCs often in proportion which exceed their population share. Some of these programmes form part of 'Bharat Nirman' and include other flagship programmes such as Integrated Child Development Services, Sarva Shiksha Abhiyan, Mid-Day Meal, National Rural Health Mission and the Mahatma Gandhi National Rural Employment Guarantee Scheme and so on.

Elimination of Manual Scavenging and Rehabilitation of Manual Scavengers
24.24. Towards rehabilitating the manual scavengers and dependents, National Scheme for Liberation and Rehabilitation of Manual Scavengers (NSLRMS) has been in operation since 1992. A total of 7.70 lakh manual scavengers are to be rehabilitated through NSLRMS. By the end of 2006, about 4.28 lakh beneficiaries were to be rehabilitated. Self-Employment Scheme for Rehabilitation of Manual Scavengers (SRMS) was introduced in January, 2007 with the objective of rehabilitating the remaining 3.42 lakh manual scavengers and their dependents by March, 2009. Under the Scheme, identified beneficiaries are provided a loan, at subsidised rate of interest (4–6 per cent per annum) and credit linked upfront capital subsidy (@50 per cent of the project cost, for projects up to ₹25,000 and @ 25 per cent for projects above ₹25,000, with a minimum of ₹12,500 and maximum of ₹20,000) for setting up self-employment projects costing up to ₹5.00 lakh. The SRMS originally envisaged rehabilitation of all manual scavengers in alternative occupations by March 2009. Subsequently this deadline was extended up to March 2010. However, 16 States and 2 UTs reported the existence of 1,18,474 manual scavengers and their dependents, who were to be rehabilitated in alternative occupations till end-March 2010. All 18 States/UTs confirmed rehabilitation of all eligible and willing beneficiaries, identified by them.

24.25. 'The Prohibition of Employment as Manual Scavengers and their Rehabilitation Bill, 2012', has been introduced in the Parliament. Survey of Manual Scavengers in the rural areas is underway as a part of the Socio-economic Caste Census (Rural). Steps for a similar survey of manual Scavengers in the urban areas have been initiated. Steps have also been taken for the revision of the Self Employment Scheme for Manual Scavengers (SRMS).

Protection Measures
24.26. Two important protective legislations in operation for people belonging to SCs are (*i*) the Protection of Civil Rights Act, 1955 and (*ii*) the Scheduled Castes and Scheduled Tribes (Prevention of Atrocities) Act, 1989. Despite these protective legislations, atrocities and crimes committed against SCs, especially against

their women, have been reported in all parts of the country in varying degrees.

24.27. The Governments of Andhra Pradesh, Bihar, Gujarat, Jharkhand, Karnataka, Kerala, Madhya Pradesh, Maharashtra, Orissa, Rajasthan, Tamil Nadu and Uttar Pradesh have identified certain atrocity prone areas in their respective States. State Governments have been specifically asked to carefully identify atrocity-prone areas and evolve special strategies as preventive measures, along with steps for their development including appropriate income generating beneficiary-oriented schemes, promotion of Self Help Groups especially for women and upgradation of infrastructure facilities like link roads.

Scheduled Castes: Strategy for the Twelfth Plan

24.28. The Twelfth Plan must strive harder to achieve the overall improvement in socio-economic conditions of the weaker sections by extending a well balanced prioritisation of efforts made for social development and economic empowerment based on the actual needs and problems of these communities. The principal goals for the Twelfth Plan, towards empowerment of the Scheduled Castes, will be:

1. To ensure the security and dignity of all persons belonging to the scheduled castes, especially women and put a complete end to all forms of 'untouchability' and discrimination against them.
2. To bring members of the SCs—both men and women—at par, to the maximum possible extent, with their non-SC/ST counterparts, in terms of all developmental indices viz.—education, health, nutrition, housing, income generation and employability.
3. To empower SCs to participate in society and in nation-building, on an equal basis with others.
4. To effectively implement SCSP as the essential instrument for accomplishing inclusive growth.

Education Development

- Education will continue to be the most important instrument to uplift the status of the SCs as it will help maximise the participation of SC students in new economic opportunities. Access to and participation of SC students should be enhanced to ensure that they have access to quality education. Special efforts need to be made to promote educational development by providing needed support in the form of scholarships for different levels of education; increasing the hostel facilities for boys and girl students; upgradation of Anganwadis by including high-quality pre-school institutions with qualified teachers; setting up a network of residential schools of high quality throughout the country so that all SC girls and boys are covered by them and receive quality education up to Class XII; ensuring that SCs are able to secure full quota of reservation and also enter the merit quota in higher education; and revising the rates of scholarships every two years, based on increase in cost of living index or Consumer Price Index (CPI). The endeavour in the Twelfth Five Year Plan will be directed towards taking up the following steps:
- The Pre-matric scholarship scheme at present exists only for children of those engaged in manual scavenging. A new pre-matric scholarship scheme has been introduced for SC students studying in Class IX and X during 2012–13. This scheme needs to be extended to SC students studying in Class I to VIII during the remaining period of the XII Five Year Plan so that all the SC students from class I to X will start getting pre-matric scholarship by the terminal year of the Twelfth Plan. Special attention needs to be paid not only to retention in schools but also to provide the children with quality education through incentives like free supply of books, mid-day meals, hostels, and so on to SC children especially the SC girls.
- The scheme of Post-Matric Scholarships for SCs provides scholarships to SC students for pursuing higher education in various courses beyond matriculation. The scheme should also have the provision for a laptop or other suitable computing device for all SC students passing Xth or XIIth Board Examination by scoring the benchmarked higher percentage in the exams, as may be fixed.
- Rajiv Gandhi National Fellowship (RGNF) for SC was increased to 2,000 students in 2010–11. There is a need to further increase the number of these fellowships.

- The number of scholarships under the scheme of 'National Overseas Scholarship' needs to be increased substantially without any restriction as regards the field of study for which the scholarship would be available.
- SC students need to be encouraged more vigorously to prepare for various competitive examinations. 'Free coaching to the SC students' should be expanded to cover Premier Entrance Exams to professional institutions like IITs, JEE, AIEEE, CPMT, CLAT, CAT, and so on under the scheme of coaching for SC students. The scheme should be comprehensively revised to make it more beneficial to SC students. Upgradation of Soft/Communication Skills for SC students is a major challenge and should be addressed suitably.
- State Governments need to upgrade the hostels to a satisfactory level using funds provided by the Finance Commission and other agencies. It is envisaged to have additional Hostel capacity of 2 Lakh seats for SC students with a minimum of 50 per cent for SC girls. Central assistance to States/UTs for construction of boys hostels need to be increased appropriately. Babu Jagjivan Ram Chhatrawas Yojana will be revised so as to provide assistance for creating additional seats for SC students in integrated hostels too, besides for constructing hostels exclusively for SC students.
- Access to good quality schools/residential schools still remains much below the actual requirement for SC students, especially for SC girls. Various steps have been taken to universalise elementary education and increase the numbers of Navodaya Vidyalayas and Kasturba Gandhi Balika Vidyalayas, along with earmarking the stipulated reservation for SCs therein. However, the problem of limited access continues. Therefore, good quality residential schools for SC boys and girls need to be set up in blocks with high SC concentration so as to ensure that all meritorious SC girls and boys have access to such residential schools, as early as possible. The percentage of SCs in such schools should be at least 50 per cent.

Economic Development

24.29. Economic empowerment through employment and income generation programmes must be given special emphasis in the Twelfth Plan. Various financial institutions viz., National Scheduled Caste Finance and Development Corporation (NSFDC), National Safai Karamcharis Finance and Development Corporation (NSKFDC) set up for promoting economic development among the respective target groups are facing major problems in channelising their funds through the States Channelising Agencies (SCAs). The loan recovery rates of these agencies are very low, but State Governments are not willing to provide the block guarantee required for advancing the loans. The national level Corporations need to consider alternative Agencies to channelise credit to SCs and Safai Karamcharis so as to meet their targets in all the States. Regarding equity support to Scheduled Castes Development Corporations (SCDCs), NSKFDC should assist at least one lakh beneficiaries under its various schemes during Twelfth Five Year Plan. A major focus should be on organising skill development programmes.

24.30. In order to implement economic development programmes with assured outcome as intended and to mobilise institutional credit at concessional rates, SCDCs need to focus on capacity building, network linking with micro-financing, risk sharing, risk mitigation and selection of viable economic ventures. Further, there is a need to devise effective mechanisms for recovery of loans to improve loan recovery. An element of professionalism in managing the SCDCs is also needed to be inculcated through continuous capacity building training of staff and computerisation. The operations of SCDCs are not economically viable at the existing rate of recovery to meet the cost of operations. Therefore, efforts need to be made to improve the functioning of SCDCs to enable them to function as viable and independent supporting financial mechanisms.

24.31. Landlessness amongst Scheduled Castes is much higher than in the non-SCs. Intensive efforts need to be made to distribute surplus government land to landless SC agricultural labourers in the rural areas. The land distribution needs to be completed in a time bound manner, so as to enable a larger number of landless SC families to improve their lot at the earliest.

24.32. Both the Central and State Governments implement various Schemes for the social and economic well-being of SCs. However, there is also a need for creating a National Fund to finance various innovative activities for their development which do not fall under any of the existing Schemes, for example development and training of talented SC artisans and artists. It would be desirable to have a National Fund for Innovative Development Activities for SCs—for supporting SC talent and potential in diverse areas, otherwise not covered under the existing Schemes. The Scheme may be implemented through National Scheduled Castes Finance and Development Corporation (NSFDC).

24.33. SC artisans and entrepreneurs face a serious problem in marketing their products. In the past, certain initiatives have been taken by the Ministry of Social Justice and Empowerment and the National Scheduled Castes Finance and Development Corporation to enable them to showcase and market their products by facilitating their participation in various fairs, exhibitions and so on. However, the ambit of such initiatives has been rather limited. There is, thus, a need to create a strong institutional mechanism to facilitate the SC entrepreneurs/artisans in marketing their products in an institutionalised manner. A National level organisation may be set up in the Twelfth Plan as a permanent marketing institution, on the lines of TRIFED, for marketing of products manufactured by Scheduled Caste entrepreneurs/artisans.

SCHEDULED TRIBES

24.34. The Scheduled Tribes (STs), with a population of 84.33 million as per 2001 Census constituted 8.2 per cent of the country's population. Unlike the SCs who are dispersed throughout the country, STs have traditionally been concentrated in about 15 per cent of the country's geographical areas, mainly forests, hills, undulating inaccessible areas. The fact that most of them live in isolated groups in relatively remote areas has made it more difficult to deliver essential services to them and has also made it much more difficult for them to benefit from the acceleration of overall growth than is the case with SCs. Out of the total ST population, 2.59 million (3.07 per cent) belong to Particularly Vulnerable Tribal Groups (PVTGs) earlier referred to as Primitive Tribal Groups (PTGs). There are 75 identified PVTGs spread across 17 States/UTs.

Scheduled Tribe Development: An Overview

24.35. Because of the remoteness of location of most of the ST population, the extent to which they can benefit from general development programmes is more limited and the need for special programmes is greater than for SCs. The need for special efforts to ensure an adequate flow of benefits to the Scheduled Tribes has been recognised in all Plans beginning with the First Plan. Over time this strategy has evolved to a multi pronged strategy culminating in the objective enunciated in the Eleventh Plan that the benefits of inclusive growth must extend fully to the STs.

24.36. The Human Development Report 2011 of the Planning Commission candidly admits that though the consumption expenditure of Scheduled Tribes has been rising overtime, the rate of increase was lower that the all India average. Further, while there has been a divergence in Monthly Per Capita Consumption Expenditure (MPCE) from the national average for STs and Muslims during 1999–2000 and 2007–08, they are also diverging from the national average in terms of female malnutrition during 1998 from the national average in terms of female malnutrition during 1998–99 and 2005–06. Only one-third STs and around half of SCs reside in pucca houses compared to 66 per cent for all India. Over time, ST households, due to a slower pace in improvement have experienced a growing divergence from the national average of households residing in pucca houses.

24.37. Poor implementation of existing schemes in the tribal regions has meant that not only poverty continues at an exceptionally high levels in these regions, but the decline in poverty has been much slower here than in the entire country, as shown in Table 24.3.

24.38. Thus the gap has been steadily rising, with the result that between 1993–94 and 2004–05 the share of the tribals amongst the poor in the country increased

TABLE 24.3
Rural Population Living Below Poverty Line (1993–94, 1999–2000 and 2004–05) (in %)

Category	1993–94	1999–2000	2004–05
Total	50.19	27.09	41.79
STs	66.02	45.86	62.28
GAP	15.83	18.77	20.49

Source: PP Division, Planning Commission.

from 15.83 to 20.49 per cent. Lagging of scheduled tribes reflects the fact that geographical seclusion has limited their access to new self-employment opportunities and as labour supply has remained abundant in the remote villages with negligible out-migration, agricultural wages for this group did not grow to the same extent as they did for the scheduled castes.

24.39. Similar gaps continue between literacy levels and health indicators of STs and the general population and have widened over the years. The continuing gap between literacy levels of STs and the general population is shown in Table 24.4 and Table 24.5.

TABLE 24.4
Literacy Rates of STs and Total Population (in %)

Category	1971	1981	1991	2001
Total Population	29.45	36.23	52.21	65.38
Scheduled Tribes	11.30	16.35	29.60	47.10
GAP	18.15	19.88	22.61	18.28

Source: Ministry of Human Resource Development.

TABLE 24.5
Female Literacy Rates of STs and Total Population (in %)

Category	1971	1981	1991	2001
All	18.69	29.85	39.29	54.16
STs	4.85	8.04	18.19	34.76
GAP	13.84	21.81	21.10	19.40

Source: Ministry of Human Resource Development.

24.40. Thus the gap in literacy levels, both for tribal men and women, has not declined significantly despite the fact that the largest proportion of centrally sponsored programmes for tribal development are related to the single sector of education. The gap would be wider if the north-eastern states are excluded from the above table, as education and health standards of tribals in that region are much above the national average. There are districts in India where the female literacy among adivasis is less than 10 per cent.

24.41. The dropout rate is a critical indicator reflecting lack of educational development and inability of a given social group to complete a specific level of education. In the case of tribals, dropout rates are still very high—31.33 per cent in Classes I to V; 58.3 per cent in Classes I to VIII; and 76.9 per cent in Classes I to X in 2008–09 (Source: Selected Educational Statistics 2008–09 of India, Ministry of Human Resource Development).

24.42. The 16th Joint Review Mission of the SSA done in 2012 notes with some concern that enrolment of SC and ST and Muslim children in the 6–14 population has reduced. Among the social categories, the enrolment rate is lowest among the scheduled tribes. As per DISE data, the enrolment of SC children has reduced from 19.81 per cent in 2009 to 19.06 per cent in 2010–11. Similarly enrolment for ST children for the same period has reduced from 10.93 per cent to 10.70 per cent. Reports of Monitoring Institutes also observed that there were noticeable gaps in learning achievement levels of SC, ST and Muslim children in almost all the states.

24.43. The health status of both SCs and STs are far worse than that of other sections of society. Since access to health care is limited for STs and SCs, barely 42 per cent of pregnant SCs could access a doctor for ante natal care and only 28 per cent could access an Auxiliary Midwife Nurse (AMN). But 64 per cent of others obtained ante natal care from a doctor. Again, since most STs live in remote rural areas, barely 18 per cent of all STs had deliveries in a health facility, compared to 51 per cent among other communities. There is, however, a failure of governance, which has multiple dimensions and is not confined to the inefficiency of the health delivery system only. See Table 24.6.

TABLE 24.6
Mortality and Undernutrition

	Mortality and Undernutrition	SC	ST	Others
1	Child Mortality (per 1,000 live births)	83	84	62
2	Infant Mortality	39	46	22
3	Proportion (per cent) of Children with Anaemia	78	79	72
4	Proportion (per cent) of Underweight Children	21	26	14

Source: Planning Commission: NFHS 2005–06 Report.

24.44. Since most of the tribal habitations are located in isolated villages and hamlets in undulating plateau lands coinciding with forest areas, they have limited access to criticalinfrastructure facilities such as roads, communication, health, education, electricity, drinking water and so on. This widens the gap between the quality of their life and the people in the country.

Education Development

24.45. Education continued to receive high priority in the Eleventh Plan to facilitate educational development among STs by providing educational facilities, incentives and support especially focusing the ST girls. The expenditure in the Eleventh Plan, compared with the allocation is given in Table 24.7.

TABLE 24.7
Eleventh Plan Allocation and Expenditure for Special Schemes for STs

		(₹ in Crores)	
		Allocation	Expenditure
1.	Post Matric Scholarship	1,496.30	2,118.36
2.	Hostels for ST girls/boys	272.96	322.00
3.	Upgradation of Merit	*	5.28
4.	Free Coaching for STs	300.00	229.76
5.	Scholarship for Top Class Education	73.80	15.96
6.	Ashram Schools	147.60	231.00
7.	Strengthening Education among ST girls	298.75	162.05
	Total	2,589.41	3,084.41

* Allocation included in Post matric Scholarship scheme

Source: Ministry of Tribal Affairs.

Post Matric Scholarship

24.46. The Post Matric Scholarship Scheme for ST Children is a centrally sponsored scheme providing financial assistance to the Scheduled Tribe students pursuing higher education beyond matriculation levels. The scholarships are awarded through the Government of the State/Union Territory where he/she is domiciled and 100 per cent Central assistance is provided to States/UTs over and above their committed liability. For North-East States committed liability is not applicable. The Scheme was revised in December, 2010. The income ceiling of parents for their children availing the scholarship has been raised from ₹1.00 lakh per annum to ₹2.00 Lakh. The Commercial Pilot License Course (CPL) is also included in the scheme and 10 Scholarships are to be given to the eligible ST students per year.

Hostels for ST Girls/Boys

24.47. The objective of the scheme is to facilitate ST students to continue their studies at distant places by extending hostel facilities to those who were otherwise unable to continue their studies due to remote location of their villages. The Eleventh Plan allocation for the hostels scheme was ₹272.96 crore. The scheme was revised on 1 April 2005 to provide 100 per cent funding for construction of hostels for both boys and girls in left wing extremism affected areas. Evaluation studies have pointed out that infrastructure facilities in most of the hostels are poor; maintenance of the buildings is also not up to the mark; and construction of hostel buildings is often hampered due to non-receipt of proper/complete proposals of the States. These problems need to be resolved in the Twelfth Plan.

Upgradation of Merit of ST Students

24.48. The objective of the scheme, which functions under the umbrella of the Post Matric Scholarship Studies, is to upgrade the merit of Scheduled Tribe students including PVTG students in classes IX to XII by providing them with facilities for all round development through education in residential schools so that they can compete with other students for admission to higher education courses and for senior administrative and technical occupations.

The Scheme was revised with effect from the financial year 2008–09. Under the Scheme, 100 per cent financial assistance is provided to the States and UTs for implementation of the scheme. A revised package grant of ₹19,500/- per student per year is provided from 2008–09 which includes the honorarium to be paid to the Principal or Experts imparting coaching and also to meet incidental charges. Coverage under the scheme reached to 1,053 ST students in the last year of the Eleventh Plan (2011–12).

Free Coaching for STs
24.49. The Scheme of Free Coaching for STs has been in operation since the Sixth Five Year Plan and provides free coaching to ST students to enhance their competitive capabilities to face various competitive examinations. Coaching is provided through State Governments/Universities/NGOs/private Coaching Institutes for competitive examinations of Group A and Group B categories in the Central/State Governments, Officers grade examinations for PSUs, Banks, and so on and soft skill development programmes for employment in private sector covering areas like call centres, BPO, retail management, information technology, and so on. Apart from coaching fee, stipend is also provided to the students @ ₹1,500/- per month for outstation students and ₹750/- per month for local students. The income ceiling under the scheme is ₹2.00 lakhs per annum.

Scholarships Scheme of Top Class Education
24.50. The Central Sector Scholarship scheme of Top Class Education for ST Students was launched in 2007–08. The scheme aims at promoting quality education amongst ST students, by providing full financial support for pursuing studies beyond XII class in premier institutions of the country. Maximum number of slots for new scholarships each year is 1,250. There are 125 institutes approved under the scheme in both the Government and private sectors covering the subjects of management, medicine, engineering, law and commercial courses. Physical coverage achieved under the scheme, is very poor as only 1,085 ST students are expected to have benefitted through the scheme in the Eleventh Plan against the target of covering 10,105 beneficiaries.

Ashram Schools
24.51. The scheme of Ashram Schools in Tribal Sub Plan areas spread over in 22 States and 2 Union Territories has been operational since 1990–91 and was revised in 2008–09. The objective is to promote and extend educational facilities to Scheduled Tribe students including PVTGs in tune with their social and cultural milieu. Ashram Schools provide education with residential facilities in an environment conducive to learning. The State Governments are eligible for 100 per cent Central Share for construction of Girls' Ashram Schools and also for construction of Boys' Ashram Schools in left wing extremism affected areas. For the other Boys' Ashram Schools, the funding to State Government is on 50:50 basis. In case of UTs, the Central Government bears the entire cost of construction of both Boys' and Girls' Ashram Schools. Ashram Schools are regular schools having the same curriculum as prescribed by the State Board of Secondary Education. The expenditure incurred on construction of hostels was ₹231.00 crore exceeding the Eleventh Plan outlay of ₹147.60 crore. The physical achievement in terms of number of seats in the Ashram School indicates nearly 5 fold increase (49,334 seats) over the Eleventh Plan Target of 10,000 seats only.

24.52. A review of the implementation of the scheme reveals that delays in construction of school buildings affects the programme and prospects of aspiring ST students adversely. Several schools are reported to be poorly maintained with little or no infrastructural facilities. Unless basic facilities are provided in Ashram Schools, children will be discouraged from continuing in these schools and their focus on education and training will be adversely affected. It is also noticed that textbooks are either not provided or are provided quite late after the session has started which defeats the purpose for which the textbooks are supplied free of cost to these students. Ideally, books and teaching medium up to the primary level should be in tribal dialects to the extent possible and the teachers should also be drawn from local tribal communities.

Strengthening Education among ST Girls

24.53. The Scheme of Educational Complexes in the Low Literacy Pockets was revised in 2008–09 and renamed as Strengthening Education among ST Girls in Low Literacy Districts. The revised scheme is being implemented in 54 identified low literacy districts where the ST population is 25 per cent or more and ST female literacy rate is below 35 per cent. The revised scheme envisages convergence with Sarva Shiksha Abhiyan (SSA) and Kasturba Gandhi Balika Vidyalaya (KGBV) schemes of the Ministry of Human Resource Development (MHRD). It meets the requirement of primary-level students as well as middle/secondary-level students and provides residential facilities to ST girl students facilitating their retention in schools. Besides formal education, the scheme also takes care of skill upgradation of ST girls in various vocations. Establishment of the District Education Support Agency (DESA) is also taken up in each low literacy district, which is required to make efforts to ensure 100 per cent enrolment and also play the role of a monitor and facilitator and support linkages with various institutions.

Rajiv Gandhi National Fellowships

24.54. The scheme of Rajiv Gandhi National Fellowships (RGNF) was launched in 2005–06 as a special incentive to extend scholarships to ST students to pursue higher studies and research degrees such as M.Phil and Ph.D. The scheme is implemented through UGC and the benefits are comparable to JRF and SRF of UGC. The scheme was revised in 2010–11 and number of fellowships has been increased from 1,333 to 2,000 to benefit more ST students.

National Overseas Scholarship

24.55. The scheme of National Overseas Scholarship launched in 1954–55 was earlier implemented as a non-Plan scheme. In the year 2007–08 the scheme was converted to a Central Sector Plan scheme whereby financial assistance is provided to meritorious ST students for pursuing higher education abroad at the level of Masters and Ph.D. The scheme envisages awarding 30 overseas scholarships every year, of these, 30 per cent are earmarked for ST finalists. Grants are given to the selected candidates on 100 per cent basis directly by the Ministry through the Indian Missions. The Eleventh Plan target was to award 50 overseas scholarships to ST students. In the first four years of the Eleventh Plan, only 8 scholarships could be awarded (2 per year). 15 scholarships were envisaged in the year 2011–12. Specified field of study under the scheme have been revised for the selected year 2010–11 in order to broaden the scope and benefit more students, the disciplines like Medicine, Pure Sciences, Engineering, agricultural science and Management have been covered under the scheme.

Tribal Research Institutes

24.56. There are 17 Tribal Research Institutes (TRIs) located in various states and UTs conducting relevant research, student surveys and training and providing necessary inputs for formulating suitable policies and programmes. The potentialities of these institutions are not being harnessed fully. TRIs with their technical and professional manpower can be directed to take up action research participatory approach, especially with respect to PVTG development and livelihood programmes. In order to ensure coordinated efforts of these TRIs, it is necessary to designate a TRI as a nodal agency representing the respective region—East, West, South, North-East and Central. There are eight sub-schemes under the umbrella scheme of TRIs (Information Technology, Monetary Evaluation and so on).

Economic Empowerment

24.57. Economic development among the tribals largely depends upon agriculture and its allied activities. Besides, forest resources and minor forest produce contribute substantially to the tribal economy. Since more than one-fifth of the ST population depends on agriculture and forests, their ability to cope with the changing economic scenario, especially in taking advantage of the new economic avenues is minimal. This calls for capacity building in diversifying their livelihood sources. Economic empowerment of the STs is being promoted through implementation of various income and employment generating programmes focusing PVTGs. The details of the economic development programmes are given below:

National Scheduled Tribes Finance and Development Corporation

24.58. National Scheduled Tribes Finance and Development Corporation (NSTFDC) is a Government of India owned undertaking under the ministry of Tribal Affairs. It provides financial assistance for income generating schemes for the economic development of scheduled tribes. The broad objectives of NSTFDC are identification of economic activities of importance to the scheduled tribes so as to generate self-employment and raise their level of income, upgradation of skills and processes used by the scheduled tribes by providing both institutional and on the job training. The eleventh plan outlay under the scheme is ₹260 crore but no expenditure was made during annual plans of 2007–08 and 2009–10 and outlay of ₹70.00 crore has also been allocated for 2011–12. Although a target of about 7.56 lakh STs were envisaged to be benefitted through NSTFDC during eleventh plan, only 3.88 lakh could be covered.

Market Development of Tribal Products

24.59. Market Development of Tribal Products/Produce is a Central Sector Scheme under which the Ministry of Tribal Affairs extends Grant-in-Aid to Tribal Cooperative Marketing Development Federation of India Limited (TRIFED) for four main activities: (*i*) Retail Marketing Development Activity; (*ii*) Minor Forest Produce (MFP) Marketing Development Activity; (*iii*) Vocational Training, Skill Up-gradation; and (*iv*) Capacity Building of ST Artisans and MFP; and Research and Development/Intellectual Property Rights (IPR) Activity.

24.60. TRIFED is now functioning both as a service provider and market developer for tribal products. Further, in its role as a capacity builder, it imparts training to ST Artisans and Minor Forest Produce (MFP) gatherers. TRIFED is marketing its products through 39 outlets (26 outlets are its own and 13 outlets are on a consignment basis in association with state-level organisations). During 2007–12, the turnover only through retail marketing activities was ₹36.96 crore.

Grants-in-aid to State Tribal Development Cooperative Corporations

24.61. The Central Sector Scheme Grants-in-Aid to State Tribal Development Cooperative Corporations (STDCCs) for Minor Forest Produce and so on for MFP Operations was launched in 1992–93 to help these State-level organisations. Grants-in-Aid are extended to these organisations under this Scheme for increasing the quantum of MFP handled by setting off operational losses; if need be; strengthening the share capital base of the Corporation for undertaking MFP operations thereby increasing the quantum of MFP presently handled; setting up of scientific warehousing facilities, wherever necessary; establishing processing industries for value addition with the objective of ensuring maximum returns on the MFPs for the tribals; giving consumption loans to the tribals; and supplementing Research and Development (R&D) activities.

Vocational Training Centre in Tribal Areas

24.62. The Scheme of Vocational Training Centre in Tribal Areas was launched in 1992–93 to develop skills among the ST youth to enable them to gain employment and self-employment opportunities and improving their socio-economic conditions by enhancing their incomes. Under the scheme, the training for trades including modern trades are being provided through ITIs Polytechnics, Computer Training Centres. Besides, training on vocational trades are being provided through institutions/organisation who are running projects affiliated under 'Modular Employable Skills' and 'Craftsmen Training Scheme'. The scheme was revised in April 2009 and provides enhanced financial norms and a time schedule for submission of proposals. The scheme makes the organisations responsible for establishing linkages with placement services and arranging easy micro-finance/loans for trained youth through financial institutions, the NSTFDC and banks.

24.63. Special Central Assistance to Tribal Sub-Plan (SCA to TSP) is a special area programme, provided by the Ministry of Tribal Development to the State Governments as an additive to the State Plan to bring about a more rapid economic development of tribals in the States (Details on SCA to TSP are furnished in the sub-chapter on SCSP and TSP).

Social Justice and Protection

24.64. Owing to their isolated existence, the tribals are not equipped to deal with the ever changing and complex socio-economic developments engulfing them. They are also susceptible to exploitation, atrocities and crimes, alienation from their land, denial of their forest rights and overall exclusion either directly or indirectly from their rightful entitlements. The PVTGs are the worst affected lot among the tribals.

24.65. The Protection of Civil Rights Act, 1955, (PCR Act) and the Scheduled Castes and Scheduled Tribes (Prevention of Atrocities) Act, 1989, (POA Act) are two important legal instruments to prevent all types of social discriminations like untouchability, exploitation and atrocities. The National Crime Records Bureau Report 2007 states that highly endemic crimes/atrocities are being reported in the states like Madhya Pradesh (27.01 per cent), Rajasthan (20.01 per cent), Andhra Pradesh (13.06 per cent), Chhattisgarh (11.01 per cent), Orissa (7.01 per cent) and Jharkhand (4.08 per cent).

24.66. In order to ensure early prosecution of cases under the SC/ST Prevention of Atrocity (Act), 1989, 151 exclusive special courts have been set up in Andhra Pradesh (12), Bihar (11), Chhattisgarh (7), Gujarat (10), Karnataka (7), Madhya Pradesh (43), Rajasthan (17), Tamil Nadu (4) and Uttar Pradesh (40). State governments, such as Bihar, Jharkhand, Madhya Pradesh and Chhattisgarh have also set up special police stations for registration of complaints of offences committed against SCs/STs; 77 such special police stations have been set up so far incidents of crime against STs registered a decline of 4.5 per cent during 2006–07.

24.67. A scheme for development of Particularly Vulnerable Tribal Groups (PVTGs) was launched in 1998–99 towards survival, protection and development of the PVTGs in view of their fragile living conditions and declining trend of their population. There are 75 identified PVTGs living in varied conditions and require PVTG specific attention to their distinct problems and needs. The scheme is, therefore, flexible in attending to diverse, living conditions of PVTGs having specific welfare and developmental needs as relevant to their socio-cultural environment. In the above lines, Conservation-cum-Development (CCD) Plan is prepared for each PVTGs. Activities undertaken include housing, land distribution, land development, agricultural development, cattle rearing, poultry, link roads, social security through insurance policy and so on An amount of ₹670.00 crore was allocated for the Eleventh Plan for the scheme against which the likely expenditure to be incurred would be ₹614.00 crore which accounts for nearly 92 per cent utilisation. Besides supporting CCD based activities 22,400 PVTG families were covered under Janashree Bima Yojana.

24.68. Grants-in-Aid under Article 275(1) as 100 per cent financial assistance is being provided to the states through the nodal Ministry of Tribal Affairs. The objective of the scheme is promotion of welfare of the STs and upgradation of the level of administration in tribal areas. The funds are released based on specific projects, such as raising critical infrastructure and enhancing Human Development Indices of STs for bridging the gaps between STs and the general population. The Eklavya Model Residential School scheme has been in operation since 1997–98; it is run out of the funds under Article 275(1) for providing quality education to ST students in the tribal areas. To improve educational infrastructure and standard of education in tribal areas, these schools are modelled on the lines of Navodaya Vidyalayas. The likely expenditure during the Eleventh Plan would be ₹3,326.04 crore which is 82 per cent of the allocation of ₹4,059.00 crore for the same period.

PESA: Panchayat Extension to Scheduled Areas Act (1996)

24.69. Article 243M of the Constitution of India states that nothing in Part IX of the Constitution relating to Panchayat shall apply to Scheduled Areas referred to in Clause (1) of Article 244, that is, areas included in the Fifth Schedule that today lie in the 9 States of Andhra Pradesh, Chhattisgarh, Gujarat, Himachal

Pradesh, Jharkhand, Madhya Pradesh, Maharashtra, Orissa and Rajasthan. However, Article 243M(4)(b) goes on to say that 'Parliament may, by law extend the provisions of this Part to the Scheduled Areas' and this was done in 1996 when Parliament enacted 'The Provisions of the Panchayats (Extension to the Scheduled Areas) Act, 1996' (PESA). However, the extension of Part IX was—subject to certain exceptions and modifications. The most significant of these relate to definition of a Village and Gram Sabha, rules, responsibilities and powers of the Gram Sabha, Principle of Subsidiarity and Consistency of other Laws with PESA.

PESA Implementation

24.70. PESA has been very poorly implemented across the nine States. One major impediment in operationalisation of PESA is the absence of a proper administrative definition of the village that is in consonance with the Act. All States, without exception, have continued with their earlier revenue definitions of the village. Thereby, not only does a village at times consist of 10–12 scattered hamlets, but several revenue villages are clubbed together to form a Gram Panchayat. This effectively precludes the functioning of a 'face to face' community as envisaged in PESA and eliminates the likelihood of a functioning Gram Sabha, which could shoulder the responsibilities of a unit of self governance. This calls for some remedial steps.

24.71. The success of PESA hinges crucially on the effective functioning of the Gram Sabha. Today, even in tribal areas, there is no automaticity to the functioning of the Gram Sabha and there is a large measure of exclusion of women. With growing socio-economic differentiation within and across Adivasi communities, there is also exclusion of those who are poorer or whose voice is weaker. To ensure that Gram Sabhas actually meet and become a vibrant fora of participatory democracy, as visualised under PESA, there is a need to facilitate this process by giving energy to it. This requires a *dedicated cadre of social mobilisers* at each GP level, specifically assigned with the task of mobilising the Gram Sabha and ensuring the effective participation of the marginalised, as also spreading greater awareness of laws such as PESA and Scheduled Tribes and Other Traditional Forest Dwellers (Recognition of Forest Rights) Act and key flagship programmes of the government.

24.72. *Land Alienation and Land Acquisition*: A clear and categorical provision should be made in the Panchayati Raj Act or the Revenue Law through a notification under Para 5(1) of the Fifth Schedule to empower the Gram Sabha to restore the unlawfully alienated land to its lawful owner.

24.73. *Community Resources*: The term 'community resources' which is used in section 4(d) of PESA has not generally been defined. Section 129c (iii) of Madhya Pradesh Panchayat Raj Act does, however, provide a definition that could be commended to other States: 'natural resources including land, water and forest within the area of the village'.

24.74. *Mines and Minerals*: The mineral rules should be amended on the pattern of Madhya Pradesh transferring all quarries with annual lease value up to ₹10 lakhs to the Gram Sabha and panchayats at different levels. This dispensation should cover all minor minerals. The consent of concerned Gram Sabha before awarding a lease should be made mandatory as per the directions of the Ministry of Mines and Minerals dated 26th December 1997. The practice of outright purchase of mineral bearing land by the mining companies should be stopped as the Mining Act envisages only a lease in these cases.

24.75. *Intoxicants*: A clear and categorical provision should be made in the Panchayati Raj Act or the excise law through a notification under para 5(1) of the Fifth Schedule to empower the Gram Sabha, on the same lines as in the Madhya Pradesh Excise Act fully empowering the Gram Sabha in all aspects mentioned in section 4(m)(i) of PESA. In all matters concerning intoxicants such as establishment of liquor shops, manufacturing units and so on, the views of women members in the Gram Sabha should be decisive, irrespective of the strength of their presence in the relevant meeting. In addition some broader changes may also be required for meaningful and effective implementation of PESA and protection of Adivasi rights.

24.76. *Non-Timber Forest Produce (NTFP)*: There is great scope to set up an NDDB-type institution (with deep pockets) to become a major player in the market for NTFPs that can support collectors of minor forest produce. Currently, in both nationalised and de/pre-nationalised regimes, these collectors are (*i*) disorganised (*ii*) very poor (*iii*) retain very little of the final value of their produce (*iv*) are at the bottom of value chains linked to fairly stable consumption patterns (for example tamarind, sal seed, mahua) but (*v*) can climb up the value chain and retain more value with appropriate interventions.

24.77. Traditional Non-Timber Forest Produce (TNTFP) policies have often been aimed at maximising state revenues and not the welfare of gatherers. The issue of bargaining power is crucial. Even where Adivasi collectors of NTFPs were organised into Self Help Groups (SHGs), they were unable to influence terms of trade for long. Local traders deployed a variety of tactics (commercial and otherwise) to ensure that SHGs were unviable as traders and gave little additional value to collectors through aggregation and collective bargaining. In some cases, where SHGs were persistent, traders, through unscrupulous tactics, ensured that these SHGs lost credibility with their own members. There is a need to visualise a new and powerful institution in the 'social entrepreneurship' mode to help primary collectors climb up the value chain and retain more value through professional sorting, grading, processing, packaging, branding and positioning. Such an institution would need to be committed to protecting Adivasi interests and must operate with great autonomy on strict business principles. Like the National Dairy Development Broad (NDDB), it must have the requisite capacity to absorb inevitable losses in initial years when it will have to take risks and counter entrenched trading interests with competitive action. It is eminently possible to come up with a road map (work in this direction is already ongoing) to make NTFPs commercially profitable for the primary gatherers while also ensuring PESA compliance.

24.78. *Effective Administrative Mechanism*: It is abundantly clear that the existing administrative structures have been found inadequate in the process of implementation of PESA. It may be time now to consider the setting up of a permanent empowered body in each Fifth Schedule Area to oversee and monitor compliance with PESA and Scheduled Tribes and Other Traditional Forest Dwellers (Recognition of Forest Rights) Act. The details of such a body, including its powers, its constituents and its precise relationship with and accountability towards existing constitutional bodies, would each need to be carefully worked out.

24.79. *Institutionalised Mechanism of Conflict Resolution*: There is also need to facilitate creation of institutional mechanisms of conflict resolution in India of the kind that exist across the world in countries which have faced conflicts over use of natural resources, especially in the context of indigenous people. A conflict resolution framework designed to suit our specific circumstances, would help mitigate conflicts before they reach a point of no return. By creating win-win scenarios for all stakeholders concerned, many conflicts that become the breeding ground for Maoism can thereby be taken care of. This would also help in moving forward the momentum of industrialisation in the hinterlands.

Scheduled Tribes and Other Traditional Forest Dwellers (Recognition of Forest Rights) Act

24.80. The Scheduled Tribes and Other Traditional Forest Dwellers (Recognition of Forest Rights) Act, 2006, popularly known as the Forests Rights Act (FRA), was enacted in 2007 through the Ministry of Tribal Affairs (MoTA) to correct the 'historic injustice done to forest-dwelling communities'. These communities were cultivating/occupying forest land and using forest produce since ages but had no tenurial security, as their rights of occupation and usage were not recorded during the settlement process. The Act recognises and vests individual forest-dwellers with forest rights to live in and cultivate forest land that was occupied before 13 Dec 2005 and grants community forest rights to manage, protect, regenerate the forest and to own and dispose minor forest products from forests where they had traditional access.

24.81. According to the findings of a government Committee[1] set up to study implementation of the Act, most States have concentrated almost entirely on implementing the provisions for individual forest rights (IFRs) and some States have achieved significant progress in granting individual rights. However, implementation of the Community Forest Rights (CFR) aspect of the FRA has been very poor in all states and therefore its potential to achieve livelihood security for collection of minor forest products and changes in forest governance along with strengthening of forest conservation, has hardly been achieved as indicated below.

Individual Titles

24.82. More than 31.3 lakh claims have been filed till 30th June, 2011, out of which 26.8 lakh (86 per cent) claims have been disposed of. A total of 11.9 lakh titles (34 per cent of those disposed of) have been distributed and the rest have been rejected. In eleven States the implementation process has not yet started. This includes the north-eastern states (except Tripura), Bihar, Uttarakhand, Himachal Pradesh and Goa. In Tamil Nadu because of restrictive orders by the High Court on a petition filed, the progress has been slow. Some states (such as Jharkhand) have lagged behind in terms of both getting a plausible number of claims and in processing the received claims.

Community Rights

24.83. The progress of implementation of the Community Forest Rights (CFR) under FRA is abysmally low. In all states, the CFR process has not even got off the ground, due to lack of awareness, amongst communities, civil society organisations, or relevant officials. The main reason is that State Governments have not adequately publicised the CFR provisions or even internalised their importance themselves. Most communities are not even aware of the groundbreaking CFR provisions in the FRA. In addition, the forms are flawed, as they do not mention the relevant sub-sections of the Act. Given the serious inadequacies in implementation of CFR at all levels, there is a need for a second phase implementation of FRA in all states with primary focus on CFR. Both MoTA and MoEF need to take the lack of implementation of CFR with the seriousness it deserves.

Checking Displacement of Tribals

24.84. Land and forest are the most important concerns of tribals. Therefore, the guiding principle should be that tribals should not be dislocated from wherever they inhabit. Should it become absolutely necessary to dislocate them, it must be by way of exception rather than rule and they; must be settled with their informed consent. Treating compensation as a panacea of all the ills associated with tribal land alienation should be discouraged completely.

24.85. The compulsory acquisition of land for public purposes and for public sector or private sector companies displaces tribals, forcing them to give up their home, assets, means of livelihood and vocation and to reside elsewhere and start their like all over again. The disproportionately large impact of displacement of tribals is evident from the fact that least 55 per cent of all displaced people are tribals and in States like Gujarat the proportion is 76 per cent. It has been an important reason for their pauperisation, often leading them to a state of shelterless and assetless destitution. The presumption that displacement is an inevitable consequence of all developmental efforts needs to be reassessed in the light of the enormous cost of human suffering in such projects. The need to avoid such large-scale displacement, particularly of tribals and in cases of unavoidable displacement, their comprehensive resettlement and rehabilitation (R&R) has become one of the central issues of the developmental process itself.

24.86. Today, project affected people are no longer in a mood to suffer passively. Consequently, there has been growing protest and militancy leading to tensions, conflict and violence. Unsatisfactory arrangements for their rehabilitation and resettlement creates opposition to acquisition of land and ultimately the costs involved in delayed acquisition of land is much more than the cost that would be incurred in case of a satisfactory compensation and rehabilitation. A well intended, liberal and comprehensive resettlement and rehabilitation policy is therefore required not only to protect the interests of the displaced or adversely affected people but also in the public interest to ensure quick acquisition and faster access to such acquired land.

24.87. Experiences of displacement and rehabilitation in India have revealed a long history of lack of rehabilitation or ill-planned, badly executed, inadequate and inappropriate rehabilitation. Even according to Government estimates only 29 per cent of the affected have been rehabilitated leaving almost 13.2 million people uprooted from their homes (Roy 1994). All that the displaced persons are left with is their labour—most often unskilled and are therefore desperate for whatever work comes their way for survival. In addition, displacement of tribals from their land amounts to violation of the Fifth Schedule of the Constitution as it deprives them of the control and ownership of natural resources and land essential for their way of life.

Condition of Tribal Women

24.88. Tribal women are among the most vulnerable people in India. They are faced with a double discrimination of being tribal and being women within the tribal households. In LWE areas women are battered and raped by both the government and the rebels and there is no system of security or redressal for the same. As tribal women move out of their households to find work as domestic workers, they are exploited in their work-space too.

24.89. The figures for literacy among tribal women are extremely low. The levels of awareness about government services, health issues like AIDS, avenues for employment and so on are also extremely low among tribal women and as a result of this, they neither are able to access the services available nor are they able to explore their potentials to the fullest.

24.90. Basic amenities are completely absent from tribal settlements. Absence of electricity and basic sanitation facilities impacts the women the most. Only 15.2 per cent of ST households have drinking water which further spells out the burden on the women.

Excise and Alcoholism

24.91. Tribal communities traditionally brew liquor from rice or other food grains for their consumption which is also related to certain rituals or social occasions and festivities. The initiation of commercial vending of liquor in tribal areas has started impoverishing the tribal population leading them to suffer from indebtedness and exploitation of various types. In 1975, the then Ministry of Social Welfare issued guidelines to the States and UTs regarding Excise Policy in Tribal Areas which included discontinuing commercial vending of liquor in tribal areas; permitting the tribal communities to brew traditional rice beer for their consumption; and weaning them away from the habit of alcohol consumption. Although the States and UTs have broadly accepted the guidelines, effective follow-up action is not taken for their implementation. More important, States with a view to augmenting their revenue tend to persist with and even extend commercial vending of liquor in the tribal areas ignoring the harmful effect on the tribal population.

Intellectual Property Rights

24.92. The tribal communities are mostly dependent on biological resources related to plants and animals/birds. Their livelihood and life style often depends upon and is shaped by these resources. Therefore, their survival and sustenance is intricately linked to conservation and utilisation of these resources. Corporate protectionism in terms of patents and intellectual property rights (IPR) arising out of various international treaties/instruments on trade and common property resources such as TRIPS under WTO represents a real threat to economic livelihood of these communities as well as a source of potential exploitation of their resource base as bio-diversity expressed in life forms and knowledge is sought to be converted into private property and treated as an open access system for free exploitation by those who want to privatise and patent it. There is an urgent need to provide appropriate legal and institutional arrangements for recognising and acknowledging the rights of tribal communities to such resources and knowledge.

Unrest in Tribal Areas: Left Wing Extremism

24.93. The majority of tribal districts are facing problems of violence during the last couple of decades. Chhattisgarh, Jharkhand, Bihar, Maharashtra, Andhra Pradesh, West Bengal, Uttar Pradesh and Madhya Pradesh are the worst-affected States. Of the 76 left-wing extremist-affected districts in the country today, 32 are PESA districts. The LWE districts extend across significant parts of

Bihar, Jharkhand, Orissa, Chhattisgarh and Andhra Pradesh, leading to the term, 'The Red Corridor'. However, some analysts pertinently argue that the analogy of 'The Speckled Band' more aptly describes the Maoists' area of influence, given they have control over some selected forested pockets in the districts stretching across the heart of central India. This includes the epicentre of the banned party's base in the Dandakaranya region, a vast forested area on the borders of Andhra Pradesh, Chhattisgarh and Orissa. While the senior leadership of the party is mostly drawn from non-tribal communities, much of the rank and file comes from local villages and has built on their grievances emanating from the non implementation of PESA.

Scheduled Tribes: Strategy for the Twelfth Plan

24.94. The perpetuation of socio-economic backwardness among the STs, inspite of the efforts made so far, presents a formidable challenge demanding effective and result-oriented steps in every developmental sector in the Twelfth Plan. The approach of the Twelfth Five Year Plan must be to achieve overall improvement in the socio-economic conditions of the Scheduled Tribes. To this end the following must be key elements:

- Relaxing the normative prescriptions about taking up a programme or a scheme in the Tribal majority areas.
- Administrative strengthening of the implementing agency so as to enable taking up implementation of these programmes in the scheduled/tribal areas. This may also require a clear cut personnel policy with regard to posting of officials in those positions, fixity of their tenure and incentivising these officials for having rendered their services in those areas for a prescribed period.
- Preferring engaging people from the tribal community itself in the areas predominantly inhabited by tribals for government efforts at spreading education, health and extension services, nutrition, public distribution, and so on. If necessary, the basic minimum qualification for such engagements could be relaxed for a specified period (say during the Twelfth Five Year Plan period). For example, engaging a +2 student from the nearby locality for teaching tribal students in primary classes.
- Sensitising officials detailed for serving in the tribal areas so that they become empathetic to the sensitivities of tribal lives and their traditions.
- Reorganising basic services such as nutritional interventions, education, health services, public distribution system, employment generating activities under MGNREGA with posting adequate staff with surety of tenure and assurance of funds to implement these programmes.
- Emphasis on education, health and livelihood support. For education, schools must be opened wherever necessary and for matriculation and above, facilities at designated places should be created. For health, necessary extension work and facilities for preventive medical-care should be ensured. For livelihood support, apart from the land and forest based activities under MGNREGA imparting of skills and creating employment opportunities near their habitations should be encouraged. For this skills relevant to the tribals should be identified on the basis of a socio-economic survey and then necessary skills training should be provided to them.
- No post in the implementing agencies in scheduled areas/areas with tribal majority should be left vacant; every post must be filled up and wherever necessary, additional posts should be created for effective implementation.
- Implementation of the schemes must be monitored closely at prescribed periodicity. Implementation should not be made to suffer on account of problems associated with transfer of funds.
- Better coverage in roads for tribal areas (population of 500–1,000), with population up to 100 being covered in LWE to be connected.
- Better connectivity through railways in LWE and tribal areas.
- Land acquisition of tribal land to be addressed as required under PESA and displaced tribal population to be resettled and rehabilitated.
- Tribal communities to have full right to minor forest produce.

- Converge MGNREGA with artisanal work to provide livelihood to tribals, many of whom are engaged in artisanal work.
- Land and Tenancy Reform: Deal with outstanding matters of tribal ownership.
- Increase coverage of the most vulnerable within the STs in the health sector. Increase cadre of health workers to better serve tribals.
- Plan within a plan of the Twelfth Plan: Suitable programmes for Central Indian Tribal Belt, border and backward areas and those who suffered discrimination like DNTs.
- Better and speedy implementation of PESA and FRA Institutional Mechanism of Conflict Resolutions.

Educational Development

24.95. A number of development projects viz. industrial, power or irrigation facilities are setup in the tribal areas. Though these projects offer tremendous opportunities for the economic advancement for the tribal people living in these areas, very little of the benefits actually accrue to tribals due to lack of adequate and eligible candidates for the jobs created. Tribal youth must be equipped with necessary education and skill abilities to take advantage of job opportunities in their areas and elsewhere. Otherwise, the opportunities will go in favour of outsiders, leaving a feeling of deprivation and discontent among the tribal youth.

24.96. Although school coverage has increased, STs continue to lag far behind the rest of the population. A special problem is that the STs use a language which is typically different from that of the State and this hampers their ability to do well in the educational system.

24.97. To deal with the low levels of literacy among tribals and to bridge the gap between dropout rates between tribals and non-tribals, there is a need to focus on elementary education. Therefore, there is a need to start a scheme of Pre-Matric Scholarship for all ST children across the country. The objectives of the proposed scheme are to support parents of ST children for education of their wards studying in classes' I–X so that the incidence of drop-out, especially in transition from the elementary to the secondary stage, is minimised.

24.98. The scheme of Vocational Training Centres in Tribal Areas is to upgrade the skills of the tribal youth in various traditional/modern vocations depending upon their educational qualification, present economic trends and the market potential, which would enable them to gain suitable employment or enable them to become self-employed. The scheme is exclusively for benefit of the Scheduled Tribes as well as PVTGs. Vocational training, including women's training, should be an important complementary part of the elementary and secondary stages. Atleast one ITI/Polytechnic should be established in each development block of TSP areas. Other training centres should include women's community polytechnics undertaking rural and community development activities through application of science and technology.

24.99. The Centrally Sponsored Scheme of Post-Matric Scholarship (PMS) to ST Students is the single intervention by the Government of India for educational empowerment of STs—involving 100 per cent central assistance to States over and above their earlier committed liability are awarded to all eligible ST students to pursue studies beyond matriculation and in all courses. The recommendations for the scheme's continuance in the Twelfth Five Year Plan include:

- The rates of scholarship and income ceiling should be revised at regular intervals in line with the price index each year. The income ceiling of parents should also be enhanced as would be appropriate from time to time.
- Possibility of paying College fees directly should be explored and students should not be asked to pay for any fees under the scheme. The fee should be paid promptly during the academic year so as to avoid any harassment to ST students.
- Scholarships to students either as day scholars or hostellers should be paid on a monthly basis to defray their expenses through an online system or remitted into the bank accounts of students.

- The number of awards allotted to each State Government per annum should be increased under the scheme of Upgradation of Merit for ST students for improving the capability of the students belonging to STs to enable them to compete more effectively for admission to professional colleges/institutions or to overcome educational deficiencies.

24.100. In order to promote education among ST girls and boys facilitating them to continue studies without dropping out of school, there is a need to expand the Scheme for Hostels for ST Girls and Boys, especially focusing the deficit areas across the States especially girls hostels. Evaluation studies have pointed out that infrastructure facilities are poor in most of the hostels; maintenance of the buildings is not up to the mark; and construction of hostel buildings is often hampered due to non-receipt of proper/complete proposals from the States. Infrastructure facilities and maintenance of the hostels needs constant improvement. There is a need to reduce the time taken for the construction of hostels from five to two years.

24.101. Under the Scheme of Ashram Schools in TSP areas, as of now, State Governments are eligible for 100 per cent central share for constructions of all Girls' Ashrams Schools and also for constructions of Boys' Ashram Schools in naxal affected areas. It is recommended that:

- It would be desirable that 100 per cent grant-in-aid is given for Establishment of Ashram Schools and Hostels for ST Boys also even in the non-Naxal areas.
- Qualified teachers belonging to the local tribal communities should be trained and placed in position as teachers in Ashram Schools.

24.102. The Rajiv Gandhi National Fellowship (RGNF) scheme for ST students was launched in 2006 with the objective of providing financial assistance to ST students pursuing M. Phil and Ph.D. Under this scheme, 667 fellowships are provided annually to ST beneficiaries. There is a justified need to increase the number of fellowship from 667 to 1,000 made available under the scheme.

24.103. The Scheme of scholarship for Institutes of Excellence/Top Class Institutes is to provide liberal financial support to a maximum 625 ST Students per year admitted in premier professional educational institutes. Larger coverage of ST candidates with special coaching would help enhance the effectiveness under the scheme as more candidates would be qualified to avail admission into the designated premier institutions.

24.104. National Overseas Scholarship (NOS) scheme for ST students awarded to 15 students for pursuing higher studies abroad leading to Master-level courses and Ph.D. programme in specific field of Engineering, Technology and Science. The number of awards under the scheme should be increased to give a fair share to ST students. Income ceiling for eligibility under the scheme should be enhanced to ₹5 lakhs per annum. The scheme should be extended so as to cover all disciplines of higher education. Orientation procedure should be facilitated at Centre, State and district level.

Health

24.105. The Tribal Affairs Ministry operates the scheme of Grant-in-aid to Voluntary Organisations (VOs) working for the Welfare of STs, to NGOs for running 10 or more bedded hospitals and Mobile dispensaries in Tribal Areas. There is also a need for taking up health programmes/projects in a big way through Public-Private Partnership especially for running Primary Health Centres in remote tribal areas.

24.106. Tribals have traditionally depended on their traditional methods of healing/treatment for minor day to day ailments and the major ones too. There is a need for evolving a new strategy of combining the indigenous tribal medicine with other medical systems. A systematic effort need to be made to document this traditional tribal knowledge of medicinal/herbal plants, standardising it and recognising it as an independent system of medicine. The local tribals especially the traditional healers can be trained and be entrusted with the responsibility of treating the people on remuneration and so on.

24.107. To prevent the problem of malnutrition, local cereals, along with pulses and oils in adequate quantity should be ensured to the tribal families. In this context, the system of public distribution should be modified appropriately in tribal areas. The management of PDS and Anganwadi Centres should involve local tribals, especially women and ensure that acceptable local food is provided to the children. The vulnerable PVTGs should be assured of food security by gradually initiating them into agriculture and other income generating activities.

24.108. Tribal areas suffer from the problems of non-availability or scarcity of safe drinking water. All tribal habitations should be provided with safe drinking water supply sources and sanitation facilities by the end of the Twelfth Plan period. Efforts also need to be made to ensure sanitation facilities to prevent health hazards envisaging from the unhygienic living conditions. To this effect, panchayat members and the community may be provided training to handle situations at the time of epidemics, to maintain sanitation and hygiene in the village and also to clean the water to make it safe for drinking.

24.109. Frequent immunisation campaigns may be taken up at regular intervals in tribal areas publicising them widely through public address system and mobile health units. Regular IEC programmes on health related behaviours, gender bias and wrong customary practices like adverse impact of early child-bearing, smoking, drug-addiction, alcohol, malnutrition factors, unsafe sex and so on.

Mahatma Gandhi National Rural Employment Guarantee

24.110. Extensive implementation of MGNREGA in tribal blocks should be ensured for extension of the benefits envisaged under it and particularly to prevent distress migration and trafficking. Effective monitoring, social audits and their reviews should be conducted specially to ensure if ST women are getting the cards and employment.

24.111. MGNREGA works should be decided by the Gram Sabha according to PESA. But, in practice, they are being decided top down by government officials and line-departments mostly targeting promotion of plantations on adivasi lands, using MGNREGS money to force down programmes of planting rubber, palm oil, biofuel, cashew nut, coffee and so on. Such actions are contrary to the policy and law and should attract punitive action.

24.112. The higher participation of the STs among the beneficiaries of the MGNREGA scheme is an indication of the fact that this section of the society needs more attention in this regard. There is need to incorporate a TSP component in the implementation of the Scheme in order to meet the objective of inclusive growth. The TSP component should not be based merely on the population share, but rather on the extent of deprivation and need arising there from.

24.113. Limit of providing maximum 100 days employment to a household in a given financial year under NREGA should be removed, as in tribal areas work of agriculture labour is available only for a period of 2-3 months during the year.

Entrepreneurship

24.114. Entrepreneurship among tribal youngsters should be developed. One of the reasons as to why tribal communities are not economically advanced in spite of their land holdings is that they have no skill in business. Efforts need to be made to encourage tribal entrepreneurship in small and large-scale businesses. Funds should be made available for them to set up enterprises in rural and urban areas. Export of tribal handicrafts should be encouraged by the government which will give more jobs to people thereby improving their economic condition.

Land

24.115. Land is the primary livelihood asset of tribals, but over decades it has been going out of their possession because of their ignorance of laws and because of deceit, coercion and other methods followed by mis-appropriators of tribal land, all in violation of laws, often in collusion with elements in the official machinery and elements in the political leadership of State Governments. The nodal Ministry needs to take necessary steps to ensure proper implementation of land alienation laws. Uncultivable land of tribals should be made cultivable under the affirmative action of MGNREGA. Irrigation is a critical input for higher productivity and higher production. Small and not-so-small irrigation projects (avoiding large projects) are required in tribal areas. Five Year Plans should be drawn up (some may exist already) for comprehensive irrigation and implementation in a staggered fashion. The irrigation schemes will not only increase agricultural productivity but also provide employment to tribal men and women. Efforts should be directed towards the hitherto neglected large tracts of agriculturally unexploited tribal areas keeping in view the advantages and merits of the indigenous seeds, practices and traditional techniques and methods.

24.116. A crash programme for providing land to the landless tribals should be undertaken. Convergence among various subsidy and loan schemes of central and state governments for STs should be ensured, so that both subsidy and low interest loans are available to STs especially their women.

24.117. Acquisition of tribal land should only be allowed with full statutory protection already existing under land alienation laws and the provisions of the Fifth Schedule. No tribal land should be acquired without explicit and informed consent of the affected tribals, keeping in mind the provisions of the PESA Act.

Atrocities on STs

24.118. Effective implementation of all legal provisions such as the Juvenile Justice Act (JJ) Act, Bonded Labour Abolition Act and Protection of Women against Domestic Violence Act, SC/ST Prevention of Atrocities Act (POA), Immoral Trafficking Prevention Act (ITPA), and so on to provide protection to tribal women and children should be ensured. For this adequate grievance redressal mechanisms should be put in place especially to deal with non-registration of FIRs and for providing time bound relief and guidance to tribals. A District Level Committee comprising of credible NGOs/Advocates and other stakeholders should be constituted to monitor and support these initiatives. NCST needs strengthening through improvements in the functioning of the Commission and placement of requisite manpower at its Headquarter and Regional offices.

Geographical Exclusion and Human Resource Management

24.119. Tribal Areas suffer from geographical exclusion which impacts upon the availability of physical and social infrastructure and quality of services rendered to the people. Social facilities do not function because service providers are unwilling to work in the area. Measures taken from time to time to incentivise these services have failed to change the situation. The main reason for persistence of this problem is centralised recruitment to various posts and eligibility conditions for competing for the posts which enable non-tribals from urban/developed areas to compete and get recruited. However, as they have no inclination to work in remote tribal areas and a centralised cadre management of these service providers. The solution lies in identifying suitable individuals from tribal areas where services are deficient and sponsor them for courses in specialities required and recruiting them on successful completion of these courses. Also, a change in the recruitment rules and eligibility criteria for this purpose is required so that local persons can acquire necessary qualifications and can get recruited.

24.120. There is a need to decentralise cadre management of these services from state level to district level and where necessary even lower. This would enable transfer and postings to take place within the district and prevent outsiders from grabbing jobs. Another suggestion is to decentralise delivery of basic services to the community. This would inter alia involve capacity building for the Gram Sabha. The Gram Sabhas should be legally and operationally empowered to conduct social audit of tribal development programmes to enforce people's participation, transparency and accountability of the implementing agencies and officials.

Protection of tribal Women

24.121. Tribal women suffer double disadvantage and intra-household disparities as well. There needs to be a concentrated effort to empower tribal women. Some suggestions are as follows. Vocational training, including women's training, should be an important complementary part of the elementary and secondary stages. At least two ITIs/Polytechnics should be established in each development block of TSP areas. Other training centres should include women's community polytechnics undertaking rural and community development activities through application of science and technology. To prevent the problem of malnutrition, local cereals, along with pulses and oils in adequate quantity should be ensured to the tribal families. In this context, the system of public distribution should be modified appropriately. The management of PDS may be handed over to the tribal community through its own institutions. In Anganwadi centres also, acceptable local food should be provided to the children. The Anganwadi Centre should be managed by local tribal women. Convergence among various subsidy and loan schemes of central and state governments for STs should be ensured, so that both subsidy and low interest loans are available to particularly ST women. Special programmes for extension and provision of agri-implements, capital and technology, particularly irrigation technology, to ST women should be commissioned. Krishi Vigyan Kendra (KVKs) under State Agriculture Universities should be deployed to promote dissemination of such practices to ST women. Mapping of the jobs in the public sector companies reserved for STs (for example drivers in Road Transport Corporation) should be undertaken and ITIs should take up special programmes for ST youth and women to provide skill trainings for those jobs.

Research, Information and Mass Education, Tribal Festivals and others

24.122. The objective of the ongoing scheme of 'Research, Information and Mass Education, Tribal Festivals and Others' is preservation and promotion of tribal culture; capacity building and awareness generation; and monitoring and evaluation of various welfare and development programmes implemented by the Ministry. During the Twelfth Plan period, the proposal is to continue focusing on the core areas and shall include preservation, protection and promotion of tribal culture; capacity building of various stake holders and advocacy; improved delivery system through effective monitoring and evaluation—forge partnership with the Traditional Tribal Institutions (TTIs)/Community Based Organisations (CBOs) where ever feasible. The scheme would cater to the needs of information and knowledge for the policy makers and implementers as well as to the beneficiaries and citizens at large.

SCHEDULED CASTE SUB PLAN (SCSP) AND TRIBAL SUB PLAN (TSP)

Background

24.123. Despite Constitutional directives and a number of legislative and executive measures taken by the Government since independence, there are large gaps between the living conditions of the general population and those of SCs and STs. Successive Five Year Plans have attempted to reduce these gaps and while there is some evidence of convergence, the gaps still remain at a level that is unacceptably high.

24.124. The persistence of socio-economic backwardness of the SCs and the STs in spite of the development efforts had warranted a special and focused strategy, inter alia, to enable them to share the benefits of overall economic growth in a more equitable manner. This has been sought to be achieved through the Special Component Plan (SCP) for Scheduled Castes, now known as Scheduled Caste Sub Plan (SCSP) and the Tribal Sub-Plan for Scheduled Tribes.

Schedule Caste Sub Plan (SCSP)

24.125. The prime objective of Scheduled Caste Sub Plan (SCSP) is to channelise funds and benefits through identified schemes, for which the States/UTs and Union Ministries have to earmark funds in proportion to the SC population in the State/UTs and the country respectively. The Special Component Plan which contains details of financial and physical targets is expected to form an integral part of Plan documents of States/UTs and Centre. Some of these schemes are envisaged to help the poor SC families through composite income generating programmes. Such family oriented programmes are expected to cover all major occupational groups amongst Scheduled Castes such as agricultural labourers, small and marginal farmers, share croppers, fishermen, sweepers and scavengers, urban unorganised labourers below the poverty line, and so on. In addition, the Special Component Plan seeks to improve the living conditions of Scheduled Castes through provision of drinking water supply, link roads, house-sites and housing improvements, establishment of such services as primary schools, health centres, veterinary centres, panchayat ghars, community halls, nutrition centres, extension of electricity, common work places, common facility centres, and so on.

Tribal Sub-Plan (TSP)

24.126. The prime object of the Tribal Sub Plan is development of tribal areas. The TSP concept, thus, aims on one hand, at the quantification of investment in the Sub-Plan areas commensurate with its size and on the other, at an all-round development of the tribal communities, in accordance with their needs. Keeping in view the distinct tribal situation, the TSP has set the twin objectives: (*i*) socio-economic development of STs; and (*ii*) protection of tribals against exploitation. Through realisation of these objectives, the ultimate aim of the TSP strategy is to narrow the development gap of the tribals with the rest of the country.

24.127. The development of tribal economy under TSP is envisaged through sectoral efforts including (*i*) Agriculture and allied activities, through provision of minor and medium irrigation facilities supplemented by programmes for animal husbandry, dairying, poultry, and so on; (*ii*) improvised credit and marketing facilities so as to ensure adequate return of the produce of the tribals in respect of agriculture and minor forest products; (*iii*) special training programmes for tribal farmers for agricultural extension supported by the provision of agricultural infrastructure; (*iv*) preparing suitable forestry programmes ensuring tribals' participation as equal partners; (*v*) promoting agricultural production through improved method of cultivation and rural electrification to promote small scale industry.

24.128. Provision of basic infrastructure for speeding up the socio-economic development of the tribal areas under TSP is another priority. Growth centres, communication network, schools, health centres, rural electrification, drinking water and other facilities and so on are being provided to the tribals. Protection of tribals against exploitation is sought to be done through land laws prohibiting transfer of tribal lands to non-tribals, law regulating money lending in tribal areas and laws for acquiring monopoly rights of collection and marketing of forest produce. The TSP pays special attention to the welfare and development of Particularly Vulnerable Tribal Groups (PVTGs) and tribals with special problems.

Special Central Assistance (SCA) to SCSP and TSP

24.129. The scheme of Special Central Assistance (SCA) to SCSP and TSP, launched in 1979, extends financial assistance to States/UTs as an additive to their SCSP and TSP programmes. It is meant to support the efforts of States/UTs for the overall development of SCs and STs. The funds provided under SCA to the States/UTs are intended to augment their efforts for economic development. SCA is a lump-sum amount received from the Planning Commission and is allocated to States/UTs by the nodal Ministries that is, Ministry of Tribal Affairs and the Ministry of Social Justice and Empowerment.

24.130. Under the Special Central Assistance (SCA) to SCSP, 100 per cent grant was initially given to fill the critical gaps by providing the missing inputs in family oriented income generating schemes. To enlarge the scope of the utilisation of SCA to SCP, new guidelines were issued in 1993. As per the new guidelines, SCA could also be used for infrastructural development in the blocks having 50 per cent or more of SC population subject to the condition that SCA allocation is made use of in such a way that it encourages larger efforts for development of SCs. SCA is released to the States/UTs on the basis of following criteria:

i) (a) On the basis of SC population of States/UTs: 40 per cent
 (b) On the basis of relative backwardness of the States/UTs: 10 per cent

ii) (a) On the basis of percentage of SC families in the States/UTs: coverage by composite economic development programmes in the Plan to enable them to cross the poverty line. — 25 per cent

(b) On the basis of the percentage of SCP to the Annual Plan as: Compared to the SC population percentage in the States/UTs. — 25 per cent

24.131. SCA to SCSP which made a modest beginning with a token provision of ₹5.00 crores in 1979–80 has been expanded to enhance its allocation to ₹2,805.00 crore in the Eleventh Plan. As per the available information, nearly 64 lakh SC families were provided with assistance to pursue viable economic activities and cross the poverty line during the first four years of the Eleventh Plan (2007–08 to 2011–12). At present, SCA is released to 27 States/UTs.

24.132. The Special Central Assistance (SCA) to TSP is extended to States/UTs as an additive to supplement and fill the gaps in their Plan outlay. It is also meant for the family-oriented income generating schemes in the sectors of agriculture, horticulture, minor irrigation, soil conservation, animal husbandry, forestry, education, cooperation, fisheries, village and small scale industries as well as the Minimum Needs Programme and so on.

24.133. The criteria for allocation of SCA to TSP have been fixed on the basis of certain norms and Integrated Tribal Development Projects (ITDPs), Modified Area Development Agency (MADA) Pockets, Particularly Vulnerable Tribal Groups and dispersed Tribal Groups. After setting apart 10 per cent of SCA for dispersed tribals, the balance amount is allocated broadly on the basis of ST population, geographical areas and inverse proportion of per-capita Net State Domestic Product. The total SCA released to States/UTs under TSP in the Eleventh Plan was in the order of ₹2,872.10 crore. About 15 lakh STs were assisted to cross the poverty line during the Eleventh Plan.

Review of Implementation of SCSP and TSP

24.134. Despite the fact that strategies of TSP and SCSP had been in operation for more than three decades, they could not be implemented as effectively as desired. The expenditure in many of the States/UTs was not even 50 per cent of the allocated funds. No proper budget heads/sub-heads were created to prevent diversion of funds. There was no controlling and monitoring mechanism and the planning and supervision was not as effective as it should be.

24.135. In order to examine the issues related to TSP and SCSP, to revitalise/re-activate these strategies, especially to ensure that population-proportionate funds flow for the development of STs and SCs, a Central Standing Tripartite Committee was constituted in May, 1999, inter alia, with the following mandate:

1. to look into the reasons for not implementing the Guidelines concerning SCSP and TSP and to suggest specific measures for their compliance;
2. to identify specific schemes which would benefit SCs and STs under various developmental sectors and their prioritisation along with earmarking of funds for them; and
3. to review the progress of implementation, impact assessment and monitoring of SCSP and TSP and utilisation of SCA to SCSP and TSP and the Grant-in-Aid under Article 275(1) and advise the Planning Commission on measures which would serve the interests of these communities more effectively.

24.136. The Committee, besides suggesting certain remedial measures, also advise the concerned Central Ministries to tie up effectively with the concerned State Governments. So far, six States, viz. Andhra Pradesh, Bihar, Madhya Pradesh, West Bengal, Punjab and Gujarat could have such Committees at their level. As the institutional set up of the CTC for monitoring the implementation of SCSP and TSP has not proved effective, it would be replaced with a new high level committee, which will be pro-active and meet at least once in a quarter to address the issues relating to SCSP/TSP.

Task Force to Examine and Revise the extant of guidelines for Implementation of SCSP and TSP
24.137. The Planning Commission constituted in 2010 a Task Force under the Chairmanship of Dr. Narendra Jadhav, Member, Planning Commission, to review the operational difficulties in implementing TSP/SCSP and suggesting necessary remedial measures by re-examining the existing guidelines and revising the same appropriately for effective and meaningful implementation in future.

24.138. The Task Force has recommended that Central Ministries/Departments should categorise Plan Expenditure under TSP and SCSP into two broad categories that is (*i*) Expenditure on poverty alleviation and individual beneficiary oriented programmes; and (*ii*) Expenditure on other schemes which are incurred in: (*a*) ST and SC concentration areas respectively, that is in the villages, blocks and districts having more than 40 per cent ST/SC population and (*b*) in other areas, in a way that demonstrably benefits the STs/SCs.

24.139. For earmarking funds under SCSP and TSP the Central Ministries/Departments have been divided into four categories that is (*i*) Ministries/Departments with no obligation for earmarking funds under TSP/SCSP; (*ii*) Ministries/Departments required to do partial earmarking; (*iii*) Ministries/Departments which will be required to earmark between 7.5 per cent to 8.2 per cent for TSP and 15 to 16.2 per cent for SCSP of their Plan Outlays; and (*iv*) Ministries/Departments which will be required to earmark more than 8.2 per cent for TSP and 16.2 per cent for SCSP of their Plan Outlays. The Task Force also recommended that administrative mechanisms in Central Ministries/Departments needs to be adequately strengthened so that they properly implement SCSP/TSP.

24.140. The Task Force recommendations are under consideration. Pending a final decision, the process of earmarking funds under SCSP and TSP has already been initiated during 2011–12. Budget Head(s) have been created as Code 789 for SCSP and Code 796 for TSP. Planning Commission and the Central Ministries/Departments have started indicating earmarked allocation under SCSP/TSP in the Statement of Budget Estimates jointly signed by the Planning Commission and the concerned Central Ministries/Departments.

SCSP and TSP: Strategy for the Twelfth Plan

Towards a Paradigm Shift: From 'Post-facto Accounting' to 'Pro-active Planning for SCSP/TSP'
24.141. In keeping with the objective of more inclusive growth, steps will be taken to reform the Scheduled Caste Sub-Plan (SCSP) and the Scheduled Tribe Sub-Plan (TSP). These Plans have the potential to become effective mechanisms in closing the development gap between the Scheduled Castes, Scheduled Tribes and other sections of the society. Towards this goal, the Twelfth Plan proposes a set of key implementation measures to strengthen the SCSP/TSP planning process. These include earmarking of SCSP/TSP funds from the total plan outlays well in advance of the commencement of the financial year, preparation of pro-active planning documents as Sub-Plans, an appraisal and approval mechanism for the Sub-Plans so formulated, and a robust mechanism for monitoring and evaluation of outcomes. An Institutional framework to effectively implement these changes will be set up in the Planning Commission. At the State level, there will be an apex body headed by the Chief Minister and designated Nodal Department, which will appraise the SC/ST Sub-Plan for the State.

24.142. The efforts made in pursuance of the Task Force recommendations have finally brought about some visible changes in the formulation and implementation of SCSP and TSP. Evidently, for the first time in 2011–12, 25 and 28 Central Ministries and Departments have categorically earmarked funds under SCSP and TSP, respectively. Having made a beginning in the Annual Plan 2011–12, there is need to further consolidate and improve upon the implementation of SCSP and TSP across sectors, ensuring not only optimal earmarking of funds under SCSP/TSP as per the guidelines, but also utilising the same in achieving the outcomes in measurable terms. The Ministries of Social Justice and Empowerment and Tribal Affairs need to spearhead the task of formulation, implementation and monitoring of SCSP/TSP as nodal coordinating agencies.

24.143. Based on the experience of implementing the SCSP/TSP by the Central Ministries/Departments, the guidelines issued by the Planning Commission will be reviewed to remove any shortcomings, so as to ensure that at least 16.2 per cent of the Central Plan outlay is earmarked under the Schemes/Programmes that benefit the SC community demonstratively, and 8.2 per cent of the Central Plan outlay is earmarked under the Schemes/Programmes that benefit the ST community demonstratively.

OTHER BACKWARD CLASSES (OBCs)

24.144. Other backward Classes (OBCs) comprise the castes and communities which are found common in the lists of the Mandal Commission Report and the Lists of the individual State Governments. The NSSO survey conducted during 2004–05 (61st Round), estimated that the OBC population constituted 41 per cent of the total population.

Constitutional Safeguards

24.145. The Constitution does not make any specific provisions for OBCs, but Article 15 of the Constitution empowers the States to make any special provision for the advancement of any socially and educationally backward classes of citizens or for the Scheduled Castes and the Scheduled Tribes. Article 16(4) also empowers the State to make provisions for reservations in appointments in favour of any backward class of citizens which in the opinion of the States is not adequately representative in the services under the State. The Directive Principles of State Policy of the Constitution (Article 46) also state that 'The State shall promote with special care the educational and economic interests of the weaker sections of the people and, in particular, of the Scheduled Castes and Scheduled Tribes and shall protect them from social injustice and all forms of exploitation.' It also empowers the State to appoint a Commission to investigate into the conditions of socially and educationally backward classes (Article 340).

Overview of OBCs: Review of the Eleventh Plan

Educational Development

24.146. The aim of the scheme of Pre-Matric Scholarship launched in 1998 was to motivate children of OBCs studying at pre-matric stage. As such, scholarships are awarded to students belonging to OBCs whose parents/guardian's income from all sources does not exceed ₹44,500 per annum. Although the rates of Pre-Matric Scholarships for OBCs have been fixed by the Central Government, there is a variation in rates among the States.

24.147. The Scheme of Post-Matric Scholarship being implemented since 1998 is intended to promote higher education by providing financial support to OBC students studying at post-matric/post-secondary levels including Ph.D. degrees. The scheme was revised in August, 2011 w.e.f 01.07.2011. As per the revised scheme, the parental income ceiling was raised from ₹44,500 to ₹1 lakh. A total of 58 lakh OBC students are estimated to have received Post-Matric Scholarships during the first four years of the Eleventh Plan. The Scheme of Assistance for Construction of Hostels was instituted in 1998 for extending better educational opportunities to students belonging to Other Backward Classes (OBCs) by providing hostel facilities to boys and girls to continue their studies and thus ensure their retention and prevent dropouts. The scheme was revised in December, 2010. A total number of 22,375 hostel seats were sanctioned in the first 4 years of the Eleventh Plan. Under the revised Scheme, priority is given to uncovered regions and districts/towns having educational institutions. An outlay of ₹180.00 crore was provided for the 'Scheme of Hostels for OBC Boys and Girls' for the Eleventh Five Year Plan (2007–12). Against the outlay provided, the expenditure anticipated was to the order of ₹126.96 crore.

Economic Development

24.148. The National Backward Classes Finance and Development Corporation (NBCFDC) was set up in the year 1992. The Corporation provides additional channel of finance to Backward Classes for economically and financially viable schemes and projects for upgrading the technological and entrepreneurial skills of individuals or groups belonging to Backward Classes. NBCFDC assists a wide range of income generating activities, which include agricultural and allied activities, artisan and traditional occupations, technical trades, small scale and tiny industry, transport services and so on. Entrepreneurs with annual income less than double the poverty line are provided concessional finance.

24.149. The major focus of the NBCFDC would be, inter alia, to address the skill requirement needs of youths belonging to the OBCs. Accordingly, a window, in the form of a new scheme, will be opened up to provide funds to the Corporation by the Ministry for this new venture.

24.150. The NBCFDC allocates a notional amount each year to State Channelising Agencies (SCAs) at the beginning of the year. However, due to weak infrastructure of the SCAs, low recovery from the SCAs and non-availability of Block Government guarantee from the State Governments, the Corporation has not been able to disburse loans as per allocation to the States.

OBCs and the Twelfth Five Year Plan; the Way Ahead

Educational Development

24.151. For ensuring educational development amongst OBCs, schemes for providing scholarships for pursuing Pre-Matric, Post-Matric and other higher education, supported with hostel facilities will be taken up on priority basis. Appropriate revision of the Pre-Matric Scholarship Scheme in respect of the sharing pattern of assistance (being raised from 50 per cent to 100 per cent), rate of scholarships and parent/guardian income limit for eligibility (from ₹44,500 p.a. to ₹1 lakh p.a.) will be given priority in the Twelfth Five Year Plan. Hostel facilities for boys and girls which are at present very limited and inadequate would be increased substantially.

24.152. National Overseas Scholarship Scheme for OBCs could also be formulated similar to those for SCs and STs so that OBC students can also go abroad for educational and professional courses which are generally not available in the country. There is a demand for Rajiv Gandhi National Fellowship (RGNF) scheme on the pattern available to the SC and ST students to be introduced for OBC students during the Twelfth Five Year Plan.

Economic Development

24.153. To meet the marketing needs and to facilitate providing a marketing platform for artisans and handicraft persons belonging to OBCs, a Marketing Federation on the lines of TRIFED may be set up. The main activities of the Federation would include cluster development of the artisans engaged particularly in arts and craft, training for upgradation of their skills, exhibition of their products to showcase their work both in India and abroad, opening of marketing outlets to appreciate, reward and popularise successful models which can be replicated by others and establishing a brand name for the products to be sold under the proposed Marketing Federation.

EMPOWERMENT OF MINORITIES

24.154. The Indian Constitution is committed to the ideas of equality and protection and assurance of rights of minorities, which cover five religious communities, viz., Muslims, Christians, Sikhs, Buddhists and Zoroastrians (Parsis). These communities accounted for 18.4 per cent of the population in 2001. The largest proportion was Muslims (13.4 per cent), followed by Christians (2.3 per cent), Sikh (1.9 per cent), Buddhists (0.8 per cent) and Zoroastrians (0.0069 per cent). Depending on their distribution across States, these communities may actually be a 'majority' in some States, for example Muslims are in majority in the Union Territory of Lakshadweep and in the State of Jammu and Kashmir as are Christians in Nagaland (90 per cent), Mizoram (87 per cent) and Meghalaya (70.03 per cent) and Sikhs in Punjab (60 per cent).

24.155. While India has experienced accelerated growth and development in recent years, not all religious communities and social groups (henceforth socio-religious communities—SRCs) have shared equally the benefits of the growth process. Among these, the Muslims, the largest minority in the country, are seriously lagging behind on all human development indices. There is also widespread disparity within different SRCs, supporting the view that each SRC is a differentiated category with multiple identities and different socio-political and economic aspirations.

Socio-economic Condition of Minorities

24.156. Until the Eleventh Five Year Plan, there were no substantive developmental programmes specifically attending to the minorities. The programmes implemented during the Eleventh Five Year Plan, have been in operation for too short a period and it is too early to estimate their impact. However, a broad assessment of the situation of religious minorities as reflected in their socio-economic status, especially regarding education, health and so on, on the basis of the available data is reflected in this section.

Poverty and Alienation

24.157. Muslims, who constitute the largest religious minority comprising about 13.4 per cent of the total population and about 73 per cent of the total Minority population of the country, lag behind others in terms of economic, health and educational indices. According to the latest Planning Commission estimates, the poverty ratio for Muslims was 33.9 per cent in urban areas, especially on account of states such as Uttar Pradesh, Gujarat, Bihar and West Bengal. In rural areas, the poverty ratio for Muslims was very high in States such as Assam, Uttar Pradesh, West Bengal and Gujarat. The literacy rate and work participation rate amongst the Muslims is low as compared to other minority communities. The majority of them are engaged in traditional and low paying professions, or are mostly small and marginal farmers, landless agricultural labourers, small traders, craftsmen and so on. Only a few of them are reported to have benefited from various developmental schemes. The other Minority communities on the whole enjoy a comparatively better socio-economic status, although there are segments among the Christians and Buddhists, Mazhabi Sikhs and even sections of Zoroastrians/Parsis who are disadvantaged.

24.158. An important concern vis-à-vis the Muslim community is the perception of discrimination and alienation. This needs to be appropriately addressed in the Twelfth Plan. Innovative steps are needed such as expanding facilitators in Muslim concentration villages and towns to act as interfaces between the community and the state institutions. Youth leadership programmes should also be initiated to strengthen this process.

Education

24.159. The importance of educational empowerment assumes special importance in the context of minorities, especially Muslims, who have been lagging behind the rest. Reports of the Sachar Committee and the Ranganath Mishra Commission have dealt at length with the educational status of the minorities, particularly Muslims. As shown in Table 24.8, the literacy rate among the Muslims is significantly lower than among other communities although it is higher than among SCs and STs. Also see Table 24.9.

24.160. The high rate of admission at primary levels shows the intense desire of the minorities to seek modern education. Lower percentages at other levels show that the community starts lagging behind from the secondary level onwards. Scholarships should thus target this band and be top-heavy, while continuing to support the primary levels. Neighbourhood schools and schools up to middle level need to be provided in minority concentrated blocks, large villages and urban minority concentrated settlements. In rural areas, schools for girls up to senior secondary level should be made mandatory to ensure that girls continue their

TABLE 24.8
Literacy Rate among Religious Communities, SCs and STs

Community/Caste	Male	Female	Total
India	75.3	53.7	64.8
Hindu	76.2	53.2	65.1
Muslim	67.6	50.1	59.1
Christian	84.4	76.2	80.3
Sikh	75.2	63.1	69.4
Buddhist	83.1	61.7	72.7
Others	60.8	33.2	47
Scheduled Castes	66.64	41.9	54.7
Scheduled Tribes	59.17	34.76	47.1

Source: Census 2001.

TABLE 24.9
Educational Levels among Different Communities

Community	Secondary Level	Sr. Secondary level	Graduation	Unclassified
All Religions	14.13	6.74	6.72	0.02
Hindus	14.25	6.92	7.01	0.01
Muslims	10.96	4.53	3.6	0.05
Christians	17.48	8.7	8.71	0.01
Sikhs	20.94	7.57	6.94	0.02
Buddhists	14.09	7.65	5.7	0.01
Others	11.24	4.55	4.35	0.01

Source: Working Group Report on the Empowerment of Minorities, Twelfth Five Year Plan.

education. There is a need for village level centres to target the rural drop out girls, or girls out of school, in the age group of 8–16 years. This should be linked to schemes such as the Rajiv Gandhi Scheme for the Empowerment of Adolescent Girls. The education level attained by different religious communities also reveals the sharp gap between the representation of Muslims in higher education and that of other communities. Moreover, student drop-out rates tend to peak at the senior secondary levels. Scholarships should, thus, target this band and be top-heavy.

Health

24.161. As per the National Family Health Survey–3 (2005–2006), the Infant Mortality Rate by community is as follows: Buddhists/Neo-Buddhists (53), Muslims (52), Sikhs (46) and Christians (42). All the figures are better than the national average of 57. Christians and Sikhs have relatively low mortality rates at all ages under five years. With respect to Perinatal Mortality, the figures are 47 for Muslims followed by 40 for Christians and 31 for Sikhs. The figure is 49 for all-India.

24.162. With respect to pregnant and lactating women, the NFHS-3 report states that Muslim women are among the least likely to purchase iron and folic acid tablets. Births in a health facility are most likely among, Buddhist/Neo-Buddhist mothers (59 per cent) and Sikh mothers (58 per cent). Births to Muslim mothers (33 per cent) are much less likely to take place in a health facility. The report also states that births to Muslim women are least likely to be followed by a postnatal check-up. This could in part reflect social and economic circumstances of Muslims, as well as their hesitation in approaching state institutions due to a real or perceived sense of discrimination. Hindu and Muslim children are about equally likely to be undernourished, but Christian and Sikh children are considerably better nourished.

24.163. Among the religious minorities, the percentage of households covered by a health scheme or health insurance is as follows: Christian (7.3), Buddhist (6.6), Sikh (6.5). It is abysmally low for Muslims at 2.1. The all-India average is 4.1 per cent. The number of women who have ever experienced domestic violence is the maximum for Buddhists at 40.9 per cent, followed by Muslims (34.6 per cent), Christians (27.8 per cent) and Sikhs (26.1 per cent). The all India average is 33.5 per cent.

Sex Ratio

24.164. As per Census 2001, the sex ratio of 1,009 for Christians, 953 for Buddhists, 936 for Muslims and 992 for other religions is above the national average of 933 for entire country. The figure however is alarmingly low for Sikhs at 893. The child sex ratio (age group 0–6) for the same period is 976 for other religions, 964 for Christians, 950 for Muslims, 942 for Buddhists, which are all above the national average of 927. It is however 786 for Sikhs, highly indicative of the disturbing trend of sex selective abortion.

Work and Employment

24.165. The Work Participation Rate (WPR) for all religious communities was 39.1 per cent in the Census of 2001. Buddhists had 40.6 per cent WPR (31.7 per cent for women), Christians 39.7 per cent (28.7 per cent for women), Sikhs 53.3 per cent (20.2 per cent) and Muslims 31.3 per cent (14.1 per cent for women). The gender gap in the work participation rate is large among Muslims (33.4 per cent points) and Sikhs (33.1 per cent points). The gender gap in WPR is 26.1 per cent points at the national level.

24.166. As per Table 24.10, 49.1 per cent Muslims, 52.8 per cent Christians and 47.3 per cent Sikhs are employed as 'other workers'. The 'other workers' category includes workers in service, manufacturing, trade and commerce and allied activities. The NSSO in their 61st Round of survey found that more than half of the workers in the rural areas were self-employed, the proportion being the highest among the Muslim workers both Males (60 per cent) and females (75 per cent). Since a large section of the Muslim, Christian and Sikhs workers are engaged in other workers category, skill development and credit related initiatives need to be tailored for the economically weak among these religious minorities.

24.167. According to the High Level Committee to Examine the Socio-Economic and Educational Status of the Muslim Community in India, the participation of Muslims in salaried jobs is low at only 13 per cent. In urban areas, less than 8 per cent are employed in the formal sector against a national average of 21 per cent. More than 12 per cent of Muslim male workers are engaged in street vending as compared to the national average of less than 8 per cent. Muslim workers are also found to be in a majority in the industrial sectors of tobacco (41 per cent), wearing apparel (30 per cent) and textiles (21 per cent). The figures indicate that Muslim workers are largely concentrated in the informal sector which is characterised by low wages, bad working conditions and little or no social security. Hence, at the macro level, policy focus on improving the lot of the economically weaker and socially marginalised sections in the unorganised workforce must be increased in order to bring in employment related dividends for Muslim workers. In the Twelfth Plan, specific interventions would need to be devised for up-gradation of skills and educational level of these workers to equip them for employment in the organised sector. To this effect, the Jan Shikshan Sansthan scheme of MHRD could be used in providing vocational training to illiterate, neo literate youth in MCDs.

Challenges for the Empowerment of Minorities

24.168. As stated earlier the eleventh Plan was the first plan to introduce a number of schemes aimed at improving the conditions of the minorities. These are listed in Box 24.1. In spite of considerable efforts made towards raising the socio-economic status of Minorities, many challenges remain which need to be addressed during the Twelfth Plan so that the lot of minorities can be improved in a time bound and effective manner.

Institutional Challenges

24.169. A programme is as good or as bad as its implementation and the quality of implementation is largely dependent on the institution implementing the programme/scheme. The Twelfth Plan should therefore consider systemic modifications to the existing system, which include participation of communities in planning and monitoring and the appointment of government 'facilitators' to improve access.

TABLE 24.10
Percentage Distribution of Workers by Category

Name of Religion	Percentage to Total Workers			
	Cultivators	Agricultural Labourers	Household Industry	Other Workers
Hindus	33.1	27.6	3.8	35.5
Muslims	20.7	22.0	8.7	49.1
Christian	29.2	15.3	2.7	52.8
Sikhs	32.4	16.8	3.4	47.3
Buddhists	20.4	37.6	2.9	39.2
Other religions	49.9	32.6	3.2	14.3
India	31.7	26.5	4.2	37.6

Source: Census 2001.

Box 24.1
Eleventh Five Year Plan Schemes

1. **Prime Minister's 15 Point Programme** was launched in 2005 with the aim of allocating 15 per cent of specified Centrally Sponsored Schemes for Minorities.
2. **Multi-sectoral Development Programme (MsDP),** formulated for 90 Minority Concentration Districts (MCDs), was designed for addressing the 'development deficits' of these districts and bring them at par with the national average. Projects taken up under MsDP involve mainly construction activities like polytechnic buildings, industrial training institutes, hostels, inter-colleges, residential schools, additional class room, health centres, water supply facilities, Anganwadi Centres, rural housing and so on.
3. **Pre-matric Scholarship Scheme** was launched in the year 2008–09, the second year of the Eleventh Five Year Plan. The scheme provides scholarships to minority students studying in Class I to X.
4. **Post-matric Scholarship Scheme** was launched in the year 2007–08. The scheme covers minority students from Class XI right upto PhD level.
5. **Merit-cum-Means Based Scholarship Scheme** was launched in the year 2007–08. The scheme covers students pursuing technical and professional courses at the UG and PG level.
6. **Maulana Azad National Fellowship for Minority Students** was launched in 2009–10 to provide integrated five year fellowships to pursue M. Phil. and Ph. D. in the Universities and institutions recognised by UGC.
7. **Grant-in-aid to Maulana Azad Education Foundation** was established in July, 1989, as a voluntary, non-political, non-profit making society registered under the Societies Registration Act, 1860, to formulate and implement educational schemes for the benefit of the educationally backward amongst the minorities. The schemes of MAEF are of two types: (*i*) Grant-in-Aid to NGOs for infrastructure development of Institutes/colleges/schools and (*ii*) scholarships to meritorious girl students.
8. **Free Coaching and Allied Scheme for Minorities** was launched to assist students through coaching institutions for enhancing their skills and capabilities to make them employable in different sectors. The review of the scheme reveals a similar discrepancy regarding physical and financial targets as with all other schemes. This will be comprehensively corrected in the Twelfth Plan.
9. **Scheme for Leadership Development of Minority Women** was launched by the Ministry in 2010, but could not be implemented due to anomalies in process of selection. A revised version of the scheme will be introduced in the Twelfth Plan.
10. **Grant-in-aid for Equity contribution to NMDFC:** an allocation of ₹500 crore was made under the Eleventh Plan for making equity contribution to NMDFC to help it fund its various schemes.
11. **Scheme of Grants-in-aid for strengthening the infrastructure of SCAs of NMDFC** aims to make SCAs a more effective instrument.
12. **Scheme for the Computerization of Records of the State/UT Wakf Boards** was introduced in order to streamline record keeping, introduce transparency, computerize the various functions/processes of the Waqf Boards and develop a single web based centralized application. The Joint Parliamentary Committee (JPC) on Waqf, in its Ninth Report submitted to Parliament on 23 October 2008, recommended computerization of the records of the State Waqf Boards with Central financial assistance. The scheme was implemented with effect from December, 2009.

24.170. As in the case of other disadvantaged communities a three-pronged strategy is needed, which will focus on (*i*) social empowerment; (*ii*) economic empowerment; and (*iii*) social justice.

Educational Empowerment

24.171. Non-availability of adequate resources and poor implementation has meant that scholarships are not provided to all eligible minority students. It is therefore imperative to ensure that financial allocations are made so that all eligible minority students are ensured much needed scholarships without any denial or deprivation. All the procedures starting from the application stage to award of scholarships, regular payment of scholarships and renewal of scholarships must be simplified so that award of scholarships to eligible students becomes automatic and hurdle-free. Assured payment of scholarships in time should be ensured through opening of Bank or Post Office accounts in the name of the awardees. Representatives of civil society, where required, should be encouraged to act as facilitators.

24.172. Under the Pre-matric scholarship scheme at present, hostellers studying in Class I–V do not receive scholarship allowances. Provision of maintenance allowance to hostellers as deemed appropriate should be considered. The rates of maintenance amounts will be revised in accordance with the changes taking place in the Consumer Price Index on a regular basis. The upward revision of the ceilings for course fees will be done rationally in order to match the actual fee costs.

24.173. In the Eleventh Five Year Plan, the Physical achievements of the Pre-matric, Post-matric and Merit-cum-Means scholarship schemes far exceed physical targets. However, financial achievements for those same years surprisingly were less than the assigned targets. This indicates that even while more students were being given scholarships, they were concentrated in groups which required less fees, or were mostly day scholars. This will be reviewed in the Twelfth Plan and scholarships equitably distributed as per demand. In the Post-matric scholarship scheme, many students were affected by scholarships not being regularly renewed. Rationalisation through integrated scholarships awards will be introduced in the Twelfth Plan, such that students do not have to drop out.

24.174. Similar scholarship schemes implemented by different Ministries follow different norms both in regard to eligibility criteria and the scholarship rates. These will be harmonised and parity in norms across Ministries implementing similar scholarship schemes will be established. The Online Scholarship Management System will be further strengthened and fully implemented during the first two years of Twelfth Five Year Plan.

24.175. School drop-out rates especially among Muslim girls are very high in Class IX and X, as they have no easy access or transport to reach distantly located institutions. Therefore, a programme through which bicycles are provided to the minority girl students to facilitate the continuance of their studies will be introduced in the Twelfth Five Year Plan. Some States are already implementing schemes to provide bicycles; the envisaged new scheme at the Central level will be rationalised and converged appropriately with the State scheme(s). Also see Box 24.2.

Recommendations for the Twelfth Five Year Plan

24.176. The empowerment of minorities in the Twelfth Plan is envisaged through their active participation in the developmental process as participants and not as passive recipients of developmental benefits. The Twelfth Plan vision for faster, more inclusive and sustainable growth mandates that bold and creative affirmative action must be undertaken to ensure inclusion of different socio-religious communities and to ensure fulfilment of their social, economic and political needs. The inclusion and empowerment of different socio-religious communities should not be viewed only as a welfare measure undertaken as a consequence of economic growth, but as a critical development imperative.

Monitorable Targets

24.177. The following monitorable targets could be adopted:

1. The literacy rate of religious minorities should be increased as quickly as possible to be at par with the national average, wherever applicable.
2. The participation of religious minorities in graduate and post graduate studies should be proportionate to their population (2011), with special focus on the economically weaker sections.
3. IMR, MMR, Institutional Deliveries, Child Immunisation and Vaccination of religious minorities should be brought at par with the national average, with special focus on the economically weaker and the socially marginalised sections.
4. Work participation rate of religious minorities in the organised sector should be increased to be at par with other communities. This is specially relevant for Muslims and other socially and economically disadvantaged groups.
5. Representation of religious minorities in all forms of Government employment should be increased in proportion to their population (2011).
6. Share of total number and total amount of bank loans given to all religious minorities, with special focus on Muslims and other economically

Box 24.2
Vision for the Twelfth Five Year Plan

The vision for the Twelfth plan consists of a series of bold and creative measures that build upon, but also go beyond the achievements of the Eleventh plan.

INCREASE ALLOCATION: Increase the scale of key interventions by greater financial outlays across the board to include MsDP and also bringing a larger number of schemes within the scope of the 15 PP, by making educational scholarships demand-driven and by initiating key pilot programmes to develop best practices for the future.

DIRECTLY TARGET MINORITIES: Re-vamp the design, expand the scope and strengthen implementation structures of key initiatives like the MsDP and 15 PP such that minority settlements and people are directly targeted; such direct targeting should be made a condition for approval of all block and district level plans.

INSTITUTIONALISE ROBUST MONITORING: Create internal accountability and impact-based monitoring systems that go beyond purely physical and financial monitoring, and also involve CSOs and peoples' groups in conducting time-bound social audits of schemes and create democratic dialogues between minority groups and state institutions at the grassroots level. All data of a district will be available with the district welfare officer (facilitator) and available in the public domain.

DEVELOP TRANSFORMATIVE LEADERSHIP: Build transformative leadership, through training and capacity building schemes, among minority communities on a large scale, especially among minority women and youth, so that they can themselves create accountability at the local level to help the State provide better neighborhoods, jobs, education, health, housing, hygiene, skills and incomes.

FOCUS ON SKILL BUILDING FOR EMPLOYABILITY: Develop skills to generate employability among minority youth in all MsDP blocks and towns through direct linkages with the National Skill Development Mission.

INITIATE PILOT SCHEMES FOR MINORITIES: Recognising that we need to constantly learn and innovate to respond to the changing needs of minorities in the context of the changing landscape of the country, the Twelfth plan should institutionalise a 'hub of innovation', through restructuring the Maulana Azad Education Foundation, wherein a range of experiments in educational and livelihood initiatives (including artisans) among minorities can be undertaken. Civil society engagement with Muslims should be revived urgently through grants-in-aid mechanisms.

weaker and socially marginalised groups, should be increased to be at par with that of the general population.

7. There should be 100 per cent financial inclusion, including access to sources of formal credit and finance for all eligible persons belonging to religious minorities.

Prime Minister's 15 Point Programme

24.178. At present, a limited number of schemes are included in the 15 Point Programme. The Twelfth Plan proposes inclusion of additional schemes from the Ministries of Small and Medium Industries, Youth Affairs, Agriculture and Rural Development (especially MGNREGA). Further, in order to ensure adequate funds and benefits reach the minorities, the existing guidelines of earmarking '15 per cent of funds wherever possible' should be revised to '15 per cent and above' in proportion to the size of the minority population. This would facilitate coverage of all minority concentrated areas under the Prime Minister's Programme, which were otherwise excluded.

24.179. All achievements under 15 PP will be disaggregated to enable monitoring and to ensure that minority settlements and beneficiaries gain directly. Monitoring guidelines will be suitably revised to ensure ground level impact-based monitoring rather than monitoring of physical and financial outlays. Annual targets and/outlays of 15 PP of the Central Ministries should be broken down to the natural settlement/hamlet/ward level, which should become the basis for reporting achievements. The Vigilance and Monitoring Committees at the Districts and the State level should have members from the minority communities to oversee effective implementation of the schemes/programmes meant for their benefit and provide the much needed feedback on the implementation of these programmes. To improve the methodology of impact evaluation, data disaggregated for SRCs should be generated across line Ministries under the PM's 15 PP. This will help evaluate the benefits accrued by individuals/families/communities across different sectors. See Box 24.3.

Multi-sectoral Development Programme (MsDP)

24.180. To ensure more focused targeting of the minorities, Blocks with minority population concentration subject to backwardness parameters as applied for Minority Concentrated Districts (MCDs) under MsDP will be adopted as the new area unit in the Multi-sectoral Development Programme. Also, the population criterion to identify MCDs will be brought down from 25 per cent to 15 per cent. MsDP programmes have left out huge minority areas including towns, urban conglomerates and isolated villages/hamlets. Additionally, the programme will adopt a *projectised* approach in order to reach individual beneficiaries among the minorities and also their localities.

24.181. For the Area Development plan, it must be a guiding principle that any assets created benefit minorities. MsDP guidelines will be revised to re-focus the programme away from topping up existing Centrally Sponsored Schemes under the 15 PP. Instead, MsDP will take up works that are need-based, rather than preferring projects that aim to saturate coverage of already existing national programmes, particularly infrastructure projects (IAY/ICDS/PHC buildings/classroom). *Revised MsDP guidelines will remove this emphasis on 15 PP and instead emphasise local need-based plans to overcome local development deficits.* This would enable poor settlements of minorities to identify what they believe are their most urgent needs and to focus resources on these, which could be drinking water, drainage, livelihoods support, electrification, support to dying vocations such as handlooms and handicrafts, innovations in skill-based education, training to artisans with backward and forward linkages into new markets, equipping technical institutes with adequate equipment and infrastructure, remedial school support for children of first-generation learners, education using new media for training and advocacy and so on. MsDP and 15 PP will work in synergy rather than the former duplicating the latter, such that 15 PP will take care of sectoral investments/ongoing CSS across the country and MsDP will fill gaps that particular communities/or settlements face and which are not being covered by existing CSS.

Box 24.3
Specific Interventions under PM's 15 PP

Following are three interventions proposed to be undertaken by line Ministries during the Twelfth Five Year Plan.

The traditional systems of education, viz., Buddhist Monastic education, training in the areas of drawing, painting, clay art and craft, music, dance, and so on needs to be preserved. To this effect, necessary support and assistance will be provided by the Ministries of Culture, Labour and Human Resource Development. As regards the modernisation of Madarsas, the ongoing schemes of Ministry of Human Resource Development with ensured support and assistance financially and otherwise will be strengthened.

Urdu assumes importance as a prominent language and medium of thought, learning, communication and culture of the nation beyond social, religious and regional boundaries. Therefore, necessary support and efforts will be made to promote Urdu as a living language. The appointment of Urdu teachers in this context will be carried out in an expanded manner with adequate funding not only to Madarsas, but also in promoting the language in more mainstream schools and colleges.

In order to provide the best quality education, the endeavour in the Twelfth Plan will be towards having one Residential School along the lines of Jawahar Navodaya Vidyalaya and Kasturba Gandhi Balika Vidyalaya. It will be established in a phased manner in minority concentration Blocks and minority concentration towns/cities. Norms in these schools need to ensure admission to at least 50 per cent children belonging to minorities. Model Schools and Inter-colleges under the existing scheme of MoHRD should also cover minority concentrated blocks and minority concentrated wards in urban areas. Efforts should also be made that MHRD schemes for interest subsidy on education loans adequately covers the minority communities.

24.182. Since the entire scheme rests on the suitability of the district plans prepared by the District level committees, these will be preceded by prior dissemination of information throughout the minority concentration areas (hamlet/ward). Such information dissemination will include traditional and locally accessible forms of communication (nukkad-nataks, community radios and so on) and not remain restricted to placement of information on the website of the concerned department/government. Further a wide and visible series of public consultations, in the minority concentration areas (hamlet/ward) of the District will now be a part of the pre-condition for plan approval by the Ministry of Minority Affairs.

24.183. MsDP and PM's new 15 PP Guidelines should mandate a specific number of social audits to be undertaken during the implementation period of each specific project. Detailed procedures and institutional support should be provided for social audits as in MGNREGA. Community/social audit conductors should have access to natural settlement/hamlet/ward annual targets and outlays. These should also be placed on websites for full transparency. Oversight and monitoring guidelines should include public accountability procedures including proactive disclosure of information at all levels (natural settlement/hamlet, block and district). Local NGOs should be formally engaged to build community-centred monitoring processes, including capacity building of local communities to conduct such monitoring on their own. Quarterly review meetings for MsDP and 15PP should also involve civil society representatives. Funds for the afore-mentioned interventions could be made available from the administrative costs for monitoring and evaluation under these programmes.

24.184. District Planning Committees (which are the same for both MsDP and PM's new 15 PP must be operationalised on a mandatory basis, with guidelines clearly instructing the inclusion of people's representatives especially from the minorities, local NGOs or development activists. In this regard, training shall also be imparted to elected representatives (ER) to PRIs, especially women and first time ERs from religious minorities. To make the implementation of the schemes transparent and involve the targeted beneficiaries, all the data of a district will be available with the district welfare officer (facilitator). It should also be available in the public domain for the benefit of elected or community representatives and civil society practitioners.

24.185. MsDP and PM's new 15 PP should also be implemented with a vision to provide all minority settlements, rural and urban, with the following minimum basic services: ICDS, health care, education and skill development, clean drinking water, individual sanitation and sewage and drainage. This assurance of basic services should be demand driven, in that the appropriate government would be responsible to provide these services, on demand from any settlement.

24.186. Direct targeting of minority populations and minority habitations (hamlets) should be made a specific condition for approval of all plans under PM's 15 pp and MsDP. It is desirable to compile socio-economic data, to the extent possible, at the level of habitations. The Assessment and Monitoring Authority may oversee this task.

24.187. In order to cover the minority concentrated pockets and villages that remain outside the identified MCDs under MsDP and are deprived of the developmental benefits, there is an urgent need to ensure that such development deficit villages and towns with 50 per cent or above minority population are provided with developmental inputs through a special programme in the Twelfth Plan. A comprehensive list of all villages and towns—with 50 per cent or above minority population and with development deficits—will be prepared and appropriate funds allocated in order to bridge the identified development deficits during the Twelfth Five Year Plan. These interventions will encompass a variety of structural, conceptual and monitoring measures to increase the pace of progress, participation and empowerment of the minorities. There is a need, however, to constantly assess these strategies against the evolving contexts and to make policies relating to the minorities—to people more generally—open to change as per the needs of those it seeks to serve.

Scheme for Life, Livelihood and Leadership Development of Minority Women

24.188. The Scheme for Leadership Development of Minority Women that was approved in the Eleventh Plan with a small allocation is yet to be rolled out. This pilot scheme will be re-designed and rolled out in the Twelfth Plan. The scheme, which involves local NGOs in its operational plan, will also go a long way in helping NGOs and civil society to overcome their lack of experience of working with Minorities as a deprived socio-economic group and begin the process of constructive and sustained engagement with these groups.

24.189. The Trade Related Entrepreneurship Assistance and Development (TREAD) Scheme of the Ministry of Micro, Small and Medium for assistance to illiterate and semi-literate women of rural and urban areas for self-employment would need to be extended to marginalised minority women under the 15 Point Programme to enable entrepreneurship development amongst women.

Implementation of the Recommendations of Sachar Committee

24.190. Report of the Justice Rajender Sachar Committee in 2006 had made special recommendations for the development of Muslims. While most of the recommendations have been translated into action in the Eleventh Plan period, there are certain recommendations that need to be put into action in the Twelfth Plan. These include (*i*) Disadvantaged minority students living in congested urban areas will be put into study centres by having the same set up as the existing school building to function after regular school hours; (*ii*) More public sector bank branches will be opened in minority concentration districts and the list of such bank branches will be placed by the Ministry of Minority Affairs on its website and (*iii*) Special programmes for providing education along with skill and vocational training in the minority concentrated towns will be initiated.

Institutional Changes:

1. **Strengthened Systems at the Centre and State levels**

    (a) The Twelfth Plan proposes the immediate augmentation and restructuring of the Ministry of Minority Affairs to address the current human resource shortages that are faced by the Ministry.

    (b) All State Governments will be asked to have a separate well endowed Department for Minorities welfare. MoUs will be signed with States so that they are able to enjoy more flexibility and assume more responsibility and accountability. In the minorities sector, an administrative chain of command should be developed with an empowered officer, who may act as a facilitator between the community, PRIs and across the various departments who will handhold the minorities in the areas of education, area development and economic advancement. Districts should have a separate Minority Welfare or Facilitation Officer, who may be the nodal officer responsible for coordination and implementation of all schemes relating to the welfare of minorities for the District. A clear chain of command and accountability should be designed right from the level of the nodal officer to the level of chief secretary of the State.

    (c) Village, block and district level Committees will be established with representations from the local government, elected representatives and minority communities to identify the development deficits and prioritise the interventions in addressing the development deficits. At the State level, separate Committees will be formed to ensure proper monitoring and effective implementation of schemes. Government functionaries involved in the implementation of schemes and the new 15 Point Programme will be sensitised as well as apprised of the various schemes and programmes of the government for minorities.

2. **Structure of implementation of MsDP**
    In order to cut down delay and establish accountability, the plan and implementation of MsDP schemes will be delegated to local authorities through the states. MoMA will perform the

role of overall management and monitoring of the Programme. This will ensure direct accountability of the major stakeholders.

3. **Skill Development**

    Schemes promoting skill development amongst minorities to enhance their potential for employment deserve special attention. The ever proliferating MsDP basket of schemes should be consolidated with greater emphasis on skill development. It is also observed that the State Governments are reluctant to accept ITI and Polytechnic schemes for the simple fact that they feel that they will become liabilities for the State exchequer right from day one. Therefore, these schemes will now have in-built provision for a lump-sum amount for maintenance/cost of these institutions for at least five years. Skilling of minorities will also be accorded priority through initiatives of the National Skill Development Coordination Board, attached to the Planning Commission.

4. **Access to resources for entrepreneurial activities**

    The National Minority Development and Finance Corporation (NMDFC) will take up skill development programmes. It will also give marketing assistance to artisans. Economic Empowerment of Minorities will be done through infusion of capital at the right levels. Priority Sector Lending (PSL) ratio has shown constant and steady rise with 10.6 per cent in 2007–08, 12.41 per cent in 2008–09, 13.01 per cent in 2009–10 and 14.16 per cent in 2010–11 of total PSL going to minority communities. There should be priority sector lending based on BPL and doubly disadvantaged BPL families. NMDFC will also be comprehensively restructured.

5. **Scholarship programmes of MoMA to be 'Demand Driven'**

    The goal will be for all eligible minority students to be covered under different scholarship schemes of MoMA in time. This will be coupled with suitable enhancement of scholarship amounts along with total simplification of procedures for fresh and reasonable cases.

6. **The Maulana Azad Education Foundation (MAEF)**

    The Maulana Azad Education Foundation (MAEF) needs to be comprehensively restructured. An evaluation study of the Maulana Azad Education Foundation (MAEF) was carried out by the Indian Social Institute, New Delhi in 2010. The findings of the study revealed that the Foundation was performing a good role in promoting education among the educationally backward minorities. However, in order to give further impetus to the functioning of the MAEF, there is a felt need for institutional restructuring of the MAEF, transforming the Foundation from its current charity/welfare mode towards empowering practices. The objective should be to turn MAEF into an independent hub of excellence for incubating innovations, pilots that may be up-scaled and dissemination of best practices for minority empowerment, cutting across sectors and schemes within the broad framework of ending social exclusion, promoting integration and citizenship rights.

24.191. The MAEF may undertake these pilot initiatives through grant-in-aid mechanisms in a broad range of educational arenas such as community based education, innovations in skill-based education, training to artisans with backward and forward linkages into new markets, training for empowerment of women and youth, equipping technical institutes with adequate equipment and infrastructure, remedial school support for children of first-generation learners, capacity building for good governance, education for civic empowerment, education for advocacy and so on. Institutional restructuring of this kind will require developing a blue print of changes in governance, including structures and processes of decision making and in the management for implementing these decisions; including the creation of a new organisational structure, roles and positions, criteria for the allocation of resources to various activities, the allotment of tasks to various units and regular performance evaluation.

7. **Sensitisation of Citizens and Functionaries at the Centre and State Levels**
    - Government functionaries involved in the implementation of schemes and the new 15 Point Programme should be sensitised as well as apprised of the various schemes and programmes for the minorities. A capacity building project will need to be introduced in the Twelfth Five Year Plan, which can support the requirements of all stakeholders.
    - NGOs with proven record of working for communal harmony will be engaged to prepare modules for democratic education. The values of the Indian Constitution will be propagated through specially designed campaigns specially targeting the younger generation from all communities. Larger social mobilisation and public education campaigns will also need to be undertaken.

8. **Data Collection and Management System**
    In order to address the needs and problems of the minorities living in diverse situations and geographical areas, especially in the Himalayan region, there is a need to have disaggregated data bases on their socio-economic conditions. To this effect, a baseline survey covering district/blocks/villages/occupational clusters/agricultural activities needs to be conducted especially at the grassroots levels, with the participation of the Ministries concerned. The developmental activities to be undertaken should be based upon the demands and needs as arise from the survey data. Employment data must also be compiled to better understand the current position of employment for minorities in the Government as well as the Private sector. This is necessary to ensure equitable representation from minority communities in civil, defense, administrative, judicial and other services, as well as in the private sector.

9. **Monitoring of Schemes and Programmes that concern Minorities**
    Social Audit needs to be built into all programmes and to make the implementation of schemes transparent all the data of a district should be available with the District Welfare Officer. It will also be available in the public domain for the benefit of elected or community representatives and civil society practitioners. The Twelfth Plan strategy for monitoring should include:
    - Development of the National Data bank, as suggested by the Sachar Committee.
    - Tracking selected Monitorable Targets disaggregated by social religious communities, in respect of beneficiary oriented programmes.
    - Suggest inclusion of socio-religious communities, especially minorities, as an agenda for review in Plan discussions with States, reviews with State Chief Ministers and State Chief Secretaries and State reviews with District Collectors and Chairpersons/CEOs of Zila Parishads.
    - Support reporting of disaggregated indicators related to minorities by the relevant flagship programmes in their existing programme review mechanisms such as Annual Common Review Missions for NHRM and SSA, half yearly/annual reviews with States and social audits such as for MGNREGA,
    - Incentivisation of States and Panchayats (through Additional Central Assistance) where social inclusion indicators related to minorities improve, with peer learning through sharing of best practices, within and across States/Districts.
    - National Resource Centre/s would need to be established, with expertise on development planning for different social religious communities—including minorities—linked to a support network of institutions, universities and voluntary agencies. This network may expand to State Resource Centre/s as needed, based on implementation experience during the Plan period.
    - Development of monitoring systems, processes and tools for assessing and reporting on the inclusiveness of growth as mentioned above.
    - An assessment of social inclusion of different socio-religious communities, including

minorities, should be conducted as part of the Mid-Term Appraisal of the Twelfth Plan.

10. The Assessment and Monitoring Authority

The Assessment and Monitoring Authority was set up following the recommendations of the Sachar Committee and anchored in the Planning Commission. This Authority needs to evaluate the extent of development benefits, which accrue to different Socio-Religious Communities (SRCs), through various programmes and perform a watch-dog function to closely monitor the participation of SRCs in programmes at all levels of governance, namely the Rural and Urban local bodies, Districts, States and the Centre. The Assessment and Monitoring Authority (AMA) also needs to institutionalise the mechanisms for assessment and monitoring at all levels, through effective generation and analysis of data and commissioning of qualitative and quantitative studies. The Authority needs to be given the requisite power and resources to monitor that necessary priority is accorded to different socio-religious communities—particularly minority communities—in policies, programmes and capacity development interventions. This will also enable effective implementation of the monitoring interventions recommended above.

New Schemes for the Twelfth Five Year Plan

24.192. The Twelfth Plan will introduce six new schemes in addition to the existing ones. These will address the issues of leadership development, preservation of culture, counseling services, education, training for civil services examinations and decline of population of the Parsi community.

1. Pilot Scheme for Leadership Training for Young Leaders among Minorities

24.193. There is a strong need for perspective building, sensitisation, community mobilisation and awareness generation among people regarding the right of equal development of minorities. Towards this end, a pilot scheme for leadership training of youth belonging to religious minorities will be introduced in the Twelfth Five Year Plan. The scheme would train 20,000 young men and women leaders across the country every year to become equipped in responding to perceptions of alienation as well as actual instances of discrimination and hostility by encouraging participation and introducing innovative ways to counter the sense of insecurity and despair. The scheme will also provide training in IT-based and new media for advocacy and communication; it will train youth as practitioners of social audit processes, develop skills to provide technical support to community mobilisation/project planning/audit and to become trainers for capacity building of members of village/district/state committees (of 15 PP/MsDP). The scheme will thus provide an active link between local government and the community towards successful implementation of government schemes. It may be linked to the Centre for the Study of Social Exclusion and Inclusive Policy set up by UGC in the Eleventh Plan period.

2. Support for students clearing Prelims under Civil Services Examination

24.194. Participation of minorities in decision making is vital for their development. Therefore, to encourage aspiring candidates from the minority communities, who clear Prelims under Civil Services Examination for Grade A and B of both UPSC as well as State Public Service Commission will be given incentives in the form of direct financial support to help them to bear the cost of coaching and other expenses.

3. Scheme for Promotion of Education in 100 Minority Concentration Towns/Cities

24.195. A sizeable minority population in towns and cities is socio-economically disadvantaged and requires a whole range of special initiatives to improve their living conditions and opportunities. It is therefore necessary to initiate special programmes for the promotion of education, including skill and vocational education, in such backward towns/cities for empowering members of minority communities, among others.

4. Pilot Scheme for Urban Youth Support Lines

24.196. There is an urgent need for intervention that helps the Youth belonging to minorities in building their human, cultural and social capital. This can best be done by leveraging technology for the rebuilding of social and institutional networks and linkages, creating space for dialogue between community and state actors and recognising and overcoming trauma/psychosocial concerns. This intervention will specifically include information dissemination on career counseling and employment opportunities to youth from poor and working class backgrounds. A pilot scheme will be introduced using a 'hub and spoke' hybrid technology model with an Urban Youth Support-line (UYSL) as the hub, supported by community outreach nodes that serve as spokes. The services that will be provided by the proposed UYSL include career guidance (education, vocational training), access to Government Schemes/Programmes, placement services, facilitation for certification, institutional linkages (financial and so on), general counseling (women's issues, health issues, legal issues, identity, security) and location based outreach services in co-ordination with NGOs/CBOs/Ward Offices.

5. Scheme for Protection and Projection of Minority Culture and Heritage

24.197. The culture of the minorities manifested in various forms—paintings, monuments, literature, artefacts, festivals, institutions and so on—gives strength and a sense of identity to people following different faiths, even as they live in different parts of the country. These expressions of culture and history of the minorities are inseparable parts of our national heritage. Therefore, efforts with adequate fund support should be made to protect and revive both material and non-material cultural traits of the minorities.

6. Linguistic Minorities

24.198. Linguistic Minorities (LMs) consist of heterogeneous linguistic groups spread across the country having concentration in the Inter-State borders. A sizeable population of LMs belongs to various occupational and artisan groups and their source of livelihood and the occupation relating thereto is closely linked to their culture. Thus, for LMs the culture and economy are inseparable. A large number of LMs remain backward socially and economically for being numerically small and marginalised. The Constitutional commitment for protecting their culture and language should therefore be attended in a comprehensive manner by not only protecting their source of livelihood, which is an integral part of their culture, but also through protective measures ensuring their all-round well-being and development.

24.199. To conclude, the interventions proposed in the Twelfth Five Year Plan encompass variety of structural, conceptual and monitoring measures to increase the pace of progress, participation and empowerment of the minorities. However, there is a need to constantly assess these strategies against the evolving contexts and to provide an enabling policy environment that is responsive to the needs of communities—particularly minorities and the most vulnerable and marginalised communities—that it seeks to serve.

OTHER VULNERABLE GROUPS

24.200. The social scenario in the country is changing rapidly due to industrialisation and the increasing flow of the rural population to the already crowded cities and towns in search of employment, leading to overcrowding, emergence of pavement/slum dwellings, breakdown of joint family system, unemployment, poverty and so on In this process of social transformation, certain categories of population, who are unable to cope with these rapid changes, have become especially vulnerable. These vulnerable groups include Persons with Disabilities (PwDs) (that is, locomotor, visual, hearing, speech and mental and so on), Older Persons, Beggars and Victims of Substance Abuse and Alcoholism. All these categories need special attention of the State because of their vulnerabilities and the disabilities that they suffer from.

PERSONS WITH DISABILITIES

An Overview

24.201. About 2.11 per cent of the population as per 2001 census comprises of persons with disabilities having one or multiple disability. Though the number is small, the need of these members of our society deserves special attention. Disabilities present probabilistic outcomes which can affect anyone and it is appropriate that society does whatever it can to assist this segment to play a full part in society. There was a paradigm shift in policy towards Persons with Disabilities since the Ninth Five Year Plan, from the earlier welfare based approach to a rights-based approach. The Tenth Five Year Plan focused on effective implementation of various provisions of legislation and National Policy for Persons with Disabilities. It advocated a multi-sectoral and multi-collaborative approach. The Eleventh Five Year Plan (2007–12) had aimed at inclusive growth. It was expected to achieve inclusiveness through significant improvements in literacy/education, health, greater employment opportunities and sharper focus on disadvantaged groups. The Eleventh Plan emphasised upon the rights-based approach to empower the PwDs inter alia through: (*i*) delineating clear cut responsibility between the concerned Ministries/Departments; (*ii*) formulating detailed rules and guidelines by concerned Ministries/Departments; and (*iii*) monitoring mechanism at various levels. A new Department, namely Department of Disability Affairs has been set up in the Ministry of Social Justice and Empowerment on Twelfth May, 2012 to act as the nodal Department for the overall policy, planning and coordination of programmes for persons with disabilities.

24.202. In consonance with the policy of providing a complete package of services and to deal effectively with the multi-dimensional problems of the disabled population, the Ministry of Social Justice and Empowerment has been implementing a variety of programmes for their treatment, rehabilitation, empowerment and development. The seven National Institutes viz., the National Institute for the Visually Handicapped, Dehradun (1979); National Institute for the Orthopedically Handicapped, Kolkata (1978); Aliyavur Jung National Institute for the Hearing Handicapped, Mumbai (1983); National Institute for the Mentally Handicapped, Secundrabad (1984); and National Institute for Multiple Disabilities, Chennai and Swami Vivekanand National Institute of Rehabilitation, Training and Research, Cuttack (1984) and Pt. Deen Dayal Upadhyaya Institute for the Physically Handicapped, New Delhi (1960) continued to develop technical manpower through full-fledged courses in various aspects of prevention, education, treatment and rehabilitation of the disabled and provide outreach and extension activities to needy areas such as slums, tribal belts, semi-urban and rural areas. In addition, a National Centre namely, Indian Sign Language Research and Training Centre has been set up in 2011 to propagate and develop Indian Sign Language.

24.203. The National Handicapped Finance and Development Corporation (NHFDC) was set up on 24th January, 1997 as an apex level body with an authorised share capital of ₹400.00 crore. The objective of the Corporation is to promote economic development activities and self-employment ventures for the benefit of Persons with Disability. The Corporation has so far released equity contribution by the Ministry as paid up capital to the extent of ₹161.80 crore. The Corporation extends credit facilities to beneficiaries through channelising agencies in States/UTs. It provides loans at concessional rate for education, skill development and self-employment ventures to Persons with Disabilities of 40 per cent or more and whose annual income does not exceed ₹5.00 lakh per annum in urban areas and ₹3.00 lakh in rural areas. NHFDC also provided loans to Parents Associations of mentally retarded persons to set up income generating activities. The Eleventh Plan outlay was ₹30.80 crore. However, on the basis of budgetary provisions made on year to year basis, a total of ₹125.00 crore was provided for the scheme in the Eleventh Plan against which the likely expenditure is ₹112.00 crore benefitting 34,461 disabled persons.

24.204. The Artificial Limbs Manufacturing Corporation of India (ALIMCO) was set up in 1972. The authorised share capital and paid up capital as on March 31, 2010 were ₹300.00 lakh and ₹196.50 lakhs respectively, for manufacturing and supplying durable, sophisticated, scientifically manufactured modern and ISI standard quality assistive aids and appliances that can promote physical, psychological, social, economic and vocational rehabilitation by reducing the effect of disabilities and enhancing potential for self-dependence. ALIMCO is the premier and the largest manufacturer of quality Aids and Appliances in entire South Asia. The Corporation has been exporting its products to Afghanistan, Angola, Bangladesh, Bhutan, Cambodia, Ghana, Hong Kong, Israel, Namibia, Nepal, Philippines, Sri Lanka, Tanzania, UAE, Uzbekistan and USA. Besides Government's efforts, NGOs are also contributing towards physical, economic and social rehabilitation of the persons with disabilities. Please refer to Box 24.4.

24.205. The scheme of setting up of Composite Regional Centres (CRCs) is a part of overall strategy to reach out to the PwDs in the country and to facilitate the creation of the required infrastructure and capacity building at Central, State and District levels and below for awareness generation, training of rehabilitation professionals, service delivery and so on. At present there are six CRCs functioning at Sundernagar, Srinagar, Lucknow, Guwahati, Patna and Bhopal. Another one has been set up at Ahmedabad (Gujarat) during the year 2010–11, which became functional from 16 August 2011 and one more CRC has been set up at Kozhikode (Kerala) on 17.02.2012. Additional Centres need to be set up at locations where the existing infrastructure for providing comprehensive services to persons with disabilities are inadequate and where such centres are needed the most.

24.206. The objective of the District Disability Rehabilitation Centres (DDRCs) is to facilitate the creation of infrastructure and capacity building at district level for awareness generation, rehabilitation, training and guiding rehabilitation professionals. The Scheme is a joint venture of the State and Central Government. The DDRCs are funded through the 'Schemes for Implementation of the Persons with Disabilities (Equal Opportunity, Protection of Rights and Full Participation) Act, 1995 for an initial period of 3 years (5 years in case of North Eastern Region, J&K, A&N Islands, Puducherry, Daman & Diu and Dadra & Nagar Haveli) and thereafter the funding is made through the Scheme of Deendayal Disabled Rehabilitation Scheme (DDRS). DDRC guidelines have been revised with effect from April 1, 2010. The revised guidelines include revision of honoraria, recurring and non recurring items of expenditure and so on 199 DDRCs have been sanctioned out of which 181 are functional and are providing rehabilitation services to persons with disabilities. 21 new DDRCs have been set up in 2010–11 In the financial year 2011–12, grant amounting to ₹196.28 lakh was released for setting up of 12 new DDRCs at Warangal (Andhra Pradesh), Supaul (Bihar), Sitamarhi (Bihar), West Champaran (Bihar), Sabarkantha (Gujarat), Banaskantha (Gujarat), Bharatpur (Rajasthan), Bhilwara (Rajasthan) Aligarh (Uttar Pradesh), Bulandshahr (Uttar Pradesh), Bardhaman (West Bengal), Purulia (West Bengal).

24.207. The main objective of the Scheme of Assistance to persons with disabilities for Purchase/Fitting of Aids/Appliances (ADIP) is to provide grant-in-aid to the various implementing agencies (NGOs/District Disability Rehabilitation Centres/ALIMCO/State Handicapped Development Corporation/other local bodies) to assist the needy disabled persons in

---

Box 24.4
The Jaipur Foot Story

The Bhagwan Mahaveer Viklang Sahayata Samiti, Limb Centre, S.M.S. Hospital/Medical College, Jaipur (hereinafter called the Society) is a non-governmental, voluntary, non-religious, non-sectarian, non-political Society for helping the handicapped, particularly the resourceless. It was set up by Mr. D.R. Mehta in March, 1975 as one of the long-term human welfare projects. It has branches in Bikaner, Jodhpur, Kota, Bharatpur, Ajmer, Pali, Udaipur, Hyderabad, Ambala, Srinagar, Indore, Chennai, Patna and Ahmadabad. The Society (Jaipur Foot/Limb and Calipers) supplements efforts in making disabled persons functional by providing artificial limbs, calipers, other aids and appliances, economic assistance free of charge. This enables them to regain their self-respect and human dignity as also to become normal and useful members of the community. The Jaipur Limb is so efficient that after this limb is fitted, a person can walk like a normal person without a stick or support, and even run, ride a bicycle and climb a tree. Many of the patients can, after the fitment, go back to work in the fields, factories, shops and offices. Jaipur Foot has also been fitted to landmine victims and others in foreign countries like Afghanistan, Bangladesh, Indonesia, Lebanon, Nigeria, Nepal, Nairobi, Pakistan, Panama, Philippines, Somalia, Sudan, Zambia, and Zimbabwe.

procuring durable, sophisticated and scientifically manufactured, modern, standard aids and appliances that can promote their physical, social and psychological rehabilitation, by reducing the effects of disabilities and enhance their economic potential. The aids and appliances supplied under the Scheme must meet ISI standards. The Scheme also envisages corrective surgeries, whenever required, before providing an assistive device. From the year 2007–08, a new approach for district–wise allocation of funds to organise camps for persons with disabilities for distribution of aids and appliance has been adopted to ensure coverage throughout the country. The procedure has been further amended for promoting the involvement of Red Cross Societies, District Disability Rehabilitation Centres and State Government Corporations/Boards.

24.208. The Scheme of Deendayal Disabled Rehabilitation Scheme (DDRS) has been implemented since 1999 with the objective of ensuring effective implementation of the Persons with Disabilities Act, 1995, by creating an enabling environment and encouraging non-governmental organisations through financial assistance for undertaking projects for the empowerment of the disabled. The DDRS guidelines, applicable since 1 April 2003, include 18 model projects covering various services provided by voluntary agencies which can be supported through grant-in-aid. The services provided include: (*i*) programmes for pre-school and early intervention; (*ii*) special education; (*iii*) vocational training and placement; (*iv*) community based rehabilitation; (*v*) manpower development; and (*vi*) psycho-social rehabilitation of persons with mental illness. The guidelines of Deendayal Disability and Rehabilitation Scheme were revised in 2009. It includes revised cost norms for honoraria, recurring items and non-recurring items of expenditure. Besides enhancement of cost-norms, rationalisation and merger of manpower categories in the various model projects have been carried out. As against 80 categories in the original Scheme, the revised list contains 66 manpower categories. 14 new trades that can be offered in Vocational Training Centres (VTCs) have been added considering the demand for new skills like computer applications and programming, web-designing, internet management, mobile repairing and so on District Disability Rehabilitation Centres set up by the Ministry are also funded under this Scheme. The outlay under the Eleventh Five Year Plan was ₹500.00 crore and likely expenditure is to the order of ₹369.10 crore accounting for 83 per cent utilisation of the allocation. Under the Scheme, 530 NGOs were assisted during 2007–11 covering an average of 2.3 lakh beneficiaries every year.

24.209. The Scheme of Incentives to Employers in the Private Sector for Providing Employment to Persons with Disabilities was launched in 2008. Under the Scheme, the Government of India provides the employer's contribution for Employees Provident Fund (EPF) and Employees State Insurance (ESI) for the first 3 years, for employees with disabilities employed in the private sector on or after 1 April 2008, with a monthly salary upto ₹25,000. Under the scheme, 392 (upto 31 March 2012) and 918 (upto 29 September 2012) persons have been registered by Employees Provident Fund Organisation (EPFO) and Employees State Insurance Corporation (ESIC) respectively till September 2010. The incentive scheme is basically voluntary in nature. Wide publicity has been given to sensitise and encourage the employers in private sector to avail the benefit of the Scheme.

Persons with Disabilities: Strategy for the Twelfth Plan

24.210. Persons with Disabilities continue to face discrimination in education, employment, transport and in terms of access to sports, recreation, and so on To counter this, the Twelfth Plan must adopt a two-pronged strategy incorporating—(*i*) service delivery and (*ii*) generation of public awareness about disability rights. In the area of service delivery the challenges to be addressed include: making a large number of products, public services and information services accessible to PwDs, improving participation and completion rates of students with disabilities at various stages of education (elementary, secondary and tertiary), reducing disproportionate incidence of poverty among the persons with disabilities, enhancing condition of nutrition, health and housing at least upto a reasonable level, identifying exclusive implementing agencies for programmes meant for persons with disabilities in States and strengthening of existing agencies. Another major area of challenge pertains to public awareness about disability rights and issues and stepping up of the level of awareness among the persons with disabilities about legislative provisions and development programmes available to them. The problems and needs of the most vulnerable among the persons with disabilities such as women, homeless and those with severe/or multiple disabilities require special and intensified focus in the Twelfth Plan.

24.211. There is need for modernisation and expansion of production units of ALIMCO to enhance the quantum of production to match/meet the demand for improved products. Efforts, therefore, need to be made to ensure provision of modernised artificial limbs and appliances for the needy persons with disabilities with greater coverage.

24.212. The Twelfth Five Year Plan will look into the three key aspects: (*i*) Recognition; of the extent to which the development, competence and emerging personal autonomy of Persons with Disabilities are enhanced through the realisation of the various agreed National and International Conventions and Programmes; (*ii*) Empowerment; in term of denoting the rights of persons with disabilities to respect their capacities and by transfer of various legal rights; (*iii*) Protection acknowledging that Persons with Disabilities have 'un-evolved' capacities as a consequence of their disabilities and thereby have rights to protection; on the part of parents, community and the State from abuse and from participation in activities likely to cause them harm. In all three cases, there are obligations on States to respect, protect and promote the right of the Persons with Disabilities.

24.213. Municipalities and Panchayats need to be specially enabled and empowered to perform their assigned role for the empowerment of Persons with Disabilities, increased sensitisation and awareness level of different stakeholders and the community; re-designing products, processes, public places and services so as to make them accessible to persons with disabilities; improved delivery and monitoring mechanism; the development of an integrated management system for the coordination of disability planning, implementation and monitoring in the various line functions at all spheres of government; and establishing of National, State and subsequent District structures that will continuously update and link strategy and policy developments with operational planning initiatives involving all role-players (District Project Officers [DPOs], government, the private sector).

24.214. To accomplish the above task, the Twelfth Plan needs to adopt the strategy of: (*i*) Involvement of Persons with Disabilities in evolving strategies of the government and involving organisations of persons with disabilities and their representatives in the decision-making processes and (*ii*) Inclusion of Persons with Disabilities in the strategies and activities of all government programmes as would be relevant.

24.215. As per the provisions of the Persons with Disabilities (Equal Opportunities, Protection of Rights and Full Participation) Act, 1995, 3 per cent reservation in employment is being provided to the persons with disabilities. All Central Ministries/Departments, especially those concerned with infrastructure, social sector and poverty alleviation corresponding Departments of State Governments and Panchayats, Municipalities and other Urban Local Bodies should earmark reasonable amounts in their Plan outlay for disability related interventions. An appropriate mechanism should be put in place for this purpose for programmes empowering PwDs and monitoring of their utilisation at all levels—Central, State, District, City/Town, Block and so on.

24.216. Education plays a pivotal role in socio-economic empowerment of Persons with Disabilities. Emphasis in the Twelfth Plan will be on educational development through: (*i*) Pre-Matric Scholarships for students with disabilities; (*ii*) Post-Matric Scholarships for students with disabilities; (*iii*) free coaching for students with disabilities; (*iv*) Special/Residential school for students with severe and multiple disabilities, in districts not having Government special schools; (*v*) Hostels for existing Government special schools not having hostels and augmentation of seats in existing hostels of Government special schools; (*vi*) Support for establishment/modernisation/capacity augmentation of Braille Presses; (*vii*) Scholarships for 'Top Class' education for students with disabilities studying in premier higher education institutes (like IITs, NITs and so on); (*viii*) Rajiv Gandhi National Fellowship for persons with disabilities; (*ix*) National Overseas Scholarship for persons with disabilities; (*x*) establishment of a college for deaf in each of the five regions of the country and (*xi*) establishment of National Accessible Library.

24.217. There is a need to give special focus on the requirement of persons with disabilities especially for Cerebral Palsy, Autism and Mental Retardation. For this purpose, the National Trust for the welfare of persons with Autism, cerebral palsy, mental retardation and multiple disabilities should emphasise on prevention, early detection, treatment and rehabilitation of the target groups in its programmes.

24.218. To make sports more accessible to Persons with Disabilities and to encourage their participation in the sports, there is a need for a Centre for Disability Sports.

24.219. In order to address the needs of differently challenged persons efforts need to be made for universal coverage of disability friendly infrastructure and facilities in Universities, Hostels and other such institutions. Adequate attention needs to be given towards providing adequate disable friendly space/facilities in all modes of transport viz. rail, buses and airplanes and so on During Twelfth Plan, efforts will be made to provide barrier free environment in important Government buildings and to make government websites accessible to persons with disabilities. A National centre will be established to facilitate and support the development of universal design and barrier free environment.

24.220. In the Twelfth Plan efforts also need to be directed to provide needed support and assistance for (*i*) Rehabilitation Centres for treating mentally ill persons; (*ii*) Model multi-disability independent living centres; (*iii*) setting up of State Spinal Injury Centres; (*iv*) provisioning accessibility in State Government institutions; (*v*) making State Governments' websites accessible; (*vi*) preparation of comprehensive database and online State depository of resources on disabilities; (*vii*) establishment of State Missions and District Coordinators; (*viii*) awareness generation and publicity; (*ix*) training of care-givers: In-service training and sensitisation of State Governments, local bodies and other service providers; (*x*) Establishment of National Institute of Mental Health Rehabilitation; (*xi*) Establishment of State Disability Resource Centres; (*xii*) Establishment of Micro-enterprises Incubation Centres for persons with disabilities; (*xiii*) grant of Association for Rehabilitation Under National Trust Initiative of Marketing (ARUNIM) for supporting its marketing activities and (*xiv*) Research on disability related technology, products and issues. Overall, the Central Ministries/Departments and State Governments need to provide adequate support to implement various programmes as per the provisions of the Persons with Disabilities (Equal Opportunities, Protection of Rights and Full Participation) Act, 1995. There is need for greater support to National Handicapped Finance Development Corporation for providing subsidies on loan for education/self-employment and grant for skill development training and so on. Further there is an urgent need to restructure and modernise ALIMCO to enable it to produce a large number of cost effective aids and assistive devices. The scheme for Incentives for Employing Persons with Disabilities in private sector needs to be suitably revamped to encourage employment and retention of persons with disabilities in private sector.

24.221. The existing laws on disability such as Persons with Disabilities (Equal Opportunities, Protection of Rights and Full Participation) Act, 1995, Rehabilitation Council of India Act, 1992, National Trust for the Welfare of Persons with Autism, Cerebral Palsy, Mental Retardation and Multiple Disabilities Act, 1999, Mental Health Act, 1987 and other laws that concern or address disability issues like Right of Children to Free and Compulsory Education Act, 2009, Protection of

Child Rights Act, 2005, The National Commission for Women Act, 1990, Apprenticeship Act, 1961, National Rural Employment Guarantee Act, 2005, Criminal Procedure Court, 1973, Indian Evidence Act, 1872 would need to be reviewed and if necessary amended or replaced in order to harmonise them with the provision of United Nations Conference on Rehabilitation of Persons with Disabilities (UNCRPD).

24.222. The existing machinery in Central and State Governments for implementing disability related programmes is generally weak both in terms of numbers and professional capability. Delivery of disability related programmes is unlikely to improve materially unless the delivery system is suitably strengthened. Therefore, the machinery attending to the rehabilitation, development and empowerment of persons with disabilities needs to be strengthened qualitatively and quantitatively.

24.223. There is a need to adopt a facilitating approach for intensive and time-bound implementation of programmes ensuring expected outcomes, dedicated implementation mechanism and management structure, adequate allocation of resources together with autonomy and accountability, intensive monitoring and regular evaluation, bringing together all concerned organisations, agencies, partners, stakeholders and community at large, high visibility through awareness generation, media, extensive use of technological inputs, and so on. To this end, National and State level Missions for Empowerment of Persons with Disabilities may be considered with full-time Mission Director and supporting staff, on the pattern of SSA, NRHM, JNNURM and so on.

24.224. All Schemes and Programmes under the envisaged Mission(s) needs to be implemented in close partnership with Panchayats, Municipalities, other Urban Local Bodies, NGOs and the community and with active involvement of persons with disabilities.

24.225. The State Mission will function in close coordination with the State Government and the State Directorate. The State Government and the Directorate will continue to have the overall administrative, regulatory and policy making role in the State. On the other hand, State Mission for Empowerment of Persons with Disabilities (SMEPwD) will be responsible for integrating and well coordinated implementation of various programmes and schemes for persons with disabilities.

24.226. To accomplish empowerment of the Persons with Disabilities, especially in making them self-reliant, independent and productive, it is imperative to ensure that they have equal and rightful access and entitlement to the services provided by the concerned Ministries/Departments of both Central and State Governments. An illustrative list of what is possible is indicated in Box 24.5. Please refer to Box 24.5.

SENIOR CITIZENS

24.227. General improvement in the health care facilities over the years has resulted in increase in life expectancy and continuing increase in proportion of population of senior citizens. The number of senior citizens of 80 years and above has been increasing. As a result the old Age Dependency Ratio has been steadily rising during the past three decades viz. 12.0 in 1981, 12.2 in 1991 and 13.1 in 2001. The needs of the older (80+) persons are different from those senior citizens in the age group of 60 years and above. Increasing attention will have to be given to this category of senior citizens. This will be addressed in the new policy for Senior Citizens which is under preparation.

24.228. The Maintenance and Welfare of Parents and Senior Citizens Act, 2007 was enacted in December 2007 to ensure need-based maintenance for parents and senior citizens and their welfare. Twenty-five States namely Andhra Pradesh, Arunachal Pradesh, Assam, Bihar, Chhattisgarh, Goa, Gujarat, Haryana, Jharkhand, Karnataka, Kerala, Madhya Pradesh, Maharashtra, Manipur, Mizoram, Nagaland, Orissa, Punjab, Rajasthan, Tamil Nadu, Tripura, Uttarakhand and West Bengal have notified the Act and all seven UTs have also notified the Act. Rest of the States which are yet to take necessary

> **Box 24.5**
> **Possible Actions by Central Government Ministries to Benefit Those with Disabilities**
>
> Actions which Central Government Ministries can take to benefit those with disabilities. Similar action could be contemplated by the States.
>
> **Ministry of Communication, Information and Technology**—Information, communications and other services, including electronic services and emergency services should be made accessible and disabled friendly.
>
> **Ministry of Civil Aviation**—The Ministry should lay down standards for safe and non-discriminatory air travel of persons with disabilities in order to implement the provisions of the UNCRPD and other air travel related international conventions. Standards for procurement of equipment, materials for ensuring safe and non-discriminatory air travel of persons with disabilities should also be laid down. Adapt buses, vessels and aircrafts in such a way as to permit easy access to persons with disabilities. Adapt toilets in vessels, aircrafts and waiting rooms in such a way as to permit the wheel chair users to use them conveniently.
>
> **Ministry of Health and Family Welfare**—The health care needs for people with disabilities include the provision of accessible hospitals and health centres, trained and sensitised human resource in the field, affordable and reasonable health insurance and establishment of community care centres.
>
> **Ministry of Human Resource Development**—As for any other group, education is critical to expanding the life prospects of people with disability. In addition, the socialisation of children with disabilities through education assumes unusually important roles in societies such as India where social exclusion of persons with disability is significant. Government schools including all Kendriya Vidyalayas and Navodaya Vidyalayas should ensure barrier free environment. School facilities such as toilets, drinking water, class rooms, furniture and fixtures, library, hostels (both boys and girls), canteens, playgrounds, labs, kitchen, auditorium, lift, extracurricular activities must be made accessible.
>
> **Ministry of Labour and Employment**—Training and development of Modular Employable Skills of people with disabilities under the Skill Development Initiative Scheme should be taken up on priority basis. The Ministry should establish an Accessible National Portal allowing people with disabilities to register and search for jobs.
>
> **Ministry of Railways**—All multi-level and multi-platform railway stations and one coach in every class of mail and express trains should be accessible and prepare rail compartments, toilets in rail compartments and waiting rooms in such a way as to permit the wheel users to use them conveniently.
>
> **Ministry of Rural Development**—Livelihood and Poverty Alleviation Programmes like Mahatma Gandhi National Rural Employment Guarantee Programme; Sampoorna Grameen Rozgar Yojana; Swarnjayanti Gram Swarozgar Yojana; New Initiative for employment in the Private Sector; Rural Housing—Bharat Nirman Indira Awas Yojana; National Social Assistance Programme and Associated Programmes.
>
> **Ministry of Women and Child Development** - The Ministry should refine the norms of WCP to prioritise the most vulnerable as beneficiaries, particularly SC, ST women, Muslim women, single women, differently-abled, and HIV-positive women, among others.

steps required under the Act such as Notification of Rules, maintenance officer, maintenance tribunal and appellate tribunal must take up the matter on priority.

24.229. The Scheme of Integrated Programme for Older Persons (IPOP) is being implemented since 1992. Under the Scheme financial assistance up to 90 per cent of the project cost is provided to non-Governmental Organisations (NGOs) for running and maintenance of Old Age Homes, Day Care Centres and Mobile Medicare Units. The Scheme has been revised w.e.f. 1 April 2008. Besides an increase in amount of financial assistance for existing projects, Governments/Panchayati Raj Institutions/Local Bodies have been made eligible for getting financial assistance. An outlay of ₹128.00 crore was provided in the Eleventh Plan and the expenditure incurred was ₹74.23 crore benefitting 1.50 lakh beneficiaries. There are three Regional Resource and Training Centres (RRTCs) functioning under the Scheme of IPOP.

Strategy for Twelfth Plan

24.230. The major focus in the Twelfth Plan will be the consolidation, expansion and strengthening of the various programmes into comprehensive coordinated systems to fulfill the aspirations of these vulnerable sections of the society. The Twelfth Plan approach and strategy sector-wise is briefly given in the subsequent paragraphs.

24.231. As a general rule, the elderly do not want to be separated from their homes and familiar surroundings and prefer to live in their own homes. But due to the widening generation gap, most elders feel lonely and need the company of peers and elders association, for active participation in life enriching activities. For such elders, day care/enrichment centre provides a meeting place to fulfill their physical, emotional and social needs and for spending their day in a meaningful way. Therefore, efforts need to be made to ensure that day care/enrichment centres for the elders receive focused attention under the scheme of Integrated Programme for Older Persons (IPOP). The scheme of IPOP needs to be revised to make it more effective so that all facilities can be provided to the elders, for example day care/enrichment centres and so on.

24.232. With the rising demand for caregivers and also to ensure quality of service of personnel employed in old age homes funded under IPOP, there has been manifold increase in training activities. Regional Resource and Training Centres (RRTCs) funded under IPOP can play an important role in this direction. Existing RRTCs funded under the IPOP need to be strengthened. In addition, steps should be taken to ensure that at least one RRTC is established in every State during the XII Plan.

24.233. A new National Policy on Senior Citizens will be formulated and implemented during the XII Plan period focusing on the following areas:

1. Mainstreaming of all the senior citizens, especially the older women and bring their concerns into the national development debate.
2. Promote the concept of 'Ageing in Place' or ageing in own home.
3.
4. It should recognise that care of senior citizens has to remain vested in the family which would partner the community, government and the private sector. Institutional care should be the last resort.
5. Schemes should be formulated for providing housing, income-security, homecare services, old age pension, access to healthcare, insurance schemes and other programmes and services to facilitate and sustain the concept of dignity in old age. The thrust of the policy would be preventive rather than curative.
6. Keeping in view the rising longevity of our population, there is a need to focus on all aspects of care for the Oldest Old (80+ years) namely, social, financial, health care and the need for shelter.
7. Since India is a signatory to the Madrid Plan of Action and Barrier Free Framework, the Policy will aim to work towards an inclusive, barrier-free and age-friendly society.
8. Recognise that senior citizens are a valuable resource for the country and create an environment that provides them with equal opportunities, protects their rights and enables their full participation in society.
9. Long term savings instruments and credit activities will be promoted to reach both rural and urban areas.
10. Employment in income generating activities after superannuation will be encouraged.
11. Organisations that provide counselling, career guidance and training services will be supported and assisted.
12. The Maintenance and Welfare of Parents and Senior Citizens Act, 2007 will be implemented effectively and Tribunals will be set up so that elderly parents, unable to maintain themselves, are not abandoned and neglected.
13. States will set up homes with assisted living facilities for abandoned senior citizens in every district of the country and will set apart adequate budgetary support for this purpose.

24.234. The National Institute of Social Defence (NISD) is the nodal training and research institute in the area of social defence. The objective of the Institute is to strengthen and provide technical inputs to the social defence programmes of the Government of India and to develop and train the manpower resources required in the area of social defence. NISD needs to be strengthened to take the lead in training the requisite human resources for caring of the senior citizens of the country, during the Twelfth Plan period.

24.235. The Maintenance and Welfare of Parents and Senior Citizens Act, 2007 was enacted to ensure need based maintenance for parents and senior citizens and their welfare. So far, 25 States and all Union Territories have notified the Act. However, it has been noticed that State Government functionaries are not fully aware of the consequential steps/actions required to be taken. Therefore, Ministry of SJ&E would prepare a suitable Action Plan in the Twelfth Plan to ensure effective implementation of the Act by creating awareness among public about the various provisions of the Act through aggressive media campaign as well as involving Panchayati Raj Institutions/Municipalities/local bodies in the campaign to reach out to rural areas as well. Workshops may be organised with State Governments, NGOs, Senior Citizens Associations, and so on to ensure that the various provisions of the Act are clearly understood and effectively implemented in letter and spirit.

24.236. In sum, with a view to ensure the well-being of senior citizens especially indigent senior citizens, by strengthening their legitimate place in society and extending support for financial and food security, health care, shelter, equitable share in development, protection against abuse and exploitation and other needs, efforts need to be made in the Twelfth Five Year Plan for: (*i*) setting up a National Commission for Senior Citizens to look into their grievances on priority for redressal and ensure that services and facilities meant for them are being provided; (*ii*) establishment of Old Age Homes for Indigent Senior Citizens with integrated multi-facility centre of varying capacity (25, 60 and 120) in 640 districts of the country, through State Government; (*iii*) setting up of a Helpline and District level help lines for older persons; (*iv*) setting up of Bureau for Socio-Economic Empowerment of Senior Citizens at district level; (*v*) creation of National Trust for the Aged; (*vi*) issue of 'Smart' Identity Cards for senior citizens; and (*vii*) health insurance for senior citizens.

NOMADIC, SEMI-NOMADIC AND DENOTIFIED TRIBES (DNTs)

24.237. The Nomadic, Semi Nomadic and De-notified Tribes cover the 200 communities that were identified by the colonial Government as 'Criminal Tribes' under a notorious legislation called 'Criminal Tribes Act (CTA) 1871.[2] CTA 1871 was annulled after Independence and communities identified under CTA, 1871 have been referred to thereafter as the De-notified, Nomadic and Semi-Nomadic Tribes (DNTs, SNTs and NTs). There is no authentic data on DNTs and no Census enumeration was conducted for them, though they are found in almost all the States and belong mostly to the OBC category in some large States. They are also spread across the SC and ST categories in other States. Some communities are not covered by any of the three SC, ST and OBC categories. Even those covered under the three categories are often not able to avail the benefits because of either not having caste certificates, or because the quotas are exhausted by the non-nomadic/non-de-notified communities in the reserved categories. A number of States have not prepared lists of the De-notified or Nomadic communities and the status of such people is unknown.

24.238. The quick and most effective way of extending developmental support for DNTs would be to provide special and relevant support and facilities for these communities within the existing facilities for ST, SC and OBC categories as applicable. Access to scholarships and hostel facilities, need to be given priority. The existing schemes for scholarships and hostel facilities need to be revised to extend their coverage to nomadic, semi-nomadic and DNTs. For economic empowerment and development of DNTs capacity building programmes for skill development and marketing, loans for economic empowerment need to be given priority. Specific strategies and mechanisms will also be put in place to ensure flow of funds for the welfare and development of nomadic, semi-nomadic and Denotified Tribes (DNTs). For social empowerment of DNTs an enabling environment needs to be created so that they are able to utilise the reservation benefits in education and employment. DNTs do not have permanent residential locations due to various social, political and cultural reasons; as a result, they are unable to avail the benefits of the various schemes of the Government. Therefore, an effective rehabilitative approach, supported with an equally effective plan for the socio-economic development of the DNTs needs to be adopted and implemented especially by establishing habitations/villages for them. This would be given emphasis during the Twelfth Plan period.

24.239. The existing legislations such as Scheduled Castes and Scheduled Tribes (Prevention of Atrocities) Act, 1989; Habitual Offenders Act, 1952; The Prevention of Begging Act, 1959; The Bombay Prevention of Begging Act, 1959; Prevention of Cruelty to Animals Act, 1986; Wildlife Protection Act, 1972 and the Forest (Conservation) Act, 1980; and Excise Law and so on need to be reviewed to ensure the dignity and the livelihood of DNTs.

Economic Empowerment

24.240. A nation-wide survey of DNT settlements needs to be conducted urgently. This could form the basis, inter alia, for introducing a suitable shelter programme for homeless DNTs. Free or subsidised housing may be provided to eligible DNT households in a phased manner—by adopting special measures like a 'Rajasthan's Gadaria Lohar Community Housing Scheme'. Given the high incidence of homelessness among DNTs, a proportion of the current outlay for Indira Awaas Yojana (IAY) should be earmarked for DNTs. Within DNTs, the nomadic communities need to be assisted financially to construct dwelling units by receiving priority under the on-going housing programmes of the Central Government. Therefore, it is suggested to create a Cluster Development Fund for assisting the DNTs for the construction of houses, for providing land to them and for creating infrastructure, and so on so that proper clusters can be developed for them.

24.241. The skill development initiatives of the States and Central Government need to give priority to cover the unemployed youth among the DNTs with a view to provide them employable skills. A suitable Action Plan for the rehabilitation of the nomadic, semi-nomadic and DNTs as well as to meet the infrastructure needs including basic amenities of their areas needs to be prepared. The requirement of funds for the purpose will be met out of the proposed Cluster Development Fund. The Finance and Development Corporations under the Ministry of Social Justice and Empowerment will be tasked to address the skill development of the DNTs.

24.242. An Integrated Infrastructure Development Programme also needs to be especially designed to provide basic amenities such as roads, schools, electricity, drinking water, community centres, and so on in the existing settlements of the DNTs.

SUBSTANCE (DRUG) ABUSE AND ALCOHOLISM

24.243. The problem of incidence of alcoholism and substance abuse is assuming alarming magnitude and poses potential threat to the society. Besides ill effects on physical and health, drug addiction is emerging as a major social problem with increasing incidence of crime among drug/alcohol addicts. Drug addiction causes immense financial and psychological problems for the addict and his/her family. This takes the issue out of the domain of individual behaviour and locates it at the centre of the community, whether it is the family or the larger society. Therefore, there is an urgent need for effective counter measures through an approach which is comprehensive and also takes up programmes in convergence mode. Further, various Central Ministries viz., Ministry of Health and Family Welfare, Ministry of Information and Broadcasting, Ministry of Home Affairs, Ministry of Rural Development, Ministry of Panchayati Raj, Ministry of Finance and Ministry of Women and Child Development are attending to different aspect relating to these vulnerable groups. A better coordination and convergence in this regard is called for. All existing schematic and non-schematic interventions made by the Ministries need to be integrated under a Mission Mode programme.

24.244. There is a need to make an accurate assessment of the extent, pattern and trends of substances abuse in the country and identify vulnerable groups and areas. Preventive measures need to be taken to reduce both supply and demand and Universal access to preventive treatment and rehabilitation of alcoholism and drug abuse.

24.245. The Narcotic Drugs and Psychotropic Substances Act, 1985, was enacted, inter alia, to curb drug abuse. Section 71 of the Act (Power of Government to establish centres for identification, treatment, and so on of addicts and for supply of narcotic drugs and psychotropic substances) provides that:

> The Government may, in its discretion, establish as many centres as it thinks fit for identification, treatment, education, after-care, rehabilitation, social reintegration of addicts and for supply, subject to such conditions and in such manner as may be prescribed, by the concerned Government of any narcotic drugs and psychotropic substances to the addicts registered with the Government and to others where such supply is a medical necessity.

24.246. Accordingly the Ministry of SJ&E has been supporting Integrated Rehabilitation Centre for Addicts (IRCAs) under the Scheme of Assistance for the Prevention of Alcoholism and Substance (Drugs) Abuse and for Social Defence Services run by voluntary organisations.

24.247. India is signatory to three United Nations Conventions, namely: (*i*) Convention on Narcotic Drugs, 1961; (*ii*) Convention on Psychotropic Substances, 1971; and (*iii*) Convention against Illicit Traffic in Narcotic Drugs and Psychotropic Substances, 1988. Thus India also has an international obligation to curb drug abuse. The demand reduction strategy consists of education, treatment, rehabilitation and social integration of drug addicts for prevention of drug abuse.

BEGGARS

24.248. There is no firm and authentic information regarding number of beggars in the country. According to the un-published data of Census 2001, there were 7.03 lakh beggars and vagrants out of which 6.31 lakh were in non-worker category. Some States viz. West Bengal, Assam, Chhattisgarh, Tripura, Orissa, Punjab, Rajasthan, Andhra Pradesh, Jammu & Kashmir, Madhya Pradesh and Uttar Pradesh have much higher population of beggars in proportion to their total population as compared to other States/UTs.

24.249. The States are responsible for taking the necessary preventive and rehabilitative steps. Neither is there any specific Central Act on prevention of begging and rehabilitation of beggars, nor is there a clear policy on how the problem is to be tackled. There are, however, general legislations having provisions for prevention of beggary. These include: Indian Penal Code (IPC), the Juvenile Justice (Care and Protection of Children) Act 2000 and Indian Railway Act 1989.

24.250. The States are responsible for taking the necessary preventive and rehabilitative steps. There is neither any Central Act on prevention of beggary and rehabilitation of beggars, nor a National Policy on beggary. There is therefore, an urgent need to formulate a National Policy so that there is uniformity of approach in dealing with the problem of beggary. Various studies and surveys have brought out that the prime reason for soliciting alms has been poverty. Significant proportions of such persons suffer from various types of disabilities, including mental illness and so on. A number of such persons are also addicted to various substances and require immediate medical/psychiatric attention. In order to be able to provide help and support to such persons, there is a need for adoption of a more humane approach. 20 States and 2 UTs have enacted their own anti-beggary laws or adopted laws enacted by other States. Even these States/UTs which have adopted anti-beggary legislation do not implement them uniformly. Further, the provisions of these legislations differ from one state to another. Therefore, there is a need to bring out a Model Legislation on Beggary at the Central level which can be suitably adapted by States/UTs.

24.251. At present, there are no central schemes directly related to beggary. However, there are programmes for welfare and development of older persons, physically challenged and drug abuse covering the issues/problems of beggary. Therefore, it would be desirable to address the problem in a holistic manner at the National Level.

24.252. Direct intervention through a new programme/scheme like the Integrated Programme for Rehabilitation of Beggars can be made. The Programme may include items like Night Shelter-cum-Work Production Centre; Multiple Skill Training; Mobile Health Care; Counselling; Awareness Generation; and Sensitisation programmes. Training of Human Resources, Research and Documentation, and so on will be given special attention in the Twelfth Five Year Plan. In addition, convergence of existing programmes for the Vulnerable Groups implemented by the Ministries of Social Justice and Empowerment, Rural Development, Urban Development and Poverty Alleviation, Women and Child Development will also need to be looked into.

PLAN OUTLAY

24.253. In the Twelfth Plan, a tentative Gross Budgetary Support of ₹32,684 crore has been earmarked for the Ministry of Social Justice and Empowerment for the welfare and development of SCs, OBCs, DNTs, PwDs and other vulnerable groups. Similarly, tentative allocations of ₹7,746 crore and ₹17,323 crore have been made for the Ministry of Tribal Affairs and Ministry of Minority Affairs, respectively for the welfare and development of STs and Minorities, The allocation indicated for the Ministry of Tribal Affairs does not include SCA to TSP and grant-in-aid under Article 275 (1) of the Constitution. In addition to this, social welfare programmes receive Plan financial Support from the State sector as well.

NOTES

1. National Committee on Scheduled Tribes and Other Traditional Forest Dwellers (Recognition of Forest Rights) Act, Ministry of Environment and Forest, December, 2010.
2. Six categories of communities were identified under CTA 1871. These included: (*i*) petty traders moving from village to village selling commodities like salt, forest produce on animal's back; (*ii*) entertainers through public performance such as musicians, dancers, singers, storytellers, acrobats, gymnasts, puppeteers and tightrope walkers and so on; (*iii*) entertainers with the help of performing animals; (*iv*) pastoral groups, hunters, gatherers, shifting cultivator communities and so on; (*v*) artisans working with bamboo, iron, clay and so on; and (*vi*) nomadic individuals who subsist on charity, fortune telling, traditional faith healing services and so on.